NORTH CAROLINA
P9-DMG-738

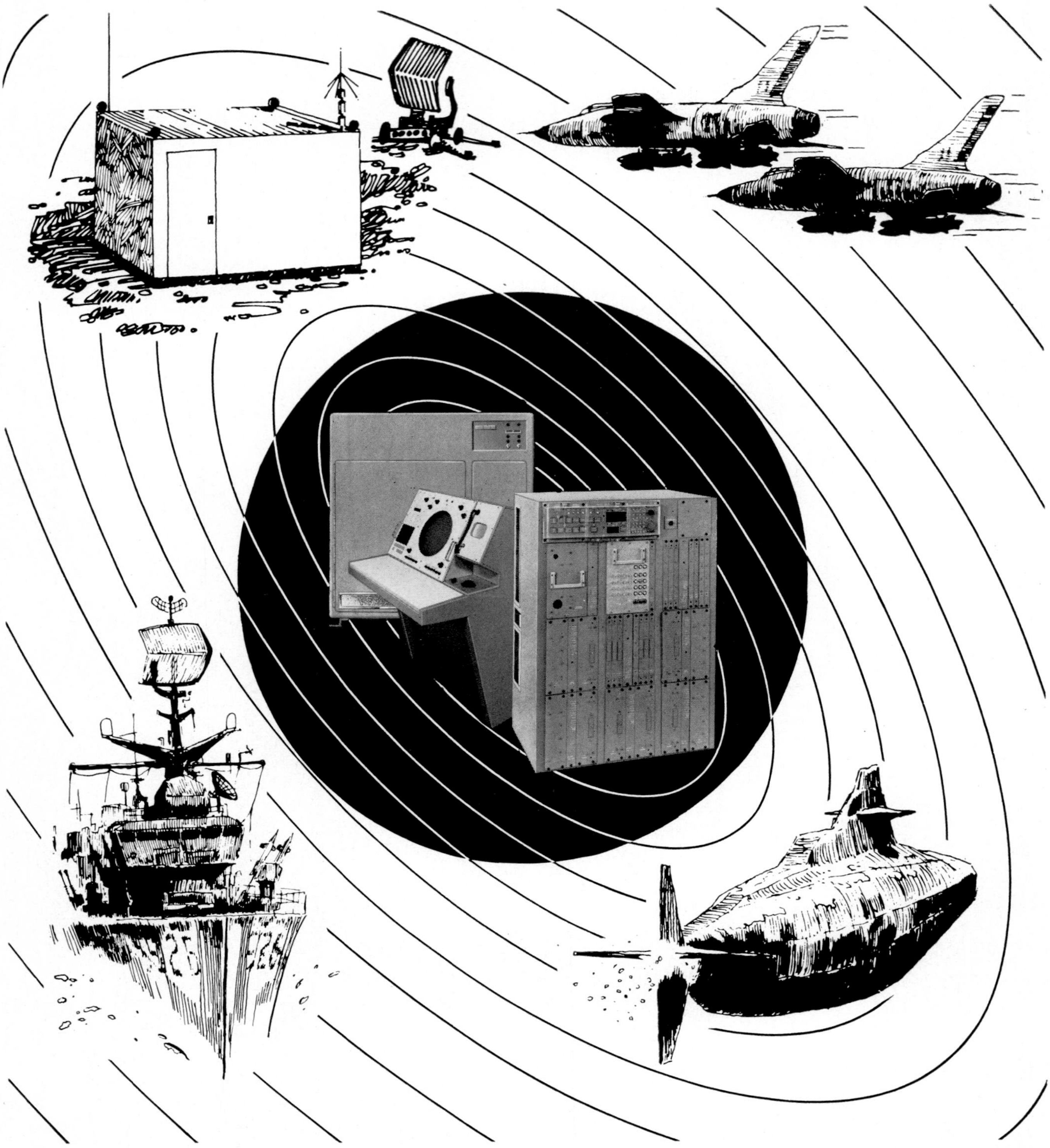

JANE'S FIGHTING SHIPS

Edited by Raymond V. B. Blackman
C.Eng., M.I.Mar.E., M.R.I.N.A.

Order of Contents

World Sales Distribution

North, Central and South America

McGraw-Hill Book Company,
330 West 42nd Street,
New York, N.Y. 10036

and

McGraw-Hill Company of Canada Ltd.
330 Progress Avenue,
Scarborough, Ontario,
Canada.

Europe, Asia, Africa and Australasia

Jane's Yearbooks,
49/50 Poland St., London, WIA 2LG.

EDITORIAL *communications should be addressed to:*

The Editor, Jane's Fighting Ships,
Jane's Yearbooks, 49/50 Poland Street, London, WIA 2LG, England
Telephone: 01-437-0686

ADVERTISEMENT *communications should be addressed to:*

Haymarket Publishing Group,
Gillow House, 5, Winsley Street, London, W.I., England
Telephone: 01-636-3600

*** Classified List of Advertisers**

The various products available from the advertisers in this edition are listed alphabetically in about 300 different headings. In order to increase the usefulness of the Classified List a section is incorporated, on tinted paper, listing the product headings in French, German, Spanish and Russian, alphabetically in those languages. The identification letter and number corresponding to the English-language listing is shown against each item.

ALPHABETICAL LIST OF ADVERTISERS

1969/70 EDITION

Now-
direct immediate display of predicted sonar ray paths

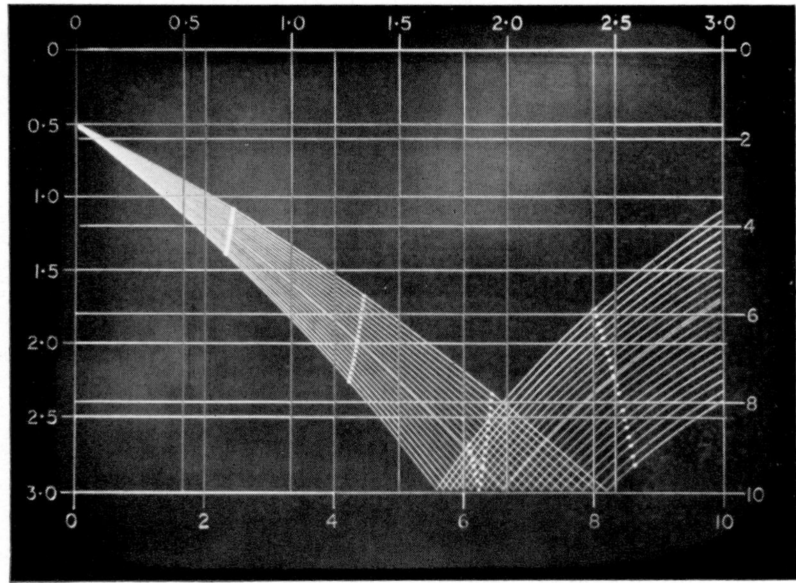

The ARTI display to the left demonstrates the vertical coverage pattern derived from the simple example of a Bathythermograph trace right.

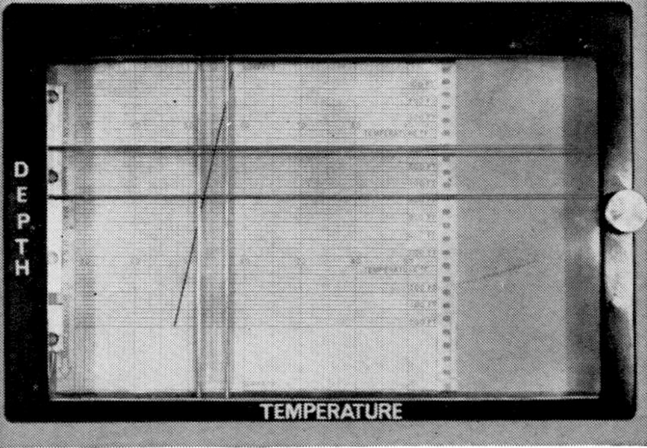

The new Acoustic Ray Trace Indicator has been developed by Plessey Marine Systems Division for the Royal Navy. This equipment provides rapid corrections to the detection range of any sonar by using temperature/depth or velocity/depth profiles. Such corrections enable targets to be located more accurately.

A.R.T.I. will receive input data from any temperature or velocity-profile source, but it is specifically designed to accept plots semi-automatically from either the R.N. Sound Velocity Recorder or the Plessey-Sippican XBT.* Expendable Bathythermograph already in service with 10 navies. The miniature analogue computer incorporated in the A.R.T.I. predicts ray paths at one degree intervals within the sonar beam. Mounted independently, it is designed so that the specific parameters of any sonar can be manually preset. The A.R.T.I. then allows the sonar ray paths to be predicted. Solid state electronic techniques makes these predictions simple, fast and accurate.

* In the U.S.A., Canada and South America, the XBT is sold and serviced by The Sippican Corporation, Maryland, Mass.

PLESSEY
Electronics

The Plessey Company Limited,
Marine Systems Division, Ilford, Essex, England.
Telephone: 01-478 3040. Telex: 23166

PE(M)24

ALPHABETICAL LIST OF ADVERTISERS—continued

CLASSIFIED LIST OF ADVERTISERS

A1. ACTION INFORMATION TRAINERS

Elliott Brother (London) Ltd.,
Trainer & Simulator Division

A 2. AIR COMPRESSORS

Hawker Siddeley Group
Western Gear Corporation

A 3. AIRCRAFT ARRESTING GEAR

A/S Horten Verft
MacTaggart, Scott & Co. Ltd.

A 4. AIRCRAFT CARRIERS

Netherlands United Shipbuilding Bureaux Ltd.
Vickers Limited

A 5. AIRCRAFT INSTRUMENTS

British Aircraft Corporation
Columbia Electronics International, Inc.
Ferranti Limited
Hawker Siddeley Group
Sperry Gyroscope Division

A 6. AIR-CUSHION VEHICLES

British Hovercraft Corporation Ltd.
Vosper Thornycroft Group, The

A 7. ALTERNATORS

Columbia Electronics International, Inc.
Electro-Dymanic Construction Co. Ltd,
Hawker Siddeley Group
Laurence, Scott & Electromotors Ltd.

A 8. AMMUNITION

AB Bofors

A 9. AMMUNITION HOISTS

Blohm + Voss AG
MacTaggart, Scott & Co. Ltd.
Vickers Limited
Western Gear Corporation

A 10. ANTI-SUBMARINE LAUNCHES

Boatservice Ltd. A/S
Brooke Marine Ltd.
Cantiere Rodriquez
Korody Marine Corporation
Netherlands United Shipbuilding Bureaux Ltd.
Vosper Thornycroft Group, The
Yarrow (Shipbuilders) Ltd.

A 11. ANTI-SUBMARINE ROCKET LAUNCHERS

AB Bofors
Vickers Limited

A 12. ANTI-SUBMARINE ROCKETS

AB Bofors
Nord Aviation
British Aircraft Corporation

A 13. ARMOUR PLATES

AB Bofors

A 14. ASSAULT CRAFT

Blohm + Voss AG
British Hovercraft Corporation
Brooke Marine Ltd.
Cantiere Rodriquez
Karlskronavarvet AB
Korody Marine Corporation
Vickers Limited
Vosper Thornycroft Group, The
Yarrow (Shipbuilders) Ltd.

A 15. ASSAULT SHIPS

Blohm + Voss AG
Boatservice Ltd. A/S
Brooke Marine Ltd.
Cantiere Rodriquez
Vickers Limited
Vosper Thornycroft Group, The
Yarrow (Shipbuilders) Ltd.

A 16. AUTOMATIC CONTROL SYSTEMS

Electro-Dynamic Construction Co. Ltd.
Ferranti Ltd.
Laurence, Scott & Electrometers Ltd.
Hollandse Signaalapparaten N.V.
Sperry Gyroscope Division
Vosper Thornycroft Group, The

A 17. AUTOMATIC STEERING

Hawker Siddeley Group
Sperry Gyroscope Division
Western Gear Corporation

A 18. AUXILIARY MACHINERY

Blohm + Voss AG
Korody-Colyer Corporation
Maybach Mercedes-Benz Motorenbau GmbH
Rolls Royce Ltd.
Western Gear Corporation

B 1. BINOCULARS

Barr & Stroud Ltd.

B 2. BOILERS

Blohm + Voss AG
Netherlands United Shipbuilding Bureaux Ltd.
Vickers Limited
Yarrow (Shipbuilders) Ltd.

B 3. BOOKS (NAVAL)

Antheil Booksellers

B 3a BOOKS (NAVAL) OUT OF PRINT

Antheil Booksellers

B 4. BULK CARRIERS

Blohm + Voss AG
Fr. Lürssen Werft
Marinens Hovedverft
Todd Shipyards Corporation
Vickers Limited

C 1. CABLE LOOMS (WITH OR WITHOUT)

McGeoch & Co. (Birmingham) Ltd.

C 2. CAISSONS

Vickers Limited
Western Gear Corporation

C 3. CAPSTANS AND WINDLASSES

MacTaggart, Scott & Co. Ltd.
Western Gear Corporation

C 4. CAR FERRIES

Blohm + Voss AG
British Hovercraft Corporation
Brooke Marine Ltd.
A/S Horten Verft
Fr. Lürssen Werft
Western Gear Corporation
Vosper Thornycroft Group, The
Yarrow (Shipbuilders) Ltd.

C 5. CARGO HANDLING EQUIPMENT

Blohm + Voss AG
British Hovercraft Corporation Ltd.
Laurence, Scott & Electromotors Ltd.
MacTaggart, Scott & Co. Ltd.
Vickers Limited

C 6. CARGO SHIPS

Blohm + Voss AG
Boatservice Ltd. A/S
Brooke Marine Ltd.
A/S Horten Verft
Fr. Lürssen Werft
Todd Shipyards Corporation
Vickers Limited
Yarrow (Shipbuilders) Ltd.

Marconi radar systems for warships

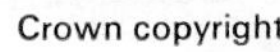

The Marconi Company Limited
Radar Division, Chelmsford, Essex, England.
Member of GEC-Marconi Electronics Limited.

LTD/S71

C 7. CARGO SPACE MONITORS

Brooke Marine Ltd.
Sperry Gyroscope Division

C 8. CASTINGS, ALUMINIUM-BRONZE

Barr & Stroud Ltd.
Vickers Limited

C 9. CASTINGS, HIGH DUTY IRON

Barr & Stroud Ltd.
Vickers Limited

C 10. CASTINGS, NON-FERROUS

Barr & Stroud Ltd.
Hawker Siddeley Group
McGeoch & Co. (Birmingham) Ltd., William
Vickers Limited

C 11. CASTINGS, SHELL, MOULDED

Ferranti Ltd.

C 12. CASTINGS S.G. IRON

Ferranti Ltd.

C 13. CASTINGS S.G. NI-RESIST IRON

Ferranti Ltd.

C 14. CASTINGS, STEEL

AB Bofors
Vickers Limited

C 15. CENTRALISED AND AUTOMATIC CONTROL

Hawker Siddeley Group
Hollandse Signaalapparaten N.V.
Maybach Mercedes-Benz Motorenbau GmbH
Sperry Gyroscope Division
Todd Shipyards Corporation
Vosper Thornycroft Group, The

C 16. COASTAL AND INSHORE MINESWEEPERS

Boatservice Ltd. A/S
Brooke Marine Ltd.
Karlskronavarvet AB
Netherlands United Shipbuilding Bureaux Ltd.
Vosper Thornycroft Group, The
Yarrow (Shipbuilders) Ltd.

C 17. COMPRESSED AIR STARTERS FOR GAS TURBINES AND DIESEL ENGINES

C 18. COMPRESSORS

Hawker Siddeley Group

C 19. COMPUTER SERVICES

Elliott Brothers (London) Ltd., Naval Division
Elliott Brothers (London) Ltd., Trainer & Simulator Division
Hollandse Signaalapparaten N.V.
Marconi Co. Ltd., The
Yarrow & Co. Ltd.

C 20. COMPUTERS

Elliott Brothers (London) Ltd., Naval Division
Elliott Brothers (London) Ltd., Trainer & Simulator Division
Ferranti Limited
General Precision Inc.—Librascope Group
Hawker Siddeley Group
Hollandse Signaalapparaten N.V.
Marconi Co. Ltd., The
Sperry Gyroscope Division
Yarrow & Co. Ltd.

C 21. CONDENSER TUBES

Vickers Limited

C 22. CONDENSERS

Blohm + Voss AG
Karlskronavarvet AB
Vickers Limited
Yarrow & Co. Ltd.

C 23. CONTAINER SHIPS

Blohm + Voss AG
Fr. Lürssen Werft
Todd Shipyards Corporation
Vickers Limited
Yarrow (Shipbuilders) Ltd.

C 24. CONTROL DESKS (ELECTRIC)

Electro-Dynamic Construction Co. Ltd.
A/S Horten Verft
Laurence Scott & Electromotors Ltd.
McGeoch & Co. (Birmingham) Ltd., William
Plessey Company Limited, The
Vosper Thornycroft Group, The

C 25. CONTROL GEAR

Columbia Electronics International, Inc.
Electro-Dynamic Construction Co. Ltd.
Laurence Scott & Electromotors Ltd.
McGeoch & Co. (Birmingham) Ltd., William
Sperry Gyroscope Division
Vosper Thornycroft Group, The

C 26. CORVETTES

Blohm + Voss AG
Brooke Marine Ltd.
A/S Horten Verft
Karlskronavarvet AB
Fr. Lürssen Werft
Netherlands United Shipbuilding Bureaux Ltd.
Western Gear Corporation
Vosper Thornycroft Group, The
Yarrow (Shipbuilders) Ltd.

C 27. CRANES, SHIPS'

Hawker Siddeley Group

C 28. CRUISERS

Cantiere Rodriquez
Netherlands United Shipbuilding Bureaux Ltd.
Vickers Limited

D 1. DECK MACHINERY

Hawker Siddeley Group
Laurence, Scott & Electromotors Ltd.
MacTaggart, Scott & Co. Ltd.
Western Gear Corporation
Vickers Limited
Vosper Thornycroft Group, The

D 2. DESTROYERS

Blohm + Voss AG
A/S Horten Verft
Karlskronavarvet AB
Netherlands United Shipbuilding Bureaux Ltd.
Vickers Limited
Vosper Thornycroft Group, The
Yarrow (Shipbuilders) Ltd.

D 3. DIESEL ENGINES, AUXILIARY

Blohm & Voss AG
Coventry Climax Engines Ltd.
C.R.M., Fabbrica Motori Marini
Hawker Siddeley Group
Korody-Colyer Corporation
Korody Marine Corporation
Maybach Mercedes-Benz Motorenbau GmbH
Netherlands United Shipbuilding Bureaux Ltd.
SACM de Mulhouse

LISTE CLASSIFIEE DES ANNONCEURS

Le numéro de référence accompagnant chaque rubrique ci-dessous indique la rubrique anglaise équivalente en pages 7 à 31

Réf.	Rubrique
E 3, E 5	Accessoires électriques
F 11	Accessoires pour navires
S 24	Acier allié et spécial
S 26	Acier au manganèse résistant à l'usure
H 4	Aéroglisseurs
G 18	Affûts de canons
N 3	Aides radio à la navigation
R 16	Ailettes anti-roulis
A 7	Alternateurs
R 1	Antennes de radar
C 25	Appareillage de commande
M 16	Appareillage de commande moteur
E 7	Appareillage de commutation électrique
S 27	Appareils de pilotage
T 22	" " "
G 19	Appareils de pointage et d'indication d'altitude
O 6	Armements
E 8	Auxiliaires électro-hydrauliques
S 5	Banc d'essais des compas magnétiques de navires
H 8	Bateau à aile portante
G 1	Bateaux à turbine à gaz
F 7	Bateaux-pompes et de sauvetage
C 3	Cabestans et treuils
E 2	Câbles électriques
C 2	Caissons
G 16	Canonnières
N 1	Canons de bord
G 17	Canons et affûts
P 4	Carénages de périscope
G 3	Carters d'engrenages
T 20	Chalutiers
F 13	Chariots élévateurs à fourche
B 2	Chaudières
W 3	Chaudières à tube d'eau
C 15	Commande centralisée et automatique
E 13	Commandes de démarrage et d'arrêt moteurs
E 12	Commandes de vitesse moteurs
G 20	Compas gyroscopiques
I 5	Composants d'instruments (Méc aniques)
P 18	Composants de pompes
C 18	Compresseurs
A 2	Compresseurs d'air
O 2	Compresseurs exempts d'huile
C 22	Condenseurs
A 17	Conduite et pilotage automatiques
S 7	Construction de systèmes pour navires
T 14	Constructeurs de vedettes lance-torpilles
S 3	Constructions et réparations de navires
S 29	Contrôle du tir dans les sous-marins
C 7	Contrôleurs de l'espace réservés au frêt
C 28	Croiseurs
C 26	Corvettes
C 17	Démarreurs à air comprimé pour turbines à gaz et moteurs Diesel
M 17	Démarreurs moteurs
D 2	Destroyers
A 3	Dispositif de freinage à la descente (Avion)
S 14	Douilles
L 1	Douilles de lampes
D 9	Dragues
M 9	Dragueurs de mines
C 16	Dragueurs de mines côtiers et d'intérieur
N 5	Dragueurs de mines non-magnétiques
H 1	Echangeurs de chaleur
D 8	Ecluses de docks
E 1	Economiseurs
P 16	Editeurs
L 5	Elévateurs hydrauliques
S 28	Elimination des tensions

Réf.	Rubrique
A 14	Embarcations d'assaut
F 6	Embarcations et autres produits en fibre de verre
R 7	Emetteurs et récepteurs radio
G 15	Engins guidés
G 9	Engrenages à denture en V
G6	Engrenages, conico-hélicoïdaux
G 13	Equipement d'entretien d'engins guidés
G 4	Engrenages divers
G 8	Engrenages droits
E 18	Engrenages épicycloidaux
G 5	Engrenages, hypoïdes
G 7	Engrenages, réducteurs-inverseurs
T 15	Enregistreurs de profondeur et de roulis des torpilles
S 1o	Ensembles à bagues collectrices
F 8,T 16	Equipement de commande et de contrôle de déviation des torpilles
D 6	Equipement d'injection de moteurs Diesel
M 5	Equipement de manutention des matériaux
T 6	Equipement de télécommunications
U 2	Equipement de télévision sous-marine
S 34	Equipement de topographie
E 9	Equipement électronique
L 8	Equipement haut-parleur
H 9	Equipement hydrographique
H 7	Equipement hydraulique
M 7	Equipement microphonique
S 15	Equipement radar ultrasonique
S 16	Equipement radar ultrasonique, appareils sur coque et systèmes hydrauliques
R 6	Equipement radio
R 5	Equipement radio d'avions
S 19	Equipement stabilisateur
S 20	Equipement stabilisateur pour le contrôle du tir
T 12	Equipement d'essai des systèmes de contrôle du tir
T 19	Equipement d'instruction
E 4	Equipement électrique
F 10	Equipement mécanique de navires
E 19	Escourteurs
I 11	Etude d'intérieurs et d'aménagements de navires
M 15	Fabricants de maquettes
H 2	Fenêtres réchauffées
F 4	Ferry-boats
C 4	Ferry-boats pour voitures
U 1	Feux de plongée sous-marine
M 21	Fiches à broches multiples
P 9	Fiches et douilles
S 13	Fiches et douilles à broches multiples
S 12	Fiches et douilles électriques étanches à l'eau
O 5	Filtres optiques
	Fondeurs de cuivre pour navires
	Foreuses de pétrole
F 15	Frégates
G 10	Génératrices électriques
R 17	Gouvernails
C 27	Grues de navires
P 13	Hélices pour navires
I 2	Indicateurs de feux de navigation
S 11	Indicateurs de fumée
H 3	Indicateurs de gouvernail
I 1	Indicateurs électriques
I 4	Injecteurs
F 16	Injecteurs de mazout
A 5	Instruments d'avions
I 10	Instruments d'équipement d'essai
I 9	Instruments de précision
I 6	Instruments électroniques
I 7	Instruments nautiques
S 2	Instruments scientifiques
M 11	Installations d'engins
E 6	Installations et réparations électriques

Code	Rubrique
R 15	Inverseurs
B 1	Jumelles
L 6	Lampes et éclairage
A 11	Lance-roquettes anti-sous-marins
T 17	Lance-torpilles latéraux
B 3	Livres de marine
B 3a	Livres de marine épuisés
A 18	Machines auxiliaires
D 1	Machines de pont
S 4	Machines de navires
P 15	Machines de propulsion
H 6	Machines hydrauliques
D 7	Matériel de plongée
I 3	Matériaux infra-rouges
S 21	Matériel classique de produ ction de vapeur
F 14	Matériel de distillation d'eau fraîche
C 5	Matériel de manutention de charges
H 5	Matériel hydraulique
S 22	Matériel nucléaire de production de vapeur
M 14	Modèliste
E 16	Moteurs à turbines à gaz
E 17	Moteurs à turbines à vapeur
E 14	Moteurs d'avions
E 15	Moteurs Diesel
D 3	Moteurs Diesel auxiliaires
D 4	Moteurs Diesel principaux de propulsion
M 19	Moteurs électriques
R 14	Moteurs réversibles actionnés à la vapeur ou à l'air comprimé
M 8	Mouilleurs de mines
A 8	Munitions
D 1o	Navires à cargaisons sèches
C 23	Navires à containers
G 14	Navires à engins guidés
M 13	Navires à missiles
P 2	Navires à passagers
C 6	Navires-cargos
T 2	Navires-citernes
T 3	Navires-citernes (petits)
A 15	Navires d'assaut
M 3	Navires d'entretien et de réparations
W 2	Navires de guerre
R 12	Navires de recherches
S 1	Navires de sauvetage et de barrage
M 6	Navires marchands
I 12	Onduleurs et chargeurs de batterie
C 20	Ordinateurs
S 35	Panneaux de commande
S 36	Panneaux de commande et appareillage de commutation
A 10	Patrouilleurs anti-sous-marins
F 1	Patrouilleurs rapides
P 3	Patrouilleurs, vedettes, ravitailleurs et péniches
L 2	Péniches de débarquement
P 5	Périscopes
S 30	Périscopes de sous-marins
F 12	Phares d'éclairage
C 14	Pièces coulées en acier
C 8	Pièces coulées en aluminium-bronze
C 11	Pièces moulées en coquille
C 9	Pièces coulées en fer à grand rendement
C 12	Pièces coulées en fer à graphite sphéroidal
C 13	Pièces coulées en fer "Ni-Resist" à graphite sphéroidal
C 10	Pièces coulées en métaux non ferreux
S 25	Pièces de forge, plaques et sections, pièces estampées
D 5	Pièces de forge, plaques et sections, pièces estampées en acier
E 11	Pièces de rechange pour moteurs Diesel
P 1 R11 P 1 E 11	Pièces pour moteurs Diesel
R 11 P 11 P 1 E 11	Pièces pour moteurs Diesel
S 17 P 11 P 1 E 11	Pièces pour moteurs Diesel
M 1	Pièces usinées en métaux ferreux
M 2	Pièces usinées en métaux non ferreux
P 8	Pistons, segments et axes de pied de bielle
A 13	Plaque de blindage
P 17	Pompes
F 9	Pompes à incendie
P 10	Pontons automoteurs
A 4	Porte-avions
F 5	Produits optiques réalisés à partir de fibres
D 11	Propriétaires de cales sèches
P 12	Propulsifs
T 5	Publications techniques
C 24	Pupitres de commande (électriques)
R 2	Radar de contrôle de tir
R 3	Radar de surveillance des ports
M 4	Radar marin
N 2	Radar naval
R 4	Radar pour la navigation, et pour l'avertissement menant à l'interception
T 11	Ravitailleurs
O 3	Réchauffeurs de combustibles
F 3	Réchauffeurs d'eau d'alimentation
P 14	Recherche relative aux hélices de navires
P 11	Récipients sous pression
R 13	Réducteurs, inverseurs, à commande à huile hydraulique
G 11	Régulateurs
E 10	Régulateurs de moteur et enregistreur de données
G 12	Régulateurs de vitesse moteur
T 21	Remorqueurs
W 1	Réparations de navires de guerre
T 4	Réservoirs de stockage de pétrole et d'eau
A 12	Roquettes anti-sous-marins
C 19	Service de calcul
F 2	Service d'étude de navires de guerre rapides
S 9	Simulateurs
T 1	Simulateurs d'entraînement tactique
W 6	Soudure à l'arc, à l'arc en atmosphère d'argon ou au gaz
S 31	Sous-marins
S 32	Sous-marins (conventionnels)
M 2o	Stabilisateurs à poids mobiles
S 6	Stabilisateurs de navires
R 8	Statoréacteurs
S 33	Surchauffeurs
W 4	Systèmes d'armements
W 5	Systèmes d'armements (Composants de radar ultrasonique)
O 4	Systèmes et brûleurs de mazout
A 16	Systèmes de commande automatiques
M 10	Systèmes de commande de missiles
T 13	Systèmes de commande de torpilles
N 4	Systèmes d'huile combustible et brûleurs
A 1	Systèmes d'instruction pour le combat
M 12	Systèmes de lancement d'engins
L 4	Systèmes Laser
T 7	Systèmes télégraphiques
I 8	Tableaux à instruments
R 10	Télécommandes
R 9	Télémètres
L 3	Télémètres à Laser
T 8	Télémoteurs
T 10	Téléphone à haut-parleur
T 9	Téléphone sans pile
L 7	Torpilles et tubes lance-torpilles
T 18	Torpilles et tubes lance-torpilles
B 4	Transporteurs en vrac
X 1	Travaux aux rayons X
W 7	Treuils
A 9	Treuils à munitions
C 21	Tubes de condenseurs
C 1	Tubes pour câbles (avec ou sans)
T 23	Turbines
T 24	Turbines à gaz d'échappement
G 2	Turbines à gaz
T 25	Turbines à gaz marines
S 23	Turbines à vapeur
T 26	Turbines à vapeur marines
P 7	Tuyaux d'eau de mer
P 6	Tuyaux en cuivre et en laiton
V 3	Vannes automatiques à plaque ou à disque
V 1	Vannes et robinets
V 2	Vannes et robinets hydrauliques
M 18	Vedettes lance-torpilles
S 18	Vedettes rapides
A 6	Véhicules à coussin d'air
Y 1	Yachts (à moteur)

INSERENTEN-BRANCHENVERZEICHNIS

Die Verweisungszahl bei jedem nachstehend aufgeführten Gegenstand gibt die entsprechende englische Überschrift auf den Seiten 7 bis 31

A1 Aktionsübermittlungs-Schulungsgeräte
E13 Anfahr- und Abstellsteuerungen für Schiffsmaschinen
C3 Ankerwinden und Auflaufhaspeln
P15 Antriebsmaschinen
P12 Antriebsmittel
I1 Anzeigegeräte, Elektrische
L5 Aufzüge, hydraulische
T19 Ausbildungsgeräte
S9 Ausbildungsgeräte (Simulatoren)
F10 Ausrüstung, Schiffs-
C4 Autofähren
A16 Automatische Regelsysteme
A17 Automatische Steuerung
D9 Bagger
M1 Bearbeitete Eisenteile
M2 Bearbeitete Nichteisenteile
C23 Behälterschiffe
H2 Beheizte Fenster
T11 Beiboote
E5 Beleuchtungskörper (Armaturen)
S1 Bergungs- und Hafensperren-Verlegungsschiffe
F11 Biegsame Leitungsummantelungen
O4 Brennölanlagen und Brenner
F16 Brennöleinspritzanlagen
B3 Bücher (nautische)
B3a Bücher (nautische) vergriffen
C20 Computer
C19 Computer, Wartung und Verkauf
S22 Dampferzeugungsanlage, Atom-
S21 Dampferzeugungsanlage, herkömmlich
B2 Dampfkessel
S23 Dampfturbinen
D1 Deckmaschinenanlagen
D6 Dieselkraftstoffeinspritzanlagen
D4 Dieselmotoren, Hauptantriebs-
D3 Dieselmotoren, Hilfs-
D5 Dieselmotoren-Ersatzteile
D8 Docktore
P11 Druckgefäße
C17 Druckluftanlasser für Gasturbinen und Dieselmotoren
S15 Echolotausrüstungen
I4 Einspritzausrüstung
E1 Ekonomiser
E4 Elektroausrüstung
E3 Elektrohilfmaschinen
E8 Elektrohydraulische Zusatzgeräte
E6 Elektroinstallation und Reparatur
E2 Elektrokabel
E9 Elektronische Ausrüstung
E7 Elektroschaltanlagen
R9 Entfernungsmesser
F2 Entwerfen von schnellen Kriegsschiffen
R11 Ersatzteile für Dieselmotoren
F4 Fähren
F5 Faseroptik
G15 Ferngelenkte Flugkörper
G13 Ferngelenkte Flugkörper, Wartungsausrüstung
G14 Ferngelenkte Flugkörper-Schiffe
B1 Ferngläser
T6 Fernmeldeanlagen
R10 Fernsteuerungen
F8 Feuerleitungs- und Schießausrüstung
F7 Feuerlösch- und Bergungsfahrzeuge
F9 Feuerlöschpumpen
T20 Fischdampfer
R5 Flugfunk
M13 Flugkörper-Schiffe
A5 Flugzeuginstrumente
A3 Flugzeuglandebremsvorrichtungen
A4 Flugzeugträger

L7 Flüssiggasbehälter (Petroleum-)
R12 Forschungsschiffe
C7 Frachtraumüberwachungsgeräte
C6 Frachtschiffe
F15 Fregatten
F14 Frischwasserdestillieranlagen
R6 Funkanlagen
R7 Funksender und -empfänger
F13 Gabelstapler
G2 Gasturbinen
G1 Gasturbinenschiffe
E19 Geleitschiffe
G10 Generatoren, Elektro-
G17 Geschütze und Lafettierung
G18 Geschützlafetten
G19 Geschützrichtaufsätze und Höhensucher
G7 Getriebe, Rückwärts-, Reduktions-,
G3 Getriebegehäuse
G4 Getrieberäder und Getriebe
F6 Glasfaserboote und andere Erzeugnisse
B4 Großtransporter
C12 Gußeisenteile, Kugelgraphit
C13 Grußeisenteile, Kugelgraphit-, Ni-Resist
C8 Gußteile, Aluminium-Bronze-
C9 Gußteile, Hochfeste Eisen-
C11 Gußteile, maskengeformte
C10 Gußteile, Nichteisen-
C14 Gußteile, Stahl-
M6 Handelsschiffe
A18 Hilfsmaschinen
H4 Hovercraft (Luftkissenfahrzeuge)
H7 Hydraulische Anlagen
H5 Hydraulische Geräte
H6 Hydraulische Maschinen
G5 Hypoidgetriebe
I3 Infrarot-Werkstoffe
I6 Instrumente, Elektronische
I10 Instrumente für Versuchseinrichtungen
I7 Instrumente, Nautische
I9 Instrumente, Präzisions-
I8 Instrumententafeln
I5 Instrumententeile (Mechanische)
Y1 Jachten (Motor-)
C1 Kabelgeflechte (mit oder ohne)
W4 Kampfanlagen
W5 Kampfanlagen (Unterwasserortungsteile)
G16 Kanonenboote
G9 Keilriemenantriebe
P8 Kolben, Kolbenringe und Kolbenbolzen
O2 Kompressoren für ölfreie Luft
C26 Korvetten
C27 Kräne, Schiffs-
G20 Kreiselkompasse
C28 Kreuzer
W2 Kriegsschiffe
W1 Kriegsschiff-Reparaturbetriebe
C16 Küsten- und Flachwasser-Mininsuchboote
C5 Ladungsumschlageinrichtungen
L6 Lampen und Beleuchtung
L1 Lampenhalter (Fassungen)
A15 Landungsboote und -schiffe
A14 Landungsfahrzeuge
L2 Landungsfahrzeuge
L3 Laser-Entfernungsmesser
L4 Lasersysteme
L8 Lautsprecheranlagen
M12 Lenkwaffenabschußsysteme
M11 Lenkwaffenanlagen
A6 Luftkissenfahrzeuge
A8 Luftverdichter

N1	Marinegeschütze
N2	Marineradar
G11	Maschinenregler
M5	Materialverladeanlagen
M21	Mehrpolstecker
M7	Mikrophonanlagen
M8	Minenleger
M9	Minensuchboote
M14	Modellhersteller
M15	Modellschleppversuchsdienst
M17	Motoranlasser
S18	Motorboote
E12	Motordrehzahlregler
G12	Motordrehzahlregler
E17	Motoren, Dampfturbinen-
E15	Motoren, Diesel-
M19	Motoren, Elektro-
E16	Motoren, Gasturbinen-
M16	Motorkontrollanlagen
E10	Motorkontrollgeräte und Datenschreiber
E11	Motorteile, Diesel-
M18	Motortorpedoboote
A8	Munition
A9	Munitionsaufzüge
N4	Nachtsichtsysteme
N3	Navigationsanlagen
H9	Nautische Vermessungsgeräte
O1	Ölbohranlagen
O5	Optische Filter
A13	Panzerplatten
P2	Passagierschiffe
P3	Patrouillenschiffe, -Barkassen, -Beiboote und -Pinassen
F1	Patrouillenschnellboote
P5	Periskope
P4	Periskopverkleidungen
E18	Planetengetriebe
P10	Pontons, selbstfahrende
I2	Positionslampen
S5	Prüftische für Schiffsmagnetkompaß
P17	Pumpen
P18	Pumpen, Einzelteile
R2	Radar für Feuerleitung
R3	Radar für Hafenaufsicht
R4	Radar für Navigation, Warnung, Abfang
R1	Radarantennen
M10	Raketensteueranlagen
S11	Rauchmarkierungsvorrichtungen
P6	Rohre, Kupfer- und Messing-
P7	Rohre, Seewasser-
X1	Röntgenarbeiten
R13	Rückwärts-Reduktionsgetriebe, ölbetrieben
H3	Rudermelder
C24	Schaltpulte (elektrische)
S35	Schalttafeln, Schaltschränke
S36	Schalttafeln (Schaltschränke) und Schaltanlagen
F12	Scheinwerfer
S7	Schiffsanlagentechnik
S3	Schiffsbauer und Instandsetzungsbetriebe
I11	Schiffsinneneinrichtung und -ausbau
S4	Schiffsmaschinen
S8	Schiffsmessinggiesserei
P14	Schiffspropeller-Forschungsdienst
M4	Schiffsradar
S10	Schleifringe
T21	Schlepper
S6	Schlingerdämpfungsanlagen
P13	Schrauben, Schiffs-
W6	Schweissen, elektrisch, Argon-Lichtbogen-oder Gas-
C2	Senkkästen
S28	Spannungsentlastung
F3	Speisewasservorwärmer
G6	Spiralzahnkegelrad
M20	Stabilisieranlagen mit verschiebbaren Massen
S19	Stabilisierungsanlagen
S20	Stabilisierungsanlagen für Feuerleitung
R16	Stabilisierungsflossen
S26	Stahl, Mangan-, widerstandsfähig gegen Abnutzung
S24	Stahl- und Speziallegierungen
S25	Stahlschmiedestücke, -platten und -teile, Preßstücke
R8	Staustrahlturbinen
S12	Steckdosen und Stecker, elektrische, wasserdicht
S13	Steckdosen und Stecker, mehrpolige Typen
S14	Stecker
P9	Stecker und Steckdosen
C25	Steuer- (Regelungs-) Anlagen
S27	Steuergeräte
R17	Steuerruder
G8	Stirnräder
N5	Suchboote für Nichtmagnetminen
T4	Tanks, Öl- und Wasservorrats-
T2	Tankschiffe
T3	Tankschiffe (klein)
D7	Tauchausrüstung
T5	Technische Veröffentlichungen
P1	Teile für Dieselmotoren
T7	Telegraphenanlagen
T8	Telemotoren
T9	Telephone, batterielose
T10	Telephone, Lautsprecher-
T12	Testgeräte für Feuerleitungsanlagen
T14	Torpedobootbauer
T18	Torpedos und Torpedorohre
T17	Torpedo-Seitenabschußvorrichtungen
T13	Torpedosteuersysteme
T16	Torpedosteuerungs und -abweichungskontrolle
T15	Torpedo-Tiefen- und Schlingeraufzeichner
H8	Tragflächenboote
O3	Treibölvorwärmer
E14	Triebwerke, Flugzeug-
D11	Trockendockinhaber
D10	Trockenfrachter
T23	Turbinen
T24	Turbinen, Auspuff-
T26	Turbinen, Schiffs-Dampf-
T25	Turbinen, Schiffs-Gas-
T22	Turbinenvorgelege
S33	Überhitzer
A10	U-Bootabwehrboote
A12	U-Bootabwehrraketen
A11	U-Bootabwehr-Raketenabschußvorrichtungen
S29	U-Boot-Feuerleitung
S30	U-Boot-Periskope
R15	Umkehrgetriebe
R14	Umkehrmotoren, dampf- und luftbetrieben
S31	Unterseeboote
S32	Unterseeboote (herkömmlich)
U2	Unterwasserfernsehgeräte
S16	Unterwasser-Schallmessanlagen, Rumpfeinbauten und hydraulische Einrichtungen für
U1	Unterwasserscheinwerfer
V3	Ventile, automatische Platten- und Teller-
V1	Ventile und Absperrvorrichtungen
V2	Ventile und Absperrvorrichtungen, hydraulische
C18	Verdichter
C22	Verflüssiger
C21	Verflüssigerrohre
P16	Verleger
S34	Vermessungsgeräte
O6	Waffen
H1	Wärmeaustauscher
M3	Wartungs- und Reparaturschiffe
W3	Wasserröhrenkessel
I12	Wechselrichter und Batterieladegeräte
A7	Wechselstromerzeuger
W7	Winden
S2	Wissenschaftliche Instrumente
C15	Zentralisierte und automatische Steuerung
D2	Zerstörer

D 4. DIESEL ENGINES, MAIN PROPULSION

Blohm + Voss AG
C.R.M., Fabbrica Motori Marini
A/S Horten Verft
Hawker Siddeley Group
Korody-Colyer Corporation
Korody Marine Corporation
Maybach Mercedes-Benz Motorenbau GmbH
Netherlands United Shipbuilding Bureaux Ltd.
SACM de Mulhouse
Vickers Limited

D 5. DIESEL ENGINE SPARE PARTS

Blohm + Voss AG
C.R.M., Fabbrica Motori Marini
Hawker Siddeley Group
A/S Horten Verft
Korody-Colyer Corporation
Korody Marine Corporation
Fr. Lürssen Wefrt
Maybach Mercedes-Benz Motorenbau GmbH
Netherlands United Shipbuilding Bureaux Ltd.
SACM de Mulhouse

D 6. DIESEL FUEL INJECTION EQUIPMENT

Korody-Colyer Corporation
Korody Marine Corporation

D 7. DIVING EQUIPMENT

Korody Marine Corporation

D 8. DOCK GATES

Vickers Limited
Vosper Thornycroft Group, The

D 9. DREDGERS

Brooke Marine Ltd.

D 10. DRY CARGO VESSELS

Blohm + Voss AG
Boatservice Ltd. A/S
Brooke Marine Ltd.
A/S Horten Verft
Fr. Lürssen Werft
Todd Shipyards Corporation
Vickers Limited
Yarrow (Shipbuilders) Ltd.

D 11. DRY DOCK PROPRIETORS

Blohm + Voss AG
A/S Horten Verft
Karlskronavarvet AB
Netherlands United Shipbuilding Bureaux Ltd.
Vickers Limited

E 1. ECONOMISERS

Netherlands United Shipbuilding Bureaux Ltd.
Yarrow & Co. Ltd.

E 2. ELECTRIC CABLES

Hawker Siddeley Group

E 3. ELECTRICAL AUXILIARIES

Electro-Dymanic Construction Co. Ltd.
Hawker Siddeley Group
Laurence Scott & Electromotors Ltd.
Vosper Thornycroft Group, The

E 4. ELECTRICAL EQUIPMENT

Columbia Electronics International, Inc.
Electro-Dynamic Construction Co. Ltd.
Hawker Siddeley Group
Laurence Scott & Electromotors Ltd.
McGeoch & Co. (Birmingham) Ltd., William
Plessey Company Limited, The
Vosper Thornycroft Group, The
Whipp & Bourne Ltd.

E 5. ELECTRICAL FITTINGS

McGeoch & Co. (Birmingham) Ltd., William
Vosper Thornycroft Group, The

E 6. ELECTRICAL INSTALLATIONS AND REPAIRS

Hawker Siddeley Group
A/S Horten Verft
Karlskronavarvet AB
Vosper Thornycroft Group, The
Yarrow (Shipbuilders) Ltd.

E 7. ELECTRICAL SWITCHGEAR

Hawker Siddeley Group
Laurence, Scott & Electromotors Ltd.
McGeoch & Co. (Birmingham) Ltd., William
Whipp & Bourne Ltd.

E 8. ELECTRO-HYDRAULIC AUXILIARIES

MacTaggart, Scott & Co. Ltd.
Sperry Gyroscope Division
Western Gear Corporation
Vosper Thornycroft Group, The

E 9. ELECTRONIC EQUIPMENT

Barr & Stroud Ltd.
British Aircrft Corporation
British Hovercraft Corporation Ltd.
Columbia Electronics International, Inc.
Decca Radar Ltd.
Edo Corporation
Ferranti Limited
General Precision Inc.—Librascope Group
Korody Marine Corporation
Laurence Scott & Electromotors Ltd.
Marconi Co. Ltd., The
McGeoch & Co. (Birmingham) Ltd., William
Nord Aviation
Plessey Company Limited, The
Sperry Gyroscope Division
Vosper Thornycroft Group, The

E 10 ENGINE MONITORS AND DATA LOGGERS

Decca Radar Ltd.
Maybach Mercedes Benz Motorenbau GmbH
Sperry Gyroscope Division
Vosper Thornycroft Group, The

E 11. ENGINE PARTS, DIESEL

C.R.M., Fabbrica Motori Marini
Hawker Siddeley Group
A/S Horton Vert
Korody-Colyer Corporation
Korody Marine Corporation
Maybach Mercedes-Benz Motorenbau GmbH
Netherlands United Shipbuilding Bureaux Ltd.
SACM de Mulhouse

E 12. ENGINE SPEED CONTROLS

Vosper Thornycroft Group, The

E 13. ENGINE START AND SHUT-DOWN CONTROLS

Elliott Brothers (London) Ltd., Naval Division
Vosper Thornycroft Group, The

E 14. ENGINES, AIRCRAFT

Maybach Mercedes Benz Motorenbau GmbH
Rolls-Royce Ltd.

E 15. ENGINES, DIESEL

Blohm + Voss AG
Coventry Climax Engines Ltd.
C.R.M., Fabbrica Motori Marini
Fiat
Hawker Siddeley Group
A/S Horton Verft
Korody-Colyer Corporation
Korody Marine Corporation
Maybach Mercedes-Benz Motorenbau GmbH
Netherlands United Shipbuilding Bureaux Ltd.
SACM de Mulhouse
Vickers Limited

E 16. ENGINES, GAS TURBINE

Rolls-Royce Ltd.

E 17. ENGINES, STEAM TURBINE

Blohm + Voss AG
A/S Horten Verft
Netherlands United Shipbuilding Bureaux Ltd.
Vickers Limited
Yarrow & Co. Ltd.

E 18. EPICYCLIC GEARS

Barr & Stroud Ltd.
Vickers Limited
Western Gear Corporation
Zahnradfabrik Friedrichshafen AG

E 19. ESCORT VESSELS

Blohm + Voss AG
Brooke Marine Ltd.
A/S Horten Verft
Fr. Lürssen Werft
Netherlands United Shipbuilding Bureaux Ltd.
Vickers Limited
Vosper Thornycroft Group, The
Yarrow (Shipbuilders) Ltd.

F 1. FAST PATROL BOATS

Boatservice Ltd. A/S
British Hovercraft Corporation
Brooke Marine Ltd.
Cantiere Rodriquez
Karlskronavarvet AB
Korody Marine Corporation
Fr. Lürssen Werft
Netherlands United Shipbuilding Bureaux Ltd.
Vosper Thornycroft Group, The
Yarrow & Co., Ltd.

F 2. FAST WARSHIP DESIGN SERVICE

Brooke Marine Ltd.
Karlskronavarvet AB
Vosper Thornycroft Group, The
Yarrow (Shipbuilders) Ltd.

F 3. FEED WATER HEATERS

Blohm + Voss AG
Vickers Limited
Yarrow & Co. Ltd.

F 4. FERRIES

British Hovercraft Corporation
Brooke Marine Ltd.
Vosper Thornycroft Group, The
Yarrow (Shipbuilders) Ltd.

F 5. FIBRE OPTICS

Barr & Stroud Ltd.
Ferranti Ltd.

F 6. FIBREGLASS VESSELS AND OTHER PRODUCTS

Blohm + Voss AG
Boatservice Ltd. A/S
Karlskronavarvet AB
Korody Marine Corporation
Netherlands United Shipbuilding Bureaux Ltd.
Vosper Thornycroft Group, The
Yarrow (Shipbuilders) Ltd.

F 7. FIRE AND SALVAGE VESSELS

Brooke Marine Ltd.
Cantiere Rodriquez
Karlskronavarvet AB
Yarrow (Shipbuilders) Ltd.

F 8. FIRE CONTROL AND GUNNERY EQUIPMENT

Barr & Stroud Ltd.
AB Bofors
Contraves AG
Elliott Brothers (London) Ltd.
Ferranti Limited
General Precision Inc.—Librascope Group
Hollandse Signaalapparaten N.V.
Laurence, Scott & Electromotors Ltd.
Marconi Co. Ltd., The
Plessey Company Limited, The
Sperry Gyroscope Division
Vickers Limited

F 9. FIRE PUMPS

Coventry Climax Engines Ltd.

F 10. FITTINGS, SHIP

McGeoch & Co. (Birmingham) Ltd., William
Vickers Limited

F 11. FLEIBLE CONDUIT COVERINGS

McGeoch & Co. (Birmingham) Ltd., William

F 12. FLOODLIGHTS

Korody Marine Corporation
McGeoch & Co. (Birmingham) Ltd. William

F 13. FORK LIFT TRUCKS

Coventry Climax Engines Ltd.
Hawker Siddeley Group

F 14. FRESH WATER DISTILLING PLANT

Netherlands United Shipbuilding Bureaux Ltd.

F 15. FRIGATES

Blohm + Voss AG
Brooke Marine Ltd.
A/S Horten Verft
Fr. Lürssen Werft
Netherlands United Shipbuilding Bureaux Ltd.
Vickers Limited
Vosper Thornycroft Group, The
Yarrow (Shipbuilders) Ltd.

F 16. FUEL OIL INJECTORS

Korody-Colyer Corporation
Korody Marine Corporation

G 1. GAS TURBINE BOATS

Blohm + Voss AG
Boatservice A/S
British Hovercraft
Brooke Marine Ltd.
Netherlands United Shipbuilding Bureaux Ltd.
Vosper Thornycroft Group, The
Yarrow (Shipbuilders) Ltd.

G 2. GAS TURBINES

Rolls-Royce Ltd.
Yarrow & Co. Ltd.

G 3. GEAR CASINGS

Vickers Limited
Yarrow & Co. Ltd.

SPERRY RAND
SPERRY IN ITS ELEMENT...
Fighting Ships' Systems
Seaslug 1 and 2 control
Seacat – shipborne control
Ikara – gyro equipment
Martel – gyro equipment
Automatic check-out equipment
Safety and Arming devices
Gunfire control systems
Integrated Systems
SINS (Ships Inertial Navigation Systems)
Gyro Compass Systems and Repeaters
Gyropilots
Central computer and back-up stores
Tracking and Surveillance Radar (including ESR)
LORAN
Engine Room Monitors
Data Loggers
Ships' Stabilisers
SPERRY
GYROSCOPE DIVISION
BRACKNELL BERKS ENGLAND

G 4. GEARS AND GEARING
Barr & Stroud Ltd.
Laurence, Scott & Electromotors Ltd.
Netherlands United Shipbuilding Bureaux Ltd.
Vickers Limited
Vosper Thornycroft Group, The
Western Gear Corporation
Yarrow & Co. Ltd.
Zahnradfabrik Friedrichshafen AG

G 5. GEARS—HYPOID
Barr & Stroud Ltd.
Western Gear Corporation

G 6. GEARS—SPIRAL BEVEL
Vosper Thornycroft Group, The
Western Gear Corporation

G 7. GEARS, REVERSE-REDUCTION
Korody-Colyer Corporation
Maybach Mercedes-Benz Motorenbau GmbH
Netherlands United Shipbuilding Bureaux Ltd.
Vickers Limited
Vosper Thornycroft Group, The
Zahnradfabrik Friedrichshafen AG

G 8. GEARS—SPUR
Barr & Stroud Ltd.

G 9. GEARS, VEE DRIVE
Vosper Thornycroft Group, The

G 10. GENERATORS, ELECTRIC
Columbia Electronics International, Inc.
Electro-Dynamic Construction Co. Ltd.
Laurence, Scott & Electromotors Ltd.

G 11. GOVERNORS
Korody-Colyer Corporation

G 12. GOVERNORS, ENGINE SPEED
Electro Dynamic Construction Co. Ltd.
Korody-Colyer Corporation

G 13. GUIDED MISSILE SERVICING EQUIPMENT
Karlskronavarvet AB
Fr. Lürssen Werft
Nord Aviation

G 14. GUIDED MISSILE SHIPS
Blohm + Voss AG
British Hovercraft Corporation
Brooke Marine Ltd.
Netherlands United Shipbuilding Bureaux Ltd.
Nord Aviation
Vickers Limited
Vosper Thornycroft Group, The
Yarrow (Shipbuilders) Ltd.

G 15. GUIDED MISSILES
British Aircraft Corporation
Contraves AG
Hawker Siddeley Group
Nord Aviation

G 16. GUN BOATS
Boatservice Ltd. A/S
Brooke Marine Ltd.
Cantiere Rodriquez
Karlskronavarvet AB
Fr. Lürssen Werft
Netherlands United Shipbuilding Bureaux Ltd.
Vickers Limited
Vosper Thornycroft Group, The
Yarrow (Shipbuilders) Ltd.

G 17. GUNS AND MOUNTINGS
AB Bofors
Contraves AG
F.M.C. Northern Ordnance Division
Vickers Limited

G 18. GUN MOUNTS
AB Bofors
F.M.C., Northern Ordnance Division

G 19. GUN-SIGHTING APARATUS AND HEIGHT FINDERS
Barr & Stroud Ltd.
British Aircraft Corporation
General Precision Inc.—Librascope Group.

G 20. GYROSCOPIC COMPASSES
British Aircraft Corporation
Ferranti Ltd.
Hawker Siddeley Group
Sperry Gyroscope Corporation

H 1. HEAT EXCHANGERS
Blohm + Voss AG
Vosper Thornycroft Group, The

H 2. HEATED WINDOWS
Barr & Stroud Ltd.

H 3. HELM INDICATORS
Hawker Siddeley Group
Sperry Gyroscope Division

H 4. HOVERCRAFT
British Hovercraft Corporation Ltd.
Vosper Thornycroft Group, The

H 5. HYDRAULIC EQUIPMENT
MacTaggart, Scott & Co. Ltd.
Vosper Thornycroft Group, The

H 6. HYDRAULIC MACHINERY
MacTaggart, Scott & Co. Ltd.
Vickers Limited
Vosper Thornycroft Group, The

H 7. HYDRAULIC PLANT
MacTaggart, Scott & Co. Ltd.

H 8. HYDROFOILS
Blohm + Voss AG
Cantiere Rodriquez

H 9. HYDROGRAPHIC SURVEY EQUIPMENT
Laurence, Scott & Electromotors Ltd.
Plessey Company Limited, The

I 1. INDICATORS, ELECTRIC
McGeoch & Co. (Birmingham) Ltd., William

I 2. INDICATORS, NAVIGATION LIGHT
McGeoch & Co. (Birmingham) Ltd., William

I 3. INFRA-RED MATERIALS
Barr & Stroud Ltd.

I 4. INJECTORS
Korody-Colyer Corporation
Korody Marine Corporation

I 5. INSTRUMENT COMPONENTS (MECHANICAL)
Columbia Electronics International, Inc.
Laurence, Scott & Electromotors Ltd.

I 6. INSTRUMENTS, ELECTRONIC
AB Bofors
British Aircraft Corporation
British Hovercraft Corporation
Columbia Electronics International, Inc.
Barr & Stroud Ltd.
Decca Radar Ltd.
Ferranti Limited
Korody Marine Corporation
Laurence, Scott & Electromotors Ltd.
Plessey Company Limited, The
Sperry Gyroscope Division
Vosper Thornycroft Group, The

I 7. INSTRUMENTS, NAUTICAL
Columbia Electronics International, Inc.
Hawker Siddeley Group
Plessey Company Limited, The

I 8. INSTRUMENT PANELS
Laurence, Scott & Electormotors Ltd.
Vosper Thornycroft Group, The

I 9. INSTRUMENTS, PRECISION
Barr & Stroud Ltd.
British Aircraft Corporation
Ferranti Limited
Hawker Siddeley Group
Laurence, Scott & Electromotors Ltd.

I 10. INSTRUMENTS, TEST EQUIPMENT
British Aircraft Corporation
Columbia Electronics International, Inc.
Ferranti Ltd.
Hollandse Signaalapparaten N.V.
Korody-Colyer Corporation
Laurence, Scott & Electromotors Ltd.
Sperry Gyroscope Division

I 11. INTERIOR DESIGN AND FURNISHING FOR SHIPS
Blohm + Voss AG
Brooke Marine Ltd.
Vosper Thornycroft Group, The

I 12. INVERTERS AND BATTERY CHARGERS
Electro-Dynamic Construction Co. Ltd.
Vosper Thornycroft Group, The

L 1. LAMPHOLDERS
McGeoch & Co. (Birmingham) Ltd. William

L 2. LANDING CRAFT
British Hovercraft Corporation
Brooke Marine Ltd.
Karlskronavarvet AB
Korody Marine Corporation
Netherlands United Shipbuilding Bureaux Ltd.
Vickers Limited
Yarrow (Shipbuilders) Ltd.

L 3. LASER RANGEFINDERS
Barr & Stroud Ltd.

L 4. LASER SYSTEMS
Barr & Stroud Ltd.
Ferranti Ltd.

L 5. LIFTS—HYDRAULIC
MacTaggart Scott & Co. Ltd.

L 6. LIGHTS AND LIGHTING
Hawker Siddeley Group
Korody Marine Corporation
McGeoch & Co. (Birmingham) Ltd. William

L 7. LIQUID PETROLEUM GAS CARRIERS
Vickers Limited

L 8. LOUDSPEAKER EQUIPMENT
Korody Marine Corporation

M 1. MACHINED PARTS, FERROUS
Blohm + Voss AG
Vickers Limited
Vosper Thornycroft Group, The
Yarrow & Co. Ltd.

M 2. MACHINED PARTS, NON-FERROUS
Barr & Stroud Ltd.
Blohm + Voss AG
Harland and Wolff Limited
Vickers Limited
Vosper Thornycroft Group, The
Yarrow & Co. Ltd.

M 3. MAINTENANCE AND REPAIR SHIPS
Brooke Marine Ltd.
Fr. Lürssen Werft
Vosper Thornycroft Group, The

M 4. MARINE RADAR
Decca Radar Limited
Marconi Co. Ltd., The
Sperry Gyroscope Division

M 5. MATERIALS HANDLING EQUIPMENT
British Hovercraft Corporation
Coventry Climax Engines Ltd.
Decca Radar Ltd.
MacTaggart, Scott & Co. Ltd.
Western Gear Corporation
Vickers Limited

M 6. MERCHANT SHIPS
Blohm + Voss AG
Boatservice Ltd. A/S
Brooke Marine Ltd.
A/S Horten Verft
Fr. Lürssen Werft
Marinens Hovedverft
Todd Shipyards Corporation
Vickers Limited
Yarrow (Shipbuilders) Ltd.

M 7. MICROPHONE EQUIPMENT
Columbia Electronics International, Inc.
Hawker Siddeley Group

M 8. MINE LAYERS
Blohm + Voss AG
Boatservice Ltd. A/S
British Hovercraft Corporation
Brooke Marine Ltd.
A/S Horten Verft
Karlskronavarvet AB
Netherlands United Shipbuilding Bureaux Ltd.
Vosper Thornycroft Group, The
Yarrow (Shipbuilders) Ltd.

M 9. MINESWEEPERS
Blohm + Voss AG
Boatservice Ltd. A/S
Brooke Marine Ltd.
Karlskronavarvet AB
Netherlands United Shipbuilding Bureaux Ltd.
Vosper Thornycroft Group, The
Yarrow (Shipbuilders) Ltd.

M 10. MISSILE CONTROL SYSTEMS
British Aircraft Corporation
Decca Radar Ltd.
Elliott Brothers (London) Ltd., Naval Division
Ferranti Ltd.
Hollandse Signaalapparaten N.V.
Marconi Co. Ltd., The
Nord Aviation
Sperry Gyroscope Division

M 11. MISSILE INSTALLATIONS
British Aircraft Corporation
Elliott Brothers (London) Ltd., Naval Division
Nord Aviation
Vosper Thornycroft Group, The

M 12. MISSILE LAUNCHING SYSTEMS
British Aircraft Corporation
F.M.C., Northern Ordnance Division
Nord Aviation

M22 weapon control system on board Royal Swedish Navy 'Spica' class MTB.

M20

Signaal's integrated weapon control systems:

ultimate compactness

Each weapon control system of the M 20 family is designed for use on board ships ranging from motorgun-boats up to destroyers. An M 20 is an autonomous weapon cell. Depending on its configuration, it controls guns, torpedoes and/or guided weapons simultaneously. Air and surface targets can be handled at the same time. The spherical radome, which covers the fully stabilized warning and tracking antenna system is now characteristic in a large number of navies.

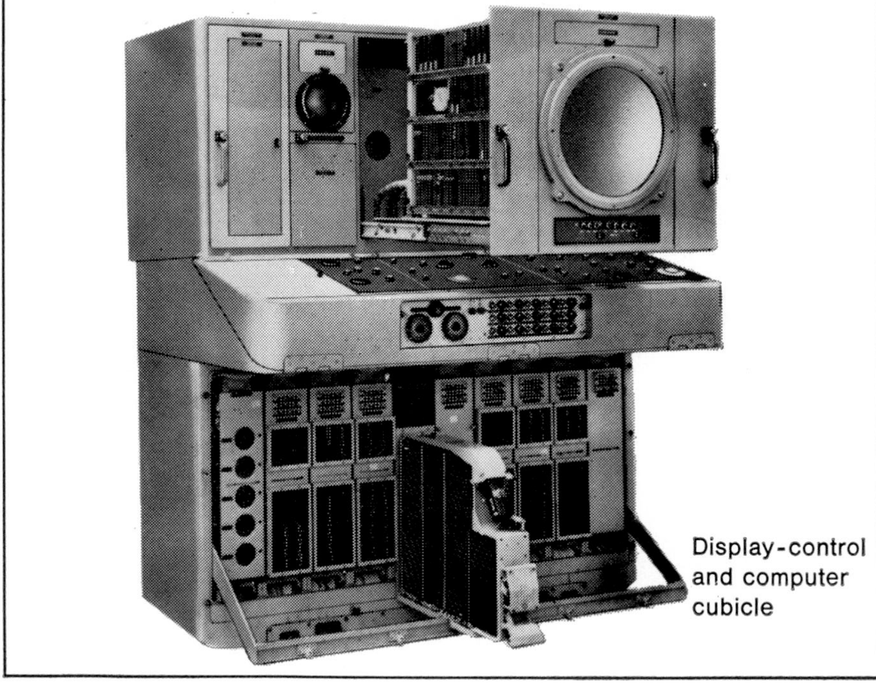

Display-control and computer cubicle

SIGNAAL

radar, weapon control, data handling and air traffic control systems

N.V. HOLLANDSE SIGNAALAPPARATEN HENGELO

M 13. MISSILE SHIPS

Blohm + Voss AG
Brooke Marine Ltd.
Fr. Lürssen Werft
Netherlands United Shipbuilding Bureaux Ltd.
Vickers Limited
Vosper Thornycroft Group, The
Yarrow (Shipbuilders) Ltd.

M 14. MODELMAKERS

Vickers Limited
Vosper Thornycroft Group, The
Yarrow (Shipbuilders) Ltd.

M 15. MODEL TEST TOWING TANK SERVICE

Vosper Thornycroft Group, The

M 16. MOTOR CONTROL GEAR

Electro-Dynamic Construction Co. Ltd.
Laurence, Scott & Electromotors, Ltd.
McGeoch & Co. (Birmingham) Ltd., William
Vosper Thornycroft Group, The

M 17. MOTOR STARTERS

Electro-Dynamic Construction Co. Ltd.
Laurence, Scott & Electromotors Ltd.
McGeouch & Co. (Birmingham) Ltd., William
Vosper Thornycroft Group, The

M 18. MOTOR TORPEDO BOATS

Boatservice Ltd. A/S
British Hovercraft Corporation
Brooke Marine Ltd.
Cantiere Rodriquez
Karlskronavarvet AB
Fr. Lürssen Werft
Vosper Thornycroft Group, The
Yarrow (Shipbuilders) Ltd.

M 19. MOTORS, ELECTRIC

Electro-Dynamic Construction Co. Ltd.
Ferranti Limited
Hawker Siddeley Group
Laurence, Scott & Electromotors Ltd.

M 20. MOVING WEIGHT STABILISERS

Vosper Thornycroft Group, The

M 21. MULTI PLAN PLUGS

McGeoch & Co. (Birmingham) Ltd., William

N 1. NAVAL GUNS

AB Bofors
Contraves AG
F.M.C., Northern Ordnance Division
Vickers Limited

N 2. NAVAL RADAR

Decca Radar Limited
Hollandse Signaalapparaten N.V.
Marconi Co. Ltd., The
Plessey Company Limited, The
Sperry Gyroscope Division

N 3. NAVIGATION AIDS

Barr & Stroud Ltd.
British Aircraft Corporation
Columbia Electronics International, Inc.
Decca Navigator Co. Ltd., The
Decca Radar Limited
Elliott Brothers (London) Ltd., Naval Division
Ferranti Limited
Hawker Siddeley Group
Laurence, Scott & Electromotors Ltd.
McGeoch & Co. (Birmingham) Ltd., William
Marconi Co. Ltd., The
Plessey Company Limited, The
Sperry Gyroscope Division

N 4. NIGHT VISION SYSTEMS

Barr & Stroud Ltd.

N 5. NON-MAGNETIC MINESWEEPERS

Boatservice Ltd. A/S
Karlskronavarvet AB
Netherlands United Shipbuilding Bureaux Ltd.
Vosper Thornycroft Group, The

O 1. OIL DRILLING RIGS

Karlskronavarvet AB

O 2. 'OILFREE' COMPRESSORS

Hawker Siddeley Group

O 3. OIL FUEL HEATERS

Blohm + Voss AG
Vosper Thornycroft Group, The

O 4. OIL FUEL SYSTEMS AND BURNERS

Todd Shipyards Corporation
Vosper Thornycroft Group, The

O 5. OPTICAL FILTERS

Barr & Stroud Ltd.

O 6. ORDNANCE

AB Bofors
F.M.C., Northern Ordnance Division
Vickers Limited

P 1. PARTS FOR DIESEL ENGINES

Blohm + Voss AG
C.R.M., Fabbrica Motori Marini
Hawker Siddeley Group
A/S Horten Verft
Korody-Colyer Corporation
Korody Marine Corporation
Maybach Mercedes-Benz Motorenbau GmbH
Netherlands United Shipbuilding Bureaux Ltd.
SACM de Mulhouse

P 2. PASSENGER SHIPS

Blohm + Voss AG
Boatservice Ltd. A/S
Brooke Marine Ltd.
Cantiere Rodriquez
Vickers Limited
Vosper Thornycroft Group, The
Yarrow (Shipbuilders) Ltd.

P 3. PATROL BOATS, LAUNCHES, TENDERS AND PINNACES

Boatservice Ltd. A/S
British Hovercraft Corporation
Brooke Marine Ltd.
Cantiere Rodriquez
Karlskronavarvet AG
Korody Marine Corporation
Fr. Lürssen Werft
Netherlands United Shipbuilding Bureaux Ltd.
Vosper Thornycroft Group, The
Yarrow (Shipbuilders) Ltd.

P 4. PERISCOPE FAIRINGS

Edo Corporation
MacTaggart, Scott & Co. Ltd.

P 5. PERISCOPES

Barr & Stroud Ltd.

P 6. PIPES, COPPER AND BRASS

Vickers Limited

P 7. PIPES, SEA WATER

Vickers Limited

P 8. PISTONS, PISTON RINGS, AND GUDGEON PINS

Korody-Colyer Corporation

P 9. PLUGS AND SOCKETS
Ferranti Limited
McGeoch & Co. (Birmingham) Ltd., William

P 10. PONTOONS, SELF PROPELLED
Brooke Marine Ltd.

P 11. PRESSURE VESSELS
Netherlands United Shipbuilding Bureaux Ltd.
Vickers Limited
Vosper Thornycroft Group, The
Yarrow & Co. Ltd.

P 12. PROPELLENTS
AB Bofors

P 13. PROPELLERS, SHIPS'
AB Bofors

P 14. PROPELLERS, SHIPS'—RESEARCH
Vosper Thornycroft Group, The

P 15. PROPULSION MACHINERY
Blohm + Voss AG
A/S Horten Verft
Korody-Colyer Corporation
Korody Marine Corporation
Laurence, Scott & Electromotors Ltd.
Maybach Mercedes-Benz Motorbauen GmbH
Netherlands United Shipbuilding Bureaux Ltd.
Rolls-Royce Ltd.
Vickers Limited
Yarrow & Co. Ltd.

P 16. PUBLISHERS
Anthiel Booksellers
B.P.C. Publishing Ltd.
McGraw-Hill Book Company
Sampson Low, Marston & Co. Ltd.

P 17. PUMPS
F.M.C., Northern Ordnance Division
Hawker Siddeley Group
MacTaggart, Scott & Co. Ltd.
Western Gear Corporation
Vickers Limited

P 18. PUMPS, COMPONENT PARTS
F.M.C., Northern Ordnance Division

R 1. RADAR AERIALS
Barr & Stroud Ltd.
British Aircraft Corporation
Decca Radar Limited
Hollandse Signaalaparaten N.V.
Marconi Co. Ltd., The
Plessey Company Limited, The
Sperry Gyroscope Division

R 2. RADAR FOR FIRE CONTROL
Contraves AG
Decca Radar Ltd.
Ferranti Ltd.
Hollandse Signaalapparaten N.V.
Marconi Co. Ltd., The
Sperry Gyroscope Division

R 3. RADAR FOR HARBOUR SUPERVISION
Decca Radar Limited
Ferranti Ltd.
Marconi Co. Ltd., The
Sperry Gyroscope Division

R 4. RADAR FOR NAVIGATION WARNING INTERCEPTION
Columbia Electronics International, Inc.
Decca Radar Limited
Ferranti Ltd.
Hollandse Signaalapparaten N.V.
Marconi Co. Ltd., The
Plessey Company Limited, The
Sperry Gyroscope Division

R 5. RADIO, AIR
Columbia Electronics International, Inc.
Marconi Co. Ltd., The
Plessey Company Limited, The

R 6. RADIO EQUIPMENT
Columbia Electronics International, Inc.
Marconi Co. Ltd., The
Plessey Company Limited, The

R 7. RADIO TRANSMITTERS AND RECEIVERS
Columbia Electronics International, Inc.
Elliott Brothers (London) Ltd., Naval Division
Imhof Ltd., Alfred
Marconi Co. Ltd., The
Plessey Company Limited, The

R 8. RAMJETS
Nord Aviation
Rolls-Royce Ltd.

R 9. RANGEFINDERS
Barr & Stroud Ltd.

R 10. REMOTE CONTROLS
Plessey Company Limited, The
Sperry Gyroscope Division
Vosper Thornycroft Group, The

R 11. REPLACEMENT PARTS FOR DIESEL ENGINES
Blohm + Voss AG
C.R.M., Fabbrica Motori Marini
Hawker Siddeley Group
A/S Horten Verft
Korody-Colyer Corporation
Korody Marine Corporation
Maybach Mercedes-Benz Motorenbau GmbH
Netherlands United Shipbuilding Bureaux Ltd.
SACM de Mulhouse

R 12. RESEARCH SHIPS
Brooke Marine Ltd.
Karlskronavarvet AB
Fr. Lürssen Werft
Vosper Thornycroft Group, The
Yarrow (Shipbuilders) Ltd.

R 13. REVERSE REDUCTION GEARS, OIL OPERATED
C.R.M., Fabbrica Motori Marini
Korody-Colyer Corporation
Maybach Mercedes-Benz Motorenbau GmbH
Vosper Thornycroft Group, The
Western Gear Corporation
Zahnradfabrik Friedrichshafen AG

R 14. REVERSING ENGINES, STEAM AND AIR OPERATED
MacTaggart, Scott & Co. Ltd.

R 15. REVERSING GEARS
C.R.M., Fabbrica Motori Marini
Korody-Colyer Corporation
Maybach Mercedes-Benz Motorenbau GmbH
Vosper Thornycroft Group, The
Western Gear Corporation
Zahnradfabrik Friedrichshafen AG

R 16. ROLL DAMPING FINS
Blohm + Voss AG
Vosper Thornycroft Group, The
Sperry Gyroscope Division

R 17. RUDDERS
Karlskronavarvet AB
Yarrow (Shipbuilders) Ltd.

S 1. SALVAGE AND BOOM VESSELS
Brooke Marine Ltd.
Vosper Thornycroft Group, The
Yarrow (Shipbuilders) Ltd.

S 2. SCIENTIFIC INSTRUMENTS
Barr & Stroud Ltd.
Decca Radar Ltd.
Ferranti Limited

S 3. SHIP BUILDERS AND SHIP REPAIRERS
Blohm + Voss AG
Boatservice Ltd. A/S
Brooke Marine Ltd.
Cantiere Rodriquez
A/S Horten Verft
Karlskronavarvet AB
Fr. Lürssen Wefrt
Netherlands United Shipbuilding Bureaux Ltd.
Todd Shipyards Corporation
Vickers Limited
Vosper Thornycroft Group, The
Yarrow (Shipbuilders) Ltd.

S 4. SHIP MACHINERY
Blohm + Voss AG
A/S Horten Verft
Maybach Mercedes-Benz Motorenbau GmbH
Netherlands United Shipbuilding Bureaux Ltd.
Rolls-Royce Ltd.
Vickers Limited
Yarrow & Co. Ltd.

S 5. SHIPS MAGNETIC COMPASS TEST TABLES
Barr & Stroud Ltd.

S 6. SHIP STABILISERS
Blohm + Voss AG
Sperry Gyroscope Division
Vosper Thornycroft Group, The

S 7. SHIP SYSTEMS ENGINEERING
Hawker Siddeley Group
Netherlands United Shipbuilding Bureaux Ltd.
Sperry Gyroscope Division
Vosper Thornycroft Group, The
Yarrow & Co. Ltd.

S 8. SHIPS' BRASSFOUNDRY
McGeoch & Co. (Birmingham) Ltd., William

S 9. SIMULATORS
Elliott Brothers (London) Ltd., Naval Division
Elliott Brothers (London) Ltd., Trainer & Simulator Division
Ferranti Limited
Laurence, Scott & Electromotors Ltd.
Sperry Gyroscope Division
Vosper Thornycroft Group, The

S 10. SLIP RING ASSEMBLIES
McGeoch & Co. (Birmingham) Ltd., William

S 11. SMOKE INDICATORS
Barr & Stroud Ltd.

S 12. SOCKETS AND PLUGS, ELECTRIC WATERTIGHT
McGeoch & Co. (Birmingham) Ltd., William
Western Gear Corporation

S 13. SOCKETS AND PLUGS, MULTI PIN PATTERNS
McGeoch & Co. (Birmingham) Ltd., William

S 14. SOCKET TERMINATIONS
McGeoch & Co. (Birmingham) Ltd., William

S 15. SONAR EQUIPMENT
British Aircraft Corporation
Columbia Electronics International, Inc.
Edo Corporation
Decca Radar Ltd.
Elliott Brothers (London) Ltd., Naval Division
Plessey Company Limited, The
Sperry Gyroscope Division

S 16. SONAR EQUIPMENT, HULL FITTINGS AND HYDRAULICS
Decca Radar Ltd.
Laurence, Scott & Electromotors Ltd.
Vosper Thornycroft Group, The

S 17. SPARE PARTS FOR DIESEL ENGINES
Blohm + Voss AG
C.R.M., Fabbrica Motori Marini
Hawker Siddeley Group
Korody-Colyer Corporation
Korody Marine Corporation
Maybach Mercedes-Benz Motorenbau GmbH
Netherlands United Shipbuilding Bureaux Ltd.

S 18. SPEED BOATS
Brooke Marine Ltd.
Boatservice Ltd. A/S
Cantiere Rodriquez
Karlskronavarvet AB
Fr. Lürssen Werft
Vosper Thornycroft Group, The
Yarrow (Shipbuilders) Ltd.

S 19. STABILISING EQUIPMENT
Blohm + Voss AG
Ferranti Ltd.
Nord Aviation
Sperry Gyroscope Division
Vosper Thornycroft Group, The

S 20. STABILISING EQUIPMENT FOR FIRE CONTROL
British Aircraft Corporation
Contraves AG.
Hollandse Signaalapparaten N.V.
Sperry Gyroscope Division

S 21. STEAM-RAISING PLANT, CONVENTIONAL
Blohm + Voss AG
Netherlands United Shipbuilding Bureaux Ltd.
Vickers Limited.
Yarrow & Co. Ltd.

S 22. STEAM-RAISING PLANT, NUCLEAR
Netherlands United Shipbuilding Bureaux Ltd.

S 23. STEAM TURBINES
Blohm + Voss AG
A/S Horten Verft
Netherlands United Shipbuilding Bureaux Ltd.
Vickers Limited
Yarrow & Co. Ltd.

S 24. STEEL, ALLOY AND SPECIAL
AB Bofors

S 25. STEEL FORGINGS, PLATES AND SECTIONS, STAMPINGS
AB Bofors
Western Gear Corporation

S 26. STEEL, MANGANESE, WEAR RESISTING
AB Bofors

S 27. STEERING GEAR
Hastie & Co. Ltd., John
MacTaggart, Scott & Co. Ltd.
Sperry Gyroscope Division
Vosper Thornycroft Group, The

S 28. STRESS RELIEVING
F.M.C., Northern Ordnance Division
Vosper Thornycroft Group, The
Yarrow & Co. Ltd.

S 29. SUBMARINE FIRE CONTROL
Electro-Dynamic Construction Co. Ltd.
Elliott Brothers (London) Ltd., Naval Division
Hollandse Signaalapparaten N.V.
Plessey Company Ltd., The
Sperry Gyroscope Division

S 30. SUBMARINE PERISCOPES
Barr & Stroud Ltd.

S 31. SUBMARINES
Karlskronavarvet AB
Netherlands United Shipbuilding Bureaux Ltd.
Vickers Limited

S 32. SUBMARINES (CONVENTIONAL)
Karlskronavarvet AB
Netherlands United Shipbuilding Bureaux Ltd.
Vickers Limited

S 33. SUPERHEATERS
Blohm + Voss AG
Yarrow & Co. Ltd.

S 34. SURVEY EQUIPMENT
British Aircraft Corporation
Elliott Brothers (London) Ltd., Naval Division

S 35. SWITCHBOARDS
Blohm + Voss AG
Electro-Dynamic Construction Co. Ltd.
Laurence, Scott & Electromotors Ltd.
McGeoch & Co. (Birmingham) Ltd., William
Vosper Thornycroft Group, The
Whipp & Bourne Ltd.

S 36. SWITCHBOARDS AND SWITCHGEAR
Electro-Dynamic Construction Co. Ltd.
Laurence, Scott & Electromotors Ltd.
McGeoch & Co. (Birmingham) Ltd., William
Vosper Thornycroft Group, The
Whipp & Bourne Ltd.

T 1. TACTICAL TRAINING SIMULATORS
Elliott Brothers (London) Ltd., Trainer & Simulator Division

T 2. TANKERS
Blohm + Voss AG
A/S Horten Verft
Fr. Lürssen Werft
Yarrow (Shipbuilders) Ltd.

T 3. TANKERS (SMALL)
Brooke Marine Ltd.
Karlskronavarvet AB
Fr. Lürssen Werft
Yarrow (Shipbuilders) Ltd.

T 4. TANKS, OIL AND WATER STORAGE
Vosper Thornycroft Group, The

T 5. TECHNICAL PUBLICATIONS
B.P.C. Publishing Ltd.
McGraw-Hill Book Company
Sampson Low, Marston & Co. Ltd.
Vickers Limited

T 6. TELECOMMUNICATION EQUIPMENT
Columbia Electronics International, Inc.
Elliott Brothers (London) Ltd., Naval Division
Ferranti Limited
Korody Marine Corporation
Marconi Co. Ltd., The

T 7. TELEGRAPH SYSTEMS
Columbia Electronics International, Inc.
Hawker Siddeley Group

T 8. TELEMOTORS
MacTaggart, Scott & Co. Ltd.

T 9. TELEPHONES, BATTERY-LESS
Columbia Electronics International, Inc.
Hawker Siddeley Group

T 10. TELEPHONES, LOUD-SPEAKING
Columbia Electronics International, Inc.
Hawker Siddeley Group
Korody Marine Corporation

T 11. TENDERS
Blohm + Voss AG
Brooke Marine Ltd.
Karlskronavarvet AB
Fr. Lürssen Werft
Vosper Thornycroft Group, The
Yarrow (Shipbuilders) Ltd.

T 12. TEST EQUIPMENT FOR FIRE CONTROL SYSTEMS
Barr & Stroud Ltd.
Columbia Electronics International, Inc.
Contraves AG.
Elliott Brothers (London) Ltd., Naval Division
Ferranti Limited
Hollandse Signaalapparaten N.V.
Laurence, Scott & Electromotors Ltd.
Sperry Gyroscope Division
Vickers Limited

T 13. TORPEDO CONTROL SYSTEMS
Elliott Brothers (London) Ltd., Naval Division

T 14. TORPEDO CRAFT BUILDERS
Boatservice Ltd. A/S
Brooke Marine Ltd.
Cantiere Rodriquez
Karlskronavarvet AB
Fr. Lürssen Werft
Netherlands United Shipbuilding Bureaux Ltd.
Vickers Limited
Vosper Thornycroft Group, The
Yarrow (Shipbuilders) Ltd.

T 15. TORPEDO DEPTH AND ROLL RECORDERS
Barr & Stroud Ltd.

T 16. TORPEDO ORDER AND DEFLECTION CONTROL
Barr & Stroud Ltd.
Laurence, Scott & Electromotors Ltd.
Vickers Limited

T 17. TORPEDO SIDE-LAUNCHERS
F.M.C., Northern Ordnance Division
Karlskronavarvet AB
Vosper Thornycroft Group, The

T 18. TORPEDOES AND TORPEDO TUBES

Karlskronavarvet AB
Netherlands United Shipbuilding Bureaux Ltd.
Plessey Company Limited, The
Vickers Limited
Vosper Thornycroft Group, The

T 19. TRAINING EQUIPMENT

Hollandse Signaalapparaten N.V.
Korody Marine Corporation
Laurence Scott & Electromotors Ltd.
Plessey Company Limited, The

T 20. TRAWLERS

Brooke Marine Ltd.
A/S Horten Verft
Karlskronavarvet AB
Vosper Thornycroft Group, The
Yarrow (Shipbuilders) Ltd.

T 21. TUGS

Brooke Marine Ltd.
Karlskronavarvet AB
Todd Shipyards Corporation
Vosper Thornycroft Group, The
Yarrow (Shipbuilders) Ltd.

T 22. TURBINE GEARS

Netherlands United Shipbuilding Bureaux Ltd.
Vickers Limited

T 23. TURBINES

Blohm + Voss AG
A/S Horten Verft
Netherlands United Shipbuilding Bureaux Ltd.
Rolls-Royce Ltd.
Vickers Limited
Yarrow & Co. Ltd.

T 24. TURBINES, EXHAUST

Netherlands United Shipbuilding Bureaux Ltd.

T 25. TURBINES, GAS MARINE

Rolls-Royce Ltd.
Yarrow & Co. Ltd.

T 26. TURBINES, STEAM MARINE

Blohm + Voss AG
A/S Horten Verft
Netherlands United Shipbuilding Bureaux Ltd.
Vickers Limited
Yarrow & Co. Ltd.

U 1. UNDERWATER LIGHTS

McGeoch & Co. (Birmingham) Ltd., William

U 2. UNDERWATER TELEVISION EQUIPMENT

Barr & Stroud Ltd.
Marconi Co. Ltd., The

V 1. VALVES AND COCKS

Metallic Valve Co. Ltd.
Vickers Limited

V 2. VALVES AND COCKS, HYDRAULIC

MacTaggart, Scott & Co. Ltd.

V 3. VALVES, AUTOMATIC PLATE OR DISC

Metallic Valve Co. Ltd.

W 1. WARSHIP REPAIRERS

Blohm + Voss AG
Brooke Marine Ltd.
A/S Horten Verft
Karlskronavarvet AB
Fr. Lürssen Werft
Netherlands United Shipbuilding Bureaux Ltd.
Todd Shipyards Corporation
Vickers Limited
Vosper Thornycroft Group, The
Yarrow (Shipbuilders) Ltd.

W 2. WARSHIPS

Blohm + Voss AG
Boatservice Ltd. A/S
Brooke Marine Ltd.
A/S Horten Verft
Karlskronavarvet AB
Fr. Lürssen Werft
Netherlands United Shipbuilding Bureaux Ltd.
Vickers Limited
Vosper Thornycroft Group, The
Yarrow (Shipbuilders) Ltd.

W 3. WATER TUBE BOILERS

Blohm + Voss AG
Netherlands United Shipbuilding Bureaux Ltd.
Vickers Limited
Yarrow (Shipbuilders) Ltd.

W 4. WEAPON SYSTEMS

AB Bofors
British Aircraft Corporation
Contraves AG.
Decca Radar Ltd.
Elliott Brothers (London) Ltd., Naval Division
Ferranti Limited
F.M.C., Northern Ordnance Division
General Precision Inc.—Librascope Group
Hollandse Signaalapparaten N.V.
Marconi Co. Ltd., The
Nord Aviation
Plessey Company Limited, The
Sperry Gyroscope Division
Vickers Limited

W 5. WEAPON SYSTEMS (SONAR COMPONENTS)

Edo Corporation
Elliott Brothers (London) Ltd., Naval Division
Laurence, Scott & Electromotors Ltd.
Plessey Company Limited, The
Sperry Gyroscope Division

W 6. WELDING, ARC, ARGON ARC OR GAS

Vosper Thornycroft Group, The
Yarrow & Co. Ltd.

W 7. WINCHES

Hawker Siddeley Group
Laurence, Scott & Electromotors Ltd.
MacTaggart, Scott & Co. Ltd.
Western Gear Corporation
Vosper Thornycroft Group, The

X 1. X-RAY WORK

Karlskronavarvet AB
Vosper Thornycroft Group, The
Yarrow & Co. Ltd.

Y 1. YACHTS (POWERED)

Boatservice Ltd. A/S
Brooke Marine Ltd.
Cantiere Rodriquez
Karlskronavarvet AB
Fr. Lürssen Werft
Vosper Thornycroft Group, The
Yarrow (Shipbuilders) Ltd.

LISTA CLASIFICADA DE ANUNCIANTES

El número de referencia de cada uno de los epígrafes abajo relacionados indica el equivalente epígrafe en inglés en las páginas 7 a 31

S 26 Acero al magneso resistente al desgaste
S 24 Aleaciones de acero y especiales
R 16 Aletas amortiguadoras de balanceo
L 8 Altavoces, equipo de
A 7 Alternadores
S 10 Anillos colectores, conjuntos de
W 5 Armamento (componentes Sonar), sistemas de
W 4 Armamento, sistemas de
O 6 Armamento y sus municiones
M 17 Arrancadores de máquinas
C 17 Arrancadores neumáticos para turbinas de gas y motores diesel
L 5 Ascensores hidráulicos
W 1 Astilleros de buques de guerra
A 3 Aviones, dispositivos para detener
A 5 Aviones, instrumentos para
E 14 Avión, motores de
C 2 Barcos-puerta
I 12 Baterías, inversores y cargadores de
B 1 Binoculares
A 13 Blindaje, planchas de
F 9 Bombas para servicio de incendio
G 20 Brújulas giroscópicas
D 7 Buceo, equipos de
F 10 Buques, accesorios de
S 8 Buques, artículos de latón para
G 1 Buques a turbina de gas
F 7 Buques-bomba y de salvamento
S 3 Buques, construcción y reparación de
A 15 Buques de asalto
C 6 Buques de carga
B 4 Buques de carga a granel
C 23 Buques de carga en containers
D 10 Buques de carga seca
E 19 Buques de escolta
W 2 Buques de guerra
F 2 Buques de guerra rápidos, servicio de diseño de
M 3 Buques de mantenimiento y reparación
P 2 Buques de pasajeros
P 3 Buques de patrulla, lanchas, falúas y pinazas
M 13 Buques de proyectiles
G 14 Buques de proyectiles teledirigidos
S 1 Buques de salvamento y posarredes
L 7 Buques de transporte de gas de petróleo líquido
I 11 Buques, diseño interior y amueblado de
M 9 Buques dragaminas
S 4 Buques, maquinaria para
M 6 Buques mercantes
M 8 Buques minadores
R 12 Buques para investigaciones técnicas
C 1 Cable (con o sin), conjuntos de
E 2 Cables eléctricos
C 3 Cabrestantes y molinetes
C 20 Calculadoras electrónicas
C 19 Calculadoras electrónicas, servicios de
B 2 Calderas
W 3 Calderas de tubos de agua
F 3 Calentadores de agua de alimentación
O 3 Calentadores de combustible
G 19 Cañones, aparatos de puntería y buscadores de elevación para
G 18 Cañones, montajes para
N 1 Cañones, navales
G 17 Cañones y montajes
C 5 Carga, equipos para manejo de
C 7 Carga, monitores de espacios de
F 13 Carretones elevadores de horquilla
A 12 Cohetes antisubmarinos
A 11 Cohetes antisubmarinos, lanzadores de
C 18 Compresores

A 2 Compresores de aire
O 2 Compresores de aire libre de aceite
C 22 Condensadores
C 21 Condensador, tubos de
F 11 Conductores flexibles, cubiertas de
C 15 Control centralizado y automático
T 12 Control de tiro, equipos de pruebas para sistema de
S 29 Control de tiro para submarinos, equipo de
F 8 Control de tiro y artillería, equipos de
A 16 Control, sistemas automáticos de
C 26 Corbetas
H 2 Cristales calentados
C 28 Cruceros
G 16 Chalupas cañoneras
F 14 Destilación de agua dulce, planta de
D 2 Destructores
D 6 Diesel, equipos de inyección de combustible
E 15 Diesel, motores
D 3 Diesel, motores auxiliares
D 4 Diesel, motores de propulsión principal
D 5, R 11, S 17 Diesel, piezas de repuesto para motores
E 11, P 1 Diesel, piezas para motores
D 8 Dique, compuertas de
D 11 Dique seco, propietarios de
C 16 Dragaminas costeros y de aguas esturiales
N 5 Dragaminas (minas no magnéticas)
D 9 Dragas
E 1 Economizadores
P 16 Editores
E 6 Eléctricas, instalaciones y reparaciones
E 7 Eléctrico, aparellaje
E 5 Eléctricos, accesorios
E 8 Electro-hidráulicos, equipos auxiliares
A 14 Embarcaciones de asalto
L 2 Embarcaciones para desembarco
S 14 Enchufes hembra M 21 Enchufes macho, tipo multiclavija
P 9 Enchufes macho y hembra
S 12 Enchufes macho y hembra, herméticos
S 13 Enchufes macho y hembra, tipo multiclavija
M 21 Enchufes múltiples
G 3 Engranajes, cajas para
G 6 Engranajes cónicos de espiral
G 8 Engranajes de dentadura recta
T 22 Engranajes de turbinas
G 9 Engranajes en "V"
E 18 Engranajes epiciclos
G 5 Engranajes hipoidales
R 15 Engranajes inversores
G 7 Engranajes reductores e inversores
R 13 Engranajes reductores e inversores accionados por aceite
G 4 Engranajes y trenes de engranajes
A 1 Entrenadores de información de combate
T 19 Equipos de instrucción
S 34 Equipos de levantamiento
M 5 Equipos de manejo de materiales
E 4 Equipos eléctricos
E 3 Equipos eléctricos auxiliares
E 9 Equipos electrónicos
T 11 Escampavías
S 28 Esfuerzos, eliminación de
S 19 Estabilizador, equipo
S 20 Estabilizador, equipo para control de tiro
S 6 Estabilizadores de buques
M 20 Estabilizadores tipo de contrapeso móvil
R 8 Estatorreactores
F 6 Fibra de vidrio, embarcaciones y otros productos de
F 15 Fragatas
S 21 Generadores convencionales de vapor
G 10 Generadores eléctricos
S 22 Generadores nucleares de vapor

A 17 Gobierno automático

S 27 Gobierno, mecanismos de

C 27 Grúas para buques

W 7 Guinches

P 13 Hélices de buques

P 14 Hélices, servicio de diseño e investigación de

H 7 Hidráulicas, instalaciones

H 6 Hidráulicas, máquinas

H 5 Hidráulicos, equipos

H 8 Hidroala, botes

H 9 Hidrográficos, equipos de estudios

H 4 Hovercraft (autodeslizadores)

S 11 Indicadores de humo

I 1 Indicadores eléctricos
I 3 Infrarrojos, materiales
S 7 Ingeniería y sistemas de a bordo

I 9 Instrumentos de precisión
I 6 Instrumentos electrónicos
I 10 Instrumentos, equipos probadores de

I 5 Instrumentos (mecánicos), componentes de
I 7 Instrumentos naúticos
I 4 Inyectores

F 16 Inyectores de fuel-oil

L 6 Lámparas y alumbrado

A 10 Lanchas antisubmarinas

S 18 Lanchas rápidas

F 1 Lanchas rápidas y de patrulla

M 18 Lanchas torpederas y de motor

L 4 Laser, sistema de

L 3 Laser, telémetros

B 3 Libros navales

B 3a Libros navales, ediciones agotadas
I 2 Luces de navegación, indicadores de las
U 1 Luces submarinas

A 18 Máquinas auxiliares

D 1 Máquinas de cubierta

M 16 Máquinas, mecanismos de gobierno de

R 14 Máquinas para inversión de marcha, accionadas por vapor y aire comprimido

C 25 Mecanismo de mando

M 7 Microfónicos, equipos

M 14 Modelos, constructores de

M 15 Modelos remolcados en tanque experimental, servicio de

E 16 Motores de turbina de gas

E 17 Motores de turbina de vapor

M 19 Motores eléctricos

E 13 Motores, mandos de arranque y parada de

E 10 Motores, monitores y registradores de datos de

E 12 Motores, reguladores de velocidad para

A 8 Municiones

A 9 Municiones, elevadores de

N 3 Navegación, ayudas de

F 5 Opticos de fibras, artículos

O 5 Opticos, filtros

O1 Perforación, equipos de.(industria petrolífera)

P 4 Periscopio, cubiertas estructurales de

P 5 Periscopios

S 30 Periscopios para submarinos

T 20 Pesqueros rastreadores

O 4 Petróleo, sistemas y quemadores de

T 2 Petroleros, buques

T 3 Petroleros (pequeños)

S 25 Piezas de acero forjado, placas y perfiles y piezas estampadas

C 14 Piezas de fundición de acero.

C 12 Piezas de fundición de hierro de grafito esferoidal

C 13 Piezas de fundición de hierro de grafito esferoidal "Ni-Resist"

C 8 Piezas fundidas de bronce/aluminio

C 9 Piezas fundidas de hierro de altas características
C 11 Piezas fundidas de moldeo en cáscara
C 10 Piezas fundidas no ferrosas

M 1 Piezas maquinadas, ferrosas

M 2 Piezas maquinadas, no ferrosas

P 8 Pistones, aros de pistón y muñequillas

P 17 Pompas

P 18 Pompas, piezas y órganos de

P 10 Pontones autopropulsores

L 1 Portalámparas

A 4 Portaviones

P 11 Presión, recipientes de

P 12 Propulsión, materiales y combustibles de

P 15 Propulsión, maquinaria de

M 11 Proyectiles, instalaciones de

M 10 Proyectiles, sistemas de control de

M 12 Proyectiles, sistemas de lanzamiento de

G 15 Proyectiles teledirigidos

G 13 Proyectiles teledirigidos, equipo de servicio de

F 12 Proyectores

T 5 Publicaciones técnicas

R 1 Radar, antenas de

R 4 Radar de navegación y aviso de intercepción

M 4 Radar marino

N 2 Radar naval

R 2 Radar para control de tiro

R 3 Radar para vigilancia de puertos

R 6 Radio, equipos de

R 5 Radios para aviones

R 7 Radio, transmisores y receptores de

X 1 Rayos X, equipos de

S 33 Recalentadores

G 11 Reguladores

G 12 Reguladores de velocidad para motores

T 21 Remolcadores

S 9 Simuladores

T 1 Simuladores de entrenamiento táctico

W 6 Soldadura al arco, al arco/argón o gas

S 15 Sonar, equipo

S 16 Sonar, equipos de casco y auxiliares hidráulicos

S 31 Submarinos

S 32 Submarinos (convencionales)

S 5 Tablas de control de compases magnéticos de buques

S 35 Tableros de control

S 36 Tableros de control y aparellaje

I 8 Tableros de instrumentos

C 24 Tableros de mando (eléctricos)

T 4 Tanques de almacenamiento de petróleo y agua

T 6 Telecomunicaciones, equipos para

T 10 Teléfonos autoparlantes

T 9 Teléfonos sin batería

T 7 Telegráficos, sistemas

R 10 Telemandos

R 9 Telémetros

T 8 Telemotores

U 2 Televisión submarina, equipos de

H 1 Termocambiadores

R 17 Timones

H 3 Timón, indicadores de ángulo de

T 14 Torpederas, constructores de embarcaciones

T 16 Torpedos, equipos de control de trayectoria y desviación de

T 17 Torpedo, rampas laterales lanza-

T 15 Torpedos, registradores de profundidad y de balanceo de

T 13 Torpedos, sistemas de control de

T 18 Torpedos y tubos lanza-torpedos

F 4 Transbordadores

C 4 Transbordadores de vehículos

P 6 Tuberías de cobre y de latón

P 7 Tuberías para agua de mar

T 23 Turbinas

G 2 Turbinas de gas

T 24 Turbinas de gases de escape

S 23 Turbinas de vapor

T 25 Turbinas marinas de gases

T 26 Turbinas marinas de vapor

V 3 Válvulas automáticas de placa o disco

V 1 Válvulas y grifos

V 2 Válvulas y grifos hidráulicos

A 6 Vehículos de cojín de aire

N 4 Visión nocturna, sistemas de

Y 1 Yates (de motor)

АЛФАВИТНО-ПРЕДМЕТНЫЙ ПЕРЕЧЕНЬ ОБЪЯВЛЕНИЙ

Ссылочный номер, поставленный перед каждым из нижеперечисленных названий, указывает заголовок на английском языке на стр. I6 - 3I.

S21 Парогенераторное оборудование, обычное.
S22 Парогенераторное оборудование, ядерное.
F4 Паромы.
S33 Пароперегреватели.
P2 Пассажирские корабли.
L1 Патроны для ламп.

G5 Передачи гипоидными зубчатыми колесами.
T22 Передачи для турбин.
G9 Передачи шевронными зубчатыми колесами.
P5 Перископы.
S30 Перископы для подводных лодок.
E18 Планетарные передачи.
M3 Плавучие мастерские.
C5 Погрузочно-разгрузочное оборудование.
M5 Погрузочно-разгрузочное оборудование.
S31 Подводные лодки.
S32 Подводные лодки (обычного типа).
U1 Подводные огни.
O3 Подогреватели жидкого топлива.
F3 Подогреватели питательной воды.
L5 Подъемники, гидравлические.
F7 Пожарные и спасательные суда.
F9 Пожарные насосы.
F11 Покрытия гибких рукавов.
P10 Понтоны, самоходные.
R3 Портовые радиолокационные станции.
P8 Поршни, поршневые кольца и поршневые пальцы.
I8 Приборные щиты.
I10 Приборы и оборудование для испытаний.
I7 Приборы, мореходные.
I9 Приборы, прецизионные.
I6 Приборы, электронные.
G19 Прицелы и высотомеры для наводки орудий.
F2 Проектирование быстрых военно-морских судов.
I11 Проектирование интерьеров судов и оснастка их мебелью.
F12 Прожекторы заливающего света.
A10 Противолодочные катера.
A12 Противолодочные ракеты.
R8 Прямоточные воздушно-реактивные двигатели.
C24 Пульты управления (электрические).
M17 Пускатели двигателей.
A11 Пусковые установки для противолодочных ракет.

R6 Радиоаппаратура.
R1 Радиолокационные антенны.
R4 Радиолокационные станции для навигации, обнаружения и наведения.
R2 Радиолокационные станции орудийной наводки.
M4 Радиолокация, судовая.
N2 Радиолокация, судовая.
R5 Радиооборудование, бортовое для самолётов.
R7 Радиопередатчики и приёмники.
P12 Ракетные топлива.
M11 Ракетные установки.
S36 Распределительные щиты и оборудование.
S35 Распредщиты.
R14 Реверсивные двигатели с паровым и пневматическим управлением.
R15 Реверсивные передачи.
G7 Реверсирующие редуктора.
R13 Реверсирующие редуктора с гидромасляным управлением.
T15 Регистраторы глубины и крена для торпед.
G11 Регуляторы.
G12 Регуляторы скорости двигателей.
T4 Резервуары для топлива и воды.
W1 Ремонт военных кораблей.
X1 Рентгенография.
L8 Репродукторное оборудование.
S27 Рулевые механизмы.
H3 Рулевые указатели.
R17 Рули.
L8 Рупоры.

W6 Сварка, дуговая, аргоно-дуговая или газовая.
P15 Силовые установки.
R10 Системы дистанционного управления.
L4 Системы лазерные.
W4 Системы оружия.
W5 Системы оружия (детали гидролокационных систем).
O4 Системы подачи жидкого топлива и форсунки.
M12 Системы пуска ракет.
N4 Системы скотопического зрения.

S29 Системы управления огнём для подводных лодок.
M10 Системы управления ракетами.
T13 Системы управления торпедами.
S28 Снятие внутренних напряжений.
S14 Соединительные муфты.
S1 Спасательные и бонозаградительные суда.
R16 Стабилизаторы бортовой качки.
S20 Стабилизаторы систем управления стрельбой.
S19 Стабилизирующее оборудование.
S24 Сталь, высоколегированная и специальная.
S26 Сталь, износостойкая марганцевая.
S25 Стальные поковки, листовая и профильная сталь, штампованные изделия.
D8 Створные ворота доков.
P3 Сторожевые суда, катера, баркасы и пинасы.
T14 Строители торпедных катеров.
L7 Суда для перевоза ожиженного нефтяного газа.
A6 Суда на воздушных подушках.
H8 Суда на подводных крыльях.
F6 Суда с корпусами из стекловолокна и другие изделия из стекловолокна.
F10 Судовая арматура.
S4 Судовые машины.
S3 Судостроители и судоремонтные предприятия.
D10 Сухогрузные грузовые суда.

S5 Таблицы для проверки судовых магнитных компасов.
T7 Телеграфные системы.
T8 Теледвигатели.
T9 Телефоны, не снабженные батареями.
T10 Телефоны с громкоговорителями.
H1 Теплообменники.
T5 Техническая литература.
S10 Токособирательные кольца.
M18 Торпедные катера.
T18 Торпеды и торпедные аппараты.
T20 Траулеры.
A1 Тренажёр для расчётов боевых данных.
S9 Тренажёры и имитаторы.
T1 Тренажёры по боевой тактике.
C21 Трубки конденсаторов.
P7 Трубы для морской воды.
P6 Трубы, медные и латунные.
T23 Турбины.
T24 Турбины, работающие на выхлопных газах.
T25 Турбины, газовые морские.
T26 Турбины, паровые морские.

T16 Управление последовательностью выпуска торпед и коррекция отклонений.
G15 Управляемые ракеты.
M20 Успокоители качки.
S6 Успокоители, судовые.
T17 Установка для бокового выпуска торпед.
O1 Установка для бурения в море.
T19 Устройства для обучения.
E12 Устройства регулирования скорости двигателя.
E13 Устройства управления пуском и остановкой двигателя.

F15 Фрегаты

H4 "Ховэркрафт" (суда на воздушных подушках).

C15 Централизованное и автоматическое управление.

G4 Шестерни и передачи.
C3 Шпили и брашпили.
P9 Штепсели и розетки.
S13 Штепсели и розетки многоштырькового типа.
S12 Штепсели и розетки, электрические водонепроницаемые.
A14 Штурмовые десантные катера.
A15 Штурмовые десантные суда.
E1 Экономайзеры.
A9 Элеваторы для боеприпасов.
E5 Электрическая арматура.
E2 Электрические кабели.
E7 Электрическое распределительное оборудование.
E8 Электро-гидравлическое вспомогательное оборудование.
M19 Электродвигатели.
E9 Электронное оборудование.
E4 Электрооборудование.
E19 Эскортные корабли.
D2 Эсминцы.
Y1 Яхты (моторные).

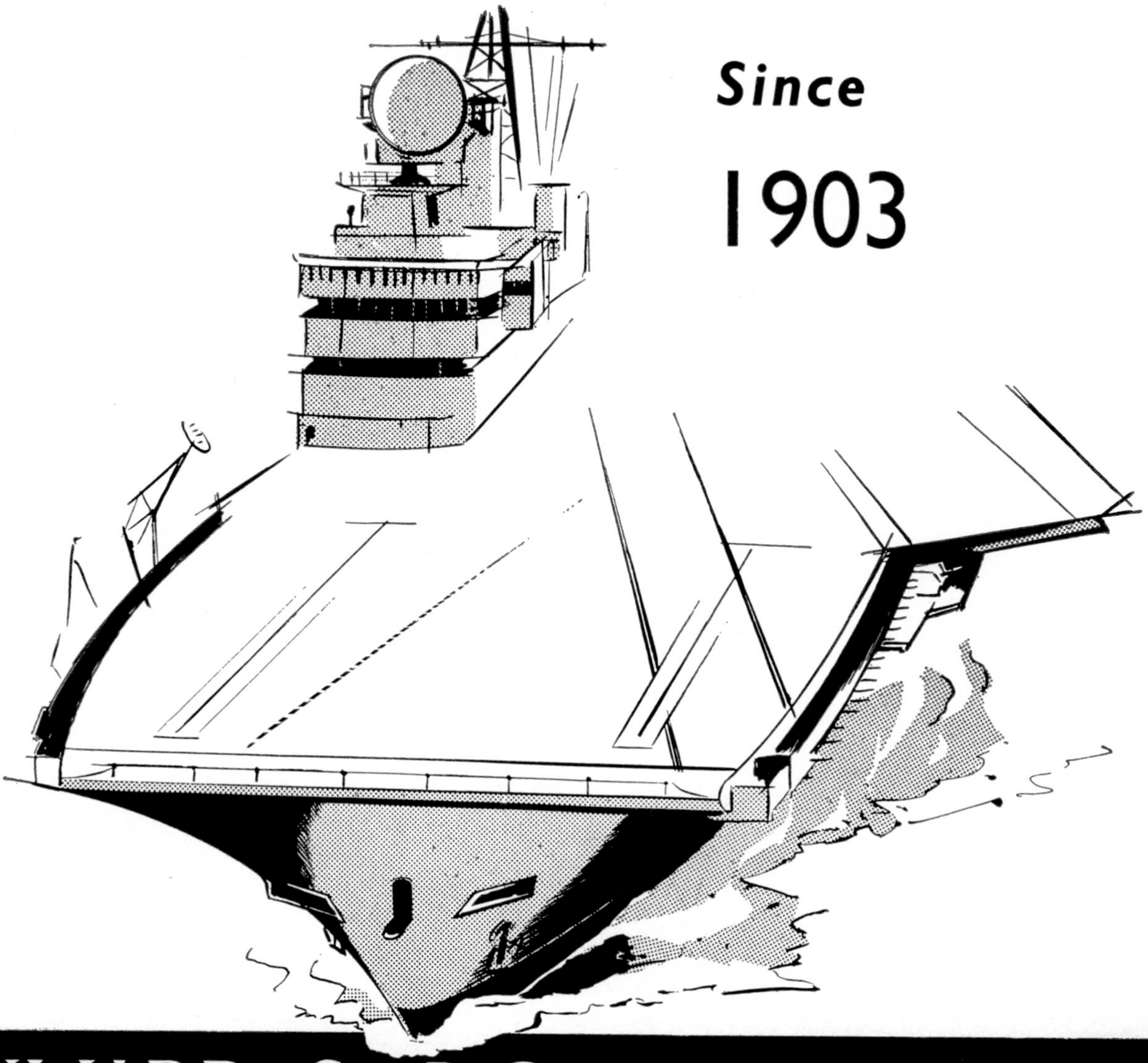

Since

1903

WHIPP & BOURNE LTD.

We have sailed a good many seas

in many a good ship . . .

Whipp & Bourne have been Marine Switchgear Specialists for over 65 years and throughout this time have kept abreast of the technical developments which are the concern of both the Engineer and the Naval Architect.

WB

ROCHDALE, LANCS.

Tel: Rochdale 32051

DIESEL ENGINES S.E.M.T. PIELSTICK

The electric generating set shown here is of the kind used in the French Navy's "Narval" type submarines. It consists of a S.E.M.T. PIELSTICK 12 PA4 185 supercharged engine to which is connected a pressurised, self-ventilating ALSTHOM generator in a closed, cooled circuit. In a French Navy test, the prototype generator set was submitted to a 2,500 hours endurance trial.

In its standard version, the 12 PA4 185 develops 1,800 hp at 1,500 rpm. In its application as part of the snorkel system (with low induction pressure and back pressure on exhaust discharge), the engine requires a supercharger mechanically linked to the crankshaft. Under these conditions, current available at the generator terminals will be 650 kW at 1,300 rpm.

The French Navy's "Daphne" type submarines are fitted with S.E.M.T. PIELSTICK 8 PA4 185 engines with a capacity of 450 kW at 1,300 rpm. These engines are also supercharged by compressors linked to the engine crankshaft.

NARVAL TYPE SUBMARINE
fitted with the 3 12 PAG 185 engines

CHANTIERS DE L'ATLANTIQUE

2, quai de Seine, SAINT-DENIS, FRANCE

A.D.A. and now C.A.A.I.S.

Royal Navy contract for Computer Assisted Action Information Systems (CAAIS) awarded to Ferranti

Ferranti Limited, Digital Systems Department, are proud to announce that they have recently been awarded a production contract for Computer-Assisted Action Information Systems (CAAIS) for the Royal Navy. This contract, awarded after competitive tender, includes Decca Limited as a sub-contractor for cathode-ray-tube display consoles: it is expected to be followed by further orders for similar systems both in the U.K. and overseas. C.A.A.I.S. will therefore join other Ferranti digital systems for the Navy of the 1970's.

C.A.A.I.S. has been carefully specified by the Ministry of Defence, in collaboration with industry, to provide an adaptable modular system especially suitable for anti-submarine Frigates and smaller craft, and at an extremely economical price so as to permit widespread fitting. Computer assistance is provided in the compilation of the tactical picture on displays, including automatic tracking of radar targets and exchange of data with other ships as well as special assistance in anti-submarine operations.

C.A.A.I.S. Computer-Assisted Action Information Systems.
Low cost modular systems specially designed for anti-submarine Frigates and smaller craft. Based on the Ferranti FM1600B microminiature computer.

Submarines
Another contract recently awarded to Ferranti was for Data Handling Systems for use in submarines. Also based on the Ferranti FM1600B microminiature computer.

A.D.A. Action Data Automation Systems.
Larger, more complex Data Handling and Weapon Control Systems as installed in H.M.S. EAGLE and COUNTY CLASS Guided Missile Destroyers, and to be fitted in H.M.S. BRISTOL (Type 82) and Type 42 Guided Missile Destroyers.

FERRANTI FM1600B COMPUTER
is a microcircuit digital computer using Ferranti Micronor 2 Integrated Circuits. Fully compatible with all other modular units in Ferranti Systems and with its big brother, the Ferranti FM1600. Conforms fully to British and N.A.T.O. Defence Specifications. FM1600B is also available for civil applications.

FERRANTI LTD., DIGITAL SYSTEMS DEPT, BRACKNELL, RG12 IRA, BERKSHIRE, ENGLAND.

DS 20

WARDEN (SR.N5) CLASS

WINCHESTER (SR.N6) CLASS

WELLINGTON (BH.7) CLASS

MOUNTBATTEN (SR.N4) CLASS

experience is the key

There is a world of difference between thinking and knowing. That difference is experience—in the case of BHC, world-wide hovercraft operating experience.

Over 70,000 hours of operation in 43 countries.

More than 2,500,000 sea miles logged.

Close on 2,000,000 fare-paying passengers carried.

Proven performance in full tropical heat and humidity.

Hundreds of high-speed sorties along fast-flowing rivers and over treacherous rapids.

Extended operations over ice and snow under Arctic conditions.

Comprehensive desert trials.

First to set up hovercraft production lines, BHC to-day has the 'Warden' (SR.N5), 'Winchester' (SR.N6) and 'Mountbatten' (SR.N4) Classes in full production. Soon to join them is the 40-ton 'Wellington' (BH.7) Class. Non-marine air-cushion applications include heavy-load road and cross-country transporters and 'FLOTALOAD' hoverpallets for industrial use.

BRITISH HOVERCRAFT—WORLD LEADERS IN THE HOVER TRANSPORT REVOLUTION

british hovercraft corporation

EAST COWES · ISLE OF WIGHT · ENGLAND

BRITISH HOVERCRAFT CORPORATION LIMITED IS A SUBSIDIARY OF WESTLAND AIRCRAFT LIMITED

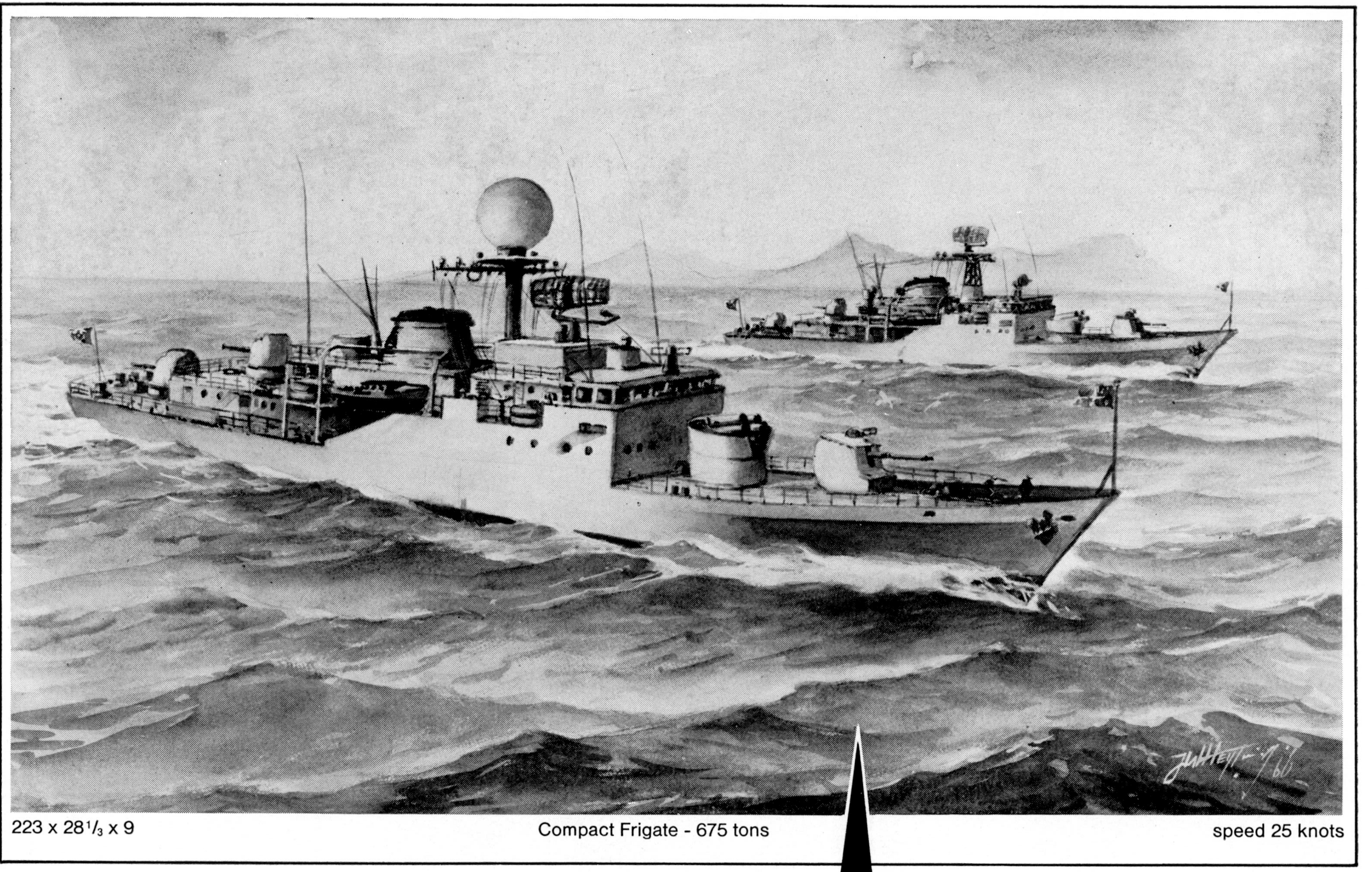
223 x 28 1/3 x 9
Compact Frigate - 675 tons
speed 25 knots

BUILDERS

6 frigates of "Van Speijk" class

DESIGNERS

Designers, builders and repairers of all types of naval vessels, turbines, boilers and Diesel engines. Torpedotubes for surface vessels and submarines.

REPAIRERS

Hr. Ms. "De Zeven Provinciën" after conversion with "Terrier" launcher (1964)

De Rotterdamsche Droogdok Mij N.V.
Rotterdam

Dok- en Werf-Mij Wilton-Fijenoord N.V.
Schiedam

Ned. Dok en Scheepsbouw Mij V.O.F.
Amsterdam

N.V. Kon. Mij „De Schelde"
Vlissingen

Werkspoor-Amsterdam N.V.
Amsterdam

N.V. Nederlandsche Vereenigde Scheepsbouw Bureaux

The Hague P.O. Box 289

Netherlands United Shipbuilding Bureaux Ltd.

Bauduin

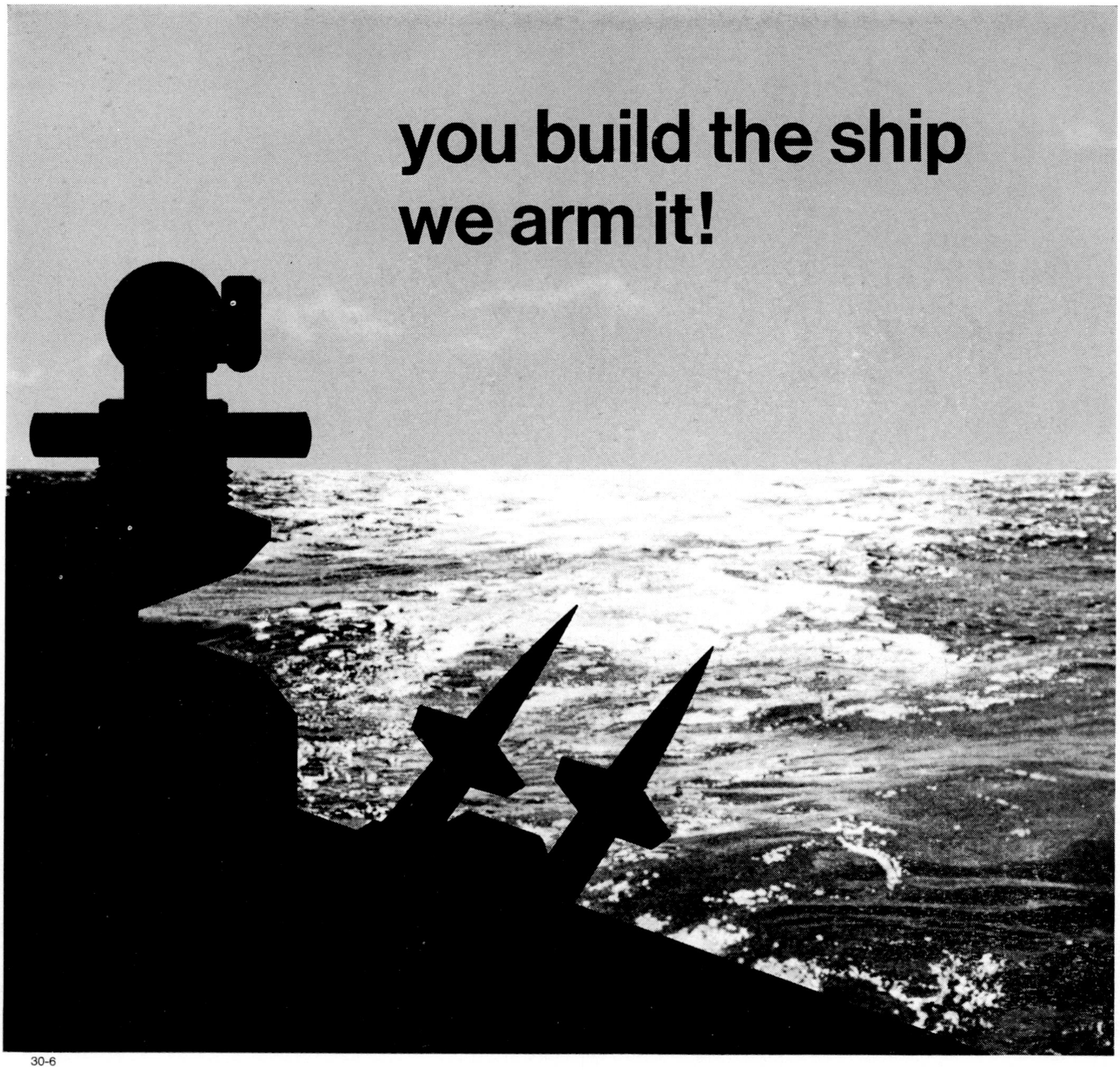
you build the ship
we arm it!

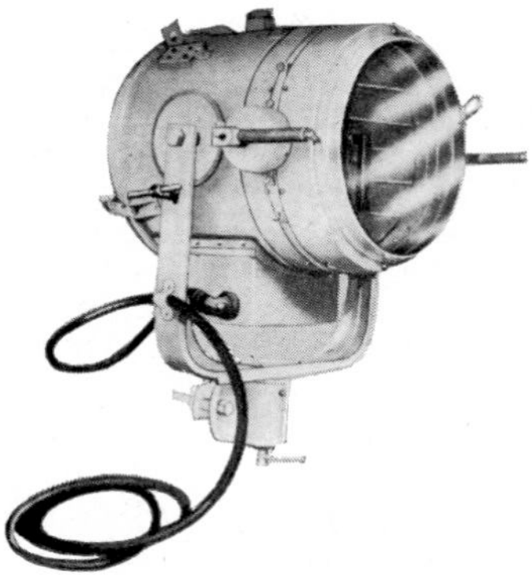

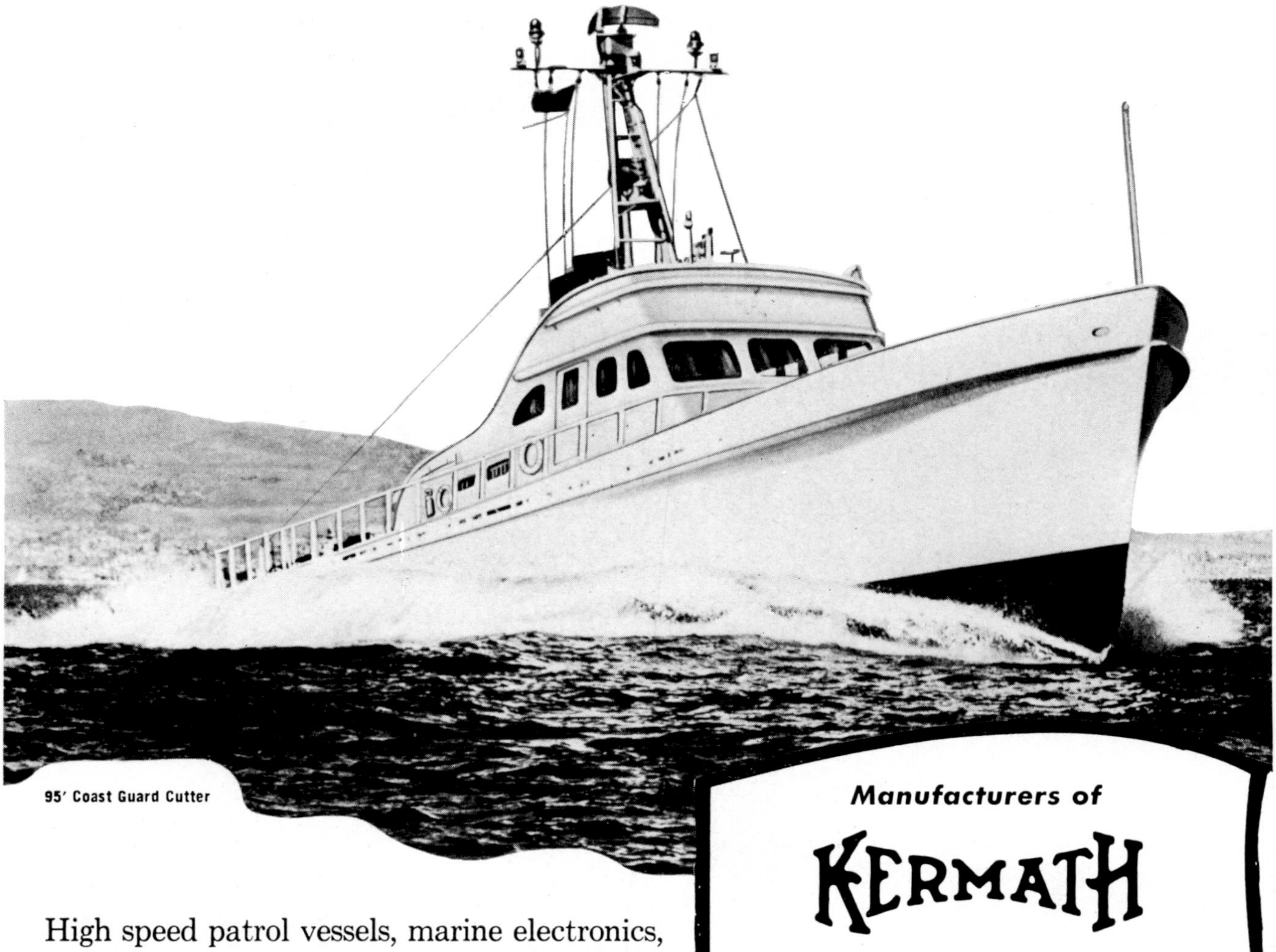

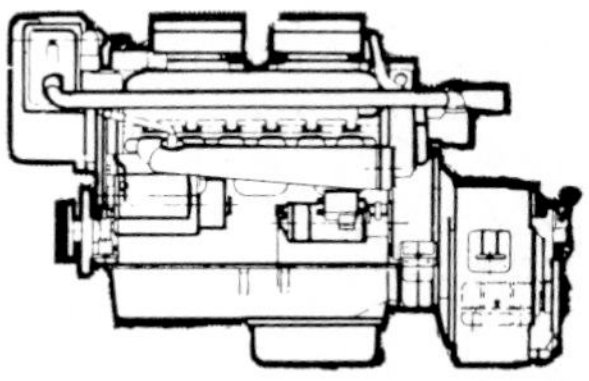

Built by Blohm+Voss

NAVAL VESSELS FROM NORWAY

Marinens Hovedverft (The Naval Dockyard)
and Boatservice Ltd. A/S
in co-operation are designers and
builders of a wide range of naval vessels.

The "OSLO" class Frigate
5 vessels delivered by Marinens Hovedverft
to the Royal Norwegian Navy

Displacement: 1800 tons full load
Speed: 25 knots

The "NASTY" class FPB
42 vessels delivered by Boatservice Ltd. A/S
to the navies of Norway, USA,
West-Germany and Greece. Another 6 being
built under licence in USA.

Displacement: 76 tons
Speed: 45 knots

Telex 1534 - HORTEN

Telex 6238 – OSLO

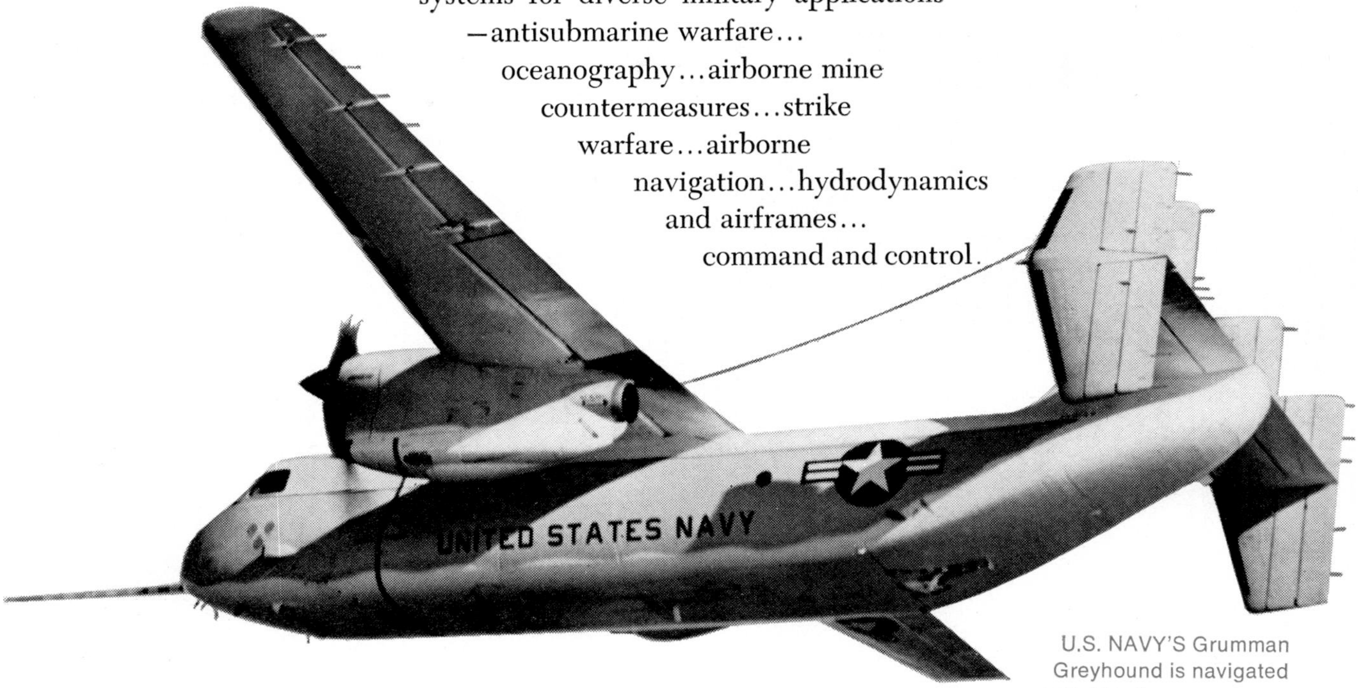

DIESEL ENGINES

C.R.M.	Cycle	No. of Cylinders	Cylinder Arrangement	Cooling	Cylinder Bore (in.)	Piston Stroke (in.)	Displacement (cu. in.)	Performance			Mean Pressure (lbs/sq. in.)	Mean Piston Speed (sec.)	Engine and Reverse Gear Overall Dimensions			Engine Weight (lbs.)	Engine Weight to H.P. Ratio (lbs/hp)	Weight of Engine with Reverse Gear to H.P. Ratio (lbs/hp)	Torque (ft./lbs)	Starting System	Remarks
								Time Rating	Output (hp)	R.P.M.			Length (in.)	Width (in.)	Height (in.)						
C.R.M. 18 D/S •	4T	18	W	water	5,91	7,09	3495	*30′ *4h cont.	1350 1250 1040	2075 2020 1900	145,47 139,35 122,29	1460,- - 2381,28 2243,52	115,82	60,63	51,33	3690 reverse gear 940	2,73 2,95 3,54	3,42 3,70 4,45	3362,- - 3203,- - 2834,- -	electric or compressed air	turbo-charged and intercooled
C.R.M. 18 D/2 •	4T	18	W	water	5,91	7,09	3495	*30′ *4h cont.	1050 950 800	1900 1800 1650	123,71 118,02 108,07	2243,52 2125,44 1948,32	115,82	52,59	53,95	3075 reverse gear 940	2,92 3,23 3,95	3,82 4,22 5,02	2855,85 2725,71 2508,81	electric or compressed air	centrifugally supercharged
C.R.M. 12 D/S •▲	4T	12	V	water	5,91	7,09	2330	*30′ *4h cont.	800 700 650	1900 1800 1700	142,20 123,71 127,98	2243,52 2125,44 2007,36	110,23	55,11	47,40	2755 reverse gear 940	3,44 3,93 4,23	4,61 5,27 5,68	2169,- - 2017,17 1973,79	electric or compressed air	turbo-charged and intercooled
C.R.M. 9 D/S •▲	4T	9	W	water	5,91	7,09	1747,5	*30′ *4h cont.	650 600 500	1950 1900 1800	149,31 142,20 123,71	2302,56 2243,52 2125,44	93,50	49,21	51,18	1760 reverse and reduction gear 1106	2,70 2,93 3,52	4,40 4,77 5,73	1720,74 1633,98 1438,77	electric or compressed air	turbo-charged and intercooled
C.R.M. 9 D/A •▲	4T	9	W	water	5,91	7,09	1747,5	*30′ *4h cont.	415 385 320	1900 1850 1750	96,69 92,43 81,85	2243,52 2184,48 2066,40	91,53	49,21	49,21	1760 940	4,24 4,82 5,50	6,50 7,01 8,43	1127,88 1070,04 947,13	electric or compressed air	natural induction

• Reduction gear with 0,561 - 0,640 - 0,730 - 0,846 ratio, or 1,181 ratio over-gear. ▲ Available optionally with reverse-reduction gear: 0,508 - 0,673 - 0,805 - 0,958 ratio * Every 10 hours in operation

C.R.M. 20121 MILANO-VIA MANZONI, 12-TEL. 708.326/708.327 TELEGR. CREMME

Shipboard tested, ready to install
Smallest, lightest
5 inch/54 caliber
automatic gun mount
The smallest, lightest, medium caliber automatic gun mount ever built for the United States Navy is now shipboard tested and ready for installation. Weighing less than 50,000 pounds, the 5 inch/54 caliber Gun Mount Mark 45 can be installed on frigates, destroyers and destroyer escorts as well as larger ships. It fits the same mounting foundation as the 5 inch/38 caliber Single Mount Mark 30.
The Mark 45 incorporates solid state logic and amplifier modules. It is remotely loaded, controlled and fired. Twenty rounds can be fired by one man at the control panel. Sustained firing beyond twenty rounds can be maintained by a crew of six.
The Mark 45 stows, loads and fires all existing types of 5 inch/54 caliber semi-fixed ammunition without adjustment.
For complete details about the Mark 45 write:
fmc
CORPORATION
NORTHERN
ORDNANCE
DIVISION
48th and N.E. Marshall
Minneapolis, Minn. 55421 U.S.A.

OTO 76/62 and 127/54 COMPACT

OTO 76/62 (3" L 62) DUAL PURPOSE COMPACT GUN
Weight 7 tons - Rate of Fire 85 Rounds/min.

OTO 127/54 (5" L 54) DUAL PURPOSE COMPACT GUN
Weight 30 tons - Rate of Fire 45 Rounds/min.

- FULLY AUTOMATIC OPERATION
- HIGHEST RELIABILITY
- MINIMUM WEIGHT AND SPACE REQUIREMENTS
- ALL WEATHER CAPABILITY
- SWITCH-TYPE AMMUNITION SELECTION
- "PLUG-IN" ON BOARD INSTALLATION
- SIMPLEST MAINTENANCE AND REPAIR
- MINIMUM CREW REQUIREMENTS
- LOW LIFE CYCLE COSTS

STUDIO GRAFICO RESTANI

 OTO MELARA S.p.A. I-19100 LA SPEZIA-ITALY TELEX 27368 (OTO) - TEL. 54041

KRÖGERWERFT
RENDSBURG
M 2680

FRONTISPIECE

United States Aircraft Carrier ENTERPRISE, Guided Missile Cruiser LONG BEACH, Guided Missile Frigate BAINBRIDGE, all nuclear powered

Soviet MOSKVA, Guided Missile Cruiser forward, Helicopter Carrier aft

British BLAKE, Conventional Cruiser forward, helicopter hangar and platform aft

JANE'S
FIGHTING SHIPS

FOUNDED IN 1897 BY FRED T. JANE

EDITED BY
RAYMOND V. B. BLACKMAN, C.Eng., M.I.Mar.E., M.R.I.N.A

1969 - 70

JANE'S YEARBOOKS

NEW YORK:
McGRAW-HILL BOOK COMPANY

Printed in Great Britain

QUEENS AWARD
TO INDUSTRY

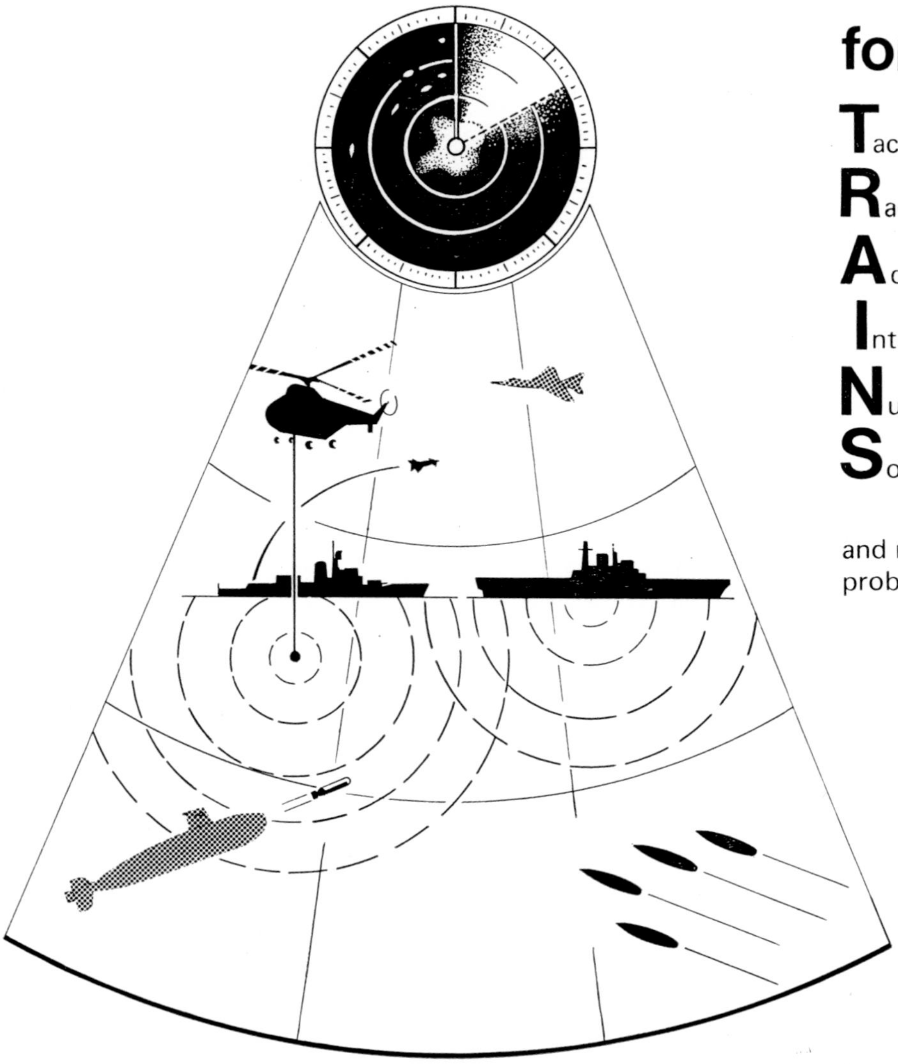

JANE'S FIGHTING SHIPS 1969-70

Compilation of the various sections of this edition has been undertaken by:

R. V. B. Blackman — EUROPE (INCLUDING TURKEY), UNITED KINGDOM, UNION OF SOVIET SOCIALIST REPUBLICS, AND CHINA

Norman Polmar — UNITED STATES OF AMERICA

Arnold Hague — OTHER COUNTRIES

J. D. R. Rawlings — NAVAL AIRCRAFT, NAVAL MISSILES

CONTENTS

MMB
Maybach Mercedes-Benz

In marine electrics experience counts

Make use of our long and specialised experience in this field

If you require

D.C. Motors
D.C. Generators
Special A.C. Motors
High Frequency Alternators

60 Hz Alternators
Frequency Changers
Rotary Converters
Servo-Motors

Electronic Controls
Stabilised Supplies
Automatic Voltage Regulators
Electronic Governors

Static Inverters
Battery Chargers
Control Gear
Switch Boards

consult **ELECTRO DYNAMIC CONSTRUCTION COMPANY LTD**

St. Mary Cray, Orpington, Kent, England.
Phone Orpington 27551 Grams ELEDAMIC St. Mary Cray.

Special constructions, including watertight, submersible and shockproof, are available on many items to meet Naval and Merchant Marine specifications.

P1833

THE NEWEST TORPEDO BOATS

for the Swedish Navy: T 124 Castor, T 125 Vega, T 126 Virgo

Length: 42.5m; breadth: 7.1m; displ: 190 tons; machinery: three Bristol Marine Proteus gas turbines with a total output of 12 300 bhp; max speed: in excess of 40 knots; weapons: six guided torpedoes, one Bofors 57 mm AA gun, remote-controlled by digital fire control equipment, 103 mm rocket flare guide rails; designed to withstand exposure to radioactivity.

have been built by **KARLSKRONAVARVET AB** Karlskrona SWEDEN

FOREWORD

A great volume of new facts and figures and a large number of pictures have been added in this edition, the 72nd year of issue of Jane's Fighting Ships.

Indeed, there is more information in this volume than in any previous edition since 1897, and it is the largest book on the navies of the world ever produced by the publishers. This is perhaps appropriate in the year when the editor has reached his majority, the present issue being the 21st edited by him. He has thus been longer in the chair than any of his four predecessors, including Fred T. Jane himself.

Apart from the physical thickness of the volume, readers will observe several new features. After many years, special articles by prominent senior officers eminent in their own spheres of specialised naval interest have been revived. The theme this year is naval developments Under the Water, Over The Water, and From The Water, with a trilogy of articles on submarine progress, naval air power, and amphibious warfare.

An entirely novel feature is the directory section, listing the naval staff hierarchies, senior command appointments, directors of departments, naval and defence attaches, and commanding officers of major warships and naval establishments of most of the navies of the world.

Springing logically from this is a new "Who's Who" section of mini-biographies of members of naval boards, commanders-in-chief, flag officers and other senior and intermediate officers in many of the world's navies. The aim is to expand this first venture into a complete list of everybody who is anybody of note in the naval world. The opportunity is taken here of thanking those Sea Lords and Chiefs of Staff who have already supplied biographies together with encouraging wishes for success in the new field.

In addition to the main alphabetical reference section of ship data there are the usual separate sections on naval aircraft and guided missiles, and a two-page-spread table at the end of the national chapters summarising the numerical strengths of 55 of the largest navies and affording a quick comparison between the maritime nations of the world.

Altogether there are some 2,400 illustrations in the book comprising about 2,000 photographs and nearly 400 scale drawings. Particulars are given of over 14,000 ships and craft in the navies or sea defence forces of 106 countries (of which three new entries appear in this edition).

There has been the usual generous response this year from keen correspondents east and west, and with the goodwill and co-operation of all but a handful of the over 100 naval and maritime authorities concerned there has been a steady inflow of information and photographs to this annual, enabling the new edition to present the latest pictorial and descriptive portraits of newly built ships, reconstructed vessels and converted units, and to maintain the tradition, established last century, of giving a comprehensive panorama of all the world's fighting ships.

USA

Fighting an attritous war on the other side of the world is not the ideal setting for the measured pace and method required in planning and developing warships of the near and medi-distant future. On the other hand things technical never develop so fast as in wartime and the USA's effort in South East Asia has given a fillip, especially as regards electronics and logistics, to developments in naval architecture and fleet operations. There must have been many lessons learned by the US Navy in recent years which will be applied and incorporated in new construction warships and vessels on the drawing board. And perhaps it can already be said that the US Navy is the only navy of any consequence which has had recent experience of operating warships in real war conditions. So qualitatively and quantitively the US Navy ought to be first and foremost among the top ten navies for several years to come.

All the same, prodigious though the recent naval shipbuilding effort has been, especially in the fields of nuclear powered submarine construction and guided missile ship development, the US Navy still has not overcome its block obsolescence problem mentioned in these pages six years ago when most of the United States' aircraft carriers, cruisers, destroyers, submarines, escorts and minesweepers built during the war were already twenty years old (a good average life for all categories of warships). Now, of course, these same warships, refitted or not, are a quarter of a century old. Broadly speaking all the USA's post-war built ships are active or operational in the main US theatres, the Far East and the Mediterranean, poles apart geographically and functionally, while most of the war-built ships are still clogging the US Reserve Fleet ports. There was a time when batches of these ships surplus to US naval requirements could be disposed of to other navies, but the countries willing to purchase warships now coming up to 30 years old in some cases are becoming fewer. The US Navy has a long tradition (which stood the USA and Britain in good stead in the Second World War emergency) of keeping old ships in reserve for as long as the hulls last and they are beyond any further possible use. But in one sense now, war potential though they could still just be, they are becoming a liability, for while the US public sees the "on paper" navy swollen by hundreds of obsolescent destroyers, submarines, escorts and minesweepers, they are not very enthusiastic about paying for the building of new ships. So for the sake of the nation and the navy it might be more politic if all the ships laid up in their neat seried rows in the reserve ports were scrapped.

This mass disposal of war-built ships might be effected very soon now, for it has been proved that the Navy, even in war conditions, is viable without them, and a substantial programme of new construction is in hand which will compensate for the inevitable withdrawal from the active fleet of those war-built ships rehabilitated for a limited term.

It is not generally realised that of the 33 large US carriers (including three rated as amphibious assault ships and two as aircraft transports) no fewer than 24 are of World War II construction though most have been refitted or modernised several times). Only one of the 35 cruisers is of post-war construction (albeit nuclear powered). Only 16 of the 100 remaining conventionally powered submarines are of post-war construction. Some 300 of the 343 destroyers and 200 of the 238 escort ships are of WWII vintage.

A Congressional survey published in Washington recently painted a startling and gloomy picture of the United States Navy being an ageing collection of warships, smaller in number and technologically inferior to those of the USSR But there is always a tendency to exaggerate to make the point, and the disclosure was doubtless designed to shock the USA itself out of an unjustified complacency engendered by an innate pride in the belief that the USA still has the largest navy in the world.

Investigators for the Armed Services Sub-Committee on Seapower stated that the Soviet Union had outpaced the United States in new construction, the Soviet Navy boasting 1,575 vessels against the United States' 894. It was pointed out that the average age of the US ships was 17½ years and that 58 per cent of them were more than 20 years old, while only one in a hundred Soviet ships was that old. The sub-committee's verdict was that the US Navy is in a serious situation primarily because of the age of its ships.

But there is a lot to be offset against this pessimistic picture, real though the block obsolescence problem is. The nine great post-war aircraft carriers including the nuclear powered *Enterprise*, are the largest and finest instruments of sea power ever devised. No fewer than 90 nuclear powered submarines have been built in an almost incredibly short term, including 41 armed with ballistic missiles. Most of the 35 frigates built in recent years can do the jobs formerly done by the much larger but now outmoded conventional cruisers: they are armed with guided missiles and the largest are nuclear powered. And the 50 new escort ships, larger than most of the destroyers, and being turned out in almost a mass production line, will go some way to compensate for the 200 overage much smaller and more elementary destroyer escorts.

Aircraft carriers continue to serve as a primary means of projecting US tactical air power overseas, with current emphasis being on their providing combat sorties in South

Vietnam, reconnaissance missions over North Vietnam, and maintaining a force in readiness to support US interests in the critical Eastern Mediterranean area. In addition aircraft carriers permit rapid deployment of tactical air power to areas where lack of land airstrips, inadequate facilities or political considerations prevent or delay the use of land-based tactical air power.

The United States Navy now is facing other crises relating directly to warships and ship construction. According to a recent statement by the Chief of Naval Operations, Admiral Thomas H. Moorer, "the most serious threat to our country today is posed by the growing strategic nuclear offensive forces threat".

This threat is exemplified in the controversies now occurring in the United States over such issues as the Anti-Ballistic Missile (ABM) system and the Multiple Independently targeted Re-entry Vehicle (MIRV) warheads for the Poseidon and Minuteman III missiles.

Currently the US Navy contributes a major share of the nation's strategic offensive forces with 41 nuclear-powered submarines, each armed with 16 Polaris A-2 or A-3 missiles. Several of these submarines have already begun conversion to fire the improved MIRV-warhead Poseidon missile, with 31 submarines planned for Poseidon conversion by the mid-1970s.

Under development by the Department of Defense is a planned test and evaluation submarine for an improved Underwater Launched Missile System (ULMS). The primary advantage of the advanced submarine missile system would be an increase in missile range.

The submarine would be "on station", i.e., capable of targeting major Soviet cities and military complexes, even before it cleared harbour and would have an operating area which includes most of the Atlantic, Pacific, and Indian Oceans. Such a deployment for a missile submarine would make such a craft virtually invulnerable to any Soviet ASW threat.

However, Defense officials are not enthusiastic about increased Navy participation in strategic warfare capabilities beyond the 31-submarine Poseidon force. There have been reports—not fully denied by Department of Defense officials—that the ten submarines retaining Polaris missiles would be phased out in the mid-1970s and that, in the existing political environment, there would be no development of the advanced ULMS concept beyond a single experimental submarine.

Secretary of Defense Melvin R. Laird recently has expressed a lack of interest in advanced sea-based strategic systems and has questioned the survivability of US missile-armed submarines beyond the early 1970s against a determined Soviet ASW effort.

Instead, the Department of Defense plans to develop a new force of 1,000 land-based Minuteman III missiles with MIRV warheads and build a new bomber force of 240 B-1A aircraft. Because land-based missiles and bomber bases could be pre-targeted by the Soviets for a first-strike attack, it is further proposed that these strategic offensive forces be defended by the Sentinel Anti-Ballistic Missile system.

Efforts to increase the size of the submarine missile force above the 41-boat level, which was determined a decade ago, and to increase the level of studies into the feasibility and possible advantages of a Sea-based Anti-Ballistic Missile Intercept System (SABMIS) as an alternative to Sentinel have been halted by the Defense Department. This attitude reflects the current American land-oriented military policy as evidenced by the high level of involvement in the ground war in Southeast Asia when compared to —for example—American use of a naval blockade in the Cuban missile crisis of 1962.

This land-oriented policy has led to the construction of what some authorities consider "permanent" facilities in Southeast Asia, particularly the military complexes at Camranh Bay in South Vietnam and bases in Thailand. The latter were, until the 1968 bombing halt, used for aircraft attacking Communist road, rail, and water supply routes in North Vietnam. Simultaneously, proposals for a naval blockade of North Vietnamese ports to halt bulk shipments of arms, petroleum, and other war supplies by Communist and "neutral" merchant shipping were repeatedly denied.

Still, the ground war in Southeast Asia has shown the continuing importance of sea power in its many and varied forms. And, despite the advent of advanced jet cargo aircraft such as the C-141A StarLifter, approximately 98 per cent of all munitions, material, provisions, and fuels going to Southeast Asia are transported by sea. Most of this shipping is merchant, but specialised US Navy logistic support ships are employed with all shipping being directed and co-ordinated by the US Navy's Military Sea Transportation Service (MSTS) and, when in the war zone, escorted by US Navy craft.

The effects of the Vietnamese War on the US Navy have been to inflict a severe strain on ships in the aircraft carrier, fleet escort, amphibious, and auxiliary categories. Although age *per se* is not directly related to ship obsolescence, the pace and nature of operations in Southeast Asia have greatly increased the deterioration of US naval ships.

New construction ships have been deferred and delayed. The last new-construction destroyer for the US Navy was delivered to the Fleet in 1964 with the next class (DD 963) *scheduled* to begin deliveries in the mid-1970s; the last guided missile frigate (destroyer leader) was commissioned in 1966 with the next DLGN *scheduled* for completion in 1973.

Two other criticisms are being voiced about US warship programmes: the lack of significant improvements in capabilities and the increasing construction time. For example, whereas several navies, notably the Soviet and the Royal Navy, are now operating large, gas-turbine warships, the US Navy has none. The DD 963 class destroyers *may* have gas turbine propulsion but a new escort ship (DE 1101) to have had gas turbines has been cancelled. There is no small ASW helicopter available for use aboard destroyer and escort ships; the new guided missile frigates, which are to be 10,000-ton warships with nuclear propuslion, will have a diminutive missile armament of only two Tartar-Standard single launchers; and the new escort ships of the "Knox" class, 4,000-ton warships, have an anti-surface/anti-aircraft armament of only one 5 inch, rapid-fire gun. There has been a notable lack of development in the areas of surface-to-surface and close-in air defence missiles until quite recently.

For a variety of reasons, construction time for US warships is continually increasing: some "Knox" class escort ships are taking four years from keel laying to completion; some nuclear powered attack submarines also are requiring four years *and more* from keel laying to completion.

All this is tempered only by limited recognition of the US Navy's continuing importance in general/limited warfare operations—*in support of land-oriented strategy*—because of numerous areas of turmoil in the world which affect American interests, the withdrawal of United Kingdom forces from several crucial areas, and the increasing Soviet naval build-up. Plans continue for sustaining a 15-ship attack carrier force with a third nuclear-powered carrier (CVAN 70) in the Fiscal Year 1970 budget and a fourth CVAN planned for Fiscal Year 1971.

Also, the previous limit of 57 first-line nuclear attack submarines has been lifted and, to counter recent Soviet progress in this field, a new class of high-speed submarines (SSN 688) is being designed as is a single ultra-quiet attack submarine (SSN 685). A follow-on class of nuclear attack submarines is planned for construction starting in the mid-1970s.

The construction of new classes of destroyers (DD and DDG) is in the offing, but there is "many a slip 'twixt cup and lip". Reportedly, the number of ships planned for these classes has already undergone several downward revisions.

New classes of amphibious warfare and replenishment ships are joining the Fleet, but in both categories the Navy still is operating ships more than 25 years old, some of which have been in almost continuous service.

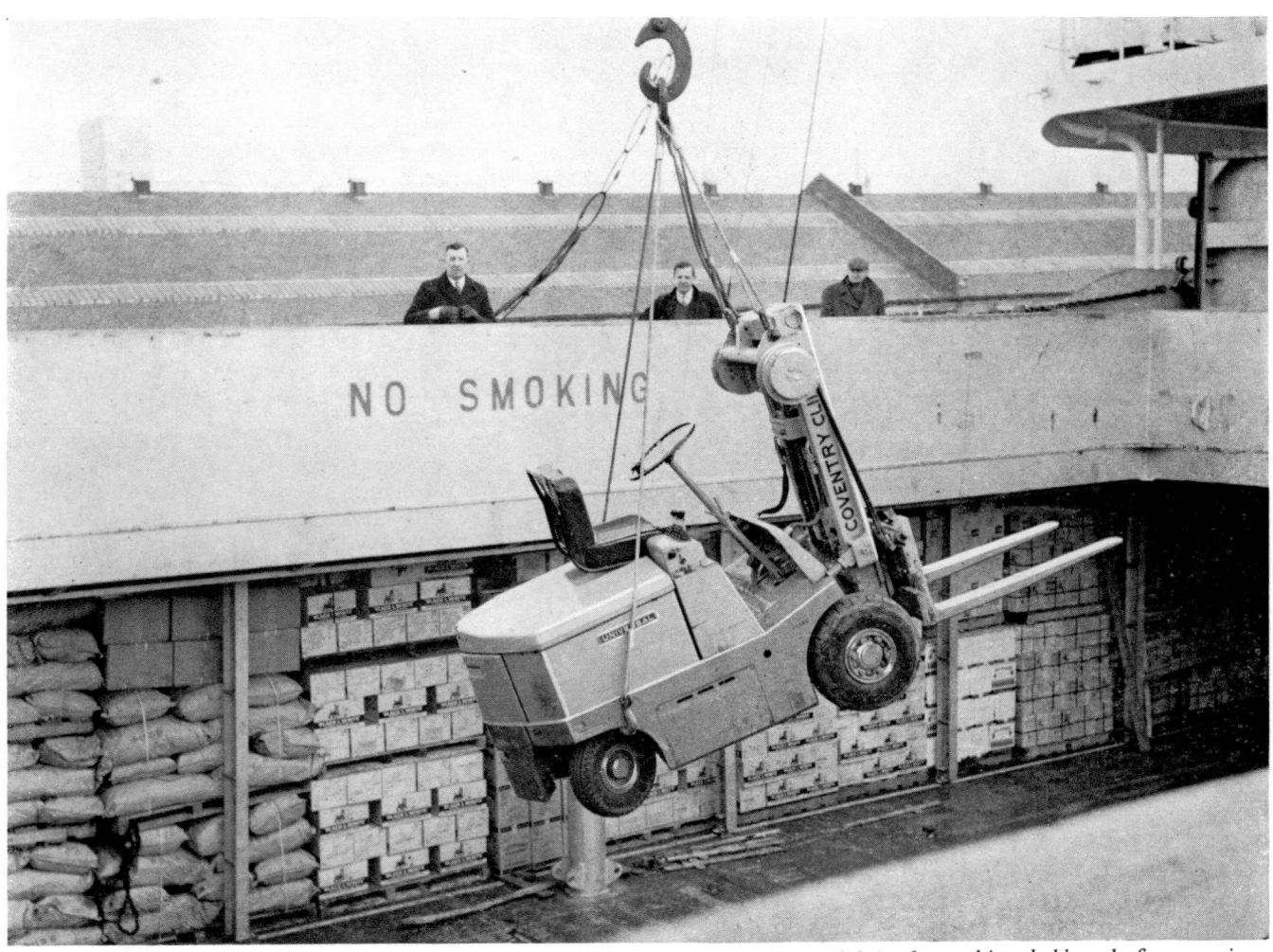

USSR

After building up her maritime forces for 20 years, but at the same time hiding her light under a bushel as far as the publicisation of her newer combatant ships was concerned, the Soviet Union has recently made a series of sorties to show the flag in the Mediterranean, in the Red Sea, in the Indian Ocean and in the Far East.

The latest and most formidable Soviet warships have in fact been seen all along, and off, the long sea route from the Baltic round the Cape to Vladivostok, and this is no phenomenon, but a justifiable and routine practice to maintain the connecting file between the USSR in the west and the USSR in the east.

Britain in her heyday had a similar chain of warships all the way from the English Channel, through the Straits of Gibraltar, the Mediterranean and the Suez Canal, now impassable, down the Red Sea, across the Indian Ocean, through the Straits of Malacca and along the coasts of South East Asia and China to, and up, the Yangstse River, and on to Dairen, to secure her physical and intangible interests. Britain has unshackled the chain and the Soviet Union has picked up the links. But she has to go by the Cape.

There is no doubt that, whether for the wide oceans or narrow waters, the Soviet Navy is now a modern and well-balanced force to be reckoned with. And it is not standing still. There was a period in the early 1950s when to save time and in the interests of economy and mass production numerically very large classes of conventional destroyers and other categories of light warships were turned out for several years by the hundred. But latterly the Soviet Navy has departed from uniformity and the assembly line and can now afford to progress on with made-to-measure warships designed for specific purposes or locations. Indeed for several years a new class has made its appearance each year and successive types of destroyers have progressed from sophistification to ingenuity, with novel missile systems and propelling machinery, and developed into what would formerly have been called light cruisers.

It has already been seen what a successful fifty-fifty compromise the Soviet Navy can make between a guided missile cruiser and a helicopter carrier in the shape of the not too massive *Moskva*, and it would not be very surprising, after the experience gained with the building of this ship and her sister, if the Soviet Navy came up with a medium sized vehicle for VTOL aircraft which would vie in utility with some of the bigger fixed-wing carriers possessed by other powers.

Although the USSR has had nuclear powered submarines for some years it has been generally reckoned that they have not approached the degree of sophistification of their opposite numbers in the American and British navies nor have been armed with missiles of the range of those foreign contemporaries. But this is a position which cannot obtain for long when it is remembered not only that the USSR has made great strides in rocketry in recent years, as witness the space travel programme, but that it was the USSR who produced the world's first nuclear powered surface ship to put to sea (the giant icebreaker *Lenin*, as heavy as *Moskva*) ten years ago. It is evident as class succeeds class, that Soviet nuclear powered and ballistic missile submarines are achieving parity.

The world's navies have also been impressed with the latest super destroyers or light cruisers armed with surface-to-air or surface-to-surface missiles, with the new classes of escorts, with the successive types of minesweepers, the constantly improving series of missile boats and torpedo boats running into hundreds, new kinds of landing ships, a variety of support ships, and many specialised auxiliaries.

Commensurate with the recent expansion of the Soviet Navy the amount of material in the Soviet section of this edition has been increased by about 33 per cent. It is estimated that the Soviet Navy now includes 65 nuclear powered submarines, 320 diesel driven submarines, 2 helicopter ships, 25 cruisers, 100 destroyers, 100 escorts, 275 patrol vessells, 350 minesweepers, 125 missile boats, 350 torpedo boats and 230 landing ships. Support ships, auxiliaries and service craft run into thousands.

A large proportion of this well-balanced and formidable. navy has been showing the flag in the Mediterranean. This force, which includes some of the Soviet Union's largest, newest and most sophisticated combatant units is demonstrably the cream of the USSR's fighting ships. It is manifestly not the sort of fleet which could be sunk within minutes of the outbreak of hostilities.

United Kingdom

The Royal Navy is undergoing a very painful process. It is having to make do and mend on very meagre funds. New construction types are being designed hopefully for one new ship to do the work of two or more old ships destined for the shipbreakers yards. If the trend continues that thin grey line which Jane's Fighting Ships foreshadowed in the 1962-63 edition will be a thinner dotted line with more gaps than dots. Of course the new ships are more sophisticated, but whether they are needed as a deterrent in peacetime or to fight in wartime it is numbers that count.

Of the ships now coming forward from recent new construction programmes, the nuclear powered submarines *Churchill* and *Revenge*, the guided missile armed destroyers *Antrim* and *Norfolk*, and six more general purposes frigates of the "Leander" class are emerging from the building yards and commissioning for service. Looking slightly further ahead, in addition to the fifth and sixth nuclear powered large fleet submarines *Conqueror* and *Superb* and the guided missile super-destroyer (or light cruiser) *Bristol* (just launched) from recent new construction programmes, there are in the pipeline two nuclear powered large fleet submarines of "Improved" Type; the first of the "Type 42" guided missile armed destroyers; the prototype of the "Type 21" frigates; and the design for the "Type 22" frigates, successors of the now almost completed programme of "Leander" class frigates.

The first of the "Type 42" destroyers, ordered in Nov 1968, will carry the Sea Dart surface-to-air missiles, and while she will be only about half the displacement of a "County" class guided missile destroyer she will carry a much more powerful anti-aircraft and anti-missile armament. The "Type 21" frigate, a Vosper-Yarrow design, will be much smaller than the "Leander" design but will carry a similar range of general purpose armament, including a helicopter.

As regards reconstruction and modernisation, the newly converted helicopter cruiser *Blake* has been commissioned after having been in dockyard hands for nearly four years; and the £30,000,000 special refit and conversion of the big aircraft carrier *Ark Royal*, enabling her to operate Phantom aircraft, is being completed.

The former symmetrical lines of HMS *Blake* have gone. For the sacrifice of more than half her armament she has gained the facility for operating up to four helicopters, which seems a modest return for the platform offered by a 566 ft cruiser and the expenditure of over £5,000,000. The smaller Italian cruiser *Vittorio Veneto* can carry nine helicopters with hangar facilities under the flight deck. A fifty-fifty compromise of cruiser and helicopter carrier on the lines of the Soviet ships *Moskva* and *Leningrad* would appear to have been a better investment. It is probably too late to alter *Tiger*, being converted on much the same lines as *Blake*, but perhaps *Lion* could be modified with hangar amidships and flight deck from hangar to stern or with a flight deck extending from the waist to the stern and hangar facilities underneath.

It is not generally appreciated that *Ark Royal*, when her modernisation and rehabilitation has been completed, must be reckoned as a mobile airstrip, a potent instrument of sea power deployable in any ocean. Assuming that nuclear deterrents will never be used this great aircraft carrier will constitute a massive proportion of Britain's sea-borne deterrent against war.

Completed in 1955, if she had merely been maintained with routine refits and no major reconstruction at all, she could have been expected to last at least until 1975, as twenty years or more is now regarded as the normal minimum life of an aircraft carrier, indeed of any warship of great size, complexity and cost.

But after having undergone such an extensive refit as she has in 1967-70 at a cost of 1½ times her original cost her span of life has been considerably extended, and in the normal course of wear and tear she should last until 1985. For she has not only been converted and strengthened to carry Phantom aircraft, but the opportunity has been taken to update to current and foreseeable future standards every department of the ship, with generously reappointed accommodation, air conditioning and insulation. It is quite inconceivable that this expensively rejuvenated highly mobile aerodrome could be phased out in 1971 after only 18 months further service at sea.

The same thesis applies to her sister ship *Eagle* which was completed in 1951 but almost entirely rebuilt during 1959 to 1964 at a cost of over £31,000,000, twice her original cost, giving her an estimated further life span until 1980. If only a further 15 per cent of that sum were spent to render her fully capable of operating the Phantom aircraft she would be an even better ship than *Ark Royal* for *Eagle* was completely redesigned only five years ago.

And to a large extent the argument is still valid for the smaller aircraft carrier *Hermes*, actually the Royal Navy's most modern carrier on a date of building basis, for completed only ten years ago she was extensively refitted at a cost of £10,000,000 in 1964-66 during which she was widened and rearmed with guided missiles.

While Britain retains these few surviving aircraft carriers she is still a first class naval power. If she sacrifices them before new types of ships are built to operate VTOL aircraft she will drop straight down to a status comparable with that of a third rate maritime country.

But the time factor involved in the replacement of fixed-wing carriers by VTOL carriers will probably be greater than is generally realised.

The "Harrier", the first operational VTOL aircraft, has a very limited payload and range and subsonic speed in its initial service form; and can only be regarded as a first generation VTOL *naval* aircraft. Not sooner than the late seventies can a fully effective naval VTOL aircraft and its equivalent carrier be in service. The below deck space requirement for such a VTOL aircraft is not much less than that needed for a present day naval combat aircraft, and the size of a VTOL carrier is likely to exceed the size of the *Moskva*.

NATO

This year saw the 20th Anniversary Review of NATO Navies by Her Majesty Queen Elizabeth II. Held on 16 May, this was a huge success by any standard, and reflected great credit on the organisers of the Fleet Assembly. It must have been a source of great pride to Admiral Sir Nigel Henderson, Chairman of the NATO Military Committee who went to some instance to point out that he was international, and only accidentally British and Naval (his post could be filled by an officer of his rank of any NATO nationality and any Service). And a matter of much satisfaction to Admiral Sir John Bush, an unblushingly British salt horse, with international connections, in seeing the fruition of a theory nurtured into practice.

This naval review was a symbolic exercise to celebrate the 20th Anniversary of the North Atlantic Treaty Organisation and to illustrate the military and political unity of the Alliance. The venue was Portsmouth, chosen for its close compass to long anchorages at Spithead where national reviews are traditionally held. No fewer than 63 ships of the 12 nations who assign forces to the Alliance were represented there, a clear indication that at the right time and in the right circumstances a mere squadron of the size of the NATO Standing Naval Force can be increased to the size and composition of a fair Navy. The well-balanced Fleet comprised an aircraft carrier, three cruisers, 36 destroyers and frigates, four submarines, a command ship, a minelayer, 14 minesweepers and three fleet replenishment ships from the navies of Belgium, Canada, Denmark, Germany, Greece, Italy, Netherlands, Norway, Portugal, Turkey, United Kingdom and USA.

The tasks of the NATO navies are to fulfil the strategy of flexibility in response by deterrents in the shape of both nuclear submarines and conventional ships, to maintain the security of the sea areas if trouble should arise, and to support the battle in Europe in case of emergency.

The object of the Standing Naval Force Atlantic (STANAVFORLANT in the modern fashion of portmanteau initials) is to maintain a force in peacetime under NATO control as a visible sign of the deterrent and a force which can be easily sent at short notice in the name of NATO as a demonstration of involvement in the case of need. The composition of the six ships of STANAVFORLANT at the time of the NATO Review was two Netherlands ships, one US, one British, one German and one Portuguese, but it has been, and could be, any combination of any of the nations in NATO. The concept for a similar force in the Mediterranean has already been agreed but has not been given much material form at the time of writing.

A very important function of the NATO navies and Maritime air forces in peacetime is surveillance, with responsibility co-ordinated by NATO.

But the allied navies at the present time are barely strong enough to carry out their tasks. Moreover, at the present rate of building new ships they certainly will not be in a few years time. It is not without significance that there is a greater proportion of new ships in the Soviet Navy, for instance, than there is in the allied navies.

No striving infant of the potential calibre, and with the aspirations, of STANAVFORLANT could but be aware of the quite miraculous use of the maritime strength of the USSR in the shape of its para-military merchant navy, its world-wide network of "research" ships, its huge fleets of "fishing" vessels, its ubiquitous intelligence trawlers, and above all its preponderant fighting navy which shows a proliferation of guided missiles and rocket projectiles. NATO could perhaps be forgiven if it did not entirely dismiss the thought that the Soviet Fleet in the Mediterranean might be there not only for political purposes to support any expansionist policies the USSR might have in the Middle East but also as a formidable counter to the United States Sixth Fleet. The NATO Military Committee is evidently resigned to the prospect of a continuing expansion of the Soviet Navy in furtherance of the spread of Soviet influence throughout the world and considers that the allies must do something if they are not to be outstripped.

The three big "A"s in the southern continents, South Africa, Argentine and Australia, are becoming increasingly and uncomfortably aware of the close proximity of the Hammer and Sickle emblem. Through a visit to South America by her Foreign Minister South Africa is reported to have made approaches to Argentina and Brazil with the object of linking South Africa and the Atlantic coast nations of South America in a defence pact to counter Communist penetration of the South Atlantic. And the Commander-in-Chief of the Argentine Navy reciprocated as a guest of the South African Defence Department. South African Navy units paid courtesy visits to Argentina and also to Australia. All these exchanges reflect the growing concern of South Africa, custodian of the today never so important sea route round the Cape, over the power vacuum in the Indian Ocean and the South Atlantic caused by the withdrawal of British forces east of Suez and from South Atlantic.

It has been suggested that there is a need south of the equator for a South Atlantic Treaty Organisation or SATO on the same lines as NATO. But why a separate SATO and NATO? Why not a combined SATO and NATO in the shape of a GATO or Greater Atlantic Treaty Organisation? It has long been a particular source of frustration to NATO that its jurisdiction is limited southwards by an arbitrarily fixed tropical line of latitude drawn on the ocean charts to exclude naval operations in the southern hemisphere even if urgent considerations required a show-the-flag foray.

Surely the logical development for the combined defence of all maritime nations in the western hemisphere would be a supreme GATO fleet under the command of an admiral divided into the three sub-commands of NATO, SATO and

METO (Mediterranean Treaty Organisation) each administered by a commodore or flag officer as circumstances dictated.

But looking ahead, even this is not the ultimate development of the banding together of a community of maritime nations for their mutual protection and preparedness. Once the principle of contributing to the common naval pool had been established by seconding ships to the GATO fleet a new principle could be introduced of contributing funds to the common wealth and setting up the GATO as a supra-national organisation which would order and build ships to its own requirements wherever it thought fit and which would select, and eventually train, its own officers and men who would owe allegiance not to any one country but to GATO. The fleet would be maintained by funds calculated on a per capita and pro rata system according to the population and wealth of the constituent countries of GATO. In this way nations who had formerly enjoyed wealth and high financial stature at the expense of other countries by not maintaining navies commensurate with their economic health and national standing would contribute their fair share for the common weal.

This supra-national GATO Navy would also have its own Reserve Fleet taking over the warships surplus to the naval requirements of countries in changed or straightened circumstances, and commissioning them in rotation from a special base in, say, the Netherlands or Belgium. In this way perfectly good ships with years of life left in them would not be lost to the shipbreakers until they had been completely expended in service. Several not so old ships spring to mind which are to be discarded in the near future but which could serve on under NATO jurisdiction, notably the British "Daring" class destroyers, only 16 years old, and the Netherlands cruiser *De Ruyter*, much admired at the NATO review. Even the arbitrarily axed aircraft carrier *Victorious*, rebuilt in 1950-58, could have become the kingpin of the NATO fleet for a few more years.

Dual Alliance

When the Royal Navy has lost its aircraft carriers and the last of its war-built ships has gone to the shipbreakers (and that time is looming up in both cases) the erstwhile Great Britain will be left with practically a small ship navy. The question might then justifiably be posed: will it be viable for overseas attenuation as well as in home and European waters? Will it have enough ships and ships with sufficient deterrent to be able to maintain patrol in brush fire danger areas in South East Asia, the East Indies, the Red Sea, the Persian Gulf, the West Indies and wherever there are emergent or frustrated nations simmering up to the boil? Will it even be able to make a token show in the Mediterranean?

With the rate of new construction not nearly keeping pace with the rate of scrapping older ships the Royal Navy must soon be smaller than at any time in the last couple of centuries. How can this be redressed? A merger with another navy with comparable interests could be the answer. A partnership between the navies of Britain and the Netherlands. Both countries are in the same boat.

Each has a sovereign. Each has lost an empire. Each is a nation of sailors and explorers for nigh on a thousand years. But probably the best argument for integration is that they like each other. Each faces the North Sea and commands the approaches to the English Channel. But neither relishes the prospect of being restricted merely to picket Europe. Rather would both navies like to maintain a Far East role despite the fact that their Governments have abdicated their East of Suez bases. The two nations are no longer rivals. Instead their interests are surprisingly intermingled. Both depend upon seaborne trade. Both have a big residue of financial interests in the Far East and both believe in sea power to sustain them. But the Netherlands has sold its one aircraft carrier and Britain is to phase out its few remaining aircraft carriers. So both navies are reduced from great power stature. How best to regain that standing? Amalgamation would go a long way. There could be a Dutch or British warship wherever there was a Dutch or British interest, be it in East Indies or West Indies, South America or South Africa, Malaysia or Indonesia, Australia or New Zealand. Already both countries have a measure of uniformity and homogeniety—there are new frigates of the very successful "Leander" class in both navies. This could be extended to common hardware and equipment in the two fleets. A merger would cut the cost of deterrent operations, fill the gaps created by savage defence cuts, and keep both nation's trade routes round the Cape open while the Suez Canal is closed.

Acknowledgements

The editor and publishers welcome this year a newcomer to *Jane's Fighting Ships:* Mr Arnold Hague, who has assisted in the compilation of the sections other than China, the USSR, the United Kingdom and the countries of Europe, including Turkey, which have remained the direct responsibility of the editor.

For the second year Mr Norman Polmar, "our man in Washington", has compiled the US chapter in direct liaison with the Navy Department of the Pentagon, evidence of which can be seen in that extensively revised section.

As usual *Fighting Ships* is much indebted to the Naval Boards, Navy Departments and Ministries of Marine and Defence who furnished information and photographs. This was facilitated by the kindness of the Ambassadors and Naval Attaches in London, including: Rear-Admiral Luis Maria Iriart, Argentine Navy; Rear-Admiral J. Brasseur-Kermadec, French Navy: Rear-Admiral Louis J. Kirn, United States Navy; Commodore Ulf E. A. Reinius, Royal Swedish Navy; Captain Haroldo Ramos, Brazilian Navy; Captain J. Thornton, Chilean Navy; Captain O. Vitikka, Finnish Navy; Captain K. T. Raedar, Federal German Navy; Captain N. A. Stathakio, Royal Hellenic Navy; Captain G. Martucci, Italian Navy; Captain Goro Yoshimura, Japanese Embassy; Captain F. de Blocq van Kuffeler, Royal Netherlands Navy; Captain O. E. Aklaksund, Royal Norwegian Navy; Captain R. Arrospide, Peruvian Navy; Captain J. C. Munoz-Delgado, Spanish Navy; Captain A. Nabanchang, Royal Thai Navy; Captain O. Karabulat, Turkish Navy; Colonel H.R.H. Prince Georg of Denmark, CVO, Royal Danish Embassy; Colonel J. Kaczorek, Polish Embassy; Commander J. B. P. Azevedo, Portuguese Navy; Commander R.D. Kingon, South African Navy; Commander Z. D. Kostic, Yugoslav Navy; Lt Colonel R Close, Belgian Embassy.

Grateful acknowledgement is made of the kind co-operation of Captain H. H. Cook, RN, Director of Public Relations (Naval), Ministry of Defence, London; Chief of Naval Information, Washington; Commandant, US Coast Guard; Commander H. E. Hetu, USN, Public Affairs Officer for the Commander-in-Chief United States Naval Forces Europe;

Captain K. D. Gray, DFC, RAN, Australian Naval Representative, London; Captain H. R. Tilley, CD, RCN, Senior Canadian Naval Liaison Officer, Canadian Defence Staff, London; Commodore K. K. Sanjana, IN, Indian Naval Adviser, London; Commander K. M. Hussain, PN, Pakistan Naval Adviser, London; Commodore E. C. Thorne, RNZN, Senior Royal New Zealand Naval Liaison Officer, London, Dr Gordon W. Stead, DSC, BCom, BA, LLD, CIMarE, Assistant Deputy Minister, Marine, Ottawa;

M. Henri le Masson, Editor of "Flottes de Combat", Herr Gerhard Albrecht, Editor of "Weyers Flottentaschenbuch"; Vice-Admiral Alberto Zamboni, Editor of "Rivista Marittima"; Captain Allan Kull, Editor of "Marinkalender"; Mr John S. Rowe, Editor "Ships and Aircraft of the US Fleet";

Dr Luigi Accorsi, Rear-Admiral M. J. Adam, CVO, CBE; Professor Alfredo Aguilera; Dr Giorgio Arra; Mr William H. Davis; Sr. Vicente Elias; Mr James C. Fahey; Dr Aldo Fraccaroli; Constructor Lt-Commander Shizuo Fukui; Dr Giorgio Giorgerini; Commander Alvin H. Grobmeier; Captain T. D. Manning, CBE, VRD, RNVR; Ing Augusto Nani; Mr C. W. E. Richardson; Captain Aluino Martins da Silva; Captain R. Steen Steensen, RDN; Herr Stefen Terzibaschitsch; Mr Godfrey H. Walker; and many others who prefer to remain anonymous.

The Editor of the United States section is grateful to the many individuals in the US armed services and in American industry who provided assistance for this year's edition, in particular: Lt Colonel Jerome Holland, USAF, and Lieutenant Kenneth Sayers, USN, of the Office of the Assistant Secretary of Defense (Public Affairs); Mr Robert Carlisle, Chief Warrant Officer Rodney Moen, and Lieutenant Douglas Strole of the Office of Information, Department of the Navy; Mr Richard Bassett, Public Affairs Officer, Naval Ship Systems Command; Lieutenant Samuel Morison, Naval History Division; Mr Lamar Holt, editor of "Sealift" magazine; Lieutenant Commander A. Marsh former Deputy Special Projects Officer of the Military Sea Transportation Service; Lieutenant Commander J. W. Duenzel, Chief Warrant Officer Joseph Greco, and Miss Elizabeth Segedi of the Public Affairs Office, US Coast Guard.

No illustration may be reproduced without permission; but the Press may reproduce information and official photographs at sight provided *Jane's Fighting Ships* is fully acknowledged. Photographs credited to professional photographers are copyright and should not be reproduced without permission. Their addresses are: Wright & Logan, Albert Road Junction, Portsmouth, England; Skyfotos, Lympne Airport, Kent, England; and A. & J. Pavia, 40 Ordnance Street, Valletta, Malta.

Photographs or information for the next edition, the preparation of which starts immediately should be sent as soon as possible to the Editor, "Janes Fighting Ships", care of Jane's Yearbooks, Sampson Low, Marston & Co, 49/50 Poland Street, London, W.1., England.

Raymond V. B. Blackman.

SPECIAL SUPPLEMENT

A TRILOGY OF NAVAL DEVELOPMENT

UNDER THE WATER

OVER THE WATER

FROM THE WATER

Articles:

THE PROGRESSION IN SUBMARINE WARFARE

By

Vice-Admiral Sir Michael P. Pollock, KCB, MVO, DSC

Flag Officer, Submarines

NAVAL AIR POWER

By

Rear-Admiral P. D. Gick, CB, OBE, DSC & Bar

(late *Flag Officer, Flying Training)*

AMPHIBIOUS WARFARE AT THE CLOSE OF THE 1960s

By

Major-General J. L. Moulton, CB, DSO, OBE

(ROYAL MARINES retired, *Chief of Amphibious Warfare,* 1957-61)

UNDER THE WATER

THE PROGRESSION IN SUBMARINE WARFARE

By

Vice-Admiral Sir Michael P. Pollock, KCB, MVO, DSC

Flag Officer, Submarines

The following article by Vice Admiral Sir Michael Pollock reflects his personal views formed both as an officer who has served most of his career in surface ships or appointments connected with them and during his present appointment as the Flag Officer Submarines. They do not necessarily reflect the views of the Ministry of Defence, London, and, indeed, the whole examination of the subject is of a general nature and has no greater reference to the Royal Navy than to any other navy.

THE PROGRESSION IN SUBMARINE WARFARE

Development History

Not surprisingly the idea of exploiting the concealment afforded by operating underwater has a long history reputedly going back as far as Alexander the Great.

The capability so to operate has a much shorter history because it has depended upon successive breakthroughs in the technologies of hull construction, propulsion and weapons. This progression continues right up to the present day.

Another continuing thread that we find throughout the history of the military use of the undersea is that it has always been the weaker maritime power which sought to develop the submarine as a weapon system—initially to break a blockade or to act as a mobile minefield in defence of its ports—and, later in its history, to break the maritime control of an opponent in an area otherwise dominated by surface or air forces. Until the submarine reached a certain level of operational capability, the limited defensive role was almost inevitable, but it was only when its offensive role became predominant that this weapon began to make a substantial impact on the conduct of the war at sea.

In the field of material, it was not until a steel hull, driven by a propulsion system stronger than a man's arms and with a weapon less suicidal than a charge on the end of a spar, was available, that it began to be apparent that here indeed was a weapon of war which must at least be countered even if not adopted for its usefulness.

It was in the nineteenth century—and particularly the second half—that, after a number of early attempts with inadequate technology, the vital technical constituents began to come together. France, USA, Germany and Russia, among others, all experimented actively with a variety of craft which ranged from what was virtually a torpedo boat which could be trimmed down in the water to make its attack while running awash, to a genuine submersible which appeared on the surface only to have a look at its target. These achieved varying degrees of success and the promise of some lethality—unfortunately not infrequently to their crew rather than target.

The Pax Britannica

This was the period in history in which "Pax Britannica" enforced by the Royal Navy was nearly complete. What then were the British doing to develop this new maritime weapon? The answer is "nothing"—not because of any inability to do so but because the Admiralty wished to give no encouragement whatever to this concept of undersea warfare which obviously could only undermine the overwhelming maritime advantage at that time held by the British Fleet.

At the beginning of the nineteenth century, when Fulton had persuaded Pitt to take an interest in his *Nautilus*—hand or sail propelled and armed only with a charge designed to be screwed to the wooden hull of a target—the appreciation of Earl St. Vincent, then First Lord of the Admiralty, was that such a development could only be to the detriment of British maritime supremacy. He refused to co-operate, saying "Pitt is the greatest fool that ever existed to encourage a mode of war which those who command the seas do not want and which, if successful, will deprive them of it". A remarkably percipient view for 1801, but one which persisted for far too long into the twentieth century and discouraged pro-submarine developments in the British Navy for many years.

By the end of the nineteenth century, however, it was becoming apparent that, with the development of electric propulsion, the Whitehead torpedo and other weapons, the submarine could no longer be safely ignored and the British Navy must at least study the submarine as a weapon in order to defeat it. For this, submarines were required and in 1901 the greatest naval power of the time had to turn to the USA to buy the designs of the Holland submarine. Five were then built in England.

Progress in European Countries

Thereafter, progress was rapid in the main European countries, who were in this decade all involved in the naval armament race which was the expensive prelude to the First World War.

By 1914 a submarine had been introduced into service in all the major navies of the world of characteristics which would have been by no means unrecognisable or inoperable by the submariners of a quarter of a century later: diesel propelled on the surface and by electric motors when submerged; armed with an outfit of Whitehead torpedoes and a small gun; fitted with ballast tanks for submergence and with hydroplanes for underwater depth keeping.

The First World War

The First World War showed that the submarine had come of age as an effective weapon system: many preconceived ideas on its use had been proved wrong and many new developments and ideas had been exploited.

It had become evident that its use as a defensive force at a port or in direct support of fleet operations was ineffective: the mobility of submarines at that period and the inadequate communications and sensory systems combined to ensure that they were seldom in the right place at the right time.

Conversely when used offensively they were the only instrument of maritime power which could operate either against warships or merchant ships in areas otherwise dominated by the opposition.

This was the chink in the armour of a maritime power—exploited on different occasions by both the Allies and the Central powers—which St. Vincent had foreseen over a hundred years before, and which in 1917 so nearly defeated the Allies by disruption of vital supply lines and the staggering losses of merchant ships.

The submarines of both sides had achieved their results with torpedoes and guns, using the latter as much as possible to conserve torpedoes, but frequently forced to use their underwater weapon by the strength of the opposition.

In the earlier part of the war there was virtually no method of detecting a submerged submarine and nets and mines constituted the main danger. By the end of it, the hydrophone and hydrostatically fired depth charge were beginning to set the pattern for the future.

Between The Wars

Between the wars the submarines of all maritime powers became larger, with longer ranges and endurance, higher speeds and greater diving depths but basically no different from their predecessors. There was no major technological breakthrough in propulsion, weapons or hull.

Several possibilities were explored. The British experimented not only with a single screw anti-submarine submarine which was years ahead of its time, but also with a steam driven "Fleet Submarine"—designed to operate ahead of the battle fleet; with a submarine seaplane carrier; with a submarine armed with a 12" gun and with another submarine armed with two twin 5.2-inch turrets designed as an ocean commerce raider.

These and similar experiments in other navies were failures: either because the tactical concept backing them was of dubious validity or the state of current technology was not adequate to support their design.

One of these experimental submarines was lost, all proved ineffective and the start of the second world war saw both sides entering the lists with patrol type submarines, armed with torpedoes and a small gun, clearly recognisable as direct descendants of the First World War vintage.

Twenty Years of Peace

During the twenty years of peace, however, the hunting forces had developed the ASDIC and better depth charges, which, for the first time gave surface forces some chance of detecting and destroying a submerged submarine not only in coastal but in open waters.

At the start of the Second World War the effectiveness of this new counter was greatly over estimated and many authorities held that the day of the submarine was over.

Events proved this not to be so, but the five years of war produced changes in tactics to meet new countermeasures and the fluctuating successes of both sides reflected the successive tactical and technological moves and counter moves as they occurred.

The Second World War

The need to reduce the detection capability of the ASDIC and to develop a tactic capable of defeating the convoy systems, initially brought the commerce raiding submarines in the North Atlantic to the surface and the bloody "Wolf Pack" battles with the escorted convoys were the result.

In these, the German U-boats operated as submersible torpedo boats using their speed on the surface to concentrate on a selected convoy, attacking on the surface by night in company, and diving only to avoid the escorting destroyers and frigates.

The development of radar and the increasing effectiveness of aircraft patrols defeated this tactic in the North Atlantic while the converse occurred in the Pacific where the use of radar by United States submarines gave them an overwhelming advantage against an enemy lagging far behind in this field and their large and efficient submarines outfought the Japanese convoy escorts.

So the seesaw of tactics and technology went up and down until, right at the end of the war in Europe, occurred a breakthrough in submarine technology comparable with the development of diesel/electrics forty years earlier.

A Revolutionary Innovation

This was the development by the Germans of a Netherlands invention, the "Schnorkel',—a method by which a submarine could recharge its batteries or make its passage submerged on its diesel engines with nothing showing above the surface except a small dome from which to suck in the necessary air and discharge the exhaust gas from the engines.

Here indeed was a revolutionary innovation: at one stroke most of the advantages conferred by overwhelming air superiority and by the efficient centimetric radar fitted in escorts and aircraft were swept away.

But it was too late to affect the outcome of the war and it will remain a fascinating speculation as to what might have happened had this development and the other far more advanced method of propulsion, the closed cycle high test peroxide engine being built into the German Mk XXVI U-boats, reached operational service in time.

Submarine Was Still A Submersible

And so the Second World War ended with the role, effectiveness, tactics and importance of the submarine not so very different from thirty years before.

The material development had been of an evolutionary rather than revolutionary nature: the submarine was still a submersible—rather more so after the development of the schnorkel, but still requiring a connection with the surface from time to time.

Its weapon was still the torpedo and the gun, the former much developed by the addition of elementary acoustic homing, "pattern running" and such refinements, but still relatively slow, relatively short ranged and, as each participant found in turn at one stage or another, a weapon of doubtful reliability.

Weapon of the Locally Weaker Power

The pattern of previous historical development had repeated itself and it was the weaker maritime power, in this case Germany, which had relied most heavily on the submarine as its principal maritime weapon and which had also led the world in the material developments in submarine propulsion—the schnorkel and the Walther hydrogen peroxide propulsion system.

These two developments arrived too late to affect the outcome; but even without them, the German submarine force had come within an ace of winning the Battle of the Atlantic but had been defeated by superior British tactics and technology and by the formidable volume of United States ship building capacity.

In the Far East, the converse had happened and the US submarine force had achieved a complete stranglehold on Japanese trade and maritime control long before the latter had been surrendered to superior air and surface forces.

Without the backing of an immense ship building programme conducted outside the range of enemy interference (as the United States had), the Japanese shipping losses reached a level at which the defeat of the country by starvation was inevitable even had the nuclear bomb not ushered in a new era of warfare at the same time as it terminated the old.

Growing Soviet Submarine Strength

At the end of the war, the USA was left with overwhelming maritime superiority but a potential opponent in her ex-ally, the USSR, already constructing a rapidly growing number of submarines.

Britain, twice in a generation nearly defeated by submarine war in the Atlantic, viewed the growing Soviet submarine strength with deep concern.

None of the victorious allies had in hand material developments in the submarine field comparable with those which were already in an advanced stage in Germany.

Immediate post-war efforts in all three countries were largely devoted to evaluating these new ideas and incorporating the principles of the Mk XXI U-boat with its high submerged speed into their existing submarine forces and immediate post-war construction.

Surprisingly little effort was directed towards improving the weapons or to developing the characteristics of hull, propulsion, sensors and weapons into one co-ordinated package as was already being found necessary in the more advanced aircraft projects.

The submarine scene was now ready for revolutionary change and the developments in technology which would make this possible were coming to fruition.

The First Nuclear Powered Vessel

In 1954, the USA completed the first nuclear powered vessel in history and called it *Nautilus* after Fulton's advanced submersible of a hundred and fifty years earlier.

A discontinuity in the course of submarine development, comparable with that achieved in the weapon field by the introduction of nuclear explosives, had occurred and every principle of submarine and anti-submarine warfare would require re-validation as a result.

It is important to understand why the introduction of this method of propulsion was so revolutionary in the field of underwater warfare while it has proved so far to have lesser advantages for surface ships and other applications.

The submarine has always been vulnerable to surface forces because of its need to have contact with the surface of the sea to replenish its atmosphere and recharge its underwater propulsion system.

There had always been a conflict in design created by the different characteristics required when operating on the surface and when operating submerged: the very shape of the hull could not be optimised for both, and because of the limited weight and space available for propulsion, the requirement for speed and endurance was not reconcilable within the same hull for both submerged and surface conditions.

The True Submarine

With nuclear power the true submarine became at last a realisable prospect. Developments were now possible in air purification and conditioning, to sophisticated navigation systems depending upon gyros and accelerometers rather than observations of astronomical or earthly reference points, to new steels, new welding techniques, new standards of precision engineering and greatly improved submerged sensors.

The dream of Jules Verne thus became capable of construction and Captain Nemo's *Nautilus* of fiction became translated into fact and sailed under the United States ensign.

With almost unlimited endurance, with a submerged speed greater than most surface ships under calm conditions and than all in rough weather, wholly divorced from contact with—and hence detection on, the surface of the sea; capable of evading the most advanced sonar by outrunning its carrier; or attacking any ship at a time of its own choosing and, if unsuccessful, of withdrawing and returning to repeat the attack; capable of following a hostile force in periods of tension until required to intervene: here was a new concept of undersea operations made possible by this revolutionary advance in technology and seeming set fair to replace all other forms of maritime power.

Search For A Weapon

Of course, it proved not to be entirely so— at least in the early years. The propulsion system proved astonishingly reliable: the vehicle met all demands made upon it. But the weapon was lacking: it was as if the Chieftain tank had been armed with a two pounder gun, the supersonic fighter with a machine gun.

The torpedo, an effective weapon for certain limited purposes, could not, by its very nature, meet some of the future applications which this remarkable war vessel had made possible, and in others could not match the performance of above water weapons.

For the same reasons that sonar is so much less effective a sensor than the comparable above water systems which depend on electro-magnetic rather than sonic emissions, so is the weapon itself limited: the sea is a less homogeneous, singularly opaque and immensely variable medium compared with the ether.

Propulsion; hull; weapons system; the trio which has always dictated the state of the art in submarine warfare. Propulsion was now far ahead of both the others; hull design and systems were adequate to support the new development for perhaps several decades: weapons lagged behind.

So there began in the late fifties a most interesting diversification of the weapons fitted in submarines which lifted them out of the tactical and into the strategic field.

Vehicle For Ballistic Missiles

As the result of the most important diversification, the "Polaris" ballistic missile system, the submarine at present provides the most invulnerable second strike capability so far devised.

In another application in the tactical field, a threat to the carrier strike force concept analogous to that presented to the battle fleets by the carrier force of thirty years ago is now also in service.

The United States Navy has led the way in the development of the strategic weapon: the Soviet Navy, as a substitute for a sea borne air strike capability, leads in the tactical application.

Following their traditional view that the submarine is primarily an anti-submarine weapon, the British have concentrated on developments in their use in this role.

The Strategic Deterrent

The strategic Polaris ballistic missile system was revolutionary, not only in sophistication and reliability but in the speed in which it was introduced into service.

The system was developed in the astonishingly short period of five years and the first missile was fired from the *George Washington* little more than two years after she had been laid down in early 1958.

The submarine has acquired a new role—that of making a vital contribution to the strategic deterrent, in which capacity its mobility and invisibility render it in the foreseeable future virtually invulnerable.

The Tactical Field

In the tactical missile field, weapon development has been led by the USSR, in pursuit of their traditional role of defence of the homeland—in this case from the potential threat of nuclear attacks launched from the carrier task forces of the Western powers.

For this role the developed weapon is a cruise type rather than ballistic missile, although they are also developing the latter for the strategic role.

Diversification of methods of defence has led them to mount such a missile in surface ships as well as submarines, and in the case of the latter, both in nuclear and conventionally powered submarines.

At present, it is necessary for a submarine to surface to launch these tactical long range missiles, but only for so short a period and at so great a distance from the force to be attacked that there can be little doubt that they pose a formidable threat even to a strongly defended surface force.

The British Contribution

The British contribution to the developments made possible by the introduction of nuclear propulsion has been in the field of silencing the propulsion machinery and fitting an excellent sonar set which can be used in direct co-operation between surface forces and a nuclear powered submarine in defence of a task force or convoy.

Until nuclear propulsion gave the submarine the capability to keep up with a surface force while remaining submerged, and until underwater communications became sufficiently reliable for continuous contact with the surface force to be maintained, close company operations between submerged and surface forces had been virtually impossible, and when essayed, had proved disastrous.

Technological progress has, once again, permitted what was impracticable and concerted operations between surface units and nuclear powered submarines are now well established practice in the British Navy.

Diversification Of Roles

In the course of the last fifteen years the submarine has therefore greatly diversified her roles to make best use of the increased capability that nuclear propulsion has provided.

The traditional roles of attack on shipping, whether merchant or warship, remain with the balance heavily tipped for the moment in favour of the nuclear powered attack submarines.

Patrol and surveillance, blockade and shadowing can all now be carried out with greatly enhanced efficiency, while to these roles have been added the totally new ones of strategic nuclear deterrence, long range tactical strike at ranges hitherto possible only for aircraft, and finally, increased capability for operations in direct support of surface forces.

The effect of this dramatic improvement in performance and diversification of capabilities is that, at this present moment, the nuclear powered submarine has far outstripped the ability of other forces to combat it: in its varied forms it is becoming the most formidable unit of the maritime power game.

The precise balance between this and other essential ships and aircraft will vary over the years and in different navies, but as advanced methods of detection and reconnaissance, by satellite or other space body, of the earth's surface become more and more effective and continuous, the possibility of concealment will become exclusive to the submarine and the balance of the larger navies will certainly shift towards the deployment of a greater proportion of their weapon systems underwater.

Exploitation Of Inner Space

A parallel trend towards a more intensive exploitation of what has been called "inner space"—that vast proportion of the earth's surface which lies under the sea—will also accelerate the pace of underwater development.

Not only is there great mineral wealth under the seabed but also the largely untapped potential for food production of the sea itself which will be developed as the human race relearns the lesson that early man learnt on land: that it is more profitable to be a farmer than a hunter.

The signposts pointing to this are already clear: whether it be in the diversification of aerospace firms into underwater projects or the growing forest of oil and gas rigs operating on suitable areas of the continental shelves at ever increasing depths.

Current progress in underwater physiology and diving expertise indicates that man may be able to live on the seabed for extended periods and divers to undertake useful work down to 1,000 feet.

The commercial impetus of these activities will create a demand for underwater vehicles of many types for a wide variety of purposes. The place of the submarine in the future seems assured.

Submarine Now Weapon of Stronger, Not Weaker Powers

In parallel with the discontinuity in tactics and warlike potential caused by the introduction of nuclear propulsion, has come a comparable break in the historical pattern of submarine development.

Through all its earlier history the submarine was the weapon of the weaker power since it offered the opportunity of operating effectively in areas under hostile control and some possibility of countering an otherwise overwhelming maritime superiority.

It is probable that this is no longer so and that the building, operating and support of nuclear powered submarines is so expensive and technologically advanced a process that they will take the place, held by the strike carrier in the 'forties and 'fifties, as the prestige and power focus only of the large navies of the world.

This will be brought about not only because of the initial monetary cost, but because the highly trained men required to maintain and operate them are not easily provided and the extensive and sophisticated installations necessary to refit and refuel even one modern nuclear powered submarine represent a formidable capital investment for any country.

Thus the nuclear powered submarine which will comprise the central strike capability of the major navies can only be included in the armoury of a nation with an advanced technology, well educated manpower and the will to devote a substantial slice of both to the operation and support of their maritime forces.

It is significant that, to date, only the USA, the USSR and the UK are building a substantial number of nuclear powered submarines and there is evidence to suggest that the effort and money required to develop and sustain a force of nuclear powered submarines could have a detrimental effect upon the balance of forces in smaller navies.

Maritime Power from Undersurface Warships

It is probable that we have now reached a point in history where the exercise of maritime power will come more and more to depend on the striking power of undersurface warships.

That, within this century, the navies of the world will all operate submerged, seems highly unlikely: the cost effectiveness equation of nuclear power and underwater passage coupled with the problems of entering, training and retaining crews to operate what would inevitably be highly complicated ships, when compared with their surface equivalents, does not produce an attractive answer in the case of merchant shipping.

Trade will therefore continue to move on, rather than under, the sea and surface warships will be needed to protect it from a variety of threats.

The Ultimate Arbiter

It is as one moves up the scale of escalation of threats that the nuclear powered submarine becomes the inescapable deterrent backing which other maritime forces must have in order to exercise maritime control: this is why they are increasingly referred to as the "capital ship"—that ultimate arbiter on which maritime strategy has always depended.

Held in successive generations by the line-of-battle-ship, by the battleship and then by the aircraft carrier, this role of the capital ship will be exercised more and more from under the surface where, for a long time to come, the elements of concealment and hence surprise will still persist, and are now allied to unlimited mobility and developing weapon systems.

The New Capital Ship

As has always been the case, the new capital ship will be expensive and hence few in number for all but the super powers.

The diversification of roles into different hulls, which has already started with the specialisation of the strategic missile carriers, may well continue and this will accelerate the process of designing the hull, propulsion and weapon systems as an integrated whole so that the characteristics and capabilities of each are in balance.

In parallel with the case for installing the nuclear powered submarine as a diversified capital ship of the future, must be examined the continuing requirement for a supporting cast of less expensive and less sophisticated ships as has always been found necessary in the past.

Exploration On The Continental Shelves

The growth of exploration and exploitation activities on the continental shelves, particularly in the shallow areas, will strengthen the requirement for a propulsion system of economic cost for the many underwater vehicles which will be required.

Both for commercial activities themselves and for requirements likely to arise out of them, such as for emergency or rescue services, the submarine will have its part to play.

If agreement should eventually be reached on international regulation of activities on the seabed, there may also be a requirement for vehicles to carry out underwater inspections: here, too, the submarine is likely to be the most suitable vehicle.

Need For Improved Conventionally Powered Submarines

Indeed, there seems every reason to believe that many of the tasks arising from developments in underwater exploitation will best be met by conventionally propelled submarines since, for many years, they will be cheaper and simpler to build and operate.

This, and military requirements, will depend upon another breakthrough in technology to replace the present diesel/battery propulsions system with one which will offer at least some of the advantages of nuclear propulsion at a far less cost and, perhaps, be capable of operation by less highly qualified officers and men.

There are many potential contenders for this breakthrough: the HTP turbine to which reference has already been made: the fuel cell to replace both battery and charging agent; or even a closed cycle diesel.

Any of these, allied to the advanced hull shapes already in use for second generation nuclear powered submarines, could produce an immense improvement in performance compared with any conventionally powered submarine at present in service or under construction.

So far none have shown sufficient saving in costs when compared with a nuclear plant to make their reduced capability acceptable, but there is undoubtedly a need for a submarine designed on these lines both to supplement the nuclear propelled capital ship of the major navies, and to provide the smaller navies with the essential benefits of a submarine capability without leading to a gross unbalance in the proportion of resources devoted to it.

Submarines of the Future

Up to the end of the century it is possible to forecast the pattern of underwater warship design with reasonable assurance.

On the assumption that there will be no agreement on a comprehensive disarmament treaty, there will be a continuing need for submarines capable of delivering strategic nuclear weapons.

The vehicle will be a "true submarine" to avoid all possibility of detection; large, to give crews good living conditions which long patrols demand; extensively automated to reduce the number of crew to a minimum: and designed to survive by concealment and evasion.

There will also be a continuing requirement for a diversified force of "capital ships" to provide support and backing for surface forces.

These, too, will be true submarines and their role will be to counter other submarines and to provide a major strike capability against surface forces.

The conventional submarines' role will be two-fold. It will remain the essential underwater component of the maritime forces of the smaller navies and, outside the military sphere, it will be used in tasks arising out of commercial exploitation of the seabed.

Until The Third Millenary

It may be argued that the foregoing is no more than the projection of current functions of a maritime power into a generally underwater environment.

This is not denied because the functions stem from the roles and the roles from the human characteristics which make warlike forces necessary: by 2,000 AD, which is as far ahead as it is sensible to project even such a vision as this, there seems little reason to suppose that either human characteristics or the principles of war will have changed to such a degree as to make some totally new concept credible.

OVER THE WATER

NAVAL AIR POWER

By

Rear-Admiral P. D. Gick, CB, OBE, DSC & Bar

(late *Flag Officer, Flying Training*)

As a pilot Rear Admiral Gick took part in the attack on the German battleship *Bismarck* by naval aircraft of 825 Squadron from the British aircraft carrier *Victorious*. He served in three other aircraft carriers, *Ark Royal*, *Vindex* and *Bulwark* (the latter as Commanding Officer), in the Western Desert, in the Pacific, and at the Admiralty. He commanded a Royal Naval Air Squadron, a destroyer, a Royal Naval Air Station, and an aircraft carrier.

The following article by Rear Admiral Gick reflects his personal views formed both as a sailor and an airman in a full career of over 30 years in the Royal Navy. These views are not necessarily those of the publishers of *Jane's Fighting Ships*.

NAVAL AIR POWER

Lessons Of History

In nearly every subject there are lessons to be learned from history and I believe the exercise of naval air power is no exception although its history may be short.

I believe therefore that if we are to plan for the future we must examine the lessons, deduce the effects which changing technology and political circumstances will have on them, and decide whether or not they are still valid.

Early Days Of Maritime Flying

In the early days of flying, despite the protestations and denials of military men and politicians alike, it was eventually accepted that aircraft might have some limited value in maritime reconnaissance.

Not long after the start of the 1914-18 war their value in attacking airships became evident and it was eventually conceded that they might also have some use in attacks against shipping.

Value In All Forms Of Warfare

By the end of the 1914-1918 war the value of aircraft in all forms of warfare had been fully demonstrated. But in the United Kingdom there were still those who felt that, once peace was restored, this untidy and difficult weapon could be dispensed with.

It was this attitude which allowed the absorption of the British naval and army air services into the Royal Air Force.

Understanding Of Naval Requirements

In theory this had much to commend it. One service supplied all the aircraft and trained all the men. It should have worked but we all know it did not. What is not so well understood is why it failed.

It has often been said that this was due to a lack of interest or understanding of naval or army requirements by the Royal Air Force. This I believe is quite untrue.

The need was understood well enough and the will to provide it was there. What was lacking was, quite simply, finance.

Between The Wars

Between the wars each of our three armed forces was given certain specific tasks and these were allotted priorities. At the same time each force was given totally inadequate finance to fulfill any of its tasks.

This led to a ludicrous and disastrous situation. The army and navy had as their top priority tasks which demanded certain types of aircraft and for these they were dependent on another service. That service meanwhile had been given priorities which put the provision of such aircraft at the bottom of its list.

I think it is grossly unfair to blame the RAF for allocating its totally inadequate finance to its two top priorities, fighter defence and long range bombing, at the expense of the maritime and army support roles which they were told were of much less importance. The blame lies squarely on the futility of the system and the ineptitude of the government of that day.

Navy's Own Aircraft Restored

At last this error was seen and at least the Navy had its power to order its own aircraft restored.

Fortunately for the United Kingdom the Germans had made the same mistake and had sadly inadequate naval air forces at the outbreak of war.

Had they had the political and strategic wisdom of the United States of America and of Japan the history of the 1939-1945 war might well have been very different, for these two nations had each allowed its navy to provide, within financial limits, the aircraft it needed.

Aircraft In The Exercise Of Maritime Power

Gradually between the wars the means of using aircraft in the exercise of maritime power had been developed, and by 1939 flying boats and shore based aircraft with long range had been designed for maritime reconnaissance and had a limited ability to attack submarines.

In the United Kingdom however, the attack of shipping by shore based aircraft had been entrusted to the high level bombers designed and built for the attack of land targets.

Only a few squadrons of bi-planes equipped to carry torpedoes were the true shore based anti-shipping strength of this country,

In the Fleet we were little better prepared. In 1936 we were still dependent for fighter defence (still regarded by many senior naval officers as a waste of time and money) upon the single or twin seat variants of the Hart bi-plane whilst the Swordfish, with a maximum cruising airspeed of 90 knots, provided the reconnaissance, torpedo attack and high level bombing capabilities.

Fighter Defence Of The Fleet

At this time the need for a faster and less vulnerable reconnaissance aircraft was being pressed and our replacement fighter, the Fulmar, was equipped to carry an observer.

By way of increasing its versatility our other fighter, the Skua, had also been designed as a dive bomber.

These additions had obvious advantages but they did not enhance the fighter defence of the Fleet.

The Swordfish too, spurred by reports of US activities, had been tried out in the dive bombing role in which it proved remarkably effective.

Meanwhile our carriers had been developed and fitted with catapults and arrester gear to cope with the faster and more heavily armed aircraft.

Vital Lessons Learned

In the early days of the 1939 war many vital lessons were learned and of these probably the most important were:—

1. However good long range shore based anti-submarine aircraft may be (and no one will deny the brilliant work of our Coastal Command aircraft) they lack the capacity for quick replacement or reinforcement.

2. Shipping is far more vulnerable to enemy attack when it has no means of destroying enemy reconnaissance aircraft immediately they are detected.

3. Shipping is infinitely more vulnerable when within range of enemy aircraft if it does not have its own fighter defence.

Merchant Aircraft Carriers

In those days these lessons were quickly learned and led to such innovations as the catapult aircraft merchant ship, the escort carrier and the merchant aircraft carrier (which unfortunately, despite the efforts of its protagonists, was introduced two years too late) and the provision of modern purely fighter aircraft in carriers.

Great Naval Air Battles

As the war progressed and the great naval air battles between the Japanese and US forces were fought out in the Pacific these lessons were reinforced and others learned.

One in particular (emphasised also in the Western Desert) was the need for the highly manoeuvrable ground attack aircraft in support of ground forces.

From this need the fighter aircraft armed with bombs or rockets grew and carrier aircraft were similarly developed to provide army support when land bases were too distant.

Perhaps a still more important lesson than the need for this type of aircraft was the need for quick response.

It was found that it was no good having army support aircraft on the ground miles away. What the army really wanted was to have its aircraft overhead fully armed and ready to be called down on to any target as it appeared or to beat off attacks by enemy aircraft. Failing this it needed these aircraft at instant readiness only a few minutes flying time away and as the war progressed, and particularly in actions involving landings from the sea, this task was more and more provided by carrier based aircraft.

These lessons were learned more than a quarter of a century ago and since then there have been vast technological advances and political changes.

East and West Military Alliances

In politics the greatest changes lie in the grouping of different peoples. When the United Nations was formed it was comprised of comparatively few quite large groups each with a single vote and most of these groups were allied to one or another of two main blocks conveniently referred to as East and West. Within these blocks military alliances were formed and attempts made to standardise weapons and tactics.

Since those days there have been defections from the alliances and the groups of peoples have disintegrated and are still disintegrating into small and often politically immature nations each with a vote in the United Nations.

The outbreak of fighting between these small nations has necessitated intervention either by United Nations' forces or by the forces of larger nations. The effect of this has been to emphasize the need for highly mobile conventional forces which are able to rely less and less on prepared shore bases.

Lethality Of Nuclear Weapons

Of the technical changes obviously the most notable has been the nuclear weapon but in my view the principal effect of this has been to cloud the judgement of both politicians and some Service officers. It is probable that its lethality is no greater than that of some of the chemical and biological weapons which have been available for the past thirty years and which, because neither side dared use them, had virtually no effect on military strategy or tactics.

The same is not quite true of the effect of nuclear warheads on maritime warfare because aircraft have been especially developed to deliver them and this has affected their capability of delivering conventional weapons but I do not believe this effect has been very great.

Nuclear Power In Aircraft Carriers

Equally spectacular has been the use of nuclear power for propulsion of ships but so far its real significance has been restricted to submarines where it has probably been the greatest advance in the whole history of this type of ship.

Its value is probably least in aircraft carriers because although it allows them to cruise indefinitely without tanker support, once these ships get into action their endurance is limited not only by their consumption of fuel for propulsion but by their prodigious use of aircraft fuel and weapons.

The Jet Engine

In aircraft the jet engine has vastly increased the speed and rate of climb of aircraft and the height at which they can operate.

Its effect on radius of action has been far less great and has generally reduced the endurance or capacity for remaining on patrols.

Advances In Electronics

Advances in electronics have given far greater radar ranges and the capacity to transmit the information obtained by radar by one ship or aircraft to the operation's rooms of others.

Communications generally have become far more reliable and limitations on distance have been virtually eliminated or will soon be.

Missiles For All Arms

Missiles have been developed for delivering conventional or nuclear war heads with accuracy and ranges far greater than all previous military weapons and capable of being used from every type of military vehicle which operates on land, sea, air or under water.

Vertical Landing And Take Off

Finally the capability of aircraft to take off and land vertically or using only small unprepared airfields has revolutionised certain aspects of warfare and will have an increasing effect on others.

Relating these technical and political changes to the main lessons of maritime warfare which I have mentioned produces some interesting facts:—

Anti-Submarine Aircraft

1. Quick reinforcement or replacement of anti-submarine aircraft. This lesson is still as valid as ever but its solution has been greatly simplified by the anti-submarine helicopter.

Operating from the decks of naval escort vessels or of merchant ships, anti-submarine helicopters can fulfil all the requirements for convoy or naval force close escort by aircraft far better than the old fixed wing aircraft and leave the long range shore based maritime aircraft to concentrate on their proper job.

Reconnaissance Aircraft

2. The destruction of enemy reconnaissance aircraft. The importance of this has certainly not diminished and I believe nothing has happened to make the task easier. Ship's radar can detect any such aircraft and shipborne missiles exist which could instantly destroy it.

Unfortunately, so far as I am aware, no device yet exists other than the human eye which can distinguish with absolute certainty between an enemy reconnaissance aircraft and a neutral civil airliner.

In this day with long range radar and absolute navigational accuracy in aircraft there is no need for the old shadowing tactics which quickly identified the enemy shadowing aircraft solely by radar plotting.

Now the reconnaissance aircraft need only continue on a steady course and return several hours later knowing that the limiting speed of ships must have retained them within an area easily covered by its radar.

It cannot be argued that neutral civil aircraft are unlikely to be met. Wars have not prevented neutral countries from continuing their shipping trade in the past and there seems no reason why in the future they should not continue to operate both their ships and aircraft. Moreover there may well be many more neutral countries in the future.

The officer in command of any force at sea in war must therefore have the means not only of detecting and destroying aircraft but of positively identifying them at long range. The only method now available is by fast intercepting aircraft and if he does not have them instantly available the vulnerability of his command will be far greater.

Defence Of Shipping

3. The defence of shipping against attack by aircraft. Missile experts these days may tell us that ships are so well equipped with guided weapons that they are immune from damage by enemy aircraft. They may be right but I am old enough to have heard this story before. In 1939 as a pilot in a Swordfish squadron I was repeatedly told that I and my fellow aircrew were wasting our time practising torpedo attacks on ships as their guns would inevitably destroy us before we could get within dropping range.

Fortunately we did not believe this and the real proof came when the German battleship *Bismarck*, which had shown her gunnery to be so much more devastating than that of the British ships, failed to beat off even one of the nine Swordfish which first attacked her.

Can we therefore be absolutely confident that ships can now rely solely upon their missile defence? If not it is just as important as ever that they should have fighter aircraft always with them or instantly available. If they do not they may be no less vulnerable than the battleship *Prince of Wales* and the battle cruiser *Repulse* who were caught at sea within range of enemy aircraft without fighter escort and were inevitably destroyed.

Aircraft Supporting Ground Forces

4. The quick response by aircraft supporting ground forces. This lesson has been re-emphasised repeatedly during the past twenty five years in Korea, at Suez and in Vietnam.

In innumerable exercises also the need has been shown for a rugged and very manoeuvrable aircraft available at a few minutes notice to destroy gun implacements, tanks or fleeting targets. In this role speed and sophistication are of far less importance than manoeuvrability, invulnerability from short range ground based weapons, the capacity to deliver a wide range of missiles with extreme accuracy and above all the ability to operate from bases close to the front line troops.

Additionally there is a recurring need for fighter aircraft to protect ground forces from attack by enemy aircraft and this is particularly necessary when troops have been brought into action from distant bases and have not had time to set up ground based anti-aircraft defences.

Four Tasks For Maritime Aircraft

These four lessons are just as valid as they were when they were first learned. Each represents a task for maritime aircraft which must be added to the traditional naval task of finding and destroying enemy shipping.

This latter task may be assisted by the nuclear powered submarine and the ship launched missile but I believe the aircraft still has a vital part to play in this role primarily in the positive identification and quick response against enemy shipping suddenly met at sea.

The Greatest Maritime Power

Without a shadow of doubt the greatest maritime power of the last twenty five years has been the United States of America. This power has been achieved not only by sheer size but by the selection of the right equipment in the right ratio.

From the very inception of aviation the US Navy has built up its own air power both shore based and carrier borne. The decision as to the ratio in which available funds should be spent on ships or aircraft was made by the Navy and, whilst there were undoubtedly bitter arguments between protagonists of various arms, all those taking part at least had the same aims.

The United States therefore entered the 1939-45 war with a reasonable proportion of their naval power airborne. Since then their increasing involvement around the world has tended to swing the balance even more towards the air.

The Other Great Naval Power

Meanwhile the other great naval power, the USSR, has been faced with an entirely different task.

Whilst the USA has been operating overseas bringing all her forces and their supplies into action by sea or air and depending largely on carriers for air bases, the USSR has had the large majority of her military power concentrated along the perimeter of or within the land mass she controls and her naval strength has been designed mainly to attack enemy shipping. For this she has relied very largely upon submarines for attacks at long range and small patrol craft for attacks on shipping approaching her shores. She relies entirely upon shore based aircraft for naval warfare.

Eight Navies With Aircraft Carriers

Of the remaining navies in the world eight have aircraft carriers capable of operating fixed wing aircraft.

Of these eight the United Kingdom has announced its intention of abandoning her fixed wing aircraft carriers in the near future. The argument for this used by the present government is that as it has (despite its previous promises to the contrary) largely withdrawn its forces from anywhere farther afield than Europe, all its air requirements can be met by land based aircraft with only helicopters operating from ships.

Certainly if British forces were never again to operate further afield than their present bases in Europe, this argument would have some logic but unfortunately British commitments extend far beyond this. Britain has defence treaties with countries all over the world and at any time may be called upon to honour these.

The Case For Carrier-Borne Aircraft

The argument is used that Britain would never have to land forces for this purpose in the face of opposition as any such landing would be made on friendly territory and suitable air bases would always be available on which she could station any aircraft she needed.

The validity of this argument relies upon the supposition that British intelligence is so dependable that it would always have sufficient warning of impending hostilities to fly in not only the required short range fighter and ground attack aircraft but also all the necessary equipment to convert a civil airfield or primitive airstrip into a first class military airfield. A more dangerous and falacious supposition is hard to imagine.

History again supports this contention. I find it hard to believe that the intelligence organisation gave many weeks warning of Germany's attacks on the Netherlands and Belgium in 1940 or the Japanese attack on Pearl Harbour. It is also relevant that the build up of the airfield at Kuwait was neither so quick or effective as the planners had envisaged.

Close Air Support

There is no doubt in my mind that if we pursue this policy we will sooner or later be confronted by a potential aggressor who will not be so foolish as to stand by and watch us land our supplies and set up our bases to defeat his aims but will decide to harass us while we try to do so.

Such harassment by guerilla forces or unsophisticated aircraft could be impossible to overcome without close air support and we would have to choose between declining to keep our promises or suffering a humiliating defeat.

The Superbly Flexible Harrier

In the Harrier vertical take off and landing aircraft we have one of the most superbly flexible weapons in the world but although one recently flew from New York to London non-stop we must not allow this great feat to delude us into thinking that such ranges are of any significance in war.

This one aircraft was supported by a fleet of tanker aircraft on this transatlantic flight and its arrival in a war zone would be valueless unless all the support installations were ready for it.

The true value of this aircraft lies not in its long range with flight refuelling but in its ability to land and refuel or re-arm on any piece of land or, still more important, on the deck of a ship.

Looking Into the Future

Looking into the future of the British Fighting Forces there is a clear demand for years to come for the type of forces we have developed. We have the ability now with our commando ships, our supporting carriers equipped with fighter and ground attack aircraft, our air transport of troops and equipment and long range reconnaissance and bombing aircraft to honour our promises by providing our allies with the help they need when and where they need it.

We can however only do this so long as we can guarantee to provide efficient air support. The only way we can give this guarantee is to maintain the capacity to operate our supporting aircraft from ships. At present we have the carriers, the aircraft and the men to do this. To replace these we must have new ships from which the RAF Harriers can operate and our existing carriers must continue until these new ships and aircraft are in service.

Falling Into The Trap

Unfortunately we find Great Britain, not for the first time, with a government which will not learn from history. Once again Britain is falling into the trap which has bedevilled her for centuries. She is laying the foundations of the next war by economising on her armed forces in peace.

FROM THE WATER

AMPHIBIOUS WARFARE AT THE CLOSE OF THE 1960s

By

Major-General J. L. Moulton, CB, DSO, OBE

(ROYAL MARINES retired, *Chief of Amphibious Warfare,* 1957-61)

AMPHIBIOUS WARFARE AT THE CLOSE OF THE 1960s.

'Let there be built great ships which can cast up on a beach, in any weather, large numbers of the heaviest of tanks'. Since Churchill's stirring minute of June 1940, a large complex range of amphibious warfare shipping has appeared in the navies of the world. Like other warships, these ships are designed to specific operational concepts, which are reflected in their material characteristics and performance, and which must be distinguished and understood if any useful evaluation and comparison is to be made.

The main distinction, clearly identifiable from the earliest days of specialised amphibious warfare shipping, is that of range and seaworthiness. In World War 2 British and United States forces in Europe faced a basically short-range problem of re-entry into continental Europe from the Mediterranean and eventually across the English Channel. Re-entry would have to be made in the face of fixed defences backed by major field forces, and would require very large land forces, fully mobile and armoured. To this problem, Churchill's dynamic influence produced the radical solution of the beaching ship: the Landing Craft Tank (LCT), which although classed as a landing craft was required to make the voyage from base to hostile shore direct and grew in size through various marks; and the Landing Ship Tank (LST), first the experimental *Maracaibos* and *Winettes* and then the real production job, the LST 3, many of which are still in service today as the US Series 1152 and earlier ships. Despite Churchill's directive, even the LST 3 shows the short-range influence, being too slow, too liable to be affected by weather and too limited in troop accommodation to be really satisfactory for long-range operations.

Unlike the problem of re-entry to Europe, the problems of the Pacific War had been foreseen and studied, by the US Navy and Marine Corps, since the early 1930s and still earlier in theory. Nevertheless, because the problems of the Pacific, and especially of the Central Pacific, were characteristically long-range, and United States forces unlikely to meet massive enemy land forces there, the methods adopted remained, until the radical solutions developed for Europe began to make themselves felt in the Pacific in the appearance there of LST, largely traditional, based on the troop ship (APA) and cargo ship (AKA) carrying minor landing craft for the final ship-to-shore movement.

Characteristically the second radical solution to the beach landing problem, the Dock Ship (LSD), although better suited than the LST to the long-range problem, originated in Europe. Symptomatically, also, the radical solution to the ship-to-shore movement, the tracked and wheeled amphibians, appeared first in the Pacific. The next, and until now the latest radical solution, the amphibious warfare helicopter carrier was a post-war development, produced by the US Marine Corps for the problem of opposed landings under nuclear threat, and later adapted by both United States and British forces for quick re-action to limited war threats. One of its favourable characteristics compared to parachute assault is its long range capability.

The range characteristic, seen in its wider shape of seaworthiness, logistic maintenance and troop and store accommodation as well as simple fuel reserves, has been dominant in amphibious warfare development, but the derivatives of other operational concepts have also to be recognized. Closely associated with the short-range continental operational concept is that of flank support in its various forms—flank landings in support of overland advance, bombardment, and raids intended to tie down superior enemy forces in coast defence. Rather similar is that of riverine operations, with a long historical record of specialised shipping reaching back to Wolseley and Kitchener on the Nile and the Yangtse gunboats.

At the other end of the range spectrum there is beginning to appear a requirement for specialised logistic shipping, notably in the form of the US Fast Deployment Logisitc Ship (FDL) project. Specialised shipping in one form or another could do a great deal to avoid the always vulnerable and sometimes near chaotic business of disembarking military forces after overseas movement by traditional civilian methods. Official failure to recognise the requirement as associated with amphibious warfare probably springs from departmental politics and from the preconception that the beach assaults of World War 2 in Europe and the Pacific are an essential concommitant of amphibious warfare.

Many amphibious warfare ships are by nature versatile, and as they become obsolete or redundant, frequently appear in other roles than those for which they were built, which may or may not be connected with amphibious warfare. Not infrequently they are connected with the logistic task. The process must be discounted in assessing amphibious warfare capability from lists of ships.

Looking then, at the varying types of amphibious warfare ships in the navies of the world, we must constantly ask ourselves the related questions: What were they built for? and, What can they do? Otherwise it is easy to reach false conclusions. In the ships themselves, the main characteristics to identify are those of range, speed, seaworthiness, load capacity and landing facility to which must often be added present usage. Along with these must be considered the availability of naval and air support, and logistic backing for them, to cover, escort and support sea movement and landing, before a realistic estimate can be made of the strategic and operational capability of a navy or a nation to deploy military forces overseas.

THE AMPHIBIOUS CAPABILITY OF THE UNITED STATES—THE MAIN LIFT

As with nuclear submarines and strike aircraft carriers, it is to the United States one must turn to see the fully developed potential of amphibious forces. Avoiding the temptation to say, 'You name it, they have it' for the more demanding task of analysis, one may identify the main elements of US amphibious warfare capability as, first, the development of two World War 2 radical solutions, the beaching ship and the dock ship, to the full long-range requirements posed by the Pacific and to a lesser degree the Atlantic; second, the bringing to full effectiveness of the inherently long-range post-World War 2 solution, the helicopter carrier; and, third, the marrying up of the three into a fully effective and versatile modern operational capability.

Landing Ships Tank (LST)

Of some eighty-five US LSTs in service or building, some forty are old World War 2 ships (full load displacement about 4,000 tons, speed now probably less than the original $11\frac{1}{2}$ knots). Fifteen are of the 1156 series (5,800 tons, 15 knots) built in the early 1950s, and seven of the 1171 series (8,000 tons, 17 knots) built in the late 1950s. The remaining seventeen are the new *Newport* class (8,300 tons, 20 knots) the first of which entered service in October 1968, the last being due in 1971. A radically redesigned bow, bow door and ramp permit these ships to reach the highest ocean going speed so far attained by a beaching ship and mark the final stage of the application of the World War 2 development to the typically US and Pacific long-range concept of amphibious operations, all but the very first stages of the process being in service today.

Landing Ships Dock (LSD) and Amphibious Transports Dock (LPD)

Six *Ashland* class (8,700 tons, 15 knots) and thirteen *Cabildo* class (9,375 tons, $15\frac{1}{2}$ knots) remain from World War 2. Eight *Thomaston* class (11,270-12,150 tons, 20 knots sustained) were built in the mid-1950s: five *Anchorage* class (13,650 tons, 20 knots) are due to enter service between December 1968 and 1970.

Meanwhile in the 1960s the LPD has appeared: three *Raleigh* class (13,900 tons, 20 knots) with accommodation for 930 troops and for amphibious force headquarters in addition to vehicles and landing craft entered service between 1960 and 1962: a total of twelve *Austin* and

Cleveland classes (16,900 tons, 20 knots, 840-930 troops) are due to do so over the period 1965-70. The difference between the two types is in the troop and headquarter accommodation of the latter provided at the expense of some dock space. Here again, all stages of the solution to the landing problems are in service simultaneously.

Helicopter Assault Ships (LPH)

The first LPH to commission, the converted and partly experimental *Thetis Bay* (11,000 tons, troop capacity 1,600 entered service in 1956, and was withdrawn ten years later. The next three, converted *Essex* class carriers (40,600 tons, 33 knots, 1,500 troops and 30 helicopters) entered service as LPH in the period 1959-60. The first ships built for the task, the seven *Iwo Jima* class (18,300 tons, 20 knots, 2,000 troops and some 30 helicopters) entered service at the rate of one a year in the period 1961-68 and show a marked improvement in economy of operation with one third increase in troop accommodation. Meanwhile improvements in helicopter performance have markedly increased their assault capability. Taking the two classes together, the development of the helicopter carrier has been the outstanding amphibious advance of the last decade, and in it the third radical solution to the amphibious warfare problem can be said to have reached maturity.

The Amphibious Assault Ship (LHA)

At the end of the 1950s the dock ships began to acquire helicopter decks, then, in the LPD troop accommodation was added. The next stage has been to bring the dock and the helicopter ship concepts together in a single large ship, the 40,000 ton LHA, speed in excess of 20 knots, range 10,000 miles. One LHA and two *Newport* class LST will together provide a twenty-knot lift for a reinforced battalion of some 1,500 men on what would appear to be generous scales. The prototype was approved for Fiscal Year 1969 after a year's delay by Congress. Two more are asked for in the Fiscal Year 1970, with the possibility of another two for the following year.

To put the main elements of a fully supported battalion landing team together in a ship large enough for prolonged troop accommodation and high speeds independent of the weather has obvious advantages. To British eyes, however, the LHA looks not only very expensive—its estimated cost is $185 million for the first and $140 million for others—but also a very high concentration of risk. Against cost it can be argued that a single ship will take the place of two or more others with the probable economies of large scale operation; while against the concentration of risk it can be said that, as the LHA does not beach and will be able to undock landing craft under way, her vulnerability is proportionately reduced. She will have the support of strike carriers, in which a greater risk is concentrated, and their escorts, and these will in any case have to establish a tactical environment in which large ships can survive.

Other Main Lift Developments

Five *Mount McKinley* class headquarter ships (12,560 tons $16\frac{1}{2}$ knots) date from World War 2. The new *Blue Ridge* (18,000 tons, 20 knots) is due to commission in 1970, and is to be followed by another ship of her class, but a third previously projected will not now be built.

The new *Charleston* class of five attack cargo ships (LKA) is due to be completed in 1969. With one exception the remaining attack cargo ships date from World War 2. Two attack transports (LPA), the *Paul Revere* class (16,800 tons, 20 knots) entered service in the late 1950s; the remainder date from World War 2 or the immediate post-war period. The class would appear to have been supplanted by the LPH and now the LHA.

A new tracked amphibian, the LVTPX12 is undergoing trials by the Marine Corps with a view to replacing in the 1970s the LVT 5 which in the late 1950s replaced the World War 2 LVT 3 and 4.

The Twenty Knot Lift

The US Navy maintains an amphibious lift for two Marine Expeditionary Forces, each of one division, corps and logistic troops and air wing, total strength 35-40,000 men in each MEF. Early in the 1960s sights were set on the target of a twenty-knot lift for these forces. The last ships to appear with less speed than twenty knots were the *Suffolk County* (Series 1171) class LST completed in 1959. By the mid-1970s, it has been announced, the whole Pacific MEF will have available twenty knot ships and two-thirds of the Atlantic MEF will be similarly lifted.

THE LOGISTIC DEVELOPMENT —THE FAST DEPLOYMENT LOGISTIC SHIP

During the 1960s a large effort has been directed to increasing the strategic airlift for the US Army and supporting air forces, with the aim of allowing a larger proportion of US forces to be retained in the homeland rather than deployed continuously abroad. Even with the C 141s now in service and the giant C 5As due to enter service in the 1970s, this will still call for forward positioning of heavy equipment and bulk supply, unless better means can be found. Positioning in bases on land is costly, inflexible, and as seen in France, politically vulnerable. An alternative has been used in the Pacific in the form of three Forward Floating Depots, modified World War 2 Victory ships stationed in the Philippines. These ships were not designed for the purpose and lack the speed, capacity and cargo handling resources required for full flexibility.

The logical next step was to design specialised ships for the task. In 1965 a programme was submitted to Congress to build some twenty Fast Deployment Logistic Ships (FDLs) during the 1970s. Although supported by all three services, the project was rejected in 1967 on the arguments that excessive deployment capability would lead to over-readiness to commit US troops abroad, that the system was cost-ineffective, and that it would lead to state competition with private enterprise shipping lines in the carriage overseas of military forces and their logistic requirements. The project was re-submitted for FY 1969 and rejected. It was again submitted for FY 1970s but its chances are said to be poor. Its fate under the new administration remains to be seen.

The design is for a 40,400 ton ship, sustained speed $24\frac{1}{2}$ knots, endurance 8,900 miles. The ship will have a full-length helicopter deck, but, unlike the similar size LHA, no dock, with consequent increase in cargo space. Nine decks below the main deck provide space for trucks, jeeps, tanks, armoured personnel carriers, guns and palletised stores, with full provision for maintenance and handling. About 70% of the cargo, it is estimated, will be discharged by helicopter, the rest by lighter. Twelve FDLs would provide the heavy equipment and supplies for a full infantry division. A range of studies of alternative methods of deployment by airlift, sealift and prepositioning has shown that the least costly method for providing for the full deployment required would be six squadrons of C 5A, fourteen squadrons of C 141 and thirty FDLs, with some prepositioning in the Pacific and the backing of cargo ships from commerce. Replacing the FDLs by C 5A would cost three times as much.

The ships will be manned by the Military Sea Transport Service, not by the US Navy, and are intended for the US Army, not the US Marine Corps, and are, therefore, not technically amphibious warfare ships in the United States usage. To British eyes the project seems vast, and, when added to the already large amphibious lift discussed above, quite out of this world. Its chief significance may be the realisation of the inescapable need to combine sea and air-lift in forward deployment. On the small scale commensurate with Britain's limited resources, this combination always occurs in operational emergency, but the customary denial of the need for it in construction programmes has severely hampered its effective development. The LHA and the FDL projects taken together with the world-wide civilian developments in roll-on roll-off and container shipping make one thing at least clear—strategic sea transport is on the move, and revolutionary developments may be expected in the 1970s.

The Support of Land Operations—Vietnam

The limited wars of the last twenty years have all been maritime in the sense that without the use of the sea by one side they could not have been waged. In addition to that the support of land armies from adjacent waters has seen extensive developments in Vietnam.

Riverine Warfare

In 1965 the US Navy to meet an immediate requirement to control the Mekong Delta deployed there four armed LCPL 4 (minor infantry landing craft) and later that year placed contracts for some 120 31-foot plastic-hulled speed boats of commercial design for use as patrol boats (PBR). These have been formed into a task force, CTF 116, the River Patrol Force, of some 200 PBR with a limited number of army helicopters in support based on four LSTs in the delta. A heavier fighting force is provided by the joint Mobile Riverine Force—CTF 117, River Assault Flotilla One, and a reinforced army brigade. CTF 117 comprises 52 LCM 6 (Landing Craft Mechanised Mark 6) converted to Armoured Troop Carriers (ATC), ten LCM 6 converted to monitors, and 32 specially built Armoured Assault Support Patrol Boats (ASPR), the whole being based on one Series 1156 LST and seven old World War 2 LST hulls plus accommodation lighters.

An early development by the South Vietnamese forces of naval Riverine Assault Groups has survived on a reduced scale, its lightly protected craft having proved vulnerable to the recoilless guns and rockets introduced in the delta by the Viet Cong in the mid 1960s. The scale and seriousness of this riverine fighting far exceeds anything in recent experience.

Bombardment Support

The US Navy has a force of four old battleships, twenty-five cruisers and eleven World War 2 landing ships, rocket, classed as fire support ships. Mostly maintained in reserve, they are available either for support of an amphibious assault or for flank bombardment. In the latter role cruisers and rocket ships have been extensively used in Vietnam, and, in 1968 the 59,000-ton *New Jersey* was taken from reserve, commissioned at something like half World War 2 complement (largely at the expense of her anti-aircraft armament) and sent to Vietnam, where she carried out her first bombardment on 30th September 1968. It is estimated that the cost of recommissioning, $21\frac{1}{2}$ million, was equal to that of twenty-one strikes by B 52 bombers without the vulnerability of the aircraft. The *New Jersey* left Vietnam in April 1969 for refit after having fired 18,000 rounds in action. She is due to return to operational duty in the autumn. Carrier-borne aircraft have, of course, been and continue to be very extensively used in Vietnam against land targets.

Landings from the Sea

The US Marine Corps 1st and 3rd Divisions deployed in 1 Corps Tactical Zone (the Northernmost zone of South Vietnam) are officially designated the IIIrd Amphibious Force, and, while most of their fighting is ashore, have frequently and successfully combined flank landings with land operations. The first of these at Van Tuong in August 1965, in which 645 Viet Cong were killed at the cost of 45 American lives, was claimed as the first major US success in Vietnam. The method continues, usually on the scale of a battalion landing team from LPH or LPD in conjunction with other units operating overland.

THE BRITISH AMPHIBIOUS LIFT

When after World War 2 was over, the lease-lend built landing ships and craft had been returned to the USA and the liners and cargo ships, that had done wartime service as Landing Ships Infantry, Headquarters Ships and Motor Transport Ships, had reverted to trade, there remained in Britain a large number of major and minor landing craft, mostly built with the Channel crossing very much in mind, and some British-built LST 3. Britain thus found herself with an essentially short-range amphibious lift. What was to prove much worse in its effect, she also found herself with an essentially short-range doctrine of amphibious operations.

For the next decade when, in hindsight at least, it is clear that Britain should have been developing a capability for small, long-range operations, Whitehall and the staff colleges, in so far as they interested themselves at all in the subject, remained obsessed with the methods of Normandy, surely by any rational assessment an unrepeatable operation. A new class of some thirty Landing Craft Tank Mark 8, LCT 8, (1,000 tons, 9 knots) was built. A few LST 3 were converted to LST 3 (A) by the addition of davits to carry six minor landing craft each so that they could substitute in exercises for the troopships that, it was envisaged, would be taken over from trade and from trooping on the outbreak of war. The rest of the LST 3 were hired to commercial firms, some working for the War Office, found odd naval jobs, or put to rust in reserve along with a large miscellaneous collection of major and minor landing craft. In the early 1950s the Amphibious Warfare Squadron was formed—one small headquarter ship, two LST 3 (A) and two LCT 8—and, exercising in the Mediterranean with the Commando Brigade, began to acquire operational as well as training significance. The three month long delay for mobilisation of amphibious resources and the subsequent ponderous methods of the Suez operation were the inevitable outcome of the practices of the decade that preceded it.

The Commando Ships

Shortly before Suez, however, the American development of the helicopter assault ship had inspired a similar British project, and two training carriers with a commando and a scratch force of helicopters embarked were used operationally at Port Said. In January 1960 the *Bulwark* (27,300 tons, 24 knots sustained, 900 troops) commissioned after permanent conversion from an aircraft carrier into a commando ship (British version of LPH), and in August 1962 her sister ship, the *Albion*, similarly converted, commissioned. Equipped with a limited number of Whirlwind helicopters the *Bulwark* was, for her first commission, very weak in landing capability. The situation was later improved by the appearance first of the Wessex 1 and later of the Wessex 5, but the British ships with a single wave lift of some 200 troops remain much inferior in this respect to their US counterparts. They are also inferior in cost-effectiveness measured in terms of the ratio of troops lifted to ship's company—900 : 1,035 for the *Bulwark*, compared to 2,090 : 528 for the *Iwo Jima*. Neither in the 1969 Defence White Paper, nor in answer to questions in the House, however, has the Government had anything to say about taking the obvious step of replacing them with ships built for the job.

It is sometimes suggested that the *Tiger* class cruisers could, after their present conversion to helicopter cruisers, stand in as amphibious warfare helicopter carriers. The very limited number of helicopters they could operate and their restricted troop accommodation would, however, so limit their effectiveness in this role, that it is difficult to think they could have more than token value.

The Assault Ships

With Suez over it was clear that either the amphibious lift must be rebuilt or amphibious warfare abandoned, at least as far as beach landing was concerned. At the time the Admiralty was luke warm; the War Office, while rather schizophrenically insisting on running its own LST, looked to some visionary breakthrough to make armoured units air portable, a vision which the Air Ministry was not disinclined to encourage. After some years in which these and other alternatives were canvassed, it was decided to build two new classes of ships, subsequently named the Landing Ship Assault and the Landing Ship Logistic. The former, the two-ship class, *Fearless* and *Intrepid* (12,120 tons, 21 knots, 400 troops and full provision for joint headquarters) commissioned in 1965 and 1967. They are, in effect, LPD and could take their place with credit alongside their US contemporaries. Compared to the Logistic Ships, they are expensive, and have in consequence been criticized as cost-ineffective, but they have flexibility and assault capability that the cheaper Logistic Ships lack.

The Logistic Ships

In the post World War 2 decade the War Office had found it convenient to run a number of LST 3 as merchant ships for the movement of vehicles and heavy stores. Like the LST 3 (A) these had been used at Suez and like them were due for replacement or scrapping. The Admiralty wished to keep clear of this sort of work, the War Office wanted to continue to have complete control over its own ships, and anyway the Director of Naval Construction was occupied with the Assault Ship. It was, therefore, acceptable to all concerned that the Logistic Ships should be designed and built for the War Office under the auspices of the Ministry of Transport. Amphibious Warfare Headquarters held a watching brief for the inclusion of limited naval characteristics and for beaching capability. Viewed at first with considerable misgivings, the method has produced a highly satisfactory class. The six *Sir Lancelot* class Landing Ships Logistic (5,500 tons displacement, 17 knots, 340 troops) can each carry 15 Chieftain tanks in addition to lorries and guns. They have good beaching characteristics, carry pontoon equipment for shallow beaches, and can hoist at need six infantry landing craft. They are cheap to build at about £2 million each, and at a complement of 70 crew, cheap to run. Entering service in the period 1964-68 they compare, except for the fact that they are civilian manned and not theoretically warships, with the United States LST of the late 1950s, but are outpaced by the new twenty-knotters. Provided their limitations are recognized, their landing craft could be used for opposed landings, or, potentially more interesting, the Stalwart amphibious load carrier be used from them for close support.

In *Statement on Defence Estimates* 1969 it is announced that the Logistic Ships will be transferred towards the end of 1969 from commercial to Royal Fleet Auxiliary management without change in their employment.

The Far East Amphibious Group and the Future

On entering service the commando ships and later the assault ships were deployed in the Far East Fleet, where by 1966 the Far East Amphibious Group was formed at a normal strength of one of each. The *Sir Lancelot*, followed by later logistic ships, was also sent to the Far East Command, where on occasion they exercise with the Amphibious Group. In September and October 1968, the *Albion*, *Intrepid*, the *Sir Geraint* and the repair ship (former aircraft carrier) *Triumph* with headquarters 3rd Commando Brigade, 40 and 42 Commandos, 29 Commando Light Regiment RA and 59 Field Squadron RE embarked carried out Exercise Coral Sands in the Shoalwater Bay training area in Queensland. About the same time the *Fearless* was at Gibraltar providing accommodation for Mr Wilson for his talks with Mr Smith. In June the *Bulwark* was in North Norway with 45 commando for Exercise Polar Express. Had these two ships and a few more logistic ships been available for Coral Sands, something like a full brigade group could have taken part. In April 1969 the *Bulwark* with 41 Commando and a battery of 95 Commando Light Regiment embarked sailed for a four-months cruise in the Mediterranean.

The forthcoming withdrawal of British forces from the Indian Ocean inevitably raises the question of the future of British amphibious forces, which, as the exercises and deployments on the NATO flanks indicate, will be used for the defence of Western Europe. For many years the US Sixth Fleet has included a reinforced Marine Corps battalion embarked in amphibious warfare shipping, but behind that has lain the full strength of the Marine Expeditionary Force, Atlantic (formerly Fleet Marine Force, Atlantic). If an embarked commando group is now to fulfil a parallel role either in the Mediterranean or on the northern flank, it should do so as a forward element of a properly constituted amphibious force; by itself it will have little significance. The sound course is clearly to transfer the Far East Amphibious Group with its associated brigade group to home waters when the time comes for it to leave the Indian Ocean.

At that time, on present programmes, the British aircraft carriers will be phased out, and amphibious and other naval operations become dependent exclusively on land-based air cover. What will be done to make that really effective remains to be seen.

OTHER WESTERN AMPHIBIOUS FORCES

The French Force Amphibie d'Intervention

The third Western amphibious force is the French. It comprises:—*Arromanches* (19,600 tons, 23½ knots, 400 troops) ex-British *Colossus*, now an amphibious warfare helicopter carrier; *Ouragan* and *Orage* (8,500 tons, 17 knots) equivalent to small LSD completed 1965-68; five *Trieux* class (4,000 ton, 11 knots) equivalent to LST completed 1961-62; eight EDIC (642 tons, 8 knots) equivalent to LCT completed 1958-68. In addition one US built World War 2 dock ship and two LST are still in service. The EDICs can be carried in the dock ships, but the speed of the force remains low. On the other hand, compared to the British amphibious ships, in alliance with which it might well operate, it will have limited carrier-borne air support available from the *Clemenceau* and *Foch* continuing after 1971.

Italy

The three *Caprera* class (980 tons, 13 knots) now recently built are equivalent to LCT. A number of ex-German landing craft equivalent to early wartime British LCT and also a number of ex-United States LCM are in the service.

Greece

A total of eight World War 2 LST (two ex-British, six ex-US), one LSD and six LSM are in service.

West Germany

Four ex-United States LSM and twenty-two LCU are in service.

The Co-ordination of NATO Amphibious Forces

The Soviet maritime activity of recent years has drawn attention to the need for countervailing NATO maritime presence in the Mediterranean and on the northern flank. For political and psychological reasons, it is important that this presence should include Western European, and if possible local elements, as well as US, which should be seen to be capable of effectively reinforcing NATO territory if threatened. Experience indicates that such reinforcement calls for the intimate combination of air transport and amphibious forces. The British amphibious force, and if they are now to return to the NATO fold, the French, could provide a valuable Western European contribution, to which other smaller Allied amphibious forces might be added indicating local commitment. World War 2 LST and similar craft can still be useful for short-range operations, but will inevitably have to be replaced one day. A lead is clearly needed from NATO in the organisation and provision of amphibious forces for the future. Britain's position as the leading maritime power of Western Europe, together with the opportunity presented in the withdrawal of her forces from the Indian Ocean, suggests that she should here set an example and foster action.

THE SOVIET UNION AND THE EASTERN BLOC

A good deal has been heard recently of Soviet amphibious warfare ships deployed in the Mediterranean and elsewhere and of the reconstitution of the Soviet naval infantry. This, while an important development and one potentially threatening if not confronted by countervailing force, must nevertheless be seen in its historical and strategic perspective. Support for the land army has always been one of the Soviet Navy's principal tasks, but in the past has not been treated as one calling for specialised forces. In the mid-1950s the fact that a modern army, even a Soviet one, could no longer fight without vehicles led to the introduction of a small range of LCT, for which the amphibious tanks already developed for river crossing would be particularly useful. As the mechanisation of the army proceeded and its projected speed of advance increased, the rather larger *Polnocny* class LCT appeared, followed by the *Alligator* class LST, and the specialised naval infantry were reconstituted. Clearly these would be valuable for a forward policy if that were to take the form of seizure of territory or bases or of participation in local conflicts, but such action would face the full maritime power of the West, including the United States strike carrier forces and attack submarines. The probable outcome of such a challenge is a general rather than a specifically amphibious question.

The Soviet amphibious lift comprises:—*Alligator* class landing ships (about 6,000 tons, 15 knots) commissioning from 1966, carrying 2,400 tons load, they appear to be quite normal LST. Unlike the British Logistic ships, they appear not to have a helicopter deck or to carry pontoon equipment nor to have troop accommodation; *Polnocny* class (about 1,000 tons, 15 knots) carrying 8 to 10 tanks, these might be called an up-to-date version of the British LCT 8, with a markedly better speed, but probably otherwise with the limitations of the class; *MP* 8 (800 tons, 15 knots) *MP* 6 (1,800 tons, 10 knots) seem essentially LCT-type ships, the former with a good speed for the type, the latter rather large for it. The smaller MP 2, 4 and 10 fit in with the general picture of development along LCT lines.

The *Moskva* and *Leningrad* were, until the former appeared in the Mediterranean in 1968, widely thought to be Soviet amphibious warfare helicopter ships equivalent to the LPH or commando ships, but have since been generally recognized as anti-submarine warfare helicopter carriers with consequent reduction in estimates of the Soviet overall amphibious warfare capability.

The amphibious ships and the 10-12,000 strong naval infantry are distributed between the four Soviet fleets, each of which could with little doubt execute a small amphibious operation with tanks, artillery and transport at short notice. Their capability for larger operations might require the inclusion of normal army divisions and the concentration of the amphibious resources of more than one fleet.

Other Eastern Bloc Countries

Of the other Warsaw Pact countries only East Germany has landing craft, and these—six *Robbe* class (800 tons, 12 knots) and twelve *Labbo* class) 200, 10 knots) follow the early Russian influence of short-range operational capability.

CONCLUSION

Space does not permit discussion of the landing ships and craft of nations outside the main East/West confrontation. In general they can be said to follow the pattern of the World War 2 LST and LCT, which, in fact, most of them are. Still useful for limited short-range operations, they are not to be compared with the fully developed types of Britain, France and USSR, let alone of the United States.

There, as has been said, the development of amphibious warfare and logistic shipping is on the march. In general terms, the 1950s saw the appearance of the modern beaching and dock ships; and the 1960s, that of the fully developed amphibious warfare helicopter ship—a type which Britain still does not possess. The 1970s will see the appearance of the 40,000-ton Amphibious Assault Ships and possibly of the similar sized Fast Deployment Logistic Ships. They are a long cry indeed from the landing ships and craft of World War 2, and a very different development, too, from that confidently predicted by the proponents of all-air lift for armies. In that, surely, there is a lesson that should not be ignored by the powers of Western Europe and especially by Britain.

J. L. Moulton.

MAIN
SHIP REFERENCE SECTION

ALBANIA

Strength of the Fleet

4 Submarines
2 Fleet Minesweepers
6 Inshore Minesweepers
12 Motor Torpedo Boats
1 Degaussing Ship
2 Oilers
16 Coastal Patrol Craft
10 Small Auxiliaries

Mercantile Marine

Lloyd's Register of Shipping:
11 vessels of 36,550 tons gross

SUBMARINES

4 Ex-USSR "W" CLASS

Displacement, tons 1 030 surface; 1 180 submerged
Dimensions, feet 240 × 22 × 15
Tubes 6—21 in (4 bow, 2 stern)
Main engines Diesels; 4 000 bhp = 17 knots surface
Electric motors; 2 500 hp = 15 knots submerged

Three of the four "W" class submarines are operational. Two were transferred from the USSR in 1960, and two others were reportedly seized from the USSR in mid-1961 upon the withdrawal of Soviet ships from their Albanian base.

FLEET MINESWEEPERS

2 Ex-USSR "T 43" CLASS

Displacement, tons 500 standard; 600 full load
Dimensions, feet 200 × 27·5 × 9
Guns 4—37 mm AA; 8—13 mm AA MG
Main engines Diesels; 2 shafts; speed = 18 knots

"T 43" class fleet minesweepers acquired from the USSR in 1960.

"T 43" Class Ex-USSR

PATROL VESSELS

4 Ex-USSR "KRONSTADT" CLASS

Displacement, tons 300 standard; 350 full load
Dimensions, feet 167·3 × 19·3 × 9
Guns 1—3·9 in; 2—37 mm AA; 3—20 mm AA
A/S weapons Depth charge projectors
Main engines Diesels; 2 shafts = 23 knots

"Krondstadt" class submarine chasers. Fitted for minelaying. Four were transferred in 1958, but two of these were exchanged for newer vessels in 1960.

"KRONSTADT" Class Ex-USSR

TORPEDO BOATS

12 Ex-USSR "P-4" CLASS

Displacement, tons 50
Dimensions, feet 85·3 × 20 × 6
Guns 4—25 mm AA MG
Tubes 2—18 in
Main engines Diesels; 2 000 bhp = 42 knots

Soviet built fast patrol boats acquired in 1955. It is reported that there are 12 motor torpedo boats in the Albanian Navy, all of the Soviet P-4 class but some may have been supplied by the Chinese.

"P-4" Class Ex-USSR

PATROL CRAFT

16 COASTAL TYPE

Displacement, tons 40
Dimensions, feet 82 × 16 × 5
Guns 2—25 mm
Main engines Speed = 30 knots

Not all of the same type. Some are of the Soviet PO-2 class.

GUNBOATS

2 ARMOURED TYPE

Displacement, tons 46
Guns 1—3 in; 2—20 mm AA
Main engines Speed = 17 knots

There are reported to be a few newer versions of this old type.

INSHORE MINESWEEPERS

6 Ex-USSR "T 301" CLASS

Displacement, tons 130 standard; 180 full load
Dimensions, feet 100 × 16 × 4·5
Guns 2—37 mm AA; 2—25 mm AA
Main engines Diesels; 2 shafts; 480 bhp = 10 knots

"T 301" class inshore minesweepers acquired from the USSR in 1957-60. Another photograph of "T 301" class appears in the 1962-63 edition.

"T 301" Class Ex-USSR

DISPOSALS
The former Yugoslavian mining tenders and inshore minesweepers, *Pasman* (ex-*Mosor*) and *Ugliano* (ex-*Marjan*), later used as small minelayers, were scrapped in 1967. The three former Soviet minesweeping boats of the "KM 4" class were stricken from the list in 1967.

"T 301" Class Ex-USSR

LANDING CRAFT

2 UTILITY TRANSPORT TYPE

Displacement, tons 225
Main engines Speed = 10 knots

Reported to be of the former German MFP type. For general utility and transport duties.

DEGAUSSING SHIP

1 Ex-USSR "SEKSTAN" CLASS

Dimensions, feet 134 × 40 × 14 max
Transferred from the USSR. Built in Finland in 1956

CONVERSION. The "Atrek" class submarine tender transferred from USSR in 1961 as a depot ship has been converted into a merchant ship.

OILERS

2 Ex-USSR "KHOBI" CLASS

Measurements, tons 1 600 deadweight
Dimensions, feet 220 × 33 × 15 max
Main engines 2 diesels; 1 600 bhp = 12 knots

Transferred from the USSR. Launched in 1956

In addition to the above there are reported to be a number of small auxiliaries,

ABU DHABI

The Sea Wing of the Abu Dhabi Defence Force was formed in 1968. The force is responsible for patrolling offshore islands and coastal oil concessions. Locally recruited, but certain ex-Royal Navy base staff initially.

PATROL CRAFT

2 "KAWKAB" TYPE

KAWKAB **THOABAN**

Displacement, tons	25
Dimensions, feet	56 oa
Guns	2—20 mm
Main engines	2 Caterpillar diesels. 800 bhp = 19 knots
Complement	11

There are five other 40 foot patrol launches operated by the Sea Wing.

KAWKAB *1969, Keith Nelson & Co. Ltd.*

THOABAN *1969, courtesy John Kinross, Esq.*

ALGERIA

Mercantile Marine
Lloyd's Register of Shipping
6 vessels of 15 644 tons gross

COASTAL ESCORTS

2 "SOI" CLASS

Displacement, tons	215 light; 250 normal
Dimensions, feet	138 pp; 147 oa × 20 × 10
Guns	4—25 mm (2 twin mounts)
Main engines	3 diesels; 3 500 bhp = 28 knots
Complement	30

Delivered by USSR on 7 and 8 Oct 1967.

MISSILE BOATS

1 "Osa" CLASS

Displacement, tons	160 standard; 200 full load
Dimensions, feet	131·5 oa × 23 × 6·5
Missiles	4 "Styx" surface to surface
Guns	4—25 mm
Main engines	3 diesels; 4 800 bhp = 35 knots

Delivered by USSR on 7 Oct 1967.

8 "KOMAR" CLASS

Displacement, tons	75 standard; 100 full load
Dimensions, feet	82 × 20 × 6
Missiles	2 "Styx" surface to surface
Guns	2—25 mm
Main engines	3 diesels; 4 800 bhp = 40 knots

Acquired in 1967 from USSR.

COASTAL MINESWEEPER

SIDI FRADJ (ex-*Darfour*)

Displacement, tons	215 standard; 270 full load
Dimensions, feet	136 oa × 24·5 × 6
Guns	1—3 in; 2—20 mm AA
Main engines	Diesels; 1 000 bhp = 13 knots

Two ex-US BYMS type coastal minesweepers were presented to Algeria by Egypt to form the nucleus of the new Algerian Navy. Both *Darfour* (ex-BYMS 2041) and *Tor* (ex-BYMS 2175) arrived in Algiers on 4 Nov 1962, being officially handed over on 6 Nov and renamed *Sidi Fradj* and *Djebel Aures*, respectively, but the latter was wrecked off Algiers in Apr 1963. Now considered obsolescent.

SIDI FRADJ Ex-*U.A.R.*

ARGENTINA

Administration

Commander in Chief of the Navy:
Pedro A. J. Gnavi

Chief of Naval Staff:
Vicealmirante Constantino G. Argueles

Operative Naval Command:
Vicealmirante Juan C. Gonzalez Llanos

Diplomatic Representation

Chief of Naval Commission in Europe and Naval Attaché in London and the Netherlands:
Contraalmirante Luis Maria Iriart

Naval Attaché in Washington:
Contraalmirante Fernando A. Milia

Strength of the Fleet

2 Aircraft Carriers
2 Submarines (Conventionally Powered)
3 Cruisers
9 Destroyers
2 Frigates
2 Corvettes
4 Coastal Minesweepers
2 Minehunters
2 Motor Torpedo Boats
9 Patrol Vessels
3 Patrol Craft
3 Survey Ships
5 Landing Ships
3 Landing Craft
1 Support Craft
1 Salvage Vessel
1 Training Ship
5 Transports
5 Oilers
1 Icebreaker (Antarctic Research)
15 Tugs

Ships

The names of all Argentine warships and naval auxiliary vessels are prefaced by "A.R.A." (Armada Republica Argentina).

Personnel

1969: 2 300 officers, 30 000 ratings (including 11 000 conscripts).

Mercantile Marine

Lloyd's Register of Shipping:
315 vessels of 1 196 817 tons gross

Silhouettes

Scale: 150 feet = 1 inch

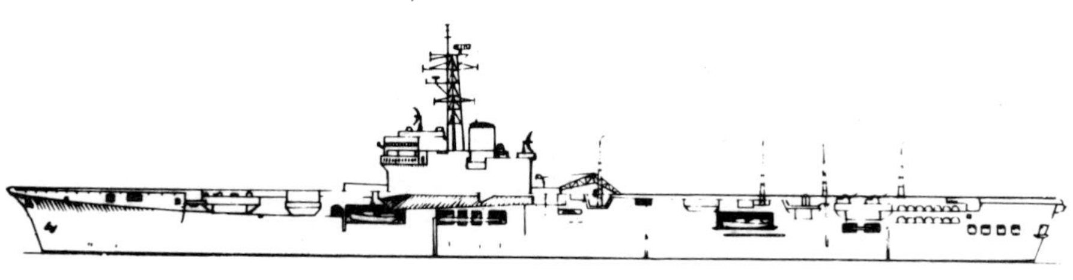

INDEPENDENCIA

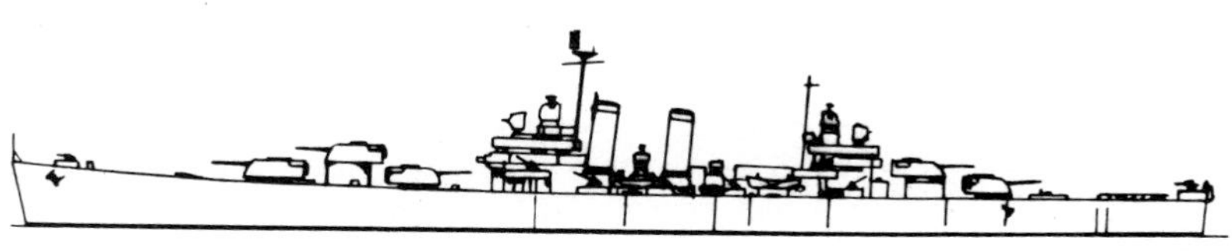

GENERAL BELGRANO, 9 DE JULIO

LA ARGENTINA

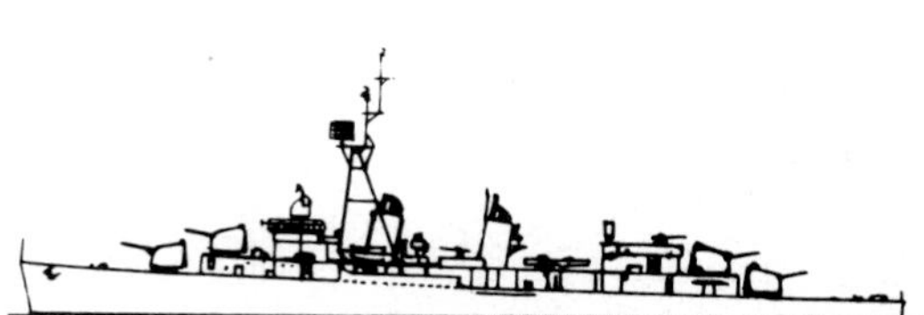

BROWN, ESPORA, ROSALES

BUENOS AIRES *Class*

COMODORO AUGUSTO LASSERE

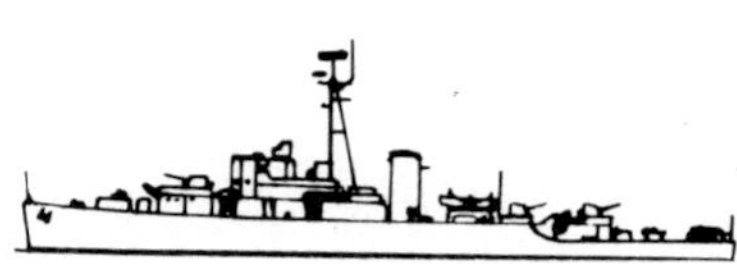

AZOPARDO, PIEDRABUENA

KING, MURATURE

AIRCRAFT CARRIERS *(Portaviones)*

Name	Builders	Laid down	Launched	Completed
VEINTICINO DE MAYO (ex-*HrMs Karel Doorman*, ex-*HMS Venerable*)	Cammell Laird & Co Ltd Birkenhead	3 Dec 1942	30 Dec 1943	17 Jan 1945

1 Ex-BRITISH "COLOSSUS" CLASS

Displacement, tons	15 892 standard; 19 896 full load
Length, feet (*metres*)	630 (*192·0*) pp 693·2 (*211·3*) oa
Beam, feet (*metres*)	80 (*24·4*)
Draught, feet (*metres*)	25 (*7·6*)
Width, feet (*metres*)	121·3 (*37·0*) overall
Hangar:	
Length, feet (*metres*)	455 (*138·7*)
Width, feet (*metres*)	52 (*15·8*)
Height, feet (*metres*)	17·5 (*5·3*)
Aircraft	Capacity 21. Official complement: 8 Tracker S2A's; 6 Seabat SH-34J helicopters
Guns, AA	10—40 mm
Guns, saluting	fitted
Boilers	4 three-drum type; working pressure 400 psi (*28·1 kg/cm²*): Superheat 700°F (*371°C*)
Main engines	Parsons geared turbines 40 000 shp; 2 shafts
Speed, knots	24·25
Radius, miles	12 000 at 14 knots
Oil fuel (tons)	3 200
Complement	1 462

Purchased from Great Britain on 1 Apr 1948. Commissioned in the Royal Netherlands Navy on 28 May 1948. Badly damaged by boilerroom fire 29 Apr 1968, sold to Argentina 15 Oct 1968 and refitted at Rotterdam by N.V. Dok en Warf Mij Wilton Fijenoord, being reboilered from *HMS Leviathan*.

RECONSTRUCTION. Underwent modernisation in 1955-58, including angled flight deck and steam catapult, mirror sight landing system and new anti-aircraft battery of ten 40 mm guns, at the Wilton-Fijenoord Shipyard, at a cost of 25 million guilders. Conversion completed in July 1958.

ENGINEERING. Engines and boilers are arranged *en echelon*, the two propelling-machinery spaces having two boilers and one set of turbines in each space, on the unit system.

APPEARANCE. With a modified island and bridge, a lattice tripod radar mast, and a tall raked funnel, she differs considerably from her former appearance and from her original sister ships in the British, French, Argentine and Brazilian Navies.

PHOTOGRAPHS. An aerial counter view appears in the 1965-66 edition. Netherlands section.

DRAWING. Port elevation and plan. Redrawn in 1966. Scale: 128 feet = 1 inch.

25 DE MAYO *1966, RNN Official*

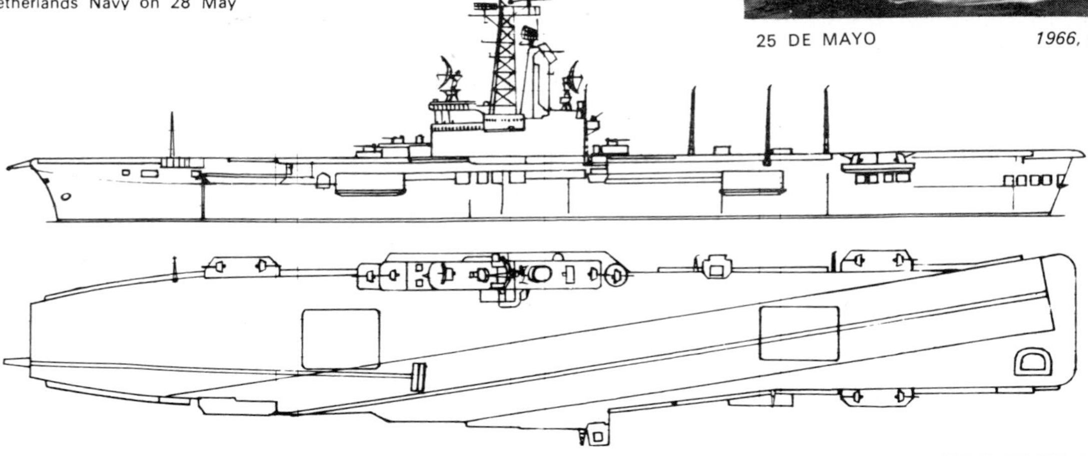

25 DE MAYO **1966 Skyfotos**

25 DE MAYO *1967, Royal Netherlands Navy, Official*

Aircraft Carriers—*Continued*

Name	*Deck No.*	*Builders*	*Laid down*	*Launched*	*Completed*
INDEPENDENCIA (ex-HMS *Warrior*)	V 1 (Formerly letter J)	Harland & Wolff, Ltd, Belfast	12 Dec 1942	20 May 1944	24 Jan 1946

Ex-BRITISH "COLOSSUS" CLASS

Displacement, tons	14 000 standard; 18 400 normal; *9 540 full load
Length, feet (*metres*)	630 (*192·0*) pp; 695 (*211·8*) oa
Beam, feet (*metres*)	80 (*24·4*)
Draught, feet (*metres*)	21·3 (*6·5*) mean; 23·5 (*7·2*) max
Width feet (*metres*)	118 (*36·0*) oa
Flight deck:	
Length, feet (*metres*)	690 (*210·3*)
Width feet (*metres*)	80 (*24·4*)
Height above wl feet, (*metres*)	39 (*11·9*)
Aircraft	Capacity 21
Guns, AA	8—40 mm
Boilers	4 Admiralty 3-drum type, working pressure 400 psi (*28·1 kg/cm²*) Max superheat 700°F (370°C)
Main engines	Parsons geared turbines 40 000 shp; 2 shafts
Speed, knots	25 designed; 24·25 sea speed
Radius, miles	12 000 at 14 knots 6 200 at 23 knots
Oil fuel (tons)	3 200
Complement	1 076 (peace); 1 300 (war)

INDEPENDENCIA *1969, Argentine Navy, Official*

Lent to the Royal Canadian Navy from 1946 to 1948. Served in the British Navy from 1948 to 1958. Modernised in 1952-53 with lattice foremast and extended and enlarged bridgework. Again modernised in 1955-56 with the partially angled flight deck and improved arrester gear. Acted as headquarters ship in the Christmas Island Atomic experiments from Feb to Oct 1957. Negotiations for the sale of the ship to the Argentine Government were concluded by the British Government in July 1958. Sailed from Portsmouth to Argentina on 10 Dec 1958. Renamed *Independencia* at Puerto Belgrano naval base on 26 Jan 1959.
Insulated for tropical service and partially air-conditioned.

ENGINEERING. Engines and boilers are arranged *en echelon*, the two propelling machinery spaces having one set of turbines and two boilers installed side by side in each space, on the unit system, so that the starboard propeller shaft is longer than the port shaft. Maximum speed is 25 knots at 225 revolutions per minute. Economical speed is 15 knots at 120 revolutions per minute.

CONSTRUCTION. The original flight deck has been strengthened to take aircraft of over 8 tons in weight. Sponsons can be dismantled to the extent of 3·5 feet on either side if necessary to allow passage through the Panama Canal. Mercantile type hull. Built to Lloyd's specification up to main deck with the original intention of converting to commercial service after the Second World War. Damage control: No great measure of vertical sub-division on the sandwich system as it was reckoned that it is better for ships to settle evenly in the event of damage and flooding than to foster capsizing.

HANGAR. Dimensions of hangar are: Length, 445 feet; width, 52 feet; clear depth, 17·5 feet. Dimensions of aircraft lifts are: 45 feet by 34 feet.

PHOTOGRAPHS. A port surface view appears in the 1957-58 to 1963-64 editions and a port bow oblique aerial view in the 1959-60 to 1963-64 editions, a starboard bow oblique aerial view in the 1964-65, 1965-66, 1967-68 and 1968-69 editions, a port quarter oblique aerial view in 1966-67 edition, and a starboard broadside aerial view in the 1964-65 to 1968-69 editions.

DRAWING
Port elevation and plan. Scale: 128 feet = 1 inch.

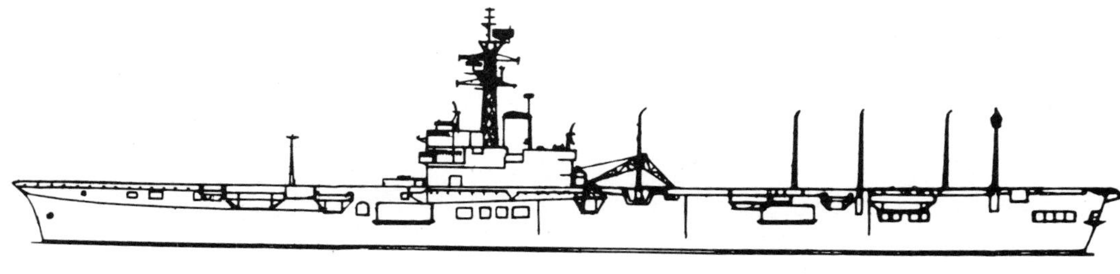

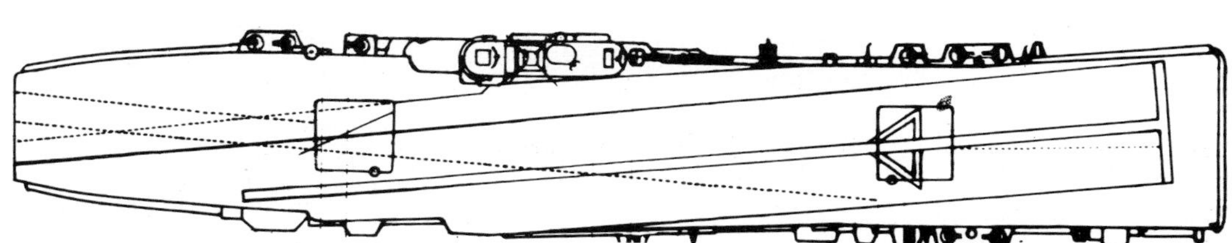

INDEPENDENCIA *1969, Argentine Navy, Official*

SUBMARINES

Name	No.	Builders	Launched	Completed	Transferred
SANTA FE (ex-USS *Lamprey*, SS 372)	S 11	Manitowoc Shipbuilding Company	18 June 1944	17 Nov 1944	27 July 1960
SANTIAGO DEL ESTERO (ex-USS *Macabi*, SS 375)	S 12	Manitowoc Shipbuilding Company	19 Sep 1944	29 Mar 1945	11 Aug 1960

2 Ex-US "BALAO" CLASS

Displacement, tons	1 526 standard; 1 816 surface; 2 425 submerged
Length, feet (*metres*)	311·5 (*94·9*)
Beam feet (*metres*)	27 (*8·2*)
Draught, feet (*metres*)	17 (*5·2*)
Torpedo tubes	10—21 in (*533 mm*); 6 bow, 4 stern. 24 Mk 14 torpedoes
Main engines	6 500 hp GM 2-stroke diesels (surface); 4 610 hp electric motors (submerged)
Speed, knots	20 on surface; 10 submerged
Radius, miles	12 000 at 10 knots
Oil fuel (tons)	300
Complement	82

Former United States submarines transferred from the USA to Argentina at Mare Island Naval Shipyard, San Francisco, in 1960 after having been refitted. Have two engine rooms instead of one to reduce size of Compartments.

PHOTOGRAPHS. Another photograph of *Santiago del Estero* appears in the 1962-63 to 1964-65 editions.

SANTIAGO DEL ESTERO — *1969, Argentine Navy, Official*

SANTA FE — *1969, Argentine Navy, Official*

CRUISERS

Name	No.	Builders	Laid down	Launched	Completed
GENERAL BELGRANO (ex-*17 de Octubre*, ex-*Phoenix*, CL 46)	C 4	New York S.B. Corp Camden	15 Apr 1935	12 Mar 1938	18 Mar 1939
NUEVE DE JULIO (ex-*Boise*, CL 47)	C 5	Newport News S.B. & D.D. Co	1 Apr 1935	3 Dec 1936	1 Feb 1939

2 Ex-US "BROOKLYN" CLASS

Displacement, tons	*Gen. Belgrano:* 10 800 standard; 12 650 normal; 13 645 full load *Nueve de Julio:* 10 500 standard 12 300 normal; 13 645 full load
Length, feet (*metres*)	608·3 (*185·4*) oa
Beam, feet (*metres*)	69 (*21·0*)
Draught, feet (*metres*)	24 (*7·3*) max
Aircraft	2 helicopters
Missiles, AA	2 quadruple "Sea Cat" launchers (*General Belgrano* only).
Guns, surface	15—6 in (*153 mm*) 47 cal; 8—5 in (*127 mm*) 25 cal.
Guns, AA	28—40 mm; 16—20 mm;
Guns, saluting	4—47 mm
Armour	Belt 4 in—1½ in (*100—38 mm*) Decks 3 in+2 in (*76+51 mm*) Turrets 5 in—3 in (*127—76 mm*) Conning Tower 8 in (*203 mm*)
Boilers	8 Babcock & Wilcox Express type
Main Engines	Westinghouse geared turbines 100 000 shp; 4 shafts
Speed, knots	32·5
Radius, miles	7 600 at 15 knots
Oil fuel (tons)	2 200
Complement	1 200

Former "light" cruisers of the United States Navy "Brooklyn" class. Superstructure was reduced, bulges added, beam increased, and mainmast derricks and catapults removed. Purchased from the United States in 1951 at a cost of $7 800 000 representing 10 per cent of their original cost ($37 000 000) plus the expense of reconditioning them. Both were transferred to the Argentine Navy on 12 Apr 1951. *General Belgrano* was commissioned under the name *17 de Octubre* at Philadelphia on 17 Oct 1951. *9 de Julio* was commissioned into the Argentine Navy at Philadelphia on 11 Mar 1952.

PHOTOGRAPHS. A starboard bow aerial view of *9 de Julio* appears in the 1954-55 to 1958-59 editions, a large port quarter surface view of *9 de Julio* in the 1957-58 edition, a port broadside view of *General Belgrano* in the 1957-58 to 1963-64 editions, and a starboard broadside surface view of *9 de Julio* in the 1964-65 and 1965-66 editions and a port broadside in the 1965-66 to 1968-69 editions.

HISTORICAL. *9 de Julio* refers to 9 July, 1816, when the Argentine provinces signed the Declaration of Independence. *17 de Octubre* was renamed *General Belgrano* in 1956 following the overthrow of President Peron the year before.

HANGAR. The hangar in the hull right aft accommodates two helicopters together with engine spares and duplicate parts, though 4 aircraft was the original complement. The incorporation of this hangar resulted in a very wide and nearly flat counter and high freeboard aft and also gave the after guns higher command. Above the hangar a revolving crane is placed at the stern extremity overhanging the hangar hatch. The two aircraft catapults, originally mounted above the hangar as far outboard as possible, and the aircraft were removed.

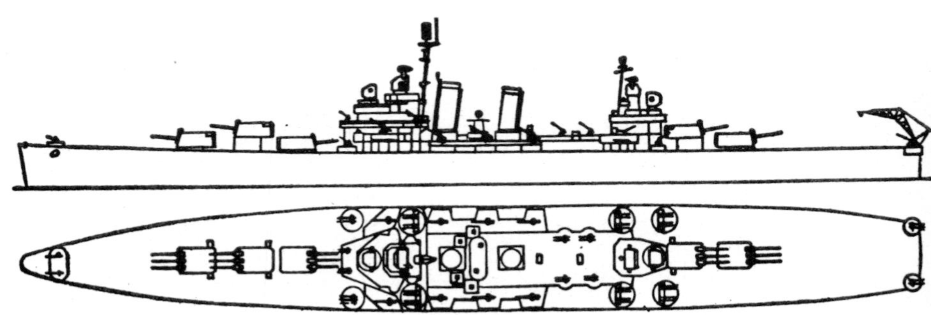

DRAWING
Port elevation and plan. Scale: 128 feet = 1 inch.

9 DE JULIO — *1969, Argentine Navy, Official*

Cruisers—*continued*

Name	No.	Builders	Laid down	Launched	Completed
LA ARGENTINA	C 3	Vickers-Armstrongs Ltd, Barrow-in Furness	Jan 1936	16 Mar 1937	31 Jan 1939

Displacement, tons	6 000 standard; 7 610 normal 8 630 full load
Length, feet (*metres*)	510 (*155·5*) pp; 541·2 (*164·9*) oa
Beam, feet (*metres*)	56·5 (*17·2*)
Draught, feet (*metres*)	16·5 (*5·0*) max
Guns, surface	9—6 in (*153 mm*)
Guns, AA	14—40 mm
Torpedo tubes	6—21 in (*533 mm*), tripled
Armour	Side and C.T. 3 in (*76 mm*); deck and gunhouses 2 in (*51 mm*)
Boilers	4 Yarrow; 300 psi (*21 kg/cm²*)
Main engines	Parsons geared turbines 54 000 shp; 4 shafts.
Speed, knots	30
Radius, miles	7 500 at 12 knots
Oil fuel (tons)	1 500
Complement	800

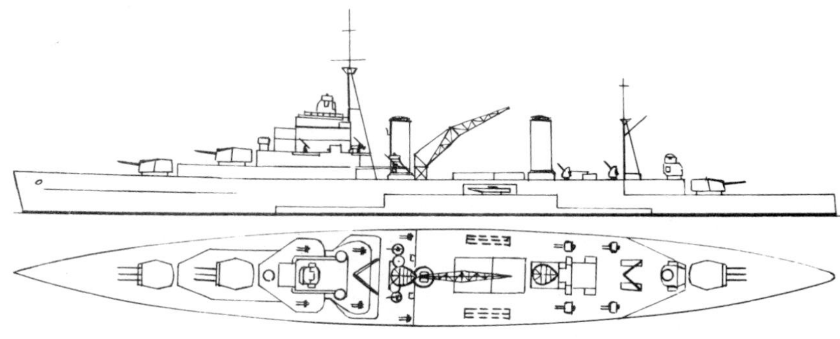

Designed as Training Cruiser. Cost 6 000 000 gold pesos (about £1 750 000). Best recent speed 25 knots.

GUNNERY. Original 4 inch guns were removed in 1950 and 40 mm guns added.

DRAWING. Port elevation and plan. Catapult and crane have been removed. Scale 128 feet = 1 inch.

LA ARGENTINA *1969, Argentine Navy, Official*

DESTROYERS

Name	No.	Builders	Laid down	Launched	Completed
BROWN (ex-USS *Heerman*, DD 532)	D 20	Bethlehem Steel Co, San Francisco	8 May 1942	5 Dec 1942	6 July 1943
ESPORA (ex-USS *Dortch*, DD 670)	D 21	Federal S.B. & D.D. Co, Port Newark	1942	20 June 1943	16 July 1943
ROSALES (ex-USS *Stembel*, DD 644)	D 22	Bath Iron Works Corporation, Bath, Maine	21 Dec 1942	8 May 1943	7 Aug 1943

3 Ex-US "FLETCHER" CLASS

Displacement, tons	2 100 standard; 3 050 full load
Length, feet (*metres*)	376·5 (*114·8*) oa
Beam, feet (*metres*)	39·5 (*12·0*)
Draught, feet (*metres*)	12·2 (*3·7*) mean; 18 (*5·5*) max
Guns, surface	4—5 in (*127 mm*) 38 cal.
Guns, AA	6—3 in (*76 mm*) 50 cal.
Torpedo tubes	5—21 in (*533 mm*) quintupled
A/S depth charges	2 fixed Hedgehogs; 1 DC rack
A/S torpedo racks	2 side-launching
Boilers	4 Babcock & Wilcox
Main engines	2 sets GE geared turbines 60 000 shp; 2 shafts
Speed, knots	35
Radius, miles	6 000 at 15 knots
Oil fuel (tons)	650
Complement	300

Brown, Espora and *Rosales* were transferred to the Argentine Navy on 1 Aug 1961. *Espora* is of the later "Fletcher" class.

PHOTOGRAPHS. A photograph of *Rosales* appears in the 1962-63 to 1964-65 editions and of *Brown* in the 1965-66 to 1968-69 editions.

TRANSFERS. The two US destroyers of the later "Fletcher" class scheduled to be transferred, *Charles J. Badger*, DD 657, and *Hickox*, DD 673, were not eventually negotiated.

ESPORA *1969, Argentine Navy, Official*

DESTROYERS—*continued*

6 "BUENOS AIRES" CLASS

Displacement, tons	1 375 standard; 1 820 to 1 850 normal; 1 980 to 2 010 full load
Length, feet (*metres*)	312 (*95·1*) pp; 320 (*97·5* wl; 323 (*98·5*) oa
Beam, feet (*metres*)	34·8 (*10·6*)
Draught, feet (*metres*)	10·7 (*3·3*) mean
Guns, surface	4—4·7 in (*120 mm*)
Guns, AA	6—40 mm; 5 MG
A/S depth charges	4—DCT
Torpedo tubes	4—21 in (*533 mm*) quadrupled
Boilers	3 three-drum type
Main engines	Parsons geared turbines 34 000 shp; 2 shafts
Speed, knots	35
Radius, miles	4 100 at 14 knots
Oil fuel (*tons*)	450
Complement	200

All laid down in 1936 and completed in Mar-Oct 1938. *Corrientes* of this class was lost by collision with the cruiser *Almirante* Brown on 3 Oct 1941. Classification changed from *Exploradores* to *Torpederos* in 1952 and to *Destructores* in 1957. One quadruple torpedo mount removed in 1956.

PHOTOGRAPHS. A photograph of *Santa Cruz* appears in the 1967-68 and 1968-69 editions, of *San Juan* in the 1953-54 to 1958-59 editions and of *Entre Rios* in the 1957-58 to 1963-64 editions.

Name	No.	Builders	Launched
BUENOS AIRES	D 6	Vickers-Armstrongs Ltd, Barrow-in-Furness	21 Sep 1937
ENTRE RIOS	D 7	Vickers-Armstrongs Ltd, Barrow-in-Furness	21 Sep 1937
MISIONES	D 11	Cammell Laird & Co Ltd, Birkenhead	23 Sep 1937
SAN JUAN	D 9	John Brown & Co Ltd, Clydebank	24 June 1937
SAN LUIS	D 10	John Brown & Co Ltd, Clydebank	24 Aug 1937
SANTA CRUZ	D 12	Cammell Laird & Co Ltd, Birkenhead	3 Nov 1937

BUENOS AIRES *1969, Argentine Navy, Official*

FRIGATES

2 "AZOPARDO" CLASS

Displacement, tons	1 160 standard; 1 220 normal; 1 400 full load
Length, feet (*metres*)	279 (*85·1*)
Beam, feet (*metres*)	31·5 (*9·6*)
Draught, feet (*metres*)	10 (*3·0*)
Guns, surface	1—4·1 in (*105 mm*)
Guns, AA	6—40 mm
A/S depth charges:	1 Hedgehog; 4 DC mortars
Boilers	2 water tube 3-drum type
Main engines	2 Parsons steam turbines 5 000 shp; 2 shafts
Speed, knots	20
Radius, miles	5 400 at 12 knots
Oil fuel (tons)	340
Complement	167

Both built at Astillero Nav. Rio Santiago. Improved "King" type. *Azopardo* is named after the Argentine naval hero.

Name	No.	Builders	Laid down	Launched	Completed
AZOPARDO	P 35	Astillero Nav. Rio Santiago	Nov 1950	11 Dec 1953	7 July 1957
PIEDRABUENA	P 36	Astillero Nav. Rio Santiago	Nov 1950	17 Dec 1954	16 Dec 1958

AZOPARDO *1966, Argentine Navy, Official*

Ex-US PF TYPE

JUAN B AZOPARDO (ex-*Hercules*, ex-USS *Asheville* ex-*HMCS Nadur*, ex-*HMS Adur*

No.	Builders	Laid down	Launched	Completed
GC 11	Canadian Vickers, Montreal	10 Mar 1942	22 Aug 1942	1 Dec 1942

Displacement, tons	1 445 standard; 1 920 normal; 2 415 full load
Length, feet (*metres*)	285·5 (*87·2*) wl; 304 (*92·7*) oa
Beam, feet (*metres*)	37·5 (*10·1*)
Draught, feet (*metres*)	13·7 (*4·2*)
Guns, AA	2—40 mm
Boilers	2 three-drum type
Main engines	Triple expansion 5 500 ihp; 2 shafts
Speed, knots	19
Radius, miles	7 800 at 12 knots
Oil fuel (tons)	700
Complement	175

Former United States patrol escort, of the "Tacoma" class. Sister ship *Santisima Trinidad*, P 34 (ex-HMS *Caicas*, ex-*Hannam*) was reclassified as a survey ship in 1963. Operated by National Maritime Prefectura and bears prefix P.N.M. to name. Maximum speed now 14 knots.

DISPOSALS
Sister ship *Heronia* (ex-USS *Reading*, PF 66) was withdrawn from active service and scrapped in 1966. *Sarandi* withdrawn from service in 1968.

JUAN B. AZOPARDO *1969, Argentine Navy, Official*

CORVETTES

2 "KING" CLASS

Displacement, tons	913 standard; 1 000 normal; 1 032 full load
Length, feet (*metres*)	252·7 (*77·0*)
Beam, feet (*metres*)	29 (*8·8*)
Draught, feet (*metres*)	7·5 (*2·3*)
Guns, surface	3—4·1 (*105 mm*)
Guns, AA	4—40 mm Bofors; 2—MG
A/S	4—DCT
Main engines	2—Werkspoor 4-stroke diesels: 2 500 bhp; 2 shafts
Speed, knots	18
Radius, miles	6 000 at 12 knots
Oil fuel (tons)	90
Complement	130

Both built at Astillero Nav. Rio Santiago. Named after Captain John King, an Irish follower of Admiral Brown, who distinguished himself in the war with Brazil, 1826-28; and Captain Murature, who performed conspicuous service against the Paraguayans at the Battle of Cuevas on Aug. 6 1865.

Name	No.	Builders	Laid down	Launched	Completed
KING	P 21	Astillero Nav. Rio Santiago	Dec 1938	Dec 1943	28 July 1946
MURATURE	P 20	Astillero Nav. Rio Santiago	June 1938	July 1945	18 Nov 1946

PHOTOGRAPHS. A photograph of *Murature* appears in the 1964-65 to 1966-67 editions.

DISPOSAL
Corvette **Republica** withdrawn from service 5 Aug 1967 and scrapped 1968.

KING *1967, Argentine Navy, Official*

COASTAL MINESWEEPERS

6 Ex-BRITISH "TON" CLASS

CHACO (ex-HMS *Rennington*) M 5
CHUBUT (ex-HMS *Santon*) M 3
FORMOSA (ex-HMS *Ilmington*) M 6
NEUQUEN (ex-HMS *Hickleton*) M 1
RIO NEGRO (ex-HMS *Tarlton*) M 2
TIERRA DEL FUEGO (ex-HMS *Bevington*) M 4

Displacement, tons	360 standard; 425 full load
Dimensions, feet	140 pp; 153 oa × 28·2 × 8·2
Guns	2—40 mm AA
Main Engines	2 diesels; 2 shafts 3000 bhp = 15 knots

Former British coastal minesweepers of the "Ton" class. Of composite wooden and non-magnetic metal construction. Purchased in 1967. In 1968 *Chaco* and *Formosa* were converted into minehunters in HM Dockyard, Portsmouth, and the other four were refitted and modernised as minesweepers by the Vosper Thornycroft Group with Vosper activated fin stabiliser equipment.

DISPOSALS
The four former minesweepers **Granville, Py, Robinson** and **Seaver** of the **Bouchard** class were deleted from the list on the 20 Nov 1967. **Py** and **Seaver** were transferred to the Paraguayan Navy.

TIERRA DEL FUEGO (sweeper) *1969, Wright & Logan*

FORMOSA (hunter) *1969, Wright & Logan*

MOTOR TORPEDO BOAT

2 Ex-US "HIGGINS" TYPE

P 82 **P 84**

Displacement, tons	45 standard; 50 full load
Dimensions, feet	71 pp; 78·8 oa × 20 × 4·5
Guns	2—40 mm AA, 2—·5 in MG
Dimensions, feet	71 pp; 78·8 oa × 20 × 4·5
Torpedoes	4 torpedo cradles
A/S weapons	2 rocket projectors
Main Engines	3 Packard engines. 4 500 hp = 40 knots
Fuel (tons)	9 aviation spirit
Radius, miles	1 000 at 20 knots
Complement	12

"Higgins" type. Built in New Orleans, USA in 1946. Originally designated as an "LT" series (1 to 9).

DISPOSALS
P 81, P 83, P 85, P 87 and P 89 were officially removed from the List in 1963, and P 86 and P 88 in 1966.

P 81 similar to P 84 and P 82

PATROL VESSELS (*Avisos*)

2 Ex-US TUG TYPE

TOMPSON (ex-US *Sombrero Key*) A 4 **GOYENA** (ex-US *Dry Tortugas*) A 3

Displacement, tons	1 863 full load
Dimensions, feet	191·3 × 37 × 18
Main engines	2 Enterprise diesels. 2 250 bhp = 12 kts
Oil fuel (tons)	532
Complement	60

Built by Pendleton Shipyard Co., New Orleans. Launched in 1943 and leased to the Argentine Navy in 1965.

2 Ex-US ATF TYPE

COMMANDANTE GENERAL IRIGOYEN (ex-USS *Cahuilla*, ATF 152) A 1
COMMANDANTE GENERAL ZAPIOLA (ex-USS *Arpaho*, ATF 68) A 2

Displacement, tons	1 235 standard; 1 675 full load
Dimensions, feet	195 wl; 205 oa × 38·2 × 15·3
Guns	1—3 in; 4—40 mm AA; 2—20 mm AA originally
Main Engines	4 sets diesels with electric drive; 3 000 bhp = 16 knots
Complement	85

Former US fleet ocean tugs of the "Apache" class. Fitted with powerful pumps and other salvage equipment. Both built by Charleston S.B. & D.D. Co., Charleston, S.C. Launched on 2 Nov. 1944 and 22 June 1942, respectively, and completed on 10 Mar. 1945 and 20 Jan. 1943. Transferred to Argentina at San Diego, California, in 1961 Classified as tugs until 1966 when they were re-rated as patrol vessels (avisos).

COMMANDANTE GENERAL IRIGOYEN *1969, Argentine Navy, Official*

4 Ex-US ATA TYPE

CHIRIGUANO (ex-US *ATA* 227) A7 **SANAVIRON** (ex-US *ATA* 228) A 8
DIAGUITA (ex-US *ATA* 124) A5 **YAMANA** (ex-US *ATA* 126) A 6

Displacement, tons	689 standard; 800 full load
Dimensions, feet	133·7 wl; 143 oa × 34 × 12
Guns	2—20 mm AA
Main Engines	Diesel-electric; 1 850 bhp = 12·5 knots
Oil fuel (tons)	154
Radius, miles	16 500
Complement	49

Former US auxiliary ocean tugs. Built by Levingstone Shipbuilding Co., Orange Texas, USA, in 1945. *Diaguita* and *Yamana* are fitted as rescue ships. All four of above ships bear names of South American Indian tribes. Classified as ocean salvage tugs until 1966 when they were re-rated as patrol vessels (avisos).

YAMANA *1969, Argentine Navy, Official*

SURVEY SHIPS (*Buques Oceanograficos*)

1 "SPIRO" TYPE

Name	*No.*	*Builders*	*Launched*
SPIRO	GC 12	Rio Santiago Navy Yard	7 June 1937

Displacement, tons 560 normal; 650 full load
Dimensions, feet 197 oa (*59·7*) × 24 (*7·32*) × 11½ (*3·5*)
Guns 4 × 40 mm
Main engines 2 MAN Diesels; 2 000 bhp = 13 knots
Complement 77

Former minesweeper of the **Bouchard** class, now operated by Prefectura Nacional Maritima. Sister ships **Py** and **Seaver** transferred to Paraguayan Navy. First warships built in Argentine yards.

SPIRO *1969, Argentine Navy, Official*

3 "LYNCH" TYPE

EREZCANO GC 23 **LYNCH** G3 21 **TOLL** GC 22

Displacement, tons 100 normal; 117 full load
Dimensions, feet 90 × 19 × 6
Guns 1 × 20 mm
Main engines 2 Maybach Diesels; 2 700 bhp = 22 knots
Complement 16

Patrol craft operated by Prefectura Nacional Maritima. Pennants GC 23, GC 21, GC 22 respectively.

LYNCH *1969, Argentine Navy, Official*

1 Ex-CANADIAN FLOWER CLASS

CAPITAN CANEPA (ex-HMCS *Barrie*) Q 8

Displacement, tons 995 standard; 1 265 full load
Dimensions, feet 208 × 33·5 × 16·5
Main Engines Triple expansion: 2 750 ihp = 15 knots
Boilers 2
Oil fuel (tons) 271
Complement 54

Former Canadian corvette (frigate) of the "Flower" class. Launched in Canada on 12 Nov. 1940. Completed on 12 May 1941. A photograph of *Capitan Canepa* appears in the 1958-59 to 1964-65 editions.

CAPITAN CANEPA *1969, Argentine Navy, Official*

1 TRANSPORT TYPE

USHUAIA No. Q 10

Displacement, tons 1 275 standard; 1 500 full load
Dimensions, feet 211 × 31·5 × 11·5
Guns Removed
Main Engines 2 sets diesels; 2 shafts; 1 200 bhp = 12·7 knots
Oil fuel (tons) 60
Radius, miles 3 500
Complement 65

Built at Rio Santiago. Launched in 1939. Named after the capital of the territory of Tierra del Fuego. Formerly rated as a transport until 1959, when she was reclassified as a survey ship. She is also a buoy ship for the laying and servicing of buoys and lights.

USHUAIA *1969, Argentine Navy, Official*

DISPOSALS

Comodoro Augusto Lassere ex- frigate *Santissima Trinidad*, ex-HMS *Caicos*, ex-USS *Hannem* discarded 1968. Photograph 1965-66 to 1968-69 editions.

1 SAIL TYPE

EL AUSTRAL (ex-US *Atlantis*) Q 7

Displacement, tons 571
Dimensions, feet 110 pp 141 oa × 27 × 20
Main engines Diesel; 400 bhp
Oil fuel (tons) 22
Complement 19

Built by Burmeister & Wain, Copenhagen. Launched and completed in 1931. Incorporated into the Argentine Navy on 30 April, 1966. Acquired from USA. Officially rated as *Buque Oceanografico*.

TANK LANDING SHIPS

5 Ex-US LST TYPE

CABO SAN BARTOLOME	BDT 1	**CABO SAN ISIDRO**	BDT 6
CABO SAN GONZALO	BDT 4	**CABO SAN PIO**	BDT 10
		CABO SAN VICENTE	BDT 14

Displacement, tons	2 366 beaching; 4 080 full load
Dimensions, feet	316 wl; 328 oa; × 50 × 14
Main Engines	2 diesels; 2 shafts; 1 800 bhp = 11 knots
Oil fuel (tons)	700
Radius, miles	9 500 at 9 knots
Complement	80

Ex-US LST's 875, 998, 872, 919, 1108. Built by Puget Sound Bridge and Dredging Co., Seattle, USA. Launched in 1944. Have two rudders. BDT 5, BDT 8, BDT 9, and BDT 12, were withdrawn from service in 1958-60, and BDT 2, BDT 7, BDT 11 and BDT 13 in 1964. *Cabo San Francisco de Paula*, BDT 3 has been used as a store ship since 1966. One BDT under construction at the Naval Shipyard in Rio Santiago to be *Cabo San Antonio*.

MEDIUM LANDING SHIP

BDM 1 Q 69

Displacement, tons	743 beaching; 1 095 full load
Dimensions, feet	196·5 wl; 203·5 oa × 33·8 × 6; (8 max)
Main Engines	2 sets diesels; 2 shafts; 2 800 bhp = 13 knots
Oil fuel, tons	170
Radius, miles	4 100 at 12 knots
Complement	60

Former American LSM's 267 and 86 respectively.

NOTE. BDM 2 converted into a Minelayer Support Vessel at the Naval Shipyard in Buenos Aires; named *Corrientes*.

INFANTRY LANDING CRAFT

BDI 1 (Q 54) **BDI 4** (Q 57) **BDI 15** (Q 68)

Displacement, tons	230 light; 387 full load
Dimensions, feet	153 wl; 159 oa × 23·2 × 5
Guns	2—20 mm AA (only in BDI 4)
Main engines	8 sets diesels; 3 200 bhp = 14 knots. Two reversible propellers
Oil fuel, tons	110
Radius, miles	6 000 at 12 knots
Complement	30

Ex-US Navy LCIL's 583, 606 and 689, BDI 3, BDI 6, BDI 8, BDI 9, BDI 11 and BDI 13 were withdrawn from service in 1958. BDI 1 and BDI 4 were given new Q numbers as shown above instead of Q 64 and 67. BDI 10 (Q 63) was converted into an oiler in 1960 and renamed *Punta Lara*. BDI 5, BDI 7, BDI 12 and BDI 14 were officially deleted from the list in 1961, and BDI 2 in 1963.

MINOR LANDING CRAFT. There are also 20 personnel and vehicle landing craft, all ex-US Navy LCVP's numbered EDVP 1, 2, 3, 4, 6, 7, 8, 9, 10, 11, 12, 13, 17, 19, 20, 21, 22, 24, 27 and 28. Displacement 12 tons. Dimensions 39·5 × 10·5 × 5·5 feet. Main engines: diesel. Speed 9 knots. Nos. 16, 23, 25 and 26 were withdrawn from service in 1959.

BDI 4 — 1960, *Giorgio Arra*

MINOR LANDING CRAFT

EDVP 1, 3 to 13, 20-29

Displacement, tons	12
Dimensions, feet	39·5 × 10·5 × 5·5
Main engines	Diesel, 9 knots

Ex-USN LCVP. Number 16, 23, 25 and 26 withdrawn from service in 1966.

SUPPORT VESSELS

CORRIENTES (ex-BDM 2)

Displacement, tons	1 095 full load
Dimensions, feet	196·5 wl; 203·5 oa × 33·8 × 8
Main engines	2 Diesel; 2 shafts; 2 800 bhp = 13 knots

Former Medium Landing Ship (ex-USN *LSM 86*). Converted at Naval Shipyard. Buenos Aires during 1968.

TRAINING SHIPS (*Buques Esquela*)

LIBERTAD Q 2

Displacement, tons	3 025 standard; 3 765 full load
Dimensions, feet	262 wl; 301 oa × 47 × 21·8
Guns	1—3 in; 4—40 mm AA; 4—47 mm saluting
Main engines	2 Sulzer diesels; 2 400 bhp = 13·5 knots
Radius	15 000 miles
Complement	370 (crew) plus 150 cadets

Built in the State-owned shipyards at Rio Santiago. Launched on 30 June 1956. The former training ship *Madryn* was removed from the list on 29 June 1967.

LIBERTAD — *1969, Argentine Navy, Official*

TRANSPORTS (*Transportes*)

BAHIA AGUIRRE **BAHIA BUEN SUCESO** **BAHIA THETIS**

Displacement, tons	3 100 standard; 5 000 full load
Dimensions, feet	334·7 × 47 × 13·8
Guns	2—4·1 in; 2—40 mm Bofors AA; 2—20 mm AA; 4—47 mm saluting
Main engines	2 sets Nordberg diesels; 2 shafts; 3 750 bhp = 16 knots
Oil fuel (tons)	500 (*Bahia Thetis*); 442 (*Bahia Buen Suceso*), 355 (*Bahia Aguirre*)
Radius, miles	15 000
Complement	100

Built in Canada by Halifax shipyards. *Bahia Buen Suceso* was completcd at Halifax, Nova Scotia, in June 1950. Nos Q 2, Q 6 and Q 8, respectively. The first two are troop transports, *Bahia Thetis* was used as a training ship and carried guns (see above).

BAHIA THETIS *Added 1967, Werner Schiefer*

BAHIA BUEN SUCESO *1969, Argentine Navy, Official*

LA PATAIA B 10

Displacement, tons	3 825 standard; 6 000 full load
Dimensions, feet	335·2 × 50·2 × 23
Main engines	2 sets diesels; 2 shafts; 3 400 bhp = 16 knots
Oil fuel (tons)	500
Radius, miles	15 000
Complement	100

Built in Italy by C. R. del Adriatico (CRDA). Laid down on 25 Apr 1948, launched on 25 June 1949, completed in June 1950, delivered 2 Oct 1951. Troop transport.

DISPOSALS. Sister ships **Le Maire** and **Les Eclaireurs** were scrapped in 1964.

LA PATAIA *Added 1964, Argentine Navy, Official*

SAN JULIAN (ex-*FS* 281) B 7

Displacement, tons	930
Dimensions, feet	176 × 32·5 × 11
Main engines	2 sets diesels; 2 shafts; 1 000 bhp = 10 knots
Oil fuel (tons)	75
Complement	40

Ex-US Army small cargo carrier. Built by Wheeler Shipbuilding Corpn. Launched in 1944. It was officially stated in May 1960 that this vessel, formerly rated as a transport was to be converted into a salvagé vessel, but in Dec 1961 it was officially stated that she would continue to be a transport ship.

SALVAGE VESSELS (*Buque de Salvamento*)

GUARDIAMARINA ZICARI (ex-*Tehuelche*, ex-HMS *Kingfisher*, ex-*King Salvor*)

Displacement, tons	1 600
Dimensions, feet	200·2 pp; 216 oa × 37·8 × 13
Main engines	Triple expansion. 2 shafts; 1 500 ihp = 12 knots
Oil fuel (tons)	310
Complement	82

Former British submarine rescue ship. Built as an Admiralty ocean salvage vessel by Wm. Simons & Co. Ltd. Renfrew, Scotland, and laid down on 17 May 1941, launched on 18 May 1942 and completed on 17 July 1942. Converted into a Submarine Rescue Bell and Target Ship in 1953-54. Paid off as Bell Rescue Ship in 1958 and subsequently employed as a Submarine Support Ship and Tender. Purchased from Great Britain in Dec. 1960, and sailed from Chatham to Argentina in Apr 1961, and renamed *Tehuelche*. Again renamed *Guardiamarina Zicari* in Apr 1963. Pennant No. Q 81. Photograph in 1962-63 to 1966-67 editions.

OILERS (*Buques Tanques*)

PUNTA MEDANOS B 18

Displacement, tons	14 352 standard; 16 331 full load
Measurement, tons	8 250 deadweight
Dimensions, feet	470 pp; 502 oa × 62 × 28·5
Main engines	Double reduction geared turbines. 2 shafts; 9 500 shp = 18 knots (over 19 knots attained on trials)
Boilers	2 Babcock & Wilcox two-drum integral furnace water-tube
Oil fuel (tons)	1 500
Radius, miles	13 700
Complement	99

Built by Swan, Hunter & Wigham Richardson Ltd, Wallsend on-Tyne. Launched on 20 Feb 1950. Completed on 10 Oct 1950. A unit of the Argentine Navy available as a training vessel for personnel. She embodied experience gained in previous fleet oilers, and was then the finest equipped and fastest of her type afloat. Fitted for fuelling warships at sea. Boilers built under licence by the Wallsend Slipway & Engineering Company. Steam conditions of 400 lb. per sq. in pressure and 750 deg F

PUNTA MEDANOS *1969, Argentine Navy, Official*

PUNTA DELGADA (ex-*Sugarland*, ex-*Nanticoke*, *AOG* 66) B 16

Displacement, tons	5 930 standard; 6 090 full load
Dimensions, feet	325 × 48·2 × 20
Main engines	Westinghouse diesel; 1 shaft; 1 400 bhp = 11·5 knots
Oil fuel, (tons)	150
Radius, miles	9 000
Complement	72

Named after geographical location. USMS type T1-M-BT1. Built by St. John's River SB Co. Launched on 7 Apr. 1945.

DISPOSALS
Two sister ships: **Punta Ninfas** (ex-**Black Bayou**, ex-**Michigamme**, AOG 65) was scrapped in 1964, and **Punta Loyola** (ex-**Capitain**, ex-**Klickitat**, AOG 64) was withdrawn from active service in 1966.

PUNTA Class *Official*

PUNTA RASA (ex-*Salt Creek*) B 20

Displacement, tons	2 055 standard; 2 253 full load
Dimensions, feet	221 × 37 × 13·8
Main engines	Diesel; 1 shaft; 800 bhp = 10 knots
Oil fuel (tons)	60
Radius, miles	3 500
Complement	37

Built by Barnes Dulath S.B. Co. Launched in 1943 and completed in 1944. Commissioned in 1947. Named after Cape. US MC type T1-M-A2.

DISPOSALS
Sister ship **Punta Ciguena** (ex-**Sulphur Bluff**) was officially deleted from the list in 1961.

PUNTA ALTA B 12

Displacement, tons	1 600 standard; 1 900 full load
Measurement, tons	800 deadweight
Dimensions, feet	210 × 33·8 × 12·5
Main engines	Diesel; 1 shaft; 1 850 bhp = 8 knots
Oil fuel (tons)	146
Radius, miles	4 700

Built at Puerto Belgrano. Launched in 1937. Named after a headland.

PUNTA LARA (ex-BDI 10, ex-USS LCIL 688)

Displacement, tons	628
Dimensions, feet	159 oa × 235 × 8·5
Main engines	8 General Motors diesels coupled to 2 shafts.

Former American Large Infantry Landing Craft. Conversion into an oiler completed 9 Sep 1960. Withdrawn from service 1961, but recommissioned 1969.

ICEBREAKERS (*Rompehielos*)

GENERAL SAN MARTIN Q 4

Displacement, tons	4 854 standard; 5 301 full load
Measurement, tons	1 600 deadweight
Dimensions, feet	279 × 61 × 21
Guns	1—4 in; 2—40 mm AA Bofors
Aircraft	1 reconnaissance aircraft and 1 helicopter
Main engines	4 diesel-electric; 2 shafts; 7 100 hp = 16 knots
Range, miles	35 000 at 10 knots
Oil fuel (tons)	1 100
Complement	160

Built by Seebeck Yard of Weser AG. Launched on 24 June 1954. Completed in Oct 1954. Used by the Antarctic Institute. Fitted for research. Specially insulated against cold.

GENERAL SAN MARTIN *1966, Argentine Navy, Official*

TUGS (*Remolcadores*)

GUAYCURU R 33 **QUILMES** R 32

Displacement, tons	368 full load
Dimensions, feet	107·2 × 24·4 × 12·5
Main engines	Skinner Unaflow engines; 645 ihp = 9 knots
Boilers	Cylindrical (Scotch)
Oil fuel (tons)	52
Radius, miles	2 200 at 7 knots
Complement	14

"Quilmes" class tugs built at Rio Santiago, Argentina, in the State Naval Shipyards. Laid down on 23 Aug and 15 Mar 1956, respectively launched on 27 Dec 1959 and 8 July 1957 and completed on 29 July and 30 Mar 1960.

PEHUENCHE R 29 **TONOCOTE** R 30

Displacement, tons	330
Dimensions, feet	105 × 24·7 × 12·5
Main engines	Triple expansion; 600 ihp = 11 knots
Boiler	2
Oil fuel (tons)	36
Radius, miles	1 200
Complement	13

Both built in Rio Santiago Naval Yard. Commissioned for service in 1954.

MATACO R 3 **TOBA** R 4

Displacement, tons	600
Measurement, tons	339 gross
Dimensions, feet	130·5 pp; 137 wl; 139 oa × 28·5 × 11·5
Main engines	Triple expansion; 2 shafts; 1 200 ihp = 12 knots
Boilers	2
Oil fuel (tons)	95 tons
Radius, miles	3 900
Complement	34

Both built by Hawthorn Leslie, Ltd, Hebburn-on-Tyne. Launched on 24 Jan 1928 and 23 Dec 1927, respectively. Both completed in Mar 1928.

HUARPE R 12 **PUELCHE** R 13

Displacement, tons	370
Dimensions, feet	107 × 27·2 × 12
Main engines	Triple expansion; 800 ihp
Boilers	1 cylindrical (Howaldt Werke)
Oil fuel (tons)	58
Complement	13

Built by Howaldt Werke in 1927. Entered service in the Argentine Navy in 1942.

QUERANDI R 2

Displacement, tons	615
Measurements, tons	345 gross
Dimensions, feet	134·5 × 30 × 11
Main engines	Triple expansion; 1 300 ihp = 12 knots
Boilers	2
Oil fuel (tons)	115
Radius, miles	2 400
Complement	34

Built by John I. Thornycroft & Co. Ltd., Woolston, Southampton. Launched in 1913.

CALCHAQUI R 6 **MOCOVI** R 5
CAPAYAN R 16 **MORCOYAN** R 19
CHULUPI R 10 **QUIQUIYAN** R 16

Displacement, tons	70
Dimensions, feet	67 × 14 × 13
Main engines	Diesel; 310 bhp = 10 knots
Oil fuel, tons	8·7
Complement	5

Built in USA.

DISPOSALS
The former tug **Ona** was deleted from the list on 11 July 1967.
The salvage tug **Ranquel** was withdrawn from service and deleted from the list in May 1960.
The salvage tug **Charrua** (ex-US Army LT 224) was officially stricken from the list in 1963. Her sister ship **Guarani** was lost without trace in the Straits of Magellan on 15 Oct 1958.

ROYAL AUSTRALIAN NAVY

Naval Board

Chairman: Minister for the Navy:
Mr. Charles R. Kelly, MP

First Naval Member and Chief of Naval Staff:
Vice Admiral Victor A. Smith, CB, CBE, DSC

Second Naval Member and Chief of Naval Personnel:
Rear-Admiral Richard I. Peek, OBE, DSC

Third Naval Member and Chief of Naval Technical Services:
Rear-Admiral Bryan J. Castles, ADC

Fourth Naval Member and Chief of Supply:
Rear-Admiral William D. Graham, CBE

Secretary, Department of the Navy:
Mr. Samuel Landau, CBE, MA

Senior Appointments

Flag Officer Commanding Australian Fleet:
Rear-Admiral Gordon J. B. Crabb, CBE, DSC

Deputy Chief of the Naval Staff:
Rear-Admiral Hugh D. Stevenson

Diplomatic Representation

Australian Naval Representative in London:
Commodore Kenneth Douglas Gray, D.F.C., R.A.N.

Naval Attaché in Washington:
Commodore Bruce H. Loxton, R.A.N.

Strength of the Fleet

2 Aircraft Carriers (1 as Transport Ship)
3 Submarines (Diesel Powered)
8 Destroyers (3 armed with guided missiles)
5 Frigates
6 Coastal Minesweepers and Minehunters
20 Patrol Boats
5 Oceanographic Research Ships
10 Fleet Support Ships and Service Craft

New Construction Programme

Construction of one submarine
Construction of two destroyer escorts

Pennant Numbers

There was a re-allocation of pennant numbers within the R.A.N. on 1 Jan 1969. Only auxiliaries now have the prefix letter painted in, submarines do not have numbers painted in.

Mercantile Marine

Lloyd's Register of Shipping:
314 vessels of 818 247 tons gross

Navy Estimates

	$A		$A
1954-55:	96 330 000	1961-62:	96 038 000
1955-56:	97 668 000	1962-63:	97 780 000
1956-57:	78 130 000	1963-64:	109 018 000
1957-58:	87 582 000	1964-65:	138 424 000
1958-59:	84 802 000	1965-66:	190 934 000
1959-60:	85 224 000	1966-67:	234 634 000 *
1960-61:	89 432 000	1967-68:	232 687 000 *
		1968-69:	223 721 500

*Includes United States Credits

Personnel

1 January 1960: 10 594 officers and sailors
1 January 1961: 10 547 officers and sailors
1 January 1962: 10 832 officers and sailors
1 January 1963: 11 228 officers and sailors
1 January 1964: 11 908 officers and sailors
1 January 1965: 12 822 officers and sailors
1 January 1966: 13 960 officers and sailors
1 January 1967: 15 247 officers and sailors
1 January 1968: 16 125 officers and sailors
1 January 1969: 16 638 officers and sailors

Ensign

On 1 Mar 1967 the British White Ensign was replaced by the Australian White Ensign. This retains the Union Jack in the top left canton but replaces the red cross of St. George with the five stars of the Southern Cross and the Federal Star, all blue, on a white background.

Silhouettes

Scale 150 feet = 1 inch

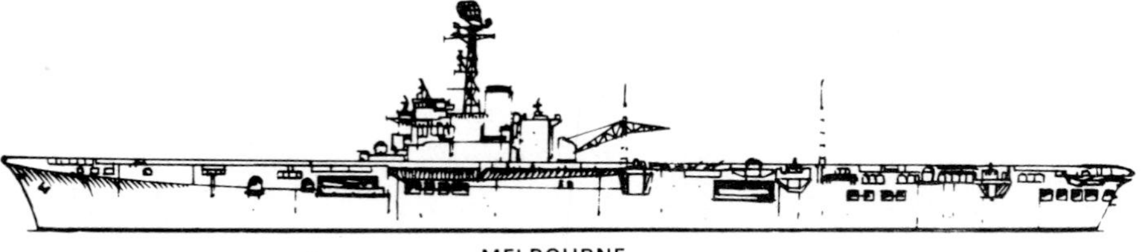

MELBOURNE

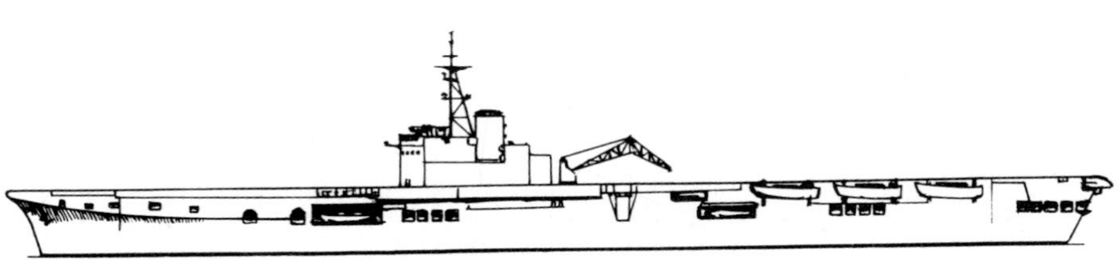

SYDNEY

BRISBANE, HOBART, PERTH

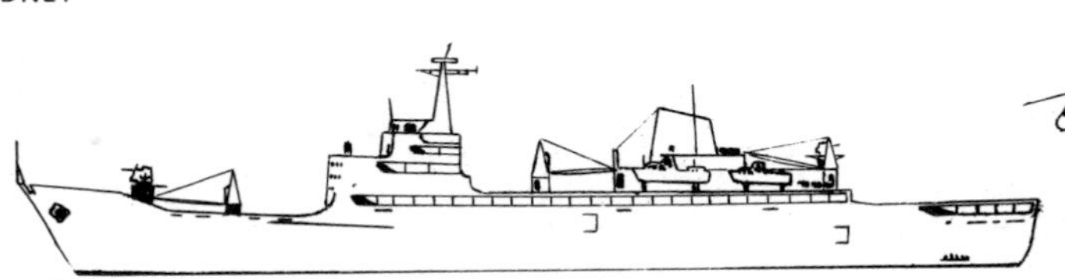

STALWART

DERWENT

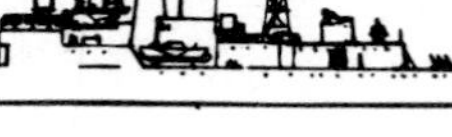

STUART

PARRAMATTA, YARRA

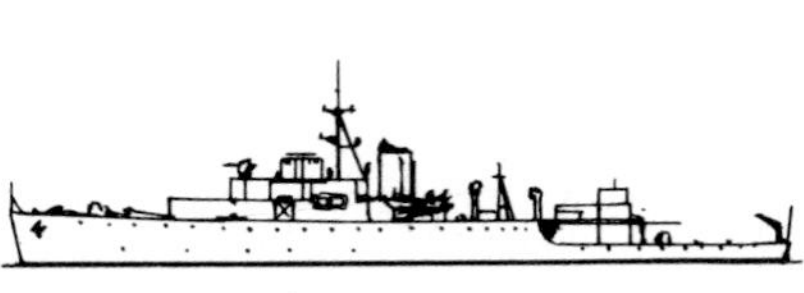

DIAMANTINA

ANZAC

QUEENBOROUGH

VENDETTA

DUCHESS

MORESBY

AIRCRAFT CARRIER

Name	*No.*	*Deck Letter*	*Builders*	*Laid down*	*Launched*	*Completed*
MELBOURNE (ex-*Majestic*)	21	M (ex-Y)	Vickers-Armstrongs, Barrow-in-Furness	15 Apr 1943	28 Feb 1945	8 Nov 1955

1 MODIFIED "MAJESTIC" CLASS

Displacement, tons	16 000 standard; 20 000 full load
Length, feet (*metres*)	650 (*198·1*) wl; 701·5 (*213·8*) oa
Beam, feet (*metres*)	80·2 (*24·5*) hull
Draught, feet (*metres*)	25 (*7·6*)
Width, feet (*metres*)	80 (*24·4*) flight deck 126 (*38·4*) oa including 6° angled deck and mirrors
Hangar, feet (*metres*)	444×52×17·5 (*135·3×15·8×5·3*)
Aircraft	4 Sky Hawk jet fighters; 6 Tracker aircraft; 10 Westland Wessex A/S helicopters (see *Aircraft* notes)
Guns, AA	12 (4 twin, 4 single) 40 mm Bofors
Boilers	4 Admiralty 3-drum type
Main engines	Parsons single reduction geared turbines; 40 000 shp; 2 shafts
Speed, knots	24; sea speed 23 max
Complement	1 354 (151 officers and 1 203 sailors)

MELBOURNE (after refit) *1969, Royal Australian Navy, Official*

At the end of the Second World War, when she was still incomplete, work on this ship was virtually brought to a standstill pending a decision as to future naval requirements. When full-scale work was resumed during 1949-55, and after her design had several times been re-cast, she underwent reconstruction and modernisation in Great Britain, including the fitting of the angled deck, the steam catapult and the mirror deck landing sights, and was transferred to RAN on completion. She was commissioned and renamed at Barrow-in-Furness on 28 Oct 1955, sailed from Portsmouth on 5 Mar 1956 and arrived at Fremantle. Australia, on 23 April 1956. She became flagship of the Royal Australian Navy at Sydney on 14 May 1956. She cost £A8 309 000.

MODERNISATION. *Melbourne* has undergone an extended refit at a cost of over $A8 750 000 (25 per cent over estimate) to enable her to operate with S2E Tracker and A4E Skyhawk aircraft, and to improve habitability.

ENGINEERING. Boilers work at a pressure of 430 lb per sq in and a temperature of 700 degrees Fahrenheit of superheat.

AIRCRAFT. The aircraft complement formerly comprised 8 Sea Venom jet fighters, 17 Gannet turbo-prop anti-submarine aircraft, and 2 Sycamore helicopters, later 4 Sea Venom, 6 Gannet and 10 Wessex A/S helicopters. Fourteen S2E Tracker anti-submarine aircraft and ten A4E Skyhawk fighter/bombers were purchased in 1966 in the USA (in service 1967) at a cost of $A46 000 000.

RADAR. The ship was fitted in 1963 with a Dutch type radar aerial on the foremast similar to that in the Type 12 frigates.

PHOTOGRAPHS. A port bow oblique aerial view of *Melbourne* appears in the 1957-58 to 1964-65 editions, a large port quarter aerial oblique view in the 1962-63 and 1963-64 editions, a port quarter surface view in the 1961-62 edition, a dead overhead aerial view showing angled deck in the 1956-57 to 1961-62 editions, a large port bow surface view in the 1955-56 to 1960-61 editions, and a port near broadside view in the 1964-65 to 1968-69 editions.

DRAWING. Starboard elevation and plan as converted with the angled deck. Scale: 128 feet = 1 inch.

MELBOURNE *1965. Royal Australian Navy. Official*

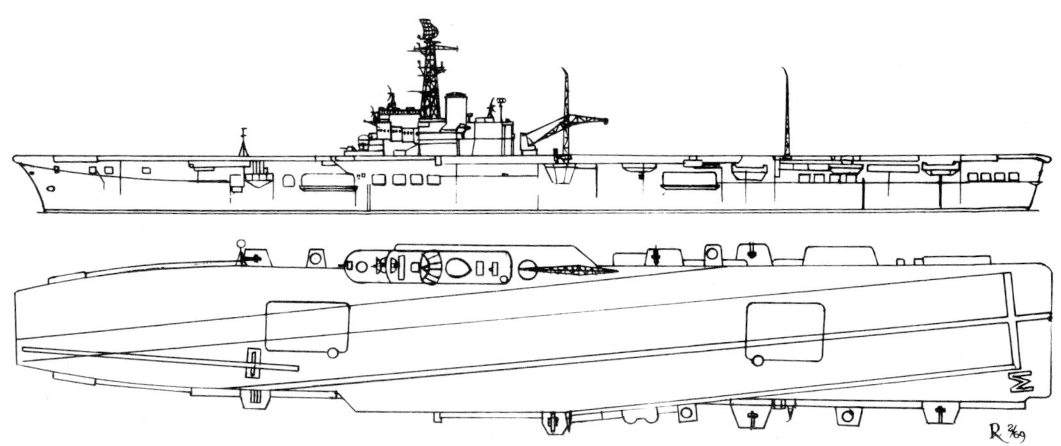

FAST TRANSPORT (*ex-Aircraft Carrier*)

Name	*No.*	*Deck Letter*	*Builders*	*Laid down*	*Launched*	*Completed*
SYDNEY (ex-*Terrible*)	A 214 (ex-R 17)	S (ex-K)	H.M. Dockyard, Devonport	19 Apr 1943	30 Sep 1944	5 Feb 1949

1 "MAJESTIC" CLASS

Displacement, tons	12 569 standard; 17 233 full load (revised official figure)
Length, feet (*metres*)	630 (*192·0*) pp; 698 (*212·8*) oa
Beam, feet (*metres*)	80 (*24·4*)
Draught, feet (*metres*)	18·25 (*5·6*) mean; 25 (*7·6*) max
Flight deck,	
Length, feet (*metres*)	690·7 (*210·5*)
Width, feet (*metres*)	112·5 (*34·3*)
Guns, AA	4—40 mm, single mountings
Boilers	4 Admiralty 3-drum; 400 psi; 700°F
Main engines	Parsons single reduction geared turbines, 40 000 shp; 2 shafts
Speed, knots	24·5
Complement	608 (40 officers, 568 sailors) nucleus as transport. Naval Reserve provide balance of ship's company in emergency.

This ship was handed over to the Royal Australian Navy on 16 Dec 1948, accepted for service on 5 Feb 1949, sailed from Devonport on 12 April and arrived in Australia in May 1949.

SYDNEY 1968, *Royal Australian Navy, Official*

ORIGINAL SCHEME. As an operational aircraft carrier she displaced 15 740 tons standard, carried Seafury fighters and Firefly anti-submarine and reconnaissance squadrons, with a stowage capacity of 37 machines, mounted 30 Bofors 40 mm AA guns, and her complement was 1 100 officers and sailors (peace), 1 300 (war).

PHOTOGRAPHS. A starboard bow oblique aerial view of *Sydney* as an aircraft carrier appears in the 1954-55 to 1961-62 editions, a port quarter surface view in the 1957-58 edition, a starboard broadside view in the 1957-58 to 1962-63 editions, and a starboard quarter oblique aerial view in the 1958-59 to 1963-64 editions. A starboard bow surface view of *Sydney* as a troop transport appears in the 1963-64 to 1965-66 editions. A port bow aerial view, as a troop transport, appears in the 1964-65 to 1967-68 editions.

TRAINING AND CONVERSION. It was officially announced on 4 Apr 1957 that she would have a flying training role, but the ship was converted to a fast military transport in 1962, and was recommissioned in 1963. She also serves as a training ship, and can operate Wessex anti-submarine helicopters.

DRAWINGS. A plan and port elevation drawing of *Sydney*, as an operational aircraft carrier, drawn to a scale of 128 feet = 1 inch, appears in the 1949-50 to 1963-64 editions, and a silhouette drawing in the 1949-50 to 1965-66 editions.

SYDNEY *1966, Royal Australian Navy, Official*

SUBMARINES

Name	*Builders*	*Laid down*	*Launched*	*Completion*
ONSLOW	Scotts' Shipbuilding & Eng Co Ltd, Greenock	4 Dec 1967	3 Dec 1968	Dec 1969
OTWAY	Scotts' Shipbuilding & Eng Co Ltd, Greenock	29 June 1965	29 Nov 1966	23 Apr 1968
OVENS	Scotts' Shipbuilding & Eng Co Ltd, Greenock	17 June 1966	4 Dec 1967	Apr 1969
OXLEY	Scotts' Shipbuilding & Eng Co Ltd, Greenock	2 July 1964	24 Sep 1965	21 Mar 1967

4 BRITISH "OBERON" CLASS

Displacement, tons	1 610 standard; 2 186 surface; 2 417 submerged (revised official figures)
Length, feet (*metres*)	241 (*73·5*) pp; 295·5 (*90·1*) oa
Beam, feet (*metres*)	26·5 (*8·1*)
Draught, feet (*metres*)	18 (*5·5*)
Torpedo tubes	8—21 in (*533 mm*) for homing torpedoes
Main engines	Admiralty Standard Range diesels, Electric drive
Complement	62 (7 officers, 55 sailors)

OXLEY *1967, Royal Australian Navy, Official*

It was officially announced by the Minister for the Navy in Canberra, Australia, on 22 Jan 1963 that four submarines of the "Oberon" class were to be built in British shipyards under Admiralty supervision at an overall cost of £A5 000 000 each, with deliveries spread over 3 years. *Oxley* commissioned 18 Apr 1967. These constitute the 1st Submarine Squadron, R.A.N.
Submarines of the Royal Navy are no longer based at Sydney, Australia, for anti-submarine training. The last unit of the Fourth Submarine Squadron of the Royal Navy, *Trump*, was withdrawn in Jan 1969.

OTWAY *1969, Royal Australian Navy, Official*

GUIDED MISSILE DESTROYERS

3 US "CHARLES F. ADAMS" CLASS

Name	No.	Builders	Laid down	Launched	Completed
BRISBANE	41	Defoe Shipbuilding Co, Bay City, Mich.	15 Feb 1965	5 May 1966	24 Jan 1968
HOBART	39	Defoe Shipbuilding Co, Bay City, Mich.	26 Oct 1962	9 Jan 1964	18 Dec 1965
PERTH	38	Defoe Shipbuilding Co, Bay City, Mich.	21 Sep 1962	26 Sep 1963	22 May 1965

Displacement, tons	3 370 standard; 4 500 full load
Length, feet (*metres*)	431 (*131·4*) wl; 437 (*132·2*) oa
Beam, feet (*metres*)	47 (*14·3*)
Draught, feet (*metres*)	20 (*6·1*)
Missiles, AA	"Tartar", single launcher
Missiles, A/S	Long range "Ikara" system with two single launchers
Guns, dual purpose	2—5 in (*127 mm*) 54 cal., single-mount, rapid fire
Torpedo tubes	6 (2 triple banks) for A/S torpedoes
Boilers	4 Foster Wheeler "D" type; 1 200 psi; 950°F
Main engines	2 GE double reduction turbines 70 000 shp; 2 shafts
Speed, knots	35
Complement	333 (21 officers, 312 sailors)

On 6 Jan 1962, in Washington, United States defence representatives and Australian military officials (on behalf of the Royal Australian Navy) and executives of the Defoe Shipbuilding Company, of Bay City, Michigan, signed a £A12 863 350 ($A25 726 700 in the new Australian decimal currency introduced in 1966) contract for the construction of two guided-missile destroyers (shipbuilding cost only). On 22 Jan 1963 it was officially announced by the Minister for the Navy in Canberra, Australia, that a third guided-missile destroyer was to be built in the United States for the Royal Australian Navy. They are the first of their kind for the Australian Navy. They constitute the 1st Destroyer Squadron, R.A.N.

DEFENCE
In addition to the "Tartar" missiles, with a range of 15 to 20 miles, they are equipped with the very latest long range anti-submarine warfare weapons.

ROLE
These versatile ships are intended to work with hunter killer groups in attacking submarines and to protect vital ocean convoys.

DESIGN
Generally similar to the United States "Charles F. Adams" class, but they differ by the addition of a broad deckhouse between the funnels enclosing the "Skara" anti-submarine torpedo-carrying missile system, and the mounting of a simple-arm launcher, instead of a twin, for the "Tartar" surface-to-air guided missiles.
As compared with previous destroyers, the ships have greater length overall, more beam and heavier displacement. They have a new hull design with aluminium superstructures. The most recent habitability improvements have been incorporated into their construction, including air conditioning of all living spaces.

COMMISSIONING
The first ship of the class, *Perth*, was commissioned and formally handed over to the Royal Australian Navy at Boston Naval Shipyard, Massachusetts, on 17 July 1965 and she steamed into an Australian port, Brisbane, for the first time on 4 March 1966. *Hobart* commissioned at Boston Naval Shipyard on 18 Dec 1965.

COST. Original estimate about £A6 400 000 to £A7 000 000 each (with missiles and electronics £A20 000 000 each). New decimal currency: about $A12 800 000 to $A14 000 000 each (with missiles and electronics $A40 000 000 each). The total cost of *Perth* is reported to be almost $A50 000 000.

BRISBANE *1969, Royal Australian Navy, Official*

PERTH *1968, Royal Australian Navy, Official*

HOBART *1969, Royal Australian Navy, Official*

DESTROYERS

3 "DARING" CLASS

Name	No.	Builders	Begun	Launched	Completed
VAMPIRE	11	Cockatoo Island Dockyard, Sydney	1 July 1952	27 Oct 1956	23 June 1959
VENDETTA	08	HMA Naval Dockyard, Williamstown	4 July 1949	3 May 1954	26 Nov 1958
DUCHESS	154	John I. Thornycroft & Co, Southampton	2 July 1948	9 Apr 1951	23 Oct 1952

Displacement, tons	2 800 standard; 3 600 full load
Length, feet (*metres*)	366 (*111·3*) pp; 388·5 (*118·4*) oa
Beam, feet (*metres*)	43 (*13·1*)
Draught, feet (*metres*)	12·8 (*3·9*)
Guns, surface	6—4·5 in (*115 mm*) in twin turrets, two forward and one aft (*Vampire* only 4—4·5 in twin, one forward one aft)
Guns, AA	6—40 mm
A/S	1 3-barrelled DC mortar (see *Design notes*)
Torpedo tubes	5—21 in (*533 mm*) in quintruple mounting
Boilers	2 Foster Wheeler; 650 psi; 850°F
Main engines	English Electric geared turbines 54 000 shp; 2 shafts
Speed, knots	30·5
Radius, miles	3 700 at 20 knots
Oil fuel (tons)	584
Complement	320 (14 officers, 306 sailors)

The above particulars refer to *Vampire* and *Vendetta*. For slightly different data applying to *Duchess*, which has Squid instead of Limbo, see under "Daring" class in United Kingdom section. The three ships constitute the 2nd Destroyer Squadron, R.A.N.

All-purpose ships, equipped for surface engagements anti-aircraft defence, and anti-submarine warfare. *Vampire* and *Vendetta* are the largest destroyers ever built in Australia. They were ordered in 1946. The ships are powerfully equipped for both offensive and defensive purposes. Their sister ship, *Voyager*, the prototype of the class, collided with the aircraft carrier *Melbourne* and sank off the southern coast of New South Wales on the night of 10 Feb 1964. She was replaced by the British destroyer *Duchess*, lent to Australia by the United Kingdom for four years, later extended to 1971.

MODERNISATION. *Vampire* and *Vendetta* have been extensively refitted, but the Australian Government has abandoned plans to install the "Ikara" anti-submarine missile system as part of the originally envisaged more costly modernisation, saving $A20 000 000.

VENDETTA *1965, Royal Australian Navy, Official*

DESIGN. *Vampire* and *Vendetta* are of similar design, including all welded construction, to that of "Daring" class, built in Great Britain, but were modified to suit Australian conditions and have "Limbo" instead of "Squid" anti-submarine mortars.

GUNNERY. The anti-aircraft guns are laid and fired by radar. "B" turret was removed from *Vampire* during her 1968 refit.

CONSTRUCTION. The superstructure is of light alloy, instead of steel, to reduce weight.

CLASS. Four large destroyers of this type were originally projected, to have been named after the Royal Australian Navy's famous "Scrap Iron Flotilla" of destroyers which won renown in the Mediterranean on the Tobruk ferry run and in other areas during the Second World War, but *Waterhen* was cancelled in 1954, and *Voyager* was lost in **1964.**

VAMPIRE (with only two 4·5 inch turrets) *1969, Royal Australian Navy, Official*

DUCHESS *1968, Royal Australian Navy Official*

Destroyers—*continued*

2 "BATTLE" CLASS

Name	No.	Builders	Laid down	Launched	Completed
ANZAC	59	Williamstown Naval Dockyard	23 Sep 1946	20 Aug 1948	22 Mar 1951
TOBRUK	37	Cockatoo Docks & Eng Co Pty Ltd	5 Aug 1946	20 Dec 1947	17 May 1950

Displacement, tons	2 400 standard; 3 450 full load
Length, feet (*metres*)	355 (*108·2*) pp 379 (*115·5*) oa
Beam, feet (*metres*)	41 (*12·5*)
Draught, feet (*metres*)	13·5 (*4·1*) mean
Guns, surface	*Tobruk:* 4—4·5 in (*115 mm*) in 2 twin turrets *Anzac:* 2—4·5 in (1 twin turret)
Guns, AA	6—40 mm
A/S	Squid 3-barrelled DC mortar
Torpedo rubes	10—21 in (*533 mm*) in *Tobruk* only
Boilers	2 Admiralty 3-drum 400 psi; 650°F
Main engines	Parsons geared turbines 50 000 shp; 2 shafts
Speed, knots	31
Complement	271 (11 officers, 260 sailors)

TOBRUK *1969, Royal Australian Navy, Official*

Ordered in 1945-46. Similar to the "Battle" class destroyers in the Royal Navy, but several alterations were incorporated, including sleeping accommodation for officers and men fore and aft, improved mess layout and other amenities, modern radar fire control, close range Staag armament (new type of twin 40 mm Bofors gun mounting) and the latest anti-submarine weapons. *Tobruk* was placed in Reserve in 1960. *Anzac* became fleet training ship, with extra deckhouse aft and director removed.

GUNNERY. *Anzac* had the first "Daring" type of 4·5 inch guns and mountings of completely Australian manufacture (weight of each twin mount is approx 50 tons). They are fully automatic, with a rate of fire of 25 rounds per minute, and an accurate range of over ten miles, firing a shell weighing 53 lb. The 4·5 inch guns for *Tobruk* were imported from Great Britain.
In 1966 "B" turret in *Anzac* was suppressed and replaced by a chartroom for training purposes.

DISPOSALS
Of the three destroyers of the "Tribal" class, **Bataan** was declared for disposal in 1957 (since scrapped), **Warramunga** in 1962, and **Arunta** in 1968, which later sank in tow 13 Feb, 1969, off W. Australia whilst in tow to breakers in Taiwan.

ANZAC ("B" turret replaced by chartroom) *1966, Royal Australian Navy, Official*

FAST ANTI-SUBMARINE FRIGATES *(Converted Destroyers)*

3 "QUEENBOROUGH" CLASS

TYPE 15

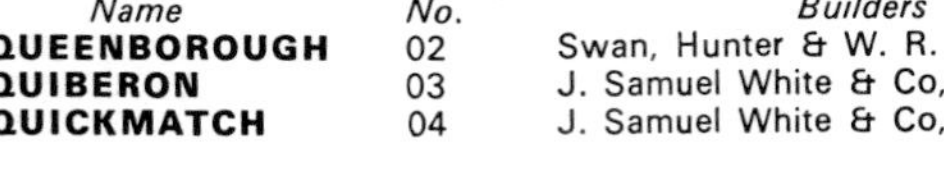

Name	No.	Builders	Laid down	Launched	Completed
QUEENBOROUGH	02	Swan, Hunter & W. R. Ltd, Wallsend	6 Nov 40	16 Jan 42	10 Dec 42
QUIBERON	03	J. Samuel White & Co, Ltd, Cowes	14 Oct 40	31 Jan 42	22 July 42
QUICKMATCH	04	J. Samuel White & Co, Ltd, Cowes	6 Feb 41	11 Apr 42	30 Sep 42

Displacement, tons	2 020 standard; 2 700 full load
Length, feet (*metres*)	358·2 (*109·2*)
Beam, feet (*metres*)	35·7 (*10·9*)
Draught, feet (*metres*)	13·2 (*4·0*) mean
Guns, surface	2—4 in (*102 mm*) twin-mount
Guns, AA	2—40 mm
A/S	2 Limbo 3-barrelled DC mortars
Boilers	2 Admiralty 3-drum; 300 psi; 650°F
Main engines	Parsons geared turbines 40 000 shp; 2 shafts
Speed, knots	31·25
Complement	146 (10 officers, 136 sailors)

QUEENBOROUGH *1968, Royal Australian Navy, Official*

Formerly in the Royal Navy. Lent to the Royal Australian Navy in 1943 (*Quiberon, Quickmatch*) and 1945 (*Quadrant, Quality, Queenborough*). Transferred permanently in June 1950 when it was announced they would be converted to fast anti-submarine frigates similar to the British Type 15, the conversions being effected at Cockatoo Island and Williamstown dockyards but only four of the ships were reconstructed (see *Disposals*). *Queenborough* completed conversion on 7 Dec 1954, *Quickmatch* on 23 Sep 1955, and *Quiberon* on 18 Dec 1957 *Queenborough* recommissioned on 28 July 1966.

PHOTOGRAPHS. A photograph of *Quickmatch* appears in the 1957-58 to 1961-62 editions and of *Quiberon* in the 1965-66 to 1967-68 editions.

DISPOSALS
Of this class, **Quality**, not converted, was declared for disposal in 1957, and **Quadrant** early in 1962.

ESCORTS *(ex-Boom Defence Vessel)*

6 "RIVER" CLASS

MODIFIED TYPE 12

Name	*No.*	*Builders*	*Launched*	*Completed*
DERWENT	49	Williamstown Naval Dockyard, Melbourne	17 Apr 1961	Apr 1964
PARRAMATTA	46	Cockatoo Island Dockyard, Sydney	31 Jan 1959	July 1961
STUART	48	Cockatoo Island Dockyard, Sydney	8 Apr 1961	June 1963
YARRA	45	Williamstown Naval Dockyard, Melbourne	30 Sep 1958	July 1961
SWAN	—	Williamstown Naval Dockyard, Melbourne	16 Dec 1967	
TORRENS	—	Cockatoo Island Dockyard, Sydney	28 Sept 1968	

Displacement, tons	2 100 standard; 2 700 full load
Length, feet (*metres*)	360 (*109·7*) pp; 370 (*112·8*) oa
Beam, feet (*metres*)	41 (*12·5*)
Draught, feet (*metres*)	12·8 (*3·9*) mean
Missiles, AA	1 quadruple launcher for "Seacat"
A/S weapons	1 launcher for "Ikara" long range system; 1 "Limbo" 3-barrelled DC mortar
Guns, dual purpose	2—4·5 in (*115 mm*)
Boilers	2 Babcock & Wilcox; 550 psi; 850°F
Main engines	2 double reduction geared turbines 30 000 shp; 2 shafts
Speed, knots	30
Complement	251 (13 officers, 238 sailors)

The design is generally similar to that of British Type 12 anti-submarine frigates, but modified by the Royal Australian Navy to incorporate improvements in equipment and habitability. The enclosed tower foremast differs from that in "Rothesay" class frigates in the Royal Navy. All six ships are being standardised to uniform armament and layout.

Stuart was the first fitted with the Ikara anti-submarine guided missile, trial ship for the system. *Derwent* was the first RAN ship to be fitted with "Seacat". Both ships are fitted with variable depth sonar.

Derwent and *Stuart* carried DE numbers for about three months but reverted to F, all six ships are now officially classed as Destroyer Escorts (1969).

PHOTOGRAPHS. Other photographs of *Parramatta* appear in the 1961-62 to 1963-64 and 1966-67 and 1968-69 editions, of *Yarra* in the 1962-63 edition, and of *Derwent* in the 1964-65 and 1965-66 and 1968-69 editions.

YARRA *John G. Callis*

PARRAMATTA *1969, Royal Australian Navy, Official*

DERWENT *1969, Royal Australian Navy, Official*

STUART *1968, Royal Australian Navy, Official*

DESTROYER TENDER

STALWART A 215

Displacement, tons	15 500
Length, feet (*metres*)	515·5 (*157·1*)
Beam, feet (*metres*)	67·5 (*20·6*)
Draught, feet (*metres*)	29·5 (*9·0*)
Guns, AA	2 twin 40 mm
Main engines	2 Scott-Sulzer 6-cylinder turbo-diesel engines; 14 400 bhp; 2 shafts
Speed, knots	18
Complement	396 (23 officers and 373 sailors)

STALWART 1968, *Royal Australian Navy, Official*

Largest naval vessel built in Australia. Built at Cockatoo Island Dockyard by Vickers (Australia) Pty Ltd, Sydney. Ordered on 11 Sep 1963. Laid down in June 1964 and launched on 7 Oct 1966. Designed to maintain destroyers and frigates and advanced weapons systems, including guided missiles. She has a helicopter flight deck and is defensively armed. High standard of habitability. Commissioned on 9 Feb 1968. Formerly rated as Escort Maintenance Ship. Redesignated Destroyer Tender in 1968. Cost officially estimated at just under $A15 000 000.

OCEANOGRAPHIC RESEARCH SHIPS (*ex-Frigates*)

DIAMANTINA	A 266 (ex-F 377)	Walkers Ltd, Maryborough, Queensland	12 Apr 43	6 Apr 44	27 Apr 45
GASCOYNE	A 276 (ex-F 354)	Morts' Dock and Engineering Co	4 June 42	20 Feb 43	20 Dec 43

Displacement, tons	1 340 standard; 2 127 full load
Length, feet (*metres*)	283 (*86·3*) pp; 301·3 (*91·8*) oa
Beam, feet (*metres*)	36·7 (*11·2*)
Draught, feet (*metres*)	12·5 (*3·8*)
Guns	1—40 mm
Boilers	2 Admiralty 3-drum
Main engines	Triple expansion 5 500 ihp; 2 shafts
Speed, knots	19·5
Complement	125 (6 officers 119 sailors)

Frigates converted in 1959-60 for survey and oceanographic research. The conversion included the provision of special laboratories and the fitting of *Gascoyne* with a helicopter platform. *Lachlan* was sold to the Royal New Zealand Navy. *Gascoyne* is in unmaintained reserve.

GUNNERY. The two 4-inch guns and two Squid A/S mortars in "B" position were removed. Forward 4-inch gun was in "A" position with 40 mm gun superimposed.

DIAMANTINA 1968, *Royal Australian Navy, Official*

DISPOSALS

Of the five other frigates of this class, **Burdekin** and **Hawkesbury** were declared for disposal in 1960, **Barwon** and **Macquarie** in 1962, and **Barcoo** in 1968. Of the four frigates of the "Bay" class, **Condamine** was declared for disposal in 1960, **Murchison** and **Shoalhaven** in 1962, and **Culgoa** in 1968.

DISPOSALS OF "SWAN" CLASS FRIGATES

Swan, latterly cadet training ship, was paid off in Nov 1962 and put up for sale in Apr 1964. **Warrego,** latterly survey ship, was paid off into reserve in Aug 1963 and put up for sale in Apr 1965.

OCEAN MINESWEEPERS. The last four ocean minesweepers of the "Bathurst" class were *Castlemaine*, immobile training ship at Flinders Naval Depot, *Colac*, now a tank cleaning vessel, *Mildura* and *Wagga*. These were survivors of a group of 32, four of which were given to New Zealand. For names and disposals of the remaining ships see 1961-62 edition.

GASCOYNE (converted for survey, with helicopter platform) 1960, *Royal Australian Navy, Official*

COASTAL MINESWEEPERS AND MINEHUNTERS

CURLEW (ex-HMS *Chediston*, ex-*Montrose*)
GULL (ex-HMS *Swanston*)
HAWK (ex-HMS *Somerleyton*, ex-*Gamston*)
IBIS (ex-HMS *Singleton*)
SNIPE (ex-HMS *Alcaston*)
TEAL (ex-HMS *Jackton*)

Displacement, tons	375 standard; 445 full load (revised official figures)
Dimensions, feet	140 pp; 152 oa × 28·8 × 8·2
Guns	2—40 mm AA, *Curlew* and *Snipe* 1—40 mm
Main engines	Napier Deltic diesels; 2 shafts; 3 000 bhp = 16 knots
Complement	4 officers; 29 sailors; Minehunters 37 (3 officers, 34 sailors)

"Ton" class coastal minesweepers. Purchased from the United Kingdom in 1961, and modified in British Dockyards to suit Australian conditions. Turned over to the Royal Australian Navy, commissioned and re-named in Britain during summer 1962. Mirrlees deisels were replaced by Napier Deltic, and ships air conditioned and fitted with stabilisers. Sailed from Portsmouth to Australia on 1 Oct 1962. Constitute the 1st Mine Countermeasures Squadron. *Curlew* and *Snipe* have been converted into minehunters.

IBIS *A. & J. Pavia*

PATROL BOATS

New Guinea **AITAPE**	**LADAVA**	**LAE**	**MADANG**	**SAMARAI**
Australia **ACUTE**	**ARCHER**	**ASSAIL**	**BANDOLIER**	**BAYONET**
ADROIT	**ARDENT**	**ATTACK**	**BARBETTE**	**BOMBARD**
ADVANCE	**ARROW**	**AWARE**	**BARRICADE**	**BUCCANEER**

Displacement, tons	146 full load
Dimensions, feet	107·5 oa × 20 × 7·3 (max)
Guns	1—40 mm; 2 medium MG
Main engines	Paxman 16 YJCM Diesels; 2 shafts = 21-24 knots
Complement	19 (3 officers, 16 sailors)

Five patrol boats for the formation of the New Guinea coastal security force and fifteen for general duties have been built. Steel construction. Builders: Evans Deakin & Co. Pty. Ltd., Brisbane, and Walkers Ltd., Maryborough. Ordered in Nov 1965. First vessel was originally scheduled for delivery in Aug 1966, but was not launched until Mar 1967. All now completed. Cost $A800 000 each.

ATTACK *1968, Royal Australian Navy, Official*

SEAWARD DEFENCE BOATS

SDB 1321 **SDB 1324** **SDB 1325**

Displacement, tons	59 standard; 64 full load
Dimensions, feet	80·2 oa × 16·1 × 5·5
Guns	1—40 mm AA
Main engines	2 Buda diesels; 2 shafts; 390 bhp max = 11 knots
Complement	12

Originally known as Harbour Defence Motor Launches (HDML) and afterwards as Seaward Defence Motor Launches (SDML). 1321 was modified with a two berth C.O.'s cabin added and covered bridge in place of an open bridge. *SDML* 1322 was stricken off in 1953. Remaining four were redesignated Seaward Defence Boats (*SDB*) in 1957. SDB 1327 was stricken from the list in 1960. Used for training.

SDB 1321 *Royal Australian Navy Official*

OCEANOGRAPHIC RESEARCH SHIP
(*ex-Boom Defence Vessel*)

KIMBLA

Displacement, tons	762 standard; 1 021 full load (revised official figures)
Dimensions, feet	150 pp; 179 oa × 32 × 12 mean
Guns	1—40 mm AA; 2—20 mm AA
Main engines	Triple expansion; Oil fuel; 12 knots
Complement	40 (4 officers and 36 sailors)

Built as a boom defence vessel by Walkers Ltd., Maryborough. Laid down on 4 Nov 1953. Launched 23 Mar 1955. Completed on 27 Mar 1956. Converted to a Trials Vessel in 1959. A photograph of *Kimbla* appears in the 1957-58 to 1965-66 editions. Is now employed on Science/Oceanography.

BOOM DEFENCE VESSELS

Of the "Kangaroo" class, *Karangi* was deleted from the list in 1965, *Kangaroo* was put up for sale in July 1966, and *Koala* was declared for disposal in 1968. *Kookaburra*, of the "Net" type, was stricken in 1965.

DIVING TENDERS

SEAL (ex-*Popham*) **OTTER** (ex-*Wintringham*)

Displacement, tons	120 standard; 159 full load
Dimensions, feet	100 pp × 22 × 5·8
Main engines	2 Paxman diesels; 1 100 bhp = 14 knots

Transferred from Royal Navy, these ex-Inshore Minesweepers were converted to Diving Tenders and attached to the Diving School at Sydney. Third ship, *HMS Neasham*, transferred 1968, not yet converted and is laid up in reserve.

GENERAL PURPOSE VESSELS

BANKS **BASS**

Displacement, tons	207 standard; 258 full load (revised official figures)
Dimensions, feet	90 pp; 101 oa × 22 × 8 mean
Main engines	Diesel; speed = 10 knots
Complement	18

"Explorer" class. Of all steel construction. *Banks* was fitted for fishery surveillance and *Bass* for surveying, but both were used for other duties. Reserve training in 1966. *Jeparit*, ex-merchant ship, will continue in RAN as a stores and ammunition supply ship.

SURVEY SHIPS

MORESBY

Displacement, tons	1 714 standard; 2 351 full load (revised official figures)
Dimensions, feet	284·5 pp; 314 oa × 42 × 13 (15 max)
Guns	2—40 mm Bofors AA (single mountings)
Aircraft	1 Westland Scout helicopter
Main engines	Diesel-electric; 2 shafts; 3 diesels; 3 990 bhp; 2 electric motors; 5 000 shp = 19 knots
Complement	123 (11 officers, 112 sailors)

The Royal Australian Navy's first specially designed survey ship. Built at the State Dockyard, Newcastle, New South Wales, at a cost of £A2 000 000. Launched on 7 Sep 1963, commissioned on 6 Mar 1964. Fitted with modern hydrographic equipment.

MORESBY *1967, Royal Australian Navy, Official*

PALUMA

Displacement, tons	336 (revised official figure)
Dimensions, feet	120 × 24 × 6·8 mean
Main engines	Diesel; Speed = 9·5 knots
Complement	3 officers and 25 sailors

A motor stores lighter of war construction converted into a small survey vessel in 1958.

FLEET OILER

SUPPLY (ex-*Tide Austral*)

Displacement, tons	15 000 standard; 25 941 full load
Measurement, tons	17 600 deadweight; 11 200 gross
Dimensions, feet	550 pp; 583 oa × 71 × 32 max
Guns	8—40 mm AA
Main engines	Double reduction geared turbines; 15 000 shp = 17·25 knots
Complement	13 officers, 187 sailors

Built for Australia by Harland & Wolf, Ltd., Belfast. Launched 1 Sep 1954, completed March 1955. British "Tide" Class. Lent to Great Britain until 1 Sep 1962, when *Tide Austral* was re-named HMAS *Supply* and commissioned in the Royal Australian Navy at Portsmouth. Sailed for Australia 1 Oct 1962.

SUPPLY *1968, Australian Navy, Official*

FLEET TUGS

SPRIGHTLY

Displacement, tons	594 standard; 869 full load
Dimensions, feet	143 × 34·5 × 12·8 mean
Guns	3—40 mm AA
Main engines	2 diesels; 2 electric motors; 4 000 bhp = 12 knots

Built at Orange Texas USA. Laid down on 6 June 1942, launched on 7 Aug 194 completed on 23 Nov 1942. Engines controllable from bridge. Now in reserve.

BRONZEWING

Displacement, tons	250
Dimensions, feet	98·8 oa × 21·2 × 8·2
Main engines	Diesel; 1 shaft; 480 bhp = 10 knots

Launched by Mort's Dock, Sydney on 2 Feb 1946 and 25 June 1946 respectivel

BELGIUM

Administration

Chief of Naval Staff
Commodore L. J. J. Lurquin

Diplomatic Representation

Naval, Military and Air Attaché in London
Colonel R. C. Close
Naval, Military and Air Attaché in Washington:
Lt. General Avi. van Rolleghens

Strength of Fleet

7 Ocean Minesweepers (Non-Magnetic)
3 Command and Logistical Support Ships
22 Coastal Minesweepers (Non-Magnetic)
16 Inshore Minesweepers
7 River Patrol Boats
2 Research Ships
13 Auxiliaries and Service Craft

Personnel

1969: 330 officers and 4,400 other ranks
1968: 335 officers and 4,800 other ranks
1967: 330 officers and 4,750 other ranks

Mercantile Marine

Lloyd's Register of Shipping:
218 vessels of 932,900 tons gross

OCEAN MINESWEEPERS

Name	*Pennant No.*	*Builders*	*Laid down*	*Launched*	*Completed*	*Transferred*
A.F. DUFOUR (ex-*Lagen*, M 950 ex-*MSO* 498)	M 903	Bellingham Shipyard Inc, Wash	1954	1955	27 Sep 1955	Summer 1966
ARTEVELDE (ex-*MSO* 503, ex-*AM* 503)	M 907	Tacoma Boatbuilding Co, Tacoma, Wash	1953	19 June 1954	15 Dec 1955	15 Dec 1955
BREYDEL (ex-*MSO* 504, ex-*AM* 504)	M 906	Tacoma Boatbuilding Co, Tacoma, Wash	1954	25 Mar 1955	15 Feb 1956	15 Feb 1956
DE BROUWER (ex-*Namsen*, M 951, ex-*MSO* 499)	M 904	Bellingham Shipyard Inc, Wash	1954	1955	1 Nov 1955	Summer 1966
F. BOVESSE (ex-*MSO* 516, ex-*AM* 516)	M 909	Tampa Shipbuilding Co Inc, Tampa, Fla.	1954	1956	25 Jan 1957	25 Jan 1957
G. TRUFFAUT (ex-*MSO* 515, ex-*AM* 515)	M 908	Tampa Shipbuilding Co Inc, Tampa, Fla.	1955	1955	12 Oct 1956	12 Oct 1956
VAN HAVERBEKE (ex-*MSO* 522)	M 902	Petersen Builders Inc, Sturgeon Bay, Wisc.	2 Mar 1959	29 Oct 1959	7 Nov 1960	9 Dec 1960

7 U.S. MSO (Ex-AM) TYPE 498

Displacement, tons	720 light; 780 full load
Length, feet (*metres*)	165 (*50·3*) wl; 172·5 (*52·6*) oa
Beam, feet (*metres*)	35 (*10·7*)
Draught, feet (*metres*)	11 (*3·4*)
Guns, AA	1—40 mm
Main engines	2 GM diesels 1 600 bhp; 2 shafts
Speed, knots	14 max
Radius, miles	2 400 at 12 knots
Oil fuel (tons)	50
Complement	72

Wooden hulls and non-magnetic equipment. Capable of sweeping mines of any type. Diesels of non-magnetic stainless steel alloy. Controllable pitch propellers.

DELIVERY. *Artevelde* and *Breydell* were transferred at Seattle, Wash. *Van Haverbeke* berthed at Ostend on 2 May 1961, *F. Bovesse* in Sep 1957, *G. Truffaut* in Aug 1957, *Breydel* in Sep 1956, and *Artvelde* in June 1956.

TRANSFERS. *A.F. Dufour* (ex-*Lagen*) and *De Brouwer* (ex-*Namsen*). handed over by USA to Norway on 27 Sep and 1 Nov 1955, respectively, were transferred to Belgium in 1966.

PHOTOGRAPHS. A photograph of *Breydel* appears in the 1966-67 edition and of *G. Truffaut* in the 1968-69 edition.

DISPOSALS OF COASTAL ESCORTS
Of the four former ocean minesweepers reclassified as coastal escorts in 1959, **A. F. Dufour** (ex-HMCS *Winnipeg*) and **De Brouwer** (ex-HMCS *Spanker*) were stricken in 1966 and **De Moor** (ex-HMS *Rosario*) and **G. Lecointe** (ex-HMCS *Wallaceburg*) were officially deleted from the list in March 1969.

DISPOSAL OF COMMAND SHIP
The command and logistical support ship for minesweepers, **Kamina** (ex-*Royal Harold*, ex-*Herman von Wissmann*), A 957 (ex-AP 907), former German submarine parent ship, was officially removed from the effective list in Sep 1967.

VAN HAVERBEKE *1969, Belgian Navy, Official*

ARTEVELDE *1968, Official*

SUPPORT SHIPS

ZINNIA A 961

Displacement, tons	1 705 light; 2 435 full load
Length, feet (*metres*)	299·2 (*91·2*) pp; 309 (*94·2*) wl; 326·4 (*99·5*) oa
Beam, feet (*metres*)	45·9 (*14·0*)
Draught, feet (*metres*)	11·8 (*3·6*)
Guns	3—40 mm AA (single)
Aircraft	1 helicopter
Main engines	2 Cockerill V 12 TR 240 CO diesels; 5 000 bhp; 1 shaft
Speed, knots	20 max; 18 sea
Oil fuel (tons)	500
Radius, miles	4 400 at 14 knots
Complement	125

Laid down at Hoboken by J. Cockerill on 8 Nov 1966. Launched on 6 May 1967. Completed on 12 Sep 1967. Controllable pitch propeller. Design includes a platform and a retractable hangar for one light liaison-helicopter. Rated as Command and Logistic Support Ship.

ZINNIA *1969, Skyfotos*

Support Ships—*continued*

GODETIA A 960

Displacement, tons	1 700 light; 2 300 full load
Dimensions, feet	289 wl; 301 oa × 46 × 11·5
Guns	4—40 mm (2 twin) AA
Aircraft	Provision for light helicopter
Main engines	4 ACEC—MAN diesels; 2 shafts; 5.400 bhp = 19 knots max
Oil fuel (tons)	500
Radius (miles)	4 500 at 15 knots
Complement	100 plus 35 spare billets

Built at Temse by J. Boel and Sons. Laid down on 15 Feb 1965, launched on 7 Dec 1965 and completed on 2 June 1966. Controllable pitch propellers. Provided with a platform which can take a light liaison-helicopter, and has Royal Apartments.

PHOTOGRAPHS. A starboard broadside view of *Godetia* appears in the 1966-67 edition, a port overhead view in the 1966-67 and 1967-68 editions, and a starboard bow surface view in the 1967-68 edition.

GODETIA *1968, Skyfotos*

1 Ex-BRITISH OCEAN MINESWEEPER

ADRIEN DE GERLACHE (ex-HMS *Liberty*) A 954

Displacement, tons	1 040 standard; 1 335 full load
Dimensions, feet	212·5 pp; 221 wl; 225 oa × 35·5 × 11
Guns	2—40 mm AA
Main engines	Geared turbines; 2 shafts; 2 000 shp = 16 knots
Boilers	2 of 3-drum type
Oil fuel (tons)	235
Radius (miles)	4 000 at 10 knots
Complement	100

Former British ocean minesweeper of the "Algerine" class, subsequently reclassified as a coastal escort and again re-rated as a Command and Logistic Support Ship for Minesweepers in 1960. Built by Harland & Wolff. Laid down on 27 Nov 1943, launched on 22 Aug 1944, and completed on 18 Jan 1945. Transferred from Royal Navy to Belgian Navy on 27 Nov 1949.

ADRIEN DE GERLACHE *1969 Belgian Navy, Official*

VERVIERS (see next column) *1969, courtesy Godfrey H. Walker, Esq.*

COASTAL MINESWEEPERS

22 U.S. MSC (ex-AMS) TYPE 60

M 923 BLANKENBERGE (ex-*MSC* 170)
M 917 CHARLEROI (ex-*MCS* 152)
M 925 DE PANNE (ex-*MSC* 131)
M 910 DIEST (ex-*MSC* 77)
M 920 DIKSMUIDE (ex-*MSC* 65)
M 911 EEKLO (ex-*MSC* 101)
M 929 HEIST
M 921 HERVE (ex-*MSC* 153)
M 931 KNOKKE
M 933 KOKSIJDE
M 924 LAROCHE (ex-*MSC* 171)
M 912 LIER (ex-*MSC* 63)
M 913 MAASEIK (ex-*MSC* 78)
M 922 MALMEDY (ex-*MSC* 154)
M 932 NIEUWPOORT
M 930 ROCHEFORT
M 918 ST. NIKLAAS (ex-*MSC* 64)
M 919 ST. TRUIDEN (ex-*MSC* 169)
M 927 SPA
M 928 STAVELOT
M 934 VERVIERS (ex-*MSC* 259)
M 935 VEURNE (ex-*MSC* 260)

Displacement, tons	330 light; 390 full load
Dimensions, feet	139 pp; 144 oa × 27·9 × 7·5 (8 max)
Guns	1—40 mm AA
Main engines	2 GM Diesels; 2 shafts; 880 bhp = 13·5 knots max
Oil fuel (tons)	28
Range, miles	2 700 at economical speed (10·5 knots)
Complement	39

Motor minesweepers with wooden hulls and constructed throughout of materials with the lowest possible magnetic attraction to attain the greatest possible safety factor when sweeping for magnetic mines. M 910-925, 934 and 935 were built in USA, under MDAP, and M 926-933 of same type were built in Belgium under MAP with machinery and equipment from USA. M 910 (ex-MSC 77, ex-AMS 77) turned over 12 May 1953, at Boston, M 919 (ex-MSC 169, ex-AMS 169) turned over 25 Feb 1954, at New York Naval Shipyard, Brooklyn, M 925 (ex-MSC 131, ex-AMS 131) transferred 28 Oct 1955, M 934 (ex-MSC 259) turned over 19 June 1956, M 935 (ex-MSC 260) was transferred on 7 Sep 1956. M 926 to 933 were all laid down in 1953-54 and launched and completed in 1954-55.

RECLASSIFICATION. *Mechelen*, M 926, former coastal minesweeper of this class was re-rated as a research ship and re-numbered A 962 in 1968 (see next page).

TRANSFERS. M 914, *Roeselaere* (ex-*MSC* 103), M 915, *Arlon* (ex-*MSC* 104) and M 916, *Bastogne* (ex-*MSC* 151) were transferred to the Royal Norwegian Navy in summer 1966 by the Belgian Naval Force.

PHOTOGRAPHS. A photograph of *Rochefort* appears in the 1961-62 to 1967-68 editions, and of *Charleroi* in the 1967-68 edition.

SPA *1968, Official*

STAVELOT *1968, Belgian Navy, Official*

HEIST *1968, Skyfotos*

INSHORE MINESWEEPERS

(Dragueurs de Mines de Petits Fonds)

16 MSI "HERSTAL" CLASS

M 485 ANDENNE (ex-*MSI* 97) May 1958
M 484 DINANT (ex-*MSI* 96) 5 Apr 1958
M 471 HASSELT 17 Nov 1956
M 478 HERSTAL (ex-*MSI* 90) 6 Aug 1956
M 479 HUY (ex-*MSI* 91) 17 Nov 1956
M 472 KORTRIJK 16 Mar 1957
M 473 LOKEREN 18 May 1957
M 476 MERKSEM 5 Apr. 1958
M 477 OUDENAERDE May 1958
M 483 OUGREE (ex *MSI* 95) 16 Nov 1957
M 480 SERAING (ex-*MSI* 92) 16 Mar 1957
M 470 TEMSE 6 Aug 1956
M 475 TONGEREN 16 Nov 1957
M 481 TOURNAI (ex-*MSI* 93) 18 May 1957
M 474 TURNHOUT 7 Sep 1957
M 482 VISE (ex-*MSI* 94) 7 Sep 1957

Displacement, tons	160 light (190 full load)
Dimensions, feet	106·7 pp; 113·2 oa × 22·3 × 6 (7 max)
Guns	1—13 mm AA
Main engines	2 diesels; 2 shafts; 1 260 bhp = 15 knots max
Oil fuel (tons)	18
Range, miles	2 300 at 10 knots
Complement	17

MSI type. Modified AMI "100-foot" class. All built in Belgium. The first four MSI were launched in 1956. *Herstal* and *Temse* were both launched at the Mercantile Marine Yard, Kruibche, on 6 Aug 1956, followed by another pair in 1956, and four more pairs in 1957 (see launch dates above). *Herstal* was completed in June 1957. The first group of eight (M 478 to 485) was a United States "off shore order", the remaining eight (M 470 to 477) being financed under the Belgian Navy Estimates.

PHOTOGRAPHS. A photograph of *Kortrijk* appears in the 1959-60 to 1964-65 editions, of *Tongeren* in the 1964-65 to 1967-68 editions, of *Seraing* in the 1963-64 to 1968-69 editions, and of *Andenne* in the 1966-67 to 1968-69 editions.

OUGREE *1968, Belgian Navy, Official*

HERSTAL *1969, Belgian Navy, Official*

TEMSE *1969, Belgian Navy, Official*

AUXILIARY CRAFT

HARBOUR CRAFT. There are three barges, namely *FN 4*, *FN 5*, and *FN 6*, displacement 300 tons, length, 105 feet, built in the Netherlands; the ammunition ship *Ekster*, displacement 140 tons, length 118 feet, built in Belgium in 1953; two diving cutters, ZM 3 and ZM 4, displacement 8 tons, length 33 feet, built in Belgium in 1953; and the harbour transport cutter *Spin*, displacement 32 tons, length 47·8 feet, with 250 bhp diesels = 8 knots and Voith-Schneider propeller, built in the Netherlands in 1958.

RIVER PATROL BOATS *(Vedettes Fluviales)*

IJZER **LEIE** **LIBERATION** **MEUSE** **SAMBRE** **SCHELDE** **SEMOIS**

Displacement, tons	25 light; 27·5 full load
Dimensions, feet	75·5 pp; 82 oa × 12·5 × 3 feet (*Liberation* 85·5 × 13·1 × 3·2)
Guns	2—13 mm MG
Main engines	2 diesels; 2 shafts; 440 bhp = 19 knots
Complement	7

Built at the Theodor Shipyards of Regensburg, Germany, in 1953, except *Liberation* in 1954. *Dender, Ourthe* and *Rupel* were officially deleted from the list in 1965.

SAMBRE *1966, Belgian Navy, Official*

RESEARCH SHIPS *(Bâtiments d'Études)*

MECHELEN A 962 (ex-M 926)

Displacement, tons	330 light; 390 full load
Dimensions, feet	139 pp; 144 oa × 27·9 × 7·5 (8 max)
Main engines	2 GM diesels; 2 shafts; 880 bhp = 13·5 knots max
Oil fuel (tons)	28
Radius (miles)	2 700 at economical speed (10·5 knots)
Complement	39

Former coastal minesweeper built in 1954. Re-rated as a research ship in 1968. A photograph of *Mechelen* as the coastal minesweeper M 926 appears in the 1968-69 edition.

MECHELEN *1969, Belgian Navy, Official*

ZENOBE GRAMME A 958

Displacement, tons	149
Dimensions, feet	92/76 × 22·5 × 7 feet
Main engines	1 MWM diesel; 1 shaft; 200 bhp = 10 knots
Complement	14

Auxiliary sail schooner. Built by J. Boel in Temse, Belgium, in 1961. Designed for scientific research. A photograph appears in the 1966-67 and 1967-68 editions.

DISPOSAL
The research ship *Eupen* (ex-*Eureka*, ex-*BYMS* 11, ex-*Young Joe*), former coastal minesweeper, was officially deleted from the list in 1964 as she had become obsolete.

TUGS *(Remorqueurs)*

SUB-LIEUTENANT VALCKE A 950

Displacement, tons	110
Dimensions, feet	78·8 pp 95 oa × 21 × 5·5
Main engines	1 diesel; 1 shaft; 600 bhp = 12 knots
Complement	14

Built in Haarlem, Netherlands in 1951. A photograph of *Sub-Lieutenant Valcke* appears in the 1966-67 to 1968-69 editions.

There are also two port tugs, *Bij* and *Krekel*, displacement 71 tons, length 57·8 feet, 2 Voith-Schneider propellers, 400 hp; three harbour tugs, *Hommel* and *Wesp*, displacement 22 tons, length 43 feet, with 300 bhp diesels and Voith-Schneider propellers; built in Germany in 1953; and *Mier*, displacement 17·5 tons, length 41 feet, with 80 bhp diesels and Voith-Schneider propellers, built in Belgium in 1962.

BRAZIL

Administration

Minister of the Navy:
Admiral Augusto Hamann Rademaker Grunewald

Chief of Naval Staff:
Admiral Adalberto de Barros Nunes

Diplomatic Representation

Naval Attaché in London:
Captain Fernando Ernesto Carneiro Ribeiro

Naval Attaché in Washington
Rear Admiral Roberto Ferreira Teixeira de Freitas

Strength of the Fleet

1 Aircraft Carrier
2 Submarines (Diesel Powered)
2 Cruisers
11 Destroyers
5 Frigates (Destroyer Escorts)
2 Coastal Minesweepers
6 Survey Ships (2 Frigate Type)
3 Seaward Defence Boats
2 River Monitors
29 Support Ships and Service Craft

1967 Ten Year Construction Programme

4 Submarines
10 Destroyer Escorts
26 Minesweepers
25 Patrol Vessels
5 River Patrol Boats
1 Dock-Ship, 1 Rescue Ship, 1 Survey Ship
1 Fleet Tug

Naval Bases

There are naval bases at Rio de Janeito, Belem, Natal, Ricife and Salvador, and a River base at Ladario.

Naval Aviation

A Fleet Air Arm was formed on 26 January 1965, exclusively of helicopters. Fixed wing aircraft afloat are operated by the Brazilian Air Force.

Personnel

1969: 4 300 officers and 50 000 men including Marines

Mercantile Marine

Lloyd's Register of Shipping:
398 vessels of 1 294 190 tons gross

Silhouettes

Scale: 150 feet = 1 inch

MINAS GERAIS

CANOPUS, SIRIUS

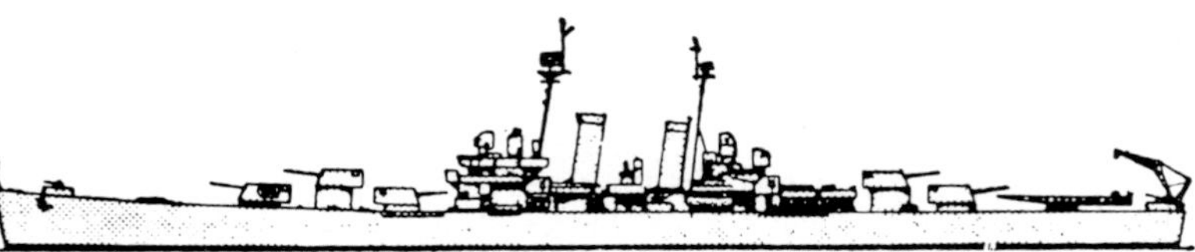

TAMANDARE

PERNAMBUCO

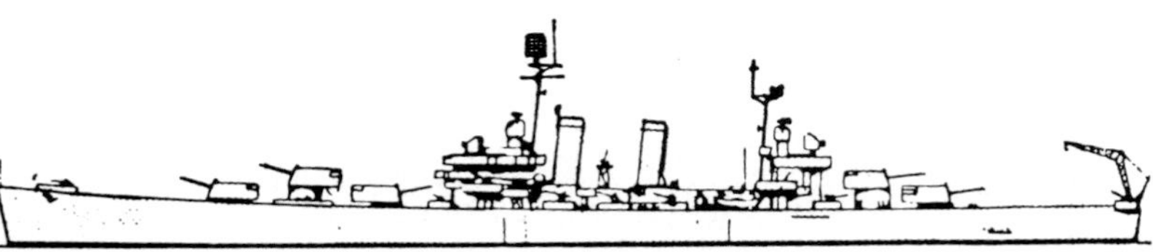

BARROSO

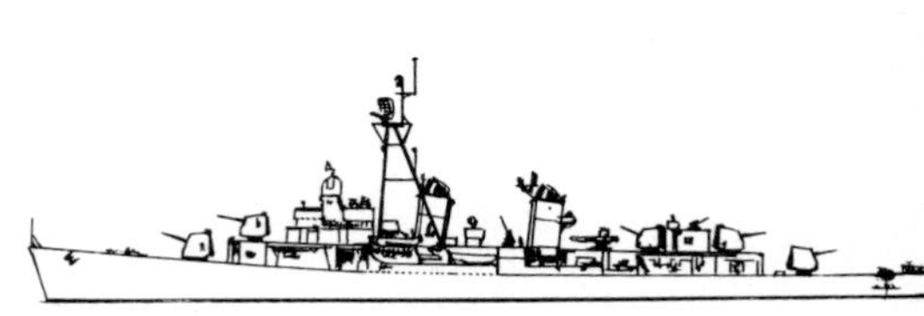

PARA *Class*

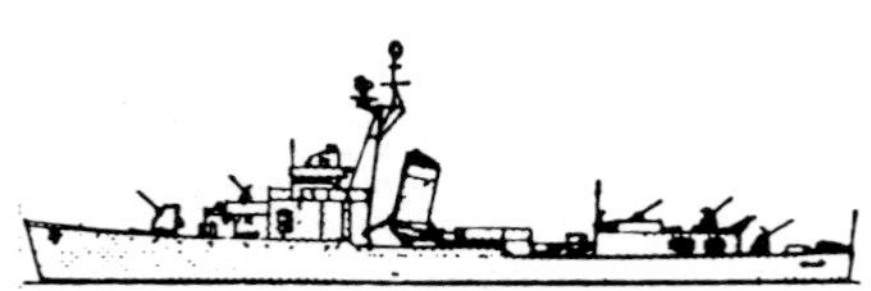

AMAZONAS *Class*

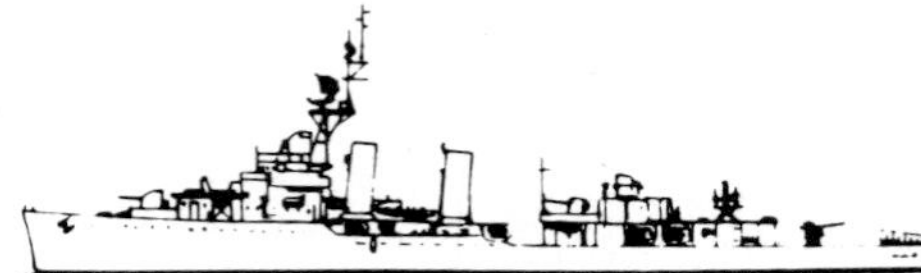

MARIZ E BARROS

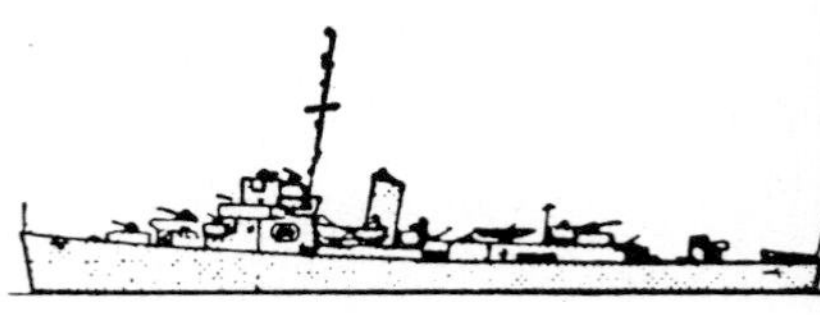

BERTIOGA *Class*

MINAS GERAIS see next page

1969, Brazilian Navy, Official

AIRCRAFT CARRIER (NAel)

	Pennant No.	*Builders*	*Laid down*	*Launched*	*Completed*	*Reconstructed*
MINAS GERAIS (ex-HMS *Vengeance*)	A 11	Swan, Hunter & Wigham Richardson, Ltd, Wallsend-on-Tyne	16 Nov 1942	23 Feb 1944	15 Jan 1945	Verolme Dock, Rotterdam, 1957-60

1 Ex-BRITISH TYPE ("COLOSSUS" CLASS)

Displacement, tons	15 890 standard; 17 500 normal; 19 890 full load (see *Displacement* note)
Length, feet (*metres*)	630 (*192·0*) pp; 695 (*211·8*) oa
Beam, feet (*metres*)	80 (*24·4*)
Draught, feet (*metres*)	21·5 (*6·6*) mean
Flight deck,	
Length, feet (*metres*)	690 (*210·3*)
Width, feet (*metres*)	121 (*37·0*) oa as reconstructed
Height, feet (*metres*)	39 (*11·9*) above water line
Catapults	1 steam
Aircraft	21 capacity
Guns, AA	10—40 mm (2 quadruple, 1 twin)
Guns, saluting	2—47 mm
Boilers	4 Admiralty 3-drum type; Working pressure 400 psi (*28 kg/cm²*); max superheat 700°F (371°C)
Main engines	Parsons geared turbines 40 000 shp; 2 shafts
Speed, knots	25; sea speed 24·25; 25·3 on trials after reconstruction (see *Engineering* note)
Radius, miles	12 000 at 14 knots 6 200 at 23 knots
Oil fuel (tons)	3 200
Complement	1 000 (1 300 with air group on board)

MINAS GERAIS — *1966, Brazilian Navy, Official*

Served in British Navy from 1945 onwards. Fitted out in late 1948-early 1949 for experimental cruise to Arctic. Lent to the Royal Australian Navy early in 1953, but was returned to the Royal Navy in August 1955. British Admiralty announced on 14 Dec 1956 the purchase of *Vengeance* by the Brazilian Government. Reconstructed at Verolme Dock, Rotterdam (Verolme United Shipyard's Rozenburg yard) from summer 1957 to Dec 1960. The conversion and overhaul included the installation of the angled deck, stream catapult, mirror sight deck landing system, and complete armament fire control and radar equipment. The ship was purchased for $9 000 000 and the reconstruction cost $27 000 000. Commissioned in Brazilian Navy at Rotterdam on 6 Dec 1960. Left Rotterdam for Rio de Janerio on her maiden voyage as *Minas Gerais* on 13 Jan 1961. Used primarily for anti-submarine warfare aircraft and helicopters.

ENGINEERING. Engines and boilers are arranged *en echelon*, the two propelling machinery spaces having one set of turbines and two boilers installed side by side in each space, on the unit system, so that the starboard propeller shaft is longer than the port shaft. Maximum speed is 25 knots at 120 revolutions per minute. Boiler capacity was increased when boilers were retubed during reconstruction in 1957-60.

ELECTRICAL. During reconstruction a complete alternating current system was built into the ship, and a total of 2 500 kW supplied by four turbo-generators and one diesel generator.

CONSTRUCTION. Damage control: No great measure of vertical sub-division on the sandwich system as it was reckoned that it is better for ships to settle evenly in the event of damage and flooding than to foster capsizing. Insulated for tropical service and partially air-conditioned.

OPERATIONAL. Arrester wires to take 20 000 lb aircraft up to 60 knots. Single track catapult for launching 20 000 lb aircraft at 60 knots. Catapult accelerator gear port side forward. Flight deck originally designed for 14 000 lb aircraft reinforced to take 20 000 lb machines.

HANGAR. Dimensions of hangar are: Length, 445 feet; width, 52 feet; clear depth, 17·5 feet. Dimensions of aircraft lifts were: 45 feet by 34 feet. During reconstruction in 1957-60 new aircraft lifts replaced the original units.

PHOTOGRAPHS. Photographs of this ship before reconstruction appear in the 1957-58 edition (port bow aerial view and starboard bow aerial view) and in the 1958-59 to 1960-61 editions (starboard bow oblique aerial view and starboard broadside view). A starboard broadside view after reconstruction appears in the 1962-63 to 1968-69 editions and a port bow surface view in the 1961-62 to 1968-69 editions.

DISPLACEMENT. The displacement before reconstruction was 13 190 tons standard and 18 010 tons full load.

DRAWING. Port elevation and plan. Scale: 128 feet = 1 inch.

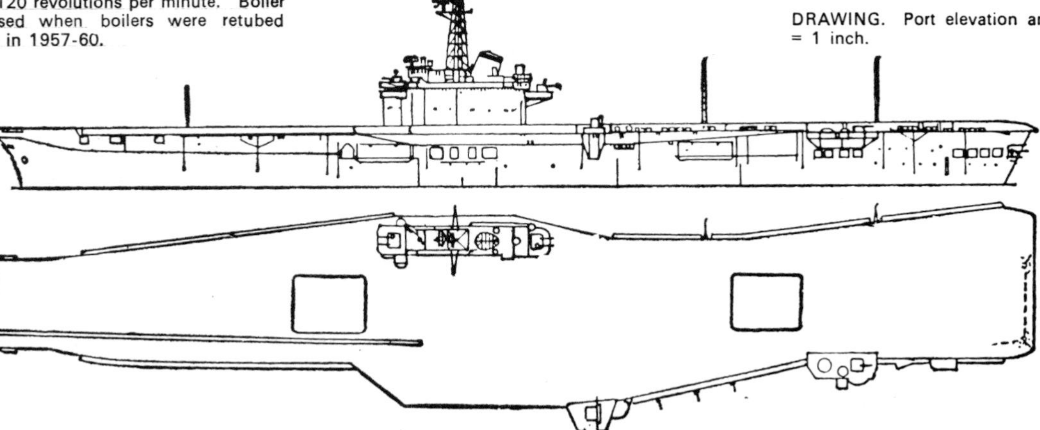

MINAS GERAIS — *1969, Brazilian Navy, Official*

SUBMARINES (*Submarinos*) (SE)

	Pennant No.	Builders	Launched	Completed
BAHIA (ex-USS *Plaice*, SS 390)	S 12	Portsmouth Naval Shipyard	15 Nov 1943	12 Feb 1944
RIO GRANDE DO SUL (ex-USS *Sand Lance*, SS 381, ex-*Orca*, ex-*Orjanco*)	S 11	Portsmouth Naval Shipyard	25 June 1943	9 Oct 1943

2 Ex-US "BALAO" CLASS

Displacement, tons	1 526 standard; 1 816 surface; 2 400 submerged
Length, feet (*metres*)	311·5 (*94·9*)
Beam, feet (*metres*)	27 (*8·2*)
Draught, feet (*metres*)	17 (*5·2*)
Torpedo tubes	10—21 in (*533 mm*); 6 bow, 4 stern
Main engines	6 500 bhp FM 2-stroke diesels; 5 500 hp electric motors
Speed, knots	20 on surface; 10 submerged
Radius, miles	12 000 at 10 knots
Oil fuel (tons)	300

Lent to Brazil for five years after overhaul at Pearl Harbour Naval Shipyard in Sep 1963.

DISPOSALS
Of the two submarines of the "GATO" class, **Humaita** S 14 (ex-US *Muskallung* SS 262) was returned to the USN in late 1967 and expended in the Pacific as a target 1968, **Riachuelo** S 15 ex-USS *Paddle* was broken up in Brazil 1968.

BAHIA — *1968, Brazilian Navy, Official*

CRUISERS (CL)

	Pennant No.	Builders	Laid down	Launched	Completed
TAMANDARÉ (ex-USS *St. Louis, CL* 49)	C 12	Newport News S.B. & DD.. Co.	10 Dec 1936	15 Apr 1938	10 Dec 1939

Displacement, tons	10 000 standard; 13 500 full load
Length, feet (*metres*)	608·5 (*185·5*) oa
Beam, feet (*metres*)	69 (*21·0*)
Draught, feet (*metres*)	24 (*7·3*) max
Aircraft	1 Helicopter (see *Hangar* notes)
Guns, surface	15—6 in (*153 mm*) 47 cal (5 triple)
Guns, dual purpose	8—5 in (*127 mm*) 38 cal (4 twin)
Guns, AA	28—40 mm, 8—20 mm
Armour, inches (*mm*)	Belt 5 in—1½ in (*127—38*); Decks 3 in+2 in (*76+51*) Turrets 5 in—3 in (*127—76*); C.T. 8 in (*203*)
Boilers	8 Babcock & Wilcox Express
Main engines	Westinghouse geared turbines 100 000 shp; 4 shafts
Speed, knots	32·5
Radius, miles	14 500 at 15 knots
Oil fuel (tons)	2 100
Complement	975

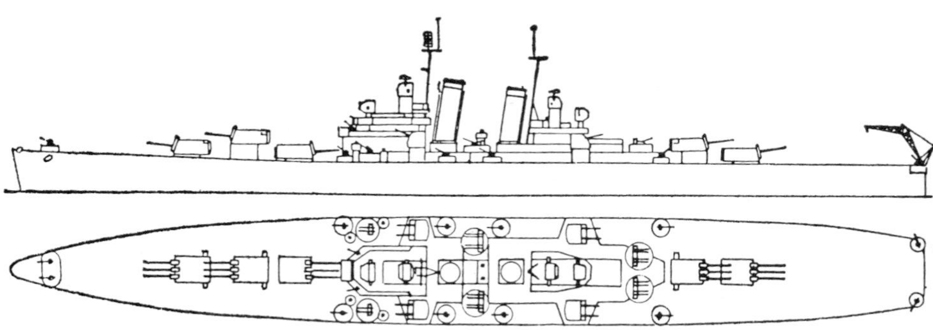

"St Louis" class. Transferred from USA on 29 Jan 1951. Differs from *Barroso* in 5-inch guns paired in roomy gunhouses on high bases, different boat stowage, small tripod mast immediately abaft 2nd funnel, and after gunnery control redistributed.

HANGAR. The hangar in the hull right aft could originally accommodate 6 aircraft if necessary together with engine spares and duplicate parts, though 4 aircraft was the normal capacity. The incorporation of this hangar resulted in a very wide and nearly flat counter and high freeboard aft and also gave the after guns higher command. Above the hangar two catapults were mounted as far outboard as possible, and a revolving crane was placed at the stern extremity overhanging the aircraft hatch.

PHOTOGRAPHS. A port bow near broadside surface view of *Tamandare* appears in the 1963-64 to 1968-69 editions.

DRAWING. Port elevation and plan: Scale. 128 feet = 1 inch.

TAMANDARE — *1969, Brazilian Navy, Official*

Cruisers—*continued*

BARROSO (ex-USS *Philadelphia*, CL 41)	*Pennant No.*	*Builders*	*Laid down*	*Launched*	*Completed*
	C 11	Philadelphia Navy Yard	28 May 1935	17 Nov 1936	28 July 1938

Displacement, tons	9 700 standard; 13 000 full load
Length, feet (*metres*)	600 (*182·9*) wl; 608·5 (*185·5*) oa
Beam, feet (*metres*)	69 (*21·0*) with bulges
Draught, feet (*metres*)	19·8 (*6·0*) mean; 24 (*7·3*) max
Aircraft	1 Helicopter
Guns, surface	15—6 in (*153 mm*) 47 cal (5 triple) 8—5 in (*127 mm*) 38 cal single
Guns, AA	28—40 mm, 20—20 mm
Armour, inches (*mm*)	Belt 4 in—1½ in (*102—38*); decks 3 in and 2 in (*76 and 51*) Turrets 5 in—3 in (*127—76*); C.T. 8 in (*203*)
Boilers	8 Babcock & Wilcox Express
Main engines	Westinghouse geared turbines 100 000 shp; 4 shafts
Speed, knots	32·5
Radius, miles	14 500 at 15 knots
Oil fuel (tons)	2 100
Complement	888

"Brooklyn" class. Purchased from the United States in 1951. Originally two catapults were mounted on the quarter deck for launching the aircraft (see *Hangar Notes* under *Tamandaré*). Commissioned in the Brazilian Navy on 21 Aug 1951.

CLASS SISTERS. Originally a sister ship of *General Belgrano* (ex-17 *de Octubre*, ex-USS *Phoenix*) and *Nueve de Julio*, ex-USS *Boise*) in the Argentine Navy, and *O'Higgins* (ex-USS *Brooklyn*) and *Prat* (ex-USS *Nashville*) in the Chilean Navy.

DRAWING. Port elevation and plan. Scale: 128 feet = 1 inch.

PHOTOGRAPHS. A starboard dead broadside view of *Barrosa* appears in the 1962-63 to 1968-69 editions.

BARROSO

1969, Brazilian Navy, Official

DESTROYERS (*Contratorpedeiros*) (CT)

4 BRITISH DESIGN "AMAZONAS" CLASS

Name	*Laid down*	*Launched*	*Completed*
ACRE	28 Dec 40	30 May 45	10 Dec 51
AMAZONAS	20 July 40	29 Nov 43	10 Nov 49
ARAGUAIA	20 July 40	24 Nov 43	3 Sep 49
ARAGUARI	28 Dec 40	14 July 46	23 June 51

Displacement, tons	1 450 standard; 1 800 full load
Length, feet (*metres*)	323 (*98·5*) oa
Beam, feet (*metres*)	35 (*10·7*)
Draught, feet (*metres*)	9 (*2·7*)
Guns, surface	3—5 in (*127 mm*) 38 cal.
Guns, AA	4—40 mm (2 twin); 2—20 mm
A/S weapons	4 DCT
Torpedo tubes	6—21 in (*533 mm*), two triple
Boilers	3 three-drum type
Main engines	Parsons geared turbines 34 000 shp;
Speed, knots	34
Radius, miles	6 000 at 15 knots
Oil fuel (tons)	150
Complement	200

All built by Ilha das Cobras, Rio de Janeiro, to a British design. Named after rivers. Refitted with tripod mast. Pennant Nos. respectively, D 10, D 12, D 14, D 15. A photograph of *Amazones* appears in the 1963-64 to 1968-69 editions.

Of this class, *Ajuricaba*, D 11, and *Apa*, D 13, were officially removed from the list in 1964.

ACRE

1969, Brazilian Navy, Official

1 "MARCILIO DIAS" CLASS

Name	*No.*	*Launched*	*Completed*
MARIZ E BARROS	D 26	28 Dec 40	1944

Displacement, tons	1 500 standard; 2 200 full load
Length, feet (*metres*)	341 (*104·0*) pp; 360 (*109·7*) oa
Beam, feet (*metres*)	35 (*10·7*)
Draught, feet (*metres*)	12 (*3·7*) max
Guns, dual purpose	2—5 in (*127 mm*) 38 cal
Guns, AA	4—40 mm
Guided Missiles	1 Seacat
A/S weapons	2 hedgehog
Torpedo tubes	4—21 in (*533 mm*) quadrupled
Boilers	4 Babcock & Wilcox Express
Main engines	GE geared turbines 42 800 shp
Speed, knots	36·5
Radius, miles	6 000 at 15 knots
Oil fuel (tons)	550
Complement	210

US design but built at Ilha das Cobras, Rio de Janeiro, with material from US. Generally similar to US destroyers and armed with US guns. Laid down in 1937 and commissioned on 29 Nov 1943.

MARIZ E BARROS

1968, Brazilian Navy, Official

GUIDED WEAPONS. British *Seacat* guided missile launcher has been installed in place of former X position 5 in gun. See photograph.

DISPOSALS

Sister ships **Greenhalgh**, D 24, and **Marcilio Dias**, D 25, were officially deleted from the list in 1966.

Destroyers—*continued*

Name	Pennant No.	Builders	Laid down	Launched	Completed
PARA (ex-USS *Guest*, DD 472)	D 27	Boston Navy Yard	27 Sep 1941	20 Feb 1942	15 Dec 1942
PARAIBA (ex-USS *Bennett*, DD 473)	D 28	Boston Navy Yard	10 Dec 1941	16 Apr 1942	9 Feb 1943
PARANA (ex-USS *Cushing*, DD 797)	D 29	Bethlehem Steel Co (Staten Island)	3 May 1943	30 Sep 1943	17 Jan 1944
PERNAMBUCO (ex-USS *Hailey*, DD 556)	D 30	Seattle-Tacoma S.B. (Corpn, Seattle)	1 Apr 1942	9 Mar 1943	30 Sep 1943
PIAUI (ex-USS *Lewis Hancock*, DD 675)	D 31	Federal S.B. & D.D. Co.		1 Aug 1943	24 Sep 1943
SANTA CATERINA (ex-USS *Irwin* DD 794)	D 32	Bethlehem Steel Co (San Pedro)		31 Oct 1943	14 Feb 1944
(ex-USS *Yarnall* DD 541)				25 July 1943	30 Dec 1943

7 Ex-US "FLETCHER" TYPE
"PARA" CLASS

Displacement, tons	2 100 standard; 3 050 full load
Length, feet (*metres*)	376·5 (*114·8*) oa
Beam, feet (*metres*)	39·3 (*12·0*)
Draught, feet (*metres*)	18 (*5·5*) max
Guns, dual purpose	5—5 in (*127 mm*) 38 cal; 4 in *Pernambuco*
Guns, AA	10—40 mm (2 quadruple and 1 twin) except in *Pernambuco:* 6—3 in (*76 mm*) 50 cal (3 twin) and *Para:* 6—40 mm (3 twin)
Torpedo tubes	5—21 in (*533 mm*)
A/S weapons	2 Hedgehogs; 1 DC rack; 2 side launching torpedo racks
Boilers	4 Babcock & Wilcox
Main engines	2 sets GE geared turbines 60 000 shp; 2 shafts
Speed, knots	35
Radius, miles	6 000 at 15 knots
Oil fuel (tons)	650
Complement	262 (15 officers, 247 men)

Cushing Lewis and *Hancock* are of the later "Fletcher" class and the other four are of the "Fletcher" class. *Bennett*, *Cushing*, *Guest* and *Hailey* were acquired from USA in 1959 on loan for five years, subsequently extended. *Guest* was transferred to Brazil on 5 June 1959, *Bennett* on 15 Dec 1959 at Bremerton, Washington, *Cushing* and *Hailey* on 20 July 1961, at Norfolk Naval Shipyard, Portsmouth, Virginia. *Piaui* (ex-USS *Lewis Hancock* DD-675) transferred 1 Aug 1967 and ex-USS *Irwin* DD-794 transferred 10 May 1968.
Sigsbee (DD-502) and *Melvin* (DD-680) were found to be beyond economical overhaul. *Yarnall* (DD-541) and *Irwin* (DD-794) were selected as replacements.

PHOTOGRAPHS. A starboard bow view of *Para* (five 5-inch) guns appears in the 1960-61 to 1962-63 editions.

PERNAMBUCO (four 5-inch guns) *1969, Brazilian Navy, Official*

PARA (five 5-inch guns) *1969, Brazilian Navy, Official*

FRIGATES (Destroyer Escorts) (Officially rated as *Avisos Oceanicos*)

Name		Laid down	Launched	Completed
BAEPENDI (ex-USS *Cannon*, DE 99)	U 27 (ex-D 17)	14 Nov 1942	25 May 1943	26 Sep 1943
BAURU (ex-USS *Reybold*, DE 177)	U 28 (ex-D 18)	17 May 1943	22 Aug 1943	11 Oct 1943
BENEVENTE (ex-USS *Christopher*, DE 100)	U 30 (ex-D 20)	7 Dec 1942	June 1943	23 Oct 1943
BOCAINA (ex-USS *Marts*, DE 174)	U 32 (ex-D 22)	26 Apr 1943	8 Aug 1943	3 Sep 1943
BRACUI (ex-USS *McAnn*, DE 179)	U 31 (ex-D 23)	3 May 1943	5 Sep 1943	24 Sep 1943

5 Ex-US DE TYPE
"BERTIOGA" CLASS

Displacement, tons	1 240 standard; 1 900 full load
Length, feet (*metres*)	306 (*93·3*) oa
Beam, feet (*metres*)	37 (*11·3*)
Draught, feet (*metres*)	12 (*3·7*)
Guns, dual purpose	3—3 in (*76 mm*)
Guns, AA	2—40 mm, 4—20 mm
Torpedo tubes	3—21 in (*533 mm*)
A/S weapons	2 DC racks
Main engines	4 GE diesels; 2 electric motors; diesel-electric drive 6 000 bhp; 2 shafts
Speed, knots	19
Radius, miles	11 500 at 11 knots
Oil fuel (tons)	300
Complement	200

BRACUI *1969, Brazilian Navy, Official*

Former US "Bostwick" class destroyer escorts, transferred in 1944. Built by Dravo, Wilmington, Del. (*Baependi*) and Federal, Port Newark (other four). Formerly designated CTE (Destroyer Escorts) but reclassified as *Avisos Oceanicos* in 1965.

PHOTOGRAPHS. A photograph of *Bocaina* appears in the 1962-63 edition.

DISPOSALS
Of this class, *Babitonga*, D 16, and *Bertioga*, D 21, were officially removed from the list in 1964, and *Beberibe* D 19, in 1968.

COASTAL MINESWEEPERS (NV)

2 Ex-US MSCo TYPE "JAVARI" CLASS

JURUENA (ex-USS *Grackle*) M 14 **JURUA** (ex-USS *Jackdaw*) M 13

Displacement, tons	270 standard; 350 full load
Dimensions, feet	136 × 24·5 × 8 max
Guns	4—20 mm in two twin mountings
A/S weapons	2 DCT
Main engines	2 GM diesels; 2 shafts; 1 000 bhp = 15 knots
Oil fuel (tons)	16
Radius, miles	2 300 at economical speed
Complement	50

Coastal motor minesweepers of wooden construction. All launched in 1942-43. Formerly known as Auxiliary Motor Minesweepers (AMS). Reclassified as Minesweepers, Coastal (old), MSC (o), in Feb 1955. *Cardinal*, MSCo4, and *Egret*, MSCo13, were transferred to Brazil by USA at Charleston Naval Shipyard on 15 Aug 1960 as the nucleus of a Brazilian mine force, and renamed after Brazilian rivers. *Jackdaw* MSCo21, was transferred in Jan 1963, and *Grackle* MSCo13, in Apr 1963. Used for patrol and escort duties, *Javari* and *Jutai* for disposal 1969.

JAVARI *1962, Brazilian Navy, Official*

SURVEY SHIPS (*Navios Hidrograficos*) (NH)

2 FRIGATE TYPE

Name	*Pennant No.*	*Laid down*	*Launched*	*Completed*
CANOPUS	H 22	13 Dec 1956	20 Nov 1957	15 Mar 1958
SIRIUS	H 21	13 Dec 1956	30 July 1957	1 Jan 1958

Displacement, tons	1 463 standard
Measurement, tons	1 600 gross
Dimensions, feet	236·2 pp; 246 wl; 255·7 oa × 39·3 × 12·2
Guns	1—3 in AA; 4—20 mm MG
Main engines	2 diesels; 2 shafts; 2 700 bhp = 15·75 knots
Radius, miles	12 000
Complement	102

Built by Ishikawajima Heavy Industries Co. Ltd., Tokyo, Japan. Helicopter platform aft. Special surveying apparatus, echo sounders, Raydist equipment, sounding machines installed and helicopter, landing craft (LCVP), jeep, and survey launches carried. All living and working spaces are air-conditioned. Controllable pitch propellers. Cruising speed 11 knots.

CANOPUS *1969, Brazilian Navy, Official*

SIRIUS *1966, Hajime Fukaya*

Survey Ships—*continued*

3 COASTAL TYPE

Name	*Pennant No.*	*Laid down*	*Launched*	*Completed*
ARGUS	H 31	12 Dec 1955	6 Dec 1957	29 Jan 1959
ORION	H 32	12 Dec 1955	5 Feb 1958	11 June 1959
TAURUS	H 33	12 Dec 1955	7 Jan 1958	23 Apr 1959

Displacement, tons	250 standard; 300 full load
Dimensions, feet	138 pp; 147·7 oa × 20 × 6·6
Main engines	2 diesels coupled to two shafts; 1 200 bhp = 15 knots
Oil fuel (tons)	35

All built by Arsenal da Marinha, Rio de Janeiro and commissioned on dates shown as completed in table above. A photograph of *Orion* appears in the 1961-62 to 1965-66 editions.

ARGUS *1966, Brazilian Navy Official*

ALMIRANTE SALDANHA U 10 (ex-NE 1)

Displacement, tons	3 325 standard; 3 825 full load
Dimensions, feet	262 pp; 307·2 oa × 52 × 18·2 mean
Main engines	Diesel; 1 400 bhp = 11 knots
Radius, miles	12 000
Complement	356

Former training ship with a total sail area of 25 990 sq ft and armed with four 4-in guns, one 3-in AA gun and four 3-pounders. Built by Vickers Armstrongs, Ltd, Barrow. Launched on 19 Dec 1933. Cost £314 500. Instructional minelaying gear was included in equipment. The single 21-in torpedo tube was suppressed. Re-classified as an Oceanographic Ship (NOc) Aug 1959, and completely remodelled by 1964. A photograph appears in the 1952-53 to 1959-60 editions.

ALMIRANTE SALDANHA *1968, Brazilian Navy, Official*

CORVETTES (*Corvetas*) (CV)

10 "IMPERIAL MARINHEIRO" CLASS

ANGOSTURA	V 20	**FORTE DE COMBRA**	V 18	**IPIRANGA**	V 17
BAHIANA	V 21	**IGUATEMI**	V 16	**MEARIM**	V 22
CABOCLO	V 19	**IMPERIAL MARINHEIRO**	V 15	**PURUS**	V 23
				SOLIMOES	V 24

Displacement, tons	911 standard
Dimensions, feet	184 × 30·5 × 11·7
Guns	1—3 in, 50 cal; 4—20 mm AA
Main engines	2 Sulzer diesels; 2 160 bhp = 16 knots
Oil fuel (tons)	135
Complement	60

All built in the Netherlands, launched in 1954-55, and incorporated into the Brazilian Navy in 1955. Actually fleet tugs. A photograph of *Imperial Marinheiro* appears in the 1956-57 and 1957-58 editions and *Ipiranga* in the 1958-59 to 1968-69 editions.

ANGOSTURA *1969, Brazilian Navy, Official*

RIVER MONITORS (*Monitores*) (M)

1 THORNYCROFT TYPE

PARNAIBA (U 17 (ex-P 2)

Displacement, tons	620 standard
Dimensions, feet	180·5 oa × 178·2 pp × 33·3 × 5 max
Guns	1—3 in, 50 cal; 2—47 mm; 2—40 mm AA; 6—20 mm AA
Armour	3 in side and partial deck protection
Main engines	2 Thornycroft triple expansion; 2 shafts; 1 300 ihp = 12 knots
Boilers	2 of 3-drum type, working pressure 250 psi
Oil fuel (tons)	70
Complement	90

Built at Rio de Janeiro. Laid down on 11 June 1936. Launched in Sep 1937, and completed in Nov 1937. In Matto Grosso Flotilla. Pennant No. U 17 (ex-P 2). Rearmed in 1960 (see guns above). For former armament see 1959-60 edition.

PARNAIBA *1967, Brazilian Navy, Official*

1 WHITE TYPE

PARAGUACU (ex-*Victoria*, ex-*Espiriot Santo*) (U 16 (ex-P 3)

Displacement, tons	430 standard
Dimensions, feet	146·5 × 34·8 × 5
Guns	1—3 in, 50 cal; 2—47 mm; 2—40 mm AA; 6—20 mm AA
Main engines	2 sets White triple expansion, 1 100 ihp = 13 knots
Boilers	2 of 3-drum type
Oil fuel (tons)	40
Complement	71

Built at Rio de Janeiro. Launched on 22 Dec 1938. In Matto Grosso Flotilla. Pennant Nos. U 16 (ex-P 3). Re-armed in 1960 (see guns above). For former armament see 1959-60 edition.

PARAGUACU ***1966, Brazilian Navy, Official***

GUNBOATS

PGM 109 **PGM 110**

Originally scheduled to be built in the United States for transfer to Brazil under MAP

SEAWARD DEFENCE BOATS (NPa)

3 "P" CLASS

PIRAJU J 28 (ex-P 1) **PIRANHA** J 30 (ex-P 3) **PIRAQUE** J 32 (ex- P4)

Displacement, tons	130 standard
Dimensions, feet	128 × 19·5 × 6
Guns	1—3 in, 23 cal.; 2—20 mm AA
A/S weapons	30 DC
Main engines	Diesels; 3 shafts; 1 890 bhp = 20 knots
Complement	30

All launched in 1947-48. Built at Rio de Janiero. The hulls are of wooden construction. A photograph of *Piranha* appears in the 1950-51 to 1960-61 editions.

Of this class *Pirambu* P 2, and *Pirapia*, P 5, were officially removed from the list in 1964, and *Pirauna*, P 6, in 1960.

DISPOSALS
The six small gunboats of the **Rio** class were deleted from the list in 1968.

PIRAQUE *1968, Brazilian Navy, Official*

REPAIR SHIPS

BELMONTE (ex-USS *Helios*, ARB 12, ex-*LST 1127*) G 24

Displacement, tons	1 625 light, 4 100 full load
Dimensions, feet	316 wl; 328 oa × 50 × 11
Guns	8—40 mm AA
Main engines	GM diesels; 2 shafts; 1 800 bhp = 11·6 knots

Former United States battle damage repair ship. Built by Maryland DD Co, Baltimore Md. Laid down on 23 Nov 1944. Launched on 14 Feb 1945. Completed on 26 Feb 1945. Loaned to Brazil by USA in Jan 1962 under MAP.

There is also *Ceara*, former US auxiliary repair dry dock *ARD 14*, transferred to Brazil and renamed: 5 200 tons displacement, 402 × 81 feet.

BELMONTE ***1969, Brazilian Navy, Official***

OILERS (*Navios-Tanques*) (NT)

NEW CONSTRUCTION

MARAJO G 26

Measurement, tons	10 500 deadweight
Dimensions, feet	440·7 × 63·3 × 24
Main engines	Diesel; one shaft = 13·6 knots
Capacity, cu metres	14 200
Complement	80

Laid down 13 Dec 1966, launched 31 Jan 1968. Construction is by Ishikawajima Do Brasil-Estaleisos SA. Completed 22 Oct 1968.

MARAJO *1969, Brazilian Navy, Official*

Name	Pennant No.	Laid down	Launched	Completed
RAZA (ex-*Klaskanine AOG 63*)	G 19 (exR 2)	21 Dec 44	3 Feb 45	26 Feb 45
RIJO (ex-*Gualula, AOG 28*)	G 20 (ex-R 1)	24 Apr 44	3 June 44	19 Aug 44

Displacement, tons	2 228 full load
Dimensions, feet	217·5 × 37 × 7
Main engines	Diesels; 850 bhp = 9 knots
Capacity, tons	1 500
Complement	41

Ex-US gasoline tankers USMC type TI-M-A2. Both built at East Coast Shipyards, Bayonne, N.J. A photograph of *Rijo* appears in the 1950-51 to 1959-60 editions.

POTENGI G 17

Displacement, tons	600
Dimensions, feet	175·5 pp; 178·8 oa × 24·5 × 6
Main engines	Diesels; 2 shafts; 550 bhp = 10 knots
Oil, tons	450
Complement	19

Built at the Papendrecht yard in the Netherlands. Launched on 16 Mar 1938. Employed in the Matto Grosso Flotilla on river service.

DISPOSALS

The following four small tankers **Anita Garibaldi**, **Gastão Moutinho**, **Mataripe** and **Taubate** and two water carriers **Itaupra** and **Paulo Afonso** were deleted from the list in 1963.

TRANSPORTS (*Navios-Auxiliares*) (NTr)

4 "PEREIRA" CLASS

Name	Pennant No.	Laid down	Launched	Completed
ARY PARREIRAS	G 21	13 Dec 1955	24 Aug 1956	29 Dec 1956
BARROSO PEREIRA	G 16	13 Dec 1953	10 Aug 1954	1 Dec 1954
CUSTÓDIO DE MELLO	U 26	13 Dec 1953	10 June 1954	30 Dec 1954
SOARES DUTRA	G 22	13 Dec 1955	13 Dec 1956	23 Mar 1957

Displacement, tons	4 800 standard; 7 300 full load
Measurement, tons	4 200 deadweight; 4 879 gross (Panama)
Dimensions, feet	362 pp; 391·8 oa × 52·5 × 20·5 max
Guns	2—20 mm AA
Main engines	Ishikawajima double reduction geared turbines; 2 shafts; 4 800 shp = 17·67 knots (sea speed 15 knots)
Boilers	2 Ishikawajima two drum water tube type, oil fuel
Complement	127 (Troop capacity 1 972)

All built in Japan by Ishikawajima Heavy Industries Co, Ltd, Tokio. Transports and cargo vessels. Flush deckers with forecastle and long poop. Elevator type helicopter landing platform laid on aft. Normal troop carrying capacity for 497 personnel, with commensurate medical, hospital and dental facilities. All working and living quarters are mechanically ventilated with partial air conditioning. Refrigerated cargo space of 15 500 cubic feet. Can carry 4 000 tons of cargo. *Barroso Pereira* and *Custódio de Mello* were incorporated into the Brazilian Navy on 22 Mar 1955 and 8 Feb 1955, respectively. Formerly armed with eight 40 mm AA guns.
Custódio de Mello has been classified as a training ship since July 1961.
A photograph of *Soares Dutra* appears in the 1958-59 to 1963-64 editions.

DISPOSAL

The training ship **Albatros** was deleted from the list in 1968.

Transports—*continued*

CUSTODIO DE MELLO *1969, Brazilian Navy, Official*

ARY PARREIRAS *1968, Brazilian Navy, Official*

TUGS (*Rebocadores*) (R)

TRIDENTE (ex-*ATA 235*) **TRITÃO** (ex-*ATA 234*) **TRIUNFO** (ex-*ATA 236*)

Displacement, tons	534 standard; 835 full load
Dimensions, feet	133·7 wl; 143 oa × 33 × 13·2
Guns	2—20 mm AA
Main engines	GM diesel-electric; 1 500 hp = 13 knots

All built by Gulfport Boiler & Welding Works, Inc, Port Arthur, Texas, and launched in 1954. Ex-US *ATRs*. Nos *Tridente* R 22, *Tritão* R 21, *Triunfo* R 23 (ex-*R* 2, R 1, R 3). A photograph of *Tridente* appears in the 1950-51 to 1957-58 editions.

TRITAO *1968, Brazilian Navy, Official*

BRUNEI

FAST PATROL BOAT

PAHLAWAN

Displacement, tons	95 standard; 114 full load
Dimensions, feet	90 pp; 96 wl; 99 oa × 25·2 × 7
Guns	1—40 mm; 2—20 mm
Main engines	3 Bristol Siddeley Proteus gas turbines; 3 shafts; 12 750 bhp = 57 knots max; 2 diesels for cruising and manoeuvring.
Radius, miles	450 at full speed; 2 300 at 10 knots
Complement.	20

Ordered from Vosper Ltd, Portsmouth, England, on 10 Dec 1965. Launched on 5 Dec 1966. Completed on 19 Oct 1967. Constructed of resin bonded timber with aluminium alloy superstructure.

PAHLAWAN *1968, Vosper Limited*

BULGARIA

Administration

Commander-in-Chief, Navy:
Vice-Admiral Dobrev

Diplomatic Representation

Naval Attaché in London:
Colonel Ivan G. Kochovski
Naval Attaché in Washington:
Colonel Tsvetko Tomov

Strength of the Fleet

2 Submarines, Conventionally Powered
2 Medium Escorts
8 Coastal Escorts
2 Fleet Minesweepers
4 Inshore Minesweepers
8 Torpedo Boats
10 Landing Craft
24 Training and Service Craft

Personnel

1969: 7 000 officers and ratings

Mercantile Marine

Lloyd's Register of Shipping
112 vessels of 548 102 tons gross

SUBMARINES

2 "W" TYPE

Displacement, tons	1 030 surface; 1 180 submerged
Length, feet (*metres*)	245 (*74·7*) oa
Beam, feet (*metres*)	23·6 (*7·2*)
Draught, feet (*metres*)	14·8 (*4·5*)
Guns, AA	4—25 mm
Torpedo tubes	6—21 in (*533 mm*), 4 bow, 2 stern
Main engines	4 000 hp diesels (surface) 2 500 hp electric motors (submerged)
Speed, knots	17 on surface, 15 submerged
Radius, miles	13 000
Complement	60

Transferred from the Soviet Navy in 1958.

The coastal submarine of the Soviet "MV" type was deleted from the list in 1967.

"W" Type *Added 1966*

The dual purpose minelayer and training ship of the Soviet type was deleted from the list in 1967.

The old destroyer *Georgi Dimitrov* (ex-*Ognevoi*) of the Soviet "Otlichny" type was deleted from the list in 1967.

MEDIUM ESCORTS

2 "RIGA" TYPE

DRUZKI **SMELI**

Displacement, tons	950 standard; 1 200 full load
Length, feet (*metres*)	295·3 (*90*) oa
Beam, feet (*metres*)	31·5 (*9·6*)
Draught, feet (*metres*)	10·2 (*3·1*)
Guns, AA	3—3·9 in (*100 mm*); 4—37 mm
Tubes	3—21 in (*533 mm*)
A/S weapons	4 DCT
Mines	50
Main engines	Geared turbines 24 000 shp; 2 shafts
Speed, knots	27

Only the above two units of the "Riga" class are reported to exist. Transferred from the Soviet Navy in 1957 and 1958.

"Riga" Type *Added 1967*

COASTAL ESCORTS

6 "SOI" TYPE

Displacement, tons	215 light; 250 normal
Dimensions	138 pp, 147 oa × 20 × 10 max
Guns	4—25 mm (2 twin)
A/S weapons	4 five-barrelled ahead throwing rocket launchers
Main engines	3 diesel; 3 500 bhp = 28 knots
Complement	30

Steel hulled patrol vessels or submarine chasers reportedly transferred from the USSR in 1963.

2 "KRONSTADT" TYPE

Displacement, tons	300 standard; 350 full load
Dimensions, feet	167 × 19·3 × 9
Guns	1—3·4 in; 2—37 mm AA; 3—20 mm AA
A/S weapons	Depth charge throwers
Main engines	Diesels; 2 shafts; 27 knots
Oil fuel (tons)	20
Complement	40

"Kronstadt" class submarine chasers transferred from the USSR in 1957.

MINESWEEPERS

2 "T 43" TYPE

Displacement, tons	500 standard; 600 full load
Dimensions, feet	200 × 27·2 × 9·5
Guns	4—37 mm AA; 8—13 mm MG
Main engines	Diesels; 2 shafts; 3,200 bhp = 18 knots
Complement	60

Three "T" class minesweepers are reported to have been transferred from the USSR in 1953, of which one was cannibalised.

INSHORE MINESWEEPERS

4 "T 301" TYPE

Displacement, tons	130 standard; 180 full load
Dimensions, feet	100 × 16 × 4·5
Guns	2—37 mm AA; 2—25 mm AA
Main engines	Diesels; 2 shafts; 480 bhp = 10 knots
Complement	30

"T" 301 class inshore minesweepers reported to have been transferred from the USSR in 1955.

TORPEDO BOATS

8 "P 4" TYPE

Displacement, tons	50
Dimensions, feet	85·3 × 20 × 6
Guns	4—25 mm AA
Torpedoes	2
Main engines	Diesels; 2 000 bhp = 42 knots

Motor torpedo boats of the "P 4" class reported to have been transferred from the USSR in 1956.
The fast patrol boats of the Soviet "PA 2" type, of which there were originally reported to have been 12, were deleted from the list in 1967.
Few of the small patrol craft of the PTC type, once numbering 30 to 50 units varying in particulars, remain in service.

MINESWEEPING BOATS

22 "PO-2" TYPE

Ex-Soviet craft. 12 are reported to have been acquired in 1950 and 12 in 1956 for harbour, coastal, inshore and estuarial employment and general purpose duties.

LANDING CRAFT

10 LCU TYPE

Displacement, tons	164 oa
Guns	1—37 mm AA

Ten utility landing craft are reported to have been built in Bulgaria in 1954. Based on a German Second World War design.

TRAINING VESSEL

VESELITZ (ex-*Asen*)

Displacement, tons	240
Guns	2—65 mm; 1 MG
Main engines	120 hp = 7 knots

Auxiliary sail training vessel. Launched in 1912. Refitted in 1933-34. *Kamicia* deleted in 1968.

TUG

A former Soviet tug of the fleet type with an overall length of 135 feet.

BURMA

Administration

Vice-Chief of Staff, Defence Services (Navy):
Commodore Thaung Tin

Personnel

1969: 300 officers and 5 900 ratings including reserves

Mercantile Marine

Lloyd's Register of Shipping:
31 vessels of 41 760 tons gross

Strength of the Fleet

1 Frigate
1 Escort Minesweeper
2 Patrol Vessels
5 Torpedo Boats
38 Gunboats
10 Support Ships and Service Craft

Diplomatic Representation

Naval, Military and Air Attaché in London:
Colonel Ye Htoon

Naval, Military and Air Attaché in Washington:
Colonel Kyi Han

FRIGATE

Name	*Builders*	*Laid down*	*Launched*	*Completed*
MAYU (ex-HMS *Fal*)	Smiths Dock Co Ltd, South Bank-on-Tees, Middlesborough, England	20 May 1942	9 Nov 1942	2 July 1943

1 Ex-BRITISH "RIVER" CLASS

Displacement, tons	1 460 standard; 2 170 full load
Length, feet (*metres*)	283 (*86·3*) pp; 301·3 (*91·8*) oa
Beam, feet (*metres*)	36·7 (*11·2*)
Draught, feet (*metres*)	12 (*3·7*)
Guns, dual purpose	1—4 in (*102 mm*)
Guns, AA	4—40 mm
Boilers	2—three drum type
Main engines	Triple expansion 5 500 ihp; 2 shafts
Speed, knots	19
Radius, miles	4 200 at 12 knots
Oil fuel (tons)	440
Complement	140

"River" class frigate. Acquired from Great Britain in 1947.

MAYU *Burmese Navy, Official*

ESCORT MINESWEEPER

Name	*Builders*	*Laid down*	*Launched*	*Completed*
YAN MYO AUNG (ex-HMS *Mariner*, ex-*Kincardine*)	Port Arthur Shipyards, Canada	26 Aug 1943	9 May 1944	23 May 1945

1 Ex-BRITISH "ALGERINE" CLASS

Displacement, tons	1 040 standard; 1 335 full load
Length, feet (*metres*)	225 (*68·6*) pp; 235 (*71·6*) oa
Beam, feet (*metres*)	35·5 (*10·8*)
Draught, feet (*metres*)	11·5 (*3·5*)
Guns, surface	1—4 in (*102 mm*)
Guns, AA	4—40 mm
Boilers	2 three-drum type
Main engines	Triple expansion 2 000 shp; 2 shafts
Speed, knots	16·5
Radius, miles	4 000
Complement	140

Former ocean minesweeper in the British Navy, of the corvette type and used as escort vessel. *Mariner*, M 380 was transferred from Great Britain in 1957. Handed over to Burma in London and renamed *Yan Myo Aung*, on 18 Apr 1958. Fitted for minelaying and can carry 16 mines, eight on each side.

YAN MYO AUNG *1964, Burmese Navy, Official*

TORPEDO BOATS

5 BRITISH-BUILT CONVERTIBLE TYPE

T 201 (ex-*PTS 101*)
T 202 (ex-*PTS 102*)
T 203 (ex-*PTS 103*)
T 204 (ex-*PTS 104*)
T 205 (ex-*PTS 105*)

Displacement, tons	50 standard; 64 full load
Dimensions, feet	67 pp; 71·5 oa × 19·5 × 6 max
Guns	As MGB: 1—4·5 in; 1—40 mm AA; As MTB: 2—20 mm AA
Tubes	As MTB: 4—21 in
Main engines	2 Napier Deltic diesels; 5 000 shp = 42 knots
Complement	13

Interchangeable motor torpedo boats/motor gunboats built by Saunders Roe (Anglesey) Ltd, England. Convertible craft of aluminium construction, with riveted skin and aluminium alloy framework. As well as main engines, auxiliary power is also provided by diesels. The Saunders-Roe slow-speed electric drive was fitted to facilitate manoeuvring in the confined inland waters where the craft may be required to operate. Armament and layout of the vessels were similar to the British fast patrol boats of the "Dark" Class. The cost including engines, equipment and spares, of the five boats was over £1 800 000. T 201 was launched 24 Mar 1956. All were completed in 1956-57. A photograph of T 201 of this class appears in the 1956-57 to 1961-62 editions.

T 202 *1966, Burmese Navy, Official*

SUPPORT GUNBOATS

4 Ex-BRITISH LCG (M) TYPE

INDAW **INLAY** **INMA** **INYA**

Displacement, tons	381
Dimensions, feet	154·5 oa × 22·5 × 7·8
Guns	2—25 pdr; 2—2 pdr
Main engines	Paxman Ricardo diesels; 2 shafts; 1 000 bhp = 13 knots
Complement	39

Former British *LCG* (M), Landing craft, gun medium. Employed as gunboats. A photograph of *Inlay* of this class appears in the 1950-51 to 1961-62 editions.

INMA *Burmese Navy, Official*

PATROL VESSELS

YAN TAING AUNG, PCE 41 (ex-USS *Farmington*, PCE 894)

Displacement, tons	640 standard; 903 full load
Dimensions, feet	180 wl; 184 oa × 33 × 9·5
Guns	1—3 in, 50 cal dp; 2—40 mm AA (1 twin); 8—20 mm AA (4 twin)
A/S weapons	1 hedgehog; 2 DCT; 2 DC tracks
Main engines	GM diesels; 2 shafts; 1 800 bhp = 15 knots

Former US patrol ship (escort). Built by Willamette Iron & Steel Corp, Portland, Oregon. Laid down 7 Dec 1942, launched 15 May 1943 completed 10 Aug 1943. Transferred 18 June 1965.

Patrol Vessels—*continued*

YAN GYI AUNG, PCE 42 (ex-USS *Creddock*, MSF 356)

Displacement, tons	650 standard; 945 full load
Dimensions, feet	180 wl; 184·5 oa × 33 × 9·8 max
Guns	1—3 in, 50 cal, single forward; 4—40 mm AA (2 twin); 4—20 mm AA (2 twin)
Main engines	Diesels; 2 shafts; 1 710 shp = 14·8 knots

Former US fleet minesweeper, steel hulled, of the "Admirable" class. Built by Willamette Iron & Steel Corp. Portland, Oregon. Laid down 10 Nov 1943, launched 22 July 1944. Transferred at San Diego 31 Mar 1967.

RIVER GUNBOATS

2 BURMESE-BUILT LARGE TYPE

NAGAKYAY **NAWARAT**

Displacement, tons	400 standard; 450 full load
Dimensions, feet	163 × 26·8 × 5·8
Guns	2—25 pdr QF; 2—40 mm AA
Main engines	2 Paxman-Ricardo turbo-charged diesels; 2 shafts; 1 160 bhp = 12 knots
Complement	43

Built at the Government Dockyard, Dawbon, Rangoon, Burma, *Nagakyay* was completed on 3 Dec 1960 and *Nawarat* on 26 Apr 1960.

NAGAKYAY *1962, Burmese Navy, Official*

10 YUGOSLAVIAN-BUILT "Y" TYPE

Y 301 Y 302 Y 303 Y 304 Y 305 Y 306 Y 307 Y 308 Y 309 Y 310

Displacement, tons	120
Dimensions, feet	100 pp; 104·8 oa × 24 × 3
Guns	2—40 mm AA; 1—2 pdr
Main engines	2 Mercedes-Benz diesels; 2 shafts; 1 000 bhp = 13 knots
Complement	29

All ten of these boats were completed in 1958 at the Shipyard "Uljanik", Pula, in Yugoslavia. For detailed building dates see 1966-67 and earlier editions.
A photogrpah of Y 301 appears in the 1962-63 and 1963-64 editions.

Y 310 *1964, Burmese Navy, Official*

9 Converted Transport Type

HINTHA **SABAN** **SAGU** **SEINDA** **SETKAYA** **SETYAHAT** **SHWEPAZUN** **SHWETHIDA** **SINMIN**

Displacement, tons	98
Dimensions, feet	94·5 × 22 × 4·5
Guns	1—40 mm; 3—20 mm
Main engines	Crossley ERL—6 diesel; 160 bhp = 12 knots
Complement	32

A photograph of *Shwepazun* appears in the 1952-53 to 1963-64 editions, and of *Saban* in the 1962-63 and 1963-64 editions.

SAGU *1964, Burmese Navy, Official*

PATROL GUNBOATS

6 US-BUILT PGM TYPE

PGM 401 PGM 402 PGM 403 PGM 404 PGM 405 PGM 406

Displacement, tons	100
Dimensions, feet	95 × 19 × 5
Guns	1—40 mm AA; 2—0·5 US Browning MG
Main engines	4 GM diesels; 2 shafts; 1 000 bhp = 16 knots
Complement	17

Built by the Marinette Marine Corporation, USA. Machinery comprises 2-stroke, 6-cylinder, tandem geared twin diesel propulsion unit—1 LH and 1 RH; 500 bhp per unit ex-US PGM 43-46, 51 and 52 respectively.

PGM 401 *1962, Burmese Navy, Official*

MOTOR GUNBOATS

7 Ex-UNITED STATES CGC TYPE

MGB 101 MGB 102 MGB 104 MGB 105 MGB 106 MGB 108 MGB 110

Displacement, tons	49 standard; 66 full load
Dimensions, feet	78 pp; 83 oa × 16 × 5·5
Guns	1—40 mm AA; 1—20 mm AA
Main engines	4 GM diesels; 2 shafts; 800 bhp = 11 knots
Complement	16

Ex-USCG 83-ft type cutters with new hulls built in Burma. Completed in 1960. For detailed building dates see 1966-67 and earlier editions. Machinery comprises 2-stroke, 6 cylinder, tandem geared, twin diesel propulsion units—1 LH and 1 RH drive; 400 bhp per unit.

MGB 102 *1962, Burmese Navy, Official*

TRANSPORT

PYIDAWAYE

Measurement, tons	2 217·31 gross
Dimensions, feet	270 × 47 × 15
Main engines	Fleming & Ferguson triple expansion 2 000 ihp
Boilers	2 Scotch (return type)
Radius, miles	2 000
Complement	88

Former passenger ship. In service since 1962. Wears the Burmese naval ensign.

PYIDAWAYE *1964, Burmese Navy, Official*

LCU 1626 (ex-USS *LCU 1626*)

Displacement, tons	200 light; 342 full load
Dimensions, feet	135·2 oa × 29 × 5·5
Main engines	Diesels; 2 shafts; 1 000 bhp = 11 knots

Former United States Navy utility landing craft. Transferred under the Military Aid Programme in 1967. Used as a transport.

LCM 701 LCM 702 LCM 703 LCM 704 LCM 705 LCM 706 LCM 707 LCM 708

Displacement, tons	28
Dimensions, feet	56 × 14 × 4
Main engines	2 Gray Marine diesels; 225 bhp

US-built LCM type landing craft. Used as local transports for stores and personnel.

CAMBODIA

Marine Royal Khmere

The Marine Royal Khmere was established on 1st March 1954.

Chief of Staff of Marine Royal Khmere (MRK):
Lieutenant Général Nhiek Tioulong.

Personnel

1969: Navy: 1 350 officers and men. Marine Corps: 150 officers and men.

Mercantile Marine

Lloyd's Register of shipping: 3 vessels of 4,230 tons gross

PATROL VESSELS

2 Ex-US PC TYPE

E 311 (ex-*Flamberge, P 631*, ex-*PC 1086*) **E 312** (ex-*L'Inconstant, P 636*, ex-*PC 1171*)

Displacement, tons	325 standard; 400 full load
Dimensions, feet	170 wl; 173·7 oa × 23 × 6·5
Guns	1—3 in dp; 1—40 mm AA, 4—20 mm AA
Main engines	2 GM diesels, 2 shafts; 3 600 bhp = 18 knots
Oil fuel (tons)	62
Radius, miles	6 000 at 10 knots
Complement	63

Former US submarine chasers of the PC type. Transferred from the US Navy to the French Navy in 1951 and served in Indo-China and again transferred to the Marine Royal Khmere in 1955-56. Built of steel.

E 312. *Official*

SUPPORT GUNBOAT

1 Ex-US LSIL TYPE

P 111 (ex-*LSIL 9039*, ex-*LSIL 875*)

Displacement, tons	230 standard; 387 full load
Dimensions, feet	169 × 23·7 × 5·7
Guns	1—3 in; 1—40 mm AA; 2—20 mm AA
Main engines	2 GM diesels; 2 shafts; 1 000 bhp = 15 knots
Oil fuel (tons)	100
Radius, miles	8 000 at 12 knots
Complement	58

Former US infantry landing ship of the LSIL type. Transferred from the US Navy to the French Navy, on 2 Mar 1951 and stationed in Indo-China; and again transferred to the Marine Royal Khmere in 1957.

TORPEDO BOATS

2 Ex-YUGOSLAV 108 TYPE

VR I **VR II**

Displacement, tons	55 standard; 60 full load
Dimensions, feet	69 pp; 78 oa × 21·3 × 7·8
Guns	1—40 mm AA; 4—12·7 mm MG
Tubes	2
Main engines	3 Packard petrol motors; 5 000 bhp = 36 knots
Complement	14

Torpedo boats presented by Yugoslavia in 1965 and numbered by the Cambodian Navy.

PATROL BOATS

2 Ex-USSR AVR TYPE

VR 3 **VR 4**

Displacement, tons	30
Dimensions, feet	63 × 13 × 4·6
Guns	4—12·7 mm MG
Main engines	GM Diesel 500 bhp = 15 knots
Complement	12

3 Ex-CHINESE CPB TYPE

VC 4 **VC 5** **VC 6**

Displacement, tons	7·7 standard; 9·7 full load
Dimensions, feet	42 × 9 × 3·9
Guns	2—12·7 mm MG
Main engines	Diesel, 300 bhp = 20 knots
Complement	10

Coastal patrol boats transferred from the People's Republic of China in Jan 1968.

VC 5, VC 4, VC 6 *1969, MRK, Official*

1 Ex-HDML TYPE

VP 212 (ex-*VP 748*, ex-*HDML 1223*)

Displacement, tons	46 standard; 54 full load
Dimensions, feet	72 oa × 16 × 5·5
Guns	2—20 mm AA; 4—7·5 mm MG
Main engines	2 diesels; 2 shafts; 300 bhp = 10 knots
Oil fuel (tons)	6
Radius, miles	2 200 at 10 knots
Complement	8

Former British harbour defence motor launch of the HDML type. Transferred from the British Navy to the French Navy in 1950 and again transferred from the French Navy to the Marine Royal Khmere in 1956. VP 749 and VP 642 were discarded in 1968.

LANDING CRAFT

3 Ex-US LCU TYPE

T 913 (ex-USS *LCU 1577*) **T 914** (ex-USS *LCU 783*) **T 915** (ex-USS *LCU 1421*)

Displacement, tons	180 standard; 360 full load
Dimensions, feet	115 wl; 119 oa × 34 × 6
Guns	2—20 mm AA
Main engines	3 diesels; 3 shafts; 675 bhp = 8 knots
Oil fuel (tons)	12
Radius, miles	750 at 7 knots
Complement	12

Former US utility landing craft of the LCU type. LCU 783 and LCU 1421 were transferred on 31 May 1962. Former LCT(6)s 9085 (ex-622) and 9091 (ex-720) were deleted from the list in 1969, with ex-LCU 9073 (ex-USS *LCU* 1420.)
There are 13 landing craft (LCM), 39 armoured craft (LCVP). There are also 3 YTL including *Pelican*, R 912 (ex-USS *YTL 555*) and *Pinquouie*, R 911 (ex-USS *YTL 556*) transferred on 15 Sep 1956 by the French.

T 913 *1969, Marine Royal Khmere, Official*

CAMEROON

Complete independence was proclaimed on 1 Jan 1960

Mercantile Marine

Lloyd's Register of Shipping: 6 vessels of 1,107 tons gross

PATROL BOATS

VIGILANTE (ex-*VC 6*, P 756)

Displacement, tons	75 standard; 82 full load
Dimensions, feet	104·2 × 15·5 × 5·5
Guns	2—20 mm AA
Main engines	Mercedes-Benz diesels; 2 shafts; 2 700 bhp = 28 knots
Radius, miles	1 500 at 15 knots
Complement	15

Former French seaward defence motor launch of the VC type. Built by Constructions Mécaniques de Normandie, Cherbourg. Completed in 1958. Transferred from France to the Republic of Cameroon on 7 Mar 1964 (officially handed over).

PATRIE DU CAMEROUN (ex-*VP 768*, ex-*HDML 1228*)

Displacement, tons	40 standard; 52 full load
Dimensions, feet	71 × 15·2 × 6
Guns	2—20 mm AA; 4 MG
Main engines	2 diesels; 2 shafts; 300 bhp = 12 knots
Radius, miles	2 200 at 10 knots
Oil fuel (tons)	6·2
Complement	11

Former British harbour defence motor launch of the HDML type. Launched in 1943. Transferred from the British Navy to the French Navy in 1950 for service in Indo-China; and again transferred from the French Navy to the Cameroon Government in 1963 to replace the ex-VP 747, ex-HDML 1423.

CANADA

Administration

Minister of National Defence:
The Hon. Leo Cadieux, MP

On 1 Aug 1964 the Naval Board was dissolved, and Naval Headquarters was integrated with Canadian Forces Headquarters. On 1 Feb 1968, the Canadian Forces Reorganization Act unified the three branches of the Canadian forces and the title Royal Canadian Navy was dropped. Maritime Command, one of six commands comprising the Canadian Armed Forces, is made up of the bulk of what was the Royal Canadian Navy plus Maritime Patrol aircraft squadrons and bases.

The Senior Naval Officer at Canadian Forces Headquarters is:—

Chief of Personnel:
Vice-Admiral R. L. Hennessy, DSC, CD

Senior Naval Appointments

Commander Maritime Command:
Vice Admiral J. C. O'Brien, CD

Commander Maritime Forces Pacific:
Rear Admiral J. A. Charles, CD

Deputy Chief Plans:
Rear Admiral R. W. Timbrell, DSC, CD

Commander Canadian Defence Liaison Staff, Washington, Canadian Forces Attaché and Senior Naval Liaison Officer, Washington:
Rear Admiral S. E. Paddon, CD

Director General Operations (Maritime):
Commodore P. F. Russell, CD

Senior Canadian Officer Afloat:
Commodore H. A. Porter, CD

Personnel

1969: 15 152 (2 258 officers and 12 894 men) in Maritime Command)

Diplomatic Representation

Senior Naval Liaison Officer, London:

Captain (N) H. R. Tilley, CD

Forces Attaché and Senior Naval Liaison Officers, Washington:
Rear Admiral S. E. Paddon, CD (see Col 1)

History

The Royal Canadian Navy officially came into being on 4 May 1910, when Royal Assent was given to the Naval Service Act.

Ships of the Royal Canadian Navy served in three wars. During the First World War the Canadian naval strength was 9 600 officers and men and 100 ships. During the Second World War the RCN expanded to 95 000 officers, men and wrens, and 392 ships, Canada's major naval effort being devoted to the Battle of the Atlantic. Canadian destroyers served in the Far East throughout the Korean War.

Flag

On 15 Feb 1965 a new Canadian flag replaced the Red, White and Blue ensigns:—

Official description: A red flag of the proportions two by length and one by width, containing in its centre a white square the width of the flag, with a single red maple leaf centred therein.

With the proclamation of the new national flag on 15 Feb 1965 Canadian ships no longer wear the Red, White or Blue Ensigns, the national flag being worn on the ensign staff aft. In Feb 1968 a naval jack was approved to be flown by Canadian Warships.

Official description: A white flag of the proportions two by length and one by width, containing in the top left corner, the Canadian flag and centred on the flag the naval crown, fouled anchor and eagle combined in dark blue.

Strength of the Fleet

1 Aircraft Carrier
4 Submarine (Diesel Powered)
22 Destroyer Escorts
1 Ocean Escort (Diving Tender)
3 Operational Support Ships (including 2 under construction)
2 Escort Maintenance Ships
6 Coastal Minesweepers
4 Patrol Craft (Submarine Chasers)
6 Oceanographic Research Vessels
1 Anti-Submarine Hydrofoil
5 Gate Vessels (Boom Defence)
40 Auxiliaries and Service Craft
2 Sailing Ketchs (Training)

Ships

Canadian naval ships carry a maple leaf on the funnel. The senior ship of a squadron wears a command broad pennant. This is a swallow-tailed pennant, white, with blue borders top and bottom, and bearing the squadron number in blue. "Barber pole" stripes are painted on the lower structure of the foremast of ships of the Fifth Canadian Escort Squadron, in the tradition of the "Barber Pole Brigade", mid-ocean escort group of the Second World War.

Navy Estimates

	$		$
1961-62:	279 900 000	1965-66:	292 565 000
1962-63:	287 466 000	1966-67:	295 000 000
1963-64:	306 184 000	1967-68:	300 000 000
1964-65:	272 892 000		
1968-69:	283 201 000 (Maritime Command)		
1969-70:	359 701 000 (Maritime Command)		

Mercantile Marine

Lloyd's Register of Shipping:
Sea: 1 022 vessels of 953 287 tons gross
Great Lakes: 274 vessels of 1 449 696 tons gross
Total 1 296 vessels of 2 402,983 tons gross

Silhouettes

Scale: 150 feet = 1 inch

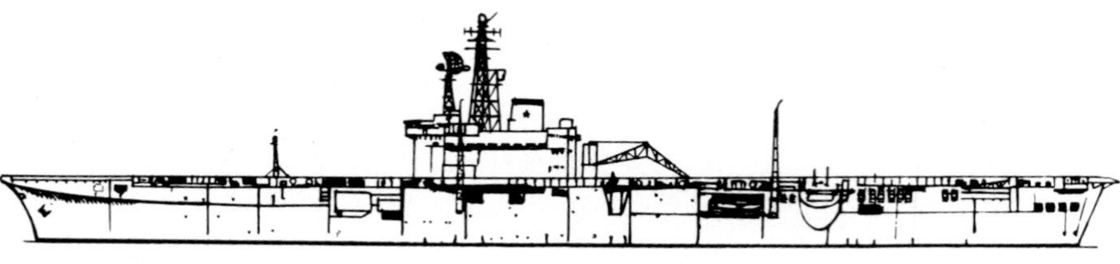

BONAVENTURE

ALGONQUIN

ANNAPOLIS *Class*

St. LAURENT (mainmast)

CRESCENT

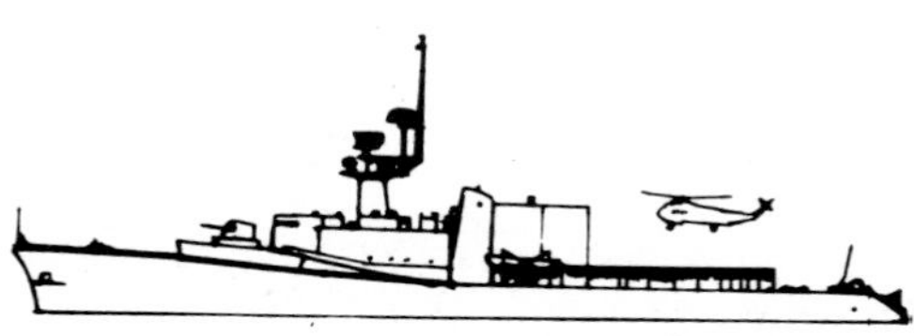

Converted St. LAURENT *Class*

Original St. LAURENT *Class*

PRESTONIAN *Class* (midship deckhouse)

RESTIGOUCHE *Class*

ATHABASKAN

PRESTONIAN (no deckhouse)

AIRCRAFT CARRIERS (CVL)

Name	No.	Builder	Laid down	Launched	Completed
BONAVENTURE (ex-*Powerful*)	CVL 22	Harland & Wolff, Ltd, Belfast	27 Nov 1943	27 Feb 1945	17 Jan 1957

1 MODIFIED "MAJESTIC" CLASS

Displacement, tons	16 000 standard; 20 000 full load
Length, feet (*metres*)	630 (*192·0*) pp; 704 (*214·6*) oa
Beam, feet (*metres*)	80 (*24·4*) hull
Width, feet (*metres*)	112·5 (*34·3*); 128 (*39·0* including angled deck and sponsons
Draught, feet (*metres*)	25 (*7·6*)
Aircraft	21 capacity CS2F-2 Tracker aircraft; CHSS-2 "Sea King" helicopters have replaced Sikorsky HO4-S-3 helicopters (one Sikorsky retained as plane guard)
Guns, dual purpose	4—3 in (*76 mm*); 2 twin mounts (4 twin mounts until 1967)
Guns, saluting	3—6 pdr.
Boilers	4 Admiralty 3-drum type, pressure 350 psi (*175 kg/cm²*)
Main engines	Parsons single-reduction geared turbines 40 000 shp; 2 shafts
Speed, knots	24·5 designed
Complement	1 370 (war)

First aircraft carrier owned by the Royal Canadian Navy. Air recognition number 22 painted on flight deck. The type designator and hull number CVL 22 follows the NATO code and signifies a small ASW aircraft carrier.

CONSTRUCTION. The former British *Powerful* was suspended in May 1946, but purchased by Canada and construction was resumed in July 1952, when she was re-named *Bonaventure*. She was fitted with the British steam catapult and angled deck redesigned to handle jet aircraft, plans being revised to provide for a modern aircraft carrier: the modification included strengthening the flight deck and elevators and improving arrester gear.

MODERNISATION. A major refit was completed in 1967, improvements included new radar, re-arrangement of operations rooms and living spaces, most modifications and better air conditioning.

PHOTOGRAPHS. Starboard bow view in the 1957-58 edition and 1966-67 to 1968-69 editions. Starboard broadside and port bow views in the 1958-59 edition. Starboard quarter oblique aerial view, showing angled deck, in the 1958-59 to 1960-61 editions. Dead overhead aerial plan view showing flight deck in the 1957-58 to 1962-63 editions. Port broadside surface view in the 1959-60 to 1963-64 editions. Port bow oblique aerial view in the 1961-62 to 1965-66 editions and 1968-69 editions. Starboard broadside aerial view in the 1963-64 to 1965-66 editions.

DRAWING. Port elevation and plan. Redrawn in 1968. Scale: 128 feet = 1 inch.

BONAVENTURE — *1969, Canadian Maritime Command, Official*

BONAVENTURE — *1968, Canadian Maritime Command, Official*

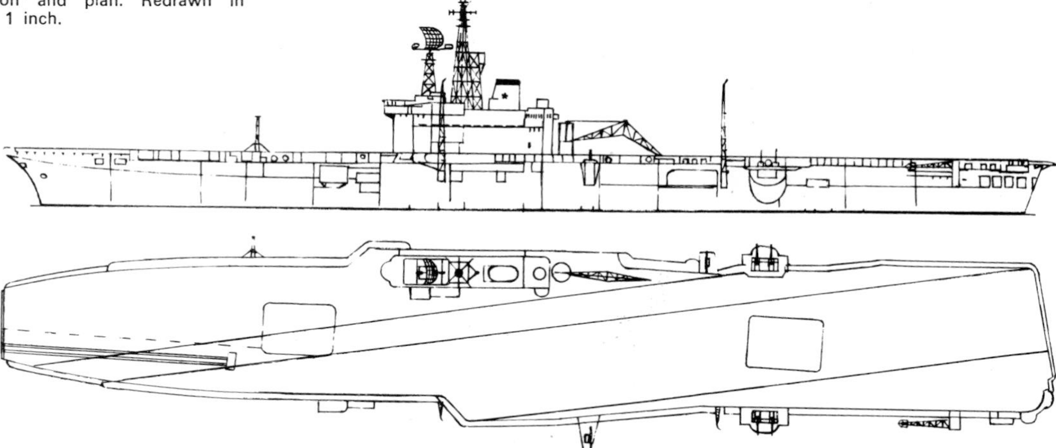

BONAVENTURE — *1968, Royal Canadian Navy, Official*

SUBMARINES (SS)

3 BRITISH-BUILT "O" TYPE

Name	No.	Builders	Laid down	Launched	Commissioned
OJIBWA (ex-*Onyx*)	72	HM Dockyard, Chatham	27 Sep 1962	29 Feb 1964	23 Sep 1965
OKANAGAN	74	HM Dockyard, Chatham	25 Mar 1965	17 Sep 1966	22 June 1968
ONONDAGA	73	HM Dockyard, Chatham	18 June 1964	25 Sep 1965	22 June 1967

Displacement, tons	2 060 full buoyancy surface; 2 200 normal surface; 2 420 submerged
Length, feet (*metres*)	241 (*73·5*) pp; 294·2 (*90·0*) oa
Beam, feet (*metres*)	26·5 (*8·1*)
Draught, feet (*metres*)	18 (*5·5*)
Torpedo tubes	8—21 in (*533 mm*), 6 bow and 2 stern
Main engines	2 400 hp Admiralty Standard Range diesels; 3 600 hp electric motors (submerged)
Speed, knots	12 on surface; 16 submerged
Complement	65 (7 officers, 58 ratings)

The procurement of three submarines for the Royal Canadian Navy was announced by the Minister of National Defence on 11 Apr 1962, all of the "Oberon" class built in Great Britain. The first of these patrol submarines was obtained by the Canadian Government from the Royal Navy construction programme. She was laid down as *Onyx* but launched as *Ojibwa*. The other two were specifically Canadian procurements. There were some design changes to meet specific new requirements including installation of RCN communications equipment and enlargement of de-icing and air-conditioning systems to meet the wide extremes of climate encountered in Canadian operating areas.

PHOTOGRAPHS. A photograph of *Ojibwa* appears in the 1966-67 and 1967-68 editions and of *Onondaga* in the 1968-69 edition.

NOMENCLATURE. The name *Ojibwa* is that of a tribe of North American Indians now widely dispersed in Canada and the USA and one of the largest remnants of aboriginal population. *Okanagan* and *Onondaga* are also well known Canadian Indian tribes. A photograph of *Ojibwa* appears in the 1967-68 edition.

OKANAGAN — *1969, Canadian Maritime Command, Official*

1 Ex-US "TENCH" CLASS

Name	No.	Builders	Laid down	Launched	Completed
RAINBOW (ex-*USS Argonaut* SS 475)	SS 75	Portsmouth Naval Shipyard	28 June 1944	1 Oct 1944	15 Jan 1945

Displacement, tons	1 526 standard; 1 800 surface; 2 500 submerged
Length, feet (*metres*)	311·2 (*95·0*)
Beam, feet (*metres*)	27·2 (*8·2*)
Draught, feet (*metres*)	17 (*5·2*)
Torpedo tubes	10—21 in (*533 mm*) 6 fwd 4 aft
Main engines	6 500 hp diesels (surface); 4 610 hp electric motors (submerged)
Speed, knots	20 on surface; 10 submerged
Radius, miles	14 000 at 10 knots
Oil fuel (tons)	300
Complement	82 (8 officers, 74 men)

Former United States submarine of the Tench class. Bought by the Canadian Armed Forces in Dec 1968 as a replacement for HMCS *Grilse*. Commissioned 2 Dec 1968. Based at Esquimalt, BC to carry out anti-submarine warfare training duties with aircraft and ships of the Pacific Maritime Command.

DISPOSAL
HMCS **Grilse** (ex-*USS Burrfish*) was returned to USN in Dec, 1968 after loan to Canada since May 1961.

RAINBOW (as USS *Argonaut*) — *Added, 1969, A. & J. Pavia*

DESTROYER HELICOPTER CARRIERS (DDH)

4 ANTI-SUBMARINE TYPE

Name	No.	Builders	
ALGONQUIN	283	Davie SB Co, Lauzon	
ATHABASKAN	282	Davie SB Co, Lauzon	
HURON	281	Marine Industries Ltd, Sorel	To complete Nov 1971
IROQUOIS	280	Marine Industries Ltd, Sorel	To complete Jan 1971

Displacement, tons	4 050 full load
Length, feet (*metres*)	398 (*121·3*); 426 (*129·8*) oa
Beam, feet (*metres*)	50 (*15·2*)
Draught, feet (*metres*)	14 (*4·3*)
Aircraft	2 "Sea King" CHSS-2 A/S helicopters
Guns, dual purpose	1—5 in (*127 mm*) LA, single
A/S	1 A/S Mortar Mk X
Torpedo tubes	2 triple for A/S homing torpedoes
Main engines	Gas turbines; 2 Pratt & Whitney FT4; 44 000 shp + 2 Pratt & Whitney FT 12 6 200 shp for cruising; 2 shafts
Speed, knots	27 designed
Radius, miles	4 500 at economical speed

It will be observed that these ships have the same hull design, dimensions and basic characteristics as the large general purpose frigates cancelled at the end of 1963 (see particulars and illustration in the 1963-64 edition). Designed as anti-submarine ships, they will be fitted as leaders, with variable depth and conventional sonar, landing deck equipped with double hauldown and bear-trap, Flume type anti-rolling tanks to stabilise the ships at low speed, pre-wetting system to counter radio-active fallout, enclosed citadel, and bridge control of machinery, which will comprise gas turbines, instead of the steam originally projected.

DESIGN. Plans have been changed over the last few years, see illustrations in the 1966-67 and 1967-68 editions.

MISSILES. Sea Sparrow anti-aircraft missile will be fitted.

DDH 280 (Modified Model) — *1968, Canadian Maritime Command, Official*

DESTROYER ESCORTS (DDH and DDE) Anti-Submarine Frigate Type

2 "ANNAPOLIS" CLASS

ANNAPOLIS **NIPIGON**

4 "MACKENZIE" CLASS

MACKENZIE **SASKATCHEWAN**
QU'APPELLE **YUKON**

7 "RESTIGOUCHE" CLASS

CHAUDIERE **GATINEAU** **RESTIGOUCHE**
COLOMBIA **KOOTENAY** **ST. CROIX**
TERRA NOVA

Name	No.	Builders	Laid down	Launched	Completed
Chaudiere	235	Halifax Shipyards Ltd, Halifax	30 July 1953	13 Nov 1957	14 Nov 1959
Gatineau	236	Davie Shipbuilding & Repairing	30 Apr 1953	3 June 1957	17 Feb 1959
St. Croix	256	Marine Industries Ltd, Sorel, Q	15 Oct 1954	17 Nov 1957	4 Oct 1958
Restigouche	257	Canadian Vickers Ltd, Montreal	15 July 1953	22 Nov 1954	7 June 1958
Kootenay	258	Burrard D.D & Shipbuilding	21 Aug 1952	15 June 1954	7 Mar 1959
Terra Nova	259	Victoria Machinery Depot Co	14 Nov 1952	21 June 1955	6 June 1959
Columbia	260	Burrard D.D. & Shipbuilding	11 June 1953	1 Nov 1956	7 Nov 1959
Mackenzie	261	Canadian Vickers Ltd, Montreal	15 Dec 1958	25 May 1961	6 Oct 1962
**Saskatchewan*	262	Victoria Machinery (and Yarrow)	July 1959	1 Feb 1961	16 Feb 1963
Yukon	263	Burrard D.D. & Shipbuilding	Oct 1959	27 July 1961	25 May 1963
Qu'Appelle	264	Davie Shipbuilding & Repairing	Jan 1960	2 May 1962	14 Sep 1963
Annapolis	265	Halifax Shipyards Ltd, Halifax	July 1960	27 Apr 1963	19 Dec 1964
Nipigon	266	Marine Industries Ltd, Sorel, Q	Apr 1960	10 Dec 1961	30 May 1964

**Saskatchewan* was launched by Victoria Machinery Depot Co Ltd, but Completed by Yarrow's Ltd.

Displacement, tons	2 366 standard; 2 900 full load
Length, feet (*metres*)	366 (*111·5*) oa
Beam, feet (*metres*)	42 (*12·8*)
Draught, feet (*metres*)	13·5 (*4·1*)
Guns, AA	2—3 in (*76 mm*) 70 cal forward (twin); 2—3 in (*76 mm*) 50 cal. aft (twin); *Qu'Appelle* has 50 cal. fore and aft; *Annapolis* and *Nipigon* 3 in 50 cal. forward only *Terra Nova* 2—3 in 70 cal. forward only
A/S weapons	2 Limbo 3-barrelled depth charge mortars in after well. 1 Limbo in *Annapolis* and *Nipigon*. ASROC in *Terra Nova*, no Limbo
Boilers	2 water tube
Main engines	Geared turbines 30 000 shp; 2 shafts
Speed, knots	28 (official figure)
Complement	246 (12 officers, 234 ratings)

These ships were developed from the original "St. Laurent" class, but there are considerable differences in the three classes. Ships fitted with helicopter hangar and landing platform are now designated DDH.

CLASS VARIATION. In providing helicopter platforms and hangars in *Annapolis* and *Nipigon*, which also incorporate variable depth sonar and cutaway stern (see photo) it was possible to mount only one Limbo and one twin 3 inch, 50 cal gun. *Saskatchewan* has different bridge (two level) from others.

DESIGN IMPROVEMENT. New features of the "Mackenzie" class include improved habitability; vinyl-asbestos tile deck covering throughout the ship; improved air-conditioning; extension of pre-wetting system (to counter radioactive fallout) to cover entire exposed area of the ship; "Dutch;" water-tight doors heated wipers for bridge windows to cope with temperature in northern waters.

CONVERSION. The "Restigouche" class is being converted to carry variable depth sonar, advanced electronics equipment and, Asroc. *Terra Nova* was the first to be taken in hand in Sep 1967. Conversion will increase the overall length to 371 feet.

CONSTRUCTION. On the prefabrication unit system ships were under construction for months before anything appeared on the ways, so it is impossible to give a true "laid down" date. The work "commencement" schedule for the "Mackenzie"/"Annapolis" group is shown in the table.

ANNAPOLIS — *1968, Canadian Maritime Command, Official*

MACKENZIE — *1968, Canadian Maritime Command, Official*

PHOTOGRAPHS. Starboard broadside view of *Restigouche* in the 1958-59 edition. Starboard bow oblique aerial view of *Terra Nova* and port quarter surface view of *Columbia* in the 1960-61 to 1962-63 editions. Port broadside aerial view of *Kootenay* in the 1959-60 to 1962-63 editions. Starboard broadside aerial view of *Saskatchewan* in the 1963-64 edition. Port quarter oblique aerial view of *Mackenzie* and port broadside surface view of *Gatineau* in the 1963-64 and 1964-65 editions. Port broadside view of *Yukon* in the 1964-65 and 1965-66 editions. Starboard quarter and starboard bow, aerial views of *Nipigon* and *Annapolis* appear in the 1965-66 to 1967-68 editions and, a starboard broadside, surface view of *Mackenzie* in the 1966-67 and 1967-68 editions.

TERRA NOVA (Note ASROC aft) — *1968, Canadian Maritime Command, Official*

Destroyer Escorts (DDH ex-DDE) Anti-Submarine Frigate Type—*continued*

7 ST. LAURENT CLASS

Name	No.	Builders	Laid down	Launched	Completed
ST. LAURENT	DDE 205	Canadian Vickers, Ltd, Montreal	22 Nov 1950	20 Nov 1951	29 Oct 1955
SAGUENAY	DDE 206	Halifax Shipyards, Ltd, Halifax	4 Apr 1951	30 July 1953	15 Dec 1956
SKEENA	DDE 207	Burrard Dry Dock & Shipbuilding	1 June 1951	19 Aug 1952	30 Mar 1957
OTTAWA	DDE 229	Canadian Vickers, Ltd, Montreal	8 June 1951	29 Apr 1953	10 Nov 1956
MARGAREE	DDE 230	Halifax Shipyards Ltd, Halifax	12 Sep 1951	29 Mar 1956	5 Oct 1957
***FRASER**	DDE 233	Yarrows, Ltd, Esquimalt, B.C.	11 Dec 1951	19 Feb 1953	28 June 1957
ASSINIBOINE	DDE 234	Marine Industries Ltd, Sorel, Q	19 May 1952	12 Feb 1954	16 Aug 1956

Displacement, tons	2 263 standard; 2 800 full load
Length, feet (*metres*)	366 (*111·5*) oa
Beam, feet (*metres*)	42 (*12·8*)
Draught, feet (*metres*)	13·2 (*4·0*)
Guns, AA	2—3 in (*76 mm*) 50 cal., twin
A/S weapons	2 Limbo 3-barrelled depth charge mortars in after well
Boilers	2 water tube
Main engines	Geared turbines 30 000 shp; 2 shafts
Speed, knots	28·5 (official figure)
Complement	250 (13 officers, 237 ratings)

Officially classed as major warships and as such were the first to be designed completely in Canada. These anti-submarine escort vessels of a high-speed type were built primarily for the detection and destruction of modern fast submarines. In evolving their design much assistance was received from the Royal Navy and the United States Navy. In function the vessels supersede the frigates of the Second World War and like the latter their design was worked out so that in the event of emergency they could be produced rapidly and in quantity. In speed, manoeuvrability and weapons the ships fulfil all the requirements of their class for modern sea warfare. The design provided for flush deck, low bridge, considerable use of aluminium instead of steel for the superstructure, fittings and furniture, and compartmented hull. The ships have long range sonar to probe for submarines and improved armament and electronic equipment as submarine chasers.

RECONSTRUCTION. All seven ships of the "St. Laurent" class have been fitted with helicopter platforms and VDS. *St. Laurent* was equipped with VDS late in 1961, and platform added later. Twin funnels were stepped to permit the forward extension of the helicopter hangar. Gunhouses are of fibreglass. In providing helicopter platforms and hangars it was possible to retain only one three barrelled Limbo mount and only one twin 3-inch 50 cal gun mount. Dates of recommissioning after conversion:—*Assiniboine* 28 June 1963, *St. Laurent* 4 Oct 1963, *Ottawa* 21 Oct 1964, *Saguenay* 14 May 1965, *Skeena* 15 Aug 1965, *Margaree* 15 Oct 1965, *Fraser* 31 Aug 1966.

PHOTOGRAPHS. Starboard quarter view of *St. Laurent* and broadside view of *Ottawa* as first completed in 1957-58 edition. Starboard quarter oblique aerial view of *Ottawa* with experimental helicopter platform laid on aft, in the 1958-59 and 1959-60 editions. Port bow oblique aerial view of *Saguenay* in the 1957-58 to 1959-60 editions. Port broadside aerial view of *Margaree* in the 1958-59 to 1961-62 editions. Port broadside view of *Skeena* in the 1962-63 to 1964-65 editions. Port broadside surface view of *Assiniboine* after reconstruction in the 1963-64 edition. Starboard bow surface view of *Assiniboine* carrying helicopter in the 1964-65 edition. Port bow surface view of *Ottawa* after conversion in the 1965-66 edition. Starboard and port broadside views of the *Saguenay* and *St Laurent* appeared in the 1967-68 editions.

GUNNERY. The original armament was 4—3 inch, 50 cal AA (2 twin), 2—40 mm AA (single), and 2 Limbos.

ENGINEERING. Propelling machinery is of British design. Yarrow & Co. Ltd., Scotstoun, Glasgow, supplied Canadian Vickers with a complete set of machinery for *St. Laurent*, the other ships being supplied with similar machinery manufactured in Canada. The main turbines and condensers are of English Electric design.

APPEARANCE. Ships of the "St. Laurent" class resemble *Annapolis* and *Nipigon* (see previous page) but there are slight variations in funnel height and rake, etc.

ASSINIBOINE — *1968, Canadian Maritime Command, Official*

FRASER — *1968, Canadian Maritime Command, Official*

ASSINIBOINE (with helicopter) — ***1965, Royal Canadian Navy, Official***

Destroyer Escorts (DDE)—*continued*

"ALGONQUIN" CLASS ("CR" TYPE)

Name	No.	Builders	Laid down	Launched	Completed
CRESCENT	DDE 226	John Brown & Co Ltd, Clydebank	16 Sep 1943	20 July 1944	21 Sep 1945

Displacement, tons	2 100 standard; 2 700 full load
Length, feet (*metres*)	339·5 (*103·5*) pp; 362·8 (*110·6*) oa
Beam, feet (*metres*)	35·5 (*10·8*)
Draught, feet (*metres*)	13·2 (*4·0*)
Guns, surface	2—4 in (*102 mm*) twin mount, forward; 2—3 in (*76 mm*) twin mount, aft (now in shield)
Guns, AA	2—40 mm Bofors
A/S	1 Limbo triple-barrelled DC mortar 3 launchers for Mark 43 A/S homing torpedoes
Boilers	2 Admiralty 3-drum type
Main engines	Parsons geared turbines 40 000 shp; 2 shafts
Speed, knots	36·75 designed; 31·25 sea speed
Radius, miles	2 800 at 20 knots
Oil fuel (tons)	580
Complement	250

CRESCENT 1968, *Canadian Maritime Command, Official*

CRESCENT
Originally a "Cr" class destroyer lent to the Royal Canadian Navy in 1945 and permanently transferred from Great Britain in 1951. Fully converted into a fast anti-submarine escort by Esquimalt Dockyard in 1956. Extensively refitted in 1958. Modified considerably in 1960 when one Limbo was removed to compensate for the weight of the variable depth sonar installed, shield fitted to 3 inch, mounting, and torpedo launchers added. Now in reserve.

APPEARANCE. *Crescent* is generally very similar to *Algonquin* except that the main armament is mounted *vice versa*, i.e. 4 inch guns are mounted forward and the 3 inch guns in the after position.

DISPOSAL
Original sister ship **Crusader**, partially converted into a fast anti-submarine escort, was declared surplus in 1963 and turned over to the Crown Assets Disposal Corporation.

"ALGONQUIN" CLASS ("V" TYPE)

Name	No.	Builders	Laid down	Launched	Completed
ALGONQUIN (ex-*Valentine*, ex-*Kempenfelt*)	DDE 224	John Brown & Co Ltd. Clydebank	8 Oct 1942	2 Sep 1943	28 Feb 1944

Displacement, tons	2 100 standard; 2 700 full load
Length, feet (*metres*)	339·5 (*103·5*) pp; 362·8 (*110·6*) oa
Beam, feet (*metres*)	35·5 (*10·8*)
Draught, feet (*metres*)	13·2 (*4·0*)
Guns, surface	2—4 in (*102 mm*) twin mount aft; 2—3 in (*76 mm*) twin mount forward
Guns, AA	2—40 mm Bofors
A/S	1 Limbo three-barrelled DC mortar 3 launchers for Mark 43 A/S homing torpedoes
Boilers	2 Admiralty 3-drum type
Main engines	Parsons geared turbines 40 000 shp; 2 shafts
Speed, knots	36·75 designed; 31·25 sea speed
Radius, miles	2 800 at 20 knots
Oil fuel (tons)	580
Complement	230

ALGONQUIN 1969, *Canadian Maritime Command, Official*

Originally a "V" class destroyer transferred from Great Britain in 1944. Fully converted into a fast anti-submarine escort by Esquimalt Dockyard in 1954. Now in reserve at Esquimalt.

CLASSIFICATION. *Algonquin* and *Crescent*, although they differ, were officially designated "Destroyer Escorts—*Algonquin* Class (DDE)" in 1956

APPEARANCE. *Algonquin* has her 4 inch twin gun mounting aft and 3 inch twin gun mounting forward instead of *vice versa* as in *Crescent* (see above). She now has a shield to her 3 inch guns.

DISPOSAL
Original sister ship **Sioux** (ex-HMS *Vixen*), partially converted into a fast anti-submarine escort, was paid off for disposal on 30 Oct 1963.

DISPOSALS OF TRIBAL CLASS
Iroquois was scrapped at Bilbao, Spain, in 1966. **Cayuga**, **Huron**, **Micmac**, **Nootka** were sold to Marine Salvage Ltd, Colbourne, Ontario, for scrap. **Haida** is a floating museum at Toronto (purchased for $20,000). **Athabaskan** (first ship of the name, built in Great Britain) was Second World War loss. **Athabaskan** (second ship of the name built in Canada) was discarded 1968.

OCEAN ESCORT (*FSE*) Diving Depot Ship

GRANBY FSE 180 (ex-*Victoriaville*, DE 320)

Displacement, tons	1 570 standard; 2 360 full load
Length, feet (*metres*)	310·5 (*91·9*) oa
Beam, feet (*metres*)	36·5 (*11·1*)
Draught, feet (*metres*)	16 (*4·9*)
Guns, surface	2—4 in (*102 mm*)
Guns, AA	6—40 mm 4 single, 1 twin
A/S	2 Squid triple barrel DC mortars
Boilers	2 Admiralty 3-drum type
Main engines	Triple expansion 5 500 ihp; 2 shafts
Speed, knots	19
Radius, miles	9 600 at 12 knots
Oil fuel (tons)	720
Complement	140

GRANBY 1968, *Canadian Maritime Command, Official*

Sole survivor of the 21 of this class, all built in Canadian shipyards, which originally of similar design to the British "River" class frigates, including three transferred to Norway, were modernised and reconstructed to flush deckers (completed anti-submarine conversion in 1953-58). All were redesignated FFE (instead of PF) in 1953. Again redesignated, as DE, in 1964 and as FSE in 1968. Seven frigates of the Fourth Canadian Escort Squadron, were fitted with a midship deckhouse to provide classroom and messing facilities for officer cadets under sea training.

DISPOSALS
Lauzon was declared surplus in 1963, **Buckingham**, **Fort Erie** and **Lanark** in 1965, **Cap de la Madeleine** **Inch Arran**, **La Hulloise** and **Outremont** in 1966, **Antigonish**, **Jonquiere**, **New Glasgow**, **New Waterford**, **Ste. Theresa**, **Stettler**, **Sussexvale** and **Swansea** in 1967, and **Beacon Hill** in 1968.

TRANSFERS. *Penetang* (ex-*Rouyn*), *Prestonian* (ex-*Beauharnois*), and *Toronto* (ex-*Gifford*) were lent to Norway in 1956, being renamed *Draug*, *Troll* and *Garm*, respectively, and transferred outright on 27 June 1958.

OPERATIONAL SUPPORT SHIPS (AOR)

2 NEW CONSTRUCTION

Name	No.	Builders	Laid down	Launched
PRESERVER	AOR 510	Saint John Dry Dock Co Ltd, Saint John, N.B.	Spring 1967	
PROTECTEUR	AOR 509	Saint John Dry Dock Co Ltd, Saint John, N.B.	Spring 1967	2 Nov 1968

Displacement, tons	9 000 light; 24 000 full load
Measurement, tons	22 000 gross; 13 250 deadweight
Length, feet (*metres*)	564 (*171·9*) oa
Guns, AA	1—3 in (*76 mm*)
A/S weapons	1 Sea Sparrow launcher (fitted for only)
Aircraft	3 helicopters (CHSS-2)
Main engines	22 000 shp
Speed, knots	20

These two new operational support ships were provided for under the Five Year Programme. Contract price $47 500 000 for both ships. In design they will be an improvement on that of the prototype *Provider.* They will increase the ability of the Canadian Navy's anti-submarine forces to remain continuously on station in emergency. Alternatively they could be used to carry spare anti-submarine helicopters, military vehicles and bulk equipment if required for sealift purposes.

PROTECTEUR *1967, Royal Canadian Navy, Official*

HELICOPTER CARRIER AND SUPPLY SHIP

Name	No.	Builders	Laid down	Launched	Completed
PROVIDER	AOR 508	Davie Shipbuilding Ltd., Lauzon, Quebec	1 May 1961	5 July 1962	28 Sep 1963

Displacement, tons	7 300 light; 22 700 full load
Measurement, tons	20 000 gross; 14 700 deadweight
Length, feet (*metres*)	523 (*159·4*) pp; 555 (*169·2*) oa
Beam, feet (*metres*)	76 (*23·2*)
Draught, feet (*metres*)	32 (*9·8*) max
Aircraft	3 HSS 2 helicopters
Boilers	2 water tube
Main engines	Double reduction geared turbine 21 000 shp; 1 shaft
Speed, knots	20
Radius, miles	5 000 at 20 knots
Oil fuel (tons)	1 200
Complement	142 (11 officers, 131 ratings)

PROVIDER *1968, Courtesy Mr. Godfrey H. Walker*

Authorised (announced) on 15 Apr 1958. Preliminary construction work began in Sep 1960. Commissioned for service on 28 Sep 1963. Cost $15 700 000.

NOMENCLATURE. *Provider* is the name borne during the Second World War by a RCN Fairmile motor launch parent ship. Formerly rated as Fleet Replenishment Ship, but reclassified as Operational Support Ship in 1965.

DESIGN. The clean, streamlined appearance of the hull follows a design to achieve high speed while fulfilling replenishments with the fleet on operations. The forward bridge structure contains the commanding officers' accommodation as well as a modern eight-berth hospital. In the superstructure also are the wheelhouse, chartroom and three positions from which there is complete control of this ship—the command control position and the two bridge wing positions. The helicopter flight deck is aft with the hangar located on this deck and immediately below the funnel. At least three Sikorsky helicopters of the type at present in service in the Royal Canadian Navy can be accommodated in the hangar space.
The flight deck is capable of receiving the largest and heaviest types of helicopter. Immediately below the flight deck are two accommodation decks for the ship's company including the main galley and combined mess-recreation spaces for chief and petty officers and men.
An unusual feature of this ship is the Self-Propelled Vehicle (SPV) fitted at number 6 station for the transfer of solid stores. A total of 20 electro-hydraulic winches are fitted on deck for ship-to-ship movement of cargo and supplies, as well as shore-to-ship requirements when alongside.

ESCORT MAINTENANCE SHIPS (ARE)

2 "CAPE" CLASS

Name	No.	Builders	Laid down	Launched	Completed
CAPE BRETON	100	Burrard Dry Dock Co, Vancouver, BC	5 July 1944	7 Oct 1944	25 Apr 1945
CAPE SCOTT	101	Burrard Dry Dock Co, Vancouver, BC	8 June 1944	27 Sep 1944	20 Mar 1945

Displacement, tons	8 580 standard; 11 270 full load
Dimensions, feet	441·5 × 57 × 20 mean at standard displacement
Main engines	Triple expansion; 1 shaft; 2 500 ihp = 11 knots
Boilers	2 Foster Wheeler
Complement	*Cape Breton* 220; *Cape Scott* 270 officers and men

CAPE SCOTT *Skyfotos*

Cape Breton formerly served in the Royal Navy as the escort maintenance ship *Flamborough Head*; but she returned from the United Kingdom in 1951 and was in turn acquired by the Royal Canadian Navy and renamed *Cape Breton* in 1953, serving as a training establishment for technical apprentices at Halifax until 1958 when she sailed for Esquimalt for conversion to her present function. On 16 Nov 1959 she commissioned on the West Coast as the second mobile repair ship; but she was paid off to reserve on 10 Feb 1964. A photograph of Cape Breton appears in the 1966-67 edition.
Cape Scott served in the Royal Navy as the *Beachy Head* until 1947, when she was lent to Royal Netherlands Navy and renamed *Vulkaan*; but she was returned to the Royal Navy in 1950, and was acquired by the Royal Canadian Navy in 1952, being renamed *Cape Scott* in 1953. On 28 Jan 1959 *Cape Scott* was commissioned at Halifax as the Royal Canadian Navy's first mobile repair ship.
Both ships are equipped with a helicopter landing platform, a decompression chamber for the ship's divers, engineering, electrical and electronic repair shops, diesel, engine repair shop, battery shop, sheet metal shop, welding shop, pipe and coppersmith's shop, plate shop and blacksmith's shop. Each ship contains an eight-berth hospital, large sick bay, operating theatre, X-ray room, small medical laboratory, dental clinic and dental laboratory.

RESEARCH VESSELS (AGOR)

BLUETHROAT (AGOR 114)

Displacement, tons	785 standard; 870 full load
Dimensions, feet	150·7 pp; 157 oa × 33 × 10
Main engines	Diesel; 2 shafts; 1 200 bhp = 13 knots

Authorised under the 1951 Programme. Built by Geo. T. Davie & Sons Ltd, Lauzon PQ. Laid down on 31 Oct 1952. Launched on 15 Sep 1955. Completed on 28 Nov 1955. Built as a Mine and Loop Layer, but under NATO standardised nomenclature listed as a Harbour Mineplanter. In 1957 she was rated as a Controlled Minelayer, No. NPC 114. Redesignated as a Cable Layer (ALC) in 1959, and as a Research Vessel (AGOR) in 1964.

BLUETHROAT *Royal Canadian Navy, Official*

SACKVILLE (AGOR 113)

Displacement, tons	1 085 standard; 1 350 full load
Dimensions, feet	190 pp; 205 oa × 33 × 14·5
Main engines	Triple expansion; 2 750 ihp = 16 knots
Boilers	2 SE

Built by St. John Dry Dock Co, St. John, NB. Launched on 15 May 1941. Completed on 30 Dec 1941. "Ex-Flower" class frigate (corvette) converted to loop layer. Employed by Naval Research Laboratories for oceanographic work. Formerly designated AN 113, but rated as ALC in 1959, as a cable layer under NATO nomenclature. Redesignated as a Research Vessel (AGOR) in 1964.

SACKVILLE *Royal Canadian Navy, Official*

FORT FRANCES (AGOR 170) **NEW LISKEARD** (AGOR 168)

Displacement, tons	1 040 standard; 1 335 full load
Dimensions, feet	225 oa × 35 × 11 max
Main engines	Triple expansion; 2 shafts; 2 000 ihp = 16·5 knots
Boilers	2, of 3-drum type
Complement	85

Built by Port Arthur Shipbuilding Co, Port Arthur, Ontario. *Fort Frances* was launched on 30 Oct 1943, *New Liskeard* on 14 Jan 1944. Former "Algerine" class Ocean Minesweepers (AM). Redesignated Coastal Escorts (FSE) in 1953. Refitted as survey ships and redesignated AGH in 1959. Again redesignated AGOR in 1964. A photograph of *Fort Frances* appears in the 1964-65 to 1966-67 editions.
Sister ship *Oshawa*, AGOR 174 disposed of when *Endeavour* commissioned. *Kapuskasing*, FSE 171, is on loan to the Dept of Mines and Technical Surveys.

NEW LISKEARD *1969, Official*

OCEANOGRAPHIC RESEARCH VESSELS

1 NEW CONSTRUCTION

		Launched
QUEST (AGOR 172)	Burrard Dry Dock Co, Vancouver	9 July 1968

Displacement, tons	2 130 (official figure)
Dimensions, feet	235 oa; 253 wl × 42 × 15·5
Aircraft	Light helicopter
Main engines	Diesel electric; 2 shafts; 2 950 shp = 16 knots max; Bow thruster propeller
Radius, miles	10 000 at 12 knots
Complement	55

Built for the Naval Research Establishment of the Defence Research Board for acoustic hydrographic and general oceanographic work, in particular as related to anti-submarine warfare. Will be capable of operating in heavy ice in the company of an icebreaker. A large 5-ton crane is fitted forward so that the jib-head can be lowered to surface level and thus reduce the swing on scientific instruments.

Design is slightly enlarged version of *Endeavour* (see below) with similar main engines, speed and range. Construction began in 1967. To be based at Halifax.

QUEST *1964, Royal Canadian Navy, Official*

ENDEAVOUR (AGOR 171)

Displacement, tons	1 560 (revised official figures)
Dimensions, feet	215 wl; 236 oa × 38·5 × 13
Aircraft	1 light helicopter
Main engines	Diesel electric; 2 shafts; 2 960 shp = 16 knots
Radius, miles	10 000 at 12 knots
Complement	10 officers, 13 scientists, 25 ratings (plus helicopter pilot and engineer)

A new research ship specifically designed to meet the scientific requirements for undertaking programmes in anti-submarine research. Flight deck 48 by 31 feet. Stiffened for operating in ice-covered areas. Designed by the Director General Ships and the Pacific Naval Laboratory. Built by Yarrows Ltd, Esquimalt, BC. Contract let in Nov 1963. Accepted for service on 9 Mar 1965. She is able to turn in 2·5 times her own length. Her crowsnest is fitted with engine and steering controls for navigation in ice. A bulbous bow reduces pitch and she has anti-roll tanks. Two 9-ton Austin-Weston telescopic cranes are fitted. There are two oceanographical winches each holding 5 000 fathoms of 5/16 in wire, two bathythermograph winches and a deep-sea anchoring and coring winch. She has acoustic insulation in her machinery spaces.

ENDEAVOUR *1965, Royal Canadian Navy, Official*

LAYMORE AGOR 516

Displacement, tons	560 gross, 262 net
Dimensions, feet	176·5 × 32 × 8
Main engines	General Motor diesels; 1 000 bhp = 10·8 knots

Former coastal supply vessel, classed as a fleet auxiliary and designated AKS. Converted to a research vessel 2 Aug 1965 to Mar 1966 and reclassified AGOR. Her original sister ship *Eastore* was sold on 30 July 1964.

COASTAL MINESWEEPERS (MCB)

6 "BAY" CLASS

Name	No.	Builders	Laid down	Launched	Completed
CHALEUR	164	Marine Industries	20 Feb 56	17 Nov 56	12 Sep 57
CHIGNECTO	160	Geo. T. Davie	25 Oct 55	26 Feb 57	1 Aug 57
COWICHAN	162	Yarrows	10 July 56	26 Feb 57	19 Dec 57
FUNDY	159	Davie Shipbuilding	7 Mar 55	14 June 56	27 Nov 56
MIRAMICHI	163	Victoria Machinery	2 Feb 56	22 Feb 57	28 Oct 57
THUNDER	161	Port Arthur	1 Sep 55	27 Oct 56	3 Oct 57

Displacement, tons	390 standard; 412 full load
Dimensions, feet	140 pp; 152 oa × 28 × 7 aft
Guns	1—40 mm
Main engine	2 GM V-12 diesels; 2 shafts; 2 400 bhp = 16 knots
Oil fuel	52 tons
Range, miles	4 500 at 11 knots
Complement	3 officers, 35 ratings

Extensively built of aluminium, including frames and decks. There were originally 14 vessels of this class. Named after Canadian straits and bays. Designation changed from AMC to MCB in 1954. Commissioned for Cadet Midshipman training during summer 1967. *Miramichi* now in reserve at Esquimalt.

PHOTOGRAPHS. A photograph of *Gaspe* appears in the 1954-55 to 1957-58 editions, and photographs of *Miramichi* appear in the 1958-59 to 1968-69 edition.

TRANSFERS. *Chaleur* (144), *Chignecto* (156), *Cowichan* (147), *Fundy* (145), *Miramichi* (150), and *Thunder* (153), of this class were transferred to the French Navy in 1954; but six more of the same class with the same names were built for the Royal Canadian Navy to replace those transferred.
Comax (146), *Gaspe* (143), *Trinity* (157), and *Ungava* (148) of this class were transferred to the Turkish Navy under Mutual Aid arrangements in 1958.

DISPOSALS
Of the "Bay" class, **Fortune**, **James Bay**, **Quinte** and **Resolute** were declared surplus in 1965. **Fortune** (renamed **Offshore**) and **James Bay** were sold for oil exploration and are active commercially.

CHALEUR — *1969, Canadian Maritime Command, Official*

GATE VESSELS (YMG)

5 "PORTE" CLASS

Name	No.	Builders	Laid down	Launched	Completed
PORTE DAUPHINE	186	Pictou Foundry	16 May 51	24 Apr 52	10 Dec 52
PORTE DE LA REINE	184	Victory Machinery	4 Mar 51	28 Dec 51	19 Sep 52
PORTE QUEBEC	185	Burrard Dry Dock	15 Feb 51	28 Aug 51	7 Oct 52
PORTE ST. JEAN	180	Geo. T. Davie	16 May 50	21 Nov 50	4 June52
PORTE ST. LOUIS	183	Geo. T. Davie	21 Mar 51	22 July 52	28 Aug 52

Displacement, tons	429 full load
Dimensions, feet	125·5 × 26·3 × 13
Guns	1—40 mm AA
Main engines	Diesel; A/C Electric; 1 shaft; 600 bhp = 11 knots
Complement	3 officers; 20 ratings

Of trawler design. Multi-purpose vessels used for operating the gates in the A/S booms, fleet auxiliaries, anti-submarine netlayers for entrances to defended harbours, Capable of being fitted for minesweeping. Designation changed from YNG to YMG in 1954. *Porte Dauphine* is on loan to the Department of Transport. *Porte St. Jean* and *Porte St. Louis* are used during the summer for the training of Reserves on the Great Lakes. Photographs of *Porte St. Jean* appear in the 1952-53 to 1960-61 and 1962-63 to 1965-66 editions, and of *Porte Quebec* in the 1961-62 edition.

PORTE ST. LOUIS — *1966, Royal Canadian Navy, Official*

ANTI-SUBMARINE HYDROFOIL (FHE)

BRAS D'OR (FHE 400)

Displacement, tons	180
Dimensions, feet	150·8 oa × 21·5 × 15 (hull depth); 23 (hull-borne draught); 7·5 (60 knots draught); foil base 90
Main engines	Pratt & Whitney FT4A—2 gas turbine when foil-borne; 22 000 shp = 50 to 60 knots Davey-Paxman diesel when hull-borne, 2 000 shp = 12 to 15 knots P & W. ST-6A gas turbine for hull-borne boost and foil-borne auxiliary power; 390 shp

De Havilland Aircraft of Canada Ltd, Toronto, designed this prototype all-weather, ocean-going hydrofoil craft. Completion was delayed by fire on 7 Nov 1966. Designated FHE for Fast Hydrofoil Escort. The supercavitating bow foil has a 22·5 ft span and the delayed cavitation main-foil has a 65 ft span. Marine Industries Ltd, Sorel, Que, were the sub-contractor for the assembly and outfitting of the vessel, of welded all-aluminium construction. Named *Bras d'Or* in recognition of early work on hydrofoils by Alexander Graham Bell and F. W. Baldwin on Bras d'Or Lake, Cape Breton Island. Photograph showing foils in the 1968-69 edition.

BRAS d'OR — *1969, Canadian Maritime Command, Official*

PATROL CRAFT (PCS)

4 "BIRD" CLASS SMALL SUBMARINE CHASERS

BLUE HERON
CORMORANT (PCS 781)
LOON (PCS 780)
MALLARD (PCS 783)

Displacement, tons	66 full load
Dimensions, feet	92 × 17 × 5·3
Guns	1—20 mm Oerlikon AA
A/S weapons	Hedgehog and depth charges
Main engines	2 diesels; 1 200 bhp = 14 knots
Complement	21

Loon, first of the class, commissioned on 14 Dec 1955. Designed for harbour patrol and training. Primarily of wood and aluminium construction. Fitted with sonar and anti-submarine apparatus. *Blue Heron* was lent to the Marine Section of the Royal Canadian Mounted Police from 1956 until 1968. A photograph of *Loon* appears in the 1956-57 to 1963-64 editions. All are now in reserve.

CORMORANT — *Official*

DIVING TENDERS

YMT 11 **YMT 12**

Displacement, tons	110
Dimensions, feet	88 × 20 × 4·8 mean
Main engines	GM diesels; 228 bhp = 10·75 knots

YMT 11 was completed in Jan 1962 and YMT 12 on 7 Aug 1963, both by Ferguson Industries Ltd, Picton, Nova Scotia. They can dive four men at a time to a depth of 250 feet and are fitted with a recompression chamber. A photograph of YMT 11 appears in the 1962-63 edition.
There are small diving tenders YMT 6, YMT 8, YMT 9 and YMT 10, 70 tons, 75 × 18·5 × 8·5 feet, 2 diesels 165 bhp, YMT 1 (46 ft) was transferred to the Naval Research Establishment as a yard craft. YMT 3 and YMT 5 were declared surplus and sold in 1963. YMT 2 and YMT 7 are 46-ft, wooden hulled single screw vessels. Two new diving tenders, YSD 1 and YSD 2, entered service in 1965.
Also torpedo recovery vessels *Nimpkish*, YMR 120, and *Songhee*, YMR 1. The yacht *Oriole*, QW 3, used for officer cadet training, has been in commission since 1953.

OILERS (AO)

(AO) 2 "DUN" CLASS

DUNDALK (AOC 50) **DUNDURN** (AOC 502)

Displacement, tons 950
Dimensions, feet 178·8 × 32·2 × 13
Main engines Diesel; 700 bhp = 10 knots

Small vessels designated tankers, and classed as fleet auxiliaries. A photograph of *Dundalk* appears in the 1949-50 to 1959-60 editions.

DUNDURN *1969, courtesy Mr. G. R. Hooper (Master)*

TUGS

3 "SAINT" CLASS

Name	*No.*	*Laid down*	*Launched*	*Completed*
SAINT ANTHONY	ATA 531	15 July 1954	2 Nov 1955	22 Feb 1957
SAINT CHARLES	ATA 533	28 Apr 1954	10 July 1956	7 June 1957
SAINT JOHN	ATA 535	1 Dec 1953	14 May 1956	23 Nov 1956

Displacement, tons 840 full load
Dimensions, feet 151·5 × 33 × 17
Guns 2—40 mm Bofors AA
Main engines Diesel; 1 shaft; 1 920 bhp = 14 knots

Ocean tugs. Authorised under the 1951 Programme. All built by the St. John Dry Dock Co. A photograph of *Saint John* appears in the 1957-58 to 1959-60 editions.

3 "TON" CLASS

CLIFTON (ATA 529) **HEATHERTON** (ATA 527) **RIVERTON** (ATA 528)

Displacement, tons 462
Dimensions, feet 104 pp; 111·2 oa × 28 × 11
Main engines Dominion Sulzer diesel; 1 000 bhp = 11 knots
Complement 17

Large harbour tugs. *Clifton* was launched on 31 July 1944. A photograph of *Heatherton* appears in the 1952-53 to 1959-60 editions.

5 "GLEN" CLASS

GLENBROOK **GLENDYNE** **GLENEVIS** **GLENLIVIT II** **GLENSIDE**

Dimensions, feet 80 × 20·7 × 7·2 (aft full load)
Main engines Diesel; 300 bhp = 9 knots

Big harbour tugs. *Glenlivit II* is loaned to Halfax Department of Public Works. Hull numbers are YTB 501 503, 502, 504 and 500, respectively. Sister tugs *Glendevon,* Y 505 and *Glendon,* Y 506 were taken out of service on 31 Mar 1964 and sold to commercial interests.

3 "WOOD" CLASS

EASTWOOD **GREENWOOD** **OAKWOOD**

Dimensions, feet 60 oa × 16 × 5 (aft full load)
Main engines 250 hp = 10 knots

Medium harbour tugs. Used as A/S Target Towing Vessels. Launched 1944. Hull numbers are YMT 550, 551 and 554 respectively. *Wildwood* was stricken from the Navy List in 1959. *Lakewood* was declared surplus in 1966.
Other medium harbour tugs are:

FT1, FT2. Employed as fire tugs, Hull numbers YMT 556 and 557 respectively. Sister fire tug FT3, YMT 558, was taken out of service on 31 Mar 1964 and transferred to Dept of Public Works, St. John's Newfoundland.

13 "VILLE" CLASS

ADAMSVILLE **BEAMSVILLE** **LAWRENCEVILLE** **LISTERVILLE** **LOGANVILLE** **MANNVILLE** **MARYSVILLE** **MERRICKVILLE** **OTTERVILLE** **PARKSVILLE** **PLAINSVILLE** **QUEENSVILLE** **YOUVILLE**

Dimensions, feet 40 × 10·5 × 4·8
Main engines Diesel; 1 shaft; 150 bhp

Small harbour tugs. Majority employed on towing duties at Esquimalt and Halifax: Hull numbers are YTS 582, 583, 584, 578, 589, 577, 585, 581, 590, 579, 587, 586 and 588 respectively. Sister tugs *Colville,* Y 576, and *Eckville,* Y 580, were taken out of service on 31 Mar 1964 for disposal. The small harbour tugs *Shoveller* and *Valliant* Nos YTS 591 and 575, were disposed of in 1966.

DISPOSAL

The diving depot ship GRANBY, YMT 180, originally a "Bangor" (Diesel) class fleet minesweeper (AM), redesignated coastal escort (FSE) in 1953 and clearance diving depot ship (YMT) in 1959 after having been employed as a submarine rescue vessel, was declared surplus in 1967 and replaced by the ocean escort **Victoriaville**, converted to a diving depot ship and renamed **Granby** (see previous page).

The supply vessel *Seatari* (ex-*Malahat*), AKS 514, was officially deleted from the list in 1969.

R.C.M.P. MARINE DIVISION

WOOD

Displacement, tons 600
Dimensions, feet 178 oa × 29 × 9
Main engines 2 Fairbanks-Morse diesels; 2 shafts; 2660 bhp = 16 knots
Complement 60

Built by Geo. T. Davie and Sons Ltd, Lauzon, Levis, Quebec. Completed in July 1958. Used for patrol on the east coast of Canada, this ship is built of steel, strengthened against ice, with aluminium superstructure.

WOOD *1966, Director of Marine Services, Official*

FORT STEELE

Displacement, tons 85
Dimensions, feet 110 wl; 118 oa × 21 × 7
Main engines Two Paxman Ventura 12 YJCM diesels; 2 shafts; Kamewa controllable pitch propellers; 2 800 bhp = over 18 knots.
Complement 16

Completed by Canadian Shipbuilding & Engineering Ltd in Nov 1958. Patrol craft on the east coast. Built of steel with aluminium superstructure. Twin rudders.

1 "BIRD" CLASS

VICTORIA

Displacement, tons 66 full load
Dimensions, feet 92 × 17 × 5·3
Main engines 2 diesels; 1 200 bhp = 14 knots
Complement 20

Victoria was built for the RCMP by Yarrows Limited, Victoria. Completed in Dec 1955. She is a steel copy of the wooden "Bird" class inshore patrol vessels, *Loon* and *Mallard.*
Blue Heron was built for the Royal Canadian Navy by Hunter Boat Works, Orilla. Launched at Barrie, Ontario, in Dec 1955. Completed on 30 July 1956. Transferred on loan to the RCMP Marine Section on 19 Nov 1956 as a sea rescue craft. Similar to *Cormorant* (see photograph on previous page). Returned to Canadian Armed Forces in 1968.

2 75 ft "DETACHMENT" CLASS

STAND OFF **NICHOLSON**

Displacement, tons 55
Dimensions, feet 75 oa × 17 × 6·5
Main engines 2 diesel; 1 400 bhp = 16 knots
Complement 5

Both of wood construction. Both built by Smith & Rhulorel, Lunenburg NS and completed in 1967 and 1968 respectively. Intended for service on the Atlantic coast.

13 65 ft "DETACHMENT" CLASS

ACADIAN **ADVERSUS** **ALERT** **BURIN** **CAPTOR** **DETECTOR** **GANGES** **INTERCEPTOR** **MASSET** **NANAIMO** **TAHSIS** **TOFINO** **WESTVIEW**

Displacement, tons 48
Dimensions, feet 65 × 15 × 4
Main engines 1 Cummins diesel; 1 shaft; 410 bhp = 12 knots

Coastal patrol police boats built for service on the east and west coasts.

LITTLE BOW II **SIDNEY**

Displacement, tons 27
Dimensions, feet 55 × 14 × 4
Main engines 2 General Motors turbojet engines; 600 bhp = 16 knots

These turbojet craft were built as an experiment and no additions are contemplated.

6 "DETACHMENT" CLASS (GREAT LAKES)

CARNDUFF II **CHILCOOT II** **CUTKNIFE II** **MOOSOMIN II** **SHAUNAVON II** **TAGISH II**

Dimensions, feet 50 × 15 × 3
Main engines 2 diesel engines; 600 bhp = over 17 knots

A class of small, fast patrol craft built for service on the Great Lakes.
There are also *Advance, Beaver, Fort Erie, Fort Francis II, Fort St. James, Fraser, Kenora III, Port Alice, Sorel* and *Valleyfield,* 26 to 36 feet in length with petrol motors, speeds up to 27 knots. Six are on the Great Lakes and four on the West Coast. In addition to these there are also the following, *Battleford, Slide Out, Dauphin, Lac La Rouge, Moose Jaw, Bruce* and *Reliance.*

CANADIAN COAST GUARD

Administration

Minister of Transport:
Hon Paul T. Hellyer, PC, MP, BA

Deputy Minister of Transport:
Mr. O. G. Stoner, BA

Assistant Deputy Minister, Marine:
Dr Gordon W. Stead, DSC, BComm, BA, LLD, MIMarE

Director Marine Operations:
Rear Admiral Anthony H. G. Storrs, DSC, CD, RCN (Ret'd)

Establishment

The Canadian Coast Guard is a civilian service, operated by the Federal Department of Transport. It has a history dating back to Confederation, when several previously established government marine organizations were brought together as a single marine service. The name "Canadian Coast Guard" was adopted in January 1962, following a period of several years during which the fleet underwent considerable expansion in the scope of its operation and in the number of its ships.

Ships

The Canadian Coast Guard is comprised of more than 140 vessels of all types, of which around 60 are of watch-keeping size. They operate in Canadian waters from the Great Lakes to the northernmost reaches of the Arctic Archipelago.

There are heavy icebreakers, icebreaking lighthouse and buoy tending ships, marine survey craft, weather-oceanographic ships and many specialized vessels for tasks such as search and rescue, cable lifting and repair, marine research and shallow-draft operations in areas such as the Mackenzie River system and some parts of the Arctic.

The Department of Defence Productions, Ship Building and Heavy Equipment Branch arranges for the design, construction and repair of Coast Guard ships and also provides this service for a number of other Canadian Government departments.

Principal bases for the ships are the department's 11 district offices, located at— St. John's, Newfoundland; Dartmouth, N.S.; Saint John, N.B.; Charlottetown, P.E.I.; Quebec and Sorel, Que.; Prescott and Parry Sound, Ont.; Victoria and Prince Rupert, B.C.; and at Hay River, on Great Slave Lake.

Duties

Canadian Coast Guard vessels maintain and supply shore-based and floating aids to navigation in Canadian waters. In winter they assist shipping in the Gulf of St. Lawrence and East Coast waters and provide flood control icebreaking service on the St. Lawrence River In summer, in addition to carrying out duties relating to aids to navigation, the fleet provides icebreaker support for the department's convoys carrying supplies to the settlements in the Arctic. Many of the vessels also serve as floating bases for scientific parties from other Canadian Government departments and agencies engaged in oceanographic, hydrographic and related marine studies.

Weather Station "Papa" in the Pacific Ocean, 900 miles west of Victoria, B.C., is maintained by two new Canadian Coast Guard weather-oceanographic ships, "Vancouver" and "Quadra". The technical and professional staffs on these ships are provided by the Department of Transport Meteorological Branch, by the Fisheries Research Board of Canada and by other Canadian Government departments with responsibilities in the realm of the marine sciences.

The Canadian Coast Guard also carries out duties as the marine element of the search and rescue organization for which the Canadian Armed Forces have the overall responsibility.

The fleet's capabilities in the realm of search and rescue are being increased by the addition of a 235 foot deep sea cutter specially designed for this service. The contract for construction was awarded to Davie Shipbuilding Limited, Lauzon, Que., in February, 1967, with delivery scheduled for June, 1969.

The vessel will have a load displacement of 2 025 tons, a maximum shaft horsepower of 9 176 and a trial speed of 18·75 knots. It will have twin screw geared diesel power and will be fitted with a helicopter deck and a telescopic hangar.

The Department of Transport is responsible for maintaining and improving the St. Lawrence River Ship Channel from Montreal to the sea. Canadian Coast Guard vessels carry out the necessary surveys. Most recent fleet addition in this field is CCGS "Nicolet", a sounding vessel delivered by Collingwood Shipyards, Collingwood, Ontario, in December, 1966. She replaces CCGS "Frontenac" and is 166 feet six inches in length with a beam of 35 feet and a load draft of 9 feet six inches. Powered by two diesels with a total of 1 350 shaft horse-power, she has a load displacement of 850 tons.

The new ship has a full load displacement of 3 096 tons, with an overall length of 231 feet, beam of 49 feet and a load draft of 16 feet. Her propulsion is diesel electric, totalling 4 250 shaft horsepower and driving two propellers. She is equipped with a helicopter deck and telescoping hangar aft.

New Construction

Scheduled for delivery in 1969 is CCGS "Louis S. St-Laurent", a triple screw icebreaker for service in eastern Canadian waters and the Canadian Arctic. Built by Canadian Vickers Limited of Montreal, the ship is the largest non-nuclear powered icebreaker in the world. She is a turbo-electric powered vessel with a total of 24 000 shaft horsepower. She carries two helicopters in a below-decks hangar, with an elevator to the flight deck. Cruising range is 16 000 miles at 13 knots.

She is 366 feet six inches long, 80 feet wide and has a draft of 31 feet.

An icebreaker for use in the Gulf of St. Lawrence. East Coast and Arctic waters, CCGS "Norman McLeod Rogers" is being built by Canadian Vickers Limited, for delivery in July, 1969. The ship measures 295 feet overall, with a width of 62 feet six inches and a draft of 20 feet.

Main engines will be four diesel and two gas turbine generators powering two electric propulsion motors, developing a total of 12 000 shaft horsepower on two propellers.

An icebreaking lighthouse and buoy vessel, named CCGS "Tracy", built at Port Weller Dry Docks, Port Weller, Ont, has been delivered. She replaces the old steamship CCGS "Safeguarder", which has been retired. The new ship is 181 feet six inches long with a beam of 38 feet and a load draft of 12 feet, her displacement being 1 270 tons. She is a twin screw vessel with two diesel engines developing a total of 2 000shp.

Two light icebreaking lighthouse and buoy tenders are being built at Marine Industries, Limited, Sorel, Que. They will replace the existing old vessels CCGS "Brant" and CCGS "Sea Beacon" at Dartmouth, N.S. and St John's Newfoundland, respectively.

Both are 189 feet three inches long, with a beam of 42 feet six inches and a load draft of 16 feet 6 inches. Propulsion will be geared diesel, driving twin controllable pitch propellers. Deliveries are scheduled for May and August, 1969, respectively.

An icebreaking lighthouse and buoy tender to replace the old tender CCGS "Grenville" sunk in ice Dec 1968, on the upper St. Lawrence River and lower Great Lakes is being built at Davie Shipbuilding Limited, Lauzon, Que. She will be 234 feet long, with a beam of 49 feet and a load draft of 15 feet. Displacement will be 2 828 tons and she will be a twin screw, diesel-electric ship with a total of 4 000 shaft horsepower. Delivery is set for August 1969.

A twin screw supply and buoy vessel for service in the Saint John, New Brunswick, marine agency is under construction at Saint John Shipbuilding and Dry Dock Company yard. The vessel will be 104 feet long with a beam of 25 feet and a load draft of seven feet. Propulsion will be geared diesel with controllable pitch propellers. The engine will develop a total of 800 shaft horsepower and delivery is scheduled for the spring of 1969.

In addition, the following ships are in varying stages of planning for construction in the future; replacements for the Northern supply vessels (converted LSTs) CCGS "Gannet" and CCGS "Puffin"; a lighthouse and buoy tender to replace CCGS "Estevan" in the Victoria, British Columbia, agency; a twin semi-submerged hull (catamaran) sounding vessel for the St. Lawrence Ship Channel, and various other smaller craft.

Strength of the fleet

Full Icebreakers	9
(including general purpose icebreaking buoy and supply vessels)	
Icebreaking Cable Repair Ship	1
Light icebreaking lighthouse and buoy tenders	9
Special Arctic Service Vessel	1
Depot ship/lighthouse and buoy tender	1
Lighthouse Supply and Buoy Vessels	12
Northern Supply Vessels	6
St. Lawrence Ship Channel Work	5
St. Lawrence River Traffic Control	1
Weatherships	2
Great Lakes Marine and Meteorology Research	1
Search and rescue Cutters	11
Mackenzie River Shallow Draft Buoy Vessels	4
Steel Landing Craft	65
Lightships	2
Marine Agency Tenders	8
Shore Based Lifeboats	4
Total Canadian Coast Guard	140
Other vessels operated by the Department of Transport	
Pilotage	16
Canals work	44
	60
Total vessels operated by the Department of Transport, including Canadian Coast Guard, Pilotage and Canals	200

WEATHER SHIPS

Name	Laid down	Launched	Completed
QUADRA	Feb 1965	4 July 1966	Mar 1967
VANCOUVER	Mar 1964	29 June 1965	4 July 1966

Displacement, tons: 5 600 full load
Dimensions, feet: 361·2 pp; 404·2 oa × 50 × 17·5
Main engines: Turbo-electric; 2 shafts; 7 500 shp = 18 knots.
Boilers: 2 automatic Babcock & Wilcox D type
Range, miles: 8 400 at 14 knots
Complement: 96

New type, turbo-electric twin screw weather and oceanographic vessels for Pacific Ocean service. Both built by Burrard Drydock Limited, North Vancouver, B.C. They replace the Coast Guard weather ships, former frigates, which have been in service for many years, on loan from the Royal Canadian Navy, for Ocean Station "Papa" 900 miles west of the British Colombia coast. They have bow water jet reaction system to assist steering at slow speeds. Flume stabilization systems are fitted. They are turbo-electric powered, with oil-fired boilers to provide the quiet operation needed for vessels housing much scientific equipment. Their complement includes 15 technical officers such as meteorologists, oceanographers and electronics technicians.

QUADRA — *1969, Canadian Coast Guard, Official*

DISPOSALS

The three former "River" class frigates, *St. Catherine*, *Stonetown* and *St. Stephen* were taken out of service in 1968 to await disposal.

CABLE REPAIR SHIP

JOHN CABOT

Displacement, tons: 6 375 full load
Dimensions, feet: 313·3 × 60 × 21·5
Main engines: Diesel-electric; 2 shafts; 9 000 shp = 15 knots
Range, miles: 10 000 at 12 knots
Complement: 85 officers and men

Combination cable repair ship and icebreaker. Built by Canadian Vickers Limited, Montreal. Laid down in May 1963, launched on 15 Apr 1964 and completed in July 1965. Designed to repair and lay cable over the bow only. For use in East Coast and Arctic waters. Bow water jet reaction manoeuvring system, heeling tanks and Flume stabilisation system. Three circular storage holds handle a total of 400 miles of submarine cable. Personnel include technicians and helicopter pilots, the ship being designed for use with that type of aircraft.

JOHN CABOT — *1966, Canadian Coast Guard, Official*

NORTHERN SUPPLY VESSELS

7 FORMER TANK LANDING CRAFT (LCT 8s)

AUK EIDER GANNET PUFFIN RAVEN SKUA

Measurement, tons: 1 083 to 1 104 gross
Dimensions, feet: 225 pp; 231·2 oa × 38 × 3
Main engines: Diesel; 1 000 shp = 9 knots

Converted LCT (8)s, acquired from Great Britain in 1957-61. Built by Harland & Wolff, Belfast (*Puffin* and *Raven*), Sir Wm. Arrol & Co Ltd, Glasgow (*Eider* and *Gannet*) and Alexander Findley, Dumbarton (*Auk*). All completed in 1946. A photograph of *Skua* appears in the 1962-63 to 1964-65 editions.
Sister ship *Nanook*, officially rated as a Northern Service Depot Ship, is in reserve.

GANNET — *1965, Canadian Coast Guard, Official*

SKUA — *Canadian Coast Guard, Official*

2 FORMER TANK LANDING CRAFT (LCT 4s)

MARMOT MINK

Displacement, tons: 586 full load
Dimensions, feet: 187·2 × 33·8 × 4
Main engines: Diesel; 920 shp = 8 knots

Converted LCT(4)s acquired from Great Britain in 1958. Completed in 1944. Officially rated as Steel Landing Craft for Northern Service.

MINK — *1963, Canadian Coast Guard, Official*

MARMOT unloading on beach at Frobisher Bay, Boffin Island — *1967, Canadian Coast Guard, Official*

FULL ICEBREAKERS

1 NEW CONSTRUCTION GULF TYPE

NORMAN MCLEOD ROGERS

Displacement, tons	6 320 full load
Dimensions, feet	295 oa × 62·5 × 20
Aircraft	1 helicopter
Landing craft	2
Main engines	4 diesels and 2 gas turbines powering 2 electric motors; 2 shafts; 12 000 shp = 15 knots *service*
Complement	55

A new type of icebreaker for use in the Gulf of St Lawrence and East Coast waters. Under construction at the yard of Canadian Vickers Limited, Montreal. This is the world's first application of gas turbine electric propulsion for booster power in an icebreaker. The ship will have a flight deck with telescopic helicopter hangar. Scheduled for completion in June 1969.

NORMAN MCLEOD ROGERS (official drawing) *1967 Canadian Coast Guard*

1 NEW CONSTRUCTION LARGE TYPE

LOUIS S. ST. LAURENT

Displacement, tons	13 000 full load
Dimensions, feet	366·5 oa 80 × 31
Aircraft	2 helicopters
Main engines	Turbo-electric; 3 shafts; 24 000 shp = 17·75 knots *trials*
Range, miles	16 000 miles at 13 knots cruising speed
Complement	Total accommodations for 216

The construction of this new icebreaker for service in the Arctic and the Gulf of St Lawrence is nearing completion at Canadian Vickers Limited, Montreal. She will be larger than any of the present Coast Guard icebreakers. This triple screw ship with a steam turbo-electric propulsion system will be the world's most powerful non-nuclear powered icebreaker. She will have a helicopter hangar below the flight deck, with an elevator to raise the two helicopters to the deck when required. She was launched on 3 Dec 1966 and entered service in 1969. She was estimated to cost $18 719 075.

LOUIS S. ST. LAURENT (Artist's impression) 1966, *Canadian Coast Guard, Official*

JOHN A. MACDONALD

Displacement, tons	9 160 full load
Measurement, tons	6 186 gross
Dimensions, feet	315 × 70 × 28
Main engines	Diesel-electric; 15 000 shp = 15·5 knots designed

Completed by Davie Shipbuilding Limited, Lauzon, Port Quebec, in Sep 1960.

JOHN A. MACDONALD *1966, Canadian Coast Guard, Official*

WOLFE

Displacement, tons	3 005 full load
Measurement, tons	2 022 gross
Dimensions, feet	220 × 48 × 16
Main engines	Steam reciprocating; 4 000 ihp = 13 knots designed

Built by Canadian Vickers Limited, Montreal. Completed in Nov 1959.

WOLFE *1963, Canadian Coast Guard, Official*

CAMSELL

Displacement, tons	3 072 full load
Measurement, tons	2 020 gross
Dimensions, feet	223·5 × 48 × 16
Main engines	Diesel-electric; 4 250 shp = 13 knots designed

Completed by Burrard Dry Dock Company Limited, Vancouver, BC in Oct 1959.

CAMSELL *1967, Canadian Coast Guard, Official*

DISPOSAL

The old icebreaker **Saurel** was removed from the Canadian Coast Guard list in 1968.

SIR HUMPHREY GILBERT

Displacement, tons	3 000 full load
Measurement, tons	1 930 gross
Dimensions, feet	220 × 48 × 16·3
Main engines	Diesel-electric; 4 250 shp = 13 knots designed

Completed by Davie Shipbuilding Limited, Lauzon, Port Quebec, in June 1959.

SIR HUMPHREY GILBERT *1963, Canadian Coast Guard Official*

Full Icebreakers—*continued*

MONTCALM

Displacement, tons 3 005 full load
Measurement, tons 2 017 gross
Dimensions, feet 220 × 48 × 16·3
Main engines Steam reciprocating; 4 000 ihp = 13 knots designed

Completed by Davie Shipbuilding Limited, Lauzon, Port Quebec, in June 1957.

MONTCALM *Jan 1967, Canadian Coast Guard, Official*

LABRADOR

Displacement, tons 6 490 full load
Measurement, tons 3 823 gross
Dimensions, feet 269 pp; 290 oa × 63·5 × 29
Aircraft Provision for 2 helicopters
Main engines Diesel-electric 10 000 shp = 16 knots designed

When commissioned in the Royal Canadian Navy was rated as Arctic Patrol Vessel, Helicopter Carrier and Icebreaker. Original designation was AGB, changed to AW. No. 50 in 1954. First naval vessel to traverse the North West Passage and circumnavigate North America, when she was Canada's largest and most modern icebreaker. High-tensile steel sides 1·6 inches thick, and heeling tanks. Aircraft hangar and flight deck aft for operating helicopters. Carries two landing craft strengthened to resist ice. Latest navigational devices, and equipped with instruments for hydrography, oceanography, meteorology, cosmic ray research, ice reconnaisssance and other scientific purposes. Fitted with Denny Brown stabilisers. Propelling machinery can be controlled from bridge. She was transferred, on loan, to the Department of Transport and subsequently acquired from the Royal Canadian Navy outright. Mounting for two 40 mm forward. Guns removed.
A photograph of *Labrador* as an Arctic Patrol Vessel in the Royal Canadian Navy appears in the 1966-67 and earlier editions.
Built by Marine Industries Limited, Sorel, Quebec. Ordered in Feb 1949, laid down on 18 Nov 1949, launched on 14 Dec 1951 and completed for the Royal Canadian Navy on 8 July 1954, but transferred to the Department of Transport in Feb 1958.

LABRADOR *1965, Canadian Coast Guard, Official*

d'IBERVILLE

Displacement, tons 9 930 full load
Measurement, tons 5 678 gross
Dimensions, feet 310 × 66·5 × 30·2
Main engines Steam reciprocating; 10 800 ihp = 15 knots designed
Completed by Davie Shipbuilding Limited, Lauzon, Port Quebec, in May 1953.

d'IBERVILLE *1967, Canadian Coast Guard, Official*

ERNEST LAPOINTE

Displacement, tons 1 675 full load
Measurement, tons 1 179 gross
Dimensions, feet 184 × 36 × 15·5
Main engines Steam reciprocating; 2 000 ihp = 13 knots designed

Completed by Davie Shipbuilding Limited, Lauzon, Port Quebec, in Feb 1941.

ERNEST LAPOINTE *1966, Canadian Coast Guard, Official*

N. B. McLEAN

Displacement, tons 5 034 full load
Measurement, tons 3 254 gross
Dimensions, feet 277 × 60·5 × 19·6
Main engines Steam reciprocating; 6 500 ihp = 13 knots max

Completed by Halifax Shipyards, Limited, Halifax, NS, in 1930.

N. B. McLEAN *1966, Canadian Coast Guard, Official*

SEARCH AND RESCUE CUTTERS

RACER **RALLY** **RAPID** **READY** **RELAY**

Measurement, tons 153 gross
Dimensions, feet 95·2 × 20 × 6·5
Main engines Diesel; 2 400 bhp = 20 knots *designed*

Built by Yarrows Ltd, Esquimalt, BC; Davie Shipbuilding Ltd, Lauzon, PQ; Ferguson Industries, Picton, NS; Burrard Dry Dock, Vancouver; and Kingston Shipyard, respectively. All completed in 1963. A photograph of *Relay* appears in the 1964-65 to 1968-69 editions.

RACER *1969, Canadian Coast Guard, Official*

Search and Rescue Cutters *(continued)*

SPINDRIFT **SPRAY** **SPUME**

Measurement, tons	57 gross
Dimensions, feet	70 × 16·8 × 4·7
Main engines	2 diesels; 1 500 bhp = 19 knots *designed*

Built by Cliff Richardson Boats Ltd, Meaford, Ont; J. J. Taylor & Sons, Ltd, Toronto; and Grew Ltd, Penetanguishene, Ont, respectively. Completed in 1963-64.

SPINDRIFT *1966, Canadian Coast Guard, Official*

LIGHT ICEBREAKERS *(Supply and Buoy Vessels)*

J. E. BERNIER

Displacement, tons	3 096
Dimensions, feet	231 × 49 × 16
Main engines	Diesel Electric; 4 250 bhp = 13·5 knots (trial speed)

Built by Davie Shipbuilding Co, Ltd, Luzon, Quebec; completed August 1967.

SIMCOE

Displacement, tons	1 300 full load
Dimensions, feet	179·5 × 38 × 12
Main engines	Diesel-electric; 2 000 shp = 12 knots

Completed by Canadian Vickers in 1962. Photograph in the 1963-64 edition.

SIMON FRASER

Displacement, tons	1 876 full load
Measurement, tons	1 357 gross
Dimensions, feet	204·5 × 42 × 14
Main engines	Diesel-electric; 2 900 shp = 13·5 knots designed

Completed by Burrard Dry Dock Company Limited, N. Vancouver in Feb 1960.

THOMAS CARLETON

Displacement, tons	1 532 full load
Dimensions, feet	180 × 42 × 13
Main engines	Diesel; 2 000 bhp = 12 knots designed

Built by Saint John Dry Dock Limited, Saint John, NB: Completed in 1960.

TUPPER

Displacement, tons	1 872 full load
Measurement, tons	1 357 gross
Dimensions, feet	204·5 × 42 × 14
Main engines	Diesel-electric; 2 900 shp = 13·5 knots designed

Built by Marine Industries Limited, Sorel, Quebec. Completed in Dec 1959.

ALEXANDER HENRY

Displacement, tons	2 497 full load
Measurement, tons	1 647 gross
Dimensions, feet	210 × 43·5 × 16
Main engines	Diesel; 3 550 bhp = 13 knots designed

Built by Port Arthur Shipbuilding Limited, Port Arthur. Completed in July 1959.

SIR WILLIAM ALEXANDER

Displacement, tons	3 555 full load
Measurement, tons	2 153 gross
Dimensions, feet	227·5 × 45 × 17·5
Main engines	Diesel electric; 4 250 shp = 15 knots designed

Built by Halifax Shipyards, Limited Halifax. Completed in June 1959. Equipped with Flume Stabilisation System.

WALTER E. FOSTER

Displacement, tons	2 715 full load
Measurement, tons	1 672 gross
Dimensions, feet	229·2 × 42·5 × 16
Main engines	Steam reciprocating; 2 000 ihp = 12·5 knots designed

Built by Canadian Vickers, Limited, Montreal. Completed in Dec 1954.

EDWARD CORNWALLIS

Displacement, tons	3 700 full load
Measurement, tons	1 965 gross
Dimensions, feet	259 × 43·5 × 18
Main engines	Steam reciprocating; 2 800 ihp = 13·5 knots designed

Built by Canadian Vickers, Limited, Montreal. Completed in Dec 1949. Photograph in the 1963-64 to 1965-66 editions.

SPECIAL ARCTIC SERVICE VESSEL

C. D. HOWE

Displacement, tons	5 170 full load
Measurement, tons	3 628 gross
Dimensions, feet	276 pp; 295 oa × 50 × 18·5
Main engines	Steam reciprocating; 4 000 ihp = 13 knots max
Range, miles	10 000 with 50 per cent reserve of fuel
Capacity	Lift of forward crane 30 000 lb

Built by Davie Shipbuilding Ltd, Lauzon, P.Q. Launched in Sep 1949. Completed in June 1950. Eastern Arctic Patrol vessel and Supply Ship. Designed as multi-purpose vessel, being icebreaker, meteorological and survey ship, hospital ship, and potential fleet auxiliary for naval use in war. With an icebreaker hull she was of novel streamlined design with the latest Arctic navigational apparatus, and reinforced for limited work in ice. See photograph at top of next column.

C. D. HOWE *1969, Canadian Coast Guard, Official*

DEPOT SHIP

NARWHAL

Measurement, tons	2 064 gross
Dimensions, feet	251·5 × 42 × 12
Main engines	Diesel 2 000 bhp
Range, miles	9 200 cruising
Complement	32

Built by Canadian Vickers, Montreal and completed July 1963.

NARWHAL *1968, Canadian Coast Guard, Official*

SUPPLY VESSELS

MONTMORENCY

Displacement, tons	1 006 full load
Measurement, tons	750 gross
Dimensions, feet	163 × 34 × 11
Main engines	Diesel; 1 200 bhp

Built by Davie Shipbuilding Limited, Lauzon, Port Quebec. Completed in Aug 1957. A photograph of *Montmorency* appears in the 1963-64 to 1968-69 editions.

ESTEVAN

Displacement, tons	2 071 full load
Dimensions, feet	200 × 38 × 12
Main engines	Steam reciprocating; 1 500 ihp

Built by Collingwood Shipyards Limited. Completed in 1912, 1 161 tons gross.

MONTMAGNY

565 tons full load, 148 × 29 × 8 feet. 1 000 bhp diesel. Built by Russel Bros, Owen Sound, Ont. Completed in May 1963.

VERENDRYE

400 tons full load, 297 tons gross, 125 × 26 × 7 feet. 760 bhp diesel. Built by Geo. T. Davie & Sons, Ltd, Lauzon. Completed in Oct 1959.

SIR JAMES DOUGLAS

730 tons full load, 564 tons gross, 150 × 30 × 10·3 feet. 1 000 bhp diesel. Built by Burrard Drydock, N. Vancouver, BC. Completed in Nov 1956.

ALEXANDER MACKENZIE

736 tons full load, 556 tons gross, 150 × 30 × 10·2 feet. 1 000 bhp diesel. Built by Burrard Drydock, N. Vancouver, BC. Completed in 1950.

C. P. EDWARDS

571 tons full load, 338 tons gross, 144·2 × 27 × 9·5. Steam reciprocating. 375 ihp. Built by Collingwood Shipyards Limited. Completed in 1946.

SAFEGUARDER

665 tons gross, 160 × 29 × 11·8 feet. Steam reciprocating. 1 350 ihp. Built at Southampton, United Kingdom. Completed in 1914.

DISPOSALS

Brant was officially listed for disposal and deleted in 1967. **Chesterfield** deleted in 1968. **Grenville** sank in the St. Lawrence river in Dec 1968 due to ice action. Wreck will be salved and disposed of in 1969.

ST. LAWRENCE SHIP CHANNEL OPERATIONS

The following Coast Guard vessels operate in this area:—*Nicolet, Beauport, Ville Marie, Detector* and *Glenada*. In addition, the *Porte Dauphine* and CG No. 111 operate in the Great Lakes on Marine and Meteorology research.

CEYLON

Administration

The Royal Ceylon Navy was formed on 9 Dec 1950 when the Navy Act was proclaimed.

Captain of the Navy:
Rear Admiral Rajanathan Kadirigamar, MVO

Naval Base

The Naval Base is established at Trincomalee, which was a British base from 1795 until 1957.

Personnel

1969: 1 980 (160 officers and 1 820 ratings

Diplomatic Representation

Services Attaché in London:
Major B. Justus Rodrigo

Strength of the Fleet

1 Frigate	27 Patrol Boats
1 Hydrofoil Craft	1 Tug

Mercantile Marine

Lloyd's Register of Shipping:
26 vessels of 9 439 tons gross

FRIGATE

1 Ex-CANADIAN "RIVER" CLASS

Name	*No.*	*Builders*	*Launched*
GAJABAHU (ex-*Misnak*, ex-HMCS *Hallowell*)	F 232	Canadian Vickers Ltd, Montreal	8 Aug 1944

Displacement, tons	1 445 standard; 2 360 full load
Length, feet (*metres*)	283 (*86·3*) pp; 295·5 (*90·1*) wl; 310·5 (*91·9*) oa
Beam, feet (*metres*)	36·5 (*11·1*)
Draught, feet (*metres*)	13·8 (*4·2*)
Guns, surface	1—4 In (*102 mm*)
Guns, AA	3—40 mm
Boilers	2 three-drum type
Main engines	Triple expansion; 5 500 ihp; 2 shafts
Speed, knots	20
Radius, miles	6 000 at 12 knots
Oil fuel, tons	585
Complement	160

Acquired by Israel in 1950 and sold by Israel to Ceylon in 1959. Guns above replaced 3—4·7 inch, 8—20 mm in 1965. Sister ship *Mahasena* (ex-*Mivtakh*, ex-Canadian *Violetta*, ex-HMCS *Orkney*) was sold early in June 1964 to a Hong Kong shipbreaker.

GAJABAHU *1967, Royal Ceylon Navy, Official*

PATROL BOATS

21 THORNYCROFT TYPE

Displacement, tons	15
Dimensions, feet	45·5 × 12 × 3
Main engines	2 boats: Thornycro. K6SMI engines; 500 bhp = 25 knots 7 boats: General Motors 6-71 Series; 560 bhp = 25 knots

Fast twin screw motor launches built by Thornycroft (Malaysia) Limited in Singapore for the Ceylon Navy. The hulls are of hard chine type with double skin teak planking. Equipped as patrol boats with radar, radio, searchlight etc. Two ordered in 1965 and completed in 1966. Seven ordered in 1966 and completed in 1967. 12 more assembled in Ceylon and completed by Sep 1968—Official.

PC 97 *1967, Royal Ceylon Navy, Official*

2 "HANSAYA" CLASS

HANSAYA **LIHINIYA**

Displacement, tons	36
Dimensions, feet	63·5 pp; 66 oa × 14 × 4
Main engines	3 General Motors diesels; 450 bhp = 16 knots

"Hansaya" class long patrol boats built for the Royal Ceylon Navy at Venice by the Korody Marine Corporation.

LIHINIYA *1967, Royal Ceylon Navy, Official*

4 "SERUWA" CLASS

DIYAKAWA **KORAWAKKA** **SERUWA** **TARAWA**

Displacement, tons	13
Dimensions, feet	46 pp; 48 oa × 12 ×3
Main engines	2 Foden FD.6 diesels; 240 bhp = 15 knots

"Seruwa" class short patrol boats. A photograph of *Diyakawa* appears in the 1957-58 to 1959-60 editions, and of *Korawakka* in the 1964-65 and 1965-66 editions

SERUWA *1967, Royal Ceylon Navy, Official*

HYDROFOIL CRAFT

1 SHORT TYPE

Dimensions, feet	22·2 × 9·9 hull; 10·2 oa. Depth over side moulded: 3; Draught at anchor: 3·7; Draught at speed: 1·7, official figures.
Main engines	2 Volvo Penta Aquamatic 100 hp engines. Total 200 hp = 40 knots

A new type of short hydrofoil craft added to the Navy List in 1964.

HYDROFOIL CRAFT *1964, Royal Ceylon Navy, Official*

TUG

ALIYA (ex-*Adept*, ex-*Empire Barbara*)

Displacement, tons	503 full load
Dimensions, feet	105 × 26·5 × 12·8
Main engines	Triple expansion; 850 ihp = 10 knots

Built by Cochrane & Sons Ltd, Selby, Yorks, England. Transferred from Great Britain. Decommissioned in 1964 to be sold, but this intention was rescinded. She was re-commissioned in 1966. and underwent major refit in 1967.

ESCORT MINESWEEPERS. *Parakrama* (ex-HMS *Pickle*) was sold in June 1964 to a Hong Kong scrapyard and *Vijaya* (ex-HMS *Flyingfish*, ex-*Tillsonburg*) was returned to Britain.

SEAWARD DEFENCE BOAT. *Kotiya* (ex-HMS *Doxford*) sank in Trincomalee Harbour during the cyclone of 22 Dec 1964, and was disposed of after salvaging.

BOOM DEFENCE VESSEL. *Baron* was purchased from Great Britain by the Colombo Port Commission.

CHILE

Administration

Minister of National Defence:
General Tulio Marambio

Commander-in-Chief of the Navy:
Admiral Fernando Porta

Chief of the Naval Staff:
Rear-Admiral Patrico Caravajal

Diplomatic Representation

Chief of the Chilean Naval Mission in Great Britain and Naval Attaché in London:
Captain Carlos Chubretovich

Chief of the Chilean Naval Mission in USA and Naval Attache in Washington:
Rear-Admiral Rául Montero

Personnel

1969: 15 000 (1 000 officers and 14 000 men)

Strength of the Fleet

2 Submarines (Diesel Powered)
2 Cruisers
4 Destroyers
4 Escort destroyers
4 Torpedo Boats
25 Support Ships and Service Craft

Mercantile Marine

Lloyd's Register of Shipping:
130 vessels of 268 641 tons gross

Silhouettes

Scale: 150 feet = 1 inch

PRAT

RIVEROS

O'HIGGINS

BLANCO ENCALADA, COCHRANE

SUBMARINES

Name	*No.*	*Builders*	*Launched*	*Completed*
SIMPSON (ex-USS *Spot*, SS 413)	SS 21	Mare Island Navy Yard	20 May 1944	3 Aug 1944
THOMSON (ex-USS *Springer*, SS 414)	SS 20	Mare Island Navy Yard	3 Aug 1944	18 Oct 1944

2 Ex-US "BALAO" CLASS

THOMSON — *1968, Chilean Navy, Official*

Displacement, tons	1,526 standard; 1 816 surface; 2 425 submerged
Length, feet (*metres*)	311·6 (*95·0*)
Beam, feet (*metres*)	27 (*8·2*)
Draught, feet (*metres*)	17 (*5·2*)
Torpedo tubes	10—21 in (*533 mm*), 6 bow and 4 stern
Main engines	6 500 hp GM 2-stroke diesels; 4 610 hp electric motors
Speed, knots	20 on surface, 10 submerged
Radius, miles	12 000 at 10 knots
Oil fuel (tons)	300
Complement	80

Thomson was transferred at San Francisco, Calif, on 23 Jan 1961. *Simpson* was transferred end of 1961. *Thomson* was completely overhauled in USA in 1966 during which a high sail was installed.

SIMPSON — *1969, Chilean Navy, Official*

O'HIGGINS (see next page) — *1969, Chilean Navy, Official*

CRUISERS (*Cruceros*)

Name	*No.*	*Builders*	*Laid down*	*Launched*	*Completed*
O'HIGGINS (ex-USS *Brooklyn*, CL 40)	CL 02	New York Navy Yard	12 Mar 1935	30 Nov 1936	18 July 1938
PRAT (ex-USS *Nashville*, CL 43)	CL 03	New York S.B. Corp.	24 Jan 1935	2 Oct 1937	25 Nov 1938

2 "PRAT" CLASS Ex-US "BROOKLYN" CLASS

Displacement, tons	
O'Higgins	9 700 standard; 13 000 full load
Prat	10 000 standard; 13 500 full load
Length, feet (*metres*)	608·3 (*185·4*) oa
Beam, feet (*metres*)	69 (*21·0*)
Draught, feet (*metres*)	24 (*7·3*) max
Aircraft	2 Helicopters (see *Hangar* notes)
Guns, surface	15—6 in (*153 mm*) 47 cal (5 triple); 8—5 in (*127 mm*) 25 cal (single)
Guns, AA	28—40 mm; 24—20 mm
Armour, inches (*mm*)	Belt 4 in—1½ in (*102—38*); Decks 3 in+2 in (*76+51*); Turrets 5 in—3 in (*127—76*); C.T. 8 in (*203*)
Boilers	8 Babcock & Wilcox Express type
Main engines	Westinghouse geared turbines 100 000 shp; 4 shafts
Speed, knots	32·5
Range, miles	14 500 at 15 knots
Oil fuel (tons)	2 100
Complement	888 to 975 (peace)

Former "light" cruisers of the US "Brooklyn" Class. Purchased from the United States in 1951 at a price representing 10 per cent of their original cost ($37 000 000) plus the expense of reconditioning them.

HANGAR. The hangar in the hull right aft could accommodate 6 aircraft if necessary together with engine spares and duplicate parts, though 4 aircraft was the normal capacity. The existence of this hangar resulted in a very wide and nearly flat counter and high freeboard aft and also gave the after guns higher command. Above the hangar two catapults were mounted as far outboard as possible, and a revolving crane was placed at the stern extremity overhanging the aircraft hatch.

DRAWING. Port elevation and plan. Scale 128 feet = 1 inch.

PRAT 1969, Chilean Navy, Official

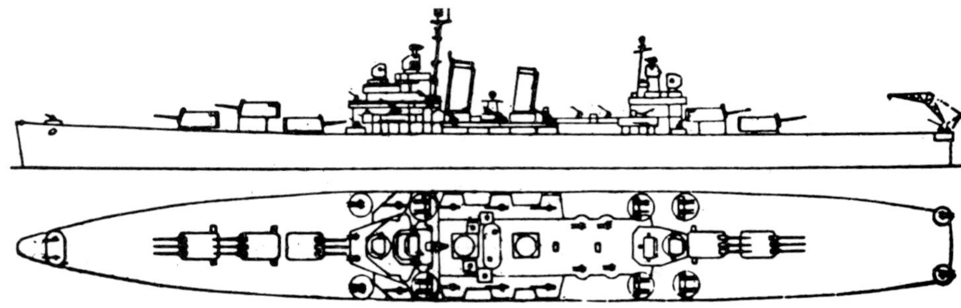

DESTROYERS (*Destructores*)

Name	*No.*	*Builders*	*Laid down*	*Launched*	*Completed*
RIVEROS	DD 18	Vickers-Armstrongs Ltd, Barrow	12 Apr 1957	12 Dec 1958	31 Dec 1960
WILLIAMS	DD 19	Vickers-Armstrongs Ltd, Barrow	20 June 1956	5 May 1958	26 Mar 1960

2 "ALMIRANTE" CLASS

Displacement, tons	2 730 standard; 3 300 full load
Length, feet (*metres*)	402 (*122·5*) oa
Beam, feet (*metres*)	43 (*13·1*)
Draught, feet (*metres*)	13·3 (*4·0*)
Missiles, AA	Quadruple launcher for "Seacat"
Guns, AA	4—4 in (*102 mm*); 6—40 mm
A/S	2 Squid 3-barrelled DC mortars
Torpedo tubes	5—21 in (*533 mm*) quintupled
Boilers	2 Babcock & Wilcox
Main engines	Parsons Pametrada geared turbine 54 000 shp; 2 shafts
Speed, knots	34·5
Range, miles	6 000 at 16 knots
Complement	266

Ordered in May 1955. Layout and general arrangements are conventional. Bunks fitted for entire crew.

OPERATIONAL. The Operations Room and other similar spaces are air-conditioned. There are twin rudders for exceptional manoeuvrability. The ventilation and heating systems have been designed to suit the Chilean coastline, extending from the tropics to Cape Horn. The latest type of warship radar is fitted, specially developed for these ships to work in conjunction with new fire control systems developed by Vickers-Armstrongs.

GUNNERY. The main armament is disposed in four single mountings, two superimposed forward and two aft. The 4-inch guns are entirely automatic with a range of 12 500 yards (11 400 metres) and an elevation of 75 degrees.

WILLIAMS 1969, Chilean Navy, Official

MISSILES. British "Seacat" radar controlled short range surface-to-air weapon installations were fitted at the Chilean Navy Yard at Talcahuano in 1964.

ELECTRICAL. The electrical system is on alternating current. Galleys are all electric. There is widespread use of fluorescent lighting. Degausing cables are fitted.

RIVEROS 1969, Chilean Navy, Official

Destroyers—*continued*

Name	*No.*	*Builder*	*Launched*	*Completed*
BLANCO ENCALADA (ex-USS *Wadleigh* DD 689)	DD 14	Bath Iron Works Corpn, Bath	7 Aug 1943	19 Oct 1943
COCHRANE (ex-USS *Rooks*, DD 804)	DD 15	Todd Pacific Shipyards	6 June 1944	2 Sep 1944

2 Ex-US "FLETCHER" CLASS

Displacement, tons	2 100 standard; 2 750 full load
Length, feet (*metres*)	376·5 (*110·5*) oa
Beam, feet (*metres*)	39·5 (*12·0*)
Draught, feet (*metres*)	18 (*5·5*) max
Guns, dual purpose	4—5 in (*127 mm*) 38 cal.
Guns, AA	6—3 in (*76 mm*) 50 cal.
Torpedo tubes	5—21 in (quintupled)
A/S	2 Hedgehogs; 2 side launching torpedo racks; 1 DC rack; 6 "K" DCT
Boilers	4 Babcock & Wilcox
Main engines	2 GE geared turbines 60 000 shp; 2 shafts
Range, miles	6 000 at 15 knots
Oil fuel (tons)	650
Speed, knots	35
Complement	250 (14 officers, 236 men). Accommodation for 324 (24 officers, 300 men)

Former United States destroyers of the "Fletcher" class. Transferred to Chile under the Military Aid Program in 1963.

TRANSFERS. Three more destroyers were scheduled for transfer from the United States Navy to the Chilean Navy under a new transfer law signed by the President of the United States in 1966 whereby the United States was lending or donating warships to friendly nations. The ships were to have been refitted and modernised and adapted to Chilean requirements before transfer to the new flag.

But priority was given to the purchase from the United States Navy in Nov 1966 of four destroyer escort transports, namely *Daniel T. Griffin*, APD 38 (ex-DE 54), *Jack C. Robinson*, APD 72 (ex-DE 671 , *Joseph E. Campbell*, APD 49 (ex-DE 70) and *Odum*, APD 71 (ex-DE 670), transferred for service in the Chilean Navy in 1967 (see under Transports on page 53).

DISPOSALS
Of the six destroyers of the "Serrano" class, all built by John Thornycroft & Co Ltd, Southampton, in 1927-29, *Hyatt*, *Orella*, *Riquelme* and *Serrano* were stricken from the Navy List in Jan 1963, and *Aldea* and *Videla* in 1958.

BLANCO ENCALADA — *1966, A. Ross*

COCHRANE — *1969, Chilean Navy, Official*

ESCORT DESTROYERS

SERRANO DE 26 (ex-USS *Odum* APD 71)
ORELLA DE 27 (ex-USS *Jack C. Robinson* APD 72)
RIQUELME DE 28 (ex-USS *Joseph E. Campbell* APD 49)
URIBE DE 29 (ex-USS *Daniel Griffin* APD 38)

Displacement, tons	1 400 standard; 2 130 full load
Dimensions, feet	300 wl; 306 oa × 37 × 12·6
Guns	1—5 in 38 cal dp; 6—40 mm AA
Main engines	GE turbo-electric; 2 shafts; 12 000 shp = 23·6 knots
Boilers	2 "D" Express

These units were purchased from the USA and arrived in Chile during 1967; they are being modernised for use as escort destroyers.

DISPOSALS
Of the three ex-Canadian frigates of the "River" class, *Baquedano* (ex-*Esmeralda*, ex-HMCS *Glace Bay*, ex-*Lauzon*) and *Iquique* (ex-HMCS *Joliette*) were officially withdrawn from service in 1965, and *Covadonga* (ex-*Seacliffe*, ex-*Megantic*) in 1968 to be disarmed and disposed of.

Of the three ex-Canadian corvettes of the "Flower" class, *Papudo* (ex-HMCS *Thorlock*, was withdrawn from service in 1965, and *Casma* (ex-*Stellarton*) and *Chipana* (ex-*Strathroy*) were officially deleted from the actual list in 1968 to be disarmed and disposed of in due course.

SERRANO — *1969, Chilean Navy, Official*

ORELLA — *1968, Chilean Navy, Official*

PATROL VESSELS

PC 1646
Authorised for construction in the USA for transfer to Chile under MAP.

	Pennant No.	Launched
LAUTARO (ex-USS *ATA 122*)	PP 62	27 Nov 1942
LIENTUR (ex-USS *ATA 177*)	PP 60	5 June 1944

Displacement, tons	534 standard; 835 full load
Dimensions, feet	134·5 wl; 143 oa × 33 × 13·2 max
Guns	1—3 in AA; 2—20 mm AA
Main engines	GM diesel-electric; 1 500 shp = 12·5 knots
Oil fuel, tons	187
Complement	33

Former United States Navy auxiliary ocean tugs of the ATA type ("Maricopa" class), originally ocean rescue tugs (ATRs), transferred to the Chilean Navy and reclassified as patrol vessels. Launch dates above. Built by Levingstone Shipbuilding Co, Orange, Texas, USA.
LOSS. Sister ship *Leucoton* (ex-USS *ATA 200*) PP 61 ran aground on a sand bank on 15 Aug 1965 and was lost as a result of a heavy coastal storm during salvage operations

LAUTARO *1969, Chilean Navy, Official*

SURVEY SHIP

YELCHO (ex-USS *Tekesta*, ATF 93) Pennant No. AGS 64

Displacement, tons	1 235 standard; 1 675 full load
Dimensions, feet	195 wl; 205 oa × 38·5 × 15·3 max
Guns	1—3 in; 4—40 mm AA; 2—20 mm AA
Main engines	4 diesels with electric drive; 3 000 bhp = 16·5 knots
Complement	85

Former United States fleet ocean tug of the ATF type ("Apache" class) fitted with powerful pumps and other salvage equipment. *Yelcho* was built by Commercial Iron Works, Portland, Oregon, laid down on 7 Sep 1942, launched on 20 Mar 1943, completed on 16 Aug 1943, and loaned to Chile by the USA on 15 May 1960, having since been employed as Antarctic research ship and surveying vessel.
LOSS. Sister ship *Janequeo* (ex-USS *Potawatomi, ATF 109*) AGS 65 sank with all hands on 15 Aug 1965 during the salvage operations of *Leucoton*, see above.

YELCHO *1969, Chilean Navy, Official*

HELICOPTER SUPPORT SHIP
(BARCAZA PORTA-HELICOPTERO)

AGUILA ARV 135 (ex-USS *Aventinus*, ARVE 3, ex-LST 1092)

Displacement, tons	1 625 light; 4 100 full load
Dimensions, feet	316 wl; 328 oa × 50 × 11·2
Guns	8—40 mm AA
Main engines	GM diesels; 2 shafts; 1 800 bhp = 11·6 knots

Former United States aircraft repair ship (engine). Built by American Bridge Co, Ambridge, Pa. Laid down on 8 Jan 1945, launched on 24 Mar 1945, and completed on 19 May 1945. Transferred to the Chilean Navy by USA in 1963 under the Military Aid Program. Also used as destroyer tender and submarine repair ship.
There is also *Mutilla*, ARD 132, former US auxiliary repair dry dock *ARD 32*, leased to Chile on 15 May 1960: 5 200 tons displacement, 492 × 84 × 5·7 to 33·2 feet.

AGUILA *1965, Chilean Navy, Official*

TORPEDO BOATS

FRESIA 81 **GUACOLDA** 80 **QUIDORA** 82 **TEGUALDA** 83

Displacement, tons	134
Dimensions, feet	118·1 × 18·4 × 7·2
Guns	2—40 mm AA
Tubes	4—21 in
Main engines	Diesels; 2 shafts; 4 800 bhp = 32 knots
Radius, miles	1 500 at 15 knots
Complement	20

Built in Spain at Cadiz to German Lürssen design. *Fresia* and *Guacolda* were delivered on 9 Dec 1965 and 30 July 1965, respectively, *Quidora* and *Tegualda* in 1966. A photograph of *Guacolda* appears in the 1968-69 edition.

QUIDORA *1969, Chilean Navy, Official*

LANDING CRAFT *(Barcazas)*

ASPIRANTE MOREL (ex-USS *Aloto, LSM 444*) LSM 92

Displacement, tons	743 standard; 1 095 full load
Dimensions, feet	196·5 wl; 203·5 oa × 34·5 × 7·3
Main engines	Diesel; 2 shafts; 2 800 bhp = 12 knots
Oil fuel (tons)	60
Radius, miles	2 500
Complement	60

Former United States medium landing ship launched in 1945. *Aspirante Morel* (ex-*Aloto*) was leased to Chile on 2 Sep 1960 at Pearl Harbour to replace the older LSM of the name.
Sister ships, *Aspirante Morel* (ex-USS *LSM 417*) was withdrawn from service in 1958, *Guardiamarine Contreras* (ex-USS *LSM 113*) in 1959, and *Aspirante Izaza* (ex-USS *LSM 259*) in 1965. *Aspirante Goicolea* (ex-USS *LSM 400*) withdrawn in 1967.

ELICURA LSM **OROMPELLO** LSM 94

Displacement, tons	290 light; 750 full load
Dimensions, feet	138 wl; 145 oa × 34 × 12·8
Main engines	Diesels; 2 shafts; 900 bhp = 10·5 knots
Oil fuel (tons)	77
Radius, miles	2 900
Complement	20

Orompello was built for the Chilean Government by Dade Drydock Corporation, Miami, Florida, and transferred on 15 Sep 1964. *Elicura* was built at Talcahuano, launched on 21 April 1967, and handed over on 10 December 1968.

GRUMETE BOLADOS LCU 95 **GRUMETE TELLEZ** LCU 93
GRUMETE DIAZ LCU 96

Displacement, tons	143 to 160 light; 309 to 329 full load
Dimensions, feet	105 wl; 119 oa × 32·7 × 5 max
Main engines	Diesel; 3 shafts; 675 bhp = 10 knots
Oil fuel (tons)	11
Radius, miles	700 at 7 knots
Complement	12

Former United States tank landing craft of the LCT (6) type. *Grumete Boladdos, Grumete Diaz* and *Grumete Tellez* are ex-LCU 1273, ex-LCU 1396 and ex-LCU 1458. Launched in 1944. Transferred in 1960.
Of the six landing craft of the "Cabo Bustos" class, *Cabo Bustos* was converted into a harbour ammunition barge and *Eduardo Llanos* and *Soldado Canaves* were officially withdrawn from service in 1965; and sister ships *Grumete Bolados, Grumete Diaz* and *Grumete Tellez were* withdrawn from service in 1959.

SMALL PATROL VESSELS

FUENTEALBA WPC 75 **ODGER** WPC 76

Displacement, tons	215 max
Dimensions, feet	80 × 21 × 9
Guns	1—20 mm AA
Main engines	One Cummins diesel 340 hp = 9 knots
Radius, miles	2 600

Both these vessels were built in Chile by Astilleros Y Maeslronzas De La Armada (ASMAR); *Fuentealba* was completed 22 July 1966 and *Odger* 21 April 1967.

FUENTEALBA *1968, Chilean Navy, Official*

TRANSPORTS

AQUILES AP-47 (ex-Danish *Tjaldur*)

Displacement, tons	2 660 registered; 1 462 net; 1 395 dw
Dimensions, feet	288 × 44 × 17
Main engines	1 Slow Burmeister and Wain Diesel; 3 600 bhp = 16 knots
Range, miles	5 500
Complement	60 crew plus 447 troops

Ex-Danish MV built in 1953 by Aalborg Verft, Denmark, bought by Chile in 1967.

AQUILES *1968, Chilean Navy, Official*

PILOTO PARDO AP 45

Displacement, tons	1 250 light; 2 000 standard; 3 000 full load
Dimensions, feet	269 × 39 × 15
Aircraft	1 helicopter
Main engines	2 diesel-electric; 2 000 hp = 14 knots
Complement	44 (plus 24 passengers)

Built by Haarlemsche Scheepsbouw Mij, Haarlem, Netherlands. Antarctic patrol ship, transport and research vessel with reinforced hull to navigate in ice. For special service in Southern Ocean. Officially listed as transport. Delivered in 1959.

The former transport *Presidente Pinto*, AKA 41 (ex-USS *Zenobia*, *AKA* 52), latterly employed as a training ship, was relegated for use as an auxiliary harbour ship in 1968. The transport *Angamos*, AP 48, was officially deleted from the list in 1968 to await disposal.

PILOTO PARDO *1969, Chilean Navy, Official*

OILERS

ARAUCANO

Displacement, tons	17 300
Measurement, tons	18 030 deadweight
Dimensions, feet	497·6 × 74·9 × 28·8
Guns	4—40 mm
Main engines	B and W diesels; 10 800 bhp = 14·5 knots (17 on trials)
Range, miles	12 000

New naval tanker built by Burmeister & Wain, Copenhagen, Denmark. Launched 21 June 1967. Sailed on 19 Jan 1967 from Copenhagen to Chile.

ARAUCANO *1968, Chilean Navy, Official*

ALMIRANTE JORGE MONTT AO 52

Displacement, tons	9 000 standard; 17 500 full load
Measurement, tons	11 800 gross; 17 750 deadweight
Dimensions, feet	548 × 67·5 × 30
Main engines	Rateau Bretagne geared turbine; 1 shaft; 6 300 shp = 14 knots
Boilers	2 Babcock & Wilcox
Radius, miles	16 500 at 14 knots

Naval squadron supply tanker. Built by Ateliers et Chantiers de la Seine Maritime, Le Trait, France. Laid down in 1954. Launched on 14 Jan 1956. Completed in Mar 1956.

ALMIRANTE JORGE MONTT *1969, Chilean Navy, Official*

TUGS

2 "CABRALES" CLASS

CABRALES ATA 71 **COLOCOLO** ATA 73

Displacement, tons	790
Dimensions, feet	126·5 × 27 × 12 mean
Main engines	Triple expansion; 1 050 shp = 11 knots
Fuel, tons	130 coal (except *Cabrales*, 135 oil)

All built by Bow, McLachlan & Co, Paisley. Formerly classed as coastguard vessels. *Cabrales* was launched on 24 Oct 1929, converted to oil firing in 1959, and reclassified as a harbour tug in 1968. Of three sister ships *Janequeo* was withdrawn from service in 1958, *Sobenes* in 1965, and *Galvarino* in 1968.

ANCUD (YT 104) **CORTEZ** (YT 128) **REYES** (YT 120)
CAUPOLICAN (YT 127) **MONREAL** (YT 105) **UGARTE** (YT 107)

Fortuna (YT 123) and *Galvez* (YT 102) were withdrawn from service in 1965, and *Moctezuma* (YT 108) in 1968. *Yagan* (YT 126) was lost in 1964 while assisting a merchant ship during a storm.
Of the two harbour tugs of the "Huemul" class, *Contramaestre Brito* (ex-*Pelantaro*) was lost, and *Huemul* was disposed of in 1968.

TRAINING SHIPS

ESMERALDA (ex-*Don Juan de Austria*) BE 43

Displacement, tons	3 040 standard; 3 673 full load
Dimensions, feet	308·8 oa; 260 pp × 43 × 23 max
Guns	2—57 mm
Sail area	Total 26 910 sq feet
Main engines	1 Fiat auxiliary diesel. 1 shaft; 1 400 bhp = 11 knots
Range, miles	8 000
Complement	271 plus 80 cadets

Four-masted schooner completed in 1952. Built in Spain by the Echevarrieta Yard, Cadiz, and originally intended for the Spanish Navy. Transferred to Chile on 12 May 1953. Near sister ship of *Juan Sebastian de Elcano* in the Spanish Navy. Similar to the Brazilian training ship *Almirante Sadanha*. Replaced transport *Presidente Pinto* as training ship.

ESMERALDA *1965, Chilean Navy, Official*

PEOPLE'S REPUBLIC OF CHINA

Administration

Commander-in-Chief of the Navy:
Vice-Admiral Hsiao

Pennant Numbers

Block numbering system:—
Submarines: 100 series; Major Surface Ships: 200 series; Amphibious Ships: 300 series.

Strength of the Fleet

33 Diesel Powered Submarines
4 Destroyers
17 Frigates and Escorts
24 Submarine Chasers (Patrol Vessels)
380 Fast Torpedo/Missile/Gunboats
22 Coast/River Defence Vessels
26 Minesweepers
70 Amphibious Types/Landing Ships
35 Auxiliaries
375 Miscellaneous Service Craft

Personnel

1969: 126 000 officers and men, including 16 000 naval air force and 28 000 marines.

Mercantile Marine

Lloyd's Register of Shipping:
239 vessels of 765 545 tons gross

SUBMARINES

1 "G" CLASS. BALLISTIC MISSILE TYPE

"G" class — *1966, col. Breyer*

Displacement, tons	2 350 surface; 2 800 submerged
Length, feet (*metres*)	320 (*97·5*)
Beam, feet (*metres*)	28 (*8·5*)
Draught, feet (*metres*)	22 (*6·7*)
Guided weapons	3 vertical tubes for missiles
Torpedo tubes	6—21 in (*533 mm*) forward
Main engines	3 diesels, total 6 000 hp (surface) Electric motors (submerged)
Speed, knots	17·6 on surface, 17 submerged
Radius, miles	22 700 surface cruising
Complement	86 (12 officers, 74 men)

Ballistic missile submarines of the Soviet "G" Class. Built at Dairen in 1964. Missiles have 380 miles range. Tubes are fitted in conning tower.

4 "R" CLASS

111 **112** **113** **114**

Four submarines of the Soviet "R" class, of the above pennant numbers, are reported to have been lent or leased. See particulars in the USSR section.

21 SOVIET "W" CLASS

Displacement, tons	1 050 standard; 1 300 surface; 1 600 submerged
Length, feet (*metres*)	245 (*74·7*) oa
Beam, feet (*metres*)	24 (*7·3*)
Draught, feet (*metres*)	14 (*4·3*)
Guns, dual purpose	2—25 mm
Torpedo tubes	6—21 in (*533 mm*); 4 forward 2 aft (20 torpedoes or 40 mines)
Main engines	Diesel-electric; 2 shafts; 4 000 bhp diesels (surface); 2 500 hp electric motors (submerged)
Speed, knots	17 on surface, 15 submerged
Radius, miles	13 000 to 16 500
Complement	60

Medium size, streamlined, long range boats similar to those built in the Soviet Union. Equipped with snort. Fitted for minelaying. Assembled from Soviet components in Chinese yards between 1956 and 1964.

4 Ex-SOVIET "S-1" CLASS

S 400 **S 401** **S 402** **S 403**

Displacement, tons	780 standard; 840 surface; 1 050 submerged
Length, feet (*metres*)	256 (*78·0*)
Beam, feet (*metres*)	21 (*6·4*)
Draught, feet (*metres*)	13 (*4·0*)
Guns, surface	1—3·9 in (*100 mm*)
Guns, AA	1—45 mm
Torpedo tubes	6—21 in (*533 mm*)
Main engines	4 200 hp diesels (surface) 2 200 hp electric motors (submerged)
Speed, knots	19 on surface; 8·5 submerged
Radius, miles	9 800 at 9 knots
Oil fuel (tons)	105
Complement	50

All launched in 1937-40. Particulars of individual boats vary slightly. Transferred from the USSR in 1954-55.

DISPOSALS
The four ex-Soviet "Shshuka" class medium type submarines (see particulars in the 1962-63 and earlier editions) were deleted from the list in 1963.

3 Ex-SOVIET "M-V" CLASS

M 201 **M 202** **M 203**

Displacement, tons	350 surface; 420 submerged
Length, feet (*metres*)	167·3 (*51·0*)
Beam, feet (*metres*)	16 (*4·9*)
Draught, feet (*metres*)	12 (*3·7*)
Guns, AA	1—45 mm; 1 MG
Torpedo tubes	2—21 in (*533 mm*)
Main engines	1 000 hp diesels (surface) 800 hp electric motors (submerged)
Speed, knots	13 on surface; 10 submerged
Radius, miles	4 000 at 8·5 knots
Oil fuel (tons)	21
Complement	24

Designed for coastal operations, now used for training and instruction. Four were transferred from the USSR in 1954-55, but *M 200* was deleted from the list in 1963.

DISPOSALS
The two smaller submarines built for coastal operations, one of the ex-Soviet "M IV" class, and one of the ex-Soviet "M 1" class, latterly used only for training and instructions, were deleted from the list in 1963.

DESTROYERS

4 Ex-SOVIET "GORDY" CLASS

ANSHAM **CHANG CHUN** **FU CHUN**

Displacement, tons	1 657 standard; 2 150 full load
Length, feet (*metres*)	357·7 (*109·0*) pp; 377 (*114·9*) oa
Beam, feet (*metres*)	33·5 (*10·2*)
Draught, feet (*metres*)	13 (*4·0*)
Guns, surface	4—5·1 in (*130 mm*)
Guns, AA	8—37 mm
A/S	8 DCT
Torpedo tubes	6—21 in (*533 mm*) tripled
Boilers	3-drum type
Main engines	Tosi geared turbines 50 000 shp; 2 shafts
Speed, knots	36
Oil fuel (tons)	500
Complement	250

CHANG CHUN — *Hajime Fukaya*

Of Odero-Terni-Orlando design. All launched in 1936-41. Fitted for minelaying. Two "Skoryi" class destroyers are also reported to have been acquired from USSR.

The old light cruiser *Pei Ching* (ex-*Huang Ho*, ex-*Victory*, ex-*Chungking*, ex-HMS *Aurora*, became a hulk. For particulars see 1959-60 and earlier deitions.

FRIGATES

1 IMPROVED "KIANGNAN" CLASS

No. 209

Displacement, tons	1 800
Length, feet (*metres*)	298 (*90·8*)
Beam, feet (*metres*)	33·5 (*10·2*)
Guns, dual purpose	6—3·9 in (*100 mm*) (3 twin)

Built at Canton in 1968 of different design to original "Kiangnan" class with two twin guns forward and one aft.

4 "KAINGNAN" CLASS ESCORTS

CH'ENG TU **KUEI YANG**
KUEI LIN **K'UN MING**

Displacement, tons	1 200 standard; 1 600 full load
Length, feet (*metres*)	295 (*89·9*) oa
Beam, feet (*metres*)	31·5 (*9·6*)
Draught, feet (*metres*)	10 (*3·0*)
Guns, dual purpose	3—3·9 in (*100 mm*) single mounts
Guns, AA	4—37 mm
A/S	4 DC projectors
Torpedo tubes	3—21 in (*533 mm*); 3 torpedoes
Mines	50 capacity, fitted with rails
Boilers	2
Main engines	Geared turbines 24 000 shp; 2 shafts
Speed, knots	28
Oil fuel (tons)	300

First of the class, launched on 28 Apr 1956 at Hutang Shipyard, Shanghai, had light tripod mast, but was later converted with heavier mast and larger bridge as in the other three. Second vessel was launched on 26 Sep 1956. Third vessel was built at Shanghai and the fourth in 1957. Somewhat similar to the Soviet "Riga" class destroyer escorts. Two were redesigned with modified superstructure.

Frigates—*continued*

2 Ex-JAPANESE ESCORT DESTROYER TYPES

"UKURU" CLASS

HUI AN (ex-*Shisaka*)

Displacement, tons	940 standard; 1 020 full load
Length, feet (*metres*)	255 (*77·7*) wl; 258·5 (*78·8*) oa
Beam, feet (*metres*)	30 (*9·1*)
Draught, feet (*metres*)	10 (*4·0*)
Guns, surface	2—4·7 in (*120 mm*); 6 MG
Main engines	2 diesels; 4 200 bhp; 2 shafts
Speed, knots	19·5
Complement	150

Ex-Japanese "Ukuru" class escort destroyer. Launched in 1943. Completed in 1945. Rearmed in 1955.

"ETOROFU" CLASS

CHANG PAI (ex-Japanese *Oki*, ex-Chinese *Ku An*)

Displacement, tons	870 standard; 1 020 full load
Length, feet (*metres*)	237·9 (*72·5*) pp; 250 (*76·0*) wl 255 (*77·7*) oa
Beam, feet (*metres*)	30 (*9·1*)
Draught, feet (*metres*)	10 (*4·0*)
Guns, surface	2—3·9 in (*100 mm*)
Guns, AA	2—45 mm
Main engines	2 diesels; 4 200 bhp; 2 shafts
Speed, knots	19·7
Complement	150

CHANG PAI *Hajime Fukaya*

Ex-Japanese Type A or "Etorofu" class. Built by Uraga Dock Co Ltd. Laid down on 27 Feb 1942. Launched on 20 Oct 1942. Completed on 31 Mar 1943. Rearmed in 1955. One raked funnel, two pole masts with tripod bases. Sister ship of *Lin An* in Taiwan (National Republic of China) Navy.

1 Ex-JAPANESE SLOOP (GUNBOAT)

NAN CHANG (ex-Chinese *Chang Chi*, ex-Japanese *Uji*)

Displacement, tons	950 standard; 1 206 full load
Length, feet (*metres*)	249·5 (*76·1*) pp; 257·5 (*78·5*) wl 264 (*80·5*) oa
Beam, feet (*metres*)	31 (*9·4*)
Draught, feet (*metres*)	8·7 (*2·6*)
Guns, surface	2—3·9 in (*100 mm*)
Guns, AA	2—3 in (*76 mm*); 4—20 mm
Boilers	2
Main engines	2 turbines; 4 600 shp; 2 shafts
Speed, knots	20·15
Radius, miles	3 460 at 14 knots
Complement	170

Former Japanese sloop or gunboat. Built at Sakurajima Works, Osaka. Launched on 25 Sep 1940. Completed in 1941. Rearmed in 1955.

NAN CHANG *K. Long*

5 Ex-JAPANESE CORVETTE TYPES

SHEN YANG (ex-*Yuang An*, ex-*Mukden*, ex-*No. 81*)

Displacement, tons	745 standard; 810 full load
Length, feet (*metres*)	206·7 (*63·0*) pp; 216·5 (*66·0*) wl; 221·5 (*67·5*) oa
Beam, feet (*metres*)	27·5 (*8·4*)
Draught, feet (*metres*)	9·5 (*2·9*)
Guns, surface	2—3·9 in (*100 mm*)
Guns, AA	4—37 mm
Main engines	2 diesels; 1 900 bhp; 2 shafts
Speed, knots	16·5
Radius, miles	6 500 at 14 knots
Complement	136

Ex-Japanese C or No. 1 type. Built in 1944-45. Rearmed in 1955. Sister ship *Chi An* became a hulk.

CHANG SHA (ex-Chinese *Chieh* 12, ex-*No. 118*)
CHI NAN (ex-*Wei Hei*, ex-*Chieh* 6, ex-*No. 194*)
HSI AN (ex-Chinese *Chieh* 14, ex-Japanese *No. 198*)
WU CHANG (ex-Chinese *Chien* 5 ex-Japanese *No. 14*)

Name	*Chang Sha*	*Hsi An*
Builders	Kawasaki Sensha Works	Mitsubishi, Zosen Co, Nagasaki
Laid down	8 June 1944	17 Jan 1945
Launched	18 Oct 1944	26 Feb 1945
Completed	27 Dec 1944	31 Mar 1945

Displacement, tons	740 standard; 900 full load
Length, feet (*metres*)	213·2 (*54·2*) pp; 223 (*56·7*) wl; 228 (*57·9*) oa
Beam, feet (*metres*)	28·2 (*8·6*)
Draught, feet (*metres*)	10 (*3·0*)
Guns, surface	2—3·9 in (*100 mm*), or 2—4·7 (*120 mm*)
Guns, AA	3—3 in (*76 mm*), or 3 or 6—37 mm; 4—25 mm, or 3—20 mm
Main engines	Steam turbine; 2 500 shp
Speed, knots	17·5
Radius, miles	4 500 at 14 knots
Complement	160

CHI NAN *Hajime Fukaya*

CHANG SHA *Hajime Fukaya*

Ex-Japanese Type D or Kaibokan Class No. 2 Type. Thin trunked funnel amidships. Pole masts with tripod bases.

1 Ex-CANADIAN CORVETTE TYPE

KUANG CHOU (ex-Chinese *Yuan Pei*, ex-HMCS *Bowmanville*, ex-*Nunney Castle*)

Displacement, tons	1 100 standard; 1 580 full load
Length, feet (*metres*)	252 (*76·8*) oa
Beam, feet (*metres*)	36·7 (*11·2*)
Draught, feet (*metres*)	15·2 (*4·6*)
Guns, surface	2—5·1 in (*130 mm*)
Guns, AA	1—45 mm
Boilers	2 three-drum type
Main engines	Triple expansion; 2 800 ihp
Speed, knots	16·5
Radius, miles	8 400 at 10 knots
Oil fuel (tons)	480
Complement	100

Built by Wm Pickersgill & Sons, Ltd, Sunderland. Laid down on 12 Aug 1943. Launched on 26 Jan 1944. Completed in 8 Oct 1944.

2 Ex-BRITISH CORVETTE TYPES

KAI FENG (ex-SS *Cloverlock*, ex-HMS *Clover*)
LIN I (ex-SS *Ziang Teh*, ex-HMS *Heliotrope*, ex-USS *Surprise*)

Displacement, tons	1 020 standard; 1 280 full load
Length, feet (*metres*)	190 (*57·9*) pp; 205 (*62·5*) oa
Beam, feet (*metres*)	33 (*10·1*)
Draught, feet (*metres*)	14·5 (*4·4*)
Guns, surface	2—3·9 in (*100 mm*)
Guns, AA	*Kai Feng:* 1—45 mm; 4—37 mm *Lin 1:* 2—37 mm
Boilers	2 S.E.
Main engines	Triple expansion; 2 750 ihp
Speed, knots	16
Radius, miles	7 000 at 10 knots
Fuel (tons)	350 coal
Complement	78

Both built in 1940-41. Converted from merchant vessels by Chinese Republicans and re-armed. Existence of sister ship, former corvette, converted, ex-*Coppercilffe* (ex-*Wan Lee*, ex-*Ta Lun*) is doubtful.

PATROL VESSELS

Ex-USSR *1969*

24 "KRONSTADT" CLASS SUBMARINE CHASERS

579 611 612 615 618 622

Displacement, tons	300
Dimensions, feet	167·5 × 19·3 × 9
Guns	1—3·9 in; 2—37 mm AA; 3—20 mm AA
Main engines	Diesels; 2 shafts; speed 27 knots

Six built in 1950-53 were received from USSR in 1956-57. Remainder were built at Shanghai and Canton, with 12 completed by 1956. The last was assembled in 1957. Flush decked, squat funnel, slightly raked, block bridge structure.
The six old former Soviet patrol vessels of the "Artillerist" class, and the three former British patrol trawlers of the "Isles" class were deleted from the list in 1967, and the two former Soviet submarine chasers of the "S.O.1." class in 1969.

The six old former Soviet patrol vessels of the "Artillerist" class, and the three former British patrol trawlers of the "Isles" class were deleted from the list in 1967, and the two former Soviet submarine chasers of the "S.O.1." class in 1969.

MISSILE BOATS

7 SOVIET "OSA" CLASS

Displacement, tons	160 standard; 200 full load
Dimensions, feet	131·5 oa × 23 × 6·5
Missiles, surface	4 "Styx" type launchers in two pairs abreast aft
Guns	4—25 mm (2 twin, 1 forward and 1 aft)
Main engines	3 diesels; 5 000 bhp = 35 knots

It was reported in Jan 1965 that one "Osa" class guided missile patrol boat had been incorporated in the Navy. Four more were acquired in 1966-67, and two in 1968.

"Osa" Class *1969*

3 SOVIET "KOMAR" CLASS

Displacement, tons	75 standard; 100 full load
Dimensions, feet	82 oa × 20 × 6
Missiles, surface	2 "Styx" type launchers with 15 miles range
Guns	2—25 mm AA (1 twin forward)
Main engines	Diesels; 2 shafts; 4 800 bhp = 40 knots

One "Komar" class guided missile boat is reported to have joined the fleet in 1965. Two more were delivered in 1967.

"Komar" Class *S. Breyer*

FLEET MINESWEEPERS

20 SOVIET "T 43" CLASS

Displacement, tons	410 standard; 530 full load
Dimensions, feet	200 × 27·2 × 9
Guns	4—37 mm AA
Main engines	Diesels = 18 knots

Two were acquired from USSR in 1954-55. Eighteen more were built in Chinese shipyards, two in 1956, and the remainder since. The construction of "T 43" class fleet minesweepers was terminated at Wuchang, but continued at Canton.

1 Ex-BRITISH "BATHURST" CLASS

Ex-SS **CHEUNG HING** (ex-HMAS *Bendigo*)

Displacement, tons	815 standard; 1 025 full load
Dimensions, feet	162 pp; 186 oa × 31 × 8·5
Guns	2—5·1 in; 2—37 mm AA
Main engines	Triple expansion; 2 shafts; 1 800 ihp = 15 knots
Boilers	2 Admiralty 3-drum small tube type
Oil fuel (tons)	170
Radius, miles	4 300 at 10 knots

Built as a fleet minesweeper but employed as an escort vessel. Launched in Mar 1941 at Sydney, Australia. Disposed of as surplus after the Second World War. Converted from a merchant vessel.

FAST GUNBOATS

100 "NEW SHANGHAI" CLASS

Displacement, tons	120 full load
Dimensions, feet	130 × 18 × 5·6
Guns	4—37 mm, 2 twin, 1 forward, 1 aft 2—25 mm, 1 twin aft of bridge
Torpedo tubes	2 (not fitted in later boats)
Main engines	4 diesels; 5 000 bhp = 30 knots

Two centreline trainable torpedo tubes mounted abaft the superstructure. Hundred boats of this class built, with construction continuing at Shanghai. Designed as interchangeable motor gunboats or fast patrol boats. Designed for series construction in China. Three units were transferred to North Korea and four to North Vietnam.

14 "SHANGHAI" TYPE

Displacement, tons	100 full load
Dimensions, feet	120 × 18 × 5·5
Guns	4—37 mm in twin mountings fore and aft
Main engines	4 diesels; 4 800 bhp = 28 knots

The prototype of these motor gun/torpedo boats appeared in 1959.

MGB *1969*

45 "SWATOW" TYPE

Displacement, tons	67 full load
Dimensions, feet	83·5 × 20 × 6
Guns	4—37 mm in twin mountings; 2—12·7 mm
A/S weapons	8 depth charges
Main engines	4 diesels; 4 800 bhp = 40 knots

"P 6" type motor torpedo boat hulls with torpedo tubes removed. In 1958 "P-6" hulls were converted to "Swatow" class motor gunboats at Dairen, Canton, and Shanghai.

MGB *1969*

TORPEDO BOATS

5 HYDROFOIL TYPE

Dimensions, feet	100 × 25 × 12 (moulded depth)
Torpedo tubes	4 fixed (two on each side)
Guns	4 light (two twin)
Complement	20

At least 25 motor torpedo boats of the hydrofoil type were reported to be in the South China Fleet in 1968. Of all-metal construction with a bridge well forward and a low superstructure extending aft. The four guns are in horizontally paired mountings, one on the main deck and one on the superstructure. Forward pair of foils can apparently be withdrawn into recesses in the hull. Painted olive green.

26 "HUCHWAN" CLASS

Displacement, tons	45
Dimensions, feet	73 × 16 × 3·1
Torpedo tubes	2—21 inch
Guns	2—12·7 mm

Hydrofoil torpedo boat, designed and built by China, at least 26 having been constructed since 1966. One unit reported transferred to North Vietnam.

70 "P4" TYPE

Displacement, tons	25
Dimensions, feet	63 × 11 × 3
Guns	2 or 4—25 mm AA
Main engines	Diesels, 2 000 bhp = 45 knots

This class have aluminium hulls. The German-built *Kual 102* was deleted from the list in 1963.

PTBs 1969

80 "P6" TYPE

Displacement, tons	66
Dimensions, feet	82 × 20 × 6
Guns	4—25 mm AA
Torpedo tubes	2—21 in
Main engines	Diesels, 5 000 bhp = 40 knots

This class have wooden hulls. "P–6" class motor torpedo boats are under construction in Chinese Republican yards. All have been built since 1956.

MTB 1969

PATROL CRAFT

8 SEAWARD DEFENCE TYPE

Dimensions, feet	50 × 12 × 3
Guns	4—37 mm (2 pairs superimposed, 1 forward, 1 aft) 4—25 mm (2 pairs superimposed, amidships)

Similar to Soviet "S.O.I." class but much smaller with no anti-submarine weapons. Low freeboard (one to three feet). The 25 mm guns are just abaft the bridge structure.

2 Ex-JAPANESE TYPE

Ex-**KWANG KUO** (ex-Japanese No. 223)

Ex-**HSIEN FENG** (ex-Chinese *Koo Ming*, ex-Japanese

Displacement, tons	135
Dimensions, feet	96 × 19 × 9

SC Type. Built in 1942-43. (The ex-British harbour defence motor launches were lost).

COASTAL MINESWEEPERS

4 Ex-US YMS TYPE

Ex-**YMS 346** Ex-**YMS 367** Ex-**YMS 393** Ex-**YMS 2017**

Displacement, tons	270 standard; 350 full load
Dimensions, feet	136 × 24·5 × 6
Guns	1—3 in; 2—20 mm; 2 DCT
Main engines	2 GM Diesels; 1 000 bhp = 13 knots

Built of wood in USA in 1942-43, and transferred to the Chinese Navy in 1948. Some are fitted as gunboats. Ex-YMS 339 was deleted from the list in 1963.

2 Ex-JAPANESE AMS TYPE

Ex-**No. 4** **No. 201** (ex No. 14)

Displacement, tons	222
Dimensions, feet	97·1 oa × 19·3 × 7·3 max
Guns	1—3·1 in; 4—25 mm (No. 201, 1—40 mm; 1—25 mm; 2—13 mm; 3—7·7 mm)
Main engines	1 Diesel; 300 bhp = 9·5 knots
Radius, miles	1 700 at 9·5 knots

Ex-Japanese auxiliary minesweepers. Trawler type No. 201, completed in 1943, was delivered to China at Tsingtau on 3 Oct 1947, and taken over by the Chinese Republic.

COAST DEFENCE VESSELS

Ex-**YUNG SUI**

Displacement, tons	650
Dimensions, feet	225 × 30 × 7 max
Guns	1—3 in AA; 1—40 mm AA; 4 MG
Main engines	Triple expansion; 2 shafts; 4 000 shp = 12 knots
Boilers	2 Yarrow; Coal fired

Built by Kiangnan Dock Co, Shanghai. Launched in 1929. Salvaged and repaired after sinking in 1949. *Yung Sui* is ex-Chinese Nationalist name.

YUNG SUI *Official*

Ex-**AN TUNG** (ex-Japanese *Ataka*, ex-*Nakosa*)

Displacement, tons	727
Dimensions, feet	222 × 32 × 7·5
Guns	2—3 in; 5—25 mm; 6 MG
Main engines	Triple expansion; 1 700 ihp = 11 knots
Boilers	2 Kampon

Former Japanese. Built at Yokohama Dock. Launched in April, 1922. Coal burinig. Ex-*Yen An*, ex-*Yung Chi*, ex-*Asuka*, ex-*Yung Chi* was discarded.

AN TUNG *Official*

Coast Defence Vessels—*continued*

3 Ex-US TYPE

Ex-**PGM 12** Ex-**PGM 14** **KAN TANG** (ex-*PGM 15*)

Displacement, tons	280 standard; 348 trial; 450 full load
Dimensions, feet	170 wl; 173·3 oa × 23 × 11 max
Guns	1—3 in 50 cal dp; 2—40 mm AA (twin)
Main engines	GM diesel; 2 shafts; 2 800 bhp = 20 knots

Former US submarine chasers or patrol vessels (gunboats).

CH'ANG CHIANG (ex-*Ming Chuan*)

Displacement, tons	464
Dimensions, feet	176·8 × 26 × 6·5 max
Guns	3 MG
Main engines	Triple expansion; 2 shafts; 2 200 ihp = 12 knots
Boilers	2 Yarrow
Coal, tons	280

Built by Kiangnan Dock Co., Shanghai, Launched in 1929.

CHIANG YUAN

Displacement, tons	550
Dimensions, feet	170 pp; 180 oa × 28 × 7
Guns	1—20 mm AA
Main engines	Triple expansion; 2 shafts; 4 000 ihp = 12 knots
Boilers	Watertube
Coal, tons	113

Built by Kawasaki Co, Kobe. Launched in 1905. Former armament removed.

CHIANG YUAN *Official*

TING HSIN **TUNG TEH**

Displacement, tons	500 standard
Guns	1—3 in; 4—47 mm
Main engines	Speed: 11 knots
Fuel	Coal

Both captured by the People's Republic of China Navy in 1949.

RIVER DEFENCE VESSELS

Ex-**YUNG AN** (ex-*Futami*) Ex-**YUNG PING** (ex-*Atami*)

Displacement, tons	170
Dimensions, feet	148·5 × 22 × 4·7
Guns	1—47 mm AA; 5—25 mm AA; 3 MG
Main engines	2 sets triple expansion; 2 shafts; 1 200 ihp = 12 knots
Boilers	2 Kampon
Oil fuel (tons)	53

Built by Tama, Fujinagata. Both launched in 1929. Former Japanese river gunboats.

YUNG PING *Official*

Ex-**CHANG TEH** (ex-*Seta*)

Displacement, tons	305
Dimensions, feet	180 × 27 × 3
Guns	2—3 in; 6 MG
Main engines	Triple expansion; 2 shafts; 2 100 ihp = 14 knots
Boilers	2 Kampon
Oil fuel (tons)	85

Japanese prize, built at Harima yard. Launched in 1923. Ex-Japanese *Katado* of the same class may still exist.

Japanese prize, built at Harima yard. Launched in 1923. Reported to have been discarded. Ex-Japanese *Katado* of the same class may still exist.

River Defence Vessels—*continued*

FU CHIANG (ex-*Chiang Feng*, ex-Chinese *Kiang Shih*, ex-Japanese *Fushima*)
Ex-**CHIANG HSI** (ex-Chinese *Nan Chang*, ex-Japanese *Sumida*)

Displacement, tons	373·6 tons, official Japanese figure, 320 standard
Dimensions, feet	159·1 pp; 164 wl; 165 oa × 32·2 × 4·1
Guns	1—3·1 in HA short cal; 8—25 mm
Main engines	2 geared turbines; 2 shafts; 2 200 shp = 16·7 knots
Boilers	2 Kampon
Radius, miles	1 496 at 14 knots

Both ships were built by Fujinagata Co, Osaka. Launched on 26 Mar 1939 and 30 October 1939, respectively. Completed on 15 July 1939 and 31 May 1940, respectively. Were the latest river gunboats in the Japanese Navy. *Fushima* bombed and bottomed at Anking on 29 Nov 1944, was salvaged and towed to Shanghai for repairs and was moored there at the end of the war. *Sumida* was at Shanghai at the end of the war; her armament has been removed for land batteries.

FU CHIANG *Official*

Ex-**YING HAO** (ex-HMS *Sandpiper*)

Displacement, tons	185
Dimensions, feet	160 × 30·7 × 2 mean
Guns	1—3·7 in howitzer; 9 smaller
Main engines	2 sets triple expansion; 2 shafts; 600 ihp = 11 knots
Boilers	1, of Admiralty 3-drum type

Built by John I. Thornycroft & Co Ltd, Southampton. Launched on 9 June 1933. Presented to Nationalist China by Great Britain in Feb 1942, and subsequently taken over by the Republicans. Now has mainmast.

Ex-**NAN CHIANG** (ex-*Ying Teh*, ex-*Lung Huan*, ex-HMS *Falcon*)

Displacement, tons	372
Dimnesions, feet	150 × 28·7 × 5 mean
Guns	1—3·7 in howitzer; 2—6 pdr; 10 MG
Main engines	Parsons geared turbines; 2 250 shp = 15 knots
Boilers	2, of Admiralty 3-drum type
Fuel oil, tons	84

Built by Yarrow & Co, Ltd, Scotstoun, Glasgow. Launched in 1931. Presented to Nationalist China by the British Government in Feb 1942, and subsequently taken over by the Republicans.

Ex-**YING SHAN** (ex-HMS *Gannet*)

Displacement, tons	310
Dimensions, feet	177 wl; 184·7 oa × 29 × 3·2
Guns	2—3 in AA; 8 MG
Main engines	Geared turbines; designed 2 250 shp = 16 knots
Boilers	Yarrow
Fuel oil (tons)	60

Designed by Yarrow. Built by Yarrow & Co, Ltd, Scotstoun, Glasgow. Launched in 1927. Presented to Nationalist China by Great Britain in Feb 1942, and subsequently taken over by the Republicans.

Ex-**MEI YUAN** (ex-USS *Tutuila*) Ex-**TAI YUAN** (ex-*Tatara*, ex-USS *Wake*, ex-*Guam*)

Displacement, tons	370 standard
Dimensions, feet	150 wl × 159·5 oa × 27 × 5·2 mean—fresh water); (6 max)
Guns	2—3 in 23 cal; 10 MG
Main engines	Triple expansion; 1 950 ihp = 12 knots
Oil fuel (tons)	75

Built by Kiangnan Dock Co, Shanghai. Launched on 14 June and 28 May 1927 respectively. *Mei Yuan* was presented to China by the US Government in March 1942. Sister ship was recovered from Japanese hands and presented to China in 1946.

TAI YUAN *Official*

River Defence Vessels—*continued*

Ex-**KIANG KUN** (ex-Japanese *Narumi*, ex-Italian *Ermanno Carlotto*)

Displacement, tons	180 standard
Dimensions, feet	160 × 24·5 × 2·8
Guns	2—3 in; 6 MG
Main engines	Designed 1 100 ihp = 14 knots max
Boilers	2 Yarrow
Oil (tons)	56

Built by Shanghai Dock & Engineering Co. Launched in 1921. Completed in 1921. Shallow draught river gunboat. Twin screws in tunnels.

Ex-**FAKU** (ex-French *Balny*)

Displacement, tons	201
Dimensions, feet	167·2; 179 oa × 23 × 5
Guns	1—3 in AA; 2—1 pdr; 4 MG
Main engines	Triple expansion; 920 ihp = 14 knots
Boilers	2 Fouche water tube
Fuel (tons)	45 coal
Range, miles	900 at 14 knots

Built by Chantiers de Bretagne, Nantes. Launched in 1920. Completed in 1921.

Ex-**HO HSEUH** (ex-Chinese *Yang Ch'i*, ex-Japanese *Toba*)

Displacement, tons	215
Dimensions, feet	180 × 27 × 2·5 mean; (4 max)
Guns	3—3 in; 3—25 mm AA; 3 MG
Main engines	Triple expansion; 2 shafts; 900 ihp = 9 knots
Boilers	2 Kampon
Coal (tons)	80

Former Japanese shallow draught river gunboat. Built by Sasebo, Japan. Launched in 1911.

HO HSEUH *Official*

BOOM DEFENCE VESSELS

1 Ex-BRITISH "BAR" TYPE

Ex-Japanese No. 101 (ex-HMS *Barlight*)

Displacement, tons	750 standard; 1 000 full load
Dimensions, feet	150 pp; 173·8 oa × 32·2 × 9·5
Guns	1—3 in dp; 6 MG
Main engines	Triple expansion; 850 ihp = 11·75 knots
Boilers	2 single-ended

Boom defence vessel of British "Bar" Class. Built by Lobnitz & Co Ltd, Renfrew. Launched on 10 Sep 1938. Captured by Japanese in 1941. Acquired by China in 1945.

5 Ex-US "TREE" CLASS

Displacement, tons	560 standard; 805 full load
Dimensions, feet	146 wl; 163 oa × 30·5 × 11·8
Guns	1—3 in AA
Main engines	Diesel-electric; 800 bhp = 13 knots

Former United States netlayers of the "Tree" class taken over by the People's Republic.

SURVEY SHIPS

Ex-**CHUNG NING** (ex-Japanese *Takebu Maru*)

Displacement, tons	200 standard
Dimensions, feet	115 × 16 × 6
Main engines	Speed; 10 knots

Former Japanese. Employed for hydrographic and general purpose duties.

Ex-**FUTING**

Displacement, tons	160 standard
Dimensions, feet	90 × 20 × 8
Main engines	Speed: 11 knots

REPAIR SHIP

TAKU SHAN (ex-*Hsing An*, ex-USS *Achilles*, *ARL* 41, ex-*LST* 455)

Displacement, tons	1 625 light; 4 100 full load
Dimensions, feet	316 wl; 328 oa × 50 × 11
Guns	1—3 in; 8—40 mm AA
Main engines	Diesel-electric; 2 shafts; 1 800 bhp = 11 knots

Launched on 17 Oct 1942. Burned and grounded in 1949, salvaged and refitted.

LANDING SHIPS

21 Ex-US LST TYPE

CHANG PAI SHAN
CHING KANG SHAN
Ex-**CHUNG 101** (ex-USS *LST* 804)
Ex-**CHUNG 102** (ex-USS *LST*)
Ex-**CHUNG 107** (ex-USS *LST* 1027)
Ex-**CHUNG 110**
Ex-**CHUNG 111** (ex-USS *LST* 805)
Ex-**CHUNG 116** (ex-USS *LST* 406)
Ex-**CHUNG 122** (ex-*Ch'ing Ling*)
Ex-**CHUNG 125**
I MENG SHAN (ex-*Chung* 106 ex-USS *LST* 589)
No. 16
No. 258
TA PIEH SHAN
TAI HSING SHAN
SZU CH'ING SHAN

Displacement, tons	1 653 standard; 4 080 full load
Dimensions, feet	316 wl; 328 oa × 50 × 14
Main engines	Diesel; 2 shafts; 1 700 bhp = 11 knots

There are now reported to be 20 ex-US LSTs in naval service, including ex-USS LST 355, and eleven other ex-US LSTs in the merchant service.

13 Ex-US LSM TYPE

Ex-**CHUAN SHIH SHUI**
Ex-**HUA 201** (ex-USS *LSM* 112)
Ex-**HUA 202** (ex-USS *LSM* 248)
Ex-**HUA 204** (ex-USS *LSM* 430)
Ex-**HUA 205** (ex-USS *LSM* 336)
Ex-**HUA 207** (ex-USS *LSM* 282)
Ex-**HUA 208** (ex-USS *LSM* 42)
Ex-**HUA 209** (ex-USS *LSM* 153)
Ex-**HUA 211**
Ex-**HUA 212**
Ex-**HUAI HO** (ex-Chinese *Wan Fu*)
Ex-**HUANG HO** (ex-Chinese *Mei Sheng*, ex-USS *LSM* 433)
Ex-**YUN HO** (ex-Chinese *Wang Chung*)

Displacement, tons	743 beaching; 1 095 full load
Dimensions, feet	196·5 wl; 203·5 oa × 34·5 × 8·8
Main engines	Diesel; 2 shafts; 2 800 = 12 knots

Built in USA in 1944-45. Some were converted for minelaying. Armament varies.

LANDING CRAFT

16 Ex-US LSIL TYPE

Ex-**CHU TIEN** (ex-Chinese *Lien Kuang* ex-USS *LCI* 517)
Ex-**KU CHOU**
Ex-USS **LCI 488**
Ex-**LIEN PI** (ex-USS *LCI* 514)
MIN 301
MIN 303
MIN 306
MIN 311
MIN 312
MIN 313
MIN 319
MIN 321
MIN 325
MIN 331
Ex-**YUNG KAN** (ex-Chinese *Lien Yung*, ex-USS *LCI* 632)

Displacement, tons	230 light; 387 full load
Dimensions, feet	159 × 23·7 × 5·7
Main engines	Diesel; 2 shafts; 1 320 bhp = 14 knots

Built in USA in 1943-45. Reported to be fitted with rocket launchers. Some are fitted as minesweepers. Armament varies.

10 Ex-US LCU (ex-LCT) TYPE

Ex-**HO CHIEN** (ex-USS *LCT* 515)
Ex-**HO YUNG** (ex-USS *LCT* 1171)

Displacement, tons	160 light; 320 full load
Dimensions, feet	105 wl; 119 oa × 33 × 5
Main engines	Diesel; 3 shafts; 475 bhp = 10 knots
Oil fuel (tons)	80

Former United States Navy Tank Landing Craft later reclassified as Utility Landing Craft. There are reported to be ten utility landing craft comprising two of the ex-British LCT (3) class and eight of the ex-US LCT (5) and LCT (6) class.

SUPPLY SHIPS

8 Ex-US ARMY FS TYPE

Ex-US Army FS 146 (ex-*Clover*)
Ex-US Army FS 155 (ex-*Violet*)
Ex-**TA CHEN** (ex-US)
Ex-US Army FS——
Ex-US Army FS——

Displacement, tons	1 000 standard
Dimensions, feet	175 oa × 32 × 10
Main engines	GM diesels; 1 000 bhp = 12 knots

Built in USA in 1944-54. Two are reported to be employed as motor torpedo boat tenders. The transport *Chiao Jen* was striken from the list in 1967.

OILERS

There are reported to be two ex-US "Mattawee" Class petrol tankers and three ex-US 174 ft yard oilers of the "YO" type.

TUGS

There are reported to be at least two tugs of the USSR type, two of the US Navy ATA type, two of the US Army type, and five of the US Army harbour tug type.
There are also reported to be 125 armed motor junks, 100 armed motor launches and 150 service craft and miscellaneous boats.

COLOMBIA

Administration

Fleet Commander
Rear Admiral Jaime Parra Ramirez

Chief of Naval Operations
Rear Admiral Eduardo Wills Olaya

Chief of Naval Staff:
Rear Admiral Jaime Barrera Larratte

Diplomatic Representation

Naval Attaché in Washington:
Captain Ciro Feinandez Gutierez

Strength of the Fleet

3 Destroyers
3 Destroyer Escort Transports
8 Coast Guard Patrol Vessels
5 River Gunboats
9 Patrol Motor Launches
23 Support Ships and Service Craft
1 Sail Training Vessel

Designation

Ships' names are prefaced by the letters "ARC" (Armada Republica de Colombia)

Personnel

1969: 700 officers and 6,500 men

Mercantile Marine

Lloyd's Register of shipping:
47 vessels of 208 846 tons gross

DESTROYERS (*Destructores*)

Name	*No.*	*Builders*	*Laid down*	*Launched*	*Completed*
SIETE DE AGOSTO	06	Götaverken, Göteberg	Nov 1955	19 June 1956	31 Oct 1958
VEINTE DE JULIO	05	Kockums Mek Verkstads A/B, Malmo	Oct 1955	26 June 1956	15 June 1958

2 MODIFIED SWEDISH "HALLAND" TYPE

Displacement, tons	2 650 standard; 3 100 full load
Length, feet (*metres*)	380·5 (*116·0*) pp; 397·2 (*121·1*) wl
Beam, feet (*metres*)	40·7 (12·4)
Draught, feet (*metres*)	12·5 (*3·8*)
Guns, surface	6—4·7 in (*120*) *mm*, 3 twin turrets
Guns, AA	4—40 mm, single mounts
Torpedo tubes	4—21 in (*533 mm*)
A/S weapons	1 quadruple DC rocket launcher
Boilers	2 Penhöet, Motala Verkstad; 568 psi; 840°F
Main engines	De Laval double reduction geared turbines; 55 000 shp; 2 shafts
Range, miles	445 at 35 knots
Oil fuel (tons)	524
Speed, knots	35 designed, 16 economical
Complement	260 (20 officers, 240 men)

7 DE AGOSTO — *1967, Colombian Navy, Official*

Modified "Halland" type ordered in 1954. The hull and machinery are similar but they have different armament (six 4·7 inch instead of four, no 57 mm guns, four 40 mm guns instead of six, and four torpedo tubes instead of eight) and different accommodation arrangements. They have an anti-submarine rocket projector, more radar and communication equipment, and air conditioned living spaces, having been designed for the tropics.

The change of name from *13 de Junio* to *7 de Agosto* was decreed by the Colombian Navy in July 1957.

PHOTOGRAPHS. A photograph of *20 de Julio* appears in the 1966-67 edition.

Name	*No.*	*Builders*	*Laid down*	*Launched*	*Completed*
ANTIOQUIA (ex-USS *Hale*, DD 642)	DD 01	Bath Iron Works Corporation, Bath, Maine	23 Nov 1942	4 Apr 1943	15 June 1943

1 Ex-US "FLETCHER" TYPE

Displacement, tons	2 100 standard; 2 952 full load
Length, feet (*metres*)	369 (*112·5*) pp; 376 (*114·8*) oa
Beam, feet (*metres*)	39·5 (*12·0*)
Draught, feet (*metres*)	12·3 (*3·8*) mean; 18·0 (*5·5*) max
Guns, surface	4—5 in (*127 mm*) 38 cal.
Guns, AA	6—3 in (*76 mm*) 50 cal.
Torpedo tubes	5—21 in (*533 mm*) quintrupled
A/S weapons	2 fixed Hedgehogs; 1 DC rack; 2 side-launching torpedo racks
Boilers	4 Babcock & Wilcox; 615 psi; 850°F
Main engines	2 sets GE geared turbines; 60 000 shp; 2 shafts
Speed, knots	35 designed, 37 max, 14 econ
Radius, miles	6 000 at 14 knots
Oil fuel (tons)	650
Complement	300 (peace); 350 (war)

ANTIOQUIA — *1963, Colombian Navy, Official*

Former United States destroyer of the "Fletcher" class. Transferred from the US Navy to the Colombian Navy at Boston Massachusetts, in 1961, and renamed *Antioquia*.

DISPOSALS

Frigates **Almirante Brion** ex-*USS Burlington PF 51* discarded 1968; **Captain Tono** ex-*USS Besbee* discarded Dec 1962 and **Almirante Padilla** ex-*USS Groton*, discarded Jan 1965. All were ships of the "Tacona" Patrol Frigate type of the USN, based on the Original British "River" class frigate.

DESTROYER TRANSPORTS

ALMIRANTE BRION (ex-*USS Barber APD 65*)
ALMIRANTE PADILLA (ex-*USS Tollberg APD* 103)
ALMIRANTE TONO (ex-*USS Bassett APD 73*)

Displacement, tons	1 400 standard; 2 130 full load
Dimensions, feet	300 wl; 306 oa × 37 × 12·7 max
Guns	1—5 in, 38 cal dp; 6—40 mm AA
Main engines	GE turbo-electric; 2 shafts; 12 000 shp = 23·6 knots
Boilers	2 "D" Express
Oil fuel (tons)	350
Radius, miles	5 500 at 15 knots
Complement	204 accommodation plus 162 troop capacity

Former US high speed transports (converted destroyer escorts). *Almirante Padilla* was built by Bethlehem SB Co, Hingham, Mass. Laid down on 30 Dec 1943, launched on 12 Feb 1944, completed on 31 Jan 1945. Transferred in 1965. *Almirante Tono* was built by Consolidated Steel Co, Orange, Tex. Laid down on 28 Nov 1943, launched on 15 Jan 1944, completed on 23 Feb 1945. Transferred at Boston, Mass, on 6 Sep 1968.

ALMIRANTE PADILLA *1969, Official*

COAST GUARD VESSELS

CARLOS E. RESTREPO **ESTEBAN JARAMILLO** **PEDRO GUAL**

Displacement, tons	123·5
Dimensions, feet	107·8 pp × 18 × 6
Guns	1—20 mm AA
Main engines	2 Maybach diesels; 2 450 bhp = 26 knots

Built by Werft Gebr. Schürenstedt KG Bardenfleth in 1964. Pennant Nos. AN 206, AN 205 and AN 204, respectively.

PEDRO GUAL *1965, Colombian Navy, Official*

OLAYA HERRERA

Displacement, tons	40
Dimensions, feet	68·8 pp × 12·8 × 3·5
Guns	1—50 Browning AA
Main engines	2 Merbens diesels; 570 bhp

Built by Astilleros Magdalena, Barranquilla, in 1960. Pennant No. AN 203.

GENERAL RAFAEL REYES **GENERAL VASQUES COBO**

Displacement, tons	146
Dimensions, feet	118 pp; 124·7 oa × 23 × 5
Guns	1—40 mm
Main engines	2 Maybach diesels; 2 400 bhp = 18 knots

Built by Lürssen Werft, Vegesack. Launched on 10 Nov and 27 Sep 1955, respectively. Delivered in May 1956. Pennant Nos. AN 01 and AN 02 respectively. Photograph of *General Vasques Cobo* in the 1957-58 to 1964-65 editions.

ESPARTANA

Displacement, tons	50
Dimensions, feet	90 wl; 96 oa × 13·5 × 4
Guns	1—20 mm AA
Main engines	2 diesels; 300 bhp = 13·5 knots

Launched on 22 June 1950 at Cartagena Naval Dockyard. Pennant No. GC 100. Photographs of *Espartana* appear in the 1953-54 to 1968-69 editions.

CAPITAN BINNEY

Displacement, tons	23
Dimensions, feet	67 × 10·7 × 3·5
Main engines	Diesels; 115 bhp = 13 knots

Built at Cartagena in 1947. Buoy and lighthouse inspection boat. Named after first head of Colombian Naval Academy, Lt-Commander Ralph Douglas Binney, RN. Pennant No. GC 101. Photograph in the 1961-62 to 1964-65 editions.

RIVER GUNBOATS

3 "ARAUCA" CLASS

ARAUCA CF 37 **LETICIA** CF 36 **RIOHACHA** CF 35

Displacement, tons	184
Dimensions, feet	163·5 oa × 23·5 × 2·8
Guns	2—3 in, dp, 50 cal; 4—20 mm
Main engines	2 Caterpillar engines; 916 bhp = 13 knots
Range, miles	1 000
Complement	43

Built by Union Industrial de Barranquilla (Unial) Colombia. Launched in 1955. Completed in 1956. Pennant Nos. CF 37, 36 and 35 respectively. A photograph of *Arauca* appears in the 1957-58 to 1960-61 editions, and of *Leticia* in the 1961-62 to 1965-66 editions. *Leticia* and one other are reported to have been disarmed and converted into floating health centres.

RIOHACHA *1966, Colombian Navy, Official*

BARRANQUILA CF 31 **CARTAGENA** CF 33

Displacement, tons	142
Dimensions, feet	130 pp; 137·8 oa × 23·5 × 2·8 max
Guns	2—3 in; 1—20 mm AA; 4 MG
Main engines	2 Gardner semi-diesels; 2 shafts; working in tunnels; 600 hp = 15·5 knots
Oil fuel (tons)	24
Complement	39

Both built by Yarrow & Co Ltd, Scotstoun, Glasgow, and launched on 10 May 1930, and 26 Mar 1930, respectively. *Barranquila* was modernised in Cartagena with new armament, engines, auxiliaries and superstructure. Photograph of *Cartagena* in the 1957-58 to 1960-61 editions. Sister ship *Santa Marta*, CF 32, was withdrawn from service in Dec 1962.

BARRANQUILA *1961, Colombian Navy, Official*

TENDERS

GORGONA FB 161

Displacement, tons	560
Dimensions, feet	135 × 29·5 × 9·3
Main engines	2 Nohab diesels; 910 bhp = 13 knots

Built by Astillero Lidingoverken. Launched in May 1954. Pennant No. FB 161. Formerly classified as a tender. Recently employed in the hydrographic service.

GORGONA *1963, Colombian Navy, Official*

RAFAEL MARTINEZ

Displacement, tons	38
Dimensions, feet	56 pp; 57·5 oa × 15 × 8
Main engines	2 six-cylinder diesels; 120 bhp

JAMARY

Dimensions, feet	146 × 25·5 × 8
Complement	43

Small tender equipped as a naval hospital ship with beds for 80 patients.

There are also *Rodriguez Zamora* (ex-USN *ARD* 28), 6 700 tons full load, 488·7 oa × 81 feet, crew 109, transferred from the United States Navy, officially rated as auxiliary floating dry dock; *Capitan Eloy Mantilla* (ex-USN *YR* 66), 516 tons standard, 150 oa × 34 feet, crew 24 transferred from the US Navy, rated as floating workshop; floating dock *Manuel Laro* and repair boat *Victor Cubillos*.

SMALL TRANSPORTS

CIUDAD DE QUIBDO TM 43

Displacement, tons	633
Dimensions, feet	165 × 23·5 × 9
Main engines	1 Mai diesel; 1 shaft; 390 bhp = 11 knots
Oil fuel (tons)	32
Complement	12

Built by Gebr. Sander Delfzijl, in the Netherlands. Photograph in the 1957-58 edition.

BELL SALTER (ex-*Souris*, ex-*Leccarmaro II*). TM 41.

Displacement, tons	60
Dimensions, feet	82 × 14 × 5·5
Main engines	2 GM diesels; 1 500 rpm; speed 8 knots

ALBERTO GOMEZ TF 53
HERNANDO GUTIERREZ TF 52
MARIO SERPA TF 51

Displacement, tons	70
Dimensions, feet	82 × 18 × 2·8
Main engines	2 GM diesels; 260 bhp = 9 knots
Oil fuel (tons)	4
Complement	10 (berths for 56 troops)

River transports. Launched at Cartagena in 1954, 1953 and 1955, respectively. Named after Army officers. Photograph of *Alberto Gomez* in the 1954-55 to 1957-58 editions.

OILERS

BARRANCABERMEJA BT 66

Displacement, tons	9 214 light; 22 316 full load
Dimension feet	602·3 × 76 × 32·1
Main engines	Rush-Sultzer diesel; 1 shaft; 10 500 bhp = 15·5 knots
Complement	65 (10 officers, 55 men)

Built by Sociedad Española de Construccion Naval, Cadiz. Laid down on 1 Feb 1965, launched on 1 Aug 1965 and completed on 1 June 1966.

COVENAS (ex-*M/T Randfonn*) BT 65

Measurement, tons	22 096 gross; 5 096 net; 14 000 deadweight
Dimensions, feet	515·3 oa × 64 × 30·5 max
Main engines	Diesel; 1 shaft; 6 000 bhp = 14·5 knots
Complement	49 (7 officers, 42 men)

Built by Gotaverken in 1950. Acquired in 1966. Capacity 136 250 barrels.

COVENAS — *1966, Colombian Navy, Official*

ANTONIO DE AREVALO (ex-*Gronland*) BT 64

Measurement, tons	22 682 gross; 5 952 net; 16 730 deadweight
Dimensions, feet	549·8 × 68 × 30 max
Main engines	1 MAN diesel; 6 650 bhp = 15 knots

Built by Deutsche Werft, Hamburg, in 1952. Purchased from commercial sources in 1959. Photograph in 1963-64 to 1965-66 editions.

MAMONAL (ex-US *Tonti*, AOG 76) BT 62
SANCHO JIMENO (ex-*Transmere*, ex-USS *Kiamichi* AOG 73) BT 63

Displacement, tons	5 984 full load
Measurement, tons	3 150 gross; 3 925 deadweight; 2 063 net
Dimensions, feet	309 wl, 325 oa × 48·2 × 21·7
Main engines	Diesel; 1 shaft; 1 400 bhp = 10 knots
Complement	33

Built by Todd Shipyard, Houston, and St. John's River S.B. Corp., Jacksonville, respectively. *Sancho Jimeno* was purchased in 1952. *Mamonal* was transferred in Jan 1965.

MAMONAL — *1965, Colombian Navy, Official*

PATROL MOTOR LAUNCHES

ALBERTO RESTREPO (1 Oct 1952)
CARLOS GALINDO (1954)
HUMBERTO CORTES (26 Nov 1952)
JUAN LUCIO (2 May 1953)

Displacement, tons	35
Dimensions, feet	76·8 pp; 81·8 oa × 12 × 2·8
Guns,	1—20 mm AA; 4 MG
Main engines	2 GM diesels; 260 bhp = 13 knots
Complement	13

Built at Cartagena. Launch dates above. Nos. LR 125, 128, 126 and 122 respectively. A photograph of *Alberto Restrepo* appears in the 1957-58 to 1964-65 editions.

HUMBERTO CORTES — *1965. Colombian Navy, Official*

ALFONSO VARGAS (3 July 1952)
FRITZ HAGALE (19 July 1952)

Displacement, tons	33
Dimensions, feet	72 pp; 76 oa × 12 × 2·8
Guns	1—20 mm AA; 4 GM
Main engines	2 GM; diesels 280 bhp = 13 knots
Complement	10

Built at Cartagena naval base. Designed for operations on rivers. Named after naval officers. Launch dates above. Pennant Nos LR 123 and 124 respectively. A photograph of *Fritz Hagale* appears in the 1956-57 to 1963-64 editions.

DILIGENTE	**PALACE**	**TRIUNFANTE**	**VENGADORA**
INDEPENDENTE	**TORMENTOSO**	**VALEROSA**	**VOLADORA**

Launched at the Naval Base, Cartagena, in 1942-54. The boats vary in detail. Pennant Nos. LR 138, 134, 130, 136, 133, 137, 139 and 135, respectively.

TUGS

PEDRO DE HEREDIA (ex-USS *Choctaw*, ATF 70) RM 72

Displacement, tons	1 235 standard; 1 764 full load
Dimensions, feet	195 wl; 205 oa × 38·5 × 15·5 max
Main engines	4 diesels, electrical drive; 3 000 bhp = 16·5 knots

Former United States ocean tug of the "Apache" class. Launched on 18 Oct 1942.

TENIENTE SORZANO

Displacement, tons	54
Dimensions, feet	60 pp; 65·7 oa × 17·5 × 9
Main engines	6-cylinder diesel; 240 bhp

ANDAGOYA RM 71

Displacement, tons	100
Main engines	Caterpillar diesel; 80 bhp = 8 knots

Launched in 1928. Re-engined in 1955. Photograph in 1957-58 edition.

ABADIA MENDEZ

Displacement, tons	39
Dimensions, feet	52·5 × 11 × 4
Main engines	Caterpillar diesel; 80 bhp = 8 knots

Built in Germany in 1924. Harbour tug. There are also the harbour tug, *La Colombiana* and the river tug *Joves Fiallo*, RR 90.

CANDIDO LEGUIZAMÓ	**CAPITAN RIGOBERTO GIRALDO**
CAPITAN HERNANDO BOCANEGRA	**CAPITAN JULIO PATINO**
CAPITAN ALVARO RUIZ	**CAPITAN VLADIMIR VALEK**
CAPITAN CASTRO	**TENIENTE LUIS BERNAL**

Displacement, tons	50
Dimensions, feet	63 × 14 × 2·5
Main engines	2 GM diesels; 260 bhp = 9 knots

TENIENTE MIGUEL SILVA

Dimensions, feet	73·3 × 17·5 × 3
Main engines	2 diesels; 260 bhp = 9 knots

River tug. Built by Union Industrial (Unial) of Barranquila. Pennant No. 89.

CONGO (*ex-Belgian*)

CONGO (ex-*President Mobuto*, ex-*General Olsen*) river boat, 260 ft oa, underwent 3 month refit, renamed 3 Sep 1967. A force for Lake Tanganyika was formed in 1967 consisting of:—2—50 ft patrol boats, 4—21 ft speed boats, 1 converted trawler, 4 other small patrol craft were reported transferred by Communist China.

CONGO (*ex-French*)

The Republic of Congo (formerly Middle Congo, of French Equatorial Africa), which became independent on 15 Aug 1960, formed a naval service, but the patrol vessel *Reine N'Galifowou* (ex-French P 754) which was transferred 16 Nov, 1962, was returned to France on 18 Feb, 1965 and then re-transferred to Senegal as *Siné Saloum*.

COSTA RICA

The Coast Guard includes two 90 ft wooden patrol boats and an armed tug.

CUBA

Strength of the Fleet

4 Frigates (1 ex-*Crucero*)
2 Escort Patrol Vessels
14 Patrol Vessels (Submarine Chasers)
18 Missile Boats
24 Torpedo Boats
13 Coast Guard Cutters
21 Auxiliaries and Service Craft.

Naval Establishments

Naval Academy: At Mariel, for Officers
Naval School: At Morro Castle, for men

Personnel

1969: 6 000 (380 officers, 220 subordinate officers, and 5 400 men)

Mercantile Marine

Lloyd's Register of Shipping:
104 vessels of 237 603 tons gross

FRIGATES (*Fragatas*)

Name	*Pennant No.*	*Builders*	*Laid down*	*Launched*	*Completed*
ANTONIO MACEO (ex-USS *Peoria*, PF 67)	F 302	Leathem D. Smith, S.B. Co, Sturgeon Bay, Wisconsin	4 June 1943	2 Oct 1943	15 Oct 1944
JOSÉ MARTI (ex-USS *Eugene*, PF 40)	F 301	Consolidated Steel, Los Angeles, California	12 June 1943	6 July 1943	15 Jan 1944
MAXIMO GOMÉZ (ex-USS *Grand Island*, PF 14)	F 303	Kaiser Cargo Inc, Richmond, California	27 Nov 1943	19 Feb 1944	27 May 1944

3 Ex-US PF TYPE

Displacement, tons	1 430 standard; 2 415 full load
Length, feet (*metres*)	285·5 (*87·0*) wl; 304·0 (*92·7*) oa
Beam, feet (*metres*)	37·5 (*11·4*)
Draught, feet (*metres*)	13·7 (*4·2*)
Guns, dual purpose	3—3 in (*76 mm*)
Guns, AA	*Ant. Maceo:* 4—40 mm; 4—12·7 mm *José Marti:* 4—40 mm; 6—20 mm *Max. Gomez:* 4—40 mm; 9—20 mm
A/S	Hedgehog; DCT; racks
Boilers	2 three-drum type
Main engines	Triple expansion 5 500 ihp; 2 shafts
Speed, knots	18
Radius, miles	9 500 at 12 knots
Complement	135 (*Jose Marti*)

MAXIMO GOMEZ *Added 1966, Cuban Navy, Official*

Acquired from the US Navy in 1947. Refitted in 1956 at Key West. *José Marti* fitted as flagship.

A photograph of *José Marti* appears in the 1955-56 to 1959-60 editions, and of *Antonio Maceo* in the 1960-61 to 1965-66 editions.

CUBA

Displacement, tons	2 055
Length, feet (*metres*)	260 (*79·3*) pp
Beam, feet (*metres*)	39 (*11·9*)
Draught, feet (*metres*)	14 (*4·3*)
Guns, surface	2—4 in (*102 mm*); 2—3 in (*76 mm*)
Guns, AA	4—57 mm; 5—20 mm
Boilers	2 Foster Wheeler 3-drum type
Main engines	Triple expansion; 6 000 ihp
Speed, knots	14

Originally rated as a *crucero* (*cruiser*). Built by Cramp, Philadelphia. Launched on 10 Aug 1911. Reconstructed in 1936-37. Converted from coal to oil burning. Completed further reconstruction in 1956.

CUBA *Added 1964, Cuban Navy, Official*

PATROL ESCORTS (*Buques de Patrulla y Escolta*)

2 Ex-US PCE TYPE ESCORT PATROL VESSELS

Name	**CARIBE** (ex-USS *PCE* 872)	**SIBONEY** (ex-USS *PCE* 893)
Pennant No.	PE 201	PE 302
Builders	Albina Eng. & Mach. Works, Portland, Oreg.	Williamette Iron & Steel Corp., Portland, Oreg.
Laid down	30 Jan 1943	27 Oct 1942
Launched	24 Mar 1943	8 May 1943
Completed	29 Nov 1943	25 July 1944

Displacement, tons	640 standard; 903 full load
Dimensions, feet	180 wl; 184·5 oa × 33 × 9·5
Guns	1—3 in dp; 3—40 mm AA; 4—20 mm AA
A/S weapons	Hedgehog; DCT and racks
Main engines	12 cylinder diesels; 2 shafts; 1 800 bhp = 14 knots
Complement	99

Built in USA. Former United States escort patrol vessels. Box deck-house amidship was removed from *Caribe* in 1953. Both completed a refit in 1956 at Key West Naval Base, when new anti-submarine armament and equipment were installed.
The old sloop *Patria*, at Mariel as a permanent installation of the Naval Academy for training midshipmen, has been removed from the effective list.

CARIBE *Cuban Navy Official*

MISSILE BOATS

18 Ex-USSR "KOMAR" TYPE

Displacement, tons	75 standard; 100 full load
Dimensions, feet	88 oa × 21 × 6
Guided weapons	2 launchers for missiles of 10 to 15 miles range
Main engines	Speed = 40 knots

Former Soviet boats. Twelve transferred in 1962. Last two arrived Dec 1966.

PATROL VESSELS (Submarine Chasers)

12 Ex-USSR "SOI" TYPE

Displacement, tons	215
Dimensions, feet	147·7 × 18 × 6·5
Guns	4—25 mm (2 twin)
A/S weapons	4 five-barrelled rocket launchers
Main engines	3 diesels; 3 500 bhp = 26 knots

Six were transferred from the USSR by Sep 1964, and six more in 1967.

6 Ex-USSR "KRONSTADT" TYPE

Displacement, tons	300 standard; 350 full load
Dimensions, feet	167·3 × 19·3 × 9
Guns	1—3·9 in; 2—37 mm AA; 3—20 mm AA; DC
Mines	6 on two racks at the stern
Main engines	2 diesels; 2 shafts; speed = 22 knots

Former Soviet submarine chasers reported transferred from the USSR in 1962.

TORPEDO BOATS

12 Ex-USSR "P 6" TYPE

Displacement, tons	75 standard; 100 full load
Dimensions, feet	88 × 21 × 6
Guns	4—25 mm AA (two twin)
Tubes	2—21 in (two single)
Main engines	Speed = 45 knots

12 Ex-USSR "P 4" TYPE

Displacement, tons	50
Dimensions, feet	85·3 × 20 × 6
Guns	4—25 mm AA (2 twin)
Main engines	Diesels; 2 000 bhp = 42 knots

Former Soviet motor torpedo boats, transferred from the USSR in 1962-64.

COAST GUARD CUTTERS (*Guardacostas*)

HABANA *GC* 107 (ex-*SC* 1291) **ORIENTE** *GC* 104 (ex-*SC* 1000)
LAS VILLAS *GC* 106 (ex-*SC* 1290) **PINAR DEL RIO** *GC* 108 (ex-*SC* 1301)

Displacement, tons 95
Dimensions, feet 107·5 wl; 111 oa × 17 × 6·5
Guns 2—20 mm AA
Main engines GM diesels; 2 shafts; 1 000 bhp = 15 knots

Built in the United States by Dingle Boat Works (*Oriente*), W. A. Robinson, Inc, Ipswich, Mass. (*Havana* and *Las Villas*), and Perkins & Vaughan, Inc, Wickford, RI (*Pinar del Rio*). *Camaguey* GC 105, was removed from the effective list in 1960.

HABANA *Cuban Navy, Official*

LEONCIO PRADO GC 101

Displacement, tons 80
Dimensions, feet 110 × 17·7 × 6·2
Guns 1—20 mm AA
Main engines 2 sets 8-cycle, 2 stroke diesels; 1 000 bhp = 15 knots
Oil 2 232 gallons for a cruising radius of 16 000 miles

Built at Havana. Launched in 1946. Of wooden hulled construction.

LEONCIO PRADO *Added 1966, Cuban Navy, Official*

GC 11 (ex-USCGC 83351) **GC 13** (ex-USCGC 83385) **GC 14** (ex-USCGC 83395)

Displacement, tons 45
Dimensions, feet 83 × 16 × 4·5
Guns 1—20 mm AA
Main engines 2 Sterling Viking petrol motors; 1 200 hp = 18 knots
Complement 12

Former *CS* of same numbers. Built in USA. Ex-Coast Guard Cutters. Launched in 1942-43. Of wooden hulled construction. Received from US Navy in March 1943. Rated as *Guardacostas*, 83 ft. GC 12 and GC 22 were disposed of.

GC 13 *Cuban Navy, Official*

GC 32 (ex-USCGC 56191) **GC 33** (ex-USCGC 56190) **GC 34** (ex-USCGC 56192)

Displacement, tons 45
Dimensions, feet 83 × 16 × 4·5
Guns 1—20 mm AA
Main engines 2 Superior diesels; 460 bhp = 12 knots
Complement 12

Built in USA. Ex-Coast Guard Cutters. Launched in 1942-43. Of wooden hulled construction. A photograph of GC 32 appears in the 1955-56 to 1959-60 editions. GC 31 was disposed of.

DONOTIVO (ex-*Capitan Fernandez Quevedo*) GC 102

Displacement, tons 130
Dimensions, feet 101 × 18 × 7
Main engines 2 sets diesels; 360 bhp = 12 knots

Built at Havana. Launched in 1932. Photograph in 1947-48 to 1959-60 editions.

MATANZAS *GC* 103

Displacement, tons 80
Dimensions, feet 100 × 18 × 6
Guns 1—1 pdr
Main engines 2 Fairbanks Morse diesels; 180 bhp = 12 knots

Wooden hulled. Built at Havana. Launched in 1912. A photograph appears in the 1947-48 to 1959-60 editions. Both of the above are rated *Guardacostas Auxiliares*.

MOTOR LAUNCHES

R 41 (ex-*PT* 715) **R 42** (ex-*PT* 716)

Displacement, tons 35
Dimensions, feet 71 × 19·2 × 5
Guns 2 MG
Main engines 2 Packard gas engines; 3 shafts; 3 600 bhp = 35 knots

Former US motor torpedo boats of the PT type. Built in the USA by Annapolis Yacht Yard Inc, Annapolis, Md. Launched on 9 July 1945 (R 41) and 17 July 1945 (R 42). Sunk during a hurricane on 5 Oct 1948, but were salvaged and put into service as sea-air rescue craft. Rated as *Buques-Auxiliares*, ex-*Torpederos*. Sister R 43 sank on 6 May 1961 after hitting a submerged object off Western Cuba.

R 41 *Added 1966, Cuban Navy, Official*

SV 7 **SV 8** **SV 9** **SV 10** **SV 12** **SV 14**

Dimensions, feet Length 40
Guns 1—50 cal MG
Main engines 2 GM diesels; speed 25 knots

Later boats of the SV type assigned to naval stations for coastal vigilance, to deal with contraband, and for auxiliary services, rescue and navigation. Equipped with radar.

SV 1 **SV 2** **SV 3** **SV 4** **SV 5** **SV 6**

Displacement, tons 6·15
Dimensions, feet 32 × 10 × 2·8
Main engines 2 Chrysler Crown; 230 bhp = 18 knots

Auxiliary patrol boats for port vigilance, launched in 1953. A photograph of *SV* 6 appears in the 1957-58 edition.

LIGHTHOUSE TENDERS (*Buque de Servicia de Faros*)

ENRIQUE COLLAZO (ex-*Joaquin Godoy*)

Displacement, tons 815
Dimensions, feet 211 × 34 × 9
Main engines Triple expansion; 2 shafts; 672 ihp = 8 knots

Built at Paisley, Scotland. Launched in 1906. Acquired in 1950 from Cuban mercantile marine. A photograph appears in the 1953-54 to 1957-58 editions.

BERTHA

Displacement, tons 98
Dimensions, feet 104 × 19 × 11
Main engines 2 Gray Marine diesels; 450 bhp = 10 knots

Launched in 1944. Pennant No. SF 10. A photograph appears in the 1957-48 edtiion.

AUXILIARY VESSELS (*Buques-Auxiliares*)

GRANMA A 11

Yacht which landed in Cuba on 2 Dec 1956 with Dr Fidel Castro and the men who began the liberation war. Historical vessel incorporated into the Navy as an auxiliary. The former Presidential Yacht *10 de Marzo* (ex-*Wakitty*) was removed from the list.

A1 **A2** **A3**

Displacement, tons 60
Dimensions, feet 74 × 15 × 5
Guns 1 MG
Main engines 2 diesel engines

Formerly yachts. A photograph of A3 appears in the 1954-55 to 1957-58 editions.

RESCUE AND SALVAGE VESSELS

10 DE OCTUBRE (ex-*ATR* 4)

Displacement, tons 852 standard; 1 315 full load
Dimensions, feet 155 wl; 165·5 oa × 33·3 × 16
Main engines Triple expansion; 1 600 ihp = 12 knots
Boilers 2 Babcock & Wilcox D-type; oil burning

Former US ocean rescue tug. Built in the USA. Launched in 1943. Largely of wooden construction. Guns removed. Pennant No. RS 210. Rated as *Buque de Rescate y Salvamento*. Sister ship *20 de Mayo* was removed from the effective list.

CYPRUS

PATROL BOATS

6 "P 4" CLASS

Displacement, tons 25
Dimensions, feet 63 × 11 × 3
Guns 2—4 25 mm
Main engines Diesels; 2 000 bhp = 45 knots

Four of these were transferred by USSR in Oct 1964 and two in Feb 1965. Also reported that two further boats transferred since that time.

2 Ex-GERMAN "R" TYPE

Displacement, tons 125
Dimensions, feet 124 × 19 × 4·5
Guns 1—40 mm; 1—20 mm
Main engines 2 MAN diesels; 1 800 bhp = 20 knots

Originally there were three of this class all taken up from mercantile use and re-armed. One was destroyed by Turkish air attack on 8 Aug 1964 at Xeros. It is also reported that there are 10 small craft of approximately 50 tons, armed with 1 or 2 20 mm guns, in service.

DENMARK

Administration

Commander in Chief:
Vice-Admiral S. Thostrup, RDN

Chief of Naval Staff:
Rear-Admiral O. Brink-Lund, RDN

Dilpomatic Representation

Defence Attaché, London:
Colonel H.R.H. Prince Georg of Denmark, CVO

Naval Attaché, Washington:
Captain O. Felding, RDN

Strength of the Fleet

4 Submarines (Diesel Powered)
6 Frigates (4 for Fishery Protection)
4 Minelayers
4 Corvettes
4 Coastal Minelayers
8 Coastal Minesweepers
9 Seaward Defence Craft
16 Motor Torpedo Boats
4 Inshore Minesweepers
9 Patrol Craft
12 Support Ships and Service craft

Navy Estimates

	Kr.		Kr.
1961-62:	177,100,000	1965-66:	291,500,000
1962-63:	210,100,000	1966-67:	371,900,000
1963-64:	231,000,000	1967-68:	376,450,000
1964-65:	279,100,000	1968-69:	390.900,000

Personnel

January 1969: 7,000 officers and men

Mercantile Marine

Lloyd's Register of Shipping:
1,140 vessels of 3,204,040 tons gross

SUBMARINES

2 "NARHVALEN" CLASS

Name	No.	Laid down	Launched	Completed
NARHVALEN	S 320	16 Feb 1965	10 Sep 1968	
NORDKAPEREN	S 321	20 Jan 1966		

Displacement, tons	370 surface; 450 submerged
Length, feet (*metres*)	144·4 (*44·0*)
Beam, feet (*metres*)	15 (*4·6*)
Draught, feet (*metres*)	12·5 (*3·8*)
Torpedo tubes	8—21 in (*533 mm*) bow, internal
Main engines	Diesels; 1 200 bhp surface; Elec. motors, 1 200 hp submerged
Speed, knots	10 surface; 17 submerged
Complement	21

These coastal submarines are similar to the German "U-4" class and are being built under licence at the Royal Dockyard, Copenhagen. They are conventionally powered, and fitted with schnorkel installation. "Tear-drop" hull. Originally numbered S 330 and S 331.

SPÆKHUGGEREN — *1968, Stefan Terzibaschitsch*

4 "DELFINEN" CLASS

Name	No.	Laid down	Launched	Completed
DELFINEN	S 326	1 July 1954	4 May 1956	16 Sep 1958
SPÆKHUGGEREN	S 327	1 Dec 1954	20 Feb 1957	27 June 1959
SPRINGEREN	S 329	3 Jan 1961	26 Apr 1963	22 Oct 1964
TUMLEREN	S 328	22 May 1956	22 May 1958	15 Jan 1960

Displacement, tons	550 standard; 595 surface 643 submerged
Length, feet (*metres*)	117·2 (54·0)
Beam, feet (*metres*)	15·4 (*4·7*)
Draught, feet (*metres*)	13·1 (*4·0*)
Torpedo tubes	4—21 in (*533 mm*)
Main engines	2 Burmeister & Wain diesels; 1 200 bhp surface; Electric motors, 1 200 hp submerged
Speed, knots	15 surface and submerged
Range, miles	4 000 at 8 knots
Complement	33

Built in the Royal Dockyard, Copenhagen. Engined with diesels of a new type. Equipped with Schnorkel.

PHOTOGRAPHS. A photograph of *Tumleren* appears in the 1966-67 and 1967-68 editions, and of *Springeren* in the 1967-68 edition.

DELFINEN — *1968, Royal Danish Navy, Official*

FAST FRIGATES

2 "PEDER SKRAM" CLASS

FF (ex-DE) TYPE

Name	No.	Builders	Laid down	Launched	Completed
HERLUF TROLLE	F 353	Helsingörs J. & M.	18 Dec 1964	8 Sep 1965	16 Apr 1967
PEDER SKRAM	F 352	Helsingörs J. &. M	25 Sep 1964	20 May 1965	30 June 1966

Displacement, tons	2 030 standard; 2 720 full load (officially revised figures)
Length, feet (*metres*)	354·3 (*108*) pp; 396·5 (*112·6*) oa
Beam, feet (*metres*)	39·5 (*12*)
Draught, feet (*metres*)	11·8 (*3·6*)
Guns, syrface	4—5 in (*127 mm*) 38 cal US
Guns, AA	4—40 mm
A/S weapons	DC
Main engines	CODAG; 2 shafts:— 2 GM 16-567 D diesels; 4 800 hp; 2 Pratt & Whitney PWA GG 4A-3 gas turbines; 44 000 hp total output
Speed, knots	28 designed; over 30 max; 18 economical sea
Complement	112

Fast frigates of Danish design built at Helsingör. They were to have been armed, additionally to guns, with three 21 inch torpedo tubes and the "Terne" anti-submarine weapon. There is space on the quarter deck for possible future surface-to-air guided missile launcher installation.

PENNANT NOS. The pennant numbers allocated originally were D 320 (see illustration in the 1963-64 to 1965-66 editions) and D 321, when they were designated DE (Destroyer Escorts). US/NATO procurement numbers PC 1644 and PC 1645, respectively.

DISPOSALS OF "HUNT" CLASS
Of the three former British fast frigates or escort destroyers of the "Hunt" class, *Rolf Krake* (ex-HMS *Calpe*) and *Valdemar Sejr* (ex-HMS *Exmoor*) were declared for disposal in 1963, and *Esbern Snare* (ex-HMS *Blackmore*) was officially stricken from the Navy List in 1966.

HERLUF TROLLE — *1968, Royal Danish Navy, Official*

PEDER SKRAM — *1969, Wright & Logan*

FRIGATES

4 "HVIDBJORNEN" CLASS

FF TYPE

Displacement, tons	1 345 standard; 1 650 full load
Length, feet (*metres*)	219·8 (*67·0*) pp; 238·2 (*72·6*) oa
Beam, feet (*metres*)	38·0 (*11·6*)
Draught, feet (*metres*)	16 (*4·9*)
Aircraft	1 Alouette III helicopter
Guns, dual purpose	1—3 in (*76 mm*)
Main engines	4 GM 16—567C diesels; 6 400 bhp; 1 shaft
Speed, knots	18
Range, miles	6 000 at 13 knots
Complement	75

Ordered in 1960-61. Of frigate type for fishery protection and surveying duties in the North Sea, Faroe Islands, and Greenland waters. They are equipped with a helicopter platform aft. The prototype ship of the class was built by Aarhus Flydedok og Maskinkompagni.

PHOTOGRAPHS. A photograph of *Vædderen* appears in the 1966-67 and 1967-68 editions and of *Hvidbjörnen* in the 1967-68 and 1968-69 editions.

Name	No.	Builders	Laid down	Launched	Completed
FYLLA	F 351	Aalborg Værft	27 June 1962	18 Dec 1962	10 July 1963
HVIDBJØRNEN	F 348	Aarhus Flydedok	4 June 1961	23 Nov 1961	15 Dec 1962
INGOLF	F 350	Svendborg Værft	5 Dec 1961	27 July 1961	27 July 1963
VÆDDEREN	F 349	Aalborg Værft	30 Oct 1961	6 Apr 1962	19 Mar 1963

INGOLF — *1968, Royal Danish Navy, Official*

FYLLA — *1969, Royal Danish Navy, Official*

DISPOSALS OF "RIVER" CLASS
Of the two former British frigates of the "River" class, *Niels Ebbesen* (ex-HMS *Annan*) was scrapped in 1963, and *Holger Danske* (ex-HMS *Monnow*) in 1959.

DISPOSALS OF "FLOWER" CLASS
The former British frigate of the "Flower" class, *Thetis* (ex-HMS *Geranium*) was discarded in 1963.

DISPOSALS OF "HUITFELDT" CLASS
Of the two patrol vessels, formerly coastal destroyers, of the "Huitfeldt" class, *Huitfeldt* (ex-*Nymfen*) was discarded in 1965, and *Willemoes* (ex-*Najaden*) was officially deleted from the Navy List in 1966. Both were scrapped at Antwerp in 1966.

CORVETTES

4 "TRITON" CLASS

Displacement, tons	760 standard; 873 full load
Length, feet (*metres*)	242·8 (*74·0*) pp; 250·3 (*76·3*) oa
Beam, feet (*metres*)	31·5 (*9·6*)
Draught, feet (*metres*)	9 (*2·7*)
Guns, surface	2—3 in (*76 mm*)
Guns, AA	1—40 mm
A/S	2 Hedgehogs; 4 DCT
Main engines	2 Ansaldo Fiat 409T diesels 4 400 bhp; 2 shafts
Speed, knots	18 designed, 20 max 16 sea
Range, miles	2 400 at 18 knots
Complement	110

All four vessels were built in Italy for the Danish Navy under the United States "offshore" account in the Mutual Defence Assistance Program.

CLASSIFICATION. Officially classified as corvettes in 1954, but have "F" pennant numbers like frigates.

PHOTOGRAPH. Of *Triton* appears in the 1956-57 to 1962-63 editions.

Name	No.	Builders	Launched	Transferred
BELLONA	F 344	Naval Meccanicia, Castellammare	9 Jan 1955	31 Jan 1957
DIANA	F 345	Cantiere del Tirreno, Riva, Trigoso	19 Dec 1954	30 July 1955
FLORA	F 346	Cantiere del Tirreno, Riva, Trigoso	25 June 1955	28 Aug 1956
TRITON	F 347	Cantiere Navali di Taranto	12 Sep 1954	10 Aug 1955

DIANA — *1968, Royal Danish Navy, Official*

MINELAYERS

4 "FALSTER" CLASS

Displacement, tons	1 900 full load
Length, feet (*metres*)	238 (*72·5*) pp; 252·6 (*77·0*) oa
Beam, feet (*metres*)	41 (*12·5*)
Draught, feet (*metres*)	10 (*3·0*)
Guns, dual purpose	4—3 in (*76 mm*), 2 twin mountings
Mines	400
Main engines	2 GM—567D 3 diesels; 4 800 shp 2 shafts
Speed, knots	17
Complement	120

Minelayers of a novel Scandinavian-NATO design. Ordered in 1960-61. All are named after Danish Islands. The steel hull is flush decked with a raking stem, a full stern, and a prominent knuckle forward. The superstructure has a block outline surmounted by a squat streamlined funnel, two light lattice masts, high angle director control towers fore and aft and whip aerials. The hull is sub-divided by watertight bulkheads and flats to isolate damage, and has been specially strengthened for ice navigation.

PHOTOGRAPHS. A photograph of *Fyen* appears in the 1967-68 edition.

Name	No.	Builders	Laid down	Launched	Completed
FALSTER	N 80	Nakskov Skibsvaerft	12 Apr 1962	19 Sep 1962	7 Nov 1963
FYEN	N 81	Frederikshavn Værft	12 Apr 1962	3 Oct 1962	18 Sep 1963
MØEN	N 82	Frederikshavn Værft	4 Oct 1962	6 Mar 1963	29 Apr 1964
SJÆLLAND	N 83	Nakskov Skibsvaerft	17 Jan 1963	14 June 1963	7 July 1964

FALSTER — *1968, Skyfotos*

COASTAL MINELAYERS

LANGELAND N 42

Displacement, tons	310 standard; 232 full load
Dimensions, feet	133·5 oa; 128·2 pp × 23·7 × 7·2
Guns	2—40 mm. 2—20 mm Madsen
Main engines	Diesel; 2 shafts; 385 bhp = 11·6 knots
Complement	37

Built at the Royal Dockyard, Copenhagen. Laid down in 1950. Launched on 17 May 1950. Completed in 1951. A photograph of *Langeland* appears in the 1951-52 to 1968-69 editions.

LOUGEN *1969, Royal Danish Navy, Official*

2 "LOUGEN" CLASS

LAALAND N 40 **LOUGEN** N 41

Displacement, tons	240 standard; 260 full load
Dimensions, feet	105·5 × 21·2 × 6·5
Guns	2—20 mm AA
Main engines	B. & W. diesel; 2 shafts; 350 bhp = 10 knots
Complement	31

Built at the Royal Dockyard, Copenhagen. Both laid down in 1940, launched in 1941 and completed in 1946. A photograph of *Lougen* appears in the 1965-66 and 1966-67 editions.

LAALAND *1968, Royal Danish Navy, Official*

LINDORMEN N 39

Displacement, tons	604 standard; 645 full load
Dimensions, feet	175·5 oa; 167·2 pp × 29 × 8
Guns	2—40 mm AA; 2 MG
Mines	150
Main engines	Triple expansion; 2 shafts; 950 ihp = 12 knots
Boilers	2 Thornycroft 3-drum type
Complement	66

Built at the Royal Dockyard, Copenhagen. Laid down in 1939. Launched on 30 Mar 1940. Completed in 1940. Scuttled in Copenhagen Harbour on 29 Aug 1943, but was salved and refitted with a new rig.

LINDORMEN *1966, Royal Danish Navy, Official*

COASTAL MINESWEEPERS

8 "SUND" CLASS

AARØSUND (ex-*AMS* 127) M 571
ALSSUND (ex-*AMS* 128) M 572
EGERNSUND (ex-*AMS* 129) M 573
GRØNSUND (ex-*MSC* 256) M 574
GULDBORGSUND (ex-*MSC* 257) M 575
OMØSUND (ex-*MSC* 221) M 576
ULVSUND (ex-*MSC* 263) M 577
VILSUND (ex-*MSC* 264) M 578

Displacement, tons	350 standard; 376 full load
Dimensions, feet	138 pp; 144 oa × 27 × 8·5
Guns	2—20 mm
Main engines	Diesels; 2 shafts; 1 200 bhp = 13 knots
Complement	35

MSC (ex-AMS) 60 class NATO coastal minesweepers all built in USA. Completed in 1954-56. Photographs of *Aarøsund* appear in the 1956-57 to 1965-66 editions. *Aarøsund* was transferred on 24 Jan 1955, *Alssund* on 5 Apr 1955, *Egernsund* on 3 Aug 1955, *Grønsund* on 21 Sep 1956, *Guldborgsund* on 11 Nov 1956. *Omøsund* on 20 June 1956, *Ulvsund* on 20 Sep 1956 and *Vilsund* on 15 Nov 1956.

A photograph of *Omøsund* appears in the 1966-67 and 1967-68 editions.

ARRØSUND *1968, Royal Danish Navy, Official*

SEAWARD DEFENCE CRAFT

9 "DAPHNE" CLASS

Name	Pennant No.	Laid down	Launched	Completed
DAPHNE	P 530	1 Apr 1960	10 Nov 1960	19 Dec 1961
DRYADEN	P 531	1 July 1960	1 Mar 1961	4 Apr 1962
HAVFRUEN	P 533	15 Mar 1961	4 Oct 1961	20 Dec 1962
HAVMANDEN	P 532	15 Nov 1960	16 May 1961	30 Aug 1962
NAJADEN	P 534	20 Sep 1961	20 June 1962	26 Apr 1963
NEPTUN	P 536	1 Sep 1962	29 May 1963	18 Dec 1963
NYMFEN	P 535	1 Apr 1962	1 Nov 1962	4 Oct 1963
RAN	P 537	1 Dec 1962	10 July 1963	15 May 1964
ROTA	P 538	19 July 1963	25 Nov 1963	20 Jan 1965

Displacement, tons	170
Dimensions, feet	121·3 × 20 × 6·5
Guns	1—40 mm AA
A/S weapons	2—51 mm rocket launchers. depth charges
Main engines	Diesels; 2 shafts; 2 600 bhp = 20 knots (plus 1 cruising engine; 100 bhp)
Complement	23

All built at the Royal Dockyard, Copenhagen. A photograph of *Havmanden* appears in the 1963-64 to 1965-66 editions, and of *Najaden* in the 1966-67 and 1967-68 editions.

DAPHNE *1968, Royal Danish Navy, Official*

ROYAL YACHT

DANNEBROG A 540

Displacement, tons	1 130
Dimensions, feet	246 oa × 34 × 11·2
Guns	2—37 mm
Main engines	2 sets Burmeister & Wain 8 cylinder; 2 cycle diesels. 1 800 bhp = 14 knots
Complement	57

Built at the Royal Dockyard, Copenhagen. Launched in 1931.

DANNEBROG *1968, Royal Danish Navy, Official*

TORPEDO BOATS (*Torpedobaade*)

6 "SØLØVEN" CLASS

Name	Pennant No.	Laid down	Launched	Completed
SØLØVEN	P 510	27 Aug 1962	19 Apr 1963	June 1964*
SØRIDDEREN	P 511	4 Oct 1962	22 Aug 1963	June 1964*
SØBJORNEN	P 512	9 July 1963	19 Aug 1964	Sep 1965
SØHESTEN	P 513	5 Sep 1963	31 Mar 1965	June 1966
SØHUNDEN	P 514	18 Aug 1964	12 Jan 1966	Dec 1966
SØULVEN	P 515	30 Mar 1965	27 Apr 1966	Mar 1967

Displacement, tons	95 standard; 114 full load
Dimensions, feet	90 pp; 96 wl; 99 oa × 25·5 × 7
Guns	2—40 mm Bofors AA
Tubes	4—21 in (side)
Main engines	3 Bristol Siddeley Proteus gas turbines; 3 shafts; 12 750 bhp = 54 knots GM diesels on wing shafts for cruising = 10 knots
Complement	29

The design is a combination of the "Brave" class hull form and "Ferocity" type construction. *Søløven* ("Sea Lion") and *Søridderen* ("Sea Knight") were built by Vosper Limited, Portsmouth, England (*delivered to the Royal Danish Navy on 12 and 10 Feb 1965, respectively); and the remaining four under licence by the Royal Dockyard, Copenhagen. A photograph of *Søløven* appears in the 1964-65 and 1965-66 editions, and of *Søridderen* in the 1966-67 and 1967-68 editions.

SØHUNDEN *1968, Royal Danish Navy, Official*

4 "FALKEN" CLASS

Name	Pennant No.	Laid down	Launched	Completed
FALKEN	P 506	1 Nov 1960	19 Dec 1961	4 Oct 1962
GLENTEN	P 507	3 Jan 1961	15 Mar 1962	15 Dec 1962
GRIBBEN	P 508	15 May 1961	18 July 1962	26 Apr 1963
HØGEN	P 509	1 Sep 1961	4 Oct 1962	6 June 1963

Displacement, tons	119
Dimensions, feet	118 × 17·8 × 6
Guns	1—40 mm AA; 1—20 mm AA
Tubes	4—21 in (side)
Main engines	3 diesels; 3 shafts; 9 000 bhp = 40 knots
Complement	23

Ordered under US offshore procurement in the Military Aid Program. All built at the Royal Dockyard, Copenhagen. Named after birds. A photograph of *Falken* appears in the 1963-64 to 1965-66 editions.

GLENTEN *1968, Royal Danish Navy, Official*

6 "FLYVEFISKEN" CLASS

FLYVEFISKEN P 500 **HAJEN** P 501 **HAVKATTEN** P 502 **LAXEN** P 503 **MAKRELEN** P 504 **SVÆRDFISKEN** P 505

Displacement, tons	110
Dimensions, feet	120 × 18 × 6
Guns	1—40 mm AA; 1—20 mm AA
Tubes	2—21 in
Main engines	3 diesels; 3 shafts; 7 500 bhp = 40 knots
Complement	22

Three built in Royal Dockyard, Copenhagen, three in Frederikssund Vaerft. All units are named after fishes. Ordered in 1952, laid down in 1953 and launched in 1954-55. A photograph of *Flyvefisken* appears in the 1956-57 to 1963-64 editions, of *Hajen* in the 1964-65 and 1965-66 editions and of *Laxen* in the 1966-67 to 1967-68 editions.

HAVKATTEN *1968, Royal Danish Navy, Official*

INSHORE MINESWEEPERS (*Minestrygere*)

4 "VIG" CLASS

Name	Pennant No.	Laid down	Launched	Completed
ASVIG	M 579	22 Apr 1959	11 May 1960	6 Sep 1961
MOSVIG	M 580	22 Apr 1959	14 Sep 1960	25 Oct 1961
SANDVIG	M 581	11 May 1960	1 Mar 1961	1 Feb 1962
SÆLVIG	M 582	14 Sep 1960	14 July 1961	30 Apr 1962

Displacement, tons	180
Dimensions, feet	113·5 × 22·5 × 6·2
Guns	2—20 mm AA
Main engines	2 diesels; 2 shafts; 11 000 bhp = 13 knots
Complement	18

All built at the Royal Dockyard, Copenhagen. A photograph of *Asvig* appears in the 1962-63 to 1965-66 editions.

ASVIG *1969, Royal Danish Navy, Official*

PATROL CRAFT (*Orlogskuttere*)

2 "MAAGEN" CLASS

MAAGEN (Y 384) **MALLEMUKKEN** (Y 385)

Displacement, tons	190
Dimensions, feet	88·5 × 21·7 × 9·5
Guns	1—40 mm AA
Main engines	385 hp; 1 shaft; speed 11 knots

Of steel construction. Built at Helsingor, laid down 15 Jan 1960, launched 1960.

1 "SKARVEN" CLASS

TEJSTEN (Y 383)

Displacement, tons	130
Dimensions, feet	82 × 20·7 × 9·4
Guns	1—37 mm
Main engines	Alfa Diesel; 180 bhp = 9 knots

Of wooden construction. Built by Holbaek Skibsbyggeri. Launched 1951. Sister ship *Skarven*, Y 382, was disabled after grounding in the Faroes on 7 May 1966 and was officially deleted from the list.

All three above for service in Greenland waters.

3 "ALHOLM" CLASS

ALHOLM Y 369 (ex-*MSK* 1) **BIRKHOLM** Y 370 (ex-*MSK* 2) **ERTHOLM** Y 371 (ex-*MSK* 3)

Displacement, tons	70
Dimensions, feet	69 × 17 × 9
Guns	1—20 mm AA
Main engines	Diesel; 120 bhp = 10 knots

Built by Frederikssund vaerft. All launched in 1945. Used as patrol vessels. A photograph of *Alholm* appears in the 1968-69 edition.

2 "FYRHOLM" CLASS

FYRHOLM Y 372 (ex-MSK 4) **LINDHOLM** Y 374 (ex-*MSK* 6)

Displacement, tons	68
Dimensions, feet	65·7 × 16·8 × 7·5
Main engines	Diesel; 120 bhp = 9 knots

Built by Sydhavns Vaerft. Launched in 1944-45. Used as patrol vessels. A photograph of *Frhyolm* appears in the 1966-67 edition. Sister boat *Græsholm* Y 373 (ex-MSK 5) was officially deleted from the list in 1968.

Of the patrol vessels, former shallow water minesweepers, *Klordyb* M 569 (ex-ML 2) and *Vejdyb* M 570 (ex-ML 3) were officially deleted from the list in May 1967, and *Graadyb* was condemned on 4 Feb 1956. For other disposals see 1963-64 edition.

LINDHOLM *1969, Royal Danish Navy, Official*

COAST GUARD CUTTERS

"ASKØ" CLASS

ASKØ MHV 81 (ex-Y 386, ex-M 560, ex-MS 2)
ENØ MHV 82 (ex-Y 388, ex-M562, ex-MS 5)
FÆNØ MHV 69 (ex-M 563, ex-MS 6)
MANØ MHV 83 (ex-Y 391, ex-M 566, ex-MS 9)

Displacement, tons	74
Dimensions, feet	78·8 × 21 × 5
Guns	1—20 mm
Main engines	Diesel; 1 shaft; 350 bhp = 11 knots

Of wooden construction. All launched in 1941. Former inshore minesweepers. Used by the Maritime Home Guard. Sister boats *Baagø* Y 387 (ex-M 561, ex-MS 3), *Hjortø* Y 389 (ex-M564, ex-MS 7) and *Lyø* Y 390 (ex-M 565, ex-MS 8) were officially deleted from the list in 1968.

FÆNO *1969, Royal Danish Navy, Official*

MHV 70 **MHV 71** **MHV 72**

Displacement, tons	76
Guns	1—20 mm AA
Main engines	200 bhp = 10 knots

Built in 1958. Patrol boats and training craft for the Naval Home Guard. Of the fishing cutter type. Formerly designated DMH, but allocated MHV numbers in 1969. A photograph of DMH 71 appears in the 1968-69 edition. In addition there are some 20 small vessels of the trawler and other types.

DISPOSALS
The surveying vessel **Freja** A 541 was officially deleted from the Navy List in Apr 1967. The utility landing craft **Balder** (ex-US LCU 715) A 543, **Brage** (ex-US LCU 810) A 544, **Hermod** (ex-US LCU 1042) A 545, **Loke** (ex-US LCU 1294) A 546, **Odin** (ex-LCU 649) A 561, **Thor** (ex-US LCU 765) A 562, **Tyr** (ex-LCU 1230) A 564, **Uller** (ex-US LCU 1373) A 565, **Vale** (ex-LCU 1383) A 566, and **Vider** (ex-US LCU 1422) A 567 were officially deleted from the Navy List in Aug 1967.

ICEBREAKERS (*Isbrydere*)

DANBJØRN **ISBJØRN**

Displacement, tons	3 685
Dimensions, feet	252 × 56 × 20
Main engines	Diesels; Electric drive; 11 880 bhp = 14 knots
Complement	34

Built in 1965. The old two-funnelled icebreaker *Isbjørn* was discarded in 1969.

ISBJORN *1969, Danish Royal Navy, Official*

ELBJØRN

Displacement, tons	893 standard; 1 400 full load
Dimensions, feet	156·5 × 40·3 × 14·5
Main engines	Diesels; electric drive; 3 600 bhp = 12 knots

Built in 1953. A photograph appears in the 1956-57 to 1960-61 editions.

STOREBJØRN

Displacement, tons	2 540
Dimensions, feet	197 × 49·2 × 19

Built in 1931. Icebreakers are controlled by the Ministry of Trade and Shipping.

LILLEBJØRN

Displacement, tons,	1 000
Dimensions, feet	144·3 × 36·5 × 18

Built in 1926. The small icebreaker *Mjolner* was stricken from the list in 1960.

DEPOT SHIPS (*Depotskibe*)

HJÆLPEREN (ex-US *LSM* 500) A 563

Displacement, tons	1 030 standard; 1 170 full load
Dimensions, feet	203·5 oa × 34·5 × 8·3
Guns	2—40 mm
Main engines	Diesels; 2 shafts; 2 800 bhp = 12 knots
Complement	60

Former United States medium landing ship. Built by Brown Shipbuilding Co, Houston, Texas. Laid down on 17 Mar 1945. Launched on 7 Apr 1945. Completed on 17 May 1945. Transferred to the Royal Danish Navy on 15 May 1953. Depot and Repair ship for motor torpedo boats.
DISPOSAL
The depot ship *Aegir*, ex-German *Tanga*, was officially deleted from the list in Jan 1967.

HJÆLPEREN *1968, Royal Danish Navy, Official*

HENRIK GERNER (ex-M/S *Hammershus*) A 542

Displacement, tons	2 200 standard
Dimensions, feet	252·7 × 40 × 18·3
Guns	6—40 mm AA
Main engines	Burmeister & Wain diesel; speed = 15 knots
Complement	230

Former Danish passenger ship. Built in 1936. Transferred to the Royal Danish Navy on 8 Jan 1964, refitted at the Royal Dockyard, Copenhagen, and commissioned as a depot ship for submarines.

HENRIK GERNER *1968, Royal Danish Navy, Official*

OILERS (*Tankfartøjer*)

IMFAXE (ex-US *YO* 226) A 568 **SKINFAXE** (ex-US *YO* 229) A 596

Displacement, tons	422 light; 1 390 full load
Dimensions, feet	174 oa × 32 × 13·2
Main engines	1 GM diesel; 560 bhp = 10 knots
Complement	23

Yard oilers transferred to the Royal Danish Navy from the USA on 2 Aug 1962. A photograph of *Rimfaxe* appears in the 1967-68 edition.

SKINFAXE *1968*

TENDERS

HOLLÆNDERDYBET (ex-*Den Lille Havfrue*) **KONGEDYBET** (ex-*Kirsten Pill*)

Displacement, tons	158 full load; 88 gross
Dimensions, feet	150 × 19 × 7·2
Main engines	Diesel

Both launched in 1935. Used for transport. Nos. A 554, A 555, respectively.

DOMINICAN REPUBLIC

Administration

Under Secretary For The Navy:
Commodore Miguel A. Cintron Romero

Chief of Naval Staff:
Commodore Ramon E. Jiménez Hijo

Vice-Chief of Naval Staff:
Captain Luis A. Pimentel

Strength of the Fleet

1 Destroyer
3 Frigates
5 Corvettes
2 Minesweepers
7 Patrol vessels
19 Auxiliary and Service Craft

Personnel

1969: 3 500 officers and men

Mercantile Marine

Lloyd's Register of Shipping
15 vessels of 11 282 tons gross

DESTROYERS (*Destructores*)

Name	*Pennant No.*	*Builders*	*Laid down*	*Launched*	*Completed*
DUARTE (ex-*Trujillo*, ex-HMS *Hotspur*)	501 (ex-D 101	Scotts' S.B. & Eng. Co. Ltd., Greenock	27 Feb 1935	23 Mar 1936	29 Dec 1936

Displacement, tons	1 340 standard; 2 020 full load
Length, feet (*metres*)	312 (*95·1*) pp; 320 (*97·5*) wl 323 (*98·5*) oa
Beam, feet (*metres*)	33 (*10·0*)
Draught, feet (*metres*)	15 (*4·6*) max (props)
Guns, surface	3—4·7 in (*120 mm*)
Guns, AA	4—20 mm
A/S	4 DCT
Torpedo tubes	4—21 in (*533 mm*)
Boilers	3 Admiralty 3-drum
Main engines	Parsons geared turbines 34 000 shp; 2 shafts
Speed, knots	36; sea speed 25
Radius, miles	5 700 at 15 knots
Oil fuel (tons)	455
Complement	145

DUARTE *Added 1966*

Former British destroyer of the "H" flotilla which served in the Royal Navy until Nov 1948 when she was purchased and renamed *Trujillo*. Renamed *Duarte* in 1962. Pennant No. was changed from D 101 to 501 in 1968. Near sister ship *Sanchez* (ex-*Generalisimo*, ex-*HMS Fame*), D 102, was discarded in 1968. Photograph in the 1961-62 to 1968-69 edition.

FRIGATES (*Fragatas*)

Name	*Pennant No.*	*Builders*	*Laid down*	*Launched*	*Completed*
CAP. GENERAL PEDRO SANTANA (ex-*Presidente Peynado*, ex-USS *Pueblo*, PF 13)	453 (ex-F 104)	Kaiser S.Y. Richmond, Cal.	14 Nov 1943	20 Jan 1944	27 May 1944
GREGORIO LUPERON (ex-*Presidente Troncoso*, ex-USS *Knoxville*, PF 64)	452 (ex-F 103)	Leatham D. Smith S.B. Co, Wis.	15 Apr 1934	10 July 1943	29 Apr 1944

2 Ex-US "RIVER" TYPE

Displacement, tons	1 430 standard; 2 415 full load
Length, feet (*metres*)	298 (*90·8*) wl; 304 (*92·7*) oa
Beam, feet (*metres*)	37·5 (*11·4*)
Draught, feet (*metres*)	12 (*3·7*)
Guns, surface	3—3 in (*76 mm*)
Guns, AA	4—40 mm (2 twin); 6—20 mm; 4—0·5 in (*12·7 mm*) MG
Boilers	2 three-drum type
Main engines	Triple expansion 5 500 ihp; 2 shafts
Speed, knots	16
Oil fuel (tons)	760
Complement	140

PENNANT NUMBERS. Pennant numbers were changed from F 104 and F 103 to 453 and 452 respectively, in 1968.

GREGORIO LUPERON *Official*

CAP GENERAL PEDRO SANTANA *1969, Dominican Navy, Official*

Frigates—*continued*

1 Ex-CANADIAN "RIVER" TYPE

MELLA (ex-*Presidente Trujillo*, ex-HMCS *Carlplace*)

Displacement, tons	1 400 standard; 2 125 full load
Length, feet (*metres*)	301·5 (*91·9*)
Beam, feet (*metres*)	36·7 (*11·2*)
Draught, feet (*metres*)	12 (*3·7*) mean
Boilers	2 three-drum
Main engines	Triple expansion 5 500 ihp; 2 shafts
Speed, knots	20
Oil fuel (tons)	645
Complement	195 (15 officers, 130 men, 50 midshipmen)

Built by Davie SB & Repairing Co, Lauzon. Launched on 6 July 1944. Completed on 13 Dec 1944. Transferred to the Dominican Navy in 1946. Original Dominican frigate. Modified for use as Presidential Yacht with extra accommodation and deck-houses built up aft. Pennant No. as a frigate was F 101, but as the Presidential Yacht she no longer wore it. Now carries pennant number 451 as training ship. Renamed *Mella* in 1962. Now used for training midshipmen.

MELLA — *1958, Official*

CORVETTES (*Corbetas*)

Name	*Pennant No.*	*Builders*	*Launched*	*Completed*
CRISTOBAL COLON (ex-HMCS *Lachute*)	401 (ex-C 101)	Morton Ltd, Quebec City, P.Q.	9 June 1944	26 Oct 1944
GERARDO JANSEN (ex-HMCS *Peterborough*)	404 (ex-C 104)	Kingston Shipbuilding Co, Kingston, Ontario	15 Jan 1944	1 June 1944
JUAN ALEJANDRO ACOSTA (ex-HMCS *Louisbourg*)	402 (ex-C 102)	Morton Ltd, Quebec City, P.Q.	13 July 1943	13 Dec 1943
JUAN BAUTISTA CAMBIASO (ex-HMCS *Belleville*)	403 (ex-C 103)	Kingston Shipbuilding Co, Kingston, Ontario	17 June 1944	19 Oct 1944
JUAN BAUTISTA MAGGIOLO (ex-HMCS *Riviere du loup*)	405 (ex-C 105)	Morton Ltd, Quebec City, P.Q.	2 July 1943	21 Nov 1943

5 Ex-CANADIAN "FLOWER" TYPE

Displacement, tons	1 060 standard; 1 350 full load
Length, feet (*metres*)	193 (*58·8*) pp; 208 (*63·4*) oa
Beam, feet (*metres*)	33 (*10·0*)
Draught, feet (*metres*)	14·5 (*4·4*) mean
Guns, surface	*C. Colon:* 1—3 in (*76 mm*); *Others:* 1—4 in (*102 mm*)
Guns, AA	*C. Colon:* 2—40 mm (twin); 6—20 mm; 4—0·5 in MG (2 twin) *Others:* 1—40 mm; 6—20 mm; 2—0·5 in MG
Boilers	2 three-drum type
Main engines	Triple expansion; 2 750 ihp
Speed, knots	16
Oil fuel (tons)	282
Complement	53

All built in Canadian shipyards under the Emergency Construction programme during the Second World War. Transferred to the Dominican Navy in 1947. The sixth ship, *Asbestos*, was wrecked *en route* from Canada. Pennant numbers were changed in 1968, 300 being added to all numbers and letter C suppressed. A photograph of *Juan Maggiolo* appears in the 1951-52 to 1957-58 editions, of *Cristobal Colon* in the 1951-52 to 1960-61 editions, and of *Gerardo Jansen* in the 1961-62 to 1965-66 editions.

JUAN BAUTISTA CAMBIASO — *1966, Official*

MINESWEEPERS

2 Ex-US MSF TYPE

SEPARACION (ex-USS *Skirmish*, MSF 302) BM 454
TORTUGERO (ex-USS *Signet*, MSF 303) BM 455

Displacement, tons	650 standard; 945 full load
Dimensions, feet	180 wl; 184·5 oa × 33 × 10
Guns	1—3 in dp; 4—40 mm AA
Main engines	Diesel; 2 shafts; 1 710 bhp = 15 knots

Former US fleet minesweepers of the "Admirable" class. Purchased on 13 Jan 1965.

PATROL VESSELS (*Patrulleros*)

3 Ex-USCG WPC TYPE

	Pennant No.	*Launched*
INDEPENDENCIA (ex-USCGC *Icarus*)	204 (ex-P 105)	1931
LIBERTAD (ex-*Rafael Atoa*, ex-USCGC *Thetis*)	205 (ex-P 106)	1931
RESTAURACION (ex-USCGC *Galathea*)	203 (ex-P 104)	1932

Displacement, tons	334-337
Dimensions, feet	165 × 25·2 × 9·5
Guns	1—3 in; 1—40 mm; 1—20 mm
Main engines	2 Diesels; 1 280 bhp = 15 knots
Complement	35 (*Independencia*, 4 officers, 25 men)

Ex-United States Coastguard Cutters. *Independencia* was completed by Bath Iron Works in 1932, and *Restauracion* by John H. Machis & Co, Camden, NJ, in 1933.

Pennant numbers were changed from P 105, P 106, P 104 to 200 series in 1968.

Of the three patrol vessels of the ex-US PC type, *27 de Febrero* (ex-*PC 613*), *Constitucion* (ex-*Cibas*, ex-*Engage*, ex-*PC 1597*) were discarded in 1968; and *Patria* (ex-*Capitan Wenceslas Arvels*, ex-*PC 1202*) in 1962.

INDEPENDENCIA — *1964, Dominican Navy, Official*

RESTAURACION — *1969, Dominican Navy, Official*

MEDIUM LANDING SHIP

(*Barcazas de Desembarco*)

1 Ex-US LSM TYPE. RATED AS AUXILIARY

(*Buque Auxiliar*)

SIRIO (ex-USS *LSM* 483) 301 (ex-BA 104)

Displacement, tons	734 standard; 1 100 full load
Dimensions, feet	196 wl; 203·5 oa × 34 × 10 mean
Main engines	2 General Motors diesels; 2 shafts; 1 800 bhp = 14 knots
Oil fuel (tons)	164
Complement	30

Ex-United States *LSM* (Medium Landing Ship). Built by Brown Shipbuilding Co, Houston, Texas. Laid down on 17 Feb 1945, launched on 10 Mar 1945 and completed on 13 April 1945. Transferred to the Dominican Navy in 1960. Pennant number changed from BA 104 to 301 in 1968.

SIRIO *1964, Dominican Navy, Official*

UTILITY LANDING CRAFT

(*Barcazas de Desembarco*)

2 LCT TYPE RATED AS AUXILIARY

(*Lanchas Auxiliares*)

ENRIQUILLO (ex-*17 de Julio*) 303 (ex-LA 3) **SAMANA** 302 (ex-LA 2)

Displacement, tons	150 standard; 310 full load
Dimensions, feet	105 wl; 119·5 oa × 36 × 3 mean
Guns	1 AA, 50 cal
Main engines	3 General Motors diesels; 441 bhp = 8 knots
Oil fuel (tons)	80
Complement,	17

Both built by Astilleros Navales Dominicanos in 1957-58. The new *Samana*, LA 2, replaced the *Samana* LA 2 lost in bad weather. *Enriquilla* (ex-*17 de Julio*) was launched on 24 Oct 1957. Renamed in 1962. Pennant numbers changed from LA 3 and LA 2 to 303 and 302, respectively, in 1968.

ENRIQUILLO *1964, Dominican Navy, Official*

COAST GUARD VESSELS (*Guardacostas*)

1 US PGM TYPE

BETELGEUSE (ex-US *PGM* 77) GC 102

Displacement, tons	107
Dimensions, feet	94·5 × 20·7 × 5
Guns	1—40 mm; 4—20 mm (2 twin); 2—0·5 in MG
Main engines	4 diesels; 2 shafts; 2 200 bhp = 21 knots
Radius, miles	1 500 at 10 knots

Built in the USA for transfer to the Dominican Republic under the Military Aid Programme. Completed in 1966 by Peterson Builders. Transferred on 14 Jan 1966.

RIGEL 101

Main engines	Speed = 18·5 knots maximum.

The former GC 102, *Las Carreras*, ex-*Sanchez*, ex-*Patria*, ex-*SC 1153*, and her sister boat GC 101, *30 de Marzo*, ex-*Mella*, ex-*Rosa*, ex-*SC 1351*, were discarded in 1966-67. *Las Calderas* (ex-*Luberon*, GC 9) and *Bahia Ocoa* (ex-*22 de Junio*, GC 10) were discarded in 1968. Sister boat *Bahia Manzanillo* GC 11 (ex-*16 de Agosto*, ex-USCG cutter 56199) was discarded in 1962.
The coastguard vessel *Trinidad*, GC 8, was also discarded in 1962, and *Boya*, GC 2, in 1960.
The training ship *Duarte* (ex-*Nueva Tioditie*), GA 1 was discarded in 1962.

RIGEL *1969, Dominican Navy, Official*

BELLATRIX GC 106 **CAPELLA** GC 108 **PROCION** GC 103

Displacement, tons	60
Dimensions, feet	85 × 18 × 5
Guns	3—·5 mg
Main engines	2 GM Diesels; 1 000 bhp = 19·5 knots

Officially added to the Dominican Republic Coast Guard list in 1969.

PROCION *1969, Dominican Navy, Official*

LIGHTHOUSE AND BUOY TENDER

(*Buque de Faros y Boyas-Boyero*)

CAPOTILLO (ex-*Camillia*) 1 (ex-FB 101)

Displacement, tons	337
Dimensions, feet	117 × 24 × 7·8
Main engines	2 Diesels; 880 bhp = 10 knots
Complement	40

Built in the United States in 1911. Acquired from the United States Coast Guard in 1949. A photograph of this ship appears in the 1957-58 edition.

MOTOR LAUNCHES (*Lanchas Auxiliare*)

MAIMON LA 5

Dimensions, feet	53 × 9 × 4
Main engines	2 motors; 500 hp = 14 knots
Complement	4

Acquired for the Hydrographic Service of the Navy in 1960.

PUERTO HERMOSO LA 7 **ATLANTIDA** LA 8

The motor launch *Altogracia*, LA-1 (ex-*Laura*), was discarded in 1960 and *Najaya*, LA 4, in 1962.

RESCUE LAUNCH (*Lancha de Rescate*)

CAPITAN ALSINA 105 (ex-LR 101)

Displacement, tons	100 standard
Dimensions, feet	92 wl; 104·8 oa × 19·2 × 5·8
Guns	2—20 mm AA; 2 MG
Main engines	Diesel; 2 shafts; 1 000 hp = 17 knots
Complement	20

Of wooden construction. Launched in 1944. Named as above in 1957. LR 102 was lost in 1956. Sister boat *Capitan Maduro*, LR 103, was discarded in 1968.

CAPITAN ALSINA *Official*

The auxiliary ships (*Buques Auxiliares*) *18 de Decembre*, BA-101 (ex-US *WPC* 587), converted patrol vessel, and *Leonor*, BA-102 (ex-*Romanita*), were discarded in 1960. The Presidential yacht *Patria* (ex-*Angelita*) was sold in 1968.

OILERS

CAPITAN W ARVELO, BT 4 (ex-USS *YO 215*)
CAPITAN BEOTEGUI, BT 5 (ex-US *YO 213*)

Displacement, tons	370 light; 1,095 full load
Dimensions, feet	156·5 × 30 × 13·3
Guns	1—20 mm
Main engines	1 Fairbanks-Morse diesel; 525 bhp = 8 knots max
Capacity	6 570 barrels
Complement	27

Former United States self propelled fuel oil barges. Both built by Ira S. Bushey & Sons, Inc, Brooklyn, New York. Loaned by the USA in Mar 1964.

CAPITAN W. ARVELO *1969, Dominican Navy, Official*

The oiler *San Carlos*, BT 102, was officially deleted from the list in Feb 1965 and *Ulises Heureaux* (ex-*24 de Octubre*, ex-YO 2) BT 101, in 1968.

TUGS (*Remolcadores*)

HERCULES 12 (ex-R 2) **GUACANAGARIX 13** (ex-R 5)

Dimensions, feet	70 × 18·5 × 9
Main engines	1 motor; 500 hp: 1 225 rpm
Complement	11

Small tugs of new construction.

ISABELA 20 (ex-R 1)

Displacement, tons	40
Dimensions, feet	65 × 14 × 9
Main engines	2 diesel motors; 300 bhp = 8 knots
Complement	8

Built in the United States. Named *Isabela* in 1957. A photograph appears in the 1951-52 to 1957-58 editions. The tug *Hercules* (ex-*Heracles*), Pennant No. R 2, transferred from the Dominican mercantile marine in 1952, was lost in 1956.

BERGANTIN R 14 **CONSUELO** R 18 **RIO HAINA** R 17
CALDERAS R 19 **MERCEDES** R 16 (ex-R 10) **SANTANA** R 15 (ex-R 7)

Small tugs for harbour and coastal use.

The tugs *Bergantin*, R-6, *Catalina*, R-3, *Leonidas*, R-8 and *Luperon*, R-4 were discarded in 1960-62.

ECUADOR

Administration

Minister of Defence:
Senor Arturo Vinueza

Commander-in-Chief of the Navy:
Rear Admiral Gonzalo Calderon Noriega

Chief of Naval Staff:
Captain Edmundo Mena S.

Diplomatic Representation

Naval Attaché in Washington:
Captain Octavio Janin

Strength of the Fleet

2 Escort Destroyers ("Hunt" Type)
1 Patrol Frigate (PF Type)
2 Escort Patrol Vessels (PCE Type)
2 Motor Gunboats (PGM Type)
6 Patrol Boats (Motor Launches)
2 Landing Craft (LSM Type)
1 Supply Ship (Cargo)
1 Survey Ship (ex-Netlayer)
1 Water Carrier (YW Type)
3 Tugs (1 Ocean, 2 Harbour)

Ships

The names of Ecuadorian naval vessels are prefaced by "BAE"

Establishments

Naval Academy: in Salinas

Naval Bases

In Galápagos Guayaquil, Salinas, and San Lorenzo

Personnel

1969: 4 000 officers and men

Mercantile Marine

Lloyd's Register of Shipping:
14 vessels of 43 000 tons gross

Name	*Pennant No.*	*Builders*	*Laid down*	*Launched*	*Completed*
GUAYAS (ex-USS *Covington*, PF 56)	E 21 (ex-E 01)	Globe S.B. Co, Superior, Wis.	1 Mar 1943	15 July 1943	7 Aug 1944

1 Ex-US PF TYPE

Displacement, tons	1 430 standard; 2 415 full load
Length, feet (*metres*)	304 (*92·6*) oa
Beam, feet (*metres*)	37·5 (*11·4*)
Draught, feet (*metres*)	13·7 (*4·2*)
Guns, surface	2—3 in (*76 mm*)
Guns, AA	2—40 mm; 4—20 mm
A/S	3 DCT
Boilers	2 small tube
Main engines	Triple expansion 5 500 ihp; 2 shafts
Speed, knots	20 designed; 16 sea
Radius, miles	7 000 at 18 knots 9 500 at 12 knots
Oil fuel (tons)	290 normal; 645 max
Complement	150

Former United States patrol frigate of the PF type. Purchased from the USA in 1947. Similar in design to British "River" class frigates.

GUAYAS *1967, Ecuadorian Navy, Official*

ESCORT DESTROYERS

Name	*Pennant No.*	*Builders*	*Laid down*	*Launched*	*Completed*
PRESIDENTE ALFARO (ex-HMS *Quantock*)	D 01	Scotts' S.B. & Eng Co Ltd, Greenock	26 July 1939	22 Apr 1940	6 Feb 1941
PRESIDENTE VELASCO IBARRA (ex-HMS *Meynell*)	D 02	Swan Hunter & Wigham Richardson, Wallsend	10 Aug 1939	7 June 1940	30 Dec 1940

2 Ex-BRITISH "HUNT" CLASS (TYPE 1) ESCORT DESTROYERS

Displacement, tons	1 000 standard; 1 490 full load
Length, feet (*metres*)	272·3 (*83·0*) pp; 280 (*85·4*) oa
Beam, feet (*metres*)	29 (*8·8*)
Draught, feet (*metres*)	14 (*4·3*)
Guns, surface	4—4 in (*102 mm*)
Guns, AA	2—20 mm
Guns, saluting	4—2 pdr.
A/S weapons	DC throwers; DC racks
Boilers	2 Admiralty 3-drum
Main engines	Parsons geared turbines (by Wallsend Slipway in *Presidente Velasco Ibarra*) 19 000 shp; 2 shafts
Speed, knots	23 sea
Radius, miles	2 000 at 12 knots 800 at 25 knots
Oil fuel (tons)	280
Complement	146

PRESIDENTE VELASCO IBARRA *1965, Ecuadorian Navy, Official*

Former British frigates (ex-escort destroyers) of the "Hunt" class, Type 1, purchased by Ecuador from Great Britain in 1955, and refitted by J. Samuel White & Co, Ltd, Cowes, Isle of Wight. *Quantock* was taken over by the Ecuadorian Navy from the Royal Navy in Portsmouth Dockyard on 16 Aug 1955, when she was renamed *Presidente Alfaro*. Sister ship *Meynell* was transferred to the Ecuadorian Navy later and renamed *Presidente Velasco Ibarra*.

25 DE JULIO (ex-*Enright* APD 66, ex-DE 216) E 12

Displacement, tons	1 400 standard; 2 130 full load
Dimensions, feet	306 pp × 37 × 12·7
Guns	1—5 in 38 cal; 4—40 mm
Boilers	2 Express
Main engines	GE Geared turbines with electrical drive; 2 shafts; 12 000 shp = 23·6 knots
Complement	204 plus 162 troops

This former US high speed transport (modified destroyer escort), launched 29 Mar 1943, was transferred 14 July 1967 under MAP.

25 DE JULIO *1968, Ecuadorian Navy, Official*

ESCORT PATROL VESSELS

2 Ex-US PCE TYPE

Name	**ESMERALDAS** (ex-USS *Eunice*, PCE 846)	**MANABI** (ex-USS *Pascagoula*, PCE 874)
Pennant No.	E 22 (ex-E 03)	E 23 (ex-E 02)
Builders	Pullman Standard Car Manufacturing Co, Chicago, Ill	Albina Eng & Mach Works, Portland, Oreg
Laid down	10 Aug 1943	1 Mar 1943
Launched	20 Dec 1943	11 May 1943
Completed	4 Mar 1944	31 Dec 1943
Transferred	29 Nov 1960	5 Dec 1960

Displacement, tons	640 standard; 903 full load
Dimensions, feet	180 wl; 184·5 oa × 33 × 9·5
Guns	1—3 in dual purpose; 6—40 mm AA
A/S weapons	4 DCT
Main engines	GM diesels; 2 shafts; 1 800 bhp = 15·4 knots
Complement	100 officers and men

Former United States patrol vessels (180 ft Escorts) transferred from the US Navy to the Ecuadorian Navy on 29 Nov and 5 Dec 1960, respectively.
A photograph of *Manabi*, appears in the 1963-64 and 1964-65 editions.

ESMERALDAS *1965, Ecuadorian Navy, Official*

GUNBOATS

2 Ex-US PGM TYPE

GUAYAQUIL (ex-US *PGM* 76) LC 73 **QUITO** (ex-US *PGM* 75) LC 71

Displacement, tons	101
Dimensions, feet	95 oa × 19 × 5
Guns	1—40 mm AA; 2—20 mm
Main engines	4 diesels; 2 shafts; 2 200 bhp = 21 knots
Radius, miles	1 500 at cruising speed
Complement	15

US built. Transferred to the Ecuadorian Navy under MAP on 30 Nov 1965.

GUAYAQUIL *1967, Ecuadorian Navy, Official*

PATROL BOATS

6 ML TYPE

LSP 1 **LSP 2** **LSP 3** **LSP 4** **LSP 5** **LSP 6**

Displacement, tons	45 standard; 64 full load
Dimensions, feet	76·8 × 13·5 × 4·2 mean (6·3 max)
Guns	Light MG AA
Main engines	Bohn & Kähler diesel; 2 shafts; 1 200 bhp = 22 knots
Range, miles	550 at 16 knots
Complement	9

Built by Hermann Havighorst, Bremen-Blumenthal. Ordered in 1954. First two were delivered in Aug 1954 and the ramainder in 1955. Pennant Nos. LP 81 to LP 86. A photograph of LP 1 appears in the 1955-56 edition.

LP 6 **1963, *Ecuadorian Navy Official***

Although not on the Navy List of Ecuador the hulls of the former US Navy high speed transports (modified destroyer escorts) *Reeves* APD 52, *Frament*, APD 77, *Crosley* APD 87, *Hunter Marshall*, APD 112, and *Walter S. Gorka*, APD 114, were transferred from the United States in July and Aug 1961 for use as floating power plants.
The auxiliary floating dock ARD 17, now renamed *Amazonas*, was also transferred on 7 Jan 1961, and dry dock companion craft YFND 20 was leased on 2 Nov 1961.

LANDING CRAFT

2 Ex-US LSM TYPE

JAMBELI (ex-USS *LSM* 539) T 31 **TARQUI** (ex-USS *LSM* 555) T 32

Displacement, tons	743 beaching; 1 095 full load
Dimensions, feet	196·5 wl; 203·5 oa × 34·5 × 8·3
Guns	2—40 mm AA
Main engines	Diesels; 2 shafts; 2 800 bhp = 12·5 knots

Former US Landing Ships, Medium. *Jambeli* was laid down by Brown S.B. Co, Houston, on 10 May 1945. *Tarqui* was laid down by the Navy Yard, Charleston, SC on 3 Mar 1945 and launched on 22 Mar 1945. Purchased from USA in 1958 and transferred to the Ecuadorian Navy at Green Cove Springs, Florida in Nov 1958. Crew 60. A photograph of *Tarqui* appears in the 1963-64 to 1966-67 editions.

JAMBELI *1967, Ecuadorian Navy, Official*

SUPPLY SHIPS

CALICUCHIMA (ex-US *FS* 525) T 42

Displacement, tons	650 light; 950 full load
Dimensions, feet	176 × 32 × 14 max
Main engines	Diesels; 2 shafts; 500 bhp = 11 knots

Former United States small cargo ship of the Army FS type. Leased to Ecuador on 8 Apr 1963. Provides service to the Galapagos Islands.

WATER CARRIERS

ATHAUALPA (ex-US *YW* 131) T 41 (ex-A 01)

Displacement, tons	415 light; 1 235 full load
Dimensions, feet	174 × 33 max
Main engines	GM diesel; 750 rpm = 11·5 knots

Built by Leatham D. Smith SB Co, Sturgeon Bay in 1945. Transferred under MAP in Mar 1963. Acquired by the Ecuadorian Navy on 2 May 1963.

SURVEY SHIPS

ORION (ex-USS *Mulberry*, AN 27) 101

Displacement, tons	560 standard; 805 full load
Dimensions, feet	146 wl; 163 oa × 30·5 × 11·8 max
Guns	1—3 in AA
Main engines	Diesel-electric; 800 bhp = 13 knots

Built by Commercial Iron Works, Portland, Oregon. Launched on 26 Mar 1941. Loaned by US under MAP. Transferred to Ecuador in Nov 1965. Crew 48.

TUGS

CAYAMBE (ex-*Los Rios*, ex-USS *Cusabo*, *ATF* 155) R 51 (ex-R 01)

Displacement, tons	1 235 standard; 1 675 full load
Dimensions, feet	195 wl; 205 oa × 38·5 × 15·5 max
Guns	1—3 in; 4—40 mm AA; 2—20 mm AA
Main engines	4 diesels with electric drive; 3 000 bhp = 16·5 knots

Former US "Apache" class fleet ocean tug. Launched on 26 Feb 1945. Fitted with powerful pumps and other salvage equipment. Transferred to Ecuador by lease on 2 Nov 1960 and renamed *Los Rios*. Again renamed *Cayambe* in 1966. Crew 85.

CAYAMBE *1966, Ecuadorian Navy, Official*

COTOPAXI (ex-*R. T. Ellis*) R 52

Displacement, tons	150
Dimensions, feet	82 × 21 × 8
Main engines	Diesel; 1 shaft; 650 bhp = 9 knots

Former American tug. Built by Equitable Building Co, Incorp. Purchased from the United States in 1947. Photograph in the 1956-57 to 1959-60 editions.

SANGAY (ex-*Loja*) R 53

Displacement, tons	295 light; 390 full load
Dimensions, feet	107 × 26 × 14
Main engines	Fairbanks Morse diesel; speed = 12 knots

Built in 1952. Acquired by the Ecuadorian Navy in 1964. Renamed in 1966.

EGYPT

Strength of the Fleet

16	Submarines	2	Corvettes
8	Destroyers	8	Patrol Boats
4	Escorts	45	Torpedo Boats
6	Minesweepers	24	Amphibious Ships
20	Missile Boats	15	Auxiliaries

Personnel

1969: 12 000 officers and men, including the Coast Guard

Mercantile Marine

Lloyd's Register of Shipping:
122 vessels of 250 075 tons gross

SUBMARINES

8 Ex-USSR "R" TYPE

Two "R" class units replaced two "W" class which returned to the USSR in May 1966. Another "R" class boat was transferred to Egypt in Feb 1966, and five "R" class had been delivered by the end of 1966. A total of eight "R" boats to be transferred by 1969. See particulars in USSR section.

"R" Type — *1968, Skyfotos*

7 Ex-USSR "W" TYPE

Displacement, tons	1 030 surface; 1 180 submerged
Length, feet (*metres*)	240 (*73·2*) oa
Beam, feet (*metres*)	22 (*6·7*)
Draught, feet (*metres*)	15 (*4·6*)
Guns, AA	4—25 mm
Torpedo tubes	6—21 in (*533 mm*); 4 forward, 2 aft
Main engines	4 000 bhp diesels; 2 500 hp electric motors
Speed, knots	17 on surface; 15 submerged
Radius, miles	13 000
Complement	60

The first "W" class units were transferred from the Soviet Navy to the Egyptian Navy in June 1957. Three more arrived at Alexandria on 24 Jan 1958. Another was transferred to Egypt at Alexandria in Jan 1962.

1 Ex-USSR "MV" TYPE

Displacement, tons	350 surface; 420 submerged
Length, feet (*metres*)	167·3 (*51·0*)
Beam, feet (*metres*)	16 (*4·9*)
Draught, feet (*metres*)	12 (*3·7*)
Guns, AA	1—45 mm; 1 MG
Torpedo tubes	2—21 in (*533 mm*)
Main engines	1 000 bhp diesels; 800 hp electric motors
Speed, knots	13 on surface; 10 submerged
Radius, miles	4 000 at 8 knots
Complement	24

Launched in 1950. Transferred from the USSR to Egypt in June 1957. There is no evidence of new construction in Egypt.

DESTROYERS

6 Ex-USSR "SKORYI" TYPE

AL NASSER
AL ZAFR
DUMYAT
SUEZ

Displacement, tons	2 600 standard; 3 500 full load
Length, feet (*metres*)	393·7 (*120·0*)pp; 420 (*128·0*) oa
Beam, feet (*metres*)	41 (*12·5*)
Draught, feet (*metres*)	13·1 (*4·0*)
Guns, surface	4—5·1 in (*130 mm*)
Guns, AA	2—3 in (*76 mm*); 7—37 mm
A/S	4 DCT
Torpedo tubes	10—21 in (*533 mm*) quintrupled
Mines	80
Boilers	3
Main engines	Geared turbines 70 000 shp; 2 shafts
Speed, knots	38
Radius, miles	4 000 at 15 knots
Complement	250

Former "Skoryi" class destroyers of the Soviet Navy. Launched in 1951. *Al Nasser* and *Al Zafr* were delivered to the Egyptian Navy on 11 June 1956 at Alexandria.

SKORYI Type — *Added 1966*

The implication of each name in Arabic is "victory". It was reported in Dec 1959 that six destroyers had been or were being transferred from the USSR to Egypt. Two were delivered at Alexandria in Jan 1962.

It is reported that the USSR will supply the Egyptian Navy with destroyers armed with 150 miles range sea-surface missiles, presumably of the "Krupny" or "Kildin" class.

2 Ex-BRITISH "Z" TYPE

EL FATEH (ex-HMS *Zenith*)
EO QAHER (ex-HMS *Myngs*)

Name	*El Fateh*	*El Qaher*
Builders	Wm. Denny & Bros Ltd, Dumbarton	Vickers-Armstrongs Ltd, Tyne
Laid down	19 May 1942	27 May 1942
Launched	5 June 1944	31 May 1943
Completed	22 Dec 1944	23 June 1944

Displacement, tons	1 730 standard; 2 575 full load
Length, feet (*metres*)	350 (*106·8*) wl; 362·8 (*110·6*) oa
Beam, feet (*metres*)	35·7 (*10·9*)
Draught, feet (*metres*)	17 (*5·2*) props
Guns, dual purpose	4—4·5 in (*115 mm*)
Guns, AA	6—40 mm
A/S	4 DCT
Boilers	2 Admiralty 3-drum
Main engines	Parsons geared turbines 40 000 shp
Speed, knots	36·75 designed; 31·25 sea speed
Radius, miles	2 800 at 20 knots
Oil fuel (tons)	580
Complement	250

Former "Z" class destroyers in the British Navy. Purchased from Great Britain in 1955. Before being taken over by Egypt *El Qaher* was refitted by J. Samuel White & Co Ltd, Cowes, Isle of Wight, and *El Fateh* refitted by John I Thornycroft & Co Ltd, Woolston, Southampton in July 1956.

MODERNISATION. Both ships were refitted and modernised by J. Samuel White & Co Ltd, at Cowes, Isle of Wight from May 1963 until July 1964.

EL QAHER — *1968*

EL FATEH — **1968**

ESCORTS

1 Ex-BRITISH "BLACK SWAN" TYPE

Name	No.	Builders	Laid down	Launched	Completed
TARIK (ex-*El Malek Farouq*, ex-HMS *Whimbrel*)	42	Yarrow & Co Ltd, Glasgow	31 Oct 1941	25 Aug 1942	13 Jan 1943

Displacement, tons 1 490 standard; 1 925 full load
Length, feet (*metres*) 283 (*86·3*) pp; 299·5 (*91·3*) oa
Beam, feet (*metres*) 38·5 (*11·7*)
Draught, feet (*metres*) 11·5 (*3·5*) mean
Guns, surface 6—4 in (*102 mm*)
Guns, AA 4—40 mm; 2—20 mm
A/S 4 DCT
Boilers 2 three-drum type
Main engines Geared turbines
4 300 shp; 2 shafts
Speed, knots 19·75 designed; 18 sea speed
Radius, miles 4 500 at 12 knots
Oil fuel (tons) 370
Complement 180

Former "Black Swan" class sloops (later re-rated as frigates) in the British Navy. Transferred from Great Britain in Nov 1949. As a flotilla leader she had a broad band painted on the funnel and a thinner flotilla band.

TARIK *Added 1966*

1 Ex-BRITISH "RIVER" TYPE

Name	No.	Builders	Laid down	Launched	Completed
RASHID (ex-HMS *Spey*)	43	Smith's Dock Co Ltd, Middlesbrough	18 July 1941	10 Dec 1941	19 May 1942

Displacement, tons 1 490 standard; 2 216 full load
Length, feet (*metres*) 283 (*86·3*) pp; 301·5 (*91·9*) oa
Beam, feet (*metres*) 36·7 (*11·2*)
Draught, feet (*metres*) 14 (*4·3*)
Guns, surface 1—4 in (*102 mm*)
Guns, AA 2—40 mm; 6—20 mm
A/S 4 DCT
Boilers 2 Admiralty 3-drum type
Main engines Triple expansion
5 500 ihp; 2 shafts
Speed, knots 18
Radius, miles 9 500 at 12 knots
Oil fuel (tons) 640
Complement 180

Former "River" class frigate of the British Navy. Purchased from Great Britain in Nov 1948. Refitted by Willoughby (Plymouth) Ltd. Sailed for Egypt in Apr 1950. Formerly mounted two 4-inch guns.

CLASS. Of her two sister ships *Abikir* (ex-HMS *Usk*) was sunk as a blockship in the Suez Canal in Nov 1956. (raised and dumped in Apr 1957); and *Domiat* (ex-HMS *Nith*) was sunk by the British cruiser *Newfoundland* off Suez on 1 Nov 1956.

RASHEED *1968*

1 Ex-BRITISH "HUNT" TYPE

Name	No.	Builders	Laid down	Launched	Completed
PORT SAID (ex-*Mohamed Ali*, ex-*Ibrahim el Awal*, ex-HMS *Cottesmore*)	11	Yarrow & Co, Ltd, Scotstoun, Glasgow	12 Dec 1939	5 Sep 1940	29 Dec 1940

Displacement, tons 1 000 standard; 1 490 full load
Length, feet (*metres*) 273 (*83·2*) wl; 280 (*85·3*) oa
Beam, feet (*metres*) 29 (*8·8*)
Draught, feet (*metres*) 14 (*4·3*) props
Guns, surface 4—4 in (*102 mm*)
Guns, AA 2—40 mm; 2—20 mm
A/S 2 DCT
Boilers 2 three-drum type
Main engines Parsons geared turbines
19 000 shp; 2 shafts
Speed, knots 25 max
Radius, miles 2 000 at 12 knots
Oil fuel (tons) 280
Complement 146

PORT SAID (ex-*Mohamed Ali*) *Added 1966*

Former British "Hunt" Class, Type 1 escort destroyer (later re-rated as frigate). Served in the British Navy from 1940. Transferred from the British Navy to the Egyptian Navy in July 1950: Sailed for Egypt in April 1951, after a nine months' refit by J. Samuel White & Co Ltd, Cowes. She was first renamed *Ibrahim el Awal* but was renamed *Mohamed Ali el Kebir* about 1951.

CLASS. Sister ship *Ibrahim el Awal* served in the British Navy as HMS *Mendip* until 1948, when she was transferred to the Chinese Navy and renamed *Lin Fu;* she was returned to the British Navy at Hong Kong a year later and reverted to her original name, but was transferred to the Egyptian Navy in Nov 1949, when she was first renamed *Mohamed Ali el Kebir* but was afterwards again renamed *Ibrahim el Awal*, exchanging names with her sister ship about 1951-52. *Ibrahim el Awal* surrendered to Israeli forces off Haifa on 31 Oct 1956; she was rehabilitated and incorporated into the Israeli Navy and renamed Haifa (see later page).

1 Ex-BRITISH "FLOWER" TYPE

Name	Builders	Laid down	Launched	Completed
EL SUDAN (ex-*Mallow*, ex-*Partizanka* ex-*Nada*, ex-HMS *Mallow*)	Harland & Wolff, Ltd, Belfast	14 Nov 1939	22 May 1940	2 July 1940

Displacement, tons 1 060 standard; 1 340 full load
Length, feet (*metres*) 190 (*57·9*) pp; 205 (*62·5*) oa
Beam, feet (*metres*) 33 (*10·0*)
Draught, feet (*metres*) 14·5 (*4·4*) max
Guns, surface 1—4 in (*102 mm*)
Guns, AA 2—20 mm
Boilers 2 SE
Main engines Triple expansion; 2 750 shp
Speed, knots 16
Radius, miles 7 000 at 10 knots
Oil fuel (tons) 230
Complement 85

Former "Flower" class corvette (later re-rated as frigate) of the British Navy. Taken over by Yugoslavia in 1943 (loaned). Returned to the British Navy early in 1949 and transferred to Egypt on 28 Oct 1949.

CLASS. Sister ship *Misr* (ex-SS *Malrouk*) was rammed and sunk by collision south of Suez 16th-17th May 1953.

None of the above four old WW2-built vessels are any longer of considerable military value.

EL SUDAN *A. & J. Pavia*

CORVETTES (ex-FLEET MINESWEEPERS)

2 Ex-BRITISH "BANGOR" TYPE

Name	Builders	Laid down	Launched	Completed
MATROUH (ex-HMS *Stornoway*)	Henry Robb, Ltd, Leith	17 July 1940	10 June 1941	17 Nov 1941
NASR (ex-HMS *Bude*)	Lobnitz & Co, Ltd, Renfrew	2 Apr 1940	4 Sep 1940	12 Dec 1941

Displacement, tons	672 standard; 900 full load
Dimensions, feet	180 oa × 28·5 × 9 5
Guns	1—4 in; 1—3 in; 2—40 mm AA; (4—20 mm in *Matrouh*)
A/S weapons	2 DCT
Main engines	Triple expansion; 2 shafts; 2 400 ihp = 16 knots (designed) sea speed 14 knots
Boilers	2 Admiralty 3-drum type
Oil fuel (tons)	170
Radius, miles	4 300 at 10 knots
Complement	60

Former "Bangor" class fleet minesweepers acquired from Great Britain. Now rated as corvettes. Sister ship *Sollum* sank in heavy weather off Alexandria on 7 Mar 1953.

MATROUH *Egyptian Navy, Official*

FLEET MINESWEEPERS

4 Ex-USSR "T 43" TYPE

BAHAIRA **CHARKIEH** **GARBIA** **MINIYA**

Displacement, tons	410 standard; 530 full load
Dimensions, feet	200 × 27·2 × 9
Guns	4—37 mm AA
Main engines	Diesel = 18 knots

Four reported to have been transferred from the Soviet Navy and delivered to Egypt in 1956, and two others later. *Hittine* and *Yarmouk* were allocated to Syria.

INSHORE MINESWEEPERS

2 Ex-USSR "T 301" TYPE

EL FAYUH **EL HANUFIEH**

Displacement, tons	130 standard; 180 full load
Dimensions, feet	100 × 16 × 4·5
Guns,	2—37 mm AA; 2—25 mm AA
Main engines	Diesels; 2 shafts; 480 bhp = 10 knots
Complement	30

Reported to have been transferred by the USSR to Egypt in 1962; possibly a third ship transferred also.

BYMS TYPE
Of the wooden coastal minesweepers, *Gaza* (ex-*BYMS* 2013) was lost on 26 July 1950. as a result of fuel-tank explosion off Mersa Matrouh, sister ships *Darfour* (ex-*BYMS* 2041) and *Tor* (ex-*BYMS* 2175) were transferred to the Algerian Navy on 6 Nov 1962, and the remaining six, *Arish* (ex-*BYMS* 2028), *Kaisaria* (ex-*BYMS* 2075), *Kordofan* (ex-*BYMS* 2212), *Malek Fuad* (ex-*BYMS* 2035), *Naharia* (ex-*BYMS* 2069) and *Rafah* (ex-*BYMS* 2149) are no more than mouldering hulks.

PATROL VESSELS

8 Ex-USSR "SOI" TYPE

Displacement, tons	215 light; 220 full load
Dimensions, feet	138 pp; 147 oa × 20 × 10 max
Guns	4—25 mm (2 twin mountings)
A/S weapons	4 five-barrelled ahead throwing rocket launchers
Main engines	3 diesels; 3 500 bhp = 28 knots

Former Soviet submarine chasers. Reported to have been transferred by the USSR to Egypt in 1962 to 1967.

ROCKET ASSAULT SHIPS

Ex-USSR "POLNOCNY" TYPE

Displacement, tons	900 to 1 000
Dimensions, feet	246 × 39·3 × 9·8
Armament	Rocket projector
Main engines	Diesels, 4 000 bhp = 15 knots

A new type of Soviet amphibious vessels basically similar to the United States medium rocket landing ships of the LSMR type. This TRV type, which can carry eight to ten tanks, was delivered by the USSR to the Egyptian Navy in 1965-66.

MISSILE BOATS

12 Ex-USSR "OSA" TYPE

Displacement, tons	160 standard; 200 full load
Dimensions, feet	121·3 pp; 131·5 oa × 23 × 6·5
Guided weapons	4 large hood type missile launchers in two pairs abreast with range of 15 to 18 miles
Guns	4—25 mm (2 twin, 1 forward, 1 aft)
Main engines	3 diesels; 4 800 bhp = 35 knots

Reported to have been delivered to Egypt by the Soviet Navy in 1966.

8 Ex-USSR "KOMAR" TYPE

Displacement, tons	75 standard; 100 full load
Dimensions, feet	88 oa × 21 × 6
Guided Missiles	2 launchers with missiles of 10 to 15 miles range
Main engines	Speed = 40 knots

Former Soviet missile patrol boats reported transferred from the USSR in 1962 to 1967. A patrol boat named *Nisr* 2, 110 tons, is reported to have been launched at Port Said on 16 May 1963 by the Castro Naval Shipyard.

KOMAR Type *1966, Col. Bjorn Borg*

TORPEDO BOATS

3 Ex-USSR "SHERSHEN" TYPE

Displacement, tons	150
Dimensions, feet	131·5 × 23 × 6·5
Guns	4—25 mm AA (2 twin)
Torpedo tubes	4—21 in (single)
Main engines	Gas turbines; speed = 40 knots

One delivered from USSR in Feb 1967 and two more (326 329) in Oct 1967.

36 Ex-USSR "P 6" TYPE

Displacement, tons	50
Dimensions, feet	85·5 × 20 × 6
Guns	4—25 mm AA MG
Tubes	2—21 in
Main engines	Speed = 42 knots

The first twelve boats were reported to have arrived at Alexandria on 19 Apr 1956. Two E-boats were destroyed by British naval aircraft on 4 Nov 1956.
The above particulars refer to the early arrivals. Six former Soviet motor torpedo boats of the "P6" class are reported to have been transferred by the USSR in 1960. See particulars in the USSR section.

6 Ex-YUGOSLAVIAN TYPE

Displacement, tons	56 full load
Dimensions, feet	78 × 20·7 × 5·2
Guns	1—40 mm AA
Tubes	4
Main engines	3 Packard motors; 3 shafts; 4 500 bhp = 35 knots

Purchased from Yugoslavia in 1956. Similar to US Higgins boats. 2 MTBs of Soviet P-153 type were sunk by Israeli destroyer *Elath* off Sinai 12 July 1967. Reported also 2 MTBs were sunk by Israeli MTBs off Sinai coast 11 July 1967.
The two motor torpedo boats of the British Fairmile "D" type, *El Naser* and *El Zafer*, are reported to have been disposed of, and the three motor launches of the British Fairmile "B" type, *Hamza* (ex-*ML* 134), *Sab el Bahr* and *Saker el Bahar* are now little more than worn out hulks.
The transport *El Quseir* (ex-*El Amira Fawzia*) and the yachts *Ntisar* (ex-*Fakhr le Bihar*) and *El Horria* (ex-Royal Yacht *Mahroussa*), latterly used as training ship, were deleted from the list in 1967.

LANDING CRAFT

Ex-USSR "MP" TYPE

Several utility landing craft of the MP-SMB 1, delivered to the Egyptian Navy in 1965.

No. 1	**No. 4**	**No. 7**	**No. 10**	**No. 13**	**No. 17**
No. 2	**No. 5**	**No. 8**	**No. 11**	**No. 14**	**No. 18**
No. 3	**No. 6**	**No. 9**	**No. 12**	**No. 16**	**No. 19**

Displacement, tons	22 light; 35 loaded
Main engines	Speed = 11 knots

Of *LCM* type. (The tank landing ship *Aka* (ex-LST 178) was sunk as a block-ship near Lake Timsah in the Suez Canal on 1 Nov 1956).

FLEET TUGS

Ex-USSR "OKHTENSKY" TYPE

A number of Soviet fleet tugs were reported transferred to the Egyptian Navy in 1966

EIRE

NEW CONSTRUCTION. It was officially stated in Feb 1969 that the Irish Government have authorised the purchase of two new vessels for the Naval Service. One will be a fast naval ship which will also have a fishery protection potential. The other will be primarily a fishery protection vessel suited for conditions off the Irish coasts. The planning, design and construction of the vessels are expected to take about two years.

CORVETTES

	Pennant No.	Laid down	Launched	Completed
CLIONA (ex-HMS *Bellwort*)	02	17 Sep 40	11 Aug 41	26 Nov 41
MACHA (ex-HMS *Borage*)	03	21 Nov 40	6 Nov 41	29 Apr 42
MAEV (ex-HMS *Oxlip*)	01	9 Dec 40	28 Aug 41	28 Dec 41

Displacement, tons	1 020 standard; 1 280 full load
Dimensions, feet	190 pp; 205 oa × 33 × 14·5
Guns	1—4 in
Main engines	Triple expansion; 2 750 ihp = 16 knots (designed); maximum sea speed now 10 to 12 knots
Boilers	2 SE
Oil fuel (tons)	230 (average bunkerage)
Complement	48 (accommodation for 78)

Formerly British "Flower" class corvettes. Purchased from Great Britain in 1946. The lattice mast was stepped in 1953. *Cliona* and *Macha* were built by George Brown & Co (Marine) Ltd, Greenock and *Maev* by A. & J. Inglis Ltd, Pointhouse, Glasgow. *Cliona* and *Macha* were refitted for fishery protection duties in 1966-67 and their secondary guns suppressed, and are no longer equipped with Hedgehog, DC or 2 pdr. Oerlikon guns. *Maev* was similarly refitted for fishery production duties in 1968-69. A photograph of *Macha* appears in the 1963-64 to 1968-69 editions.

MAEV (before refit) *Added 1969, Official*

TENDERS

JOHN ADAMS

Measurement, tons	94 gross
Dimensions, feet	85 × 18·5 × 7
Main engines	Diesel; 125 bhp = 8 knots

Built by Richard Dunston, Ltd, Thorne, Doncaster, Yorks. Launched in 1934.

GENERAL McHARDY

Measurement, tons	100 gross
Dimensions, feet	76·5 × 18 × 9·5
Main engines	Compound reciprocating; 200 ihp = 9 knots

Built by Philip & Son, Ltd, Dartmouth, Devon, launched in 1928. Ferry tender.

DISPOSAL

The tender **Wyndham** was sold in 1968 and subsequently broken up.

EL SALVADOR

PATROL BOATS

GC 1 (ex-*Fle-Ja-Lis*) **GC 2** (ex-*Nohaba*)

Displacement, tons	46
Dimensions, feet	72 oa × 16 × 5·5
Guns	1—20 mm
Main engines	2 diesels; 2 shafts; speed = 12 knots
Complement	16

Former British HDML type. Purchased from commercial sources in 1959.

ETHIOPIA

Administration

The Imperial Ethiopian Navy, founded in 1955, is one of the three Services under the Ministry of National Defence. The Commander-in-Chief is His Imperial Majesty. The Deputy Commander-in-Chief has his Naval Headquarters in Addis Ababa.
Deputy Commander-in-Chief of the Imperial Ethiopian Navy:
Commander H.I.H. Prince Alexander Desta
Assistant Minister: Colonel Mebratu Fisseha
Naval Advisers:
Captain W. C. Simpson, OBE, DSC, RN
Commandant J. P. Billard
Haile Selassie I Naval Base Commander:
Commander H. Stern

Naval Establishments

"Haile Selassie I", Massawa: Naval College, established in 1956
Dongollo: Naval School and Training Centre
Embaticalla: Marine Commando Training School
Assab: Naval Base, expanding to include a ship repair facility.

Personnel

1969: 210 National officers and cadets. 980 National enlisted men

TRAINING SHIP

ETHIOPIA (ex-USS *Orca*, AVP 49) A 01

Displacement, tons	1 766 standard; 2 800 full load
Dimensions, feet	300 wl; 310·8 oa × 41 × 13·5 max
Guns	1—5 in 38 cal; 5—40 mm AA (but guns vary)
Main engines	2 sets diesels; 2 shafts; 6 080 bhp = 18·2 knots
Complement	215

Former United States seaplane tender. Built by Lake Washington Shipyard, Houghton Wash. Laid down 13 July 1942, launched on 4 Oct 1942 and completed on 23 Jan 1944. Transferred from the US Navy in Jan 1962.

ETHIOPIA *1967, Imperial Ethiopian Navy, Official*

TORPEDO BOATS

BARRACUDA P 22 **SHARK** P 21

Displacement, tons	60
Dimensions, feet	69 pp; 78 oa × 21·3 × 7
Guns	1—40 mm AA; 2—12·7 mm MG
Tubes	2
Main engines	3 Packard petrol motors; speed 40 knots
Complement	17

Former Yugoslavian motor torpedo boats built late in 1951. Received by Ethiopia in Jan 1960, and given fish names.

SHARK (*Barracuda* behind) 1963, *Imperial Ethiopian Navy, Official*

PATROL BOATS

PC 11 (ex-USCG *WVP* 95304)
PC 12 (ex-USCG *WVP* 95310)
PC 13 (ex-USN *PGM* 53)
PC 14 (ex-USN *PGM* 54)
PC 15 (ex-USN *PGM* 58)

Displacement, tons	101
Dimensions, feet	95 oa × 19 × 5
Guns	1—40 mm AA; 1—·50 cal MG
Main engines	4 diesels; 2 shafts; 2 200 bhp = 21 knots
Radius, miles	1 500 at cruising speed
Complement	15

Ex-WVP 95304 and WVP 95310 are former US Coast Guard cutters transferred in 1958. Ex-*PGM* 53 and Ex-*PGM* 54 are motor gunboats of the same type built by Petersen Builders for transfer on 25 Aug 1961 ex-*PGM 58* built by Marinette and transferred 19 July 1962. Ex-*PGM* 58 was transferred under MAP in June 1962. All are steel-hulled and twin-screwed. Photograph of PC 14 in 1962-63 to 1966-67 editions. There are also four new construction boats, length 40 feet, guns 2— 50 cal (one forward, one aft), speed 25 knots, crew 1 officer, 3 men. First two are named *Caroline* and *John*, GB 21.

PC 11 *1967, Imperial Ethiopian Navy, Official*

LANDING CRAFT

There are 2 of the US LCM type and 2 of the US LCVP type, all acquired in 1963.

FINLAND

Administration

Commander-in-Chief, Finnish Navy:
Rear-Admiral J. Pirhonen

Diplomatic Representation

Naval Attaché in London:
Captain Kai Ruusuvuori, FN

Naval Attaché in Washington:
Colonel Martti Frick

Strength of the Fleet

3 Frigates (1 for Training)
2 Coastal Minelayers
2 Corvettes (Fast Gunboats)
15 Fast Patrol Boats
4 Coast Guard Patrol Vessels
13 Motor Patrol Boats
5 Inshore Minesweepers
1 Cable Ship
22 Support Ships and Service Craft

Treaty Limitations

The Finnish Navy is limited by the treaty of Paris 1947 to 10,000 tons of ships and 4 500 personnel. Submarines and motor torpedo boats are prohibited.

Personnel

1969: 2,000 officers and ratings

Mercantile Marine

Lloyd's Register of Shipping:
399 vessels of 1,127,896 tons gross

FRIGATES (*SAATTAJAT*)

2 "UUSIMAA" CLASS

HÄMEENMAA **UUSIMAA**

Displacement, tons	950 standard; 1 350 full load
Length, feet (*metres*)	278·8 (*85·0*) pp; 295·2 (*90·0*) oa
Beam, feet (*metres*)	32·2 (*9·8*)
Draught, feet (*metres*)	11 (*3·4*)
Guns, dual purpose	3—3·9 in (*100 mm*) single
Guns, AA	2—40 mm
A/S	1 Hedgehog; 4 DC projectors
Torpedo tubes	3—21 in (*533 mm*)
Mines	50 (capacity)
Boilers	2
Main engines	Geared turbines 25 000 shp; 2 shafts
Speed, knots	28
Complement	150

Former Soviet frigates of the "Riga" class. Purchased from the Soviet Union, and transferred to the Finnish Navy on 28 Apr 1964 and 12 May 1964, respectively.

UUSIMAA *1969, Finnish Navy, Official*

PHOTOGRAPHS. A starboard near broadside view of *Hameenmaa* appears in the 1967-68 edition and a starboard quarter oblique view of *Hameenmaa* showing minelaying stern in the 1968-69 edition.

TRAINING FRIGATE (*KOULULAIVA*)

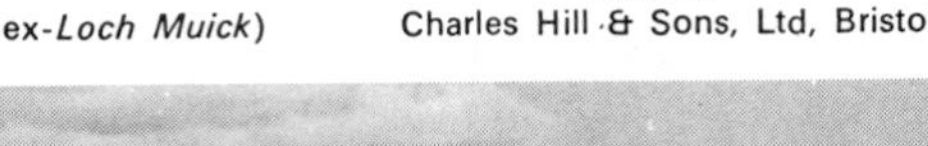

Name	*Builders*	*Laid down*	*Launched*	*Completed*
MATTI KURKI (ex-HMS *Porlock* Bay, ex-*Loch Sea-forth*, ex-*Loch Muick*)	Charles Hill & Sons, Ltd, Bristol	22 Nov 1944	14 June 1945	8 Mar 1946

1 Ex-BRITISH "BAY" CLASS

Displacement, tons	1 580 standard; 2 420 full load
Length, feet (*metres*)	286 (*87·2*) pp; 307·5 (*93·7*) oa
Beam, feet (*metres*)	38·5 (*11·7*)
Draught, feet (*metres*)	15·2 (*4·6*)
Guns, surface	4—4 in (*102 mm*)
Guns, AA	6—40 mm
Boilers	2 Admiralty 3-drum
Main engines	Triple expansion 5 500 ihp; 2 shafts
Speed, knots	18
Radius, miles	9 500 at 12 knots
Oil fuel (tons)	724
Complement	160

Former British frigate of the "Bay" class. Transferred from the Royal Navy to the Finnish Navy in March 1962. Employed as a training ship.

MATTI KURKI *1969, Finnish Navy, Official*

COASTAL MINELAYERS (*MIINALAIVAT*)

KEIHÄSSALMI

Displacement, tons	**360**
Dimensions, feet	**168 × 23 × 6 (officially revised figures)**
Guns	**2—40 mm AA; 2—20 mm AA**
Mines	**100**
Main engines	**2 MAN diesels; 2 shafts; 1 600 bhp = 15 knots**
Complement	**60**

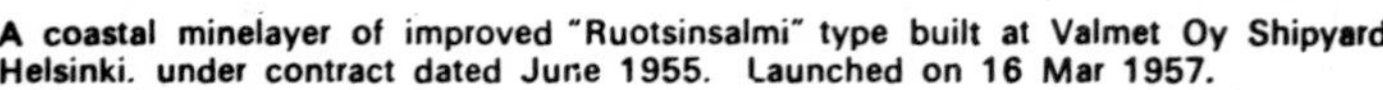

A coastal minelayer of improved "Ruotsinsalmi" type built at Valmet Oy Shipyard, Helsinki, under contract dated June 1955. Launched on 16 Mar 1957.

KEIHASSALMI ***1967, Finnish Navy, Official***

COASTAL MINELAYERS —*continued*

RUOTSINSALMI

Displacement, tons 310
Dimensions, feet 150 × 23 × 5 (officially revised figure)
Guns 2—40 mm AA; 2—20 mm AA
Mines 100
Main engines 2 Rateau diesels; 2 shafts; 1 200 bhp = 15 knots
Complement 60

Built by Crichton-Vulcan Shipyard, Turku. Laid down in 1937. Launched in May 1940. Completed in Feb 1941.

RUOTSINSALMI *1969, Finnish Navy, Official*

CORVETTES (*Tykkiveneet*)

2 FAST GUNBOAT TYPE

KARJALA TURUNMAA

Displacement, tons 650 (officially revised figure)
Dimensions, feet 243·1 × 25·6 × 7·9
Guns 1—4·7 in automatic dp forward; 2—40 mm AA (single; 2—30 mm AA (1 twin) aft
A/S weapons Depth charge projectors
Main engines CODOG (combined diesel or gas turbine). Rolls Royce Olympus gas turbine; 22 000 hp = 35 knots
Complement 70

Fast gunboats for trade protection ordered by the Finnish Navy on 23 Feb 1965 from Wärtsilä-yhtymä Oy Shipyard, Helsinki, Flush decked, raked bow, simple and clean superstructure. Rocket flare guide rails on sides of 4·7 in turret. Fitted with Vosper Thornycroft fin stabiliser equipment. *Karjala* was launched on 16 Aug 1967 and completed on 21 Oct 1968. *Turunmaa* was launched on 11 July 1967 and completed on 29 Aug 1968.

TURUNMAA *1969, Finnish Navy, Official*

PATROL VESSELS (*Vartiolaivat*)

SILMÄ

Displacement, tons 500
Dimensions, feet 160·8 × 27·2 × 11·8 (officially revised figures)
Main engines 1 800 bhp = 15 knots

Coast guard vessel built by Laivateollisuus Oy, Turku, in 1962-63. Another ship of the "Silmä" class is projected.

SILMÄ *1964, Finnish Navy, Official*

UISKO

Displacement, tons 400
Dimensions, feet 141 × 24 × 12·8 (officially revised figures)
Main engines 1 800 bhp = 15 knots

Coast guard patrol vessel built by Valmet Oy, Helsinki. Launched in 1958. Completed in 1959. A photograph of *Uisko* appears in the 1964-65 to 1967-68 editions.

TURSAS

Displacement, tons 400
Dimensions, feet 131·2 × 23·5 × 14
Guns 1—3 in; 1—40 mm AA; 2—20 mm AA
Main engines Diesel; 620 bhp = 12 knots

Built by Crichton-Vulkan. Launched in 1933. Coast Guard, under Ministry of Interior.

TURSAS *1968, Finnish Navy, Official*

AURA

Displacement, tons 350
Dimensions, feet 131·2 × 23·3 × 13·8 (officially revised figures)
Guns 1—3 in, 2—20 mm AA
Main engines Triple expansion; 700 ihp = 10 knots

Launched in 1907. Belongs to the Coast Guard, under the Ministry of the Interior.

FAST PATROL BOATS (*NOPEAT VARTIOVENEET*)

13 "NOULI" CLASS

NUOLI 1 **NUOLI 2** **NUOLI 3** **NUOLI 4** **NUOLI 5** **NUOLI 6** **NUOLI 7** **NUOLI 8** **NUOLI 9** **NUOLI 10** **NUOLI 11** **NUOLI 12** **NUOLI 13**

Displacement, tons 40
Dimensions, feet 72·2 × 21·7 × 5
Guns 1—40 mm; 1—20 mm AA
Main engines 3 diesels; 2 700 bhp = 40 knots
Complement 15

Designed and built by Laivateollisuus Oy, Turku. First four were launched in 1961, five more in 1962, and two more in 1963. A photograph of *Nuoli 1* appears in the 1962-63 to 1968-69 editions, and another photograph of *Nuoli 6* in the 1965-66 to 1968-69 editions.

NUOLI 10 *1969, Finnish Navy, Official*

NUOLI 6 *Finnish Navy, Official*

2 "VASAMA" CLASS

VASAMA 1 **VASAMA 2**

Displacement, tons	70
Dimensions, feet	67 pp; 71·5 oa × 19·5 × 6
Guns	2—40 mm AA
Main engines	2 Napier Deltic diesels; 5 000 bhp = 42 knots
Complement	20

British "Dark" type built by Saunders Roe (Anglesey) Ltd, Beaumaris, England, in 1955-57. A photograph of *Vasama 2* appears in the 1963-64 to 1966-67 editions.

VASAMA *1967, Finnish Navy, Official*

DISPOSALS

The former Italian fast patrol boats *Hurja* 1, *Hurja* 2, *Hurja* 3, *Hurja* 4 and *Hurja* 5 we scrapped in 1963

Of the fast patrol boats of the "Taisto" class, *Taisto* 2, *Taisto* 4 and *Taisto* 5 were scrappe in 1963 and *Taisto* 3, *Taisto* 6, *Taisto* 7 and *Taisto* 8 were removed from the effectiv list in 1966.

The coast guard vessel *Merikotka* was officially deleted from the list in 1960.

PATROL BOATS (*VARTIOMOOTTORIVENEET*)

VIIMA

Displacement, tons	135
Dimensions, feet	118·1 × 21·7 × 7·5 (officially revised figures)
Guns	1—20 mm AA
Main engines	3 diesels; 4 050 bhp = 24 knots

Coast guard patrol boat built by Laivateollisuus Oy Ab, Turku, Finland in 1964.

VIIMA *1969, Finnish Navy, Official*

8 "KOSKELO" CLASS

KAAKKURI **KOSKELO** **TELKKA** **KURKI**
KIILSA **KUOVI** **KUIKKA** **TAVI**

Displacement, tons	75 standard; 97 full load
Dimensions, feet	95·1 × 16·4 × 4·9 (officially revised figures)
Guns	2—20 mm AA
Main engines	2 Mercedes-Benz diesels; 2 shafts; 1 000 bhp = 16 knots
Complement	8

Built of steel and strengthened against ice, *Koskelo* and *Kuikka* were completed in 1956. Remaining six were completed in 1958-60.
A photograph of *Koskelo* appears in the 1957-58 to 1963-64 editions and of *Tavi* in the 1964-65 to 1967-68 editions.

KUIKKA *1968, Finnish Navy, Official*

VMV 19 **VMV 20**

Displacement, tons	27
Dimensions	69 × 13·5 × 4
Guns	1—20 mm
Main engines	Speed = 13 knots

Built in Finland. Launched in 1943. Ex-motor launches *SP* 41, 42. *VM* 18 (ex-*SP* 1) was stricken from the list in 1958. For other disposals see 1966-67 edition.

VMV 11 **VMV 13**

Displacement, tons	35
Dimensions, feet	82 × 13·8 × 3·2
Guns	1—20 mm
Main engines	Semi-diesel; 1 200 bhp = 25 knots
Complement	9

Built in Finland. Launched in 1935. All the above motor patrol boats (*Viima*, "Koskelo" class, and *VMSs*) belong to the Coast Guard which is under the Ministry of the Interior.

CABLE SHIPS (*Kaapelialus*)

PUTSAARI

Displacement, tons	430
Dimensions, feet	147·6 × 38·5 × 9·8 (officially revised figures)
Main engines	Diesel; 450 bhp = 10 knots

Built by Rauma-Repola Oy Shipyard, Rauma. Launched in Dec 1965.

PUTSAARI *1968, Finnish Navy Official*

INSHORE MINESWEEPERS (*Raivaajat*)

5 "R" CLASS

RAISIO	RIHTNIEMI	RÖYTTA	RUISSALO	RYMATTYLA
(No. 4)	(No. 1)	(No. 5)	(No. 3)	(No. 2)

Displacement, tons	110 standard; 130 full load
Dimensions, feet	108·7 × 18·3 × 6
Guns	1—40 mm Bofors; 1—20 mm Masden
Main engines	2 Mercedes-Benz diesels; 1 400 bhp = 15 knots

Rihtniemi and *Rymättylä* were ordered in July 1955 and launched in 1956. Built by Rauma-Repela Oy Shipyard, Rauma, Finland. Delivered on 20 May 1957. Variable pitch propellers. *Raislo, Röyttä* and *Ruissalo* were built by Laivateollisuus, Turku, in 1959. A photograph of *Rymättylä* appears in the 1960-61 to 1963-64 editions, of *Ruissalo* in the 1967-68 edition, and of *Raisio* in the 1965-66 to 1968-69 editions.

RIHTNIEMI *1968, Finnish Navy, Official*

RÖYTTA *1969, Finnish Navy, Official*

Inshore Minesweepers—*continued*

DISPOSALS (COASTAL MINESWEEPERS)
Of the four ex-US BYMS type coastal minesweepers, *Tammenpaä* and *Vahterpää* were sold for scrap in 1958. *Purunpää* was discarded as unfit for further service in 1959, and *Katanpää* was scrapped in 1960.

DISPOSALS (MOTOR MINESWEEPING BOATS)
The motor minesweeping boat *Kallanpää* was scrapped in 1963, and her sister ship *Ajonpää* was scrapped in 1959.

Of the motor minesweeping boats of the "Kuha" class, *Kuha* 2, *Kuha* 5, *Kuha* 7, *Kuha* 8, *Kuha* 12, *Kuha* 13, *Kuha* 14, *Kuha* 15, *Kuha* 16, *Kuha* 17 and *Kuha* 18 were scrapped in 1963, *Kuha* 10 and *Kuha* 11 were scrapped in 1961, and *Kuha* 1, *Kuha* 4 and *Kuha* 9 were scrapped in 1959-60.

Of the motor minesweeping boats of the "Ahven" class, *Ahven* 2, *Ahven* 3, *Ahven* 4 and *Ahven* 6 were scrapped in 1963. *Ahven* 1 and *Ahven* 5 were scrapped in 1961.

STAFF SHIPS

KORSHOLM

Displacement, tons	650
Dimensions, feet	160·8 × 27·9 × 10·8
Speed, knots	10·5

Adapted merchant ship of the small passenger and cargo type. Built in 1931.

ICEBREAKERS (*JÄÄNMURTAJAT*)

3 "TARMO" CLASS

TARMO **VARMA** **No. III**

Displacement, tons	4 890
Dimensions, feet	281 × 71 × 21
Main engines	Wärtsilä-Sulzer diesels; electric drive; 4 shafts (2 screws forward 2 screws aft); 12 000 bhp = 17 knots

Built by Wärtsilä-yhtymä Oy Shipyard, Helsinki. *Tarmo* was completed in 1963 and *Varma* in 1968 (launched 29 Mar). It was officially stated in March 1969 that a third ship of the "Tarmo" class was under construction.

TARMO *1968, Finnish Navy, Official*

3 (4) "KARHU" CLASS

KARHU **MURTAJA** **SAMPO**

Displacement, tons	3 540
Dimensions, feet	243·2 × 57 × 20
Main engines	Diesel-electric; 4 shafts; 7 500 bhp = 16 knots

Built by Wärtsilä-yhtymä Oy Shipyard, Helsinki. *Karhu* was launched on 22 Oct 1957, and completed at the end of 1958. *Murtaja* was launched on 23 Sep 1958. *Sampo* was completed in 1960. There is also the combined Finnish/West German owned, Finnish manned, icebreaker *HANSA*, of the "Sampo" class, completed on 25 Nov 1966, which operates off Germany in winter and off Finland otherwise.
A photograph of *Sampo* appears in the 1963-64 to 1967-68 editions.

KARHU *1968*

MURTAJA *1968*

VOIMA

Displacement, tons	4 415
Dimensions, feet	254·8 wl; 274 oa × 63·7; 61·3 wl × 20·3
Main engines	Diesels with electric drive; 4 shafts; 14 000 bhp = 16·5 knots
Oil fuel (tons)	740

Built by Wärtsilä-yhtymä Oy Shipyard, Helsinki. Launched and completed in 1953. Built for deep-sea work. Two propellers forward and aft. Transferred to the Board of Navigation in 1956.

VOIMA *1968, Finnish Navy, Official*

SISU

Displacement, tons	2 075
Dimensions, feet	194·8 wl; 210·2 oa × 46·5 × 16·8
Guns	2—3·9 in AA
Main engines	3 sets Atlas Polar Diesels with electric drive; 2 shafts and a bow propeller; 4 000 hp = 16 knots
Complement	100

Built by Wärtsilä-yhtymä Oy Shipyard, Helsinki. Launched on 24 Sep 1938.

SISU *1968, Finnish Navy, Official*

OTSO

Displacement, tons	900
Dimensions, feet	134·5 pp; 144·3 oa × 37·5 × 16·5
Main engines	Triple expansion, with bow propeller; 1 860 iph = 13 knots
Oil fuel, tons	60

Launched in 1936. Belongs to the town of Helsinki. Photograph in the 1953-54 and earlier editions.

APU (ex-*Tarmo*, ex-*Sampo II*)

Displacement, tons	2 300
Dimensions, feet	210·5 wl; 220 oa × 47 × 18·2
Main engines	Triple expansion; 2 shafts; 3 850 ihp = 12 knots
Complement	43

Built by Armstrong & Co Ltd, Newcastle-on-Tyne. Launched in 1907. (Her name was changed when *Sampo* and *Tarmo* were allocated successively as names for new icebreakers). A photograph of this ship (as *Tarmo*) appears in the 1958-59 to 1963-64 editions.
It was officially stated in March 1969 that the icebreaker *Apu* was steaming her last winter period and would be scrapped or at least removed from the effective list.

All the above icebreakers belong to the Board of Navigation, except the *Otso*, which belongs to the town of Helsinki.

DISPOSALS
The old and less powerful icebreakers *Apu* and *Murtaja* were scrapped in Spring 1959 and 1958, respectively. The old icebreaker *Sampo* was scrapped in 1961.

TRANSPORT CRAFT (*KULJETUSALUKSET*)

6 "KALA" CLASS

KALA 1 **KALA 2** **KALA 3** **KALA 4** **KALA 5** **KALA 6**

Displacement, tons	60
Dimensions, feet	81·8 × 26·2 × 6
Main engines	2 diesels; 370 bhp = 9 knots

Launched in 1956. Completed in 1959. Of LCU (utility landing craft) type. Officially classed as transport craft. A photograph of *Kala* 2 appears in the 1959-60 to 1962-63 editions.

KALA 6 *1963, Finnish Navy, Official*

SEILI ex-F 177)

Displacement, tons	180
Dimensions, feet	143 × 20 × 4 (officially revised figures)
Guns	1—1·4 in (*105 mm*)
Main engines	Speed = 10 knots

Former German MFP type landing craft converted and armoured. Launched in 1942. *Lonna* was scrapped in 1963.

3 "PANSIO" CLASS (TUG TYPE)

PANSIO (1947) **PORKKALA** (1940) **PUKKIO** (1929)

Displacement, tons	162
Dimensions, feet	92 × 21·5 × 9
Guns	1—40 mm; 1—20 mm AA
Main engines	Diesel; 300 bhp = 10 knots

Built by Valmet Oy, Turku. Launch dates above. Vessels of the tug type used as transports, minesweeping tenders, minelayers and patrol vessels. Can carry 20 mines. A photograph of *Porkkala* appears in the 1962-63 edition.

TRAINING SHIP

The training ship *Suomen Joutsen* (ex-*Oldenburg*, ex-*Laennec*) was converted into a stationary seaman's school ship, and sold to the Finnish Mercantile School in 1960.

TUGS (*HINAAJAT*)

3 "PIRTTISAARI" CLASS

PIRTTISAARI (ex-*DR* 7) **PYHTÄÄ** (ex-*DR* 2) **PURHA** (ex-*DR* 10)

Displacement, tons	106
Dimensions, feet	69 × 20 × 8·5
Guns	1—20 mm
Main engines	Speed = 8 knots

Former United States Army Tugs. Launched in 1943-44. General purpose vessels used as minesweepers, minelayers, patrol vessels, tenders, tugs or personnel transports. *DR* 2 and *DR* 7 were adapted as the Coast Artilery transports *Pyhtää* and *Pirttisaari* in 1958 and 1959, respectively. A photograph of *Pyhtää* (DR 2) appears in the 1953-54 to 1962-63 editions.

FRANCE

Administration

Chief of the Naval Staff:
Amiral Andre Patou

Assistant Chief of Naval Staff:
Vice-Amiral Storelli

Diplomatic Representation

Naval Attaché in London:
Contre-Amiral Jean Brasseur-Kermadec

Naval Attaché in Washington:
Contre-Amiral N. M. Houot

Strength of the Fleet

3 Aircraft Carriers (1 Training)
1 Helicopter Carrier (Training/Commando)
19 Submarines (Diesel Powered)
2 Cruisers (1 Fleet Command Ship)
2 Guided Missile Armed Frigates
4 Guided Missile Armed Destroyers
14 Destroyers (A/S, AD, and Command)
28 Frigates
15 Ocean Minesweepers
71 Coastal Minesweepers
14 Patrol Vessels
15 Inshore Minesweepers
9 Survey Ships (2 Former Frigates)
50 Support Ships and Service Craft

1969-70 New Construction Plan

2 Nuclear Powered Ballistic Missile Submarines
1 Nuclear Powered Fleet Submarine
3 Guided Missile Frigates ("Corvettes") "C 67" Type
1 Guided Missile Frigate ("Corvette") "Aconit" Type
5 Minehunters
2 Avisos

Personnel

1969: 70,200 (5,400 officers, 64,800 ratings)

Mercantile Marine

Lloyd's Register of Shipping:
1,495 vessels of 5,796,360 tons gross

FRENCH CARRIER-BORNE AIRCRAFT

Name	*Maker*	*Type*	*Dimensions*	*Power Plant*	*Armament*	*Performance*
ETENDARD IV-M	Dassault	Single-Seat Interceptor and Fighter-Bomber	Wing Span 31 ft 6 in Length 47 ft 3 in	One SNECMA Atar 8 turbojet	Two 30 mm cannon, 3 000 lb of bombs or missiles	Max speed 673 mph at 36 000 ft. Range 370-1 000 miles
ETENDARD IV-P	Dassault	Single-Seat Reconnaissance/ Flight Refuelling Tanker Aircraft	Wing Span 31 ft 6 in	One SNECMA Atar 8 turbojet	Cameras in nose and underfuselage pack	Max speed 673 mph at 36 000 ft. Range 370-1 000 miles
Br 1050 ALIZÉ	Breguet	Three-Seat Anti-Submarine Aircraft	Wing Span 51 ft 2 in Folded 22 ft 11 in Length 45 ft 6 in	One Rolls-Royce Dart R. Da. 7 turboprop	Two ASM torpedoes. Up to five depth charges Six rockets or two missiles	Max speed 322 mph. Normal endurance 4 hr 30 min.
SA 321G SUPER FRELON	Sud-Aviation	Anti-Submarine and Transport Helicopter	Rotor dia 62 ft. Length (blades and tail folded), 56 ft.	Three Turboméca Turmo III C3 shaft turbines	Anti-Submarine attack weapons	Max speed 165 mph. Range 584 miles

French carriers also equipped with US-built F-8E (FN) Crusader fighters and French-built Sikorsky SH-34 (HSS-1) helicopters.

FRENCH NAVAL GUIDED MISSILES

Type	*Name*	*Maker*	*Length ft*	*Propulsion*	*Speed Mach.*	*Range miles*	*Guidance System*	*Notes*
SURFACE-TO-SURFACE	Malafon	Latécoère	19.66	Two solid boosters only. Unpowered in cruise	0.6	11	Command	Aeroplane configuration. Built around 21in. acoustic homing torpedo. In service.
SURFACE-TO-AIR	Masurca Mk 2	Ruelle Arsenal	28.2	Two-stage solid propellent	2.5	25	Semi-active radar	To be standard naval anti-aircraft armament
UNDER-WATER-TO-SURFACE	MSBS	S.E.R.E.B.		Two-stage solid propellent		1 250 to 1 600	Inertial	Sixteen to be carried by each SNLE submarine. Under development. Nuclear warhead

PENNANT NUMBERS

R Aircraft Carriers
S Submarines (*Sous-marins*)

C Cruisers and Command Ships
D Destroyers (*Escorteurs d'Escadre* and *Lance-Engins*)

F Frigates (*Escorteurs and Avisos*)
M Minesweepers (*Dragueurs*)
P Patrol Vessels (*Patrouilleurs*)

L Landing Ships
A Auxiliaries (including Support Ships and Survey Ships)

R Flag Superior:

95 Arromanches
97 Jeanne d'Arc
98 Clemenceau
99 Foch

S Flag Superior:

610 Le Foudroyant
611 Le Redoutable
612 Le Terrible
631 Narval
632 Marsouin
633 Dauphin
634 Requin
635 Aréthuse
636 Argonaute
637 Espadon
638 Morse
639 Amazone
640 Ariane
641 Daphné
642 Diane
643 Doris
644 Eurydice
645 Flore
646 Galatée
648 Junon
649 Venus
650 Psyche
651 Sirene
655 Gymnote

C Flag Superior:

610 de Grasse
611 Colbert

D Flag Superior:

602 Suffren
603 Duquesne
621 Surcouf
622 Kersaint
623 Cassard
624 Bouvet
625 Dupetit Thouars
626 Chevalier Paul
627 Maillé Brézé
628 Vauquelin
629 D'Estrées
630 Du Chayla
631 Casabianca
632 Guépratte
634 La Bourdonnais
635 Forbin
636 Tartu
637 Jauréguiberry
638 La Galissonniere

F Flag Superior:

703 Aconit
725 Victor Schoelcher
726 Commandant Bory
727 Amiral Charner
728 Doudart de Legrée
729 Balny
733 Commandant Riviére
740 Commandante Bourdais
748 Protet
749 Ensigne de Vaisseau Henry
761 Le Corse
762 Le Brestois
763 Le Boulonnais
764 Le Bordelais
765 Le Normand
766 Le Picard
767 Le Gascon

F Flag Superior:—*continued*

768 Le Lorrain
769 Le Bourguignon
770 Le Champenois
771 Le Savoyard
772 Le Breton
773 Le Basque
774 L'Agenais
775 Le Béarnais
776 L'Alsacien
777 Le Provencal
778 Le Vendéen

M Flag Superior:

609 Narvik
610 Ouistreham
612 Alençon
613 Berneval
614 Bir Hacheim
615 Cantho
616 Dompaire
617 Garigliano
618 Mytho
619 Vinh-long
620 Berlaimont
621 Origny
622 Autun
623 Baccarat
624 Colmar
631 Pavot
632 Pervenche
633 Pivoine
634 Renoncule
635 Réséda
638 Acacia
639 Acanthe
640 Marjolaine
667 Ajonc
668 Azalée
669 Begonia
670 Bleuet
671 Camélia
672 Chrysanthéme
673 Coquelicot
674 Cyclamen
675 Eglantine
676 Gardénia
677 Giroflée
678 Glaieul
679 Glycine
681 Laurier
680 Jacinthe
682 Lilas
683 Liseron
684 Lobelia
685 Magnolia
687 Mimosa
688 Muguet
701 Sirius
702 Rigel
703 Antarès
704 Algol
705 Aldebaran
706 Régulus
707 Véga
708 Castor
709 Pollux
710 Pégase
712 Cybele
713 Calliope
714 Clio
715 Circe
726 La Dunkerquoise
727 La Malouine
728 La Bayonnaise
729 La Paimpolaise
730 La Dieppoise
731 La Lorientaise
734 Croix du Sud
735 Etoile Polaire
736 Altair

M Flag Superior—*continued*

737 Capricorne
740 Cassiopée
741 Eridan
742 Orion
743 Sagittaire
744 Achernar
745 Procyon
746 Arcturus
747 Bételgeuse
748 Persée
749 Phénix
750 Bellatrix
751 Dénébola
752 Centaure
753 Fomalhaut
754 Canopus
755 Capella
756 Céphée
757 Verseau
758 Aries
759 Lyre
765 Mercure
771 Tulipe
772 Armoise
773 Violette
774 Oeillet
775 Paquerette
776 Jasmin
781 Aubepine
782 Capucine
783 Hortensia
784 Geranium
785 Hibiscus
786 Dahlia
787 Jonquille
788 Myosotis
889 Petunia

P Flag Superior:

630 L'Intrépide
635 L'Ardent
637 L'Etourdi
638 L'Effronté
639 Le Frondeur
640 Le Fringant
641 Le Fougueux
642 L'Opiniâtre
643 L'Agile
644 L'Adroit
645 L'Alerte
646 L'Attentif
647 L'Enjoué
648 Le Hardi
730 La Combattante
780 Oiseau des Isles

L Flag Superior:

9003 Argens
9004 Bidassoa
9006 Cheliff
9007 Trieux
9008 Dives
9009 Blavet
9021 Ouragan
9022 Orage
9097 Issole

A Flag Superior

603 Henry Poincaré
607 Arago
608 Moselle
610 Ile d'Oléron
611 Maine
612 Médoc

A Flag Superior —*continued*

613 Morvan
614 Falleron
615 Loire
617 Garonne
618 Rance
619 Aber Wrac'h
620 Acheron
621 Rhin
622 Rhone
626 La Charente
627 La Seine
628 La Saone
629 Lac Chambon
630 Lac Tonle Sap
631 Lac Tchad
633 Duperré
634 Verdon
635 Rummel
637 Maurienne
638 Sahel
641 Gustave Zédé
643 Aunis
644 Berry
645 Anjou
646 Triton
647 Ingénieur Elie Monnier
648 Archimede
649 Etoile
650 Belle Poule
652 Mutin
653 La Grande
660 Hippotarne
661 Infatigable
665 Goliath
666 Eléphant
667 Hercule
668 Rhinocéros
669 Tenace
670 Implacable
673 Luffeur
674 Acharné
675 Isére
678 La Coquille
682 Alidade
683 Octant
684 Coolie
685 Robuste
686 Actif
687 Laborieux
688 Valeureux
692 Travailleur
698 Petrel
699 Pelican
700 Buffle
706 Courageux
718 Pachyderme
719 Bélier
724 Belouga
727 Araignée
728 Scorpion
729 Tarentule
733 Saintonge
735 Guyenne
740 Hanap
750 Liamone
755 Commandant Robert Giraud
756 L'Esperance
757 D'Entrecasteaux
758 La Recherche
759 Marcel Le Bihan
760 Cigale
761 Criquet
762 Fourmi
763 Grillon
764 Scarabée
765 Locuste
771 Tarn
777 Luciole
780 Astrolabe
781 Boussole
785 Zelee
791 Corail

Aircraft Carriers

Silhouettes

Cruisers

Scale: 150 feet = 1 inch

1 : 1800

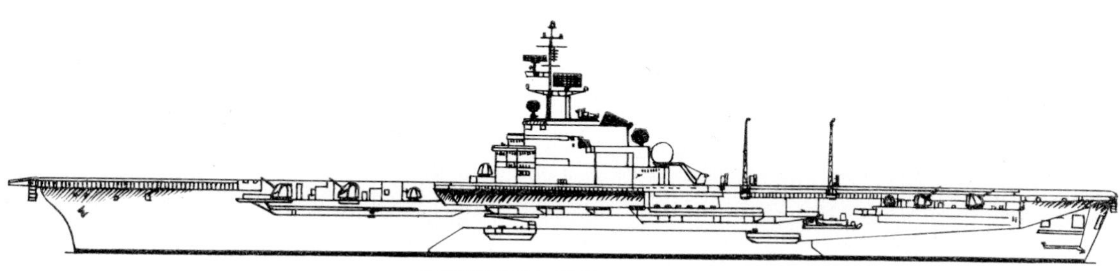

CLEMENCEAU, FOCH

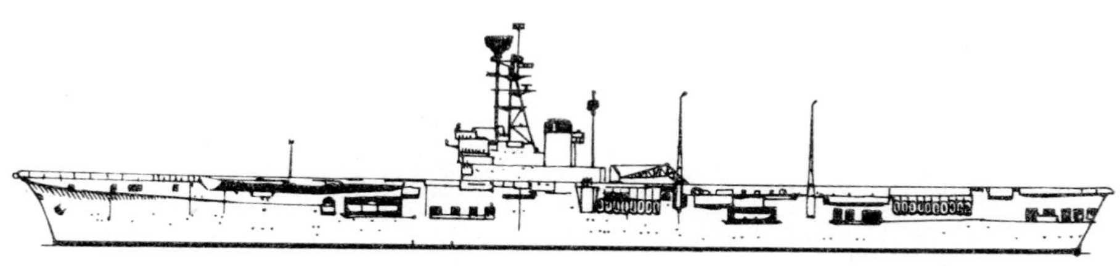

ARROMANCHES

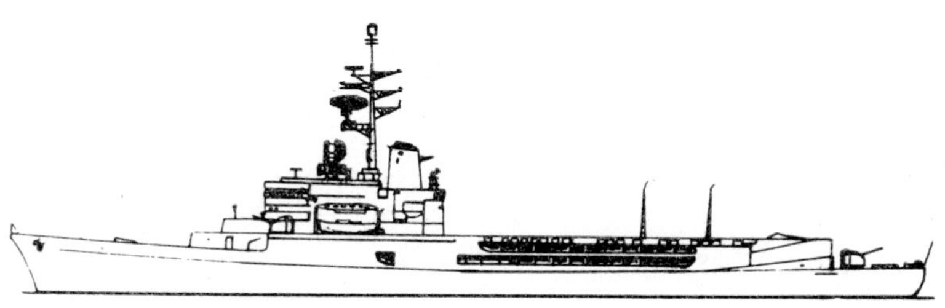

JEANNE D'ARC

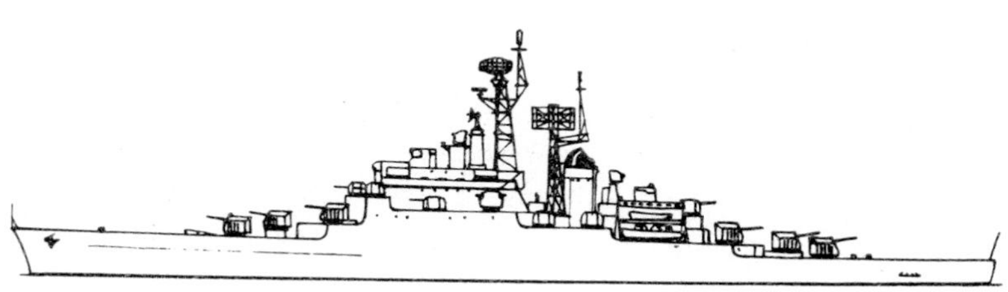

COLBERT

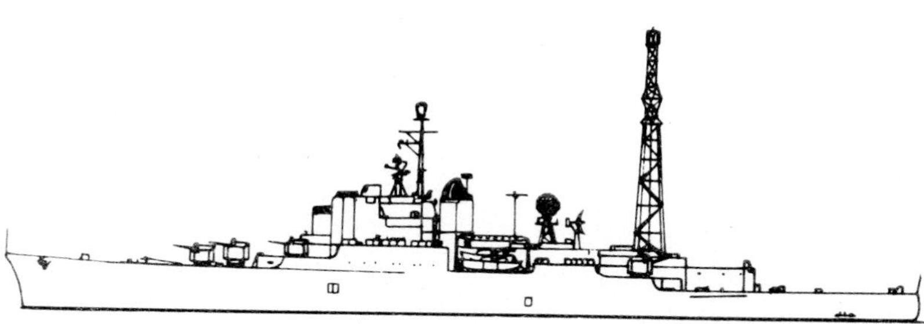

DE GRASSE

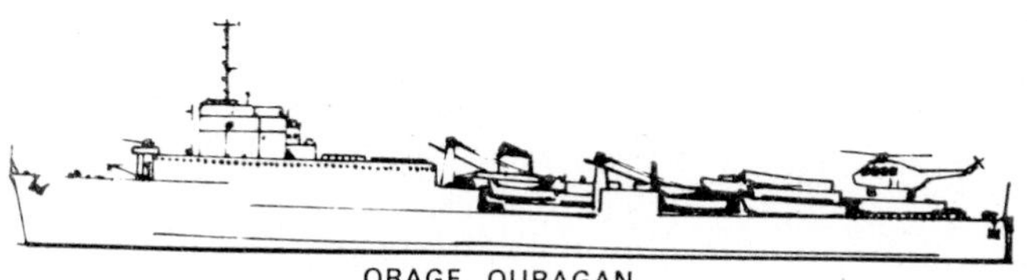

ORAGE, OURAGAN

DUQUESNE, SUFFREN

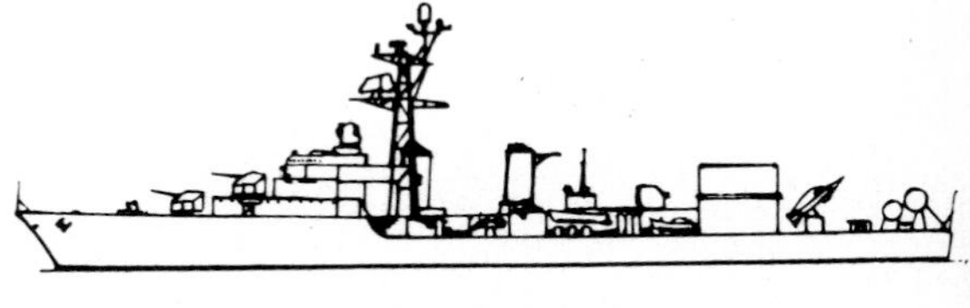
LA GALISSONNIERE

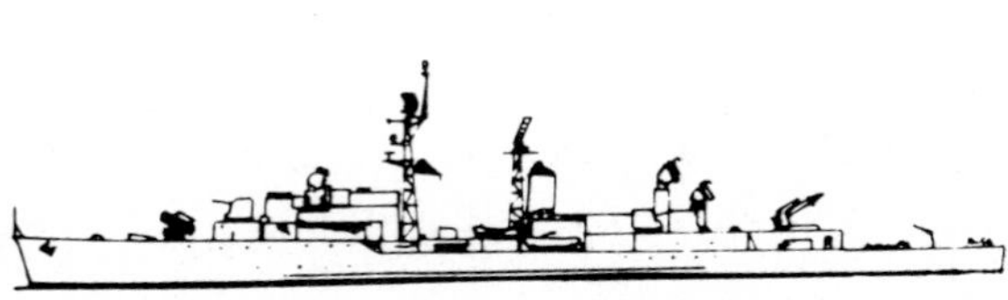
DU CHAYLA *Class.* Guided Missile Type

COMMANDANT RIVIÉRE *Class*

DE Type (ARAGO Modified)

FORBIN *Class.* T. 53 R Type

L'ALSACIEN, LE PROVENCAL, LE VENDEEN

LE BOURGUIGNON

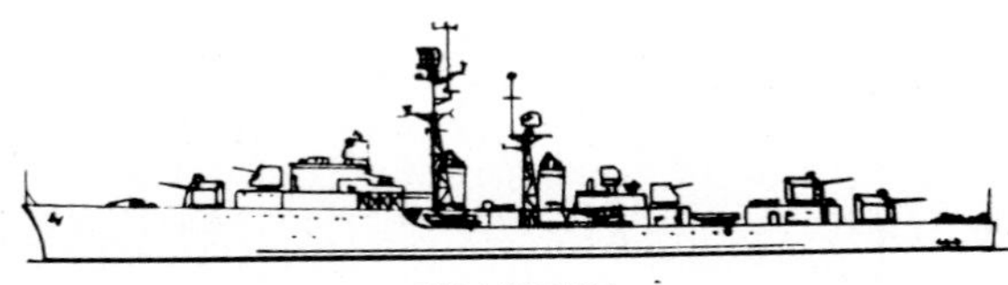
CASABIANCA

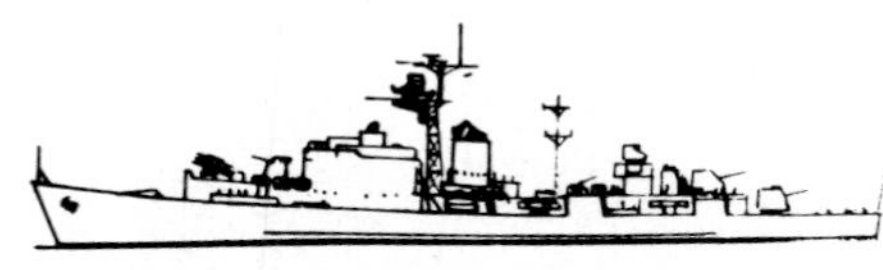
L'AGENAIS, LE BÉARNAIS, LE BRETON

ROBERT GIRAUD *Class*

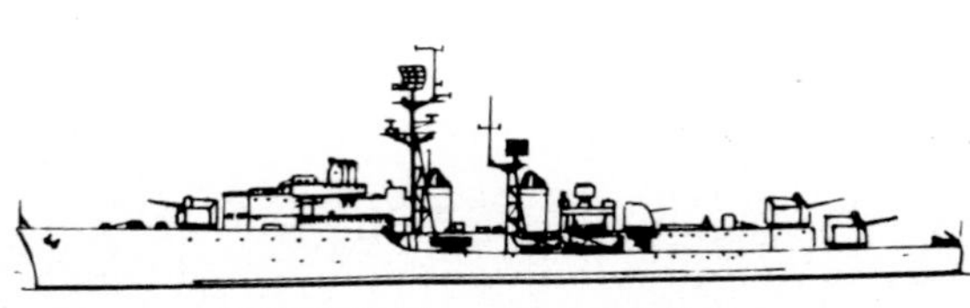
SURCOUF *Class.* Command Type

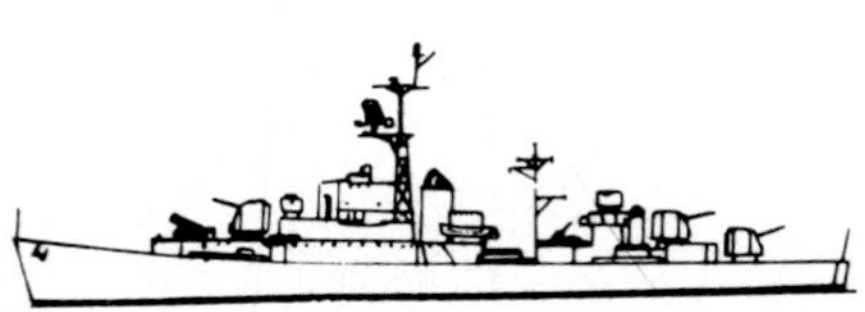
LE NORMAND *Class* E 52 Type

GUSTAVE ZÉDÉ

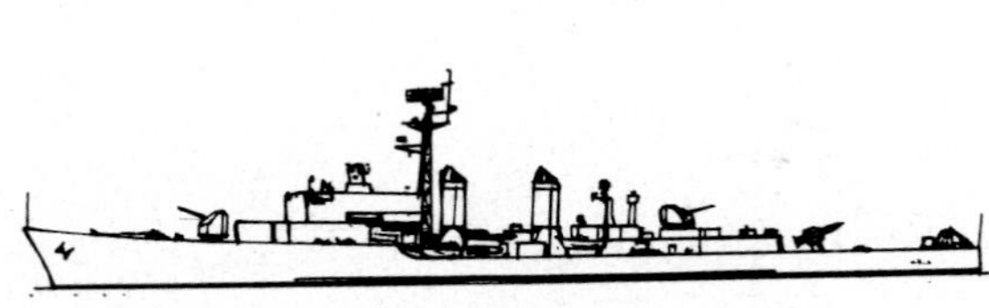
D'ESTRÉES (VDS aft)

LE CORSE *Class,* E 50 Type

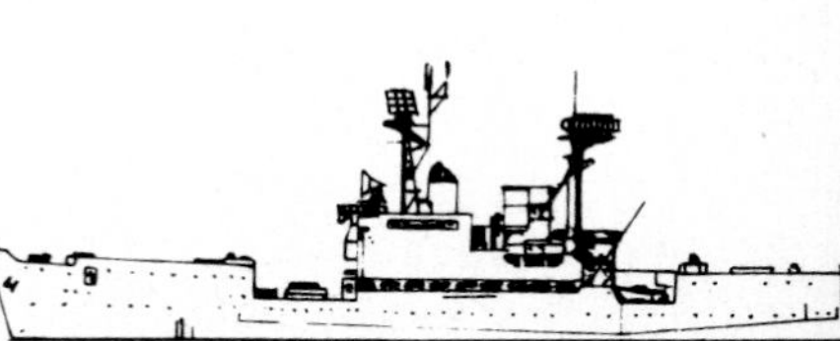
ILE d'OLÉRON

AIRCRAFT CARRIERS (*Porte-Avions*)

2 "CLEMENCEAU" CLASS

Name	No.	Builders	Laid down	Launched	Completed
CLEMENCEAU (PA 54)	R 98	Brest	Nov 1955	21 Dec 1957	22 Nov 1961
FOCH (PA 55)	R 99	Penhoët-Loire & Brest	Feb 1957	23 July 1960	15 July 1963

Displacement, tons	22 000 standard; 32 800 full load
Length, feet (*metres*)	780·8 (*238·0*) pp (864·8 (*263·6*) oa
Beam, feet (*metres*)	104·1 (*31·7*) hull with bulges
Width, feet (*metres*)	168 (*51·2*) oa
Draught, feet (*metres*)	25·3 (*7·7*); 28 (*8·56*) screws
Catapults	2 Mitchell-Brown steam, Mk BS 5
Aircraft	Capacity 30, including jet aircraft. Each carries 3 Flights—1 of *Etendard IV*, 1 of *Crusader*, 1 of Breguet *Alizé*. See *Aircraft* notes
Armour	Flight deck, island superstructure and bridges, hull (over machinery spaces and magazines)
Guns, AA	8—3·9 in (*100 mm*) automatic in single turrets
Boilers	6; steam pressure 640 psi (*45 kg/cm²*), superheat 842°F (450°C)
Main engines	2 sets Parsons geared turbines 126 000 shp; 2 shafts
Speed, knots	31 max (33·4 trials); 24 sustained sea
Radius, miles	6,400 at 18 knots 3 500 at full power
Oil fuel (tons)	3 600
Complement	2 150

The first aircraft carriers designed as such and built from the keel to be completed in France. Authorised in 1953 and 1955 respectively. *Clemenceau* was ordered from Brest Dockyard on 28 May 1954 and begun in Nov 1955. *Foch* began construction at Chantiers de l'Atlantique a St. Nazaire, Penhoet-Loire, in a special dry dock (the contract provided for the construction of the hull and propelling machinery) and was completed by Brest Dockyard.

CLEMENCEAU — 1969, French Navy, Official

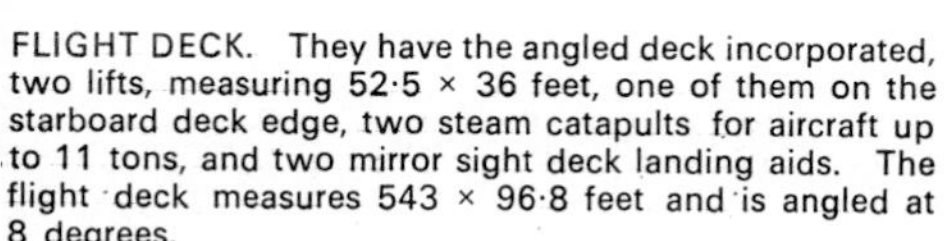

FLIGHT DECK. They have the angled deck incorporated, two lifts, measuring 52·5 × 36 feet, one of them on the starboard deck edge, two steam catapults for aircraft up to 11 tons, and two mirror sight deck landing aids. The flight deck measures 543 × 96·8 feet and is angled at 8 degrees.

HANGAR. Dimensions of the hangar are: 497·7 × 87 × 28 feet.

GUNNERY. These aircraft carriers were originally to have been of the light fleet type with an armament of 24—2·25 inch guns in twin mountings, but the armament was revised to 12—3·9 inch (*100 mm*) in 1956 and to 8—3·9 inch (*100 mm*) in 1958. The 100 mm guns are of a new design. Rate of fire 60 rounds per minute.

BULGES. *Foch* was completed with bulges. These having proved successful during trials, *Clemenceau* was modified similarly during her first refit, increasing her beam by 6 feet.

DRAWING. Port elevation and plan. Drawn in 1969. Scale: 125 feet = 1 inch (1 : 1 500).

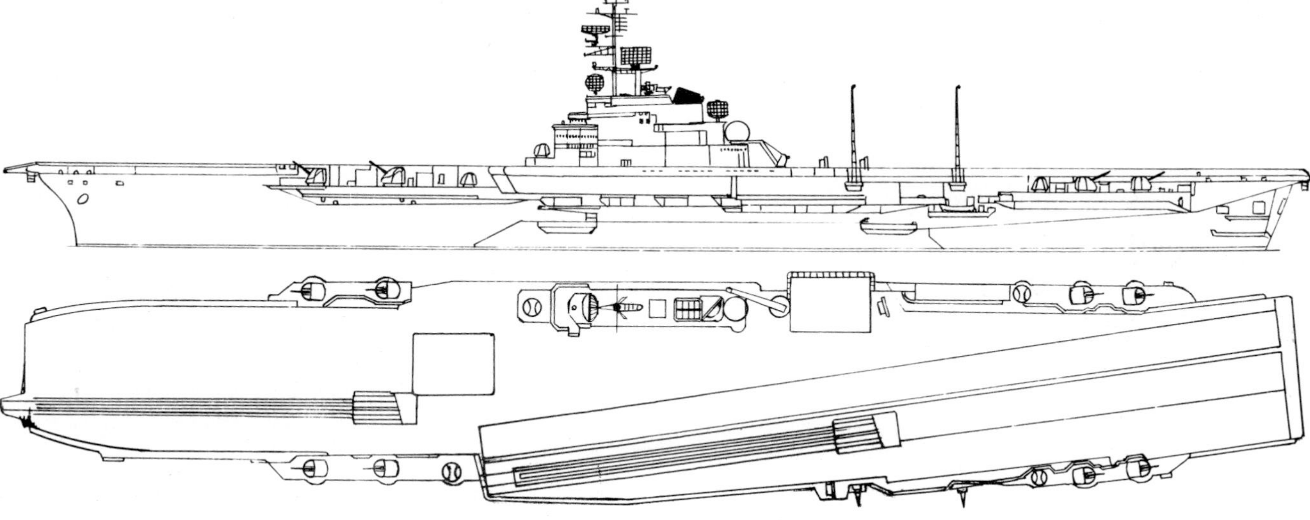

FOCH — 1969, French Navy, Official

Aircraft Carriers—*continued*

Name	*Pennant No.*	*Builders*	*Laid down*	*Launched*	*Completed*
ARROMANCHES (ex-HMS *Colossus*)	R 95	Vickers-Armstrongs Ltd, Newcastle-on-Tyne	1 June 1942	30 Sep 1943	16 Dec 1944

1 Ex-BRITISH "COLOSSUS" CLASS

Displacement, tons	14 000 standard; 19 600 full load
Length, feet (*metres*)	694·5 (*211·7*) oa
Beam, feet (*metres*)	80·2 (*24·5*)
Width, feet (*metres*)	118 (*36·0*) oa
Draught, feet (*metres*)	23 (*7·0*)
Aircraft	24 (variable) including Helicopters
Boilers	4 three-drum type; 400 psi *28 kg/cm²*); 680°F (360°C)
Main engines	Parsons geared turbines 40 000 shp; 2 shafts
Speed, knots	23·5
Radius, miles	12 000 at 14 knots
Oil fuel (tons)	3 200
Complement	1 019 (42 officers and 777 men, plus 200 for air service)

This ship was lent to the French Navy for five years from August 1946 with the option of purchase in 1951. This was taken up, and she was permanently transferred from Great Britain in that year. Extensively refitted 1950-51; and again refitted in 1957-58.

RECONSTRUCTION. Modernised and partially rebuilt in 1957-58 with the angled deck at 4 degrees, and mirror sight deck landing aid sponsons, the overall width being increased from 112·5 feet to just over 118 feet (*36 metres*). In consequence of these modifications the ship was able to receive Breguet Alizé ASM aircraft of the 1050 type.

ENGINEERING. Engines and boilers are arranged *en echelon*, one set of turbines and two boilers being installed side by side in each of the two main propelling machinery spaces, on the unit system, so that the starboard propeller shaft is longer than the port.

GUNNERY. She formerly mounted 43—40 mm AA guns (as refitted) but these were removed when she became a training and helicopter carrier.

DRAWING. Port elevation and plan. Scale: 128 feet = 1 inch.

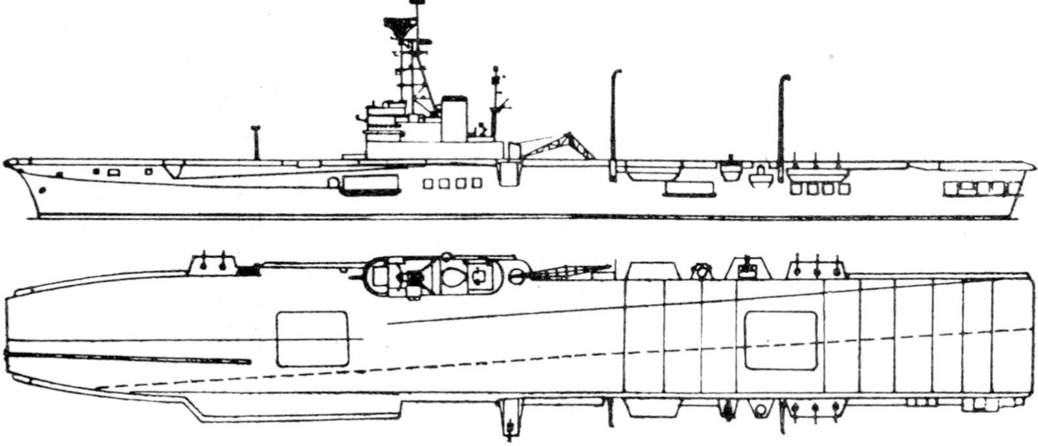

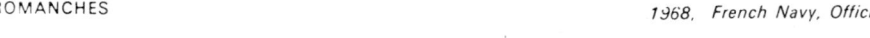

ARROMANCHES 1968, *French Navy, Official*

ARROMANCHES *1969, Official*

ARROMANCHES *French Navy Official*

HELICOPTER CARRIER (*Croiseur Porte-Hélicoptères*)

Name	*No.*	*Builders*	*Ordered*	*Laid down*	*Launched*	*Completed*
JEANNE D'ARC (ex-*La Résolue*)	R 97	Brest Dockyard	8 Mar 1957	7 July 1960	30 Sep 1961	1 July 1963 (trials) 30 June 1964 (service)

1 TRAINING/COMMANDO TYPE

Displacement, tons	10 000 standard; 12 360 full load
Length, feet (*metres*)	597·1 (*182·0*) oa
Beam, feet (*metres*)	78·7 (*24·0*) hull
Draught, feet (*metres*)	21·6 (*6·6*) max
Flight deck	230 × 85 ft (*70 × 26 m*)
Aircraft	Heavy A/S helicopters (4 in peacetime as training ship 8 in wartime)
Guns, AA	4—3·9 in (*100 mm*) single
Boilers	4; working pressure 640 psi (*45 kg/cm²*); 842°F (*450°C*)
Main engines	Rateau-Bretagne geared turbines 40 000 shp; 2 shafts
Speed, knots	26·5 designed
Radius, miles	6 000 at 15 knots
Oil fuel (tons)	1 360
Complement	906 (44 officers, 670 ratings and 192 cadets)

Authorised under the 1957 estimates. Used for training officer cadets in peacetime in place of the old training cruiser *Jeanne d'Arc* (which was decommissioned on 28 July 1964 and sold for scrap in Dec 1965 at Brest). In wartime, after rapid modification, she would be used as a commando ship, helicopter carrier or troop transport with commando equipment and a battalion of 700 men. The lift has a capacity ot 12 tons. The ship is almost entirely air-conditioned.

GUNNERY. She was originally designed to mount six 100 mm (3·9 inch) guns (now four).

ELECTRONICS. The ship is almost as well equipped with electronic apparatus as the aircraft carrier *Clemenceau*. She also has long range sonar gear.

NOMENCLATURE. The name *La Résolue* was only a temporary one until the decommissioning of the training cruiser *Jeanne d'Arc* which was relieved by *La Résolue* in 1964 when the latter ship took the name *Jeanne d'Arc*, on 16 July.

MODIFICATIONS. Between first steaming trials and completion for operational service the ship was modified with a taller funnel to clear the superstructure and obviate the smoke and exhaust gases swirling on to the bridges. After completion, in 1964, the whaleboat emplacement was plated in.

PHOTOGRAPHS of *Jeanne d'Arc* (as *La Résolue*), before modification with taller funnel, appear in the 1963-64 edition: near broadside surface view, starboard quarter surface view, and port quarter oblique aerial view showing hangar open. The latter view also appears in the 1964-65 edition. A port bow view and a starboard quarter view, both before the whaleboat emplacement was plated in, appear in the 1964-65 and 1965-66 editions. A starboard quarter oblique aerial view appears in the 1965-66 to 1968-69 editions.

RETURN OF ESCORT CARRIER
The auxiliary aircraft carrier *Dixmude* (ex-HMS *Biter*, ex-*Rio Parana*), officially rated as *Transport d'Aviation*, former US escort carrier, reduced to a hulk in 1960 and used as a barracks, was returned to the USA in 1965 and sunk as a target. (For disposals of Fast Light Fleet Aircraft Carriers, Battleships, Cruisers and Light Cruisers, see 1964-65 edition).

JEANNE D'ARC — *1969, French Navy, Official*

JEANNE D'ARC — *1966 courtesy Admiral M. Adam*

JEANNE D'ARC (whaleboat emplacement plated in) — ***1966, French Navy, Official***

SUBMARINES

Name	No.	Builders	Laid down	Launched	Completion	Operational
LE REDOUTABLE	SNLE 1 (S 611)	Cherbourg Naval Dockyard	30 Mar 1964	29 Mar 1967	Estimated 1969	Estimated 1970
LE TERRIBLE	SNLE 2 (S 612)	Cherbourg Naval Dockyard	24 June 1967	Estimated 1969	Estimated 1971	Estimated 1972
LE FOUDROYANT	SNLE 3 (S 610)					Estimated 1975

NUCLEAR POWERED BALLISTIC MISSILE TYPE

Displacement, tons	7 900 surface; 9 000 submerged
Length, feet (*metres*)	420 (*128·0*)
Beam, feet (*metres*)	34·8 (*10·6*)
Draught, feet (*metres*)	32·8 (*10·0*)
Missiles, surface	16 tubes amidships for "Polaris" type ICBM's; range 1 900 miles
Torpedo tubes	4
Nuclear reactors	1 pressurised water-cooled
Main engines	2 turbo-alternators; 1 electric motor; 15 000 hp; 1 shaft
Auxiliary propulsion	1 diesel
Speed, knots	20 on surface; 25 submerged (conservative estimate)
Complement	135 (14 officers, 121 men); two alternating crews

LE REDOUTABLE — *1968, French Navy, Official*

Le Redoutable is the first French nuclear powered, ballistic missile armed submarine and prototype of the *"Force de dissuasion"* of four, or five, such vessels which the Navy plans to have in the 1970s. The vessels have a 3 months submerged cruise duration. The ballistic missiles are comparable with the United States "Polaris" weapons, but are of French manufacture with a weight of 15 tons. The diesel has bunkerage for a range of 5 000 miles. The decision to build a fourth unit of this class was officially announced on 7 Dec 1967.

1 EXPERIMENTAL MISSILE TYPE

Name	No.	Builders	Laid down	Launched	Completed
GYMNOTE	S 655	Cherbourg Naval Dockyard	17 Mar 1963	17 Mar 1964	17 Oct 1966

Displacement tons	3 800
Length, feet (*metres*)	275·6 (*84·0*)
Beam, feet (*metres*)	34·7 (*10·6*)
Draught feet (*metres*)	25 (*7·6*)
Missiles, surface	4 tubes for "Polaris" type ICBM's
Main engines	2 600 hp diesels and electric motors; 2 shafts
Speed, knots	11 on surface; 10 submerged
Complement	70 (8 officers, 62 men) plus 40 technicians and engineers

An experimental platform for testing ballistic missiles destined for the first French nuclear powered "Polaris" type submarine, and for use as an underwater laboratory to prove equipment and arms for nuclear submarines.

Gymnote is the hull that was laid down in 1958 as the nuclear powered submarine Q 244 which was cancelled in 1959. The hull however was still available when a trials vessel for the French Polaris type missiles was required and was then completed as *Gymnote*.

POSTPONEMENT. The projected nuclear powered fleet submarine of a new hunter Killer type, allocated the name *Rubis*, was officially taken out of the list, *pro tem*, in 1968.

GYMNOTE — *1969, French Navy, Official*

8 + 2 "DAPHNE" CLASS

Name	No.	Launched	Completed.
DAPHNÉ	S 641	20 June 1959	1 June 1964
DIANE	S 642	4 Oct 1960	20 June 1964
DORIS	S 643	14 May 1960	26 Aug 1964
EURYDICE	S 644	19 June 1962	26 Sep 1964
FLORE	S 645	21 Dec 1960	21 May 1964
GALATÉE	S 646	22 Sep 1961	25 July 1964
JUNON	S 648	11 May 1964	25 Feb 1966
VENUS	S 649	24 Sep 1964	1 Jan 1966
PSYCHÉ	S 650	July 1969	(est) 1970
SIRENE	S 651	July 1969	(est) 1970

Displacement, tons	850 surface; 1 040 submerged
Length, feet (*metres*)	190·3 (*58·0*)
Beam, feet (*metres*)	22·3 (*6·8*)
Draught, feet (*metres*)	15·4 (*4·7*)
Torpedo tubes	12—21·7 in (*550 mm*) (8 bow, 4 stern)
Main engines	SEMT-Pielstick diesel-electric 1 300 bhp surface, 1 600 hp motors submerged; 2 shafts
Speed, knots	16 surface and submerged
Complement	45 (6 officers, 39 men)

BUILDERS. *Daphné* and *Diane* were built by Dubigeon, Nantes, and *Doris, Eurydice, Flore, Galatée, Junon* and *Venus* by Cherbourg.

COMPLETION. The revised completion dates given above are the actual dates of "admission to active service" announced officially.

PHOTOGRAPHS. A photograph of *Flore* appears in the 1961-62 edition, and a starboard dead broadside surface view of *Galatée* in the 1965-66 to 1967-68 editions.

LOSS. *Minerve*, S 647, of the "Daphne" class was lost in the Western Mediterranean on 27 Jan 1968.

VENUS — *1968, French Navy, Official*

EURYDICE — *1969, A. & J. Pavia*

GALATÉE — *1968, Skyfotos*

Submarines—*continued*

4 "ARETHUSE" CLASS

Name	No.	Programme	Builders	Laid down	Launched	Completed
AMAZONE	S 639	1954	Cherbourg	Dec 1955	3 Apr 1958	1 July 1959
ARÉTHUSE	S 635	1953	Cherbourg	Mar 1955	9 Nov 1957	23 Oct 1958
ARGONAUTE	S 636	1653	Cherbourg	Mar 1955	29 June 1957	11 Feb 1959
ARIANE	S 640	1954	Cherbourg	Dec 1955	12 Sep 1958	16 Mar 1960

Displacement, tons: 400 standard; 529 surface; 650 submerged
Length, feet (*metres*): 164 (*50·0*)
Beam, feet (*metres*): 19 (*5·8*)
Draught, feet (*metres*): 12·8 (*3·9*)
Torpedo tubes: 4—21·7 in (*550 mm*) bow
Main engines: 12-cyl. SEMT-Pielstick diesel-electric; 1 060 bhp surface; 1 300 hp motors submerged; 1 shaft
Speed, knots: 16 on surface; 18 submerged
Complement: 45 (6 officers, 39 men)

All built at Cherbourg. Submarine-killer type for hunting enemy submarines. Streamlined hull, silent motors, and up-to-date electronic and detection equipment.

PHOTOGRAPHS. A photograph of *Argonaute* appears in the 1959-60 to 1963-64 editions, of *Amazone* in the 1964-65 and 1965-66 editions, and of *Ariane* in the 1966-67 edition.

ARETHUSE — *1967, French Navy, Official*

6 "NARVAL" CLASS

Name	No.	Programme	Builders	Laid down	Launched	Completed
DAUPHIN	S 633	1950	Cherbourg	Jan 1952	17 Sep 1955	1 Aug 1958
ESPADON	S 637	1954	Normand	Mar 1957	15 Sep 1958	2 Apr 1960
MARSOUIN	S 632	1949	Cherbourg	Nov 1951	21 May 1955	1 Oct 1957
MORSE	S 638	1954	Seine Maritime	Dec 1956	10 Dec 1958	2 May 1960
NARVAL	S 631	1949	Cherbourg	Oct 1951	11 Dec 1954	1 Dec 1957
REQUIN	S 634	1950	Cherbourg	Feb 1952	3 Dec 1955	1 Aug 1958

Displacement: 1 200 standard; 1 640 surface; 1 910 submerged
Length, feet (*metres*): 256 (*78·0*)
Beam, feet (*metres*): 23·6 (*7·2*)
Draught, feet (*metres*): 18 (*5·5*)
Torpedo tubes: 8—21·7 in (*550 mm*) quick loading (6 bow, 2 stern); 22 torpedoes
Main engines: 4 000 bhp Schneider 7-cylinder 2-stroke diesels; 5 000 hp electric motors (submerged); 2 shafts
Speed, knots: 16 on surface, 18 submerged
Radius, miles: 15 000 at 8 knots with schnorkel
Complement: 68 (7 officers, 61 men)

Designed as oceangoing submarines. Improved versions of the German XXI type. *Dauphin, Marsouin, Narval* and *Requin* were built in seven prefabricated parts each of 10 metres in length.

NOMENCLATURE. *Dauphin* means Dolphin, *Espadon* means *Swordfish, Marsouin* means Porpoise, *Morse* means Walrus, *Narval* means Narwhal, and *Requin* means Shark.

REQUIN (as reconstructed) — *1969, French Navy, Official*

PHOTOGRAPHS of *Narval* as first completed without bulbous bow appear in the 1957-58 edition, a photograph of *Requin* appears in the 1959-60 and 1960-61 editions, and of *Narval* with bulbous bow and of *Dauphin* in the 1957-58 to 1965-66 editions.

RECONSTRUCTION. It was announced in 1965 that these submarines would be reconstructed and given a new propulsion plant. The refit of *Requin, Espadon* and *Morse* at Lorient has been completed. It is reported that this reconstruction has been very successful. See altered appearance of *Requin* in top photograph.

MORSE — *1966, French Navy, Official*

ENGINEERING. New main machinery installed on reconstruction includes diesel-electric drive on the surface with SEMT-Pielstick diesels.

MARSOUIN — *1966, French Navy, Official*

DISPOSALS OF "LA CRÉOLE" CLASS
Of "La Créole" class *L'Africaine* was withdrawn from active service on 1 July 1961 (she was reported to be worn out), *La Créole* was officially deleted from the list in Mar 1963, *L'Andromède* and *L'Astrée* in 1965, and *L'Artémis* in 1966.

DISPOSALS OF "S" CLASS
Of the former British submarines of the "S" class, *Siréne* was returned to Great Britain at Gosport on 24 Oct 1958. and reverted to the original name *Spiteful*, and *Sultane* was returned to Great Britain at Rosyth on 5 Nov 1959, and reverted to her original name *Statesman*. *Saphir* (ex-*Satyr*) was also returned to Great Britain on 11 Aug 1961 to await disposal at Rosyth. *Sibylle* (ex-*Sportsman*) was lost accidentally with all hands on 23 Sep 1952, near Toulon.

DISPOSALS OF GERMAN TYPES
Blaison (ex-U 123), former German Type IX B, was discarded in 1957. *Bouan* (ex-U 510), former German Type IXC, was scrapped in 1958.
Of the two former German Type VII C boats, *Laubie* (ex-U 766) was withdrawn on 17 Oct 1961 (seriously damaged by collision and scrapped) and *Mille* (ex-U 471) in Aug 1963.
Roland Morillot (ex-U 2518) S 613, former German oceangoing Type XXI, was officially deleted from the list in 1968.

ESPADON — *1967, Wright & Logan*

ANTI-AIRCRAFT CRUISERS (*Croiseurs Anti-Aérien*)

Name	*Pennant No.*	*Builders*	*Laid down*	*Launched*	*Completed*	*Commissioned*
COLBERT	C 611	Brest Dockyard	Dec 1953	24 Mar 1956 (floated out of dry dock)	1958 (trials end of 1957)	5 May 1959

Displacement, tons	9 080 standard; 11 100 full load
Length, feet (*metres*)	574·2 (*175·0*) pp; 593·2 (*180·8*) oa
Beam, feet (*metres*)	64·9 (*19·8*)
Draught, feet (*metres*)	21·7 (*6·6*); 25·2 (*7·7*) screws
Aircraft	1 Helicopter
Guns, dual purpose	16—5 in (*127 mm*), 8 twin mountings
Guns, AA	20—57 mm Bofors; 10 twin mountings
Armour	Has some protection. See notes
Boilers	4 Indret multiturbular; 640 psi (*45 kg/cm²*); 842°F (*450°C*)
Main engines	2 sets CEM-Parsons geared turbines; 86 000 shp; 2 shafts
Speed, knots	32·4 max (33·7 trials); 15 economical sea
Radius, miles	4 000 at 25 knots
Oil fuel (tons)	1 492
Complement	777 (46 officers, 731 men) in peacetime; 964 (61 officers, 903 men) in wartime

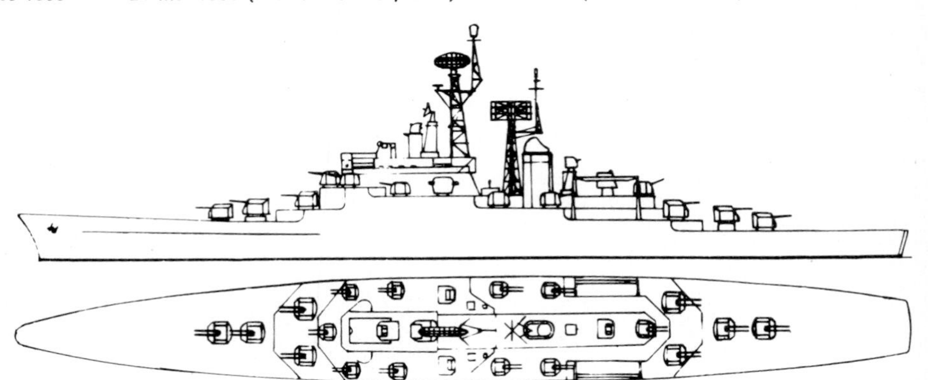

COLBERT (whaleboat emplacement suppressed) *1966, French Navy, Official*

Provision was made in the design so that she can be fitted eventually with guided missiles. Has a new scheme of protection, and a platform for a helicopter. Equipped as a fleet command ship and for radar control of air strikes. As a fast transport she could carry 2 400 men and equipment. Refitted from Oct 1962 to 1963.

GUNNERY. Guns are radar controlled with stabilised gunlayers for automatic tracking.

PHOTOGRAPHS of *Colbert* before modifications and the suppression of the whaleboat emplacement appear in the 1965-66 and earlier editions.

DRAWING. Port elevation and plan. Redrawn in 1967. Scale 128 feet = 1 inch.

RECONSTRUCTION. *Colbert* will undergo a major refit in January 1970, it is officially stated. Her existing armament will be replaced by an anti-aircraft "Masurca" guided missile system and six 3·9 inch (100 *mm*) guns. The ship will be operational in 1972.

Name	*Pennant No.*	*Builders*	*Laid down*	*Launched*	*Completed*	*Commissioned*
DE GRASSE	C 610	Lorient Dockyard and Brest Dockyard (see notes)	Nov 1938	11 Sep 1946	Aug 1955 (trials)	3 Sep 1956 (operational)

Displacement, tons	10 238 light; 12 350 full load
Length, feet (*metres*)	617·8 (*188·3*) oa
Beam, feet (*metres*)	69·9 (*21·3*)
Draught, feet (*metres*)	21·4 (*6·53*) aft
Guns, dual purpose	12—5 in (*127 mm*); 6 twin mountings
Boilers	4 A & C de B Indret multitubular; 500 psi (*35 kg/cm²*); 725°F (*385°C*)
Main engines	2 sets Rateau-Chantiers de Bretagne geared turbines 105 000 shp; 2 shafts
Speed, knots	33 max (33·8 trials); 18 cruising
Radius, miles	5 200 at 18 knots; 2 500 at full power
Oil fuel (tons)	1 900 normal
Complement	651 (38 officers, 615 men) in peacetime; 952 (58 officers, 894 men) in wartime

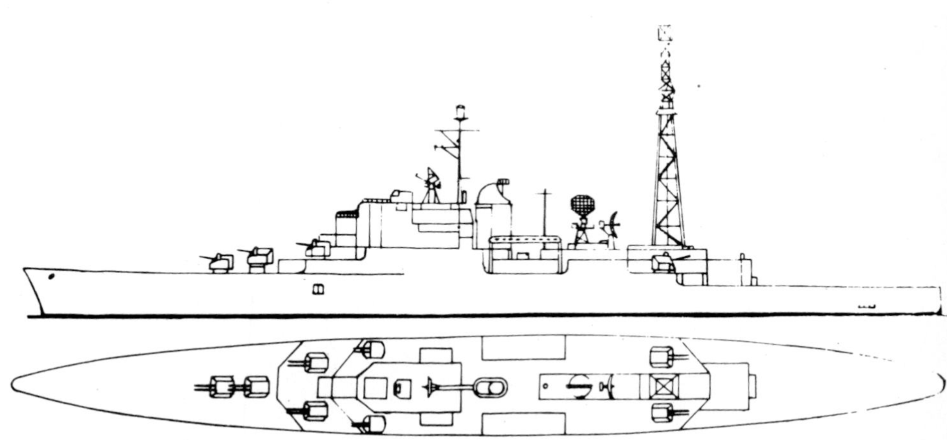

Ordered under the 1937 Estimates. Her construction was suspended during the German occupation of Lorient, but was resumed in 1946 until her launch when building was stopped. Construction was again resumed on 9 Jan 1951. Completed in Brest Dockyard as an anti-aircraft cruiser to a modified design. She is equipped as a fleet command ship and for radar control of air strikes.

MODIFICATIONS. Refitted at Brest as Flagship of the Pacific Experimental Nuclear Centre in 1966. Signal department enlarged, and several turrets suppressed.

GUNNERY. Guns are radar controlled with stabilised gunlayers. All the 57 mm Bofors AA guns (six twin mountings) and two twin 5 inch guns were suppressed during the conversion as flagship of the Pacific Experimental Centre.

PHOTOGRAPHS of *De Grasse* before conversion from anti-aircraft cruiser to command ship appear in the 1965-66 and earlier editions.

DRAWING. Port elevation and plan. Redrawn in 1967. Scale: 128 feet = 1 inch.

DE GRASSE *1967, French Navy, Official*

GUIDED MISSILE FRIGATES (*Fregates Lance-Engins*)

2 "SUFFREN" CLASS (FLE 60 TYPE)

Name	No.	Builders	Laid down	Launched	Trials	Operational
DUQUESNE	D 603	Brest Dockyard	Nov 1964	12 Feb 1966	Oct 1968	Jan 1969
SUFFREN	D 602	Lorient Dockyard	Dec 1962	15 May 1965	Dec 1965	July 1968

Displacement, tons	4 700 standard; 5 700 full load
Length, feet (*metres*)	485·5 (*148·0*) pp; 518·4 (*158·0*) oa
Beam, feet (*metres*)	50·8 (*15·5*)
Draught, feet (*metres*)	19·5 (*5·9*)
Missiles, AA	"Masurca", twin launcher
A/S	"Malafon" rocket/homing torpedo single launcher 13 missiles carried
Guns, AA	2—3·9 in (*100 mm*) automatic, single 2—30 mm (automatic, single)
Torpedo launchers	4 (2 each side) for A/S homing torpedoes
Boilers	4 automatic; working pressure 640 psi (*45 kg/cm²*); superheat 842°F (450°C)
Main engines	Double reduction geared turbines 70 000 shp; 2 shafts
Speed, knots	34
Radius, miles	5 000 at 18 knots
Complement	446 (39 officers, 407 men)

DUQUESNE *1969, French Navy, Official*

Ordered under the 1960 Programme. The structure of the ship provides the best possible resistance to atomic blast. Fitted with up-to-date detection devices (radar and sonar), two sonars including VDS, and SENIT tactical information system. Carefully studied habitability is a feature of the design. Equipped with stabilisers. Originally to have carried an anti-submarine helicopter.

SUFFREN *1968, French Navy, Official*

1 NEW CONSTRUCTION "ACONIT" CLASS

ACONIT

Displacement, tons	3 200 standard; 3,560 full load;
Length, feet (*metres*)	416·7 (*127·0*) oa
Beam, feet (*metres*)	44·0 (*13·4*)
Missiles, A/S	"Malafon" rocket/homing torpedo
Guns, AA	2—3·9 in (*100 mm*)
A/S weapons	1 quadruple 12in (305*mm*) mortar
Torpedo tubes	Auto-guided torpedoes
Main engines	Geared turbines; 27 200 shp; 1 shaft
Speed, knots	26·5 max
Radius, miles	5 000 at 18 knots
Complement	252 (22 officers, 230 men)

ACONIT *1967, French Navy, Official*

Officially rated as "Corvettes" but from their size and armament they can logically be described as frigates.

Laid down at Lorient Dockyard in Jan 1966 for trials in 1970 and operations in 1971.

2 ENLARGED "ACONIT" CLASS (67 TYPE)

Displacement, tons	5 080 standard; 5 580 full load
Length, feet (*metres*)	467·5 (*142·50*)
Beam, feet (*metres*)	50·2 (*15·30*)
Missiles A/S	"Malafon" rocket/homing torpedoes
Guns, AA	3—3·9 in (*100 mm*)
A/S weapons	1 sextuple rocket launcher
Torpedo Tubes	Auto-guided torpedoes
Aircraft	2 Franco-British WG 13 ON ASW helicopters
Main engines	Geared Turbines; 57 300 shp; 2 shafts
Radius, miles	5 000 at 18 knots
Complement	300 (26 officers, 274 men)

Laid down at Lorient in Jan and July 1968. Trials in 1972. Operational in 1973. This class will comprise several ships. The later units will be gas turbine powered. Officially rated as corvettes, but will be comparable with the "Suffren" class frigates.

EXPERIMENTAL GUIDED MISSILE SHIP (*ex-Transport*)

ILE d'OLERON (ex-*München*, ex-*Mur*)

Displacement, tons	3 280 standard; 7 500 full load
Length, feet (*metres*)	350 (*106·7*) pp; 377·5 (*115·2*) oa
Beam, feet (*metres*)	50 (*15·2*)
Draught, feet (*metres*)	21·3 (*6·5*)
Main engines	MAN 6-cylinder diesels 3 500 bhp, 1 shaft
Speed, knots	14·5
Oil fuel (tons)	340
Radius, miles	7 200 at 12 knots
Complement	195 (15 officers, 180 men)

Launched in Germany in 1939. Taken as a war prize. Formerly rated as a transport. Converted into an experimental guided missiles ship in 1957-58 by Chantiers de Provence et l'Arsenal de Toulon. Commissioned as a test bed early in 1959. Equipped with stabilisers.

ILE d'OLÉRON *1967, courtesy Dr. Giorgio Arra*

EXPERIMENTAL. When converted she was designed for experiments with two launchers for ship to air missiles, the medium range "Masurca" and the long range "Masalca", and one launcher for ship to shore missiles, the "Malaface". Latterly fitted with one launcher for target planes.

DESTROYERS *(Rated as Escorteurs d'Escadre)*

Name	*Pennant No.*	*Builders*	*Laid down*	*Launched*	*Completed*
LA GALISSONNIÈRE	D 638	Lorient Naval Dockyard	Nov 1958	12 Mar 1960	July 1962

1 ANTI-SUBMARINE (T 56) TYPE

Displacement, tons	2 750 standard; 3 910 full load;
Length, feet (*metres*)	435·7 (*132·8*) oa
Beam, feet (*metres*)	41·7 (*12·7*)
Draught, feet (*metres*)	15·4 (*4·7*) aft; 18·0 (*5·5*) screws
Aircraft	1 A/S helicopter
A/S	"Malafon" rocket/homing torpedoes, 1 launcher
Guns, AA	2—3·9 in (*100 mm*) automatic, single
Torpedo tubes	6—21·7 in (*550 mm*) ASM, 2 triple
Boilers	4 A & C de B Indret; 500 psi (*35 kg/cm²*); 716°F (*380°C*)
Main engines	2 sets geared turbines 63 000 shp (72 000 on trials, light) 2 shafts
Speed, knots	34·5 (38·2 on trials, light), 15 sea
Radius, miles	4 900 at 18 knots
Oil fuel (tons)	725
Complement	333 (20 officers, 313 men)

Designed as a squadron escort and flotilla leader. She has extensive sonar and anti-submarine apparatus, including variable depth sonar and homing torpedoes. Particularly well developed anti-aircraft and radar equipment. T 56 type. Same characteristics as regards hull and machinery as T 47 and T 53 R types, but different armament. She has a hangar and a platform for landing a helicopter. When first commissioned she was used as an experimental ship for new sonars and anti-submarine weapons.

ARMAMENT. She is fitted with French marks of guided missiles and was the first French combatant ship to be so armed. This is the reason for the two 3·9 in (*100 mm*) guns instead of the 3 or 4 previously planned. As re-designed she was France's first operational guided missile ship.

PHOTOGRAPHS of *La Galissonniere* as first completed appear in the 1962-63 edition, and a starboard bow view in the 1963-64 to 1965-66 editions.

LA GALISSONNIÈRE — *1969, French Navy, Official*

Name	*Pennant No.*	*Builders*	*Laid down*	*Launched*	*Completed (commissioned)*
DUPERRÈ	A 633	Lorient Naval Dockyard	Nov 1954	2 July 1955	8 Oct 1957
FORBIN	D 635	Brest Naval Dockyard	Aug 1954	15 Oct 1955	1 Feb 1958
JAURÈGUIBERRY	D 637	Forges et Chantiers de la Gironde	Sep 1954	5 Nov 1955	July 1958
LA BOURDONNAIS	D 634	Brest Naval Dockyard	Aug 1954	15 Oct 1955	Mar 1958
TARTU	D 636	Ateliers et Chantiers de Bretagne	Nov 1954	2 Dec 1955	5 Feb 1958

4 AIRCRAFT DIRECTION (T53) TYPE

1 EXPERIMENTAL ("DUPERRÈ")

Displacement, tons	2 750 standard; 3 750 full load
Length, feet (*metres*)	422 (*128·6*) oa
Beam, feet (*metres*)	41·7 (*12·7*)
Draught, feet (*metres*)	15·0 (*4·6*) aft; 17·7 (*5·4*) screws
Guns, dual purpose	6—5 in (*127 mm*), twin mounts
Guns, AA	6—2·25 in (*57 mm*) Bofors 2 or 4—20 mm
A/S	Sextuple Bofors *lance roquettes* howitzer
Torpedo tubes	6—21·7 in (*550 mm*) ASM, 2 triple (also able to launch ordinary torpedoes)
Boilers	4 Indret or A & C de B in two boiler rooms separated by turbine compartment. Working pressure 500 psi (*35·2 kg/cm²*); superheat 725°F (*385°C*)
Main engines	2 ACL geared turbines 63 000 shp; 2 shafts
Speed, knots	34 max (35 trials)
Radius, miles	5 000 at 18 knots
Oil fuel (tons)	700
Complement	281 (19 officers, 262 men)

LA BOURDONNAIS — *1966, Dr. Giorgio Arra*

Radar Picket Destroyers. Modified "Surcouf" Class or "T 53 R" Type fitted as aircraft direction and command ships. Radar equipment more comprehensive and prominent than in the original "Surcouf" or "T 47" Anti-Aircraft Type. Classed as Escorteurs Rapides in 1953, but re-rated as Escorteurs in 1955. Latest electronic appliances. Named after famous sailors *Duperré* was reclassified as trials ship in 1967, all armament removed.

CONSTRUCTION. Hull entirely welded. Light alloys used extensively for upperworks.

GUNNERY. The 5 inch guns are able to use standard American ammunition.

PHOTOGRAPHS of *Forbin* appear in the 1958-59 to 1962-63 editions, of *Duperré* in the 1962-63 to 1965-66

TARTU — *French Navy, Official*

Destroyers—*continued*

12 "SURCOUF" CLASS

Bouvet *Du Chayla* *Dupetit Thouars* *Kersaint*	Rearmed with guided missiles
Cassard *Chevalier Paul* *Surcouf*	Converted to command ships
Casabianca *D'Estrées* *Guépratte* *Maillé Brézé* *Vauquelin*	Original anti-aircraft T 47 type converted to anti-submarine

Name	*No.*	*Builders*	*Laid down*	*Launched*	*Completed*
BOUVET	D 624	Lorient Naval Dockyard	June 1952	3 Oct 1953	13 May 1956
CASABIANCA	D 631	A. C. Bretagne	Oct 1953	13 Nov 1954	4 May 1957
CASSARD	D 623	A. C. Bretagne	Nov 1951	12 May 1953	14 Apr 1956
CHEVALIER PAUL	D 626	F. C. Gironde	Feb 1952	28 July 1953	22 Dec 1956
D'ESTRÉES	D 629	Brest Naval Dockyard	May 1953	27 Nov 1954	19 Mar 1957
DU CHAYLA	D 630	Brest Naval Dockyard	July 1953	27 Nov 1954	4 June 1957
DUPETIT THOUARS	D 625	Brest Naval Dockyard	Mar 1952	4 Feb 1954	15 Sep 1956
GUÉPRATTE	D 632	F. C. Gironde	Aug 1953	9 Nov 1954	6 June 1957
KERSAINT	D 622	Lorient Naval Dockyard	Nov 1951	3 Oct 1953	20 Mar 1956
MAILLÉ BRÉZÉ	D 627	Lorient Naval Dockyard	Oct 1953	26 Sep 1954	4 May 1957
SURCOUF	D 621	Lorient Naval Dockyard	July 1951	3 Oct 1953	1 Nov 1955
VAUQUELIN	D 628	Lorient Naval Dockyard	Mar 1953	26 Sep 1954	3 Nov 1956

Displacement, tons	2 750 standard; 3 850 full load
Length, feet (*metres*)	421·3 (*128·4*) oa
Beam, feet (*metres*)	42·6 (*13·0*)
Draught, feet (*metres*)	15·8 (*4·8*) aft; 18·3 (*5·6*) screws
Missiles, AA	Single "Tartar" Mark 13 (40 missiles) in *Bouvet, Du Chayla, Dupetit Thouars* and *Kersaint* only
Guns, dual purpose	6—5 in (*127 mm*), twin mounts (see *Conversion* and *Gunnery* notes)
Guns, AA	6—57 mm; 6—20 mm
Torpedo tubes	12—21·7 in (*550 mm*) in 4 triple mounte, (6 ordinary, 6 ASM)
Boilers	4 Indret; 500 psi (*35·2 kg/cm²*); superheat 725°F (385°C)
Main engines	2 Parsons geared turbines 63 000 shp; 2 shafts
Speed, knots	35 max
Radius, miles	5 000 at 18 knots
Oil fuel (tons)	800
Complement	293 (336 with command staff)

Designed as Escorteurs Rapides Anti-aériens but re-rated Escorteurs Prèmiere Classe in 1951, Escorteurs Rapides in 1953 and Escorteurs d'Escadre in 1955. Named after famous French sailors.

CONSTRUCTION. Hull entirely welded, assembled from 84 prefabricated sections with a total weight of 1 100 tons. Light alloys used extensively for upper-works. Two boiler rooms alternate with two turbine.

GUNNERY. The semi-automatic 5 inch guns were chosen to use standard US ammunition. The four SAM conversions lost all their 5 inch guns.

COMMAND. *Cassard, Chevalier Paul* and *Surcouf*, refitted as flotilla leaders, retained their 6—5 inch guns but only 4—57 mm AA and 6 tubes for ASM torpedoes.

CONVERSION. In Jan 1966-1968 *D'Estrées* was converted into an anti-submarine vessel, followed in order by *Maillé Brézé* Jan 1967-Apr 1969, *Vauquelin, Casabianca* and *Guépratte*. New armament: 2—3·9 in (*100 mm*) AA, 1 Malafon missile launcher, 6 A/S tubes (2 triple), 1 Bofors rocket launcher, variable depth sonar and bow sonar.

MAILLÉ BRÉZÉ — *1968, French Navy, Official*

BOUVET (missile launcher aft) — *1967, French Navy, Official*

PHOTOGRAPHS. A Photograph of *Vauquelin* appears in the 1957-58 to 1962-63 editions, *Guépratte* in the 1959-60 to 1961-62 editions, *Cassard* in the 1962-63 to 1965-66 editions, *D Estrées* in the 1963-64 to 1965-66 editions, and *Dupetit Thouars* (firing guided missiles) in the 1966-67 and 1967-68 editions.

D'ESTREES (as converted to anti-submarine) — *1969, French Navy, Official*

SURCOUF (command type) — *1966, Dr. Giorgio Arra*

DUAL PURPOSE FRIGATES (Rated as *Avisos Escorteurs*)

9 "COMMANDANT" RIVIERE CLASS

	Launched	*Completed*
AMIRAL CHARNER	12 Mar 60	15 Dec 62
BALNY	17 Mar 62	31 Mar 69
COMMANDANT BORY	11 Oct 58	5 Mar 64
COMMANDANT BOURDAIS	15 Apr 61	1 Mar 63
COMMANDANT RIVIÈRE	11 Oct 58	4 Dec 62
DOUDART DE LAGRÉE	15 Apr 61	1 Mar 63
ENSEIGNE DE VAISSEAU HENRY	14 Dec 63	1 Jan 65
PROTET	7 Dec 62	1 May 64
VICTOR SCHOELCHER	11 Oct 58	15 Oct 62

Displacement, tons	1 750 standard; 1 950 full load
Length, feet (*metres*)	321·5 (*98·0*) pp; 338 (*103*) oa
Beam, feet (*metres*)	37·8 (*11·5*)
Draught, feet (*metres*)	12·5 (*3·8*) mean; 14·1 (*4·3*) max
Aircraft	1 light helicopter can land aft
Guns, AA	3—3·9 in (*100 mm*) automatic, singles; 2—30 mm
A/S	1—12in (*305mm*) quadruple mortar
Torpedo tubes	6—21 in (*533 mm*) ASM
Main engines	4 SEMT-Pielstick diesels; 16 000 bhp; 2 shafts; except *Commandant Bory:* Sigma free piston generators and gas turbines; *Balny:* CODAG; 1 shaft; (trials 1969)
Speed, knots	25·4 max (26·4 trials)
Radius, miles	4 500 at 15 knots
Complement	214 (15 officers, 199 men)

All built by Lorient Naval Dockyard. *Commandant Rivière* started assembly on slip in Nov 1956 and preliminary sea trials on 1 Apr 1959. Formerly classed as *Escorteurs d'Union Francaise*. Officially rerated as *Avisos Escorteurs* on 1 Apr 1959. Designed to serve as *avisos* in peace and frigates in war. *Commandant Bourdais* commissioned as fishery protection ship for Newfoundland and Greenland in Mar 1963. *Victor Schoelcher* acts as training ship.

BALNY (CODAG propulsion system) — *1969, Official*

PROTET — *1968, French Navy, Official*

PHOTOGRAPHS. A photograph of *Commandant Rivière* appears in the 1960-61 to 1964-65 editions, of *Doudart de la Grée* in the 1964-65 and 1965-66 editions, of *Enseigne de Vaisseau Henry* in the 1965-66 to 1967-68 editions, of *Commandant Bory* in the 1966-67 to 1968-69 editions.

FAST FRIGATES (Rated as *Escorteurs Rapides*)

14 "LE NORMAND" CLASS (E 52 TYPE)

Name	*No.*	*Builders*	*Laid down*	*Launched*	*Completed*
LE NORMAND	F 765	F. Ch. de la Medit	July 1953	13 Feb 1954	3 Nov 1956
LE LORRAIN	F 768	F. Ch. de la Medit	Feb 1954	19 June 1954	1 Jan 1957
LE PICARD	F 766	A. C. Loire	Nov 1953	31 May 1954	20 Sep 1956
LE GASCON	F 767	A. C. Loire	Feb 1954	23 Oct 1954	29 Mar 1957
LE CHAMPENOIS	F 770	A. C. Loire	May 1954	12 Mar 1955	1 June 1957
LE SAVOYARD	F 771	F. Ch. de la Medit	Nov 1953	7 May 1955	14 June 1956
LE BOURGUIGNON	F 769	Penhoët	Jan 1954	28 Jan 1956	11 July 1957
LE BRETON	F 772	Lorient Navy Yard	June 1954	2 Apr 1955	20 Aug 1957
LE BASQUE	F 773	Lorient Navy Yard	Dec 1954	25 Feb 1956	18 Oct 1957
L'AGENAIS	F 774	Lorient Navy Yard	Aug 1955	23 June 1956	14 May 1958
LE BÈARNAIS	F 775	Lorient Navy Yard	Dec 1955	23 June 1956	18 Oct 1958
L'ALSACIEN	F 776	Lorient Navy Yard	July 1956	26 Jan 1957	27 Aug 1960
LE PROVENCAL	F 777	Lorient Navy Yard	Feb 1957	5 Oct 1957	6 Nov 1959
LE VENDÈEN	F 778	F. Ch. de la Medit	Mar 1957	27 July 1957	1 Oct 1960

Displacement, tons	1 295 standard; 1 795 full load
Length, feet (*metres*)	311·7 (*95·0*) pp; 325·8 (*99·3*) oa
Beam, feet (*metres*)	33·8 (*10·3*)
Draught, feet (*metres*)	11·2 (*3·4*) aft; 13·5 (*4·1*) screws
Guns, AA	6—2·25 in (*57 mm*), in twin mountings (4 only in F 776, 777, 778); 2—20 mm
A/S	Heavy sextuple Bofors ASM (*lance-roquettes*) mortar of Hedgehog type forward (*except* F 776, 777, 778 with 1—12 in (*305 mm*) quadruple mortar) 2 DC mortars; 1 DC rack
Torpedo tubes	12 ASM (4 triple mountings aft) for homing torpedoes
Boilers	2 Indret; pressure 500 psi (*35·2 kg/cm²*); superheat 725°F (385°C)
Main engines	Parsons or Rateau geared turbines 20 000 shp
Speed, knots	28 (on trials they exceeded 29 kts)
Radius, miles	4 500 at 12 knots
Oil fuel (tons)	310
Complement	175 peace; 200 war

The E 52a type have similar characteristics to the E 50 type as regards hull and machinery but are easily distinguished in that they have the ASM tubes aft and the heavy hedgehog or ASM howitzer forward while the E 50 type have the ASM torpedo tubes forward. *L'Agenais, L'Alsacien, Le Béarnais, Le Provençal* and *Le Vendèen* have a different arrangement of bridges. *L'Alsacien, Le Provençal,* and *Le Vendéen* have the Strombos-Velensi type modified funnel cap, and differ in armament, with a 12-inch quadruple mortar in place of the sextuple Bofors' howitzer and only 4—57 mm AA guns.

PHOTOGRAPHS of *Le Gascon* appear in the 1957-58 to 1959-60 editions, of *L'Agenais* in the 1958-59 and 1960-61 to 1963-64 editions, of *Le Bourguignon* in the 1962-63 and 1963-64 editions, of *Le Savoyard* in the 1964-65 and 1695-66 editions, of *Le Vendeen* in the 1964-65 to 1966-67 editions, and of *Le Breton* in the 1966-67 edition.

DISPOSALS OF EX-BRITISH "RIVER" TYPE
Of the *"L'Aventure"* class, *La Decouverte* (ex-HMS *Windrush* was condemned in May 1961 and *La Croix de Lorraine* (ex-HMS *Strule*, ex-*Glenarm*), *L'Ailette* (ex-*L'Escarmouche*, ex-HMS *Frome*) and *La Confiance* (ex-*Toniknois*, ex-HMS *Malaya*) in Sep 1961. *L'Aventure* was withdrawn from service on 15 Dec 1961. *La Surprise* was sold to Morocco in June 1964.
La Decouverte replaced *Lucifer* (ex-German M 277 as experimental ship at Cherbourg.

LE LORRAIN and LE BOURGUIGNON — *1968, Skyfotos*

LE CHAMPENOIS — *1967, Wright & Logan*

FAST FRIGATES (Rated as *Escorteurs Rapides*)

4 "LE CORSE" CLASS (E 50 TYPE)

Name	No.	Builders	Laid down	Launched	Completed
LE BORDELAIS	F 764	F. Ch. de la Medit	May 1952	11 July 1953	7 Apr 1955
LE BOULONNAIS	F 763	A. C. Loire	Mar 1952	12 May 1953	5 Aug 1955
LE BRESTOIS	F 762	Lorient Navy Yard	Nov 1951	16 Aug 1952	19 Jan 1956
LE CORSE	F 761	Lorient Navy Yard	Oct 1951	5 Aug 1952	15 Apr 1955

Displacement, tons	1 290 standard; 1 528 for trials; 1 680 full load (official revised figures)
Length, feet (*metres*)	311·7 (*95·0*) pp; 325·5 (*99·2*) oa
Beam, feet (*metres*)	33·8 (*10·3*)
Draught, feet (*metres*)	11·2 (*3·4*) aft; 13·5 (*4·1*) screws
Guns, AA	6—2·25 in (*57 mm*), twin mounts 2—20 mm
A/S	2 mortars; 1 DC rack; 1 sextuple "lance roquettes"
Torpedo tubes	12 ASM tubes (four triple mounts forward) for homing torpedoes
Boilers	2 Indret; pressure 500 psi (*35·2 kg/cm²*); superheat 725°F (385°C)
Main engines	Rateau A & C de B geared turbines 20 000 shp
Speed, knots	28·5 max, 28·9 trials (*Bordelais* 29·5 on trials); economical sea speed 14
Radius, miles	4 000 at 15 knots
Complement	174 peace, 198 war
Oil fuel (tons)	292
Complement	174 peace, 198 war

Intended as seagoing convoy escort vessels with a large radius of action. Designed as Escorteurs Rapides Anti-Sousmarins. Re-rated as Escorteurs de Deuxième Classe in 1951, as Escorteurs in 1953, and as Escorteurs Rapides in 1955. First four laid down are E 50 type, remainder E 52 type. *Le Bordelais* has Strombos-Velensi type modified funnel cap. *Le Brestois* has similar mainmast to that in *Le Provencal*.

GUNNERY. Le Brestois had a single 3·9 in (*100 mm*) automatic AA gun mounted in place of the after twin mounting for experimental purpose, and after her refit completed in 1963 she retains this mounting.

LE BRESTOIS *1969, Official*

STATUS. *Le Boulonnais* and *Le Corse* normal reserve status on 1 Dec 1964, *Le Bordelais* since Aug 1966.

PHOTOGRAPHS of *Le Boulonnais* appear in the 1956-57, 1957-58, 1963-64, 1964-65 and 1965-66 editions, and of *Le Bordelais* in the 1966-67 to 1968-69 editions.

EX-FRIGATES (Rated as *Avisos*) Ex-*Escorteurs*

Ex-US DESTROYER ESCORT TYPE

1 "ARABE" CLASS

Name	No.	Builders	Launched	Completed
ARAGO (ex-*Somali*, ex-USS DE 111)	A 607	Dravo Corp, Willmington	12 Feb 1944	9 Apr 1944

Displacement, tons	1 300 standard; 1 650 full load
Length, feet (*metres*)	300 (*91·4*) pp; 306 (*93·3*) wl
Beam, feet (*metres*)	36·8 (*11·2*)
Draught, feet (*metres*)	10·7 (*3·3*)
Guns	All removed
Main engines	4 GE diesels, 2 electric motors; diesel-electric drive 6 000 bhp; 2 shafts
Speed, knots	19 (economical speed 12 kts)
Radius, miles	11 500 at 11 knots
Complement	150 peace;

Sole survivor of 14 "Bostwick" class destroyer escorts acquired from the United States in 1944-1952, formerly rated as Torpilleurs d'Escorte, but re-rated Escorteurs de Deuxieme Classe in 1951, Escorteurs in 1953 and Avisos in 1964.

EXPERIMENTAL. *Arago* was converted into an experimental vessel in 1956 and her armament landed, her pennant number subsequently being changed from F 703 to A 607. Her name was changed from *Somali* to *Arago* on 1 Apr 1968.

DISPOSALS
Sister ships *Arabe* (ex-*Samuel S. Miles, DE* 183), *Berbere* (ex-*Clarence L. Evans, DE* 113, *Hova* (ex-*DE* 110), *Marocain* (ex-*DE* 109), *Sakalave* (ex-*Wingfield, DE* 194), and *Tunisien* (ex-*Crosley, DE* 108) of the 1st Group, and were officially stricken from the list in 1960, and *Bambara* (ex-*Swearer, DE* 186, *Kayble* (ex-*Riddle*, DE 185), *Oise* (ex-*Algérien*, ex-*Cronin, DE* 107), *Soundanais* (ex-*Cates, DE* 763), *Touareg* (ex-*Bright, DE* 747) and *Yser* (ex-*Sénégalais*, ex-*Corbesier, DE* 106) in 1965, and *Malgache* (ex-USS *Baker, DE* 190) in 1969.

ARAGO (ex-*Somali*) *1968, French Navy, Official*

LE CORSE (see above) *1966, Stefan Terzibaschitsch*

Ex Frigates—*continued*

COMMANDANT ROBERT GIRAUD
(ex-*Immelmann*) A 755 (ex-F 755)

Displacement, tons	1 000 standard; 1 380 full load
Length, feet (*metres*)	239 (*72·9*) pp; 256 (*78·0*) oa
Beam, feet (*metres*)	36 (*11·0*)
Draught, feet (*metres*)	12 (*3·7*)
Main engines	4 MAN diesels 8 800 bhp; 2 shafts
Speed, knots	20·5
Radius, miles	7 800 at 12 knots
Oil fuel (tons)	236

Former dépanneur d'hydravions, ex-German aircraft tender. Built by Norderwerft, Hamburg. Launched in 1941. Completed in Dec 1941. Transferred by Great Britain in Aug 1946, with *Paul Goffeny*. Re-rated as Escorteur de Deuxième Classe early in 1953, as Aviso Escorteur on 11 Aug 1953, as Aviso in 1955, as *Gabarre* in 1963, and *Aviso Hydrograph* in 1969. Formerly used as patrol and escort vessel, support gunboat and carrier for commandos. The four diesels are coupled two by two by hydraulic transmission on two shafts.
Sister ship *Paul Goffeny* was officially deleted from the list in 1969.

COMMANDANT ROBERT GIRAUD *1969, Official*

Of the ex-frigates serving as *Avisos Hydrographes*, *Amiral Mouchez*, F 752, was condemned in Sep 1965, and *Beautemps,-Beaupré* A 752 (ex-F 751) and *La Pérouse* A 753 (ex-F 750) were officially deleted from the list in 1969.

COMMAND SHIP (*Bâtiment de Commandement*)

GUSTAVE ZEDE (ex-*Saar*) A 641

Displacement, tons	2 895 standard; 3 230 full load
Length, feet (metres)	308 (*93·9*)
Beam, feet (*metres*)	44·5 (*13·5*)
Draught, feet (*metres*)	14 (*4·3*)
Guns, surface	3—4·1 in (*105 mm*)
Guns, AA	4—40 mm; 8—20 mm
Main engines	2 Krupp diesels 3 700 bhp; 2 shafts
Speed, knots	16
Radius, miles	9 400 at 11 knots
Oil fuel (tons)	336
Complement	364

Former German submarine school depot ship, built by Krupp-Germania and launched on 5 Apr 1934. Acquired from the US Navy in Oct 1947. Recommissioned in 1949 as a Ravitailleur-pour-Sousmarins (submarine Depot Ship). Alterations were made to the bridge and foremast in 1952. Formerly Flagship of the 3rd FER (3e flotille d'escorteurs rapides) or Groupe d'action anti-submarine (Anti-submarine Group).

GUSTAVE ZÉDÉ *1966, French Navy, Official*

ASSAULT LANDING SHIPS (*Transports de chalands de debarquement*)

ORAGE TCD 2 **OURAGAN** TCD 1

Displacement, tons	5 800 light; 8 500 full load; 15 000 when fully immersed
Length, feet (*metres*)	489 (*149·0*)
Beam, feet (*metres*)	70·5 (*21·5*)
Draught, feet (*metres*)	15 (*4·6*); 28·5 (8·7) max
Guns, surface	2—4·7 in (*120 mm*) mortars
Guns, AA	6—30 mm
Main engines	2 diesels; 8 000 bhp; 2 shafts
Speed, knots	17
Radius, miles	8 000 at 15 knots
Complement	341 (14 officers, 327 men)

Built at Brest Dockyard. *Ouragan* was laid down in June 1962, launched on 9 Nov 1963, completed for trials in 1964, and commissioned in Jan 1965. Bridge is on the starboard side. Fitted with a platform for three heavy helicopters. Able to carry EDICs loaded with eleven light tanks each, or 18 loaded LCMs, also 1 500 tons of material and equipment handled by two 35 tons cranes. Allocated to the Pacific Nuclear Experimental Centre. *Orage* was launched on 22 Apr 1967 and completed in Mar 1968.

OURAGAN *1967 French Navy Official*

ORAGE *1969, French Navy, Official*

MINEHUNTERS (*Chasseurs de Mines*)

5 NEW CONSTRUCTION "CIRCE" CLASS

CALLIOPE **CIRCE** **CLIO** **CYBELE**

Displacement, tons	460 standard; 495 normal; 510 full load
Guns	1—20 mm
Main engines	Diesels; single axial screw; designed for 15 knots
Radius, miles	3 000 at 12 knots

A new design. Officially rated as *Chasseurs de Mines*. The ships will have a special rudder on each side for working up at slow speeds. Ordered in 1968. Formerly published name *Ceres* for the fifth unit was officially suppressed in 1969.

CIRCE *1968, courtesy M Henry Le Masson*

OCEAN MINESWEEPERS

15 US MSO (ex-AM) TYPE "BERNEVAL" CLASS

ALENCON (ex-*AM* 453)
AUTUN (ex-*AM* 502)
BACCARAT (ex-*AM* 505)
BERLAIMONT (ex-*AM* 500)
BERNEVAL (ex-*AM* 450)
BIR HACHEIM (ex-*AM* 451)
CANTHO (ex-*AM* 476)
COLMAR (ex-*AM* 514)
DOMPAIRE (ex-*AM* 454)
GARIGLIANO (ex-*AM* 452)
MYTHO (ex-*AM* 475)
NARVIK (ex-*AM* 512)
ORIGNY (ex-*AM* 501)
OUISTREHAM (ex-*AM* 513)
VINH LONG (ex-*AM* 477)

Displacement, tons	700 standard; 795 full load
Dimensions, feet	165 wl; 171 oa × 35 × 10·3
Guns	1—40 mm AA
Main engines	2 General Motors diesels; 2 shafts; 1 600 bhp = 13·5 knots designed; 14 knots on trials
Radius, miles	3 000 at 10 knots
Complement	54

The USA agreed in Sep 1952 to transfer to France eight new AMs in 1953, and four in 1954. Three more transferred in 1956. *Bir Hacheim* transferred in Feb 1954, *Garigliano* in Apr 1954 and *Vinh Long* in 1955. *Origny* was launched on 25 Feb 1955. *Autun* on 6 May 1955, *Baccarat* on 6 Aug 1955 and *Berlaimont* on 7 Jan 1955. *Origny* is classified and fitted as an oceanographic research vessel but is Navy owned and manned.

APPEARANCE. *Autun, Baccarat, Berlaimont, Colmar, Narvik, Origny* and *Ouistreham* are somewhat different from the others and have a taller funnel.

PHOTOGRAPHS. An aerial port quarter view of *Garigliano* appears in the 1955-56 edition, a broadside surface view of *Alençon* in the 1956-57 to 1958-59 editions, a starboard bow view of *Narvik* in the 1959-60 edition, a port broadside view of *Vinh Long* in the 1960-61 to 1963-64 editions, a starboard quarter oblique aerial view of *Colmar* in the 1962-63 to 1966-67 editions, a starboard broadside view of *Berneval* in the 1964-65 to 1968-69 editions.

MYTHO (short funnel type) *1969, French Navy, Official*

BERLAIMONT (tall funnel type) *1967, courtesy Admiral M. Adam*

COASTAL MINESWEEPERS (*Dragueurs Côtiers*)

34 BRITISH TYPE. "SIRIUS" CLASS

ACHERNAR (12 Aug 54)
ALDÉBARAN (27 June 53)
ALGOL (15 Apr 53)
ALTAIR (27 Mar 56)
ANTARÈS (21 Jan 54)
ARCTURUS (12 Mar 54)
ARIES (13 Mar 56)
BELLATRIX (21 July 55)
BÉTELGEUSE (12 July 54)
CANOPUS (31 Dec 53)
CAPELLA (6 Sep 55)
CAPRICORNE (8 Aug 56)
CASSIOPÉE (16 Nov 53)
CASTOR (19 Nov 53)
CENTAURE (8 Mar 55)
CÉPHÉE (3 Jan 56)
CROIX DU SUD (13 June 56)
DÉNÉBOLA (12 July 56)
ERIDAN (18 May 54)
ETOILE POLAIRE (5 Mar 57)
FOMALHAUT (24 Apr 55)
LYRE (3 May 56)
ORION (20 Nov 53)
PEGASE (21 June 55)
PERSÉE (23 May 55)
PHÉNIX (23 May 55)
POLLUX (16 July 54)
PROCYON (12 Dec 54)
RÉGULUS (18 Nov 52)
RIGEL (13 May 53)
SAGITTAIRE (12 Jan 55)
SIRIUS (6 Oct 52)
VEGA (14 Jan 53)
VERSEAU (26 Apr 56)

Displacement, tons	365 standard; 424 full load
Dimensions, feet	140 pp; 152 oa × 28 × 8·2
Guns	1—40 mm Bofors AA; 1—20 mm Oerlikon AA (several have 2—20 mm AA)
Main engines	SIGMA free piston generators and Alsthom or Rateau-Bretagne gas turbines or SEMT-Pielstick 16-cyl fast diesels; 2 shafts; 2 000 bhp = 15 knots (11·5 knots when sweeping)
Oil fuel (tons)	48
Radius, miles	3 000 at 15 knots
Complement	38

Of wooden and aluminium alloy construction. Launch dates above. Of same general characteristics as the British "Coniston" class, but of different hull construction. Propelled by Alsthom or Rateau gas turbine with SIGMA free piston generator, except *Altair, Arcturus, Aries, Bételgeuse, Canopus, Capella, Capricorne, Céphée, Croix du Sud, Etoile Polaire, Lyre, Phénix* and *Verseau*, which have SEMT-Pielstick light diesels. Similar to those built in Great Britain and the Netherlands of which the plans were basically similar for all. The original design of this type of craft was developed in close collaboration with John I. Thornycroft & Co. Ltd, Southampton, and the Royal Navy. 16 of these vessels were built under the "off-shore" procurement programme. *Altair, Arcturus* and *Croix de Sud* have been station-ships in the West Indies since 1960. D 25, D 26 and D 27 were allocated to Yugoslavia.

PHOTOGRAPHS. A large starboard bow view of *Régulus* appears in the 1957-58 to 1959-60 editions, a starboard broadside view of *Vega* in the 1954-55 to 1963-64 editions, and a starboard bow near broadside surface view of *Altair* in the 1964-65 to 1966-67 editions.

ALDEBARAN *1967, French Navy, Official*

29 US MSC (Ex-AMS) TYPE. "ACACIA" CLASS

ACACIA (ex-*AMS* 69)
ACANTHE (ex-*AMS* 70)
ACONIT (ex-*AMS* 66)
AJONC (ex-*AMS* 71)
AZALÉE (ex-*AMS* 67)
BEGONIA (ex-*AMS* 83)
BLEUÈT (ex-*AMS* 116)
CAMÉLIA (ex-*AMS* 68)
CHRYSANTHEME (ex-*AMS* 113)
COQUELICOT (ex-*AMS* 84)
CYCLAMEN (ex-*AMS* 119)
EGLANTINE (ex-*AMS* 117)
GARDÉNIA (ex-*AMS* 114)
GIROFLÉE (ex-*AMS* 85)
GLAIEUL (ex-*AMS* 120)
GLYCINE (ex-*AMS* 118)
JACINTHE (ex-*AMS* 115)
LAURIER (ex-*AMS* 86)
LILAS (ex-*AMS* 93)
LISERON (ex-*AMS* 98)
LOBELIA (ex-*AMS* 96)
MAGNOLIA (ex-*AMS* 87)
MIMOSA (ex-*AMS* 99)
MUGUET (ex-*AMS* 97)
PAVOT (ex-*AMS* 124)
PERVENCHE (ex-*AMS* 141)
PIVOINE (ex-*AMS* 125)
RENONCULE (ex-*AMS* 142)
RÉSÈDA (ex-*AMS* 126)

Displacement, tons	370 standard; 405 full load
Dimensions, feet	136·2 pp; 141 oa × 26 × 8·3
Guns	2—20 mm AA
Main engines	2 General Motors diesels; 2 shafts; 1 200 bhp = 13 knots (8 knots when sweeping)
Oil fuel (tons)	40
Radius, miles	2 500 at 10 knots
Complement	38 (3 officers, 35 men)

The USA agreed in Sep 1952 to allocate to France in 1953, 36 new AMS (later re-designated MSC) under the Mutual Defense Assistance Programme, but only 30 were finally transferred to France in 1953-55. Three were returned to the USA after delivery to Saigon for Indo-China, and two of these were allocated to Japan (AMS 95 and 144). Three (AMS 139, 140, 143) were not delivered, having been allocated to Spain. Auxiliary motor minesweepers constructed throughout of wood or other materials with the lowest possible magnetic attraction to attain the greatest possible safety factor when sweeping for magnetic mines. All named after flowers. *Aconit* was renamed *Marjolaine* in 1967 (name *Aconit* assigned to new frigate). All built in the United States in 1951-54. *Marguerite* (ex-*AMS* 94) was officially deleted from the list in 1969.

PHOTOGRAPHS. A larger port broadside view of *Coquelicot* appears in the 1954-55 to 1959-60 editions, a starboard view of *Pervenche* in the 1961-62 to 1964-65 editions, and a starboard broadside view of *Pavot* in the 1965-66 to 1967-68 editions. See photograph of *Laurier* at the top of column 1, next page.

Coastal Minesweepers—*continued*

LAURIER *1968, French Navy, Official*

1 SPECIAL TYPE

MERCURE

Displacement, tons	333 light; 362 normal; 380 full load
Dimensions, feet	137·8 pp; 145·5 oa × 27 × 8·5
Guns	2—20 mm AA
Main engines	2 Mercedes-Benz diesels; 2 shafts; Kamewa variable pitch propellers; 4 000 bhp = 15 knots
Oil fuel (tons)	48
Radius, miles	3 000 at 15 knots
Complement	48

Ordered in France from Mécaniques de Normandie (who have built six sister ships for the Federal German Navy) under the "off-shore" programme. Laid down in Jan 1955. Launched on 21 Dec 1957. Completed in Dec 1958. Somewhat different from the "Sirius" class and with the same method of construction as the United States-built "Acacia" class. Stated to be a very successful model.

MERCURE *1968, French Navy, Official*

6 Ex-CANADIAN "BAY" TYPE "LA DUNKERQUOISE" CLASS

LA BAYONNAISE (ex-*Chignecto*)
LE DIEPPOISE (ex-*Chaleur*)
LA DUNKERQUOISE (ex-*Fundy*)
LA LORIENTAISE (ex-*Miramachi*)
LA MALOUINE (ex-*Cowichan*)
LA PAIMPOLAISE (ex-*Thunder*)

Displacement, tons	390 standard; 412 full load
Dimensions, feet	140 pp; 152 oa × 28 × 8·7
Guns	1—40 mm AA
Main engines	General Motors diesels; 2 shafts; 2 400 bhp = 16 knots max
Oil fuel (tons)	52
Radius, miles	4 500 at 11 knots
Complement	43 (4 officers, 39 men)

La Bayonnaise (launched 12 May 1952) *La Malouine* (launched 12 Nov 1951) and *La Paimpolaise* (launched 17 July 1953) were tranferred to the French flag at Halifax on 1 Apr 1954, *La Dunkerquoise* (launched Apr 1953) on 30 Apr 1954, and *La Dieppoise* (launched 21 June 1952) and *La Lorientoise* (launched in 1953) on 10 Oct 1954. All similar to the "Bay" class in the Royal Canadian Navy. *La Bayonnaise* and *La Dunkerquoise* left Brest in Apr 1961 for the Pacific to relieve *Lotus* and *Tiare* in New Caledonia and Tahiti, respectively. *La Dieppoise* is at Djibouti. *La Malouine* is at Diego Saurez, and *La Lorientaise* and *La Paimpolaise* are in New Caledonia and Tahiti, respectively. As these ships are used on "colonial" service they have been air conditioned.

LA DUNKERQUOISE *1968, French Navy, Official*

PATROL VESSELS (*Escorteurs Cotiers*)

14 "LE FOUGUEUX" CLASS

L'ADROIT (6 Sep 1958)
L'AGILE (26 June 1954)
L'ALERTE (5 Oct 1957)
L'ATTENTIF (10 July 1958)
L'ARDENT (17 July 1958)
L'EFFRONTÉ (27 Jan 1959)
L'ENJOUE (5 Oct 1957)
L'ETOURDI (5 Feb 1958)
LE FOUGUEUX (31 May 1954)
LE FRINGANT (6 Feb 1958)
LE FRONDEUR (26 Feb 1959)
LE HARDI (17 Sep 1958)
L'INTRÉPIDE (12 Dec 1958)
L'OPINIATRE (4 May 1954)

Displacement, tons	325 standard; 400 full load
Dimensions, feet	170 pp × 23 × 6·5
Guns	2—40 mm Bofors AA; 2—20 mm AA
A/S weapons	1 hedgehog; 4 DC mortars (and 2 DC racks); Sonar in *L'Agile, Le Fougueux, L'Opiniatre*; others have a new 120 mm ASM mortar forward; 2 DCT; 1 DC rack
Tubes	*L'Intrépide* has a tube mounted on the stern
Main engines	4 SEMT-Pielstick light and fast diesel engines coupled 2 by 2; 3 240 bhp = 18·7 knots (22 knots on trial)
Radius, miles	3 000 at 12 knots; 2 000 at 15 knots
Complement	62 (4 officers, 58 men)

L'Agile, Le Fougueux and *L'Opiniatre* were built in France under a USA offshore order. Five more were built under the 1955 and six under the 1956 estimates. These have a different armament, slightly different appearance, and modified bridge. *L'Agile* is employed on fishery protection duties in the North Sea, English Channel, Bristol Channel, off Shetland and Orkney Islands and Norway.

PHOTOGRAPHS. A photograph of *L'Opiniatre* appears in the 1958-59 and 1959-60 editions, and of *L'Adroit* in the 1960-61 to 1966-67 editions.

LE FOUGUEUX *1967, French Navy, Official*

LA COMBATTANTE

Displacement, tons	182 standard; 201 full load
Dimensions, feet	147·8 × 24·2 × 6·5
Guns	1—40 mm AA
Guided weapons	1 rocket launcher for SS 11
Main engines	2 SEMT-Pielstick diesels; 2 shafts; variable pitch propellers 3 200 bhp = 23 knots
Radius, miles	2 000 at 12 knots
Complement	25

Patrouilleur garde-côte or light patrol vessel. Authorised under the 1960 Programme. Built by Construction Mécaniques de Normandie. Laid down in Apr 1962, launched on 20 June 1963, and completed on 1 Mar 1964. Of wooden and plastic laminated non-magnetic construction.

LA COMBATTANTE *1968, French Navy, Official*

PATROL LAUNCH (*Chasseurs de Sousmarins*)

1 Ex-US SC TYPE

M 691 (ex-*CH* 101, ex-*SC* 524)

Displacement, tons	110 standard; 138 full load
Dimensions, feet	107·5 wl; 110·6 oa × 18·8 × 6·5
Main engines	2 GM diesels; 2 shafts; 1 000 bhp = 15 knots

Of wooden construction. Launched in 1943. Acquired from the USN in 1944. Formerly rated as Submarine Chasers, but re-rated as patrol vessels in 1951. *P* 690, 691, 695, 696, 697, 711, 713, 714, 715 were converted into inshore minesweepers in 1954, but were discarded as such in 1958-59. P 706 was officially deleted from the list in 1969. For full list of disposals see 1967-68 and earlier editions.

TRANSFERS
P 699 was transferred to the Ivory Coast Republic and re-named *Patience* and P 700 was transferred to the Senegalian Republic and re-named *Senegal*.

1 FAIRMILE ML TYPE

OISEAU DES ILES P 780

This former Fairmile motor launch was seized by the Customs Authority and allocated to the Navy for training frogmen.

MAINTENANCE SHIPS

5 LOGISTIC SUPPORT TYPE

GARONNE Repair Workshop (*Bâtiment de soutien logistique, version Atelier*)
LOIRE Minesweeper Support (*Bâtiment de soutien logistique, version Dragueurs*)
RANCE Damage Control (*Bâtiment de soutien logistique, version Sécurité*)
RHIN Electronic Service (*Bâtiment de soutien logistique, version Électronique*)
RHONE Submarine Depot (*Bâtiment de soutien logistique, version Sousmarins*)

Displacement, tons	2 075 standard; 2 375 full load; see notes
Dimensions, feet	300 × 43 × 12 (*Garonne* 333 × 45·2 × 12·7)
Guns	3—40 mm AA
Aircraft	2 Alouette helicopters
Landing craft	2 (LCP)
Main engines	2 SEMT-Pielstick diesels; 1 shaft; 3 300 bhp = 16 knots
Radius, miles	6 000 at 12 knots
Complement	71 (5 officers, 66 men) plus *circa* 100 technicians, except *Garonne* 221 (10 officers, 211 men)

All these maintenance and logistic support ships have the same basic characteristics, hull and machinery, differing only in their respective specialisation, except *Garonne* which has one more deck, larger workshops and a heavier displacement of 2 320 tons standard, as a repair ship for the Pacific Nuclear Experimental Station (CEP), and *Rance*, radiological security ship (radioactive decontamination) with extended bridge and different silhouette and hangar for three helicopters. All were built by Lorient Dockyard. A photograph of *Rhin* appears in the 1963-64 to 1965-66 editions and of *Garonne* in the 1966-67 and 1967-68 editions.

Name	*No.*	*Programme*	*Laid down*	*Launched*	*Completed*
Garonne	A 617	1963	Nov 1963	8 Aug 1964	1 Sep 1965
Loire	A 615	1962	July 1965	1 Oct 1966	1967
Rance	A 618	1963	Aug 1964	15 May 1965	5 Feb 1966
Rhin	A 621	1959	May 1961	17 Mar 1962	1 Mar 1964
Rhone	A 622	1960	Feb 1962	8 Dec 1962	1 Dec 1964

LA LOIRE *1968, French Navy, Official*

RHIN *1969, French Navy, Official*

RANCE *1969, French Navy, Official*

RHIN *1969, French Navy, Official*

5 CONVERTED LINERS

MAINE (ex-*El Mansour*) A 611

Displacement, tons	5 420
Measurement, tons	5 818 gross; 1 320 deadweight
Dimensions, feet	399·2 × 53·8 × 18
Main engines	2 Parsons turbines; 2 shafts; 7 500 shp = 15 knots
Boilers	2 (2 landed)
Complement	115 (9 officers, 106 men)

MEDOC (ex-*Sidi Ferruch*) A 612

Displacement, tons	4 430
Measurement, tons	3 988 gross
Dimensions, feet	372·2 × 49·2 × 23
Main engines	2 Rateau turbines; 2 shafts; 4 750 shp = 15 knots
Boilers	2
Complement	123 (8 officers, 115 men)

MEDOC *1969, French Navy, Official*

MORVAN (ex-*Sidi Mabrouk*) A 613

Displacement, tons	4 090
Measurement, tons	3 760 gross
Dimensions, feet	371·8 × 51 × 23·8
Main engines	2 Parsons turbines; 2 shafts; 4 600 shp = 15 knots
Boilers	2
Complement	120 (8 officers, 112 men)

These three passenger vessels designed and built for Algeria by F. C. Medit. (22 Oct 32) *Maine*, Bretagne/Loire (14 May 1949) *Medoc*, J. S. White (22 Apr 1948) were purchased in Sep 1963 and fitted out as barrack and accommodation ships for the maintenance of the Nuclear Establishment of Polynesia, the experimental base in the Pacific where they are manned by naval Personnel. A photograph of *Maine* appears in the 1965-66 edition.

MORVAN *1969, French Navy, Official*

MAURIENNE (ex-M/S *Brazza*) A 637 **MOSELLE** (ex-*Foucauld*) A 608

Displacement, tons	8 700 standard; 9 100 full load
Measurement, tons	9 065 gross; 5 946 deadweight
Dimensions, feet	480 oa × 62 × 22·3
Main engines	2 Doxford diesels; 2 shafts; 8 800 bhp = 17·5 knots

Former motor passenger ships of the *Chargeurs Réunis* (West Africa Coast Service). Built by Swan, Hunter & Wigham Richardson Ltd, Wallsend-on-Tyne. Launched on 14 Oct and 17 July 1947. Completed in 1948. *Maurienne* was purchased in Nov 1964, converted at Brest in 1965 and admitted to active service on 8 Mar 1966 (left Brest the following day for the Pacific Nuclear Experimental Centre), helicopter landing platform aft. *Moselle* was converted in 1967 (no platform).

MAURIENNE *9 Mar 1966, courtesy Admiral M. Adam*

SURVEY SHIPS (*Annexes Hydrographiques*)

1 NEW CONSTRUCTION

OCEANOGRAPHER D'ENTRECASTEAUX A 757

Displacement, tons	2 200
Dimensions, feet	295·2 × 42·7 × 12·8
Main engines	2 diesel-electric; 1 000 Kw; 2 variable pitch propellers; Speed = 15 knots
Auxiliary engines	2 Schottel orientable and removal
Complement	125 (8 officers, 79 men + 38 scientists)

This ship was specially designed for oceanographic surveys. She will be completed in 1971.

BOUSSOLE 1969, *Official*

2 TROPICAL TYPE

ASTROLABE A 780 (ex-P 681) **BOUSSOLE** A 781 (ex-P 680)

Displacement, tons	350 standard
Dimensions, feet	137·8 × 27 × 8·2
Guns	1—40 mm AA; 2 MG
Main engines	2 Baudouin DV.8 diesels, 1 shaft; variable pitch propeller; 800 bhp = 13 knots max
Radius, miles	4 000
Complement	34 (3 officers, 31 men)

Authorised under the 1961 Programme. Specially designed for the Hydrographic Service for surveys in tropical waters. Built by Chantiers de la Seine Maritime, Le Trait. Laid down in 1962, launched on 27 May and 11 Apr 1963 respectively, and commissioned in 1964.

ASTROLABE 1966, *French Navy, Official*

AIRCRAFT TENDER TYPE. *Paul Goffeny* was officially deleted from the list in 1969, but her sister ship *Commandant Robert Giraud* was reinstated in her place as a survey ship, see earlier page.

1 RESEARCH TYPE

LA RECHERCHE (ex-*Guyane*) A 758 (ex-P 660)

Displacement, tons	780 standard; 1 047 full load
Measurement, tons	965 gross
Dimensions, feet	203·5 pp; 221·5 oa × 34·2 × 13
Main engines	1 Werkspoor diesel; 1 535 bhp = 13·5 knots
Complement	72 (5 officers and 67 men)

Former passenger motor vessel built by Chantiers Zeigler at Dunkirk. Launched on 17 Sep 1951. Purchased in 1960 and converted by Cherbourg Dockyard into a surveying ship. Commissioned into the French Navy in Mar 1961 and her name changed from *Guyane* to *La Recherche*. To improve stability she was fitted with bulges.

LA RECHERCHE 1964, *French Navy, Official*

2 CONVERTED TRAWLER TYPE

L'ESPERANCE (ex-*Jacques Coeur*) A 756 (ex-*Jacques Cartier*)

Displacement, tons	800
Main engines	MAN diesels. Speed = 15 knots

Former trawlers purchased in 1968-69 and adapted as survey ships.

1 EXPERIMENTAL TYPE

LA COQUILLE (ex-*Atlantic Dolphin*) A 678

Displacement, tons	349
Dimensions, feet	121·3 × 26·2
Main engines	Paxman diesel-electric; 1 shaft; speed 12 knots

Former British trawler. Built by J. S. Doig, Grimsby, in 1963. Purchased in May 1965 and converted by Cherbourg Dockyard as a survey and scientific research ship for the Pacific Nuclear Experimental Centre.

OCTANT 1969, *Official*

2 TENDER TYPE

ALIDADE (ex-*Evelyne Marie*) P 682 **OCTANT** (ex-*Michel Marie*) P 683

Displacement, tons	120 approx
Dimensions, feet	Length 78
Main engines	2 diesels; 1 shaft; variable pitch; 1 250 bhp = 9 knots
Complement	11 men

Two small fishing trawlers purchased by the Navy and converted into surveying vessels of a new type by the Constructions Mécaniques de Normandie at Cherbourg to act as tenders to *La Recherche* (see above). Wooden hull and steel upperworks. *Alidade* was set afloat after conversion on 15 Nov 1962 and *Octant* on 20 Dec 1962. Commissioned in 1963.

ALIDADE 1969, *Official*

LARGER SURVEY SHIPS. The former frigates *Beautemps-Beaupré*, A 752 (ex-F 751), and *La Pérouse*, A 753 (ex-F 750), latterly used as survey ships, were officially deleted from the list in 1969.
The old survey ship of the frigate type, *Amiral Mouchez*, F 752, was discarded in 1965.

AMMUNITION SHIP

1 NEW CONSTRUCTION

ACHERON A 620

Displacement, tons	6 485 standard; 10 250 full load
Dimensions, feet	482·2 × 70·5 × 21·3
Main engines	2 SEMT-Pielstick diesels; 1 shaft; 11 500 bhp = 18 knots

Provided for under the 1961 Programme. Under construction at Brest Dockyard. To be launched in 1970 and completed in 1972.

TORPEDO RECOVERY CRAFT

PELICAN (ex-*Kerfany*) **PETREL** (ex-*Cap Lopez*)

Measurement, tons	395 (*Pelican*); 263 (*Petrel*)

Purchased and converted from tuna clippers into torpedo recovery craft.

SEAWARD PATROL CRAFT

4 VC Type (*Vedettes de Surveillance Côtière*)

VC 1 P 751 **VC 2** P 752 **VC 3** P 753 **VC 10** P 760

Displacement, tons	75 standard; 82 full load
Dimensions, feet	104·2 × 15·5 × 5·5
Guns	2—20 mm AA
Main engines	2 Mercedes-Benz diesels; 2 shafts; 2 700 bhp = 28 knots
Radius, miles	1 500 at 15 knots
Complement	15

Seaward defence motor launches of new type. All completed in 1958 and 1959. Built by the Construction Mécaniques de Normandie, Cherbourg (VC 3 and 10), and Lürrsens in Germany (VC 1 and 2). A photograph of VC 3 appears in the 1967-68 and 1968-69 editions.

TRANSFERS
VC 11 (P 761) was transferred to the Tunisian Navy on 22 Sep 1959; VC 12 (P 762) to the Royal Moroccan Navy on 15 Nov 1960 and renamed *Es Sabiq*; VC 4 (P 754) to the Republic of the Congo on 16 Nov 1962; VC 5 (P 755) to Senegal on 19 Jan 1963; VC 9 (P 759) to Cote d'Ivoire (Ivory Coast) in 1963; VC 8 (P 758) to Madagascar in 1963 and renamed *Mailaka*; VC 6 (P 756) to Cameroon on 7 Mar 1964, VC 7 (P 757) to Mauritania in 1966.

VC 2 1968

INSHORE MINESWEEPERS

(*Dragueurs de Rade et d'Estuaire*)

ARMOISE (ex-*Wexham*)	M 772	**JASMIN** (ex-*Stedham*)	M 766
AUBEPINE (ex-*Rendlesham*)	M 781	**JONQUILLE** (ex-*Sulham*)	M 787
CAPUCINE (ex-*Petersham*)	M 782	**MYOSOTIS** (ex-*Ripplingham*)	M 788
DAHLIA (ex-*Whippingham*)	M 786	**OEILLET** (ex-*Isham*)	M 774
GERANIUM (ex-*Tibenham*)	M 784	**PAQUERETTE** (ex-*Kingham*)	M 775
HIBISCUS (ex-*Sparham*)	M 785	**PETUNIA** (ex-*Pineham*)	M 789
HORTENSIA (ex-*Mileham*)	M 783	**TULIPE** (ex-*Frettenham*)	M 771
		VIOLETTE (ex-*Mersham*)	M 773

Displacement, tons	120 standard; 140 full load
Dimensions, feet	100 pp; 106·5 oa × 21·2 × 5·5
Guns	1—40 mm Bofors AA or 1—20 mm Oerlikon AA forward
Main engines	2 Paxman diesels; 550 bhp = 14 knots (9 knots when sweeping)
Oil fuel (tons)	15
Complement	12 (2 officers, 10 men)

Former British inshore minesweepers of the "Ham" class transferred to France under the American "off-shore" procurement program. First, M 771, was delivered in Dec 1954. Last, M 789 was handed over at Hythe on 10 Nov 1955.

ARMOISE *1969, courtesy Dr. Giorgio Arra*

VIOLETTE *M. Henri Le Masson*

TRANSPORTS

ANJOU (ex-*Leoville*) A 645 **BERRY** (ex-M/*S Médoc*) A 644

Displacement, tons	2 700
Measurement, tons	1 203 gross; 1 552 deadweight
Dimensions, feet	284·5 oa × 38 × 15
Main engines	2 MWM diesels coupled on one shaft; 2 400 bhp = 15 knots

Built by Roland Werft, Bremen, Launched on 10 Sep and 10 May 1958, respectively. Purchased in Jan 1966 and Oct 1964 from Cie. Worms for the Pacific experimental station, renamed in 1966 and 1964 and refitted in 1966 and 1965. Classed as refrigerated transports. For CEP (Centre Experimental Pacific).

BERRY *1969, French Navy, Official*

AUNIS (ex-*Regina Pacis*) A 643

Displacement, tons	2 700 full load
Measurement, tons	1 250 gross
Dimensions, feet	284·5 × 31 × 15
Main engines	2 4-str 8-cyl oil geared to 1 shaft; 2 000 bhp = 16·6 knots

Built by Roland Werft, Bremen. Launched on 3 July 1956. Purchased in Nov 1966 from Seatto, Ambrosino & Pugliese for Pacific Experimental Station.

LUTIN (ex-*George Clemenceau*)

Displacement, tons	68
Main engines	400 hp = 10 knots

Purchased in 1965. Ex-vedette. Detection school, Toulon.

VERDON (ex-*Josta*) A 634

Displacement, tons	6 500
Measurement, tons	3 100 gross; 4 275 deadweight
Dimensions, feet	344·8 × 48·8 × 20
Main engines	1 B & W 5-cyl diesel; 1 shaft

Former Norwegian motor ship. Built in 1952. Purchased in June 1964 by the Army white and light products carrier service but manned and commissioned by the Navy for CEP.

TARN (ex-*Orgeval*, ex-*Colomb Bechar*, ex-*Maria Laetitia*) A 771

Displacement, tons	2 660
Measurement, tons	2 392 gross; 3 748 deadweight
Dimensions, feet	330·8 × 47·5 × 19
Main engines	Reciprocating engine with exhaust turbine; 1 shaft; 1 900 shp = 12 knots
Boilers	2

Built by Ateliers et Chantiers de Bretagne at Nantes. Launched on 23 June 1951. Completed in 1952. Purchased in Apr 1965 from Beringuier Ltd. Converted in 1965-66 into a general purpose cargo ship, ammunition carrier, transport and store-ship and fitted out as a logistic support ship for the Pacific Centre (bâtiment magasin du CEP).

ARIEL Y 604 **KORRIGAN** Y 661

Displacement, tons	225 full load
Dimensions, feet	132·8 × 24·5 × 10·8
Main engines	MGO diesels; 2 shafts; 1 640 bhp = 16 knots

SSBN TENDER. A 1 200-ton service lighter of 1 000 hp for nuclear fuel elements of SSBNs was launched on 26 Oct 1967 for delivery in May 1968.

SYLPHE Y 710

Displacement, tons	171 standard; 189 full load
Dimensions, feet	126·5 × 22·7 × 8·2
Main engines	MGO diesel; 1 shaft; 600 bhp = 12 knots

Small transports for personnel, built by Chantiers Franco-Belge in 1959-60 (*Sylphe*) and 1963-64 (*Ariel* and *Korrigan*).

FALLERON (ex-German *Welle*) A 614

Displacement, tons	150; 247 full load
Main engines	Diesels; speed = 7 knots

Herault was removed from the effective list in 1955. *Alphée* became a station ship in 1958. *Cap Ferrat* was stricken in 1960. *Ter* (ex-German *Heinrich*) was condemned in 1964 *Moléne* (ex-German B 262, ex-*V* 620, ex-*Köln*) was officially deleted from the list in Aug 1963, and *Gapeau* (ex-German B 264, ex-V 625, ex-*Johan Schultz*) in 1969.

MELUSINE **MERLIN**

Small transports for personnel built in 1966 by Chantiers Navals Franco-Belges at Chalon sur Saône. Their home port is Toulon.

TRÉBÉRON (ex-*B* 254) Y 712

Displacement, tons	120
Dimensions, feet	82 × 20 × 9
Main engines	Diesel; 120 bhp = 8·5 knots

Former German danlayer used as small personnel transport for local service. Rated as Patrol Craft. Sister ship *Rachgoun* was scrapped in 1957.

SAINTONGE (ex-*Santa Maria*) A 733

Measurement, tons	294 gross; 500 deadweight
Dimensions, feet	177 × 28 × 10·5
Main engines	1 diesel; 1 shaft; 520 bhp = 9 knots

Built by Chantiers Duchesne et Bossière, Le Havre, for a Norwegian owner under the name of *Sven Germa*. Launched on 12 July 1956. Purchased in Apr 1965 from the firm of H. Beal & Co, Fort de France for the Pacific Nuclear Experimental Centre.

GUYENNE (ex-*Douce France*, ex-*Sunfarer*) A 735

Displacement, tons	375 light; 800 full load
Measurement, tons	300 gross; 580 deadweight
Dimensions, feet	177 × 27·5 × 11
Main engines	1 diesel; 1 shaft; 580 bhp = 10·5 knots

Built in 1954-55 by D. W. Kremer und Sohn, Elmshorn. Purchased in May 1965 from Cie Marseille Fret for the Pacific Experimental Station facilities.

EXPERIMENTAL SHIP

(*Bâtiment-Réceptacle d'Engines d'Experimention*)

HENRI POINCARE (ex-*Maina Marasso*) A 603

Displacement, tons	20 000 full load
Measurement, tons	12 885 gross
Dimensions, feet	565 × 74 × 31
Main engines	1 double reduction turbine; 1 shaft; speed = 15 knots
Boilers	2 high pressure water tube

Built by Cantieri Riuniti de Adriatico, Monfalcone. Launched in Oct 1960. Former Italian tanker. Purchased in Sep 1964. Arrived in Brest dockyard on 1 Oct 1964 to undergo conversion into a radar picket ship and guidance vessel for the experimental guided missile station in the Landes (SW France). The conversion was completed in March 1968. Named after the mathematician and scientist.

HENRI POINCARE *1969, French Navy, Official*

DIVING TENDERS

(*Bâtiment de Récherches Sous Marines*)

INGENIEUR ÉLIE MONNIER (ex-German trawler *Albatros*) A 647

Displacement, tons	280 standard; 350 full load
Dimensions, feet	111·5 × 24 × 10
Main engines	Diesel; 1 shaft; Speed 12 knots
Range, miles	1 500
Complement	19

Former German trawler. Built by D. W. Kremer Schiffwert Elmshom in 1944. Fitted for ocean research. Photograph in the 1957-58 to 1961-62 editions.

BELOUGA (ex-*Cote d'Argent*)

Tuna clipper purchased in 1966 for conversion into a diving tender.

TRITON A 646

Displacement, tons	1 300
Dimensions, feet	223·1 × 39·4 × 11·8
Main engines	Diesels 2 Voith Schneider = 13 knots
Radius, miles	4 000
Complement	50 (4 officers, 29 men + 17 scientists)

Under construction. Under sea recovery and trials ship to replace *Élie Monnier*. To be equipped with a helicopter.

PORT DEPOT SHIPS

Former warships, now obsolete, are class·d as port depot ships:—
There are the heavy cruiser *Ocean* (ex-*Suffren*) and the light cruiser *Montcalm* at Toulon, all used as barracks; Also the flotilla leaders (ex-light cruisers) *Chateaurenault* and *Guichen*, and a number of other ships including *Voltigeur*.

PATROL BOATS (*Ex-Flotilla du Rhin*)

P 9785 **P 9786**

Displacement, tons	45
Dimensions, feet	79·3 × 14·8 × 4·2
Guns	8—0·5 MG (four twin mountings)
Main engines	2 Daimler-Benz diesels; 2 shafts; 1 000 bhp = 18 knots

Built by Burmeister-Brême (P 9785) and Bodenwerft-Kressbronn. Completed in 1954. Sister boats P 9783, P 9784, P 9787 and P 9788 were officially deleted from the list in 1969.

DISPOSALS
The auxiliary patrol launch *Rambervillers* was deleted from the list in 1963. She was a war prize with the *Ormont* which was retired from service in Feb 1958. The former Rhine Flotilla support ships *Hoche*, L 981, *Kleber*, L 982, and *Marceau*, L 980, were officially deleted from the list in 1965. The former Rhine Flotilla patrol boats P 9781 and P 9782 (35 tons, duralumin hull), P 9796 (ex-41), P 9787 (ex-42) and P 9798 (ex-43), all 23 tons, P 9740, P 9741, P 9742 and P 9743 (12 tons, peralumin hull), P 9794 (10 tons, hydrofoil), and P 9790 and P9791 (2 tons, fixed foils) were also officially deleted from the list in 1965, and P 9792 and P 9793 (6 tons, fixed foils) in 1966. The patrol boats *Enclume* A 790, old German LCM, and *Amiral Exelmans* (ex-*Germania*), A 73, ex-river passenger boat used for training pilots, were officially deleted from the list in 1969.

TRANSFERS
Nine control patrol launches of 10·2 tons, Y 6642-Y 5550, one river tug, and 9 landing craft (LCM) were transferred to the Bundeswehr in 1957-58. Repair ship *Les Volges* (ex-*Washington*, ex-*Brunehilde*), was transferred to the Bundeswehr in Dec 1957).

TRAINING SHIPS (*Voiliers-École*)

LA BELLE-POULE A 650 **L'ÉTOILE** A 649

Displacement, tons	227
Dimensions, feet	128 oa × 23·7 × 11·8
Main engines	Sulzer diesel; 120 bhp = 6 knots

Auxiliary sail vessels. Built by Chantiers de Normandie (Fécamp) in 1932. Accommodation for 3 officers, 30 cadets, 5 petty officers, 12 men. Attached to Navy School.

LA GRANDE HERMINE (ex-*Menestral*) A 753

Ex-fishing boat, built in 1936. Purchased in 1963 in replacement for *Dolphin* (ex-*Simone Marcelle*) as the School of Manoeuvre Training ship.

MUTIN A 652

A small coastal tender attached to *l'École de pilotage* (the School of Pilotage).

WATER CARRIERS

HANAP (ex-*Stjordels Fjord*) A 740 **LIAMONE** (ex-*Arrosoir*) A750

Displacement, tons	450 light; 1 369 full load
Dimensions, feet	184 × 28·9 × 13·8
Main engines	Sulzer diesels; 1 000 bhp = 11·5 knots

Rated as regional supply ships. Crew 27. *Arrosoir* was renamed *Liamone* in Mar 1954. Photograph of *Liamone* in 1957-58 edition. Sister ship *Giboulée* was officially deleted from the list in 1969.

RUMMEL A 635 **SAHEL** A 638

Displacement, tons	630 light; 1 450 full load
Measurement, tons	650 deadweight
Dimensions, feet	176·2 × 29·5 × 14·5
Guns	2—20 mm AA
Main engines	2 diesels; 700 bhp = 12 knots

Sahel was completed in Aug 1951, *Rummel* in 1952 by Chantiers Naval de Caen. Photograph of *Sahel* in 1957-58 and earlier editions.

OASIS

Displacement, tons	335 standard; 683 full load
Displacement, feet	164·8 × 27 × 9
Guns	2—20 mm AA
Main engines	Triple expansion; 1 shaft; 800 ihp = 10 knots

Built by A. C. Bretagne. No. A 751. Sister *Torrent* was scrapped in 1964.

AVERSE **CATARACTE** **DELUGE** **FONTAINE** **FORMENE** **MIRAGE** **ONDEE**

Small water carriers of various displacements (*Cataracte* 330 tons), *Formene* carries fuel. *Cascade*, *Durance* and *Fraiche* were scrapped in 1957, *Aube* in 1958, *Ardèche* in 1960, *Casamance* and *Zöghouan* in 1963, *Aiguade* in 1964, *Benzene* in 1967, *Bruine* in 1969.

CHÉLIFF (ex-US *LST* 874) **ODET** (ex-US *LST* 815)

Displacement, tons	1 625 standard; 4 030 full load
Dimensions, feet	316 wl; 328 oa × 50 × 14 max
Main engines	GM diesels; 2 shafts; 1 700 bhp = 11 knots

Former US tank landing ship, converted and used as transport. Scheduled to be withdrawn from active service in 1961, but restored to the Navy List in 1963 with *Odet* (ex-US *LST* 815) which was officially deleted in 1969.

CHÉLIFF *1969, E. Laidlaw*

Landing Ships —*continued*

ARGENS BDC 2 **BIDASSOA** BDC 5 **DIVES** BDC 4
BLAVET BDC 3 **TRIEUX** BDC 1

Displacement, tons	1 400 standard; 1 765 normal; 4 000 full load
Dimensions, feet	328 oa × 50 × 14
Guns	2—40 mm AA; 2—40 mm AA (*Bidassoa, Blavet, Dives,* 1—4·7 in mortar); 3—40 mm AA
Main engines	SEMT-Pielstick diesels; 2 shafts; 2 000 bhp = 11 knots
Radius, miles	18 500 at 10 knots
Complement	85 (6 officers and 79 men). Plus 170 troops (normal)

Built by Chantiers Seine Maritime (*Bidassoa, Dives*) and Chantiers de Bretagne, Nantes (others). Launched on 7 Apr 1959, 30 Dec 1960, 15 Jan 1960, 29 June 1960 and 6 Dec 1958, respectively. All commissioned in 1960-61. Can carry: 4 LCVP's, 1 800 tons of freight, 335 (up to 870 if required) troops (329 in bunks, 552 in hammocks). *Blavet* and *Trieux* are fitted with a helicopter platform. A photograph of *Trieux* appears in the 1960-61 to 1966-67 editions.

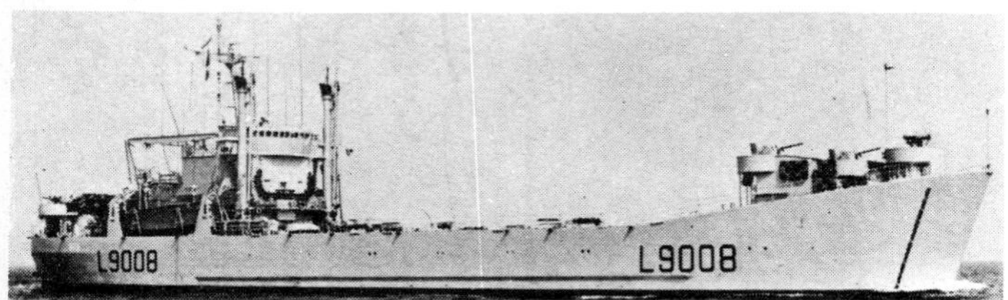

DIVES *1967, French Navy, Official*

LANDING SHIP DOCK. The dock landing ship FOUDRE (ex-Greek *Okeanos*, ex-British *Oceanway*, ex US *LSD* 12), A 646, was officially deleted from the list in 1969.

LANDING CRAFT

9 EDIC (*ENGINS DE DEBARQUEMENT INFANTERIE (CHARS)*)

EDIC 1 (7 Jan 1958) **EDIC 4** (24 July 1958) **EDIC 7** (30 Oct 1967)
EDIC 2 (21 Feb 1958) **EDIC 5** (11 Apr 1958) **EDIC 8** (30 Jan 1968)
EDIC 3 (17 Apr 1958) **EDIC 6** (11 Oct 1958) **EDIC 9**

Displacement, tons	292 standard; 642 full load
Dimensions, feet	193·5 × 39·2 × 4·5
Guns	2—20 mm AA
Main engines	MGO diesels; 2 shafts; 1 000 bhp = 8 knots
Complement	16 (1 officer, and 15 men)

EDIC 1, 4, 7 were built by C. N. Franco Belges, 5, 6 by Toulon Dockyard, 8 by La Perrière. Launch dates above. Nos. L9091-96, L9070-71. EDIC 9 was ordered in Dec 1967.

EDIC 1 *1967, French Navy, Official*

4 EDA (*Engins de Debarquement Ateliers*)

Same hull and engine characteristics as the EDIC type, but equipped as repair ships. Built in 1964 and 1965. No names allocated.

ISSOLE L 9097

Displacement, tons	600 full load
Dimensions, feet	160·8 × 23 × 7·2
Main engines	2 diesels; 1 000 bhp = 12 knots

Built at Toulon in 1957-58. Coaster with bow doors and ramp.

ISSOLE *1969, courtesy Godfrey H. Walker, Esq.*

LCT 9099

Former British tank landing craft. *LCT* 9098 was purchased in 1963. *LCT* 9099 was fitted as a workshop on 1964. *LCT* 9062, *LCT* 9063 (ex-*Alkyon*) and *LCT* 9064 (ex-*Salvor*) were officially deleted from the list in 1969.

LCT 9061 (ex-HMS *Buttress*, LCT(8) 4099)

Former British tank landing craft purchased in July 1965, see LCT(8)s, UK section.

L 9081 and **L 9082** are *bâtiments-annexe atelier* (B.A.A.)
L 9083 is *bâtiment-annexe-électronique* (B.A.E.)
L 9084 is *bâtiment-annexe-magasin électrique* (B.A.M.E.)

BOOM DEFENCE VESSELS

LA FIDÉLE **LA PERSÉVÉRANTE** **LA PRUDENTE**

Dimensions, feet	148 × 32·9 × 9·2
Main engines	Badouin diesels; 2 shafts, 720 bhp

Net layers and tenders being built by A. C. La Manche, Dieppe, La Rochelle, L. Pallice.

5 "GRILLON" CLASS

CIGALE (ex-*AN* 98) **FOURMI** (ex-*AN* 97) **SCARABÉE** (ex-*AN* 94)
CRIQUET (ex-*AN* 96) **GRILLON** (ex-*AN* 95)

Displacement, tons	560 standard; 770 full load
Dimensions, feet	149·3 × 33·5 × 10·5
Guns	1—40 mm Bofors; 4—20 mm AA
Main engines	2, 4-stroke diesels, electric drive; 1 600 bhp = 12 knots

US AN type "Off-shore" orders. Sister ship *G* 6 was allocated to Spain. *Criquet* was launched on 3 June 1954, *Cigale* on 23 Sep 1954, *Fourmi* on 6 July 1954, *Grillon* on 18 Feb 1954 and *Scarabée* on 21 Nov 1953. Rated as Garbarres (Mouilleur de Filets). A photograph of *Criquet* appears in the 1957-58 to 1964-65 editions, and of *Cigale* in the 1965-66 to 1967-68 editions.

SCARABÉE *1968, French Navy, Official*

5 Ex-US AN TYPE NETLAYERS

ARAIGNÉE (ex-*Hackberry*, ex-*Maple*, *AN* 727)
LOCUSTE (ex-*Locust*, *AN* 765)
LUCIOLE (ex-*Sandalwood*, *AN* 32)
SCORPION (ex-*Yew*, *AN* 37)
TARENTULE (ex-*Pepperwood*, ex-*Walnut*, *AN* 729)

Displacement, tons	560 standard; 850 full load
Dimensions, feet	146 wl; 163 oa × 30·5 × 11·7
Guns	1—3 in AA; some MG
Main engines	2 GM diesels; 2 shafts; 4 400 bhp = 16 knots
Radius, miles	2 000 at 13 knots

Launched on 6 Mar 1941, 1 Feb 1941, 6 Mar 1941, 25 Sep 1941 and 25 Aug 1941, respectively. *Locuste* was purchased in 1966 and *Luciole* in 1967. The three others were transferred in 1944. Photographs of *Araignee* appear in the 1954-55 to 1967-68 editions.

MARCEL LE BIHAN (ex-German *Giref*) A 759

Displacement, tons	800 standard; 1 000 full load
Dimensions, feet	236·2 × 34·8 × 10·5 max
Guns	4—20 mm AA
Main engines	2 GM diesels; 2 shafts, 4 400 bhp = 16 knots
Radius, miles	2 000 at 13 knots

Former German aircraft tender. Built by Lubecker Fleudewerke. Launched in 1936. Completed in 1937. Transferred by USA in Feb 1948. Re-rated Escorteur de Deuxième Classe early 1953, Aviso Escorteur 11 Aug 1953, Aviso 1955 and Gabarre 1 Nov 1959, 4·1 in gun and 2—40 mm removed. Tender for bathysphere *Archimede*.

REINSTATEMENT. *Commandant Robert Giraud* (ex-German *Immelmann*), A 755, former German aircraft tender, escort vessel and boom defence vessel successively was reinstated as a survey ship in 1969 in place of her sister ship *Paul Guffeny*.

MARCEL LE BIHAN *1965, French Navy, Official*

PATIENTE **PERSISTANTE**

Patiente 450 tons. *Persistante* 350 tons. *Girafe* and *Persévérante* were scrapped in 1957, *Fidéle* in 1958, *Puissant* in 1960, *Agissante* in 1961, *Victorieuse* in 1964.

OILERS (*Transports Petroliers*)

LA CHARENTE (ex-*Beaufort*) A 626

Displacement, tons	7 084 light; 26 000 full load
Measurement, tons	12 373 gross; 18 800 deadweight
Dimensions, feet	587·2 × 72 × 30·3
Main engines	1 General Electric geared turbine
Boilers	2

Former Norwegian tanker built by Kaldnes Mek. Verksted Tönsberg, in 1957. Purchased by the French Navy in May 1965 and adapted for the Pacific Experimental Station.

LA CHARENTE *1969, courtesy Admiral M. Adam*

ISERE (ex-*La Mayenne*, ex-*Caltex-Strasbourg*)

Displacement, tons	10 172 light
Measurement, tons	18 000 deadweight
Dimensions, feet	559 × 71·2 × 30·3
Main engines	1 single geared Parsons turbine; 8 260 shp = 16 knots
Boilers	2

Built by Seine Maritime. Launched on 22 June 1959. Former French tanker. Purchased late in 1964 for the Pacific Nuclear Experimental Centre.

LAC CHAMBON (ex-*Anticline*) A 629 **LAC TONLÉ-SAP** (ex-*Pumper*) A 630
LAC TCHAD (ex-*Syncline*) A 631

Displacement, tons	800 light, 2 670 full load
Dimensions, feet	235 × 37 × 15·8
Guns	3—20 mm AA
Main engines	2 Fairbanks-Morse diesels; 1 150 bhp = 11 knots

Ex-US oil barges. Acquired in Dec 1944 and Mar 1945. *Lac Noir* scrapped in 1951, *Lac Pavin* in 1953. Photograph of *Lac Tonle Sap* in 1965-66 to 1967-68 editions.

LAC TCHAD *1968, French Navy, Official*

LA SAÔNE A 628 **LA SEINE** A 627

Displacement, tons	7 350 light; 23 800 full load
Measurement, tons	16 870 deadweight
Dimensions, feet	525 × 72·5 × 33
Main engines	Parsons geared turbines; 2 shafts; 15 800 shp = 17 knots
Boilers	3 Penhoët

Ordered as fleet tankers. After the war completed as merchant tankers. Returned to French Navy from charter company Sep 1953. *La Seine* was fitted as a fleet replenishment ship in 1961, *La Saône* in 1962. Now rated as Petroliers Rivatailleurs d'Escadre. They carry 11 500 tons of fuel, 300 tons of food, and have 75 000 l. tanks of wine. Photograph of *La Seine* in 1962-63 to 1967-68 editions.

LA SAÔNE *1968*

ABER-WRAC'H (ex-*CA* 1) A 619

Displacement, tons	1 380 standard; 3 400 full load
Dimensions, feet	262·5 pp; 284 oa × 40 × 15·8
Guns	1—40 mm AA
Main engines	1 diesel; variable pitch propeller; 2 000 bhp = 12 knots

Built at Cherbourg. Authorised in 1956. Ordered in 1959. Laid down in 1961. The after part with engine room was launched on 24 Apr 1963. The fore part was built on the vacated slip, launched and welded to the after part. Complete hull floated up on 21 Nov 1963. Commissioned in 1964. A photograph appears in the 1967-68 and 1968-69 editions.

FLEET TUGS

ACTIF **HERCULE** **LUTTEUR** **TRAVAILLEUR**
COURAGEUX **LABORIEUX** **ROBUSTE** **VALEUREUX**

Displacement, tons	230
Dimensions, feet	92 × 26 × 13
Main engines	1 MGO diesel; 1 050 bhp = 11 knots
Radius, miles	2 400 nautical
Complement	15

Courageux, Hercule, Robuste and *Valeureux* were completed in 1960 and the other four in 1962-63 at Le Havre, F. Ch. de la Mediterranee for service at Cherbourg (*Lutteur*), Toulon (*Actif* and *Travailleur*) and Brest (*Laborieux*).

HIPPOPOTAME (ex-*Utrecht*)

Measurement, tons	524 gross
Main engines	Diesel-electric; 2 600 shp

Former Netherlands high sea tug. Built in 1943. Purchased by the French Navy in Jan 1964 to be used at the Experimental Base in the Pacific. Admitted to active service on 5 Mar 1964.

BELIER **PACHYDERME**

Displacement, tons	900 standard; 1 185 and 1 115 full load, respectively
Main engines	2 000 ihp = 12 knots
Oil fuel (tons)	180
Radius, miles	3 000

A photograph of *Pachyderme* appears in the 1957-58 edition.

BUFFLE

Displacement, tons	900 standard; 1 180 full load
Dimensions, feet	167·5 × 33 × 10
Main engines	2 sets triple expansion; 2 000 ihp = 12 knots
Complement	32

Launched on 4 May 1939. *Erable* was officially deleted from the list in 1969.

ACHARNÉ

Displacement, tons	500 to 682 full load
Dimensions, feet	114·8 × 27·8 × 10
Main engines	Triple expansion; 1 000 ihp = 10 to 11 knots

Both laid down in 1937-38. *Acharné* by Brest, *Utile* by F. & C. de la Gironde, Bordeaux, *Actif, Applique* and *Capét* were scrapped in 1957-58. *Contentin* was withdrawn from service in 1960. *Champion* was condemned in 1961, *Obstiné* in 1965, *Enténté* and *Tetu* in 1966, *Utile* in 1969.

INFATIGABLE (ex-*Polangen*)

Displacement, tons	540
Main engines	1 200 ihp = 11 knots

Coolie was officially deleted from the list in 1969 and sister tug *Malabar* in 1969.

IMPLACABLE (ex-*Fohn II*)

Displacement, tons	620
Main engines	1 600 ihp = 11 knots

DISPOSALS
Intraitable (ex-*Nordergrunde*) was condemned in Mar 1961, and *Mammouth* in July 1963. *Imbattable* (ex-*Nesserland*) was officially deleted in 1965.

ÉLÉPHANT (ex-*Bar*)

Displacement, tons	850; 1 180 full load
Main engines	1 800 ihp = 12 knots

The tug *Samson* (ex-German *Suder Hever*) was officially condemned Mar 1961.

RHINOCÉROS

Displacement, tons	700
Main engines	Diesels; 1 850 bhp = 12 knots

A photograph of *Rhinocéros* appears in the 1953-54 to 1957-58 editions.

TENACE (ex-*ATA* 226)

Displacement, tons	400
Main engines	Diesels; 1 200 bhp = 10 knots

DISPOSALS. *Locmine* was condemned in 1964, and *Efficace* was officially deleted from the list in 1966.

HARBOUR TUGS. *Acajou, Balsa Bouleau Charme, Chene, Cormier, Equeurdreville, Erable, Frene, Hetre, Hevea, Latanier, Meleze, Merisier Okoume, Olivier Peuplier Pin, Platane, Saule, Sycomore.*

Chataignier, Manguier, Marronnier, Noyer, Paletuvier, Papayer:
Built at Cherbourg in 1967 for service at Brest (*Chataignier, Manguier, Papayer*) Toulon (*Marronnier, Noyer*) and Cherbourg (*Paletuvier*) 700 hp.

Ana, Bengali, Eider, Grand Duc, Macreuse Marabont, Martin Pecheur:
All eight 60·2 × 18·8 × 9 feet, diesel 250 hp = 9 knots. Five based at Lorient, three at St. Malo. *Alouette, Sarcelle, Vanneau* and three more ordered in Oct 1967.

GERMANY

Bundesmarine Administration

Chief of Naval Staff, Federal German Navy:
Vice-Admiral Gert Jeschonnek

Commander-in-Chief of the Fleet:
Vice-Admiral Karl Hetz

Diplomatic Representation

Naval Attaché in London:
Captain Karl Theodor Raeder

Naval Attaché in Washington:
Captain Paul Brasack

Strength of the Fleet

12 Submarines (Diesel Powered)
11 Destroyers (Two Missile)
8 Frigates (Six Fast)
13 Escort and Support Ships
1 Training Ship (Cruiser Type)
6 Corvettes (Chaser Type)
24 Coastal Minesweepers
30 Fast Minesweepers
21 Inshore Minesweepers
40 Torpedo Boats
2 Minelayers (ex-Landing Ships)
26 Landing Craft
42 Supply Ships and Auxiliaries
28 Service Craft

New Construction

Guided missile ships planned include:
4 Frigates of 3 500 tons (full load)
10 fast patrol boats of 300 tons

Personnel

1961: 23 100 (2 100 officers, 21 000 men)
1962: 29 000 (2 636 officers, 26 364 men)
1965: 33 000 (3 000 officers, 30 000 men)
1968: 36 600 (3 300 officers, 33 270 men)
1969: 37 500 (3 750 officers, 33 750 men)

Mercantile Marine

Lloyd's Register of Shipping:
2 732 vessels of 6 527 946 tons gross

Silhouettes

Scale: 150 feet = 1 inch

DEUTSCHLAND

HAMBURG, SCHLESWIG-HOLSTEIN

BAYERN, HESSEN

SCHARNHORST

GNEISENAU

FLETCHER *Class*

KÖLN *Class*

LAHN, LECH

SUBMARINES

6 NEW CONSTRUCTION HUNTER-KILLER TYPE

U 25 **U 26** **U 27** **U 28** **U 29** **U 30**

Displacement, tons 1 000
Torpedo tubes For homing
Main engines Diesels; Electric motors
Complement 60

Construction of six ocean going hunter-killer U-boats displacing up to 1 000 tons was authorised on 9 Oct 1963 for delivery from German shipyards by 1967, but this schedule was not implemented.

12 NEW CONSTRUCTION

U 13 **U 15** **U 17** **U 19** **U 21** **U 23**
U 14 **U 16** **U 18** **U 20** **U 22** **U 24**

Displacement, tons 400 surface

U 13-24 are reported to be of similar design to U 4-9. Construction scheduled to start in 1969.

11 COASTAL TYPE

U 1 (21 Oct 1961) S 180
U 2 (25 Jan 1962) S 181
U 4 (22 Aug 1962) S 183
U 5 (22 Nov 1962) S 184
U 6 (22 Apr 1963) S 185
U 7 (29 May 1963) S 186
U 8 (11 Oct 1963) S 187
U 9 (20 Oct 1966) S 188
U 10 (20 July 1967) S 189
U 11 (9 Feb 1968) S 190
U 12 (10 Sep 1968) S 191

Displacement, tons 370 surface; 450 submerged
Length, feet (*metres*) 142·7 (*43·5*) oa
Beam, feet (*metres*) 15·1 (*4·6*)
Torpedo tubes 8 in bow
Main engines 2 MB diesels; total 1 200 bhp
2 electric motors, total 1 700 bhp
Speed, knots 10 on surface; 17 submerged
Complement 21

All built by Howaldtswerke, Kiel in floating docks. Original launch dates above. "Teardrop" Hull. Fitted with schnorkel. First submarines designed and built by Germany since the end of the Second World War.

DESIGN IMPROVEMENT. U 4-12 were built to a heavier and improved design, U 1 and U 2 were modified accordingly and refloated on 17 Feb 1967 and 15 July 1966, respectively. U 1 was completely reconstructed from late 1963 to 4 Mar 1965. (See original appearance in the 1962-63 and 1963-64 editions). U 4-8 are sheathed with zinc. U-9-12 have hulls of different steel alloys of non-magnetic propensity. U 7 and U 11 were put into service on 22 May 1968 and 21 June 1968, respectively.

PHOTOGRAPHS. A photograph of U 2 appears in the 1962-63 and 1963-64 editions and photographs of U 6 appear in the 1964-65 to 1967-68 editions.

U 9 *1968, Official*

U 8 *1968, Stefan Terzibaschitsch*

DISPOSALS
U 3 of this class lent to Norway on 10 July 1962 and temporarily named *Kobben* (S 310), was returned to Germany in 1964 and decommissioned on 15 Sep 1967 for disposal.

Submarines—*continued*

1 CONVERTED TYPE XXI

WILHELM BAUER (ex-U 2540) Y 880

Displacement, tons	1 620 surface; 1 820 submerged
Length, feet (*metres*)	252·7 (*77·0*) pp
Beam, feet (*metres*)	21·7 (*6·6*)
Draught, feet (*metres*)	20·3 (*6·2*)
Torpedo tubes	4—21 in (*533 mm*) in bow
Main engines	Diesel-electric drive 2 diesels total 4 200 bhp 2 electric motors total 5 000 hp
Speed, knots	15·5 surface; 17·5 submerged

German Second World War Type XXI. Launched in 1944 by Blohm and Voss, Hamburg. Sunk on 3 May 1945. Raised in 1957. Rebuilt in 1958-59 at Howaldtswerke, Kiel, for commissioning on 1 Sep 1960. Used for experimental purposes on electronic equipment machinery and outfit in the *Erpobungsstelle fur Marinewaffen* (Experimental Station for Naval Weapons). Conning tower has been modified.

WILHELM BAUER *1968, Official*

DISPOSAL
The Type XXIII coastal submarine *Hecht* (Pike), S 171, ex-*UW* 21, ex-U 2367, was removed from the effective list on 30 Sep. 1968.

LOSS. Sister ship *Hai* (Shark), S 170, ex-*UW* 20, ex-*U* 2365 was lost off the Dogger Bank on 14 Sep 1966 and although raised has not been rehabilitated.

GUIDED MISSILE ARMED DESTROYERS

Name	*No.*	*Builders*	*Laid down*	*Launched*	*Completion*
LÜTJENS	D 185 (ex-DDG 28)	Bath Iron Works Corp	1 Mar 1966	11 Aug 1967	12 Mar 1969
MÖLDERS	D 186 (ex-DDG 29)	Bath Iron Works Corp	12 Apr 1966	13 Apr 1968	30 Aug 1969
ROMMEL	D 187 (ex-DDG 30)	Bath Iron Works Corp	22 Aug 1967	1 Feb 1969	30 Mar 1970

3 NEW CONSTRUCTION

"CHARLES F. ADAMS" CLASS

Displacement, tons	4 000 normal; 5 000 full load
Length, feet (*metres*)	431 (*131·4*) wl; 440 (*134·1*) oa
Beam, feet (*metres*)	47 (*14·3*)
Draught, feet (*metres*)	15 (*4·6*) mean; 20 (*6·1*) max
Aircraft	Provision for helicopter
Missiles, AA	"Tartar" launcher
Guns, dual purpose	2—5 in (*127 mm*) single mount, rapid fire
A/S	"Asroc" launcher; 2 triple torpedo launchers; 1 DCT
Boilers	4 Combustion Engineering; 1 200 psi (*84·4 kg/cm²*)
Main engines	Geared steam turbines 70 000 shp; 2 shafts
Speed, knots	36
Complement	337

LÜTJENS *1969, Official*

In 1964 it was decided that three "Charles F. Adams" class destroyers would be built in United States Shipyards and another five in West German shipyards.
In 1965 the contract for the first three, assigned the US Navy numbers DDG 28, DDG 29 and DDG 30, was awarded to Bath Iron Works Corp. Cost $43 754 000.

In 1968 the intention to build five sister ships in Germany was rescinded.

DESTROYERS

Name	*No.*	*Builders*	*Laid down*	*Launched*	*Completed*
BAYERN	D 183	H. C. Stülcken Sohn, Hamburg	1962	14 Aug 1962	6 July 1965
HAMBURG	D 181	H. C. Stülcken Sohn, Hamburg	1959	26 Mar 1960	23 Mar 1964
HESSEN	D 184	H. C. Stülcken Sohn, Hamburg	1962	4 May 1963	31 Oct 1968
SCHLESWIG-HOLSTEIN	D 182	H. C. Stülcken Sohn, Hamburg	1959	20 Aug 1960	12 Oct 1964

4 "HAMBURG" CLASS

Displacement, tons	3 340 standard; 4 330 full load
Length, feet (*metres*)	420 (*128*) wl; 439·7 (*134·0*) oa
Beam, feet (*metres*)	44 (*13·4*)
Draught, feet (*metres*)	17 (*5·2*)
Guns, dual purpose	4—3·9 in (*100 mm*)
Guns, AA	8—40 mm, 4 twin mounts
A/S	2 Bofors 4-barrel DC Mortars (rocket launchers)
Torpedo tubes	5—21 in (*533 mm*), 3 bow and 2 stern; 2 tubes for ASW torpedoes
Boilers	4 Wahodag; 910 psi (*64 km/cm²*), 860°F (460°C)
Main engines	2 Wahodag double reduction geared turbines; 68 000 shp; 2 shafts
Speed, knots	35·8 max; 18 economical sea
Radius, miles	920 at full power
Oil fuel, tons	674
Complement	282 (17 officers, 265 men)

All named after countries of the German Federal Republic. Completion was delayed while recent technical developments were incorporated.
PHOTOGRAPHS. A photograph of *Bayern* appears in the 1966-67 to 1968-69 editions, and of *Hamburg* in the 1967-68 and 1968-69 editions.

HESSEN *1969, Official*

SCHLESWIG-HOLSTEIN *1969, Official*

Destroyers—*continued*

Name	No.	Builders	Laid down	Launched	Completed	German commissioned
Z 1 (ex-USS *Anthony, DD* 515)	D 170	Bath Iron Works Corporation, Maine	17 Aug 1942	20 Dec 1942	26 Feb 1943	17 Jan 1958
Z 2 (ex-USS *Ringgold, DD* 500)	D 171	Federal SB & DD Co, Port Newark	25 June 1942	11 Nov 1942	24 Dec 1942	14 July 1959
Z 3 (ex-USS *Wadsworth, DD* 516)	D 172	Bath Iron Works Corporation, Maine	18 Aug 1942	10 Jan 1943	16 Mar 1943	6 Oct 1959
Z 4 (ex-USS *Claxton, DD* 571)	D 178	Consolidated Steel Corporation, Orange	25 June 1941	1 Apr 1942	8 Dec 1942	15 Dec 1959
Z 5 (ex-USS *Dyson, DD* 572)	D 179	Consolidated Steel Corporation, Orange	25 June 1941	15 Apr 1942	30 Dec 1942	23 Feb 1960

5 Ex-US "FLETCHER" CLASS

Displacement, tons	2 100 standard; 2 750 full load
Lenght, feet (*metres*)	368·4 (*112·3*) wl; 376·5 (*114·8*) oa
Beam, feet (*metres*)	39·5 (12)
Draught, feet (*metres*)	18 (*5·5*) max
Guns, dual purpose	4—5 in (*127 mm*) 38 cal.
Guns, AA	6—3 in (*76 mm*) 50 cal., 3 twin mountings
A/S	2 hedgehogs; 1 DC rack
Torpedo tubes	5—21 in (*533 mm*), quintuple bank; 2 ASW tubes *No tubes in* Z6
Boilers	4 Babcock & Wilcox; 569 psi (*40 kg/cm²*); 851°F (*455°C*)
Main engines	2 sets GE geared turbines 60 000 shp; 2 shafts
Speed, knots	34 max; 17 economical sea speed
Radius, miles	6 000 at 15 knots
Oil fuel (tons)	650
Complement	280

Former American "Fletcher" class destroyers. On loan from the United States for five years. *Anthony*, now Z 1 (NATO *Pennant No.* D 170) arrived at Bremerhaven on 14 Apr 1958. *Ringgold* was transferred by the USA at Charleston, S.C., on 14 July 1959.

PHOTOGRAPHS. A starboard broadside surface view at sea of Z 1 appears in the 1958-59 to 1961-62 editions, a similar photograph of Z 5, a dead broadside view showing radar fitted on after funnel, in the 1962-63 edition, a silhouette view of Z 5 in the 1963-64 to 1966-67 editions, a port rear broadside oblique aerial view of Z 6 in the 1967-68 edition, and a starboard bow surface view of Z 4 in the 1967-68 edition.

DISPOSALS
Z6, No. D 180 (ex-USS *Charles Ausburn*, DD 570) was decommissioned on 15 Dec 1967 and is to be scrapped, it was officially confirmed in 1969.

Z 2 *1968*

Z 3 *1968*

FAST FRIGATES

Name	No.	Builders	Launched	Completed
AUGSBURG	F 222	H. C. Stülcken Sohn, Hamburg	15 Aug 1959	7 Apr 1962
BRAUNSCHWEIG	F 225	H. C. Stülcken Sohn, Hamburg	3 Feb 1962	16 June 1964
EMDEN	F 221	H. C. Stülcken Sohn, Hamburg	21 Mar 1959	24 Oct 1961
KARLSRUHE	F 223	H. C. Stülcken Sohn, Hamburg	24 Oct 1959	15 Dec 1962
KÖLN	F 220	H. C. Stülcken Sohn, Hamburg	6 Dec 1958	15 Apr 1961
LUBECK	F 224	H. C. Stülcken Sohn, Hamburg	23 July 1960	6 July 1963

6 "KOLN" CLASS

Displacement, tons	2 100 standard; 2 550 full load
Length, feet (*metres*)	360·9 (*110*)
Beam, feet (*metres*)	36·1 (*11·0*)
Draught, feet (*metres*)	11·2 (*3·4*)
Guns, dual purpose	2—3·9 in (*100 mm*)
Guns, AA	6—40 mm; 2 twin and 2 single
A/S	2 Bofors 4-barrel DC mortars (rocket launchers)
Torpedo tubes	2 for ASW torpedoes
Main engines	Combined diesel and gas turbine plant: 4 MAN 16-cyl. diesels, total 12 000 bhp; 2 Brown-Boveri gas turbines, 26 000 bhp 38 000 shp; 2 shafts
Speed, knots	30 max; 23 economical sea speed;
Radius, miles	920 at full power
Oil fuel, tons	333
Complement	210

A new type of fast anti-submarine frigates or escort destroyers. All built by H. C. Stülcken Sohn, Hamburg. Ordered in Mar 1957. All ships of this class are named after towns of West Germany. Classed as *Geleitboote*.

MODERNISATION: All ships of the "Koln" class are to be refitted, since they did not prove to be strong enough in heavy North Sea weather. The first ship, *Koln* completed refit on 31 May 1967. *Augsburg* was decommissioned on 9 Jan 1967 for refit and modernisation.

ENGINEERING. Each of the two shafts is driven by two diesels coupled and geared to one BBC gas turbine. Variable pitch propellers.

CATEGORY. Formerly designated *Geleitboote*, but now rated as *Fregatten*.

PHOTOGRAPHS. A photograph of *Köln* appears in the 1961-62 to 1966-67 editions, of *Augsburg* in the 1965-66 edition, of *Emden* in the 1966-67 and 1967-68 editions, and of *Karlsruhe* in the 1967-68 edition.

LUBECK *1968, Skyfotos*

BRAUNSCHWEIG *1968, Stefan Terzibaschitsch*

GUIDED MISSILE FRIGATES

4 NEW CONSTRUCTION ORIGINALLY RATED AS CORVETTES

Displacement, tons	3 200 standard; 3 500 full load
Length, feet (*metres*)	426·5 (*130·0*)
Beam, feet (*metres*)	44·9 (*13·7*)
Draught, feet (*metres*)	13·1 (*4·0*)
Gun, dual purpose	4—3 in (*76 mm*)
Missile launchers	1 "Tartar" single
Torpedo tubes	4
Main engines	Diesel and gas turbine
Speed, knots	30
Complement	250 approx (official figure)

Officially reclassified as "Class 121" (Fregatte 70). Still in the planning and design stages but approved by Parliament in Jan 1969. Originally ten ships of this type were planned, but the project was reduced to four units, it was officially stated in 1968. Although designated "corvettes" in the scheduled new construction programme they approximated nearly to frigates in design, size and armament, even at the first envisaged standard displacement of 2 000 tons, and now that their dimensions have been revised upwards their higher category is more apparent. The tabulated particulars and the sketch above were officially furnished.

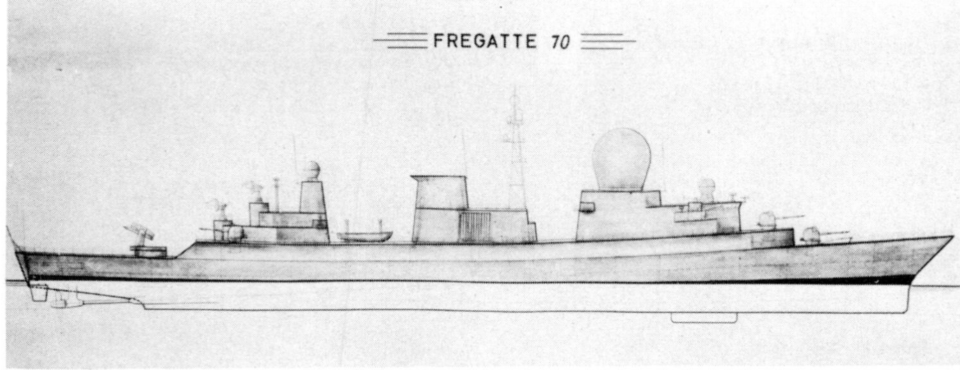

SCHEME FOR FREGATTEN *1969, Official*

FRIGATE (ex-Escort Destroyer)

Name	*No.*	*Builders*	*Laid down*	*Launched*	*Completed*
GNEISENAU (ex-HMS *Oakley*, ex-*Tickham*)	F 212	Yarrow & Co Ltd, Scotstoun, Glasgow	19 Aug 1940	15 Jan 1942	7 May 1942

1 Ex-BRITISH "HUNT" CLASS TYPE II

Displacement, tons	1 050 standard; 1 610 full load
Length, feet (*metres*)	264·2 (*80·5*) pp; 280 (*85·3*) oa
Beam, feet (*metres*)	31·5 (*9·6*)
Draught, feet (*metres*)	14 (*4·3*)
Guns, dual purpose	1—3·9 in (*100 mm*)
Guns, AA	4—40 mm
Boilers	2 Admiralty 3-drum; 299 psi (*21 km/cm²*); 660°F (*350°C*)
Main engines	2 Parsons double reduction geared turbines; 19 000 shp; 2 shafts
Speed, knots	25·5 max, 12 economical sea speed
Radius, miles	3 600 at 14 knots
Oil fuel (tons)	345
Complement	130

Former British frigate (ex-escort destroyer) of the "Blankney" class ("Hunt" class, Type II). Purchased in Nov 1957. Officially taken over after refit in Great Britain, at Langton Branch Dock, Harland & Wolff Ltd, Liverpool, 2 Oct 1958. Commissioned and renamed at Bremerhaven on 18 Oct 1958. Fitted with stabiliser, radar and cowl funnel. Employed as a training ship by the Gunnery School. Modified in 1961. Anti-Submarine weapons removed. Underwent further reconstruction by Howaldtswerke, Hamburg, in 1962-64. Placed in reserve in 1968. To be disposed of in due course.

GNEISENAU *1967, Official*

DISPOSALS
The two former British frigates (ex-escort destroyers) of the "Hunt" class, Type III, **Brommy** (ex-HMS *Eggesford*), F 218, and **Raule** (ex-HMS *Albrighton*), F 217, were decommissioned in 1968 and are being scrapped, it was officially conformed in 1969.

FRIGATE (ex-Sloop)

Name	*No.*	*Builders*	*Laid down*	*Launched*	*Completed*
SCHARNHORST (ex-HMS *Mermaid*)	F 213	Wm Denny & Bros Ltd, Dumbarton	8 Sep 1942	11 Nov 1943	12 May 1944

1 Ex-BRITISH "BLACK SWAN" CLASS

Displacement, tons	1 490 standard; 1 975 full load
Length, feet (*metres*)	283 (*86·3*) pp; 300 (*91·44*) oa
Beam, feet (*metres*)	38·5 (*11·7*)
Draught, feet (*metres*)	11·5 (*3·5*) mean
Guns, dual purpose	2—3·9 in (*100 mm*)
Guns, AA	4—40 mm
A/S	1 DCT; 1 DC rack; 40 DC
Boilers	2 Admiralty 3-drum; 250 psi (*17·5 km/cm²*); 400°F (*205°C*)
Main engines	2 Parsons double reduction geared turbines; 4 300 shp; 2 shafts
Speed, knots	18
Radius, miles	4 500 at 12 knots
Oil fuel (tons)	370
Complement	180

Former British frigate (ex-sloop) of the Modified "Black Swan" class. Under the economy programme announced by the German Navy in Sep 1967 *Scharnhorst* was scheduled to be placed in reserve on 15 Mar 1968. This was rescinded, but she will be disposed of in due course.

TRANSFER. *Scharnhorst* was handed over at Vickers-Armstrongs, Tyne, on 5 May 1959.

SCHARNHORST *1968, Official*

TRAINING. *Scharnhorst* was latterly employed for gunnery training.

CONVERSION. *Scharnhorst* was converted by Stülcken Sohn, Hamburg, from June 1961 to July 1962, with French type 100 mm guns (her former armament was 6—4 inch AA, 2—40 mm AA).

Of this class *Graf Spee* (ex-HMS *Flamingo*), F 215, and *Hipper* (ex-HMS *Actaeon*), F 214 were officially stricken from the active list on 31 July 1964 and scheduled to be scrapped. *Scheer* (ex-HMS *Hart*), F 216, converted into a radar picket training ship, was decommissioned in 1968 and scheduled to be scrapped.

ESCORT AND SUPPORT SHIPS

13 "RHEIN" CLASS

DONAU	69	**LECH**	56	**RHEIN**	58
ELBE	61	**MAIN**	63	**RUHR**	64
ISAR	64	**MOSEL**	67	**SAAR**	65
LAHN	55	**NECKAR**	66	**WERRA**	68
				WESER	62

Displacement, tons	2 370 standard; 2 540 full load except *Lahn* and *Lech* 2 460 standard; 2 680 full load
Length, feet (*metres*)	304·5 (*92·8*) wl; 323·5 (*98·6*) oa
Beam, feet (*metres*)	38·8 (*11·8*)
Draught, feet (*metres*)	11·2 (*3·4*)
Guns, AA	2—3·9 in (*100 mm*); none in *Lahn, Lech*; 4—40 mm
Main engines	6 Maybach or Daimler diesels; Diesel-electric drive in *Isar, Lahn, Lech, Mosel, Saar* 11 400 bhp; 2 shafts
Speed, knots	21·7 max, 15 economical sea speed
Radius, miles	1 625 at 15 knots
Oil fuel, tons	334
Complement	110 (accommodation for 200)

Elbe, Mosel, Rhein, and *Ruhr* were built by Schlieker-werft, Hamburg, *Isar* by Blohm & Voss, Hamburg, *Weser* by Elsflether Werft, *Neckar* by Lürssen, Bremen-Vegesack, *Saar* by Norderwerft, Hamburg, *Donau* by Schlichting, Travemünde, *Lahn* and *Lech* by Flender, Lübeck, *Main, Werra* by Lindenau, Kiel-Friedrichsort. All completed in 1961-64. Rated as *Belgleitschiffe* (tenders) for mine-sweepers (*Isar, Mosel, Saar*), submarines (*Lahn, Lech*), training (*Donau, Ruhr, Weser*), and motor torpedo boats (others) but these handsome and symmetrical ships of very interesting design, with their 3·9 in (100 mm) guns and comparatively high speed could obviously be used in lieu of frigates, although their flag superior is A.

CONVERSION. *Mosel* and *Saar* were scheduled to become *Flugsicherungsschiffe* with helicopter platform, aft and hospital installations, but this project was cancelled in 1969.

STATUS. Six of these comparatively new ships, namely *Donau, Isar, Lech, Mosel, Saar* and *Weser*, were scheduled to be decommissioned and placed in reserve by July 1968 it was officially stated. This was part of the economy programme announced by the Federal German Navy in Sep 1967.

PHOTOGRAPHS. A photograph of *Rhein* appears in the 1962-63 edition, of *Weser* in the 1963-64 edition, of *Elbe* in the 1964-65 to 1967-68 editions, and of *Lahn* and *Ruhr* in the 1967-68 edition.

MOSEL *1968, Wright & Logan*

SAAR *1968, courtesy Mr Michael D. J. Lennon*

LECH *1968, John G. Callis*

TRAINING SHIP

1 LIGHT CRUISER TYPE

Name	*No.*	*Builders*	*Laid down*	*Launched*	*Completed*
DEUTSCHLAND	A 59	Nobiskrug, Rendsburg	1959	5 Nov 1960	25 May 1963

Displacement, tons	4 800 normal; 5 500 full load
Length, feet (*metres*)	452·8 (*138·0*) pp; 475·8 (*145·0*) oa
Beam, feet (*metres*)	59 (*18·0*)
Draught, feet (*metres*)	14·8 (*4·5*)
A/S	2 Bofors 4-barrel rocket launchers
Guns, dual purpose	4—3·9 in (*100 mm*) single mounts
Guns, AA	6—40 mm; 2 twin and 2 single
Torpedo tubes	4 for A/S torpedoes; 2 for surface torpedoes
Main engines	6 680 bhp diesels (2 Daimler-Benz and 2 Maybach); 2 shafts 8 000 shp double reduction MAN geared turbines; 1 shaft
Boilers	2 Wahodag; 768 psi (54 *km/cm²*); 870°F (*465°C*)
Speed, knots	21·9 max (3 shafts); 17 (2 shafts) 14 economical sea (1 shaft)
Radius, miles	1 715 at 17 knots
Oil fuel, tons	230 furnace; 411 diesel
Complement	334 (29 officers, 305 men) plus 231 cadets.

First West German naval ship to exceed the post-war limit of 3 000 tons. Large frigate or light cruiser type. Can also be employed as a minelayer. Designed with armament and machinery of different types for training purposes. The name originally planned for this ship was *Berlin*. Ordered in 1956. Carried out her first machinery sea trials on 15 Jan 1963.

DEUTSCHLAND *1968*

CORVETTES

HANS BÜRKNER Y 879

Displacement, tons	982 standard; 1 100 full load
Dimensions, feet	265·2 oa × 30·8 × 10
Guns	2—40 mm AA (twin mounting)
Tubes	2—18 in anti-submarine homing
A/S weapons	1 DC mortar (four-barrelled); 2 DC racks
Main Engines	4 MAN diesels; 2 shafts; 13 600 shp = 25 knots
Complement	50

Large PCE type. Rated as Type B Torpedofangboote. Built by Atlaswerke, Bremen. Launched on 16 July 1961. Completed on 18 May 1963. Named after the designer of the German pre-First World War battleships. Serving for trials and manned by civilians.

HANS BÜRKNER *Official*

5 "THETIS" CLASS

HERMES P 6112
NAJADE P 6113
THESEUS P 6115
THETIS P 6111
TRITON P 6114

Displacement, tons	564 standard; 680 full load
Dimensions, feet	229·7 × 27 × 7·5
Guns	2—40 mm AA (twin mounting)
A/S weapons	Bofors DC mortar (*Hermes* 2 tubes)
Main engines	2 MAN diesels; 2 shafts; 6 800 bhp = 24 knots
Complement	48

Built by Roland Werft, Bremen-Hemelingen. Some have a computer house before the bridge structure. *Thetis* commissioned on 1 July 1961, *Hermes* on 16 Dec 1961, *Najade* on 12 May 1962, *Triton* on 10 Nov 1962, and *Theseus* on 15 Aug 1963.
These Torpedofangboote of advanced type would be used as submarine chasers in wartime.

PHOTOGRAPHS. Photographs of *Najade* appear in the 1963-64 to 1967-68 editions (starboard quarter and port broadside surface views).

TRITON *1968, Skyfotos*

THETIS *1968, courtesy Mr Godfrey H. Walker*

HERMES *1968, Skyfotos*

MISSILE BOATS

10 PROJECTED

Displacement, tons	*circa* 300 (officially revised figure)
Guided weapons	Launcher for "Tartar" missiles
Guns	2—76 mm AA

Designed as fast patrol boats. Projected under the new construction programme. Reported will have a launching system for surface-to-surface missiles.

TORPEDO BOATS

40 "JAGUAR" CLASS

ALBATROS	P 6069	**HERMELIN**	P 6095	**PANTHER**	P 6064
ALK	P 6084	**HYÄNE**	P 6099	**PELIKAN**	P 6086
BUSSARD	P 6074	**ILTIS**	P 6058	**PINGUIN**	P 6090
DACHS	P 6094	**JAGUAR**	P 6059	**PUMA**	P 6097
DOMMEL	P 6091	**KONDOR**	P 6070	**REIHER**	P 6089
ELSTER	P 6088	**KORMORAN**	P 6077	**SEEADLER**	P 6068
FALKE	P 6072	**KRANICH**	P 6083	**SPERBER**	P 6076
FRETTCHEN	P 6100	**LEOPARD**	P 6060	**STORCH**	P 6085
FUCHS	P 6066	**LÖWE**	P 6065	**TIGER**	P 6063
GEIER	P 6073	**LUCHS**	P 6061	**WEIHE**	P 6082
GEPARD	P 6098	**MARDER**	P 6067	**WIESEL**	P 6093
GREIF	P 6071	**NERZ**	P 6096	**WOLF**	P 6062
HABICHT	P 6075	**OZELOT**	P 6101	**ZOBEL**	P 6092
HÄHER	P 6087				

Displacement, tons	160 standard; 190 full load
Dimensions, feet	138 × 22 × 5
Guns	2—40 mm AA (single)
Tubes	4—21 in (2 torpedo tubes can be removed for 4 mines)
Main Engines	Mercedes-Benz or Maybach 20 cyl diesels; 4 shafts; 12 000 bhp = 42 knots
Complement	33

32 boats were built by Fr. Lürssen, Bremen-Vegessack in 1957-62 and eight by Kröger-werft, Rendsburg in 1958-64. Of composite construction, with steel frames, mahogany diagonal carvel hulls, alloy bulkheads and superstructure. *Dachs, Frettchen, Gepard, Hermelin, Hyäne, Nerz, Ozelot, Puma, Wiesel* and *Zobel* are of improved type with a different bridge.

PHOTOGRAPHS. A photograph of *Jaguar* appears in the 1958-59 to 1961-62 editions, of *Häher* in the 1962-63 to 1966-67 editions, of *Gepard* in the 1964-65 to 1966-67 editions, of *Wolf* in the 1964-65 to 1967-68 editions, and of *Zobel* in the 1967-68 edition.

ARMAMENT CONVERSION. Ten units of the *"Jaguar"* class will be fitted with missiles as in the new fast patrol boats.

DACHS *1968, Wright & Logan*

HABICHT *1968, Stephan Terzibaschitsch*

GEIER *1968, Official*

Torpedo Boats—*continued*

TRANSFERS. The two motor torpedo boats built by Vosper Ltd, Portsmouth, *Strahl* (Beam) P 6194 of the modified "Brave" type, and *Pfeil* (Arrow) P 6193 of the modified "Ferocity" type, were sold to Greece in Feb 1967. They arrived at Vospers for refit in Jan 1967 and were scheduled to be delivered to Greece in the late summer 1968. They are renamed *Astrapi* and *Aiolos*, respectively.
The two motor torpedo boats of the Norwegian "Nasty" type, *Hugin*, P 6191, and *Munin* P 6192, lent to Turkey in Aug 1964 were later transferred outright and renamed *Dogan* and *Marti* respectively.

DISPOSALS

Of the six motor torpedo boats of the German S-boote type, "Silbermowe" Class, **Eismöwe** P 6055 (ex-S 1), **Raumpöwe** P 6056 (ex-S 2), **Silbermöwe** P 6052 (ex-**Silver Gull**), **Sturmmöwe** P 6053 (ex-**Storm Gull**) and **Wildschwan** P 6054 (ex-**Wild Swan**) were decommissioned on 15 Mar 1967, stricken on 31 May 1967 and scrapped, and **Seeschwalbe** P 6057 (ex-S 3), renamed UW 9 as a training vessel in 1961, was decommissioned on 31 Jan 1964.
The former motor torpedo boats re-rated as training vessels, UW 10 (ex-FPB 5030, ex-S 130) and UW 11 (ex-FPB 5208) were deleted from the list in 1964.
The submarine chaser or small corvette of the US PC type, UW 12, No. W 51 (ex-*PC* 1618, ex-*P* 9) was decommissioned on 15 Dec 1967 and listed for scrap.

COASTAL MINESWEEPERS

18 "LINDAU" CLASS

CUXHAVEN	M 1078	**KONSTANZ**	M 1081	**TÜBINGEN**	M 1074
DÜREN	M 1079	**LINDAU**	M 1072	**ULM**	M 1083
FLENSBURG	M 1084	**MARBURG**	M 1080	**VÖLKLINGEN**	M 1087
FULDA	M 1068	**MINDEN**	M 1085	**WEILHEIM**	M 1077
GÖTTINGEN	M 1070	**PADERBORN**	M 1076	**WETZLAR**	M 1075
KOBLENZ	M 1071	**SCHLESWIG**	M 1073	**WOLFSBURG**	M 1082

Displacement, tons	370 standard; 425 full load
Dimensions, feet	137·8 pp; 147·7 oa × 27·2 × 8·5
Guns	1—40 mm AA
Main Engines	Maybach diesels; 2 shafts; 4 000 bhp = 17 knots
Complement	46

Lindau, first German-built vessel for the Federal German Navy since the Second World War, launched on 16 Feb 1957. Built by Yacht- & Bootswerft, Burmester, Bremen-Burg. Seventeen similar Kustenmineensuchboote were built in German yards in 1958-60. The hull is of wooden construction, laminated with plastic glue. The engines are of non-magnetic materials. The first six, *Göttingen, Koblenz, Lindau, Schleswig, Tübingen* and *Wetzlar*, were modified with lower bridges in 1958-59. *Schleswig* was lengthened by 6·8 feet in 1960, and all others in 1960-64. *Flensburg* and *Fulda* were converted into minehunters in 1968-69.

PHOTOGRAPHS. Photographs of *Weilheim* appear in the 1959-60 to 1961-62 editions, and of *Schleswig* in the 1962-63 to 1967-68 editions.

ULM — *1968, John G. Callis*

LINDAU — *1968*

TUBINGEN — *1968, John G. Callis*

6 "VEGESACK" CLASS

DETMOLD	M 1252	**PASSAU**	M 1255	**VEGESACK**	M 1250
HAMELN	M 1251	**SIEGEN**	M 1254	**WORMS**	M 1253

Displacement, tons	362 standard; 378 full load
Dimensions, feet	137·8 pp; 144·3 oa × 26·2 × 9
Guns	2—20 mm AA
Main Engines	2 Mercedes-Benz diesels; 2 shafts; 1,500 bhp = 15 knots Kamewa controllable pitch propellers

Built in Cherbourg, under the "off-shore" programme. All launched and completed in 1959-60. In reserve. A photograph of *Vegesack* appears in the 1960-61 to 1963-64 editions, of *Hamelin* in the 1964-65 to 1966-67 editions, and of *Detmold* in the 1967-68 edition.

PASSAU — *1969, Official*

FAST MINESWEEPERS

30 "SCHUTZE" CLASS

ALGOL	M 1068	**MARS**	M 1058	**SCHUTZE**	M 1062
ATAIR	M 1067	**MIRA**	M 1050	**SIRIUS**	M 1055
CAPELLA	M 1098	**NEPTUN**	M 1093	**SKORPION**	M 1060
CASTOR	M 1051	**ORION**	M 1053	**SPICA**	M 1059
DENEB	M 1064	**PEGASUS**	M 1066	**STEINBACK**	M 1091
FISCHE	M 1096	**PERSEUS**	M 1090	**STIER**	M 1061
GEMMA	M 1097	**POLLUX**	M 1054	**URANUS**	M 1099
HERKULES	M 1095	**PLUTO**	M 1092	**WAAGE**	M 1063
JUPITER	M 1065	**REGULUS**	M 1057	**WEGA**	M 1069
KREBS	M 1055	**RIGEL**	M 1056	**WIDDER**	M 1094

Displacement, tons	200 standard; 226 full load
Dimensions, feet	144·5 pp; 154·5 oa × 22·3 × 7·2
Guns	1—40 mm AA (some still have the designed 2—40 mm) *Pegasus* have 2—40 mm
Main engines	Maybach diesels; 2 shafts; Escher-Wyss propellers 3 600 bhp = 24·5 knots
Complement	39

Algol, Capella, Castor, Fische, Gemma, Krebs, Mars, Mira, Orion, Pollux, Regulus, Rigel, Schütze, Sirius, Skorpion, Spica, Steinback, Stier, Waage and *Wega* were built by Abeking & Rasmussen, Lemwerder; *Deneb, Jupiter, Pluto, Uranus* and *Widder* by Schurenstedt, Bardenfl; *Atair, Herkules, Neptun, Pegasus* and *Perseus* by Schlichting, Travemünde. The design is a development of the "R" boats of the Second World War. All this class are named after stars. *Stier* carries no weapons, but has a decompression chamber, being security vessel for submarines. All completed in 1959-64. Formerly classified as inshore minesweepers, but re-rated as fast minesweepers in 1966.

PHOTOGRAPHS. A photograph of *Schultze* appears in the 1959-60 edition, of *Gemma* in the 1960-61 to 1962-63 editions, of *Pegasus* in the 1963-64 to 1966-67 editions, of *Jupiter* in the 1966-67 and 1967-68 editions, and of *Pluto* in the 1967-68 edition.

SCHÜTZE — *1968, Official*

DENEB — *1968, Wright & Logan*

Fast Minesweepers—*continued*

GEMMA *1968, courtesy Dr Giorgio Arra*

DISPOSALS

Of the remaining fast minesweepers of the "R" types **Alderbaran** M 1088 (ex-R 131, ex-R 91), mine-diving vessel; **Merkur** W 68 (ex-M 1066, ex-R 134), security vessel for submarines; OT 1, W 52 (ex-*Jupiter*, ex-R 146), for sonar training duties; UW 4 (ex-R 149, ex-R 102) and UW 5, W 47 (ex-R 150) both training vessels for the submarine weapons school, were all stricken from the active list, it is officially stated, and when not required for ancillary purposes will be scrapped.

COASTAL PATROL BOATS. Of the remaining coastal patrol boats FM 1 (ex-W 7, ex-*Pierre Mené*) and FM 2 (ex- W 8, ex-*Malgré Tout*), both for telecommunications training; TM 1 (ex-UW 3, ex-W 12, ex-No. 186) and TM 2 (ex-UW 2, ex-W 11, ex-*Miss Andrée*) both for diving training; UW 1 (ex-W 10, ex- *Adrien Magnier*) for underwater training, all of the motor minesweeper (MMS 1) type; KW 15, KW 16, KW 17, KW 18, KW 19 (gunnery training) and KW 20, of the frontier patrol boat type; and KW 1, KW 2, KW 3, KW 6, KW 7 and KW 8, of the harbour defence boat type, were all officially stricken from the active list in 1968 as they are either scrapped or serving as experimental vessels, training hulks and barges for various agencies. KW 4, KW 5, KW 9 and KW 10 were given to Tanzania (shipped on 8 Dec 1963) and handed over to commercial interests.

INSHORE MINESWEEPERS

10 "FRAUENLOB" CLASS

ACHERON	M 2680	**FRAUENLOB**	M 2671	**MEDUSA**	M 2674
ATLANTIS	M 2679	**GEFION**	M 2673	**MINERVA**	M 2676
DIANA	M 2677	**LORELEY**	M 2678	**NAUTILUS**	M 2672
				UNDINE	M 2675

Displacement, tons	204 standard; 230 tons full load
Dimensions, feet	124·7 × 27·2 × 7·2
Guns	1—40 mm AA
Main engines	Diesels = 14 knots
Complement	24

Built by Kröger Werft, Rendsburg. Launched in 1965-67. Completed in 1965-68. Originally designed as *Küstenwachboote* or coastguard boats with "W" pennant numbers: W 31 to W 38 (*Frauenlob, Nautilus, Gefion, Medusa, Undine, Minerva, Diana, Loreley*, respectively) and rated as patrol boats of the seaward defence craft type; but officially re-rated as inshore minesweepers in 1968.

MINERVA *1968, Official*

HOLNIS M 2651

Displacement, tons	180
Dimensions, feet	116·8 × 24·3 × 6·9
Guns	1—20 mm AA
Main engines	2 Mercedes-Benz diesels; 2 shafts; 2 000 bhp = 14·5 knots
Complement	21

Now serving for test and evaluation purposes, *Holnis* was launched on 22 May 1965 and completed in 1966 by Abeking & Rasmussen, Lemwerde, as the prototype of a new design of *Binnenminensuchboote* projected as a class of 20 such vessels but she is the only unit of this type, the other 19 boats having been cancelled.

HOLNIS *1969, Official*

HANSA W 22 (18 Nov 1957) **NIOBE** W 21 (18 Aug 1957)

Displacement, tons	150 standard; 180 full load
Dimensions, feet	115·2 × 21·3 × 5·6
Guns	1—40 mm AA
Main engines	*Hansa:* 1 Mercedes-Benz diesel; 1 shaft; 950 bhp = 14 knots *Niobe:* 2 Mercedes-Benz diesels; 2 shafts; 1 900 bhp = 16 knots
Complement	*Hansa* 19; *Niobe* 22

Built by Kröger Werft, Rendsburg. Launch dates above. Completed in 1958. The post-war prototype vessels of the category, formerly designated *Küstenwachboote* or coastal patrol vessels but re-rated as *Binnenminensuchboote* or inshore minesweepers in 1966. Named after former cruisers. *Hansa* serves as support ship for minedivers. *Niobe* (photograph in the 1967-68 edition) serves for test and evaluation purposes.

HANSA *1968*

8 ARIADNE CLASS

AMAZONE (27 Feb 1963)	**FREYA** (25 June 1966)	**NIXE** (3 Dec 1962)
ARIADNE (23 Apr 1960)	**GAZELLE** (14 Aug 1963)	**NIYMPHE** (20 Nov 1962)
	HERTHA (18 Feb 1961)	**VNETA** (17 Sep 1960)

Displacement, tons	184 standard; 210 full load
Dimensions, feet	124·3 × 27·2 × 6·6
Guns	1—40 mm AA
Main engines	2 Mercedes-Benz diesels; 2 shafts; 2 000 bhp = 14 knots
Complement	23

Launch dates above. Pennant Nos. W 29, 23, 24, 30, 26, 28, 27, 25 respectively. All completed by Krögerwerft, Rendsburg, in 1960-63. Some have minesweeping gear. All named after former large or small cruisers, 1897- 1900. Formerly classified as patrol boats (*Küstenwachboote*) but re-rated as inshore minesweepers in 1966.

AMAZONE *1968*

ARIADNE *1968, Stefan Terzibaschitsch*

MINELAYERS

BOCHUM (ex-USS *Rice County*, *LST* 1089) *N* 120 (ex-A 1404)
BOTTROP (ex-USS *Saline County*, *LST* 1101) *N* 121 (ex-A 1504)

Displacement, tons	1 653 standard; 4 080 full load
Dimensions, feet	316 wl; 328 oa × 50 × 14
Guns	6—40 mm (2 twin, 2 single)
Main Engines	2 GM diesels; 2 shafts; 1 700 bhp = 11 knots
Oil fuel (tons)	600
Radius, miles	15 000 at 9 knots

Former United States tank landing ships of the 511-1152 series transferred in 1961. and converted into minelayers. Commissioned on 6 Feb 1964. The third ship of this type, *Bamberg*, N 122 (ex-A 1403, ex-USS *Greer County*, LST 799) was scrapped in 1968.

BOTTROP *1967, Col. Breyor*

BOCHUM *1969, Official*

MEDIUM LANDING SHIPS

4 Ex-US LSM TYPE

EIDECHSE (ex-USS *LSM* 491) L 751 **SALAMANDER** (ex-USS *LSM* 553) L 752
KROKODIL (ex-USS *LSM* 537) L 750 **VIPER** (ex-USS *LSM* 558) L 753

Displacement, tons	743 light; 1 095 full load
Dimensions, feet	196·5 wl; 203·5 oa × 34·5 × 8·3
Guns	2—40 mm AA (1 twin)
Main engines	GM diesel; 2 shafts; 2 800 bhp = 12·5 knots

Rated as Lundungsboote. Six medium landing ships (two LSM(R) and four LSM) were purchased from USA for about $6 000 000 and transferred to Germany on 5 Sep 1958 at Charleston SC. Refitted in 1959. The four remaining ships constitute the German Landungsgeschwader No. 1. A starboard bow surface view of *Salamander* appears in the 1960-61 and 1961-62 editions, and a starboard broadside surface view of *Eidechse* in the 1967-68 edition.

DISPOSALS

The two medium landing ships (rocket) o₁ the US LSMR type, **Natter** L 755 (ex-*Thames River*, LSM(R) 534) and **Otter** L 754 (ex-*Smyrna River*, LSM(R) 532). were decommissioned on 15 Dec 1967 and are being scrapped.

CANCELLATION. The project to build six large landing craft or medium landing ships of 1,000 tons has been abandoned, it was officially stated in 1968.

KROKODIL (helicopter deck aft) *Wright & Logan*

VIPER *LSM*

LANDING CRAFT

22 LCU TYPE

BARBE	L 790	**FELCHEN**	L 793	**LACHS**	L 762	**SALM**	L 799
BRASSE	L 789	**FLUNDER**	L 760	**MAKRELE**	L 796	**SCHLEIE**	L 765
BUTT	L 788	**FORELLE**	L 794	**MURANE**	L 797	**STOR**	L 766
DELPHIN	L 791	**INGER**	L 795	**PLOTZE**	L 763	**TUMMLER**	L 767
DORSCH	L 792	**KARPFEN**	L 761	**RENKE**	L 798	**WELS**	L 768
				ROCHEN	L 764	**ZANDER**	L 769

Displacement, tons	200 light; 403 full load
Dimensions, feet	136·5 × 28·9 × 5·2
Guns	1—20 mm AA
Main engines	GM diesels; 2 shafts; 1 380 bhp = 12 knots

Similar to the United States LCU (Landing Craft, Utility) type. Provided with bow and stern ramp. Built by Howaldt, Hamburg, all launched in 1965-66.

DISPOSALS

The utility landing craft LCU 1 (ex-USS LCU 779, ex-LCT(6) 779), transferred from the USA under MAP was scrapped in 1968.

DELPHIN *1967, Official*

REPAIR SHIPS

ODIN (ex-USS *Diomedes*, *ARB* 11, ex-*LST* 1119) A 512
WOTAN (ex-USS *Ulysses*, *ARB* 9, ex-*LST* 967) A 513

Displacement, tons	1 625 light; 4 100 full load
Dimensions, feet	316 wl; 328 oa × 50 × 11
Guns	8—40 mm AA
Main Engines	2 GM diesels; 2 shafts; 1 800 bhp = 11·6 knots
Oil fuel (tons)	600
Radius, miles	15 000 at 9 knots

Transferred under MAP in June 1961. *Odin* commissioned in Jan 1966 and *Wotan* on 2 Dec 1965.

The two landing ships of the former United States LST type, ex-USS *Millard County*, LST 987, and ex-USS *Montgomery County*, LST 1041, purchased in 1960 for conversion into repair ships similar to the US ARB type, above, were scrapped in 1968. The other two repair ships, *Wieland* Y 804, rated as a *Schwimmwerkstattschiff* or floating workshop, and *Memmert* Y 805 (ex-USN 106, ex-*India*, ex-BP 34), rated as a *Torpedoklarmachschiff* or torpedo repair ship, salvage vessel with a derrick, were officially stricken from the active list in 1968.

ODIN *1968, Stefan Terzibaschitsch*

WOTAN *1968, Stefan Terzibaschitsch*

EIDER (ex-*Catherine*, ex-*Dochet*) A 50 **TRAVE** (ex-*Caroline*, ex-*Flint*) A 51

Displacement, tons	480 standard; 750 full load
Dimensions, feet	164 pp; 177·2 oa × 27·5 × 14
Guns	1—40 mm AA; 1—20 mm AA
Main Engines	*Eider:* Triple expansion; 1 shaft; 750 ihp = 12 knots *Trave:* Mercedes-Benz diesels; 1 shaft; 900 bhp = 12 knots
Fuel (tons)	*Trave:* 153; *Eider:* 130

Former British "Isles" type minesweeping trawlers. Built in Canada by Davie & Sons, Lauzon, in 1942. *Trave* was converted from steam (triple expansion) to diesel-electric propulsion in 1952-54. *Eider* is employed as a mine clearance training vessel.

TRAVE *Wright & Logan*

EIDER *1969, Official*

DEPOT SHIPS AND TENDERS

OSTE (ex-USN 101, *Puddefjord*) A 52

Measurement, tons	567 gross
Dimensions, feet	160 × 29·7 × 17
Guns	2—20 mm AA
Main Engines	2 Sulzer diesels; 1 shaft; 1 400 bhp = 14 knots

Built in 1943 at Akers Mekaniske Vaerkstad, Oslo. Taken over from the US Navy.

OSTE *1968*

DISPOSALS

The depot ship WS 1 (ex-*City of Havana*, ex-*José Marti*, ex-*Northway*, ex-*LSD* 11), former US Landing Ship, Dock, then a West Indian fruit carrier, latterly employed by the West German Navy as an accommodation ship, was sold to Greek mercantile interests in 1966.
The depot ship **Ems** (ex-USN 104, ex-*Hunte*) A 53 was officially stricken from the active list in 1968.
The tenders **Friedrich Voge** (ex-*Kurefjord*) Y 888, former tug; **Karl Kolls** (ex-*Salmo*, ex-*Gerda* **1**, ex-*Margarethe*, ex-*Nora*) Y 887, former small freighter; **Otto Meycke**, Y 882, former trawler; **Walther von Ledebur**, wooden hulled vessel; SP 1 and SP 2 (**Wilhelm Pullwer**) were all officially deleted in 1968 as none of them are on the Navy List, all being manned by civilians as experimental vessels for various agencies. See particulars in the 1967-68 edition.

SUPPLY SHIPS (*Tross-Schiffe*)

3 PROJECTED HEAVY TYPE

Displacement, tons	6 000
Dimensions, feet	360·9 × 52·5 × 19·7
Guns	2—3 in (*76 mm*)
Main Engines	Speed = 17 knots designed

Rated as *Grosse Versorger* or heavy maintenance, support, and provision ship.

CANCELLATION. The project for a *Torpedotransporter*, designed as a supply ship and transport for torpedoes, etc, was abandoned in 1968.

2 NEW CONSTRUCTION MINE TYPE

SACHSENWALD A 1437 **STEIGERWALD** A 1438

Displacement, tons	3 000
Dimensions, feet	363·5 × 45·6 × 11·2
Guns	4—40 mm AA (two twin mountings)
Main engines	2 diesels; 2 shafts; 3 080 bhp = 18·3 knots (official figures)
Radius, miles	3 500 nautical

Built by Blohm & Voss, Hamburg as mine transports. Laid down on 1 Aug 1966 and 9 May 1966. Launched on 10 Dec 1966 and 10 Mar 1967. Scheduled to be commissioned in July 1969. Rated as *Minentransporter*. Have mine ports in the stern and can be used as minelayers.

2 "WESTERWALD" CLASS

ODENWALD A 1436 **WESTERWALD** A 1435

Displacement, tons	3 460
Dimensions, feet	347·8 × 46 × 12·2
Guns	4—40 mm AA
Main engines	Diesels; 5 600 bhp = 17 knots
Complement	60

Ammunition transports of a new type built by Lübecker Masch in 1966-67. *Odenwald* was commissioned on 20 Mar 1968 and *Westerwald* on 1 Feb 1967. Rated as *Munitionstransporter*.

WESTERWALD *1968, Official*

Supply Ships—*continued*

8 "LÜNEBURG" CLASS

COBURG	A 1412	**LÜNEBURG**	A 1411	**OFFENBURG**	A 1417
FREIBURG	A 1413	**MEERSBURG**	A 1418	**SAARBURG**	A 1415
GLÜCKSBURG	A 1414	**NIENBURG**	A 1416		

Displacement, tons	3 254
Dimensions, feet	341·2 × 43·3 × 13·8
Guns	4—40 mm AA
Main engines	2 Maybach diesels; 2 shafts; 5 600 bhp = 17 knots
Complement	103

Lüneburg, Coburg, Glücksburg, Meersburg and *Nienburg* were built by Flensburger Schiffbau and Vulkan, Bremen, others by Blohm & Voss, Hamburg. Commissioned on 9 July, 27 May, 9 July, 9 July, 25 June, 1 Aug, 27 May and 30 July, respectively, 1968.

LÜNEBURG *1968, Stefan Terzibaschitsch*

2 "ANGELN" CLASS

ANGELN (ex-*Borée*) A 1408 **DITHMARSCHEN** (ex-*Hébé*) A 1409

Measurement, tons	2 111 gross
Dimensions, feet	296·9 × 43·6 × 20·3
Main engines	Pielstick diesels; 1 shaft; 3 000 bhp = 17 knots
Complement	57

Both built by Ateliers et Chantiers de Bretagne, Nantes. Purchased from shipowners S. N. Caënnaise, Caen. Launched in 1954-55. Commissioned on 27 Nov 1959 and 19 Dec 1959, respectively. Rated as Materialtransporter.

ANGELN *1968*

DITHMARSCHEN *1968, Stefan Terzibaschitsch*

PFÄLZERLAND (ex-*Lucetta*) Y 831

Measurement, tons	299 gross; 521 deadweight
Dimensions, feet	156·1 × 26 × 8·2
Main Engines	2 MWM diesels; 2 shafts; 300 bhp = 10·5 knots

Built by W. & E. Sielaff Büsum. Completed in 1956. Purchased in 1960 for service with the armed forces' supply organisation. In service 1960.

SIEGERLAND (ex-*Leuchtenburg* 3) Y 832

Measurement, tons	280 gross; 350 deadweight
Main engines	Designed for 8 knots

Built in 1952 Cargo ship (*Material-Versorger*) and depot ship (*Depotschiffe*).

SCHWARZWALD (ex-*Amalthee*) A 1400

Measurement, tons	1 103 gross
Dimensions, feet	263·1 × 39 × 15·1
Guns	4—40 mm AA Bofors
Main engines	Sulzer diesel; 3 000 bhp = 17 knots

Built by Ch. Dubigeon, Nantes. Launched 31 Jan 1956. Purchased from Soc Navale Caënnaise in Feb 1960. Commissioned as ammunition transport. A dead broadside view appears in the 1967-68 edition.

SCHWARZWALD *1967, Official*

SAUERLAND (ex-*Rolandseck*) Y 830

Measurement, tons	1 299 gross; 1 755 deadweight
Dimensions, feet	233·2 × 36·2 × 16·5
Main Engines	MAN diesel; 1 380 bhp = 12 knots

Built by Atlas Werke, Bremen. Completed in 1953. Purchased in 1960 for service with the armed forces' supply organisation. In service 1960.

SAUERLAND *1968, Official*

SAIL TRAINING SHIPS

GORCH FOCK

Displacement, tons	1 760 standard; 1 870 full load
Dimensions, feet	229·7 wl; 257 oa × 39·2 × 15·8
Main Engines	Auxiliary MAN diesel; 800 bhp = 11 knots
Sail area, sq ft	21 141 (speed of up to 15 knots under sail)
Radius, miles	1 990
Complement	206 (10 officers, 56 ratings, 140 cadets)

Sail training ship of the improved "Horst Wessel" type. Barque rig. Launched by Blohm & Voss, Hamburg, on 23 Aug 1958 and commissioned on 17 Dec 1958.

GORCH FOCK *1968, courtesy Mr. Martin E. Holbrook*

NORDWIND

Displacement, tons	100
Dimensions, feet	78·8 × 22 × 9
Main Engines	Diesel; 150 bhp = 8 knots. (Sail area 2 037·5 sq ft)

Ketch, ex-Kreigsfischkutter (KFK). Photograph in the 1954-55 edition. There are other vessels of various sailing types: *Achat, Argonaut, Borasco, Diamont, Dompfaff, Flibustier, Freibeuter, Geuse, Gödicke Michel, Gunnar, Hadubrand, Hunding, Kaper, Klipper, Korsar, Kuckuck, Likendeeler, Magellan, Mime, Mistral, Monsun, Nachtigall, Ortwin, Ostwind, Pampero, Samum, Schirocco, Seeteufel, Siegmund, Störtebecker, Taifun, Tornado, Westwind, Wiking, Vitalienbrüder.*

EXPERIMENTAL VESSELS

4 Ex-COASTAL MINESWEEPERS

ADOLF BESTELMEYER (ex-*BYMS* 2213) **HERMAN VON HELMOLTZ**
H. C. OERSTED (ex-*Vinstra*, ex-*NYMS* 247) **RUDOLF DIESEL** (ex-*BYMS* 2279)

Displacement, tons	270 standard; 350 full load
Dimensions, feet	136 × 24·5 × 8
Main Engines	2 diesels; 2 shafts; 1 000 bhp = 15 knots;

Of US YMS type. Built in 1943. *Adolf Bestelmeyer*, Y 881, and *Rudolph Diesel*, Y 889, are used for gunnery purposes. *H. C. Oersted*, Y 877, was acquired from the Royal Norwegian Navy. *Herman von Helmholtz*, Y 878, commissioned on 18 Dec 1962, is used as a degaussing ship. A photograph of *H. C. Oersted* appears in the 1967-68 edition.

ADOLF BESTELMEYER *1968*

SURVEYING VESSELS include *Planet* (1967), military research ship temporarily commissioned as a survey ship, Y 843, in the Bundesmarine; and *Meteor* (1964), *Süderoog, Gauss, Hooge, Ruden, Atair, Runghol̈t, Alkor* and *Wega*, administered by the Federal Ministry of Transport.

TRIALS VESSELS include *Viktoria* (ex-*Herzog Friederich*) Y 808; TF 101 (Y 883), TF 102 (Y 884), TF 103 (Y 885), TF 104 (Y886) and TF 105 (Y 835); TF 25 (Y 806) and TF 26 (Y 807); and EF 1 (ex-*Süderoog*) Y 890, but these were all officially deleted from the strength in 1968 as none of them are on the Navy List, all being manned by civilians as experimental vessels for various agencies, as are the four YMS type vessels above which are retained in this edition, however, since as former minesweepers they are still naval defence potential.

FISHERY PROTECTION VESSELS include *Poseidon, Anton Dohrn, Meerkatze, Frithjof Walther Herwig* and *Uthorn*, administered by the Federal Ministry for Agriculture and Fisheries.

TANK CLEANING VESSELS include *Forde* and *Jade* of 1 100 tons completed in late 1967.

RESCUE LAUNCHES

4 "KW" TYPE

FL 5 Y 857 (ex-W 11) **FL 7** Y 859 (ex-W 13)
FL 6 Y 858 (ex-W 12) **FL 8** Y 860 (ex-W 14)

Displacement, tons	45 standard; 60 full load
Dimensions, feet	83 pp; 93·5 oa × 15·5 × 4
Main Engines	2 Mercedes-Benz diesels; 2 000 bhp = 25 knots
Complement	14

Built 1951-52. All are similar to US Coast Guard 93-ft type. Formerly rated as harbour defence vessels, but re-rated as Flugsicherungsboote (employed as air/sea rescue launches) in 1959. Guns removed. Formerly H 11 (ex-P 1), H 12 (ex-P 2), H 13 (ex-P3) and H 14 (ex-P 4) respectively.

DISPOSALS
FL 1 (ex-*FL* 51, ex-*MSM* 2) was disposed of in 1962. **FL 4** (ex-*Falke*, ex-*FL* 4), a smaller type of aircraft rescue boat, was also disposed of in 1962.
FL 2 (ex-*FL* 52, ex-*MSM* 3) and **FL 3** (ex-*FL* 50, ex-*MSM* 1), ex-German Air Force sea rescue launches, were disposed of on 2 Aug and 1 Aug 1963 respectively.

FL 6 *1968, Official*

FL 9 Y 861 (ex-D 2763) **FL 10** Y 862 (ex-D 2765) **FL 11** Y 963 (ex-D 2766)

Displacement, tons	70
Dimensions, feet	95·2 × 16·5 × 4·2
Main Engines	Maybach diesels; 2 shafts; 3 200 bhp = 30 knots
Radius, miles	600 at 20 knots

Built by Kröger, Rendsburg. Former Flugsicherungsboote of the RAF station List/Sylt. Commissioned on 1 Sep 1961.

OILERS

4 NEW CONSTRUCTION

AMMERSEE A 1425 **WALCHENSEE** A 1424
TEGERNSEE A 1426 **WESTENSEE** A 1427

Displacement, tons	1 898
Dimensions, feet	233 × 36·7 × 13·5
Main engines	Diesels; 2 shafts; 1 400 bhp = 12·6 knots

Built by Lindenau, Friedrichsort. *Walchensee* was launched on 10 July 1965. Commissioned on 2 Mar 1967, 23 Mar 1967, 29 June 1966 and 6 Oct 1967, respectively.

CANCELLATION. The project to build five larger oilers rated as *Grosse Betriebsstoff-transporter* of 5 999 tons and 334·6 × 45·9 × 19·7 feet was officially abandoned in 1968.

TEGERNSEE *1968, Skyfotos*

EIFEL (ex-*Friedrich Jung*) A 1429

Displacement, tons	2 279 light; 4 700 full load
Measurement, tons	3 444 gross; 4 720 deadweight
Dimensions, feet	334 × 47·2 × 23·3
Main Engines	3 360 hp = 14 knots

Built in 1958 by Norder-Werft, Hamburg. Purchased in 1963 for service as an oiler in the Bundesmarine. Commissioned on 27 May 1963. A photograph appears in the 1964-65 to 1967-68 editions.

HARZ (ex-*Claere Jung*) A 1428

Displacement, tons	1 308 light; 3 696 full load
Measurement, tons	2 594 gross; 3 755 deadweight
Dimensions, feet	303·2 × 43·5 × 21·7
Main Engines	2 520 hp = 13 knots

Built in 1953 by Norder-Werft, Hamburg. Purchased in 1963 for service as an oiler in the Bundesmarine. Commissioned on 27 May 1963.

FRANKENLAND (ex-*Münsterland*, ex-*Powell*) Y 827

Displacement, tons	16 310
Measurement, tons	11 700 gross
Dimensions, feet	521·8 × 70·2 × 37·5
Main Engines	Diesels; 5 800 bhp = 13·5 knots

Built by Lithgows, Glasgow. Launched in 1950. Commissioned on 29 Apr 1959.

FRANKENLAND *1968, courtesy Mr Godfrey H. Walker*

BODENSEE (ex-*Unkas*) A 1406 **WITTENSEE** (ex-*Sioux*) A 1407

Displacement, tons	1 200
Measurement, tons	1 230 deadweight: 980 gross
Dimensions, feet	208·3 × 32·5 × 15
Main Engines	Diesels; 1 050—1 250 bhp = 12 knots

Built by P. Lindenau, Kiel-Friedrichsort. Launched on 19 Nov 1955 and an 23 Sep 1958, respectively. Commissioned on 26 Mar 1959. These ships are nearly identical.

BODENSEE *1968*

Oilers—*continued*

BORKUM (ex-USN 105, ex- *Borkum*) Y 824

Displacement, tons	450
Measurement, tons	265 gross
Dimensions, feet	124·7 × 26·5 × 12
Main Engines	Diesels; Speed = 6 knots

Built by Flender Lübeck. Launched in 1939. Former German motor tanker.

EUTIN (ex-*Ramsöy*) Y 825

Displacement, tons	410
Main engines	Speed = 6 knots

Built by Menzer, Geesthact. Launched in 1943. Commissioned on 1 July 1956.

EMSLAND (ex-*Antonio Zotti*) Y 828 **MÜNSTERLAND** (ex-*Angela Germona*) Y 829

Measurement, tons	6 200 gross (*Emsland*); 6 191 (*Münsterland*)
Dimensions, feet	461 × 54·2 × 25·8
Main Engines	Diesel; CRDA; 4 800 bhp (*Emsland*); Fiat 5 500 bhp (*Münsterland*) = 13 knots

Built by CRDA Monfalcone, and Ansaldo, Genoa, respectively. Both launched in 1943. Completed in 1947 and 1946, respectively. Purchased in 1960 from Italian owners. Converted in 1960-61 by Schliekerwerft, Hamburg, and Howaldswerke, Hamburg, respectively. Commissioned 7 Nov 1961 and 16 Oct 1961. Civilian crew. A photograph of *Emsland* appears in the 1965-66 to 1967-68 editions.

MUNSTERLAND *1968, Skyfotos*

FW 1 **FW 2** **FW 3** **FW 4** **FW 5** **FW 6**

Displacement, tons	350
Dimensions, feet	144·4 × 25·6 × 8·2
Main engines	MWM diesel, 230 bhp = 9 knots

Built by Germania in 1963-64. Actually employed as Frischwasserboote.

DISPOSAL

The oiler **Jeverland** (ex-*Ammerland*, ex-*Kongsdal*) Y 826 was removed from the effective list on 30 Sep 1968.

TUGS

BALTRUM **JUIST** **LANGEOOG** **NORDERNEY** **SPIEKEROOG** **WANGEROOGE**

Displacement, tons	854 standard; 1 024 full load
Dimensions, feet	170·6 × 39·4 × 12·8
Guns	1—40 mm AA
Main engines	Diesel-electric; 2 400 hp = 13·6 knots

Built by Schichau, Bremerhaven. *Wangerooge*, prototype, salvage tug, was launched on 4 July 1966. *Wangerooge* commissioned on 9 Apr 1968, *Langeoog* and *Spiekeroog* on 14 Aug 1968, *Baltrum* on 8 Oct 1968.

FEHMARN A 1458 **HELGOLAND** A 1457

Displacement, tons	1 310 standard; 1 619 full load
Dimensions, feet	223·1 × 41·7 × 14·4
Guns	1—40 mm AA
Main engines	Diesel-electric; 4 MWM diesels; 2 shafts; 3 800 hp = 16·6 knots

Bergungsschlepper or salvage tugs. Built by Unterweser, Bremerhaven. Launched on 25 Nov 1965 and 8 Apr 1965 and commissioned on 1 Jan 1967 and 8 June 1966,

FEHMARN *1968, Official*

AMRUM Y 822 **FÖHR** Y 821 **NEUWERK** Y 823 **SYLT** Y 820

Displacement, tons	262 standard
Dimensions, feet	100·7 oa × 25·2
Main Engines	1 Deutz diesel 800 bhp = 12 knots

Built by Fr. Schichau, Bremerhaven. Launched in 1961. All completed in 1962-63.

DISPOSALS

Passat (ex-USN 103, ex-*Passat*) Y 800 was deleted from the list and scrapped in 1968. **Pellworm** (ex-USN 102, ex-*Pellworm*) Y 801 was stricken from the active list in 1968.

PLÖN (ex-*Bombay*, ex-*Bodden*) Y 802

Measurement, tons	101 gross
Main engines	350 hp

Tug for Kiel purchased in 1956. Yard craft for harbour and canal duties generally. There are also nine small harbour tugs all completed in 1958-60:—*Blauort* Y 803, *Knechtsand* Y 814, *Langeness* Y 819, *Lütje Hörn* Y 812, *Mellum* Y 813, *Nordstrand* Y 817, *Scharhörn* Y 815, *Trischen* Y 818 and *Vogelsand* Y 816.

ICEBREAKERS

HANSE

Displacement, tons	3 700
Dimensions, feet	243·2 × 57 × 20
Main engines	Diesel-electric; 4 shafts; 7 500 bhp = 16 knots

Built by Wärtsilä Oy, Helsinki, Finland. Laid down on 12 Jan 1965. Launched on 17 Oct 1966. Completed on 25 Nov 1966. Commissioned on 13 Dec 1966. Although owned by West Germany she sails under the Finnish flag, manned by a Finnish crew. Only when the winter is so severe that icebreakers are needed in the southern Baltic will she be transferred under the German flag and command. She is of improved "Karhu" class.

EISBÄR A 1402 **EISVOGEL** A 1401

Displacement, tons	560 standard
Dimensions, feet	125·3 oa × 31·2 × 7·9 (15·1 max)
Guns	Can carry 1—40 mm AA Bofors
Main Engines	2 Maybach diesels; 2 shafts; 2 400 bhp = 13 knots

Built by J. G. Hitzler, Lauenburg. Launched on 9 June and 28 Apr 1960, and commissioned on 1 Nov and 11 Mar 1961, respectively. Icebreakers and tugs.

GERMANY (EAST)

Administration

Commander-in-Chief, Volksmarine:
Vice Admiral Willi Ehm

Chief of Naval Staff:
Rear Admiral Johannes Streubel

Strength of the Fleet

4 Escorts
22 Minesweepers
24 Inshore Minesweepers
12 Missile Boats
24 Patrol Vessels
60 Torpedo Boats
60 Coastguard Boats
18 Landing Craft
30 Auxiliary Vessels
10 Tugs

Personnel

1969: 16 000 officers and men

Mercantile Marine

Lloyd's Register of Shipping:
361 vessels of 806 074 tons gross

ESCORTS

4 Ex-USSR "RIGA" TYPE

ERNST THÄLMANN 121 **KARL LIEBKNECHT** 123
FRIEDRICH ENGELS 124 **KARL MARX** 122

Displacement, tons	1 050 standard; 1 350 full load
Dimensions, feet	278·9 oa × 31·2 × 9
Guns	3—3·9 in single; 4—37 mm AA paired vertically
Tubes	3—21 in
A/S weapons	4 depth charge projectors
Main Engines	Geared turbines; 2 shafts; 24 000 shp = 28 knots
Oil fuel (tons)	300
Complement	190

Designed to carry 50 miles. A fifth ship of this type was burnt out at the end of 1959 and became a total wreck.

The training ship *Albin Köbis* (ex-escort *Ernst Thälmann*, ex-*Dorsch*, ex-Danish fishery protection ship *Hvidbjornen*, was deleted from the list in 1968.

1965, Werner Kähling

ERNST THÄLMANN

MINESWEEPERS

10 "KRAKE" CLASS

221 **222** **223** **224** **225** **241** **242** **243** **244** **245**

Displacement, tons	650
Dimensions, feet	229·7 × 26·5 × 12·2
Guns	1—3·4 in; 10—25 mm AA paired vertically
A/S weapons	4 DCT
Main Engines	Diesels; 2 shafts; 34 000 bhp = 18 knots
Complement	80 (peace) 96 (war)

Built in 1956-58 at Peenewerft, Wolgast. The first four were completed in 1958, originally for Poland, but not delivered. Appearance is different compared with the first type, the squat wide funnel being close to the bridge work with a lattice mast and radar. Fitted for minelaying. On 1 Mar 1961 they were given the names of the capitals of districts etc, of Eastern Germany.

"Krake" Class *Added 1968*

6 "HABICHT II" CLASS

211 **212** **217** **218** **219** **220**

Displacement, tons	550
Dimensions, feet	213 oa × 26·5 × 11·8
Guns	1—3·4 in; 8—25 mm AA paired vertically
A/S weapons	4 DCT
Main Engines	2 diesels; 2 shafts; 2 800 bhp = 18 knots

These are a modification of the "Habicht 1" class, but lengthened by 20 feet amidships. Built at Wolgast Peene Yard. All completed in 1955-56. All welded. Fitted for minelaying.

"Habicht II" Class *1969*

6 "HABICHT I" CLASS

213 **214** **215** **216** **R11** **R 21**

Displacement, tons	500 standard
Dimensions, feet	193·5 oa × 26·2 × 11·8
Guns	1—3·4 in; 8—25 mm AA; 2—20 mm AA
A/S weapons	4 DCT
Main Engines	Diesels; 2 shafts; 2 400 bhp = 17 knots

Modified German M 40 type minesweepers but with diesel propulsion. Prefabricated in five sections and assembled at Volkswerft, Stralsund. Laid down in 1952-53, launched in 1952-54 and completed in 1952-54. All welded. Fitted to carry 18 mines. MLR 6-33 sank early in 1958 but was salvaged and repaired in 1959 and serves as a rescue ship. Four ships are employed as patrol escort ships as well as minesweepers, the other two having been converted to rescue ships in 1961 and numbered R 11 and R 21. "Habicht" means Hawk.

"Habicht I" Class *1963, Erich Groner*

R 21 *1968, Werner Kähling*

MISSILE BOATS

12 USSR "OSA" CLASS

ALBERT GAST
ALBIN KÖBIS
FRITZ GAST
KARL MESEBERGER
MAX REICHPIETSCH
PAUL WIECZOREK
RICHARD SORGE
RUDOLF EGELHUFER

Displacement, tons	160 standard; 200 full load
Dimensions, feet	121·3 pp; 131·5 oa × 28 × 6·5 max
Guided weapons	4 large hooded missile launchers in 2 pairs abreast
Guns	4—25 mm (2 twin, 1 forward, 1 aft)
Main Engines	3 diesels; speed = 35 knots

A development of the hybrid fast patrol boat—motor torpedo boat—motor gunboat type. Reported to have been launched in 1964 onwards.

OSA Type 1965, *Reinecke*

PATROL VESSELS

12 USSR "SOI" TYPE

ADLER
BUSSARD
FALKE
HABICHT
KRANICH
MÖWE
REIHER
WEIHE

Displacement, tons	215 standard; 250 full load
Dimensions, feet	138 pp; 147·7 oa × 20 × 10 max
Guns	4—25 mm AA (2 twin mounts)
A/S weapons	4 ahead throwing launchers; 2 DCT
Main Engines	3 diesels; 3 500 bhp = 28 knots
Complement	30

Submarine chasers. Fitted with mine rails. Pennant numbers run in a 400 series.

No. 411 1964, *courtesy Herr Werner Kähling*

12 "HAI" CLASS

Displacement, tons	300 standard; 370 full load
Dimensions, feet	174 pp; 187 oa × 19 × 10
Main Engines	Diesels and gas turbines; speed 25 knots

Submarine chasers built at Peenewerft, Wolgast. The prototype completed construction in 1963. Four in service by the end of 1964. Pennant numbers are in the 400 series.

HAI III Type 1968, *Col Breyer*

TRAINING SHIPS

WILHELM PIECK

Displacement, tons	200
Main Engines	Diesel; 1 shaft; 106 bhp = 8 knots

Brigantine employed as a school ship. Built in 1951. Photo in 1955-56 edition. Also yachts, *Ernst Thälmann*, 150 tons, *Jonny Scheer*, 120 tons, *Max Riechpietsch* and *Knechtsand*.

DISPOSALS
The fishery protection vessels **Robert Koch**, **Professor Henking** (ex-*Neues Deutschland*) and **Dr Friedrich Wolf** were deleted from the list in 1968.
The tenders H 41 and H 43, the netlayer H 42, and the experimental vessels *Karl* **Liebknecht**, **Rosa Luxemburg** and **Saturn** were also stricken off in 1968.

TORPEDO BOATS

33 "ILTIS" CLASS

Displacement, tons	28 to 30
Length, feet	60
Tubes	2—21 in (torpedoes fired over stern)
Main engines	Designed for 30 knots

Newly constructed *Leiche Torpedoschnellboote* or light torpedo boats of the PT type. No anti-aircraft guns. Reported to be numbered in a 900 series.

No. 914 1968

27 Ex-USSR "P6" CLASS

Displacement, tons	75
Dimensions, feet	85·3 × 20 × 6 max
Guns	4—25 mm (2 twin mountings)
Tubes	2—21 in
Main Engines	4 diesels; 4 800 bhp = 43 knots max

Interchangeable torpedo/gunboats acquired in 1957-60 from the USSR. Wooden hull. Pennant numbers now run in an 800 series.

DISPOSALS
The motor torpedo boats of the "PA 3" Class were deleted from the list in 1968.

No 808 1968

P 6 Class 1960, *Erich Gröner*

No. 306 1965, *Werner Kähling*

1965, *Werner Kähling*

INSHORE MINESWEEPERS

24 "SCHWALBE II" CLASS

Displacement, tons 100 standard
Dimensions, feet 105 oa × 18 × 3·5 max
Main Engines 2 diesels; 380 bhp = 12·5 knots

Small minesweepers of medium speed built in 1955-57 at VEB Yachtwerft, Berlin. Pennant numbers now run in a 300 series. A number of units of this class are used as torpedo retrievers, buoy tenders and in the Coast Guard.

DISPOSALS
The minesweeping boats of the "Schwalbe" class were deleted from the list in 1968.

No. 34 1968

"SCHWALBE" Class

LANDING CRAFT

6 "ROBBE" CLASS

Displacement, tons 600 standard; 800 full load
Dimensions, feet 196·8 × 32·8 × 6·6
Guns 2—45 mm AA (1 twin); 4—25 mm AA (2 twin)
Main Engines Diesels = 12 knots

Amphibious vessels of a new type midway between the landing ship and landing craft categories. Reported to have been launched in 1963.

"ROBBE" Class *1965, Reinecke*

12 "LABO" CLASS

Displacement, tons 150 standard; 200 full load
Dimensions, feet 131·2 × 27·9 × 5·9
Guns 4—25 mm AA (2 twin)
Main engines Diesels = 10 knots

Landing craft of a new light type. Built by Peenewerft, Wolgast. Reported to have been launched in 1959-60 and 1961-63.

"LABO" Class *1969, S. Breyer*

COAST GUARD BOATS

2 "FORELLE" CLASS

Displacement, tons 55
Dimensions, feet 88·5 × 20 × 5·5
Guns 2—25 mm AA; 4—15 mm AA
Tubes 2—21 in
Main Engines 2 diesels; 5 000 bhp = 40 knots

First launched in 1956 at Schiffswerft, Rosslau. These boats now belong to the *Grenzbrigade Kuste* or Coast Guard. All the boats used by this force are called "gun-boats" and have the prefix "G" before the pennant numbers. The force comprises:—2 boats of the "Forelle" class, some 30 boats of the "Delphin"/"Tummler" group, about 20 boats of the "KS 1" class, and 7 boats of the "Schwalbe II" class.

30 "DELPHIN/TUMMLER" CLASS

Displacement, tons 50
Guns 2—25 mm AA or 4—15 mm AA. Also carry 4 DC
Main Engines Jumo diesels; 1 000 bhp = 25 knots

Küsten-und Reede Schutzboote (Coastal and harbour defence boats) of all metal construction. Twelve operational and remainder for training. A photograph of this KRS type appears in the 1963-64 to 1968-69 editions.

The coastal defence boats of the "Sperber" class were deleted from the list in 1968.

PIONIER 1969

PARTISAN **PIONIER**

Displacement, tons 79
Main engines Speed = 13 knots

Built in 1957. Coastal boats rated as *schulschiffe* or training vessels.

SURVEY VESSELS

JOHANN L. KRÜGER (1951) **HELMUT JUST** (1952)

Displacement, tons 475
Measurement, tons 260 gross
Dimensions, feet 128 × 24 × 11
Main engines Diesel; 400 bhp = 10·5 knots

Built at VEB Rosslauer Shipyard, Rosslau. River Elbe. Launch dates above.
Also *Alfred Merz* and *Karl F. Gauss* (1952-55), 200 tons, 9·5 knots (seiner type); *Jordan* and *Magnetologe* (1954), 135 tons 10 knots, (German KFK type); *Arkona*, *Darsser Ort* and *Stubbenkammer* (1956), 55 tons, 10 knots (cutter type); and *Flaggtief* (ex-*Stralsund*) and *Hydrograph* (1953) 30 tons, 8 knots.
Hydrograph is also reported as an electronic intelligence collection trawler based at Warnemuende and employed in the Baltic.
The surveying vessel *Meteor* was deleted from the list in 1968 as she is not on the Navy List, being civilian manned and administered. See particulars in the 1967-68 edition.

OILERS

HIDDENSEE **POEL** **RIEMS**

Displacement, tons	1 000 full load
Dimensions, feet	195 oa × 29·5 × 12·5 max
Main Engines	2 diesels; 2 800 bhp = 14 knots

Built at Peenewerft, Wolgast, in 1960-61. Crew 26. Speed in service 9 knots.

Three new oilers were built by Matthias-Thesen -W, Wismar, 585 tons, 9 knots.

RIEMS *1968*

TUGS

There are at least ten tugs of various types all with the prefix "A" before the pennant numbers.

GHANA

Administration

Commander, Navy: Commodore P. F. Quaye

Personnel

1969: 800 (90 officers, 710 ratings)

Mercantile Marine

Lloyd's Register of Shipping: 57 vessels of 120 486 gross tons

CORVETTES

2 "KROMANTSE" CLASS

KROMANTSE F 17 — **KETA** F 18

Displacement, tons	380 light; 440 standard; 500 full load
Dimensions, feet	162 wl; 177 oa × 28·5 × 13 (props)
Guns	1—4 in, 1—40 mm AA (see notes)
A/S weapons	1 Squid triple-barrelled depth charge mortar
Main engines	2 Bristol Siddeley Maybach diesels; 2 shafts; 390 rpm; 7 100 bhp = 20 knots (5 700 hp = 18 knots sea)
Oil fuel, tons	60
Radius, miles	2 000 at 16 knots
Complement	54 (6 + 3 officers, 45 ratings)

Anti-submarine vessels of a novel type designed by Vosper Ltd, Portsmouth, a joint venture with Vickers-Armstrongs, Ltd, one ship being built by each company. Comprehensively fitted with sonar, air and surface warning radar. Vosper roll damping fins, and air conditioning throughout excepting machinery spaces. Generators 360 kW. The electrical power supply is 440 volts, 60 cycles ac. The originally proposed twin 40 mm mounting was suppressed to save top weight. A very interesting patrol vessel design, an example of what can be achieved on a comparatively small platform to produce an inexpensive and quickly built anti-submarine vessel. *Kromantse* was launched by Vosper Ltd at the Camber Shipyard, Portsmouth, on 5 Sep 1963, and commissioned on 27 July 1964. *Keta* was launched at Newcastle on 18 Jan 1965 and commissioned on 18 May 1965.

RESCINDMENT. The order to Yarrow & Co Ltd, Scotstoun, Glasgow for the construction of a frigate (see full particulars and photograph of the model in the 1966-67 edition) was rescinded in 1966, but the ship was launched without ceremony or name on Clydeside on 29 Dec 1966 and completed in 1968 for sale.

KETA — *1966, Wright & Logan*

KROMANTSE — *1969, Ghana Navy, Official*

COASTAL MINESWEEPERS

1 "TON" CLASS

EJURA (ex-*Aldington*) M 16

Displacement, tons	360 standard; 425 full load
Dimensions, feet	140 pp; 153 oa × 28·8 × 8·2
Guns	1—40 mm AA forward; 2—20 mm AA aft
Main Engines	Deltic diesels; 2 shafts; 3 000 bhp = 15 knots max
Oil fuel (tons)	45
Complement	27

Former Royal Navy non-magnetic type vessel. Lent to Ghana by Britain in 1964.

EJURA — *1964, Ghana Navy, Official*

PATROL BOATS

4 USSR BUILT

P 20 — **P 21** — **P 22** — **P 23**

Displacement, tons	86 standard; 91 full load
Dimensions, feet	98 pp × 15 × 4·8
Guns, AA	2—14·5 mm (twin mounting)
Main engines	2 Model M50-3 diesels; 2 shafts; 1 600 rpm; 1 200 bhp = 18 knots
Oil fuel, tons	9·25
Radius, miles	460 at 17 knots
Complement	16 (2 officers, 14 ratings)

Built in the USSR. Completed in Aug 1963. Acquired in 1967.

P 23 — *1969, Ghana Navy, Official*

INSHORE MINESWEEPERS

AFADZATO (ex-*Ottringham*) M 12 — **YOGAGA** (ex-*Malham*) M 11

Displacement, tons	120 standard; 159 full load
Dimensions, feet	100 pp; 107·5 oa × 22 × 5·8
Guns	1—40 mm AA
Main Engines	2 Paxman diesels; 1 000 bhp = 14 knots
Oil fuel, tons	15
Complement	22

Malham, commissioned on 2 Oct 1959, and *Ottringham*, commissioned on 30 Oct 1959, sailed for Ghana on 31 Oct 1959, and were officially transferred from the Royal Navy to the Ghana Navy at Takoradi at the end of Nov 1959 and renamed after hills in Ghana. Now fitted with funnel.

A photograph of *Afadzato* appears in the 1964-65 and 1965-66 editions.

YOGAGA — *1966, Ghana Navy, Official*

SEAWARD DEFENCE BOATS

2 "FORD" CLASS

ELMINA P 13 — **KOMENDA** P 14

Displacement, tons	120 standard; 160 full load
Dimensions, feet	100 wl; 117·5 oa × 20·5 × 5
Guns	1—40 mm, 60 cal Bofors AA
A/S weapons	Depth charge throwers
Main engines	2 Davey Paxman diesels; 2 shafts; 1 000 bhp = 16·5 knots
Complement	19

Built for Ghana by Yarrow & Co Ltd, Scotstoun, Glasgow. Both laid down on 18 Oct 1961. *Komenda* was launched on 17 May 1962 and commissioned on 1 Nov 1962. *Elmina* was commissioned on 29 Nov 1962. Fitted with roll damping fins. It was officially stated in 1967 that the Foden diesel and centre shaft have been removed.

KOMENDA — *1969, Ghana Navy, Official*

ELMINA — *1966, Ghana Navy, Official*

TRAINING SHIP

ACHIMOTA (ex-*Kantamento*, ex-*Radiant*) A 15

Displacement, tons	600
Dimensions, feet	174 oa × 28 × 14
Main Engines	Diesels; 2 shafts; speed = 13 knots max
Oil fuel tons	60
Complement	35 (with additional accommodation for 30)

Built in 1927 by Camper & Nicholsons, Ltd, England for the Commodore of the Royal Yacht Squadron. Converted into an anti-submarine vessel during the Second World War. After hostilities sold to the Abingdon Steamship Co Ltd, for Mediterranean cruises. Later re-engined and modernised. The Ghana Government then purchased her for use as a State Yacht. In Feb 1963 she was transferred to the Ghana Navy and converted into Training Depot Ship. She also serves as Flagship.

ACHIMOTA *1968, Ghana Navy, Official*

MAINTENANCE REPAIR CRAFT

ASUANTSI (ex-*MRC* 1122)

Displacement, tons	657
Dimensions, feet	225 pp; 231·3 oa × 39 × 3·3 forward, 5 aft
Main engines	4 Paxman, 1 840 bhp = 9 knots cruising

Acquired from Britain in 1965 and arrived in Ghana waters in July 1965. Used as a base workshop at Tema Naval Base. Is kept operational, and does a fair amount of seatime in general training and exercise tasks.

ASUANTSI *1966, Ghana Navy, Official*

ROYAL HELLENIC NAVY

Administration

Commander-in-Chief, Royal Hellenic Navy:
Vice-Admiral K. Margaritis, R.H.N.

Diplomatic Representation

Naval Attaché in London:
Captain N. Stathakis. RHN

Naval Attaché in Washington:
Commodore D. Evgenidis, RHN

Strength of the Fleet

2 Submarines (Diesel Powered)
8 Destroyers
4 Frigates (Destroyer Escorts)
5 Escort Minesweepers (Corvettes)
7 Patrol Vessels
2 Minelayers
7 Patrol Vessels
14 Coastal Minesweepers
7 Fast Patrol Boats (Torpedo Boats)
14 Landing Ships (6 Medium)
43 Support Ships and Service Craft

Personnel

1969: 17 800 (1 620 officers and 16 180 ratings) (conscript, 18 months or enlistment)

Mercantile Marine

Lloyd's Register of Shipping:
1 634 vessels of 7 415 984 tons gross

Silhouettes

Scale: 150 feet = 1 inch

NAVARINON, THYELLA

ASPIS, LONCHI, SFENDONI, VELOS

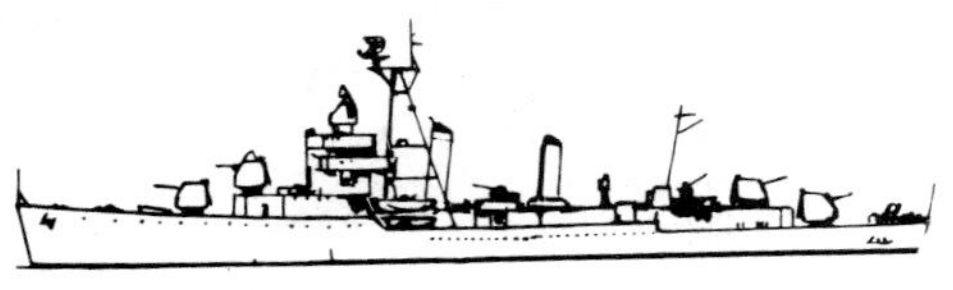
DOXA, NIKI

AETOS, IERAX, LEON, PANTHIR

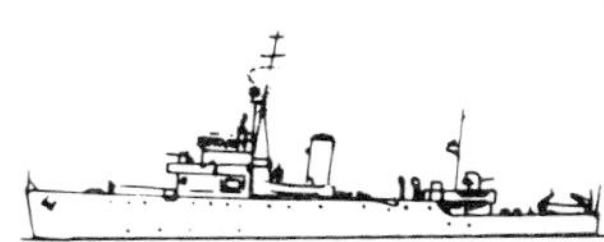
PIRPOLITIS

SUBMARINES

1 Ex-US "BALAO" CLASS

Name	No.	Builders	Launched	Completed
TRIAINA (ex-USS *Scabbardfish*, SS 397)	S 86	Portsmouth Navy Yard	27 Jan 1944	29 Apr 1944

Displacement, tons	1 526 standard; 1 816 surface; 2 425 submerged
Length, feet (*metres*)	311·5 (*94·9*) oa
Beam, feet (*metres*)	27 (*8·2*)
Draught, feet (*metres*)	17 (*5·2*)
Torpedo tubes	10—21 in (*533 mm*), 6 bow, 4 stern
Main engines	6 500 bhp diesels (surface) 4 610 hp electric motors (submerged)
Speed, knots	20 on surface, 10 submerged
Radius, miles	12 000 at 10 knots
Oil fuel (tons)	300
Complement	80

Transferred on 26 Feb 1965 at San Francisco (loaned by US in 1964 under MAP).

TRIAINA *1968, A. & J. Pavia*

Name	No.	Builder	Laid down	Launched	Completed
POSEIDON (ex-*Lapon*)	S 78 (ex -Y 16)	Electric Boat Div, Gen Dynamics Corp	21 Feb 1942	27 Oct 1942	23 Jan 1943

1 Ex-US "GATO" CLASS

Displacement, tons	1 525 standard; 1 816 surface; 2 425 submerged
Length, feet (*metres*)	311·7 (*95·0*)
Beam, feet (*metres*)	27 (*8·2*)
Draught, feet (*metres*)	17 (*5·2*)
Guns, dual purpose	1—5 in (*127 mm*) 25 cal.
Torpedo tubes	10—21 In (*533 mm*), 6 bow, 4 stern
Main engines	6 500 bhp GM 2-stroke diesels (surface); 2 750 hp electric motors (submerged)
Speed, knots	21 on surface; 10 submerged
Complement	85

Loaned from the United States in 1957 under the Military Aid Program. Has two engine rooms instead of one to reduce the size of the compartments. *Lapon* was transferred to the Royal Hellenic Navy on 8 Aug 1957.

PHOTOGRAPHS. A larger photograph of *Poseidon* appears in the 1964-65 and 1965-66 editions.

POSEIDON *1969, Royal Hellenic Navy, Official*

POSEIDON *1969, Royal Hellenic Navy, Official*

DISPOSAL

Sister submarine **Amfitriti** (ex-USS *Jack*, SS 259) was returned to US custody and expended as a target in Sep 1967.

DESTROYERS

Name	No.	Builder	Laid down	Launched	Completed
ASPIS (ex-USS *Conner, DD* 582)	D 06	Boston Navy Yard	16 Apr 1942	18 July 1942	8 June 1943
LONCHI (ex-USS *Hall, DD* 583)	D 56	Boston Navy Yard	16 Apr 1942	18 July 1942	6 July 1943
NAVARINON (ex-USS *Brown, DD* 546)	D 63	Bethlehem (S. Pedro)	27 June 1942	22 Feb 1943	10 July 1943
SFENDONI (ex-USS *Aulick, DD* 569)	D 85	Consolidated Steel Corp, Texas	14 May 1941	2 Mar 1942	27 Oct 1942
THYELLA (ex-USS *Bradford, DD* 545)	D 28	Bethlehem (S. Pedro)	28 Apr 1942	12 Dec 1942	12 June 1943
VELOS (ex-USS *Charette, DD* 581)	D 16	Boston Navy Yard	20 Feb 1941	3 June 1942	18 May 1943

6 Ex-US DD TYPE

"FLETCHER" CLASS

Displacement, tons	2 100 standard, 3 050 full load
Length, feet (*metres*)	376·5 (*114·6*) oa
Beam, feet (*metres*)	39·5 (*12·0*)
Draught, feet (*metres*)	12·2 (*3·7*) mean; 18 (*5·5*) max
Guns, dual purpose	5—5 in (*127 mm*) 38 cal. in D63 and D28; 4 only in remainder
Guns, AA	10—40 mm, 2 quadruple, 1 twin, in D63, D28; 6—3 in (*76 mm*) 3 twin, in remainder
A/S weapons	Hedgehogs; DC's
Torpedo tubes	None in D63 and D28; 5—21 in (*533 mm*), quintuple bank, in others
Torpedo racks	Side-launching for A/S torpedoes
Boilers	4 Babcock & Wilcox or Foster Wheeler; 615 psi (*43·3 km/cm²*) 800°F (*427°C*)
Main engines	2 sets GE geared turbines 60 000 shp; 2 shafts
Speed, knots	34 max
Radius, miles	6 000 at 15 knots; 1 285 at 32 knots
Oil fuel (tons)	506
Complement	300

Transferred from USA to Greece under the Mutual Defence Assistance Programme, *Aspis, Lanchi* and *Velos* at Long Beach, California, on 15 Sep 1959, 9 Feb 1960 and 15 June 1959, respectively, *Sfendoni* at Philadelphia on 21 Aug 1959, *Navarinon* and *Thyella* at Seattle, Washington, on 27 Sep 1962. *Aspis* means Shield.

PHOTOGRAPHS. A photograph of *Sfendoni* appears in the 1960-61 to 1965-66 editions, of *Thyella* in the 1963-64 to 1967-68 editions, and of *Aspis* in the 1967-68 editions.

DISPOSAL OF CRUISER
The light cruiser **Elli**, formerly the Italian *Eugenio di Savoia*, was officially deleted from the list in 1964.

VELOS — *1968, A. & J. Pavia*

LONCHI — *1968, A. & J. Pavia*

Name	No.	NATO No.	Builders	Laid down	Launched	Completed
DOXA (ex-USS *Ludlow, DD* 438)	20	D 220	Bath Iron Works Corpn	18 Dec 1939	11 Nov 1940	5 Mar 1941
NIKI (ex-USS *Eberle, DD* 430)	65	D 225	Bath Iron Works Corpn	12 Apr 1939	14 Sep 1940	4 Dec 1940

2 Ex-US DD TYPE

"GLEAVES" CLASS

Displacement, tons	1 630 standard; 2 572 full load
Length, feet (*metres*)	341 (*103·9*) wl; 348·2 (*106·1*) oa
Beam, feet (*metres*)	36·1 (*11·0*)
Draught, feet (*metres*)	18 (*5·5*) max
Guns, surface	4—5 in (*127 mm*), 38 cal.
Guns, AA	12—40 mm, 2 quadruple, 1 twin (see *Gunnery* notes)
A/S weapons	Hedgehogs; DC's
Torpedo tubes	Removed
Torpedo racks	Side-launching for A/S torpedoes
Boilers	4 Babcock & Wilcox; 580 psi (*40·8 kg cm²*); 850°F (*455°C*)
Main engines	2 sets GE geared turbines 50 000 shp; 2 shafts
Speed, knots	35 max
Radius, miles	5 000 at 15 knots; 1 564 at 30 knots
Oil fuel (tons)	440
Complement	250 (war); 188 peace

Taken over from the United States Navy on 18 Apr 1951. As modernised, now have tripod foremast. For former appearance, with pole foremast see photograph of *Niki* in the 1956-57 to 1964-65 editions. Names mean "Glory" and "Victory" respectively.

GUNNERY. The six 20 mm AA guns were removed in 1962.

TORPEDO TUBES. The 5—21 in torpedo tubes originally mounted in a quintuple bank were removed.

PHOTOGRAPHS. A port quarter oblique view of *Doxa* appears in the 1965-66 to 1968-69 editions.

NIKI — *1969, Royal Hellenic Navy, Official*

DOXA — *Official*

FRIGATES (Destroyer Escorts)

Name	No.	NATO No.	Builders	Laid down	Launched	Completed
AETOS (ex-USS *Slater*, DE 766)	01	D 212	Tampa SB Co	9 Mar 1943	13 Feb 1944	1 May 1944
IERAX (ex-USS *Elbert*, DE 768)	31	D 213	Tampa SB Co	1 Apr 1943	23 May 1944	12 July 1944
LEON (ex-USS *Eldridge*, DE 173)	54	D 217	Federal SB & DD Co	22 Feb 1943	25 June 1943	27 Aug 1943
PANTHIR (ex-USS *Garfield Thomas*, DE 193)	67	D 227	Federal SB & DD Co	23 Sep 1943	12 Dec 1943	24 Jan 1944

4 Ex-US DE TYPE "BOSTWICK" CLASS

Displacement, tons	1 240 standard; 1 900 full load
Length, feet (*metres*)	306 (*93·3*) oa
Beam, feet (*metres*)	36·7 (*11·2*)
Draught, feet (*metres*)	14 (*4·3*)
Guns, dual purpose	3—3 in (*76 mm*) 50 cal.
Guns, AA	6—40 *mm*, 3 twin; 14—20 *mm*, 7 twin
A/S weapons	Hedgehog; 8 DCT; 1 DC rack
Torpedo racks	Side launching for A/S torpedoes
Main engines	4 sets GM diesel-electric; 6 000 bhp; 2 shafts
Speed, knots	19·25 max
Radius, miles	11 500 at 11 knots; 6 920 at 17·5 knots
Oil fuel (tons)	316
Complement	220 (war)

Aetos and *Ierax* were transferred on 15 Mar 1951, *Leon* and *Panthir* on 15 Jan 1951. Their 3—21 inch torpedo tubes (triple mount) were removed. Meanings of names are Eagle, Falcon, Lion and Panther, respectively.

PHOTOGRAPHS. A photograph of *Leon* appears in the 1962-63 to 1965-66 editions, and of *Panthir* in the 1967-68 editions.

DISPOSALS OF "HUNT" CLASSES
Of the ex-British "Hunt" Type III frigates (escort destroyers). **Adrias** (ex-*Bordef*), was scrapped after a mine blew away her forecastle on 22 Oct 1943: **Kanaris** (ex-*Hatherleigh*) and **Pindos** (ex-*Bolebroke*) were returned to Great Britain on 12 Dec 1959 and sold for scrap in Greece, **Miaoulis** (ex-*Modbury*) was similarly disposed of in 1960; **Adrios** (ex-*Tanatside*) and **Astings** (ex-*Catterick*) were discarded in 1963 and sold by the British Admiralty.
The ex-British "Hunt" Type II frigates (escort destroyers). **Aegaion** (ex-*Lauderdale*); **Kriti** (ex-*Hursley*) and **Themistocles** (ex-*Bramham*) were returned to Great Britain on 12 Dec 1959 and sold for scrap in Greece.

IERAX — *1968, A. & J. Pavia*

AETOS — *1968, A. & J. Pavia*

MINESWEEPERS RATED AS CORVETTES

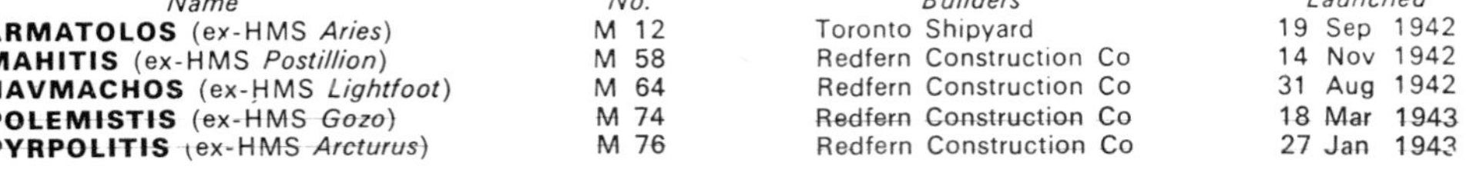

Name	No.	Builders	Launched
ARMATOLOS (ex-HMS *Aries*)	M 12	Toronto Shipyard	19 Sep 1942
MAHITIS (ex-HMS *Postillion*)	M 58	Redfern Construction Co	14 Nov 1942
NAVMACHOS (ex-HMS *Lightfoot*)	M 64	Redfern Construction Co	31 Aug 1942
POLEMISTIS (ex-HMS *Gozo*)	M 74	Redfern Construction Co	18 Mar 1943
PYRPOLITIS (ex-HMS *Arcturus*)	M 76	Redfern Construction Co	27 Jan 1943

5 Ex-BRITISH "ALGERINE" TYPE OCEAN MINESWEEPERS (OFFICIALLY CLASSED AS CORVETTES)

Displacement, tons	1 030 standard; 1 325 full load
Length, feet (*metres*)	225 (*68·6*) oa
Beam, feet (*metres*)	35·5 (*10·8*)
Draught, feet (*metres*)	11·5 (*3·5*) max
Guns, dual purpose	2—3 in (*76 mm*) US Mark 21 (1 in *Pirpolitis*, none in *Mahitis*)
Guns, AA	4—20 mm (US), 2MG
A/S weapons	2 to 4 DCT
Main engines	2 triple expansion; 2 shafts; 2 700 ihp = 16 knots max
Boilers	2 Yarrow, 250 psi (*17·6 kg cm²*)
Oil fuel, tons	235
Radius, miles	5 000 at 10 knots; 2 270 at 14·5 knots
Complement	85

Acquired from the Executive Committee of surplus Allied Material. Formerly employed as corvettes. The armament of *Mahitis* was removed when she became a training ship. *Armatolos*, *Mahitis* and *Navmachos* were used as auxiliaries. All act as personnel transports.

PYRPOLITIS — *1969, Royal Hellenic Navy, Official*

MINELAYERS

AKTION (ex-*LSM* 301) N 04 **AMVRAKIA** (ex-*LSM* 303) N 05

Displacement, tons	720 standard; 1 100 full load
Dimensions, feet	196·5 wl; 203·5 oa × 34·5 × 8·3 max
Guns	8—40 mm dp (4 twin); 6—20 mm AA (single)
Mines	Capacity 100 to 130
Main Engines	2 diesels; 2 shafts; 3 600 bhp = 12·5 knots
Radius, miles	3 000 at 12 knots
Complement	65

Former US Landing Ships Medium. Both built at Charleston Naval Shipyard. *Aktion* was launched on 1 Jan 1945 and *Amvrakia* on 14 Nov 1944. Converted in the USA into all purpose seagoing minelayers for the Royal Hellenic Navy under the Mutual Defence Assistance Programme. Underwent extensive rebuilding from the deck up. Twin rudders. The Greek flag was hoisted on 1 Dec 1953.
A photograph of *Aktion* appears in the 1965-66 to 1967-68 editions.

AMVRAKIA — *1968*

PATROL VESSELS

ANTIPLOIARKHOS LASKOS (ex-*PGM* 16, ex-*PC* 1148) P 53
ANTIPLOIARKHOS PEZOPOULOS (ex-*PGM* 21, ex-*PC* 1552) P 70
PLOIARKHOS MELETOPOULUS (ex-*PGM* 22, ex-*PC* 1553) P 57
PLOTARKHIS ARSLANOGLOU (ex-*PGM* 25, ex-*PC* 1556) P 14
PLOTARKHIS CHANTZIKONSTANDIS (ex-*PGM* 29, ex-*PC* 1565) P 96

Displacement, tons	335 standard; 439 full load
Dimensions, feet	170 wl; 174·7 oa × 23; (10·8 max)
Guns	1—3 in; 6—20 mm AA (see *Gunnery* notes)
A/S weapons	Hedgehog; side launching torpedo racks; depth charges
Main Engines	2 GM 2 str diesels; 2 shafts; 3 600 bhp = 19 knots

All launched in 1943-44. Presented from the US Navy in Aug 1947. The two 40 mm AA guns were removed and a hedgehog was installed in 1963.

Sister ship *Plotarkhis Blessas* (ex-*PGM* 28, ex-*PC* 1559) P 61, was sold in 1963.

PLOTARKHIS ARSLANOGLOU *1969, Royal Hellenic Navy, Official*

PLOTARKHIS MARIDAKIS (ex-USS *LSSL* 65) 14 Nov 1944 P 94
PLOTARKHIS VLACHAVAS (ex-USS *LSSL* 35) 17 Sep 1944 P 95

Displacement, tons	257 standard; 395 full load
Dimensions, feet	157 × 23·2 × 5·7
Guns	1—3 in; 4—40 mm AA (2 twins); 4—20 mm AA
Main Engines	Diesel; 2 shafts; 1 600 bhp = 14·4 knots

Built by Albina Engine & Machinery Works Inc, Portland, Oreg, and Commercial Iron Works, Portland, respectively. *Plotarkhis Vlachavas* was transferred from USA on 12 Aug 1957 and *Plotarkhis Maridakis* in June 1958.

PLOTARKHIS VLACHAVAS *1969, Royal Hellenic Navy, Official*

TORPEDO BOATS

ANDROMEDA P 21 **KASTOR** P 23 **KYKONOS** P 24 **PIGASSOS** P 25 **TOXOTIS** P 26

Displacement, tons	69 standard; 76 full load
Dimensions, feet	75 pp; 80·4 oa × 24·6 × 6·9
Torpedo tubes	4—21 In
Guns	2—40 mm AA
Main engines	2 Napier Deltic T 18-37 K diesels; 3 100 bhp = 43 knots
Complement	22

Andromeda was taken over in Feb 1967 from Mandal, Norway. *Kastor* and *Kykonos*, and the third pair, *Pigassos* and *Toxotis*, were delivered in succession within the year. *Iniohos* was officially deleted from the list in 1969.

INIOHOS *1967, Royal Hellenic Navy, Official*

ASTRAPI P 20 (ex-*Strahl* P 6194)

Displacement, tons	95 standard; 110 full load
Dimensions, feet	96 (full); 99 oa × 25 × 7 (props)
Torpedo chutes	4—21 in side launching
Guns	2—40 mm AA
Main engines	3 Bristol Siddeley Marine Proteus gas turbines; 3 shafts; 12 750 bhp = 55·5 knots

Built by Vosper Ltd, Portsmouth. Launched on 10 Jan 1962. Commissioned in the Federal German Navy on 21 Nov 1962. Transferred to the Royal Hellenic Navy in Apr 1967. Refitted by Vosper Ltd. in 1968. Of similar design to the "Brave" class fast patrol boats in the British Navy.

ASTRAPI *1969, Royal Hellenic Navy, Official*

AIOLOS P 19 (ex-*Pfeil* P 6193)

Displacement, tons	75 standard; 80 full load
Dimensions, feet	92 wl; 95 oa × 23·9 × 6·5
Torpedo chutes	4—21 in side launching
Guns	2—40 mm AA
Main engines	2 Bristol Siddeley Marine Proteus gas turbines; 2 shafts; 8 500 bhp = 50 knots

Built by Vosper Ltd, Portsmouth. Launched on 26 Oct 1961. Commissioned in the Federal German Navy on 27 June 1962. Transferred to the Royal Hellenic Navy in Apr 1967. Refitted by Vosper Ltd in 1968. Based on the design of *Ferocity*, the Vosper private venture prototype.

AIOLOS *1969, Royal Hellenic Navy, Official*

COASTAL MINESWEEPERS

AIDON (ex-*MSC* 310) M 248
AIGLI (ex-*MSC* 299) M 246
ARGO (ex-*MSC* 317) M 213
AVRA (ex-*MSC* 318) M 214
DAPHNI (ex-*MSC* 307) M 247
DORIS (ex-*MSC* 298) M 245
KICHLI (ex-*MSC* 308) M 241
KISSA (ex-*MSC* 309) M 242

Displacement, tons	320 light; 370 full load
Dimensions, feet	138 pp; 144 oa × 28 × 8·5
Guns	2—20 mm AA
Main Engines	2 General Motors diesels; 2 shafts; 880 bhp = 13 knots
Oil fuel (tons)	25
Radius, miles	2 500 at 10 knots
Complement	39

Built in the USA for Greece. The first six, *Aidon, Aigli, Daphni, Doris, Kichli* and *Kissa*, were completed and transferred in 1964-65, two more, *Argo* and *Avra*, in 1968. Built of wood and materials with the lowest magnetic attraction to obtain the greatest safety factor when sweeping magnetic mines. MSC 314 and MSC 319 are building in USA for transfer under MAP. A photograph of *Kichli*, M 241 appears in the 1966-67 edition.

DAPHNI *1967, A. & J. Pavia*

Coastal Minesweepers—*continued*

AFROESSA (ex-*BYMS* 2185) M 209
KALYMNOS (ex-*BYMS* 2033) M 201
KARTERIA (ex-*BYMS* 2065) M 203
KERKYRA (ex-*BYMS* 2172) M 208
PARALOS (ex-*BYMS* 2066) M 204
ZAKYNTHOS (ex-*BYMS* 2209) M 212

Displacement, tons	270 standard; 350 full load
Dimensions, feet	136 × 24·5 × 8
Guns	1—3 in; 2—20 mm AA; 4 MG; 2 DCT
Main Engines	Diesel; 1 000 bhp = 12 knots
Complement	33

Of wooden construction. All the names are conventional and are not mentioned in signals or correspondence. Known by numbers, *Karteria* was launched on 21 Dec 1942. *Ithaki* (ex-*BYMS* 2240), *Kefallinia* (ex-*BYMS* 2171), *Lefkas* (ex-*BYMS* 2086), *Patmos* (ex-*BYMS* 2229), *Salaminia* (ex-*BYMS* 2067), and *Simi* (ex-*BYMS* 2190) were deleted from the list in 1966 and *Leros* (ex-*BYMS* 2186) and *Paxi* (ex-*BYMS* 2056) in 1969. A photograph of *Paralos* appears in the 1955-56 to 1962-63 editions, and of *Leros* in the 1963-64 to 1965-66 editions.

TANK LANDING SHIPS

PINIOS L 171 (ex-*LST* 3506)

Displacement, tons	2 256 standard; 4 980 full load
Dimensions, feet	330 wl; 347 oa × 55 × 14·5 max
Guns	10—20 mm AA
Main Engines	Triple expansion; 2 shafts; 5 500 bhp = 13 knots
Oil fuel (tons)	1 950

Original LST (3) type landing ship. Launched in 1943. On loan from Great Britain. *Alfios* (ex-*LST* 3020), *Axios* (ex-*LST* 3007) and *Strymon* (ex-*LST* 3502) were returned to the Royal Navy, refitted at Malta and taken over by the Ministry of Transport. *Acheloos* and *Aliakmon* L 104 (ex-*LST* 3002) were officially deleted from the list in 1969.

IKARIA (ex-USS *Potter County, LST* 1086) L 154
LESBOS (ex-USS *Boone County, LST* 389) L 172
RODOS (ex-USS *Bowman County, LST* 391) L 157
SYROS (ex-USS *LST* 325) L 144

Displacement, tons	1 653 standard; 4 080 full load
Dimensions, feet	316 wl; 328 oa × 50 × 14 max
Guns	8—40 mm AA; 6—20 mm AA; (*Rodos:* 10—40 mm)
Main Engines	GM diesels; 2 shafts; 1 700 bhp = 11·6 knots
Complement	119 (accommodation for 266)

Former United States tank landing ships. *Ikaria, Lesbos* and *Rodos* were transferred to the Royal Hellenic Navy on 9 Aug 1960. *Syros* was transferred on 29 May 1964 at Portsmouth, Virginia, under MAP. Cargo capacity 2 100 tons.

SYROS *1969, Royal Hellenic Navy, Official*

CHIOS L 195 (ex-*LST* 35) **LIMNOS** L 158 (ex-*LST* 36) **SAMOS** L 179 (ex-*LST* 33)

Displacement, tons	1 625 standard; 4 080 full load
Dimensions, feet	316 wl; 328 oa × 50 × 14 max
Guns	1—3 in; 6—20 mm AA
Main Engines	Diesel; 2 shafts; 1 700 bhp = 11 knots
Oil fuel (tons)	595
Complement	119

All launched in 1943. Acquired from the US Navy in 1943, on Lend-lease terms. *Lesvos* (ex-*LST* 322) was returned to the British Government in 1953. A photograph of *Chios* appears in the 1952-53 to 1960-61 editions.

SAMOS *1969, Royal Hellenic Navy, Official*

MEDIUM LANDING SHIPS

IPOPLIARKHOS CRYSTALIDIS (ex-USS *LSM* 541) L 165
IPOPLIARKHOS DANIOLOS (ex-USS *LSM* 227) L 163
IPOPLIARKHOS GRIGOROPOULOS (ex-USS *LSM* 45) L 161
IPOPLIARKHOS MERLIN (ex-USS *LSM* 577) L 166
IPOPLIARKHOS ROUSSEN (ex-USS *LSM* 399) L 164
IPOPLIARKHOS TOURNAS (ex-USS *LSM* 102) L 162

Displacement, tons	743 beaching; 1 095 full load
Dimensions, feet	196·5 wl; 203·5 oa × 34·2 × 8·3
Guns	2—40 mm AA; 8—20 mm AA
Main Engines	Diesel direct drive; 2 shafts; 3 600 bhp = 13 knots

Former United States Medium Landing Ships. *LSM* 541 and *LSM* 557 were handed over to the Royal Hellenic Navy at Salamis on 30 Oct 1958. *LSM* 45, *LSM* 102, *LSM* 227 and *LSM* 399 were transferred to Greece at Portsmouth, Virginia on 3 Nov 1958. All were renamed after naval heroes killed during the Second World War.

IPOPLIARKHOS GRIGOROPOULOS *1967, Royal Hellenic Navy, Official*

DOCK LANDING SHIP

NAFKRATOUSSA (ex-*Hyperion*, ex-*LSD* 9)

Displacement, tons	4 790 standard; 9 375 full load
Dimensions, feet	454 wl; 457·8 oa × 72·2 × 18 max
Guns	1—3 in; 8—40 mm AA
Main Engines	Geared turbines; 2 shafts; 7 000 shp = 15 knots

Launched by Newport News Shipbuilding & Dry Dock Co on 21 May 1943. Taken over by Royal Hellenic Navy in 1953. Headquarters ship of Captain, Landing Forces.

NAFKRATOUSSA *1967, Royal Hellenic Navy, Official*

LANDING CRAFT

LCU 763 **LCU 766** **LCU 827** **LCU 852** **LCU 971** **LCU 1229** **LCU 1379** **LCU 1382**

Displacement, tons	143 standard; 309 full load
Dimensions, feet	105 wl; 119 oa × 32·7 × 5 max
Guns	2—20 mm AA
Main Engines	Diesel; 3 shafts; 440 bhp = 8 knots
Complement	13

Former US Utility Landing craft of the *LCU* (ex-*LST* (6)) type. *Sciathos* and *Scopelos* were acquired in 1959. *Kea, Kitnos* and *Sifnos* were transferred from USA in 1961, and three more in 1962. These LCUs are referred to by their hull numbers and not by name.

MINOR LANDING CRAFT. There are also **13 LCMs** and **34 LCVPs,** all transferred from the United States.

REPAIR SHIP

SAKIPIS (ex-*KNM Ellida*, ex-USS *ARB* 13, ex-USS *LST* 50) A 329

Displacement, tons	3 800 standard; 5 000 full load
Dimensions, feet	316 wl; 328 oa × 50 × 11 max
Guns	12—40 mm AA; 12—20 mm AA
Main Engines	GM diesels; 2 shafts; 1 800 bhp = 10 knots
Complement	200

Former US tank landing ship. Built by Dravo Corporation, Pittsburgh. Laid down on 29 Aug 1943, launched on 16 Oct 1943, completed on 27 Nov 1943. Converted to a battle damage repair ship in 1952 by Puget Sound Bridge & Dry Dock Co. Taken over by the Royal Norwegian Navy at Seattle on 14 Nov 1952 to serve as a battle damage repair ship for surface vessels. Returned to the US Navy on 1 July 1960. Transferred to Greece on 16 Sep 1960 at Bergen, Norway.

SAKIPIS *1969, Royal Hellenic Navy, Official*

MINESWEEPER DEPOT SHIP

HERMES (ex-*Product*, ex-*Port Jackson*) A 324

Displacement, tons	550 standard; 650 full load
Dimensions, feet	133 × 27·8 × 11
Main Engines	Diesel; 4-stroke; 560 bhp = 11 knots

Former British trawler. Launched on 1941. On loan from Great Britain.

HERMES *1969, Royal Hellenic Navy, Official*

BOOM DEFENCE VESSELS

THETIS (ex-USS *AN* 103) A 307

Displacement, tons	680 standard; 805 full load
Dimensions, feet	146 wl; 169·5 oa × 33·5 × 11·8 max
Guns	1—40 mm AA; 4—20 mm AA
Main engines	MAN diesels; 1 shaft; 1 400 bhp = 12 knots
Complement	48

Netlayer of the US type. Built by Kröger, Rendsburg, as a US offshore order. Launched in 1959. Taken over by the Royal Hellenic Navy on 9 Apr 1960.

THETIS *Royal Hellenic Navy, Official*

OCEAN SALVAGE VESSELS

SOTIR (ex-*Salventure*) A 384

Displacement, tons	1,440 standard; 1 700 full load
Measurement, tons	1 112 gross
Dimensions, feet	216 oa × 37·8 × 13 max
Main Engines	Triple expansion; 2 shafts; 1 500 ihp = 12 knots
Oil fuel (tons)	310
Complement	60

Former British Royal Fleet Auxiliary ocean salvage vessel of the "Salv" class. On loan from Great Britain. Equipped with a decompression chamber.

SOTIR *1969, Royal Hellenic Navy, Official*

LIGHTHOUSE TENDERS

ST LYKOUDIS (ex-*Chania*, ex-HMS *Nasturtium*) A 481

Displacement, tons	1 020 standard; 1,280 full load
Dimensions, feet	190 pp; 205 oa × 33 × 14·5
Main Engines	Triple expansion; 2 750 ihp = 14 knots
Boilers	2 SE
Oil fuel (tons)	230

Former corvette of the British "Flower" type. Launched in 1940. Sold to Greece as a merchant ship in 1948.

SKYROS A 485

Displacement, tons 350

SERRAI (ex-*Anna Raeder*) A 487

Displacement, tons 725

ST. LYKOUDIS *1969, Royal Hellenic Navy, Official*

WATER CARRIERS

ILIKI **KALIROE** **KASTORIA** **STYMPHALIA** **TRIHONIS** **VOLVI**

Capacity 120 tons, except *Trihonis* 300, *Volvi* 350, *Kastoria* 520 tons.

COASTAL SURVEY CRAFT

ARIADNE (ex-*BYMS* 2058) **VEGAS** (ex-*BYMS* 2078)

Former coastal minesweepers of the wooden hulled BYMS type, see sister craft on previous page. The survey craft *Alykoni* was discarded in 1961. Of seven sister craft used as coastal patrol vessels *Aura* (ex-*BYMS* 2054) was deleted from the list in 1962, *Andromeda* (ex-*BYMS* 2261), *Kleio* (ex-*BYMS* 2152) and *Thalia* (ex-*BYMS* 2252) in 1967, and *Lambadias* (ex-*BYMS* 2182), *Pigassos* (ex-*BYMS* 2221) and *Prokyon* (ex-*BYMS* 2076) in 1968.

ANEMOS

Officially added to the Royal Hellenic Navy List in 1969.

OILERS

ARETHOUSA (ex-USS *Natchaug*, AOG 54) A 377

Displacement, tons	1 850 light; 4 335 full load
Measurement, tons	2 575 deadweight; cargo capacity 2 040
Dimensions, feet	292 wl; 310·8 oa × 48·5 × 15·7 max
Guns	4—3 in dp; 50 cal
Main engines	GM diesels; 2 shafts; 3 300 bhp = 14 knots
Complement	43 (6 officiers, 37 men)

Former US petrol carrier. Built by Cargill Inc, Savage, Minn. Laid down on 15 Aug 1944. Launched on 6 Dec 1944. Transferred from the USA to Greece under the Mutual Defense Assistance Program at Pearl Harbour, Hawaii, in July 1959.

ARETHOUSA *1968, A. & J. Pavia*

ZEUS (ex-YOG 98) A 372

Dimensions, feet 165 × 35 × 10

Former US yard petrol carrier. Launched in 1944. Capacity 900 tons.

SIRIOS (ex-*Poseidon*, ex-*Empire Faun*) A 345

Formerly on loan from Great Britain, but purchased outright in 1962. This ship was renamed *Sirios* when the name *Poseidon* was given to the submarine *Lapon* acquired from the USA in 1958 (see earlier page). Capacity 850 tons.

VIVIIS A 471

Originally a water carrier but now employed as an oiler. Capacity 687 tons.

PROMETHEUS A 374

Small yard oil tanker. Launched in 1959. Capacity 520 tons.

KRONOS (ex-*Islay*, ex-*Dresden*) A 373

Displacement, tons 311

Capacity 110 tons. *Khalki* and *Xanthi* were officially stricken from the list in 1958.

ORION (ex-US tanker Y 126) A 376

Formerly small United States yard tanker. Capacity 700 tons.

ORION *1969, Royal Hellenic Navy, Official*

FLEET TUGS

ACCHILEUS (ex-*Confident*)
AEGEVS
AIAS
ANTAIOS (ex-*Busy*)
ATLAS (ex-*F* 5)
ATROMITOS A 410
CIGAS
MINOTAVROS (ex-*Theseus*, ex-*ST* 539)
PERSEUS (ex-*ST*772)
ROMALEOS
TITAN
SAMSON (ex-*F* 16)

Heraklis was officially deleted from the list in 1966, *Aegeus* in 1968, and *Kentravros* in 1969.

GABOON

Mercantile Marine

Lloyd's Register of Shipping: 2 vessels of 625 tons gross

PATROL BOAT

BOUET-WILLAUMEZ (ex-*VP* 775, ex-*VP* 25, ex-*HDML* 1021)

Displacement, tons	40 standard; 52 full load
Dimensions, feet	72 oa × 15·2 × 6
Guns	2—20 mm AA; 2 MG
Main Engines	2 diesels; 2 shafts; 300 bhp = 12 knots

Former French vedette de port, ex-British harbour defence motor launch, transferred from the French Navy to Gaboon in 1961. Named after the Admiral who signed the first Franco-Gabonese Treaty.

BOUET-WILLAUMEZ *1964, Gabonese Armed Forces, Official*

GUATEMALA

Mercantile Marine

Lloyd's Register of Shipping: 2 vessels of 3 629 tons gross

PATROL VESSEL

JOSÉ FRANCISCO BARRUNDIA (ex-*Snapphanen*)

Displacement, tons	310 standard; 370 full load
Dimensions, feet	170·8 × 19·8 × 9·2
Guns	2—3 in; 2—25 mm AA
Main Engines	De Laval geared turbines; 2 shafts; 3 600 shp = 23 knots
Boilers	2 Vancon-Normand
Oil fuel (tons)	50
Complement	40

Built by Karlskrona Dockyard. Launched on 2 Nov 1933. Former minesweeper in the Royal Swedish Navy until 1959 when she was transferred to the new Guatemalan Navy as the first warship. Now has lower mast (lattice), bridge and funnel (squat, thicker and streamlined) and shields on her 12-pounder guns. One of the 25 mm guns was moved aft. She is painted a very light grey, nearly white. In 1964 she was reported to be inoperative.

On 5th Jan 1959 Guatemala announced the establishment of a navy, with the primary duty of routing poaching fishing boats and smugglers. In addition to the patrol vessel above there are four small patrol craft (ex-US 40 ft coastguard cutters). A 63 ft aircraft rescue boat (AVR) was transferred from the US to Guatemala on 8 Oct 1964. Personnel: 85 officers and men.

JOSÉ FRANCISCO BARRUNDIA *1959, Official*

GUINEA

COAST GUARD

Mercantile Marine

Lloyd's Register of Shipping: 4 vessels of 11 854 tons gross

2 "P-6" class MTBs were delivered at Conakry July 1967 making a total of 6 to 8 of this class received since Aug 1967.

GUYANA

Mercantile Marine

Lloyd's Register of Shipping: 34 vessels of 10 003 tons gross

PATROL LAUNCHES

Dimensions, feet	44·5 × 11·5 × 6·3;
Guns	7·62 mm general purpose machine guns
Main engines	D 336A diesels

It was officially reported that four launches for this force were launched on 15 Feb 1968. They have steel hulls with aluminium superstructures.

HAITI

COAST GUARD PATROL VESSELS

DESSALINES (ex-USS *Tonawanda, AN* 89) GC 10

Displacement, tons	650 standard; 785 full load
Dimensions, feet	168·5 × 33 × 10·8
Main Engines	Busch-Sulzer diesel-electric; 1 500 shp = 12 knots

Former United States Navy netlayer of the "Cohoes" class. Built by Leatham D. Smith S.B. Co. Launched on 14 Nov 1944. Loaned to Haiti in 1960 for five years.

LA CRETE A PIERROT (ex-USCG 95315) GC 8 **VERTIERES** GC 9

Displacement, tons	100
Dimensions, feet	95 × 19 × 5
Guns	1—40 mm AA
Main Engines	4 diesels; 2 shafts; 2 200 bhp = 21 knots
Radius, miles	1 500
Complement	15

Former US Coast Guard steel cutters. Built at US Coast Guard Yard, Curtiss Bay, Maryland. *La Crete a Pierrot* was acquired on 26 Feb 1956. *Vertieres* was transferred to Haiti at Norfolk, Virginia, in Oct 1956 and commissioned in Dec 1956.

AMIRAL KILLICK (ex-USCG *Black Rock, WAGL* 367) GC 7

Displacement, tons	160
Dimensions, feet	Length 114

Former buoy tender purchased from the US Coast Guard in 1955, commissioned in Jan 1956. A photograph appears in the 1957-58 to 1963-64 editions.

16 AOUT 1946 (ex-*SC* 453) GC 2

Displacement, tons	110 standard; 138 full load
Dimensions, feet	110·5 × 18·8 × 6·5
Guns	2—40 mm; 2—20 mm
Main Engines	Diesels; 2 shafts; 1 000 bhp = 15 knots

Submarine chaser of the SC type acquired during 1947 from the US Navy. Launched in 1943. Laid up in reserve. *Amiral Killick*, GC 4, was discarded in 1954, *Toussaint L'Ouverture* (ex-SC 1064) was sold in 1959.

SAVANNAH GC 1

Displacement, tons	47
Dimensions, feet	83 × 16 × 4·2
Main Engines	Diesels; 2 shafts; 200 bhp = 9 knots
Complement	12

Ex-USCG cutter 56200, built in the USA in 1944 and acquired in 1944.

ARTIBONITE (ex-US *LCT*) GC 5

Displacement, tons	134 standard; 285 full load
Dimensions, feet	120·3 oa × 32 × 4·2
Main Engines	3 diesels; 675 bhp = 8 knots
Complement	12

Former US tank landing craft. Salvaged by Haitian Coast Guard after grounding and converted. Laid up in reserve having been damaged by grounding in Mar 1956. *Vertieres* GC 6 (ex-USS *APC* 92) was lost at sea.

SANS SOUCI (ex-*Captain James Taylor*)

Displacement, tons	161
Main Engines	Diesels; 2 shafts; 300 bhp = 10 knots

Employed, when required, as the Presidential Yacht.

HONDURAS

Coast Guard

A frigate was adapted for mercantile use. There are three small coastguard cutters.

Mercantile Marine

Lloyd's Register of Shipping: 45 vessels of 68 958 tons gross

HUNGARY

Mercantile Marine

Lloyd's Register of Shipping: 20 vessels of 28 438 tons gross

River Service

Until 1968 naval vessels listed included the river patrol vessel *Baya* (ex-*Barsch*), the depot ship *Csobanc*, the training ship *Badacsony*, ten patrol launches, ten river minesweepers, and two minesweeping launches (see full particulars of all these vessels in the 1968-69 and earlier editions); but in March 1969 it was officially stated by the Hungarian Embassy in London that there are no longer any fighting ships in Hungary since the small fleet has been dispersed.

ICELAND

Administration

Minister of Justice:
Mr. Johann Hafstein

Director, Coast Guard Service
Mr. Petur Sigurdsson

Deputy Director, Coast Guard Service:
Mr. Gunnar Bergsteinsson

The Coast Guard Service (Landhelgisgaezlan) deals with fishery protection, salvage, hydrographic research and surveying.

Strength of the Coast Guard

5 Patrol Vessels; Prefix: v/s; colour: dark grey.

Mercantile Marine

Lloyd's Register of Shipping:
295 vessels of 133 162 tons gross

COAST GUARD PATROL VESSELS

ÆGIR

Displacement, tons	1 150 (officially revised figure)
Dimensions, feet	204 × 33 × 13
Guns	1—57 mm
Main engines	2 diesels; 2 shafts; 8 000 bhp = 19 knots
Complement	22

The first new construction patrol vessel for the Icelandic Coast Guard Service for about eight years. Projected in Feb 1965. Built by Aalborg Vaerft, Denmark. Laid down in May 1967. Completed in 1968.

ÆGIR *1969, Icelandic Coast Guard Service, Official*

ODINN

Measurements, tons	1 000
Dimensions, feet	187 pp × 33 × 13
Guns	1—57 mm
Main Engines	2 diesels; 2 shafts; 5 000 bhp = 18 knots
Complement	22.

Designed as a coast guard vessel. Built at Aalborg Vaerft A/S, Denmark. Laid down in Jan 1959. Launched in Sep 1959. Completed in Jan 1960.

ODINN *1967, Icelandic Coast Guard Service, Official*

ALBERT

Measurement, tons	200 gross
Dimensions, feet	Length: 111·2
Guns	1—47 mm
Main engines	1 Nohab diesel; 650 bhp = 12·5 knots
Complement	15

Launched in 1956. Completed and commissioned for service in Apr 1957.

ALBERT *1967, Icelandic Coast Guard Service, Official*

THOR

Displacement, tons	920
Dimensions, feet	183·3 pp; 206 oa × 31·2 × 13
Guns	1—57 mm
Main engines	2 diesels; 3 200 bhp = 17 knots
Complement	22

Built at Aalborg, Denmark. Launched in 1951. Completed and commissioned in late 1951. Rated as coastal inspection and salvage vessel.

THOR *1969, Icelandic Coast Guard Service, Official*

ARVAKUR

Displacement, tons	716
Dimensions, feet	106 × 33 × 13
Guns	none at present
Main engines	1 diesel; 1 000 bhp = 12 knots
Complement	12

New in the Coast Guard Service. Built as a lighthouse tender in the Netherlands in 1962. Acquired for duty in 1969.

LOSS. The fishery protection patrol vessel and lighthouse tender *Hermodur* foundered off the south-west coast of Iceland on 17 Feb 1959.

DISPOSALS

Gautur (ex-*Odinn*) was officially deleted from the Coast Guard List on 1 Jan 1963, **Tyr** in 1964, and **Sæbjorg** in Aug 1965. The old **Aegir** (built in 1929) was broken up in 1968, and the small **Maria Julia** was sold in 1969.

ARVAKUR *1969, Icelandic Coast Guard Service, Official*

INDIA

Administration

Chief of the Naval Staff:
Admiral Adhar Kumar Chatterjee

Flag Officer C in C, West Coast:
Vice-Admiral Sardarilal Mathrades Nanda

Flag Officer Commanding Western Fleet:
Rear-Admiral Vasudeva Anant Kamath

Flag Officer C in C, East Coast:
Rear-Admiral Kesavapillai Ramakrishnan Nair

Strength of the Fleet

1 Aircraft Carrier
4 Submarines (Diesel Powered)
2 Cruisers
3 Destroyers
14 Frigates
2 Escorts
4 Survey Ships (3 ex-Frigates)
1 Ocean Minesweeper
4 Coastal Minesweepers
2 Inshore Minesweepers
15 Patrol Craft (Seaward Defence)
14 Support Ships and Service Craft

Diplomatic Representation

Naval Adviser in London:
Commodore Khushru Kaikobad Sanjana

Naval Attaché in Washington:
Brigadier F. Mehta

Personnel

1969 20 000 (1 800 officers, 18 200 ratings)

Naval Bases

Calcutta, Cochin and Madras

Naval Establishments

Bombay, Goa, Jamnagar, Lonavla, Vizagapatam. The latter being developed as the I.N. Submarine base.

Mercantile Marine

Lloyd's Register of Shipping:
383 vessels of 1 945 037 tons gross

Silhouettes

Scale: 150 feet = 1 inch

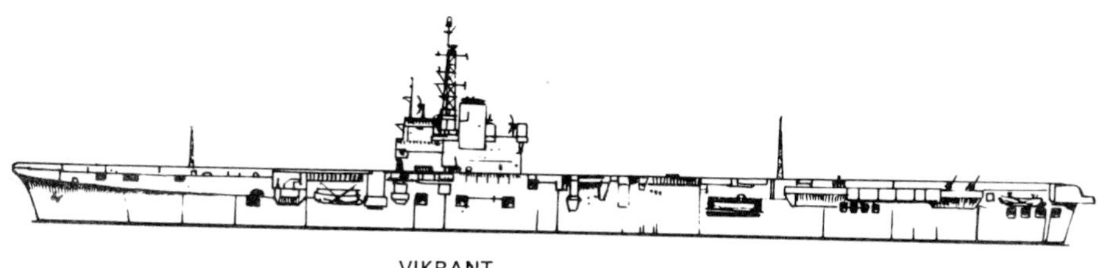
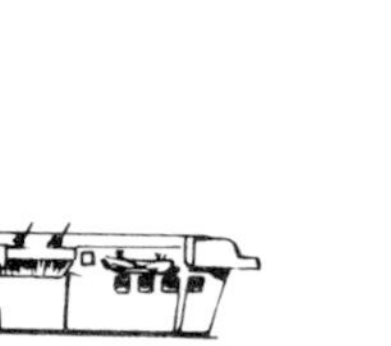

VIKRANT

DARSHAK

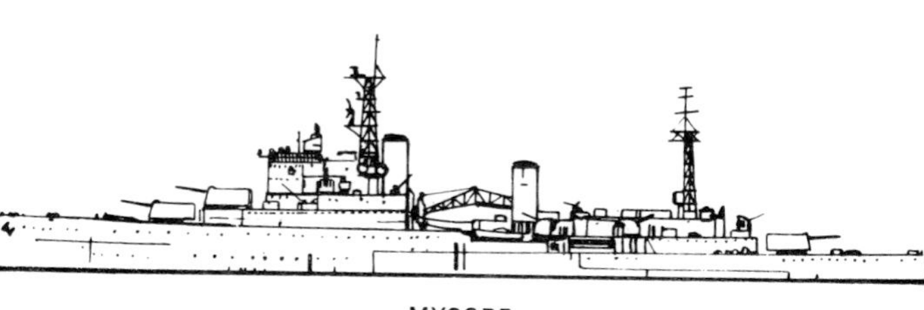

MYSORE

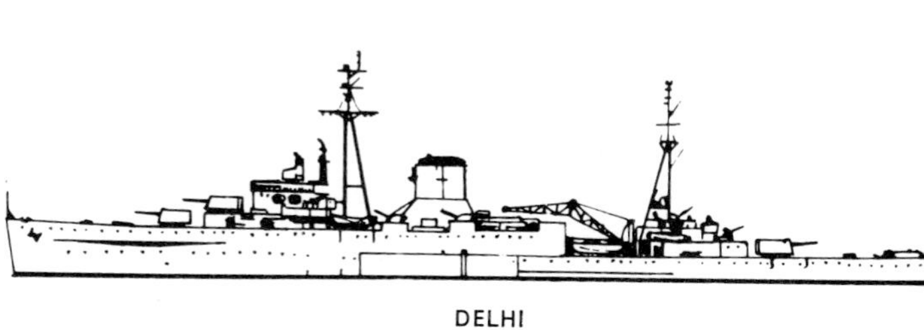

DELHI

RANA, RAJPUT, RANJIT

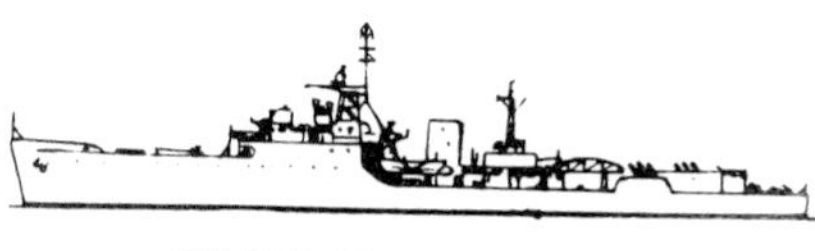

KHUKRI, KIRPAN, KUTHAR

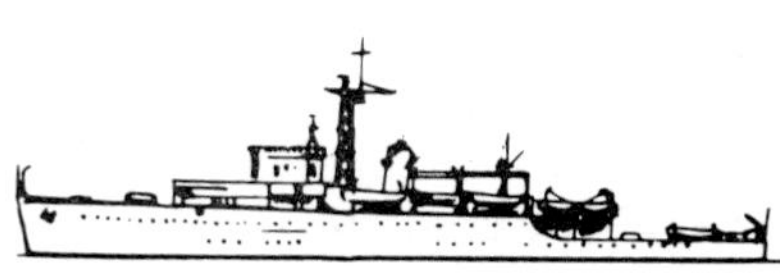

JUMNA, SUTLEJ

TALWAR, TRISHUL

GANGA, GODAVARI, GOMATI

TIR

BEAS, BETWA, BRAHMAPUTRA

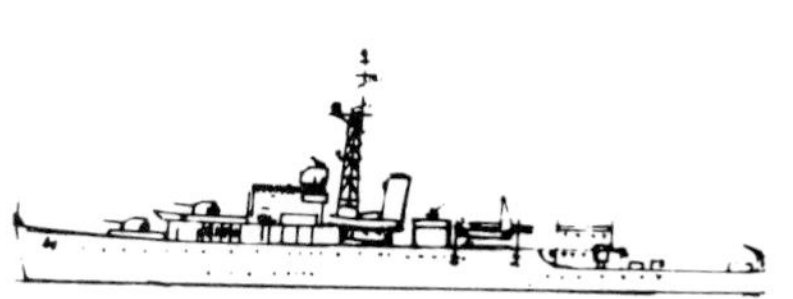

KAVERI, KISTNA

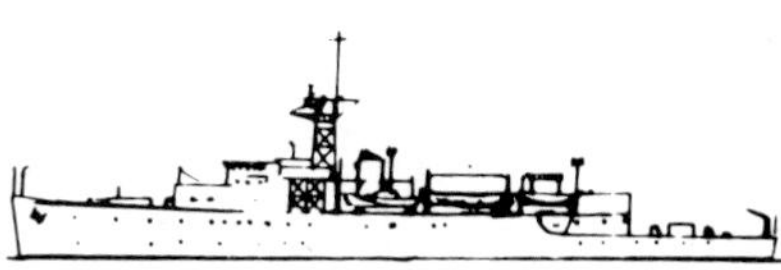

INVESTIGATOR

AIRCRAFT CARRIER

Name	No.	Builders	Engineers	Laid down	Launched	Completed
VIKRANT (ex-HMS *Hercules*)	R 11	Vickers-Armstrong Ltd, Tyne	Parsons Marine Steam Turbine Co	14 Oct 1943	22 Sep 1945	4 Mar 1961

1 Ex-BRITISH "MAJESTIC" CLASS

Displacement, tons	16 000 standard; 19 500 full load
Length, feet (*metres*)	630 (*192·0*) pp; 700 (*213·4*) oa
Beam, feet (*metres*)	80 (*24·4*) hull
Width, feet (*metres*)	128 (*39·0*)
Draught, feet (*metres*)	24 (*7·3*)
Aircraft	21 capacity
Guns, AA	15—40 mm; 4 twin, 7 single
Boilers	4 Admiralty 3-drum; 400 psi; 700°F
Main engines	Parsons single reduction geared turbines; 40 000 shp; 2 shafts
Speed, knots	24·5 designed
Complement	1 343, designed accommodation

Acquired from Great Britain in Jan 1957 after having been suspended in May 1946 when structurally almost complete and 75% fitted out. Taken in hand by Harland & Wolff Ltd, Belfast, in Apr. 1957 for completion in 1961 when she was commissioned on 4 Mar and renamed *Vikrant*.

HABITABILITY. Partially air-conditioned and insulated for tropical service, the ship's sides being sprayed with asbestos cement instead of being lagged. Separate messes and dining halls.

ENGINEERING. Engines and boilers are arranged *en echelon*, one set of turbines and two boilers being installed side by side in each of the two propelling machinery spaces, on the unit system, so that the starboard propeller shaft is longer than the port.

FLIGHT DECK. The aircraft, including 10 Seahawk strike, 2 Alouette, and 4 Breguet Alize anti-submarine aircraft, operate from an angled deck, with steam catapult, landing sights and two electrically operated lifts.

VIKRANT — *courtesy Godfrey H. Walker, Esq*

CLASS. Originally a sister ship of *Leviathan* (structurally almost finished and 80 per cent fitted out but never wholly completed) and *Magnificent* (which served in the Royal Canadian Navy 1946-57) of the Royal Navy; *Sydney* (ex-*Terrible*) and *Melbourne* (ex-*Majestic*) in the Royal Australian Navy; and *Bonaventure* (ex-*Powerful*) in the Royal Canadian Navy.

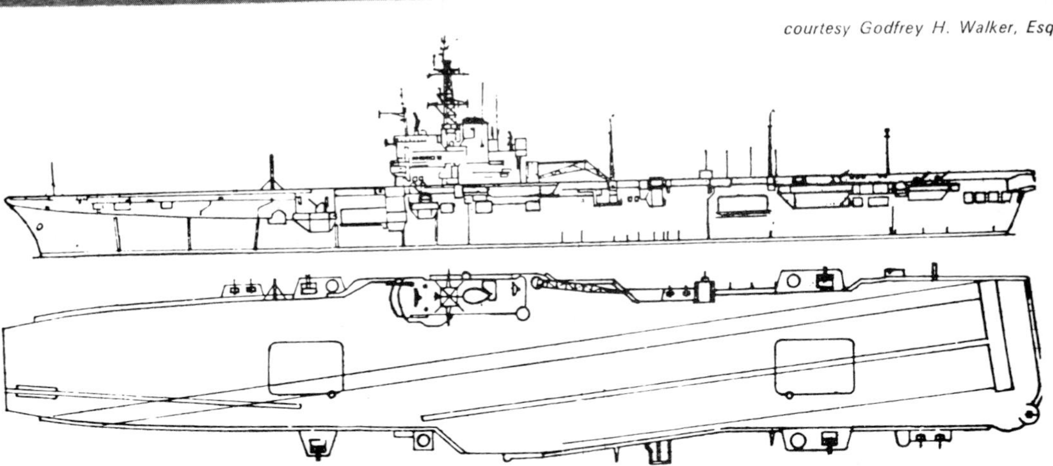

DRAWING. Port elevation and plan. Drawn in 1962. Scale: 128 feet = 1 inch.

VIKRANT — *Added 1966, courtesy Godfrey H. Walker, Esq*

SUBMARINES

Ex-SOVIET "F" CLASS

KALVARI **KANDHERI** **KHADERI**

Displacement, tons	2 000 surface; 2 300 submerged
Dimensions, feet	300 × 27 × 19
Tubes	8—21 in (20 torpedoes carried)
Main engines	Diesel 3 shaft 10 000 bhp = 20 knots surface Electric motors 4 000 hp = 15 knots submerged

Kalvasi arrived in India in July 1968 and *Kandheri* and *Khaderi* in 1969.

KHADERI — *1969, courtesy Dr. Louis Th. Bergé*

CRUISERS

Name	*No.*	*Builders*	*Engineers*	*Laid down*	*Launched*	*Completed*
MYSORE (ex- HMS *Nigeria*)	C 60	Vickers-Armstrongs, Ltd, Tyne	Parsons	8 Feb 1938	18 July 1939	23 Sep 1940

Displacement, tons	8 700 standard; 11 040 full load
Length, feet (*metres*)	538 (*164·0*) pp; 549 (*167·3*) wl 555·5 (*169·3*) oa
Beam, feet (*metres*)	62 (*18·9*)
Draught, feet (*metres*)	21 (*6·4*) max
Guns, surface	9—6 in (*152 mm*)
Guns, AA	8—4 in (*102 mm*) 12—40 mm; 5 twin and 2 single
Armour	Side 4½ in—3 in (*114—76 mm*); Deck 2 in (*51 mm*); Conning tower 4 in (*102 mm*); Turrets 2 in (*51 mm*)
Boilers	4 Admiralty 3-drum
Main engines	Parsons geared turbines 72 500 shp; 4 shafts
Speed, knots	31·5
Complement	800

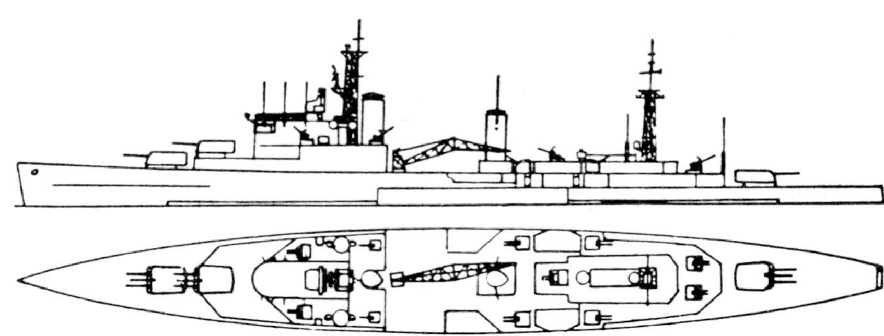

Formerly a "Colony" class cruiser in the Royal Navy. Purchased from Great Britain (announced 8 Apr 1954) for £300 000. Underwent extensive refit and reconstruction by Cammell Laird & Co Ltd, Birkenhead, before commissioning. Formerly handed over to the Indian Navy at Birkenhead and renamed *Mysore* on 29 Aug 1957.

RECONSTRUCTION. Ship formerly had tripod masts. During reconstruction the triple 6 inch turret in "X" position and the 6—21 inch torpedo tubes (tripled) were removed, the bridge was modified, two lattice masts were stepped, all electrical equipment was replaced and the engine room and other parts of the ship were refitted.

DRAWING. Port elevation and plan. Scale 128 feet = 1 inch.

PHOTOGRAPHS. A port bow surface view of *Mysore* appears in the 1957-58 to 1960-61 editions, and an oblique aerial view in the 1961-62 to 1965-66 editions.

MYSORE

1966, Indian Navy, Official

Name	*No.*	*Builders*	*Laid down*	*Launched*	*Completed*
DELHI (ex HMS *Achilles*)	C 74	Cammell Laird & Co Ltd, Birkenhead	11 June 1931	1 Sep 1932	5 Oct 1933

Displacement, tons	7 114 standard; 9 740 full load
Length, feet (*metres*)	522 pp; 544·5 oa
Beam, feet (*metres*)	55·2
Draught, feet (*metres*)	20 max
Guns, surface	6—6 in (*152 mm*)
Guns, AA	8—4 in (*102 mm*); 14—40 mm
Guns, saluting	4—3 pdr
Armour	4 in-2 in side, 1 in gunhouses, 1 in bridge, 2 in deck
Main engines	Parsons geared turbines; 4 shafts 72 000 shp = 32 knots
Boilers	4 Admiralty 3-drum type
Oil fuel, tons	1 800
Complement	800

Formerly a "Leander" class light cruiser in the Royal Navy. Purchased from Great Britain and delivered on 5 July 1948. Refitted in 1955.

TORPEDO TUBES. In 1958 the original eight 21 inch torpedo tubes, in two quadruple banks, were removed, their emplacement, their replacement suppressed, and the forecastle deck plating was consequently extended aft to the twin 40 mm AA guns abreast the boat stowage.

HISTORICAL. As HMS *Achilles*, then lent to the Royal New Zealand Navy, this ship, with HMS *Ajax* and HMS *Exeter*, defeated the German battleship *Admiral Graf Spee* in the Battle of the River Plate on 17 Dec 1939.

DELHI

Added 1966, A. & J. Pavia

DESTROYERS

Name	No.	Builders	Bebun	Launched	Completed	Transferred
RANA (ex-HMS *Raider*)	D 115	Cammell Laird & Co Ltd, Birkenhead	16 Apr 1941	1 Apr 1942	16 Nov 1942	10 Sep 1949
RAIPUT (ex-HMS *Rotherham*)	D 209	John Brown & Co Ltd, Clydebank	10 Apr 1941	21 Mar 1942	27 Aug 1942	29 July 1949
RANJIT (ex-HMS *Redoubt*)	D 141	John Brown & Co Ltd, Clydebank	19 June 1941	2 May 1942	1 Oct 1942	4 July 1949

Displacement, tons	1 725 standard; 2 424 full load
Dimensions, feet	339·5 wl; 362 oa × 35·7 × 16 max
Guns, surface	4—4·7 in (*120 mm*)
Guns, AA	4—40 mm
A/S weapons	4 DCT
Torpedo tubes	8—21 inch (2 quadruple) still mounted in *Rana*
Main engines	Parsons geared turbines; 2 shafts 40 000 shp = 32 knots
Boilers	2 Admiralty 3-drum type
Oil fuel (tons)	490
Radius, miles	2 500 at 20 knots
Complement	240

These, the first British destroyers with officers' accommodation forward instead of aft, were refitted and modernised prior to transfer. All three arrived in Indian waters in Jan 1950. They constitute the 11th Destroyer Squadron of which *Rajput* is Leader.

TORPEDO TUBES. These ships formerly mounted eight 21-inch torpedo tubes in two quadruple banks.

PHOTOGRAPHS. Photographs of *Rana* appear in the 1953-54 to 1957-58 editions. A photograph of *Ranjit* appears in the 1966-67 edition.

RAJPUT *Added 1967*

ESCORT DESTROYERS (Frigates)

Name	No.	Builders	Laid down	Launched	Completed
GANGA (ex-HMS *Chiddingfold*)	D 94	Scott's Shipbuilding & Engineering Co Ltd, Greenock	1 Mar 1940	10 Mar 1941	16 Oct 1941
GODAVARI (ex-HMS *Bedale*, ex-*Slazak*, ex-*Bedale*)	D 92	R. & W. Hawthorn, Leslie & Co Ltd, Hebburn	29 May 1940	5 Sep 1941	18 June 1944
GOMATI (ex-HMS *Lamerton*)	D 93	Swan, Hunter & Wigham Richardson Ltd, Wallsend	10 Apr 1949	14 Dec 1940	16 Aug 1944

3 "HUNT" CLASS. TYPE II

Displacement, tons	1 050 standard; 1 610 full load
Length, feet (*metres*)	264·2 (*80·5*) pp 280 (*85·3*) oa
Beam, feet (*metres*)	31·5 (*9·6*)
Draught, feet (*metres*)	14 (*4·3*)
Guns, dual purpose	6—4 in (*102 mm*)
Guns, AA	4—20 mm
Boilers	2 Admiralty 3-drum
Main engines	Parsons geared turbines 19 000 shp; 2 shafts
Speed, knots	25
Radius, miles	3 700 at 14 knots
Oil fuel (tons)	280
Complement	150

Former "Hunt" class, Type II frigates F 131, F 126 and F 88, respectively, (ex-Escort Destroyers). Transferred from Great Britain in Apr/May 1953. Lent to the Indian Navy for three years, subject to extension by agreement. Officially rated as destroyers with D pennant Nos. and constitute the 22nd Destroyer Squadron. *Godavari* is the Leader.

GOMATI *Added 1966, A. & J. Pavia*

A photograph of *Godavari* appears in the 1953-54 to 1955-56 editions, and of *Ganga* in the 1954-55 to 1959-60 editions.

GENERAL PURPOSE FRIGATES

3 NEW CONSTRUCTION "LEANDER" CLASS

NILGIRI

Displacement, tons	2 450 standard; 2 800 full load
Dimensions, feet (*metres*)	360 (*109·7*) wl; 372 (*113·4*) oa × 43 (*13·1*) × 18 (*5·5*)
Aircraft	1 Wasp helicopter
Missiles, AA	"Seacat" quadruple launcher
Guns, dual purpose	2—4·5 in (*115 mm*) twin
A/S	1 Limbo 3 barrelled DC mortar
Boilers	2
Main engines	2 d.r. geared turbines
Speed, knots	30
Oil fuel, tons	460

First major warships built in Indian yards. Similar design to later (broad beam) "Leander" class of Royal Navy. All ordered from Mazagon Docks Ltd, Bombay. *Nilgiri* was laid down in Oct 1966 and launched on 23 Oct 1968.

ANTI-AIRCRAFT FRIGATES

Name	No.	Builders	Launched	Completed
BEAS	F 137	Vickers-Armstrongs Ltd, Newcastle-on-Tyne	9 Oct 1958	24 May 1960
BETWA	F 139	Vickers-Armstrongs Ltd, Newcastle-on-tyne	15 Sep 1959	8 Dec 1960
BRAHMAPUTRA (ex-*Panther*)	F 31	John Brown & Co Ltd, Clydebank	15 Mar 1957	28 Mar 1958

3 "LEOPARD" CLASS

Displacement, tons	2 251 standard; 2 515 full load
Dimensions, feet	320 pp; 330 wl; 339·8 oa × 40 × 12·7 max
Guns, surface	4—4·5 in (*114 mm*), 2 twin turrets
Guns, AA	4—40 mm
A/S weapons	1 Squid 3-barrelled DC mortar
Main engines	Admiralty standard range diesels 2 shafts; 12 380 bhp = 25 knots
Oil fuel (tons)	230
Complement	210

Brahmaputra (Leader) originally, ordered as *Panther* for the Royal Navy on 28 *June* 1951, was the first major warship to be built in Great Britain for the Indian Navy since India became independent. All three ships are generally similar to the British frigates of the "Leapard" class, but modified to suit Indian conditions.

BEAS *Added 1966, Official*

PHOTOGRAPHS. A larger port near broadside view of *Brahmaputra* appears in the 1958-59 to 1960-61 editions, and a starboard bow view of *Betwa* in the 1961-62 to 1965-66 editions.

ANTI-SUBMARINE FRIGATES

2 "WHITBY" CLASS. 1st RATE

Name	No.	Builders	Launched	Completed
TALWAR	F 140	Cammell Laird & Co Ltd, Bitkenhead	18 July 1958	1960
TRISHUL (*Leader*)	F 143	Harland & Wolff Ltd, Belfast	18 June 1959	1960

Displacement, tons	2 144 standard; *Talwar* 2 545 full load; *Trishul* 2 557 full load
Length, feet (*metres*)	360 (*109·7*) pp; 369·8) (*112·7*) oa
Beam, feet (*metres*)	41 (*12·5*)
Draught, feet (*metres*)	17·8 (*5·4*)
Guns, surface	2—4·5 in (*115 mm*)
Guns, AA	4—40 mm; twin before Limbos, singles abaft funnel
A/S	2 Limbo 3-barrel DC mortars
Boilers	2 Babcock & Wilcox
Main engines	2 sets geared turbines 30 000 shp; 2 shafts
Speed, knots	30
Oil fuel (tons)	400
Complement	231 (11 officers, 220 men)

TALWAR — *Added 1966, Official*

Built in Great Britain and generally similar to the British frigates of the "Whitby" class, but modified to suit Indian conditions. Talwar is a common type of weapon in India.

TORPEDO TUBES. Provision was made in the original design for twelve 21 inch (eight single A/S and two twin) but they were not fitted.

PHOTOGRAPHS. A larger photograph of *Trishul* appears in the 1960-61 edition, and a port quarter oblique aerial view of *Talwar* in the 1961-62 to 1965-66 editions.

3 "BLACKWOOD" CLASS 2nd RATE

Name	No.	Builders	Launched	Completed
KHUKRI	F 149	J. Samuel White & Co Ltd, Cowes, Isle of Wight	20 Nov 1956	16 July 1958
KIRPAN	F 144	Alex Stephen & Sons Ltd, Govan, Glasgow	19 Aug 1958	July 1959
KUTHAR	F 146	J. Samuel White & Co Ltd, Cowes, Isle of Wight	14 Oct 1958	1959

Displacement, tons	1 180 standard; 1 456 full load
Length, feet (*metres*)	300 (*91·4*) pp; 310 (*94·5*) oa
Beam, feet (*metres*)	33 (*10·0*)
Draught, feet (*metres*)	15·5 (*4·7*)
Guns, AA	3—40 mm
A/S	2 Limbo 3-barrel DC mortars
Boilers	Babcock & Wilcox
Main engines	1 set geared turbines 15 000 shp; 1 shaft
Speed, knots	27·8 max; 24·5 sustained sea speed
Oil fuel (tons)	300
Complement	150

KUTHAR — *Added 1966, Wright & Logan*

Built in Great Britain, and generally similar to the British frigates of the "Blackwood" class; but slightly modified to suit Indian requirements. Kirpan means Sword.

TORPEDO TUBES. Provision was made for four 21-inch (2 twin) but they were not fitted.

PHOTOGRAPHS of *Khukri* appear in the 1958-59 to 1965-66 editions.

FRIGATES (ex-Sloops)

2 "KISTNA" CLASS

Name	No.	Builders	Laid down	Launched	Completed
KAVERI	F 110	Yarrow & Co, Ltd, Scotstoun, Glasgow	28 Oct 1942	15 June 1943	21 Oct 1943
KISTNA	F 46	Yarrow & Co, Ltd, Scotstoun, Glasgow	14 July 1942	22 Apr 1943	23 Aug 1943

Displacement, tons	1 470 standard; 1 925 full load
Length, feet (*metres*)	283 (*86·3*) pp; 295·5 (*90·1*) wl 299·5 (*91·3*) oa
Beam, feet (*metres*)	38·5 (*11·7*)
Draught, feet (*metres*)	11·2 (*3·4*)
Guns, surface	4—4 in (*102 mm*)
Guns, AA	4—40 mm
A/S weapons	2 DCT
Boilers	2 three-drum type
Main engines	Parsons geared turbines 4 300 shp; 2 shafts
Speed, knots	19
Radius, miles	4 500 at 12 knots
Oil fuel (tons)	370
Complement	210

Former sloops of the British "Black Swan" type built for India and modified to suit Indian conditions. *Cauvery* was renamed *Kaveri* in 1968 (in accordance with the policy of Indianisation of names). A photograph of *Kaveri* appears in the 1955-56 to 1959-60 editions.

KISTNA — *1962, Edward Rodwell*

TRAINING FRIGATE

1 "RIVER" CLASS

Name	No.	Builders	Laid down	Launched	Completed
TIR (ex-HMS *Bann*)	F 256	Charles Hill & Sons Ltd, Bristol	18 June 1942	29 Dec 1942	7 May 1943

Displacement, tons	1 463 standard; 1 934 full load
Length, feet (*metres*)	283 (*86·3*) pp; 303 (*92·4*) oa
Beam, feet (*metres*)	36·7 (*11·2*)
Draught, feet (*metres*)	14·5 (*4·4*)
Guns, surface	1—4 in (*102 mm*)
Guns, AA	1—40 mm; 2—20 mm
Boilers	2 Admiralty 3-drum
Main engines	Triple expansion 5 500 ihp; 2 shafts
Speed, knots	18
Radius, miles	3 100 at 12 knots
Oil fuel (tons)	385
Complement	120

Former "River" class frigate in the Royal Navy. Converted to a Midshipman's Training Frigate by Bombay Dockyard in 1948. Originally the sister ship of *Investigator*, see under Survey Ships.

TIR — ***1964, Indian Navy, Official***

2 Ex-SOVIET "PETYA" CLASS

KADMATH **KAMORTA**

Displacement, tons	1 050 standard; 1 200 full load
Length, feet (*metres*)	250 (*76·2*) wl; 262·5 (*80*) oa
Beam, feet (*metres*)	32 (*9·8*)
Draught, feet (*metres*)	9·8 (*3·0*)
Guns, dual purpose	4—3 in (*76 mm*) 2 twin
Torpedo tubes	5—21 in (*533 mm*)
Main engines	2 diesels, 4 000 hp 2 gas turbines, 10 000 hp 2 shafts
Speed, knots	30

Transferred to Indian Navy, early 1969. Reported that four other units may be acquired.

SURVEY SHIPS

1 INDIAN BUILT

Name	*Builders*	*Launched*	*Commissioned*
DARSHAK	Hindustan Shipyard, Vizagapatam	2 Nov 1959	28 Dec 1964

Displacement, tons	2 790
Length, feet (*metres*)	319 (*97·2*) oa
Beam, feet (*metres*)	49 (*14·9*)
Draught, feet (*metres*)	28·8 (*8·8*)
Aircraft	1 Helicopter
Main engines	2 diesel-electric units, 3 000 bhp
Speed, knots	16
Complement	150

This ship marked a new stage in Indian shipbuilding. She was the first ship to be built by the Hindustan Shipyard for the Navy. The ship is operated by the Navy's hydrographic branch and is undertaking a marine survey of the Indian coastline and harbours. She was fitted with the latest surveying and navigational equipment, and equipped with several surveying boats and motor launches. Provision was also to operate a helicopter. The ship is all welded.

DARSHAK *1967, Official*

1 "RIVER" CLASS (Ex-FRIGATE)

Name	*No.*	*Builders*	*Laid down*	*Launched*	*Completed*
INVESTIGATOR (ex-*Khukri*, ex-HMS *Trent*)	F 243	Charles Hill & Sons Ltd, Bristol	31 Jan 1942	10 Oct 1942	15 Feb 1943

Displacement, tons	1 460 standard; 1 930 full load
Length, feet (*metres*)	283 (*86·3*) pp; 303 (*92·4*) oa
Beam, feet (*metres*)	36·7 (*11·2*)
Draught, feet (*metres*)	14 (*4·3*)
Boilers	2 Admiralty 3-drum
Main engines	Triple expansion 5 500 shp; 2 shafts
Speed, knots	18 max
Radius, miles	5 000 at 10 knots
Oil fuel, (tons)	400
Complement	120

Former "River" class frigate in the Royal Navy. Converted to a survey ship and renamed *Investigator* in 1951. Originally the sister ship of the training frigate *Tir*, see previous page.

INVESTIGATOR *1965, Indian Navy, Official*

2 "SUTLEJ" CLASS

(Ex-FRIGATES Ex-SLOOPS)

Name	*No.*	*Builders*	*Laid down*	*Launched*	*Completed*
JUMNA	F 11	Wm. Denny & Bros Ltd, Dumbarton	20 Feb 1940	16 Nov 1940	13 May 1941
SUTLEJ	F 95	Wm Denny & Bros Ltd, Dumbarton	4 Jan 1940	1 Oct 1940	23 Apr 1941

Displacement, tons	1 300 standard; 1 750 full load
Length, feet (*metres*)	276 (*84·1*) wl; 292·5 (*89·2*) oa
Beam, feet (*metres*)	37·5 (*11·4*)
Draught, feet (*metres*)	11·5 (*3·5*)
Boilers	2 Admiralty 3-drum
Main engines	Parsons geared turbines 3 600 shp; 2 shafts
Speed, knots	18
Radius, miles	5 600 at 12 knots
Oil fuel (tons)	370
Complement	150

Former frigates employed as survey ships since 1957 and 1955 respectively. Both ships are generally similar to the former British frigates of the "Egret" class. *Jumna* and *Sutlej* together with *Kaveri* and *Kistna* (see previous page) formerly constituted the 12th Frigate Squadron.

JUMNA *A. & J. Pavia*

SUTLEJ *Official*

DISPOSAL

Afonso de Albuquerque, former Portuguese frigate disabled and taken in the Goa conquest in Dec 1961, was sold for scrap late 1966.

Bengal was deleted from the Navy List in 1967 (see full particulars and photographs of these ships in the 1959-60 edition, and of **Konkan** on the next page).

OCEAN MINESWEEPER

1 "BANGOR" CLASS

KONKAN (ex-HMS *Tilbury*) M 228

Displacement, tons	656 standard; 825 full load
Dimensions, feet	171·5 pp; 180 oa × 28·5 × 9·5
Guns	1—2 pdr; 4 MG
Main Engines	Triple expansion; 2 shafts; 2 000 ihp = 16·5 knots
Boilers	2 Admiralty 3-drum
Complement	87

Built by Lobnitz & Co Ltd, Renfrew. Laid down on 15 Aug 1941. Launched on 18 Feb 1942. Completed on 12 June 1942. Scheduled for decommissioning for the last several years, but still in the Navy List in Spring 1967 as operational.
Three ocean minesweepers of the "Bathurst" class, *Bengal*, *Bombay* and *Madras*, all reciprocating type, built in Sydney, Australia, and three of the "Bangor" class, *Rohilkhand*, turbine type, *Konkan* and *Rajputana*, all built in Scotland, constituted the 31st Minesweeping Squadron.
Rajputana and *Rohilkhand* were disposed of in 1960 and *Bombay* and *Madras* in 1962. *Bengal* was still in the 1966 navy list, in reserve.

KONKAN *Official*

INSHORE MINESWEEPERS

2 "HAM" CLASS

BASSEIN (ex-*Littleham*) M 2707 **BIMLIPTAN** (ex-*Hildersham*) M 2705

Displacement, tons	120 standard; 170 full load
Dimensions, feet	98 pp; 107 oa × 22 × 6·7
Guns	1—20 mm AA
Main Engines	2 Paxman diesels; 550 bhp = 14 knots (9 knots sweeping)
Oil fuel (tons)	15
Complement	16

"Ham" class inshore minesweepers of wooden construction built for the Royal Navy but transferred from Great Britain to the Indian Navy in 1955. *Bassein* was built by Brooke Marine Ltd, Oulton Broad, Lowestoft, and launched on 4 May 1954; *Bimlipitan* was built by Vosper Ltd, Portsmouth, and launched on 5 Feb 1954.

Barq (ex-*MMS* 132), *MMS* 130 and *MMS* 154, former British motor minesweepers of the "105 ft" type, of wooden construction, transferred from Great Britain, are employed as yard craft. *MMS* 1632 and *MMS* 1654 are yard craft in Bombay.

BIMLIPITAN *Added 1966, A. & J. Pavia*

BASSEIN *Indian Navy, Official*

COASTAL MINESWEEPERS

4 "TON" CLASS

CANNANORE (ex-*Whitton*) M 1191 **KAKINADA** (ex-*Durweston*) M 1201
CUDDALORE (ex-*Wennington*) M 1190 **KARWAR** (ex-*Overton*) Leader M 1197

Displacement, tons	360 standard; 425 full load
Dimensions, feet	140 pp; 153 oa × 28·8 × 8·2
Guns	1—40 mm AA, 2—20 mm AA
Main Engines	Napier Deltic diesels; 2 shafts; 1 250 bhp = 15 knots
Oil fuel (tons)	45
Complement	40

"Ton" class coastal minesweepers of wooden construction built for the Royal Navy, but transferred from Great Britain to the Indian Navy in 1956. *Cannanore* was built by Fleetlands Shipyard, Ltd, Gosport and launched 30 Jan 1956; *Karwar* was built by Camper & Nicholson ,Ltd, Gosport, and launched 30 Jan 1956. *Cuddalore*, built by J. S. Doig Ltd, Grimsby, and *Kakinada*, built by Dorset Yacht Co Ltd, Hamworthy were taken over in Aug 1956, and sailed for India in Nov/Dec 1956. Named after minor ports in India. Constitute the 18th MCM Squadron, together with the inshore minesweepers. Four more are to be acquired. Coastal minesweepers will first be built at the dockyards acquired by the Indian Navy in Bombay and Calcutta.

A photograph of *Cannanore* appears in the 1957-58 to 1963-64 editions and of *Karwar* in the 1964-65 to 1966-67 editions.

CUDDALORE *Added 1965, J. W. Kennedy*

KAKINADA *Added 1967*

PATROL CRAFT

6 SOVIET "POLUCHAT 1" CLASS

Displacement, tons	*circa* 100
Dimensions, feet	97 × 20 × 6

Six were ordered from USSR five of which were reportedly delivered in 1967.

4 HDML TYPE

SPC 3110 (ex-*HDML* 1110) **SPC 3117** (ex-*HDML* 1117)
SPC 3112 (ex-*HDML* 1112) **SPC 3118** (ex-*HDML* 1118)

Displacement, tons	48 standard; 54 full load
Dimensions, feet	72 oa × 16 × 4·7
Guns	2—20 mm AA
Main Engines	Diesel; 2 shafts; 320 bhp = 12 knots
Complement	14

Former British Harbour Defence Motor Launches. These boats, formerly known as Seaward Defence Motor Launches, constitute the 321st Sea/Land Patrol Craft Squadron.

The seaward patrol craft *SPC* 6420 (ex-*ML* 6420, ex-*ML* 420) of the Fairmile "B" motor launch type, was stricken from the Navy list in 1963.

SPC 3112 *Indian Navy, Official*

SEAWARD DEFENCE BOATS

3 "AJAY" CLASS

ABHAY **AJAY** **AKSHAY**

Displacement, tons	120 standard; 151 full load (*Ajay* 146)
Dimensions, feet	110 pp; 117·2 oa × 20 × 5
Guns	1—40 mm AA
Main Engines	2 diesels; speed = 18 knots

Generally similar to the "Ford" class in the Royal Navy. *Ajay* was built by Garden Reach Workshop, Calcutta and commissioned on 21 Sep 1960. *Abhay* and *Akshay* were both built by Hoogly Docking and Engineering Company Ltd, Calcutta and commissioned on 13 Nov 1961 and 8 Jan 1962, respectively.

AJAY *1964, Indian Navy, Official*

2 "SHARADA" CLASS

SHARADA SDB 3133 **SUKANYA** SDB 3132

Displacement, tons	86
Dimensions, feet	103·2, length
Guns	Small arms
Main Engines	Diesels

Built in Yugoslavia. Commissioned on 5 Dec 1959 and 12 Dec 1959, respectively.

SHARADA *1964, Indian Navy, Official*

4 "SAVITRI" CLASS

SAVITRI SDB 3123 **SHARYU** SDB 3129 **SUBHADRA** SBD 3130 **SUVARNA** SDB 3131

Displacement, tons	63
Dimensions, feet	85·3 pp; 90·2 oa × 20 × 5
Guns	Small Arms
Main Engines	2 diesels; 2 shafts; 1 900 bhp = 21 knots

Built in Italy. Commissioned on 6 Feb 1958, 28 Oct 1957, 20 Aug 1957 and 28 Aug 1957, respectively. Constitute the 322nd SDB Squadron. *Sharyu* is Leader.

SAVITRI *1964, Indian Navy, Official*

REPAIR SHIP

DHARINI (ex-*Hermine*)

Displacement, tons	4 625
Dimensions, feet	328 × 46 × 19
Main Engines	Triple expansion
Oil fuel (tons)	621

Cargo ship converted to a tender. Officially rated as a repair and store ship. Commissioned in May 1960. Pennant number A 306.

DHARINI *1964, Indian Navy, Official*

MOTOR TORPEDO BOATS

6 SOVIET TYPE

MTB 1 **MTB 2** **MTB 3** **MTB 4** **MTB 5** **MTB 6**

Six motor torpedo boats are reported to be scheduled for transfer from the USSR to India in the near future.

LANDING SHIP

MAGAR (ex-HMS *Avenger*, LST (3) 3011)

Displacement, tons	2 256 light; 4 980 full load
Dimensions, feet	347·5 oa × 55·2 × 11·2
Guns	2—40 mm AA; 6—20 mm AA; (2 twin, 2 single)
Main Engines	Triple expansion; 2 shafts; 5 500 ihp = 13 knots
Complement	180

Former British tank landing ship of the LST (3) type transferred in 1949.

MAGAR *Added 1964, A. & J. Pavia*

LANDING CRAFT

2 SOVIET "POLOCNY" CLASS

LSMR 1 **LSMR 2**

Displacement, tons	900 to 1 000
Dimensions, feet	246 × 39·3 × 9·8
Armament	Rocket projector
Main Engines	Diesels; 4 000 bhp = 15 knots

Two landing crafts, a new type of amphibious vessel basically similar to the US medium landing ships, rocket (LSMR) are reported to have been received from the USSR in 1966.

POLNOCNY class *1967, col. Breyer*

LCT 4294 (Ex-LCT 1294)

Displacement, tons	200
Dimensions, feet	187·2 × 38·8 × 3·5
Main Engines	Speed 9·5 knots

3 000 added to original numbers. LCT 4117, 4298, 4315, 4358 and 4360 were discarded in 1957, and LCT 4310 in 1961. LCT 4294 is employed as a yard craft.

SUBMARINE TENDER

AMBAA 14

One submarine tender is scheduled to be received from the USSR.

OILERS

SHAKTI

Displacement, tons	3 500
Dimensions, feet	323 × 44 × 20
Main Engines	Diesel; speed: 13 knots max; 9 knots economical

Rated as Fleet Replenishment Group Tanker. Acquired from Italy in Nov 1953. Pennant Number A 136.

CHILKA **SAMBHAR**

Displacement, tons	1 530 (oil capacity 1 000)
Dimensions, feet	202 × 30·7 × 13
Main Engines	Triple expansion; 809 ihp = 9 knots

Chilka built by Blythwood Shipbuilding Co, Scotstoun. *Sambhar* by A. & J. Inglis, Ltd, Glasgow, launched 1942. Both acquired in 1948. Engined by David Rowan & Co. Two steam dynamos, two steam pumps, ballast pump. Rated as yard craft.

DEEPAK A 1750
On charter to Indian Navy from Mogul Lines. Fleet replenishment tanker. Fitted with a helicopter landing platform aft, but no hangar.

TUG

HATHI

Displacement, tons	668
Dimensions, feet	147·5 × 23·7 × 15
Main Engines	Triple expansion; speed = 13 knots

Built by the Taikoo Dock & Engineering Company, Hong Kong. Launched in 1932.

INDONESIA

Administration

Commander-in-Chief of the Navy/Chief of the Naval Staff:
Admiral R. Muljadi

Deputy Commander-in-Chief of the Navy/C in C of the Marine Commando Corps:
Lieutenant-General Hartono (Marine Commando Corps)

Deputy Chief of the Naval Staff (Operations):
Rear Admiral R. Subono

Inspector General of the Navy:
Rear Admiral R. Sudomo

Commander-in-Chief Indonesian Fleet:
Rear Admiral L. M. Abdul Kadir

Strength of the Fleet

12	Diesel Powered Submarines
1	Cruiser
7	Destroyers
11	Frigates
1	Corvette (Ocean Minesweeper)
12	Patrol Vessels
31	Motor Torpedo Boats
6	Fleet Minesweepers
15	Coastal Minesweepers
23	Patrol Boats
18	Motor Gunboats
25	Seaward Defence Craft
6	Landing Ships
7	Landing Craft
70	Support Ships and Service Craft

Diplomatic Representation

Naval Attaché in London:
Colonel Atomodjo Brotodarmodjo

Naval and Air Attaché in Washington:
Brigadier General Imam Soetomo

Personnel

Navy: 25 000; Total: 40 000 (including Fleet Air Arm); and 14 000 Marine Commando Corps

Mercantile Marine

Lloyd's Register of Shipping
479 vessels of 711 500 tons gross

SUBMARINES

12 Ex-USSR "W" CLASS

ALUGORO 512 **NANGGALA** 402 **TJAKRA** 401

Displacement, tons	1 030 surface; 1 180 submerged
Length, feet (*metres*)	240 (*73·1*) oa
Beam, feet (*metres*)	22 (*6·7*)
Draught, feet (*metres*)	15 (*4·6*) max
Guns, AA	2—2·4 in (*57 mm*); 2—25 mm
Torpedo tubes	6—21 in (*533 mm*) 4 forward, 2 aft; 14 torpedoes carried
Mines	40, or 20 additional torpedoes
Main engines	4 000 bhp diesels; 2 500 hp electric motors, diesel-electric drive; 2 shafts
Speed, knots	17 on surface; 15 submerged
Radius, miles	13 000 to 16 500
Complement	60

TJAKRA *Indonesian Navy, Official*

Former Soviet submarines of the medium sized, long range "W" class. *Nanggala* and *Tjakra* were purchased from Poland and transferred to the Indonesian Navy in Aug 1959. *Nanggala* was overhauled at Surabaja in 1960. The four Soviet Submarines of the "W" class, which arrived in Indonesia on 28 June 1962, brought the total number of this class transferred to Indonesia by the USSR to 14 units, but it was reported that only six would be maintained operational, while six would be kept in reserve and two used for spare parts.

CRUISER

1 Ex-USSR "SVERDLOV" CLASS

IRIAN (ex-*Ordzhonikidze*) 201

Displacement, tons	15 450 standard; 19 200 full load
Length, feet (*metres*)	650 (*198·0*) pp; 689 (*210·0*) oa
Beam, feet (*metres*)	70 (*21·3*)
Draught, feet (*metres*)	16 (*4·9*) mean; 24·5 (*7·5*) max
Guns, surface	12—6 in (*152 mm*), 4 triple; 12—3·9 in (*100 mm*), 6 twin
Guns, AA	32—37 mm, 16 twin mounts
Torpedo tubes	10—21 in (*533 mm*), 2 quintuple
Mines	140 to 250 capacity
Armour	Belt 4 in to 1½ in (*100* to *38 mm*); CT 6 in (*150 mm*); turrets 5 in (*125 mm*); deck 3 in to 1 in (*75* to *25 mm*)
Boilers	6
Main engines	Geared steam turbines; 130 000 shp; 2 shafts
Speed, knots	34·5
Radius, miles	5 000 at 20 knots
Oil fuel (tons)	4 000
Complement	1050

Irian was transferred from the USSR to Indonesia where she arrived in Oct 1962. A second Soviet cruiser was to have been acquired by the end of 1963, according to the Indonesian (then) Deputy Chief of Naval Staff. She was being modified to suit Indonesian requirements and conditions in the equatorial climate, and her armament was to be different from that of her sister ship. But in fact only one "Sverdlov" class cruiser has been transferred from the USSR to Indonesia by 1969.

IRIAN *Added 1963, Wright & Logan*

DESTROYERS

7 Ex-USSR "SKORI" CLASS

BRAWIDJAJA
DIPONEGORO
ISKANDARMUDA
SANDJAJA 203
SAWUNGGALING 204
SILIWANGI 201
SINGAMANGARADJA 202

Displacement, tons	2 600 standard; 3 500 full load
Length, feet (*metres*)	393·8 (*120·0*) pp; 420 (*128·0*) oa
Beam, feet (*metres*)	41 (*12·5*)
Draught, feet (*metres*)	13·1 (*4·0*)
Guns, surface	4—5·1 in (*130 mm*), 2 twin
Guns, AA	2—3 in (*76 mm*); 7—37 mm; certain ships have 8—37 mm in twin mounts
A/S	4 DCT
Torpedo tubes	10—21 in (*533 mm*)
Mines	80
Boilers	3
Main engines	Geared turbines 70 000 shp; 2 shafts
Speed, knots	38
Radius, miles	4 000 at 15 knots
Complement	250

DIPONEGORO *1968, Indonesian Navy, Official*

Former Soviet destroyers of the "Skori" type. Built in 1951-56. Four (201, 202, 203, 204) were purchased from Poland and transferred to the Indonesian Navy in 1959. Pennant No. of *Singamangaradja* (which means Gannet) was reported in 1963 as 302. *Sawunggaling* was originally named *Sarwadjala*. *Iskandandarmuda* was transferred in 1962 and *Brawidjaja* and *Diponegoro* in 1964.

PHOTOGRAPHS. A starboard broadside surface view of *Siliwangi* appears in the 1963-64 to 1967-68 editions.

SANDJAJA *Indonesian Navy, Officia!*

FRIGATES

7 Ex-USSR "RIGA" CLASS

405 **406**

Displacement, tons	1 200 standard; 1 600 full load
Length, feet (*metres*)	278·8 (*85·0*) pp; 295 (*90·0*) oa
Beam, feet (*metres*)	34·5 (*10·5*)
Draught, feet (*metres*)	9·5 (*2·9*)
Guns, dual purpose	3—3·9 in (*100 mm*) single mounts
Guns, AA	4—37 mm
A/S	4 DC projectors
Torpedo tubes	3—21 in (*533 mm*)
Mines	Fitted with mine rails
Boilers	2
Main engines	Geared steam turbines 25 000 shp; 2 shafts
Speed, knots	28

Two "Riga" class frigates, pennant Nos. 405 and 406, were transferred from the USSR to Indonesia with the cruiser *Irian* in Sep. 1962. Two more were transferred the following year and three more a year later.

RIGA Class *Sergei Romanov*

2 "SURAPATI" CLASS

Name	*No.*	*Builders*	*Laid down*	*Launched*	*Completed*
IMAN BONDJOL	250	Ansaldo, Leghorn	8 Jan 1956	5 May 1956	19 May 1958
SURAPATI	251	Ansaldo, Leghorn	Jan 1956	5 May 1956	28 May 1958

Displacement, tons	1 150 standard; 1 500 full load
Length, feet (*metres*)	295·2 (*90·0*) pp 325 (*99·0*) oa
Beam, feet (*metres*)	36 (*11·0*)
Draught, feet (*metres*)	8·5 (*2·6*)
Guns, AA	4—4 in (*102 mm*) 46 cal., 2 twin mounts; 6—30 mm, 3 twin; 6—20 mm, 3 twin
A/S	2 Hedgehogs; 4 DCT
Torpedo tubes	3—21 (*533 mm*)
Boilers	2 Foster Wheeler
Main engines	2 sets Parsons geared turbines 24 000 shp; 2 shafts
Speed, knots	32
Radius, miles	2 800 at 22 knots cruising speed
Oil fuel (tons)	350
Complement	200

Fast frigate or light destroyer type. A photograph of *Surapati* appears in the 1959-60 to 1966-67 editions.

IMAN BONDJOL *courtesy Dr Ing Luigi Accorsi*

Frigates—*continued*

2 "PATTIMURA" CLASS

Name	*No.*	*Builders*	*Laid down*	*Launched*	*Completed*
PATTIMURA	252	Ansaldo, Leghorn	8 Jan 1956	1 July 1956	28 Jan 1958
SULTAN HASANUDIN	253	Ansaldo, Leghorn	8 Jan 1956	24 Mar 1957	8 Mar 1958

Displacement, tons	950 standard; 2 200 full load
Length, feet (*metres*)	246 (*75·0*) pp; 270·2 (*82·4*) oa
Beam, feet (*metres*)	34 (*10·4*)
Draught, feet (*metres*)	9 (*2·7*)
Guns, AA	2—3 in (*76 mm*) 40 cal. 2—30 mm 70 cal twin
A/S	2 Hedgehogs; 4 DCT
Main engines	3 Ansaldo-Fiat diesels 6 900 bhp; 3 shafts
Speed, knots	22
Radius, miles	2 400 at 18 knots cruising speed
Oil fuel (tons)	100
Complement	110

Small sloop or fast corvette type. A photograph of *Sultan Hasanudin* appears in the 1963-64 to 1965-66 editions.

PATTIMURA — *Added 1966, courtesy Dr Ing Luigi Accorsi*

PATROL VESSELS

8 Ex-USSR "KRONSTADT" TYPE

KATULA **LADJURA** **LAPAI** **LUMBA-LUMBA** **MADIDIHANG** **MOMARE** **TJUTJUT** **TONGKOL**

Displacement, tons	300
Dimensions, feet	167·3 × 19·3 × 9
Guns	1—3·9 in; 2—37 mm AA; 3—20 mm AA
A/S weapons	Depth bomb projectors
Mines	Fitted for laying
Main Engines	Diesels; 2 shafts; bhp = 27 knots
Oil fuel (tons)	20
Complement	40

Former Soviet submarine chasers of the "Kronstadt" type. Built in 1951-54. Transferred to the Indonesian Navy on 30 Dec 1958. Pennant Nos. 301 and 308.

"Kronstadt" Class — *1961, Indonesian Navy, Official*

4 Ex-US PC TYPE

HUI (ex-USS *Malvern, PC* 580) **TJAKALANG** (ex-USS *Pierre, PC* 1141)
TENGGIRI (ex-USS *PC* 1183) **TORANI** (ex-USS *Manville, PC* 581)

Displacement, tons	280 standard; 450 full load
Dimensions, feet	170 wl; 173·7 oa × 23 × 10·8 max
Guns	1—3 in; 1—40 mm AA; 2—20 mm AA; 4 DCT
Main Engines	2 GM diesels; 2 shafts; 2 880 bhp = 20 knots
Oil fuel (tons)	60
Radius, miles	5 000 at 10 knots
Complement	54 (4 officers, 50 men)

Former American submarine chasers of the steel-hulled PC type. Built in 1942-43. *Pierre* transferred from the US Navy at Pearl Harbour, Hawaii in Oct 1958 and *Malvern* and *Manville* in Mar 1960. Pennant Nos. 318, 309, 313 and 317, respectively.

Sister ship *Alu-Alu* (ex-USS *PC* 787) removed from the effective list in 1961.

TINGGIRI — *1966, Indonesian Navy, Official*

CORVETTE

1 "BANTENG" CLASS (OCEAN MINESWEEPER)

PATI UNUS (ex-*Tidore*, ex-HMAS *Tamworth*) 256

Displacement, tons	815 standard; 1 025 full load
Dimensions, feet	162 pp; 186 oa × 31 × 8·3
Guns	1—4 in; 1—40 mm AA; 4—20 mm AA
Main engines	Triple expansion; 2 shafts; 2 000 ihp = 15·5 knots
Boilers	2 of 3-drum type
Oil fuel (tons)	170
Radius, miles	4 300 at 10 knots
Complement	56 to 70

Built in Australia as an ocean minesweeper by Walkers, Maryborough, *Hang Tuah* by Evans Deakin, Brisbane, and *Radjawali* by Cockatoo Docks and Eng Co. Launched on 14 Mar 1942. *Hang Tuah* and *Pati Unus* were transferred from the Royal Netherlands Navy on 28 Dec 1949, *Banteng* and *Radjawali* on 6 Apr 1950. *Hang Tuah* (ex-*Morotai*, ex-*Ipswich*) was reported sunk by rebel planes off Balikpapan, East Borneo, on 28 Apr 1958. *Pati Unus* has been transferred to the Training Establishment for ratings. Sister ships *Banteng* and *Radjawali* arrived in Hong Kong in Apr 1968 for scrapping. A photograph of *Radjawali* appears in the 1955-56 to 1960-61 editions.

TORPEDO BOATS

7 GERMAN-BUILT "JAGUAR" TYPE

ADJAK **ANOA** **BIRUANG** **HARIMAU** **MADJAN KUMBANG** **SERIGALA** **SINGA**

Displacement, tons	150
Dimensions, feet	131 pp; 138 oa × 25 × 5
Guns	2—40 mm AA (single)
Torpedo tubes	4—21 in
Main engines	4 Daimler-Benz diesels; 4 shafts; 12 000 bhp = 40 knots
Complement	39

Built for the Indonesian Navy by Lürssen, Bremen-Vegesack in 1959-60. The first four boats had wooden hulls, but the second four were built of steel. Pennant Nos. 601, 602, 603, 604, 605, 607 and 608. A photograph of *Harimou* appears in the 1960-61 edition, and of *Singa* in the 1961-62 to 1967-68 editions. *Matjan Tutul* 606 of this class was sunk on 15 Jan 1962 by Dutch warships off Borneo

24 Ex-USSR "P 6" TYPE

ANGIN KUMBANG

Displacement, tons	75 standard; 100 full load
Dimensions, feet	88 × 21 × 5·2
Guns	4—25 mm AA (two twin)
Tubes	2—21 in (two single)
Main engines	Diesels; speed 42 knots max

Former Soviet interchangeable gun torpedo boats of the "P 6" class. A total of 24 reported delivered since 1961, including eight in 1961, and six in 1962. Only one name, *Angin Kumbang*, No. 1613, has been notified.

ANGIN KUMBANG — *1968, Indonesian Navy, Official*

FLEET MINESWEEPERS

6 Ex-USSR "T 43" TYPE

Displacement, tons	500 standard; 600 full load
Dimensions, feet	200 × 27·2 × 9
Guns	4—37 mm AA; 8—13 mm AA
Main Engines	Diesels; 2 shafts; speed = 17 knots

Former Soviet fleet minesweepers of the "T 43" type transferred to Indonesia by the USSR, four in 1962 and two in 1964.

COASTAL MINESWEEPERS

10 "R" CLASS (RAUM-BOATS)

PALAU RASS 503 **PALAU RANGSANG** 506 **PALAU RAU** 501 **PALAU REMPANG** 508 **PALAU RENGAT** 509 **PALAU RINDJA** 507 **PALAU ROMA** 502 **PALAU ROTI** 504 **PALAU RUPAT** 505 **PALAU RUSA** 510

Displacement, tons	139·4 standard
Dimensions, feet	129 × 18·7 × 5
Guns	1—40 mm AA; 2—20 mm AA
Main engines	2 MAN diesels; 12 cyl; 2 800 bhp = 24·6 knots
Complement	26

Built by Abeking & Rasmussen Yacht-und Bootswerft, Lemwerder IO in 1945-57. These boats have a framework of light metal covered with wood.

PALAU ROTI *Indonesian Navy, Official*

DJAMPEA **DJOMBANG** **ENGGANO** (ex-*Hino Maru*) **FLORES**

Displacement, tons	175
Dimensions, feet	106·7 pp; 113·7 (*Flores*) 114·1 oa × 18·8 × 6·2
Main Engines	1 Enterprise diesel; 360 bhp = 12·5 knots

First three were commissioned in 1941. *Flores* was completed by the Japanese during the occupation of Java. First two were built at Droogdak Maatschappij, and the other two at Droogdok Mij, Tandjorg Priok. Used as auxiliary minesweepers by the Royal Netherlands Navy. *Enggano* was re-named by Japanese. These ships were recovered after the war.

1 Ex-USSR "T 301" CLASS

Displacement, tons	130
Dimensions, feet	100 × 16 × 4·5
Guns	2—37 mm AA
Main Engines	Diesels; 480 bhp = 10 knots

Former Soviet inshore minesweeper of the "T 301" type reported to have been transferred from the USSR to Indonesia in 1962.

PATROL BOATS

6 Ex-YUGOSLAVIAN "KRALJEVICA" TYPE

BUBARA **DORANG** **JAJANG** **KRAPU** **LEMADANG** **TODAK**

Displacement, tons	190 standard; 245 full load
Dimensions, feet	134·5 × 20·8 × 7
Guns	1—3 in; 1—40 mm AA; 6—20 mm AA
A/S weapons	DC
Main Engines	2 MAN diesels; 2 shafts; 3 300 bhp = 20 knots
Oil fuel (tons)	15
Radius, miles	1 500 at 12 knots
Complement	54

Former Yugoslavian submarine chasers of the "Kraljevica" class. Purchased and transferred on 27th Dec 1958. Nos 310 to 312 and 314 to 316. A photograph of *Lajang* appears in the 1961-62 to 1967-68 editions.

DORANG *1968, Indonesian Navy, Official*

5 "MAWER" CLASS. NEW CONSTRUCTION

Displacement, tons	147
Guns	40 mm AA
Main engines	2 diesels; speed 21 knots

Indonesia was reported to be building five submarine chasers of the "Mawar" class in her own yards. Similar to the prototype *Kelabang*. At least two, *Kelalang* and *Kalahitam*, have been completed.

KALAHITAM *1968, Indonesian Navy, Official*

MISSILE BOATS

12 Ex-USSR "KOMAR" CLASS

Displacement, tons	75 standard; 100 full load
Dimensions, feet	88 × 21 × 5·2
Guns	2—25 mm AA (1 twin)
Guided weapons	2 launchers in twin housing with missiles of 10 to 15 nautical miles range
Main engines	Diesels; speed = 40 knots

Former Soviet guided missile patrol boats of the "Komar" class. Six were transferred to Indonesia in 1961-63, four more in Sep 1964 and two in 1965.

MOTOR GUNBOATS

18 Ex-USSR "BK" CLASS

Displacement, tons	120
Dimensions, feet	124·7 × 19 × 4·6
Guns,	1—85 mm; 4—25 mm AA
Main engines	Diesels; speed 20 knots

Reported to have been transferred from the USSR to Indonesia in 1962. Fitted with large gun mounting.
Ten Soviet-built gunboats were reported to have been transferred to Indonesia at Djakarta 11 Oct 1961.

PGM TYPE. Three USN PGM type, 55-57 were intended for transfer to Indonesia as *Silungkang*, *Waitatire* and *Kalukuang* respectively, but were handed over to Philippines instead as *Yacha*, *Yanga* and *Yundi* in 1965.

SEAWARD DEFENCE BOATS

25 Ex-HDML PATROL BOAT TYPES

PP 01 **PP 02** **PP 03** **PP 04** **PP 05** **PP 06** **PP 07** **PP 08** **PP 09** **PP 10** **PP 011** **PP 012** **PP 013** **PP 014** **PP 015** **PP 016** **PP 017** **PP 018** **PP 019** **PP 020** **PP 021** **PP 022** **PP 023** **PP 024** **PP 025**

Displacement, tons	46 standard; 54 full load
Dimensions, feet	72 × 16 × 5·5
Guns	1—37 mm; 2—20 mm Oerlikon MG
Main Engines	2 diesels; 2 shafts; 300 bhp = 11 knots
Complement	10

All ex-Netherlands patrol boats. Built in 1943-46. Formerly British HDML type *RP* 109, *RP* 111, *RP* 112, *RP* 114, and *RP* 118 ex-*HDML* 1451, *HDML* 1472, *HDML* 1473, *HDML* 1454 and *HDML* 1449).

Displacement, tons	44 standard; 56 full load
Dimensions, feet	62 oa × 18·3 × 4
Guns	1—20 mm AA; 1 MG
Main Engines	1 diesel; 165 bhp = 10 knots
Complement	10

Built in 1945-46. Former American Higgins type motor launches, later Netherlands *RP* 120, *RP* 121, *RP* 122, *RP* 125, *RP* 127, *RP* 128, *RP* 130, *RP* 134, and *RP* 136, transferred to Indonesia in 1950.

Displacement, tons	54
Guns	1—40 mm AA; 2—20 mm AA
A/S weapons	3 DCT
Main Engines	Speed = 11 knots
Complement	10

Former Netherlands motor launch *RP* 138. transferred by the Royal Netherlands Navy in 1950. A photograph of this type appears in the 1951-52 to 1960-61 editions.

TRAINING SHIPS

NANUSA

Displacement, tons	14 320
Dimensions, feet	441·7 × 58·3 × 26·3
Guns	1—3 in; 1—40 mm; 2—37 mm; 4—20 mm; 6—12·7 mm MG
Main Engines	Triple expansion; 1 shaft; 2 800 ihp = 9 knots
Boilers	3
Complement	100 (accommodation for 350 ratings under training)

Transferred to the Indonesian Navy in 1958. A converted freighter.

DEWARUTJI

Displacement, tons	810 standard; 1 500 full load
Dimensions, feet	191·2 oa; 136·2 pp × 31·2 × 13·9
Main Engines	MAN diesel engines; 600 bhp = 10·5 knots
Complement	110 (32 + 78 midshipmen)

Training ship for Indonesian Navy, built in Germany by H. C. Stülcken & Sohn, Hamburg. Launched on 24 Jan 1953. Completed on 9 July 1953. Barquentine of iron construction. Sail area, 1 305 sq yds (*1 091 sq metres*). Speed with sails 12·8 knots.

A photograph appears in the 1967-68 edition.

SUBMARINE SUPPORT SHIPS

MULTATULI

Displacement, tons	3 220
Dimensions, feet	338 pp; 365·3 oa × 52·5 × 23
Guns	1—85 mm; 4—40 mm (single mountings)
Main engines	B & W diesel; 5 500 bhp = 18·5 knot max
Oil fuel (tons)	1 400
Radius, miles	6 000 at 16 knots cruising speed
Complement	134

Built in Japan by Ishikawajima-Harima Heavy Industries Co Ltd, as a submarine tender. Launched on 15 May 1961. Delivered to Indonesia in Aug 1961. Pennant No. 476. Flush decker. Capacity for replenishment at sea (fuel oil, fresh water, provisions, ammunition, naval stores and personnel). Medical and hospital facilities. Equipment for supplying compressed air, electric power and distilled water to submarines. Air conditioning and mechanical ventilation arrangements for all living and working quarters. A photograph of *Multatuli* appears in the 1962-63 to 1967-68 editions.

1 Ex-USSR "DON" CLASS

RATULANGI

Displacement, tons	4 750 standard; 6 000 full load
Dimensions, feet	450 × 49 × 17
Guns	4—3·9 in; 12—37 mm AA
Main Engines	Diesels; speed = 21 knots approx
Complement	300

A submarine support ship, escort vessel and maintenance tender of the "Don" class, transferred from the USSR to Indonesia in 1962, arriving in Indonesia in July with Soviet pennant No. 441.

RATULANGI *1968, Indonesian Navy, Official*

1 Ex-USSR "ATREK" CLASS

THAMRIN

Displacement, tons	3 500 standard
Measurement, tons	3 258 gross
Dimensions, feet	336 × 49 × 20
Main Engines	Steam expansion and exhaust turbine; 2 450 ihp = 13 knots
Boilers	2
Radius	3 500 miles

Former Soviet advanced submarine parent ship of the smaller tender type. Built in 1955-57 and converted to naval use from a mercantile freighter. Arrived in Indonesia on 28 June 1962 as a transfer from the USSR "Atrek" class.

SURVEY SHIPS

BURUDJULASAD

Displacement, tons	2 150 max
Dimensions, feet	269·5 × 37·4
Machinery	Twin diesels = 19·1 knots
Complement	78

Launched in 1966, her equipment includes laboratories for oceanic and meteorological research, a cartographic room, and a helicopter.

BURUDJULASAD *1968, Indonesian Navy, Official*

BURDIAMHAL

Displacement, tons	1 200
Dimensions, feet	211·7 oa; 192 pp × 33·2 × 10
Main Engines	2 Werkspoor diesel engines; 1 160 bhp = 10 knots
Complement	90

Built by Scheepswerf De Waal, Zalthomme. Launched on 6 Sep 1952. Completed on 6 July 1953. A photograph of this ship appears in the 1954-55 to 1960-61 editions.

SAMUDERA

Measurement, tons	200 gross
Dimensions, feet	125·2 × 21·5 × 9·8
Main Engines	Werkspoor diesel engine; 450 bhp

Built by Ferus Smit, Foxol. Launched on 28 May 1952. Completed on 28 Aug 1952. Same type as "Bango" class motor patrol vessels. Equipped as a laboratory ship, used for deep sea exploration in Indonesian waters. A photograph of this vessel appears in the 1953-54 to 1960-61 editions.

LANDING SHIPS

5 Ex-US LST "511-1152" TYPE

TANDJUNG NUSANIE, LST 1 (ex-USS *Lawrence County, LST* 887)
TELUK BAYUR, LST 870 (ex-USS *LST* 616)
TELUK KAU, LST 871 (ex-USS *LST* 652)
TELUK LANGSA, LST 868 (ex-USS *Solano County,* LST 1128)
TELUK MENADO, LST 872 (ex-USS *LST* 657)

Displacememt, tons	1 653 standard; 4 080 full load
Dimensions, feet	316 wl; 328 oa × 50 × 14
Guns	7—40 mm AA; 2—20 mm AA
Main Engines	GM diesels; 2 shafts; 1 700 bhp = 11·6 knots
Oil fuel (tons)	600
Radius, miles	7 200 at 10 knots
Cargo capacity	2 100 tons
Complement	119 (accommodation for 266)

Teluk Langsa was transferred by the United States at Seattle, Washington, on 31 Mar 1960. *Tandjung Nusanie* and *Tandjung Radja* were transferred on 27 Dec 1960, and *Teluk Bayur, Teluk Kau* and *Teluk Menado* on 17 June 1961.
Tandjung Radja was badly damaged by grounding and was discarded in 1963.

TELUK LANGSA *1961, Indonesian Navy, Official*

1 JAPANESE TYPE

TELUK AMBOINA LST 869

Displacement, tons	2 200 standard; 4 800 full load
Dimensions, feet	327 × 50 × 15
Guns	2—85 mm; 4—40 mm
Main Engines	MAN diesels; 2 shafts; 3 000 bhp = 13·1 knots
Oil fuel (tons)	1 200
Radius, miles	4 000 at 13·1 knots
Complement	88 (accommodation for 300)

Built in Japan. Launched on 17 Mar 1961 and transferred in June 1961.

LANDING CRAFT

3 Ex-US LCI TYPE

AMAHAI (ex-*Tropenvogel, LCI* 467) 864
MARICH (ex-*Zeemeeuw*) 866
PIRU (ex-*Zeearend, LCI* 420) 868

Displacement, tons	250 standard; 381 full load
Dimensions, feet	158 × 23 × 7
Guns	1—37 mm; 2 Vickers MG
Main engines	GM diesels; 1 800 bhp = 15 knots
Complement	60

Former US infantry landing craft. Turned over from Netherlands East Indies Government on formation of Indonesian Navy in 1950. Sister ships *Baruna* (ex-*Jjsvogel,* LCI 948) and *Namlea* (ex-*Stormvogel*) *LCI* 588, were rerated as pilot ship and light ship in 1961.

4 Ex-YUGOSLAVIAN LCT TYPE

TELUKKATURAI **TELUKWADJO** **TELUKWEDA** **TELUKWORI**

Displacement, tons	110 standard; 250 full load
Dimensions, feet	166 × 21·5 × 5·5
Guns	1—40 mm; 2—20 mm
Main engines	2 diesels; 2 shafts; 375 bhp = 7 knots
Oil fuel (tons)	6
Complement	15

Transferred from Yugoslavia on 1 Nov 1958. Nos 862, 860, 861 and 863.

CABLE SHIP

BIDUK

Displacement, tons	1 250 standard
Dimensions, feet	213·2 oa × 39·5 × 11·5
Main Engines	1 Triple expansion engine; 1 600 ihp = 12 knots
Complement	66

Cable Layer, Lighthouse Tender, and multi-purpose naval auxiliary. Built by J. & K. Smit, Kinderijk. Launched on 30 Oct 1951. Completed on 30 July 1952. A photograph of this ship appears in the 1953-54 to 1960-61 editions.

TRANSPORTS

2 "BANGGAI" TYPE

BANGGAI (ex-*Biscaya*) **NUSA TELU** (ex-*Casa Blanca*)

Measurement, tons 750
Dimensions, feet 168 × 27·9 × 7·8

Dual purpose troop and cargo ships. Renamed in 1961. Pennant Nos 925, 924.

MOROTAI TYPE. The transports *Halmahera*, No 921, and *Merotai*, No. 922, reverted to the Merchant Navy as *Djati Roto* and *Djati Bono* in 1968. Acquired from merchant service on 23 Nov 1957. A photograph of *Moratai* appears in the 1961-62 to 1968-69 editions.

AUXILIARY PATROL CRAFT

5 DKN TYPE

DKN 901 **DKN 902** **DKN 903** **DKN 904** **DKN 905**

Displacement, tons 140
Dimensions, feet 128 × 19 × 5·2
Guns 4—20 mm AA
Main Engines Maybach diesels; 2 shafts; 3 000 bhp = 24·5 knots

Patrol craft and police boats. Projected as a class of ten units. 901, 902 and 904 were built by Lürssen, Vergesack, 903 and 905 by Abeking & Rasmussen Lemwerder.

1 + 1 KELABANG TYPE

KELABANG

Displacement, tons 147
Main engines 2 diesels; speed 21 knots

Launched on 22 Aug 1960 at Surabja. A sister ship was scheduled to be built.

6 "PAT" CLASS

PAT 01 **PAT 02** **PAT 03** **PAT 04** **PAT 05** **PAT 06**

Dimensions, feet 91·9 pp; 100 oa × 17 × 6
Main Engines 2 Caterpillar diesels; 340 bhp

6 "BALAM" CLASS

BALAM **BARAU** **BEKAKA** **BELATIK** **BENDALU** **BOGA**

Measurement, tons 200 gross
Dimensions, feet 125·2 oa × 21·3 × 6·5
Main Engines Werkspoor diesel engine; 400-430 bhp = 11 knots

All launched in 1953. *Balam* and others were commissioned for service in 1953.

7 "BANGO" CLASS

BANGO **BABUT** **BEO** **BETTET** **BIDO** **BLEKOK** **BLIBIS**

Measurement, tons 194 gross
Dimensions, feet 120·5 pp; 125·2 oa × 21·3 × 6·6
Main Engines Werkspoor diesel engine; 430 bhp = 11 knots

All launched in 1952. A photograph of *Bettet* appears in the 1953-54 to 1960-61 editions.

7 "DURIAN" CLASS

DAIK **DAGONG** **DAMARA** **DATA** **DUATA** **DUKU** **DURIAN**

Displacement, tons 90
Dimensions, feet 78·2 × 16 × 6·8
Main Engines Caterpillar diesel; 190 bhp

All launched in 1952.

12 "ALKAI" CLASS

ALKAI **ALULU** **AMPIS** **ANKANG** **ANTANG** **ARYAT**
ALLAP **AMPOK** **ANDIS** **ANKLOENG** **AROKWES** **ATTAT**

Displacement, tons 143; 247 full load
Dimensions, feet 124·3 × 18·5 × 5·5
Guns 1—37 mm AA; 4 MG
Main engines Enterprise diesel; 400-450 = 12 knots
Complement 20

Built in the Netherlands. *Ampok* and *Alkai* were shipped to Indonesia on 17 Mar 1950.

3 Ex-US SC TYPE

BHAYAMKARA 1 **BHAYAMKARA II** **BHAYAMKARA III**

Displacement, tons 116 (trials); 148 full load
Dimensions, feet 107·5 wl; 110·8 oa × 17 × 6·5
Main Engines Diesel; 800 bhp = 15·5 knots

Former US submarine chasers of the 110 SC type. Operated by Indonesian Marine Police. A photograph appears in the 1954-55 to 1960-61 editions.

2 MERABU TYPE

MERABU (ex-*Merbaboe*) **RINDJANI**

Displacement, tons 80
Dimensions, feet 74·5 × 14·5 × 5
Main Engines Diesel; 135 bhp = 10 knots
Complement 20

OILERS

2 Ex-USSR TYPE

BUNJU **SAMBU**

Displacement, tons 2 170 standard; 6 170 full load
Dimensions, feet 350·5 × 49·2 × 20·2
Guns 2—20 mm
Main Engines Polar diesel; 1 shaft; 2 650 bhp = 10 knots
Oil fuel (tons) 390
Cargo capacity 4 739 tons
Complement 71

Former Soviet tankers transferred to the Indonesian Navy on 29 June 1959. Pennant Nos. 904 and 903.

SAMBU *1961, Indonesian Navy, Official*

TJEPU (ex-*Scandus*, ex-*Nordhem*)

Displacement, tons 1 372
Measurement, tons 1 042 gross
Dimensions, feet 226·5 × 34 × 14·2
Main Engines Polar diesel; 1 shaft; 850 bhp = 11 knots

Built in Sweden in 1949. Acquired in 1951. Pennant No. 901.

PLĄDJU

Displacement, tons 1 412 standard; 4 062 full load
Dimensions, feet 294·7 × 42·2 × 15·5
Guns 2—20 mm
Main Engines Compound engines; 1 700 ihp = 10 knots
Oil fuel (tons) 449
Cargo capacity, tons 3 132
Complement 70

Purchased from Singapore in 1958. Pennant No. 902.

SALVAGE VESSELS

TRITON (ex-*Mutsunoura Maru*)

Displacement, tons 384
Measurement, tons 383 gross
Dimensions, feet 182·5 × 30 × 15
Main Engines Triple expansion reciprocating; 700 ihp = 7 knots
Complement 43

Former Japanese vessel renamed. Launched in 1941. Pennant No. 926.

TUGS

RAKATA (ex-USS *Menominee*, *ATF* 73)

Displacement, tons 1,235 standard; 1,675 full load
Dimensions, feet 195 wl; 205 oa × 38·5 × 15·5 max
Guns 1—3 in; 4—40 mm AA; 2—20 mm AA
Main engines 4 diesels with electric drive; 3 000 bhp = 16 5 knots
Complement 85

Former American fleet ocean tug of the "Apache" class. Launched on 14 Feb 1942. Transferred from the United States Navy to the Indonesian Navy at San Diego in Mar 1961. Pennant No. 928.

LAMPO BATANG

Displacement, tons 250
Dimensions, feet 92·3 oa; 86·7 pp × 23·2 × 11·3
Main engines 2 diesels; 1 200 bhp = 11 knots
Oil fuel (tons) 18
Radius, miles 1 000 at 11 knots
Complement 43

Ocean tug. Built in Japan. Launched in April 1961. Delivered in Nov 1961. Pennant No. 934.

GANDENG

Measurement, tons 610 gross
Main Engines Speed = 7·5 knots

Launched in 1940. Reported to have been given a new Indonesian name.

BROMO **TAMBORA**

Displacement, tons 150
Dimensions, feet 71·7 wl; 79 oa × 21·7 × 9·7
Main Engines MAN diesel; 2 shafts; 600 bhp = 10·5 knots
Oil fuel (tons) 9
Radius, miles 690 at 10·5 knots
Complement 15

Harbour tugs. Built in Japan. Launched in June 1961. Delivered in Aug 1961. Pennant Nos 936 and 935.

IRAN (PERSIA)

Strength of the Fleet

1 Destroyer	23 Patrol Boats
5 Frigate	4 Landing Craft
5 Corvettes	1 Support Ship
6 Minesweepers	8 Auxiliaries

Administration

Commander-in-Chief Imperial Iranian Navy:
Admiral Fazlollah Rassaie

Mercantile Marine

Lloyd's Register of Shipping:
37 vessels of 74 448 tons

Diplomatic Representation

Naval, Military and Air Attaché in London:
Colonel G. H. Aghakhani Afshar

Naval, Military and Air Attaché in Washington:
Lieutemant Colonel Abbas Eshraghi

DESTROYER

Name	*Builders*	*Laid down*	*Launched*	*Completed*
ARTEMIS (ex-HMS *Sluys*, D 60)	Cammell Laird & Co Ltd, Birkenhead	24 Nov 1943	28 Feb 1945	30 Sep 1946

1 Ex-BRITISH "BATTLE" CLASS

Displacement, tons	2 325 standard; 3 361 full load
Length, feet (*metres*)	355 (*107·2*) pp; 379 (*115·5*) oa
Beam, feet (*metres*)	40·3 (*12·3*)
Draught, feet (*metres*)	17 (*5·2*) props
Guns, surface	4—4·5 in (*115 mm*); 2 twin turrets forward
Guns, AA	8—40 mm
Missile launchers	1 quadruple "Seacat"
Main engines	Parsons geared turgines; 2 shafts; 50 000 shp
Speed, knots	31 sustained sea

Handed over to the Imperial Iranian Navy at Southampton on 26 Jan 1967, and taken in hand for 2-year major refit and modernisation by the Vosper Thornycroft Group, see new appearance on completion.

ARTEMIZ — *1969, Wright & Logan*

FRIGATES

Name	*Builders*	*Laid down*	*Launched*
ROSTAM	Vickers, Newcastle		4 Mar, 1969
SAAM	Vosper Thornycroft, Woolston	22 May 1967	25 July 1968
	Vosper Thornycroft, Woolston		
ZAAL	Vickers, Barrow		4 Mar 1969

4 "SAAM" CLASS

Displacement, tons	1 200 approx, official figure
Length, feet (*metres*)	310 (*94·4*) oa
Main engines	2 Bristol Siddeley "Olympus" gas turbines; 2 Paxman diesels; 2 shafts
Missile launchers	1 quadruple "Seacat"
A/S weapons	Depth charge projector

It was announced on 25 Aug 1966 that Vosper Ltd, Portsmouth, had received an order for four "destroyers" for the Iranian Navy Of small frigate type, one main gun forward, two secondary guns aft, anti-aircraft and anti-submarine weapons, high speed from gas turbines, with diesels for long range cruising. Air conditioned throughout, and fitted with Vosper stabilisers. *Rostam* was towed to Barrow for completion.

Mk 5 Frigate — *1967, courtesy Vosper Ltd, Portsmouth*

Name	*Builders*	*Laid down*	*Launched*	*Completed*
BABR (ex-HMS *Derby Haven*, ex-*Loch Assynt*)	Swan, Hunter & Wigham Richardson, Ltd Wallsend on-Tyne	11 Feb 1944	14 Dec 1944	2 Aug 1945

1 Ex-BRITISH "LOCH" TYPE

Displacement, tons	1 650 standard; 2 160 full load
Length, feet (*metres*)	286 (*87·2*) pp; 309 (*94·2*) oa
Beam, feet (*metres*)	38·5 (*11·7*)
Draught, feet (*metres*)	14·5 (*4·4*) max
Guns, surface	2—4 in (*102 mm*)
Guns, AA	4—40 mm
Boilers	2 Admiralty 3-drum
Main engines	Triple expansion 5 500 ihp; 2 shafts
Speed, knots	19·5
Radius, miles	9 500 at 12 knots
Oil fuel (tons)	725
Complement	140

Modified "Loch" class frigate acquired from Great Britain in 1949 "Babr" means "Panther".

BABR — *Added 1966, courtesy Dr Giorgio Arra*

CORVETTES

4 US PF TYPE

BAYANDOR F 25
KAHNAMUIE F 28
NAGHDI F 26
MILANIAN F 27

Displacement, tons	900 standard; 1 135 full load
Length, feet (*metres*)	275 (*83·8*) oa
Beam, feet (*metres*)	33 (*10·0*)
Draught, feet (*metres*)	10 (*3·0*)
Guns, surface	2—3 in (*76 mm*)
Guns, AA	2—40 mm
A/S weapons	Hedgehog
Main engine	F-M diesels; 6 000 bhp
Speed, knots	20
Complement	140

Built by Levingstone Shipbuilding Co, *Bayandor*, PF 103, laid down 20 Aug 1962, launch July 1963, transfer 18 May 1964. *Naghdi*, PF 104, laid down 12 Sep 1962, launch Oct 1963, transfer 22 July 1964. *Milanian*, PF 105, and *Kahnamuie*, PF 106, laid down on 1 May 1967, 12 June 1967, launched 4 Jan 1968, 4 Apr 1968 respectively, *Milanian* completed 6 Dec 1968. A photograph of *Byandor* appears in the 1964-65 to 1968-69 editions

NAGHDI — *1969, Imperial Iranian Navy, Official*

Corvettes—*continued*

	Name	Builders	Laid down	Launched	Completed
1 Ex-BRITISH "ALGERINE" TYPE	**PALANG** (ex-HMS *Fly*)	Lobnitz & Co Ltd, Renfrew	6 Oct 1941	1 June 1942	10 Oct 1942

ESCORT MINESWEEPER

Displacement, tons	1 040 standard; 1 235 full load
Length, feet (*metres*)	225 (*68·6*) oa
Beam, feet (*metres*)	35·5 (*10·8*)
Draught, feet (*metres*)	13 (*4·0*)
Guns, surface	2—4 in (*102 mm*)
Guns, AA	4—40 mm
A/S depth charges	2 DCT
Main engines	Triple expansion 2 000 ihp; 2 shafts
Speed, knots	16·5
Radius, miles	5 000 at 10 knots
Oil fuel (tons)	270
Complement	85

Former "Algerine" class ocean minesweeper and escort vessel acquired from Great Britain in 1949. "Palang" means "Tiger"

PALANG — *1966, Official*

COASTAL MINESWEEPERS

4 MSC TYPE

KARKAS (ex-USS *MSC* 292) 34 — **SHAHROKH** (ex-USS *MSC* 276) 31
SHAHBAZ (ex-USS *MSC* 275) 32 — **SIMORGH** (ex-USS *MSC* 291) 33

Displacement, tons	320 light; 378 full load
Dimensions, feet	138 pp; 145·8 oa × 28 × 8·3
Guns	1—20 mm
Main Engines	2 GM diesels; 2 shafts; 890 bhp = 12·8 knots
Oil fuel (tons)	27
Radius, miles	2 400 at 11 knots
Complement	40 (4 officers, 2 midshipmen, 34 men)

Built by Bellingham Shipyards Co (*Shahbaz* and *Shakrokh*), Petersen Builders Inc. (*Karkas*) and Tacoma Boatbuilding Co, (*Simorgh*). Of wooden construction. Launched in 1958-61 and transported from US to Iran under MAP in 1959-62. "Shahbaz" means Eagle and "Shahrokh" means Bird of Prey.

SHAHROKH — *1969, A. & J. Pavia*

INSHORE MINESWEEPERS

2 US MSI TYPE

HARISCHI (ex-*Kahnamuie*) 301 (ex-*MSI* 14) — **RIAZI** 302 (ex-*MSI* 13)

Displacement, tons	180 standard; 235 full load
Dimensions, feet	111 × 23 × 6
Main Engines	Diesels; 650 bhp = 13 knots
Complement	23 (5 officers, 18 men)

Built in USA by Tacoma Boat Building Co for delivery to Iran under MAP. Laid down on 22 June 1962 and 1 Feb 1963, and transferred at Seattle, Washington, on 3 Sep 1964 and 15 Oct 1964, respectively. In Aug 1967 *Kahnamuie* was renamed *Harischi* as the name *Kahnamuie* was required for one of the new US PFs under construction, see previous page.
In Aug 1967 *Kahnamuie* was renamed *Harischi* as the name *Kahnamuie* was required for one of the new US PFs under construction, see previous page.

HARISCHI — *1969, Imperial Iranian Navy, Official*

COAST GUARD CUTTERS

9 "AZAR" CLASS

AZAR **DARAKHSH** **PEYKAN** **TONDAR** **TOUSAN**
CHAHAB **NAVAK** **TONDBAD** **TOUFAN**

Displacement, tons	65 standard; 90 full load
Dimensions, feet	90 × 16 × 9
Guns	MG
Main Engines	2 diesels; speed = 22 knots

Built by Cant Nav INMA, La Spezia. Transferred to the Coast Guard in 1958. A photograph of *Azar* appears in the 1955-56 to 1963-64 editions.

CGC — *A. F.*

PATROL VESSELS

4 PGM TYPE

KEYVAN (MDA1) **MAHAN** 64 **MEHRAN** **TIRAN**

Displacement, tons	85 standard; 107 full load
Dimensions, feet	90 pp; 95 oa × 20·2 × 6·8 max
Guns,	1—40 mm AA
A/S weapons	8-barrelled 7·2 in projector, 8—300 lb depth charges
Main Engines	4 Cummins diesels; 2 shafts; 2 200 bhp = 20 knots
Radius, miles	1 500 cruising range
Complement	15

Keyvan, built in USA in 1955, was delivered to Iran on 14 Jan 1956. In the Persian Gulf. *Tiran* was built by the US Coast Guard at Curtis Bay, Maryland, and transferred to Iran in 1957. *Mahan* and *Mehran* were delivered to Iran in 1959. PGM 103 and PGM 112 are building in USA for transfer to Iran under MAP.

MAHAN — *1969, Imperial Iranian Navy, Official*

REPAIR SHIP

1 Ex-US ARL (Ex-LST) TYPE

SOHRAB (ex-USS *Gordlus*, *ARL* 36, ex-*LST* 1145)

Displacement, tons	1 625 light; 4 100 full load
Dimensions, feet	316 wl; 328 oa × 50 × 11·2
Guns	8—40 mm AA
Main Engines	GM diesels; 2 shafts; 1 800 bhp = 11·6 knots

Former US repair ship for landing craft. Built by Chicago Bridge & Iron Co, Seneca Ill. Laid down on 5 Feb 1945. Launched on 7 May 1945. Completed on 18 May 1945. Transferred by the USA under the Military Aid Programme in Sep 1961.

Repair Ships—*continued*

SOHRAB *1964, Official*

HYDROFOILS

Iran is reported to have ordered:—
6 Hydrofoils of the "Fast Attack Type", SRN 6; 9 tons; and "Logistic Amphibious Type", BH7; 40 tons.

LANDING CRAFT

3 Ex-US LSIL TYPE

GHASM (ex-USS *LSIL*) **LARAK** (ex-USS *LSIL* 710) 42
HENGAM (ex-French *LSIL* 9037, ex-USS *LSIL* 768) 41

Displacement, tons	210 light; 393 full load
Dimensions, feet	153 wl; 159 oa × 23·7 × 5·7 max
Guns	4—20 mm AA
Main Engines	GM diesels; 2 shafts; 1 800 bhp = 14·4 knots
Oil fuel (tons)	80
Radius, miles	5 000 at 12 knots
Complement	40

Former US Landing Ships, Infantry, Large, built in 1944. LSIL 768 was ceded by USA to France in 1953 for service in Indo-China, given back to USA in 1957 and then transferred to Iran. LSIL 710 was loaned by USA in 1959. *Ghasm* was added to the fleet in 1964.

GHESHNE (ex-USS *LCU* 1431)

LCU 1431 was transferred to Iran by US in 1964. See details in US section.

HENGAM *1963, Official*

SEAWARD DEFENCE CRAFT

2 EX-BRITISH HDML TYPE

ASALON (ex-HMS *SML* 323, ex-*HDML* 1081)
TAHMADOU FDB 65 (ex-*FDB* 58, ex-HMS *SDML* 1389)

Displacement, tons	46 standard; 58 full load
Dimensions, feet	72 × 16 × 5
Guns	8 MG
Main Engines	Diesel; 320 bhp = 12 knots
Complement	10

Former British motor launches of the harbour (seaward) defence type. *SML* 323 (last employed on survey duties) was transferred from the British Navy to the Iranian Navy at Khorramshahr on 21 June 1956. Employed as despatch boats. A photo graph of *Asalon* appears in the 1957-58 to 1968-69 editions.

ASALON *1957, Official*

COASTAL LAUNCHES

3 CASPIAN TYPE

BABOLSAR **GORGAN** **SEFIDROUDE**

Displacement, tons	28 to 32
Dimensions, feet	68·5 × 12·5 × 5·2
Guns	1—47 mm (Skoda); 1 MG
Main Engines	2 Krupp diesels; 2 shafts; 300 bhp = 14 knots

Built in 1935 by Cant Nav Riuniti Palermo, Italy. Employed in the Caspian Sea.

6 HARBOUR TYPE

MAHNAVI-HAMRAZ **MAHNAVI-VAHEDI** **MORVARID**
MAHNAVI-TAHERI **MARDJAN** **SADAF**

Displacement, tons	10
Dimensions, feet	40 × 11 × 3·7
Guns	MG
Main Engines	2 GM diesels.

Small launches for port duties. Not all in service in 1969.

IMPERIAL YACHT

CHASAVAR

Displacement, tons	530
Dimensions, feet	176 × 25·3 × 10·5
Main Engines	2 sets diesels; 1 300 bhp

Built by N. V. Boele's Scheepwerven, Boines, Netherlands. Engined by Gebr Stork of Hengelo. Launched in 1936. In the Caspian Sea.

CHAHSAVAR *1958, Imperial Iranian Navy, Official*

OILERS

HORMUZ 43

Displacement, tons	1 250 standard; 1 700 full load
Dimensions, feet	171·2 wl; 178·3 oa × 32·2 × 14
Main Engines	1 Ansaldo Q 370, 4 cycle diesel

Hormuz was built by Cantiere Castellamare di Stabia. Own oil fuel: 25 tons. Cargo oil capacity: 5 000 to 6 000 barrels. A photograph of *Hormuz* appears in the 1957-58 to 1959-60 editions.

WATER CARRIER

LENGEH 46 (ex-USS *YW* 88)

Transferred to Iran by US in 1964. Similar to oiler *Hormuz* above.

LENGEH *1969, Official*

TENDER

SIRRY (ex-*MVF* 1513)

Purchased from Great Britain in 1949. Rated as a 90 ft "Fire Extinguishing Boat".

TUGS

YADAK BAR (ex-*Neyrou*)

Displacement, tons	226
Dimensions, feet	81 pp; 88·5 oa × 22 × 10
Main Engines	Triple expansion; 600 ihp = 11 knots

Built by Cant Nav Riuniti, Ancona. Launched on 9 Dec 1944. In Persian Gulf

BAHMANSHIR 45
Harbour tug (ex-US Army ST 2001), 150 tons, transferred in 1962.

IRAQ

Mercantile Marine

Lloyds' Register of Shipping:
35 vessels of 36 547 tons gross

PATROL VESSELS

3 Ex-USSR "SOI" TYPE

Displacement, tons	215 light; 220 normal
Dimensions, feet	138 pp; 147 oa × 20 × 10 max
Guns	4—25 mm AA
A/S weapons	4 five-barrelled ahead-throwing rocket launchers.
Main Engines	3 diesels; 3 500 bhp = 25 knots

Former Soviet submarine chasers delivered by the USSR to Iraq in 1962.

TORPEDO BOATS

12 Ex-USSR "P 6" TYPE

Displacement, tons	50
Dimensions, feet	82 × 20 × 6
Guns	4—13 mm AA MG
Tubes	2—21 in
Main Engines	Speed = 40 knots

Presented by the USSR. Two were received in 1959, four in Nov 1960, and six in Jan 1961. Some remain non-operational.

PATROL BOATS

No. 1 **No. 2** **No. 3** **No. 4**

Displacement, tons	67
Dimensions, feet	100 × 17 × 3 mean
Guns	1—3·7 in howitzer; 2—3 in mortars; 4 MG
Main Engines	2 Thornycroft diesels; 2 shafts; 280 bhp = 12 knots

Protected by bullet-proof plating. All built by John I. Thornycroft & Co Ltd, Woolston, Southampton. All launched, completed and delivered in 1937.

No. 1 *John I. Thornycroft & Co. Ltd*

6 Ex-USSR SMALL TYPE

Six small patrol boats are also reported to have been delivered by the USSR.

8 PORTS ADMINISTRATION TYPE

Eight patrol boats of 36 feet in length with a diesel of 125 bhp were built by John I. Thornycroft & Co for the Iraqi Ports Administration.

4 PILOT DESPATCH TYPE

Four 21 ft pilot despatch launches with a diesel of 40 bhp were built by John I. Thornycroft & Co for the Iraqi Ports Administration.

LIGHTHOUSE TENDER

FAISAL 1 (ex-*Sans Peur*, ex-*Restless*)

Displacement, tons	1 025
Dimensions, feet	186 × 29·5 × 14·5
Main Engines	Triple expansion; 2 shafts; 850 ihp = 13 knots
Boilers	1 oil-fired

Former Royal Yacht. Designed by G. L. Watson Ltd. Built by John Brown & Co Ltd, Clydebank. Launched in 1923. A photograph appears in the 1937 to 1959-60 editions.

PRESIDENTIAL YACHT

AL THAWRA (ex-*Melike Aliye*)

Displacement, tons	746
Main Engines	Diesels; 2 shafts; 1 800 shp = 14 knots

Royal Yacht before assassination of King Faisal II in 1958, after which she was renamed *Al Thawra* (*The Revolution*) instead of *Malike Aliye* (*Queen Aliyah*)

AL THAWRA *Added 1966, Aldo Fraccaroli*

TUG

ALARM (ex-*St Ewe*)

Displacement, tons	570 standard; 820 full load
Dimensions, feet	135 × 30 × 14·5
Main Engines	Triple expansion; 1 shaft; 1 200 ihp = 12 knots
Boilers	2 oil-fired

Former British "Rescue" type tug of the "Saint" class. Built by Murdock & Murray. Launched in 1919.

ISRAEL

Strength of the Fleet

4 Submarines (Diesel Powered)
2 Destroyers (1 Escort Type)
9 Torpedo Boats
7 Fast Gunboats
5 Patrol Vessels (1 Submarine Chaser)
6 Landing Craft

Diplomatic Representation

Naval, Military and Air Attaché in London:
Colonel A. Avnon

Naval, Military and Air Attaché in Washington:
Brigadier-General D. Carmon

Administration

Commander-in-Chief of the Israeli Navy:
Rear Admiral A. Botzer

Mercantile Marine

Lloyds' Register of Shipping:
111 vessels of 722 951 tons gross

SUBMARINES

2 Ex-BRITISH "T" CLASS

Name	*Builders*	*Laid down*	*Launched*	*Completed*
LEVIATHAN (ex-HMS *Turpin*)	HM Dockyard Chatham	24 May 1943	5 Aug 1944	18 Dec 1944
DOLPHIN (ex-HMS *Truncheon*)	HM Dockyard Devonport	5 Nov 1942	22 Feb 1944	25 May 1945

Displacement, tons	*Dolphin:* 1 310 standard; 1 535 surface; 1 740 submerged *Leviathan:* 1 280 standard; 1 505 surface; 1 700 submerged
Length, feet (*metres*)	*Dolphin:* 293·5 (*89·5*) oa; *Leviathan:* 285·5 (*87·0*) oa
Speed, knots	15·25 on surface; 15 submerged
Complement	65 to 69

Leviathan (whale) was acquired from Great Britain (announced Nov 1964) and handed over to Israel after refit in HM Dockyard, Portsmouth, 19 May 1967. *Dolphin* was handed over to Israel at Gosport on 9 Jan 1968 and arrived on 31 Jan 1968 in Israel for refit.

LOSS. Sister ship *Dakar* (ex-HMS *Totem*) lost in eastern Mediterranean 25 Jan 1968 had been handed over by Royal Navy on 10 Nov 1967.

LEVIATHAN (reconstructed) *1967, Skyfotos*

2 Ex-BRITISH "S" CLASS

Name	*No.*	*Builders*	*Laid down*	*Launched*	*Completed*
RAHAV (ex HMS *Sanguine*)	73	Cammell Laird Birkenhead	10 Jan 1944	15 Feb 1945	13 May 1945
TANIN (ex-HMS *Springer*)	71	Cammell Laird Birkenhead	8 May 1944	14 May 1945	2 Aug 1945

Displacement, tons	715 standard; 814 surface; 1 000 submerged
Length, feet (*metres*)	202·5 (*61·7*) pp; 217 (*66·2*) oa
Beam, feet (*metres*)	23·8 (*7·2*)
Draught, feet (*metres*)	10·5 (*3·2*)
Guns, surface	1—4 in (*102 mm*)
Torpedo tubes	6—21 in (*533 mm*)
Main engines	1 900 hp diesels (surface); 1 300 hp electric motors (submerged)
Speed, knots	14·7 on surface; 9 submerged
Complement	57

Purchased by Israel in Oct 1958. *Springer* was handed over to the Israeli Navy at Portsmouth on 9 Oct 1958 and renamed *Tanin* (Crocodile). Both were refitted in Great Britain before delivery to Israel in May 1960 (*Rahav*) and Dec 1959 (*Tanin*). They are fitted with "Snort" mast and sonar domes. A photograph of *Tanin* appears in the 1961-62 to 1965-66 editions.

RAHAV *1966, Israeli Navy, Official*

DESTROYERS

1 Ex-BRITISH "Z" CLASS

Name	*No.*	*Builders*	*Laid down*	*Launched*	*Completed*
YAFFO (ex-HMS *Zodiac*)	42	John I. Thornycroft & Co, Ltd Southampton	7 Nov 1942	11 Mar 1944	25 Oct 1944

Displacement, tons	1 710 standard; 2 555 full load
Length, feet (*metres*)	362·2 (*110·4*) oa
Beam, feet (*metres*)	35·5 (*10·8*)
Draught, feet (*metres*)	17 (*5·2*)
Guns, dual purpose	4—4·5 in (*115 mm*)
Guns, AA	6—40 mm
A/S	4 DCT
Torpedo tubes	8—21 in (*533 mm*)
Boilers	2 Admiralty 3-drum
Main engines	Parsons geared turbines 40 000 shp; 2 shafts
Speed, knots	31
Complement	250

Transferred to Israel on 15 July in Cardiff Docks. Refitted before going to Israel in 1956, *Yaffo* by Crichtons in Trafalgar Dock, Liverpool. A photograph of *Yaffo* appears in the 1964-65 to 1966-67 editions.
LOSS. Sister ship *Elath* sunk off Sinia coast 21 Oct 1967 as a result of UAR missile patrol boat rocket attack.

YAFFO *1968, A. & J. Pavia*

1 Ex-EGYPTIAN "HUNT" CLASS ESCORT

Name	*No.*	*Builders*	*Laid down*	*Launched*	*Completed*
HAIFA (ex-*Ibrahim el Awal*, ex-*Lin Fu*, ex-*Mendip*)	38	Swan, Hunter & Wigham Richardson, Ltd Wallsend	10 Aug 1939	9 Apr 1940	12 Oct 1940

Displacement, tons	1 000 standard; 1 490 full load
Length, feet (*metres*)	273·3 (*83·3*) pp; 280 (*00·0*) oa
Beam, feet (*metres*)	29 (*8·8*)
Draught, feet (*metres*)	7·8 (*2·4*) mean; 14 (*4·3*) max
Guns, surface	4—4 in (*102 mm*)
Guns, AA	2—40 mm; 3—20 mm
A/S	2 DCT
Boilers	2 three-drum type
Main engines	Parsons geared turbines 19 000 shp; 2 shafts
Speed, knots	25
Complement	190

HAIFA *1966, Israeli Navy, Official*

Destroyers—*continued*

Former escort destroyer, later reclassified as anti-aircraft frigate of the British "Hunt" class, Type 1. Engined by the Wallsend Slipway & Engineering Co Ltd, Wallsend-on-Tyne. Classified by Israel as a destroyer.

HISTORY: This ship, first named *Mendip*, served with the British Navy from Oct 1940 until May 1948 when she was transferred to the Chinese Navy and renamed *Lin Fu*. She was returned to the British Navy at Hong Kong a year later and reverted to the name *Mendip* but was transferred to the Egyptian Navy in Nov 1949 and renamed *Mohamed Ali el Kebir* but was again renamed *Ibrahim el Awal* in 1951. She was captured from Egypt off Haifa by Israeli forces on 31 Oct 1956 and renamed *Haifa*. Commissioned in the Israeli Navy in Jan 1957.

FAST GUN BOATS

7 NEW CONSTRUCTION "SAAR" TYPE

Displacement, tons	220 standard; 240 full load
Dimensions, feet	147·6 oa × 23 × 5·9
Missiles launcher	"Gabriel" surface-to-air
Guns, AA	3—40 mm
Torpedo armament	2 side launchers for 21 inch torpedoes (surface or anti-submarine)
Main engines	4 diesels; 13 500 bhp total = 45 knots
Range, cruising	800 miles at 30 knots
Complement	40

It was officially stated in Mar 1967 that Israel was building some high speed gur boats which will be known as "Saar" type. French built hulls and Italian electronic equipment.

PATROL VESSELS

NOGAH (ex-USS *PC* 1188) P 22

Displacement, tons	295 standard; 450 full load
Dimensions, feet	170 pp; 173·7 oa × 23 × 10
Guns	1—4 in; 1—40 mm AA; 3—20 mm AA
A/S	4 DCT
Main Engines	2 diesels; 2 shafts; 1 764 bhp = 18 knots
Complement	70

Former United States patrol vessel (submarine chaser) of the Steel hulled PC type.

NOGAH *1966, Israeli Navy, Official*

TORPEDO BOATS

OPHIR T 150 **SHVA** T 151 **TARSHISH** T 152

Displacement, tons	40
Dimensions, feet	70 × 17 × 5
Guns,	1—40 mm AA; 2—20 mm AA
Torpedoes	2—17·7 in
Main Engines	High octane petrol engines; 4 000 bhp = 40 knots.

Motor Torpedo Boats/Gunboats built for the Israeli Navy by Cantieri Baglieto, Varrazze, Italy, in 1956-57.

SHVA *1964, Israeli Navy, Official*

AYAH T 200 **BAZ** T 201 **DAYA** T 202 **PERESS** T 203 **TAHMASS** T 204 **YASOOR** T 205

Displacement, tons	62 standard
Dimensions, feet	85·3 oa × 20·7 × 5
Guns	1—40 mm; 4—20 mm AA
Torpedoes	2—17·7 in
Main Engines	2 Napier Deltic diesels; 2 shafts; 4 600 bhp = 42 knots
Complement	15

Built by Chantiers de Meulan, France. Launched in 1950-56. Photographs appeai of T 208 in the 1953-54 to 1957-58 editions, of T 207 in the 1953-54 to 1960-61 editions, and of *Peress* in the 1961-62 to 1964-65 editions.
The three old motor torpedo boats *Lilitt*, T 209; *Shaldagg*, T 210; and *Tinshemett*, T 212, built by Vosper Ltd, Portsmouth, in 1942, are reported to be no longer in service.

TAHMASS *1965, Israeli Navy, Official*

PATROL BOATS

YARDEN 42 **YARKON** 44

Displacement, tons	96 standard; 109 full load
Dimensions, feet	100 × 20 × 6
Guns,	2—20 mm AA
Main Engines	Diesels; 2 shafts; speed 22 knots
Complement	16

Both built by Yacht & Bootswerft, Burmester Bremen-Burg, Germany. *Yarkon* was launched on 25 July 1956 and *Yarden* in 1957. A photograph of *Yarden* appears in the 1961-62 to 1965-66 editions.

YARKON *1966, Israeli Navy Official*

DROR 21 **TIRTSA** 25

Displacement, tons	46 standard; 54 full load
Dimensions, feet	72 oa × 16 × 5·5
Guns	2—20 mm AA
A/S	8 DC
Main Engines	2 diesels; 2 shafts; 320 bhp = 12 knots
Complement	12

Former British harbour defence motor launches. Built in Great Britain in 1943.

LANDING CRAFT

3 ISRAELI NEW CONSTRUCTION

ASHDOD *1968, Israeli Navy, Official*

ASHDOD (61) **ASHKELON** (63) **ACHZIV** (65)

Displacement, tons	400 standard; 730 full load
Dimensions, metres	55 pp; 61·4 oa × 10 × 1·78
Guns	2—20 mm
Main engines	3 × MWM diesels, shp 3 × 19 000 3 shafts = 10·5 knots
Oil fuel, tons	37
Complement	20

These three landing craft were completed during 1966-67 by Israel Shipyards, Haifa.

LC 51 **LC 53** **LC 55**

Displacement, tons	122
Dimensions, feet	100 × 19·4 × 4
Guns, AA	2—20 mm
Main Engines	2 diesels; 1 280 bhp = 10 knots
Complement	12

It was officially stated in Mar 1967 that in lieu of the landing craft of the LCI and LCT types, which were taken out of commission for disposal (with the exception of one LCT, which was given to the Israeli National Museum in Haifa) three new landing craft have been built in the Israeli Dockyard.

LC *1967, Israeli Navy, Official*

LCM

Displacement, tons	22 tons standard; 60 full load
Dimensions, feet	50 × 14 × 3·2
Main Engines	2 diesels; 450 bhp = 11 knots

Former United States vessels of the LCM (Landing Craft Mechanised) type.

ITALY

Administration

Chief of Naval Staff:
Ammiraglio di Squadra Virgilio Spigai

Commander, Allied Naval Forces, Southern Europe (Commander Navy South, Malta):
Ammiraglio di Squadra Giuseppe Roselli Lorenzini

Commander-in Chief of Fleet:
Ammiraglio di Squadra Gino Birindelli

Director General Navy Personnel:
Ammiraglio Divisione Ennio Ciuffo

Deputy Chief of Naval Staff:
Ammiraglio di Squadra Francesco Brunetti

Diplomatic Representation

Naval Attaché in London:
Captain Giuseppe Martucci, ItN

Naval Attaché in Washington:
Captain Arrigo Barbi, ItN

Strength of the Fleet

8 Diesel Powered Submarines
4 Guided Missile Armed Cruisers
2 Guided Missile Armed Destroyers
2 Destroyer Leaders (ex-Light Cruisers)
4 Destroyers
13 Frigates
24 Corvettes
4 Ocean Minesweepers
37 Coastal Minesweepers
8 Motor Gunboats
8 Motor Torpedo Boats
20 Inshore Minesweepers
140 Support Ships and Service Craft

New Construction Programme

2 Guided Missile Armed Destroyers
5 Missile Boats
1 Nuclear Powered Fast Fleet Replenishment Ship of new design

Navy Estimates

1964: 87,375,934,000 Lire
1965: 177,633,679,000 Lire
1966: 201,333,181,000 Lire
1967: 213,557,581,000 Lire
1968: 82,700,000,000 Lire *
1969: 91,500,000,000 Lire *

*Under the Defence budget reorganisation the Navy now has direct control only of sufficient funds to modernise and operate the Fleet. The cost of all other requirements is the direct responsibility of the Defence Ministry.

Personnel

1964: 38,000 officers and ratings
1965: 39,000 officers and ratings
1966: 39,000 officers and ratings
1967: 40,000 officers and ratings
1968: 40,000 officers and ratings
1969: 40,000 officers and ratings

Mercantile Marine

Lloyd's Register of Shipping:
1,490 vessels of 6,623,643 tons gross

Silhouettes

Scale: 150 feet = 1 inch (1 : 1800)

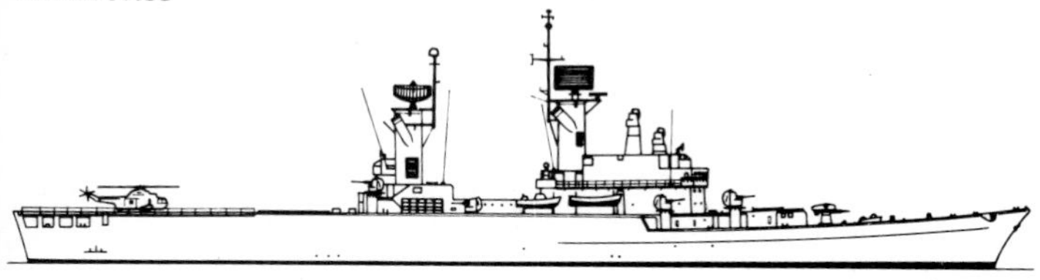
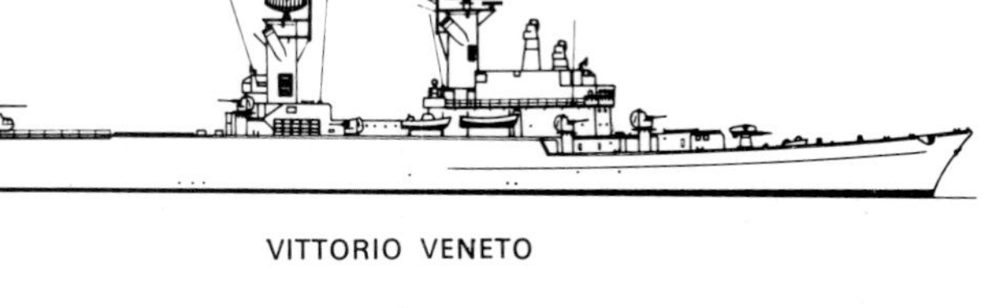

VITTORIO VENETO

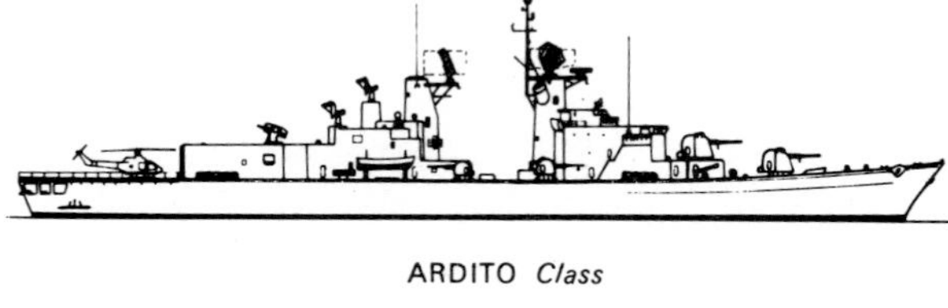

ARDITO *Class*

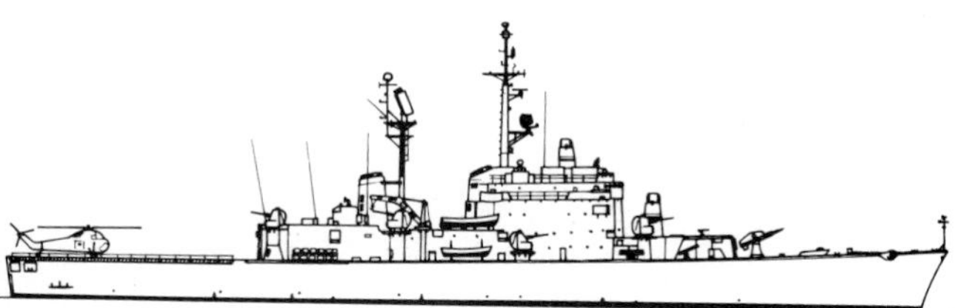

ANDREA DORIA, CAIO DUILIO

SAN MARCO

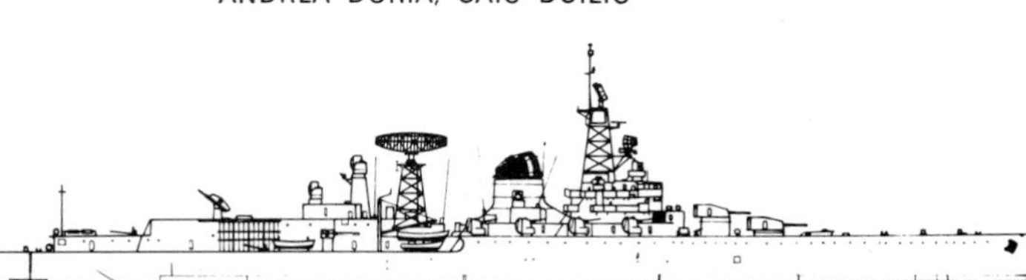

GIUSEPPE GARIBALDI

SAN GIORGIO

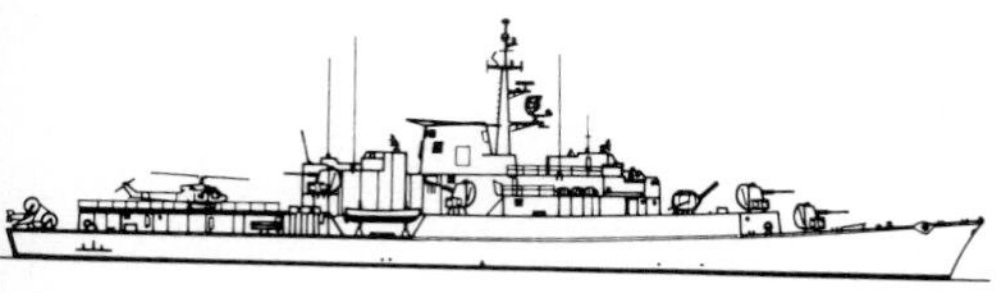

ALPINO, CARABINIERE

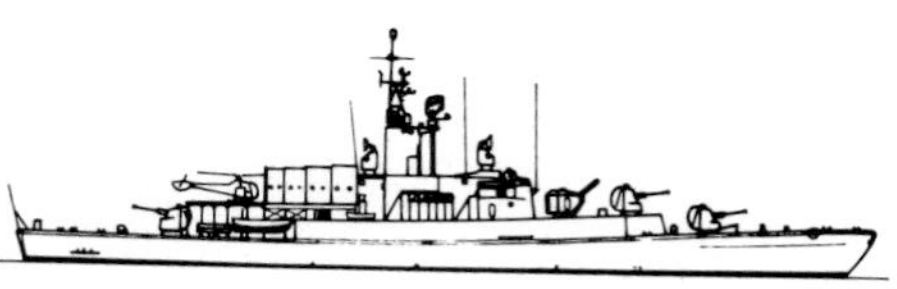

BERGAMINI *Class*

ALTAIR *Class*

IMPAVADO, INTREPIDO

CENTAURO *Class* as converted

ALBATROS *Class*

IMPETUOSO, INDOMITO

DE CRISTOFARO *Class*

CENTAURO *Class* original

SUBMARINES

4 "TOTI" CLASS (NEW CONSTRUCTION)

Name	No.	Builders	Laid down	Launched	Completed
BAGNOLINI	S 505	CRDA Monfalcone	15 Apr 1965	26 Aug 1967	16 June 1968
DANDOLO	S 513	CRDA Monfalcone	10 Mar 1967	16 Dec 1967	25 Sep 1968
MOCENIGO	S 514	CRDA Monfalcone	12 June 1967	20 Apr 1968	11 Jan 1969
TOTI	S 506	CRDA Monfalcone	15 Apr 1965	12 Mar 1967	22 Jan 1968

Displacement, tons	460 standard; 524 surface; 582 submerged
Length, feet (*metres*)	153·2 (*46·7*)
Beam, feet (*metres*)	15·4 (*4·7*)
Draught, feet (*metres*)	13·1 (*4·0*)
Torpedo tubes	4—21 in
Main engines	2 Fiat MB 820 N/I diesels, 1 electric motor, Diesel-electric drive; 2 200 hp; 1 shaft
Speed, knots	9 on surface; 14 submerged
Radius, miles	3 000 at 5 knots
Complement	24

BAGNOLINI *1969, Italian Navy, Official*

Italy's first native-built submarines since the Second World War. The design was recast several times, being finalised as coastal submarines of the hunter-killer type. The above figures were officially revised in 1969.

RESCINDMENT. The two projected oceangoing hunter-killer submarines of 1 370 tons were officially deleted from the New Construction Programme in 1968.

TOTI on speed trials *1968, Italian Navy, Official*

3 Ex-US "BALAO" CLASS

Name	No.	Builders	Launched	Completed	Transferred
ALFREDO CAPPELLINI (ex-USS *Capitaine, SS* 336)	S 513	Electric Boat Div, General Dynamics Corpn	1 Oct 1944	26 Jan 1945	5 Mar 1966
EVANGELISTA TORRICELLI (ex-USS *Lizardfish, SS* 373)	S 512	Manitowoc SB Co, Manitowoc, Wisconsin	16 July 1944	30 Dec. 1944	9 Jan 1960
FRANCESCO MOROSINI (ex-USS *Besugo, SS* 321)	S 514	Electric Boat Div, General Dynamics Corpn	27 Feb 1944	19 June 1944	31 Mar 1966

Displacenemt, tons	1 600 standard; 1 816 surface; 2 425 submerged
Length, feet (*metres*)	311·5 (*95·0*)
Beam, feet (*metres*)	27 (*8·2*))
Draught, feet (*metres*)	17 (*5·2*)
Torpedo tubes	10—21 in (*533 mm*) 6 bow and 4 stern
Main engines	4 GM 16/278 diesels, 6 000 hp; 4 electric motors; 2 750 hp
Speed, knots	18 on surface; 10 submerged
Radius, miles	14 000 at 10 knots
Oil fuel (tons)	300
Complement	85

Former United States oceangoing submarines. *Lizardfish* was originally to have been renamed *Luigi Torelli*. The 3-inch gun is no longer mounted. Photographs of *Evangelista Torricelli* appear in the 1960-61 to 1967-68 editions.

ALFREDO CAPPELLINI *1968, Italian Navy, Official*

2 Ex-US "GATO" CLASS

Name	No.	Builders	Laid down	Launched	Completed	Transferred
LEONARDO DA VINCI (ex-USS *Dace, SS* 247)	S 510	Electric Boat Div, General Dynamics Corpn	22 July 1942	25 Apr 1943	23 July 1943	15 Dec 1954
ENRICO TAZZOLI (ex-USS *Barb, SS* 220)	S 511	Electric Boat Div, General Dynamics Corpn	7 June 1941	2 Apr 1942	8 July 1942	31 Jan 1955

Displacement, tons	1 525 standard; 1 816 surface; 2 425 submerged
Length, feet (*metres*)	307·4 (*93·7*)
Beam, feet (*metres*)	27·3 (*8·3*)
Draught, feet (*metres*)	17 (*5·2*)
Torpedo tubes	10—21 in (*533 mm*) 6 bow and 4 stern
Main engines	4 GM diesels, 6 000 hp; 2 electric motors, 2 750 hp
Speed, knots	18 on surface; 10 submerged
Radius, miles	12 000 at 10 knots
Oil fuel (tons)	300 tons
Complement	85

LEONARDO DA VINCI *1968, Aldo Fraccaroli*

Former United States oceangoing submarines. Transferred to Italy by the USA after conversion to guppy snorkel in 1953-54. Modified structure and fairwater. Loan by US was extended for 5 years in 1959.

A photograph of *Enrico Tazzoli* appears in the 1963-64 to 1965-66 editions.

1 "FLUTTO" CLASS

Name	No.	Builders	Laid down	Launched	Completed	Rebuilt
PIETRO CALVI (ex-*Bario*, ex-*Uit 7*, ex-*Bario*)	S 503	CRDA Trieste (1944); CN Taranto (1961)	15 Mar 1943	23 Jan 1944	Dec 1957	1961

Displacement, tons	800 standard; 905 surface 1 107 submerged
Length, feet (*metres*)	216·5 (*66·0*)
Beam, feet (*metres*)	23 (*7·0*)
Draught, feet (*metres*)	13·2 (*4·0*)
Torpedo tubes	4—21 in (*533 mm*)
Main engines	2 MAN diesels, 2 700 hp; 3 electric motors; 1 shaft
Speed, knots	14 on surface; 14 submerged
Radius, miles	10 000 at 8 knots
Complement	60

Sunk by Allied air-raid on 16 Mar 1945 after having been renamed *Uit* 7. She was reconstructed with a tear drop bow and modernised during 1957-59, being re-launched on 21 June 1959. In Mar 1961 her original name *Bario* was changed to *Pietro Calvi*.

PIETRO CALVI *1967, Aldo Fraccaroli*

DISPOSALS. The submarine *Vortice* of the "Flutto" class was officially deleted from the list in 1967.

The submarine *Giada* of the "Acciaio" class was removed from the effective list in 1965.

GUIDED MISSILE CRUISERS (CG)

Name	No.	Builders	Laid down	Launched	Completed
VITTORIO VENETO	C 550	Navalmeccanica Castellammare di Stabia	10 June 1965	5 Feb 1967	30 Apr 1969

1 NEW CONSTRUCTION

Displacement, tons	8 850 full load
Length, feet (*metres*)	557·7 (*170·0*) oa
Beam, feet (*metres*)	63·6 (*19·4*)
Draught, feet (*metres*)	17·2 (*5·2*)
Aircraft	9 A/B 240B ASW helicopters
Missiles, AA	1 "Terrier"/"Asroc" twin launcher forward
Guns, AA	8—3 in (*76 mm*) 62 cal.
Torpedo tubes	2 triple for A/S torpedoes
Boilers	4 Foster-Wheeler; 711 psi (*50 kg/cm²*); 842°F (*450°C*)
Main engines	2 Tosi double reduction geared turbines; 73 000 shp; 2 shafts
Speed, knots	32 designed
Radius, miles	6 000 at 20 knots
Oil fuel, tons	1 200
Complement	550

Multi-purpose guided missile armed cruiser and helicopter carrier. Developed from the "Doria" class, but with much larger helicopter squadron and improved facilities for anti-submarine operations. Projected under the 1959-60 New Construction Programme, but her design has been recast several times, see official artist's impression in the 1963-64 to 1966-67 editions.

RESCINDMENT. The projected improved guided missile cruiser helicopter carrier/assault ship *Trieste* (ex-*Italia*) was officially deleted from the New Construction Programme in 1968.

VITTORIO VENETO — *1969, Italian Navy, Official*

VITTORIO VENETO — *1969, Italian Navy, Official*

DRAWING. Scale: 75 feet = 1 inch (1 : 900)

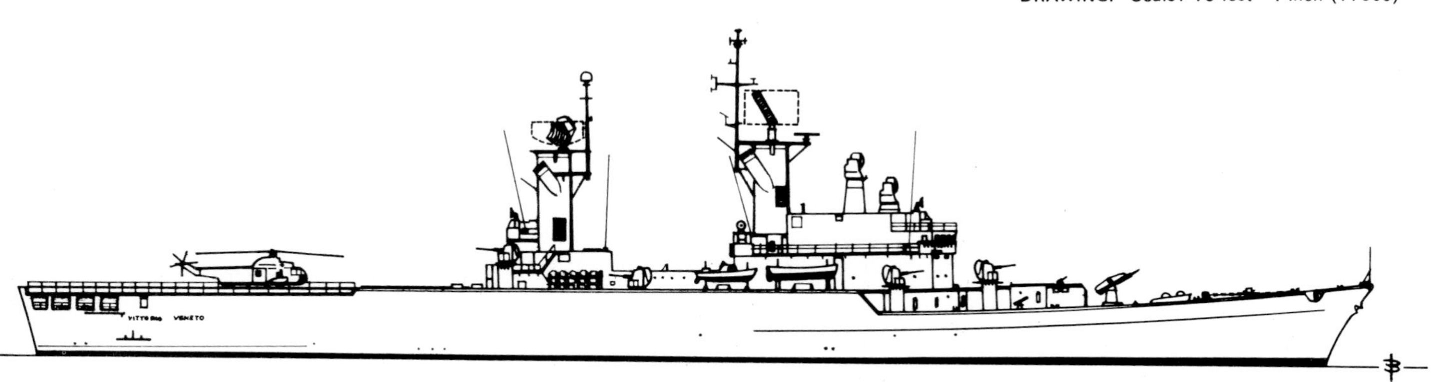

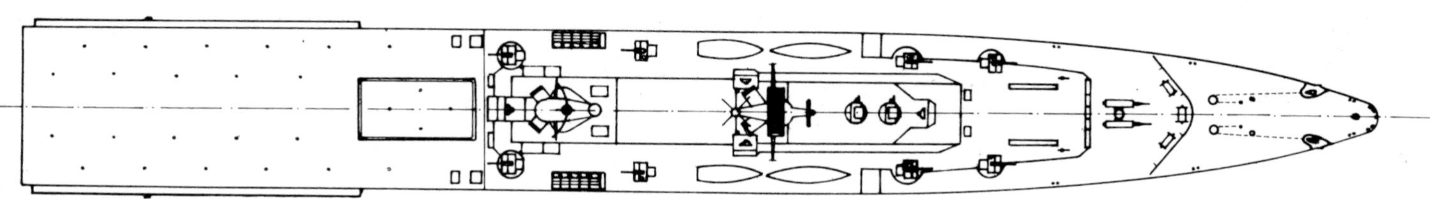

GUIDED MISSILE ESCORT CRUISERS (CG)

Name	No.	Builders	Laid down	Launched	Completed
ANDREA DORIA	553	Cantieri del Tirreno, Riva Trigoso	11 May 1958	27 Feb 1963	23 Feb 1964
CAIO DUILIO	554	Navalmeccanica Castellammare di Stabia	16 May 1958	22 Dec 1962	30 Nov 1964

2 "ANDREA DORIA" CLASS

(officially rated as *Incrociatori di Scorta*)

Displacement, tons	6 500 full load
Length, feet (*metres*)	489·8 (*149·3*) oa
Beam, feet (*metres*)	56·4 (*17·2*)
Draught, feet (*metres*)	16·4 (*5·0*)
Aircraft	4 A/B 204B ASW helicopters
Missiles, AA	1 "Terrier" twin launcher forward
Guns, AA	8—3 in (*76 mm*) 62 cal.
Torpedo tubes	2 triple for 12 in (*305 mm*) A/S torpedoes
Boilers	4 Foster-Wheeler; 711 psi (*50 kg/cm²*); 842°F (*450°C*)
Main engines	2 double reduction geared turbines 60 000 shp; 2 shafts
Speed, knots	31 designed, 30 sustained
Radius, miles	6 000 at 20 knots
Oil fuel, tons	1 100
Complement	478 (53 officers, 425 men)

Escort cruisers of an entirely new design, extraordinarily beamy in relation to their length. *Enrico Dandolo* was the name originally allocated to *Andrea Doria*.

GUNNERY. The anti-aircraft battery includes eight 3-inch fully automatic guns of a new pattern, disposed in single turrets, four on each side amidships abreast the funnels and the bridge.

HELICOPTER PLATFORM. Helicopters operate from a large platform aft measuring 98·5 feet by 52·5 feet (*30 by 16 metres*).

ROLL DAMPING. Both ships have Gyrofin-Salmoiraghi stabilisers.

VTOL HARRIER. The Harrier, the world's first operational VTOL close support fighter aircraft, designed and built by Hawker Siddeley, demonstrated its capabilities of operating from shipborne platforms when it completed a two-day demonstration watched by Italian service chiefs, with a vertical landing on the comparatively small helicopter flight deck of the *Andrea Doria* over which it had arrived at almost the speed of sound and from which it took off again vertically to fly back to England via Pisa, see adjacent photograph.

ANDREA DORIA *1969, Dr. Aldo Fraccaroli*

CAIO DUILIO *1968, Italian Navy, Official*

ANDREA DORIA showing most of the flight deck and HARRIER vertically landed *1969*

ANDREA DORIA *1968, Dr Giorgio Arra*

GUIDED MISSILE LIGHT CRUISER *(CG)*

Name	*No.*	*Builders*	*Laid down*	*Launched*	*Completed*	*Converted*
GIUSEPPE GARIBALDI	C 551	C.R. dell'Adriatico, Trieste	Dec 1933	21 Apr 1936	Dec 1937	Dec 1957-1962

Displacement, tons	9 800 standard; 11 335 full load
Length, feet *(metres)*	593 *(180·7)* wl; 613·5 *(187·0)* oa
Beam, feet *(metres)*	61·7 *(18·8)* oa
Draught, feet *(metres)*	22 *(6·7)*
Missiles, surface	4 tubes for ICBM's aft in "Y" position. see *Guided Weapons* notes
Missiles, AA	1 "Terrier" twin launcher
Guns, dual purpose	4—5·3 in *(135 mm)*, 53 cal., 2 twin, see *Gunnery* notes
Guns, AA	8—3 in *(76 mm)* 62 cal., singles
Armour	Belt 4·5 in *(115 mm)*; deck 2·25 in *(57·5 mm)*; turrets 4 in *(100 mm)*; CT 5 in *(125 mm)*
Boilers	6 CRDA Yarrow three-drum type; 356 psi *(25 kg/cm²)*; 608°F *(320°C)*
Main engines	2 Parsons single reduction geared turbines; 100 000 shp; 2 shafts
Speed, knots	30
Radius, miles	4 000 at 20 knots
Oil fuel (tons)	1 700
Complement	694 (43 officers, 651 men)

Originally a sister ship of the light cruiser *Luigi di Savoia Duca degli Abruzzi* (removed from the effective list in Apr 1961), she was converted into a guided missile cruiser. The appearance of the ship was completely altered, with a single large trunked funnel and lattice masts. She was commissioned for operational service in Nov 1962, and became Flagship of the Commander-in-Chief.

MISSILE SYSTEMS. The ballistic missile tubes are installed aft in "Y" position the "Terrier" system being superimposed in "X" position, a deck higher. *Giuseppe Garibaldi* launched mock "Terriers" and ballistic missiles off La Spezia in late 1961 and 1962. Her initial launches were made in the Caribbean Sea on 8 Nov 1962 first with "Terriers" and then with ballistic missiles.

CONVERSION. The modernisation and conversion of *Giuseppe Garibaldi* into an Anti-Submarine Warfare Command Ship was under consideration, but was rescinded due to lack of funds.

GUNNERY. The armament includes four 5·3 inch dual purpose guns of a new automatic model disposed in two twin turrets forward, and an anti-aircraft battery of eight 3-inch automatic guns, also of a new pattern, built by O.T.O. La Spezia, disposed in single turrets, four on each side amidships abreast the funnel and bridge.

ENGINEERING. On her original trials this ship developed 104 030 shp and a speed of 33·6 knots. During reconstruction her machinery was completely refitted.

FUNNEL. Early in 1963 the top of the funnel cowl was modified, increasing the height.

OPERATIONAL. *Giuseppi Garibaldi*, with the guided missile armed destroyers *Impavido* and *Intrepido*, form the 4th Naval Division.

PHOTOGRAPHS. A starboard broadside view and a port quarter oblique view, both before the funnel was heightened, appear in the 1962-63 edition; and a port quarter view of the ship, firing a Polaris-type fleet ballistic missile from a vertical tube aft, appears in the Addenda (page 450) of the 1963-64 edition. A starboard dead broadside surface view appears in the 1964-65 and 1965-66 editions, a port quarter oblique surface view in the 1965-66 edition, a stern view of the ship, firing a "Terrier" missile, in the 1966-67 edition, a port broadside surface view in the 1966-67 and 1967-68 editions, a port quarter oblique aerial view in the 1967-68 edition, and a starboard bow oblique aerial view in the 1968-69 edition.

DRAWING. Starboard elevation and plan. Drawn in 1969. Scale: 125 feet = 1 inch (1 : 1500)

GIUSEPPE GARIBALDI (missiles aft silhouetted) *1969, Italian Navy, Official*

GIUSEPPE GARIBALDI (showing stern tubes for 4 ballistic missiles) 1963, *Captain Aldo Fraccaroli*

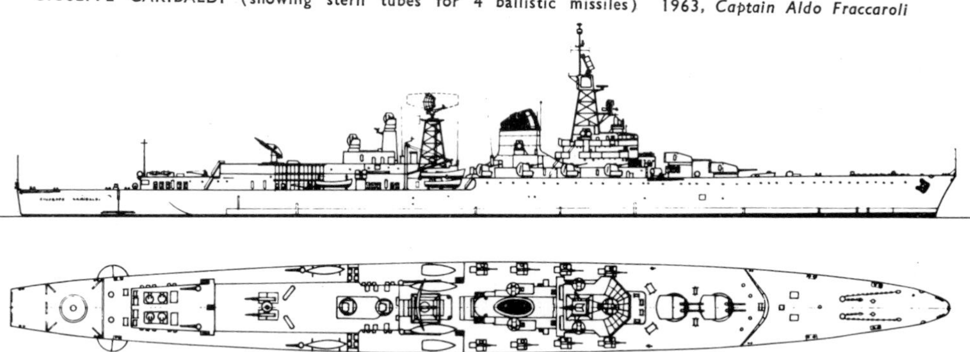

GIUSEPPE GARIBALDI *1968, Dr. Giorgio Arra*

GUIDED MISSILE ARMED DESTROYERS *(DDG)*

2 "AUDACE" CLASS NEW CONSTRUCTION

ARDITO **AUDACE**

Displacement, tons	4 400 full load
Length, feet (*metres*)	446·4 (*136·6*)
Beam, feet (*metres*)	46·7 (*14·2*)
Draught, feet (*metres*)	15 (*4·6*)
Aircraft	2 light A/S helicopters
Missiles, AA	1 "Tartar" launcher aft
Guns, dual purpose	2—5 in (*127 mm*) 54 cal single
Guns, AA	4—3 in (*76 mm*) 62 cal
Torpedo tubes	6 A/S (two tripled)
Boilers	4
Main engines	2 geared turbines; 73 000 shp
Speed, knots	33

It was announced in Apr 1966 that two new guided missile armed destroyers would be built. They will be basically similar to, but an improvement in design on that of, the "Impavido" class, but will be measurably larger, with an extended flight platform so that they can operate more than one A/B 204 B ASW helicopters. Officially rated as *Caccia Lanciamissile* and designated DDG.

Name	*No.*	*Builders*	*Ordered*	*Laid down*	*Launched*	*Completed*
IMPAVIDO	D 570	Cantieri del Tirreno, Riva Trigoso	Jan 1957	10 June 1957	25 May 1962	16 Nov 1963
INTREPIDO	D 571	Ansaldo, Leghorn	1959	16 May 1959	21 Oct 1962	30 Oct 1964

2 "IMPAVIDO" CLASS

Displacement, tons	3 201 standard; 3 941 full load
Length, feet (*metres*)	429·5 (*130·9*)
Beam, feet (*metres*)	44·7 (*13·6*)
Draught, feet (*metres*)	14·8 (*4·5*)
Aircraft	1 A/S light helicopter
Missiles, AA	1 "Tartar" launcher, aft
Guns, AA	2—5 in (*127 mm*) 38 cal. forward 4—3 in (*76 mm*) 62 cal.
Torpedo tubes	2 triple for A/S torpedoes
Boilers	4 Foster Wheeler; 711 psi (*50 kg/cm²*); 842°F (*450°C*)
Main engines	2 double teduction geared turbines 70 000 shp; 2 shafts
Speed, knots	34 designed, see *Engineering*
Radius, miles	3 300 at 20 knots
Oil fuel, tons	650
Complement	344 (15 officers, 319 men)

Rated as *Caccia Lanciamissili*. Built under the 1956-57 and 1958-59 programmes, respectively. Both ships have stabilisers.

ANTI-SUBMARINE WARFARE. The helicopters are of the weapons carrier type (Italian).

ENGINEERING. On preliminary full power trials *Impavido*, at light displacement, reached 34·5 knots (33 knots max at normal load). Sustained sea speed: 30 knots.

IMPAVIDO *1968, Aldo Fraccaroli*

INTREPIDO *1968, Dr. Giorgio Arra*

GIUSEPPE GARIBALDI *1968, Dr. Giorgio Arra*

DESTROYER LEADERS (*ex-LIGHT CRUISERS*) DL

Name	*No.*	*Builders*	*Laid down*	*Launched*	*Completed*
SAN GIORGIO (ex-*Pompeo Magno*)	D 562	Cantieri N. Riuniti Ancona	23 Sep 1939	28 Aug 1941	24 June 1943
SAN MARCO (ex-*Giulio Germanico*)	D 563	Navalmeccanica Castellammare de Stabia	11 May 1940	20 July 1941	19 Jan 1956

Displacement, tons	*San Marco:* 5 257 full load *San Giorgio:* 4 450 full load
Length, feet (*metres*)	455·2 (*138·8*) wl; 466·5 (142·3) oa
Beam, feet (*metres*)	47·2 (*14·4*)
Draught, feet (*metres*)	21 (*6·4*)
Guns, surface	*San Marco:* 6—5 in (*127 mm*) 38 *San Giorgio:* 4—5 in (*127 mm*) 38
Guns, AA	*San Marco:* 20—40 mm, 56 cal. *San Giorgio:* 3—3 in (*76 mm*) 62
A/S	*San Marco:* 1 three-barrel mortar; 4 DCT; 1 DC rack *San Giorgio:* 1 three-barrel mortar: 2 triple torpedo tubes
Boilers	*San Marco* only: 4 three-drum type; 412 psi (*29 kg/cm²*); 608°F (*320°C*)
Main engines	*San Marco:* 2 single reduction Geared steam turbines, 110 000 shp; 2 shafts *San Giorgio:* 2 Tosi Metrovick gas turbines, 15 000 hp; and 4 Fiat diesels; 16 600 bhp; 2 shafts
Speed, knots	*San Marco:* 38·5; *San Giorgio:* 20 (diesels only), 28 (diesel and gas)
Radius, miles	*San Marco:* 3 080 at 20 knots; *San Giorgio:* 4 800 at 20 knots
Oil fuel (tons)	*San Marco:* 1 380; *San Giorgio:* 500 (diesel oil)
Complement	*San Giorgio:* 348 (23 officers, 325 men) *San Marco:* 494 (30 officers, 464 men)

SAN GIORGIO *1969, A. F. Nicholas*

Built as *Esploratori Oceanici* (Ocean Scouts), but re-rated light cruisers of the Roman Captains (*Capitani Romani*) class. *Guillio Germanico* sunk by Germans in Sep 1943 before completion, but re-floated in 1947. Both converted into fleet destroyers in 1951-56 by Cantieri del Tirreno, Genova and Navalmeccanica Castellammare di Stabia, *San Giorgio* being completed 1 July 1955 and *San Marco* 20 Feb 1956. Re-rated *Esploratori* (scouts) in 1957 ,and *Cacciatorpediniere Conduttori* (destroyer leaders in 1958. *San Giorgio* underwent complete re-construction at the Naval Dockyard, La Spezia, in 1963-65. The modernisation included her adaptation as a Training Ship for 130 cadets of the Accademia Navale. Changes were made in the armament (she was formerly armed like *San Marco*) and new machinery fitted, gas turbines and diesels replacing steam turbines and boilers.

SAN MARCO *1968, Aldo Fraccaroli*

DESTROYERS

Name	*No.*	*Builders*	*Ordered*	*Laid down*	*Launched*	*Completed*
IMPETUOSO	D 558	Cantieri del Tirreno, Riva Trigoso	Nov 1950	7 May 1952	16 Sep 1956	25 Jan 1958
INDOMITO	D 559	Ansaldo, Leghorn (formerly OTO)	Nov 1950	24 Apr 1952	7 Aug 1955	23 Feb 1958

2 "IMPETUOSO" CLASS

Displacement, tons	2 755 standard; 3 800 full load
Length, feet (*metres*)	405 (*123·4*) pp; 418·7 (*127·6*) oa
Beam, feet (*metres*)	43·5 (*13·3*)
Draught, feet (*metres*)	17·5 (*5·3*)
Guns, AA	4—5 in (*127 mm*) 38 cal. 16—40 mm, 56 cal.
A/S	1 three-barrel mortar; 4 DCT; 1 DC rack
Torpedo tubes	2 triple for A/S torpedoes
Boilers	4 Foster-Wheeler; 711 psi (50 *kg/cm²*) working pressure; 842°F (*450°C*) superheat temperature
Main engines	2 double reduction geared turbines 65 000 shp; 2 shafts
Speed, knots	34, see *Engineering* notes
Radius, miles	3 400 at 20 knots
Oil fuel (tons)	650
Complement	393 (25 officers, 368 men)

Italy's first destroyers constructed since the Second World War. Officially rated as Cacciatorpediniere or torpedo boat destroyers.

ENGINEERING. On their initial sea trials these ships attained a speed of 35 knots at full load.

CONVERSION. The modernisation and conversion of these ships to guided missile armed destroyers, with single "Tartar" launcher aft in place of the 5 inch gun mounting, is under consideration, but the decision has been postponed pending provision of funds.

INDOMITO *1968, Aldo Fraccaroli*

IMPETUOSO *Added 1967, Aldo Fraccaroli*

DESTROYERS —*continued*

Name	No.	Builders	Laid down	Launched	Completed
ARTIGLIERE (ex-USS *Woodworth, DD* 460)	D 553	Bethlehem, San Francisco	13 Jan 1941	29 Nov 1941	30 Apr 1942

Displacement, tons 2 575 full load
Length, feet (*metres*) 347·3 (*105·9*) oa
Beam, feet (*metres*) 36·1 (*11·0*)
Draught, feet (*metres*) 18 (*5·5*) max
Guns, surface 4—5 in (*127 mm*) 38 cal.
Guns, AA 12—40 mm, 56 cal.
6—20 mm, 70 cal.
A/S 4 DC throwers; 2 DC racks
Boilers 4 high pressure
Main engines Geared turbines
50 000 shp; 2 shafts
Speed, knots 31
Radius, miles 6 000 at 12 knots
Oil fuel (tons) 600
Complement 250

ARTIGLIERE *1969, Aldo Fraccaroli*

Former United States "Mayo" class destroyer (DD). Used as command ship of motor torpedo boat flotillas.

TRANSFER. Both transferred from USA and commissioned on 25 May 1951. Officially turned over to Italy on 11 June 1951. The 5—21 inch torpedo tubes were removed.

APPEARANCE. *Artigiere* has flat funnels and shielded "X" 5 inch mounting, but *Aviere* has round funnels and no shield to "X" 5 inch gun mounting, and has extra tier on bridge, see photographs above and below.

Name	No.	Builders	Laid down	Launched	Completed
AVIERE (ex-USS *Nicholson, DD* 442)	D 554	Boston Navy Yard	1 Nov 1939	31 May 1940	3 June 1941

Displacement, tons 2 580 full load
Length, feet (*metres*) 341 (*103·9*) wl; 348·2 (*106·1*) oa
Beam, feet (*metres*) 36·1 (*11·0*)
Draught, feet (*metres*) 18 (*5·5*) max
Guns, surface 4—5 in (*127 mm*) 38 cal.
Guns, AA 12—40 mm; 6—20 mm
A/S 4—DC throwers; 2 DC racks
Boilers 4 Babcock & Wilcox
Main engines GE geared turbines
50 000 shp; 2 shafts
Speed, knots 31
Radius, miles 6 000 at 12 knots
Oil fuel (tons) 600
Complement 250

AVIERE *1969, Italian Navy, Official*

Former United States "Gleaves" class destroyer (DD). See TRANSFER and APPEARANCE above.

Name	No.	Builders	Laid down	Launched	Completed
ALPINÒ (ex-*Circe*)	F 580	Cantiere Navali del Tirreno, Riva Trigoso	27 Feb 1963	10 June 1967	14 Jan 1968
CARABINIERE (ex-*Climene*)	F 581	Cantiere Navali del Tirreno, Riva Trigoso	9 Jan 1965	30 Sep 1967	1968

FRIGATES (*Fregate*)

2 "ALPINO" CLASS NEW CONSTRUCTION

Displacement, tons 2 700 full load
Length, feet (*metres*) 349·0 (*106·4*) pp; 352·0 (*107·3*) wl; 371·7 (*113·3*) oa
Beam, feet (*metres*) 43 (*13·1*)
Draught, feet (*metres*) 12·7 (*3·9*)
Aircraft 2 A/B 204B ASW helicopters
Guns dual purpose 6—3 in (*76 mm*) 62 cal single
A/S 1 single-barrelled DC mortar
Tubes 2 triple 12 In (*305 mm*) for A/S torpedoes
Main engines 4 Tosi diesels = 16 800 hp; 2 Tosi Metrovick gas turbines = 15 000 hp; 31 800 hp; 2 shafts
Speed, knots 22 (diesel only), 28 (diesel and gas)
Radius, miles 4 200 at 18 knots
Oil fuel (tons) 275
Complement 254 (21 officers, 233 men)

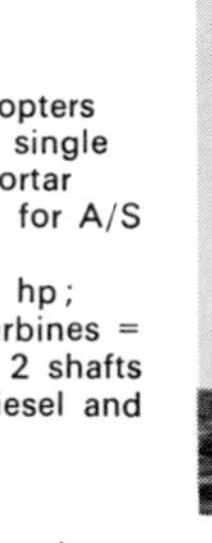

CARABINIERE *1968, Dr. Ing. Luigi Accorsi*

Circe and *Climene* were provided for under the 1959-60 programme. The original "Circe" class project was modified in 1962, in respect of both machinery and armament. The originally allocated names *Circe* and *Climene* were changed to *Alpino* and *Carabiniere*, respectively in June 1965. The new design is an improved version of that of the "Centauro" class combined with that of the "Bergamini" class. They have similar basic characteristics but a heavier displacement and increased engine power. Two other ships of the same type, to have been named *Perseo* and *Polluce* were provided for under the 1960-61 programme, but they were suspended owing to fiscal considerations, and new names reported are *Bersagliere* and *Granatiere*.

Name	No.	Builders	Laid down	Launched	Completed
ALDEBARAN (ex-USS *Thornhill, DE* 195)	F 590	Federal SB & DD Co, P. Newark	7 Oct 1943	30 Dec 1943	1 Feb 1944
ALTAIR (ex-USS *Gandy, DE* 764)	F 591	Tampa SB Co	1 Mar 1943	12 Dec 1943	7 Feb 1944
ANDROMEDA (ex-USS *Wesson, DE* 184)	F 592	Federal SB & DD Co, P. Newark	29 July 1943	17 Oct 1943	11 Nov 1943

3 Ex-US DE TYPE "ALTAIR" CLASS

Displacement, tons 1 900 full load
Length, feet (*metres*) 306 (*93·3*) oa
Beam, feet (*metres*) 36·7 (*11·2*)
Draught, feet (*metres*) 14 (*4·3*)
Guns, surface 3—3 in (*76 mm*) 50 cal.
Guns, AA 6—40 mm; 18—20 mm
A/S 1 Hedgehog; 8 DCT; 2 DC racks
Main engines 6 000 hp GM diesel-electric, 2 shafts
Speed, knots 21; 17·5 sea speed
Radius, miles 11 500 at 11 knots
Oil fuel (tons) 300
Complement 160

Ex-US destroyer escorts of the "Bostwick" class ceded by USA under MDAP. Transferred on 10 Jan 1951. In 1956 a pentapod foremast was stepped in place of the former polemast. A photograph of *Aldebaran* appears in the 1967-68 edition.

ALTAIR ***1968, Aldo Fraccaroli***

Frigates—*continued*

4 "CENTAURO" CLASS

Name	No.	Builders	Laid down	Launched	Completed
CANOPO	F 552 (ex-D 570)	Cantieri Navali di Taranto	15 May 1952	20 Feb 1955	1 Apr 1958
CENTAURO	F 554 (ex-D 571)	Ansaldo, Leghorn	31 May 1952	4 Apr 1954	5 May 1957
CIGNO	F 555 (ex-D 572)	Cantieri Navali di Taranto	10 Feb 1954	20 Mar 1955	7 Mar 1957
CASTORE	F 553 (ex-D 573)	Cantieri Navali di Taranto	14 Mar 1955	8 July 1956	14 July 1957

Displacement, tons	1 807 standard; 2 196 full load (revised official figures)
Length, feet (*metres*)	308·4 (*94*) pp; 338·4 (*103·1*) oa
Beam, feet (*metres*)	39·5 (*12*)
Draught, feet (*metres*)	12·6 (*3·8*)
Guns, AA	3—3 in (*76 mm*) 62 cal single
A/S	1 three-barrelled depth charge mortar 6 torpedo launchers (2 triple)
Main engines	2 double reduction geared turbines 2 shafts; 22 000 shp
Speed, knots	26
Boilers	2 Foster Wheeler; 626 psi (44 *kg/cm*^{2}) working pressure; 842°F (*450°C*) superheat temperature
Oil fuel, tons	400
Radius, miles	2 500 at 20 knots
Complement	255 (16 officers, 239 men)

The above refers to *Castore*, see *Conversion.*

Cigno (US hull No. DE 1020) and *Castore* (DE 1031) were built to Italian plans and specifications under the US off-shore programme. All four ships have automatic anti-submarine and medium anti-aircraft armament, and are fitted with US sonar gear.

PENNANT NOS. In 1960 these four ships, which originally had D pennant numbers, were given F Nos. The originally allocated F number of *Canopo* was 551.

CONVERSION. *Castore* underwent medium anti-aircraft conversion in 1966-67 and the other three ships are being similarly converted. See former particulars in the 1966-67 and earlier editions. The changes include the mounting of three 3-inch 62 cal single guns, replacing the two 2 barrelled 76/62 and the four 40 mm 70 cal AA.

GUNNERY. The 3 inch guns originally mounted were in twin gunhouses of a new type with the two barrels in the vertical plane, one superfiring over the other. They were Italian designed and built by OTO, La Spezia. Their rate of fire was 60 rounds per minute with 3 200 feet per second muzzle velocity.

PHOTOGRAPHS Several differing views of *Cigno* appear in the 1957-58 to 1965-66 editions.

CENTAURO *1967, Italian Navy, Official*

CASTORE *1967, Italian Navy, Official*

4 "BERGAMINI" CLASS

Name	No.	Builders	Laid down	Launched	Completed
CARLO BERGAMINI	F 593	San Marco, CRDA Trieste	19 May 1957	16 June 1960	23 June 1962
CARLO MARGOTTINI	F 595	Navalmeccanica, Castellammare	26 May 1957	12 June 1960	5 May 1962
LUIGI RIZZO	F 596	Navalmeccanica, Castellammare	26 May 1957	6 Mar 1957	15 Dec 1961
VIRGINIO FASAN	F 594	Navalmeccanica, Castellammare	6 Mar 1960	9 Oct 1960	10 Oct 1962

Displacement, tons	1 650 full load
Length, feet (*metres*)	308·4 (*94*) oa
Beam, feet (*metres*)	37·4 (*11·4*)
Draught, feet (*metres*)	10·2 (*3·1*)
Guns, AA	3—3 in (*76 mm*) 62 cal single
A/S	1 single-barrelled depth charge mortar; 6—12 in torpedo launchers (2 triple)
Aircraft	1 A/B-47-J3 helicopter
Main engines	4 diesels (Fiat in *Fasan* and *Margottini*, Tosi in others); 2 shafts; 15 000 bhp
Speed, knots	26 max; 24·5 sustained
Radius, miles	4 000 at 10 knots

Light frigates of new type with diesel instead of steam propulsion. Originally rated as *Corvette Veloci.*

CONSTRUCTION. *Carlo Bergamini* was originally to have been built by Cantieri Navali di Taranto: but the order was cancelled and she was begun at CRDA di Trieste Yard in May 1959 (built until launch in San Marco yard, Trieste, but completed in Monfalcone yard, both of CRDA).

ANTI-SUBMARINE WARFARE. The single-barrelled automatic depth charge mortars have a range of 1 000 yards. Rate of fire 15 DC per minute. The 12-inch torpedoes have a life of six minutes at 30 knots.

ENGINEERING. The diesels are coupled to the shafts by reduction gearing and Vulcan joints.

ROLL DAMPING. Two Denny-Brown stabilisers reduce inclination in heavy seas from 20 to 5 degrees.

PHOTOGRAPHS. A starboard broadside view of *Carlo Margottini* appears in the 1963-64 to 1965-66 editions.

PHOTOGRAPHS. A starboard broadside view of *Carlo Margottini* appears in the 1963-64 to 1965-66 editions, and a starboard bow surface view of *Carlo Bergamini* in the 1966-67 and 1967-68 editions.

VIRGINIO FASAN *1968, Italian Navy, Official*

LUIGI RIZZO *1966, Aldo Fraccaroli*

CORVETTES

Name	No.	Builders	Laid down	Launched	Completed
LICIO VISINTINI	F 546	CRDA Monfalcone	30 Sep 1963	30 May 1965	25 Aug 1966
PIETRO DE CRISTOFARO	F 540	Cantiere Navali de Tirreho, Riva Tregoso	30 Apr 1963	29 May 1965	19 Dec 1965
SALVATORE TODARO	F 550	Cantiere Ansaldo, Leghorn	21 Oct 1962	24 Oct 1964	25 Apr 1966
UMBERTO GROSSO	F 541	Cantiere Ansaldo, Leghorn	21 Oct 1962	12 Dec. 1964	25 Apr. 1966

4 "DE CRISTOFARO" CLASS

Displacement, tons	850 standard; 940 full load
Length, feet (*metres*)	246 (*75·0*) pp; 263·2 (*80·2*) oa
Beam, feet (*metres*)	33·7 (*10·3*)
Draught, feet (*metres*)	9 (*2·7*)
Guns, dual purpose	2—3 in (*76 mm*), 62 cal, single
A/S	1 single-barrel DC mortar
Torpedo tubes	2 triple for A/S torpedoes
Main engines	2 diesels = 8 400 bhp; 2 shafts
Speed, knots	23·5 max; 21·5 sustained sea
Radius, miles	4 000 at 18 knots
Oil fuel, tons	100
Complement	131 (8 officers, 123 men)

The design is an improved version of that of the "Albatros" class.

PHOTOGRAPHS. A photograph of *Pietro de Cristofaro* appears in the 1966-67 and 1967-68 editions.

UMBERTO GROSSO *1968, A. & J. Pavia*

RESCINDMENT. The projected improved "corvette" of this type, *circa* 1 200 tons, gas turbines, 20 000 hp, 30-31 knots, was officially deleted from the New Construction Programme in 1968.

Name	No.	Builders	Launched	Completed
AIRONE (ex-*PCE* 1921)	F 545	Navalmeccanica, Castellammare di Stabia	21 Nov 1954	29 Dec 1955
ALBATROS (ex-*PCE* 1919)	F 543	Navalmeccanica, Castellammare di Stabia	18 July 1954	1 June 1955
ALCIONE (ex-*PCE* 1920	F 544	Navalmeccanica, Castellammare di Stabia	19 Sep 1954	23 Oct 1955
AQUILA (ex-*Lynx*, ex-*PCE* 1626)	F 542	Breda Marghera Yard, Mestre, Venice	31 July 1954	2 Oct 1956

4 "ALBATROS" CLASS

Displacement, tons	800 standard; 950 full load
Length, feet (*metres*)	250·3 (*76·3*) oa
Beam, feet (*metres*)	31·5 (*9·6*)
Draught, feet (*metres*)	9·2 (*2·8*)
Guns, AA	4—40 mm 70 cal. Bofors (see *Gunnery*)
A/S	2 Hedgehogs Mk II; 2 DCT; 1 DC rack (see *Tubes*)
Main engines	2 Fiat diesels = 5 200 bhp; 2 shafts
Speed, knots	19
Radius, miles	2 400 at 18 knots
Oil fuel (tons)	100
Complement	109

Airone, *Albatros* and *Alcione* were built in Italy. Four identical ships were built in Italian yards to the offshore construction order of the USA for MDP account and handed over to Denmark.

GUNNERY. The two 3-inch guns originally mounted, one forward and one aft, were temporarily replaced by two 40 mm guns in 1963. The ultimate armament will include two 3-inch guns of the OTO Malera model.

TRANSFER. *Aquila*, built in Italy (laid down on 25 July 1953), but initially given to the Netherlands, was ceded to the Italian Navy on 18 Oct 1961 at Den Helder.

TUBES. All four ships will receive two triple ASW torpedo tubes.

PHOTOGRAPHS. A photograph of *Airone* appears in the 1959-60 to 1961-62 editions.

AQUILA *1967, Aldo Fraccaroli*

15 "APE" CLASS

BAIONETTA	F 578	**GABBIANO**	F 571
BOMBARDA	F 549	**GRU**	F 566
CHIMERA	F 569	**IBIS**	F 561
CORMORANO	F 575	**PELLICANO**	F 574
CRISALIDE	F 547	**SCIMITARRA**	F 564
FARFALLA	F 548	**SFINGE**	F 579
FLORA	F 572	**SIBILLA**	F 565
		URANIA	F 570

Displacement, tons	670 standard; 771 full load
Length, feet (*metres*)	192·8 (*58·8*) wl; 212·6 (*64·8*) oa
Beam, feet (*metres*)	28·5 (*8·7*)
Draught, feet (*metres*)	8·9 (*2·7*)
Guns, AA	4—40 mm 56 cal in 6 ships; 3—40 mm 56 cal in 8 ships; 2—40 mm 56 cal in 2 ships, see *Gunnery*
A/S	1 Hedgehog Mk 10 (see notes); 4 DCT; 1 DC rack
Torpedo tubes	2—17·7 in (*450 mm*), see notes
Main engines	2 Fiat diesels = 3 500 bhp; 2 shafts
Speed, knots	15
Radius, miles	2 800 at 15 knots
Oil fuel (tons)	64
Complement	100

All launched in 1942-48. Originally fitted for minesweeping. Armament is frequently changed. All modified with navigating bridge. The eight vessels attached to Command Training School carried torpedo tubes.

GUNNERY. *Chimera*, *Cormorano*, *Flora*, *Pellicano*, *Sibilla* and *Sfinge* carry 4—40 mm 56 cal AA. *Bombarda* and *Gabbiano* carry 2—40 mm 56 cal AA and 2—20 mm 70 cal AA. Remainder have 3—40 mm 56 cal AA. *Cormorano* and *Sibilla* have no hedgehog.

PHOTOGRAPHS. A photograph of *Gru* appears in the 1955-56 and 1956-57 editions, of *Scimitarra* in the 1957-58 edition, of *Pellicano* in the 1960-61, 1961-62 and 1962-63 editions, and of *Cormorano* in the 1963-64, 1964-65 and 1965-66 editions.

DISPOSALS

Ape, F 567, **Fenice**, F 577, **Folaga**, F 576, and **Pomona**, F 573, were officially deleted from the list in 1965, **Driade**, F 568, on 1 Aug 1966, **Danaide**, F 563 in 1968, **Minerva**, F 562, in 1969.

CRISALIDE *1966, Italian Navy, Official*

SFINGE *1968, Aldo Fracaroli*

OCEAN MINESWEEPERS

4 "SALMONE" CLASS (Ex-US MSO TYPE)

SALMONE (ex-*MSO* 507) M 5430
SGOMBRO (ex-*MSO* 517) M 5432
SQUALO (ex-*MSO* 518) M 5433
STORIONE (ex-*MSO* 506) M 5431

Displacement, tons	665 standard; 750 full load
Dimensions, feet	165 wl; 173 oa × 35 × 10
Guns	1—40 mm; 56 cal AA
Main Engines	2 diesels; 2 shafts; 1 600 bhp = 14 knots
Oil fuel (tons)	46
Range, miles	3 000 at 10 knots

Former US "Agile" class. Wooden hulls and non-magnetic equipment, diesels of non-magnetic stainless steel alloy. Controllable pitch propellers. *Storione*, launched on 13 Nov 1954, was built by Martinolich SB Company, San Diego, and transferred on 23 Feb, 1956. *Salmone*, launched on 19 Feb 1955 was built by Martinolich SB Co, and transferred at San Diego, Calif, on 17 June 1956 under MDAP. *Sgombro* and *Squalo* were delivered in June 1957.

A much larger photograph of *Storione* appears in the 1957-58 to 1959-60 editions, and a starboard bow view in the 1960-61 to 1965-66 editions. A photograph of *Squalo* appears in the 1963-64 to 1967-68 editions, and of *Sgombro* in the 1966-67 to 1968-69 editions.

STORIONE *1969, Italian Navy, Official*

SALMONE *1968, Italian Navy, Official*

SUPPORT GUNBOATS *(Cannoniere d'appoggio)*

6 "ALANO" CLASS
(Ex-US LANDING SHIPS, SUPPORT/LARGE)

ALANO (ex-*LSSL* 34)
BRACCO (ex-*LSSL* 38)
MASTINO (ex-*LSSL* 62)
MOLOSSO (ex-*LSSL* 63)
SEGUGIO (ex-*LSSL* 64)
SPINONE (ex-*LSSL* 118)

Displacement, tons	246 standard; 430 full load
Dimensions, feet	153 wl; 158·5 oa × 23·7 × 5·7
Guns	5—40 mm; 56 cal; 4—20 mm, 70 cal; 4—12·7 mm
Main Engines	8 Gray Marine diesels; 2 shafts; 1 800 bhp = 12 knots
Oil fuel (tons)	87
Radius, miles	8 000 at 10 knots

Transferred from the USA on 25 July 1951, under the Mutual Defense Assistance Program. NATO pennant numbers L 9851 to L 9856, respectively.
A photograph of *Alano* appears in the 1955-56 to 1957-58 editions, of *Segugio* in the 1967-68 to 1962-63 editions and of *Mastino* in the 1963-64 to 1967-68 editions.

SPINONE *1968, Italian Navy, Official*

MISSILE BOATS

5 NEW CONSTRUCTION

Displacement, tons	300
Missile launchers	Surface-to-surface system
Main engines	All gas turbine propulsion

Vessels of the large MGB type projected under the 1969 new construction programme.

PATROL VESSEL

VEDETTA (ex-*Belay Deress*, ex-USS *PC* 1616) F 597

Displacement, tons	325 standard; 450 full load
Dimensions, feet	170 pp; 174 oa × 23 × 10
Guns	2—40 mm; 56 cal Bofors AA; 2—20 mm AA
Main Engines	4 diesels; 2 shafts; 3 240 bhp = 19 knots
A/S	1 Hedgehog; 4 DCT; 2 DC racks
Range, miles	3 000 at 12 knots
Complement	60

Built at Brest, France, as a United States off-shore order under the Mutual Defense Assistance Program. Laid down on 17 Dec 1953. Launched on 30 Sep 1954. Completed on 23 Aug 1955. Originally intended for Germany, but a change in US plans resulted in the ship never being delivered, and she was finally given to Ethiopia under the Military Aid Programme. Transferred to Ethiopia at Bremerhaven, Germany, by the US Navy in Jan 1957. Officially taken over from the US flag at Massawa, Ethiopia, in mid-1957. Later, the ship was found to be too sophisticated for Ethiopia, and she was returned to the US Navy. She was then sold to Italy, being transferred on 3 Feb 1959, and officially classified as a *nave pattuglia* (patrol vessel). Air-conditioning equipment is installed. Refitted in La Spezia Navy Yard in 1959. Employed as a Fishery Protection Vessel.

VEDETTA *1969, Italian Navy, Official*

TORPEDO BOATS *(Motosiluranti)*

MS 441 (ex-841) **MS 443** (ex-843) **MS 453** (ex-853)

Displacement, tons	64 full load
Dimensions, feet	78 × 20 × 6
Guns	1—40 mm, 56 cal; 2 or 3—20 mm, 70 cal
Torpedoes	2—17·7 in (no tubes)
Main engines	3 petrol motors; 3 shafts; 4 500 bhp = 34 knots
Radius, miles	1 000 at 20 knots

Former US PT boats of Higgins type. Refitted in Italy in 1949-53. New radar installed. MS 441 converted into a fast transport for commandos and frogmen.
MS 442 (ex-842), MS 451 (ex-851) and MS 452 (ex-852) transferred to Customs in 1966, and MS 444 (ex-844) was removed from the effective list in 1966.

MS 453 *1969, Italian Navy, Official*

MS 472 (ex-612) **MS 473** (ex-813) **MS 474** (ex-614) **MS 481** (ex-615)

Displacement, tons	72 full load
Dimensions, feet	92 × 15 × 5
Guns	1 or 2—40 mm, 56 cal
Tubes	2—17·7 in
Main Engines	Petrol motors; 3 shafts; 3 450 bhp = 27 knots
Radius, miles	600 at 16 knots

Built in 1942-43 at CRDA Monfalcone yard; converted as MV (motovedette) with no tubes under the Peace Treaty. Reconverted in 1951-53. MS 472 and MS 473 were refitted as convertible boats in 1960 and MS 474 and MS 481 in 1961.
MS 482 (ex-616), MS 483 (ex-617) and MS 484 (ex-618) were removed from the effective list in 1963, and MS 471 (ex-611) and MS 475 (ex-619) in 1965.
The British MTBs *Dark Avenger*, *Dark Biter*, *Dark Hunter* and *Dark Invader* were taken over in 1967 for the Guardia di Finanza.

MS 473 *1966, Giorgio Arra*

COASTAL MINESWEEPERS

18 "ABETE" CLASS

ABETE	M 5501	**FAGGIO**	M 5507	**OLMO**	M 5512
ACACIA	M 5502	**FRASSINO**	M 5508	**ONTANO**	M 5513
BETULLA	M 5503	**GELSO**	M 5509	**PINO**	M 5514
CASTAGNO	M 5504	**LARICE**	M 5510	**PIOPPO**	M 5515
CEDRO	M 5505	**MANDORLO**	M 5519	**PLATANO**	M 5516
CILIEGIO	M 5506	**NOCE**	M 5511	**QUERCIA**	M 5517

Displacement, tons	378 standard; 405 full load
Dimensions, feet	138 pp; 144 oa × 26·5 × 8·5
Guns	2—20 mm, 70 cal AA
Main Engines	2 diesels; 2 shafts; 1 200 bhp = 13·5 knots
Oil fuel (tons)	25
Radius, miles	2 500 at 10 knots

Wooden hulled Dragomine Costieri constructed throughout of materials with the lowest possible magnetic attraction to attain the greatest safety factor when sweeping for magnetic mines. All transferred by the US in 1953-54. Original hull numbers AMS 72-76, 79-82, 88-90, 133-137.
Mandorlo (ex-*Salice*, ex-USS *MSC* 280), transferred at Seattle on 16 Dec 1960, is of slightly different type and is used as MHC (minehunter).
A photograph of *Cilegio* appears in the 1956-57 to 1961-62 editions, and of *Frassino* in the 1965-66 edition. A port bow view of *Mandorlo* appears in the 1962-63 to 1965-66 editions, and a starboard view in the 1966-67 to 1968-69 editions.

PIOPPO *1969, Italian Navy, Official*

19 "AGAVE" CLASS

AGAVE	M 5531	**GLICINE**	M 5537	**BAMBÙ**	*M 5521
ALLORO	M 5532	**LOTO**	M 5538	**EBANO**	*M 5522
EDERA	M 5533	**MIRTO**	M 5539	**MANGO**	*M 5523
GAGGIA	M 5534	**TIMO**	M 5540	**MOGANO**	*M 5524
GELSOMINO	M 5535	**TRIFOGLIO**	M 5541	**PALMA**	*M 5525
GIAGGIOLO	M 5536	**VISCHIO**	M 5542	**ROVERE**	*M 5526
				SANDALO	*M 5527

Displacement, tons	375 standard; 405 full load
Dimensions, feet	144 oa × 26·5 × 8·5
Guns	2—20 mm; 70 cal AA
Main Engines	2 diesels; 2 shafts: 1 200 bhp = 13·5 knots
Oil fuel (tons)	25
Radius, miles	2 500 at 10 knots

Non-magnetic minesweepers of composite wooden and alloy construction similar to those transferred from the US but built in Italian yards. *Last 7 were built by CRDA, Monfalcone, and launched in 1956.
A photogrpah of *Alloro* appears in the 1959-60 to 1961-62 editions, of *Sandalo* in the 1962-63 to 1965-66 editions, of *Gaggia* and *Palma* in the 1966-67 to 1968-69 editions.

BAMBU *1969, Italian Navy, Official*

AGAVE *1969, Italian Navy, Official*

MOTOR GUNBOATS *(Motocannoniere)*

4 "FRECCIA" CLASS CONVERTIBLE TYPE

DARDO (ex-*MC* 592, ex-493)	P 495	**SAETTA** (ex-*MC* 591)	P 494
FRECCIA (ex-*MC* 590)	P 493	**STRALE** (ex-*MC* 593, ex-494)	P 496

Displacement, tons	188 standard; 215 full load
Dimensions, feet	150 × 23·8 × 5·5
Guns	*As Gunboat:* 3—40 mm, 70 cal or 2—40 mm, 70 cal *As Fast Minelayer:* 1—40 mm AA with 8 mines *As Torpedo Boat:* 1—40 mm, 70 cal
Tubes	*As Torpedo Boat:* 2—21 in
Main engines	2 diesels; 7 600 bhp; 1 Bristol Siddeley Proteus gas turbine. 4 250 shp; Total hp 11 850 = 40 knots

Freccia was laid down by Cantiere del Tirreno, Riva Trigosa on 30 Apr 1963, launched on 9 Jan 1965 and commissioned on 6 July 1965. *Saetta* was laid down by CRDA, Monfalcone on 11 June 1963, launched on 11 Apr 1965. and completed in 1966. *Dardo* was laid down by Taranto Navy Yard on 10 May 1964. Special convertible version designed to carry mines or depth charges. Can be converted in 24 hours to gunboat, torpedo boat, fast minelayer, or missile boat. *Saetta* has been experimentally armed with 5 short range missiles (range 10 000 metres). A photograph of *Saetta* appears in the 1967-68 and 1968-69 editions.

FRECCIA *1969, Dr. Aldo Fraccaroli*

2 "LAMPO" CLASS CONVERTIBLE TYPE

BALENO (ex-*MC* 492) P 492 **LAMPO** (ex-*MC* 491) P 491

Displacement, tons	170 standard; 206 full load
Dimensions, feet	131·5 × 21 × 5
Guns	*As Gunboat:* 3—40 mm, 70 cal or 2—40 mm, 70 cal *As Torpedo Boat:* 1—40 mm, 70 cal
Tubes	*As Torpedo Boat:* 2—21 in
Main engines	2 Fiat diesels, 1 Metrovick gas turbine; 3 shafts; total 11 700 hp = 39 knots.

A new type of convertible gunboats, improved version of the *Folgore* prototype. Both built by Arsenale MM Taranto. *Lampo* was laid down on 4 Jan 1958, launched on 22 Nov 1960 and commissioned in July 1963. A photograph of her as gunboat appears in the 1965-66 to 1967-68 editions and as torpedo boat in the 1968-69 edition. *Baleno* was laid-down on the same slip on 22 Nov 1960, launched on 10 May 1964 and commissioned on 16 July 1965. She has been converted to an improved design.

BALENO *1969, Italian Navy, Official*

FOLGORE (ex-*MC* 490) P 490

Displacement, tons	160 standard; 190 full load
Dimensions, feet	129·5 × 19·7 × 5
Guns	2—40 mm AA
Tubes	2—21 in
Main Engines	4 diesels; 4 shafts; 10 000 bhp = 38 knots (accelerating from 20 knots to full speed very rapidly)

Authorised in Nov 1950, launched on 21 Jan 1954 from CRDA Monfalcone Yard, and commissioned on 21 July 1955. Two rudders. A port quarter oblique aerial view of *Folgore* appears in the 1963-64 to 1966-67 editions, and a port broadside view in the 1967-68 and 1968-69 editions.
The old motor gunboat MC 485 (ex-*MS* 621, ex-*Toros*), former German S-boat, was officially deleted from the list in 1965.

FOLGORE *1969, Dr. Aldo Fraccaroli*

Motor Gunboats —*continued*

1 SUBMARINE CHASER

FULMINE (ex-*Sentinella* ex-*VAS* 470) P499 (ex-F 598)

Displacement, tons	300 standard; 340 full load
Dimensions, feet	154 pp; 163 oa × 21·7 × 7
Guns	1—3 in, 62 cal forward; 2—40 mm 56 cal AA
Main engines	4 diesels; 2 shafts; 9 000 bhp = 30 knots
Oil fuel (tons)	28
Complement	60

Ordered in 1952 and laid down on 21 June 1954 at CRDA Monfalcone Yard. Launched on 14 Nov 1955. Commissioned on 20 Sep 1956 as a submarine chaser, and rated specifically as a corvette under the generic category of coastal escort vessels. Assigned to motor torpedo boat flotillas as leader. Re-rated as a gunboat, re-named and re-numbered at the end of 1965. Formerly armed with Hedgehog, depth charge throwers and D.C. rack. 3 inch gun mounted in 1967 and the two 17·7 inch torpedoes removed.

FULMINE *1969, Dr. Aldo Fraccaroli*

INSHORE MINESWEEPERS
(Dragamine Litoranei)

20 "ARAGOSTA" CLASS

ARAGOSTA	M 5450	**GAMBERO**	M 5457	**POLIPO**	M 5463
ARSELLA	M 5451	**GRANCHIO**	M 5458	**PORPORA**	M 5464
ASTICE	M 5452	**MITILO**	M 5459	**RICCIO**	M 5465
ATTINIA	M 5453	**OSTRICA**	M 5460	**SCAMPO**	M 5466
CALAMARO	M 5454	**PAGURO**	M 5461	**SEPPIA**	M 5467
CONCHIGLIA	M 5455	**PINNA**	M 5462	**TELLINA**	M 5468
DROMIA	M 5456			**TOTANO**	M 5469

Displacement, tons	119 standard; 130 full load
Dimensions, feet	106 × 21 × 6
Main Engines	2 diesels; 1 000 bhp = 14 knots
Oil fuel (tons)	15
Radius, miles	2 000 at 9 knots
Complement	14

Similar to the British "Ham" class. NATO order. All constructed in Italian yards in 1955-57. All names of small sea inhabitants. Designed armament of one 20 mm gun not mounted. *Polipo* was originally named *Polpo*.
A photograph of *Ricco* appears in the 1958-59 to 1961-62 edirions, of *Aragosta* in the 1962-63 and 1963-64 editions, of *Arsella* in the 1964-65 to 1966-67 editions.

TELLINA *1969, Dr. Aldo Fraccaroli*

DISPOSALS OF BYMS TYPE
Of the 17 coastal minesweepers of the BYMS type, **Begonia** and **Dalia** were transferred to the Custom House Guard Sea Service in Apr 1966, and the other nine vessels of the "Azalea" class (one funnel), **Azalea**, **Fiordaliso**, **Gardinia**, **Gladiolo**, **Magnolia**, **Orchidea**, **Primula**, **Tulipano**, **Verbena**, were removed from the effective list at the end of 1966 with the six units of the "Anemone" class (two funnels), **Anemone**, **Biancospino**, **Geranio**, **Mughetto**, **Narciso** and **Oleandro**, see full particulars in the 1966-67 and earlier editions.

FAST REPLENISHMENT SHIP (AOR)

1 NEW CONSTRUCTION NUCLEAR POWERED TYPE

ENRICO FERMI

Displacement, tons	18 000
Dimensions, feet	574·2 × 72·2 × 26·3
Aircraft	8 helicopters
Main engines	Nuclear reactor; steam turbines = 21 knots
Range, cruising	300 000 miles
Complement	350 officers and ratings

Italy's first nuclear powered ship. Scheduled to come into service in 1970-71. A Fiat-Ansaldo project, with Fiat building the reactor and some of the main components, under the aegis of the Italian Navy which will be responsible for her operation. A hangar for all types of helicopters will be built aft, and a large workshop constructed on the forecastle for the maintenance of submarines. Will carry 4 850 tons of black oil, 1 550 tons of diesel oil, 340 tons of petrol and 150 tons of aviation spirit.

SURVEY SHIPS (*Navi Idrografiche*)

1 Ex-BRITISH "FLOWER" TYPE

STAFFETTA (ex-*Elbano*, ex-USS *Prudent*, PG 96, ex-HMS *Privet*) A 5307

Displacement, tons	1 020 standard; 1 280 full load
Dimensions, feet	205 oa × 33 × 14·5
Guns	2—20 mm AA
Main Engines	Triple expansion; 2 750 ihp = 15 knots
Boiler	2 cylindrical
Oil fuel (tons)	250
Radius, miles	5 500 at 8 knots

Former British "Flower" class corvette (later re-rated frigate). Built by Morton Engine & DD Co, Montreal, Canada, engined by Port Arthur SB Co. Laid down on 14 Aug 1942. Launched on 4 Dec 1942. Completed on 16 Aug 1943. Converted for hydrographic duties and commissioned in 1953.
The oceanographic vessel *Bannock* (ex-USS *Bannock*, *ATF* 81), former US fleet ocean tug was converted and is manned by the National Research Council and is not on the Navy List; she wears the mercantile flag. (See data in the 1964-65 edition.)

STAFFETTA *1968, Italian Navy, Official*

The survey ship **Daino** (ex-*B* 2, ex-*M* 802), former German coal-burning minesweeper, was removed from the effective list in 1966.

NETLAYERS (*Posareti*)

2 "ALICUDI" CLASS

ALICUDI A 5304 (ex-USS AN 99) **FILICUDI** A 5305 (ex-USS AN 100)

Displacement, tons	680 standard; 834 full load
Dimensions, feet	151·8 pp; 165·3 oa × 33·5 × 10·5
Guns	1—40 mm, 70 cal AA; 4—20 mm, 70 cal AA
Main Engines	Diesel-electric; 1 200 hp = 12 knots

Built to the order of NATO. Laid down on 22 Apr 1954 and 19 July 1954, respectively by Ansaldo, Leghorn, launched on 11 July 1954 and 26 Sep 1954.

ALICUDI *Italian Navy, Official*

LANDING SHIPS

CAPRERA **MARSALA** **QUARTO**

Displacement, tons	764 standard; 930 to 980 full load
Dimensions, feet	226·4 × 31·3 × 6
Guns	4—40 mm AA (2 twin)
Main engines	3 diesels, 2 300 bhp = 13 knots
Radius, miles	1 300 at 13 knots

A new type of landing ships. Quarto was laid down on 19 Mar 1966 at Taranto Naval Shipyard and launched on 18 Mar 1967. *Marsala* was laid down on 18 Mar 1967. The design is intermediate between that of LSM and LCT. Two more ships of this class, *Lombardo* and *Piemonte*, were officially deleted from the New Construction Programme in 1968.

QUARTO *1969, Italian Navy, Official*

TROOP TRANSPORT (COMMAND SHIP)

ANDREA BAFILE (ex-USS *St. George*, AV 16)

Displacement, tons	8 510 standard; 14 000 full load
Dimensions, feet	492 oa × 69·5 × 26 max
Main engines	Allis-Chalmers geared turbines; 1 shaft; 8 500 shp = 18·7 knots
Boilers	2 Foster-Wheeler

Former US seaplane carrier, launched on 14 Feb 1944. Purchased in 1969 and modified.

SUPPORT SHIP (*Nave appogio*)

PIETRO CAVEZZALE (ex-USS *Oyster Bay*, *AVP* 28, ex-*AGP* 6) A 5301

Displacement, tons	1 766 standard; 2 800 full load
Dimensions, feet	300 wl; 311·8 oa × 41 × 13·5 max
Guns	2—40 mm, 56 cal AA
Main Engines	2 sets diesels; 2 shafts; 6 080 bhp = 16 knots
Oil fuel (tons)	400
Radius, miles	10 000 at 11 knots
Complement	200

Former United States seaplane tender (previously motor torpedo boat tender) of the "Barnegat" class, built at Lake Washington Shipyard and launched on 7 Sep 1942. Transferred to the Italian Navy on 23 Oct 1957 and renamed.

PIETRO CAVEZZALE *1968, Italian Navy, Official*

SALVAGE SHIP (*Nave Salvataggio*)

PROTEO (ex-*Perseo*, ex-*Proteo*) A 5310

Displacement, tons	1 865 standard; 2 147 full load
Dimensions, feet	220·5 pp; 248 oa × 38 × 21 max
Main Engines	2 diesels; 4 800 bhp = 16 knots (see Notes)
Radius, miles	7 500 at 13 knots

Laid down at Cantieri Navali Riuniti, Ancona, in 1943. Suspended in 1944. Seized by Germans and transferred to Trieste. Construction recommenced at Cantieri Navali Riuniti, Ancona, in 1949. Diesels at 250 rpm drive a single propeller through hydraulic couplings and reduction gearing. Formerly mounted one 3·9 inch AA gun and two 20 mm, 70 cal AA guns.

PROTEO *1969, Italian Navy, Official*

REPAIR CRAFT (*Motoofficine Costiere*)

MOC 1201 **MOC 1202** **MOC 1203** **MOC 1204** **MOC 1205** **MOC 1207** **MOC 1208**

Displacement, tons	350 standard; 640 full load
Dimensions, feet	192 × 31 × 7
Guns	2—40 mm; 2—20 mm (2 ships have 2—40 mm and 1 ship has 3—20 mm)
Main Engines	Diesel = 8 knots

Former British LCT (3) type landing craft converted to repair craft. MOC 1207 and 1208 are ammunition transports. NATO Nos.: A 5331 to 5338, respectively.

A photograph of MOC 1201 appears in the 1955-56 to 1966-67 editions, and of MOC 1208 in the 1967-68 and 1968-69 editions.

MOC 1202 *1969, Italian Navy, Official*

TRANSPORTS (*Navi Trasporto*)

STROMBOLI A 5329 **VESUVIO** A 5329

Displacement, tons	2 848 light; 4 713 standard; 6 160 full load
Dimensions, feet	334·1 oa × 46 × 21·7
Guns	*Stromboli:* 1—3·9 in; 4—40 mm, 56 cal *Vesuvio:* 2—40 mm AA; forward only
Main engines	1 double reduction geared turbine; 3 000 shp = 15 knots
Boilers	3 water tube
Radius, miles	3 340 at 11 knots

Both built by Odero-Terni-Orlando yard, La Spezia. *Stromboli* was completed in 1948 and *Vesuvio* in 1954. *Stromboli* is Flagship of the Logistic Support Group. The 3·9 inch gun aft was removed from *Vesuvio*, converted into a tender for helicopters served by a hangar abaft the funnel and a flight deck laid on right aft.

VESUVIO *1968, Aldo Fraccaroli*

STROMBOLI *1968, Aldo Fraccaroli*

ETNA (ex-USS *Whitley*, *AKA* 91) A 5328

Displacement, tons	7 430 light; 14 200 full load
Measurement, tons	5 145 gross; 7 700 deadweight
Dimensions, feet	435 wl; 459·2 oa × 63 × 26·3 max
Main Engines	GE geared turbines; 1 shaft; 6 000 shp = 16·5 knots
Boilers	2 Combustion Engineering

Former US attack cargo ship of the "Andromeda" class. Built by Moore DD Co, Oakland, California, launched on 22 June 1944. Completed on 21 Sep 1944. C2—S—B 1 type. Transferred to Italy in Feb 1962. Rated as *Nave trasporto mezzi da sbarco.*

ETNA *1967, Italian Navy, Official*

ANTEO (ex-USS *Alameda County*, AVB 1, ex-*LST* 32) A 5306

Displacement, tons	1 625 light; 2 366 beaching; 4 080 full load
Dimensions, feet	316 wl; 328 oa × 50 × 14 max
Guns	7—40 mm AA; 2—20 mm AA
Main Engines	GM diesels; 2 shafts; 1 700 bhp = 11·6 knots max

Former US tank landing ship. Built by Dravo Corp, Neville Island, Pa. Laid down on 17 Feb 1943. Launched on 23 May 1943. Completed on 12 July 1943. Reclassified from LST 32 to AVB 1 (Advance Aviation Base ship) on 28 Sep 1957. Transferred to the Italian Navy in Nov 1962 as a transport.

ANTEO *1967, Aldo Fraccaroli*

TRAINING SHIPS *(Navi Scuola)*

AMERIGO VESPUCCI A 5312

Displacement, tons	3 543 standard; 4 146 full load
Dimensions, feet	229·5 pp; 270 oa hull; 330 oa bowsprit × 51 × 22
Guns	4—3 in, 50 cal; 1—20 mm
Main Engines	Two Fiat diesels with electric drive to 2 Marelli motors. 1 shaft; 2 000 hp = 10 knots
Sail area	22 604 square feet
Endurance	5 450 miles at 6·5 knots
Complement, tons	400 + 150 midshipmen

Built at Castellammare. Launched on 22 March 1930 and completed in 1931. Hull, masts and yards are of steel. Loud speakers and echo-sounding gear are included in her equipment. Extensively refitted at La Spezia Naval Dockyard in 1964.

AMERICO VESPUCCI — *1968, Italian Navy, Official*

PALINURO (ex-*Commandant Louis Richard*) A 5311.

Displacement, tons	1 042 standard; 1 450 full load
Measurement, tons	858 gross
Dimensions, feet	204 pp; 226·3 oa × 32 × 18·7
Main engines	1 diesel; 1 shaft; 450 bhp = 7·5 knots
Endurance, miles	5 390 at 7·5 knots
Sail area, square feet	1 152

Barquentine, Ex-French, launched in 1920. Purchased in 1950. Rebuilt and commissioned in Italian Navy on 16 July 1955.

PALINURO — *1968, Italian Navy, Official*

CORSARO II

Measurement, tons	41
Dimensions, feet	68·6 × 15·4 × 9·5
Auxiliary engines	1 Mercedes-Benz diesel, 96 bhp
Sail area	2117 square feet

Special yacht for sail training and oceanic navigation. RORC class. Built by Costaguta Yard, Voltri, in 1959-60.

STELLA POLARE

Measurement, tons	47
Dimensions, feet	6 9 × 15·4 × 9·8
Sail area, square feet	2 200
Complement	14

Yawl. Built by Santgerm. Chiavari in 1964-65 as a sail training vessel for the Italian Navy.

DISPOSAL

The training ship **Gazzella** (ex-*B* 3, ex-*M* 801), former German fleet minesweeper, subsequently used as an auxiliary ship, then a patrol ship, later a coastal escort (*corvette*) and finally *navi idrografiche*, was removed from the effective list in 1966.

MOTOR TRANSPORTS *(Mototrasporti)*

13 Ex-GERMAN MFP TYPE

MTC 1001	**MTC 1005**	**MTC 1008**	**MTC 1101**	**MTC 1103**
MTC 1003	**MTC 1006**	**MTC 1009**	**MTC 1102**	**MTC 1104**
MTC 1004	**MTC 1007**	**MTC 1010**		

Displacement, tons	240 standard
Dimensions, feet	164 × 21·3 × 5·7
Guns	2 or 3—20 or 37 mm
Main Engines	2 or 3 diesels; 500 bhp = 10 knots

Moto-Trasporti Costieri, MTC 1001 to 1010 are Italian MZ (*Motozattere*) type. MTC 1101 to 1104 are ex-German built in Italy. NATO Pennant Nos.: A 5341 and A 5343 to A 5359, respectively, MTC 1002 was removed from the effective list in 1964.

MTC 1003 — *1965, Italian Navy, Official*

19 Ex-US LCM TYPE

MTM 9901	**MTM 9905**	**MTM 9910**	**MTM 9914**	**MTM 9918**
MTM 9902	**MTM 9906**	**MTM 9911**	**MTM 9915**	**MTM 9919**
MTM 9903	**MTM 9908**	**MTM 9912**	**MTM 9916**	**MTM 9920**
MTM 9904	**MTM 9909**	**MTM 9913**	**MTM 9917**	

Displacement, tons	20 standard
Dimensions, feet	49·5 × 14·8 × 4·2
Guns	2—20 mm AA
Main Engines	Diesels; speed 10 knots

Rated as *Moto-Trasporti Medi*. Former US landing craft of the LCM type. MTM 9907 was removed from the effective list in 1967.

28 Ex-US LCVP TYPE

MTP 9701	**MTP 9707**	**MTP 9713**	**MTP 9719**	**MTP 9727**
MTP 9702	**MTP 9708**	**MTP 9714**	**MTP 9720**	**MTP 9728**
MTP 9703	**MTP 9709**	**MTP 9715**	**MTP 9721**	**MTP 9729**
MTP 9704	**MTP 9710**	**MTP 9716**	**MPT 9722**	**MTP 9730**
MTP 9705	**MTP 9711**	**MTP 9717**	**MTP 9723**	
MTP 9706	**MTP 9712**	**MTP 9718**	**MTP 9724**	

Displacement, tons	8 standard
Dimensions, feet	36·5 × 10·8 × 3
Guns	2 MG
Main Engines	Diesels; Speed: 10 knots

Rated as *Moto-Trasporti Piccoli*. Former US landing craft of the LCVP type. MTP 9726 of 10 tons displacement and similar characteristics is of Italian construction. MTP 9725 was officially removed from the effective list in 1963.

LIGHTHOUSE TENDERS

BUFFOLUTO A 5327

Displacement, tons	930 standard
Dimensions, feet	172·5 pp; 184·2 oa × 29·5 × 11
Main Engines	2 triple expansion; 1 400 ihp = 10 knots
Boilers	2 Thornycroft

Built by S. Giorgio, La Spezia. Launched in 1922. Sister ship *Panigaglia* blew up in July 1947.

RAMPINO A 5309

Displacement, tons	350 standard; 645 full load
Dimensions, feet	158·8 × 24·2 × 13
Main Engines	Triple expansion = 7 knots

Buoy tender. Of netlayer type. Built at Osaka. Classed as *Nave Ausiliarie*.

3 Ex-BRITISH LCT(3) TYPE

MTF 1301	**MTF 1302**	**MTF 1303**

Displacement, tons	296 light; 700 full load
Dimensions, feet	192 × 31 × 7
Guns	1—40 mm, 56 cal AA; 2—20 mm, 70 cal AA
Main Engines	Diesel; 1 shaft; speed = 8 knots

Converted landing craft of the British LCT (3) type. Lighthouse motor transports (Moto-Trasporti Fari). NATO Pennant Nos.: A 5361, A 5362 and A 5363.

MFT 1301 — *1968, Italian Navy, Official*

OILERS *(Navi Cisterna per Nafta)*

STEROPE (ex-*Enrico Insom*) A 5368

Displacement, tons	5 350 light; 21 800 full load
Dimensions, feet	523·5 oa × 68 × 30·8
Main Engines	Turbo-electric; 6 000 shp = 15 knots
Boilers	2 Babcock & Wilcox

Former United States built oiler of the T 2 type acquired by the Italian Navy in 1959 and refitted at La Spezia Navy Yard in April 1959.

STEROPE *1967, Italian Navy, Official*

DALMAZIA A 5367

Displacement, tons	1 466 light; 3 216 standard; 5 000 full load
Dimensions, feet	260 × 32·5 × 15·2
Guns	1—4·7 in; 2—20 mm AA
Main Engines	Triple expansion; 2 shafts; 1 450 ihp = 10 knots
Boilers	2 Thornycroft oil-fired
Cargo, tons	1 800

Built by Quarnaro Yard, Fiume, launched in 1922. Formerly classified as a water carrier. Reclassified as a fleet oiler in 1958. A photograph of *Dalmazia* appears in the 1967-68 and earlier editions.

There is also ex-USS YO 247, a small oiler transferred from the United States to Italy under the Military Aid Programme.

WATER CARRIERS *(Navi Cisterna per Acqua)*

PO A 5365 **VOLTURNO** A 5366

Displacement, tons	1 556 light; 3 541 standard; 6 000 full load
Dimensions, feet	270·7 × 38·8 × 16·8
Guns	1—4 in, 35 cal; 2—40 mm; 2—20 mm (*Po*) 1—4·7 in, 45 cal; 2—40 mm; 2—20 mm AA (*Volturno*)
Main Engines	Triple expansion; 1 700 ihp = 11·5 knots
Boilers	2 oil-fired watertube
Oil fuel (tons)	226
Cargo capacity, tons	2 200

Po was launched by Cant Nav Riuniti, Ancona, on 21 Dec 1936. *Volturno* was built by Cantieri del Tirreno, Riva, Trigoso, in 1936-37, and rebuilding was completed in 1951. *Volturno* has radar mast. A photograph of *Volturno* appears in the 1967-68 and earlier editions.

ADIGE (ex-*YW* 92) **ISONZO** (ex-*YW* 77) **TICINO** (ex-*YW* 79)
FLEGETONTE (ex-*YW* 95) **TANARO** (ex-*YW* 99)

Displacement, tons	436 standard; 1 470 full load
Guns	3—20 mm, 70 cal AA
Main engines	2 diesels; 315 hp = 8 knots
Water capacity, tons	850

Ex-US Army YW type. NATO Pennant Nos.: A 5369, A 5371, A 5372, A 5376 and A 5377, respectively.

SESIA A 5375

Displacement, tons	1 050
Dimensions, feet	213·2 × 33 × 11·2
Guns	3—20 mm, 70 cal AA
Main Engines	Fiat diesels; 2 shafts; 600 bhp = 8 knots

Built by Adriatico. Launched in 1933. Fitted for minelaying.

METAURO A 5373

Displacement, tons	592
Dimensions, feet	133·2 × 26·5 × 10·5
Guns	1—20 mm, 70 cal AA
Main Engines	Tosi diesels; 400 bhp = 8 knots

Built by C. N. Quarnaro-Fiume. Launched in 1933

METAURO *1968, Aldo Fraccaroli*

Water Carriers—*continued*

ARNO A 5370

Displacement, tons	634
Dimensions, feet	138·8 × 26 × 10
Guns,	1—20 mm, 70 cal AA
Main Engines	1 Fiat diesel; 350 bhp = 8 knots

Built by Odero-Terni-Orlando, La Spezia. Launched in 1929.

MINCIO A 5374

Displacement, tons	645
Dimensions, feet	138·5 × 26·2 × 10
Guns	1—20 mm, 70 cal AA
Main Engines	Tosi diesels; 350 bhp = 8 knots

Built in Venice. Launched in 1929.

TIMAVO

Displacement, tons	265
Main Engines	1 Tosi diesel; 200 bhp = 8 knots

Built by COMI, Venezia, 1926. Sister ship *Vipacco* was removed from the effective list in 1961.

FRIGIDO (ex-*Fukuiu Maru*)

Displacement, tons	398
Dimensions, feet	116·5 × 21·5 × 10
Guns	2 MG
Main Engines	Triple expansion; 221 ihp = 7 knots
Boilers	1 cylindrical

Built by Osaka. Launched in 1912. Purchased in 1916.

OFANTO

Displacement, tons	250
Dimensions, feet	105·5 × 19·7 × 7·5
Main Engines	1 Triple expansion; 165 ihp = 6 knots
Boilers	1

Built by SEB, Riva Trigoso, 1913-14.

LENO **SIMETO** **SPRUGOLA** **STURA** **TRONTO**
Small water carriers of 270, 167, 212, 126 and 110 tons displacement, respectively.

TUGS *(Rimorchiatori)*

CIRCEO **TAVOLARA**
Both completed in 1955. Minor tugs for local and general purposes.

AUSONIA **PANARIA**

Displacement, tons	240

Both launched in 1948. Coastal tugs for general utility duties.

CICLOPE A 5319 **TITANO** A 5320

Displacement, tons	1 200
Dimensions, feet	157·5 × 32·5 × 13
Main Engines	Triple expansion; 1 shaft; 1 000 ihp = 8 knots

Both were launched in 1948. Sister ship *Nereo* was discarded in 1957.

MISENO **MONTE CRISTO**

Displacement, tons	285

Former United States Navy harbour tugs.

GAGLIARDO A 5322 **ROBUSTO** A 5323

Displacement, tons	389 standard; 506 full load
Main Engines	1 000 ihp = 8 knots

Both launched in 1939.

PORTO EMPEDOCLE

Displacement, tons	330 standard
Main Engines	500 ihp = 11 knots

Launched in 1934. Employed as a harbour tug. Armament of 1—3 in gun removed.

PORTO FOSSONE **PORTO RECANATI** **PORTO VECCHIO**
PORTO PISANO **PORTO TORRES** **SALVORE**
TINO

Displacement, tons	226 to 270
Dimensions, feet	88·8 × 22 × 10
Main Engines	600 ihp = 9 knots

All launched in 1936-37, except *Tino*, 1931. Principally employed as harbour tugs. Armament of 1—3 inch gun removed. *Porto Rosso* was deleted from the list in 1965.

ATLETA (ex-*LT* 152) **FORTE** (ex-*LT* 159)
COLOSSO (ex-*LT* 214) **TENACE** (ex-*LT* 154)

Displacement, tons	525 standard; 835 full load
Dimensions, feet	142·8 × 32·8 × 11
Main Engines	2 diesel-electric; 690 hp = 11 knots

Ex-US Army. Pennant Nos.: A 5318, A 5320, A 5321, A 5324, respectively.

ATLANTE A 5317

Displacement, tons	355
Dimensions, feet	212·3 × 23 × 9
Main Engines	900 ihp = 11 knots

Launched in 1928. Sunk by collision in harbour at Genoa in Jan 1948, but later salvaged. Armament of 1—3 inch gun removed.

LIPARI **VENTIMIGLIA**

Displacement, tons	254 (*Lipari*); 230 (*Ventimiglia*)
Dimensions, feet	108·2 × 23 × 7·2 *(Lipari)*
Main Engines	(*Lipari*) 500 hp = 9 knots; (*Ventimiglia*) 550 = 10 knots

Lipari was built in 1917. There are also 55 harbour tugs, ferry tugs, lagoon tugs, numbered tugs and minor tugs.

IVORY COAST

PATROL BOATS

1 FRANCO-BELGE TYPE

LE VIGILANT

Displacement, tons	235 normal
Dimensions, feet	149·3 pp; 155·8 oa × 23·6 × 8·2
Guns	2—40 mm AA
Main engines	2 diesels; 1 shaft; 2 400 bhp
Speed, knots	18·5
Range, miles	2 000 at 18 knots
Complement	25 (3 officers and 22 men)

Built by Franco-Belge. Laid down in Feb 1967. Launched on 23 May 1967. Scheduled for completion in 1968. Sister ship to *Malaika* of Madagascan Navy.

1 Ex-FRENCH VC TYPE

PERSEVERANCE (ex-*VC* 9, *P* 759)

Displacement, tons	75 standard; 82 full load
Dimensions, feet	104·5 × 17 × 6
Guns	2—20 mm AA
Main Engines	2 Mercedes-Benz diesels; 2 shafts; 2 700 bhp = 28 knots
Oil fuel (tons)	10
Radius, miles	1 100 at 16·5 knots; 800 at 21 knots
Complement	15

Former French seaward defence motor launch. Built by Constructions Mecaniques de Normandie, Cherbourg. Completed in 1958. Transferred from France to Ivory Coast in 1963.

PERSEVERANCE *1964, Ivory Coast Armed Forces, Official*

1 Ex-US SC TYPE

PATIENCE (ex-*P* 699, ex-*CH* 71, ex-US *SC* 1337)

Displacement, tons	110 standard; 138 full load
Dimensions, feet	107·5 wl; 110·8 oa × 17 × 6·5
Guns	1—40 mm AA; 3—20 mm AA
Main Engines	2 GM diesels; 2 shafts; 1 000 bhp = 15 knots
Oil fuel (tons)	15
Radius, miles	2 000 at 10 knots; 1 150 at 15 knots
Complement	25

Former United States wooden submarine chaser. Transferred from the USA to France on 29 Dec 1943, and from France to Ivory Coast in 1961.

PATIENCE *1964, Ivory Coast Armed Forces, Official*

LANDING CRAFT

There are two landing craft of the LCVP type, 7 tons, 9 knots, 2 machine guns, 200 hp.

JAMAICA

Defence Force Coast Guard

Jamaica, which became independent within the Commonwealth, on 6 Aug 1962, formed the Coast Guard as the Maritime Arm of the Defence Force.
The Jamaican Government signed an agreement with the USA for the transfer of a small number of coastguard vessels for the new navy.
Great Britain lent several RN petty officers for technical assistance. The British Mission included a technical team to survey sites for the establishment of local naval bases.

Administration

Officer Commanding Jamaican Defence Force Coast Guard:
Lieutenant-Commander G. B. L. Copland

Personnel

1969: 9 officers, 43 men

Mercantile Marine

Lloyd's Register of Shipping: 6 vessels of 13,012 tons gross

PATROL BOATS

DISCOVERY BAY P 4 **HOLLAND BAY** P 5 **MANATEE BAY** P 6

Displacement, tons	60
Dimensions, feet	85 × 18·8 × 5·9
Guns	3—·50 cal Browning
Main Engines	2 GM 16 V71 N diesels; 2 shafts; 700 bhp = 21 knots
Oil fuel, tons	13
Radius, miles	500 at 12 knots
Complement	10

Built by Sewart Seacraft Inc, Berwick, La, USA. All aluminium construction. *Discovery Bay*, the prototype was launched in Aug 1966 and named and commissioned on 3 Nov 1966. *Holland Bay*, commissioned 4 Apr 1967, and *Manatee Bay*, commissioned 9 Aug 1967, were supplied under the US Military Assistance Programme.

DISCOVERY BAY *1968, Jamaica Coast Guard*

DISCOVERY BAY *1967, courtesy ALCOA*

AVR TYPE
The former ex-US AVR type patrol boats, *Mandingo* P 1 and *Coromantee* P 2 have been disposed of.

JORDON

Coastal Guard

It is officially stated in 1969 that Jordan has no naval force known as such, but the Jordan Coastal Guard, sometime called the Jordan Sea Force, is commanded by Major Fuad Haddaden who takes his orders direct from the Director of Operations at General Headquarters.
The force of two Bertram fibre glass patrol boats, two Polson aluminium motor boats and four wooden motor boats is based at Aqaba. There is no flotilla in the Dead Sea.

JAPAN

Administration

Chief of the Maritime Staff, Defence Agency:
Admiral Takaichi Itaya

Commander-in-Chief, Self-Defence Fleet:
Vice Admiral Shoichi Ibuki

Chief Administration, Maritime Staff Office:
Rear Admiral Tatsuhiko Ishikuma

Diplomatic Representation

Defence (Naval) Attaché in London:
Captain Goro Yoshimura

Defence (Naval) Attaché in Washington:
Captain Fumiro Shimizu

Five Year Defence Build-up Plan

Under the third 5-year defence programme (from 1968 to 1972). Japan planned to build 56 new warships aggregating 48,000 tons, including 2 destroyers (equipped with anti-submarine helicopters) of 4,700 tons, 1 destroyer (with surface-to-air missiles) of 3,900 tons, 3 destroyers of 2,000 tons, 8 destroyer escorts of 1,450 tons and 5 submarines of 1,800 tons.

New Construction Programmes

1969:
1 Destroyer (2,100 tons)
1 Destroyer (1,450 tons)
1 Submarine (1,800 tons)
2 Coastal Minesweepers (380 tons)
1 Minelayer (2,000 tons)
1 Minesweeper Tender (2,000 tons)

1968:
1 Destroyer (4,700 tons new type)
2 Destroyers (1 450 tons)
1 Submarine (1 800 tons)
2 Coastal Minesweepers (380 tons)

1967:
1 Destroyer (2 000 tons)
1 Destroyer (1 450 tons new type)
1 Submarine (1 800 tons)
1 Submarine Rescue Vessel (1 500 tons)
1 Training Support Ship (2 000 tons)
1 Surveying Ship (1 500 tons)
2 Coastal Minesweepers (380 tons)

1966:
1 Destroyer (3 000 tons)
1 Destroyer (2 000 tons)
1 Submarine (1 600 tons killer type)
1 Training Ship (3 500 tons)

Strength of the Fleet

10 Submarines (Diesel Powered)
28 Destroyers (1 Guided Missile Type)
16 Frigates
20 Fast Patrol Vessels
2 Minelayers
40 Coastal Minesweepers
10 Motor Torpedo Boats
3 Landing Ships
100 Support Ships and Service Craft

Personnel

1969: 42,572 (6,974 officers, 30,839 men, 4,759 civil)
1967: 41,626 (6,589 officers, 30,002 men, 5,035 civil)
1966: 40,160 (6,300 officers, 28,880 men, 4,980 civil)
1965: 39,943 (6,210 officers, 28,832 men, 4,901 civil)

Coast Guard

87 patrol vessels, 42 patrol craft, 169 coastal craft, 26 surveying vessels, 26 tenders.

Mercantile Marine

Lloyd's Register of Shipping:
6,877 vessels of 19,586,902 tons gross

Silhouettes

Scale: 150 feet = 1 inch

KIKUZUKI, TAKATSUKI

ASAGUMO, MAKIGUMO, YAMAGUMO

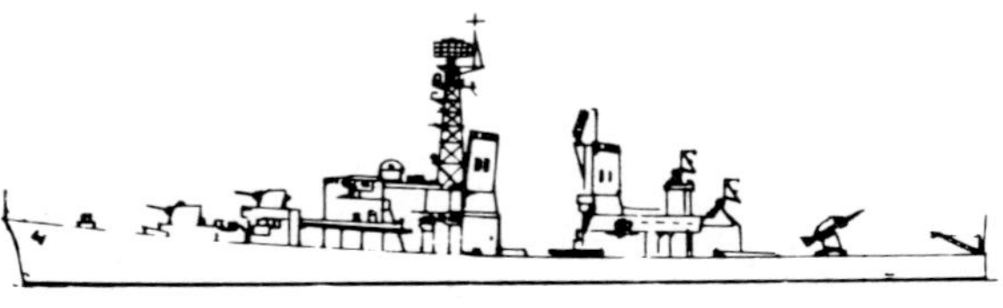
AMATSUKAZE

KITAKAMI, OOI

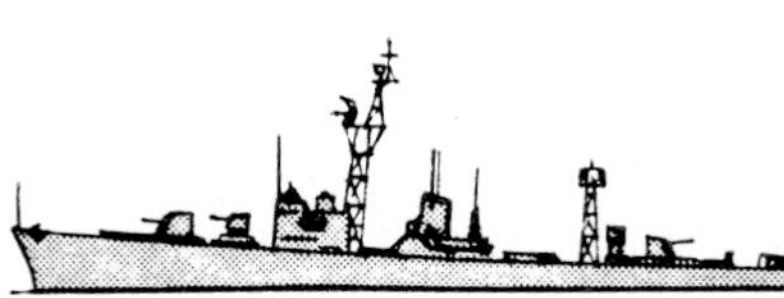
ISUZU, MOGAMI

AKIZUKI, TERUZUKI

ARIAKE

IKAZUCHI, INAZUMA

HARUSAME, MURASAME, YUDACHI

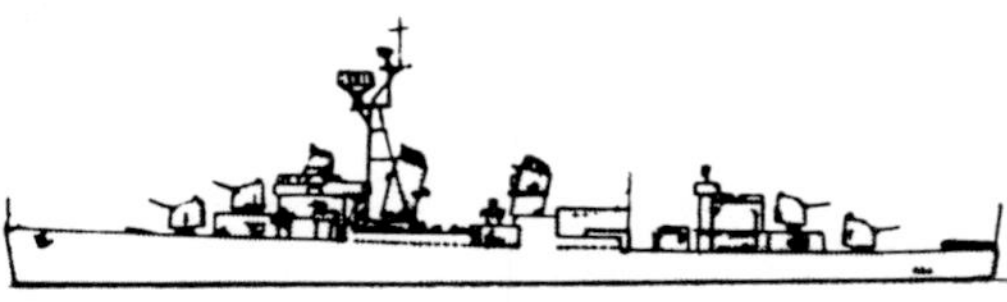
YUGURE

AKEBONO

AYANAMI *Class*

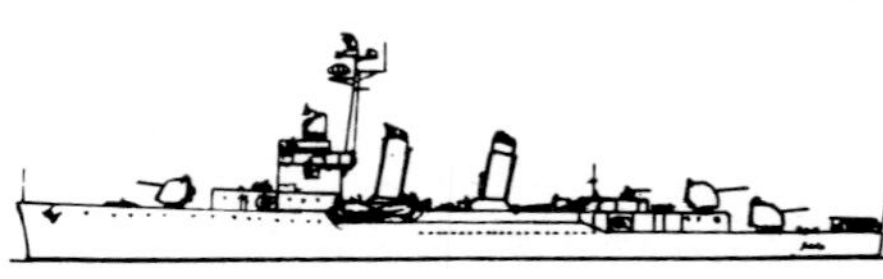
ASAKAZE, HATAKAZE

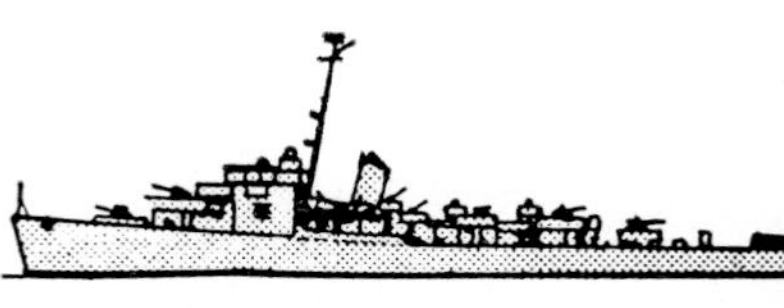
ASAHI, HATSUHI

HARUKAZE, YUKIKAZE

WAKABA

KAYA *Class*

SUBMARINES

5 "OSHIO" CLASS

Name	No.	Builders	Laid down	Launched	Completed
ARASHIO	SS 565	Mitsubishi Jyuko, Kobe	5 July 1967	24 Oct 1968	30 July 1969
ASASHIO	SS 562	Kawasaki Jyuko Co, Kobe	10 Oct 1964	27 Nov 1965	13 Oct 1966
HARUSHIO	SS 563	Mitsubishi Jyuko Co, Kobe	12 Oct 1965	25 Feb 1967	
ŌSHIO	SS 561	Mitsubishi Jyuko Co, Kobe	29 June 1963	30 Apr 1964	10 Apr 1965
MICHISHIO	SS 564	Kawasaki Jyuko, Kobe	26 July 1966	5 Dec 1967	27 Sep 1968

Displacement, tons	1 600 standard
Length, feet (*metres*)	288·7 (*88·0*)
Beam, feet (*metres*)	27 (*8·2*)
Draught, feet (*metres*)	15·4 (*4·7*)
Torpedo tubes	8—21 in (*533 mm*); 6 bow, 2 stern
Main engines	2 Kawasaki MAN diesels; 2 300 bhp; 2 electric motors 6 300 hp; 2 shafts
Speed, knots	14 on surface, 18 submerged
Complement	80

Ōshio was built under the 1961 fiscal year new construction programme. Cost $5 600 000. A bigger design to obtain improved seaworthiness, a larger torpedo capacity and more comprehensive sonar and electronic devices. She is capable of deep diving, the first submarine of this propensity of all submarines built before or after the Second World War in Japanese yards. *Asashio* means "Morning Tide" and *Ōshio* means "Flood Tide" or "Big Tide". *Asashio* was built under the 1963 programme.

PHOTOGRAPHS. A photograph of *Oshio* appears in the 1965-66 to 1967-68 editions, and of *Asashio* in the 1968-69 edition.

HARUSHIO *1969, Japanese Maritime Sefl-Defence Force Official*

ASASHIO *1968, Japanese Maritime Self-Defence Force, Official*

4 "HAYASHIO" CLASS

Name	No.	Builders	Laid down	Launched	Completed
FUYUSHIO	SS 524	Kawasaki Jyuko Co, Kobe	6 Dec 1961	14 Dec 1962	17 Sep 1963
HAYASHIO	SS 521	Shin Mitsubishi Jyuko Co, Kobe	6 June 1960	31 July 1961	30 June 1962
NATSUSHIO	SS 523	Shin Mitsubishi Jyuko Co, Kobe	5 Dec 1961	18 Sep 1962	29 June 1963
WAKASHIO	SS 522	Kawasaki Jyuko Co, Kobe	7 June 1960	28 Aug 1961	17 Aug 1962

Displacement, tons	750 standard (SS 521, 522); 780 standard (SS 523, 524) officially revised figures
Length, feet (*metres*)	193·6 (*59·0*) oa (SS 521, 522); 200·1 (*61·0*) oa (SS 523, 524)
Beam, feet (*metres*)	21·3 (*6·5*)
Draught, feet (*metres*)	13·5 (*4·1*)
Torpedo tubes	3—21 In (*533 mm*); bow
Main engines	2 diesels, total 1 350 hp; 2 shafts 2 electric motors, total 1 700 hp
Speed, knots	11 on surface; 14 submerged
Complement	40

Medium submarines of improved type, with more efficient sonar devices, giving them slightly increased displacement. Very handy and successful boats, with a large safety factor, complete air conditioning and good habitability.

CONSTRUCTION. *Hayashio* and *Wakishio* were built under the 1959 fiscal year new construction programme and *Natsushio* and *Fuyushio* under the 1961 programme.

NOMENCLATURE. *Fuyushio* means "Winter Tide", *Hayashio* "Swift Tide", *Natsushio* "Summer Tide", and *Wakashio* "Young Tide".

PHOTOGRAPHS. A photograph of *Wakashio* appears in the 1964-65 to 1966-67 editions.

HAYASHIO *1968, Japanese Maritime Self-Defence Force, Official*

FUYUSHIO *1965, Japanese Maritime Self-Defence Force, Official*

1 "OYASHIO" CLASS

OYASHIO SS 511

Displacement, tons	1 130 surface; 1 420 submerged
Length, feet (*metres*)	258·5 (*78·8*)
Beam, feet (*metres*)	23 (*7·0*)
Draught, feet (*metres*)	15·2 (*4·6*)
Torpedo tubes	4—21 in (*533 mm*); 10 torpedoes
Main engines	2 diesels, total 2 700 hp 2 electric motors, total 5 960 hp
Speed, knots	13 on surface; 19 submerged
Radius, miles	5 000 at 10 knots
Complement	65

Ordered under the 1956 Programme. Built by Kawasaki Jyuko Co Kobe. Laid down on 25 Dec 1957, launched on 25 May 1959 and completed on 30 June 1960. The first submarine built in a Japanese shipyard after the Second World War, *Oyashio* is the name of a tide stream in the Pacific off Honshu. First estimated to cost £2 718 000, but this figure was exceeded.

An oblique aerial view of *Oyashio* appears in the 1961-62 to 1965-66 editions.

OYASHIO *1969, Japanese Maritime Self-Defence Force, Official*

NUCLEAR POWER STUDY
The Director of the Japanese Defence Agency stated on 5 May 1955 that Japan was studying the possibility of building a nuclear powered submarine. In the meantime, conventional submarines would be ordered.

"GATO" CLASS

The former United States submarine of the "Gato" class, *Kuroshio*, SS 501 (ex-USS *Mingo*, SS 261) was officially taken out of commission on 31 Mar 1966.

DESTROYERS

NEW CONSTRUCTION

ANTI-SUBMARINE TYPE

3+1 IMPROVED "MOON" CLASS

Name	No	Builders	Laid down	Lauuched	Completed
KIKUZUKI	DD 165	Mitsubishi Jyuko Co, Nagasaki	15 Mar 1966	25 Mar 1967	Feb 1968
MOCHIZUKI	DD 166	Ishikawajima Jyuko Co, Tokyo	25 Nov 1966	15 Mar 1968	
TAKATSUKI	DD 164	Ishikawajima Jyuko Co, Tokyo	8 Oct 1964	7 Jan 1966	15 Mar 1967

Displacement, tons	3 050 (official figure)
Length, feet (*metres*)	446·2 (*136·0*) oa
Beam, feet (*metres*)	44·0 (*13·4*)
Draught, feet (*metres*)	14·5 (*4·4*)
Aircraft	DASH helicopter
A/S	Octuple Asroc; 1 four barrelled rocket launcher
Guns, dual purpose	2—5 in (*127 mm*) 54 cal. single
Torpedo launchers	2 triple for A/S homing torpedoes
Boilers	2 Mitsubishi CE
Main engines	2 Mitsubishi WH geared turbines 60 000 shp; 2 shafts
Speed, knots	32
Complement	270

Takutski was provided for under the 1963 fiscal year new construction programme. She is equipped with a drone anti-submarine helicopter with hangar. *Takatsuki* means "High Moon". *Kikuzuki* completed. *Mochizuki* nearing completion; fourth ship ordered under 1966 Construction programme. A port bow view of *Takatsuki* appears in the 1968-69 edition.

KIKUZUKI *1969, Japanese Maritime Self-Defence Force, Official*

NEW CONSTRUCTION

DIESEL TYPE

4+3 "CLOUD" CLASS

Name	No.	Builders	Laid down	Launched	Completed
ASAZUMO	DD 115	Maizuru Jyuko Co, Maizuru	24 June 1965	25 Nov 1966	
MAKIZUMO	DD 114	Uraga Dock Co, Yokosukia	10 June 1964	26 July 1965	29 Nov 1966
YAMAZUMO	DD 113	Mitsui Zozen Co, Tamano	23 Mar 1964	27 Feb 1965	30 Oct 1966
MINEZUMO	DD 116	Mitsui Zozen Co, Tamano	14 Mar 1967	18 Dec 1967	1968

Displacement, tons	2 050 (official figure)
Length feet (*metres*)	374 (*114·0*)
Beam, feet (*metres*)	38·7 (*11·8*)
Draught, feet (*metres*)	12·8 (*3·9*)
A/S	Octuple Asroc; 1 four-barrelled rocket launcher
Guns, AA	4—3 in (*76 mm*) 50 cal., 2 twin
Torpedo launchers	2 triple for A/S homing torpedoes
Main engines	6 Mitsui (*Yamazumo*), Mitsubishi (*Asazumo, Makizumo*) B & W diesels; 26 500 bhp; 2 shafts
Speed, knots	27
Complement	210

MINEZUMO *1969, Japanese Maritime Self-Defence Force, Official*

Yamazumo was ordered under the 1962 fiscal year new construction programme. *Makizumo* under the 1963 programme, and *Asazumo* under the 1964 programme. *Makizumo* means "Rolling Cloud", and *Yamazumo* means "Mountain Cloud". *Asazumo* completed. *Minezumo* nearing completion; other three ships ordered under 1965, 1966 and 1967 Construction Programmes.

PHOTOGRAPHS. A photograph of *Makizumo* appears in the 1966-67 and 1967-68 editions and of *Asazumo* in the 1968-69 edition.

YAMAZUMO *1969, Japanese Maritime Self-Defence Force, Official*

1 GUIDED MISSILE ARMED TYPE

AMATSUKAZE DD 163

Displacement, tons	3 050 standard; 4 000 full load
Length, feet (*metres*)	429·8 (*131·0*)
Beam, feet (*metres*)	44 (*13·4*)
Draught, feet (*metres*)	13·8 (*4·2*)
Missiles, A/A	1 single "Tartar" launcher
Guns, AA	4—3 in (*76 mm*) 50 cal., 2 twin
A/S	2 hedgehogs
Torpedo dropping gear	1 each side for A/S short torpedoes
Boilers	2 Ishikawajima Foster Wheeler
Main engines	2 Ishikawajima GE geared turbines 60 000 shp; 2 shafts
Speed, knots	33
Oil fuel (tons)	900
Complement	290

AMATSUKAZE *1967, Japanese Maritime Self-Defence Force, Official*

Ordered under the 1960 fiscal year new construction programme. Built by Mitsubishi, Nagasaki. Laid down on 29 Nov 1962, launched on 5 Oct 1963 and completed on 15 Feb 1965. The largest naval vessel completed in Japan after the Second World War, and the first to be armed with guided missiles. Distinguished by clean lines, flush deck and minimum superstructure. Equipped with "Tartar" surface-to-air guided missiles supplied from the USA. Designed to carry and operate a helicopter. *Amatsukaze* means "Heaven Wind".

Destroyers—*continued*

2 "MOON" CLASS (US "OFF-SHORE" PROGRAMME)

Name	*No.*	*Builders*	*Laid down*	*Launched*	*Completed*
AKIZUKI	DD 161	Mitsubishi Zosen Co, Nagasaki	31 July 1958	26 June 1959	13 Feb 1960
TERUZUKI	DD 162	Shin Mitsubishi Jyuko Co, Kobe	15 Aug 1958	24 June 1959	29 Feb 1960

Displacement, tons 2 350 standard; 2 890 full load
Length, feet (metres) 387·2 (*118·0*) oa
Beam, feet (*metres*) 39·4 (*12·0*)
Draught, feet (*metres*) 13·1 (*4·0*)
Guns, dual purpose 3—5 in (*127 mm*) 54 cal. single
Guns, AA 4—3 in (*76 mm*) 50 cal., 2 twin
Torpedo tubes 4—21 In (*533 mm*) quadrupled
A/S 1—US model Mk 108 rocket launcher; 2 hedgehogs; 2 Y-mortars; 2 DCT
Boilers 2 Mitsubishi CE type
Main engines 2 geared turbines:— *Akizuki:* Mitsubishi Escher-Weiss *Teruzuki:* Westinghouse 45 000 shp, 2 shafts
Speed, knots 32
Complement 330

AKIZUKI *1969, Japanese Maritime Self-Defence Force, Official*

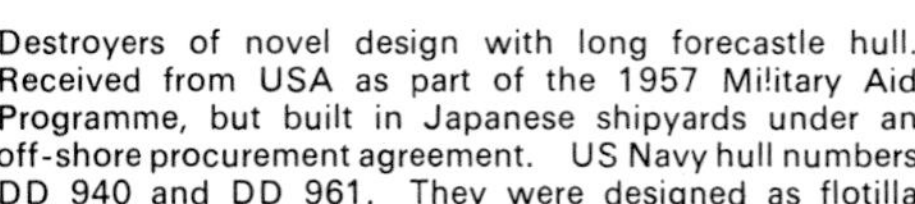

Destroyers of novel design with long forecastle hull. Received from USA as part of the 1957 Military Aid Programme, but built in Japanese shipyards under an off-shore procurement agreement. US Navy hull numbers DD 940 and DD 961. They were designed as flotilla leaders to serve as senior officers' ships, and are equipped with two homing torpedo launchers, two radar systems and two sonar installations. *Akizuki* means "Autumn Moon"; *Teruzuki* means "Shining Moon".

PHOTOGRAPHS. A port bow oblique aerial view of *Akizuki* appears in the 1961-62 to 1965-66 editions. and a starboard broadside view of *Terezuki* in the 1966-67 to 1968-69 editions.

ANTI-SUBMARINE ("A" TYPE DDK) 7 "WAVE" CLASS

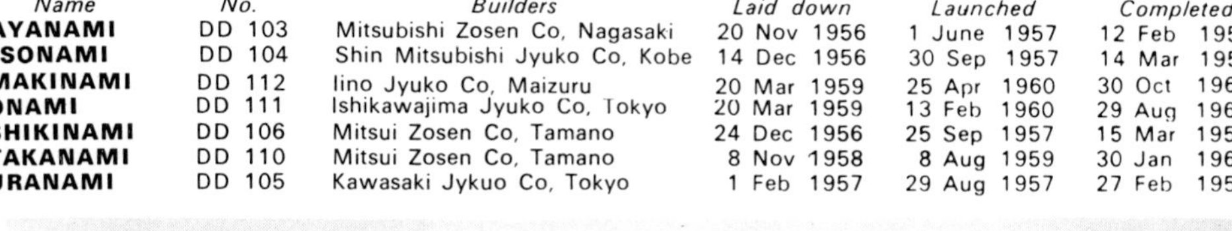

Name	*No.*	*Builders*	*Laid down*	*Launched*	*Completed*
AYANAMI	DD 103	Mitsubishi Zosen Co, Nagasaki	20 Nov 1956	1 June 1957	12 Feb 1958
ISONAMI	DD 104	Shin Mitsubishi Jyuko Co, Kobe	14 Dec 1956	30 Sep 1957	14 Mar 1958
MAKINAMI	DD 112	Iino Jyuko Co, Maizuru	20 Mar 1959	25 Apr 1960	30 Oct 1960
ŌNAMI	DD 111	Ishikawajima Jyuko Co, Tokyo	20 Mar 1959	13 Feb 1960	29 Aug 1960
SHIKINAMI	DD 106	Mitsui Zosen Co, Tamano	24 Dec 1956	25 Sep 1957	15 Mar 1958
TAKANAMI	DD 110	Mitsui Zosen Co, Tamano	8 Nov 1958	8 Aug 1959	30 Jan 1960
URANAMI	DD 105	Kawasaki Jykuo Co, Tokyo	1 Feb 1957	29 Aug 1957	27 Feb 1958

Displacement, tons 1 700 standard; 2 500 full load
Length, feet (*metres*) 357·6 (*109·0*) oa
Beam, feet (*metres*) 35·1 (*10·7*)
Draught, feet (*metres*) 12 (*3·7*) max
Guns, AA 6—3 in (*76 mm*) 50 cal. 3 twin
A/S 2 US Model Mk 15 Hedgehogs; 2 Y-mortars
Torpedo tubes 4—21 in (*533 mm*) quadrupled
Torpedo launchers 4 fixed, for A/S homing torpedoes
Boilers 2 (see *Engineering*)
Main engines 2 Mitsubishi Escher-Weiss geared turbines 35 000 shp; 2 shafts
Speed, knots 32
Complement 230

Built under the 1955 Programme (*Ayanami, Isonami, Shikinami, Uranami*); 1957 Programme (*Takanami*) and 1958 Programme (*Ōnami, Makinami*).

ANTI-SUBMARINE. The Hedgehog type depth charge throwers are mounted on turntables before the bridge. Four torpedoe loading racks are mounted in pairs abreast the after funnel. Droppers for anti-submarine homing torpedoes are mounted on the quarter deck.

GUNNERY. To facilitate ammunition supply the armament was designed to take standard US shell.

ENGINEERING. Types of boilers installed are as follows: Mitsubishi CE in *Ayanami, Isonami* and *Uranami*; Hitachi Babcock & Wilcox in *Ōnami, Shikinami* and *Takanami*; Kawasaki Jyuko BD in *Makinami.*

CLASS. Reported to be very successful ships. The largest batch of destroyers of a single design put in hand since the Second World War.

NOMENCLATURE. *Ayanami* means "Weave Wave", *Isonami* means "Shore Wave", *Shikinami* means "Spread Wave", *Takanami* means "High Wave", *Uranami* means "Small Bay Wave", *Ōnami* means "Billow Wave" and *Makinami* means "Roller Wave".

PHOTOGRAPHS of *Uranami* appear in the 1958-59 to 1960-61 editions, of *Isonami* and *Murasame* (Addenda) in the 1959-60 editions, of *Ōnami* (Addenda) in the 1960-61 edition and the 1966-67 to 1968-69 editions and of *Takanami* in the 1961-62 and 1962-63 editions and the 1966-67 to 1968-69 editions. A starboard broadside surface view, of *Makinami* appears in the 1963-64 to 1965-66 editions, and a port broadside view in the 1966-67 to 1968-69 editions.

AYANAMI *1969, Japanese Maritime Self-Defence Force, Official*

SHIKINAMI *1969, Japanese Maritime Self-Defence Force, Official*

URANAMI *1969, Japanese Maritime Self-Defence Force, Official*

Destroyers—*continued*

ANTI-AIRCRAFT TYPE

3 "RAIN" CLASS

Name	*No.*	*Builders*	*Laid down*	*Launched*	*Completed*
HARUSAME	DD 109	Uraga Dock Co, Yokosuka	17 June 1958	18 June 1959	15 Dec 1959
MURASAME	DD 107	Mitsubishi Zosen Co, Nagasaki	17 Dec 1957	31 July 1958	28 Feb 1959
YŪDACHI	DD 108	Ishakawajima Jyuko Co, Tokyo	16 Dec 1957	29 July 1958	25 Mar 1959

Displacement, tons	1 800 standard; 2 500 full load
Length, feet (*metres*)	354·3 (*108·0*) oa
Beam, feet (*metres*)	36 (*11·0*) oa
Draught, feet (*metres*)	12·2 (*3·7*)
Guns, dual purpose	3—5 in (*127 mm*) 54 cal.
Guns, AA	4—3 in (*76 mm*) 50 cal., 2 twin
A/S	8 short torpedoes; 1 Hedgehog; 1 DC rack; 1 Y-gun
Boilers	2 (see *Engineering* notes)
Main engines	2 sets geared turbines 30 000 shp; 2 shafts
Speed, knots	30
Complement	250

Murasame and *Yūdachi* were built under the 1956 Programme, *Harusame* 1957 Programme. *Harusame* means "Spring Rain" *Murasame* means "Shower".

A photograph of *Harusame* appears in the 1960-61 to 1962-63 editions, and of *Murasame* in the 1963-64 to 1965-66 editions.

YŪDACHI *1966, Japanese Maritime Self-Defence Force, Official*

ENGINEERING. *Murusame* has Mitsubishi Jyuko turbines and Mitsubishi CE boilers; and the other two have Ishikawajima Harima Jyuko turbines and Ishikawajima FW-D boilers.

2 "WIND" CLASS

Name	*No.*	*Builders*	*Laid down*	*Launched*	Completed
HARUKAZE	DD 101	Mitsubishi Zosen Co, Nagasaki	15 Dec 1954	20 Sep 1955	26 Apr 1956
YŪKIKAZE	DD 102	Mitsubishi Jyuko Co, Kobe	17 Nov 1954	20 Aug 1955	31 July 1956

Displacement, tons	1 700 standard; 2 340 full load
Length, feet (*metres*)	347·8 (*106·0*) wl; 358·5 (*109·3*) oa
Beam, feet (*metres*)	34·5 (*10·5*)
Draught, feet (*metres*)	12·0 (*3·7*)
Guns, dual purpose	3—5 in (*127 mm*) 38 cal.
Guns, AA	8—40 mm (2 quadruple)
A/S	Tubes for short homing torpedoes; 2 Hedgehogs; 1 DC rack; 4 K-guns
Boilers	*Harukaze:* 2 Hitachi-Babcock *Yukikaze:* 2 Combustion Engineering
Main engines	2 sets geared turbines; *Harukaze:* 2 Mitsubishi Escher Weiss *Yukikaze:* 2 Westinghouse 30 000 shp; 2 shafts
Speed, knots	30
Radius, miles	6 000 at 18 knots
Oil fuel (tons)	557
Complement	240

YŪKIKAZE *1968, Japanese Maritime Self-Defence Force, Official*

Authorised under the 1953 fiscal year programme. First destroyer hulled vessels built in Japan after the Second World War. Electric welding was extensively adopted in hull construction; development and usage of weldable high tension steel in main hull and light alloy in superstructure were also novel. Nearly all armament was supplied from the USA under the MSA clause. *Harukaze* means "Spring Wind", *Yūkikaze* means "Snow Wind".

Armament was modified in Mar. 1959 when homing torpedo tubes were mounted and depth charge equipment correspondingly reduced.

Photographs of *Harukaze* appear in the 1956-57 to 1961-62 editions and 1963-64 to 1965-66 editions.

US LATER "FLETCHER" TYPE

2 "TWILIGHT" CLASS

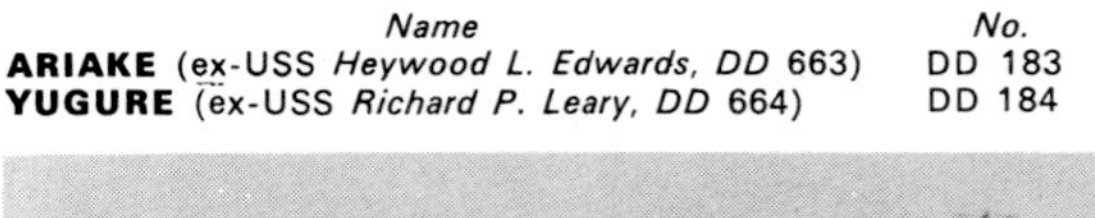

Name	*No.*	*Builders*	*Launched*	*Completed*
ARIAKE (ex-USS *Heywood L. Edwards, DD* 663)	DD 183	Boston Navy Yard	6 Oct 1943	26 Jan 1944
YUGURE (ex-USS *Richard P. Leary, DD* 664)	DD 184	Boston Navy Yard	6 Oct 1943	23 Feb 1944

Displacement, tons	2 050 standard; 3 040 full load
Length, feet (*metres*)	376·5 (*114·8*)
Beam, feet (*metres*)	39·3 (*12·0*)
Draught, feet (*metres*)	18 (*5·5*) max
Guns, dual purpose	*Ariake:* 3—5 in (*127 mm*) 38 cal. *Yugure:* 4—5 in (*127 mm*) 38 cal.
Guns AA	10—40 mm
A/S	*Ariake:* Mk 108 rocket launcher (Weapon A); dropping gear for short homing torpedoes on each side; *Yugure* 2 Hedgehogs
Boilers	4 Foster Wheeler
Main engines	GE geared turbines 60 000 shp; 2 shafts
Speed, knots	35
Complement	300

Transferred on loan from the US Navy on 10 Mar 1959 and towed to Japan for refit, during which No. 3 5 inch gun was removed. *Ariake* means "Dawn Twilight" *Yugure* means "Evening Dusk".

ARIAKE *1966, Japanese Maritime Self-Defence Force, Official*

CONVERSION. Both ships completed conversion in Mar 1962 with improved bridges, larger combat information centre, newer radar aerials and tripod masts. No. 2 5 inch gun in *Ariake* was replaced by Weapon A.

A photograph of *Yugure* appears in the 1964-65 and 1965-66 editions.

US "GLEAVES-LIVERMORE" TYPE

2 "BREEZE" CLASS

Name	*No.*	*Builders*	*Laid down*	*Launched*	*Completed*
ASAKAZE (ex-USS *Ellyson*)	DD 181	Federal SB & DD Co	2 Dec 1940	25 July 1941	28 Nov 1941
HATAKAZE (ex-USS *Macomb*)	DD 182	Bath Iron Works Corpn	3 Sep 1940	22 Sep 1941	26 Jan 1942

Displacement, tons	1 630 standard; 2 775 full load
Length, feet (*metres*)	341 (*104·0*) wl; 348·3 (*106·2*) oa
Beam, feet (*metres*)	36 (*11·0*)
Draught, feet (*metres*)	18 (*5·5*) max
Guns, dual purpose	3—5 in (*127 mm*) 38 cal.
Guns, AA	8—40 mm; 4—20 mm
A/S	2 DC racks
Boilers	4 Babcock & Wilcox
Main engines	Geared turbines 50 000 shp; 2 shafts
Speed, knots	36 designed; 30 present
Complement	270

ASAKAZE *1966, Japanese Maritime Self-Defence Force, Official*

Former US destroyers DD 454 (ex-DMS 19) and DD 458 (ex-DMS 23) respectively. Taken over from the USA on 19 Oct 1954. Names mean "Morning Breeze" and "Flag-fluttering Breeze", respectively.

A photograph of *Hatakaze* appears in the 1963-64 to 1965-66 editions.

FRIGATES

DESTROYER ESCORT TYPE (DE)

4 "RIVER" CLASS

Name	No.	Builders	Laid down	Launched	Completed
ISUZU	DE 211	Mitsui Zosen Co, Tamano	16 Apr 1960	17 Jan 1961	29 July 1961
KITAKAMI	DE 213	Ishikawajima-Harima Co, Tokyo	7 June 1962	21 June 1963	27 Feb 1964
MOGAMI	DE 212	Mitsubishi Zosen Co, Nagasaki	4 Aug 1960	7 Mar 1961	28 Oct 1961
ŌI	DE 214	Maizuru (former Iino) Co, Maizuru	10 June 1962	15 June 1963	22 Jan 1964

Displacement, tons	1 490 standard; 1 700 full load
Length, feet (*metres*)	308·5 (*94·0*) oa
Beam, feet (*metres*)	34·2 (*10·4*)
Draught, feet (*metres*)	11·5 (*3·5*)
Guns, dual purpose	4—3 in (*76 mm*) 50 cal. 2 twin
A/S	1 4-barrelled rocket launcher; 1 DCT; 1 DC rack
Torpedo tubes	4—21 in (*533 mm*) quadrupled
Torpedo launchers	2 triple for A/S homing torpedoes
Main engines	4 diesels, Mitsui in *Oi, Isuzu,* Mitsubishi in *Kitakami, Mogami;* 16 000 hp; 2 shafts
Speed, knots	25
Complement	180

Isuzu and *Mogami* were built under the 1959 fiscal year new construction programme and *Kitakami* and *Ōi* were built under the 1961 fiscal year new construction programme.

CLASS VARIATION. The second pair of this type, *Kitakami* and *Ōi*, have a number of improvements in armament and other equipment and are reported to be of slightly different dimensions.

NOMENCLATURE. All new frigates of the destroyer escort (DE) type are named after rivers, like the old light cruisers. This naming system applied on 1 Oct 1960.

PHOTOGRAPHS. A photograph of *Mogami* appears in the 1961-62 edition, and of *Isuzu* in the 1962-63 to 1966-67 editions.

KITAKAMI — *1967, Ishikawajima-Harima Heavy Industries Co, Ltd*

ŌI — *1967, Maizura Heavy Industries*

DIESEL "B" TYPE ESCORT

2 "THUNDER" CLASS

Name	No.	Builders	Laid down	Launched	Completed
IKAZUCHI	DE 202	Kawasaki Jyuko Co, Kobe	18 Dec 1954	6 Sep 1955	29 May 1956
INAZUMA	DE 203	Mitsui Zosen Co Tamano	25 Dec 1954	4 Aug 1955	5 Mar 1956

Displacement, tons	1 070 standard; 1 300 full load
Length, feet (*metres*)	287 (*87·5*) wl; 288·7 (*88·0* oa)
Beam, feet (*metres*)	28·5 (*8·7*)
Draught, feet (*metres*)	10·2 (*3·1*)
Guns, dual purpose	2—3 in (*76 mm*) 50 cal.
Guns, AA	2—40 mm
A/S	1 Hedgehog; 8 K-guns; 2 DC racks
Main engines	12 000 hp diesels; Mitsubishi in *Ikazuchi*; Mitsui B & W in *Inazuma*; 2 shafts
Speed, knots	25
Complement	160

Diesel powered "B" type DE Escort Vessels. Authorised by Congress under 1953 fiscal year programme. Unlike the turbine boat, *Akebono* (see below) which has two funnels, these diesels boat have only one funnel.

NOMENCLATURE. *Ikazuchi* means "Thunder" and *Inazuma* means "Thunderbolt".

GUNNERY. The original 2—3 inch guns and 4—40 mm guns were removed in Mar 1959 and replaced by 2—3 inch quick firing guns and 2—40 mm guns.

PHOTOGRAPHS. A dead broadside view of *Inazuma* appears in the 1961-62 to 1966-67 editions.

IKAZUCHI — *1967, Japanese Maritime Self-Defence Force, Official*

INAZUMA — *1967, Japanese Maritime Self-Defence Force, Official*

STEAM TURBINE "B" TYPE ESCORT

Name	No.	Builders	Laid down	Launched	Completed
AKEBONO	DE 201	Ishikawajima Jyuko Co, Tokyo	10 Dec 1954	15 Oct 1955	20 Mar 1956

Displacement, tons	1 060 standard; 1 350 full load
Length, feet (*metres*)	295 (*90·0*) oa
Beam, feet (*metres*)	28·5 (*8·7*)
Draught, feet (*metres*)	11 (*3·4*) max
Guns, AA	2—3 in (*76 mm*) 50 cal.
Boilers	2 Ishikawajima-Foster Wheeler
Main engines	Ishikawajima geared turbines 18 000 shp; 2 shafts
Speed knots,	28
Complement	190

The only steam powered DE. Rated as "B" type Escort Vessel. Built under the 1953 Programme. Ordered on 20 Nov 1954. *Akebono* means "Dawn".

GUNNERY. The original 2—3 inch guns and 4—40 mm guns were removed in March 1959 when 2—3 inch quick firing guns were mounted.

AKEBONO — *1967, Japanese Maritime Self-Defence Force, Official*

Frigates—*continued*

EXPERIMENTAL SHIP

FORMER ESCORT DESTROYER

Name	*No.*	*Builders*	*Laid down*	*Launched*	*Completed*
WAKABA (ex-*Nashi*)	DE 261	Kawasaki, Kobe	1 Sep 1944	17 Jan 1945	15 Mar 1945

Displacement, tons 1 250 standard; 1 560 full load
Length, feet (*metres*) 322·2 (*98·2*) pp 329·8 (*100·5*) oa
Beam, feet (*metres*) 31·2 (*9·5*)
Draught, feet (*metres*) 10·7 (*3·3*)
Guns, AA 2—3 in (*76 mm*) 50 cal. aft
A/S 1 Hedgehog; 4 K-guns; 2 DCT
Boilers 2 Kanpon
Main engines 2 geared turbines; 14 000 shp; 2 shafts
Speed, knots 26 designed; 24 present
Radius, miles 4 680 at 16 knots
Oil fuel (tons) 395
Complement 175

WAKABA *1967, Japanese Maritime Self-Defence Force, Official*

This former escort destroyer, *Nashi* was built under the, War Programme of 1943 as one of the Modified "Matsu" type. She was sunk on 28 July 1945 off Hatajiri Point, Inland Sea, by carrier borne aircraft. She was officially scrapped on 15 Sep 1945, but was subsequently raised and repaired and purchased by the Maritime Self-Defence Force. She completed her first reconstruction at Kure Zosen on 12 May 1956, being renamed and commissioned on 31 May. *Wakaba* means "Young Leaf". She was to be used as a training ship, but was converted into a radar, picket. Her second reconstruction commenced at Uraga Dock Co on 10 Sep 1957 and was completed on 28 Mar 1958. Her lattice foremast and tripod mainmast were stepped in 1958. In 1961 she had a large radar aerial fitted aft. In 1968 she was re-classified as an Experimental Ship.

A port broadside view of *Wakaba* appears in the 1961-62 to 1966-67 editions.

Name	*No.*	*Builders*	*Laid down*	*Launched*	*Completed*
ASAHI (ex-USS *Amick, DE* 168)	DE 262	Federal Port Newark	30 Nov 1942	27 May 1943	26 July 1943
HATSUHI (ex-USS *Atherton, DE* 169)	DE 263	Federal Port Newark	14 Jan 1943	27 May 1943	29 Aug 1943

US "BOSTWICK" TYPE

DESTROYER ESCORTS

2 "SUN" CLASS

Displacement, tons 1 250 standard; 1 510 normal; 1 900 full load
Length, feet (*metres*) 306 (*93·3*) oa
Beam, feet (*metres*) 36·1 (*11·0*)
Draught, feet (*metres*) 12 (*3·7*) max
Guns, dual purpose 3—3 in (*76 mm*) 50 cal.
Guns, AA 6—40 mm; 8—20 mm
A/S 8 K-guns; 1 DCT
Main engines GM diesels, electric drive 6 000 hp; 2 shafts
Speed, knots 20
Complement 220

Taken over from the US Navy on 14 June 1955. *Asohi* means "Morning Sun"; *Hatsuhi* means "First Sun of the Year".

A photograph of *Asahi* appears in the 1961-62 to 1966-67 editions.

HATSUHI *1967, Japanese Maritime Self-Defence Force, Official*

US "TACOMA" TYPE PATROL

FRIGATES

6 "TREE" CLASS

KAYA (ex-USS *San Pedro, PF* 37) P F 288
KEYAKI (ex-USS *Evansville, PF* 70) P F 295
KIRI (ex-USS *Everett, PF* 8) P F 291
NIRE (ex-USS *Sandusky, PF* 54) P F 287
SHII (ex-USS *Long Beach, PF* 34) P F 297
SUGI (ex-USS *Coronado, PF* 38) P F 285

Displacement, tons 1 450 standard; 2 415 full load
Length, feet (*metres*) 285·5 (*87·0*) wl; 304 (*92·7*) oa
Beam, feet (*metres*) 37·5 (*11·4*)
Draught, feet (*metres*) 13·7 (*4·2*) max
Guns, dual purpose 3—3 in (*76 mm*) 50 cal.
Guns, AA 2—40 mm; 9—20 mm
A/S 1 Hedgehog; 8 K-guns; 2 DC racks.
Boilers 2 three-drum type; 240 psi (*16·9 kg/cm²*)
Main engines Triple expansion 5 500 shp; 2 shafts
Speed, knots 18
Radius, miles 9 500 at 12 knots
Oil fuel (tons) 645
Complement 170

All launched in 1943. Transferred on loan from the United States in 1953. All were technically returned to the US on 28 Aug 1962, but were transferred outright to the Japanese Government the same day and became Japanese ships. Named after trees. *Kaede* and *Keyaki* have a deckhouse added abaft the mainmast.

Ten sister ships, *Buna*, on 1 Feb 1965, *Kashi, Moni, Tochi* and *Ume* on 1 Apr 1965, and *Kaede, Maki, Matsu, Nara* and *Sakura* on 31 Mar 1966, were reclassified from escort vessels to training ships (moored).

Kusu was converted to Drone Target Carrier in 1964. Photographs of *Kiri, Nora, Nire* and *Sugi* appear in the 1953-54 to 1962-63 editions, a photograph of *Kaya* in the 1963-64 to 1966-67 editions and of *Keyaki* in the 1966-67 and 1967-68 editions.

SHII *1967, Japanese Maritime Self-Defence Force, Official*

KATORI *Japanese Maritime Self-Defence Force, Official*

A medium size training ship of 3,372 tons was ordered under the 1966 Construction Programme from Ishikawajima-Hexima, Tokyo. Armament appears to include 4—3 in (76 mm) 50 calibre AA guns, 1 four-barrelled AS rocket launcher and 2 triple torpedo launchers. A landing deck has been provided for helicopters. Launched 19 Nov 1968.

FAST PATROL VESSELS

10 "MIZUTORI" CLASS SUBMARINE CHASERS (PC)

Name	No.	Builders	Laid down	Launched	Completed
MIZUTORI	311	Kawasaki, Kobe	13 Mar 1959	22 Sep 1959	27 Feb 1960
YAMADORI	312	Fujinagata, Osaka	14 Mar 1959	22 Oct 1959	15 Mar 1960
ŌTORI	313	Kure Shipyard	16 Dec 1959	27 May 1960	13 Oct 1960
KASASAGI	314	Fujinagata, Osaka	18 Dec 1959	31 May 1960	31 Oct 1960
HATSUKARI	315	Sasebo Shipyard	25 Jan 1960	24 June 1960	15 Nov 1960
UMIDORI	316	Sasebo Shipyard	15 Feb 1962	15 Oct 1962	30 Mar 1963
WAKATAKA	317	Kure Shipyard	5 Mar 1962	13 Nov 1962	30 Mar 1963
KUMATAKA	318	Fujinagata, Osaka	20 Mar 1963	21 Oct 1963	25 Mar 1964
SHIRATORI	319	Sasebo Shipyard	29 Feb 1964	8 Oct 1964	27 Feb 1965
HIYODORI	320	Sasebo Shipyard	29 Feb 1965	25 Sep 1965	28 Feb 1966

Displacement, tons	420 to 450 standard
Dimensions, feet	197 × 23·3 × 7·5
Guns	2—40 mm (1 twin)
A/S weapons	1 hedgehog; 1 DC rack; 2 homing torpedo launchers
Main Engines	2 MAN diesels; 2 shafts; 3 800 bhp = 20 knots
Oil fuel (tons)	24·5
Complement	70

Mizutori and *Yamadori* built under 1958 programme, *Ōtori, Kasasagi* and *Hatsukari* 1959, *Umidori* (Sea Bird) and *Wahataka* (Young Hawk) 1961, *Kumataka* 1962, *Shiratori* (White Bird) 1963, *Hiyodori* 1964. A photograph of *Otori* appears in the 1961-62 to 1966-67 editions.

HIYODORI *1967, Japanese Maritime Self-Defence Force, Official*

2 "UMITAKA" CLASS SUBMARINE CHASERS (PC)

	No.	Builders	Laid down	Launched	Completed
UMITAKA	309	Kawasaki, Kobe	13 Mar 1959	25 July 1959	30 Nov 1959
ŌTAKA	310	Kure Shipyard	18 Mar 1959	3 Sep 1959	14 Jan 1960

Displacement, tons	440 to 480 standard
Dimensions, feet	197 × 23·3 × 8
Guns	2—40 mm (1 twin)
A/S weapons	1 hedgehog, 1 DC rack; 2 triple A/S torpedo launchers
Main Engines	2 B & W diesels; 2 shafts; 4 000 bhp = 20 knots
Oil fuel (tons)	24
Radius, miles	2 000 at 12 knots
Complement	70

Built under the 1957 programme. Design emphasised good sea-keeping qualities. *Ōtaka* means Great Hawk. *Umitaka* Sea Hawk. A port bow oblique aerial view of *Ōtaka* appears in the 1960-61 to 1966-67 editions.

ŌTAKA *1967, Hajime Fukaya*

1 GAS TURBIBE TYPE SUBMARINE CHASER (PC)

HAYABUSA 308

Displacement, tons	380 standard
Dimensions, feet	190·2 × 25·7 × 7
Guns	2—40 mm AA (1 twin)
A/S weapons	1 Hedgehog; 2 DC throwers; 2 DC racks
Main engines	1 Gas turbine 5,000 hp; 2 diesels 4,000 bhp; 3 shafts Total 9 000 hp = 26 knots
Complement	75

Built under the 1954 fiscal year programme by Mitsubishi Shipbuilding & Engineering Co Ltd, Nagasaki. Laid down on 23 May 1956. Launched on 20 Nov 1956. Completed on 10 June 1957. The gas turbine was installed in Mar 1962.

HAYABUSA *1967, Japanese Maritime Self-Defence Force, Official*

Fast Patrol Vessels—*continued*

7 DIESEL TYPE SUBMARINE CHASERS (PC)

Name	No.	Builders	Laid down	Launched	Completed
KAMOME	305	Uraga	27 Jan 1956	3 Sep 1956	14 Jan 1957
KARI	301	Fujimagata, Osaka	18 Jan 1956	26 Sep 1956	8 Feb 1957
KIJI	302	Iino, Maizuru	14 Dec 1955	11 Sep 1956	29 Jan 1957
MISAGO	307	Uraga	27 Jan 1956	1 Nov 1956	11 Feb 1957
TAKA	303	Fujimagata, Osaka	18 Jan 1956	17 Nov 1956	11 Mar 1957
TSUBAME	306	Kure Shipyard	15 Mar 1956	10 Oct 1956	31 Jan 1957
WASHI	304	Iino, Maizuru	14 Dec 1955	12 Nov 1956	20 Mar 1957

Displacement, tons	330 standard; (*Kari, Kiji, Taka, Washi*, 310)
Dimensions, feet	173·3 oa × 21·8 × 6·8
Guns	2—40 mm (1 twin)
A/S weapons	1 hedgehog; 2-Y guns; 2 DC racks
Main Engines	2 diesels (*Kari, Kiji, Taka* and *Washi*, Kawasaki-MAN; others Mitsui-Burmeister & Wain). 2 shafts; 4 000 bhp = 20 knots
Oil fuel (tons)	21·5
Complement	70

Authorised under the 1954 programme. At the time they were an entirely new type of fast patrol vessels or submarine chasers, reminiscent of the United States PC type but modified and improved in many ways. *Kamome* means "Seagull". A photograph of *Kamome* appears in the 1957-58 to 1965-66 editions.

MISAGO *1966, Japanese Maritime Self Defence Force, Official*

MINELAYERS

MINELAYER AND CABLE LAYER (ARC)

TSUGARU 481

Displacement, tons	950 standard
Dimensions, feet	216·3 × 34·1 × 11
Guns	1—3 in, 50 cal dp; 2—20 mm AA;
A/S weapons	4 K-guns (DC mortars)
Mines	4 mine launchers, capacity of 40 mines
Main Engines	Diesel; 2 shafts; 3 200 bhp = 16 knots
Complement	100

Dual purpose cable layer and coastal minelayer. Built under the 1953 programme by Yokohama Shipyard & Engine Works, Mitsubishi Nippon-Heavy Industries Ltd. Laid down on 18 Dec 1954. Launched on 19 July 1955. Completed on 15 Dec 1955.

TSUGARU *1966, Japanese Maritime Self-Defence Force, Official*

MINELAYER AND MINESWEEPER (AMC)

ERIMO 491

Displacement, tons	630 standard
Dimensions, feet	210 × 26 × 8
Guns	2—40 mm AA; 2—20 mm AA
A/S weapons	1 hedgehog; 2 K-guns; 2 DC racks
Main Engines	Diesel; 2 shafts; 2 500 bhp = 18 knots
Complement	80

Multi-purpose minelayer, ocean minesweeper (non-magnetic) and submarine chaser. Authorised under 1953 fiscal programme. Built by Uraga Dock Co. Laid down on 10 Dec 1954. Launched on 12 July 1955. Completed on 28 Dec 1955.

ERIMO ***1968, Japanese Maritime Self-Defence Force, Official***

COASTAL MINESWEEPERS

26 "KASADO" CLASS

Name	No.	Laid down	Launched	Completed
KASADO	MSC 604	9 July 1956	19 Mar 1958	26 June 1958
SHISAKA	MSC 605	20 July 1956	20 Mar 1958	16 Aug 1958
KANAWA	MSC 606	25 Aug 1958	22 Apr 1959	24 July 1959
SAKITO	MSC 607	16 Aug 1958	22 Apr 1959	25 Aug 1959
HABUSHI	MAC 608	24 Mar 1959	19 June 1959	22 Sep 1959
KOOZU	MSC 609	30 Mar 1959	12 Nov 1959	26 Feb 1960
TATARA	MSC 610	25 Aug 1958	14 Jan 1960	26 Mar 1960
TSUKUMI	MSC 611	24 Mar 1959	12 Jan 1960	27 Apr 1960
MIKURA	MSC 612	30 Mar 1959	14 Mar 1960	27 May 1960
SHIKINE	MSC 613	12 Jan 1960	22 July 1960	15 Nov 1960
HIRADO	MSC 614	14 Mar 1960	3 Oct 1960	17 Dec 1960
KOSHIKI	MSC 615	20 Mar 1961	9 Nov 1961	29 Jan 1962
HOTAKA	MSC 616	22 Mar 1961	23 Oct 1961	24 Feb 1962
KARATO	MSC 617	15 Mar 1962	11 Dec 1962	23 Mar 1963
HARIO	MSC 618	19 Mar 1962	10 Dec 1962	27 Mar 1963
MUTSURE	MSC 619	28 Mar 1963	16 Dec 1963	24 Mar 1964
CHIBURI	MSC 620	27 Mar 1963	29 Nov 1963	25 Mar 1964
OOTSU	MSC 621	25 Mar 1964	5 Nov 1964	24 Feb 1965
KUDAKO	MSC 622	17 Mar 1964	8 Dec 1964	24 Mar 1965
RISHIRI	MSC 623	9 Mar 1964	22 Nov 1965	5 Mar 1966
REBUN	MSC 624	27 Mar 1965	7 Dec 1965	25 Mar 1966
AMAMI	MSC 625	1 Mar 1966	31 Oct 1966	3 Mar 1967
URUME	MSC 626	1 Feb 1966	12 Nov 1966	30 Jan 1967
MINASE	MSC 627	1 Feb 1966	10 Jan 1967	25 Mar 1967
IBUKI	MSC 628	27 Feb 1967	2 Dec 1967	27 Feb 1968
KATSURA	MSC 629	10 Feb 1967	18 Sep 1967	18 Feb 1968

Displacement, tons	340
Dimensions, feet	151 × 27·5 × 17·5
Guns	1—20 mm AA
Main Engines	2 diesels; 2 shafts; 1 200 bhp = 14 knots

Hull is of wooden construction. Otherwise built of non-magnetic materials. *Habushi, Kanawa* and *Kasado* were built by Hitachi, Kanawaga Works, *Shishaka* and *Sakito* by Nippon Steel Tube Co, Tsurumi. *Kasado* and *Shisaka* were ordered under the 1955 programme, *Habushi, Kanawa* and *Sakito* 1957, four 1958, two 1959, two 1960, two 1961, two 1962, two 1963, two 1964, three 1965. A photograph of *Shisaka* appears in the 1961-62 to 1966-67 editions. A photograph of *Rishiri* appears in the 1967-68 edition.

KATSURA *1968, Japanese Maritime Self-Defence Force, Official*

YASHIRO MSC 603

Displacement, tons	230 standard; 255 full load
Dimensions, feet	118 pp × 22·7 × 6·2
Guns	1—20 mm AA
Main Engines	Diesel; 2 shafts; 1 200 bhp = 13 knots

Built under the 1953 Programme by the Nippon Kokan Co, Tsurumi. Laid down on 22 June 1955, launched on 26 Mar 1956 and completed on 10 July 1956.

YASHIRO *1967, Japanese Maritime Self-Defence Force, Official*

2 "ATADA" CLASS

Name	No.	Laid down	Launched	Completed
ATADA	MSC 601	20 June 1955	12 Mar 1956	30 Apr 1956
ITSUKI	MSC 602	22 June 1955	12 Mar 1956	20 June 1956

Displacement, tons	240 standard; 260 full load
Dimensions, feet	118 pp; 123·3 oa × 21 × 6·8
Guns	1—20 mm AA
Main Engines	Diesel; 2 shafts; 1 200 bhp = 13 knots

Of wood and light metal construction. Authorised under the 1953 fiscal year programme. Built by the Hitachi Zosen Co. Named after small islands. A photograph of *Itsuki* appears in the 1960-61 to 1966-67 editions.

Coastal Minesweepers—*continued*

ATADA *1967, Japanese Maritime Self-Defence Force, Official*

4 "YASHIMA" CLASS

HASHIMA (ex-USS *AMS* 95)
TOSHIMA (ex-USS *MSC* 258)
TSUSHIMA (ex-USS MSC, ex-*AMS* 255)
YASHIMA (ex-USS *AMS* 144)

Displacement, tons	335 standard; 375 full load
Dimensions, feet	138 pp; 144 oa × 26·5 × 8·3
Guns	1—20 mm AA
Main engines	2 GM diesels; 880 bhp = 13 knots

Former US auxiliary minesweepers of non-magnetic construction. Transferred on 3 June 1955 (*Hashima*, MSC 652), 1 Feb 1957 (*Toshima*, MSC 654), 18 July 1956 (*Tsushima*, MSC 652), and 16 Dec 1954 (*Yashima*, MSC 651). A photograph of *Yashima* appears in the 1961-62 to 1965-66 editions.

TOSHIMA *1966, Japanese Maritime Self-Defence Force, Official*

1 "UJISHIMA" CLASS

YAKUSHIMA (ex-USS *Osprey, AMS* 28)

Displacement, tons	310 standard; 350 full load
Dimensions	136 × 24·5 × 8 max
Guns	1—40 mm AA; 2—20 mm AA
Main engines	2 GM diesels; 1 000 bhp = 12 knots

Former US "Albatros" class of wooden construction, formerly auxiliary motor minesweepers (AMS) but reclassified as Minesweepers, Coastal (old) or MSC (o) in Feb 1955.

Yakushima is now used for training.

DISPOSALS

Former sister ships **Moroshima, Ogishima, Ninoshima, Yugeshima, Nuwajima, Yurishima** were officially deleted from the list in 1967; **Etajima** and **Ujishima** in 1966.

MINESWEEPING BOATS (*Sookaitei*)

No. 1 **No. 2** **No. 3** **No. 4** **No. 5** **No. 6**

Displacement, tons	40
Dimensions, feet	57·2 wl; 62·3 oa × 16 × 4
Main Engines	Diesels; 2 shafts; 320 bhp = 10 knots
Complement	10

Nos. 1, 2 and 3 were launched in Jan and Feb 1957 and completed in Mar and Apr 1957. No. 4 was launched in Apr 1957 and completed in June 1957. Nos. 5 and 6 were laid down in Aug 1958 and completed in Feb-Mar 1959. Nos. 1 and 2 were built by Hitachi, Kanagawa; and the others by Nihon Kohan, Tsurumi. Named *Sokaitel* Nos. 1 to 6 and numbered MSB 701 to 706.

MB 5 *1963, Official*

MOTOR TORPEDO BOATS *(Gyoraitei)*

PT 10

Displacement, tons	90 standard; 120 full load
Dimensions, feet	105 × 27·8 × 3·7
Guns	2—40 mm AA (1 forward, 1 aft)
Tubes	4—21 in (single, amidships)
Main Engines	3 Napier Deltic diesels; 9 400 bhp = 40 knots
Complement	26

1960 programme. Built by Mitsubishi, Shimonoseki. Laid down on 30 Jan 1961. Launched on 28 July 1961. Completed on 25 May 1962. Light metal hull.

PT 10 *1964, Mitsubishi Shipbuilding & Engineering Co Ltd.*

PT9

Displacement, tons	55
Dimensions, feet	71·3 × 19·8 × 6
Tubes	2—21 in
Main Engines	2 Napier Deltic diesels; 5 000 bhp = 40 knots
Complement	14

Basically similar to the British "Dark" class MTBs. Built by Saunders-Roe (Anglesey) Ltd, Beaumaris. Delivered to Yokosuka Naval Base on 29 July 1957. Accepted into service on 2 Sep 1957. Has mounting for 1—40 mm AA (gun not fitted).

PT 9 *Saunders-Roe (Anglesey) Ltd*

PT 7 **PT 8**

Displacement, tons	100
Dimensions, feet	112 × 24·7 × 4
Guns	2—40 mm AA
Tubes	4—21 in
Main Engines	3 Mitsubishi diesels; 3 shafts; 6 000 bhp = 33 knots
Complement	30

Authorised in the 1954 fiscal year. Built by Mitsubishi Zosen Co, Shimonoseki Works. Both laid down on 23 Aug 1956, launched on 2 Feb and 20 July 1957, respectively, and completed on 19 Dec 1957 and 10 Jan 1958. Light metal hulls.

PT 8 *1966, Japanese Maritime Self-Defence Force, Official*

PT 1 **PT 2** **PT 3** **PT 4** **PT 5** **PT 6**

Displacement, tons	75 (Nos 3 and 4: 70)
Dimensions, feet	82 × 20 × 6
Guns	1—40 mm AA
Tubes	2—21 in torpedo launchers
Main Engines	2 diesel engines; 4 000 bhp = 31 knots
Complement	18

Authorised under the 1953 fiscal year programme. Nos. 1 and 2 have wooden hulls, Nos. 5 and 6 have steel hulls, and Nos. 3 and 4 have light metal hulls. Builders: Azuma Zosen Co (Nos 5 and 6), Hitachi Zosen Co (Nos. 1 and 2), and Mitsubishi Zosen Co (Nos. 3 and 4). Numbers 801 to 809 were assigned on 1 Sep 1957.

PT 1 *1969 Japanese Maritime Self Defence Force, Official*

SUBMARINE RESCUE VESSEL (ASR)

CHIHAYA ASR 401

Displacement, tons	1 340 standard
Dimensions, feet	239·5 × 39·3 × 12·7
Main Engines	Diesels; 2 700 bhp = 15 knots
Complement	90

Authorised under the 1959 fiscal year programme. The first vessel of her kind to be built in Japan. Laid down on 15 Mar 1960. Launched by Mitsubishi Nippon Heavy Industries Co, Yokohama on 4 Oct 1960. Completed on 15 Mar 1961. Has rescue chamber, decompression chamber, and four-point mooring equipment.

CHIHAYA *1968, Japanese Maritime Self-Defence Force, Official*

DRONE TARGET CARRIER

KUSU (ex-USS *Ogden*, PF 39) PF 281

Displacement, tons	1 450 standard; 2 415 full load
Dimensions, feet	285·5 wl, 304 oa × 37·5 × 13·7 max
Guns, AA	2—40 mm; 6—20 mm
A/S weapons	1 Hedgehog
Main engines	Triple expansion; 2 shafts; 5 500 ihp = 18 knots
Boilers	2 three-drum type; 240 psi
Oil fuel, tons	645
Complement	170

Former frigate of the "Tree" class, ex-US "Tacoma" type patrol frigate, see earlier page. Converted to a Drone Target Carrier in 1964.

DISPOSAL

The drone target carrier **Hamagiku** (ex-415, ex-USS *LSSL* 87), former American landing ship support, large, was deleted from the list in 1967.

ICEBREAKER (AGB)

FUJI 5001

Displacement, tons	5 250 standard; 7 760 normal; 8 566 full load
Dimensions, feet	328 × 72·2 × 29
Aircraft	3 helicopters
Main engines	4 diesel-electric; 2 shafts; 12 000 shp = 16 knots
Radius, miles	5 000 at 15 knots
Complement	200 plus 35 scientists and observers

Icebreaker and Antarctic Support Ship. Built by Tsurumi Shipyard, Yokohama, Nippon Kokan Kabushiki Kaisha. Laid down on 28 Aug 1964, launched on 18 Mar 1965 and delivered on 15 July 1965. Equipped with hangar and flight deck aft. Named after the mountain.

FUJI *1968, Japanese Maritime Self-Defence Force, Official*

SALVAGE VESSEL

SHOBO 41

Displacement, tons	45
Dimensions, feet	75 × 18 × 3·3
Main engines	4 diesels; Speed = 19 knots

A new fire defence boat. Built by Azumo Zosen, Yokosuka. Completed 28 Feb 1964.

PATROL BOATS

SHOOKAI 1, 2, 3, 4, 5, 6, 7 **SHOOKAI 11, 12, 13, 14, 15, 16, 17**

Displacement, tons	18
Dimensions, feet	45·5 × 13·7 × 3·2
Main Engines	2 diesels; 450 bhp = 16 knots

These vessels were transferred to Japan under the MAP programme in 1958.

TANK LANDING SHIPS

OOSUMI 4001 **SHIMOKITA** 4002 **SHIRETOKO** 4003

Displacement, tons	1 650 standard; 4 080 full load
Dimensions, feet	316 wl; 348 oa × 50 × 14
Guns	7—40 mm AA; 2—20 mm AA
Main engines	GM diesels; 2 shafts; 1 700 bhp = 11 knots
Complement	70

Former US tank landing ships *Daggett County, LST* 689, *Hillsdale County, LST* 835, and *Nansemond County, LST* 1064, built by Jeffersonville B. & M. Co, Jeffersonville, Ind; American Bridge Co, Ambridge, Pa; and Bethlehem Steel Co, Hingham, Mass. respectively, in 1944-45. Transferred from USA and commissioned in the Japanese MSDF on 1 Apr 1961. Named after homeland peninsulars. A photograph of *Oosumi* appears in the 1962-63 to 1966-67 editions.

SHIRETOKO 1967, *Japanese Maritime Self-Defence Force, Official*

MEDIUM LANDING SHIP

LSM 3001 (ex-French *LSM* 9013, ex-USS *LSM* 125)

Displacement, tons	743 beaching; 1 095 full load
Dimensions, feet	196·5 wl; 203·5 oa × 34·5 × 5·2 beaching; (8·5 max)
Guns	2—40 mm AA; 6—20 mm AA
Main Engines	Diesels; 2 shafts; 2 800 bhp = 12 knots
Complement	50

Transferred from the US Navy to the French Navy in 1954 for use in Indo-China. She was returned by the French in 1957 to the US Navy, and then transferred to the Japanese in 1958..

LSM 3001 *1966, Japanese Maritime Self-Defence Force Official*

LANDING CRAFT

LCU 2001 LCU 2002 LCU 2003 LCU 2004 LCU 2005 LCU 2006

Displacement, tons 187

Former US Navy LCU 1602, 1603, 1604, 1605, 1606 and 1607 transferred under MAP

42 Ex-U.S. LCM TYPE

LCM 1001—1042

Displacement, tons 22

55 landing craft comprising 6 LCUs of 187 tons, 29 LCMs of 22 tons and 20 LCVPs of 8 tons were transferred from the United States on 2 June 1955. 13 LCMs, Nos 1030—1042, were transferred from the United States under MAP in 1961.

HIGH SPEED BOATS *(Kosoku)*

KOSOKU 4 **KOSOKU 5**

Displacement, tons	26
Dimensions, feet	75·5 × 18 × 2·5
Main Engines	2 Packard engines; 3 000 bhp = 40 knots

Of aluminium construction. Laid down on 10 Oct 1958 and 11 Dec 1958 at Mitsubishi, Shimonoseki Works under the 1957 and 1958 Programme, launched on 11 Dec 1958 and 2 Mar 1959, and completed on 11 May 1959 and 12 June 1959. respectivley. Pennant Nos. ASH 04 and 05.

KOSOKU 1 **KOSOKU 2** **KOSOKU 3**

Displacement, tons	30
Dimensions, feet	65·7 × 17 × 2·7
Main Engines	2 Packard petrol engines; 3 000 bhp = 42 knots

ASH category. Of wooden construction. Former names of Kosoku 1 and 2 were YS 03, YS 04 as service craft. All are Maritime Delf-Sefence Force auxiliaries.

KOSOKU 22, 23, 24, 25, 26, 27, 28, 30

Displacement, tons	30
Dimensions, feet	63·2 × 15·2 × 6
Main Engines	2 petrol engines; 1 200 bhp = 33·5 knots

ASH 22-26 transferred under MAP in 1958-59, 27-30 in 1961-62.

MINESWEEPER TENDERS (MST)

HAYATOMO (ex-USS *Hamilton County, LST* 802) MST 461

Displacement, tons	1 650 standard; 4 080 full load
Dimensions, feet	316 wl; 328 oa × 50 × 14
Guns	7—40 mm AA; 2—20 mm AA (original armament)
Main engines	GM diesels; 2 shafts; 1 700 bhp = 11 knots
Complement	70

Former US tank landing ship. Built by Jeffersonville B. & M. Co, Jeffersonville, Ind. Laid down on 2 Sep 1944, launched on 19 Oct 1944 and completed on 13 Nov 1944. Purchased from the US Navy on 30 June 1960. Rated as MSC Tender.

HAYATOMO *1963, Tatuo Kamino*

2 "MIHO" CLASS

MIHO (ex-USS *FS* 524) **NASAMI** (ex-USS *FS* 408)

Displacement, tons	706
Dimensions, feet	177 × 30 × 10
Main Engines	Diesels; 2 shafts; 1 000 bhp = 11 knots

Transferred from the United States in 1955. *Nasami* is rated as a minesweeper tender (MST), *Miho*, formerly rated as ASS, was refitted as an inshore minesweeper depot ship in August 1959. A photograph of *Nasami* appears in the 1957-58 edition.

OILERS (AO)

HAMANA

Displacenemt, tons	2 900 light; 7 550 full load
Dimensions, feet	420 × 51·5 × 20·5
Guns	2—40 mm AA
Main Engines	Diesel; 5 000 bhp = 16 knots

Built by Uraga Dock Co under the 1960 programme. Laid down on 17 Apr 1961 launched on 24 Oct 1961, and completed on 10 Mar 1962. Named after the lake.

HAMANA *Japanese Maritime Self-Defence Force, Official*

TOBA

Displacement, tons	390
Dimensions, feet	126·7 × 28 × 12
Main Engines	1 diesel; 1 200 bhp = 11 knots

AST category. Of wooden construction. Former name was LT 392.

SUMA

Displacement, tons	115
Dimensions, feet	70·5 × 19 × 5
Main Engines	1 diesel; 600 bhp = 12 knots

ATR category. Steel construction. Former name YLT 749. The small harbour tugs YTL 162, 167, 203, 244, 748, 749 and 750 were transferred by the USA.

MARITIME SAFETY AGENCY

Established in May 1948. *Director General:* Mitsuo Sato Personnel 1968: 11 236

LARGE PATROL VESSELS

1+1 "IZU" CLASS

IZU PL 31

Displacement, tons	2 080 normal
Dimensions, feet	295·3 wl × 38 × 17·8
Main engines	Diesels; 2 shafts; 10 400 bhp = 21·6 knots
Radius, miles	14 700 at 12·7 knots; 1 500 at 20·3 knots
Complement	72

Laid down in Aug 1966, launched in Jan 1967 and completed in July 1967. This ship is to be employed in long range rescue and patrol and weather observation duties. As such she is equipped with weather observation radar, various types of marine instruments and has an ice proof hull for winter work. A sister ship *Miura*, is now under construction and will be completed in 1969.

IZU *1968, Japanese Maritime Safety Agency, Official*

ERIMO PL 13 **SATSUMA** PL 14

Displacement, tons	1 009 normal (official figures)
Dimensions, feet	239·5 wl × 30·2 × 9·9
Guns	1—3 in, 50 cal; 1—20 mm AA
Main Engines	Diesels; 2 shafts; 4 800 bhp = 19·78 knots

Both built by Hitachi Zosen Co Ltd. *Erimo* was laid down on 29 Mar 1965, launched on 14 Aug 1965 and completed on 30 Nov 1965. Her structure is strengthened against ice. Employed as a patrol vessel off northern Japan. *Satsuma*, completed on 30 July 1966, is assigned to guard and rescue south of Japan; she is not particularly strengthened against ice.

ERIMO *1966, Japanese Maritime Safety Agency, Official*

KOJIMA PL 21

Displacement, tons	1 100
Dimensions, feet	228·3 × 33·8 × 10·5
Guns	1—3 In; 1—40 mm AA; 1—20 mm AA
Main Engines	Diesels; 2 600 hp = 17 knots
Complement	17 officers, 42 men, 47 cadets

Maritime Safety Agency training ship. Completed on 21 May 1964 at Kure Zosen.

KOJIMA *1965, Japanese Maritime Safety Agency, Official*

2 "NOJIMA" CLASS

NOJIMA PL 11 **OJIKA** PL 12

Displacement, tons	950 standard; 980 normal; 1 100 full load
Dimensions, feet	208·8 pp; 226·5 oa × 30·2 × 10·5
Main Engines	2 sets diesels; 3 000 bhp = 17·5 knots
Complement	51

Nojima was built by Uraga Dock Co Ltd. Laid down on 27 Oct 1961, launched on 12 Feb 1962, and completed on 30 Apr 1962. *Ojika* was completed on 10 June 1963. Both employed as patrol vessels and weather ships.

NOJIMA *1968, Japanese Maritime Safety Agency, Official*

Large Patrol Vessels *continued*

2 "MUROTO" CLASS

DAIO PL 02 **MUROTO** PL 01

Displacement, tons	750 standard; 840 normal
Dimensions, feet	182 pp; 200 oa × 30·5 × 10·2
Guns	1—3 in, 50 cal; 2—20 mm AA
Main engines	2—4 cycle single acting diesels; 1 500 bhp = 15·37 knots

Muroto, built by Uraga Dock Company Ltd, Tokyo, was laid down on 16 Aug 1949, launched on 5 Dec 1949, and delivered on 20 Mar 1950. Vertical tubular donkey boiler, three generators, wireless, radar, direction finder, echo-sounder, streamlined bridge wings.

MUROTO *1968, Japanese Maritime Safety Agency, Official*

SOYA PL 107

Displacement, tons	4 364 normal; 4 818 full load
Dimensions, feet	259·2 wl × 51·9 (*including bulge*) × 18·9
Aircraft	4 helicopters (see *Notes*)
Main Engines	2 sets diesels; 4 800 bhp = 12·5 knots on trials
Radius, miles	16 400 at 11 knots
Complement	96

Originally a Lighthouse Supply Ship and Navigational Aid Vessel (LL) but converted by Asano Dockyard of Nippon Steel Tube Co Ltd into a South Pole Research Ship. Her first conversion, begun on 12 Mar 1956 was completed on 10 Oct. 1956. The second conversion, begun on 1 July 1957, was completed on 30 Sep 1957. The third conversion was completed on 5 Oct 1958. She carried two Sikorsky S—58 helicopters and two Bell 47G-2 helicopters on a flight platform laid on the quarter deck for exploration and surveying in the Antarctic. She was designed for breaking ice more than 4 feet thick. Upon completion of her Antarctic research mission in 1963 she was assigned to guard and rescue service as a patrol vessel.

SOYA *1959, Japanese Maritime Safety Agency, Official*

MEDIUM PATROL VESSELS

5 "CHIFURI" CLASS

CHIFURI PM 18
KUROKAMI PM 19
KOZU PM 20
SHIKINE PM 21
DAITO PM 22

Displacement, tons	465 standard; 483 normal
Dimensions, feet	169 pp; 177 wl × 25·2 × 8·5 (normal)
Guns	1—3 in 50 cal; 1—20 mm AA
Main engines	2 sets diesels; 1 300 bhp = 15·8 knots
Radius, miles	4 400 at 12 knots

A photograph of *Chifuri* appears in the 1962-63 to 1965-66 editions.

DAITO *1966, Eiichi Aoki*

14 "REBUN" CLASS

REBUN	PM 04	**HACHIJO**	PM 08	**NOTO**	PM 13
IKI	PM 05	**AMAKUSA**	PM 09	**HEKURA**	PM 14
OKI	PM 06	**OKUSHIRI**	PM 10	**MIKURA**	PM 15
GENKAI	PM 07	**KUSAKAKI**	PM 11	**KOSHIKI**	PM 16
		RISHIRI	PM 12	**HIRADO**	PM 17

Displacement, tons	450 standard; 488 trials; 495 normal
Dimensions, feet	155·2 pp; 164 wl; 170 oa × 26·5 × 8·5
Guns	1—3 in 50 cal; 1—20 mm AA
Main engines	2 sets diesels; 1 300 bhp = 15 knots
Radius, miles	3 000 at 12 knots

Medium Patrol Vessels—*continued*

A development of the original "Awaji" class design. All completed in 1951.
A photograph of *Mikura* appears in the 1961-62 to 1964-65 editions, and of *Genkai* in the 1963-64 to 1965-66 editions.

HACHIJO — *1968, Japanese Maritime Safety Agency, Official*

3 "AWAJI" CLASS

AWAJI PM 01 **MIYAKE** PM 02 **SADO** PM 03

Displacement, tons	510 standard; 550 normal
Dimensions, feet	172 oa × 26·7 × 9·2
Guns	1—3 in 50 cal; 1—20 mm AA
Main engines	2 sets diesels; 1 300 bhp = 15 knots
Radius, miles	3 000 at 12 knots

Of a design resembling United States Coast Guard Cutters. All completed in 1950.
A photograph of *Awaji* appears in the 1962-63 and 1963-64 editions.

SADO — *1966, Eiichi Aoki*

SMALL PATROL VESSELS

5 "MATSUURA" CLASS

AMAMI PS 62 **MATSUURA** PS 60 **SENDAI** PS 61
KARATSU PS 64 **NATORI** PS 63

Displacement, tons	420 standard; 425 normal
Dimensions, feet	163·3 pp; 181·5 oa × 23 × 7·5
Guns	1—20 mm AA
Main engines	2 sets diesels; 1 400 bhp = 16·5 knots (*Matsuura, Sendai*); 1 800 bhp = 16·8 knots (*Amami, Natori*); 2 600 bhp (*Karatsu*)
Radius, miles	3 500 at 13 knots
Complement	37

Matsuura and *Sendai* were built by Osaka Shipbuilding Co Ltd. *Matsuura* was laid down on 16 Oct 1960, launched on 24 Dec 1960 and completed on 18 Mar 1961. *Sendai* was laid down on 23 Aug 1961, launched on 18 Jan 1962 and completed on 21 Apr 1962. *Amami*, completed on 29 Mar 1965, *Natori*, completed in 1966, and *Karatsu*, delivered to MSA on 31 Mar 1967, were built by Hitachi Zosen Co Ltd.

MATSUURA — *1966, Eiichi Aoki*

1 "TESHIO" CLASS

TESHIO PS 53

Displacement, tons	421·5 normal
Dimensions, feet	149·4 pp; 159 wl × 23 × 8·2
Guns	1—40 mm AA
Main engines	2 sets diesels; 1 400 bhp = 15·71 knots
Radius, miles	3 690 at 12 knots
Complement	37

Built by Uraga Dock Co Ltd. Laid down on 15 Sep 1954, launched on 12 Jan 1955 and completed on 19 Mar 1955.
A photograph of *Teshio* appears in the 1962-63 to 1965-66 editions.

6 "YAHAGI" CLASS

CHITOSE PS 56 **SORACHI** PS 57 **YAHAGI** PS 54
HORONAI PS 59 **SUMIDA** PS 55 **YUBARI** PS 58

Displacement, tons	333·15 standard; 375·7 normal
Dimensions, feet	147·3 pp; 157·2 wl × 24 × 7·4 (normal)
Guns	1—40 mm AA
Main engines	2 sets diesels; 1 400 bhp = 15·5 knots
Radius, miles	4 000 at 12 knots
Complement	37

Small Patrol Vessels—*continued*

All built by Niigata Engineering Co Ltd. *Yahagi* was laid down on 9 Dec 1955, launched on 19 May 1956 and completed on 31 July 1956. *Sumida* was completed on 30 June 1957. *Chitose* was laid down on 20 Sep 1957, launched on 24 Feb 1958 and completed on 30 Apr 1958. *Sorachi* was completed in Mar 1959, *Yubari* on 15 Mar 1960, *Horonai* on 4 Feb 1961. A photograph of *Yahagi* appears in the 1959-60 and 1960-61 editions, and of *Chitose* in the 1961-62 to 1966-67 editions.

HORONAI — *1967, Japanese Maritime Safety Agency, Official*

2 "TOKACHI" CLASS

TOKACHI PS 51 **TATSUTA** PS 52

Displacement, tons	336 standard; 381 normal (*Tokachi*) 324 standard; 369 normal (*Tatsuta*)
Dimensions, feet	157·5 pp; 164 wl; 170 oa × 21·9 × 11·2
Guns	1—40 mm AA
Main engines	2 sets of 4 cycle single acting diesels 1 500 bhp = 16 knots (max); 12 knots (service) (*Tokachi*) 1 400 bhp = 15 knots (max); 12 knots (service) (*Tatsuta*)
Radius, miles	3 824 at 12 knots (*Takachi*); 3 930 at 12 knots (*Tatsuta*)
Complement	37

Tokachi was built by Harima Dockyard, Kure. Laid down on 14 Nov 1953, launched on 8 May 1954 and completed on 31 July 1954. *Tatsuta* was completed on 10 Sep 1954. A photograph of *Tokachi* appears in the 1962-63 to 1966-67 editions.

TATSUTA — *1967, Japanese Maritime Safety Agency, Official*

3 "NAGARA" CLASS

NAGARA PS 18 **TONE** PS 19 **KITAKAMI** PS 20

Displacement, tons	260
Dimensions, feet	131·2 × 23 × 7·2
Guns	1—40 mm AA
Main engines	2 diesels; 2 shafts; 800 bhp = 13·5 knots
Radius, miles	2 000 at 12 knots
Complement	35

Improved versions of the "Kuma" class. All launched and completed in 1952.

NAGARA — *1966, Eiichi Aoki*

17 "KUMA" CLASS

KUMA	PS 01	**SAGAMI**	PS 06	**YOSHINO**	PS 12
FUJI	PS 02	**OYODO**	PS 07	**NOSHIRO**	PS 13
TENRYU	PS 03	**ABUKUMA**	PS 08	**KISO**	PS 14
ISUZU	PS 04	**KUZURYU**	PS 09	**SHINANO**	PS 15
ISHIKARI	PS 05	**KIKUCHI**	PS 10	**CHIKUGO**	PS 16
		MOGAMI	PS 11	**KUMANO**	PS 17

Displacement, tons	258 standard; 275 normal
Dimensions, feet	122 pp; 126·3 wl; 132·2 oa × 23 × 7·5
Guns	1—40 mm AA
Main engines	2 sets diesels; 800 bhp = 13·6 knots
Radius, miles	2 000 at 12 knots
Complement	35

Small Patrol Vessels—*continued*

Kuma was built by Nihon Kokan Ltd, Tsurumi Dockyard, laid down on 29 Sep 1950, launched on 12 Jan 1951 and completed on 24 Mar 1951.

MOGAMI *1966, Eiichi Aoki*

1 "KABASHIMA" TYPE

KABASHIMA PS 100

Small patrol vessel displacing about 100 tons. Of this group *Fujitaka*, PS 151, and *Hayabusa*, PS 153, were deleted from the list in 1965, and *Komadori*, PS 152, in 1966.

6 "KAWACHIDORI" CLASS

HAMACHIDORI	PS 102	**MIOCHIDORI**	PS 104	**SAWACHIDORI**	PS 107
ASACHIDORI	PS 103	**TOMOCHIDORI**	PS 105	**HARUCHIDORI**	PS 115

Former naval aircraft rescue vessels, employed as local patrol vessel. A photograph of *Hamachidori* appears in the 1959-60 to 1963-64 editions. *Namichidori*, PS 110, and *Sayochidori*, PS 113, were officially deleted from the list in 1965, *Okichidori*, PS 106 and *Shimachidori*, PS 112, in 1966, *Kawachidori*, PS 101, *Murachidori*, PS 109, and *Iwachidori*, PS 114, in 1967 and *Wakachidori*, PS 108 and *Isochidori*, PS 111 in 1968.

ASACHIDORI *1964, Kohji Ishiwata*

13 "HIDAKA" CLASS

ASHITAKA	PS 43	**IBUKI**	PS 45	**ROKKO**	PS 35
AKIYOSHI	PS 37	**KAMUI**	PS 41	**TAKANAWA**	PS 36
HIDAKA	PS 32	**KUNIMI**	PS 38	**TAKATSUKI**	PS 39
HIMAYA	PS 33	**KURAMA**	PS 44	**TOUMI**	PS 46
				TSURUGI	PS 34

Displacement, tons	166·2 to 164·4 standard; 169·4 normal
Dimensions, feet	100 pp; 111 oa × 20·8 × 5·5
Main engines	1 set diesels; 1 shaft; 690 to 700 bhp = 13·5 knots
Radius, miles	1 100 at 12 knots

Hidaka was built by Azuma Shipbuilding Co, Laid down on 4 Oct 1961, launched on 2 Mar 1962 and completed on 23 Apr 1962. Both *Hiyama* and *Tsurugi* were completed in Mar 1963 by Hitachi Shipbuilding Co. *Kunimi* was built under the 1964 fiscal year programme by Hayashikane Shipbuilding & Engineering Co, Shimoneseki, laid down on 15 Nov 1964, launched on 19 Dec 1964 and completed on 15 Feb 1965. Three more local patrol ships were completed in 1965, two in 1966, two in 1967 and two in 1968. A photograph of *Hidaka* appears in the 1963-64 to 1965-66 editions.

TSURUGI *1966, Eiichi Aoki*

Small Patrol Vessels—*continued*

3 SPECIAL RESCUE TYPE

AKAGI PS 40 **TSUKUBA** PS 31

Displacement, tons	65 (*Akagi* 41·9 normal)
Dimensions, feet	80·5 × 21·5 × 3·7; *Akagi* 78·8 oa × 17·8 × 3·2
Main engines	2 Niigata diesels; 900 bhp = 18·44 knots trials; *Akagi* 2 Mercedes Benz diesels; 1 100 bhp = 28 knots
Radius, miles	300 at 12 knots; *Akagi* 260 at 28 knots

Akagi and *Tsukuba* (photograph in the 1963-64 to 1965-66 editions) were built by Hitachi Zosen, Kanagawa, and completed in 1965 and on 30 Mar 1962 respectively.

BIZAN PS 42

Displacement, tons	39·8 normal
Dimensions, feet	80·5 × 18·3 × 2·8
Guns	1 MG aft
Main engines	2 Mitsubishi diesels; 1 140 bhp = 21·6 knots
Radius, miles	400 at 18 knots

Built by Shimonoseki Shipyard & Engine Works, Mitsubishi Heavy Industries Ltd. Completed in Mar 1966. Of light metal construction.

BIZAN *1967, Japanese Maritime Safety Agency, Official*

PATROL CRAFT

7 "SHINONOME" CLASS 3 "HANAYUKI" CLASS

SHINONOME	PC 30	**NATSUGUMO**	PC 35
HATAGUMO	PC 31	**TATSUGUMO**	PC 36
MAKIGUMO	PC 32	**HANAYUKI**	PC 37
YAEGUMO	PC 33	**MINEYUKI**	PC 38
ASAGUMO	PC 34	**ISOYUKI**	PC 39

Displacement, tons	43 to 46 normal (*Hanayuki* 37 to 40)
Dimensions, feet	69 × 17·2 × 3·2 (*Hatagumo, Makigumo, Shinonome, Yaegumo, Asagumo, Natsugumo, Tatsugumo*) 68·9 oa × 16·7 × 3·1 (*Hanayuki, Mineyuki, Isoyuki*)
Main engines	2 diesels; 1 400 bhp = 20 knots 2 diesels; 1 000 bhp = 18 8 knots (*Shinonome*) 2 diesels; 1 500 bhp = 21 knots (*Hanayuki* class) 3 diesels; 2 200 bhp = 25 knots (*Yamayuki, Komoyuki*)
Complement	9 to 10

Isoyuki on 29 Feb 1960, *Hanayuki* and *Mineyuki* in Mar 1959, *Asagumo* on 15 Mar 1955, *Natsugumo* on 31 Mar 1955, *Tatsugumo* on 31 May 1955 and the others before Oct 1954. Of light alloy framework and wooden hulls.

HANAYUKI *1963, Official*

8 "MATSUYUKI" CLASS

MATSUYUKI	PC 40	**YAMAYUKI**	PC 44
SHIMAYUKI	PC 41	**KOMAYUKI**	PC 45
TAMAYUKI	PC 42	**UMIGIRI**	PC 46
HAMAYUKI	PC 43	**ASAGIRI**	PC 47

Displacement, tons	40 normal
Dimensions, feet	65·6 wl × 16·7 × 3·2
Guns	One 13 mm AA
Main engines	Two Mercedes Benz diesels; 2 200 bhp = 25·8 knots
Radius, miles	244 at 24·8 knots
Complement	10

Since 1964 two or three craft of this type have been built per year by Hitachi Kanagawa Factory, *Yamayuki* and *Komoyuki* in 1966-67. Built of light alloy frame-work and wooden hulls to give considerably reduced weight and increased speed.

Patrol Craft—*continued*

HIRYU PC 109

Displacement, tons	33·5 normal
Dimensions, feet	71·5 wl × 18·2 × 4·8
Main engines	2 Packard engines; 1 200 bhp = 15 knots

Former US motor torpedo boat of the PT type which served in the US Navy in the Second World War. Built by Annapolis Yacht Yard Inc, Annapolis, Ind, in 1943. Acquired from USA in 1957. Converted to a patrol craft by Azuma Shipbuilding Co, Yokosuka, engines being replaced. Rated as inshore patrol boat.

HIRYU *1968, Japanese Maritime Safety Agency, Official*

24 "HATSUNAMI" CLASS

HATSUNAMI	PC 01	**CHIYONAMI**	PC 09	**TERUZUKI**	PC 17
AYANAMI	PC 02	**HAYANAMI**	PC 10	**URAZUKI**	PC 18
ISONAMI	PC 03	**HATSUZUKI**	PC 11	**WAKAZUKI**	PC 19
URANAMI	PC 04	**HANAZUKI**	PC 12	**YAMAZUKI**	PC 20
KYONAMI	PC 05	**KIYOZUKI**	PC 13	**HARUZUKI**	PC 21
OKINAMI	PC 06	**MOCHIZUKI**	PC 14	**NATSUZUKI**	PC 22
TAMANAMI	PC 07	**NIIZUKI**	PC 15	**AKIZUKI**	PC 23
SUZUNAMI	PC 08	**SUZUTSUKI**	PC 16	**FUYUZUKI**	PC 24

Displacement, tons	45 normal
Dimensions, feet	75·5 oa × 15·1 × 3·1
Main engines	2 diesels; 700 bhp = 14 knots

Rated as local patrol boats. Seaward defence patrol craft and small submarine-chaser type. A photograph of *Suzutsuki* appears in the 1953-54 to 1960-61 editions.

AYANAMI *1968, Japanese Maritime Safety Agency, Official*

MUTSUKI PC 25

Displacement, tons	55 normal
Dimensions, feet	83·7 oa × 16 × 3·2
Main engines	2 diesels; 1 000 bhp = 15 knots

A small general purpose vessel officially rated as a local craft.

SURVEYING VESSELS

TENYO HM 05

Displacement, tons	181
Dimensions, feet	95 × 19·2 × 9·2
Main engines	Diesels; 230 bhp = 10 knots
Radius, miles	3 160 at 10 knots

HEIYO HM 04

Displacement, tons	69
Dimensions, feet	73·5 × 14·5 × 8
Main engines	Diesel; 150 bhp = 9 knots
Radius, miles	670 at 9 knots

Completed by Shimuzu Dockyard of Nippon Steel Tube Co Ltd, in Mar 1955.
There are 21 other smaller vessels of HS type ranging from 5 to 8 tons displacement.

MEIYO HL 03

Displacement, tons	486 normal
Measurement, tons	360 gross
Dimensions, feet	133 wl; 146 oa × 26·5 × 9·5
Main engines	1 set diesel; 700 bhp = 12 knots
Radius, miles	4 500 at 10 knots
Complement	40

Built by Nagoya Shipbuilding & Engineering Co, Nagoya. Laid down on 14 Sep 1962, launched 22 Dec 1962, completed 15 Mar 1963. Controllable pitch propeller.
The former *Meiyo* (HL 01) was discarded on 1 Mar 1963 due to old age, and replaced by the new *Meiyo*, HL 03.

Surveying Vessels—*continued*

TAKUYO HL 02

Displacement, tons	880 standard; 930 normal
Dimensions, feet	185 pp; 192·8 wl × 31·2 × 10·7 normal
Main engines	2 sets diesels; 1 300 bhp = 14 knots max
Radius, miles	8 000 at 12 knots

Built for the Maritime Safety Agency, by Niigata Engineering Co Ltd. Laid down on 19 May 1956, launched on 19 Dec 1956, and completed in March 1957.

TAKUYO *Japanese Maritime Safety Agency, Official*

KAIYO HM 06

Displacement, tons	378 normal
Dimensions, feet	132·5 wl; 146 oa × 26·5 × 7·8
Main engines	1 set diesels; 450 bhp = 12 knots
Radius, miles	6 100 at 11 knots

Built by Nagoya Shipbuilding & Engineering Co, Nagoya. Completed on 14 Mar 1964. Rated as Medium Surveying Vessel. Controllable pitch propeller.

TENDERS

WAKAKUSA LL 01

Displacement, tons	1 815
Dimensions, feet	204 × 32·2 × 19·1
Main engines	1 850 hp

Built by Hitachi Innoshima Dockyard in Mar 1946. Purchased from Osaka Shosen Kaisha, in Jan 1956. Rated as Navigation Aid Vessel (Lighthouse Supply Ship).

GINGA LL 12 **HOKUTO** LL 11 **KAIO** LL 13

Displacement, tons	500
Dimensions	128·7 × 31·2 × 13·9
Main engines	2 diesels; 420 bhp = 11·26 knots
Radius, miles	2 800 miles at 10 knots

The above three are not sister ships. The above particulars refer to *Ginga* which was built by Osaka Shipbuilding Co Ltd. Laid down on 11 Nov 1953, launched on 6 May 1954 and completed on 30 June 1954. Equipped with 15 ton derrick for laying buoys. Rated as Navigation Aid Vessels (Buoy Tenders). A photograph of *Ginga* appears in the 1955-56 to 1964-65 editions.
There are also 7 LMs (LM 101 to LM 109) and 15 navigation and buoy tenders for miscellaneous service.

NEW CONSTRUCTION

New buoy tender will be the first catamaran type for the Maritime Safety Agency. Designed for installing, exchanging and adjusting position of floating aids to navigation. 100 ft, 300 bhp diesel engines.

COASTAL PATROL CRAFT

43 MOTOR LAUNCH TYPE

HARUSAME	CL 01	**SACHIKAZE**	CL 16	**KOTOKAZE**	CL 31
MURASAME	CL 02	**HATAKAZE**	CL 17	**KITAKAZE**	CL 32
SOYOKAZE	CL 03	**MATSUKAZE**	CL 18	**ISOKAZE**	CL 33
SAWAKAZE	CL 04	**IWAKAZE**	CL 19	**KISOKAZE**	CL 34
OKIKAZE	CL 05	**NATSUKAZE**	CL 20	**MICHIKAZE**	CL 35
YAMAKAZE	CL 06	**YUKEKAZE**	CL 21	**TSURUKAZE**	CL 36
MINEKAZE	CL 07	**SHIMAKAZE**	CL 22	**AMATSUKAZE**	CL 37
UMIKAZE	CL 08	**YUKAZE**	CL 23	**KUKIKAZE**	CL 38
NOKAZE	CL 09	**YODOKAZE**	CL 24	**SAGIKAZE**	CL 39
NUMAKAZE	CL 10	**ASAKAZE**	CL 25	**SHIOKAZE**	CL 40
KAWAKAZE	CL 11	**YAKAZE**	CL 26	**NIIKAZE**	CL 41
TANIKAZE	CL 12	**KIYAKAZE**	CL 27	**TOMOKAZE**	CL 42
HATSUKAZE	CL 13	**IYOKAZE**	CL 28	**WAKAKAZE**	CL 43
ARAKAZE	CL 14	**FUSAKAZE**	CL 29		
HARUKAZE	CL 15	**TACHIKAZE**	CL 30		

Arakaze is constructed of light alloy, welding having been used for approx 40 per cent of the hull; she was laid down on 11 Nov 1953, launched on 11 Feb 1954 and completed on 29 Mar 1954. A photograph of *Arakaze* appears in the 1958-59 to 1964-65 editions and of *Kawakaze* in the 1953-54 to 1960-61 editions. The others are of wooden construction. *Natsukaze* was completed on 15 Feb 1960.
There are 34 other CLs, CL 101 to CL 157 for coastal patrol,

HARBOUR PATROL CRAFT

CS 01 to **CS 58** (58 boats) and **CS 102** to **CS 126** (22 boats).
For harbour patrol and seaward defence duties. Of various types and displacements. A photograph of this type, Isagiku CS 63, appears in the 1960-61 to 1964-65 editions.

SERVICE CRAFT
CR 01 to **CR 18** (18 boats) and **CR 51** for rescue service.

SALVAGE CRAFT
CF 01 to **CF 07** (7 boats) for fire-fighting service

UTILITY LAUNCHES
There are 15 local and miscellaneous boats of various sizes and employment.

KENYA

Establishment

The Kenya Navy, which is based in Mombasa, was inaugurated on 12 Dec 1964 the first anniversary of Kenya's independence.

Administration

Commander, Kenya Navy: Commander Anthony Allen Pearse, R.N.

SEAWARD DEFENCE BOATS

1 BRITISH "FORD" CLASS

NYATI (ex-HMS *Aberford*)

Displacement, tons	120 standard; 160 full load
Dimensions, feet	110 pp; 117·5 oa × 20 × 5
Guns	1—40 mm Bofors AA
Main engines	Davey Paxman diesels; 1 100 bhp = 15 knots max

Transferred on loan from Great Britain in 1964, but acquired outright in 1967 and now belongs to Kenya. A starboard bow view of *Nyati* appears in the 1965-66 edition and a port broadside view in the 1966-67 to 1968-69 editions. *Nyati* means *Buffalo*.

NYATI *1969, Kenya Navy, Official*

PATROL CRAFT

3 BRITISH VOSPER TYPE

CHUI P 3112 **NDOVU** P 3117 **SIMBA** P 3110

Displacement, tons	96 standard; 109 full load
Dimensions, feet	95 wl; 103 oa × 19·8 × 5·8
Guns	2—40 mm Bofors AA
Main engines	Paxman Ventura diesels; 2 800 bhp = 24 knots
Radius, miles	1 500 at economical speed
Complement	23 (3 officers and 20 ratings)

The first ships specially built for the Kenya Navy. Designed and built by Vosper Ltd, Portsmouth. Ordered on 28 Oct 1964 for delivery in mid-1966. *Simba* was launched on 9 Sep 1965 and completed on 23 May 1966, *Chui* was handed over on 7 July 1966 and *Ndovu* was handed over on 27 July 1966. All three left Portsmouth on 22 Aug 1966 and arrived at their base in Mombasa on 4 Oct 1966. Air conditioned and fitted with modern radar and communications equipment and roll damping fins. *Chu* means Leopard, *Ndovu* means Elephant, *Simba* means *Lion*.

SIMBA *1969, Kenya Navy, Official*

CHUI *1967, A. & J. Pavia*

NDOVU *1967, A. & J. Pavia*

KUWAIT

PATROL BOATS

8 "78 ft" TYPE. NEW CONSTRUCTION

AL-SALEMI	**AMAN**	**MASHHOOR**	**MURSHED**
AL-MUBARAKI	**MARZOOK**	**MAYMOON**	**WATHAH**

Dimensions, feet	78 oa × 15·5 × 4·5 mean
Main engines	2 Rolls Royce 8-cylinder 90° V form marine diesels. 1 340 shp at 1 800 rpm, 1 116 shp at 1 700 rpm = 20 knots
Range	700 nautical miles at 15 knots cruising speed
Complement	12 (5 officers, 7 men)

Two were built by Thornycroft before the merger and six by Vosper aftarwards (first two of which were ordered from the Group on 12 Sep 1966). Designed and built by John I. Thornycroft & Co Ltd, Woolston, Southampton, *Al-Salemi* and *Al-Mubaraki* were ordered in Aug 1965 and shipped to Kuwait on 8 Sep 1966. Specially designed for operational duties in the Arabian Gulf. Hulls are of welded steel construction, with superstructures of aluminium alloy. Twin hydraulically operated rudders, giving good manoeuvrability. Decca type D.202 radar. Two Lister Blackstone air-cooled diesel generators, 220 volts.

AL-MUBARAKI *1969, Vosper-Thornycroft*

AL-SALEMI *1967, courtesy Vosper Thornycroft Group*

PATROL LAUNCHES

Built by the Singapore yard of Thornycroft (Malaysia) Limited, now part of the Vosper-Thornycroft Group. Known as 50-foot patrol craft. Completed in 1962.

KOREA (NORTH)

Administration

Commander of the Navy: Rear Admiral Yu Chang Kwon

Personnel

1969: 9,000 (800 officers and 8,200 men)

Mercantile Marine

Lloyd's Register of Shipping:
6 vessels of 16,484 tons gross

SUBMARINES

2 Ex-USSR "W" CLASS

Displacement, tons	1 030 surface; 1 180 submerged
Dimensions, feet	240 × 12 × 15
Tubes	6—21 in (4 bow, 2 stern); 18 torpedoes carried normally (or up to 40 mines)
Main engines	Diesel-electric; 2 shafts; Diesels: 4 000 bhp = 17 knots surface; Electric motors: 2,500 hp = 15 knots submerged
Radius, miles	13 000 to 16 500
Complement	60 to 70

FLEET MINESWEEPERS

2 Ex-USSR "T 43" TYPE

Displacement, tons	500 standard; 600 full load
Dimensions, feet	200 oa × 27·5 × 9

Fleet Minesweepers received by the North Korean Navy from the USSR. Built 1954.

8 Ex-USSR "FUGAS" TYPE

Displacement, tons	440 standard; 550 full load
Dimensions, feet	203·5 oa × 23·7 × 8
Guns	1—3·9 in; 1—37 mm AA
Main engines	Diesels; 2 shafts; 2 800 bhp = 18 knots

Former Soviet minesweepers built in 1935-42. Fitted for minelaying. A photograph appears in the 1964-65 to 1967-68 editions.

"FUGAS" CLASS *Ziro Kimata*

PATROL VESSELS

2 Ex-USSR "ARTILLERIST TYPE

Displacement, tons	240 standard; 280 full load
Dimensions, feet	160·8 × 19 × 6·7
Guns	1—3·9 in; 2—37 mm AA
A/S weapons	2 depth charge throwers
Main engines	Diesels; 2 shafts; 3 300 bhp = 22 knots

Former Soviet patrol vessels or coastal escorts, rated submarine chasers. Built in 1943.

4 "SHANGHAI" TYPE

Displacement, tons	100 full load
Dimensions, feet	120 × 18 × 5·5
Guns	4—37 mm (2 twin); 2—25 mm (1 twin)

Fast patrol boats or motor gunboats reported acquired from China in 1967.

2 NEW CONSTRUCTION

Displacement, tons	circa 160
Dimensions, feet	Length 125

Two fast submarine chasers of medium size built for the North Korean Navy.

10 PATROL TYPE

Displacement, tons	*circa* 130
Dimensions, feet	Length 100

Small craft for seaward defence and local duties, rated as submarine chasers.

4 Ex-USSR "MO 1" TYPE

Displacement, tons	50
Dimensions, feet	85·5 × 13 × 4·5
Guns	2—13 mm AA MG
Main engines	2 petrol engines; 2 shafts; 1 300 bhp

Former Soviet motor launches transferred in 1954. Rated as submarine chasers.

TORPEDO BOATS

3 PTF TYPE

Fast patrol craft of the motor torpedo boat type commissioned for service in 1967-68.

39 Ex-USSR "P 4" TYPE

Displacement, tons	50
Dimensions, feet	85·5 × 20 × 6
Guns	4—25 mm AA
Main engines	Diesels; 2 000 bhp = 42 knots

Former Soviet motor torpedo boats. Built in 1951-57. Aluminium hulls.

MOTOR GUNBOATS

7 MGB TYPE

Reported to have been incorporated into the North Korean Navy since 1 Jan 1967.

4 PTG TYPE

Larger vessels of the patrol gunboat type reported to have been acquired in 1967-68.

MINESWEEPING BOATS

24 INSHORE TYPE

Displacement, tons	20
Dimensions, feet	Length, 50

Very small minesweeping craft for inshore, coastal, estuarial and general utility.

KOREA

Administration

Chief of Naval Operations:
Vice-Admiral Kim, Yong-Kwan

Vice Chief of Naval Operations:
Rear Admiral Kim, Chum Tae

Commander-in-Chief of Fleet:
Rear Admiral Chang, Chi Soo

Personnel

1969: 16,600 (2,300 officers, 14,300 men)

Strength of the Fleet

3 Destroyers
7 Frigates (3 Destroyer Escort Type)
6 Fast Transports (ex-Destroyer Escorts)
11 Escort Vessels (3 ex-Fleet Minesweepers)
6 Patrol Vessels (Submarine Chasers)
11 Coastal Minesweepers
8 Tank Landing Ships
12 Medium Landing Ships
1 Survey Ship
13 Fleet Support Ships and Service Craft.

Diplomatic Representation

Naval Attaché in London:
Colonel Sang Sup Rim
Naval Attaché in Washington:
Commodore Chan Kuk Pak

Mercantile Marine

Lloyd's Register of Shipping
232 vessels of 473,991 tons gross

DESTROYERS

Name	*No.*	*Builders*	*Laid down*	*Launched*	*Completed*
CHUNG MU (ex-USS *Erben*, DD 631)	DD 91	Bath Iron Works Corpn, Bath, Maine	28 Oct 1942	21 Mar 1943	28 May 1943
SEOUL (ex-USS *Halsey Powell*, DD 686)	DD 92	Bethlehem Co., Staten Island		30 June 1943	25 Oct 1943
PUSAN (ex-USS *Hickox*, DD 673)	DD 93	Federal SB-DD Co, Port Newark		4 July 1943	10 Sep 1943

3 Ex-US "FLETCHER" TYPE

Displacement, tons	2 100 standard; 3 050 full load
Length, feet (*metres*)	360·9 (*110·0*) wl; 376·5 (*114·8*) oa
Beam, feet (*metres*)	39·5 (*12·0*)
Draught, feet (*metres*)	18 (*5·5*) max
Guns, dual purpose	5—5 in (*127* mm) 38 cal.
Guns, AA	6—40 mm Bofors
A/S	2 fixed Hedgehogs; 1 DC rack
Torpedo tubes	5—21 in (*533 mm*) quintupled
Torpedo racks	2 side launching for A/S torpedoes
Boilers	4 Babcock & Wilcox; 634 psi (*44·6 kg/cm²*); 850°F (*454°C*)
Main engines	2 GE geared turbines 60 000 shp; 2 shafts
Speed, knots	35 max; 12 economical sea
Radius, miles	6 000 at 15 knots
Oil fuel (tons)	650
Complement	300 (18 officers, 282 men)

Former United States destroyers of the "Fletcher" class, transferred to Korea in May 1963, 27 April 1968 and 15 Nov 1968.

PHOTOGRAPHS. A starboard near broadside surface view of *Kyong Ki* appears in the 1963-64 to 1966-67 editions.

CHUNG MU *1967, Korean Navy, Official*

FRIGATES

2 Ex-US "BOSTWICK" TYPE DESTROYER ESCORTS

Name	*No.*	*Builders*	*Launched*	*Completed*
KANG WON (ex-USS *Sutton, DE* 771)	DE 72	Tampa S.B. Co	6 Aug 1944	22 Dec 1944
KYONG KI (ex-USS *Muir, DE* 770)	DE 71	Tampa S.B. Co	4 June 1944	20 Aug 1944

Displacement, tons	1 240 standard; 1 900 full load
Length, feet (*metres*)	306 (*93·2*) oa
Beam, feet (*metres*)	36·8 (*11·2*)
Draught, feet (*metres*)	14 (*4·3*) max
Guns, dual purpose	3—3 in (*76 mm*) 50 cal.
Guns, AA	3—40 mm; 8—20 mm
A/S weapons	8 depth charge throwers
Torpedo tubes	Removed (see notes)
Main engines	GM diesels, electric drive 6 000 hp; 2 shafts
Speed, knots	20
Radius, miles	11 500 at 11 knots
Oil fuel (tons)	300
Complement	208

Former United States destroyer escorts, DE, of the "Bostwick" class. Transferred from the United States Navy at Boston in 1956 under the Mutual Defense Assistance Program. Renamed after Korean States.

TORPEDO TUBES. These ships formerly carried three 21 inch torpedo tubes in a triple mounting, since removed.

PHOTOGRAPHS. A starboard near broadside surface view of *Kyong Ki* appears in the 1963-64 to 1966-67 editions.

KANG WON *1967, Korean Navy, Official*

Frigates—*continued*

1 Ex-US "RUDDEROW" TYPE

DESTROYER ESCORT

Name	*No.*	*Builders*	*Launched*	*Completed*
CHUNG NAM (ex-USS *Holt, DE* 706)	DE 73	Defoe Shipbuilding Co, Bay City	15 Dec 1943	9 June 1944

Displacement, tons	1 450 standard; 2 230 full load
Length, feet (*metres*)	306 (*93·2*) oa
Beam, feet (*metres*)	36·8 (*11·2*)
Draught, feet (*metres*)	14 (*4·3*) max
Guns, surface	2—5 in (*127 mm*) 38 cal.
Guns, AA	2—40 mm; 6—20 mm
A/S	DCT
Boilers	2 Combustion Engineering
Main engines	GE geared turbines, electric drive 12 000 shp; 2 shafts
Speed, knots	24
Radius, miles	5 000 at 15 knots
Oil fuel (tons)	378
Complement	186 (6 officers, 180 men)

Former United States destroyer escort of the "Rudderow" class transferred to Korea at Seattle, Washington, on 16 June 1963 and renamed.

CHUNG NAM — *1967, Korean Navy, Official*

Name	*No.*	*Builders*	*Laid down*	*Launched*	*Completed*
DUMAN (ex-USS *Muskogee, PF* 49)	PF 61	Consolidated Steel Corpn	18 Sep 1943	18 Oct 1943	16 Mar 1944
IMCHIN (ex-USS *Sausalito, PF* 4)	PF 66	Kaiser Cargo Inc	7 Apr 1943	20 July 1943	4 Mar 1944
NAKTONG (ex-USS *Hoquiam, PF* 5)	PF 65	Permanente Metals Corpn	10 Apr 1943	31 July 1943	8 May 1944
TAE DONG (ex-USS *Tacoma, PF* 3)	PF 63	Permanente Metals Corpn	10 Mar 1943	7 July 1943	6 Nov 1944

4 Ex-US "TACOMA" TYPE

Displacement, tons	1 430 standard; 2 435 full load
Length, feet (*metres*)	285·5 (*87·0*) wl; 304 (*92·7*) oa
Beam, feet (*metres*)	37·5 (*11·4*)
Draught, feet (*metres*)	13·7 (*4·2*)
Guns, dual purpose	3—3 in (*76 mm*) 50 cal.
Guns, AA	2—40 mm; 9—20 mm
A/S weapons	6 depth charge throwers
Boilers	2; 250 psi (*17·6 kg/cm²*); 425°F (*218°C*)
Main engines	Triple expansion 5 500 ihp; 2 shafts
Speed, knots	18
Radius, miles	9 500 at 12 knots
Oil fuel (tons)	645
Complement	181 (10 officers, 171 men)

Former United States patrol frigates, PF, of the "Tacoma" class. Transferred to the USSR under the Lend-Lease scheme during the Second World War. Returned to USA after hostilities and laid up at Yokosuka naval base. Reactivated on the outbreak of the Korean War. *Apnok* and *Duman* were loaned to the Korean Navy and commissioned on 5 Nov 1950. *Naktong* and *Taedong* were transferred on 8 Oct 1951 at Yokosuka. *Apnok*, ex-USS *Rockford* (PF 48), in collision on 21 May 1952, was decommissioned, returned to the USN and expended as a target in 1953. She was replaced by *Imchin*.

NAK TONG — *1967, Korean Navy, Official*

PHOTOGRAPHS. A photograph of *Tae Dong* appears in the 1963-64 to 1966-67 editions.

Note: *USS Pasco* PF6, towed to Korea in Jan 1969, probably for cannibalisaion for existing frigates. Reported *USS Gloucester* may also be similarly handed over.

ESCORT TRANSPORTS

6 Ex-USAPD (ex-DE) TYPE

ASAN (ex-USS *Harry L. Corl*, APD 108, ex-*DE* 598) APD 82
KYONG NAM (ex-USS *Cavallero*, APD 128, ex-*DE* 712) APD 81
UNG PO (ex-USS *Julius A. Raven*, APD 110, ex-*DE* 600) APD 83
KYONG BUK (ex USS *Kephart* APD 61 ex DE 207) PG 85
CHR JU (ex USS *William M. Hobby* APD 95 ex DE 236) PG 87
CHUN NAM (ex USS *Hayter* APD 80 ex DE 212) PG 86

Displacement, tons	1 400 standard; 2 130 full load
Dimensions, feet	300 wl; 306 oa × 37 × 12·6
Guns	1—5 in, 38 cal dp; 6—40 mm AA
Main engines	GE turbines with electric drive; 2 shafts; 12 000 bhp = 23 knots
Boilers	2 "D" Express
Oil fuel (tons)	350
Radius, miles	5 500 at 15 knots
Complement	210 plus 162 troops

Former United States high speed transports, APD, modified destroyer escorts. *Kyong Nam* was built by the Defoe Shipbuilding Co, Bay City, Mich. Laid down on 28 Mar 1944. Launched on 15 June 1954. Completed on 13 Mar 1945. Transferred in 1959. *Asan*, laid down on 19 Jan 1944 and launched on 1 Mar 1944, and *Ung Po*, laid down on 26 Jan 1944 and launched on 3 Mar 1944, both by Bethlehem S.B. Co, Hingham, Mass, were transferred in 1966. Ex-USS *Kephart*, launched 6 Sep 1943, and ex-USS *William M. Hobby*, launched 11 Feb 1944, both transferred May 1967 under MAP. *Chun Nam* transferred Aug 1967.

KYONG NAM — *1967, Korean Navy, Official*

ESCORTS

3 Ex-US "AUK" CLASS MSF TYPE

SHIN SONG (ex-USS *Ptarmigan*, MSF 376) PCE 1001
SUNCHON (ex-USS *Speed*, MSF 116) PCE 1002
KOJE (ex-USS *Dextrous*, MSF 341) PCE 1003

Displacement, tons	890 standard; 1 250 full load
Dimensions, feet	215 wl; 221 oa × 32·2 × 10·8 max
Guns	2—3 in, 50 cal dp (single); 4—40 mm AA (2 twin); 4—20 mm AA (2 pairs)
Tubes	3—21 In (pyramided)
A/S weapons	4 DCT (single) 2 DC tracks; 1 hedgehog
Main engines	2 GM diesel electric; 2 shafts; 3 532 bhp = 18 knots
Complement	117 total accommodation

Former United States steel-hulled fleet minesweepers. *Shin Song* was built by the Savannah Machinery & Foundry Co. Laid down on 9 Mar 1944, launched on 15 July 1944 and completed on 15 Jan 1945. Transferred from the US to the Republic of Korea Navy on 25 July 1963 at Seattle, Washington. Employed as a patrol escort ship (PCE). The other two were scheduled to be transferred to Korea in 1967.

SHIN SONG — *1964, Korean Navy, Official*

Escorts—*continued*

8 Ex US "180ft." STEEL PCE TYPE

HAN SAN (ex-USS *PCEC* 873)	PCEC 53
KOJIN (ex USS *Report* MSF 289)	PCEC 50
MYONG RYANG (ex-USS *PCEC* 896)	PCEC 52
OK PO (ex-USS *PCEC* 898)	PCEC 55
PYOK PA (ex-USS *Dania, PCE* 870)	PCE 57
RO RYANG (ex-USS *PCEC* 882)	PCEC 51
RYUL PO (ex-USS *Somerset PCE* 892)	PCE 58
SA CHON (ex-USS *Batesburg, PCE* 903)	PCE 59

Displacement, tons	640 standard; 967 full load
Dimensions, feet	180 wl; 184·5 oa × 33·1 × 10 max
Guns	1—3 in 50 cal, dp; 3—40 mm AA; 8—20 mm AA
Main engines	Diesels; 2 shafts; 2 000 bhp = 14·3 knots
Oil fuel (tons)	260
Radius, miles	4 300 at 10 knots
Complement	104

Former United States patrol ships, escorts, PCE (four were later redesignated control escorts, PCEC, on assignment to amphibious forces). Built in 1942-45 by Albina Engine and Machine Works, Portland, Oregon (*Han San, Pyok Pa, Ro Ryang*), and Willamette Iron & Steel Corp, Portland, Oregon (*Myong Ryang, Ok Po, Ryul Po, Sa Chan*). Transferred from the United States Navy in Feb 1955 (*Myong Ryang, Ro Ryang*), on loan, in 1956 (*Han San, Ok Po*) and 1961 (*Pyok Pa, Ryul Po, Sa Chon, Tang Po*). Sister ship *Tang Po*, PCE 56 (ex-USS *Maria*, PCE 842) was sunk by North Korean coastal batteries north of the demarcation line on 19 Jan 1967. A photograph of *Han San* appears in the 1959-60 and 1960-61 editions, and of *Ok Po* in the 1961-62 to 1966-67 editions.

RO RYANG *1967 Korean Navy, Official*

PATROL VESSELS

2 NEW CONSTRUCTION

On trials recently were two 100-ft patrol boats built in Korea for the Korean Navy equipped with Vosper stabilisers.

4 Ex-US "173 ft." STEEL PC TYPE

KUM CHONG SAN (ex-USS *Grosse Point*, PC 1546)	PC 708
MYO HYANG SAN (ex-*PC* 600)	PC 706
O TAE SAN (ex-USS *Winnemucca, PC* 1145)	PC 707
SOL AK (ex-USS *Chadron, PC* 546)	PC 709

Displacement, tons	280 standard; 450 full load
Dimensions, feet	170 wl; 173·7 oa × 23 × 10·8 max
Guns	1—3 in, 50 cal, dp; 1—40 mm AA; 4—20 mm
A/S weapons	2 ASW rocket launchers, mousetrap
Main engines	Diesels; 2 shafts; 2 880 bhp = 20 knots
Complement	71

Former United States submarine chasers, PC, of steel construction, built in 1941-42. *Kum Chong San* and *O Tae San* were transferred on loan at Seattle on 21 Nov 1960 and Nov 1 1960 respectively. *Pak Tu San*, PC 701 (ex *Ensign-Whitehead*, ex-PC 823), *Kum Kang San*, PC 702 (ex-*PC* 810) and *Sam Kak San*, PC 703 (ex-PC 802) were decommissioned on 21 Aug 1960 and scrapped. *Chirisan* PC 704, was mined and sank off Wonson, Korea, on 26 Dec 1951. *Han Ra San*, PC 705 (ex-USS PC 485) was sunk in a typhoon at Guam in Nov 1962 and although raised was scrapped in 1964. *Sol Ak* (ex-USS *Chadron*) was transferred at Guam on 22 Jan 1964.
A photograph of *Myo Hyang San* appears in the 1957-58 edition, and of *Sol Ak* in the 1964-65 to 1966-67 editions.

KUM CHONG SAM *1967, Korean Navy, Official*

Patrol Vessels—*continued*

2 Ex-US "136 ft" WOODEN PCS TYPE

HWA SEONG PCS 205 (ex-*PCS* 1448) **KUM SEONG** PCS 202 (ex-*PCS* 1445)

Displacement, tons	251 standard; 338 full load
Dimensions, feet	130 wl; 136 oa × 24·5 × 8·5
Guns	1—40 mm; 2—20 mm
Main engines	2 GM diesels; 2 shafts; 800 bhp = 14 knots

Former United States submarine chasers, *PSC* type, of wooden construction, built in 1943-44. Acquired by Korea in 1952. *Suseong* PCS 201 (ex-USS *PCS* 1426) was returned to USA in Apr 1963. *Mok Seong* lent to the Hydrographic Office in Jan 1964, was returned to USN and discarded in Sept 1967.

MOK SEONG *1967 Korean Navy, Official*

COASTAL MINESWEEPERS

7 Ex-US MSC TYPE

HA DONG MSC 527 (ex-*MSC* 296)
KO HUNG MSC 523 (ex-*MSC* 285)
KUM KOK MSC 525 (ex-*MSC* 286)
KUM SAN MSC 522 (ex-*MSC* 284)
NAM YANG MSC 526 (ex-*MSC* 295)

Displacement, tons	320 standard; 370 full load
Dimensions, feet	138 pp; 144 oa × 28 × 9 max
Guns	2—20 mm AA
Main engines	2 diesels; 2 shafts; 1 200 bhp = 14 knots
Complement	43

"Bluebird" class specially built by USA for transfer under the Military Aid Program. *Ko Hung* and *Kum San* were transferred to Korea in 1959, followed by *Kum Kok*, transferred at Long Beach, California, on 10 Nov 1959. *Ha Dong* and *Nam Yang* were transferred at Boston, Mass on 16 Nov 1963 and 7 Oct 1963, respectively. Both were built by Petersen Builders, Inc, Sturgeon Bay, Wisc. MSC 302 and MSC 316 are building in USA for transfer to Korea under MAP.
A photograph of *Kum Kok* appears in the 1961-62 to 1966-67 editions.
MSB 2 was transferred from the US Navy to the Korean Navy on 1 Dec 1961.

KUM SAN *1967, Korean Navy, Official*

5 Ex-US YMS TYPE

KUM HWA MSC(O) 519 (ex-USS *Curlew*, ex-*MSC(O)* 8, ex-*YMS* 218)
KIM PO MSC(O) 520 (ex-USS *Kite*, ex-*MSC(O)* 22, ex-*AMS* 22, ex-*YMS* 369)
KOCHANG MSC(O) 521 (ex-USS *Mockingbird*, ex-*MSC(O)* 22, ex-*YMS* 419)
KWANG CHE MSC(O) 503 **KIM CHON** MSC(O) 513

Displacement, tons	270 standard; 350 full load
Dimensions, feet	136 oa × 24·5 × 8 max
Guns	1—40 mm, 50 cal; 2—20 mm AA
Main engines	Diesels; 1 000 bhp = 15 knots
Complement	50

Former United States auxiliary motor minesweepers of wooden construction, built in 1941-42. All ex-YMS type. *Kum Hwa, Kim Po* and *Kochang* were transferred from the US Navy on 6 Sept 1956. *Kyong Chu*, MSC (O) 502 was decommissioned on 10 May 1962. *Kang Kyong* MSC(O) 510 was scrapped in 1964.

KOCHANG *1967, Korean Navy, Official*

TANK LANDING SHIPS

8 Ex-US LST TYPE

BI BONG LST 809 (ex-USS *LST* 218)
BUK HAN LST 815 (ex-USS *Lynn County LSC* 900)
DUK BONG LST 808 (ex-*LST* 227)
HWA SAN LST 816 (ex-USS *Pendet County LST* 1080)
KAE BONG LST 810 (ex-USS *Berkshire County, LST* 288)
SU YONG LST 813 (ex-USS *Kane County LST* 853)
UN BONG LST 807 (ex-USS *LST* 1010)
WEE BONG LST 812 (ex-USS *Johnson County LST* 849)

Displacement, tons	1 635 standard; 2 366 beaching; 4 080 full load
Dimensions, feet	316 wl; 328 oa × 50 × 14 max
Guns	7 to 10—40 mm AA; 6 or 8—20 mm AA
Main engines	Diesel; 2 shafts; 1 700 bhp = 11 knots
Cargo capacity, tons	2 100
Complement	113

Former United States tank landing ships. *Duk Bong* and *Un Bong* were transferred on 22 Mar 1955 at S. Diego, *Kae Bong* on 5 May 1956 at Seattle, *Buk Han, Su Yong* and *Wee Bong* on 2 Dec 1958, 22 Dec 1958 and 13 Jan 1959, respectively, at Seattle, and *Hwa San* was transferred on 30 Oct 1958 at Long Beach.

SU YONG *1967, Korean Navy, Official*

ROCKET LANDING SHIP

SI HUNG LSMR 311 (ex-USS *St Joseph River, LSMR* 527)

Displacement, tons	1 102 standard; 1 280 full load
Dimensions, feet	203·5 oa × 34·5 × 8·3 max
Guns	1—5 in; 2—40 mm AA; 2—20 mm AA
Launchers	8—5 in rocket projectors
Main engines	Diesels; 2 shafts; 2 800 bhp = 13 knots
Complement	142

Former US medium landing ship (rocket). Transferred to the Korean Navy at San Diego, Cal. on 15 Sep 1960. *Si Hung* means "The Beginning of Prosperity."

SI HUNG *1967, Korean Navy, Official*

MEDIUM LANDING SHIPS

11 Ex-US LSM TYPE

BIYOUP LSM 607 (ex-USS *LSM* 96)
KA DUK LSM 605 (ex-USS *LSM* 462)
KI RIN LSM 610 (ex-USS *LSM* 19)
KU MOON LSM 606 (ex-USS *LSM* 30)
NEUNG RA LSM 611 (ex-USS *LSM* 84)
PUNG DO LSM(F)608 (ex-USS *LSM* 54)
SIN-MI LSM 612 (ex-USS *LSM* 316)
TAE CHO LSM 601 (ex-USS *LSM* 546)
ULRYUNG LSM 613 (ex-USS *LSM* 17)
WOLMI LSM 609 (ex-USS *LSM* 57)
YEU DO LSM 602 (ex-USS *LSM* 268)

Displacement, tons	743 beaching; 1 095 full load
Dimensions, feet	196·5 wl; 203·5 oa × 34·5 × 8·5 max
Guns	1—40 mm AA; 4—20 mm AA
Main engines	Diesels, direct drive; 2 shafts; 2 880 bhp = 12·5 knots
Complement	62

LSM 19, 30, 54, 84 and 96 were transferred to the Korean Navy at Seattle in 1956. LSM 19, 84 transferred on 3 July 1956, LSM 17 on 18 Oct 1956, LSM 316 on 18 Nov 1956. *Pun Do*, (*LSM(F)* 608) was converted into a Mine Force Flagship. *Dok Do*, LSM 603 (ex-USS *LSM* 419) was decommissioned on 26 Feb 1963.
A photograph of *Ku Moon* appears in the 1963-64 to 1966-67 editions.

YEO DO *1967, Korean Navy, Official*

SURVEY SHIP

Hydrographic Survey Ship No. 3 (ex-USC and GSS *Hodgson*) transferred to Korea at Seattle, Washington, March 1968. This ex-YMS type, of 267 tons, 137 feet, built in 1943, is assigned to the Korean Hydrographic Office and may not be rated as a Navy ship.

LANDING CRAFT REPAIR SHIP

DUK SOO (ex-USS *Minotaur, ARL* 15, ex-*LST* 645)

Displacement, tons	2 366 standard; 4 100 full load
Dimensions, feet	316 wl; 328 oa × 50 × 11·2
Guns	2—40 mm AA
Main engines	GM diesels; 2 shafts; 1 800 bhp = 11·5 knots
Complement	277

Former United States landing craft repair ship. Built by Chicago Bridge & Iron Co Seneca, Del. Laid down on 20 June 1944. Launched on 20 Sep 1944. Completed on 30 Sep 1944

DUK SOO *1963, Korean Navy, Official*

SUPPLY SHIPS

KIMHAE AKL 902
KUN SAN AKL 908 (ex-USS *Sharps, AKL* 10)
WAEKWAN AKL 903
MA SAN AKL 909 (ex-USS *AKL* 35)
MOCK PO AKL 907 (ex-USCGC *Trillium, WAK* 170)

Displacement, tons	520
Dimensions, feet	179 oa × 32 × 10 max
Guns	1—40 mm AA; 2—30 mm AA
Main engines	Diesel; 2 shafts; 1 000 shp = 13 knots
Complement	43 *Kimhae*; 49 others

AKL 35 was transferred from the USA on 6 Sep 1956, *Kun San* on 3 Apr 1956, *Ma San* on 9 Sep 1956, and *Mack Po* in 1956. Ex-USS Army FS craft.

OILERS

CHUN-JI (ex-*Birk*) AO 2 **PUJON** (ex-*Hassel*) AO 3

Displacement, tons	1 400 standard; 4 160 full load
Measurement, tons	2 257 and 2 256 gross, respectively
Dimensions, feet	275 pp × 44·5 × 18·2
Guns	1—40 mm AA; 2—20 mm AA
Complement	73

Former Norwegian tankers. Both built by A/S Berken Mek Verks Bergen, Norway. in 1951. Taken over by Korean Navy at Rotterdam, Sep and July 1953, respectively.

KU RYONG YO 1, ex-YO 106 (ex-USS *YO* 118)

Displacement, tons	428 standard; 1 126 full load
Dimensions, feet	174 oa × 33 × 13 max
Main engines	Union diesel; 1 shaft; 500 shp = 7 knots
Complement	36

Former US self-propelled fuel oil barge. Transferred to Korea on 3 Dec 1946.

HWA CHON YO 5 (ex-*Paek Yeon*, AO 5, ex-USS *Derrick, YO* 59)

Displacement, tons	893 standard; 2 700 full load
Dimensions, feet	236 oa × 38 × 15 max
Guns	3—20 mm AA
Main engines	Fairbanks-Morse diesel; 1 shaft; 1 150 bhp = 10·5 knots
Complement	46

Former US self-propelled fuel oil barge. Loaned to Korea on 14 Oct 1955.

TUGS

DO BONG ATA 3 (ex-USS *Pinola, ATA* 206)
YONG MUN ATA 2 (ex-USS *Keosanqua, ATA* 198)

Displacement, tons	538 standard; 838 full load
Dimensions, feet	134·5 wl; 143 oa × 34 × 13·2 max
Guns	1—3 in; 4—20 mm AA
Main engines	GM diesel-electric; 1 shaft; 1 500 hp = 13·5 knots

Former United States auxiliary ocean tugs of the "Maricopa" class, ATA type. Built by Gulfport Boiler and Welding Works, Inc, Port Arthur, Texas (*Do Bong*) and Levingston Shipbuilding Co, Orange, in 1944-45. Transferred on 2 Jan 1962.

YONG MUN *1967, Korean Navy, Official*

LAOS

Administration

Chief of Naval Staff: Colonel Prince Sintnanarong Kindarong

RIVER PATROL CRAFT

7	LCM (6) Type	28 tons	4 in commission, 3 in reserve
6	Cabin Type	21 tons	3 in commission, 3 in reserve
1	Chris Craft Type	15 tons	1 in commission
12	11 metre Type	10 tons	3 in commission, 9 in reserve
8	8 metre Type	6 tons	8 in reserve

It is officially stated that the above river squadrons have been formed since 1968.

LEBANON

Diplomatic Representation

Naval, Military and Air Attache in London: Brigadier Nicolas Samaha

Mercantile Marine

Lloyds Register of Shipping: 122 vessels of 443 881 tons gross

PATROL BOATS

TARABLOUS

Displacement, tons	105 standard
Dimensions, feet	124·7 × 18 × 5·8
Guns	2—40 mm
Main engines	2 Mercedes-Benz diesels; 2 shafts; 2 700 bhp = 27 knots
Radius, miles	1 500
Complement	19 (3 officers, 16 men)

Tarablous was built by Ch. Navals de l'Estérel. Laid down in June 1958. Launched in June 1959. Completed in 1959.

TARABLOUS *1968 Lebanese Navy, Official*

3 "BYBLOS" CLASS

BYBLOS 11 **SIDON** 12 **BEYROUTH** (ex-*T/R*) 13

Displacement, tons	28 standard
Dimensions, feet	66 × 13·5 × 4
Guns	1—20 mm AA; 2 MG
Main engines	General Motors diesels; 2 shafts; 530 bhp = 18·5 knots

French built ML type craft. Built by Ch. Navals de l'Estérel. Launched in 1954-55.

BYBLOS *1968, Lebanese Navy, Official*

FISHERY PROTECTION VESSEL

SEHTA

Built in 1962 and employed on fishery protection and general coastguard duties.

LANDING CRAFT

SOUR (ex-LCU 1474)

Displacement, tons	180 standard; 360 full load
Dimensions, feet	115 × 34 × 6
Guns	2—20 mm AA
Main engines	3 diesels; 3 shafts; 675 bhp = 10 knots

Former United States utility landing craft built in 1957, transferred in Nov 1958.

SOUR *1968, Lebanese Navy, Official*

LIBERIA

Personnel

The small naval service of coast guard has about 200 officers and men

Mercantile Marine

Lloyd's Register of Shipping: 1 613 vessels of 25 719 642 tons gross

MOTOR GUNBOATS

PGM 69 **PGM 102**

Displacement, tons	100
Dimensions, feet	95 oa × 19 × 5
Guns	1—40 mm AA
Main engines	4 diesels; 2 shafts; 2 200 bhp = 21 knots
Complement	15

PGM 102 (US number) is being built in the United States for transfer under the Military Aid Programme. PGM 69, sister boat, was the prototype for Liberia from USA.

PRESIDENTIAL YACHT

LIBERIAN (ex-*Virginia*)

Measurement, tons	742 (*Thomas*); 692·27 gross; 341·6 net
Dimensions, feet	173 wl; 209 oa × 29·7 × 13·1

Motor yacht of 742 tons (yacht measurement) built in 1930 by William Beardmore & Co Ltd, Dalmuir. Purchased by Liberia for use as the Presidential yacht in 1957. (Her previous owners were the Trustees of the Estate of the late Viscount Camrose). Extensively refitted by Cammell Laird & Co Ltd, Birkenhead, at the end of 1962.

LIBERIAN *1964, Official*

PATROL BOATS

ML 4001 **ML 4002**

Displacement, tons	11·5
Dimensions, feet	40·5 oa × 11·5 × 3·5
Guns	2 MG
Main engines	2 GM diesels; 2 shafts; 380 bhp = 23 knots max

Coastguard cutters built at the United States Coast Guard Yard, Curtis Bay, Maryland. presented by the USA and transferred during 1957.

ML 4002 *courtesy Dr Giorgio Arra*

LANDING CRAFT

Landing craft reported to be used for transport and general utility purposes.

LIBYA

Establishment

The Royal Libyan Navy was established in Nov 1962 when a British Naval Mission was formed and first recruits were trained at HMS *St Angelo,* Malta. Cadets were also trained at the Britannia Royal Naval College, Dartmouth, and technical ratings at HMS *Sultan*, Gosport, and HMS *Collingwood*, Fareham, England.

Administration

Head of the Armed Forces of Libya: General Nuri es Sadik
Senior Officer, Royal Libyan Navy:
Lieutenant-Commander Mansur Bader, RLN
Head of the British Naval Mission:
Captain W. H. Hoyle, RN

Mercantile Marine

Lloyd's Register of Shipping: 7 vessels of 3,184 tons gross

FRIGATE

1 NEW CONSTRUCTION

Displacement, tons	*circa* 1 500
Dimensions, feet	310 pp; 330 oa × 36 × 11
Guns	1—4·5 in; 2—40 mm
Aircraft	1 helicopter
Missile launchers	2 triple "Seacat" close range ship-to-air
Main engines	2 Rolls Royce Olympus gas turbines = 37·5 knots max 2 Paxman diesels = 17 knots max
Range, miles	5 700

An order was placed with Vosper Thornycroft on 6 Feb 1968 for a Mark 7 Fast Frigate. She will be generally similar in design to the two Iranian destroyers, at present under construction by this firm, but larger and with a different armament.

VOSPER THORNYCROFT MARK 7 FAST FRIGATE *1968, Vosper Thornycroft*

LOGISTIC SUPPORT SHIP

ZELTIN

Displacement, tons	2 200 standard; 2 470 full load
Dimensions, feet	300 wl; 324 oa × 48 × 10; 19 aft when flooded
Guns	2—40 mm AA
Main engines	2 Paxman diesels 16 cyl = 15 knots
Range, miles	3 000 at 14 knots
Complement	As Senior Officer Ship 15 officers, 86 ratings

ZELTIN *1969, Official*

The Vosper-Thornycroft Group received the order for this ship on 31 Jan 1957 (announced) for delivery in late 1968. She was designed and built by John I. Thornycroft & Co Ltd, at the Group's Woolston Shipyard. She provides full logistic support, including mobile docking maintenance and repair facilities for the Libyan fleet and acts as parent ship for the corvette *Tobruk* and the three fast patrol boats just built. Craft up to 120 ft can be docked. Launched on 29 Feb 1968. Commissioned (with *Sirte* and *Susa*) on 23 Jan 1969.

ZELTIN *1969, Vosper Thornycroft*

CORVETTES

TOBRUK

Displacement, tons	440 standard; 500 full load
Dimensions, feet	162 wl; 177 oa × 28·5 × 10 mean (13 props)
Guns	1—4 in; 4—40 mm AA (single)
Main engines	2 Paxman Ventura 16 YJCM diesels; 2 shafts; 3 800 bhp = 18 knots
Radius, miles	2 900 at 14 knots
Complement	63 (5 officers and 58 ratings)

Designed and built by Vosper Limited, Portsmouth, in association with Vickers Limited. Launched on 29 July 1965, completed on 30 Mar 1966, commissioned for service at Portsmouth on 20 Apr 1966, sailed for Libya on 30 May 1966 and arrived in Tripoli on 15 June 1966. A gun corvette fitted with surface warning radar, Vosper roll damping fins and air-conditioning. Duties for which she was designed include protection of shipping from air and sea attack, training officers and men of the Royal Libyan Navy, and State visiting. A suite of State apartments is included in the accommodation.

TOBRUK *1966, courtesy Vosper Limited, Portsmouth, Builders*

MAINTENANCE REPAIR CRAFT

ZLEITEN (ex-*MRC* 1013, ex-LCT)

Displacement, tons	657
Dimensions, feet	225 pp, 231·3 oa × 39 × 3·3 forward, 5 aft
Main engines	4 Paxman diesels; 1 840 bhp = 9 knots cruising

Purchased from Great Britain on 5 Sep 1966. Depot ship for minesweepers.

COAST GUARD VESSELS

SECURITY PATROL VESSELS. *Ar-Rakib* and *Farwa* were completed on 4 May 1967 by John I Thornycroft, Woolston, 100 tons, 100 × 21 × 5·5 feet, 3 Rolls Royce DV8TLM diesels, 1 740 bhp = 18 knots, 1—20 mm gun, 1 800 miles range at 14 knots, fuel 20 tons. Designed specifically for operation in North African waters. Welded steel construction. Four similar craft were ordered from the Vosper Thornycroft Group (announced on 3 Jan 1968).

CUSTOMS LAUNCHES

There are also three fast patrol launches for customs and fishery protection, see full particulars in the 1963-64 and 1964-65 editions.

FAST PATROL BOATS

SUSA discharging one of her eight Nord-Aviation missiles — *1969, Vosper*

SEBHA — *1969, Wright & Logan*

SIRTE — *1969, Wright & Logan*

3 NEW CONSTRUCTION

SEBHA (ex-*Sokna*) **SIRTE** **SUSA**

Displacement, tons	95 standard; 114 full load
Dimensions, feet	90 pp; 96 wl; 99 oa × 25·5 × 7
Main engines	3 Bristol Siddeley Proteus gas turbines; 3 shafts; 12 750 bhp = 54 knots

The order for these three fast patrol boats from Vosper Limited, Portsmouth, England, was announced on 12 Oct 1966. The are generally similar to the motor torpedo boats designed and built by Vosper for the Royal Danish Navy. Built at the Vosper-Thornycroft Group's Portchester shipyard. Fitted with air conditioning and modern radar and radio equipment. *Susa* launched 31 Aug 1967, *Sirte* 10 Jan 1968, *Sokna* (renamed *Sebha*) 29 Feb 1968. First operational vessels in the world to be armed with Nord-Aviation SS 12(M) guided weapons with sighting turret installation and other equipment developed jointly by Vosper and Nord. These weapons, of which eight can be fired by each boat without reloading, have a destructive power equivalent to a six-inch shell.

FARWA (see previous page) — *1969, Thornycroft*

INSHORE MINESWEEPERS

BRAK — *A. & J. Pavia*

ZUARA — *1967, A. & J. Pavia*

2 BRITISH "HAM" TYPE

BRAK (ex-HMS *Harpham*) **ZUARA** (ex-HMS *Greetham*)

Displacement, tons	120 standard; 159 full load
Dimensions, feet	100 pp; 106 oa × 21·2 × 5·5
Guns	1—20 mm AA
Main engines	2 Paxman diesels; 1 100 bhp = 14 knots
Complement	15 to 22

Lent to Great Britain in 1963 to form the nucleus of a navy for Libya, and given outright to the Royal Libyan Navy in 1966. Given Libyan names in Sep 1966.

SUSA docked in ZELTIN (see previous page) — *1969, Thornycroft*

MALAWI

It is reported that Great Britain is to supply Malawi with at least three gunboats to patrol the disputed waters of Lake Malawi (which has an extent of 11,460 sq miles and a length of 360 miles with an outlet to the River Zambesi)

MALAYSIA

Administration

Chief of the Naval Staff:
Commodore K. Thanabalasingam, AMN, RMN

Diplomatic Representation

Military Adviser in London:
Brigadier General Unku Ahmed bin Abdul Rahman, KMN

Strength of the Fleet

1 Frigate +1 (New Construction)
6 Coastal Minesweepers
2 Inshore Minesweepers
4 Fast Patrol Boats
24 Patrol craft
1 Survey Vessel
1 Seaward Defence Boat
22 Minor Landing Craft

Personnel

1969: 4 000 officers and ratings

Ships

The names of Malaysian warships are prefixed by K.D. (Kapal Diraja) Royal Ship

Mercantile Marine

Lloyd's Register of Shipping:
85 vessels of 40 465 tons

FRIGATES

1 NEW CONSTRUCTION YARROW TYPE

HANG JEBAT F 24

Displacement, tons	1 600
Length, feet (*metres*)	308 (*93·9*) oa
Beam, feet (*metres*)	34 (*10·4*)
Draught, feet (*metres*)	14·7 (*4·5*)
Aircraft	1 helicopter
Missiles, AA	1 quadruple "Seacat" launcher
Guns, dual purpose	1—4·5 in (*114 mm*)
Guns, AA	2—40 mm
A/S weapons	1 Limbo three-barrelled depth charge mortar
Main engines	1 Bristol-Siddeley Olympus gas turbine, 19 500 shp; Crossley Pielstick diesel; 3 850 bhp
Speed, knots	27
Complement	140

NEW FRIGATE (Model) *1966, Yarrow & Co, Ltd, Scotstoun, Glasgow*

An order was placed with Yarrow & Co Ltd, Scotstoun, Glasgow, on 11 Feb 1966 for a general purpose frigate. A long range vessel of a new design developed by Yarrow, resulting in a comparatively low cost ship with an armament-displacement ratio superior to that of any comparable warship. The ship is fully automatic with a consequent saving in complement. Launched on 18 Dec 1967. Scheduled to be ready for delivery in 1969. Cost estimated at £4 000 000.

NOMENCLATURE. *Hang Jebat* is the name of a Malay warrior in the 15th century.

1 Ex-BRITISH "LOCH" CLASS

Name	*No*	*Builders*	*Laid down*	*Launched*	*Completed*
HANG TUAH (ex-HMS *Loch Insh*)	F 433	Henry Robb Ltd, Leith	17 Nov 1943	10 May 1944	20 Oct 1944

Displacement, tons	1 575 standard; 2 400 full load
Length, feet (*metres*)	286 (*87·2*) pp; 297·2 (*90·6*) wl 307 (*91·7*) oa
Beam, feet (*metres*)	38·5 (*11·7*)
Draught, feet (*metres*)	14·9 (*4·5*) max
Guns, dual purpose	2—4 in (*102 mm*)
Guns, AA	6—40 mm
A/S	2 Squid 3-barrelled DC mortars
Boilers	2 Admiralty 3-drum; 225 psi (*15·8 kg/cm²*)
Main engines	2 sets triple expansion; 5 500 ihp; 2 shafts
Speed, knots	19·5 designed; 17 max
Radius, miles	9 500 at 12 knots
Complement	148 (10 officers, 138 ratings)

On transfer to the Royal Malaysian Navy she was refitted with a helicopter landing deck, air-conditioned throughout, modern radar, and extra accommodation, in HM Dockyard, Portsmouth, from whence she sailed for Singapore on 12 Nov 1964.

NOMENCLATURE. *Hang Tuah* is the name of a Malay Admiral and warrior in the 15th century.

HANG TUAH *1969, Royal Malaysian Navy, Official*

COASTAL MINESWEEPERS

6 Ex-BRITISH "TON" CLASS

BRINCHANG (ex-*Thankerton*) M 1172
JERAI (ex-*Dilston*) M 1168
KINABALU (ex-*Essington*) M 1134
LEDANG (ex-*Hexton*) M 1143
MAHAMIRU (ex-*Darlaston*) M 1127
TAHAN (ex-*Lullington*) M 1163

Displacement, tons	360 standard; 425 full load
Dimensions, feet	140 pp; 152 oa × 28·8 × 8·2
Guns	1—40 mm AA forward; 2—20 mm AA aft
Main engines	Diesels; 2 shafts; 2 500 bhp = 15 knots max
Oil fuel, tons	45
Complement	39

Mahamiru was transferred from the Royal Navy in 1960 under the Defence Agreement. *Ledang* was refitted at HM Dockyard, Chatham before transfer, and was commissioned and sailed for Malaysia in Oct 1963. *Jerai* and *Kinabalu* were refitted in Great Britain and arrived in Malaysia in summer 1964. *Brinchang* and *Tahan* were refitted in Singapore and transferred to the Royal Malaysian Navy in May and Apr 1966, respectively. A photograph of *Ledang* appears in the 1964-65 to 1966-67 editions, of *Mahamiru* in the 1967-68 edition and of *Kinabalu* in the 1968-69 edition.

JERAI *1969, Michael D. J. Lennon*

INSHORE MINESWEEPERS

2 Ex-BRITISH "HAM" CLASS

JERONG (ex-HMS *Felmersham*) M 2627 **TODAK** (ex-HMS *Boreham*) M 2610

Displacement, tons	120 standard; 159 full load
Dimensions, feet	100 pp; 106·5 oa × 21·2 × 5·5
Guns	1—40 mm AA forward; 2—20 mm AA aft (see notes)
Main engines	2 Paxman diesels; 1 100 bhp = 14 knots max
Oil fuel, tons	15
Complement	22

M 2601 Series *Jerong* and *Todak* were transferred from the Royal Navy at Singapore in Jan and Mar 1966, respectively. As a temporary measure they have been armed with two single 20 mm AA guns aft instead of sweeping gear. Of four sister boats transferred from Great Britain in 1958 and 1959, *Temasek* (ex-HMS *Brantingham*) M 2612 paid off in 1966, and *Langka Suka* (ex-HMS *Bedham*) M 2606, *Sri Johor* (ex-HMS *Altham*) M 2602 and *Sri Perlis* (ex-HMS *Asheldham*) M 2604 in 1967.

JERONG *Royal Malaysian Navy, Official*

FAST PATROL BOATS

4 "PERKASA" CLASS

GEMPITA P 152 **HANDALAN** P 151 **PENDEKAR** P 153 **PERKASA** P 150

Displacement, tons	95 standard; 114 full load
Dimensions, feet	90 pp; 96 wl; 99 oa × 25·5 × 7
Guns	1—40 mm AA; 1—20 mm AA
Torpedoes	4—21 in Mk 2 side launchers
Main engines	3 Rolls Royce Proteus gas turbines; 3 shafts; 12 750 bhp = 54 knots GM diesels on wing shafts for cruising = 10 knots

The design is a combination of the "Brave" class hull form and "Ferocity" type construction. Ordered from Vosper Limited, Portsmouth, England, on 22 Oct 1964. Generally similar to the motor torpedo boats built by Vosper for the Royal Danish Navy. They can also operate in the gunboat rôle or a minelaying rôle. *Perkasa* (Valiant) was launched on 26 Oct 1965, *Handalan* (Reliant) on 18 Jan 1966, *Gempita* (Thunderer) on 6 Apr 1966, and *Pendekar* (Champion) on 24 June 1966. The hull is entirely of glued wooden construction, with upperworks of aluminium alloy. Equipment includes Rover gas turbine generating sets, full air conditioning, Decca radar, and comprehensive navigation and communications system. The craft were shipped to Mala/sia in mid-1967.

PENDEKAR *1968, Royal Malaysian Navy, Official*

PATROL CRAFT

6 "KEDAH" CLASS

SRI KEDAH P 3138 **SRI PAHANG** P 3141 **SRI SELANGOR** P 3139
SRI KELANTAN P 3142 **SRI PERAK** P 3140 **SRI TRENGGANU** P 3143

4 "SABAH" CLASS

SRI MELAKA P 3147 **SRI SABAH** P 3144
SRI NEGRI SEMBILAN P 3146 **SRI SARAWAK** P 3145

14 "KRIS" CLASS

BADEK P 37 **KRIS** P 34 **SERAMPANG** P 41
BELADAU P 44 **LEMBING** P 40 **SRI JOHOR** P 49
KELEWANG P 45 **PANAH** P 42 **SRI PERLIS** P 47
KERAMBIT P 43 **RENCHONG** P 38 **SUNDANG** P 36
RENTAKA P 46 **TOMBAK** P 39

Displacement, tons	96 standard; 109 full load
Dimensions, feet	95 wl; 103 oa × 19·8 × 5·5
Guns	2—40 mm; 70 cal AA
Main engines	2 Bristol Siddeley Maybach MD 655/18 diesels; 3 500 bhp = 27 knots max
Radius, miles	1 400 (*Sabah* class 1 660) at 14 knots
Complement	22 (3 officers, 19 ratings)

All 24 craft were built by Vosper Limited, Portsmouth. The first six boats, constituting the "Kedah" class were ordered in 1961 for delivery in 1963. The four boats of the "Sabah" class were ordered in 1963 for delivery in 1964. The remaining 14 boats of the "Kris" class were ordered in 1965 for delivery between 1966 and 1968. All are of prefabricated steel construction and are fitted with Decca radar, air conditioning and Vosper roll damping equipment. The difference between the three classes are minor, the later ones having improved radar, communications, evaporators and engines of Maybach, as opposed to Bristol Siddeley construction. *Sri Johor*, the last of the 14 boats of the "Kris" class, was launched on 22 June 1967. Originally the pennant numbers allocated were in a "3100" series, but the later boats were numbered in a two figure run as shown above. A photogrpah of *Sri Kedah* appears in the 1963-64 to 1965-66 editions, of *Sri Pahang* in the 1964-65 and 1965-66 editions, and of *Sri Perak* in the 1964-65 to 1966-67 editions.

SRI SARAWAK ("Sabah" Class) *1967, Wright & Logan*

SRI KEDAH ("Kedah" Class) *Added 1969, Vosper Ltd.*

SEAWARD DEFENCE BOAT

SDML 3502 (ex-*Sri Trengganu*, ex-*SDML* 3502)

Displacement, tons	46 standard; 54 full load
Dimensions, feet	72 oa × 16 × 5·5
Guns	2—20 mm AA
Main engines	2 Gardner diesels; 2 shafts; 320 bhp = 12 knots

Former British harbour defence motor launch (HDML) later known as seaward defence motor launch (SDML). Of the original seven craft of this type *Sri Kedah* (ex-*SDML* 3501) was scrapped in 1959, and *Sri Selangor* (ex-*SDML* 1509) in 1961, SDML 3505 (ex-*Sri Pahang*, ex-*SDML* 3505) and SDML 3508 (ex-*Sri Kelantan*, ex-*SDML* 3508) in 1965. SDML 3506 (ex-*Sri Negri Sembilan*, ex-*SDML* 3506) and SDML 3507 (ex-*Sri Perak*, ex-*SDML* 3507) were offered for sale in 1966. These motor launches all reverted to their numbers in turn as the new patrol craft (see above) took their names.

KELEWANG ("Kris" Class) *1969, John G. Callis*

SURVEY VESSEL

PERANTAU (ex-HMS *Myrmidon*, ex-HMS *Edderton*) A 151

Displacement, tons	360 standard; 420 full load
Dimensions, feet	153 oa × 28·8 × 8·5
Main engines	Diesels; 2 shafts; 3 000 bhp = 15 knots
Endurance, miles	2 300 at 13 knots
Complement	26

A former Coastal minesweeper of the "Ton" type, converted by the Royal Navy into a survey ship and commissioned for service 20 July 1964. Paid off in 1968 and purchased by Malaysia in 1969. To be in service in Malaysian waters in mid 1970 *Perantau* means "a rover".

PERANTAU *Skyfotos*

DISPOSALS
The landing craft *Sri Perlis* (ex-HMS *Pelandok*, ex-*LGC*(L) 450), and the trawler type controlled minelayer *Sri Johor* (ex-HMS *Penyu*, ex-HMS *Dabchick*, ex-*Thorney*), were paid off in 1959 and sold. The auxiliary *Panji* was returned to Singapore in 1965. The patrol craft *Sri Tanjong Merang* was paid off October 1966 and returned to the Marine Dept, Malaya. The maintenance repair craft *MRC* 1401 (ex-*Sri Melaka*, ex-HMMS *Malaya*, ex-MRC 1401, ex-LCT (E) 341) was scrapped in 1967. The former Tank Landing Craft *Sri Langkawi* (ex-HMS *Counterguard*, ex-*LCT* (8) 4043) was sold in February 1968. The Despatch and Survey Vessel *Mutiara* was paid off March 1969, and is to be disposed of.

MEXICO

Administration

Secretary of the Navy:
Admiral Antonio Vazquez del Mercado

Under-Secretary of the Navy:
Vice-Admiral Antonio J. Aznar Zetina

Commander-in-Chief of the Navy:
Vice-Admiral C. G. Gabriel Lagos Beltrán

Chief of the Naval Staff:
Vice-Admiral C. G. Federico Romero Ceballos

Director of Services:
Rear-Admiral C. G. Angel Ramos Ramirez

Personnel

1969: Total 11 100 (2 300 officers and 8 000 men including marines)

Strength of the Fleet

8 Frigates and Gunboats
22 Escorts and Minesweepers
8 Patrol Boats and Launches
4 Support Ships and Auxiliaries

Mercantile Marine

Lloyd's Register of Shipping:
114 vessels of 403 573 tons gross

FRIGATES

Name	*No.*	*Builders*	*Laid down*	*Launched*	*Completed*
CALIFORNIA (ex-USS *Belet*, APD 109, ex-*DE* 599)	B 3 (ex-H 3)	Bethlehem SB Co, Hingham	26 June 1944	3 Mar 1944	15 June 1945
PAPALOAPAN (ex-USS *Earhart*, APD 113, ex-*DE* 603)	B 4 (ex-H 4)	Bethlehem SB Co, Hingham	20 Mar 1945	12 May 1945	26 July 1945
TEHUANTEPEC (ex-USS *Joseph M. Auman*, APD 117, ex-DE 74)	B 5 (ex-H 5)	Consolidated Steel Co, Orange	8 Nov 1943	5 Feb 1944	25 Apr 1945
USUMACINTA (ex-USS *Don O. Woods*, APD 118, ex-DE 721)	B 6 (ex-H 6)	Consolidated Steel Co, Orange	1 Dec 1943	19 Feb 1944	28 May 1945

4 Ex-US "RUDDEROW" CLASS

RATED AS FRAGATAS TRANSPORTES

Displacement, tons	1 400 standard; 2 130 full load
Length, feet (*metres*)	300 (*91·5*) wl; 306 (*93·3*) oa
Beam, feet (*metres*)	37 (*11·3*)
Draught, feet (*metres*)	12·7 (*3·9*)
Guns, dual purpose	1—5 in (*127 mm*) 38 cal.
Guns, AA	6—40 mm, 3 twin; 6—20 mm
Boilers	2 Foster Wheeler "D" with superheater; 475 psi (*33·4 kg/cm^2*); 750°F (*399°C*)
Main engines	GE turbo-electric 12 000 shp; 2 shafts
Speed, knots	23·6; 13 economical sea
Radius, miles	5 500 at 15 knots
Oil fuel (tons)	350
Complement	204 plus 162 troops

Former US converted destroyer escorts rated as high speed transports (APD) in the US Navy. Purchased by Mexico on 12 Dec 1963. They replaced the four ex-US "Tacoma" type frigates bearing the same names, which were stricken in June and Aug 1964. Photographs of *Papaloapan* appear in the 1965-66 to 1968-69 editions.

CALIFORNIA and *Papaloapan* (from *Guanarjuato*) *1969, Mexican Navy, Official*

1 "DURANGO" TYPE

RATED AS TRANSPORTE DE GUERRA

Name	*No.*	*Builders*	*Launched*	*Completed*
DURANGO	B—1 (ex-128)	Union Naval de Levante, Valencia	28 June 1935	**1936**

Displacement, tons	1 600 standard; 2 000 full load
Length, feet (*metres*)	282 (*86·0*) pp; 303 (*92·4*) oa
Beam, feet (*metres*)	40 (*12·2*)
Draught, feet (*metres*)	10 (*3·1*)
Guns, surface	2—4 in (*102 mm*); 2—2·24 in (*57 mm*)
Guns, AA	2—25 mm, twin; 4—20 mm
Main engines	2 Enterprise DMR-38 diesels, 5 000 bhp; electric drive; 2 shafts
Speed, knots	18 max, 12 sea (cruising)
Radius, miles	3 000 at 12 knots
Oil fuel (tons)	140
Complement	149 (24 officers and 125 men)

Originally designed primarily as an armed transport with accommodation for 20 officers and 450 men. The two Yarrow boilers and Parsons geared turbines of 6 500 shp installed when first built were replaced with two 2 500 bhp diesels in 1967 when the ship was re-rigged with remodelled funnel (see new appearance in photograph). Carries a lighter armament than the "Guanajuato" class (see below) which besides troop carrying and transport capacity are equivalent to frigates in many ways. *Durango* replaced *Zaragoza* as training ship in Mar 1964.

DURANGO *1969, Mexican Navy, Official*

3 "GUANAJUATO" CLASS

RATED AS CANONEROS (GUNBOATS)

Name	*No.*	*Builders*	*Launched*
GUANAJUATO	C-7	Sociedad Espanol de Construction Naval, Ferrol	29 May 1934
POTOSI	C-9	Sociedad Espanol de Construction Naval, Motagorda, Cadiz	24 Aug 1934
QUERETARO	C-8	Sociedad Espanol de Construction Naval, Ferrol	29 June 1934

Displacement, tons	1 300 standard; 1 950 full load
Length, feet (*metres*)	264 (*80·5*) oa
Beam, feet (*metres*)	37·8 (*11·5*)
Draught, feet (*metres*)	10 (*3·0*)
Guns, surface	3—4 in (*102 mm*) singles
Guns, AA	6—20 mm, singles
Main engines	2 Enterprise DMR-38 diesels 5 000 bhp; 2 shafts
Speed, knots	14
Oil fuel (tons)	140
Complement	140 (20 officers and 120 men)

Officially classified as gunboats (canoneros), but can be used as transports with berths for 120 troops. The Parsons geared turbines (2 shafts, 5 000 shp = 19 knots) and Yarrow boilers installed when originally built in 1934 were replaced with two diesels each of 2 500 bhp: *Querétaro* in 1958, *Potosi* in 1961, and *Guanajuato* in 1964. Former pennent numbers: *Querétaro* H 9 (ex-43); *Potosi* H 8 (ex-44). A photograph of *Querétaro* appears in the 1964-65 and 1965-66 editions and of *Potosi* in the 1966-67 to 1968-69 editions.

GUANAJUATO *1969, Mexican Navy Official*

ESCORT MINESWEEPERS

20 Ex-US MSF TYPE *(RATED AS DRAGAMINAS)*

Name	No.	Ex-US Name & No.		Name	No.	Ex-US Name & No.	
DM-01	D-1	*Jubilant*	255	**DM-11**	E-1	*Device*	220
DM-02	D-2	*Hilarity*	241	**DM-12**	E-2	*Ransom*	283
DM-03	D-3	*Execute*	232	**DM-13**	E-3	*Knave*	256
DM-04	D-4	*Facility*	233	**DM-14**	E-4	*Rebel*	284
DM-05	D-5	*Scuffle*	298	**DM-15**	E-5	*Crag*	214
DM-06	D-6	*Eager*	224	**DM-16**	E-6	*Dour*	223
DM-07	D-7	*Recruit*	285	**DM-17**	E-7	*Diploma*	221
DM-08	D-8	*Success*	310	**DM-18**	E-8	*Invade*	254
DM-09	D-9	*Scout*	296	**DM-19**	E-9	*Intrigue*	253
DM-10	D-0	*Instill*	252	**DM-20**	E-0	*Harlequin*	365

Displacement, tons	650 standard; 945 full load
Displacement, feet	180 wl; 184·5 oa × 33 × 10
Guns	1—3 in, 50 cal dp; 4—40 mm AA
Main engines	2 diesels; 2 shafts; 1 710 bhp = 15 knots
Complement	104

Former US steel-hulled "180-ft" fleet minesweepers of the "Admirable" class, MSF, ex-AM type. All completed in 1943-44. Transferred at Orange, Texas, on 2 Oct 1962. Of the twenty vessels ten are designated *dragaminas* for minesweeping duties, with D pennant numbers, and ten are designated *escoltas* for escort and general purpose duties with E pennant numbers.

DM 11 — *1966, Mexican Navy, Official*

DM 16 — *1966, Mexican Navy, Official*

DM 02 — *Mexican Navy, Official*

DM 19 — *Mexican Navy, Official*

PATROL VESSELS

TOMAS MARIN (ex-*PCE* 875) C 3

Displacement, tons	600 standard; 903 full load
Dimensions, feet	180 wl; 184·5 oa × 33·1 × 9·5
Guns	1—3 in, 50 cal; 6—40 mm AA (3 twin); 4—20 mm AA (single)
A/S weapons	2 DCT
Main engines	GM diesels; 2 shafts; 1 800 bhp = 15 knots
Complement	80

Sole survivor of five former US patrol vessels of the PCE type, all completed in 1943-44 and purchased from the US Navy in 1947. Rated as *Corbeta*. Sister ships *Blass Godinez* (ex-*PCE* 871) C 2, *David Porter* (ex-*PCE* 847) C 4, *Pedro Saina de Baranda* (ex-*PCE* 844) C 1, and *Virgilio Uribe* (ex-*PCE* 868) C 5 were scrapped in 1965.

TOMAS MARIN — *1966, Mexican Navy, Official*

GC 38 (ex-USS *PC* 1210) G 8

Displacement, tons	280 standard; 450 full load
Dimensions, feet	170 wl; 173·7 oa × 23 × 11
Guns	1—3 in; 2—20 mm AA
A/S weapons	4 DCT
Main engines	2 diesels; 2 shafts; 2 880 bhp = 19 knots
Oil fuel, tons	60
Radius, miles	5 000 at 10 knots (cruising speed)
Complement	65

Sole survivor of nine former US submarine chasers of the "173-ft" steel PC type, launched in 1942-44, completed in USA in 1942-45, and purchased as surplus in USA in 1952. Rated as *Guardacosta*. Of this class GC 31 (ex-USS *PC* 820) GC 32 (ex-USS *PC* 608), GC 34 (ex-USS *PC* 794) and GC 36 (ex-USS *PC* 1224) were officially deleted from the list in Mar 1964 for scrapping, and GC 30 (ex-USS *PC* 820), GC 33 (ex-USS *PC* 813), GC 35 (ex-USS *PC* 824) and GC 37 (ex-USS *PC* 819) were scrapped in 1966.

Of the nine patrol vessels of the "G 20" class, G 29 was scrapped in 1952, G 20, G 21, G 23 G 26 and G 27 in 1954, G 22 and G 25 in 1956, and G 28 in 1966.

PATROL BOATS

2 "AZUETA" CLASS

AZUETA G 9 — **VILLAPANDO** G 6

Displacement, tons	80 standard
Dimensions, feet	85 × 16 × 7
Guns	2—13·2 mm AA (twin)
Main engines	Superior motors; 600 bhp = 12 knots

Of all steel construction. Built at Astilleros de Tampico in 1959 and 1960, respectively.

VILLAPANDO — *1966, Mexican Navy, Official*

AZUETA — *Mexican Navy, Official*

5 RIVER TYPE

AM 4 **AM 5** **AM 6** **AM 7** **AM 8**

Displacement, tons	35
Main engines	Diesel; speed = 10 knots

River patrol craft of steel construction. Built in Tampico and Veracruz. Entered service from 1960 to 1962.

Patrol Boats—*continued*

POLIMAR 1 G 1 **POLIMAR 2** G 2 **POLIMAR 3** G 3

Displacement, tons	37 standard
Dimensions, feet	60 × 15 × 4
Main engines	2 diesels; 456 bhp = 16 knots

Small patrol craft of steel construction. *Polimar 1* was built at Astilleros de Tampico in 1961 and entered service on 1 Oct 1962. *Polimar 2* and *Polimar* 3 were built at Icacas Shipyard, Guerrero and entered service in 1966.

POLIMAR 1 *1969, Mexican Navy, Official*

TRANSPORT

ZACATECAS B 2

Displacement, tons	780 standard
Dimensions, feet	158 × 27·2 × 9
Guns	1—40 mm AA; 2—20 mm AA (single)
Main engines	1 MAN diesel; 560 hp = 10 knots
Complement	50 (13 officers and 37 men)

Built at Ulua Shipyard, Veracruz. Launched in 1959. Cargo ship type. The hull is of welded steel construction.

ZACATECAS *1966, Mexican Navy, Official*

The training ship *Zaragoza* (ex-*Orizaba*), ex-*Southern Cross*, ex-*Rover*, former Presidential Yacht, was officially stricken from the Navy List for disposal in Mar 1964. The six landing craft of the US LCT (LCU) type were officially deleted from the Navy List in 1966. The auxiliary ocean tug of the US "Maricopa" class, *Sotoyomo* (ex-USS *ATA* 121), loaned to Mexico under MAP, was removed from the list in 1966, as were *Nereida*, former patrol boat adapted as a tug and fire fighting craft, and three small tugs.

OILERS

1 Ex-US YOG TYPE

AGUASCALIENTES (ex-YOG 6) 1 5

Displacement, tons	440 light; 1 480 full load
Dimensions, feet	174·5 oa × 33 × 11·8 max
Main engines	Union diesel direct; 500 bhp = 8 knots
Capacity	6 570 barrels
Complement	26 (5 officers and 21 ratings)

Former US self-propelled fuel oil barge. Built by Geo. H. Mathis Co Ltd, Camden, N.J. in 1943. Purchased in 1964. Entered service in Nov 1964.

1 Ex-US YO TYPE

TLAXCALA (ex-YO 107) I 6

Displacement, tons	440 light; 1 800 full load
Dimensions, feet	174·5 oa × 33 × 11·8 max
Main engines	Union diesel direct; 500 bhp = 8 knots
Capacity	6 570 barrels
Complement	26 (5 officers and 21 ratings)

Former US self-propelled fuel oil barge. Built by Geo Lawley & Son, Neponset, Mass. in 1943. Purchased in 1964. Entered service in Nov 1964.

TLAXCALA *1966, Mexican Navy, Official*

SURVEY SHIP

SOTAVENTO 1 A

Displacement, tons	300 standard; 400 full load
Dimensions, feet	165·5 × 28 × 10
Main engines	Diesels; 1 800 bhp = 17 knots

Built by Higgins, New Orleans. Launched in 1947. Handsome, symmetrical and low-lying. Streamlined, with truncated funnel. Air conditioned and equipped with radar. Formerly the Presidential Yacht, but officially reclassified as *Buque Hidrografico* in 1966.

SOTAVENTO *1967, Mexican Navy, Official*

MADAGASCAR

(MALAGASY REPUBLIC)

The *République Malgache* became an independent state on 26 June 1960.

PATROL VESSELS

MALAIKA

Displacement, tons	235 light
Dimensions, feet	149·3 pp; 155·8 oa × 23·6 × 8·2
Guns	2—40 mm AA
Main engines	2 MGO diesels; 1 shaft; 2,400 bhp = 18·5 knots
Radius, miles	2 000 at 18 knots
Complement	25 (3 officers and 22 men)

Ordered by the French Navy to be built by Chantiers Navals Franco-Belges for delivery to Madagascar. Laid down in Nov 1966, launched on 22 Mar 1967 and completed in Dec 1967.

TANAMASOANDRO (ex-*Marjolaine*, ex-*D* 337, ex-*YMS* **69**)

Displacement, tons	280 standard; 325 full load
Dimensions, feet	134·5 × 24·2 × 12
Guns	1—3 in, dp 2—20 mm AA; 2 MG
Main engines	2 diesels; 2 shafts; 1 000 bhp = 15 knots
Oil fuels, ton	36
Radius, miles	3 000 at 10 knots

Former French patrol vessel, ex-coastal minesweeper of the US YMS type, transferred from the French Navy to the new Malgache Navy at Diego Suarez on 18 Feb 1961 and name changed from *Marjalaine* to *Tanamasoandro* (which means Sunray). To be discarded as soon as the new patrol vessel is in full operational service.

FANANTENANA (ex-*Richelieu*)

Displacement, tons	1 040 standard; 1 200 full load
Dimensions, feet	183·7 pp; 206·4 oa × 30 × 14·8
Guns	2—40 mm AA
Main engines	2 Deutz diesels; 1 shaft; 1 060 + 500 bhp = 12 knots

Trawler purchased and converted in 1966-67 to Coast Guard and training ship. 691 tons gross. Built in 1959 by A. G. Weser, Bremen, Germany.

JASMINE

Former coastal minesweeper of the YMS type acquired from France on 19 Aug 1965 as a light tender. Same type originally as *Tanamasoandra* above.

TRANSFER. The patrol vessel *Mailaka* (ex-*P* 758, *VC* 8) was returned to the French Navy in 1967.

MAURITANIA

PATROL BOATS

IM RAQ'NI (ex-VC 7, P 757)

Displacement, tons	75 standard; 82 full load
Dimensions, feet	104·3 × 15·4 × 5·5
Guns	2—20 mm AA
Main engines	2 Mercedes-Benz diesels; 2 shafts; 2 700 bhp = 28 knots
Radius, miles	1 500 at 15 knots
Complement	15

Built by construction Mécaniques de Normandie, Cherbourg. Launched on 10 Dec 1957. Transferred from France in 1966.

NATO

North Atlantic Treaty Organisation (NATO) Naval Forces are:—

BELGIUM, CANADA, DENMARK, GERMAN FEDERAL REPUBLIC, GREECE, ICELAND, ITALY, NETHERLANDS, NORWAY, PORTUGAL, TURKEY, UNITED KINGDOM, UNITED STATES. (France withdrew from NATO on 1 July 1966.)

MOROCCO

Mercantile Marine

Lloyd's Register of shipping: 38 vessels of 70 066 tons gross

FRIGATES

Name	*Builders*	*Laid down*	*Launched*	*Completed*
AL MAOUNA (ex-*La Surprise*, ex-HMS-*Torridge*) 31 (ex-033)	Blyth Dry Docks & Ship building Co	17 Oct 1942	16 Aug 1943	6 Apr 1944

Displacement, tons	1 450 standard; 2 150 full load
Length, feet (*metres*)	283 (*86·3*) pp; 301·3 (*91·8*) oa
Beam, feet (*metres*)	36·5 (*11·1*)
Draught, feet (*metres*)	12·5 (*3·8*)
Guns, surface	2—4·1 in (*105 mm*)
Guns, AA	3—40 mm; 2—20 mm; 2—37 mm saluting
A/S	1 Hedgehog; 4 DCT; 2 DC racks
Aircraft	1 helicopter
Boilers	2 Admiralty 3-drum
Main engines	Triple expansion 5 500 ihp; 2 shafts
Speed, knots	18
Radius, miles	7 700 at 12 knots
Oil fuel (tons)	645
Complement	123 (10 officers, 113 men)

Originally a British frigate of the "River" class, purchased by France in 1944. Sold to Morocco in June 1964 when she was converted as flagship and Royal yacht by Chantiers Dubigeon at Brest. Accepted on 5 Mar 1965. A helicopter landing deck and extra accommodation have been provided aft.

AL MOUNA — *1968, Royal Moroccan Navy, Official*

PATROL VESSELS

(*Escorteur Cotier*)

AL BACHIR 22 (ex-12)

Displacement, tons	125 light; 154 full load
Dimensions, feet	124·7 pp; 133·2 oa × 20·8 × 4·7
Guns	AA and MG
Main engines	2 SEMT-Pielstick diesels; 2 shafts; 3 600 bhp = 25 knots
Oil fuel, tons	21
Radius, miles	2 000 at 15 knots

Ordered in 1964 from Constructions Mécaniques de Normandie, Cherbourg, launched 25 Feb 1967, delivered 30 Mar 1967.

AL BACHIR — *1967, Royal Moroccan Navy, Official*

LIEUTENANT RIFFI 32

Displacement, tons	325 standard; 374 full load
Dimensions, feet	170 wl; 173·8 oa × 23 × 6·3
Guns	1—3 in dp; 2—40 mm AA
A/S weapons	2 ASM mortars; 1 DC rack
Main engines	SEMT-Pielstick diesels; 2 shafts; 3 600 bhp = 19 knots
Radius, miles	3 000 at 12 knots; 2 000 at 15 knots
Complement	59 (4 officers, 55 men)

Of modified "Fougueux" design. Built by Constructions Mécaniques de Normandie, Cherbourg. Laid down in May 1963. Launched on 1 Mar 1964. Completed in May 1964. Controllable pitch propellers.

LIEUTENANT RIFFI — *1969, Royal Moroccan Navy, Official*

The corvette (*aviso*) *El Lahiq* (ex-*Chamois*, ex-*Annamite*) is no longer in service with the Royal Moroccan Navy. She was transferred from the French Navy on 7 Nov 1961. The patrol vessel **Agadir** (ex-French *Gaumier*, ex-USS *PC* 545) was returned to France on 19 Aug 1964 and became Q 390. Sold for scrap at Brest on 15 Nov 1965.

SEAWARD PATROL CRAFT

(*Vedette de Port*)

ES SABIQ (ex-*P* 762, *VC* 12) 11

Displacement, tons	75 standard; 82 full load
Dimensions, feet	104·5 × 15·5 × 5·5
Guns	2—20 mm AA
Main engines	Mercedes-Benz diesels; 2 shafts; 2 700 bhp = 28 knots
Radius, miles	1 500 at 15 knots
Complement	17

Former French seaward defence motor launch of the VC type. Built by Chantiers Navals d'Estérel. Launched on 13 Aug 1957. Completed in 1958. Transferred from the French Navy to the Moroccan Navy on 15 Nov 1960 and renamed *Es Sabiq*.

VC — *Official*

UTILITY LANDING CRAFT

LIEUTENANT MALGHAGH 21

Displacement, tons	292 light; 642 full load
Dimensions, feet	193·5 × 39·2 × 4·5
Guns	2—12·7 mm Browning
Main engines	2 MGO diesels; 2 shafts; 1 000 bhp = 8 knots
Complement	20 (2 officers, 18 men)

Ordered early in 1963 from the Chantiers Navals Franco-Belges and completed in 1964. Similar to the French landing craft of the EDIC type built at the same yard.

LIEUTENANT MALGHAGH — *1968, Royal Moroccan Navy, Official*

NATIONALIST CHINA

Administration

Commander-in-Chief Chinese Nationalist Navy:
Vice-Admiral Feng Chi-Chung

Fleet Commander:
Vice-Admiral Li Tan-Chien

Diplomatic Representation

Naval Attaché in Washington:
Rear Admiral Chien Tsou

Strength of the Fleet

7	Destroyers	48	Coastal Craft
15	Frigates	6	Transports
2	Escort Transports	5	Oilers
5	Escort Vessels	21	LSTs
3	Fleet Minesweepers	15	LSMs
1	Minelayer	5	LSIs
23	Submarine Chasers	3	LSLs
1	Gunboat	30	LSUs
7	Coastal Minesweepers	8	Support Ships

Personnel

1969: Naval 35 000 officers and ratings: Marine 27 000 officers and men.

The Navy underwent training with the United States Military Assistance Advisory Group on Taiwan. United States Marine Corps advisers trained Chinese Nationalist marines in amphibious operations.

Ships

Chinese (Nationalist) ship's names are prefaced by "RCN" (Republic of China Navy).

Acquisition Programme

1 ex-US Destroyer
2 Fast Transports, US APD (ex-DEs)

Mercantile Marine

Lloyd's Register of Shipping
187 vessels of 762 515 tons gross

DESTROYERS

Name	*No.*	*Builders*	*Laid down*	*Launched*	*Completed*
AN YANG (ex-USS *Kimberley*, DD 521)	18	Bethlehem Co. Staten Island	27 July 1942	4 Feb 1943	22 May 1943
KUN YANG (ex-USS *Yarnall*, DD 541)	19	Bethlehem Co., San Francisco	5 Dec 1942	25 July 1943	30 Dec 1943

Kimberley was recommissioned at Boston, Mass 1967 and transferred under MAP in June 1967. *Yarnall* was purchased on 10 June 1968. Armament under review. See details under "Fletcher" class in US section.

Displacement, tons	2 100 standard; 3 050 full load
Length, feet (*metres*)	376·2 (*114·7*)
Beam, feet (*metres*)	39·7 (*12·1*)
Draught, feet (*metres*)	
Boilers	4 Babcock & Wilcox
Main engines	2 GE turbines; 60 000 shp
Speed, knots	35
Complement	250

Name	*No.*	*Builders*	*Laid down*	*Launched*	*Completed*
HSUEN YANG (ex-USS *Rodman*, DD 456, ex-DMS 21)	16	Federal SB & DD Co	2 Dec 1940	26 Sep 1941	27 Jan 1942
NAN YANG (ex-USS *Plunkett*, DD 431)	17	Federal SB & DD Co	1 Mar 1939	9 Mar 1940	16 July 1940

2 Ex-US "GLEAVES" CLASS

Displacement, tons	1 630 (*Nan Yang* 1 700) standard; 2 575 full load
Length, feet (*metres*)	341 (*104·0*) wl; 348·3 (*106·2*) oa
Beam, feet (*metres*)	36 (*11·0*)
Draught, feet (*metres*)	18 (*5·5*)
Guns, surface	3—5 in (*127 mm*) 38 cal.; *Nan Yang* 4—5 in, 38 cal
Guns, AA	4—40 mm; 4—20 mm
Torpedo tubes	5—21 in (*533 mm*) in *Nan Yang*
Boilers	4 Babcock & Wilcox
Main engines	GE geared turbines 50 000 shp; 2 shafts
Speed, knots	34
Radius, miles	5 000 at 15 knots
Oil fuel (tons)	600
Complement	250

Transferred on loan from the US Navy, *Rodman* on 28 July 1955 and *Plunkett* on 16 Feb 1959.

NAN YANG *1962, courtesy Mr W. H. Davis*

PHOTOGRAPHS. An official photograph of the destroyer *Hsuen Yang*, former US destroyer minesweeper, afterwards reclassified as a destroyer, a port quarter oblique view, appears in the 1956-57 to 1961-62 editions, showing a different scheme of main armament with a modified layout.

Name	*No.*	*Builders*	*Laid down*	*Launched*	*Completed*
HAN YANG (ex-USS *Hilary P. Jones*, DD 427)	15	Philadelphia Navy Yard	16 Nov 1938	14 Dec 1939	7 Sep 1940
LO YANG (ex-USS *Benson*, DD 421)	14	Bethlehem (Quincy)	16 May 1938	15 Nov 1939	25 July 1940

2 Ex-US "MAYO" CLASS

Displacement, tons	1 620 standard; 2 450 full load
Length, feet (*metres*)	340 (*103·6*) wl; 348·2 (*106·2*) oa
Beam, feet (*metres*)	35·3 (*10·8*)
Draught, feet (*metres*)	18 (*5·5*)
Guns, surface	4—5 in (*127 mm*) 38 cal.
Guns, AA	4—40 mm; 6—20 mm
A/S	DC mortar; DC throwers
Boilers	4 high pressure
Main engines	2 sets GE geared turbines 50 000 shp; 2 shafts
Speed, knots	34
Radius, miles	5 000 at 15 knots
Oil fuel (tons)	600
Complement	250

Presented by USA. Transferred to China (Taiwan) at Charleston, South Carolina, on 26 Feb 1954.

PHOTOGRAPHS. A photograph of *Lo Yang* appears in the 1954-55 to 1957-58 editions.

HAN YANG *Added 1957, Official*

1 Ex-JAPANESE "KAGERO" TYPE

Name	*No.*	*Builders*	*Launched*	*Completed*
TAN YANG (ex-*Yukikaze*)	12	Sasebo, Japan	1939	1940

Displacement, tons	2 050 standard; 2 490 full load
Length, feet (*metres*)	388 (*118·3*) oa
Beam, feet (*metres*)	35·5 (*10·8*)
Draught, feet (*metres*)	12·3 (*3·8*)
Guns, dual purpose	3—5 in (*127 mm*) 38 cal. in open mounts in "A", "X" and "Y" positions. 2—3 in (*76 mm*) in open mounts, one on deck in "P" position, one in deckhouse in "Q" position.
Guns, AA	10—40 mm distributed fore and aft
A/S	DC racks
Boilers	3 Kampon
Main engines	2 geared turbines 52 000 shp; 2 shafts
Speed, knots	27 (see *General Notes*)
Radius, miles	5 000 at 18 knots
Complement	290

TA YANG *1962, Official*

The largest combatant unit in the Navy. Extensively refitted in 1951-52. On trials in Feb 1953, 27·5 knots was reached. Rearmed with US guns in 1959. Reported to have been discarded in 1968.

FRIGATES

1 Ex-US "RUDDEROW" TYPE

TAIYUAN (ex-*USS Riley*), DE 579

Displacement, tons	1 450 standard; 2 230 full load
Dimensions, feet (*metres*)	306 (*93·3*) × 37 (*11·3*) × 14 (*4·3*)
Guns	2—5 in 38 cal DP; 4—40 mm, 6—20 mm
Main engines	Turbo electric drive 12 000 shp
Speed, knots	24

Built by Bethlehem-Hingham. Launched 29 Dec 1943, completed 13 Mar 1944. Transferred at Seattle, Wash, 10 July 1968.

4 Ex-US "BOSTWICK" TYPE

Displacement, tons	1 240 standard; 1 900 full load
Length, feet (*metres*)	306 (*92·3*) oa
Beam, feet (*metres*)	36·8 (*11·2*)
Draught, feet (*metres*)	12 (*3·7*)
Guns, dual purpose	4—3 in (*76 mm*) 50 cal.
Guns, AA	3 or 4—40 mm; 9 or 10—20 mm
A/S	8 DCT
Torpedo tubes	3—21 in (*533 mm*) in triple mounting
Main engines	Diesel-electric 6 000 bhp; 2 shafts
Speed, knots	19
Radius, miles	11 500 at 11 knots
Oil fuel (tons)	300
Complement	220

Former United States destroyer escorts. Transferred on 31 Dec 1948. Two underwent overhaul in Japanese yards, late in 1952.

TAI HO Type

Added 1964. Official

Name	*No.*	*Launched*	*Completed*
TAI CHAO (ex-USS *Carter*, DE 112)	26	29 Feb 1944	2 May 1944
TAI HO (ex-USS *Thomas*, DE 102)	23	31 July 1943	21 Nov 1943
TAI HU (ex-USS *Breeman*, DE 104)	25	31 July 1943	12 Dec 1943
TAI TSANG (ex-*Bostwick*, DE 103)	24	30 Aug 1943	21 Dec 1943

1 Ex-US "EVARTS" TYPE

Name	*No.*	*Builders*	*Launched*	*Completed*
TAI KANG (ex-US *Wyffels*, DE 6)	21	Boston Navy Yard	1943	21 Apr 1943

Displacement, tons	1 150 standard; 1 430 full load
Length, feet (*metres*)	283·5 (*86·4*) wl; 289·5 (*88·2*) oa
Beam, feet (*metres*)	35 (*10·7*)
Draught, feet (*metres*)	10·7 (*3·3*)
Guns, dual purpose	3—3 in (*76 mm*) 50 cal.
Guns, AA	4—40 mm; 11—20 mm
A/S	9 DCT
Main engines	Diesel-electric 6 000 bhp; 2 shafts
Speed, knots	19
Radius, miles	5 500 at 14 knots
Complement	120

Former United States destroyer escort. Presented to China in 1946. Sister ship *Tai Ping* (ex-USS *Decker*, DE 47), was torpedoed and sunk by Chinese Republican motor torpedo boats off Tachen islands on 14 Nov 1954.

TAI KANG

Official

The following frigates were scrapped in 1964:— *Hsin Yang* (ex-*Hatsume*), ex-Japanese "Hagi" Type, modified "Matsu" class (sister ships *Hon Yang*, *Hua Yang* and *Hui Yang* were already hulked or discarded as beyond economical repair); *Yung Ching* (ex-*Salshu*), ex-Japanese Minelaying Type, formerly rated as a light minelayer and latterly as a destroyer escort.

The following frigates were discarded in 1963:— *Cheng An* (ex-*Hsueh Feng*, ex-*Wei Tai*, ex-*Yashiro*), ex-Japanese "Mikura" Type; *Lin An* (ex-*Tsushima*), ex-Japanese "Etorofu" type; *Chen An* (ex-Japanese No. 40) and *Tai An* (ex-Japanese No. 104), former Japanese turbine "Kaiboken" Type (sister ships *Tsi Nan* and *Tung An* were already discarded); *Chao An* (ex-Japanese No. 107) and *Jui An* (ex-*Ying Kan*, ex-Japanese No. 67), former Japanese diesel "Kaibokan" Type (sister ships *Chang An* and *Tsing Pai* were already hulked).

"CASTLE TYPE"
Of the former Canadian frigates (corvettes) of the "Castle" class, *Kao-An* (ex-*Chin Chin*, ex-HMCS *Tillsonburg*, ex-HMS *Pembroke Castle*), was discarded in 1963, and *Te-An* (ex-*Hsi Lin*, ex-HMCS *Orangeville*, ex-HMS *Hedingham Castle*) was discarded in 1967.

Modified Destroyer Escorts

11 Ex-US APD TYPE

CHUNG SHAN (ex-*Blessman*, APD 48, ex-*DE* 69)
LU SHAN PF 36 (ex-*Bull*, *APD* 78, ex-*DE* 693)
HWA SHAN PF 33 (ex-*Donald W. Wolf*, *APD* 129, ex-*DE* 713)
WEN SHAN PF 34 (ex-*Gantner*, *APD* 42, ex-*DE* 60)
KANG SHAN PF 43 (ex-*George W. Ingram*, *APD* 43, ex-*DE* 62)
YO SHAN (ex-*Kinzer*, *APD* 91, ex-DE 232)
SHOA SHAN PF 37 (ex-*Kline*, *APD* 120, ex-DE 687)
HENG SHAN PF 39 (ex-*Raymond W. Herndon*, *APD* 121, ex-*DE* 688)
TAI SHAN PF 38 (ex-*Register*, *APD* 92, ex-*DE* 233)
FU SHAN PF 35 (ex-*Truxton*, *AP* 98, ex-*DE* 282)
TIEN SHAN 315 (ex-*Kleinsmith*, *APD* 134, ex-*DE* 718)

Displacement, tons	1 400 standard; 2 130 full load
Length, feet (*metres*)	300 (*91·4*) wl; 306 (*93·3*) oa
Beam, feet (*metres*)	37 (*11·3*)
Draught, feet (*metres*)	12·7 (*3·9*)
Guns, dual purpose	1—5 in (*127 mm*) 38 cal.
Guns, AA	6—40 mm
Boilers	2 Express
Main engines	GE geared turbines, electric drive 12 000 shp; 2 shafts
Speed, knots	23
Radius, miles	5 500 at 15 knots
Oil fuel (tons)	350
Complement	204

TIEN SHAN

1962. Official

Former destroyer escorts converted by the USA and officially rated as High Speed Transports. *Kleinsmith* was transferred from the United States Navy to Nationalist China at Tsoyin, Taiwan, on 16 May 1960. Her new name *Tien Shan* means Heavenly Mountain. *Gantner* and *Walter B. Cobb* were transferred to Taiwan on 15 Mar 1966 at San Francisco, California, but *Walter B. Cobb* was lost at sea while under tow to Taiwan, and was replaced by *Bull*. *Donald W. Wolf*, *Kinzer*, *Kline*, and *Truxtun*, were transferred in 1966, *Raymond W. Herndon* and *Register* in Sep 1966, *Blessman* and *George W. Ingram* on 3 July 1967. Only *Chung Shan* and *Tien Shan* are rated as APD, the others as frigates. *Rednour* APD 102, (ex-DE 592) was not in the event transferred.

ESCORT PATROL VESSELS

1 Ex-US PCE TYPE

WEI YUAN (ex-*Yung Hsiang*, ex-*PCE* 869, 6 Feb 1943) 42

Displacement, tons	640 standard; 903 full load
Dimensions, feet	180 wl; 184·5 oa × 33 × 9·5 max
Guns	2—3 in dp; 3—40 mm AA; 6—20 mm AA
Main engines	Diesel; 2 shafts; 1 800 bhp = 17 knots
Complement	110

Launch dates above. Built by Albina Engine and Machinery Works, Portland, Ore. One 3 inch, 50 cal gun was added in 1955. Rated as gunboats. These may be replaced by *I Men* (PCE 63) and *Chin Lan* (PCE 64). *Yung Tai*, PCE 62 (ex-41, ex-USS *PCE* 867) was damaged in action on 14 Nov 1965 and later discarded.

YUNG TAI *1963, Official*

4 Ex-US MSF TYPE

CHU YUNG (ex-USS *Waxwing*, *MSF* 389) PCE 67
WU SHENG (ex-USS *Redstart*, *MSF* 378) PCE 66
MO LING (ex-USS *Roselle MSF* 359) PCE 68
PING CHING (ex-USS *Steady*, *MSF* 118) PCE 70

Displacement, tons	890 standard; 1 250 full load
Dimensions, feet	215 wl; 221·2 oa × 32·5 × 10·8 max
Guns	2—3 in, 50 cal (single); 4—40 mm AA (2 twin); 4—20 mm AA (2 twin)
A/S weapons	1 ASW projector, 1 triple ASW torpedo tube mounting, 2 DC projectors; 2 DCT
Main engines	2 shafts; 3 530 bhp = 18 knots
Complement	95

Former US Fleet Minesweepers of the "Auk" Class. Steel hulled. Built by American SB Co, Cleveland, Ohio (*Waxwing*) and Savannah Mach & Foundry Co (*Redstart*) Launched and completed in 1964-65. Minesweeping gear removed so that the ships can be employed as Escort Patrol Vessels. *Redstart* and *Waxwing* were transferred on 22 July 1965 and 14 Oct 1965, respectively, at Seattle, Washington. *Steady* was purchased on 15 Aug 1967 and transferred in 1968.
Chein Men (ex-USS *Toucan*, MSF 387) PCE 45, transferred from the US Navy to the Taiwan Navy on 22 Dec 1964, was sunk by Communist Chinese warships south of Quemoy on 6 Aug 1965.

FLEET MINESWEEPERS

3 Ex-US MSF (ex-AM) TYPE

47 YUNG CHIA	(ex-USS *Implicit*, *AM* 246, 6 Sep 1943)	*2 rated as*
48 YUNG HSIU	(ex-USS *Pinnacle*, *AM* 274, 11 Sep 1943)	*Minesweepers*
50 YUNG FENG	(ex-USS *Prime*, *AM* 279, 22 Jan 1944)	(*Minelayer*)

Displacement, tons	650 standard; 945 full load
Dimensions, feet	180 wl; 184·5 oa × 33 × 9·8 max
Guns	1—3 in dp; 3—40 mm AA; 6—20 mm AA
Main engines	Diesel; 2 shafts; 1 710 bhp = 14·8 knots
Complement	104

All MSF (ex-AM) type fleet minesweepers acquired from the US Navy. Launch dates above. *Yung Feng* is fitted for minelaying with tracks on her stern and is rated as a coastal minelayer. *Yung Hsing* served as a maritime customs vessel. *Yung Ting* was converted to a survey ship, see later page.
Sister ships *Yung Chun* No. 52 (ex-USS *Gavia*, AM 363), *Yung Ho*, No. 53 (ex-USS *Delegate*, AM 217) and *Yung Kang*, No. 54 (ex-USS *Elusive*, AM 225), all rated as gunboats, and *Yung Hsing*, No. A 4 (ex-USS *Embattle*, AM 226) in the Coastguard, were scrapped in 1964. *Yung Ning*, No. 46 (ex-USS *Magnet*, AM 260), rated as a minesweeper, was discarded in 1963. *Yung Sheng*, No. 43 (ex-*USS Lance*, AM 257), *Yung Shou* (ex-USS *Pivot*, AM 276) and *Yung Shun* (ex-USS *Logic*, AM 258) rated as minesweepers, were discarded in 1968.
Yung Chang (ex-USS *Refresh*, AM 287) 51, of this class, rated as a gunboat, was sunk off Southern China on 14 Nov 1965 by a Chinese Communist escort.

YUNG CHANG *1962, Official*

SUBMARINE CHASERS

14 EX-US PC TYPE

105 FUKIANG	(ex-*Hwangpu*, ex-US *PC* 492) 29 Dec 1941
108 HSIANG KIANG	(ex-US *PC* 786) 6 Feb 1943
109 CHIH KIANG	(ex-US *PC* 1078), 8 Aug 1942
111 LI KIANG	(ex-US *PC* 1208), 15 Sep 1943
113 KUNG KIANG	(ex-US *PC* 1233), 11 Jan 1943)
114 PO KIANG	(ex-US *PC* 1254), 31 Oct 1942
115 CHUNG KIANG	(ex-US *PC* 1262), 27 Mar 1943
116 CHING KIANG	(ex-US *PC* 1168), 3 July 1943
119 TUNG KIANG	(ex-USS *Placerville*, ex-*PC* 1087)
120 HSI KIANG	(ex-USS *Susanville*, ex-*PC* 1149)
122 PEI KIANG	(ex-USS *Hanford*, ex-*PC* 1142)
123 LIU KIANG	(ex-USS *Escondido*, ex-*PC* 1169)
124 HAN KIANG	(ex-USS *Vandalia*, ex-*PC* 1175)
125 TO KIANG	(ex-USS *Milledgeville*, ex-*PC* 1263)

Displacement, tons	280 standard; 450 full load
Dimensions, feet	173·7 oa × 23 × 10·8 max
Guns	1—3 in, 50 cal; 1—40 mm AA; 5—20 mm AA
Main engines	Diesel; 2 880 bhp = 20 knots
Oil fuel, tons	60
Radius, miles	5 000 at 10 knots
Complement	65

Launch dates above, *Hanford*, *Placerville*, *Escondido* and *Vandalia* transferred from the US Navy on 15 July 1957 and *Milledgeville* in July 1959. *Chien Fang* and *Wu Sung* were discarded in 1951-52, and *Chialing* (ex-US *PC* 1247) in 1964. *Yuan Kiang* was officially deleted from the list in 1966. *Chang Kiang* (ex-US *PC* 1232) *PC* 118, was sunk by Communist China warships south of Quemoy on 6 Aug 1965.

CHUNG KIANG *United States Navy, Official*

9 Ex-US SC TYPE

SC 502 (ex-*Chu Chien*, ex-*SC* 708)
SC 503 (ex-103 *Chu Chien*, ex-*SC* 698)
Ex-**SC 518**, Ex-**SC 648**, Ex-**SC 722**, Ex-**SC 735**
Ex-**SC 637**, Ex-**SC 703**, Ex-**SC 723**

Displacement, tons	95 standard; 148 full load
Dimensions, feet	107·5 wl; 110·9 oa × 17 × 6·5
Guns	1—40 mm AA
Main engines	Diesel; 2 shafts; 800 bhp = 15·5 knots
Complement	28

COASTAL MINESWEEPERS

7 Ex-US MSC TYPE

YUNG AN,	MSC 56 (ex-USS *MSC* 140)
YUNG CHI,	MSC 160 (ex-USS *MSC* 300)
YUNG CHUAN,	MSC 58 (ex-USS *MSC* 278)
YUNG HSIN,	MSC 59 (ex-USS *MSC* 302)
YUNG LO,	MSC 161 (ex-USS *MSC* 306)
YUNG NIEN,	MSC 57 (ex-USS *MSC* 277)
YUNG PING,	MSC 55 (ex-USS *MSC* 123)

Displacement, tons	335 light; 378 full load
Dimensions, feet	138 pp; 145 oa × 27 × 8·5
Guns	2—20 mm AA
Main engines	2 GM diesels; 2 shafts; 880 bhp = 14 knots
Complement	40 (5 officers, 35 men)

"Bluebird" class non-magnetic and wooden hull construction. Built in USA. MSC 123 and MSC 140 were transferred to Taiwan on 4 June 1955. MSC 227, launched on 30 June 1958, and MSC 278, launched on 1 Aug 1958, both built by the Tacoma Boatbuilding Co, were transferred at Seattle on 10 June and 10 July respectively, in 1959. MSC 302 transferred on 5 Mar 1965, MSC 300 on 15 Apr 1965, MSC 306 on 18 May 1966. MSC 307 is being built for transfer by USA.

YUNG NIEN *1963, Official*

JAPANESE TYPE

The coastal minesweepers *Chiang*, No. 541, and *Chiang Yung*, No. 542, rormerJapanese auxiliary minesweepers No. 22 and No. 19, respectively, were discarded in 1968.

GUNBOATS

1 Ex-US PGM TYPE

117 CHU KIANG (ex-USS PGM 31, ex-*PC* 1567)

Displacement, tons	295 standard; 470 full load
Dimensions, feet	173·7 oa; 170 wl × 23 × 11 max
Guns	1—3 in; 1—40 mm AA; 4—20 mm AA
Main engines	2 GM diesels; 2 800 bhp = 20 knots
Complement	80

Built by Leatham D. Smith SB Co, Sturgeon Bay, Wis. Laid down on 18 July 1944, launched on 23 Sep 1944 and completed on 17 Jan 1945. Transferred from the US Navy in 1954. 103 *Ling Chiang* (ex-*Tung Ting*, ex-USS *PGM* 13) was torpedoed and sunk by Chinese Republican motor torpedo boats on 10 Jan 1955. 101 *Ying Chiang* (ex-*Pao Ying*, ex-USS *PGM* 20) was torpedoed by Republican motor torpedo boats on 20 Jan 1955, and was subsequently scrapped as beyond economical repair.

Sister ship *Ou Chang*, No 102 (ex-*Hung Tse*, ex-USS *PGM* 26), *Chu Chiang*, No. 106 (ex-*Ya Ling*, ex-49, ex-*Hai Hung*, SC 401), ex-Japanese type and the very old gunboat *Chu Kuan*, No. 75, Japanese built were scrapped in 1964.
The old gunboat *Yung Hsiang*, also Japanese built and the old auxiliary minelayer *Chieh 29* (ex-*Kuroshimu*), Japanese built, were previously deleted from the active list.

CHU KIANG *1962, Official*

DOCK LANDING SHIP

1 Ex-US "ASHLAND" CLASS

TUNG HAI LSD 191 (ex-USS *White Marsh*, LSD 8)

Displacement, tons	4 790 standard; 8 700 full load
Dimensions, feet	454 wl; 457·8 oa × 72 × 18
Guns	12—40 mm AA
Main engines	Skinner Unaflow; 2 shafts; 7 400 ihp = 15·6 knots
Boilers	2, of 2-drum type
Complement	326 (total accommodation)

Built by Moore Dry Dock Co. Launched on 19 July 1943. Designed to serve as parent ship for landing craft and coastal craft. Transferred from the US Navy to the Chinese (Taiwan) Navy on 17 Nov 1960 at Long Beach, California, under the Military Aid Programme.

TUNG HAI *1965, Official*

REPAIR SHIP ARL

336 SHUNG SHAN (ex-*Vulcain*, ex-USS *Agenor*, ARL 3, ex-*LST 490*)

Displacement, tons	1 625 light; 4 080 full load
Dimensions, feet	328 oa × 50 × 14·5
Guns	8—40 mm AA; 8—20 mm AA
Main engines	2 diesels; 1 700 bhp = 10·8 knots
Oil fuel, tons	1 060
Radius, miles	6 000 at 9 knots

Former US ocean tank carrier with bow doors. Built by Kaiser Co, Inc, Vancouver, Wash. Laid down on 24 Jan 1943. Launched on 3 Apr 1943. Completed on 20 Aug 1943. Transferred from the US Navy to France in 1951 for service in Indo-China. Returned to the USA by France, and then transferred to (Taiwan) China by the USA on 15 Sep 1957.

The repair ship *Soung Shan*, 335 (ex-*LST* 202, ex-USS *LST* 1030) was deleted from the list in 1969.

AMPHIBIOUS FORCE FLAGSHIPS

2 Ex-US LST TYPE

AGC 1 **KAO HSIUNG** (ex-LST *Chung Hsi*, ex-USS *LST 735 USS Dukes County*)
AGC 2 ex-LST *Chung Shi*, ex-USS *LST 1010*

Converted from LST type, *Kao Hsiung* in 1964, AGC 2 in 1968

KAO SHIUNG (ex-Chung Hai) *Official*

TANK LANDING SHIPS

21 Ex-US LST TYPE

216 CHUNG KUANG (ex-USS *LST* 503)
227 CHUNG MING (ex-USS *Sweetwater County, LST* 1152)
231 CHUNG YEA (ex-USS *Sublette County, LST* 1144)
218 CHUNG CHIH (ex-USS *Berkeley County, LST* 279)
221 CHUNG CH'UAN (ex-*Wan Yiu*, ex-*Lu Yi*, ex-*LST* 640)
224 CHUNG CHENG (ex-USS *Lafayette County, LST* 859)
206 CHUNG CHI (ex-*LST* 1017)
205 CHUNG CHIEN (ex-*LST* 716)
225 CHUNG CHIANG (ex-USS *San Bernadino County, LST* 1110)
230 CHUNG BANG (ex-USS *LST* 578)
223 CHUNG FU (ex-USS *Iron County, LST* 840)
201 CHUNG HAI (ex-*LST* 755)
204 CHUNG HSING (ex-*LST* 557
208 CHUNG SHUN (ex-*Wan Kuo*, ex-*LST* 732)
209 CHUNG LIEN (ex-*LST* 1050)
222 CHUNG SHENG (ex-*LST* 1033)
228 CHUNG SUO (ex-USS *Bradley County, LST* 400
203 CHUNG TING (ex-*LST* 537)
229 CHUNG WAN (ex-*LST* 535)
215 CHUNG YU (ex-*Wan Li*, ex-*LST* 520
210 CHUNG YUNG (ex-*LST* 574)

Displacement, tons	1 653 standard; 4 080 full load
Dimensions, feet	316 wl; 328 oa × 50 × 14 max
Guns	6—40 mm AA; 12—20 mm AA
Main engines	Diesel; 2 shafts; 1 700 bhp = 11 knots
Complement	119

LST 218, 400 and 735 transferred to Nationalist China at San Diego, in July 1955 and 1960 (*Dukes County*), LST 216 at San Diego 29 April 1955, LST 226 and LST 227 at Seattle on 21 Oct 1958, LST 520, 535 and 578 in Sep 1958, LST 213, 224 and 225 in 1958, LST 231 at Charleston, SC, on 21 Sep 1961. Ex-US LST 732 and ex-US LST 1152 are on loan to US with Chinese crews. An LST was torpedoed and sunk by Chinese Republican torpedo boats off Quemoy on 25 Aug 1958. LST 208 *Chung Shun* (ex-*LST* 993) is believed to have been lost, since a newly acquired LST has been numbered 208. Five of above (200, 202, 308, 313, 315) were acquired from the merchant service in 1955. LST 313 *Chung Kung* (ex-*Chung* ex-*LST* 945) was scrapped in 1956, LST 207 *Chung Cheng* in 1958. *Chung Hsi* ex-LST 219, ex-USS *LST* 735 and *Chung Shih*, ex-LST 236, ex-USS *LST* 1010, both converted to Amphibious Force Flagships

MEDIUM LANDING SHIPS

15 Ex-US LSM TYPE

241 MEI CHIN (ex-*LSM* 155)
245 MEI HENG (ex-*LSM* 456)
248 MEI HO (ex-*LSM* 13)
244 MEI PENG (ex-*LSM* 431)
246 MEI HUNG (ex-*LSM* 442)
247 MEI SUNG (ex-*LSM* 457)
243 MEI I (ex-*LSM* 285)
249 MEI CHIEN (ex-*LSM*) 76
250 MEI HWA (ex-*LSM*) 256
251 MEI CHEN (ex-*LSM*) 422
252 MEI KUN (ex-*LSM*) 478
253 MEI PING (ex-USS *LSM*)
254 MEI WEN (ex-*LSM* 472)
255 MEI HAN (ex-*LSM* 474)
256 MEI LO (ex-USS *LSM* 362)

Displacement, tons	743 standard; 1 095 full load
Dimensions, feet	196·5 wl; 203·5 oa × 34·5 × 7·3
Guns	2—40 mm AA; 4—20 mm AA
Main engines	Diesel; 2 shafts; 2 800 bhp = 12 knots
Complement	59 (*Mei Lo* 6 officers and 46 men)

Mei Lo 242 (ex-*LSM* 157) was destroyed by Chinese Communist artillery and beached on Quemoy Island on 8 Sep 1958. *Mei Wen*, 254, and *Mei Han*, 255, were transferred from the United States Navy at Seattle, Wn, on 6 Feb 1959. LSM 242, LSM 471 and LSM 478 were also loaned to Nationalist China by the USA in 1959. *Mei Lo* 256 (ex-*LSM* 362) was transferred at Bremeston, Wash in May 1962.

MEI KUN *1962. Official*

LANDING CRAFT

5 LSIL TYPE

264 LIEN CHENG (ex-*LCI* (*M*) 630)
265 LIEN HUA (ex-*LCI* (*G*) 631)
261 LIEN CHU (ex-*LCI* (*G*) 233)
262 LIEN LI (ex-*LCI* (*G*) 417)
263 LIEN SHENG (ex-*LCI* (*G*) 418)

Displacement, tons	227 standard; 387 full load
Dimensions, feet	159 × 23·7 × 5·7
Guns	2—20 mm AA
Main engines	Diesel; 2 shafts; 1 320 bhp = 14 knots
Complement	28

Former United States Landing Craft Infantry (Gunboat), and Landing Craft Infantry (Mortar). Armament varies. China (Taiwan) received ex-US LSIL 818, 1017, 1092 from the United States under MDAP (they were formerly on loan to France from the USA for service in Indo-China) to be used only for cannibalization.

LIEN HUA — *1963, Official*

3 LSSL TYPE

271 LIEN CHIH (ex-USS *LSSL* 56)
272 LIEN JEN (ex-USS *LSSL* 81)
273 LIEN YUNG (ex-USS *LSSL* 95)

Displacement, tons	227 standard; 387 full load
Dimensions, feet	153 wl; 158 oa × 28·7 × 5·7
Guns	6—40 mm AA (twin); 10 rocket launchers
Main engines	GM diesels; 2 shafts; 1,320 bhp = 14·4 knots
Complement	78

Ex-US LSSL's formerly LCS(L) 3, Landing Craft Support (Large) transferred at Yokosuka, Japan, on 19 Feb 1954. Taiwan received ex-US LSSL 2 and 28 from USA under MDAP (they were formerly on loan to France from USA for service in Indo-China) to be used for cannibalization.

30 LCU (Ex-LCT) TYPE

405 HO CHANG (ex-*LCT* 512)
406 HO CHEN (ex-*LCT* 1145)
403 HO CHENG (ex-*LCT* 1143)
407 HO CHIH (ex-*LCT*)
401 HO CHUN (ex-*LCT* 892)
404 HO CHUNG (ex-*LCT* 849)
402 HO CH'UNG (ex-*LCT* 1213)

Displacement, tons	143 standard; 285 full load
Dimensions, feet	114·2 × 32·7 × 3·5
Guns	2—20 mm AA
Main engines	Diesel; 3 shafts; 675 bhp = 10 knots
Complement	11

Additional craft were transferred, including 5 LCU (craft formerly on loan to France from the USA for use in Indo-China). Those listed were ex-LCU 290, 292, 638, 700, 1225, 1271, 1596, 1597, 1598, 1600 and 1601. In 1964 ex-LCU 1212, 1218, 1224, 1367, 1397, 1429 and 1452 transferred from USA under MAP.

SURVEY SHIPS

362 YANG MING (ex-45 *Yung Ting*, ex-USS *Lucid, AM* 259)

Displacement, tons	650 standard; 945 full load
Dimensions, feet	180 wl; 184·5 oa × 33 × 9·8 max
Main engines	Diesels; 2 shafts; 1 710 bhp = 14·8 knots

Former US fleet minesweeper converted into a survey ship. Launched 5 June 1943.

266 LIEN CHING

Former US LSIL type converted into a survey ship. See particulars above.

PATROL CRAFT

521 HAI LI	**546 CHIANG LIEN**	**591 P'AO 111**	**635 P'AO 5**
522 HAI NING	**547 CHIANG P'ING**	**592 P'AO 112**	**636 P'AO 6**
523 HAI YAO	**548 CHIANG FENG**	**593 P'AO 113**	**637 P'AO 7**
524 HAI WEI	**549 CHIANG KUNG**	**594 P'AO 114**	**638 P'AO 8**
525 HAI AN	**550 CHIANG LUN**	**595 P'AO 115**	**639 P'AO 9**
526 HAI CHING	**551 CHIANG CH'ENG**	**596 P'AO 116**	**640 P'AO 10**
542 CHIANG YUNG	**581 P'AO 101**	**631 P'AO 1**	**641 P'AO 11**
543 CHIANG HSIU	**584 P'AO 104**	**632 P'AO 2**	**642 P'AO 12**
544 CHIANG TING	**587 P'AO 107**	**633 P'AO 3**	**643 P'AO 13**
545 CHIANG MING	**588 P'AO 408**	**634 P'AO 4**	**646 P'AO 16**

6 Ex-HDML TYPE

681 FANG I · **682 FANG SAN** · **684 FANG SEU** · **685 FANG CHI** · **686 FANG LIU** · **687 FANG PA**

Displacement, tons	46 standard; 54 full load
Dimensions, feet	72 × 15·9 × 4·8
Guns	1—40 mm; 1—20 mm; 4 MG
Main engines	2 Diesels; 320 bhp = 11 knots

Former harbour defence motor launches. Built in Great Britain in 1942-43.

2 MTB TYPE

FU CHOU (PT 511) — **HSUEH CHIH** (PT 512)
Built by Mitsubishi Zosen Co, Japan in 1957. Armed with 18-inch torpedo tubes and 1—20 mm AA gun aft.

OILERS

307 CHANG PEI (ex-USS *Pecatonica*, AOG 57)

Displacement, tons	1 850 light; 4 335 full load
Measurement, tons	2 575 deadweight
Dimensions, feet	292 wl; 310·8 oa × 48·5 × 15·7 max
Guns	4—3 in dp 50 cal
Main engines	Diesel-electric; 2 shafts; 3 300 bhp = 14 knots

Former US petrol carrier of the "Patapsco" class. Built by Cargill, Inc, Savage, Minn. Laid down on 6 Dec 1944. Launched on 17 Mar 1945. Transferred to Taiwan China under MAP on 24 Apr 1961 at Tsoying, Taiwan. Crew 124.

306 KUAI CHI (ex-*Soviet Tuapse*)
Petrol Tanker. Captured in 1954. Commissiorred in Nationalist Navy in Feb 1956.

304 SZU MING (ex-USS *YO* 198)

Displacement, tons	1 400 full load
Dimensions, feet	174 oa × 32 × 15
Guns	1—25 mm; 2—20 mm; 2 MG
Main engines	Diesel; 560 bhp = 11 knots

Built in USA in 1945 by Manitowoc SB Co, Wis. Capacity 6 570 barrels.

302 HSIN KAO (ex-*Tai Hwa*, ex-USS *Towaliga, AOG* 42)

Displacement, tons	700 standard; 2 700 full load
Measurement, tons	1 453 deadweight
Dimensions, feet	212·5 wl; 220·5 oa × 37 × 12·8
Guns	1—3 in; 2—40 mm AA; 3—20 mm AA
Main engines	Diesel; 1 shaft; 800 bhp = 10 knots

Ex-US. TI-M-A2 type, "Mettawee" class. Launched by East Coast Shipyards on 29 Oct 1944. Sister ship *Yu Chuan*, No. 303 (ex-*Wautanga*, AOG 22, ex-*Conrol*, ex-USS *Sakatonchee, YOG* 52) and the oiler *Ho Lan*, No 305 (ex-Polish oiler *Praca*) were scrapped in 1964.
Ex-USS YO 175 was transferred under MAP in March 1967.

DISPOSAL
The oiler *Omei* was scrapped at Kaoshiung Naval Base Aug to Sept 1967.

TRANSPORTS

311 WULING (ex-*Shirasaki*)

Displacement, tons	950
Dimensions, feet	203 × 31·2 × 10·2
Guns	1—3 in; 1—40 mm AA; 8—25 mm AA; 4 MG
Main engines	2 diesels; 600 bhp = 15 knots

Former Japanese. Refrigerated cargo ship. Destroyer hull.

313 TIEN CHU · **316 TIEN TAI** · **315 CHIU HUA** · **317 CHUNG SHAN** · **HUEI FENG**

Displacements and other particulars vary in individual ships. *Tien Chu* is ex-Polish cargo ship *Prezedent Gottwald* captured by China while trading with the Communists.

TUGS

TA TUNG (ex-USS *Chickasaw, ATF* 83)

Displacement, fons,	1 235 standard; 1 675 full load
Dimensions, feet	195 wl; 205 oa × 38·5 × 15·4 max
Guns	1—3 in; 2—20 mm
Main engines	GM diesel electric; 1 shaft; 3 000 bhp = 16·5 knots

US fleet ocean tug of the "Apache" class transferred on loan in Jan 1966.

342 TA WU (ex-*Wu Kung*, ex-*Pei Chi* No. 1, ex-*LT*) **343 TA MING** (ex-*LT* 200)

Displacement, tons	570 light; 967 full load
Dimensions, feet	149 oa × 33 × 15
Guns	1—40 mm; 2—20 mm
Main engines	Reciprocating. Oil fuel. 1 200 hp = 12 knots

Built in USA in 1943. *Ta Ch'ing* reported decommissioned on 1 June 1951.

345 TA YU (ex-*LT* 310) **347 TA SHUEH** (ex-USS *Tonkowa, ATA* 176)

Displacement. tons	534 standard; 835 full load
Dimensions, feet	133·7 wl; 143 oa × 33·9 × 13·2
Guns	2—25 mm; 2 MG; (*Ta Sueh* 1—3 in)
Main engines	Diesel-electric; 1 500 hp = 12·5 knots

Ta Yu is a former US Army tug. *Ta Shueh* is a former US Navy tug of the "Marikopa" class built by Levingstone SB Co, Orange, Texas, completed on 19 Aug 1944, and transferred on 5 Apr 1962.
(There are small harbour tugs YTL 427, YTL 428, YTL 454, YTL 584 and YTL 585 transferred by USA in 1963-64).
Floating Drydock, ex-USS *Ard* 9 May be transferred under MAP.

ROYAL NETHERLANDS NAVY

Organisation

The top policy making body of the Royal Netherlands Navy is the Admiralty Board. The senior naval officer is the Chief of Naval Staff, who also holds the appointment of Commandor-in-Chief. Under him all ships, aircraft and establishments in the Netherlands are commanded by the Admiral Netherlands. Ships of the sea-going fleet form "Task Group 5", which normally consist of one or two cruisers, from 5 to 8 destroyers and frigates, 2 or 3 submarines and a number of shorebased aircraft. Other submarines, aircraft, minesweepers, etc come under their respective type-commanders.

The Netherlands Naval Air Service—comprising just under 100 aircraft—carries out both maritime patrol (Neptunes—Atlantics) and shipboard (helicopters) operations. Also available are search and rescue, communications and training aircraft.

The Netherlands Marine Corps consists of about 3 000 men.

The defence of the Netherlands Antilles (West Indies) is entirely a naval responsibility under the "Admiral Netherlands Antilles". A destroyer, some small craft, a naval air squadron and R. Neth. Marine units are normally available, and could be quickly re-inforced if needed.

Administration

Minister of Defence:
W. den Toom

Chairman Joint Chiefs of Staff:
Vice-Admiral H. M. van den Wall Bake

Secretary of State for Defence (Navy):
A. van Es

Chief of the Naval Staff and Commander-in-Chief:
Vice-Admiral J. B. M. J. Maas

Flag Officer Naval Personnel:
Vice-Admiral Jonkheer W. C. M. de Jonge van Ellemeet

Flag Officer Naval Material:
Rear-Admiral J. Doorenbos

Command

Admiral Netherlands:
Rear-Admiral A. van der Moer

Commander Netherlands Task Group 5:
Commodore O. Cramwinckel

Commandant Royal Netherlands Marine Corps:
Major-General A. M. Luyk

Admiral Netherlands Antilles:
Commodore F. Visee

Diplomatic Representation

Naval Attaché in London:
Captain F. de Blocq van Kuffeler

Naval Attaché in Washington:
Rear-Admiral E. van Rees

Ships

Warships are painted greyish blue except submarines, which are dark grey overall. Ships of the Royal Netherlands Navy are referred to by the prefix "Hr. Ms."

Strength of the Fleet

6 Submarines (Diesel Powered)
2 Cruisers (1 Guided Missile Armed)
12 Destroyers (Anti-Submarine Type)
6 Frigates (General Purpose Type)
6 Corvettes (Patrol Escort Type)
3 Escorts (ex-Ocean Minesweepers)
3 MCM ships (ex-Ocean Minesweepers)
5 Patrol Vessels (Submarine Chasers)
39 Coastal Minesweepers (Non-Magnetic)
2 Coastal Minehunters (Non-Magnetic)
5 Diving Vessels (Converted Minesweepers)
16 Inshore Minesweepers (Non-Magnetic)
44 Support Ships and Service Craft

Aircraft Carrier

The Netherlands aircraft carrier, H. Ms. *Karel Doorman* (ex-HMS *Venerable*), was officially transferred to the Argentine Navy on 15 October 1968 and renamed *25 de Mayo*.

New Construction Programme

1 nuclear powered fleet submarine, building postponed
2 diesel powered submarines, ocean-going type.
2 guided missile frigates, DDG type

Conversion Programmes

2 coastal minesweepers to minehunters (1967)
2 coastal minesweepers to minehunters (1968)

Naval Aircraft

Brequet Atlantic
Lockheed Neptune
Grumman Tracker (both US and Canadian versions)
Augusta Bell 204B
Sikorsky Seabat
Westland Wasp
Various training aircraft
("Atlantic" maritime patrol aircraft are in the New Construction Programme)

Missiles

Surface to air: US: Terrier
British: Sea-Cat
Air to surface: French: A.S.12

Personnel

1 January 1969: 20 755 officers and ratings (including the Navy Air Service, Royal Netherlands Marine Corps and about 300 officers and women of the W.R.NL.N.S.)

Navy Estimates

1960: f 390 000 000	1965: f 660 000 000
1961: f 445 000 000	1966: f 702 000 000
1962: f 564 000 000	1967: f 727 000 000
1963: f 542 000 000	1968: f 775 000 000
1964: f 627 000 000	1969: f 824 000 000

(officially revised figures)

Mercantile Marine

Lloyd's Register of Shipping:
1 721 vessels of 5 267 681 tons gross

Silhouettes

Scale: 150 feet = 1 inch

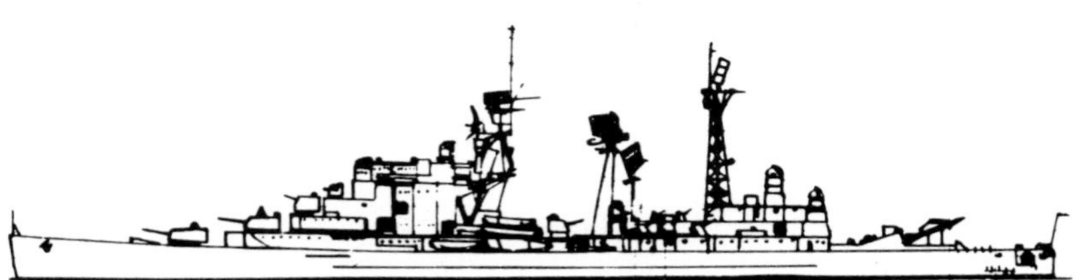

DE ZEVEN PROVINCIEN

FRIESLAND *Class*

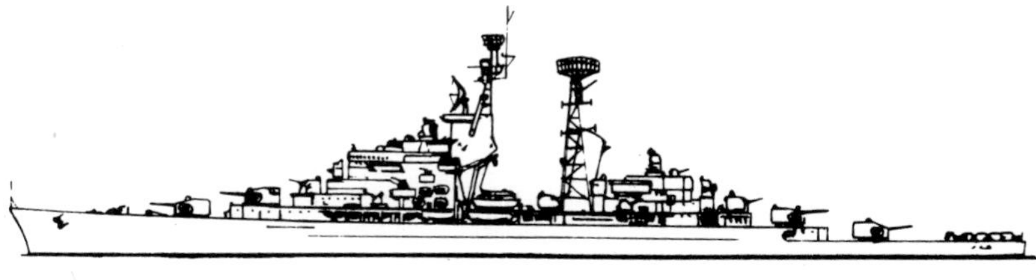

DE RUYTER

HOLLAND *Class*

VAN SPEIJK *Class*

WOLFF *Class*

SNELLIUS *Class*

LIST OF PENNANT NUMBERS

Submarines:

S 802 Walrus
S 803 Zeeleeuw
S 804 Potvis
S 805 Tonijn
S 808 Dolfijn
S 809 Zeehond

Cruisers:

C 801 De Ruyter
C 802 De Zeven Provinciën

Destroyers:

D 808 Holland
D 809 Zeeland
D 810 Noord Brabant
D 811 Gelderland
D 812 Friesland
D 813 Groningen
D 814 Limburg
D 815 Overijssel
D 816 Drenthe
D 817 Utrecht
D 818 Rotterdam
D 819 Amsterdam

Frigates:

F 802 Van Speijk
F 803 Van Galen
F 804 Tjerk Hiddes
F 805 Van Nes
F 814 Isaac Sweers
F 815 Evertsen
F 817 Wolf
F 818 Fret
F 819 Hermelijn
F 820 Vos
F 821 Panter
F 822 Jaguar

Patrol Vessels:

P 802 Balder
P 803 Bulgia
P 804 Freijer
P 805 Hadda
P 806 Hefring

Mine Warfare Ships:

M 801 Dokkum
M 802 Hoogezand
M 803 Wildervank
M 804 Steenwijk
M 805 Gieten
M 806 Roermond
M 807 Waalwijk
M 808 Axel
M 809 Naaldwijk
M 810 Abcoude
M 811 Aalsmeer
M 812 Drachten
M 813 Ommen
M 814 Meppel
M 815 Giethoorn
M 816 Lochem
M 817 Venlo
M 818 Drunen
M 819 Goes
M 820 Woerden
M 822 Leersum
M 823 Naarden
M 824 Sneek
M 826 Grijpskerk
M 827 Hoogeveen
M 828 Staphorst
M 829 Elst
M 830 Sittard
M 841 Gemert
M 842 Veere
M 843 Lisse
M 844 Rhenen
M 845 Beemster
M 846 Bolsward
M 847 Bedum
M 848 Beilen
M 849 Borculo
M 850 Borne
M 851 Brummen
M 852 Breukelen
M 853 Blaricum
M 854 Brielle
M 855 Breskens
M 856 Bruinisse
M 857 Boxtel
M 858 Brouwershaven
M 868 Alblas
M 869 Bussemaker
M 870 Lacomblé
M 871 Van Hamel
M 872 Van Straelen
M 873 Van Moppes
M 874 Chömpff
M 875 Van Well Groeneveld
M 876 Schuiling
M 877 Van Versendaal
M 878 Van Der Wel
M 879 Van 't Hoff
M880 Mahu
M 881 Staverman
M 882 Houtepen
M 883 Zomer

Auxiliary Ships:

A 829 Mercuur
A 830 Pelikaan
A 832 Woendi
A 835 Poolster
A 847 Argus
A 848 Triton
A 849 Nautilus
A 850 Hydra
A 854 Onversaagd
A 855 Onbevreesd
A 856 Onverschrokken
A 857 Onvermoeid
A 858 Onvervaard
A 859 Onverdroten
A 870 Wamandai
A 871 Wambrau
A 872 Westgat
A 873 Wielingen
A 895 Cerberus
A 902 Luymes
A 903 Zeefakkel
A 907 Snellius
A 909 Dreg 1
A 910 Dreg 2
A 911 Dreg 3
A 912 Dreg 4

Nos. 879 to 892 are allocated to stationary accommodation hulks.

GUIDED MISSILE FRIGATE DVG TYPE, under construction *1969, Courtesy N.V. Hollandse Signaalapparaten*

SUBMARINES *(Onderzeeboten)*

Name	*No.*	*Builders*	*Laid down*	*Launched*	*Completed*
POTVIS	S 804	Wilton-Fijenoord, Schiedam	17 Sep 1962	12 Jan 1965	2 Nov 1965
TONIJN	S 805	Wilton-Fijenoord, Schiedam	27 Nov 1962	14 June 1965	24 Feb 1966
DOLFIJN	S 808	Rotterdamse Droogdok Mij, Rotterdam	30 Dec 1954	20 May 1959	16 Dec 1960
ZEEHOND	S 809	Rotterdamse Droogdok Mij, Rotterdam	30 Dec 1954	20 Feb 1960	16 Mar 1961

2 "POTVIS" CLASS
2 "DOLFIJN" CLASS

Displacement, tons	1 140 standard; 1 494 surface: 1 826 submerged
Length, feet *(metres)*	260·9 *(79·5)*
Beam, feet *(metres)*	25·8 *(7·8)*
Draught, feet *(metres)*	15·8 *(4·8)*
Torpedo tubes	8—21 in *(533 mm)*
Main engines	2 MAN diesels, total 3 100 bhp Electric motors, 4 200 hp; 2 shafts
Speed, knots	14·5 on surface; 17 submerged
Complement	64

These submarines are of a triple-hulled design. Maximum depth 980 feet *(300 metres)*. *Potvis* and *Tonijn*, originally voted for in 1949 with the other pair, but suspended for some years, have several modifications compared with *Dolfijn* and *Zeehond* and are officially considered to be a separate class.

CONSTRUCTION. The hull consists of three cylinders arranged in a triangular shape. The upper cylinder accommodates the crew, navigational equipment and armament. The lower two cylinders house the propulsion machinery comprising diesel engines, batteries and electric motors. See Frontispiece of the 1959-1960 edition for scale models—cutaway longitudinal section showing double decker roominess, and cross section showing triple hull permitting greater diving depth.

PROJECTED NUCLEAR POWERED TYPE. In the "defence note" issued in June 1964 the construction of nuclear powered submarines was announced. In the defence note 1968 it was still considered that the nuclear vessel is the submarine of the future, but when one can be obtained is uncertain in view of presently available defence funds and required overall investments, and nuclear submarines are not considered within the present short term plans (official).

POTVIS 1968, *Skyfotos*

DOLFIJN *1969, Royal Netherlands Navy, Official*

ZEEHOND *1967, Royal Netherlands Navy Official*

TONIJN *1969, Royal Netherlands Navy, Official*

2 NEW CONSTRUCTION

TIJGERHAAI ZWAARDVIS

Displacement, tons	1 800 surface; 2 300 submerged
Length, feet *(metres)*	216·5 *(66·0)*
Beam, feet *(metres)*	27·5 *(8·4)*
Draught, feet *(metres)*	23·3 *(7·1)*
Torpedo tubes	6—21 in *(533 mm)*
Main engines	Diesel-electric; 1 shaft
Speed, knots	15 on surface; 25 submerged
Complement	68

In the 1964 Navy Estimates a first instalment was approved for the construction of two conventionally powered submarines. Ordered from Rotterdam DD Co on 24 Dec 1965 and laid down on 14 July 1966.

Name	*No.*	*Builders*	*Laid down*	*Launched*	*Completed*	*Converted*	*Transferred*
WALRUS (ex-*Icefish*)	S 802	Manitowoc SB Co, Wisconsin	1943	20 Feb 1944	10 June 1944	1952	21 Feb 1953
ZEELEEUW (ex-*Hawkbill*)	S 803	Manitowoc SB Co, Wisconsin	1943	9 Jan 1944	17 May 1944	1952	21 Apr 1953

2 "WALRUS" CLASS

Displacement, tons	1 420 standard; 1 525 surface; 2 425 submerged
Length, feet *(metres)*	309 *(94·2)* oa
Beam, feet *(metres)*	27 *(8·2)*
Draught, feet *(metres)*	17 *(5·2)*
Torpedo tubes	10—21 in *(533 mm)*, 6 bow and 4 stern
Main engines	4 GM 2-stroke diesels, total 6 500 bhp; Electric motors, 2 700 hp
Speed, knots	20 on surface; 10 submerged
Radius, miles	12 000 at 10 knots
Oil fuel (tons)	300
Complement	79

Former "Balao" Class submarines, acquired on loan from the US Navy (for a period of five years, subsequently extended by regular periods) after having been converted and streamlined with enclosed conning tower "fin". 24 torpedoes can be carried.

DISPOSALS OF "T" CLASS. Of the two submarines of the former British "T" class, *Zwaardvis* (ex-HMS *Talent*) was withdrawn from service on 15 Jan 1963 and scrapped in July 1963 and *Tijgerhaai* (ex-HMS *Tarn*) was deleted from the list in 1966.

DISPOSALS OF "O" CLASS. O 27 was stricken from the list in Dec 1959 and sold. O 24, removed from the list in 1956 and used for instruction until discarded in 1962, was sold for scrap in June 1963 and broken up at Flushing. O 21 was sold for scrap on 24 Jan 1958.

WALRUS *1969, Royal Netherlands Navy, Official*

ZEELEEUW *1969, Royal Netherlands Navy, Official*

CRUISERS *(Kruisers)*

Name	*No.*	*Builders*	*Laid down*	*Launched*	*Completed*
DE RUYTER (ex-*Zeven Provincien*)	C 801	Wilton-Fijenoord, Schiedam	5 Sep 1939	24 Dec 1944	18 Nov 1953
DE ZEVEN PROVINCIEN (ex-*De Ruyter*, ex-*Eendracht*, ex-*Kijkduin*)	C 802	Rotterdam Drydock Co	19 May 1939	22 Aug 1950	17 Dec 1953

Displacement, tons	9 529 standard; 11 850 full load (*C 802:* 9 850 std; 12 250 load)
Length, feet (*metres*)	590·5 (*180·0*) pp; *C801:* 614·5 (*190·3*) oa; *C802:* 609 (*188·7*) oa
Beam, feet (*metres*)	56·7 (*17·3*)
Draught, feet (*metres*)	22 (*6·7*) max
Missiles, AA	*De Zeven Provincien* (*C802*) *only:* 1 twin "Terrier" launcher aft
Guns, surface	*C801:* 8—6 in (*152 mm*) in twin turrets; *C802:* 4—6 in (*152 mm*) in twin turrets
Guns, AA	*C801:* 8—57 mm in twin turrets; 8—40 mm; *C802:* 6—57 mm in twin turrets; 4—40 mm
Boilers	4 Werkspoor-Yarrow
Main engines	2 De Schelde-Parsons geared turbines; 85 000 shp; 2 shafts
Speed, knots	32
Complement	*De Ruyter:* 926 *De Zeven Provincien:* 940

Machinery by K. M. de Schelde. Construction resumed in 1946. Both hulls were nameless in 1945 and since the name *De Ruyter* was wanted back in the Navy as soon as possible that name was given to the hull already launched and therefore the most advanced. Tripod mast, originally abaft after funnel, is now before after funnel.

GUIDED MISSILE CONVERSION. *De Zeven Provincien* was converted in 1962-64 by Rotterdamsche Droogdok Mij. Rotterdam. wtih"Terrier" installation by NV Dok en Werf Mij Wilton-Fijenoord, Schiedam. *De Ruyter* will not be converted. She will be replaced in 1975 by two frigates (DDG) whose construction will commence in 1969.

GUNNERY. Main armament has 60 degrees elevation. All guns are fully automatic and radar controlled. The 6 inch guns have a rate of fire of 15 rounds per minute.

DRAWING. Represents *De Zeven Provincien*. Port elevation and plan. *De Ruyter* has curved bow which accounts for the variation in overall length. Scale 128 feet = 1 inch. A port elevation and plan drawing of *De Ruyter* appears in the 1953-54 to 1965-66 editions.

TRANSFER OF AIRCRAFT CARRIER. H.NL.M.S. *Karel Doorman* was sold to Argentina in Oct 1968 and renamed *Veinticinco de Mayo*.

DE ZEVEN PROVINCIEN *1968, Royal Netherlands Navy, Official*

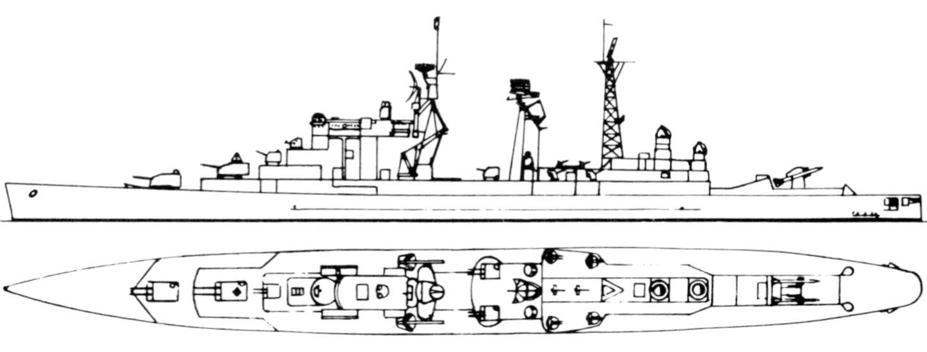

DE RUYTER *1969, Stefan Terzibaschitsch*

DE ZEVEN PROVINCIEN converted with guide missile launcher aft *1967, Royal Netherlands Navy, Official*

GUIDED MISSILE FRIGATES

2 NEW CONSTRUCTION DDG TYPE

Displacement, tons: 4 300 standard; 5 400 full load
Dimensions, feet: 453·1 oa; 429·5 pp × 48·5 × 15
Guns: 2—4·7 in (twin turret)
Guided weapons: 1 Tartar Launcher aft; Point defence missile system
Aircraft: 1 light weight helicopter armed with homing torpedoes
Main engines: Main gas turbines (2×20 000 hp) Cruising gas turbines (2 × 4 000 hp)
Complement: 310

First design allowance was voted for in 1967 estimates. Ships will be ordered in 1969 to replace *"De Ruyter"* in 1975. Hangar and helicopter spot landing platform aft. See artist's impression of the ship operating at sea on the second page of the Netherlands section.

FRIGATES (*Fregatten*)

Name	*No.*	*Builders*	*Laid down*	*Launched*	*Completed*
TJERK HIDDES	F 804	Nederlandse Dok en Scheepsbouw Mij, Amsterdam	1 June 1964	17 Dec 1965	16 Aug 1967
VAN GALEN	F 803	Koninklijke Maatschappij De Schelde, Flushing	25 July 1963	19 June 1965	1 Mar 1967
VAN NES	F 805	Koninklijke Maatschappij De Schelde, Flushing	25 July 1963	26 Mar 1966	9 Aug 1967
VAN SPEIJK	F 802	Nederlandse Dok en Scheepsbouw Mij, Amsterdam	1 Oct 1963	5 Mar 1965	14 Feb 1967
EVERTSEN	F 815	Koninklijke Maatschappij De Schelde, Flushing	6 July 1965	18 June 1966	21 Dec 1967
ISAAC SWEERS	F 814	Nederlandse Dok en Scheepsbouw Mij, Amsterdam	5 May 1965	10 Mar 1967	15 May 1968

6 "Van Speijk" Class

Displacement, tons: 2 200 standard; 2 850 full load
Dimensions, feet: 360 wl, 372 oa × 41 × 18
Guns: 2—4·5 in (twin turret)
Guided weapons: 2 quadruple launchers for "Seacat"
A/S: 1 three-barrelled depth charge mortar
Aircraft: 1 lightweight helicopter armed with homing torpedoes
Boilers: 2 Babcock & Wilcox
Main engines: 2 double reduction geared turbines; 2 shafts; 30 000 shp = 28·5 knots
Complement: 254

Built as replacements for the six frigates of the "Van Amstel" class which were returned to the US and subsequently scrapped. Basically similar to the British "Leander" class. Four ships were ordered in Oct 1962 and the other two later.

EQUIPMENT. To avoid delay these ships were fitted with equipment available at short notice and instead of that still in the development stage.

CONSTRUCTION. As far as possible equipment of Netherlands manufacture was installed, and this resulted in a number of changes in the ships' superstructure.

DESIGN. Although in general they are based on the design of the British Improved Type 12, they have small modifications in accordance with the requirements of the Royal Netherlands Navy.

PHOTOGRAPHS. Starboard broadside surface views of *Van Speijk* appear in the 1967-68 and 1968-69 editions, and a photograph of *Tjerk Hiddes* appears in the 1968-69 edition.

DISPOSALS OF DE TYPE
The six frigates or destroyer escorts of the "Van Amstel" class, **De Bitter** (ex-USS *Rinehart, DE 196*) F 807, **De Zeeuw** (ex-USS *Eisner, DE 192*) F810, **Dubois** (ex-USS *O'Neill, DE 188*) F 809, **Van Amstel** (ex-USS *Burrows, DE 195*) F 806, **Van Ewijck** (ex-USS *Gustafson, DE 182*) F 808, and **Van Zijll** (ex-USS *Stern, DE 187*) F 811, were returned to the US Navy and sold for scrap in Dec 1967.

VAN NES — *1969, Royal Netherlands Navy, Official*

VAN GALEN — *1969, Royal Netherlands Navy, Official*

EVERTSEN — *1968, Wright & Logan*

VAN SPEIJK — *1969, Royal Netherlands Navy, Official*

ANTI-SUBMARINE DESTROYERS DDE (*Onderzeebootjagers*)

Name	*No.*	*Builders*	*Laid down*	*Launched*	*Completed*
FRIESLAND	D 812	Nederlandse Dok en Scheepsbouw Mij, Amsterdam	17 Dec 1951	21 Feb 1953	22 Mar 1956
GRONINGEN	D 813	Nederlandse Dok en Scheepsbouw Mij, Amsterdam	21 Feb 1952	9 Jan 1954	12 Sep 1956
LIMBURG	D 814	Koninklijke Maatschappij De Schelde, Flushing	28 Nov 1953	5 Sep 1955	31 Oct 1956
OVERIJSSEL	D 815	Dok-en-Werfmaatschappij Wilton-Fijenoord	15 Oct 1953	8 Aug 1955	4 Oct 1957
DRENTHE	D 816	Nederlandse Dok en Scheepsbouw Mij, Amsterdam	9 Jan 1954	26 Mar 1955	1 Aug 1957
UTRECHT	D 817	Koninklijke Maatschappij De Schelde, Flushing	15 Feb 1954	2 June 1956	1 Oct 1957
ROTTERDAM	D 818	Rotterdamse Droogdok Mij, Rotterdam	7 Jan 1954	26 Jan 1956	28 Feb 1957
AMSTERDAM	D 819	Nederlandse Dok en Scheepsbouw Mij, Amsterdam	26 Mar 1955	25 Aug 1956	10 Aug 1958

8 "FRIESLAND" CLASS

Displacement, tons	2 497 standard ; 3 070 full load
Length, feet (*metres*)	370 (*112·8*) pp ; 380·5 (*116·0*) oa
Beam, feet (*metres*)	38·5 (*11·7*)
Draught, feet (*metres*)	17 (*5·2*)
Guns, surface	4—4·7 in (120 *mm*) twin turrets
Guns, AA	4—40 mm (2 removed during recent refits)
A/S	2 four-barrelled depth charge mortars
Boilers	4
Main engines	2 Werkspoor geared turbine, 60 000 shp ; 2 shafts
Speed, knots	36
Complement	284

These ships have some side armour as well as deck protection, like light cruisers. They have "Limbo" type anti-submarine rocket throwers. Twin rudders. Propellers 370 rpm. Named after provinces of the Netherlands, and the two principal cities.

GUNNERY. The 4·7 inch guns are fully automatic with a rate of fire of 50 rounds per minute. All guns are radar controlled. Originally six 40 mm guns were mounted.

TORPEDO TUBES. *Utrecht* was equipped with eight 21 inch A/S torpedo tubes (single, four on each side) in 1960 and *Overijssel* in 1961, and the others were to have been, but the project was dropped and tubes already fitted were removed.

PHOTOGRAPHS. A photograph of *Friesland* appears in the 1956-57 to 1958-59 editions, of *Overijssel* in the 1958-59 to 1963-64 editions, of *Rotterdam* in the 1964-65 to 1966-67 editions, of *Utrecht* in the 1967-68 and 1968-69 editions.

AMSTERDAM — *1969, Royal Netherlands Navy, Official*

FRIESLAND — *1967, courtesy Godfrey H. Walker, Esq*

OVERIJSSEL — *1969, Wright & Logan*

DRENTHE — *1968, Royal Netherlands Navy, Official*

ANTI-SUBMARINE DESTROYERS —*continued*

Name	*No.*	*Builders*	*Laid down*	*Launched*	*Completed*
HOLLAND	D 808	Rotterdamse Droogdok Mij, Rotterdam	21 Apr 1950	11 Apr 1953	31 Dec 1954
ZEELAND	D 809	Koninklijke Maatschappji De Schelde, Flushing	12 Jan 1951	27 June 1953	1 Mar 1955
NOORD BRABANT	D 810	Koninklijke Maatschappji De Schelde, Flushing	1 Mar 1951	28 Nov 1953	1 June 1955
GELDERLAND	D 811	Dok-en-Werfmaatschappij Wilton-Fijenoord	10 Mar 1951	19 Sep 1953	17 Aug 1955

4 "Holland" Class

Displacement, tons	2 215 standard; 2 765 full load
Length, feet (*metres*)	360·5 (*109·9*) pp; 371 (*113·1*) oa
Beam, feet (*metres*)	37·5 (*11·4*)
Draught, feet (*metres*)	16·8 (*5·1*)
Guns, surface	4—4·7 in (*120 mm*) twin turrets
Guns, AA	1—40 mm
A/S	2 four-barrelled depth charge mortars
Boilers	4
Main engines	Werkspoor Parsons geared turbine, 4 500 shp; 2 shafts
Speed, knots	32
Complement	247

Equipped with the engine installations of destroyers which were to have been built by the Germans in Holland. These engines were completed although the hulls were never built. (*Tjerk Hiddes*, completed by Germany as ZH 1, and *Isaac Sweers*, completed in Britain; of the "Callenburgh" class of four ships were actually commissioned with their original engines in 1941. The Germans ordered more engines of identical design for ships which they wanted to build in Netherlands yards but which were never laid down. At the end of the war four complete installations, now in the "Holland" class, were found).

TUBES. Unlike most orthodox destroyers these never had tubes.

GUNNERY. The 4·7 inch guns are fully automatic with a rate of fire of 50 rounds per minute. All guns are radar controlled.

PHOTOGRAPHS. A photograph of *Noord Brabant* appears in the 1957-58 edition and of *Zeeland* in the 1958-59 to 1960-61 editions.

NOORD BRABANT *1969, Royal Netherlands Navy, Official*

ZEELAND *1969, courtesy Sub-Lieutenant K. M. Napier, R.N.*

GELDERLAND *1968, courtesy Godfrey H. Walker, Esq*

CORVETTES

Name	*No.*	*Builders*	*Laid down*	*Launched*	*Completed*
FRET (ex-*PCE* 1604)	F 818	General Shipbuilding and Engineering Works, Boston	18 Dec 1952	30 July 1953	4 May 1954
HERMELIJN (ex-*PCE* 1605)	F 819	General Shipbuilding and Engineering Works, Boston	2 Mar 1953	6 Mar 1954	5 Aug 1954
JAGUAR (ex-*PCE* 1609)	F 822	Avondale Marine Ways, Inc, New Orleans, Louisiana	10 Dec 1952	20 Mar 1954	11 June 1954
PANTER (ex-*PCE* 1608)	F 821	Avondale Marine Ways, Inc, New Orleans, Louisiana	1 Dec 1952	30 Jan 1954	11 June 1954
VOS (ex-*PCE* 1606)	F 820	General Shipbuilding and Engineering Works, Boston	3 Aug 1952	1 May 1954	2 Dec 1954
WOLF (ex-*PCE* 1607)	F 817	Avondale Marine Ways, Inc, New Orleans, Louisiana	15 Nov 1952	2 Jan 1954	26 Mar 1954

6 "Wolf" Class

Displacement, tons	808 standard; 975 full load
Length, feet (*metres*)	180 (*54·9*) pp; 184·5 (*56·2*) oa
Beam, feet (*metres*)	33 (*10·0*)
Draught, feet (*metres*)	9·5 (*2·9*) mean; 14·5 (*4·4*) max
Guns, dual purpose	1—3 in (*76 mm*)
Guns, AA	6—40 mm (*Jaguar, Panter:* 4—40 mm); 8—20 mm
A/S	1 Hedgehog; 2 DCT (*Jaguar, Panter:* 4); 2 DC racks
Main engines	2 GM diesels; 1 600 bhp; 2 shafts
Speed, knots	15
Complement	96

Corvettes (PCE type escorts) built in the United States under the Mutual Defence Assistance Programme.

PHOTOGRAPHS. A photograph of *Fret* appears in the 1957-58 to 1960-61 editions, of *Jaguar* in the 1961-62 to 1967-68 editions, and of *Panther* in the 1962-63 to 1967-68 editions.

TRANSFER
Lynx (ex-*PCE* 1626) was handed over to the Italian Navy on 18 Oct 1961 under MDAP and renamed *Aquila*.

WOLF *1968, Royal Netherlands Navy, Official*

MCM SUPPORT SHIPS (*Onderstenningsschepen*) and ESCORTS (*Escortevaartuigen*)

6 US AM TYPE

Name	*No.*	*Laid down*	*Completed*
ONVERSAAGD (ex-AM 480)	A 854 (ex-M 884)	1952	27 May 1954
ONBEVREESD (ex-AM 481)	A 855 (ex-M 885)	1952	21 Sep 1954
ONVERSCHROKKEN (ex-AM 483)	A 856 (ex-M 886)	1952	22 July 1954
ONVERMOEID (ex-AM 484)	A 857 (ex-M 887)	1952	23 Sep 1954
ONVERVAARD (ex-AM 482)	A 858 (ex-M 888)	1952	31 Mar 1955
ONVERDROTEN (ex-AM 485)	A 859 (ex-M 889)	1952	22 Nov 1954

Displacement, tons	735 standard; 790 full load
Dimensions, feet	165 pp; 172 oa × 36 × 10 max
Guns	1—40 mm AA
A/S	2 DC
Main engines	Diesel; 1 600 bhp = 15·5 knots
Oil fuel, tons	46
Radius, miles	2 400 at 12 knots
Complement	67

Built in USA for the Netherlands under MDAP. *Onversaagd*, *Onbevreesd* and *Onvervaard* were built by Astoria Marine Construction Co and the remaining three by Peterson, Builders, Wisconsin. Of wooden and non-magnetic construction.

RECLASSIFICATION. Originally designed as Ocean Minesweepers (*Oceanmijnenvegers*) but used as Escorts and re-numbered with "A" pennants in 1966. Reclassified in 1968 as Escorts (*Escorte vartuigen*) for *Onversaagd*, *Onbevreesd* and *Onverschrokken*, and MCM Group HQ and Support Ships (*Hoofdkwartier-ondersteuningsachepen voor M. B. Gropen*) other three.

PHOTOGRAPHS. Photographs of *Onverdroten* appear in the 1957-58 to 1965-66 editions. Starboard bow oblique aerial view of *Onvervaard* in the 1966-67 to 1968-69 editions.

ONVERVAARD *1969, Royal, Netherlands Navy, Official*

PATROL VESSELS (*Patrouillevaartuigen*)

5 US SC TYPE SUBMARINE CHASERS

Name	*No.*	*Laid down*	*Launched*	*Completed*
BALDER	P 802	12 Sep 1953	24 Feb 1954	6 Aug 1954
BULGIA	P 803	10 Oct 1953	24 Apr 1954	9 Aug 1954
FREYR	P 804	24 Feb 1954	21 July 1954	1 Dec 1954
HADDA	P 805	24 Apr 1954	2 Oct 1954	3 Feb 1955
HEFRING	P 806	21 July 1954	1 Dec 1954	23 Mar 1955

Displacement, tons	149 standard; 225 full load
Dimensions, feet	114·9 pp; 119·1 oa × 20·2 × 5·9
Guns	1—40 mm; 3—20 mm
A/S	2 DCT, Mousetrap
Main engines	Diesels; 2 shafts; 1 050 shp = 15·5 knots
Radius, miles	1 000
Complement	27

Built in the Netherlands by Rijkswerf Willemsoord with USA funds under MDAP as an off-shore procurement. US SC Nos 1627-1631.

PHOTOGRAPHS. A photograph of *Hadda* appears in the 1960-61 edition, and of *Balder* in the 1955-56 to 1959-60 and 1961-62 to 1965-66 editions.

FREYR *1966, Royal Netherlands Navy, Official*

COASTAL MINESWEEPERS (*Kustmijnenvegers*) and MINE HUNTERS (*Mijnenjagers*)

18 "DOKKUM" CLASS

ABCOUDE	M 810	**HOOGEZAND**	M 802	**ROERMOND**	M 806
DOKKUM	M 801	**HOOGEVEEN**	M 827	**SITTARD**	M 830
DRACHTEN	M 812	**NAALDWIJK**	M 809	**STAPHORST**	M 828
DRUNEN	M 818	**NAARDEN**	M 823	**VEERE**	M 842
GEMERT	M 841	**OMMEN**	M 813	**VENLO**	M 817
GIETHOORN	M 815	**RHENEN***	M 844	**WOERDEN***	M 820

14 "WILDERVANK" CLASS

AALSMEER	M 811	**GOES**	M 819	**MEPPEL**	M 814
AXEL	M 808	**GRIJPSKERK**	M 826	**SNEEK**	M 824
ELST	M 829	**LEERSUM***	M 822	**STEENWIJK**	M 804
GIETEN	M 805	**LISSE***	M 843	**WAALWIJK***	M 807
		LOCHEM	M 816	**WILDERVANK**	M 803

Displacement, tons	373 standard; 417 full load
Dimensions, feet	149·8 oa × 28 × 6·5
Guns	2—40 mm
Main engines	2 diesels; Fyenoord MAN or Werkspoor; 2 500 bhp = 16 knots
Complement	38

Of 32 Western Union type non-magnetic coastal minesweepers built in the Netherlands, 18 were offshore procurement (on US account under MDAP) known as the "Dokkum" class, with MAN engines, and 14 were built on Netherlands account, known as the "Wildervank" class, with Werkspoor engines. All launched in 1954-56 and completed in 1955-56. Named after small towns in the Netherlands. *Dokkum* and *Drunen* converted to minehunters in 1968-69. Two more conversions in 1969 programme. Total of nine to be converted. **Leersum, Lisse, Rhenen, Waalwijk* and *Woerden* were re-rated as MCM diving vessels in 1962-65, and *Roermond* was converted in 1968 to replace *Lisse*. The minesweepers of the "Wildervank" class are in low grade reserve and on the sales list. A photograph of *Dokkum* appears in the 1956-57 to 1961-62 editions, of *Venlo* in the 1961-62 to 1965-66 editions, of *Aalsmeer* in the 1962-63 to 1966-67 editions, of *Meppel* in the 1966-67 to 1968-69 editions, of *Naaldwijk* in the 1967-68 and 1968-69 editions.

HOOGESAND ("Wildervank" Class) *1969, Wright & Logan*

SNEEK ("Dokkum" Class) *1969, Royal Netherlands Navy, Official*

14 "BEEMSTER" CLASS

BEEMSTER (ex-*AMS* 105)	M 845	**BREUKELEN** (ex-*AMS* 100)	M 852
BOLSWARD (ex-*AMS* 109)	M 846	**BLARICUM** (ex-*AMS* 112)	M 853
BEDUM (ex-*Beerta* ex-*AMS* 106)	M 847	**BRIELLE** (ex-*AMS* 167)	M 854
BEILEN (ex-*AMS* 110)	M 848	**BRESKENS** (ex-*AMS* 148)	M 855
BORCULO (ex-*AMS* 107)	M 849	**BRUINISSE** (ex-*AMS* 168)	M 856
BORNE (ex-*AMS* 108)	M 850	**BOXTEL** (ex-*AMS* 149)	M 857
BRUMMEN (ex-*AMS* 111)	M 851	**BROUWERSHAVEN** ex-*AMS* 150)	M 858

Displacement, tons	330 standard; 384 full load
Dimensions, feet	138 pp; 144·7 oa × 27·9 × 7·5
Guns	2—20 mm AA
Main engines	2 diesels; 880 bhp = 13·6 knots
Complement	37

MSC (ex-*AMS*) type. Of non-magnetic construction. All completed and transferred from USA in 1953-54. Named after small towns in the Netherlands. A photograph of *Beemster* appears in the 1955-56 to 1960-61 editions, of *Brouwershaven* in the 1961-62 to 1965-66 editions, of *Brummen* in the 1966-67 and 1967-68 editions.

BORCULO *1968, Royal Netherlands Navy, Official*

INSHORE MINESWEEPERS

(*Ondiepwater mijnenvegers*)

16 "VAN STRAELEN" CLASS

ALBLAS	M 868	**MAHU**	M 880	**VAN MOPPES**	M 873
BUSSEMAKER	M 869	**SCHUILING**	M 876	**VAN STRAELEN**	M 872
CHÖMPFF	M 874	**STAVERMAN**	M 881	**VAN VERSENDAAL**	M 877
HOUTEPEN	M 882	**VAN DER WEL**	M 878	**VAN WELL GROENEVALD**	M 875
LACOMBLÉ	M 870	**VAN HAMEL**	M 871		
		VAN 'T HOFF	M 879	**ZOMER**	M 883

Displacement, tons	151 light; 169 full load
Dimensions, feet	90 pp; 99·3 oa × 18·2 × 5·2
Guns	1—20 mm AA
Main engines	Werkspoor diesels; 2 shafts; 1 100 bhp = 13 knots
Complement	12

USA and Netherlands signed an agreement for the construction of 16 inshore minesweepers for the Royal Netherlands Navy at a cost of $16 900 000, 6 by Werf de Noord at Albasserdam; 5 by N.V. de Arnhemse Scheepsbouw Maatschappij at Arnhem; and 5 by Amsterdamsche Scheepswerf G. de Vries Lentsch Jr at Amsterdam. Eight were built under the offshore procurement programme, with MDAP funds, and the remaining eight were paid for by Netherlands. All ordered in mid-1957. Built of non-magnetic materials. *Alblas*, the first, was laid down at Werf de Noord N.V. at Albasserdam on 26 Feb 1958, launched on 29 June 1959, started trials on 15 Jan 1960 and completed on 12 Mar 1960. All the others were laid down in 1958-61, launched in 1958-61 and commissioned in 1960-62. The first nine ships built are named after naval personnel decorated with the Military Willems Order" (the equivalent of the British V.C.) during the Second World War. The remaining seven are named after naval personnel who also distinguished themselves during this war and were also decorated posthumously. A photograph of *Alblas* appears in the 1960-61 edition, of *Bussemaker* in the 1961-62 to 1965-66 editions, of *Van Straelen* in the 1966-67 to 1968-69 editions.

VAN HAMEL *1969, Royal Netherlands Navy, Official*

ACCOMMODATION SHIPS (*Logementschepen*)

A 880 *Willem van der Zaan*, former minesweeper support ship, former frigate, former minelayer. A 879 *Jacob van Heemskerck*, former light cruiser, A 891 *Soemba*, former radar training ship, A 881 *Neptunus*, A 882 *Schorpioen*, A 884 *Buffel*, A 886 *Cornolis Drebbel*, A 887 *Haarlemmermeer* and A 888 *Hertog Hendrik* (old ships). The hulls of A 877 (ex-*Flores*), former gunboat, and A 878 *Tromp*, former light cruiser, were scrapped in 1968. Further hulls are being scrapped in 1969.

SUPPLY SHIPS (*Voorraadschepen*)

1 Ex-US LST TYPE

WOENDI (ex-*Steven van der Hagen*, ex-*LST V*, ex-*LST* 1034) A 832

Displacement, tons	1,625 light; 3,770 standard; 4 145 full load
Dimensions, feet	316 wl; 328 oa × 50 × 14 max
Guns	4—40 mm AA; 6—20 mm AA
Main engines	Diesel; 2 shafts; 1 800 bhp = 11 knots
Complement	105

Built at Boston, Mass, in 1944. Seagoing store ship at Den Helder.

Zuiderkrius (ex-*Granston Victory*) A 853 was paid off and sold in 1968 on completion of the first part of the new naval barracks at Den Helder.

1 Ex-BRITISH LST TYPE

PELIKAAN (ex-HMS *Thruster*, ex-*LST*) A 830

Displacement, tons	2 840 light; 4 250 standard; 6 538 full load
Dimensions, feet	390 × 49 × 13
Guns	2—40 mm AA; 10—20 mm AA
Main engines	Turbine; 7 000 shp = 17 knots
Oil fuel, tons	2 100 max
Complement	127

Built by Harland & Wolff Ltd, Belfast. Laid down on 31 July 1941. Launched on 24 Sep 1942. Completed on 14 Mar 1943. Purchased and taken over from Great Britain in 1947. Commissioned in the Royal Netherlands Navy in July 1948. Used as a store and accommodation ship at Den Helder. Photograph in the 1957-58 edition.

PELIKAAN *1969, Royal Netherlands Navy, Official*

SURVEY SHIPS (*Opnemingsvaartuigen*)

2 SLOOP TYPE

Name	*No.*	*Builders*	*Laid down*	*Launched*	*Completed*
LUYMES	A 902	Gusto, Schiedam	4 Apr 1949	21 Apr 1951	4 May 1952
SNELLIUS	A 907	P. Smit, Jr, Rotterdam	3 Jan 1949	14 Apr 1951	4 Feb 1952

Displacement, tons	1 100 standard; 1 538 full load
Dimensions, feet	234·2 × 35·5 × 7 max
Guns	1—40 mm AA; 2—20 mm AA
A/S	2 DCT; 1 Mousetrap
Main engines	Two 6-cycle, 4 stroke Stork diesels; 2 shafts; 2 000 bhp = 15 knots
Complement	108

Fitted for service in the tropics with special upper deck access and habitability.

LUYMES *1968, A & J. Pavia*

SNELLIUS *1966, Skyfotos*

1 PATROL TYPE

ZEEFAKKEL A 903

Displacement, tons	355 standard; 384 full load
Dimensions, feet	149 oa; 24·7 × 7 max
Guns	1—3 in AA; 1—40 mm AA
Main engines	Two 8-cycle 4-stroke Smit MAN diesels; 2 shafts; 640 bhp = 12 knots
Complement	29

Originally ordered from Vuyk but her construction was transferred later to J. & K Smit Kinderdijk where she was laid down in Sep 1949, launched on 21 July 1950 and completed on 22 Mar 1951. Commissioned on 23 Mar 1951, for local service. Photographs appear in the 1957-58 to 1967-68 editions.

4 INSHORE TYPE

DREG 1 A 909 **DREG II** A 910 **DREG III** A 919 **DREG IV** A 920

Displacement, tons	46 standard; 48 full load
Dimensions, feet	65·7 × 15 × 5
Main engines	120 hp × 9·5 knots
Complement	10

Dreg I and *Dreg II* were launched on 15 May 1950 and completed in July 1950.

DIVING VESSELS (*Duikvaartuigen*)

The five diving vessels (ex-coastal minesweepers) of the US BYMS type, were sold in 1962 and replaced by five coastal minesweepers of the "*Dokkum*" class, LEERSUM, LISSE, RHENEN, WAALWIJK and WOERDEN acting as diving vessels.
The four small diving vessels, *Keeten*, *Jakhals*, *Mastgat* and *Zijpe* scrapped in 1962 were replaced by *Argus*, A 843, *Hydra*, A 850, *Nautilus*, A 849 and *Triton*, A 848.

WEATHER SHIP

WEATHER SHIPS. The weather observation ships *Cirrus* (ex-USS *Abilene*, PF 58) and *Cumulus* (ex-USS *Forsyth*, PF 102), former patrol frigates, were replaced by a new weather observation ship, *Cumulus*, specially built for this work. In May 1962 her keel was laid at the yard of the NV Gebr van der Werf at Deest (near Nijmegen). Launched on 22 Dec 1962. Taken over on 18 Apr 1963. Measurement: 1 974 tons gross. Dimensions: Length 233·7 oa; 203·5 pp. Beam 41 feet. Draught 15 feet. Main engines: 6-cyl Werkspoor diesel; 1 400 bhp = 12 knots. Crew 62. She is operated by the Ministry of Transport and manned by mercantile personnel.

FAST COMBAT SUPPORT SHIP

POOLSTER A 835

Displacement, tons	16 800 full load
Measurement, tons	10 000 deadweight
Dimensions, feet	515 pp; 552·2 oa × 66·7 × 27
Guns	2—40 mm AA
Aircraft	Capacity: 5 helicopters (official complement 3 SH-34 J)
Main engines	22 500 shp turbines = 21 knots (18 service).

Fast fleet repenlishment ship (*Bevoorradingsschip*). Built by Rotterdam Dry Dock Co. Laid down on 18 Sep 1962. Launched on 16 Oct 1963. Trials mid-1964. Commissioned on 10 Sep 1964. Helicopter deck aft. Funnel heightened by 4·5 m.

POOLSTER *1969, Skyfotos*

LANDING CRAFT (*Landingsvaartuigen*)

L 9609 (ex-*Kais*)

Measurement, tons	468 gross
Dimensions, feet	137 × 36·2 × 4·5
Guns	4—20 mm AA
Main engines	2 Kromhout diesel engines; 540 bhp = 8·5 knots
Complement	22

Built in 1954 by Arnhedmsche Scheepsbouw Mij, Arnhem. Taken over from Nederl. Nieuw Guinea Petroleum Mij on 4 June 1960. Stationed in the Netherlands Antliles. A photograph of L 9609 appears in the 1965 66 to 1968-69 editions.

L 9521 **L 9526**

Displacement, tons	20
Dimensions, feet	50 × 11·8 × 5·8
Main engines	2 Kromhout diesels; 75 bhp = 8 knots
Complement	3

Now officially rated as LCA Type.

L 9510 **L 9512** **L 9514** **L 9517** **L 9520**
L 9511 **L 9513** **L 9515** **L 9518** **L 9522**

Displacement, tons	13·6
Dimensions, feet	46·2 × 11·5 × 6
Main engines	Rolls Royce diesel; Schottel propeller; 200 bhp = 12 knots
Complement	3

New landing craft made of plastic (polyester), all commissioned in 1962-63, except L 9520 in 1964.

L 9510 *1969, Royal Netherlands Navy, Official*

DIVING TENDER (*Duikwerkschip*)

CERBERUS A 895

Displacement, tons	780 standard; 902 full load
Dimensions, feet	165 × 33 × 10
Guns	1—3 in; 4—20 mm AA
Main engines	Diesel electric; 1 shaft; 1 500 bhp = 12·8 knots
Complement	51

Former netlayer and boom defence vessel. Built by Bethlehem Steel Company, Staten Island. Launched in May 1952. Completed on 10 Nov 1952. Transferred from the US in Dec 1952. Equipped as salvage vessel and diving tender in 1961, but she retains her netlaying capability.

1968, Royal Netherlands Navy, Official

TRAINING SHIPS *Opleidingsvaartuigen*)

HENDRIK KARSSEN (ex-*Y* 807, ex-*RC* 11, ex-*De Mok* 1) Y 8102

Displacement, tons	172 standard; 185 full load
Dimensions, feet	137·8 oa; 114 pp × 20·7 × 5·5
Guns	2—20 mm AA
Main engines	2 Kromhout diesels; 180 bhp = 11 knots
Complement	18

Built by Rijkswerft Willemsoord. Launched in 1939. Equipped with water monitors for fire fighting. Renamed *Hendrik Karssen* in 1954. Training and ferry vessel for local use at Den Helder. A photograph appears in the 1966-67 and 1967-68 editions.

HOBEIN (ex-*Doornbos*, ex-German *Dornbusch*) Y 8101

Displacement, tons	132
Dimensions, feet	92 oa; 83·3 pp × 19·7 × 5·5
Guns	1—40 mm AA; 1—20 mm AA
Main engines	Diesel; 250 bhp = 8·5 knots
Complement	10

Navigational training ship for midshipmen and other naval personnel, and ferry vessel for local use at Den Helder. Renamed *Hobein* in July 1952.

URANIA (ex-*Tromp*) Y 8050

Displacement, tons	38
Dimensions, feet	72 × 16·3 × 10
Main engines	Diesel; 65 hp
Complement	15

Schooner used for training in seamanship. Commissioned on 23 Apr 1938. (*van Kinsbergen*, former frigate, ex-gunboat, is stationary hulk for instruction at the Technical Training Centre in Amsterdam).

TENDERS (*Hulpschepen*)

VAN BOCHOVE A 923

Displacement, tons	150
Dimensions, feet	97·2 × 18·2 × 6
Main engines	Kromhout diesel; Schottel propeller; 140 bhp = 8 knots
Complement	8

Torpedo recovery vessel. Built by Zaanlandse Scheepsbouw Mij, Zaandam. Ordered Oct 1961, launched on 20 July 1962 and completed in Aug 1962.

VAN BOCHOVE *1968, Royal Netherlands Navy, Official*

MERCUUR A 829

Displacement, tons	274 standard; 290 full load
Dimensions, feet	137·5 pp; 140 oa × 23 × 9
Main engines	Diesels engine; 375 bhp = 12 knots (see *Notes*)
Complement	35

Built by Rijkswerf Willemsoord. Launched on 26 Feb 1936. Torpedo trials vessel. Rebuilt in 1960, triple expansion replaced by diesel, and guns removed.

TUGS (*Sleepboten*)

WESTGAT A 872 **WIELINGEN** A 873

Displacement, tons	185
Dimensions, feet	90·6 × 22·7 × 7·7
Guns	2—20 mm AA
Main engines	Bolnes diesel; 720 bhp = 12 knots

Built by Rijkswerf, Willemsoord in 1967-68. Equipped with salvage pumps and fire fighting equipment. Stationed at Den Helder.
The tug *Hercules* (ex-*Walcheren* XII, ex-*Atlas*) A 828, is out of naval service, it was officially stated in 1968.

WAMANDAI A 870 (ex-Y 8035)

Displacement, tons	159 standard; 185 full load
Dimensions, feet	89·2 × 21·3 × 7·5
Guns	2—20 mm AA
Main engines	Diesel; 500 bhp = 11 knots

Built by Rijkswerf, Willemsoord, Den Helder. Launched on 28 May 1960. Equipped with salvage pumps and fire fighting equipment. In the Netherlands Antilles since 1964.

WAMBRAU A 871

Displacement, tons	154 standard; 184 full load
Dimensions, feet	86·5 oa × 20·7 × 7·5
Guns	2—20 mm AA
Main engines	Werkspoor diesel and Kort nozzle; 500 bhp = 10·8 knots

Built by Rijkswerf Willemsoord. Launched on 27 Aug 1956. Completed on 8 Jan 1957. Equipped with salvage pumps and fire fighting equipment. Stationed at Den Helder.

BERKEL Y 8037 **DINTEL** Y 8038 **DOMMEL** Y 8039 **IJSSEL** Y 8040

Displacement, tons	139 standard; 163 full load
Dimensions, feet	82 oa × 20·5 × 7·3
Main engines	Werkspoor diesel and Kort nozzle; 500 bhp

Harbour tugs built by H. H. Bodewes, Millingen. Specially designed for use at Den Helder. Completed in 1956-57.

ROYAL NEW ZEALAND NAVY

Naval Board

Chairman: (Minister of Defence):
The Hon David Thomson, MC, ED, MP

First Naval Member and Chief of Naval Staff:
Rear Admiral J. O'C. Ross, CB, CBE

Second Naval Member (Personnel):
Commodore L. G. Carr DSC, ADC

Third Naval Member (Technical Supply Transport and Works):
Commodore L. B. Carey, MSc, C.Eng, MIEE, AMNZIM

Deputy Secretary of Defence (Navy):
Mr. A. B. Cole, DSC

Diplomatic Representation

Head of New Zealand Defence Liaison Staff, London and Senior Naval Liaison Officer:
Commodore E. C. Thorne

Naval Attaché in Washington:
Commodore J. W. H. F. Dickie, RNZN

Personnel

January 1964: 3 059 officers and ratings
January 1965: 2 818 officers and ratings
January 1966: 2 950 officers and ratings
January 1967: 2 920 officers and ratings
January 1968: 2 953 officers and ratings
January 1969: 2 959 officers and ratings

Strength of the Fleet

2 General Purpose Frigate
3 Anti-Submarine Frigates
1 Survey Ship (Former Frigate)
2 Escort Minesweepers (Ocean)
12 Seaward Patrol Craft
1 Antarctic Support Ship
2 Tenders

Mercantile Marine

Lloyd's Register of Shipping:
127 vessels of 191 618 tons gross

Silhouettes

Scale: 150 feet = 1 inch

WAIKATO

OTAGO, TARANAKI

BLACKPOOL

GENERAL PURPOSE FRIGATES

2 "LEANDER" CLASS

IMPROVED TYPE 12

Name	*No.*	*Builders*	*Laid down*	*Launched*	*Completed*
CANTERBURY		Yarrow Ltd, Clyde	June 1969		
WAIKATO	F 55	Harland & Wolff Ltd, Belfast	10 Jan 1964	18 Feb 1965	19 Sep 1966

Displacement, tons	2 305 standard; 2 640 normal; 2 800 full load
Length, feet (*metres*)	360 (*109·7*) pp; 372 (*113·4*) oa
Beam, feet (*metres*)	41 (*12·5*)
Draught, feet (*metres*)	13·8 (*4·2*)
Aircraft	1 Wasp helicopter armed with homing torpedoes
Missiles, AA	1 "Seacat" quadruple launcher
Guns, surface	2—4·5 in (*155 mm*) in twin turret; 2—20 mm
A/S	1 Limbo 3-barrelled DC mortar
Boilers	2 Babcock & Wilcox
Main engines	2 sets d.r. geared turbines 30 000 shp; 2 shafts
Speed, knots	30
Complement	248 (14 officers, 234 ratings)

Ordered on 14 June 1963 (announced by the High Commission for New Zealand in London). Commissioned on 16 Sep 1966. Trials in the United Kingdom until spring 1967. Arrived in New Zealand waters in May 1967. *Canterbury* ordered August 1968, to replace *Blackpool* on delivery.

WAIKATO *1969, Royal New Zealand Navy, Official*

ANTI-SUBMARINE FRIGATE

1 "WHITBY" CLASS. TYPE 12

Name	*No.*	*Builders*	*Laid down*	*Launched*	*Completed*
BLACKPOOL	F 77	Harland & Wolff Ltd, Belfast	20 Dec 1954	14 Feb 1957	13 Aug 1958

Displacement, tons	2 150 standard; 2 560 full load
Length, feet (*metres*)	360 (*109·7*) wl; 369·8 (*112·7*) oa
Beam, feet (*metres*)	41 (*12·5*)
Draught, feet (*metres*)	17·5 (*5·3*) max
Guns, surface	2—4·5 in (*115 mm*) in twin turret
Guns, AA	1—40 mm Bofors
A/S	2 Limbo 3-barrelled DC mortars
Boilers	2 Babcock & Wilcox
Main engines	2 sets d.r. geared turbines 30 430 shp; 2 shafts
Speed, knots	31 max
Oil fuel (tons)	370
Complement	228 (13 officers, 234 ratings)

It was announced on 30 Mar 1966 that the New Zealand Government would hire HMS *Blackpool* for four to five years until a new frigate for New Zealand was built. *Blackpool* was commissioned as a unit of the Royal New Zealand Navy on 16 June 1966. To be replaced in 1971 by *Canterbury*.

BLACKPOOL *1969, Royal New Zealand Navy, Official*

ANTI-SUBMARINE FRIGATES

Name	No.	Builders	Launched	Completed
OTAGO (ex-*Hastings*)	F 111	John I. Thornycroft & Co, Ltd Woolston, Southampton	11 Dec 1958	22 June 1960
TARANAKI	F 148	J. Samuel White & Co Ltd, Cowes, Isle of Wight	19 Aug 1959	28 Mar 1961

2 "ROTHESAY" CLASS TYPE 12

Displacement, tons	2 144 standard; 2 557 full load
Length, feet (*metres*)	360 (*109·7*) pp; 370 (*112·8*) oa
Beam, feet (*metres*)	41 (*12·5*)
Draught, feet (*metres*)	12 (*3·7*)
Missiles, AA	1 "Seacat" quadruple launcher
Guns surface	2—4·5 in (*115 mm*) in twin turret; 2—40 mm (*Taranaki* only)
A S	2 Limbo 3-barrelled DC mortars
Torpedo tubes	Originally 12—21 in (*533 mm*), 8 single A/S, 2 twin (now suppressed)
Boilers	2 Babcock & Wilcox
Main engines	2 sets d.r. geared turbines 30 430 shp; 2 shafts
Speed, knots	over 30
Complement	240 (13 officers, 227 ratings)

Taranaki was ordered direct (announced by J. Samuel White & Co on 22 Feb 1957). For *Otago* New Zealand took over the contract (officially stated on 26 Feb 1957) for *Hastings* originally ordered from John I. Thornycroft & Co in Feb 1956 for the Royal Navy). Both vessels are generally similar to those in the Royal Navy, but were modified to suit New Zealand conditions. *Otago* has enclosed foremast service 1967 refit; *Taranaki* to be similarly fitted during 1969.

OTAGO *1966, Royal New Zealand Navy, Official*

DISPOSALS
Of the six anti-submarine frigates of the "Loch" class, purchased from Great Britain in 1948, and renamed after New Zealand lakes, *Taupo* and *Tutira* were sold for scrap on 15 Dec 1961, *Hawea* and *Pukaki* were sold for scrap at Hong Kong in Sep 1965, *Rotoiti* was taken out of commission on 29 July 1965 and *Kanieri*, latterly used as an alongside training ship at Auckland, were scrapped in Hong Kong in Sept 1966.

TARANAKI ("Seacat" guided missile launcher on step of after superstructure) *1966, Royal New Zealand Navy, Official*

ESCORT MINESWEEPERS

2 "BATHURST" CLASS

Displacement, tons	790 standard; 1 025 full load
Length, feet (*metres*)	162 (*49·4*) pp; 186 (*56·7*) oa
Beam, feet (*metres*)	31 (*9·4*)
Draught, feet (*metres*)	9·5 (*2·9*)
Guns AA	2—40 mm
Boilers	2 Admiralty 3-drum small tube
Main engines	Triple expansion, 1 800 ihp; 2 shafts
Speed, knots	15
Complement	71

Name	No.	Builders	Laid down	Launched	Completed
INVERELL	M 233	Mort's Dock, Sydney	7 Dec 1941	2 May 1942	2 May 1943
KIAMA	M 353	Evans Deakins, Brisbane	2 Nov 1942	3 July 1943	26 Jan 1944

Originally four vessels were given to New Zealand by Australia in 1952. *Stawell* now in reserve.

Kiama was recommissioned on 15 Mar 1966 for training and fishery protection duties, her 4-inch gun being replaced by a 40 mm AA gun, and a deckhouse being built aft.

Inverell was recommissioned on 15 Aug 1965 as a training ship for new entry ratings, replacing the frigate *Rotoiti*. Her sweeping gear was removed and her deckhouse extended further aft. 4-inch gun replaced by 40 mm.

DISPOSALS
Echuca was scrapped at Auckland in April 1968, and *Stawell* in Aug 1968.

PHOTOGRAPHS. A photograph of *Kiama* appears in the 1953-54, 1954-55 and 1955-56 editions, of *Echuca* in the 1953-54 to 1959-1960 editions, and of *Stawell* in the 1956-57 to 1965-66 editions.

COASTAL MINESWEEPERS. The Royal Navy coastal minesweepers HICKLETON and SANTON, which were manned by the Royal New Zealand Navy, commissioning at Singapore on 10 Apr 1965 for patrol duties in Malaysian waters, reverted to the Royal Navy in late 1966 and returned to the United Kingdom.

INVERELL *1969, Royal New Zealand Navy, Official*

DISPOSALS OF LIGHT CRUISERS
Of the two light cruisers of the improved "Dido" class lent to New Zealand by Great Britain, *Black Prince* reverted to Royal Navy control in Dec 1961 and was scrapped in Japan in May 1962, and *Royalist* was taken out of commission on 4 July 1966 and reverted to the control of the Royal Navy, prior to sale for scrapping in Japan, towed from Auckland Jan 1968.

SURVEY SHIP (Ex-Frigate)

1 "RIVER" CLASS

Name	No.	Builders	Launched	Transferred
LACHLAN	F 364	Mort's Dock, Sydney, NSW	25 Mar 1944	1962

Displacement, tons — 1 420 standard; 2 220 full load
Length, feet (*metres*) — 301·2 (*91·8*)
Beam, feet (*metres*) — 36·7 (*11·2*)
Draught, feet (*metres*) — 12 (*3·7*)
Boilers — 2 Admiralty 3-drum
Main engines — Triple expansion 5 500 ihp; 2 shafts
Speed, knots — 20
Complement — 143

Former Australian "River" class frigate. On loan until she was purchased outright in 1962. She is employed surveying the New Zealand coast. Her forecastle deck was subsequently extended aft from the shelter deck to the quarter deck. Guns were removed on conversion for survey duties. A helicopter platform 50 feet by 30 feet, standing 7 feet above the quarter deck, was added in 1966.

LACHLAN *1967, Royal New Zealand Navy, Official*

SEAWARD PATROL CRAFT

12 HDML TYPE

HAKU P 3565 (ex-*Wakefield* ex-Q 1197)
KAHAWAI P3553 (ex-*Tamaki*)
KOURA P 3564 (ex-*Toroa* ex-Q 1350)
KUPARU P 3563 (ex-*Pegasus* ex-Q 1349)
MAKO P3551 (ex-Q 1183)
MANGA P3567 (ex-Q 1185)
MARORO P3554 (ex-*Irirangi* ex-Q 1192)
PAEA P3552 (ex-Q 1184)
PARORE P3562 (ex-Q 1190 ex *Olphert*)
TAKAPU P3556 (ex-Q 1188)
TAMURE P3555 (ex-*Ngapona* ex-Q 1193)
TARAPUNGA (P 3566 ex-Q 1387)

Displacement, tons — 46 standard; 54 full load
Dimensions, feet — 72 × 16 × 5·5
Guns — 1—20 mm AA; several MG (not fitted at present)
Main engines — Diesel; 2 shafts; 320 bhp = 12 knots
Complement — 9

Originally known as Harbour Defence Motor Launches. All built in various yards in the United States and Canada and shipped to New Zealand.

Takapu and *Tarapunga* are commissioned as surveying MLs and operate with *Lachlan*. All others have been converted with lattice masts surmounted by a radar aerial, *Mako*, *Paea*, *Maroro*, *Kahawai* and *Haku* are employed on Fishery Protection duties, others are attached to RNZNVR Divisions.

A photograph of *Mako* appears in the 1958-59 to 1962-63 editions, and of *Paea* in the 1963-64 to 1965-66 editions.

MANGA (lattice mast and radar) *1966, Royal New Zealand Navy, Official*

TAMURE *1969, Royal New Zealand Navy, Official*

PATROL VESSELS

Of the two patrol vessels of the "Bird" class (anti-submarine and minesweeping trawlers of the corvette type, *Kiwi* was sold in 1962 and broken up at Auckland in 1965, and sister ship *Tui* was taken out of service in Dec 1967 and was awaiting disposal in 1969

TENDERS

ARATAKI **MANAWANUI**

Dimensions, feet — Length: 75
Main engines — Diesel

Steel tugs. *Arataki* is used as a dockyard tug and *Manawanui* as a diving tender.

DISPOSALS
The lighthouse tender *Hauraki* (ex-*Endeavour*) was officially deleted from the list in 1964.

Of the two naval stores vessels, *Lander 1* was officially deleted from the list in 1964, and *Coastguard* was sold as a fishing boat on 7 July 1961.
The two Fairmile "B" Type motor launches *Maori* and *Philomel*, converted to local naval transports and passenger harbour craft, were officially deleted from the list in 1964.

ANTARCTIC SUPPORT SHIPS

ENDEAVOUR (ex-USS *Namakagon*, AOG 53) A 184

Displacement, tons — 1 850 light; 4 335 full load
Dimensions, feet — 292 wl; 310·8 oa × 48·7 × 15·7
Main engines — GM diesels; 2 shafts; 3 300 bhp = 14 knots
Complement — 72 officers and ratings

Former US "Patapsco" class petrol carrier. Built by Cargill, Inc, Savage, Minn. Laid down on 1 Aug 1944. Launched on 4 Nov 1944. Refitted and strengthened for service in ice and transferred on loan to the Royal New Zealand Navy in Oct 1962 under the Military Aid Program and re-named *Endeavour*.

ENDEAVOUR *1968, Royal New Zealand Navy, Official*

ENDEAVOUR *Royal New Zealand Navy, Official*

DISPOSALS OF FORMER ANTARCTIC SUPPORT SHIP
HMNZS *Endeavour* (ex-MV *John Briscoe*, ex-HMS *Pretext*, ex-USS *AN* 76), former netlayer, boom defence vessel, survey ship, and Antarctic support ship in turn, was declared surplus and sold in 1961.

NICARAGUA

Coast Guard

The Coast Guard is under the authority of the National Guard. It comprises small patrol boats on the east and west coasts to prevent smuggling.

Mercantile Marine

Lloyd's Register of Shipping: 8 vessels of 15 492 tons gross

COAST GUARD BOATS (*Guardacostas*)

RIO CRUTA

Dimensions, feet — Length: 85
Guns — 1—20 mm automatic cannon in bow
Main engines — Diesels; speed = 9 knots maximum
Complement — 11

Guardacosta of the Marine Section of the Guardia Nacional of Nicaragua. Of wooden construction. Another *guardacosta* with no name or number is a diesel powered launch of approx 26 ft length mounting a 20 mm cannon and theoretically capable of 25 knots crewed by 5 or 6. There were also reported to be six wooden patrol boats, four 90 ft and two about 80 ft long, and a former patrol boat, 75 ft, wooden, built in 1925, used for training.

NIGERIA

Administration

Commodore Commanding Nigerian Navy:
Rear-Admiral Joseph Etim Akinwole Wey, OFR
Chief of the Naval Staff:
Rear-Admiral Joseph Etim Akinwole Wey, OFR

Naval Attaché in London:
Commander Apayi Emmanuel Joe

Strength of the Fleet

1 Frigate, 1 Patrol Vessel, 7 Seaward Defence Boats, 3 Fast Patrol Boats 1 Landing Craft, 3 Survey Craf'

Personnel

1968: 100 Officers and 1 200 ratings (official figures)
1969: 120 Officers and 1 600 ratings

FRIGATE

1 A S AND AA TYPE

Name	*No.*	*Builders*	*Laid down*	*Launched*	*Completed*
NIGERIA	F 87	Wilton, Fijenoord NV	9 Apr 1964	12 Apr 1965	16 Sep 1965

Displacement, tons	1 724 standard; 2 000 full load
Length, feet (*metres*)	341·2 (*104·0*) pp; 360·2 (*109·8*) oa
Beam, feet (*metres*)	37 (*11·3*)
Draught, feet (*metres*)	11 (*3·3*)
Guns, dual purpose	2—4 in (*102 mm*) twin mounting.
Guns AA	5—40 mm single mountings
A/S	1—triple-barrel DCM
Main engines	4 MAN diesels 16 000 bhp; 2 shafts
Speed, knots	26
Complement	216

Anti-aircraft and anti-submarine frigate built in the Netherlands. Cost £3 500 000. Commissioned in Sep 1965. Helicopter platform laid on aft.

NIGERIA *Wright & Logan*

PATROL VESSEL

OGOJA (ex-*Queen Wilhelmina*, ex-USS *PC* 468)

Displacement, tons	320 standard; 413 full load
Dimensions, feet	165 wl; 173·7 oa × 23 × 6·5
Guns	1—3 in dp; 1—40 mm AA; 5—20 mm AA
Main engines	Fairbanks diesel; 2 shafts; 2 880 bhp = 20 knots
Oil fuel, tons	60
Complement	70

Given by the Royal Netherlands Navy to the Nigerian Navy. Former US submarine chaser built by Geo Lawley & Sons, Neponset, Mass, launched on 30 Apr 1942.

OGOJA *1965, Nigerian Navy, Official*

SEAWARD DEFENCE BOATS

7 "FORD" CLASS

BENIN (ex-HMS *Hinksford*)
BONNY (ex-HMS *Gifford*) P 3111
ENUGU P 3137
IBADAN (ex-HMS *Montford*)
KADUNA (ex-HMS *Axford*)
SAPELE (ex-HMS *Dubford*) P 3119
IBADAN II (ex-HMS *Bryansford*)

Displacement, tons	120 standard; 160 full load
Dimensions, feet	110 pp; 117·2 oa × 20 × 5
Guns	1—40 mm Bofors AA; 2—20 mm Oerlikon
A/S weapons	DC rails and DC
Main engines	Davey Paxman diesels; Foden engine on centre shaft; 1 100 bhp = 18 knots max; 15 knots sea speed
Complement	26

Enugu was the first warship built for the Nigerian Navy. Ordered from Camper and Nicholson's, Gosport, in 1960. Completed on 14 Dec 1961. Sailed from Portsmouth for Nigeria on 10 Apr 1962. Fitted with Vosper roll damping fins. *Benin, Ibadan* and *Kaduna* were purchased from Great Britain on 1 July 1966 and transferred at Devonport on 9 Sep 1966. *Ibadan* was seized by the Eastern Region prior to its declaration of independence as the Republic of Biafra on 30 May 1967 and renamed *Vigilance* but was sunk at Port Harcourt on 10 Sep 1967 by Nigerian Navy, salved and recommissioned. *Dubford* and *Gifford* were purchased from Great Britain during 1967-68 and *Bryansford* in 1968-69.

ENUGU *1965, courtesy Dr Giorgio Arra*

Kaduna (ex HMS *SDML* 3515) was officially deleted from the Navy List in 1965. Presidential Yacht *Valiant* transferred to Inland Waterways Department in 1966. Of the two minesweeping launches, *Sapele* (ex-MSML 2217) was disposed of in Feb 1967 and *Calabar* (ex-MSML 2223) was officially deleted from the list in 1969.

FAST PATROL BOATS

3 Ex-SOVIET "P 6" CLASS

EKPEN **EKUN** **ELOLE**

Displacement, tons	69·6 standard; 79·5 full load
Dimensions, feet	83·7 × 20 × 9
Guns	4 × 25 mm (2 twin)
A/S Weapons	2 DCT; 2 DC racks
Engines	4 12 cyl diesels; 4 800 bhp = 38·5 knots
Complement	24

Soviet built fast patrol boats of the small submarine chaser type purchased from the USSR in 1967.

EKPEN *1969, Nigerian Navy, Official*

LANDING CRAFT

LOKOJA (ex-*LCT* (4) 1213)

Displacement, tons	350 standard; 586 full load,
Dimensions, feet	187·5 × 38·8 × 4·5
Guns	2—20 mm AA
Main engines	2 Paxman diesels; 920 bhp = 10 knots

Purchased from Great Britain in 1959. Allocated the name *Lokoja* in 1961. Underwent a major refit in 1966-67, including complete replating of the bottom.

LOKOJA *1965, Nigerian Navy, Official*

SURVEY CRAFT

PATHFINDER P 06

Measurement, tons	544 gross
Dimensions, feet	154·2 × 27 × 11
Guns	1—40 mm AA
Main engines	2 triple expansion; 200 ihp = 8 knots

Built by J. Samuel White & Co Ltd, Cowes, Isle of Wight, in 1954.

PENELOPE P 11

Measurement, tons	79 gross
Dimensions, feet	79·5 × 7·8 × 4·5
Main engines	2 Gardner diesels; speed 10 knots

Built by Aldous Successors, Brightlingsea in 1958. Used for local survey duties.

CHALLENGER P 10

Measurement, tons	114 gross
Dimensions, feet	110·5 × 18·5 × 5
Guns	1—40 mm AA Bofors AA
Main engines	3 Gleniffer diesels; speed 13 knots

Built by Aldous Successors, Brightlingsea in 1955. Customs preventive duties.

ROYAL NORWEGIAN NAVY

Administration

Permanent Under-Secretary: Mr Erik Himle

Commander-in-Chief:
Vice-Admiral Magne Braadland, CVO, RNoN

Deputy Commander-in-Chief:
Rear Admiral Hans Sigurd Skjong, RNoN

Commander Coastal Fleet:
Commodore Øivind Schau, RNoN

Chief of Staff (Operations):
Captain Ole Birger Hatlem, RNoN

Diplomatic Representation

Defence Attaché in London:
Captain Ole Andreas Aslaksrud, RNoN

Naval Attaché in Washington:
Captain Charles Oluf Herlofson, DSC, RNoN

Naval Attaché in Moscow:
Captain Bjorn Erling Ytterhorn, RNoN

Strength of the Fleet

15 Coastal Submarines (Diesel Powered)
5 Frigates (Destroyer Escort Type)
4 Coastal Minelayers (ex-Ocean Minesweepers)
2 Patrol Vessels (Submarine Chasers)
10 Coastal Minesweepers (Non-Magnetic)
26 Torpedo Boats
21 Gunboats (Fast Patrol Boats)
14 Fleet Support Ships and Service Craft

Ships

Norwegian warships are referred to officially with the prefix KNM, equivalent to HMS. Since Mar 1959 the suffix "RNoN" has been used instead of "RNorN".

Personnel

1969: 6 000 officers and ratings
1968: 6 000 officers and ratings
1967: 6 000 officers and ratings
1966: 6 200 officers and ratings
1965: 6 000 officers and ratings
1964: 6 300 officers and ratings
1963: 6 300 officers and ratings
1962: 5 200 officers and ratings

Mercantile Marine

Lloyd's Register of Shipping:
2 881 ships of 19 667 441 tons gross

Silhouettes

Scale: 150 feet = 1 inch

OSLO *Class*

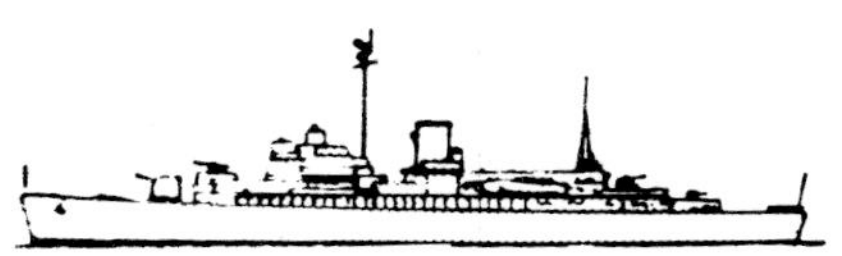
HAAKON VII

BRAGE, GOR, TYR, ULLER

SUBMARINES *(Undervannsbater)*

15 "KOBBEN" CLASS

Name	*No.*	*Launched*	*Completed*
KAURA	S 315	16 Oct 1964	5 Feb 1965
KINN	S 316	30 Nov 1963	8 Apr 1964
KOBBEN	S 318	25 Apr 1964	17 Aug 1964
KUNNA	S 319	16 July 1964	1 Oct 1964
KYA	S 317	20 Feb 1964	15 June 1964
SKLINNA	S 305	21 Jan 1966	27 May 1966
SKOLPEN	S 306	24 Mar 1966	17 Aug 1966
STADT	S 307	10 June 1966	15 Nov 1966
STORD	S 308	2 Sep 1966	9 Feb 1967
SVENNER	S 309	27 Jan 1967	1 July 1967
ULA	S 300	19 Dec 1964	7 May 1965
UTHAUG	S 304	8 Oct 1965	16 Feb 1966
UTSIRA	S 301	11 Mar 1965	1 July 1965
UTSTEIN	S 302	19 May 1965	9 Sep 1965
UTVAER	S 303	30 June 1965	1 Dec 1965

Displacement, tons	350 standard; 472 submerged
Length, feet (*metres*)	149 (*45·4*)
Beam, feet (*metres*)	15 (*4·6*)
Draught, feet (*metres*)	14 (*4·3*)
Tubes	8—21 in (*533 mm*) bow
Main engines	2 MB 820 Maybach-Mercedes-Benz diesels; 1 200 bhp; electric drive; 1 200 hp; 1 shaft
Speed, knots	17
Complement	18 (5 officers, 13 men)

It was announced in July 1959 that the USA and Norway would share equally the cost of these submarines ordered under a modernisation programme, for delivery in 1964-67. All were built by Rheinstahl-Nordseewerke in Emden, West Germany. Of the same type as the German U 4 class but with stronger hulls to dive deeper.

NOMENCLATURE. These boats were given names perpetuating those of submarines which recently served in the Royal Norwegian Navy but have been discarded (see *Disposals* below), and some new names.

The "U" group were named after features of the Norwegian seaboard, *Ula* being the name of the birthplace of Ulabrand the navigator.

TRANSFER. The German submarine U 3, lent to the Royal Norwegian Navy in 1962 for training and temporarily named *Kobben*, S 310, was returned to the Federal German Navy in 1964. A new submarine for the Royal Norwegian Navy named *Kobben*, S 318 was completed in 1964 (see above).

DISPOSALS
Of the former British "U" class, *Utsira* (ex-HMS *Variance*) was stricken from the Navy List in Dec 1962, *Utstein* (ex-HMS *Venturer*) in Jan 1964, *Ula* (ex-HMS *Varne*) in July 1964, *Utvaer* (ex-HMS *Viking*) in Dec 1964, and *Uthang* (ex-HMS *Votary*) in Oct 1965.

DISPOSALS OF EX-GERMAN VII C TYPE
Of the ex-German VII C type, *Kinn* (ex-U 1202) was removed from the Royal Norwegian Navy List on 1 June 1961, *Kaura* (ex-U 995) in Jan 1963, and *Kya* (ex-U 926) in Mar 1964.

SKOLPEN *1968, John G. Callis*

ULA *1969, Royal Norwegian Navy, Official*

STADT *1969, courtesy Godfrey H. Walker, Esq.*

FRIGATES

5 "OSLO" CLASS

DESTROYER ESCORT TYPE

Name	No.	Builders	Laid down	Launched	Completed
BERGEN	F 301	Marinens Hovedverft, Horten	1964	23 Aug 1965	15 June 1967
NARVIK	F 304	Marinens Hovedverft, Horten	1964	8 Jan 1965	30 Nov 1966
OSLO	F 300	Marinens Hovedverft, Horten	1963	17 Jan 1964	29 Jan 1966
STAVANGER	F 303	Marinens Hovedverft, Horten	1965	4 Feb 1966	1 Dec 1967
TRONDHEIM	F 302	Marinens Hovedverft, Horten	1963	4 Sep 1964	2 June 1966

Displacement, tons	1 450 standard; 1 745 full load
Length, feet (*metres*)	308 (*93·9*) pp; 317 (*96·6*) oa
Beam, feet (*metres*)	36·7 (*11·2*)
Draught, feet (*metres*)	17·4 (*5·3*)
Guns, dual purpose	4—3 in (*76 mm*) 2 twin mounts
A/S weapons	"Terne" system
Torpedo launchers	2
Boilers	2 Babcock & Wilcox
Main engines	1 set De Laval Ljungstron double reduction geared turbines; 1 shaft; 20 000 shp
Speed, knots	25
Complement	151 (11 officers, 140 ratings)

Built under the five-year naval construction programme accepted by the Norwegian "Storting" (Parliament) late in 1960. Although all the ships were constructed in the Norwegian Naval Dockyard, half the cost was borne by Norway and the other half by the United States. The design of these ships is similar to that of the "Dealey" class destroyer escorts in the United States Navy. They have traditional Norwegian destroyer or torpedo boat names.

ENGINEERING. The main turbines, of a new type, and auxiliary machinery were all built by De Laval Ljungstrom, Sweden, at the company's works in Stockholm-Nacka.

PHOTOGRAPHS. A photograph of *Oslo* appears in the 1966-67 to 1968-69 editions.

DISPOSALS OF "Cr" CLASS

Of the former British destroyers of the "Cr" class, *Trondheim* (ex-HMS *Croziers*) was removed from the Navy List on 1 May 1961. *D 303* (ex-*Oslo*, ex-HMS *Crown*) was removed from the list and scrapped in 1966, and *Bergen* (ex-HMS *Cromwell*, ex-*Cretan*) and *Stavanger* (ex-HMS *Crystal*) were stricken from the Navy List on 1 Jan 1967.

DISPOSAL OF "S" CLASS

The former British destroyer *Stord* (ex-HMS *Success*) of the "S" class, purchased from Great Britain in 1946 was stricken from the Navy List in 1959.

DISPOSALS OF "HUNT" CLASS

Of the three former British escort destroyers or frigates of the "Hunt" Class, Type II, *Haugesund* (ex-HMS *Beaufort*) and *Tromso* (ex-HMS *Zetland*) were removed from the list in 1965 and sold, and *Arendal* (ex-HMS *Badsworth*) was removed from the list on 1 May 1961. The former British escort destroyer *Narvik* (ex-HMS *Glaisdale*) of the "Hunt" class, Type III, was removed from the list on 1 May 1961.

DISPOSALS OF "RIVER" CLASS

Of the three former Canadian frigates of the "River" Class, *Draug* (ex-HMCS *Penetang*) was removed from the list and sold in 1966, and *Garm* (ex-HMCS *Toronto*) and *Troll* (ex-HMCS *Prestonian*) were converted, respectively, into Torpedo Boat Depot Ship and Submarine Depot Ship in 1964 and 1965 and renamed *Valkyrien* and *Horten*; see later page.

TRONDHEIM *1967, Royal Norwegian Navy, Official*

OSLO *1966, Royal Norwegian Navy, Official*

NARVIK *1969, courtesy Lieut. K. M. Napier, RN*

Name	*No.*
HAAKON VII (ex-US *Gardiners Bay*, *AVP* 39)	A 537

Displacement, tons	1 766 standard; 2 800 full load
Length, feet (*metres*)	300 (*91·4*) wl; 310·8 (*94·7*) oa
Beam, feet (*metres*)	41·2 (*12·7*)
Draught, feet (*metres*)	13·5 (*4·1*) max
Guns, surface	1—5 in (*127 mm*)
Guns, AA	8—40 mm; 4—20 mm
Main engines	2 F-M diesels 6 080 bhp; 2 shafts
Speed, knots	18·2
Complement	215, plus 86 officer cadets and petty officer apprentices

Former US seaplane tender (small) of the AVP type. Built by Lake Washington Shipyard, Houghton, Wash. Laid down on 14 Mar 1944, launched on 2 Dec 1944 and completed on 11 Feb 1945. Transferred from the US Navy to the Royal Norwegian Navy on 17 May 1958 and converted and rearmed as a training ship for mid-naval cadets. Accommodation for 367.

HAAKON VII *1968, Wright & Logan*

COASTAL MINELAYERS

4 "GOR" CLASS

BRAGE (ex-USS *Triumph*, MMC 3, ex-*MSF* 323, ex-*AM* 323) transferred 1960
GOR (ex-USS *Strive*, MMC 1 ex-*MSF* 117, ex-*AM* 117) transferred 1959
TYR (ex-USS *Sustain*, MMC 2, ex-*MSF* 119, ex-*AM* 119) transferred 1959
ULLER (ex-USS *Seer*, MMC 5, ex-*MSF* 112, ex-*AM* 112) transferred 1960

Displacement, tons	890 standard; 1 250 full load
Dimensions, feet	215 wl; 221·2 oa × 32·2 × 16 max
Guns	*Brage, Gor, Tyr:* 1—3 in, 50 cal; 4—20 mm AA (2 twin); *Uller:* 1—3 in, 50 cal; 1—40 mm AA
A/S weapons	*Brage, Gor, Tyr:* 2 Hedgehogs; 3 DCT *Uller:* "Terne" ASW system; 1 DCT
Main engines	GM diesels with electric drive; 2 shafts 2 070 bhp = 16 knots
Complement	83

Former US Coastal Minelayers (MMC) originally built as Ocean Minesweepers (AM) of the steel-hulled large type ("Auk" class) reclassified as Fleet Minesweepers (MSF) in Feb 1955. *Gor, Tyr* and *Uller* were built by American Shipbuilding Co, Cleveland Ohio, and *Brage* by Associated Shipbuilders. *Gor* and *Tyr* converted into coastal minelayers at Charleston Naval Shipyard in 1959, and *Brage* at the same yard in 1960, but *Uller* was converted at a Norwegian shipyard. A photograph of *Gor* appears in the 1960-61 to 1967-68 editions.

Name	*No.*	*Laid down*	*Launched*	*Completed*
Brage	N 49	27 Oct 1942	25 Feb 1943	3 Feb 1944
Gor	N 48	17 Nov 1941	16 May 1942	27 Oct 1942
Tyr	N 47	17 Nov 1941	23 June 1942	9 Nov 1942
Uller	N 50	28 Nov 1941	23 May 1942	21 Oct 1942

BRAGE *1968, Skyfotos*

TYR *1969, Royal Norwegian Navy, Official*

BRAGE *1968, Wright & Logan*

CONTROLLED MINELAYERS

BORGEN N 51

Displacement, tons	282 standard
Dimensions, feet	94·5 pp; 102·5 oa × 26·2 × 11
Main engines	2 GM diesels; 2 Voith-Schneider propellers; 330 bhp = 9 knots

PATROL VESSELS

2 "SLEIPNER" CLASS CORVETTE TYPE

AEGER P 951 **SLEIPNER** P 950

Displacement, tons	600 standard; 780 full load
Dimensions, feet	227·8 oa × 26·2
Guns	1—3 in; 1—40 mm
A/S weapons	"Terne" ASW system
Main engines	4 Maybach diesels; 2 shafts; 9 000 bhp = over 20 knots
Complement	62

Submarine chasers of the corvette type. Under the five-year programme only two instead of the originally planned five new patrol vessels were built. *Sleipner* was launched on 9 Nov 1963 at the Nylands Verksted shipyard, Oslo, and completed on 29 Apr 1965. *Aeger*, originally to have been named *Balder*, was launched on 24 Sep 1965. and completed on 31 Mar 1967.

AEGER *1968, Royal Norwegian Navy, Official*

SLEIPNER *1969, Royal New Zealand Navy, Official*

COASTAL MINESWEEPERS

10 "SAUDA" CLASS

ALTA (ex-*Arlon* M 915, ex-*MSC* 104)	M 314	
GLOMMA (ex-*Bastogne* M 916, ex-*MSC* 151)	M 317	
KVINA	M 332	21 July 1954
OGNA	M 315	18 June 1954
SAUDA (ex-USS *AMS* 102)	M 311	July 1953
SIRA (ex-USS *MSC* 132)	M 312	
TANA (ex-*Roeselaere* M 914, ex-*MSC* 103)	M 313	
TISTA	M 331	1 June 1954
UTLA	M 334	2 Mar 1955
VOSSO	M 316	16 June 1954

Sauda, built by Hodgeson Bros, Gowdy & Stevens, East Boothbay, Maine, was completed on 25 Aug 1953 and *Sira* on 28 Nov 1955. Hull of wooden construction. Five coastal minesweepers of the non-magnetic type were built in Norway with US engines. Launch dates above. Completed on 5 Mar 1955 (*Ogna*), 16 Mar 1955 (*Vosso*), 27 Apr 1955 (*Tista*), 12 July 1955 (*Kvina*) and 15 Nov 1955 (*Utla*). *Kvina, Ogna* and *Utla* were built by Båtservice Ltd, Mandal, *Tista* by Forende Batbyggeriex, Risör, and *Vosso* by Skaaluren Skibsbyggeri, Rosendal.

Alta, Glomma and *Tana* were taken over from the Royal Belgian Navy in May, Sep and Mar 1966, respectively, having been exchanged for two Norwegian ocean minesweepers of the US MSO type, *Lagen* (ex-*MSO* 498) and *Namsen* (ex-*MSO* 499).

UTLA *Skyfotos*

TORPEDO BOATS

6 NEW CONSTRUCTION

Six steel hulled torpedo boats of a new design ordered from Båtservice Verft, A/S, Mandal, Norway, have hulls similar to those of the "Storm" class gunboats, see next column. They will replace the six boats of the "Rapp" class, see below.

"Tjeld" Class, SEL leading — *1969, Royal Norwegian Navy, Official*

20 "TJELD" CLASS

DELFIN	P 386	**HAI**	P 381	**LAKS**	P 384	**SKARV**	P 344
ERLE	P 390	**HAUK**	P 349	**LOM**	P 347	**SKREI**	P 380
FALK	P 350	**HVAL**	P 383	**LYR**	P 387	**STEGG**	P 348
GEIR	P 389	**JO**	P 346	**RAVN**	P 357	**TEIST**	P 345
GRIBB	P 388	**KNURR**	P 385	**SEL**	P 382	**TJELD**	P 343

Displacement, tons	64 light; 70 standard; 82 full load
Dimensions, feet	75·5 pp; 80·3 oa × 24·5 × 6·8 max
Guns	1—40 mm AA; 1—20 mm AA
Tubes	4—21 in
Main engines	2 Napier Deltic Turboblown diesels; 2 shafts; 6 200 bhp = 45 knots
Radius, miles	450 at 40 knots; 600 at 25 knots
Complement	18 to 22

Built by Boatservice Ltd, Oslo. The first boat, *Tjeld* commissioned in June 1960, and the last of the first group of twelve in 1962. The first of the second group of eight built under the five year programme, *Sel*, was launched on 7 Mar 1963 and the last *Delfin* on 7 Jan 1966 (commissioned on 20 May 1966). A photograph of *Tjeld* appears in the 1961-62 and 1962-63 editions, of *Gribb* in the 1963-64 to 1965-66 editions of *Teist* in the 1966-67 to 1968-69 editions.

JO — *1967, Royal Norwegian Navy, Official*

SKARV — *1969, Wright & Logan*

6 "RAPP" CLASS

KJAPP	P 354	**RAPP**	P 351	**SNAR**	P 355
KVIKK	P 353	**RASK**	P 352	**SNÖGG**	P 356

Displacement, tons	72 standard
Dimensions, feet	87 × 23 × 5
Guns	1—40 mm; 1—20 mm AA
Tubes	4—21 in
Main engines	4 Packard petrol; 2 shafts; 4 800 bhp = 32 knots
Complement	18

Built by Boatservice Ltd. Wood construction. *Rapp*, prototype, laid down in Aug 1951, launched on 7 May 1952, completed on 18 Nov 1952. Five more built in 1953-56.

RAPP — ***1968, Royal Norwegian Navy, Official***

GUNBOATS

21 "STORM" CLASS

ARG	P 968	**DJERV**	P 966	**LYN**	P 980	**SKUDD**	P 967
BLINK	P 961	**GLIMT**	P 962	**ODD**	P 975	**STEIL**	P 969
BRANN	P 970	**GNIST**	P 979	**PIL**	P 976	**STORM**	P 960
BRASK	P 977	**HVASS**	P 972	**ROKK**	P 978	**TRAUST**	P 973
BROTT	P 974	**KJEKK**	P 965	**SKJOLD**	P 963	**TROSS**	P 971
						TRYGG	P 964

Displacement, tons	100 standard; 125 full load
Dimensions, feet	118 × 19·8 × 5
Guns	1—3 in; 1—40 mm
A/S weapons	Rocket throwers
Main engines	2 Maybach diesels; 7 200 bhp = over 30 knots
Complement	15

The first of the 20 (instead of the 23 originally planned) gunboats of a new design built under the five-year programme was *Storm*, launched on 8 Feb 1963, and completed on 31 May 1963, but this prototype was largely experimental and subject to design modifications. The first of the production boats was *Blink*, launched on 28 June 1965 and completed on 18 Dec 1965. Formerly known as Motor Gunboats, but officially reclassified as Gunboats in 1965.

GLIMT — *1969, Royal Norwegian Navy, Official*

BLINK — *1966, Royal Norwegian Navy, Official*

DEPOT SHIPS

2 Ex-CANADIAN FRIGATE TYPE

HORTEN (ex-*Troll*, ex-*Prestonian*) Pennant No. 1530 (ex-F 314)
VALKYRIEN (ex-*Garm*, ex-*Toronto*) Pennant No. A 535 (ex-F 315)

Displacement, tons	1,570 standard; 2 240 full load
Dimensions, feet	301·3 × 36·5 × 16
Guns	*Horten:* 3—40 mm; *Valkyrien:* 2—4 in, 2—40 mm
Main engines	Triple expansion; 2 shafts; 5 500 ihp = 19 knots
Complement	*Horten:* 86; *Valkyrien:* 104

Former Canadian modernised "River" class frigates. Both built by Davie Shipbuilding Co., Lauzon, Port Quebec, Canada. Launched on 22 June 1944 and 18 Sep 1943, and completed on 13 Sep 1944 and 6 May 1944, respectively. Loaned to Norway on 10 Mar 1956 and renamed, transferred outright early in 1959, and converted for use as depot ships and again renamed in 1965 and 1964, respectively. *Horten* for submarine support, and *Valkyrien* as parent ship for torpedo boats and gunboats.

HORTEN — *1969, Royal Norwegian Navy, Official*

FORMER DEPOT SHIPS
The former depot ship for torpedo boats, *Valkyrien*, ex-commercial coastal passenger mail and freight carrier, was removed from the Navy List on 17 Dec 1963. The former depot ship and support tender for submarines, *Sarpen*, ex-German *Königsau*, was removed from the Navy List on 12 Dec 1964.

FORMER AUXILIARIES
The battle damage repair ship of the converted American tank landing ship type, *Ellida* (ex-USS *ARB* 13, ex-USS *LST* 50), was returned to the US Navy on 1 July 1960, and transferred to the Royal Hellenic Navy on 16 Sep 1960 and renamed *Sakipis*. The former US utility landing craft *LCU* 1478 was removed from the Navy List in 1964.

FISHERY PROTECTION SHIPS

NORNEN

Measurement, tons	930 gross
Dimensions, feet	201·8 × 32·8 × 15·8
Guns	1—3 in (*76 mm*)
Main engines	4 diesels; 3 500 bhp = 17 knots
Complement	32

Built by Mjellem & Karlsen, Bergen, Norway. Launched and completed in 1963. This ship demonstrated, on 14 May 1968, the British Decca Navigator System fitted in fishery patrol vessels.

FARM **HEIMDAL**

Measurement, tons	600 gross
Dimensions, feet	177 × 26·2 × 16·5
Guns	1—3 in (*76 mm*)
Main engines	2 diesels; 2 700 bhp = 16 knots
Complement	29

Farm built by Ankerlökken Veft, Fiorö; *Heimdal* by Bolsones Verft, Molde, in 1962.

HEIMDAL *1966, Royal Norwegian Navy, Official*

ANDENES **NORDKAPP** **SENJA**

Measurement, tons	500 gross
Dimensions, feet	186 × 31 × 16
Guns	1—3 in (*76 mm*)
Main engines	MAN diesel; 2 300 bhp = 16 knots
Complement	29

All three built in the Netherlands in 1957 as whalers. Acquired by Norway in 1965 and converted into Fishery Protection Ships.

ANDENES *1966, Royal Norwegian Navy, Official*

WEATHER SHIPS

POLARFRONT I (ex-*Saxifrage*) **POLARFRONT II** (ex-*Bryony*)

Displacement, tons	1 060 standard; 1 300 full load
Dimensions, feet	205 oa × 33 × 14·5 max
Main engines	Triple expansion; 2 750 ihp = 16·5 knots
Boilers	2 SE
Oil fuel (tons)	350
Radius, miles	7 000 at 10 knots
Complement	46

Former British "Flower" class corvettes (later re-rated as frigates). Built by Charles Hill & Sons Ltd, Bristol (*Saxifrage*) and Harland & Wolff Ltd, Belfast (*Bryony*). Laid down on 1 Feb 1941 and 16 Nov 1940, launched on 24 Oct 1941 and 15 Mar 1941, and completed on 6 Feb 1942 and 16 June 1942, respectively. Transferred to Norway and employed as weather ships, but not on the Navy List.

POLARFRONT II *K. Knudsen & Co, A/S Bergen, courtesy RNoN*

OCEANOGRAPHIC RESEARCH SHIP

H. U. SVERDRUP

Displacement, tons	400
Measurement, tons	295 gross
Dimensions, feet	127·7 oa; 111·5 pp × 25 × 13
Main engines	Wichmann diesel; 600 bhp = 11·5 knots
Oil fuel (tons)	65
Radius, miles	5 000 at 10 knots cruising speed
Complement	10 crew; 9 scientists

Built by Örens Mekaniske Vërksted, Trondheim. Laid down in Sep 1959, launched in Feb 1960, completed on 15 June 1960. Financed by the US Mutual Weapon Development Programme and operated by the Norwegian Defence Research Establishment. Steel hull, welded construction, controllable pitch propeller. She does not belong to the Royal Norwegian Navy, but is a Defence project.

H. U. SVERDRUP *1964, Norwegian Defence Research Establishment*

ROYAL YACHT

NORGE (ex-*Philante*) A 533

Measurement, tons	1 686 (*Thames yacht measurement*)
Dimensions, feet	250·2 pp; 263 oa × 28 × 15·2
Main engines	8-cyl diesels; 2 shafts; 3 000 bhp = 17 knots

Built by Camper & Nicholson's Ltd, Gosport, England, to the order of the late Mr T. O. M. Sopwith as escort and store vessel for the yachts *Endeavour I* and *Endeavour II*. Launched on 17 Feb 1937. Served in the British Navy as an anti-submarine escort during the Second World War, after which she was purchased by the Norwegian people for King Haakon at a cost of nearly £250 000 and reconditioned as a Royal Yacht at Southampton. Can accommodate about 50 people in addition to crew.

NORGE *1965, Royal Norwegian Navy, Official*

ICEBREAKER

A new naval icebreaker is planned under the new construction programme, but she is not being proceeded with for the time being.

PANAMA

Base

Under the 1955 Treaty the United States occupied the Rio Hato base.

Mercantile Marine

Lloyd's Register of Shipping: 798 ships of 5 096 956 tons gross

COAST GUARD PATROL VESSELS

2 US SMALL CG UTILITY TYPE

Displacement, tons	35
Dimensions, feet	69 × 14 × 5
Guns	1 MG
Main engines	400 hp = 13 knots
Complement	10

Two coast guard utility boats were transferred to Panama by the USA at the US Naval Station, Rodman, Canal Zone, in June 1962.
There is a Navy fire-fighting tug. One or two US service boats are also reported.

PAKISTAN

Administration

Commander-in-Chief, Pakistan Navy, and Chief of the Naval Staff:
Vice-Admiral S. M. Ahsan, HQA, SPk, DSC

Deputy Chief of Naval Staff (Operations):
Commodore M. Sharriff, SK, PN

Commodore Commanding P. N. Flotilla:
Commodore Rashid Ahmad, SK, TQA, PN

Strength of the Fleet

1 Submarine (Conventional)
1 Light Cruiser
5 Destroyers
2 Frigates
8 Coastal Minesweepers
6 Patrol Boats
1 Survey Ship
7 Auxiliaries

Diplomatic Representation

Naval Adviser, High Commission, London:
Commander K. M. Hussain, PN

Naval Attaché in Washington
Captain Zafar Shamsie PN

Personnel

1963: 7,700 (700 officers; 7,000 ratings)
1964: 8,250 (750 officers; 7,500 ratings)
1965: 8,350 (790 officers; 7,560 ratings)
1966: 8,680 (820 officers; 7,860 ratings)
1967: 9,000 (820 officers; 8,180 ratings)
1968: 9,050 (800 officers; 8,250 ratings)
1969: 9,200 (850 officers; 8,350 ratings)

Mercantile Marine

Lloyd's Register of Shipping:
170 vessels of 540,551 tons gross

Silhouettes

Scale: 150 feet = 1 inch

BABUR

SHAH JAHAN

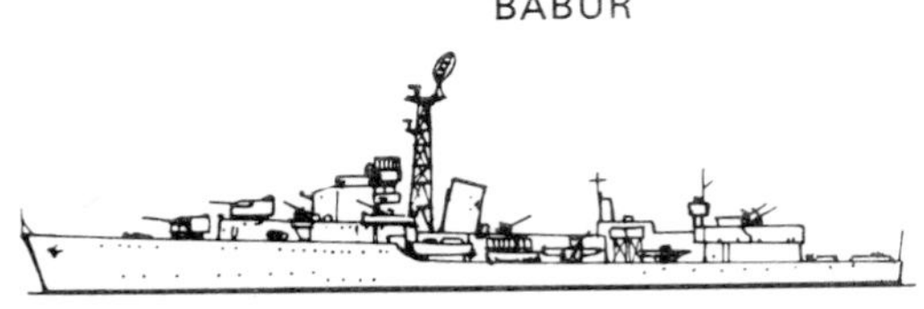

BADR, KHAIBAR

TIPPU SULTAN, TUGHRIL

ALAMGIR, JAHANGIR

ZULFIQUAR

SUBMARINES

Name	No.	Builders	Launched	Completed
GHAZI (ex-USS *Diablo* AGSS ex-*SS* 479)	S 130	Portsmouth Naval Shipyard	30 Nov 1944	31 Mar 1945

1 "TENCH" CLASS

Displacement, tons	1 570 standard; 1 864 surface 2 410 submerged
Length, feet (*metres*)	311·7 (*95·0*) oa
Beam, feet (*metres*)	27·3 (*8·3*)
Draught, feet (*metres*)	16·3 (*5·0*)
Torpedo tubes	10—21 in (*533 mm*); 6 bow, 4 stern
Main engines	4 diesels, total 6 500 bhp; 4 electric motors, total 4 610 shp
Speed, knots	20 on surface; 10 submerged
Radius, miles	14 000 at 10 knots
Oil fuel (tons)	300
Complement	89

Transferred on loan from the US Navy after extensive overhaul and refit at the Philadelphia Naval Shipyard, converting her into a Fleet Snorkel Type. Commissioned at the USN Submarine Base, New London, Connecticut on 1 June 1964. The name *Ghazi* means Defender of the Faith.

3 NEW CONSTRUCTION

It was reported in May 1967 that three submarines of the French "Daphne" class had been ordered, with two to be built by C. N. La Ciotat, Le Trait. All three are now under construction; the third is being built at Brest. The two building at Le Trait were laid down on 1 Dec 1967 and 8 July 1968.

GHAZI *1966, Pakistan Navy, Official*

LIGHT CRUISER (*Cadet Training Ship*)

Name	No.	Builders and Engineers	Laid down	Launched	Completed
BABUR (ex-HMS *Diadem*)	84	R. & W. Hawthorn Leslie & Co Ltd, Hebburn-on-Tyne	15 Nov 1939	26 Aug 1942	6 Jan 1944

Displacement, tons	5 900 standard; 7 560 full load
Length, feet (*metres*)	485 (*147·9*) pp; 512 (*156·1*) oa
Beam, feet (*metres*)	52 (*15·8*)
Draught, feet (*metres*)	18·5 (*5·6*)
Guns, surface	8—5·25 in (*133 mm*)
Guns, AA	14—40 mm
Torpedo tubes	6—21 in (*533 mm*) tripled
Armour	3 in (*76 mm*) sides; 2 in (*51 mm*) decks and turrets
Boilers	4 Admiralty 3-drum
Main engines	Parsons s.r. geared turbines 62 000 shp; 4 shafts
Speed, knots	32
Oil fuel, tons	1 100
Complement	588

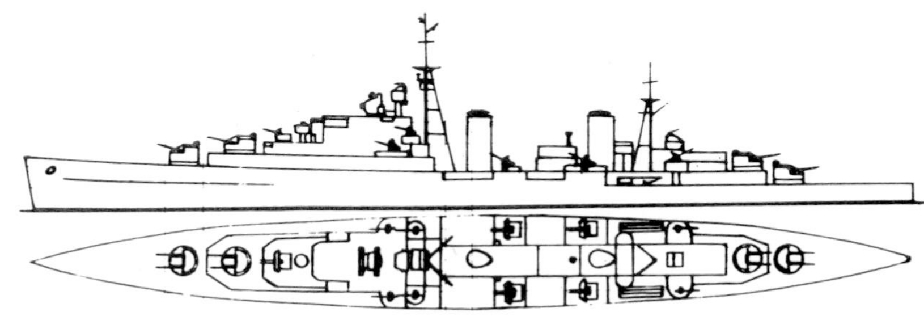

Former British "Dido" class anti-aircraft light cruiser. Sold to Pakistan on 29 Feb 1956 (announced by Admiralty). Refitted at HM Dockyard, Portsmouth in 1957, with new radar and revised secondary armament. Officially turned over to the Pakistan Navy and renamed *Babur* at Portsmouth on 5 July, 1957.

NOMENCLATURE. Renamed after Babur, the founder of the Mogul Empire. (*Diadem* means emblem of sovereignty).
Prefix C was dropped from the pennant number in 1963.

CONVERSION. Adapted as cadet training ship in 1961.

DRAWING. Port elevation and plan. Redrawn in 1966. Scale: 128 feet = 1 inch.

Light Cruiser—*continued*

BABUR

1966. Pakistan Navy, Official

DESTROYERS

Name	*No.*	*Builders*	*Laid down*	*Launched*	*Completed*
BADR (ex-HMS *Gabbard*)	161 (ex-D 47)	Swan, Hunter & Wigham Richardson Ltd, Wallsend-on-Tyne	2 Feb 1944	16 Mar 1945	10 Dec 1946
KHAIBAR (ex-HMS *Cadiz*)	163 (ex-D 79)	Fairfield Shipbuilding & Engineering Co Ltd, Govan, Glasgow	10 May 1943	16 Sep 1944	12 Apr 1946

2 "BATTLE" CLASS

Displacement, tons	2 325 standard; 3 361 full load
Length, feet (*metres*)	355 (*108·2*) pp; 379 (*115·5*) oa
Beam, feet (*metres*)	40·2 (*12;3*)
Draught, feet (*metres*)	17 (*5·2*)
Guns, surface	4—4·5 (*115 mm*)
Guns, AA	10—40 mm
A/S	"Squid" Triple DC mortar
Torpedo tubes	8—21 in (*533 mm*) quadrupled
Boilers	2 Admiralty 3-drum
Main engines	Parsons geared turbines 50 000 shp; 2 shafts
Speed, knots	35·75 designed; 31 sea speed
Radius, miles	3 000 at 20 knots
Oil fuel (tons)	680
Complement	270

Sold by Great Britain to Pakistan (announced) on 29 Feb 1956. Modernised with US funds under MDAP. *Badr* was refitted at Palmers Hebburn, Yarrow, handed over to the Pakistan Navy on 24 Jan 1957 and sailed from Portsmouth for Karachi on 17 Feb 1957. *Khaibar* was refitted at Alex Stephen & Son Ltd, Govan, Glasgow, and handed over to the Pakistan Navy on 1 Feb 1957.

BADR

1966. Pakistan Navy, Official

PENNANT NOS. Were changed from D 47 and D 79 to 161 and 163, respectively, in 1963.

NOMENCLATURE. *Khaibar* was named in commemoration of a famous battle in the history of Islam which Prophet Mohammed won in Arabia over 1,350 years ago.

KHAIBAR

1964, Pakistan Navy, Official

Name	*No.*	*Builders*	*Laid down*	*Launched*	*Completed*
SHAH JAHAN (ex-HMS *Charity*)	164 (ex-D 29)	John I. Thornycroft & Co Ltd, Woolston, Southampton	9 July 1943	30 Nov 1944	19 Nov 1945

1 "CH" CLASS

Displacement, tons	1 710 standard; 2 545 full load
Length, feet (*metres*)	350 (*106·7*) wl; 362·7 (*110·5*) oa
Beam, feet (*metres*)	35·7 (*10·9*)
Draught, feet (*metres*)	17 (*5·2*)
Guns, surface	3—4·5 in (*1,15 mm*)
Guns, AA	6—40 mm
A/S	2 "Squid" triple DC mortars
Torpedo tubes	4—21 in (*533 mm*) quadrupled
Boilers	2 Admiralty 3-drum
Main engines	Parsons geared turbines 40 000 shp; 2 shafts
Speed, knots	36·75 designed; 31·25 sea speed
Complement	200

Purchased from Great Britain by USA and, under MDAP, handed over to Pakistan on 16 Dec 1958 at J. Samuel White & Co Ltd, Cowes, who refitted her, and renamed *Shah Jahan* ("Emperor of the World") after the Fifth Emperor of the Mughal Dynasty who was ruler at the height of prosperity of the Mughal Empire.

SHAH JAHAN

1963, Pakistan Navy, Official

PENNANT No. changed from D 29 to 164 in 1963.

DISPOSAL
Sister ship *Taimur* (ex-HMS *Chivalrous*) was returned to the Royal Navy and scrapped in 1960-61.

Destroyers—*continued*

Name	*No.*	*Builders*	*Laid down*	*Launched*	*Completed*
ALAMGIR (ex-HMS *Creole*)	160 (ex-D 82)	J. Samuel White & Co Ltd, Cowes	3 Aug 1944	22 Nov 1945	14 Oct 1946
JAHANGIR (ex-HMS *Crispin*, ex-*Craccher*)	162 (ex-D 168)	J. Samuel White & Co Ltd, Cowes	1 Feb 1944	23 June 1945	10 July 1946

2 "CR" CLASS

Displacement, tons	1 730 standard; 2 560 full load
Length, feet (*metres*)	350 (*106·7*) wl 362·8 (*110·5*) oa
Beam, feet (*metres*)	35·7 (*10·9*)
Draught, feet (*metres*)	17 (*5·2*)
Guns, surface	3—4·5 in (*115 mm*)
Guns, AA	6—40 mm
A S	2 "Squid" triple DC mortars
Torpedo tubes	4—21 in (*533 mm*) quadrupled
Boilers	2 Admiralty 3-drum
Main engines	Parsons geared turbines 40 000 shp; 2 shafts
Speed, knots	36·75 designed; 31·25 sea speed
Radius, miles	2 800 at 20 knots
Oil fuel (tons)	580
Complement	200

ALAMGIR *1965, Pakistan Navy, Official*

Sold to Pakistan (announced by the Royal Navy) on 29 Feb 1956. Refitted and modernised in Great Britain by John I. Thornycroft & Co Ltd, Woolston, Southampton, in 1957-58 with US funds under MDAP. Turned over to the Pakistan Navy at Southampton in 1958 (*Crispin* on 18 Mar) and renamed.

GUNNERY. They formerly had a W/T cabin in place of "B" gun and a gun in "X" position but during the refit before joining the Pakistan Navy the 4·5 inch gun was restored to "B" position, the 4·5 inch gun in "X" position was suppressed and two Squids substituted.

PENNANT NOS. Changed from D 82 and D 168 to 160 and 162, respectively, in 1963.

JAHANGIR *1963, Pakistan Navy, Official*

FAST ANTI-SUBMARINE FRIGATES (*Ex-Destroyers*)

Name	*No.*	*Builders*	*Laid down*	*Launched*	*Completed*
TIPPU SULTAN (ex-HMS *Onslow*, ex-*Pakenham*)	260 (ex-F 249)	John Brown & Co Ltd, Clydebank	1 July 1940	31 Mar 1941	8 Oct 1941
TUGHRIL (ex-HMS *Onslaught*, ex-*Pathfinder*)	261 (ex-F 204)	Fairfield SB & Eng Co Ltd, Glasgow	14 Jan 1941	9 Oct 1941	19 June 1942

2 LIMITED CONVERSION TYPE 16

Displacement, tons	1 800 standard; 2 300 full load
Length, feet (*metres*)	328·7 (*100·2*) pp; 345 (*105·2*) oa
Beam, feet (*metres*)	35 (*10·7*)
Draught, feet (*metres*)	15·7 (*4·8*)
Guns, dual purpose	2—4 in (*102 mm*)
Guns, AA	5—40 mm
A, S	2 "Squid" triple DC mortars
Torpedo tubes	4—21 in (*533 mm*)
Boilers	2 Admiralty 3-drum
Main engines	Parsons geared turbines 40 000 shp; 2 shafts
Speed, knots	34
Complement	170

TIPPU SULTAN *1963, Pakistan Navy, Official*

Originally three "O" class destroyers were acquired from Great Britain, *Tippu Sultan* being handed over on 30 Sep 1949; *Tariq* on 3 Nov 1949; and *Tughril* on 6 Mar 1951. An agreement was signed in London between Great Britain and USA for refit and conversion in the United Kingdom of *Tippu Sultan* and *Tughril* (announced 29 Apr 1957) with US funds. All three ships were scheduled for conversion into fast anti-submarine frigates. *Tippu Sultan* and *Tughril* were converted at Liverpool by Grayson Rolls & Clover Docks Ltd, Birkenhead, and C. & H. Crighton Ltd, respectively. *Tariq* was not converted. She was handed back to Great Britain at Portsmouth on 10 July 1959 for disposal. Pennant Nos were changed from D 49 and D 204 to F 249 and F 204 respectively, in 1959, and to 260 and 261 in 1963.

SURVEY SHIP (*Ex-Frigate*)

Name	*No.*	*Builders*	*Laid down*	*Launched*	*Completed*
ZULFIQUAR (ex-*Dhanush*, ex-*Deveron*)	262 (ex-F 265)	Smith's Dock Co Ltd, South Bank-on-Tees	16 Apr 1942	12 Oct 1942	2 Mar 1943

1 "RIVER" CLASS

Displacement, tons	1 370 standard; 2 100 full load
Length, feet (*metres*)	283 (*86·3*) pp; 301·5 (*91·9*) oa
Beam, feet (*metres*)	36·7 (*11·2*)
Draught, feet (*metres*)	12·5 (*3·8*)
Guns, surface	1—4 in (*102 mm*)
Guns, AA	2—40 mm
Boilers	2 Admiralty 3-drum
Main engines	Triple expansion; 5 500 ihp
Speed, knots	20
Radius, miles	3 000 at 12 knots
Oil fuel (tons)	400
Complement	150

Former British "River" class frigate, converted into a survey ship, with additional charthouse aft. She has strengthened davits and carries survey motor boats. The after 4-inch gun was removed.

PENNANT NUMBER was changed from F 265 to 262 in 1963.

DISPOSAL
Sister ship *Shamsher* (ex-*Nadder*) (training ship) of the "River" class was disposed of in 1960.

ZULFIQUAR *1965, Pakistan Navy, Official*

COASTAL MINESWEEPERS

8 MSC TYPE

MAHMOOD	(ex-*MSC* 267)	**MUHAFIZ**	(ex-*AMS* 138)
MOMIN	(ex-*MSC* 293)	**MUJAHID**	(ex-*MSC* 261)
MOSHAL	(ex-*MSC* 294)	**MUKHTAR**	(ex-*MSC* 274)
MUBARAK	(ex-*MSC* 262)	**MUNSIF**	(ex-*MSC* 273)

Displacement, tons	335 light; 375 full load
Dimensions, feet	138 pp; 144 oa × 27 × 8·5
Guns	2—20 mm
Main engines	GM diesels; 2 shafts; 880 bhp = 14 knots
Complement	39

Transferred to Pakistan by the US under MAP. *Mukhtar* and *Munsif* on 25 June 1959, *Muhafiz* on 25 Feb 1955, *Mujahid* in Nov 1956, *Mahmood*, M 160, in May 1957, *Mubarak* in 1957, *Momin* in Aug 1962 and *Moshal* M 167, on 13 July 1963. A photograph of *Momin* appears in the 1964-65 edition.

MAHMOOD *1963, Pakistan Navy, Official*

PATROL CRAFT

4 "TOWN" CLASS

COMILLA P 142 **JESSORE** P 141 **RAJSHAHI** P 140 **SYLHET** P 143

Displacement, tons	115 standard; 143 full load
Dimensions, feet	100 wl; 107 oa × 20 × 5
Guns	2—40 mm; 70 cal Bofors AA
Main engines	2 Maybach/Mercedes MD 655/18 diesels; 3 400 bhp (tropical) = 24 knots
Complement	19

These fast patrol craft, named after towns in East Pakistan, were built by Brooke Marine Limited, Lowestoft, England, to the order of the Pakistan Government. The contract was placed on 5th Oct 1963, *Jessore* and *Comilla* were commissioned on 20th May, 1965 and *Rajshahi* and *Sylhet* on 2 Aug 1965. The hulls are of special design longitudinally and transversely strengthened. All-welded steel construction with superstructures of all welded sea resistant aluminium alloy.

COMILLA *1965, Pakistan Navy, Official*

SEAWARD DEFENCE MOTOR LAUNCHES

2 SDML TYPE

SDML 3517 (ex-*SDML* 1261) **SDML 3520** (ex-*SDML* 1266)

Displacement, tons	46 standard; 54 full load
Dimensions, feet	72 oa × 15·8 × 15·3
Guns	1—3 pdr; 1—20 mm AA
Main engines	Diesels; 2 shafts; 320 bhp = 12 knots
Complement	14

Former British Harbour Defence Motor Launches of wooden construction, built under the emergency programme during the Second World War, and re-designated Seaward Defence Motor Launches after the war. SDML 3518 and SDML 3519 were scrapped in 1965. A photograph of SDML 3517 appears in the 1963-64 and 1964-65 editions.

SDML 3520 *1965, Pakistan Navy, Official*

OILERS

DACCA (ex-USNS *Mission Santa Clara*, AO 132) A 41

Displacement, tons	5 730 light; 22 380 full load
Dimensions, feet	503 wl; 523·5 oa × 68 × 30·9 max
Main engines	Turbo-electric; 6 000 shp = 15 knots
Boilers	2 Babcock & Wilcox
Oil capacity	20,000 tons (official figure); 134,000 barrel capacity
Complement	160 (15 officers and 145 men)

Former US fleet tanker of the "T2-SE-A1" Type ("Mission" Class). Transferred on loan to Pakistan under MDAP. Handed over from the US on 17 Jan 1963.

DACCA *1964, Pakistan Navy, Official*

ATTOCK

Displacement, tons	600 standard; 1,255 full load
Dimensions, feet	177·2 oa × 32 × 15 max
Main engines	Direct coupled diesel; speed 8·5 knots
Complement	26

A harbour oiler of 6,500 barrels capacity built in Trieste, Italy, in 1960 for the Pakistan Navy, under the Mutual Defence Assistance Programme of USA.

ATTOCK *1963, Giorgio Arra*

WATER CARRIERS

ZUM ZUM YW 15

Built in Italy under US off-shore procurement of the MDA Programme.

TUGS

MADADGAR (ex-USS *Yuma, ATF* 94)

Displacement, tons	1 235 standard; 1 675 full load
Dimensions, feet	195 wl; 205 oa × 38·5 × 15·3 max
Main engines	4 GM diesels; electric drive; 1 shaft; 3 000 bhp = 16·5 knots
Complement	85

Ocean-going salvage tug. Built by Commercial Iron Works, Portland, Oregon. Laid down on 13 Feb 1943. Launched on 17 July 1943. Completed on 31 Aug 1943. Transferred from the US Navy to the Pakistan Navy on 25 Mar 1959 under MDAP. Fitted with powerful pumps and other salvage equipment.

MADADGAR *1965, Pakistan Navy, Official*

RUSTOM

Dimensions, feet	105 × 30 × 11
Main engines	Crossley diesel; 1 000 bhp = 9·5 knots (max)
Radius, miles	1 500 endurance
Complement	21

General purpose tug for the Pakistan Navy originally ordered from Werf-Zeeland at Hansweert, Netherlands, in Aug 1952, but after the liquidation of this yard the order was transferred to Worst & Dutmer at Meppel. Launched on 29 Nov 1955. A photograph appears in the 1964-65 edition.

BHOLU **GAMA**

These are small harbour tugs built under an "off-shore" order by Costaguta-Voltz.

PERU

Administration

Minister of Marine:
Rear Admiral Vice-Admiral Raul Delgado E

Chief of Naval Operations:
Vice-Admiral Jorge Luna F

Chief of Naval Staff:
Rear Admiral Fernando Elias A

Commander-in-Chief of the Fleet:
Rear Admiral Jose Rivarula Rojas

Strength of the Fleet

4 Submarines (Diesel Powered)
2 Cruisers
2 Destroyers
3 Destroyer Escorts
2 Patrol Vessels (Corvettes)
6 Coastal Patrol Boats
2 Coastal Minesweepers
4 Landing Ships (2 Medium)
8 River Gunboats
3 Patrol Launches
16 Support Ships and Service Craft

Diplomatic Representation

Naval Attaché in London:
Captain Ramon Arrospide

Naval Attaché in Washington:
Rear Admiral Luis Rivero Romainville

Personnel

1969: 7 680 (680 officers, 7 000 men)

Mercantile Marine

Lloyd's Register of Shipping:
275 vessels of 287 843 tons gross

SUBMARINES

Name	*No.*	*Laid down*	*Launched*	*Completed*
ABTAO (ex-*Tiburon*)	42	12 May 1952	27 Oct 1953	20 Feb 1954
ANGAMOS (ex-*Atun*)	43	27 Oct 1955	5 Feb 1957	1 July 1957
DOS DE MAYO (ex-*Lobo*)	41	12 May 1952	6 Feb 1954	14 June 1954
IQUIQUE (ex-*Merlin*)	44	27 Oct 1955	5 Feb 1957	1 Oct 1957

4 "ABTAO" CLASS (US BUILT)

Displacement, tons	**825 standard; 1 400 submerged**
Length, feet (*metres*)	**243 (*74·1*) oa**
Beam, feet (*metres*)	**22 (*6·7*)**
Draught, feet (*metres*)	**14 (*4·3*)**
Guns, surface	1—5 in (*127 mm*) 25 cal (*Abtao* and 2 *de Mayo*)
Torpedo tubes	6—21 in (*533 mm*); 4 bow, 2 stern
Main engines	2 GM 278A diesels; 2 400 bhp; Electric motors; 2 shafts
Speed, knots	16 on surface; 10 submerged
Radius, miles	5 000 at 10 knots
Oil fuel (tons)	45
Complement	40

All built by Electric Boat Division, General Dynamics Corporation, Groton, Connecticut. They are of modified US "Mackerel" class.

NOMENCLATURE. The names of all Peruvian submarines were changed in Apr 1957 by a supreme decree of the President of the Republic of Peru. The names now used are in honour of famous Peruvian naval battles. Previous names: *Lobo* means wolf, *Tiburon* shark.

PENNANT NUMBERS were changed from 5, 7, 6 and 8 to SS 2, SS 3, SS 1 and SS 4 respectively in 1959, and were again changed to 42, 43, 41 and 44 respectively in 1960.

PHOTOGRAPHS. A photograph of all four submarines of this class together appears in the 1959-60 edition, of *Iquique* in the 1964-65 and 1965-66 editions and of *Abtao* in the 1966-67 and 1967-68 editions.

"R" CLASS
The four old submarines of the "R" class, *Arica* (ex-R 4), *Casma* (ex-R 2), *Islay* (ex-R 1) and *Pacocha* (ex-R 3) were scrapped in 1960.

ANGAMOS — *1968, Peruvian Navy, Official*

DOS DE MAYO — *1968, Peruvian Navy, Official*

CRUISERS

Name	*No.*	*Builders*	*Laid down*	*Launched*	*Completed*
ALMIRANTE GRAU (ex-HMS *Newfoundland*)	81	Swan, Hunter & Wigham Richardson, Ltd, Wallsend on-tyne	9 Nov 1939	19 Dec 1941	31 Dec 1942
CORONEL BOLOGNESI (ex-HMS *Ceylon*)	82	Alexander Stephen & Sons, Ltd, Govan, Glasgow	27 Apr 1939	30 July 1942	13 July 1943

2 "ALMIRANTE GRAU" CLASS

Displacement, tons	*Almirante Grau:* **8 800 standard; 11 090 full load** *Col. Bolognesi:* **8 781 standard; 11 110 full load**
Length, feet (*metres*)	**538 (*164·0*) wl; 549 (*167·4*) wl; 555·5 (*169·3*) oa**
Beam, feet (*metres*)	**63·6 (*19·4*)**
Draught, feet (*metres*)	**16·5 (*5·0*) mean; 20·5 (*6·2*) max**
Guns, surface	**9—6 in (*152 mm*)**
Guns, AA	**12—40 mm *Almirante Grau*** **18—40 mm *Col. Bolognesi***
Armour	**4 in (*102 mm*) sides and CT; 2 in (*51 mm*) turrets and deck**
Boilers	**4 Admiralty 3-drum; 400 psi (*28 kg/cm²*); 720°F (*382°C*)**
Main engines	**Parsons s.r. geared turbines 72 500 shp; 4 shafts**
Speed, knots	**31·5**
Radius, miles	**6 000 at 13 knots; 2 800 at full power**
Oil fuel (tons)	**1 620**
Complement	***Almirante Grau:* 743** ***Col Bolognesi:* 766**

Former British cruisers of the "Ceylon" class, a modification of the original 8 000-ton "Colony" class design, one 6-inch turret having been suppressed, and the number of light AA. guns augmented *Almirante Grau* was engined by Wallsend Slipway & Engineering Co Ltd.

RECONSTRUCTION. *Almirante Grau* was reconstructed in 1951-53 at HM Dockyard, Devonport, with two lattice masts, new bridge and improved AA armament, her torpedo tubes being removed. *Coronel Bolognesi* was refitted with lattice foremast and covered modified bridge in 1955-56, and her torpedo tubes were removed.

GUNNERY. The 4 inch guns of *Coronel Bolognesi* are radar-controlled.

TORPEDO TUBES. Each ship originally mounted 6—21 inch torpedo tubes.

APPEARANCE. *Almirante Grau* has HA director mounted on either side of bridge. *Coronel Bolognesi* was refitted with a lattice foremast and a tripod mainmast, whereas *Almirante Grau* was reconstructed with two lattice masts.

TRANSFER. *Almirante Grau* (incorporated in the Peruvian Navy on 19 Dec 1959) was formally transferred from the British Navy at Portsmouth on 30 Dec 1959 and *Coronel Bolognesi* was transferred from the British Navy at Portsmouth on 9 Feb 1960.

UPPER DRAWING. Port elevation and plan of *Almirante Grau*. Scale 128 feet = 1 inch.

LOWER DRAWING. Port elevation and plan of *Coronel Bolognesi*. Scale: 128 feet = 1 inch.

Cruisers—*continued*

ALMIRANTE GRAU *1967, Peruvian Navy, Official*

CORONEL BOLOGNESI *1966, Peruvian Navy, Official*

DESTROYERS

Name	*No.*	*Builders*	*Launched*	*Completed*
GUISE (ex-USS *Isherwood, DD* 520)	72	Bethlehem Steel Co, Staten Island	24 Nov 1942	10 Apr 1943
VILLAR (ex-USS *Benham, DD* 796)	71	Bethlehem Steel Co, Staten Island	29 Aug 1943	20 Dec 1943

2 "VILLAR" CLASS

Ex-US "FLETCHER" CLASS

Displscement, tons,	2 120 standard; 2 715 normal; 3 050 full load
Length, feet (*metres*)	360·2 (*109·8*) pp; 370 (*112·8*) wl; 376·2 (*114·7*) oa
Beam, feet (*metres*)	39·7 (*12·1*)
Draught, feet (*metres*)	12·2 (*3·7*) mean; 18 (*5·5*) max
Guns, dual purpose	4—5 in (*127 mm*) 38 cal.
Guns, AA	6—3 in (*76 mm*) 50 cal., 3 twin
A/S weapons	2 fixed Hedgehogs; 1 DC rack
Torpedo tubes	5—21 in (*533 mm*) quintupled
Torpedo racks	2 side-launching for A/S torpedoes
Boilers	4 Babcock & Wilcox; 600 psi (*42 kg/cm²*); 850°F (*455°C*)
Main engines	2 GE impulse reaction geared turbines; 60 000 shp; 2 shafts
Speed, knots	34 max; 15 economical sea
Radius, miles	6 000 at 15 knots; 900 at full power
Oil fuel (tons)	650
Complement	Allowance; 245 (15 officers and 230 men) Max accommodation: 275 (15 officers and 260 men) revised official figures

GUISE *1964, Peruvian Navy, Official*

Former United States destroyers of the later "Fletcher" class (*Villar*) and "Fletcher" class (*Guise*).

TRANSFER. Transferred from the United States Navy to the Peruvian Navy at Boston, Massachusetts, on 15 Dec 1960, and at San Diego, California, on 8 Oct 1961 respectively.

VILLAR *1967, Peruvian Navy, Official*

DESTROYER ESCORTS

3 "CASTILLA" CLASS

Ex-US "BOSTWICK" CLASS

Name	No.	Launched	Completed
AGUIRRE (ex-USS, *Waterman, DE* 740)	62	4 July 1943	31 Dec 1943
CASTILLA (ex-USS *Bangust, DE* 739)	61	6 June 1943	30 Oct 1943
RODRIGUEZ (ex-USS *Weaver, DE* 741)	63	20 June 1943	30 Nov 1943

Displacement, tons	1 240 standard; 1 900 full load
Length, feet (*metres*)	300 (*91·4*) pp; 302·2 (*92·1*) wl; 306 (*93·3*) oa
Beam, feet (*metres*)	36·9 (*11·2*)
Draught, feet (*metres*)	12 (*3·6*) mean; 14·1 (*4·3*) max
Guns, dual purpose	3—3 in (*76 mm*) 50 cal.
Guns, AA	6—40 mm, 3 twin; 10—20 mm
A/S weapons	1 Mk 10 ahead-throwing mortar; 8 K mortars; 2 DC racks aft
Torpedo tubes	Removed
Main engines	4 GM diesel-electric sets 60 000 hp; 2 shafts
Speed, knots	21 designed; 19 max continuous
Radius, miles	10 500 at 12 knots; 3 000 at full power
Oil fuel (tons)	322
Complement	Allowance: 172 (12 officers and 160 men); Max accommodation: 212 (12 officers and 200 men) revised official figures

CASTILLA — *1964, Peruvian Navy, Official*

Former United States destroyer escorts DE, of the "Bostwick" class. All built by the Western Pipe & Steel Co, San Pedro, California, in 1943. Transferred to Peru on 26 Oct 1951, under the Mutual Defense Assistance Program. Reconditioned and modernised at Green Cove Springs and Jacksonville, Flor. Actually arrived in Peru on 24 May 1952.

AGUIRRE — *1967, Peruvian Navy, Official*

PENNANT NUMBERS. Given "DE" instead of "D" pennant numbers in 1959. Pennant numbers were changed from 2, 1 and 3 to 62, 61 and 63 respectively, in 1960.

TORPEDO TUBES. The original three 21 inch torpedo tubes in a triple mounting were removed.

RODRIGUEZ — *1967, Peruvian Navy, Official*

PHOTOGRAPHS. A starboard quarter oblique aerial view of *Castilla* appears in the 1953-54 to 1959-60 editions, a port broadside surface view of *Rodriguez* in the 1960-61 to 1963-64 editions, a port bow surface view of *Aguirre* in the 1960-61 to 1965-66 editions, a starboard bow oblique aerial view of *Rodriguez* in the 1966-67 edition.

RIVER CLASS
The two frigates of the "Palacios" Class, *Ferré* (ex-HMCS *Poundmaker*) and *Palacios* (ex-HMCS *St. Pierre*), former frigates of the Canadian "River" class, were officially stricken from the Navy List in 1966.
The frigate *Galvez* (ex-USS *Woonsocket PF* 32), former patrol frigate of the United States "Tacoma" class, was scrapped in 1961.

PATROL VESSELS (*Corvettes*)

Name	No.	Laid down	Launched	Completed
DIEZ CANSECO (ex-USS *Shoveler, MSF* 382)	69	1 Apr 1944	10 Dec 1944	28 June 1945
GALVEZ (ex-USS *Ruddy, MSF* 380)	68	24 Feb 1944	29 Oct 1944	28 Apr 1945

2 "GALVEZ" CLASS. Ex-US MSF TYPE

Displacement, tons	890 standard; 1 250 full load
Dimensions, feet	215 wl; 221·2 oa × 32·2 × 11 max
Guns	1—3 in, 50 cal dp; 2—40 mm AA
A/S weapons	1 hedgehog
Main engines	Diesel electric; 2 shafts; 3 532 bhp = 18 knots
Complement	100

Former US "Auk" class fleet minesweepers, MSF (ex-ocean minesweepers, AM), of the large steel hulled type. Both built by Gulf Shipbuilding Corp. Activated at San Diego, California, and transferred to the Peruvian Navy under the Mutual Defense Assistance Program on 1 Nov 1960. Minesweeping gear was removed and sonar equipment fitted so that they could be used as patrol vessels. The 3 inch gun director was also removed. A photograph of *Diez Canseco* appears in the 1961-62 to 1964-65 editions.

GALVEZ — *1967, Peruvian Navy, Official*

FAST PATROL CRAFT

6 VOSPER TYPE

DE LOS HEROS 23
HERRERA 24
LARREA 25
SANCHEZ CARRION 26
SANTILLANA 22
VELARDE 21

Displacement, tons	100
Dimensions, feet	103·7 wl; 109·7 oa × 21 × 5·7
Guns	2—20 mm AA
Main engines	2 Napier Deltic 18 cyl, turbocharged diesels; 6 200 bhp = 30 knots
Complement	25 (4 officers and 21 ratings)

Ordered in 1963. Designed and built by Vosper Ltd, Portsmouth, England, for the Peruvian Navy. Of all-welded steel construction with aluminium upperworks. Designed for coastal patrol, air sea-rescue, and fishery protection. Equipped with Vosper roll damping fins, Decca Type 707 true motion radar, comprehensive radio, up-to-date navigation aids, and air-conditioning. The first boat, *Velarde*, was launched on 10 July 1964, the last, *Sanchez Carrion*, on 18 Feb 1965. Can be armed as gunboat, torpedo boat (provision was made to ship four side-launched torpedoes) or minelayer. As an alternative to the gun armament a twin rocket projector can be fitted forward. Fitted with sonar equipment and depth charges in racks aft.

VELARDE *1966, Vosper Ltd, Portsmouth, England, Builders*

COASTAL MINESWEEPERS

2 "BONDY" CLASS

BONDY (ex-*YMS* 25) 137
SAN MARTIN (ex-*YMS* 35) 138

Displacement, tons	300 standard; 325 full load
Dimensions, feet	136 × 24·5 × 6
Guns	1—3 in; 2—20 mm AA
Main engines	2 GM diesels; 1 000 bhp = 13 knots; 11 knots econ)
Complement	30

Former US motor minesweepers of the YMS type. Of wooden construction, *Bondy* was built by Greenport Basin & Construction Co, Long Island, NY, and launched on 28 Jan 1943, *San Martin* was built by C. Hiltebrandt Drydock Co, Kingston, NY, and acquired from the USA in 1947. Formerly known as *Alferez de Fragata Bondy* and *Guardiamarina San Martin*. Pennant Nos. were changed from 27 and 29 to 137 and 06 respectively, in 1964 and the latter to 138 in 1965.
A photograph of *San Martin* appears in the 1958-59 to 1965-66 editions.

BONDY *1966, Peruvian Navy, Official*

PATROL LAUNCHES

3 "RIO" CLASS

RIO PIURA 04
RIO TUMBES 02
RIO ZARUMILLA 01

Displacement, tons	37 full load
Dimensions, feet	65·7 × 17 × 3·2
Guns	2—40 mm
Main engines	2 GM diesels; 2 shafts; 1 200 bhp = 18 knots

Built by Viareggio, Italy. Ordered in 1959, laid down on 15 July 1959, and entered service on 5 Sep 1960. *Rio el Salto*, 03, was deleted from the list in 1966.
There are also the ex-US small patrol craft *YP 99, YP 242* and *YP 243*.

RIO PIURA *1967, Peruvian Navy, Official*

GUNBOATS

RIO SAMA PC 11 (ex-USS *PGM 78*) (ex-*PGM 711*)

Displacement, tons	145·5
Dimensions, feet	101 × 21 × 7
Guns	2—20 mm, 2—0·5 MG
Main engines	Diesel = 18 knots
Complement	15

Transferred in Sept 1966 from the United States under MA programme.

RIVER GUNBOATS

2 "MARANON" CLASS

MARAÑÓN	13	John I. Thornycroft & Co Ltd, Southampton, England	23 Apr 1951	July 1951
UCAYALI	14		7 Mar 1951	June 1951

Displacement, tons	365 full load
Dimensions, feet	154·8 wl × 32 × 4 max
Guns	2—3 in, 50 cal dp; 7—20 mm AA (2 twin, 3 single)
Main engines	British Polar M 441 diesels; 800 bhp = 12 knots
Range, miles	6 000 without refuelling
Complement	40

Ordered early in 1950. Employed on police duties in Upper Amazon. Specially designed for carrying naval officers and men under tropical conditions. Very shallow draught. Superstructure of aluminium alloy. Mechanical ventilation. Based on Iquitos.

MARANON *1962, Peruvian Navy, Official*

2 "LORETO" CLASS

AMAZONAS 11
LORETO 12

Displacement, tons	250 standard
Dimensions, feet	145 × 22 × 4
Guns	2—3 in; 1—47 mm; 2—20 mm AA
Main engines	Diesel; 750 bhp = 15 knots
Complement	35

Designed and built by the Electric Boat Co, Groton, Conn. Launched in 1934.
A photograph of *Loreto* appears in the 1958-59 edition.

AMAZONAS *Peruvian Navy, Official*

NAPO 301

Displacement, tons	98
Dimensions, feet	100 pp; 101·5 oa × 18 × 3
Guns	3—47 mm (3 pdr); 2 MG AA
Main engines	Triple expansion; 250 ihp = 12 knots
Boilers	Yarrow
Complement	22

Built by Yarrow Co Ltd, Scotstoun, Glasgow. Launched in 1920. Of steel construction. Converted from wood to oil fuel burning. In the Upper Amazon Flotilla. Pennant No. 16 was changed to 301 in 1967.

AMERICA 15

Displacement, tons	240
Dimensions, feet	133 × 19·5 × 4·5
Guns	2—3 pdr; 4—12·7 mm AA
Main engines	Triple expansion; 350 ihp = 14 knots
Complement	26

Built by Tranmere Bay Development Co Ltd, Birkenhead. Launched and completed in 1904. Of steel construction. Converted from coal to oil fuel burning. In the Upper Amazon Flotilla.

The old river gunboat *Iquitos* was deleted from the list in 1967 after 92 years service.

LANDING SHIPS

CHIMBOTE (ex-M/S *Rawhiti*, ex-USS *LST* 283) 34

Displacement, tons	1 625 standard; 4 050 full load
Dimensions, feet	316 wl; 328 oa × 50 × 14·1
Guns	1—3 in
Main engines	GM diesels; 2 shafts; 1 700 bhp = 10 knots
Oil fuel, tons	600 oil tanks; 1 100 ballast tanks
Radius, miles	24 000 at 9 knots
Complement	Accommodation for 16 officers and 130 men

Former US tank landing ship of the 1-510 Series. Built by American Bridge Co, Ambridge, Pennsylvania. Laid down on 2 Aug 1943, launched on 10 Oct 1943 and completed on 18 Nov 1943. Sold to Peru by a British firm in 1951.

CHIMBOTE *1965, Peruvian Navy, Official*

PAITA (ex-USS *Burnett County*, *LST* 512) 35 (ex-*AT* 4)

Displacement, tons	1 653 standard; 4 080 full load
Dimensions, feet	316 wl; 328 oa × 50 × 14·5 max
Guns	6—40 mm AA; 6—20 mm AA
Main engines	GM diesels; 2 shafts; 1 700 bhp = 10 knots
Complement	13 officers, 106 men

Former US tank landing ship of the 511-1152 Series. Built by Chicago Bridge & Iron Co, Seneca, Illinois. Laid down on 29 July 1943. Launched on 10 Dec 1943 and completed on 8 Jan 1944. Purchased by Peru in 1957.

PAITA *1966, Peruvian Navy, Official*

2 "LOMAS" CLASS

ATICO (ex-USS *LSM* 554) **LOMAS** (ex-USS *LSM* 396)

Displacement, tons	513 standard; 913 full load
Dimensions, feet	196·5 wl; 203·5 oa × 34·5 × 7
Guns	2—40 mm AA; 4—20 mm AA
Main engines	Diesels; 800 rpm; 2 shafts; 3 600 bhp = 12 knots
Oil fuel, tons	165 oil tanks
Complement	Accommodation for 116 (10 officers and 106 men)

Former US medium landing ships of the LSM type. Both built by Charleston Navy Yard, Charleston, SC, USA. Purchased in 1959. A photograph of *Atico* appears in ths 1960-61 to 1966-67 editions.

Name	*No.*	*Laid down*	*Launched*	*Completed*
Atico	37	3 Mar 1945	22 Mar 1945	14 Sep 1945
Lomas	36	13 Dec 1944	2 Jan 1945	23 Mar 1945

LOMAS *1967, Peruvian Navy, Official*

FLOATING DOCKS

The former United States auxiliary floating dry dock *ARD 8* was transferred to Peru in Feb 1961: displacement 5 200 tons; length 492 feet; beam 84 feet; draught 5·7 to 33·2 feet. Pennant No. changed from WY 20 to ADF 112 in 1964.

The former United States floating dock *AFDL* 33 launched in Oct 1964 was transferred to Peru in July 1959: displacement 1 900 tons; length 288 feet; beam 64 feet, draught 8·2 to 31·5 feet. Pennant No. changed from WY 19 to ADF 111 in 1964.

TRANSPORTS

INDEPENDENCIA (ex-USS *Bellatrix*, *AKA* 3, ex-*Raven*, *AKA* 20) 21

Displacement, tons	6 194 light
Measurement, tons	Maritime Commission deadweight, 8 656
Guns	1—5 in 38 cal; 3—3 in 50 cal. 10—20 mm
Dimensions, feet	435 wl; 459 oa × 63 × 26·5
Main Engines	1 Nordberg diesel; 1 shaft; 6 000 bhp = 16·5 knots

Former US attack cargo ship. Built by Tampa Shipbuilding Co, Tampa, Florida, in 1941. Transferred to Peru at Bremerton, Washington on 20 July 1963 under the Military Aid Program. Training ship for the Peruvian Naval Academy.

INDEPENDENCIA *1966, Peruvian Navy, Official*

ILO (ex-*Norlindo*) 133

Displacement, tons	8 385 full load
Dimensions, feet	388·5 × 50·2 × 9
Main engines	Diesels; 1 shaft; 1 700 bhp = 10·5 knots

Built at Sturgeon Bay, Wis, USA, by Leatham D. Smith Shipbuilding Co, in 1945. Acquired by the Peruvian Navy from Benham and Boyesen Inc. Norway in 1959. Pennant No. changed from 33 to 133 in 1964.

ILO *1962, Peruvian Navy, Official*

CALLAO (ex-*Monserrate*) 132

Displacement, tons	7 790 full load
Measurement, tons	5 578 gross
Dimensions, feet	459 × 56 × 22
Main engines	2 diesel motors; speed = 14 knots
Complement	100 (13 officers, 87 ratings)

Former Hamburg America liner. Built by Bremen Vulkan Yard, Bremen-Vegesack. Launched in 1938. Salved and seized on 1 Apr 1941 by the Peruvian Government, after scuttling by the Germans. Employed as a troop transport and cargo carrier. Pennant No. changed from 32 to 132 in 1964.

CALLAO *1965, Peruvian Navy, Official*

The German type transport *Rimac* (ex-*Eten*, ex-*Rhakotis*) was scrapped in July 1960. The fleet supply ships and oilers *Cabo Blanco* (ex-*Mariscall Castilla*, ex-*Preserver*) and *Organus* (ex-*Olaya*) of the Canadian type, were scrapped in 1961.

WATER CARRIERS

MANTILLA (ex-US *YW* 122) 141

Displacement, tons	1 235 full load
Dimensions, feet	174 × 32
Guns	1 MG forward
Capacity, gallons	200,000

Former US water barge. Built by Henry C. Grebe & Co Inc, Chicago, Ill. Lent to Peru in July 1963.

OILERS

3 "SECHURA" CLASS

LOBITOS 159 **SECHURA** 154 **ZORRITOS** 158

Displacement, tons	8 700
Measurement, tons	4 300 gross; 6 000 deadweight
Dimensions, feet	360 wl; 385 oa × 52 × 21·2 max
Main engines	Burmeister & Wain diesel; 2 400 bhp = 12 knots (13·25 knots on trials)
Boilers	2 Scotch with Thornycroft oil burners for cargo tank cleaning

Sechura, built by John I. Thornycroft & Co Ltd, Woolston Southampton, England, was laid down late in 1952, launched on 12 Nov 1954 and completed in Feb 1955. Designed for transferring fuel to warships at sea. *Zorritos*, built by Servicio Industrial de la Marina in the Arsenal Naval del Callao, Peru, was laid down on 8 Oct 1955, and launched on 8 Oct 1958. Pennant Nos were changed from 54 and 58 to 154 and 158, respectively, in 1964. A photograph of *Sechura* appears in the 1956-57 to 1963-64 editions. *Lobitos*, built by Servicio Industrial de la Marina in the Arsenal Naval del Callao, Peru, was launched in May 1965.

LOBITOS *1967, Peruvian Navy, Official*

TALARA 153

Displacement, tons	7 000
Measurement, tons	4 800 deadweight; (about 35 000 barrels)
Dimensions, feet	336·2 × 50·9 × 22·5
Main engines	Burmeister & Wain diesel; Type 562, *VT*-F115, 2 400 bhp = 12 knots

Built to requirements of Lloyd's Register. Laid down in 1953 by Burmeister & Wain's Maskin-Og Skibsbygger, Copenhagen. Completed in 1955. No. changed from 53 to 153 in 1964. A photograph appears in the 1955-56 to 1966-67 editions.

MOLLENDO (ex-*Amalienborg*) ATP 151

Displacement, tons	6 084 standard; 25 670 full load
Dimensions, feet	534·8 × 72·2 × 30
Main engines	674-VTFS-160 diesels; 7 500 bhp = 14·5 knots

This Japanese built tanker, completed Sep 1962, was acquired by Peru in Apr 1967.

MOLLENDO *1968, Peruvian Navy, Official*

TUGS

RIOS (ex-USS *Pinto, ATF* 90) 123

Displacement, tons	1 235 standard; 1 675 full load
Measurement, tons	195 wl; 205 oa × 38·5 × 15·5 max
Main engines	4 GM diesel electric; 3 000 bhp = 16·5 knots

Former United States fleet ocean tug of the "Apache" class. Launched on 5 Jan 1943. Transferred to Peru in 1960 and delivered in Jan 1961. Fitted with powerful pumps and other salvage equipment.

RIOS *1967, Peruvian Navy, Official*

UNANUE (ex-USS *Wateree, ATA* 174) 136

Displacement, tons	534 standard; 852 full load; official revised figure
Dimensions, feet	133·7 wl; 143 oa × 33·9 × 13·2
Main engines	GM diesel-electric; 1 500 bhp = 13 knots

Former United States auxiliary ocean tug of the "Maricopa" class. Built by Levingston SB Co, Orange, Texas. Laid down on 5 Oct 1943, launched on 18 Nov 1943 and completed on 20 July, 1944. Purchased from the USA in Nov 1961 under MAP.

PARAGUAY

Strength of the Fleet

4 River Gunboats, 2 Patrol Launches, 4 River Patrol Boats

Personnel

1969: 1,900 officers and men, including coastguard and marines

Mercantile Marine

Lloyd's Register of Shipping: 26 vessels of 22,165 tons gross

RIVER GUNBOATS *(Canoneros)*

HUMAITA (ex-*Capitan Cabral*) C 2 **PARAGUAY** (ex-*Comodor Meya*) C 1

Displacement, tons	636 standard; 865 full load
Dimensions, feet	231 × 35 × 5·3
Guns	4—4·7 in; 4—3 in AA; 2 MG
Mines	6
Armour	·5 in side amidships; ·3 in deck; ·8 in CT
Main engines	Parsons geared turbines; 2 shafts; 3 800 shp = 17 knots
Boilers	2
Oil fuel, tons	150
Radius, miles	1 700 at 16 knots
Complement	86

Rated as gunboats but also fitted for minelaying. The armour is of high tensile steel. Both built by Odero, Genoa, laid down in Apr 1929, launched in 1930, and completed in May 1931.

PARAGUAY *Official*

BOUCHARD M 7 **PARKER** M 11

Displacement, tons	450 standard; 620 normal; 650 full load
Dimensions, feet	164 pp; 197 oa × 24 × 8·5 max
Guns	4—40 mm Bofors AA; 2 MG
Main engines	2 sets MAN 2-cycle diesels; 2 000 bhp = 16 knots
Oil fuel, tons	50
Radius, miles	3 000 at 12 knots
Complement	70

Former Argentinian minesweepers of the "Bouchard" class. Built at Rio Santiago Naval Shipyard and Sanchez Shipyard, San Fernando, respectively. Laid down in 1935 and 1936. Launched on 20 Mar 1936 and 2 May 1937. Can carry mines. Transferred from the Argentinian Navy to the Paraguayan Navy in Apr 1964.

PATROL LAUNCHES *(Launchas Patrulleras)*

P1 (ex-USCGC 20417) **P 2** (ex-USCGC 20418)

Displacement, tons	16
Dimensions, feet	45·5 oa × 13·5 × 3·5
Guns	2—20 mm AA
Main engines	2 petrol motors; 2 shafts; 190 hp = 20 knots
Complement	10

Of wooden construction. Built in the United States in 1944. Acquired from the United States Coast Guard in 1944.

RIVER PATROL BOATS *(Avisos de Guerra)*

CORONEL MARTINEZ A 2

Displacement, tons	80
Dimensions, feet	71·5 × 18 × 8·2
Guns	1—3 in; 2—37 mm
Main engines	150 ihp = 6·5 knots

Medium type of river patrol boat, military transport, and general utility craft.

CAPITAN CABRAL (ex-*Adolfo Riquelme*) A 1

Displacement, tons	180 standard; 206 full load
Dimensions, feet	98·5 pp; 107·2 oa × 23·5 × 9·8
Guns	1—3 in Vickers; 2—37 mm Vickers; 4 MG
Main engines	Triple expansion; 1 shaft; 300 ihp = 9 knots
Complement,	47

Former tug. Built by Werf-Conrad, Haarlem. Launched in 1907. Of wooden construction. A photograph appears in the 1954-55 to 1963-64 editions.

TENIENTE HERREROS A 3

Displacement, tons	41
Dimensions, feet	63·2 × 11 × 6·8
Guns	4 MG
Main engines	300 ihp = 5·5 knots

Small type of river patrol boat and service craft. Built in the Netherlands in 1908.

YLT 559 A 4

Dimensions, feet	66·2 × 17 × 5
Main engines	Diesel; 300 bhp

Small harbour tug YTL 559 transferred to Paraguay by the USA under the Military Aid Program in May 1963. Built by Everett Pacific SB & DD Co, Wash.

PHILIPPINES

Administration

Flag Officer in Command, Philippine Navy:
Commodore Ismael C. Lomibao, PN

Diplomatic Representation

Naval, Military and Air Attaché in London:
Jose D. Regala

Personnel

1969: 5 000 officers and men

Strength of the Fleet

7 Escort Vessels
7 Patrol Vessels
3 Command Ships
2 Coastal Minesweepers
28 Patrol Boats
35 Support Ships, etc

Coast Guard

Established Oct 1967 as a specialised branch within the Navy.

Commandant: Commodore Dioscero E. Papa

Ships

Names are those of geographical locations, mostly provinces, and are prefixed by RPS (Republic of Philippines Ship).

Mercantile Marine

Lloyd's Register of shipping: 278 vessels of 854 256 tons

ESCORT VESSELS

CEBU (ex-*PCE* 881) PS 28
ILOILO (ex-*PCE* 879) PS 32
LEYTE (ex-*PCE* 885) PS 30
NEGROS OCCIDENTAL (ex-*PCE* 884) PS 29
PANGASINAN (ex-*PCE* 891) PS 31

Displacement, tons	640 standard; 903 full load
Dimensions, feet	180 wl; 184·5 oa × 33 × 9·5
Guns	1—3 in; 3—40 mm (E31, 6—40 mm); 4—20 mm
Main engines	2 GM diesels; 2 shafts; 1 800 bhp = 15 knots

Former US escorts. Built in Portland, Oregon, USA, by Albina Eng & Mach Works (28, 29, 30) and Willamette Iron & Steel Corp (31, 32). All launched in 1943-44. A photograph of *Leyte* appears in the 1956-57 to 1964-65 editions and of *Negros Occidental* in the 1965-66 to 1968-69 editions.

ILOILO *1969, Philippine Navy, Official*

QUEZON (ex-USS *Vigilance, MSF* 324, ex-*AM* 324) PS 70
RIZAL (ex-USS *Murrelet, MSF* 372, ex-*AM* 372) PS 69

Displacement, tons	890 standard; 1 250 full load
Dimensions, feet	215 wl; 221 oa × 32·2 × 10·8 max
Guns	2—3 in, 50 cal (single); 4—40 mm AA (2 twin)
A/S	1 mortar; 2 DCT
Main engines	Diesel-electric; 2 shafts; 3 532 bhp = 18 knots

Former US fleet minesweepers of the "Auk" class. *Rizal* was built by Savannah Machine & Foundry Co. Launched on 24 Dec 1944. Transferred on 18 June 1965. Minesweeping gear removed. *Quezon* was transferred on 19 Aug 1967 at Seattle, Washington.

QUEZON *1969, Philippine Navy, Official*

PATROL VESSELS

BATANGAS (ex-*PC* 1134) PS 24
BOHOL (ex-*PC* 1131) PS 22
CAPIZ (ex-*PC* 1564) PS 27
NUEVA ECIJA (ex-*PC* 1241) PS 25
NUEVA VISCAYA (ex-USS *Altus PC 568*) PS 80

Displacement, tons	330 standard; 450 full load
Dimensions, feet	173·7 oa × 23 × 10·8
Guns	1—3 in dp; 1—40 mm AA; 5—20 mm AA
Main engines	2 GM diesels; 2 shafts; 3 600 bhp = 18 knots

Former US submarine chasers of steel construction. Built in 1942-44. Transferred in 1947-48. *Negros Oriental*, C 26 (ex-PC 1563), sank in a typhoon at Guam in Nov 1962, was raised, but stricken on 24 Jan 1963. *Nueva Viscaya* transferred 1968, after service with US Air Force, stricken from USN 15 Mar 1963.

BOHOL *1968, Philippine Navy, Official*

LAGUNA (ex-*PCS* 1403) PG 12 **TARLAC** (ex-*PCS* 1399, ex-*YMS* 450) PG 11

Displacement, tons	230 standard; 300 full load
Dimensions, feet	136 oa × 24·5 × 8·5
Guns	1—3 in; 4—20 mm
Main engines	2 GM diesels; 2 shafts; 800 bhp = 14 knots

Former US submarine chasers of wooden construction. Built in 1943-44. Transferred in Jan 1948. Photograph of *Laguna* in the 1956-57 to 1961-62 edition.

LAGUNA *1969, Philippine Navy, Official*

COMMAND SHIPS

THE PRESIDENT (ex-*Roxas*, ex-*Lapulapu*) TP 777

Measurement, tons	2 200 gross
Guns	2—40 mm; 2—20 mm AA
Main engines	B. & W. diesels; 2 shafts; 5 000 bhp = 16·5 knots

Formerly the Presidential Yacht. Acquired from Japan as reparation. Built at Ishakawajima, Japan. Launched in 1958 and completed in 1959. Originally named *Lapu-Lapu* after the chief who killed Magellan. On 9 Oct 1962 the ship was recommissioned and renamed *Roxas* after the late Manuel Roxas, first President of the Philippine Republic. Renamed *The President* in 1967.
The command ship *Rajah Soliman* D 66 (ex-USS *Bowers*, APD 40, ex-DE 637) sank in a typhoon at Bataan National Shipyard in June 1964, was raised, but stricken on 3 Dec 1964.

THE PRESIDENT *1968, Philippine Navy, Official*

Command Ships—*Continued*

DATU KALANTIAN (ex-USS *Booth* DE 170) DE 76

Displacement, tons	1 240 standard; 1 900 full load
Dimensions, feet	306 × 36·6 × 14
Guns	2—3 in AA; 6—40 mm (3 twin) 2—20 mm
ASW weapons	2 triple launchers
Main engines	Diesel Electric 6 000 shp = 21 knots
Complement	11 Officers, 154 men

Former US "Bestwick" class destroyer escort transferred to Philippine Navy 15 Dec 1967 at Philadelphia. Numbered as Destroyer Escort but also rated as Command Ship.

MOUNT SAMAT (ex-*Pagasa*, ex-*Santa Maria*, ex-*Pagasa*, ex-*Apo* 21, ex-USS *Quest*, *AM* 281) TP 21

Displacement, tons	650 standard; 945 full load
Dimensions, feet	180 wl; 184 ·5 oa × 33 × 9·8
Guns	1—3 in; 4—20 mm AA
Main engines	Diesel; 2 shafts; 1 710 bhp = 14 knots

Former US fleet minesweeper. Built by Gulf SB Corpn. Launched on 16 Mar 1944. Converted into Presidential Yacht. Renamed *Mount Samat* in 1967.

MOUNT SAMAT *1965, Philippine Navy, Official*

COASTAL MINESWEEPERS

ZAMBALES (ex-USS *MSC* 218) PM 55
ZAMBOANGA DEL NORTE (ex-USS *MSC* 210) PM 56

Displacement, tons	335 standard; 375 full load
Dimensions, feet	138 pp; 144 oa × 27 × 8·3
Main engines	GM diesels; 2 shafts; 880 bhp = 14 knots

Non-magnetic coastal minesweepers of the US "Bluebird" class. *Zambales* was built by Bellingham Shipyard Co, Washington, laid down in Aug 1954 and launched on 25 Feb 1955. Transferred on 7 Mar and 23 Apr 1956, respectively.

ZAMBALES *1969, Philippine Navy, Official*

PATROL BOATS

AGUSAN (ex-*PGM* 39) G 61
ANTIQUE (ex-*PGM* 36) G 51
CAMARINES SUR (ex-*PGM* 33) G 48
CATAN DUANES (ex-*PGM* 40) G 62
LA UNION (ex-*PGM* 35) G 50
MASBATE (ex-*PGM* 37) G 52
MISAMIS OCCIDENTAL (ex-*PGM* 38) G 53
PALAWAN (ex-*PGM* 42) G 64
ROMBLON (ex-*PGM* 41) G 63
SULU (ex-*PGM* 34) G 49
YACHI (ex-*PGM*) 55 G 57
YANGA (ex-*PGM* 56) G 59
YUNDI (ex-*PGM* 57) G 60

Displacement, tons	95 standard; 143 full load
Dimensions, feet	110 × 17 × 6·5
Guns	1—60 mm mortar; 2—40 mm AA; 4—50 cal MG
Main engines	Diesels; 2 shafts; 1 540 bhp = 18 knots

G 48-53 were built by Georgia Shipbuilding Co, St Mary's Georgia. Motor gunboats with the basic design of the former 110 ft SC type of the US Navy. The first four were delivered to the Philippine Navy in 1955 and G 52 and G 53 in 1956. G 61-64 were built by Tacoma Boatbuilding Co, Tacoma, Washington, for transfer under MAP. All steel, G 61, completed in Aug 1959, and G 62 were transported to the Philippines aboard ship in Feb 1960, followed by G 63 and G 64 in Apr 1960. A photograph of *Camarines Sur* appears in the 1956-57 to 1961-62 editions.

ROMBLON *1968, Philippine Navy, Official*

ALERT (ex-*SC* 1267) P 16
CAVITE (ex-*SC* 981) P 19
MALAMPAY SOUND (ex-*SC* 1274) P 20
MOUNTAIN PROVINCE (ex *SC* 736) P 15
SURIGAO (ex-*SC* 747) P 17

Displacement, tons	85 standard; 130 full load
Dimensions, feet	111 oa × 17 × 6
Guns	1—40 mm AA; 3—20 mm AA
Main engines	Diesels; 2 shafts; 1 000 bhp = 14·18 knots

Former US small submarine chasers of wooden construction. Built in 1942-43. Transferred in 1946-48.

6 US PCF TYPE

306 (ex-USS *PCF 33*)
307 (ex-USS *PCF 34*)
308 (ex-USS *PCF 83*)
309 (ex-USS *PCF 84*)
310 (ex-USS *PCF 85*)
311 (ex-USS *PCF 86*)

Displacement, tons	22 full load
Dimensions, feat	50 × 13 × 3·5
Guns	2·50 cal mg
Main engines	2 geared diesels; 960 shp = 25 knots

PATROL BOAT 310 *1969, Philippine Navy, Official*

HYDROFOIL PATROL BOATS

CAMIGUIN H 72
SIQUIJOR H 73

Displacement, tons	28
Measurement, tons	60 gross
Dimensions, feet	68·5 × 15·8 (24·3 foils) × 7
Guns	1—20 mm AA
A/S weapons	1 torpedo launcher
Main engines	Mercedes Benz diesel (MB 20, 12 cyl); 2 shafts; 1 250 bhp = 38 knots

Built by Cantiere Navale Leopaldo Rodriquez, Messina, Sicily. Laid down on 26 May and 28 Oct 1964. Completed in Apr 1965. For military and police patrol.

CAMIGUIN *1969, Philippine Navy, Official*

BALER H 75 **BONTOC** H 74

Displacement, tons	32 full load
Measurement, tons	60 gross
Dimensions, feet	68·9 × 15·7 × 24·6 over foils
Guns	MG fore and aft
Main engines	Ikegai-Mercedes Benz diesel; 3 200 bhp = 37·8 knots (32 cruising). Also auxiliary engine
Complement	15 (3 officers, 12 ratings)

Built by Hitachi Zosen, Kanagawa, Japan. Completed in Dec 1966. For smuggling prevention.

REPAIR SHIP

AKLAN (ex-USS *Romulus*, ARL 22, ex-*LST* 926)

Displacement, tons	1 625 light; 4 100 full load
Dimensions, feet	316 wl; 328 oa × 50 × 11
Guns	8—40 mm AA
Main engines	GM diesels; 2 shafts; 1 800 bhp = 11·6 knots

Former US landing craft repair ship transferred under MAP in Nov 1961.

AKLAN *1968, Philippine Navy, Official*

LANDING SHIPS

ALBAY (ex-*LST* 865) LT 39 **BULACAN** (ex-*LST* 843) LT 38 **MISAMIS ORIENTAL** (ex-*LST* 875) LT 40

Displacement, tons	1 625 light; 4 080 full load
Dimensions, feet	316 wl; 328 oa × 50 × 14 max
Guns	7—40 mm AA; 2—20 mm AA
Main engines	Diesel; 2 shafts; 1 800 bhp = 12 knots

Former US landing ships of the LST type. LST 72 and LCU 117 were sold.

MISAMIS ORIENTAL *1968, Philippine Navy, Official*

BATANES (ex-USS *LSM* 236) LP 65 **ISABELA** (ex-USS *LSM* 463) LP 41 **ORIENTAL MINDORO** (ex-US *LSM* 320) LP 68

Displacement, tons	743 beaching; 912 full load
Dimensions, feet	196·5 wl; 204 oa × 34·5 × 8·3
Guns	2—40 mm AA
Main engines	Direct drive diesel; 2 shafts; 2 800 bhp = 12·5 knots

Former medium landing ships. *Batanes* was transferred on 15 Sep 1960. *Isabella* was refloated on 1 Jan 1964 after being aground since Sep 1963.

BATANES *1962, courtesy Mr W. H. Davis*

OILERS

LAKE NAUJAN (ex-US *YO* 173) Y 43

Displacement, tons	521 standard; 1 400 full load
Dimensions, feet	174 oa × 32 × 13·2
Guns	2—20 mm
Main engines	Diesel; 560 bhp = 8 knots

Ex-US YO type. A photograph appears in the 1953-54 to 1960-61 editions. Ex-US YO 67 was transferred under MAP Mar 1967.

SUPPLY SHIP

LIMASAWA (ex-USCGC *Nettle WAK 169*) 79

Displacement, tons	728
Dimensions, feet	176·5 × 32 × 10
Main engines	Diesel; 2 shafts; 1 000 bhp = 11 knots

Same basic design (USN FS type) as *Bojeadour* and *Lauis Ledge*. Transferred from USCG at Manilla 1968.

LIGHTHOUSE TENDERS

BOJEADUR (ex-US *FS* 203) L 46 **LAUIS LEDGE** (ex-US *FS* 185) L 45

Displacement, tons	470 standard; 811 full load
Dimensions, feet	180 oa × 32 × 10
Main engines	Diesel; 2 shafts; 1 000 bhp = 11 knots

Ex-US FS type.

LAUIS LEDGE *1969, Philippine Navy, Official*

PEARL BANK (ex-US *OL* 4) L 47

Displacement, tons	162 standard; 301 full load
Dimensions, feet	120 oa × 24 × 8
Guns	2—20 mm AA
Main engines	Diesel; 2 shafts; 240 bhp = 6 knots

Ex-OL type. A photograph appears in the 1953-54 to 1957-58 editions.

WATER CARRIER

LAKE LANAO (ex-US *YW* 125) Y 42

Displacement, tons	1 235 full load
Dimensions, feet	174 oa × 32 × 15
Guns	2—20 mm AA
Main engines	Diesel; 640 bhp = 9 knots

LAKE LANAO *1969, Philippine Navy, Official*

TUGS

IFUGAO (ex-US *ATR* 96) R 44

Displacement, tons	534 standard; 852 full load
Dimensions, feet	134·5 wl; 413 oa × 33 × 13·5
Guns	1—3 in; 2—20 mm
Main engines	Diesel-electric; 1 500 bhp = 13 knots

Rescue tug returned to US from United Kingdom, and then transferred to the Philippines. Photograph in the 1956-57 to 1957-58 editions.

IGOROT (ex-*YTL* 572) 222 **MARANAO** (ex-*YTL* 574) 221 **MANGYAN** (ex-*ST* 1312) 223

Small harbour tugs. US YTL 429 and 449 were transferred under MAP in 1963.

COASTGUARD UTILITY BOATS. 15 ex-US CG Cutters, Nos 100-114. No names assigned.

A small auxiliary floating dry dock, AFDL 44, was transferred by US in 1968 under MAP.

FLEET MINESWEEPERS (*TRALOWCE*)

12 "KROGULEC" CLASS

ALBATROS 618	**KORMORAN** 616		**619**	**622**
CZAPLA 617	**KROGULEC** 614	**TUKAN**	**620**	**623**
JASTRAB 615	**ORLIK** 613		**621**	**624**

Displacement, tons	500
Dimensions, feet	190·3 × 24·6 × 8·2
Guns	6—25 mm AA
Main engines	Diesels; speed = 16 knots

Flushdecked minesweepers of a new type built at the Stocznia Yard from 1963 onwards. *Jastrab* and *Orlik* commissioned in 1964.
A photograph of *Jastrab* appears in the 1966-67 and 1967-68 editions.

ALBATROS *1968, Official*

12 Ex-USSR "T 43" TYPE

BIZON 605	**DZIK** 604	**MORS** 610	**TUR** 602
BOBR 606	**FOKA** 609	**ROSOMAK** 607	**ZBIK** 612
DELFIN 608	**LOS** 603	**RYS** 611	**ZUBR** 601

Displacement, tons	500 standard; 600 full load
Dimensions, feet	200 × 27·2 × 9
Guns	4—37 mm AA; 8—13 mm MG AA
Main engines	Diesels; 2 shafts; speed = 18 knots
Complement	60

Soviet "T43" type but built in Poland at Stocznia Gdynska. Gdynia in 1957-62.
A photograph of *Tur* appears in the 1958-59 edition, and of *Los* in the 1959-60 to 1964-65 editions.

DELFIN *1969, Royal Polish Navy, Official*

COASTAL CRAFT (*Ex-MINESWEEPERS*)

4 "BIRD" CLASS

CZAIKA (10 Apr 1935) 325
MEWA (1935) 326
RYBITWA (26 Apr 1935) 327
KOMPAS, ex-*Zuaw* (22 Aug 1938)

Displacement, tons	140 standard; 183 full load
Dimensions, feet	139·5 × 21·3 × 5·5
Main engines	Diesel; 1 040 bhp = 15 knots
Complement	30

All built in Poland, *Mewa* and *Kompas* at Gdynia, *Czajka* and *Rybitwa* at Modlin. Launch dates above. Recovered from German hands in 1945. *Czajka* (Lapwing) had been renamed *Westerplatte*. *Mewa* (Seagull) and *Rybitwa* (Tern were numbered MT 6 and 7 respectively, by the Germans. They are no longer used for minesweeping, nor classified as coastal minesweepers but as miscellaneous auxiliaries. All armament has been removed. *Kompas* is used as a surveying vessel. A photograph of *Mewa* appears in the 1958-59 to 1964-65 editions.

D 46 *1969, Official*

MISSILE BOATS

12 USSR "OSA" TYPE

Displacement, tons	160 standard; 200 full load
Dimensions, feet	121·3 pp; 131·5 oa × 20 × 6·5
Guided weapons	4 large hood type missile launchers in two pairs abreast
Guns	4—25 mm (2 twin, 1 forward, 1 aft)
Main engines	3 diesels; 4 800 bhp = 35 knots
Complement	25

Fast vessels of the motor torpedo boat type but with a large hull and four missile launchers in two pairs abreast the superstructure. Reported to have a surface-to-surface missile range of about 15 miles.

"Osa" class No. 164 *1969, Official*

"Osa" class No. 080 *1966, Col Borg*

PATROL VESSELS

8 Ex-USSR "KRONSTADT" CLASS

CZUINY 368	**NIEUGIETY** 361	**ZAWZIETY** 363	**ZWINNY** 365
GROZNY 362	**WYTRWALY** 367	**ZRECZNY** 366	**ZWROTNY** 364

Displacement, tons	300 standard; 350 full load
Dimensions, feet	167·3 × 19·3 × 9
Guns	1—3·9 in; 2—37 mm AA; 4—13 mm MG AA
Main engines	2 diesels; speed = 27 knots
Complement	40

Former Soviet submarine chasers. Four built in 1953 were acquired by Poland in 1957. *Grozny*, *Wytrwaly*, *Zrecany* and *Zwinny* (Strong, Energetic, Clever and Speedy), were delivered on 15 Dec 1957. A photograph of *Zwrotny* appears in the 1958-59 to 1964-65 editions.

ZAWZIETY *1968, Official*

NIEUGIETY *Official*

PATROL BOATS

4 "OKSYWIE" CLASS

OP 301 **OP 302** **OP 303** **OP 304**

Displacement, tons	170 standard
Dimensions, feet	134·5 × 19 × 6·9
Guns	2 twin 37 mm
A/S weapons	Depth charge racks
Main engines	Diesels; Speed = 20 knots

In series construction. Are an improved version of the earlier patrol boats of this type.

OP 301 *1969, Official*

5 "OBLUZE" CLASS

321 **322** **323** **324** **325**

Displacement, tons	170
Dimensions, feet	134 × 19 × 7
Guns	2—37 mm AA

In series production since 1965 at Oksywie Shipyard. Some hulls differ.

9 "GDANSK" CLASS

311 **313** **315** **317** **319**
312 **314** **316** **318**

Displacement, tons	120
Dimensions, feet	124·7 × 19·2 × 5
Guns	2—37 mm AA
A/S	Depth charges
Main engines	Diesels; speed 20 knots

Nine submarine chasers of the "Gdansk" class were built in 1960.

20 "KP" TYPE

KP 118 **KP 120** **KP 122** **KP 124** **KP 126**
KP 119 **KP 121** **KP 123** **KP 125**

Displacement, tons	60
Guns	2 MG AA (in twin mounting)
Main Engines	3 motors; speed 15 knots

Small patrol boats reported to be under the jurisdiction of the Frontier Guard.

TORPEDO BOATS (*Scigacze torpedowe*)

20 Ex-USSR "P 6" TYPE

401 **404** **407** **410** **413** **417**
402 **405** **408** **411** **414** **418**
403 **406** **409** **412** **415** **419**
416 **420**

Displacement, tons	68 full load
Dimensions, feet	83 × 20 × 6 max
Guns	4—25 mm AA; 8 DC
Tubes	2—12 in
Main engines	4 diesels; 4 800 bhp = 43 knots

Acquired from the USSR in 1957-58. (A new series of MTB's of Polish design, with gas turbines, is reported to have been constructed in Polish yards).

No. 410 *1969, Official*

Nos. 418 and 419
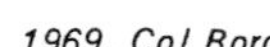
1969, Col Borg

No. 414 *1968, Official*

No. 409 *1965, Polish Navy, Official*

No. 405 *1966, Col Borg*

LANDING SHIPS

16 "POLNOCNY" CLASS

Displacement, tons	900 to 1 000
Dimensions, feet	246 × 39·3 × 9·8
Armament	Rocket projectors
Main engines	Diesels; 4 000 bhp = 15 knots

Polish built, in Gdansk, but same as the Soviet "Polnocny" type. Pennant numbers run in an 800 series.

LSMR 894 — *1969, Official*

LANDING CRAFT

10 US LCT(5) TYPE

Displacement, tons	286 standard
Dimensions, feet	177·5 × 32 × 4 max
Main engines	3 diesels; 670 bhp = 8 knots
Complement	15

Tank landing craft of American LCT type for mechanised vehicles and stores.

MINESWEEPING BOATS

7 "TR 40" CLASS

Polish built minesweeping boats numbered in 800 series.

20 "K 8" CLASS

Minesweeping boats built in Poland. Pennant numbers run in 800 and 900 series.

TRAINING SHIPS

(Okrety szkolne)

GRYF (ex-*Zetempowiec*, ex-*Opplem*, ex-*Omsk*, ex-*Empire Contees*, ex-*Irene Oldendorf*)

Measurement, tons	1 959 gross
Dimensions, feet	282·2 × 44·2 × 18·8
Guns	2—3·9 in; 4—37 mm AA
Main engines	Steam; 1 200 hp = 10 knots

Former German "Hansa" class ship. Built by Burmeister & Wain. Launched in 1944. Taken over in 1947. Transferred to the Navy in 1949. The name was changed from *Zetempowiec* to *Gryf* in 1957. Reported to be used as a hospital ship.

GRYF — *1969, Official*

ISKRA (ex-*Pigmy*, ex-*Iskra*, ex-*St Blanc*, ex-*Vlissinghr*)

Displacement, tons	560
Dimensions, feet	128 × 25 × 10
Main engines	Diesels; 250 bhp = 7·5 knots
Complement	30, plus 40 cadets

A three masted schooner with auxiliary engines. Built by Muller, Foxhol, Holland. Launched in 1917.

ISKRA — *1969, Official*

Dar Pomorza (ex-*Prinz Eitel Freidrich*), 1 560 tons, see full details in the 1961-62 edition, is an auxiliary motored full rigged sail training ship of the Polish Merchant Marine.

DAR POMORZA — *Skyfotos*

SURVEYING VESSELS

(Okret hydrograficzne)

BALTYK

Displacement, tons	1 000
Measurement, tons	658 gross; 450 deadweight
Dimensions, feet	194·3 oa; 175·3 pp × 29·5 × 14
Main engines	Steam; 1 000 hp = 11 knots

Trawler of B-10 type. Built in 1944 in Glansk. Converted and structure altered. The hydrographic vessels *Zodiac* and *Koziorozec* (see details in the 1961-62 edition) are no longer on the Navy List. They belong to the Shipping Board of Gdansk.

BALTYK *1968, Official*

OILERS *(Ropowiec)*

ZOLW (ex-*Stutthof*) Z 4

Displacement: 450 tons. Name changed from *Stutthof* to *Zolw* (Turtle) in 1961.

KRAB Z 1 **SLIMAK** Z 3

Measurement 300 tons deadweight. *Krab* means Crab and *Slimak* means snail. Small tankers built in 1958 at Gdansk.

MEDUZA Z 2

Dimensions, feet	98 × 15 × 8
Complement	8

Fuel oil and replenishment vessel for ships in ports and local waters.

Z 5 **Z 6** **Z 7**

Lighters of 300 tons gross with diesels, converted into tankers for coastal service.

CABLE SHIP

KABLOWIEC

Measurement, tons	800 gross
Dimensions, feet	130 × 15 × 5

Cable ship and general naval auxiliary, converted from a freighter-bunker ship.

DEGAUSSING VESSELS

URAN **URANIA**

Displacement, tons	254
Main engines	Speed = 8 knots

Degaussing vessels of the British MMS 11 type, classed as auxiliaries.

ICEBREAKER

PERKUM

Displacement, tons	800
Main engines	Diesel-electric; 2 shafts; 3 500 bhp = 12 knots

Icebreaker, twin screw, built in 1962 by P. K. Harris & Sons, Appledore, Devon, England.

Not a naval vessel but can be employed with and for the Navy.

PORTUGAL

Administration

Minister of Marine:
Rear-Admiral Manuel Pereira Crespo

Chief of Naval Staff:
Vice-Admiral Armando Julio de Roboredo e Silva

Diplomatic Representation

Naval Attaché in London:
Commander J. B. Pinheiro Azevedo, PoN

Naval Attaché in Washington:
Commander Vasco Antonio Martins Rodrigues, PoN

Strength of the Fleet

4 Submarines (Diesel Powered)
12 Frigates
14 Patrol Vessels (1 Corvette, 1 Gunboat)
5 Ocean Minesweepers (1 Trawler)
12 Coastal Minesweepers
6 Survey Ships and Launches
3 Training Ships
42 Patrol Boats
63 Support Ships and Service Craft

Personnel

1969: 17 730 (1 630 officers and 16 100 men) including marines

Navy Estimates

1962: Escudos 605 496 335
1963: Escudos 1 056 903 256
1964: Escudos 1 250 324 896
1965: Escudos 1 278 093 329
1966: Escudos 1 746 984 109
1967: Escudos 2 012 275 632
1968: Escudos 2 266 012 273
1969: Escudos 2 423 004 584

Mercantile Marine

Lloyd's Register of Shipping:
348 vessels of 755,000 tons gross

Silhouettes

Scale 150 feet = 1 inch

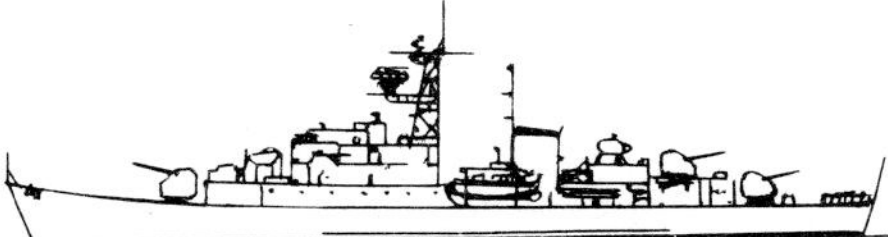

COMANDANTE JOAO BELO *Class*

ALVARES CABRAL *Class*

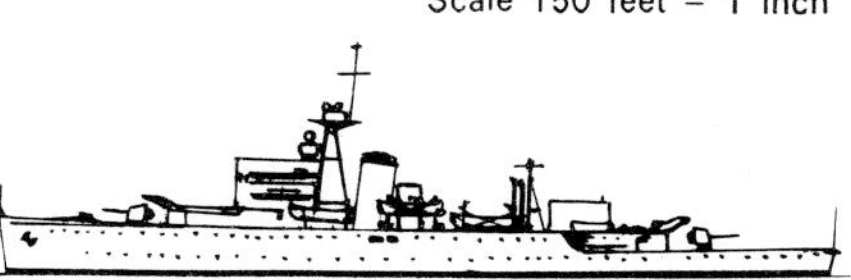

S. CRISTOVÃO (ex-*Bartolomeu Dias*)

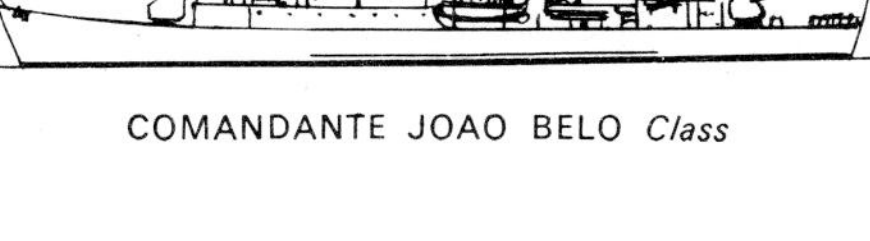

ALMIRANTE PEREIRA DA SILVA *Class*

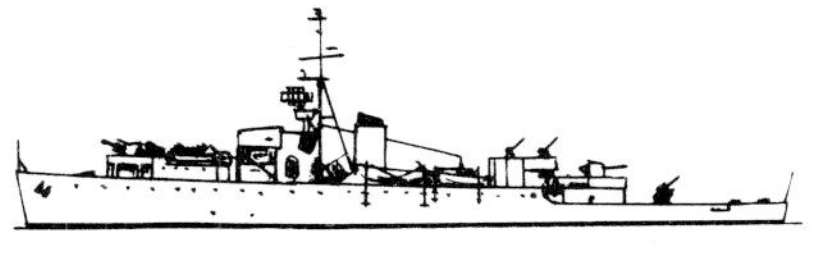

NUNO TRISTÃO

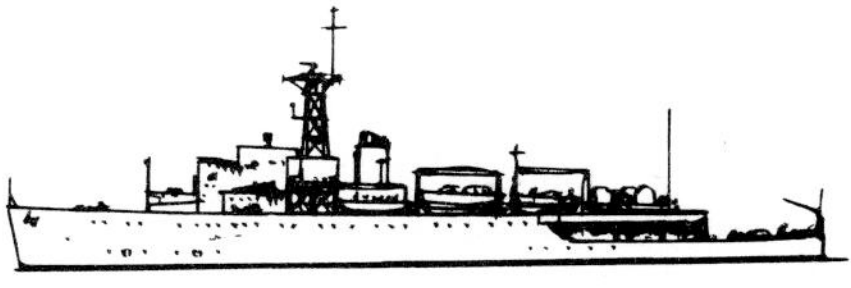

AFONSO DE ALBUQUERQUE

PERO ESCOBAR

D. FERNANDO (ex-*Diogo Gomes*)

PEDRO NUNES

SUBMARINES (*Submersiveis*)

4 "ALBACORA" CLASS

(FRENCH "DAPHNE" TYPE)

Name	*No.*	*Builders*	*Laid down*	*Launched*	*Completed*
ALBACORA	S 163	Dubigeon-Normandie	6 Sep 1965	13 Oct 1966	1 Oct 1967
BARRACUDA	S 164	Dubigeon-Normandie	19 Oct 1965	24 Apr 1967	4 May 1968
CACHALOTE	S 165	Dubigeon-Normandie	27 Oct 1966	16 Feb 1968	25 Jan 1969
DELFIM	S 166	Dubigeon-Normandie	12 May 1967	23 Sep 1968	1 Oct 1969

Displacement, tons	869 surface; 1 043 submerged
Length, feet (*metres*)	190·2 (*58·0*)
Beam, feet (*metres*)	22·7 (*6·9*)
Draft, feet (*metres*)	15·5 (*4·7*)
Torpedo tubes	12—21·7 in (*550 mm*), 8 bow, 4 stern
Main engines	SEMT-Pielstick diesels, 1 300 hp Electric motors, 1 600 hp. 2 shafts
Speed, knots	16 on surface and submerged
Radius, miles	3 000 at 7 knots
Oil fuel (tons)	90
Complement	45 (6 officers; 39 men)

The prefabricated construction of these submarines was begun on 1 Oct 1964 at Dubigeon-Normandie Shipyard, Nantes, France. They are basically similar to the French "Daphne" type.

ALBACORA — *1969, Portuguese Navy, Official*

1 "NARVAL" CLASS

(Ex-BRITISH "S" CLASS)

Name	*No.*	*Builders*	*Laid down*	*Launched*	*Completed*
NARVAL (ex-HMS *Spur*)	S 160	Cammell Laird	1 Oct 1943	17 Nov 1944	18 Feb 1945

Displacement, tons	715 standard; 859 surface; 1 008 submerged
Length, feet (*metres*)	217 (*66·2*) oa
Beam, feet (*metres*)	23·8 (*7·2*)
Draft, feet (*metres*)	10·5 (*3·2*)
Guns, dual purpose	1—4 in (*102 mm*)
Torpedo tubes	6—21 in (*533 mm*) in bow 12 torpedoes carried
Main engines	Diesels, 1 900 hp Electric motors, 1 300 hp
Speed, knots	14·75 on surface; 9 submerged
Radius, miles	5 000 at 10 knots
Oil fuel, (tons)	87
Complement	46 (5 officers, 41 men)

"S" Class patrol submarine purchased from Great Britain in 1948. Built by Cammell Laird & Co Ltd, Birkenhead. Designed for offensive operations in confined waters.

GUNNERY. The 20 mm Oerlikon anti-aircraft gun and three Vickers gas operated machine guns formerly carried were removed in 1961.

NARVAL — *1968, Portuguese Navy, Official*

DISPOSALS
Of two sister ships, *Neptuno* (ex-HMS *Spearhead*) was discarded on 1 Sep 1967 and *Nautilo* (ex-HMS *Saga*) on 25 Jan 1969.

FAST FRIGATES (*Fragatas*)

Name	No.	Builders	Laid down	Launched	Completed
COMANDANTE HERMENEGILDO CAPELO	F 481	At et Ch de Nantes	13 May 1966	29 Nov 1966	26 Apr 1968
COMANDANTE JOÃO BELO	F 480	At et Ch de Nantes	6 Sep 1965	22 Mar 1966	1 July 1967
COMANDANTE ROBERTO IVENS	F 482	At et Ch de Nantes	13 Dec 1966	8 Aug 1967	23 Nov 1968
COMANDANTE SACADURA CABRAL	F 483	At et Ch de Nantes	18 Aug 1967	1 Apr 1968	1 July 1969

4 "COMANDANTE JOÃO BELO" CLASS (FRENCH "COMMANDANT RIVIERE" TYPE)

Displacement, tons	1 650 standard; 2 180 full load
Length, feet (*metres*)	321·5 (*98*) pp; 338 (*103·0*) oa
Beam, feet (*metres*)	37·7 (*11·5*)
Draft, feet (*metres*)	12·5 (*3·8*) mean
Guns, AA	3—3·9 in (*100 mm*) singles; 2—40 mm
A/S	1—12 in (*305 mm*) quadruple
Torpedo tubes	6—21·7 in (*550 mm*) ASM, 2 triple
Main engines	SEMT-Pielstick diesels 16 200 bhp; 2 shafts
Speed, knots	25 (*26·5* max)
Radius, miles	4 500 at 15 knots
Complement	214

The prefabricated construction of these ships was begun on 1 Oct 1964 at the Ateliers et Chantiers de Nantes, France. They are similar to the French "Commandant Riviere" type except the 30 mm AA guns which will be replaced by 40 mm AA guns

COMANDANTE JOÃO BELO *1969, Portuguese Navy, Official*

DISPOSALS OF DESTROYERS
Of the five destroyers of the "Vouga" class, the only unconverted ship **Douro,** was discarded in Dec 1959. Of the converted ships **Dao** was discarded on 29 Nov 1960, **Tejo** on 9 Feb 1965, **Lima** on 16 Oct 1965, and **Vouga** on 3 June 1967.

DISPOSALS OF DESTROYER ESCORTS
Of the two fast frigates of the "Diogo Cão" class (former U.S. destroyer escorts of the "John C. Butler" type) **Corto Real** (ex-USS *McCoy Reynolds*, DE 440) was discarded on 21 Oct 1968 and **Diogo Cao** (ex-USS *Formoe*, DE 509) on 19 Nov 1968.

COMANDANTE JOÃO BELO *1968, Portuguese Navy, Official*

Name	No.	Builders	Laid down	Launched	Completed
ALMIRANTE GAGO COUTINHO	F 473 (ex-US DE 1042)	Estaleiros Navais Lisnave, Lisbon	2 Dec 1963	30 Aug 1965	1 Aug 1967
ALMIRANTE MAGALHÃES CORREIA	F 474 (ex-US DE 1046)	Estaleiros Navais de Viana do Castelo	1 Sep 1963	26 Apr 1965	1 Dec 1967
ALMIRANTE PEREIRA DA SILVA	F 472 (ex-US DE 1039)	Estalerois Navais Lisnave, Lisbon	14 June 1962	2 Dec 1963	20 Dec 1966

3 "ALMIRANTE PEREIRA DA SILVA" CLASS

Displacement, tons	1 450 standard; 1 950 full load
Length, feet (*metres*)	314·6 (*95·9*)
Beam, feet (*metres*)	37 (*11·3*)
Draft, feet (*metres*)	14 (*4·3*)
Guns, dual purpose	4—3 in (*76 mm*) 50 cal.
A/S	2 Bofors 4-barrelled mortars; 2 DC throwers
Torpedo tubes	6 (2 triple) for A/S torpedoes
Boilers	2 Foster Wheeler, 300 psi, 850°F
Main engines	De Laval dr geared turbines 20 000 shp; 1 shaft
Speed, knots	26 designed
Radius, miles	4 500 at 15 knots
Oil fuel (tons)	400
Complement	166 (12 officers, 154 men)

US "Dealey" type escort ships. Prefabrication of 472, 473 was begun in 1961 at Lisnave (formerly Navalis Shipyard, Lisbon) and of 474 in 1962.

ALMIRANTE PEREIRA DA SILVA *1968, Portuguese Navy, Official*

Name	No.	Builders	Laid down	Launched	Completed
PERO ESCOBAR	F 335	Navalmeccanica, Castellammare di Stabia, Italy	7 Jan 1955	25 Sep 1955	1 July 1957

Displacement, tons	1 250 standard; 1 600 full load
Length, feet (*metres*)	295·2 (*90·0*) pp; 306·7 (*93·5*) wl; 321·5 (*98·0*) oa
Beam, feet (*metres*)	35·5 (*10·8*)
Draft, feet (*metres*)	10 (*3·0*)
Guns, dual purpose	4—3 in (*76 mm*) 50 cal.
A/S	2 "Squid" triple DC mortars
Torpedo tubes	6 (2 triple) for A/S torpedoes
Boilers	2 Ansoldo-Foster Wheeler "D" *32 kg/cm²*, 400°C
Main engines	2 Ansaldo-Genova sr geared turbines; 24 000 shp; 2 shafts
Speed, knots	32·6 max
Radius, miles	2 800 at 13·5 knots
Oil fuel (tons)	236
Complement	165 (10 officers, 155 men)

A "light destroyer" or fast anti-submarine escort built to the order of NATO for the Portuguese Navy.

GUNNERY. The armament before modernisation comprised two single 3 inch guns, two 40 mm AA (twin mount), four 20 mm AA (two twin mounts) and three 21 inch torpedo tubes.

MODERNISATION. Modernised in 1968-69, the alterations including the fitting of new guns, sonar and anti-submarine torpedo tubes similar to those in the "Almirante Pereira da Silva" class frigates

PERO ESCOBAR *1969, Portuguese Navy, Official*

FRIGATES (*Fragatas*)

Name	No.	Builders	Laid down	Launched	Completed
ALVARES CABRAL (ex-HMS *Burghead Bay*)	F 336	Charles Hill & Sons Ltd, Bristol	21 Sep 1944	3 Mar 1945	20 Sep 1945
D. FRANCISCO DE ALMEIDA (ex-HMS *Morecambe Bay*)	F 479	Wm. Pickersgill Ltd, Sunderland T	30 Apr 1944	1 Nov 1944	22 Feb 1949
PACHECO PEREIRA (ex-HMS *Bigbury Bay*)	F 337	Hall Russell & Co Ltd, Aberdeen	30 May 1944	16 Nov 1944	10 July 1945
VASCO DA GAMA (ex-HMS *Mounts Bay*)	F 478	Wm. Pickersgill Ltd, Sunderland W	23 Oct 1944	8 June 1945	11 Apr 1949

T=Completed by John I. Thornycroft & Co Ltd, Woolston, Southampton.   W=Completed by J. Samuel White & Co Ltd, Cowes, Isle of Wight.

4 "ALVARES CABRAL" CLASS
(Ex-BRITISH "BAY" CLASS)

Displacement, tons	1 600 standard; 2 580 full load
Length, feet (*metres*)	286 (*87·2*) pp; 307·5 (*93·7*) oa
Beam, feet (*metres*)	38·5 (*11·7*)
Draft, feet (*metres*)	15·5 (*4·7*)
Guns, surface	4—4 in (*102 mm*)
Guns, AA	6—40 mm
A/S	1 Hedgehog; 4 DCT; 2 DC racks
Boilers	2 Admiralty 3-drum, 225 psi
Main engines	Triple expansion 5 500 ihp; 2 shafts
Speed, knots	19·5
Radius, miles	7 500 at 10 knots
Oil fuel (tons)	680
Complement	168 (11 officers, 157 men)

Former British frigates of the "Bay" class, designed primarily for anti-aircraft escort duties.

TRANSFER. *Alvares Cabral* and *Pacheco Pereira* were purchased from Great Britain in Apr 1959 and officially transferred to the Portuguese Navy at Plymouth on 11 May 1959. *D. Francisco de Almeida* and *Vasco da Gama* were purchased from Great Britain in May 1961 and modernised before delivery by John I. Thornycroft & Co Ltd, Woolston, Southampton, where they were commissioned in the Portuguese Navy on 3 Aug 1961.

PHOTOGRAPHS. A photograph of *D Francisco de Almeida* appears in the 1963-64 to 1965-66 editions and of *Alvares Cabral* in the 1966-67 to 1968-69 editions.

PACHECO PEREIRA — *1969, Portuguese Navy, Official*

VASCO DA GAMA — *1968, Portuguese Navy, Official*

Name	No.	Builders	Laid down	Launched	Completed
D. FERNANDO (ex-*Diogo Gomes*, ex-HMS *Awe*)	F 331	Fleming & Ferguson Ltd, Paisley	27 May 1943	28 Dec 1943	21 Apr 1944
NUNO TRISTÃO (ex-HMS *Avon*)	F 332	Charles Hill & Sons, Bristol	8 Jan 1943	19 June 1943	18 Sep 1943

2 "DIOGO GOMES" CLASS
(Ex-BRITISH "RIVER" CLASS

Displacement, tons	1 460 standard; 2 450 full load
Length, feet (*metres*)	283 (*86·3*) pp; 301·5 (*91·9*) oa
Beam, feet (*metres*)	36·7 (*11·2*)
Draft, feet (*metres*)	12 (*3·7*); 15 (*4·6*) max
Guns, surface	2—4 in (*102 mm*)
Guns, AA	6—40 mm
A/S	2 Squid triple DC mortars; 2 DC racks
Boilers	2 Admiralty 3-drum, 210 psi
Main engines	Triple expansion 5 500 ihp; 2 shafts
Speed, knots	18 max, 16 sustained
Radius, miles	7 000 at 10 knots
Oil fuel (tons)	600
Complement	175 ((11 officers, 164 men)

Purchased from Great Britain in 1948 and transferred to Portugal in May 1949. Refitted in 1959 when the anti-submarine capabilities were improved by the installation of two squid triple-barrelled depth charge mortars, the four side thrown depth charge projectors were removed and only two depth charge racks were retained.

TRAINING. *Diogo Gomes*, renamed *D. Fernando* has been employed as a training ship since 31 Oct 1968 and her main armament has been removed.

PHOTOGRAPHS. A port bow view of *Diogo Gomes* appears in the 1958-59 to 1960-61 editions.

NUNO TRISTÃO (Squid in "B" position) — *1966, Portuguese Navy, Official*

D. FERNANDO (as *Diogo Gomes*) — *1969, Portuguese Navy, Official*

DEPOT SHIP *(Navio Deposito) Ex-Frigate*

Name	*No.*	*Builders*	*Laid down*	*Launched*	*Completed*
S. CRISTOVÃO (ex-*Bartolomeu Dias*)	A 5208 (ex-F 471)	R. & W. Hawthorn Leslie & Co Ltd, Hebburn-on Tyne	24 May 1933	10 Oct 1934	May 1935

Displacement, tons	1 788 standard; 2 439 full load
Length, feet (*metres*)	314 (*95·7*) pp 334·5 (*101·9*) wl 338·6 (*103·2*) oa
Beam, feet (*metres*)	44·2 (*13·5*)
Draft, feet (*metres*)	12·5 (*3·8*)
Guns, surface	2—4·7 in (*120 mm*) 50 cal.
Boilers	2 Yarrow, 300 psi
Main engines	2 Parsons sr geared turbines 8 000 shp
Speed, knots	21·8 max
Radius, miles	10 000 at 10 knots
Oil fuel (tons)	580
Complement	71 (6 officers, 65 men)

Formerly designated "Bartolomeu Dias" class and rated as Aviso de Primeiro Classe, when she was armed with four 4·7 inch, two 3 inch and eight 20 mm guns, with a capacity of 40 mines, but in Feb 1967 she was converted into a depot ship and rated as Navio Deposito.
Sister ship *Afonso de Albuquerque* was lost in action on 18 Dec 1961 during the Indian invasion of Goa.

S. CRISTOVÃO *1968, Portuguese Navy, Official*

CORVETTES

6 NEW CONSTRUCTION

"JOÃO COUTINHO" CLASS

Name	
ANTÓNIO ENES	Empresa Nacional Bazan de Construcciones Navales Militares, Spain
AUGUSTO CASTILHO	Empresa Nacional Bazan de Construcciones Navales Militares, Spain
GENERAL PEREIRA D'ECA	Blohm and Voss A.G., Hamburg, Germany
HONORIO BARRETO	Empresa Nacional Bazan de Construcciones Navales Militares, Spain
JACINTO CANDIDO	Blohm and Voss A.G., Hamburg, Germany
JOÃO COUTINHO	Blohm and Voss A.G., Hamburg, Germany

Displacement, tons	1 252 standard; 1 400 full load
Length, feet (*metres*)	227·5 (*84·6*)
Beam, feet (*metres*)	33·8 (*10·3*)
Draught, feet (*metres*)	10·0 (*3·07*)
Guns, AA	2—3 in (*76 mm*); 2—40 mm
A/S weapons	1 Hedgehog; 2 DC throwers; 2 DC tracks
Main engines	2 OEW 12 cyl. Pielstick diesels; 10 560 bhp
Speed, knots	22·3
Radius, miles	6 250 at 14 knots
Complement	97

These six corvettes or escorts of the small frigate type are projected under the new construction programme. The three being built in Germany were ordered in Apr 1968 for delivery in Jan, Apr and Aug 1970.

CACHEU (ex-*Comandate Almeida Carvalho*, ex-*Fort York*, ex-*Mingon*) F-470 (ex-A 527)

Displacement, tons	672 standard; 900 full load
Length, feet (*metres*)	171·5 (*52·3*) pp; 180 (*54·9*) oa
Beam, feet (*metres*)	28·5 (*8·7*)
Draft feet (*metres*)	9·5 (*2·9*) max
Guns, dual purpose	1—3 in (*76 mm*)
Guns, AA	2—20 mm
Boilers	2 three-drum small tube type
Main engines	Triple expansion 2 400 ihp; 2 shafts
Speed, knots	16
Oil fuel (tons)	160
Complement	83 (8 officers, 75 men)

Former British fleet minesweeper of the "Bangor" class. Originally a sister ship of *Almirante Lacerda*, see next page. Launched in Canada on 24 Aug 1941. Purchased from Great Britain in 1950. Served as a survey ship until 1965 when she was converted into a corvette and her name and number changed from *Comandante Alneida Carvalho*, A 527, to *Cacheu*, F 470.

S. CRISTOVÄA *1969, Portuguese Navy, Official*

SURVEY SHIPS *(Navios Hidrograficos) Ex-Frigate*

AFONSO DU ALBUQUERQUE (ex-HMS *Dalrymple*, ex-*Luce Bay*, ex-*Loch Glass*) A 526

Displacement, tons	1 600 standard; 2 230 full load
Length, feet (*metres*)	286 (*87·2*) pp; 307 (*93·6*) oa
Beam, feet (*metres*)	38·5 (*11·7*)
Draught, feet (*metres*)	14·2 (*4·3*)
Boilers	2 Admiralty 3-drum
Main engines	4-cylinder triple expansion 5 500 ihp; 2 shafts
Speed, knots	19·5
Radius, miles	5 000 at 10 knots
Oil fuel (tons)	580
Complement	140 (10 officers, 130 men)

Modified frigate of the "Bay" class. Built by Wm. Pickersgill & Sons Ltd, Sunderland, but completed at HM Dockyard, Devonport. Laid down on 29 Apr 1944. launched on 12 Apr 1945, and completed on 10 Feb 1949. Equipped with radar and sonar. Purchased by Portugal from Great Britain in Apr 1966.
The main machinery was manufactured by George Clark Ltd, Sunderland.
Power at 220 volts DC, is from two 120 kw turbo-generators and two 150 kw diesel generators.

AFONSO DE ALBUQUERQUE *1968, Portuguese Navy, Official*

Survey Ships—*continued*

1 "PEDRO NUNES" CLASS (Ex-SLOOP)

PEDRO NUNES A 528

Displacement, tons	1 090 standard; 1 197 full load
Dimensions, feet	223 pp × 32·8 × 9·5
Guns	1—4·7 in, 50 cal; 4—20 mm AA (see *Gunnery*)
Main engines	2 sets MAN 8 cyl diesels; 2 400 bhp = 16·5 knots
Oil fuel, tons	110 normal; 126 max
Radius, miles	6 000 at 13 knots
Complement	51 (7 officers, 44 men)

Built as a second class sloop (aviso de segundo classe) at Lisbon Naval Yard. Laid down on 5 Nov 1931, launched on 17 Mar 1934 and completed on 11 Apr 1935. Converted into a survey ship (navio hidrografico) in 1956.

GUNNERY. The forward 4·7 inch gun was removed from *Pedro Nunes* in 1956. when she was converted into a survey ship.

DISPOSAL
Sister ship **Joao de Lisboa** (ex-*Infante D. Henrique*), A 5200, was discarded on 17 Aug 1966.

PEDRO NUNES *1968, Portuguese Navy, Official*

1 Ex-BRITISH "FLOWER" CLASS FRIGATE

CARVALHO ARAUJO (ex-*Terje Ten*, ex-*Commandant Drogou*, ex-*Chrysanthemum*) A 524

Displacement, tons	1 020 standard; 1 340 full load
Dimensions, feet	190 pp; 205 oa × 33 × 16·5
Guns	1—3 inch; 4—20 mm AA
Main engines	Triple expansion; 2 750 ihp = 16 knots
Boilers	2 cylindrical
Oil fuel, tons	288
Complement	48 (7 officers and 41 men)

Former British corvette (later re-rated as a frigate) of the "Flower" class. Built by Harland & Wolff Ltd, Belfast. Laid down on 17 Dec 1940, launched on 11 Apr 1941, and completed on 26 Jan 1942. Served in the French Navy during the Second World War. Sold out of the service after hostilities. Purchased by Portugal from the Hector Whaling Company, at Capetown, in Mar 1959, and later equipped as a survey ship for the Portuguese Navy to replace the former *Corvalho Araújo* (ex-British "Flower" class minesweeping sloop *Jonquil*) which was discarded in 1959.

DISPOSAL
The survey ship **Salvador Correia** former minesweeper and patrol vessel **Baldaque da Silva**, ex-minesweeping trawler **Ruskholm** of the British "Isles" class, was discarded on 27 Mar 1967.

CARVALHO ARUJO *Added 1968, Admiral M. Adam*

Ex-BRITISH "BANGOR" CLASS FLEET MINESWEEPER

ALMIRANTE LACERDA (ex-*Caroquet*) A 525

Displacement, tons	672 standard; 900 full load
Dimensions, feet	171·5 pp; 180 oa × 28·5 × 9·5 max
Guns	1—3 in; 2—20 mm AA
Main engines	Triple expansion; 2 shafts; 2 400 ihp = 16 knots
Boilers	2, of 3-drum small-tube type
Oil fuel, tons	160
Complement	49 (7 officers, 42 men)

Former British fleet minesweeper of the "Bangor" class, steam type. Built in Canada, launched on 2 June 1941, and purchased from Great Britain in 1946.

Survey Ships—*continued*

ALMIRANTE LACERDA *1969, Portuguese Navy, Official*

SURVEY LAUNCHES

CRUZEIRO DO SUL (ex-*Giroflée*)

Displacement, tons	100 standard
Dimensions, feet	93·2 × 17·8 × 8
Main engines	2 Gleenifer diesels; 320 bhp = 12 knots max
Radius, miles	2 000 at 10 knots (economical speed)
Complement	6

MIRA (ex-*Formalhaut*, ex-*Arrabida*)

Displacement, tons	23 standard
Dimensions, feet	62·9 × 15·2 × 4
Main engines	3 Perkins diesels; 300 bhp = 15 knots max
Radius, miles	650 at 8 knots (economical speed)
Complement	6

OCEAN MINESWEEPERS

(*Draga-minas oceânicos*)

4 "S. JORGE" CLASS

CORVO (ex-USS *MSO* 487) M 418
GRACIOSA (ex-USS *MSO* 486) M 417
PICO (ex-USS *MSO* 479) M 416
S. JORGE (ex-USS *MSO* 478) M 415

Displacement, tons	665 standard; 750 full load
Dimensions, feet	165 pp; 172 oa × 35 × 10 mean
Guns	1—40 mm AA
Main engines	2 GM diesels; 2 shafts; 1 600 bhp = 13·5 knots max
Oil fuel, tons	46
Radius, miles	3 800 at 10 knots (economical speed)
Complement	69

"MSO 421" class ocean minesweepers built in the USA under the Mutual Defense Assistance Programme by Burger Boat Co, Maniowoc, Wisconsin and Bellingham Shipyard Co. Constructed of wooden and non-magnetic materials. The diesels of non-magnetic stainless steel alloy, are model 8-278A, two stroke cycle, non-reversible 8-cylinder V engines. Controllable pitch propellers are fitted. Photographs of *S. Jorge* appear in the 1956-57 to 1960-61 editions.

Name	*Builders*	*Laid down*	*Launched*	*Completed*
Corvo	Burger Boat Co	18 Aug 1953	28 July 1954	23 Nov 1955
Graciosa	Burger Boat Co	16 May 1953	19 Nov 1953	15 Aug 1955
Pico	Bellingham SY	1 Oct 1953	18 June 1954	1 June 1955
S. Jorge	Bellingham SY	26 Aug 1953	30 Apr 1954	24 Apr 1955

PICO *1967, Portuguese Navy, Official*

CORVO *Portuguese Navy, Official*

PATROL VESSELS (*Patrulhas*)

5 PORTUGUESE BUILT "MAIO" CLASS

Name	No.	Builders	Launched	Completed
BOAVISTA	P 592	Est Nav do Mondego	10 July 1956	17 May 1957
BRAVA	P 590	EN de Viana do Castelo	2 May 1956	27 Dec 1956
FOGO	P 591	EN de Viana do Castelo	2 May 1956	11 Apr 1957
SANTA LUZIA	P 594	Arsenal do Alfeite	17 Jan 1957	24 Oct 1958
SANTO ANTÃO	P 593	Arsenal do Alfeite	8 June 1956	30 Dec 1957

Displacement, tons	366 standard; 400 full load
Dimensions, feet	170 pp; 173·8 oa × 23 × 10 mean
Guns	2—40 mm AA; 2—20 mm AA
A/S weapons	1 Hedgehog; 4 DCT; 2 depth charge tracks
Main engines	4 SEMT-Pielstick diesels (4-stroke, 14 cylinder V); 2 shafts; 3 500 bhp = 19 knots
Oil fuel, tons	45
Radius, miles	3 900 at 19 knots
Complement	62 (5 officers, 57 men)

Built in Portugal under the US off-shore procurement programme. Of all-welded construction. A photograph of *Brava* appears in the 1958-59 to 1962-63 editions and of *Santo Antão* in the 1963-64 to 1967-68 editions.

SANTO LUZIA 1968

3 FRENCH BUILT "MAIO" CLASS

Name	No.	Builders	Launched
MAIO (ex-*Funchal*, ex-*P* 4)	P 587	Dubigeon, Nantes	27 Sep 1954
PORTO SANTO (ex-*P* 5)	P 588	Normand (Le Havre)	9 Feb 1955
S NICOLAU (ex-*P* 8)	P 589	Normand (Le Havre)	7 June 1955

Displacement, tons	366 standard; 400 full load
Dimensions, feet	170 pp; 173·7 oa × 23 × 10
Guns	2—40 mm AA; 2—20 mm AA
A/S weapons	1 Hedgehog; 4 DCT; 2 depth charge tracks
Main engines	4 SEMT-Pielstick diesels; 2 shafts; 3 240 bhp = 17·5 knots
Radius, miles	4 000 at 10 knots
Complement	62 (5 officers, 57 men)

Of PC design, but built in France as a US offshore procurement order under the Mutual Defense Assistance Programme. Fitted with two mine rails.

S. NICOLAU *1967, Portuguese Navy, Official*

4 "PRINCIPE" CLASS

PRINCIPE (ex-*Flores*, ex-*PC* 812) P 581 **S. TOMÉ** (ex-*PC* 1256) P 585
MADEIRA (ex-*PC* 811) P 582 **S. VICENTE** (ex-*PC* 1259) P 586

Displacement, tons	318 standard; 357 full load
Dimensions, feet	170 wl; 173·7 oa × 23 × 11 max
Guns	1—40 mm AA; 3—20 mm AA
A/S weapons	1 Hedgehog; 4 DCT; 2 depth charge tracks
Main engines	2 Hamilton diesels; 2 shafts; 3 500 bhp = 19 knots
Complement	62 (5 officers, 57 men)

Submarine chasers of the PC type purchased from USA in 1948. Named after Portuguese Atlantic Islands. For patrol and Air/Sea Rescue duties in the Azores, Maderia, and off the Portuguese coast. The armament was modified in 1957, anti-submarine weapons added and the 3 inch guns and two 20 mm guns removed. A photograph of *Madeira* appears in the 1966-67 to 1968-69 editions. Of sister ships, *Santiago* was decommissioned on 1 July 1967, and *Sal* on 31 Aug 1968.

PRINCIPE *1969, Portuguese Navy, Official*

COASTAL MINESWEEPERS

(*Draga-Minas Costeiros*)

4 "S. ROQUE" CLASS (BRITISH "TON" TYPE)

Name	No.	Launched	Completed
LAGOA	M 403	15 Sep 1955	10 Aug 1956
RIBEIRA GRANDE	M 402	14 Oct 1955	8 Feb 1957
ROSARIO	M 404	29 Nov 1955	8 Feb 1956
S ROQUE	M 401	5 Sep 1955	4 June 1956

Displacement, tons	360 standard; 425 full load
Dimensions, feet	140 pp; 152 oa × 28·8 × 7
Guns	1—40 mm AA; 2—20 mm AA (twin mount)
Main engines	2 Mirrlees diesels; 2 shafts; 2 500 bhp = 15 knots
Complement	47 (4 officers, 43 men)

Similar to the British "Ton" class coastal minesweepers, but built in Portugal. All laid down at CUF Shipyard, Lisbon, on 7 Sep 1954, under the OSP-MAP. *Lagoa* and *S Roque* were financed by USA and the other two by Portugal. A photograph of *Lagoa* appears in the 1958-59 to 1960-61 ediitons, of *Ribeira Grande* in the 1961-62 to 1965-66 editions and of *S. Roque* in the 1966-67 to 1968-69 editions.

ROSARIO *1969, Portuguese Navy, Official*

8 "PONTA DELGADA" CLASS

ANGRA DO HEROISMO	(ex-*AMS* 62)	M 407
HORTA	(ex-*AMS* 61)	M 406
LAJES	(ex-*AMS* 146)	M 411
PONTA DELGADA	(ex-*Adjutant, AMS* 60)	M 405
SANTA CRUZ	(ex-*AMS* 92)	M 409
S. PEDRO	(ex-*AMS* 147)	M 412
VELAS	(ex-*AMS* 145)	M 410
VILA DO PORTO	(ex-*AMS* 91)	M 408

Displacement, tons	375 standard; 405 full load
Dimensions, feet	138 pp; 144 oa × 27 × 8
Guns	2—20 mm AA (twin mount)
Main engines	GM diesels; 900 bhp = 14 knots
Complement	40 (4 officers, 36 men)

Of wooden and non-magnetic construction. *Ponta Delgada* was transferred from the US on 7 Apr 1953. Four more were delivered in 1953-54 and the remaining three in 1955. A photograph of *Horta* appears in the 1957-58 to 1960-61 editions, of *S. Pedro* in the 1961-62 to 1965-66 editions and of *Santa Cruz* in the 1966-67 to 1968-69 editions.

LAJES *1969, Portuguese Navy, Official*

FISHERY PROTECTION LAUNCHES

5 "AZEVIA" CLASS (*Lanchas de Fiscalizacão da Pesca*)

AZEVIA P595 **BICUDA** P596 **CORVINA** P 597 **DOURADA** P598 **ESPADILHA** P599

Displacement, tons	230; 270 full load
Dimensions, feet	134·5 pp; 139·8 oa × 21·3 × 7
Guns	2—20 mm AA
Main engines	2 7-cyl 2-stroke Sulzer diesels except first pair; 2 10-cyl 4-stroke MAN diesels; 2 shafts; 2 400 bhp = 17 knots
Oil fuel, tons	25
Radius, miles	3 700 at 11 knots; 850 at 17 knots
Complement	30 (2 officers, 28 men)

All launched in 1941-42. Photograph of *Bicuda* in the 1953-54 to 1959-60 editions.

AZEVIA *1968, Portuguese Navy, Official*

COASTAL PATROL VESSELS

(Navio Patrulhas)

8 + 4 "CACINE" CLASS

CACINE	**GEBA**	**QUANZA**	**ZAIRE**
CUNENE	**MANDOVI**	**ROVUMA**	**ZAMBEZE**

Displacement, tons	310 full load
Dimensions, feet	144 oa × 25·2 × 7·1
Guns	2—40 mm AA 1—32 barrelled rocket-launcher 37 mm
Main engines	2 Maybach diesels; 2 000 bhp = 20 knots
Complement	33 (3 officers, 30 men)

The first four were built in Arsenal do Alfeite, the others in Estaleiros Navais do Mondego. Four more are being built.

10 "ARGOS" CLASS

ARGOS	P 372	**DRAGÃO**	P 374	**LIRA**	P 361		
CASSIOPEIA	P 373	**ESCORPIÃO**	P 375	**ORION**	P 362		
CENTAURO	P 1130	**HIDRA**	P 376	**PEGASO**	P 379		
				SAGITARIO	P 1134		

Displacement, tons	180 standard; 210 full load
Dimensions, feet	131·2 pp; 136·8 oa × 20·5 × 7
Guns	2—40 mm AA
Main engines	2 Maybach diesels; 1 200 bhp = 17 knots
Oil fuel, tons	16
Complement	24 (2 officers, 22 men)

Six built by Arsenal do Alfeite, Lisbon, and four by Estaleiros Navais de Viana do Castelo. All completed June 1963 to Sep 1965. Named after constellations. A photograph of *Dragão* appears in the 1964-65 to 1966-67 editions.

ARGOS *1967, Portuguese Navy, Official*

PATROL LAUNCHES

2 "D. ALEIXO" CLASS

D. ALEIXO **D. JEREMIAS**

Displacement, tons	60 full load
Dimensions, feet	82·1 oa × 17 × 5·2
Guns	1—20 mm AA
Main engines	2 Cummins diesels; 1 270 bhp = 16 knots
Complement	10 (1 officer)

D. *Aleixo* was commissioned on 7 Dec 1967. *D. Jeremias* on 22 Dec 1967.

DOM ALEIXO *1969, Portuguese Navy, Official*

3 "ALVOR" CLASS

ALBUFEIRA P 1157 **ALJEZUR** P 1158 **ALVOR** P 1156

Displacement, tons	35·7 full load
Dimensions, feet	68 oa × 18 × 5·1
Guns	1—20 mm AA
Main engines	2 Cummins diesels; 235 bhp = 12·3 knots
Complement	7 (1 officer)

They were all built at Arsenal do Alfeite and commissioned in 1967-68.

ALVOR *1968, Portuguese Navy, Official*

13 "BELLATRIX" CLASS

ALDEBARAN		**CANOPUS**	P 364	**POLLUX**	P 368
ALTAIR	P 377	**DENEB**	P 365	**PROCION**	
ARCTURUS		**ESPIGA**	P 366	**RIGEL**	P 378
BELLATRIX	P 363	**FOMALHAUT**	P 367	**SIRIUS**	
				VEGA	

Displacement, tons	23 light; 29 full load
Dimensions, feet	62·8 wl; 68 oa × 15·2 × 4
Guns	1—20 mm Oerlikon AA
Main engines	2 Cummins diesels; 470 bhp = 15 knots
Complement	7

The first eight were completed in 1961-62 in Germany by Beyerische Schiffbaugesellschaft and the last five (*Arcturus, Aldebaran* and *Procion*, commissioned on 17 May 1968, *Sirius* and *Vega*) were built in Arsenal do Alfeite, Lisbon. A photograph of *Bellatrix* appears in the 1962-63 to 1967-68 editions.

ESPIGA *1969, Portuguese Navy, Official*

6 "JUPITER" CLASS

JUPITER	P 1132	**MERCURIO**	P 1135	**URANO**	P 1137
MARTE	P 1134	**SATURNO**	P 1136	**VENUS**	P 1133

Displacement, tons	32 full load
Dimensions, feet	69 oa × 16·5 × 4·3
Guns	1—20 mm Oerlikon AA
Main engines	2 Cummins diesels; 1 270 bhp = 20 knots
Complement	8

Built during 1964-65. All commissioned between 10 Mar and 12 Aug 1965.

JUPITER *1967, Portuguese Navy, Official*

ALGOL P 1138

Displacement, tons	24
Dimensions, feet	50·3 × 13·3 × 2·5
Guns	2 MG
Main engines	2 Cummins diesels; 244 bhp

Built by Argibay, Lisbon in 1964. Crew varies, normally seven.

ALGOL *1969, Portuguese Navy, Official*

CASTOR P 580

Displacement, tons	22
Dimensions, feet	53·5 wl; 58 oa × 13·1 × 3·3
Guns	1—20 mm Oerlikon AA
Main engines	2 Cummins diesels; 500 bhp = 15 knots
Complement	7

Built at the Estaleiros Navais do Mondego and commissioned on 3 Feb 1964.

Patrol Launchers—*continued*

2 "ANTARES" CLASS

ANTARES P 360 **REGULUS** P 369

Displacement, tons	18
Dimensions, feet	56 oa; 51·5 wl × 15·2 × 4 aft
Guns	1—20 mm Oerlikon quick firing AA
Main engines	2 Cummins diesels; 2 shafts; 460 bhp = 18·2 knots
Complement	7

Antares was built in 1959 by James Taylor (Shipbuilders) Ltd, Shoreham, Sussex, England. Hull of Deborine resinglass fibre moulding. *Regulus* was built in Portugal by Navalis Shipyard, the hull being imported from England. Completed 27 Jan 1962. Photographs of *Antares* appear in the 1960-61 to 1966-67 editions.
Of this class, *Sirius* and *Vega* were lost in action in Dec 1961 during the Indian invasion of Goa.

RIO MINHO P 370

Displacement, tons	13·5
Dimensions, feet	49·2 × 10·5 × 2·3
Guns	2 MG
Main engines	2 Alfa Romeo engines; 130 bhp = 9 knots
Complement	8

Built at Arsenal do Alfeite in 1955-57 for the River Minho on Spanish border.

TETE P 371

Displacement, tons	100
Dimensions, feet	76·7 × 20 × 2·2
Guns	2—47 mm; 2 MG
Main engines	Stern-wheel propulsion; 70 hp = 8 knots
Boilers	1 Yarrow

Built by Yarrow & Co Ltd, Scotstoun, Glasgow. Launched in 1918. Re-launched at Chinde in 1920. Employed on Zambesi River. Formerly river gunboat (lancha canhoneira) but re-rated patrol boat (lancha de fiscalizaçao) with 6 crew in 1960.

GUNBOAT (*Canhoneira*)

DIO A 5205

Displacement, tons	397 standard; 492 full load
Dimensions, feet	147·7 × 27·2 × 7
Guns	2—3 in, 40 cal (Armstrong); 2—47 mm
Main engines	Triple expansion; 2 shafts; 700 hp = 13 knots
Boilers	Yarrow (fired by coal, 85 tons)
Complement	58 (5 officers, 53 men)

Built at Lisbon Dockyard. Launched in Oct 1929. Used as reserve training ship

DIO *1964, Portuguese Navy, Official*

MINESWEEPER (*Caça-Mina*)

SANTA MARIA (ex-*P 4*, ex-*Whalsay*) M 392

Displacement, tons	560 standard; 770 full load
Dimensions, feet	164 × 27·5 × 15
Guns	1—3 in; 2—20 mm AA; DC carried
Main engines	Triple expansion; 850 ihp = 12 knots
Complement	52 (3 officers and 49 men)

"Isles" class trawler. Built by Cook, Welton & Gemmel, laid down 19 Dec 1941, launched 4 Apr 1942, completed 4 Sep 1942. Purchased from Great Britain in 1947, and named after island in the Azores. Originally classified as patrol vessel but later rated as minesweeper. Of five sister ships, *Miguel* (ex-*Brurey*) was discarded in 1956, *Terceira* (ex-*Haling*) in 1957, *Salvador Correia* (ex-*Saltarelo*) in 1961, and *Faial* (ex-*Mangrove*) M 391 was decommissioned in 27 Mar 1967. *Baldaque da Silva* (ex-*Ruskholm*) changed her name to *Salvador Correia* and was reclassified as a survey ship.

SANTA MARIA *1966, Portuguese Navy, Official*

LANDING CRAFT (*Lanchas de desembarque*)

5 LDG

ALFANGE **BOMBARDA** **ARIETE** **CIMITARRA** **MONTANTE**

Displacement, tons	500
Dimensions, feet	Length: 187
Main engines	2 diesels; 1 000 bhp
Complement	20

Landing craft similar to the LCT (4) type built at the Estaleiros Navais do Mondego and commissioned during 1965 (first four) and 1969 (*Bombarda*).

ALFANGE *1968, Portuguese Navy, Official*

9 LDM 400 CLASS

LDM 401 **LDM 402** **LDM 403** **LDM 404** **LDM 405** **LDM 406** **LDM 407** **LDM 408** **LDM 409**

13 LDM 300 CLASS

LDM 301 **LDM 302** **LDM 303** **LDM 304** **LDM 305** **LDM 306** **LDM 307** **LDM 308** **LDM 309** **LDM 310** **LDM 311** **LDM 312** **LDM 313**

5 LDM 200 CLASS

LDM 201 **LDM 202** **LDM 203** **LDM 204** **LDM 205**

5 LDM 100 CLASS

LDM 101 **LDM 102** **LDM 103** **LDM 104** **LDM 105**

Displacement, tons	50 full load
Dimensions, feet	Length: 50 feet
Main engines	2 diesels; 450 bhp

29 LCM type landing craft were commissioned in 1964 to 1966 setting up four classes in LDM 100, 200, 300, and 400 series as above. All built at the Estaleiros Navais do Mondego.

4 LDP 300 (Ex-LD) CLASS

LDP 301 **LDP 302** **LDP 303** **LDP 304**

17 LDP 200 CLASS

LDP 201 **LDP 202** **LDP 203** **LDP 204** **LDP 205** **LDP 206** **LDP 207** **LDP 208** **LDP 209** **LDP 210** **LDP 211** **LDP 212** **LDP 213** **LDP 214** **LDP 215** **LDP 216** **LDP 217**

5 LDP 100 (Ex-LD) CLASS

LDP 103 **LDP 105** **LDP 107** **LDP 108** **LDP 109**

Displacement, tons	12 light; 18 full load
Dimensions, feet	Length: 46 oa
Main engines	2 diesels; 180 bhp

The nine LD class landing craft (of the LCA type) were redesignated LDP 103, 105, 107, 108 and 109 and LDP 301, 302, 303 and 304. Built at the Estaleiros Navais do Mondego and commissioned on 16 June 1961 (LDP 103), 22 Feb 1963 (LDP 105), 1964 (LDP 107, 108, 109, 301, 302, 303, 304).
Thirteen LDP 200 class were commissioned in 1965-67, four in Jan-Feb 1969.

TRAINING SHIP (*Navio-Escola*)

SAGRES (ex-*Guanabara*, ex-*Albert Leo Schlageter*) A 520

Displacement, tons	1 415 standard; 1 869 full load
Dimensions, feet	229·7 pp; 249 oa × 39·3 × 17
Main engines	2 MAN auxiliary diesels; 1 shaft; 750 bhp = 10 knots
Oil fuel, tons	52
Radius, miles	3 500 at 10 knots
Complement	280

Former German sail training ship. Built by Blohm & Voss, Hamburg. Launched in June 1937 and completed on 1 Feb 1938. Sister of US Coast Guard training ship *Eagle* (ex-German *Horst Wessel*). Taken by USA as a reparation after the Second World War in 1945 and sold to Brazil in 1948. Purchased from Brazil and commissioned in the Portuguese Navy on 2 Feb 1962 at Rio de Janeiro and renamed *Sagres*. Sail area 20 793 sq ft. Height of mast 142 ft. A photograph of *Sagres* appears in the 1964-65 to 1967-68 editions.

Launching Ship—*continued*

SAGRES *1969, Portuguese Navy, Official*

DEPOT SHIP (*Navio Deposito*) Former Training Ship

SANTO ANDRÉ (ex-*Sagres*, ex-*Flores*, ex-*Max*, ex-*Rickmer Rickmers*) A 5207

Displacement, tons	3 067 standard; 3 176 full load
Dimensions, feet	263·5 × 40·3 × 19
Guns	4—47 mm saluting
Main engines	2 Krupp diesels; 2 shafts; 700 bhp = 8 knots

Former German sailing vessel. Built at Bremerhaven. Launched in 1896. Captured during the First World War. Re-rigged as a barque and adapted as a naval training ship during 1924-27. Auxiliary motors were fitted in 1931. Reclassified as a depot ship and renamed *Santo André* by decree of 31 Jan 1962. Replaced on 8 Feb 1962 by the training ship *Guanabara*, purchased from Brazil which took the name and number of the former *Sagres*.

FLEET OILER (*Navio Petroleiro*)

S. GABRIEL A 5206

Displacement, tons	9 000 standard; 14 200 full load
Measurement, tons	9 500 gross; 9 000 deadweight
Dimensions, feet	452·8 pp; 479 oa × 59·8 × 26·2
Main engines	1 Pametrada geared turbine; 1 shaft; 9 500 shp = 17 knots
Boilers	2
Radius, miles	6 000 at 15 knots
Complement	102 (9 officers, 93 men)

Built at Estaleiros de Viana do Castelo. Commissioned on 27 Mar 1963.

S. GABRIEL *1969, Portuguese Navy, Official*

LOGISTIC SHIP (*Navio de apoio Logistico*)

S. RAFAEL (ex-*Medusa*, ex-USS *Portunus, ARC* 1, ex-*LSM* 275, ex-*LCT* (7) 1773) A 5214

Displacement, tons	743 standard; 1 220 full load
Dimensions, feet	196·5 pp; 221·1 oa × 34·5 × 10·5
Guns	2—40 mm; 2—20 mm
Main engines	GM direct drive diesel; 2 shafts; 2 800 bhp = 12 knots
Radius, miles	5 240 at 10 knots
Complement	44

Former US medium landing ship, LSM type. Built by Federal Shipbuilding and Drydock Co, Newark, New Jersey. Laid down on 1 Aug 1944. launched on 11 Sep 1944, and completed on 6 Oct 1944. Converted to a cable repairing or laying ship the US Navy in 1952. Transferred to the Portuguese Navy under MAP in 1959. Delivered to Portugal on 16 Nov and commissioned on 18 Nov as a diving tender (*navio-apoio de mergulhadores*). A photograph of *S. Rafael* as such appears in the 1960-61 to 1967-68 editions. Converted to a logistic ship in 1969 and guns mounted as above.

Logistic Ship—*continued*

S. RAFAEL (as *Medusa*) *Portuguese Navy, Official*

SAM BRAS A 523

Displacement, tons	2 460 light; 5 600 standard; 7 375 full load
Measurement, tons	7 000 gross; 3 500 deadweight
Dimensions, feet	336·2 pp; 356·8 oa × 50·8 × 18
Guns	1—3 in (*76 mm*); 2—40 mm; 2—20 mm
Main engines	B. & W. 2-stroke diesel; 1 shaft; 2 820 bhp = 12 knots
Oil fuel, tons	568
Radius, miles	11 000 at 12 knots
Complement	70

Built at Arsenal do Alfeite. Laid down on 22 Feb 1941. Launched on 17 Mar 1942. Former fleet oiler converted to logistic ship and armed as above in Arsenal do Alfeite. A photograph of *Sam Bras* appears in the 1960-61 to 1967-68 editions.

S. BRAS *1969, Portuguese Navy, Official*

LIGHTHOUSE TENDER (*Navio Balizador*)

ALMIRANTE SCHULTZ A 521

Displacement, tons	538
Dimensions, feet	131·2 × 31 × 10·8
Main engines	2 Rateau diesels; 2 shafts; 500 bhp = 9 knots
Oil fuel, tons	21
Complement	47 (4 officers and 43 men)

Launched at Penhoët dockyard in 1929. Photograph in 1953-54 to 1957-58 editions.

ALMIRANTE SCHULTZ *Official*

RUMANIA

Diplomatic Representation

Naval ,Military and Air Attaché in London:
Colonel George I. Popa

Naval, Military and Air Attaché in Washington:
Colonel Nicolae Gheorghe Plesa

Strength of the Fleet

4 Fleet Minesweepers
5 Missile Boats
3 Patrol Vessels
8 Torpedo Boats
22 Inshore Minesweepers
8 Minesweeping Boats
2 Training Ships
30 Auxiliary Vessels

Personnel

1969: Total 8 000 officers and ratings

Mercantile Marine

Lloyd's Register of shipping:
56 vessels of 324 999 tons gross

MINESWEEPERS

4 Ex-GERMAN "M 40" TYPE

DESCATUSARIA DESROBIERA DEMOCRATIA DREPTATEA

Displacement, tons	543 standard; 775 full load
Dimensions, feet	188 pp; 203·5 oa × 28 × 7·5 (max)
Guns	6—37 mm AA (twin)
A/S weapons	2 DCT
Main engines	Triple expansion; 2 shafts; 2 400 ihp = 17 knots
Boilers	2 three-drum water tube
Fuel, tons	152 coal
Radius, miles	4 000 at 10 knots
Complement	80

Former German "M 40" type coal-burning minesweepers. Built in 1943. Taken over by USSR at the end of the Second World War. Transferred to Rumania in 1956-1957. Pennant numbers DB-13, DB-14, DB-15 and DB-16.

DB-15 and DB-16 *1968*

DB-14 and DB-15 *1964, P. H. Silverstone*

MISSILE BOATS

4 Ex-USSR "OSA" CLASS

Displacement, tons	160 standard, 200 full load
Dimensions, feet	131·5 oa × 23 × 6·5
Missile launchers	4 large hood type in two pairs abreast
Guns, AA	4—25 mm (2 twin, 1 forward, 1 aft)
Main engines	3 diesels; 4 800 bhp = 35 knots

Built since 1959. Reported to have a surface-to-surface range of 15 to 18 miles.

PATROL VESSELS

3 Ex-USSR "KRONSTADT" CLASS

V-1 V-2 V-3

Displacement, tons	300 standard; 350 full load
Dimensions, feet	167·3 × 19·3 × 9
Guns	1—3·4 in dual purpose forward; 2—37 mm AA single aft; 6—12·7 mm in twin mounts
A/S weapons	2 ahead throwing launchers; 2 side projectors; 2 depth charge tracks
Main engines	Diesels; 2 shafts; speed = 27 knots

Former Soviet submarine chasers transferred to Rumania from the USSR.

TORPEDO BOATS

8 Ex-USSR "P 4" CLASS

Displacement, tons	50
Dimensions, feet	85·3 × 20 × 6
Guns	4—25 mm AA
Tubes	2—21 in
Main engines	Speed = 42 knots

Former Soviet motor torpedo boats transferred to Rumania from the USSR.

INSHORE MINESWEEPERS

22 Ex-USSR "T 301" CLASS

Displacement, tons	130
Dimensions, feet	100 × 16 × 4·5
Guns	2—45 mm AA; 4—12·7 mm MG
Main engines	Diesel; 480 bhp = 10 knots
Complement	30

Former Soviet coastal Minesweepers transferred to Rumania by the USSR in 1956-60.

There are some launches on the Danube and some patrol boats in the Black Sea. Reports mention two surveying vessels, three landing ships (one LST and two LSM), ten landing craft (2 LCI and 8 LCT), ten transports and three oilers.

TRAINING SHIPS (*Navă Scoălă*)

MIRCEA

Displacement, tons	1 604
Dimensions, feet	239·5 oa; 267·3 (with bowsprit) × 39·3 × 16·5
Sail area	18 830 sq ft
Main engines	Auxiliary MAN; 6-cylinder Diesel; 500 bhp = 9·5 knots
Complement	83 + 140 midshipmen for training

Built by Blohm & Voss, Hamburg. Laid down on 30 Apr 1938. Launched on 22 Sep 1938. Completed on 29 Mar 1939 (delivered). Sail training ship. Refitted at Hamburg in 1966.

RASARITUL (ex-*Taifun*)

Measurement, tons	34 (*Thames* measurement)
Dimensions, feet	54 × 12·5 × 3
Main engines	2 petrol motors; 2 shafts.

Built by J. Samuel White & Co Ltd, Cowes, Isle of Wight, England. Launched in 1938. Of wooden construction. Yacht used as sail training ship. The training ship *Liberatea* (ex-*Luceafarul*, ex-*Nahlin*), former Royal Yacht was removed from the List in 1968.

MINESWEEPING BOATS

8 "TR-40 CLASS"

VD-241 VD-242 VD-243 VD-244 VD-245 VD-246 VD-247 VD-248

Eight "TR-40" Class minesweeping boats are employed on shallow water and river duties.

The medium escorts of the Soviet "Riga" class previously listed were apparently never more than on a mission to the Rumanian Navy.

The eight former Soviet submarines; the Rumanian built submarines *Requinul* (S 1) and *Marsuinul* (S 2); and the four former Soviet coastal submarines of the "M V" Type, were all deleted from the list in 1967. Most were over age and obsolescent and were discarded.

The very old destroyers *D 9* (ex-D 21, ex-*Letuchi*, ex-*Regina Maria*) and *D 10* (ex-D 22, ex-*Likhol*, ex-*Regele Ferdinand*), over age and obsolescent, were also deleted from the list in 1967.

The well over-age and obsolete destroyers *Marasti* (ex-Italian *Sparvieto*) and *Marasesti* (ex-Italian *Nibbio*) were discarded. One was scrapped at Constanta and the other reduced to a hulk.

The old minelayer *Amiral Murgescu*, latterly used as a training ship was deleted from the list in 1967. She was worn out and not worth refitting.

The old light cruiser *Kertch* (ex-*Stalingrad*, ex-Z 15, ex-*Emanuele Filiberto Duca D'Aosta*) was reported to have been lent by USSR to the Rumanian Navy. But in 1961 it was reported that she was being scrapped.

The two old patrol vessels rated as gunboats (canoniere), *Locotenent-Comandor Stiki Eugen* (ex-French *Friponne*) and *Sublocotenent Ghiculescu* (ex-French *Mignonne*), were deleted due to being over age and obsolete.

The two very old patrol boats, former Austrian torpedo boats (torpiloare), *Sborul* (ex-*T* 81) and *Smeul* (ex-*T* 83), considered to be of no further military value, were discarded to be scrapped.

Some of the old river monitors *Ardeal*, *Basarabia*, *Bratianu* and *Bucovina* are reported to still exist, but *Lahoorai* and the old river gunboats *Closca*, *Cusan* and *Horia* have been discarded.

The training ships *Constanta* (former submarine depot ship) and *Liberatea* (former Royal Yacht) were removed from the list in 1968.

SAUDI ARABIA

Mercantile Marine

Lloyd's Register of Shipping: 39 vessels of 49 625 tons gross

PATROL BOAT

RIYADH

Displacement, tons	102
Length, feet	95
Guns	1—40 mm AA
Speed	21 knots

Steel-hulled patrol boat of United States Coast Guard design transferred to Saudi Arabia in 1960.

MINESWEEPERS

A US Navy "Auk" class minesweeper is not now to be transferred to the Saudi Arabian Navy, but other minesweepers may be acquired.

MOTOR LAUNCHES

22 patrol boats, length 45 ft, with diesels have been ordered from Whittingham & Mitchel, Chertsey, England.

SENEGAL

Mercantile Marine

Lloyd's Register of Shipping: 39 vessels of 49 625 tons gross

PATROL BOATS

2 Ex-FRENCH "VC" TYPE

CASAMANCE (ex-*VC* 5, *P* 755)
SINE-SALOUM (ex-*Reine N'Galifourou*, ex-*VC* 4, *P* 754)

Displacement, tons	75 standard; 82 full load
Dimensions, feet	104·5 × 15·5 × 5·5
Guns	2—20 mm AA
Main engines	2 Mercedes-Benz diesels; 2 shafts; 2 700 bhp = 28 knots max

Former French patrol craft (Vedettes de Surveillance Côtière). Built by the Constructions Mécaniques de Normandie, Cherbourg. Completed in 1958. *Casamance* was transferred from France to Senegal in 1963. *Sine-Saloum* was given to Senegal on 24 Aug 1965 after having been returned to France bv the Congo in Feb 1965.

SINE-SALOUM *1967, Senegalese Navy, Official*

1 Ex-US "SC" TYPE

SÉNÉGAL (ex-*P* 700, ex-*CH* 62, ex-US *SC* 1344)

Displacement, tons	110 standard; 138 full load
Dimensions, feet	107·5 wl; 110·9 × 17 × 6·5
Guns	1—40 mm AA; 3—20 mm AA
Main engines	2 GM diesels; 2 shafts; 1 000 bhp = 13 knots max
Complement	25

Former US submarine chaser transferred to France on 19 Nov 1943, and from France to Senegal on 12 July 1961. First ship of Senegalese naval force.

SENEGAL *1967, Senegalese Navy, Official*

SIERRA LEONE

Mercantile Marine

Lloyd's Register of Shipping: 5 vessels of 4 438 tons gross

PATROL VESSELS

It has been officially stated that Sierra Leone is acquiring at least one fighting vessel (Sierra Leone became independent on 27 Apr 1961).

SINGAPORE

Mercantile Marine

Lloyd's Register of Shipping: 73 vessels of 133 855 tons gross

FAST PATROL CRAFT

6 NEW CONSTRUCTION

VOSPER THORNYCROFT TYPE

Displacement, tons	100
Dimensions, feet	110 × 21 × 6
Guns	2—20 mm AA (under review)
Main engines	2 Maybach diesels; 3 500 bhp; = 30 knots (max)
Complement	22 to 25

On 21 May 1968 the Vosper Thornycroft Group announced the receipt of an order for six of their 110-foot fast patrol boats for the Republic of Singapore. Two boats are being built at the Group's Portsmouth Yard and four at Vosper Thornycroft Uniteers Yard in Singapore. The total value of the order is £4 000 000. This is the first time that such advanced patrol craft have been built in the Group's Singapore Yard. It marks a significant step towards meeting further requirements for these very specialised craft in South East Asia. In design these vessels are of a hybrid type between that of the fast patrol craft built for the Malaysian Navy and those built for the Peruvian Navy.

SEAWARD DEFENCE BOAT

1 "FORD" TYPE

PANGLIMA P 48

Displacement, tons	119 standard; 131 full load
Dimensions, feet	117 oa × 20 × 6
Guns	1—40 mm, 60 cal forward
Main engines	Paxman YHAXM supercharged B 12 diesels = 14 knots
Oil fuel, tons	15
Complement	15 officers and men

Built by United Engineers, Singapore. Laid down in 1954. Launched on 14 Jan 1956. Accepted by the Singapore Government in May 1956. Similar to the British seaward defence boats of the "Ford" class. Transferred to the Royal Malaysian Navy on the formation of Malaysia. Transferred to the Singapore Government (independent Republic of Singapore) in 1967.

PANGLIMA *1964, Official*

SOMALIA

Somalia became an independent as the Somali Republic on 1 July 1960.

Mercantile Marine

Lloyd's Register of Shipping: 15 vessels of 58 677 tons gross

PATROL BOATS

2 Ex-USSR "POLUCHATI I" CLASS

12 of more ex-USSR "P-6" type were to be transferred by the USSR or UAR.

SOUTHERN YEMEN

Mercantile Marine

Lloyd's Register of Shipping: 3 vessels of 1,012 tons gross

INSHORE MINESWEEPERS

3 "HAM" CLASS

Displacement, tons	120 standard; 160 full load
Dimensions, feet	106·5 oa × 21·2 × 5·5
Guns	1—20 mm AA
Main engines	2 Paxman diesels; 1 100 bhp = 14 knots
Oil fuel, tons	15
Complement	15 officers and men

The British inshore minesweepers *Bodenham*, *Blunham* and *Elsenham* were transferred to the South Arabian Navy established by the Federal Government.

SOUTH AFRICA

Administration

Commander Maritime Defence and Chief of the Navy:
Vice-Admiral H. H. Bierman SSA, SM

Chief of Naval Staff:
Rear-Admiral N. R. Terry-Lloyd, SM

Armed Forces Attaché in London:
Brigadier S. P. Palmer, SM, DFC, SAAF

Diplomatic Representation

Naval Attaché in London:
Commander R. D. Kingdom, SAN

Naval, Military and Air Attaché in Washington:
Brigadier H. J. P. Burger, SM

Strength of the Fleet

2 Destroyers (Helicopter Carrying)
6 Anti-Submarine Frigates
1 Escort Minesweeper (Training)
10 Coastal Minesweepers (Non-Magnetic)
6 Seaward Defence Craft
4 Support Ships and Auxiliaries

New Construction Programme

3 Submarines (French "Daphne" Class),
1 Diving and Torpedo Recovery vessel, 1 Tug

Personnel

1969: 390 officers and 3 050 ratings

Naval Base

HM Dockyard at Simonstown was transferred to the Republic of South Africa on 2 Apr 1957.

Mercantile Marine

Lloyd's Register of Shipping:
244 vessels of 470 078 tons gross

SUBMARINES

3 FRENCH "DAPHNE" TYPE

Of the same basic characteristics as those of the "Daphne" type in the French Navy, also ordered by Pakistan and Portugal.

Name	*Builders*	*Laid down*	*Launched*	*Completion*
MARIA VAN RIEBECK	Dubigeon—Normandie	14 Mar 1968	18 Mar 1969	1970
JOHANNA VAN DER MERWE	Dubigeon—Normandie	18 Nov 1968		1971
EMILY HOBHOUSE	Dubigeon—Normandie			1971

DESTROYERS

2 FORMER BRITISH "W" CLASS

Name	*No.*	*Builders*	*Laid down*	*Launched*	*Completed*
JAN VAN RIEBEECK (ex-HMS *Wessex*, ex-*Zenith*)	D 278	Fairfield SB & Eng Co Ltd, Govan, Glasgow	20 Oct 1942	2 Sep 1943	11 May 1944
SIMON VAN DER STEL (ex-HMS *Whelp*)	D 237	R. & W. Hawthorn Leslie & Co Ltd	1 May 1942	3 June 1943	25 Apr 1944

Displacement, tons	2 105 standard; 2 750 full load
Length, feet (*metres*)	339·5 (*103·6*) pp; 362·8 (*110·6*) oa
Beam, feet (*metres*)	35·7 (*10·9*)
Draught, feet (*metres*)	17 (*5·2*) max (props)
Aircraft	2 Westland Wasp helicopters
Guns, surface	4—4 in (*102 mm*) (two twin)
Guns, AA	4—40 mm (single)
Guns, saluting	4—3 pdr.
Torpedo tubes	4—21 in (quadruple)
A/S	2 DCT; 2 DC racks
Boilers	2 Admiralty 3-drum; 300 psi; 670°F
Main engines	2 Parsons sr geared turbines 40 000 shp; 2 shafts
Speed, knots	36·75 designed; 31·25 sea speed
Radius, miles,	3 262 at 14 knots
Oil fuel, tons	579 (95%)
Complement	192 (11 officers, 181 men)

Purchased from Great Britain, *Jan van Riebeeck* was transferred to South Africa on 29 Mar 1950, and *Simon van der Stel* early in 1952. *Jan van Riebeeck* now in reserve.

GUNNERY. Main armament formerly comprised 4—4·7 inch guns.

JAN VAN RIEBEECK (after modernisation) *1967, South African Navy, Official*

MODERNISATION. *Simon van der Stel* was modernised in 1962-64 and *Jan van Riebeeck* in 1964-66.

PHOTOGRAPHS. A photograph of *Simon van der Stel* appears in the 1964-65 to 1966-67 editions.

ANTI-SUBMARINE FRIGATES

3 "PRESIDENT" CLASS. TYPE 12

Name	*No.*	*Builders*	*Laid down*	*Launched*	*Completed*
PRESIDENT KRUGER	F 150	Yarrow & Co, Scotstoun	6 Apr 1959	20 Oct 1960	1 Oct 1962
PRESIDENT PRETORIUS	F 145	Yarrow & Co, Scotstoun	21 Nov 1960	28 Sep 1962	4 Mar 1964
PRESIDENT STEYN	F 147	Alex Stephen & Sons, Govan	20 May 1960	23 Nov 1961	25 Apr 1963

Displacement, tons	2 144 standard; 2 557 full load
Length, feet (*metres*)	360 (*109·7*) wl; 370 (*112·8*) oa
Beam, feet (*metres*)	41 (*12·5*)
Draught, feet (*metres*)	17 (*5·2*) max (props)
Guns, surface	2—4·5 in (*115 mm*), twin
Guns, AA	2—40 mm Bofors
Guns, saluting	4—3 pdr.
A/S	2 Limbo 3-barrel DC mortars
Boilers	2 Babcock & Wilcox, 550 psi, 850°F
Main engines	2 sets double reduction geared turbines; 30 000 shp; 2 shafts
Speed, knots	over 30 max, 28 sustained
Radius, miles	4 500 at 15 knots
Oil fuel, tons	431
Complement	203 (13 officers, 190 men)

PRESIDENT KRUGER *1969, South African Navy, Official*

"Whitby" type built in the United Kingdom as a part of the expansion programme. *President Kruger* arrived in South Africa on 27 Mar 1963.

GUNNERY. The two 40 mm guns are on the main deck, a deck lower than in the "Whitby" class.

ENGINEERING. Geared turbines of advanced design and high power start on a cruising turbine and automatically switch over to the main turbine as a predetermined speed.

ELECTRICAL. System is alternating current, 440 volts, three phase, 60 cycles per second.

NAMES. Kruger was the last President of the Transvaal Republic. Steyn was the last President of old Orange Free State. Pretorius was the first President of the Transvaal Rapublic: he built and named the capital Pretoria after his father, one of the "Great Trek" leaders.

PHOTOGRAPHS. A photograph of *President Pretorius* appears in the 1967-68 to 1968-69 editions.

PRESIDENT STEYN *1966, South African Navy, Official*

Frigates—*continued*

1 FORMER BRITISH TYPE 15

VRYSTAAT (ex-HMS *Wrangler*) F 157

Displacement, tons	2 160 standard; 2 710 full load
Length, feet (*metres*)	339·5 (*103·6*)pp; 362·8 (*110·6*)oa
Beam, feet (*metres*)	35·7 (*10·9*)
Draught, feet (*metres*)	17 (*5·2*) max props
Guns, surface	2—4 in (*102 mm*)
Guns, AA	2—40 mm Bofors
Guns, saluting	4—3 pdr.
A/S	2 Squid triple DC mortars
Boilers	2 Admiralty 3-drum; 300 psi; 675°F
Main engines	Parsons single reduction geared turbines; 40 000 shp; 2 shafts
Speed, knots	36·75 designed; 31·25 sea speed
Radius, miles	3 200 at 14 knots
Oil fuel, tons	505
Complement	195 (13 officers, 182 men)

Built by Vickers-Armstrongs Ltd, Barrow-in-Furness. Laid down on 23 Sep 1942, launched on 30 Dec 1943, completed on 14 June 1944. Fully converted into a Type 15 fast anti-submarine frigate from a fleet destroyer of the "W" class in 1951-52 by Harland & Wolff Ltd, Belfast. Refitted by the Mount Stuart Dry Dock Ltd, Cardiff, and taken over from the Royal Navy on 29 Nov 1956 as a unit of the South African Navy and renamed *Vrystaat*. Sailed for South Africa at the end of Jan 1957. Originally a sister ship of *Jan van Riebeeck* and *Simon van der Stel* (see previous page).

VRYSTAAT — *1966, South African Navy, Official*

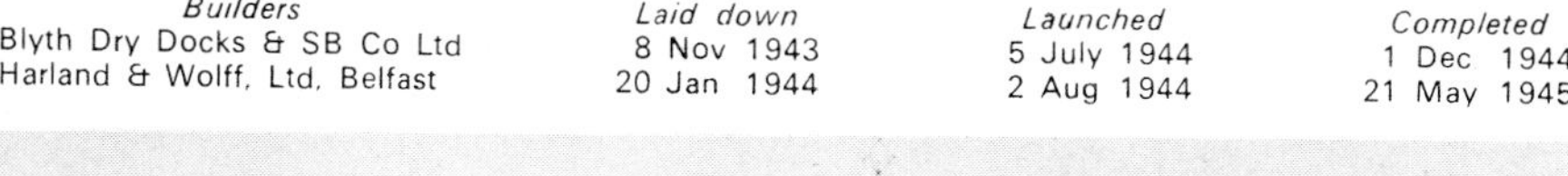

Name	*No.*	*Builders*	*Laid down*	*Launched*	*Completed*
GOOD HOPE (ex-HMS *Loch Boisdale*)	F 432	Blyth Dry Docks & SB Co Ltd	8 Nov 1943	5 July 1944	1 Dec 1944
TRANSVAAL (ex-HMS *Loch Ard*)	F 602	Harland & Wolff, Ltd, Belfast	20 Jan 1944	2 Aug 1944	21 May 1945

2 FORMER BRITISH "LOCH" CLASS

Displacement, tons	1 610 standard; 2 450 full load
Length, feet (*metres*)	286 (*87·2*) pp; 307 (*93·6*) oa
Beam, feet (*metres*)	38·5 (*11·7*)
Draught, feet (*metres*)	15 (*4·6*) max
Guns, surface	2—4 in (*102 mm*)
Guns, AA	*Transvaal:* 6—40 mm Bofors *Good Hope:* 2—40 mm Bofors
Guns, saluting	*Good Hope:* 4—3 pdr.
A/S	2 Squid triple DC mortars
Boilers	2 Admiralty 3-drum; 225 psi
Main engines	2 sets triple expansion 5 500 ihp; 2 shafts
Speed, knots	19·5 max (designed)
Radius, miles	9 500 at 12 knots
Oil fuel (tons)	724
Complement	165 (10 officers, 155 men)

These two "Loch" class anti-submarine frigates, and a sister ship, *Natal*, were presented to South Africa by Great Britain in 1944-45.

GOOD HOPE — *1969, South African Navy, Official*

CONSTRUCTION. *Transvaal* was completed by Lobnitz & Co Ltd, Renfrew.

MODIFICATION. When *Transvaal* was modernised she had her forecastle deck extended aft to provide extra accommodation (see photograph).

CONVERSIONS. *Good Hope* was converted to a despatch vessel in 1955 as Administrative Flagship of the South African Navy. She has deckhouse superstructure for extra cabins, and reception platform above built on aft, and mainmast. Refitted in 1961. Sister ship *Natal* was converted into a survey ship in 1957, see next page.

TRANSVAAL — *South African Navy, Official*

ESCORT MINESWEEPER

1 FORMER BRITISH "ALGERINE" CLASS

PIETERMARITZBURG (ex-HMS *Pelorus*) M 291

Displacement, tons	1 040 standard; 1 330 full load
Length, feet (*metres*)	212·5 (*64·8*) pp; 225 (*68·6*) oa
Beam, feet (*metres*)	35·5 (*10·8*)
Draught, feet (*metres*)	11·5 (*3·5*)
Guns, surface	2—4 in (*102 mm*)
Guns, AA	2—40 mm Bofors
A/S	4 DCT
Boilers	2 three-drum type; 250 psi
Main engines	2 sets triple expansion 2 400 ihp; 2 shafts
Speed, knots	16 max, 14 sustained
Radius, miles	5 500 at 10 knots
Oil fuel (tons)	270
Complement	115 (8 officers, 107 men)

Built as ocean minesweeper by Lobnitz & Co Ltd, Renfrew. Laid down on 8 Oct 1942, launched on 18 June 1943, completed on 7 Oct 1943. Also used as escort vessel. Purchased from Great Britain in 1947. Re-commissioned as midshipmen's training ship on 30 Aug 1962.

Sister ship *Bloemfontein* (ex-HMS *Rosamund*) was sunk on 5 June 1967 off Simonstown as a target by *Johannesburg* and *President Kruger*.

PIETERMARITZBURG — *1969, South African Navy, Official*

SURVEY SHIP (*ex-Frigate*)

NATAL (ex-HMS *Loch Cree*) A 301

Displacement, tons	1 435 standard; 2 260 full load
Length, feet (*metres*)	286 (*87·2*) pp; 307 (*93·6*) oa
Beam, feet (*metres*)	38·5 (*11·7*)
Draught, feet (*metres*)	12 (*3·7*) mean; 14·7 (*4·5*) max
Boilers	2 Admiralty 3-drum
Main engines	Triple expansion 5 500 ihp; 2 shafts
Speed, knots	19·5 max (designed)
Radius, miles	9 500 at 12 knots
Oil fuel (tons)	724
Complement	124

"Loch" class frigate built by Swan, Hunter & Wigham Richardson Ltd, Wallsend on Tyne. Laid down on 18 Oct 1943, launched on 19 June 1944, completed on 8 Mar 1945. Presented by Great Britain in 1945. Converted into a survey ship in 1957, when guns and A/S weapons were removed. Sister ship of *Good Hope* and *Transvaal*, see previous page.

NATAL *South African Navy, Official*

COASTAL MINESWEEPERS

10 BRITISH "TON" CLASS

DURBAN	M 1499	**MOSSELBAAI** (ex-*Oakington*)	M 1213
EAST LONDON (ex-*Chilton*)	M 1215	**PORT ELIZABETH** (*Dumbleton*)	M 1212
JOHANNESBURG (*Castleton*)	M 1207	**PRETORIA** (ex-*Dunkerton*)	M 1144
KAAPSTAD (ex-*Hazleton*)	M 1142	**WALVISBAAI** (ex-*Packington*)	M 1214
KIMBERLEY (ex-*Stratton*)	M 1210	**WINDHOEK**	M 1498

Displacement, tons	360 standard; 425 full load
Dimensions, feet	140 pp; 152 oa × 28·8 × 8·2
Guns	1—40 mm Bofors AA; 2—20 mm AA
Main engines	Diesels (Mirrlees in *Kaapstad* and *Pretoria*; 2 500 bhp. Deltic in remainder; 3 000 bhp = 15 knots
Complement	27

Kaapstad and *Pretoria*, which have lattice masts and open bridge, were purchased in 1955. *Windhoek*, with frigate bridge and tripod mast, was launched at John I. Thornycroft & Co Ltd, Woolston, Southampton, on 27 June 1957. *Durban*, which has a covered bridge and tripod mast, was launched at Camper & Nicholson's Gosport, on 12 June 1957. *East London* and *Port Elizabeth* were transferred from the Royal Navy at Hythe, Southampton, on 27 Oct 1958, and sailed for South Africa in Nov 1958. *Johannesburg*, *Kimberley* and *Mosselbaai* were delivered in 1959. *Walvisbaai* was launched by Harland & Wolff, Belfast on 10 Dec 1958 and delivered in 1959. A photograph of *Pretoria* appears in the 1956-57 to 1962-63 editions, of *Windhoek* in the 1958-59 to 1963-64 editions, of *Kimberley* in the 1962-63 to 1966-67 editions.

WALVISBAAI *1967, Wright & Logan*

SEAWARD DEFENCE LAUNCH

SDML 1204

Displacement, tons	46 standard; 54 full load
Dimensions, feet	72 oa × 15·9 × 5·3
Main engines	2 Gardner 8-cylinder diesels; 130 bhp = 11 knots
Complement	11 to 14

Sole survivor of the former HDMLs (Harbour Defence Motor Launches) later designated Seaward Defence Motor Launches. Built in South Africa. Guns were removed. Used as tender to South African Naval Base. SDML 1202 was converted to a gunnery practice target. SDML 1330 and 1331 were stricken off in 1953 and SDML 1199 and 1201 in 1955. SDML 1198 was scrapped in 1956, SDML 1332 on 11 Feb 1958 and SDMLs 1197, 1200, 1202 and 1203 in 1968.

FLEET REPLENISHMENT SHIP

TAFELBERG (ex-*Annam*)

Measurement, tons	12 500 gross; 18 430 deadweight
Speed, knots	15·5
Complement	100 as naval vessel (40 as tanker)

Built as Danish East Asiatic Co.'s tanker by Nakskovs Skibsvaerf. Launched on 20 June 1958. Purchased by the South African Navy in 1965. Accommodation re-habilitated by Barens Shipbuilding and Engineering Co, Durban with extra accommodation, air conditioning, re-wiring for additional equipment, new upper RAS (replenishment at sea) deck built to contain gantries, re-fuelling pipes. Provision for helicopters. Remainder of conversion carried out by Jowies, Brown and Hamer, Durban. Name means Table Mountain.

TAFELBERG *1968, South African Navy, Official*

SEAWARD DEFENCE BOATS

5 BRITISH "FORD" CLASS

GELDERLAND (ex-HMS *Brayford*)	P 3105	**NAUTILUS** (ex-HMS *Glassford*)	P 3120
		OOSTERLAND	P 3127
HAERLEM	P 3126	**RIJGER**	P 3125

Displacement, tons	120 standard; 160 full load
Dimensions, feet	110 wl; 117·2 oa × 20 × 4·5
Guns	1—40 mm AA
A/S weapons	2 DCT in *Haerlem*, *Oosterland* and *Rijger*
Main engines	2 Davey Paxman diesels. Foden engine on centre shaft. 1 100 bhp = 18 knots max; sea speed: 15 knots
Complement	24

Gelderland was purchased from Great Britain in 1954, being handed over to the South African Navy at Portsmouth on 30 Aug 1954. They were a new design of naval vessel, their purpose being to detect, locate and destroy submarines, including midget submarines, in the approaches of defended ports. They have modern electronic equipment for armament, and a comprehensive electrical installation. *Gelderland* was built by A. & J. Inglis Ltd, Glasgow. Second ship, *Nautilus*, was purchased in 1955, *Rijger* was launched on 6 Feb 1958, *Haerlem* on 18 June 1958, *Oosterland* on 27 Jan 1959. All three of these later ships, built by Vosper Ltd, Portsmouth, are fitted with roll damping fins developed and manufactured by Vosper. *Haerlem* had a charthouse added aft as an inshore survey boat. A photograph of *Gelderland* appears in the 1955-56 edition, of *Nautilus* in the 1956-57 to 1959-60 edition, and of *Rijger* in the 1964-65 and 1965-66 editions.

HAERLEM (charthouse added aft) *1966, South African Navy, Official*

BOOM DEFENCE VESSEL

SOMERSET (ex-HMS *Barcross*) P 285

Displacement, tons	750 standard; 960 full load
Dimensions, feet	150 pp; 182 oa × 32·2 × 11·5
Main engines	Triple expansion; 850 ihp = 11 knots
Boilers	2 SE
Oil fuel, tons	186
Complement	32

Built by Blyth Dry Dock & SB Co Ltd. Laid down on 15 Apr 1941, launched on 21 Oct 1941, completed on 14 Apr 1942. Engined by Swan, Hunter & Wigham Richardson Ltd, Wallsend-on-Tyne. "Bar" class. Transferred from Great Britain. Renamed in 1951 after Dick King's horse. Sister ship *Fleur* (ex-HMS *Barbrake*) P 273 was expended as a target and sunk in False Bay on 8th Oct 1965.

SOMERSET *R. M. Scott*

NAVAL TUG

DE NOORDE

Displacement, tons	170
Dimensions, feet	104·5 × 25
Main engines	2 Lister Blackstone diesels; 2 shafts

Built by Globe Engineering Works Ltd, Cape Town. Completed in Dec 1961.

SPAIN

Administration

Minister of Marine:
Admiral Excmo Sr Don Pedro Nieto Antunez

Chief of Naval Staff:
Admiral Excmo Sr Don Adolfo Baturone Colombo

Deputy Chief of Naval Staff:
Vice-Admiral Excmo Sr Don Ignacio Martel Viniegra.

Commander-in-Chief of the Fleet:
Vice-Admiral Excmo Sr Don Juan Romero Manso

Diplomatic Representation

Naval Attaché in London:
Captain Sr Don Juan Carlos Muñoz-Delgado

Naval Attaché in Washington:
Captain Sr Don Jorge Garcia-Parreño Kaden

Strength of the Fleet

1 Helicopter Carrier
8 Submarines (Diesel Powered)
1 Heavy Cruiser
19 Destroyers (15 Anti-Submarine)
6 Frigates
6 Frigate Minelayers
6 Corvettes
13 Fleet Minesweepers
12 Coastal Minesweepers
17 Patrol Vessels
3 Torpedo Boats
11 Landing Craft
40 Support Ships and Service craft

Building Programme

New construction projected includes 5 frigates of US design and 2 submarines of French design.

Personnel

1969: Total 51 200 (4 400 officers, 36 000 ratings, 4 800 civil branch, 6 000 marines)

Navy Estimates

1960: 2 655 833 903.00 pesetas
1961: 2 658 479 733.00 pesetas
1962: 3 314 590 252.00 pesetas
1963: 3 559 743 625.00 pesetas
1964: 3 904 880 558.00 pesetas
1965: 4 000 000 000.00 pesetas
1966: 4 500 000 000.00 pesetas
1967: 5 000 000 000.00 pesetas
1968: 6 800 000 000.00 pesetas
1969: 6 800 000 000.00 pesetas

Mercantile Marine

Lloyd's Register of Shipping:
2 046 vessels of 2 820 784 tons gross

Silhouettes

Scale 150 feet = 1 inch

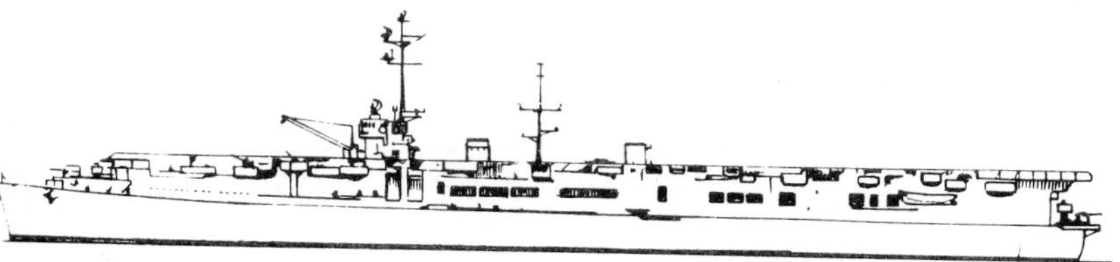

DÉDALO

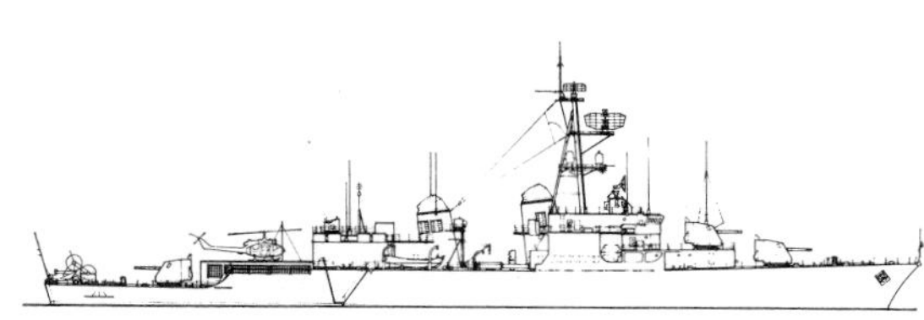

MARQUES DE LA ENSENADA, ROGER DE LAURIA

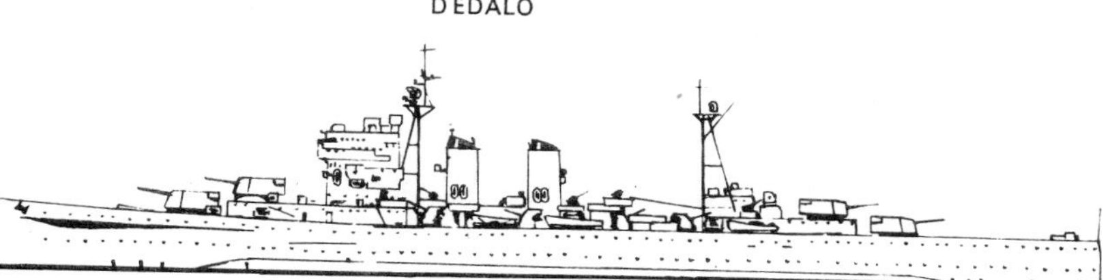

CANARIAS

ALCALA GALIANO, JORGE JUAN

ALMIRANTE FERRANDIZ

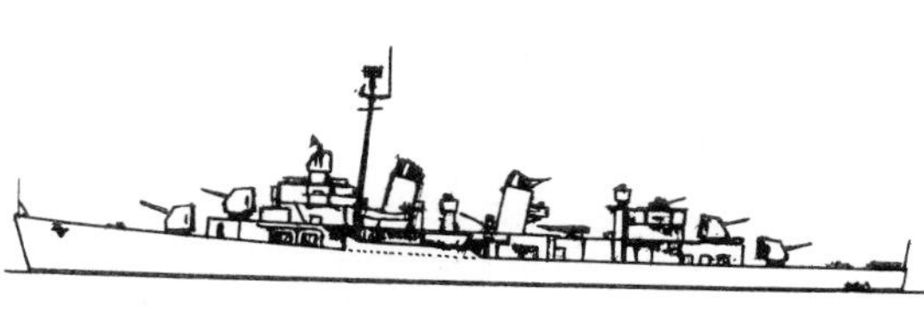

ALMIRANTE VALDES

LEPANTO

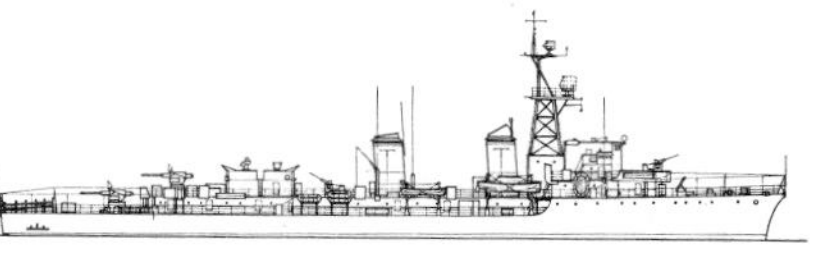

AUDAZ *Class*

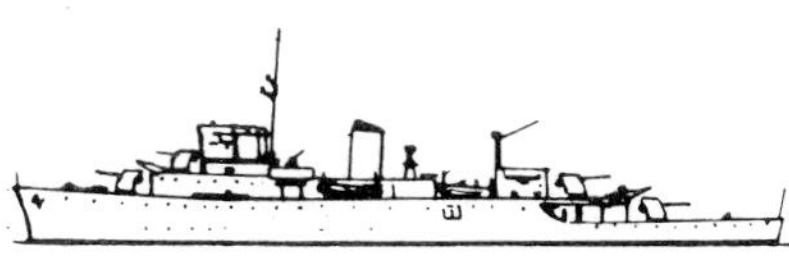

EOLO, TRITON

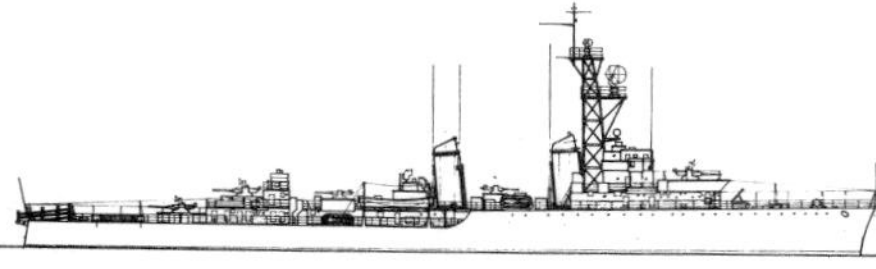

ALAVA, LINIERS

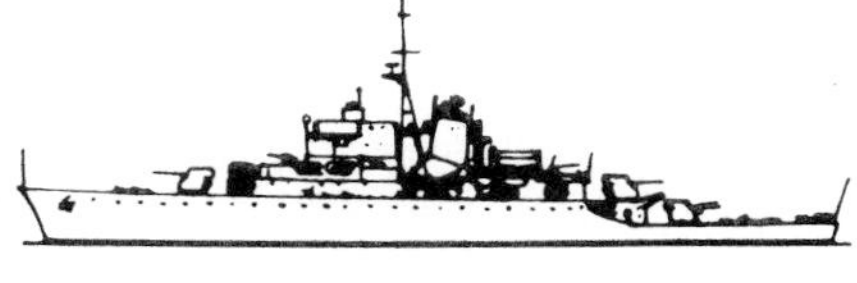

PIZARRO *Class*

MARTE, NEPTUNO

ALMIRANTE ANTEQUERA *Class*

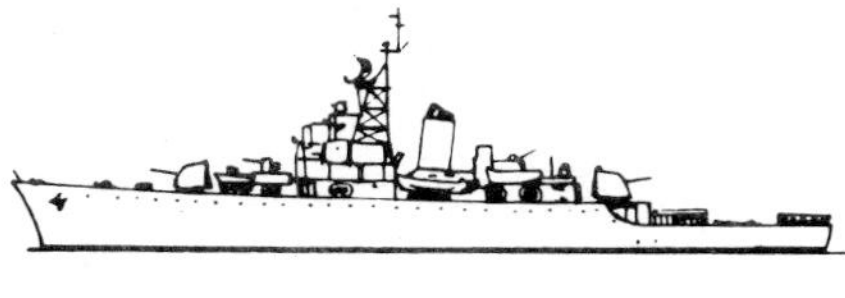

LEGAZPI, VICENTE YANEZ PINZON

DESCUBIERTA

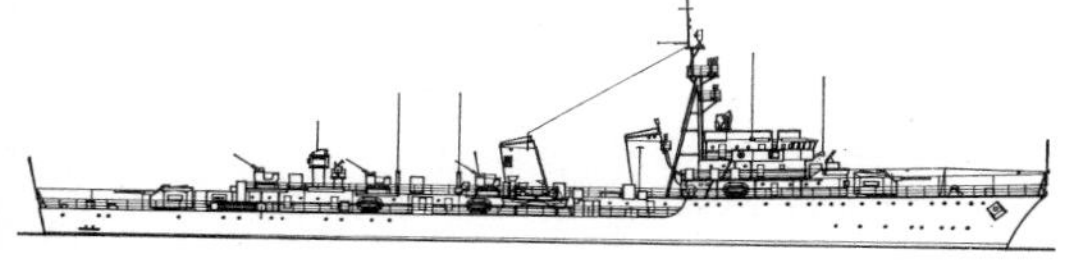

OQUENDO

JUPITER, VULCANO

ATREVIDA *Class*

HELICOPTER CARRIER

Name	No.	Builders	Laid down	Launched	Completed
DÉDALO (ex-USS *Cabot*, ex-*Wilmington*, AVT 3, ex-CVL 28)	PH 01	New York Shipbuilding Corporation	16 Aug 1942	4 Apr 1943	24 July 1943

Ex-AIRCRAFT TRANSPORT (AVT)
FORMER AIRCRAFT CARRIER ("CVL")

Displacement, tons	11 000 standard; 15 800 full load
Length, feet (*metres*)	600 (*182·9*) wl; 623 (*189·9*) oa
Beam, feet (*metres*)	71·5 (*21·8*) hull
Draught, feet (*metres*)	26 (*7·9*)
Width, feet (*metres*)	109 (*33·2*) extreme
Aircraft	20 anti-submarine helicopters
Boilers	4 Babcock & Wilcox
Main engines	GE geared turbines 100 000 shp; 4 shafts
Speed, knots	32
Complement	800 (50 officers, 750 men)

Completed as an aircraft carrier after having been laid down as a cruiser of the "Cleveland" class. Originally carried over 40 aircraft. Converted to ASW, i.e. modified to specialise in anti-submarine warfare, and classed as a "Hunter-Killer Carrier" with strengthened flight and hangar decks, large port side catapult, revised magazine arrangements, new electronic gear, corrected stability to counter added top weight, and a maximum of 26 aircraft. As an aircraft carrier the original complement was 1 109 (159 officers and 950 men). Originally designed to include 4—5 inch guns in armament. Latterly mounted 28—40 mm AA. Since conversion has only two of her original four funnels.

US approval to loan *Thetis Bay*, LPH 6, former assault helicopter carrier CVHA 1, converted escort aircraft carrier CVE 90, to Spain for five years was rescinded, and instead *Cabot* was reactivated and modernised at Philadelphia Naval Shipyard, where she was transferred to Spain on 30 Aug 1967, on loan for five years.

DÉDALO *Official*

DÉDALO *1969, Official*

DÉDALO *1969, Spanish Navy, Official*

SUBMARINES

2 NEW CONSTRUCTION FRENCH "DAPHNE" TYPE

Displacement, tons	850 surface; 1 040 submerged
Dimensions, feet	190·2 × 22·2 × 15·5
Tubes	12—21·7 in (8 bow, 4 stern)

Two submarines basically similar to the French "Daphne" class are being built by France for Spain in the Cartagena Yard.

Name	*No.*	*Builders*	*Launched*	*Completed*
ALMIRANTE GARCIA DE LOS REYES E 1 (ex-USS *Kraken, SS* 370)	S 31	Manitowoc SB Co	30 Apr 1944	8 Sep 1944

1 Ex-US "BALAO" TYPE

Displacement, tons	1 526 standard; 1 880 surface; 2 059 submerged
Length, feet (*metres*)	306·2 (*93·3*)
Beam, feet (*metres*)	27 (*8·2*)
Draught, feet (*metres*)	17 (*5·2*)
Torpedo tubes	10—21 in (*533 mm*)
Main engines	4 diesels, total 6 400 bhp Electric motors, 4 600 hp
Speed, knots	20 on surface; 10 submerged

Ex-US "Balao" class. Transferred on 24 Oct 1959 after modernisation and overhaul at Pearl Harbour.

ALMIRANTE GARCIA DE LOS REYES *1969, Spanish Navy, Official*

2 "D" CLASS

	No.	*Laid down*	*Launched*	*Completed*
D 2	S 21	Sep 1934	12 Dec1944	2 Apr 1951
D 3	S 22	Sep 1945	20 Feb1952	20 Feb 1954

Displacement, tons	1 099 standard; 1 200 surface; 1 480 submerged
Length, feet (*metres*)	276·5 (*84·3*)
Beam, feet (*metres*)	22 (*6·7*)
Draught, feet (*metres*)	13 (*4·0*)
Torpedo tubes	6—21 in (*533 mm*), 4 fwd, 2 aft
Main engines	2 Sulzer diesels, 5 000 hp Electric motors, 1 300 hp
Speed, knots	20·5 on surface; 9·5 submerged
Radius, miles	9 000 on surface
Complement	75

Ordered under the 1926 Programme. Both built at the Sociedad Española de Construction Naval, Cartagena. Diving limit, 50 fathoms. *D* 2 (S 21) and D 3 (S 22) were delivered after modernisation on 10 Dec and 14 Mar 1963, respectively. Allocated S pennant numbers in 1961. Sister ship D 1 (S 11), not modernised, was deleted from the list in 1966.

D 2 *1966, Spanish Navy, Official*

D 3 *1968, Spanish Navy, Official*

1 Ex-GERMAN TYPE

G 7 (ex-U 537

Displacement, tons	711 standard; 757 surface; 865 submerged
Length, feet (*metres*)	227·5 (*69·3*)
Beam, feet (*metres*)	20·5 (*6·3*)
Draught, feet (*metres*)	14·8 (*4·5*)
Guns, surface	1—3·5 in (*90 mm*)
Torpedo tubes	5—21 in (*522 mm*); 4 fwd, 1 aft
Main engines	Diesels, 2 800 hp Electric motors 750 hp
Speed, knots	17·9 on surface; 8·5 submerged
Radius, miles	6 500 on surface
Complement	58

Former German U-boat of the VII type, built by Blohm & Voss, Hamburg. Interned in Spain in 1942. Purchased from Germany the following year. Allocated pennant number S 01 in 1961.

G 7 *1966, Spanish Navy, Official*

2 "TIBURON" CLASS

SA 51 **SA 52**

Displacement, tons	78 surface; 81 submerged
Length, feet (*metres*)	70·5 (*21·5*)
Beam, feet (*metres*)	9 (*2·7*)
Draught, feet (*metres*)	9 (*2·7*)
Torpedo tubes	2—21 in (*533 mm*)
Main engines	Pegaso diesels, 400 hp Electric motors, 400 hp
Speed, knots	10 on surface; 14·5 submerged
Complement	5

Midget submarines launched in 1958. All four originally rated Submarinos Experimentales, but in 1963 designated Assault Submarines with "SA" numbers.

ENGINEERING. The diesels were constructed by the ENASA (former Hispano-Suiza) Barcelona, 200 hp each, at 2 000 rpm, with reduction gear on the single screw disposed in a nozzle in continuation of the conic after hull.

SA 51 *1966. Spanish Navy, Official*

2 "FOCA" CLASS

SA 41 (F 1) **SA 42** (F 2)

Displacement, tons	16 surface; 20 submerged
Length, feet (*metres*)	45·4 (*13·9*)
Beam, feet (*metres*)	6 (*1·8*)
Draught, feet (*metres*)	5 (*1·5*)
Torpedo tubes	2—21 in (*533 mm*)
Main engines	Pegaso diesel, 160 hp Siemens electric motor 110 hp
Speed, knots	9·2 on surface; 12 submerged
Complement	3

Midget submarines launched in 1957 and numbered in 1958. A photograph of F-2 (SA 42) appears in the 1966-67 to 1968-69 editions.

SA 41 *1969, Spanish Navy, Official*

CRUISER

Name	No.	Builders	Laid down	Launched	Completed
CANARIAS	C 21	Sociedad Espanola de Construction Naval, El Ferrol	15 Aug 1928	28 May 1931	1 Oct 1936

(Rated as Crucero Type 2)

Displacement, tons	10 670 standard; 13 500 full load
Length, feet (*metres*)	636·5 (*194·0*)
Beam, feet (*metres*)	64 (*19·5*)
Draught, feet (*metres*)	21·3 (*6·5*)
Guns, surface	8—8 in (*203 mm*) 50 cal. 8—4·7 in (*120 mm*) 45 cal.
Guns, AA	4—1·5 in (*38 mm*) 70 cal.; 4—37 mm; 2—20 mm
Armour	sides 1·5—2 in (*38—50 mm*); turrets 1 in (*25 mm*); magazines 4 in (*100 mm*)
Boilers	8 Yarrow
Main engines	Parsons geared turbines 92 000 shp; 2 shafts
Speed, knots	31 max, 11 economical sea
Radius, miles	7 800 at 11 knots
Oil fuel (tons)	2 794
Complement	1 022 (40 officers, 982 men)

DESIGN. This ship was designed by the late Sir Philip Watts on the basic pattern of the contemporary British heavy cruisers of the later "County" classes. From initial completion until 1952 she had trunked funnels, but she emerged from refit early in 1953 with two separate funnels, this being a reversion to the original design which had never been carried out.

MODERNISATION. To be completely overhauled as Flagship of the Spanish Navy, under the Spanish Naval Modernisation Programme (United States Military Aid Programme).

TORPEDO TUBES. The 12—21 inch torpedo tubes in triple mountings which she formerly carried, were removed in 1960.

GUNNERY. The maximum elevation of the 8 inch guns is 70 degrees.

CLASS. Sister ship *Baleares* was torpedoed and sunk on 6 Mar 1938 during the Spanish Civil War.

DISPOSALS
"Galicia" Class cruisers:—**Almirante Cervera**, **Galicia** and **Miguel de Cervantes** were stricken from the Navy List in 1966. The anti-aircraft cruiser **Mendez Nuñez** was stricken in 1963, and the light cruiser **Navarra** in 1956.

1969, Spanish Navy, Official

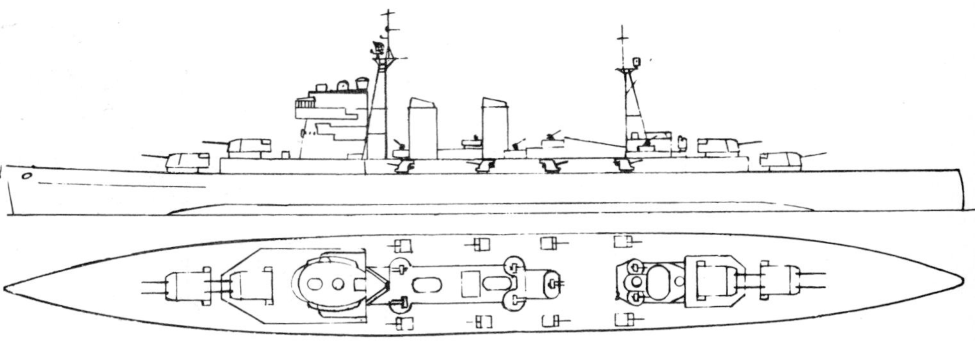

NOMENCLATURE. *Canarias* is named after the Canary Islands.

DRAWING. Port elevation and plan. Redrawn in 1968. Scale 128 feet = 1 inch.

CANARIAS

1966, Spanish Navy, Official

CANARIAS

1964, Spanish Navy, Official

ANTI-SUBMARINE DESTROYERS (*Destructores Caza Submarinas*)

8 "AUDAZ" CLASS

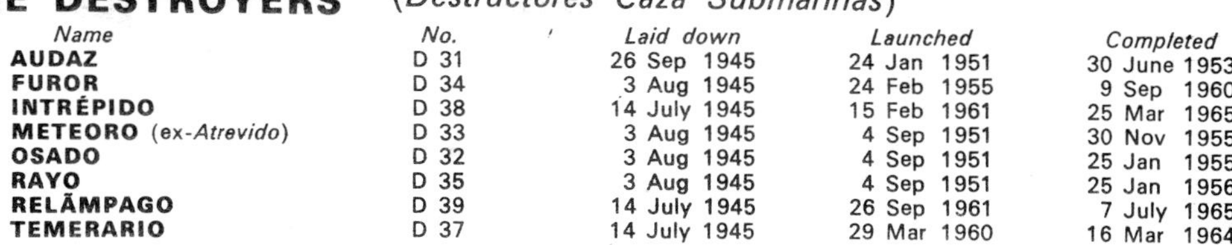

Name	No.	Laid down	Launched	Completed
AUDAZ	D 31	26 Sep 1945	24 Jan 1951	30 June 1953
FUROR	D 34	3 Aug 1945	24 Feb 1955	9 Sep 1960
INTRÉPIDO	D 38	14 July 1945	15 Feb 1961	25 Mar 1965
METEORO (ex-*Atrevido*)	D 33	3 Aug 1945	4 Sep 1951	30 Nov 1955
OSADO	D 32	3 Aug 1945	4 Sep 1951	25 Jan 1955
RAYO	D 35	3 Aug 1945	4 Sep 1951	25 Jan 1956
RELÃMPAGO	D 39	14 July 1945	26 Sep 1961	7 July 1965
TEMERARIO	D 37	14 July 1945	29 Mar 1960	16 Mar 1964

Displacement, tons	1 227 standard; 1 548 full load
Length, feet (*metres*)	295·2 (*90·0*) pp; 308·2 (*94·0*) oa
Beam, feet (*metres*)	30·5 (*9·3*)
Draught, feet (*metres*)	17 (*5·2*) max
Guns, AA	2—3 in (*76 mm*) 50 cal. 2—40 mm, 70 cal.
A/S	2 Hedgehogs; 8 mortars; 2 DC racks
Torpedo racks	2 side launching for A/S torpedoes (6 torpedoes)
Boilers	3 La Seine 3-drum type
Main engines	Rateau-Bretagne geared turbines 28 000 shp; 2 shafts
Speed, knots	31·6
Radius, miles	3,200 at 14 knots
Oil fuel (tons)	290
Complement	191

Based on the design of the French "Le Fier" type. All built at Ferrol. Allocated D Pennant numbers in 1961. but still referred to officially and unofficially as fast frigates, see *Classification* note below.

MODERNISATION. Dates of delivery after modernisation: *Audaz* 28 June 1961, *Furor* 9 Sep 1960, *Meteoro* 21 Feb 1963, *Osado* Aug 1961, *Rayo* 21 Feb 1963. All fitted with US electronic and ASW equipment under MAP.

GUNNERY. Before rearmament and modernisation these ships mounted 3—4·1 inch guns, 4—37 mm AA guns and 8—20 mm AA guns.

ENGINEERING. The boilers are in two compartments separated by the engine rooms. Steam is superheated to 375 degrees Fahrenheit. Working pressure is 500 lb. per sq in. Engines have developed 30 800 shp on trials and 32,500 shp max = 33 knots.

CLASSIFICATION. These ships were originally projected as conventional destroyers but their classification was changed to fast frigates in 1955. they were again re-rated, as anti-submarine frigates, in 1956, and as anti-submarine destroyers in 1961.

NOMENCLATURE. Meanings of names: *Audaz*, audacious; *Furor*, Fury; *Intrépido*, fearless; *Meteoro*, meteor; *Osado*, daring; *Rayo*, thunderbolt; *Relámpago*, lightning flash; *Temerario*, venturesome.

PHOTOGRAPHS. Photographs of *Audaz* appear in the 1952-53 to 1955-56, 1957-58 and 1962-63 to 1965-66 editions, of *Osada* in the 1956-57 and 1957-58 editions, of *Meteoro* in the 1956-57 to 1960-61 editions, of *Rayo* in the 1956-57 to 1961-62 editions, of *Furor* in the 1961-62 edition, and of *Ariete* in the 1962-63 to 1965-66 editions.

LOSS. Sister ship *Ariete* (battering ram) grounded on 25 Feb 1966 and was declared a total loss.

INTREPIDO — *1969, Spanish Navy, Official*

FUROR — *1966, Spanish Navy, Official*

TEMERARIO — *1966, Spanish Navy, Official*

ROGER DE LAURIA (see next page) — *1969, Spanish Navy, Official*

Anti-Submarine Destroyers— *continued*

1 "OQUENDO" TYPE

2 MODIFIED "OQUENDO" TYPE

Name	No.	Laid down	Launched	Completed
MARQUÉS DE LA ENSENADA	D 43	4 Sep 1951	15 July 1959	30 Dec 1969
OQUENDO	D 41	15 June 1951	5 Sep 1956	22 Dec 1964
ROGER DE LAURIA	D 42	4 Sep 1951	12 Nov 1958	22 Dec 1969

Displacement, tons	*D 42, D 43:* 3 000 standard; 3 587 full load; *D 41:* 2 582 standard; 3 005 full load
Length, feet (*metres*)	391·5 (*119·3*); *D 41:* 382 (*116·4*)
Beam, feet (*metres*)	42·7 (*13·0*); *D41:* 36·5 (*11·1*)
Draught, feet (*metres*)	18 (*5·6*); *D41:* 12·5 (*3·8*)
Aircraft	*D 42, D 43:* 1 A/S helicopter
Guns, surface	*D 41,* 4—4·7 (*120 mm*) (2 twin); *D 42, D 43:* 6—5 in (*127 mm*) 38 cal (3 twin)
Guns, AA	*D41 only:* 6—40 mm, 70 cal.
A/S	*D41:* 2 Hedgehogs, 2 TT racks
Torpedo tubes	*D42 ,43:* 2 triple for A/S torpedoes 2—21 in single
Boilers	3 three-drum type
Main engines	2 Rateau-Bretagne geared turbines; 2 shafts; 60 000 shp
Speed, knots	*D 42, D 43:* 31; *D 41* 32·4 max
Oil fuel, tons	673 (*Oquendo* 659)
Radius, miles	4 500 at 15 knots
Complement	303 (*Oquendo* 249)

All ordered at Ferrol in 1947-48. *Oquendo* was initially completed on 13 Sep 1960, and completed modernisation on 22 Dec 1964.

OQUENDO 1968, *Spanish Navy, Official*

CONSTRUCTION. Designed as conventional destroyers but modified during construction. The seven 21-inch torpedo tubes and two depth charge throwers were suppressed in favour of more modern anti-submarine weapons.
Roger de Lauria and *Marqués de la Ensenada* were towed to Cartagena for reconstruction to a new design and are scheduled to be delivered to the Spanish Navy in the latter half of 1969. Sisters *Bias de Laao, Blasco de Garay, Bonifaz, Gelmirez, Langara* and *Recalde* were cancelled in 1953.

CLASSIFICATION. These three ships were re-classified as anti-submarine frigates in 1955, again re-rated as fast frigates in 1956, and as anti-submarine destroyers in 1961.

Name	No.	Builders	Laid down	Launched	Completed
ALCALA GALIANO (ex-USS *Jarvis,* DD 799)	D 24	Todd Pacific Shipyards	—	14 Feb 1944	3 June 1944
ALMIRANTE FERRANDIZ (ex-USS *David W. Taylor* DD 551)	D 22	Gulf SB Corpn, Chickasaw, Ala	12 June 1941	4 July 1942	18 Sep 1943
ALMIRANTE VALDÉS (ex-USS *Converse,* DD 509)	D 23	Bath Iron Works Corp, Maine	23 Feb 1942	30 Aug 1942	8 June 1943
JORGE JUAN (ex-USS *McGowan,* DD 678)	D 25	Federal SB & DD Co	—	14 Nov 1943	20 Dec 1943
LEPANTO (ex-USS *Capps,* DD 550)	D 21	Gulf SB Corpn, Chickasaw, Ala	12 June 1941	31 May 1942	23 June 1943

5 "Lepanto" Class

Displacement, tons	2 080 standard; 2 750 normal; 3 050 standard
Length, feet (*metres*)	376·5 (*114·8*) oa
Beam, feet (*metres*)	39·5 (*12·0*)
Draught, feet (*metres*)	18 (*5·5*)
Guns, surface	*D21, D22:* 5—5 in (*127 mm*) 38 cal.; *Others:* 4—5 in (*127 mm*) single mounts
Guns, AA	*D21, D22:* 6—40 mm Bofors; *D21:* 12—20 mm Oerlikon (6 in *D22*); *Others:* 6—3 in (*76 mm*) 50 cal., 3 twin
A/S	2 Hedgehogs; 6 DCT; 2 DC racks
Torpedo tubes	5—21 in (*533 mm*) quintupled
Torpedo racks	2 side launching for A/S torpedoes
Boilers	4 Babcock & Wilcox
Main engines	Allis Chalmers geared turbines 60 000 shp; 2 shafts
Speed, knots	36 max, 16 economical sea
Radius, miles	5 800 at 16 knots
Oil fuel (tons)	650
Complement	290 (17 officers, 273 men)

Former United States fleet destroyers. *Capps,* renamed *Lepanto,* and *David W. Taylor,* renamed *Almirante Ferrandiz,* were the first units of the "Fletcher" class to be transferred to a foreign government: loaned to Spain for a period of five years, they were reconditioned at San Francisco and turned over to the Spanish Navy at San Francisco, California, on 15 May 1957, sailing for Spain on 1 July 1957. *Converse,* renamed *Almirante Valdes,* was transferred to the Spanish Navy at Philadelphia on 1 July 1959. *McGowan,* renamed *Jorge Juan,* was transferred at Barcelona on 1 Dec 1960 and *Jarvis* at Philadelphia on 3 Nov 1960, both being of the Later "Fletcher" class and transferred on a five year renewable loan basis, under the Military Aid Programme. All five ships were allocated D pennant numbers in 1961.

JORGE JUAN (four 5 inch, tripod mast) 1969, *Spanish Navy, Official*

ALMIRANTE FERRANDIZ (five 5 inch, tripod mast) 1969, *Spanish Navy, Official*

PHOTOGRAPHS. A port bow oblique aerial view of *Almirante Ferrandiz* appears in the 1958-59 and 1959-60 editions, a port dead broadside surface view of *Lepanto* in the 1958-59 to 1961-62 editions, a starboard bow view of *Almirante Veldes* (as re-armed) appears in the 1960-61 edition, starboard bow surface view of *Alcalá Galiano* in the 1961-62 to 1965-66 editions, a port broadside surface view of *Almieante Ferrandiz* in the 1962-63 to 1965-66 editions, a port quarter oblique surface view of *Jorge Juan* and a port near broadside-quarter view of *Lepanto* in the 1966-67 to 1968-69 editions.

APPEARANCE. *Alcala Galiano, Almirante Ferrandiz* and *Jorge Juan* have tripod mast, *Almirante Valdés* and *Lepanto* have pole mast. See also differing number of 5 inch guns in data table above.

ALMIRANTE VALDÉS (four 5 inch, pole mast) 1966, *Spanish Navy, Official*

DESTROYERS (*Destructores*)

Name	*No.*	*Builders*	*Laid down*	*Launched*	*Completed*	*Modernised*
ALAVA	D 52 (ex-23)	Cartagena	21 Dec 1944	19 May 1947	21 Dec 1950	17 Jan 1962
LINIERS	D 51 (ex-21)	Cartagena	1 Jan 1945	1 May 1946	27 Jan 1951	18 Sep 1962

2 "ALAVA" CLASS

Displacement, tons	1 842 standard; 2 287 full load
Length, feet (*metres*)	336·3 (*102·5*)
Beam, feet (*metres*)	31·5 (*9·6*)
Draught, feet (*metres*)	19·7 (*6·0*)
Guns, AA	3—3 in (*76 mm*) 50 cal., Mk 22; 3—40 mm, 70 cal.
A/S	2 Hedgehogs; 8 DC mortars; 6 DC racks
Torpedo racks	2 side launching, 6 A/S torpedoes
Boilers	3 Yarrow 3-drum type
Main engines	Parsons geared turbines 31 500 shp; 2 shafts
Speed, knots	29 max, 12 economical sea
Radius, miles	3 500 at 16 knots
Oil fuel (tons)	370
Complement	224 (17 officers, 207 men)

CONSTRUCTION. These two destroyers, a development of the *Churruca* design were ordered in 1936, but construction was held up by the Civil War. After being resumed, it was again suspended in 1940, but restarted at the Empresa Nacional Bazan, Cartagena in 1944.

LINIERS — *1966, Spanish Navy, Official*

PHOTOGRAPHS. Photographs of *Alava* appear in the 1953-54 to 1965-66 editions.

GUNNERY. Before modernisation on the lines of fast frigates these ships mounted 4—4·7 inch, 6—37 mm AA and 3—20 mm AA guns.

TORPEDO TUBES. This class have had no torpedo tubes since they were modernised in 1962. They formerly carried 6—21 inch (tripled), but now have torpedo racks for six homing torpedoes instead of tubes.

2 "ALMIRANTE" ANTEQUERA CLASS ("CHURRUCA" GROUP 2)

Name	*No.*	*Launched*	*Completed*
ALMIRANTE ANTEQUERA	D 14	29 Dec 1930	30 May 1935
ALMIRANTE MIRANDA	D 15	20 Oct 1931	30 May 1935

Displacement, tons	1 590 standard; 2 130 full load
Length, feet (*metres*)	320 (*97·5*) pp; 333 (*101·5*) oa
Beam, feet (*metres*)	31·8 (*9·7*)
Draught, feet (*metres*)	19·7 (*6·0*)
Guns, surface	4—4·7 (*120 mm*) 45 cal.
Guns, AA	2—20 mm
A/S	4 DCT
Torpedo racks	Side launching for A/S torpedoes
Boilers	4 Yarrow
Main engines	2 sets Parsons geared turbines 42 000 shp; 2 shafts
Speed, knots	27 max, 13 economical sea
Radius, miles	2 100 at 13 knots
Oil fuel (tons)	500
Complement	202 (10 officers, 192 men)

Built at Cartagena by Sociedad Española de Construccion Naval. This class is a later version of the *"Sanchez Barcaiztegui"* design. Now have D pennant numbers painted on bows which replaced the former numbers in 1961. *Almirante Antequera* was withdrawn from active service on 12 Nov 1965.

PHOTOGRAPHS. A photograph of *Almirante Antequera* appears in the 1965-66 to 1967-68 editions.

ALMIRANTE MIRANDA — *1968, Spanish Navy, Official*

DISPOSALS

Of the "Churruca" Group 2, **Ciscar**, sunk in the Civil War in Oct 1937, but salved and refitted in 1938-39, ran aground in fog and broke her back off El Ferrol on 17 Oct 1957, and was discarded in 1958. **Jorge Juan** was removed from the Navy List in 1959, and **Escaño, Gravina** and **Ulloa** in 1964.

Of the "Churruca" Group 1, **Lepanto, Alcala Galiano** and **Almirante Valdes** were removed from the list in 1957, **Churruca** in 1964, **Sanchez Barcaiztegui** in 1965, and **Jose Luiz Diez** in 1966.

Of the *"Alsedo"* class **Alsedo** and **Velasco** were removed from the list in 1957, and **Lazaga** in 1961.

FRIGATES (rated as *Fragatas*)

5 NEW CONSTRUCTION GUIDED MISSILE ARMED US DEG TYPE

DEG 7 DEG 8 DEG 9 DEG 10 DEG 11

Displacement, tons	2 643 standard; 3 426 full load
Length, feet (*metres*)	414·5 (*126·3*) oa
Beam, feet (*metres*)	44 (*13·4*)
Draught, feet (*metres*)	24 (*7·3*) max
Missiles, AA	1 "Tartar" launcher
Guns	1—5 in

CONSTRUCTION. In June 1966 Spain and USA signed an agreement for construction of five frigates in Spain with technical and material assistance by USA. Being built at EL Ferrol del Caudille. Generally similar to the US guided missile escort ships of the "Brooke" class. Equipped with weapons and electronic equipment furnished by the United States, including anti-submarine warfare torpedoes and rockets.

6 "PIZARRO" CLASS

Name	*No.*	*Launched*	*Completed*
HERNAN CORTES	F 32	3 Aug 1944	18 Sep 1947
LEGAZPI	F 42	8 Aug 1944	8 Aug 1951
MAGALLANES	F 35	8 Aug 1944	20 Dec 1948
SARMIENTO DE GAMBOA	F 36	8 Aug 1944	2 May 1950
VASCO NUÑEZ DE BALBOA	F 33	3 Aug 1944	15 Mar 1947
VICENTE YAÑEZ PINZON	F 41	3 Aug 1944	5 Aug 1949

Displacement, tons	1 924 standard; 2 228 full load
Length, feet (*metres*)	279 (*85·0*) pp 312·5 (*95·30*) oa
Beam, feet (*metres*)	39·5 (*12·0*)
Draught, feet (*metres*)	17·7 (*5·4*)
Guns, surface	*F41, F42:* 2—5 in (*127 mm*) 38 cal. *Others:* 6—4·7 in (*120 mm*) 3 twin
Guns, AA	*F41, F42:* 4—40 mm, 70 cal. *Others:* 8—37 mm; 6—20 mm
A/S	*F41, F42:* 2 Hedgehogs; 8 mortars; 2 racks; *Others:* 4 DCT
Torpedo racks	*F41, F42:* 2 side launching for A/S torpedoes
Mines	30 can be carried
Boilers	2 Yarrow
Main engines	2 sets Parsons geared turbines 6 000 shp; 2 shafts
Speed, knots	18·5
Radius, miles	4 000 at 14 knots
Oil fuel (tons)	390
Complement	291 (14 officers, 277 men)

All built at Ferrol. Designed to carry 30 mines. Rated as *Canoneras* (Gunboats) until 1958 when they were re-rated as *Fragatas*. Allocated F pennant numbers in 1961. *Legazpi* and *Vicente Yañez Pinzon* completed modernisation on 14 Jan and 25 Mar 1960 respectively. A photograph of *Vicente Yañez Pinzon* after modernisation appears in the 1962-63 to 1965-66 editions. Sister ships *Martin Aloñso Pinzon* and *Pizarro* were officially removed from the list in 1968.

MAGALLANES — *1969, Spanish Navy, Official*

FRIGATE MINELAYERS (*Minadores*)

2 "EOLO" CLASS

Name	No.	Launched	Completed
EOLO	F 21	30 Sep 1939	1 Jan 1942
TRITON	F 22	26 Feb 1940	18 Oct 1943

Displacement, tons	1 723 standard; 1 942 full load
Length, feet (*metres*)	291·7 (*88·9*) oa
Beam, feet (*metres*)	38·5 (*11·7*)
Draught, feet (*metres*)	17·7 (*5·4*) max
Guns, dual purpose	4—4·1 in (*105 mm*)
Guns, AA	4—37 mm
A/S	2 DCT
Mines	Stowage for 170 *Eolo*, 180 ***Tritón***
Boilers	2 Yarrow
Main engines	Parsons geared turbines 5 000 shp; 2 shafts
Speed, knots	19·5 max, 12 economical sea
Oil fuel (tons)	300
Complement	224 (9 officers, 215 men)

EOLO — *1967, Spanish Navy, Official*

Both built by the Sociadad Española de Construccion Naval, Ferrol.
Dual purpose frigates or gunboats and minelayers.

Allocated F pennant numbers in 1961.
A photograph of *Tritón* appears in the 1962-63 to 1966-67 editions.

4 "JUPITER" CLASS

Name	No.	Launched	Completed
JUPITER	F 11	14 Sep 1935	1937
MARTE	F 01	19 June 1936	1937
NEPTUNO	F 02	17 Dec 1937	1939
VULCANO	F 12	12 Oct 1935	1937

Displacement, tons	2 103 standard; 2 245 full load
Length, feet (*metres*)	302·8 (*92·3*) pp; 328 (*100·0*) oa
Beam, feet (*metres*)	41·5 (*12·6*)
Draught, feet (*metres*)	11·5 (*3·5*)
Guns, surface	*F 01* and *F 02* only: 4—4·7 in (*120 mm*)
Guns, AA	*F 01:* 4—2·5 in (*63 mm*); 4—20 mm; *F 02:* 4—37 mm; 3—20 mm *F 11* and *F 12* as modernised:— 4—3 in (*76 mm*) Mk 26, single; 4—40 mm, 70 cal.
A/S	*F 11* and *F 12* as modernised:— 2 Hedgehogs; 8 mortars; 2 DC racks
Mines	Stowage for 264 but normally less
Boilers	2 Yarrow
Main engines	2 sets Parsons geared turbines 5 000 shp; 2 shafts
Speed, knots	17·4 max, 10 economical sea
Oil fuel (tons)	280
Complement	243 (16 officers, 227 men)

All built by the Sociedad Española de Construccion Naval, Ferrol. Multi-purpose frigates or gunboats and cruising type minelayers. *Neptuno* is midshipmen's training ship. The modernisation of *Jupiter* was completed on 28 Oct 1960, and of *Vulcano* on 28 Feb 1961. All allocated F pennant numbers in 1961.

PHOTOGRAPHS. A port broadside view of *Neptuno* appears in the 1956-57 to 1963-64 editions, a port bow view of *Jupiter* as modernised in the 1961-62 editions, a port broadside view of *Vulcano* as modernised in the 1962-63 to 1965-66 editions, a starboard quarter view of *Jupiter* in the 1964-65 and 1965-66 editions, a starboard quarter view of *Neptuno* in the 1966-67 and 1967-68 editions, a starboard quarter view of *Vulcano* in the 1966-67 to 1968-69 editions.

NEPTUNO — *1968, Spanish Navy, Official*

JUPITER (four 3 inch, lattice mast) — *1969, Spanish Navy, Official*

DISPOSALS
The frigate **Canovas del Castillo** was stricken from the list in 1959, and the larger frigate **Calvo Sotelo** (ex-*Zacatecas*) in 1957.

CORVETTES (*Corbetas*)

6 "ATREVIDA" CLASS

Name	No.	Laid down	Launched	Completed
ATREVIDA	F 61	26 June 1950	2 Dec 1952	19 Aug 1954
DESCUBIERTA	F 51	26 June 1950	9 June 1952	1 Feb 1955
DIANA	F 63	27 July 1953	29 Apr 1955	13 May 1960
NAUTILUS	F 64	27 July 1953	23 Aug 1956	15 Dec 1959
PRINCESA	F 62	18 Mar 1953	31 Mar 1956	3 Oct 1959
VILLA DE BILBAO	F 65	18 Mar 1953	19 Feb 1958	2 July 1960

Displacement, tons	997 standard; 1 135 full load
Length, feet (*metres*)	247·8 (*75·5*) oa
Beam, feet (*metres*)	33·5 (*10·2*)
Draught, feet (*metres*)	9 (*2·7*)
Guns, dual purpose	*F 51* only: 1—4·1 in (*105* mm) 45 cal. *Remainder:* 1—3 in (*76 mm*) 50 cal. Mk 26
Guns, AA	*F* 51 only: 4—37 mm, 80 cal. *Remainder:* 3—40 mm, 70 cal.
A/S	*F* 51 only: 4 DCT *Remainder:* 2 Hedgehogs 8 mortars; 2 DC racks
Mines	20 can be carried
Main engines	Sulzer diesels 3 200 bhp; 2 shafts
Speed, knots	18·5
Radius, miles	8 000 at 7 knots
Oil fuel (tons)	100
Complement	132 (10 officers, 122 men)

Atrevida commissioned on 19 Aug 1954, *Descubierta* in 1955. All except *Descubierta* have been modernised since 1959. *Princesa* was delivered on 3 Oct 1959. *Nautilus* on 15 Dec 1959. *Diana* on 13 May 1960. *Atrevida* on 14 June 1960 and *Villa de Bilbao* on 2 July 1960. Allocated F pennant numbers in 1961.

PHOTOGRAPHS. A photograph of *Descubierta* appears in the 1955-56 to 1959-60 editions, of *Diana* rearmed with lattice mast in the 1960-61 edition, of *Villa de Bilbao* as modernised in the 1961-62 to 1965-66 editions, of *Princesa* in the 1967-68 and 1968-69 editions.

NAUTILUS — *1969, Spanish Navy, Official*

FLEET MINESWEEPERS (*Dragaminas*)

7 "ALMANZORA" CLASS

Name	*No.*	*Builders*	*Launched*	*Completed*	*Modernised*
ALMANZORA	M 14	Cartagena	27 July 1953	Nov 1954	20 May 1960
EO	M 17	Cadiz	22 Sep 1953	Mar 1955	22 Mar 1961
EUME	M 13	Cartagena	27 July 1953	Dec 1953	20 July 1960
GUADALHORCE	M 16	Cartagena	18 Feb 1953	Dec 1953	18 Feb 1960
GUARDIARO	M 11	Cartagena	26 June 1950	Apr 1953	14 Dec 1959
NAVIA	M 15	Cadiz	28 July 1953	Mar 1955	22 Nov 1960
TINTO	M 12	Cartagena	26 June 1950	May 1953	28 July 1959

Displacement, tons	671 standard; 770 full load
Dimensions, feet	243·8 × 33·5 × 12·3 max
Guns	2—20 mm AA
Main engines	Triple expansion and exhaust turbines; 2 shafts; 2 400 hp = 16 knots
Boilers	2 Yarrow
Oil fuel, tons	90
Radius, miles	1 000 at 6 knots
Complement	79

Former Pennant Nos were DM 11, 13, 10, 14, 8, 12, 9, respectively. Allocated new M Pennant Nos in 1961. Until modernisation the armament also included 1—3·5 in gun and 1—37 mm AA gun. A photograph of *Eume* appears in the 1962-63 and 1963-64 editions, of *Almanzora* in the 1964-65 to 1966-67 editions, and of *Navia* in the 1967-68 and 1968-69 editions.

EO — *1969, A. & J. Pavia*

6 "BIDASOA" CLASS

Name	*No.*	*Builders*	*Launched*	*Completed*
BIDASOA	M 01	Cartagena	15 Sep 1943	5 Apr 1946
LEREZ	M 03	Cartagena	21 Dec 1944	12 Feb 1947
NERVION	M 02	Cartagena	15 Apr 1944	4 June 1946
SEGURA	M 05	Cartagena	6 Oct 1948	20 Dec 1948
TAMBRE	M 04	El Ferrol	18 Oct 1944	21 July 1946
TER	M 06	Cartagena	18 Feb 1948	22 July 1948

Displacement, tons	555 standard; 470 full load
Dimensions, feet	200·5 × 28 × 12 max
Guns	1—4·1 in; 1—37 mm AA; 2—20 mm AA
Main engines	Triple expansion and exhaust turbines; 2 shafts; 2 400 hp = 16·5 knots
Boilers	2 Yarrow
Oil fuel, tons	135
Radius, miles	1 060 at 10 knots
Complement	82

German M-Boote 40 type. Named after rivers. Formerly carried pennant numbers DM 1, 5, 3, 2, 6, 4, 7, respectively. Allocated new M pennant numbers in 1961. *Guadalete*, of this class, which was employed as a coastguard vessel, sank in a gale 20 miles east of Gibraltar on 25 Mar 1954. A photograph of *Bidasoa* appears in the 1964-65 to 1967-68 editions.

TAMBRE — *1968, Spanish Navy, Official*

PATROL BOAT

CABO FRADERA

Displacement, tons	25 standard; 28 full load
Dimensions, feet	58·5 × 14 × 5·2
Main engines	2 diesels; 760 bhp = 12 knots
Complement	9

Built at La Carraca, in 1963. (River patrol boat *Cabo Fradera* was disposed of).

PATROL VESSELS (*Patrulleros*)

JAVIER QUIROGA (ex-*Blue Arrow*, ex-USS *PC* 1211)

Displacement, tons	362 standard; 440 full load
Dimensions, feet	170 wl; 172·7 oa × 23 × 10·8
Guns	2—37 mm
Main engines	2 diesels; 2 shafts; 3 500 bhp = 20 knots

Former US submarine chaser of the "173 ft" steel type. Built by Luders Marine Construction Co, Stamford, Conn. Laid down on 11 Aug 1942, launched on 12 Mar 1943, and completed on 16 Aug 1943. Transferred on 24 Oct 1956.

JAVIER QUIROGA — *1968, Spanish Navy, Official*

CANDIDO PEREZ (ex-*SC* 679)

Displacement, tons	108 standard; 138 full load
Dimensions, feet	107·5 wl; 111 oa × 19 × 7
Guns	1—40 mm AA; 3—20 mm
A/S weapons	2 DCT
Main engines	GM diesels; 2 shafts; 1 000 bhp = 15·6 knots
Radius, miles	2 300

Former United States submarine chaser of the "110 ft" wooden type. Built by Walter E. Abrams Shipyard, Inc. Laid down on 4 mar 1942. Launched on 29 Aug 1942. Completed on 19 Dec 1942. Transferred to Spain in 1957.

CANDIDO PEREZ — *Spanish Navy, Official*

COASTAL MINESWEEPERS

12 Ex-US AMS TYPE

DUERO (ex-*Spoonbill, MSC* 202)	M 28	**NALÓN** (ex-*AMS* 139)	M 21
EBRO (ex-*MSC* 269)	M 26	**ODIEL** (ex-*MSC* 288)	M 32
GENIL (ex-*MSC* 279)	M 31	**SIL** (ex-*Redwing, MSC* 200)	M 29
JUCAR (ex-*AMS* 220)	M 23	**TAJO** (ex-*MSC* 287)	M 30
LLOBREGAT (ex-*AMS* 143)	M 22	**TURIA** (ex-*AMS* 130)	M 27
MIÑO (ex-*AMS* 266)	M 22	**ULLA** (ex-*AMS* 265)	M 24

Displacement, tons	355 standard; 384 full load
Dimensions, feet	138 pp; 144 oa × 27·2 × 8
Guns	1—20 mm AA
Main engines	2 diesels; 2 shafts; 900 bhp = 14 knots
Oil fuel, tons	30
Radius, miles	2 700 at 10 knots
Complement	39

Anti-magnetic minesweepers transferred from the USA. *Nalón* on 16 Feb 1954, *Llobragat* on 5 Nov 1954, *Turia* on 1 June 1955, *Jucar* on 22 June 1956, *Ulla* on 24 July 1956, *Miño* on 25 Oct 1956, *Redwing* and *Spoonbill* on 16 June 1959, *Ebro* on 19 Dec 1958, *Genil* on 11 Sep 1959, *Tajo* on 9 July 1959 and *Odiel*, 9 Oct 1959. A photograph of *Odiel* appears in the 1961-62 edition, of *Ulla* in the 1962-63 to 1967-68 editions, and of *Tajo* in the 1968-69 edition.

LLOBREGAT — *1969, A. & J. Pavia*

TORPEDO BOATS (*Lanchas Torpederas*)

LT 30 **LT 31** **LT 32**

Displacement, tons	100 standard; 116 full load
Dimensions, feet	114 × 16·8 × 5
Guns	1—20 mm AA
Tubes	2—21 in
Main engines	3 diesel; 3 shafts; 7 500 bhp = 41 knots
Oil fuel, tons	20
Radius, miles	650 at 30 knots
Complement	26

Built at La Carraca, Cadiz, to the design of Lurssens of Bremen. LT 31 was commissioned on 21 July 1956. L 32 was launched in 1956. (photograph in 1960-61 to 1966-67 editions). LT 27, LT 28 and LT 29 were discarded in 1963.

LT 30 *1967, Spanish Navy, Official*

LANDING SHIPS (*Borcazas de Desembarco*)

LSM 1 (ex-USS *LSM* 329) **LSM 2** (ex-USS *LSM* 331) **LSM 3** (ex-USS *LSM* 343)

Displacement, tons	930 standard; 1 094 full load
Dimensions, feet	196·5 wl × 203·5 oa × 34·5 × 8·3
Guns	1—40 mm AA; 2—40 mm AA
Main engines	2 diesels; 2 shafts; 3 600 bhp = 12·5 knots
Complement	59

Medium landing ships transferred at Bremerton, Washington ,on 25 Mar 1960.

A photograph of LSM 2 appears in the 1965-66 to 1967-68 editions.

LSM 3 *1969, Official*

K 1 **K 2** **K 3** **K 4** **K 5**

Displacement, tons	481 standard; 868 full load
Dimensions, feet	187 × 38·8 × 5·5
Main engines	2 diesels; 1 000 bhp = 7 knots

Built by Bazan, Ferrol. Of British LCT (4) Type, (There are also 13 LCMs (Lanchas de Desembarco), LCM 1 to LCM 13, and 5 LCPs, LCP 1 to LCP 5).

K 5 *1969, Spanish Navy, Official*

K 1 *1968, Spanish Navy Official*

SURVEY SHIPS (*Buques Hidrografos*)

CASTOR H 4 **POLLUX** H 5

Displacement, tons	327 standard; 383 full load
Dimensions, feet	111 pp; 125·9 oa × 24·9 × 8·9
Main engines	1 Sulzer 4TD-36 diesel; 720 hp = 11·7 knots
Radius, miles	3 620
Complement	36

Built by E. N. Bazan La Carraca. Completed on 10 Nov 1966 and 6 Dec 1966.

MALASPINA (ex-*Bausa*) **TOFIÑO**

Displacement, tons	998 standard; 1 255 full load
Dimensions, feet	224·5 × 35 × 11
Guns	1—37 mm
Main engines	Triple expansion; 2 shafts; 810 ihp = 12·5 knots
Boilers	2 Yarrow
Complement	181

Built by Matagorda, Cadiz and Ferrol, respectively. Launched on 13 Sep 1935 and 21 Aug 1933, respectively.

TOFINO *1965, Spanish Navy, Official*

MALASPINA *1969, Spanish Navy, Official*

JUAN DE LA COSA (ex-*Artabro*)

Displacement, tons	770 standard; 1 100 full load
Dimensions, feet	188 × 35·5 × 8·8
Main engines	B. & W diesels; electric drive; 500 bhp = 9 knots

Launched by UNL, Valence in 1935. The small survey craft **H 2** and **H 3** were withdrawn from the active list in 1968.

JUAN DE LA COSA *1969, Spanish Navy, Official*

H 3 *1969, Official*

TRANSPORTS

ALMIRANTE LOBO (ex-*Torrelaguna*)

Displacement, tons	5 662 standard; 8 038 full load
Dimensions, feet	362·5 × 48·2 × 25·7
Guns	2—37 mm, 60 cal
Main engines	1 triple expansion; 2 000 ihp = 12 knots

Ex-cargo vessel. Built at Astilleros Echevarrieta, Cadiz. Commissioned 4 Oct 1954.

ALMIRANTE LOBO *Official*

ARAGON (ex-USS *Noble*), APA 218) TA 11

Displacement, tons	6 720 light; 12 450 full load
Dimensions, feet	436·5 wl; 455 oa × 63·5 × 24 max
Main engines	Geared turbines; 8 500 shp = 17 knots
Boilers	2 Babcock & Wilcox

Former US Attack Transport, transferred at San Francisco on 19 Dec 1964.

ARAGON *1968, Spanish Navy, Official*

CASTILLA (ex-USS *Achernar*, AKA 53) TA 21

Displacement, tons	7,430 light; 11 416 full load
Dimensions, feet	435 wl; 457·8 oa × 63 × 24
Guns	1—5 in, 38 cal; 8—40 mm, 60 cal
Main engines	2 GE geared turbines; 12 000 shp = 16 knots
Boilers	2 Foster-Wheeler

Former US Attack Cargo Ship, transferred at New York on 2 Feb 1965.

CASTILLA *1966, courtesy Professor Alfredo Aguilera*

PATROL VESSELS (*Guardacostas*)

CENTINELA **SERVIOLA**

Displacement, tons	255 standard; 282 full load
Dimensions, feet	117·5 × 22·5 × 9·8
Guns	2—37 mm..
Main engines	1 diesel; 430 bhp = 12 knots

Completed at Ferrol, in 1953. Rated as Fishery Protection Vessels (Guardapescas).

SERVIOLA *1969, Spanish Navy, Official*

Patrol Vessels—*continued*

PEGASO **PROCYON**

Displacement, tons	436 standard; 498 full load
Dimensions, feet	137·8 × 27 × 9·5
Guns	2—20 mm AA
Main engines	1 shaft; 532 bhp = 12 knots

Both commissioned at Cartegena in Jan 1951. Rated as Coastguard Vessels (Guardacostas). Photograph of *Pegaso* in the 1961-62 to 1965-66 editions.

PROCYON *1966, Spanish Navy, Official*

AZOR

Displacement, tons	442 standard; 486 full load
Dimensions, feet	153 × 25·2 × 12·5
Main engines	2 diesels; 1 200 bhp = 12 knots

Fishery Protection Launch (Lancha Guardapescas). Used as the Caudillo's yacht.

AZOR *1969, Spanish Navy, Official*

CIES **SALVORA**

Displacement, tons	180 standard; 275 full load
Dimensions, feet	107 × 20·5 × 9
Guns	1 MG
Main engines	1 Sulzer diesel; 400 bhp = 12 knots

Purchased in Dec 1952. Rated as Fishery Protection Vessels (Guardapescas).

SALVORA *1969, Spanish Navy, Official*

ARCILA (ex-*William Doak*) **XAUEN** (ex-*Henry Cramwell*)

Displacement, tons	462 standard; 692 full load
Dimensions, feet	138·5 pp; 148·5 oa × 23·8 × 14·7
Guns	2—3 in (*Xauen*, 1—3 in; 1—47 mm AA)
Main engines	500 ihp = 10 knots
Coal, tons	200
Complement	57

"Mersey" type trawlers. Launched in 1918 by Goole SB & Rep Co, and Lobnitz. *Arcila* is rated as a guardacosta and *Xauen* as an oceanographicos.

DISPOSALS

The patrol vessel (trawler) **Uad Kert** (ex-*Rother*, ex-*Anthony Aslett*) was officially deleted from the list in 1968.

ARCILLA *1969, Spanish Navy, Official*

BOOM DEFENCE VESSEL (*Cola-Redes*)

CR 1 (ex-*G* 6)

Displacement, tons	630 standard; 831 full load
Dimensions, feet	165·5 × 34 × 10·5
Guns	1—40 mm AA; 1—20 mm AA
Main engines	2 diesels with electric drive; 1 500 bhp = 12 knots

Built by Penhoët, France, as a US off-shore order. Launched on 28 Sep 1954. Transferred from the US in 1955 under MDAP.

CR 1 — *1968, Professor Alfredo Aguilera*

OILERS

TEIDE

Displacement, tons	2 747 light; 8 030 full load
Dimensions, feet	385·5 × 48·5 × 20·3
Guns	1—4·1 in
Main engines	2 diesels; 3 360 bhp = 12 knots

Ordered from Factoria de Bazan, Cartegana, in December 1952. Laid down on 11 Nov 1954. Launched on 20 June 1955. In service October 1956.

TEIDE — 1968, *Spanish Navy, Official*

PLUTON (ex-*Campilo*) BP 01

Displacement, tons	4 550 light; 7 550 full load
Dimensions, feet	342·5 × 53·8 × 19·5
Main engines	2 sets B & W diesels; 2 600 bhp = 13·5 knots

Built at Valencia. Diesels built at Barcelona. Launched in 1931. Purchased in Dec 1934. A photograph appears in the 1954-55 to 1961-62 editions.

PLUTON — *1969, Official*

PP 1 **PP 2**

Displacement, tons	470
Dimensions, feet	138 pp; 147·5 oa × 25 × 9·5
Main engines	Deutz diesel; 220 bhp = 10 knots
Complement	12

Both built at Santander and launched in 1939. Small service tankers.

LANDING CRAFT

K 6 **K 7** **K 8**

Displacement, tons	315 standard; 665 full load
Dimensions, feet	193·5 × 39 × 5
Guns	1—20 mm AA; 2—12·7 mm MG
Main engines	2 diesels; 1 040 bhp = 9·5 knots
Radius, miles	1 500
Complement	17

Landing craft of the French EDIC type built at La Carraca. Completed in Dec 1966.

JUAN SEBASTIAN DE ELCANO — *1969, Spanish Navy, Official*

TRAINING SHIPS (*Buque-Escuela*)

JUAN SEBASTIAN DE ELCANO

Displacement, tons	3 420 standard; 3 754 full load
Dimensions, feet	269·2 pp; 308·5 oa × 43 × 23 full load
Guns	2—37 mm
Main engines	1 Sulzer diesel; 1 shaft; 1 500 bhp = 9·5 knots
Oil fuel, tons	230
Endurance, miles	10,000 at 9·5 knots
Complement	224 + 80 cadets

Four-masted schooner. Named after the first circumnavigator of the world (1519-26) who succeeded to the command of the expedition led by Magallanes after the latter's death. Built by Echevarrieta Yard, Cadiz. Launched on 5 Mar 1927. Completed in 1928. A photograph appears in the 1952-53 to 1957-58 editions.

COASTAL LAUNCHES (*Lanchas de Vigilancia*)

	Displacement	Guns	Speed
V 2	22 tons	1—7 mm	6·7 knots
V 3	10 tons	1—7 mm	7·5 knots
V 4	65 tons	1—7 mm	9 knots
V 5	4·5 tons	1—7 mm	5 knots
V 7	20 tons	1—7 mm	8·5 knots
V 8	26·5 tons	1—7 mm	7·8 knots
V 9	15·6 tons	1—7 mm	9 knots
V 10	11·69 tons	1—7 mm	9·5 knots
V 11	11·69 tons	1—7 mm	9·5 knots
V 12	28 tons	1—7 mm	7·8 knots
V 13	45·1 tons	1—7 mm	7·8 knots
V 17	110·9 tons	1—13 mm	10·5 knots
V 18	116 tons	1—13 mm	6 knots
V 21	16 tons	1—13 mm	17·6 knots

LANZON (V 18) — *1969, Spanish Navy, Official*

There are also V 1 and V 6. Coastal launches employed on surveillance and fishery protection duties, lanchos guardapescas, except V 17, rated as patrullero. V 4 is named *Alcatraz*, V 12 *Esturian* and V 18 *Lanzon*. V 19 was officially stricken from the list in 1963, and V 20 in 1965.

V 21 — *1969, Spanish Navy, Official*

AUXILIARY PATROL VESSELS

RR 10 **RR 19** **RR 20** **RR 28** **R 29**

Displacement, tons 364 standard; 498 full load
Dimensions, feet 124 × 29 × 10
Guns 1—47 mm; 1—20 mm AA
Main engines Triple expansion; 1 shaft; 800 ihp = 11·5 knots
Coal, tons 200
Radius, miles 620 at 10 knots

Former tugs. All launched in 1941-42. A photograph appears in the 1957-58 edition.

RR 19 *1969, Spanish Navy, Official*

TUGS (*Remolcadores*)

RR 50 **RR 51** **RR 52** **RR 53** **RR 54** **RR 55**

Displacement, tons 227
Dimensions, feet 91·2 × 23 × 11
Main engines 1 shaft; 1 400 shp

All built at Cartagena for naval service in 1963-66.

BS 1 (ex-RA 6) **RA 4** **RA 5**

Displacement, tons 951 standard; 1 069 full load
Dimensions, feet 183·5 × 32·8 × 15·8
Main engines 2 Sulzer diesels; 3 200 bhp = 15 knots

All built at La Carraca, in 1963. RA 6 was renumbered BS 1 when she became a frogman base.

BS 1 (ex-RA 6) *1969, courtesy Professor Alfredo Aguilera*

RA 1 **RA 2**

Displacement, tons 757 standard; 1 039 full load
Dimensions, feet 184 × 33·5 × 12
Guns 2 MG
Main engines 2 Sulzer diesels; 3 200 bhp = 15 knots

Ordered in 1949. Built at Factoria de Bazan, Cartagena. Launched on 2 Sep 1954 and 5 Oct 1954, commissioned on 9 July 1955 and 12 Sep 1955, respectively.

RA 2 *1969, Spanish Navy, Official*

RA 3 (ex-*Metinda III*)

Displacement, tons 762 standard; 1 080 full load
Dimensions, feet 137 × 33·1 × 15·5
Main engines Triple expansion; 12 knots max; 10 knots service

RA 3 *1969, Official*

RR 15 **RR 16**

Displacement, tons 434
Dimensions, feet 124 × 27·5 × 10
Main engines 800 ihp = 11·5 knots

Of this class RR 17 was officially deleted from the Navy List in 1968.

RR 11

Displacement, tons 279
Dimensions, feet 111·5 × 20 × 10
Main engines 600 ihp = 11 knots

ROYAL SWEDISH NAVY

Administration

Commander-in-Chief of the Navy (including Coast Artillery):
Vice-Admiral A. F. Lindemalm

President of the Navy Technical and Administrative Board:
Commodore (E) Harry Hallberg

Commander-in-Chief of Active Fleet:
Rear-Admiral D. Arvas

Diplomatic Representation

Naval Attaché in London:
Captain S. L. Ahrin

Naval Attaché in Washington:
Commodore Nils-Gustaf Gynning

Strength of the Fleet

24 Submarines (Diesel Powered)
1 Cruiser
8 Destroyers
7 Fast Anti-submarine Frigates
1 Minelayer and Sea Training Ship
1 Submarine Support Ship
42 Torpedo Boats
6 Minesweepers (Steel)
18 Coastal Minesweepers (Wooden)
17 Inshore Minesweepers
10 Mining Tenders
1 Staff Communications Ship
2 Training Ships
31 Patrol Boats
12 Surveying Vessels
23 Landing Craft
4 Icebreakers
15 Support Ships and Service Craft

New Construction Programme

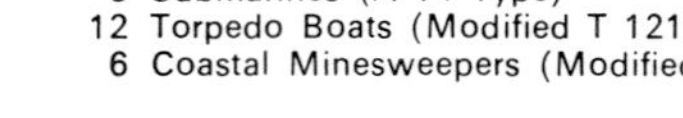

Plan "ÖB—67" comprises:—
5 Submarines (A 14 Type)
12 Torpedo Boats (Modified T 121 type)
6 Coastal Minesweepers (Modified M 69 type)

Personnel

1969: Active list of Navy and Coast Artillery, 16 000 officers and men, including conscripts

Navy Estimates

	kr.		kr.
1960-61:	389 500 000	1964-65:	490 250 000
1961-62:	409 000 000	1965-66:	532 770 000
1962-63:	423 000 000	1966-67:	652 300 000
1963-64:	469 000 000	1967-68:	672 000 000
		1968-69:	670 000 000

Mercantile Marine

Lloyd's Register of Shipping:
1 074 vessels of 4 865 365 tons gross

Silhouettes

Scale: 150 feet = 1 inch

GÖTA LEJON

SÖDERMANLAND

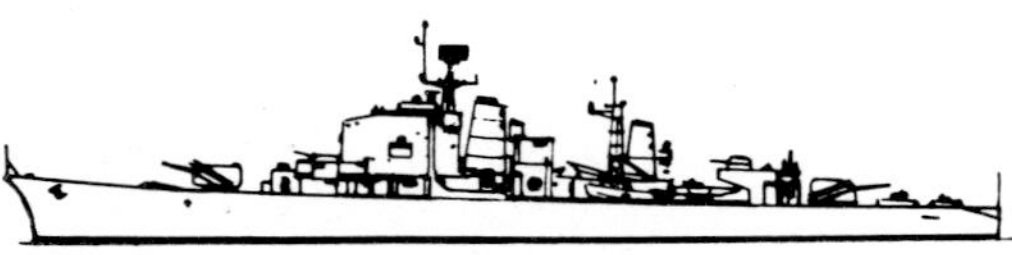

OSTERGOTLAND *Class*

KARLSKRONA

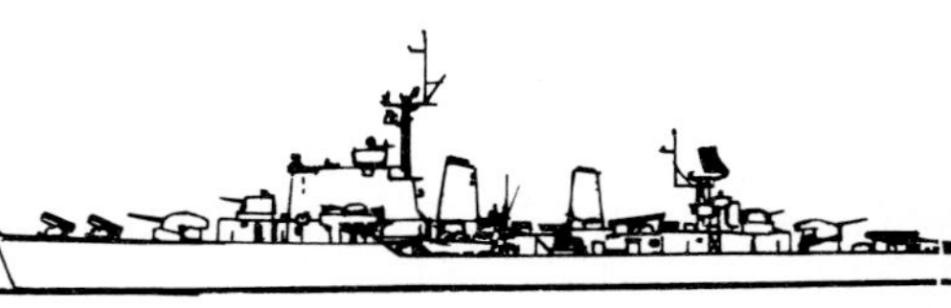

HALLAND *Class*

ÖLAND

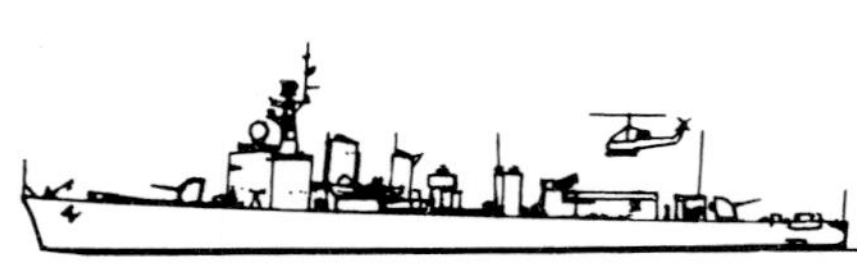

VISBY *Class*

MJÖLNER *Class*

UPPLAND

KALMAR

ÄLVSNABBEN

SJOBJORNEN *1969 Royal Swedish Navy, Official*

NORDKAPAREN *1969, Official*

SUBMARINES

NEW CONSTRUCTION
5 + 5 "SJOORMEN" CLASS

Name	*Builders*	*Launched*	*Completed*
SJÖORMEN	Kockums	25 Jan 67	June 67
SJÖLEJONET	Kockums	29 June 67	Mar 68
SJÖHUNDEN	Kockums	21 Mar 68	Sep 68
SJÖHÄSTEN	Karlskrona	Sep 68	Mar 69
SJÖBJÖRNEN	Karlskrona	9 Jan 68	June 68

Displacement, tons	700 standard; 800 surface; 1 110 submerged
Length, feet (*metres*)	167·3 (*51*)
Beam, feet (*metres*)	20 (*6·1*)
Draught, feet (*metres*)	19·7 (6·0)
Torpedo tubes	21 in (*533 mm*)
Main engines	Diesels; electric motors

Three building by Kockums, two by Karlskrona (now a civilian yard). *Sjöbjörnen* means Seabea·, *Sjöormen* Seaserpent, *Sjöhästen* Seahorse, *Sjöhunden* Seadog, and *Sjölejonet* Sealion. Conning tower letters: Sor, Sbj, She, Shu, Sle.

Five more submarines of a new highly streamlined, long-range type, are included in the new construction programme. They will be conventional but with engines enabling them to stay submerged for a long time.

6 "DRAKEN" CLASS

Name	*Builders*	*Launched*	*Completed*
DELFINEN	Karlskrona	7 Mar 61	7 June 62
DRAKEN	Kockums	1 Apr 60	4 Apr 62
GRIPEN	Karlskrona	31 May 60	28 Apr 62
NORDKAPAREN	Kockums	8 Mar 61	4 Apr 62
SPRINGAREN	Kockums	31 Aug 61	7 Nov 62
VARGEN	Kockums	20 May 60	15 Nov 61

Displacement, tons	770 standard; 835 surface
Length, feet (*metres*)	229·7 (*70*)
Beam, feet (*metres*)	16·7 (*5·1*)
Draught, feet (*metres*)	16·7 (*5·1*)
Torpedo tubes	4—21 in (*533 mm*) bow
Main engines	Diesels; electric motors
Speed, knots	16·75 on surface; 25 submerged

DIVING. These six submarines have fast-diving capabilities.

NOMENCLATURE. *Draken* means Dragon, *Gripen* Griffon, *Vargen* Wolf.

APPEARANCE. Distinctive letters painted on the conning tower are: Del. *Delfinen;* Dra. *Draken*; Gri. *Gripen;* Nor. *Nordkaparen*; Spr. *Springaren*. Vgn. *Vargen*.

PHOTOGRAPHS. A photograph of *Draken* appears in the 1962-63 to 1964-65 editions and of *Gripen* in the 1967-68 and 1968-69 editions.

6 "HAJEN" CLASS

Name	*Builders*	*Launched*	*Completed*
BÃVERN	Kockums	11 Dec 1954	1956
HAJEN	Karlskrona	21 Apr 1955	1957
ILLERN	Kockums	3 Oct 1955	1957
SÃLEN	Kockums	14 Nov 1957	1959
UTTERN	Kockums	3 Feb 1958	1959
VALEN	Kockums	14 Nov 1958	1960

Displacement, tons	720 standard; 785 surface
Length, feet (*metres*)	216·5 (*64·5*)
Beam, feet (*metres*)	16·7 (*5·1*)
Draught, feet (*metres*)	14·8 (*4·5*)
Guns, AA	1—20 mm
Torpedo tubes	4—21 in (*533 mm*) bow (8 torpedoes)
Main engines	SEMT-Pielstick diesels; 1 700 bhp; Electric motors; electric drive on surface
Speed, knots	16 on surface, 20 submerged
Complement	44

All built by Kockums Mekaniska Verkstads Aktiebolag, Malmo, except *Valen* built by the Royal Swedish Naval Dockyard, Karlskrona.

OPERATIONAL. Equipped with Schnorkel, and have fast-diving capabilities.

NOMENCLATURE. *Bävern* means Beaver, *Hajen* Shark, *Illern* Polecat, *Sälen* Seal, *Uttern* Otter and *Valen* Whale.

APPEARANCE. Distinctive letters painted on the conning tower are: Bav, *Bävern*; Haj, *Hajen*; Iln *Illern*; Sal, *Sälen*; Utn, *Uttern*; Val, *Valen*.

PHOTOGRAPHS. A photograph of *Hajen* appears in the 1957-58 to 1959-60 editions, of *Bävern* in the 1960-61 to 1965-66 editions, of *Illern* in the 1964-65 to 1966-67 editions, of *Uttern* in the 1966-67 to 1968-69 editions, of *Valen* in the 1967-68 and 1968-69 editions.

DISPOSALS

Of the nine old submarines of the "Sjölejonet" class, **Dykaren** (Diver), **Sjöborren** (Sea-urchin), **Sjöhunden** (Seadog), **Sjölejonet** (Sealion) and **Svärdfisken** (Swordfish) were stricken in 1960 and scrapped; and **Sjöbjörnen** (Seabear), **Sjöhästen** (Seahorse), **Sjöormen** (Seaserpent) and **Tumlaren** (Porpoise) were discarded on 1 Jan 1964. The three old submarines of the "Najad" class, **Nacken** (Neck), **Najad** (Naiad) and **Neptun** (Neptune) were discarded in 1967.

SJÖORMEN *1968, Royal Swedish Navy, Official*

SPRINGAREN *1968, Royal Swedish Navy, Official*

DELFINEN *1969, Royal Swedish Navy, Official*

VARGEN *Royal Swedish Navy, Official*

SALEN *1969, Royal Swedish Navy, Official*

Submarines—*continued*

6 "ABBORREN" CLASS

ABBORREN (ex-U5) **LAXEN** (ex-U8)
FORELLEN (ex-U4) **MAKRILLEN** (ex-U9)
GÄDDAN (ex-U7) **SIKEN** (ex-U6)

Displacement, tons	420 standard; 430 surface; 460 submerged
Length, feet (*metres*)	164 (*50·0*)
Beam, feet (*metres*)	17·5 (*5·3*)
Draught, feet (*metres*)	17·5 (*5·3*)
Torpedo tubes	4—21 in (*533 mm*) 3 bow and 1 stern
Main engines	2 MAN diesels, total 1 500 hp Electric motor, 750 hp
Speed, knots	14 on surface; 9 submerged
Complement	23

All were built by Kockums Mek. Verkstads, Malmö (*U* 4, 5 June 1943, *U* 5, 8 July 1963, *U* 6 ,18 Aug 1943, *U* 7, 23 Nov 1943), and by Karlskrona Naval Dockyard (*U* 8, 25 Apr 1944, *U* 9, 23 May 1944) (original launch dates). Reconstructed in 1960-64. Launching dates after reconstruction: *Abborren* 1962, *Makrillen* 1963, *Forellen* 1963, *Laxen* 1964, *Gäddan* 1963, *Siken* 1964. All have been streamlined. Officially rated as *Kustubåtar* (coastal submarines). Distinctive letters Abb, For, Gad, Lax, Mak, Sik.

PHOTOGRAPHS. A photograph of *Laxen* appears in the 1965-66 to 1967-68 editions, of *Abborren* in the 1967-68 and 1968-69 editions.

DISPOSALS
Of three sister boats, **U 1** was scrapped in 1961, **U 2** was for sale in 1962, and **U 3** in 1964.

MAKRILLEN *1969, Royal Swedish Navy, Official*

SIKEN *1968, Royal Swedish Navy, Official*

1 Ex-BRITISH "MIDGET" TYPE

Displacement, tons	36 surface; 41 submerged
Length, feet (*metres*)	50·7 (*15·5*) pp; 53·9 (*16·4*) oa
Beam, feet (*metres*)	6·3 (*1·9*)
Draught, feet (*metres*)	7·5 (*2·3*)
Main engines	Perkins 6-cyl diesels Electric motors
Speed, knots	7 on surface; 6 submerged
Complement	5

Former British X-craft. Built by Vickers-Armstrongs Ltd, Barrow. Launched on 1 Oct 1954. Refitted in 1957-58. Purchased from Great Britain on 15 July 1958. Distinctive letters: Spg. "Spiggen" means "Stickleback"

SPIGGEN *1968, Royal Swedish Navy, Official*

CRUISER (*Kryssare*)

1 THE "KRONOR" CLASS

Name	Builders	Laid down	Launched	Completed
GÖTA LEJON	Eriksberg Mekaniska Verkstad, Göteborg	27 Sep 1943	17 Nov 1945	15 Dec 1947

Displacement, tons	8 200 standard; 9 200 full load
Length, feet (*metres*)	571 (*174·0*) pp; 590·5 (*180·0*) wl 597 (*182·0*) oa
Beam, feet (*metres*)	54 (*16·5*)
Draught, feet (*metres*)	19·5 (*6·0*) mean; 21·5 (*6·6*) max
Guns, surface	7—6 in (*150 mm*) 53 cal.
Guns, AA	4—57 mm Bofors; 11—40 mm Bofors
Armour	Exceptionally strong, 3 in—5 in (*75—125 mm*)
Boilers	4 Swedish 4-drum type
Main engines	2 sets De Laval geared turbines 100 000 shp; 2 shafts
Speed, knots	33
Complement	610

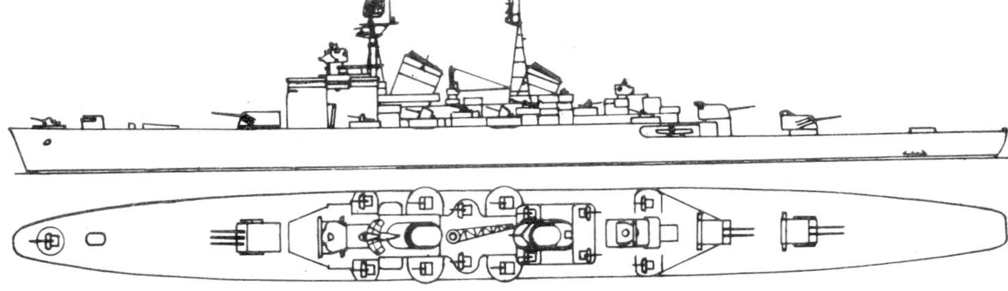

DRAWING. Port elevation and plan. Scale: 128 feet = 1 inch.

Cost was estimated at 74 000 000 kronor. Radar control arrangements were installed for 6-inch guns. Fitted for minelaying with a capacity of 120 mines. Reconstructed in 1951-52. Modernised in 1958, with new radar, 57 mm guns, etc.

GUNNERY. The 6 inch guns are high angle automatic anti-aircraft weapons with an elevation of 70 degrees. The 9—25 mm AA formerly mounted were suppressed in 1951 and 7—40 mm AA added.

APPEARANCE. Light tripod masts have been stepped as shown in photo. Enclosed tower bridge structure.

DISPOSALS
Sister ship **Tre Kronor** was discarded on 1 Jan 1964. The old anti-aircraft cruiser **Gotland** was sold in 1961.

GÖTA LEJON *1969, Royal Swedish Navy, Official*

DESTROYERS (*Jagare*)

4 "ÖSTERGÖTLAND" CLASS

Name	No.	Builders	Laid down	Launched	Completed
GÄSTRIKLAND	J 22	Götaverken, Göteborg	1 Oct 1955	6 June 1956	14 Jan 1959
HÄLSINGLAND	J 23	Kockums Mek Verkstads A/B	1 Oct 1955	14 Jan 1957	17 June 1959
ÖSTERGÖTLAND	J 20	Götaverken, Göteborg	1 Sep 1955	8 May 1956	3 Mar 1958
SÖDERMANLAND	J 21	Eriksberg Mekaniska Verkstad	1 June 1955	28 May 1956	27 June 1959

Displacement, tons	2 150 standard; 2 600 full load
Length, feet (*metres*)	367·5 (*112·0*) pp; 380 (*115·8*) oa
Beam, feet (*metres*)	36·8 (*11·2*)
Draught, feet (*metres*)	12 (*3·7*)
Missile launchers	"Seacat" surface-to-air
Guns, surface	4—4·7 in (*120 mm*)
Guns, AA	*Östergötland:* 7—40 mm *Hälsingland:* 5—40 mm *Others:* 4—40 mm
A/S	Triple barrelled DC mortar
Torpedo tubes	6—21 in (*533 mm*)
Mines	60 can be carried
Boilers	2 Babcock & Wilcox
Main engines	De Laval turbines 40 000 shp; 2 shafts
Speed, knots	35
Radius, miles	2 200 at 20 knots
Oil fuel (tons)	330
Complement	244

These ships have improved anti-aircraft defence and anti-submarine weapons of the Bofors type.

MODERNISATION. *Södermanland* was modernised in 1962, and *Gästrikland* and *Östergötland* in 1963.

GÄSTRIKLAND *1967, Royal Swedish Navy, Official*

PHOTOGRAPHS. A photograph of *Östergötland* appears in the 1962-63 to 1965-66 editions and of *Hälsingland* in the 1965-66 and 1966-67 editions.

PENNANT NUMBERS. J (for *Jagare*) painted on bows with number in 1966.

SÖDERMANLAND *1968, Royal Swedish Navy, Official*

2 "HALLAND" CLASS

Name	No.	Builders	Laid down	Launched	Completed
HALLAND	J 18	Götaverken, Göteborg	1951	16 July 1952	8 June 1955
SMALAND	J 19	Eriksberg Mekaniska Verkstad, Göteborg	1951	23 Oct 1952	12 Jan 1956

Displacement, tons	2 650 standard; 3 200 full load
Length, feet (*metres*)	380·5 (*116·0*) wl; 397·2 (*121·0*) oa
Beam, feet (*metres*)	41·3 (*12·6*)
Draught, feet (*metres*)	14·8 (*4·5*)
Missiles, surface	1 rocket launcher
Guns, dual purpose	4—4·7 in (*120 mm*)
Guns, AA	2—57 mm; 6—40 mm
A/S	2 four-barrelled DC mortars
Torpedo tubes	8—21 in (*533 mm*)
Mines	Can be fitted for minelaying
Boilers	2
Main engines	De Laval double reduction geared turbines; 58 000 shp; 2 shafts
Speed, knots	35
Radius, miles	3 000 at 20 knots
Oil fuel (tons)	500
Complement	290

Both ordered in 1948. The first Swedish destroyers of post-war design and construction. These large destroyers have fully automatic gun turrets forward and aft, ahead throwing anti-submarine weapons of the Bofors type, forward and ship-to-ship guided missiles launcher abaft the after funnel.

SMÅLAND *1968, Royal Swedish Navy, Official*

HALLAND *1968, Royal Swedish Navy, Official*

Destroyers—*continued*

Name	No.	Builders	Laid down	Launched	Completed	Modernised
ÖLAND	J 16	Kockums Mek Verkstads A/B, Malmö	1943	15 Dec 1945	5 Dec 1947	1960
UPPLAND	J 17	Karlskrona Dockyard	1943	5 Nov 1946	31 Jan 1949	1963

2 "ÖLAND" CLASS

Displacement, tons	2 000 standard; 2 400 full load
Length, feet (*metres*)	351 (*107·0*) pp; 364·2 (*111·0*) oa
Beam, feet (*metres*)	36·8 (*11·2*)
Draught, feet (*metres*)	11·2 (*3·4*)
Guns, dual purpose	4—4·7 in (*120 mm*)
Guns, AA	6—40 mm
A/S weapons	1 triple-barrelled depth charge mortar
Torpedo tubes	6—21 in (*533 mm*) tripled
Mines	60
Boilers	2 Penhoët
Main engines	De Laval geared turbines 44 000 shp; 2 shafts
Speed, knots	35
Radius, miles	2 500 at 20 knots
Oil fuel (tons)	300
Complement	210

The superstructure and machinery spaces are lightly armoured. Fitted for minelaying.

GUNNERY. The 4·7 inch guns are semi-automatic with an elevation of 80 degrees. The 40 mm AA gun near the jackstaff was removed in 1962, and the eight 20 mm AA guns were suppressed in 1964.

RECONSTRUCTION. *Öland* was modernised in 1960 with a new bridge, and *Uppland* was modernised with a new bridge and a helicopter platform in 1963, see new photograph.

PENNANT NUMBERS. J (for *Jagare*) painted on bows with number in 1966.

PHOTOGRAPHS. A port near broadside view of *Uppland* before reconstruction, appears in the 1955-56 to 1961-62 editions, a starboard bow near broadside view of *Öland* in the 1962-63 to 1965-66 editions, and a starboard bow surface view of *Uppland* in the 1965-66 and 1966-67 editions.

DISPOSALS OF OLDER DESTROYERS

Klas Horn was discarded in 1958. **Ehrensköld** and **Nordensköld** were discarded on 1 Apr 1963.

UPPLAND *1969, Royal Swedish Navy, Official*

ÖLAND *1969, Royal Swedish Navy, Official*

FAST ANTI-SUBMARINE FRIGATES (ex-Destroyers) Rated as *Fregatter*

Displacement, tons	1 250 standard; 1 400 full load
Length, feet (*metres*)	304 (*92·7*) wl; 310·5 (*94·6*) oa
Beam, feet (*metres*)	29·5 (*9·0*)
Draught, feet (*metres*)	12·5 (*3·8*)
Guns, dual purpose	3—4·7 in (*120 mm*);
Guns, AA	4—40 mm
A/S weapons	2 triple-barrelled DC mortars
Boilers	3 Penhoët
Main engines	De Laval geared turbines 32 000 shp; 2 shafts
Speed, knots	39
Radius, miles	1 200 at 20 knots
Oil fuel (tons)	150
Complement	130

Name	No.	Builders	Launched	Completed	Converted
KARLSKRONA	F 79	Karlskrona	16 June 1939	1940	1963

Former torpedo boat destroyer. Originally carried 20 to 60 mines. Refitted for anti-submarine warfare, and officially reclassified as frigate on 1 Jan 1961. F for *Fregatter*) painted on bows with number in 1966.

DISPOSALS

Of this class **Göteborg** was discarded in 1958, **Stockholm** on 1 Jan 1964, **Malmö** and **Norrköping** in 1967, and **Gavle** in 1969.

KARLSKRONA *1967, Royal Swedish Navy, Official*

2 "MJOLNER" CLASS

Name	No.	Builders	Launched	Completed
MODE	73	Götaverken	11 Apr 1942	1955
MUNIN	75	Öresundsvarvet	27 May 1942	1955

Displacement, tons	760 standard; 960 full load
Length, feet (*metres*)	243·8 (*74·3*) wl; 256 (*78·0*) oa
Beam, feet (*metres*)	26·2 (*8·0*)
Draught, feet (*metres*)	7·5 (*2·3*)
Guns, dual purpose	2—4·1 in (*105 mm*)
Guns, AA	2—40 mm
Boilers	2 three-drum type
Main engines	2 sets De Laval geared turbines 16 000 shp; 2 shafts
Speed, knots	30
Oil fuel (tons)	190
Complement	100

MUNIN *1969, Royal Swedish Navy, Official*

Both laid down in Sep 1941 and completed in 1942. Formerly rated as seagoing torpedo boats or coastal destroyers (kustjagare). Originally fitted for minelaying, but converted into fast anti-sumbarine frigates and the 3—21 inch torpedo tubes removed.

PHOTOGRAPHS. A photograph of *Mode* appears in the 1967-68 and 1968-69 editions.

DISPOSALS

Sister ships *Magne* and *Mjolner* were officially deleted from the list in 1967.

Fast Anti-Submarine Frigates—*continued*

4 "VISBY" CLASS

Name	*No.*	*Builders*	*Launched*	*Completed*
HÄLSINGBORG	13	Götaverken	23 Mar 43	1943
KALMAR	14	Eriksberg	20 July 43	1944
SUNDSVALL	F 12	Eriksberg	20 Oct 42	1943
VISBY	F 11	Götaverken	16 Oct 42	1943

Displacement, tons	1 150 standard; 1 320 full load
Length, feet (*metres*)	310 (*94·5*) wl; 320 (*97·5*) oa
Beam, feet (*metres*)	30 (*9·1*)
Draught, feet (*metres*)	12·5 (*3·8*)
Aircraft	*Nos. 11, 12:* I helicopter
Guns, dual purpose	*Nos. 13, 14:* 3—4·7 in (*120 mm*)
Guns, AA	*Nos. 11, 12*: 2—57 mm; *Nos. 13, 14*: 3—40 mm
A/S	1 four-barrelled DC mortar
Torpedo tubes	*Nos. 13 and 14:* 5—21 in (*533 mm*) quintupled
Boilers	3 three-drum type
Main engines	De Laval geared turbines 36 000 shp; 2 shafts
Speed, knots	39
Radius, miles	1 600 at 20 knots
Oil fuel (tons)	150
Complement	140

Former destroyers. *Kalmar* was laid down on 16 Nov 1942, and *Visby* on 29 Apr 1942. All were originally fitted for minelaying.

VISBY — *1969, Royal Swedish Navy, Official*

RECLASSIFICATION. Officially re-rated as frigates on 1 Jan 1965.

PENNANT NUMBERS. F (for *Fregatter*) painted on bows of *Sundsvall* and *Visby* with number in 1966.

PHOTOGRAPHS. A photograph of *Kalmar* appears in the 1962-63 to 1966-67 editions, of *Hälsingborg*, in the 1963-64 to 1966-67 edition and of *Sundsvaal* in the 1967-68 and 1968-69 editions.

MINELAYER AND SUBMARINE DEPOT SHIP

1 NEW CONSTRUCTION

ÄLVSBORG

Displacement, tons	2 700
Length, feet (*metres*)	302·5 (*92·2*)
Beam, feet (*metres*)	49·2 (*15·0*)
Draught, feet (*metres*)	13·1 (*4·0*)
Guns, AA	3—57 mm Bofors
Speed, knots	15
Cost	Estimated about 34 000 000 kr total
Complement	90 (accommodation for 210 more)

This new combined minelayer and submarine depot ship was ordered in 1968 from the Naval Dockyard in Karslkrona.

The novel ship will replace both the minelayer *Alvsnabben*, and the submarine depot ship *Patricia*.

The adjacent artist's impression shows the unique multiple minelaying rail sloping transom.

ÄLVSBORG — *1969, Royal Swedish Navy, Official*

MINELAYER (*Minfartyg*) Cadets' Seagoing Training Ship

ALVSNABBEN

Displacement, tons	4 250 standard;
Length, feet (*metres*)	317·5 (*96·8*) wl; 334·7 (*102·0*) oa
Beam, feet (*metres*)	44·5 (*13·5*)
Draught, feet (*metres*)	16 (*4·9*)
Guns, surface	2—6 in (*152 mm*)
Guns, AA	2—57 mm Bofors; 2—40 mm (+ mounts for 2 twin 40 mm)
Guns, saluting	4—35 mm
Main engines	Diesels, 1 shaft
Speed, knots	14
Complement	255 (63 cadets)

Built on a mercantile hull by Eriksberg Mekaniska Verkstad Göteborg. Laid down in Oct 1942, launched on 19 Jan 1943, completed in Apr 1943. Employed as a training ship during 1953-58, and relieved the anti-aircraft cruiser *Gotland* as Cadet's Seagoing Training Ship in 1959. Re-armed in 1961. Formerly carried 4—6 inch, 8—40 mm AA, 6—20 mm AA.

ÄLVSNABBEN — *1969 Royal Swedish Navy, Official*

SUBMARINE DEPOT SHIP (*Ubåts depåfartyg*)

PATRICIA (ex- *Patris II*) A 206

Displacement, tons	4 950 standard;
Length, feet (*metres*)	335 (*102·0*)
Beam, feet (*metres*)	47·5 (*14·5*)
Draught, feet (*metres*)	20 (*6·0*)
Guns, AA	8—40 mm; 2—20 mm
Boilers	2
Main engines	2 shafts; 2 450 ihp
Speed, knots	14
Complement	Accommodation for 500

Former Swedish-Lloyd merchant liner. Built by Swan, Hunter & Wigham Richardson Ltd, Wallsend-on-Tyne. Launched and completed in 1926. Acquired in 1940. She was reconstructed to increase the accommodation for about 500 men and to maintain and administer nine submarines.

PATRICIA — *1966, Royal Swedish Navy, Official*

TORPEDO BOATS (TORPEDBATAR)

6 + 12 NEW CONSTRUCTION

CAPELLA 123	**SIRIUS 122**	**VEGA 125**	**T 127**	**T 129**	**T 131**
CASTOR 124	**SPICA 121**	**VIRGO 126**	**T 128**	**T 130**	**T 132**

Displacement, tons	190 standard; 200 normal
Dimensions, feet	139·5 hull; 141 oa × 23·3
Guns	1—57 mm Bofors AA
Tubes	6—21 in (single, fixed)
Guided weapons	Light rocket launchers
Main engines	3 Bristol Siddeley Proteus 1274 gas turbines; 3 shafts 12 720 shp = 40 knots
Complement	28 (4 officers, 3 warrant officers, 7 petty officers, 14 ratings)

The lead vessel of a class of six, constituting the first group, *Spica* was completed in 1966 by Götaverken, Göteborg, who shared the contract for the series with Karlskronavarvet. The largest craft of their type. Designed to operate in areas contaminated by nuclear fall-out. *Sirius* and *Capella* built by Götaverken; *Castor, Vega* and *Virgo* by Karlskronavarvet. Six more projected.

GUNNERY. The 57 mm gun is in a power operated turret controlled by a radar equipped director, with a 57 mm rocket flare projector placed before, and a 10·3 mm launcher on each side, of the totally enclosed bridge. The turret is mounted in the centre of a long foredeck to give wide and clear arcs of fire.

CASTOR — *1969, Royal Swedish Navy, Official*

SPICA — *1968, Royal Swedish Navy, Official*

SIRIUS — *1968, Royal Swedish Navy, Official*

11 MTB—MGB CONVERTIBLES

ALDEBARAN	T 107	**ARCTURUS**	T 110	**POLARIS**	T 103
ALTAIR	T 108	**ARGO**	T 111	**POLLUX**	T 104
ANTARES	T 109	**ASTREA**	T 112	**REGULUS**	T 105
		PLEJAD	T 102	**RIGEL**	T 106

Displacement, tons	155 standard; 170 ful load
Dimensions, feet	157·5 × 18·3
Guns	2—40 mm Bofors AA
Tubes	6—21 in (2 forward, 4 aft)
Main engines	3 Mercedes-Benz diesels; 3 shafts; 9 000 bhp = 37·5 knots
Range, miles	600 at 30 knots
Complement	33

All built at Lurssen, Vegesack, launched between 1954 and 1959 and completed by 1960.

PHOTOGRAPHS. A photograph of *Plejad* emerging from camouflaged nuclear bomb-proof shelter appears in the 1962-63 to 1964-65 editions, of *Antares* in the 1960-61 to 1964-65 editions, and of *Polaris* in the 1965-66 to 1967-68 editions.

DISPOSAL

Perseus, T 101, built at Karlskrona, completed in 1951, the first of a convertible type of torpedo and gunboat of experimental design, re-engined with Götaverken machinery to give greater power, differing in appearance from the other boats, but funnel later removed, was discarded in 1967.

Torpedo Boats—*continued*

REGULUS — *1969, Royal Swedish Navy, Official*

RIGEL — *1968, Royal Swedish Navy, Official*

15 "T 42" TYPE

T 42	**T 45**	**T 48**	**T 51**	**T 54**
T 43	**T 46**	**T 49**	**T 52**	**T 55**
T 44	**T 47**	**T 50**	**T 53**	**T 56**

Displacement, tons	40 standard
Dimensions, feet	75·5 × 19·4 × 4·6
Guns	1—40 mm Bofors AA
Tubes	2—21 in
Main engines	Diesels; speed = 45 knots

Built by Kockums Mekaniska Verkstads Aktiebolag, Malmö. All launched between 1956 and 1959 and completed by 1960.

PHOTOGRAPHS. A photograph of T 56 appears in the 1964-65 to 1966-67 editions and of T 42 in the 1967-68 and 1968-69 editions.

T 49 — *1969, Royal Swedish Navy, Official*

10 "T 32" TYPE

T 32	**T 34**	**T 36**	**T 38**	**T 40**
T 33	**T 35**	**T 37**	**T 39**	**T 41**

Displacement, tons	40 standard
Dimensions, feet	75·5 × 18·4 × 4·5
Guns	1—40 mm Bofors AA; 2 MG
Tubes	2—21 in
Main engines	Diesels; Speed 40 knots

Launched in 1950-52. Built by Kockums Mekaniska Verkstads Aktiebolag, Malmö. Of all welded steel construction. T 41, of slightly different design, provided under the 1952 Programme, was launched and completed in 1962.

PHOTOGRAPHS. A photograph of T 38 appears in the 1953-54 to 1962-63 editions, of T 40 in the 1963-64 to 1966-67 editions, of T 41 in the 1966-67 to 1968-69 editions.

DISPOSALS

Of the small type of motor torpedo boats, **T 21**, **T 22**, **T 23**, **T 24**, **T 25**, **T 26** and **T 27** were scrapped in 1959, and **T 28**, **T 29**, **T 30** and **T 31** were scrapped in 1960. The older motor torpedo boats, **T 15**, **T 16**, **T 17** and **T 18** were discarded in 1957.

T 32 — *1967, Royal Swedish Navy, Official*

COASTAL MINESWEEPERS

12 "ARKÖ" CLASS

ARKÖ M 57
ASPÖ M 63
BLIDÖ M 68
HASSLÖ M 64
IGGÖ M 60
KARLSÖ M 59
NÄMDÖ M 67
SKAFTÖ M 62
SPÅRÖ M 58
STYRSÖ M 61
VÅLLÖ M 66
VINÖ M 65

Displacement, tons	300 standard
Dimensions, feet	131 pp; 144·5 oa × 23 × 8
Guns	1—40 mm AA
Main engines	Mercedes-Benz diesels; 2 shafts; 2 000 bhp = 14·5 knots

Of wooden construction. There is a small difference in the deck-line between M 57-59 and M60-68. *Arkö* was launched on 21 Jan 1957. *Arkö, Karlsö* and *Spårö* were completed in 1957, *Iggö* in 1960. *Skaftö* in 1961. *Aspö, Haåslö, Vinö* and *Styrsö* in 1952. *Vållö* in 1963, *Bildö* and *Nämdö* in 1964. Six more are in the new construction programme. A photograph of *Arkö* appears in the 1959-60 to 1965-66 editions and of *Aspö* in the 1966-67 to 1968-69 editions.

STYRSÖ *1968, Royal Swedish Navy, Official*

VALLÖ *1969, Royal Swedish Navy, Official*

6 "HANÖ" CLASS

HANÖ M 51
ORNÖ M 55
STURKÖ M 54
TÄRNÖ M 52
TJURKÖ M 53
UTÖ M 56

Displacement, tons	270 standard
Dimensions, feet	131·2 × 23 × 8
Guns	2—40 mm AA
Main engines	Diesels; 2 shafts; 2 400 bhp = 14·5 knots

All the minesweepers of this class were built at Karlskrona and launched in 1953.

HANÖ *1967 Royal Swedish Navy, Official*

ORNÖ *1968, Royal Swedish Navy, Official*

MINING TENDERS (*Minutlaggare*)

MUL 12 (1952)
MUL 13 (1952)
MUL 14 (1953)
MUL 15 (1953)
MUL 16 (1956)
MUL 17 (1956)
MUL 18 (1956)
MUL 19 (1956)

Displacement, tons	245 standard
Dimensions, feet	102·3 × 25 × 10·2
Guns	1—40 mm
Main engines	1 Diesel-electric; 360 bhp = 10·5 knots

Launch dates above. Coastal Artillery personnel. A photograph of *MUL* 15 appears in the 1963-64 to 1966-67 editions and of *MUL* 12 in the 1967-68 and 1968-69 editions.

MUL 11 (1946)

Displacement, tons	200 standard
Dimensions, feet	98·8 × 23·7 × 11
Guns	2—20 mm
Main engines	2 diesels; speed = 10 knots

MUL 10 (1939)

Displacement, tons	166 standard
Dimensions, feet	90 × 18·3 × 7·5
Guns	4 MG
Main engines	Deisel; speed = 9·5 knots

MUL 12 *1967, Royal Swedish Navy, Official*

DISPOSALS OF MINESWEEPERS

Of the "Bredskär" class, **Ven** was scrapped in 1960, **Grönscär** was removed from the effective list on 1 Apr 1963, **Halmön Koster**, **Sandön** and **Vingo** were discarded on 1 Jan 1964, **Bredskär**, **Bremön**, **Kullen**, **Arskär** and **Ramskär** by the end of 1967, and **Ulvön** in 1968. Of the "Arholma" class, **Arholma** was scrapped in 1959 and **Landsort** was officially discarded on 1 Jan 1964. Of the "Jägaren" class, **Snapphanen** was transferred to the Guatemalan Navy in 1959, and **Jägaren**, **Kaparen** and **Vaktaren** were scrapped in 1958.

STAFF SHIP (*Stabsfartyg*)

MARIEHOLM A 201

Displacement, tons	1 445 standard
Dimensions, feet	210 × 32·5 × 14
Aircraft	1 helicopter
Guns	2 MG
Main engines	Steam reciprocating; speed = 12 knots

Former passenger ship. Completed in 1934. Converted during the Second World War to serve as a Base Communication Centre for the Commander-in-Chief of the Active Fleet. Recently used as a Staff Ship for the Commander-in-Chief in winter time, flying his flag. The ship had her mainmast removed and a helicopter platform installed aft in 1959 for employment as flagship of the Active Fleet (the "Coast Fleet"). The 40 mm Bofors on the forecastle has been landed for the time being.

MARIEHOLM *1967, Royal Swedish Navy, Official*

TRAINING SHIPS (*Skonerter*)

FALKEN (12 June 1947)
GLADAN (14 Nov 1946)

Displacement, tons	220 standard
Dimensions, feet	93 wl; 129·5 oa × 23·5 × 13·5
Main engines	Auxiliary diesel; 50 bhp

Sail training ships. Schooners. Launch dates above. Sail area 5 511 square feet.

INSHORE MINESWEEPERS

6 "ORUST" CLASS

BLACKAN	M 44	**GILLÖGA**	M 47	**RÖDLÖGA**	M 48
DÄMMAN	M 45	**HISINGEN**	M 43	**SVARTLÖGA**	M 49
GALTEN	M 46	**ORUST**	M 41	**TJÖRN**	M 42

Displacement, tons	*Orust, Tjörn:* 110 standard; others 140
Dimensions, feet	*Orust, Tjörn:* 62·3 × 19·7 × 4·5; others 76·2 × 21 × 4·7
Guns	*Orust, Tjörn:* 1—20 mm AA; others 1—40 mm AA
Main engines	2 diesels; 600 bhp = 9 knots

Orust and *Tjörn* were launched in 1948. Of the fishing cutter type. *Blackan, Dämman, Galten* and *Hisingen* were launched in 1957. Three more authorised in Apr 1962 were built in 1964. A photograph of *Galten* appears in the 1963-64 to 1966-67 editions.

HISINGEN — *1967, Royal Swedish Navy, Official*

8 LARGE MOTOR LAUNCH TYPE

M 15	**M 21**	**M 23**	**M 25**
M 16	**M 22**	**M 24**	**M 26**

Displacement, tons	70 standard
Dimensions, feet	85·3 × 16·5 × 4·5
Guns	1—20 mm
Main engines	Diesel; 600 bhp = 13 knots

All launched in 1941. M 17 and M 18 of this type were rerated as tenders and renamed *Lommen* and *Spoven*, respectively, see later page. M 19 and M 20 were officially deleted from the list in 1969.

M 22 — *1969, Royal Swedish Navy, Official*

SALVAGE VESSEL (*Bärgningsfartyg*)

BELOS A 211

Displacement, tons	950 standard
Dimensions, feet	204 × 27 × 12
Aircraft	1 helicopter
Main engines	Diesel; 2 shafts; 1 200 bhp = 13 knots

A new salvage vessel built to succeed and take the name of the old *Belos*. Launched on 15 Nov 1961. Completed on 29 May 1963. Equipped with a decompression chamber. The old salvage vessel *Belos* (launched in 1885), then the world's oldest naval vessel in service (she helped to raise the 334-year old warship *Vasa* in 1961) was discarded on 1 Aug 1963.

BELOS — *1969, Royal Swedish Navy, Official*

PATROL BOATS (*Vedettbåtar*)

V 57

Displacement, tons	115 standard
Dimensions, feet	98 pp; 105 oa × 17·3 × 7·5
Guns	2—20 mm AA
Main engines	Diesel; 500 bhp = 13·5 knots
Complement	12

Built at Stockholm. Launched in 1953. Fitted for minelaying. In Coast Artillery.

DISPOSALS

V 51, V 52, V 53, V 54, V 55 and **V 56**, 125 tons coal burning triple expansion steam engined type manned by Coast Artillery, were officially discarded in 1967.

71 72 73 74 75 76 77

Displacement, tons	28 standard
Dimensions, feet	69 × 15 × 5
Guns	1—20 mm
Main engines	Diesel; speed = 18 knots

Launched in 1966-67 and completed in 1968. Rated as *Bevakningsbåtar*.

V 57 — *1962, A. Kull*

61 62 63 64 65 66 67 68 69 70

Displacement, tons	30 standard
Dimensions, feet	62·3 × 15 × 4
Guns	1—20 mm
Main engines	Diesel; speed = 19 knots

Guard boats of the coast artillery (Bevakningsbåt) launched in 1960-61.

62 — *1967, Royal Swedish Navy, Official*

SVK 1 SVK 2 SVK 3 SVK 4 SVK 5

Displacement, tons	19
Dimensions, feet	55·8 × 12 × 4
Guns	1—20 mm AA
Speed	11 knots

Patrol launches of the Sjövärnskårens type. All launched in 1944. Sjövärnskåren = RNVR. *Tumlaren*, a small fishing cutter, also belongs to the SVK.

M 7 M 8

Displacement, tons	50 standard
Dimensions, feet	78·8 × 16·5 × 4·5
Guns	1—20 mm
Main engines	Diesel: 400 bhp = 13 knots

Former inshore minesweepers of the medium motor launch type, taken over as patrol boats.

FRYKEN A 217

Displacement, tons	307 standard
Dimensions, feet	105 × 19 × 9
Main engines	Speed = 10 knots

A new construction water carrier. Launched in 1959 and completed in 1960. Former pennant number was 263.

UNDEN A 216

Displacement, tons	500
Dimensions, feet	121·3 × 23·3 × 14
Speed, knots	10

Launched in 1946. The pennant number of *Unden* was formerly 268.

GÄLNAN

Displacement, tons	100
Dimensions, feet	95 × 19 × 9
Main engines	Speed = 8 knots

Launched in 1942. Small water tanker for harbour and local services.

SURVEY SHIPS (*Sjömätningsfartyg*)

JOHAN MÅNSSON

Displacement, tons	900
Dimensions, feet	183·7 × 36 × 8·5
Main engines	Speed = 15 knots

Launched on 14 Jan 1966. A new survey ship is planned in the near future.

JOHAN MANSSON *1968, Royal Swedish Navy, Official*

RAN

Displacement, tons	285 standard
Dimensions, feet	98·5 × 23 × 8·5

Ran was launched in 1945 and completed and commissioned for service in 1946

GUSTAV AF KLINT

Displacement, tons	750 standard
Dimensions, feet	170·5 × 28·5 × 15·5
Main engines	Diesel; speed = 10 knots

Launched in 1941. Reconstructed in 1963. She formerly displaced 650 tons, length 154 feet. A photograph appears in the 1953-54 to 1963-64 editions.

GUSTAV AF KLINT *1966, Royal Swedish Navy, Official*

ANDEN (ex-*M* 9) **GRISSLAN** (ex-*M* 6) **MÅSEN** (ex-*M* 3) **SVÄRTAN** (ex-*M* 5) **TÄRNAN** (ex-*M* 4) **VIGGEN** (ex-*M* 10)

Displacement, tons	50 standard
Dimensions, feet	78·8 × 16·5 × 4·5
Main engines	Diesel; 400 bhp = 13 knots

Former inshore minesweepers of the motor launch type, launched in 1940 and subsequently converted into survey craft. M 7 and M 8 were taken over as patrol boats.

JOHAN NORDENANKAR (1924)

Displacement, tons	260 standard
Dimensions, feet	98·5 × 22·3 × 8·2
Main engines	Speed = 8 knots

PETTER GEDDA (1924)

Displacement, tons	135 standard
Dimensions, feet	82 × 18 × 7
Main engines	Speed = 6 knots

EJDERN (1916)

Displacement, tons	95 standard
Dimensions, feet	78·8 × 15·8 × 17·5
Main engines	Speed = 8 knots

NILS STRÖMCRONA (1894)

Displacement, tons	140 standard
Dimensions, feet	90 × 17 × 8·2
Guns	None in peacetime
Main engines	Speed = 9 knots

Launch dates above. The older survey ships will eventually be replaced.

SUPPLY SHIP

FREJA A2 21

Displacement, tons	300 standard; 450 full load
Dimensions, feet	160·8 × 27·5 × 10
Main engines	Speed = 11 knots

Built by Kroger, Rendsburg. Launched in 1953. Employed as a provision ship.

ICEBREAKERS (*Isbrytarfartyg*)

1 New Construction

NIORD

Displacement, tons	5 260 standard
Dimensions, feet	260·8 pp; 283·8 oa × 69·6 × 20·3
Main engines	Wärtsilä diesel-electric; 12 000 hp = 18 knots

Built by Wärtsilä, Finland. Scheduled to be completed in Dec 1969. Near sister ship of *Tor*.

TOR

Displacement, tons	4 980 standard
Dimensions, feet	254·3 pp; 277·2 oa × 69·5 × 20·3
Main engines	Wärtsilä-Sulzer diesel-electric; 4 shafts; 2 forward; 2 aft; 12 000 hp = 18 knots

Launched from Wärtsilä's Crichton-Vulcan yard, Turku, on 25 May 1963. Towed to Sandvikens Skeppsdocka, Helsingfors, for completion. Delivered on 31 Jan 1964. Larger but generally similar to *Oden*, and a near-sister to *Tarmo* built for Finland.

TOR *1968, Royal Swedish Navy, Official*

ODEN

Displacement, tons	4 950 standard
Dimensions, feet	256 pp; 273·5 oa × 63·7 × 22·7
Main engines	Diesel-electric; 4 shafts; 10 500 bhp = 17 knots
Oil fuel, tons	740
Complement	75

Similar to the Finnish *Voima* and 3 Soviet icebreakers. 4 screws, 2 forward, 2 aft. Built at Sandviken, Helsingfors. Launched on 16 Oct 1956. Completed in 1958.

ODEN *1969, Royal Swedish Navy, Official*

THULE

Displacement, tons	2 200 standard
Dimensions, feet	187 wl; 204·2 oa × 50 × 19 max
Main engines	Diesel-electric; 3 shafts (1 for'd); 4 800 bhp = 16 knots
Complement	43

Launched at the Naval Dockyard, Karlskrona, in 1951. Completed in 1953.

THULE *1969, Royal Swedish Navy, Official*

Icebreakers—*continued*

YMER *1969, Royal Swedish Navy, Official*

YMER

Displacement, tons	4 330 standard
Dimensions, feet	240 wl; 258 oa × 63·1 × 22·3
Guns	4—3 in AA; 1—40 mm AA; 4—25 mm AA
Main engines	6 Atlas diesel-electric; 9 000 hp = 16 knots
Complement	44

Launched by Kockums MV A/B, Malmö in 1932. First large icebreaker with diesel-electric propulsion. Designed to carry a seaplane for ice spotting and survey.

DISPOSAL

The icebreaker **Atle** was officially discarded in 1967.

LANDING CRAFT

BORE **GRIM** **HEIMDAL**

Displacement, tons	380
Dimensions, feet	116·5 × 28 × 8·5
Main engines	Speed = 12 knots

General utility landing craft of improved design. Launched in 1961 (*Grim*) and 1966. A photograph of *Grim* appears in the 1966-67 to 1968-69 editions.

BORE *1969, Royal Swedish Navy, Official*

SKAGUL A 333 **SLEIPNER** A 335

Displacement, tons	355 standard
Dimensions, feet	118 × 28 × 8·5
Main engines	Speed = 12 knots

Sleipner was launched in 1959 and completed in 1960. *Skagul* was launched and completed in 1960. A photograph of *Skagul* appears in the 1962-63 to 1966-67 editions

Nos. 201-204 **205-238** **239-243**

Displacement, tons	31
Dimensions, feet	69 × 13·8 × 4·2
Main engines	Speed = 18 knots

A series of 43 landing craft rated as Landstigningfarkoster. Launched in 1957 *et seq.*

200 Series *1967, Royal Swedish Navy, Official*

L 51 **L 52** **L 53** **L 54** **L 55**

Displacement, tons	32 standard (officially revised figure)
Dimensions, feet	50·8 × 16 × 3·2
Main engines	Diesel; 140 bhp = 8 knots

Landing craft of general utility type. Launched in 1948, L 53 and L 54 laid up 1960.

ANE **BALDER** **LOKE** **RING**

Displacement, tons	135 (*Loke* 145)
Dimensions, feet	91·9 × 26·2 × 5; (*Loke* 6)
Main engines	Speed = 8·5 knots; (*Loke* 9·2 knots)

Artillery transport craft for general purpose duties. Launched in 1943-45.

OILERS (*Tankfartyg*)

OLJAREN (ex-*Martha*) A 227

Displacement, tons	1 100 standard
Cargo capacity	695 tons
Dimensions, feet	179 × 28 × 11
Guns	2—25 mm AA
Main engines	Speed = 9 knots

Launched in 1939. The pennant number of *Oljaren* was formerly 267, changed recently.

OLJAREM *1969, Royal Swedish Navy, Official*

ELDAREN (ex-*Muron*) A 226

Displacement, tons	585 standard
Cargo capacity	535 tons
Dimensions, feet	169 × 25·8 × 10
Guns	2—25 mm AA
Main engines	Speed = 9·5 knots

Launched in 1938. The pennant number of *Eldaren* was formerly 266. The oiler *Tankaren* (ex-*Lister*) 269 has been deleted from the list.

MINE TRANSPORT

FÄLLAREN A 236 **MINÖREN** A 237

Displacement, tons	165 standard
Dimensions, feet	105 × 20·3 × 7·2
Main engines	Speed = 9 knots

Launched in 1941 and 1940 respectively. Rated as *Mintransportfartyg*.

TENDERS

PELIKANEN A 247

Displacement, tons	100 standard
Dimensions, feet	108·2 × 19 × 6
Main engines	Speed = 15 knots

Torpedo recovery and rocket trials vessel. Launched in 1964.

ACHILLES A 251 **AJAX** A 252

Displacement, tons	450
Dimensions, feet	108·2 × 28·9 × 12

Achilles was launched in 1962 and *Ajax* in 1963. Both are icebreaking tugs. Former pennant numbers were 276 and 277, respectively.

SIGRUN A 256

Displacement, tons	250 standard
Dimensions, feet	105 × 22·3 × 11·8
Main engines	Speed = 11 knots

Launched in 1961. Rated as *Tvättbytesfartyg*.

HERMES A 253

Displacement, tons	185
Dimensions, feet	75·5 × 22·3 × 13
Main engines	Speed = 11·5 knots

Launched in 1957. Pennant number was changed from 318.

HÄGERN (ex-*Torpedbärgaren*) A 246

Displacement, tons	50 standard
Dimensions, feet	92 × 16·5 × 6

Hägern was launched in 1951. Pennant number changed from 274.

LOMMEN (ex-*M* 17) A 231 **SPOVEN** (ex-*M* 18) A 232

Displacement, tons	70 standard
Dimensions, feet	85·3 × 16·5 × 4·5
Main engines	Diesel; 600 bhp = 13 knots

Former inshore minesweepers of the large motor launch type. Both launched in 1941.

SUDAN

Establishment

The Navy was established in 1962 to guard the Red Sea coast.

Mercantile Marine

Lloyd's Register of Shipping: 7 vessels of 15 620 tons gross

PATROL BOATS

GIHAD PB 1 **HORRIYA** PB 2 **ISTIGLAL** PB 3 **SHAAB** PB 4

Displacement, tons	100
Dimensions, feet	115 × 16·5 × 5·2
Guns	1—40 mm AA; 1—20 mm AA; 2—7·6 mm MG
Main engines	Mercedes-Benz diesels; 2 shafts; 1 800 bhp = 20 knots
Radius, miles	1 400
Complement	20 officers and men

Built by Mosor Shipyard, Trogir, Yugoslavia, in 1961-62. Of steel construction. First craft acquired by the newly established Sudanese Navy. A photograph of *Horriya, Istiglal* and *Shaab* in company appears in the 1962-63 to 1965-66 editions, of *Gihad* in the 1962-63 to 1966-67 editions, and of *Istiglal* and *Shaab* together in the 1967-68 and 1968-69 editions.

GIHAD *Sudan Navy, Official*

HORRIYA *Sudan Navy, Official*

SYRIA

New Construction

The construction is planned of patrol vessels of 150 tons with a speed of 27 knots; motor torpedo boats; and seaward defence boats of 60 tons with a speed of 23 knots.

Acquisition Programme

One destroyer, two small submarines of the "M" type and six motor torpedo boats were expected from the USSR. Several small craft were received from France.

Mercantile Marine

Lloyd's Register of Shipping: 3 vessels of 728 tons gross

MINESWEEPERS

2 Ex-U.S.S.R. "T 43" Type

HITTINE **YARMOUK**

Displacement, tons	500 standard; 600 full load
Dimensions, feet	200 × 27·2 × 9
Guns	4—37 mm AA; 8—13 mm AA
Main engines	Diesel motors; 2 shafts; speed = 18 knots

Reported in 1962 to have transferred from the Soviet Navy to the Syrian Navy.

PATROL VESSELS

3 Ex-French "Ch" Type

Name	*Builders*	*Laid down*	*Launched*	*Completed*
AKABA BEN NASEH	A. C. de France	1938	Jan 1940	Apr 1940
AL HARISSI	A.C. Seine Maut	1938	1939	1940
TAREK BEN SAID	A.C. Seine Maut	1938	1939	1940

Displacement, tons	107 standard; 131 full load
Dimensions, feet	116·5 pp; 121·8 oa × 17·5 × 6·5
Guns	1—3 in; 2—20 mm AA
A/S weapons	Depth charges
Main engines	MAN diesels; 2 shafts; 1 130 bhp = 16 knots
Oil fuel, tons	5
Radius, miles	1 200 at 8 knots; 680 at 13 knots
Complement	28

These former French submarine chasers were transferred in 1962 to form the nucleus of the Syrian Navy. Respectively ex-*Ch* 10, ex-*Ch* 19, and ex-*Ch* 130.

"Ch" Type *M Henri Le Masson*

MISSILE BOATS

10 Ex-USSR "KOMAR" CLASS

Former Soviet missile patrol boats. See particulars in USSR section.

TORPEDO BOATS

15 Ex-USSR TYPE

Displacement, tons,	50
Tubes	2—21 in
Main engines	Speed = 40 knots

Five motor torpedo boats were transferred from the USSR at Latakia on 7 Feb 1957, and others subsequently.

TANZANIA

COASTAL PATROL

There are reported to be four small patrol boats, two of 50 tons and two of 27 tons.
It was officially stated in 1967 that the four küstenuachboote loaned to the Tanzania Government by the Federal Republic of Germany, KW 4, KW 5, KW 9 and KW 10, shipped from West Germany on 8 Dec 1963, and renamed *Rafiki, Papa, Uhura* and *Salama*, respectively, see full particulars in the 1966-67 edition, have since been handed over to the Southern Engineering Company of Mombasa, Kenya.
There are reported to be four other small patrol boats, two of 50 tons and two of 27 tons.

ROYAL THAI NAVY

Administration

Commander-in-Chief of the Navy:
Admiral Charoon Chalermtiarana

Chief of the Naval Staff:
Admiral Thavil Rayananon

Diplomatic Representation

Naval Attaché in London:
Captain Ampol Nabangchang

Naval Attaché in Washington:
Captain Tada Ditbanjong

Personnel

1969: *Navy*, 15 000 (2 000 officers) and 13 000 ratings)
Marine Corps: 6 400 (400 officers and 6 000 men)

Strength of the Fleet

1 Destroyer Escort
4 Frigates
1 Escort Minesweeper
1 Armoured Gunboats
2 Coastal Minelayers
18 Patrol Vessels
4 Coastal Minesweepers
10 Patrol Boats
5 Gunboats
5 CG Vessels
6 Landing Ships
8 Landing Craft
1 Survey Ship
15 Auxiliaries

DESTROYER ESCORT

Name	*No.*	*Builders*	*Launched*	*Completed*
PIN KLAO (ex-USS *Hemminger, DE* 746)	DE 3 (ex-1)	Western Pipe & Steel Co	12 Sep 1943	30 May 1944

1 Ex-US "BOSTWICK" CLASS

Displacement, tons	1 240 standard; 1 900 full load
Length, feet (*metres*)	306 (*93·3*) oa
Beam, feet (*metres*)	37 (*11·3*)
Draught, feet (*metres*)	14 (*4·3*)
Guns, dual purpose	3—3 in (*76 mm*) 50 cal.
Guns, AA	6—40 mm
A/S	8 DCT
Torpedo tubes	6 (2 triple mounts) for A/S torpedoes
Main engines	GM diesels with electric drive 6 000 bhp; 2 shafts
Speed, knots	20
Radius, miles	11 500 at 11 knots
Oil fuel (tons)	300
Complement	220

Transferred from the United States Navy to the Royal Thai Navy at New York Naval Shipyard in July 1959 under the Mutual Defence Assistance Programme and given the new Thai name *Pin Klao*.

ARMAMENT. The 3—21 in torpedo tubes were removed, and the 4—20 mm AA guns were replaced by 4—40 mm AA. The six ASW torpedo tubes were fitted in 1966.

PIN KLAO *1966, Royal Thai Navy, Official*

FRIGATES

Name	*No.*	*Builders*	*Laid down*	*Launched*	*Completed*
PRASAE (ex-USS *Gallup, PF* 47)	2	Consolidated Steel Corpn, Los Angeles	18 Aug 1943	17 Sep 1943	29 Feb 1944
TAHCHIN (ex-USS *Glendale, PF* 36)	1	Consolidated Steel Corpn, Los Angeles	6 Apr 1943	28 May 1943	1 Oct 1943

Ex-US PF TYPE

2 "PRASAE" CLASS

Displacement, tons	1 430 standard; 2 100 full load
Length, feet (*metres*)	304 (*92·7*) oa
Beam, feet (*metres*)	37·5 (*11·4*)
Draught, feet (*metres*)	13·7 (*4·2*)
Guns, dual purpose	3—3 in (*76 mm*) 50 cal.
Guns, AA	2—40 mm; 9—20 mm
A/S	8 DCT
Boilers	2 small water tube 3-drum type
Main engines	Triple expansion 5 500 ihp; 2 shafts
Speed, knots	19
Radius, miles	9 500 at 12 knots
Oil fuel (tons)	685
Complement	180

Former United States patrol frigates of the "Tacoma" class. Delivered to the Royal Thai Navy on 29 Oct 1951. They were of similar design to the British frigates of the "River" class.

PHOTOGRAPHS. A photograph of *Prasae* appears in the 1965-66 to 1968-69 editions.

TACHIN *1969, Royal Thai Navy, Official*

Name	*No.*	*Builders*	*Laid down*	*Launched*	*Completed*
BANGPAKONG (ex-*Gondwana*, ex-HMS *Burnet*)	PF 4	Ferguson Bros Ltd, Port Glasgow	2 Nov 1942	31 May 1943	23 Sep 1943

1 Ex-BRITISH "FLOWER" CLASS

Displacement, tons	1 060 standard; 1 350 full load
Length, feet (*metres*)	193 (*58·8*) pp; 203·2 (*61·9*) oa
Beam, feet (*metres*)	33 (*10·0*)
Draught, feet (*metres*)	14·5 (*4·4*)
Guns, dual purpose	1—3 in (*76 mm*) 50 cal.
Guns, AA	1—40 mm; 6—20 mm
A/S	4 DCT
Boilers	2 three-drum type
Main engines	Triple expansion; 2 880 ihp
Speed, knots	16
Radius, miles	4 800 at 12 knots
Oil fuel (tons)	282
Complement	100

Served in the Indian Navy before transfer to the Royal Thai Navy. The 3 inch gun replaced a 4 inch gun, and the 40 mm gun replaced a 20 mm gun in 1966. Sister ship *Prasae* (ex-*Sind*, ex-*Betony*) was lost in the Korean War on 13 Jan 1951.

BANGPAKONG *Royal Thai Navy, Official*

Frigates—*continued*

Name	*No.*	*Builders*	*Laid down*	*Launched*	*Completed*
MAEKLONG	3	Uraga Dock Co, Japan	1936	27 Nov 1936	June 1937

1 SLOOP TYPE

Displacement, tons	1 400 standard; 2 000 full load
Length, feet (*metres*)	269 (*82·0*)
Beam, feet (*metres*)	34 (*10·4*)
Draught, feet (*metres*)	10·5 (*3·2*)
Guns, surface	4—4·7 in (*120 mm*)
Guns, AA	3—40 mm; 3—20 mm
Boilers	2 water tube
Main engines	Triple expansion 2 500 ihp; 2 shafts
Speed, knots	14
Radius, miles	8 000 at 12 knots
Oil fuel (tons)	487
Complement	155 as training ship

Ordered in 1934. Designed as a dual-purpose sloop and torpedo boat. Fitted for minesweeping. Employed as a training ship. The 4—18 inch torpedo tubes were removed. The 40 mm and 20 mm AA guns were each increased from two to three in 1966. Sister ship *Tachin* was heavily damaged during the Second World War on 1 June 1945 and eventually scrapped. To be rearmed with 3 inch 50 cal in 1969.

MAEKLONG *1967, Royal Thai Navy, Official*

ESCORT MINESWEEPER

Name	*No.*	*Builders*	*Laid down*	*Launched*	*Completed*
PHOSAMTON (ex-HMS *Minstrel*)	MSF 1	Redfern Construction Co	1943	5 Oct 1944	1945

1 Ex-BRITISH "ALGERINE" CLASS

Displacement, tons	1 040 standard; 1 335 full load
Length, feet (*metres*)	225 (*68·6*) oa
Beam, feet (*metres*)	35·5 (*10·8*)
Draught, feet (*metres*)	10·5 (*3·2*)
Guns, surface	1—4 in (*102 mm*)
Guns, AA	6—20 mm
A/S	4 DCT
Boilers	2 three-drum type
Main engines	Triple expansion 2 000 ihp; 2 shafts
Speed, knots	16
Radius, miles	5 000 at 10 knots
Oil fuel (tons)	270
Complement	103

Former British "Algerine" class minesweeper of ocean-going type capable of fleet sweeping and escort duties. The 20 mm AA guns were increased from 3 to 6, and the DCTs from 2 to 4 in 1966.

PHOSAMTON *1965, Royal Thai Navy, Official*

ARMOURED GUNBOAT

SUKOTHAI	Vickers Armstrong	Dec 1928	19 Nov 1929	Dec 1930

1 COAST DEFENCE TYPE

Displacement, tons	886 standard; 1 000 full load
Length, feet (*metres*)	160 (*48·8*) pp; 173 (*52·7*) oa
Beam, feet (*metres*)	37 (*11·3*)
Draught, feet (*metres*)	10·8 (*3·3*)
Guns, surface	2—6 in (*152 mm*)
Guns, dual purpose	4—3 in (*76 mm*)
Guns, AA	2—40 mm; 3—20 mm
Armour	Sides: 2½ in (*63 mm*) midship, 1¼ in (*32 mm*), ends; Barbette rings 2½ in (*63 mm*); CT 4¾ in (*120 mm*); Upper deck 1½ in—¾ in (*38—19 mm*)
Boilers	2 water tube; 225 psi (*15·8 kg/cm²*)
Main engines	Triple expansion 850 ihp; 2 shafts
Speed, knots	12
Radius, miles	2 000 at 10 knots
Oil fuel (tons)	96
Complement	103

Sister ship *Ratanakosindra* was withdrawn from service in 1968. A photograph appears in the 1966-67 to 1968-69 editions.

SUKOTHAI *1969, Royal Thai Navy, Official*

COASTAL MINELAYERS

2 "BANGRACHAN" CLASS

BANGRACHAN (No. 1) **NHONG SARHAI** (No. 2)

Displacement, tons	368 standard; 408 full load
Dimensions, feet	160·8 × 26 × 7·2
Guns	2—3 in AA; 2—20 mm AA
Mines	142 capacity
Main engines	Burmeister & Wain diesels; 2 shafts; 540 bhp = 12 knots
Oil fuel, tons	18
Radius, miles	2 700
Complement	55

Launched by Cantiere dell'Adriatico, Monfalcone in 1936, *Nhong Sarhai* on 22 July. A photograph of *Nhong Sarhai* appears in the 1961-62 to 1965-66 editions.

BANGRACHAN *Royal Thai Navy, Official*

PATROL VESSELS

7 "TRAD" CLASS

CHANDHABURI 16 Dec 1936 No. 22
CHUMPORN 18 Jan 1937 No. 31
PATTANI 16 Oct 1936 No. 13
PUKET 28 Sep 1935 No. 12
RAYONG 11 Jan 1937 No. 23
SURASDRA 28 Nov 1936 No. 21
TRAD 26 Oct 1935 No. 11

Displacement, tons	318 standard; 470 full load
Dimensions, feet	219 pp; 223 oa × 21 × 7
Guns	2—3 in AA; 1—40 mm AA; 2—20 mm AA; *Chumporn* 2—40 mm
Tubes	4—18 in (2 twin); *Chumporn* 2—18 in (1 twin)
Main engines	Parsons geared turbines; 2 shafts; 9 000 hp = 31 knots
Boilers	2 Yarrow
Oil fuel, tons	102
Radius, miles	1 700 at 15 knots
Complement	70

Designed as torpedo boats, *Puket* and *Trad* laid down on 8 Feb 1935 by Cantieri Riuniti dell'Adriatico, Monfalcone, for delivery by end of 1935. Launch dates above. Armament supplied by Vickers-Armstrongs Ltd. First boat reached 32-34 knots on trials with 10 000 hp. All delivered by summer 1937. The 2 single 18 inch torpedo tubes and the 4—8 mm guns were removed. A photograph of *Trad* appears in the 1956-57 to 1964-65 editions. 3 more ships to be modified like *Chumporn*.

CHANDHABURI *1965, Royal Thai Navy, Official*

4 "SATTAHIB" CLASS

KANTANG No. 7 **KLONGYAI** No. 5 **SATTAHIB** No. 8 **TAKBAI** No. 6

Displacement, tons	110 standard; 135 full load
Dimensions, feet	131·5 × 15·5 × 4
Guns	1—3 in; 1—20 mm
Tubes	2—18 in
Main engines	Geared turbines; 2 shafts; 1 000 shp = 19 knots
Boilers	2 water-tube
Oil fuel, tons	18
Complement	31

Sattahib was built by the Royal Naval Dockyard, Bangkok, laid down on 21 Nov 1956, launched on 28 Oct 1957, completed in 1958. The other three were built by Ishikawajima Co, Japan, all launched on 26 Mar 1937 and completed on 21 June 1937. A photograph of *Klongyai* appears in the 1956-57 to 1964-65 editions.

SATTAHIB *1965, Royal Thai Navy, Official*

7 "LIULOM" CLASS

LIULOM (ex-*PC* 1253)
LONGLOM (ex-*PC* 570)
PHALI (ex-*PC* 1185)
SARASIN (ex-*PC* 495)
SUKRIP (ex-*PC* 1218)
THAYANCHON (ex-*PC* 575)
TONGPLIU (ex-*PC* 616)

Displacement, tons	280 standard; 400 full load
Dimensions, feet	174 oa × 23·2 × 6
Guns	1—3 in AA; 1—40 mm AA; 5—20 mm AA
A/S weapons	2 ASW torpedo tubes (except *Sarasin*)
Main engines	Diesel; 2 shafts; 3 600 bhp = 19 knots
Oil fuel, tons	60
Radius, miles	6,000 at 10 knots
Complement	62 to 71, *Sukeip* 69 (10 officers, 59 men)

Former US submarine chasers. Launched in 1941-43. Nos. PC 7, 8, 4, 1, 5, 2 and 6, respectively. A photograph of *Sukrip* appears in the 1956-57 to 1964-65 editions, and of *Longlom* in the 1965-66 to 1968-69 editions.

THAYANCHON *1969, Royal Thai Navy, Official*

SURVEY SHIP

CHANTHARA

Displacement, tons	870 standard; 996 full load
Dimensions, feet	229·2 oa × 34·5 × 10
Guns	1—20 mm AA
Main engines	2 diesels; 2 shafts; 1 000 bhp = 13·25 knots
Radius	10 000 miles (cruising)
Complement	69

Built by C. Melchers & Co, Bremen, Germany. Laid down on 27 Sep 1960. Launched on 17 Dec 1960. Can also be used as training ship and yacht.

CHANTHARA *1962, Royal Thai Navy, Official*

COASTAL MINESWEEPERS

BANGKEO (ex-USS *MSC* 303) 6
DONCHEDI (ex-USS *MSC* 313) 8
LADYA (ex-USS *MSC* 297) 5
TADINDENG (ex-USS *MSC* 301) 7

Displacement, tons	330 standard; 362 full load
Dimensions, feet	145·3 oa × 27 × 8·5
Guns	2—20 mm AA
Main engines	4 GM diesels; 2 shafts; 1 000 bhp = 13 knots
Complement	43 (7 officers and 36 men)

Built by Peterson Builders Inc, Sturgeon Bay, Wisc, (*Ladya* and *Donchedi*), Tacoma Boat building Co Tacoma, Wash. (*Tadindeng*) and Dorchester Shipbuilding Corp, Camden (*Bangkeo*). *Ladya* was transferred on 14 Dec 1963, *Bangkeo* on 9 July 1965, *Tadindeng* on 26 Aug 1965, and *Donchedi* on 17 Sep 1965 (last three launched in 1964, 1 July, 11 Apr, 22 Dec). A photograph of *Ladya* appears in the 1964-65 to 1966-67 editions and of *Tadindeng* in the 1967-68 to 1968-69 editions. Of the ex-US *YMS* type, *Bangkeo* (ex-*YMS* 384), *Ladya* (ex-*YMS* 138) and *Tadindeng* (ex-*YMS* 21) were removed from the effective ist in 1964 and 1965.

DONCHEDI *1969, Royal Thai Navy, Official*

PATROL BOATS

SC 7 (ex-*SC* 31, ex-US *SC* 1632) **SC 8** (ex-*SC* 32, ex-US *SC* 1633)

Displacement, tons	110 light; 125 full load
Dimensions feet,	111 × 17 × 6
Guns	1—40 mm; 3—20 mm
A/S weapons	Depth Charges, Mousetrap
Main engines	High-speed diesel = 18 knots

Former US wooden submarine chasers. Built by South Coast Co, Newport Reach, California, in 1954-65. SC 33 (ex-*SC* 1634) was scrapped 8 Mar 1962.

SC 8 *Royal Thai Navy, Official*

GUNBOATS

T 91

Displacement, tons	87·5
Dimensions, feet	104·3 × 17·5
Guns	1—40 mm, 1—20 mm
Main engines	Diesels; 1 600 bhp = 25 knots
Compliment	21

T 11 (ex-US *PGM* 71) **T 12** (ex-US *PGM* 79) **T 13** (ex-US *PGM* 107)

Displacement, tons	130 standard; 147 full load
Dimensions, feet	99 wl; 101 oa × 21 × 6
Guns	1—40 mm AA; 4—20 mm AA; 2—·50 cal
Main Engines	Diesels; 2 shafts; 1 800 bhp = 18·5 knots
Complement	30

T 11 was built by Peterson Builders Inc, launched on 5 May 1965, transferred to the Royal Thai Navy on 1 Feb 1966. T 13 transferred 28 Aug 1967.

T 12 *1969, Royal Thai Navy, Official*

NAKA LSSL 3 (ex.-U.S.S. *LSSL* 102)

Displacement, tons	233 standard; 287 full load
Dimensions, feet	153 wl; 158 oa × 23 × 4·25
Guns	1—3 inch; 4—40 mm AA; 4—20 mm AA; 4—81 mm mortar
Main engines	Diesels; 2 shafts; 1 320 bhp = 15 knots

Transferred in 1966. Acquired when Japan returned her to U.S.A. Support gunboat.

COAST GUARD VESSELS

CGC 13 **CGC 14** **CGC 15** **CGC 16**

Displacement, tons	95
Dimensions, feet	95 × 20·2 × 5
Guns	1—20 mm AA
A/S weapons	2 D.C. racks; 2 mousetraps
Main engines	4 diesels; 2 shafts; 2 200 bhp = 21 knots
Boilers	1 500 miles cruising range
Complement	15

U.S. coastguard cutters transferred in 1954. Similar to those built for U.S.C.G. by U.S. Coast Guard Yard, Curtis Bay, in 1953. Cost £475,000 each.

CGC 14 *Royal Thai Navy Official*

CGC 11

Displacement, tons	44·5
Dimensions, feet	83·1 × 16 × 4·5
Guns	1—20 mm AA
A/S weapons	2 DC racks; 2 mousetraps
Main engines	2 Viking petrol engines; 1 300 bhp = 20·5 knots

Former US Coast Guard cutter of the YP class. Of wooden hulled construction. A photograph on CGC 12 appears in the 1959-60 to 1966-67 editions, she was decommissioned in 1968.

CGC 11 *1967, Royal Thai Navy Official*

TRAINING SHIP (*Ex-Fleet Minesweeper*)

CHOW PRAYA (ex-H.M.S. *Havant*)

Displacement, tons	680 standard; 840 full load
Dimensions, feet	220 × 28·2 × 7·5
Guns	2—57 mm AA; 1—40 mm AA
Main engines	Triple expansion; 2 shafts; 1 hp; 2 200 = 16 knots
Boilers	Yarrow, converted to burn oil
Oil fuel (tons)	160
Radius, miles	1 750 at 15 knots
Complement	65

Former British fleet minesweeper of the "Racecourse" class. Built by Eltringhams, South Shields. Launched in Nov. 1918. Purchased in 1923 and reconstructed by John I. Thornycroft & Co. Ltd., Southampton. Guns are interchangeable for training.

CHOW PRAYA *Royal Navy Thai Official*

LANDING SHIPS

3 Ex-US LST TYPE

ANGTHONG (ex-USS *LST* 294) LST 1
CHANG (ex-U.S.S. *Lincoln County LST* 898) LST 2
PANGAN (ex-U.S.S. *Stark County LST* 1134) LST 3

Displacement, tons	1 625 standard; 4 080 full load
Dimensions, feet	316 wl; 328 oa × 50 × 14
Guns:	6—40 mm; 4—20 mm
Main engines	GM diesels; 2 shafts; 1 700 bhp = 11 knots
Complement	80

Angthong is employed as a transport. *Chang*, transferred to Thailand in 1962, was built by Dravo Corp., laid down on 15 Oct 1944, launched on 25 Nov 1944 and completed on 29 Dec 1944. *Pangan* was transferred on 16 May 1966. A photograph of *Angthong* appears in the 1956-57 to 1964-65 edtions.

CHANG *1965, Royal Thai Navy, Official*

3 Ex-US LSM TYPE

KRAM (ex-USS *LSM* 469) LSM 3 **KUT** (ex-USS *LSM* 333) LSM 5
PAI (ex-USS *LSM* 338) LSM 2

Displacement, tons	743 standard; 1 095 full load
Dimensions, feet	196·5 wl; 203·5 oa × 34·5 × 8·3
Guns	2—40 mm AA
Main engines	Diesel direct drive; 2 shafts; 2 800 bhp = 12·5 knots
Complement	55

Former United States landing ship of the LCM, later LSM (Medium Landing Ship), type. *Kram* was transferred to Thailand under MAP at Seattle, Wash. on 25 May 1962; she was built by Brown Shipbuilding Col, Houston, Tex., laid down on 27 Jan 1945, launched on 17 Feb 1945, and completed on 17 Mar 1945. A photograph of *Kut* appears in the 1956-57 to 1964-65 editions.

KRAM *1965, Royal Thai Navy, Official*

LANDING CRAFT

2 Ex-US LCI TYPE

PRAB (ex-*LCI* 670) LC1 1 — **SATAKUT** (ex-*LCI* 739) LCI 2

Displacement, tons	230 standard; 387 full load
Dimensions, feet	157 × 23 × 6
Guns	2—20 mm AA
Main engines	Diesel; 2 shafts; 1 320 bhp = 14 knots
Complement	54

Former United States landing craft of the LCI (Infantry Landing Craft) type. A photograph of *Prab* appears in the 1957-58 and earlier editions.

SATAKUT — *Royal Thai Navy, Official*

6 LCU Ex-US LCT (6) TYPE

ARDANG (LCU 10) **MATAPHON** (LCU 8) **RAWI** (LCU 9)
KOLUM (LCU 12) **PHETRA** (LCU 11) **TALIBONG** (LCU 13)

Displacement, tons	134 standard; 279 full load
Dimensions, feet	112 × 32 × 4
Guns	2—20 mm AA
Main engines	Diesel; 3 shafts; 675 bhp = 10 knots
Complement:	37

Former United States landing craft of the LCT(6) type. Employed as transport ferries A photograph of *Mataphon* appears in the 1950-51 to 1961-62 editions.

FAST PATROL CRAFT

T 21 **T 22**

Displacement, tons	20 standard; 22 full load
Dimensions, feet	50 × 13
Guns	2—0·50 cal (1 twin)
Main engines	Diesels; 2 shafts; 480 bhp = 25 knots
Complement	5

RIVER PATROL CRAFT

T 31 **T 32** **T 33** **T 34** **T 35** **T 36**

Displacement, tons	10·4 standard; 13·05 full load
Dimensions, feet	35 × 10
Guns	2—0·50 cal (1 twin); 2—0·30 cal
Main engines	Diesels; 2 shafts; 225 bhp = 14 knots
Complement	7

TRANSPORTS

SICHANG AKL 1

Displacement, tons	815 standard
Dimensions, feet	160 × 28 × 16
Main Engines	Diesel; 2 shafts; 550 bhp = 16 knots
Complement	30

Built by Harima Co, Japan. *Sichang* was launched on 10 Nov 1937. Completed in Jan 1938. A photograph of this ship appears in the 1953-54 to 1959-60 editions. Sister ship *Pangan* was deleted from the list in 1962.

KLED KEO A 7
Reefer ship reported to be operating as a naval auxiliary and transport.

OILERS

SAMED

Displacement, tons	305 standard; 485 full load
Dimensions, feet	108 × 20 × 10 feet
Main Engines	Diesel; 500 bhp = 11 knots

Built by Royal Thai Naval Dockyard, Bangkok. Launched on 8 July 1966.

CHULA AO 2

Displacement, tons	2 395 standard
Dimensions, feet	328 × 43·2 × 25 feet
Main Engines	Steam turbine

This tanker and *Matra* (see below) were acquired for naval oiling and supply duties.

CHULA — *1969, Royal Thai Navy, Official*

MATRA AO 3

Displacement, tons	4 744
Dimensions, feet	328 × 45·2 × 20
Main Engines	Steam turbine

Employed as a freighting and fleet replenishment tanker and naval supply ship.

SAMUI YO 4

Displacement, tons	422 standard
Dimensions, feet	174·5 × 32 × 15
Main Engines	Diesel; 2 shafts; 600 bhp = 8 knots
Complement	49

Small tanker of the ex-YOG type. Employed as a fleet auxiliary attendant oiler.

SAMUI — *Royal Thai Navy, Official*

PRONG

Displacement, tons	150 standard
Dimensions, feet	95 × 18 × 7·5
Main Engines	Diesel; 150 bhp = 10 knots
Complement	14

Launched in 1938. Employed as a small naval auxiliary servicing tanker.

RANG KWIEN MCS 11

Displacement, tons	586 standard
Dimensions, feet	162·3 × 31·2 × 13
Main Engines	Triple expansion steam engine; Speed = 10 knots

This ship is not employed as a tug but as a mine countermeasures support ship (MCS).

RANG KWIEN — *1969, Royal Thai Navy, Official*

WATER CARRIERS

CHUANG

Displacement, tons	305 standard; 485 full load
Dimensions, feet	98 × 18 × 7·2 (official figures)
Main Engines	GM diesel; 500 bhp = 11 knots
Complement:	29

Built by the Royal Thai Naval Dockyard, Bangkok. Launched on 14 Jan 1965.

CHAN YW 6

Displacement, tons	355 standard
Dimensions, feet	139·5 × 24 × 10
Main Engines	Diesel; Speed = 6 knots

A photograph of this ship appears in the 1956-57 to 1959-60 editions.

TUGS

SAMAESAN (ex-*Empire Vincent*)

Displacement, tons	503 full load
Dimensions, feet	105 × 26·5 × 13
Main Engines	Triple expansion; 850 ihp = 10·5 knots
Complement	27

Built by Cochrane & Sons Ltd, Selby, Yorks, England. A photograph appears in the 1957-58 and earlier editions. Pennant No. YTB 7.

KLUENG BADAN **MARN VICHAI**

Displacement, tons	63 standard
Dimensions, feet	64·7 × 16·5 × 6
Main Engines	Diesel; Speed = 8 knots

RAD

Displacement, tons	52 standard
Dimensions, feet	60·7 × 17·5 × 5
Main Engines	Diesel; Speed = 6 knots

TOGO

Mercantile Marine

Lloyd's Register of Shipping: 1 vessel of 150 tons gross

PATROL BOATS

It is reported that Togo, which proclaimed independence on 27 April 1960, has acquired 3 steel 100 ft. motor patrol boats and 1 steel 95 ft. river gunboat and may have in the near future 1 steel 130 ft. patrol vessel.

TRINIDAD & TOBAGO

COAST GUARD

Personnel

125 officers and men

Mercantile Marine

Lloyd's Register of Shipping: 21 vessels of 20 096 tons gross

PATROL CRAFT

2 VOSPER 95 ft TYPE

COURLAND BAY CG 2 — **TRINITY** CG 1

Displacement, tons	96 standard; 123 full load
Dimensions, feet	95 wl; 102·6 oa × 19·7 × 5·5
Guns:	1—40 mm Bofors
Main Engines	2 12-cyl Vee-form Paxman Ventura YJCM turbo-charged diesels; 2 910 bhp = 24·5 knots (max.)
Oil fuel (tons)	18
Radius, miles	1 800 at 13·5 knots
Complement	17 (3 officers; 14 ratings)

Designed and built by Vosper Limited, Portsmouth. Of steel construction with aluminium alloy superstructure. Up-to-date radar and navigation equipment is fitted, and the boats are air-conditioned throughout except the engine room. Vosper roll-damping equipment is fitted for improved sea-keeping and greater efficiency and comfort of the crews. Laid down Oct 1963. *Trinity* was launched on 14 Apr 1964. Both were commissioned at Portsmouth on 20 Feb 1965. *Trinity* is named after Trinity Hills, so named by Columbus on making his landfall in 1498, and *Courland Bay* after a bay in Tobago where a settlement was founded by the Duke of Courland in the 17th century.

COURLAND BAY — *1968 Trinidad and Tobago Coast Guard, Official*

TRINITY — *1969, Trinidad and Tobago Coastguard, Official*

1 60 ft TYPE

SEA HAWK

Built by J. Taylor (Shipbuilders) Ltd, Shoreham-by-Sea. Under extensive refit 1969.

1 46 ft TYPE

SEA SCOUT

Built by J. Taylor (Shipbuilders) Ltd Shoreham-by-sea.

SEA SCOUT — *1969, Trinidad and Tobago Coast Guard. Official*

TUNISIA

Mercantile Marine

Lloyd's Register of Shipping: 16 vessels of 21 518 tons gross

CORVETTE *(Aviso)*

DUSTUR (ex-*Chevreuil* F 735) E 71

Displacement, tons	647 standard; 920 full load
Dimensions, feet	257 × 28·5 × 10·5
Guns	1—4·1 inch; 1—40 mm; 4—20 mm
A/S weapons	4 DCT; 2 DC racks
Main engines	Sulzer diesels; 2 shafts; 4 000 vhp = 20 knots
Oil fuel (tons)	105
Radius, miles	10 000 at 9 knots; 5 200 at 15 knots
Complement	100 (8 officers, 92 men)

Built at Lorient Dockyard. Laid down in Apr 1937, launched on 17 June 1939 and completed in Oct 1939. Transferred from the French Navy on 13 Oct 1959 and renamed.

DUSTUR — *1964 A. & J. Pavia*

PATROL CRAFT *(Vedette de Port)*

ISTIQLAL (ex-*VC* 11, *P* 761)

Displacement, tons	75 standard; 82 full load
Dimensions, feet	104·5 × 15·5 × 5·5
Guns	2—20 mm AA
Main Engines	2 Mercedes-Benz diesels; 2 shafts; 2 700 bh = 28 knots
Radius, miles	1 400 at 15 knots
Complement	17

Seaward defence motor launch of the VC type. Completed in 1958. Built by Lurssens in Germany. Transferred from the French Navy on 22 Sep 1959.

ISTIQLAL — Ex-*VC* 11

SEAWARD DEFENCE CRAFT

Displacement, tons	250
Dimensions, feet	157 ft 6 in AA × 23·4
Missiles, surface	8 S 12M missiles
Guns	2 × 40 mm
Main engines	Twin diesel 4 800 bhp = 23 knots

Two seaward defence craft were ordered early in 1969 from Ch Navales Franco-Belge (Villeneuve la Garenne).

TURKEY

Administration

Commander-in-Chief, Turkish Naval Forces:
Oramiral (Senior Admiral) Celal Eyiceoglu

Chief of Staff, Turkish Naval Forces:
Koramiral (Admiral) Turgut Kunter

Commander of the Turkish Fleet:
Koramiral (Admiral) Kemal Kayacan

Strength of the Fleet

10 Submarines
10 Destroyers
1 Minelayer
18 Escorts
8 Torpedo Boats
6 Coastal Minelayers
6 Patrol Vessels
13 Coastal Minesweepers
3 Inshore Minesweepers
30 Motor Launches
6 Boom Vessels
10 Support Ships

Personnel

1969: 36,200 (2,730 officers and 33,470 ratings)

Diplomatic Representation

Naval Attaché in London:
Captain Orhan Karabulat

Naval Attaché in Washington:
Captain Seref Batbay

Mercantile Marine

Lloyd's Register of Shipping:
298 vessels of 648,171 tons gross

Silhouettes

Scale: 150 feet = 1 inch

ALP ARSLAN *Class*

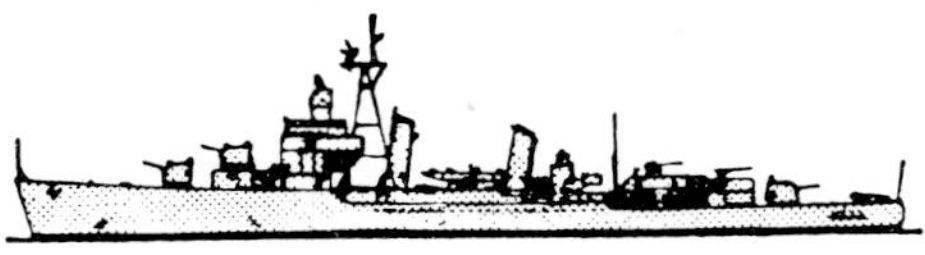

GELIBOLU, GIRESUN

NUSRET

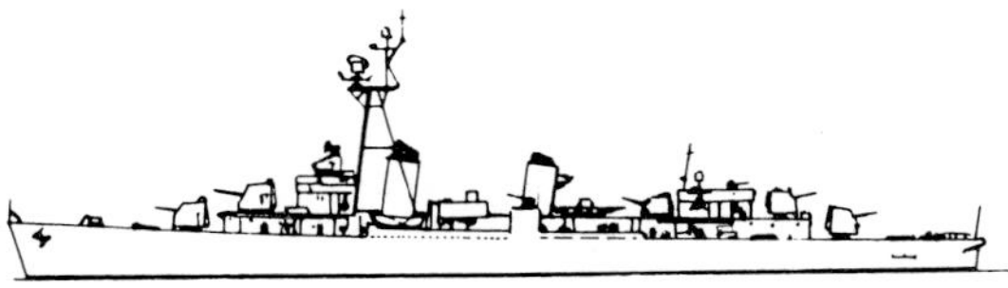

ISTANBUL, IZMIR

GAZIANTEP, GEMLIK

CANDARLI *Class*

SUBMARINES

Name	*Nato No.*	*Turk No.*	*Builders*	*Launched*	*Completed*
BIRINCI INÖNÜ (ex-USS *Brill, SS* 330)	S 330	—	Electric Boat Co	25 June 1944	26 Oct 1944
CANAKKALE (ex-USS *Bumper, SS* 333)	S 333	21	Electric Boat Co	6 Aug 1944	9 Dec 1944
CERBE (ex-USS *Hammerhead, SS* 364)	S 341	03	Manitowoc SB Co	27 Oct 1943	1 Mar 1944
GÜR (ex-USS *Chub,* ex-*Bonat, SS* 329)	S 334	20	Electric Boat Co	7 May 1944	28 Apr 1945
HIZIR REIS (ex-USS *Mero, SS* 378)	S 344	—	Manitowoc SB Co	17 Jan 1945	17 Aug 1945
IKINCI INÖNÜ (ex-USS *Blueback, SS* 326)	S 331	17	Electric Boat Co	21 May 1944	23 Sep 1944
PIRI REIS (ex-USS *Mapiro, SS* 376)	S 343	—	Manitowoc SB Co	9 Nov 1944	30 Apr 1945
PREVEZE (ex-USS *Guitarro, SS* 363)	S 340	22	Manitowoc SB Co	26 Sep 1943	16 Jan 1944
SAKARYA (ex-USS *Boarfish, SS* 327)	S 332	—	Electric Boat Co	18 June 1944	21 Oct 1944
TURGUT REIS (ex-USS *Bergall, SS* 320)	S 342	—	Electric Boat Co	16 Feb 1944	12 June 1944

10 "GUR" CLASS

Displacement, tons	1 526 standard; 1 829 surface; 2 424 submerged
Length, feet (*metres*)	311·8 (*95·0*)
Beam, feet (*metres*)	27·2 (*8·3*)
Draught, feet (*metres*)	13·8 (*4·2*)
Guns, surface	1—5 in (*127 mm*) 25 cal., removed from most boats
Torpedo tubes	10—21 in (*533 mm*), 6 bow and 4 stern; 24 torpedoes carried
Main engines	GM 2-stroke diesels, total 6 500 hp Electric motors, total 2 750 hp
Speed, knots	20 on surface; 10 submerged
Radius, miles	12 000 at 10 knots
Oil fuel (tons)	300
Complement	85

Former US submarines of the "Balao" type acquired by Turkey in 1948-60. All built by the Electric Boat Company, Groton, Connecticut, except *Cerbe, Hizir, Reis, Piri Reis* and *Preveze*, by Manitowoc Shipbuilding Co. Of all-welded construction. High standard of accommodation including separate messing and sleeping compartments. *Canakkale*, officially transferred in 1950, was semi-streamlined before delivery. *Dumlupinar* (ex-*Blower*) was lost in the Dardanelles on 4 Apr 1953. *Preveze* semi-streamlined and *Cerbe*, fully streamlined, were transferred on 7 Aug 1954 and Oct 1954 respectively. *Cerbe* and *Preveze* are "guppy snorkel" conversions. Their loan was extended for five years in 1959, *Sakarya* was overhauled by the Electric Boat Division of the General Dynamics Corporation (formerly known as the Electric Boat Company), Groton, in 1957. *Turgut Reis* was transferred in Oct 1958 and *Hizar Reis* and *Piri Reis* on 20 Apr 1960 and 18 Mar 1960 at San Francisco Naval Shipyard.

PHOTOGRAPHS. A photograph of *Gür* appears in the 1958-59 to 1961-62 editions, of *Canakkale* in the 1962-63 and 1963-64 editions, of *Piri Reis* in the 1962-63 to 1965-66 editions, of *Turgut Reis* in the 1959-60 to 1965-66 editions, of *Hizir Reis* in the 1964-65 to 1967-68 editions, of *Sakarya* and *Ikinci Inonu* in the 1966-67 to 1968-69 editions.

OLDER SUBMARINES
Burak Reis, Murat Reis and *Oruc Reis*, of the "Burak Reis" class, and *Saldiray* and *Yildiray* of the "Saldiray" class, were discarded in 1957.

BATTLE CRUISER. The very old Turkish (former German) battle cruiser *Yavuz* (ex-*Goeben*), decommissioned in 1960, was still at Golcuk naval base in 1969.

CERBE *1968, Turkish Navy, Official*

BIRINCI INONU *1969, Official*

PREVESE *1969, Official*

PIRI REIS *1966, Turkish Navy, official*

DESTROYERS

Name	No.	Builders	Laid down	Launched	Completed
ALP ARSLAN (ex-HMS *Milne*)	D 348	Scotts Shipbuilding & Eng Co Ltd, Greenock	24 Jan 1940	30 Dec 1941	6 Aug 1942
KILIC ALI PASA (ex-HMS *Matchless*)	D 350	Alex Stephen & Sons Ltd, Govan, Glasgow	14 Sep 1940	4 Sep 1941	26 Feb 1942
MARESAL FEVZI ÇAKMAK (ex-HMS *Marne*)	D 349	Vickers Armstrongs, Ltd, Newcastle on-Tyne	23 Oct 1940	30 Oct 1940	2 Dec 1941
PIYALE PASA (ex-HMS *Meteor*)	D 351	Alex Stephen & Sons Ltd, Govan, Glasgow	14 Sep 1940	3 Nov 1941	12 Aug 1942

Ex-BRITISH "MILNE" TYPE

4 "ALP ARSLAN" CLASS

Displacement, tons	2 115 standard; 2 840 full load
Length, feet (*metres*)	354 (*107·9*) pp; 362·5 (*110·5*) oa
Beam, feet (*metres*)	36·8 (*11·2*)
Draught, feet (*metres*)	16·2 (*5·0*)
Guns, surface	6—4·7 in (*120 mm*)
Guns, AA	6—40 mm (1 twin, 4 single)
Guns, saluting	2—3 pdr
A/S	1 Squid triple-barrel DC mortar
Torpedo tubes	4—21 in (*533 mm*)
Boilers	2 Admiralty 3-drum
Main engines	Parsons geared turbines 48 000 shp; 2 shafts
Speed, knots	36
Radius, miles	1 700 at 20 knots
Oil fuel (tons)	500
Complement	240

Former "Milne" class, one of the most successful and handsome types which ever served in the Royal Navy. The first British destroyers with three power worked turrets. Transferred to Turkey under an agreement signed in Ankara on 16 Aug 1957. Nominally handed over to the Turkish Navy at Portsmouth on 29 June 1959 after refit in British shipyards, where the after tubes and secondary armament were removed and replaced by deckhouse ,"Squid" and 40 mm guns. Renamed after famous generals and 16-18th century admirals.

PHOTOGRAPHS. A photograph of *Killic Ali Pasa* appears in the 1962-63 to 1965-66 editions and of *Maresal Fevzi Cakmak* in the 1966-67 to 1968-69 editions.

OLDER DESTROYERS
Gayret was officially deleted from the list in 1965. *Demishiar, Muavenet* and *Sultanhisar* were discarded in 1960, and *Tinaztepe* and *Zafer* in 1957.

ALP ARSLAN

1969, Official

PIYALE PASA

1966, Turkish Navy, Official

Name	No.	Builders	Laid down	Launched	Completed
GAZIANTEP (ex-USS *Lansdowne*, DD 486)	D 344	Federal SB & DD Co, Port Newark	July 1941	20 Feb 1942	29 Apr 1942
GELIBOLU (ex-USS *Buchanan*, DD 484)	D 346	Federal SB & DD Co, Port Newark	11 Feb 1941	22 Nov 1941	21 Mar 1942
GEMLIK (ex-USS *Lardner*, DD 487)	D 347	Federal SB & DD Co, Port Newark	July 1941	20 Mar 1942	13 May 1942
GIRESUN (ex-USS *McCalla*, DD 488)	D 345	Federal SB & DD Co, Port Newark	July 1941	20 Mar 1942	27 May 1942

4 "GELIBOLU" CLASS

Displacement, tons	1 810 standard; 2 580 full load
Length, feet (*metres*)	341 (*103·9*) wl; 348·5 (*106·2*) oa
Beam, feet (*metres*)	36 (*11·0*)
Draught, feet (*metres*)	18 (*5·5*)
Guns, surface	*D345, D346:* 3—5 in (*127 mm*) 38 cal.; *D344, D347:* 4—5 in (*127 mm*) 38 cal.
Guns, AA	*D345, D346:* 4—3 in (*76 mm*) *D344, D347:* 4—40 mm
A/S	2 Hedgehogs; homing torpedoes; 4 DCT
Torpedo tubes	5—21 in (*533 mm*)
Boilers	4 Babcock & Wilcox
Main engines	GE geared turbines 50 000 shp; 2 shafts
Speed, knots	37 designed; 34 max
Radius, miles	5 000 at 15 knots
Oil fuel (tons)	600
Complement	250

Former US destroyers of the "Gleaves" class acquired by Turkey early in 1949. *Gelibolu* and *Giresun* were formerly taken over on 29 Apr 1949, and *Gaziantep* and *Gemlik* in 1950. Modernised in USA in 1957-58 and fitted with tripod, instead of pole, foremast and raised bridge.

GEMLIK

1968, A. & J. Pavia

GUNNERY. The 5 inch gun in "X" position, 40 mm AA guns and 20 mm AA guns in *Gelibolu* and *Giresun* were replaced by four 3-inch AA guns in two twin mountings.

PHOTOGRAPHS. A photograph of *Giresun* appears in the 1966-67 and 1967-68 editions.

Name	No.	Builders	Launched	Completed
ISTANBUL (ex-USS *Clarence K. Bronson*, DD 668)	D 340	Federal SB & DD Co, Port Newark	18 Apr 1943	11 June 1943
IZMIR (ex-USS *Van Valkenburgh*, DD 656)	D 341	Gulf Shipbuilding Corporation	19 Dec 1943	2 Aug 1944

Displacement, tons	2 050 standard; 3 050 full load
Length, feet (*metres*)	376·2 (*114·7*) oa
Beam, feet (*metres*)	39·7 (*12·1*)
Draft, feet (*metres*)	18 (*5·5*)
Guns, surface	5—5 in (*127 mm*) 38 cal
Guns, AA	10—40 mm
A/S weapons	2 Hedgehogs
Torpedo tubes	5—21 in (*533 mm*) quintupled
Boilers	4 Babcock & Wilcox
Main engines	GE geared turbines; 60 000 shp; 2 shafts
Speed, knots	34
Radius, miles	6 000 at 15 knots
Oil fuel, tons	650
Complement	18 officers, 320 men

Transferred from the US Navy at Philadelphia on 14 Jan and 28 Feb 1967, respectively. A photograph of *Istanbul* appears in the 1967-68 and 1968-69 editions.

ISMIR

1969, Official

MINELAYER

1 "SCANATO" TYPE

NUSRET N 108

Displacement, tons	1 880 standard
Length, feet (*metres*)	246 (*75·0*) pp; 252·7 (*77·0*) oa
Beam, feet (*metres*)	41 (*12·6*)
Draught, feet (*metres*)	11 (*3·4*)
Guns, dual purpose	4—3 in (*76 mm*), 2 twin mountings
Mines	400 capacity
Main engines	GM diesels, 4 800 hp; 2 shafts
Speed, knots	18
Complement	130

A new type of minelayer of special Scandinavian-NATO design. Built at Frederikshaven Dockyard, Denmark. Laid down in 1962, launched in 1964, and completed in 1965. Commissioned on 16 Sep 1964 at Copenhagen.

NUSRET *1969, Official*

ESCORT MINESWEEPERS

6 "CANDARLI" CLASS

CANDARLI (ex-*Frolic*, 22 July 1943)	AGS	2
CARDAK (ex-*Tourmaline*, 4 Oct, 1942)	A	596
CARSAMBA (ex-*Tattoo*, 27 Jan 1943)	AGS	1
CESME (ex-*Elfreda*, 25 Jan 1943)	A	595
EDINCIK (ex-*Grecian*, 1943)	A	598
EREGLI (ex-*Pique*, 26 Oct 1942)	A	592

Displacement, tons	1 010 standard; 1 250 full load
Length, feet (*metres*)	215 (*61·4*) wl; 221 (*67·4*) oa
Beam, feet (*metres*)	32 (*9·8*)
Draught, feet (*metres*)	10·8 (*3·3*)
Guns, dual purpose	1—3 in (*76 mm*)
Guns, AA	6—40 mm
A/S	4 DCT
Main engines	Diesels, with electric drive 3 500 bhp; 2 shafts
Speed, knots	18
Complement	105

Former US steel hulled fleet minesweepers of the "Auk" type. Transferred to Great Britain while under construction. Served in the Royal Navy. Retransferred to Turkey in Apr 1947. Built by Associated Shipbuilders, Cleveland (*Carsamba*, *Cesme* and *Edincik*); General Engineering & DD Co, Alameda (*Candarli*) and Gulf Shipbuilding Corporation, Houston (*Cardak* and *Eregli*).

EREGLI *1968, Turkish Navy, Official*

Launch dates above. Named after Turkish ports. *Erdemli* (ex-*Catherine*) was withdrawn from active service in 1963, and *Edremit* (ex-*Chance*) in 1965.

Cesme and *Cardak* are Headquarter Ships. *Eregli* is Logistic Support Ship, *Edincik* and *Erdemli* are Training Ships, *Carsanba* and *Candarli* are Survey Ships.

Ex-BRITISH "BATHURST" TYPE
3 "ALANYA" CLASS

Name	*No.*	*Builders*	*Launched*
ALANYA (ex-*Broome*)	M 501	Evans Deakin, Brisbane	6 Oct 1941
AMASRA (ex-*Pirie*)	M 502	Broken Hill, Whyalla	Dec 1941
AYVALIK (ex- *Antalya*, ex-*Geraldton*)	M 500	Poole & Steele, Sydney	16 Aug 1941

Displacement, tons	790 standard; 1 025 full load
Length, feet (*metres*)	162 (*49·4*) pp; 186 (*56·7*) oa
Beam, feet (*metres*)	31 (*9·4*)
Draught, feet (*metres*)	8·5 (*2·6*)
Guns, surface	1—4 in (*102 mm*)
Guns, AA	1—40 mm; 4—20 mm
A/S	2 DCT
Main engines	Triple expansion 1 800 ihp; 2 shafts
Speed, knots	15·5
Radius, miles	4 500 at 10 knots
Oil fuel (tons)	170
Complement	85

All Australian built, 1940-42. Served in the Royal Navy. Acquired from Great Britain in Aug 1946. Named after Turkish ports. All are now Logistic Support Ships. *Hamit Naci* (ex-*Ayancik*, ex-*Launceston*) was withdrawn from service in 1965, and *Ayvalik* (ex-*Gawler*) in 1963. A photograph of *Alanya* appears in the 1951-52 to 1963-64 editions and of *Amasra* in the 1964-65 to 1968-69 editions.

AYVALIK *1968, Official*

TRAINING SHIP

SAVARONA

Displacement, tons	5 100
Length, feet (*metres*)	349·5 (*106·5*)wl; 408·5 (*124·5*)oa
Beam, feet (*metres*)	53 (*16·2*)
Draught, feet (*metres*)	20·5 (*6·2*) mean
Guns, surface	4—3 in (*76 mm*)
Guns, AA	2—40 mm; 2—20 mm
Boilers	4 watertube; 400 psi
Main engines	6 geared turbines 10 750 shp; 2 shafts
Speed, knots	21 designed; about 18 now
Radius, miles	9 000 at 15 knots
Oil fuel (tons)	2 100
Complement	132 + 81 midshipmen

Built by Blohm & Voss, Hamburg. Launched on 28 Feb 1931. Formerly probably the most sumptuously fitted yacht afloat. Equipment includes Sperry gyro-stabilisers. Converted into a training ship in 1952, the saloons and dining rooms being adapted as classrooms, workshops and libraries for 120 midshipmen.

SAVARONA *1968, A. & J. Pavia*

COASTAL ESCORTS (*ex-Fleet Minesweepers*)

Ex-CANADIAN "BANGOR" TYPE

9 "BAFRA" CLASS

Name	No.	Launched
BAFRA (ex-HMCS *Nipigon, FSE* 188)	P 121	30 Sep 1940
BANDIRMA (ex-HMCS *Kenora, FSE* 191)	P 129	20 Dec 1941
BARTIN (ex-HMCS *Kentville, FSE* 182)	P 130	18 Apr 1942
BEYKOZ (ex-HMCS *Blairmore, FSE* 193)	P 122	14 May 1942
BEYLERBEYI (ex-HMCS *Mahone, FSE* 192)	P 123	15 Nov 1940
BODREM (ex-HMCS *Fort William, FSE* 195)	P 125	30 Dec 1941
BORNOVA (ex-HMCS *Westmount, FSE* 187)	P 126	14 Mar 1942
BOZCAADA (ex-HMCS *Swift Current, FSE* 185)	P 127	29 May 1941
BUYUKDERE (ex-HMCS *Sarnia, FSE* 190)	P 128	21 Jan 1942

Displacement, tons	672 standard; 900 full load
Length, feet (*metres*)	171·5 (*52·3*) pp; 180 (*54·8*) oa
Beam, feet (*metres*)	28·5 (*8·7*)
Draught, feet (*metres*)	12·5 (*3·8*) max
Guns, AA	1—40 mm; 6—20 mm
A/S	1 Hedgehog; 4 DCT
Boilers	2 Admiralty 3 drum
Main engines	Triple expansion; 2 400 ihp; 2 shafts
Speed, knots	16·5
Complement	70

Former Canadian fleet minesweepers, rerated coastal escorts in 1953. Transferred to Turkey in 1957. *Bafra Bandirma, Bartin* and *Bodrum* were turned over 29 Nov 1957 at Point Edward Naval Base, Sydney, NS, and *Beykoz, Beylerbeyi, Barnova, Bozcaada* and *Buyukdere* early 1958. All sailed from Canada to Turkey on 19 May 1958. *Biga* (ex-MHCS *Medicine Hat, FSE* 197) was withdrawn from service in 1963.

PHOTOGRAPHS. A photograph of *Beykoz* appears in the 1963-64 to 1965-66 editions and of *Bandirma* in the 1966-67 to 1968-69 editions.

BARTIN *1969, Official*

COASTAL MINESWEEPERS

SAMSUN M 257 (ex-U.S.A. *MSC* 268)
SAPANCA M 266 (ex-U.S.S. *MSC* 312)
SARIYER M 267 (ex-U.S.S. *MSC* 315)
SAROS M 264 (ex-U.S.S. *MSC* 305)
SEDDULBAHIR M 260 (ex-*MSC* 272)
SIGACIK M 265 (ex-U.S.S. *MSC* 311)
SILIFKE M 263 (ex-U.S.S. *MSC* 304)
SINOP M 258 (ex-U.S.S. *MSC* 270)
SURMENE M 259 (ex-U.S.S. *MSC* 271)

Displacement, tons	320 standard 370 full load
Dimensions, feet	138 pp; 144 oa × 28 × 9
Guns	2—20 mm AA
Main Engines	2 diesels; 2 shafts; 1 200 bhp = 14 knots
Oil fuel (tons)	25
Radius, miles	2,500 at 10 knots
Complement	38 (4 officers, 34 men)

Built of non-magnetic materials. Transferred on 30 Sep 1958, 26 July 1965, 8 Sep 1967, 8 Nov 1965, 9 July 1959, 29 May 1965, 25 Oct 1965, 30 Jan 1959, 27 Mar 1959, respectively. A photograph of *Sinop* appears in the 1961-62 to 1965-66 editions, and of *Seddulbahir* in the 1965-67 to 1968-69 editions.

SAMSUN *1969, Official*

TIREBOLU M 524 (ex-H.M.C.S. *Comax*)
TEKIRDAG M 525 (ex-H.M.C.S. *Ungava*)
TERME M 523 (ex-H.M.C.S. *Trinity*)
TRABZON M 522 (ex-H.M.C.S. *Gaspe*)

Displacement, tons	390 standard; 412 full load
Dimensions, feet	140 pp; 152 oa × 28 × 7
Guns	1—40 mm
Main Engines	Diesels; 2 shafts; 2 400 bhp = 16 knots
Oil fuel (tons)	52
Radius, miles	4 500 at 11 knots
Complement	40

Ex-Canadian MCBs. Sailed from Sydney, Nova Scotia, to Turkey on 19 May 1958. A photograph of *Terme* appears in the 1959-60 to 1966-67 editions.

TRABZON *1967, Turkish Navy, Official*

INSHORE MINESWEEPERS

FETHIYE (ex-*MSI* 16)
FINIKE M 503 (ex-*MSI* 18)
FOCA (ex-*MSI* 15)

Built in US and transferred under MAP at Boston, Mass, Aug-Sep 1967. *Finike* delivered by Peterson Builders Inc, 8 Nov 1967. See particulars in US section.

COASTAL MINELAYERS

MARMARIS (ex-*LSM* 481) N 100
MERIC (ex-*LSM* 490) N 102
MERSIN (ex-*LSM* 492) N 103
MORDOGAN (ex-*LSM* 494) N 101
MUREFTE (ex-*LSM* 493) N 104

Displacement, tons	743 standard; 1 100 full load
Dimensions, feet	196·5 wl; 203·2 oa × 34·5 × 8·5
Guns	2—40 mm AA; 2—20 mm AA
Main Engines	Diesels; 2 shafts; 2 880 bhp = 12 knots
Oil fuel (tons)	60
Radius, miles	2 500 at 10 knots
Complement	70

Ex-U.S. Landing Ships Medium. All launched in 1945, converted into coastal minelayers by the U.S. Navy in 1952 and taken over by the Turkish Navy (LSM 481, 484 and 490) and the Norwegian Navy (LSM 492 and 493) in Oct 1952 under MAP. LSM 492 (*Vale*) and LSM 493 (*Vidar*) were retransferred to the Turkish Navy on 1 Nov 1960 at Bergen, Norway.

PHOTOGRAPHS. A photograph of *Marmaris* appears in the 1955-56 to 1968-69 editions.

MERSIN *1969, Official*

MEHMEDCIK (ex-U.S.S. *YMP* 3) N 105

Displacement, tons	540 full load
Dimensions, feet	130 × 35 × 6
Main Engines	Diesels; 2 shafts; 600 bhp = 10 knots
Complement	22

Former U.S. motor mine planter. Built by Higgins Inc, New Orleans. Completed in 1958. Steel hulled. Transferred under MAP in 1958. For harbour defence.

"K" CLASS
Of the "K" class, former US *YMS* type, *Kas* (ex-*YMS* 79) and *Kilimli* (ex-*YMS* 289) were withdrawn from service in 1963, *Kozlu* (ex-*YMS* 375) and *Kusadasi* (ex- *YMS* 468) in 1965, and *Karamursel* (ex-*Kulluck*, ex-*YMS* 348), *Kemer* (ex-*YMS* 228), *Kerempe* (ex-*YMS* 239) and *Kirte* (ex-*YMS* 307) in 1966.

MEHMEDCIK 1969, *Official*

PATROL VESSELS

6 "AKHISAR" CLASS

AKHISAR P 114 (ex-*PC* 1641)
DEMIRHISAR P 112 (ex-*PC* 1639)
KOCHISAR P 116 (ex-*PC* 1643)
SIVRIHISAR P 115 (ex-*PC* 1642)
SULTANHISAR P 111 (ex-*PC* 1638)
YARHISAR P 113 (ex-*PC* 1640)

Displacement, tons	280 standard; 412 full load
Dimensions, feet	170 wl; 173·7 oa × 23 × 10·2
Guns	1—3 inch dp; 1—40 mm AA
A/S weapons	4 DCT
Main Engines	2 FM Diesels; 2 shafts; 2 800 bhp = 19 knots
Complement	65 (5 officers and 60 men)

Similar to U.S. 173 ft. class submarine chasers. Built by Gunderson Bros. Engineering Co, Portland, Oregon, except *Kochisar* built in Gölcük Dockyard, Turkey. Transferred on 3 Dec 1964, 22 Apr 1965, 22 Apr 1965, 2 May 1964, 24 Sep 1964 and 22 Apr 1965 respectively. PC 1645 is building in U.S.A.

PHOTOGRAPHS. A photograph of *Sultanhisar* appears in the 1966-67 to 1968-69 editions.

GUNBOATS PGM 72, 104, 105, 106, 108 building in U.S.A. for transfer to Turkey.

KOCHISAR — *1969, Official*

TORPEDO BOATS

6 "KARTAL" CLASS

ATMACA P 335
DENIZKUSU P 336
KARTAL P 333
KASIRGA P 338
MELTEM P 337
SAHIN P 334

Displacement, tons	160 standard; 180 full load
Dimensions, feet	140·5 × 23·5 × 7·2
Guns	2—40 mm AA
Tubes	4—21 inch
Main Engines	4 Maybach diesels; 4 shafts; 12 000 bhp = 12 knots

Of the German "Jaguar" type. Built by Lürssen, Vegesack, in 1966-67.

KARTAL — *1967, Turkish Navy, Official*

DOGAN (ex-*Hugin*)
MARTI (ex-*Munin*)

Displacement, tons	70 standard; 75 full load
Dimensions, feet	75·5 pp; 80·3 oa × 24·5 × 6·8
Guns	1—40 mm AA
Tubes	2—21 inch
Main Engines	2 Napier Deltic turbo blown diesels; 6 200 bhp = 43 knots

Transferred under a German-Turkish war reparations plan from West Germany and renamed. "Nasty" type, built by Boat Services Ltd, A/S in 1959-60. A photograph of *Dogan* appears in the 1966-67 edition.

REPAIR SHIPS

BASARAN (ex-*Patroclus, ARL* 19, ex-*LST* 955) A 582
ONARAN (ex-*Alecto, AGP* 14, ex-*LST* 558) A 581

Displacement, tons	1 625 standard; 3 960 to full load
Dimensions, feet	316 wl; 328 oa × 50 × 11
Guns	2—40 mm AA; 8—20 mm AA
Main Engines	Diesel; 2 shafts; 1 700 bhp = 11 knots
Oil fuel (tons)	1 000
Radius, miles	6 000 at 9 knots

Former U.S. repair ship and MTB tender, respectively, of the LST type. *Basaran* was launched on 22 Oct 1944 by Bethlehem Hingham Shipyard, *Onaran* on 14 Apr 1944 by Missouri Valley Bridge & Iron Co. Acquired from the U.S.A. in 1952 and 1947, respectively. Photograph of *Basaran* in the 1965-66 and 1966-67 editions.

ONARAN — *1967, Turkish Navy, Official*

MOTOR LAUNCHES

J 12 J 13 J 14 J 15 J 16 J 17 J 18 J 19 J 20

Displacement, tons	70
Dimensions, feet	95 × 15·5 × 4·2
Main Engines	4 MB diesels; 2 shafts; 2 700 bhp = 29 knots

Cutters of U.S.C.G. type built in 1960-61 by Schweers, Bardenfleth. A photograph of J 12 appears in the 1962-63 to 1965-66 editions.

J 19 — *1966, Turkish Navy, Official*

AB 1 (ex-*ML* 386) P 321
AB 2 (ex-*ML* 584) P 322
AB 3 (ex-*ML* 836) P 323
AB 4 (ex-*ML* 837) P 324
AB 6 (ex-*ML* 842) P 326
AB 7 (ex-*ML* 862) P 327

Displacement, tons	85 standard; 115 full load
Dimensions, feet	112 × 17·8 × 4
Guns	1—3 pdr; 2—20 mm AA; 4 MG
Main Engines	2 Hall-Scott engines; 1 120 bhp = 21 knots
Oil fuel (tons)	12
Complement	18

Fairmile B type. Launched in 1940-42. Transferred in 1947. NATO pennant numbers above. A photograph of AB 2 appears in the 1947-48 to 1960-61 editions, and of AB 7 in the 1961-62 to 1965-66 editions. AB 5 and AB 8 were scrapped, it was officially stated in 1969.

AB 6 — *1966, Turkish Navy, Official*

LS 9 P 339 **LS 10** P 308 **LS 11** P 309 **LS 12** P 310

Displacement, tons	63
Dimensions, feet	83 × 14 × 5
Guns	1—20 mm AA
Main Engines	2 Cummins; 1 100 bhp

Ex-US type, transferred on 25 June 1953. NATO pennant numbers (P) above. A photograph of LS 12 (P 310) appears in the 1961-62 to 1967-68 editions.

LS 10 — *1968, Aldo Fraccaroli*

MTB 1 P 311
MTB 2 P 312
MTB 3 P 313
MTB 4 P 314
MTB 6 P 316
MTB 7 P 317
MTB 8 P 318
MTB 9 P 319
MTB 10 P 320

Displacement, tons	70
Dimensions, feet	71·5 × 13·8 × 8·5 (max)
Main Engines	Diesel; 2 000 bhp = 10 knots

All launched in 1942. General purpose craft. P pennant numbers (NATO) above Photograph of MTB 9 in the 1957-58 edition. MTB 5 (P 315) was scrapped.

SUBMARINE RESCUE SHIP

KURTARAN (ex-*Bluebird*, ASR 19, ex-*Yurak*) A 584

Displacement, tons	1 294 standard; 1 675 full load
Dimensions, feet	205 oa × 38·5 × 12
Guns	1—3 inch; 2—40 mm AA
Main Engines	Diesel-electric; 3 000 bhp = 16 knots

Built by Charleston S.B. & D.D. Co. Launched in 1946. Former salvage tug, adapted as a submarine rescue vessel in 1947. Transferred from the US Navy on 15 Aug 1950.

KURTARAN *1966, Turkish Navy, Official*

BOOM DEFENCE VESSELS

AG 5 P 306

Displacement, tons	680 standard; 960 full load
Dimensions, feet	148·7 pp; 173·8 oa × 35 × 13·5
Guns	1—40 mm AA; 3—20 mm AA
Main Engines	4 MAN diesels; 2 shafts; 1 450 bhp = 12 knots

Netlayer AN 104 built in US off-shore programme by Kröger, Rebdsburg for Turkey. Launched on 20 Oct 1960. Delivered on 25 Feb 1961. A photograph of AG 5 appears in the 1964-65 to 1968-69 editions.

AG 4 (ex-*Larch*, ex-*AN* 21) P 304

Displacement, tons	560 standard; 805 full load
Dimensions, feet	146 wl; 163 oa × 30·5 × 10·5
Guns	1—3 inch AA
Main Engines	Diesel-electric; 800 bhp = 12 knots

Former U.S. netlayer of the "Aloe" class. Built by American S.B. Co, Cleveland. Laid down in 1940. Launched on 2 July 1941. Completed in 1941. Acquired in 1947.

AG 4. *1969, Official*

AG 1 (ex-*Barbarian*, 21 Oct 1937) P301 **AG 2** (ex-*Barbette*, 15 Dec 1937) P 302 **AG 3** (ex-*Barfair*, 21 May 1938) P 303

Displacement, tons	750 standard; 1 000 full load
Dimensions, feet	150 pp; 173·8 oa × 32·2 × 9·5
Guns	1—3 inch AA
Main Engines	Triple expansion; 850 ihp = 11·5 knots
Boilers	2 SE

Former British boom defence vessels. First two built by Blyth S.B. Co, third by J Lewis & Sons. Launch dates above. A photograph of AG 1 appears in the 1957-58 edition. and of AG 2 in the 1966-67 edition.

KALDIRAY P 305

Measurement, tons	732 gross
Main Engines	Steam reciprocating; 500 ihp = 10 knots
Complement	97

Built in 1938. Former French vessel. Purchased in 1964.

KALDIRAY *1967, Turkish Nav., Official*

TENDERS

ISIN (ex-*Imia Layteri*) A 570

Displacement, tons	390 full load
Dimensions, feet	110 × 24 × 7
Guns	1 MG
Main Engines	Crossley diesel; 330 bhp
Oil fuel (tons)	32

Built by James Pollock, Sons & Co, Faversham, England. Launched in 1941. Coaster type. Formerly employed in charging the batteries of submarines. Now a main diving ship. A photograph of *Isin* appears in the 1957-58 and earlier editions. The tenders *Akin* and *Dalgie* have been discarded, it is officially stated.

GATE VESSELS. The gate vessels ex-YNG 45, 46 and 47 were built by US for transfer to Turkey under MAP.

PRESIDENTIAL YACHT

HALAS (ex-*Umur*)

Completed and commissioned for service in 1956. Renamed *Halas* in 1961.

OILERS

ALBAY HAKKI BURAK A 572

Displacement, tons	3 800 full load
Dimensions, feet	251·3 pp; 274·7 oa × 40·2 × 18
Main Engines	2 GM diesels; electric drive; 4 400 bhp = 16 knots
Complement	88

Two new tankers for the Turkish Navy were ordered from Gölcük Dockyard, Izmit. *Alban Burak* was built in 1964.

ALBAY HAKKI BURAK *1967, Turkish Navy, Official*

YUZBASI TOLUNAY A 586

Displacement, tons	2 500 standard; 3 500 full load
Dimensions, feet	260 × 41 × 19·5
Main Engines	Atlas Polar-diesels; 2 shafts; 1 920 bhp = 14 knots

Built at Taskizak by Haskoy Naval D.Y., Istanbul. Launched on 22 Aug 1950.

YUZBASI TOLUNAY *1967, Turkish Navy, Official*

AKAR (ex-*Istanvul*, ex-*Adour*) A 580

Displacement, tons	4 289 light; 13 200 full load
Dimensions, feet	433 × 52·7 × 27 feet
Main Engines	Parsons geared turbines; 5 200 shp = 15 knots

A photograph of *Akar* appears in the 1959-60 to 1966-67 editions.

AKPINAR (ex-*Chiwaukum*) A 574

Displacement, tons	700 light; 2 700 full load
Measurement, feet	1 453 deadweight
Dimensions, feet	212·5 wl; 220·5 oa × 37 × 12·8
Main Engines	Diesel; 800 bhp = 10 knots

Formerly the United States oiler *AOG 26*. Built by East Coast S.Y. Inc., Bayonne. Laid down on 2 Apr 1944. Launched on 5 May 1944. Completed on 22 July 1944. Transferred to Turkey in 1949. A photograph appears in the 1957-58 edition.

GOLCUK A 573

Displacement, tons	1 255
Measurement, feet	750 deadweight
Dimensions, feet	185 × 31·1 × 10
Main Engines	B. & W. diesel; 700 bhp = 12·5 knots

Built by Gölcük Dockyard, Ismot. Launched on 4 Nov 1935. A photograph appears in the 1957-58 and earlier editions.

The U.S. harbour tugs ex-YTL 155, 751 were transferred under MAP.

THE ROYAL NAVY

Admiralty Board

Secretary of State for Defence (Chairman):
The Right Honourable Denis W. Healey, MBE, MP
Minister of Defence for Administration (Vice-Chairman):

Minister of Defence for Equipment (Vice-Chairman)
Mr. J. Morris, MP
Parliamentary Under-Secretary of State for Defence for the Royal Navy:
Dr David A. L. Owen, MP
Chief of the Naval Staff and First Sea Lord:
Admiral Sir Michael Le Fanu, GCB, DSC
Chief of Naval Personnel and Second Sea Lord:
Admiral Sir Frank Roddam Twiss, KCB, DSC
Controller of the Navy:
Admiral Sir Horace Rochfort Law, KCB, OBE, DSC
Chief of Fleet Support:
Vice-Admiral Arthur Francis Turner, CB, DSC
Vice-Chief of the Naval Staff:
Vice-Admiral Edward Beckwith Ashmore, CB, DSC
Chief Scientist (Royal Navy):
Mr. Basil Wilfred Lythall, CB, MA
Second Permanent Under-Secretary for Administration:
Sir Arthur Drew, KCB, JP
Second Permanent Under-Secretary for Equipment:
Sir Martin Flett, KCB

Commanders-in-Chief

Commander-in-Chief, Naval Home Command:
Admiral Sir John Byng Frewen, KCB
Commander-in-Chief, Western Fleet:
Admiral Sir John Fitzroy Duyland Bush, KCB, DSC and 2 Bars
Commander-in-Chief, Far East:
Admiral Sir Peter John Hill-Norton, KCB

Flag Officers

Commander, Far East Fleet:
Vice-Admiral Leslie Derek Empson
Flag Officer, Naval Air Command:
Vice-Admiral Hugh Richard Benest Janvrin, CB, DSC
Flag Officer, Scotland and Northern Ireland:
Vice-Admiral Sir Ian Lachlan Mackay McGeoch, KCB, DSO, DSC
Flag Officer, Submarines:
Vice-Admiral Sir Michael Patrick Pollock, KCB, MVO, DSC
Flag Officer, Aircraft Carriers and Amphibious Ships:
Vice-Admiral Michael Frampton Fell, CB, DSO, DSC & Bar
Flag Officer, Flotillas, Western Fleet:
Rear-Admiral John Ernle Pope (*November 1969*)
Flag Officer, Medway, and Admiral Superintendent, H.M. Dockyard, Chatham:
Vice-Admiral Wilfred John Parker, CB, OBE, DSC
Flag Officer, Plymouth:
Vice-Admiral Anthony Templer Frederick Griffith Griffin, CB
Flag Officer, Naval Flying Training:
Rear-Admiral Cedric Kenelm Roberts, DSO
Flag Officer, Second-in-Command, Far East Fleet:
Rear-Admiral Terence Thornton Lewin, MVO, DSC
Flag Officer, Sea Training and in command Portland Naval Base:
Rear Admiral John Anthony Rose Troup, DSC & Bar
Flag Officer, Malta:
Rear-Admiral Derrick George Kent
Flag Officer, Gibraltar, and Admiral Superintendent, H.M. Dockyard, Gibraltar:
Rear-Admiral Arthur Rodney Barry Sturdee (*October 1969*)
Flag Officer, Spithead and Admiral Superintendent, H.M, Dockyard, Portsmouth:
Rear-Admiral Arthur Mackenzie Power, MBE
Admiral Superintendent, H.M. Dockyard, Devonport:
Rear-Admiral Denis Bryan Harvey Wildish, CB, CEng, MIMarE
Admiral Superintendent, H.M. Dockyard, Rosyth:
Rear-Admiral William Terence Colborne Ridley, CB, OBE, CEng, AMIMechE, MIMarE

General Officers, Royal Marines

Commandant-General, Royal Marines:
Lieutenant-General Peter William Cradock Hellings, CB, DSC, MC
Chief of Staff to Commandant-General, Royal Marines:
Major-General Ian Stewart Harrison
General Officer Commanding Portsmouth Group, Royal Marines:
Major-General Basil Ian Spencer Gourlay, OBE, MC
General Officer Commanding, Plymouth Group, Royal Marines:
Major-General Anthony Patrick Willasey-Wilsey, MBE, MC

Senior Appointments

Director-General Ships, Chief Naval Engineer Officer, and Senior Naval Representative, Bath:
Vice-Admiral Robert George Raper, CB, CEng, MIMechE, MIMarE
Director-General Aircraft (Naval):
Rear-Admiral John Bayley Holt, BSc, CEng, MIEE
Director-General Weapons (Naval):
Rear-Admiral Ian Stewart McIntosh, DSO, MBE, DSC
Assistant Controller (Polaris):
Rear-Admiral George Francis Allan Trewby, GEng, MIMechE, MIMarE, MRINA
Director of Warship Design:
Mr Charles Edgar Sherwin, CEng, MRINA, RCNC

Dilpomatic Representation

British Naval Attaché in Washington:
Rear-Admiral Colin Charles Harrison Dunlop, CBE
American Naval Attaché in London:
Rear-Admiral Louis Joseph Kirn, US Navy

1969-70 New Construction Programme

1 Frigate. Interim "Type 21". Order announced 26 Mar 1969
Lead Items for Frigate. Standard "Type 22". Announced 26 Mar 1969.

1969-70 Conversion Programme

1 Cruiser. *Lion*. Conversion to operate helicopters.
1 Conventionally Powered Patrol Submarine. For training.

1968-69 New Construction Programme

1 Nuclear Powered Fleet Submarine. "Improved" Design. Ordered end 1968.
1 Guided Missile Armed Destroyer. "Type 42". Ordered 14 Nov 1968.
Design Study for Patrol Frigate. Announced 27 Feb 1968.
Lead Items for Minesweepers. New Design.
1 Experimental Trials Vessel. Order announced 3 Dec 1968.
3 Anti-Fast Patrol Boat Training Craft
? Ocean Tugs

1968-69 Conversion Programme

1 Conventionally Powered Patrol Submarine. For training.
1 Destroyer. For Trials.
1 Store Carrier. As Torpedo Recovery Vessel.

1967-68 New Construction Programme

1 Nuclear Powered Fleet Submarine. "Improved" Design. Announced 16 Feb 1967. Ordered Nov 1967.
2 General Purpose Frigates. "Leander Class". Ordered (announced) 29 July 1968.
3 Small Fleet Tankers. New Design. Ordered Jan 1968.

1967-68 Conversion Programme

1 Aircraft Carrier. *Ark Royal*. 3-year, £30m special refit and modernisation.
1 Cruiser. *Tiger*. Conversion to operate Helicopters.
6 Minehunters. "Ton" Class. Conversion from Coastal Minesweepers.
1 Ice Patrol Ship. *Endurance* (ex-*Anita Dan*). Conversion from commercial ice operating ship.

1966-67 New Construction Programme

1 Aircraft Carrier. CVA 01. Cancelled.
2 Nuclear Powered Fleet Submarines. "Valiant" Class. Ordered 9 Aug 1966 (*Conqueror*) and 1 Mar 1967 (*Superb*).
2 General Purpose Frigates. "Leander" Class. Ordered 8 Mar 1967.

1966-67 Conversion Programme

1 Gas Turbine Powered Anti-Submarine Frigate. *Exmouth*. Conversion from steam.
3 Minehunters. "Ton" Class. Conversion from Coastal Minesweepers.

1965-66 New Construction Programme

1 Guided Missile Armed Destroyer. "Type 82". Ordered 4 Oct 1966.
1 Nuclear Powered Fleet Submarine. *Churchill*. Ordered 15 Oct 1965.
3 General Purpose Frigates. "Leander" Class.
2 Medium Berthing Tugs.
2 Landing Craft Mechanised. Mk 9.

1965-66 Conversion Programme

1 Cruiser. *Blake*. Conversion to operate helicopters.
2 Minehunters. "Ton" Class. Conversion from Coastal Minesweepers.

1964-65 New Construction Programme

1 Diesel-Electric Powered Patrol Submarine. *Onyx*.
2 Guided Missile Armed Destroyers. "County" Class
3 General Purpose Frigates. "Leander" Class.
1 Exercise Minelayer. *Abdiel*. Ordered 28 May 1965.
6 Coastal Survey Ships. "Fawn" Class. 2 rescinded.
1 Stores Support Ship. "Lyness" Class.
1 Replenishment Oiler. "Olynthus" Class.
5 Fleet Tenders. "Aberdovey" Class.
5 Medium Berthing Tugs.
5 Landing Craft Mechanised. Mk 9.

1964-65 Conversion Programme

1 Helicopter Support Ship. *Lofoten*. Conversion from Tank Landing Ship.
2 Minehunters. "Ton" Class. Conversion from Coastal Minesweepers.
3 Degaussing Vessels. "Ham" Class. Conversion from Inshore Minesweepers.

1963-64 New Construction Programme

4 Nuclear Powered "Polaris" Ballistic Missile Submarines. "Resolution Class".
3 General Purpose Frigates. "Leander" Class.
2 Survey Ships. "Hecla" Class.
1 Patrol Survey and Scientific Support Icebreaker. *Terra Nova*. Cancelled 1966.
2 Stores Support Ships. "Lyness" Class.
1 Fleet Replenishment Ship. "Regent" Class.
1 Replenishment Oiler. "Olynthus" Class.
6 Fleet Tenders. "Aberdovey" Class.
5 Landing Craft Mechanised Mk 9.

1963-64 Conversion Programme

1 Minehunter. "Ton" Class. Prototype conversion from Coastal Minesweepers.
2 Coastal Survey Vessels. "Ton" Class. Conversion from Coastal Minesweepers.
2 Inshore Survey Craft. "Ham" Class. Conversion from Inshore Minesweepers.

Navy Estimates

1960-61: £397 500 010	1965-66: £589 040 000
1961-62: £406 073 400	1966-67: £597 129 000
1962-63: £422 273 000	1967-68: £648 043 500
1963-64: £439 951 600	1968-69: £668 743 000
1964-65: £487 690 000	1969-70: £645 624 000

Personnel

1959-60: 106 000	1963-64: 100 000	1966-67: 103 000
1960-61: 102 000	1964-65: 103 000	1967-68: 100 500
1961-62: 100 000	1965-66: 104 000	1968-69: 98 000
1962-63: 100 000		1969-70: 95 500

Mercantile Marine

Lloyd's Register of Shipping: 4 020 vessels of 21 920 980 tons gross

Strength of the Fleet

4 Aircraft Carriers (1 Accommodation Ship)
2 Commando Carriers
4 Nuclear Powered Polaris Submarines
4 Nuclear Powered Fleet Submarines
33 Diesel Powered Patrol Submarines
2 Assault Ships
3 Cruisers
8 Guided Missile Armed Destroyers
11 Destroyers
68 Frigates
1 Training Ship (Minesweeper Support Ship)
1 Helicopter Support Ship
1 Ice Patrol Ship

1 Heavy Repair Ship
2 Submarine Parent Ships
1 Destroyer Depot Ship
4 Maintenance Ships
4 Survey Ships
9 Survey Craft
66 Coastal Minesweepers (and Hunters)
22 Inshore Minesweepers (20 Auxiliary)
5 Coastal Minelayers
2 Tank Landing Ships
26 Tank Landing Craft
43 Minor Landing Craft
7 Experimental Vessels

4 Fast Patrol Boats
4 Seaward Defence Boats
11 Fleet Supply Ships
38 Fleet Oilers
20 Boom Defence Vessels
5 Ocean Salvage Vessels
6 Coastal Salvage Vessels
2 Cable Vessels
14 Fleet Tenders
12 Armament Carriers
16 Water Carriers
70 Fleet and Berthing Tugs
88 Service Craft

British Carrier Borne Aircraft

Name	*Maker*	*Type*	*Dimensions*	*Power Plant*	*Armament*	*Performance*
PHANTOM II (F-4K)	McDonnell (USA)	Two-Seat All-Weather Interceptor and Attack Fighter	Wing Span 38 ft 5 in Folded 27 ft 6·5 in Length 58 ft 3 in	Two Rolls-Royce Spey 25 R Turbojets with afterburners	Sidewinder and Sparrow AAM's, bombs, rockets	Maximum Speed, over Mach 2
SEA VIXEN FAW Mks. 1 and 2	Hawker Siddeley	Two-Seat Day and Night All-Weather Fighter	Wing Span 50 ft Folded 22 ft 3 in Length 53 ft 7 in	Two Rolls-Royce Avon 208 Turbojets	Firestreak or Red Top, bombs, rockets, Bullpup	Maximum Speed, approx 700 mph
BUCCANEER S. Mks 1 and 2	Hawker Siddeley	Two-Seat All-Weather Strike Aircraft	Wing Span 42 ft 4 in Folded 19 ft 11 in Length 63 ft 5 in	Two Bristol Siddeley Gyron Junior 101 or R-R Spey Turbojets	Nuclear Weapons Bombs, rockets, Bullpup missiles, Martel ASMs and Sidewinder	Speed in transonic range at low altitudes
GANNET AEW. Mk 3	Westland	Three-Seat Early Warning Aircraft	Wing Span 54 ft 4 in Folded 19 ft 11 in Length 44 ft	One Bristol Siddeley Double Mamba 102 Turboprop	None	Maximum Speed, approx 250 mph
SEA KING SH-3D	Westland	Multi-Seat All-Weather Anti-Submaірne Helicopter	Rotor dia 62 ft Length 72 ft 8 in Width Folded 16 ft 4 in Height 16 ft 10 in	Two RR Bristol Gnome 1400 engines	Up to 840 lb of weapons including homing torpedoes	Maximum Speed 135 knots (155 mph) Cruising speed for max range 188 knots Range with max fuel 550 nautical miles
WESSEX HAS Mk 3	Westland	Multi-seat Anti-Submarine Helicopter	Rotor dia 56 ft	One Rolls-Royce Gazelle 165	Anti-Submarine weapons	Maximum Speed 115 knots (133 mph)
WESSEX HAS Mk 1	Westland	Multi-Seat Anti-Submarine and Transport Helicopter	Rotor dia 56 ft Fueslage Length 48 ft 4·5 in	One Napier Gazelle 161 Shaft-Turbine Engine	Anti-Submarine Weapons SS 11 missiles	Maximum speed, 132 mph Range, 390 miles
WESSEX HU Mk 5	Westland	Commando assault transport	Rotor dia 56 ft Fuselage Length 48 ft 4·5 in	Two coupled Bristol Siddeley Gnome Shaft-turbines	SS 11 missiles, guns, rockets	Maximum Speed, 132 mph Range, 478 miles
WASP HAS Mk 1	Westland	Five-Seat Anti-Submarine Helicopter	Rotor dia 32 ft 3 in Overall length (blades folded) 30 ft 4 in	One Bristol Siddeley Nimbus Shaft-turbine	Anti-Submarine homing torpedoes or missiles	Maximum Speed, 120 mph Range, 270 miles

British Naval Guided Missiles

Type	*Name*	*Maker*	*Length ft*	*Propulsion*	*Speed Mach*	*Range miles*	*Guidence System*	*Notes*
SURFACE-TO-AIR	Seacat	Short Bros & Harland	4·85	Solid Propellent			Radio command	Close range anti-aircraft missile
	Seadart	Hawker Siddeley	14·3	BS Odin ramjet, Solid propellent booster				Test firing began 1965
	Seaslug	Hawker Siddeley	19·65	ICI Solid propellent and solid boosters			Beamrider	Carried by County Class destroyers. Capable of engaging ship targets
	Seawolf (PX 430)	British Aircraft Corporation						Close range anti-aircraft missile. Also designed for use against ships and hovercraft
AIR-TO-AIR	Firestreak	Hawker Siddeley	10·5	Solid propellent	2·0+	0·75—5	Infra-red	Carried by Sea Vixen Mk 1 fighters
	Sparrow	Raytheon	12	Solid propellent	2·2		Semi-active	Carried by Phantom II, F-4K
	Red top	Hawker Siddelyy	11·5	Solid propellent	3·0	7	Infra-red	Carried by Sea Vixen Mk II fighters
	Sidewinder	NOTS (USA)	9·2	Solid propellent	2·5	2	Infra-red	Carried by Phantom II fighters, Buccaneers
AIR-TO-SURFACE	Bullpup	Martin, Maxson (USA) and European consortium	10·5	Liquid propellent	1·8	7	Radio Command	Carried by Phantom II, Buccaneer, Sea Vixen
	Martel	Anglo-French						Carried by Buccaneers
	SS 11	Nord-Aviation (France)	3·9	Solid propellent	335 mph	1·75	Wire guidance	Carried by Wessex helicopters
ANTI-SUBMARINE	Ikara	British Aircraft Corporation	11	Solid propellent			Carries homing torpedoes	To be mounted in Type 82 guided missile destroyer

LIST OF PENNANT NUMBERS

A few of the ships listed below are on the sales list or have been earmarked for disposal, but their pennant numbers have been retained in this edition for reference and identification until they are actually broken up; and a few ships listed are not yet completed.

Submarines, Aircraft Carriers, Cruisers, Destroyers, Frigates, Minelayers, Helicopter Support Ships

S Flag Superior:

S 01 Porpoise
S 02 Rorqual
S 03 Narwhal
S 04 Grampus
S 05 Finwhale
S 06 Cachalot
S 07 Sealion
S 08 Walrus
S 09 Oberon
S 10 Odin
S 11 Orpheus
S 12 Olympus
S 13 Osiris
S 14 Onslaught
S 15 Otter
S 16 Oracle
S 17 Ocelot
S 18 Otus
S 19 Opossum
S 20 Opportune
S 21 Onyx
S 22 Resolution
S 23 Repulse
S 26 Renown
S 27 Revenge
S 32 Tiptoe
S 33 Trump
S 34 Taciturn
S 37 Talent
S 41 Alaric
S 42 Tabard
S 43 Amphion
S 47 Astute
S 49 Artemis
S 55 Thermopylae
S 61 Acheron
S 63 Andrew
S 64 Anchorite
S 65 Alcide
S 66 Alderney
S 67 Alliance
S 68 Ambush
S 69 Auriga
S 72 Aeneas
S 96 Artful
S 101 Dreadnought
S 102 Valiant
S 103 Warspite
S 104 Churchill
S 105 Conqueror
S 106 Superb

R Flag Superior:

R 05 Eagle
R 06 Centaur
R 07 Albion
R 08 Bulwark
R 09 Ark Royal
R 12 Hermes
R 38 Victorious

C Flag Superior:

C 20 Tiger
C 34 Lion
C 35 Belfast
C 99 Blake

D Flag Superior:

D 01 Caprice
D 02 Devonshire
D 05 Daring
D 06 Hampshire
D 07 Caesar
D 09 Dunkirk
D 10 Cassandra
D 12 Kent
D 15 Cavendish
D 16 London
D 18 Antrim
D 19 Glamorgan
D 20 Fife
D 21 Norfolk
D 22 Aisne
D 25 Carysfort
D 31 Broadsword
D 32 Camperdown
D 35 Diamond
D 43 Matapan
D 44 Lagos
D 61 Chequers
D 64 Scorpion
D 68 Barrosa
D 70 Solebay
D 73 Cavalier
D 77 Trafalgar
D 84 Saintes
D 85 Cambrian
D 86 Agincourt
D 96 Crossbow
D 97 Corunna
D 106 Decoy
D 108 Dainty
D 114 Defender
D 119 Delight
D 126 Diana
D 154 Duchess

F Flag Superior

F 08 Urania
F 09 Troubridge
F 10 Aurora
F 12 Achilles
F 14 Leopard
F 15 Euryalus
F 16 Diomede
F 18 Galatea
F 19 Terpsichore
F 27 Lynx
F 28 Cleopatra
F 29 Verulam
F 32 Salisbury
F 34 Puma
F 36 Whitby
F 37 Jaguar
F 38 Arethusa
F 39 Naiad
F 40 Sirius
F 41 Volage
F 42 Phoebe
F 43 Torquay
F 45 Minerva
F 47 Danae
F 48 Dundas
F 50 Venus
F 51 Grafton
F 52 Juno
F 53 Undaunted
F 54 Hardy
F 56 Argonaut
F 57 Andromeda
F 58 Hermione
F 59 Chichester
F 60 Jupiter
F 61 Llandaff
F 62 Pellew
F 63 Scarborough
F 65 Tenby
F 69 Bacchante
F 71 Scylla
F 72 Wizard
F 73 Eastbourne
F 75 Charybdis
F 76 Virago
F 77 Blackpool
F 78 Blackwood
F 80 Duncan
F 83 Ulster
F 84 Exmouth
F 85 Keppel

F Flag Superior:

F 88 Malcolm
F 91 Murray
F 94 Palliser
F 97 Russell
F 99 Lincoln
F 101 Yarmouth
F 102 Zest
F 103 Lowestoft
F 104 Dido
F 106 Brighton
F 107 Rothesay
F 108 Londonderry
F 109 Leander
F 113 Falmouth
F 114 Ajax
F 115 Berwick
F 117 Ashanti
F 119 Eskimo
F 121 Tumult
F 122 Gurkha
F 124 Zulu
F 125 Mohawk
F 126 Plymouth
F 127 Penelope
F 129 Rhyl
F 131 Nubian
F 133 Tartar
F 138 Rapid
F 156 Tuscan
F 159 Wakeful
F 185 Relentless
F 187 Whirlwind
F 189 Termagant
F 193 Rocket
F 196 Urchin
F 197 Grenville
F 200 Ursa
F 390 Loch Fada

N Flag Superior:

N 11 Minstrel
N 12 Gossamer
N 13 Miner III
N 16 Miner VI
N 17 Miner VII
N 18 Mindful
N 21 Abdiel
N 26 Plover
N 70 Manxman

K Flag Superior:

K 07 Lofoten
K 08 Engadine

PENNANT NUMBERS—*continued*

DGV
Converted to
Degaussing Vessels

PAS
Employed in the
Port Auxiliary Service

RNXS
Adapted for the
Royal Naval Auxiliary Service

TRV
Converted to
Torpedo Recovery Vessels

Support Ships, Boom Defence Vessels, Landing Ships, Coastal Minesweepers, Inshore Minsweepers

A Flag Superior:

A 00 Britannia
A 84 Reliant
A 108 Triumph
A 133 Hecla
A 134 Rame Head
A 137 Hecate
A 144 Hydra
A 146 Protector
A 154 Mermaid
A 158 Duncansby Head
A 160 Fort Dunvegan
A 164 Adamant
A 185 Maidstone
A 186 Fort Rosalie
A 187 Forth
A 191 Berry Head
A 194 Tyne
A 200 Vidal
A 225 Mull of Kintyre
A 229 Fort Duquesne
A 230 Fort Langley
A 231 Reclaim
A 236 Fort Charlotte
A 262 Hartland Point
A 280 Resurgent
A 303 Dampier
A 307 Cook
A 311 Owen
A 316 Fort Sandusky
A 329 Retainer
A 339 Lyness
A 334 Stromness
A 335 Tarbatness
A 387 Girdle Ness
A 480 Resource
A 486 Regent

P Flag Superior:

P 190 Laymoor
P 191 Layburn
P 192 Mandarin
P 193 Pintail
P 194 Garganey
P 195 Goldeneye
P 200 Barfoss
P 201 Barbain
P 202 Barfoot
P 214 Barbecue
P 216 Barglow
P 232 Barmond
P 241 Barnard
P 243 Barbican

P Flag Superior:

P 244 Barfield
P 254 Barrage
P 259 Barrington
P 261 Bartizan
P 282 Barfoam
P 284 Moorsman
P 294 Barfoil
P 297 Barnestone

L Flag Superior:

L 10 Fearless
L 11 Intrepid
L 3003 Anzio
L 3016 Dieppe
L 3043 Messina
L 3044 Narvik
L 3515 Stalker
L 3516 Striker

M Flag Superior:

M 304 Waterwitch
M 1101 Coniston
M 1103 Kilmorey
M 1104 Alverton
M 1105 Clyde
M 1106 Appleton
M 1107 Beachampton
M 1109 Killiecrankie
M 1110 Bildeston
M 1112 Boulston
M 1113 Brereton
M 1114 Brinton
M 1115 Bronington
M 1116 Burnaston
M 1117 Thames
M 1118 Calton
M 1119 Carhampton
M 1120 Caunton
M 1122 Chilcompton
M 1123 Clarbeston
M 1124 St. David
M 1125 Cuxton
M 1126 Montrose
M 1128 Derriton
M 1129 Oulston
M 1130 Highburton
M 1132 Blaxton
M 1133 Bossington
M 1135 Fenton
M 1136 Curzon
M 1137 Flockton
M 1138 Floriston
M 1140 Gavington

M Flag Superior:

M 1141 Glasserton
M 1145 Dufton
M 1146 Venturer
M 1147 Hubberston
M 1149 Badminton
M 1150 Invermoriston
M 1151 Iveston
M 1153 Kedelston
M 1154 Kellington
M 1155 Monkton
M 1156 Kemerton
M 1157 Kirkliston
M 1158 Laleston
M 1159 Lanton
M 1160 Letterston
M 1161 Leverton
M 1162 Kildarton
M 1164 Maddiston
M 1165 Maxton
M 1166 Nurton
M 1167 Repton
M 1169 Penston
M 1170 Picton
M 1173 Mersey
M 1174 Puncheston
M 1175 Northumbria
M 1177 Roddington
M 1179 Sefton
M 1180 Shavington
M 1181 Sheraton
M 1182 Shoulton
M 1187 Upton
M 1188 Walkerton
M 1189 Wasperton
M 1192 Wilkieston
M 1193 Wolverton
M 1194 Woolaston
M 1195 Wotton
M 1196 Yarnton
M 1198 Ashton
M 1199 Belton
M 1200 Soberton
M 1202 Maryton
M 1203 Dartington
M 1204 Stubbington
M 1205 Wiston
M 1206 Fiskerton
M 1208 Lewiston
M 1209 Chawton
M 1211 Houghton
M 1216 Solent

M Flag Superior.

M 2001 Dingley
M 2002 Aveley
M 2003 Brearley
M 2004 Brenchley
M 2005 Brinkley
M 2007 Watchful
M 2008 Squirrel
M 2009 Chailey
M 2010 Isis
M 2603 Arlingham PAS
M 2614 Bucklesham TRV
M 2616 Chelsham
M 2618 Cobham
M 2619 Darsham
M 2620 Davenham
M 2621 Dittisham TRV
M 2622 Downham TRV
M 2624 Elsenham TRV
M 2626 Everingham PAS
M 2628 Flintham TRV
M 2629 Damerham
M 2630 Fritham TRV
M 2631 Glentham
M 2635 Haversham TRV
M 2636 Lasham TRV
M 2637 Hovingham
M 2706 Ledsham
M 2708 Ludham
M 2713 Nettleham
M 2714 Ockham
M 2716 Pagham RNXS
M 2717 Fordham DGV
M 2722 Rackham
M 2726 Shipham RNXS
M 2727 Saxlingham
M 2728 Shrivenham
M 2733 Thakeham RNXS
M 2735 Tongham PAS
M 2737 Warmington DGV
M 2778 Woldingham PAS
M 2780 Woodlark
M 2781 Portisham RNXS
M 2783 Odiham RNXS
M 2784 Puttenham RNXS
M 2785 Birdham RNXS
M 2787 Abbotsham
M 2788 Georgeham
M 2790 Thatcham DGV
M 2791 Sandringham
M 2792 Polsham
M 2793 Thornham

Silhouettes | **Aircraft Carriers** | Scale: 150 feet = 1 inch

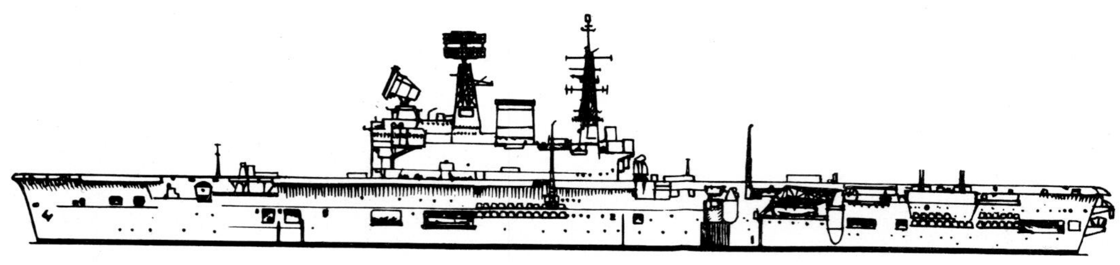

EAGLE

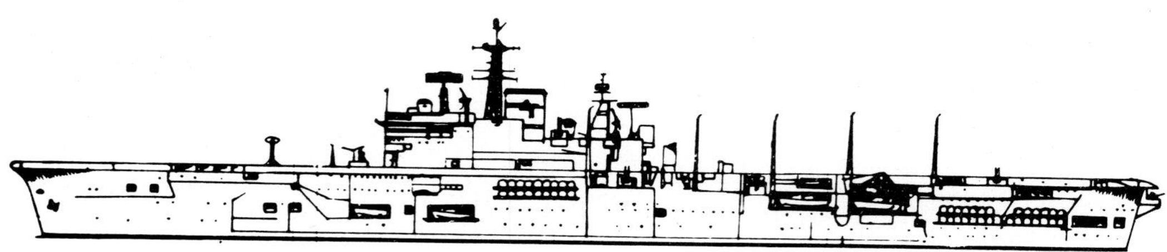

ARK ROYAL

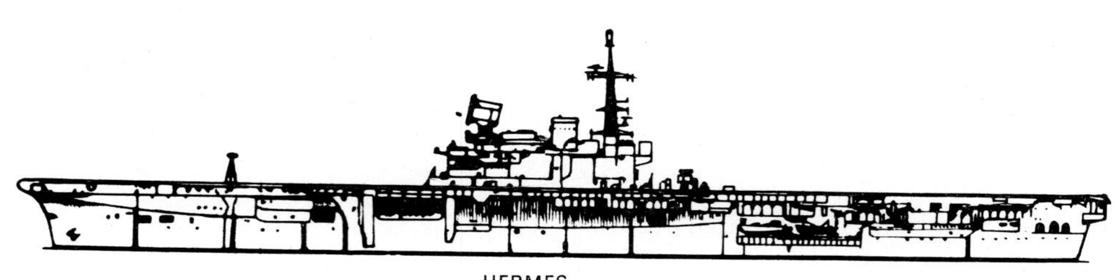

HERMES

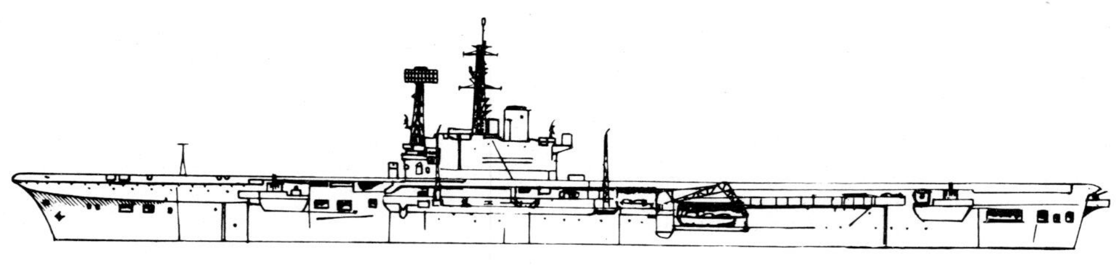

CENTAUR

Commando Carriers

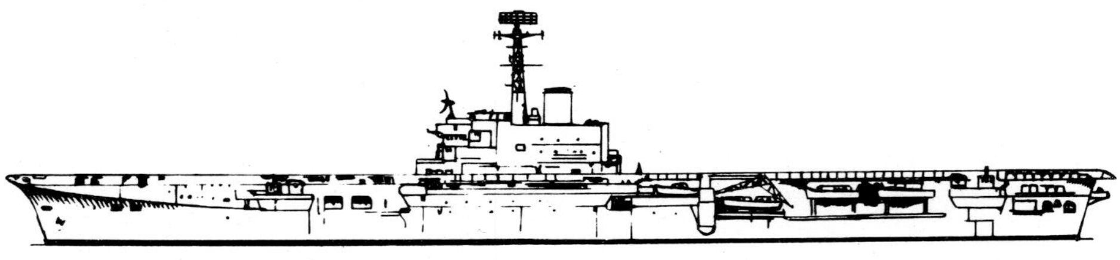

ALBION

BULWARK

Silhouettes—contd.

Cruisers, Guided Missile Destroyers, Destroyers, Support Ships

Scale: 150 feet = 1 inch

BLAKE with Sea King helicopter

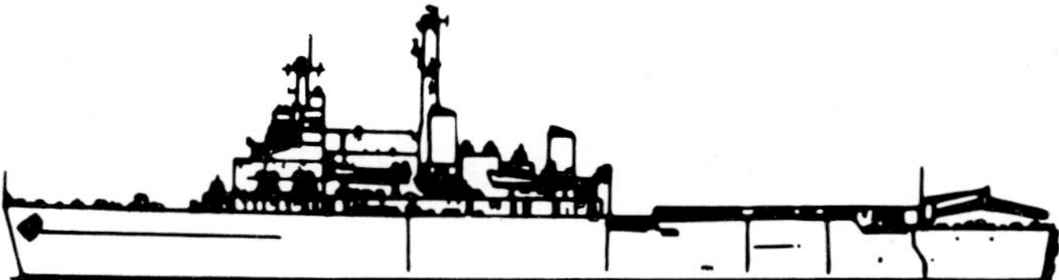

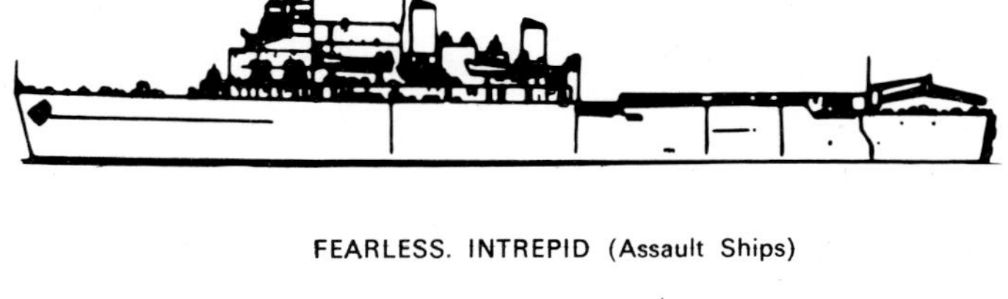

FEARLESS. INTREPID (Assault Ships)

FIFE, GLAMORGAN

FORTH (Nuclear Submarine Support Ship)

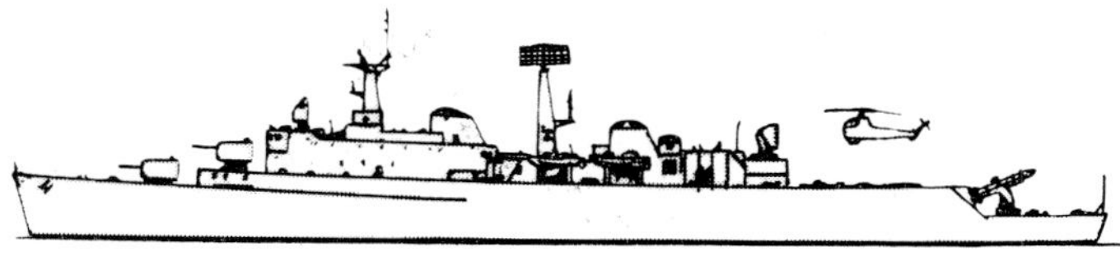

KENT, LONDON

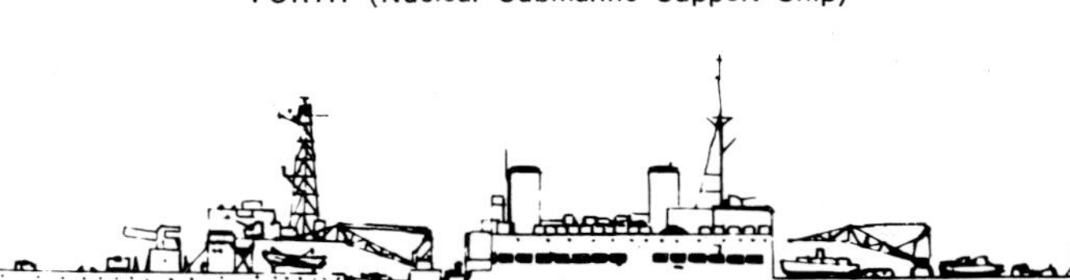

MAIDSTONE (Nuclear Submarine Support Ship)

DEVONSHIRE, HAMPSHIRE

HARTLAND POINT (Escort Maintenance Ship)

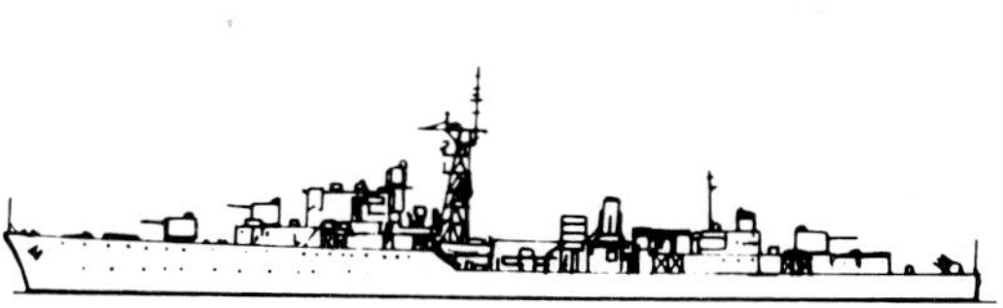

DECOY, DIAMOND, DIANA, DUCHESS

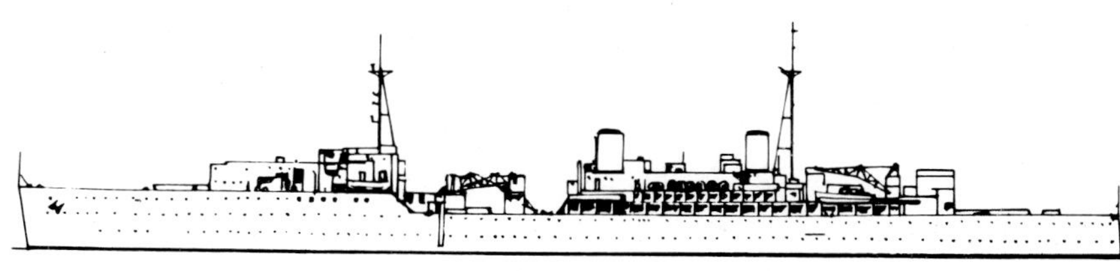

ADAMANT (Submarine Support Ship)

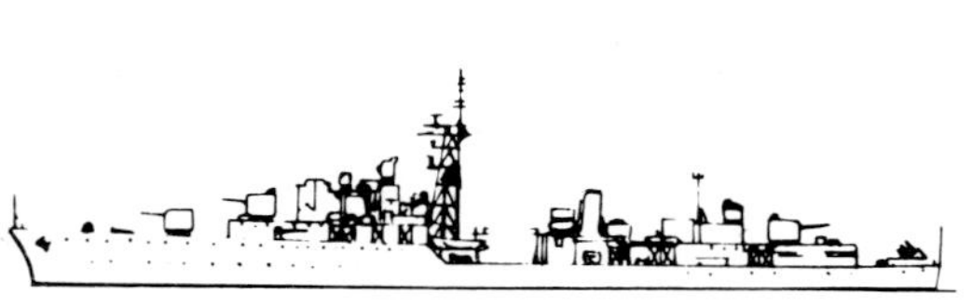

DAINTY, DARING, DEFENDER, DELIGHT

TYNE (Destroyer Depot Ship)

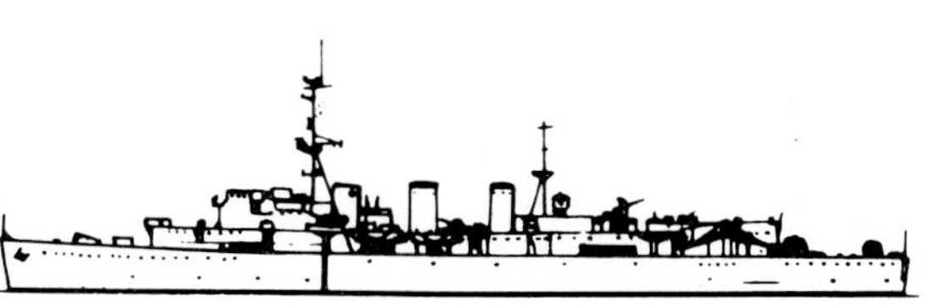

MANXMAN (Engineering Training Ship)

BELFAST (ex-Cruiser, Harbour Accommodation Ship)

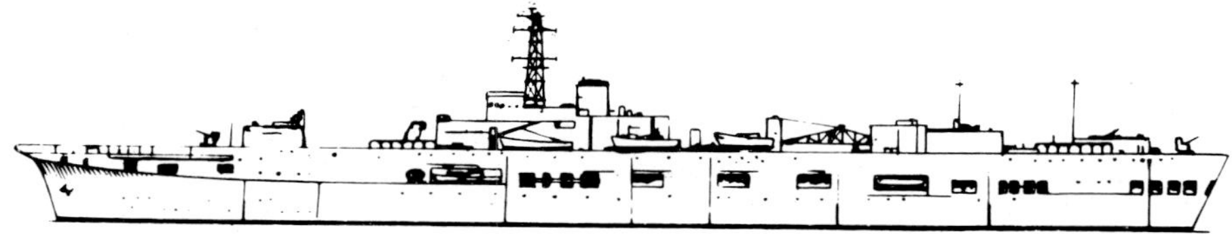

TRIUMPH (ex-Aircraft Carrier, Heavy Repair and Escort Maintenance Ship)

Silhouettes—contd.

Scale: 150 feet = 1 inch

Radar Pickets, Destroyers, Frigates, Survey Ships, Ice Patrol Ship

BARROSA ("BATTLE" *Class*) Radar Picket

Converted ROTHESAY *Class*

TROUBRIDGE, ULSTER

AGINCOURT, AISNE, CORUNNA ("BATTLE" *Class*)

ROTHESAY *Class*

GRENVILLE, UNDAUNTED, helideck aft

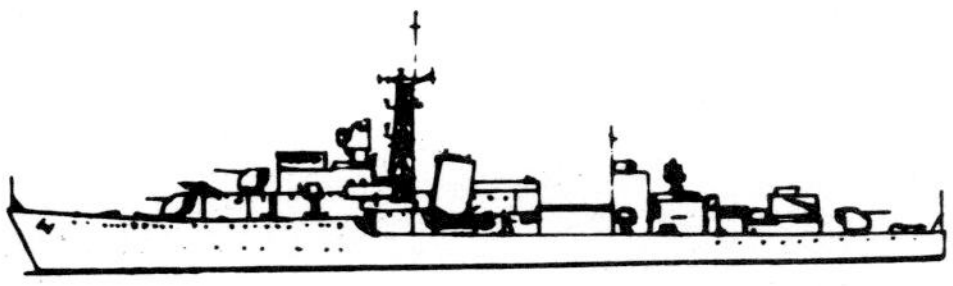

CAPRICE

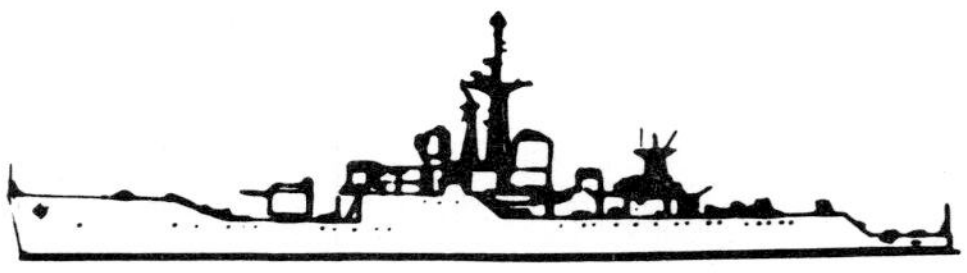

WHITBY *Class*

WAKEFUL

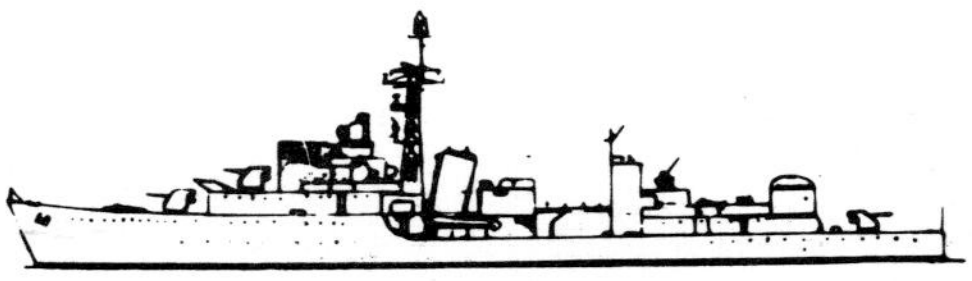

CAMBRIAN, CARYSFORT

JAGUAR, LEOPARD, LYNX, PUMA

EXMOUTH

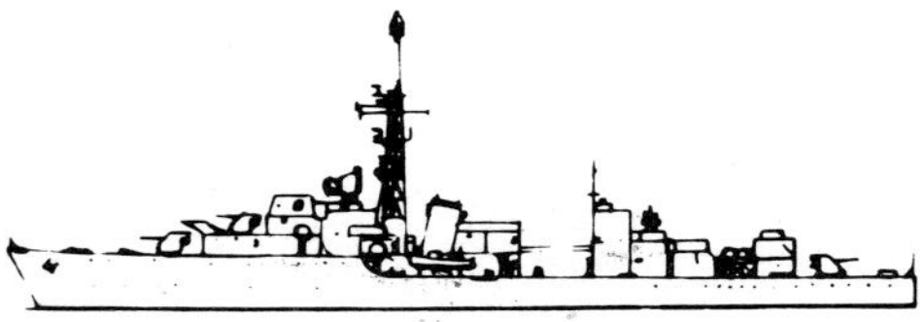

CAVALIER

CHICHESTER, LLANDAFF

RAPID

Later LEANDER *Class* with "Seacat"

SALISBURY

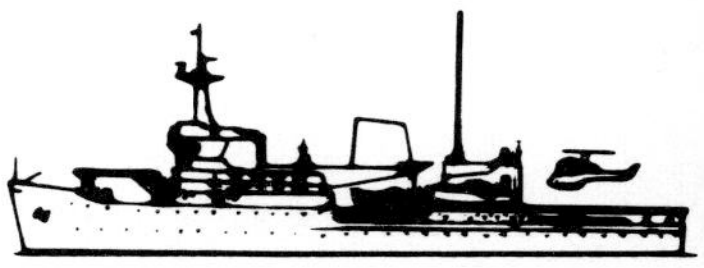

HECATE, HECLA, HYDRA (Survey)

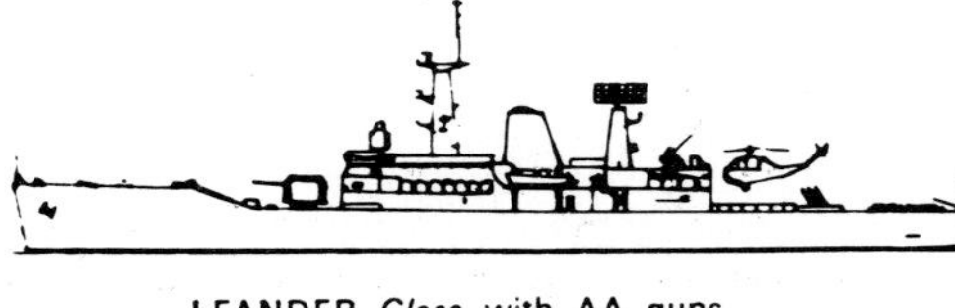

LEANDER *Class* with AA guns

LINCOLN

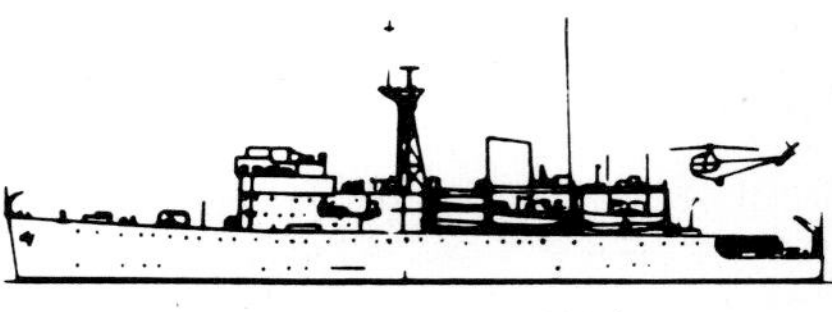

VIDAL (Survey Ship)

"TRIBAL" *Class*

BLACKWOOD *Class*

ENDURANCE (Ice Patrol Ship)

AIRCRAFT CARRIERS

Name	*Deck Letter*	*No.*	*Builders*	*Laid down*	*Launched*	*Completed*
HERMES (ex-*Elephant*)	H	R 12	Vickers-Armstrongs, Barrow-in-Furness	21 June 1944	16 Feb 1953	18 Nov 1959

Displacement, tons	23 900 standard; 28 700 full load
Length, feet (*metres*)	650 (*198·1*) pp; 744·3 (*226.9*) oa
Beam, feet (*metres*)	90 (*27·4*) hull
Draught, feet (*metres*)	29 (*8·8*)
Width, feet (*metres*)	160 (*48·8*) overall
Catapults	2 improved steam
Aircraft	20 fixed wing + 8 helicopters
Armour	+ in flight deck
Missile launchers	2 quadruple "Seacat" surface-to-air systems
Boilers	4 Admiralty 3-drum
Main engines	Parsons geared turbines; 2 shafts 76 000 shp
Speed, knots	28 designed maximum
Oil fuel, tons	3 880 furnace; 320 diesel; 1 000 avgas
Complement	1 830 (190 officers, 1 640 men) 2 100 with air squadrons

Originally the name ship of a class including *Albion, Bulwark* and *Centaur*, see following pages, but her design was modified to a different type, more advanced and incorporating new equipment and improved arrangements, including five post-war developments—angled deck, steam catapult, landing sight, 3-D radar, and deck-edge lift. Air-conditioned throughout. Manned for trials on 23 Oct 1959, accepted from builders on 18 Nov 1959, commissioned on 25 Nov 1959, embarked air squadrons and joined the Fleet summer 1960. Long refit 1964 to 1966, costing £10 000 000, during which the "Alaskan Highway" was stepped out on the starboard side of the island, adding 15·5 feet to the overall breadth, all ten 40 mm AA guns in five twin mountings were suppressed and two "Seacat" guided weapons systems installed, and living accommodation improved. Refit 1969.

HERMES 1968, *Official*

FLIGHT DECK. Angled 6·5 degrees off centre line of ship, the biggest angle that can be contrived in an aircraft carrier of the size. Strengthened to take Harrier aircraft.

ENGINEERING. Remote control for engines, coupled with automatic feed for boilers, whereby with entire complement of officers and men under cover and protected in "the citadel", a self-contained section proof against radio-active fall-out, the ship can be steamed through an atomic cloud.

ELECTRICAL. The plant is 440 volt, 3 phase, 60 cycle AC with a generating capacity of 5 440 kW.

DRAWING. Port elevation and plan. Scale: 128 feet = 1 inch.

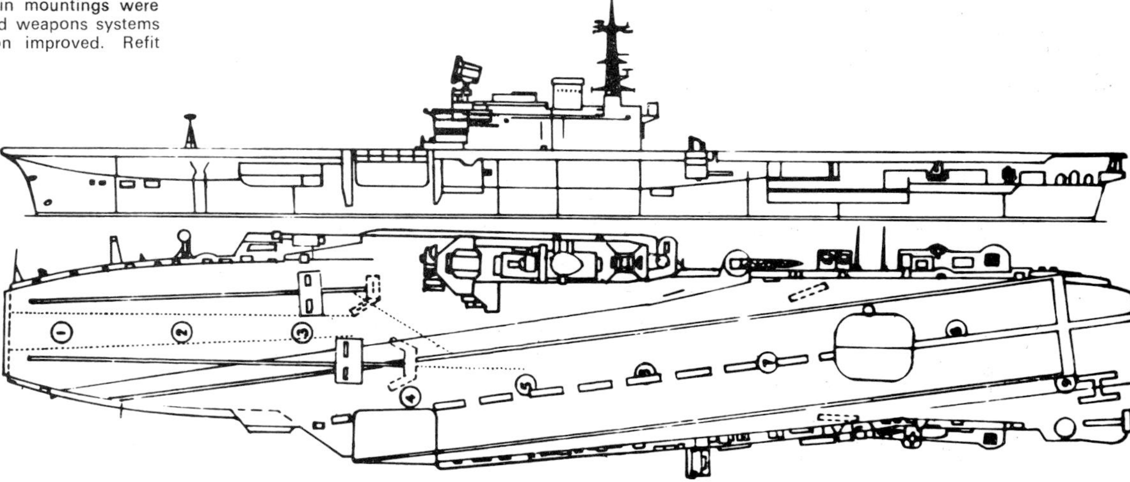

HERMES 1969, *Official*

HERMES 1967, *Official*

Aircraft Carriers—*continued*

Name	*Deck Letter*	*No.*	*Builders*	*Laid down*	*Launched*	*Completed*
ARK ROYAL (ex-*Irresistible*)	R	R 09	Cammell Laird, Birkenhead	3 May 1943	3 May 1950	25 Feb 1955

Displacement, tons	43 000 standard; 50 786 full load
Length, feet (*metres*)	720 (*219·5*) pp; 845·0 (*257·6*) oa, revised official figures
Beam, feet (*metres*)	112·8 (*34·4*) hull
Draught, feet (*metres*)	36 (*11·0*)
Width, feet (*metres*)	166·0 (*50·6*) official figures
Catapults	2 improved steam
Aircraft	30 fixed wing + 6 helicopters
Missile launchers	4 quadruple "Seacat" surface-to-air systems
Armour	4·5in belt; 4·5in flight deck; 2·5in hangar deck; 1·5in hangar side
Boilers	8 Admiralty 3 drum; pressure 400 psi (*28·1 kg/cm²*); superheat 600°F (316°C)
Main engines	Parsons single reduction geared turbines; 152 000 shp; 4 shafts
Speed, knots	31·5 designed maximum
Oil fuel (tons)	5 500 capacity
Complement	260 officers (as Flagship) 2 380 ratings (with Air Staff)

Ship has 5·5 degrees angled deck, two centre line lifts, more effective deck landing aid, new type arrester gear, and improved hangar ventilation. First British aircraft carrier with steam catapults. Had first side lift in a British aircraft carrier, situated amidships on the port side and serving the upper hangar but in 1959 this was removed, the deck park provided by the angled deck having obviated its necessity, and a lattice stump mast for larger radar scanner stepped abaft the bridge. In 1961, the deck landing projector sight, "Hilo" long range guidance system, and more powerful steam catapults were installed. Ship originally cost £21 428 000. A three-years "special refit" and modernisation costing £30 000 000, commenced in Mar 1967 for recommissioning in July 1970. Island superstructure similar to that of *Eagle*. New steam catapults fitted which project 20 feet over bows and angled deck.

ARK ROYAL *Added 1969, Official*

GUNNERY. Originally mounted 16—4·5 inch guns in eight twin turrets, two on each beam forward and two on each beam aft, but the four on port side forward, were removed in 1956, the four on starboard side forward in 1959, four in two forward turrets on after sponsons in 1964 and the four aft in 1969.

DRAWING. Port elevation and plan. Drawn in 1965 before present refit. Scale: 128 feet = 1 inch.

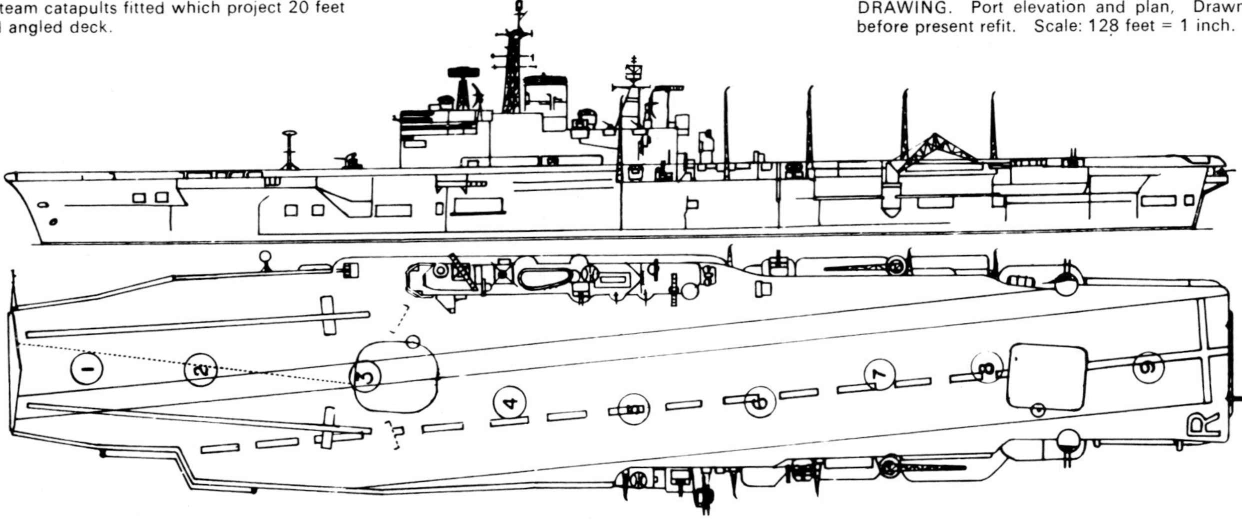

ARK ROYAL *1967, Official*

ARK ROYAL ***Added 1968, Official***

Aircraft Carriers—*continued*

Name	*Deck Letter*	*No.*	*Builders*	*Laid down*	*Launched*	*Completed*	*Reconstructed*
EAGLE (ex-*Audacious*)	E	R 05	Harland & Wolff, Belfast	24 Oct 1942	19 Mar 1946	1 Oct 1951	HM Dockyard Devonport, 1959-64

Displacement, tons	43 000 standard; 50 536 full load
Length, feet (*metres*)	720 (*219·5*) pp; 811·8 (*247·4*) oa
Beam, feet (*metres*)	112·8 (34·4) hull
Draught, feet (*metres*)	36 (*11·0*)
Width, feet (*metres*)	171 (*52·1*) overall
Catapults	2 steam (see *Reconstruction* note)
Aircraft	34 plus 10 helicopters
Missiles, AA	6 quadruple launchers for "Seacat" (3 starboard, 2 port, 1 aft)
Guns, dual purpose	8—4·5 in (*115 mm*), (2 twin starboard, 2 twin port)
Armour	4·5 in belt; 4 in flight deck; 2·5 in hangar deck; 1·5 in hangar side
Boilers	8 Admiralty 3-drum
Main engines	Parsons s.r. geared turbines 152 000 shp; 4 shafts
Speed, knots	31·5
Complement	1 745 including ship's air staff; 2 750 max with air squadrons

Ordered on 19 May 1942. Accepted into the Royal Navy on 1 Mar 1952. Of 90 per cent welded construction. Damage control arrangements are exceptionally complete. Originally cost £15 795 000. Modernisation cost £31 000 000.

RECONSTRUCTION. Fully angled flight deck at 8·5 degrees, new flight deck armour, and Type 984 radar. Two steam (instead of hydraulic) catapults for launching the latest naval aircraft. Superstructure half as long again as former island, and lattice mast shorter and thicker than previously stepped. The most up-to-date living accommodation was also incorporated. Reconstruction commenced at the end of 1959, and was completed in 1964. Commissioned on 14 May 1964.

REFIT. During the refit at HM Dockyard, Devonport, from Sep 1966 to Apr 1967, more powerful catapults and arrester gear were installed to receive the new Phantom aircraft. Recommissioned 6 Apr 1967.

ANTI-CONTAMINATION. Equipped with an improved and built-in pre-wetting system to counteract contamination in the event of fallout or chemical hazard.

ELECTRICAL. During reconstruction the generating capacity of the ship was increased to 8 250 kW.

CLASS. Sister ship of *Ark Royal*, see previous page. Two more large aircraft carriers of this type, *Africa* and original *Eagle* were cancelled at the end of the Second World War. Three much larger aircraft carriers, to have been named *Gibraltar*, *Malta* and *New Zealand*, were also cancelled.

PHOTOGRAPHS. A port bow oblique aerial view and an overhead plan view appear in the 1964-65 to 1966-67 editions, and a starboard broadside surface view in the 1966-67 edition.

DRAWING. Port elevation and plan after reconstruction. Drawn in 1964. Scale: 128 feet = 1 inch.

EAGLE with *Phantom* touching down — 1969, *Official*

EAGLE — *1969, Official*

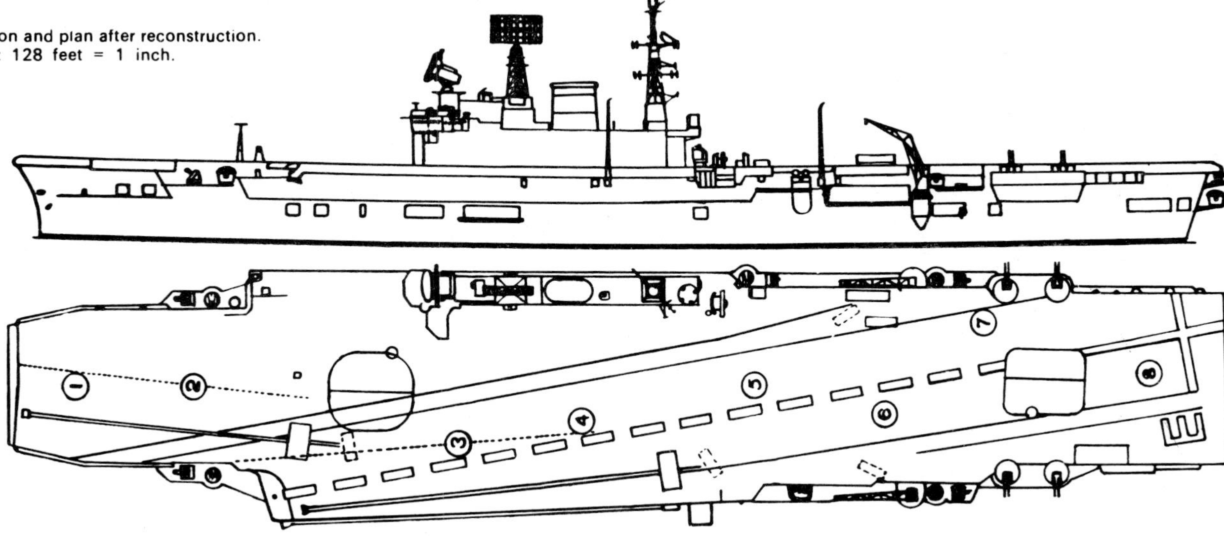

EAGLE with *Phantom* landing on — *1969, Official*

Aircraft Carriers—*continued*

Name	*Deck Letter*	*No.*	*Builders*	*Laid down*	*Launched*	*Completed*
CENTAUR	C	R 06	Harland & Wolff, Belfast	30 May 1944	22 Apr 1947	1 Sep 1953

Displacement, tons	23 670 standard; 27 000 full load
Length, feet (*metres*)	650 (*198·1*) pp; 685 (*208·8*); 737·8 (*224·9*) oa
Beam, feet (*metres*)	90 (*27·4*) hull
Draught, feet (*metres*)	27 (*8·2*)
Width, feet (*metres*)	123 (*37·5*) overall
Catapults	2 steam
Aircraft	18 plus 8 helicopters
Guns, AA	10—40 mm, 4 twin, 2 single
Boilers	4 Admiralty 3-drum
Main engines	Parsons geared turbines 78 000 shp; 2 shafts
Speed, knots	28 (29·5 on trials)
Oil fuel (tons)	4 200 (plus 1 000 avgas)
Complement	1 028 including ship's air staff 1 330 to 1 390 with air squadrons

Improvements incorporated during construction increased the originally designed displacement from 18 300 tons standard. Cost £10 434 000 excluding guns, aircraft and equipment. An "interim" (5·5 degrees) angled deck was installed which necessitated the removal of three twin 40 mm mounts and the extension of the flight deck on the port side amidships. Five arrester wires spaced equally along the angled deck. Equipped with steam catapults and new arrester gear in 1957. Two propellers 15·5 ft (4·7 m) diameter, 235 rpm. Completed an extensive refit in Mar 1961, a small sponson being fitted on the port side right aft. Refitted in 1963 with Type 965 single "bedstead" aerial on a small lattice tower in place of the light tripod mast at the forward end of the island. The 6-barrelled 40 mm AA gun abaft the island, a twin 40 mm mounting and two single 40 mm guns were removed. *Centaur* has latterly been used as an accommodation ship for aircraft carriers refitting.

DRAWING. Port elevation and plan. Drawn in 1967. Scale: 128 feet = 1 inch.

CLASS. Of two sister ships, *Bulwark* was converted into a commando carrier in 1959-60, and *Albion* was similarly converted in 1961-62, see later page. Of the other five ships of this class originally ordered, *Arrogant*, original *Hermes*, *Monmouth* and *Polyphemus* were cancelled in 1945; and *Hermes* (ex-*Elephant*) was completed to a modified design (see previous page).

VICTORIOUS
The aircraft carrier *Victorious* was decommissioned on 13 Mar 1968 and was still laid up in 1969.

"MAJESTIC" CLASS
Magnificent (lent to Canada from 1946 to 1957) was scrapped in 1965. *Powerful* (renamed *Bonaventure*) was completed for Canada; *Majestic* (renamed *Melbourne*) was completed for Australia; and *Terrible* (renamed *Sydney*) was sold to Australia. *Hercules* was sold to India in 1957 for completion and modernisation and commissioned and renamed *Vikrant* in Mar 1961. *Leviathan* (suspended in 1946 and never completed) was towed away from Portsmouth on 23 May 1968 and arrived in the Firth of Clyde on 27 May to be broken up at Faslane.

"COLOSSUS" CLASS
Venerable (renamed *Karel Doorman*) was sold to Netherlands in 1948 and was sold to Argentina in 1968 and renamed *25 de Mayo*; *Colossus* (renamed *Arromanches*) was sold to France in 1951; two were completed as maintenance aircraft carriers—*Perseus* (scrapped in 1958) and *Pioneer* (scrapped in 1954). *Vengeance* was sold to Brazil in 1956 and after being modernised was commissioned under new name *Minas Gerais* in Dec 1960. *Warrior* was sold to Argentine in July 1958 and was commissioned under new name *Independencia* in Jan 1959. *Glory* was scrapped in 1961 and *Ocean* and *Theseus* in 1962. *Triumph* was converted into a heavy repair ship, see later page.

CENTAUR *Added 1968, Official*

CENTAUR *Added 1969, Official*

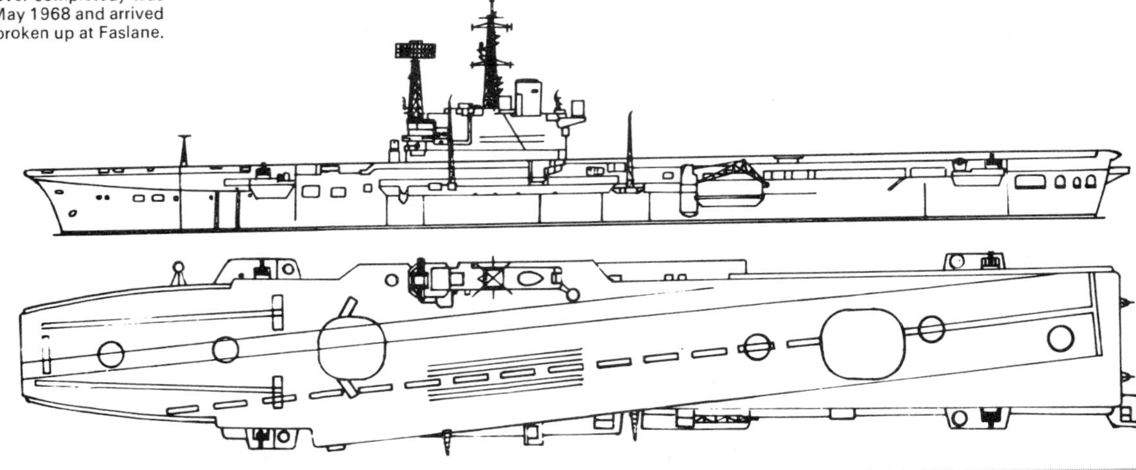

CENTAUR ***Added 1968, courtesy Dr. Giorgio Arra***

COMMANDO CARRIERS

Name	Deck Letter	No.	Builders	Laid down	Launched	Completed	Converted
ALBION	A	R 07	Swan, Hunter & Wigham Richardsom	23 Mar 1944	6 May 1947	26 May 1954	1961-62
BULWARK	B	R 08	Harland & Wolff Ltd, Belfast	10 May 1945	22 June 1948	4 Nov 1954	1959-60

2 MODIFIED "CENTAUR" CLASS

Displacement, tons	23 300 standard; 27 300 full load
Length, feet (*metres*)	650 (*198·1*) pp; 737·8 (*224·9*) oa
Beam, feet (*metres*)	90 (*27·4*) hull
Draught, feet (*metres*)	28 (*8·5*)
Width, feet (*metres*)	123·5 (*37·7*) overall
Aircraft	16 helicopters
Landing craft	4 LCVP
Guns, AA	8—40 mm; 4 twin
Boilers	4 Admiralty 3 drum
Main engines	Parsons geared turbines 76 000 shp; 2 shafts
Speed, knots	28
Oil fuel, tons	3 880 furnace; 320 diesel
Complement	1 035 plus 733 Royal Marine Commando and troops (900 in *Bulwark*); Accommodation for 1 923 to 1 937 officers and men

ALBION *1969, Official*

ALBION *1969, John G. Callis*

Former sister ships of *Centaur*, see previous page. Originally cost £9 836 000 and £10 386 000, respectively, excluding guns, aircraft and equipment. Converted into commando carriers at Portsmouth Dockyard, Feb 1961 to 1 Aug 1962 (*Albion*) and 1959 to 19 Jan 1960 (*Bulwark*). A full strength commando is available, which the ships can quickly transport and land with equipment. Their helicopters are also able to disembark the commando's vehicles. The ships have sufficient stores and fuel to support the commandos in operations ashore, and can re-embark the unit speedily. They not only reinforce the traditionally close association of the Corps of Royal Marines with the Royal Navy, but give these versatile troops greater mobility and usefulness, and enable them to be fully self-supporting. The ships are fully convertible to the anti-submarine role. They are able, at short notice, and entirely within their own resources to adapt their helicopters for anti-submarine work. *Bulwark* was the first ship of her kind in the Royal Navy.

GUNNERY. Eight 40 mm AA guns were removed during the initial conversion of *Bulwark* to provide space for four vehicle personnel landing craft carried at built-in gantries, leaving her with 18—40 mm AA. guns. As converted *Albion* has one twin 40 mm mounting in each quadrant; and *Bulwark* has since also been reduced to this armament.

ENGINEERING. The three-bladed propeller in *Bulwark* was replaced by a four-bladed propeller. At 28 knots the propellers work at 230 revolutions per minute. *Albion* was engined by Walsend Slipway & Engineering Co Ltd, Tyne, and *Bulwark* by her builders.

CONVERSION. Basically *Bulwark* was not changed during her initial conversion, although the fixed wing capability, arrester wires and catapults were removed. Alterations and modifications were made to render the ship suitable as an all-helicopter troop carrier with 16 Westland Whirlwind aircraft, replaced at a later date by the Wessex, and four landing craft (vehicle or personnel). The ship was fitted with the most extensive air conditioning system in the Royal Navy. In 1963 *Bulwark* was further refitted to the same standard as *Albion*, with slight variation in air conditioning. In her initial conversion *Albion* embodied a number of improvements and was able to carry Wessex helicopters and a larger military force. Her extensive modifications included alteration to the angled flight deck and the removal of catapult and arrester gear.

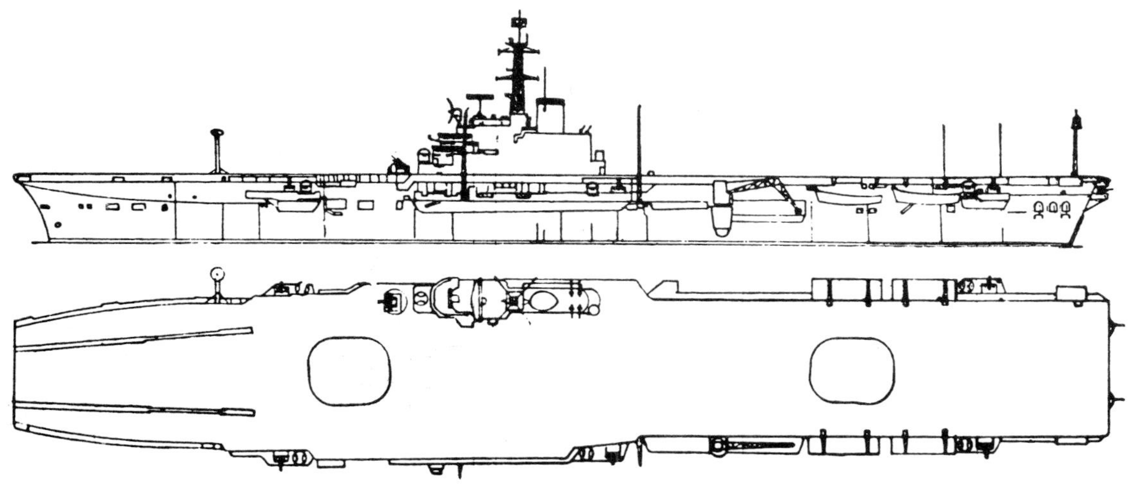

PHOTOGRAPHS. A port broadside aerial veiw of *Bulwark* with Whirlwind helicopters flying above appears in the 1961-62 to 1963-64 editions, a starboard broadside aerial view with helicopter formation in the 1962-63 and 1963-64 editions, a port broadside view of *Albion* in the 1962-63 edition (Addenda), a starboard quarter surface view in the 1962-63 and 1963-64 editions, a port broadside surface view of *Bulwark* in the 1964-65 and 1965-66 editions and a starboard quarter oblique aerial view in the 1966-67 to 1968-69 editions; and a port bow oblique overhead view of *Albion* showing helicopters ranged on deck in the 1964-65 to 1966-67 editions and a port bow oblique aerial view with helicopters overhead in the 1967-68 and 1968-69 editions.

DRAWING. Port elevation and plan of *Bulwark*. Scale: 128 feet = 1 inch.

BULWARK ***1969 Official***

SUBMARINES

Name	No.	Builders	Laid down	Launched	Accepted
RENOWN	S 26	Cammell Laird & Co Ltd, Birkenhead	25 June 1964	25 Feb 1967	Feb 1969
REPULSE	S 23	Vickers-Armstrongs Ltd, Barrow-in-Furness	12 Mar 1965	4 Nov 1967	Oct 1968
RESOLUTION	S 22	Vickers-Armstrongs Ltd, Barrow-in-Furness	26 Feb 1964	15 Sep 1966	Oct 1967
REVENGE	S 27	Cammell Laird & Co Ltd, Birkenhead	19 May 1965	15 Mar 1968	

Nuclear Powered Ballistic Missile Submarines (SSBN)

4 "RESOLUTION" CLASS

Displacement, tons	7 500 surface; 8 400 submerged
Length, feet (*metres*)	360 (*109·7*) pp; 425 (*129·5*) oa
Beam, feet (*metres*)	33 (*10·1*)
Draught, feet (*metres*)	30 (*9·1*)
Missiles, surface	16 tubes amidships for "Polaris" A—3 ICBM's, range 2 500 nautical miles
Torpedo tubes	6—21 in (*533 mm*) forward
Nuclear reactors	1 pressurised water cooled
Main engines	Geared steam turbines; 1 shaft
Speed, knots	20 on surface; 25 submerged
Complement	141 (13 officers, 128 ratings); 2 crews (see *Personnel*)

In Feb 1963 it was officially stated that it was intended to order four or five 7 000 ton nuclear powered submarines, each to carry 16 "Polaris" missiles, and it was planned that the first would be on patrol in 1968. Their hulls and machinery would be of British design. As well as building two submarines Vickers-Armstrongs would give lead yard service (ie act as the "parent" firm) to the builders of the other two. Four "Polaris" submarines were in fact ordered on 8 May 1963 (date of official announcement). The intention to build a fifth Polaris submarine was confirmed by the then Ministry of Defence on 26 Feb 1964, but this intention was rescinded by a new Ministry of Defence on 15 Feb 1965. Britain's first "Polaris" armed submarine, *Resolution*, put to sea on 22 June 1967 and completed 6 weeks trial in the Firth of Clyde and Atlantic on 17 Aug 1967.

DESIGN. These submarines, the largest ever built for the Royal Navy differ in several respects from United States "Polaris" submarines, notably in having six torpedoe tubes instead of four and modified habitability.

PERSONNEL. Each submarine, which has accommodation for 19 officers and 135 ratings is manned on a two-crew basis, in order to get maximum operational time at sea on the pattern of the system in the United States "Polaris" submarines in which two complete crews relieve each other approximately every three months.

COST. Originally officially estimated to cost (contract value) £15 000 000 each (shipbuilders' statement); £40 240 000, *Resolution*, £39 950 000, *Renown* £37 500 00, *Repulse*, completed ships (Navy Estimates) excluding missiles; £52 000 000, *Resolution*, £55 000 000, *Renown*, including weapon system; and £70 000 000 each total with initial design, projection and development. The full Polaris programme including all shore and support facilities cost £350 000 000 (official statement).

RESOLUTION (operational) *1968, Official*

REVENGE *1969, Official*

REPULSE *1969, Official*

RENOWN *1969, Official*

Submarines—*continued*

Name	*No.*	*Builder*	*Ordered*	*Laid down*	*Launched*	*Completed (Commissioned)*
CHURCHILL	S 104	Vickers Ltd Shipbuilding Group, Barrow	21 Oct 1965	30 June 1967		
CONQUEROR	S 105	Cammell Laird & Co Ltd, Birkenhead	9 Aug 1966	5 Dec 1967		
VALIANT	S 102	Vickers Ltd Shipbuilding Group, Barrow	31 Aug 1960	22 Jan 1962	3 Dec 1963	18 July 1966
WARSPITE	S 103	Vickers Ltd Shipbuilding Group, Barrow	12 Dec 1962	10 Dec 1963	25 Sep 1965	18 Apr 1967
	S 106	Vickers Ltd Shipbuilding Group, Barrow				
	S 107	Vickers Ltd Shipbuilding Group, Barrow				
	S 108					

VALIANT *1968, Official*

Nuclear Powered Fleet Submarines (SSN)

5 "VALIANT" CLASS
+ 2 "IMPROVED"

Displacement, tons	3 500 standard; 4 500 submerged
Length, feet (*metres*)	285 (*86·9*)
Beam, feet (*metres*)	33·2 (*10·1*)
Draught, feet (*metres*)	27 (*8·2*)
Torpedo tubes	6—21 in (*533 mm*) homing
Nuclear reactors	1 pressurised water-cooled, British prototype
Main engines	EE Geared steam turbines; 1 shaft
Speed, knots	30 approx
Complement	103 (13 officers, 90 men)

It was announced on 31 Aug 1960 that the contract for a second nuclear powered submarine (*Valiant*) had been awarded to Vickers-Armstrongs (Shipbuilders Ltd), the principal sub-contractors being Vickers-Armstrongs (Engineers) Ltd, for the machinery and its installation, and Rolls Royce and Associates for the nuclear steam raising plant. Her hull is broadly of the same design as that of *Dreadnaught*, but she is slightly larger. She was originally scheduled to be completed in Sep 1965, but work was held up by the "Polaris" programme. The Intention to order the third nuclear powered submarine (*Warspite*) from Vickers-Armstrongs Ltd was announced by the Ministry of Defence on 10 Aug 1962, the intention to order the fourth (*Churchill*) on 13 Mar 1965, a fifth (*Conqueror*) on 4 Mar 1966, and a sixth (*Superb*) on 9 Nov 1966. The proposed order for a seventh nuclear powered fleet submarine, of "Improved" type, was published in the Statement on the 1967-68 Defence Estimates and for the eighth in 1968.

ENDURANCE. On 25 Apr 1967 *Valiant* completed the 12,000-mile homeward voyage from Singapore, the record submerged passage by a British submarine, after 28 days non-stop.

ANTI-SUBMARINE WARFARE. *Valiant* and her sister ships are equipped to hunt and kill enemy submarines and surface warships, with sonar gear to detect at much greater ranges than that fitted in British Conventional submarines.

ENGINEERING. *Valiant's* reactor core was made in Great Britain, with machinery of British design and manufacture similar to the shore prototype installed in the Admiralty Reactor Test Establishment at Dounreay. The main steam turbines and condensers were designed and manufactured by the English Electric Company, Rugby, and the electrical propulsion machinery and control gear by Laurence, Scott & Electromotors Ltd.

NOMENCLATURE. All the names given to British nuclear powered submarines (except *Churchill*, named after the late Sir Winston Churchill, First Lord of the Admiralty during the early part of both World Wars, famous wartime leader, and greatest Prime Minister) are former battleship names of the first and second world wars. The name originally chosen for the second nuclear submarine (*Valiant*) was *Inflexible*.

CHURCHILL (launch) *Dec 1968, Official*

WARSPITE with *Wessex*
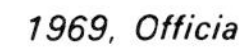
1969, Official

WARSPITE *1969, Official*

Submarines—*continued*

Name	*No.*	*Builders*	*Engineers*	*Laid down*	*Launched*	*Commissioned*
DREADNOUGHT	S 101	Vickers-Armstrongs, Barrow	Rolls-Royce and Westinghouse	12 June 1959	21 Oct 1960	17 April, 1963

1 PROTOTYPE NUCLEAR POWERED

Displacement, tons	3 000 standard; 3 500 surface; 4 000 submerged
Length, feet (*metres*)	265·8 (*81·0*)
Beam, feet (*metres*)	32·2 (*9·8*)
Draught, feet (*metres*)	26 (*7·9*)
Torpedo tubes	6—21 in (*533 mm*) bow, all internal
Nuclear reactor	1 S5W pressurised water-cooled
Main engines	Geared steam turbines; 1 shaft
Speed, knots	30 approx
Complement	88 (11 officers, 77 men)

DREADNOUGHT *1967, Official*

The Royal Navy's first nuclear powered submarine, specially designed to hunt and destroy enemy underwater craft. A prominent feature of her design is her whale-shaped hull, the near-perfect streamlining giving maximum underwater efficiency, while the fin-like conning tower is also aimed at reducing "drag" to a minimum. She is capable of continuous high underwater speed and has long endurance. Her hull is British built, but her nuclear plant was manufactured in the United States. It was announced by the Navy on 10 Aug 1959 that the General Dynamics Corporation, USA had been awarded a contract for help in her construction. *Cost:* £18,455,000.

OFFICIAL STATEMENT. As originally planned *Dreadnought* was to have been fitted with a British designed and built nuclear reactor, but in 1958 an agreement was concluded with the United States Government for the purchase of a complete set of propulsion machinery of the type fitted in USS *Skipjack*. This agreement enabled the submarine to be launched far earlier. The supply of this machinery was made under a contract between the Westinghouse Electric Corporation and Rolls-Royce. The latter were also supplied with design and manufacturing details of the reactor and with safety information and set up a factory in this country to manufacture similar cores. *Dreadnought* has a hull of British design both as regards structural strength and hydrodynamic features, although the latter are based on the pioneering work of the US Navy in *Skipjack* and *Albacore*. From about amidships aft, the hull lines closely resemble *Skipjack* to accommodate the propulsion machinery. The forward end is wholly British in concept. In the Control Room and Attack Centre the instruments are fitted into consoles. Almost every electrical and mechanical part of the propulsion machinery is installed in duplicate to minimise the inconvenience of breakdowns. In addition, every control feature of the power plant and of the boat is duplicated. These innovations ensure an extremely high standard of reliability which, combined with the need to refuel at only very long intervals, give her the ability to undertake patrols of particularly long endurance at continued high underwater speeds.
Accommodation for her crew is of a standard impossible to attain in any previous submarine. The improved water distilling plant for the first time provides unlimited fresh water for shower baths and for washing machines in the fully equipped laundry. Separate mess spaces are provided for senior and junior ratings, arranged on either side of a large galley, equipped for serving meals on the cafeteria system. Particular attention was paid to the decoration and furnishing of living quarters and to recreational facilities which include cinema equipment, an extensive library and tape recordings, features which help to offset the monotony associated with prolonged underwater voyages.
She is fitted with an inertial navigation system and with means of measuring her depth below ice.

ROLE. Her primary role is as a submarine hunter killer for which purpose she is equipped with the latest developments in underwater weapons and detection.

MANOEUVRABILITY. This submarine manoeuvres and travels underwater with movements similar to those of an aircraft banking in flight, as she has similar controls.

ENGINEERING. A complete nuclear reactor for installation in *Dreadnought* was purchased in the USA. The General Dynamics Corporation Provided design, material and technical assistance in the installation of the propulsion system. The propulsion plant itself was placed under contract to Westinghouse Electric Corporation by Rolls-Royce acting as agents for the Royal Navy.

REFUELLING and REFIT. On 30 Jan 1969 the Royal Navy announced at Rosyth Dockyard that the first refuelling of a nuclear powered submarine had been completed on schedule in HMS *Dreadnought*.
It is officially stated that her refit will be completed in 1970.

DREADNOUGHT *courtesy Godfrey H. Walker, Esq.*

VALIANT (see previous page) *1969, Wright & Llogan*

Patrol Submarines

13 "OBERON" CLASS

Displacement, tons	1 610 standard; 2 030 surface; 2 410 submerged
Length, feet (*metres*)	241 (*73·5*) pp; 295·2 (*90·0*) oa
Beam, feet (*metres*)	26·5 (*8·1*)
Draught, feet (*metres*)	18 (*5·5*)
Torpedo tubes	8—21 in (*533 mm*) for homing torpedoes
Main engines	2 ASR 1, 16 VMS diesels; 3 680 bhp; 2 electric motors; 6 000 shp; 2 shafts; electric drive
Speed, knots	12 surface, 17 submerged
Complement	68 (6 officers, 62 men)

Name	*No.*	*Builders*	*Laid down*	*Launched*	*Completed*
OBERON	S 09	H.M. Dockyard, Chatham	28 Nov 1957	18 July 1959	24 Feb 1961
OCELOT	S 17	H.M. Dockyard, Chatham	17 Nov 1960	5 May 1962	31 Jan 1964
ODIN	S 10	Cammell Laird & Co Ltd, Birkenhead	27 Apr 1959	4 Nov 1960	3 May 1962
OLYMPUS	S 12	Vickers-Armstrongs Ltd, Barrow	4 Mar 1960	14 June 1961	7 July 1962
ONSLAUGHT	S 14	H.M. Dockyard, Chatham	8 Apr 1959	24 Sep 1960	14 Aug 1962
ONYX *	S 21	Cammell Laird & Co Ltd, Birkenhead	16 Nov 1964	18 Aug 1966	20 Nov 1967
OPOSSUM	S 19	Cammell Laird & Co Ltd, Birkenhead	21 Dec 1961	23 May 1963	5 June 1964
OPPORTUNE	S 20	Scotts' S.B. & Eng Co Ltd, Greenock	26 Oct 1962	14 Feb 1964	29 Dec 1964
ORACLE	S 16	Cammell Laird & Co Ltd, Birkenhead	26 Apr 1960	26 Sep 1961	14 Feb 1963
ORPHEUS	S 11	Vickers-Armstrongs Ltd, Barrow	16 Apr 1959	17 Nov 1959	25 Nov 1960
OSIRIS	S 13	Vickers-Armstrongs Ltd, Barrow	26 Jan 1962	29 Nov 1962	11 Jan 1964
OTTER	S 15	Scotts' S.B. & Eng Co Ltd, Greenock	14 Jan 1960	15 May 1961	20 Aug 1962
OTUS	S 18	Scotts' S.B. & Eng Co Ltd, Greenock	31 May 1961	17 Oct 1962	5 Oct 1963

This class have improved detection equipment and are capable of high underwater speeds. They are able to maintain continuous submerged patrols in any part of the world and are equipped to fire homing torpedoes.

CONSTRUCTION. For the first time in British submarines plastic was used in the superstructure construction. Before and abaft the bridge the superstructure is mainly of glass fibre laminate in most units of this class. The superstructure of *Orpheus* is of light alloy aluminium.

*The submarine of this class laid down on 27 Sep 1962 at HM Dockyard, Chatham, as *Onyx* for the Royal Navy was launched on 29 Feb 1964 as *Ojibwa* for the Royal Canadian Navy. She was replaced by another "Oberon" class submarine named *Onyx* for the Royal Navy built by Cammell Laird, Birkenhead.

GUNNERY. "O" class submarines serving in the Far East carry a small surface gun.

MODIFICATION. *Oberon* is being modified with deeper casing to house equipment for the initial training of personnel for nuclear powered submarines.

PHOTOGRAPHS. A photograph of *Orpheus* appears in the 1961-62 and 1962-63 editions, of *Otter* in the 1963-64 to 1966-67 editions, of *Opportune* in the 1965-66 and 1966-67 editions, of *Onslaught* in the 1967-68 editions, and of *Ocelot, Oracle, Osiris* and *Otus* in the 1967-68 and 1968-69 editions.

DISPOSALS OF "S" CLASS
Sidon, which sank after a torpedo explosion forward in Portland Harbour on 16 June 1955, but was salved a week later, was towed out of Portland Harbour and sunk off Portland on 14 June 1957 in 20 to 25 fathoms to be used by the Navy as a target on the sea bottom. *Selene* was discarded in 1957 and subsequently scrapped. *Sleuth* and *Sturdy* were scrapped in 1958, *Subtle* in 1959, *Seneschal* and *Scythian* in 1960, *Solent* in 1961, *Satyr, Scorcher* and *Sentinel* in 1962, *Spiteful* and *Statesman* in 1963, and *Scotsman* in 1964. *Sea Devil*, the last operational submarine of this class at sea, was scrapped in 1965, *Seascout* for disposal in mid-Aug 1962, and *Serpah* in 1963 were towed to the shipbreakers in Dec 1965. *Sirdar*, expended in experiments by the Naval Construction Research Establishment at Rosyth, was sold for scrap in 1965.

TRANSFERS OF "S" CLASS. *Saga, Spearhead* and *Spur* were sold to the Portuguese Navy in 1948 and renamed *Nautilo, Neptune* and *Narval*, respectively. *Satyr, Spiteful, Sportsman* (lost 23 Sep 1962 under the French name *Sibylle*) and *Statesman* were transferred to the French Navy, Oct 1951 to July 1952; but *Spiteful* (on loan under the name *Sirene*) was returned to the Royal Navy on 24 Oct 1958 and towed from Portsmouth to be scrapped on 9 July 1963; *Statesman* (on loan under the name *Sultane*) was returned on 5 Nov 1959; and *Satyr* (on loan under the name *Saphir*) was returned in Aug 1961. *Sanguine* and *Springer* were sold to Israel in Oct 1958. *Springer* was handed over to the Israel Navy at Portsmouth on 9 Oct and renamed *Tanin* (Crocodile) and delivered to Israel in Dec 1959. *Sanguine*, renamed *Rahav*, was delivered to Israel in May 1960.

ONYX (latest of class) *1968, Official*

OBERON *1969, Official*

OPOSSUM surfaced in pack ice *Added 1969, Official*

OLYMPUS *1969, Official*

Submarines—*continued*

Patrol Submarines

8 "PORPOISE" CLASS

Name	*No.*	*Builders*	*Laid down*	*Launched*	*Completed*
CACHALOT	S 06	Scotts S.B. & Eng Co Ltd, Greenock	1 Aug 1955	11 Dec 1957	1 Sep 1959
FINWHALE	S 05	Cammell Laird & Co Ltd, Birkenhead	18 Sep 1956	21 July 1959	19 Aug 1960
GRAMPUS	S 04	Cammell Laird & Co Ltd, Birkenhead	16 Apr 1955	30 May 1957	19 Dec 1958
NARWHAL	S 03	Vickers-Armstrongs Ltd, Barrow	15 Mar 1956	25 Oct 1957	4 May 1959
PORPOISE	S 01	Vickers-Armstrongs Ltd, Barrow	15 June 1954	25 Apr 1956	17 Apr 1958
RORQUAL	S 02	Vickers-Armstrongs Ltd, Barrow	15 Jan 1955	5 Dec 1956	24 Oct 1958
SEALION	S 07	Cammell Laird & Co Ltd, Birkenhead	5 June 1958	31 Dec 1959	25 July 1961
WALRUS	S 08	Scotts' S.B. & Eng Co Ltd, Greenock	12 Feb 1958	22 Sep 1959	10 Feb 1961

Displacement, tons	1 605 standard; 2 030 surfece; 2 405 submerged
Length, feet (*metres*)	241 (*73·5*) pp; 295·2 (*90·0*) oa
Beam, feet (*metres*)	26·5 (*8·1*)
Draught, feet (*metres*)	18 (*5·5*)
Torpedo tubes	8—21 in (*533 mm*), 6 bow, 2 stern; 30 torpedoes carried
Main engines	2 ASR-1, 16 VMS diesel-electric sets, total 3 680 bhp; 2 shafts; 2 main batteries; electric drive; 6 000 shp
Speed, knots	12 on surface; 17 submerged
Complement	71 (6 officers, 65 men)

Porpoise was the first operational submarine designed since the Second World War to be accepted into service. Able to undertake continuous submerged patrol in any part of the world. The design of hull and superstructure gives capabilities of high underwater speed and great diving depth. Stress was also laid on long endurance, both on the surface and submerged, whether on batteries or snorting. Propelled on the surface, or when snorting by diesel-electric drive from Admiralty Standard Range diesels, and from large batteries driving the motors when submerged. The snort equipment was designed to give maximum snort-charging facilities and to operate in rough sea conditions. Both air and surface warning radar can be operated at periscope depth as well as when surfaced. The general habitability is of the highest standard, with strip lighting and air conditioning plant which provides drying and either heating or cooling of the air for arctic or tropical service. Oxygen replenishment and carbon dioxide and hydrogen eliminators make it possible to remain totally submerged without even using snort for several days. Apparatus to distil fresh water from sea water for drinking, and stowage for large quantities of stores and provisions enable the boats to remain on patrol for months without outside support.

ENGINEERING. The propelling machinery was made by the builders except in *Cachalot* and *Walrus*, by HM Dockyard, Chatham.

ELECTRICAL. The electric propulsion system in all eight boats was manufactured by The English Electric Co Ltd, Rugby, and was of more advanced design than hitherto.

PHOTOGRAPHS. A photograph of *Sealion* appears in the 1966-67 and 1967-68 editions and of *Finwhale*, *Narwhal* and *Porpoise* in the 1967-68 and 1968-69 editions.

DISPOSALS OF "EX" CLASS
Of the two experimental fast submarines with propelling machinery employing high test peroxide, the first submarines of post-war design to be built for the Royal Navy. *Explorer*, S 30, was discraded in 1963 and scrapped at Barrow in Feb 1965, and *Excalibur*, S 40, was listed for disposal by scrapping in 1965.

DISPOSALS OF MIDGET CLASS
The three "Midget" Type (X-craft), namely *Minnow* (X-54), *Shrimp* (X-52) and *Sprat* (X-53), were placed on the disposal list in 1961. Sister boat *Stickleback* (X-51) was sold to Sweden on 15 July 1958 and renamed *Spiggen* (Swedish equivalent of "*Stickleback*").

GRAMPUS *1968, John G. Callis*

RORQUAL *1969, Official*

WALRUS *1969, Official*

CACHALOT *1969, courtesy Mr. John R. Mortimer*

Submarines—*continued*

Patrol Submarines

10 "A" CLASS

Displacement, tons,	1 120 standard; 1 385 surfece; 1 620 submerged
Length, feet (*metres*)	221 (*67·4*) pp; 283 (*86·3*) oa
Beam, feet (*metres*)	22·2 (*6·8*)
Draught, feet (*metres*)	17 (*5·2*)
Guns	Removed (see *Gunnery* notes)
Torpedo tubes	6—21 (*533 mm*) internal, 4 bow, 2 stern; 16 torpedoes carried External tubes removed (see notes)
Main engines	8-cyl. diesel, 4 300 bhp Electric motors, 1 250 hp
Speed, knots	19 on surface, 8 submerged
Oil fuel (tons)	159
Complement	60 to 68 (5 officers, 63 men)

Name	No.	Builders	Laid down	Launched	Completed
ACHERON	S 61	H.M. Dockyard, Chatham	26 Aug 1944	25 Mar 1947	17 Apr 1948
AENEAS	S 72	Cammell Laird & Co Ltd, Birkenhead	10 Oct 1944	25 Oct 1945	31 July 1946
ALARIC	S 41	Cammell Laird & Co Ltd, Birkenhead	31 May 1944	18 Feb 1946	11 Dec 1946
ALCIDE	S 65	Vickers-Armstrongs Ltd, Barrow	2 Jan 1945	12 Apr 1945	18 Oct 1946
ALLIANCE	S 67	Vickers-Armstrongs Ltd, Barrow	13 Mar 1945	28 July 1945	14 May 1947
AMBUSH	S 68	Vickers-Armstrongs Ltd, Barrow	17 May 1945	24 Sep 1945	22 July 1947
ANDREW	S 63	Vickers-Armstrongs Ltd, Barrow	13 Aug 1945	6 Apr 1946	16 Mar 1948
ARTEMIS	S 49	Scotts' S.B. & Eng Co Ltd, Greenock	28 Feb 1944	26 Aug 1946	15 Aug 1947
ASTUTE	S 47	Vickers-Armstrongs Ltd, Barrow	4 Apr 1944	30 Jan 1945	30 June 1945
AURIGA	S 69	Vickers-Armstrongs Ltd, Barrow	7 June 1944	29 Mar 1945	12 Jan 1946

These submarines were originally designed for service in the Pacific, and had a different hull from the "T" class. Construction was entirely welded. All have "Snort" breathing equipment. *Alliance* and *Ambush*, so fitted, remained submerged for record periods in 1947-48. On 15 June 1953, *Andrew* completed a 2 500 sea miles underwater voyage from Bermuda to the English Channel in 15 days, a record for "snorting" in the Royal Navy.

GUNNERY. Some boats of this class had the 4-inch guns removed before reconstruction. Others mounted the 4-inch gun temporarily after reconstruction. Some are fitted with a mounting for a gun. *Aeneas* had a 4-inch gun mounted in Feb 1960 and again carried a gun before the conning tower in 1966. *Artemis* mounted a 4-inch gun in 1960, after reconstruction. *Andrew* and *Auriga* carried a gun while in the Far East.

CONVERSION. The "A" class were rebuilt and streamlined with an enclosed fin conning tower 26·5 feet high. *Artful* was the first to undergo reconstruction in 1955 followed by the remainder of this class.

TORPEDO TUBES. Originally mounted 10—21 inch (4 external) as designed, and carried 20 torpedoes. External tubes (two bow and two stern) were removed.

PHOTOGRAPHS. A photograph of *Acheron* (before reconstruction) appears in the 1958-59 edition, of *Artemis* (after reconstruction) with gun in the 1960-61 and 1961-62 editions, of *Alaric* (before reconstruction) in the 1958-59 to 1961-62 editions, of *Auriga* without gun in the 1960-61 to 1962-63 editions, of *Artemis* without gun in the 1962-63 to 1968-69 editions, of *Acheron* and *Aeneas* without gun in the 1964-65 to 1966-67 editions, and of *Aeneas, Alaric* and *Astute* in the 1967-68 and 1968-69 editions.

CLASS. The following 30 units were cancelled, though some had actually been launched. *Abalard, Acasta, Ace, Achates, Adept, Admirable, Adversary, Agate, Aggressor, Agile, Aladdin, Alcestis, Andromache, Answer, Antaeus, Antagonist, Anzac, Aphrodite, Approach, Arcadian, Argent, Argosy, Asgard, Asperity, Assurance, Astarte, Atlantis, Austere, Awake, Aztec*. *Affray* was lost in the English Channel on 17 April 1951.

PENNANT NOS. The pennant numbers of most of the "A" Class submarines (and all "O" class submarines) were changed on 1 May 1961.

DISPOSALS
Aurochs, the only one of the class not conv[illegible], was listed for disposal in Sep 1965, towed away from Portsmouth on 9 May 1966, and broken up at Troon in Feb 1967. *Alderney* and *Anchorite* were officially listed in Feb 1968 for disposal by scrapping, and *Amphion* and *Artful* in Feb 1969.

ALCIDE — *1969, Official*

AURIGA with gun — *1969, Official*

ARTEMIS — *1969, A. & J. Pavia*

ANDREW with gun — *1969, Official*

ALLIANCE — *1969, Wright & Logan*

Submarines—*continued*

Patrol Submarines

4 "T" CLASS

Name	No.	Builders	Laid down	Launched	Completed
TABARD*	S 42	Scotts' S.B. & Eng Co, Greenock	6 Sep 1944	21 Nov 1945	25 June 1946
TACITURN	S 34	Vickers-Armstrongs Ltd, Barrow	9 Mar 1943	7 June 1944	7 Oct 1944
TIPTOE	S 32	Vickers-Armstrongs Ltd, Barrow	10 Nov 1942	25 Feb 1944	13 June 1944
TRUMP*	S 33	Vickers-Armstrongs Ltd, Barrow	31 Dec 1942	25 Mar 1944	9 July 1944

Displacement, tons	
Taciturn	1 280 standard; 1 505 surface; 1 700 submerged
Tabard, Tiptoe, and Trump	1 310 standard; 1 535 surface; 1 740 submerged
Length, feet (*metres*)	
Taciturn	287·5 (*87·6*) oa
Tabard, Tiptoe, and Trump	293·5 (*89·5*) oa
Beam, feet (*metres*)	26·5 (*8·1*)
Draught, feet (*metres*)	14·8 (*4·5*)
Guns	Removed. Originally carried. 1—4 in (*102 mm*) (see *Reconstruction*)
Torpedo tubes	6—21 in (*533 mm*), 4 bow, 2 stern 20 homing torpedoes carried (see *Torpedo* notes)
Main engines	Diesels, 2 500 bhp Electric motors, 4 = 2 900 hp
Speed, knots	15·25 on surface; 15 to 18 submerged
Oil fuel (tons)	250
Complement	65 (6 officers, 59 men)

TIPTOE — *1968, Wright & Logan*

Officially described as "Patrol" submarines for general service. Of saddle-tank design, they originally had an endurance equal to a 42-day patrol. All were subsequently fitted with "Snort" equipment. Eight of the surviving boats of this class were converted and rebuilt into the most advanced submarines. From them were developed the "Porpoise" and "Oberon" classes.

RECONSTRUCTION. Rebuilding of the eight boats of the "conversion" type in 1951-56 was drastic. The pressure hull was severed at the engine-room section, the two halves moved apart and a new section built in. The extra space accommodated a second pair of electric motors, clutches between which and the original motors made diesel-electric drive possible, and a fourth battery section was added to give a submerged speed of 15 knots. All guns and external torpedo tubes were removed. Improved periscopes, sonar and radar were installed with a periscopic snort mast. *Tabard* and *Trump* had the bridge built into the fin, which housed two periscopes, two radar masts, two snort masts, and an aerial. In the other six the bridge was reduced to a cramped cab before the fin. Alteration of the five boats of the "modernised" type in 1955-60 was less radical. They were streamlined with the formerly prominent periscope standards and aerials enclosed in a conning tower "fin" or "sail" which also contained the bridge. All guns, external torpedo tubes and obstructions were removed, and the resulting streamlining improved speed without increase in engine power. They were also much more silent under water and could use their improved sonar with enhanced efficiency. For specific operations a gun could be quickly mounted.

There was a considerable difference between the super "T" class "Conversions" which had welded pressure hulls and had an additional section of about 20 feet built into them (*Taciturn* was lengthened by 14 feet) and the "T" class "Streamlines" which were riveted hulled boats and therefore did not undergo the full conversion. Underwater speed of conversion types (after reconstruction, streamlined hull, more motors, greater batteries) is 15 knots and *Taciturn* is reported to have developed more than twice her previous maximum underwater speed.

TORPEDO TUBES. Originally mounted 11—21 inch (3 external) as designed. External tubes removed.

APPEARANCE. The appearance of submarines, with or without guns, etc, is liable to change frequently and quickly according to operational and experimental requirements.

TRANSFERS. *Talent* (renamed (*Zwaardvis*) and *Tarn* (renamed *Tijgerhaai*) were transferred to the Royal Netherlands Navy. Two lent to the Royal Netherlands Navy in June 1948 were returned to the Royal Navy in 1953, *Tapir* (Netherlands name *Zeehond*) on July 16 and *Taurus* (Netherlands name *Dolfijn*) on Dec 8. *Totem* and *Turpin* (converted boats) were transferred to the Israeli Navy in 1965 and renamed *Dakar* (Shark) and *Leviathan* (Whale), respectively. (*Dakar* was lost in the eastern Mediterranean on 25 Jan 1968). *Truncheon* (converted boat) was transferred to the Israeli Navy on 9 Jan 1968 and renamed *Dolphin*.

SECOND WORLD WAR LOSSES: *Talisman, Tempest, Thorn, Thunderbolt* (ex-*Thetis*), *Tigais, Tarpon, Traveller, Trooper, Tetrach, Thistle, Triad, Triton, Triumph, Turbulent, P 311.* Cancelled: *Talent* (1) (*P 343*), *Theban, Thor, Threat, Tiara.*

TRUMP — *1969, courtesy Mr. John R. Mortimer*

TACITURN — *1967, Official*

DISPOSALS
Truculent sank after collision in the Thames Estuary on 12 Jan 1950, was salvaged on 14 Mar, but was scrapped on 5 Apr 1950. *Tantalus, Tantivy* and *Templar* were discarded in 1950. *Tradewind* was scrapped in 1955. *Taurus* and *Thorough* were approved to be scrapped in 1958 when they awaited tow to the shipbreakers or disposal otherwise as targets in 1960. *Telemachus* and *Trespasser* were scrapped in 1961, *Thule* (damaged in collision in 1960) in 1962, *Tactician, Trenchant* and *Tudor* in 1963. *Tally Ho* (latterly harbour training), *Tapir* and *Tireless* ("Streamlines") were for disposal in 1964 (and removed from the list in 1968). *Teredo* ("Streamline") was sold for scrap in 1965. *Thermopylae* (converted boat) and *Talent* and *Token* ("Streamlines") were approved for disposal by scrapping in 1968.
**Tabard* and *Trump* were listed for disposal in 1969, but *Tabard* was used as a training boat in 1969 and *Trump* was refitted.

TABARD — *1967, Official*

ASSAULT SHIPS

Name	*No.*	*Builders*	*Ordered*	*Laid down*	*Launched*	*Completion*
FEARLESS	L 10 (ex-L 3004)	Harland & Wolff Ltd, Belfast	1 Dec 1961	25 July 1962	19 Dec 1963	25 Nov 1965
INTREPID	L 11 (ex-L 3005)	John Brown & Co, (Clydebank) Ltd	1 May 1962	19 Dec 1962	25 June 1964	11 Mar 1967

2 AMPHIBIOUS CRUISER TYPE

Displacement, tons	11 060 standard; 12 120 full load 16 950 ballasted
Length, feet (*metres*)	500 (*152·4*) wl; 520 (*158·5*) oa
Beam, feet (*metres*)	80 (*24·4*)
Draught, feet (*metres*)	20·5 (*6·2*)
Draught, ballasted	32 (*9·8*) aft; 23 (*7·0*) fwd; 27·5 (*8·4*) mean
Landing craft	4 LCM(9) in dock; 4 LCVP at davits
Vehicles	*Specimen load:* 15 tanks, 7 three-ton and 20 quarter-ton trucks (20 three tonners on flight deck)
Aircraft	Flight deck facilities for 5 Wessex helicopters (6 operable)
Missiles, AA	4 "Seacat" systems
Guns, AA	2—40 mm Bofors
Boilers	2 Babcock & Wilcox
Main engines	2 EE turbines 22 000 shp; 2 shafts
Speed, knots	21
Complement	556 (36 officers, 520 men) 111 Royal Marines and Army

INTREPID 1969, Official

Assault ships of a new design, which, with commando carriers, replace the former ships of the Amphibious Warfare Squadron. They carry landing craft which can be floated through the open stern by flooding compartments of the ship and lowering her in the water; are able to deploy tanks, vehicles and men; have seakeeping qualities much superior to those of tank landing ships, and their speed and range is greater. Capable of operating independently. Also able to serve as Command Ships at sea for transit operations and as Headquarters Ships in the assault area. Another valuable feature is a helicopter platform which is also the deckhead of the covered well or dock from which the landing craft are floated out. The vessels have a new type of hull combining features of both an escort aircraft carrier and a troop transport with the basic lines of a cruiser and a dock landing ship. Officially estimated building cost: *Fearless* £11 250 000; *Intrepid* £10 300 000.

ENGINEERING. The two funnels are staggered across the beam of the ship, indicating that the engines and boilers are arranged *en echelon*, two machinery spaces having one turbine and one boiler installed in each space, the starboard shaft being longer than the port. The main machinery is arranged in two self contained units, each driving one shaft. The turbines were manufactured by the English Electric Co, Rugby, the gearing by David Brown & Co Huddersfield. Boilers work at a pressure of 550 lbs per sq in and a temperature of 850 deg F.

ELECTRICAL. Power at 440V 60 c/s 3-phase a.c. is supplied by four 1 000 kW AE1 turbo-alternators.

OPERATIONAL. Each ship is fitted out as a Naval Assault Group/Brigade Headquarters with an Assault Operations Room from which naval and military personnel, working in close co-operation, can mount and control the progress of an assault operation. Equipped with latest radio aids so that the Admiralty Board can send teleprinter messages wherever ships are operating. H.F. transmitters enable ships to communicate with Commonwealth or Allied receiving stations. Also able to maintain contact with other ships, aircraft, military authorities and associated landing craft which may be operating with them. Each ship operates with a Royal Marine Commando or infantry battalion.
In the Defence Estimates these assault ships are listed after aircraft carriers and commando ships and before cruisers and destroyers.

FEARLESS 1968, Skyfotos

TROOPS. Each ship can carry 380 to 400 troops at ship's company standards, and an overload of 700 marines and military personnel can be accommodated for short periods.

SATELLITE SYSTEM. The Royal Navy fitted its first operational satellite communication system in *Intrepid* in 1969, the contract having been awarded to Plessey Radar.

FEARLESS 1969, Official

CRUISERS

3 "TIGER" CLASS

Name	No.	Builders and Engineers	Laid down	Launched	Completed
BLAKE (ex-*Tiger*, ex-*Blake*)	C 99	Fairfield SB & Eng Govan	17 Aug 42	20 Dec 45	8 Mar 61
LION (ex-*Defence*)	C 34	Scotts' SB & Eng, Greenock*	24 June 42	2 Sep 44	20 July 60
TIGER (ex-*Bellerophon*)	C 20	John Brown, Clydebank	1 Oct 41	25 Oct 45	18 Mar 59

*To launching stage. Completed by Swan, Hunter & Wigham Richardson Ltd, Wallsend-on-Tyne: Main machinery completed by the Wallsend Slipway & Engineering Co Ltd, Wallsend-on-Tyne.

Displacement, tons	9 500 standard; 12 080 full load
Length, feet (*metres*)	538 (*164·0*) pp; 550 (*167·6*) wl 566·5 (*172·8*) oa official figures as converted
Beam, feet (*metres*)	64 (*19·5*)
Draught, feet (*metres*)	23 (*7·0*)
Aircraft	4 helicopters in *Blake*
Missile launchers	2 quadruple "Seacat" surface-to-air systems in *Blake, Tiger*
Guns	As helicopter ships; 2—6 in (*152 mm*) 1 twin; 2—3 in (*76 mm*) 1 twin. As cruisers; 4—6 in (*152 mm*); 2 twin; 6—3 in (*76 mm*); 3 twin
Armour	Belt 3·5 in—3·2 in (*89—83 mm*); deck 2 in (*51 mm*); turrets 3 in—1 in (*76—25 mm*)
Boilers	4 Admiralty 3-drum
Main engines	4 Parsons geared turbines; 4 shafts; 80 000 shp
Speed, knots	31·5
Radius, miles	2 100 at full power; 4 000 at 20 knots; 6 500 at 13 knots
Oil fuel (tons)	1 850
Complement	*Blake:* 85 officers, 800 ratings

Originally designed to provide close cover and anti-aircraft support for convoys, aircraft carrier groups and assault landings. Other rôles included military and policing duties in any part of the world. Original designed displacement: 8 000 tons. Work on ships stopped in July 1946, for eight years. Decision to complete them announced 15 Oct 1954. Dismantled for resumption to new design in 1955. *Tiger* cost £13 113 000, *Lion* £14 375 000, *Blake* £14 940 0000 (helicopter conversion £5 500 000).

CONVERSION. Early in 1965 *Blake* was taken in hand for conversion to the rôle of command helicopter cruiser at HM Dockyard, Portsmouth. She recommissioned on 23 Apr 1969. The reconstruction involved the suppression of the after twin 6 inch turret and the two midship twin 3 inch turrets and the provision of a raised flight deck at the stern and hangar for operating Sea King anti-submarine helicopters. *Tiger* is being converted, and in the 1969-70 Estimates it was stated it is planned to convert *Lion* later on.

GUNNERY. As originally designed guns included nine 6 inch, ten 4 inch. The 6 inch fully automatic guns of advanced design are equally effective in surface and anti-aircraft rôles. Rate of fire is twenty rounds per minute, more than twice that of any previous cruiser. The 3 inch guns are capable of 90 rpm. The guns are fitted with a comprehensive direction system which enables all turrets to be controlled by radar. Each Mk 26 6 inch turret weighs 163 tons and each Mk 6 3 inch turret 38·5 tons.

OPERATIONAL. Ships are conned from totally enclosed bridge, the first fitted in British cruisers. A 200-line automatic telephone exchange facilitates internal communications.

ENGINEERING. The main machinery is largely automatic and can be remotely controlled. Steam conditions at 400 psi pressure and 640°F. Propellers 11 ft dia. 285 rpm.

ELECTRICAL. Four turbo-generators provide over 4 000 kilowatts of alternating current, the first time this type of power was used in British cruisers.

TORPEDOES. Originally designed to mount eight 21-inch torpedo tubes in two quadruple banks.

HABITABILITY. Complete air-conditioning is installed. Generous electrical equipment is provided for all domestic and recreational purposes. Accommodation is of a much higher standard than in previous cruisers.

CLASS. *Hawke* of this class, laid down at HM Dockyard, Portsmouth in Aug 1944, was cancelled in 1946, as was *Bellerophon* (ex-*Tiger*) a cruiser of enlarged design ordered from Vickers-Armstrongs.

BLAKE after conversion — *1969, Official*

TIGER before conversion — *Added 1969, Wright & Logan*

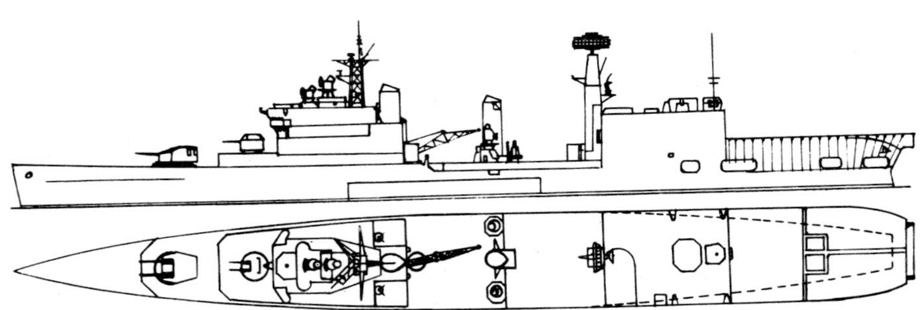

NOMENCLATURE. The name of *Defence* was changed to *Lion* in 1957 (announced 8 Oct 1957).

DRAWING. Port elevation and plan of *Blake* after conversion. Scale 1 : 1 500.

BLAKE showing conversion aft — *1969 Official*

Cruisers—*continued*

Name	*No.*	*Builders*	*Laid down*	*Launched*	*Completed*
BELFAST	C 35	Harland & Wolff, Ltd, Belfast	10 Dec 1936	17 Mar 1938	3 Aug 1939

Displacement, tons	11 550 standard; 14 930 full load
Length, feet (*metres*)	579 (*176·5*) pp; 606 (*184·7*) wl; 613·5 (*187·0*) oa
Beam, feet (*metres*)	69 (*21·0*)
Draught, feet (*metres*)	23 (*7·0*)
Guns, surface	12—6 in (*152 mm*)
Guns, AA	8—4 in (*102 mm*); 8—40 mm
Armour	Side 4·5 in—3 in (*114—76 mm*); turrets 2·5 in (*63 mm*); deck 2 in—3 in (*51—76 mm*)
Torpedo tubes	Removed (see *Torpedoes*)
Boilers	4 Admiralty 3-drum
Main engines	Parsons geared turbines 80 000 shp; 4 shafts
Speed, knots	32·5
Radius, miles	6 500 at 14 knots
Oil fuel (tons)	2 260
Complement	710 (52 officers, 658 men)

Improved "Southampton" type. The largest cruiser in the Royal Navy. Designed displacement was 10 000 tons with beam of 63·5 feet. Built under the 1936 Navy Estimates. Internal subdivision is exceptionally complete. Was rebuilt after being heavily damaged by a mine early in the Second World War, beam being increased and other alterations made. Refitted at Devonport early in 1963 and placed in Reserve. Arrived at Portsmouth on 4 May 1966 to relieve *Sheffield* as Headquarters of the Commodore Reserve Ships and was reclassified as harbour accommodation ship on 15 June 1966. There are plans afoot to preserve *Belfast* as a permanent floating naval museum.

GUNNERY. Until her 1956-59 reconstruction the light anti-aircraft armament comprised two 8-barrelled 2 pdr and nine single 40 mm.

PROTECTION. Designed to withstand 8-inch shellfire. The armour extends over the length of the citadel, and the protective deck across the ship's breadth above the magazines.

PHOTOGRAPHS. A starboard broadside view before second reconstruction appears in the 1957-58 and 1958-59 editions, a port broadside view after reconstruction in the 1959-60 to 1961-62 editions, a port oblique aerial view in the 1962-63 edition, and a starboard near broadside view in the 1963-64 to 1968-69 editions.

BELFAST — *Added 1969, Official*

TORPEDOES. The 6—21 inch torpedo tubes originally mounted in triple banks were removed during 1956-59 refit.

FIRST RECONSTRUCTION. When she was mined her back was broken, and in the course of repairs, to strengthen her, she was fitted with an external bulge adding approximately 3 feet each side. This bulge roughly covered the same areas as the armour belt above the water line. Besides providing additional under-water protection, it improved the ship's stability, thereby enabling her to retain her entire 6-inch armament despite extra top weight having been added.

SECOND RECONSTRUCTION. In 1956 *Belfast* began her second reconstruction and modernisation. This was completed on 12 May, 1959. Extensive modifications included lattice masts, a new operations room, new type covered bridge, modernised armament and improved habitability. This reconstruction cost £5 553 000.

CLASS. Sister ship *Edinburgh* was lost in action on 2 May 1942.

"SOUTHAMPTON" CLASS. *Glasgow* and *Liverpool* were scrapped in 1958, *Newcastle* in 1959, *Birmingham* in 1960 and *Sheffield* in 1967. Sister ships *Gloucester*, *Manchester* and *Southampton* were lost during the Second World War.

"COLONY" CLASS. *Jamaica* was scrapped in 1960, *Kenya* in 1962, *Bermuda* and *Mauritius* in 1965, and *Gambia* in 1968. Of this class, *Nigeria* was sold to the Indian Navy in 1954 and renamed *Mysore*. Two others, *Fiji* and *Trinidad*, were lost in action during the Second World War.

"CEYLON "CLASS. *Newfoundland* was transferred to the Peruvian Navy at Portsmouth on 30 Dec 1959 and renamed *Almirante Grau*, and *Ceylon* was transferred to the Peruvian Navy at Portsmouth on 9 Feb 1960 and renamed *Colonel Bolognesi*.

LATER CRUISERS. *Superb* was scrapped in 1960, and *Swiftsure* in Oct 1962.

BELFAST — *Added 1967, Wright & Logan*

LION (see previous page) — *Added 1969, John G. Callis*

GUIDED MISSILE ARMED DESTROYERS *(Gas Turbine)*

"TYPE 42". NEW CONSTRUCTION

Displacement, tons	3 500
Aircraft	1 twin engined WG 13 anti-submarine helicopter
Missile launchers	1 "Sea Dart" twin medium range surface-to-air (surface-to-surface capability)
Guns	1—4·5 in automatic, new type, high rate of fire; 2—20 mm; 2 saluting
A/S weapons	Torpedoes carried by helicopter
Main engines	Rolls Royce Olympus gas turbines for full power; Rolls Royce Tyne gas turbines for cruising; 2 shafts; reversible pitch propellers for manoeuvring
Speed, knots	30 designed
Complement	270 officers and ratings (accommodation for 312)

The first "Type 42" all-gas-turbine propelled destroyer with the Sea Dart guided missile as her main armament was ordered from Vickers Limited Shipbuilding Group, Barrow-in-Furness (announced 14 Nov 1968) for service in 1973. Smaller version of the original "Type 82" design. Equipped with the most up-to-date sonar systems. The helicopter will carry an air-to-surface weapon for use against lightly defended surface ship targets such as fast patrol boats. The gas turbine installation is a development of the system in the small frigate Exmouth. Benefits include rapid ability to reach maximum speed, reduction in space and weight, and 25 per cent reduction in technical manpower. High standard of accommodation, with living and working spaces fully air-conditioned. To cost £17 000 000.

TYPE 42 model *1969, Official*

TYPE 42, artist's impression *1969, Vickers Limited*

TYPE 42 model *1969, Official*

GUIDED MISSILE ARMED DESTROYERS

1 NEW CONSTRUCTION "TYPE 82"

BRISTOL

Displacement, tons	5 650 standard (approx); 6 750 full load
Length, feet (*metres*)	490 (*149·4*) wl; 507 (*154·5*) oa
Beam, feet (*metres*)	55 (*16·8*)
Draught, feet (*metres*)	22·5 (*6·9*)
Aircraft	Facilities for 1 light helicopter
Missiles, AA	1 "Seadart" GWS 30 twin launcher aft
Missiles, A/S	1 "Ikara" single launcher forward
Guns, dual purpose	1—4·5 in (*115 mm*) forward
Guns, AA	2—40 mm
Guns, saluting	4
A/S	1 Limbo 3-barrel DC mortar aft
Boilers	2
Main engines	Combined steam and gas turbines. 2 sets Standard Range geared steam turbines, 30 000 shp. 2 Bristol-Siddeley marine "Olympus" gas turbines, 44 600 shp. Total 74 600 shp; 2 shafts
Speed, knots	28 deep load; 32 max
Range, miles	5 000 at 18 knots
Complement	433 (33 officers, 400 ratings)

The design was originally intended to be an enlarged version of that of the "Leander" class general purpose frigate as a vehicle for the new "Seadart" guided weapons system, but the design turned out larger than that of the "County" class guided missile armed destroyers and has been referred to as escort cruiser.

BRISTOL model — *1969, Official*

Designed around a powerful new weapons system. Hull capable of sea-keeping and high speeds in all weathers. Fully stsbilised to present a steady weapon platform. Sleek, modern appearance. The gas turbines provide emergency power and high speed boost. The machinery is remotely from a ship control centre. Automatic steering, obviating the need for a quartermaster. Many labour-saving items of equipment fitted to make the most efficient and economical use of manpower resulting in a smaller ships' company for tonnage than any previous warship. Living conditions highest obtainable in a warship, with full air-conditioning, modern electric galleys, multi-choice cafeteria messing, television and individual bunk sleeping in comfortable mess-decks. Capable of steaming and fighting without discomfort to her crew when shut-down against nuclear fallout. Fitted with Action Data Automation Weapon System to compute information from the new 3D radar and other censors, and control their various weapons to engage the targets selected, the latest Sonar system to provide the long-range information required for the Seadart and Ikara weapons.

The Seadart ship missile system, developed to meet the air threat of the 1970's and 1980's, also has a reasonable antiship capability. Its main advantages over the Seaslug system fitted in the "County" Class are: Considerably improved surface-to-air performance, particularly at very high and very low levels. Quicker reaction time. Considerably improved target handling capacity. It is lighter and takes up less space.

Ikara is a long-range anti-submarine weapon system developed in Australia, designed to deliver homing torpedoes to a position where they can attack submarine targets. It is propelled by a rocket motor providing the missile with its long-range capability.

It was officially stated on 23 Feb 1966 that Type 82 ships were expected to be ordered later that year, but only one was ordered (announced 4 Oct 1966) from Swan Hunter Group (Wallsend) Associated Shipbuilders and laid down on 15 Nov 1967.

BRISTOL, artist's impression — *1969, Official*

BRISTOL model — *1969, Official*

Guided Missile Armed Destroyers—*continued*

8 "COUNTY" CLASS

Displacement, tons	5 440 standard; 6 200 full load
Length, feet (*metres*)	505 (*153·9*) wl; 520·5 (*158·7*) oa
Beam, feet (*metres*)	54 (*16·5*)
Draught, feet (*metres*)	20 (*6·1*) max (props)
Aircraft	1 Westland Wessex helicopter
Missiles, AA	1 "Seaslug" twin launcher aft; 2 "Seacat" quadruple launchers abaft after funnel
Guns, dual purpose	4—4·5 in (*115 mm*), 2 twin turrets forward; 2—20 mm, single
Boilers	2 Babcock & Wilcox
Main engines	Combined steam and gas turbine. 2 sets geared steam turbines, 30 000 shp; 4 gas turbines, 30 000 shp. Total 60 000 shp; 2 shafts (see *Engineering* notes)
Speed, knots	32·5
Complement	471 (33 officers, 438 men)

Name	*No.*	*Builders*	*Laid down*	*Launched*	*Completed*
ANTRIM	D 18	Fairfield SB & Eng Co Ltd, Govan	20 Jan 66	19 Oct 67	
DEVONSHIRE	D 02	Cammell Laird & Co Ltd, Birkenhead	9 Mar 59	10 June 60	15 Nov 62
FIFE	D 20	Fairfield SB & Eng Co Ltd, Govan	1 June 62	9 July 64	21 June 66
GLAMORGAN	D 19	Vickers-Armstrongs Ltd, Newcastle-on-Tyne	13 Sep 62	9 July 64	11 Oct 66
HAMPSHIRE	D 06	John Brown & Co (Clydebank) Ltd, Glasgow	26 Mar 59	16 Mar 61	15 Mar 63
KENT	D 12	Harland & Wolff Ltd, Belfast	1 Mar 60	27 Sep 61	15 Aug 63
LONDON	D 16	Swan, Hunter & Wigham Richardson, Wallsend	26 Feb 60	7 Dec 61	14 Nov 63
NORFOLK	D 21	Swan, Hunter & Wigham Richardson, Wallsend	15 Mar 66	16 Nov 67	

Devonshire and *Hampshire*, designed to embody developments in the destroyer field, were projected under the 1955-56 Estimates, and it was later found possible to arm this super-destroyer type with guided weapons instead of anti-aircraft guns, and to carry modern anti-submarines, rader and communication equipment. *Kent* and *London*, provided under the 1956-57 Estimates, have mainmast stepped further aft. *Fife* and *Glamorgan* 1961-62 Estimates and *Antrim* and *Norfolk* 1964-65 Estimates have the more powerful "Seaslug II" system, later to be fitted in the first four. All fitted with stabilisers. Their endurance gives them a considerable capacity for operating independently like cruisers. Photographs of *Devonshire* firing "Seaslug" appear in the 1962-63 to 1964-65 editions.

ANTI-SUBMARINE. In addition to anti-submarine homing torpedoes dropped by an anti-submarine helicopter the ships are fitted with modern underwater detection equipment for anti-submarine work.

OPERATIONAL. Ships of this class have three main roles:—Escort duties with a task group, including the ability to provide anti-aircraft defence for the group and to augment its anti-submarine capability; Operations as part of a task unit of light forces with the ability to bombard in support of land forces and to attack light forces with gunfire; Police duties in any part of the world. The ships are designed to operate in "fall out" areas. As many deck installations are under cover, the ships have clean lines, facilitiatng "washing down" in the event of nuclear attack.

GUNNERY. The 4—4·5 inch guns are radar controlled, fully automatic dual-purpose quick-firing for attack and defence against ships and aircraft. The 20 mm guns were added for picket duties in S.E. Asia.

ENGINEERING. These are the first ships of their size to have COSAG (combined steam and gas) turbine machinery. This is of exceptionally compact and light design, enabling the amount of fighting equipment to be increased. Boilers work at a pressure of 700 psi and a temperature of 950 deg F. The steam and gas turbines are geared to the same shaft. Each shaft set consists of a high pressure and low pressure steam turbine of 15 000 shp combined output plus two G.6 gas turbines each of 7 500 shp. The gas turbines provide a high concentration of compact power and are used to supplement the steam power for high speed work. They are also able to develop their full power from cold within a few minutes, providing unprecedented mobility, and enabling ships lying in harbour without steam to get under way instantly in emergency.

HELICOPTER. The helicopter is the first to be fitted as a complete "hunter killer". It carries dipping sonar and homing torpedoes.

ELECTRICAL. Two 1 000 kW turbo-alternators and three gas turbine alternators, total 3 750 kW, at 440 V.a.c.

RADAR. Each ship is exceptionally well equipped with the latest "watching" and "warning" radar.

HABITABILITY. All vessels have the latest accommodation standards and are fully air-conditioned.

GLAMORGAN *1969, Official*

FIFE *1969, courtesy Michael D. J. Lennon, Esq.*

HAMPSHIRE *1969, courtesy Godfrey H. Walker, Esq*

LONDON *1969, Wright & Logan*

Guided Missile Armed Destroyers—*continued*

KENT *1969, Official*

GLAMORGAN *1969, Wright & Logan*

FIFE *1969, Official*

DEVONSHIRE *1969, courtesy Dr. Giorgio Arra*

DESTROYERS

5 "DARING" CLASS

Name	No.	Builders	Laid down	Launched	Completed
DAINTY	D 108	J. Samuel White & Co Ltd, Cowes	17 Dec 45	16 Aug 50	26 Feb 53
DECOY	D 106	Yarrow & Co Ltd, Scotstoun	22 Sep 46	29 Mar 49	28 Apr 53
DEFENDER	D 114	Alex Stephen & Sons Ltd, Govan	22 Mar 49	27 July 50	5 Dec 52
DIAMOND	D 35	John Brown & Co Ltd, Clydebank	15 Mar 49	14 June 50	21 Feb 52
DIANA	D 126	Yarrow & Co Ltd, Scotstoun	3 Apr 47	8 May 52	29 Mar 54

(*Duchess* is lent to the Royal Australian Navy)

Displacement, tons	2 800 standard; 3 600 full load
Length, feet (*metres*)	366 (*111·7*) pp; 375 (*114·3*) wl; 390 (*118·9*) oa
Beam, feet (*metres*)	43 (*13·1*)
Draught, feet (*metres*)	18 (*5·5*) max
Guns, surface	6—4·5 in (*115 mm*), 2 twin fwd, 1 twin aft, Mk VI
Guns, AA	6—40 mm 3 twin, Mk V in *Dainty, Daring, Defender, Delight*; 2—40 mm singles in remainder
A/S	1 Squid 3-barrelled DC mortar
Torpedo tubes	*Decoy, Diamond, Diana, Duchess:* 5—21 in (*533 mm*) in pentad mount
Boilers	2 Babcock & Wilcox in *Daring, Decoy, Delight* and *Diana*. 2 Foster Wheeler in remainder. Pressure 650 psi (*45·7 kg/cm²*); Superheat 850°F (454°C)
Main engines	Parsons d.r. geared turbines; EE design in *Decoy, Diana* 54 000 shp; 2 shafts
Speed, knots	34·75 designed; 31·5 deep
Radius, miles	1 700 at full power 4 400 at 20 knots
Oil fuel (tons)	580
Complement	297 (12 officers, 285 ratings)

These destroyers were designed for several roles including cruiser reconnaissance, and anti-submarine or anti-ship patrol. All fitted as leaders. They were the largest destroyers built for the Royal Navy. Of all-welded construction. An ingenious and comprehensive light warship class. Habitability and accommodation of high standard. Improved anti-aircraft and anti submarine systems. Cost, £2 047 000 to £2 880 000 each.

MISSILES. *Decoy* was temporarily fitted with "Seacat" aft. *Diamond, Diana* and *Duchess* were to have been similarly fitted but in 1963 it was decided that the "Daring" class would not carry "Seacat".

GUNNERY. The 4·5 inch turrets are fully automatic. radar controlled. In 1959 Decoy had her after twin 40 mm replaced by a deckhouse support for "Seacat".

TORPEDOES. Originally mounted ten 21 inch tubes, but the after bank of five was in 1958-59 replaced by a deckhouse for extra accommodation, and the forward pentad mounting was suppressed in *Dainty, Daring, Defender* and *Delight* in 1963-64 refit.

ENGINEERING. The propelling machinery of advanced design was developed by PAMETRADA (Parsons and Marine Engineering Turbine Research and Development Association). Steam conditions were the highest used in ships of the Royal Navy, the boilers being designed for superheat control. Propellers 300 rpm, 12 ft diameter.

ELECTRICAL. All-electric galleys, laundry and fluorescent lighting. *Decoy, Diamond, Diana* and *Duchess* differed from previous ships in having alternating current, operating at 440 volts, 3-phase, 60-cycles per second. *Dainty, Daring, Defender* and *Delight* had direct current at 220 volts.

APPEARANCE. In *Decoy* the deckhouse replacing the after tubes was built out with a platform reaching the ship's sides, supported by stanchions, for "Seacat" support.

NOMENCLATURE. Originally allocated other names:—*Decoy* (ex-*Dragon*), *Defender* (ex-*Dogstar*), *Delight*, (ex-*Disdain*, ex-*Ypres*) and *Diana* (ex-*Druid*).

CLASS. Eight of this class ordered under the Second World War Construction Programme were cancelled after cessation of hostilities:—*Danae*, original *Decoy*, original *Delight, Demon, Dervish, Desire, Desperate, Doughty*.

DISPOSALS
Daring and *Delight* were officially approved for disposal by scrapping during 1968-69.

PHOTOGRAPHS. A photograph of *Diana* (with ten tubes) appears in the 1960-61 edition, of *Decoy* fitted with "Seacat" in the 1962-63 and 1963-64 editions, and of *Decoy* without "Seacat" in the 1967-68 and 1968-69 editions.

DEFENDER — *1969, Official*

DIANA — *1969, Wright & Logan*

DIAMOND — *1969, Official*

DAINTY — *1969, Skyfotos*

Fleet Radar Pickets

4 LATER "BATTLE" CLASS

Displacement, tons	2 780 standard; 3 430 full load
Length, feet (*metres*)	355 (*108·2*) pp; 364 (*110·9*) wl 379 (*115·5*) oa
Beam, feet (*metres*)	40·5 (*12·3*)
Draught, feet (*metres*)	17·5 (*5·3*) max (props)
Missiles, AA	"Seacat "quadruple launcher aft
Guns, dual purpose	4—4·5 in (*115 mm*) 2 twin forward
A/S	1 Squid 3-barrelled DC mortar
Boilers	2 Admiralty 3 drum type Pressure 400 psi (*28·1 kg/cm²*) Temperature 650°F (343°C)
Main engines	Parsons geared turbines 50 000 shp; 2 shafts
Speed, knots	35·75 designed; 30·5 sea speed
Radius, miles	1 300 at full power 3 000 at 20 knots 4 400 at 12 knots
Oil fuel (tons)	680
Complement	268 (12 officers, 256 ratings)

Apart from heavier main armament this class embodied improvements on earlier destroyers. Before conversion they mounted ten 21-inch torpedo tubes in two quintuple banks on the centre line abaft the funnel, and eight 40 mm anti-aircraft guns in four twin mountings.

CONVERSION. Known as "Battle class AD Conversions" (aircraft direction destroyers). Little remains of the original destroyers except hull, engines and boilers. Internally the ships were completely rebuilt to give a higher standard of living and fighting efficiency. The operations room is one of the most complex and compact ever contrived in destroyers. All four ships completed conversion in Jan to May 1962.

ENGINEERING. Two three-bladed propellers, 11·5 ft. diameter, 320 rpm.

GUIDED MISSILES. During conversion a guided weapons system was fitted to mount the "Seacat" launcher on the after superstructure, which, with the complex radar and gunnery systems, needs alternating current generators (the ships normally use direct current).

RADAR. Fitted with a beam to beam lattice foremast straddling the ship, similar to an electric grid tower, for the 293 type radar on its platform and five more aerials. The ships also have a mainmast carrying 27 aerials. Most prominent feature is the 965 radar, described as a double bedstead, twice the size of the normal air warning radar scanner.

Destroyers—*continued*

Name	*No.*	*Builders*	*Laid down*	*Launched*	*Completed*
AGINCOURT	D 86	R. & W. Hawthorn Leslie, Hebburn	12 Dec 1943	29 Jan 1945	25 June 1947
AISNE	D 22	Vickers-Armstrongs Ltd, Newcastle	26 Aug 1943	12 May 1945	20 Mar 1947
BARROSA	D 68	John Brown & Co Ltd, Clydebank	28 Dec 1943	17 Jan 1945	14 Feb 1947
CORUNNA	D 97	Swan, Hunter & Wigham Richardson	12 Apr 1944	29 May 1945	6 June 1947

AGINCOURT

1969, Skyfotos

AISNE

1969, John G. Callis

LATER "BATTLE" CLASS
Alamein, Dunkirk and *Jutland* were scrapped in 1965. **Matapan** (see particulars in 1961-62 edition), laid up in reserve ever since, is scheduled to be converted into a Trials Ship.

"WEAPON" CLASS
Radar Picket Destroyers. *Battleaxe* scrapped in 1964, *Scorpion* in 1966. *Broadswood* expended as target in 1968. *Crossbow* used as harbour training ship since 1967 (see particulars in 1965-66 edition).

CORUNNA

1969, John G. Callis

BARROSA

1969, Official

Destroyers—*continued*

4 "CA" CLASS

Name	No.	Builders	Laid down	Launched	Completed
CAMBRIAN	D 85	Scotts SB & Eng Co, Greenock	14 Aug 1942	10 Dec 1943	17 July 1944
CAPRICE	D 01	Yarrow & Co Ltd, Scotstoun	28 Sep 1942	16 Sep 1943	5 Apr 1944
CARYSFORT	D 25	J. Samuel White & Co Ltd, Cowes	12 May 1943	25 July 1944	20 Feb 1945
CAVALIER	D 73	J. Samuel White & Co Ltd, Cowes	28 Feb 1943	7 Apr 1944	22 Nov 1944

Displacement, tons	2 106 standard; 2 749 full load
Length, feet (*metres*)	339·5 (*103·5*) pp; 350 (*106·7*) wl; 362·8 (*110·6*) oa
Beam, feet (*metres*)	35·7 (*10·9*)
Draught, feet (*metres*)	17 (*5·2*) max (props)
Missiles, AA	"Seacat" in *Caprice, Cavalier*
Guns, dual purpose	3—4·5 (*115 mm*)
Guns, AA	4—40 mm
A/S	2 Squid triple-barrelled DC mortars in "X" position
Torpedo tubes	4—21 in (*533 mm*) quadrupled; Removed in *Cambrian, Carysfort*
Boilers	2 Admiralty 3 drum Pressure 300 psi (*211 kg/cm²*) Temperature 640°F (*338°C*)
Main engines	Parsons geared turbines 40 000 shp; 2 shafts
Speed, knots	36·75 designed; 31·25 sea speed
Radius, miles	1 300 at full power 2 800 at 20 knots
Oil fuel (tons)	580
Complement	186 (10 officers, 176 ratings)

The "C" group of destroyers were built as 4 flotillas, ie: "Caesar", "Chequers", "Cossack" and "Crescent" classes.

RECONSTRUCTION. Extensively refitted and modernised, with superstructure extended aft and modified bridge. *Carysfort* and *Cavalier* have different bridges from *Cambrian* and *Caprice* which have "Leopard" type.

GUNNERY. Former armament was 4—4·5 inch and 6—40 mm guns (also 8—21 inch torpedo tubes). The 4·5 inch gun in "X" position was removed.

NOMENCLATURE. Originally allocated other names:—*Cambrian* (ex-*Spitfire*), *Caprice* (ex-*Swallow*).

TRANSFERS. Of the "Cr" class, *Crescent* and *Crusader* were transferred to the Royal Canadian Navy in 1945, *Cromwell, Crown, Croziers* and *Crystal* were sold to Norway in 1946, and *Creole* and *Crispin* were sold to Pakistan in 1956. Of the "Ch" class, *Chivalrous* was transferred to Pakistan in 1953 and *Charity* in 1958.

CAMBRIAN — *1969, courtesy Dr. Giorgio Arra*

CARYSFORT — *1969, A & J. Pavia*

Caesar, Carron, Cassandra and *Cavendish* were scrapped in 1967. *Cambrian* and *Carysfort* are in reserve but are approved for disposal.

For disposals of the destroyers of the "Ch", "Co" and "Cr" classes, early "Battle" class, and older destroyers, see 1966-67 edition.

CAVALIER ("Seacat" on after superstructure) — *1969, courtesy C. E. Taylor, Esq.*

CAPRICE — *1969, Official*

FAST FRIGATES (*Gas Turbine*)

"TYPE 21". NEW CONSTRUCTION

Displacement, tons: 2,500
Length, feet:
Aircraft: 1 twin engined WG 13 anti-submarine helicopter
Missile launchers: 1 quadruple "Seacat" surface-to-air system
Guns: 1—4·5 in Mark 8; 2—20 mm
A/S weapons: Torpedoes dropped by helicopter
Main engines: Rolls Royce "Olympus" gas turbines for very high speed; Rolls Royce "Tyne" gas turbines for normal cruising; 2 shafts; controllable pitch propellers for astern
Speed, knots: *circa* 40 estimated
Complement: 170 officers and ratings

The Navy Department of the Ministry of Defence awarded Vosper Thornycroft, Portsmouth and Southampton, a contract for the design of a patrol frigate to be prepared in the fullest collaboration with Yarrow Ltd, Scotstoun (announced on 27 Feb 1968). The resulting first "Type 21" all-gas-turbine powered frigate was ordered from Vosper Ltd (announced on 26 Mar 1969) to be built at Woolston Yard, Hants. for completion in the summer of 1972. This is the first custom built gas turbine frigate (designed and constructed as such from the keel up, as opposed to conversion) and the first war ship designed by commercial firms for many years. The helicopter will be armed with wire guided missiles. Estimated to cost £7 000 000 to £8 000 000.

"TYPE 22". PROJECTED

Displacement, tons: 3 000 (unofficial estimate)
Aircraft: 1 helicopter
Missile launchers: "Sea Wolf" close range self-defence surface-to-air guided weapon system
Main engines: Rolls Royce gas turbines
Speed, knots: 30 plus

The new class known as "Type 22" frigates were designed as successors to the "Leander" class general purpose frigates the construction of which will cease with the completion of the scheduled programme of 26 ships.

TYPE 21 model — *1969, Vosper Thornycroft Group*

TYPE 21 model — *1969, Vosper Thornycroft Group*

TYPE 21 model — *1969, Vosper Thornycroft Group*

TYPE 21 artist's impression — *1969, Vosper Thornycroft Group*

GENERAL PURPOSE FRIGATES *(Anti-Submarine Versatile Type)*

"LEANDER" CLASS
TYPE 12 IMPROVED

24 + 2 NEW CONSTRUCTION
1st RATE

Displacement, tons	2 450 standard; 2 860 full load
Length, feet (*metres*)	360 (*109·7*) wl; 372 (*113·4*) oa
Beam, feet (*metres*)	41/43 (*12·5/13·1*) see *Design*
Draught, feet (*metres*)	18 (*5·5*) max (props)
Aircraft	1 Wasp helicopter armed with homing torpedoes
Missiles, AA	"Seacat" quadruple launcher in *Naiad* and later ships (see notes)
Guns, dual purpose	2—4·5 in (*115 mm*), twin
Guns, AA	2—40 mm, single; 2—20 mm, single in "Seacat" ships
A/S	1 Limbo 3-barrelled DC mortar
Boilers	2
Main engines	2 d.r. geared turbines 30 000 shp; 2 shafts
Speed, knots	30
Oil fuel, tons	460
Complement	263 (17 officers, 246 ratings)

Name	No.	Builders	Laid down	Launched	Completed
AJAX	F 114	Cammell Laird & Co Ltd, Birkenhead	12 Oct 59	16 Aug 62	10 Dec 63
DIDO	F 104	Yarrow & Co Ltd, Scotstoun, Glasgow	2 Dec 59	22 Dec 61	18 Sep 63
LEANDER	F 109	Harland & Wolff Ltd, Belfast	10 Apr 59	28 June 61	27 Mar 63
PENELOPE	F 127	Vickers-Armstrongs Ltd, Tyne	14 Mar 61	17 Aug 62	31 Oct 63
AURORA	F 10	John Brown & Co (Clydebank) Ltd	1 June 61	28 Nov 62	9 Apr 64
EURYALUS	F 15	Scotts' Shipbuilding & Eng, Greenock	2 Nov 61	6 June 63	16 Sep 64
GALATEA	F 18	Swan, Hunter & Wigham Richardson, Tyne	29 Dec 61	23 May 63	25 Apr 64
ARETHUSA	F 38	J. Samuel White & Co Ltd, Cowes	7 Sep 62	5 Nov 63	24 Nov 65
NAIAD	F 39	Yarrow & Co Ltd, Scotstoun, Glasgow	30 Oct 62	4 Nov 63	15 Mar 65
CLEOPATRA	F 28	HM Dockyard, Devonport	19 June 63	25 Mar 64	4 Jan 66
SIRIUS	F 40	HM Dockyard, Portsmouth	9 Aug 63	22 Sep 64	15 June 66
MINERVA	F 45	Vickers-Armstrongs Ltd, Tyne	25 July 63	19 Dec 64	14 May 66
PHOEBE	F 42	Alex Stephen & Sons Ltd, Glasgow	3 June 63	8 July 64	15 Apr 66
DANAE	F 47	HM Dockyard, Devonport	16 Dec 64	31 Oct 65	7 Sep 67
JUNO	F 52	John I. Thornycroft Ltd, Woolston	16 July 64	24 Nov 65	18 July 67
ARGONAUT	F 56	Hawthorn Leslie, Ltd, Hebburn-on-Tyne	27 Nov 64	8 Feb 66	17 Aug 67
ANDROMEDA	F 57	HM Dockyard, Portsmouth	25 May 66	24 May 67	6 Jan 69
JUPITER	F 60	Yarrow & Co Ltd, Scotstoun, Glasgow	3 Oct 66	4 Sep 67	24 June 69
HERMIONE	F 58	Alex Stephen & Sons Ltd, Glasgow	6 Dec 65	26 Apr 67	27 June 69
BACCHANTE	F 69	Vickers Ltd, High Walker, Newcastle	27 Oct 66	29 Feb 68	5 Aug 69
SCYLLA	F 71	HM Dockyard, Devonport	17 May 67	8 Aug 68	16 Dec 69
CHARYBDIS	F 75	Harland & Wolff Ltd, Belfast	27 Jan 67	28 Feb 68	15 July 69
ACHILLES	F 12	Yarrow & Co Ltd, Scotstoun	1 Dec 67	21 Nov 68	9 June 70
DIOMEDE	F 16	Yarrow & Co Ltd, Scotstoun	30 Jan 68	15 Apr 69	16 Oct 70

This class exploits the qualities of the successful "Whitby" class anti-submarine frigates in a more versatile improved Type 12. The main new features are long-range air warning radar, "Seacat" anti-aircraft missiles improved anti-submarine detection equipment and a lightweight helicopter armed with homing torpedoes. Air conditioning and better living conditions were also provided in this mainly anti-submarine but flexible and all-purpose type. Seven ships initially provided for, three more ordered in 1961-62 Estimates, three in 1962-63 programme, three 1963-64, three 1964-65 (*Hermione* was completed by Yarrow), three 1965-66, two 1966-67. The last two were ordered from Yarrow (announced) on 29 July 1968.

GUIDED WEAPONS. *Naiad* was the first of the class to be completed with "Seacat", followed by *Arethusa, Cleopatra, Phoebe, Minerva, Sirius, Juno, Argonaut, Danae*. The 40 mm guns mounted in the earlier ships will be replaced by "Seacat".

DESIGN. Has hull and machinery similar to "Whitby" class, but plans revised for a composite anti-submarine, anti-aircraft and air direction role. Equipped with VDS (Varaible Depth Sonar). Later ships have beam of 43 feet to improve stability. *Andromeda* was the first, followed by *Jupiter, Hermione, Bacchante, Charybdis, Scylla, Achilles, Diomede*.

ELECTRICAL. Alternating current, 440 volts, 60 cycles, 1 900 kW in early vessels, 2 500 kW in later vessels.

NOMENCLATURE. *Ajax, Dido, Leander* were originally to have been the last three of the "Rothesay" class, *Fowey, Hastings, Weymouth*, respectively. *Penelope* was to have been the fifth of the "Salisbury" class, *Coventry*.

PHOTOGRAPHS. A photograph of *Leander* appears in the 1963-64 and 1964-65 editions, of *Ajax* and *Penelope* in the 1964-65 editions, of *Euryalus* in the 1965-66 and 1966-67 editions, of *Arethusa* and *Minerva* in the 1967-68 and 1968-69 editions.

DIDO *1969, Skyfotos*

JUNO *1968, Official*

ARGONAUT *1969, courtesy Godfrey H. Walker, Esq.*

General Purpose Frigates—*continued* **Improved Type 12**

GALATEA *1969, Official*

NAIAD *1969, Official*

SIRIUS *1969, Wright & Logan*

CLEOPATRA *1969, Official*

ANDROMEDA *1969, Official*

GENERAL PURPOSE FRIGATES (*Gas Turbine*)

7 "TRIBAL" CLASS. TYPE 81

Name	No.	Builders	Laid down	Launched	Completed
ASHANTI	F 117	Yarrow & Co Ltd, Scotstoun	15 Jan 1958	9 Mar 1959	23 Nov 1961
ESKIMO	F 119	J. Samuel White & Co Ltd, Cowes	22 Oct 1958	20 Mar 1960	21 Feb 1963
GURKHA	F 122	J. I. Thornycroft & Co Ltd ,Woolston	3 Nov 1958	11 July 1960	13 Feb 1963
MOHAWK	F 125	Vickers-Armstrongs Ltd, Barrow	23 Dec 1960	5 Apr 1962	29 Nov 1963
NUBIAN	F 131	HM Dockyard, Portsmouth	7 Sep 1959	6 Sep 1960	9 Oct 1962
TARTAR	F 133	HM Dockyard, Devonport	22 Oct 1959	19 Sep 1960	26 Feb 1962
ZULU	F 124	Alex Stephen & Sons Ltd, Govan	13 Dec 1960	3 July 1962	17 Apr 1964

Displacement, tons	2 300 standard; 2 700 full load
Length, feet (*metres*)	350 (*106·7*) wl; 360 (*109·7*) oa
Beam, feet (*metres*)	42·3 (*12·9*)
Draught, feet (*metres*)	17·5 (*5·3*) max (props)
Aircraft	1 Westland Wasp helicopter
Missiles, AA	**2 "Seacat" quadruple launchers in *Zulu* (which also has 2 sextuple launchers and 2—20 mm AA guns)**
Guns, dual purpose	2—4·5 in (*115 mm*) single
Guns, AA	2—40 mm, single
A/S depth charges	1 Limbo 3-barrelled DC mortar
Boilers	1 Babcock & Wilcox (plus 1 auxiliary boiler)
Main engines	Combined steam and gas turbine: Metrovick steam turbine; 12 500 shp. Metrovick gas turbine; 7 500 shp; 20 000 shp; 1 shaft
Speed, knots	28
Complement	253 (13 officers, 240 ratings)

Designed to fulfil economically all functions of frigates rather than for outstanding performance in any one specialised rôle, but capable of meeting the main escort functions of anti-submarine protection, anti-aircraft defence, and aircraft direction. *Ashanti, Eskimo* and *Gurkha* were ordered under the 1955-56 Navy Estimates *Nubian* and *Tartar* in the 1956-57 programme and *Mohawk* and *Zulu* 1957-58 programme These versatile ships were designed as self-contained units for service in such areas as the Persian Gulf. They are fully air conditioned in all accommodation and most working spaces. *Ashanti* cost £5 220 000

ENGINEERING. These ships have COSAG (combined steam and gas) turbine machinery. The engines are right aft. The principle employed is that of highly efficient steam turbines and gas turbines geared to the same propeller shaft. The gas turbines provide a high concentration of power in a very compact form and are used to boost the steam turbines for sustained bursts of high speed. They are also able to develop full power from cold within a few minutes, providing un-precedented mobility. The steam turbine provides power for normal cruising and manoeuvring. The gas turbine driving on the same propeller shaft provides additional power for high speed, and also enables the ship lying in harbour without steam up to get under way instantly in emergency. The machinery is remotely controlled at all powers. The main boiler works at a pressure of 550 psi and a temperature of 850 deg F. Five-bladed propeller, 11·75 ft diameter, 280 rpm. The machinery installations were designed by the Yarrow-Admiralty Research Department. Metropolitan-Vickers designed and manufactured the steam turbines, gas turbines, gearing and control gear. This lightweight and compact machinery enabled more fighting equipment to be carried than with orthodox machinery. The forward funnel serves the boiler, the after one the gas turbine.

ANTI-SUBMARINE. The first frigates designed to carry a helicopter for anti-submarine reconnaissance.

OPERATIONAL. The ships have a totally enclosed bridge and an air-conditioned operations room. They are equipped with warning radar of the most modern design, are fitted with stabilisers, and have twin rudders.

PHOTOGRAPHS. A photograph of *Nubian* appears in the 1968-69 edition and of *Gurkha and Tartar* in the 1967-68 and 1968-69 editions.

ELECTRICAL. Generator capacity of 1 500 kW. Fluorescent lighting in all living accommodation.

HABITABILITY. High standard of living accommodation. All manned compartments air-conditioned.

CONSTRUCTION. Ships are of all-welded prefabricated construction. The structural arrangements were designed to provide a robust hull with special emphasis on prevention of corrosion. Denny Brown stabilisers are fitted to reduce rolling in heavy seas. Good seakeeping qualities enable ships to maintain high speed in rough weather.

MOHAWK — *1969, Official*

ASHANTI — *1969, A. & J. Pavia*

ESKIMO — *1969, Wright & Logan*

ZULU (rearmed with multiple missile launchers) — *1968 Wright & Logan*

9 "ROTHESAY" CLASS. MODIFIED TYPE 12 1st RATE

(*Anti-Submarine Quality Type*)

Displacement, tons	2 200 standard; 2 600 full load (as originally completed); 2 380 standard; 2 800 full load (as converted)
Length, feet (*metres*)	360 (*109·7*) wl; 370 (*112·8*) oa
Beam, feet (*metres*)	41 (*12·5*)
Draught, feet (*metres*)	17·3 (*5·3*) max (props)
Aircraft	1 Wasp helicopter armed with homing torpedoes (in *Rothesay, Yarmouth, Plymouth, Rhyl.*
Missile launchers	1 quadruple for "Seacat" in *Rothesay, Yarmouth, Plymouth, Rhyl.*
Guns, dual purpose	2—4·5 in (*115 mm*), twin
Guns, AA	1—40 mm in unconverted ships
A/S weapons	2 Limbo 3-barrelled DC mortars (1 in *Rothesay, Yarmouth, Plymouth*)
Boilers	2 Babcock & Wilcox
Main engines	2 double reduction geared turbines; 30 000 shp; 2 shafts
Speed, knots	30 maximum
Oil fuel (tons)	400 approx
Complement	235 (15 officers, 220 ratings)

Provided under the 1954-55 programme. Basically similar to the "Whitby" class but with modifications in layout as a result of experience gained with the earlier Type 12. There were several differences, including the single 40 mm-gun and the build up of the after superstructure around the mainmast

MISSILES. The "Rothesay" class, as opportunity offers during conversion or routine refits, (*Londonderry* and *Lowestoft* in 1969, remainder in 1970) are being fitted with "Seacat" surface-to-air guided missiles as secondary armament in place of Bofors close range anti-aircraft guns. The single 40 mm gun mounted as a temporary measure is being replaced by a "Seacat" launcher and director.

CONVERSION. *Rothesay* was taken in control at HM Dockyard, Rosyth, in May 1966 for a two-year reconstruction and modernisation during which she was equipped to operate a Wessex Wasp lightweight anti-submarine helicopter armed with homing torpedoes, and fitted with "dipping" sonar. A flight deck and hangar were built on aft, necessitating the removal of one of her anti-submarine mortars. A "Seacat" replaced the 40 mm gun. *Rhyl, Yarmouth* and *Plymouth* also underwent conversion with a hangar aft, and the remaining ships of this class will be similarly converted when they come into dockyard for extended overhaul, on the pattern of the very successful general purpose frigates of the "Leander" class, except mainmast with long range air warning set.

PHOTOGRAPHS. A photograph of *Rhyl* appears in the 1963-64 and 1964-65 editions, of *Falmouth* in the 1963-64 to 1966-67 editions, of *Londonderry* (large starboard bow oblique aerial view) in the 1967-68 and 1968-69 editions.

NOMENCLATURE. The "Rothesay" (and "Whitby") classes were named after seaside resorts and coastal towns. The ships laid down as *Fowey, Hastings* and *Weymouth* were re-designed as general purpose frigates of the "Leander" class and re-named *Ajax, Dido* and *Leander*, respectively, see earlier page.

IMPROVEMENT. Although basically similar to the "Whitby" class, opportunity was taken during construction to incorporate in the "Rothesay" class modifications which extensive experience with earlier ships had shown to be advantageous.

ENGINEERING. Two Admiralty Standard Range turbines each rated at 15 000 shp. Propeller revolutions 220 rpm. Steam conditions vary, but the average is 550 psi (*38·7 kg/cm²*) pressure and 850°F (454°C) temperature.

ELECTRICAL. Two turbo generators and two diesel generators in all ships. Total 1 140 kW. Alternating current, 440 volts, three phase, 60 cycles per second.

ANTI-SUBMARINE FRIGATES

Name	*No.*	*Builders*	*Laid down*	*Launched*	*Completed*
BERWICK	F 115	Harland & Wolff Ltd, Belfast	16 June 1958	15 Dec 1959	1 June 1961
BRIGHTON	F 106	Yarrow & Co Ltd, Scotstoun	23 July 1957	30 Oct 1959	28 Sep 1961
FALMOUTH	F 113	Swan Hunter, Wigham Richardson	23 Nov 1957	15 Dec 1959	25 July 1961
LONDONDERRY	F 108	J. Samuel White & Co Ltd, Cowes	15 Nov 1956	20 May 1958	22 July 1960
LOWESTOFT	F 103	Alex Stephen & Sons Ltd, Govan	9 June 1958	23 June 1960	18 Oct 1961
PLYMOUTH	F 126	HM Dockyard, Devonport	1 July 1958	20 July 1959	11 May 1961
RHYL	F 129	HM Dockyard, Portsmouth	29 Jan 1958	23 Apr 1959	31 Oct 1960
ROTHESAY	F 107	Yarrow & Co Ltd, Scotstoun	6 Nov 1956	9 Dec 1957	23 Apr 1960
YARMOUTH	F 101	John Brown & Co Ltd, Clydebank	29 Nov 1957	23 Mar 1959	26 Mar 1960

YARMOUTH (after conversion) *1969, Official*

LOWESTOFT *1967, Wright & Logan*

BRIGHTON *1967, Wright & Logan*

BERWICK *1967, Skyfotos*

Anti-Submarine Frigates—*continued* Converted Type 12

ROTHESAY after conversion *1969, Official*

PLYMOUTH after conversion *1969, Wright & Logan*

ROTHESAY *Wessex* Mk 3 refuelling, *Wasp* about to land *1969, Official*

ROTHESAY *Wasp* landed *Wessex* above *1969, Official*

Anti-Submarine Frigates—*continued*

6 "WHITBY" CLASS. TYPE 12

1st RATE

(ANTI-SUBMARINE QUALITY TYPE)

Displacement, tons	2 150 standard; 2 560 full load
Length, feet (*metres*)	360 (*109·7*) wl; 369·8 (*112·7*) oa
Beam, feet (*metres*)	41 (*12·5*)
Draught, feet (*metres*)	17 (*5·2*) max (props)
Guns, dual purpose	2—4·5 in (*115 mm*), twin
Guns, AA	2—40 mm Bofors, twin
A/S	2 Limbo 3-barrelled DC mortars
Boilers	2 Babcock & Wilcox Pressure 550 psi (*38·7 kg/cm²*) Temperature 850°F (454°C)
Main engines	2 sets d.r. geared turbines 30 430 shp; 2 shafts
Speed, knots	31 (29 sea speed)
Oil fuel (tons)	370
Complement	221 (11 officers, 210 ratings)

Ordered in 1951. Primarily designed for the location and destruction of modern submarines, these frigates were fitted with the latest underwater detection equipment and anti-submarine weapons of post-war development. Good sea-keeping qualities enable the vessels to maintain their high speed in rough seas. Their twin-rudders improve manoeuvrability. They are all welded and the structural arrangements were specially designed to achieve the lightest possible structure. The designed full load displacement was 2 440 tons.

ENGINEERING. Propelling machinery fitted included geared turbines of Y.100 design and high power. Double reduction gearing allows low propeller revolutions of 220 rpm at high power and the propeller efficiency is correspondingly high. This, coupled with improvements in hull design, enables these frigates to achieve over 30 knots on only 75 per cent of the power required by older destroyers of comparable displacement. Arrangement of the engine room machinery is outstandingly good.

ANTI-SUBMARINE WARFARE. Have modern equipment for hunting and killing submarines and facilities for directing anti-submarine aircraft.

TORPEDO MOUNTINGS. Provision was made in the design for mounting 12 A/S torpedo tubes (8 single, 2 twin), but later ships never carried them, and they were removed from earlier ships. *Scarborough* was the first to be fitted with tubes (four fixed on each side, and two swivel mountings).

ELECTRICAL. The electrical system is alternating current, 440 volts, three phase, 60 cycles per second. Two turbo alternators and two diesel alternators. Total 1 140 kilowatts.

OPERATIONAL. When completed they were considered to be the most useful class of ships of their size ever put into service. With high fo'c'sle and clean lines they ride well in a sea-way and are exceptionally dry. The enclosed bridge is spacious, with splendid vision, heated windows in the fore of the bridge being an asset in Arctic waters. Internal communications satisfied every demand placed upon them. The operations room was the finest ever put into a ship of the size.

APPEARANCE. Later ships were completed with a thicker, raked back funnel with a dome cap (actually there are two stacks inside the funnel) and early ships of the class, which had a vertical funnel, were taken in hand for similar alterations as opportunities offered.

TRAINING. *Eastbourne, Scarborough, Tenby* and *Torquay*, Dartmouth Training Squadron, are now slightly different in appearance.

PHOTOGRAPHS. A photograph of *Blackpool* appears in the 1966-67 edition (see also New Zealand section) and of *Tenby* in the 1967-68 and 1968-69 editions.

Name	*No.*	*Builders*	*Laid down*	*Launched*	*Completed*
BLACKPOOL*	F 77	Harland & Wolff Ltd ,Belfast	20 Dec 1954	14 Feb 1957	13 Aug 1958
EASTBOURNE†	F 73	Vickers-Armstrongs Ltd Tyne	13 Jan 1954	29 Dec 1955	9 Jan 1958
SCARBOROUGH	F 63	Vickers-Armstrongs Ltd, Tyne	11 Sep 1953	4 Apr 1955	10 May 1957
TENBY	F 65	Cammell Laird & Co Ltd, Birkenhead	23 June 1953	4 Oct 1955	18 Dec 1957
TORQUAY	F 43	Harland & Wolff Ltd, Belfast	11 Mar 1953	1 July 1954	10 May 1956
WHITBY	F 36	Cammell Laird & Co Ltd, Birkenhead	30 Sep 1952	2 July 1954	19 July 1956

*(*Blackpool* is lent to the Royal New Zealand Navy)

† Completed at Barrow

TORQUAY — *1969, A. & J. Pavia*

WHITBY — *1968, courtesy Mr. Michael D. J. Lennon*

SCARBOROUGH — *1967, Wright & Logan*

EASTBOURNE — *1967, Official*

Anti-Submarine Frigates—*continued*

10 "BLACKWOOD" CLASS. TYPE 14

2nd RATE

(ANTI-SUBMARINE UTILITY TYPE)

Displacement, tons	1 180 standard; 1 456 full load
Length, feet (*metres*)	300 (*91·4*) wl; 310 (*94·5*) oa
Beam, feet (*metres*)	33 (*10·1*)
Draught, feet (*metres*)	15·5 (*4·7*) max (props)
Guns, AA	2—40 mm Bofors (see *Gunnery*)
A/S	2 Limbo 3-barrelled DC mortars
Boilers	2 Babcock & Wilcox Pressure 550 psi (*38·7 kg/cm²*) Temperature 850°F (454°C)
Main engines	1 set geared turbines; 15 000 shp; 1 shaft (see Machinery Conversion)
Speed, knots	27·8 max; 24·5 sea speed
Radius, miles	4 000 at 12 knots
Oil fuel, tons	275
Complement	140 (8 officers, 132 ratings)

Name	*No.*	*Builders*	*Laid down*	*Launched*	*Completed*
BLACKWOOD	F 78	John I. Thornycroft & Co, Woolston	14 Sep 1953	4 Oct 1955	22 Aug 1957
DUNCAN	F 80	John I. Thornycroft & Co, Woolston	17 Dec 1953	30 May 1957	21 Oct 1958
DUNDAS	F 48	J. Samuel White & Co Ltd, Cowes	17 Oct 1952	25 Sep 1953	16 Mar 1956
EXMOUTH	F 84	J. Samuel White & Co Ltd, Cowes	24 Mar 1954	16 Nov 1955	20 Dec 1957
HARDY	F 54	Yarrow & Co Ltd, Scotstoun	4 Feb 1953	25 Nov 1953	15 Dec 1955
KEPPEL	F 85	Yarrow & Co Ltd, Scotstoun	27 Mar 1953	31 Aug 1954	6 July 1956
MALCOLM	F 88	Yarrow & Co Ltd, Scotstoun	1 Feb 1954	18 Oct 1955	12 Dec 1957
MURRAY	F 91	Alex Stephen & Sons Ltd, Govan	30 Nov 1953	22 Feb 1955	5 June 1956
PALLISER	F 94	Alex Stephen & Sons Ltd, Govan	15 Mar 1955	10 May 1956	13 Dec 1957
RUSSELL	F 97	Swam, Hunter & Wighan Richardson	11 Nov 1953	10 Dec 1954	7 Feb 1957

Very lightly gunned. Designed for a mainly anti-submarine rôle. Of comparatively simple construction. Built in pre-fabricated sections. In 1958-59 their hulls were strengthened to withstand severe and prolonged sea and weather conditions on fishery protection in Icelandic waters.

ANTI-SUBMARINE WEAPONS. The Limbos each fire with great accuracy a pattern of large depth charges set to explode at a predetermined depth. They are trained over a wider arc than previous types of anti-submarine mortars, and have a much greater and more accurate range.

GUNNERY. The original gun armament was three 40 mm Bofors AA guns, but one was removed.

TORPEDOES. 4—21 inch tubes (2 twin) mounted in *Blackwood*, *Exmouth*, *Malcolm* and *Palliser* were removed.

ENGINEERING. All engined by their builders, except *Pellew* and *Russell*, by Wallsend Slipway & Eng Co Ltd, and *Grafton* and *Malcolm* by Parsons Marine Steam Turbine Co Ltd, Wallsend-on-Tyne. The turbines were of advanced design. The propelling machinery of *Hardy* and *Keppel* includes turbines of English Electric Co design. Four-bladed, 12 ft diameter propeller, 220 rpm.

FISHERY PROTECTION. *Duncan* (on completion as Leader in 1958), *Malcolm* (in 1959) *Palliser* (Apr 1958) and *Russell* (Jan 1958) originally formed the 1st Division of the Fishery Protection Squadron (now incorporated in the Western Fleet).

PHOTOGRAPHS. A photograph of *Keppel* appears in the 1956-57 and 1957-58 editions, of *Palliser* in the 1959-60 edition, of *Duncan* in the 1961-62 to 1963-64 editions, of *Grafton* in the 1964-65 edition, of *Blackwood* and *Dundas* in the 1967-68 edition., of *Pellew* in the 1967-68 and 1968-69 editions.

NOMENCLATURE. Named after famous Captains of British naval history.

CLASS. Sister ships *Grafton* and *Pellew* were officially approved for disposal in 1968-69.

TRAINING. *Blackwood* was also earmarked for disposal but it was officially stated in 1969 that she had arrived at Portsmouth to join *Crossbow* as harbour training ship for the shore establishments *Sultan* and *Collingwood*.

MACHINERY CONVERSION. Conversion of *Exmouth* (announced on 10 Feb 1966) to all-gas turbine propulsion at HM Dockyard, Chatham, was completed on 20 July 1968. She provided the Royal Navy with the first major warship propelled entirely by gas turbines, heralding a new era in naval marine engineering. *Exmouth* has one BSE Olympus for full power, with two Proteus engines for cruising. The Olympus engine develops 22 500 hp and the two Proteus engines 3 250 each = 6 500 hp but only one system or the other will propel; they cannot be used together or for boost. Both these engines are marine versions of well-known and proven aircraft gas turbines and their use in warships benefits from the extensive research and development already completed for aircraft use, and from which they have evolved. The Olympus will be used in new classes of frigates and destroyers to come into service in the early 1970's. In the meantime *Exmouth* took the Olympus to sea as a main propulsion plant some years earlier and enables the operational characteristics and benefits of all-gas turbine propulsion to be fully evaluated in the rigours of naval service. These benefits include significant reductions in weight and space of machinery and fuel, and in operating and maintenance staffs. Gas turbine machinery installations in *Exmouth* and in future ships will be operated and controlled entirely from the bridge. Other new features in *Exmouth* are the use of a gas turbine developed by Centrax Ltd of Newton Abbot, Devon, for driving the main electric generator, and this incorporates a waste heat boiler to produce steam for auxiliary and domestic purposes. A controllable pitch propeller by Stone Manganese Marine Ltd, of Deptford, is fitted for astern operation. The new installation for *Exmouth* was designed by the Yarrow-Admiralty Research Department in conjunction with Bristol Siddeley Engines Ltd, under the overall direction of the Navy Department.

EXMOUTH *1969, Wright & Logan*

RUSSELL *1968, John G. Callis*

MALCOLM *1969, Wright & Logan*

HARDY *1968, John G. Callis*

ANTI-AIRCRAFT FRIGATES

4 "LEOPARD" CLASS. TYPE 41

(*Diesel Anti-Aircraft Type*)

Displacement, tons	2 300 standard, 2 520 full load
Length, feet (*metres*)	320 (*97·5*) pp; 330 (*100·6*) wl; 339·8 (*103·6*) oa
Beam, feet (*metres*)	40 (*12·2*)
Draught, feet (*metres*)	16 (*4·9*) max (props)
Guns, dual purpose	4—4·5 in (*115 mm*), 2 twin turrets
Guns, AA	1—40 mm
A/S	Squid 3-barrelled DC mortar
Main engines	8 Admiralty Standard Range 1 diesels in three engine rooms; 12 380 bhp; 2 shafts; 4 engines geared to each shaft
Speed, knots	25
Radius, miles	2 300 at full power 7 500 at 16 knots
Oil fuel (tons)	220
Complement	205 (10 officers, 195 ratings)

Name	No.	Builders	Laid down	Launched	Completed
JAGUAR	F 37	Wm Denny & Bros Ltd, Dumbarton	2 Nov 1953	30 July 1957	12 Dec 1959
LEOPARD	F 14	H.M. Dockyard, Portsmouth	25 Mar 1953	23 May 1955	30 Sep 1958
LYNX	F 27	John Brown & Co Ltd, Clydebank	13 Aug 1953	12 Jan 1955	14 Mar 1957
PUMA	F 34	Scotts' SB & Eng Co Ltd, Greenock	16 Nov 1953	30 June 1954	24 Apr 1957

Designed primarily for the protection of convoys against aircraft, but can also serve as a medium type of destroyers in offensive operations.

CONSTRUCTION. All welded. The structural arrangements represented the latest in the development of modern technique, opportunity, having been taken in their building to study the problems associated with rapid production in emergency conditions. *Jaguar*, *Lynx* and *Puma* were ordered on 28 June 1951. Fitted with stabilisers. The construction of another ship ordered under the 1956-57 Navy Estimates to have been named *Panther*, was cancelled in the 1957 defence economies.

ENGINEERING. The propelling machinery consists of Admiralty Standard Range 1 heavy oil engines coupled to the propeller shafting through hydraulic gear boxes. These diesels are of low weight, about 17 lb/shp. *Puma's* engines, of the latest Admiralty design, were manufactured by HM Dockyard, Chatham, and Polar Engines, Ltd, Glasgow, the installation being by Scotts' Shipbuilding and Engineering Co Ltd. Engines of similar design are used for driving the ship's electric generators, and these were manufactured by Peter Brotherhood & Co Ltd, Peterborough. The engines of *Lynx* were manufactured by Crossley Brothers, Manchester, and British Polar Engines, Glasgow, the installation being by John Brown & Co Ltd, and the ship's electric generators were by Vickers-Armstrongs. The engines of *Leopard* were manufactured by Vickers-Armstrongs, Ltd, Barrow, and the engines of *Jaguar* by Crossley Motors Ltd, Manchester. *Jaguar* is the only ship of class to be fitted with controllable pitch propellers, 12 ft diameter, 200 rpm.

The fuel tanks have a compensating system, so that sea water replaces oil fuel as it is used.

RECONSTRUCTION. *Lynx* underwent extended refit in 1963 with new main "mack" (combined mast/stack), *Puma* was similarly refitted in 1964, and *Leopard* in Oct 1964-Feb 1966, followed by *Jaguar*.

DISPLACEMENT. The original design called for a standard displacement of about 1 800 tons, but with improvements and additions incorporated during construction the ships turned out heavier (1 950 tons light displacement.)

NOMENCLATURE. All the ships of this class are named after big cats. The fifth and intended sixth ships of the class were successively to have been named *Panther* (see *Constru'.ion* notes above and *Class* notes below).

CLASS. A ship of this class, originally to have been named *Panther*, built by John Brown & Co Ltd, Clydebank, intended for the Royal Navy, was transferred to the Indian Navy and renamed *Brahmaputra*, see Indian section. Another *Panther* was projected to take her place, but this ship was not built as a unit of this class or under that name (see *Nomenclature* notes on following page).

GUNNERY. The main armament of two Mk 6 twin 4·5 inch gun mountings and the gunnery armament control are similar to those mounted in the "Daring" class destroyers. The secondary armament, initially consisting of a Mk 2 twin 40 mm mounting, will eventually be replaced by "Seacat" ship-to-air guided missiles.

PUMA — *1969, Official*

LYNX — *1968, Skyfotos*

LEOPARD — *1968, courtesy Mr. Michael D. J. Lennon*

JAGUAR — *1968. Official*

AIRCRAFT DIRECTION FRIGATES

4 "SALISBURY" CLASS. TYPE 61

(*Diesel Aircraft Direction Type*)

Name	No.	Builders	Laid down	Launched	Completed
CHICHESTER	F 59	Fairfield SB & Eng Co Ltd, Govan	25 Jan 1953	21 Apr 1955	16 May 1958
LINCOLN	F 99	Fairfield SB & Eng Co Ltd, Govan	20 May 1955	6 Apr 1959	7 July 1960
LLANDAFF	F 61	Hawthorn Leslie Ltd, Hebburn-on-Tyne	27 Aug 1953	30 Nov 1955	11 Apr 1958
SALISBURY	F 32	HM Dockyard, Devonport	23 Jan 1952	25 June 1953	27 Feb 1957

Displacement, tons	2 170 standard; 2 350 full load
Length, feet (*metres*)	320 (*97·5*) pp; 330 (*100·6*) wl; 339·8 (*103·6*) oa
Beam, feet (*metres*)	40 (*12·2*)
Draught, feet (*metres*)	15·5 (*4·7*) max (props)
Guns, dual purpose	2—4·5 in (*115 mm*)
Guns, AA	2—40 mm (1—40 mm in *Lincoln*, see *Guided Missile* note)
A/S	Squid triple-barrelled DC mortar
Main engines	8 Admiralty Standard Range diesels in three engine rooms; 12 380 bhp; 2 shafts
Speed, knots	25
Radius, miles	2 300 at full power 7 500 at 16 knots
Oil fuel (tons)	2 300
Complement	207 (9 officers, 198 ratings)

Designed primarily for the direction of carrier-borne and shore based aircraft, but can also serve as a lighter type of destroyer in offensive operations.

CONSTRUCTION. Ordered on 28 June 1951 except *Salisbury*, the prototype ship. Construction was all welded and the design largely prefabricated in such a manner as to allow for rapid building in emergency. The construction of the fifth ship, *Exeter*, ordered under the 1956-57 Navy Estimates, was cancelled in the 1957 defence economies. Fitted with stabilisers (except *Lincoln*).

ENGINEERING. *Salisbury* has twin screws and is powered by Admiralty Standard Range 1 heavy oil engines coupled to the propeller shafts through hydraulic couplings and oil operated reverse and reduction gear boxes. These engines designed to develop 1940 bhp at 920 rpm, were manufactured by Messrs Vickers-Armstrongs, Barrow, who also made the engines of similar design for driving the ship's four 360 kW electric generators. Other ships have four 500 kW generators. *Llandaff* has similar main engines manufactured by British Polar, of Glasgow. Engines of similar design for driving the ship's electric generators were manufactured by Vickers-Armstrongs, Barrow-in-Furness. *Llandaff* is the only Type 61 frigate to have a 500 kW gas-turbine alternator and three diesel generators. This new gas-turbine alternator was manufactured by W. H. Allen & Sons, Bedford. *Lincoln* is fitted with controllable pitch propellers, rotating at 200 rpm, which are 12 feet in diameter, manufactured by Stone Marine & Engineering Co Ltd. The full tanks have a compensating system whereby sea water replaces oil fuel as it is consumed.

RECONSTRUCTION. *Salisbury* underwent extended refit in 1962. Her after funnel and lattice mast combination was replaced by a single tall funnel with Type 985 aerial on top, reminiscent of the US combined mast and stack or "mack". *Chichester* underwent similar refit in 1964 but with both fore and main "macks". *Llandaff* completed conversion with fore and main "macks" in 1966.

RADAR. All four ships have highly developed electronic equipment, *Chichester* was fitted with a new type of radar display on the foremast and mainmast. The radar on the foremast consists of a "spoked" aerial of the "cartwheel" type (without rim).

GUIDED MISSILE ARMAMENT. A single 40 mm AA gun, mounted in *Lincoln*, as a temporary measure, will eventually be replaced by a "Seacat" guided missile launcher and director.

NOMENCLATURE. All ships of this class are named after cathedral cities. A fifth ship was to have been named *Exeter*. A sixth ship, to have been named *Coventry*, was originally ordered as *Panther* and was built as *Penelope* (see *Nomenclature* notes under "Leander" class and "Leopard" class on preceding pages). A seventh ship was to have been named *Gloucester*.

DISPLACEMENT. The originally designed light displacement was 1 738 tons, but with modifications and additions during construction the ships turned out heavier.

CHICHESTER — *1969, Official*

SALISBURY — *1969, Official*

LINCOLN — *1969, Official*

LLANDAFF — *1967, Official*

FAST ANTI-SUBMARINE FRIGATES (*ex-Destroyers*)

6 "TYPE 15" 1st RATE

"T" "U" "V" "W" CLASSES

(*Fully Converted from Destroyers*)

Name	No.	Builders	Laid down	Launched	Completed
GRENVILLE	F 197	Swan, Hunter & Wigham Richardson, Ltd	1 Nov 41	12 Oct 42	27 May 43
TROUBRIDGE	F 09	John Brown & Co Ltd, Clydebank	10 Nov 41	23 Sep 42	8 Mar 43
ULSTER	F 83	Swan, Hunter & Wigham Richardson, Ltd	12 Nov 41	9 Nov 42	30 June 43
UNDAUNTED	F 53	Cammell Laird & Co Ltd, Birkenhead	8 Sep 42	19 July 43	3 Mar 44
VERULAM	F 29	Fairfield SB & Eng Co Ltd, Govan	26 Jan 42	22 Apr 43	10 Dec 43
WAKEFUL	F 159	Fairfield SB & Eng Co Ltd, Govan	3 June 42	30 June 43	17 Feb 44

Displacement, tons	2 240 standard; 2 880 full load
Length, feet (*metres*)	339·5 (*103·5*) pp; 350 (*106·7*) wl; 362·8 (*110·6*) oa
Beam, feet (*metres*)	35·7 (*10·9*)
Draught, feet (*metres*)	17 (*5·2*)
Guns, surface	2—4 in (*102 mm*), twin
Guns, AA	2—40 mm, twin
A/S	*Troubridge* and *"U" class:* 2 Limbo 3-barrelled DC mortars. *Verulam* and *Wakeful:* Provision for tubes.
Torpedo tubes	8 (4 each side) for homing torpedoes were fitted in *Ulster*
Boilers	2 Admiralty 3 drum Pressure 300 psi (*21·1 kg/cm²*) Superheat 640°F (*338°C*)
Main engines	Parsons geared turbines 40 000 shp; 2 shafts
Speed, knots	36·75 designed; 31·25 sea speed
Radius, miles	1 300 at full power 2 800 to 3 000 at 20 knots
Oil fuel (tons)	570 to 600
Complement	195 (15 officers, 180 men)

UNDAUNTED — *1969, Official*

"W" CLASS. *Wakeful*, ex-*Zebra*, converted by Scott's Shipbuilding & Engineering Co Ltd, Greenock, in 1952-53, was refitted with higher open bridge in 1959 for Portsmouth Squadron duties, her 4 inch gun mounting being removed and replaced by a deckhouse; and in 1967 an experimental satellite terminal was installed in her for trials. Of the original flotilla of eight "W" class destroyers *Wessex* and *Whelp* were transferred to the South African Navy in 1950-52 and renamed *Jan van Riebeeck* and *Simon von Stel*, respectively, and *Kempenfelt* and *Wager* were sold to Yugoslavia in 1957 and renamed *Kotor* and *Pula*, respectively. Of those converted into frigates *Wrangler* was transferred to the South African Navy on 29 Nov 1956 and renamed *Vrystaat*, and *Whirlwind* and *Wizard* were scheduled for disposal in 1966. *Wakeful* is being paid off and relieved by *Grenville*.

"V" CLASS. *Verulam* was converted by HM Dockyard, Portsmouth, but she is now without 4 inch, Bofors, Squids or director as trials ship for new A/S equipment. Of the original flotilla of eight "V" class destroyers, *Valentine* and *Vixen* were transferred to the Royal Canadian Navy in 1944 and renamed *Algonquin* and *Sioux*, respectively, and the leader *Hardy* was lost in the Second World War. Of those converted into frigates *Vigilant* and *Virago* were sold for scrap in 1965. *Venus* was scheduled for disposal by scrapping in 1965, and *Volage* was on the disposal list in 1966 (used as Harbour Training Ship, RM).

A photograph of *Verulam* appears in the 1967-68 and 1968-69 editions.

"U" CLASS. Converted in 1952-54, *Ulster* at HM Dockyard, Chatham, *Undaunted* by J. Samuel White & Co Ltd, Cowes. *Ulster* has a bowl-shaped sponson at the break and "Leopard" type bridge, *Grenville* and *Undaunted* are fitted with helicopter platform aft. In July 1966 the 20 × 30 ft section from the stern of *Urchin* was fitted to *Ulster*, damaged in May, at HM Dockyard, Devonport. Sister ships *Ulysses*, *Undine* and *Urchin* were all listed for disposal by scrapping in 1965 and *Urania* and *Ursa* in 1968.

TROUBRIDGE. Different from early Type 15's. Her conversion was started by HM Dockyard, Portsmouth, in 1955, but completed by J. Samuel White & Co Ltd, Cowes, on 29 July 1957. Has "Leopard" type bridge and 40 mm mounting on the break of the forecastle

"Z" CLASS. *Zest* was officially approved for disposal in 1969. See photograph and full particulars in the 1968-69 and earlier editions.

ULSTER — *1969, Wright & Logan*

WAKEFUL — *1969, John G. Callis*

TROUBRIDGE — *1968, John G. Callis*

GRENVILLE — *1968, John G. Callis*

Fast Anti-Submarine Frigates (*ex-Destroyers*)—*continued*

2 Early "Type 15" 1st Rate "R" Class (*Fully Converted from Destroyers*)

Name	*No.*	*Builders*	*Laid down*	*Launched*	*Completed*
RAPID	F 138	Cammell Laird & Co, Birkenhead	16 June 1941	16 July 1942	20 Feb 1943
RELENTLESS	F 185	John Brown & Co Ltd, Clydebank	20 June 1941	15 July 1942	30 Nov 1942

Displacement, tons	2 200 standard; 2 710 full load
Length, feet (*metres*)	339·5 (*103·5*) pp; 350 (*106·7*) wl; 358·2 (*109·2*) oa
Beam, feet (*metres*)	35·7 (*10·9*)
Draught, feet (*metres*)	17 (*5·2*) max
Guns, surface	2—4 in (*102 mm*) twin
Guns, AA	2—40 mm Bofors
A/S	2 Limbo 3-barrelled DC mortars
Boilers	2 Admiralty 3-drum type
Main engines	Parsons geared turbines 40 000 shp; 2 shafts
Speed, knots	36·75 designed; 31·25 sea speed
Radius, miles	2 800 at 20 knots
Oil fuel (tons)	580
Complement	180

Former fleet destroyers, converted to prototype fast frigates. Bridges, funnel, masts, superstructure, 4—4·7 inch guns in single mountings, 4—2 pdr pompons, 8—20 mm AA guns and 8—21 inch tubes in quadruple mountings, were removed entirely and each ship was stripped down to the bare hull. The forecastle deck was then extended aft, extensive use being made of aluminium to reduce top weight. A new superstructure was built up, two short lattice masts stepped, short raked funnel erected, and two anti-submarine mortars arranged *en echelon*, mounted in the after shelter deck. They had a completely new armament, and represented rhe new conception of frigate submarine-killers. Conversion of *Relentless* at HM Dockyard, Portsmouth, was completed in July 1951. She was originally fitted with torpedo tubes for experimental purposes. Refitted in 1955-56. *Rapid* was converted by Alex Stephen & Sons, Ltd, Govan, Glasgow, in 1952-53.

CLASS. Of four original sister ships *Racehorse* was scrapped (as destroyer) in 1950, and *Raider, Redoubt* and *Rotherham* (Leader) were transferred to the Indian Navy (as destroyers) in 1949 and renamed *Rana, Ranjit* and *Rajput*, respectively.

Sister ships (as frigates) *Roebuck* and *Rocket* were on the list for disposal by scrapping in 1965, and *Rapid* was on the sales list in 1965. In Mar 1966 *Rapid* carried out speed trials in the Solent in prospect of transfer from the Royal Navy to the Ecuadorian Navy, but the deal was not effected, and she is now seagoing training ship for engine room artificer apprentices at HMS Caledonia, Rosyth. *Roebuck* was expended as a target in 1969.

RAPID *1969, Official*

F185

RELENTLESS *1969, A. & J. Pavia*

Of the seven Type 16 1st Rate fast anti-submarine frigates of the "T" class (limited conversion destroyers), *Teazer, Tenacious, Termagant, Tyrian* and *Tumult* were broken up in 1965, *Tuscan* and *Terpsichore* in 1966.

Of the three fast anti-submarine frigates of the Smaller "Type 16", Limited Conversion from Destroyers, *Paladin* was scrapped in 1962, *Orwell* in 1965, and *Petard* (ex-*Persistent*) was for disposal in 1965.

FRIGATES

1 "Loch" Class. 2nd Rate (*Anti-Submarine Type*)

Name	*No.*	*Builders*	*Laid down*	*Launched*	*Completed*
LOCH FADA	F 390	John Brown & Co Ltd, Clydebank	8 June 1943	14 Dec 1943	10 Apr 1944

Displacement, tons	1 610 standard; 2 449 full load
Length, feet (*metres*)	286 (*87·2*) pp; 297·2 (*90·6*) wl; 307 (*93·6*) oa
Beam, feet (*metres*)	38·5 (*11·7*)
Draught, feet (*metres*)	14·7 (*4·5*) max
Guns, surface	2—4 in (*102 mm*)
Guns, AA	6—40 mm
A/S	2 Squid 3-barrelled DC mortars
Boilers	2 Admiralty 3-drum; 225 psi
Main engines	2 4-cyl triple expansion 5 500 ihp; 2 shafts
Speed, knots	19·5
Radius, miles	9 500 at 12 knots
Oil fuel (tons)	753
Complement	124 to 140

Designed mainly for anti-submarine escort. Originally displaced 1 435 tons standard (2 260 tons full load). When modernised she was air-conditioned for service in the Persion Gulf.

GUNNERY. Before modernisation she mounted 1—4 inch, 4—40 mm AA and 4—2 pdr guns.

TRANSFERS. *Loch Ard, Loch Boisdale* and *Loch Cree* were presented to the South African Navy in 1944-45, and renamed *Transvaal, Good Hope*, and *Natal*, respectively, and *Loch Achanalt, Loch Achray, Loch Eck, Loch Katrine, Loch Morlich* and *Loch Shin* were sold to the Royal New Zealand Navy in 1948 and renamed *Pukaki, Kaniere, Hawea, Rotoiti, Tutira* and *Taupo*, respectively. *Loch Insh* was transferred to the Royal Malaysian Navy in 1964 and renamed *Hang Tuah*.

CLASS. *Loch Glendhu* and *Loch Quoich* were scrapped in 1957, *Loch Scavaig* and *Loch Tarbert* in 1959, *Loch Arkaig, Loch Dunvegan* and *Loch Killin* in 1960, *Loch Gorm* in 1962. *Loch Craggie, Loch More, Loch Tralaig* in 1963. *Loch Alvie* and *Loch Veyatie* in 1965 and *Loch Ruthven* in 1966. *Loch Lomond* was listed for disposal in 1966 and *Loch Killisport* in 1968. *Loch Fyne* was listed as target ship in 1969. *Loch Fada* is for disposal in the near future.

MODIFIED "LOCH" CLASS
Woodbridge Haven (ex-*Loch Torridon*), built as a "Loch" class frigate but converted into a Submarine Depot and Repair Ship and reclassified as a Minesweeper Support Ship in 1960 was broken up at Blyth in Aug 1965. Sister ship *Derby Haven* (ex-*Loch Assynt*) was transferred as a frigate to the Imperial Iranian Navy (Persia) in 1949 and renamed *Babr* (*Panther*)

LOCH FADA *1964, Official*

Of the two Flag Frigates (Despatch Vessels) of the Modified "Loch-Bay" Type, *Surprise* (ex-*Gerrans Bay*, ex-*Loch Carron*) was scrapped in 1965 (towed from Portsmouth on 26 June to the shipbreakers' yard on the Firth of Forth); and *Alert* (ex-*Dundrum Bay*, ex-*Loch Scamadale*) was paid off in 1964 for disposal in due course.

"HUNT "TYPE 1
Brocklesby, last survivor of the famous "Hunt" group in the Royal Navy (designed as "fast escort vessels", but rated as destroyers until 1947, when they were re-classified as anti-aircraft frigates) was paid off on 21 June 1963 (she had latterly been Sonar Trials and Training Ship) and listed for scrap in 1965. *Mendip*, transferred to China in May, 1948, was returned to the Royal Navy a year later, but transferred to Egypt in 1949 and captured by Israel in 1956. *Cottesmore* was also transferred to Egypt in 1951. *Meynell* and *Quantock* were purchased by Ecuador in 1955. *Liddesdale* was discarded. *Cotswold* and *Hambledon* were used as artificial harbour at Harwich. *Eglinton, Fernie, Holderness, Pytchley* and *Southdown* were scrapped in 1956, *Blencathra, Cleveland, Atherstone, Cattistock* in 1957. *Garth* in 1958 and *Whaddon* in 1959. *Berkeley, Exmoor, Quorn* and *Tynedale* were Second World War losses. For disposal of "Hunt" types II, III, and IV see 1959-60 to 1966-67 editions.

"BAY" CLASS
Whitesand Bay was scrapped in 1956. *Enard Bay* and *Widemouth Bay* in 1957, *Largo Bay* and *Start Bay* in 1958, *Carnarvon Bay, Cawsand Bay, Padstow Bay, St Austell Bay, Tremadoc Bay, Veryan Bay* and *Wigtown Bay* in 1959, *Cardigan Bay* and *St Brides Bay* in 1962. *Bigbury Bay* and *Burghead Bay* were transferred to Portugal at Plymouth on 11 May 1959 and renamed *Pacheco Perèira* and *Alvares Cobral* respectively; and *Morecambe Bay* and *Mounts Bay* were transferred to Portugal in 1961 after refit at John I. Thornycroft & Co Ltd, Southampton and renamed *Vasco da Gama* and *D. Francisco de Almeida*. *Porlock Bay* transferred to Finland in April 1962.

"BLACK SWAN" CLASS
Woodcock was scrapped in 1955, *Cygnet, Wild Goose, Wren, Alacrity, Black Swan* in 1956, *Amethyst* in 1957, *Hind, Nereide, Peacock* and *Sparrow* in 1958, *Magpie* in 1959, *Opossum, Redpole* and *Snipe* in 1960, *Modeste* in 1961, *Pheasant* in 1963, *Crane* in 1964, *Starling* was scrapped in 1965 (towed from Portsmouth on 6 July to be broken up at Sheerness). *Whimbrel* was transferred to Egypt in 1949, *Actaeon, Flamingo, Hart* and *Mermaid* were allocated to West Germany in 1957, and delivered in 1958 and 1959. *Erne* was reduced to a hulk for Solent Division RNR in 1952 and renamed *Wessex*, but reverted to name *Erne* in 1964 and scrapped in 1965. *Ibis* and *Woodpecker* were Second World War losses.

HELICOPTER SUPPORT SHIPS

ENGADINE *1969, Official*

ENGADINE K 08

Measurement, tons	*circa* 8 000 deadweight (official figure)
Dimensions, feet	424 oa × 58
Aircraft	Accommodation for 4 Wessex and 2 Wasp or 2 Sea King helicopters
Main engines	1 Sulzer two stroke, 5 cyl turbo charged 5RD68 diesel; 4 400 bhp = 16 knots
Complement	RFA: 61 (15 officers and 46 ratings); RN: 14 (2 officers and 12 ratings) Accommodation for a further RN complement of 113 (29 officers and 84 ratings)

Projected under the 1964-65 Navy Estimates. Built by Henry Robb Ltd, Leith. Ordered on 18 Aug 1964. Laid down on 9 Aug 1965. Officially named on 15 Sep 1966 (high winds caused postponement of the launching ceremony). Accepted into service on 15 Dec 1967. Largest ship so far to be built by the company. Intended for the training of helicopter crews in deep water operations against submarines. Fitted with Denny Brown stabilisers to provide greater ship control during helicopter operations, the only RFA vessel so equipped.

ENGADINE *Added 1969, J. W. Kennedy*

ENGADINE *1969, Official*

MINELAYER

ABDIEL

Displacement, tons	1 375 standard; 1 500 full load
Dimensions, feet	244·5 pp; 265 oa × 38·5 × 10
Main engines	2 Paxman Ventura 16 cyl pressure charged diesels; 1 250 rpm; 2 690 bhp = 16 knots
Complement	123 (14 officers, 109 ratings)

Exercise minelayer for the Royal Navy ordered in June 1965 from John I Thornycroft & Co Ltd, Woolston, Southampton. Laid down on 23 May 1966. Launched on 27 Jan 1967. Completed 17 Oct 1967. Main machinery manufactured by Davey Paxman, Colchester. Main gearing supplied by Messrs Wisemans. Her function is to support mine counter-measure forces, maintain these forces when they are operating away from their shore bases, and lay exercise mines. She replaced aging vessels previously employed on this work. Living accommodation is of a high standard. Cost £1 500 000. The helicopter support ship *Lofoten*, K 07, converted LST(3) 3027, was officially approved for disposal during 1968-69.

ABDIEL *1969, Official*

ENGINEERS' TRAINING SHIP (former *Minesweeper Support Ship* ex-Fast Minelayer)

Name	*No.*	*Builders*	*Laid down*	*Launched*	*Completed*	*Converted*
MANXMAN	N 70	Alex Stephen, Glasgow	24 Mar 1939	5 Sep 1940	20 June 1941	1960-1963

Displacement, tons	3 000 standard; 4 000 full load
Length, feet (*metres*)	400·5 (*122·1*) pp; 410 (*125·0*) wl; 418 (*127·4*) oa
Beam, feet (*metres*)	40 (*12·2*)
Draught, feet (*metres*)	15 (*4·6*)
Guns, AA	6—40 mm Bofors, 1 twin, 4 single
Boilers	2 Admiralty 3-drum; 300 psi; 640°F
Main engines	Parsons geared turbines 36 000 shp; 2 shafts
Speed, knots	26
Radius, miles	2 000 at 20 knots
Oil fuel (tons)	750
Complement	238 (11 officers, 227 men)

Built under the 1938 Estimates. Torpedoed by an enemy submarine and badly damaged in Nov 1942.

CONVERSION. Recommissioned on 23 Feb 1963 after conversion into a Minesweeper Support Ship at HM Dockyard, Chatham, at a cost of £1 000 000 to serve as parent ship for eight coastal minesweepers East of Suez. Her four 4-inch guns forward were suppressed; and two boilers forward removed for the installation of additional generators and evaporators, her shp being halved; but her forward funnel was retained for use as a ventilator and for diesel exhaust trunking. Part of the mining flat, which had an original capacity of 156 mines, was altered to take stores and spare minesweeping equipment. The stern mining doors were used for the exchange of sweeping gear. Returned from her Far East tour in 1968 but is retained in service, having been converted in Apr-May 1969 for the sea training of marine engineer officers.

CLASS. Of two sister fast minelayers *Apollo* was scrapped in 1962, and *Ariadne* in 1963. The fast minelayers *Abdiel*, *Latona* and *Welshman* of this class were lost during the Second World War.

MANXMAN — *Added 1969, Official*

MANXMAN — *1969, Official*

ICE PATROL SHIP

ENDURANCE (ex-*Anita Dan*) A 171

Displacement, tons	*circa* 3 600 (official)
Measurement, tons	2 641 gross
Length, feet (*metres*)	300 (*91·44*) oa; 305 (*92·96*) including helicopter deck extension
Beam, feet (*metres*)	46 (*14·02*)
Draught, feet (*metres*)	16·5 (*5·03*); 18 (*5·5*) max
Aircraft	2 Whirlwind Mk IX helicopters
Guns	2—20 mm
Main engines	B & W 550 VTBF diesels; 3 220 ihp; 1 shaft
Speed knots	14·5
Range, miles	12 000 at 14·5 knots
Complement	119 (13 officers, 106 men, including a small Royal Marine detachment) plus 12 spare berths for scientists

Ten year old ship purchased from J. Lauritzen Lines, Copenhagen (announced on 20 Feb 1967). Strengthened for operation in ice. Converted by Harland & Wolff, Belfast, into an ice patrol ship in southern waters to replace *Protector*, undertaking hydrographic and oceanographic surveys for the Royal Navy, as support ship and guard vessel. New name *Endurance* was announced 27 July, 1967.

The new ice patrol ship was ready for deployment in the Antarctic for the 1968 season by Oct. An unusual feature for one of HM ships is her hull painted a vivid red for easy identification in the ice, particularly from the air. Her upperworks and funnel are the traditional white and buff of the naval surveying fleet. Another feature is that the ship can be controlled from the crow's nest so as to give her officers the furthest view of channels through the ice. Refitted May to Oct during the Antarctic winter.

"PROTECTOR" CLASS. The ice patrol ship *Protector*, A 146, converted netlayer, was paid off in 1968 after 13 years service in the Antarctic and was officially approved for disposal in 1969 but she is still laid up in mid 1969. The original sister ship of *Protector*, the netlayer *Guardian*, was disposed of in 1962.

ENDURANCE — *1969, Official*

ENDURANCE in pack ice off Grahamland, Antarctic — *1969, Official*

HEAVY REPAIR SHIP (Former *Aircraft Carrier*)

Name	*No.*	*Builders*	*Laid down*	*Launched*	*Completed*	*Converted*
TRIUMPH	A 108 (ex-*R* 16)	R & W Hawthorn Leslie, Hebburn	27 Jan 1943	2 Oct 1944	9 Apr 1946	HM Dockyard, Portsmouth 1 Jan 1958 to 7 Jan 1965

Displacement, tons	13 350 standard; 17 000 full load
Length, feet (*metres*)	630 (*192·0*) pp; 650 (*198·1*) wl; 699 (*213·1*) oa
Beam, feet (*metres*)	80 (*24·4*)
Draught, feet (*metres*)	23·5 (*7·2*)
Width, feet (*metres*)	112·5 (*34·3*) overall
Aircraft	3 helicopters in flight deck hangar
Guns, AA	4—40 mm
Guns, saluting	3
Boilers	4 Admiralty 3-drum Pressure 400 psi (*28·1 kg/cm²*) Temperature 700°F (371°C)
Main engines	Parsons geared turbines 40 000 shp; 2 shafts
Speed, knots	24·25
Radius, miles	10 000 at 14 knots; 5 500 at full speed
Oil fuel (tons)	3 000
Complement	500 (27 officers, 473 men) plus 285 (15 officers, 270 men) maintenance staff

TRIUMPH *1969, courtesy Mr. John C. Jeremy*

Insulated for tropical service and partially air-conditioned. When she was still an aircraft carrier of the "Colossus" class her accommodation was modified in 1953 to fit her for employment as officer cadets' training ship, but she was converted into a heavy repair ship under the 1956-57 Estimates, and her sponsons removed. Commissioned for service after conversion on 7 Jan 1965. Sailed for portsmouth on 1 Feb 1965 for the Far East where she is employed as an escort maintenance ship.

CONVERSION. Her reconstruction spanned a period of seven years, but the work actually took less time as her conversion was suspended for about 2·5 years while dockyard commitments of higher priority were met. Although intended for heavy repair the special machinery in the comprehensive workshops for this in the former hangar, 445 feet (*135·6 metres*) long, 52 feet (*15·8 metres*) wide, and 17·5 feet (*5·3 metres*) in depth, is placed in a state of preservation and her main role is escort maintenance, but she has space and facilities to undertake a variety of tasks including the carrying and maintenance of helicopters. She can take four destroyers and frigates alongside, two on each beam. Cost of conversion: £10 200 000, including capital expenditure on the heavy repair plant carried and dockyard and expenses over a protracted period

CONSTRUCTION. As an aircraft carrier the flight deck, 690 feet (*210·3 metres*) long, 80 feet (*24·4 metres*) wide, and 39 feet (*11·9 metres*) above the water line, was strengthened to take aircraft of over 8 tons in weight. Sponsons could be dismantled to the extent of 3·5 feet on either side if necessary to allow for passage through Panama Canal. Mercantile type hull. Built to Lloyd's specifications up to main deck with the original intention of converting to commercial service after the war. Damage control: No great measure of vertical subdivision on the sandwich system as it was reckoned that it is better for ships to settle evenly in the event of damage and flooding than to foster capsizing.

ENGINEERING. Engines and boilers are arranged *en echelon*, one set of turbines and two boilers being installed side by side in each of the two main propelling machinery spaces, on the unit system, so that the starboard propeller shaft is longer than the port shaft. The maximum designed speed was 25 knots, at 225 rpm. The economical speed is 15 knots at 120 rpm.

APPEARANCE. Distinguished from aircraft carriers by generally lighter appearance, thin funnel, distinctive shape of ship's side forward, absence of sponsons, and block deckhouses on the former flight deck.

PHOTOGRAPHS. A starboard quarter view and a dead broadside surface view of *Triumph* appear in the 1965-66 and 1966-67 editions.

CLASS. Of her original sister aircraft carriers, the *Venerable* (renamed *Karel Doorman*) was sold to the Royal Netherlands Navy in 1948; *Colossus* (renamed *Arromanches*) was sold to the French Navy in 1951; and two were completed as maintenance aircraft carriers, *Perseus* (scrapped in 1958) and *Pioneer* (scrapped in 1954). *Vengeance* was lent to the Royal Australian Navy early in 1953, but was returned to the Royal Navy in August 1955, and sold to the Brazilian Navy in 1956 (announced by Admiralty on 14 Dec); she was modernised in 1957-60 and commissioned in 1961 under the name *Minas Gerais*. *Warrior* was sold to the Argentine Navy in July 1958 and commissioned under the name *Independencia* in Jan 1959.

CLASS. Of *Triumph's* sister ships, *Glory* was broken up in 1961, and *Ocean* and *Theseus* in 1962. Half-sister *Perseus*, also *Unicorn*, were scrapped in 1958-59. (*Unicorn* arrived at Dalmuir on 15 June 1959).

TRIUMPH ***1967, Official***

DESTROYER DEPOT SHIP

Name	*No.*	*Builders*	*Laid down*	*Launched*	*Completed*
TYNE	A 194	Scotts' SB & Eng Co Ltd, Greenock	15 July 1938	28 Feb 1940	28 Feb 1941

Displacement, tons	11 000 standard; 14 600 full load
Length, feet (*metres*)	585 (*178·3*) pp; 613 (*186·8*) wl; 621 (*189·3*) oa
Beam, feet (*metres*)	66 (*20·1*)
Draught, feet (*metres*)	20·8 (*6·3*)
Guns, surface	8—4·5 in (*115 mm*)
Guns, AA	7—40 mm
Boilers	4 three-drum type
Main engines	Parsons geared turbines 7 500 shp; 2 shafts
Speed, knots	17
Oil fuel (tons)	1 400
Complement	520 (normal) as depot ship 820 as flagship Accommodation for 1 000

Built under the 1937 Estimates. Equipment includes two furnaces, each capable of melting 500 lb of metal at any temperature up to 1 500 degrees centigrade; a foundry and machine shops with milling and grinding machines. Refitted from late 1956 to early 1958 with enclosed lower bridge and improved operations room and internal arrangements, etc, seven 40 mm guns replacing former smaller anti-aircraft guns. Was flagship of Home fleet from Autumn 1954 to August 1956, and again from April 1958 to 1960. Also parent ship of the 2nd Submarine Squadron in 1960, and Flagship of the Flag Officer, Flotillas, Home Fleet, until Apr 1961, when she became accommodation ship for Fleet Maintenance Units personnel at Portsmouth, from whence she was towed to Devonport on 18 July 1961 and placed in reserve and used as a living ship.

TYNE ***Added 1968, courtesy Mr. Godfrey H. Walker***

SUBMARINE DEPOT SHIPS

Name	No.	Builders	Laid down	Launched	Completed
ADAMANT	A 164	Harland & Wolff, Ltd, Belfast	18 May 1939	30 Nov 1940	28 Feb 1942

Displacement, tons	12 700 standard; 16 500 full load
Length, feet (*metres*)	620 (*189·0*) pp; 646 (*196·9*) wl; 658 (*200·6*) oa
Beam, feet (*metres*)	70·5 (*21·5*)
Draught, feet (*metres*)	21·2 (*6·5*)
Guns, saluting	4—3 pdr
Boilers	4 three-drum type
Main engines	Parsons geared turbines 8 000 shp; 2 shafts
Speed, knots	17
Radius, miles	4 000 at 13·5 knots
Oil fuel (tons)	2 600
Complement	750 (ships company + repair staff)

Ordered under the 1938 Estimates. Equipment includes a foundry, fitters', patternmakers', coppersmiths', and shipwrights' shops; light and heavy machine shops; torpedo and electrical shops; and submarine repair capacity of all kinds. When originally built she had facilities for nine submarines and accommodation for their complements. She has total accommodation for 800 officers and men of the ship and 550 from the submarines. Her eight 4·5 inch and twelve 40 mm guns have been removed. On disposal list in 1968.

ADAMANT 1966 courtesy Dr Giorgio Arra,

Nuclear Powered Submarine Support Ships

2 "MAIDSTONE" CLASS

Name	No.	Builders	Laid down	Launched	Completed	Reconstructed
FORTH	A 187	John Brown, Clydebank	30 June 1937	11 Aug 1938	14 May 1939	1962-1966
MAIDSTONE	A 185	John Brown, Clydebank	17 Aug 1936	21 Oct 1937	5 May 1938	1958-1962

Displacement, tons	10 000 standard; 13 000 full load
Length, feet (*metres*)	497 (*151·5*) pp; 531 (*161·8*) oa
Beam, feet (*metres*)	73 (*22·3*)
Draught, feet (*metres*)	21·2 (*6·5*)
Guns, AA	5—40 mm Bofors (see *Gunnery*)
Boilers	4 Admiralty 3-drum
Main engines	Geared turbines (Brown Curtis in *Forth;* Parsons in *Maidstone*) 7 000 shp; 2 shafts
Speed, knots	16
Oil fuel (tons)	2 300
Complement	695 (45 officers, 650 men) Accommodation for 1 159 (119 officers, 1 040 men) normal; over 1 500 max

Parent Ships for Submarines. *Maidstone* was ordered on 17 Aug 1936 under the 1935 Estimates. She originally cost £993 000. *Forth* was laid down under the 1937 Estimates. Equipment includes a foundry, coppersmith's, plumbers' and carpenters' shops; heavy and light machine shops; electrical and torpedo repair shop; and plant for charging submarine batteries. Designed for looking after nine operational submarines, and capable of supplying over 140 torpedoes and a similar number of mines when required. Besides large workshops there are repair facilities on board for all material in the attached submarines, and extensive diving and salvage equipment is carried. There are steam laundry, cinema, hospital, chapel, two canteens, bakery, barber shops, fully equipped operating theatre and dental surgery. *Maidstone* was the Flagship of the Commander-in-Chief Home Fleet from 16 Aug 1956 until 31 Mar 1958. From 1962 to 1968 she was depot ship for the Third Submarine Squadron but when her function was taken over by the new Clyde Submarine Base, HMS *Neptune*, at Taslane, she became surplus to naval requirements, and she was officially approved for disposal by scrapping during 1968-69. In mid-1969 she was still laid up at Portsmouth

MAIDSTONE 1969, Official

RECONSTRUCTION. *Maidstone* was extensively reconstructed in HM Dockyard, Portsmouth in 1958-62 as a nuclear-powered submarine support ship, with a lattice foremast and additional superstructure amidships. The conversion and modernisation included refitting for acting as parent ship for the nuclear-powered submarine *Dreadnought*. *Forth* was similarly modernsied and converted into a nuclear-powered submarine support ship in HM Dockyard Chatham, in 1962-66.

GUNNERY. As originally designed both ships mounted eight 4·5 inch guns in four twin housings, one forward, one aft, and one sponsored on either beam between the funnels, but these were removed during their conversion into nuclear submarines support ships. *Maidstone* formerly also had a light AA gun in the bows, and she carried a 4-inch gun on a submarine pattern mounting, for training purposes only, on the starboard side just aft of the midships 4·5 inch turret.

PHOTOGRAPHS. A starboard bow surface view of *Maidstone* before reconstruction appears in the 1960-61 and 1961-62 editions, and a larger port view, in the 1957-58 to 1959-60 editions. A port bow view after reconstruction appears in the 1962-63 edition, and a larger starboard broadside view in the 1963-64 to 1965-66 editions. A starboard broadside view of *Forth* before reconstruction appears in the 1960-61 to 1962-63 editions, and a starboard bow view in the 1963-64 to 1965-66 editions.

FORTH 1969, Official

MAINTENANCE SHIPS

1 "POINT" CLASS

Displacement, tons	8 580 standard; 10 200 full load
Length, feet (*metres*)	416 (*126·8*) pp; 441·5 (*134·6*) oa
Beam, feet (*metres*)	57·5 (*17·5*)
Draught, feet (*metres*)	21 (*6·4*)
Guns, AA	11—40 mm
Main engines	Triple expan; 2 500 ihp; 76 rpm; Pressure 250 psi (*17·6 kg/cm²*) Temperature 600°F (316°C)

Name	*No.*	*Builders*	*Laid down*	*Launched*	*Completed*
HARTLAND POINT	A 262	Burrard Dry Dock N Vancouver	18 July 1944	4 Nov 1944	11 July 1945

Speed, knots	10
Oil fuel (tons)	1 000
Complement	445 (25 officers, 420 men)

Former Landing Ship Maintenance. Extensively refitted externally and internally and modernised as an Escort Maintenance Ship in 1959-60, with lattice foremast, modified bridge, novel short funnel, additional deckhouses, modern cranes, and new armament, messing arrangements and air conditioning. Her task was the maintenance of destroyers and frigates in the Far East which she carried out at any port required or where the fleet was concentrated. Returned to United Kingdom in May 1965. Sister ship *Dodman Point* disposed of in 1962.

HARTLAND POINT *1963, Official*

BERRY HEAD *1969, Wright & Logan*

3 "HEAD" CLASS

Displacement, tons	9 000 standard; 11 270 full load
Length, feet (*metres*)	416 (*126·8*) pp; 441·5 (134·6) oa
Beam, feet (*metres*)	57·5 (*17·5*)
Draught, feet (*metres*)	22·5 (*6·9*)
Guns, AA	11—40 mm (*Berry Head, Rame Head*)
Boilers	2 Foster Wheeler
Main engines	Triple expansipn; 2 500 ihp
Speed, knots	10
Oil fuel (tons)	1 600

Name	*No.*	*Builders*	*Laid down*	*Launched*	*Completed*
BERRY HEAD	A 191	North Vancouver Ship Repairs	15 June 1944	21 Oct 1944	30 May 1945
DUNCANSBY HEAD	A 158	Burrard DD, N Vancouver	29 July 1944	17 Nov 1944	8 Aug 1945
RAME HEAD	A 134	Burrard DD, N Vancouver	12 July 1944	22 Nov 1944	18 Aug 1945

Escort Maintenance Ships, *Rame Head* refitted and modernised in 1960-63. *Duncansby Head* on 1 Dec 1962 became "half" of HMS *Cochrane* (Senior Officer Reserve Ships, Rosyth) jointly with *Girdleness*. In 1963 *Rame Head* became HQ ship (Senior Officer Reserve Ships, Portsmouth) but is now accommodation ship in Belfast. *Berry Head* was refitted in 1968-69 to relieve HMS *Triumph* in the Far East.

"MULL" CLASS. *Mull of Galloway* was scrapped in 1965 and *Mull of Kintyre* was in reserve in 1969 for disposal.

"NESS" CLASS. *Buchan Ness* was scrapped in 1959 and *Girdleness* was officially approved for disposal in 1969.

RAME HEAD *1969, Official*

DUNCANSBY HEAD *Dr. Giorgio Arra*

SURVEY SHIPS

3 "HECLA" CLASS

Name	No.	Builders	Laid down	Launched	Completed
HECATE	A 137	Yarrow & Co Ltd, Scotstoun	26 Oct 1964	31 Mar 1965	20 Dec 1965
HECLA	A 133	Yarrow & Co and Blythswood	6 May 1964	21 Dec 1964	9 Sep 1965
HYDRA	A 144	Yarrow & Co and Blythswood	14 May 1964	14 July 1965	5 May1966

Displacement, tons	1 915 light; 2 733 full load
Measurement, tons	2 898 gross
Length, feet (*metres*)	235 (*71·6*) pp; 260·1 (*79·3*) oa
Beam, feet (*metres*)	49·1 (*15·0*)
Draught, feet (*metres*)	15·6 (*4·7*)
Aircraft	1 Wasp helicopter
Main engines	Diesel-electric drive; 1 shaft. 3 Paxman "Ventura" 12-cyl Vee turbocharged diesels; 3,840 bhp. 1 electric motor; 2 000 shp
Speed, knots	14·35 on trials
Radius, miles	20 000 at 9 knots
Oil fuel, tons	450
Complement	118 (14 officers, 104 ratings)
Accommodation	123 (19 officers, 104 ratings)

New dual purpose deep ocean survey ships for the Royal Navy. The first to be designed with a combined oceanographical and hydrographical role, and the first to be built on commercial lines without a supplementary naval function. Of merchant ship design and similar in many respects to the Royal Research ship *Discovery*, they have range and endurance to fit them for their specialised work. The hull is strengthened for navigation in ice, and a propeller built into a transverse tunnel in the bow for good manoeuvrability. The fore end of the superstructure incorporates a Landrover garage and the after end a helicopter hangar with adjacent flight deck. Equipped with chartroom, drawing office and photographic studio; two laboratories, dry and wet; electrical, engineering and shipwright workshops, and large storerooms. Capable of operating independently of shore support for long periods. High standard of habitability, with library, canteen, laundry, cinema, and hospital. Air conditioned throughout. Ordered from Yarrow & Co Ltd, Scotstoun, in Feb 1964 (Blythswood Shipbuilding Co Ltd, Glasgow, collaborating on two of the three hulls). *Hecla* and *Hecate* were launched from the Blythswood yard.

MODIFIED "BAY" CLASS SURVEY SHIPS. Of the four survey ships of the "Bay" class (modified frigates), *Cook* (ex-*Pegwell Bay*, ex-*Loch Mockrum*) was for disposal in 1965, *Owen* (ex-*Thurso Bay*, ex-*Loch Muick*) in 1966, *Dalrymple* (ex-*Luce Bay*, ex-*Loch Class*) was sold to Portugal in Apr 1966 and renamed *Afonso de Albuquerque*, and *Dampier* (ex-*Herne Bay*, ex-*Loch Eil*) was approved for disposal by scrapping in 1968.

HECLA *1969, Official*

HYDRA *1967, Official*

HECATE *1969, Official*

1 ADMIRALTY DESIGN

Name	No.	Builders	Laid down	Launched	Completed
VIDAL	A 200	HM Dockyard, Chatham	5 July 1950	31 July 1951	29 Mar 1954

Displacement, tons	1 940 standard; 2 200 full load
Length, feet (*metres*)	297 (*90·5*) pp; 315·2 (*96·1*) oa
Beam, feet (*metres*)	40 (*12·2*)
Draught, feet (*metres*)	11 (*3·4*) forward; 13·2 (*4·0*) aft
Aircraft	1 helicopter
Main engines	4 ASR-1 diesels (see *Engineering*) 2 940 shp; 2 shafts
Speed, knots	15·9
Radius, miles	9 500 at 10 knots
Complement	191 (19 officers, 172 ratings)
Accommodation	197 (20 officers, 177 ratings)

Designed by the Royal Navy from the start for hydrographic surveying and chart production. First survey ship to be equipped with a helicopter flight deck and a hangar, designed to enable a helicopter to land on and fly off for air survey photography and transport of personnel to shore observation stations. Air conditioning plant is installed to meet equatorial and polar climatic conditions. The ship carries three survey motor launches equipped with echo sounding apparatus. First British naval vessel to be built equipped from the beginning for cafeteria messing. Cost £1 345 000. Refitted with enclosed bridge in 1961, but the bridge wings were left open. Again refitted in 1962.

ELECTRICAL. The latest electronic aids to surveying and navigation are incorporated. Electrical power is provided from 360 kw 220 volt dc diesel generating sets.

HELICOPTER OPERATION. The after end of the forecastle deck extension is a landing apron for the helicopter, housed in the after deck house hangar on the same level.

ENGINEERING. The main propelling machinery was designed in HM Dockyard, Chatham. The four ASR 1 diesels drive two shafts through reverse and reduction gear boxes. Each engine is of the 12 cylinder vee unsupercharged type with a rating of 1 050 hp at 920 rpm.

APPEARANCE. Funnel and fore bridge are pear shaped in plan.

VIDAL *1969, Official*

COASTAL MINESWEEPERS AND MINEHUNTERS

64 "TON" CLASS

ALVERTON (ex-*Thames*, ex-*Alverton*)
APPLETON
ASHTON
BEACHAMPTON
BELTON
BILDESTON
BLAXTON
BOSSINGTON (ex-*Embleton*)
BOULSTON (ex-*Warsash*, ex-*Boulston*)
BRERETON (ex-*St. David*, ex-*Brereton*)
BRINTON
BRONINGTON (ex-*Humber*, ex-*Bronington*)
BURNASTON
BUTTINGTON (ex-*Thames*, ex-*Buttington*, ex-*Venturer* ex-*Buttington*)
CHILCOMPTON
CHAWTON
CLYDE (ex-*Amerton*, ex-*Mersey*, ex-*Amerton*)
CONISTON
CURZON (ex-*Fittleton*)
CUXTON
DARTINGTON
FISKERTON
GAVINGTON
GLASSERTON
HIGHBURTON
HOUGHTON
HUBBERSTON
IVESTON
KEDLESTON
KELLINGTON
KILLIECRANKIE (ex-*Bickington*, ex-*Curzon*, ex-*Bickington*)
KILMOREY (ex-*Alfriston*, ex-*Warsash*, ex-*Alfriston*)
KIRKLISTON (ex-*Kilmorey*, ex-*Kirkliston*)
LALESTON
LETTERSTON
LEVERTON
LEWISTON
MADDISTON
MAXTON
MERSEY (ex-*Pollington*)
MONKTON (ex-*Kelton*)
MONTROSE (ex-*Dalswinton*)
NORTHUMBRIA (ex-*Quainton*)
NURTON (ex-*Montrose*, ex-*Nurton*)
OULSTON
PUNCHESTON
REPTON (ex-*Ossington*)
ST. DAVID (ex-*Crichton*, ex-*Clyde*, ex-*Crichton*)
SHAVINGTON
SHERATON
SHOULTON
SOBERTON
SOLENT (*ex-Croften*)
STUBBINGTON
UPTON
VENTURER (ex-*Hodgeston*, ex-*Northumbria*, ex-*Hodgeston*)
WALKERTON
WASPERTON
WILKIESTON
WISTON
WOLVERTON
WOOLASTON
WOTTON
YARNTON

Displacement, tons	360 standard; 425 full load
Dimensions, feet	140pp; 153 oa × 28·8 × 8·2
Guns	1—40 mm AA (removed in some); 2—20 mm AA (minehunters 2—40 mm)
Main Engines	2 diesels; 2 shafts; 2 500 (JVSS 12 Mirrlees), 3 000 (18A-7A Deltic) bhp = 15 knots (max); See *Engineering*
Oil fuel (tons)	45
Radius, miles	2 300 at 13 knots
Complement	27 (minehunters 5 officers, 31 ratings)

These were a new type with double mahogany hull and constructed of aluminium alloy and other materials with the lowest possible magnetic attraction to attain the greatest possible safety factor when sweeping. John I Thornycroft & Co Ltd, Southampton, were the "parent" firm for the group which built this class of uniform design capable of sweeping both contact and influence type mines and dealing with mines operated magnetically and acoustically. The last, *Lewiston*, was completed in 1960, and the first, *Coniston*, in Feb 1953; she has Vosper stabilisers, and the whole class are being so fitted. *Stubbington* and others have fibre-glass bottom sheathing.

DIVING CONVERSION *Laleston* was converted into diving trials ship (recommissioned on 22 Mar 1967).

SURVEY CONVERSIONS. *Edderton* and *Sullington* of this class were converted into coastal survey ships in 1964 and renamed *Myrmidon* and *Mermaid*, respectively. (*Myrmidon* was sold to Malaysia and *Mermaid* approved for disposal in 1968-69).

CLASS. *Calton, Fenton, Floriston* and *Sefton* were officially approved for disposal by scrapping in 1966-67; *Badminton, Caunton* and *Lanton* in 1967-68, *Carhampton, Clarbeston, Derriton, Dufton, Flockton, Kemerton, Kildarton, Maryton, Penston, Picton* nd *Roddington* in 1968-69.

NOMENCLATURE. Named after villages with the suffix "ton". Since 1954 some have been renamed on being allocated to the Royal Naval Reserve, taking the traditional names associated with the divisions (see below). Ships are not permanently attached to one division; on becoming due for refit they revert to their original names and might then be re-allocated to a different division or return to general service. The former Royal Navy and Royal Naval Reserve names are shown in parenthesis above.

ENGINEERING. High speed diesels, standardised to simplify maintenance. The earlier vessels had Mirrlees diesels, but most of the later units had Napier Deltic light weight diesels. *Highburton*, the first with Deltic diesels was accepted on 21 Apr 1955. Some early ships have undergone conversion from Mirrlees to Deltic diesels. The generators for electrical power are in a separate engine room. Three-bladed propellers, 6 ft diameter, 400 rpm. *Shoulton*, refitted 1965-67 (recommissioned 5 Apr), has pumpjet propulsion.

APPEARANCE. *Ashton, Chawton, Fiskerton, Houghton, Lewiston, Mersey* (ex-*Pollington*), *Nurton, Puncheston, Northumbria* (ex-*Quainton*), *Repton, Sheraton, Soberton, Stubbington, Walkerton, Wilkieston, Wiston* and others are fitted with an enclosed or frigate bridge and tripod mast. *Appleton* and *Shoulton* covered bridge.

MINEHUNTING. *Shoulton* was fitted with unique mine-hunting equipment, an all-British Sonar development which enables her to locate and classify any mine-like objects on the sea bed with accuracy and range previously impossible. Since then *Bossington, Brereton, Bronington, Derriton, Glasserton, Highburton, Hubberston, Iveston, Kellington, Kirkliston, Sheraton* and others have been refitted as minehunters, with active rudders incorporating electric motors for manoeuvring at slow speed. *Highburton* and *Glasserton* fitted with Osbourne mine destroyer units.

ROLE VARIATIONS. Of this class *Belton, Soberton, Wasperton* and *Wotton* constituted a division of the Fishery Protection Squadron. *Iveston* was converted to night guard aircraft ship. **INVERMORISTON** modified for SAR duties, PAS manned.

PHOTOGRAPHS. A photograph of *Coniston* appears in the 1953-54 to 1957-58 editions, of *Appleton* in the 1958-59 and 1959-60 editions, of *Bildeston* in the 1954-55 and 1955-56 editions, of *Highburton* in the 1957-58 edition, of *Bossington* and *Repton* in the 1958-59 and 1959-60 editions, of *Houghton* in the 1959-60 edition, of *Wilkieston* in the 1960-61 edition, of *Monkton* in the 1960-61 to 1964-65 editions, of *Wolverton* in the 1961-62 to 1964-65 editions, of *Burnaston* in the 1963-64 and 1964-65 editions, of *Lewiston* in the 1963-64 to 1966-67 editions, of *Shavington* and *Sheraton* in the 1965-66 to 1967-68 editions, of *Beachampton* and *Laleston* in the 1967-68 and 1968-69 editions.

TRANSFERS. *Dunkerton* and *Hazleton* were transferred to South Africa in 1955 and renamed *Pretoria* and *Kaapstad*, respectively. *Durweston, Overton, Whitton* and *Wennington* to India in 1956, and renamed *Kakinada, Karwar, Connamore* and *Cuddalore*, respectively. *Castleton, Chilton, Dumbleton, Oakington, Packington* and *Stratton* to South Africa in 1958-59 and renamed *Johannesburg, East London, Port Elizabeth, Mosselbaai, Walvisbaai* and *Kimberley*, respectively, with *Durban* and *Windhoek*. *Darlaston* was sold to Malaysia in 1960 and renamed *Mahamiru*, *Hexton* in 1963 and renamed *Ledang*, *Dilston* and *Essington* in 1964 and renamed *Jerai* and *Kinabalu*, respectively, and *Lullington* and *Thankerton* in 1966 and renamed *Tahan* and *Brinchang*, respectively. *Alcaston, Chediston, Jackton, Singleton, Somerleyton* and *Swanston* were transferred to Australia in 1962, and renamed *Snipe, Curlew, Teal, Ibis, Hawk,* and *Gull*, respectively. *Aldington* to Ghana in 1964 and renamed *Ejura*, *Bevington, Hickleton, Ilmington, Rennington, Santon* and *Tarlton* to Argentina in 1968 and renamed *Tierra del Fuego, Neuquen, Formosa, Chaco, Chubut* and *Rio Negro*, respectively, *Myrmidon* (ex-*Edderton*) to Malaysia in 1968.

ROYAL NAVAL RESERVE. Eleven units were renamed and attached to Royal Naval Reserve Division Headquarters as follows (Division under *Name*):—

Thames	*Curzon*	*Warsash*	*Venturer*	*St. David*	*Mersey*
London	Sussex	Solent	Severn	S. Wales	Mersey
Kilmorey	*Clyde*	*Montrose*	*Killiecrankie*	*Northumbria*	
Ulster	Clyde	Tay	Forth	Tyne	

(The Humber Division was disbanded in 1958 and HMS *Humber* reverted to her original name *Bronington*). *Woolaston* is London RNR temporarily.

KIRKLISTON (Minehunter) *1969, Dr. Giorgio Arra*

SHOULTON (Minehunter) *1968, Wright & Logan*

IVESTON (Minehunter) *1969, Official*

BRONINGTON (Minehunter) *1969, Official*

BOULSTON *1969, courtesy, Michael D. J. Lennon, Esq*

WISTON *1968, John G. Callis*

INSHORE MINESWEEPERS

20 "HAM" CLASS

M 2601 M 2701 AND M 2777 SERIES

ARLINGHAM	PAS	**FORDHAM**	DGV	**PUTTENHAM**	RNXS
BIRDHAM	RNXS	**FRITHAM**	TRV	**SHIPHAM**	RNXS
BUCKLESHAM	TRV	**HAVERSHAM**	TRV	**THAKEHAM**	RNXS
DITTISHAM *	TRV	**LASHAM**	TRV	**THATCHAM**	DGV
DOWNHAM	TRV	**ODIHAM**	RNXS	**TONGHAM**	PAS
EVERINGHAM	PAS	**PAGHAM**	RNXS	**WARMINGHAM**	DGV
FLINTHAM *	TRV	**PORTISHAM**	RNXS		

Displacement, tons	120 standard; 159 full load
Dimensions, feet	2601 Series: 100 pp; 106·5 oa × 21·2 × 5·5 2701 Series: 100 pp; 107 oa × 21·7 × 5·7 2777 *et seq:* 100 pp; 107·5 oa × 22 × 5·8
Guns	1—40 mm Bofors AA or 1—20 mm Oerlikon AA forward (see *Gunnery*)
Main engines	2 Paxman diesels; 1 100 bhp = 14 knots max (9 knots sea speed) see *Engineering*
Oil fuel (tons)	15
Complement	15 (2 officers, 13 ratings)

Designed to operate in shallow waters, rivers and estuaries. When built they were an entirely new type of vessel embodying novel features resulting from lessons learned during the war and in course of subsequent developments. Named after villages with the suffix "ham". The first inshore minesweeper, *Inglesham*, was launched by J Samuel White & Co Ltd, Cowes, on 23 Apr 1952. The 2701 series were of wooden construction, whereas the 2601 series were of composite construction. All the M 2701 series had a rubbing strake, unlike the M 2601 and M 2001 series.

DGV:—Converted to Degaussing Vessels.
PAS:—Employed in the Port Auxiliary Service.
RNXS:—Adapted for the Royal Naval Auxiliary Service
TRV:—Converted to Torpedo Recovery Vessels.

**Dittisham* and *Flintham* are in full commission as HM ships and training tenders to H.M.S. *Ganges*.

GUNNERY. Most of the M 2601 series had the 40 mm gun replaced by a 20 mm gun. All the M 2701 series had a 20 mm gun (armament as minesweepers).

ENGINEERING. The main machinery was manufactured by Davey Paxman & Co Ltd, Colchester, or by Ruston & Hornsby Ltd, Lincoln, Foden Ltd, Sanbach, Cheshire, or Ransomes, Sims and Jeffries Ltd, Ipswich, under licence from Davey Paxman. Three-bladed propellers, 600 r.p.m.

NOMENCLATURE. *Fordham* was originally to have been named *Pavenham*.

PHOTOGRAPHS
A photograph of *Altham* appears in the 1957-58 and 1958-59 editions, of *Chillingham* in the 1958-59 and 1959-60 editions, of *Darsham* in the 1959-60 edition, of *Woldingham* in the 1960-61 to 1964-65 editions, and of *Polsham* in the 1963-64 to 1966-67 editions.

EVERINGHAM — *1967 A & J Pavia*

AUXILIARY SERVICE. *Birdham, Odiham, Pagham, Portisham, Puttenham, Shipham, Thakeham* were adapted for the Royal Naval Auxiliary Service. *Arlingham, Everingham, Tongham* and *Woldingham* were employed in the Port Auxiliary Service, but *Woldingham* was deleted from the list in 1968.
Bucklesham, Dittisham, Downham, Flintham, Fritham, Haversham and *Lasham* were adapted for service as Torpedo Recovery vessels.
Fordham, Thatcham and *Warmingham* have been converted into Degaussing Vessels to replace the older degaussing vessels of the converted MMS 1001 type.

COASTAL COMMAND. *Chelsham* and *Bottisham* were transferred to the RAF in 1966 for service at Plymouth as Coastal Command range and recovery vessels and numbered HMFA 5000 and HMFA 5001, discarding their former names.

SURVEY CONVERSIONS. *Powderham* and *Yaxham* were converted into inshore survey craft in 1964 and renamed *Waterwitch* and *Woodlark*, respectively.

DITTISHAM — *1969, Official*

Inshore Minesweepers—*continued*

"HAM" CLASS—*continued*

TRANSFERS
Frettenham, Isham, Kingham, Mersham, Mileham, Petersham, Pineham, Rendlesham, Riplingham, Sparham, Stedham, Sulham, Tibenham, Wexham and *Whippingham* were transferred to France in 1954-55; *Hildersham* and *Littlesham* to India in 1955 and renamed *Bimlipitan* and *Bassein*, respectively; *Bassingham* to East Africa on 25 June 1958, but returned on 9 Oct 1961; *Bedham* to Malaysia in 1958 and renamed *Lanka Suka*. *Cardingham* and *Etchingham* to Hong Kong R.N.V.R. in 1959, but returned on 1 Apr 1966; *Altham, Asheldham* and *Brantingham* to Malaysia in 1959 and renamed *Sri Johar, Sri Perlis* and *Temasek*, respectively, *Malham* and *Ottringham* to Ghana at the end of 1959, and renamed *Yogoda* and *Afadzato* respectively; and *Harpham* and *Greetham* to Libya in 1963, and renamed *Brak* and *Zuara*, respectively; *Boreham* and *Felmersham* to Malaysia in 1966 and renamed *Jerong* and *Todak*, respectively; *Popham* and *Wintringham* to Australia on 9 June 1966 and renamed *Otter* and *Seal*, respectively; *Blunham, Bodenham* and *Elsenham* to South Arabia in 1967; *Neasham* to Australia in 1968.

CLASS. *Bisham* and *Edlingham* damaged by fire on 29 Sep 1956 were scrapped in 1959. *Bassingham, Brigham, Chillingham, Cranham, Halsham, Inglesham, Mickleham, Pulham*, (renamed *Isis* while attached to London RNR), *Rampisham* (renamed *Squirrel* while on *Fishery Protection*), *Reedham, Sidlesham, Tresham* and *Wrentham* were on the disposal list in 1964, *Cobham, Damerham, Darsham, Davenham, Glentham* and *Hovingham* were listed for disposal by scrapping in 1965, *Abbotsham, Georgeham, Ledsham, Ludham, Nettleham, Rackham, Sandringham, Saxlingham, Shrivenham* and *Thornham* were officially approved for disposal by scrapping in 1966 (but *Thornham* is attached to Aberdeen University RN Unit) and *Ockham* and *Polsham* in 1967).

ODIHAM — *Added 1964, J W Kennedy*

2 "LEY" CLASS. M 2001 SERIES

AVELEY — **ISIS** (ex-*Cradley*)

Displacement, tons	123 standard; 164 full load
Dimensions, feet	100 pp; 107 oa × 21·8 × 5·5
Guns	1—40 mm AA or 1—20 mm AA forward
Main Engines	2 Paxman diesels; 700 bhp = 13 knots
Oil fuel (tons)	15
Complement	15 (2 officers, 13 ratings)

The "Ley" class differed from the "Ham" class. They were of composite (non-magnetic metal and wooden) construction, instead of all wooden construction. Their superstructure and other features also differed considerably. They had no winch and sweeping gear, as they were mine hunters, not sweepers. They had smaller engines as less towing power was needed. *Aveley* is attached to Plymouth.

ROYAL NAVAL RESERVE
Cradley was allocated to the London Division R.N.R. in 1963 and renamed *Isis*, relieving *Pulham* (renamed *Isis* from 1956 to 1963 while in London R.N.R.).

CLASS. *Broadley*, damaged by fire on 29 Sep 1956, was scrapped in 1959. *Brenchley* and *Brinkley* were for disposal by scrapping in 1965. *Chailey* was on the Sales List in 1965. *Squirrel* and *Warchful* (originally named *Burley* and *Broomley*, respectively, until allocated to Fishery protection in 1960 and 1958) were approved for disposal by scrapping in 1966, *Dingley* in 1967, *Brearley* in 1969.

AVELEY — *Added 1969, Official*

ISIS — *1967, Skyfotos*

CONTROLLED MINELAYERS

4 "MINER" CLASS

Name	Pennant No.	Laid down	Launched	Completed
GOSSAMER (ex-*Miner II*)	N 12	22 Dec 38	18 Aug 39	19 Jan 40
MINER III	N 13	18 Jan 39	16 Nov 39	16 Mar 40
BRITANNIC (ex-*Miner V*)	Ex-N 15	22 Apr 40	2 Nov 40	26 June 41
STEADY (ex-*Miner VII*)	Ex-N 17	31 Mar 43	29 Jan 44	31 Mar 44

Displacement, tons	300 standard; (346 to 355 full load)
Dimensions, feet	110·2 × 26·5 × 8
Main Engines	Ruston & Hornsby diesels; 2 shafts; 360 bhp = 10 knots

All built by Philip & Son Ltd, Dartmouth, and all engined by Ruston & Hornsby Ltd, Lincoln. *Gossamer*, latterly an experimental torpedo trials vessel and no longer capable of minelaying is on the disposal list. *Miner V* was converted into a cable lighter and renamed *Britannic* in 1960 and is now with PAS as store carrier. *Miner VII* was adapted as a stabilisation trials ship at Portsmouth and renamed *Steady* in 1960 and is now with PAS. *Miner III* was a tender for Clearance Diving Teams attached to HMS *Vernon* shore establishment but was relieved by the coastal minesweeper *Laleston* as diving trials ship in 1967.

PHOTOGRAPHS. A photograph of *Gossamer* (aerial view) appears in the 1957-58 and earlier editions.

BRITANNIC *1969, courtesy Dr Giorgio Arra*

MINER III *1969, courtesy Dr Giorgio Arra*

COASTAL MINELAYER. The coastal minelayer *Plover* paid off at HMS *Lochinvar*, Port Edgar base in Dec 1967 and sailed on her last voyage across the Forth to Rosyth Dockyard for disposal in 1968.

CONTROLLED MINELAYERS. Of the "Miner" class *Miner IV* and *Mindful* (ex-*Miner VIII*), formerly tender to the experimental submarine *Explorer*, were sold in 1965. *Minstrel* (ex-*Miner I*), formerly accommodation ship for the experimental submarine *Excalibur*, was listed for disposal by scrapping in 1965 and *Miner VI* was removed from the list in 1968.

The controlled minelaying trawler *Redshank* was scrapped in 1958. The controlled minelayer *Penyu* was disposed of in 1959 and *Linnet* was sold for scrap in 1964.

STALKER *Added 1969, Dr Ian S. Pearsall*

SEAWARD DEFENCE BOATS

4 "FORD" CLASS

ABERFORD P 3102 **DEE** (ex-*Beckford*) P 3104 **DROXFORD** P 3113 **KINGSFORD** P 3117

Displacement, tons	120 standard; 160 full load
Dimensions, feet	110 wl; 117·2 oa × 20 × 7 props
Guns	1—40 mm Bofors AA
A/S weapons	DC rails and large and small DC
Main Engines	Davey Paxman diesels. Foden engine on centre shaft. 1,100 bhp = 18 knots max; 15 knots continuous sea
Oil fuel (tons)	23
Complement	19

Originally designed to detect, locate and destroy submarines, including midget submarines, in the approaches to defended ports. All built in 1953-57. Had modern electronic equipment, depth charge release gear and flares, and comprehensive electrical installations. *Droxford*, formerly attached to H.M.S. *St. Vincent*, now closed down, is on the sales list.

ROYAL NAVAL RESERVE. *Beckford* (renamed *Dee* in 1969) and *Kingsford* were transferred to Mersey and Clyde divisions, respectively, in Dec 1964.

TRANSFERS
Brayford was sold to South African Navy in 1954 and *Glassford* in 1955. *Desford* was transferred to Ceylon in 1955. *Elmina* and *Komenda* were built for Ghana in 1962. *Axford*, *Hinksford* and *Montford* were sold to Nigeria 1 July 1966. *Dubford* and *Gifford* in 1968, and *Bryansford* in 1969.

CLASS. *Camberford, Greatford, Ickford, Marlingford, Mayford, Shalford* and *Tilford* were officially approved for disposal during 1966-67.

DROXFORD *1967, Wright & Logan*

CANCELLATION. The construction of the projected multi-purpose icebreaker, patrol ship, survey vessel and scientific support ship, *Terra Nova*, was cancelled in 1966 (see full particulars and artist's impression in the 1964-65 to 1966-67 editions.

LANDING SHIPS

2 LST (3) TYPE

STALKER (ex-*LST* (3) 3515) **TRACKER** (ex-*LST* (3) 3522)

Displacement, tons	2 140 light; 5 000 full load
Dimensions, feet	330 pp; 347·5 oa × 55·2 × 4·7 (forward); 12 (max)
Guns	8—20 mm Oerlikon AA
Main Engines	Triple expansion; 2 shafts; 5 500 ihp = 13 knots (10 knots cruising)
Boilers	2 Admiralty 3-drum type
Oil fuel (tons)	1 400
Complement	115 officers and ratings

Stalker was designated submarine support ship in 1958. *Lofoten*, designated harbour accommodation ship in 1958, was converted into the Royal Navy's first helicopter support ship in 1964 (for disposal in 1969). *Tracker*, designated harbour accommodation ship in 1958, was converted into a net and boom carrier in 1964.

TRANSFER
Sister ship *Avenger* was transferred to the Indian Navy in 1949 and renamed *Magar*.

NOMENCLATURE
When commercially chartered *Charger* became *Empire Nordic*, *Fighter* became *Empire Grebe*, *Hunter* became *Empire Curlew*, *Trouncer* became *Empire Gull*, *Trumpeter* became *Empire Fulmar* and *Walcheren* became *Empire Guillimot*, *Attacker* was renamed *Empire Cymric* on commercial charter in 1954.

CLASS. *Smiter* was wrecked off Lagos on 25 Apr 1949. *Searcher* was scrapped in 1949. *Bruiser* was stricken in 1959. *Reggio, Salerno, Suvla* and *Vagso* in 1960. *Puncher* and *Raveger* in 1961, and *Hunter* in 1962. *Chaser*, designated as a submarine support ship in 1958, was listed for disposal in 1962. *Zeebrugge*, employed as a harbour accommodation ship since 1958, was placed on the disposal list in 1963. *Dieppe*, designated as a harbour accommodation ship in 1967, was officially approved for disposal by scrapping in 1968, but she was still shown in the spring 1969 Navy List.

TRACKER *Added 1968, A. & J. Pavia*

LST(A) TYPE
Anzio (ex-LST(A) 3003) was officially approved for disposal by scrapping in 1966 (de-equipped ready for tow in 1967) and *Striker* (ex-LST(A) 3516) in 1967. For disposals of the other ships of this class see 1966-67 edition.

LST(C) TYPE
Of the two LST(C) type tank landing ships, *Narvik* (ex-LST(C) 3044) was officially approved for disposal by scrapping in 1968-69, and *Messina* (ex-*LST(C)* 3043) was de-equipped in 1967 for tow to shipbreakers.

"BEN" CLASS
Of the two LST(Q) type tank landing ships, *Ben Nevis*, L 3101 (ex-*LST(Q)* 1, ex-*LST(3)* 3012) was listed for disposal in 1965, and *Ben Lomond*, L 3102 (ex-*LST(Q)* 2, ex-*LST(3)* 3013 was sold out of the Service in 1960.)

LANDING CRAFT

12 LCT (8) TYPE

AACHEN L 4062	**AKYAB** (ex-*Rampart*) L 4037	**AREZZO** L 4128
ABBEVILLE L 4041	**ANDALNES** L 4097	**ARAKAN** L 4164
AGEDABIA L 4085	**ANTWERP** L 4074	**ARROMANCHES** L 4086
AGHEILA L 4002	**ARDENNES** L 4073	**AUDEMER** L 4061

Displacement, tons	657 light; 895 to 1 017 loaded
Dimensions, feet	225 pp; 231·2 oa × 39 × 3·2 forward; 5 aft Beaching draughts
Main Engines	4 Paxman engines; 1 840 bhp 12·6 knots (9 knots cruising)
Complement	33 to 37

Akyab **has lattice mast aft and deckhouse forward.** *LCT* **(8) 4002 (*Agheila*), 4037 (*Akyab*, ex-*Rampart*), 4041 (*Abbeville*), 4061 (*Audemer*), 4062 (*Aachen*), 4073 (*Ardennes*), 4074 (*Antwerp*), 4085 (*Agedabia*), 4086 (*Arromanches*), which has a large lattice mast forward, 4097 (*Andalnes*), 4182 (*Arezzo*) and 4164 (*Arakan*) were transferred from the Royal Navy to the Army.**

PHOTOGRAPHS. A photograph of *Arromanches* appears in the 1960-61 and 1961-62 editions and of *Akyab* in the 1965-66 to 1967-68 editions.

CLASS. *LCT (8)* 4042, 4045, 4050, 4148, 4156 and 4165 were stricken from the list in 1958, and 4025, 4049, 4063 and 4098 in 1960. *LCT (8)* 4063, *Jawada*, on loan to a commercial company, was for disposal at Bahrein. *Redoubt*, L 4001, and *Sallyport*, L 4064, were listed for disposal by scrapping in 1965. *Counterguard*, L 4043, was sold to Malaysia in 1965 and renamed *Sri Langkawi*. *Buttress*, L 4099, was sold to France, in July 1965 and renamed L 9061. *Parapet*, L 4039, was sold to La Société Maseline Ltd (Merchants), Sark, in 1966. *Bastion*, L 4040, was sold to Zambia on 15 Sep 1966. *Citadel*, L 4038, and *Portcullis*, L 4044, which were to have been converted into fleet degaussing vessels, were deleted from the Spring 1969 Navy List.

ANDALNES *1969, Skyfotos*

AUDEMER *1968, Skyfotos*

AGHEILA *1968, John G. Callis*

L 3507 (see Col 2) *1969, courtesy Dr Giorgio Arra*

Landing Craft—*continued*

14 LCM (9) TYPE

LCM (9) 700	**LCM (9) 703**	**LCM (9) 706**	**LCM (9) 710**
LCM (9) 701	**LCM (9) 704**	**LCM (9) 707**	**LCM (9) 711**
LCM (9) 702	**LCM (9) 705**	**LCM (9) 708**	**LCM (9) 3507**
		LCM (9) 709	**LCM (9) 3508**

Displacement, tons	75 light; 176 loaded
Dimensions, feet	77 pp; 85 oa × 21·5 × 5·5
Capacity	2 battle tanks or 100 tons of vehicles
Main Engines	2 Paxman 6 cyl. YHXAM diesels; 2 shafts; 624 bhp 10 knots Screws enclosed in Kort nozzles to improve manoeuvrability.

LCM (9) 3507 and LCM (9) 3508 were the first operational minor landing craft to be built since the Second World War. Ramped in the traditional manner forward, a completely enclosed radar-fitted wheelhouse is positioned aft. Upon completion they carried out familiarisation trials to perfect the new techniques required in launching and recovering LCMs from the flooded sterns of the parent assault ships. Four each of the 700 Series allocated to assault ships.

CONSTRUCTION. The prototype, L 3507, was laid down in Apr. 1962 and accepted on 19 Mar 1963. L 3508 was begun in May 1962 and handed over on 6 June 1963. Both built by Vosper Ltd, Portsmouth. Twelve more of these craft have since been built, 700, 701, 702 and 703 by Brook Marine Ltd, Lowestoft (launched in 1965), 704, 705, 706, 707, 708 and 709 by Richard Dunston Ltd, Thorne (launched in 1965-66), and 710 and 711 by J. Bolson & Sons, Ltd, Poole (launched in Oct 1966).

DESIGN. A new type of Landing Craft Mechanized for operation with the Assault Ships recently built for the Royal Navy. Designed by Vosper Ltd in collaboration with the Royal Navy. The design was evolved as the result of the most exhaustive tank trials ever carried out on a landing craft. Scale models were made and operated by remote control in the Admiralty Experiment Works test tank at Haslar, using simulated wave conditions to prove the design in the roughest possible sea conditions, resulting in a design incorporating new standards of landing craft stability.

ENGINEERING. The Davey Paxman diesels are of the A6YHXAM type, the shafts being geared by a Vee-drive to enable the propulsion machinery to be placed as far aft as possible, an arrangement which provides a clear well deck for tanks and heavy transport carried in the new assault ships.

STEERING. Fitted with Kort rudders, which consist of a swivelling ring surrounding each of the two propellers and which replace conventional rudders. The Kort rudders produce more precise steering and control when going ahead or astern. The ring enclosing each propeller also provides protection when beaching in shallow water during disembarkation or recovery of tanks and heavy transport.

L 702 (F3) *1967, Wright & Logan*

10 MRC (Ex-LCT)

MEDWAY (MRC 1110) **SIMBANG** (MRC 1100)

Maintenance and Repair Craft, former Tank Landing Craft, *Cana*, rated as Naval Servicing Craft (Engineering) was in Singapore reserve, now for disposal. *Medway* (see photograph on page 280, 1966-67 edition) a Submarine Support Ship, was base ship Seventh Submarine Division, until relieved by *Forth* in 1966, but she is still shown in the 1968 Navy List. *Simbang*, nominal depot ship, RN Air Station, Singapore. Also *MRC* 1013, 1015, 1023, 1097, 1098, 1119 (for disposal), 1120, and 1413 (ex-LCT (E) 413) used as a power and workshop, Malta, *MRC* 1122 was sold to Ghana in July 1956 and renamed *Asuantsi*. *Cana* (MRC 1109) was removed from the Navy List in 1968.

2 LCM (7) 7,000 SERIES (and NSB)

Displacement, tons	28 light; 63 loaded
Dimensions, feet	60·2 × 16 × 3·7
Main Engines	290 bhp = 9·8 knots

Nos. 7037, 7100. Three are employed as naval servicing boats and store carriers: 7037 (NSB 351), 7100 (NSB 359), 7104 (NSB 358). Some of the LCM (7) type were re-engined with Gray Marine diesels. 7087 and 7104 were removed from the list in 1968 and 7016 in 1969.

29 LCVP 100 SERIES

Displacement, tons	8·5 light; 13·5 full load; LCVP (ex-LCA (2)s 11·5 light; 16 full load
Dimensions, feet	41·5 LCVP (2)s; 43 × 10 × 2·5
Main Engines	130 bhp = 8 knots; LCVP (2)s: 2 Foden diesels, 200 bhp = 10 knots

There are 15 LCVP (1)s Nos 101 to 136 (103 and 118 were deleted from the list in 1969) and 14 LCVP (2)s, Nos 137 to 150. There were also a number of variations and prototypes of about the same length (43 feet).

Raiding Landing Craft, including LCR 5507 and 5508, and Navigational Landing Craft, including LCN 604 (ex-LCR 5505). LCA (1) 1275, 1330, 1481, 1485, 1644, 1678, 1705, 1712, 1733, 1745, 1779 and 1787 were for disposal in 1961, eleven more in 1963, and 1272, 1543, 1639, 1972 and 1891 in 1964, 1485 and 1700 in 1968. LCVP (2)s carried by *Intrepid* and *Fearless* can carry 35 troops or 2 Land Rovers. Crew 4. LCA (2)s were redesignated LCVPs (Landing Craft Vehicle and Personnel) in 1966.

2 LCP (L)3 500 SERIES

Displacement, tons	6·5 light; 10 loaded
Dimensions, feet	37 × 11 × 3·2
Main Engines	225 bhp = 12 knots

There are two LCP (L) 3s Nos 501 and 503. Aurora gas turbines were installed in LCP (L) 3 No. 502.
LCP (L) No. 556 (6·5 tons light, 10 tons full load, 37 × 11 × 3·2 feet, 225 bhp, speed 12 knots) was officially deleted from the list in 1969.

FAST PATROL BOATS

2 "BRAVE" CLASS

(Gas Turbine Type Convertible Torpedo Gunboats)

BRAVE BORDERER P 1011 **BRAVE SWORDSMAN** P 1012

Displacement, tons	89 standard; 114 full load
Dimensions, feet	90 wl; 96 hull; 98·8 oa × 25·5 × 7 props
Armament	As MGB: 2—40 mm single guns in power operated mountings; 2—21 inch side launched torpedoes As MTB: 4—21 inch torpedoes; 1—40 mm gun
Main Engines	3 Bristol Siddeley Proteus 1 250 gas turbines; 3 shafts; 10 500 shp = 52 knots max, 46 knots continuous. Fixed pitch propellers 1 700 rpm
Fuel capacity, tons	25
Complement	20 (3 officers, 17 ratings)

Built by Vosper Ltd, Portsmouth. The hull is framed in welded aluminium with double skinned planking of mahogany and sheathed with glass fibre below the waterline. An hydraulic operated flap fitted on the transom maintains the running trim. Very beamy in relation to length, the ratio being less than 1:4 only. *Brave Borderer*, was launched on 7 Jan 1958 and accepted on 26 Jan 1960. Cost: £880,000. *Brave Swordsman* was launched on 22 May 1958 and was handed over on 20 July 1960. Cost: £640,000.

ENGINEERING. Powered with Proteus gas turbines, originally designed for aircraft use, but adapted for marine purposes by Bristol Siddeley Engines Ltd, Filton, in association with W H Allen, Sons & Co Ltd, Bedford, who supplied the primary reduction gears and the reverse reduction gearboxes. Rover gas turbines driving Metro-Vickers 40 kw generators provide electrical power. No diesel machinery. Both Proteus and Rover turbines run on diesel fuel. Authorised maximum rating of Proteus is 3 500 shp and maximum continuous rating 2 800 shp. A striking feature is that with the primary reduction gearbox the Proteus gives one hp for every 0.83 lbs of its weight, and including the reverse reduction gearbox, one hp for every 1·6 lbs of its weight. Designed for offensive operations against enemy warships and merchant ships in coastal, inshore and shoal waters, where high speed is essential. The propellers are relatively small and of high speed. This was a novel and unusual feature resulting from joint research carried out out by the Royal Navy and Vosper Ltd. using the firm's cavitation tunnel. Gas turbines give an increase of 35 per cent in total power combined with a reduction of 50 per cent in machinery and a saving of 25 per cent in machinery space.

ELECTRICAL. The electrical system incorporates experimental light weight equipment designed and installed by Vosper Ltd, to make an overall contribution to weight reduction. The generators comprise two Rover gas turbines, each of 40 kW.

DESIGN. The design studies were carried out by Vosper with Royal Navy departments and co-ordinated by the Director General, Ships, whose extensive research facilities were available at all stages in design. Both craft underwent extensive evaluation trials and the design proved to be very satisfactory.

ARMAMENT. The originally designed armament, functioning as Motor Gun Boats, comprised one 3·3 inch turret mounted gun specially developed for these craft, with a stabilisation system capable of dealing with the motion experienced in such high speed craft. With the 3·3 inch gun was one 40 mm gun and two 21 inch torpedoes.

FUNCTIONAL. In addition to their roles as gunboats or torpedo boats these craft can also be employed as minelayers or high speed raiding craft for Commandos.

EXPERIMENTAL. Both were initially in the Coastal Forces Trials and Special Service Squadron, at H.M.S. *Dolphin II*, formerly H.M.S. *Hornet*, shore base at Gosport.

FISHERY PROTECTION. In Aug 1962 both were attached to the Fishery Protection Squadron in British waters to achieve greater surprise in areas where poaching was likely, a role for which with their high speed they are eminently suitable.

PHOTOGRAPHS. Photographs as torpedo boats (carrying four torpedoes) appear in the 1960-61 to 1962-63 editions (*Brave Borderer*) and 1961-62 and 1962-63 editions (*Brave Swordsman*). A starboard broadside view of *Brave Swordsman* as gunboat (two torpedoes) at speed appears in the 1963-64 to 1966-67 editions, a starboard bow oblique aerial view of *Brave Borderer* as gunboat in the 1964-65 to 1967-68 editions, a bow view of *Brave Borderer* and *Brave Swordsman* in company at sea in the 1967-68 and 1968-69 editions.

BRAVE SWORDSMAN and BRAVE BORDERER — *1968, Official*

BRAVE SWORDSMAN — *1969, Skyfotos*

Fast Patrol Boats—*continued*

3 NEW CONSTRUCTION. ANTI-FPB TYPE

Three anti-fast patrol boat training craft are in the current new construction programme.

2 "DARK" CLASS

(Convertible Motor Torpedo Boats and Motor Gunboats)

DARK GLADIATOR P 1114 **DARK HERO** P 1115

Displacement, tons	50 standard; 70 full load
Dimensions, feet	67 wl; 71·5 oa × 19·8 × 6·1 max
Armament	As MGB: 1—4·5 inch gun; 1—40 mm AA gun (or 2—40 mm AA guns) As MTB: 4—21 inch torpedo tubes; 1—40 mm AA
Main Engines	2 Napier Deltic diesels; 5 000 shp = 46 knots (designed); 35 to 37 knots sea speed
Fuel capacity (tons)	8
Complement	15

Of composite construction, aluminium alloy being used for the framing and deck. Hulls are painted black. Cost £325,000 to £338,000 each. The design was not entirely successful. The boats were overweight, and it was not possible to develop full engine power owing to vibration, unsatisfactory propellers, and intake and exhaust restrictions. Can also be employed as minelayers (*Dark Antagonist* carried six ground mines).

ENGINEERING. A new design of diesel machinery which for its power was the lightest unit so far designed. The Napier Deltic, an opposed piston two-stroke engine, of high performance, constructed in triangular form with three crankshafts, an arrangement new to engineering. It was designed and developed for the Royal Navy by D. Napier & Son Ltd, London, on behalf of their parent company, the English Electric Company Ltd. The type I8-11B develops 2 500 shp at 2 000 rpm. The engine and reverse gear weighs only 10 500 lbs and therefore gives one hp for every 4·2 lbs of its weight. This is the best power-weight ratio ever achieved in a marine diesel. All power is provided by diesel machinery. A Foden FD. 4 two-stroke diesel drives the 35 kw. auxiliary generator set and bilge pump.

EXPERIMENTAL. Unlike earlier craft, of composite wood planking on aluminium framing, *Dark Scout*, last of the 18 boats, built by Saunders-Roe (Anglesey) Ltd, Beaumaris, was of all-welded aluminium throughout. The hull was of hard chine form, developed to give good seagoing qualities with high maximum and cruising speeds.

TRANSFERS. Five boats of the "Dark" type were purchased by Burma and two by Finland. In Feb 1968 *Dark Avenger*, *Dark Biter*, *Dark Hunter* and *Dark Invader* were sold to Italy.

PHOTOGRAPHS. A photograph of *Dark Hussar* appears in the 1959-60 edition, of *Dark Adventurer* (as gunboat) in the 1955-56 to 1958-59 editions, of *Dark Antagonist* and *Dark Highwayman* in the 1960-61 to 1967-68 editions.

CANCELLATION. The construction of the 19th boat, *Dark Horseman* was abandoned.

CLASS. *Dark Aggressor*, *Dark Killer*, *Dark Rover* and *Dark Scout* were disposed of *Dark Antagonist*, *Dark Buccaneer*, *Dark Clipper*, *Dark Fighter*, *Dark Highwayman*, in the 1967 Navy List, were scheduled to be scrapped. *Dark Adventurer*, *Dark Hussar* and *Dark Intruder* in the 1968 Navy List are for sale. *Dark Intruder* was in commission in 1966, *Dark Hero* was in commission in 1966 to 1968 and *Dark Gladiator* was in commission in 1967 to 1969 (in the 1st FPB Squadron with *Brave Borderer* and *Brave Swordsman*).

"BOLD" CLASS

Bold Pathfinder was disposed of in 1962 and *Bold Pioneer* in 1958.

"GAY" CLASS

Gay Brusier, *Gay Centurion*, *Gay Dragoon* and *Gay Forester* were on the sales list in 1961. *Gay Archer*, *Gay Bombadier*, *Gay Bowman*, *Gay Caribineer* and *Gay Cavalier* were on the disposal list in 1963. *Gay Charger*, *Gay Charioteer* and *Gay Fencer*, were latterly employed as fast target towing boats, and *Gay Charrioteer* is still in the Spring 1969 Navy List.

DARK INTRUDER — *1968, John G. Callis*

DARK GLADIATOR — *1968, courtesy Mr. Godfrey H. Walker*

In June-July 1967 the Royal Navy found it necessary to charter for three weeks the Vosper fast patrol boat *Ferocity* (built as a private venture in 1960) while one of the "Brave" class fast patrol boats was being overhauled, and she was temporarily commissioned into the Royal Navy as HMS *Ferocity*. Particulars in 1968-69 edition. Vosper Thornycroft have built another private venture fast patrol boat, TENACITY, see later page.

COASTAL SURVEY SHIPS

FAWN *1969, Wright & Logan*

BEAGLE *1969, Official*

FOX *1969, Official*

4 "FAWN" CLASS. NEW CONSTRUCTION

BEAGLE **BULLDOG** **FAWN** **FOX**

Displacement, tons	800 approx standard (official figure); 990 full load
Dimensions, feet	189 oa × 37·5 × 12
Main Engines	4 Lister Blackstone ERS8M, 8 cyl. 4 str. diesels, coupled to 2 shafts, 2 000 bhp = 15 knots max designed, controllable pitch propellers
Range, miles	4 000 at 12 knots cruising
Complement	38 (4 officers, 34 ratings)

A new class of coastal survey ships planned for the charting and re-charting of shallow waters. Designed for duty overseas, working in pairs. *Fawn* and *Fox* replace the coastal minesweeper conversions. The names originally allocated were *Albacore, Albatross, Barracouta, Bulldog, Fawn* and *Fox*, but these were changed in 1965 to *Beagle, Bulldog, Fawn, Fox, Pelican* and *Porcupine*, and the two latter were cancelled in 1967. The first ship of the class launched was *Bulldog* on 12 July 1967 at Brooke Marine Ltd, Lowestoft, followed by *Beagle* on 7 Sep 1967, *Fox* on 6 Nov 1967 and *Fawn* on 29 Feb 1968. *Bulldog* was commissioned on 21 Mar 1968 and the others by the end of 1968. Built to commercial standards. Lloyd's class 100 A1 and additionally to naval standards where applicable. Fitted with passive tank stabilizer to reduce rolling, most modern echo sounders, precision ranging radar, Decca "Hifix" system, automatic steering. Air conditioned throughout. Carries 28·5 ft survey motor launch in davits. Capable of hydrographic survey anywhere in the world. Designed for maximum habitability.

BULLDOG *1968, Wright & Logan*

"TON" CLASS
Of the two coastal survey ships of the "Ton" class, modified coastal minesweepers, *Myrmidon* (ex-*Edderton*) was sold to Malaysia in 1968, and *Mermaid* (ex-*Sullington*) was officially approved for disposal by scrapping in 1968-69.

INSHORE SURVEY CRAFT

EGERIA *1969, courtesy Dr. Ian S. Pearsall*

3 "E" CLASS

ECHO A 70 **EGERIA** A 72 **ENTERPRISE** A 71

Displacement, tons	160
Dimensions, feet	100 pp; 106·8 oa × 22 × 5·6 fwd, 6·8 aft
Main Engines	2 Paxman diesels; 2 shafts; Controllable pitch propellers. 700 bhp = 14 knots max; 12 knots normal
Oil fuel (tons)	15
Endurance, miles	1 600 at 10 knots
Complement	18 (2 officers, 16 ratings)
Accommodation	22 (4 officers, 18 ratings)

Echo, the first Inshore Survey Craft, was built by J. Samuel White & Co Ltd, Cowes, launched on 1 May 1957, and commissioned on 12 Sep 1958. *Egeria* was built by Wm Weatherhead & Sons Ltd, Cockenzie, and *Enterprise* by M. W. Blackmore & Sons Ltd, Bideford. Of all-wood construction with glued laminated members. *Echo's* main machinery was manufactured by Davey Paxman & Co Ltd, Colchester. No armament, but was fitted with a 40 mm gun for trials and retains her gun seat. In wartime she could be used as an armed inshore minehunter on which her design was based. All built for coastal and harbour hydrographic surveys around the British Isles. Ability to navigate in shoal water, to obtain depths and detect wrecks on the sea bed, and to fix the position with accuracy. Equipped with two echo sounding machines and sonar for wreck location, and survey equipment for triangulation ashore. Modern radar, wire sweep gear, echo sounding launch, and modern chart room.

PHOTOGRAPHS. A larger photograph of *Echo*, without armament appears in the 1959-60 edition, and a photograph as built with gun in the 1960-61 to 1967-68 editions.

ECHO *1968, John G. Callis*

2 "HAM" CLASS

MODIFIED INSHORE MINESWEEPERS

WATERWITCH (ex-*Powderham*) M 304 **WOODLARK** (ex-*Yaxham*) M 2780

Displacement, tons	120 standard; 160 full load
Dimensions, feet	107·5 oa × 22 × 5·5
Main Engines	Diesels; 2 shafts; 1 100 bhp = 14 knots
Endurance, miles	1 500 at 12 knots
Complement	18 (2 officers, 16 ratings)

Former inshore minesweepers of the "Ham" class converted to replace the old survey motor launches *Meda* and *Medusa* for operation in inshore waters at home. *Waterwitch* was seconded to Port Auxiliary Service in 1968.

WOODLARK (ex-*Yaxham*) *Wright & Logan*

FLEET SUPPLY SHIPS

3 NEW CONSTRUCTION STORES SUPPORT SHIPS (AFS)

LYNESS A 339 **STROMNESS** A 344 **TARBATNESS** A 345

Displacement, tons	*circa* 16 500 laden (official figure)
Measurements, tons	12 359 gross; 4 744 net; 7 782 deadweight
Dimensions, feet	490 pp; 524 oa × 72 × 25·5
Aircraft	Facilities for helicopters
Main Engines	Wallsend-Sulzer 8-cyl RD.76 diesel; 11 520 bhp = 17 knots
Complement	184

Ordered on 7 Dec 1964. Designed and built by Swan Hunter & Wigham Richardson Ltd, Wallsend-on-Tyne to meet specific requirements. All fitted with Sulzer type main machinery remotely controlled, and auxiliary machinery manufactured by Wallsend Slipway & Engineering Co Ltd. Lifts and mobile appliances provided for handling stores internally, and a new replenishment at sea system and a helicopter landing platform for transferring loads at sea. A novel feature of the ships is the use of closed circuit television to monitor the movement of stores. All air-conditioned. *Lyness* was launched on 7 Apr 1966, *Stromness* on 16 Sep 1966, and *Tarbatness* on 27 Feb 1967. *Lyness* was completed on 22 Dec 1966, *Stromness* on 21 Mar 1967.

LYNESS *1969, Official*

STROMNESS *1967, Official*

1 AIR STORES SUPPORT SHIP

RELIANT (ex-*Somersby*) A 84

Displacement, tons	4 447 light as built; 13 737 full load
Measurement, tons	9 290 deadweight (summer), 8 460 gross
Dimensions, feet	440 pp; 468·8 oa × 61·5 × 26·2
Main Engines	Doxford 6 cyl. diesel; 8 250 bhp = 18 knots
Complement	110 officers and men

Built by Sir James Laing & Sons Ltd, Sunderland. Launched on 9 Sep 1953. Engined by Hawthorn Leslie. Completed in 1954. Former grain carrier which traded for two years, working between the Gulf of Mexico and the United Kingdom, before purchase from the Ropner Shipping Company. Converted for her now role at North Shields. Sailed from Chatham on 4 Nov 1958 for the Far East as the Royal Navy's first air/victualling stores issuing ship capable of replenishing aircraft carriers at sea. Has an endurance of 50 days steaming at 16 knots, and carries 40 000 different patterns of aircraft spares and general naval stores. Has six holds and the latest automatic tensioning winch for transfer of stores to aircraft carriers in unfavourable weather. Fully air-conditioned for service in the tropics. Her conversion was based on the concept that aircraft carriers should be able to spend more time at sea, independent of shore bases. Originally named *Somersby*. Renamed *Reliant* in 1958. As refitted she has a helicopter landing platform built over the poop deckhouse with netting surrounds.

RELIANT *1967, A & J Pavia*

2 NEW CONSTRUCTION REPLENISHMENT SHIPS

REGENT A 486 **RESOURCE** A 480

Displacement, tons	19 000 full load (deep departure)
Measurement, tons	18 029 gross
Dimensions, feet	600 pp; 640 oa × 77·2 × 26·1
Aircraft	1 Wessex helicopter embarked
Guns	2—40 mm Bofors (single)
Main Engines	Steam turbines (by Associated Electrical Industries)
Complement	119 R.F.A. service and Merchant Navy officers and ratings; 52 Navy Department industrial and non-industrial civil servants; 11 Royal Navy (1 officer and 10 ratings) for helicopter flying and maintenance.

It was officially announced on 24 Jan. 1963 that two 19 000-ton replenishment ships would be ordered. On 13 Aug. the builders were named: Scott's Shipbuilding & Engineering Co, Greenock; and Harland & Wolff, Belfast. They have lifts for armaments and stores, and helicopter platforms for transferring loads at sea. Designed from the outset as Fleet Replenishment Ships (previous ships have been converted merchant vessels). Air conditioned. *Resource* was launched at Greenock on 11 Feb 1966. *Regent* was launched at Belfast on 9 Mar 1966.

RESOURCE *1969, Official*

REGENT *1968, Official*

2 FLEET REPLENISHMENT SHIPS

RESURGENT (ex-*Changchow*) A 280 **RETAINER** (ex-*Chungking*) A 329

Displacement, tons	14 000 (approx) official estimate
Measurement, tons	*Resurgent* 9 511 gross; *Retainer* 9 301 gross
Dimensions, feet	451 pp; 477·2 oa × 62 × 29 max
Main Engines	Doxford diesel; 1 shaft; 6 500 bhp = 15 knots
Oil fuel (tons)	925

Former passenger and cargo motor vessels, both built for the China Navigation Co by Scotts' Shipbuilding and Engineering Co Ltd, Greenock, and completed in 1951 and 1950, respectively. *Retainer* was formerly a passenger and cargo liner along the China coast. She was purchased in 1952 and converted into a naval storeship during autumn 1954-April 1955 by Palmers Hebburn Co Ltd, where further conversion was carried out Mar-Aug 1957 to extend her facilities as a stores ship, including the fitting out of holds to carry naval stores, the installation of lifts for stores, the provision of extra cargo handling gear and new bridge wings. *Resurgent* was taken over on completion for employment as a fleet replenishment ship.

RESURGENT *1969, Official*

RETAINER *Added 1966, Wright & Logan*

ARMAMENT SUPPORT SHIPS

3 FORT CLASS

FORT LANGLEY A 230 | **FORT ROSALIE** A 186 | **FORT SANDUSKY** A 316

Displacement, tons	5 250 light; 9 788 normal (13 820 full load)
Measurement, tons	8 570 deadweight; 7 201 to 7 332 gross
Dimensions, feet	416 pp; 424·5 wl; 441·5 oa × 57 × 27
Main Engines	Triple expansion; 2 500 ihp = 11 knots
Boilers	2 Babcock & Wilcox

All launched in 1944. *Fort Langley, Fort Rosalie* and *Fort Sandusky* are Armament Support Ships. Rated as Royal Fleet Auxiliaries. Similar in type to the Maintenance Ships of the "Mull" and "Head" Classes, see earlier page.

PHOTOGRAPHS. A photograph of *Fort Dunvegan* appears in the 1960-61 to 1966-67 editions, and of *Fort Duquesne* in the 1967-68 edition.

CLASS. *Fort Beauharnois* and *Fort Constantine* were stricken from the list in 1963. *Fort Charlotte* and *Fort Duquesne* were sold in 1968, and *Fort Dunvegan* in 1969.

FORT LANGLEY *1969, Official*

FORT SANDUSKY *1966, A & J Pavia*

FORT ROSALIE *1968, A. & J. Pavia*

STORE CARRIERS

2 "BACCHUS" CLASS

BACCHUS A 404 | **HEBE** A 406

Displacement, tons	2 740 light; 7 958 full load
Measurement, tons	4 823 gross; 2 441 net; 5 218 deadweight
Dimensions, feet	350 pp; 379 oa × 55 × 22 max
Main Engines	Swan Hunter Sulzer diesel; 1 shaft; 5 500 bhp = 15 knots
Oil fuel, tons	720
Complement	57

Built by Henry Robb Ltd, Leith, for the British India Steam Navigation Co. Taken over by the Royal Navy on completion on long term bare boat charter and operated as Royal Fleet Auxiliaries. Rated as dry cargo ships. *Bacchus* was completed in Sep 1962, *Hebe* in May 1962. Crew accommodation and engines aft as in tankers.

BACCHUS *1967, Wright & Logan*

ROYAL YACHT

BRITANNIA A 00

Displacement, tons	3 990 light; 4 961 full load
Measurement, tons	5 769 gross
Dimensions, feet	Length: 360 pp; 380 wl; 412·2 oa; Beam: 55. Draught: 15·6 (mean at load), 17 max.
Main Engines	Single reduction geared steam turbines; 2 shafts; 12 000 shp = 21 knots approx continuous cruising speed; 22·75 knots max (trials)
Boilers	2
Radius, miles	2 100 at 20 knots; 2 400 at the economical speed of 18 knots; 3 000 miles at 15 knots
Oil fuel (tons)	330 (can be increased to 490 with auxiliary fuel tanks)
Complement	271

This vessel was designed as a medium sized naval hospital ship to be used by Her Majesty The Queen in time of peace as a Royal Yacht. Built by John Brown & Co Ltd, Clydebank. Ordered in Feb 1952. Laid down on 16 June 1952. Launched on 16 Apr 1953. Completed on 14 Jan 1954. She has endurance sufficient to enable her to undertake long ocean voyages, modified cruiser stern, and raked bow. Her construction conforms to mercantile practice. The complete bridge structure, and the funnel, are constructed of aluminium. The ship is fitted with Denny-Brown single fin stabilisers to reduce roll in bad weather from 20 deg to 6 deg. Cost £2,098,000. To enable her to pass under the bridges of the St. Lawrence Seaway when she visited Canada, the top 20 feet of her mainmast and the wireless aerial on her foremast were hinged in Nov 1958 so that they can be lowered as required.

BRITANNIA *1969, Wright & Logan*

TRAWLERS

8 "ISLES" CLASS (TANK CLEANING VESSELS)

2 *Ardrossan Dockyard Co Ltd, Ardrossan*	
COLL	7 Apr 1942
GRAEMSAY	3 Aug 1942
2 *Cook, Welton & Gemmell Ltd, Beverley*	
BERN	2 May 1942
LUNDY	29 Aug 1942
1 *A. & J. Inglis Ltd, Glasgow*	
SWITHA	3 Apr 1942
3 *John Lewis & Sons Ltd., Aberdeen*	
CALDY	31 Aug 1943
FOULNESS	23 Mar 1943
SKOMER	17 June 1943

Displacement, tons	560 standard; 770 full load
Dimensions, feet	150 pp; 164 oa × 27·5 × 14
Main Engines	Triple expansion; 1 shaft; 850 ihp = 12 knots
Boilers	1 cylindrical
Coal, tons	183
Radius, miles	4 200 at 8 knots

Launch dates above. Former minesweeping trawlers converted to tank cleaning vessels. Classed as port auxiliary service craft and have "A" pennant numbers. Sister ship *Bardsey*, also converted, was taken over by Malta Dockyard. For transfers, disposals and other particulars of "Isles" class trawlers see 1961-62 edition.

PHOTOGRAPHS. A large photograph of *Graemsay* appears in the 1959-60 to 1961-62 editions and a port broadside view of *Skomer* in the 1962-63 to 1966-67 editions.

SWITHA *1967, J. W. Kennedy*

HEBE (see Col. 1) *1969, Official*

FLEET REPLENISHMENT OILERS

3 "OL" CLASS

Name	No	Builders	Launched	Completed
OLMEDA (ex-*Oleander*)	A 124	Swan Hunter, Wallsend	19 Nov 1964	18 Oct 1965
OLNA	A 123	Hawthorn Leslie, Hebburn	28 July 1965	1 Apr 1966
OLWEN (ex-*Olynthus*)	A 122	Hawthorn Leslie, Hebburn	10 July 1964	21 June 1965

Displacement, tons — 10 890 light; 33 240 full load
Measurement, tons — 22 350 deadweight; 18 600 gross
Dimensions, feet — 611·1 pp; 648 oa × 84 × 34
Aircraft — 2 Wessex helicopters (can carry 3)
Main Engines — Pametrada double reduction geared turbines; 26 500 shp = 19 knots; 21·2 on trials
Boilers — 2 Babcock & Wilcox, 750 lbs sq in, 950 deg F
Complement — 87 (25 officers and 62 ratings)

Largest and fastest ships to join the Royal Fleet Auxiliary Service. Of an entirely new class designed by Hawthorn Leslie and Swan Hunter to meet specified requirements. Machinery for *Olmeda* was manufactured by Wallsend Slipway & Engineering Co Ltd, and for *Olna* and *Olwen* by Hawthorn Leslie (Engineers) Ltd. Designed for support of the Fleet, they are fitted with handling gear for transferring fuels and stores by jackstay and derricks whilst steaming at speed. A helicopter landing platform and hangar are provided to enable helicopter carrying ships to collect stores by air. Sophisticated machinery control systems are incorporated, including bridge control of ahead revolutions. Specially strengthened for operations in ice. Accommodation of a very high standard is fully air conditioned. Additionally, *Olna* is fitted with a transverse bow thrust unit for improved manoeuvrability in confined waters and with a new design of replenishment at sea system. *Olynthus* was renamed *Olwen* in Sep. 1967 to obviate confusion with the submarine *Olympus*, in correspondence and by telephone and *Oleander* was renamed *Olmeda* to avoid confusion with the frigate *Leander*.

OLWEN — *1969, Skyfotos*

OLNA — *1969, Official*

OLMEDA — *1969, Official*

2 LATER "TIDE" CLASS

TIDESPRING A 75 — **TIDEPOOL** A 76

Displacement, tons — 8 531 light; 25 931 full load
Measurement, tons — 17 400 deadweight; 14 130 gross
Dimensions, feet — 550 pp; 583 oa × 71 × 32
Main Engines — Double reduction geared turbines; 15 000 shp = 17 knots
Boilers — 2 Babcock & Wilcox
Complement — 115 (30 officers and 85 ratings)

Built by Hawthorn Leslie, Hebburn. The machinery was installed by Hawthorn Leslie (Engineers) Ltd. Highly specialised ships for the fuelling (13 000 tons cargo fuel) and storing of naval vessels at sea and capable of high performance under rigorous service conditions. Their all-round capability is enhanced by the provision of a helicopter landing platform and hangar. *Tidespring* was laid down on 24 July 1961, launched on 3 May 1962, and accepted into service on 18 Jan 1963. *Tidepool* was laid down on 4 Dec 1961 and launched on 11 Dec 1962. A photograph of *Tidespring* appears in the 1963-64 to 1966-67 editions.

TIDEPOOL — *1967, Official*

Fleet Replenishment Oilers—*continued*

TIDESPRING — *1969, Official*

3 "TIDE" CLASS

TIDEFLOW (ex-*Tiderace*) A 97 — **TIDESURGE** (ex-*Tiderange*) A 98 — **TIDEREACH** A 96

Displacement, tons — 9 040 light; 25 940 full load
Measurement, tons — 16 900 deadweight; 13 700 gross
Dimensions, feet — 550 pp; 583 oa × 71 × 32 max.
Main Engines — Double reduction geared turbines; 15 000 shp = 17 knots

Tidereach, launched by Swan, Hunter & Wigham Richardson Ltd, Wallsend-on-Tyne, on 2 June 1954, and completed on 30 Aug 1955, was the first of the new Fleet Replenishment Tankers. The main machinery was manufactured by the Wallsend Slipway Co. Designed for the support of the Fleet and replenishment under way at sea. Capacious (15 000 tons of fuel cargo) and fitted with modern handling gear for transferring food, stores, ammunition, oil and jet aircraft fuels by jackstay and derricks. Oil cargo can be discharged at high rate to ships on either beam or astern, while steaming at speed. *Tiderange* (renamed *Tidesurge*) in 1958 was launched at I. L. Thompson & Sons Ltd, Sunderland, on 30 Aug 1954. the main machinery of both being manufactured by North Eastern Marine Engineering Co Ltd, Wallsend. A fourth ship, *Tide Austral*, built for Australia, was renamed *Supply* on 7 Sep 1962. A photograph of *Tidereach* appears in the 1959-60 and earlier editions.

TIDEREACH refuelling *Hermes* — *1969, Official*

TIDEFLOW — *1969, Wright & Logan*

TIDESURGE — *1966, A. & J. Pavia*

Oilers—*continued*

7 "LEAF" GROUP

APPLELEAF (ex-M.V. *George Lyras*) A 83

Displacement, tons	22 980 full load
Measurement, tons	16 850 deadweight; 11 588 gross; 6 559 net
Dimensions, feet	526 pp; 577·5 oa × 68 × 29·8 mean summer draught
Main Engines	Doxford 6-cyl diesel, 119 rpm; 6 800 bhp = 14 knots
Oil fuel (tons)	1 480
Complement	67

The M.V. *George Lyras*, built by Bartram & Co Ltd, and formerly owned by Marine Enterprises Ltd, was launched on 22 Apr 1955, completed in Sep 1955, and taken over by the Royal Navy on 17 Apr 1959 on a long term bareboat charter for service as a Royal Fleet Auxiliary and renamed *Appleleaf*.

APPLELEAF *1968, Wright & Logan*

BAYLEAF (ex-*London Integrity*) A 79 **BRAMBLELEAF** (ex-*London Loyalty*) A 81

Measurement, tons	17 960 deadweight; 12 123 gross; 7 042 net
Dimensions, feet	526 pp; 556·7 oa × 71·3 × 30
Main Engines	Doxford 6-cyl. diesel; 6 800 bhp = 14·5 knots (*Bayleaf*); 14 knots (*Brambleleaf*)
Oil fuel (tons)	1 470

Both built by Furness S.B. Co Ltd. *Bayleaf* was launched on 28 Oct 1954 and completed in Apr 1955. *Brambleleaf* was completed in Jan 1954. Both from London & Overseas Freighters Ltd, 22 May 1959.

BAYLEAF *Tom Molland Ltd*

BRAMBLELEAF *1969, Wright & Logan*

ORANGELEAF (ex-M.V. *Southern Satellite*) A 80

Measurement, tons	17 475 deadweight; 12 481 gross; 6 949 net
Dimensions, feet	525 pp; 556·5 oa × 71·7 × 30·5 mean
Main Engines	Doxford 6-cyl. diesel; 6 800 bhp = 15 knots
Oil fuel (tons)	1 610

Built by Furness Shipbuilding Co Ltd, Haverton Hill on Tees. Launched on 8 Feb 1955. Completed June 1955. From South Georgia Co Ltd, 25 May 1959.

All "Leaf" class tankers have astern fuelling capabilities. *Orangeleaf*, *Pearleaf* and *Plumleaf* have abeam fuelling capabilities also.

CLASS. The oiler *Cherryleaf*, A 82 (ex- MV *Laurelwood*) was returned to her owners (Molasses & General Transport Co Ltd) in 1966. Sold to Greek interests.

ORANGELEAF *1967, Skyfotos*

"Leaf" Group—*continued*

PEARLEAF A 77

Displacement, tons	24 900 full load
Measurement, tons	18 045 deadweight; 12 139 gross; 7 216 net
Dimensions, feet	535 pp; 568 oa × 71·7 × 30
Main Engines	Rowan Doxford 6-cyl. diesels; 8 800 bhp = 15·8 knots

Built by Scotstoun Yard of Blythswood Shipbuilding Co Ltd, for Jacobs and Partners Ltd, London. Launched on 15 Oct 1959 and completed in Jan 1960. Chartered by the Royal Navy on completion. Can carry three different grades of cargo.

PEARLEAF *1966, Wright & Logan*

PLUMLEAF A 78

Displacement, tons	24 920 full load
Measurement, tons	18 562 deadweight; 12 692 gross
Dimensions, feet	534 pp; 560 oa × 72 × 30
Main Engines	N.E. Doxford 6-cyl diesels; 9 350 bhp = 15·5 knots

Built by Blyth DD & Eng Co Ltd. Launched 29 Mar 1960. Completed July 1960.

PLUMLEAF *1969, Wright & Logan*

2 "EDDY" CLASS

Name	*No*	*Builders*	*Launched*	*Completed*
EDDYFIRTH	A 261	Lobnitz & Co Ltd, Renfrew	10 Sep 53	10 Feb 54
EDDYNESS	A 295	Blyth Dry Docks & Shipbuilding Co	22 Oct 53	11 Oct 54

Displacement, tons	1 960 light; 4 160 full load
Measurement, tons	2 157 to 2 300 gross; 2 095 to 2 200 deadweight
Dimensions, feet	270 pp; 286 oa × 44 × 17·2
Main Engines	1 set triple expansion; 1 shaft; 1 750 ihp = 12 knots
Boilers	2 oil burning cylindrical

Royal Fleet Auxiliaries. Launch dates above. Constructed on the combined transverse and longitudinal system of framing and classed 100 A1 at Lloyd's for the carriage of petroleum in bulk. Cargo capacity: 1 650 tons oil. Only *Eddifirth* appears in the 1969 Navy List. *Eddyness* is in reserve.

ENGINEERING. The main propelling machinery was built by Lobnitz & Co Ltd, Renfrew and boilers by Caledon Shipbuilding & Engineering Co Ltd, Dundee.

CLASS. *Eddybay, Eddybeach, Eddycliffe, Eddycreek* and *Eddyreef* were disposed of in 1963 and 1964. *Eddyrock* was sold in 1967.
For disposal of older and other classes of oilers, including the old "Dale" class, see 1966-67 and earlier editions. *Bishopdale* was for sale in 1967.

EDDYFIRTH *1967, Skyfotos*

EDDYNESS *Wright & Logan*

Oilers—*continued*

3 "Dale" Group

DEWDALE *1968, Official*

DERWENTDALE (ex-M.V. *Halcyon Breeze*)

Measurement, tons 67 700 deadweight
Main Engines B. & W. diesels; 20 700 bhp

DEWDALE (ex-M.V. *Edenfield*)

Measurement, tons 60 600 deadweight
Main Engines B. & W. diesels; 17 000 bhp

ENNERDALE (ex-M.V. *Naess Scotsman*)

Measurement, tons 47 270 deadweight
Dimensions, feet 710 × 98 × 40
Main Engines B. & W. diesels, 16 800 bhp
Complement 51

The Ministry of Defence (Navy) chartered the above three large tankers (announced 13 July 1967) for service East of Suez, and renamed them, re-introducing famous "Dale" class names. After limited modifications the ships operate in the Indian Ocean area. Manned by Royal Fleet Auxiliary personnel and wear the Blue Ensign.

DERWENTDALE refuelling *Bulwark* *1969, Official*

DEWDALE *1969, Wright & Logan*

2 "Surf" Class

SURF PATROL (ex-*Tatry*) A 357 **SURF PIONEER** (ex-*Beskidy*) A 365

Displacement, tons 15 800
Measurement, tons 7 742 gross; 11 500 deadweight
Dimensions, feet 445 pp; 469·5 oa × 60·5 × 27·5 max
Main Engines Doxford 4-cyl diesels; 4 250 bhp = 13·75 knots

Taken over whilst under construction by Bartram's, Sunderland, for Poland, at the time of the Korean War. Launched on 7 Feb and 23 Apr 1951, respectively. Both in reserve.

SURF PATROL *1969, Wright & Logan*

SURF PIONEER *Added 1969, John G. Callis*

Oilers—*continued*

3 NEW CONSTRUCTION. "ROVER" CLASS

GREEN ROVER **GREY ROVER** **BLUE ROVER**

Measurement, tons 7 000 *deadweight*
Dimensions, feet 461 × 63
Main engines 2 Ruston & Hornsby 16 cyl. uni-directional diesels; 1 shaft; controllable pitch propeller.
Complement 42 or 43 officers and men of the Royal Fleet Auxiliary

Small fleet tankers designed to replenish HM ships at sea with fuel, fresh water, limited dry cargo and refrigerated stores under all conditions while underway. A helicopter landing platform is provided, served by a stores lift, to enable stores to be transferred at sea by helicopter. Built at Swan Hunter, Hebbern-on-Tyne, Green Rover was launched on 19 Dec 1968 and Grey Rover on 17 Apr 1969.

6 "WAVE" CLASS

Name	*No.*	*Builders*	*Launched*
WAVE BARON (ex-*Empire Flodden*)	A 242	Furness SB Co Ltd,	19 Feb 1946
WAVE RULER (ex-*Empire Evesham*)	A 212	Haverton Hill on Tees	17 Jan 1946
WAVE CHIEF (ex-*Empire Edgehill*)	A 265	Harland & Wolff, Ltd (Govan), Glasgow	4 Apr 1956
WAVE DUKE (ex-*Empire Mars*)	A 246	Sir James Laing	16 Nov 1944
WAVE LAIRD (ex-*Empire Dunbar*)	A 119	& Sons Ltd.	3 Apr 1946
WAVE PRINCE (ex-*Empire Herald*)	A 207	Sunderland	27 July 1945

Displacement, tons 4 750 light; 8 200 standard; 16 485 full load
Measurement, tons 11 900 *deadweight*; 8 187 to 8 447 *gross*
Dimensions, feet 465·3 pp; 492·5 oa × 64·5 × 28·5
Main engines Double reduction geared turbines; 6 800 shp = 14·5 knots
Boilers Three-drum type

Classed as Royal Fleet Auxiliaries. Launch dates above. *Wave Baron, Wave Chief,* and *Wave Ruler* are fleet replenishment tankers, others being freighters. Turbines of Metrovick type in *Wave Baron, Wave Chief, Wave Duke* and *Wave Laird*, Parsons in others. *Wave Baron* and *Wave Prince* were modernised in 1961-62. *Wave Victor* lent to Air Ministry as hulk at Gan Island. *Wave Duke* and *Wave Laird* in reserve.

WAVE BARON *1969, Official*

WAVE PRINCE *1969, courtesy Dr. Giorgio Arra*

WAVE CHIEF *1966, A. & J. Pavia*

WAVE RULER *1967, courtesy Dr. Aldo Fraccaroli*

CLASS. *Wave Commander* and *Wave Liberator* scrapped in 1959. *Wave Conqueror* and *Wave King* sold in 1960 when *Wave Emperor, Wave Governor* and *Wave Premier* were stricken from the list. *Wave Protector* hulked at Malta, *Wave Regent* broken up and *Wave Monarch* sold to foreign interests in 1961. *Wave Knight* and *Wave Master* disposed of in 1963-64. *Wave Sovereign* sold in 1967.

Oilers—*continued*

4 LATER "ÓL" CLASS

BIRCHOL (19 Feb 1946) A 127
OAKOL (28 Aug 1946) A 300
ROWANOL (ex-*Cedarol*, ex-*Ebonol* 15 May 1946) A 284
TEAKOL (14 Nov 1956) A 167

Displacement, tons	2 670
Measurement, tons	1 638 deadweight; 1 440 gross
Dimensions, feet	218 pp; 232 oa × 39 × 15·8
Main Engines	Triple expansion; 1 140 ihp = 11 knots
Complement	26

All built by Lobnitz & Co Ltd, Renfrew. Launch dates above. *Rowanol* is in the 1969 Navy List, the other three being in reserve.

TEAKOL *1967, courtesy Godfrey H. Walker, Esq.*

BIRCHOL *Added 1969, Official*

OAKOL *Wright & Logan*

ROWANOL *courtesy, Dr. Aldo Fraccaroli.*

6 COASTAL TYPE NEW CONSTRUCTION

Six coastal tankers of 250 tons were ordered on 10 May 1967 from Appledore.

Oilers—*continued*

4 "RANGER" CLASS

BLACK RANGER (22 Aug 1940) A 163
BLUE RANGER (29 Jan 1941) A 157
BROWN RANGER (12 Dec 1940) A 169
GOLD RANGER (12 Mar 1941) A 130

Measurement, tons	3 313 to 3 417 gross. *Gold Ranger* 3 788 deadweight, others 3 435 to 3 781 deadweight
Dimensions, feet	*Gold Ranger* 339·5 pp; 355·2 oa × 47 × 20 Others 349·5 pp; 365·8 oa × 47 × 20
Main Engines	Burmeister & Wain diesels; 2 750 bhp = 12 knots

Classed as Royal Fleet Auxiliaries. Built by Harland & Wolff Ltd, Govan, Glasgow, except *Gold Ranger* by Caledon S.B. & Eng Co Ltd, Dundee. Launch dates above. The funnel in these ships is on the port side. All are fitted with special derrick on the beam to facilitate fuelling at sea. *Gray Ranger* was lost during the Second World War. *Black Ranger, Brown Ranger* and *Gold Ranger* are in the 1969 Navy List, and *Blue Ranger* is in reserve.

CLASS. Sister ship *Green Ranger* was officially deleted from the list in 1965.

BLACK RANGER *1967, courtesy Godfrey H. Walker, Esq.*

GOLD RANGER *1969, Official*

BROWN RANGER *1969, courtesy Dr. Giorgio Arra*

BLUE RANGER *Added 1969, A. & J. Pavia*

EARLY "DALE" CLASS
It is officially stated that the old oil tanker *Bishopdale* of the Early "Dale" class, discarded some years ago, is for disposal by sale in 1969.

BOOM DEFENCE VESSELS

4 "Wild Duck" Class

GARGANEY P 194 **GOLDENEYE** P 195 **MANDARIN** P 192 **PINTAIL** P193

Displacement, tons	950
Measurement, tons	283 deadweight
Dimensions, feet	150 pp; 168·2 excluding horns × 36·5 × 10·8
Main Engines	2 Davey Paxman 16 cyl diesels; 1 shaft; controllable pitch propeller; 1 100 bhp = 14 knots
Complement	24 (6 officers, 6 petty officers, 12 ratings)

Mandarin was the first of a new class of marine service vessels. Launched on 17 Sep 1963 and handed over on 5 Mar 1964. *Pintail* was launched on 3 Dec 1963. Both built by Cammell Laird & Co Ltd, Birkenhead. Designed to be used for mooring, salvage and boom work. Previously these three tasks were separately undertaken by specialist vessels, but the new type is able to give all three services. Capable of laying out and servicing the heaviest moorings used by the Fleet and also maintaining booms for harbour defence. Heavy lifting equipment enables a wide range of salvage operations to be performed, especially in harbour clearance work. The special heavy winches have an ability for tidal lifts over the apron of 200 tons. *Garganey* and *Goldeneye* (port auxiliary service, civilian crew) were built in 1966-67 by Brooke Marine Ltd, Lowestoft.

GOLDENEYE *1967, Wright & Logan*

MANDARIN *1969, Official*

GARGANEY *1969, Official*

LAYBURN *1967, A. & J. Pavia*

2 "Lay" Class

LAYBURN P 191 **LAYMOOR** P 190

Displacement, tons	800 standard; 1 050 full load
Dimensions, feet	160 pp; 192·7 oa × 34·5 × 11·5 feet
Main Engines	Triple expansion; 2 shafts; 1 300 ihp = 14 knots
Boilers	2 Foster Wheeler "D" type; 200 psi
Complement	2 officers; 29 to 34 ratings

Both built by Wm. Simons & Co Ltd (Simons-Lobnitz Ltd). The first boom defence vessels designed and built since the Second World War. *Laymoor* was the first and "name" ship of her class. *Layburn*, which cost £565,000 was launched on 14 Apr 1960 and completed on 7 July 1960. *Laymoor* which cost £562,000 was launched on 6 Aug 1959 and accepted on 9 Dec 1959. In addition to minor salvage work and towing net sections, can lay and maintain the latest types of underwater and surface boom defences, first class moorings and navigational buoys. Detailed specifications of the propulsion plant appear in the 1966-67 and earlier editions. Designed for naval or civilian manning. Lifting capacity is greater than that of predecessors, improvement in accommodation enables them to be operated in any climate. A photograph of *Laymoor* appears in the 1964-65 to 1966-67 editions.

LAYMOOR *1969, courtesy Dr. Giorgio Arra*

4 "Moor" Class

MOORHEN A 489 **MOORLAND** A 491 **MOORSMAN** P 284 **MOORPOUT** P 223

Displacement, tons	*Moorhen, Moorpout:* 650 standard; 900 full load; *Moorland,* 600 standard; 800 full load
Dimensions, feet	*Moorhen, Moorpout:* 149 pp; 159 oa hull × 30 × 12 (196 oa horns;) *Moorland:* 135 pp; 145 oa hull × 30 × 12
Main Engines	500 ihp = 9 knots

Built in 1938-46. Displacement and dimensions vary. Employed as Boom Defence Vessels, Boom Working Vessels, Mooring Vessels and Salvage Vessels. Fitted with salvage pumps, air compressors and diving equipment. *Moorsman* and *Moorpout* are of the larger type built by H.M. Dockyard, Chatham. *Moorland* was built by Goole Shipbuilding & Repair Co Ltd. *Moorhen, Moorland* and *Moorpout* are Port Auxiliary Service Craft at Malta, Gibraltar and Devonport, respectively. *Moorsman*, in the Clyde, also civilian manned, is in the 1969 Navy List. *Moorpout* was earmarked for disposal in 1968. A photograph of *Moorpout* appears in the 1963-64 to 1966-67 editions.

CLASS. *Moordale* was sold in 1961. *Moorburn, Moorcock, Moorfield, Moorfire, Moorgrass, Moorhill, Moormyrtle* and *Moorside* were for disposal in 1962, *Mooress* and *Moorfowl* in 1963. *Moorfly* and *Moorgrieve* were also sold.

MOORHEN *1967, Wright & Logan*

BARNARD *1967, Dr. Giorgio Arra*

Boom Defence Vessels—*continued*

13 "BAR" CLASS

Name	*No*	*Launched*	*Name*	*No*	*Launched*
2 Ardrosson Dockyard Co Ltd			*4 John Lewis & Sons Ltd, Aberdeen*		
BARBECUE	P 214	19 Dec 1944	**BARFIELD**	P 244	28 July 1938
			BARFOOT	P 202	25 Sep 1942
3 Blyth D.D. & S.B. Co			**BARGLOW**	P 216	9 Nov 1942
BARBAIN	P 201	8 Jan 1940	**BARNARD**	P 241	1 July 1942
			2 Lobnitz & Co Ltd, Renfrew		
BARNSTONE	P 297	25 Nov 1939	**BARNDALE**	P 215	30 Nov 1939
			1 Philip & Son Ltd, Dartmouth		
1 Ferguson Bros Ltd, Port Glasgow			**BARFOIL**	P 294	18 July 1942
BARHILL	P 204	26 Nov 1942	*4 Wm Simons & Co Ltd, Renfrew*		
1 Hall Russell & Co Ltd, Aberdeen			**BARMOND**	P 232	24 Dec 1942
BARRAGE	P 254	2 Dec 1937	**BARRINGTON**	P 259	15 Nov 1940

Displacement, tons	750 standard; 919 to 1 000 full load
Dimensions, feet	150 pp; 173·8 oa; 182 horns × 32·2 × 11·5
Main Engines	Triple expansion; 850 ihp = 11 knots. Sea speed 9 knots
Boilers	2 S.E. (200 lbs per sq in)
Fuel, tons	214 coal (*Barfoam* and *Barmond* converted to oil in 1966)
Radius, miles	3 000
Complement	32

Built under the 1936, 1937, 1939 and Second World War Estimates. Bow lift of 27 to 70 tons. *Barcarole, Barcliff, Barhill* and *Barndale* are Port Auxiliary Service Craft. *Barbecue, Barfield, Barfoot, Barfoss* and *Barglow* are also civilian manned. *Barfoss* is a Degaussing Rangelaying vessel. Second World War losses: *Barflake, Barlight.* A photograph of *Barfoss* appears in the 1963-64 to 1966-67 editions and of *Barndale* in the 1965-66 to 1967-68 editions.

TRANSFERS. *Barbrake* and *Barcross* were transferred to South Africa, *Barbarian, Barbette* (first of this name in the class, launched on 15 Dec 1937) and *Barfair* to Turkey, *Baron* to Ceylon in 1958 (purchased by the Colombo Port Commission).

CLASS. *Barbour, Bardell* and *Barricade* were discarded. *Barberry, Barbrook, Barcombe, Barford, Baritone, Barlane, Barlow, Barmill, Barneath* and *Barnwell* were for disposal in 1958, *Barilla* and *Baronia* in 1959, *Barholm* and *Barstoke* in 1960, *Barbette* (second of this name in the class, accepted into service on 12 July 1943), *Barbridge, Barcastle, Barcock, Barcote, Barcroft, Bardolf, Barlake, Barsing, Barsound, Barthorpe* and *Barrier* in 1962. *Barbourne, Barclose, Barking, Barspear* and *Barwind* in 1963, *Barbastel, Barfount, Barkis, Barleycorn, Barmouth, Barnaby, Barnehurst, Barova, Barranca* and *Barrhead* in 1964, *Bartisan* in 1966, *Barcarole, Barcliffe, Barbican, Barfoam* and *Barfoss* in 1969. *Barnstone* and *Barrington* are for disposal in 1970.

BARRINGTON *1968, Dr. Giorgio Arra*

BARRAGE *1969, courtesy Dr. Giorgio Arra*

OCEAN SALVAGE VESSELS

SALVEDA

Displacement, tons	1 250 standard; 1 360 full load
Dimensions, feet	184 pp; 194 oa × 34·5 × 11·2 mean
Main Engines	1 200 hp = 12 knots
Oil fuel, tons	150
Complement	62

Built by Cammell Laird & Co Ltd, Birkenhead, and launched on 9 Feb 1943. Formerly a Royal Fleet Auxiliary ocean salvage vessel on charter to Metal Industries Ltd. In the Spring 1967 Navy List, in reserve.

Ocean Salvage Vessels—*continued*

4 "SALV" CLASS

SALVALOUR
SALVESTOR
SALVICTOR
SEA SALVOR

Displacement, tons	1 440 standard; 1 700 full load
Measurement, tons	1 114 to 1 122 gross
Dimensions, feet	200·2 pp; 216 oa × 37·8 × 13 max
Main Engines	Triple expansion; 2 shafts; 1 500 ihp = 12 knots
Oil fuel, tons	310
Complement	52 to 72

Ocean salvage vessels. All launched in 1942-45. *Salvalour* and *Sea Salvor* were built by Goole Shipbuilding & Repair Co Ltd, and launched on 8 Mar 1943, 2 Nov 1944 and 22 Apr 1943, respectively. *Salvestor* and *Salvictor* were built by Wm. Simons & Co Ltd, Renfrew, and launched on 28 Aug 1942 and 11 Mar 1944 respectively. *Sea Salvor* is a Royal Fleet Auxiliary. A photograph of *Salvictor* appears in the 1966-67 to 1968-69 editions.

TRANSFERS. *Salventure* is on loan ro the Royal Hellenic Navy and renamed *Sotir.*

CLASS
King Salvor was converted to a submarine rescue bell ship in 1953-54 and renamed *Kingfisher* and was sold to Argentina in Dec 1960, sailing to Argentina in Apr 1961 under the new name *Tehuelche* (again renamed *Guardiamarina Zicari* in 1963). *Salvage Duke,* formerly on charter to Turkish Salvage Administration (renamed *Imroz*), was gutted by fire in 1959.

Ocean Salvor and *Salviola* were disposed of in 1960, and *Prince Salvor* and *Salvigil* were sold in 1968.

SEA SALVOR *1967, courtesy Dr. Giorgio Arra*

COASTAL SALVAGE VESSELS

6 "KIN" CLASS

KINBRACE 17 Jan 45	**KINLOSS** 14 Apr 45	**SWIN** 25 Mar 44
KINGARTH 22 May 44	**SUCCOUR** 18 Aug 43	**UPLIFTER** 29 Nov 43

Displacement, tons	950 standard; 1 050 full load
Measurement, tons	775 gross; 261·6 register
Dimensions, feet	150 pp; 179·2 oa × 35·2 × 9·5 mean; 12 max
Main Engines	Triple expansion; 1 shaft; 600 ihp = 9 knots
Boilers	1 return tube cylindrical (30 ton)
Complement	34

Coastal salvage vessels. Launch dates above. Equipped with horns and heavy rollers. Can lift 200 tons dead weight over the bow. *Kinbrace, Kingarth, Kinloss* and *Swin* were built by A. Hall, Aberdeen, *Succour* by Smith's Dock. *Uplifter,* built by Smith's Dock Co Ltd, was the only salvage vessel wearing the White Ensign. She was laid down on 13 Feb 1943, and completed on 6 Apr 1944. (*Kingarth* wore the White Ensign in 1957). *Dispenser* is on charter to Liverpool & Glasgow Salvage Association. *Succour* and *Swin* are Royal Fleet Auxiliaries wearing the Blue Ensign. *Kinloss* is in the Port Auxiliary Service as a mooring vessel. *Kinbrace, Kingarth* and *Uplifter* were refitted with diesel engines in 1966-67.
A photograph of *Kingarth* appears in the 1959-60 and earlier editions, of *Swin* in the 1956-57 and earlier editions, and of *Uplifter* in the 1960-61 to 1962-63 editions.

CLASS. Sister *Help* was disposed of. *Lifeline* was on the disposal list in 1960.

KINLOSS *1966, Wright & Logan*

SUCCOUR *1969, John G. Callis*

DIVING TRIALS SHIP

Modified Ocean Salvage Vessel

RECLAIM (ex-*Salverdant*) A 231

Displacement, tons	1 200 standard; 1 800 full load
Dimensions, feet	200 pp; 217·8 oa × 38 × 15·5
Main Engines	Triple expansion; 2 shafts: 1 500 ihp = 12 knots
Oil fuel, tons	310
Radius, miles	3 000
Complement	84

CONSTRUCTION. Built by Wm. Simons & Co Ltd, Renfrew. Engined by Aitchison Blair Ltd. Laid down on 9 Apr 1946. Launched on 12 Mar 1948. Completed in Oct 1948. Her construction was based on the design of a "King Salvor" class naval ocean salvage vessel. She was the first deep diving and submarine rescue vessel built as such for the Royal Navy. She is fitted with sonar, radar, echo-sounding apparatus for detection of sunken wrecks, and equipped for submarine rescue work.
RECLASSIFICATION. Formerly a tender to H.M.S. *Vernon* shore establishment at Portsmouth for deep diving experiments, and subsequently a deep diving vessel in the Portsmouth Squadron. Reclassified as a Mine Countermeasure Support and Diving Trials Ship in 1960, and attached to HMS *Lochinvar*, the minesweeping base at Port Edgar, but her mine countermeasures functions were taken over in 1968 by the minelayer *Abdiel*. Carried out deep diving experiments in the Canary Islands in Jan to Mar 1961.

RECLAIM *1967, Wright & Logan*

CABLE SHIPS

2 "Bull" Class

BULLFINCH (19 Aug 1940) **ST. MARGARETS** (13 Oct 1943)

Displacement, tons	1 300 light; 2 500 full load
Measurement, tons	1 524 gross; 1 200 deadweight
Dimensions, feet	228·8 pp; 252 oa × 36·5 × 16·3 mean
Main Engines	Triple expansion; 2 shafts; 1 250 ihp = 12 knots

Royal Fleet Auxiliaries. Both built by Swan, Hunter & Wigham Richardson Ltd. Launch dates above. *Bullfrog* and *Bullhead* of this type were transferred to Cable and Wireless service in 1947. Provision was made for mounting one 4 inch gun and four 20 mm AA guns but no armament is fitted.

BULLFINCH *1966, Official*

ST. MARGARETS *1967, A. & J. Pavia*

HOVERCRAFT

1 SRN 6 Civil Type

Dimensions, feet	48 length × 23 beam
Main Engines	Rolls Royce Marine Gnome, 900 hp = 50 knots
Range, miles	200

It was officially announced on 16 June 1967 that:—"A civilian type SRN 6 Hovercraft has been ordered by the Ministry of Defence and will be delivered by the British Hovercraft Corporation within the next few weeks, when the Royal Navy's first operational Hovercraft Unit will be formed. It will be taken in hand for modification for Service use at the Royal Naval Aircraft Yard, Fleetlands, Gosport, including the installation of radar and military communications equipment for its primary role of a fast amphibious communication craft to support Royal Marine units. It will not be armed as its role will not involve belligerent use."
It was stated by the Minister of Technology on 4 Apr 1968 that the Government would order a BH-7 hovercraft as a naval patrol vessel.

EXPERIMENTAL TRIALS VESSEL

1 NEW CONSTRUCTION

An experimental trials vessel is in the current new construction programme to replace *Sarepta*.

WHIMBREL (ex-*NSC* (E) 1012)

Displacement, tons	300 (official figure)
Dimensions, feet	190 × 30 × 4·5

Experimental Trials Vessel. Basically of the tank landing craft LCT(3) Type.

WHIMBREL *1968, A. & J. Pavia*

ICEWHALE

Displacement, tons	289 standard; 350 full load
Dimensions, feet	120 × 24 × 9
Main Engines	Speed = 9 knots
Complement	12 (Master, Mate and 10 ratings)

Experimental Trials Vessel for the Underwater Weapons Establishment, Portland.

ICEWHALE *1968, John G. Callis*

SAREPTA (ex-*Frieda Peters*)

Displacement, tons	465 standard
Dimensions, feet	150 pp; 157 oa × 27·5 × 12
Tubes	4—21 inch

Ex-German vessel. Launched in 1920. Multi-purpose torpedo experimental, firing, and recovery vessel. Reclassified as TRV in 1956. A photograph of *Sarepta* appears in the 1951-52 to 1957-58 editions. *TRV 1, TRV 3, TRV 4, Choctaw* (TRC 5817) and *Mortar* are also employed as recovery vessels. *TRV 6* is an experimental trials vessel.

FLEET TENDERS

20 "ABERDOVEY" CLASS

ABERDOVEY	**ALNMOUTH**	**BEAULIEU**	**BIBURY**
ABINGER	**APPLEBY**	**BEDDGELERT**	**BLAKENEY**
ALNESS	**ASHCOTT**	**BEMBRIDGE**	**BRODICK**

Measurement, tons	70 gross register
Dimensions, feet	75 pp; 79·2 oa × 18 × 5·5
Main Engines	1 Lister Blackstone 4-cyl diesel; 210 bhp = 10·5 knots

Built in 1963-65 by Isaac Pimblott & Sons, Northwich, and J. S. Doig Ltd, Grimsby, six by each yard. Built Lloyd's Register requirements. Designed to carry 25 tons deadweight (or up to 3,000 cu ft) of stores or 200 standing passengers in addition to two 21 inch torpedoes each weighing 1·8 tons. Sixty fleet tenders are being built over ten years to replace the old MFVs. Six more were ordered from Pimblott & Sons in 1967. A photograph of *Beaulieu* appears in the 1965-66 to 1967-68 editions.

ALNESS *1968, Dr. Giorgio Arra*

70 MFV TYPES

MFV 2, 7, 9, 15, 43, 45, 57, 63, 64, 65, 74, 84, 88, 93, 96, 97, 119, 123, 133, 136, 139, 140, 158, 175, 205, 237, 256, 278, 289, 323
Length: 61·5 feet — 30 in port auxiliary service

MFV 627, 642, 657, 658, 673, 686, 687, 715, 737, 740, 742, 767, 773, 775, 815, 816, 867, 911, 944 Length: 45 feet — 19 in port auxiliary service

MFV 1015, 1033, 1037, 1048, 1051, 1057, 1062, 1077, 1079, 1151, 1164, 1190, 1206, 1215, 1219, 1254, 1255, 1256, 1257
Length: 75 feet — 19 in port auxiliary service

MV 1527, 1544 Length: 90 feet — 2 in port auxiliary service

Employed for subsidiary duties serving warships and dockyards. *MFV 1151, Squirrel* and *MFV 1080, Watchful* were used as Fishery Protection Gunboats until replaced. *MFVs* 105, 1021 and 1528 were deleted from the list in 1969.

STORE CARRIERS

THOMAS GRANT

Displacement, tons 209 light; 461 full load
Measurement, tons 252 deadweight; 218 gross
Dimensions, feet 113·5 × 25·5 × 8·8
Main Engines 2 diesels; Speed = 9 knots

Built as a local store carrier. Completed in 1953 by Charles Hill & Sons Ltd, Bristol. Turned over to the Port Auxiliary Service in 1959 under Dockyard administration at Portsmouth. Converted into a torpedo recovery vessel in 1968.

THOMAS GRANT *Added 1969, Official*

ROBERT DUNDAS A 204 **ROBERT MIDDLETON** A 241

Displacement, tons 900 light; 1 900 full load
Measurement, tons 1 000 deadweight; 1 125 gross
Dimensions, feet 210 pp; 222·5 oa × 35 × 13·5 mean
Main Engines Atlas Polar Diesel; 1 shaft; 960 bhp = 10·5 knots
Oil fuel, tons 60
Complement 17

Coastal store carriers. Both built by Grangemouth Dockyard Co Ltd. Machinery by British Auxiliaries Ltd, Govan. Launched on 28 July and 29 June 1938, respectively. *Robert Middleton* 220 ft oa. Royal Fleet Auxiliaries. A photograph of *Robert Dundas* appears in the 1966-67 to 1968-69 editions.
The degaussing vessels DGV 400, 401 and 403 (ex-MMS 1002, 1003 and 1011, respectively) were deleted from the list in 1969, having been replaced by IMS *Fordham, Thatcham* and *Warmingham*. DGV 402 (ex-MMS 1004) was stricken in 1963.

ROBERT MIDDLETON *1969, courtesy Godfrey H. Walker Esq.*

ARMAMENT CARRIERS

KINTERBURY A 378 **THROSK**

Displacement, tons 1 490 standard; 1,770 full load
Measurement, tons 600 deadweight
Dimensions, feet 185 pp; 199·8 × 34·3 × 13
Main Engines Triple expansion; 1 shaft; 900 ihp = 11 knots
Coal, tons 154

Launched in 1943 and 1944, respectively. Both built by Philip & Son Ltd. Rated as naval armament carriers. Converted in 1959 with hold stowage and a derrick for handling guided missiles for attending and servicing the guided weapons trials ship *Girdle Ness*.
A photograph of *Kinterbury* appears in the 1963-64 to 1966-67 editions.

THROSK *1968, John G. Callis*

BALLISTA **CATAPULT** **MATCHLOCK**
BOWSTRING **FLINTLOCK** **SPEAR**

Of various displacements and particulars. In PAS . *Blowpipe* and *Obus* sold.

Armament Carriers—*Continued*

ENFIELD A 395 **MAXIM** A 377
GATLING A 376 **NORDENFELT** A 135

Displacement, tons 604 to 663
Measurement, tons 340 deadweight
Dimensions, feet 131·5 to 144·5 × 25 × 8
Main Engines Reciprocating; 500 ihp = 9 knots
Complement 13

All built by Lobnitz & Co Ltd, Renfrew. *Chattenden* was reduced in 1961 to a dumb derrick lighter. *Snider* was disposed of in 1968.

GATLING *1969, John G. Callis*

WATER CARRIERS

4 "WATER" CLASS

WATERFALL **WATERSHED** **WATERSIDE** **WATERSPOUT**

Measurement, tons 285 gross
Dimensions, feet 123 pp, 131·5 oa × 24·8 × 8
Main engines Diesels; 1 shaft; 1 100 bhp = 11 knots

Built in 1966 by Drypool Engineering & Drydock Co, Hull.

WATERSHED *1969, Wright & Logan*

5 "SPA" CLASS

2 *Charles Hill & Sons Ltd, Bristol*
SPALAKE (10 Aug 46) A 260
SPAPOOL (28 Feb 46) A 222

3 *Philip & Son Ltd, Dartmouth*
SPA (11 Oct 41) A 192
SPABROOK (24 Aug 44) A 224
SPABURN (5 Jan 46) A 257

Displacement, tons 1 219 full load
Measurement, tons 630 deadweight; 672 to 719 gross
Dimensions, feet 160 pp; 172 oa × 30 × 12
Main Engines Triple expansion; 675 ihp = 9 knots
Coal, tons 90

Spabeck, high test peroxide carrier for the experimental submarine *Explorer*, was disposed of in May 1966. *Spapool* is with PAS. A photograph of *Spa* appears in the 1963-64 to 1966-67 editions.

SPALAKE *1967, courtesy Dr. Giorgio Arra*

7 "FRESH" CLASS

FRESHBURN **FRESHLAKE** **FRESHMERE** **FRESHPOOL**
FRESHENER **FRESHPOND** **FRESHSPRING**

Displacement, tons 594
Dimensions, feet 126·2 × 25·5 × 10·8 max
Main Engines Triple expansion; 450 ihp = 9 knots

Freshener and *Freshspring* converted from coal to oil fuel, in 1961. A photograph of *Freshpond* appears in the 1951-52 to 1953-54 editions and of *Freshlake* in the 1963-64 to 1965-66 editions. *Freshbrook* and *Freshnet* were stricken in 1963, *Freshwater* and *Freshwell* sold in 1968, and *Freshford, Freshspray* and *Freshtarn* in 1969.

FRESHPOOL *1966, courtesy Dr. Giorgio Arra*

TUGS

2 NEW CONSTRUCTION

Two ocean tugs are being built under the 1969 new construction programme.

TYPHOON A 95

Displacement, tons	800 standard; 1 380 full load
Dimensions, feet	200 oa; 181 pp × 40 × 13
Main Engines	2 12-cyl turbocharged vee type diesels; 1 shaft; 2 750 bhp = over 16 knots

Royal Fleet Auxiliary. Built by Henry Robb & Co Ltd, Leith. Launched on 14 Oct 1958. Completed in 1960. Diesels manufactured by Vickers-Armstrongs Ltd, Barrow-in-Furness. The machinery arrangement of two diesels geared to a single shaft was an innovation for naval ocean tugs. Controllable pitch propeller, 150 rpm. Fitted for fire fighting, salvage and ocean rescue, with a heavy mainmast and derrick attached. Bollard pull 32 tons.

TYPHOON *1966, Skyfotos*

2 "CON" CLASS

CONFIANCE (15 Nov 1955) A 289 **CONFIDENT** (17 Jan 1956) A 290

Displacement, tons	760 loaded
Dimensions, feet	140 pp; 154·8 oa × 35 × 11
Main Engines	4 Paxman diesels; 2 shafts; 1 600 bhp = 13 knots
Complement	29 plus 13 salvage party

Built by A. & J. Inglis Ltd, Glasgow. Launch dates above. *Confiance* was completed on 27 Mar 1956. Fitted with 2·50 m diam Stone Kamewa controllable pitch propellers.

CONFIANCE *1967, Wright & Logan*

CONFIDENT *1969, courtesy Michael D. J. Lennon Esq.*

1 "Envoy" Class

ENCORE A 379

Displacement, tons	868 standard; 1 332 full load
Measurement, tons	762 gross
Dimensions, feet	160 pp; 174·5 oa × 34·5 × 15·7 max
Main Engines	Triple expansion; 1 700 ihp = 12 knots
Boilers	2 cylindrical
Oil fuel, tons	398
Complement	33

Built by Cochrane & Sons Ltd, Selby. Launched in Dec 1944. In wartime carried 1—3 inch AA gun, 2—20 mm AA guns, and 2 MG. *Enticer* was lost on 21 Dec 1946. *Enforcer* and *Enigma* were stricken from the list in 1963. *Envoy* was sold in 1968, and *Encore* was put up for sale.

Tugs—*continued*

3 "SAMSON" CLASS

SAMSON (14 May 1953) A 390 **SEA GIANT** (2 June 1954) A 288 **SUPERMAN** (23 Nov 1953)

Displacement, tons	1 200 full load
Measurement, tons	850 gross
Dimensions, feet	165 pp; 180 oa × 37 × 14
Main Engines	Triple expansion; 2 shafts; 3 000 ihp = 15 knots

All built and engined by Alexander Hall & Co Ltd, Aberdeen. Launch dates above. A photograph of *Samson* appears in the 1957-58 and earlier editions.

SUPERMAN *Added 1969, Official*

SEA GIANT *1963, A. & J. Pavia*

4 "NIMBLE" CLASS

CAPABLE (22 Nov 1945) A 508 **EXPERT** (1944) A 172
CAREFUL (23 Oct 1945) A 293 **NIMBLE** (4 Dec 1941) A 223

Displacement, tons	890 standard; 1 190 full load
Dimensions, feet	165 pp 175 oa × 35·8 × 13·8
Main Engines	Triple expansion; 2 shafts; 3 500 ihp = 16 knots
Boilers	2 of 3-drum type
Oil fuel, tons	300

Capable was built by Hall Russell, *Careful* by A. Hall & Co, *Expert* and *Nimble* by Fleming & Ferguson. Launch dates above. *Capable* was fitted experimentally with controllable pitch propellers. *Expert* is for sale in 1969. A photograph of *Expert* appears in the 1963-64 to 1966-67 editions.

NIMBLE *1969, A. & J. Pavia*

CAPABLE *1967, Skyfotos*

Tugs—*continued*

5 "BUSTLER" CLASS

BUSTLER (4 Dec 1941) A 240
CYCLONE (ex-*Growler*, 10 Sep 1942) A 111
REWARD (13 Oct 1944) A 264
SAMSONIA (1 Apr 1942) A 218
WARDEN (28 June 1945) A 309

Displacement, tons	1 118 standard; 1 630 full load
Dimensions, feet	190 pp; 205 oa × 40·2 × 16·8
Main Engines	2 Atlas Polar 8-cyl diesels; 1 shaft; 4 000 bhp = 16 knots
Oil fuel, tons	405
Range, miles	17 000
Complement	42

All built by Henry Robb Ltd, Leith. Launch dates above. *Growler*, temporarily renamed *Caroline Moller* while on long term charter, then renamed *Castle Peak*, was returned to R.F.A. service in 1957, then renamed *Welshman* and chartered to the United Towing Co Ltd, and again renamed *Cyclone* on return to Royal Fleet Auxiliary service in 1964. Most of this class, including *Reward*, to United Towing Co Ltd in 1963, and *Turmoil*, to Overseas Towage & Salvage Co, were chartered by commercial undertakings. *Bustler* wears the Blue Ensign. Of this class, *Hesperia* was lost during the Second World War, and HMS *Meditator* the last tug to sail under the White Ensign and not the Blue Ensign of the Royal Fleet Auxiliary Service, was paid off in 1964 to be sold. *Turmoil* was sold in 1968. A photograph of *Reward* appears in the 1964-65 to 1967-68 editions.

CYCLONE *1969, A. & J. Pavia*

BUSTLER *1968, Mr. Michael D. J. Lennon*

1 "ASSURANCE" CLASS

ANTIC A 141

Displacement, tons	700 standard; 1 055 full load
Measurement, tons	597 gross
Dimensions, feet	142·5 pp; 157 oa × 33 × 14·8
Main Engines	Triple expansion; 1 350 ihp = 12 knots
Boiler	1 cylindrical
Oil fuel, tons	262
Complement	31

Built by Cochrane & Sons Ltd, Selby. Launched in May 1943. In wartime carried 1—3 inch AA gun, 1—20 mm AA gun and 2 MG. Second World War losses of the class were *Adept*, *Adherent* (original), *Assurance*, *Horsa* and *Sesame*. *Assiduous* was transferred to Ceylon in 1959, *Adherent* (the second) and *Tryphon* were disposed of in 1960. *Alligator* was sold in 1961. *Allegiance* was lost in a typhoon on 4 Sep 1962 while under charter. Sister ships *Cautious*, *Earner*, *Hengist*, *Jaunty*, *Prosperous*, *Restive* and *Saucy* were sold in 1968.

BOXER ("Dog" Class) *1969, Skyfotos*

Tugs—*continued*

FORCEFUL *1969, courtesy, Dr. Giorgio Arra*

Tugs employed on harbour service and in H.M. Dockyards, include the diesel-electric paddle tugs *Dextrous*, *Director*, *Faithful*, *Favourite*, *Forceful*, *Grinder* and *Griper*: twin screw diesel dockyard tugs *Accord*, *Adept*, *Agile* and *Advice*: medium berthing tugs *Airedale*, *Alsation*, *Boxer*, *Cairn*, *Dalmation*, *Pointer* ("Dog" class); and harbour berthing tugs *Agatha*, *Agnes*, *Alice*, *Audrey* and *Betty* ("Girl" class). The building of "Dog" and "Girl" class tugs continues to replace older vessels. Five "Dog" class were ordered from Appledore and four "Girl" class from Dunstan in Dec 1967.

AGILE *1969, Wright & Llgan*

Small fleet servicing and coastal harbour tugs include *Empire Ace* (ex-*Diligent*), *Empire Demon*, *Empire Fred*, *Empire Netta*, *Empire Rosa*, *Energetic* (ex-*Empire Edward*) and *Frisky* (ex-*Empire Rita*), but not all are of the same type. *Empire Plane* was sold in 1958, and *Empire Zona* was deleted from the list.

EXPELLER *1969, Skyfotos*

Tugs in the Port Auxiliary Service include:—*Bombshell*, *Cannon*, *Chainshot*, *Destiny*, *Diver*, *Driver*, *Eminent*, *Energy*, *Expeller*, *Fidget*, *Flamer*, *Foremost*, *Freedom*, *Grapeshot*, *Handmaid*, *Impetus*, *Integrity*, *Prompt*, *Regard*, *Resolve*, *Security*, *Tampeon*, *Trunnion*, *Vagrant* and *Weasel*.

REGARD *1969, Wright & Logan*

GUIDED MISSILE GAS TURBINE PATROL BOATS

(*Private Venture*)

TENACITY model — *1969, Vosper Thornycroft*

1 VOSPER THORNYCROFT MISSILE BOAT

(*TRIPLE SCREW*)

TENACITY

Displacement, tons 165 standard; 200 full load
Length, feet (*metres*) 130 (*39·62*) wl; 142 (*43·28*) deck; 144·5 (*44·04*) oa
Beam, feet (*metres*) 26·54 (*8·09*)
Draught, feet (*metres*) 7·75 (*2·36*)
Missile launchers 2 twin "Sea Killer" surface-to-surface
Guns, dual purpose 2—35 mm (1 twin mounting)
Main engines 3 Rolls Royce Proteus gas turbines; 3 shafts; 12 750 bhp = 39 knots
2 Maybach diesels on wing shafts for cruising = 16 knots
Complement 27 (3 officers, 24 ratings)

Built as a private venture by Vosper Thornycroft. Launched on 18 Feb 1969 at Camber Shipyard, Portsmouth. Steel hull and aluminium alloy superstructure. Fully air-conditioned quarters. Range of 2 500 miles at cruising speed of 15 knots.

Quadruple screw version showing 76 mm gun forward and rotating quintuple Sea Killer mounting aft — *1969, Vosper Thornycroft*

Gas turbine version with 2 twin Sea Killer launchers and a twin 35 mm Oerlikon — *1969, Vosper Thornycroft*

Gas turbine version with 4 Sea Killer missiles aft in two fixed launchers and twin 35 mm gun forward — *1969, Vosper Thornycroft*

Quadruple screw diesel version with 3 inch gun and 5 Sea Killer missiles — *1969, Vosper Thornycroft*

Artist's impression of diesel version with Otto Melara gun and quintuple Sea Killer — *1969, Vosper Thornycroft*

HMS VICTORY

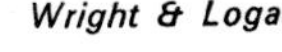

Wright & Logan

HMS VICTORY *Wright & Logan*

TWO VIEWS

OF

HMS VICTORY

LAUNCHED 1765

NELSON'S FLAGSHIP

AT TRAFALGAR 1805

1969 FLAGSHIP

AT PORTSMOUTH

OF

ADMIRAL SIR JOHN FREWEN, GCB,

FIRST AND PRINCIPAL

NAVAL AIDE-DE-CAMP

TO THE QUEEN,

COMMANDER-IN-CHIEF

NAVAL HOME COMMAND

UNITED STATES NAVY

Compiled and Edited by Norman Polmar

ORGANISATION

The ships and aircraft of the United States Navy are assigned to two major naval commands, the Atlantic Fleet and the Pacific Fleet.
Each of these fleets has two distinct organisational structures. The administrative or "type" commands and the operational or "task" commands. The type commands prescribe or recommend standard shipboard organisation, training requirements, inspection standards, material allowances, and other administrative matters for their particular ships. The type commands in the Atlantic Fleet and Pacific Fleet which have administrative control of ships are: Naval Air Force (aircraft carriers), Cruiser-Destroyer Force, Submarine Force, Amphibious Force, Mine Force, and Service Force.

Within these type commands are various subordinate flotillas, groups, squadrons, and divisions. A ship remains in a given type command (and subordinate organisations) regardless of which "task" organisation to which the ship is assigned or the operation in which engaged. (In addition, each of the fleets have an Anti-Submarine Warfare Force which co-ordinates ASW activities and a Fleet Marine Force which is responsible for the Marine ground and air units in the ocean area).

The major operational commands within the Atlantic Fleet are the Sixth Fleet in the Mediterranean and the Second Fleet in the Atlantic; the major operational commands within the Pacific Fleet are the Seventh Fleet in the Western Pacific and the First Fleet in the Eastern Pacific.

The fleets in the Atlantic area have national and NATO responsibilities. The Commander-in-Chief Atlantic Fleet is also Supreme Allied Commander Atlantic; the Commander Second Fleet is also Commander Striking Fleet Atlantic; and the Commander Sixth Fleet is also Commander Naval Striking and Support Forces Southern Europe. In his national role the Commander Sixth Fleet reports to the Commander-in-Chief US Naval Forces Europe (ashore in London); in his NATO role the Commander Sixth Fleet reports to the Commander-in-Chief Allied Forces Southern Europe (at Naples). (The Commander Sixth Fleet has a NATO deputy at Naples to carry out his NATO planning and co-ordination).

The main task forces of the Sixth Fleet in the Mediterranean are Attack Carrier Striking Force (TF 60) with two attack carriers, screening cruisers, frigates, and destroyers; Amphibious Force (TF 61) with amphibious ships to transport and land a reinforced Marine battalion, and supporting minesweepers; Fleet Marine Force (TF 62), a reinforced Marine battalion landing team with some 1 800 men with tanks, atrillery, trucks, and helicopters; and Service Force (TF 63) consisting of underway replenishment ships, tenders, and repair ships. Also assigned are several attack submarines (TF 68; the fleet ballistic missile submarine in the Mediterranean comprise TF 69). Periodically the Sixth Fleet is augmented by an Anti-Submarine Force (TF 66) with one carrier and screening destroyers.

Similarly, the Seventh Fleet in the Western Pacific has an Attack Carrier Striking Force (TF 77), Amphibious Force (TF 76), Fleet Marine Force (TF 79), and Mobile Logistics Support Force (TF 73). The Seventh Fleet organisation also contains a separate Taiwan Patrol Force (TF 72), anti-Submarine Group (TG 70.4), and Cruiser-Destroyer Group (TG 70.8), the last a shore-bombardment force designated Operation SEA DRAGON.

Almost all of the ships and aircraft squadrons assigned to the Sixth Fleet in the Mediterranean and the Seventh Fleet in the Western Pacific are based in the United States and deploy overseas for specific periods of time, rotating with ships and aircraft squadrons of the Second and First Fleets, respectively.

NAVAL AVIATION

The US Navy and Marine Corps currently operate some 8 600 fixed-wing aircraft and helicopters. The principal tactical organisations are:

Sixteen Attack Carrier Air Wings with a total of 1 650 fixed-wing aircraft (including shore-based squadrons which periodically deploy aircraft aboard carriers). Each Wing normally consists of two fighter and three or four attack squadrons plus detachments of photographic, reconnaissance, airborne early warning, aerial tanker, and electronic countermeasure aircraft. One Wing is assigned to each Attack Aircraft Carrier (CVA) and to one ASW Support Aircraft Carrier (CVS) which operates as a "limited CVA" in the Vietnam conflict.

Seven ASW Air Groups with a total of some 350 fixed-wing aircraft and helicopters. Each Group normally consists of two fixed-wing ASW squadrons and one helicopter ASW squadron plus detachments of airborne early warning and, in some ships, fighter aircraft. One Group is assigned to each ASW Support Aircraft Carrier.

Thirty Patrol Squadrons, each with nine P-3 Orion or 12 P-2 Neptune maritime reconnaissance/ASW aircraft. More than half of these squadrons now have P-3 aircraft, which eventually will replace all Neptunes.

Three Marine Aircraft Wings with a total of approximately 1 200 fixed-wing aircraft and helicopters. Each Wing has several fighter/attack (F-4 Phantom) and attack (A-4 Skyhawk, A-6 Intruder) squadrons, one refueller/transport squadron (C-130 Hercules), one observation squadron (UH-1 Huey), two heavy helicopter squadrons (CH-53 Seastallion), four medium helicopter squadrons (CH-46 Sea Knight), and one light helicopter squadron (UH-1 Huey, AH-1 Huey Cobra). Each Wing normally is assigned in support of a Marine division; however, there are now four Marine divisions in active service and certain additional squadrons have been formed to support the additional division, but have not been organised as an aircraft wing.

In addition, there are a number of Navy special mission and training squadrons. The former include six Fleet Tactical Support Squadrons which fly 71 transport and cargo aircraft including 37 which operate aboard carriers (C-1 Trader, C-2 Greyhound); one Light Attack Squadron (OV-10 Bronco) for counter-insurgency operations; one Special Attack Squadron (AP-2H Neptune) which conducts night interdiction missions in Vietnam; one Helicopter Light Attack Squadron (UH-1 Huey) which supports riverine operations in South Vietnam; seven Helicopter Combat Support Squadrons which provide helicopters to underway replenishment ships and certain other naval activities; and five Development, Test, and Evaluation Squadrons which fly a variety of special-purpose and test aircraft. There are 20 Navy training squadrons which train Navy, Marine Corps, and Coast Guard aviators. (In addition, there are Navy and Marine Corps air reserve units; their aircraft are not included in the above totals).

PERSONNEL

Administration

Commander-in Chief:
The President of the United States

Secretary of Defense:
Melvin R. Laird

Secretary of the Navy:
John H. Chafee

Under Secretary of the Navy:
John W. Warner

Command

Chairman, Joint Chiefs of Staff:
General Earle G. Wheeler, USA

Chief of Naval Operations:
Admiral Thomas H. Moorer, USN

Vice Chief of Naval Operations:
Admiral Bernard A Clarey, USN

**Commander-in-Chief Atlantic and Commander-in-Chief Atlantic Fleet:*
Admiral Ephraim P. Holmes, USN

**Commander-in-Chief Pacific:*
Admiral John S. McCain, Jr., USN

Commander-in-Chief Pacific Fleet:
Admiral John J. Hyland, USN

Commander First Fleet:
Vice Admiral Bernard F. Roeder, USN

Commander Second Fleet:
Vice Admiral Benedict J. Semmes, Jr. USN

Commander Sixth Fleet:
Vice Admiral David C. Richardson, USN

Commander Seventh Fleet:
Vice Vdmiral William F. Bringle, USN

Commander Military Sea Transportation Service
Vice Admiral Lawson P. Ramage, USN

Oceanographer of the Navy:
Rear Admiral Odale D. Waters, Jr, USN

Commandant of the Marine Corps:
General Leonard F. Chapman, Jr USMC

Assistant Commandant of the Marine Corps:
General Lewis W. Walt, USMC

Material

Chief of Naval Material:
Admiral Ignatius J. Galantin USN

Commander Naval Air Systems Command:
Rear Admiral Thomas J. Walker, USN

Commander Naval Electronic Systems Command:
Rear Admiral Joseph E. Rice (ED), USN

Commander Naval Facilities Engineering Command:
Rear Admiral Alexander C. Husband, CEC, USN

Commander Naval Ordnance Systems Command:
Rear Admiral Mark W. Woods, USN

Commander Naval Ship Systems Command:
Rear Admiral Nathan Sonenshein (ED), USN

Commander Naval Supply Systems Command:
Rear Admiral Bernhard H. Bieri, Jr, SC, USN

Deputy Commander for Nuclear Propulsion, Naval Ship Systems Command and Director Division of Naval Reactors, US Atomic Energy Commission:
Vice Admiral Hyman G. Rickover, USN (Ret)

Diplomatic

US Naval Attaché and Naval Attaché for Air in London:
Rear Admiral Lewis J. Kirn, USN

NOTE: *Unified Command with the Commander-in-Chief directing all US Army, Navy, and Air Force activities in the area.

Personnel —*continued*

Active Personnel (Estimated)

	30 June 1969	30 June 1970
Navy		
Officers	90,730	85,992
Enlisted men	699,577	676,236
Naval Academy midshipmen	4,243	4,243
Marine Corps		
Officers	26,187	25,000
Enlisted men	280,248	289,000

Mercantile Marine

Lloyd's Register of Shipping:
Total 3,232 vessels of 19,668,421 tons, gross

SPECIAL NOTES

For classifications through the listings for Amphibious Warfare Ships those ships which are in active commission are indicated by an (*) next to the particular ship's name at the head of each class. It should be noted that this marking for active ships applies ONLY to the United States section of *Jane's Fighting Ships.*

The introductory passages in the United States section of this edition are based primarily on official United States government statements and Congressional hearings on the Fiscal Year 1970-1974 Defence Programme and the Fiscal Year 1970 Defence Budget. Any interpretation of these statements and hearings is solely the responsibility of the Compiler and Editor of the United States section, Mr. Norman Polmar.

NEW JERSEY (BB 62) *1969, US Navy, PH2 Monty Tipton*

ALBANY (CG 10) *1969, United States Navy*

WHALE (SSN 638)

Surfaced at North Pole on 6 Apr 1969; note position of sail-mounted diving planes which are rotated to a vertical axis to facilitate breaking through ice; rudder can be seen protruding through ice at far right of photograph.
United States Navy, PHC B. M. Anderson

BARRY (DD 933)

At sea after completion of conversion to ASW configuration; because of deletion of DASH the ASROC launcher was moved from proposed position between funnels to former helicopter deck; raked stem because of bow-mounted SQS-23 sonar; other ships have SQS-23 sonar further aft. *United States Navy*

GLOVER (AGDE 1)

At sea after modifications; note fantail configuration in comparison to earlier photographs. *United States Navy*

THOMAS (DD 833)

As modified to test nuclear-biological-chemical warfare defences; all bridge and lookout positions enclosed and ship "sealed" to protect personnel; deckhouse on starboard 01 level (below ASROC) houses air conditioning equipment *United States Navy*

ADVANCED GUN DESIGNS (from left): 8 inch Major Calibre Light Weight Gun (MCLWG) proposed for LFS; 5 inch 54 cal Mk 42 gun for DD 931 class destroyers; 5 inch/54 cal Mk 45 gun for DD 963 class destroyers; 5 inch/54 cal Mk 65 gun for possible use on later destroyers; 3 inch/70 cal light-weight gun. *United States Navy*

X-1 (Midget Submarine)

Undergoing maintenance at Naval Ship Research and Development Centre in Annapolis, Maryland
1969, United States Navy

DOLPHIN (AGSS 555)

At sea on trials; note narrow deck and stepped sail structure.
1969, United States Navy

RUCHAMKIN (LPR 89)

One of the few surviving Amphibious Transports (Small). Her FRAM II features include improved electronics, extended deckhouse forward of bridge, triple ASW torpedo launchers, and tripod mast. Several ships of this type serve in Asian and South American navies.
United States Navy

MILWAUKEE (AOR 2)

Being fitted out at Quincy, Massachusetts. Note the resemblance to the larger AOE type underway replenishment ships. Their functions are similar.
1969, General Dynamics/Quincy Division

NEWPORT (LST 1179) being fitted out at Philidalphia Naval Shipyard after launching

1969, United States Navy

STRENGTH OF THE FLEET

The following table provides a tabulation of the ship strength of the United States Navy and an index to the ship listings within the United States section of this edition. Ship arrangement is based on function and employment; the official arrangement of ship types is contained in the "List of classifications of naval ships and service craft" which appears on a later page in this section. Numbers of ships listed in the table are estimated as of 1 Sep 1969 based on official and unofficial sources. Active ships in categories through Fire Support Ships are indicated by an asterisk in the individual ship listings. This scheme of identifying active ships applies *only* to *the United States Section*. Notes appear at the end of the table.

Category-Type	*Active* a	*Building-Conversion* b	*Reserve*
STRATEGIC WARFARE SHIPS			
Polaris Missile Submarines (SSBN)	41	—	—
COMMAND AND COMMUNICATION SHIPS			
Command Ships (CC-AGF)	3	—	—
Communication Ships (AGMR)	2	—	—
AIRCRAFT CARRIERS			
Attack Aircraft Carriers (CVA-CVAN)	15	3	—
ASW Aircraft Carriers (CVS)	7	—	4
Training Aircraft Carriers (AVT)	1	—	—
FLEET ESCORT SHIPS			
Guided Missile Cruisers (CG-CGN)	4	—	—
G.M. Light Cruisers (CLG)	5	—	1
Guided Missile Frigates (DLG-DLGN)	30	2	—
Frigates (DL)	3	—	—
Guided Missile Destroyers (DDG)	29	—	—
Destroyers (DD)	181	—	106
Guided Missile Escort Ships (DEG)	6	—	—
Research Escort Ship (AGDE)	1	—	—
Escort Ships (DE)	36	43	134
Radar Picket Escort Ships (DER)	9	—	15
SUBMARINES			
First-line Attack Submarines (SSN)	35	22	—
Attack and Fleet Submarines (SS-SSN)	67	—	3
Auxiliary Submarines (AGSS)	12	—	2
Transport Submarines (LPSS)	2		—
Training Submarines (SST)	3	—	—
FIRE SUPPORT SHIPS			
Battleships (BB)	1	—	3
Heavy Cruisers (CA)	4	—	13
Light Cruisers (CL)	—	—	6
Inshore Fire Support Ships (LFR)	4	—	8
AMPHIBIOUS WARFARE SHIPS			
Amphibious Command Ships (LCC)	5	2	—
Amphibious Assault Ships (LPH)	9	1	—
Amphibious Transport Docks (LPD)	12	3	—
Dock Landing Ships (LSD)	34	4	—
Amphibious Cargo Ships (LKA)	15	1	5
Amphibious Transports (LPA)	10	—	3
Amphibious Transports (Small) (LPR)	5	—	8
Tank Landing Ships (LST)	61	15	3
Landing Craft			
PATROL COASTAL AND RIVERINE CRAFT			
Patrol Gunboats (PG)	9	8	—
Hydrofoil Patrol Gunboats (PGH)	2	—	—
Fast Patrol Boats (PTF)	18	—	—
Fast Patrol Craft (PCF)			
Riverine Craft (ASPB-ATC-CCB-MON-MSD-MSM-MSR)			
Patrol Air Cushion Vehicles (PACV)			
MINE WARFARE SHIPS			
Mine Countermeasures Ships (MCS)	2	—	—
Fleet Minelayers (MMF)	—	—	1
Fast Minelayers (MMD)	—	—	10
Ocean Minesweepers (MSO)	62	—	—
Coastal Minesweepers (MSC-MSCO)	14	—	16
Fleet Minesweepers (MSF)	—	—	29
Special Minesweepers (MSS)	1	—	—
Inshore Minesweepers (MSI)	2	—	—
Minesweeping Boats (MSB)	39	—	2
Minesweeping Launches (MSL)			
UNDERWAY REPLENISHMENT SHIPS	87	13	3
FLEET SUPPORT SHIPS	120	7	37
FLOATING DRY DOCKS	29	—	18
LOGISTIC SUPPORT SHIPS	117	—	24
EXPERIMENTAL, RESEARCH AND SURVEYING SHIPS	71	6	4 c
SPECIALISED AUXILIARY SHIPS AND SERVICE CRAFT			
DEEP SUBMERGENCE VEHICLES			

NOTES: a includes ships undergoing overhaul, modernisation, and refuelling in the case of nuclear-powered ships; b includes ships authorised through Fiscal Year 1969 programmes; c includes one ex-cruiser planned for conversion to sonar test ship; one ex-cruiser hulk; one damaged technical research ship; and a former aircraft carrier (AVT) used as an electronics test ship. *Operational* Naval Reserve Training Ships are included in the active category.

SHIP PROGRAMMES

Fiscal Year 1970 New Construction Programme

1 Nuclear-Powered Attack Carrier (CVAN)
1 Nuclear-Powered Fleet Escort Ship (DXGN)
5 Destroyers (DD)
2 Nuclear-Powered Attack Submarines (SSN)
2 Amphibious Assault Ships (LHA)
3 Fast Deployment Logistic Ships (FDL)

Fiscal Year 1970 Conversion Programme

6 Nuclear-powered Fleet Ballistic Missile Submarines (SSBN) to Poseidon capability
2 Guided Missile Frigates (DLG) to improved AAW capability

Fiscal Year 1969 New Construction Programme

5 Destroyers, DX
2 Nuclear-powered Attack Submarines, SSN
1 Amphibious Assault Ship, LHA
4 Fast Deployment Logistic Ships, FDL

Fiscal Year 1969 Conversion Programme

2 Nuclear-Powered Fleet Ballistic Missile Submarines, SSBN, to Poseidon capability
1 Guided Missile Frigate, DLG, to Terrier HT
1 Submarine Tender, AS, to Poseidon support
1 Cargo Ship, T-AK, to Poseidon support
1 Range Instrumentation Ship, T-AGM, to support Poseidon

Of the original FY 1969 programmes, the following ships were either deferred or cancelled; new construction: 5 destroyers (DX), 1 All-Weather Patrol Boat (PB), 1 Destroyer Tender (AD), 1 Submarine Tender (AS), 4 Fast Deployment Logistic Ships (FDL); conversions: 4 Fleet Ballistic Missile Submarines (SSBM) to Poseidon capability, 10 Ocean Minesweepers (MSO).

Fiscal Year 1968 New Construction Programme

2 Nuclear-Powered Attack Submarines, SSN
1 Nuclear-Powered Attack Submarine, SSN, electric drive
1 Nuclear-Powered Guided Missile Frigate, DLGN
2 Ammunition Ships, AE
1 Fast Combat Support Ship, AOE
2 Oceanographic Research Ships, AGOR
1 Submarine Rescue Ship, ASR

Fiscal Year 1968 Conversion Programme

1 Guided Missile Frigate, DLG, to Terrier HT
9 Ocean Minesweepers, MSO
1 Submarine Tender, AS, to Poseidon support
6 Destroyers, DD, improved ASW

Of the original FY 1968 programmes, the following ships were either deferred or cancelled: new construction: 10 Escort Ships (DE), 7 Ocean Minesweepers (MSO), 9 All-Weather Patrol Boats (WPB); conversion: 3 Fleet Ballistic Missile Submarines (SSBN) to Poseidon capability; 1 Destroyer (DD) to improved ASW capability.

Fiscal Year 1966 New Construction Programme

6 Nuclear-Powered Attack Submarines, SSN
1 Nuclear-Powered Guided Missile Frigate, DLGN
1 Amphibious Assault Ship, LPH
1 Amphibious Transport Dock, LPD
10 Escort Ships, DE
1 Amphibious Force Flagship, AGC
3 Dock Landing Ships, LSD
8 Tank Landing Ships, LST
4 Ocean Minesweepers MSO (deferred)
1 Submarine Tender, AS
1 Destroyer Tender, AD (deferred)
10 Motor Gunboats, PGM
2 Hydrofoil Gunboats, PGH
1 Attack Cargo Ship, AKA
2 Ammunition Ships, AE
1 Combat Stores Ship, AFS
1 Fast Combat Support Ship, AOE
2 Replenishment Fleet Oilers, AOR
2 Fast Deployment Logistics Ships, FDL (deferred)
2 Oceanographic Research Ships, AGOR
1 Surveying Ship, AGS
1 Salvage Tug, ATS

Fiscal Year 1966 Conversion Programme

1 Attack Aircraft Carrier, CVA
1 Guided Missile Cruiser, CG
2 Guided Missile Frigates, DLG, to Terrier HT
5 Destroyers, DD, improved ASW
1 Special Minesweeper, MSS
2 MSTS Tankers, T-AO (deferred)

UNITED STATES SHIP-BASED AIRCRAFT

(Dimensions and performance characteristics will be found in the Naval Aircraft listings, beginning on page)

Name	*Manufacturer*	*Models*	*Mission (crew)*	*Engines*	*Notes*
SKYWARRIOR	Mc-Donnell Douglas	EA-3A, EA-3B KA-3B EKA-3B RA-3B	electronic countermeasures (4-7) tanker TACOS (Tanker Aircraft/Countermeasures Or Strike) Photographic reconnaissance (3-5)	2 Pratt & Whitney J57	Loaded weight approx 82 000 lbs; guns removed; Skywarrior detachments on deployed attack carriers; flown only by Navy
SKYHAWK	McDonnell-Douglas	A-4B, A-4C TA-4B A-4E, A-4F TA-4F	light attack (1) light attack trainer (2) light attack (1) light attack trainer (2)	1 Wright J65 1 Wright J65 1 Pratt & Whitney J52 1 Pratt & Whitney J52	Loaded weight approx 24 500 lbs with 11 000+ lbs bombs, rockets, missiles for A-4F; 2 20 mm cannon (1 gun replaced by ECM gear in Vietnam); A-4C with 2 Sidewinder missiles used as CVS fighter; flown by Navy and Marines; TA-4J will carry Shrike, Bullpup, "buddy store" fuel, improved avionics
VIGILANTE	North American	RA-5C	reconnaissance (2)	2 General Electric J79	Multi-sensor, all weather reconnaissance; loaded weight approx 61 700 lbs; most remanufactured A-5A, A-5B; RA-5C production reopened 1967-1969; flown by Navy from larger attack carriers
INTRUDER	Grumman	A-6A, A-6B EA-6A EA-6B	all-weather attack (2) electronic countermeasures (2) electronic surveillance & ECM (4)	2 Pratt & Whitney J52	Loaded weight approx 60 600 lbs with 15 000 lbs bombs, missiles for A-6A; A-6B carries Standard ARM; flown by Navy and Marines; KA-6D tanker variant will replace Skywarrior
CORSAIR II	Ling-Temco-Vought	A-7A, A-7B, A-7E	light attack (1)	1 Pratt & Whitney TF30	Loaded weight approx 38 000 lbs with 8 200 lbs bombs, rockets, missiles (including 2 air-to-air) for A-7A; 2 20 mm cannon in A-7A, A-7B; 1 20 mm M61 Gatling gun in A-7E; flown primarily by Navy; Marine procurement deferred
PHANTOM II	McDonnell-Douglas	F-4B, F-4J RF-4B, RF-4J	all-weather fighter (2) photographic reconnaissance (2)	2 General Electric J79	Loaded weight approx 54 000 lbs with 13 000+ lbs bombs, rockets, missile for F-4B; no guns; recon variants flown only by Marines; fighters by Navy and Marines (on larger attack carriers); F-4J has improved avionics, pulse doppler radar (AWG-10)
CRUSADER	Ling-Temco-Vought	F-8H, F-8J F-8K, F-8L RF-8A, RF-8G	fighter (1) fighter (1) photographic reconnaissance (1)	1 Pratt & Whitney J57	All except FR-8A remanufactured from earlier models; 4 20 mm cannon in fighters plus four air-to-air missiles and limited bomb/rocket capability (to 4 000 lbs); flown only by Navy from "Essex" class attack carriers; pulse doppler mode APQ-49 radar in F-8J
	Grumman	F-14A F-14B, F-14C	all-weather fighter (2)	2 Pratt & Whitney TF30 2 TF-400 series	Formerly VFX/VFAX designs; replacement for F-111B; F-14A to be operational mid-1973; improved engines in F-14B/C; improved avionics in F-14C; 1 20 mm M61 Gatling gun, 4 Sparrow missiles in F-14A; all later will have Phoenix air-to-air missile; to be flown by Navy and Marines
	General Dynamics-Grumman	F-111B	all-weather fighter (2)	2 Pratt & Whitney TF30	Procurement as Navy-Marine fighter cancelled because of overweight; six prototypes remain; to have carried six Phoenix air-to-air missiles in attack carrier defence role
KESTREL	Hawker-Siddeley		V/STOL fighter (1)	1 Rolls-Royce Bristol Pegasus 101	12 aircraft procured for Marines in Fiscal Year 1970; previously tested aboard LPD amphibious ships as XV-6A; no guns; approx 5 000 lbs bombs, rockets, missiles with STOL weight of 23 000 lbs
TRACKER	Grumman	S-2E	anti-submarine (4)	2 Wright R-1820	Loaded weight approx 29 000 lbs; no guns; variety of bombs, depth charges, torpedoes; flown by Navy from ASW carriers
	Grumman	S-3A	anti-submarine (4)	2 TF34 turbofan	Former VSX; replacement for Tracker for use on ASW carriers; improved sensors and data processing equipment
TRACER	Grumman	E-1B	airborne early warning (4)	2 Wright R-1820	Loaded weight approx 27 000 lbs; no guns; detachments operate from ASW carriers; flown by Navy; saucer-shaped APS-82 radar atop fuselage
HAWKEYE	Grumman	E-2A, E-2B, E-2C	airborne early warning (5)	2 Allison T56	Loaded weight approx 49 000 lb; no guns; detachments operate from attack carriers; flown by Navy, rotating saucer-shaped APS-96 radar atop fuselage; improved avionics in E-2B, E-2C
TRADER	Grumman	C-1A	light transport (2+9 passengers)	2 Wright R-1820	Carrier On-board Delivery (COD) transport version of Tracker/Tracer series; flown by Navy
GREYHOUND	Grumman	C-2A	light transport (3+33 passengers)	2 Allison T56	COD transport; wings, engines, subsystems, same as Hawkeye; rear-loading cargo compartment; flown primarily by Navy, few in Marine service
HUEY (Official name IROQUOIS)	Bell	UH-1B, UH-1E UH-1L	utility/gunship helicopter (2+7 troops) utility/transport (2+7 troops)	1 Lycoming T53	Loaded weight approx 9 500 lbs; UH-1B/1E have armour; normal armament 2 7·62 mm M60 MG and two pods of 2·75" rockets; flown by Navy and Marines
HUEYCOBRA	Bell	AH-1J	helicopter gunship (2)	1 Lycoming T53	Loaded weight approx 9 500 lbs; modified Huey design; rapid-fire 20 mm cannon in chin turret; stub wings for additional guns, rockets, missiles; gun improvement planned; flown by Marines
SEASPRITE	Kaman	UH-2A, UH-2B HH-2C, UH-2C	utility/rescue (2+11 passengers) utility/rescue (2-3+10 passengers)	1 General Electric T58 2 General Electric T58	Loaded weight approx 8 600 lbs for UH-2A/B, 10 000 for -2C variants; -2B has auxiliary fuel tanks fitted and some avionics deleted; 12 HH-2C have 7·62 mm MG in chin turret and two waiste MG for Vietnam rescue; flown by Navy
SEA KING	Sikorsky	RH-3A SH-3A, SH-3D HH-3A	minesweeping helicopter anti-submarine helicopter (4) rescue helicopter	2 General Electric T58	Loaded weight approx 18 600 lbs for SH-3D; SH-3A/D have dunking sonar, carry 840 lbs of torpedoes; 6 RH-3A built, 2 assigned each MCS; SH-3A/D assigned to ASW carriers; HH-3A has 7·62 mm MG in turret; flown by Navy

UNITED STATES SHIP-BASED AIRCRAFT —*Continued*

(Dimensions and performance characteristics will be found in the Naval Aircraft listings)

Name	*Manufacturer*	*Models*	*Mission (crew)*	*Engines*	*Notes*
SEAHORSE	Sikorsky	LH-34D, UH-34E, UH-34G	utility helicopter (2-4+ up to 12 troops)	1 Wright R-1820	SH-34 anti-submarine variants discarded by US Navy; LH-34D for Antarctic operations; UH-34D has fired Bullpup missile; no guns, flown by Navy and Marines; few remain
SEA KNIGHT	Boeing Vertol	CH-46A, CH-46D UH-46A, UH-46D	cargo/transport helicopter (3+25 troops) utility/replenishment helicopter (3)	2 General Electric T58	Loaded weight approx 21 400 lbs for -46A variants, 23 000 lbs for -46D variants; 4 000 lbs cargo in -46A; CH-46 variants flown by Marines as medium helicopter; UH-46 variants flown by Navy for Vertical Replenishment (VERTREP); no guns; CH-46F will have improved navigation gear and avionics
SEA STALLION	Sikorsky	CH-53A	cargo/transport helicopter (3+38 troops)	2 General Electric T64	Loaded weight approx 37 000 lbs; 8 000 lbs cargo; no guns; flown by Marines as heavy lift helicopter

UNITED STATES NAVY MISSILES

Category	*Name*	*Maker*	*Overall length Ft*	*Propulsion*	*Speed Mach*	*Range Miles*	*Guidance*	*Notes*
AIR TO AIR								
	SPARROW IIIB AIM-7E AIM-7F	Raytheon	12	Rocketdyne Solid propellent	2+	8	Semi-active homing	Arms carrier fighters; -7E used as Sea Sparrow in Basic Point Defence Missile System (BPDMS)
	SIDEWINDER 1A AIM-9B	Philco and General Electric	9·4	Naval Powder Plant Solid propellent	2·5	2	Infra-red-homing	
	SIDEWINDER 1C AIM-9D	Raytheon	9·5	Solid propellent			Infra-red-homing	Improved range over -9b
	PHOENIX AIM-54A	Hughes	13	Solid propellent			Radar-homing	Intended for F-111B; will be used by F 14's two-stage; fitted with electronic countermeasures capability
AIR TO SURFACE								
	BULLPUP A AGM-12B	Martin and Maxson	11	Thiokol storable liquid	1·8	6	Command	250-lb warhead
	BULLPUP B AGM-12C	Maxson	13·6	Storable liquid		9	Command	1 000-lb warhead
	SHRIKE AGM-45A	Texas Instrument-Sperry	10	Rocketdyne Solid propellent		approx 10	Passive-radar homing	Anti-radar missile used by A-4 and A-7
	CONDOR AGM-53A	North American				approx 40	Television from aircraft	In "operational development" status; conventional warhead; for use by A-6
	WALLEYE AGM-62A	Martin	11·3	Nil (glide bomb)			Television from aircraft	1 000-lb warhead
	STANDARD ARM AGM-78A	General Dynamics	14				Radar homing	Homes on enemy radar beams

United States Ship Based Aircraft—*continued*

Category	Name	Maker	Overall length Ft	Propulsion	Speed Mach	Range Miles	Guidance	Notes
SURFACE TO AIR								
TALOS 6BW1/RIM-8D 6C1/RIM-8E RIM-8F	Bendix		33	Bendix ramjet solid propellent booster	2·5+	65+ slant	Beam-riding cruise phase; semi-active homing	Carried by cruisers; high explosive or nuclear war head
STANDARD (ER) RIM-67A	General Dynamics		27	Solid propellent		30+ slant	Semi-active homing	Terrier replacement; compatible with existing launchers; 2 stage (Extended Range)
STANDARD (MR) RIM-66A	General Dynamics		14	Solid Propellent		10+ slant	Semi-active homing	Tartar replacement; compatible with existing launchers; as ER without booster stage
ADVANCED TERRIER RIM-2F	General Dynamics		26·5	Allegany Ballistics solid propellent (both stages)	3·0	approx 35 slant	Homing all the way	Carried by frigates; carriers, cruisers; replaces earlier Terrier BW and BT series
FLEET BALLISTIC								
IMPROVED TARTAR RIM-24B	General Dynamics		15	Aerojet General solid propellent	2·5	approx 12·5 slant	Semi-active homing	Carried by destroyers, escorts, and CG cruisers; replaces RIM-24A model
POLARIS A-2 UGM-27B •	Lockheed		31	Aerojet General or Hercules Powder solid propellent		1 725		A-2 in "Lafayette" class SSBN to be replaced by Poseidon; A-3 being fitted in all 10 "George Washington" and "Ethan Allen" FBM submarines; Polaris A-1 discarded; nuclear warheads; 2 stages
POLARIS A-3 UGM-27C	Lockheed		31	(as above)		2 875		
POSEIDON B-3 UGM-73A	Lockheed		34·2	Hercules Powder and Thiokol solid propellent		approx 2 900		To replace Polaris in 31 "Lafayette" class submarines; increased accuracy and payload including multiple independent re-entry vehicle (MIRV) containing several warheads and penetration aids (PENAIDS) weight 65 000 lbs; 2 stages

UNITED STATES ANTI-SUBMARINE WEAPONS

WEAPON ALFA RUR-4A	A 12·75 in. anti-submarine rocket weighing 500 lbs. fired at a detected submarine from a launcher with an almost circular field of fire. Uses Mk 108 launcher.
ASROC (Anti Submarine Rocket) RUR-5A	Ballistic ASW rocket developed by Honeywell, operational since 1961. Payload can be either a Gen Electric Mk 44 acoustic-homing torpedo or nuclear depth charge, which enters water after aerial trajectory to vicinity of target. Length 15 ft. Weight approx 1,000 lb. Launched from eight-tube "pepper box" launcher or combination Terrier/ASROC launcher on surface ships.
SUBROC (Submarine Rocket) UUM-44A	Developed by Goodyear Aerospace Corporation, a 4 000 lb rocket-propelled missile about 21 ft. in length launched from submarine torpedo tubes, emerges from the water and is guided by self-containing inertial guidance system in aerial trajectory to the vicinity of the target to dive on enemy submarines. Has range considerably greater than present ASW weapons (20+ miles). Nuclear warhead. Carried by "Thresher" and later classes of attack submarines which have BQQ-2 sonar.
DASH QH-50C	Drone anti-submarine helicopter. Helicopter carries two ASW torpedoes released remotely by launching ship after being positioned over target. To be replaced by manned ASW helicopter; now carried only by FRAM II destroyers. Reconnaissance version "snoopy dash" also in use.
Mk 37 Torpedo	Electric-propulsion torpedo launched from surface ships (Mk 23 and Mk 25 torpedo tubes or submarines. Mod 0 is ASW and anti-shipping torpedo with passive or active homing guidance; 11·25 ft in length, 19 in. diameter, 1 430 lb. Mod 1 is wire-guided ASW torpedo; 13·5 ft in length, 19 in. diameter, 1 690 lb.
Mk 44 Torpedo	Electric propulsion ASW torpedo with active homing guidance. Launched from surface ships (ASROC payload, Mk 32 tubes) or aircraft including DASH. Mod 0 is 8·33 ft. in length, 12·75 in. diameter, 422 lb. Mod 1 is 8·5 ft in length, 12·75 in. diameter, 433 lb.
Mk 45 Anti-Submarine Torpedo (ASTOR)	Electric propulsion-torpedo launched from submarines; nuclear warhead. Mod 0 is wire-guided ASW torpedo. Mod 1 is anti-shipping or ASW torpedo. Range 10+ miles. Both Mods 19·9 ft. in length, 19 in. diameter, 2 400 lbs.
Mk 46 Torpedo	ASW torpedo, successor to Mk 44, launched from surface ships or aircraft. Mod 0 is solid-propellent, 8·4 ft. in length, 12·75 in. diameter, 570 lbs. Mod 1 is liquid mono-propellent (same size).
Mk 48 Torpedo	**ASW torpedo, successor to Mk 37, launched from surface ships (Mk 25 tubes) or submarines.** For use against high-speed, deep-diving submarines. Liquid **mono-propellent fuel. Delayed** by development problems with procurement starting in 1969. Anti-shipping version under development.

LIST OF CLASSIFICATIONS OF NAVAL SHIPS AND SERVICE CRAFT

Every vessel on the Navy List has a distinctive serial number, prefaced by letters denoting the category to which she belongs.

The following is the official US Navy list of classifications of naval ships and service craft as promulgated by the Secretary of the Navy. The arrangement within categories and subcategories is alphabetical by symbol. In actual usage, symbols preceded by the letter "E" indicates the ship or craft is being used in experimental work; the prefix "T" indicates that the ship is assigned to the Navy's Military Sea Transportation Service and is civilian manned; and the prefix "F" indicates a ship being constructed by the United States for a foreign government.

COMBATANT SHIPS

(1) Warships

Cruisers:	
Battleship	BB
Heavy Cruiser	CA
Guided Missile Cruiser	CG
Guided Missile Cruiser (nuclear propulsion)	CGN
Light Cruiser	CL
Guided Missile Light Cruiser	CLG
Command Ship	CC
Aircraft Carriers:	
Attack Aircraft Carrier	CVA
Attack Aircraft Carrier (nuclear propulsion)	CVAN
ASW Support Aircraft Carrier	CVS
Training Aircraft Carrier	CVT
Destroyers:	
Destroyer	DD
Guided Missile Destroyer	DDG
Radar Picket Destroyer	DDR
Frigate	DL
Guided Missile Frigate	DLG
Guided Missile Frigate (nuclear propulsion)	DLGN
Ocean Escorts:	
Escort Ship	DE
Guided Missile Escort Ship	DEG
Radar Picket Escort Ship	DER
Submarines:	
Submarine	SS
Submarine (nuclear propulsion)	SSN
Fleet Ballistic Missile Submarine (nuclear propulsion)	SSBN
Guided Missile Submarine	SSG
Patrol Ships:	
Patrol Escort	PCE
Patrol Rescue Escort	PCER
Patrol Gunboat	PG

(2) Amphibious Warfare Ships

Amphibious Command Ship	LCC
Inshore Fire Support Ship	LFR
Amphibious Fire Support Ship	LFS
Amphibious Assault Ship (general purpose)	LHA
Amphibious Cargo Ship	LKA
Amphibious Transport	LPA
Amphibious Transport Dock	LPD
Amphibious Assault Ship	LPH
Amphibious Transport (small)	LPR
Amphibious Transport Submarine	LPSS
Dock Landing Ship	LSD
Tank Landing Ship	LST

(3) Mine Warfare Ships

Mine Countermeasures Ship	MCS
Minehunter, Coastal	MHC
Minelayer, Coastal	MMC
Minelayer, Fast	MMD
Minelayer, Fleet	MMF
Minesweeper, Coastal (non-magnetic)	MSC
Minesweeper, Coastal (old)	MSCO
Minesweeper, Fleet (steel hulled)	MSF
Minesweeper, Ocean (non-magnetic)	MSO
Minesweeper, Special (device)	MSS

COMBATANT CRAFT

(1) Patrol Craft	
Patrol Craft (hydrofoil)	PCH
Patrol Craft, Submarine	PCS
Patrol Gunboat (hydrofoil)	PGH
Fast Patrol Craft	PTF
(2) Landing Craft	
Landing Craft, Assault	LCA
Landing Craft, Mechanised	LCM
Landing Craft, Personnel, Large	LCPL
Landing Craft, Personnel, Ramped	LCPR
Landing Craft, Utility	LCU
Landing Craft, Vehicle, Personnel	LCVP
Amphibious Warping Tug	LWT
(3) Mine Countermeasures Craft	
Minehunter, Auxiliary	MHA
Minesweeper, Auxiliary	MSA
Minesweeping Boat	MSB
Minesweeper, Drone	MSD
Minesweeper, Inshore	MSI
Minesweeping Launch	MSL
Minesweeper, River	MSM
Minesweeper, Patrol	MSR
(4) Riverine Warfare Craft	
Assault Support Patrol Boat	ASPB
Armoured Troop Carrier	ATC
Command and Control Boat	CCB
Monitor	MON
Patrol Air Cushion Vehicle	PACV
River Patrol Boat	PBR
Patrol Craft, Inshore	PCF

AUXILIARY SHIPS

Destroyer Tender	AD
Degaussing Ship	ADG
Ammunition Ship	AE
Store Ship	AF
Combat Store Ship	AFS
Miscellaneous	AG
Escort Research Ship	AGDE
Hydrofoil Research Ship	AGEH
Environmental Research Ship	AGER
Miscellaneous Command Ship	AGF
Missile Range Instrumentation Ship	AGM
Major Communications Relay Ship	AGMR
Oceanographic Research Ship	AGOR
Radar Picket Ship	AGR
Surveying Ship	AGS
Satellite Launching Ship	AGSL
Auxiliary Submarine	AGSS
Technical Research Ship	AGTR
Hospital Ship	AH
Cargo Ship	AK
Cargo Ship, Dock	AKD
Light Cargo Ship	AKL
Vehicle Cargo Ship	AKR
Stores Issue Ship	AKS
Cargo Ship and Aircraft Ferry	AKV
Net Laying Ship	ANL
Oiler	AO
Fast Combat Support Ship	AOE
Gasoline Tanker	AOG
Replenishment Oiler	AOR
Transport	AP
Self-propelled Barracks Ship	APB
Small Coastal Transport	APC
Repair Ship	AR
Battle Damage Repair Ship	ARB
Cable Repairing Ship	ARC
Internal Combustion Engine Repair Ship	ARG
Landing Craft Repair Ship	ARL
Salvage Ship	ARS
Salvage Lifting Ship	ARSD
Salvage Craft Tender	ARST
Aircraft Repair Ship (Aircraft)	ARVA
Aircraft Repair Ship (Engine)	ARVE
Aircraft Repair Ship (Helicopter)	ARVH
Submarine Tender	AS
Submarine Rescue Ship	ASR
Auxiliary Ocean Tug	ATA
Fleet Ocean Tug	ATF
Salvage Tug	ATS
Seaplane Tender	AV
Advance Aviation Base Ship	AVB
Guided Missile Ship	AVM
Aviation Supply Ship	AVS
Auxiliary Aircraft Transport	AVT
Distilling Ship	AW
Fast Deployment Logistics Ship	FDL
Unclassified Miscellaneous	IX

SERVICE CRAFT

Large Auxiliary Floating Dry Dock	AFDB
Small Auxiliary Floating Dry Dock	AFDL
Medium Auxiliary Floating Dry Dock	AFDM
Barracks Craft (non-self-propelled)	APL
Auxiliary Repair Dry Dock	ARD
Medium Auxiliary Repair Dry Dock	ARDM
Submersible Research Vehicle (nuclear propulsion)	NR
Target and Training Submarine	SST
Submersible Craft	X
Miscellaneous Auxiliary	YAG
Open lighter	YC
Car Float	YCF
Aircraft Transportation Lighter	YCV
Floating Crane	YD
Diving Tender	YDT
Covered Lighter (self-propelled)	YF
Ferryboat or Launch	YFB
Yard Floating Dry Dock	YFD
Covered Lighter (non-self-propelled)	YFN
Large Covered Lighter	YFNB
Dry Dock Companion Craft	YFND
Lighter (special purpose)	YFNX
Floating Power Barge	YFP
Refrigerated Covered Lighter (self-propelled)	YFR
Refrigerated Covered Lighter (non-self-propelled)	YFRN
Covered Lighter (Range Tender)	YFRT
Harbour Utility Craft	YFU
Garbage Lighter (self-propelled)	YG
Garbage Lighter (non-self-propelled)	YGN
Salvage Lift Craft, Heavy (non-self-propelled)	YHLC
Salvage Lift Craft, Light (non-self-propelled)	YLLC
Dredge	YM
Salvage Lift Craft, Medium (non-self-propelled)	YMLC
Gate Craft	YNG
Fuel Oil Barge (self-propelled)	YO
Gasoline Barge (self-propelled)	YOG
Gasoline Barge (non-self-propelled)	YOGN
Fuel Oil Barge (non-self-propelled)	YON
Oil Storage Barge (non-self-propelled)	YOS
·ol Craft	YP
..ting Pile Driver	YPD
Floating Workshop	YR
Repair and Berthing Barge	YRB
Repair, Berthing and Messing Barge	YRBM
Repair, Berthing and Messing Barge (Large)	YRBML
Floating Dry Dock Workshop (Hull)	YRDH
Floating Dry Dock Workshop (Machine)	YRDM
Radiological Repair Barge	YRR
Salvage Craft Tender (non-self-propelled)	YRST
Seaplane Wrecking Derrick	YSD
Sludge Removal Barge	YSR
Large Harbour Tug	YTB
Small Harbour Tug	YTL
Medium Harbour Tug	YTM
Drone Aircraft Catapult Control Craft	YV
Water Barge (self-propelled)	YW
Water Barge (non-self-propelled)	YWN

UNITED STATES SERIAL NUMBERS

(Arranged in accordance with ship listings)

Strategic Warfare Ships

SSBN—Nuclear Powered Fleet Ballistic Missile Submarines

598 George Washington
599 Patrick Henry
600 Theodore Roosevelt
601 Robert E. Lee
602 Abraham Lincoln
608 Ethan Allen
609 Sam Houston
610 Thomas A. Edison
611 John Marshall
616 Lafayette
617 Alexander Hamilton
618 Thomas Jefferson
619 Andrew Jackson
620 John Adams
622 James Monroe
623 Nathan Hale
624 Woodrow Wilson
625 Henry Clay
626 Daniel Webster
627 James Madison
628 Tecumseh
629 Daniel Boone
630 John C. Calhoun
631 Ulysses S. Grant
632 Von Steuben
633 Casimir Pulaski
634 Stonewall Jackson
635 Sam Rayburn
636 Nathanael Greene
640 Benjamin Franklin
641 Simon Bolivar
642 Kamehameha
643 George Bancroft
644 Lewis and Clark
645 James K. Polk
654 George C. Marshall
655 Henry L. Stimson
656 George Washington Carver
657 Francis Scott Key
658 Mariano G. Vallejo
659 Will Rogers

Command and Communications Ships

CC—Command Ships

1 Northampton
(ex-CLC 1, ex-CA 125)
2 Wright
(ex-AVT 7, ex-CVL 49)

AGF—Miscellaneous Flagship

1 Valcour (ex-AVP 55)

AGMR—Major Communications Relay Ships

1 Annapolis (ex-Gilbert Islands, ex-AKV 39, ex-CVE 107)
2 Arlington (ex-Saipan, ex-CC 3, ex-AVT 6, ex-CVL 48)

Aircraft Carriers

CVAN—Nuclear Powered Attack Aircraft Carriers

65 Enterprise
68 Nimitz
69

CVA—Attack Aircraft Carriers

14 Ticondedoga
19 Hancock
31 Bon Homme Richard
34 Oriskany
41 Midway
42 Franklin D. Roosevelt
43 Coral Sea
59 Forrestal
60 Saratoga
61 Ranger
62 Independence
63 Kitty Hawk
64 Constellation
66 America
67 John F. Kennedy

CVS—Anti-Submarine Warfare Support Aircraft Carriers

9 Essex
10 Yorktown
11 Intrepid
12 Hornet
15 Randolph
18 Wasp
20 Bennington
33 Kearsarge
36 Antietam
38 Shangri-La
39 Lake Champlain

CVT—Training Aircraft Carrier

16 Lexington

CG—Guided Missile Cruisers

10 Albany (ex-CA 123)
11 Chicago (ex-CA 136)
12 Columbus (ex-CA 74)

CGN—Nuclear Powered Guided Missile Cruiser

9 Long Beach

CLG—Guided Missile Light Cruisers

3 Galveston (ex-CL 93)
4 Little Rock (ex-CL 92)
5 Oklahoma City (ex-CL 91)
6 Providence (ex-CL 82)
7 Springfield (ex-CL 66)
8 Topeka (ex-CL 67)

DLGN—Nuclear Powered Guided Missile Frigates

25 Bainbridge
35 Truxtun
36
37

DLG—Guided Missile Frigates

6 Farragut
7 Luce
8 Macdonough
9 Coontz
10 King
11 Mahan
12 Dahlgren
13 William V. Pratt
14 Dewey
15 Preble
16 Leahy
17 Harry E. Yarnell
18 Worden
19 Dale
20 Richmond K. Turner
21 Gridley
22 England
23 Halsey
24 Reeves
26 Belknap
27 Josephus Daniels
28 Wainwright
29 Jouett
30 Horne
31 Sterett
32 William H. Standley
33 Fox
34 Biddle

DL—Frigates

1 Norfolk
4 Willis A. Lee
5 Wilkinson

DDG—Guided Missile Destroyers

2 Charles F. Adams
3 John King
4 Lawrence
5 Claude V. Ricketts (ex-Biddle)
6 Barney
7 Henry B. Wilson
8 Lynde McCormick
9 Towers
10 Sampson
11 Sellers
12 Robinson
13 Hoel
14 Buchanan

DDG—Guided Missile Destroyers—*continued*

15 Berkeley
16 Joseph Strauss
17 Conygham
18 Semmes
19 Tattnall
20 Goldsborough
21 Cochrane
22 Benjamin Stoddert
23 Richard E. Byrd
24 Waddell
31 Decatur (ex-DD 936)
32 John Paul Jones
(ex-DD 932)
33 Parsons (ex-DD 933)
34 Somers (ex-DD 947)
35 Mitscher (ex-DL 2)
36 John S. McCain (ex-DL 3)

DD—Destroyers

422 Mayo
423 Gleaves
432 Kearny
435 Grayson
437 Woolsey
440 Ericsson
441 Wilkes
443 Swanson
445 Fletcher
446 Radford

448 La Vallette
449 Nicholas
450 O'Bannon
455 Hambledon
462 Fitch
466 Waller
475 Hudson
478 Stanley
479 Stevens
490 Quick
491 Farenholt
493 Carmick
494 Doyle
495 Endicott
496 McCook
497 Frankford
499 Renshaw
501 Schroeder
502 Sigsbee
507 Conway

511 Foote
513 Terry
519 Daly
528 Mullany
530 Trathen
531 Hazelwood
534 McCord
535 Miller
536 Owen
537 Sullivans
538 Stephen Potter
540 Twining
544 Boyd
547 Cowell
554 Franks
558 Laws
561 Pritchett
562 Robinson
563 Ross
564 Rowe
566 Stoddard
567 Watts
568 Wren
575 McKee
578 Wickes
585 Haraden
587 Bell
588 Burns
589 Izard
594 Hart
595 Metcalfe
596 Shields
598 Bancroft
600 Boyle

DD—Destroyers—*continued*

601 Champlin
602 Meade
603 Murphy
604 Parker
606 Coghlan
607 Frazier
608 Gansevoort
609 Gillespie
610 Hobby
613 Laub
614 Mackenzie
615 McLanahan
616 Nields
617 Ordronaux
618 Davison
619 Edwards
621 Jeffers
626 Satterlee
627 Thompson
629 Abbott
630 Braine
632 Cowie
634 Doran
635 Earle
637 Gerhardi
638 Herndon
641 Tillman
643 Sigourney
646 Stockton
647 Thorn
649 Albert W. Grant
650 Caperton
651 Cogswell
652 Ingersoll
653 Knapp
654 Bears
658 Colahan
659 Dashiell
660 Bullard
661 Kidd
662 Bennion
665 Bryant
666 Black
667 Chauncey
669 Cotton
671 Gatling
672 Healy
674 Hunt

679 McNair
680 Melvin
681 Hopewell
682 Porterfield
683 Stockham
684 Wedderburn
685 Picking
687 Uhlmann
688 Remey
690 Norman Scott
691 Mertz
692 Allen M. Sumner
693 Moale
694 Ingraham
696 English
697 Charles S. Sperry
698 Ault
699 Waldron
700 Haynsworth
701 John W. Weeks
702 Hank
703 Wallace L. Lind
704 Borie
705 Compton
706 Gainard
707 Soley
708 Harlan R. Dickson
709 Hugh Purvis
710 Gearing
711 Eugene A. Greene
712 Gyatt (ex-DDG 1, ex-DDG 712)
713 Kenneth D. Bailey
714 William R. Rush
715 William M. Wood
716 Wiltsie
717 Theo E. Chandler
718 Hammer
719 Epperson
723 Walke
724 Laffey
725 O'Brien
727 De Haven
728 Mansfield
729 Lyman K. Swenson
730 Collett
731 Maddox
732 Hyman
734 Purdy
742 Frank Knox
743 Southerland
744 Blue
745 Brush
746 Taussig

DD—Destroyers—*continued*

747 Samuel L. Moore
748 Harry E. Hubbard
752 Alfred A. Cunningham
753 John R. Pierce
755 John A. Bole
756 Beatty
757 Putnam
758 Strong
759 Lofberg
760 John W. Thomason
761 Buck
762 Henley
763 William C. Lawe
764 Lloyd Thomas
765 Keppler
770 Lowry
775 Willard Keith
776 James C. Owens
777 Zellars
778 Massey
779 Douglas H. Fox
780 Stormes
781 Robert K. Huntington
782 Rowan
783 Gurke
784 McKean
785 Henderson
786 Richard B. Anderson
787 James K. Kyes
788 Hollister
789 Eversole
790 Shelton
793 Cassin Young
795 Preston
800 Porter
805 Chevalier
806 Higbee
807 Benner
808 Dennis J. Buckley
817 Corry
818 New
819 Holder
820 Rich
821 Johnston
822 Robert H. McCard
823 Samuel B. Roberts
824 Basilone
825 Carpenter
826 Agerholm
827 Robert A. Owens
829 Myles C. Fox
830 Everett F. Larson
831 Goodrich
832 Hanson
833 Herbert J. Thomas
834 Turner
835 Charles P. Cecil
836 Georges K. Mackenzie
837 Sarsfield
838 Ernest G. Small
839 Power
840 Glennon
841 Noa
842 Fiske
843 Warrington
844 Perry
845 Bausell
846 Ozbourn
847 Robert L. Wilson
849 Richard E. Kraus
850 Joseph P. Kennedy Jr.
851 Rupertus
852 Leonard F. Mason
853 Charles A. Roan
857 Bristol
858 Fred T. Berry
859 Norris
860 McCaffery
861 Harwood
862 Vogelgesang
863 Steinaker
864 Harold J. Ellison
865 Charles R. Ware
866 Cone
867 Stribling
868 Brownson
869 Arnold J. Isbell
870 Fechteler
871 Damato
872 Forrest Royal
873 Hawkins
874 Duncan
875 Henry W. Tucker
876 Rogers
877 Perkins
878 Vesole
879 Leary
880 Dyess
881 Bordelon
882 Furse
883 Newman K. Perry
884 Floyd B. Parks
885 John R. Craig
886 Orleck
887 Brinkley Bass
888 Stickell
889 O'Hare
890 Meredith

DD—Destroyers—*continued*

931 Forrest Sherman
933 Barry
937 George F. Davis
938 Jonas Ingram
940 Manley
941 Dupont
942 Bigelow
943 Blandy
944 Mullinnix
945 Hull
946 Edson
948 Morton
950 Richard S. Edwards
951 Turner Joy

DEG—Guided Missile Escort Ships

1 Brooke
2 Ramsey
3 Schofield
4 Talbot
5 Richard L. Page
6 Julius A. Furer

AGDE—Escort Research Ship

1 Glover

DE—Escort Ships/DER—Radar Picket Escort Ships

129 Edsall
130 Jacob Jones
131 Hammann
134 Pope
137 Herbert C. Jones
138 Douglas L. Howard
139 Farquhar
140 J.R.Y. Blakeley
141 Hill
145 Huse
146 Inch
147 Blair/DER
149 Chatelain
150 Neunzer
151 Poole
152 Peterson
153 Reuben James
162 Levy
163 McConnell
164 Osterhaus
165 Parks
167 Acree
172 Cooner
180 Trumpeter
181 Straub
191 Coffman
202 Eichenberger
210 Otter
217 Coolbaugh
219 J. Douglas Blackwood
220 Francis M. Robinson
224 Rudderow
231 Hodges
238 Stewart
239 Sturtevant/DER
240 Moore
241 Keith
242 Tomich
244 Otterstetter/DER
245 Sloat
247 Stanton
248 Swasey
249 Marchand
250 Hurst
251 Camp/DER
253 Pettit
254 Ricketts
317 Joyce/DER
318 Kirkapatrick/DER
320 Menges
321 Mosley
323 Pride
324 Falgout/DER
326 Thomas J. Gary/DER
328 Finch/DER
329 Kretchmer/DER
330 O'Reilly
332 Price/DER
333 Strickland/DER
334 Forster/DER
335 Daniel

DE—Escort Ship—*continued*

336 Roy O. Hale/DER
337 Dale W. Peterson
339 John C. Butler
340 O'Flaherty
341 Raymond
342 Richard A. Suesens
346 Edwin A. Howard
348 Key
349 Gentry
353 Doyle C. Barnes
354 Kenneth M. Willett
356 Lloyd E. Acree
357 George E. Davis
358 Mack
360 Johnnie Hutchins
362 Rolf
363 Pratt
364 Rombach
367 French
370 John L. Williamson
382 Ramsden/DER
383 Mills/DER
384 Rhodes/DER
386 Savage/DER
387 Vance/DER
388 Lansing/DER
389 Durant/DER
390 Calcaterra/DER
391 Chambers/DER
392 Merrill
394 Swenning
395 Willis
396 Janssen
398 Cockrill
399 Stockdale
400 Hissem/DER
405 Dennis
406 Edmonds
409 La Prade
411 Stafford
414 Le Ray Wilson
415 Lawrence C. Taylor
416 Melvin R. Nawman
417 Oliver Mitchell
418 Tabberer
419 Robert F. Keller
420 Leland E. Thomas
421 Chester T. O'Brien
423 Dufilho
438 Corbesier
439 Conklin
441 William Seiverling
443 Kendall C. Campbell
444 Goss
449 Hanna
450 Joseph E. Connolly
508 Gilligan
531 Edward H. Allen
532 Tweedy
533 Howard F. Clark
534 Silverstein
537 Rizzi
538 Osberg
539 Wagner/DER
540 Vandivier/DER
577 Alexander J. Luke
580 Leslie L. B. Knox
581 McNulty
586 Lough
587 Thomas F. Nickel
589 Tinsman
639 Gendreau
640 Fieberling
641 William C. Cole
642 Paul G. Barker
643 Damon M. Cummings
667 Wiseman
681 Gillette
683 Henry R. Kenyon
685 Coates
696 Spangler
697 George
699 Marsh
701 Osmus
703 Holton
704 Cronin
705 Frybarger
700 Jobb
708 Parle
742 Hibert
743 Lamons
744 Kyne
745 Snyder
750 McClelland
765 Earl K. Olsen
767 Oswald
795 Gunason
796 Major
798 Varian
800 Jack W. Wilke
1006 Dealey
1014 Cromwell
1015 Hammerberg

DE—Escort Ships—*continued*

1021 Courtney
1022 Lester
1023 Evans
1024 Bridget
1025 Bauer
1026 Hopper
1027 John Willis
1028 van Voorhis
1029 Hartley
1030 Joseph K. Taussig
1033 Claud Jones
1034 John P. Perry
1035 Charles Berry
1036 McMorris
1037 Bronstein
1038 McCloy
1040 Garcia
1041 Bradley
1043 Edward McDonnell
1044 Brumby
1045 Davidson
1047 Voge
1048 Sample
1049 Koelsch
1050 Albert David
1051 O'Callahan
1052 Knox
1053 Roark
1054 Gray
1055 Hepburn
1056 Connole
1057 Rathburne
1058 Mayerkord
1059 W. S. Sims
1060 Lang
1061 Patterson
1062 Whipple
1063 Reasoner
1064 Lockwood
1065 Stein
1066 Marvin Shields
1067 Francis Hammond
1068 Vreeland
1069
1070 Downes
1071 Badger
1072 Blakely
1073
1074 Harold E. Holt
1075 Trippe
1076 Fanning
1077 Ouellet
1078 Joseph Hewes
1079 Bowen
1080 Paul
1081
1082
1083
1084
1085
1086
1087
1088
1089
1090
1091
1092
1093
1904
1095
1096
1097

Submarines

SSN—Nuclear Powered Attack Submarines

571 Nautilus
575 Seawolf
578 Skate
579 Swordfish
583 Sargo
584 Seadragon
585 Skipjack
586 Triton (ex-SSRN)
587 Halibut (ex-SSGN)
588 Scamp
590 Sculpin
591 Shark
592 Snook
594 Permit
595 Plunger
596 Barb
597 Tullibee
603 Pollack
604 Haddo
605 Jack
606 Tinosa
607 Dace
612 Guardfish
613 Flasher
614 Greenling
615 Gato

SSN—Submarines—*continued*

621 Haddock
637 Sturgeon
638 Whale
639 Tautog
646 Grayling
647 Pogy
648 Aspro
649 Sunfish
650 Pargo
651 Queenfish
652 Puffer
653 Ray
660 Sand Lance
661 Lapon
662 Gurnard
663 Hammerhead
664 Sea Devil
665 Guitarro
666 Hawkbill
667 Bergall
668 Spadefish
669 Seahorse
670 Finback
671 Narwhal
672 Pintado
673 Flying Fish
674 Trepang
675 Bluefish
676 Billfish
677 Drum
678
679
680
681
682
683
684
685
686
687

SS—Submarines/ AGSS—Auxiliary Submarines/ LPSS—Transport Submarines

224 Cod AGSS (T)
236 Silversides AGSS (T)
240 Angler AGSS (es-SSK) (T)
241 Bashaw AGSS (ex-SSK)
244 Cavalla AGSS (ex-SSK) (T)
245 Cobia AGSS (T)
246 Croaker (ex-SSK) (T)
270 Raton AGSS (ex-SSR) (T)
272 Redfin AGSS (ex-SSR) (T)
274 Rock AGSS (ex-SSR)
286 Billfish AGSS
287 Bowfin AGSS (T)
297 Ling AGSS (T)
298 Lionfish AGSS (T)
303 Sablefish AGSS
313 Perch LPSS (T)
315 Sealion LPSS
318 Baya AGSS
319 Becuna
322 Blackfin
323 Caiman
324 Blenny
328 Charr AGSS (T)
331 Bugara AGSS
334 Cabezon AGSS (T)
337 Carbonero (ex-SSG) AGSS
338 Carp AGSS (T)
339 Catfish

348 Cusk AGSS
377 Menhaden
382 Picuda
383 Pampanito AGSS (T)
384 Parche AGSS (T)
385 Bang AGSS
391 Pomfret
394 Razorback
396 Ronquil
398 Segundo
402 Sea Fox
403 Atule
405 Sea Owl AGSS
406 Sea Poacher
407 Sea Robin
409 Piper AGSS (T)
410 Threadfin
416 Tiru
417 Tench
418 Thornback
419 Tigrone (ex-SSR) AGSS
420 Tirante
421 Trutta
423 Torsk AGSS (T)

SS—Submarines—*continued*

424 Quillback
425 Trumpetfish
426 Tusk
476 Runner AGSS (T)
478 Cutlass
480 Medregal AGSS
481 Requin (ex-SSR) AGSS (T)
482 Irex AGSS
483 Sea Leopard
484 Odax
485 Sirago
486 Pomodon
487 Remora
489 Spinax AGSS (ex-SSR)
490 Volador
522 Amberjack
523 Grampus
524 Pickerel
525 Grenadier
555 Dolphin AGSS
563 Tang
564 Trigger
565 Wahoo
566 Trout
567 Gudgeon
568 Harder
569 Albacore AGSS
572 Sailfish (ex-SSR)
573 Salmon (ex-AGSS, ex-SSR)
547 Grayback LPSS (ex-SSG)
576 Darter
577 Growler (ex-SSG)
580 Barbel
581 Blueback
582 Bonefish

SST—Training Submarines

1 Mackerel
2 Marlin
3 Barracuda (ex-SSK 1)

X—Submersible Craft
1 (unnamed)

Fire Support Ships

BB—Battleships

61 Iowa
62 New Jersey
63 Missouri
64 Wisconsin

CA—Heavy Cruisers

68 Baltimore
69 Boston (ex-CAG 1)
70 Canberra (ex-CAG 2)
71 Quincy
72 Pittsburgh
73 St. Paul
75 Helena
122 Oregon City
124 Rochester
130 Bremerton
131 Fall River
132 Macon
133 Toledo
134 Des Moines
135 Los Angeles
139 Salem
148 Newport News

CL—Light Cruisers

65 Pasadena
90 Astoria
101 Amsterdam
102 Portsmouth
103 Wilkes Barre
106 Fargo
144 Worcester
145 Roanoke

LFR—Inshore Fire Support Ship (ex-IFS, ex-LSMR)

1 Carronade
401 Big Black River
405 Broadkill River
409 Clarion River
412 Des Plaines River
512 Lamoille River
513 Laramie River
515 Owyhee River
522 Red River
525 St Francis River
531 Smokey Hill River
536 White River

Amphibious Warfare Ships

LCC—Amphibious Command Ships (ex-AGC)

7 Mount McKinley
11 Eldorado
12 Estes
16 Pocono
17 Taconic
19 Blue Ridge
20

LPH-1—Amphibious Assault Ships

2 Iwo Jima
3 Okinawa
4 Boxer (ex-CVS 21)
5 Princeton (ex-CVS 37)
7 Guadalcanal
8 Valley Forge (ex-CVS 45)
9 Guam
10 Tripoli
11 New Orleans
12 Inchon

LPD—Amphibious Transports Dock

1 Raleigh
2 Vancouver
3 La Salle
4 Austin
5 Ogden
6 Duluth
7 Cleveland
8 Dubuque
9 Denver
10 Juneau
11 Coronado
12 Shreveport
13 Nashville
14 Trenton
15 Ponce

LSD—Dock Landing Ships

1 Ashland
2 Belle Grove
3 Carter Hall
5 Gunston Hall
6 Lindenwald
7 Oak Hill
13 Casa Grande
14 Rushmore
15 Shadwell
16 Cabildo
17 Catamount
18 Colonial
19 Comstock
20 Donner
21 Fort Mandan
22 Fort Marion
25 San Marcos
26 Tortuga
27 Whetstone
28 Thomaston
29 Plymouth Rock
30 Fort Snelling
31 Point Defiance
32 Spiegel Grove
33 Alamo
34 Hermitage
35 Monticello
36 Anchorage
37
38
39
40

COAST GUARD

WHEC—High Endurance Cutters

31 Bibb
32 Campbell
33 Duane
35 Ingham
36 Spencer
37 Taney
39 Owasco
40 Winnebago
41 Chautauqua
42 Sebago
44 Wachusett
64 Escanaba
65 Winona
66 Klamath
67 Minnetonka
68 Androscoggin
69 Mendota
70 Pontchartrain
371 Mackinac
372 Humboldt
373 Matagorda
374 Absecon
375 Chincoteague
377 Rockway
378 Half Moon
379 Unimac
380 Yakutat
381 Bartaria
382 Bering Strait
383 Castle Rock
384 Cook Inlet
385 Dexter
386 McCulloch
387 Gresham
715 Hamilton
716 Dallas
717 Mellon
718 Chase
719 Boutwell
720 Sherman
721 Gallatin
722 Morganthan
723 Rush
724
725

WAGO—Oceanographic Cutter

377 Rockaway (ex-WHEC)

WMEC—Medium Endurance Cutters

147 Morris

615 Reliance
616 Diligence
617 Vigilant
618 Active
619 Confidence
620 Resolute
621 Valiant
622 Courageous
623 Steadfast
624 Dauntless
625 Venturous
626 Dependable
627 Vigorous
628 Durable
629 Decisive
630 Alert

WAGB—Icebreakers

4 Glacier
38 Storis
83 Mackinaw
278 Staten Island (ex-AGB 3)
279 Eastwind
280 Southwind (ex-AGB 3)
281 Westwind
282 Northwind
283 Burton Island (ex-AGB 1)
284 Edisto (ex-AGB 2)

Silhouettes Scale: 150 feet = 1 inch **Aircraft Carriers**

Many detail changes of appearance of most vessels shown here have occurred during the Vietnamese war, particularly on antenna. It is intended that a complete updating of these drawings be undertaken for the next edition.

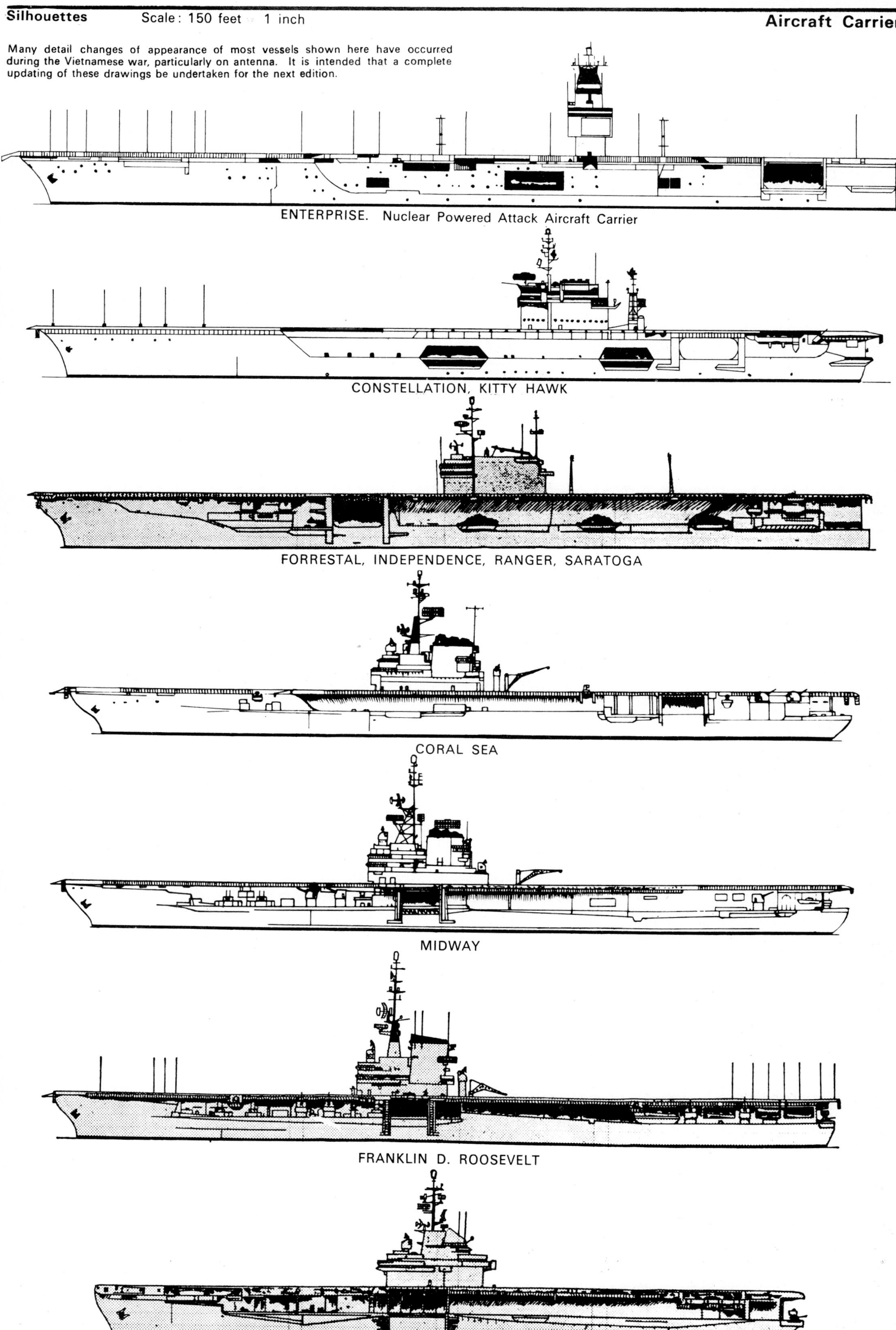

ENTERPRISE. Nuclear Powered Attack Aircraft Carrier

CONSTELLATION, KITTY HAWK

FORRESTAL, INDEPENDENCE, RANGER, SARATOGA

CORAL SEA

MIDWAY

FRANKLIN D. ROOSEVELT

ESSEX *Class* with angled deck and enclosed bow

Heavy Cruisers, Command Ships

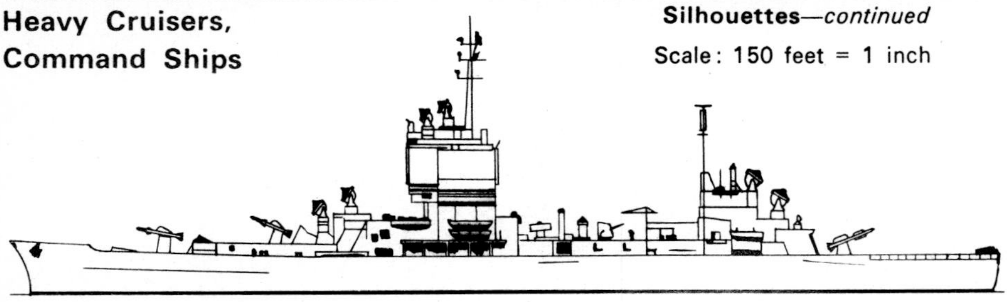

Silhouettes—*continued*

Scale: 150 feet = 1 inch

LONG BEACH. Nuclear Powered Guided Missile Cruiser

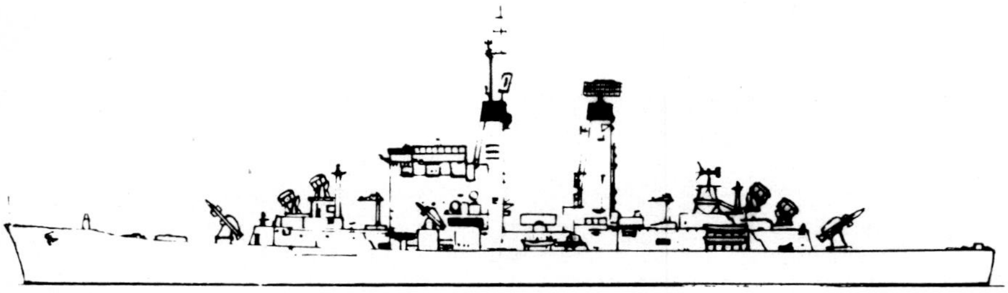

ALBANY, CHICAGO COLUMBUS. Guided Missile Cruisers, converted Heavy Cruisers

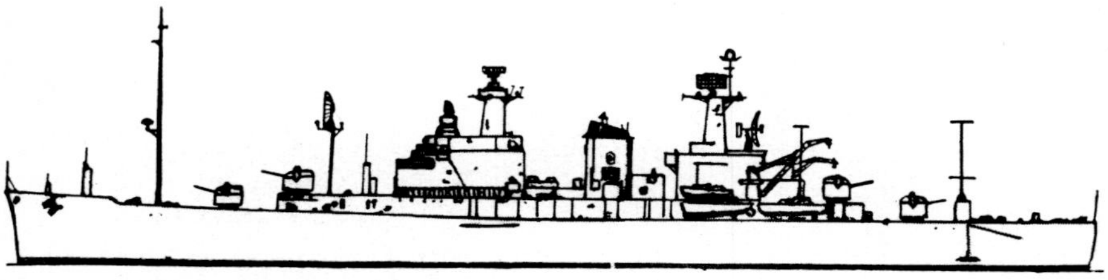

NORTHAMPTON. Command ship. Originally designed as a Heavy Cruiser

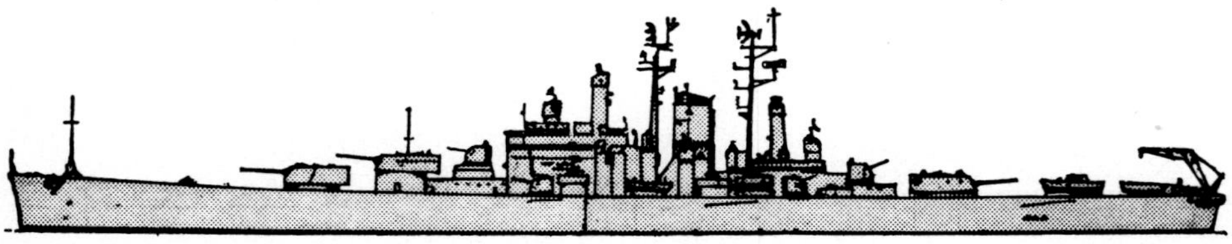

NEWPORT NEWS

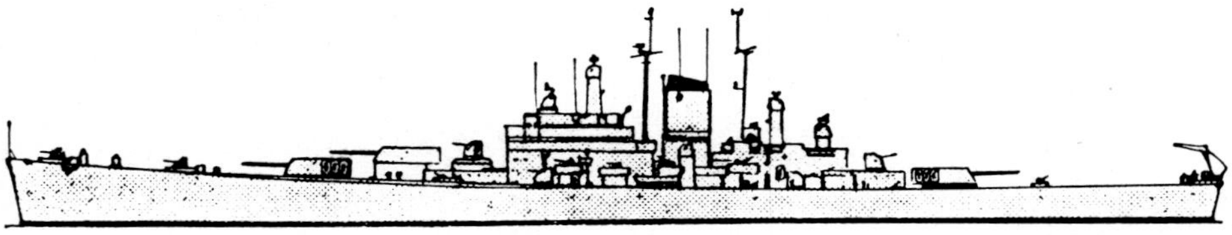

DES MOINES, SALEM

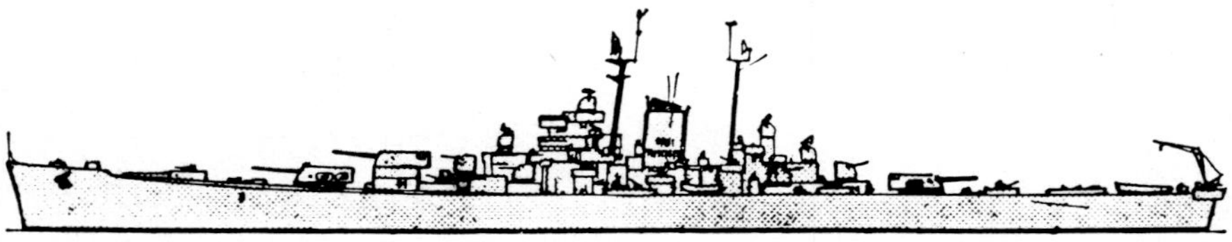

OREGON CITY, ROCHESTER

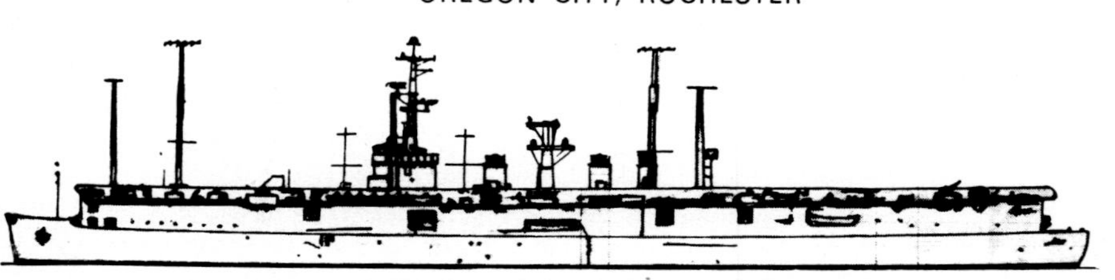

WRIGHT. Command Ship. Converted Aircraft Carrier

IWO JIMA *Class*. Amphibious Assault Ship (Helicopter Commando Carrier)

Destroyers

CARPENTER *Class* FRAM II conversions

CARPENTER *Class*

Converted GEARING *Class* FRAM I

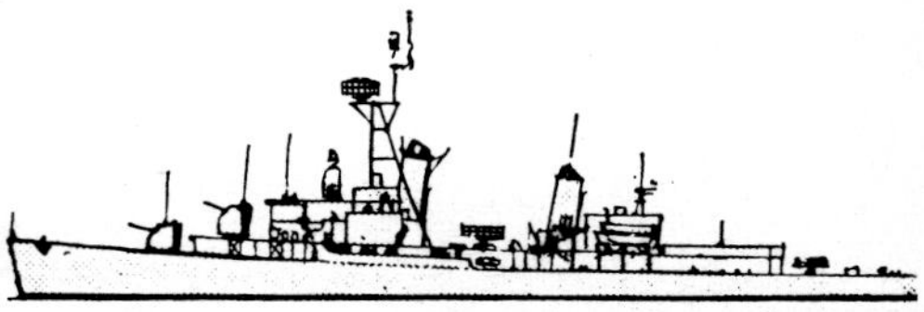

GEARING *Class* FRAM conversions

GEARING *Class* with tripod mast

GEARING *Class* Radar Pickets

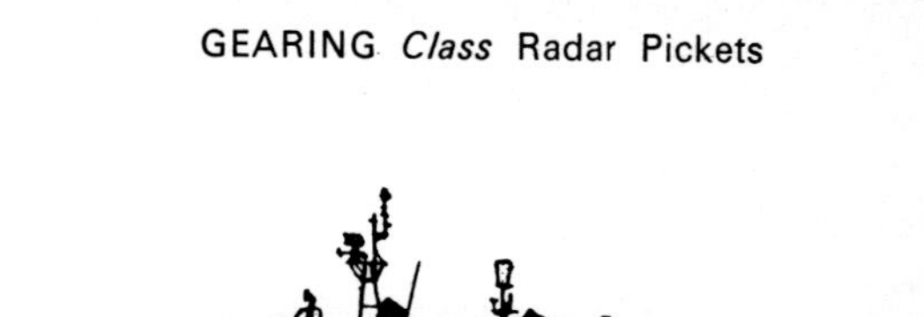

GEARING *Class* Radar Pickets with mainmast

ALLEN M. SUMNER *Class* with tripod

Cruisers

Silhouettes—*continued*

Scale: 150 feet = 1 inch

Destroyers

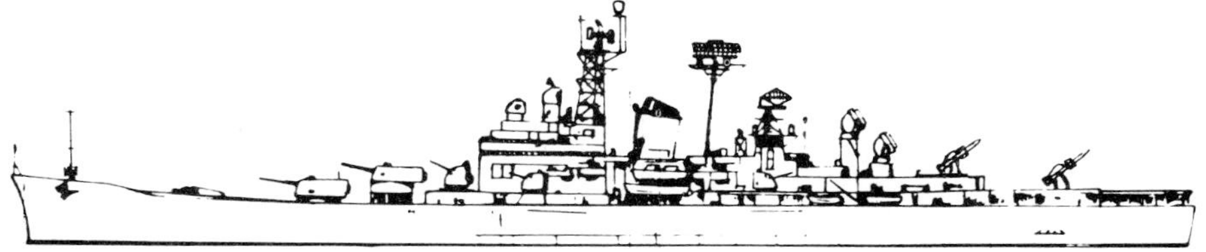

BOSTON (no helo deck), CANBERRA. Guided Missile Heavy Cruisers. Converted

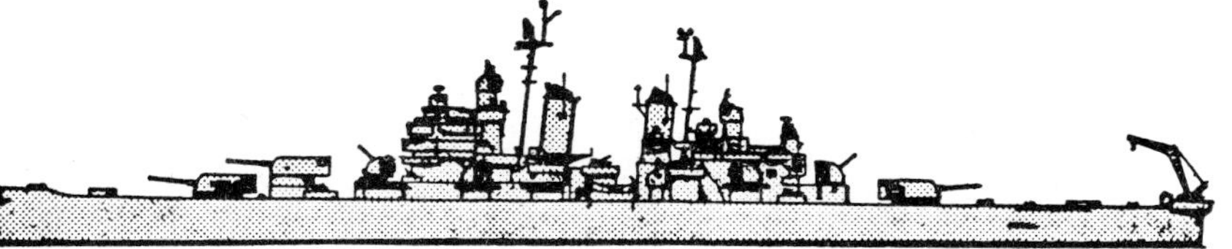

BALTIMORE *Class*. Heavy Cruisers

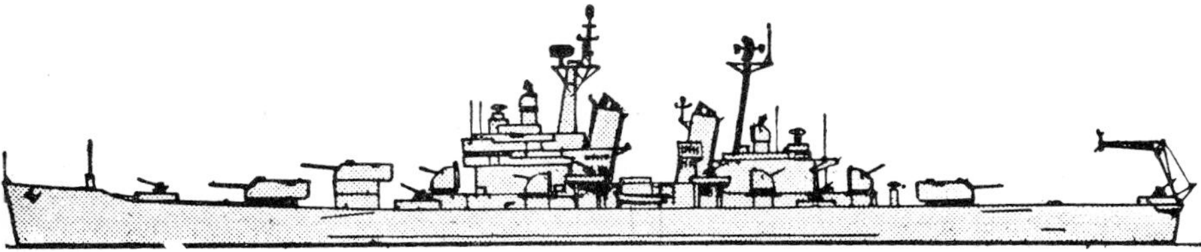

HELENA, ST. PAUL. Heavy Cruisers

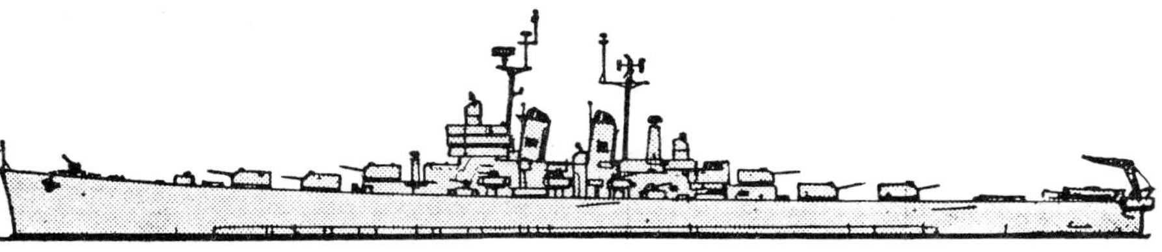

ROANOKE, WORCESTER. Large Light Cruisers

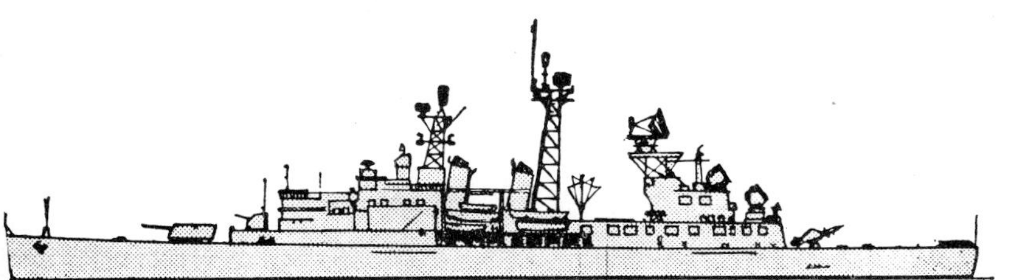

LITTLE ROCK, OKLAHOMA CITY. Guided Missile Light Cruisers. Converted

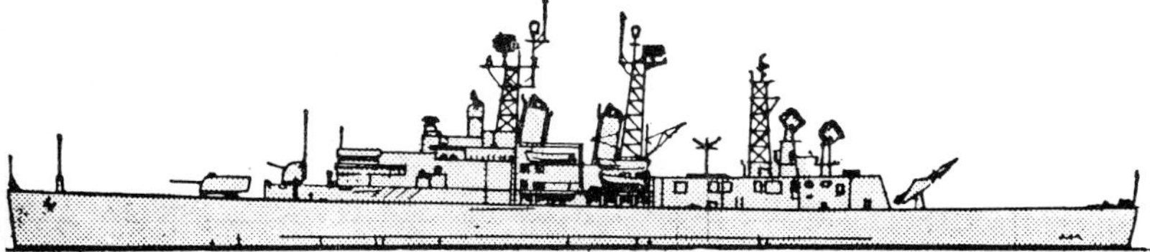

PROVIDENCE, SPRINGFIELD. Guided Missile Light Cruisers, Converted

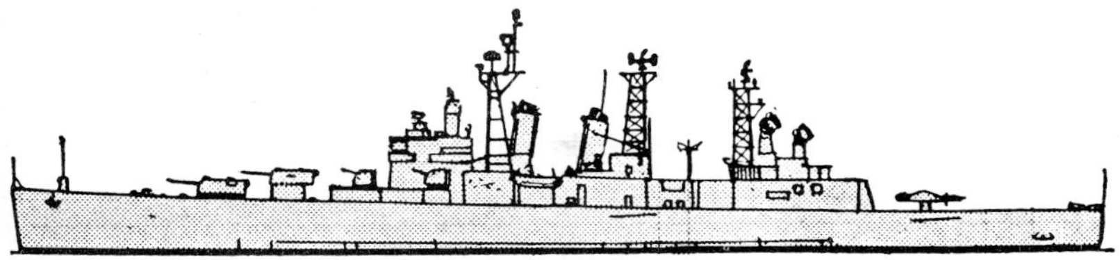

TOPEKA. Guided Missile Light Cruiser. Converted

GALVESTON. Guided Missile Light Cruiser. Converted

Converted FLETCHER *Class* FRAM

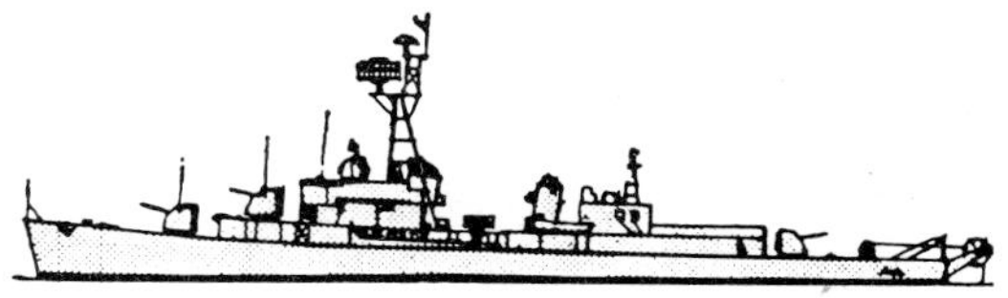

ALLEN M. SUMNER *Class* FRAM

FLETCHER *Class* FRAM Conversions

FLETCHER *Class* with 4—5" guns

FLETCHER *Class* with 5—5" guns

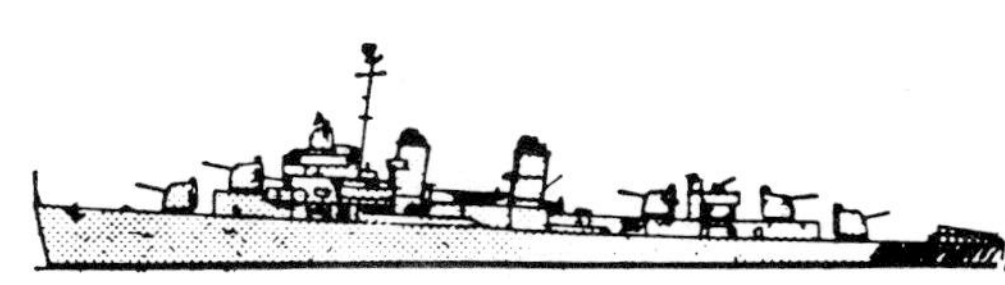

Later FLETCHER *Class*

Converted FLETCHER *Class* with polemast

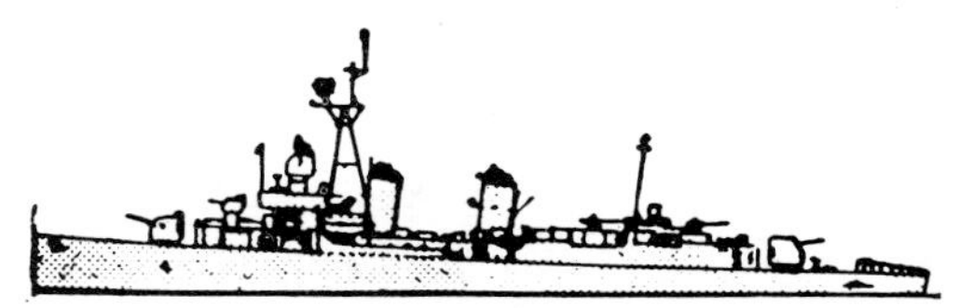

Converted FLETCHER *Class* with tripod mast

Cruisers, Destroyers **Silhouettes**—*oued* Scale: 150 feet = 1 inch **Escort Ships**

FARGO. Light Cruiser

CLEVELAND *Class.* Light Cruisers

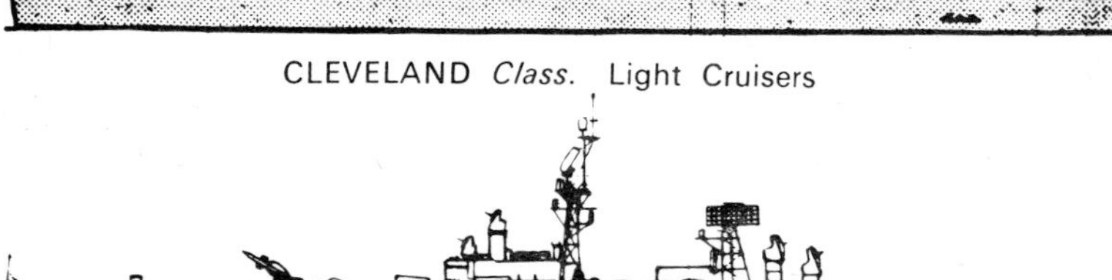

BAINBRIDGE. Nuclear Powered Guided Missile Frigate (Destroyer Leader)

NORFOLK. Frigate. ex-Anti-Submarine Light Cruiser

BELKNAP *Class.* Guided Missile Frigates (Destroyer Leaders)

LEAHY *Class.* Guided Missile Frigates (Destroyer Leaders)

COONTZ *Class.* Guided Missile Frigates (Destroyer Leaders)

MITSCHER *Class.* Frigates, ex-Destroyer Leaders

FORREST SHERMAN *Class.* Large Destroyers

CHARLES F. ADAMS *Class.* Guided Missile Armed Destroyers

BROOKE *Class* Guided Missile Escort Ships

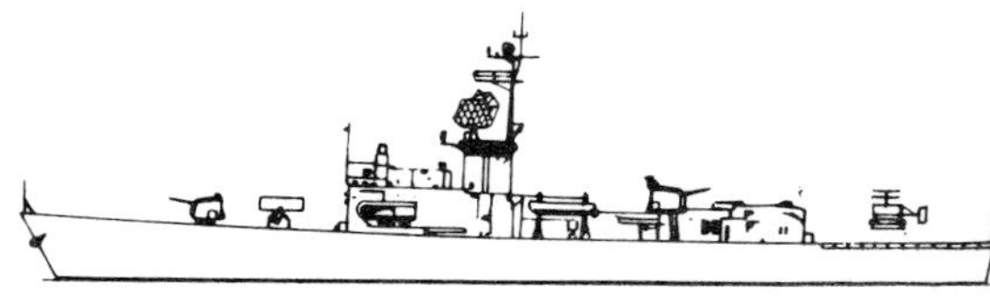

GARCIA *Class.* A/S Escort Ships

BRONSTEIN *Class*

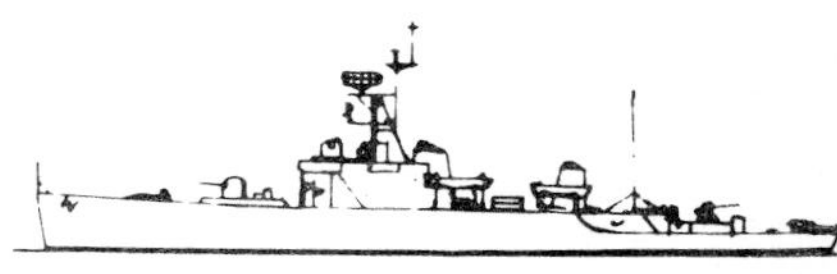

CLAUDE JONES *Class*

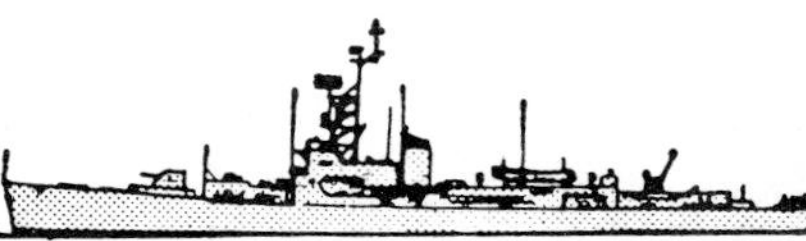

DEALEY *Class*

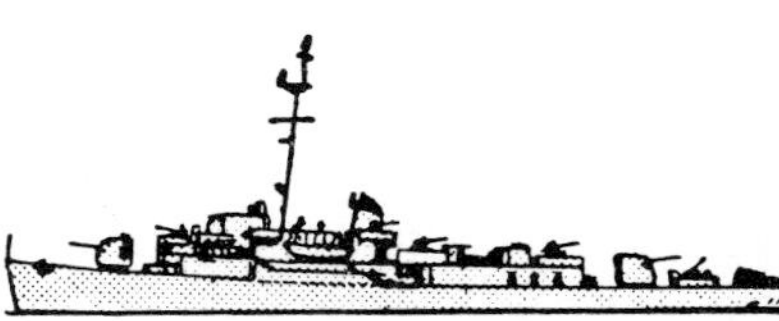

RUDDEROW *Class*

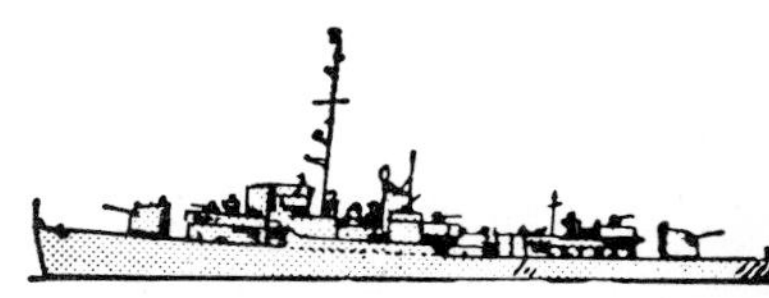

JOHN C. BUTLER *Class*

BUCKLEY *Class* with 5" guns

BUCKLEY *Class* as Radar Picket

EDSALL *Type* as Radar Picket

STRATEGIC WARFARE SHIPS

The United States has begun conversion of its Polaris Fleet Ballistic Missile (FBM) force to the improved, multiple-warhead Poseidon missile. As initially completed, the US Navy's 41-submarine FBM force consisted of five submarines armed with the Polaris A-1 missile (1,370-statute-mile range), 13 with the A-2 missile (1 700 miles), and 23 with the A-3 missile (2 875 miles). The five "George Washington" class submarines armed with the A-1 missile have been converted to fire the A-3 version as will the five "Ethan Allen" class submarines built with an A-2 missile capability. The remaining 31 submarines of the "Lafayette" class (with A-2 or A-3 capability) all will be rearmed with the Poseidon C-3, a larger, more-powerful missile. Of the 41-submarine FBM force, more than half is on deterrent patrol at any given time. The remaining submarines are alongside tenders undergoing a 28-day replenishment and refit between deterrent patrols, or are undergoing overhauls in US shipyards.

Thus, the Polaris submarine force is capable of providing a deterrent force of approximately 25 submarines carrying some 400 missiles at sea on a continuous basis. During periods of crisis the number of submarines at sea can be increased by delaying and shortening refit periods.

POSEIDON. Conversion of the first "Lafayette" class submarine to fire the improved Poseidon missile has begun, wth two ships funded under the Fiscal Year 1968 programme, two in FY 1969, six planned for FY 1970, seven in FY 1971, six in FY 1972, five in FY 1973, and three in FY 1974.

The Poseidon C-3 missile is based on Polaris experience and considerably advance technologies. According to official statements, the Poseidon has double the payload and twice the accuracy of the Polaris A-3 missile. The new missile's effectiveness is enhanced by the use of the Multiple Independently targeted Re-entry Vehicle (MIRV) concept in which the Poseidon warhead consists of several separate thermo-nuclear explosive packages which are each guided to separate targets. Unofficial estimates have credited each Poseidon with 10 to 14 separate "warheads".

Range of the Poseidon will vary with warhead configuration, but is similar to that of the Polaris A-3 missile. The first flight of a Poseidon test vehicle was made on 16 Aug 1968 from Cape Kennedy, Florida, with the missile travelling "in excess of 1 000 miles" down the Atlantic test range before impacting. Additional Poseidon flight tests have been conducted from Cape Kennedy with at-sea test firings beginning in August 1969 from the USS *Observation Island* (AG 154). Some 15 to 20 test launches from the *Observation Island* are scheduled.

Initial deployment of the Poseidon is scheduled for January 1971 in the FBM submarine *James Madison*, with several Poseidon-armed submarines going to sea later in 1971. Total cost of developing, producing, and deploying the Poseidon missiles in 31 submarines is estimated to be $3·3 *billion*. The ten submarines of the "George Washington" and "Ethan Allen" classes will not be modified to Poseidon configuration because of their design limitations, but will operate with the Polaris A-3.

POLARIS A-3. Improved variants of the Polaris A-3 missiles are now operational. Project ANTELOPE, completed in 1966, provided the A-3 missile with improved penetration aids and engine modifications. Reports that the A-3 missile was being fitted with multiple warheads were confirmed in an unclassified statement by Senator Henry M. Jackson on 10 May 1968. The A-3 missile, capable of delivering an explosive force of between 0·7 and one megaton, apparently has three separate warheads which are not independently targeted (ie, MIRV), but impact within a small area of a single target.

UNDERSEA LONG-RANGE MISSILE SYSTEM. A new, improved submarine-launched strategic missile system is in the advanced development stage. Now known as ULMS for Undersea Long-Range Missile System, this would be a follow-on to the Polaris-Poseidon submarine force. The system involves a longer range missile and a more efficient, quieter, nuclear-powered launching submarine. The longer range missile, according to the Secretary of Defence, could be a completely new weapon or an improved version of the Poseidon C-3. The latter missile configuration would reduce development schedule and cost of the ULMS missile. Because of the modified-Poseidon option, current efforts are directed toward the ULMS submarine, the long-lead-time component of the system. (Additional data on the proposed submarine is listed below).

The longer range of the ULMS missile would provide the submarine with a greater operating area from which Soviet cities and military activities could be targeted, thus complicating Soviet anti-submarine efforts.

Concept formulation of ULMS is being conducted in Fiscal Years 1969-1970, with $5 000 000 provided in the Fiscal year 1969 defense programms and $20 000 000 in the FY 1970 programme. Actual design of ULMS is planned for Fiscal Years 1970-1971, with a research and development prototype of the ULMS submarine proposed for construction in the mid 1970s. Should the decision be made to deploy ULMS the first advanced submarine could be operational as early as 1980, according to the Chief of Naval Operations.

BALLISTIC MISSILE SHIP. Periodically the Navy has studied the feasibility of installing strategic missiles in surface ships, both merchant-type vessels and warships. The "Albany" and "Long Beach" cruiser classes at one time were scheduled to carry the Polaris FBM, but this project was deferred. (These ships are described in the listing for Fleet Escort Ships).

A 1966-1967 study of candidates for future strategic missile systems (STRAT-X) proposed two sea-based candidates, ULMS (described above) and the Ship-based Long-Range Missile System (SLMS), now commonly referred to as the Ballistic Missile Ship (BMS) concept. According to a statement in 1968 by the Secretary of the Navy, a surface missile ship "could provide survivable payloads of long-range missiles. Basing such missiles on a surface ship would permit utilisation of large ocean areas. In such a world-wide deployment, the missiles would be continually within range of targets, even while in port. The ships can be designed to accept any of the missiles now contemplated for development in the 1975-1985 decade". However, there is apparently no active effort on this scheme at this time.

HUNLEY (AS 31), THOMAS A. EDISON (SSBN 610) *United States Navy*

ANTI-BALLISTIC MISSILE SHIP. The Navy also is studying a Sea-based Anti-Ballistic Missile Intercept System (SABMIS). The SABMIS concept is offered by the Navy as a supplement and possibly alternate to the "thin" Safeguard/Nike-X Anti-Ballistic Missile (ABM) system proposed by the Nixon Administration. Although certain factions within the Navy and in the Congress have advocated a comparative analysis of the proposed SABMIS and Safeguard concepts, the official policy of the Departments of Defence and Navy has been to consider SABMIS only as a study for a backup or "in depth" complement to the Safeguard system. Reportedly, approximately $3 000 000 has been spent on SABMIS compared to approximately $4 *billion* on Safeguard/Nike-X studies, research, and development.

In view of the existing political situation with President Nixon's Administration firmly committed to a policy of deploying the Safeguard system, it appears unlikely that SABMIS could be developed so long as there is any interest in the Safeguard system. The proposed SABMIS ship is described on a subsequent page of the listings for Strategic Warfare Ships.

PHOTOGRAPHS. The photograph above shows the FBM submarine *Thomas A. Edison* in Holy Loch, Scotland, alongside the submarine tender *Hunley* (AS 31). The tender is offloading a Polaris missile for test and inspection. Names, normally painted on both sides of a submarine aft, and sail identification numbers are removed from FBM submarines while deployed on deterrent patrols. The differences in the external appearance of the various classes of FBM submarines are virtually nil.

ROBERT E. LEE (SSBN 601) *1966, United States Navy*

Strategic Warfare Ships—*Continued*

PROTOTYPE UNDERSEA LONG-RANGE MISSILE SYSTEM (ULMS) SUBMARINE: PROPOSED

Displacement, tons — approx 8 000 surface
Length, feet — approx 450 oa
Main engines — steam turbines, 1 shaft
Reactor — 1 pressurised-water cooled
Missiles — long-range, advanced ballistic missiles

The construction of a "dedicated research and development submarine for the ULMS prototype, which could be retained for use in on-going research and development programmes after the ULMS development was complete," has been proposed by the Department of Defence.
Preliminary design of the ULMS submarine will be undertaken by the Electric Boat Division of the General Dynamics Corp. The ULMS submarine would incorporate the latest advances in nuclear submarine technology, especially in the areas of noise-reduction, crew habitability, communications, and modular construction and maintenance. The last feature would greatly facilitate maintenance, overhaul, and subsequent modernisation, with a resulting reduction in non-operational time for the submarine. There have been major advances in all of these areas since the "Lafayette" class FBM submarines was designed in the late 1950s.

31 FLEET BALLISTIC MISSILE SUBMARINES (FBM): "LAFAYETTE" CLASS

Name	*No.*	*Builder*	*Laid down*	*Launched*	*Commissioned*
***LAFAYETTE**	SSBN 616	General Dynamics (Electric Boat Div)	17 Jan 1961	8 May 1962	23 Apr 1963
***ALEXANDER HAMILTON**	SSBN 617	General Dynamics (Electric Boat Div)	26 June 1961	18 Aug 1962	27 June 1963
***ANDREW JACKSON**	SSBN 619	Mare Island Naval Shipyard	26 Apr 1961	15 Sep 1962	3 July 1963
***JOHN ADAMS**	SSBN 620	Portsmouth Naval Shipyard	19 May 1961	12 Jan 1963	12 May 1964
***JAMES MONROE**	SSBN 622	Newport News Shipbuilding & DD Co	31 July 1961	4 Aug 1962	7 Dec 1963
***NATHAN HALE**	SSBN 623	General Dynamics (Electric Boat Div)	2 Oct 1961	12 Jan 1963	23 Nov 1963
***WOODROW WILSON**	SSBN 624	Mare Island Naval Shipyard	13 Sep 1961	22 Feb 1963	27 Dec 1963
***HENRY CLAY**	SSBN 625	Newport News Shipbuilding & DD Co	23 Oct 1961	30 Nov 1962	20 Feb 1964
***DANIEL WEBSTER**	SSBN 626	General Dynamics (Electric Boat Div)	28 Dec 1961	27 Apr 1963	9 Apr 1964
***JAMES MADISON**	SSBN 627	Newport News Shipbuilding & DD Co	5 Mar 1962	15 Mar 1963	28 July 1964
***TECUMSEH**	SSBN 628	General Dynamics (Electric Boat Div)	1 June 1962	22 June 1963	29 May 1964
***DANIEL BOONE**	SSBN 629	Mare Island Naval Shipyard	6 Feb 1962	22 June 1963	23 Apr 1964
***JOHN C. CALHOUN**	SSBN 630	Newport News Shipbuilding & DD Co	4 June 1962	22 June 1963	15 Sep 1964
***ULYSSES S. GRANT**	SSBN 631	General Dynamics (Electric Boat Div)	18 Aug 1962	2 Nov 1963	17 July 1964
***VON STEUBEN**	SSBN 632	Newport News Shipbuilding & DD Co	4 Sep 1962	18 Oct 1963	30 Sep 1964
***CASIMIR PULASKI**	SSBN 633	General Dynamics (Electric Boat Div)	12 Jan 1963	1 Feb 1964	14 Aug 1964
***STONEWALL JACKSON**	SSBN 634	Mare Island Naval Shipyard	4 July 1962	30 Nov 1963	26 Aug 1964
***SAM RAYBURN**	SSBN 635	Newport News Shipbuilding & DD Co	3 Dec 1962	20 Dec 1963	2 Dec 1964
***NATHANAEL GREENE**	SSBN 636	Portsmouth Naval Shipyard	21 May 1962	12 May 1964	19 Dec 1964
***BENJAMIN FRANKLIN**	SSBN 640	General Dynamics (Electric Boat Div)	25 May 1963	5 Dec 1964	22 Oct 1965
***SIMON BOLIVAR**	SSBN 641	Newport News Shipbuilding & DD Co	17 Apr 1963	22 Aug 1964	29 Oct 1965
***KAMEHAMEHA**	SSBN 642	Mare Island Naval Shipyard	2 May 1963	16 Jan 1965	10 Dec 1965
***GEORGE BANCROFT**	SSBN 643	General Dynamics (Electric Boat Div)	24 Aug 1963	20 Mar 1965	22 Jan 1966
***LEWIS AND CLARK**	SSBN 644	Newport News Shipbuilding & DD Co	29 July 1963	21 Nov 1964	22 Dec 1965
***JAMES K. POLK**	SSBN 645	General Dynamics (Electric Boat Div)	23 Nov 1963	22 May 1965	16 Apr 1966
***GEORGE C. MARSHALL**	SSBN 654	Newport News Shipbuilding & DD Co	2 Mar 1964	21 May 1965	29 Apr 1966
***HENRY L. STIMSON**	SSBN 655	General Dynamics (Electric Boat Div)	4 Apr 1964	13 Nov 1965	20 Aug 1966
***GEORGE WASHINGTON CARVER**	SSBN 656	Newport News Shipbuilding & DD Co	24 Aug 1964	14 Aug 1965	15 June 1956
***FRANCIS SCOTT KEY**	SSBN 657	General Dynamics (Electric Boat Div)	5 Dec 1964	23 Apr 1966	3 Dec 1966
***MARIANO G. VALLEJO**	SSBN 658	Mare Island Naval Shipyard	7 July 1964	23 Oct 1965	16 Dec 1966
***WILL ROGERS**	SSBN 659	General Dynamics (Electric Boat Div)	20 Mar 1965	21 July 1966	1 Apr 1967

Displacement, tons — 6 650 light surface; 7 320 standard surface; 8 250 submerged
Length, feet (*metres*) — 425 (*129·5*) oa
Beam, feet (*metres*) — 33 (*10·1*)
Draft, feet (*metres*) — 31·5 (*9·6*)
Missiles — 16 tubes for Polaris A-2 in SSBN 616, 617, 619, 620, 622-625 (eight submarines); 16 tubes for Polaris A-3 in others except *James Madison* and *Daniel Boone* converting to Poseidon missiles (see *Missile* notes)
Torpedo tubes — 4—21 in (*533 mm*) forward
Nuclear reactor — 1 pressurised-water cooled S5W (Westinghouse)
Main engines — 2 geared turbines 15 000 shp; 1 shaft
Speed, knots — 20 surface; approx 30 submerged
Complement — 140 (14 officers, 126 enlisted men)

These Fleet Ballistic Missile (FBM) submarines are the largest undersea craft ever built. Construction plans and design were awarded to the Electric Boat Division of the General Dynamics Corp., Groton, Connecticut, on 24 Mar 1960. The first four SSBNs of this class were authorised in the Fiscal Year 1961 shipbuilding programme with five additional submarines (SSBN 622-626) authorised in a supplemental FY 1961 programme; SSBN 627-636 (ten) in FY 1962, SSBN 640-645 (six) in FY 1963, and SSBN 654-659 (six) in FY 1964. Cost for the earlier ships of this class was approximately $109 500 000 per ship.

CLASSIFICATION. The *Benjamin Franklin* and later submarines officially are considered a separate class; however, differences are minimal (eg, quieter machinery) and all 31 submarines generally are considered as a single class.

DESIGN. The *Daniel Webster* has her diving planes mounted at bow instead of on sail structure as do all other SSBNs. Although this arrangement has proved successful, no change is anticipated in existing or planned nuclear-powered submarines with sail diving planes. This class incorporates a modified "tear-drop" hull design based on the experimental submarine *Albacore* (AGSS 569).

ENGINEERING. The *Benjamin Franklin* and subsequent ships of this class have been re-engined with quieter machinery. All SSBNs have diesel-electric stand-by machinery, snorkels, and "outboard" auxiliary propeller for emergency use.

MISSILES. The first eight ships of this class were fitted with the Polaris A-2 missile (1 725 statute mile range) and the 23 later ships with the Polaris A-3 missile (2 880 statute mile range). All are being rearmed with the improved Poseidon C-3 missile.

LAFAYETTE (SSBN 616) — *1968, United States Navy*

WILL ROGERS (SSBN 659) — *1967, United States Navy*

Strategic Warfare Ships—*Continued*

"LAFAYETTE" CLASS *continued*

The *James Madison* began Poseidon refit in Feb 1969 at Electric Boat and the *Daniel Boone* on 11 May 1969 at Newport News. . Reportedly, the eight FY 1969-1970 submarines to undergo Poseidon refit are the *Von Steuben, John C. Calhoun, Ulysses S. Grant, Tecumseh, Casimir Pulaski, Sam Rayburn, Nathanael Greene,* and *Sam Rayburn,* all to begin late in 1969 or early 1970.
Poseidon refit and reactor refuelling are conducted simultaneously during an overhaul of approximately 15 months. The *James Madison* is scheduled to complete overhaul late in June 1970 and the *Daniel Boone* in mid-August 1970.
The missiles are launched from 16 vertical tubes within the submarine's hull. The SSBN 616, 617, 619, 620, 622 and 623 launch their Polaris missiles by compressed air (with the missile's solid-fuel rocket engine igniting after it leaves the water); the 25 later ships have a gas-steam generator launching system in which a small solid rocket motor produces extremely hot gasses into a water-filled chamber to produce steam to launch the missile. The *Andrew Jackson* launched the first Polaris A-3 missile fired from a submarine on 26 Oct 1963. The *Daniel Webster* was the first submarine to deploy with the A-3 missile, beginning her first patrol on 28 Sep 1964. The *Daniel Boone* was the first Polaris submarine to deploy to the Pacific, beginning her first patrol with the A-3 missile on 25 Dec 1964.
These submarines have Mk 84 fire control systems (Polaris).

NAVIGATION. FBM submarines are equipped with an elaborate Ship's Inertial Navigation System (SINS), a system of gyroscopes and accelerometers which relates movement of the ship in all directions, true speed through the water and over the ocean floor, and true north to give a continuous report of the submarine's position. The system includes the capability of both optical and electronic checks. Navigation data produced by SINS can be provided to each missile's guidance package until the instant the missile is fired.
The first 19 submarines have three Mk 2 SINS and the 12 later submarines have two Mk 2 SINS; all have navigational satellite receivers.

NOMENCLATURE. FBM submarines are named for "famous Americans", including South American and Hawaiian leaders as well as Europeans who aided the United States war for independence. The lead ship of the class is named after the French aristocrat who served with George Washington in the American Revolution.

TECUMSEH (SSBN 628) *United States Navy*

PERSONNEL. Each FBM submarine is assigned two alternating crews designed "Blue" and "Gold". Each crew mans the submarine during a 60-day patrol and partially assists during the intermediate 28-day refit alongside a Polaris tender. The "off-duty" crew is undergoing training or is on leave. All FBM submarines are fully air conditioned and the newer ships have elaborate crew study and recreation facilities.

FRANCIS SCOTT KEY (SSBN 657) After launching *United States Navy*

DANIEL WEBSTER (SSBN 626) *United States Navy*

WOODROW WILSON (SSBN 624) *United States Navy*

Strategic Warfare Ships—*Continued*

5 FLEET BALLISTIC MISSILE SUBMARINES (SSBN): "ETHAN ALLEN" CLASS

Name	*No.*	*Builder*	*Laid down*	*Launched*	*Commissioned*
***ETHAN ALLEN**	SSBN 608	General Dynamics (Electric Boat Div, Groton)	14 Sep 1959	22 Nov 1960	8 Aug 1961
***SAM HOUSTON**	SSBN 609	Newport News Shipbuilding & DD Co	28 Dec 1959	2 Feb 1961	6 Mar 1962
***THOMAS A. EDISON**	SSBN 610	General Dynamics (Electric Boat Div, Groton)	15 Mar 1960	15 June 1961	10 Mar 1962
***JOHN MARSHALL**	SSBN 611	Newport News Shipbuilding & DD Co	4 Apr 1960	15 July 1961	21 May 1962
***THOMAS JEFFERSON**	SSBN 618	Newport News Shipbuilding & DD Co	3 Feb 1961	24 Feb 1962	4 Jan 1963

Displacement tons	6 900 standard surface; 7 900 submerged
Length feet (*metres*)	410·5 (*125·1*) oa
Beam, feet (*metres*)	33 (*10·1*)
Draft, feet (*metres*)	30 (*9·4*)
Missiles	16 tubes for Polaris A-2 (see *Missile* notes)
Torpedo tubes	4—21 in (*533 mm*) forward
Nuclear reactor	1 pressurised-water cooled S5W (Westinghouse)
Main engines	1 geared turbine (General Electric) 15 000 shp, 1 shaft
Speed, knots	20 surface; approx 30 submerged
Complement	112 (12 officers, 100 enlisted men)

These submarines were designed specifically for the FBM role and are larger and better arranged than the earlier "George Washington" class submarines. The first four ships of this class were authorised in the Fiscal Year 1959 programme; the *Thomas Jefferson* (which is out of numerical sequence) was in the FY 1961 programme.

DESIGN. These submarines and the subsequent "Lafayette" class are deep-diving submarines with a depth capability similar to the "Thresher" class attack submarines; pressure hulls of HY-80 steel.

MISSILES. These ships were initially armed with the Polaris A-2 missile (1 725 statute mile range). The *Ethan Allan* launched the first A-2 missile fired from a submarine on 23 Oct 1961. She was the first submarine to deploy with the A-2 missile, beginning her first patrol on 26 June 1962. The *Ethan Allen* fired a Polaris A-2 missile in the Christmas Island Pacific Test Area on 6 May 1962 in what was the first complete US test of a ballistic missile including detonation of the nuclear warhead. All five of these ships are being modified to fire the A-3 missile (2 880 statute mile range).
Fitted with Mk 80 fire control system and compressed air missile ejectors; to have Mk 84 fire control systems and gas-steam missile ejectors with A-3 missile.

NAVIGATION. Fitted with two Mk 2 Ship's Inertial Navigation Systems (SINS) and navigational satellite receiver.

PERSONNEL. Alternating "Blue" and "Gold" crews as in "Lafayette" class submarines.

JOHN MARSHALL (SSBN 611) — *1967, United States Navy*

ETHAN ALLEN (SSBN 608) — *1967, US Navy, Joc Harold Wise*

5 FLEET BALLISTIC MISSILE SUBMARINES (SSBN): "GEORGE WASHINGTON" CLASS

Name	*No.*	*Builder*	*Laid down*	*Launched*	*Commissioned*
***GEORGE WASHINGTON**	SSBN 598	General Dynamics (Electric Boat Div, Groton)	1 Nov 1957	9 June 1959	30 Dec 1959
***PATRICK HENRY**	SSBN 599	General Dynamics (Electric Boat Div, Groton)	27 May 1958	22 Sep 1959	9 Apr 1960
***THEODORE ROOSEVELT**	SSBN 600	Mare Island Naval Shipyard	20 May 1958	3 Oct 1959	13 Feb 1961
***ROBERT E. LEE**	SSBN 601	Newport News Shipbuilding & DD Co	25 Aug 1958	18 Dec 1959	16 Sep 1960
***ABRAHAM LINCOLN**	SSBN 602	Portsmouth Naval Shipyard	1 Nov 1958	14 May 1960	11 Mar 1961

Displacement, tons	5 900 standard surface; 6 700 submerged
Length, feet (*metres*)	381·7 (*115·8*) oa
Beam, feet (*metres*)	33 (*10·1*)
Draft, feet (*metres*)	29 (*8·8*)
Missiles	16 tubes for Polaris A-3
Torpedo tubes	6—21 in (*533 mm*) forward
Nuclear reactor	1 pressurised-water cooled S5W (Westinghouse)
Main engines	1 geared turbine (General Electric) 15 000 shp, 1 shaft
Speed, knots	20 surface; approx 30 submerged
Complement	112 (12 officers 100 enlisted men)

The *George Washington* was the West's first ship to be armed with ballistic missiles. A supplement to the Fiscal Year 1958 new construction programme signed on 11 Feb 1958 provided for the construction of the first three Fleet Ballistic Missile (FBM) submarines. The Navy had already ordered the just-begun attack submarine *Scorpion* (SSN 589) to be completed as a missile submarine on 31 Dec 1957; the hull was redesignated SSBN 598 and completed as the *George Washington*. The *Theodore Roosevelt* similarly was reordered on the last day of 1957, her materials having originally been intended for the not-yet-started SSN 590. These submarines and three sister ships (two authorised in FY 1959) were built to a modified "Skipjack" class design with almost 130 feet being added to the original design to accommodate two rows of eight missile tubes, fire control and navigation equipment, and auxiliary machinery.

GEORGE WASHINGTON (SSBN 598) — *United States Navy*

MISSILES. These ships were initially armed with the Polaris A-1 missile (1 380 statute mile range). The *George Washington* successfully fired two Polaris A-1 missiles while submerged off Cape Canaveral (Kennedy) on 20 July 1960 in the first underwater launching of a ballistic missile from a US submarine. She departed on her initial patrol on 15 Nov 1960 and remained submerged for 66 days, 10 hours. All five submarines of this class have been refitted to fire the improved Polaris A-3 missile (2 880 statute mile range). Missile refit and first reactor

Strategic Warfare Ships—*Continued*

"GEORGE WASHINGTON" CLASS *continued*

refuelling were accomplished simultaneously during overhaul: *George Washington* from 20 June 1964 to 2 Feb 1966, *Patrick Henry* from 4 Jan 1965 to 21 July 1966, *Theodore Roosevelt* from 28 July 1965 to 14 Jan 1967, *Robert E. Lee* from 23 Feb 1965 to 2 July 1966, and *Abraham Lincoln* from 25 Oct 1965 to 3 June 1967; four at Electric Boat yard in Groton, Connecticut, and *Robert E. Lee* at Mare Island Naval Shipyard.
These submarines all have Mk 84 fire control systems and gas-steam missile ejectors (originally fitted with Mk 80 fire control systems and compressed air missile ejectors; changed during A-3 missile refit).

ENGINEERING. The *George Washington* was the first FBM submarine to be overhauled and "refuelled". During her 4½ years of operation on her initial reactor core she carried out 15 submerged missile patrols and steamed more than 100 000 miles.

NAVIGATION. Fitted with three Mk 2 Ship's Inertial Navigation Systems (SINS) and navigational satellite receiver.

PERSONNEL. Alternating "Blue" and "Gold" crews as in "Lafayette" class submarines.

ABRAHAM LINCOLN (SSBN 602) *United States Navy*

THEODORE ROOSEVELT (SSBN 600) *United States Navy*

CRUISER-TYPE ANTI-BALLISTIC MISSILE SHIPS: PROPOSED

Displacement, tons	20 000-30 000 full load
Length, feet (*metres*)	approx 700 (*214·0*)
Missiles	approx 40-60 ABM several Point Defense Missile System (PDMS) launchers
Nuclear reactors	2 pressurised-water cooled
Main engines	Geared turbines, 2 shafts

The US Navy has studied the feasibility of a Sea-based Anti-Ballistic Missile Intercept System (SABMIS) to provide an effective and *relatively* low cost defence against intercontinental ballistic missiles. The SABMIS concept provides for tracking/missile ships which could be deployed to intercept enemy ICBMs early in their flight, before multiple warheads and penetration decoys break away from the launching rocket. Thus, a sea-based ABM would have one target per enemy ICBM whereas a land-based ABM system in the target area would have to cope with several re-entry packages for every enemy missile which is fired.
The radar to detect an enemy ICBM launching, the fire control computers, missile guidance, and the ABM missile launchers would all be mounted in a single ship under the SABMIS concept. It is anticipated that an extremely small number of ships could provide the capability of intercepting the approximately 40 inter-continental missiles which Communist China would be able to launch against the United States in the mid-1970s. Also, the SABMIS concept could provide a low-cost "thin" defence against an "accidental" Soviet ICBM launching of a small number of missiles against the United States. (Most authorities agree there is today no possiblity of providing defence against an all-out Soviet ICBM strike against the United States).
However, even against a threat of this size a force of several SABMIS ships may be desired to provide for survivability in the event of war and for normal overhaul and training. Still, a multi-ship SABMIS force, with nuclear powered-escort ships, is expected to cost considerably less than the $8 to 40 billion Safeguard/Nike-X "thin" ABM defence now being proposed for the United States.
A sea-based ABM would appear to offer several major advantages over a land-based system:

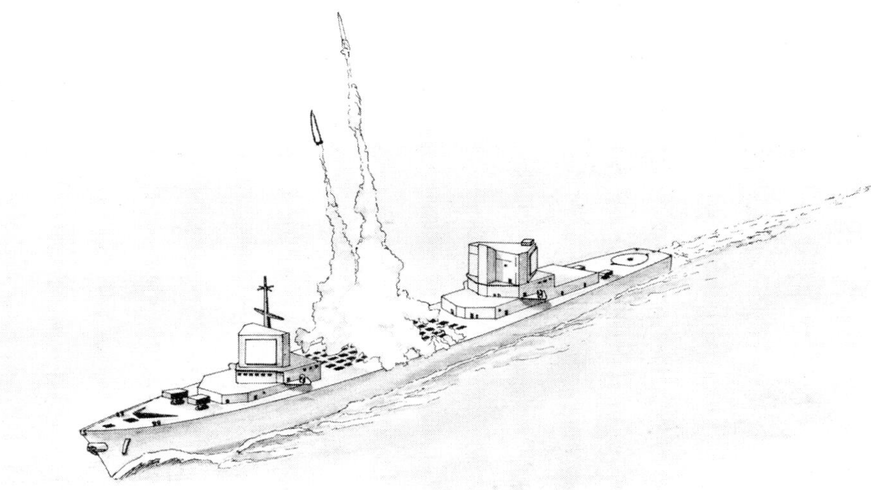

ARTIST'S CONCEPT OF SABMIS *Jane's Fighting Ships*

- The problems of detecting and destroying an ICBM during the launch-boost stage is far less complicated than seeking to locate and destroy several re-entry packages (warheads and decoys).
- The Safeguard/Nike-X ABM is a "sector system" with each of the planned 12 missile sites defending a sector of the United States. Thus, each site must have the capability of intercepting all intercontinental missiles which China is expected to have available in the mid-1970s. However, a single SABMIS ship could be positioned to intercept virtually all missiles being fired at the United States because of the limited China-to-United States ICBM trajectory spectrum.
- A sea-based system would not increase the number of strategic targets within the United States which would be attacked in a nuclear conflict.
- The mobility of a sea-based ABM will enable the defence to be shifted as the threat changes. For example, an ABM system in the United States could not provide for defence against ICBMs aimed at Japan. A sea-based ABM could counter Chinese ICBMs being launched against virtually any Asian target.
- Should the opposition develop an anti-ABM system (in the same manner that anti-radar missiles have been developed) the sea-based ABM ships probably would be less vulnerable than the land-based ABM and enemy "misses" would not devastate the continental United States.
- Shipboard systems appear to have a longer life than do fixed weapon complexes on land, a result of the feasibility of adopting a given ship hull to changing missions and equipment.

COMMAND AND COMMUNICATION SHIPS

The US Navy operates two command ships as part of the National Military Command System. This organization provides national authorities (eg, the President and the Joint Chiefs of Staff) with the facilities for exercising strategic and broad operational direction of the armed forces under varying conditions such as cold war, limited war, and general nuclear war.

The National Military Command System consists of a command centre at the Pentagon in Washington, D.C., an alternate underground command centre, several airborne command posts, and the command ships *Northampton* and *Wright*, both of which are designated as National Emergency Command Posts Afloat (NECPA). Both command ships operate off the Atlantic coast of the United States. They are supported by tropospheric scatter communications stations at Lewes, Delaware; Otis Air Force Base in Massachusetts; and Lola, North Carolina.

The *Northampton*, a converted cruiser, and the *Wright*, a converted aircraft carrier, have been extensively modified for their role as command ships. These ships, and the flagship *Valcour* (listed below), which serves a multi-service unified command, should not be confused with Navy flagships which carry fleet and task force commanders.

Two major communications relay ships (designated AGMR) are operated by the Navy to provide mobile communications for Navy and other service commanders where shore-based communication facilities are inadequate or do not exist.

The command and the radio relay ships are totally different in concept, although both can be used to support national authorities. The command ships *Northampton* and *Wright* are floating command headquarters and their communication facilities are for transmitting and receiving large volumes of voice and teletype communications (as well as electronic data). The radio relay ships *Annapolis* and *Arlington* are fitted to relay large volumes of teletype communications. Further, the two radio relay ships do not have the command centres, data display facilities, message centres, and staff accommodations which are the keys to the command ships' capabilities.

The converted seaplane tender *Valcour* is classified as a miscellaneous flagship (AGF) and operates in the Indian Ocean area to provide afloat faciltiies for the US Commander Middle East Force. (While undergoing overhaul at the Norfolk Naval Shipyard in 1968-1969 she was replaced by a guided missile frigate, a much more impressive ship for representating US interests in the area).

ANTENNA MASTS ON ARLINGTON (AGMR 2) *1969, US Navy, JOSN W. R. Griffin*

1 COMMAND SHIP (CC): CONVERTED CRUISER

Name	*No.*	*Builder*	*Laid down*	*Launched*	*Commissioned*
***NORTHAMPTON**	CC 1 (ex-CLC 1, ex-CA 125)	Bethlehem Steel Co (Quincy)	31 Aug 1944	27 Jan 1951	7 Mar 1953

Displacement, tons	14 700 standard; 17 200 full load
Length, feet (*metres*)	664 (*202·4*) wl; 676 (*206·0*) oa
Beam, feet (*metres*)	71 (*21·6*)
Draft, feet (*metres*)	29 (*8·8*)
Guns	2—5 in (*127 mm*) 54 cal dual-purpose (see *Gunnery* notes)
Helicopters	2 normally carried
Armour	Side 6 in (*152 mm*); Decks 3 in + 2 in (*76 + 51 mm*)
Main engines	4 geared turbines (General Electric); 120 000 shp; 4 shafts
Boilers	4 (Babcock & Wilcox)
Speed, knots	33
Complement	1 240 (62 officers, approx 1 175 enlisted men); accommodations for 1 657 (227 officers, 1 450 enlisted men)

The *Northampton* was begun as a heavy cruiser of the "Oregon City" class, numbered CA 125. She was cancelled on 11 Aug 1945 when 56·2 per cent complete. She was re-ordered as a command ship on 1 July 1948 and designated CLC 1 (Task Force Command Ship and later Tactical Command Ship). As CLC 1 she was configured for use primarily by fast carrier force commanders and fitted with an elaborate combat information centre (CIC), electronic equipment, and flag accommodations. She was largely employed as flagship for Commander Second Fleet in the Atlantic prior to her being made available for use by national authorities. Her designation was changed to CC (Command Ship) on 15 April 1961 and she was relieved as Second Fleet flagship on October 1961.

DESIGN. The *Northampton* is one deck higher than other US heavy cruisers to provide additional office and equipment space. Her foremast is the tallest unsupported mast afloat (125 feet). All living and working spaces are air conditioned.

ELECTRONICS. Advanced communications, electronic data processing equipment, and data displays are installed; tropospheric scatter and satellite relay communications facilities. As CLC 1 the *Northampton* carried what was believed the largest radar antenna afloat (see 1968-1969 and earlier editions); removed in 1961 and temporarily installed on missile cruiser *Little Rock*.

GUNNERY. As built the *Northampton* mounted 4—5 inch and 8—3 inch weapons. The 5 inch guns are 54 calibre weapons capable of firing up to 54 rounds per minute. (Similar weapons are installed in US destroyer-type ships built since World War II). The original 3 inch/50 calibre guns in open twin mounts were replaced by twin 3 inch/70 calibre rapid-fire guns in closed mounts. The latter were removed in 1962 because of high maintenance requirements; removal of the guns and their ammunition hoists, *et cetera*, provided additional space for berthing, offices, and electronic equipment.

NORTHAMPTON (CC 1) *United States Navy*

Command and Communication Ships—*Continued*

1 COMMAND SHIP (CC)
1 MAJOR COMMUNICATIONS RELAY SHIP (AGMR)
CONVERTED AIRCRAFT CARRIERS

Name	*No.*	*Builder*	*Laid down*	*Launched*	*CVL Comm*	*CC-AGMR Comm.*
*WRIGHT	CC 2 (ex-AVT 7, ex-CVL 49)	New York SB Corp	21 Aug 1944	1 Sep 1945	9 Feb 1947	11 May 1963
*ARLINGTON	AGMR 2 (ex-AVT 6, ex-CVL 48)	New York SB Corp	10 July 1944	8 July 1944	14 July 1945	27 Aug 1966

Displacement, tons	14 500 standard; 19 600 full load
Length, feet (*metres*)	664 (*202·4*) wl; 683·6 (*208·4*) oa
Beam, feet (*metres*)	76·8 (*23·6*)
Draft, feet (*metres*)	28 (*8·5*)
Flight deck width, feet (*metres*)	109 (*33·2*)
Guns	*Wright* 8—40 mm anti-aircraft (twin); *Arlington* 8—3 in (*76 mm*) 50 calibre (twin)
Helicopters	5 or 6 carried by *Wright*
Main engines	4 geared turbines (General Electric); 120 000 shp; 4 shafts
Boilers	4 (Babcock & Wilcox)
Speed, knots	33
Complement	746 plus approx 1 000 on command or communications staff

These ships were built as the light carriers *Saipan* (CVL 48) and *Wright* (CVL 49), respectively. They served as experimental and training carriers for a decade before being mothballed in 1957. Both were reclassified as Auxiliary Aircraft Transports on 15 May 1959, being designated AVT 6 (*Saipan*) and AVT 7 (*Wright*). The *Wright* was converted to a command ship at the Puget Sound Naval Shipyard, 1962-1963; the *Saipan* was to have been similarly converted, but the requirement for an additional ship of this category was cancelled. The *Saipan* subsequently was converted to a major communications relay ship at the Alabama Drydock and Shipbuilding Company in 1963-1965, and renamed *Arlington*. See Conversion and Nomenclature notes. (The survivors of the "Independence" class of light carriers, converted from cruisers during World War II, are now rated as Aircraft Transports (AVT) and are listed under Logistic Support Ships).

DESIGN. Although both of these ships were laid down with the specific intention of being constructed as aircraft carriers, their hulls and machinery duplicate the design of the "Baltimore" class heavy cruisers. As built they had small island bridge structures and four small funnels aft of the island trunked out at right angles. When aircraft carriers they could operate approximately 50 contemporary aircraft including jets.

CONVERSION. The *Wright* was converted to a command ship under the Fiscal Year 1962 authorisation at a cost of $25 000 000. Like the *Northampton*, she is fitted with elaborate communications, data processing, and display facilities for use by national authorities. The command spaces include presentation theatres similar to those at command posts ashore. The *Wright* has the most powerful transmitting antennas ever installed on a ship. They are mounted on glass masts to reduce interference with electronic transmissions. The tallest mast is 83 feet high and is designed to withstand 100-mph winds. She was reclassified from AVT 7 to CC 2 on 1 Sep 1962.
The *Saipan* was converted to a major communications relay ship at a cost of $26 886 424. She actually began conversion to a command ship (CC 3) and work was halted in February 1964. Work was resumed for her conversion to a communications ship later that year. She is fitted with elaborate communications relay equipment for the support of major commands afloat or ashore. The *Saipan* was reclassified from AVT 6 to CC 3 on 1 Jan 1964, and to AGMR 2 on 3 Sep 1964; she was renamed *Arlington* in April 1965.
The flat, unencumbered deck of an aircraft carrier-type ship facilitates antenna placement for optimum electromagnetic wave propagation. The new "Blue Ridge" class of amphibious command ships has a similar appearance.

NOMENCLATURE. The Navy's two communications ships are named for the naval radio stations at Arlington, Virginia, and Annapolis, Maryland.

WRIGHT (CC 2) — *1968, US Navy, PH 1 Arnold A. Clemons*

PHOTOGRAPHS. The *Wright* has a large pylon mast supporting radar antennas amidships and two pole antenna masts; *Arlington* has two 3 inch gun mounts at forward and after ends of flight deck. Also, *Arlington* has letters "GMR" preceeding hull number, following identification scheme of deleting initial letter "L" or "A" for US amphibious and auxiliary ships. Note open bow configurations of *Wright* and *Arlington* in comparison with enclosed bow of *Annapolis* (AGMR 1) on following page.

ARLINGTON (AGMR 2) — *1967, United States Navy*

Command and Communication Ships—*Continued*

1 MAJOR COMMUNICATIONS RELAY SHIP (AGMR): CONVERTED ESCORT CARRIER

Name	*No.*	*Builder*	*Laid down*	*Launched*	*CVE Comm.*	*AGMR Comm.*
***ANNAPOLIS**	AGMR 1 (ex-AKV 39, ex-CVE 107)	Todd Shipyards (Tacoma)	29 Nov 1943	20 July 1944	5 Feb 1945	7 Mar 1964

Displacement, tons	11 473 standard; 22 500 full load
Length, feet (*metres*)	525 (*160·0*) wl; 563 (*171·6*) oa
Beam, feet (*metres*)	75 (*22·9*)
Draft, feet (*metres*)	30·6 (*9·3*)
Flight deck width, feet (*metres*)	106 (*32·5*)
Guns	8—3 in (*76 mm*) 50 calibre anti-aircraft (twin)
Main engines	2 turbines (Allis Chalmers); 16 000 shp; 2 shafts
Boilers	4 (Combustion Engineering)
Speed, knots	18
Complement	710 (44 officers, 666 enlisted men)

The *Annapolis* was built as the escort aircraft carrier *Gilbert Islands* (CVE 107). She was decommissioned on 21 May 1946 and placed in reserve; again active as a CVE from Sep 1951 to Jan 1955 when she was again decommissioned. While in reserve, on 7 May 1959 she was reclassified as a Cargo Ship and Aircraft Ferry (AKV 39). Converted into a communications ship by the New York Naval Shipyard, 1962-1964.

CONVERSION. During conversion the ship was fitted with elaborate communications relay equipment including approximately 30 transmitters providing frequency band coverage from low frequency to ultra-high frequency. The power outputs of the transmitters vary from 10 to 10 000 watts. Numerous radio receivers also were installed as were five large antenna towers. The ship was renamed *Annapolis* and reclassified AGMR 1 on 1 June 1963.
The former escort carrier *Vella Gulf* (AKV 11, ex-CVHE 111, ex-CVE 111) was to have been converted to the AGMR 2; her conversion never began because of the availability of the larger carrier *Saipan* for use in this role.

DESIGN. The *Gilbert Islands* was one of 19 "Commencement Bay" class escort carriers built during the latter part of World War II. The surviving ships of this type are classified as cargo ships (AKV) and are listed in the section on Logistic Support Ships.

ANNAPOLIS (AGMR 1) *1964, United States Navy*

PHOTOGRAPHS. Note enclosed "hurricane bow" installed during conversion to AGMR to improve rough-sea operation. She has a small helicopter landing area on the port side of the former flight deck.

ANNAPOLIS (AGMR 1) *1966, United States Navy*

1 MISCELLANEOUS FLAGSHIP (AGF): CONVERTED SEAPLANE TENDER

Name	*No.*	*Builder*	*Laid down*	*Launched*	*Commissioned*
***VALCOUR**	AGF 1 (ex-AVP 55)	Lake Washington Shipyard	21 Dec 1942	5 June 1943	5 July 1946

Displacement, tons	1 766 standard; 2 800 full load
Length, feet (*metres*)	300 (*91·4*) wl; 310·8 (*94·7*) oa
Beam, feet (*metres*)	41·1 (*12·5*)
Draft, feet (*metres*)	13 (*4·0*)
Guns	8—40 mm anti-aircraft (1 quad forward, 2 twin amidships)
Main engines	2 diesels (Fairbanks, Morse); 6 080 bhp; 2 shafts
Speed, knots	18
Complement	215

The *Valcour* serves as flagship for the US Commander Middle East Force, operating in the Persion Gulf, Arabian Sea, and Indian Ocean. From 1950 to 1965 the *Valcour* rotated this duty with her sister ships *Duxbury Bay* (AVP 38) and *Greenwich Bay* (AVP 41). All three were fitted with additional communications, radar, and electronic countermeasures (ECM) equipment; painted white, and partially air conditioned. The *Valcour* was reclassified from AVP 55 to AGF 1 of 15 Dec 1965 and is now permanently assigned to the Middle East area.

DESIGN. The *Valcour* was one of 35 "Barnegat" class small seaplane tenders built during World War II. Several survive as Navy auxiliaries and Coast Guard cutters.

VALCOUR (AGF 1) *1966, United States Navy*

AIRCRAFT CARRIERS

Aircraft carriers continue to serve as a primary means of projecting US tactical air power overseas, with current emphasis being on their providing combat sorties in South Vietnam, reconnaissance missions over North Vietnam, and maintaining a force in readiness to support US interests in the crisis-torn Eastern Mediterranean area. In addition, aircraft carriers permit rapid deployment of tactical air power to areas where the lack of land bases, inadequate support facilities or political considerations prevent or delay the use of land-based tactical air power. (For example, US aircraft carriers were deployed off Korea after the North Koreans seized the intelligence ship *Pueblo* in January 1968 and again when the North Koreans shot down a Navy EC-121M reconnaissance plane in April of 1969).

To meet these requirements the US Navy currently operates 15 Attack Aircraft Carriers (CVA) and seven ASW Support Aircraft Carriers (CVS). In addition, a Training Aircraft Carrier (CVT) is employed in training Navy and Marine Corps pilots.

ATTACK AIRCRAFT CARRIERS. The force level of 15 attack carriers has been predicated on having two carriers continually deployed in the Mediterranean and three deployed in the Western Pacific. However, the Vietnamese War has required that the United States maintain five of these ships in Asian waters. Two or three of these ships normally conduct strikes against Vietnam while the other carriers are replenished at sea or are in Asian ports for courtesy calls and minor maintenance. The two or three ships not "on the line" regularly rotate with those attack carriers flying strikes and thus constitute a ready reserve in the event of expanded hostilities in the area or to support US policy elsewhere in the Western Pacific.

The normal deployment of two attack carriers in the Mediterranean and three in the Western Pacific requires a total force of 15 attack carriers to provide for overhaul, training, and operational commitments in the Atlantic and Eastern Pacific areas. The requirements for five CVAs in the Western Pacific during the past few years has been met by extending normal carrier deployments, reducing the number of carriers available in the Atlantic, and by employing an ASW carrier as a "limited" attack carrier in South East Asia.

The current 15-ship attack carrier force is composed of the nuclear-powered carrier *Enterprise*, eight ships of the "Forrestal" design, two "Midway" class carriers, and four modified "Essex/Hancock" class ships. A second nuclear-powered carrier, the *Nimitz*, is now under construction and two more ships of this type are planned. It is anticipated that these three ships and the carrier *Midway*, which is now being modernised, will replace the four "Essex" type carriers now employed in the attack role. Thus, by the mid-1970s the US Navy will possess four nuclear and eight conventional attack carriers of post-war construction plus three extensively modernised "Midway" class ships (originally completed 1945-1947).

Each attack carrier normally operates a carrier air wing of 70 to 85 aircraft, the number depending upon the class of carrier in which embarked; air wing compositions vary. However, a "typical" air wing has two fighter squadrons (F-4 Phantoms in the larger ships; F-8 Crusaders in the "Hancock" type); two light attack squadrons (A-4 Skyhawks and/or A-7 Corsairs); an all-weather attack squadron (A-6 Intruders); and special-mission aircraft (RA-5C Vigilante or RF-8G Crusaders reconnaissance planes; E-2A Hawkeye or E-1B Tracer early warning aircraft; KA-3B and EKA-3B Skywarrior in-flight tankers; C-1A Trader or C-2A Greyhound cargo planes; and utility helicopters).

This "mix" of aircraft and the multi-mission capability of specific aircraft types such as the F-4 Phantom fighter enable the attack carrier and her embarked air wing to provide a potent force for a wide spectrum of combat operations, varying from counter-insurgency support to general nuclear war.

ASW SUPPORT AIRCRAFT CARRIERS. The Navy now operates seven ASW support carriers, all of which are modernised ships of the "Essex" class. An eighth ship of this type, the *Lexington*, is employed in the Gulf of Mexico as a training carrier (CVT).

Each CVS normally operates two squadrons of fixed-wing aircraft (S-2 Trackers) and one squadron of helicopters (SH-3 Sea Kings) plus a detachment of radar warning aircraft (E-1B Tracers). In addition, ASW carriers operating in the Western Pacific are normally assigned four A-4 Skyhawks for limited air defense (the A-4C variant being armed with two 20-mm cannon and two air-to-air missiles).

Recent studies have indicated that ASW carriers are expensive to operate in relationship to their effectiveness compared with other ASW "platforms" (eg, land-based aircraft, destroyer-type ships, attack submarines). Accordingly it is tentatively planned to reduce the ASW carrier force to four ships (two in Atlantic and two in Pacific) when the Vietnamese War is "concluded". However, this plan is subject to several variables including the availability of a new carrier-based ASW aircraft (the S-3A/VSX) and the nature of the Soviet and Communist Chinese submarine threat in the 1970s.

TRAINING AIRCRAFT CARRIER. No aircraft are assigned to the training carrier *Lexington*. However, in an emergency situation she could embark an active or reserve ASW air group. Her ability to support effectively ASW operations would depend upon the degree to which she could be outfitted with aircraft stores, spare parts, and maintenance facilities prior to being deployed.

PHOTOGRAPH. The photograph on this page shows the USS *America* on Yankee Station in the Gulf of Tonkin, steaming into the wind to launch aircraft. On her forward catapults are an A-6A Intruder attack plane and an E-2A Hawkeye early warning aircraft; on her angled-deck catapults are an EKA-3B Skywarrior and F-4 Phantom.

2 + 1 NUCLEAR-POWERED ATTACK AIRCRAFT CARRIERS (CVAN): "NIMITZ" TYPE

Displacement, tons	95 100 full load
Length, feet (*metres*)	1 040 (*317·0*) wl; 1 092 (*332·0*) oa
Beam, feet (*metres*)	134 (*40·8*)
Catapults	4
Aircraft	approx 90
Main engines	Geared steam turbines
Nuclear reactors	2 pressurised-water cooled
Speed, knots	30+
Missiles	3 Basic Point Defence Missile System (BPDMS) launchers with Sea Sparrow missiles

Name	*No.*	*Builder*	*Ordered*	*Status*
NIMITZ	CVAN 68	Newport News SB & DD Co	31 Mar 1967	Under construction
(Unnamed)	CVAN 69			Proposed
(Unnamed)	CVAN 70			Proposed

The lead ship for this class and the world's second nuclear-powered aircraft carrier was ordered 9½ years after the first such ship, the USS *Enterprise*. The *Nimitz* was authorised in the Fiscal Year 1967 new construction programme. Estimated cost of the *Nimitz* is $536 000 000 twice that of the last conventional (non-nuclear) carrier built by the United States, the *John F. Kennedy*. The CVAN 69 authorised in FY 1970 has an estimated cost of $510 000 000, the lesser cost reflecting both ships being built with the same design plans. A third ship of this class is planned for the FY 1971 new construction programme. All to be built by the Newport News Shipbuilding & Dry Dock Co, the only US shipyard now capable of constructing large carriers.

The *Nimitz* was laid down on 22 June 1968; scheduled to be launched in October 1970 and completed in 1972-1973.

ELECTRONICS. These ships will have the Naval Tactical Data System (NTDS) and the following radars: SPS-10 surface search, SPS-43A two-dimensional air search, and SPS-48 three-dimensional air search. It is not envisioned that these carriers will be fitted with sonar as were the last conventionally powered aircraft carriers (the *America* and *John F. Kennedy*).

ENGINEERING. These carriers will each have only two nuclear reactors compared to the eight reactors required for the carrier *Enterprise*. The nuclear cores for the reactors in these ships are expected to provide sufficient energy for the ships to each steam for at least 13 years, an estimated 800 000 to 1 million miles between "refuelling"

NOMENCLATURE. The *Nimitz* honours Fleet Admiral Chester W. Nimitz who was Commander-in-Chief Pacific Fleet and Commander-in-Chief Pacific Ocean Areas during World War II, and Chief of Naval Operations from December 1945 to December 1947.

4 ATTACK AIRCRAFT CARRIERS (CVA): "KITTY HAWK" CLASS

Name	*No.*	*Builder*	*Laid down*	*Launched*	*Commissioned*
***KITTY HAWK**	CVA 63	New York SB Corp, Camden, NJ	27 Dec 1956	21 May 1960	29 Apr 1961
***CONSTELLATION**	CVA 64	New York Naval Shipyard	14 Sep 1957	8 Oct 1960	27 Oct 1961
***AMERICA**	CVA 66	Newport News SB & DD Co	9 Jan 1961	1 Feb 1964	23 Jan 1965
***JOHN F. KENNEDY**	CVA 67	Newport News SB & DD Co	22 Oct 1964	27 May 1967	7 Sep 1968

Displacement, tons	
Kitty Hawk	60 100 standard; 75 200 full load
Constellation	60 100 standard; 75 200 full load
America	60 300 standard; 78 250 full load
John F. Kennedy	61 000 standard; 83 000 full load
Length, feet (*metres*)	990 (*301·8*) wl
Kitty Hawk	1 062·5 (*323·9*) oa
Constellation	1 072·5 (*326·9*) oa
America, J.F.K.	1 047·5 (*319·3*) oa
Beam, feet (*metres*)	
Kitty Hawk, Constellation	129·5 (*38·5*)
America, J.F.K.	130 (*39·6*)
Flight deck width, feet (*metres*)	
Constellation	260 (*79·2*) maximum
Others	252 (*76·8*) maximum
Catapults	4 steam
Aircraft	70 to 90, according to type
Missiles	2 twin Terrier surface-to-air launchers in *Kitty Hawk, Constellation, America*; *John F. Kennedy* has provision for 3 Basic Point Defence Missile System (BPDMS) launchers with Sea Sparrow missiles
Main engines	4 geared turbines (Westinghouse) 280 000 shp; 4 shafts
Boilers	8—1 200 psi (*83·4 kg/cm²*) (Foster Wheeler)
Speed	35 knots

AMERICA (CVA 66) *1968, United States Navy*

Aircraft Carriers—*Continued*

"KITTY HAWK" CLASS *continued*

Complement	2 700 (120 officers, approx 2 600 enlisted men) plus approx 2 000 assigned to attack air wing for a total of 4 700 to 5 000 officers and enlisted men per ship

These ships were built to an improved "Forrestal" design and are easily recognised by their smaller island structure which is set further aft than the superstructure in the four "Forrestal" class ships. Lift arrangement also differs (see design notes). The *Kitty Hawk* was authorised in Fiscal Year 1956 new construction programme, the *Constellation* in FY 1957, the *America* in FY 1961, and the *John F. Kennedy* in FY 1963. Completion of the *Constellation* was delayed because of a fire which ravaged her in the New York Naval Shipyard in December 1960. Construction of the *John F. Kennedy* was delayed because of debate over whether to provide her with conventional or nuclear propulsion.
Estimated construction costs were $217 963 000 for *Kitty Hawk*, $247 620 000 for *Constellation*, and $277 000 000 for *John F. Kennedy*.

CLASSIFICATION. Officially known as the "Kitty Hawk" class; generally referred to as improved "Forrestals".

JOHN F. KENNEDY (CVA 67) — *1968, United States Navy*

DESIGN. These ships are officially considered to be of a different design than the "Forrestal" class by the Navy's Ship Characteristics Board. The island structure is smaller and set further aft in the newer ships with two deck-edge lifts forward of the superstructure, a third lift aft of the structure, and the port-side left on the after quarter (compared with two lifts aft of the island and the port-side lift at the forward end of the angled deck in the earlier ships). This lift arrangement considerably improves flight deck operations. All four of these ships also have a small radar mast aft of the island structure.

ELECTRONICS. All four ships of this class have highly sophisticated electronic equipment and the Naval Tactical Data System (NTDS). The *America* and *John F. Kennedy* have bow-mounted SQS-23 sonar, the first US attack carriers with anti-submarine sonar (several ASW carriers have been fitted with sonar during modernisations).

MODERNISATION. The *Constellation* was extensively modified during her 1965 overhaul with her displacement and overall length being increased to the dimensions noted above.

NOMENCLATURE. US aircraft carriers are generally named after battles and historic ships. However, the *Kitty Hawk* better honours the site where the Wright brothers made their historic flights than the converted aircraft ferry of that name which served in World War II. The *Constellation* remembers a frigate built in 1797 and a later ship still afloat at Baltimore, Maryland, although no longer in Navy commission. The name "America" was previously carried by a 74-gun ship-of-the line launched in 1782 and presented to France, by the racing schooner which gave her name to the America's Cup, and by the German liner *Amerika* which was taken over by the US Navy in World War I, renamed, and used as a troop transport. The *John F. Kennedy* remembers the martyred president who was assassinated in 1963. The destroyer *Joseph P. Kennedy Jr.* (DD 850) honours his older brother who was killed in a bomber explosion over England in World War II.

PHOTOGRAPHS. A close-up view of the *John F. Kennedy's* island structure and the ship's unusual angled funnel appears in the 1968-1969 edition. The *Kitty Hawk*, below, is launching an E-2A Hawkeye early-warning aircraft as she cruises on Yankee station in the Gulf of Tonkin. The *America* is shown fueling destroyers in the Mediterranean.

KITTY HAWK (CVA 63) — *1968, United States Navy*

RICHARD E. BYRD (DDG 23), AMERICA (CVA 66), WILLIAM R. RUSH (DD 714) — *1967, US Navy, PH1 R. L. Campbell*

Aircraft Carriers—*Continued*

1 NUCLEAR-POWERED ATTACK AIRCRAFT CARRIER (CVAN): "ENTERPRISE" TYPE

Name	*No.*	*Builder*	*Laid down*	*Launched*	*Commissioned*
***ENTERPRISE**	CVAN 65	Newport News Shipbuilding & Dry Dock Co	4 Feb 1958	24 Sep 1960	25 Nov 1961

Displacement, tons	75 700 standard; 83 350 full load
Length, feet (*metres*)	1 040 (*317·0*) wl; 1 123 (*341·3*) oa
Beam, feet (*metres*)	133 (*40·5*)
Draft, feet (*metres*)	25 (*7·6*)
Flight deck width, feet (*metres*)	257 (*78·3*) maximum
Catapults	4 steam
Aircraft	70 to 100, according to type.
Missiles	2 Basic Point Defense Missile System (BPDMS) launchers with Sea Sparrow missiles (see *Armament* notes)
Main engines	4 geared steam turbines (Westinghouse); approx 300 000 shp; 4 shafts
Nuclear reactors	8 pressurised-water cooled A2W (Westinghouse)
Speed, knots	35
Complement	2 870 (120 officers, approx 2 750 enlisted men) plus over 2 000 assigned to attack air wing for a total of over 5 000

The *Enterprise* was the largest warship ever built at the time of her construction and will be rivalled in size only by the nuclear-powered carrier *Nimitz*. The *Enterprise* was authorised in the Fiscal Year 1958 new construction programme. She was launched only 19 months after her keel was laid down. During her first year of operation the *Enterprise* made a six-month deployment to the Mediterranean and took part in the Cuban quarantine of 1962. During that year she recorded more than 12 000 arrested landings a record for non-combat operations. The *Enterprise* was flagship of Task Force One during Operation Sea Orbit when the carrier, the nuclear-powered cruiser *Long Beach* (CGN 9), and the nuclear-powered frigate *Bainbridge* (DLGN 25) circumnavigated the world, in 1964, cruising more than 30 000 miles in 64 days (underway 57 days) without refuelling.
The estimated cost of the *Enterprise* was $393 167 000. The Fiscal Year 1960 budget provided $35 000 000 to prepare plans and place orders for components of a second nuclear-powered carrier, but the money was spent otherwise.

ARMAMENT. The *Enterprise* — "the world's largest warship"—was completed without any armament in an effort to hold down construction costs. Space for Terrier missile system was provided. Short-range Sea Sparrow BPDMS was installed in 1967 because of danger to ship while operating in Gulf of Tonkin. A third Sea Sparrow launcher will be installed during the ship's 1970-1971 overhaul.
The BPDMS launcher is a modified eight-tube ASROC missile launcher; the launchers are visible in the overhead view on the following page.

DESIGN. Built to a modified "Forrestal" Class design. The most distinctive feature is the island structure. Nuclear propulsion eliminated requirement for smoke stack and boiler air intakes, reducing size of superstructure, and reducing vulnerability to battle damage, radioactivity, and biological agents. Rectangular fixed-array radar antennas ("billboards") are mounted on sides of island; electronic countermeasure (ECM) antennas ring cone-shaped upper levels of island structure. Fixed antennas have increased range and performance (see

ENTERPRISE (CVAN 65) *1969, US Navy PH1 W. R. Dappen*

ENTERPRISE (CVAN 65) *1968, US Navy PH1 P. Plouffe*

ENTERPRISE (CVAN 65) *1968, United States Navy*

Aircraft Carriers—*Continued*

"ENTERPRISE" TYPE *continued*

listing for cruiser *Long Beach*). The *Enterprise* has four deck-edge lifts, two forward of island and one aft on starboard side and one aft on port side (as in improved "Kitty Hawk" class).

ELECTRONICS. Fitted with the Naval Tactical Data System (NTDS)

ENGINEERING. The *Enterprise* is the world's second nuclear-powered warship (the cruiser *Long Beach* was completed a few months earlier). Design of the first nuclear powered aircraft carrier began in 1950 and work continued until 1953 when the programme was deferred pending further work on the submarine reactor programme. The large ship reactor project was reinstated in 1954 on the basis of technological advancements made in the previous 14 months. The Atomic Energy Commission's Bettis Atomic Power Laboratory was given prime responsibility for developing the nuclear power plant.
Construction of a land-based prototype plant (designated A1W) began in April 1956 at the National Reactor Testing Station in Idaho. This plant consisted of two reactors and the associated steam generating equipment to drive one shaft of an aircraft carrier. The first reactor core was installed on 8 Aug 1958 and criticality was achieved on 21 Oct 1958. The second reactor achieved initial criticality on 10 July 1959 and the two-reactor plant was first operated at full power on 15 Sep 1959, demonstrating the feasibility of nuclear propulsion for large ships.
The first of the eight reactors installed in the *Enterprise* achieved initial criticality on 2 Dec 1960, shortly after the carrier was launched. After three years of operation during which she steamed more than 207 000 miles, the *Enterprise* was overhauled and refuelled from November 1964 to July 1965. Her second set of cores have about 25 per cent greater life. The eight cores initially installed in the *Enterprise* cost $64 000 000; the second set cost about $20 000 000. The *Enterprise* will be refuelled during her 1970-1971 overhaul.
In addition to virtually unlimited high-speed endurance nuclear propulsion for aircraft carriers provides additional space for aviation fuels and ordnance, elimination of stack gases and smoke which have corrosive effects on electronic antennas and aircraft, virtually unlimited electrical power, and the ability to quickly change speed without affecting the number of personnel on watch in the engineering spaces.
There are two reactors for each of the ship's four shafts. The eight reactors feed 32 heat exchangers. The *Enterprise* developed more horsepower during her propulsion trials than any other ship in history (officially "in excess of 200 000 shaft horsepower").

NOMENCLATURE. Eight US Navy ships have carried the name *Enterprise*. The first was a British supply sloop captured in 1775 and armed for use on Lake Champlain. The seventh *Enterprise* (CV 6) was the most famous US carrier of World War II. She earned 20 battle stars. That "Big E" was sold in 1958 and scrapped.

ENTERPRISE (CVAN 65) — *1968, US Navy, PH1 R. L. Fitzgerald*

PHOTOGRAPHS. The photograph above shows the *Enterprise* departing the Naval Air Station at Alameda (San Francisco), California, on 2 Jan 1968; note aircraft cargo ship (AKV) at upper right. Aircraft parked at the stern of the *Enterprise* include (from left) an EKA-3B Skywarrior, F-4 Phantoms, an A-4 Skyhawk, an SH-3 Sea King helicopter, and an RA-5C Vigilante.

ENTERPRISE (CVAN 65) — *1968, United States Navy*

ENTERPRISE (CVAN 65) — *United States Navy*

Aircraft Carriers—*Continued*

4 ATTACK AIRCRAFT CARRIERS (CVA): "FORRESTAL" CLASS

Name	*No.*	*Builder*	*Laid down*	*Launched*	*Commissioned*
***FORRESTAL**	CVA 59	Newport News SB & DD Co	14 July 1952	11 Dec 1954	1 Oct 1955
***SARATOGA**	CVA 60	New York Naval Shipyard	16 Dec 1952	8 Oct 1955	14 Apr 1956
***RANGER**	CVA 61	Newport News SB & DD Co	2 Aug 1954	29 Sep 1956	10 Aug 1957
***INDEPENDENCE**	CVA 62	New York Naval Shipyard	1 July 1955	6 June 1958	10 Jan 1959

Displacement, tons	
Forrestal	59 650 standard; 78 000 full load
Others	60 000 standard; 78 000 full load
Length, feet (*metres*)	990 (*301·8*) wl
Forrestal, Saratoga, Ranger	1 039 (*316·7*) oa
Independence	1 046·5 (*319·0*) oa
Beam, feet (*metres*)	129.5 (*38·5*)
Draft, feet (*metres*)	37 (*11·3*)
Flight deck width, feet (*metres*)	
Ranger	260 (*79·2*) maximum
Others	252 (*76·8*) maximum
Catapults	4 steam
Aircraft	70 to 90, according to type
Guns	4—5 in (*127 mm*) dual-purpose; removed from *Forrestal* (see *Gunnery* notes)
Missiles	1 Basic Point Defence Missile System (BPDMS) launcher with Sea Sparrow missiles in *Forrestal*
Main engines	4 geared turbines (Westinghouse) 4 shafts 260 000 shp in *Forrestal* 280 000 shp in others
Boilers	8 (Babcock & Wilcox) 600 psi (*41·7 kg/cm²*) in *Forrestal* 1 200 psi (*83·4 kg/cm²*) in others
Speed, knots	
Forrestal	33
Others	35
Complement	2 700 (120 officers, approx 2 600 enlisted men) plus approx 2 000 assigned to attack air wing for a total of 4 700+ per ship

FORRESTAL (CVA 59) *1968, United States Navy*

The *Forrestal* was the world's first aircraft carrier designed and built after World War II. The *Forrestal* design drew heavily from the aircraft carrier *United States* (CVA 58) which was cancelled immediately after being laid down in April 1949. The *Forrestal* was authorised in the Fiscal Year 1952 new construction programme; the *Saratoga* followed in the FY 1953 programme, the *Ranger* in FY 1954, and *Independence* in FY 1955.

Estimated construction costs are $189 463 000 for *Forrestal*, $214 387 000 for *Saratoga*, $182 162 000 for *Ranger*, and $222 796 000 for *Independence*.

CLASSIFICATION. The *Forrestal* and *Saratoga* were initially classified as Large Aircraft Carriers CVB 59 and 60, respectively; reclassified as Attack Aircraft Carriers (CVA) in October 1952 to reflect their purpose rather than size. The ill-fated *United States* was a "heavy" carrier (CVA).

DESIGN. The "Forrestal" Class ships were the first aircraft carriers designed and built specifically to operate jet-propelled aircraft. The *Forrestal* was redesigned early in construction to incorporate British-developed angled flight deck and steam catapults. These were the first US aircraft carriers built with an enclosed flight deck to improve seaworthiness. Four large deck-edge lifts are fitted, one forward of island structure to starboard, two aft of island structure to starboard and one at forward edge of angled flight deck to port. Other features include armoured flight deck and advanced underwater protection and internal compartmentation to reduce effects of con-

RANGER (CVA 61) *1967, US Navy, LT (jg) L. N. Wilson*

INDEPENDENCE (CVA 62) *1968, US Navy, PHC R. I. Campbell*

Aircraft Carriers—*Continued*

ventional and nuclear attack. Mast configuration differ; the *Forrestal* originally had two masts, one of which was removed in 1967.

ENGINEERING. The *Saratoga* and later ships have an improved steam plant; increased machinery weight of the improved plant is more than compensated by increased performance and decreased fuel consumption.

GUNNERY. All four ships initially mounted 8—5 inch guns in single mounts, two mounts on each quarter. The forward sponsons carrying the guns interfered with ship operations in rough weather, tending to slow the ships down. The forward sponsons and guns were subsequently removed, reducing armament to four guns per ship. The guns are 5 inch/54 calibre, rapid-fire, dual-purpose weapons.

The four after 5 inch guns were removed from the *Forrestal* late in 1967 and a single BPDMS launcher for Sea Sparrow missiles was installed forward on the starboard side. Two additional launchers will be installed. (BPDMS launcher is just visible in photograph on previous page).

MODERNISATION. During an overhaul in 1963-1964 the width of the *Ranger's* angled flight deck was extended eight feet to accommodate newer aircraft.

NOMENCLATURE. The *Forrestal* honours James V. Forrestal, Secretary of the Navy from 1944 until he was appointed the first US Secretary of Defense in 1947, a post he held until shortly before his death in 1949. The *Saratoga* commemorates the battle at Saratoga, New York, in the American Revolution and five earlier US warships including a carrier of World War II fame (CV 3). The first USS *Ranger* was a sloop built in 1777 and a later ship of that name was the first US built-for-the-purpose carrier (CV 4). The first USS *Independence* was a sloop built in 1775 and a later ship of that name was a light carrier (CVL 22) which saw extensive combat in World War II.

PHOTOGRAPHS. The *Ranger* retains her forward sponsons; they probably will be removed in her next major overhaul.

RANGER (CVA 61) — *1968, United States Navy*

3 ATTACK AIRCRAFT CARRIERS (CVA): "MIDWAY" CLASS

Name	*No.*	*Builder*	*Laid down*	*Launched*	*Commissioned*
MIDWAY	CVA 41	Newport News SB & DD Co	27 Oct 1943	20 Mar 1945	10 Sep 1945
***FRANKLIN D. ROOSEVELT**	CVA 42	New York Navy Yard	1 Dec 1943	29 Apr 1945	3 Nov 1945
***CORAL SEA**	CVA 43	Newport News SB & DD Co	10 July 1944	2 Apr 1946	1 Oct 1947

Displacement, tons	
Midway	51 000 standard; 64 000 full load
F.D. Roosevelt	51 000 standard; 62 674 full load
Coral Sea	52 500 standard; 63 400 full load
Length, feet (*metres*)	900 (*274·3*) wl; 979 (*298·4*) oa
Beam, feet (*metres*)	121 (*36·9*)
Draft, feet (*metres*)	36 (*11·0*)
Flight deck width, feet (*metres*)	222 (*67·7*) maximum
Catapults	3 steam in *Midway* and *Coral Sea*; 2 steam in *F. D. Roosevelt*
Aircraft	60 to 75, according to type
Guns	4—5 in (*127 mm*) dual-purpose in *F. D. Roosevelt*; three guns in *Midway* and *Coral Sea* (see *Gunnery* notes)
Main engines	4 geared turbines (Westinghouse in *Midway* and *Coral Sea*; General Electric in *F. D. Roosevelt*); 212 200 shp; 4 shafts
Boilers	12—600 psi (*41·7 kg/cm²*) (Babcock & Wilcox)
Speed, knots	33
Complement	2 600 (112 officers, approx 2 500 enlisted men) plus approx 1 500 assigned to attack air wing for a total of 4 000+ per ship

These carriers were the largest US warships constructed during World War II. Completed too late for service in that conflict, they were the backbone of US naval strength for the first decade of the Cold War. Beginning in 1949 they were modified to store, assemble, and load nuclear weapons, making them the world's first warships with a nuclear strike capability. (P2V-3C Neptunes and AJ-1 Savages were the first delivery aircraft). All three ships operated in the Atlantic and Mediterranean during the Korean War, but subsequently they have operated in the Pacific. The entire class has been in active service (except for overhaul and modernisation) since the ships were completed more than 24 years ago.

CLASSIFICATION. These ships were initially classified as Large Aircraft Carriers CVB 41-43, respectively; reclassified as Attack Aircraft Carriers (CVA) in October 1952.

DESIGN. These ships were built to the same design with a standard displacement of 45 000 tons, full load displacement of 60 100 tons, and an overall length of 968 feet. They have been extensively modified since completion (see notes below). These ships were the first US aircraft carriers with an armoured flight deck and the first US warships with a designed width too large to enable them to pass through the Panama Canal.

CORAL SEA (CVA 43) — *United States Navy*

"Midway" Class—*continued*

Aircraft Carriers—*Continued*

GUNNERY. As built these ships mounted 18—5 inch guns (14 in *Coral Sea*), 84—40 mm guns, and 28—20 mm guns. Armament reduced periodically with 3 inch guns replacing lighter weapons. Minimal 5 inch armament remains. The 5 inch guns are 54 calibre, essentially modified 5 inch/38 calibre with a longer barrel for greater range; not to be confused with rapid-fire 5 inch/54s of newer US warships.

MISSILES. During the 1950s these ships were fitted with the Regulus I surface-to-surface missile. Fired by carriers, cruisers, and submarines, the Regulus I had a speed of approx 500 mph, a 500-mile range, and could carry a nuclear warhead.

MODERNISATION. All three "Midway" Class carriers have been extensively modernised. Their most extensive conversion "package" gave them angled flight decks, steam catapults, enclosed "hurricane" bows, new electronics, and new lift arrangement (*Franklin D. Roosevelt* from 1953 to 1956, *Midway* from 1954 to 1957, and *Coral Sea* from 1956 to 1960; all at Puget Sound Naval Shipyard). Lift arrangement was changed in *Franklin D. Roosevelt* and *Midway* to one centreline lift forward, one deck-edge lift aft of island on starboard side, and one deck-edge lift at forward end of angled deck on port side. The *Coral Sea* has an improved arrangement with one lift forward and one aft of island on starboard side and third lift outboard on port side aft. The *Midway* began another extensive modernisation at the San Francisco Bay Naval Shipyard in February 1966; she is scheduled to recommission in January 1970. The modernisation included provisions for handling newer aircraft, new catapults, new lifts (arranged as in *Coral Sea*), and new electronics. A similar modernisation planned for the *Franklin D. Roosevelt*, to have begun in Fiscal Year 1970, has been cancelled because the *Midway* modernisation is taking longer and costing more than originally estimated (24 months and $88 000 000 was planned; actual work is requiring approximately 48 months and $178 000 000). The *Franklin D. Roosevelt* completed an austere overhaul in June 1969 which enables her to operate the new A-6 Intruder and A-7 Corsair II attack aircraft.

NOMENCLATURE. The *Midway* and *Coral Sea* recall the first carrier-versus-carrier battles in history. Outnumbered US carriers stopped the Japanese Navy in both engagements of 1942. The CVA/CVB 42 was originally named *Coral Sea*; renamed on 8 May 1945 after death of President Franklin D. Roosevelt on 12 Apr 1945.

PHOTOGRAPHS. Note the forward sponson configuration of the *Franklin D. Roosevelt* and the absence of sponsons in the more-updated *Coral Sea*. In her latest configuration the *Midway* resembles the *Coral Sea* in deck arrangement, but retains her tripod mast structure in lieu of the pylon masts in her sister ships. A photograph of the *Midway* taken prior to her conversion appears in the 1968-1969 edition.

CORAL SEA (CVA 43) *1968, United States Navy*

FRANKLIN D. ROOSEVELT (CVA 42) *1966, United States Navy*

FRANKLIN D. ROOSEVELT (CVA 42) *1967, US Navy, PH1 J. D. Goss*

Aircraft Carriers—*Continued*

MIDWAY (CVA 41) At San Francisco Bay NSY
Port side extension to flight deck not completed

1969, US Navy

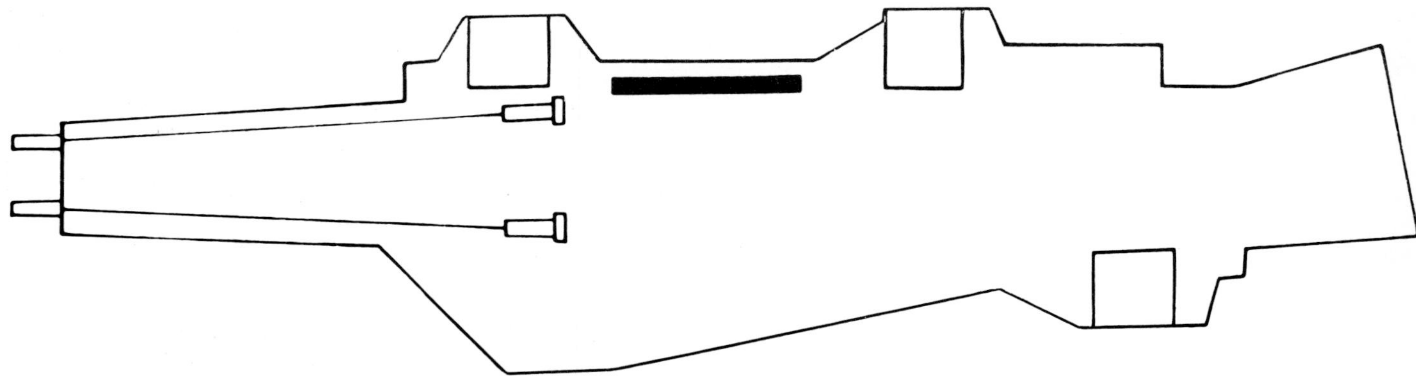

MIDWAY (CVA 41)

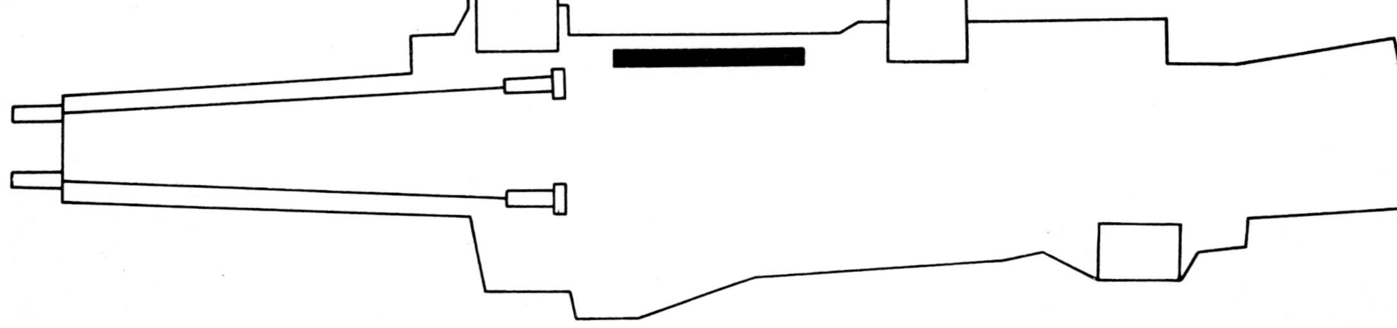

CORAL SEA (CVA 43)

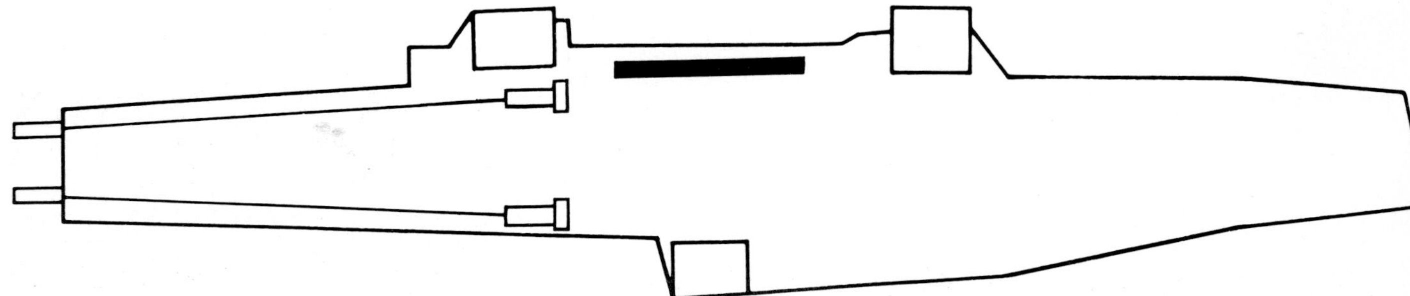

FRANKLIN D ROOSEVELT (CVA 42)

Aircraft Carriers—*Continued*

4 ATTACK AIRCRAFT CARRIERS (CVA): "HANCOCK" CLASS

Name	*No.*	*Builder*	*Laid down*	*Launched*	*Commissioned*
***TICONDEROGA**	CVA 14	Newport News SB & DD Co	1 Feb 1943	7 Feb 1944	10 Sep 1945
***HANCOCK**	CVA 19	Bethlehem Steel Co (Quincy)	26 Jan 1943	24 Jan 1944	15 Apr 1944
***BON HOMME RICHARD**	CVA 31	New York Navy Yard	1 Feb 1943	29 Apr 1944	26 Nov 1944
***ORISKANY**	CVA 34	New York Navy Yard	1 May 1944	13 Oct 1945	25 Sep 1950

Displacement, tons	
Oriskany	33 250 standard; 42 625 full load
Others	32 800 standard; 41 726 full load
Length, feet (*metres*)	820 (*249·9*) wl
Oriskany	890 (*271·3*) oa
Others	894·5 (*272·6*) oa
Beam, feet (*metres*)	
Oriskany	106·5 (*32·5*)
Others	103 (*30·8*)
Draft, feet (*metres*)	31 (*9·4*)
Flight deck width, feet (*metres*)	
Oriskany	195 (*59·5*) maximum
Others	192 (*58·5*) maximum
Catapults	2 steam
Aircraft	60 to 70, according to type
Guns	4—5 in. (*127 mm*) 38 cal dual-purpose (single)
Main engines	4 geared turbines (Westinghouse) 150 000 shp; 4 shafts
Boilers	8—600 psi (*41·7 kg/cm²*) (Babcock & Wilcox)
Speed, knots	33
Complement	2 000 (100 officers, approx 1 900 enlisted men) plus approx 1 500 assigned to attack air wing for a total of 3 500 per ship

Twenty-three "Essex" class aircraft carriers were completed between 1943 and 1946, and the modified *Oriskany* was completed in 1950. Fourteen of these ships fought in World War II; many saw combat in the Korean War and Vietnamese War.

TICONDEROGA (CVA 14) *1967, United States Navy*

Two additional ships of this class were cancelled while under construction, the *Reprisal* (CV 35) and *Iwo Jima* (CV 46), and six others were cancelled prior to keel laying, the unnamed CV 50-55.

CLASSIFICATION. These ships were initially classified as "aircraft" carriers (CV); reclassified as Attack Aircraft Carriers (CVA) in October 1952. The remaining ships of this type officially are known as the "Hancock" class.

DESIGN. All 24 ships were built to the same basic design with a standard displacement of 27 100 tons, full load displacement of 36 380 tons, and an overall length of 888 or 872 feet. These were the first aircraft carriers built with a deck-edge lift (in addition to two centreline lifts) except for a small outboard platform lift in the carrier *Wasp* (CV 7) launched in 1939.

ELECTRONICS. The *Oriskany* and the frigates *King* (DLG 10) and *Mahan* (DLG 11) conducted the initial sea trials of the Naval Tactical Data System (NTDS) in 1961-1962. NTDS is a highly automated system for collecting, processing, exchanging, and evaluating data on tactical situations. Priorities are assigned to enemy threats and possible courses of action are presented to the commander. The system is intended primarily to deal with the threat of high performance aircraft.

GUNNERY. As built, except for the *Oriskany*, these ships mounted 12—5 inch guns, 68 or 72—40 mm guns, and 52—20 mm guns; the *Oriskany* completed with only 10—5 inch guns and 44—40 mm guns. Armament reduced periodically with 3 inch guns replacing lighter weapons. Minimal 5 inch armament remains on ships in service as carriers (CVA/CVS).

MISSILES. During the 1950s six "Essex" class ships were fitted with the Regulus I surface-to-surface missile (*Randolph, Lexington, Hancock, Bennington, Bon Homme Richard*, and *Shangri-La*).

MODERNISATION. The completion of the *Oriskany* was delayed after World War II, allowing her to be completed with heavier catapults, improved elevators, reinforced flight deck, increased aviation fuel storage, and other features for operating jets. All of these ships subsequently have been modernised to enable them to operate advanced aircraft including the Mach 1·7 Crusader fighter and 35-ton KA-3B Skywarrior aerial tanker.

NOMENCLATURE. All 24 "Essex" class carriers are named for early American ships or battles except for *Shangri-La*, which is named for the imaginary locale in James Hilton's novel which President Roosevelt told the press was the base for the Doolittle-Halsey raid against Japan in 1942. Several ships renamed during construction to carry on names of carriers lost in battle. The *Hancock* and *Ticonderoga* exchanged names during construction.

PHOTOGRAPHS. Overhead view of *Oriskany*, showing the ship in the Gulf of Tonkin, has propeller-driven A-1 Skyraiders parked forward; the planes have since been discarded by the Navy. The *Oriskany's* island structure is barely visible (two E-1B Tracer AEN aircraft are parked next to the island); two F-8 Crusader fighters are parked on starboard deck-edge elevator. Note folding antenna mast aft of island structure on the *Ticonderoga*.

ORISKANY (CVA 34) *1968, US Navy, PHC Neal Crowe*

Aircraft Carriers—*Continued*

11 ASW SUPPORT AIRCRAFT CARRIERS (CVS)
1 TRAINING AIRCRAFT CARRIER (CVT)

"ESSEX" CLASS

Name	*No.*	*Builder*	*Laid down*	*Launched*	*Commissioned*
ESSEX	CVS 9	Newport News SB & DD Co	28 Apr 1941	31 July 1942	31 Dec 1942
***YORKTOWN**	CVS 10	Newport News SB & DD Co	1 Dec 1941	21 Jan 1943	15 Apr 1943
***INTREPID**	CVS 11	Newport News SB & DD Co	1 Dec 1941	26 Apr 1943	16 Aug 1943
***HORNET**	CVS 12	Newport News SB & DD Co	3 Aug 1942	29 Aug 1943	29 Nov 1943
RANDOLPH	CVS 15	Newport News SB & DD Co	10 May 1943	28 June 1944	9 Oct 1944
***LEXINGTON**	CVT 16 (ex-CVS 16)	Bethlehem Steel Co (Quincy)	15 July 1941	26 Sep 1942	17 Mar 1943
***WASP**	CVS 18	Bethlehem Steel Co (Quincy)	18 Mar 1942	17 Aug 1943	24 Nov 1943
***BENNINGTON**	CVS 20	New York Navy Yard	15 Dec 1942	26 Feb 1944	6 Aug 1944
***KEARSARGE**	CVS 33	New York Navy Yard	1 Mar 1944	5 May 1945	2 Mar 1946
ANTIETAM	CVS 36	Philadelphia Navy Yard	15 Mar 1943	20 Aug 1944	28 Jan 1945
***SHANGRI-LA**	CVS 38	Norfolk Navy Yard	15 Jan 1943	24 Feb 1944	15 Sep 1944
LAKE CHAMPLAIN	CVS 39	Norfolk Navy Yard	15 Mar 1943	2 Nov 1944	3 June 1945

Displacement, tons	
Intrepid, Shangri-La	32 800 standard; 41 726 full load
Lake Champlain	30 800 standard; 40 600 full load
Antietam	approx 30 000 standard; approx 38 000 full load
Others	approx 33 000 standard; 40 600 full load
Length, feet (*metres*)	820 (*249·9*) wl
Intrepid, Shangri-La	894·5 (*272·6*) oa
Lake Champlain	899 (*274·0*) oa
Antietan	888 (*270·7*) oa
Others	890 (*271·3*) oa
Beam, feet (*metres*)	
Intrepid, Shangri-La	103 (*31·4*)
Antietam	93 (*28·4*)
Others	102 (*31*)
Draft, feet (*metres*)	31 (*9·4*)
Flight deck width, feet (*metres*)	
Intrepid, Lexington, Shangri-La	192 (*58·5*) maximum
Lake Champlain	152 (*46·3*) maximum
Antietam	154 (*47·0*) maximum
Others	196 (*59·7*) maximum
Catapults	
Intrepid, Lexington, Shangri-La	2 steam
Others	2 hydraulic
Aircraft	40 to 47 (including 16 to 18 helicopters)
Guns	4—5 in (*127 mm*) 38 cal dual-purpose (single)
Main engines	4 geared turbines (Westinghouse) 150 000 shp; 4 shafts
Boilers	8—600 psi (*41·7 kg/cm²*) (Babcock & Wilcox)
Speed, knots	33
Complement	1 615 (115 officers, approx 1 500 enlisted men) plus approx 800 assigned to ASW air group for a total of 2 400 per ship

ESSEX (CVS 9) *1967, US Navy, PHCS W. A. Jackman*

LAKE CHAMPLAIN (CVS 39) *United States Navy*

Eight of these ships are in service, seven serving with anti-submarine groups and the *Lexington* as a training carrier. Active ships are indicated by asterisk. The *Lexington* relieved the *Antietam* as training carrier in May 1962, the latter subsequently being mothballed. The *Lake Champlain* was mothballed in 1965, the last US straight-deck carrier to operate fixed-wing aircraft. See previous listing for "Hancock" class attack carriers for general class notes.
The *Randolph* was decommissioned in Nov 1968 and placed in reserve; the *Essex* was decommissioned in June 1969 and placed in reserve, the latter ship in active service for 22 years (1943-1947, 1951-1969).
The *Intrepid* operated as a "limited attack carrier" from 1966 to 1969, carrying an air wing of fighter and light attack aircraft; she reverted to ASW status in August 1969 when she replaced the inactivated *Essex*.

ANGLED DECK. The *Antietam* was the world's first carrier to have an angled flight deck. The angled deck, a British invention, was provided by adding a small triangular section of flight deck on the port side, rearranging the arresting wires, and repainting the landing lanes. The installation was made at the New York Naval Shipyard, September-December 1952. The scheme greatly increases efficiency and safety of high-speed carrier operations.

(Initial angled deck landing trials were conducted on the British light carrier *Triumph* and then the US large carrier *Midway*, with a simulated angled deck landing lane being painted on their standard flight decks).

CLASSIFICATION. These ships were initially classified as "aircraft carriers" (CV). All were redesignated Attack Aircraft Carriers (CVA) in October 1952 and subsequently became ASW Support Aircraft Carriers (CVS): *Antietam* in July 1953, *Wasp* on 1 Nov 1955, *Lake Champlain* on 1 Aug 1957, *Yorktown* on 1 Sep 1957, *Hornet* on 27 June 1958, *Kearsarge* on 1 Oct 1958, *Randolph* on 31 Mar 1959, *Bennington* on 30 June 1959, *Essex* on 8 Mar 1960, *Intrepid* on 31 Mar 1962, *Lexington* on 1 Oct 1962, *Shangri-La* on 30 June 1969. Their places in the CVA ranks were taken by new-construction ships. The *Lexington*, a training ship since May 1962, was officially designated as a Training Aircraft Carrier (CVT) on 1 Jan 1969.

ELECTRONICS. ASW sonar fitted in eight carriers which have undergone FRAM II work (see Modernisation notes).

ENGINEERING. The *Lake Champlain* made an Atlantic crossing from Gibraltar to Newport News, Virginia, in 4 days, 9 hours in November 1945, averaging 32 knots. The *Philippine Sea* of this class (former CV 47) made a Pacific crossing from Yokohama to San Francisco in 7 days, 13 hours, averaging 25·2 knots.

MODERNISATION. Except for the *Antietam*, all of these ships were extensively modernised while in an attack carrier status; all but the *Lake Champlain* received angled flight decks. While in a CVS status the *Essex, Yorktown, Intrepid, Hornet, Randolph, Wasp, Bennington,* and *Kearsarge* were extensively overhauled under the so-called Fleet Rehabilitation and Modernisation (FRAM II) programme. They received new electronic equipment (including sonar), remodeled combat information centres

Aircraft Carriers—*Continued*

"Essex" Class—*continued*

(CIC), and other features to extend their useful life and improve their ASW capabilities.

One of these ships will be modernised in Fiscal Year 1972 and one in FY 1974 to permit operation of the Planned S-3A (VSX) aircraft.

NOMENCLATURE. Ships renamed during construction were *Yorktown*, ex-*Bon Homme Richard; Hornet*, ex-*Kearsarge; Lexington*, ex-*Cabot;* and *Wasp*, ex-*Oriskany*.

DISPOSALS

Five "straight-deck" carriers of this class have been stricken: **Franklin** (AVT 8, ex-CVS 13) stricken from the Navy List on 1 Oct 1964; **Bunker Hill** (AVT 9, ex-CVS 17) stricken on 1 Nov 1966, but retained as moored electronics test ship at San Diego, California; **Tarawa** (AVT 12, ex-CVS 40) stricken on 1 June 1967; **Leyte** (AVT 10, ex-CVS 32) and **Philippine Sea** (AVT 11, ex-CVS 47) stricken in 1969.

BENNINGTON (CVS 20), TAPPAHANNOCK (AD 43), McKEAN (DD 784) *1968, United States Navy*

HORNET (CVS 12) *1968, United States Navy*

KEARSARGE (CVS 33) *1968, US Navy, PH3 S. R. Mcrnis, PH 2 J. D. Turner*

FLEET ESCORT SHIPS

The US Navy's fleet escort force is comprised of those ships which have Anti-Submarine Warfare (ASW) and Anti-Air Warfare (AAW) capabilities. In addition, most of these ships are capable of performing other missions such as patrol and fire support.
The ship types which are included in the broad category of fleet escort ships are cruisers (CG, CGN, CLG), frigates (DL, DLG, DLGN), destroyers (DD, DDG,) and escort ships (DE, DEG, DER).
Of the nine cruisers currently in the Fleet Escort Force, only the nuclear-powered *Long Beach* (CGN 9) is scheduled to remain in service beyond the mid-1970s. The other ships, three all-missile cruisers of the "Albany" class and five gun-missile cruisers, are considered too expensive to operate and of too limited capabilities for future anti-air warfare requirements. An additional gun-missile cruiser, the *Topeka* (CLG 8), is in reserve (decommissioned on 5 June 1969).
Similarly, the gun-missile cruisers *Boston* (formerly CAG 1) and *Canberra* (formerly CAG 2) have been reclassified as heavy cruisers (CA 69 and CA 70, respectively) because of the limited effectiveness of their Terrier BW-1 missiles in task force defence. These two cruisers are listed in the section on Fire Support Ships.
Conventional and nuclear-powered frigates with both anti-air and anti-submarine capabilities are replacing these cruisers in the fleet escort role.
Current plans provide for a force of 239 fleet escort ships in service by the late 1970s, all of post-World War II construction. Of this number, nine would be nuclear powered to provide all-nuclear escorts for two of the Navy's four nuclear attack carriers (with one nuclear escort normally in overhaul). These nuclear escorts would be the CGN 9 *Long Beach*, DLGN 25 *Bainbridge*, DLGN 35 *Truxtun*, DLGN 36, DLGN 37, and the four ships now designated DXGN.
The more-capable ships armed with guided missiles would be assigned to the attack carrier forces since they represent the highest target value in the Fleet. Destroyer-type ASW escorts would be assigned to amphibious groups because their mission would require fire support as well as ASW. However, in view of the Soviet submarine-launched missile threat to amphibious groups, missile-armed escorts would be assigned to these groups. Since amphibious groups would not be employed continuously, escorts allocated to this role could also be used for underway replenishment groups and convoys. To meet the requirements for convoying merchant ships the US Navy plans to rely on destroyer-type ships in the reserve fleet and in allied navies.)

NEW CONSTRUCTION. Four classes of destroyer-type ships are now under construction.
Four large, nuclear-powered ships now designated DXGN will be built during the Fiscal Year 1970-1973 period to provide two all-nuclear carrier task groups (one carrier and four escorts per group).
The Department of Defence has estimated that the additional costs to provide escorts for four all-nuclear carrier task groups (a total of 16 escorts) would cost more than $400 000 000 more to build and operate over a ten-year period than would two all-nuclear groups and two groups with nuclear carriers but conventional escorts.
Reportedly, a total of 62 destroyers will be built during the FY 1970-1975 period. These ships will be of two similar classes, one armed with missiles and guns (DDG) and one armed with a point-defence missile system and guns (DD).
The "Knox" (DE 1052) class of ocean escorts will be completed through 1972. This class now numbers 46 ships, with all ten ships of the FY 1968 programme (DE 1908-1107) having been cancelled. One of the cut ships, the DE 1101, was to have had the first gas-turbine propulsion system mounted in a large US warship.

CONVERSIONS. The 19 guided missile frigates of the "Coontz" and "Leahy" classes are undergoing extensive AAW modernisations. They are receiving improved radars, missile fire control systems, and command and control facilities, and increased electric power capabilities. Plans to convert the "Mitscher" class frigates and "Forrest Sherman" class destroyers to missile or improved ASW configurations have been cut back because of increasing costs.

HELICOPTERS. The Drone Anti-Submarine Helicopter (DASH) has lost favour in the US Navy and is now operated in the ASW role only from the FRAM II destroyers which do not have the ASROC long-range anti-submarine weapon. However, the unmanned helicopters have been used from other ships in the Vietnam conflict as reconnaissance vehicles, having been fitted with special electronic/optical sensors.
A helicopter development effort began in FY 1970. This programme will result in a Light Airborne Multi-Purpose System (LAMPS) capable of performing a number of missions off a destroyer, especially reconnaissance and anti-submarine tasks. Presumably, these manned helicopters will be capable of operating from ships which could operate DASH.

3 GUIDED MISSILE CRUISERS (CG): "ALBANY" CLASS

Name	*No.*	*Builder*	*Laid down*	*Launched*	*Commissioned*	*CG Comm.*
* **ALBANY**	CG 10 (ex-CA 123)	Bethlehem Steel Co (Quincy)	6 Mar 1944	30 June 1945	15 June 1946	3 Nov 1962
* **CHICAGO**	CG 11 (ex-CA 136)	Philadelphia Navy Yard	28 July 1943	20 Aug 1944	1 Jan 1945	2 May 1964
* **COLUMBUS**	CG 12 (ex-CA 74)	Bethlehem Steel Co (Quincy)	28 June 1943	30 Nov 1944	8 June 1945	1 Dec 1962

Displacement, tons	13 700 standard; 17 500 full load
Length, feet (*metres*)	664 (*202·4*) wl; 673 (*205·3*) oa
Beam, feet (*metres*)	70 (*21·6*)
Draft, feet (*metres*)	27 (*8·2*)
Missiles	2 twin Talos surface-to-air launchers; 2 twin Tartar surface-to-air launchers
Guns	2—5 in (*127 mm*) 38 calibre dual-purpose (see *Gunnery* notes)
ASW Weapons	1 ASROC 8-tube launcher 2 triple torpedo launchers (Mk 32)
Main engines	4 geared turbines (General Electric); 120 000 shp; 4 shafts
Boilers	4 (Babcock & Wilcox) 565 psi
Speed, knots	33
Complement	1 000 (60 officers, approx 940 enlisted men)

These ships were fully converted from heavy cruisers, the *Albany* having been a unit of the "Oregon City" class and the *Chicago* and *Columbus* of the "Baltimore" class. Although the two heavy cruiser classes differ in appearance (see Fire Support Ships), they have the same hull dimensions and machinery. These three missile ships now form a new, homogeneous class.
The cruiser *Fall River* (CA 131) was originally scheduled for missile conversion, but was replaced by the *Columbus*. Proposals to convert two additional "Baltimore" class cruisers to missile ships (CG 13 and CG 14) were dropped, primarily because of high conversion costs and improved capabilities of newer missile-armed frigates.

COLUMBUS (CG 12) *1965, United States Navy*

CONVERSION. During conversion to missile configuration these ships were stripped down to their main hulls with all cruiser armament and superstructure being removed. New superstructures make extensive use of aluminium to reduce weight and improve stability. Former masts and stacks were replaced by "macks" which support electronic antennas and have machinery exhausts vented from sides near top. These "macks" are covered with plastic material to reduce expansion and contraction with ambient temperature changes which could change

CHICAGO (CG 11) *1968, United States Navy*

Fleet Escort Ships—*Continued*

"ALBANY" CLASS—*continued*

alignment of radar and other electronic antennas. Side vents direct exhausts away from electronic gear.

The *Albany* was converted at the Boston Naval Shipyard between January 1959 and November 1962; the *Columbus* at Puget Sound Naval Shipyard from June 1959 to March 1963; and *Chicago* at San Francisco Naval Shipyard from July 1959 to September 1964.

ELECTRONICS. These ships are fitted with SQS-23 sonar which is linked to the ASROC fire control system. The Naval Tactical Data System (NTDS) is fitted in the *Albany* and *Chicago*.

GUNNERY. No guns were fitted when these ships were converted to missile cruisers. Two single, *open-mount* 5 inch guns were fitted subsequently to provide minimal defence against low-flying, subsonic aircraft or torpedo boat attacks.

Two Mk 56 directors installed.

MISSILES. One twin Talos launcher is forward and one aft; a twin Tartar launcher is on each side of the main bridge structure. During conversion space was allocated amidships for installation of eight Polaris missile tubes, but the plan to install ballistic missiles in cruisers was cancelled in mid-1959. Reportedly, 92 Talos and 80 Tartar missiles are carried.

MODERNISATION. The *Albany* underwent an extensive anti-air warfare modernisation at the Boston Naval Shipyard; "conversion" began on 1 Feb 1967 and was completed in August 1969. She was formerly recommissioned on 9 Nov 1968. The *Chicago* and *Columbus* will not have AAW modernisations because of plan to discard all conventionally powered cruisers during the 1970s.

The *Albany's* AAW conversion included installation of NTDS, a digital Talos fire-control system which provides faster and more-reliable operation, and improved SPS-48 and SPS-30 air search radars (the *Albany* also has an SPS-43 long-range and SPS-10 short-range search radars, and SPG-51C fire-control radar).

NOMENCLATURE. US cruisers are named for American cities.

1 NUCLEAR-POWERED GUIDED MISSILE CRUISER (CGN): "LONG BEACH" TYPE

Name	*No.*	*Builder*	*Laid down*	*Launched*	*Commissioned*
*LONG BEACH	CGN 9 (ex-CGN 160, CLGN 160)	Bethlehem Steel Co. (Quincy)	2 Dec 1957	14 July 1959	9 Sep 1961

Displacement, tons	14 200 standard; 17 350 full load
Length, feet (*metres*)	721·2 (*220*) oa
Beam, feet (*metres*)	73·2 (*22·3*)
Draft, feet (*metres*)	29 (*8·8*)
Missiles	1 twin Talos surface-to-air launcher; 2 twin Terrier surface-to-air launchers
Guns	2—5 in (*127 mm*) 38 calibre dual-purpose (see *Gunnery* notes)
ASW Weapons	1 ASROC 8-tube launcher; 2 triple torpedo launchers (Mk 32)
Main engines	2 geared turbines (General Electric); approx 80 000 shp; 2 shafts
Reactors	2 pressurised-water cooled C1W (Westinghouse)
Speed, knots	approx 35
Complement	1 000 (60 officers, approx 950 enlisted men)

LONG BEACH CGN 9) *1968, US Navy, PHCM, L. P. Bodine*

The *Long Beach* was the first ship to be designed and constructed from the keel up as a cruiser for the United States since the end of World War II. She is the world's first nuclear-powered surface warship and the first warship to have a guided missile main battery. She was authorised in the Fiscal Year 1957 new construction programme. Estimated construction cost was $332 850 000. Construction was delayed because of shipyard strike.

No additional new-construction cruisers are planned because of the capabilities of new guided-missile frigates (DLG and DLGN), which are approaching the size of World War II-era light cruisers.

CLASSIFICATION. The *Long Beach* was ordered as a Guided Missile Light Cruiser (CLGN 160) on 15 Oct 1956; reclassified as a Guided Missile Cruiser (CGN 160) early in 1957 and renumbered (CGN 9) on 1 July 1957.

DESIGN. The *Long Beach* was initially planned as a large destroyer or "frigate" of about 7 800 tons (standard displacement) to test the feasibility of a nuclear powered surface warship. Early in 1956 the decision was made to capitalise on the capabilities of nuclear propulsion and her displacement was increased to 11 000 tons and a second Terrier missile launcher was added to the design. A Talos missile launcher was also added to the design which, with other features, increased displacement to 14 000 tons by the time the contract was signed for her construction on 15 October 1956.

ELECTRONICS. The *Long Beach* has fixed-array ("billboard") radar which provides increased range over rotating antennas. Horizontal antennas on bridge superstructure are for SPS-32 bearing and range radar; vertical antennas are for SPS-33 target tracking radar. She is equipped with Naval Tactical Data System (NTDS) and SQS-23 sonar.

GUNNERY. Completed with an all-missile armament. Two single 5 inch mounts were fitted during 1962-1963 yard period to provide defence against low-flying, subsonic aircraft and torpedo boats.

ENGINEERING. The reactors are similar to those of the nuclear-powered aircraft carrier *Enterprise* (CVAN 65). The *Long Beach* first got underway on nuclear power on 5 July 1961. After four years of operation and having steamed more than 167 000 miles she underwent her first overhaul and refuelling at the Newport News Shipbuilding and Dry Dock Company from August 1965 to February 1966.

MISSILES. Initial plans provided for installation of the Regulus II surface-to-surface missile, a transonic missile which carried a nuclear warhead and had a 1 000-mile range. Upon cancellation of the Regulus II programme, provision was made for providing eight Polaris missile tubes, but they were never installed. Plans to provide Polaris were dropped early in 1961 in an effort to reduce construction costs.

Reportedly, the *Long Beach* carries 40 Talos and 240 Terrier missiles.

LONG BEACH (CGN 9) *1968, United States Navy, PH1 W. A. Clayton*

Fleet Escort Ships—*Continued*

6 GUIDED MISSILE LIGHT CRUISERS (CLG): CONVERTED "CLEVELAND" CLASS

Name	*No.*	*Builder*	*Laid down*	*Launched*	*Commissioned*	*CLG Comm.*
***GALVESTON**	CLG 3 (ex-CL 93)	Cramp Shipbuilding (Philadelphia)	20 Feb 1944	22 Apr 1945	24 May 1946	28 May 1958
***LITTLE ROCK**	CLG 4 (ex-CL 92)	Cramp Shipbuilding (Philadelphia)	6 Mar 1943	27 Aug 1944	17 June 1945	3 June 1960
***OKLAHOMA CITY**	CLG 5 (ex-CL 91)	Cramp Shipbuilding (Philadelphia)	8 Mar 1942	20 Feb 1944	22 Dec 1944	7 Sep 1960
***PROVIDENCE**	CLG 6 (ex-CL 82)	Bethlehem Steel Co (Quincy)	27 July 1943	28 Dec 1944	15 May 1945	17 Sep 1959
***SPRINGFIELD**	CLG 7 (ex-CL 66)	Bethlehem Steel Co (Quincy)	13 Feb 1943	9 Mar 1944	9 Sep 1944	2 July 1960
TOPEKA	CLG 8 (ex-CL 67)	Bethlehem Steel Co (Quincy)	21 Apr 1943	19 Apr 1944	23 Dec 1944	26 Mar 1960

Displacement, tons	10 670 standard; 14 600 full load
Length, feet (*metres*)	600 (*182·9*) wl; 610 (*185·9*) oa
Beam, feet (*metres*)	66·3 (*20·2*)
Draft, feet (*metres*)	25 (*7·6*)
Missiles CLG 3, 4, 5:	1 twin Talos launcher
CLG 6, 7, 8:	1 twin Terrier launcher
Guns CLG 4-7:	3—6 in (*152 mm*) 47 cal; 2—5 in (*127 mm*) 38 cal dual-purpose
CLG 3, 8:	6—6 in (*152 mm*) 47 cal; 6—5 in (*127 mm*) 38 cal dual-purpose
Main engines	4 geared turbines (General Electric); 100 000 shp; 4 shafts
Boilers	4 (Babcock & Wilcox)
Speed	31·6 knots
Complement CLG 4-7:	1 680 officers and enlisted men (including fleet staff)
CLG 3,8:	1 200 officers and enlisted men

These ships were converted from light cruisers of the "Cleveland" class (see Fire Support Ships). Although generally similar, the six ships are of four distinct designs: the *Galveston* armed with Talos missiles; the *Little Rock* and *Oklahoma City* armed with Talos and fitted as fleet flagships; the *Providence* and *Springfield* armed with Terrier and fitted as fleet flagships; and the *Topeka* armed with Terrier. The flagships normally rotate as flagships of the Sixth Fleet in the Mediterranean and the Seventh Fleet in the Western Pacific. *Topeka* decommissioned on 5 June 1969

CLASSIFICATION. The *Galveston* was reclassified CLG 93 on 4 Feb 1956 and CLG 3 on 23 May 1957. All US Navy guided missile cruisers were numbered in a single series, the CAG 1 and CAG 2 having been the *Boston* (now CA 69) and *Canberra* (CA 70), respectively.

CONVERSION. All six of these ships had their two after 6 inch gun turrets replaced by a twin surface-to-air missile launcher, superstructure enlarged to support missile fire control equipment, lattice masts fitted to carry antennas, 5 inch battery reduced (from original 12 guns), and all 40 mm and 20 mm light anti-aircraft guns removed. The four ships fitted as fleet flagships additionally had their No. 2 turret of 6 inch guns removed and their forward superstructure enlarged to provide command and communications spaces for the flag staff.

The *Galveston* began conversion at the Philadelphia Naval Shipyard in August 1956 and was completed in September 1958; the *Little Rock* began conversion at the New York Shipbuilding Corp (Camden, New Jersey) in January 1957 and was completed in June 1960; the *Oklahoma City* began conversion at the Bethlehem Steel shipyard in San Francisco in May 1957 and was completed in September 1960; the *Providence* began conversion at the Boston Naval Shipyard in June 1957 and was completed in September 1959; the *Springfield* began conversion at the Bethlehem Steel shipyard in Quincy, Massachusetts, in August 1957, but was moved to the Boston Naval Shipyard in March 1960 for completion in July 1960; and the *Topeka* was converted at the New York Naval Shipyard between August 1957 and March 1960.

MISSILES. Reportedly, the three ships armed with Terrier each carry 120 missiles and the three ships armed with Talos each carry 46 missiles.

PHOTOGRAPHS. The four flagships (CLG 4-7) can be identified by their single 6 inch gun turret forward; the ships armed with the Terrier missile have three lattice masts while those with Talos have a short radar-supporting platform in lieu of the third mast.

OKLAHOMA CITY (CLG 5) — *1967, United States Navy*

PROVIDENCE (CLG 6) — *1966, United States Navy*

GALVESTON (CLG 3) — *1966, United States Navy*

Fleet Escort Ships—*continued*

TOPEKA (CLG 8) *1968, United States Navy*

1 + 3 NUCLEAR-POWERED FLEET ESCORT SHIPS (DXGN)

Displacement, tons	approx 10 000 full load
Length, feet (*metres*)	approx 600 (*183*) oa
Missiles, 2 combination	tartar—D/ARSOC Launchers
Guns	5 in (*127 mm*) dual-purpose
Main engines	2 geared turbines; 2 shafts
Reactors	2 pressurised-water cooled

The Department of Defense had proposed the construction of five advanced nuclear-powered, guided missile fleet escort ships. The Department had proposed to use the $134 800 000 previously authorised for construction of the DLGN 37 and the $20 000 000 authorised for long-lead time (reactor) procurement of the DLGN 38 plus additional funding to construct these five ships. Under this scheme the ships would be built by the total package procurement concept with one ship being funded under the Fiscal Year 1968 programme (DXGN/DLGN 37), two in FY 1970, and two in FY 1971. Estimated total cost for this five-ship programme were $625 000 000 (Defence) and $726 000 000 (Navy).
However, yielding to Congressional pressure President Johnson approved construction of the already funded DLGN 37, reducing the DXGN programme to four ships.
The Department of Defence now plans to build one DXGN per year in the FY 1970-1973 programmes. The cost of the first DXGN was estimated at $22 000 000 with the succeeding ships to cost approximately $180 000 000 to $190 000 000 each (Dec 1968 estimate).
The FY 1969 programme provided $52 000 000 for procurement of long-lead time components for the first two DXGNs. The FY 1970 programme requested $196 000 000 to complete funding of the first ship plus $68 000 000 for advance procurement which would complete funding of nuclear components of all four ships and fire control systems for three ships.

CLASSIFICATION. When their final characteristics are determined it is expected that these ships will be classified as frigates (DLGN).

2 NUCLEAR-POWERED GUIDED MISSILE FRIGATES (DLGN): NEW CONSTRUCTION

Displacement, tons	10 150 full load
Length, feet (*metres*)	596 (*181·7*) oa
Beam, feet (*metres*)	61 (*18·6*)
Missiles	TD 2G (General Electric) Tartar-D surface-to-air-launchers
Guns	2—5 in (*127 mm*) 54 calibre dual-purpose
ASW Weapons	torpedo launchers; 1 ASROC 8-tube launcher
Main engines	2 geared turbines; 2 shafts
Reactors	2 pressurised-water cooled D 2G (General Electric)

No	*Builder*	*Laid down*	*Launch*	*Commission*
DLGN 36	Newport News SB & DD Co	late 1969	1971	mid-1972
DLGN 37	Newport News SB & DD Co	late 1970	1972	mid-1973

The DLGN 36 was authorised by the Congress in the Fiscal Year 1967 budget with $20 000 000 being funded in FY 1966 for long-lead time (reactor) components and $130 500 000 being funded in FY 1967. The DLGN 37 and DLGN 38 were authorised in FY 1968 with the requirement that "the contracts for the construction of the two nuclear powered guided missile frigates shall be entered into as soon as practicable unless the President fully advises the Congress that their construction is not in the national interest"; DLGN 37 was funded with $20 000 000 in FY 1967 for long-lead time procurement and $114 800 000 in FY 1968; DLGN 38 was funded with $20 000 000 for long-lead time procurement in FY 1968.
The rising costs of warship construction and the proposed DXGN programme (see above) caused cancellation of the proposed DLGN 38 (only partially funded).
The compromise solution to the DXGN/DLGN situation was explained by Secretary of Defence Clark M. Clifford in a memorandum to the President dated 25 March 1968: "As you recall, the programme which the Secretary of Defence (McNamara) recommended last December would provide six new nuclear escorts, the last being funded in FY 1971. These six ships, in combination with the three nuclear escorts we already have, would give us two all-nuclear attack carrier groups. He also recommended that options for further nuclear escort construction be obtained in the event that we should later decide to move to a total of four all-nuclear groups. Of the six new nuclear escorts, one would be DLGN 36, and the remaining five would be a new class tentatively called the DXGN. (The DXGN is smaller than the DLGN, has one missile system rather than two, and would cost $40 000 000-$54 000 000 million less, depending on how many we built). Under this plan we would build neither DLGN 37 nor DLGN 38. "The Navy recommends an alternative under which we would build DLGN 36 and DLGN 37 (but not DLGN 38) and four DXGNs, also maintaining the option for further construction in the future. On balance, I believe that the Navy's proposal has merit. In the long run, building one more DLGN and one less DXGN would cost us roughly $50 000 000 more. On the other hand, it would give us the ship we need to round out our first all-nuclear attack carrier task group roughly 18 months sooner, since DLGN 37 is essentially ready for construction, while the DXGN design is not".

DLGN 36 *Official Navy Model*

Fleet Escort Ships– *continued*

1 NUCLEAR-POWERED GUIDED MISSILE FRIGATE (DLGN): "TRUXTUN" TYPE

Name	*No.*	*Builder*	*Laid down*	*Launched*	*Commissioned*
***TRUXTUN**	DLGN 35	New York Shipbuilding Corp (Camden)	17 June 1963	19 Dec 1964	27 May 1967

Displacement, tons	8 200 standard ; 9 200 full load
Length, feet (*metres*)	564 (*171·9*) oa
Beam, feet (*metres*)	58 (*17·7*)
Draft, feet (*metres*)	31 (*9·4*)
Missiles	1 twin Terrier/ASROC launcher (see *Missile* notes)
Guns	1—5 in (*127 mm*) 54 calibre dual-purpose ; 2—3 in (*76 mm*) 50 calibre anti-aircraft (single)
ASW Torpedos	2 triple torpedo launchers (Mk 32) 2 fixed torpedo tubes (stern) (Mk 25)
Helicopters	Facilities for helicopters
Main engines	2 geared turbines ; 60 000 shp ; 2 shafts
Reactors	2 pressurised-water cooled D2G (General Electric)
Speed, knots	30+
Complement	approx 500 (35 officers, 465 enlisted men)

The *Truxtun* was the US Navy's fourth nuclear-powered surface warship. The Navy had requested seven oil-burning frigates in the Fiscal 1962 shipbuilding programme; the Congress authorised seven ships, but stipulated that one must be nuclear powered.
Estimated construction cost was $138 667 000.

ELECTRONICS. The *Truxton* has bow-mounted SQS-26 sonar and the Naval Tactical Data System (NTDS).

ENGINEERING. Power plant is identical to that of the frigate *Bainbridge*.

MISSILES. The twin missile launcher aft can fire both Terrier anti-aircraft missiles and ASROC anti-submarine rockets.

PHOTOGRAPHS. The *Truxtun* can be readily identified by her squared lattice radar masts, empty "B" gun position, and lack of funnel. The later DLGN 36 design has solid mass structures which somewhat resemble those of the Soviet *Kynda* class missile ships (which are considerably smaller than the US nuclear-powered frigates).

CANCELLATION. A DLGN to be armed with the Typhon missile system was authorised and funded in the FY 1963 programme. When the missile system was cancelled because of high costs the ship also was cancelled. No hull number had been assigned. Announced characteristics included a full load displacement of more than 9 000 tons, overall length exceeding 600 feet, one twin launcher for long-range Typhon missiles, two single launchers for short-range Typhon missiles, two 5 inch guns, ASW torpedo launchers, ASROC, and Naval Tactical Data System (NTDS). See guided missile ship *Norton Sound* (AVM 1) for additional data.

NOMENCLATURE. Frigates are named primarily for admirals and commodores of the US Navy. The *Truxtun* is the fifth ship to be named for Commodore Thomas Truxton (sic) who commanded the frigate *Constellation* (38 guns) in her successful encounter with the French frigate *L'Insurgente* (44) in 1799.
The *Bainbridge*, fourth ship of that name, honours Commodore William Bainbridge who commanded the frigate *Constitution* (38) in her historic victories over the British frigates *Guerriere* (49) and *Java* (38) in 1812. The US Navy's lone "Admiral of the Navy", George Dewey, is honoured by a frigate (DLG 14) as are three of the Navy's four Fleet Admirals: Ernest J. King (DLG 10), William D. Leahy (DLG 16), and William F Halsey (DLG 23); Fleet Admiral Chester W. Nimitz is remembered with a nuclear-powered aircraft carrier (CVAN 68).
The *Josephus Daniels* (DLG 27) is named for the Secretary of the Navy during World War I.
"State" names are reported to be under consideration for subsequent nuclear-powered frigates, in particular the names *Montana* and California

TRUXTUN (DLGN 35) — *1967, United States Navy*

TRUXTUN (DLGN 35) — *1967, United States Navy*

TRUXTUN (DLGN 35) — *1968, United States Navy, J01 J– es Johnston*

Fleet Escort Ships– *continued*

9 GUIDED MISSILE FRIGATES (DLG): "BELKNAP" CLASS

Displacement, tons	6 570 standard; 7 930 full load
Length, feet (*metres*)	547 (*166·7*) oa
Beam, feet (*metres*)	54·8 (*16·7*)
Draft, feet (*metres*)	28·8 (*8·7*)
Missiles	1 Twin terrier/ASROC launcher
ASW Weapons	ASROC (see *Missiles* notes) 2 triple torpedo launchers (Mk 32)
Guns	1—5 in (*127 mm*) 54 cal dual-purpose; 2—3 in (*76 mm*) 50 cal anti-aircraft
Helicopters	Facilities for helicopters
Main engines	2 geared turbines (General Electric in DLG 26-28, 32, 34; De Laval in DLG 29-31, 33); 85 000 shp; 2 shafts
Boilers	4 (Babcock & Wilcox in DLG 26-28, 32, 34; Combustion Engineering in DLG 29-31, 33)
Speed, knots	34
Complement	418 (31 officers, 387 enlisted men) including squadron staff

Name	*No.*	*Builder*	*Laid down*	*Launched*	*Commissioned*
*BELKNAP	DLG 26	Bath Iron Works Corp	5 Feb 1962	20 July 1963	7 Nov 1964
*JOSEPHUS DANIELS	DLG 27	Bath Iron Works Corp	23 Apr 1962	2 Dec 1963	8 May 1965
*WAINWRIGHT	DLG 28	Bath Iron Works Corp	2 July 1962	25 Apr 1964	8 Jan 1966
*JOUETT	DLG 29	Puget Sound Naval Yard	25 Sep 1962	30 June 1964	3 Dec 1966
*HORNE	DLG 30	San Francisco Naval Yard	12 Dec 1962	30 Oct 1964	15 Apr 1967
*STERETT	DLG 31	Puget Sound Naval Yard	25 Sep 1962	30 June 1964	8 Apr 1967
*WILLIAM H. STANDLEY	DLG 32	Bath Iron Works Corp	29 July 1963	19 Dec 1964	9 July 1966
*FOX	DLG 33	Todd Shipyard Corp	15 Jan 1963	21 Nov 1964	8 May 1966
*BIDDLE	DLG 34	Bath Iron Works Corp	9 Dec 1963	2 July 1965	21 Jan 1967

These ships are considered excellent anti-submarine and anti-air warfare ships, intended to screen fast carrier task forces. The DLG 26-28 were authorised in the Fiscal Year 1961 new construction programme; the DLG 29-34 in FY 1962 programme.

DESIGN. These ships are distinctive by having their single missile launcher forward and 5 inch gun mount aft. This arrangement allowed missile stowage in the larger bow section and provided space aft of the superstructure for a helicopter hangar and platform. The reverse gun-missile arrangement, preferred by some commanding officers, is found in the *Truxtun*. The "Belknap" class ships have their masts and stacks combined into "mack" structures.

ELECTRONICS. SQS-26 bow-mounted sonar installed. These ships have the Naval Tactical Data System (NTDS).

ENGINEERING. These ships have twin 6-bladed screws and a large single rudder providing an excellent degree of manoeuvrability for ships of their size.

GUNNERY. The 5 inch guns were installed previously on forward sponsons of the "Forrestal" class carriers.

HELICOPTERS. These ships were to have operated Drone Anti-Submarine Helicopters (DASH). Although control and maintenance facilities have been removed, these ships can still support helicopters.

MISSILES. The *Truxtun* and "Belknap" class ships have a twin Terrier/ASROC Mk 10 missile launcher. A "triple-ring" rotating magazine stocks both Terrier anti-aircraft missiles and ASROC anti-submarine rockets, feeding either weapon to the launcher's two firing arms. The rate of fire and reliability of the launcher provide a potent AAW/ASW capability to these ships.

TORPEDOES. As built, these ships each had two 21 inch tubes for anti-submarine torpedoes installed in the structure immediately forward of the 5 inch mount, one tube angled out to port and one to starboard; subsequently removed.

JOSEPHUS DANIELS (DLG 27) — *1965, United States Navy*

BELKNAP (DLG 26) — *1964, United States Navy*

HORNE (DLG 30) — *1968, United States Navy*

Fleet Escort Ships—*continued*

1 NUCLEAR-POWERED GUIDED MISSILE FRIGATE (DLGN): "BAINBRIDGE" TYPE

Displacement, tons	7 600 standard; 8 580 full load
Length, feet (*metres*)	550 (*167·6* wl; 565 (*172·5*) oa
Beam, fee (*metres*)	57·9 (*17·6*)
Draft, feet (*metres*)	29 (*7·9*)
Missiles	2 twin Terrier surface-to-air launchers
Guns	4—3 in (*76 mm*) 50 calibre anti-aircraft (twin)
ASW Weapons	1 ASROC 8-tube launcher 2 triple torpedo launchers Mk 32
Main engines	2 geared turbines; approx 60 000 shp; 2 shafts
Reactors	2 pressurised-water cooled D2G (General Electric)
Speed, knots	30+
Complement	approx 450 (26 officers, approx 425 enlisted men)

Name	*No.*	*Builder*	*Laid down*	*Launched*	*Commissioned*
BAINBRIDGE	DLGN 25	Bethlehem Steel Co (Quincy)	15 May 1959	15 Apr 1961	6 Oct 1962

The *Bainbridge* was the US Navy's third nuclear-powered surface warship and the world's first "destroyer type" ship to have nuclear propulsion. She is larger than the light anti-aircraft cruisers the United States built during World War II. Authorised in Fiscal Year 1956 shipbuilding programme.
Estimated construction cost was $163 610 000.

DESIGN. Two heavy lattice radar masts are fitted in place of conventional masts and funnels; can be distinguished easily from the *Truxtun* by twin missile launchers forward and aft whereas later ship has 5 inch gun forward.

ELECTRONICS. Fitted with SQS-26 bow-mounted sonar and Naval Tactical Data System (NTDS).

ENGINEERING. Development of a nuclear power plant suitable for use in a large "destroyer type" warship began in 1957. The Atomic Energy Commission's Knolls Atomic Power Laboratory undertook development of the destroyer power plant (designated D1G/D2G). Because of the developmental nature of this plant, a land-based prototype was constructed in the 225-foot diameter sphere at West Milton, New York, which previously housed the sodium-cooled propulsion plant developed in conjunction with the submarine *Seawolf* (SSN 575). The D1G plant constructed at West Milton consisted of the reactor and machinery for one of the frigate's two shafts. Initial criticality was achieved on 28 Mar 1962 and the reactor first operated at full power on 9 May 1962.

BAINBRIDGE (DLGN 25) — *1968, USN, PHC, L. A. Hyatt*

BAINBRIDGE (DLGN 25) — *1968, United States Navy, PHC L. A. Hyatt*

LEAHY (DLG 16) — *1968, United States Navy, Joseph P. Garfinkel*

Fleet Escort Ships—*continued*

9 GUIDED MISSILE FRIGATES (DLG:) "LEAHY" CLASS

Displacement, tons: 5 670 standard; 7 800 full load
Length, feet (*metres*): 533 (*162·5*) oa
Beam, feet (*metres*): 54·9 (*16·6*)
Draft, feet (*metres*): 24·5 (*7·4*)
Missiles: 2 twin Terrier launchers
Guns: 4—3 in (*76 mm*) 50 cal anti-aircraft (twin).
ASW Weapons: 1 ASROC 8-tube launcher; 2 triple torpedo launchers (Mk 32)
Main engines: 2 geared turbines (see *Engineering* notes); 85 000 shp; 2 shafts
Boilers: 4 (Babcock & Wilcox in DLG 16-18; Foster Wheeler in DLG 19-24)
Speed, knots: 34
Complement: 396 (31 officers, 365 enlisted men) including squadron staff

Name	*No.*	*Builders*	*Laid down*	*Launched*	*Commissioned*
***LEAHY**	DLG 16	Bath Iron Works Corp	3 Dec 1959	1 July 1961	4 Aug 1962
***HARRY E. YARNELL**	DLG 17	Bath Iron Works Corp	31 May 1960	9 Dec 1961	2 Feb 1963
***WORDEN**	DLG 18	Bath Iron Works Corp	19 Sep 1960	2 June 1962	3 Aug 1963
***DALE**	DLG 19	New York SB Corp	6 Sep 1960	28 July 1962	23 Nov 1963
***RICHMOND K. TURNER**	DLG 20	New York SB Corp	9 Jan 1961	6 Apr 1963	13 June 1964
***GRIDLEY**	DLG 21	Puget Sound B & D Co	15 July 1960	31 July 1961	25 May 1963
***ENGLAND**	DLG 22	Todd Shipyards Corp	4 Oct 1960	6 Mar 1962	7 Dec 1963
***HALSEY**	DLG 23	San Francisco Naval Yard	26 Aug 1960	15 Jan 1962	20 July 1963
***REEVES**	DLG 24	Puget Sound Naval Yard	1 July 1960	12 May 1962	16 May 1964

These ships are "double-end" missile frigates, especially designed to screen fast carrier task forces. They are limited in having only 3 inch guns in comparison with 5 inch guns of other DLG classes. The DLG 16-18 authorised in the Fiscal Year 1958 new construction programme; DLG 19-24 in the FY 1959 programme.

DESIGN. These ships are distinctive in having twin missile launchers forward and aft with ASROC "pepper box" launcher between the forward missile launcher and bridge. Masts and stacks combined into "macks".

ELECTRONICS. These ships are being fitted with the Naval Tactical Data System (NTDS) during AAW modernisation. SQS-26 bow mounted sonar installed. *Warden*, *Richard K. Turner* and *Reeves* have only two missile directors; other ships have four.

ENGINEERING. General Electric turbines in DLG 16-18; De Laval turbines in DLG 19-22; and Allis-Chalmers turbines in DLG 23 and DLG 24.

MODERNISATION. All of these ships are undergoing AAW modernisation to improve the effectiveness of their command-control and missile systems. The modernisation includes installation of NTDS, SPS-48 air-search radar, Mk 76 fire control system for Terrier missiles, and larger ship's service turbo generators; improvements also are being made to the Terrier missile system.
The *Leahy* was modernised at the Philadelphia Naval Shipyard from Feb 1967 to Aug 1968; *Yarnell* at Bath Iron Works Corp, Bath, Maine, from Feb 1968 to May 1969; *Gridley* at Bath from Sep 1968 to late 1969; *Reeves* at Bath from Apr 1969 to mid-1970. The remaining ships of this class are scheduled for modernisation at Bath.

PHOTOGRAPHS. Note built up section between the *Leahy's* "macks", different radar and mast configurations; antenna pylon on forecastle.

NOMENCLATURE. The *England* is the second US warship to honour a sailor killed at Pearl Harbour on 7 Dec 1941; the first *England* (DE 635) sank six Japanese submarines in just 12 days during May of 1944.

LEAHY (DLG 16) — *1968, US Navy, Joseph P. Garfinkel*

WORDEN (DLG 18) — *1965, United States Navy*

HARRY E. YARNELL (DLG 17) — *1964, United States Navy*

Fleet Escort Ships—*Continued*

10 GUIDED MISSILE FRIGATES (DLG): "COONTZ" CLASS

Displacement, tons	4 700 standard; 5 800 full load
Length, feet (*metres*)	512·5 (*156·2*) oa
Beam, feet (*metres*)	52·5 (*15·9*)
Draft, feet (*metres*)	25 (*7·6*)
Missiles	1 twin Terrier launcher
Guns	1—5 in (*127 mm*) 54 cal dual purpose; 4—3 in (*76 mm*) 50 cal anti-aircraft (twin)
ASW Weapons	1 ASROC 8-tube launcher 2 triple torpedo launchers (Mk 32)
Main engines	2 geared turbines (see *Engineering* notes); 85 000 shp; 2 shafts
Boilers	4 (Foster Wheeler in DLG 6-8; Babcock & Wilcox in DLG 9-15)
Speed, knots	34
Complement	375 (28 officers, 347 enlisted men)

Name	*No.*	*Builder*	*Laid down*	*Launched*	*Commissioned*
***FARRAGUT**	DLG 6	Bethlehem Co, Quincy	3 June 1967	18 July 1958	10 Dec 1966
***LUCE**	DLG 7	Bethlehem Co, Quincy	1 Oct 1957	11 Dec 1958	20 May 1961
***MACDONOUGH**	DLG 8	Bethlehem Co, Quincy	15 Apr 1958	9 July 1959	4 Nov 1961
***COONTZ**	DLG 9	Puget Sound Naval Yard	1 Mar 1957	6 Dec 1958	15 July 1960
***KING**	DLG 10	Puget Sound Naval Yard	1 Mar 1957	6 Dec 1958	17 Nov 1960
***MAHAN**	DLG 11	San Francisco Naval Yard	31 July 1957	7 Oct 1959	25 Aug 1960
***DAHLGREN**	DLG 12	Philadelphia Naval Yard	1 Mar 1958	16 Mar 1960	8 Apr 1961
***WILLIAM V. PRATT**	DLG 13	Philadelphia Naval Yard	1 Mar 1958	16 Mar 1960	4 Nov 1961
***DEWEY**	DLG 14	Bath Iron Works, Maine	10 Aug 1957	30 Nov 1958	7 Dec 1959
***PREBLE**	DLG 15	Bath Iron Works, Maine	16 Dec 1957	23 May 1959	9 May 1960

These ships are "single-end" missile frigates intended to screen fast carrier task forces. Their design is based on the "Mitscher" class (DL/DDG). The DLG 6-11 were authorised in the Fiscal Year 1956 shipbuilding programme; the DLG 12-15 in FY 1957 programme. Estimated cost per ship was $51 000 000.

CLASSIFICATION. The *Farragut* and *Luce* initially were classified as DL 6 and DL 7, respectively. These ships are known officially as the "Coontz" class; the *Coontz* was the first to be ordered as a DLG (DLG 9-11 ordered on 18 Nov 1955; DLG 6-8 ordered on 27 Jan 1956).

DESIGN. These ships are the only US guided missile "frigates" with separate masts and funnels. They have aluminium superstructures to reduce weight and improve stability. Early designs for this class had a second 5 inch gun mount in the "B" position; design revised when ASROC "pepper box" was developed.

ELECTRONICS. The *King* and *Mahan* along with the aircraft carrier *Oriskany* (CVA 34) were the first ships fitted with the Naval Tactical Data System (NTDS), conducting operational evaluation of the equipment in 1961-1962. NTDS is a computerised system of collecting, processing, exchanging, and evaluating data on tactical situations. Priorities are assigned to enemy threats and alternative courses of action are presented to the commander. The system is intended primarily to deal with the threat of high-performance aircraft.
The *Coontz* was fitted with the SSM-5 Test Evaluation and Monitoring Syatem (TEAMS) in 1968 for operational evaluation of the electronic check-out system. See *Knox* (DE 1052) for details.

ENGINEERING. De Laval turbines in DLG 6-8 and DLG 15; Allis-Chalmers turbines in DLG 9-14.

MISSILES. The first five ships of this class were built with Terrier BW-1 beam-riding missile systems; five later ships built with Terrier BT-3 homing missile systems.

See *Modernisation* notes for conversion of earlier ships to improve missile capability. Reportedly, each ship carries 40 missiles.

MODERNISATION. These ships are undergoing AAW modernisations to improve the effectiveness of their electronic and missile system; NTDS installed. The *Farragut* was modernised at the Philadelphia Naval Shipyard from May 1968 to Oct 1969; *Preble* from Feb 1969 to early 1970 (Philadelphia); *Dewey* from Aug 1969 to late 1970 (Philadelphia).

NOMENCLATURE. The DLG 7 was to have been named *Dewey;* named *Luce* in 1957.

PHOTOGRAPHS. Note gun-missile arrangement; ASROC "pepper box" in "B" position on 01 level; tripod and lattice masts supporting radar and other antennas.

FARRAGUT (DLG 6) *1967, United States Navy*

DEWEY (DLG 14) *1968, US Navy, PHCM Louis P. Bodine*

DEWEY (DLG 14) *1968, United States Navy*

Fleet Escort Ships—*continued*

2 FRIGATES (DL)
2 GUIDED MISSILE DESTROYERS (DDG)
"MITSCHER" CLASS

Name	*No.*	*Builder*	*Laid down*	*Launched*	*DL Comm.*	*DDG Comm.*
***MITSCHER**	DDG 35 (ex-DL 2)	Bath Iron Works	3 Oct 1949	26 Jan 1952	15 May 1953	29 June 1968
***JOHN S. McCAIN**	DDG 36 (ex-DL 3)	Bath Iron Works	24 Oct 1949	12 July 1952	12 Oct 1953	21 June 1969
***WILLIS A. LEE**	DL 4	Bethlehem Steel Co. (Quincy)	1 Nov 1949	26 Jan 1952	5 Oct 1954	
***WILKINSON**	DL 5	Bethlehem Steel Co (Quincy)	1 Feb 1950	23 Apr 1952	3 Aug 1954	

Displacement, tons	3675 standard; 4 730 full load
Length, feet (*metres*)	493 (*150·3*) oa
Beam, feet (*metres*)	50 (*15·2*)
Draft, feet (*metres*)	26 (*7·9*)
Missiles DDG	1 single Tartar surface-to-air launcher
Guns DL/DDG	2—5 in (*127 mm*) 54 calibre dual-purpose
ASW Weapons DDG	1 ASROC 8-tube launcher
DL/DDG	2 triple torpedo launchers (Mk 32)
DL	4 torpedo tubes (Mk 23)
Helicopters DL	Facilities for helicopters
Main engines	2 geared turbines (General Electric in DDG 35 and DDG 36; Westinghouse in DL 4 and DL 5); 80 000 shp; 2 shafts
Speed, knots	35
Boilers DDG	4—1 225 psi (*86·1 kg/cm²*) (Combustion Engineering)
DL	4—1 200 psi (*84·4 kg/cm²*) Foster Wheeler)
Complement DDG	336 (18 officers, 318 enlisted men)

CLASSIFICATION. These ships were originally classified as Destroyers (DD 927-930, respectively); reclassified as Destroyer Leaders (DL 2-5) on 9 Feb 1951 while under construction; the symbol DL was changed to Frigate on 1 Jan 1955. The *Mitscher* and *John S. McCain* were reclassified as the DDG 35 and DDG 36 on 15 Mar 1967.

DESIGN. The "Mitscher" class was the first group of destroyer-type ships built by the United States after World War II. The design provided for potent anti-air and anti-submarine capabilities in a ship which could accompany fast carrier task forces. Accommodations and communications equipment provided for a destroyer flotilla or squadron commander.

GUNNERY. As built these ships each mounted two 5 inch/54 calibre guns and four 3 inch/50 calibre guns (plus two 12·75 inch Weapon Able ASW rocket launchers and four fixed 21 inch ASW torpedo tubes). Rapid-fire 3 inch/70 calibre guns were mounted in place of the original 3 inch weapons in 1957-1958. After twin 3 inch mount removed to provide helicopter platform; forward twin 3 inch mount subsequently deleted, leaving only 5 inch armament.

ELECTRONCIS. SQS-26 bow-mounted sonar installed. In *Willis A. Lee* and *Wilkinson*; SQS-23. Sonar in *Mitscher* and *John S. McCain*.

HELICOPTERS. The first at-sea landing aboard a US ship of an unmanned (drone) helicopter is believed to have been made by a DSN-1 on the *Mitscher* in August 1960. (A pilot was aboard the drone as a safety precaution, but did not handle the controls).

PHOTOGRAPHS. Note that both 5 inch guns were retained in DDG conversions; ASROC launcher installed in forward of bridge ("B") position and Tartar launcher fitted aft ("X" position); new lattice radar masts fitted; ASW torpedo launchers retained just behind second funnel on each side.

CONVERSION. The *Mitscher* and *John S. McCain* were converted to guided missile destroyers at the Philadelphia Naval Shipyard. The *Mitscher* began her conversion in March 1966 and the *John S. McCain* in June 1966. The *Willis A. Lee* and *Wilkinson* have not been scheduled for missile conversion.

MITSCHER (DDG 35) *1969, United States Navy*

MITSCHER (DDG 35) *1969, United States Navy*

WILKINSON (DL 5) *1968, United States Navy*

Fleet Escort Ships—*continued*

1 FRIGATE (DL): "NORFOLK" TYPE

Displacement, tons	5 600 standard; 7 300 full load
Length, feet (*metres*)	540·2 (*164·6*) oa
Beam, feet (*metres*)	54·2 (*16·5*)
Draft, feet (*metres*)	26 (*7·9*)
Guns	8—3 in (*76 mm*) 70 cal. dual purpose
ASW Weapons	1 ASROC 8-tube launcher 2 triple torpedo launchers (Mk 32)
Main engines	2 geared turbines (General Electric); 80 000 shp; 2 shafts
Boilers	4—1 200 psi (*84·4 kg/cm²*) (Babcock & Wilcox)
Speed, knots	32
Complement	411 (26 officers, 385 enlisted men)

Name	*No.*	*Builder*	*Laid down*	*Launched*	*Commissioned*
*NORFOLK	DL 1 (ex-CLK 1)	New York Shipbuilding Corp	1 Sep 1949	29 Dec 1951	4 Mar 1953

NORFOLK (DL 1) *United States Navy*

The Norfolk was one of two cruiser-size anti-submarine ("killer") ships authorised in 1948. Their size was to provide a rough-weather, long-range ASW capability. Construction of the CLK 2 was deferred on 2 Mar 1949 and cancelled on 9 Feb 1951; her keel was not laid down. She was to have been named *New Haven*.

ASW WEAPONS. The *Norfolk* was originally armed with four Weapon Alfa (formerly Weapon Able) rocket launchers. The two launchers aft of the second funnel have been replaced by an ASROC rocket launcher. The *Norfolk* has served as test ship for ASW equipment and was the primary test ship for ASROC. (Original armament included fixed torpedo tubes, but not the two triple torpedo launchers now installed on the main deck alongside the bridge structure).

CLASSIFICATION. The *Norfolk* was reclassified as a Destroyer Leader (DL 1) on 9 Feb 1951 while under construction; the symbol DL was changed to Frigate on 1 Jan 1955. While engaged in experimental work she was designated EDL 1.

DESIGN. The *Norfolk* was the first ship fully designed and built by the US Navy after World War II. She has a cruiser hull similar to the anti-aircraft cruisers (CLAA) of about the same dimensions built during the war, but with a clipper bow and a more streamlined superstructure.

ELECTRONICS. An advanced SQS-23 anti-submarine sonar was installed in 1958, the first ship so fitted.

ENGINEERING. The *Norfolk* reached 35 knots on trials; six-bladed propellers.

GUNNERY. Original gun armament consisted of eight 3 inch/50 calibre guns in twin open mounts and eight 20 mm guns. Faster-firing 3 inch/70s in enclosed mounts were fitted and the lighter weapons were removed.

MISSILES. Conversion to a Terrier DLG configuration was considered, but dropped.

NOMENCLATURE. The *Norfolk* retains her cruiser name; the only ship in the destroyer "family" named for a city.

PHOTOGRAPHS. Note "bug-eye" 3 inch gun mounts, Weapon Alfa rocket launchers in front of bridge, uneven stacks, ASROC rocket launcher aft of second stack and fire-control director. Stern view shows ASROC firing.

NORFOLK (DL 1) *1965, United States Navy*

BUCHANAN (DDG 14) *1966, United States Navy*

Fleet Escort Ships—*continued*

23 GUIDED MISSILE DESTROYERS (DDG): "CHARLES F. ADAMS" CLASS

Displacement, tons	3 370 standard; 4 500 full load
Length, feet (*metres*)	437 (*132·8*) oa
Beam, feet (*metres*)	47 (*14·3*)
Draft, feet (*metres*)	20 (*6·1*)
Missiles DDG 2-14	1 twin Tartar launcher
DDG 15-24	1 single Tartar launcher
Guns	2—5 in (*127 mm*) 54 cal dual-purpose
ASW Weapons	1 ASROC 8-tube launcher 2 triple torpedo launchers (Mk 32)
Main engines	2 geared steam turbines (General Electric in DDG 2, 3, 7, 8, 10-13, 15-22; Westinghouse in DDG 4-6, 9, 14, 23, 24); 70 000 shp; 2 shafts
Boilers	4 (Babcock & Wilcox in DDG 2, 3, 7, 8, 10-13, 20-22; Foster Wheeler in DDG 4-6, 9, 14; Combustion Engineering in DDG 15-19)
Speed, knots	35
Complement	354 (24 officers, 330 enlisted men)

Name	*No.*	*Builder*	*Laid down*	*Launched*	*Commissioned*
***CHARLES F. ADAMS**	DDG 2	Bath Iron Wotks	16 June 1958	8 Sep 1959	10 Sep 1960
***JOHN KING**	DDG 3	Bath Iron Works	25 Aug 1958	30 Jan 1960	4 Feb 1961
***LAWRENCE**	DDG 4	New York Shipbuilding Corp	27 Oct 1958	27 Feb 1960	6 Jan 1962
***CLAUDE V. RICKETTS**	DDG 5	New York Shipbuilding Corp	18 May 1959	4 June 1960	6 Jan 1962
***BARNEY**	DDG 6	New York Shipbuilding Corp	18 May 1959	10 Dec 1960	11 Aug 1962
***HENRY B. WILSON**	DDG 7	Defoe Shipbuilding Co	28 Feb 1958	23 Apr 1959	17 Dec 1960
***LYNDE McCORMICK**	DDG 8	Defoe Shipbuilding Co	4 Apr 1958	9 Sep 1960	3 June 1961
***TOWERS**	DDG 9	Todd Shipyards Inc, Seattle	1 Apr 1958	23 Apr 1959	6 June 1961
***SAMPSON**	DDG 10	Bath Iron Works	2 Mar 1959	9 Sep 1960	24 June 1961
***SELLERS**	DDG 11	Bath Iron Works	3 Aug 1959	9 Sep 1960	28 Oct 1961
***ROBISON**	DDG 12	Defoe Shipbuilding Co	23 Apr 1959	27 Apr 1960	9 Dec 1961
***HOEL**	DDG 13	Defoe Shipbuilding Co	1 June 1960	4 Aug 1960	16 June 1962
***BUCHANAN**	DDG 14	Todd Shipyards Inc, Seattle	23 Apr 1959	11 May 1960	7 Feb 1962
***BERKELEY**	DDG 15	New York Shipbuilding Corp	1 June 1960	29 July 1961	15 Dec 1962
***JOSEPH STRAUSS**	DDG 16	New York Shipbuilding Corp	27 Dec 1960	9 Dec 1961	20 Apr 1963
***CONYNGHAM**	DDG 17	New York Shipbuilding Corp	1 May 1961	19 May 1962	13 July 1963
***SEMMES**	DDG 18	Avondale Marine Ways Inc	18 Aug 1960	20 May 1961	10 Dec 1962
***TATTNALL**	DDG 19	Avondale Marine Ways Inc	14 Nov 1960	26 Aug 1961	13 Apr 1963
***GOLDSBOROUGH**	DDG 20	Puget Sound B & DD Co	3 Jan 1961	15 Dec 1961	9 Nov 1963
***COCHRANE**	DDG 21	Puget Sound B & DD Co	31 July 1961	18 July 1962	21 Mar 1964
***BENJAMIN STODDERT**	DDG 22	Puget Sound B & DD Co	11 June 1962	8 Jan 1963	12 Sep 1964
***RICHARD E. BYRD**	DDG 23	Todd Shipyards Inc, Seattle	12 Apr 1961	6 Feb 1962	7 Mar 1964
***WADDELL**	DDG 24	Todd Shipyards Inc, Seattle	6 Feb 1962	26 Feb 1963	28 Aug 1964

These destroyers are considered excellent multi-purpose ships. The DDG 2-9 were authorised in the Fiscal Year 1957 new construction programme, DDG 10-14 in FY 1958, DDG 15-19 in FY 1959, DDG 20-22 in FY 1960, DDG 23 and DDG 24 in FY 1961. Three additional ships of this design have been built in US shipyards for Australia (DDG 25-27) and three for West Germany (DDG 28-30).

CLASSIFICATION. The first eight ships were initially assigned hull numbers in the standard DD series (DDG 952-959); renumbered while under construction. The DDG 1 was the *Gyatt* (ex-DD 712), which operated as a missile destroyer from 1956 to 1962.

DESIGN. These ships were built to an improved "Forrest Sherman" class design with aluminium superstructures and a high level of habitability including air conditioning in all living spaces. They do not have the second radar trellis mast nor secondary gun battery of the earlier class. DDG 20-24 have stem anchors because of sonar arrangement.

ELECTRONICS. The DDG 20-24 have bow-mounted SQS-26 sonar; earlier ships have SQS-23. SPS-39 three-dimensional, air-search radar is mounted on second stack.

MISSILES. The DDG 2-14 have a twin Mk 11 Tartar missile launcher while the DDG 15-24 have a single Mk 13 Tartar launcher. The Mk 11 launcher installation weighs 165 240 pounds while the Mk 13 weighs only 132 561 pounds. Reportedly, their magazine capacities are 42 and 40 missiles, respectively, and ships equipped with either launcher can load, direct, and fire about six missiles per minute. (The twin Mk 11 launcher is installed in the cruisers CG 10-12; the "Mitscher" and "Forrest Sherman" DDG conversions have a similar Mk 13 launcher which weighs approximately 135 000 pounds).

NOMENCLATURE. US destroyers are named for officers and enlisted personnel of the Navy and Marine Corps, Secretaries of the Navy, members of Congress who have influenced naval affairs, and inventors. The DDG 5 was originally named *Biddle;* renamed *Claude, V. Ricketts* on 28 July 1964 to honour the late Vice Chief of Naval Operations who had supported multi-national NATO manning of ballistic missile surface ships. (The name *Biddle* subsequently was assigned to the DLG 34).

BARNEY (DDG 6) *1968, United States Navy*

LAWRENCE (DDG 4) *1968, United States Navy*

RICHARD E. BYRD (DDG 23) *1965, United States Navy*

Fleet Escort Ships—*continued*

5 + 57 (?) DESTROYERS (DD AND DDG): FORMER DX/DXG SERIES DESTROYERS

No.
DD 963
DD 964
DD 965
DD 966
DD 967

Displacement, tons	approx 6 000 full load
Length, feet (*metres*)	approx 500 (*152·0*) oa
Missiles DDG	1 twin Tartar-D surface-to-air launcher
DD	Basic Point Defence Missile System (BPDMS)
Guns DDG	1 or 2—5 inch (*127 mm*) 54 calibre dual-purpose (see *Gunnery* notes)
DD	2—5 inch (*127 mm*) 54 calibre dual-purpose
ASW weapons DD/DDG	ASROC; torpedo launchers
Main engines	gas turbines; 2 shafts
Speed, knots	30+

These ships are intended as replacements for the large number of World War II-built destroyers which have undergone extensive modernisation (FRAM) to enable them to serve into the 1970s. The number of ships in this series has been reduced from initial plans because of increasing ship construction costs.

The Fiscal Year 1969 new construction programme proposed by the Department of Defence requested funds for the first five destroyers; however, funds were denied by Congress because of design status. Five ships (DD 963-967) were funded in the FY 1970 programme. Fifty-seven additional DD/DDG ships of this series are believed planned for the FY 1971-1975 programmes.

For FY 1969 the Congress approved $25 000 000 for long-lead time components for five ships; FY 1970 funding is $335 000 000 for construction of the first five ships plus long-lead time components for eight additional ships for an average cost of approximately $60 000 000 per ship in the FY 1970 programme.

CONSTRUCTION. The Navy made contract definition awards for the DD 963 class on 3 July 1968 to three shipbuilders: Bath Iron Works Corp, Bath, Maine ($10 500 000); General Dynamics Corp, Quincy, Massachusetts ($9 000 000); and Litton Industries, Pascagoula, Mississippi ($9 000 000). Based on their design and cost proposals, a contract for the development and production of the *entire* DD 963 class will be awarded to one of the firms in Nov 1969. Awarding the contract to build the more than 30 ships of the DD 963 class to a single shipyard is expected to facilitate shipyard modernisation, standardisation of the ships, and reduction of construction costs.

Proposals from qualified shipyards for development and construction of the missile-armed ships (DDG) will be requested early in 1970.

CLASSIFICATION. During the early proposal stage these ships were designated as the DX and DXG projects, the letter "X" signifying that their characteristics were not fully defined.

The last "straight" destroyer built for the US Navy was the DD 951 of the "Forrest Sherman" class. Hull numbers DD 952-959 initially were assigned to the missile-armed DDG 2-9; DD 960 and DD 961 were assigned to the Japanese *Akizuki* and *Teruzuki*, respectively built with US military aid; DD 962 was assigned to HMS *Charity*, purchased from Great Britain in 1958 and transferred to Pakistan (*Shah Jahan*).

DESIGN. The DDG configuration will be slightly larger than the DD design, but both types are similar to the greatest extent possible. Extensive use of the modular concept is used to facilitate initial construction and bloc modernisation of the ships. Emphasis is also placed on use of equipment which can be installed easily for specialised destroyer missions such as space capsule recovery and electronic intelligence (ELINT).

ELECTRONICS. These ships will have SQS-26 sonar and will be the first US warships with a completely digital command and control system, which will reduce complexity and speed up production. (Most existing systems have a mixture of digital and analog components). Advanced electronic countermeasure (ECM) equipment will be fitted.

ENGINEERING Gas turbine propulsion is planned, the first in a large US warship.

Controllable-pitch propeller may be fitted.

GUNNERY. These ships may have the 5 inch/54 calibre, light-weight Mk 45 gun. An improved, 5 inch/54 calibre Mk 65 gun is being considered for use on later ships of this series. Both weapons are rapid fire and have no personnel in the above-deck mount (see listing for experimental ship *Norton Sound*, AVM 1).

MISSILES. The DDG will have a Tartar-D missile system firing the new Standard missile to provide area air defense. The DD will have the Sea Sparrow BPDMS for close-in air defense.

14 DESTROYERS (DD)
4 GUIDED MISSILE DESTROYERS
"FORREST SHERMAN" CLASS

Name	*No.*	*Builder*	*Laid down*	*Launched*	*DD Comm.*	*DDG Comm*
***FORREST SHERMAN**	DD 931	Bath Iron Works	27 Oct 1953	5 Feb 1955	9 Nov 1955	
***BARRY**	DD 933	Bath Iron Works	15 Mar 1954	1 Oct 1955	31 Aug 1956	
***DAVIS**	DD 937	Bethlehem Steel Co (Quincy)	1 Feb 1955	28 Mar 1956	28 Feb 1957	
***JONAS INGRAM**	DD 938	Bethlehem Steel Co (Quincy)	15 June 1955	8 July 1956	19 July 1957	
***MANLEY**	DD 940	Bath Iron Works	10 Feb 1955	12 Apr 1956	1 Feb 1957	
***DU PONT**	DD 941	Bath Iron Works	11 May 1955	8 Sep 1956	1 July 1957	
***BIGELOW**	DD 942	Bath Iron Works	6 July 1955	2 Feb 1957	8 Nov 1957	
***BLANDY**	DD 943	Bethlehem Steel Co (Quincy)	29 Dec 1955	19 Dec 1956	26 Nov 1957	
***MULLINNIX**	DD 944	Bethlehem Steel Co (Quincy)	5 Apr 1956	18 Mar 1957	7 Mar 1958	
***HULL**	DD 945	Bath Iron Works	12 Sep 1956	10 Aug 1957	3 July 1958	
***EDSON**	DD 946	Bath Iron Works	3 Dec 1956	1 Jan 1958	7 Nov 1958	
***MORTON**	DD 948	Ingalls Shipbuilding Corp	4 Mar 1957	23 May 1958	26 May 1959	
***RICHARD S. EDWARDS**	DD 950	Puget Sound Bridge & DD Co	20 Dec 1956	24 Sep 1957	5 Feb 1959	
***TURNER JOY**	DD 951	Puget Sound Bridge & DD Co.	30 Sep 1957	5 May 1958	3 Aug 1959	
***DECATUR**	DDG 31 (ex-DD 936)	Bethlehem Steel Co (Quincy)	13 Sep 1954	15 Dec 1955	7 Dec 1956	29 Apr 1967
***JOHN PAUL JONES**	DDG 32 (ex-DD 932)	Bath Iron Works	18 Jan 1954	7 May 1955	5 Apr 1956	23 Sep 1967
***PARSONS**	DDG 33 (ex-DD 949)	Igalls Shipbuilding Corp	17 June 1957	19 Aug 1958	29 Oct 1959	3 Nov 1967
***SOMERS**	DDG 34 (ex-DD 947)	Bath Iron Works	4 Mar 1957	30 May 1958	3 Apr 1959	10 Feb 1968

Displacement tons	
DD 931-944	2 780 standard; 3 950 full load
DD 945-951	2 850 standard; 4 050 full load
Length, feet (*metres*)	
DD 931-944	418·4 (*127·5*) oa
DD 945-951	418 (*127·4*) oa
Beam, feet (*metres*)	
DD 931-944	45·2 (*13·8*)
DD 945-951	45 (*13·7*)
Draft, feet (*metres*)	20 (*6·1*)
Missiles DDG	1 single Tartar surface-to-air launcher
Guns DD (ASW Mod)	2—5 in (*127 mm*) 54 calibre dual-purpose
DDG	1—5 in (*127 mm*) 54 calibre dual-purpose
DD	2—5 in (*127 mm*) 54 calibre dual-purpose; 4—3 in (*76 mm*) 50 calibre anti-aircraft (twin)
ASW DDG/ASW Mod	1 ASROC 8-tube launcher; 2 triple torpedo launchers (Mk 32)
DD	2 hedgehogs; depth charges; 2 triple torpedo launchers (Mk 32)
Main engines	2 geared turbines (Westinghouse in DD 931-933; General Electric in others); 70 000 shp; 2 shafts
Boilers	4 (Babcock & Wilcox in DD 931-933, 940-942, 945-947, 950-951; Foster Wheeler in others)
Speed	33 knots

These ships were the first US destroyers of post-World War II design and construction. They have all had their anti-submarine capabilities improved and four have been fitted with an anti-aircraft missile system (see below). They were authorised in the Fiscal Year 1952-1956 new construction programmes.

(The hull number DD 934 was reserved for the ex-Japanese *Hanazuki*, DD 935 for the ex-German *T-35*, and DD 939 for the ex-German *Z-39*, all 1945 war prizes which were discarded).

DECATUR (DDG 31) — *1968, United States Navy*

"FORREST SHERMAN" CLASS *continued*

Fleet Escort Ships—*continued*

ARMAMENT. As built all 18 ships of this class had three single 5 inch guns, two twin 3 inch mounts, four fixed 21 inch ASW torpedo tubes (amidships); two ASW hedgehogs (forward of bridge), and depth charge racks.

CONVERSION. Four of these ships have been converted to guided missile destroyers, the *Decatur* beginning conversion at the Boston Naval Shipyard on 15 June 1965, the *John Paul Jones* at the Philadelphia Naval Shipyard on 2 Dec 1965, the *Parsons* at the Long Beach (California) Naval Shipyard on 30 June 1965, and the *Somers* at the San Francisco Bay Naval Shipyard on 30 Mar 1966. During conversion all existing armament was removed except forward 5 inch gun; two triple ASW torpedo launchers installed forward of bridge; two heavy lattice radar masts fitted; ASROC mounted aft of second stack; single Tartar Mk 13 launcher installed aft (system weighs approximately 135 000 pounds). Plans for additional "Forrest Sherman" class DDG conversions were dropped; *Turner Joy* was to have been the next DDG.
Original DDG conversion plans provided for Drone Anti-Submarine Helicopter (DASH) facilities; however, ASROC substituted in all four ships as DASH lost favour with the Navy.

CLASSIFICATION. The *Decatur* was reclassified as DDG 31 on 15 Sep 1966; the *John Paul Jones, Somers*, and *Parsons* to DDG on 15 Mar 1967.

DESIGN. The entire superstructures of these ships are of aluminium to obtain maximum stability with minimum displacement. All living spaces are air conditioned. The *Decatur* and later ships have higher bows; the *Hull* and later ships have slightly different bow designs. The *Barry* had her sonar dome moved forward in 1959 and a stem anchor fitted.

ELECTRONICS. SQS-23 sonar installed. Radars vary, even after modernisation.

GUNNERY. With original armament of one 5 inch mount forward and two 5 inch mounts aft, these were the first US warships with more firepower aft than forward.

MODERNISATION. The 14 non-missile-armed ships of this class all were to have been fitted with "improved ASW systems (to) greatly enhance the effectiveness of these ships against modern high-speed submarines", according to official statements.
The *Barry* was modernised with FY 1964 funds at the Boston Naval Shipyard in 1967-1968. Five additional ships were to undergo ASW modernisation in the FY 1966 conversion programme (DD 931, 937, 938, 943, 944); eight others in FY 1967-1968. The DD 941 and DD 943 reprogrammed for FY 1967 funds; DD 937, 938, 940, 945, and 948 reprogrammed for FY 1968 funds. Six ships (DD 931, 942, 944, 946, 950, and 951) will not undergo modernisation because "the estimated cost of converting these ships hasris en substantially since they were originally programmed", according to official statements. During ASW modernisation these ships are being fitted with ASROC and two triple ASW torpedo launchers.

NOMENCLATURE. DD 951 was originally named *Joy*; renamed *Turner Joy* on 26 July 1957. The *John Paul Jones* honours the Scottish-born father of the American Navy who later served as a rear-admiral in the Russian Navy (1788).

DECATUR (DDG 31) *1968, United States Navy*

PARSONS (DDG 33) *1968, United States Navy*

RICHARD S. EDWARDS (DD 950) *United States Navy*

Fleet Escort Ships—*continued*

75 DESTROYERS (DD): MODERNISED "GEARING" CLASS (FRAM 1)

Displacement, tons	2 425 standard; 3 480 to 3 520 full load
Length, feet (*metres*)	390·5 (*119·0*) oa
Beam, feet (*metres*)	40·9 (*12·4*)
Draft, feet (*metres*)	19 (*5·8*)
Guns	4—5 in (*127 mm*) 38 calibre dual-purpose
ASW Weapons	1 ASROC 8-tube launcher 2 triple torpedo launchers (Mk 32) facilities for DASH
Main engines	2 geared turbines (General Electric or Westinghouse); 60 000 shp 2 shafts
Boilers	4 (Babcock & Wilcox or combination Babcock & Wilcox and Foster-Wheeler)
Speed, knots	34
Complement	274 (14 officers, 260 enlisted men)

Name	*No.*	*Builder*	*Launched*	*Commissioned*
***GEARING**	DD 710	Federal SB & DD Co	18 Feb 1945	3 May 1945
***WILTSIE**	DD 716	Federal SB & DD Co	31 Aug 1945	12 Jan 1946
***THEODORE E. CHANDLER**	DD 717	Federal SB & DD Co	20 Oct 1945	22 Mar 1946
***HAMNER**	DD 718	Federal SB & DD Co	24 Nov 1945	11 July 1946
***WILLIAM C. LAWE**	DD 763	Bethlehem (San Francisco)	21 May 1945	18 Dec 1946
***ROWAN**	DD 782	Todd Pacific Shipyards	29 Dec 1944	31 Mar 1945
***GURKE**	DD 783	Todd Pacific Shipyards	15 Feb 1945	12 May 1945
***HENDERSON**	DD 785	Todd Pacific Shipyards	28 May 1945	4 Aug 1945
***RICHARD B. ANDERSON**	DD 786	Todd Pacific Shipyards	7 July 1945	26 Oct 1945
***JAMES E. KYES**	DD 787	Todd Pacific Shipyards	4 Aug 1945	8 Feb 1946
***HOLLISTER**	DD 788	Todd Pacific Shipyards	9 Oct 1945	26 Mar 1946
***EVERSOLE**	DD 789	Todd Pacific Shipyards	8 Jan 1946	10 July 1946
***SHELTON**	DD 790	Todd Pacific Shipyards	8 Mar 1946	21 June 1946
***JOHNSTON**	DD 821	Consolidated Steel Corp	19 Oct 1945	10 Oct 1945
***ROBERT H. McCARD**	DD 822	Consolidated Steel Corp	9 Nov 1945	26 Oct 1946
***SAMUEL B. ROBERTS**	DD 823	Consolidated Steel Corp	30 Nov 1945	20 Dec 1946
***AGERHOLM**	DD 826	Bath Iron Works Corp	30 Mar 1946	20 June 1946
***GEORGE K. MacKENZIE**	DD 836	Bath Iron Works Corp	13 May 1945	13 July 1945
***SARSFIELD**	DD 837	Bath Iron Works Corp	27 May 1945	31 July 1945
***POWER**	DD 839	Bath Iron Works Corp	30 June 1945	13 Sep 1945
***GLENNON**	DD 840	Bath Iron Works Corp	14 July 1945	4 Oct 1945
***NOA**	DD 841	Bath Iron Works Corp	30 July 1945	2 Nov 1945
***WARRINGTON**	DD 843	Bath Iron Works Corp	27 Sep 1945	20 Dec 1945
***PERRY**	DD 844	Bath Iron Works Corp	25 Nov 1945	17 Jan 1946
***BAUSELL**	DD 845	Bath Iron Works Corp	19 Nov 1945	7 Feb 1947
***OZBOURN**	DD 846	Bath Iron Works Corp	22 Dec 1945	5 Mar 1946
***RICHARD E. KRAUS** (ex-AG 151)	DD 849	Bath Iron Works Corp	2 Mar 1946	23 May 1946
***JOSEPH P. KENNEDY Jr**	DD 850	Bethlehem (Quincy)	26 July 1945	15 Dec 1945
***RUPERTUS**	DD 851	Bethlehem (Quincy)	21 Sep 1945	8 Mar 1946
***LEONARD F. MASON**	DD 852	Bethlehem (Quincy)	4 Jan 1946	28 June 1946
***CHARLES H. ROAN**	DD 853	Bethlehem (Quincy)	15 Mar 1945	12 Sep 1946
***VOGELGESANG**	DD 862	Bethlehem (Staten Island)	15 Jan 1945	28 Apr 1945
***HAROLD J. ELLISON**	DD 864	Bethlehem (Staten Island)	14 Mar 1945	23 June 1945
***CHARLES R. WARE**	DD 865	Bethlehem (Staten Island)	12 Apr 1945	21 July 1945
***CONE**	DD 866	Bethlehem (Staten Island)	10 May 1945	18 Aug 1945
***STRIBLING**	DD 867	Bethlehem (Staten Island)	8 June 1945	29 Sep 1945
***BROWNSON**	DD 868	Bethlehem (Staten Island)	15 Mar 1945	17 Nov 1945
***ARNOLD J. ISBELL**	DD 869	Bethlehem (Staten Island)	6 Aug 1945	17 Nov 1945
***FORREST ROYAL**	DD 872	Bethlehem (Staten Island)	17 Jan 1946	29 June 1946
***FLOYD B. PARKS**	DD 884	Consolidated Steel Corp	31 Mar 1945	31 July 1945
***JOHN R. CRAIG**	DD 885	Consolidated Steel Corp	14 Apr 1945	20 Aug 1945
***ORLECK**	DD 886	Consolidated Steel Corp	12 May 1945	15 Sep 1945
***BRINKLEY BASS**	DD 887	Consolidated Steel Corp	26 May 1945	1 Oct 1945
***MEREDITH**	DD 890	Consolidated Steel Corp	28 June 1945	31 Dec 1945
		(Former Escort Destroyers, ex-DDE)		
***NEW**	DD 818	Consolidated Steel Corp	18 Aug 1945	5 Apr 1946
***HOLDER**	DD 819	Consolidated Steel Corp	25 Aug 1945	18 May 1946
***RICH**	DD 820	Consolidated Steel Corp	5 Oct 1945	4 July 1946
***ROBERT L. WILSON**	DD 847	Bath Iron Works Corp	5 Jan 1946	28 Mar 1946
***DAMATO**	DD 871	Bethlehem (Staten Island)	21 Nov 1945	27 Apr 1946
		(Former Radar Picket Destroyers, ex-DDR)		
***EUGENE A. GREENE**	DD 711	Federal SB & DD Co	18 Mar 1945	8 June 1945
***WILLIAM R. RUSH**	DD 714	Federal SB & DD Co	8 July 1945	21 Sep 1945
***WILLIAM M. WOOD**	DD 715	Federal SB & DD Co	29 July 1945	24 Nov 1945
***SOUTHERLAND**	DD 743	Bath Iron Works Corp	5 Oct 1944	22 Dec 1944
***McKEAN**	DD 784	Todd Pacific Shipyards	31 Mar 1945	9 June 1945
***HIGBEE**	DD 806	Bath Iron Works Corp	12 Nov 1944	27 Jan 1945
***DENNIS J. BUCKLEY**	DD 808	Bath Iron Works Corp	20 Dec 1944	2 Mar 1945
***CORRY**	DD 817	Consolidated Steel Corp	28 July 1945	26 Feb 1946
***MYLES C. FOX**	DD 829	Bath Iron Works Corp	13 Jan 1945	20 Mar 1945
***HANSON**	DD 832	Bath Iron Works Corp	11 Mar 1945	11 May 1945
***HERBERT J. THOMAS**	DD 833	Bath Iron Works Corp	25 Mar 1945	29 May 1945
***CHARLES P. CECIL**	DD 835	Bath Iron Works Corp	22 Apr 1945	29 June 1945
***FISKE**	DD 842	Bath Iron Works Corp	8 Sep 1945	28 Nov 1945
***STEINAKER**	DD 863	Bethlehem (Staten Island)	13 Feb 1945	26 May 1945
***FECHTELER**	DD 870	Bethlehem (Staten Island)	19 Sep 1945	2 Mar 1946
***HAWKINS**	DD 873	Consolidated Steel Corp	7 Oct 1944	10 Feb 1945
***HENRY W. TUCKER**	DD 875	Consolidated Steel Corp	8 Nov 1944	12 Mar 1945
***ROGERS**	DD 876	Consolidated Steel Corp	20 Nov 1944	26 Mar 1945
***VESOLE**	DD 878	Consolidated Steel Corp	29 Dec 1944	23 Apr 1945
***LEARY**	DD 879	Consolidated Steel Corp	20 Jan 1945	7 May 1945
***DYESS**	DD 880	Consolidated Steel Corp	26 Jan 1945	21 May 1945
***BORDELON**	DD 881	Consolidated Steel Corp	3 Mar 1945	5 June 1945
***FURSE**	DD 882	Consolidated Steel Corp	9 Mar 1945	10 July 1945
***NEWMAN K. PERRY**	DD 883	Consolidated Steel Corp	17 Mar 1945	26 July 1945
***STICKELL**	DD 888	Consolidated Steel Corp	16 June 1945	30 Oct 1945
***O'HARE**	DD 889	Consolidated Steel Corp	22 June 1945	29 Nov 1945

These ships are enlarged versions of the "Allen M. Sumner" class with an additional 14-foot section amidships for additional fuel tanks. All of the above listed ships have been extensively modernised under the FRAM 1 programme (see *Modernisation* notes). The *Richard E. Kraus* (ex-AG 151) and *Sarsfield* are used for experimental work (EDD). (The former ship was designated AG 151 from 24 Aug 1949 to 11 Dec 1953).

Eleven "Gearing" class ships were modified in 1949 and 1950 for specialised anti-submarine operations and four others were completed to specialised ASW configurations. Five of these ships which were reclassified as "escort" destroyers (DDE) on 4 March 1960 and subsequently reclassified as "straight" destroyers (DD) on 30 June 1962 are listed above. These ships have undergone FRAM I modernisation. The ten other ships of the basic "Gearing" design which were modified or completed to specialised ASW designs are listed separately.
Thirty-six "Gearing" class ships were modified for radar picket operations after World War II. These ships were reclassified DDR between 1949 and 1953. All have been modernised under the FRAM schemes. Twenty-six FRAM 1 ex-DDRs are listed here; ten FRAM II ex-DDRs are listed separately.

ARMAMENT-DESIGN. As built these ships had a pole mast and carried an armament of six 5 inch guns (twin mounts), 12 40 mm AA guns (2 quad, 2 twin), 11 20 mm AA guns (single), and 10 21 inch torpedo tubes (quin). After World War II the after bank of tubes was replaced by an additional quad 40 mm mount. All 40 mm and 20 mm guns were replaced subsequently by six 3 inch guns (2 twin, 2 single) and a tripod mast was installed to support heavier radar antennas. The 3 inch guns and remaining torpedo tubes were removed during FRAM conversion.
The "Gearing" class initially covered hull numbers DD 710-721, 742, 743, 763-769, 782-791, 805-926. Forty-nine of these ships were cancelled in 1945 (DD 768, 769, 809-816, 854-856, and 891-926); four ships were never completed and were scrapped in the 1950s: *Castle* (DD 720), *Woodrow R. Thompson* (DD 721), *Lansdale* (DD 766), and *Seymour D. Owens* (DD 767).

GUNNERY. The "B" twin 5 inch mount was removed from the experimental destroyer *Sarsfield* in 1959. The other ships lost their "B" or "Y" (after) 5 inch mount during FRAM conversion.

HELICOPTERS. These ships no longer operate drone helicopters, but rely on ASROC and tube-launched torpedoes for anti-submarine weapons.

CHARLES H. ROAN (DD 853) *1967, United States Navy*

Fleet Escort Ships—*continued*

"GEARING" CLASS (FRAM I)
continued

MODERNISATION. All of these ships have undergone extensive modernisation under the Fleet Rehabilitation and Modernisation (FRAM I) programme. They were stripped of all armament except two 5 inch mounts, new anti-submarine weapons were installed including facilities for operating ASW helicopters, new electronic equipment was installed, machinery was overhauled, living and working spaces were rehabilitiated. For budgeting reasons FRAM I work was officially considered a "conversion". The *Perry* was the first ship to undergo FRAM I conversion, the work being accomplished at the Boston Naval Shipyard from May 1959 to April 1960; her FRAM I cost an estimated $7 700 000.

PHOTOGRAPHS. Note normal position of triple torpedo launchers in place of "B" mount compared to arrangement of guns and torpedo launchers in *Shelton* shown in destroyer "nest" on a later page. These ships are easily distinguished from the "Allen M Sumner" and "Gearing" FRAM II classes by the ASROC launcher between their funnels.
The *Vogelgesang* is shown with an SH-3A helicopter hovering overhead.

DISPOSAL
Timmerman (DD 828) reclassified as an experimental ship (AG 152) and stricken after tests of light-weight machinery.

VOGELGESAND (DD 862) *United States Navy*

BORDELON (DD 881) *1964, United States Navy*

1 EXPERIMENTAL DESTROYER (DD): "GYATT" TYPE

Displacement, tons:	2 400 standard; 3 480 full load
Length, feet (*metres*)	390·5 (*119·0*) oa
Beam, feet (*metres*)	40·9 (*12·4*)
Draft, feet (*metres*)	19 (*5·8*)
Guns	4—5 in (*127 mm*) 38 calibre dual purpose 4—3 in (*76 mm*) 50 calibre anti-aircraft
ASW Weapons	2 triple torpedo launchers (Mk 32) 2 hedgehogs
Main engines	2 geared turbines (General Electric); 60 000 shp; 2 shafts
Boilers	4 (Babcock & Wilcox)

Name	*No.*	*Builder*	*Launched*	*Commissioned*
*GYATT	DD 712 (ex-DDG 1)	Federal SB & DD Co	15 Apr 1945	2 July 1945

The *Gyatt* was completed as standard "Gearing" class destroyer. She was converted to the world's first guided missile destroyer but later reverted to DD status (missiles removed). The *Gyatt* is now an operational Naval Reserve training ship, based at Washington, DC.

CLASSIFICATION. The *Gyatt* was reclassified to DDG 1 on 1 Dec 1955; to DDG 712 on 30 Dec 1956; back to DDG 1 on 23 May 1957 and reverted to DD 712 on 1 Oct 1962.

CONVERSION. The *Gyatt* was the US Navy's third guided missile warship (after the cruisers *Boston* and *Canberra*) and the world's first guided missile destroyer. She was converted to a missile ship at the Boston Naval Shipyard in 1955-1956. A twin Terrier surface-to-air missile launcher was installed aft (Y position) and two rotating missile magazines were installed in a deck house aft on the main deck level (14 missiles being stowed). During conversion she was fitted with the first US Navy installation of a fin stabilisation system (British Denny-Brown retractable fin stabilisers). The Terrier was found unsuitable for a ship of this size and, with the availability of newer missile-armed ships, the Terrier installation was removed in 1962.

DISPOSAL
The experimental destroyer **Witek** DD 848, was stricken on 17 Sep 1968 (described in 1968-1969 and previous editions).

GYATT (DD 712) *1964, United States Navy*

Fleet Escort Ships—*continued*

2 DESTROYERS (DD): "CARPENTER" TYPE (FRAM I)

Displacement, tons	2 425 standard; 3 410 full load
Length, feet (*metres*)	390·5 (*119·0*) oa
Beam, feet (*metres*)	40·9 (*12·4*)
Draft, feet (*metres*)	19 (*5·8*)
Guns	2—5 in (*127 mm*) 38 calibre dual-purpose (twin)
ASW Weapons	1 ASROC 8-tube launcher 2 triple torpedo launchers (Mk 32) facilities for DASH
Main engines	2 geared turbines (Westinghouse in *Carpenter*, General Electric in *Robert A. Owens*); 60 000 shp; 2 shafts
Boilers	4 (Babcock & Wilcox)
Speed, knots	34
Complement	264 (14 officers, 250 enlisted men)

Name	*No.*	*Builder*	*Launched*	*Commissioned*
***CARPENTER**	DD 825	Consolidated Steel Corp	30 Dec 1945	15 Dec 1946
***ROBERT A. OWENS**	DD 827	Bath Iron Works Corp	15 July 1946	5 Nov 1949

These ships were laid down as units of the "Gearing" class. Their construction was suspended after World War II until 1947 when they were towed to the Newport News Shipbuilding and Drydock Co for completion as "hunter-killer" destroyers (DDK). As specialised ASW ships they mounted 3 inch (76 mm) guns in place of 5 inch mounts and were armed with improved ahead-firing anti-submarine weapons (hedgehogs and Weapon Able/Alfa); special sonar equipment installed. The DDK and DDE classifications were merged in 1950 with both of these ships being designated DDE on 4 March 1950. Upon being modernised to the FRAM I configuration they were reclassified DD on 30 June 1962.
Drone helicopters are no longer carried.

ROBERT A. OWENS (DD 827) *1964, United States Navy*

2 DESTROYERS (DD): "EPPERSON" TYPE (FRAM I)

Displacement, tons	2 425 standard; 3 500 full load
Length, feet (*metres*)	390·5 (*119·0*) oa
Beam, feet (*metres*)	40·9 (*12·4*)
Draft, feet (*metres*)	19 (*5·8*)
Guns	4—5 in (*127 mm*) 38 calibre dual-purpose
ASW Weapons	1 ASROC 8-tube launcher 2 triple torpedo launchers (Mk 32) facilities for DASH
Main engines	2 geared turbines (General Electric in *Epperson*, Westinghouse in *Basilone*); 60 000 shp; 2 shafts
Boilers	4 (Babcock & Wilcox)
Speed, knots	34
Complement	264 (14 officers, 250 enlisted men)

Name	*No.*	*Builder*	*Launched*	*Commissioned*
***EPPERSON**	DD 719	Federal SB & DD Co	22 Dec 1945	19 Mar 1949
***BASILONE**	DD 824	Consolidated Steel Corp	21 Dec 1945	26 July 1949

These ships were laid down as units of the "Gearing" class. Their construction was suspended after World War II until they were towed to the Bath Iron Works Corp for completion as specialised "escort" destroyers (DDE). They carried improved sonar and ASW weapons. Upon being modernised to the FRAM I configuration they were reclassified DD on 1 July 1962.
Drone helicopters are no longer carried.

PHOTOGRAPHS. The *Basilone* and *Epperson* differ from the two "Carpenter" type destroyers in having a second twin 5 inch gun mount (aft) and having a short antenna mast atop the after deckhouse vice the small tripod antenna mast forward of the second funnel in the *Carpenter* and *Robert A. Owens*; bridge configurations differ.

BASILONE (DD 824) *1966, United States Navy*

BENNER (DD 807) *United States Navy*

Fleet Escort Ships—*continued*

16 DESTROYERS (DD): MODERNISED "GEARING" CLASS (FRAM II)

Displacement, tons: 2 425 standard; approx 3 500 full load
Length, feet (*metres*): 390·5 (*119·0*) oa
Beam, feet (*metres*): 40·9 (*12·4*)
Draft, feet (*metres*): 19 (*5·8*)
Guns: ex-DDE 4—5 inch (*127 mm*) 38 calibre dual-purpose; ex-DDR 6—5 inch (*127 mm*) 38 calibre dual-purpose
ASW Weapons: 2 triple torpedo launchers (Mk 32); 2 fixed torpedo tubes (Mk 25); 2 Drone Anti-Submarine Helicopters (DASH) (see notes)
Main engines: 2 geared turbines; 60 000 shp; 2 shafts
Boilers: 4 (Babcock & Wilcox)
Speed: 34 knots
Complement: 275 (15 officers, 260 enlisted men)

Name	*No.*	*Builder*	*Launched*	*Commissioned*
(Former Escort Destroyers, ex-DDE; former Hunter-Killer Destroyers, ex-DDK)				
***LLOYD THOMAS**	DD 764	Bethlehem (San Francisco)	5 Oct 1945	21 Mar 1947
***KEPPLER**	DD 765	Bethlehem (San Francisco)	24 June 1946	23 May 1947
***FRED T. BERRY**	DD 858	Bethlehem (San Pedro)	28 Jan 1945	12 May 1945
***NORRIS**	DD 859	Bethlehem (San Pedro)	25 Feb 1945	9 June 1945
***McCAFFERY**	DD 860	Bethlehem (San Pedro)	12 Apr 1945	26 July 1945
***HARWOOD**	DD 861	Bethlehem (San Pedro)	24 May 1945	28 Sep 1945
(Former Radar Picket Destroyers, ex-DDR)				
***KENNETH D. BAILEY**	DD 713	Federal SB & DD Co	17 June 1945	31 July 1945
***FRANK KNOX**	DD 742	Bath Iron Works Corp	17 Sep 1944	11 Dec 1944
***CHEVALIER**	DD 805	Bath Iron Works Corp	29 Oct 1944	9 Jan 1945
***BENNER**	DD 807	Bath Iron Works Corp	20 Nov 1966	13 Feb 1945
***EVERETT F. LARSON**	DD 830	Bath Iron Works Corp	28 Jan 1945	6 Apr 1945
***GOODRICH**	DD 831	Bath Iron Worps Corp	25 Feb 1945	24 Apr 1945
***TURNER**	DD 834	Bath Iron Works Corp	8 Apr 1945	12 June 1945
***ERNEST G. SMALL**	DD 838	Bath Iron Works Corp	9 June 1945	21 Aug 1945
***DUNCAN**	DD 874	Consolidated Steel Corp	27 Oct 1944	25 Feb 1945
***PERKINS**	DD 877	Consolidated Steel Corp	7 Dec 1944	5 Apr 1945

All of these ships were formerly of the "Gearing" class, with most of the former escort destroyers having been completed with only four 5 inch guns (vice standard six guns).

Six of these ships were modified for ASW in 1949-1950 and reclassified as "hunter-killer" destroyers (DDK) and then changed to "escort" destroyers (DDE) on 4 March 1950. As DDK/DDE ships they carried improved ahead-firing anti-submarine weapons. They were reclassified as "straight" destroyers (DD) on 30 June 1962 with FRAM II modernisation. (Virtually identical to FRAM I configuration less ASROC but with variable depth sonar (VDS) installed on fantail).

The former radar picket destroyers were completed as standard six-gun destroyers of the "Gearing" class (some with only five torpedo tubes). After World War II about two dozen "Gearing" class ships were fitted with a tripod mainmast forward of their second funnel to support a large air-search radar antenna. In this configuration they served as long-range pickets in support of carrier task forces to provide early warning of enemy air attacks and to control fighter aircraft intercepts.

These ships and a dozen additional "Gearing" class ships subsequently were fitted with a TACAN (Tactical Air Navigation) "beehive" antenna on a short tripod mast forward of their second funnel and a large radar antenna atop their after deckhouse These 36 ships were redesignated radar picket destroyers (DDR) in 1949-1953. Sixteen DDRs were modernised under the FRAM I programme and reverted to the standard DD configuration and designation.

Four ships, the *Chevalier, Benner, Everett F. Larson,* and *Perkins,* underwent FRAM II modernisation, losing their special radar installations but retaining six 5 inch guns (VDS and DASH provided); upon modernisation they were reclassified as "straight" destroyers (DD).

Six other radar picket destroyers undersent modified FRAM II process, the *Kenneth D. Bailey, Frank Knox, Goodrich, Turner, Ernest G. Small,* and *Duncan.* Their special electronic equipment was retained and a DASH capability was not provided. These six ships were not redesignated as "straight" destroyers (DD) until 1 Jan 1969.

PHOTOGRAPHS. Note the DASH on helicopter deck of the *Perkins*; tripod radar mast and antenna on after deckhouse of *Turner*. The *Perkins* and *Benner* (on previous page) do not have VDS installed in these photographs. Compare distances between funnels in views *Benner* ("Gearing" class) and *Wallace L. Lind* ("Sumner" class), and the "nest" of destroyers on the following page.

TURNER (DD 834) *1965, United States Navy*

PERKINS (DD 877) *1966, United States Navy*

WALLACE L. LIND (DD 703) (see following page) *1966, United States Navy*

Fleet Escort Ships—*continued*

32 DESTROYERS (DD): MODERNISED "ALLEN M. SUMNER" CLASS (FRAM II)

Displacement, tons	2 200 standard; 3 320 full load
Length, feet (*metres*)	376·5 (*114·8*) oa
Beam, feet (*metres*)	40·9 (*12·4*)
Draft, feet (*metres*)	19 (*5·8*)
Guns	6—5 in (*127 mm*) 38 calibre dual-purpose
ASW Weapons	2 triple torpedo launchers (Mk 32) 2 fixed torpedo tubes (Mk 25) 2 ahead-firing hedgehogs 2 Drone Anti-Submarine Helicopters (DASH)
Main engines	2 geared turbines; 60 000 shp; 2 shafts.
Boilers	4
Speed, knots	34
Complement	274 (14 officers, 260 enlisted men)

The above 33 ships have been extensively modernised under the FRAM II programme. See the following class listing for basic data.

The *Robert K. Huntington* became an operational Naval Reserve training ship in 1969, the first FRAM destroyer to be so assigned.

Frank E. Evans (DD 754) cut in half by Australian carrier *Melbourne* on 2 June 1969; bow section sank with loss of 74 crew. Officially stricken from the Navy List on 1 July 1969.

MODERNISATION. All of these ships have been modernised under the Fleet Rehabilitation and Modernisation (FRAM II) programme. New ASW torpedo launchers were installed as were facilities for operating ASW helicopters and variable depth sonar (VDS). Machinery was overhauled, new electronic equipment was installed, and living and working spaces were rehabilitated.

Name	*No.*	*Builder*	*Launched*	*Commissioned*
ALLEN M SUMNER	DD 692	Federal SB & DD Co	15 Dec 1943	26 Jan 1944
MOALE	DD 693	Federal SB & DD Co	16 Jan 1944	26 Feb 1944
INGRAHAM	DD 694	Federal SB & DD Co	16 Jan 1944	10 Mar 1944
CHARLES S. SPERRY	DD 697	Federal SB P DD Co	13 Mar 1944	17 May 1944
AULT	DD 698	Federal SB & DD Co	26 Mar 1944	31 May 1944
WALDRON	DD 699	Federal SB & DD Co	26 Mar 1944	8 June 1944
WALLACE L. LIND	DD 703	Federal SB & DD Co	14 June 1944	8 Sep 1944
BORIE	DD 704	Federal SB & DD Co	4 July 1944	21 Sep 1944
HUGH PURVIS	DD 709	Federal SB & DD Co	17 Dec 1944	1 Mar 1945
WALKE	DD 723	Bath Iron Works Corp	27 Oct 1943	21 Jan 1944
LAFFEY	DD 724	Bath Iron Works Corp	21 Nov 1943	8 Feb 1944
O'BRIEN	DD 725	Bath Iron Works Corp	8 Dec 1943	25 Feb 1944
DE HAVEN	DD 727	Bath Iron Works Corp	9 Jan 1944	31 Mar 1944
MANSFIELD	DD 728	Bath Iron Works Corp	29 Jan 1944	14 Apr 1944
LYMAN K. SWENSON	DD 729	Bath Iron Works Corp	12 Feb 1944	2 May 1944
COLLETT	DD 730	Bath Iron Works Corp	5 Mar 1944	16 May 1944
BLUE	DD 744	Bethlehem (Staten Island)	28 Nov 1943	20 Mar 1944
TAUSSIG	DD 746	Bethlehem (Staten Island)	25 Jan 1944	20 May 1944
ALFRED A. CUNNINGHAM	DD 752	Bethlehem (Staten Island)	3 Aug 1944	23 Nov 1944
JOHN A. BOLE	DD 755	Bethlehem (Staten Island)	1 Nov 1944	3 Mar 1945
PUTNAM	DD 757	Bethlehem (San Francisco)	26 Mar 1944	12 Oct 1944
STRONG	DD 758	Bethlehem (San Francisco)	23 Apr 1944	8 Mar 1945
LOFBERG	DD 759	Bethlehem (San Francisco)	12 Aug 1944	26 Apr 1945
JOHN W. THOMASON	DD 760	Bethlehem (San Francisco)	30 Sep 1944	11 Oct 1945
BUCK	DD 761	Bethlehem (San Francisco)	11 Mar 1945	28 June 1946
LOWRY	DD 770	Bethlehem (San Pedro)	6 Feb 1944	23 July 1944
JAMES C. OWENS	DD 776	Bethlehem (San Pedro)	1 Oct 1944	17 Feb 1945
ZELLARS	DD 777	Todd Pacific Shipyards	19 July 1944	25 Oct 1944
MASSEY	DD 778	Todd Pacific Shipyards	19 Aug 1944	24 Nov 1944
DOUGLAS H. FOX	DD 779	Todd Pacific Shipyards	30 Sep 1944	26 Dec 1944
STORMES	DD 780	Todd Pacific Shipyards	4 Nov 1944	27 Jan 1945
ROBERT K. HUNTINGTON	DD 781	Todd Pacific Shipyards	5 Dec 1944	3 Mar 1945

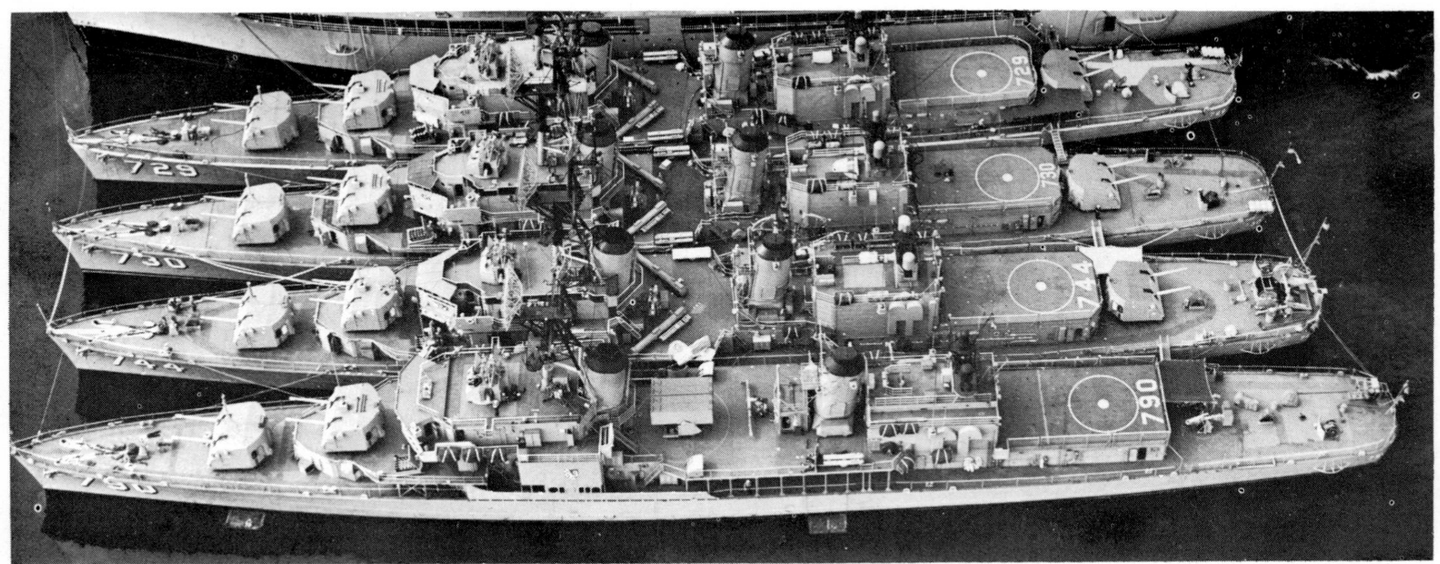

SHELTON (DD 790), BLUE (DD 744), COLLETT (DD 730) LAYMAN K. SWENSON (DD 729) *United States Navy*

BRUSH (DD 745) *1963, United States Navy*

Fleet Escort Ships—*continued*

19 DESTROYERS (DD): "ALLEN M. SUMNER" CLASS

Displacement, tons	2 200 standard; 3 320 full load
Length, feet (*metres*)	376·5 (*114·8* oa)
Beam, feet (*metres*)	40·9 (*12·4*)
Draft, feet (*metres*)	19 (*5·8*)
Guns	6—5 inch (*127 mm*) 38 calibre dual-purpose (twin) 4—3 inch (*76 mm*) 50 calibre AA (twin)
ASW weapons	2 fixed hedgehogs; depth charges 2 triple torpedo launchers (Mk 32)
Main engines	2 geared turbines; 60 000 shp; 2 shafts
Boilers	4
Speed, knots	34
Complement	274 (14 officers, 260 enlisted men) (designed wartime 345)

Name	*No.*	*Builder*	*Launched*	*Commissioned*
***ENGLISH**	DD 696	Federal SB & DD Co	27 Feb 1944	4 May 1944
***HAYNSWORTH**	DD 700	Federal SB & DD Co	15 Apr 1944	22 June 1944
***JOHN W. WEEKS**	DD 701	Federal SB & DD Co	21 May 1944	21 July 1944
***HANK**	DD 702	Federal SB & DD Co	21 May 1944	28 Aug 1944
***COMPTON**	DD 705	Federal SB & DD Co	17 Sep 1944	4 Nov 1944
***GAINARD**	DD 706	Federal SB & DD Co	17 Sep 1944	23 Nov 1944
***SOLEY**	DD 707	Federal SB & DD Co	8 Sep 1944	7 Dec 1944
***HARLAN R. DICKSON**	DD 708	Federal SB & DD Co	17 Dec 1944	17 Feb 1945
MADDOX	DD 731	Bath Iron Works Corp	19 Mar 1944	2 June 1944
***HYMAN**	DD 732	Bath Iron Works Corp	8 Apr 1944	16 June 1944
***PURDY**	DD 734	Bath Iron Works Corp	7 May 1944	18 July 1944
***BRUSH**	DD 745	Bethlehem (Staten Island)	28 Dec 1943	17 Apr 1944
***SAMUEL N. MOORE**	DD 747	Bethlehem (Staten Island)	23 Feb 1944	24 June 1944
***HARRY E. HUBBARD**	DD 748	Bethlehem (Staten Island)	24 Mar 1944	22 July 1944
***JOHN R. PIERCE**	DD 753	Bethlehem (Staten Island)	1 Sep 1944	30 Dec 1944
***BEATTY**	DD 756	Bethlehem (Staten Island)	30 Nov 1944	31 Mar 1945
***HENLEY**	DD 762	Bethlehem (San Francisco)	8 Apr 1945	8 Oct 1946
***WILLARD KEITH**	DD 775	Bethlehem (San Pedro)	29 Aug 1944	27 Dec 1944
***BRISTOL**	DD 857	Bethlehem (San Pedro)	29 Oct 1944	17 Mar 1945

Fifty-eight destroyers of this class were completed in 1944-1945 with an additional 12 ships completed in 1944 as Light Minelayers (DM). The minelayers are listed in the section on Mine Warfare Ships and 33 destroyers modernised under the FRAM II programme are listed on the previous page.
Sixteen of these destroyers are operational Naval Reserve training ships; the *John W. Weeks* and *Gainard* are in full commission with the Atlantic Fleet.

ARMAMENT-DESIGN. The "Allen M. Sumner" class introduced the 5 inch gun, dual-purpose twin mount on US destroyers.
The 13 US Navy "destroyer leaders" (DD 356-363, 381, 383, 394-396) built during the 1930s had twin 5 inch gun mounts, but they were not capable of sufficient elevation for anti-aircraft fire.
One-hundred six-gun destroyers were planned in the first six-gun destroyer series (DD 692-791); 31 of these were re-ordered as lengthened "Gearing" class. The "later" DD 857 is a short-hull "Sumner".

As built, all ships of this class mounted six 5 inch guns, twelve 40 mm AA guns, several 20 mm guns, and ten 21 inch torpedo tubes. A twin 40 mm mount was installed on bridge wings on both sides of the forward funnel, and two quad 40 mm mounts were installed aft of the second funnel; a five-tube torpedo bank was between the funnels and a second five-tube bank was at the end of the deck house (immediately forward of the No. 3 5 inch mount). After the war all ships had the after torpedo bank replaced by a quad 40 mm mount and the 20 mm guns were removed (providing a total of 16 40 mm guns). During the early 1950s most of these ships had the 40 mm guns replaced by two single and two twin 3 inch gun mounts (single mounts on bridge wings and twin mounts aft of second funnel in tandem arrangement) and a tripod radar mast replaced the original pole mast.

During the early 1960s most of these ships were modernised under the FRAM II programme. The non-modernised ships (listed above and in disposals) had their remaining bank of torpedo tubes removed along with the two single 3 inch gun mounts, and two triple Mk 32 launchers for ASW torpedoes were installed.

WAR LOSSES. *Cooper* (DD 695), *Meredith* (DD 726), *Mannert L. Abele* (DD 733), and *Drexler* (DD 741).

DISPOSALS

Hugh W. Hadley, DD 774, heavily damaged by suicide plane attack, was scrapped after World War II; **Barton**, DD 722, stricken on 1 Oct 1968.

12 DESTROYERS (DD): MODERNISED "FLETCHER" CLASS (3 FRAM II)

Displacement, tons,	2 080 standard; 2 940 full load
Length, feet (*metres*)	376·5 (*114·3*) oa
Beam, feet (*metres*)	39·5 (*12·0*)
Draft, feet (*metres*)	18 (*5·5*)
Guns FRAM II ships	2—5 in (*127 mm*) 38 cal DP
Others	2—5 in (*127 mm*) 38 cal DP 4—3 in (*76 mm*) 50 cal AA
ASW Weapons	
FRAM II ships	1 Weapon Alfa (Mk 108) 2 fixed hedgehogs 2 triple torpedo launchers (Mk 32) 2 Drone Anti-Submarine Helicopters (DASH)
Others	1 Weapon Alfa (Mk 108) or trainable hedgehog 2 fixed hedgehogs 2 triple torpedo launchers (Mk 32) depth charges
Main engines	2 geared turbines; 60 000 shp, 2 shafts
Boilers	2 (Babcock & Wilcox)
Speed, knots	35
Complement	249 (14 officers, 235 enlisted men)

Name	*No.*	*Builder*	*Laid down*	*Launched*	*Commissioned*
					9 Oct 1942
***CONWAY**	DD 507	Bath Iron Works Corpn	5 Nov 1941	16 Aug 1942	9 Oct 1942
***CONY**	DD 508	Bath Iron Works Corpn	24 Dec 1941	16 Aug 1942	30 Oct 1942
***EATON**	DD 510	Bath Iron Works Corpn	17 Mar 1942	20 Sep 1942	4 Dec 1942
FLETCHER	DD 445	Federal SB & DD Co	2 Oct 1941	3 May 1942	30 June 1942
JENKINS	DD 447	Federal SB & DD Co	22 Nov 1941	21 June 1942	31 July 1942
***NICHOLAS**	DD 449	Bath Iron Works Corpn	3 Mar 1942	19 Feb 1942	4 June 1942
***O'BANNON**	DD 450	Bath Iron Works Corpn	3 Mar 1941	19 Feb 1942	26 June 1942
***RADFORD**	DD 446	Federal SB & DD Co	2 Oct 1941	3 May 1942	21 July 1943
***RENSHAW**	DD 499	Federal SB & DD Co	7 May 1942	13 Oct 1942	5 Dec 1942
TAYLOR	DD 468	Bath Iron Works Corpn	28 Aug 1941	7 June 1942	28 Aug 1942
WALKER	DD 517	Bath Iron Works Corpn	31 Aug 1942	31 Jan 1943	3 Apr 1943
WALLER	DD 466	Federal SB & DD Co	12 Feb 1942	15 Aug 1942	1 Oct 1942

All of these ships were originally standard "Fletcher" class destroyers (see next listing). Eighteen ships were converted 1948-1951 to serve as close convoy escort and were classified Escort Destroyers (DDE) in 1949-1951. All reclassified DD on 1 July 1962. Three ships subsequently modernised under the FRAM II programme (see *Modernisation*) notes.
Five ships of this class were placed in reserve in 1969.

MODERNISATION. The *Jenkins, Nicholas,* and *Radford* were modernised in 1960 under the FRAM II programme. They were extensively rehabilitated and fitted with a hangar and flight deck to operate DASH and with variable depth sonar (VDS). All 18 ships of this type were to undergo FRAM II modification, but the plan was dropped in December 1961 in favour of new-construction escort ships.

DISPOSALS

Saufley, DD 465, stricken on 1 Sep 1966 and expended as target; **Bache**, DD 470, ran aground off Rhodes, Greece, on 6 Feb 1968 and stricken on 1 Mar 1968; **Murray**, DD 576, stricken on 1 June 1965; **Beale**, DD 471, **Philip**, DD 498, **Sproston**, DD 577, stricken on 1 Oct 1968.

EATON (DD 510) *1964, United States Navy*

Fleet Escort Ships—*continued*

RADFORD (DD 446) *United States Navy*

O'BANNON (DD 450) *1963, United States Navy*

32 DESTROYERS (DD): LATER "FLETCHER" CLASS

Displacement, tons	2 050 standard; 3 500 full load
Length, feet (*metres*)	376·5 (*114·7*) oa
Beam, feet (*metres*)	39·5 (*11·9*)
Draft, feet (*metres*)	18 (*5·5*)
Guns	4 or 5—5 inch (*127 mm*) 38 calibre dual-purpose; 10—40 mm AA (twin) or 6—3 in (*76 mm*) AA (twin) see *Armament* notes)
ASW weapons	depth charges; 2 fixed hedgehogs. 2 triple torpedo launchers (Mk 32) in some active ships
Torpedo tubes	5 or 10—21 inch (*533 mm*) quintuple (removed from some active ships)
Main engines	2 geared turbines; 60 000 shp; 2 shafts
Boilers	4
Speed, knots	35
Complement	250 (14 officers, 236 enlisted men) (designed wartime 329)

Fifty-six destroyers of this class were completed in 1943-1944. They are essentially the same as the original "Fletcher" class

ARMAMENT-DESIGN. As built, these ships each mounted five 5 inch guns, ten 40 mm AA guns, several 20 mm guns, and ten 21 inch torpedo tubes. The twin 40 mm gun mounts were installed just forward of and below the bridge, alongside the second funnel, and atop the after deckhouse.

Name	*No.*	*Builder*	*Launched*	*Commissioned*
ALBERT W GRANT	DD 649	Charleston Navy Yard	29 May 1943	24 Nov 1943
BEARSS	DD 654	Gulf SB Corpn	25 July 1943	12 Apr 1944
BENNION	DD 662	Boston Navy Yard	4 July 1943	14 Dec 1943
BLACK	DD 666	Federal SB & DD Co	28 Mar 1943	21 May 1943
BULLARD	DD 660	Federal SB & DD Co	28 Feb 1943	9 Apr 1943
BRYANT	DD 665	Charleston Navy Yard	29 May 1943	4 Dec 1943
CAPERTON	DD 650	Bath Iron Works Corpn	24 July 1943	30 July 1943
CASSIN YOUNG	DD 793	Bethlehem Co San Pedro	12 Sep 1943	31 Dec 1943
CHAUNCEY	DD 667	Federal SB & DD Co	28 Mar 1943	31 May 1943
***COGSWELL**	DD 651	Bath Iron Works Corpn	5 June 1943	17 Aug 1943
COTTEN	DD 669	Federal SB & DD Co	12 June 1943	24 July 1943
DASHIELL	DD 659	Federal SB & DD Co	6 Feb 1943	20 Mar 1943
***HALSEY POWELL**	DD 686	Bethlehem Co Staten Island	30 June 1943	25 Oct 1943
HEALY	DD 672	Federal SB & DD Co	4 July 1943	3 Sep 1943
***HOPEWELL**	DD 681	Bethlehem Co San Pedro	2 May 1943	30 Sep 1943
HUNT	DD 674	Federal SB & DD Co	1 Aug 1943	22 Sep 1943
***INGERSOLL**	DD 652	Bath Iron Works Corpn	28 June 1943	31 Aug 1943
JOHN HOOD	DD 655	Gulf SB Corpn	23 Oct 1943	7 June 1944
KIDD	DD 661	Federal SB & DD Co	28 Feb 1943	23 Apr 1944
KNAPP	DD 653	Bath Iron Works Corpn	10 July 1943	16 Sep 1943
McNAIR	DD 679	Federal SB & DD Co	14 Nov 1943	30 Dec 1943
MELVIN	DD 680	Federal SB & DD Co	17 Oct 1943	24 Nov 1943
MERTZ	DD 691	Bath Iron Works Corpn	11 Sep 1943	19 Nov 1943
NORMAN SCOTT	DD 690	Bath Iron Works Corpn	28 Aug 1943	5 Nov 1943
***PICKING**	DD 685	Bethlehem Co Staten Island	31 May 1943	21 Sep 1943
PORTER	DD 800	Todd Pacific Shipyards	13 Mar 1944	24 June 1944
PORTERFIELD	DD 682	Bethlehem Co San Pedro	13 June 1943	30 Oct 1943
***PRESTON**	DD 795	Bethlehem Co San Pedro	12 Dec 1943	20 Mar 1944
REMEY	DD 688	Bath Iron Works Corpn	24 July 1943	30 Sep 1943
STOCKHAM	DD 683	Bethlehem Co, San Francisco	25 June 1943	11 Feb 1944
***UHLMANN**	DD 687	Bethlehem Co, Staten Island	30 July 1943	22 Nov 1943
***WEDDERBURN**	DD 684	Bethlehem Co, San Francisco	1 Aug 1943	9 Mar 1944

COGSWELL (DD 851) NP 243 ENTERPRISE (CVAN 65)

Fleet Escort Ships—*continued*

LATER "FLETCHER" CLASS DD

continued

After World War II a large number of these ships had their pole mast replaced by a tripod mast and five torpedo tubes between funnels were removed. All 20 mm guns also were removed. Twenty ships had their No. 3 ("Q") 5 inch mount removed and the 40 mm guns replaced by six 3 inch guns (twin), the latter installed between funnels and atop after deckhouse. Four-gun destroyers remaining on the Navy List are: *Black, Cogswell, Dashiell, Hopewell, Hunt, Ingersoll, McNair, Picking, Preston* and *Uhlmann*.
Most active ships of this class have Mk 32 launchers for ASW torpedoes.

WAR LOSSES. *Callaghan* (DD 792), *Colhoun* (DD 801), and *Little* (DD 803).

PHOTOGRAPHS. The *Cogswell*, on previous page, is a "four-gun" destroyer with a secondary battery of three twin 3 inch gun mounts (two between funnels and one atop after deckhouse). The *Porterfield* retains five 5 inch mounts but has had secondary gun battery removed. Both ships have triple Mk 32 torpedo launchers; those in *Cogswell*, just aft of her second funnel, are covered.

TRANSFERS
Heywood L. Edwards, DD 663, **Richard P. Leary**, DD 664, transferred to Japan in 1959; **Benham**, DD 796, transferred to Peru in 1960; **Jarvis**, DD 799, **McGowan**, DD 768, transferred to Spain in 1960; **Cushing**, DD 797, transferred to Brazil in 1961; **Dortch**, DD 670, transferred to Argentina in 1961; **Rooks**, DD 804, **Wadleigh**, DD 689, transferred to Chile in 1963; **Hickox**, DD 673, transferred to South Korea on 11 Nov 1968; **Halsey Powell**, DD 686, to South Korea in 1969.

DISPOSALS
Monssen, DD 798, stricken on 1 Feb 1963; **McDermut**, DD 677, stricken on 1 Apr 1965; **Callahan**, DD 658, stricken on 1 Aug 1966 and expended as target.
Gregory, DD 802, stricken on 1 May 1966, but retained as a non-sea-going training ship at San Diego (renamed *Indoctrinator*).

PORTERFIELD (DD 682) *1965, United States Navy*

41 DESTROYERS (DD): "FLETCHER" CLASS

Displacement, tons	2 100 standard; 3 050 full load
Length, feet (*metres*)	376·5 (*114·7*) oa
Beam, feet (*metres*)	39·5 (*11·9*)
Draft, feet (*metres*)	18 (*5·5*)
Guns	4 or 5—5 inch (*127 mm*) 38 calibre dual-purpose 6—40 mm AA (twin) or 6—3 inch (*76 mm*) AA (twin) (see *Armament* notes)
ASW weapons	depth charges 2 fixed hedgehogs 2 triple torpedo launchers (Mk 32) in some active ships
Torpedo tubes	5 or 10—21 inch (*533 mm*) quintuple
Main engines	2 geared turbines; 60 000 shp; 2 shafts
Boilers	4
Speed, knots	35
Complement	249 (14 officers, 235 enlisted men) (designed wartime 329)

One hundred ninteen ships of this class were completed in 1942-45. Eighteen ships subsequently were converted to Escort Destroyers (DDE) and are listed separately. Eleven ships of this class were cancelled: DD 505, 506, 523-525, 542, 543, 548, 549, *Percival* (DD 542), and *Watson* (DD 482). The last two were to have been 2 100-ton destroyers with experimental power plants. (The experimental ships DD 503 and DD 504, of an unspecified type, were cancelled in 1941).
The *Shields* and *Twining* are operational Naval Reserve training ships.

ARMAMENT-DESIGN. These ships marked reversion to flush-deck destroyers by the US Navy after several broken-deck designs built during the 1930s and early 1940s. This design was extremely successful and 56 additional ships of this class were constructed (listed separately).

As built, these ships each mounted five 5 inch guns, six 40 mm AA guns, several 20 mm AA guns, and ten 21 inch torpedo tubes. The twin 40 mm gun mounts were installed on each side of the second funnel and atop the after deckhouse.

After World War II a large number of these ships had their pole mast replaced by a tripod mast and the five torpedo tubes between funnels were removed. All 20 mm guns also removed. Twenty-one ships had their No. 3 ("Q") 5 inch mount removed and the 40 mm guns replaced by six 3 inch guns (twin), the latter installed between funnels and atop after deckhouse. Four-gun destroyers remaining on the Navy List are: *Abbot, Boyd, Braine, Cowell, Daly, Mullany, Pritchett, Ross, Rowe, Stoddard,* and *Trathen*.
Most active ships of this class have Mk 32 launchers for ASW torpedoes.

HELICOPTERS. The *Hazelwood* was extensively modified to serve as test ship for the Drone Anti-Submarine Helicopter (DASH) programme. Her gun armament was reduced to three 5 inch mounts and a helicopter hangar and platform were fitted amidships (see photograph).

Name	*No.*	*Builder*	*Laid down*	*Launched*	*Completed*
ABBOT	DD 629	Bath Iron Works Corpn	21 Sep 1942	17 Feb 1943	23 Apr 1943
BELL	DD 587	Charleston Navy Yard	24 Feb 1942	24 June 1942	4 Mar 1943
***BOYD**	DD 544	Bethlehem Co, San Pedro	2 Apr 1942	29 Oct 1942	8 May 1943
***BRAINE**	DD 630	Bath Iron Works Corpn	12 Oct 1942	7 Mar 1943	11 May 1943
BURNS	DD 588	Charleston Navy Yard	9 May 1942	8 Aug 1942	3 Apr 1943
***COWELL**	DD 547	Bethlehem Co, San Pedro	7 Sep 1942	18 Apr 1943	23 Aug 1943
DALEY	DD 519	Bethlehem Co, Staten Island	29 Apr 1942	24 Oct 1942	10 Mar 1943
FOOTE	DD 511	Bath Iron Works Corpn	14 Apr 1942	11 Oct 1942	22 Dec 1942
FRANKS	DD 554	Seattle-Tacoma SB Corpn	8 Mar 1942	7 Dec 1942	30 July 1943
HARADEN	DD 585	Boston Navy Yard	3 June 1942	19 Mar 1943	16 Sep 1943
HART	DD 594	Puget Sound Navy Yard	10 Aug 1943	25 Sep 1944	4 Nov 1944
HAZELWOOD	DD 531	Bethlehem Co, San Francisco	11 Apr 1942	20 Nov 1942	18 June 1943
HUDSON	DD 475	Boston Navy Yard	23 Feb 1942	3 June 1942	13 Apr 1943
IZARD	DD 589	Charleston Navy Yard	9 May 1942	8 Oct 1942	15 May 1943
LA VALLETTE	DD 448	Federal SB & DD Co	27 Nov 1941	21 June 1942	12 Aug 1942
LAWS	DD 558	Seattle-Tacoma SB Corpn	19 May 1942	22 Apr 1943	18 Nov 1943
METCALF	DD 595	Puget Sound Navy Yard	10 Aug 1943	25 Sep 1944	18 Nov 1944
MILLER	DD 535	Bethlehem Co, San Francisco	18 Aug 1942	7 Mar 1943	31 Aug 1943
***MULLANY**	DD 528	Bethlehem Co, San Francisco	15 Jan 1942	12 Oct 1942	23 Apr 1943
McCORD	DD 534	Bethlehem Co, San Francisco	17 Mar 1942	10 Jan 1943	19 Aug 1943
McKEE	DD 575	Consolidated Steel Corpn	2 Mar 1942	2 Aug 1942	31 Mar 1943
OWEN	DD 536	Bethlehem Co, San Francisco	17 Sep 1942	21 Mar 1943	20 Sep 1943
***PRICHETT**	DD 561	Seattle-Tacoma SB Corpn	20 July 1942	31 July 1943	15 Jan 1944
ROBINSON	DD 562	Seattle-Tacoma SB Corpn	12 Aug 1942	28 Aug 1943	31 Jan 1944
ROSS	DD 563	Seattle-Tacoma SB Corpn	7 Sep 1942	10 Sep 1943	21 Feb 1944
ROWE	DD 564	Seattle-Tacoma SB Corpn	7 Dec 1942	30 Sep 1943	13 Mar 1944
SCHROEDER	DD 501	Federal SB & DD Co	25 June 1942	11 Nov 1942	1 Jan 1943
***SHIELDS**	DD 596	Puget Sound Navy Yard	10 Aug 1943	25 Sep 1944	8 Feb 1945
SIGOURNEY	DD 643	Bath Iron Works Corpn	7 Dec 1942	24 Apr 1943	29 June 1943
SIGSBEE	DD 502	Federal SB & DD Co	22 July 1942	7 Dec 1942	23 Jan 1943
STANLY	DD 478	Charleston Navy Yard	30 Dec 1941	2 May 1942	15 Oct 1942
STEPHEN POTTER	DD 538	Bethlehem Co, San Francisco	27 Oct 1942	28 Apr 1943	21 Oct 1943
STEVENS	DD 479	Charleston Navy Yard	30 Dec 1941	24 June 1942	1 Feb 1943
***STODDARD**	DD 566	Seattle-Tacoma SB Corpn	10 Mar 1943	19 Nov 1943	15 Apr 1944
TERRY	DD 513	Bath Iron Works Corpn	8 June 1942	22 Nov 1942	26 Jan 1943
THE SULLIVANS	DD 537	Bethlehem Co, San Francisco	10 Oct 1942	4 Apr 1943	30 Sep 1943
***TRATHEN**	DD 530	Bethlehem Co, San Francisco	17 Mar 1942	22 Oct 1942	28 May 1943
***TWINING**	DD 540	Bethlehem Co, San Francisco	20 Nov 1942	11 July 1943	1 Dec 1943
WATTS	DD 567	Seattle-Tacoma SB Corpn	26 Mar 1943	31 Dec 1943	29 Apr 1944
WICKES	DD 578	Consolidated Steel Corpn	15 Apr 1942	13 Sep 1942	16 June 1943
WREN	DD 568	Seattle-Tacoma SB Corpn	24 Apr 1943	29 Jan 1944	22 May 1944

MULLANY (DD 528) *1968, United States Navy*

"FLETCHER" CLASS *continued*

Fleet Escort Ships—*continued*

NOMENCLATURE. Three ships were renamed while building: DD 528 ex-*Beatty*, DD 537 ex-*Putnam*, DD 594 ex-*Mansfield*.

WAR LOSSES. *Chevalier* (DD 451), *Strong* (DD 467), *De Haven* (DD 469), *Pringle* (DD 477), *Spence* (DD 512), *Brownson* (DD 518), *Luce* (DD 522), *Abner Read* (DD 526), *Bush* (DD 529), *Hoel* (DD 533), *Johnston* (DD 557), *Longshaw* (DD 559), *Morrison* (DD 560), *William D. Porter* (DD 579), *Halligan* (DD 584), and *Twiggs* (DD 591).

PHOTOGRAPHS. The *Shields*, a Naval Reserve training ship, has five 5 inch gun mounts and one twin 40 mm mount (atop after deckhouse); the *Mullany*, on previous page, has lost one 5 inch mount but has three twin 3 inch mounts (two between funnels and one atop after deckhouse). Note absence of secondary gun battery and depth charge rack in the *Hazelwood's* helicopter-deck configuration.

HAZELWOOD (DD 531) *United States Navy*

TRANSFERS
Anthony, DD 515, **Charles Ausburn**, DD 570, **Claxton**, DD 571, **Dyson**, DD 572, **Ringgold**, DD 500, **Wadsworth**, DD 516, transferred to German Federal Republic in 1957-1960; **Capps**, DD 550, **David W. Taylor**, DD 551, transferred to Spain in 1957; **Aulick**, DD 569, **Charette**, DD 581, **Conner**, DD 508, transferred to Greece in 1959; **Converse**, DD 509, transferred to Spain in 1959; **Bennett**, DD 743, **Guest**, DD 472, transferred to Brazil in 1959; **Hall**, DD 583, transferred to Greece in 1960; **Hailey**, DD 556, transferred to Brazil in 1961; **Hale**, DD 642, transferred to Columbia in 1961; **Heerman**, DD 532, **Stembel**, DD 644, transferred to Argentina in 1961; **Isherwood**, DD 250, transferred to Peru in 1961; **Bradford**, DD 545, **Brown**, DD 546, transferred to Greece in 1962; **Erben**, DD 631, transferred to South Korea in 1963; **Yarnall**, DD 541, to Brazil in 1966; **Kimberly**, DD 521, to Taiwan China in 1967.

DISPOSALS
Ammen, DD 527, stricken in 1960 after being damaged in collision; **Howarth**, DD 529, stricken on 1 June 1961 and expended as target; **Fullham**, DD 474, stricken on 1 June 1962 and expended as target; **Killen**, DD 593, stricken on 1 Jan 1963 and expended as target; **Smalley**, DD 565, stricken on 1 Apr 1965; **Tingey**, DD 539, stricken on 1 Nov 1965; **Halford**, DD 480, **Harrison**, DD 573, **John D. Henley**, DD 553, **John Rodgers**, DD 574, **Paul Hamilton**, DD 590, **Wiley**, DD 597, **Young**, DD 580, stricken on 1 May 1968.

SHIELDS (DD 596) *1966, United States Navy*

28 DESTROYERS (DD): "GLEAVES-LIVERMORE" CLASS

Displacement, tons	1 700 standard; 2 580 full load
Length, feet (*metres*)	348·2 (*106·1*) oa (see *Design* notes)
Beam, feet (*metres*)	36 (*11·0*)
Draft, feet (*metres*)	18 (*5·5*)
Guns	3 or 4—5 inch (*127 mm*) 38 calibre dual-purpose 4—40 mm AA (twin) 4 to 7—20 mm AA (single)
ASW weapons	depth charges (removed in former DMS type)
Torpedo tubes	5—21 inch (*533 mm*) quintuple (removed in former DMS type)
Main engines	2 geared turbines; 50 000 shp; 2 shafts
Boilers	4 (Babcock & Wilcox)
Speed, knots	37·6
Complement	240 (designed wartime 276 in DD type; 272 in former DMS type)

Name	*No.*	*Builder*	*Laid down*	*Launched*	*Commissioned*
CARMICK	DD 493	Seattle-Tacoma SB Corpn	29 May 1941	8 Mar 1942	28 Dec 1942
COWIE	DD 632	Boston Navy Yard	18 Mar 1941	27 Sep 1941	1 June 1942
DAVISON	DD 618	Federal SB & DD Co	26 Feb 1942	19 July 1942	11 Sep 1942
DORAN	DD 634	Boston Navy Yard	14 June 1941	10 Dec 1941	4 Aug 1942
DOYLE	DD 494	Seattle-Tacoma SB Corpn	29 May 1941	17 Mar 1942	27 Jan 1943
EARLE	DD 635	Boston Navy Yard	14 June 1941	10 Dec 1941	1 Sep 1942
EDWARDS	DD 619	Federal SB & DD Co	26 Feb 1942	19 July 1942	18 Sep 1942
ENDICOTT	DD 495	Seattle-Tacoma SB Corpn	1 May 1941	6 Apr 1942	25 Feb 1943
ERICSSON	DD 440	Federal SB & DD Co	18 Mar 1940	23 Nov 1940	31 Mar 1941
FITCH	DD 462	Boston Navy Yard	6 Jan 1941	14 June 1941	3 Feb 1943
FRANKFORD	DD 497	Seattle-Tacoma SB Corpn	5 June 1941	18 May 1942	31 Mar 1943
GHERARDI	DD 637	Philadelphia Navy Yard	16 Sep 1941	12 Feb 1942	15 Sep 1942
GLEAVES	DD 423	Bath Iron Works Corpn	16 May 1938	9 Dec 1939	14 June 1940
GRAYSON	DD 435	Charleston Navy Yard	17 July 1939	7 Aug 1940	14 Feb 1941
HAMBLETON	DD 455	Federal SB & DD Co	16 Dec 1940	26 Sep 1941	22 Dec 1941
HERNDON	DD 638	Norfolk Navy Yard	26 Aug 1941	5 Feb 1942	20 Dec 1942
JEFFERS	DD 621	Federal SB & DD Co	25 Mar 1942	26 Aug 1942	4 Nov 1942
KEARNY	DD 432	Federal SB & DD Co	1 Mar 1939	9 Mar 1940	13 Sep 1940
McCOOK	DD 496	Seattle-Tacoma SB Corpn	1 May 1941	30 Apr 1942	15 Mar 1943
QUICK	DD 490	Seattle-Tacoma SB Corpn	3 Nov 1941	3 May 1942	3 July 1942
SATTERLEE	DD 626	Seattle-Tacoma SB Corpn	10 Sep 1941	17 July 1942	1 July 1943
STOCKTON	DD 646	Federal SB & DD Co	24 July 1942	11 Nov 1942	11 Jan 1943
SWANSON	DD 443	Charleston Navy Yard	15 Nov 1939	2 Nov 1940	29 May 1941
THOMPSON	DD 627	Seattle-Tacoma SB Corpn	22 Sep 1941	15 July 1942	10 July 1943
THORN	DD 647	Federal SB & DD Co	15 Nov 1942	28 Feb 1943	1 Apr 1943
TILLMAN	DD 641	Charleston Navy Yard	1 May 1941	20 Dec 1941	4 June 1942
(ex-**WILKES**)	DD 441	Boston Navy Yard	1 Nov 1939	31 May 1940	22 Apr 1941
WOOLSEY	DD 437	Bath Iron Works Corpn	9 Oct 1939	12 Feb 1940	7 May 1941

Sixty-six destroyers of this class were completed in 1940-1943. Twelve subsequently were converted to High Speed Minesweepers (DMS) in 1944 and another 12 in 1945. This class saw extensive service in World War II with 13 ships being lost to enemy action. The surviving "straight" destroyers (DD) were laid up in reserve in 1946-1948; some of the converted minesweepers remained in service into 1956. The 19 remaining DMS were reclassified DD in 1954-1955.
The *Hobson* (DMS 26, ex-DD 464) was sunk on 26 Apr 1952 in a night collision with the carrier *Wasp* (CVA 18).

CONVERSION. The 24 ships converted to minesweepers had their aftermost 5 inch gun, all torpedo tubes, and depth charge racks and projectors removed. Minesweeping equipment fitted aft. Of the remaining ships of this class, the following are former minesweepers: *Hambleton* (ex-DMS 20), *Fitch* (ex-DMS 25), *Quick* (ex-DMS 32), *Carmick* (ex-DMS 33), *Doyle* (ex-DMS 34), *Endicott* (ex-DMS 35), *McCook* (ex-DMS 36), *Davison* (ex-DMS 37), *Jeffers* (ex-DMS 27), *Thompson* (ex-DMS 38), *Cowie* (ex-DMS 39), *Doran* (ex-DMS 41), *Earle* (ex-DMS 42), and *Gherardi* (ex-DMS 30).

DESIGN. This class was built to plans prepared by Gibbs and Cox and differs slightly from the previous "Benson-Mayo" class. (These ships have rounded funnels). Within this class, the DD 423, 424, 429-444 are 348·3 feet overall and the other ships are 348·2 feet overall.

GUNNERY. The DD 423, 424, 429-444 were armed with five 5 inch guns when completed; subsequently reduced to four guns.

TORPEDOES. The first 18 ships were completed with ten torpedo tubes; subsequently reduced to five.

NOMENCLATURE. The name *Wilkes* was withdrawn from the DD 441 on 16 July 1968 for assignment to the surveying ship AGS 33. Charles Wilkes, an American naval officer, undertook extensive ocean explorations in 1838-1842 and is credited with the discovery of the Antarctic Continent.

WAR LOSSES. *Gwin* (DD 433), *Meredith* (DD 434), *Monssen* (DD 436), *Ingraham* (DD 444), *Bristol* (DD 453), *Emmons* (DD 457/DMS 22), *Corry* (DD 463), *Aaron Ward* (DD 483), *Duncan* (DD 485), *Glennon* (DD 620), *Maddox* (DD 622), *Beatty* (DD 640, *Turner* (DD 648).

TRANSFERS
Buchanan, DD 484, **McCalla**, DD 488, transferred to

Fleet Escort Ships—*continued*

"GLEAVES-LIVERMORE" CLASS
continued

Turkey in 1949; **Landsdowne**, DD 486, **Lardner**, DD 487, to Turkey in 1950; **Eberle**, DD 430, **Ludlow**, DD 438, transferred to Greece in 1951; **Nicholson**, DD 442, transferred to Italy in 1951; **Ellyson**, DMS 19/DD 454, **Macomb**, DMS 23/DD 458, transferred to Japan in May 1954; **Rodman**, DMS 21/DD 456, transferred to Taiwan China on 28 July 1955; **Plunkett**, DD 431, to Taiwan China on 16 Feb 1959.

DISPOSALS
Four heavily damaged ships were scrapped shortly after World War II: **Shubrick**, DD 639, **Forrest**, DMS 24/DD 461, **Harding**, DMS 28/DD 625, **Butler**, DMS 29/DD 636; **Livermore**, DD 429, stricken on 19 July 1956 and expended in tests during 1957-58; **Baldwin** DD 624, stricken on 1 June 1961 (she went aground while under tow, was salvaged, and scuttled on 5 June 1961); **Edison**, DD 439, stricken on 1 Apr 1966; **Knight**, DD 633, stricken on 1 Jan 1967, and expended as target; **Nelson**, DD 623, **Wells**, DD 628, stricken on 1 Mar 1968; **Bailey**, DD 492, **Charles F. Hughes**, DD 428, **Kalk**, DD 611, **Madison**, DD 425, stricken on 1 June 1968.

CARMICK (DD 493, ex-DMS 33) — *United States Navy*

GHERARDI (DD 637, ex-DMS 30) — *A. & J. Pavia*

18 DESTROYERS (DD): "BENSON-MAYO" CLASS

Displacement, tons	1 620 standard; 2 575 full load
Length, feet (*metres*)	347·7 (*105·9*) oa
Beam, feet (*metres*)	36 (*10·9*)
Draft, feet (*metres*)	18 (*5·5*)
Guns	4—5 inch (*127 mm*) 38 calibre dual-purpose 4—40 mm AA (twin) 7—20 mm AA (single)
ASW weapons	depth charges
Torpedo tubes	5 or 10—21 inch (*533 mm*) quintuple
Main engines	2 geared turbines (Bethlehem); 50 000 shp; 2 shafts
Boilers	4 (Babcock & Wilcox)
Speed, knots	37·6
Complement	230 (designed wartime 276)

Name	*No.*	*Builder*	*Laid down*	*Launched*	*Commissioned*
BANCROFT	DD 598	Bethlehem, Quincy	1 May 1941	31 Dec 1941	30 Apr 1943
BOYLE	DD 600	Bethlehem, Quincy	31 Dec 1941	15 June 1942	15 Aug 1942
CHAMPLIN	DD 601	Bethlehem, Quincy	31 Jan 1942	25 July 1942	12 Sep 1942
COGHLAN	DD 606	Bethlehem, San Francisco	28 Mar 1941	12 Feb 1942	10 July 1942
FARENHOLT	DD 491	Bethlehem, Staten Island	11 Dec 1940	19 Nov 1941	2 Apr 1942
FRAZIER	DD 607	Bethlehem, San Francisco	5 July 1941	17 Mar 1942	30 July 1942
GANSEVOORT	DD 608	Bethlehem, San Francisco	16 June 1941	11 Apr 1942	26 Aug 1942
GILLESPIE	DD 609	Bethlehem, San Francisco	16 June 1941	8 May 1942	18 Sep 1942
HOBBY	DD 610	Bethlehem, San Francisco	30 June 1941	4 June 1942	18 Nov 1942
LAUB	DD 613	Bethlehem, San Pedro	1 May 1941	28 Apr 1942	24 Oct 1942
McLANAHAN	DD 615	Bethlehem, San Pedro	29 May 1941	7 Sep 1942	19 Dec 1942
MACKENZIE	DD 614	Bethlehem, San Pedro	29 May 1941	27 June 1942	21 Nov 1942
MAYO	DD 422	Bethlehem, Quincy	16 May 1938	26 Mar 1940	18 Sep 1940
MEADE	DD 602	Bethlehem, Staten Island	25 Mar 1941	15 Feb 1942	22 June 1942
MURPHY	DD 603	Bethlehem, Staten Island	19 May 1941	29 Apr 1942	25 July 1942
NIELDS	DD 616	Bethlehem, Quincy	15 June 1942	1 Oct 1942	15 Jan 1943
ORDRONAUX	DD 617	Bethlehem, Quincy	25 July 1942	9 Nov 1942	13 Feb 1943
PARKER	DD 604	Bethlehem, Staten Island	9 June 1941	12 May 1942	31 Aug 1942

Thirty destroyers of this class were completed in 1940-1943. They saw extensive service in World War II, with three ships being sunk by enemy action. The survivors were laid up in reserve in 1946-1948.

CONVERSION. After World War II two of these ships were to have been converted to Corvettes (DDC) as prototypes for conversion of this and the "Gleaves-Livermore" classes. Conversion plans provided for removal of two boilers and installation of improved sonar. The ships would be employed as fast convoy escorts. Conversion rescinded.

DESIGN. All of this class were built to Bethlehem-prepared plans and have square funnels.

ENGINEERING. The principal innovation of this class was the alternate grouping of boiler and engine rooms, an arrangement reflected in their separate funnels and greatly increasing their capacity to survive serious damage.

GUNNERY. The first six ships of this class (DD 421, 422, 425-428) initially were armed with five 5 inch guns; subsequently reduced to four guns.

TORPEDOES. The first six ships of this class also were completed with ten tubes; later ships built with five tubes. This class introduced quintuple torpedo tube mounts to United States destroyers.

WAR LOSSES. *Lansdale* (DD 426), *Laffey* (DD 459), *Barton* (DD 599).

PHOTOGRAPH. The *Woolsey* of the "Gleaves-Livermore" class is shown underway four months after joining the Fleet. The contemporary classes described on this page were identical except for funnel configuration and other minor design details. The *Woolsey* has two quintuple banks of torpedo tubes; the destroyer-minesweepers shown above lost their torpedo tubes and aftermost ("Y") 5 inch gun mounts. The ships of these classes completed with five mounts had an open, forward-facing 5 inch mount between the after bank of torpedo tubes and No. 4 ("X") gun mount.

TRANSFERS
Woodworth, DD 460, transferred to Italy in 1951; **Benson**, DD 421, **Hilary P. Jones**, DD 427, transferred to Taiwan China in 1954.

DISPOSALS
Caldwell, DD 605, stricken on 1 May 1965; **Kendrick**, DD 612, stricken on 1 May 1966; **Bailey**, DD 492, **Charles F. Hughes**, DD 428, **Kalk**, DD 611, **Madison**, DD 425, stricken on 1 June 1968.

WOOLSEY (DD 437) — *1941, Charles W. Hatch*

Fleet Escort Ships—*Continued*

46 ESCORT SHIPS (DE): "KNOX" CLASS

Displacement, tons	3 011 standard; 4 100 full load
Length, feet (*metres*)	438 (*133·5*) oa
Beam, feet (*metres*)	46·75
Draft, feet (*metres*)	24·75
Guns	1—5 inch (*127 mm*) 54 calibre dual-purpose
ASW Weapons	1 ASROC 8-tube launcher 4 fixed torpedo launchers (Mk 32) facilities for small ASW helicopter
Missiles	Space reserved for Basic Point Defence Missile System (BPDMS) (see *Missile* notes)
Main engines	1 geared turbine (Westinghouse), 35 000 shp; 1 shaft
Boilers	2
Speed, knots	27+
Complement	220 (15 officers, 205 enlisted men)

Name	*No.*	*Builder*	*Laid down*	*Launched*	*Commission*
***KNOX**	DE 1052	Todd Shipyards (Seattle)	5 Oct 1965	19 Nov 1966	12 Apr 1969
ROARK	DE 1053	Todd Shipyards (Seattle)	2 Feb 1966	24 Apr 1967	Jan 1970
GRAY	DE 1054	Todd Shipyards (Seattle)	19 Nov 1966	3 Nov 1967	May 1970
***HEPBURN**	DE 1055	Todd Shipyards (San Pedro)	1 June 1966	25 Mar 1967	July 1969
***CONNOLE**	DE 1056	Avondale Shipyards	23 Mar 1967	20 July 1968	Aug 1969
RATHBURNE	DE 1057	Avondale Shipyards	8 Jan 1968	2 May 1969	mid-1970
MEYERKORD	DE 1058	Todd Shipyards (San Pedro)	1 Sep 1966	15 July 1967	Feb 1970
W. S. SIMS	DE 1059	Avondale Shipyards	10 Apr 1967	4 Jan 1969	Dec 1969
LANG	DE 1060	Todd Shipyards (San Pedro)	25 Mar 1967	17 Feb 1968	mid-1970
PATTERSON	DE 1061	Avondale Shipyards	12 Oct 1967	3 May 1969	Mar 1970
WHIPPLE	DE 1062	Todd Shipyards (Seattle)	24 Apr 1967	12 Apr 1968	late 1970
REASONER	DE 1063	Lockheed SB & Constn Co	6 Jan 1969	Mar 1970	mid-1971
LOCKWOOD	DE 1064	Todd Shipyards (Seattle)	3 Nov 1967	5 Sep 1964	early 1971
STEIN	DE 1065	Lockheed SB & Constn Co	Nov 1969	Aug 1970	late 1971
MARVIN SHIELDS	DE 1066	Todd Shipyards (Seattle)	12 Apr 1968	Nov 1969	mid-1971
FRANCIS HAMMOND	DE 1067	Todd Shipyards (San Pedro)	15 July 1967	11 May 1968	late 1970
VREELAND	DE 1068	Avondale Shipyards	20 Mar 1968	June 1969	mid-1970
	DE 1069	Lockheed SB & Constn Co	Apr 1970	late 1970	early 1972
DOWNES	DE 1070	Todd Shipyards (Seattle)	5 Sep 1968	Dec 1969	late 1971
BADGER	DE 1071	Todd Shipyards (Seattle)	17 Feb 1968	7 Dec 1968	early 1971
BLAKELY	DE 1072	Avondale Shipyards	3 June 1968	Oct 1969	July 1970
	DE 1073	Lockheed SB & Constn Co	July 1970	early 1971	mid-1972
HAROLD E. HOLT	DE 1074	Todd Shipyards (San Pedro)	11 May 1968	3 May 1969	June 1971
TRIPPE	DE 1075	Avondale Shipyards	29 July 1968	Dec 1969	late 1970
FANNING	DE 1076	Todd Shipyards (San Pedro)	7 Dec 1968	Oct 1969	late 1971
OUELLET	DE 1077	Avondale Shipyards	15 Jan 1969	Feb 1970	late 1970
JOSEPH HEWES	DE 1078	Avondale Shipyards	May 1969	Feb 1970	late 1970
BOWEN	DE 1079	Avondale Shipyards	July 1969	Mar 1970	early 1971
PAUL	DE 1080	Avondale Shipyatds	Sep 1969	May 1970	early 1971
	DE 1081	Avondale Shipyards	Nov 1969	July 1970	mid-1971
	DE 1082	Avondale Shipyards	Dec 1969	Aug 1970	mid-1971
	DE 1083	Avondale Shipyards	Feb 1970	late 1970	mid-1971
	DE 1084	Avondale Shipyards	Apr 1970	late 1970	late 1971
	DE 1085	Avondale Shipyards	May 1970	early 1971	late 1971
	DE 1086	Avondale Shipyards	July 1970	early 1971	early 1972
	DE 1087	Avondale Shipyards	Aug 1970	early 1971	early 1972
	DE 1088	Avondale Shipyards	Oct 1970	mid-1971	early 1972
	DE 1089	Avondale Shipyards	Dec 1970	mid-1971	mid-1972
	DE 1099-1092	Avondale Shipyards	1971	late 1971	1972
	DE 1093-1097	Avondale Shipyards	1972	1972	1973

The 46 "Knox" class escort ships comprise the largest group of destroyer-type warships built to the same design in the West since the end of World War II. These ships are almost identical in design to the previous "Garcia" and "Brooke" classes, but slightly larger. (See those class listings for basic design data). DE 1052-1061 (10 ships) were authorised in the Fiscal Year 1964 new construction programme, DE 1062-1077 (16 ships) in FY 1965, DE 1078-1087 (10 ships) in FY 1966, DE 1088-1097 (10 ships) in FY 1967, and DE 1098-1107 (10 ships) in FY 1968. However, construction of six ships (DE 1102-1107) was deferred in 1968 as US Navy emphasis shifted to the more-versatile and faster DX/DXG ships; three additional ships (DE 1099-1101) were deferred late in 1968 to finance cost overruns of FY 1968 nuclear-powered attack submarines and to comply with a Congressional mandate to reduce expenditures; the last ship of the FY 1968 programme (DE 1098) was deferred early in 1969. According to Secretary of Defence Melvin Laird, the DE 1098, intended as an experimental gas-turbine ship, would not be needed because of the decision to use gas-turbine propulsion in the DD 963-class (DX) destroyers.

ELECTRONICS. SQS-26CX bow-mounted sonar is installed and there are provisions for SQA-13 variable depth sonar (VDS). These ships are being fitted with the SSM-5 Test Evaluation and Monitoring System (TEAMS) which continuously checks shipboard radar and sonar systems. If TEAMS detects a malfunction an automatic search will be conducted throughout the subsystems until the fault is found and the defective component identified for repair or replacement. Up to 5 000 test points in 10 radar and sonar systems can be monitored by TEAMS on a 15-minute cycle with "real time" indication of whether the system is working, not working, or failing but still working. TEAMS can also test itself for malfunction and has a mean time to repair of 10 minutes.

ENGINEERING. The DE 1098 was to have had gas turbine propulsion plant.

HELICOPTERS. These ships were designed to operate drone ASW helicopters. It now appears likely the US Navy will adopt a manned Light Airborne ASW Vehicle (LAAV) for use in destroyer-type ships by the early 1970s.

MISSILES. Original planning provided for these ships to have the Sea Mauler, a short-range anti-aircraft missile adapted from a missile being developed by the US Army. However, technical problems forced the Army to abandon the Mauler, terminating the Sea Mauler programme. Weight and space are reserved for eventual installation of a Basic Point Defense Missile System to provide close-in defence against aircraft.

TORPEDOES. Improved ASROC-torpedo reloading capability as in some ships of previous "Garcia" class (note slanting face of bridge structure immediately behind ASROC "pepper box"). Four Mk 32 torpedo tubes are fixed in the amidships structure, two to a side angled out at 45 degrees. The arrangement provides improved loading capability over exposed triple Mk 32 launchers. Fixed Mk 25 torpedo tubes in stern are believed deleted.

STATUS. These ships are considerably behind schedule, partially because of shipyard labour strikes and delays in Navy acceptance. The Fiscal Year 1964 ships are taking $2\frac{1}{2}$ to 4 years to build; some FY 1965 ships were not to be laid down until 1970, more than four years after the FY 1964 ships.
These ships have been criticised by some authorities as being inferior to their foreign contemporaries. Critics note the delay in providing variable depth sonar and a helicopter capability, the minimal gun armament, and the use of conventional propulsion vice gas turbines or combination diesel-gas turbines.

NOMENCLATURE. Escort ships are generally named for US Navy, Marine Corps, and Coast Guard personnel. The *Harold E. Holt* honours the late Prime Minister Harold E. Holt of Australia, a firm supporter of American policy in Southeast Asia during the Vietnamese War. The lead ship remembers naval historian Dudley W. Knox (the DD 742 is named for Frank Knox who was Secretary of the Navy from 1940 to 1944).

KNOX (DE 1052) *1969, Courtesy Comdr. William A. Lamm, U.S.N.*

KNOX (DE 1052) *1969, Courtesy Comdr. William A. Lamm*

Fleet Escort Ships—*continued*

10 ESCORT SHIPS (DE)
6 GUIDED MISSILE ESCORT SHIPS (DEG)
"GARCIA" AND "BROOKE" CLASSES

Displacement, tons	
DE	2 620 standard; 3 400 full load
DEG	2 640 standard; 3 425 full load
Length, feet (*metres*)	414·5 (*126·3*) oa
Beam, feet (*metres*)	44·2 (*13·5*)
Draft, feet (*metres*)	24 (*7·3*)
Missiles DEG	1 single Tartar surface-to-air launcher
Guns DEG	1—5 in (*127 mm*) 38 calibre dual-purpose
DE	2—5 in (*127 mm*) 38 calibre dual-purpose
ASW Weapons	1 ASROC 8-tube launcher 2 triple torpedo launchers (Mk 32) 2 fixed torpedo tubes (stern) (Mk 25)
Main engines	1 geared turbine (Westinghouse); 35 000 shp; 1 shaft
Boilers	2 — 1 200 psi (*83·4 kg/cm²*) (Foster Wheeler)
Speed, knots	27
Complement DEG	241 (16 officers, 225 enlisted men)

Name	*No.*	*Builder*	*Laid down*	*Launched*	*Commissioned*
***GARCIA**	DE 1040	Bethlehem Steel (San Francisco)	16 Oct 1962	31 Oct 1963	21 Dec 1964
***BRADLEY**	DE 1041	Bethlehem Steel (San Francisco)	17 Jan 1963	26 Mar 1964	15 May 1965
***EDWARD McDONNELL**	DE 1043	Avondale Shipyards	1 Apr 1963	15 Feb 1964	15 Feb 1965
***BRUMBY**	DE 1044	Avondale Shipyards	1 Aug 1963	6 June 1964	5 Aug 1965
***DAVIDSON**	DE 1045	Avondale Shipyards	30 Sep 1963	2 Oct 1964	7 Dec 1965
***VOGE**	DE 1047	Defoe Shipbuilding Co	21 Nov 1963	4 Feb 1965	25 Nov 1966
***SAMPLE**	DE 1048	Lockheed SB & Construction Co	19 July 1963	28 Apr 1964	23 Mar 1968
***KOELSCH**	DE 1049	Defoe Shipbuilding Co	19 Feb 1964	8 June 1965	10 June 1967
***ALBERT DAVID**	DE 1050	Lockheed SB & Construction Co	29 Apr 1964	19 Dec 1964	19 Oct 1968
***O'CALLAHAN**	DE 1051	Defoe Shipbuilding Co	19 Feb 1964	20 Oct 1965	13 July 1968
***BROOKE**	DEG 1	Lockheed SB & Construction Co	10 Dec 1962	19 July 1963	12 Mar 1966
***RAMSEY**	DEG 2	Lockheed SB & Construction Co	4 Feb 1963	15 Oct 1963	3 June 1967
***SCHOFIELD**	DEG 3	Lockheed SB & Construction Co	15 Apr 1963	7 Dec 1963	20 Apr 1968
***TALBOT**	DEG 4	Bath Iron Works Corp	4 May 1964	6 Jan 1966	22 Apr 1967
***RICHARD L. PAGE**	DEG 5	Bath Iron Works Corp	4 Jan 1965	4 Apr 1966	5 Aug 1967
***JULIUS A. FURER**	DEG 6	Bath Iron Works Corp	12 July 1965	22 July 1966	11 Nov 1967

These ships are intended primarily for ASW with those of the "Brooke" class being fitted with an anti-aircraft missile system in lieu of a second 5 inch gun. They exceed many of the world's destroyers in size and ASW capability, but are designated escort ships by virtue of their single propeller shaft and limited speed. The DE 1040 and DE 1041 were authorised in the Fiscal Year 1961 new construction programme. DE 1043-1045 and DEG 1-3 in FY 1962, and DE 1047-1051 and DEG 4-6 in FY 1963. Plans for ten additional DEGs in FY 1964 and possibly three more DEGs in a later programme were dropped because of $11 000 000 additional cost of DEG over DE.

CLASSIFICATION. Hull numbers DE 1042 and DE 1046 were assigned to frigates built overseas for Portugal; DEG 7-11 are guided missile frigates being built in Spain with US assistance.

DESIGN. These ships are an enlargement of the previous "Bronstein" design. They have a flush deck, radically raked stem, stem anchor, and mast and stack combined into a "mack" structure. Anchors are mounted at stem and on portside, just forward of 5 inch gun. Fitted with gyrostabilising fins.

ELECTRONICS. SQS-26 bow-mounted sonar installed. All DEGs have improved SPS-52 air-search radar.

The *Voge* and *Koelsch* have been fitted with a specialised ASW Naval Tactical Data System (NTDS); they conducted operational evaluation of the system with the ASW carrier *Wasp*.

ENGINEERING. These ships have an advanced "pressure-fired steam generating plant" which generates 70 percent more power than previous steam plants of the same size and weight. Each boiler has an integrated supercharger and associated control system which provides automatic regulation of fuel, air, and water. The boilers can use JP-5 jet fuel or diesel oil which facilitates boiler maintenance and cleaning, and ballasting empty fuel tanks with sea water. Finally, fewer engineering personnel are required to operate the plant.
A small auxiliary boiler is provided to supply steam when in port. Special noise-reduction features are provided.

GUNNERY. Early designs for these ships included a 5 inch/54 calibre gun but existing 5 inch/38 calibre weapons were installed to hold down costs. The older gun is a reliable weapon but has less range and a slower rate of fire than the 5 inch/54, significant factors in the missile ships which have only one gun.

HELICOPTERS. The Drone Anti-Submarine Helicopter (DASH) programme was cut back before these ships were provided with helicopters. Reportedly, only the *Bradley* actually operated with DASH.

MISSILES. The six DEGs have a single Tartar Mk 22 launching system which weighs 92 395 pounds. Reportedly, the system has a rate of fire similar to the larger Mk 11 and Mk 13 systems installed in guided missile destroyers, but the DEG system has a considerably smaller magazine capacity.
The DEGs have a single Mk 74-2 missile fire control system whereas the larger DDGs have two such systems providing a considerably greater anti-air warfare capability. The *Bradley* was fitted with a Sea Sparrow Basic Point Defense Missile System (BPDMS) in 1967-1968; removed for installation in the carrier *Forrestal*. The BPDMS "pepperbox" was fitted between funnel and after 5 inch mount.

The *Voge* and later DEs and DEG 4-6 have automatic ASROC loading system (note angled base of bridge structure aft of ASROC "pepper box" in these ships).

TORPEDOES. Most of these ships were built with two Mk 25 torpedo tubes built into their tansom for launching wire-guided ASW torpedoes. However, they have been removed from the earlier ships and deleted in the later ships.

VOGE (DE 1047) — *1966, United States Navy*

BROOKE (DEG 1) — *1967, US Navy by PHC R. C. Veeder*

RAMSEY (DEG 2) — *1967, Lockheed SB & Construction Co*

Fleet Escort Ships—*continued*

1 ESCORT RESEARCH SHIP (AGDE): "GLOVER" TYPE

Displacement, tons	2 643 standard; 3 426 full load
Length, feet (*metres*)	414·5 (*126·3*) oa
Beam, feet (*metres*)	44·2 (*13·5*)
Draft, feet (*metres*)	14·5 (*4·3*)
Guns	1—5 in (*127 mm*) 38 calibre dual purpose
ASW Weapons	1 ASROC 8-tube launcher; 2 triple torpedo launchers (Mk 32)
Main engines	1 geared turbine (Westinghouse); 35 000 shp; 1 shaft
Boilers	2—1 200 psi (*83·4 kg/cm²*) (Foster Wheeler)
Speed, knots	27
Complement	225 (14 officers, 211 enlisted men)

Name	*No.*	*Builder*	*Laid down*	*Launched*	*Commissioned*
***GLOVER**	AGDE 1 (ex-AG 163)	Bath Iron Works	29 July 1963	17 Apr 1965	13 Nov 1965

The *Glover* was built to test an advanced hull design and propulsion system, much the same as the *Albacore* (AGSS 569) embodied advanced submarine design concepts. However, unlike the *Albacore*, the *Glover* has a full combat capability.
The ship was originally authorised in the Fiscal Year 1960 new construction programme, but was postponed and re-introduced in the FY 1961 programme. Estimated construction cost was $29 330 000.

ARMAMENT. Not fitted with Tartar missile system as stated in previous editions.

ACCOMMODATIONS. Provision for approximately 30 civilian scientists and technicians in addition to naval complement.

DESIGN. The *Glover* has a massive bow sonar dome integral with her hull and extending well forward underwater; another "pod" or "nacelle" aft supports counter-rotating propellers mounted on a single shaft. The "pods" at both ends of the ship reduce ship motion at high speeds and move propeller turbulence as far as possible from the bow sonar to increase sonar efficiency. Above the waterline the *Glover* is identical to the "Garcia" class escort ships.

ELECTRONICS. The *Glover* has bow-mounted SQS-26 sonar and variable depth sonar (VDS) housed in the bottom of the ship.

PHOTOGRAPH. Stern configuration differs from "Garcia" class escort ships.

GLOVER (ADGE 1) — *1968, United States Navy*

2 ESCORT SHIPS (DE): "BRONSTEIN" CLASS

Displacement, tons	2 360 standard; 2 650 full load
Length, feet (*metres*)	371·5 (*113·2*) oa
Beam, feet (*metres*)	40·5 (*12·3*)
Draft, feet (*metres*)	23 (*7·0*)
Guns	3—3 in (*76 mm*) 50 calibre anti-aircraft
ASW Weapons	1 ASROC 8-tube launcher; 2 triple torpedo launchers (Mk 32); 2 Drone Anti-Submarine Helicopters (DASH)
Main engines	1 geared turbine (De Laval); 20 000 shp; 1 shaft
Boilers	2 (Foster Wheeler)
Speed, knots	26
Complement	220

Name	*No.*	*Builder*	*Laid down*	*Launched*	*Commissioned*
***BRONSTEIN**	DE 1037	Avondale Shipyards	16 May 1961	31 Mar 1962	15 June 1963
***McCLOY**	DE 1038	Avondale Shipyards	15 Sep 1961	9 June 1962	21 Oct 1963

BRONSTEIN (DE 1037) — *United States Navy, Official*

These two ships may be considered the first of the "second generation" of post-World War II escort ships which are comparable in size and ASW capabilities to conventional destroyers. The *Bronstein* and *McCloy* have several features such as hull design, large sonar, and ASW weapons which subsequently were incorporated into the mass-produced "Garcia", "Brooke", and "Knox" classes.
Both ships were built under the Fiscal Year 1960 new construction programme.

DESIGN. These ships have a radically raked stem, stem anchor, and mast and stacks combined in a "mack" structure. Position of stem anchor and portside anchor (just forward of gun mount) necessitated by large bow sonar dome.

ELECTRONICS. SQS-26 bow-mounted sonar installed.

GUNNERY. A twin 3 inch closed mount is forward and a single 3 inch open mount aft.

PHOTOGRAPHS. Note location of helicopter deck forward of after gun mount; later DEs have helicopter deck aft of second gun or missile launcher.

McCLOY (DE 1038) — *1968, United States Navy by PH1 A. Clemens*

Fleet Escort Ships—*Continued*

4 ESCORT SHIPS (DE): "CLAUD JONES" CLASS

Displacement, tons	1 450 standard; 1 750 full load
Length, feet (*metres*)	310 (*95·0*) oa
Beam, feet (*metres*)	37 (*11·3*)
Draft, feet (*metres*)	18 (*5·5*)
Guns	1 or 2 —3in (*76 mm*) 50 cal
ASW Weapons	2 triple torpedo launchers (Mk 32)
Main engines	4 diesels (Fairbanks Morse), 9 200 shp; 1 shaft
Speed, knots	22
Complement	175 (15 officers, 160 enlisted men)

Name	*No.*	*Builder*	*Laid down*	*Launched*	*Commissioned*
***CLAUD JONES**	DE 1033	Avondale Marine Ways, Inc	1 June 1957	27 May 1958	10 Feb 1959
***JOHN R. PERRY**	DE 1034	Avondale Marine Ways, Inc	1 Oct 1957	29 July 1958	5 May 1959
***CHARLES BERRY**	DE 1035	Avondale Marine Ways, Inc	29 Oct 1958	17 Mar 1959	25 Nov 1959
***McMORRIS**	DE 1036	Avondale Marine Ways, Inc	5 Nov 1958	26 May 1959	4 Mar 1960

These diesel-powered escorts were built in an effort to develop an economical DE suitable for mass production; however, they cannot carry the sonar and weapons necessary to cope with modern submarines.
The *Claud Jones* and *John R. Perry* were authorised in the Fiscal Year 1956 shipbuilding programme and the *Charles Berry* and *McMorris* in the FY 1957 programme. The two later ships were ordered originally from the American Shipbuilding Co (Lorain, Ohio) but were completed by Avondale Marine Ways.

ARMAMENT: As built these ships each had two 3 inch guns (single closed mount forward and open mount aft), two ahead-firing hedgehog launchers, two torpedo tubes (Mk 32), and one depth charge rack. The *Charles Berry* and *McMorris* had their hedgehogs removed and were fitted with the Norwegian-developed Terne III ASW missile launcher from 1961 to 1964. Fixed torpedo tubes removed from all ships and triple torpedo launchers installed. After 3 inch gun and depth charges are being removed (see *Modernisation* notes).

DESIGN. These are the only diesel-powered destroyer-type ships built by the US Navy since World War II. They have aluminium superstructure, tripod mast forward and pole mast amidships, and two funnels.

MODERNISATION. These ships are being modernised with deckhouse being built up between forward gun and bridge, and after gun and depth charge racks being removed for installation of variable depth sonar (VDS); see photograph of *Charles Berry*.

CHARLES BERRY (DE 1035) *United States Navy*

13 ESCORT SHIPS (DE): "DEALEY" AND "COURTNEY" CLASSES

Displacement, tons	1 450 standard; 1 914 full load
Length, feet (*metres*)	314·5 (*95·9*) oa
Beam, feet (*metres*)	36·8 (*11·2*)
Draft, feet (*metres*)	13·6 (*4·2*)
Guns	2 or 4—3 in (*76 mm*) 50 calibre
ASW Weapons	1 Weapon Alfa rocket launcher (Mk 108); 2 triple torpedo launchers (Mk 32); 2 Drone Anti-Submarine Helicopters (DASH) in ships with 2 guns (see *Modernisation* notes)
Main engines	1 geared turbine (De Laval); 20 000 shp; 1 shaft
Boilers	2 (Foster Wheeler)
Speed, knots	25
Complement	149 (9 officers, 140 enlisted men) to 170 (11 officers, 159 enlisted men)

Name	*No.*	*Builder*	*Laid down*	*Launched*	*Commissioned*
***DEALEY**	DE 1006	Bath Iron Works Corpn	15 Dec 1952	8 Nov 1953	3 June 1954
***CROMWELL**	DE 10014	Bath Iron Works Corpn	3 Aug 1953	4 June 1954	24 Nov 1954
***HAMMERBERG**	DE 10015	Bath Iron Works Corpn	12 Nov 1953	20 Aug 1954	2 Mat 1955
***COURTNEY**	DE 1021	Defoe SB Co, Bay City, Mich	2 Sep 1954	2 Nov 1955	24 Sep 1956
***LESTER**	DE 1022	Defoe SB Co, Bay City, Mich	2 Sep 1954	5 Jan 1956	14 June 1957
***EVANS**	DE 1023	Puget Sound B & D Co	8 Apr 1955	14 Sep 1955	14 June 1957
***BRIDGET**	DE 1024	Puget Sound B & D Co	19 Sep 1955	25 Apr 1956	24 Oct 1957
***BAUER**	DE 1025	Bethlehem, San Francisco	1 Dec 1955	4 June 1957	21 Nov 1957
***HOOPER**	DE 1026	Bethlehem, San Francisco	4 Jan 1956	1 Aug 1957	18 Mar 1958
***JOHN WILLIS**	DE 1027	New York SB Corpn	5 July 1955	4 Feb 1956	21 Feb 1957
***VAN VOORHIS**	DE 1028	New York SB Corpn	29 Aug 1955	28 July 1956	22 Apr 1957
***HARTLEY**	DE 1029	New York SB Corpn	31 Oct 1955	24 Nov 1956	26 June 1957
***JOSEPH K. TAUSSIG**	DE 1030	New York SB Corpn	3 Jan 1956	3 Jan 1957	10 Sep 1957

The *Dealey* was the prototype for the first post-World War II escort ships built by the US Navy. The first three ships are known as the "Dealey" class and the ten others as the "Courtney" class. They were designed for fast convoy escort.
Dealey authorised in the Fiscal Year 1952 shipbuilding programme; DE 1014 and DE 1015 in FY 1953; DE 1021 and DE 1022 in FY 1954; DE 1023-1030 in FY 1955. The *Dealey* cost an estimated $15 000 000.
The *Evans, Bridget, Bauer*, and *Hooper* are operational Naval Reserve training ships.

ARMAMENT. As built each ship mounted four 3 inch guns (twin closed mount forward, twin open mount aft), one Weapon Able/Alfa rocket launcher, two torpedo tubes (Mk 32), and depth charge racks and projectors. The *Dealey* conducted tests with British "Squid" depth charge launchers (in place of Weapon Alfa). Fixed torpedo tubes have been replaced in all ships by two triple torpedo launchers, depth charge racks removed from most ships.

CLASSIFICATION. The hull numbers DE 1007-1013 were assigned to *Le Normand* class (Type E-52) frigates built in French shipyards with funds from the US Military Defence Assistance Programme (MDAP); DE 1016-1019 were *Le Corse* class (Type E-50) frigates built in French yards under MDAP; DE 1020 and 1031 were *Centauro* class frigates built in Italian yards under MDAP; DE 1032 was built in an Italian yard for Portugal (*Pero Escobar*). All officially transferred upon completion.

DESIGN. These ships differ radically from the "destroyer escorts" (DE) built by the US Navy during World War II. They have all-aluminium superstructures, lattice masts to support extensive electronic antennas, and are single-screw ships. Intended for mass production in wartime. Light displacement is 1 280 tons.

JOSEPH K. TAUSSIG (DE 1030) *1968, United States Navy*

MODERNISATION. All but the *Dealey* (12 ships) are being modernised with a helicopter hangar and landing platform being installed amidships and removal of after 3 inch gun mount.

PHOTOGRAPHS. Note helicopter hangar and platform in view of *Joseph K. Taussig*; a depth charge rack is retained aft. *Courtney*, on following page, retains open 5 inch twin mount aft. Both ships have Mk 32 torpedo launchers abaft funnel.

NOMENCLATURE. *Hooper* ex-*Gatch*, was renamed on 19 July 1956.

Fleet Escort Ships—*continued*

COURTNEY (DE 1021) — *1967, United States Navy*

45 ESCORT SHIPS (DE): "JOHN C. BUTLER" CLASS

Displacement, tons	1 350 standard; 2 100 full load
Length, feet (*metres*)	306 (*93·3*) oa
Beam, feet (*metres*)	36·6 (*11·3*)
Draft, feet (*metres*)	11 (*3·4*)
Guns	2—5 in (*127 mm*) 38 cal DP 2—40 mm AA
ASW Weapons	hedgehogs; depth charges
Main engines	2 geared turbines (General Electric or Westinghouse); 12 000 shp; 2 shafts
Boilers	2 (Babcock & Wilcox or Combustion Engineering)
Speed, knots	24
Complement	190

These ships were originally rated as Destroyer Escorts (DE). The *Tweedy* remains in service as an operational Naval Reserve training ship.

ARMAMENT. Designed armament for this class was two 5 inch guns, ten 40 mm guns (one quad, three twin), six 20 mm guns, and one bank of three 21 inch torpedo tubes. (With full armament the designed wartime complement was 15 officers and 207 enlisted men).

CONVERSIONS. The *Wagner* (DE 539) and *Vandivier* (DE 539) of this class were completed as radar picket ships and are listed separately. The *Tweedy* (listed above) and *Lewis* (DE 535; now stricken) were converted to special ASW configurations; the *Tweedy* is distinguished by enlarged bridge structure, removal of "gun tubs" amidships, installation of ahead-firing hedgehogs atop bridge, deletion of depth charge rack, and short second mast (see photograph on following page).

DESIGN. This class is officially the WGT design group, the WGT symbol indicating geared turbine drive.

LOSSES. The *Eversole* (DE 404), *Oberrender* (DE 344), *Samuel B. Roberts* (DD 413), and *Shelton* (DE 407) of this class were lost in World War II.

Name	*No.*	*Builder*	*Launched*	*Commissioned*
CHESTER T. O'BRIEN	DE 421	Brown SB Co, Houston	29 Feb 1944	3 July 1944
CONKLIN	DE 439	Federal SB & DD Co, Pt Newark	13 Feb 1944	21 Apr 1944
CORBESIER	DE 438	Federal SB & DD Co, Pt Newark	13 Feb 1944	31 Mar 1944
DENNIS	DE 405	Brown SB Co, Houston	4 Dec 1943	20 Mar 1944
DOYLE C. BARNES	DE 353	Consolidated Steel Corpn, Orange	4 Mar 1944	13 July 1944
DUFILHO	DE 423	Brown SB Co, Houston	9 Mar 1944	21 July 1944
EDMONDS	DE 406	Brown SB Co, Houston	17 Dec 1943	3 Apr 1944
EDWARD H. ALLEN	DE 531	Boston Naval Shipyard	17 Oct 1943	16 Dec 1943
EDWIN A. HOWARD	DE 346	Consolidated Steel Corpn, Orange	25 Jan 1944	25 May 1944
FRENCH	DE 367	Consolidated Steel Corpn, Orange	17 June 1944	9 Oct 1944
GENTRY	DE 349	Consolidated Steel Corpn, Orange	15 Feb 1944	14 June 1944
GEORGE E. DAVIS	DE 357	Consolidated Steel Corpn, Orange	8 Apr 1944	11 Aug 1944
GILLIGAN	DE 508	Federal SB & DD Co, Pt Newark	22 Feb 1944	12 May 1944
GOSS	DE 444	Federal SB & DD Co, Pt Newark	19 Mar 1944	26 Aug 1944
HANNA	DE 449	Federal SB & DD Co, Pt Newark	4 July 1944	27 Jan 1945
HOWARD F. CLARK	DE 533	Boston Naval Shipyard	8 Nov 1943	25 May 1944
JOHN C. BUTLER	DE 339	Consolidated Steel Corpn, Orange	11 Dec 1943	31 Mar 1944
JOHN L. WILLIAMSON	DE 370	Consolidated Steel Corpn, Orange	29 Aug 1944	31 Oct 1944
JOHNNIE HUTCHINS	DE 360	Consolidated Steel Corpn, Orange	2 May 1944	28 Aug 1944
JOSEPH E. CONNOLLY	DE 450	Federal SB & DD Co, Pt Newark	6 Aug 1944	28 Feb 1945
KENDALL C. CAMPBELL	DE 443	Federal SB & DD Co, Pt Newark	19 Mar 1944	31 July 1944
KENNETH M. WILLETT	DE 354	Consolidated Steel Corpn, Orange	7 May 1944	19 July 1944
KEY	DE 348	Consolidated Steel Corpn, Orange	12 Feb 1944	5 June 1944
LA PRADE	DE 409	Brown SB Co, Houston	31 Dec 1943	20 Apr 1944
LAWRENCE C. TAYLOR	DE 415	Brown SB Co, Houston	29 Jan 1944	13 May 1944
LE RAY WILSON	DE 414	Brown SB Co, Houston	28 Jan 1944	10 May 1944
LELAND E. THOMAS	DE 420	Brown SB Co, Houston	28 Feb 1944	19 June 1944
LLOYD E. ACREE	DE 356	Consolidated Steel Corpn, Orange	21 Mar 1944	1 Aug 1944
MACK	DE 358	Consolidated Steel Corpn, Orange	11 Apr 1944	16 Aug 1944
MELVIN R. NAWMAN	DE 416	Brown SB Co, Houston	7 Feb 1944	16 May 1944
O'FLAHERTY	DE 340	Consolidated Steel Corpn, Orange	14 Dec 1944	8 Apr 1944
OLIVER MITCHELL	DE 417	Brown SB Co, Houston	8 Feb 1944	14 June 1944
OSBERG	DE 538	Boston Naval Shipyard	7 Dec 1943	17 Dec 1945
PRATT	DE 363	Consolidated Steel Corpn, Orange	1 June 1944	18 Sep 1944
RAYMOND	DE 341	Consolidated Steel Corpn, Orange	8 Jan 1944	15 Apr 1944
RICHARD W. SUESENS	DE 342	Consolidated Steel Corpn, Orange	11 Jan 1944	26 Apr 1944
RIZZI	DE 537	Boston Naval Shipyard	7 Dec 1943	30 June 1944
ROBERT BRAZIER	DE 345	Consolidated Steel Corpn, Orange	22 Jan 1944	18 May 1944
ROBERT F. KELLER	DE 419	Brown SB Co, Houston	11 Feb 1944	17 June 1944
ROLF	DE 362	Consolidated Steel Corpn, Orange	23 May 1944	7 Sep 1944
ROMBACH	DE 364	Consolidated Steel Corpn, Orange	6 June 1944	20 Sep 1944
SILVERSTEIN	DE 534	Boston Naval Shipyard	8 Nov 1943	14 July 1944
STAFFORD	DE 411	Brown SB Co, Houston	11 Jan 1944	19 Apr 1944
TABBERER	DE 418	Brown SB Co, Houston	18 Feb 1944	23 May 1944
***TWEEDY**	DE 532	Boston Naval Shipyard	7 Oct 1943	12 Feb 1944
WILLIAM SEIEVERLING	DE 441	Federal SB & DD Co, Pt Newark	7 Mar 1944	1 June 1944

DISPOSALS AND TRANSFERS

The incomplete **Oswald A. Powers** (DE 542) and **Sheeham** (DE 541) were scrapped; **Woodson** (DE 359) stricken on 1 July 1965; **Douglas A. Munro** (DE 422) stricken on 1 Dec 1965 and expended as target; **Ulvert M. Moore** stricken on 1 Dec 1965 and expended as target; **Lewis** (DE 535) and **Naifeh** (DE 352) stricken on 1 Jan 1966 and expended as targets; **Heyliger** (DE 510), **Maurice J. Manuel** (DE 351), **Straus** (DE 408) stricken on 1 May 1966, **Cross** (DE 448) and **Hass** (DE 424) stricken on 1 July 1966; **Williams** (DE 372), **Cecil J. Doyle** (DE 368), and **Traw** (DE 350) stricken on 1 July 1967 and expended as targets; **Thaddeus Parker** (DE 369) stricken on 1 Sep 1967 and scrapped; **Jaccard** (DE 355) stricken on 1 Nov 1967 and expended as target; **Abercrombie** (DE 343) stricken in 1967 and scrapped; **Robert Brazier** (DE 345) and **Jesse Rutherford** (DE 347) stricken on 1 Jan 1968 and expended as targets. **Bivin** (DE 536), **Grady** (DE 445), **Jack Miller** (DE 410), **Presley** (DE 371), **Richard M. Rowell** (DE 403), **Richard S. Bull** (DE 402), **Walter C. Wann** (DE 412), stricken on 30 June 1968; **Albert T. Harris** (DE 447), **Alvin C. Cockrell** (DE 366), **Charles E. Brannon** (DE 446), **McGinty** (DE 365), **Walton** (DE 361), stricken on 23 Sep 1968. **McCoy** (DE 440) transferred to Portugal on 1 Nov 1968; **Formoe** (DE 509) transferred to Portugal on 1 Oct 1968.

ROBERT F. KELLER (DE 419) — *1962, United States Navy*

Fleet Escort Ships—*Continued*

TWEEDY (DE 532) *US Navy*

ALVIN C. COCKRELL (DE 366) (now stricken) *US Navy*

2 RADAR PICKET ESCORT SHIPS (DER): CONVERTED "JOHN C. BUTLER" CLASS

Name	No.	Builder	Laid down	Launched	Commissioned
VANDIVIER	DER 540	Boston Naval Shipyard	8 Nov 1943	27 Dec 1943	1 Dec 1955
WAGNER	DER 539	Boston Naval Shipyard	8 Nov 1943	27 Dec 1943	31 Dec 1955

Displacement, tons	1 745 standard; 2 100 full load
Length, feet (*metres*)	306 (*93·3*) oa
Beam, feet (*metres*)	36·6 (*11·2*)
Draft, feet (*metres*)	11 (*3·4*)
Guns	2—5 in (*127 mm*) 38 cal DP
ASW Weapons	1 trainable hedgehog; depth charges
Main engines	2 geared turbines (Westinghouse) 12 000 shp; 2 shafts
Boilers	2 (Babcock & Wilcox)
Speed, knots	24
Complement	187

These two ships were begun as standard Destroyer Escorts (DE); construction suspended in 1946. Work resumed in 1954 and they were completed as Radar Picket Escort Ships (DER) at the Boston Naval Shipyard. Light displacement 1 260 tons. Both ships are in reserve.

ENGINEERING. These are the US Navy's only steam-driven radar picket escort ships; all others have diesel propulsion.

PHOTOGRAPH. Note TACAN navigation "bee-hive" antenna on second mast and SPS-8 height-finding radar antenna atop after deckhouse.

VANDIVIER (DER 540) *United States Navy*

10 ESCORT SHIPS (DE): "RUDDEROW" CLASS

Name	No.	Builder	Launched	Commissioned
***COATES**	DE 685	Bethlehem, Quincy	12 Dec 1943	24 Jan 1944
HODGES	DE 231	Charleston Navy Yard	9 Dec 1943	27 May 1944
JOBB	DE 707	Defoe SB & Co, Bay City	4 Mar 1944	4 July 1944
LESLIE L. B. KNOX	DE 580	Bethlehem-Hingham	8 Jan 1944	22 Mar 1944
LOUGH	DE 586	Bethlehem-Hingham	22 Jan 1944	2 May 1944
McNULTY	DE 581	Bethlehem-Hingham	8 Jan 1944	31 Mar 1944
***PARLE**	DE 708	Defoe SB & Co, Bay City	25 Mar 1944	29 July 1944
RUDDEROW	DE 224	Philadelphia Navy Yard	14 Oct 1943	15 May 1944
THOMAS F. NICKEL	DE 587	Bethlehem-Hingham	22 Jan 1944	9 June 1944
TINSMAN	DE 589	Bethlehem-Hingham	29 Jan 1944	26 June 1944

Displacement, tons	1 450 standard; 2 230 full load
Length, feet (*metres*)	306 (93·3) oa
Beam, feet (*metres*)	37 (*11·3*)
Draft, feet (*metres*)	14 (*4·3*)
Guns	2—5 in (*127 mm*) 38 cal DP; 4—40 mm AA (10 in *De Long*)
ASW Weapons	hedgehogs; depth charges
Main engines	turbo-electric drive (General Electric geared turbines) 12 000 shp; 2 shafts
Boilers	2 (Foster Wheeler in DE 580-589; Babcock & Wilcox in DE 224; Combustion Engineering in others)
Speed, knots	24
Complement	180

These ships were originally rated as Destroyer Escorts (DE). Sixty-two ships of this type were built; most converted to High Speed Transports (APD). Those ships remaining in service are operational Naval Reserve training ships (indicated by asterisk).

ARMAMENT. Designed armament for this class was two 5 inch guns, ten 40 mm guns (one quad, three twin), six 20 mm guns, and one bank of three 21 inch torpedo tubes. (With full armament the designed wartime complement was 15 officers and 206 enlisted men).

CONVERSIONS. The following ships of this class were converted to high speed transports (see Amphibious Warfare ships): DE 226-229, 232-237, 590-606, 687-692, and 710-722.

DESIGN. This class is similar to the "Buckley" class of escort ships, the principal difference being the main battery of two 5 inch guns in this class in place of three 3 inch guns in the "Buckley" class ships. The "John C. Butler" class is officially the TEV design group, the TEV symbol indicating turbine-electric drive with 5 inch guns.

DE LONG *United States Navy, Official*

DISPOSALS AND TRANSFERS

Daniel A. Joy (DE 585) stricken on 15 May 1965; **George A. Johnson** (DE 583) stricken on 1 Nov 1965; **Peiffer** (DE 588) stricken on 1 Dec 1966 and expended as target in May 1967; **Holt** (DE 706) transferred to South Korea in 1963; **Riley** (DE 579), transferred to Taiwan China in 1968; **Charles J. Kimmel** (DE 584), **Eugene E. Elmore** (DE 686), **Metivier** (DE 582), **Day** (DE 225), stricken on 30 June 1968 (last sunk as target) **De Long** (DE 684) stricken on 8 Aug 1969.

Fleet Escort Ships—*continued*

16 ESCORT SHIPS (DE): "BOSTWICK" CLASS

Displacement, tons	1 240 standard; 1 900 full load
Length, feet (*metres*)	306 (*93·3*) oa
Beam, feet (*metres*)	36·6 (*11·2*)
Draft, feet (*metres*)	14 (*4·3*)
Guns	3—3 in (*76 mm*) 50 cal AA 2—40 mm AA
ASW Weapons	hedgehogs; depth charges
Main engines	Diesel-electric (4 General Motors diesels); 6 000 shp; 2 shafts
Speed, knots	21
Complement	150

These ships were originally rated as Destroyer Escorts (DE). Fifty ships of this type have been transferred to Allied navies (see below).

ARMAMENT. Designed armament for this class was three 3 inch guns, six 40 mm guns (three twin), several 20 mm guns, and a bank of three 21 inch torpedo tubes. Torpedo tubes removed and light AA guns reduced. (With full armament the designed wartime complement was 15 officers and 201 enlisted men).

DESIGN. This class is officially the DET design group, the DET symbol indicating diesel-electric tandem motor drive.

TRANSFERS. Fourteen ships of this class have been transferred to France, eight to Brazil, six to the Netherlands, four to Nationalist China (Taiwan), four to Greece, three to Italy, three to Peru, two to South Korea, two to Japan and the Philippines and one each to Uruguay and Thailand.

DISPOSALS
Carroll (DE 171) and **Micka** (DE 176) were stricken in 1965; **Neal A. Scott** (DE 769) stricken on 1 June 1968; **Tills** (DE 748), **Roberts** (DE 749), stricken on 23 Sep 1968.

Name	*No*	*Builder*	*Launched*	*Commissioned*
ACREE	DE 167	Federal SB & DD Co, Pt Newark	9 May 1943	19 July 1943
COFFMAN	DE 191	Federal SB & DD Co, Pt Newark	28 Nov 1943	27 Dec 1943
COONER	DE 172	Federal SB & DD Co, Pt Newark	25 July 1943	21 Aug 1943
EARL K. OLSEN	DE 765	Tampa SB Co	13 Feb 1944	10 Apr 1944
HILBERT	DE 742	Western Pipe & Steel Co	18 July 1943	4 Feb 1944
KYNE	DE 744	Western Pipe & Steel Co	15 Aug 1943	4 Apr 1944
LAMONS	DE 743	Western Pipe & Steel Co	1 Aug 1943	29 Feb 1944
LEVY	DE 162	Federal SB & DD Co, Pt Newark	28 Mar 1943	13 May 1943
McCLELLAND	DE 750	Western Pipe & Steel Co	28 Nov 1944	19 Sep 1944
McDONNELL	DE 153	Federal SB & DD Co, Pt Newark	28 Mar 1943	28 May 1943
OSTERHOUS	DE 164	Federal SB & DD Co, Pt Newark	18 Apr 1943	12 June 1943
OSWALD	DE 767	Tampa SB Co	25 Apr 1944	12 June 1944
PARKS	DE 165	Federal SB & DD Co, Pt Newark	18 Apr 1943	22 June 1944
SNYDER	DE 745	Western Pipe & Steel Co	29 Aug 1943	5 May 1944
STRAUB	DE 181	Federal SB & DD Co, Pt Newark	18 Sep 1943	25 Oct 1943
TRUMPETER	DE 180	Federal SB & DD Co, Pt Newark	18 Sep 1943	25 Oct 1943

ROBERTS (DE 749) (now stricken) *1963, United States Navy*

27 ESCORT SHIPS (DE): "BUCKLEY" CLASS

Displacement, tons	1 400 standard; 2 170 full load
Length, feet (*metres*)	306 (*93·3*) oa
Beam, feet (*metres*)	37 (*11·3*)
Draft, feet (*metres*)	14 (*4·3*)
Guns varies	11 ships have 2—5 in (*127 mm*) 38 cal DP; others have 2 or 3—3 in (*76 mm*) 50 cal AA up to 8—40 mm AA per ship (removed entirely from some ships)
ASW Weapons	hedgehogs; depth chargers
Main engines	Turbo-electric drive (General Electric turbines); 12 000 shp; 2 shafts
Boilers	2 (Babcock & Wilcox, Combustion Engineering or Foster Wheeler)
Speed, knots	23·5
Complement	180 (185 in ex-DER)

These ships were originally rated as Destroyer Escorts (DE). Forty-six ships of this type were transferred to the Royal Navy in 1944 under the Lend-Lease where they served as frigates; six of these ships were lost and the remainder were returned to the United States and scrapped.

Only the *J. Douglas Blackwood* remains in service, employed as an operational Naval Reserve Training Ship.

ARMAMENT. Designed armament for this class was three 3 inch guns, six 40 mm guns (three twin), several 20 mm guns, and one bank of three 21 inch torpedo tubes. However, 20 ships were fitted with a 5 inch main battery in lieu of 3 inch guns. Torpedo tubes removed and 40 mm and 20 mm weapons reduced. (With full armament the designed wartime complement was 15 officers and 198 enlisted men).

CONVERSIONS. Fifty ships of this type were convertec to high speed transports (see Amphibious Warfare ships). The *Cronin, Frybarger,* and *Raby* were modified after World War II to direct boat waves during amphibious landings and were designated amphibious control vessels (DEC); all three were mothballed in 1953-1954 and reclassified DE on 27 Dec 1957.

Seven ships of this type were converted to rader picket ships in 1949-1950; they reverted to DE status in Oct 1954 and were mothballed as more efficient radar picket escorts became available. Only two former DERs remain, the *Alexander J. Luke* and *Robert I. Paine*. (See 1968-1969 and earlier editions for photographs showing DER configuration).

DESIGN. This class is officially the TE design group, the TE symbol indicating turbine-electric drive with 3 inch guns.

ENGINEERING. The *Marsh, Wiseman,* and *Whitehurst* have been modified to provide electrical power to shore activities and each has two large reels for power cables amidships. (See photograph of *Marsh* on following page).

EXPERIMENTAL. The *Vammen* was modified for ASW operations; the *Maloy* was employed as an experimental ship (EDE) until decommissioned in 1965 as were the *Francis M. Robinson* and *Jack W. Wilke* before they were decommissioned in 1960.

Name	*No.*	*Builder*	*Launched*	*Commissioned*
ALEXANDER J. LUKE (ex-DER)	577	Bethlehem-Hingham	28 Dec 1943	19 Feb 1944
COOLBAUGH	217	Philadelphia Navy Yard	29 May 1943	15 Oct 1943
CRONIN	704	Defoe Co, Bay City, Mich	5 Jan 1944	5 May 1944
DAMON M. CUMMINGS	643	Bethleham, San Francisco	18 Apr 1944	29 June 1944
EICHENBERGER	202	Charleston Navy Yard	22 July 1943	17 Nov 1943
FIEBERLING	640	Bethlehem, San Francisco	2 Mar 1944	11 Apr 1944
FRANCIS M. ROBINSON	220	Philadelphia Navy Yard	29 May 1943	15 Jan 1944
FRYBARGER	705	Defoe Co, Bay City, Mich	25 Jan 1944	18 May 1944
GENDREAU	639	Bethlehem, San Francisco	12 Dec 1943	17 Mar 1944
GEORGE	697	Defoe Co, Bay City, Mich	16 Feb 1943	20 Nov 1943
GILLETTE	681	Bethlehem, Quincy	25 Sep 1943	27 Oct 1943
GUNASON	795	Consolidated Steel Corpn, Orange	17 Oct 1943	1 Feb 1944
HENRY R. KENYON	683	Bethlehem, Quincy	30 Oct 1943	30 Nov 1943
HOLTON	703	Defoe Co, Bay City, Mich	15 Dec 1943	1 May 1944
JACK W. WILKE	800	Consolidated Steel Corpn, Orange	18 Dec 1943	7 Mar 1944
***J. DOUGLAS BLACKWOOD**	219	Philadelphia Navy Yard	29 May 1943	15 Dec 1943
MAJOR	796	Consolidated Steel Corpn, Orange	23 Oct 1943	12 Feb 1944
MARSH	699	Defoe Co, Bay City, Mich	29 Jan 1943	12 Jan 1944
OSMUS	701	Defoe Co, Bay City, Mich	4 Nov 1943	23 Feb 1944
OTTER	210	Charleston Navy Yard	23 Oct 1943	21 Feb 1944
PAUL G. BAKER	642	Bethlehem, San Francisco	12 Mar 1944	25 May 1944
ROBERT I. PAINE (ex-DER)	578	Bethlehem-Hingham	30 Dec 1943	28 Feb 1944
SPANGLER	696	Defoe Co, Bay City, Mich	15 July 1943	31 Oct 1943
VAMMEN	644	Bethlehem, San Francisco	21 May 1944	27 July 1944
VARIAN	798	Consolidated Steel Corpn, Orange	6 Nov 1943	29 Feb 1944
WILLIAM C. COLE	641	Bethlehem, San Francisco	28 Dec 1943	12 May 1944
WISEMAN	667	Dravo Corpn, Pittsburgh	6 Nov 1943	4 Apr 1944

DARBY (DE 218) (5 inch guns; now stricken) *1962, United States Navy*

LOSSES. The *Fechteler* (DE 157) and *Underhill* (DE 682) of this class were lost during World War II. The *Solar* (DE 221) was destroyed by internal explosion on 30 Apr 1946.

DISPOSALS
Ahrens (DE 575), **Borum** (DE 790), **Durik** (DE 666), **Foreman** (DE 633), **Foss** (DE 59), **Fowler** (DE 222), **Harmon** (DE 678), **Maloy** (DE 791), **Scott** (DE 214), and **Scroggins** (DE 799), stricken in 1965; **Jenks** (DE 665), **Currier** (DE 700, and **Willmarth** (DE 638), stricken in 1966; **Earl V. Johnson** (DE 702), **Greenwood** (DE 679, **Lovelace** (DE 198), **Neundorf** (DE 200), stricken in 1967; **Fogg** (DE/DER 57), **Spangenburg** (DE/DER 223), **William T. Powell** (DE/DER 213), stricken in 1965; **Buckley** (DE/DER 51), **Raby** (DE698), stricken on 1 June 1968; **James E. Craig** (DE 201), **Thomason** (DE 203), **Weeden** (DE 797), **Reuben James** (DE/DER 153), stricken on 30 June 1968; **Manning** (DE 199), stricken on 30 July 1968; **Darby** (DE 218), **Loeser** (DE 680), stricken on 23 Sep 1968.
Whitehurst (DE 634) stricken on 12 July, 1969.

Fleet Escort Ships—*continued*

MARSH (DE 699) (Power transmission type) *United States Navy*

VAMMEN (DE 644) (ASW modification) *United States Navy*

38 ESCORT SHIPS (DE): "EDSALL" CLASS

Displacement, tons	1 200 standard; 1 850 full load
Length, feet (*metres*)	306 (*93·3*) oa
Beam, feet (*metres*)	36·6 (*11·3*)
Draft, feet (*metres*)	11 (*3·4*)
Guns	3—3 in (*76 mm*) 50 cal AA up to 8—40 mm AA (removed entirely from some ships)
ASW Weapons	hedgehogs; depth charges
Main engines	4 diesels (Fairbanks Morse); 6 000 shp; 2 shafts
Speed, knots	21
Complement	149

These ships were originally rated as Destroyer Escorts. Thirty-six ships of this type have been converted to radar picket ships (DER) and are listed separately.
The *Richey* served in the US Coast Guard as WDE 485 from 1952 to 1954.
None of these ships are in commission; all in reserve.

ARMAMENT. Designed armament for this class was three 3 inch guns, eight 40 mm guns (one quad, two twin), several 20 mm guns, and a bank of three 21 inch torpedo tubes. Rearmament with two 5 inch guns in place of the 3 inch battery was planned but not carried out. Torpedo tubes removed after World War II and anti-aircraft guns reduced in some ships. (With full armament the designed wartime complement was 15 officers and 201 enlisted men).

CONVERSION. The *Peterson* was modified to a special ASW configuration in 1951-1952; two trainable hedgehogs fitted in the "B" position forward of the bridge, additional sonar installed, and a short pole mainmast fitted; all light AA guns were removed. She was decommissioned in 1965.

DESIGN. This class is officially the FMR design group, the FMR symbol indicating Fairbanks Morse diesel reverse gear drive.

ENGINEERING. The *Mills* (DE 383) was to have been fitted with two British RM 60 gas turbines in place of her diesel engines. The machinery was to reduce plant weight by approximately 15 per cent while providing 67 per cent more power. The conversion was proposed in the Fiscal Year 1955 programme, but the project was abandoned and the *Mills* became a radar picket (DER).

EXPERIMENTAL. The *Brough* (EDE 146), now stricken, and *Huse* (EDE 145) were used for experimental work.

LOSSES. The *Fiske* (DE 143), *Frederick C. Davis* (DE 136), *Holder* (DE 401), and *Leopold* (DE 319) were lost during World War II.

DISPOSALS
Flaherty (DE 135), **Frost** (DE 144), and **Brough** (DE 148) stricken in 1965; **Marten H. Ray** (DE 338) and **Robert E. Peary** (DE 132) stricken in 1966; **J. Richard Ward** (DE 243) stricken in 1967. **Richey** (DE 385) stricken on 30 June 1968 and expended as target; **Howard D. Crow** (DE 252), **Snowden** (DE 246), stricken on 23 Sep 1968.

Name	*No.*	*Builders*	*Launched*	*Commissioned*
CHATELAIN	DE 149	Consolidated Steel Corpn	21 Aug 1943	22 Sep 1943
COCKRILL	DE 398	Brown SB Co, Houston	29 Oct 1943	24 Dec 1943
DALE W. PETERSEN	DE 337	Consolidated Steel Corpn	22 Dec 1943	17 Feb 1944
DANIEL	DE 335	Consolidated Steel Corpn	16 Nov 1943	24 Jan 1944
DOUGLAS L. HOWARD	DE 138	Consolidated Steel Corpn	25 Jan 1943	29 July 1943
EDSALL	DE 129	Consolidated Steel Corpn	1 Nov 1942	10 Apr 1943
FARQUHAR	DE 139	Consolidated Steel Corpn	13 Feb 1943	5 Aug 1943
HAMMANN (ex-*Langley*)	DE 131	Consolidated Steel Corpn	13 Dec 1942	17 May 1943
HERBERT C. JONES	DE 137	Consolidated Steel Corpn	19 Jan 1943	21 July 1943
HILL	DE 141	Consolidated Steel Corpn	28 Feb 1943	16 Aug 1943
HURST	DE 250	Brown SB Co, Houston	14 Apr 1943	30 Aug 1943
HUSE	DE 145	Consolidated Steel Corpn	23 Mar 1943	30 Aug 1943
INCH	DE 146	Consolidated Steel Corpn	4 Apr 1943	8 Sep 1943
JACOB JONES	DE 130	Consolidated Steel Corpn	29 Nov 1942	29 Apr 1943
JANSSEN	DE 396	Brown SB Co, Houston	10 Oct 1943	18 Dec 1943
J. R. Y. BLAKELEY	DE 140	Consolidated Steel Corpn	7 Mar 1943	16 Aug 1943
KEITH	DE 241	Brown SB Co, Houston	21 Dec 1942	19 July 1943
MARCHAND	DE 249	Brown SB Co, Houston	20 Mar 1943	8 Sep 1943
MENGES	DE 320	Consolidated Steel Corpn	15 June 1943	26 Oct 1943
MERRILL	DE 392	Brown SB Co, Houston	29 Aug 1943	27 Nov 1943
MOORE	DE 240	Brown SB Co, Houston	21 Dec 1942	1 July 1943
MOSLEY	DE 321	Consolidated Steel Corpn	26 June 1943	30 Oct 1943
NEUNZER	DE 150	Consolidated Steel Corpn	27 Apr 1943	27 Sep 1943
O'REILLY	DE 330	Consolidated Steel Corpn	2 Sep 1943	28 Dec 1943
PETERSON	DE 152	Consolidated Steel Corpn	15 May 1943	29 Sep 1943
PETTIT	DE 253	Brown SB Co, Houston	28 Apr 1943	23 Sep 1943
POOLE	DE 151	Consolidated Steel Corpn	8 May 1943	29 Sep 1943
POPE	DE 134	Consolidated Steel Corpn	12 Jan 1943	25 June 1943
PRIDE	DE 323	Consolidated Steel Corpn	3 July 1943	13 Nov 1943
RICKETTS	DE 254	Brown SB Co, Houston	10 May 1943	5 Oct 1943
SLOAT	DE 245	Brown SB Co, Houston	21 Jan 1943	16 Aug 1943
STANTON	DE 247	Brown SB Co, Houston	28 Feb 1943	7 Aug 1943
STEWART	DE 238	Brown SB Co, Houston	22 Nov 1942	31 May 1943
STOCKDALE	DE 399	Brown SB Co, Houston	30 Oct 1943	31 Dec 1943
SWASEY	DE 248	Brown SB Co, Houston	18 Mar 1943	31 Aug 1943
SWENNING	DE 394	Brown SB Co, Houston	13 Sep 1943	1 Dec 1943
TOMICH	DE 242	Brown SB Co, Houston	28 Dec 1942	27 July 1943
WILLIS	DE 395	Brown SB Co, Houston	14 Sep 1943	10 Dec 1943

HUSE (DE 145) *Skyphotos*

Fleet Escort Ships—*continued*

24 RADAR PICKET ESCORT SHIPS (DER): CONVERTED "EDSALL" CLASS

Displacement, tons	1 590 standard; 1 850 full load
Length, feet (*metres*)	306 (*93·3*) oa
Beam, feet (*metres*)	36·6 (*11·1*)
Draft, feet (*metres*)	14 (*4·3*)
Guns	2—3 in (*76 mm*) 50 cal AA
ASW Weapons	2 triple torpedo launchers (Mk 32) in active ships; 1 trainable hedgehog; depth charges
Main engines	4 diesels (Fairbanks Morse), 6 000 shp; 2 shafts
Speed, knots	21
Complement	169 (19 officers, 150 enlisted men)

Name	*No.*	*Builder*	*Launched*	*Commissioned*
BLAIR	DER 147	Consolidated Steel Corpn	6 Apr 1943	13 Sep 1943
***CALCATERRA**	DER 390	Brown SB Co, Houston	16 Aug 1943	17 Nov 1943
***CAMP**	DER 251	Brown SB Co, Houston	16 Apr 1943	16 Sep 1943
CHAMBERS	DER 391	Brown SB Co, Houston	17 Aug 1943	22 Nov 1943
DURANT	DER 389	Brown SB Co, Houston	3 Aug 1943	16 Nov 1943
FALGOUT	DER 324	Consolidated Steel Corpn	24 July 1943	15 Nov 1943
***FINCH**	DER 328	Consolidated Steel Corpn	28 Aug 1943	13 Dec 1943
***FORSTER**	DER 334	Consolidated Steel Corpn	13 Nov 1943	25 Jan 1944
***HISSEM**	DER 400	Brown SB Co, Houston	26 Dec 1943	13 Jan 1944
JOYCE	DER 317	Consolidated Steel Corpn	26 May 1943	30 Sep 1943
KIRKPATRICK	DER 318	Consolidated Steel Corpn	5 June 1943	23 Oct 1943
***KRETCHMER**	DER 329	Consolidated Steel Corpn	31 Aug 1943	13 Dec 1943
LANSING	DER 388	Brown SB Co, Houston	3 Aug 1943	10 Nov 1943
***MILLS**	DER 383	Brown SB Co, Houston	26 May 1943	12 Oct 1943
OTTERSTETTER	DER 244	Brown SB Co, Houston	19 Jan 1943	6 Aug 1943
PRICE	DER 332	Consolidated Steel Corpn	30 Oct 1943	12 Jan 1944
RAMSDEN	DER 382	Brown SB Co, Houston	24 May 1943	19 Oct 1943
RHODES	DER 384	Brown SB Co, Houston	29 June 1943	25 Oct 1943
ROY O. HALE	DER 336	Consolidated Steel Corpn	20 Nov 1943	3 Feb 1944
***SAVAGE**	DER 386	Brown SB Co, Houston	15 July 1943	29 Oct 1943
STRICKLAND	DER 333	Consolidated Steel Corpn	2 Nov 1943	10 Jan 1944
STURTEVANT	DER 239	Brown SB Co, Houston	3 Dec 1942	16 June 1943
***THOMAS J. GARY**	DER 326	Consolidated Steel Corpn	21 Aug 1943	27 Nov 1943
VANCE	DER 387	Brown SB Co, Houston	16 July 1943	1 Nov 1943

Thirty-six ships of this type were converted to radar picket ships between 1951 and 1958; redesignated DER (See *Conversion* notes). Eleven of these ships were on loan to the US Coast Guard from 1951 to 1954 (they retained Navy names and were designated WDE with hull numbers upped by one hundred to avoid confusion with Coast Guard numbering series): DE 322-325, 328, 331, 334, 382, 387-389, and 391.
Most active ships are used in Operation MARKET TIME in the South China Sea and Gulf of Tonkin to halt Communist infiltration of men and arms to South Vietnam; while engaged in MARKET TIME several ·50 calibre machineguns are mounted. *Mills* became an operational Naval Reserve training ship in 1968 (at Baltimore, Maryland).

ARMAMENT. Upon conversion to radar picket ships these ships were fitted with six 20 mm guns; subsequently removed. See "Edsall" class listing for details of original DE configuration.

CONVERSION. Conversion to radar picket escorts included removal of conventional torpedo tubes and 40 mm guns; installation of mess compartment on main deck and other habitability improvements; fitting of two tripod masts to support radar antennas and TACAN navigation "bee-hive" antenna; installation of SPS-8 height-finding radar antenna atop after deckhouse; combat information centre (CIC) expanded and improved; and aluminium superstructure installed. Note trainable hedgehog fitted in "B" position in place of second 3 inch mount. TACAN and SPS-8 removed from active ships when sea ward radar picket barrier was ended in 1965. (See photographs in 1968-1969 and earlier editions for previous configuration).

GUNNERY. There ships have closed 3 inch mounts forward and open or closed mounts aft.

DISPOSALS
Pillsbury (DER 133), **Fessenden** (DER 142), stricken in 1965 and expended as targets; **Sellstrom** (DER 255) stricken in 1965 and scrapped; **Haverson** (DER 316) stricken in 1966 and expended as targets **Newell** (DER 322), **Lowe** (DER 325), **Brister** (DER 327), **Koiner** (DER 331) stricken on 23 Sep 1968 and scrapped, **Haverfield** (DER 393) stricken on 2 June 1969, **Wilhoite** (DER 397) stricken on 2 July 1969.

SAVAGE (DER 386) *1968, United States Navy*

FORSTER (DER 334) *1968, US Navy, by PHCM L. P. Bodine*

RADAR PICKET SHIPS
From 1956 to 1965 the US Navy operated a number of Radar Picket Ships (AGR) converted from Liberty-type merchant hulls to provide radar coverage of the seaward approaches to the United States as part of the continental air defence system. These ships operated in conjunction with the DER-type ships. Sixteen radar picket ships were converted under the Fiscal Year 1955-1959 programmes. Conversion included installation of air and surface search radar, communication equipment, combat information centre (CIC), and suitable berthing and recreation facilities.
The first four ships were initially designated Miscellaneous Auxiliary Craft (YAG); subsequently all were designated Ocean Radar Station Ships (YAGR); and on 28 Sep 1958 they were redesignated Radar Picket Ships (AGR). Names and hull numbers as YAGR/AGR remained the same.
All 16 ships were stricken in 1965 when the seaward extension of the radar barrier was disestablished; they were stripped of electronic equipment and returned to Maritime Administration custody: **Guardian** (AGR 1, ex-YAG 41), **Lookout** (AGR 2, ex-YAG 42), **Skywatcher** (AGR 3, ex-YAG 43), **Searcher** (AGR 4, ex-YAGR 44), **Scanner** (AGR 5), **Locator** (AGR 6), **Picket** (AGR 7), **Interceptor** (AGR 8), **Investigator** (AGR 9), **Outpost** (AGR 10), **Protector** (AGR 11), **Vigil** (AGR 12), **Interdictor** (AGR 13), **Interpreter** (AGR 14), **Tracer** (ex-*Interrupter*), AGR 15, **Watchman** (AGR 16). All in reserve.

CAMP (DER 251) *1968, US Navy by Lt T. S. Storek*

SUBMARINES

The US Navy's submarine force consists of two principal categories: fleet ballistic missile submarines (SSBN) and attack submarines (SSN and SS). The missile submarines are considered a component of the Strategic Warfare forces and are described at the beginning of the United States listings.

The attack submarines are a component of the General Warfare forces and have a primary mission of anti-submarine warfare—seeking out and destroying enemy submarines. Current force levels provide for 105 attack submarines. However, in mid-1969 the attack submarine force level was only 102 (41 SSN and 61 SS). The shortage was caused by the loss of the *Scorpion*, the decommissioning of the *Triton*, and the delay in completion of the *Pogy* (all nuclear powered). A force level of 105 attack submarines is expected to be reached in mid-1970 (47 SSN and 58 SS).

Through 1968 the Department of Defense had stated that 57 "first line" nuclear-powered attack submarines were required in the 1970s (in addition to nine older nuclear-powered submarines). This goal has been reassessed in the light of Soviet submarine developments; in particular, a Soviet nuclear submarine capable of relatively high speeds was detected in 1968. Accordingly, the United States has initiated a new class of high speed nuclear attack submarines (SSN 688 class) and an experimental "quiet" submarine (SSN 685). In addition, an advanced attack submarine design should be ready for construction in the Fiscal Year 1973 programme (CONFORM project).

These projects, if adequately endorsed and funded, should insure United States superiority in this most vital warship category. Superiority is contingent on quality and on quality. The Chief of Naval Operations, on 23 Jan 1969, stated that: "At this time our submarines requirements are based on our plans for using submarines, and we don't look on this necessarily as a one-for-one problem [vis-à-vis the Soviet Navy], because ASW is a combination of the use of undersea warfare forces—that is, submarines, surface ships, and air.

"We feel now that we need more [nuclear] submarines—and if we build five a year, since we only have about 65 authorised now—it would take a number of years to even replace the 35 diesels [attack submarines] that we still operate."

Supporting the missile and attack submarine forces are several auxiliary submarines (AGSS) employed for training research, and test activities. They are not included in the attack submarine force level (ie, 105); they are included within this section because of the numerical sequence of their hull numbers and their similarity to combat submarines. Similarly, the transport submarines (LPSS, formerly APSS) are included in this section although they are officially classified as Amphibious Warfare Ships.

HADDO (SSN 604) *United States Navy*

2+ NUCLEAR POWERED ATTACK SUBMARINES (SSN): HIGH SPEED DESIGN

No.	*Builder*
SSN 688	Newport News SB & DD Co
SSN 689	

ASW Weapons	SUBROC and ASW torpedoes
Main engines	2 geared turbines; 1 shaft
Nuclear reactor	1 pressurised-water cooled
Speed, knots	approx 40 submerged

A new class of attack submarines characterised by high submerged speed. The speed increases initially provided by the S5W reactor plant have been partially negated by the installation of heavier and more sophisticated equipment in the submarines, increasing their displacement and preventing optimum hull shapes which have resulted in reduced speeds.

Three submarines (SSN 688-690) were proposed in the original Fiscal Year 1970 shipbuilding programme of the Johnson Administration (to cost $504 500 000 in addition to $31 500 000 of FY 1969 advanced procurement funds). The Nixon Administration in March 1969 proposed a change in the FY 1970 new construction programme, providing for construction of only two submarines (SSN 688 and 689), deferring the third submarine (SSN 690) until the FY 1971 programme. Of the $152 000 000 originally planned for SSN 690 construction in the FY 1970 programme, $47 200 000 would be allowed for advanced procurement of long-lead time components of the submarine and $105 500 000 would be deferred to FY 1971.

In addition, the revised FY 1970 programme provides $72 000 000 for advanced procurement of long-lead time components for "several" more submarines of this class to be funded in FY 1971. Unofficial sources estimate that as many as 20 submarines of this class may be built in the FY 1970-1972 programmes.

DESIGN. These submarines apparently will be larger than the previous "Sturgeon" class. All construction features, including sail size, hull shape, proplusion plant design, machinery mounting techniques, auxiliary machinery, etc, will be designed to provide the maximum degree of quietness possible. Their sound level will be similar to the "Sturgeon" class when both submarines are travelling at comparable speeds.

ENGINEERING. Unofficial sources indicate that a modified surface ship nuclear reactor plant may be used in this class to attain underwater speeds of approximately 40 knots.

1 NUCLEAR-POWERED ATTACK SUBMARINE (SSN): "NARWHAL" TYPE

Displacement, tons	4 640 full load
Length, feet (*metres*)	314 (*95·7*) oa
Beam, feet (*metres*)	38 (*11·5*)
Draft, feet (*metres*)	26 (*7·9*)
Torpedo tubes	4—21 in (*533 mm*) amidships
ASW weapons	SUBROC and ASW torpedoes
Main engine	2 steam turbines; approx 17 000 shp; 1 shaft
Nuclear reactor	1 pressurised-water cooled S5W (Westinghouse) except modified S5WA reactor in one FY 1968 submarine
Speed, knots	20 surface; 30+ submerged
Complement	107 (12 officers, 95 enlisted men)

Name	*No.*	*Builder*	*Laid down*	*Launched*	*Commissioned*
***NARWHAL**	SSN 671	General Dynamics (Electric Boat)	17 Jan 1966	9 Sep 1967	14 June 1969

The *Narwhal* is a large attack submarine with an improved propulsion system. She is the largest "straight" nuclear-powered attack submarine yet built by the US Navy (slightly shorter than the pioneers *Nautilus* and *Seawolf* but wider, deeper, and heavier). Authorised in the Fiscal Year 1964 new construction programme.

DESIGN. The *Narwhal* is similar to the "Sturgeon" class submarines in design.

ELECTRONICS. Fitted with BQQ-2 sonar system.

ENGINEERING. The *Narwhal* is fitted with the prototype sea-going S5G Natural Circulation Reactor. According to Vice Admiral H. G. Rickover, the Natural Circulation Reactor "offers promise of increased reactor plant reliability, simplicity, and noise reduction due to the elimination of the need for large reactor coolant pumps and associated electrical and control equipment by taking maximum advantage of natural convection to circulate the reactor coolant".

NARWHAL (SSN 671) *1967, General Dynamics/Electric Boat*

Natural circulation eliminates the requirement for primary coolant pumps, the second noisiest component of a pressurised-water propulsion system after the steam turbines.

The Atomic Energy Commission's Knolls Atomic Power Laboratory was given prime responsibility for development of the power plant. Construction of a land-based prototype plant began in May 1961 at the National Reactor Testing Station in Idaho. The reactor achieved initial criticality on 12 Sep 1965.

Submarines—*continued*

1 NUCLEAR POWERED ATTACK SUBMARINE (SSN): QUIET DESIGN

No.	*Builder*	*Comm.*
SSN 685	General Dynamics (Electric Boat)	1973

ASW Weapons: SUBROC and ASW torpedoes
Main engines: Turbine-electric drive (General Electric); 1 shaft
Nuclear reactor: 1 pressurised-water cooled S5WA (Westinghouse)
Speed, knots: approx 25 submerged

The Turbine-Electric Drive Submarine (TEDS) is being built to test "a combination of advanced silencing techniques" involving "a new kind of propulsion system, and new and quieter machinery of various kinds", according to the Department of Defense. The noise level produced by an operating submarine is an important factor in its ability to remain undetected by an opponent's passive listening devices and its own ability to detect the opponent.

The TEDS project will permit an at-sea evaluation of improvements in ASW effectiveness due to noise reduction. The SSN 685 will be slightly larger than "Sturgeon" class submarines and somewhat slower.
No class of turbine-electric nuclear submarines is planned at this time. Rather, quieting features developed in the SSN 685 which do not detract from speed probably will be incorporated in the SSN 688 design and subsequent SSN classes. (The TEDS design is several years ahead of the SSN 688 design).
Authorised in the Fiscal Year 1968 new construction programme; estimated construction cost will be between $150 000 000 and $200 000 000.

Design of an advanced submarine specifically intended for quiet operation began with Navy studies which commenced in October 1964. Approval to construct the submarine was revoked on at least one occasion by the Department of Defense in an effort to combine several desired characteristics in a single submarine design. However, high speed and silent operation apparently are not compatible with available technology.
Final Department of Defense approval for construction of the turbine-electric drive submarine was announced on 25 Oct 1968.

ENGINEERING. Turbine-electric drive eliminates the noisy reduction gears of standard steam turbine power plants, the major source of noise in a nuclear-powered submarine. The turbine-electric power plant is larger and heavier than comparable steam turbine submarine machinery.
The *Tullibee* (SSN 597) was an earlier effort at noise reduction through a turbine-electric nuclear plant.

SEA DEVIL (SSN 664) — *1968, Newport News SB & DD by B. J. Nixon*

WHALE (SSN 638) — *1968, General Dynamics Quincy Division*

Submarines—*continued*

37 NUCLEAR-POWERED ATTACK SUBMARINES (SSN): "STURGEON" CLASS

Displacement, tons	3 860 standard; 4 630 submerged
Length, feet (*metres*)	292·2 (*89·0*) oa
Beam, feet (*metres*)	31·7 (*9·5*)
Draft, feet (*metres*)	26 (*7·9*)
Torpedo tubes	4—21 in (*533 mm*) amidships
ASW weapons	SUBROC and ASW torpedoes
Main engines	2 steam turbines; approx 15 000 shp; 1 shaft
Nuclear reactor	1 pressurised-water cooled S5W (Westinghouse)
Speed, knots	approx 20 surface; approx 30 submerged
Complement	107 (12 officers, 95 enlisted men)

Name	*No.*	*Builder*	*Laid down*	*Launched*	*Commissioned*
*STURGEON	SSN 637	General Dynamics (Electric Boat)	10 Aug 1963	26 Feb 1966	3 Mar 1967
*WHALE	SSN 638	General Dynamics (Quincy)	27 May 1964	14 Oct 1966	12 Oct 1968
*TAUTOG	SSN 639	Ingalls Shipbuilding Corp	27 Jan 1964	15 Apr 1967	17 Aug 1968
*GRAYLING	SSN 646	Portsmouth Naval Shipyard	12 May 1964	22 June 1967	31 May 1969
POGY	SSN 647	Ingalls Shipbuilding Corp	4 May 1964	3 June 1967	late 1970
*ASPRO	SSN 648	Ingalls Shipbuilding Corp	23 Nov 1964	29 Nov 1967	20 Feb 1969
*SUNFISH	SSN 649	General Dynamics (Quincy)	15 Jan 1965	14 Oct 1966	15 Mar 1969
*PARGO	SSN 650	General Dynamics (Electric Boat)	3 June 1964	17 Sep 1966	5 Dec 1967
*QUEENFISH	SSN 651	Newport News SB & DD Co	11 May 1965	25 Feb 1966	6 Dec 1966
*PUFFER	SSN 652	Ingalls Shipbuilding Corp	8 Feb 1965	30 Mar 1968	Aug 1969
*RAY	SSN 653	Newport News SB & DD Co	1 Apr 1965	21 June 1966	12 Apr 1967
SAND LANCE	SSN 660	Portsmouth Naval Shipyard	15 Jan 1965	late 1969	late 1970
*LAPON	SSN 661	Newport News SB & DD Co	26 July 1965	16 Dec 1966	14 Dec 1967
*GURNARD	SSN 662	San Francisco NSY (Mare Island)	22 Dec 1964	20 May 1967	6 Dec 1968
*HAMMERHEAD	SSN 663	Newport News SB & DD Co	29 Nov 1965	14 Apr 1967	28 June 1968
SEA DEVIL	SSN 664	Newport News SB & DD Co	12 Apr 1966	5 Oct 1967	30 Jan 1969
GUITARRO	SSN 665	San Francisco NSY (Mare Island)	9 Dec 1965	27 July 1968	early 1990
HAWKBILL	SSN 666	San Francisco NSY (Mare Island)	12 Sep 1966	12 Apr 1969	Mar 1970
*BERGALL	SSN 667	General Dynamics (Electric Boat)	16 Apr 1966	17 Feb 1968	31 May 1969
*SPADEFISH	SSN 668	Newport News SB & DD Co	21 Dec 1966	15 May 1968	31 July 1969
*SEAHORSE	SSN 669	General Dynamics (Electric Boat)	13 Aug 1966	15 June 1968	30 Aug 1969
FINBACK	SSN 670	Newport News SB & DD Co	26 June 1967	7 Dec 1968	Dec 1969
PINTADO	SSN 672	San Francisco NSY (Mare Island)	27 Oct 1967	Aug 1969	July 1970
FLYING FISH	SSN 673	General Dynamics (Electric Boat)	30 June 1967	17 May 1969	May 1970
TREPANG	SSN 674	General Dynamics (Electric Boat)	28 Oct 1967	Sep 1969	Sep 1970
BLUEFISH	SSN 675	General Dynamics (Electric Boat)	13 Mar 1968	Jan 1970	early 1971
BILLFISH	SSN 676	General Dynamics (Electric Boat)	20 Sep 1968	May 1970	early 1971
DRUM	SSN 677	San Francisco NSY (Mare Island)	20 Aug 1968	May 1970	early 1971
ARCHERFISH	SSN 678	General Dynamics (Electric Boat)	31 May 1969	early 1971	early 1972
	SSN 679	General Dynamics (Electric Boat)	Sep 1969	mid 1971	mid 1972
REDFISH	SSN 680	Ingalls Shipbuilding (Litton)	26 May 1969	early 1971	mid 1972
	SSN 681	General Dynamics (Electric Boat)	Jan 1970	late 1971	late 1972
	SSN 682	Ingalls Shipbuilding (Litton)	Sep 1969	late 1971	late 1972
	SSN 683	Ingalls Shipbuilding (Litton)	Jan 1970	early 1972	1973
	SSN 684	General Dynamics (Electric Boat)	May 1970	early 1972	1973
	SSN 686				
	SSN 687				

The 37 "Sturgeon" class attack submarines comprise the largest group of nuclear-powered ships built to the same design (followed in the US Navy by the 31 "Lafayette" class missile submarines). These submarines are intended to seek out and destroy enemy submarines. They are similar in design to the previous "Permit" (ex-"Thresher") class but are slightly larger. SSN 637-639 (3 ships) were authorised in the Fiscal Year 1962 new construction programme, SSN 646-653 (8 ships) in FY 1963, SSN 660-664 (5 ships) in FY 1964, SSN 665-670 (6 ships) in FY 1965, SSN 672-677 (6 ships) in FY 1966, SSN 678-682 (5 ships) in FY 1967, SSN 683-684 (2 ships) in FY 1968, and SSN 686 and SSN 687 in FY 1969. The estimated construction cost of the two submarines of this class in the FY 1969 programme is $81 300 000 per ship.

The *Guittaro* sank in 35 feet of water on 15 May 1969 while being fitted out at the San Francisco Bay Naval Shipyard. According to congressional report, the sinking, caused by shipyard workers, was "wholly avoidable". Subsequently raised; damage estimated at $25 000 000 to repair due to interior flooding.

CONSTRUCTION. The *Pogy* was begun by the New York Shipbuilding Corp (Camden, New Jersey), but was towed to Ingalls Shipbuilding Corp for completion; contract with the New York Shipbuilding Corp was terminated on 1 June 1967; contract for completion awarded to Ingalls Shipbuilding Corp on 7 Dec 1967.

DESIGN. These submarines are slightly larger than the previous "Permit" (ex-"Thresher") class and can be identified by their taller sail structure and the lower position of their diving planes on the sail (to improve control at periscope depth). These ships incorporate modifications of the submarine safety (SUBSAFE) programme established after the loss of the *Thresher*. These submarines probably are slightly slower than the previous "Permit" and "Skipjack" classes because of their increased size with the same propulsion system as in the earlier classes.

ELECTRONICS. These submarines are fitted with the advanced BQQ-2 sonar system. Principal components of the BQQ-2 include the BQS-6 active sonar, with transducers mounted in a 15-foot diameter sonar sphere, and BQR-7 passive sonar, with hydrophones in a conformal array on sides of forward hull. The active sonar sphere is fitted in the optimum bow position, requiring placement of torpedo tubes amidships. These submarines also have BQS-8 and BQS-13 active/passive sonars; transducers for the former are in small, fin-like domes aft of sail structure. BQS-8 sonar is intended primarily for under-ice-navigation.

NOMENCLATURE. Submarines are generally named for fish and marine life. Most nuclear-powered attack submarines carry on the names of famous World War II "boats".

PHOTOGRAPHS. Note small vertical fins on horizontal control surfaces of *Grayling* in photograph on next page showing her being launched bow first; fins improve control during high-speed manoeuvres. Propeller was not fitted to *Grayling* at time of launching. The *Queenfish*, below, has three of her antenna masts raised from her sail structure. Dark rectangles on sail are sonars.

STURGEON (SSN 637) — *1967, United States Navy*

QUEENFISH (SSN 651) — *1967, US Navy, by PH3 A R Foss*

Submarines—*continued*

GUARDFISH (SSN 612) *1965, US Navy*

GRAYLING (SSN 646) *1967, US Navy*

13 NUCLEAR-POWERED ATTACK SUBMARINES (SSN): "PERMIT" CLASS

Name	*No.*	*Builder*	*Laid down*	*Launched*	*Commissioned*
***PERMIT**	SSN 594	Mare Island Naval Shipyard	16 July 1959	1 July 1961	29 May 1962
***PLUNGER**	SSN 595	Mare Island Naval Shipyard	2 Mar 1960	9 Dec 1961	21 Nov 1962
***BARB**	SSN 596	Ingalls Shipbuilding Corp	9 Nov 1959	12 Feb 1962	24 Aug 1963
***POLLACK**	SSN 603	New York Shipbuilding Corp	14 Mar 1960	17 Mar 1962	26 May 1964
***HADDO**	SSN 604	New York Shipbuilding Cotp	9 Sep 1960	18 Aug 1962	16 Dec 1964
***JACK**	SSN 605	Portsmouth Naval Shipyard	16 Sep 1960	24 Apr 1963	31 Mar 1967
***TINOSA**	SSN 606	Portsmouth Naval Shipyard	24 Nov 1959	9 Dec 1961	17 Oct 1964
***DACE**	SSN 607	Ingalls Shipbuilding Corp	6 June 1960	18 Aug 1962	4 Apr 1964
***GUARDFISH**	SSN 612	New York Shipbuilding Corp	28 Feb 1961	15 May 1965	20 Dec 1966
***FLASHER**	SSN 613	General Dynamics (Electric Boat)	14 Apr 1961	22 June 1963	22 July 1966
***GREENLING**	SSN 614	General Dynamics (Electric Boat)	15 Aug 1961	4 Apr 1964	3 Nov 1967
***GATO**	SSN 615	Ingalls Shipbuilding Corp	15 Dec 1961	14 May 1964	25 Jan 1968
***HADDOCK**	SSN 621	Ingalls Shipbuilding Corp	24 Apr 1961	21 May 1966	22 Dec 1967

Displacement, tons	3 750 standard, *Flasher, Greenling,* and *Gato* 3 800 tons; 4 300 submerged except *Jack* 4 500, submerged, *Flasher, Greenling,* and *Gato* 4 600 submerged
Length, feet (*metres*)	278·5 (*84·9*) oa except *Jack* 295·7 *Flasher, Greenling* and *Gato* 292·2(*89·1*)
Beam, feet (*metres*)	31·7 (*9·6*)
Draft, feet (*metres*)	25·2 (*7·6*)
Torpedo tubes	4—21 in (*533 mm*) amidships
ASW weapons	SUBROC and ASW torpedoes
Main engines	2 steam turbines, approx 15 000 shp; 1 shaft
Nuclear reactor	1 pressurised-water cooled S5W (Westinghouse)
Speed, knots	20 surface; 30+ submerged
Complement	107 (12 officers, 95 enlisted men)

These submarines were the first of a series of advanced attack submarines intended to seek out and destroy enemy submarines. They have a greater depth capability than previous nuclear-powered submarines and are the first to combine the SUBROC anti-submarine missile capability with the advanced BQQ-2 sonar system. The lead ship of the class, the ill-fated *Thresher* (SSN 593), was authorised in the Fiscal Year 1957 new construction programme, the SSN 594-596 (3 ships) in FY 1958, SSN 603-607 (5 ships) in FY 1959, SSN 612-615 (4 ships) in FY 1960, and SSN 621 in FY 1961. Four of these submarines were intended as guided missile submarines (see *Design* notes).

The *Thresher* (SSN 593) was lost off the coast of New England on 10 Apr 1963 while on post-overhaul trials. She went down with 129 men on board (108 crewmen plus four naval officers and 17 civilians on board for trials).

Later submarines of this and subsequent classes were delayed because of safety programme (SUBSAFE) modifications, increased quality control of submarine construction, and specific problems at the New York Shipbuilding Corp and the Portsmouth Naval Shipyard.

CLASS. These submarines are officially listed as belonging to the "Thresher" class in the Naval Vessels Register; generally referred to as the "Permit" class after loss of the *Thresher* in1963.

CONSTRUCTION. *Greenling* and *Gato* were launched by the Electric Boat Division of the General Dynamics Corp (Groton, Connecticut); towed to Quincy Division (Massachusetts) for lengthening and completion.

DESIGN. The *Plunger, Barb, Pollack,* and *Dace* were ordered as guided missile submarines (SSGN) and were to each carry four Regulus II missiles. They were re-ordered as "Thresher" class attack submarines after the Regulus II programme was cancelled on 18 Dec 1958 (retaining numerical sequence in the submarine series).

The *Jack* was built to a modified design to test a different power plant (see *Engineering* notes).

The *Flasher, Gato,* and *Greenling* were modified during construction; fitted with SUBSAFE features, heavier machinery, and larger sail structures.

These submarines have a modified "tear-drop" hull design. Their bows are devoted to sonar and their four torpedo tubes are amidships, angled out, two to port and two to starboard.

ELECTRONICS. These submarines are fitted with the advanced BQQ-2 sonar system (first installed in the *Tullibee*, SSN 597). Principal components of the BQQ-2 include the BQS-6 active sonar, with transducers mounted in a 15-foot diameter sonar sphere, and BQR-7 passive sonar, with hydrophones in a conformal array along sides of forward hull. The active sonar sphere is fitted in the optimum bow position, requiring placement of torpedo tubes amidships. Reportedly, the advanced BQS-13 active/passive sonar will be fitted in these submarines.

PLUNGER (SSN 595) *U.S. Navy*

ENGINEERING. The *Jack* is fitted with two propellers on essentially one shaft (actually a single shaft within a sleeve-like shaft) and a counter-rotating turbine without a reduction gear. Both innovations are designed to reduce operating noises. To accommodate the larger turbine the engine spaces were lengthened ten feet and the shaft structure was lengthened seven feet to mount the two propellers. The propellers are of different size and are smaller than in the other submarines of this class. The *Jack's* propulsion arrangement provides a ten per cent increase in power efficiency, but no increase in speed. All submarines of this and subsequent classes have special machinery mountings to reduce self-generated noise levels. The *Jack's* counter-rotating propellers were intended originally to reduce operating noise.

NAVIGATION. These submarines are fitted with the Ship's Inertial Navigation System (SINS).

NOMENCLATURE. Names changed during construction: *Plunger* ex-*Pollack; Barb* ex-*Pollack*, ex-*Plunger; Pollack* ex-*Barb*.

PHOTOGRAPHS. Note smooth hull surfaces when underway at sea; all bits, cleats, capstans, etc., are hinged, retractable, or removable. In the photograph on the previous page the *Plunger* has her deck equipment "up" as she steams off Hawaii. The *Guardfish* has two multi-antenna masts raised slightly out of her sail structure. The sails in these submarines are shorter than in the earlier "Skipjack" class; compare position of sail-mounted diving planes with the later "Sturgeon" class submarines.

Submarines—*continued*

1 NUCLEAR-POWERED ATTACK SUBMARINE (SSN): "TULLIBEE" TYPE

Displacement, tons	2 317 standard; 2 640 submerged
Length, feet (*metres*)	273 (*83·2*) oa
Beam, feet (*metres*)	23·3 (*7·1*)
Draft, feet (*metres*)	21 (*6·4*)
Torpedo tubes	4—21 in (*533 mm*) amidships
ASW weapons	ASW torpedoes
Main engines	Turbo-electric drive with steam turbine (Westinghouse), 2 500 shp; 1 shaft (Combustion Engineering)
Speed, knots	15 surface; 20 submerged
Complement	56 (6 officers, 50 enlisted men)

Name	*No.*	*Builder*	*Laid down*	*Launched*	*Commissioned*
***TULLIBEE**	SSN 597	General Dynamics (Electric Boat)	26 May 1958	27 Apr 1960	9 Nov 1960

The *Tullibee* was designed specifically for anti-submarine operations and was the first US submarine with the optimum bow position devoted entirely to sonar. No additional submarines of this type were constructed because of the success of the larger, more-versatile "Thresher" class. The *Tullibee* was authorised in the Fiscal Year 1958 new construction programme. She is no longer considered a "first line" submarine.

DESIGN. The *Tullibee* has a modified, elongated "tear-drop" hull design. Originally she was planned as a 1 000-ton craft, but reactor requirements and other considerations increased her size during design and construction.
The *Tullibee* has four amidships torpedo tubes angled out from the centreline, two to port and two to starboard. However, she is not fitted to fire the SUBROC anti-submarine missile. She cannot match the "Thresher" and later SSN classes in underwater speed or manoeuvrability.

TULLIBEE (SSN 597) *United States Navy*

ELECTRONICS. The *Tullibee* was the first submarine fitted with the advanced BQQ-2 sonar system (see "Thresher" class listing for details). The two fin-like sonar domes are PUFFs for BQG-4 passive fire control sonar; a third dome is in the submarine's superstructure. PUFF is an ancronym for Passive Underwater Fire-control Feasibility study.

ENGINEERING. The *Tullibee* has a small nuclear power plant designed and developed by the Combustion Engineering Company. Construction of a land-based prototype plant began at the Atomic Energy Commission's Windsor, Connecticut, test site in June of 1957 and the plant was operated at full power for the first time on 19 Dec 1959.

The *Tullibee* propulsion system features turbo-electric drive rather than conventional steam turbines with reduction gears in an effort to reduce operating noises.

NAVIGATION. The *Tullibee* is fitted with Ships Inertial Navigation System (SINS).

5 NUCLEAR-POWERED ATTACK SUBMARINES (SSN): "SKIPJACK" CLASS

Displacement, tons	3 075 standard; 3 500 submerged
Length, feet (*metres*)	251·7 (*76·7*) oa
Beam, feet (*metres*)	31·5 (*9·6*)
Draft, feet (*metres*)	28 (*8·5*)
Torpedo tubes	6—21 in (*533 mm*) forward
ASW weapons	ASW torpedoes
Main engines	2 steam turbines (Westinghouse in *Skipjack*; General Electric in others); approx 15 000 shp; 1 shaft
Nuclear reactor	1 pressurised-water cooled S5W (Westinghouse)
Speed, knots	20 surface; 30+ submerged
Complement	93 (8 officers, 85 enlisted men)

Name	*No.*	*Builder*	*Laid down*	*Launched*	*Commissioned*
***SKIPJACK**	SSN 585	General Dynamics (Electric Boat)	29 May 1956	26 May 1958	15 Apr 1959
***SCAMP**	SSN 588	Mare Island Naval Shipyard	23 Jan 1959	8 Oct 1960	5 June 1961
***SCULPIN**	SSN 590	Ingalls Shipbuilding Corp	3 Feb 1958	31 Mar 1960	1 June 1961
***SHARK**	SSN 591	Newport News SB & DD Co	24 Feb 1958	16 Mar 1960	9 Feb 1961
***SNOOK**	SSN 592	Ingalls Shipbuilding Corp	7 Apr 1958	31 Oct 1960	24 Oct 1961

The "Skipjack" class combines the high-speed endurance of nuclear propulsion with the high-speed "tear-drop" hull design tested in the conventionally powered submarine *Albacore* (AGSS 569). (See *Design* and *Engineering* notes). The *Skipjack* was authorised in the Fiscal Year 1956 new construction programme; the five other submarines of this class were authorised in FY 1957. Although they are now nearing their first decade of service, these submarines are still considered suitable for "first line" service.
Each submarine cost approximately $40 000 000.

The *Scorpion* (SSN 589) of this class was lost some 400 miles southwest of the Azores while en route from the Mediterranean to Norfolk, Virginia, in May 1968. She went down with 99 men on board.

CONSTRUCTION. The *Scorpion's* keel was laid down twice: the original keel laid down on 1 Nov 1957 was renumbered SSBN 598 and became the Polaris submarine *George Washington*; the second SSN 589 keel became the *Scorpion*. The *Scamp's* keel laying was delayed when material for her was diverted to the SSBN 599 (*Patrick Henry*).
This class introduced the Newport News Shipbuilding and Dry Dock Company and the Ingalls Shipbuilding Corporation to nuclear submarine construction. Newport News had not previously built any submarine since before World War I; Ingalls previously had built only one submarine, the *Blueback* (SS 581) launched in 1959.

SNOOK (SSN 592) *1964, United States Navy*

DESIGN. The *Skipjack* was the first modern US submarine built to the "tear-drop" or modified spindle hull design which improves underwater performance. Her length-to-beam ratio is 7·8 : 1 compared to a ratio of 10·7 : 1 for the "Skate" class. (The conventionally powered attack submarine *Barbel* was built to a similar design at the same time as the *Skipjack*). These submarines have a single propeller shaft (vice two in earlier nuclear submarines) and their diving planes are mounted on sail structures to improve underwater manoeuvrability. No after torpedo tubes are fitted because of their tapering sterns.

ELECTRONICS. Original sonar equipment was modified to provide improved ASW capabilities.

ENDURANCE. The *Scorpion* set an endurance record in 1962 when she maintained a sealed atmosphere for 70 consecutive days.

ENGINEERING. The "Skipjack" class introduced the S5W fast attack submarine propulsion plant which has been used in all subsequent attack and missile submarines except the *Narwhal*. The plant was developed by the Bettis Atomic Power Laboratory. No land-based prototype was constructed because of the data available from the earlier S3W and S4W nuclear power plants.

PHOTOGRAPHS. Note streamlined shape and lack of projections; all equipment outside of the hull is either recessed or retractable.

Submarines—*continued*

SHARK (SSN 591) *1968, U.S. Navy PHC RM Anderson.*

1 NUCLEAR-POWERED ATTACK SUBMARINE (SSN): FORMER GUIDED MISSILE SUBMARINE

Name	*No.*	*Builder*	*Laid down*	*Launched*	*Commissioned*
***HALIBUT**	SSN 587 (ex-SSGN 587)	Mare Island Naval Shipyard	11 Apr 1957	9 Jan 1959	4 Jan 1960

Displacement, tons	3 850 standard; 5 000 submerged
Length, feet (*metres*)	350 (*106·6*) oa
Beam, feet (*metres*)	29.5 (*8·9*)
Draft, feet (*metres*)	21·5 (*6·5*)
Torpedo tubes	6—21 in (*533 mm*) 4 forward; 2 aft
ASW Weapons	ASW torpedoes
Main engines	2 steam turbines (Westinghouse), approx 6 000 shp; 2 shafts
Nuclear reactor	1 pressurised-water cooled S3W (Westinghouse)
Speed, knots	15 surface; 20 submerged
Complement as SSN	97 (9 officers, 88 enlisted men)
as SSGN	119 (11 officers, 108 enlisted men)

The *Halibut* is believed to have been the first submarine designed and constructed specifically to fire guided missiles. She was originally intended to have diesel-electric propulsion but on 27 Feb 1956 the Navy announced she would have nuclear propulsion. She was the US Navy's only nuclear-powered *guided* missile submarine (SSGN) to be completed. Authorised in the Fiscal Year 1956 new construction programme and built for an estimated cost of $45 000 000.
The *Halibut* was reclassifed as an attack submarine on 25 July 1965 after the Navy discarded the Regulus submarine-launched missile force. Her missile equipment was removed; she is no longer considered a "first line" submarine and is employed in experimental work. The submarine's large missile compartment makes her an excellent ship for underwater projects.

DESIGN. The *Halibut* was built with a large missile hangar faired into her bow. Her hull was intended primarily to provide a stable launching platform rather than for speed or manoeuvrability.

MISSILES. The *Halibut* was designed to carry two Regulus II surface-to-surface missiles. The Regulus II was a transonic missile which could carry a nuclear warhead and had a range of 1 000 miles. The Regulus II was cancelled before becoming operational and the *Halibut* operated from 1960 to 1964 carrying five Regulus I missiles, subsonic cruise missiles which could deliver a nuclear warhead on targets 500 miles from the launching ship or submarine.

NAVIGATION. The *Halibut* is fitted with Ship's Inertial Navigation System (SINS).

HALIBUT (SSN 587) *1968, U.S. Navy PHCM L. P. Bodine*

Submarines—*continued*

1 NUCLEAR-POWERED ATTACK SUBMARINE (SSN): FORMER RADAR PICKET SUBMARINE

Name	*No.*	*Builder*	*Laid down*	*Launched*	*Commissioned*
TRITON	SSN 586 (ex-SSRN 586)	General Dynamics Corp (Electric Boat)	29 May 1956	19 Aug 1958	10 Nov 1959

Displacement, tons	5 940 standard; 7 780 submerged
Length, feet (*metres*)	447·5 (*136·3*) oa
Beam, feet (*metres*)	37 (*11·3*)
Draft, feet (*metres*)	24 (*7·3*)
Torpedo tubes	6—21 in (*533 mm*) 4 forward; 2 aft
ASW weapons	ASW torpedoes
Main engines	2 steam turbines (General Electric); approx 34 000 shp; 2 shafts
Nuclear reactors	2 pressurised-water cooled S4G (General Electric)
Speed, knots	27 surface; 20 submerged
Complement as SSRN	172 (16 officers, 156 enlisted men)

The *Triton* was designed and constructed to serve as a radar picket submarine to operate in conjunction with surface carrier task forces. She is the longest submarine ever constructed and is exceeded in displacement only by the later Polaris missile submarines. Authorised in the Fiscal Year 1956 new construction programme and built for an estimated cost of $109 000 000.

The *Triton* circumnavigated the globe in 1960, remaining submerged except when her sail structure broke the surface to enable an ill sailor to be taken off near the Falkland Islands. The 41 500-mile cruise took 83 days and was made at an average speed of 18 knots.

The underwater giant was reclassified as an attack submarine (SSN) on 1 Mar 1961 as the Navy dropped the radar picket submarine programme. She is no longer considered a "first line" submarine and was decommissioned on 3 May 1969 and became the first US nuclear submarine to be relegated to the "mothball fleet". There had been proposals to operate the *Triton* as an underwater national command post afloat, but no funds were provided and there were major operational/technical problems involved in this concept because of the difficulty in communications with a submerged submarine.

DESIGN. The *Triton* was designed to operate as a surface radar picket, submerging when in danger of enemy attack. She was fitted with an elaborate combat information centre and large radar antenna which retractad into the sail structure.

ENGINEERING. The *Triton* is the only US submarine with two nuclear reactors. The Atomic Energy Commission's Knolls Atomic Power Laboratory was given prime responsibility for development of the power plant. Construction of a land-based prototype plant began in October 1955 at West Milton, New York. The prototype plant's single reactor achieved criticality on 18 Aug 1958. After 2½ years of operation, during which she steamed more than 110 000 miles, the *Triton* was overhauled and refuelled from July 1962 to March 1964.

PHOTOGRAPH. Note size of sail structure; recess opening for surface radar antenna.

TRITON (SSN 586) *United States Navy*

4 NUCLEAR-POWERED ATTACK SUBMARINES (SSN): "SKATE" CLASS

Displacement, tons	2 570 standard; 2 861 submerged
Length, feet (*metres*)	267·7 (*81·5*) oa
Beam, feet (*metres*)	25 (*7·6*)
Draft, feet (*metres*)	21 (*6·4*)
Torpedo tubes	6—21 in (*533 mm*) 4 forward; 2 aft
ASW weapons	ASW torpedoes
Main engines	2 steam turbines (Westinghouse) approx 6 600 shp; 2 shafts
Nuclear reactor	1 pressurised-water cooled S3W (Westinghouse) in *Skate* and *Sargo*; 1 pressurised-water cooled S4W (Westinghouse) in *Swordfish* and *Seadragon*
Speed, knots	20 surface; approx 25 submerged
Complement	95 (8 officers, 78 enlisted men)

Name	*No*	*Builder*	*Laid down*	*Launched*	*Commissioned*
***SKATE**	SSN 578	General Dynamics (Electric Boat)	21 July 1955	16 May 1957	23 Dec 1957
***SWORDFISH**	SSN 579	Portsmouth Naval Shipyard	25 Jan 1956	27 Aug 1957	15 Sep 1958
***SARGO**	SSN 583	Mare Island Naval Shipyard	21 Feb 1956	10 Oct 1957	1 Oct 1958
***SEADRAGON**	SSN 584	Portsmouth Naval Shipyard	20 June 1956	16 Aug 1958	5 Dec 1959

SEADRAGON (SSN 584) *United States Navy*

SARGO (SSN 583) *United States Navy*

The "Skate" class submarines were the first production model nuclear-powered submarines. They are similar in design to the *Nautilus*, but smaller. The *Skate* and *Swordfish* were authorised in the Fiscal Year 1955 new construction programme, and the *Sargo* and *Seadragon* in FY 1956.

The *Skate* was the first submarine to make a completely submerged transatlantic crossing; in 1958 she established a (then) record of 31 days submerged with a sealed atmosphere; on 11 Aug 1958 she passed under the North Pole during a polar cruise; and on 17 Mar 1959 she became the first submarine to surface at the North Pole. The *Sargo* undertook a polar cruise during January-February 1960 and surfaced at the North Pole on 9 Feb 1960. The *Seadragon* transited from the Atlantic to the Pacific via the Northwest Passage (Lancaster Sound, Barrow and McClure Straits) in August 1960. The *Skate*, operating from New London, Connecticut, and the *Seadragon*, based at Pearl Harbour, rendezvoused under the North Pole on 2 Aug 1962 and then conducted anti-submarine exercises under the polar ice pack and surfaced together at the North Pole.

These submarines are no longer considered "first line" submarines.

DESIGN. The "Skate" design is similar to the *Nautilus*-*Seawolf* design with GUPPY hull, bow diving planes, and twin propellers.

ENGINEERING. After the land-based prototype of the *Nautilus* reactor plant was placed in operation work was begun on a similar but smaller plant suitable for use in smaller submarines. Developed by the Atomic Energy Commission's Bettis Atomic Power Laboratory, the new propulsion system was similar to that of the *Nautilus* but considerably simplified with improved operation and maintenance. No land-based prototype was constructed because of the similarity to the *Nautilus* plant. The final propulsion plant developed under this programme had two arrangements, the S3W configuration in the *Skate*, *Sargo* and *Halibut*, and the S4W configuration in the *Swordfish* and *Seadragon*. Both arrangements have proven satisfactory.

The *Skate* began her first overhaul and refuelling in January 1961 after steaming 120 862 miles on her initial reactor core during three years of operation. The *Swordfish* began her first overhaul and refuelling in early 1962 after more than three years of operation in which time she steamed 112 000 miles.

Submarines *continued*—

1 NUCLEAR-POWERED ATTACK SUBMARINE (SSN): "SEAWOLF" TYPE

Displacement, tons	3 720 standard; 4 280 submerged
Length, feet (*metres*)	337·5 (*102·9*) oa
Beam, feet (*metres*)	27·7 (*8·4*)
Draft, feet (*metres*)	22 (*6·7*)
Torpedo tubes	6—21 in (*533 mm*) forward
ASW weapons	ASW torpedoes
Main engines	2 steam turbines (General Electric), approx 15 000 shp; 2 shafts
Nuclear reactor	1 pressurised-water cooled S2Wa (Westinghouse)
Speed, knots	20 surface; 20 submerged
Complement	105 (10 officers, 95 enlisted men)

Name	*No.*	*Builder*	*Laid down*	*Launched*	*Commissioned*
***SEAWOLF**	SSN 575	General Dynamics (Electric Boat)	15 Sep 1953	21 July 1955	30 Mar 1957

The *Seawolf* was the world's second nuclear-propelled vehicle; she was constructed almost simultaneously with the *Nautilus* to test a competitive reactor design. Funds for the *Seawolf* were authorised in the Fiscal Year 1952 new construction programme.
The *Seawolf* established a submerged endurance record in 1958 when she remained submerged for 60 consecutive days, travelling a distance of 13 761 miles with a completely sealed atmosphere. She is no longer considered a "first line" submarine.

ENGINEERING. Initial work in the development of naval nuclear propulsion plants investigated a number of concepts, two of which were of sufficient interest to warrant full development: the pressurised water and liquid metal (sodium). The *Nautilus* was provided a pressurised-water reactor plant and the *Seawolf* was fitted initially with a liquid-metal reactor.
Originally known as the Submarine Intermediate Reactor (SIR), the liquid-metal plant was developed by the Atomic Energy Commission's Knolls Atomic Power Laboratory. A land-based prototype designated SIR Mark I was constructed at the Laboratory's West Milton New York, site. The plant attained initial criticality on 20 Mar 1955 and was operated until dismantled in early 1957.
The SIR Mark II was installed in the *Seawolf*. (The reactor plants were later redesignated SIG and S2G, respectively). The Mark II/S2G in the *Seawolf* achieved initial criticality on 25 June 1956. Steam leaks developed during the dockside testing. The plant was shut down and it was determined that the leaks were caused by sodium-potassium alloy which had entered the superheater steam piping. After repairs and testing the *Seawolf* began sea trials on 21 Jan 1957. The trials were run at reduced power and after two years of operation the *Seawolf* entered the Electric Boat yard for removal of her sodium-cooled plant and installation of a pressurised-water plant similar to that installed in the *Nautilus* (designated S2Wa). When the original *Seawolf* plant was shut down in December 1958 the submarine had steamed a total of 71 611 miles. She was recommissioned on 30 Sep 1960. The pressurised-water reactor was refuelled for the first between May 1965 and August 1967, having propelled the *Seawolf* for more than 161 000 miles on its initial fuel core.

SEAWOLF (SSN 575) — *Electric Boat Division, General Dynamics Corp*

1 NUCLEAR POWERED SUBMARINE (SSN): "NAUTILUS" TYPE

Displacement, tons	3 530 standard; 4 040 submerged
Length, feet (*metres*)	323·7 (*98·6*) oa
Beam, feet (*metres*)	27·6 (*8·4*)
Draft, feet (*metres*)	22 (*6·7*)
Torpedo tubes	6—21 in (*533 mm*) forward
ASW weapons	ASW torpedoes
Main engines	2 steam turbines (Westinghouse), approx 15 000 shp; 2 shafts
Nuclear reactor	1 pressurised-water cooled S2W (Westinghouse)
Speed, knots	20 surface; 20+ submerged
Complement	105 (10 officers, 95 enlisted men)

Name	*No.*	*Builder*	*Laid down*	*Launched*	*Commissioned*
***NAUTILUS**	SSN 571	General Dynamics (Electric Boat)	14 June 1952	21 Jan 1954	30 Sep 1954

The *Nautilus* was the world's first nuclear-propelled vehicle. The Chief of Naval Operations established a requirement for a nuclear-propelled submarine in August 1949 and specified a "ready-for-sea" date of January 1955. The funds for construction of the *Nautilus* were authorised in the Fiscal Year 1952 budget. The *Nautilus* put to sea for the first time on 17 Jan 1955 and signalled the historic message: "Underway on nuclear power".
On her shakedown cruise in May 1955 the *Nautilus* steamed submerged from New London, Connecticut, to San Juan, Puerto Rico, travelling more than 1 300 miles in 84 hours at an average speed of almost 16 knots; she later steamed submerged from Key West, Florida, to New London, a distance of 1 397 miles, at an average speed of more than 20 knots.

During 1958 the *Nautilus* undertook extensive operations under the Arctic ice pack and in August she made history's first polar transit from the Pacific to the Atlantic, steaming from Pearl Harbour to Portland, England. She passed under the Geographic North Pole on 3 Aug 1958.
The *Nautilus* is no longer considered a "first line" submarine.

DESIGN. The *Nautilus* and *Seawolf* have GUPPY-type hull configurations. The *Seawolf* has a stepped sail and a slight rise at the bow.

ENGINEERING. In January 1948 the Department of Defense requested the Atomic Energy Commission to undertake the design, development, and construction of a nuclear reactor for submarine propulsion. Initial research and conceptual design of the Submarine Thermal Reactor (STR) was undertaken by the Argonne National Laboratory. Subsequently the Atomic Energy Commission's Bettis Atomic Power Laboratory, operated by the Westinghouse Electric Corporation, undertook development of the first nuclear propulsion plant.
Construction of a land-based prototype plant (STR Mark I) began in August 1950 at the reactor test station in Idaho. The STR Mark I was constructed inside a submarine hull, with a surrounding tank of water, to simulate actual submarine operating conditions. Initial criticality was attained on 30 Mar 1953. That June the STR Mark I reached full power and made a simulated 96-hour, full-power crossing of the Atlantic.
A virtually identical STR Mark II reactor plant was installed in the *Nautilus*. (The reactor plants were later redesignated S1W and S2W, respectively). The *Nautilus* Mark II/S2W plant was first operated at power on 20 Dec 1954 and first developed full power on 3 Jan 1955.
After more than two years of operation, during which she steamed 62 562 miles, the *Nautilus* began an overhaul which included refuelling in April 1957. She was again refuelled in 1959 after steaming 91 324 miles on her second fuel core, and again in 1964 after steaming approximately 150 000 miles on her third fuel core. (The prototype Mark I/S1W plant was refuelled in 1955, 1958, 1960, and 1967; it remains in operation as an experimental and training facility).

NAUTILUS (SSN 571) — *United States Navy*

Submarines—*continued*

3 ATTACK SUBMARINES (SS): "BARBEL" CLASS

Displacement, tons: 2 150 surface; 2 895 submerged
Length, feet (*metres*): 219·5 (*66·8*) oa
Beam, feet (*metres*): 29 (*8·8*)
Draft, feet (*metres*): 28 (*8·5*) max
Torpedo tubes: 6—21 in (*533 mm*) forward
Main engines: 3 diesels 4 800 hp (Fairbanks Morse); electric motors (General Electric); 1 shaft
Speed, knots: 15 on surface; 25 submerged
Complement: 77 (8 officers, 69 men)

Name	*No.*	*Builder*	*Laid down*	*Launched*	*Commissioned*
***BARBEL**	SS 580	Portsmouth Naval Shipyard	18 May 1956	19 July 1958	17 Jan 1959
***BLUEBACK**	SS 581	Ingalls Shipbuilding Corporation	15 Apr 1957	16 May 1959	15 Oct 1959
***BONEFISH**	SS 582	New York Shipbuilding Corp	3 June 1957	22 Nov 1958	9 July 1959

These submarines were the last non-nuclear combatant submarines built by the US Navy. All three were authorised in the Fiscal Year 1956 new construction programme.

DESIGN. These submarines have the "tear-drop" or modified spindle hull design which was tested in the experimental submarine *Albacore*. As built their diving planes were bow-mounted; subsequently relocated to the sail structure.

CONSTRUCTION. The *Blueback* was the first submarine built by the Ingalls Shipbuilding Corp at Pascagoula, Mississippi, and the *Bonefish* was the first constructed at the New York Shipbuilding Corp yard in Camden, New Jersey.

BONEFISH (SS 582) *1962, United States Navy*

BARBEL (SS 580) *1962, United States Navy*

1 ATTACK SUBMARINE (SS): "DARTER" TYPE

Displacement, tons: 1 720 surface; 2 388 submerged
Length, feet (*metres*): 268·6 (*81·9*) oa
Beam, feet (*metres*): 27·2 (*8·3*)
Draft, feet (*metres*): 19 (*5·8*)
Torpedo tubes: 8—21 in (*533 mm*) 6 fwd; 2 aft
Main engines: 3 diesels (Fairbanks Morse); 4 500 shp; 1 electric motor (Elliott); 2 shafts
Speed, knots: 17 surface; 25 submerged
Complement: 83 (8 officers, 75 men)

Name	*No.*	*Builder*	*Laid down*	*Launched*	*Commissioned*
***DARTER**	SS 576	General Dynamics Corp (Electric Boat)	10 Nov 1954	28 May 1956	20 Oct 1956

Designed for high submerged speed with quiet machinery. Planned sister submarines *Growler* and *Grayback* were completed to missile-launching configuration. Authorised in Fiscal Year 1954 shipbuilding programme. No additional submarines of this type were built because of shift to high-speed hull design and nuclear propulsion.

DARTER (SS 576) *courtesy Giorgio Ghiglione*

1 AMPHIBIOUS TRANSPORT SUBMARINE (LPSS)
1 ATTACK SUBMARINE (SS)
FORMER MISSILE SUBMARINES

Name	*No.*	*Builder*	*Laid down*	*Launched*	*Commissioned*	*LPSS Comm.*
***GRAYBACK**	LPSS 574 (ex-SSG 574)	Mare Island Naval Shipyard	1 July 1954	2 July 1957	7 Mar 1958	9 May 1969
GROWLER	SS 577 (ex-SSG 577)	Portsmouth Naval Shipyard	15 Feb 1955	5 Apr 1959	30 Apr 1958	

Displacement, tons
Grayback: 2 670 standard; 3 650 submerged
Growler: 2 540 standard; 3 515 submerged
Length, feet (*metres*)
Grayback: 334 (*101·8*) oa as LPSS
Growler: 317·6 (*96·8*) oa
Beam, feet (*metres*)
Grayback: 30 (*9·0*)
Growler: 27·2 (*8·2*)
Draft, feet (*metres*): 19 (*5·8*)
Torpedo tubes: 8—21 inch (*533 mm*) 6 fwd; 2 aft
Main engines: 3 diesels (Fairbanks Morse); 4 500 shp/2 electric motors (Elliott); 5 600 shp; 2 shafts
Speed, knots: 20 surface; 17 submerged
Complement as SSG: 84
Troops as LPSS: 67 (7 officers, 60 enlisted men)

These submarines are former Regulus guided missile submarines. They were originally intended to be attack submarines but in 1956 their design was modified to provide a missile-launching capability. The *Grayback* was authorised in the Fiscal Year 1953 new construction programme and the *Growler* in FY 1955.
When the Regulus submarine missile programme ended in 1964 the *Grayback* and *Growler* were withdrawn from service. The *Grayback* subsequently was converted to an Amphibious Transport Submarine (LPSS); the *Growler* was scheduled to undergo a similar conversion when the *Grayback* was completed; however, the *Growler* conversion was deferred late in 1968 because of rising ship conversion costs. The *Grayback* conversion was originally estimated at $15 200 000, but was actually about $30 000 000. As a transport submarine the *Grayback* carries commando, reconnaissance, or "frogman" units on covert missions. The *Growler* is out of service. Above data, except where indicated, for SSG configuration.

DESIGN. These submarines initially were designed as attack submarines similar to the *Darter*. Upon redesign as missile submarines they were cut in half on the building ways and were lengthened approximately 50 ft; two cylindrical hangars, each 11 ft high and 70 ft long, were superimposed on their bows; a missile launcher was installed between the hangars and conning towers; elaborate navigation systems fitted for missile firing.

CLASSIFICATION. The *Grayback* was redesignated from SSG to LPSS on 30 Aug 1968 (never officially designated APSS).

Submarines—*continued*

FORMER MISSILE SUBMARINES
continued

CONVERSION. The *Grayback* was converted to a troop submarine to replace the older, less-capable *Tunny* (LPSS 282) and *Perch* (LPS 313). As a transport she can berth and mess 67 troops and carry their equipment including landing craft or swimmer delivery vehicles (SDV). Her torpedo tubes and hence an attack capability are retained; improved electronic equipment installed. As completed (SSG) the *Grayback* had an overall length of 322 ft 4 inch; lengthened 12 ft during LPSS conversion. Conversion of the *Grayback* was authorised in Fiscal Year 1965 programme. She arrived at the San Francisco Bay Naval Shipyard (Mare Island) on 15 May 1967 and began conversion in Nov 1967; completed in June 1969. The conversion was delayed because of higher priorities being allocated to other submarine projects.

CORRECTION. Torpedo tube data in previous editions was in error.

MISSILES. The *Grayback* and *Growler* were built to each carry two Regulus II surface-to-surface missiles. The Regulus II was a transonic missile which could deliver a nuclear warhead on targets 1 000 miles from the launching ship. The Regulus II was cancelled before becoming operational and these submarines operated from 1958 to 1964 armed with the Regulus I missile. The latter was a subsonic cruise missile which could deliver a nuclear warhead on targets 500 miles away. Each submarine could carry four Regulus I missiles.

PHOTOGRAPHS. Note differences in configuration between the *Grayback* and *Growler*. In the drawing the *Grayback* is launching swimmer delivery vehicles; sonar PUFFs are fitted to her in the LPSS configuration.

GRAYBACK (as LPSS 574) *Official United States Navy drawing*

GRAYBACK (left), GROWLER (right) *1964, United States Navy*

2 ATTACK SUBMARINES (SS): CONVERTED RADAR PICKET SUBMARINES

Displacement, tons	2 625 surface; 3 168 submerged
Length, feet (*metres*)	350·5 (*106·8*) oa
Beam, feet (*metres*)	29·0 (*8·8*)
Draft, feet (*metres*)	18 (*5·5*) max
Torpedo tubes	6—21 in (*533 mm*) forward
Main engines	4 diesels (Fairbanks Morse); 9 600 shp/2 electric motors (Elliott); 8,200 shp; 2 shafts
Speed, knots	20·5 on surface; 15 submerged
Complement	96 (11 officers, 85 men)

Name	*No.*	*Builder*	*Laid down*	*Launched*	*Commissioned*
***SAILFISH**	SS 572 (ex-SSR 572)	Portsmouth Naval Shipyard	8 Dec 1953	7 Sep 1955	14 Apr 1956
***SALMON**	SS 573 (ex-AGSS 573, ex-SSR 573)	Portsmouth Naval Shipyard	10 Mar 1954	25 Feb 1956	25 Aug 1956

Largest non-nuclear submarines built by the US Navy since the *Narwhal* (SS 167) and *Nautilus* (SS 168) completed in 1930. The *Sailfish* and *Salmon* were built as radar picket submarines (SSR) with air-search radar antennas on deck and elaborate air control centres. Both submarines underwent FRAM II modernisation. Authorised in Fiscal Year 1952 programme.

CLASSIFICATION. Reclassified from radar picket submarines (SSR) to SS on 1 Mar 1961; *Salmon* reclassified AGSS on 29 June 1968 to serve as test and evaluation submarine for Navy's Deep Submergence Rescue Vehicle (DSRV). However, the DSRV programme has been delayed and the *Salmon* reverted to SS designation on 30 June 1969
As a mother submarine test platform she will evaluate the DSRV's ability to "land on" and "take off" from a moving submarine. (In actual operation the mother submarine would transport the DSRV "piggyback" while travelling submerged to the rescue or work area; see section on Deep Submergence Vehicles). The PUFF sonar antennas will be removed from the *Salmon* during the trials; she retains all other combat capabilities (as will DSRV support submarines).

SAILFISH (SS 572) *1966, United States Navy*

SALMON (AGSS 573) *1965, United States Navy*

Submarines—*continued*

1 EXPERIMENTAL SUBMARINE (AGSS): "ALBACORE" TYPE

Displacement, tons	1 500 surface; 1 850 submerged
Length, feet (*metres*)	204 (*62·2*) oa
Beam, feet (*metres*)	27·5 (*8·4*)
Draft, feet (*metres*)	18·5 (*5·6*)
Torpedo tubes	None
Main engines	2 diesels, radial pancake type (General Motors)/electric motor (Westinghouse) 15 000 shp; 1 shaft
Speed, knots	25 on surface; 33 submerged
Complement	52 (5 officers, 47 men)

Name	*No.*	*Builder*	*Laid down*	*Launched*	*Commissioned*
***ALBACORE**	AGSS 569	Portsmouth Naval Shipyard	15 Mar 1952	1 Aug 1953	5 Dec 1953

High speed experimental submarine. Conventionally powered submarine of radical design with new hull form which makes her faster and more manoeuvrable than any other conventional submarine. Officially described as a hydrodynamic test vehicle. Streamlined, whale-shaped without the naval flat-topped deck. Conning tower resembles a fish's dorsal fin.

ALBACORE (AGSS 569) *United States Navy*

CONVERSIONS. Phase I (1953): cruciform stern. Phase II (1956): open stern, plastic sonar bow. Phase III (1959): improved sonar system, enlarged dorsal rudder, dive brakes on after sail section. Phase IV (1961): Electrical Drive, contra-rotating motors and 2 propellers contra-rotating about the same axis. A high capacity, long endurance silver zinc battery providing power to drive her at 30+ knots submerged (commenced in Dec 1962, completed on 20 Feb 1965). Conversions were carried out at Portsmouth Naval Shipyard.

6 ATTACK SUBMARINES (SS): "TANG" CLASS

Displacement, tons	2 100 surface; 2 400 submerged
Length, feet (*metres*)	287 (*87·4*) oa
Beam, feet (*metres*)	27·3 (*8·3*)
Draft, feet (*metres*)	19 (*6·2*)
Torpedo tubes	8—21 in (*533 mm*) 6 fwd, 2 aft
Main engines	3 diesels (Fairbanks-Morse); 4 500 shp/2 electric motors; 5 600 shp
Speed, knots	20 on surface; 18 submerged
Complement	83 (8 officers, 75 men)

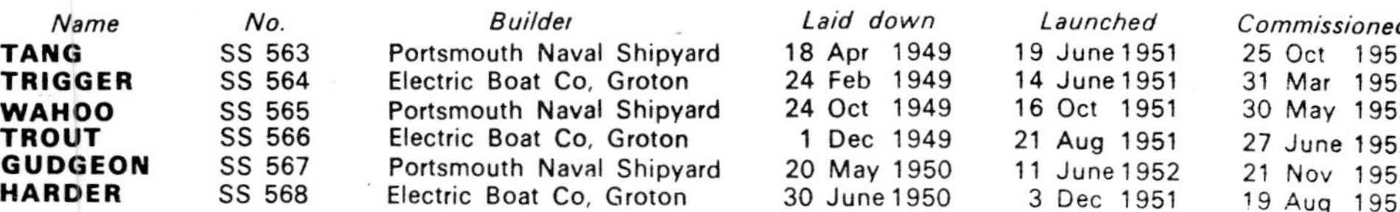

Name	*No.*	*Builder*	*Laid down*	*Launched*	*Commissioned*
***TANG**	SS 563	Portsmouth Naval Shipyard	18 Apr 1949	19 June 1951	25 Oct 1951
***TRIGGER**	SS 564	Electric Boat Co, Groton	24 Feb 1949	14 June 1951	31 Mar 1952
***WAHOO**	SS 565	Portsmouth Naval Shipyard	24 Oct 1949	16 Oct 1951	30 May 1952
***TROUT**	SS 566	Electric Boat Co, Groton	1 Dec 1949	21 Aug 1951	27 June 1952
***GUDGEON**	SS 567	Portsmouth Naval Shipyard	20 May 1950	11 June 1952	21 Nov 1952
***HARDER**	SS 568	Electric Boat Co, Groton	30 June 1950	3 Dec 1951	19 Aug 1952

This design embodied various improvements to give higher submerged speed, with a development of the Schnorkel. They are streamlined deep-diving submarines but have comparatively short hulls. *Trigger* was the first submarine of the post-war programme to be laid down. *Tang* was the first of the new class to be completed. *Tang* and *Trigger* authorised in Fiscal Year 1947 new construction programme, *Wahoo* and *Trout* in FY 1948, and *Gudgeon* and *Harder* in FY 1949.
The *Gudgeon* was the first United States submarine to circumnavigate the world during Sep 1957-Feb 1958.

GUDGEON (SS 567) *1968, United States Navy*

ENGINEERING. *Tang, Trigger, Trout* and *Wahoo* were originally powered by a compact, radial type engine produced after five years of development work, comprising a 16-cylinder 2-cycle plant, mounted vertically with four rows of cylinders radially arranged. These new engines were half the weight and two-thirds the size of the engines previously available for submarines. They proved to be unsatisfactory and were replaced by machinery similar to that in *Gudgeon* and *Harder* which have a Fairbanks-Morse high speed lightweight engine mounted horizontally. The electric motors are Elliott in *Tang* and *Trigger*, General Electric in *Wahoo* and *Trout*, Westinghouse in *Gudgeon* and *Harder*.

WAHOO (SS 565) *1968, United States Navy, PH1 W. A. Clayton*

RECONSTRUCTION. All six submarines of this class were built with an overall length of 269 ft 2 in. The *Tang, Trigger, Trout*, and *Wahoo* had their original diesel engines replaced during the late 1950s. During the process they were cut in half and a 9 ft section inserted amidships. All six submarines were modernised during the 1960s with the installation of improved electronic equipment and other features; additional sections were added to give an overall length of 287 ft.

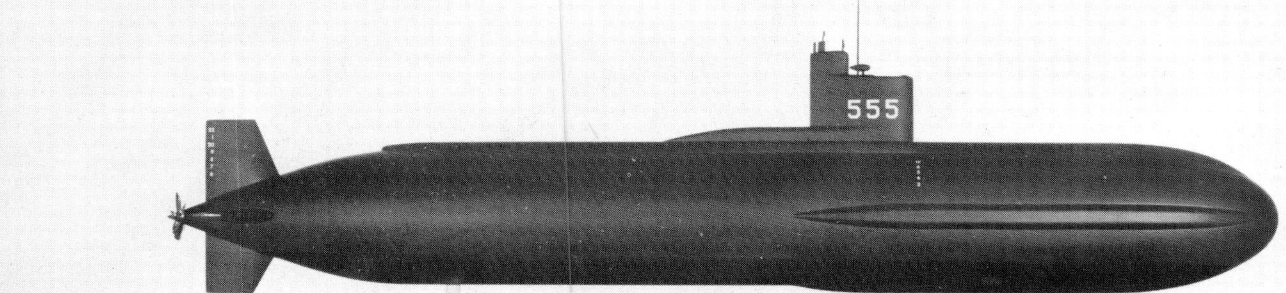

DOLPHIN (AGSS 555) (see following page) *Official design model*

Submarines—*continued*

1 EXPERIMENTAL SUBMARINE (AGSS): "DOLPHIN" TYPE

Displacement, tons	approx 600 standard; approx 900 submerged
Length, feet (*metres*)	152 (*46·3*) oa
Beam, feet (*metres*)	19 (*5·8*)
Torpedo tube	1 (experimental)
Main engines	diesel/electric; 1 shaft
Complement	23 (3 officers and 20 enlisted men) plus up to seven scientists

Name	*No.*	*Builder*	*Laid down*	*Launched*	*Commissioned*
***DOLPHIN**	AGSS 555	Portsmouth Naval Shipyard	9 Nov 1962	8 June 1968	17 Aug 1968

The *Dolphin* is an auxiliary submarine specifically designed for deep-diving operations. Authorised in Fiscal year 1961 new construction programme, but delayed because of changes in mission and equipment coupled with higher priorities being given to other submarine projects. Operating depth is greater than combatant submarines. Underwater endurance is limited (endurance and habitability were considered of secondary importance in design).

The *Dolphin* is fitted for deep-ocean sonar and oceanographic research. She is highly automated and has three computer-operated systems: a safety system, hovering system, and one that is classified. The digital-computer submarine safety system monitors equipment and provides data on closed-circuit television screens; malfunctions in equipment or trends toward potentially dangerous situations set off an alarm and if they are not corrected within the prescribed time the system, unless overrriden by an operator, automatically brings the submarine to the surface. There are several research stations for scientists in the *Dolphin* and she is fitted to take water samples down to her operating (test) depth.

CLASSIFICATION. The *Dolphin*'s number was taken from a block (551-562) authorised but cancelled late in World War II with no construction being assigned. (Submarines built in Norway and Denmark were assigned the hull numbers SS 553 and SS 554, respectively, for financial accounting purposes; hull numbers SS 551 and SS 552 in this series were assigned to the late hunter-killer submarines *Bass*, ex-SSK 2, and *Bonita* ex-SSK 3, respectively).

DESIGN. The *Dolphin* has a constant diameter, cylindrical pressure hull approximately 15 feet in outer diameter, closed at both ends with hemispherical heads. Pressure hull fabricated of HY-80 steel with aluminium and fibreglass used in secondary structures to reduce weight, a critical factor in retaining buoyancy at deep depths. No conventional diving planes are mounted; improved rudder design and other features provide manoeuvring control and hovering capability.

STATUS. Completed in early 1969, approximately five years behind official schedule at time of keel laying. The *Dolphin* is in commission and has a commanding officer (correction to previous edition).

DOLPHIN (AGSS 555) *Official design model*

PHOTOGRAPHS. The *Dolphin* is shown above as launched bow first into the Piscataqua River. Note her constant diameter hull, narrow deck and sail structure, and lack of bow or sail diving planes. The model on the previous page shows her small propeller and stepped sail structure.

9 ATTACK SUBMARINES (SS): GUPPY III TYPE

Displacement, tons	1 975 standard; 2 540 submerged
Length, feet (*metres*)	326·5 (*99·4*) oa
Beam, feet (*metres*)	27 (*8·2*)
Draft, feet (*metres*)	17 (*5·2*)
Torpedo tubes	10—21 in (*533 mm*); 6 fwd, 4 aft
Main engines	4 diesels; 6 400 shp/2 electric motors; 5 400 shp; 2 shafts
Speed, knots	20 surface; 15 submerged
Complement	approx 86

Name	*No.*	*Builder*	*Laid down*	*Launched*	*Commissioned*
***CLAMAGORE**	SS 343	Electric Boat Co	16 Mar 1944	25 Feb 1945	21 Oct 1944
***COBBLER**	SS 344	Electric Boat Co	3 Apr 1944	1 Apr 1945	8 Aug 1945
***CORPORAL**	SS 346	Electric Boat Co	27 Apr 1944	10 June 1945	9 Nov 1945
***GREENFISH**	SS 351	Electric Boat Co	29 June 1944	21 Dec 1945	7 June 1946
***TIRU**	SS 416	Mare Island Navy Yard	17 Apr 1944	16 Sep 1947	1 Sep 1948
***TRUMPETFISH**	SS 425	Cramp Shipbuilding Co	23 Aug 1943	13 May 1945	29 Jan 1946
***REMORA**	SS 487	Portsmouth Navy Yard	5 Mar 1945	12 July 1945	3 Jan 1946
***VOLADOR**	SS 490	Portsmouth Navy Yard	15 June 1945	17 Jan 1946	10 Jan 1948
***PICKEREL**	SS 524	Boston Navy Yard	8 Feb 1944	15 Dec 1944	4 Apr 1949

Nine submarines of the "Balao" and "Tench" classes were modernised under the GUPPY III programme in 1960-1962 (see *Design* notes). All previously were GUPPY II submarines. Plans for 15 additional GUPPY III modernisations were dropped in favour of new construction, nuclear-powered submarines.

DESIGN. The Greater Underwater Propulsion Programme (GUPPY) evolved after World War II as a method to improve underwater performance of existing US submarines. The GUPPY concept was based on the German Type XXI submarines which were mass produced in 1944-1945. The Type XXI characteristics included a streamlined hull and superstructure, snorkel, and increased battery power.

The US Navy's GUPPY conversions have similar features, with resulting increases in underwater speed and endurance, plus improved fire control and electronic equipment over their unmodernised sister submarines.

ELECTRONICS. GUPPY submarines are fitted with BQR-2 array sonar.

ENGINEERING. The GUPPY III submarines have two increased capacity, 126-cell electric batteries as do GUPPY IIA and IA submarines. All GUPPY submarines are fitted with snorkel to permit operation of diesel engines to charge batteries and for propulsion while at Periscope depth. The *Tiru* has only three diesel engines (4 800 shp).

PHOTOGRAPHS. Small, fin-like structures on submarines are hydrophones (referred to as PUFFS—acronym for Passive Underwater Fire-control Feasibility Study, an anti-submarine targeting system). GUPPY conversions have rounded bows as opposed to "ship bows in streamlined fleet-type submarines.

TRUMPETFISH (SS 425)  *1965, United States Navy*

Submarines—*continued*

PICKEREZ (SS 524) — *United States Navy*

14 ATTACK SUBMARINES (SS): GUPPY II TYPE

Displacement, tons	1 870 standard; 2 420 submerged
Length, feet (*metres*)	307·5 (*93·6*) oa
Beam, feet (*metres*)	27·2 (*8·3*)
Draft, feet (*metres*)	18 (*5·5*)
Torpedo tubes	10—21 in (*533 mm*); 6 fwd, 4 aft
Main engines	3 diesels; 4 800 shp/2 electric motors; 5 400 shp; 2 shafts
Speed, knots	18 surface; 15 submerged
Complement	Approx 82

Name	*No.*	*Builder*	*Laid down*	*Launched*	*Commissioned*
***CATFISH**	SS 339	Electric Boat Co	6 Jan 1944	19 Nov 1944	19 Mar 1945
***CUBERA**	SS 347	Electric Boat Co	11 May 1944	17 June 1945	19 Dec 1945
***DIODON**	SS 349	Electric Boat Co	1 June 1944	10 Sep 1945	18 Mar 1946
***DOGFISH**	SS 350	Electric Boat Co	22 June 1944	27 Oct 1945	29 Apr 1946
***HALFBEAK**	SS 352	Electric Boat Co	6 July 1944	19 Feb 1946	22 July 1946
***TUSK**	SS 426	Cramp Shipbuilding Co	23 Aug 1943	8 July 1945	11 Apr 1946
***CUTLASS**	SS 478	Portsmouth Navy Yard	22 July 1944	5 Nov 1944	17 Mar 1945
***SEA LEOPARD**	SS 483	Portsmouth Navy Yard	7 Nov 1944	2 Mar 1945	11 June 1945
***ODAX**	SS 484	Portsmouth Navy Yard	4 Dec 1944	10 Apr 1945	11 July 1945
***SIRAGO**	SS 485	Portsmouth Navy Yard	3 Jan 1945	5 May 1945	13 Aug 1945
***POMODON**	SS 486	Portsmouth Navy Yard	29 Jan 1945	12 June 1945	11 Sep 1946
***AMBERJACK**	SS 522	Boston Navy Yard	8 Feb 1944	15 Dec 1944	4 Mar 1946
***GRAMPUS**	SS 523	Boston Navy Yard	8 Feb 1944	15 Dec 1944	26 Oct 1949
***GRENADIER**	SS 525	Boston Navy Yard	8 Feb 1944	15 Dec 1944	2 Oct 1951

Fifteen submarines of the "Balao" and "Tench" classes were modernised under the GUPPY II programme in 1948-1950. The *Odax* and *Pomodon* were initially modernised to a GUPPY I configuration; subsequently updated to GUPPY II. The *Cochino* (SS 345) of this type was lost off Norway on a training cruise on 26 Aug 1949 (one civilian on board was lost; no naval personnel aboard *Cochino* were lost but another submarine assisting her had several men washed overboard and lost). General GUPPY notes are found in the GUPPY III listing.

ENGINEERING. GUPPY II submarines have four 126-cell electric batteries. The *Pomodon* has only two 1 600 hp diesels and is fitted with a special 1 500-hp diesel for snorkel operations.

DOGFISH (SS 350) — *1965, United States Navy*

SIRAGO (SS 485) — *1965, United States Navy*

POMFREY (SS 391) (GUPPY IIA) — *1968, United States Navy, PHC R. G. Dahson*

Submarines—*continued*

15 ATTACK SUBMARINES (SS): GUPPY IIA TYPE

Displacement, tons	1 840 standard; 2 445 submerged
Length, feet (*metres*)	306 (*93·2*) oa
Beam, feet (*metres*)	27 (*8·2*)
Draft, feet (*metres*)	17 (*5·2*)
Torpedo tubes	10—21 in (*533 mm*); 6 fwd; 4 aft
Main engines	3 diesels; 4 800 shp/2 electric motors; 5 400 shp; 2 shafts
Speed, knots	18 surface; 15 submerged
Complement	Approx 84

Sixteen submarines of the "Balao" and "Tench" classes were modernised under the GUPPY IIA programme in 1952-1954. The *Stickleback* (SS 415) of this type was rammed by US escort ship and sunk off Hawaii on 29 May 1958 (no crewmen lost). General GUPPY conversion notes are found in the GUPPY III listing.

PHOTOGRAPHS. Note differing superstructure designs; stepped structures in some submarines are being replaced with more streamlined structures of light-weight materials as in *Pomfrey*.

Name	*No.*	*Builder*	*Laid down*	*Launched*	*Commissioned*
*ENTEMEDOR	SS 340	Electric Boat Co	3 Feb 1944	17 Dec 1944	6 Apr 1945
*HARDHEAD	SS 365	Manitowoc Shipbuilding Co	7 July 1943	12 Dec 1943	18 Apr 1944
*JALLAO	SS 368	Manitowoc Shipbuilding Co	29 Sep 1943	12 Mar 1944	8 July 1944
*MENHADEN	SS 377	Manitowoc Shipbuilding Co	21 June 1944	20 Dec 1944	22 June 1945
*PICUDA	SS 382	Portsmouth Navy Yard	15 Mar 1943	12 July 1943	16 Oct 1943
*BANG	SS 385	Portsmouth Navy Yard	30 Apr 1943	30 Aug 1943	4 Dec 1943
*POMFRET	SS 391	Portsmouth Navy Yard	14 July 1943	27 Oct 1943	19 Feb 1944
*RAZORBACK	SS 394	Portsmouth Navy Yard	9 Sep 1943	27 Jan 1944	3 Apr 1944
*RONQUIL	SS 396	Portsmouth Navy Yard	9 Sep 1943	27 Jan 1944	22 Apr 1944
*SEA FOX	SS 402	Portsmouth Navy Yard	2 Nov 1943	28 Mar 1944	13 June 1944
*THREADFIN	SS 410	Portsmouth Navy Yard	18 Mar 1944	26 June 1944	30 Aug 1944
*THORNBACK	SS 418	Portsmouth Navy Yard	5 Apr 1944	7 July 1944	13 Oct 1944
*TIRANTE	SS 420	Portsmouth Navy Yard	28 Apr 1944	9 Aug 1944	6 Nov 1944
*TRUTTA	SS 421	Portsmouth Navy Yard	22 May 1944	18 Aug 1944	16 Nov 1944
*QUILLBACK	SS 424	Portsmouth Navy Yard	27 June 1944	1 Oct 1944	29 Dec 1944

TIRANTE (SS 420) *1965, United States Navy*

10 ATTACK SUBMARINES (SS): GUPPY IA TYPE

Displacement, tons	1 870 standard; 2 440 submerged
Length, feet (*metres*)	308 (*93·8*) oa
Beam, feet (*metres*)	27 (*8·2*)
Draft, feet (*metres*)	17 (*5·2*)
Torpedo tubes	10—21 in (*533 mm*); 6 fwd, 4 aft
Main engines	3 diesels; 4 800 shp/2 electric motors; 5 400 shp; 2 shafts
Speed, knots	18 surface; 15 submerged
Complement	approx 84

Name	*No.*	*Builder*	*Laid down*	*Launched*	*Commissioned*
*BECUNA	SS 319	Electric Boat Co	29 Apr 1943	30 Jan 1944	27 May 1944
*BLACKFIN	SS 322	Electric Boat Co	10 June 1943	12 Mar 1944	4 July 1944
*CAIMAN	SS 323	Electric Boat Co	24 June 1943	30 Mar 1944	17 July 1944
*BLENNY	SS 324	Electric Boat Co	8 July 1943	9 Apr 1944	27 July 1944
*CHIVO	SS 341	Electric Boat Co	21 Feb 1944	14 Jan 1945	28 Apr 1945
CHOPPER	SS 342	Electric Boat Co	2 Mar 1944	4 Feb 1945	25 May 1945
*ATULE	SS 403	Portsmouth Navy Yard	2 Dec 1943	6 Mar 1944	21 June 1944
*SEA POACHER	SS 406	Portsmouth Navy Yard	23 Feb 1944	20 May 1944	31 July 1944
*SEA ROBIN	SS 407	Portsmouth Navy Yard	1 Mar 1944	25 May 1944	7 Aug 1944
*TENCH	SS 417	Portsmouth Navy Yard	1 Apr 1944	7 July 1944	6 Oct 1944

Ten submarines of the "Balao" and "Tench" classes were modernised under the GUPPY IA programme in 1951. General GUPPY conversion notes are found in the GUPPY III listing.

PHOTOGRAPHS. *Blenny* has later sail structure and three PUFF sonar antennae

STATUS. The *Chopper* was decommissioned in 1969, after having experienced a control casualty on 11 Feb 1969 during operations in the Caribbean Sea. The casualty resulted in a sharp-angle descent followed by an abrupt-angle ascent as her crew fought to halt the dive and bring the submarine back to the surface. Reportedly, the submarine's bow reached a depth of approximately 1 000 feet before the descent was halted. (The designed operating (test) depth of this class is 412 feet).
After the accident the *Chopper* returned on the surface to the US Naval Base at Guantanamo Bay, Cuba, for repairs, and then transited safely to her homeport of Key West, Florida.

BLENNY (SS 324) *1966, United States Navy*

TENCH (SS 417) *1968, United States Navy*

Submarines—*continued*

4 FLEET SUBMARINES (AGSS): "TENCH" CLASS

Displacement, tons	1 840 standard; 2 400 submerged
Length, feet (*metres*)	312 (*95·1*) oa
Beam, feet (*metres*)	27·2 (*8·3*)
Draft, feet (*metres*)	16·5 (*5·0*)
Torpedo tubes	10—21 in (*533 mm*); 6 fwd, 4 aft
Main engines	4 diesels; 6 400 shp/2 electric motors; 5 400 shp; 2 shafts
Speed, knots	20 surface; 10 submerged
Complement	approx 85

Name	*No.*	*Builder*	*Laid down*	*Launched*	*Commissioned*
TIGRONE	AGSS 419	Portsmouth Navy Yard	8 May 1944	20 July 1944	25 Oct 1944
***MEDREGAL**	AGSS 480	Portsmouth Navy Yard	21 Aug 1944	15 Dec 1944	14 Apr 1945
IREX	AGSS 482	Portsmouth Navy Yard	2 Oct 1944	26 Jan 1945	14 May 1945
***SPINAX**	AGSS 489	Portsmouth Navy Yard	14 May 1945	20 Nov 1945	20 Sep 1946

Twenty-seven "Tench" class submarines were completed as fleet submarines in 1944-1946 and four others were completed to GUPPY configurations in 1949-1950. Fourteen of the older boats subsequently were converted under the various GUPPY programmes. A further 101 submarines of this design were cancelled in 1944-1945 (see below).
Only four non-GUPPY submarines of this class remain on the Navy List, among them two former radar picket submarines (see *Conversion* notes).

CANCELLATIONS. Cancelled units were *Unicorn* (SS 429), *Vandace* (SS 430), *Walrus* (SS 431), *Whitefish* (SS 432), *Whiting* (SS 433), *Wolffish* (SS 434), unnamed SS 438-474, 495-515, 517-521, *Dorado* (SS 526) *Comber* (SS 527), *Sea Panther* (SS 528), *Tibourn* (SS 529), unnamed SS 530-544, 548-550, 545-547, *Pompano* (SS 491), *Grayling* (SS 492), *Needlefish* (SS 493), *Sculpin* (SS 494), and *Wahoo* (SS 516). The hulls of the uncompleted *Unicorn* and *Walrus* were not stricken until 1957. Construction of the *Turbot* (SS 427) and *Ulua* (SS 428) were "deferred" in August 1945 and their unfinished hulls were used in machinery experiments.

CLASSIFICATION. *Tigrone* to AGSS on 1 Dec 1963, *Medregal* to AGSS on 1 May 1967. *Irex* and *Spinax* to AGSS in *1969*

CONVERSIONS. The *Tigrone*, and *Spinax* were converted to radar picket submarines in 1947-1948 and reclassified SSR, *Tigrone* on 31 Mar 1948 and the *Spinax* on 19 Jan 1948; fitted with elaborate air search radar and air control centre; reclassified SS on 15 Aug 1959 with end of radar picket submarine programme.

DESIGN. These ships were originally of an improved "Balao" class design, slightly larger and with a deeper operating capability. As built the fleet types carried deck guns of varying size and number (authorised gun armament was one 5 inch 25 calibre mount and a single 40 mm mount plus MG). Several of the surviving fleet-type have been fitted with streamlined superstructures but can be differentiated from GUPPY conversions by their ship-like prows.

ENGINEERING. All surviving submarines of this type have snorkel installations.

DISPOSALS AND TRANSFERS
Toro (SS 422), **Corsair** (SS 435) and **Conger** (SS 477) stricken from Navy List in 1963, **Diablo** (SS 479) sold to Pakistan in 1964, and **Sarda** (SS 488) stricken in 1964 and scrapped (not transferred to Spain), **Argonaut** (SS 475) stricken on 2 Dec 1968 and transferred to Canada.

TRAINING. Three submarines of this type are employed as dockside trainers: *Torsk* (AGSS 423), *Runner* (AGSS 476), and *Requin* (AGSS 481).

REQUIN (SS481) (now dockside trainer) *1966, United States Navy*

MEDREGAL (AGSS480) *1963, United States Navy*

SPINAX (AGSS489) *1965, United States Navy*

7 FLEET SUBMARINES (SS/AGSS): "BALAO" CLASS

Displacement, tons	1 450 standard; 2 400 submerged
Length, feet (*metres*)	312 (*95·1*) oa
Beam, feet (*metres*)	27·2 (*8·25*)
Draft, feet (*metres*)	17·2 (*5·25*)
Torpedo tubes	10—21 in (*533 mm*); 6 fwd, 4 aft
Main engines	4 diesels; 6 400 shp/2 electric motors; 5 400 shp; 2 shafts
Speed, knots	20 surface; 10 submerged
Complement	approx 85

Name	*No.*	*Builder*	*Laid down*	*Launched*	*Commissioned*
***SABALO**	SS 302	Cramp Shipbuilding (Phila)	5 June 1943	4 June 1944	19 June 1945
***SABLEFISH**	AGSS 303	Cramp Shipbuilding (Phila)	5 June 1943	4 June 1944	18 Dec 1945
***BUGARA**	AGSS 331	Electric Boat Company	21 Oct 1943	2 July 1944	15 Nov 1944
***CARBONERO**	AGSS 337	Electric Boat Company	16 Dec 1943	15 Oct 1944	7 Feb 1945
***CUSK**	AGSS 348	Electric Boat Company	25 May 1944	28 July 1945	5 Feb 1946
***SEGUNDO**	SS 398	Portsmouth Navy Yard	14 Oct 1943	5 Feb 1944	9 May 1944
***SEA OWL**	AGSS 405	Portsmouth Navy Yard	7 Feb 1944	7 May 1944	17 July 1944

One hundred-twenty "Balao" class submarines were completed in 1943-1948, most of which were operational during World War II. Thirty-one submarines were converted to GUPPY configurations. Ten submarines of this type were cancelled in 1944 and the SS 353-355 were renumbered SS 435-437. Numerous war losses, transfers, conversions, and disposals are listed below. Three stricken submarines were used as target ships in the 1946 atomic bomb tests at Bikini: *Skate* (SS 305), *Apogon* (SS 308), *Pilotfish* (SS 386).
Twenty non-GUPPY "Balao" class submarines remain on the Navy List: seven boats listed above, two conversions listed separately, and 11 immobilised dockside trainers (see *Training* note).

CANCELLATIONS. Cancelled units were *Jawfish* (SS 356), *Ono* (SS 357), *Garlopa* (SS 358), *Garruda* (SS 359), *Goldring* (SS 360), *Needlefish* (SS 379), *Nerka* (SS 380), *Dugong* (SS 353), *Eel* (SS 354), and *Espada* (SS 355). The hull of the uncompleted *Lancetfish* (SS 296) was stricken in 1957.

CUSK (SS 348) *United States Navy*

Submarines—*continued*

"BALAO" CLASS *continued*

STATUS. *Sablefish, Bugara, Carbonero, Cusk,* and *Sea Owl* to AGSS on 30 June 1969.

CONVERSIONS. *Carbonero* (SS 337) converted to fire guided missiles but not reclassified; *Cusk* (SS 348) converted to fire guided missiles, to SSG in 1948 (reverted to SS in 1954).

DESIGN. As built these submarines carried deck guns of varying size and number. Authorised armament included one 5 inch 25 calibre gun and a single 40 mm mount plus 20 mm and ·50 calibre machine guns; several submarines carried two 5 inch guns, two 40 mm guns, and several MG. Original configuration provided for carrying 24 contemporary torpedoes (including ten in tubes). Streamlined superstructures fitted to some fleet boats.

ENGINEERING. All surviving fleet type submarines of this class have snorkel installations.

TRAINING. Eleven of the submarines of this type are immobilised dockside training ships for the Naval reserve. Their torpedo tubes are welded shut, propellers removed, berthnig spaces converted to classrooms. *Bowfin* (AGSS 287), *Ling* (AGSS 297), *Lionfish* (AGSS 298), *Batfish* (AGSS 310), *Perch* (LPSS 313), *Charr* (AGSS 328), *Cabezon* (AGSS 334), *Carp* (AGSS 338) *Pampanito* (AGSS 383), *Parche* (AGSS 384), *Piper* (AGSS 409).

WAR LOSSES. Ten submarines of this class were lost during World War II: *Capelin* (SS 289), *Cisco* (SS 290), *Esoclar* (SS 294), *Tank* (SS 306), *Shark* (SS 314), *Barbel* (SS 316), *Bullhead* (SS 332), *Golet* (SS 361), *Kete* (SS 369), *Lagarto* (SS 371).

DISPOSALS AND TRANSFERS
Balao (AGSS 285 stricken in 1963, **Devilfish** (AGSS 292) stricken in 1967 and sunk as targets, **Hackleback** (AGSS 295) stricken in 1966, **Lancetfish** (SS 296) stricken in 1958, **Manta** (AGSS 299), **Moray** (AGSS 300), and **Seahorse** (AGSS 304) stricken in 1967, **Skate** (SS 305) sunk in 1948, **Tilefish** (SS 307) transferred to Venezuala in 1965, **Apogon** (SS 308) sunk at Bikini in 1946 (stricken 1947), **Aspro** (AGSS 309) stricken in 1962, **Burrfish** (SS 312) to Canada in 1961, returned to USA in 1968 and scrapped, **Barbero** (SSG 317) stricken in 1964, **Bergall** (SS 320) to Turkey in 1959, **Besugo** (AGSS 321) to Italy in 1966, **Blower** (SS 325), **Blueback** (SS 326), **Boarfish** (SS 327), **Chub** (SS 329), and **Brill** (SS 330) to Turkey in 1948, **Bumper** (SS 333) to Turkey in 1950, **Dentuda** (AGSS 335) stricken in 1967, **Capitaine** (SS 336) to Italy in 1966, **Guavina** (AOSS 362) stricken in 1967 (expended as target), **Guitarro** (SS 363) and **Hammerhead** (SS 364) to Turkey in 1954, **Hawkbill** (SS 366) and **Icefish** (SS 367) to Netherlands in 1953, **Kraken** (SS 370) to Spain in 1959, **Lamprey** (SS 372) to Argentina in 1960, **Lizardfish** (SS 373) to Italy in 1960, **Loggerhead** (AGSS 374) stricken in 1967, **Macabi** (SS 375) to Argentina in 1960, **Mapiro** (SS 376) and **Mero** (SS 378) to Turkey in 1960, **Sand Lance** (SS 381) to Brazil in 1963, **Pilotfish** (SS 386) stricken in 1947, **Pintado** (AGSS 387), **Pipefish** (AGSS 388), and **Piranha** (AGSS 389) stricken in 1967, **Plaice** (SS 390) to Brazil in 1963, **Queenfish** (AGSS 393) stricken in 1963, **Redfish** (AGSS 395) stricken in 1965, **Scabbardfish** (AGSS 397) to Greece in 1965, **Sea Devil** (AGSS 400) stricken in 1964, **Spikefish** (AGSS 404) stricken in 1963 **Spadefish** (AGSS 411) and **Trepang** (AGSS 412) stricken in 1967, **Spot** (SS 413) and **Springer** (SS 414) to Chile in 1962 and 1961, respectively. **Crevalle** (AGSS 291) stricken on 15 Apr 1968, **Sennet** (SS 408) stricken on 2 Dec 1968, **Sea Dog** (AGSS 401) stricken on 2 Dec 1968, **Archerfish** (AGSS 311) stricken on 1 May 1968 expended as target), **Sea Cat** (AGSS 399) stricken on 2 Sep 1968, **Cabrilla** (AGSS 288) stricken on 30 June 1968, **Sterlet** (S 392) stricken on 1 Oct 1968, **Roncador** (AGSS 301) stricken in 1969.

SEGUNDO (SS 398) *1966, United States Navy*

SEA OWL (SS 405) *1967, United States Navy*

1 AMPHIBIOUS TRANSPORT SUBMARINE (LPSS): "SEALION" TYPE

Displacement, tons	2 145 surface; 2 500 submerged
Length, feet (*metres*)	311·5 (*95·0*)
Beam, feet (*metres*)	27 (*8·2*)
Draft, feet (*metres*)	17 (*5·2*)
Guns,	2—40 mm AA
Main engines	2 diesels (General Motors), 2 305 hp/4 electric motors; 2 shafts
Speed, knots	13 surface; 10 submerged
Complement	74 (6 officers, 68 men)
Troops	160

Name	*No.*	*Builder*	*Laid down*	*Launched*	*Commissioned*
*SEALION	LPSS 315	Electric Boat Company, Groton	25 Feb 1943	31 Oct 1943	8 Mar 1944

The *Sealion* and *Perch* (LPSS 313) were converted from "Balao" class submarines to underwater transports used to deliver Marines, commandos, frogmen or other passengers in covert operations or where surface ships would be too vulnerable. The *Perch* was declared unsuitable for underway operations in 1967 and became an immobilised Naval Reserve training ship at San Diego. The former Regulus missile submarine *Tunny* (ex-SSG 282) was quickly modified to provide an interim replacement until conversion of the more-effective *Grayback* (LPSS 574) was completed. *Tunny* (LPSS 282) was stricken from the Navy List on 30 June 1969. *Sealion* was to have been replaced by conversion of *Growler* c(SS 577) to transport, submarine; however *Growler* conversion to LPSS cancelled because of high cost.

CLASSIFICATION. *Sealion* was redesignated APSS upon conversion to transport configuration; redesignated LPSS on 1 Jan 1969 (*Tunny* same date).

CONVERSION. The *Sealion* was converted to a submarine transport at the San Francisco Naval Shipyard in 1948. All torpedo tubes and half of diesel propulsion plant were removed to provide berthing for 160 troops; stowage provided for rubber rafts and other equipment in deck aft of conning tower.

PERCH (LPSS 313) now dockside trainer,) *1965, United States Navy*

"SEALION" TYPE *continued*

STATUS. In 1960 the *Sealion* was assigned to operational reserve training duties; recommissioned late in 1961 with increase of US conventional warfare capabilities.

PHOTOGRAPHS. Note hull bulges abaft conning tower. Older photograph shows 5 inch/25 calibre gun forward of conning tower; since removed and second 40 mm gun installed.

1 EXPERIMENTAL SUBMARINE (AGSS): "BAYA" TYPE

Name	*No.*	*Builder*	*Laid down*	*Launched*	*Commissioned*
***BAYA**	AGSS 318	Electric Boat Company, Groton	9 Apr 1943	2 Jan 1944	20 May 1944

Displacement, tons	1 900 surface; 2 625 submerged
Length, feet (*metres*)	334·8 (*102·0*) oa
Beam, feet (*metres*)	27 (*8·2*)
Draft, feet (*metres*)	17 (*5·2*)
Torpedo tubes	4 aft
Main engines	2 diesels (General Motors)/4 electric motors; 2 shafts
Speed, knots	10·5 surface; 8 submerged
Complement	76 (8 officers, 68 men)

Originally a "Balao" class submarine; decommissioned in May 1946 and placed in reserve until reactivated in 1948 for use as an electronics laboratory; re-commissioned on 10 Feb 1948. Currently assigned to Submarine Development Group One at San Diego.

CONVERSION. The *Baya* underwent a limited conversion to an electronics laboratory in 1948-1949, being re-designated AGSS on 12 Aug 1949. Underwent more extensive conversion at San Francisco Naval Shipyard in 1958-1959. At that time the *Baya* was cut in half and a 23-foot section was added between the forward torpedo room and forward battery room; fitted with two booms forward which extended to position sonar equipment; bow modified to house experimental electronic equipment; forward torpedo tubes removed; 4 000-pound mushroom anchor installed in bottom of hull; extensive electronic research equipment provided. Much of the *Bay's* work is in support of the Naval Electronics Laboratory Centre at San Diego.

BAYA (AGSS 318) *United States Navy*

2 AUXILIARY SUBMARINES (AGSS): "GATO" CLASS

Name	*No.*	*Builder*	*Launched*	*Commissioned*
***BASHAW**	AGSS 241 (ex-SSK)	Electric Boat Co	25 July 1943	25 Oct 1943
***ROCK**	AGSS 274 (ex-SSR)	Manitowic Ship- building (Wisconsin)	20 June 1943	26 Oct 1943

Displacement, tons		1 800 standard
	Bashaw	2 425 submerged
	Rock	2 500 submerged
Length, feet (metres)	*Bashaw*	312 (95·1) oa
	Rock	343 (104·5) oa
Beam, feet (metres)		27·2 (*8·3*)
Draft, feet (metres)	*Bashaw*	15 (*4·6*)
	Rock	17 (*5·2*)
Torpedo tubes	*Bashaw*	8—21 inch (*533 mm*) 4 fwd, 4 aft;
	Rock	6—21 inch (*533 mm*) fwd
Main engines	*Bashaw*	3 diesels, 4 800 shp/4 electric motors, 4 600 shp; 2 shafts;
	Rock	4 diesels, 6 400 shp/4 electric motors, 4 600 shp; 2 shafts
Speed, knots	*Bashaw*	17 surface/10 submerged
	Rock	21 surface/10 submerged
Complement		approx 85

The *Gato* (SS 212), lead submarine of this class, was commissioned on the last day of 1941; 72 sisters completed in 1942-1943. The *Bashaw* and *Rock* are the only submarines of this class remaining in active US service. Seven immobilized sister submarines serve as dockside training craft for naval reservists.

CLASSIFICATION. *Bashaw* reclassified from SSK to AGSS on 1 Sep 1962; *Rock* from SSR to AGSS in Dec 1959.

CONVERSION. *Bashaw* converted to hunter-killer submarine, reclassified SSK on 18 Feb 1953. Fitted with improved BQR-2 and BQR-4 anti-submarine sonars, improved torpedoes, noise-reduction features, and snorkel. Two forward torpedo tubes removed to provide space for sonar equipment. Reverted to SS classification on 15 Aug 1959. *Rock* was converted to a radar picket submarine, reclassified SSR on 18 July 1952. Cut in half and lengthened to provide space for additional electronic equipment, stern torpedo tubes removed, air search radar antennas fitted on deck and sail structure. Classification changed to AGSS in 1959 with end of submarine radar picket programme.

DESIGN. Almost identical to previous US submarine classes built on the eve of World War II. Authorised armament included one 5 inch 25 calibre gun and a single 40 mm mount plus machine guns; generally increased in submarines of this class during World War II.

TRAINING. Submarines of this type used as immobilised dockside trainers for Naval Reserve are *Cod* (AGSS 224), *Angler* (AGSS 240), *Cavalla* (AGSS 244), *Cobia* (AGSS 245), *Croaker* (AGSS 246), *Rasher* (AGSS 269) and *Redfin* (AGSS 272).

BASHAW (AGSS 241) *United States Navy*

WAR LOSSES. Nineteen submarines of the "Gato" class were lost during World War II: *Growler* (SS 215), *Grunion* (SS 216), *Albacore* (SS 218), *Amberjack* (SS 219), *Bonefish* (SS 223), *Corvina* (SS 226), *Darter* (SS 227), *Herring* (SS 233), *Trigger* (SS 237), *Wahoo* (SS 238), *Dorado* (SS 248), *Flier* (SS 250), *Harder* (SS 257), *Robalo* (SS 273), *Runner* (SS 275), *Scamp* (SS 277), *Scorpion* (SS 278), *Snook* (SS 279), *Tullibee* (SS 284).

DISPOSALS AND TRANSFERS

Guardfish (SS 217), **Gato** (SS 212), **Greenling** (SS 213), stricken in 1960, **Barb** (SS 220) transferred to Italy in 1954, **Blackfish** (SS 221) and **Bluefish** (SS 222) stricken in 1958, **Cero** (AGSS 225) stricken in 1957, **Drum** (AGSS 228) stricken in 1968, **Finback** (SS 230) stricken in 1959, **Haddock** (SS 231) stricken in 1960, **Halibut** (SS 232) stricken in 1947, **Kingfish** (SS 234), **Shad** (SS 235), and **Whale** (SS 239) stricken in 1960, **Dace** (SS 247) to Italy in 1954, **Flounder** (SS 251), **Gabilan** (SS 252), and **Gurnard** (SS 254) stricken in 1960, **Gunnel** (SS 253) stricken in 1959, **Haddo** (SS 255) stricken in 1958, **Hake** (AGSS 256) stricken in 1968, **Hoe** (SS 258) stricken in 1960, **Jack** (SS 259) and **Lapon** (SS 260) to Greece in 1957, **Mingo** (SS 261) to Japan in 1955, **Muskallunge** (SS 262) and **Paddle** (SS 263) to Brazil in 1957, **Pargo** (SS 264), **Peto** (SS 265), **Pompon** (SSR 267), **Puffer** (SS 268), **Ray** (SSR 271), **Sawfish** (SS 276), **Steelhead** (SS 280), and **Sunfish** (SS 281) stricken in 1960, **Pogy** (SS 266) and **Tinosa** (SS 283) stricken in 1958. **Grouper** (AGSS 214) stricken on 2 Dec 1968, **Bluegill** (AGSS 242), **Bream** (AGSS 243), **Raton** (AGSS 270), **Tunny** (LPSS 282, ex-SSG 282), **Silversides** (AGSS 236) stricken in 1969.

Submarines—*continued*

2 TRAINING SUBMARINES (SST): "MACKEREL" TYPE

Displacement, tons	303 surface; 347 submerged
Length, feet (*metres*)	131·2 (*40·0*) oa
Beam, feet (*metres*)	13·5 (*4·1*)
Draft, feet (*metres*)	12·2 (*3·7*)
Torpedo tubes	1 forward
Main engines	2 GM diesels; 1 shaft 1 electric motor; 380 hp
Speed, knots	8 surface; 9·5 submerged
Complement	18 (2 officers, 16 men)

The *Mackerel* and *Marlin* were authorised in the Fiscal Year 1951 and 1952 shipbuilding programmes, respectively. They are the smallest US submarines built since the "C" class of 1909; intended specifically for anti-submarine training. Estimated construction cost was $3 000 000 per submarine.

CLASSIFICATION. The *Mackerel* was ordered as AGSS 570; both submarines were designated SST during construction.

NOMENCLATURE. Renamed in 1956: *Mackerel* ex-T-1, *Marlin* ex-T-2.

Name	*No.*	*Builder*	*Laid down*	*Launched*	*Commissioned*
***MACKEREL** (ex-T 1)	SST 1	Electric Boat Co, Groton	12 May 1952	14 Oct 1953	20 Nov 1953
***MARLIN** (ex-T 2)	SST 2	Electric Boat Co, Groton	1 Apr 1952	17 July 1953	9 Oct 1953

MACKEREL (SST 1) *United States Navy*

1 TRAINING SUBMARINE (SST): "BARRACUDA" TYPE

Displacement, tons	765 surface; 1 160 submerged
Length, feet (*metres*)	196 (*59·7*) oa
Beam, feet (*metres*)	24·8 (*7·5*)
Draft, feet (*metres*)	16 (*4·9*)
Torpedo tubes	4—21 in (*533 mm*), 2 fwd, 2 aft
Main engines	3 diesels (General Motors); 1 050 shp/2 electric motors (General Electric); 2 shafts
Speed, knots	10 surface; 8 submerged
Complement	50 (5 officers, 45 men)

Authorised in Fiscal Year 1948 shipbuilding programme. Medium sized, quiet, and handy design specifically built for anti-submarine operations. Had letter and number instead of name until 15 Dec 1955 when "B" name was substituted for "K" number. Originally had an ungainly prow housing large BQR-4 passive submarine detection sonar; very quiet boat and small to reduce target size and increase manoeuvrability in submarine-versus-submarine encounters. By 1959 this class was considered to be wanting as hunter killer craft. They lacked speed, range, and endurance for effective ASW operations.

CLASSIFICATION. SSK 1 designation changed to SST 1 in 1959 (simultaneously SSK 2 and SSK 3 were redesignated SS 551 and SS 552, respectively; see *Disposals*).

DISPOSALS
Sister boats **Bass**, SS 551 (ex-K 2) and **Bonita**, SS 552 (ex-K3) were stricken from the Navy List on 1 Apr 1965.

Name	*No.*	*Builder*	*Laid down*	*Launched*	*Commissioned*
***BARRACUDA**	(ex-K 1) SST3 (ex-SSK 1)	Electric Boat Co, Groton	1 July 1949	2 Mar 1951	10 Nov 1951

BARRACUDA (SST 3) *United States Navy*

1 MIDGET SUBMARINE: "X" TYPE

Name	*Builder*	*Laid down*	*Launched*	*In Service*
***X-1**	Fairchild Engine & Airplane Corp	8 June 1954	7 Sep 1955	7 Oct 1955

Displacement, tons	31·5 surface; 36·3 submerged
Length, feet (*metres*)	49 7 in oa
Beam, feet (*metres*)	7 (*2·1*)
Draft, feet (*metres*)	6 9 in
Main engines	1 diesel (Hercules) / 1 electric motor; 1 shaft
Complement	4

The only "midget" submarine built for the US Navy. Prototype for small submarines intended to penetrate harbours undetected to seek out and destroy enemy shipping with demolition charges. Provisions were made to set and release explosive charges from within the submarine or to lock-out and recover underwater swimmers who would plant ot attach the explosives. Designed to be towed to operational area by larger submarine. In service vice being in commission; commanded by an officer-in-charge.

STATUS. Underwent extensive tests and evaluation in 1956-1957. An internal explosion while the *X-1* was at the Portsmouth Naval Shipyard in February 1958 blew off the craft's forward section; remainder of submarine remained intact and was backed away from burning bow section and pier. In reserve from 1958-1960; reactivated in 1960 for experimental work. Based at Naval Ship Research and Development Centre in Annapolis, Maryland; operates in Chesapeake Bay in support of studies relating to origin and structure of waves, heat balance between water and atmosphere, light penetration of water, underwater visibility, and mixing factors of water. The *X-1* is painted orange for safety considerations because of merchant shipping and pleasure craft in the area.

X 1 *1962, United States Navy*

DESIGN. Modified tear-drop hull design; aircraft type controls; forward diving planes mounted on superstructure forward (just above draft numbers in photograph).

ENDURANCE. Designed for ten-day missions with crew of four, can carry six men for shorter missions.

ENGINEERING. Originally fitted with diesel/hydrogen-peroxide system which permitted operation of diesel engine while submerged. Small electric "creeping" motor was fitted to diesel for very slow speeds and for battery charging. Hydrogen-peroxide components removed in 1960 and electric motor fitted in 1962 for underwater propulsion ("creeping" motor was retained). Fitted with single five-bladed, five-foot propeller, snorkel installed.

Submarines—*continued*

21 IMMOBILIZED TRAINING SUBMARINES (AGSS/LPSS)

No.	*Name*	*Location*
AGSS 224	**COD**	Cleveland, Ohio
AGSS 240	**ANGLER**	Philadelphia
AGSS 244	**CAVALLA**	Houston, Texas
AGSS 245	**COBIA**	Milwaukee, Wisc
AGSS 246	**CROAKER**	Portsmouth, NH
AGSS 269	**RASHER**	Portland, Ore
AGSS 272	**REDFIN**	Baltimore
AGSS 287	**BOWFIN**	Seattle, Wash
AGSS 297	**LING**	New York City
AGSS 298	**LIONFISH**	Providence, R I
AGSS 310	**BATFISH**	New Orleans
LPSS 313	**PERCH**	San Diego, Calif
AGSS 328	**CHARR**	San Pedro, Calif
AGSS 334	**CABEZON**	Tacoma, Wash
AGSS 338	**CARP**	Boston
AGSS 383	**PAMPANITO**	Vallejo, Calif
AGSS 384	**PARCHE**	Alameda, Calif
AGSS 409	**PIPER**	Detroit
AGSS 423	**TORSK**	Washington, DC
AGSS 476	**RUNNER**	Chicago
AGSS 481	**REQUIN**	St Petersburg, Fla

These submarines are immobilised dockside training vessels employed to train Naval Reserve personnel. Their propellers are removed and their torpedo tubes are welded shut. The reservists undergo periodic at-sea training on operational diesel-powered submarines.

CLASSIFICATION. All designated AGSS except *Perch*; she was changed from APSS to LPSS on 1 Jan 1969.

PIPER (AGSS 409) (now dockside trainer) *1964, United States Navy*

FIRE SUPPORT SHIPS

The US Navy's fire support force comprises a battleship, four 8 inch gun cruisers, and four rocket ships which are used for shore bombardment in the Vietnamese War. In addition, a number of cruisers and destroyers in the Fleet Escort Force which are armed with 6 inch and 5 inch guns have been used effectively for gunfire support.

BATTLESHIPS. A page describing battleships returned to *Jane's Fighting Ships* with the 1968-69 edition after a six-year absence. The return of a full-scale listing for the "Iowa" class dreadnoughts followed the decision to reactivate the USS *New Jersey* to "provide an extended range and increased destructive power to the . . . Seventh Fleet bombardment group".
The US Navy had tenaciously retained the four 45 000-ton "Iowa" class ships long after all other navies had scrapped or disarmed their battleships. Several proposals had been put forward to convert the "Iowa" class ships to underway replenishment ships, combination command-bombardment-assault ships, *et cetera*, but they were retained in their existing configuration in the reserve (mothball) fleet.

The activation of the *New Jersey* to serve as a fire support ship was announced on 1 Aug 1967. She deployed to the Vietnam combat zone from early September 1968 to late March 1969, after which she returned to her home-port of Long Beach, California, for maintenance and refresher training.
A second deployment to the combat zone was scheduled for the fall of 1969, "contingent upon the status of operations at that time".
The battleships *Iowa*, *Missouri*, and *Wisconsin* remain in the reserve fleet. There are no plans at this writing to return them to active service.

CRUISERS. The US Navy's surviving all-gun cruisers are listed as Fire Support Ships because of their limited capabilities for performing other missions. Only extensive modification has enabled the all-gun *Newport News* and *Saint Paul* to continue as fleet flagships. The gun-missile cruisers *Boston* and *Canberra* have been reclassified as heavy cruisers (CA vice CAG) reflecting the limited capability of their Terrier BW missiles for task force defense. They are also listed as Fire Support Ships, the role in which they have been used extensively in the Vietnamese War.

FIRE SUPPORT SHIPS. The specialised fire support ships in the US Navy consist of several modified World War II-built landing ships and a single prototype fire support ship built during the Korean War.
A new Amphibious Fire Support Ship (LFS) is being designed which will combine in one hull an armament of large-calibre guns and rocket launchers. The guns would provide long range, accuracy, and destructive power while the rockets would provide saturation fire. The LFS main battery is expected to consist of three or four 8 inch Major Calibre Light Weight Guns (MCLWG) which will fire conventional and rocket-assisted projectiles. The latter may have a range of as much as 100 miles.
The ship's secondary gun battery probably will consist of twin 5 inch/54 caliber Mark 65 mounts, a variation of the rapid-fire 5 inch gun being evaluated in the *Norton Sound* (AVM 1).
This ship would replace the Navy's gun cruisers, which are old and expensive to operate, and the slow rocket ships.
The Fiscal Year 1969 budget provided funds to have industry access and propose solutions to the technical problems of designing and building the new fire support ship (contract definition). However, this work is behind schedule. At this writing the Navy planned to construct these new fire support ships during the Fiscal Year 1971-1973 period.

Fire Support Ships—*continued*

4 BATTLESHIPS (BB): "IOWA" CLASS

Displacement, tons	45 000 standard; 59 000 full load
Length, feet (*metres*)	860 (*262·1*) wl; 887·2 (*270·4*) oa except *New Jersey* 887·6 (*270·5*)
Beam, feet (*metres*)	108·2 (*33·0*)
Draft, feet (*metres*)	38 (*11·6*)
Guns	9—16 inch (*406 mm*) 50 cal. 20—5 inch (*127 mm*) 38 cal. dual purpose.
Main engines	4 geared turbines (General Electric in BB 61 and BB 63; Westinghouse in BB 62 and BB 64); 212 000 shp; 4 shafts
Boilers	8 (Babcock & Wilcox)
Speed, knots	33 (all have reached 35 knots in service)
Complement	designed complement varied, averaging 169 officers and 2 689 enlisted men in wartime; *New Jersey* now manned by 70 officers and 1 556 enlisted men (requirements reduced with removal of all light anti-aircraft weapons, floatplanes, and reduced operational requirements)

Name	*No.*	*Builder*	*Laid down*	*Launched*	*Commissioned*
IOWA	BB 61	New York Navy Yard	27 June 1940	27 Aug 1942	22 Feb 1943
***NEW JERSEY**	BB 62	Philadelphia Navy Yard	16 Sep 1940	7 Dec 1942	23 May 1943
MISSOURI	BB 63	New York Navy Yard	6 Jan 1941	29 Jan 1944	11 June 1944
WISCONSIN	BB 64	Philadelphia Navy Yard	25 Jan 1941	7 Dec 1943	16 Apr 1944

NEW JERSEY (BB 62) *1968, US Navy AN E. J. Bonner*

These ships were the largest battleships ever built except for the Japanese *Yamato* and *Musashi* (64 170 tons standard, 863 feet overall, 9—18·1 inch guns.) All four "Iowa" class ships were in action in the Pacific during World War II, primarily screening fast carriers and bombarding amphibious invasion objectives. Three were mothballed after the war with the *Missouri* being retained in service as a training ship. All four ships again were in service during the Korean War (1950-1953) as shore-bombardment ships; all mothballed 1954-1958.

The *New Jersey* began reactivation in mid-1967 at a cost of approximately $21 000 000; recommissioned on 6 Apr 1968. The *Iowa* and *Wisconsin* remain in reserve at the Philadelphia Naval Shipyard where the *New Jersey* had been berthed and reactivated; the mothballed *Missouri* is at the Puget Sound Naval Shipyard, Bremerton, Washington.

Two additional ships of this class were laid down, but never completed: *Illinois* (BB 65), laid down 15 Jan 1945, and *Kentucky* (BB 66), laid down 6 Dec 1944. The *Illinois* was 22 percent complete when cancelled on 11 Aug 1945. The *Kentucky* was 69·2 percent complete when construction was suspended late in the war; floated from its building dock on 20 Jan 1950. Conversion to a missile ship (BBG) was proposed, but no work was undertaken and she was stricken on 9 June 1958 and broken up for scrap.

Approximate construction cost was $114 485 000 for *Missouri*; other ships cost slightly less.

AIRCRAFT. As built, each ship carried three floatplanes for scouting and gunfire spotting and had two quarterdeck catapults. Catapults removed and helicopters carried during the Korean War.

ARMOUR. These battleships are the most heavily armoured US warships ever constructed, being designed to survive ship-to-ship combat with enemy ships armed with 16 inch guns. The main armour belt consists of Class A steel armour 12·1 inches thick tapering vertically to 1·62 inches; a lower armour belt aft of Turret No. 3 to protect propeller shafts is 13·5 inches; turret faces are 17 inches; turret tops are 7·25 inches; turret backs are 12 inches; barbetts have a maximum of 11·6 inches of armour; second deck armour is 6 inches; and the three-level conning tower sides are 17·3 inches with an armoured roof 7·25 inches (the conning tower levels are pilot house, navigation bridge, and flag-signal bridge).

DESIGN. These ships carried same armament as six previous US battleships but had increased protection and larger engines accounting for additional displacement and increased speed. Design includes clipper bow and long foredeck, with graceful sheer (see photographs). All fitted as fleet flagships with additional accommodations and bridge level for admiral and staff.

GUNNERY. The 16 inch guns in these ships can fire projectiles weighing up to 2 700 pounds (*1 225 kg*) (armour piercing) a maximum distance of 23 miles (*39 km*). As built, these ships had 80—40 mm and 49 to 60 —20 mm anti-aircraft guns (except *Iowa*, only 19 quad 40 mm mounts); all 20 mm guns removed and a reduced number of 40 mm weapons remain on the mothballed ships.

MODERNISATION. The *New Jersey* underwent an "austere" modernisation in 1967-1968, with installation of modern communications equipment, electronic countermeasure (ECM) equipment, a fog foam firefighting system in engine rooms, air conditioning in living spaces, a new target-designating system, and a helicopter platform.

NOMENCLATURE. US battleships are generally named for states; the exception was the *Kearsarge*, BB 5 launched in 1899 (later *Crane Ship No. 1*, AB 1).

DISPOSALS

Eight World War II-built battleships and large (battle) cruisers have been stricken: **North Carolina** (BB 55), **Washington** (BB 56), **Alaska** (CB 1), and **Guam** (CB 2) on 1 June 1960; **South Dakota** (BB 57), **Indiana** (BB 58), **Massachusetts** (BB 59), and **Alabama** (BB 60) on 1 June 1962. **North Carolina, Massachusetts** and **Alabama** to their states as memorials; others scrapped. Plans to convert the unfinished **Hawaii** (CB 3) to a command ship (CBC 1) were dropped and she was stricken on 9 June 1958.

The five battleships of the "Montana" class authorised on the eve of World War II were never begun and formally were cancelled on 21 July 1943 (60 500 tons standard displacement, 921·25 feet overall, 12—16 inch guns).

NEW JERSEY (BB 62) *1968, United States Navy by PHC Harold Wise*

Fire Support Ships—*continued*

2 Heavy Cruisers (CA): "Boston-Canberra" Type (ex-CAG)

Name	*No.*	*Builder*	*Laid down*	*Launched*	*Commissioned*	*CAG Comm.*
***BOSTON**	CA 69 (ex-CAG 1)	Bethlehem Steel Co (Quincy)	30 June 1941	26 May 1942	30 June 1943	1 Nov 1955
***CANBERRA**	CA 70 (ex-CAG 2)	Bethlehem Steel Co (Quincy)	3 Sep 1941	19 Apr 1943	14 Oct 1943	15 June 1956

Displacement, tons	13 300 standard; 17 500 full load
Length, feet (*metres*)	664 (*222·3*) wl; 673·5 (*205·3*) oa
Beam, feet (*metres*)	70·8 (*21·6*)
Draft, feet (*metres*)	26 (*7·9*)
Missiles	2 twin Terrier launchers
Guns	6—8 in (*203 mm*) 55 cal 10—5 in (*127 mm*) 38 cal dual-purpose 8—3 in (*76 mm*) 50 cal anti-aircraft
Main engines	4 geared turbines (General Electric), 120 000 shp; 4 shafts
Boilers	4 (Babcock & Wilcox)
Speed, knots	33
Complement	1 273 (73 officers; 1 200 enlisted men)

These were the world's first guided missile warships. Originally heavy cruisers (CA) of the "Baltimore" class. Converted 1952-1956 to combination gun-missile configuration and reclassified CAG. Subsequently reclassified as CA on 1 May 1968, reverting to original hull numbers. They both retain Terrier missile armament but have early BW-1 missile systems which are no longer considered suitable for task force defence against high-performance aircraft.

Retention of 8 inch guns forward have made these ships invaluable in the fire support role during the Vietnamese conflict.

CONVERSION. Both ships were converted to a missile configuration at the New York Shipbuilding Corp, Camden, New Jersey. *Boston* conversion ordered on 4 Dec 1951 and *Canberra* on 28 Jan 1952. Conversion included removal of after 8-inch gun turret (143 tons) and after twin 5-inch mount; all 40 mm and 20 mm guns replaced by six 3-inch twin mounts (subsequently reduced to four mounts). Superstructure modified and twin funnels replaced by single large funnel (as in "Oregon City" class cruisers). Forward pole mast replaced by lattice radar mast and radar platform fitted aft of second

Polemast. Missile system installation includes rotating magazines below decks, loading and check-out equipment, and two large directors aft. Estimated conversion cost was £30,000,000 for two ships.

BOSTON (CA 69) *1968, United States Navy, PH3 D. R. Hyden*

MISSILES. Reportedly, each ship carries 144 missiles in two, rotating magazines. Each launcher can load and fire two missiles every 30 seconds; loading is completely automatic with missiles sliding onto launchers in the vertical position.

NOMENCLATURE. The *Canberra* was originally named *Pittsburgh*: she was renamed while under construction to honour an Australian cruiser of that name which was sunk with several US Navy Ships in the Battle of Savo Island in August 1942. She is the only US warship named for a foreign capital city.

PHOTOGRAPHS. Twin 3-inch gun mounts abaft missile directors have been removed from both ships. The Photograph of the *Boston*, taken in April 1968, Oahu, Hawaii, show her still carrying the "1" of her late CAG 1 designation.

CANBERRA (CA70) *1968, United States Navy, PH2 R. E. Duggan*

Fire Support Ships—*continued*

3 HEAVY CRUISERS (CA): "SALEM" CLASS

Name	No.	Builder	Laid down	Launched	Commissioned
DES MOINES	CA 134	Bethlehem Steel Co (Quincy)	28 May 1945	27 Sep 1946	17 Nov 1948
SALEM	CA 139	Bethlehem Steel Co (Quincy)	4 June 1945	25 Mar 1947	9 May 1949
***NEWPORT NEWS**	CA 148	Newport News SB & DD Co	1 Oct 1945	6 Mar 1947	29 Jan 1949

Displacement, tons	17 000 standard; 21 500 full load
Length, feet (*metres*)	700 (*213·4*) wl; 716·5 (*218·4*) oa
Beam, feet (*metres*)	76·3 (*23·3*)
Draft, feet (*metres*)	26 (*7·9*)
Guns CA 148	9—8 in (*203 mm*) 55 calibre 12—5 in (*127 mm*) 38 calibre dual-purpose 8—3 in (*76 mm*) 50 calibre anti-aircraft) (see *Gunnery* notes)
Main engines	4 geared turbines (General Electric); 120 000 shp; 4 shafts
Boilers	4 (Babcock & Wilcox)
Speed, knots	33
Complement CA 148	approx 1 200

These ships were the largest and most powerful 8 inch-gun cruisers ever built. Completed too late for World War II, they were employed primarily as flagships for the Sixth Fleet in the Mediterranean and the Second Fleet in the Atlantic. The *Salem* was decommissioned on 30 Jan 1959 and the *Des Moines* on 14 July 1961. The *Newport News* remains in commission; normally flagship of the Second Fleet, she was employed as a fire support ship off Vietnam in 1967-1968.

AIRCRAFT. As completed the *Des Moines* had two stern catapults and carried four floatplanes; catapults removed.

DESIGN. These ships are an improved version of the previous "Oregon City" class. The newer cruisers have automatic main batteries, larger main turrets, taller fire control towers, and larger bridges. The *Des Moines* and *Newport News* are fully air conditioned.

Nine additional ships of this class were cancelled: the *Dallas* (CA 140) and the unnamed CA 141-142, CA 149-153.

GUNNERY. The cruisers were the first ships to be armed with fully automatic 8 inch guns firing cased ammunition. The guns can be loaded at any elevation from —5 to +41 degrees; rate of fire is four times faster than earlier 8 inch guns. As built these ships mounted 12 5 inch guns, 20 3 inch guns (in twin mounts with provision for 24 guns), and 12 20 mm guns (single mounts). The 20 mm guns were removed almost immediately and the 3 inch battery was reduced gradually as ships were overhauled. (With full armament the designed wartime complement was 1 860).

MODERNISATION. The *Newport News* has been extensively modified to provide improved flagship facilities; note elaborate antennas on masts, forecastle, atop turrets, and atop stern crane superstructure expanded outward on both sides between forward 3 inch twin mounts and secondary battery directors.

DES MOINES (CA 148) *1967, United States Navy, JO1 W. B. Bass*

DES MOINES (CA 148) *1967, United States Navy, JO1 W. B. Bass*

SALEM (CA 139) *United States Navy*

2 HEAVY CRUISERS (CA): "OREGON CITY" CLASS

Name	No.	Builder	Laid down	Launched	Commissioned
OREGON CITY	CA 122	Bethlehem Steel Co (Quincy)	8 Apr 1944	9 Feb 1945	16 Feb 1946
ROCHESTER	CA 124	Bethlehem Steel Co (Quincy)	29 May 1944	28 Aug 1945	20 Dec 1946

Displacement, tons	13 700 standard; 17 500 full load
Length, feet (*metres*)	664 (*202·4*) wl; 673·5 (*205·3*) oa
Beam, feet (*metres*)	70·9 (*21·6*)
Draft, feet (*metres*)	26 (*7·9*)
Guns	9—8 in (*203 mm*) 55 calibre; 12—5 in (*127 mm*) 38 calibre dual-purpose; 40—40 mm anti-aircraft in *Oregon City*; 20—3 in (*127 mm*) 50 calibre AA in *Rochester* (see *Gunnery* notes)
Main engines	4 geared turbines (General Electric); 120 000 shp; 4 shafts
Boilers	4 (Babcock & Wilcox)
Speed, knots	33
Complement	1 700 (designed wartime)

These cruisers are similar to the previous "Baltimore" class ships but have a single funnel and more compact superstructure. Three ships of this class were completed; the *Albany* (CA 123) was converted to a guided missile cruiser (CG 10) in 1958-1962. The *Oregon City* was mothballed in 1947, shortly after completion, and the *Rochester* in 1961.

ROCHESTER (CA 124) *United States Navy*

Fire Support Ships—*continued*

AIRCRAFT. As completed these ships had two stern catapults and carried four floatplanes; catapults removed from the *Rochester*.

DESIGN. These ships are identical in design to the "Baltimore" class except for their superstructure. Seven additional ships of this class were cancelled: the *Northampton* (CA 125), *Cambridge* (CA 126), *Bridgeport* (CA 127), *Kansas* (CA 128), *Tulsa* (CA 129), *Norfolk* (CA 137), and *Scranton* (CA 138); the *Northampton* was later re-ordered as a command ship (CLC 1, now CC 1).

GUNNERY. These ships were designed to mount nine 8 inch guns, 12 5 inch guns, 48 40 mm guns (11 quad and two twin mounts), and 24 20 mm guns. Lighter weapons were replaced by twin 3 inch mounts in *Rochester*.

OREGON CITY (CA 122) — *1946, United States Navy*

10 HEAVY CRUISERS (CA): "BALTIMORE" CLASS

Name	No.	Builders	Laid down	Launched	Commissioned
BALTIMORE	CA 68	Bethlehem Steel Company, Quincy	26 May 1941	28 July 1942	15 Apr 1943
QUINCY	CA 71	Bethlehem Steel Company, Quincy	9 Oct 1941	23 June 1943	15 Dec 1943
PITTSBURG	CA 72	Bethlehem Steel Company, Quincy	3 Feb 1943	22 Feb 1944	10 Oct 1944
***ST. PAUL**	CA 73	Bethlehem Steel Company, Quincy	3 Feb 1943	16 Sep 1944	17 Feb 1945
HELENA	CA 75	Bethlehem Steel Company, Quincy	9 Sep 1943	28 Apr 1945	4 Sep 1945
BREMERTON	CA 130	New York Shipbuilding Corporation	1 Feb 1943	2 July 1944	29 Apr 1945
FALL RIVER	CA 131	New York Shipbuilding Corporation	12 Apr 1943	13 Aug 1944	1 July 1945
MACON	CA 132	New York Shipbuilding Corporation	14 June 1943	15 Oct 1944	26 Aug 1945
TOLEDO	CA 133	New York Shipbuilding Corporation	13 Sep 1943	6 May 1945	27 Oct 1946
LOS ANGELES	CA 135	Philadelphia Naval Shipyard	28 July 1943	20 Aug 1944	22 July 1945

Displacement, tons	13 600 standard; 17 200 full load
Length, feet (*metres*)	664 (*202·4*) wl; 673·5 (*205·3*) oa
Beam, feet (*metres*)	70·9 (*21·6*)
Draft, feet (*metres*)	26 (*7·9*)
Guns: *Saint Paul*	9—8 in (*203 mm*) 55 calibre 10—5 in (*127 mm*) 38 calibre dual purpose 12—3 in (*76 mm*) 50 calibre anti-aircraft (see *Gunnery* notes)
Main engines	4 geared turbines (General Electric); 120 000 shp; 4 shafts
Boilers	4 (Babcock & Wilcox)
Speed, knots	33
Complement	1 146 (61 officers, 1,085 enlisted men) in *Saint Paul*; designed wartime complement 1 772 in *Baltimore* and *Quincy*, 1 969 in later ships

Fourteen ships of this class were completed; four of the ships have been converted to guided missile cruisers: the *Boston* (CA 69/CAG 1), *Canberra* (CA 70/CAG 2), *Columbus* (CA 74, now CG 12), and *Chicago* (CA 136, now CG 11). The *Fall River* was scheduled for missile conversion, but was replaced by the *Columbus*. The remaining all-gun cruisers were phased out of the active fleet as missile ships became available. The *Baltimore* was mothballed in 1955, *Quincy* in 1954, *Pittsburg* in 1955, *Helena* in 1963, *Bremerton* in 1960, *Fall River* in 1947, *Macon* in 1961, *Toledo* in 1960, and *Los Angeles* in 1966. Only the *Saint Paul* remains in service as an all-gun cruiser.

AIRCRAFT. As completed these ships had two stern catapults and carried four floatplanes; catapults removed after World War II.

GUNNERY. These ships were completed with nine 8 inch guns, 12—5 inch inch guns, 48—40 mm guns (12 quad mounts in CA 68-71, 11 quad and two twin mounts in later ships), and 23—20 mm guns. All 20 mm weapons were removed and the 40 mm guns were replaced by 20—3 inch guns (twin mounts) in all but the *Fall River* and *Quincy*. The number of 3 inch guns was reduced subsequently in some ships before they were mothballed. (The *Helena* had only 14—3 inch guns when decommissioned; the *Saint Paul* retains only 12). The *Saint Paul* also lost the twin 5 inch mount forward of her bridge.

MODERNISATION. The *Saint Paul*, *Helena*, *Macon*, and *Los Angeles* have been modified to improve their flagship facilities; advanced electronic equipment fitted and pole foremast replaced by a pylon mast to support additional antennas including "bee-hive" TACAN (Tactical Air Navigation system to guide aircraft).

NOMENCLATURE. Ships renamed during construction were *Quincy*, ex-*Saint Paul; Pittsburg*, ex-*Albany; Saint Paul*, ex-*Rochester;* and *Helena*, ex-*Des Moines*.

SAINT PAUL (CA 73) — *1967, United States Navy, PH 1. D. Granthom*

SAINT PAUL (CA 73) — *1967, United States Navy, JO1 B. S. Whitehead*

HELENA (CA 75) — *1961, United States Navy*

Fire Support Ships—*continued*

SAINT PAUL (CA 73) *1967, United States Navy, JO1 B. S. Whitehead*

2 LIGHT CRUISERS (CL): "WORCESTER" CLASS

Name	*No.*	*Builders*	*Laid down*	*Launched*	*Commissioned*
ROANOKE	CL 145	New York Shipbuilding Corporation	15 May 1945	16 June 1947	4 Apr 1948
WORCESTER	CL 144	New York Shipbuilding Corporation	29 Jan 1945	4 Feb 1947	25 June 1948

Displacement, tons	14 700 standard; 18 500 full load
Length, feet (*metres*)	664 (*202·4*) wl; (679·5 (*207·1*) oa
Beam, feet (*metres*)	70·7 (*21·5*)
Draft, feet (*metres*)	25 (*7·6*)
Guns	12—6 in (*152 mm*) 47 calibre dual-purpose; 24—3 in (*127 mm*) 50 calibre AA in *Roanoke*; 12—3 in (*127 mm*) 50 calibre AA in *Worcester*
Main engines	4 geared turbines (General Electric); 120 000 shp; 4 shafts
Boilers	4 (Babcock & Wilcox)
Speed, knots	32
Complement	1 170 (peacetime; designed war time complement 1 700)

These ships are amongst the largest cruisers ever constructed and are ranked as "light" cruisers only because of their 6 inch main battery. They served in the active fleet for a decade. often paired to an 8 inch-gunned "Salem" class heavy cruiser in two-ship cruiser divisions. Both the *Worcester* and *Roanoke* were decommissioned and placed in mothballs late in 1958, giving them the distinction of being the last all-gun light cruisers to serve in the United States Navy.

ROANOKE (CL 145)  *United States Navy*

DESIGN. These ships have their 12—6 inch guns arranged in six twin turrets vice 12 guns in four triple turrets of other US light cruisers of the World War II era. The *Worcester* and *Roanoke* are also the only US cruisers of World War II design without 5 inch guns.

Eight additional ships of this class were cancelled: the *Vallejo* (CL 146), *Gary* (CL 147), and the unnamed CL 154-159.

GUNNERY. The 6 inch guns in these ships are automatic weapons suitable for use against air as well as surface targets. Their original design provided for a secondary battery of 48—40 mm AA guns (11 quad and two twin mounts). As completed, both ships had 24—3 inch guns (11 twin and two single mounts), 12—40 mm guns, and 12—20 mm guns. The lighter guns were removed soon after completion; the *Worcester's* 3 inch battery was reduced prior to her being decommissioned.

1 LIGHT CRUISER (CL): "FARGO" CLASS

Name	*No.*	*Builder*	*Laid down*	*Launched*	*Commissioned*
FARGO	CL 106	New York Shipbuilding Corporation	23 Aug 1943	25 Feb 1945	9 Dec 1945

Displacement, tons	10 500 standard; 14 055 full load
Length, feet (*metres*)	600 (*182·9*) wl; 610 (*185·9*) oa
Beam, feet (*metres*)	66·3 (*20·2*)
Draft, feet (*metres*)	25 (*7·6*)
Guns	12—6 in (*152 mm*) 47 calibre 12—5 in (*127 mm*) 38 calibre dual-purpose 28—40 mm anti-aircraft
Main engines	4 geared turbines (General Electric), 100 000 shp; 4 shafts
Boilers	4 (Babcock & Wilcox)
Speed, knots	32·5
Complement	916 (peacetime; designed war-time complement 1 426)

The *Fargo* was one of two modified "Cleveland" class cruisers completed shortly after World War II. She was mothballed in 1949; her sister ship *Huntington* (CL 107) was stricken on 1 Sep 1962.

AIRCRAFT. The *Fargo* and *Huntington* were completed with two stern catapults and carried four floatplanes.

DESIGN. The *Fargo* is almost identical to the previous "Cleveland" class except for a single funnel in place of the two funnels in the earlier class.

Eleven additional ships of this class were cancelled: *Newark* (CL 108), *New Haven* (CL 109), *Buffalo* (CL 110), *Wilmington* (CL 111), *Roanoake* (CL 114), *Tallahassee* (CL 116), *Cheyenne* (CL 117), *Chattanooga* (CL 118), and the unnamed CL 112, CL 113, and CL 115.

GUNNERY. The 40 mm weapons are mounted in six quad and two twin mounts, the latter in stern "tubs". As built 19—20 mm AA guns were also installed; they were removed after completion.

FARGO (CL 106) *Marius Bar*

Fire Support Ships—*continued*

5 LIGHT CRUISERS (CL): "CLEVELAND" CLASS

Displacement, tons	10 500 standard; 13 750 full load
Length, feet (*metres*)	600 (*182·9*) wl; 610 (*185·9*) oa
Beam, feet (*metres*)	66·3 (*20·2*)
Draft, feet (*metres*)	25 (*7·6*)
Guns	12—6 in (*152 mm*) 47 calibre 12—5 in (*127 mm*) 38 calibre dual-purpose 28—40 mm anti-aircraft
Main engines	4 geared turbines (General Electric); 100 000 shp; 4 shafts
Boilers	4 (Babcock & Wilcox)
Speed	33 knots
Complement	916 (peacetime; designed wartime complement varied, up to 1 475 in later ships)

The "Cleveland" class was numerically the largest group of cruisers ever planned with 39 hull numbers being assigned to this class. Only 27 were completed as light cruisers; five of these survive as all-gun ships in reserve, six as gun-missile ships (CLG), and one as an experimental ship (*Atlanta*, ex-CL 104, now IX 304). All ships completed as light cruisers were mothballed by the outbreak of the Korean War in 1950 except for the *Manchester* (CL 83) which was decommissioned in 1956.

Name	*No.*	*Builder*	*Laid down*	*Launched*	*Commissioned*
PASADENA	CL 65	Bethlehem Steel Co (Quincy)	6 Feb 1943	28 Dec 1943	8 June 1944
ASTORIA	CL 90	Cramp Shipbuilding Co	6 Sep 1941	6 Mar 1943	17 May 1944
AMSTERDAM	CL 101	Newport News SB & DD Co	3 Mar 1943	25 Apr 1944	8 Jan 1945
PORTSMOUTH	CL 102	Newport News SB & DD Co	28 June 1943	20 Sep 1944	25 June 1945
WILKES-BARRE	CL 103	New York Shipbuilding Corp	14 Dec 1942	24 Dec 1943	1 July 1944

AIRCRAFT. As completed these ships had two stern catapults and carried four floatplanes.

GUNNERY. The 28—40 mm guns were arranged in four quad and six twin mounts; two twin mounts removed from some ships before decommissioning. The *Manchester* had her light AA guns replaced by 20—3 inch guns in twin mounts during the Korean War. As built each ship also had 19—20mm AA weapons.

NOMENCLATURE. *Astoria* ex-*Wilkes-Barre*.

DISPOSALS AND CONVERSIONS
Cleveland (CL 55), **Columbia** (CL 56), **Montpelier** (CL 57), **Denver** (CL 58), stricken from Navy List in 1959 and scrapped; **CL 59** completed as light carrier CVL 22; **Santa Fe** (CL 60) stricken in 1959; **CL 61** completed as CVL 23; **Birmingham** (CL 62), **Mobile** (CL 63), stricken in 1959; **Vincennes** (CL 64) stricken in 1966; **Springfield** (CL 65) converted to CLG 7; **Topeka** (CL 66) converted to CLG 8; **CL 76-79** completed as CVL 24-28, respectively; **Biloxi** (CL 80) stricken in 1961; **Houston** (CL 81) stricken in 1959; **Providence** (CL 82) converted to CLG 6; **Manchester** (CL 83) stricken in 1960; **CL 84** cancelled in 1940; **CL 85** completed as CVL 27; **Vicksburg** (CL 86) stricken in 1962; **Duluth** (CL 87) stricken in 1960; **CL 88** cancelled in 1940; **Miami** (CL 89) stricken in 1961; **Oklahoma City** (CL 91) converted to CLG 5; **Little Rock** (CL 92) converted to CLG 4; **Galveston** (CL 93) converted to CLG 3; **Youngstown** (CL 94) cancelled in 1945; **CL 99** completed as CVL 29; **CL 100** completed as CVL 30; **Atlanta** (CL 104) stricken in 1962, but returned to Navy List in 1964 as IX 304; **Dayton** (CL 105) stricken in 1961.

The World War II-era "anti-aircraft cruisers" have all been stricken or reclassified: **San Diego** (CLAA 53), **San Juan** (CLAA 54), **Oakland** (CLAA 95), **Reno** (CLAA 96) stricken in 1959; **Flint** (CLAA 97) stricken in 1965; **Tucson** (CLAA 98) stricken in 1966; **Juneau** (CLAA 119) stricken in 1959; **Spokane** (CLAA 120) classified as sonar test ship T-AG 191; **Fresno** (CLAA 121) stricken in 1965.

PORTSMOUTH (CL 102) — *1946, United States Navy*

1 INSHORE FIRE SUPPORT SHIP (LFR): "CARRONADE" TYPE

Name	*No.*	*Builder*	*Commissioned*
***CARRONADE**	IFS 1	Puget Sound Bridge	25 May 1955

Displacement, tons	1 040 standard; 1 500 full load
Dimensions, feet	245 oa × 38·5 × 10
Guns	1—5 in 38 cal dual-purpose 4—40 mm AA (twin)
Rockets	8 rapid-fire launchers for 5 inch rockets
Main engines	2 diesels (Fairbanks-Morse); 3 100 shp; 2 shafts
Speed, knots	15
Complement	139 (9 officers, 130 enlisted men)

The *Carronade* was specifically designed to provide fire support for amphibious landings; she is an improvement over the World War II-era LSMR but lacks big-gun firepower. Built by Puget Sound Bridge & Dredging Co; laid down 19 Nov 1952; launched 26 May 1953. Mothballed from 1960 to 1965 when recommissioned for duty off Vietnam. Designation changed from IFS-1 to LFR-1 on 1 Jan 1969 (both Inshore Fire Support Ship).

ENGINEERING. Fitted with controllable-pitch propellers.

CARRONADE (LFR 1) — *1967, United States Navy*

11 INSHORE FIRE SUPPORT SHIPS (LFR): FORMER LSMR

Name	*No.*	*Builder*	*Commissioned*
BIG BLACK RIVER	LFR 401	Charleston Navy Yard	7 Apr 1945
BROADKILL RIVER	LFR 405	Charleston Navy Yard	2 May 1945
***CLARION RIVER**	LFR 409	Charleston Navy Yard	16 May 1945
DES PLAINES RIVER	LFR 412	Charleston Navy Yard	23 May 1945
LAMOILLE RIVER	LFR 512	Brown Shipbuilding	5 July 1945
LARAMIE RIVER	LFR 513	Brown Shipbuilding	9 July 1945
OWYHEE RIVER	LFR 515	Brown Shipbuilding	16 July 1945
RED RIVER	LFR 522	Brown Shipbuilding	6 Aug 1945
***ST FRANCIS RIVER**	LFR 525	Brown Shipbuilding	15 Aug 1945
SMOKY HILL RIVER	LFR 531	Brown Shipbuilding	25 Sep 1945
***WHITE RIVER**	LFR 536	Brown Shipbuilding	28 Nov 1945

Displacement, tons	994 standard; 1 084 full load
Dimensions, feet	LSMR 401-412 197·2 wl; 203·5 oa × 34·5 × 10 LSMR 501-536 204·5 wl; 206·2 oa × 34·5 × 10
Guns	1—5 in 38 cal dual-purpose; 4—40 mm AA (twin)
Rockets	8 twin launchers for 5 in rockets
Main engines	2 diesel (General Motors); 2 800 shp; 2 shafts
Speed, knots	12·6
Complement	137 (7 officers, 130 enlisted men)

These ships were redesigned during construction to provide fire support for amphibious landings. They have pointed bows, bridge structure aft, and 5 inch mount forward of bridge (earlier LSMRs had 5 inch gun aft of bridge). Built by Charleston Navy Yard and Brown Shipbuilding Company, Houston, Texas; originally 48 ships in these series (LSMR 401-412 and LSMR 501-536); all launched 1945; completed 1945-1946. All mothballed after World War II; named for rivers on 1 Oct 1955; three ships recommissioned in 1965 for duty off Vietnam. Original designation of Medium Landing Ship—Rocket (LSMR) changed to Inshore Fire Support Ship (LFR) for 11 surviving ships on 1 Jan 1969.

CLARION RIVER (LFR 409) — *1967, United States Navy*

ROCKETS. The automatic rocket launchers each fire 30 spin-stabilised rockets per minute.

RECLASSIFICATIONS AND DISPOSALS
Full list of stricken ships in 1967-68 edition; one ship remains on Navy List with other designation: **Elk River** (ex-LSMR 501) as ocean engineering range support ship (IX 501). The only "straight" LSM remaining in service is the civilian-manned AG 335, former LSM 335, operated by the Military Sea Transportation Service (see Logistic Support Ships). **Targeteer**, YV 3, formerly the *Gunnison River* (LSMR 508), was stricken in 1969; **Catapult**, YV 1, ex-LSM 445, and **Launcher**, YV 2, ex-LSM 446, were stricken in 1960.

AMPHIBIOUS WARFARE SHIPS

The US Navy now seeks to provide a 20-knot amphibious lift capability for one Marine division/aircraft wing team in the Pacific and two-thirds of a division/wing team in the Atlantic. This is an increase in the 20-knot lift capability planned previously for the Atlantic. In addition, with a delay of comparatively few days, a predesignated group of amphibious ships in the Pacific could enter the Atlantic to provide lift for a complete division/wing team. (A Marine division/wing team, designated Marine Expeditionary Force, numbers some 35 000 to 45 000 officers and enlisted men).

The 20-knot amphibious ships now in service plus construction of additional multi-purpose amphibious assault ships (LHA) and tank landing ships (LST) will provide the required high-speed lift capability. When the new ships have been delivered the amphibious warfare force will consist almost entirely of post-World War II construction. A number of older ships will be kept in Category Bravo reserve for rapid activation in the event a capability to lift two full Marine division/wing teams simultaneously is required.

The new LHA represents the latest design in the evolution of specialised amphibious warfare ships which began with British development of the LST in World War II. The first major improvements in amphibious ship design came in the late 1950s with development of the Amphibious Assault Ship (LPH), in essence a troop ship with a flight deck for the operation of helicopters, and the Amphibious Transport Dock (LPD), which is an improved variant of the Dock Landing Ship (LSD) with more vehicle and troop spaces at the expence of docking well space (and hence smaller landing craft capacity).

These two ships replaced the Amphibious Transports (LPA, former APA) and, to a limited extent, LSDs and Amphibious Cargo Ships (LKA, former LKA). However, new LSD and LKA type ships are still required for amphibious operations.

The new Amphibious Assault Ship (LHA) is intended to carry as many troops and helicopters as an LPH, as much cargo as an LKA, and as many landing craft as an LSD. The LHA is also intended to overcome a reported shortcoming of specialised amphibious shipping: the imbalance which occurs when one of the specialised ships is lost. The LHA would carry a more-balanced load of men, troops, equipment, vehicles, and supplies. It is anticipated that an LHA together with one or two LSTs could put ashore (by helicopter and landing craft) a Marine battalion landing team of some 1 800 men, a task which now requires five older amphibious ships.

With procurement of the new LHA no further amphibious ships will be procured except tank landing ships and possibly a few additional dock landing ships.

The LST continues to be a key ship in naval operations. The Vietnamese War has forced the US Navy to activate all available mothballed LSTs and increase the construction of these ships. They are being employed in Southeast Asia for amphibious assault operations, for cargo hauling, for unloading merchantmen when docking facilities are not available, and for replenishment and support of riverine and coastal forces. (In addition to the LSTs listed in the section on Amphibious Warfare Ships, a number of civilian manned T-LSTs operated by the Navy's Military Sea Transportation Service are listed with Logistic Support Ships).

HARNETT COUNTY (LST 821) *1968, US Navy, JOSN J. W. Fletcher*

Fire Support Ship (LFS vice LSMR), Amphibious Cargo Ship (LKA vice AKA), Amphibious Transport (LPA vice APA), Amphibious Transport (small) (LPR vice APD), and Amphibious Transport Submarine (LPSS vice APSS). The various fire support ships are listed in the section on Fire Support Ships and the amphibious transport submarines are listed in the section on Submarines.

CLASSIFICATION. As predicted in the 1968-1969 edition, the US Navy has revised amphibious ship designations to have all designations in this category begin with the letter "L"; the ships affected were: Amphibious Command Ship (now LCC vice AGC), Inshore Fire Support Ship (LFR vice IFS), Amphibious Fire Support Ship (LFS vice LSMR), Amphibious Cargo Ship (LKA vice AKA), Amphibious Transport (LPA vice APA), Amphibious Transport (small) (LPR vice APD), and Amphibious Transport Submarine (LPSS vice APSS). The various fire support ships are listed in the section on Fire Support Ships and the amphibious transport submarines are listed in the section on Submarines.

PHOTOGRAPHS. The *Harnett County* (LST 821) lies at anchor in South Vietnam's Bassac River while serving as base for Navy river patrol boats and UH-1B "Seawolf" helicopters. Four LSTs have been outfitted to support these boats and helicopters employed in river patrol.

5 AMPHIBIOUS COMMAND SHIPS (LCC): "MOUNT McKINLEY" CLASS

Displacement, tons	7 510 light; 12 560 full load
Length, feet (*metres*)	435 (*132·2*) wl; 495·3 (*150·5*) oa
Beam, feet (*metres*)	63 (*19·2*)
Draft, feet (*metres*)	28·2 (*8·5*)
Guns	1—5 in (*127 mm*) 38 cal DP 4—40 mm AA (twin mounts)
Main engines	1 turbine (General Electric); 6 000 shp; 1 shaft
Boilers	2 (Babcock & Wilcox in AGC 7; Combustion Engineering in others)
Speed, knots	16·4
Complement (ship)	517 (36 officers, 486 enlisted men)

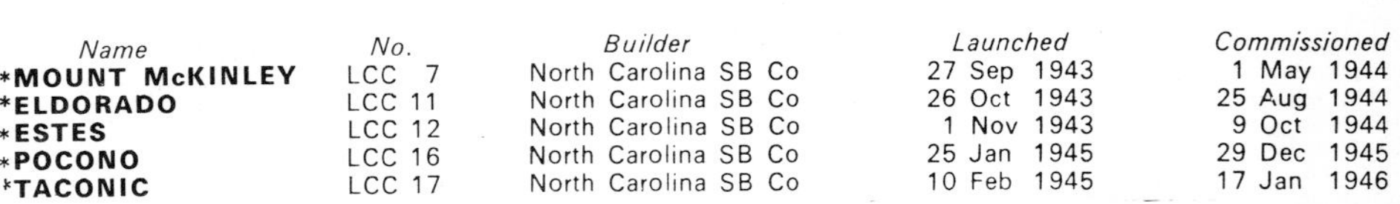

Name	*No.*	*Builder*	*Launched*	*Commissioned*
***MOUNT McKINLEY**	LCC 7	North Carolina SB Co	27 Sep 1943	1 May 1944
***ELDORADO**	LCC 11	North Carolina SB Co	26 Oct 1943	25 Aug 1944
***ESTES**	LCC 12	North Carolina SB Co	1 Nov 1943	9 Oct 1944
***POCONO**	LCC 16	North Carolina SB Co	25 Jan 1945	29 Dec 1945
***TACONIC**	LCC 17	North Carolina SB Co	10 Feb 1945	17 Jan 1946

Acquired by the Navy in 1943-1944 while under construction to Maritime Commission C2-S-AJ1 design. After 5 inch gun and two twin 40 mm mounts replaced by helicopter platform. Forward 5 inch gun also removed in some ships. The *Pocono* and *Taconic* have a single mast aft in lieu of after king-post in earlier ships.

NOMENCLATURE. Amphibious command ships are named for mountain ranges.

CLASSIFICATION. Originally referred to as Auxiliary Combined Operations and Communications Headquarters Ships, but designated Amphibious Force Flagships (AGC); five surviving ships redesignated Amphibious Command Ships (LCC) on 1 Jan 1969.

POCONO (AGC 16) *United States Navy*

DISPOSALS

Thirteen World War II amphibious force flagships have been stricken from the Navy List: **Appalachian** (AGC 1) on 1 Mar 1959; **Blue Ridge** (AGC 2), **Rocky Mount** (AGC 3) on 1 Jan 1960; **Ancon** (AGC 4) on 25 Feb 1946; **Catoctin** (AGC 5) on 1 Mar 1959; **Mount Olympus** (AGC 8) in 1961; **Wasatch** (AGC 9) on 1 Jan 1960; **Auburn** (AGC 10), **Panamint** (AGC 13) in late 1960; **Teton** (AGC 14), **Adirondack** (AGC 15) in 1961; **Biscayne** (AGC 18, ex-AVP 11) transferred to US Coast Guard on 19 July 1946. The **Duane** (AGC 6) was retained by the Coast Guard. All except the **Ancon**, **Duane**, and **Biscayne** were converted C2 merchant hulls. The yacht **Williamsburg** (ex-*Aras*, ex-PG 56) was designated AGC 369 in 1945; served as presidential yacht until stricken in 1962 (converted to oceanographic research ship, renamed *Anton Bruun*).

Amphibious Warfare Ships—*continued*

2 AMPHIBIOUS COMMAND SHIPS (LCC): "BLUE RIDGE" CLASS

Displacement, tons	17 100 full load
Length, feet (*metres*)	620 (*000·0*) oa
Beam, feet (*metres*)	82 (*25·3*)
Draft, feet (*metres*)	27 (*8·2*)
Guns	8—3 in (*76 mm*) 60 cal AA
Main engines	1 turbine (General Electric); 22 000 shp; 1 shaft
Boilers	2 (Foster Wheeler)
Speed, knots	20

Name	*No.*	*Builder*	*Laid down*	*Launched*	*Commission*
BLUE RIDGE	LCC 19	Philadelphia Naval Shipyard	27 Feb 1967	4 Jan 1969	Nov 1970
MOUNT WHITNEY	LCC 20	Newport News SB & DD Co	8 Jan 1969	Jan 1970	1971

Complement	732 (52 officers, 680 enlisted men)
Flag accommodations	688 (217 officers, 471 enlisted men)

These are the first amphibious force flagships of post-World War II design. They will provide integrated commarfd and control facilities for sea, air, and land commanders in amphibious operations. The *Blue Ridge* was authorised in the Fiscal Year 1965 new construction programme, the AGC 20 in FY 1966. An AGC 21 was planned for the FY 1970 programme but cancelled late in 1968. It was proposed that the ship combine fleet as well as amphibious force command-control facilities.

CLASSIFICATION. Originally designated Amphibious Force Flagships (AGC); redesignated Amphibious Command Ships (LCC) on 10 Jan 1969.

BLUE RIDGE (AGC 19) *Official Navy Model*

3 + 5 AMPHIBIOUS ASSAULT SHIPS (LHA): NEW CONSTRUCTION

No.	*Builder*
LHA 1	Litton Systems
LHA 2	Litton Systems
LHA 3	Litton Systems

Displacement, tons	approx 40 000 full load
Length, feet	796 oa
Beam, feet	106
Main engines	Turbines; 2 shafts
Speed, knots	20+
Troops	Approx 2 000

These are the first ships to be procured by the US Navy with the acquisition processes known as Concept Formulation, Contract Defination, and Total Package Procurement. The proposals of Litton Systems Inc and two other shipbuilding firms were submitted in response to specific performance criteria related to the ships mission. The firms submitted detailed designs and cost estimates for series production of not less than five ships of this type.

The Department of Defence first requested construction funds for the LHA in the Fiscal Year 1968 shipbuilding programme, but these were denied by the Congress because of the uncertain state of the LHA design at that time. The FY 1969 programme provided $153 000 000 for LHA procurement: $123 000 000 for the first LHA with the remainder to be applied to future LHA costs or, if the programme is cancelled, forefeited to the shipbuilding firm.

Current LHA cost estimates are $185 000 000 for the first ship and $1 012 500 000 for the entire nine-ship programme.

LHA 1 authorised in Fiscal Year 1969 Shipbuilding Programme; two each in the FY1970-1973 programmes.

LHA *Official artist's concept*

The LHA will be the first class of ship to be designed and produced under the new Department of Defense acquisition process termed Concept Formulation / Contract Definition, in which the entire class construction contract is awarded to a single shipbuilder as Total Package Procurement.

DESIGN. Similar in design to the built-for-the-purpose LPH ships but larger, fitted with a docking well, and with one deck-edge helicopter lift to port and a second lift at the after end of the flight deck. Armament will probably include new, light-weight 5 inch/54 cal gun (Mk 45) and Basic Point Defense Missile System (BPDMS), both of which are shown at stern of LHA in artist's concept.

CONSTRUCTION. Litton Systems operates the Ingalls Shipbuilding Corp at Pascagoula, Mississippi, but will construct a new shipyard in the area for producing these ships.

PERSONNEL. These ships will have a high degree of automation to reduce operating personnel requirements.

TRIPOLI (LPH 10) *United States Navy*

Amphibious Warfare Ships—*continued*

7 AMPHIBIOUS ASSAULT SHIPS (LPH): "IWO JIMA" CLASS

Displacement, tons	17 000 light; 18 300 full load
Length, feet (*metres*)	592 (*180·0*) oa
Beam, feet (*metres*)	84 (*25·6*)
Draft, feet (*metres*)	26 (*7·9*)
Flight deck width, feet (*metres*)	105 (*31·9*) maximum
Helicopters	20-24 medium (CH-46) 4 heavy (CH-53) 4 observation (HU-1)
Guns	8—3 in (*76 mm*) 50 cal AA
Main engines	1 geared turbine, 23 000 shp; 1 shaft
Boilers	2—655 psi (Combustion Engineering in LPH 2, LPH 3, LPH 7; Babcock & Wilcox in LPH 9)
Speed, knots	20 (sustained)
Complement	528 (48 officers, 480 enlisted men)
Troops	2 090 (190 officers, 1 900 enlisted men)

Name	*No.*	*Builder*	*Laid down*	*Launched*	*Commissioned*
***IWO JIMA**	LPH 2	Puget Sound Naval Shipyard	2 Apr 1959	17 Sep 1960	26 Aug 1961
***OKINAWA**	LPH 3	Philadelphia Naval Shipyard	1 Apr 1960	19 Aug 1961	14 Apr 1962
***GUADALCANAL**	LPH 7	Philadelphia Naval Shipyard	1 Sep 1961	16 Mar 1963	20 July 1963
***GUAM**	LPH 9	Philadelphia Naval Shipyard	15 Nov 1962	22 Aug 1964	16 Jan 1965
***TRIPOLI**	LPH 10	Ingalls Shipbuilding Corp	15 June 1964	31 July 1965	6 Aug 1966
***NEW ORLEANS**	LPH 11	Philadelphia Naval Shipyard	1 Mar 1966	3 Feb 1968	16 Nov 1968
INCHON	LPH 12	Ingalls Shipbuilding Corp	8 Apr 1968	24 May 1969	Oct 1969

The *Iwo Jima* was the world's first ship designed and constructed specifically to operate helicopters. These ships correspond to Commando Ships in the Royal Navy, except that the US ships do not carry landing craft. (This shortcoming is rectified in the new LHA). Each LPH can carry a Marine battalion landing team, its guns, vehicles, and equipment, plus a reinforced squadron of transport helicopters and various support personnel.
The *Iwo Jima* was authorised in the Fiscal Year 1958 new construction programme, the *Okinawa* in FY 1959, *Guadalcanal* in FY 1960, *Guam* in FY 1962, *Tripoli* in FY 1963, *New Orleans* in FY 1965, and *Inchon* in FY 1966. No additional ships of this type are planned in view of the new LHA capabilities.
Estimated cost of the *Iwo Jima* is $40 000 000.

DESIGN. These ships resemble World War II-era escort carriers in size but have massive bridge structures, hull continued up to flight deck providing enclosed bows, and rounded flight decks. Each ship has two deck-edge lifts, one to port opposite the bridge and one to starboard aft of island. Full hangars are provided; no arresting wires or catapults. Two small elevators carry cargo from holds to flight deck.

GUNNERY. Guns are in four twin mounts, two forward of island structure and two at stern, "notched" into flight deck. The *New Orleans* has closed mounts forward of her island.

MEDICAL. These ships are fitted with extensive medical facilities including operating room, X-ray room, hospital ward, isolation ward, laboratory, pharmacy, dental operating room, and medical store rooms.

NOMENCLATURE. Amphibious assault ships are named for battles in Marine Corps history. Iwo Jima, Okinawa, Guadalcanal, and Guam were World War II campaigns; the Marines fought Barbary pirates at Tripoli in 1801 and helped stop the British at New Orleans in 1814. There was also a naval battle at New Orleans during the American Civil War. Inchon was the near-perfect 1950 Amphibious assault in Korea.

DISPOSALS
The **Thetis Bay** (LPH 6, ex-CVHA 1, ex- CVE 90) was stricken in 1966. The **Block Island** (originally CVE 106) was reclassified LPH 1 on 22 Dec 1957 but conversion was cancelled and she reverted to CVE status on 17 Jan 1959; subsequently stricken (as AKV 38) and scrapped.

TRIPOLI (LPH 10) *1966, United States Navy*

GUADALCANAL (LPH 7) *United States Navy*

BOXER (LPH 4) *United States Navy*

Amphibious Warfare Ships—*continued*

3 AMPHIBIOUS ASSAULT SHIPS (LPH): "ESSEX" CLASS (EX-CVA/CVS)

Name	*No.*	*Builder*	*Laid down*	*Launched*	*Commissioned*
***BOXER**	LPH 4 (ex-CVS 21)	Newport News SB & DD Co	13 Sep 1943	14 Dec 1944	16 Apr 1945
***PRINCETON**	LPH 5 (ex-CVS 37)	Philadelphia Navy Yard	14 Sep 1943	8 July 1945	18 Nov 1945
***VALLEY FORGE**	LPH 8 (ex-CVS 45)	Philadelphia Navy Yard	7 Sep 1944	18 Nov 1945	3 Nov 1946

Displacement, tons	30 800 standard; 40 600 full load
Length, feet (*metres*)	820 (*249·2*) wl; 888 (*270·7*) oa
Beam, feet (*metres*)	93 (*28·3*)
Draft, feet (*metres*)	31 (*9·4*)
Flight deck width, feet (*metres*)	147·5 (*44·7*) maximum
Helicopters	approx 30
Guns *Boxer*	8—5 in (*127 mm*) 38 cal DP
Princeton, Valley Forge	6—5 in (*127 mm*) 38 cal DP
Main engines	4 geared turbines (Westinghouse) 150 000 shp; 4 shafts
Boilers	8—600 psi (Babcock & Wilcox)
Speed, knots	33
Complement	approx 1 000
Troops	approx 1 500

These ships are former "Essex" class attack/ASW carriers, relegated to an amphibious warfare role. See listing for modified "Essex" class attack carriers for general class notes. These ships will probably be replaced in the active fleet by the new LHA-type ships when the latter become available in the early 1970s.

CLASSIFICATION. These ships were initially classified as "aircraft carriers" (CV). All were redesignated Attack Aircraft Carriers (CVA) in October 1952 and subsequently became ASW Support Aircraft Carriers (CVS) and Amphibious Assault Ships (LPH): *Boxer* to CVS on 1 Feb 1956 and LPH on 30 Jan 1959; *Princeton* to CVS in Jan 1954 and LPH on 2 Mar 1959; *Valley Forge* to CVS in Jan 1954 and LPH on 3 June 1961.

GUNNERY. These are the only "Essex" class carriers in service which have 5 inch gun mounts on their flight decks. The *Boxer* has four twin mounts; others have two with two single 5 inch guns on port side of flight deck.

NOMENCLATURE. The *Princeton* was renamed during construction, ex-*Valley Forge*.

VALLEY FORGE (LPH 8) *1968 United States Navy*

PRINCETON (LPH 5) *1968, United States Navy, JO1 R. D. Egnor*

5 AMPHIBIOUS CARGO SHIPS (LKA): "CHARLESTON" CLASS

Name	*No.*	*Laid down*	*Launched*	*Commissioned*
***CHARLESTON**	LKA 113	5 Dec 1966	2 Dec 1967	14 Dec 1968
***DURHAM**	LKA 114	10 July 1967	29 Mar 1968	24 May 1969
***MOBILE**	LKA 115	15 Jan 1968	19 Oct 1968	July 1969
***ST. LOUIS**	LKA 116	3 Apr 1968	4 Jan 1969	Aug 1969
EL PASO	LKA 117	22 Oct 1968	May 1969	Dec 1969

Displacement, tons	20 700 full load
Dimensions, feet	575·5 oa × 82 × 25·5
Main engines	1 steam turbine; 22 000 shp; 1 shaft = 20+ knots
Boilers	2
Guns	8—3 inch (*76 mm*) 50 cal AA (twin)
Complement	334 (24 officers, 310 enlisted men)
Troops	approx 300

These ships are designed specifically for the attack cargo ship role; they carry 18 landing craft (LCM) and supplies for amphibious operations. Design includes two heavy-lift cranes with a 78·4-ton capacity and helicopter deck aft.
The LKA 113-116 were authorised in the Fiscal Year 1965 shipbuilding programme; LKA 117 in FY 1966 programme.
All built by Newport News Shipbuilding and Dry Dock Co, Virginia.

ENGINEERING. These are the first US Navy ships with a fully automated main propulsion plant; control of plant is from bridge or central machinery space console. This automation enabled a 45-man reduction in complement.

CLASSIFICATION. Originally designated Attack Cargo Ship (AKA). *Charleston* redesignated Amphibious Cargo Ship (LKA) on 1 Jan 1969; others to LKA on 10 Jan 1969.

CHARLESTON (LKA 113) *1968, United States Navy, PH2 D. Bayse*

1 AMPHIBIOUS CARGO SHIP (LKA): "TULARE" TYPE

***TULARE** (ex- *Evergreen Mariner*) LKA 112

Displacement, tons	12 000 light; 15 970 full load
Measurement, tons	9 200 gross; 13 400 deadweight
Dimensions, feet	564 oa × 76 × 26
Guns	12—3 inch 50 cal AA (twin)
Main engines	Turbine; 1 shaft; 22 000 shp = 20 knots
Boilers	2
Complement	38 officers, 399 men
Troops	approx 135.

Built by Bethlehem, San Francisco. Laid down on 16 Feb 1953, launched on 22 Dec 1953: Acquired by Navy during construction. Commissioned on 13 Jan 1956. C4-S-1 B type. Has helicopter landing platform and booms capable of lifting 60-ton landing craft. Carries 9 LCM-6 landing craft. Designation changed from AKA 112 to LKA 112 on 1 Jan 1969.

TULARE (LKA 112) *United States Navy*

6 AMPHIBIOUS CARGO SHIPS (LKA): "RANKIN" CLASS

Name	*No.*	*Launched*	*Commissioned*
***RANKIN**	LKA 103	22 Dec 1944	25 Feb 1945
***SEMINOLE**	LKA 104	28 Dec 1944	8 Mar 1945
SKAGIT	LKA 105	28 Nov 1944	2 May 1945
UNION	LKA 106	23 Nov 1944	25 Apr 1945
***VERMILLION**	LKA 107	12 Dec 1944	23 June 1945
WASHBURN	LKA 108	12 Dec 1944	17 May 1945

Amphibious Warfare Ships—*continued*

"RANKIN" CLASS *continued*

Displacement, tons 6 456 light; 14 160 full load
Dimensions, feet 459·2 oa × 63 × 26·3
Guns 8—40 mm AA (twin)
Main engines Geared turbines; 1 shaft; 6 000 shp = 16·5 knots
Boilers 2
Complement 247

C2-S-AJ3 type. Laid down in 1944 and commissioned in 1945. Launch dates above. Combat load 4 500 tons. The removed 5-inch gun is scheduled to be replaced by a twin 3-inch mountings. Ten 20 mm AA guns removed. Designation changed from AKA to LKA on 1 Jan 1969.
Skagit, Union, Washburn decommissioned in 1969.

VERMILLION (LKA 107) *1963, United States Navy*

9 AMPHIBIOUS CARGO SHIPS (LKA): "ANDROMEDA" CLASS

Name	*No.*	*Launched*	*Commissioned*
THUBAN	LKA 19	26 Apr 1943	10 June 1943
***ALGOL** (ex-*James Baines*)	LKA 54	17 Feb 1943	21 July 1944
***ARNEB** (ex-*Mischief*)	LKA 56	6 July 1943	28 Apr 1944
***CAPRICORNUS** (ex-*Spitfire*)	LKA 57	14 Aug 1943	31 May 1944
***MULIPHEN**	LKA 61	26 Aug 1944	23 Oct 1944
UVALDE (ex-*Wild Pigeon*)	LKA 88	20 May 1944	18 Aug 1944
***YANCEY**	LKA 93	8 July 1944	11 Oct 1944
***WINSTONE**	LKA 94	30 Nov 1944	19 Jan 1945
***MERRICK**	LKA 97	28 Jan 1945	31 Mar 1945

Displacement, tons 7 430 light; 14 000 full load
Dimensions, feet 435 wl; 459·2 oa × 63 × 24 max
Guns 8—40 mm AA (twin)
Main engines Geared turbines; 1 shaft; 6 000 shp = 15·5 knots
Boilers 2 (Foster Wheeler)
Complement 247

C2-S-B1 type. Can carry over 5 200 tons of cargo and 2 200 tons of tanks. *Arneb* completed refit for Arctic service on 15 Mar 1949. *Wyandot*, AKA 92, assigned to the Navy's Military Sea Transportation Service and manned by a civilian crew since 1963, was redesignated T-AK 283 on 1 Jan 1969. Designation of other ships remaining on Navy List changed from AKA to LKA on 1 Jan 1969.

TRANSFERS. *Whitley* AKA 91, was transferred to Italy in 1962, and *Achernar* AKA 53, to Spain on 2 Feb 1965.

DISPOSALS

Alshain AKA 55, **Andromeda** AKA 15, **Chara** AKA 58, **Leo** AKA 60, **Marquette** AKA 95, **Montagu** AKA 98, **Rolette** AKA 99, were disposed of in 1961. **Diphda** AKA 59, **Virgo** AKA 20, **Warrick** AKA 89, and **Whiteside** AKA 90, were stricken from the Navy List and transferred to the Maritime Administration Reserve Fleet in 1961 but **Chara** and **Virgo** were reacquired in 1965 and reclassified as ammunition ships AE 30 and AE 31 respectively; see section on Underway Replenishment Ships. **Matthews** AKA 96, **Oglethrope** AKA 100 stricken on 1 Nov 1968. **Uvalde** AKA 88 stricken 1 Dec 1968.

DISPOSALS OF OTHER CLASSES
Of the "Libra" class, **Libra** AKA 12 and **Oberon** AKA 14 were disposed of in 1961, and **Titania** AKA 13 was stricken from the Navy List and transferred to the Maritime Administration Reserve Fleet in 1961.
Of the "Bellatrix" class, **Bellatrix** AKA 3, was disposed of in 1961, but reacquired and transferred to Peru in 1963; and **Electra** AKA 4, was stricken from the Navy List and transferred to the Maritime Administration Reserve Fleet in 1961.

ARNEB (LKA 56) *1965, United States Navy*

2 AMPHIBIOUS TRANSPORTS (LPA): "PAUL REVERE" CLASS

Name	*No.*	*Launched*	*Commissioned*
***PAUL REVERE** (ex-*Diamond Mariner*)	LPA 248	13 Feb 1954	3 Sep 1958
***FRANCIS MARION** (ex-*Prairie Mariner*)	LPA 249	11 Apr 1953	6 July 1961

Displacement, tons 10 709 light; 16 838 full load
Dimensions, feet 528 pp; 563·5 oa × 76 × 27 max
Guns 8—3 inch 50 cal AA (twin)
Main engines Geared turbines; 1 shaft; 19 250 shp = 20 knots
Boilers 2
Complement 414 (35 officers, 379 men)

Paul Revere is a C4-S-1 type cargo vessel converted into an Attack Transport by Todd Shipyard Corp, San Pedro, Calif, under the Fiscal Year 1957 Conversion programme. Fitted with helicopter platform. *Francis Marion* was a similar "Mariner" type hull converted into an APA by Bethlehem Steel, Key Highway Yard, Baltimore, Md, under the Fiscal Year 1959 programme. Both ships were originally built by New York Shipbuilding Corporation, Camden, *Francis Marion* in 1954 and *Paul Revere* in 1953. Designation changed from APA to LPA on 1 Jan 1969.

FRANCIS MARION (LPA 249) *United States Navy*

8 AMPHIBIOUS TRANSPORTS (LPA): "HASKELL" CLASS

Name	*No.*	*Launched*	*Commissioned*
***SANDOVAL**	LPA 194	11 Sep 1944	7 Oct 1944
TALLADEGA	LPA 208	17 Aug 1944	31 Oct 1944
***MONTROSE**	LPA 212	13 Sep 1944	2 Nov 1944
***MOUNTRAIL**	LPA 213	20 Sep 1944	16 Nov 1944
***NAVARRO**	LPA 215	3 Oct 1944	15 Nov 1944
***OKANOGAN**	LPA 220	22 Oct 1944	3 Dec 1944
***PICKAWAY**	LPA 222	5 Nov 1944	12 Dec 1944
BEXAR	LPA 237	25 July 1945	9 Oct 1945

Displacement, tons 6 720 light; 10 470 full load
Dimensions, feet 436·5 wl; 455 oa × 62 × 24
Guns 12—40 mm AA (1 quad, 4 twin)
Main engines Geared turbines; 1 shaft; 8 500 shp = 17·7 knots
Boilers 2 (Babcock & Wilcox)
Complement 536
Troops 1 560

VC 2-S-AP 5 "Victory" type, all launched in 1944-45. All have County names. 3 000 tons cargo. Designation of ships remaining on Navy List changed from APA to LPA on 1 Jan 1969.

GUNNERY. The 5-inch gun was removed.

TRANSFER. *Noble* APA 218 was decommissioned on 1 July 1964 and transferred to Spain.

PAUL REVERE (APA 248) *United States Navy*

Amphibious Warfare Ships—*continued*

"HASKELL" CLASS

DISPOSALS

Arenac APA 128, **Barnwell** APA 132, **Bronx** APA 236, **Brookings** APA 140, **Clinton** APA 144, **Crockett** APA 148, **Dane** APA 238, **Edgecombe** APA 164, **Gage** APA 168, **Grimes** APA 172, **Kershaw** APA 176, **Lavaca** APA 180, **Lubbock** APA 197, **McCracken** APA 198, **Menifee** APA 202, **Meriweather** APA 203, **Mifflin** APA 207, **Missoula** APA 211, **Natrona** APA 214, **Neshoba** APA 216, **New Kent** APA 217, **Okaloosa** APA 219, **Oneida** APA 221, **Rawlins** APA 226, **Rockingham** APA 229, **Rutland** APA 192, **San Saba** APA 232, **Sherburne** APA 205, **Sibley** APA 206 and **Tazewell** APA 209, were stricken from the Navy List and transferred to the Maritime Administration Reserve Fleet in 1959, **Deuel** APA 160, **Logan** APA 196, **Rockwall** APA 130, in 1960. **Deuel** and **Rockwall** were stricken on 1 Dec 1958. **Glynn** APA 239, **Latimer** APA 152, **Menard** APA 201, **Olmstead** APA 188, **Randall** APA 224, **Sanborn** APA 193, **Sarasota** APA 204, in 1961. **Botetourt** APA 136, **Bottineau** APA 235, **Menard** APA 201, were stricken from the Navy List and transferred to the Maritime Administration Reserve Fleet in 1961. **Lenawee** APA 195 and **Renville** APA 227 in 1967. **Magoffin** APA 199, stricken 16 May 1968.

OKANOGAN (LPA 220) *1967, United States Navy*

3 AMPHIBIOUS TRANSPORTS (LPA): "BAYFIELD" CLASS

Name	*No.*	*Launched*	*Commissioned*
***CAMBRIA** (ex-*Sea Swallow*)	LPA 36	10 Nov 1942	10 Nov 1943
***CHILTON** (ex-*Sea Needle*)	LPA 38	24 Dec 1942	7 Dec 1943
FREMONT (ex-*Sea Corsair*)	LPA 44	31 Mar 1943	23 Nov 1943

Displacement, tons	8 100 light; 15 200 full load
Dimensions, feet	465 wl × 69·5 × 26·5
Guns	1— or 2—5 inch DP; 12— or 8—40 mm AA (quad)
Main engines	Geared turbines; 1 shaft; 8 500 shp = 18·4 knots
Boilers	2 (Combustion Engineering)
Complement	250 (554 total accommodation)

C3-S-A2 type.
Cambria and *Chilton* built by Western Pipe & Steel Co, San Francisco; *Fremont* built by Ingalls Shipbuilding Corp, Pascagola, Mississippi. Designation changed from APA to LPA on 1 Jan 1969.

PHOTOGRAPHS. *Cambria* has 5 inch guns forward and aft; *Fremont* has quad 40 mm mount in place of forward 5 inch gun.

DISPOSALS

Bayfield APA 33, **Cavalier** APA 37, stricken on 1 Oct 1968. **Henrico** APA 45 stricken on 21 Feb 1968; transferred to Maritime Administration (to LPA 45 on 1 Jan 1969).

CAMBRIA (LPA 36) *1968, United States Navy*

FREMONT (LPA 44) *1966, United States Navy*

DISPOSALS OF OTHER CLASSES

Arthur Middleton APA 25, and **Samuel Chase** APA 26 of the "Arthur Middleton" class, and **President Adams** APA 19, **President Hayes** APA 20, **President Jackson** APA 18 and **Thomas Jefferson** (ex-*President Garfield*) APA 30 (of the "President" class) were stricken from the Navy List in 1959 and transferred to the Maritime Administration Reserve Fleet. **George Clymer** APA 27 of the "Arthur Middleton" class stricken 1 Nov 1967 and transferred to Maritime Administration Reserve Fleet. **Charles Carroll** APA 28 and **Cresent City** APA 21, were stricken from the Navy List in 1959, and transferred to the Maritime Administration Reserve Fleet. **Calvert** APA 22, stricken in Aug 1966, is employed as training hulk for cargo handling at Oakland, Calif. **Monrovia** APA 31, stricken 1 Nov 1968.

12 AMPHIBIOUS TRANSPORT DOCKS (LPD): "AUSTIN" CLASS

Name	*No.*	*Laid down*	*Launched*	*Commissioned*
***AUSTIN**	LPD 4	4 Feb 1963	27 June 1964	6 Feb 1965
***OGDEN**	LPD 5	4 Feb 1963	27 June 1964	19 June 1965
***DULUTH**	LPD 6	18 Dec 1963	14 Aug 1965	12 Apr 1966
***CLEVELAND**	LPD 7	30 Nov 1964	7 May 1966	21 Apr 1967
***DUBUQUE**	LPD 8	25 Jan 1965	6 Aug 1966	1 Sep 1967
***DENVER**	LPD 9	7 Feb 1964	23 Jan 1965	26 Oct 1968
***JUNEAU**	LPD 10	23 Jan 1965	12 Feb 1966	June 1969
***CORONADO**	LPD 11	3 May 1965	30 July 1966	1969
***SHREVEPORT**	LPD 12	27 Dec 1965	22 Oct 1966	1969
NASHVILLE	LPD 13	14 Mar 1966	7 Oct 1967	1969
TRENTON	LPD 14	8 Aug 1966	25 May 1968	1970
PONCE	LPD 15	31 Oct 1966	3 Aug 1968	1970

Displacement, tons	10 000 light; 16 900 full load
Length, feet (*metres*)	570 (*173·3*) oa
Beam, feet (*metres*)	84 (*25·6*)
Draft, feet (*metres*)	23 (*7·0*)
Guns	8—3 in (*76 mm*) 50 cal AA (twin)
Helicopters	6 UH-34 or CH-46 (see *Helicopter* notes)
Main engines	2 steam turbines; 2 shafts; 24 000 shp = 20 knots
Boilers	2
Complement	490 (30 officers, 460 enlisted men)
Troops	930 in LPD 4-6 and LPD 14-16; 840 in LPD 7-13
Flag accommodations	Approx 90 in LPD 7-13

These ships are enlarged versions of the previous "Raleigh" class; most notes for the "Raleigh" class apply to these ships. All 12 of these ships are officially considered in a single class; earlier references to separate classes was based on contract awards to builders.
The LPD 4-6 were authorised in the Fiscal Year 1962 new construction programme, LPD 7-10 in FY 1963, LPD 11-13 in FY 1964, LPD 14 and LPD 15 in FY 1965, and LPD 16 in FY 1966. LPD 16 was deferred in favour of LHA programme. No additional ships of this type are planned in view of the LHA capabilities.
LPD 4-6 built by New York Naval Shipyard; LPD 7-8 built by Ingalls Shipbuilding Corp; LPD 9-15 built by Lockheed Shipbuilding & Construction Co, Seattle, Washington.

DESIGN. These ships are 48 feet longer than the previous "Raleigh" class with the additional space used to carry more cargo, especially vehicles, and more fuel oil. The *Cleveland* and six later ships differ from the first three and last three in detail (ie, flagship facilities for amphibious squadron commander in LPD 7-13).

HELICOPTERS. These ships do not have integral hangars or aircraft maintenance facilities. The *Cleveland* and *Dubuque* were fitted with telescopic helicopter hangars late in 1967; similar hangars later fitted to all other LPDs. The telescopic hangars extend from 25 feet in length to 62 feet.

NOMENCLATURE. Amphibious transport docks are named for United States cities the namesake of which were explorers and developers of America. Some of the names previously were borne by cruisers.

PHOTOGRAPHS. Note additional bridge level in *Cleveland* compared to *Ogden*, on following page, identifying the former as a flagship. Hangar is visible in stern view of *Cleveland*.

CLEVELAND (LPD 7) *1967, United States Navy, PHCM L. P. Bodine*

CLEVELAND (LPD 7) *1967, United States Navy*

Amphibious Warfare Ships—*continued*

OGDEN (LPD 5) *1965, United States Navy*

3 AMPHIBIOUS TRANSPORT DOCKS (LPD): "RALEIGH" CLASS

Name	*No.*	*Laid down*	*Launched*	*Commissioned*
***RALEIGH**	LPD 1	23 June 1960	17 Mar 1962	8 Sep 1962
***VANCOUVER**	LPD 2	19 Nov 1960	15 Sep 1962	11 May 1963
***LA SALLE**	LPD 3	2 Apr 1962	3 Aug 1963	22 Feb 1964

Displacement, tons	8 040 light; 13 900 full load
Length, feet (*metres*)	500 (*152·0*) wl 521·8 (*158·4*) oa
Beam, feet (*metres*)	84 (*25·6*)
Draft, feet (*metres*)	21 (*6·4*)
Guns	8—3 in (*76 mm*) 50 cal AA
Helicopters	6 UH-34 or CH-46 (see *Helicopter* notes)
Main engines	2 steam turbines; 24 000 shp; 2 shafts
Boilers	2
Speed, knots	20 sustained; 23 maximum
Complement	490 (30 officers, 460 enlisted men)
Troops	930 except 860 in *La Salle*
Flag accommodations	90 in *La Salle*

The amphibious transport dock was developed from the dock landing ship (LSD) concept but provides more versatility. The LPD replaces the Amphibious Transport (LPA) and, in part, the Amphibious Cargo Ship (LKA) and dock landing ship. The LPD can carry a "balanced load" of assault troops and their equipment, has a docking well for landing craft, a helicopter deck, cargo holds and vehicle garages. The *Raleigh* was authorised in the Fiscal Year 1959 new construction programme, the *Vancouver* in FY 1960, and *La Salle* in FY 1961. Built by New York Naval Shipyard. Approximate construction cost was $29 000 000 per ship.

DESIGN. These ships resemble dock landing ships (LSD) but have fully enclosed docking well with the roof forming a permanent helicopter platform. The docking well is 168 feet long and 50 feet wide, less than half the length of wells in newer LSDs; the LPD design provides more space for vehicles, cargo, and troops. Ramps allow vehicles to be driven between helicopter deck, parking area, and docking well; side ports provide roll-on/roll off capability when docks are available. An overhead monorail in the docking well with six cranes facilitates loading landing craft.
The *La Salle* has an additional superstructure level to provide accommodations and facilities for an amphibious squadron commander and his staff. *La Salle* has modified pole mast atop bridge and lighter pole mast amidships; *Raleigh* and *Vancouver* have tripod mast.

HELICOPTERS. These ships are not normally assigned helicopters because they lack integral hangars and maintenance facilities. It is intended that helicopters from a nearby amphibious assault ship (LHA or LPH) would provide helicopters during an amphibious operation. The *La Salle* has successfully operated six SH-3A Sea King helicopters for an extended period. Hangars being fitted (see "Austin" class).

LANDING CRAFT. The docking well in these ships can hold one LCU and three LCM-6s or four LCM-8s or 20 LVTs (amphibious tractors). In addition, two LCM-6s or two LCPLs are carried on the boat deck which are lowered by crane.

PHOTOGRAPHS. Note staggered funnels. A Hawker vertical take-off/landing P.1127 Harrier is lifting off the *Raleigh* (designated XV-6A for US evaluation).

13 AMPHIBIOUS TRANSPORTS (SMALL) (LPR): CONVERTED DE TYPE

Name	*No.*	*Launched*	*Commissioned*
LANING	LPR 55 ex-DE 159	4 July 1943	1 Aug 1943
HOLLIS	LPR 86 ex-DE 794	11 Sep 1943	24 Jan 1943
***RUCHAMKIN**	LPR 89 ex-DE 228	15 June 1944	16 Sep 1945
KIRWIN	LPR 90 ex-DE 229	16 June 1944	4 Nov 1945
RINGNESS	LPR 100 ex-DE 590	5 Feb 1944	25 Oct 1944
KNUDSON	LPR 101 ex-DE 591	5 Feb 1944	25 Nov 1944
***BEVERLY W. REID**	LPR 119 ex-DE 722	4 Mar 1944	25 June 1945
***DIACHENKO**	LPR 123 ex-DE 690	15 Aug 1944	8 Dec 1944
HORACE A. BASS	LPR 124 ex-DE 691	12 Sep 1944	21 Dec 1944
BEGOR	LPR 127 ex-DE 711	25 May 1944	14 Mar 1945
***COOK**	LPR 130 ex-DE 714	26 Aug 1944	25 Apr 1945
BALDUCK	LPR 132 ex-DE 716	27 Oct 1944	7 May 1945
***WEISS**	LPR 135 ex-DE 719	17 Feb 1945	7 July 1945

Displacement, tons	1 400 standard; 2 130 full load
Dimensions, feet	300 wl; 306 oa × 37 × 12·6
Guns	1—5 in (*127 mm*) 38 cal DP; 4—40 mm AA (twin) in active ships; 8—40 mm AA (twin) in others
ASW weapons	2 triple torpedo launchers (Mk 32) in active ships; depth charges in others
Main engines	Geared turbines (General Electric) with electric drive; 12 000 shp; 2 shafts = 23·6 knots
Boilers	2 ("D" Express)
Complement	204 (designed wartime; 12 or 15 officers, 189 or 192 enlisted men, depending upon DE type)
Troops	162 (12 officers, 150 enlisted men)

These ships are former Destroyer Escorts (DE), converted during World War II to carry commandoes, reconnaissance troops, or frogmen and classified as High Speed Transports (APD). Designation of surviving 13 ships changed to Amphibious Transports (Small) and reclassified LPR on 1 January 1969. These ships were of the TE and TEV escort types. Fitted to carry four LCVP landing craft.

MODERNISATION. Several of these ships, including all in active status, were modernised under the FRAM II programme. They have new bridge configuration, additional electronic equipment, tripod mast (in place of original pole mast), improved habitability, ASW torpedo launchers, and retain only two twin 40 mm mounts (aft).

WAR LOSS. *Bates* (APD 47).

DISPOSALS

Chase, APD 54, **England**, APD 41, and **Witter**, APD 58, were scrapped soon after the Second World War, **Wantuck**, APD 125, was stricken from the Navy List on 4 Mar 1958 after collision. **Carpellotti**, APD 136, was stricken on 1 Dec 1960. **Amesbury**, APD 46, **Barr**, APD 39, **Bray**, APD 139, **Brock** APD 93, **Cread**, APD 88, **Crosley**, APD 87, **Frament**, APD 77, **Haines**, APD 84, **Hunter Marshall**, APD 112, **Ira Jeffrey**, APD 44, **John Q. Roberts**, APD 94, **Myers**, APD 105, **Ray K. Edwards**, APD 96, **Reeves**, APD 52, **Roger Blood**, APD 105, **Runels**, APD 85, **Sims**, APD 50, **Tatum**, APD 81, **Upham**, APD 99, **Walter S. Gorka**, APD 114, **Webber**, APD 75, and **William J. Pattison**, APD 104, were stricken at the end of 1960, and **Walter X. Young**, APD 131, in 1962 (used as target ship), **Bray** APD 139, was expended as a target on 26 Mar 1963. **Arthur L. Bristol**, APD 97, **Bunch**, APD 79, **Francovich**, APD 116, **Gosselin**, APD 126, and **Yokes** APD 69, were stricken on 1 Apr 1964. **Charles Lawrence**, APD 37, **Earle B. Hall**, APD 107, **Hopping**, APD 51, **Lee Fox** APD 45, **Loy**, APD 56, and **Newman**, APD 59, were stricken in 1965. **Burdo**, APD 133, and **Cofer**, APD 62 were stricken on 1 Apr 1966, and **Lloyd**, APD 63, on 1 June 1966, **Joseph E. Campbell** on 1 Dec 1966, **Liddle**, APD 60, stricken on 18 Mar 1967. **Rendour**, APD 102, in Mar 1967. **Hubbard**, APD 53, and **Walsh**, APD 111, on 1 May 1967. **Barber** APD 57, stricken 27 Nov 1968. **Burke** APD 65 stricken 1 June 1968.

TRANSFERS. *Cavallero*, APD 128, was transferred to Korea in Oct 1959, *Kleinsmith*, APD 134, was *Enright*, APD 66 to Ecuador in 1967, *George W. Ingram*, APD 43, *Blessman*, APD 48, and *Joseph E. Campbell*, APD 49, to Taiwan China in 1967, *Schmitt*, APD 76, to Taiwan China 1968. *Kephart*, APD 61, *Hayter*, APD 80, and *William M. Hobby*, APD 95, to South Korea in 1967. *Basset*, APD 73 and *Tolberg*, APD 103, to Columbia in 1968. *John P. Gray*, APD 74, to Chile.

5 DOCK LANDING SHIPS (LSD): NEW CONSTRUCTION

Name	*No.*	*Laid down*	*Launched*	*Commissioned*
***ANCHORAGE**	LSD 36	13 Mar 1967	5 May 1968	15 Mar 1969
PORTLAND	LSD 37	21 Sep 1967	Sep 1969	late 1970
PENSACOLA	LSD 38	12 Mar 1969	early 1970	early 1971
	LSD 39	Sep 1969	late 1970	late 1971
	LSD 40	Mar 1970	early 1971	early 1972

Displacement, tons	13 650 full load
Dimensions, feet (*metres*)	553 (*162·8*) oa × 84 (*25·6*)
Guns	8—3 in (*76 mm*) 50 cal AA (twin)
Main engines	2 geared turbines; 2 shafts = 20+ knots
Complement	793 (51 officers, 742 enlisted men)

Improved dock landing ships, slightly larger than previous class; designed to replace earlier LSDs which are unable to meet 20-knot amphibious lift requirement. Similar

RALEIGH (LPD 1) *1966, United States Navy*

Amphibious Warfare Ships—*continued*

(LSD): NEW CONSTRUCTION

in appearance to earlier classes but with a tripod mast. Helicopter platform aft with docking well partially open.
LSD 36 was authorised in Fiscal Year 1965 shipbuilding programme; LSD 37-39 in FY 1966 programme; LSD 40 in FY 1967 programme. *Anchorage* built by Ingalls Shipbuilding; LSD 37-40 by General Dynamics (Quincy).

ANCHORAGE (LSD 36) *1969, Ingalls Shipbuilding*

8 DOCK LANDING SHIPS (LSD): "THOMASTON" CLASS

Name	*No.*	*Launched*	*Commissioned*
***THOMASTON**	LSD 28	9 Feb 1954	17 Sep 1954
***PLYMOUTH ROCK**	LSD 29	7 May 1954	24 Jan 1955
***FORT SNELLING**	LSD 30	16 July 1954	24 Jan 1955
***POINT DEFIANCE**	LSD 31	28 Sep 1954	31 Mar 1955
***SPIEGEL GROVE**	LSD 32	10 Nov 1955	8 June 1956
***ALAMO**	LSD 33	20 Jan 1956	24 Aug 1956
***HERMITAGE**	LSD 34	12 June 1956	17 Dec 1956
***MONTICELLO**	LSD 35	10 Aug 1956	29 Mar 1957

Displacement, tons	6 880 light; 11 270 full load; *Alamo, Hermitage, Monticello, Spiegel Grove:* 12 150 full load
Dimensions, feet	510 oa × 84 × 19 max
Guns	12—3 inch 50 cal AA (twin)
Main engines	Steam turbines: 2 shafts: 23 000 shp = 24 knots
Boilers	2
Complement	305 plus 100 marines

Larger and faster than earlier types. Built by Ingalls Shipbuilding Corp. Fitted with helicopter landing platforms; two 50 ton cranes; 21 LCM (6) or 3 LCU and 6 LCM can be carried.

FORT SNELLING (LSD 30) *United States Navy*

MONTICELLO (LSD 35), LCU 1476 *1967, United States Navy*

SPIEGEL GROVE (LSD 32) *1968, United States Navy*

13 DOCK LANDING SHIPS (LSD): "CASA GRANDE" CLASS

Name	*No.*	*Launched*	*Commissioned*
***CASA GRANDE** (ex-*Spear*, ex-*Portway*)	LSD 13	11 Apr 1944	5 June 1944
***RUSHMORE** (ex-*Sword*, ex-*Swashway*)	LSD 14	10 May 1944	3 July 1944
***SHADWELL** (ex-*Tomahawk*, ex-*Waterway*)	LSD 15	24 May 1944	24 July 1944
***CABILDO**	LSD 16	28 Dec 1944	15 Mar 1945
***CATAMOUNT**	LSD 17	27 Jan 1945	9 Apr 1945
***COLONIAL**	LSD 18	28 Feb 1945	15 May 1945
***COMSTOCK**	LSD 19	28 Apr 1945	2 July 1945
***DONNER**	LSD 20	6 Apr 1945	31 July 1945
***FORT MANDAN**	LSD 21	2 June 1945	31 Oct 1945
***FORT MARION**	LSD 22	22 May 1945	29 Jan 1946
***SAN MARCOS**	LSD 25	10 Jan 1945	15 Apr 1945
***TORTUGA**	LSD 26	21 Jan 1945	8 June 1945
***WHETSTONE**	LSD 27	18 July 1945	12 Feb 1946

Displacement, tons	4 790 standard; 9 375 ufll load
Dimensions, feet	475·4 oa × 76·2 × 18 max
Guns	8— or 12—40 mm AA (2 quad, 2 twin in some ships)
Main engines	Geared turbines; 2 shafts; 7 000 shp = 15.4 knots
Boilers	2, two-drum single pass
Complement	265 (15 officers, 250 men)

LSD 13-19 built by Newport News SB & DD Co, Virginia; LSD 20, 21, 26, 27 by Boston Navy Yard; LSD 22 by Gulf SB Corp, Chickasaw, Alabama; LSD 25 by Philadelphia Navy Yard. *Fort Snelling*, LSD 23, and *Point Defiance*, LSD 24, cancelled in 1945; former ship completed for merchant service, reacquired by Navy as cargo ship *Taurus*, T-AK 273, T-AKR 8 (stricken in 1968.) LSD 9-12 of this class transferred to Britain in 1943-1944.
Can carry 3 LCUs or 18 LCMs. The 5-inch gun and all 20 mm guns have been removed. All ships are fitted with helicopter platforms.
Catamount LSD 17, *Colonial* LSD 18, *Donner* LSD 20, *Fort Mandan* LSD 21, and *Fort Marion* LSD 22, were modernised under the FRAM II programme in 1960-1962. Fitted with helicopter platforms on docking well.

ARMAMENT. Arrangement differs; all ships have two quad 40 mm mounts on forward superstructure; some have two twin 40 mm mounts on dock walls aft.

DONNER (LSD 20) *1968, United States Navy*

COMSTOCK (LSD 19), LCU 1481 *1965, United States Navy*

Amphibious Warfare Ships—*continued*

5 DOCK LANDING SHIPS (LSD): "ASHLAND" CLASS

Name	*No.*	*Launched*	*Commissioned*
***ASHLAND**	LSD 1	21 Dec 1942	5 June 1943
***BELLE GROVE**	LSD 2	17 Feb 1942	9 Aug 1943
***CARTER HALL**	LSD 3	4 Mar 1943	18 Sep 1943
***GUNSTON HALL**	LSD 5	1 May 1943	10 Nov 1943
***OAK HILL**	LSD 7	25 June 1943	5 Jan 1944

Displacement, tons	4 790 standard; 8 700 limit; *Guston Hall*, 5 480 standard; 9 200 full load
Dimensions, feet	454 wl; 457·8 oa × 72·2 × 18
Guns	12—40 mm AA (two quad, two twin)
Main engines	2 Skinner Unaflow; 2 shafts; 7 400 shp = 15 knots
Boilers	2
Complement	15 officers, 250 men

All built by Moore Dry Dock Co. Designed to serve as parent ships for landing and coastal craft. The 5-inch gun and all 20 mm guns were removed. All carry 18 flat nosed LCMs (Landing Craft Medium) or 3 LCUs in their well deck running three-quarters of their length. Length of well in open 252 feet, width of well 44 feet. All fitted with a helicopter landing platform over the well-deck.
Oak Hill, LSD 7, was modernised under the FRAM II programme in 1960 and *Belle Grove* in 1961.

TRANSFER. *White Marsh*, LSD 8, was transferred to Taiwan, China on 17 Nov 1960.

DISPOSAL Lindenwald, LSD 6, was stricken on 1 Dec 1967.

CONVERSION. *Epping Forest* (ex-LSD 4) was converted to a minecraft tender, MCS 7 stricken 1 Nov 1968.

CARTER HALL (LSD 3) *1968, United States Navy*

20 + 7 TANK LANDING SHIPS (LST): "NEWPORT" CLASS

Name	*No.*	*Laid down*	*Launched*	*Commissioned*
***NEWPORT**	LST 1179	1 Nov 1966	3 Feb 1968	7 June 1969
***MANITOWOC**	LST 1180	27 Feb 1967	4 Jan 1969	June 1969
SUMTER	LST 1181	14 Nov 1967	July 1969	Sep 1969
***FRESNO**	LST 1182	16 Dec 1967	28 Sep 1968	July 1969
***PEORIA**	LST 1183	22 Feb 1968	23 Nov 1968	Aug 1969
FREDERICK	LST 1184	13 Apr 1968	8 Mar 1969	Nov 1969
SCHENECTADY	LST 1185	2 Aug 1968	May 1969	early 1970
CAYUGA	LST 1186	28 Sep 1968	July 1969	1970
TUSCALOOSA	LST 1187	23 Nov 1968	Sep 1969	1970
	LST 1188		1970	1970
	LST 1189		1970	1970
	LST 1190-1195		1970	1971
	LST 1196-1198		1971	1974

Displacement, tons	8 342 full load
Dimensions, feet (*metres*)	522·3 (*158·7*) oa × 69·5 (*21·0*) × 15 (*4·5*) (aft)
Guns	4—3 inch (*76 mm*) 50 cal AA (twin)
Main engines	6 diesels (Alco); 2 shafts = 20 knots (sustained)
Complement	231 (14 officers, 217 enlisted men)
Troops	430

These ships are of an entirely new design, larger and faster than previous tank landing ships. They will operate with 20-knot LHA/LPD/LSD amphibious squadrons to transport tanks, other heavy vehicles, engineer equipment, and supplies which cannot be readily landed by helicopters or landing craft. Seven additional ships of this type are planned for the Fiscal Year 1971 new construction programme.
The *Newport* was authorised in the Fiscal Year 1965 new construction programme, LST 1180-1187 (8 ships) in FY 1966, and LST 1188-1198 (11 ships) in FY 1967. LST 1179-1181 built by Philadelphia Naval Shipyard; LST 1182-1198 built by National Steel & Shipbuilding Co, San Diego, California.

DESIGN. These ships are the first LSTs to depart from the bow-door design developed by the British early in World War II. The hull form required to achieve 20 knots would not permit bow doors, thus these ships unload by a 112-foot ramp over their bow; the ramp is supported by twin derrick arms. A ramp just forward of the super structure connects the lower tank deck with the main deck and a vehicle passage through the superstructure provides access to the parking area amidships. A stern gate to the tank deck permits unloading of amphibious tractors into the water, or unloading of other vehicles into an LCU or onto a pier. Vehicle stowage is rated at 500 tons and 19 000 square feet (5 000 sq ft more than previous LSTs). Full load draft is 15 feet aft and six feet forward.

NEWPORT (LST 1179) *1968, United States Navy*

7 TANK LANDING SHIPS (LST): "SUFFOLK COUNTY" CLASS

Name	*No.*	*Builder*	*Launched*
***DE SOTO COUNTY**	LST 1171	Avondale, New Orleans	28 Feb 1957
***SUFFOLK COUNTY**	LST 1173	Boston Navy Yard	5 Sep 1956
***GRANT COUNTY**	LST 1174	Avondale, New Orleans	12 Oct 1956
***YORK COUNTY**	LST 1175	Newport News SB & DD Co	5 Mar 1957
***GRAHAM COUNTY**	LST 1176	Newport News SB & DD Co	19 Sep 1957
***LORAIN COUNTY**	LST 1177	American SB Co, Lorrain	22 June 1957
***WOOD COUNTY**	LST 1178	American SB Co, Lorrain	14 Dec 1957

Displacement, tons	4 164 light; 8 000 full load
Dimensions, feet	445 oa × 62 × 16·5
Guns	6—3 in, 50 cal (3 twin)
Main engines	Diesels; 2 shafts; controllable pitch propellers; 14 400 bhp (except *Graham County*, 9 600 bhp) = 17·5 knots (except *Graham County*, 14·5 knots); see *Engineering* notes.
Complement	184 (10 officers, 174 men)
Troops	Vary. Approx 575 per ship except *York County* and *Graham County* only 430 troops; see *Design* notes.

Improved LSTs with greater speed and troop capacity than earlier ships of this category; considered the "ultimate" design attainable with traditional LST bow door configuration. Contract for LST 1172 not awarded. *De Soto County* commissioned on 10 June 1958, *Suffolk County* on 15 Aug 1957, *Grant County* on 17 Dec 1957, *York County* on 8 Nov 1957, *Graham County* on 17 Apr 1958, *Lorain County* on 3 Oct 1958, *Wood County* on 5 Aug 1959. *Lorain County* delivered to Todd Shipyards on 11 July 1958 for trials and completion.

LST 1179 DESIGN

Amphibious Warfare Ships—*continued*

DESIGN. High degree of habitability with all crew and troop living spaces air conditioned. Can carry 23 medium tanks or vehicles up to 75 tons on 288-foot-long (lower) tank deck. Davits for four LCVP-type landing craft. Liquid cargo capacity of 170 000 gallons (US) diesel or jet fuel plus 7 000 gallons (US) of petrol for embarked vehicles; two ships have reduced troop spaces and carry additional 250 000 gallons (US) of aviation petrol for pumping ashore or to other ships.

ENGINEERING. All except *Graham County* built with six Nordberg diesels. *Graham County* has four Fairbanks Morse diesels, hydraulic couplings and controllable-pitch propellers (9 600 bhp = 14·5 knots). First four ships now have six Fairbanks Morse diesels, electric couplings and reduction gears (14 400 bhp = 17·5 knots). *Lorain County* and *Wood County* now have six Cooper Bessemer diesels, electric couplings and reduction gears (14 400 bhp = 17·5 knots).

PHOTOGRAPHS. The "Suffolk County" class LSTs are identified by their twin fire control towers forward; note the pontoons being carried on the sides of the *Graham County*.

GRANT COUNTY (LST 1174) 1966, *United States Navy*

GRAHAM COUNTY 1967, *United States Navy*

15 TANK LANDING SHIPS (LST): "TERREBONNE PARISH" CLASS

Name	No.	Launched	Commissioned
* **TERREBONNE PARISH**	LST 1156	9 Aug 1952	21 Nov 1952
* **TERRELL COUNTY**	LST 1157	6 Dec 1952	19 Mar 1953
TIOGA COUNTY	LST 1158	11 Apr 1953	20 June 1953
* **TOM GREEN COUNTY**	LST 1159	2 July 1953	12 Sep 1953
* **TRAVERSE COUNTY**	LST 1160	3 Oct 1953	19 Dec 1953
* **VERNON COUNTY**	LST 1161	25 Nov 1952	18 May 1953
* **WAHKIAKUM COUNTY**	LST 1162	23 Jan 1953	13 Aug 1953
* **WALDO COUNTY**	LST 1163	17 Mar 1953	17 Sep 1953
* **WALWORTH COUNTY**	LST 1164	18 May 1953	26 Oct 1953
* **WASHOE COUNTY**	LST 1165	14 July 1953	30 Nov 1953
* **WASHTENAW COUNTY**	LST 1166	22 Nov 1952	29 Oct 1953
* **WESTCHESTER COUNTY**	LST 1167	18 Apr 1953	10 Mar 1954
* **WEXFORD COUNTY**	LST 1168	28 Nov 1953	15 June 1954
* **WHITFIELD COUNTY**	LST 1169	22 Aug 1953	14 Sep 1954
* **WINDHAM COUNTY**	LST 1170	22 May 1954	15 Dec 1954

Displacement, tons	2 590 light; 5 800 full load
Dimensions, feet	384 oa × 55 × 17
Guns	6—3 in, 50 cal (twin)
Main engines	4 GM diesels; 2 shafts; controllable pitch propellers; 6 000 bhp = 15 knots
Complement	116
Troops	395

Design is modification of that of two experimental ships constructed after the Second World War. LST 1156-1160 were built by Bath Iron Works, 1166-1170 by Christy Corporation, and 1161-1165 by Ingalls Shipbuilding Corporation. *Tioga County* decommissioned in 1969.

WALDO COUNTY (LST 1163) *United States Navy*

VERNON COUNTY (LST 1161) *1965, United States Navy*

1 TANK LANDING SHIP (LST): "TALBOT COUNTY" TYPE

TALBOT COUNTY LST 1153

Displacement, tons	2 324; 6 000 full load
Dimensions, feet	368 wl; 382 oa × 54 × 17
Guns	2—5 in, 38 cal; 4—40 mm AA
Main engines	Geared turbines; 2 shafts; 6 000 shp = 14 knots
Complement	82
Troops	197

The *Talbot County* and her sister ship *Tallahatchie County* (LST 1154) were the only steam-driven LSTs built for the US Navy. Built by Boston Navy Yard; *Talbot County* launched on 24 Apr 1947 and commissioned on 3 Sep 1947. Improved arrangements and greater cargo capacity than the war-built LSTs.

CONVERSION. *Tallahatchie County* converted to advance Aviation Base Ship (AVB 2); listed with Fleet Support Ships.

TALBOT COUNTY (LST 1153) *A. & J. Pavia*

39 TANK LANDING SHIPS (LST): 511-1152 SERIES

* **CADDO PARISH**	515	* **LITCHFIELD COUNTY**	901
* **CAROLINE COUNTY**	525	* **LUZERNE COUNTY**	902
CHEBOYGAN COUNTY	533	* **MADERA COUNTY**	905
* **CHURCHILL COUNTY**	583	* **MEEKER COUNTY**	980
* **CLARKE COUNTY**	601	**MIDDLESEX COUNTY**	983
* **COCONINO COUNTY**	603	* **MONMOUTH COUNTY**	1032
DODGE COUNTY	722	* **OUTAGAMIE COUNTY**	1073
DUVAL COUNTY	758	* **PAGE COUNTY**	1076
* **FLOYD COUNTY**	762	* **PARK COUNTY**	1077
* **GARRETT COUNTY**	786	* **PITKIN COUNTY**	1082
* **HAMPSHIRE COUNTY**	819	* **POLK COUNTY**	1084
HARNETT COUNTY	821	**ST CLAIR COUNTY**	1096
HENRY COUNTY	824	* **SAN JOAQUIN COUNTY**	1122
* **HICKMAN COUNTY**	825	* **SEDGWICK COUNTY**	1123
* **HOLMES COUNTY**	836	**SNOHOMISH COUNTY**	1126
* **HUNTERDON COUNTY**	838	* **STONE COUNTY**	1141
* **IREDELL COUNTY**	839	**SUMMIT COUNTY**	1146
* **JENNINGS COUNTY**	846	**SUMNER COUNTY**	1148
* **JEROME COUNTY**	848	* **SUTTER COUNTY**	1150
* **KEMPER COUNTY**	854		

Displacement, tons	1 653 standard; 2 366 beaching; 4 080 full load
Dimensions, feet	316 wl; 328 oa × 50 × 14
Guns	8—40 mm AA (twin)
Main engines	GM diesels; 2 shafts; 1 700 bhp = 11·6 knots
Complement	119
Troops	147

Amphibious Warfare Ships—*continued*

"SUFFOLK" COUNTY *continued*

LSTs which previously carried numbers only, were named on 1 July 1955. Cargo capacity 2 100 tons. All reserve LSTs (17 ships) were recommissioned in 1965-1966. Ten ships decommissioned in 1969.

Four of these ships have been modified to support river patrol operations in South Vietnam: *Garrett County, Jennings County, Hunterdon County,* and *Harnett County.* Changes include installation of 10-ton capacity boom forward of superstructure on starboard side to lift PBR patrol craft, enlargement of cargo hatch to 16 feet by 34 feet to permit lowering of PBRs to tank deck for repairs or transport, strengthening of main deck for operation of UH-1B "Huey" helicopters, and installation of additional communications equipment, helicopter and boat fueling systems, helicopter deck lighting, additional workshops and storerooms, modification of ammunition magazines, and boat booms to permit small craft to moor alongside. (*Harnett County* was one of the LSTs decommissioned in 1969).

Forty-two of the war-built LSTs are operated by the Navy's Military Sea Transportation Service and are listed with the Logistic Support Ships. The *Clearwater County* (LST 602) is operated by the US Air Force. (The only LSM, remaining in US service now designated AG 335, is also described in the section on Logistic Support Ships).

MODERNISATION. *Holmes County,* LST 836, *Polk County* LST 1084, *Stone County* LST 1141, *Sumner County* LST 1148, were modernised in the 1960 FRAM II programme.

TRANSFERS. LST 1010 was transferred to Korea on 22 Mar 1955, *Iron County* LST 840, *Lafayette County* LST 859, *San Bernadino County* LST 1110, *Sagadahoe County* LST 1091, and *Sweetwater County* LST 1152 to Nationalist China in 1958; *Johnson County* LST 849, *Kane County* LST 853, *Lynn County* LST 900 and *Pender County* LST 1080 to Korea in 1958; *Burnett County* LST 512 to Peru in 1958, *Solana County* LST 1128, to Indonesia in 1960; *Hamilton County* LST 802 to Japan in 1960; *Potter County* LST 1086, to Greece in 1960; LST 849 to Korea, LST 520, LST 535, LST 578 and LST 735 to Taiwan, *Greer County* LST 799, *Rice County* LST 1089, and *Saline County* LST 1101 to West Germany in 1961, *Lawrence County* LST 887 and *Russell County* LST 1090 to Indonesia; *Doggett County* LST 689, *Hillsdale County* LST 835 and *Nansemond County* LST 1064 to Japan in 1961, *Sublette County* LST 1144 to Taiwan China in Jan 1961; *Millard County* LST 987 amd *Montgomery County* LST 1041 to West Germany in 1961; LST 616, LST 652 and LST 657 to Indonesia in 1961; *Lincoln County* LST 898 to Thailand in 1962, *Marricopa County* LST 938 and *Marion County* LST 975 to Vietnam in 1962, and *Cayuga County* LST 529 in 1963, *Stark County* LST 1134 to Thailand on 16 May 1966.

DISPOSALS

Mineral County LST 983 was destroyed as a target for gunfire, **Ford County** LST 772, **Kent County** LST 855 and **Orange County** LST 1068 were disposed of in 1957, **Cassia County** LST 527, **Hampden County** LST 803 and **Hillsborough County** LST 827 in 1958, **Chittenden County** LST 561 after grounding at Kauai, Hawaii, in Mar 1958, (salvaged but torpedoed by the nuclear Submarine *Sargo* off Oahu in Nov 1958) **Lyman County** LST 903 and **Lyon County** LST 904, were sunk as targets in 1959. **Calaveras County** LST 516, **Crook County** LST 611, **Eddy County** LST 759, **Esmeralda County** LST 761, **Garfield County** LST 784, **Gibson County** LST 794 were stricken in 1959, **Cape May County** LST 521, **Catahouia Parish** LST 528, **Chelan County** LST 542, **Curry County** LST 685, **Douglas County** LST 731, **Juniata County** LST 850, **Lake County** LST 880, **Lamoure County** LST 883, **Lee County** LST 888, **Mahoning County** LST 914, **Marinette County** LST 593, **Morgan County** LST 1048, **Ouachita County** LST 1071, **Overton County** LST 1074, **Payette County** LST 1079, **Pima County** LST 1081, **Somervell County** LST 1129 and **Stratford County** LST 1142, between 1 June and 30 June 1960. **King County** AG 157 (ex-LST 857) and LST 618 in 1960, **Jefferson County** LST 845, **Steuben County** LST 1138 and **Dunn County** LST 742 were stricken in 1961, **Calhoun County** LST 519 in Nov 1962, **Mahnomen County** LST 912, was stricken on 31 Jan 1967 after grounding in Vietnam, **Coconino County** LST 603 transferred to South Vietnam on 4 April 1969.

SUMNER COUNTY (LST 1148 — *1968, United States Navy, PH3 R. Ferraro*

SNOHOMISH COUNTY (LST 1126) — *1964, United States Navy*

BLANCO COUNTY (LST 344) — *courtesy "Our Navy"*

2 TANK LANDING SHIPS (LST): 1-510 SERIES

*BLANCO COUNTY LST 344 — *BULLOCH COUNTY LST 509

Displacement, tons	1 625 light; 2 366 beaching; 4 050 full load
Dimensions, feet	328 oa × 50 × 14·3 max
Guns	8—40 mm AA
Main engines	GM diesels; 2 shafts; 1 700 bhp = 10·8 knots
Complement	80 to 119
Troops	147

These ships are ocean tank carriers with bow doors built during World War II, *Blanco County* and *Bulloch County* recommissioned in 1965.

TRANSFERS. LST 53 was transferred to Korea, *Berkeley County* LST 227 and *Bradley County* LST 400 to Taiwan China, LST 503 to Taiwan on 29 Apr 1955, LST 218 and LST 227 to Korea in 1955 and *Berkshire County* LST 288 on 5 Mar 1956, LST 503 to Taiwan, *Boon County* LST 389 and *Bowman County* LST 391, to Greece in 1960, *Alameda County* reclassified from LST 32 to AVB 1 (Advance Aviation Base Ship) to Italy in Nov 1962, LST 325 to Greece on 29 May 1964.

DISPOSALS

LST 291 was stricken after grounding in 1954. **Addison County** LST 31, **Armstrong County** LST 57, **Branch County** LST 482, **Brewster County** LST 483 and **Buchanan County** LST 405 were stricken on 11 Aug 1955 and used as targets, **Atchison County** LST 60, **Bamberg County** LST 209, **Benton County** LST 263, **Benzie County** LST 266, **Bernalilo County** LST 306, **Bledsoe County** LST 356 and **Buncombe County** LST 510 on 1 June 1959 and 30 June 1960.

LANDING CRAFT

26+9 UTILITY LANDING CRAFT: LCU 1610 SERIES

LCU 1610	**LCU 1615**	**LCU 1620**	**LCU 1625**	**LCU 1631**
LCU 1611	**LCU 1616**	**LCU 1621**	**LCU 1627**	**LCU 1632**
LCU 1612	**LCU 1617**	**LCU 1622**	**LCU 1628**	**LCU 1633**
LCU 1613	**LCU 1618**	**LCU 1623**	**LCU 1629**	**LCU 1534**
LCU 1614	**LCU 1619**	**LCU 1624**	**LCU 1630**	**LCU 1635**
				LCU 1636

Displacement, tons	200 light; 375 full load
Dimensions, feet	135·2 oa × 29 × 5·5
Guns	2—20 mm AA
Main engines	Diesels; 2 000 bhp; 2 shafts = 11 knots (see *Engineering* notes)
Complement	12

Improved landing craft, larger than previous series. Can carry three M-103A tanks or six M-42 tanks or three M-48 tanks.

LCU 1610-1612 built by Christy Corp, Sturgeon Bay, Wisconsin; LCU 1613-1619, 1623, 1624 built by Gunderson Bros Engineering Corp, Portland, Oregon; LCU 1620, 1621, 1625, 1626, 1629, 1630 built by Southern Shipbuilding Corp, Slidell, Louisiana; LCU 1622 built by Weaver Shipyards, Texas; LCU 1627, 1628, 1631-1636 built by General Ship and Engine Works (last six units completed in 1968). LCU 1637-1645 are under construction.

ENGINEERING. LCU 1620 has two 500-hp engines on vertical shafts fitted with vertical-axis cycloidal, six-bladed propellers. LCU 1621 is fitted with two right-angle drive propulsion units, port and starboard, which rotate through 360 degrees, providing thrust in any direction; the two units can be locked together or operated independently, and obviate the need for rudders and shafts. LCU 1622 equipped with Kort-nozzle propellers. LCU 1625 equipped with cycloid propellers. LCU 1622 was to have had gas-turbine propulsion machinery, but project was cancelled.

TRANSFERS. LCU 1626 was transferred to Burma in 1967.

PHOTOGRAPHS. Note amidships, right-side "island" structure of LCU 1614; LCU 1625 differs with built-up structure aft.

LANDING CRAFT *continued*

LCU 1614 *1965, United States Navy*

LCU 1625 *United States Navy*

42 UTILITY LANDING CRAFT: LCU 1466 SERIES

LCU 1466	**LCU 1475**	**LCU 1486**	**LCU 1494**	**LCU 1537**
LCU 1467	**LCU 1476**	**LCU 1487**	**LCU 1495**	**LCU 1539**
LCU 1468	**LCU 1477**	**LCU 1488**	**LCU 1497**	**LCU 1547**
LCU 1469	**LCU 1481**	**LCU 1489**	**LCU 1498**	**LCU 1548**
LCU 1470	**LCU 1482**	**LCU 1490**	**LCU 1499**	**LCU 1559**
LCU 1471	**LCU 1483**	**LCU 1491**	**LCU 1500**	**LCU 1576**
LCU 1472	**LCU 1484**	**LCU 1492**	**LCU 1525**	**LCU 1582**
LCU 1473	**LCU 1485**	**LCU 1493**	**LCU 1535**	**LCU 1608**
			LCU 1536	**LCU 1609**

Displacement, tons	180 light; 360 full load
Dimensions, feet	115 wl; 119 oa × 34 × 6 max
Guns	2—20 mm
Main engines	3 diesels; 3 shafts; 675 bhp = 10 knots
Complement	14

These are enlarged versions of the World War II-built LCTs; constructed during the early 1950s. LCU 1608 and 1609 have modified propulsion systems; LCU 1582 and later craft have Kort nozzle propellers. LCU 1496 reclassified as YFU 69 on 1 Mar 1966.

CLASSIFICATION. The earlier craft of this series were initially designated as Utility Landing Ships (LSU); redesignated Utility Landing Craft (LCU) on 15 Apr 1952 and classified as service craft.

DISPOSALS AND TRANSFERS

LCU 1478 was transferred to Norway and **LCU 1479, 1480, 1501, 1502** were transferred to South Vietnam upon completion; **LCU 1504-1593** were built under US Navy contract for US Army; **LCU 1594-1607** were built in Japan for the Japanese and Nationalist Chinese (Taiwan) navies; **LCU 1503** lost accidentally in Aug 1953.

LCU 1483 *1965, United States Navy*

LCU 1488 *1965, United States Navy*

26 UTILITY LANDING CRAFT: LCU 501 SERIES

LCU 539	**LCU 660**	**LCU 768**	**LCU 1045**	**LCU 1387**
LCU 588	**LCU 666**	**LCU 780**	**LCU 1124**	**LCU 1430**
LCU 599	**LCU 667**	**LCU 803**	**LCU 1241**	**LCU 1451**
LCU 608	**LCU 674**	**LCU 871**	**LCU 1348**	**LCU 1459**
LCU 654	**LCU 742**	**LCU 893**	**LCU 1348**	**LCU 1462**

Displacement, tons	143 to 160 light; 309 to 320 full load
Dimensions, feet	105 wl; 119 oa × 32·7 × 5 max
Guns	2—20 mm
Main engines	Gray Marine diesels; 3 shafts; 675 bhp = 10 knots
Complement	13

Formerly LCT(6) 501-1465 series; built in 1943-1944. Can carry four tanks or 200 tons of cargo. LCUs 1273, 1330, 1363, 1452, 1463, and 1374 modified for Arctic service in 1948-1949. LCU 524, 529, 550, 562, 592, 600, 629, 664, 666, 668, 677, 686, 742, 764, 776, 788, 840, 869, 877, 960, 973, 974, 979, 980, 1056, 1082, 1086, 1124, 1136, 1156, 1159, 1162, 1195, 1224, 1236, 1250, 1283, 1286, 1363, 1376, 1378, 1384, 1386, 1398, 1411, and 1430 reclassified as YFU 1 through 46, respectively, on 18 May 1958; LCU 1040 reclassified YFB 82 on 18 May 1958; LCU 1446 reclassified YFU 53 in 1964; LCU 509, 637, 646, 709, 716, 776, 851, 916, 973, 989, 1126, 1165, 1203, 1232, 1385, and 1388 reclassified as YFU 54 through 69, respectively, on 1 Mar 1966; YFU 9 reverted to LCU 666 on 1 Jan 1962; changes reflect employment as general cargo craft assigned to shore commands (see section on Special Auxiliary Ships and Service Craft).

CLASSIFICATION. Originally rated as Landing Craft, Tank (LCT(6)); redesignated Utility Landing Ships (LSU) in 1949 to reflect varied employment; designation changed to Utility Landing Craft (LCU) on 15 Apr 1952 and classified as service craft.

WAR LOSSES. LCT(6) 548, 579, 582, 593, 597, 612, 714, 777, 823, 961, 963, 983, 984, 988, 998.

DISPOSALS AND TRANSFERS

LCT(6) 555, 703 stricken in 1944 and scrapped; **LCT(6) 627, 629** transferred to Britain on 21 Jan 1944; 30 units expended as target ships in 1946 Bikini atomic bomb tests; **LCU 1460** lost at sea in 1952; **LCU 815** stricken in 1956; **LCU 569, 676, 767, 1258, 1288, 1362, 1447, 1453, 1454** stricken in 1957; **LCU 638, 700, 779, 1174, 1225, 1271, 1278** stricken in 1958; **LCU 1538** stricken in 1959; **LCU 1212, 1244, 1367, 1429** transferred under Military Aid Programme in 1959; **LCU 1530** stricken in 1960.

MECHANISED LANDING CRAFT: LCM 8 TYPE

Displacement, tons	113 full load (steel)
Dimensions, feet	73·7 oa × 21 × 5·2
Main engines	2 diesels; 2 shafts; 650 shp = 9 knots

Constructed of welded-steel and (later units) aluminium. Can carry one M-48 or M-60 tank. Also operated in large numbers by the US army.

LCM-8 *1967, United States Navy*

MECHANISED LANDING CRAFT: LCM 6 TYPE

Displacement, tons	55 full load
Dimensions, feet	56·2 oa × 14 × 3·9
Main engines	2 diesels; 2 shafts; 450 shp = 9 knots

Welded-steel construction.

LANDING CRAFT VEHICLE AND PERSONNEL (LCVP)

Displacement, tons	13·5 full load
Dimensions, feet	35·8 oa × 10·5 × 3·5
Main engines	diesel; 1 shaft; 225 shp = 9 knots

Constructed of wood or fibreglass-reinforced plastic. Fitted with ·30-calibre machine guns when in combat areas.

LCVP *1966, United States Navy*

PATROL, COASTAL AND RIVERINE CRAFT

The US Navy continues to operate a large number of patrol, coastal, and riverine craft in Southeast Asia to support ground operations in South Vietnam and naval missions along the strife-torn country's coasts and inland waterways. The South Vietnamese Navy is undertaking a larger portion of these activities. During 1968-1969 the United States transferred 18 "Swift" boats (PCF), two Coast Guard Patrol Craft (WPB), 23 River Patrol Boats (PBR), and two River Assault Squadrons (100 riverine craft) to South Vietnam. However, the majority of the naval operations in South Vietnam are still conducted by the US Navy and Coast Guard.

In October 1968 the US Navy initiated Operation SEA LORDS which integrates patrol, surveillance, and river assault forces into small task groups to interdict Viet Cong infiltration routes from Cambodia to the Mekong Delta, to pacify and clear the Bassac River islands, to control the major trans-delta canals, and to harass the Viet Cong. According to the Chief of Naval Operations statement on 1 Apr 1969: "The operation has been successful in penetrating areas which have not previously known a continuing (South Vietnamese) government or US presence". Three major task forces have been established for US inshore warfare operations in South Vietnam. Under the direction of the Commander US Naval Forces Vietnam, these task forces are:

- Coastal Surveillance Force (Task Force 115) which is responsible for halting Communist infiltration of men and arms into South Vietnam by Sea. This force conducts Operation MARKET TIME, a barrier of ships, small craft, and aircraft along the 1 000-mile coast of South Vietnam. The small craft are primarily "Swift" Fast Patrol Craft (PCF) and Coast Guard Patrol Boats (WPB) along with a lesser number of Coastal Minesweepers (MSC), Ocean Minesweepers (MSO), and Patrol Gunboats (PG). Completing the barrier are a small number of Radar Picket Escort Ships (DER) and larger Coast Guard cutters. Air support for this operation is provided by P-2 Neptune and P-3 Orion patrol aircraft based at Cam Ranh Bay in South Vietnam; Utapno, Thailand; and Sangley Point in the Philippines. Maintenance and logistic support for MARKET TIME are provided by Landing Craft Repair Ships (ARL), Barracks Craft (APL), and Tank Landing Ships (LST).

- River Patrol Force (Task Force 116) which is responsible for preventing Communist use of waterways in the Mekong Delta area and keeping the waterways open to Allied shipping. This force conducts Operation GAME WARDEN in the delta area of approximately 7 000 square miles. The principal small craft of this force are the River Patrol Boats (PBR). Air Support for GAME WARDEN is provided by a squadron of HU-1B "Huey" helicopters operating from the LSTs modified to service the patrol boats and from several small land bases. The PBRs are also supported by specially configured barges.

- River Assault Force (Task Force 117) which is responsible for transporting and supporting US and South Vietnamese troops in the Mekong Delta area. This force, administratively designated River Assault Flotilla One, and US Army infantry units comprise the Mobile Riverine Force. TF 117's combat craft consist of multi-purpose Assault Support Patrol Boats (ASPB), Command and Control Boats (CCB), Armoured Troop Carriers (ATC), Monitors, (MON), and various minesweepers (MSM-MSD-MSR). All naval personnel and some Army battalions are embarked in Self-Propelled Barrack Ships (APB) and Non-Self-Propelled Barracks Craft (APL). Maintenance and logistic support for the riverine craft are provided by ARLs and LSTs.

The US Navy currently has two river assault squadrons in South Vietnam Each squadron normally consists of 16 Assault Support Patrol Boats, five Monitors, two Command and Control Boats, and 27 Armoured Troop Carriers (some fitted with helicopter decks and are employed as a refueler to provide petrol to other boats and helicopters).

Also operating under Commander US Naval Forces Vietnam are Minesweeping Boats (MSB) and numerous lesser patrol and support craft.
The specialised PCF, PBR, ASPB, CCB, ATC, Monitor, and minesweeper designs were all developed or adopted specifically for operations in Southeast Asian waters. Riverine warfare craft are now being completed or modified to the so-called Programme V configuration. Programme V refers to a fiscal phase. Armament has been revised to reflect combat experience in Vietnam, and special armour and flotation material added. Bar armour resembling steel cages has been fitted to riverine craft to trigger enemy projectiles, especially shaped rounds, before they strike the craft's conventional armour. The space between this "stand-off" armour and the conventional armour often is filled with sand bags to further reduce damage. LCM landing craft modified to riverine configurations have been widened with buoyancy material being added to the new side sections to increase flotation if the craft takes on water due to enemy damage. Finally, the helicopter flight decks added to some Armoured Troop Carriers provides additional protection against enemy mortar fire.
The larger Patrol Gunboats (PG, formerly PGM) were designed earlier. The lack of suitable coastal patrol craft has required the use of Coast Guard patrol boats in the combat area (under Navy operational control)

In addition to the above inshore warfare craft, the Navy is evaluating two Patrol Gunboats-Hydrofoil (PGH) designs for possible procurement in large numbers.

Evaluation of the Navy's three air cushion patrol craft included two combat deployments to South Vietnam. It does not appear likely that these craft will remain in Navy service.

Finally, some consideration is being given to developing a small missile-launching craft armed with surface-to-surface missiles. Interest in this type has been increased because of the success of Soviet-supplied Egyptian missile boats in sinking the Israeli destroyer *Eilat* in October 1967. Adaptions of the *Asheville* class patrol gunboat and the *Tucumcari* type hydrofoil gunboat to missile-launching configurations have been mentioned.

The ten All-Weather Patrol Boats (designated PB) authorised in the Fiscal Year 1968 (eight boats) and FY 1969 (one boat) programmes have been dropped. These boats were to have been about 100 feet long, displace about 100 tons, and have a relatively high endurance and all-weather operating capability. Secretary of Defence Robert S. McNamara was the principal advocate of these craft and upon his leaving the funds for these boats were allocated to other programmes by the Navy.
The nine 95-foot Patrol Craft (WPB) and two 82-foot Patrol Craft (WPB) transferred from the US Coast Guard to the US Navy subsequently were retransferred to the South Korean and South Vietnamese navies, respectively.

17 PATROL GUNBOATS (PG): "ASHEVILLE" CLASS

Name	No.	Builder	Commissioned
ASHEVILLE	PG 84	Tacoma Boatbuilding	6 Aug 1966
GALLUP	PG 85	Tacoma Boatbuilding	22 Oct 1966
ANTELOPE	PG 86	Tacoma Boatbuilding	4 Nov 1967
READY	PG 87	Tacoma Boatbuilding	6 Jan 1968
CROCKETT	PG 88	Tacoma Boatbuilding	24 June 1967
MARATHON	PG 89	Tacoma Boatbuilding	11 May 1968
CANON	PG 90	Tacoma Boatbuilding	26 July 1968
TACOMA	PG 92	Tacoma Boatbuilding	June 1969
WELCH	PG 93	Petersen Buildiers	July 1969
CHEHALIS	PG 94	Tacoma Boatbuilding	July 1969
DEFIANCE	PG 95	Petersen Builders	Aug 1969
BENICIA	PG 96	Tacoma Boatbuilding	Dec 1969
SURPRISE	PG 97	Petersen Builders	Sep 1969
GRAND RAPIDS	PG 98	Tacoma Boatbuilders	Jan 1970
BEACON	PG 99	Petersen Builders	Oct 1969
DOUGLAS	PG 100	Tacoma Boatbuilders	Feb 1970
GREEN BAY	PG 101	Petersen Builders	Nov 1969

Displacement, tons	225 standard; 240 full load
Dimensions, feet	164·5 oa × 23·8 × 9·5
Guns	1—3 in (*76 mm*) 50 cal (forward); 1—40 mm (aft); 4—·50 cal MG (twin)
Main engines	CODAG: 2 diesels (Cummins); 1 450 shp; 2 shafts = 16 knots 1 gas turbine (General Electric); 13 300 shp; 2 shafts = 40+ knots
Complement	24 (3 officers, 21 enlisted men)

These are the largest patrol-type craft built by the US Navy since World War II and the first US Navy ships with gas-turbine propulsion plants. They were designed to perform patrol, blockade, surveillance, perimeter defence, and support missions. No anti-submarine capability.
Built by Tacoma Boatbuilding Co of Tacoma, Washington, and Petersen Builders of Sturgeon Bay, Wisconsin. PG 84 and PG 85 authorised in Fiscal Year 1963 new construction programme; PG 86 and PG 87 in FY 1964; PG 88-90 in FY 1965; PG 92-101 in FY 1966. *Ashville* was laid down on 15 Apr 1964 and launched on 1 May 1965; later ships approximately 18 months from keel laying to completion. Estimated cost per ship approximately $5 000 000.
The *Benicia* was virtually destroyed by a shipyard fire in August 1968; material being assembled for the *Grand Rapids* and *Douglas* was extensively damaged. All three ships delayed.

CLASSIFICATION. These ships were originally classified as Motor Gunboats (PGM); reclassified Patrol Gunboats (PG) with same hull numbers on 1 Apr 1967. The term motor gunboats is now applied primarily to 100-foot, 117-ton craft built for allied navies (PGM 39-83, 91, and 102-122). PGM 1-32 were submarine chasers modified during World War II; PGM 33-38 were post war craft built for foreign navies.

DESIGN. All-aluminium hull and aluminium-fibreglass superstructure. Because of the heat-transmitting qualities of the aluminium hull and the amount of waste heat produced by a gas turbine engine the ships are completely air conditioned.

ENGINEERING. These ships have a Combination Diesel and Gas turbine (CODAG) propulsion system with twin diesel engines for cruising and a gas turbine for high-speed operations. The gas turbine is an LM1500 with the gas generator essentially the same as the J-79-8 aircraft engine (used in the F-4 Phantom and other aircraft). The transfer from diesel to gas turbine propulsion (or vice versa) can be accomplished while underway with no loss of speed. From full stop these ships can attain 40 knots in one minute; maneuvrability is excellent due in part to controllable-pitch propellers. Speed and propeller pitch is controlled directly from the pilot house console. Either JP-5 or diesel fuel can be used for both the gas turbine and diesels.

MARATHON (PG 89) *1968, United States Navy*

MARATHON (PG 89) *1968, United States Navy*

GUNNERY. The *Antelope* and *Ready* have the Mk 87 weapons control system for rapid acquisition and tracking of fast-moving targets; the system can also direct and fire appropriate weapons automatically. The Mk 87 can operate in a radar mode or with a stabilised optical sight on the weather decks. No further procurement of this advanced fire control system is planned in the Navy although it is being fitted to a number of foreign warships.
Other ships have Mk 63 Mod 29 Gunfire Control System with SPG-50 fire control radar.

PHOTOGRAPHS. Note Mk 87 antenna sphere on the *Antelope*. The gas turbine air intake is immediately aft of the bridge structure, the adjacent large funnel is the turbine exhaust with a smaller diesel exhaust to either side.

Patrol, Coastal, and Riverine Craft—*continued*

ANTELOPE (PG 86) *1967, United States Navy*

1 HYDROFOIL GUNBOAT (PGH): "TUCUMCARI" TYPE

TUCUMCARI PGH 2

Displacement, tons	58
Dimensions, feet	71·8 oa × 19·5 × 4·5 (hull borne)
Guns	1—40 mm; 4—50 cal MG (twin); 1—81 mm mortar
Main engines	foil borne: 1 gas turbine (Proteus); 3 100 hp; water-jet propulsion = 40+ knots hull borne: 1 diesel (General Motors); 150 shp; water-jet propulsion
Complement	13 (1 officer, 12 enlisted men)

The *Tucumcari* is one of two hydrofoil gunboats built by the US Navy as competitive prototypes. Built by Boeing Company in Seattle, Washington, with hull fabricated by Gunderson Brothers of Portland, Oregon. Laid down on 1 Sep 1966, launched on 15 July 1967, placed in service on 7 Mar 1968. Estimated construction cost was $4 000 000. Hydrofoil gunboats are "in service" rather than being in commission.

DESIGN. The *Tucumcari* has the canard foil configuration with approximately 30 per cent of the boat's weight supported by the forward foil and 70 per cent by the aft set of foils. The forward foil assembly provides steering by means of rotating the strut about its vertical axis. The foil-borne operation is automatic with a wave-height sensing system to maintain the hull clear of the sea. The foils are fully retractable for hull-borne operations. Aluminium construction.

ENGINEERING. During foil-borne operations the craft's gas turbine drives a water-jet pump instead of a propeller. Water is taken in from the sea through openings in the main pods and carried in ducts within the foil struts to the pump inlet. The water—at the rate of approximately 27 000 gallons (100 tons) per minute—is then pumped out through nozzles under the craft's stern to obtain thrust. The jet pump has a thrust rating comparable to the 18 000-pound thrust of commercial aircraft engines. Hull-borne operation is by means of a diesel-driven water-jet pump.

TUCUMCARI (PGH 2) *1969, Boeing Company*

TUCUMCARI (PGH 2) *1969, United States Navy*

1 HYDROFOIL GUNBOAT (PGH): "FLAGSTAFF" TYPE

FLAGSTAFF PGH 1

Displacement, tons	57
Dimensions, feet	74·4 oa × 21·4 × 4·2 (hull borne)
Guns	1—40 mm; 4—·50 cal MG (twin); 1—81 mm mortar
Main engines	foil borne: 1 gas turbine (Rolls-Royce); 3 600 hp; controllable pitch propeller = 40+ knots hull borne: 2 diesels (General Motors); 300 hp; water-jet propulsion
Complement	13 (1 officer, 12 enlisted men)

The *Flagstaff* is a competitive prototype being evaluated with the *Tucumcari*. Built by Grumman Aircraft Corporation in Stuart, Florida. Laid down on 15 July 1966, launched on 9 Jan 1968, placed in service in July 1968. Estimated construction cost was $3 600 000.

DESIGN. The *Flagstaff* has a conventional foil arrangement with 70 per cent of the craft's weight supported by the forward set of foils and 30 per cent of the weight supported by the stern foil. Steering is accomplished by movement of the stern strut about its vertical axis. Foil-borne operation is automatically controlled by a wave-height sensing system. The foils are fully retractable for hull-borne operations. Aluminium construction.

ENGINEERING. During foil-borne operations the propeller is driven by a geared transmission system contained in the tail strut and in the pod located at the strut-foil connection. During hull-borne operations two diesel engines drive a water-jet propulsion system. Water enters the pump inlets through openings in the hull and the thrust is exerted by water flow though nozzles in the transome. Steering in the hull-borne mode is by deflection vanes in the water stream.

EXPERIMENTAL HYDROFOILS. Two experimental hydrofoils are listed in the section on Experimental, Research and Surveying Ships, the *High Point* (PCH 1) and *Plainview* (AGEH 1). Although both are armed, they are not considered combat vessels as are the *Flagstaff* and *Tucumcari*.

FLAGSTAFF (PGH 1) *Grumman*

FLAGSTAFF (PGH 1) *Grumman*

Patrol, Coastal, and Riverine Craft—*continued*

10 FAST PATROL BOATS (PTF): NEW CONSTRUCTION

PTF 17	**PTF 19**	**PTF 21**	**PTF 23**	**PTF 25**
PTF 18	**PTF 20**	**PTF 22**	**PTF 24**	**PTF 26**

Dimensions, feet	80·3 oa × 24·5 × 6·8
Guns (varies)	1—81 mm mortar; 1—40 mm; 2—20 mm (single); 1—·50 cal MG (mounted over mortar)
Main engines	2 diesels (Napier-Deltic); 6 200 shp; 2 shafts

PTF 17-22 built by John Trumpy & Sons, Annapolis, Maryland; lead boat completed in late 1967, others in 1968. PTF 23-26 built by Stewart Seacraft Division of Teledyne Inc of Berwick, Louisiana; lead boat completed in late 1967, others 1968. Based on "Nasty" design.

These craft are used on clandestine missions in Southeast Asia.

PTF 13 *United States Navy*

8 FAST PATROL BOATS (PTF): "NASTY" TYPE

PTF 3 (ex-PT 812)	**PTF 6**	**PTF 10**	**PTF 12**
PTF 5	**PTF 7**	**PTF 11**	**PTF 13**

Displacement, tons	64 light; 69 standard; 76 full load
Dimensions, feet	80·3 oa × 24·5 × 6·8
Guns (varies)	2—40 mm (single); 2—20 mm (single)
Main engines	2 diesels (Napier-Deltic); 6 200 shp; 2 shafts = 45 knots
Complement	19 (3 officers, 16 enlisted men)

PTF 3-16 of the "Nasty" type were built by Boatservice Ltd A/S of Mandal, Norway. Same design as the Norwegian Navy's "Tjeld" class torpedo boats. PTF 3 and PTF 4 delivered to USA in December 1962, PTF 5-8 in April 1964, and PTF 9-16 in September 1964. Hulls made of two layers of mahogany which sandwich a layer of fibreglass. British engines.

DISPOSALS
PTF 4 (ex-PT 813) stricken from Navy List in 1965; **PTF 8**, **PTF 9**, **PTF 14**, **PTF 15**, and **PTF 16** stricken in 1966. **PTF 1** and **PTF 2** (former PT 810 and PT 811, respectively), stricken in 1965 and expended as targets.

PTF *United States Navy*

FAST PATROL CRAFT (PCF): "SWIFT" TYPE

PCF 1—104 series

Displacement, tons	22·5 full load
Dimensions, feet	50 oa × 13 × 3·5
Guns	1—81 mm mortar; 3—50 cal MG (twin MG mount atop pilot house and single MG mounted over mortar)
Main engines	2 geared diesels (General Motors); 960 shp; 2 shafts = 28 knots (maximum)
Complement	6 (1 officer, 5 enlisted men); three crews are provided for every two boats when deployed in Southeast Asia

The "Swift" design is adapted from the all-metal crew boat which is used to support off-shore drilling rigs in the Gulf of Mexico. Original order of 50 boats followed by additional 54 of "Swift" Mk 1 (above) and eight similar Mk II;
All Mk I boats built by Stewart Seacraft Inc, Berwick, Louisiana, 1965-1966.

LOSSES. PCF 4, 41, and 97 lost to enemy action off South Vietnam; PCF 77 lost in heavy weather off South Vietnam in November 1966; PCF 14 and 76 lost in heavy weather off South Vietnam in Oct 1967; PCF 19 sunk off South Vietnam on 16 June 1968 in accidental attack by US Air Force aircraft.

TRANSFERS. PCF 33, 34, and 83-86 transferred to the Philippines in 1966. Additional PCFs of this type constructed specifically for transfer to Thailand, the Philippines, and South Korea; not assigned US hull numbers in the PCF series.
In addition, 18 PCFs were transferred to South Vietnam 1968-69.

NEW CONSTRUCTION. Thirteen additional PCFs for the US Navy are being built with Fiscal Year 1969 Funds.

PCF 38 *1966, United States Navy*

RIVER PATROL BOATS (PBR): MARK II

PBR 161—241 series

Displacement, tons	8
Dimensions, feet	32 oa × 11·5
Guns	3—·50 cal MG (twin mount forward; single aft); 1—40 mm grenade launcher
Main engines	2 geared diesels (General Motors); water jets = 25+ knots
Complement	4 or 5 (enlisted men)

An improved PBR design; fibreglass hull. Built in 1967-68. Forward ·50 cal MG mount is lower than in Mk 1 boats.

River Patrol Boat Mk II (PBR) *United States Navy*

RIVER PATROL BOATS (PBR): MARK I

PBR 1—160 series

Displacement, tone	7·5
Dimensions, feet	31 oa × 10·9 × 2·2
Guns	3—·50 cal MG (twin mount forward) single aft; 1—40 mm grenade launcher
Main engines	2 geared diesels (General Motors); 440 hp; water jets = 25 + knots
Complement	4 (enlisted men)

The PBR design is adapted from a commercial fibreglass-hull (plastic) boat; especially suited for shallow-water operations with trainable water jet nozzles in lieu of conventional propeller or rudders. Original design provided for single ·30 cal MG aft; replaced by single ·50 cal MG. The 160 Mk I PBRs built by United Boat Builders, Bellingham, Washington, 1965-1966. PBR 20 sunk in collision in 1967; PBR 30 stricken in 1967 after being damaged; PBR 55 stricken in 1966 after being damaged; PBR 113 destroyed after being damaged by Viet Cong grenades in 1967; all in South Vietnam area.

Patrol, Coastal, and Riverine Craft—*continued*

ASSAULT SUPPORT PATROL BOATS (ASPB): MARK 2 DESIGNS

Dimensions, feet	50 oa × 20
Guns	1—105 mm howitzer; 2—30 mm; 2—7·62 mm MG; 1—40 mm grenade launcher (see notes)
Main engines	3 gas turbines (United Aircraft of Canada) driving three water jets (Buehler Corp) = approx 40 knots

The Sikorsky Aircraft Division of United Aircraft Corp. and the Stewart Seacraft Division of Teledyne, Inc. have developed prototype advanced ASPBs for the Navy (designated Mark 2). The Sikorsky craft is described above and shown on trials during March-April 1969 in Long Island Sound. It has a light-weight 105 mm howitzer and two 20 mm cannon mounted in a tank-like turret which has a 360 degree field of fire. The smaller, forward mount is remote controlled and initially contains two 7·62 mm MG and a 40 mm grenade launcher, but Sikorsky has proposed replacing the machine-guns with two 20 mm cannon. Also fitted for minesweeping; note position of radar on tripod mast aft. The Stewart Seacraft ASPB is similar, but initially has an 81 mm mortar in lieu of the 105 mm howitzer. Both craft are heavily armoured with the main turret and engines on shock springs to reduce effects of mine explosions. No photographs of the Stewart Seacraft were available when this page closed.

ASPB/MK2 *1969, Sikorsky, United Aircraft*

ASPB/MK2 *1969, Sikorsky, United Aircraft*

ASSAULT SUPPORT PATROL BOATS (ASPB): PROGRAMME V

Displacement, tons	36·25 full load
Dimensions, feet	50 oa × 17 × 4·5
Guns (varies)	1 or 2—20mm (with 2—·50 cal MG in boats with one 20 mm); 2—·30 cal MG; 2—40 mm high-velocity grenade launchers
Main engines	2 diesels; 2 shafts = 15 knots
Complement	6

The ASPB was designed specifically for riverine operations and serves as an escort for other Navy river craft, provides mine countermeasures during river operations, and intercepts enemy river traffic. Welded-steel hulls. Armament changed to above configuration in 1968; some boats have twin- ·50 cal MG "turret" forward in place of single 20 mm gun.

Note that open stern well is plated over in the ASPB pictured here (A-131-2); a view of an ASPB with 81 mm mortar/·50 cal MG aft appears in the 1968-1969 edition (programme IV ASPB). The ASPB below (A-92-5) has two ·50 cal MG in the forward "turret".

ASPBs followed by Monitor *1968, United States Navy*

ASSAULT SUPPORT PATROL BOAT (ASPB) *1968, United States Navy*

MONITORS (MON): PROGRAMME V

Displacement, tons	80 to 90 full load
Dimensions, feet	60 oa × 17·5 × 4·5
Guns	1—105 mm howitzer; 2—20 mm; 3—·30 cal MG; 2—40 mm high-velocity grenade launchers
Main engines	2 diesels; 2 shafts = 8 knots
Complement	11 (enlisted)

These craft provide fire support for riverine operations as well as security for afloat bases. Heavily armoured. Some have two Army M10-8 flame throwers in lieu of one 20 mm gun and howitzer; these craft are dubbed "zippo" monitors. Armament changed to above configuration in 1968. Converted from LCM-6 landing craft. Popularly referred to as the "battleships" of the riverine fleet.

MONITOR (MON) *1968, United States Navy*

ARMOURED TROOP CARRIERS (ATC): PROGRAMME V

Displacement, tons	66 full load
Dimensions, feet	56 oa × 17·5 × 4·5
Guns	1 or 2—20mm; 2—·50 cal MG; 2 to 6—·30 cal MG; 1—40 mm high-velocity grenade launcher; 2—40 mm low-velocity grenade launchers
Main engines	2 diesels; 2 shafts = 8 knots
Complement	7
Troops	approx 40

These craft were converted from LCM-6 landing craft to transport troops, small vehicles field artillery, and supplies. Heavily armoured. Several have been fitted with light steel helicopter platforms to facilitate evacuation of wounded personnel. Armament changed to the above configuration in 1968.
Note winch on fantail for chain drag equipment used to sweep for command detonated underwater mines. ATCs equipped with helicopter platforms are unofficially referred to as ATC(H).

ARMOURED TROOP CARRIER (ATC) *1968, United States Navy*

COMMAND AND CONTROL BOATS (CCB): PROGRAMME V

Displacement, tons	80 full load
Dimensions, feet	60 oa × 17·5 × 4·5
Guns	2—20 mm; 2—·30 cal MG; 2—40 mm high-velocity grenade launchers
Main engines	2 diesels; 2 shafts = 8 knots
Complement	11

These craft serve as afloat command posts providing command and communications facilities for ground force and boat group commanders. Heavily armoured. Armament changed to above configuration in 1968. Converted from LCM-6 landing craft.

Patrol, Coastal, and Riverine Craft—*continued*

COMMAND AND CONTROL BOAT (CCB) *1968, United States Navy*

PATROL MINESWEEPERS (MSR): MODIFIED ASPB

Dimensions, feet	50 oa × 17
Guns	2—·50 cal MG
Main engines	2 diesels; 2 shafts = 20 knots

Modified ASPB design fitted with bow mine deflector and minesweeping gear to sweep moored and bottom mines in shallow water.

RIVER MINESWEEPERS (MSM): PROGRAMME V

Dimensions, feet	56 × 17·5 × 4·5
Guns	2—20 mm; 1—50 cal MG; 2—40 mm grenade launchers
Main engines	2 diesels; 2 shafts = 10 knots (maximum; minesweeping speed is 8 knots)
Complement	4 or 5 (enlisted)

These craft were converted from LCM-6 landing craft for river minesweeping. Heavily armoured. The 20 mm guns are in amidships "turrets", one to port and one to starboard. These craft can sweep moored and bottom mines in shallow water.

RIVER MINESWEEPER (MSM) *1968, United States Navy*

RIVER MINESWEEPER (MSM) *1968, United States Navy*

DRONE MINESWEEPERS (MSD)

Displacement, tons	2·5
Dimensions, feet	23 oa × 8 × 1·5
Main engines	Gasoline engine with outboard drive; 250 hp = 15 to 20 knots in unmanned operation; 30+ knots with operator on board

Small, fibreglass minesweeping launch intended for unmanned (drone) operations in river areas; radio controlled.

DRONE MINESWEEPER (MSD) *1968, United States Navy*

3 PATROL AIR CUSHION VEHICLES (PACV): SK-5 TYPE

PACV 1 **PACV 2** **PACV 3**

Weight, tons	8·5 normal gross; 10 overload gross
Dimensions, feet	38·8 oa × 23·8 × 16 (height)
Guns	2—·50 cal MG (twin mount); 2—7·62 mm MG (single); 2 grenade launchers
Main engines	1 gas turbine (General Electric); 1 150 shp; 1 three-bladed, variable-pitch aircraft propeller = 60 knots
Complement	6 (2 officers, 4 enlisted men)

These are Americanised versions of the British-developed SR.N5 hovercraft. Built as the SK-5 by Bell Aerosystems of Buffalo, New York, under licence from Saunders-Roe Division of Westland Aircraft Limited. Three SK-5 hovercraft have also been acquired by the US Army for evaluation.

The PACV 1-3 were twice deployed to South Vietnam in 1966-1969. The craft encountered mixed success in their two combat deployments; they were found lacking in coastal operations but were highly successful in the marshy Plain of Reeds during the wet season. After their return to the United States in May 1969 the Navy stated the air cushion vehicles "would not be active in the next calendar year". Unofficial reports indicate the three PACVs will be transferred to the Army.

DESIGN. The hard bottom of the PACVs travel on a cushion of air more than four feet thick. Flexible, air-actuated trunks provide obstacle clearance and ditch crossing capability over land and improved riding qualities over water. A large buoyancy chamber subdivided into watertight compartments, provides flotation on water. Some 20 troops can be carried in cabin and on deck.

ENGINEERING. A General Electric 7LM-100 marine gas turbine engine drives both the lift fan, which forces air downward to create the air cushion beneath the craft, and the aft-mounted propeller which provides propulsion.

GUNNERY. Above armament as modified for 1968-1969 deployment in South Vietnam.

Patrol Air Cushion Vehicle (PACV) *1967, United States Navy*

PATROL AIR CUSHION VEHICLE (PACV) *1968, United States Navy*

MINE WARFARE SHIPS

The US Navy is engaged in a major programme to modernise its mine countermeasure ships. Two large Mine Countermeasures Ships (MCS) were recently completed (*Catskill* and *Ozark*) and two new ships of this type are planned for construction in Fiscal Years 1971-1972. These ships carry and support minesweeping launches and helicopters.
The existing force of 63 Ocean Minesweepers (MSO) is being modernised.
Funds were provided in Fiscal Years 1966-1968 for the construction of 16 new ocean minesweepers (which would also have the capabilities of coastal minehunters). However, difficulties in their design and procurement procedures led to postponement of construction. These ships are tentatively planned for construction in the Fiscal Year 1971-1973 period.
Upon completion of the ocean minesweeper modernisation/construction programmes, the surviving coastal minesweepers (MSC) will be relegated to training or experimental duties.
In addition to the ships and craft listed in this section, a large number of smaller craft are employed for minesweeping operations in Vietnamese rivers. These are listed in the section on Patrol, Coastal and Riverine Craft.

PHOTOGRAPH. The ocean minesweeper *Loyalty* (MSO 457) inspects a junk for contraband arms or supplies during Operation MARKET TIME off the coast of South Vietnam. The larger minesweepers operating in the Western Pacific are regularly employed in this role and, with their wood hulls and maneuverability, are well suited for such tasks.

LOYALTY (MSO 457) *United States Navy*

2 MINE COUNTERMEASURES SHIPS (MCS): "CATSKILL" CLASS

Name	*No.*	*Builder*	*Laid down*	*Launched*	*LSV Comm*	*MCS Comm*
CATSKILL	MCS 1 (ex-LSV 1, ex-CM 6, ex-AP 106)	Willamette Iron & Steel	12 July 1941	19 May 1942	30 June 1944	6 Oct 1967
OZARK	MCS 2 (ex-LSV 2, ex-CM 7, ex-AP 107)	Willamette Iron & Steel	12 July 1941	15 June 1942	23 Sep 1944	24 June 1966

Displacement, tons	5 875 standard; 9 040 full load
Length, feet (*metres*)	440 (*134·1*) wl; 455·5 (*138·8*) oa
Beam, feet (*metres*)	60·2 (*18·4*)
Draft, feet (*metres*)	20 (*6·1*)
Guns, dual purpose	2—5 in (*127 mm*) 38 cal.
Guns, AA	8—40 mm
Boilers	4 Combustion Eng. "D" type
Main engines	GE geared turbines 11 000 shp; 2 shafts
Speed, knots	20·3
Complement	564 (114 officers, 450 men)

These are the first ships to be totally converted to carry and support minesweeping launches and helicopters. Heretofore this role was performed by modified tank and landing ships. The *Catskill* and *Ozark* are fitted with navigation and communications equipment for vectoring minesweeping launches and helicopters; also fitted with command and communication facilities for mine force commander and staff. They are intended for use in support of amphibious operations.

CLASSIFICATION. Designed as large minelayers (CM), redesignated transports (AP), and completed as vehicle landing ships (LSV). Reclassified as Mine Warfare Command and Support Ships (MCS) in 1955; changed to Mine Countermeasures and Support Ships (MCS) in 1958; and to Mine Countermeasures Support Ships (MCS) on 25 Aug 1960. Stricken from the Navy List on 1 Sep 1961, but reinstated on 1 Oct 1963 (*Ozark*) and 1 June 1964 (*Catskill*) and converted to mine warfare configuration. MCS classification changed to Mine Countermeasures Ship on 14 Aug 1968.

CONSTRUCTION. Both ships built by Willamette Iron & Steel Corp, Portland, Washington. As vehicle landing ships they carried amphibious tractors and tanks, unloaded by stern ramp. Original armament consisted of two 5 inch guns and eight 40 mm AA guns.

CONVERSION. Converted to mine warfare ships under the Fiscal Year 1963 (*Ozark*) and 1964 (*Catskill*) Shipbuilding and Conversion Programmes. *Ozark* converted by Norfolk Shipbuilding & Dry Dock Corp, Norfolk, Virginia, from Sep 1963 to June 1966; *Catskill* converted by Boland Machine & Manufacturing Co, New Orleans, Louisiana, from July 1964 to Sep 1967.
Each ship was converted to carry and support twenty 36-foot minesweeping launches (MSL) and two minesweeping helicopters. Maintanance shops, minesweeping equipment stowage, and berthing spaces for minesweeper crews are provided.

HELICOPTERS. Each ship operates two RH-3A helicopters. The helicopters, an adaptation of the SH-3A Sea King, can stream and recover minesweeping gear.

MINELAYING. These ships can be modified to carry several hundred influence mines. Approximately ten days in a major industrial facility would be required to configure them for minelaying. (Moored contact mines could not be carried).

CATSKILL (MCS 1) *1968, United States Navy*

PHOTOGRAPHS. Note davits for holding Minesweeping Launches (MSL) in photographs on this and following pages; ships' boats carried on davits alongside bridge structure. Boom aft of funnels can lift launches and helicopters from maintenance area.

DISPOSALS

Of the three vessels of the original netlayer type converted into vehicle landing ships, **Saugus**, MCS 4 (ex-LSV 4, ex-AN 4) was stricken from the Navy List on 1 July 1961, and **Monitor**, MCS 5 (ex-LSV 5, ex-AN 5) and **Osage**, MCS 3 (ex-LSV 3, ex-AN 3), were stricken on 1 Sep 1961.
The netlayer **Galilea** (ex-*Montauk*), AKN 6 (ex-LSV 6, ex-AN 2, ex-AP 161) was stricken from the Navy List on 1 Sep 1960.
The mine countermeasures support ship **Orleans Parish,** MCS 6 (ex-LST 1069), was redesignated as an LST on 1 June 1966 and is operated by the Navy's Military Sea Transportation Service (see Logistic Support Ships).
The **Epping Forest,** MCS 7 (ex-LSD 4), was stricken from the Navy List on 1 Nov 1968.

Mine Warfare Ships—*continued*

OZARK (MCS 2) *1966, United States Navy*

1 FLEET MINELAYER (MMF): "TERROR" TYPE

Name	*No.*	*Builder*	*Laid down*	*Launched*	*Commissioned*
TERROR	MMF 5 (ex-MM 5, ex-CM 5)	Philadelphia Navy Yard	3 Sep 1940	6 June 1941	15 July 1942

Displacement, tons	5 875 standard; 8 640 full load
Length, feet (*metres*)	454·9 (*138·4*)
Beam, feet (*metres*)	60·2 (*18·4*)
Draft, feet (*metres*)	20 (*6·1*)
Guns	4—5 in (*127 mm*) 38 cal. (single) 24—40 mm AA (quad); several 20 mm AA
Mines	930 capacity
Boilers	4 (Combustion Engineering)
Main engines	2 geared turbines (General Electric); 11 000 shp; 2 shafts
Speed, knots	20
Complement	481 (25 officers, 456 enlisted men)

Authorised under the Fiscal Year 1938 new construction programme. Mine ports in stern. Cruiser type hull with high freeboard. Decommissioned on 1 Dec 1947 and placed in Atlantic Reserve Fleet at Philadelphia.

RECLASSIFICATION. Formerly classified as a Large (Cruiser) Minelayer (CM) but reclassified as a Fleet Minelayer (MM) in Feb 1955 and redesignated MMF in 1956.

TERROR (MMF 5) *United States Navy, Official*

10 FAST MINELAYERS (MMD): "SMITH" CLASS

Name	*No.*	*Builder*	*Launched*	*Commissioned*
ADAMS	MMD 27	Bath Iron Works Corp	23 July 1944	10 Oct 1944
GWIN	MMD 33	Bethlehem, San Pedro	9 Apr 1944	30 Sep 1944
HARRY F. BAUER	MMD 26	Bath Iron Works Corp	3 July 1944	22 Sep 1944
HENRY A. WILEY	MMD 29	Bethlehem, Staten Island	21 Apr 1944	31 Aug 1944
LINDSEY	MMD 32	Bethlehem, San Pedro	5 Mar 1944	20 Aug 1944
ROBERT H. SMITH	MMD 23	Bath Iron Works Corp	25 May 1944	4 Aug 1944
SHANNON	MMD 25	Bath Iron Works Corp	24 June 1944	8 Sep 1944
SHEA	MMD 30	Bethlehem, Staten Island	20 May 1944	30 Sep 1944
THOMAS E. FRASER	MMD 24	Bath Iron Works Corp	10 June 1944	22 Aug 1944
TOLMAN	MMD 28	Bath Iron Works Corp	13 Aug 1944	27 Oct 1944

Displacement, tons	2 250 standard; 3 375 full load
Length, feet (*metres*)	375·5 (*114·8*)
Beam, feet (*metres*)	40·9 (*12·5*)
Draft, feet (*metres*)	19 (*5·8*)
Guns, surface	6—5 in (*127 mm*) 38 cal.
Guns, AA	12—40 mm AA (2 quad, 2 twin); 11—20 mm AA (single); (some ships rearmed with 6—3 in (*76 mm*) in place of 40 mm and 20 mm)
Mines	80
Boilers	4 (Babcock & Wilcox)
Main engines	2 geared turbines 60 000 shp; 2 shafts
Speed, knots	34
Complement	275 (15 officers, 260 men; designed wartime 363)

Modified destroyers of the "Allen M. Sumner" class. Later fitted with tripod masts. All out of commission, in reserve.

RECLASSIFICATION. Formerly classified as Light Minelayers (DM); reclassified as Destroyer Minelayers (DM) in Feb 1955, and changed to MMD on 1 Jan 1969.

DISPOSALS
J. William Ditter, DM 31, and **Aaron Ward,** DM 34 were scrapped.

PHOTOGRAPH. The *Robert H. Smith* is shown in her World War II configuration with pole mast. Note mines on rails along starboard side of 01 level; she has another mine track on port side. Twin 40 mm mounts alongside bridge are covered; two 40 mm quad mounts are aft of second funnel.

Mine Warfare Ships—*continued*

OCEAN MINESWEEPERS (MSO): PROPOSED

This is a new class of ships combining the capabilities of Ocean Minesweepers (MSO) and Coastal Minehunters (MHC). They will be similar in design to the "Ability" class, but larger. Planned displacement is approximately 1 000 tons (full load) and length 200 feet (oa); to be diesel powered with wooden hulls.
Four ships of this design were originally authorised in the Fiscal Year 1964 shipbuilding programme, five in FY 1967, and seven in FY 1968. However, of the $139 000 000 appropriated for their construction, $43 000 000 was allocated to the nuclear frigate programme (DLGN) and the remaining $96 000 000 was rescinded by the Congress in the FY 1969 budget because of difficulties encountered in design and contracting procedures. The Department of Defense now plans tentatively to request funding for the 16 minesweepers in the FY 1971-73 shipbuilding programmes. Estimated cost per ship is about $9 000 000.
To be numbered MSO 523-538.

3 OCEAN MINESWEEPERS (MSO): "ABILITY" CLASS

		Launched			*Launched*
ABILITY	MSO 519	29 Dec 1956	**ALACRITY**	MSO 520	8 June 1957
			ASSURANCE	MSO 521	31 Aug 1957

Displacement, tons	810 light; 934 full load
Dimensions, feet	190 × 36 × 14·5
Guns	1—40 mm AA; 2—·50 cal MG
Main engines	2 GM diesels; 2 shafts; controllable pitch propellers; 2 700 bhp = 15 knots
Complement	71 (6 officers, 65 men)

Non-magnetic, wooden hulled vessels built by Petersen Builders Inc, Sturgeon Bay, Wisc. Fitted as mine division commander's flagships. Equipped for all types of mine countermeasures operations. Laid down on 5 Mar 1956, 3 May 1956 and 28 Jan 1957 respectively. Launch dates above. *Ability* commissioned on 4 Aug 1958. *Assurance* commissioned on 22 Nov 1958. *Alacrity* on 2 Oct 1958. Fitted with VQS-1 mine detecting sonor. Endurance is 3 200 miles at 12 knots.
These ships will be modernised; see notes for "Acme" class.

ABILITY (MSO 519) *A. & J. Pavia*

4 OCEAN MINESWEEPERS (MSO): "ACME" CLASS

		Launched			*Launched*
ACME	MSO 508	23 June 1955	**ADVANCE**	MSO 510	12 July 1957
ADROIT	MSO 509	20 Aug 1955	**AFFRAY**	MSO 511	18 Dec 1956

Displacement, tons	720 light; 780 full load
Dimensions, feet	173 oa × 35 × 10
Guns	1—40 mm AA; 2—·50 cal MG
Main engines	4 Packard diesels; 2 shafts; 2 800 bhp = 14 knots
Complement	74

This class is different from the "Agile" type but have similar basic particulars. *Acme* commissioned on 27 Sep 1956, *Adroit* commissioned on 4 Mar 1957, *Advance* commissioned on 16 June 1958, *Affray* commissioned on 8 Dec 1958.

MODERNISATION. These ships are being modernised: 4 Waukesha Motor Co diesel engines replace original engines, improved SQQ-14 mine-detecting sonar fitted, 40 mm gun replaced by single or twin 20 mm mount, communication equipment and habitability improved (air conditioning for living spaces); complement after modernisation is 6 officers and 70 enlisted men. Note built up structure aft of bridge in photograph of *Advance*; single 20 mm gun fitted forward of bridge. Photograph of *Affray* in next column shows original configuration.

TRANSFERS. MSO 506 and MSO 507 were transferred to Italy in 1956; MSO 512 class, was transferred to Belgium in Dec 1960.

ADVANCE (MSO 510) *1968, US Navy*

AFFRAY (MSO 511) *A. & J. Pavia*

56 OCEAN MINESWEEPERS (MSO): "AGILE" CLASS

	MSO		MSO
AGILE (19 Nov 1955)	421	**IMPERVIOUS** (29 Aug 1952)	449
AGGRESSIVE (4 Oct 1952)	422	**IMPLICIT** (1 Aug 1953)	455
AVENGE (15 Mar 1953)	423	**INFLICT** (6 Oct 1953)	456
BOLD (14 Mar 1953)	424	**LOYALTY** (22 Nov 1953)	457
BULWARK (14 Mar 1953)	425	**LUCID** (14 Nov 1953)	458
CONFLICT (16 Dec 1952)	426	**NIMBLE** (6 Aug 1954)	459
CONSTANT (14 Feb 1952)	427	**NOTABLE** (15 Oct 1954)	460
DASH (20 Sep 1952)	428	**OBSERVER** (19 Oct 1954)	461
DETECTOR (5 Dec 1952)	429	**PINNACLE** (3 Jan 1955)	462
DIRECT (27 May 1953)	430	**PIVOT** (9 Jan 1954)	463
DOMINANT (5 Nov 1953)	431	**PLUCK** (6 Feb 1954)	464
DYNAMIC (17 Dec 1952)	432	**PRIME** (27 May 1954)	466
ENGAGE (ex-*Elusive*, 18 June 1953)	433	**REAPER** (25 June 1954)	467
EMBATTLE (27 Aug 1953)	434	**RIVAL** (15 Aug 1953)	468
ENDURANCE (9 Aug 1952)	435	**SAGACITY** (20 Feb 1954)	469
ENERGY (13 Feb 1953)	436	**SALUTE** (14 Aug 1954)	470
ENHANCE (11 Oct 1952)	437	**SKILL** (23 Apr 1955)	471
ESTEEM (20 Dec 1952)	438	**VALOR** (13 May 1953)	472
EXCEL (25 Sep 1953)	439	**VIGOR** (24 June 1953)	473
EXPLOIT (10 Apr 1953)	440	**VITAL** (12 Aug 1953)	474
EXULTANT (6 June 1953)	441	**CONQUEST** (20 May 1954)	488
FEARLESS (17 July 1953)	442	**GALLANT** (4 June 1954)	489
FIDELITY (21 Aug 1953)	443	**LEADER** (15 Sep 1954)	490
FIRM (15 Apr 1953)	444	**PERSISTANT** (23 Apr 1955)	491
FORCE (26 June 1953)	445	**PLEDGE** (20 July 1955)	492
FORTIFY (14 Feb 1953)	446	**STURDY** (28 Jan 1956)	494
GUIDE (17 Apr 1954)	446	**SWERVE** (1 Nov 1955)	495
ILLUSIVE (12 July 1952)	448	**VENTURE** (27 Nov 1956)	496

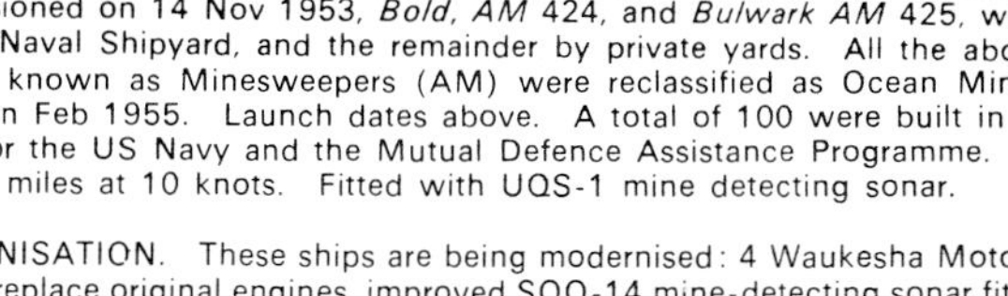

Displacement, tons	665 light; 750 full load
Dimensions, feet	165 wl; 172 × 36 × 13·6
Guns	1—40 mm AA; 2—·50 cal MG
Main engines	4 Packard diesels; 2 shafts; controllable pitch propellers; 2 280 bhp = 15·5 knots; *Dash, Detector, Direct* and *Dominant*, have 4 GM diesels, 1 520 bhp
Complement	72 to 75

These ships have wooden hulls and non-magnetic equipment, with diesels of non-magnetic stainless steel alloy. *Aggressive, AM* 422, was built by Luders Marine Const Co, Stamford, Conn. Cost $3 500 000. Laid down on 25 May 1951, commissioned on 25 Nov 1953. *Illusive, AM* 448, was built by Martinlock SB Co, San Diego, and commissioned on 14 Nov 1953. *Bold, AM* 424, and *Bulwark AM* 425, were built by Norfolk Naval Shipyard, and the remainder by private yards. All the above vessels, formerly known as Minesweepers (AM) were reclassified as Ocean Minesweepers, (MSO) in Feb 1955. Launch dates above. A total of 100 were built in the United States for the US Navy and the Mutual Defence Assistance Programme. Endurance is 2 400 miles at 10 knots. Fitted with UQS-1 mine detecting sonar.

MODERNISATION. These ships are being modernised: 4 Waukesha Motor Co diesel engines replace original engines, improved SQQ-14 mine-detecting sonar fitted, 40 mm gun replaced by twin 20 mm mount or combination ·50 calibre MG/81 mm mortar, communication equipment and habitability improved; complement, in modernised ships is 6 officers and 70 enlisted men. Modernised ships can be identified by built-up structure aft of bridge, as in photographs of *Persistant, Pivot*, and *Lucid*.

TRANSFERS. MSO 450-454, 475-487, 498-507, 512-518 were built for foreign countries under the Military Aid Programme and no US names were allocated. 8 were transferred to France, 6 to the Netherlands, 4 to Portugal, 4 to Belgium, 2 to Norway, and 2 to Italy.

CASUALTIES. *Prestige* MSO 465, was stranded in the Naruto Straits, Inland Sea, Japan, on 23 Aug 1958, abandoned as a total loss and stricken from the Navy List. *Exultant* caught fire after an explosion off the coast of Savannah, Georgia, on 12 Aug 1960 but has been repaired. *Stalwart* MSO 493, capsized and sank as a result of fire at San Juan, Puerto Rico, in June 1966; subsequently stricken.

PIVOT (MSO 463) *1968, US Navy*

Mine Warfare Ships—*continued*

PERSISTANT (MSO 491) *1967, United States Navy*

ENERGY (MSO 436) *1968, United States Navy*

LUCID (MSO 458) *1968, United States Navy*

22 COASTAL MINESWEEPERS (MSC): "BLUEBIRD" CLASS

	MSC		MSC		MSC
BLUEBIRD	T 121	**LIMPKIN**	T 195	**THRUSH**	T 204
CORMORANT	T 122	**MEADOW LARK**	T 196	**VIREO**	205
FALCON	T 190	**PARROT**	T 197	**WARBLER**	206
FRIGATE BIRD	T 191	**PEACOCK**	198	**WHIPPOORWILL**	207
HUMMING BIRD	T 192	**PHOEBE**	199	**WIDGEON**	208
JACANA	T 193	**SHRIKE**	T 201	**WOODPECKER**	209
KING BIRD	T 194	**THRASHER**	T 203	**ALBATROSS**	289
				GANNET	290

Displacement, tons	320 light; 370 full load
Dimensions, feet	138 pp; 144 oa × 28 × 8·2
Guns	2—20 mm (twin)
Main engines	2 GM diesels; 2 shafts; 880 bhp = 12 knots (MSC 200-209); Packard engines; 2 shafts; 1 200 bhp = 12·5 knots; (MSC 121, 122, 190-199) *Albatross* and *Gannet* have 4 Harnischfeger 6-cyl diesels = 12 knots
Oil fuel, tons	25
Radius, miles	2 500 at 10 knots
Complement	39

Constructed throughout of wood and other materials with the lowest possible magnetic attraction to attain the greatest possible safety factor when sweeping for magnetic mines. *Bluebird* and *Cormorant* (commissioned 14 Aug 1953) built by Mare Island Naval Shipyard, 310 tons light. Only named vessels AMS 121, 122, 190-209 were commissioned into the US Navy. Remainder, 60-120, 123-154, 167-171, 218-221, 255-288 were built for NATO or foreign countries under MDAP. Thirteen of these minesweepers are assigned to operational Naval Reserve training (indicated by letter "T").

CONSTRUCTION. Bellingham Shipyards Company, Washington, built MSC 268-272 and MSC 273-288 for foreign countries under the Military Assistance Programme. Two were built by Tacoma Boatbuilding Co, Tacoma, Washington:—*Albatross*, laid down on 26 Feb 1959, launched on 26 Mar 1960, and completed on 24 Apr 1961, and *Gannet*, laid down on 1 May 1959, launched on 2 June 1960, and completed on 14 July 1961. MSC 291 was launched on 3 Mar 1961 at Tacoma for MDAP. Two were built by Petersen Builders Inc, Sturgeon Bay, Wisc, with 4 diesels driving two fixed-pitch propellers, and gas turbine generators for power minesweeping (MSC 292 and 293, for MAP) and MSC 294, 295, 296 and 297 for MAP, 145 × 27 feet, 362 tons full load. Tacoma Boatbuilding Co built MSC 298-301; Stowman shipbuilding Corp, NJ, built MSC 302-306; Petersen Builders built MSC 307-315. MSC 315 was launched on 12 Jan 1966; 145·5 × 27·2 feet, 2 shafts, 4 diesels = 1 000 hp.

TRANSFERS. 18 to Italy: AMS 72-76, 79-82, 88-90, 113-137, 280. 18 to Belgium: AMS 63-65, 77, 78, 101, 103, 104, 131, 151-154, 169-171, 259, 260. 8 to Denmark: AMS 127, 128, 129, MSC 221, 256, 257, 263, 264. 30 to France: AMS 66-71, 83-87, 93, 94, 96-99, 113-120, 124-126, 141-142. 14 to Netherlands: AMS 100, 105-112, 148-150, 167, 168. 2 to Norway: AMS 102, 132. 8 to Portugal: AMS 60 (ex-USS *Adjutant*), 61, 62, 91, 92, 145-147. 12 to Spain: AMS 130, 139, 143, 220, 265, 266, MSC 200 (ex-USS *Redwing*), MSC 202 (ex-USS *Spoonbill*), MSC 269, 279, 287, 288. 4 to Japan: AMS 95, 144, 255, 258. 8 to Pakistan: AMS 138, 261, 262, 267, 273, 274, 293, 294. 9 to Turkey: 268, 270, 271, 272, 304, 305, 311, 312, 316. 4 to Iran: MSC 275, 276, 291, 292. 8 to Taiwan, China: AMS 123, 140, MSC 277, 278, 300, 302, 306, 307. 3 to Vietnam: MSC 281, 282, 283. 6 to Korea: MSC 284, 285, 286, 295, 296, 316. 2 to Philippines: MSC 218, 219. 8 to Greece: MSC 298, 299, 308, 309, 310, 314, 317, 318. 4 to Thailand: MSC 297, 301, 303, 313.

CANCELLATION. AMS 155 to 166 were reserved for German built vessels, but the order and numbers were cancelled.

CLASSIFICATION. All the early vessels formerly known as Auxiliary Motor minesweepers (AMS) were reclassified as Coastal Minesweepers, (MSC) in Feb 1955.

PEACOCK (MSC 198) *United States Navy*

BLUEBIRD (MSC 121) *1967, United States Navy*

KINGBIRD (MSC 194) *United States Navy*

Mine Warfare Ships—*continued*

25 FLEET MINESWEEPERS (MSF): "AUK" CLASS

4 American SB Co	MSF	*Gulf SB Corpn*	MSF
SPRIG (15 Sep 1944)	384	**ROSELLE** (29 Aug 1945)	379
TERCEL (16 Dec 1944)	386	**SCOTER** (26 Sep 1945)	381
WHEATEAR (21 Apr 1945)	390	**VELOCITY** (19 Apr 1942)	128
Associated Shipbuilders		*John H. Mathis Co*	
SPEAR (25 Feb 1943)	322	**SWAY** (29 Sep 1942)	120
		SWIFT (5 Dec 1942)	122
Defoe B & M Works		*Pennsylvania Shipyard*	
BROADBILL (21 May 1942)	58	**PILOT** (5 July 1942)	104
General Engineering & DD Co		**PIONEER** (26 July 1942)	105
ARDENT (22 June 1943)	340		
CHAMPION (12 Dec 1942)	314	**SYMBOL** (2 July 1942)	123
CHIEF (5 Jan 1943)	315	**THREAT** (15 Aug 1942)	124
COMPETENT (9 Jan 1943)	316		
DEFENSE (18 Feb 1943)	317		
DEVASTATOR (19 Apr 1943)	318	*Winslow Marine Ry & SB Co*	
GLADIATOR (7 May 1943)	319	**SAGE** (21 Nov 1942)	111
HERALD (4 July 1942)	101		
IMPECCABLE (21 May 1943)	320		
STARLING (11 Apr 1942)	64		

Displacement, tons	890 standard; 1 250 full load
Dimensions, feet	215 wl; 221·2 oa × 32·2 × 10·8
Guns	1—3 in, 50 cal dp; 2 mm AA (single); 4—40 mm AA (twin) in MSF 314-341 series
Main engines	Diesel electric; 2 shafts; 3 118-3 532 bhp = 18·1 knots
Complement	9 officers and 96 enlisted men in ships numbered up to MSF 340; 10 officers and 107 enlisted men in later ships.

Steel hulled. Launch dates above. All are in the Reserve Fleet.

RECLASSIFICATION. All the above, formerly known as Ocean Minesweepers (AM) were reclassified as Fleet Minesweepers, (steel-hulled) MSF in Feb 1955. *Prevail (AM* 107), *Pursuit* (AM 108), *Requisite* (*AM* 109) and *Sheldrake* (*AM* 62) were reclassified as survey ships (AGS) in 1952 and *Towhee* (MSF 388) in Apr 1964. *Surfbird* (MSF 383) was reclassified as a degaussing vessel (ADG) on 18 May 1957. *Tanager*, MSF 385, was transferred to the Coast Guard on 1 Nov 1963. Designation of *Peregrine*, MSF 373, was changed to AG 176 on 1 Apr 1964.

TRANSFERS. *Strive*, MSF 17, *Sustain* MSF 119, *Seer* MSF 112, and *Triumph* MSF 323, converted and reclassified as coastal minelayers MMC 1, MMC 2, MMC 5, and MMC 3, respectively, transferred to Norway in 1959-60, *Ruddy* MSF 380 and *Shoveler* MSF 382 to Peru in 1960, *Ptarmigan* MSF 376 to Korea on 25 July 1963, *Murrelet* MSF 372 to Philippines in June 1965, *Redstart* MSF 378, *Toucan* MSF 387 to Taiwan on 22 Dec 1964 and *Waxwing* MSF 389, in Aug 1965, *Chickadee* MSF 59 to Uruguay in Aug 1966, *Dextrous*, MSF 341 and *Speed* MSF 116 to Korea in 1967, *Vigilance* MSF 324 to Philippines in 1967.

DISPOSALS
Auk MSF 57 was stricken from the list of naval vessels on 1 Aug 1959, and **Raven** MSF 55, **Nuthatch** MSF 60, **Heed** MSF 100, **Pheasant** MSF 51, **Motive**, MSF 102 (expended as target off San Diego, Calif), **Oracle** MSF 103, **Revenge** MSF 110, **Staff** MSF 114, **Token** MSF 126, **Zeal** MSF 131, **Pigeon** MSF 374, **Pochard** MSF 375 and **Quail** MSF 377 in 1967.
Tumult, MSF 127, stricken on 1 May 1967.

WAXWING (MSF 389) *Ted Stone*

4 FLEET MINESWEEPERS (MSF): "ADMIRABLE" CLASS

Associated Shipbuilders	MSF	*Tampa SB Co*	MSF
		CRUISE (21 Mar 1943)	215
SPECTRE (15 Feb 1944)	306		
SUPERIOR (11 May 1944)	311	*Williamette Iron & Steel Corpn*	
		COUNSEL (17 Feb 1943)	165

Displacement, tons	650 standard; 945 full load
Dimensions, feet	180 wl; 184·5 oa × 33 × 10
Main engines	2 diesels; 1 701 shp; 2 shafts = 15 knots
Guns	1—3 in 50 cal dp; 4—40 mm AA
Complement	104

Steel Hulled. Launch dates above. Appearance varies according to the builders. Some have a funnel. *Cruise*, completed by Charleston Navy Yard, was armed with only 2—40 mm guns. All in the Atlantic Reserve Fleet except *Counsel*, Pacific Reserve Fleet. *Prowess*, MSF 280, employed as a naval reserve training ship and redesignated IX 305 on 18 Feb 1966.

RECLASSIFICATION. All the above minesweepers, formerly known as Fleet Minesweepers (AM) were reclassified as Fleet Minesweepers MSF in Feb 1955.

TRANSFERS. 34 of this class were transferred to the Soviet Navy in 1943, and 13 to the Chinese Navy. *Gayety*, MSF 329 and *Sentry* MSF 299 were transferred to the Vietnamese Navy in June 1962 and Aug 1962, respectively, and *Serene*, MSF 300 and *Shelter* MSF 301, in Jan 1964, *Crag* MSF 214, *Device* MSF 220, *Diploma* MSF 221, *Dour* MSF 223, *Eager* MSF 224, *Execute* MSF 232, *Facility* MSF 233, *Hilarity* MSF 241, *Instill* MSF 252, *Intrigue* MSF 253, *Invade* MSF 254, *Jubilant* MSF 255, *Knave* MSF 256, *Ransom* MSF 283, *Rebel* MSF 284, *Recruit* MSF 285, *Scout* MAF 296, *Scuffle* MSF 298, *Success* MSF 310 and *Harlequin* MSF 365, to Mexico in Oct 1962. *Report* MSF 289 was transferred to the army in Apr 1963. *Craddock* MSF 356, to Burma on 31 Mar 1967, *Signet* MSF 302 and *Skirmish* MSF 303 to the Dominican Republic in 13 Jan 1965.

LOSSES. *Salute* AM 294, was lost in the Second World War. *Pirate* (AM 275) and *Pledge* (AM 277) of this class struck mines and sank off Wonsan, Korean east coast, on 12 Oct 1950.

DISPOSALS
Control MSF 164, was stricken from the Navy List on 13 Mar 1948 and disposed of in 1959, **Clamour** MSF 160, **Climax** MSF 161, **Compel** MSF 162, **Concise** MSF 163, **Incredible** MSF 249, **Mainstay** MSF 261, **Reign** MSF 288, **Dipper** MSF 357 and **Harrier** MSF 366, on 1 Dec 1959, **Change** MSF 159, **Density** MSF 218, **Design** MSF 219, **Garland** MSF 238, **Opponent** MSF 269 and **Scrimmage** MSF 297, at the end of 1960, **Inaugural** MSF 242 in 1961, **Gadwall** MSF 362 on 1 Nov 1966. **Scurry** MSF 304 stricken 1 May 1967. **Hazard** MSF 240 stricken 1 Nov 1967. **Staunch** MSF 307, **Strategy** MSF 308, **Strength** MSF 309, stricken 1 Apr 1967. **Graylag** MSF 364 stricken 1 Oct 1967.

8 COASTAL MINESWEEPERS (MSCO): "ALBATROSS" CLASS

FULMAR	(ex-*YMS* 193)	MSCO 47	**REEDBIRD**	(ex-*YMS* 291)	MSCO 51
LINNET	(ex-*YMS* 395)	MSCO 24	**RUFF**	(ex-*YMS* 327)	MSCO 54
LORIKEET	(ex-*YMS* 271)	MSCO 49	**SISKIN**	(ex-*YMS* 425)	MSCO 58
PLOVER	(ex-*YMS* 442)	MSCO 33	**TURKEY**	(ex-*YMS* 444)	MSCO 56

Displacement, tons	270 standard; 250 full load
Cimensions, feet	136 × 24·5 × 8
Guns	1—40 mm or 3 in/50 calibre AA
Main engines	2 GM diesels; 2 shafts; 1 000 bhp = 15 knots
Complement	50

Of wooden construction. All launched in 1942-1943. Formerly known as Auxiliary Motor Minesweepers (AMS). Reclassified as Minesweepers, Coastal (old), MSCo, in Feb 1955. *Magpie* (AMS 25) and *Partridge* (AMS 31) of this class struck floating mines and sank off the Korean east coast on 1 Oct 1950 and 2 Feb 1951, respectively. *Bobolink, Bunting, Gull, Merganser, Redhead, Sanderling* and *Waxbill* were converted into coastal minehunters in 1945-1955. Only one-funnelled ships in this class now, the two-funnelled ships and the no-funnel ships having been stricken. The *Ruff* is employed as an operational Naval Reserve training ship at Everett, Washington; others in reserve.

DISPOSALS
Albatross MSCO 1 and **Hawk** MSCO 17 were stricken from the Navy List in 1958, **Redpoll** MSCO 57, on 1 July 1959, **Cardinal** MSCO 4, **Courser** MSCO 6, **Crow** MSCO 7, **Flamingo** MSCO 11, **Goldfinch** MSCO 12, **Grosbeak** MSCO 14, **Hornbill** MSCO 19, **Ostrich** MSCO 29, **Swan** MSCO 37, **Verdin** MSCO 38, **Barbet** MSCO 41, **Brambling** MSCO 42, **Brant** MSCO 43, **Courlan** MSCO 44, **Crossbill** MSCO 45, **Egret** MSCO 46, **Lapwing** MSCO 48, **Nightingale** MSCO 50, **Rheda** MSCO 52, and **Seagull** MSCO 55, on 1 Nov 1959, **Flicker** MSCO 9, and **Jackdaw** MSCO 21 on 1 Jan 1960, **Robin** MSCO 53 in Aug 1961. **Grouse** MSCO 15, was destroyed after grounding on 21 Sep 1963.

SEAGULL (MSCO 55) *United States Navy*

DISPOSALS OF OTHER CLASSES

All 29 of the converted minehunters of the underwater locator type (8 former coastal minesweepers of the YMS class and 21 former large infantry landing ships of the LSIL class) were stricken on 1 Nov 1959 or 1 Jan 1960. See names, former numbers, and full particulars on page 433 of the 1959-1960 edition. **Bittern** (MHC 43), a prototype Coastal Mine Hunter built in 1955-1957 has been on loan to commercial operator since July 1966; she remains on Navy List.

1 SPECIAL MINESWEEPER (MSS)

MSS 1 (ex-*Harry L. Glucksman*)

Dimensions, feet	441·5 oa × 57
Main engines	5 outboard deck mounted diesels = 10 knots
Complement	9 (1 officer, 8 enlisted men)

A "Liberty" ship converted to explode pressure mines. Specially modified to withstand mine explosions and remain afloat and underway. Conversion authorised in Fiscal Year 1966 and work began at American Shipbuilding Co, Lorain, Ohio, in Aug 1966; completed late in May 1969. Two additional "Liberty" hull conversions to MSS are planned. EC2-S-C1 design.

(Ten "Liberty" ships were partially modified in 1952-1953 to explode pressure mines. Only one ship placed in service, the ex-*John L. Sullivan* as YAG-37. Fitted with four T-34 turbo-prop aircraft engines on deck and stuffed with buoyancy material. She was employed in mine countermeasures experiments until reduced to a floating wreck; scrapped in 1958).

Mine Warfare Ships—*continued*

2 INSHORE MINESWEEPERS (MSI): "COVE" CLASS

COVE MSI 1 — **CAPE** MSI 2

Displacement, tons	120 light; 240 full load
Dimensions, feet	105 × 22 × 10
Main engines	2 GM diesels; 1 shaft; 650 bhp = 12 knots
Complement	21 (3 officers, 18 men)
Guns	1—·50 calibre MG

Provided under the 1956 programme. Prototypes for inshore minesweeping. Cost $750 000 plus $350 000 for equipment. Both built at Bethlehem Shipyards Co Bellingham, Washington. Laid down on 1 Feb 1957 and 1 May 1957, respectively, launched on 8 Feb 1958 and 5 Apr 1958 and placed in service on 20 Nov 1958 and 27 Feb 1959, respectively. Both active.

MSI 3-10 were built in the Netherlands for the Dutch Navy under US Military Assistance Programme; MSI 11 and MSI 12 built in Denmark under MAP; MSI 13 and MSI 14 built in United States for Iran; MSI 15-19 built in United States for Turkey.

CAPE MSI 2 — *1968, United States Navy*

41 MINESWEEPING BOATS (MSB)

MSB 5	**MSB 13**	**MSB 21**	**MSB 31**	**MSB 38**	**MSB 47**
MSB 6	**MSB 15**	**MSB 25**	**MSB 32**	**MSB 39**	**MSB 48**
MSB 7	**MSB 16**	**MSB 26**	**MSB 33**	**MSB 40**	**MSB 50**
MSB 8	**MSB 17**	**MSB 27**	**MSB 34**	**MSB 41**	**MSB 51**
MSB 9	**MSB 18**	**MSB 28**	**MSB 35**	**MSB 42**	**MSB 52**
MSB 10	**MSB 19**	**MSB 29**	**MSB 36**	**MSB 44**	**MSB 53**
MSB 11	**MSB 20**	**MSB 30**	**MSB 37**	**MSB 46**	

Displacement, tons	30 light; 39 full load except MSB 29, 80 full load
Dimensions, feet	57·2 × 15·5 × 4 except MSB 29, 82 × 19 × 5·5
Guns	several MG (Vietnam configuration)
Main engines	2 geared diesels (Packard); 2 shafts; 600 hp = 12 knots
Complement	6 (enlisted; increased to 7 when deployed)

Wooden-hull minesweepers intended to be carried to theatre of operations by large assault ships; however, they are too large to be easily handled by cranes and are assigned to sweeping harbours and, since 1966, to river operations in South Vietnam. MSB 1-4 were ex-Army minesweepers built in 1946 (since discarded); MSB 5-54 (less MSB 24) were completed in 1952-1956. MSB 24 was not built. MSB 29 built to enlarged design by John Trumpy & Sons, Annapolis, Maryland, in an effort to improve seakeeping ability.

MSB 5 and MSB 27 are in reserve; others are operational with several deployed to South Vietnam. Normally commanded by chief petty officer or petty officer first class.

ENGINEERING. MSB 5 was the first vessel built for the US Navy with gas turbine engines (to provide power for the boat's generators). 48 MSBs fitted with gas turbine generators.

LOSSES AND DISPOSALS

MSB 23 destroyed by fire on 2 Feb 1955 while under construction; rebuilt as experimental glass-reinforced plastic and delivered in Aug 1956; never operational and used at Naval Ship Research & Development Laboratory, Panama City, Florida.
MSB 1 and **MSB 3** stricken on 1 Nov 1958; **MSB 2** and **MSB 4** transferred to South Korea and Taiwan China, respectively, in Dec 1961; **MSB** 12 stricken on 1 Apr 1964; **MSB 14** sunk in Long Tau River, South Vietnam, after collision with merchant ship on 14 Jan 1967; **MSB 22** stricken in Jan 1968; **MSB** 43 struck dolphin and sank at Charleston, South Carolina, on 20 Jan 1967; **MSB 45** destroyed by mine near Saigon on 15 Feb 1967; **MSB 49** stricken in Sep 1967 (previously damaged by mine); **MSB 54** sunk by mine in Long Tau River on 31 Oct 1966.

MODIFICATION. MSBs serving in South Vietnam are fitted with several machine guns and removable fibreglass armour.

MSB in South China Sea — *1967, United States Navy*

MSB 32 — *1968, US Navy, LT Ted Storck*

MINESWEEPING LAUNCHES (MSL)

Displacement, pounds	18 500 hoisting; 23 100 full load
Dimensions, feet	36 oa × 11·6 × 3·7
Main engines	Gas turbine; 1 shaft; 200 shp = 12 knots or geared diesel; 1 shaft; 160 shp = 10 knots
Complement	4 to 6 enlisted men

Versatile minesweeping craft intended to sweep for acoustic, magnetic, and moored mines in inshore waters and in advance of landing craft. Twenty MSLs and two minesweeping helicopters are carried by each Mine Countermeasures Support Ship (MCS); MSLs are also carried by large amphibious ships operating in areas where MCS support is not available.

CONSTRUCTION: MSL 1-4 completed in 1946 (wood hull, gas turbine); MSL 5-29 completed in 1948 (wood hull, gas turbine); MSL 30 completed in 1948 (plastic hull, gas turbine); MSL 31-56 completed in 1966 (plastic hull, geared diesel); three wood hull boats converted to geared diesel in 1967.

MSL 11, MSL 17, MSL 14 — *1967, United States Navy*

KILAUEA (AE 26) (see following page) — *1968, Laurence Lowry/General Dynamics*

UNDERWAY REPLENISHMENT SHIPS

8 AMMUNITION SHIPS (AE): NEW CONSTRUCTION

Name	*No.*	*Laid down*	*Launched*	*Commissioned*
KILAUEA	AE 26	10 Mar 1966	9 Aug 1967	10 Aug 1968
BUTTE	AE 27	21 July 1966	9 Aug 1967	29 Nov 1968
SANTA BARBARA	AE 28	20 Dec 1966	23 Jan 1968	Feb 1970
MOUNT HOOD	AE 29	8 May 1967	17 July 1968	July 1970
	AE 32			1971
	AE 33			1971
	AE 34			1971
	AE 35			1971

Displacement, tons	20 500 full load
Dimensions, feet	565 oa × 81 × 25·7
Guns	8—3 in 50 cal
Main engines	Geared turbines; 1 shaft = 20+ knots
Boilers	2
Complement	401 (28 Officers, 373 enlisted men)

A new class of improved ammunition ships, easily identified by amidships position of superstructure. Fitted with helicopter facilities aft and the Fast Automatic Shuttle Transfer (FAST) system for underway replenishment of missiles to combatant ships. Estimated cost per ship is $32 700 000. AE 26 and 27 authorised in Fiscal Year 1965 shipbuilding programme; AE 28 and 29 in FY 1966, AE 32 and 33 in FY 1967, and AE 34 and 35 in FY 1968. *Kilauea* and *Butte* built by General Dynamics Corp, Quincy Division; *Mount Hood* and *Santa Barbara* by Bethlehem Steel Corp, Sparrows Point, Maryland; AE 32-35 being built by Ingalls shipbuilding Corp (Litton Systems), Pascagoula.

GUNNERY. 3 inch guns in twin mounts, two closed mounts forward and two open mounts amidships.

HALEAKALA (AE 25) *1968, United States Navy*

NITRO (AE 23) *1965, United States Navy*

BUTTE (AE27) *1968, General Dynamics (Quincy)*

5 AMMUNITION SHIPS (AE): "SURIBACHI" CLASS

Name	*No.*	*Laid down*	*Launched*	*Completed*
HALEAKALA	AE 25	10 Mar 1958	17 Feb 1959	3 Nov 1959
MAUNA KEA	AE 22	16 May 1955	3 May 1956	30 Mar 1957
NITRO	AE 23	20 May 1957	25 June 1958	1 May 1959
PYRO	AE 24	21 Oct 1957	5 Nov 1958	24 July 1959
SURIBACHI	AE 21	31 Jan 1955	2 Nov 1955	17 Nov 1956

Displacement, tons	7 470 light; 10 000 standard; 17 500 full load
Measurement, tons	7 500 deadweight
Dimensions, feet	512 oa × 72 × 29
Guns	4 or 8—3 in, 50 cal AA (twin)
Main engines	Steam turbines; 1 shaft; 16 000 hp = 21 knots
Boilers	2
Complement	316 (18 officers, 298 men)

CONSTRUCTION. Designed especially to meet the strenuous requirements of rapid replenishment at sea. Built from the hull up as Navy Ships. Elevators fitted for internal handling of ammunition and explosives, up-to-date methods of stowage, air conditioning, improved crew quarters. All built by Bethlehem, Sparrows Point, Md Shipyard. Another ship of this class to have been built under the 1959 programme was cancelled. All of these ships are active.

CONVERSION. The two "FAST" (Fast Automatic Shuttle Transfer) conversions in the 1963 Programme. *Haleakala* and *Suribachi*, were the first of this class to be modernised for the rapid handling and transfer of missiles up to the size of "Talos". This conversion provides for three holds to be rigged for missile stowage; completely mechanised handling facilities to transfer missiles from stowage to transfer stations; and the installation of the fast automatic shuttle transfer system. This modernisation results in safer missile handling and a greatly reduced transfer time. The two after mountings were removed for installation of a helicopter platform. The remaining three ships underwent the "FAST" conversion in the 1964 conversion programme. Note in photographs as the *Haleakala* has two after 5 inch mounts replaced by helicopter platform; 1965 view of *Nitro* taken prior to fitting of helicopter platform.

7 AMMUNITION SHIPS (AE): "WRANGELL" CLASS

Name	*No.*	*Launched*	*Commissioned*
WRANGELL (*ex-Midnight*)	AE 12	14 Apr 1944	28 May 1944
FIREDRAKE (*ex-Winged Racer*)	AE 14	12 May 1944	27 Dec 1944
VESUVIUS (*ex-Gamecock*)	AE 15	26 May 1944	3 July 1944
MOUNT KATMAI	AE 16	6 Jan 1945	21 July 1945
GREAT SITKIN	AE 17	20 Jan 1945	11 Aug 1945
PARICUTIN	AE 18	30 Jan 1945	25 July 1945
DIAMOND HEAD	AE 19	3 Feb 1945	9 Aug 1945

Displacement, tons	6 350 light; 15 295 full load
Dimensions, feet	435 wl; 459·2 oa × 63 × 28·2
Guns	2 or 4—3 in, 50 cal AA (single)
Main engines	Geared turbines; 6 000 shp = 16·4 knots
Boilers	2
Complement	267

C2 type. The 5 inch gun and four 40 mm AA guns were removed. Some ships fitted with helicopter platform aft.

All built by North Carolina SB Co, Wilmington, North Carolina. All of these ships are active.

FIREDRAKE (AE 14) *1967, United States Navy*

Underway Replenishment Ships—*continued*

2 AMMUNITION SHIPS (AE): CONVERTED AKA

Name	No.	Launched	Commissioned
VIRGO	AE 30 (ex-AKA 20, ex-AK 69)	4 June 1943	16 July 1943
CHARA	AE 31 (ex-AKA 58)	15 Mar 1944	14 June 1944

Displacement, tons	7 430 light; 14 000 full load
Dimensions, feet	434 wl; 459·2 oa × 63 × 24
Guns	4—3 in 50 cal (single)
Main engines	Geared turbines; 6 000 shp = 15·5 knots
Boilers	2 Foster-Wheeler

Former Attack Cargo Ships. Transferred to Maritime Administration Reserve Fleet in 1961; reacquired by Navy in 1965 and refitted as ammunition ships; recommissioned in 1966. Built by Federal SB & DD Co, Kearney, New Jersey. Both of these ships are active.

CHARA (AE 31) *1967, United States Navy*

4 AMMUNITION SHIPS (AE): "LASSEN" CLASS

Name	No.	Launched	Commissioned
MOUNT BAKER (ex-*Kilauea*, ex-*Surprise*)	AE 4	6 Aug 1940	20 Mar 1941
RAINER (ex-*Rainbow*)	AE 5	1 Mar 1941	21 Dec 1941
SHASTA (ex-*Comet*)	AE 6	9 July 1941	25 Mar 1943
MAUNA LOA	AE 8	14 Apr 1943	27 Oct 1943
MAZAMA	AE 9	15 Aug 1943	10 Mar 1944

Displacement, tons	5 220 light; 14 225 full load
Dimensions, feet	435 wl; 459·2 oa × 63 × 26·5
Guns	2 or 4—3 in, 50 cal AA (single)
Main engines	2 Nordberg diesels; 6 000 bhp = 15·3 knots
Complement	281

All built by Tampa SB Co. Modified C2 type, converted by Navy. Carries 5 000 tons cargo. War loss: *Mount Hood* AE 11. *Akutan* AE 13 was disposed of in 1961. *Mazuma* and *Mauna Loa* were reacquired and returned to the Navy in Sep 1961 and recommissioned on 27 Nov 1961. Some ships fitted with helicopter platform aft. *Lassen* AE 3, transferred to Maritime Administration in 1961. All remaining ships are active except *Shasta*, decommissioned in 1969.

Note helicopter platform in photograph of *Mauna Loa*; shadow from overhang of forward 3 inch gun "tubs".

DISPOSALS

Of the two ammunition ships of the "Sangay" class, **Sangay**, AE 10, was stricken in 1961 and *Formalhaut*, AE 20 ex-AK 22, transferred to Maritime Administration in Sep 1962.

MAUNA LOA (AE 8) *1965, United States Navy*

6 STORE SHIPS (AF): R2-S-BV1 TYPE

Name	No.	Launched	Commissioned
ALSTEDE (ex-*Ocean Chief*)	AF 48	28 Nov 1944	17 May 1946
ZELIMA (ex-*Golden Rocket*)	AF 49	2 Mar 1945	27 July 1946
ARCTURUS (ex-*Golden Eagle*)	AF 52	15 Mar 1942	18 Nov 1951
PICTOR (ex-*Great Republic*)	AF 54	4 June 1942	13 Sep 1950
ALUDRA (ex-*Matchless*)	AF 55	14 Oct 1944	7 July 1952
PROCYON (ex-*Flying Scud*)	AF 61	1 July 1942	24 Nov 1961

Displacement, tons	6 914 light; 15 500 full load
Dimensions, feet	459·2 oa × 63 × 28
Boilers	2
Complement	17 officers, 275 men
Guns	4—40 mm (twin); *Aludra:* 8—3 in 50 cal (twin)
Main engines	Geared turbines; 6 000 shp = 16·4 knots

All built by Moore Dry Dock Co and launched in 1945 and 1946. R2-S-BV1 design reefer type. *Aludra* was acquired for conversion by the Navy. *Pictor* was transferred from Maritime Administration to US Navy. C2-S-B1 type similar to R2-S-BV1 design, except that R2s were built as reefers and C2s as cargo ships. Same type as "Eagle" class. *Procyon* was acquired from the Maritime Administration and commissioned in Nov 1961. *Sirius* AF 60 was transferred to the Maritime Administration Reserve Fleet in 1965. *Bellatrix*, AF 62, stricken on 1 Oct 1968 (scrapped). All of these ships are active.

ARCTURUS (AF 52) *United States Navy*

2 STORE SHIPS (AF): R3-S-4A TYPE

Name	No.	Launched	Commissioned
RIGEL	AF 58	15 Mar 1955	2 Sep 1955
VEGA	AF 59	26 Apr 1955	10 Nov 1955

Displacement, tons	7 950 light; 15 540 full load
Measurement, tons	10 850 gross
Dimensions, feet	475 wl; 502 oa × 72 × 29 max
Guns	4—3 in, 50 cal AA (twin)
Main engines	Steam turbine; 1 shaft; 12 500 shp = 18 knots

Built by Ingalls Shipbuilding Co, Pascagoula. R3-S-4A type. Cost $12 440 000 each. Helicopter platform fitted (two after twin 3 inch mounts removed). 360 000 cu ft of refrigerated space. Both of these ships are active.

RIGEL (AF 58) *1968, United States Navy*

2 STORE SHIPS (AF): "VICTORY" TYPE

Name	No.	Launched	Commissioned
DENEBOLA (ex-*Hibbing Victory*)	AF 56	10 June 1944	20 Jan 1954
REGULUS (ex-*Escanaba Victory*)	AF 57	7 June 1944	3 Feb 1954

Displacement, tons	6 700 light; 12 130 full load
Measurement, tons	8 000 deadweight
Dimensions, feet	455·2 × 62 × 28·5
Guns	4—3 in, 50 cal AA, (twin)
Main engines	Westinghouse geared turbines; 1 shaft; 8 500 shp = 17 knots
Boilers	2
Complement	225

Helicopter platforms fitted aft (two 3 inch twin mounts removed). Both of these ships are active.

Underway Replenishment Ships—*continued*

DENEBOLA (AF 56) *United States Navy*

2 STORE SHIPS (AF): C2-S-E1 TYPE

Name	*No.*	*Launched*	*Commissioned*
HYADES (ex-*Iberville*)	AF 28	12 June 1943	30 Sep 1943
GRAFFIAS (ex-*Topa Topa*)	AF 29	12 Dec 1943	18 Feb 1944

Displacement, tons	6 313 light; 15 300 full load
Dimensions, feet	463·6 oa × 63 × 28
Guns	4—3 in, 50 cal single
Main engines	Geared turbines; 6 000 shp = 15·5 knots
Boilers	2 (Babcock & Wilcox)
Complement	252

Cargo capacity 5 300 tons. The 5 inch gun was removed. Both of these ships are active.

DISPOSALS OF OTHER CLASSES

Aldebaran, AF 10, transferred to Maritime Administration (decommissioned in June 1968).

HYADES (AF 28) *Ing Augusti Nani*

7 COMBAT STORE SHIPS (AFS): "MARS" CLASS

Name	*No.*	*Laid down*	*Launched*	*Commissioned*
MARS	AFS 1	5 May 1962	15 June 1963	21 Dec 1963
SYLVANIA	AFS 2	18 Aug 1962	15 Aug 1963	11 July 1964
NIAGARA FALLS	AFS 3	22 May 1965	26 Mar 1966	29 Apr 1967
WHITE PLAINS	AFS 4	2 Oct 1965	23 July 1966	23 Nov 1968
CONCORD	AFS 5	26 Mar 1966	17 Dec 1966	27 Nov 1968
SAN DIEGO	AFS 6	11 Mar 1965	13 Apr 1968	Apr 1969
SAN JOSE	AFS 7		Nov 1969	July 1970

Displacement, tons	16 500 full load
Dimensions, feet	581 oa × 79 × 24
Guns	8—3 in, 50 cal (twin)
Aircraft	2 helicopters (UH-46A Sea Knight)
Main engines	Steam turbines; 1 shaft; 22 000 shp = 20 knots
Boilers	3 (Babcock & Wilcox) (one spare)
Radius, miles	10 000 at 18·5 knots
Complement	430 (30 officers, 400 enlisted men; designed 486)

All built by National Steel & Shipbuilding, San Diego, California. Of a new design with a completely new replenishment at sea system. "M" frames replace conventional king posts and booms, which are equipped with automatic tensioning devices to maintain transfer lines taut between the ship and the warships being replenished despite rolling and yawing. Computers provide up-to-the-minute data on stock status with data displayed by closed-circuit television. Fire holds (one refrigerated). Helicopters are carried to provide vertical replenishment ships in a task force spread over a wide area.

Mars authorised in Fiscal Year 1961 shipbuilding programme, *Sylvania* in FY 1962, *Niagara Falls* in FY 1964, *White Plains* and *Concord* in FY 1965, *San Diego* in FY 1966, *San Jose* in FY 1967.

NOMENCLATURE. Combat store ships are named for American cities.

SYLVANIA (AFS 2) *1967, United States Navy*

MARS (AFS 1) *1965, United States Navy*

DISPOSALS OF STORES ISSUE SHIPS (AKS)

Of this type **Mercury** AKS 20 (ex-AK 42) was stricken in 1960.
All five of the LST type **Chimon** AKS 31 (ex-AG 150, ex-LST 1102), **Colington** AKS 29 (ex-AG 140, ex-LST 1085), **Electron** AKS 27 (ex-AG 146, ex-LST 1070), **League Island** AKS 30 (ex-AG 149, ex-LST 1097), and **Proton**, AKS 28 (ex-AG 147, ex-LST 1078) were stricken in 1960.
All six of the "Island" class, **Avery Island** AKS 24, **Belle Isle** AKS 21, **Coaster's Harbor** AKS 22, **Cuttyhunk Island** AKS 23, **Indian Island** AKS 25 and **Kent Island** AKS 26, were also stricken in 1960.
The C-2 cargo type **Castor**, AKS 1, and **Pollux**, AKS 4 ex-AK 54, were stricken on 1 Dec 1968 and 1 Jan 1969, respectively.
The Victory type **Altair**, AKS 32 ex-AK 257, was stricken in 1969.

6 OILERS (AO): "NEOSHO" CLASS

Name	*No.*	*Launched*	*Commissioned*
NEOSHO	AO 143	10 Nov 1953	24 Sep 1954
MISSISSINEWA	AO 144	12 June 1954	18 Jan 1955
HASSAYAMPA	AO 145	12 Sep 1954	19 Apr 1955
KAWISHIWI	AO 146	11 Dec 1954	6 July 1955
TRUCKEE	AO 147	10 Mar 1955	23 Nov 1955
PONCHATOULA	AO 148	9 July 1955	12 Jan 1956

Displacement, tons	11 600 light; 38 000 to 40 000 full load
Dimensions, feet	640 wl; 655 oa × 86 × 35
Guns	12—3 in, 50 cal (twin)
Main engines	GE Turbines; 2 shafts; 28 000 shp = 20 knots
Complement	300 (fitted to carry squadron staff of 12 officers)

AO 143, built by Bethlehem Steel Company, Quincy, Mass. AO 144-148 by New York Shipbuilding Corporation, Camden, New Jersey. Largest Navy oilers built. Carry 180 000 barrels in 24 tanks. The 2—5 inch, 38 cal guns were removed in 1960. A helicopter platform was installed in place of the after 5 inch gun in AO 143, 144 and 147. These ships are fitted to carry a service force commander and staff. All of these ships are active.

NOMENCLATURE. Oilers are named after American rivers with Indian names.

NEOSHO (AO 143) *1968, United States Navy*

5 OILERS (AO): T3-S2-A3

Name	*No.*	*Launched*	*Commissioned*
MISPILLION	AO 105	10 Aug 1945	29 Dec 1945
NAVASOTA	AO 106	30 Aug 1945	27 Feb 1946
PASSUMPSIC	AO 107	31 Oct 1945	1 Apr 1946
PAWCATUCK	AO 108	19 Feb 1945	10 May 1946
WACCAMAW	AO 109	30 Mar 1946	25 June 1946

Displacement, tons	11 000 light; 34 750 full load
Dimensions, feet	646 oa × 75 × 35·5
Guns	4—3 in, 50 cal AA (single)
Main engines	Turbines; 2 shafts; 13 500 shp = 16 knots
Boilers	4
Complement	290 (16 officers, 274 men)

Navasota and *Waccamaw*, jumboised under the 1963 programme, (recommissioned on 28 Dec 1964 and 26 Feb 1965), other three under the 1964 programme. Conversion increased the oil cargo capacity from 100 000 to 150 000 barrels. Helicopter platform fitted forward. All of these ships are active. (Photograph on following page).

Underway Replenishment Ships—*continued*

NAVASOTA (AO 106) (with UH-46A Sea Knight) *1965, United States Navy*

4 OILERS (AO): T2-A TYPE

Name	No.	Launched	Commissioned
KENENBEC (ex-*Corsicana*)	AO 36	19 Apr 1941	4 Feb 1942
MATTAPONI (ex-*Kalkay*)	AO 41	7 Jan 1942	11 May 1942
TAPPAHANNOCK (ex-*Jorkay*)	AO 43	18 Apr 1942	22 June 1942
NECHES (ex-*Askal*)	AO 47	11 Oct 1941	16 Sep 1942

Displacement, tons	6 013 light; 21 850 full load
Dimensions, feet	502 oa × 68 × 30·8
Guns	2 or 4—3 in, 50 cal AA (single)
Main engines	2 (Babcock & Wilcox)

Cargo capacity 126 000 barrels. The *Kankakee* (AO 39) was decommissioned on 27 June 1968 and transferred to Maritime Administration reserve on 27 Nov 1968. The remaining ships are active.

23 OILERS (AO): T3-S2-A1 TYPE

Name	No.	Launched	Commissioned
PLATTE	AO 24	8 July 1939	1 Dec 1939
SABINE (ex-*Esso Albany*)	AO 25	27 Apr 1940	25 Sep 1940
SALAMONIE (ex-*Esso Columbia*)	AO 26	18 Sep 1940	28 Apr 1941
KASKASKIA (ex-*Esso Richmond*)	AO 27	29 Sep 1939	29 Oct 1940
CHEMUNG (ex-*Esso Annapolis*)	AO 30	9 Sep 1939	3 July 1941
GUADALUPE (ex-*Esso Raleigh*)	AO 32	26 Jan 1940	5 June 1941
ASHTABULA	AO 51	22 May 1943	7 Aug 1943
CACAPON	AO 52	6 June 1943	21 Sep 1943
CALIENTE	AO 53	26 Aug 1943	22 Oct 1943
CHIKASKIA	AO 54	2 Oct 1943	10 Nov 1943
ELOKOMIN	AO 55	19 Oct 1943	30 Nov 1943
AUCILLA (ex-*Escanaba*)	AO 56	20 Nov 1943	22 Dec 1943
MARIAS	AO 57	21 Dec 1943	12 Feb 1944
MANATEE	AO 58	19 Feb 1944	6 Apr 1944
NANTAHALA	AO 60	29 Apr 1944	19 June 1944
SEVERN	AO 61	31 May 1944	19 July 1944
TALUGA	AO 62	10 July 1944	25 Aug 1944
CHIPOLA	AO 63	21 Oct 1944	30 Nov 1944
TOLOVANA	AO 64	6 Jan 1945	24 Feb 1945
CALOOSAHATCHEE	AO 88	2 June 1945	10 Oct 1945
ALLAGASH	AO 97	14 Apr 1945	21 Aug 1945
CANISTEO	AO 99	6 July 1945	3 Dec 1945
CHUKAWAN	AO 100	28 Aug 1945	22 Jan 1946

Displacement, tons	25 525 full load; Jumboised ships 34 700 full load
Dimensions, feet	553 or 644 oa × 75 × 31·5
Guns	1—5 in; 4—3 in (*Chemung, Guadalupe, Kaskaskia, Sabine, Platte, Salamonie*, 3—5 in; *Cacapon*, 4—3 in, 50 cal; *Chipola Guadalupe*, 2—3 in, 50 cal); 8—3 in (twin) in Jumboised ships
Main engines	Geared turbines; 2 shafts; 13 500 shp = 18 knots
Boilers	4 Foster Wheeler
Complement	64

War Losses. *Mississinewa, Neosho.* Three ships of this class, the *Ashtabula, Caloosahatchee* and *Canisteo*, have been "Jumboised" and re-armed with 8—3 inch, 50 cal guns in 4 twin mounts, two forward and two aft. A new central tank section increases length to 644 feet and displacement to 34 700 tons. Cargo capacity as built was 141 600 barrels. *Sabine* and *Salamonie* are in Navy reserve fleet; all others are active.

DISPOSALS
"T3-S-A1" type: **Enoree** AO 69 and **Niobrara** AO 72 were stricken in Dec 1958. "T2-A" type: **Merrimack** AO 37 and **Monagahela** AO 42 were stricken in Dec 1958. Distilling ships, ex-oilers, of the "Pasig" class **Abatan** AW 4 (ex-*Mission San Lorenzo* AO 92) and **Pasig** AW 3 (ex-*Mission San Xavier* AO 91) transferred to the Maritime National Defence Reserve Fleet in 1960-61, but **Abatan** was reacquired in Sep 1962 and returned to Maritime Administration in Nov 1962 (now at Guatanamo Bay, Cuba, in service status with the distilling plant activated). **Cimarron**, AO 22, was transferred to Portugal on 1 Oct 1968.

NANTAHALA (AO 60) *1964, United States Navy*

CIMARRON (AO 22) (to Portugal) *1965, US Navy*

5 FAST COMBAT SUPPORT SHIPS (AOE): "SACRAMENTO" CLASS

Name	No.	Laid down	Launched	Commissioned
SACRAMENTO	AOE 1	30 June 1961	14 Sep 1963	14 Mar 1964
CAMDEN	AOE 2	17 Feb 1964	29 May 1965	1 Apr 1967
SEATTLE	AOE 3	1 Oct 1965	2 Mar 1968	Apr 1969
DETROIT	AOE 4	29 Nov 1966	May 1969	Apr 1970
	AOE 5			

Displacement, tons	19 200 light; 53 600 full load
Dimensions, feet	793 oa × 107 × 39·3
Guns	8—3 in, 50 cal (twin)
Aircraft	2 cargo helicopters (UH 46 Sea Knight)
Main engines	Geared turbines; 2 shafts; 100 000 shp = 26 knots sustained speed
Boilers	4
Complement	600 (33 officers, 567 men)

The Fast Combat Support Ships (AOE) are designed to supply task forces. Fitted with "FAST". They combine the functions of ammunition ships, cargo ships and fleet oilers. They carry one fifth more fuel than the latest fleet oilers (black oil, diesel oil and aviation spirit), and one quarter the capacity of the latest ammunition ship, including guided missiles, as well as 250 tons of dry cargo and 250 tons of frozen food. Oil capacity 177 000 barrels. *Detroit, Seattle* and *Sacramento* were built by Puget Sound Naval Shipyard, *Camden* was built by New York Shipbuilding Corporation, Camden, New Jersey.

Sacramento authorised in Fiscal Year 1961 shipbuilding programme, *Camden* in FY 1963, *Seattle* in FY 1965, *Detroit* in FY 1966. AOE 5 in FY 1968. Awarding of construction contract for last ship delayed.

ENGINEERING. *Sacramento* and *Camden* have machinery intended for cancelled battleship *Kentucky* (BB 66).

NOMENCLATURE. Fast combat support ships are named for American cities.

PATAPSCO (AOG 1) *1966, United States Navy*

Underway Replenishment Ships—*continued*

MARS (AFS 1), SACRAMENTO (AOE 1), WALKE (DD 723)

1964, United States Navy

8 GASOLINE TANKERS (AOG): "PATAPSCO" CLASS

Name	*No.*	*Launched*	*Commissioned*
PATAPSCO	AOG 1	18 Aug 1942	4 Feb 1943
ELKHORN	AOG 7	15 May 1943	12 Feb 1944
GENESEE	AOG 8	23 Sep 1943	27 May 1944
KISHWAUKEE	AOG 9	24 July 1943	27 May 1944
TOMBIGBEE	AOG 11	18 Nov 1943	13 July 1944
CHEWAUCAN	AOG 50	22 July 1944	19 Feb 1945
NESPELEN	AOG 55	10 Apr 1945	
NOXUBEE	AOG 56	3 Apr 1945	

Displacement, tons	1 850 light; 4 570 full load
Dimensions, feet	292 wl; 310·8 oa × 48·5 × 15·7 max
Guns	3—3 in dp, 50 cal (single)
Main engines	Diesel-electric; 2 shafts; 3 100 bhp = 14 knots
Complement	81 (6 officers, 75 men)

Navy designed small fuel ships originally intended to carry diesel and aviation fuels. All built by Cargill Inc, Savage, Minnesota. Cargo capacity 17 775 barrels. *Kishwaukee Noxubee* and *Patapsco* were reacquired from the Maritime Administration and re-commissioned in 1966. All are active.

DISPOSALS
Maquoketa T-AOG 51 was stricken, **Kern** AOG 2, **Wabash** AOG 4, and **Maquoketa** AOG 51 were transferred to Maritime Administration in 1958 and **Susquehanna** AOG 5 in 1959-60. **Ontonagon** AOG 36 was stricken from the Navy List and returned to Maritime Administration on 13 Nov 1957. **Agawam** AOG 6, **Nemasket** AOG 10, and **Rio Grande** AOG 3 were disposed of in 1961. **Chestatee** AOG 49 and **Wacissa** AOG 59 were stricken in 1963 and scrapped. **Mattabesset**, AOG 52, stricken on 1 Oct 1968 and transferred to Maritime Administration.

TRANSFER. *Natchoug* AOG 54 was transferred to Greece under the MDAP on 1 Aug 1959. *Pinnebog* AOG 58 is on loan to the US Air Force. *Pecatonica* AOG 57 was transferred to Taiwan China in Apr 1962. *Namakagon* AOG 53 was loaned to New Zealand in 1963.

6 REPLENISHMENT OILERS (AOR): "WICHITA" CLASS

Name	*No.*	*Laid down*	*Launched*	*Commissioned*
WICHITA	AOR 1	18 June 1966	16 Mar 1968	**17 June** 1969
MILWAUKEE	AOR 2	29 Nov 1966	17 Jan 1969	Oct 1969
KANSAS CITY	AOR 3	20 Apr 1968	**28 June** 1969	June 1970
	AOR 4	22 Jan 1969		1970
	AOR 5	Aug 1969		1971
	AOR 6	Feb 1970		1971

Displacement, tons	38 100 full load
Dimensions, feet	659 oa × 96 × 35
Guns	8—3 in., 50 cal., (twin)
Main engines	Geared turbines; 2 shafts; = 20 knots, 18 knots on 2 boilers
Boilers	3
Complement	345 (20 officers, 325 men)
Helicopters	2 (UH-46 Sea Knight)

Fitted with helicopter platform. These ships provide rapid replenishment at sea of petroleum products, ammunition, provisions and fleet freight to task forces. All built by General Dynamics Corporation Quincy.

Wichita and **Milwaukee** authorised in Fiscal Year 1965, new construction programme, **Kansas City** and AOR 4 in FY 1966, AOR 5 and AOR 6 in FY 1967.

DISPOSALS
"Fleet Tanker" **Conecuh** (AOR 110, ex-AO 110, ex-IX 301, former German U-boat tender) stricken 1 June 1960; carried mixed cargoes with fuels; prototype multi-store underway replenishment ship.

NOMENCLATURE. Replenishment oilers are named after American cities.

WICHITA (AOR 1)

1969, General Dynamics (Quincy Division)

Fleet Support Ships—*continued*

2 DESTROYER TENDERS (AD): NEW CONSTRUCTION

Name	No.	Laid down	Launched	Commissioned
SAMUEL GOMPERS	AD 37	9 July 1964	14 May 1966	1 July 1967
PUGET SOUND	AD 38	15 Feb 1965	16 Sep 1966	27 Apr 1968

Displacement, tons	20 500 to 21 600 full load
Dimensions, feet	643 × 85
Guns	1—5 in, 38 cal
Main engines	20 000 hp = over 18 knots
Complement	1 803 (135 officers, 1 668 men)

Samuel Gompers is the first destroyer tender of post-Second World War design. These ships have repair, supply and support facilities for new destroyer types, missile systems, anti-submarine warfare weapons and equipments, advanced communications and electronic systems and nuclear propulsion plants. They are able to furnish in port service to six guided missile destroyers alongside simultaneously. *Samuel Gompers* was authorised under the Fiscal Year 1964 new construction programme; *Puget Sound* in the 1965 programme. Both built by Puget Sound Naval Shipyard. AD 39 in FY 1969 programme was cancelled on 27 Mar 1969 to provide funds for overruns in FY 1969 and FY 1970 programmes (estimated saving was $72 500 000).

NOMENCLATURE. Destroyer tenders generally are named for geographic areas; Samuel Gompers was an American labour leader.

SAMUEL GOMPERS (AD 37) *1968, United States Navy*

PUGET SOUND (AD 38) *1968, United States Navy*

GRAND CANYON (AD 28) *1968, United States Navy*

9 DESTROYER TENDERS (AD): "KLONDIKE" CLASS

Name	No.	Launched	Commissioned
ARCADIA	AD 23	19 Nov 1944	13 Sep 1945
EVERGLADES	AD 24	28 Jan 1945	25 May 1951
FRONTIER	AD 25	25 Mar 1945	2 Mar 1946
SHENANDOAH	AD 26	29 Mar 1945	13 Aug 1945
YELLOWSTONE	AD 27	12 Apr 1945	15 Jan 1946
GRAND CANYON	AD 28	27 Apr 1945	5 Apr 1946
ISLE ROYALE	AD 29	19 Sep 1945	9 June 1962
TIDEWATER	AD 31	30 June 1945	19 Feb 1946
BRYCE CANYON	AD 36	7 Mar 1946	15 Sep 1950

Displacement, tons	8 165 standard: 16 635 to 16 900 full load
Dimensions, feet	465 wl; 492 oa × 69·5 × 27·2
Guns	1—5 in, 38 cal dp
Main engines	Geared turbines; 1 shaft; 8 500 shp = 18·4 knots
Boilers	2 (Foster-Wheeler or Babcock & Wilcox)
Complement	778 to 918

Constructed by Todd Shipyards (*Arcadia, Grand Canyon, Shenandoah, Yellowstone*), Charleston Navy Yard (*Bryce Canyon, Tidewater*), Los Angeles SB & DD Co (*Everglades, Frontier*) and Tacoma-Pacific Shipyard (*Isle Royale*). Three other ships (*Arrowhead, Canopus, New England*) were cancelled in 1945, and a fourth (*Great Lakes*) sold. C 3 type. Ships vary in appearance. *Tidewater* originally ordered as submarine tender (AS 30). Sister ship *Klondike*, AD 22, recommissioned in 1959, and was reclassified as AR 22 on 20 Feb 1960. *Arcadia* and *Frontier* decommissioned in 1968 and placed in reserve; all other ships are active.

CONSTRUCTION. *Isle Royale* which had been in reserve status almost ever since she was built by Tacoma-Pacific Shipyard, Inc, Seattle, Washington, and first commissioned on 26 Mar 1946 was brought forward for rehabilitation in Jan 1962, recommissioned on 9 June 1962. overhauled in the Long Beach Navy Shipyard, and became ready for fleet service on 1 Jan 1963.

MODERNISATION. Most of these ships have been modernised under the FRAM II programme to service modernised destroyers fitted with ASROC, improved electronics, helicopters, etc. The tenders' shops were improved and four 3 inch and four 40 mm guns removed.

SHENANDOAH (AD 26) *1964, United States Navy*

1 DESTROYER TENDER (AD): "CASCADE" TYPE

CASCADE AD 16

Displacement, tons	9 800 standard; 16 600 full load
Dimensions, feet	492 oa × 69·5 × 27·2
Guns	1—5 in, 38 cal dp
Main engines	Turbines; 8 500 shp = 18·4 knots
Boilers	2
Complement	857

Built by Western Pipe & Steel Co, San Francisco, C3-S1-N2 type. Launched on 7 June 1942 and commissioned on 12 Mar 1943. Modernised to service FRAM destroyers. Six 40 mm guns removed during modernisation.
The *Cascade* is in active service.

CASCADE (AD 16) *1968, United States Navy*

Fleet Support Ships—*continued*

5 DESTROYER TENDERS (AD): "DIXIE" CLASS

Name	*No.*	*Launched*	*Commissioned*
DIXIE	AD 14	27 May 1939	25 Apr 1940
PRAIRIE	AD 15	9 Dec 1939	5 Aug 1940
PIEDMONT	AD 17	7 Dec 1942	5 Jan 1944
SIERRA	AD 18	23 Feb 1943	20 Mar 1944
YOSEMITE	AD 19	16 May 1943	25 May 1944

Displacement, tons	9 450 standard; 17 176 full load
Dimensions, feet	520 wl; 530·5 oa × 73·3 × 25·5
Guns	1 or 2—5 in, 38 cal dp
Main engines	Geared turbines; 2 shafts; 11 000 shp = 19·6 knots
Boilers	2
Complement	1 076 to 1 698 (total accommodation)

Dixie and *Prairie* built by New York Shipbuilding Corp, Camden, New Jersey; others by Tampa Shipbuilding Co, Florida. All five ships are active. The two after 5 inch guns and the eight 40 mm AA guns were removed.

MODERNISATION. All of these ships have been modernised under the FRAM II programme to service destroyers fitted with ASROC, improved electronics, helicopters, etc. Two or three 5 inch guns and eight 40 mm guns removed during modernisation.

YOSEMITE (AD 19) *1968, United States Navy*

YOSEMITE (AD 19) *1968, United States Navy*

1 DEGAUSSING SHIP (ADG): Ex-MINESWEEPER

SURFBIRD (ex-*MSF* 383) ADG 383

Displacement, tons	890 standard; 1 250 full load
Dimensions, feet	215 wl; 221·2 oa × 32·2 × 10·8
Main engines	Diesel electric; 2 shafts; 3 532 bhp = 18 knots
Complement	70

Built by American Shipbuilding Co, Lorain, Ohio. Laid down on 15 Feb 1944. Launched on 31 Aug 1944. Completed (first commissioned) on 25 Nov 1944. Former Fleet Minesweeper of the steel-hulled type, MSF (ex-AM), reclassified as ADG on 18 May 1957. In active status in the Far East.

SURFBIRD (ADG 383) *United States Navy*

3 DEGAUSSING SHIPS (ADG): Ex-PCE

DEPERM (ex-*PCE* 883, 14 Jan 1944)	ADG 10
LODESTONE (ex-*PCE* 876, 30 Sep 1943)	ADG 8
MAGNET (ex-*PCE* 879, 1 Sep 1943)	ADG 9

Displacement, tons	640 standard; 900 full load
Dimensions, feet	184·5 oa × 33 × 9·5
Main engines	Diesel; 2 shafts; 2 400 bhp = 16 knots

Launch dates above. Named on 1 Feb 1955. All out of commission, in reserve. Sister ship *Ampere* ADG 11 (ex-*Drake* AM 359) was stricken from the Navy List on 1 July 1961.

2 HOSPITAL SHIPS (AH): "HAVEN" TYPE

Name	*No.*	*Launched*	*Commissioned*
REPOSE (ex-*Marine Beaver*)	AH 16	8 Aug 1944	26 May 1945
SANCTUARY (ex-*Marine Owl*)	AH 17	15 Aug 1944	20 June 1945

Displacement, tons	11 141 standard; 15 400 full load
Dimensions, feet	496 wl; 520 oa × 71·5 × 24
Main engines	Geared turbines (General Electric); 1 shaft; 9 000 shp = 18 3
Boilers	2 (Babcock & Wilcox)
Complement	Accommodation for 626 to 698

Built by the Sun SB & DD Co, Chester, Pa. Maritime Commission C 4-S-B2 Type. Beds for approximately 700 patients. Air conditioned throughout. *Consolation* (AH 15) was chartered to a private group, operated by American President Lines, as a floating laboratory and medical school since 1961; she was renamed *Hope* by the People to People Health Foundation Inc. *Benevolence* (AH 13) sank after a collision with a freighter off San Francisco in Aug 1950. *Tranquility* (AH 14) transferred to the Maritime Administration Reserve Fleet in 1961 and *Haven* (AH 12) on 1 Mar 1967. *Repose* was in Sep 1962 transferred to Maritime Administration, but was reacquired and recommissioned on 16 Oct 1965 at San Francisco for naval service with complement of 54 officers, 29 nurses and 543 men and 922 bed capacity. *Sancutary*, was reacquired from Maritime Administration in 1966 and recommissioned on 15 Nov 1966 for naval service. After modernisation by Avondale Shipyard, New Orleans, she has helo platform aft, 760 bed hospital, with 319 staff (24 doctors, 29 nurses, 3 dentists, 263 enlisted hospital corpsmen) and 375 crew (17 officers, 358 men). Both ships are active.

NOMENCLATURE. Hospital ships are named with words implying comfort and help.

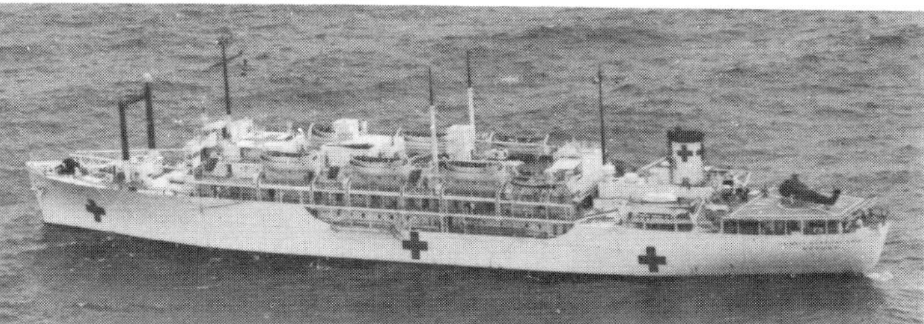

REPOSE (AH 16) *1967, United States Navy*

1 NET LAYING SHIP (ANL): "COHOES" CLASS

COHOES ANL 78 (ex-AN 78)

Displacement, tons	650 standard; 855 full load
Dimensions, feet	146 wl; 168·5 oa × 33·8 × 11·7
Guns	3—20 mm AA (single)
Main engines	Busch-Sulzer diesel-electric; 1 shaft; 1 200 shp = 12 knots
Complement	46 (4 officers, 42 men)

Both built by Commercial Iron Works, Portland, Oregon. Launched 29 Nov 1944; commissioned 23 Mar 1945. Designation changed from Netlayer (AN) to Net Laying Ship (ANL) on 1 Jan 1969.

TRANSFERS. *Tonawanda* AN 89, was transferred to Haiti in 1960, *Marietta* AN 82 to Venezuela in Jan 1961, *Tunxis* AN 90, and *Waxsaw* AN 91 to Venezuela in Jan 1963, *Nahaut* AN 83 to Uruguay in 1968.

DISPOSALS

Manayunk AN 81, **Naubuc** AN 84, **Suncock** AN 80 and **Tunxis** AN 90, were stricken from the Navy List in Sep 1962, **Etlah** AN 79, **Oneota** AN 85, **Passaconaway** AN 86, **Passaic** AN 87, **Shakamaxon** AN 88 and **Yazoo** AN 92, in July 1963. **Suncock** AN 80 was retransferred to the Bureau of Mines in Oct 1964. **Cohoes** AN 78 was reacquired from Maritime Administration in Mar 1967 for conversion to river/harbour as salvage tender; redesignated YRST 4 on 1 Apr 1968 (see section on Specialised Auxiliary Ships and Service Craft).

NOMENCLATURE. Net laying ships are named for trees.

COHOES (ANL 78) *1968, United States Navy*

Fleet Support Ships—*continued*

1 NET LAYING SHIP (ANL): "TREE" CLASS

BUTTERNUT ANL 9 (ex-AN 9, ex-YN 4)

Displacement, tons	560 standard; 760 full load
Dimensions, feet	146 wl; 163 oa × 30·5 × 11·8 max
Guns	4—20 mm AA (single)
Main engines	Diesel-electric; 1 shaft; 1 000 bhp = 11·5 knots
Complement	48 (4 officers, 44 men)

Former YN. Steel Hull. Built by Lake Washington Shipyards Houghton. Laid down 11 Mar 1941, launched 10 May 1941, placed in service 3 Sep 1941. Originally designated Net Tender (YN); subsequently changed to Netlayer (AN) and to Net Laying Ship (ANL) on 1 Jan 1969.

TRANSFERS. *Hackberry* AN 25, *Pepperwood* AN 36 and *Yew* AN 37 were transferred to France in 1944, *Larch* AN 21 to Turkey in 1947. *Mulberry* AN 27 to Ecuador in 1965 (on loan), *Locust* AN 22 to France in 1966 (sold). *Rosewood* AN 31 to France.

Mimosa AN 26, **Palm** AN 28, **Hazel** AN 29, **Redwood** AN 30, **Sandalwood** AN 32, **Nutmeg** AN 33 and **Teak** AN 35, stricken from the Navy List in Sep 1962. **Teaberry** AN 34 stricken in 1961 became MS **Pacific Salvor** in 1962. **Buckeye** AN 13 and **Buckthorn** AN 14 stricken in July 1963 and transferred to Maritime Administration Reserve.

BUTTERNUT (AN 9) *United States Navy*

8 SELF-PROPELLED BARRACKS SHIPS (APB)

Name	*No.*	*Launched*
BENEWAH	APB 35 (ex-APL 35)	6 May 1945
COLLETON	APB 36 (ex-APL 36)	30 July 1945
ECHOLS	APB 36 (ex-APL 37)	30 July 1945
MERCER	APB 39 (ex-APL 39)	17 Nov 1944
NUECES	APB 40 (ex-APL 40)	6 May 1945
DORCHESTER	APB 46 (ex-AKS 17, ex-LST 1112)	12 Apr 1945
KINGMAN	APB 47 (ex-AKS 18, ex-LST 1113)	17 Apr 1945
VANDENBURGH	APB 48 (ex-AKS 19, ex-LST 1114)	20 Apr 1945

Displacement, tons	2 189 light; 4 080 full load
Dimensions, feet	316 wl; 328 oa × 50 × 11
Guns	Vary (see notes)
Main engines	Diesels (General Motors); 2 shafts; 1 600 to 1 800 bhp = 12 knots (*APB* 41-50); 10 knots (*APB* 35-40)

Officially rated as Self-Propelled Barracks Ships (APB). All ex-LST type ships of the same basic characteristics. *Benewah* and *Colleton* recommissioned on 28 Jan 1967 for service in Vietnam; *Mercer* and *Nueces* recommissioned in 1968 for service in Vietnam. However, *Colleton* decommissioned in 1969 as US riverine forces in South Vietnam reduced. All others in reserve.
These most-useful ships support the joint Army-Navy Mobile Riverine Force in the Mekong Delta region of South Vietnam (Navy River Assault Flotilla 1/Task Force 117/ River Support Squadron 7). Complement of each ship in this role is 12 officers and 186 enlisted men, and 900 troops and boat crew personnel are carried. These two ships have an armament of two 3 inch guns (single), eight 40 mm guns (two quad mounts), eight ·50 cal MG, and ten ·30 cal MG. They each have troop berthing and messing facilities, evaporators which produce up to 40 000 gallons of fresh water per day, a 16-bed hosiptal, X-ray room, dental room, bacteriological laboratory, pharmacy, laundry, library, and tailor shop; living and most working spaces are air conditioned. Most ships not activated for Vietnam have eight 40 mm AA guns (quad).

DISPOSALS
Sister ships **Accomac** APB 49, **Cameron** APB 50, **Presque Isle** APB 44, **Wythe** APB 41, **Yavapai** APB 42 and **Yola** APB 43, were stricken from the Navy List in 1959, **Blackford** APB 45 (ex-AKS 16, ex-LST 1111) in 1960, and **Marlboro** APB 38, on 1 Dec 1963.
The barracks ship **Dupage** APB 51 (ex-SS *John R. Weeks*), converted "Liberty" type merchant vessel, was stricken on 1 June 1959.

BENEWAH (APB 35) *1967, United States Navy*

1 REPAIR SHIP (AR): Ex-DESTROYER TENDER

MARKAB (ex-*Mormacpenn*) AR 23 (ex-AD 21, ex-AK 31)

Displacement, tons	8 560 standard; 14 800 full load
Dimensions, feet	465 wl; 492·5 oa × 69·8 × 24·8
Guns	4—3 in, 50 cal AA
Main engines	Geared turbines (General Electric); 1 shaft; 8 500 shp = 18·4 knots
Boilers	2 (Foster-Wheeler)

Built by Ingalls SB Co, Pascagoula, Mass. Launched on 21 Dec 1940; commissioned on 15 June 1941. Former destroyer tender, reclassified as repair ship on 15 Apr 1960 and designation changed from AD to AR. The 5 inch and 4—40 mm guns were removed. The *Markab* is in active service.

MARKAB (AR 23) *United States Navy*

1 REPAIR SHIP (AR): Ex-DESTROYER TENDER

KLONDYKE AR 22 (ex-AD 22)

Displacement, tons	8 165 standard; 16 635 full load
Dimensions, feet	465 wl; 492 oa × 69·5 × 27·2
Guns	2—3 in, 50 cal AA
Main engines	Geared turbines (General Electric); 1 shaft; 8 500 shp = 18·4 knots
Boilers	2 (Babcock & Wilcox)
Complement	Accommodation for 826

Sister ship of "Arcadia" class destroyer tenders, reclassified as a repair ship on 20 Feb 1960 and designation changed from AD 22 to AR 22. Built by Los Angeles Shipbuilding Corp; launched on 12 Aug 1944 and commissioned on 30 July 1945. The *Klondike* is in active service.
Armament reduced: 5 inch gun; two 3 inch guns, 4—40 mm guns removed

KLONDIKE (AR 22) *1965, United States Navy*

2 REPAIR SHIPS (AR): "AMPHION" CLASS

Name	*No.*	*Launched*	*Commissioned*
AMPHION	AR 13	15 May 1945	30 Jan 1946
CADMUS	AR 14	5 Aug 1945	23 Apr 1946

Displacement, tons	7 826 standard; 14 490 full load
Dimensions, feet	456 wl; 492 oa × 70 × 27·5
Guns	2—3 in, 50 cal AA
Main engines	Turbines (Westinghouse); 1 shaft; 8 500 shp = 16.5 knots
Boilers	2 (Foster-Wheeler)
Complement	Accommodation for 921

Built by Tampa Shipbuilding Co. C 3 cargo type. Designed armament was two 5 inch guns and eight 40 mm guns (quad). Both of these ships are active.

CADMUS (AR 14) *A. & J. Pavia*

Fleet Support Ships—*continued*

2 REPAIR SHIPS AR): "DELTA" CLASS

Name	*No.*	*Commissioned*
DELTA (ex-*Hawaiian Packer*)	AR 9 (ex-AK 29)	16 June 1941
BRIAREUS (ex-*Hawaiian Planter*)	AR 12	15 Nov 1943

Displacement, tons	8 975 standard; 14 500 full load
Dimensions, feet	465·5 pp; 490·5 oa × 69·5 × 24·3
Guns	4—3 in, 50 cal AA
Main engines	Geared turbines; 8 500 shp = 17 knots
Boilers	2 Foster-Wheeler and 2 Babcock & Wilcox, respectively

Both launched in 1941. C 3 type. The 5 inch and 4—40 mm guns were removed. *Delta* is active; the *Briareus* was decommissioned and placed in reserve in Sep 1955.

NOMENCLATURE. Repair ships generally are named after mythological characters.

DELTA (AR 9) *United States Navy*

4 REPAIR SHIPS (AR): "VULCAN" CLASS

Name	*No.*	*Launched*	*Commissioned*
VULCAN	AR 5	14 Dec 1940	16 June 1941
AJAX	AR 6	22 Aug 1942	30 Oct 1942
HECTOR	AR 7	11 Nov 1942	7 Feb 1944
JASON	AR 8	3 Apr 1943	19 June 1944

Displacement, tons	9 140 standard; 16 200 full load
Dimensions, feet	520 wl; 529·3 oa × 73·3 × 23·3
Guns	4—5 in, 38 cal dp
Main engines	Geared turbines; 2 shafts; 11 000 shp = 19·2 knots
Boilers	4 (Babcock & Wilcox 3-drum)
Complement	950

Vulcan was built by New York SB Corpn under the 1939 programme and the other three by Los Angeles SB & DD Corpn under the 1940 Programme. All carry a most elaborate equipment of machine tools to undertake repairs of every description. *Jason*, originally designated ARH 1 and rated as heavy hull repair ship, was reclassified AR 8 on 9 Sep 1957. Eight 40 mm AA guns (twin) have been removed.
All of these ships are active.

JASON (AR 8) *United States Navy*

HECTOR (AR 7) *United States Navy*

1 ENGINE REPAIR SHIP (ARG): "LIBERTY" TYPE

TUTUILA (ex-*Arthur P. Gorman*) ARG 4

Displacement, tons	5 766 standard; 14 350 full load
Dimensions, feet	416 wl; 441·5 oa × 57 × 23
Guns	3—3 in, 50 cal AA
Main engines	Triple expansion (General Machinery Corp); 1 shaft; 2 500 hp = 12·5 knots
Boilers	2 (Babcock & Wilcox)

Liberty ship. "EC 2" type. Built by Bethlehem Steel Co, Fairfield Yard Baltimore, Md. Launched on 12 Sep 1943; commissioned on 8 Apr 1944. Armament reduced with removal of 5 inch gun and four 40 mm guns (twin). The *Tutuila* is active.

DISPOSALS
Oglala ARG 1 (ex-CM 4), **Beaver** ARG 19 (ex-AS 5), and **Otus** ARG 20 (ex-A 20) stricken after World War II. **Luzon** ARG 2, **Mindanao** ARG 3 **Oahu** ARG 5, **Cebu** ARG 6, **Culebra Island** ARG 7, **Mavi** ARG 8, **Mona Island** ARG 9, **Palawan** ARG 10, **Samar** ARG 11, **Chourre** ARV 1 (ex-ARG 14), **Webster** ARV 2 (ex-ARG 15), **Kermit Roosevelt** ARG 16, **Hooper Island** ARG 17 all stricken from Navy List between 1959-1963. (ARG 12 and ARG 13 to AG 68 and AG 69 respectively).

TUTUILA (ARG 4) *United States Navy*

18 REPAIR SHIPS: CONVERTED LST TYPE

(Battle damage Repair Ships)

ZEUS	ARB 4 (ex-LST 132)	**SARPEDON**	ARB 7 (ex-LST 956)
MIDAS	ARB 5 (ex-LST 524)	**TELAMON**	ARB 8 (ex-LST 957)

(Landing Craft Repair Ships)

ACHELOUS	ARL 1 (ex-LST 10)	**SATYR**	ARL 23 (ex-LST 852)
AMYCUS	ARL 2 (ex-LST 489)	**SPHINX**	ARL 24 (ex-LST 963)
ATLAS	ARL 7 (ex-LST 231)	**ASKARI**	ARL 30 (ex-LST 1131)
EGERIA	ARL 8 (ex-LST 136)	**BELLEROPHON**	ARL 31 (ex-LST 1132)
ENDYMION	ARL 9 (ex-LST 513)	**INDRA**	ARL 37 (ex-LST 1147)
		KRISHNA	ARL 38 (ex-LST 1149)

(Aircraft Repair Ships — Aircraft)

FABIUS	ARVA 5 (ex-LST 1093)	**MEGARA**	ARVA 6 (ex-LST 1095)

(Aircraft Repair Ship — Engine)

CHLORIS ARVE 4 (ex-LST 1094

Displacement, tons	1 625 light; 4 100 full load
Dimensions, feet	316 wl; 328 oa × 50 × 11
Guns	8—40 mm AA (quad)
Main engines	Diesels (General Motors); 2 shafts; 1 800 bhp = 11·6 knots
Complement	251 to 286 (see notes)

All launched in 1942-1945.

Indra, *Askari*, *Satyr*, and *Sphinx* activated for service in Vietnam; all others except *Krishna* are in reserve. Photographs show *Askari* in Mekong Delta, South Vietnam, servicing small craft of River Flotilla One. Note LST stern anchor, topside clutter of parts and stores, crane for lifting riverine craft, tripod lattice mast.

TRANSFERS. *Agenor* ARL 3 (ex-LST 490) to France on 2 Mar 1951, *Patrolcus* ARL 19 (ex-LST 955) to Turkey in 1952, *Minotaur* ARL 15 (ex-LST 645) to Korea on 3 Oct 1955, *Romulus* ARL 22, to Philippines in 1961, *Diomedes* ARB 11 and *Ulyssss* ARB 9, to West Germany in June 1961, *Gordius* ARL 36 to Iran in Sep 1961, *Hellas* ARB 12 to Brazil in Jan 1962, *Quirinus* ARL 39 (ex-LST 1151) to Venezuela in June 1962, *Aventinus* ARVE 3 (ex-LST 1092) to Chile in 1963.

DISPOSALS
Demeter ARB 10 (ex-LST 1121), was stricken from the list on 1 Mar 1959, **Adonis** ARL 4, **Daedalus** ARL 35, **Minos** ARL 14, **Pentheus** ARL 20 and **Proserpine** ARL 21, **Crean** ARL 11, **Menelaus** ARL 13, **Myrmidon** ARL 16, **Numitar** ARL 17, **Stentor** ARL 26 and **Typhoon** ARL 28 in 1960, **Amphritrite** ARL 29, **Aristaeus** ARB 1, **Chimaera** ARL 33, **Caronis** ARL 10, **Oceanus** ARB 2, **Phaon** ARB 3, and **Poseidon** ARL 12 on 1 July 1961, **Pandemus** ARL 18 stricken on 1 Oct 1968.

ASKARI (ARL 30) *1967, United States Navy*

Fleet Support Ships—*continued*

ASKARI (ARL 30) *1967, United States Navy*

13 SALVAGE SHIPS (ARS): "DIVER" CLASS

Name	*No*	*Launched*	*Commissioned*
ESCAPE	ARS 6	22 Nov 1942	20 Nov 1943
GRAPPLE	ARS 7	31 Dec 1942	16 Dec 1943
PRESERVER	ARS 8	1 Apr 1943	11 Jan 1944
CURRENT	ARS 22	25 Sep 1943	14 June 1944
DELIVER	ARS 23	25 Sep 1943	18 July 1944
GRASP	ARS 24	31 July 1943	22 Aug 1944
SAFEGUARD	ARS 25	20 Nov 1943	31 Oct 1944
BOLSTER	ARS 38	23 Dec 1944	1 May 1945
CONSERVER	ARS 39	27 Jan 1945	9 June 1945
HOIST	ARS 40	31 Mar 1945	21 July 1945
OPPORTUNE	ARS 41	31 Mar 1945	5 Oct 1945
RECLAIMER	ARS 42	25 June 1945	20 Dec 1945
RECOVERY	ARS 43	4 Aug 1945	15 May 1946

Displacement, tons	1 530 standard; 1 900 full load
Dimensions, feet	207 wl; 213·5 oa × 39 × 43 × 13
Guns	1—40 mm AA; 2—·50 cal MG
Main engines	Diesel-electric; 2 shafts; 2 440 shp = 14 knots
Complement	85

These ships are fitted for salvage and towing; equipped with compressed air diving facilities. Note position of 40 mm gun forward of funnel. 20 ton and 10 ton capacity booms.
Built by Basalt Rock Co. *Cable* ARS 19, *Curb* ARS 21 and *Gear* ARS 34 are on loan to private operators; they remain on the Navy List and support naval requirements as needed. All others are active with Navy crews.

Chain and *Snatch* were converted into Oceanographic Research Ships in 1958-1960. *Chain* ARS 20, converted by the Savannah Machine & Foundry, was assigned to the Woods Hole Oceanographic Institute by the Office of Naval Research (now AGOR 17). *Snatch* ARS 27 converted by Puget Sound Bridge and Drydock Co was assigned to the Scripps Institution of Oceanography by the ONR.

Clamp (ex-*Atlantic Salvor*) ARS 33 was stricken in July 1963.

NOMENCLATURE. Salvage ships are named for words relating to salvage activities.

GRASP (ARS 24) *1967, United States Navy*

2 SALVAGE LIFTING SHIPS (ARSD): CONVERTED LSM

GYPSY ARSD 1 (ex-*LSM* 549) **MENDER** ARSD 2 (ex-*LSM* 550)

Displacement, tons	740 standard; 1 095 full load
Dimensions, feet	224·2 × 34 × 7
Guns	2—20 mm AA
Main engines	Diesel; 2 shafts; 2 800 bhp = 13 knots
Complement	65.

Used as diving tenders. Both launched on 7 Dec 1945. In the Pacific Reserve Fleet. Sister ships *Salvager* (ex-LSM 551) ARSD 3 and *Windlass* (ex-LSM 552) ARSD 4 were reclassified as YMLC 3 and YMLC 4, respectively, on 1 Nov 1967; they are no longer self-propelled.

2 SALVAGE TENDERS (ARST): CONVERTED LST

LAYSAN ISLAND ARST 1 (ex-*LST* 1098) **PALMYRA** ARST 3 (ex-*LST* 1100)

Displacement, tons	1 653 standard; 4 080 full load
Dimensions, feet	328 × 50 × 11; 14·3 max
Main engines	Diesel; 2 shafts; 1 800 bhp = 11 knots

Former Tank Landing Ships. Out of commission, in reserve.

2 SUBMARINE TENDERS (AS): NEW CONSTRUCTION

Name	*No*	*Laid down*	*Launched*	*Commission*
L. Y. SPEAR	AS 36	5 May 1966	7 Sep 1968	early 1970
DIXON	AS 37	7 Sep 1967	Nov 1969	early 1971

Displacement, tons	13 000 standard; 22 640 full load
Dimensions, feet	643 × 85
Guns	2—5 in

Both ships built by General Dynamics Corp, Quincy, Massachusetts. *L. Y. Spear* authorised in Fiscal Year 1965 new construction programme; *Dixon* in FY 1966 programme. AS 38 of FY 1969 programme was cancelled on 27 Mar 1969 to provide funds for overruns in FY 1969 and FY 1970 programmes (estimated saving was $68 600 000.
These ships are especially equipped to support and replenish nuclear-powered attack submarines, providing alongside services to as many as four submarines simultaneously.

NOMENCLATURE. Submarine tenders generally are named after pioneers in submarine development and mythological characters. Howard W. Gilmore was a submarine commander who lost his life in World War II (subsequently awarded Medal of Honour).

2 SUBMARINE TENDERS (AS): "SIMON LAKE" CLASS

Name	*No.*	*Laid down*	*Launched*	*Commissioned*
SIMON LAKE	AS 33	7 Jan 1963	8 Feb 1964	7 Nov 1964
CANOPUS	AS 34	2 Mar 1964	12 Feb 1965	4 Nov 1965

Displacement, tons	21 450 to 22 250 full load
Dimensions, feet	643·7 × 85 × 30
Guns	4—3 in, 50 cal AA (twin)
Main engines	Steam turbines; 1 shaft; 20 000 hp = 18 knots
Boilers	2 (Combustion Engineering)
Complement	1 075 (55 officers, 1 020 men)

These ships are designed specifically to service Fleet Ballistic Missile Submarines (SSBM), with as many as three submarines alongside being supported simultaneously. The *Simon Lake* was authorised in the Fiscal Year 1963 new construction programme and built by the Puget Sound Naval Shipyard; the *Canopus* was authorised in FY 1964 and built by Ingalls Shipbuilding Corp. AS 35 was authorised in FY 1965 programme, but her construction was deferred. The last ship would have permitted one tender to be assigned to each of five FBM submarine squadrons with a sixth ship available to rotate when another was in overhaul; however, only four SSBN squadrons were established. All serve as squadron flagships.
Note cranes amidships, funnel location (flanked by gun mounts, and helicopter platform); stern anchor resembles LST arrangement.

CANOPUS (AS 34) *1965, United States Navy*

SIMON LAKE (AS 33) *1965 United States Navy*

Fleet Support Ships—*continued*

2 SUBMARINE TENDERS (AS): "HUNLEY" CLASS

Name	*No.*	*Laid down*	*Launched*	*Commissioned*
HUNLEY	AS 31	28 Nov 1960	28 Sep 1961	16 June 1962
HOLLAND	AS 32	5 Mar 1962	19 Jan 1963	7 Sep 1963

Displacement, tons	10 500 standard; 18 300 full load
Dimensions, feet	599 × 83 × 24
Guns	4—3 in, 50 cal, AA (twin)
Main engines	Diesel-electric (10 Fairbanks-Morse diesels); 1 shaft; 15 000 bhp = 19 knots
Complement	1 081 (58 officers, 1 023 men) plus accommodation for 30 officers and 270 men from submarines

Tenders for serving FBM submarines. *Hunley* was authorised in the Fiscal Year 1960 new construction programme and built by Newport News Shipbuilding & Drydock Co, Newport, Virginia. She provides weapon and nuclear logistic support for ballistic missile submarines. A large hammerhead crane of 32 ton capacity with athwartships bridge travel, the first of its kind aboard a ship, is installed to on and off missiles from submarines. *Holland* was authorised under the 1962 programme and built by Ingalls Shipbuilding Corp for $24 359 800. Equipped with 52 workshops and a helicopter platform. Note amidships funnel position compared to later class of FBM submarine tenders.

NOMENCLATURE. *Holland* is named after John Philip Holland, an Irish emigrant to the United States, who became "the father of the submarine". One of his submarines was accepted by the US Navy in 1900 and became Submarine Torpedo Boat No 1, named *Holland*, the first successful Navy submarine.

HUNLEY (AS 31) *United States Navy*

HUNLEY (AS 31) *United States Navy*

1 SUBMARINE TENDER (AS): "AEGIR" CLASS

AEGIR AS 23

Displacement, tons	8 100 standard; 16 100 full load
Dimensions, feet	492 oa × 69·5 × 26·5
Guns	1—5 in, 38 cal; 4—3 in, 50 cal AA
Main engines	Geared turbines (Westinghouse); 1 shaft; 8 500 shp = 14·4 knots
Boilers	2 (Foster-Wheeler "D")
Complement	1 460 (82 officers, 1 378 enlisted men)

Launched in 1943 and commissioned on 8 Sep 1944. Built by Ingalls Shipbuilding Corp. CS-3-A2 type. Accommodation, headquarters and berthing ship for the San Diego reserve group.

DISPOSALS

Of three sister ships, **Anthedon**, AS 24 and **Clytle** AS 26 were stricken from the Navy List on 1 Sep 1961, and **Apollo** AS 25, transferred to the Maritime Administration in 1963, was stricken in 1964. **Anthedon** transferred to Turkey on 7 Feb 1969.

1 SUBMARINE TENDER (AS): "EURYALE" CLASS

EURYALE (ex-SS *Hawaiian Merchant*) AS 22

Displacement, tons	8 282 standard; 15 400 full load
Dimensions, feet	492·5 oa × 69·5 × 25
Guns	1—5 in, 38 cal; 4—3 in, 50 cal AA
Main engines	Geared turbines (De Laval); 1 shaft; 8 500 shp = 16·5 knots
Boilers	2 (Foster-Wheeler "D")
Complement	1 304 (90 officers, 1 313 enlisted men)

Launched in 1941 and commissioned on 2 Dec 1943. Built by Federal SB & DD Co, Kearny, New Jersey. Modified C3 type. In the Pacific Reserve Fleet as Headquarters ship at Bermerton, Wash.

2 SUBMARINE TENDERS (AS): "GRIFFIN" CLASS

Name	*No.*	*Launched*	*Commissioned*
GRIFFIN (ex-*Marmacpenn*)	AS 13	10 Nov 1939	31 July 1941
PELIAS (ex-*Mormacyork*)	AS 14	14 Nov 1939	5 Sep 1941

Displacement, tons	8 600 standard; 14 500 full load
Dimensions, feet	492 × 69·5 × 24·2
Guns	4—3 in, 50 cal AA
Main engines	Diesel (Busch-Sulzer); 1 shaft; 8 500 bhp = 16·5 knots
Complement	1 511 and 1 067 respectively

C3 Cargo type. Built by Sun SB & DD Co, Chester, Pennsylvania. Both in the Pacific Reserve Fleet. *Pelias* is Accommodation/Berthing ship at Mare Island, California.

7 SUBMARINE TENDERS (AS): "FULTON" CLASS

Name	*No.*	*Launched*	*Commissioned*
FULTON	AS 11	27 Dec 1940	12 Sep 1941
SPERRY	AS 12	17 Dec 1941	1 May 1942
BUSHNELL	AS 15	14 Sep 1942	10 Apr 1943
HOWARD W. GILMORE (ex-*Neptune*)	AS 16	16 Sep 1943	24 May 1944
NEREUS	AS 17	12 Feb 1945	27 Oct 1945
ORION	AS 18	14 Oct 1942	30 Sep 1943
PROTEUS	AS 19	12 Nov 1942	31 Jan 1944

Displacement, tons	9 734 standard; 18 000 full load *Proteus:* 10 234 standard; 18 500 full load
Dimensions, feet	530·5; *Proteus* 574·5 oa × 73·3 × 25·5
Guns	2—5 in, 38 cal (one gun in *Proteus*)
Main engines	11 200 bhp = 15·4 knots
Complement	approx 1 300

Ships vary in detail. *Orion* and *Proteus* built by Moore Dry Dock Co, Oakland, California, others by Mare Island Navy Yard, California. Each ship has two 20 ton capacity booms, except *Proteus*.

CONVERSION. *Proteus*, AS 19 was converted at the Charleston Naval Shipyard, under the Fiscal Year 1959 conversion programme, at a cost of $23 000 000 to service nuclear powered Fleet Ballistic Missile Submarine (SSBN) squadron. Conversion was started on 19 Jan 1959 and she was recommissioned on 8 July 1960. She was lengthened by adding a section amidships 44 feet in length, and the bare hull weight of this 6-deck high insertion was approximately 500 tons. Three 5 inch guns were removed and her upper decks extended aft to provide additional workshops.

MODERNISATION. *Bushnell, Fulton, Howard W. Gilmore, Nereus, Orion* and *Sperry* have undergone FRAM II modernisation to service nuclear powered attack submarines. Additional maintenance shops provided to service nuclear plant components and advanced electronic equipment and weapons. After two 5 inch guns and eight 40 mm guns (twin) removed.

FULTON (AS 11) *1965, United States Navy*

SPERRY (AS 12) *United States Navy*

PROTEUS (AS 19) *United States Navy*

Fleet Support Ships—*continued*

2 SUBMARINE RESCUE SHIPS (ASR): NEW CONSTRUCTION

Name	*No.*	*Builder*	*Launch*	*Commission*
PIGEON	ASR 21	Alabama DD & SB Co (Mobile)	Sep 1969	late 1970
ORTOLAN	**ASR 22**	Alabama DD & XB Co (Mobile)	Nov 1969	early 1971

Displacement, tons 3 411 full load
Dimensions, feet 251 oa × 86 (see *Design* notes)
Guns 2—3 in (*76 mm*) 50 cal AA; 4—·50 cal MG
Main engines 4 diesels; 6 000 shp; 2 shafts = 15 knots
Complement 115 (6 officers, 109 enlisted men)
Staff accommodation 14 (4 officers, 10 enlisted men)
Submersible operators 24 (4 officers, 20 enlisted men)

These are the world's first ships designed specifically for this role, all other ASR designs being adaptations of tug types. The ASR 21 class ships will serve as (1) surface support ships for the Deep Submergence Rescue Vehicles (DSRV), (2) rescue ships employing the existing McCann rescue chamber, (3) major deep-sea diving support ships, and (4) operational control ships for salvage operations.
The Navy has announced plans to replace the current 10-ship ASR force with new construction ASRs. ASR 21 authorised in Fiscal Year 1967 new construction programme; ASR 22 in FY 1968 programme. Estimated cost per ship is approximately $17 000 000.

DESIGN. These ships will have twin, catamaran hulls, the first ocean-going catamaran ships to be built for the US Navy since Robert Fulton's steam gunboat *Demologus* of 1812. The design will provide a large deck working area, facilities for raising and lowering submersibles and underwater equipment and improved stability when operating equipment at great depths. Each of the twin hulls is 251 feet long and 26 feet wide. The well between the hulls will be 34 feet across, giving the ASR a maximum beam of 86 feet. Fitted with helicopter platform.

ENGINEERING. Space and weight are reserved for future installation of a ducted thruster in each bow to enable the ship to maintain precise position while stopped or at slow speeds.

ELECTRONICS. Fitted with precision three-dimensional sonar system for tracking submersibles.

DIVING. These ships will be fitted with the Mk 2 Deep Diving System to support conventional or saturation divers operating at depths to 850 feet. The system consists of two decompression chambers, two personnel transfer capsules to transport divers between the ship and ocean floor, and the associated controls, winches, cables, gas supplies, *et cetera*. Submarine rescue ships are the US Navy's primary diving ships and the only ones fitted for helium-oxygen diving.

SALVAGE. During major salvage operations the ASR can carry a mobile Salvage Operational Control Centre (SOCC) which will serve as a command post for the salvage master. Equipment in the SOCC will provide data on the position of the object being raised, the lift pontoons, divers, and other components of the operation. A computer will calculate the force required to break ocean-floor suction on the object and the necessary lift forces for each stage of the operation.

SUBMERSIBLES. Each ASR will be capable of transporting, servicing, lowering, and raising two Deep Submergence Rescue Vehicles (DSRV) (see section on Deep Submergence Vehicles).

NOMENCLATURE. Submarine rescue ships traditionally have carried bird names (the US Navy's first six ARSs were converted "Bird" class minesweepers).

ASR 21 *Official Navy Drawing*

2 SUBMARINE RESCUE SHIPS (ASR): "PENGUIN" CLASS

Name	*No.*	*Launched*
PENGUIN (ex-*Chetco*)	ASR 12 (ex-AT 99)	20 July 1943
SKYLARK (ex-*Yustaga*)	ASR 20 (ex-AFT 165)	19 Mar 1946

Displacement, tons 1 235 standard; 1 740 full load
Dimensions, feet 195 wl; 205 oa × 38·5 × 15·3
Main engines Diesel-electric (Busch-Sulzer diesels in *Penguin*, General Motors in *Skylark*); 1 shaft; 3 000 bhp = 14 knots
Complement 85

Former fleet tugs, converted in 1947. Built by Charleston SB & DD Co, Charleston, SC. *Bluebird* ASR 19 of this type was transferred to Turkey on 15 Aug 1950. These ships are equipped with powerful pumps, heavy air compressors, and submarine rescue chambers. Fitted for helium-oxygen diving. Guns removed; formerly armed with one 3 inch gun. See "Chanticleer" class for additional notes applicable to this class.

8 SUBMARINE RESCUE SHIPS (ASR): "CHANTICLEER" CLASS

	ASR	*Launched*		ASR	*Launched*
CHANTICLEER	7	29 May 1942	**KITTIWAKE**	13	10 July 1945
COUCAL	8	29 May 1942	**PETREL**	14	26 Sep 1945
FLORIKAN	9	14 June 1942	**SUNBIRD**	15	3 Apr 1945
GREENLET	10	12 July 1942	**TRINGA**	16	25 June 1945

Displacement, tons 1 653 standard; 2 290 full load
Dimensions, feet 240 wl; 251·5 oa × 42 × 14·9
Main engines Diesel-electric (Alco in first 4 ships, GM in others); 1 shaft; 3 000 bhp = 14·9 knots
Complement 85

ASR 7-10 built by Moore SB & DD Co, Oakland, California; and ASR 13-16 by Savannah Machine & Foundry Co, Georgia. All equipped with powerful pumps, heavy air compressors and submarine rescue chambers. Fitted for helium-oxygen diving. Guns removed 1957-1958. Built with two 3 inch guns. All are active; one ship normally deployed to Western Pacific, one to Mediterranean, with others at US submarine bases. Note mooring buoys ("spuds") alongside funnels and anchors forward and aft for laying four-point moor required for salvage and rescue operations. ARSs have diver "fish" symbol on bow.

FLORIKAN (ASR 9) *1966, United States Navy*

TRINGA (ASR 16) *1966, United States Navy*

17 AUXILIARY TUGS (ATA): "MARICOPA" CLASS

	ATA	*Launched*		ATA	*Launched*
ACCOKEEK	181	27 July 1944	**STALLION**	193	24 Nov 1944
KALMIA	184	29 Aug 1944	**TATNUCK**	195	14 Dec 1944
KOKA	185	11 Sep 1944	**MAHOPAC**	196	21 Dec 1944
CAHOKIA	186	18 Sep 1944	**SUNNADIN**	197	6 Jan 1945
SALISH	187	29 Sep 1944	**WANDANK**	206	9 Nov 1944
PENOBSCOT	188	12 Oct 1944	**SAGAMORE**	208	19 Jan 1945
SAMOSET	190	26 Oct 1944	**UMPQUA**	209	2 Feb 1945
TILLAMOOK	192	15 Nov 1944	**CATAWBA**	210	15 Feb 1945
			KEYWADIN	213	9 Apr 1945

Displacement, tons 534 standard; 835 full load
Dimensions, feet 134·5 wl; 143 oa × 33·9 × 13
Guns 1—3 in, 50 cal
Main engines 2 GM diesel-electric; 1 shaft; 1 500 bhp = 13 knots
Complement 45 (5 officers, 40 men)

Formerly designated Rescue Tugs (ATR). *Bagaduce* ATA 194 was transferred to the US Coast Guard in 1959, and *Wampanoag* ATA 202 in 1959, *Algorma* ATA 212, *Challenge* ATA 201, *Geronimo* ATA 207, *Iuka* ATA 123, *Navajo* ATA 211, *Navigator* ATA 203, *Nottoway* ATA 183, *Reindeer* ATA 189, *Sciota* ATA 205, *Sonoma* ATA 175, *Tunica* ATA 178, *Tuscarora* ATA 245, (ex-YTB 341), *Unadilla* ATA 182 and *Undanted* ATA 199, to the Maritime Administration National Defence Reserve Fleet in 1962. *Wateree* ATA 174 to Peru in Nov 1961. *Keosanqua* ATA 198 and *Pinola* ATA 206 to Korea on 1 Feb 1962. *Tankowa* ATA 176 to Taiwan China on 5 Apr 1962, *Geromino* ATA 207 to US Fish and Wild Life Service, *Sotoyomo* ATA 121, to Mexico in July 1963. *Undaunted* ATA 199 to Bureau of Commercial Fisheries in July 1964, *Geronimo* transferred from MarAd to Taiwan China in 1968.
Allagheny ATA 179, employed in oceanographic research for Office of Naval Reserach, **was stricken on 14 Dec 1968. All in active service.**

Fire Support Ships—*continued*

TILLAMOOK (ATA 192) *1965, United States Navy*

1 AUXILIARY TUG (ATA): Ex-US ARMY

ATA 240 (ex-US Army *LT* 455)

Displacement, tons	534 standard; 835 full load
Dimensions, feet	143 oa × 33·3 × 13·9 max
Main engines	Diesel-electric; 1 500 bhp = 13 knots

ATA 240 is out of commission, in reserve.
T-ATA 239 (ex-LT 532) was returned to US Army. T-ATA 244 (ex-LT 156) was stricken on 1 Nov 1959. T-ATA 241 (ex-LT 60), T-ATA 242 (ex-LT 132) and T-ATA 243 (ex-LT 646) were transferred to Maritime Administration in 1962.

ATAKAPA (ATF 149) *1967, United States Navy*

30 FLEET TUGS (ATF): "APACHE" CLASS

	ATF	Launched		ATF	Launched
ABNAKI	96	22 Apr 1943	**MUNSEE**	107	21 Jan 1943
APACHE	67	8 May 1942	**NIPMUC**	157	12 Apr 1945
ARIKARA	98	22 June 1943	**PAKANA**	108	3 Mar 1943
ATAKAPA	149	11 July 1944	**PAIUTE**	159	4 June 1945
CHOWANOC	100	20 Aug 1943	**PAPAGO**	160	21 June 1945
COCOPA	101	5 Oct 1943	**QUAPAW**	110	15 May 1943
CREE	84	17 Aug 1942	**SALINAN**	161	20 July 1945
HITCHITI	103	29 Jan 1944	**SENECA**	91	2 Feb 1943
KIOWA	72	5 Nov 1942	**SHAKORI**	162	9 Aug 1945
LIPAN	85	17 Sep 1942	**SIOUX**	75	27 May 1942
LUISENO	156	17 Mar 1945	**TAKELMA**	113	18 Sep 1943
MATACO	86	14 Oct 1942	**TAWAKONI**	114	28 Oct 1943
MOCTOBI	105	25 Mar 1944	**TAWASA**	92	22 Feb 1943
MOLALA	106	23 Dec 1942	**UTE**	76	24 June 1942
MOSOSPELEA	158	7 Mar 1945	**UTINA**	163	31 Aug 1945

Displacement, tons	1 235 standard; 1 675 full load
Dimensions, feet	195 wl; 205 oa × 38·5 × 15·5 max
Guns	1—3 in, 50 cal dp
Main engines	Diesel-electric drive; 1 shaft; 3 000 bhp = 15 knots
Complement	85 (5 officers, 80 enlisted men)

Launch dates above. Fitted with powerful pumps and other salvage equipment. *Wateree* ATF 117 lost, *Sarsi* ATF 111 sank after striking a mine off Korea, 22 Aug 1952. *Chippewa* ATF 69, *Moreno* ATF 87, *Narragansett* ATF 88, *Achomawl* ATF 148, *Alsea* ATF 97, *Pawnee* ATF 74, *Tenino* ATF 115 and *Wenatchee* ATF 118 were stricken in 1961 and *Carib* ATF 82, *Chawasha* ATF 181, *Chimariko* ATF 154, *Hidatsa* ATF 102, *Hopi* ATF 71, *Ilcarlla* ATF 104, and *Pakana* ATF 108 in 1963. *Avoyel* ATF 150 and *Chilula* ATF 152 were transferred to the Coast Guard in 1956. *Serrano* ATF 112 was reclassified as surveying ship, AGS 24. *Chetco* ATF 99, *Yurok* ATF 164, *Yustaga* ATF 165 converted to submarine rescue ships ASR 12, 19, 20. *Yuma* ATF 94 was transferred to Pakistan on 25 Mar 1959. *Tekesta* ATF 93 to Chile in 1960, *Cusabo* ATF 155 to Ecuador in 1960, *Choctaw* AFT 70 to Columbia in 1961, *Menominee* ATF 73 to Indonesia in 1961, *Pinto* AFT 90 to Peru in 1961, *Arapaho* ATF 68 and *Cahuilla* ATF 152 to Argentina in 1961, *Tolowa* ATF 116 to Venezuela in Feb 1962, *Potawatomi* ATF 109 to Chile in 1963, *Bannock* ATF 81 to Italy in 1954, *Chickasaw* ATF 83, to Taiwan China in 1966. *Pakana* reinstated on Navy List in 1967.
All remaining ships are active.
Note electronic equipment fitted to *Atakapa's* tripod mast.

NOMENCLATURE. US tugs of World War II construction and previous classes were named for Indian tribes and words.

MOSOPELEA (ATF 158) *1968, United States Navy*

3 SALVAGE TUGS (ATS): NEW CONSTRUCTION

Name	*No.*	*Laid down*	*Launched*	*Commission*
EDENTON	ATS 1	1 Apr 1967	15 May 1968	Sep 1969
BEAUFORT	ATS 2	19 Feb 1968	20 Dec 1968	early 1970
BRUNSWICK	ATS 3	5 June 1968	Apr 1969	early 1970

Displacement, tons	2 650 full load
Dimensions, feet	232·6 × 50 × 14·5
Main engines	4 diesels; 6 000 shp; 2 shafts = 16 knots

These tugs are designed specifically for salvage operations and will be capable of (1) ocean towing, (2) supporting diver operations to depths of 850 feet, (3) lifting submerged objects weighing as much as 600 000 pounds from a depth of 120 feet, (4) fighting ship fires, and (5) performing general salvage operations.
The ATS 1 was authorised in the Fiscal year 1966 shipbuilding programme; ATS 2 and ATS 3 in the FY 1967 programme. All three ships are under construction at Brooke Marine, Lowestoft, England. ATS 4 and ATS 5 planned for FY 1970 programme were deferred.

DIVING. These ships can carry the air-transportable Mk 1 Deep Diving System to support four divers working in two-man shifts at depths of 850 feet. The system consists of a double-chamber decompression chamber, a personnel transfer capsule to transport divers between the ships and ocean floor, and the associated controls, winches, cables, gas supplies, *et cetera*. The ships' organic diving capability is compressed air.

ENGINEERING. Fitted with controllable-pitch propellers.

NOMENCLATURE. Salvage tugs are being named for small American cities.

EDENTON (ATS 1) *Artist's concept, photograph by Charles Hodge*

EDENTON (ATS 1) *1968, Ford Jenkins*

Fleet Support Ships—*continued*

1 HELICOPTER REPAIR SHIP (ARVH): CONVERTED SEAPLANE TENDER

CORPUS CHRISTI BAY (ex-*Albermarle*) T-ARVH 1 (ex-AV 5)

Displacement, tons	8 671 standard; 13 475 full load
Length, feet (*metres*)	508 (*154·8*) wl; 537 (*163·7*) oa
Beam, feet (*metres*)	69·2 (*21·1*)
Draft, feet (*metres*)	21·3 (*6·5*)
Main engines	Geared turbines (Parsons); 12 000 shp; 2 shafts
Boilers	4 (Babcock & Wilcox)
Speed, knots	19·7
Complement	128 (22 officers, 106 men) plus 400 Army personnel

Built as a large seaplane tender by the New York Shipbuilding Corp, Camden, New Jersey, under the Fiscal Year 1937 shipbuilding Programme; laid down on 12 June 1939, launched on 13 July 1940, commissioned on 20 Dec 1940. She was modernised in 1956-1957 and subsequently converted to a helicopter repair ship in 1964-1965 (see *Conversion* notes).

DESIGN. As built the *Albermarle* and her sister ship *Curtiss* (AV 4) resembled the "Curritück" class configuration, but with twin funnels. Both of these large seaplane tender designs provided extensive maintenance shops and spare parts, munition, and petrol stowage to support seaplane squadrons; space provided for squadron flight crews and Fleet Air Wing staff; aircraft hangar amidships, open deck aft, and two large aircraft cranes (20-ton capacity in "Curtiss" class; 30-ton capacity in "Currituck" class). As built the *Albermarle* had an armament of 4 5 inch DP guns and 16 40 mm AA guns.

STATUS. The *Corpus Christi Bay* is in service, operated by the Military Sea Transportation Service and manned by a civilian operating crew and army helicopter maintenance battalion.

CONVERSION. The *Albermerle* was converted under the Fiscal Year 1956 programme at the Philadelphia Naval Shipyard to support the P6M Seamaster jet-propelled seaplane. Recommissioned on 21 Oct 1957. Decommissioned in 1960 and placed in the Maritime Administration Reserve Fleet. Stricken from the Navy List in Sep 1962. Reacquired by the Navy in Aug 1964 for conversion to a helicopter repair ship.
The *Albermarle* was converted to an aircraft repair ship (helicopter) at the Charleston Naval Shipyard in 1964-1965; fitted with 33 maintenance shops specialising in helicopter repairs, closed-circuit television provided for rapid transmission of drawings and blueprints from central technical library, automatic boiler controls to reduce operating crew, flight control tower (installed on flying bridge), and improved habitability features; amidships hangar structure extended aft and topped with a 50 × 150 ft helicopter platform with four-part steel hatch to permit helicopters to be lowered into hangars; two 20-ton capacity cranes installed aft of second funnel; smaller helicopter deck installed forward. All armament removed. Renamed *Corpus Christi Bay* and designated T-ARVH 1 on 27 Mar 1965. Deployed to South Vietnam to repair Army light fixed-wing aircraft and helicopters.

DISPOSALS

The **Curtiss** (AV 4) was stricken from the Navy List and transferred to the Maritime Administration in 1963. (She was modified for scientific work in 1951 and subsequently served mainly in support of Atomic Energy Commission experiments until decommissioned in Sep 1957).
For disposals of the "Kenneth Whiting" and "Tangier" classes of seaplanes tender see the 1966-1967 and earlier editions.

CORPUS CHRISTI BAY (T-ARUH 1) — *US Navy (MSTS)*

CORPUS CHRISTI BAY (T-ARUH 1) — *US Navy (MSTS)*

3 SEAPLANE TENDERS (AV): "CURRITUCK" CLASS

Name	*No.*	*Launched*	*Commissioned*
CURRITUCK	AV 7	11 Sep 1943	6 June 1944
PINE ISLAND	AV 12	26 Feb 1944	26 Apr 1945
SALISBURY SOUND (ex-*Puget Sound*)	AV 13	18 June 1944	26 Nov 1945

Displacement, tons	9 106 standard; 15 092 full load
Length, feet (*metres*)	520 (*158·5*) wl; 540·4 (*164·7*) oa
Beam, feet (*metres*)	69·2 (21·1)
Draft, feet (*metres*)	26 (*7·9*)
Guns	4—5 in (*127 mm*) 38 cal DP
Main engines	Geared turbines (Parsons in *Currituck*; Allis Chalmers in others); 12 000 shp; 2 shafts;
Boilers	4 (Babcock & Wilcox)
Speed, knots	19·2
Complement	approx 555 (30 officers, 525 enlisted men, peacetime; designed wartime complement was 1 247—162 officers, 1 085 enlisted men)

The *Currituck* was built by the New York Shipbuilding Corp, Camden, New Jersey; *Pine Island* and *Salisbury Sound* by Todd Shipyards Corp, San Pedro, California; A fourth ship of this class, the *Norton Sound* (ex-AV 11) serves as a missile test ship (AVM 1). All three ships listed above remain on the Navy List out of commission in reserve, but are assigned to Maritime Administration Reserve Fleets. The *Currituck* was the last to decommission, being placed in "mothballs" in 1967 when the Navy phased out the last P5M Marline seaplane patrol squadron.

ARMAMENT. As built these ships mounted up to 20 40 mm AA guns (four twin, three quad mounts); all removed during post-World War II service.

CONVERSION. The *Currituck* was converted under the Fiscal Year 1957 programme at the Philadelphia Naval Shipyard to support the P6M Seamaster jet-propelled seaplane. Recommissioned on 20 Aug 1960 after the P6M project was cancelled.

PHOTOGRAPH. A P5M Martin patrol plane is shown on the deck of the *Salisbury Sound* in Camranh Bay, South Vietnam. Note 5 inch gun mounts atop aircraft hangar. A broadside view of the *Currituck* is in the 1968-1969 edition, as does a photo of the *Chandeleur*

SALISBURY SOUND (AU13) — *US Navy*

1 SEAPLANE TENDER (AV): "CHANDELEUR" TYPE

CHANDELEUR AV 10

Displacement, tons	9 031 standard; 14 200 full load
Length, feet (*metres*)	492 (*000·0*) oa
Beam, feet (*metres*)	69·5 (*00·0*)
Draft, feet (*metres*)	23·8 (*00·0*)
Guns	1—5 in (*127 mm*) 38 cal DP; 4—3 in (*76 mm*) 50 cal A
Main engines	Geared turbines (General Electric); 8 500 shp; 1 shaft
Boilers	2 (Foster-Wheeler)
Speed	18·4 knots
Complement	1 075 (120 officers, 955 enlisted men; designed wartime

Built by Western Pipe & Steel Co, San Francisco, Calif; launched on 29 Nov 1941 commissioned on 19 Nov 1942. Maritime Commission type C3-S1-B1. Fitted wit 22-ton capacity crane aft. Decommissioned in 1947; retained as accommodatio ship for reserve group at Philadelphia.

1 ADVANCED AVIATION BASE SHIP (AVB): CONVERTED TANK LANDING SHIP

TALLAHATCHIE COUNTY AVB 2 (ex-LST 1154)

Displacement, tons	6 000 full load
Dimensions, feet	368 wl; 382 oa × 54 × 17
Guns	1—5 in (*127 mm*) 38 cal; 4—40 mm AA (twin)
Main engines	Geared turbines; 6 000 shp; 2 shafts = 14 knots
Complement	215 (15 officers, 200 enlisted men)

Built by the Boston Navy Yard; launched on 19 July 1946 and commissioned on June 1949. One of a two-ship class of steam-powered LSTs (sister ship is *Talbc County*, LST 1153). Active in the Mediterranean.

CONVERSION. The *Tallahatchie County* was converted to an advanced aviatic base ship at the Naval Shipyard, Charleston, South Carolina, under the 1960 conversio programme; recommissioned on 20 Jan 1962. Designed to provide airfield facilitie at advanced bases in the Mediterranean area. Fitted with enlarged, all-aluminiu superstructure, maintenance shops, communications equipment, briefing room accommodations for 270 aircraft squadron personnel; carries portable airfield towe airfield vehicles, portable lighting system, aviation fuel, spare parts and ordnance.

TRANSFER. *Alameda County* (AVB 1, ex-LST 32) was transferred to Italy in Novemb 1962.

Fleet Support Ships—*continued*

TALLAHATCHIE COUNTY (AVB 2) *1967, US Navy*

TALLAHATCHIE (AVB 2) *US Navy*

FLOATING DRY DOCKS

FLOATING DRY DOCKS

The US Navy operates a number of floating dry docks to supplement dry dock facilities at major naval activities, to support fleet ballistic missile submarines (SSBN) at advanced bases, and to provide repair capabilities in forward combat areas (such as South Vietnam).

The larger floating dry docks are made sectional to facilitate movement overseas and to render them self docking. The ARD-type docks have the forward end of their docking well closed by a structure resembling the bow of a ship to facilitate towing.

well closed by a structure resembling the bow of a ship to facilitate towing. Berthing facilities, repair shops, and machinery are housed in sides of larger docks. None is self-propelled.

Twenty-nine floating dry docks are in US Navy service (including one partial dock), 18 are out of service in reserve (including one partial dock), 32 are on lease to commercial firms for private use, and 15 are on loan to other US services or foreign navies (including one partial dock). Asterisks indicate docks in active US service.

ABRAHAM LINCOLN (SSBN 602) in LOS ALAMOS *1963, US Navy*

Name-No.	*Capacity*	*Construction*	*Notes*
***AFDL 1**	1 000 tons	Steel	Guantanamo Bay, Cuba
AFDL 2	1 000 tons	Steel	Reserve
***AFDL 6**	1 000 tons	Steel	Little Creek, Virginia
AFDL 7	1 900 tons	Steel	Reserve
AFDL 8	1 000 tons	Steel	Commercial lease
AFDL 9	1 000 tons	Steel	Commercial lease
***AFDL 10**	1 000 tons	Steel	Subic Bay Philippines
***AFDL 11**	1 000 tons	Steel	Subic Bay, Philippines
AFDL 12	1 000 tons	Steel	Reserve
AFDL 15	1 000 tons	Steel	Commercial lease
AFDL 16	1 000 tons	Steel	Commercial lease
AFDL 17	1 000 tons	Steel	Reserve
AFDL 19	1 000 tons	Steel	Commercial lease
AFDL 20	1 000 tons	Steel	Loan to Philippines
***AFDL 21**	1 000 tons	Steel	Guam, Marianas
***AFDL 22**	1 900 tons	Steel	Danang, South Vietnam
***AFDL 23**	1 900 tons	Steel	Danang, South Vietnam
AFDL 25	1 000 tons	Steel	Reserve
AFDL 26	1 000 tons	Steel	Loan to Paraguay
***AFDL 28**	1 000 tons	Steel	Key West, Florida
AFDL 29	1 000 tons	Steel	Commercial lease
AFDL 30	1 000 tons	Steel	Commercial lease
AFDL 33	1 900 tons	Steel	Loan to Peru
AFDL 35	2 800 tons	Concrete	Reserve
AFDL 37	2 800 tons	Concrete	Commercial lease
AFDL 38	2 800 tons	Concrete	Commercial lease
AFDL 39	2 800 tons	Concrete	Loan to Brazil
AFDL 40	2 800 tons	Concrete	Commercial lease
AFDL 41	2 800 tons	Concrete	Commercial lease
***AFDL 42**	2 800 tons	Concrete	Long Beach NavShipyard
AFDL 43	2 800 tons	Concrete	Commercial lease
AFDL 44	2 800 tons	Concrete	Reserve
AFDL 45	2 800 tons	Concrete	Commercial lease
AFDL 47	6 500 tons	Steel	Commercial lease
***AFDL 48**	4 000 tons	Concrete	Long Beach Nav Shipyard
***ARD 5**	3 000 tons	Steel	New London, Connecticut
ARD 6	3 000 tons	Steel	Loan to Pakistan
***ARD 7**	3 000 tons	Steel	New London, Connecticut
ARD 8	3 000 tons	Steel	Loan to Peru
ARD 9	3 000 tons	Steel	Reserve
ARD 10	3 000 tons	Steel	Reserve
***ARD 11**	3 000 tons	Steel	Key West, Florida
***ARD 12**	3 000 tons	Steel	Charleston NavShipyard
ARD 13	3 000 tons	Steel	Loan to Venezuela
ARD 14	3 000 tons	Steel	Loan to Brazil
***ARD 15**	3 000 tons	Steel	Charleston NavShipyard
***ARD 16**	3 000 tons	Steel	Davisville, Rhode Island
ARD 17	3 000 tons	Steel	Loan to Ecuador
***ARD 18**	3 000 tons	Steel	
***OAK RIDGE** ARDM 1 (ex-ARD 19)		Steel	Rota, Spain
***WHITE SANDS** ARD 20	3 000 tons	Steel	San Diego, California
***WINDSOR** ARD 22	3 000 tons	Steel	Subic Bay, Philippines
ARD 23	3 000 tons	Steel	Loan to Argentina
ARD 24	3 000 tons	Steel	Reserve
ARD 25	3 000 tons	Steel	Reserve
ALAMAGORDO ARDM 2 (ex-ARD 26)		Steel	Charleston South Carolina
ARD 27	3 000 tons	Steel	Reserve
ARD 28	3 000 tons	Steel	Loan to Columbia
***ARCO** ARD 29	3 000 tons	Steel	Guam, Marianas
***ARD 30**	3 000 tons	Steel	Pearl Harbour NavShipyard
***ARD 31**	3 000 tons	Steel	US Air Force
ARD 32	3 000 tons	Steel	Loan to Chile
YFD 7	18 000 tons	Steel (3)	Commercial lease
YFD 8	20 000 tons	Wood	Commercial lease
YFD 9	16 000 tons	Wood	Commercial lease
YFD 15	6 500 tons	Wood	Commercial lease
YFD 23	10 500 tons	Wood	Commercial lease
YFD 42	1 000 tons	Wood	Commercial lease
YFD 54	5 000 tons	Wood	Commercial lease
YFD 55	10 500 tons	Wood	Commercial lease
YFD 68	14 000 tons	Steel (3)	Commercial lease
YFD 69	14 000 tons	Steel (3)	Commercial lease
YFD 70	14 000 tons	Steel (3)	Commercial lease
YFD 71	14 000 tons	Steel (3)	Commercial lease
***YFD 82** (ex-ARD 1)	1 500 tons	Steel	Portsmouth NavShipyard
***YFD 83** (ex-AFDL 31)	1 000 tons	Steel	US Coast Guard
***AFDB 1**	90 000 tons	Steel (10)	Guam, Marianas
AFDB 2	90 000 tons	Steel (10)	Reserve
AFDB 3	81 000 tons	Steel (9)	Reserve
AFDB 4	55 000 tons	Steel (7)	Reserve
AFDB 5	55 000 tons	Steel (7)	Reserve
AFDB 6	55 000 tons	Steel (7)	Reserve
AFDB 7 (partial)		Steel (2)	Reserve
***AFDB 7** (partial)	10 000 tons	Steel (1)	US Army
***LOS ALAMOS** AFDB 7 (partial)	40 000 tons	Steel (4)	Holy Loch, Scotland
AFDM 1 (ex-YFD 3)	15 000 tons	Steel (3)	Commercial lease
AFDM 2 (ex-YFD 4)	15 000 tons	Steel (3)	Commercial lease
AFDM 3 (ex-YFD 6)	18 000 tons	Steel (3)	Commercial lease
***AFDM 5** (ex-YFD 21)	18 000 tons	Steel (3)	Subic Bay, Philippines
***AFDM 6** (ex-YFD 62)	18 000 tons	Steel (3)	Subic Bay, Philippines
AFDM 7 (ex-YFD 63)	18 000 tons	Steel (3)	Commercial lease
***AFDM 8** (ex-YFD 64)	18 000 tons	Steel (3)	Guam, Marianas
AFDM 9 (ex-YFD 65)	18 000 tons	Steel (3)	Commercial lease
AFDM 10	18 000 tons	Steel (3)	Commercial lease

Figures in parenthesis indicate the number of sections for sectional docks. Each section of the AFDB docks have a lifting capacity of about 10 000 tons. Four sections of the AFDB 7 form the floating dry dock *Los Alamos* at Holy Loch, Scotland, one section is used at Kwajalein atoll by the US Army in support of the Nike-X missile project, and two sections are in reserve.

The *White Sands* (ARD 20) is employed in support of the deep-diving bathyscaph *Trieste II* (see section on Deep Submergence Vehicles). Early in 1969 the *White Sands*, with *Trieste II* on board, was towed to the Azores to support investigation of the remains of the nuclear-powered submarine *Scorpion*. The ARD 18 is being modified at the Newport News SB & DD Co.

All floating dry docks were built during World War II except the YFD 82 (ex-ARD 1) which was built in 1934.

LOGISTIC SUPPORT SHIPS

Most of the Logistic Support Ships of the US Navy which are in service are operated by the Military Sea Transportation Service (MSTS) which provides ocean transportation for the Department of Defence. The MSTS nucleus fleet, described below, consists of those cargo ships, tankers, aircraft ferries, and other logistic support ships which are actually owned and managed by MSTS. These ships are civilian manned with their crews either merchant seamen or under Civil Service regulations. Four cargo ships are Navy Manned. A number of ships are manned by Japanese and South Korean personnel. (Also listed in this section are several "aircraft carriers" which are suitable only for use as cargo ships and transports; should they be returned to active service they would probably be manned by MSTS personnel).

In addition to logistic support ships, MSTS operates a number of so-called Special Projects ships which are employed primarily in research, surveying, and missile-space range support. These ships are listed in the section on Experimental, Research, and Surveying Ships. Also MSTS operates the helicopter repair ship *Corpus Christi Bay* (T-ARVH 1), listed in the section on Fleet Support Ships and the cable ship *Albert J. Myer* (T-ARC 6), listed in the section on Specialised Auxiliary Ships and Service Craft.

In addition to the below listed government owned and manned ships, MSTS directs the operations of ships in two other categories which provide logistic support for the US government: (1) General Agency Agreement ships, which are government-owned merchantmen reactivated from the Maritime Administration's National Defence Reserve Fleet for the build up in Southeast Asia and operated for MSTS by commercial shipping lines; and (2) merchantmen which are owned by shipping lines or private parties and are on charter to MSTS with the Navy renting cargo space (part or all) in these ships.

ARMAMENT. No MSTS ships are armed.

CLASSIFICATION. MSTS nucleus fleet ships are assigned standard US Navy hull designations with the added prefix "T". Ships in this category are prefixed "USNS" (United States Naval Ship) vice "USS" (United States Ship), which is used only by Navy-manned ships.

COMMAND. The direction of MSTS is a joint Navy-civilian effort with the Commander MSTS and the various MSTS area commanders being officers of flag rank of the regular Navy.

STATUS. Unless otherwise indicated, all ships within this category are in active service.

NORWALK (T-AK 279) replenishes HUNLEY (AS 31) and REARMS FBM SUBMARINE AT HOLY LOCH — *US Navy*

2 STORE SHIPS (AF): "VICTORY" TYPE

ASTERION (ex-*Arcadia Victory*) T-AF 63 **PERSEUS** (ex-*Union Victory*) T-AF 64

Displacement, tons	6 700 light; 12 130 full load
Measurement, tons	8 000 deadweight
Dimensions, feet	455·2 × 62 × 28·5
Main engines	Geared turbines (Westinghouse); 1 shaft; 8 500 shp = 17 knots
Boilers	2
Complement	56

Victory ships (VC 2-S-AP 3 type). Acquired from the Maritime Administration in 1962, and converted at Portland, Oregon, by Willamette Iron & Steel Co under the 1962 Programme. Of the same type as the Navy-manned replenishment ships *Denebola* and *Regulus*, except they are unarmed and manned by Civilian crews.

ASTERION (T-AF 63) — *United States Navy (MSTS)*

2 STORE SHIPS (AF): "EAGLE" CLASS

BALD EAGLE T-AF 50 **BLUE JACKET** T-AF 51

Displacement, tons	7 430 light; 12 800 full load
Dimensions, feet	459·2 oa × 63 × 24
Main engines	Turbine; 1 shaft; 6 000 shp = 16·4 knots
Boilers	2

Both built by Moore Dry Dock Co. Launched in 1942. C 2-S-B1 type. Sister ship *Golden Eagle* is a Navy-manned replenishment ship (renamed *Arcturus*).

BALD EAGLE (T-AF 50) — *United States Navy (MSTS)*

2 STORE SHIPS (AF): "ADRIA" CLASS

Name	*No.*	*Launched*
BONDIA	T-AF 42	9 Nov 1944
LAURENTIA (ex-*Wall* and *Crown*)	T-AF 44	12 Dec 1944

Displacement, tons	3 139 light; 7 435 full load
Dimensions, feet	320 wl; 338·5 oa × 50 × 21 max
Main engines	Nordberg diesel; 1 700 bhp = 11·5 knots

2 100 tons cargo. R1-M-AV 3 type. Both built by Pennsylvania Shipyard, Beaumont, Texas. The following ships of this type have been stricken from the Navy List and transferred to the Maritime Administration: *Adria* AF 30, *Arequipa* AF 31, *Corduba* AF 32, *Karin* AF 33, *Kerstin* AF 34, *Latona* AF 35, *Lioba* AF [illegible] *Malabar* AF 37, *Merapi* AF 38, and *Valentine* AF 47.

BONDIA (T-AF 42) — *Skyfotos*

1 CARGO SHIP (AG): Ex-LSM

AG 335 **T-AG 335**

Displacement, tons	743 beaching; 1 095 full load
Dimensions, feet	196·5 wl; 204·5 oa × 34·5 × 8·3
Main engines	Diesel direct drive; 2 shafts; 2 800 bhp = 12·5 knots

The AG 335 is the only medium landing ship remaining in US service, stationed at Okinawa. Formerly LSM 335, redesignated AG 335 on 1 Jan 1969. This class could carry 5 medium tanks. Launched on 10 Nov 1944.

NOMENCLATURE. LSM 161, 175, 373 and 540 were named *Kodiak*, *Oceanside*, *Lakeland* and *Raritan* respectively, on 14 Oct 1959, see *Transfers* and *Disposals*. The name *Kodiak* was cancelled on 22 Mar 1965 and reassigned to YF 866.

TRANSFERS. LSM 500 was transferred to Denmark on 15 May 1953. LSM 17, 19, 30, 54, 57, 84, 96, 268, 316, 419, 462 and 546 to Korea in 1956, LSM 491, LSM 537, LSM 553 and LSM 558 to West Germany on 15 Aug 1959 (first two) and 5 Sep 1958 (other two), LSM 472 and LSM 474 to Taiwan China at Seattle on 3 Feb 1959, LSM 539 and LSM 555 to Ecuador in 1959, LSM 444 *Aloto* to Chile in 1960. LSM 236 to the Philippines on 15 Sep 1960, LSM 483 to the Dominican Republic in 1960, *Oceanside* LSM 175 and LSM 313 to Vietnam in 1961, LSM 320 and LSM 463 to the Philippines on 17 Mar 1961, LSM 469 to Thailand in 1962, LSM 362 to Taiwan China in May 1962, LSM 276 to Vietnam in Mar 1963.

LSM DISPOSALS

All LSMs were stricken from the Navy List by 1957 except 13 LSMs and the two YVs. **LSM 455**, **491**, **533**, **537**, **541**, **557** and **558** were stricken in 1958-1959, **Lakeland** LSM 373 and **Raritan** LSM 540 in 1960, **Catapult** YV 1, ex-LSM 445 and **Launcher** YV 2, ex-LSM 446 in 1960, **Hunting** EAG 398 (ex-*LSM* 398) on 1 Nov 1962. **Targeteer** YV 1 ex-LSMR 508 stricken in 1969. LSM 161 (ex-*Kodiak*) stricken on 1 June 1965.

Logistic Support Ships—*continued*

3 CARGO SHIPS (AG): FORMER DEPOT SHIPS

PHOENIX (ex-*Arizona*, ex-*Capitol Victory*) T-AG 172
PROVO (ex-*Utah*, ex-*Drew Victory*) T-AG 173
CHEYENNE (ex-*Wyoming*, ex-*Middlesex Victory*) T-AG 174

Displacement, tons	6 700 light; 2 400 full load
Dimensions, feet	455 × 62
Main engines	Geared turbines; 1 shaft; 6 000 shp = 15·5 knots
Boilers	2

These ships were acquired in 1963 from the Maritime Administration. Initially they were employed as forward depot ships; now used as general cargo ships. Korean manned.

RESCINDED ACQUISITIONS. The twelve "Victory" ships planned as forward depot ships were not acquired from the Maritime Administration Reserve Fleet on 1 Feb 1966 as requested and redesignated T-AG 179 to 190 and given new Navy names (see complete list in the 1966-1967 edition) but were chartered to and operated by commercial shipping companies in Vietnam service under their original "Victory" names.

PHOENIX (T-AG 172) *United States Navy (MSTS)*

1 CARGO SHIP (AK): Ex-AKA TYPE

WYANDOT T-AK 283 (ex-T-AKA 92)

Displacement, tons	7 430 light; 14 000 full load
Dimensions, feet	435 wl; 459·2 oa × 63 × 24
Main engines	Geared turbines (General Electric); 1 shaft; 6 000 shp = 16·5 knots
Boilers	2 (Combustion Engineering)

The *Wyandot* is a winterised cargo ship; formerly an Attack Cargo Ship (AKA) of the "Andromeda" class. Built by Moore Dry Dock Co, Oakland, California; launched on 28 June 1944; commissioned on 30 Sep 1944 as AKA 92. Assigned to MSTS and manned by civilian crew since 1963 (T-AKA 92). Designation changed to T-AK 283 on 1 Jan 1969.
Original armament of one 5 inch gun and eight 40 mm guns (twin) removed.

3 FBM CARGO SHIPS (AK): "VICTORY" TYPE

NORWALK (ex-*Norwalk Victory*) T-AK 279
FURMAN (ex-*Furman Victory*) T-AK 280
VICTORIA (ex-*Ethiopia Victory*) T-AK 281

Displacement, tons	11 150 full load
Dimensions, feet	455 × 62
Main engines	Geared turbine; 1 shaft; 8 500 shp = 16·5 knots
Boilers	2
Complement	75

Fleet ballistic missile resupply cargo ships AK (FBM). VC 2-S-AP 3 type. Designed as a one-stop cargo ship to provide complete resupply of a deployed fleet ballistic missile submarine tender. The logistic support includes "Polaris" missiles, submarine torpedoes, technical spares, packaged petroleum products, bottled gas, black oil and diesel fuel, general cargo, and frozen and dry provisions. No. 3 hold converted to carry 16 Polaris missiles in vertical position, 355 000 gallons of diesel oil and 430 000 gallons of fuel oil carried.
Operated as an independent unit wtih a civilian (MSTS) crew and with a Navy unit embarked. The *Norwalk* was converted from a "Victory" cargo ship by Boland Machine and Mfg Co, and accepted on 30 Dec 1963. Conversion of *Furman* was completed by American Shipbuilding Co in Oct 1964. Conversion of *Victoria* completed by Philadelphia Naval Shipyard in Oct 1965. All acquired from the Maritime Administration reserve fleet.

1 FBM CARGO SHIP (AK): "VICTORY" TYPE

BETELGEUSE (ex-*Colombia Victory*) AK 260

Displacement, tons	4 420 Navy Light; 15 580 full load (Maritime Commission deadweight 10 850 tons)
Dimensions, feet	455·2 oa × 62 × 28·5
Guns	8—40 mm AA (twin)
Main engines	Geared turbines; 1 shaft; 8 500 shp = 16·5 knots

VC2-S-AP3 type. Reactivated for the Navy in 1951 from the Maritime Administration reserve fleet. Fitted with special equipment to transport material and supplies for fleet ballistic missile submarines (details as in *Norwalk*, above). Navy manned, not MSTS.

DISPOSALS
Of the "Alcona" class, **Sussex** AK 213, was stricken on 1 Jan 1960, and **Alcona** AK 157, **Beltrami** AK 162, **Faribaulr** AK 179, and **Grainger** AK 184, end 1960. All six vessels of the "Alchiba" class, namely **Alchiba** (ex-*Charles E. Winsor*), **Algorab** (ex-*Elisha Whitney*), **Aquarius** (ex-*John D. Whitney*), **Centaurus** (ex-*Nathanial Brown*), **Cepheus** (ex-*Richard W. Dixie*) and **Serpens** (ex-*William Lester*) AK 261 to 266, respectively, were stricken on 1 Feb 1960.

BETELGEUSE (AK 260) *United States Navy*

1 CARGO SHIP (AK): "BLAND" TYPE

SCHUYLER OTIS BLAND T-AK 277

Displacement, tons	8 918 gross; 10 516 deadweight
Dimensions, feet	478 × 66 × 30
Main engines	Steam turbine; 1 shaft; speed = 18·5 knots
Boilers	2

Acquired from the Maritime Administration by the Military Sea Transportation Service in July 1961. The only ship of the type (C3-S-DX2).

SCHUYLER OTIS BLAND (T-AK 277) *United States Navy (MSTS)*

6 CARGO SHIPS (AK): "O'BRIEN" TYPE

COLONEL WILLIAM J. O'BRIEN (ex-*Maiden's Eye*) T-AK 246
SHORT SPLICE T-AK 249
PRIVATE FRANK J. PETRARCA (ex-*Long Splice*) T-AK 250
FENTRESS (ex-V 206) T-AK 180
HERKIMER (ex-V 203) T-AK 188
MUSKINGUM (ex-V 208) T-SK 198

Displacement, tons	2 460 light; 7 450 full load
Dimensions, feet	338·7 × 50 × 21
Main engines	Diesel; 1 shaft; 1 750 bhp = 11·5 knots

C1-M-AV1 Type. *Colonel William J. O'Brien* and *Short Splice* were converted to heavy lift ships with two 80-ton capacity cranes.

TRANSFERS. *Pembina* T-AK 200 and *Captain Ario L. Olsen* T-AK 245 (ex-*Bell Ringer*) were transferred to the Maritime Administration in 1958. *Pembina* T-AK 200, and *Private John F. Thorson* T-AK 247, were stricken from the Navy List in 1959. *Sergeant George Peterson*, T-AK 248, was transferred to the Maritime Administration by the MSTS. *Pvt Frank J. Petrarca* T-AK 250, was stricken on 9 Apr 1959, but was reacquired by the MSTS in 1960. *Hennepin* T-AK 187 (ex-V 205) and *Sergeant George Peterson* T-AK 248, stricken on 27 Mar 1959 were transferred to the Maritime Administration.
The *Short Splice* is Korean manned.

HERKIMER (T-AK 188) *United States Navy (MSTS)*

1 CARGO SHIP (AK): "ELTANIN" TYPE

Displacement, tons	2 036 light; 4 942 full load
Measurement, tons	2 486 gross, 1 300 deadweight
Dimensions, feet	256·8 wl; 262·2 oa × 51·5 × 18·7
Main engines	2 ALCO diesels with Westinghouse electric motors; 2 shafts; 3 200 bhp = 13 knots

Built for MSTS by Avondale Marine Ways, New Orleans, La. Designed for Arctic operation with hull strengthened against ice. C1-M E2-13a type. Launched on 5 Aug 1957. Note icebreaking prow in photo on next page.

CONVERSION. Two other ships of this class converted for oceanographic research: *Eltanin*, reclassified from T-AK 270 to T-AGOR 8 on 15 Nov 1962. *Mizar* T-AK 272 was reclassified T-AGOR 11 on 15 Apr 1964.

Logistic Support Ships—*continued*

MIRFAK (T-AK 271) *United States Navy (MSTS)*

5 CARGO SHIPS (AK): "VICTORY" TYPE

GREENVILLE VICTORY T-AK 237
LIEUTENANT JAMES E. ROBINSON (ex-T-AG 170, ex-T-AK 274, ex-*Czechoslovakia Victory*) T-AK 274
PRIVATE JOHN R. TOWLE (ex-*Appleton Victory*) T-AK 240
PRIVATE JOSEPH F. MERRELL (ex-*Grange Victory*) T-AK 275
SERGEANT JACK J. PENDLETON T-AK 276

Displacement, tons	6 720 light; 12 450 full load
Dimensions, feet	455 oa × 62 × 24
Main engines	Turbine; 1 shaft; 8 500 shp = 16·5 to 17·7 knots
Boilers	2

VC2-S-AP3 type. *Greenville Victory* has been winterised.

RECLASSIFICATION. The former Military Sea Transportation Service Aircraft Cargo and Ferry Ships *Lieut. James E. Robinson, Private Joseph F. Merrell* and *Sergeant Jack J. Pendleton*, AKV 3, AKV 4 and AKV 5, respectively, were reclassified as Cargo Ships, AK 274, AK 275 and AK 276 on 7 May 1959. *Kingsport Victory* T-AK 239, was renamed and reclassified *Kingsport* T-AG 164 in 1962 for Project "Advent". *Lieut. James E. Robinson* T-AK 274, was to have been transferred to the Maritime Administration, but was modified for special project work and reclassified as T-AG 170 in 1963, and reverted to the original classification T-AK 274 on 1 July 1964.

Haiti Victory T-AK 238 and *Dalton Victory* T-AK 256 converted to satellite tracking and recovery ships, reclassified and renamed, *Longview* T-AGM 3 and *Sunnyvale* T-AGM 5, respectively.

LIEUTENANT JAMES E. ROBINSON (T-AK 274) *US Navy (MSTS)*

2 HEAVY LIFT SHIPS (AK): "BROSTROM" TYPE

PVT. LEONARD C. BROSTROM (ex-*Marine Eagle*) T-AK 255
MARINE FIDDLER T-AK 267

Dimensions, feet	520 oa × 72 × 33
Main engines	Geared turbine; 1 shaft; 9 000 shp = 15·8 knots
Boilers	2

C4-S-B1 and C4-S-B5 Types, respectively. *Marine Fiddler* was built in 1945, and acquired from the Maritime Administration Reserve Fleet in 1952. Both were converted to heavy lift ships for carrying locomotives and general cargo in 1954.

MARINE FIDDLER (T-AK 267) *United States Navy*

7 CARGO SHIPS (AK): "VICTORY" TYPE

PRIVATE FRANCIS X. McGRAW (ex-*Wabash Victory*) T-AK 241
SERGEANT ANDREW MILLER (ex-*Radcliffe Victory*) T-AK 242
SERGEANT ARCHER T. GAMMON (ex-*Yale Victory*) T-AK 243
SERGEANT MORRIS E. CRAIN (ex-*Mills Victory*) T-AK 244
LT. GEORGE W. G. BOYCE (ex-*Waterville Victory*) T-AK 251
LT. ROBERT CRAIG (ex-*Bowling Green Victory*) T-AK 252
SERGEANT TRUMAN KIMBRO T-AK 254

Displacement, tons	6 700 light; 12 400 full load
Dimensions, feet	455 × 62 × 24
Main engines	Geared turbines; 1 shaft; 6 000 shp = 15·5 knots
Boilers	2

T-AK 251, 252, and 254 are VC2-S-AP2, the others VC2-S-AP3 type. (AK-278 authorised in Aug 1962 for the Military Sea Transportation Service, was assigned a new designation and hull number, T-LSV 9, *Sea Lift*; subsequently changed to T-AKR 9).

Victory Type—*continued*

Pvt. Joe E. Mann T-AK 253, ex-*Owensboro Victory*, was fitted out as a range instrumentation and telemetry ship for the Pacific Missile Range in Oct 1958 and renamed *Richfield* T-AGM 4.
Sagita T-AK 87 (ex-SS *Moses Pike*) and *Vela* T-AK 89 (ex-SS *Charles A. Roulett*) transferred to the Maritime Administration in July 1961 and on 3 Apr 1959 respectively.

LIEUTENANT ROBERT CRAIG (T-AK 252) *United States Navy (MSTS)*

1 DOCK CARGO SHIP (AKD)

POINT BARROW T-AKD 1

Displacement, tons	5 940 light; 9 415 standard; 14 094 full load
Measurement, tons	12 000 gross; 4 020 deadweight
Dimensions, feet	475 wl; 492 oa × 78 × 22
Main engines	Turbine; 2 shafts; 6 000 shp = 18 knots
Boilers	2
Complement	66 plus 42 transients

Built for MSTS by Maryland Shipbuilding & Dry Dock Co. Laid down on 18 Sep 1956, launched on 25 May 1957 and commissioned on 28 Feb 1958. Delivered to MSTS on 29 May 1958. S2-ST-23A type. Originally a Roll-on, Roll-off ship to load vehicles on ramp. Winterised for Arctic service. Ballasting arrangements permit embarking and debarking landing craft as in dock landing ships.
Subsequently refitted with hangar over docking well and employed in transport of large booster rockets to Cape Kennedy space centre.

POINT BARROW (T-AKD 1) *US Navy (MSTS)*

1 LIGHT CARGO SHIP (AKL)

REDBUD T-AKL 398. Launched 11 Sep 1943

Displacement, tons	approx 700
Dimensions, feet	180 oa × 37 × 13·7
Main engines	1 diesel; 1 shaft = 10 knots

Built in 1943 by Marine Iron & Shipbuilding Co, Duluth, Minnesota. Launched on 11 Sep 1943. Former US Coast Guard buoy tender WAGL 398; transferred to Navy for transport and supply work in the Greenland area on 20 Feb 1952. Operated by MSTS as multi-purpose freighter, icebreaker, and communications ship. Now in reserve.

REDBUD (T-AKL 398) *United States Navy (MSTS)*

Logistic Support Ships—*continued*

4 LIGHT CARGO SHIPS (AKL)

Name	*No.*
MARK (ex-FS 214, ex-AG 143)	AKL 12
AKL 17 (ex-*New Bedford*, ex-FS 289)	AKL 17
BRAULE (ex-FS 370)	AKL 28
AKL 31 (ex-FS 407)	T-AKL 31

Displacement, tons	approx 700
Dimensions, feet	176·5 oa × 32·8 × 10
Main engines	1 diesel; 1 000 shp; 1 shaft = 10 knots
Guns	20 mm AA in *Mark* and *Braule*
Complement	varies 21 (designed)

Small cargo ships (freight and supply) acquired from the Army. AKL 17 is operated by the Naval Torpedo Station, Keyport, Washington. Note differences in superstructure and masts.

CONVERSIONS. *Banner* (AKL 25), *Pueblo* (AKL 44), and *Palm Beach* (AKL 45) of this type were converted to reconnaissance ships and reclassified as Environmental Research Ships, AGER 1-3, respectively, on 1 June 1967. They are listed with Experimental, Research, and Surveying Ships.

DISPOSALS AND TRANSFERS

AKL 13, **T-AKL 13**, **15**, **16**, **18**, **19**, **21**, **23**, **24**, **26**, **34**, **36** stricken in 1959; **AKL 1**, **5**, **6**, **14**, **T-AKL 29** stricken in 1960; **AKL 2**, **9**, **T-AKL 20**, **22**, **30**, **32** stricken in 1961; **T-AKL 43** stricken in 1963; **T-AKL 27** stricken in 1966 and used for salvage training; **T-AKL 35** transferred to Korea in 1956; Korean manned **T-AKL 37-42** formerly transferred to Korea in 1960.

MARK (AKL 12) *1966, United States Navy*

AKL 17 *1966, United States Navy*

T-AKL 31 *United States Navy (MSTS)*

1 VEHICLE CARGO SHIP (AKR): "SEA LIFT" TYPE

SEA LIFT T-AKR 9 (ex-T-LSV 9)

Displacement, tons	11 130 light; 16 940 standard; 21 700 full load
Measurement, tons	15 750 gross; 12 100 deadweight
Dimensions, feet	540 oa × 83 × 29
Main engines	Geared steam turbines; 2 shafts; 19 400 shp = 20 knots
Boilers	2
Complement	62 plus 12 Passengers

Improved roll-on/roll-off vehicle cargo ship. Maritime Administration C4-ST-67a type. Built by the Puget Sound Bridge & Dry Dock Co. (now Lockheed Shipbuilding and Construction Co), Seattle, Wash, at a cost of $15 895 500. Authorised under the Fiscal Year 1963 programme. Laid down on 19 May 1964 and launched on 18 Apr 1965. Delivered to Navy on 25 Apr 1967 and to MSTS on 19 May 1967. Designed for point-to-point sea transportation of Department of Defense self-propelled, fully-loaded, wheeled, tracked and amphibious vehicles and general cargo. Her configuration of internal ramps, stern ramp and side openings will provide for quick loading and unloading. A second ship was requested under the 1964 programme, but not approved; requested again in 1965 but again funds not provided.
Designation changed from T-LSV toT-AKR on 1 Jan 1969.

SEA LIFT (T-AKR 9) *1966, Lockheed Shipbuilding*

SEA LIFT (T-AKR 9) *1966, Lockheed Shipbuilding*

1 VEHICLE CARGO SHIP (AKR): "COMET" TYPE

COMET T-AKR 7 (ex-T-LSV 7, ex-T-AK 269)

Displacement, tons	7 605 light; 18 150 full load
Measurement, tons	12 750 gross; 6 500 deadweight
Dimensions, feet	465 pp; 499 oa × 78 × 28·8
Main engines	Geared turbines (General Electric); 2 shafts; 13 200 shp = 18 knots
Boilers	2 (Babcock & Wilcox)
Complement	73

Roll-on/roll-off vehicle carrier built for MSTS by Sun Shipbuilding & Dry Dock Co. C3-ST-14A type. Laid down on 15 May 1956. Launched on 31 July 1957. Completed on 27 Jan 1958. Has ramp system for loading and discharging. The hull is strengthened against ice. Fitted with stern ramp. Can accommodate 700 vehicles in two after holds. The forward holds are for general cargo. Equipped with Denny-Brown Stabilisers. Reclassified from T-AK to T-LSV on 1 June 1963, and changed to T-AKR on 1 Jan 1969.
LSV 1-6 were World War II-built amphibious ships, subsequently redesignated as Mine Warfare ships (MCS) or Net Cargo Ship (AKN)

DISPOSAL

Taurus (T-AKR 8, ex-T-LSV 8, ex-AK 273, ex-LSD 23) deactivated in 1968 pending disposal.
Galilea (AKN 6, ex-LSV 6, ex-AP 161) transferred to Maritime Administration, stricken from the Navy List.

COMET (T-AKR 7) *United States Navy*

Logistic Support Ships—*continued*

11 CARGO AND AIRCRAFT FERRY SHIPS (AKV): "COMMENCEMENT BAY" CLASS

Name	*No.*	*Laid down*	*Launched*	*Commissioned*
COMMENCEMENT BAY (ex-*St Joseph's Bay*)	AKV 37 (ex-CVHE 105)	23 Sep 1943	9 May 1944	27 Nov 1944
KULA GULF (ex-*Vermilion Bay*)	T-AKV 8 (ex-CVE 108)	16 Dec 1943	15 Aug 1944	12 May 1945
CAPE GLOUCESTER (ex-*Willapa Bay*)	AKV 9 (ex-CVHE 109)	10 Jan 1944	12 Sep 1944	3 Mar 1945
VELLA GULF (ex-*Totem Bay*)	AKV 11 (ex-CVHE 111)	7 Mar 1944	19 Oct 1944	9 Apr 1945
SIBONEY (ex-*Frosty Bay*)	AKV 12 (ex-CVE 112)	1 Apr 1944	9 Nov 1944	14 May 1945
RENDOVA (ex-*Mosser Bay*)	AKV 14 (ex-CVE 114)	15 June 1944	28 Dec 1944	22 Oct 1945
BADOENG STRAIT (ex-*San Alberto Bay*)	AKV 16 (ex-CVE 116)	18 Aug 1944	15 Feb 1945	14 Nov 1845
SAIDOR (ex-*Saltery Bay*)	AKV 17 (ex-CVHE 117)	29 Sep 1944	17 Mar 1945	4 Sep 1945
POINT CRUZ (ex-*Trocadero Bay*)	T-AKV 19 (ex-CVE 119)	4 Dec 1944	18 May 1945	16 Oct 1946
RABAUL	AKV 21 (ex-CVHE 121)	29 Jan 1945	14 July 1945	30 Aug 1946
TINIAN	AKV 23 (ex-CVHE 123)	20 Mar 1945	5 Sep 1945	30 July 1946

Displacement, tons	11 473 standard; 24 275 full load
Length, feet (*metres*)	557 (*169·8*) oa
Beam, feet (*metres*)	75 (*22·9*) hull
Draft, feet (*metres*)	30·7 (*9·3*)
Width, feet (*metres*)	105 (*32·0*) extreme
Aircraft	Originally carried 34
Guns,	1—5 in (*127 mm*) 38 cal DP; 24—40 mm AA (guns removed in active ships)
Boilers	4
Main engines	Geared turbines 16 000 shp; 2 shafts
Speed knots	18
Complement	*Kula Gulf* and *Point Cruz:* 140

All built by Todd Pacific Shipyard, Tacoma. As escort aircraft carriers their complement was 924 officers and men (peace) and over 1 000 (war). *Kula Gulf* and *Point Cruz* were reactivated in 1965 for MSTS operation and designated T-AKV, USNS, unarmed with civil service crew. Others in reserve.

GUNNERY. Designed armament for these ships was two 5 inch guns and 36 40 mm guns (three quad and 12 twin) plus 20 mm guns.

CONVERSION. *Gilbert Islands* (AKV 39, CVE 107) was converted into a Major Communications Relay Ship (AGMR 1) in 1963.

RECLASSIFICATION. Seven Escort Aircraft Carriers (CVE) of this class were reclassified as Escort Helicopter Aircraft Carriers (CVHE) on 12 June 1955: *Block Island* was reclassified as LPH on 22 Dec 1957, but in 1958 her conversion to Helicopter Amphibious Assault Ship was cancelled and she was reclassified as an AKV on 7 May 1959, when all the remaining 18 ships of the class were also reclassified as AKVs, and stricken on 1 July 1959.

POINT CRUZ (T-AKV 19) As aircraft carrier *1954, United States Navy*

CLASS. Sixteen more ships of this class, *Bastogne* CVE 124, *Eniwetok* CVE 125, *Lingayen* CVE 126, *Okinawa* CVE 127, and CVE Nos 128 to 139, were cancelled in Aug 1945.

DISPOSALS
Block Island, AKV 38 (ex-*LPH* 1, CVE 106) was stricken on 1 July 1959, **Mindoro** AKV 20 (ex-CVE 120) on 1 Dec 1959 and **Bairoko**, AKV 15 (ex-CVE 115), **Palau** AKV 22 (ex-*CVE* 122), **Puget Sound**, AKV 13 (ex-CVHE 113) and **Vella Gulf**, AKV 11 (ex-CVHE 111) in 1960, **Sicily**, AKV 18 (ex-CVE 118) in 1961 and **Gilbert Islands**, AKV 39 (ex-CVE 107) and **Salerno Bay** AKV 10 (ex-CVE 110) on 1 June 1961. **Vella Gulf** and **Gilbert Islands**, however, were reinstated on the Navy List on 1 Nov 1961.

4 CARGO AND AIRCRAFT FERRY SHIPS (AKV): "BOGUE" CLASS

Name	*No.*	*Laid down*	*Launched*	*Commissioned*
CARD	T—AKV 40 (ex-CVU 11, ex-CVHE 11)	27 Oct 1941	21 Feb 1942	8 Nov 1942
CORE	T—AKV 41 (ex-CVU 13, ex-CVHE 13)	2 Jan 1942	15 May 1942	10 Dec 1942
BRETON	T—AKV 42 (ex-CVU 23, ex-CVHE 23)	25 Feb 1942	27 June 1942	12 Apr 1943
CROATAN	T—AKV 43 (ex-CVU 25, ex-CVHE 25)	15 Apr 1942	3 Aug 1942	28 Apr 1943

Displacement, tons,	9 800 standard; 15 700 full load
Length, feet (*metres*)	496 (*151·2*) oa
Beam, feet (*metres*)	69·5 (*21·2*) hull
Draft, feet (*metres*)	26 (*7·9*)
Width, feet (*metres*)	112 (*34·1*) extreme
Flight deck, feet (*metres*)	450 (*137·2*)
Aircraft	See *General* notes
Guns	See *Gunnery* notes
Boilers	2 (Foster Wheeler)
Main engines	Westinghouse geared turbines; 1 shaft; 8 500 shp
Speed, knots	18
Complement	75

All converted from mercantile hulls built by Seattle-Tacoma Shipbuilding Corpn. Vary slightly in appearance. As escort carriers they carried 30 aircraft and had a complement of 800 officers and men. Named after sounds. Equipped with derricks for loading and unloading aircraft at the pierside.

RECLASSIFICATION. Reclassified from Escort Aircraft Carriers (CVE) to Escort Helicopter Aircraft Carriers (CVHE) on 12 June 1955, to CVU on allocation as MSTS aircraft ferries on 1 July 1958 and to AKV on 7 May 1959.

GUNNERY. Unarmed while designated USNS with civil crews. Formerly mounted one or two 5-inch guns, 16—40 mm AA guns, and 20-20 mm AA guns.

DISPOSALS
Sister ships **Altamaha** CVHE 18, **Barnes**, CVHE 20, **Bogue**, CVHE 9, **Copahee**, CVHE 12, and **Nassau**, CVHE 16 also half-sister **Prince William**, CVHE 31 were stricken from the list in 1 Mar 1959 when **Chenango**, CVHE 28, **Santtee** CVHE 29, and **Suwannee**, CVHE 27, of the "Suwanee" class, were also stricken. The last survivor of the 50 former escort aircraft carriers of the "Anzio" class, **Thetis Bay** LPH6, ex-CVHA 1, ex-CVE 90, was sold for scrap in 1967.

CARD (T-AKV 40) *United States Navy*

Logistic Support Ships—*continued*

1 TANKER (AO): "EXPLORER" TYPE

AMERICAN EXPLORER T-AO 165

Measurement, tons	16 500 gross; 22 525 deadweignt
Dimensions, feet	615 oa × 80 ×44·5
Main engines	Steam turbines; 1 shaft; 22 000 shp = 20 knots

T5-S-RM2a type. Laid down on 9 July 1957; launched on 11 Apr 1958. Built by Ingalls Shipbuilding Corporation, Pascagoula, for the Maritime Administration, but acquired MSTS. Cargo capacity 190 300 barrels.

AMERICAN EXPLORER (T-AO 165) *United States Navy*

3 TANKERS (AO): "MAUMEE" CLASS

Name	*No.*	*Launched*
MAUMEE	T-AO 149	16 Feb 1956
SHOSHONE	T-AO 151	17 Jan 1957
YUKON	T-AO 152	16 Mar 1956

Displacement, tons	7 950 light
Measurement, tons	16 500 gross; 25 000 deadweight
Dimensions, feet	591 wl; 620 oa × 83·5 × 32
Main engines	Turbine; 1 shaft; 20 460 shp = 18 knots
Cargo	203 216 barrels

Yukon, laid down 16 May 1955 by Ingalls, Pascagoula, delivered May 1957. *Maumee* laid down 8 Mar 1955, delivered Dec 1956. *Shoshone* laid down 15 Aug 1955 by Sun Shipbuilding, Chester, delivered Apr 1957. T5-S-12A type. *Potomac* T-AO 150 sank at Morehead, North Carolina, after explosion on 26-27 Sep 1961, but was rebuilt in 1963-1964, renamed SS *Shenandoah* and chartered to MSTS.

SHOSHONE (T-AO 151) *United States Navy*

16 TANKERS (AO): "MISSION" CLASS

	T-AO
CACHE (ex-*Stillwater* 1942)	67
CHEPACHET (ex-*Eutaw Springs*, 1943)	78
COSSATOT (ex-*Fort Necessity*, 1942)	77
COWANESQUE (ex-*Fort Duquesne*, 1942)	79
MISSION BUENAVENTURA	111
MILLICOMA (ex-*Conastoga*, 1943)	73
MISSION SAN RAFAEL	130
MISSION SANTA CRUZ	133
MISSION SANTA YNEX	134
PECOS (ex-*Corsicana*, 1942)	65
PIONEER VALLEY	140
SAUGATUCK (ex-*Newton*, 1942)	75
SCHUYLKILL ex-*Louisburg*, 1943)	76
SHAWNEE TRAIL	142
SUAMICO (ex-*Harlem Heights*, 1941)	49
TALLUAH (ex-*Valley Forge*, 1944)	50

Displacement, tons	5 730 light; 22 380 full load
Dimensions, feet	503 wl; 523·5 oa × 68 × 31
Main engines	A 1 type Turbo-electric; 6 000 shp = 15 knots A 2 type; 1 000 shp = 16 knots
Boilers	2 Babcock & Wilcox
Cargo	141 158 barrels

T2-S E-A1 and T2-S E-A2 design. These are Navy-owned tankers, operated by commercial shipping firms under contract to the Navy. Several are equipped with an aluminium portable aircraft cargo deck. *Mission Santa Clara* T-AO 132, was loaned to Pakistan in Jan 1963. *Shawnee Trail* T-AO 142 was reacquired from Maritime Administration on 20 Jan 1965 to replace *Mission San Antonio* which was stricken.

CONVERSION. *Mission Capistrano* AO 112, converted into a sound testing experimental ship (T-AG 162).

MISSION SAN RAFAEL (T-AO 130) *Skyfotos*

2 GASOLINE TANKERS (AOG): "ALATNA" CLASS

Name	*No.*	*Launched*
ALATNA	T-AOG 81	6 Sep 1956
CHATTAHOOCHEE	T-AOG 82	4 Dec 1956

Displacement, tons	5 720
Measurement, tons	3 200 gross; 3 445 deadweight
Dimensions, feet	302 oa × 16 × 19
Main engines	Diesel-electric; 2 shafts; 3 400 hp = 12 knots
Cargo	30 000 barrels

T1-MET-24a type. Built for MSTS by Bethlehem Steel, Staten Island, NY. Laid down on 16 Mar 1956 and 1 May 1956, respectively. Delivered in June and August 1957. Bows strengthened for navigation in ice; equipped with helicopter flight deck aft.

ALATNA (T-AOG 81) *United States Navy*

4 GASOLINE TANKERS (AOG): "PECONIC" CLASS

	T-AOG
NODAWAY (*ex-Belridge*)	78
PETALUMA (*ex-Raccoon Bend*)	79
PISCATAQUA (ex-*Cisne*)	80
RINCON	77

Displacement, tons	2 060 light; 6 000 full load
Dimensions, feet	325 oa × 48 × 19 max
Main engines	Diesel; 1 shaft; 1 400 bhp = 10 knots
Complement	33
Cargo	30 000 barrels

T1-M-BT2 design. All built by Todd, Houston. *Nodaway* was reacquired from the Maritime Administration in 1965.

TRANSFERS. *Tonti* AOG 76, of this class was transferred to Colombia in 1965.

DISPOSALS
Peconic AOG 68, was transferred to Maritime Administration in 1960.

RINCON (T-AOG 77) *United States Navy (MSTS)*

3 TRANSPORTS (AP): "BARRETT" CLASS

		Launched	*Completed*
BARRETT (ex-*President Jackson*)	T-AP 196	27 June 1950	15 Dec 1951
GEIGER (ex-*President Adams*)	T-AP 197	9 Oct 1950	13 Sep 1952
UPSHUR (ex-*President Hayes*)	T-AP 198	19 Jan 1951	20 Dec 1952

Displacement, tons	17 600 standard; 19 600 full load
Measurement, tons	12 660 gross; 10 600 deadweight
Dimensions, feet	533 oa × 73 × 27
Main engines	Geared turbines; 1 shaft; 13 750 shp = 19 to 20 knots (cruising), see *Engineering*
Troops	1 900 (400 officers, 1 500 men)

Maritime Administration type P2-S1-DNI. All three were built by the New York Shipbuilding Corporation, New Jersey. Originally laid down as passenger ships for the American President Lines but taken over by the Navy to be completed as troop transports, and were all assigned to the Military Sea Transportation Service as US Naval Ships (non-commissioned naval vessels). Troop carrying capacity of 1 500 plus 396 cabin berths for officers and dependants. Troop lift can be increased by at least 1 000 men if necessary by converting recreation areas into berthing spaces. All spaces, compartments and holds are air-conditioned except the engine room and bridge.

The *Barrett* and *Geiger* are the only US Navy troop transports in service; the *Upshur* is in reserve.

ENGINEERING. On sea trials *Barrett* attained a speed of 21·5 knots at full power.

Logistic Support Ships—*continued*

UPSHUR (T-AP 198) *Skyfotos*

GENERAL ALEXANDER M. PATCH (T-AP 122) *Skyfotos*

5 TRANSPORTS (AP): "ADMIRAL" CLASS

GENERAL ALEXANDER M. PATCH (ex-*Admiral R. E. Coontz*)	T-AP 122
GENERAL SIMON B. BUCKNER (ex-*Admiral E. W. Eberle*)	T-AP 123
GENERAL NELSON M. WALKER (ex-*Admiral H. T. Mayo*)	T-AP 125
GENERAL MAURICE ROSE (ex-*Admiral Hugh Rodman*)	T-AP 126
GENERAL WILLIAM O. DARBY (ex-*Admiral W. S. Sims*)	T-AP 127

Displacement, tons	9 676 standard; 20 120 full load
Dimensions, feet	609 oa × 75·5 × 26·5 (29 max)
Main engines	2 GE Turbo-electric; 2 shafts; 18 000 shp = 19 knots
Boilers	4 (Combustion Engineering "D" type)
Complement	367 (37 officers, 330 enlisted men)
Troops	4 680 (280 officers, 4 400 enlisted men)

MC Type P 2-SE2-R1. Ex-"Admiral" Class. All built by Bethlehem-Alameda in 1944-1945. T-AP 125 *General Nelson M. Walker* was transferred to the Maritime Administration in 1958, but was reacquired by the Navy as a result of the Lebanon landings in July 1958. She was stricken from the Navy List on 20 Jan 1959, and transferred to the Maritime Administration as excess to MSTS requirements, but was reacquired from Maritime Administration in Sep 1965.
All remaining ships in reserve.

DISPOSALS
Of this class the **General Daniel I. Sultan** T-AP 120 transferred to Maritime Administration on 7 Nov 1968, **General Hugh J. Gaffey** T-AP 121 to MarAd on 27 Nov 1968, **General Edwin D. Patrick** T-AP 124 to MarAd on 20 Sep 1968.
Of the C-4 "General" class, the **General R. M. Blatchford** T-AP 153 and **General Le Roy Eltinge** T-AP 154 transferred to MarAd on 17 Sep 1968.

VC3 types. *Frederick Funston* T-AP 178, *James O'Hara* T-AP 179, *David C. Shanks* T-AP 180, *Fred C. Ainsworth* T-AP 181, *George W. Goethals* T-AP 182, and *Henry Gibbins* T-AP 183, were transferred to the Maritime Administration in 1960. (*Henry Gibbins* was turned over to the New York Maritime College at Fort Schuyler as a training vessel on a loan basis).
T-AP 186 *Sergeant Charles E. Mower*, was transferred in 1960. Sister ship T-AP 185 *Private William H. Thomas* (ex-*Rixey*) and T-AP 184 *Private Eldon H. Johnson* (ex-*Kinkney*) were transferred to the Maritime Administration late in 1957.
T-AP 202 *Marine Serpent*, returned to Maritime Administration in 1955. T-AP 193 *Marine Adder*, T-AP *Marine Lynx*, T-AP 195 *Marine Phoenix* and T-AP 199 *Marine Carp* transferred to the Maritime Administration in 1958.

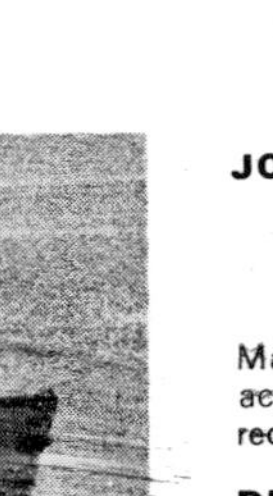

GENERAL MAURICE ROSE (T AP 126) *United States Navy (MSTS)*

3 TRANSPORTS (AP): P-2 "GENERAL" CLASS

Name	*No.*	*Launched*
GENERAL JOHN POPE	T-AP 110	21 Mar 1945
GENERAL W. H. GORDON	T-AP 117	7 May 1944
GENERAL WILLIAM WEIGEL	T-AP 119	3 Sep 1944

Displacement, tons	11 828 standard; 20 175 full load
Dimensions, feet	573 wl; 622·5 oa × 75·5 × 25·5 max
Main engines	De Laval geared turbines; 2 shafts; 17 000 shp = 20·6 knots
Boilers	4 (Foster-Wheeler)
Troops	5 240 (320 officers, 4 920 enlisted men)
Complement	476 (43 officers, 433 enlisted men)

All built by Federal SB & DD Co at Kearny. *General W. H. Gordon*, was reacquired from the Maritime Administration, returned to the Navy, and assigned to the MSTS in 1961, being manned by a civil service crew. The three ships manned by Navy crews, were transferred to the Maritime Administration in 1965 and 1966, see *Transfers* below. They were replaced by *General John Pope*, *General William Weigel* and *General Nelson M. Walker*. All in reserve.

TRANSFERS. *General A. E. Anderson*, AP 111, *General John Pope* AP 110, *General M. C. Meigs* AP 116, and *General William Weigel* AP 119, were transferred to the Maritime Administration Reserve Fleet in 1958; but *General John Pope* and *General William Weigel* were reacquired by the Navy in 1965 and designated USNS. *General H. W. Butner* T-AP 113, was transferred to the Maritime Administration in May 1961, *General G. M. Randall* T-AP 115, in Sep 1962, *General J. C. Breckinbridge* T-AP 176, *General W. A. Mann* T-AP 112 and *General William Mitchell* T-AP 114, on 1 Dec 1966

GENERAL JOHN POPE (T-AP 110) *United States Navy (MSTS)*

1 COASTAL TRANSPORT (APC)

JONAH E. KELLEY (ex-*Link Splice*) T-APC 116

Displacement, tons	2 460 light; 7 460 full load
Dimensions, feet	338·8 × 50 × 21
Main engines	Diesel; 1 750 bhp = 11·5 knots

Maritime Administration C1-M-AV1 Type. *Private Jose F. Valdez* (APC 119) reacquired from the Maritime Administration, returned to the Navy in Aug 1961, and reclassified as T-AG 169 in 1963. T-APC 116 is in reserve.

DISPOSALS
Of this type, **Sergeant George D. Keathley** T-APC 117 (ex-*Acorn Knot*, ex-*Alexander R. Niminger, Sr*), and **Sergeant Joseph E. Muller** T-APC 118 (ex-*Check Knot*), were transferred to the Maritime Administration in 1959, but the latter was reacquired in 1962 and reclassified as T-AG 171 in 1963 and the former was reacquired in 1966 and redesignated T-AGS 35 on 1 Dec 1966.

2 AIRCRAFT TRANSPORTS (AVT): "INDEPENDENCE" CLASS

Name	*No.*	*Builder*	*Laid down*	*Launched*	*Commissioned*
MONTEREY (ex-*Dayton*)	AVT 2 (ex-CVL 26)	New York SB Corpn	29 Dec 1941	28 Feb 1943	17 June 1943
SAN JACINTO (ex-*Reprisal*, ex-*Newark*)	AVT 5 (ex-CVL 30)	New York SB Corpn	26 Oct 1942	26 Sep 1943	15 Dec 1943

Displacement, tons	11 000 standard; 15 800 full load
Length, feet (*metres*)	600 (*182·9*) wl; 623 (*189·9*) oa
Beam, feet (*metres*)	71·5 (*21·8*) hull
Draft, feet (*metres*)	26 (*7·9*)
Width, feet (*metres*)	109 (*33·2*) extreme
Aircraft	40+
Guns	28—40 mm
Boilers	4 (Babcock & Wilcox)
Main engines	GE geared turbines; 4 shafts; 100 000 shp
Speed, knots	32

Completed as aircraft carriers after having been laid down as cruisers of the "Cleveland" class. Both ships are in reserve.
As aircraft carriers the original complement was 1 569 (159 officers and 1 410 enlisted men). *Princeton* (ex-*Tallahassee*) CVL 23, of this class, was lost in action in 1944.

GUNNERY. Originally designed to include 4—5 inch guns in armament, but subsequently mounted 16—40 mm AA guns and 40—20 mm AA guns.

TRANSFERS. *Langley* (CVL 27) was transferred to the French Navy in 1951 under the Mutual Defence Assistance Programme but was returned to the USA in Mar 1963, stricken from the Navy List in June 1963, and later scrapped. *Belleau Wood* (CVL 24), transferred to France in Sep 1953 on loan for five years, subsequently extended for five more, was returned to the USA in Sep 1960 and stricken.

Cabot (CVL 28) was transferred to Spain in 1967 (helicopter carrier).

RECLASSIFICATION. The ships of this class were reclassified from Small Aircraft Carriers (CVL) to Auxiliary Aircraft Transports (AVT) on 15 May 1959.

FUNNELS. *Monterey* has only two of her original four funnels.

DISPOSALS
Bataan (AVT 4 ex-CVL 29), was stricken from the Navy list on 1 Sep 1959 and **Cowpens**, (AVT 1 ex-CVL 25), on 1 Nov 1959. **Independence** (CVL 22) was expended in atom bomb and radiographical experiments from July 1946 to Jan 1951.

The five "Essex" class aircraft carriers classified as aircraft transports have been stricken from the Navy List: The **Franklin** (AVT 8 ex-CVS 13) was stricken on 1 Oct 1964, and the **Bunker Hill** (AVT 9, ex-CVS 17) on 1 Nov 1966; both ships had been severely damaged late in World War II and had not been returned to operational status before being "mothballed" in the reserve fleet early in 1947. The **Bunker Hill** is retained as an electronic test platform (see section on Experimental, Research and Surveying Ships). The **Tarawa** (AVT 12, ex-CVS 40) stricken on 1 June 1967 and scrapped. **Leyte** (AVT 10, ex-CVS 32) and **Philippine Sea** (AVT 11, ex-CVS 47) both stricken in 1969.

Logistic Support Ships—*continued*

MONTEREY (AVT 2) As aircraft carrier (see previous page). *United States Navy*

PROPOSED FAST DEPLOYMENT LOGISTIC SHIPS (FDL):

Displacement, tons	40 500 full load
Dimensions, feet	855 oa × 104 × 28
Main engines	Steam turbines; 6 000 shp, 2 shafts = 24+ knots

These ships are intended to carry pre-loaded Army combat equipment to overseas areas where the equipment would be "married" to troops flown overseas. Presumably, some of the ships always would be deployed overseas as floating depots. According to the Department of Defense, the most cost-effective number of FDL ships necessary to meet anticipated requirements in the 1970s would be 30 operating in conjunction with 14 squadrons of C-141 jet cargo aircraft and six squadrons of C-5 jet cargo aircraft. However, continued reluctance by the Congress to authorize the FDL programme led to a revised proposal by the Department of Defense in 1968 to build only 15 FDLs and obtain the balance of the sealift requirement through the long-term charter of up to 30 new cargo ships to be privately built according to design criteria specified by the Navy's Military Sea Transportation Service.

The first FDLs originally were requested in the Fiscal Year 1966 shipbuilding programme and each year since then, but at this writing had not been funded by the Congress.

The Fiscal Year 1970 programme requests $187 000 000 for the construction of three ships with the remaining 12 ships planned for FY 1971-1973 (four ships per year). Estimated cost per ship is $52 000 000.

CARGO. Each ship could lift 11 100 tons of material including tanks, helicopters, and heavy engineering equipment. Twelve FDLs could lift the equipment of a reinforced infantry division a task which would otherwise require 33 C-5 merchant ships (Department of Defense estimate).

CONSTRUCTION. Litton Systems Inc of Culver City, California, won the design competition for these ships, submitting the best technical proposal which included the factors of ship design efficiency and ship life cycle cost. Should the Congress approve construction of these ships the Navy would enter into contract negotiations with Litton for the actual construction of the ships; if negotiations with Litton were unsatisfactory there would be open competition amongst eligible shipbuilders. (Litton owns the Ingalls shipbuilding yard in Pascagoula but is also constructing a new yard in the area to build the LHA amphibious assault ship; presumably Litton would also construct the FDL ships at the new yard).

DESIGN. These ships have their superstructure aft with the forward deck suitable for operating cargo-carrying helicopters. There is a stern ramp for unloading amphibious vehicles and side entries for roll-on roll-off loading and unloading when piers are available. Vehicles and other equipment are stowed under dehumidified conditions and special fuel distribution and ventilation systems allow the vehicles to be fueled or defueled in any of the vehicle holds. Cranes, elevators, and ramps will speed loading and unloading.

ENGINEERING. A bow thruster and stern thruster are provided to assist docking operations when tugs are not available.

PERSONNEL. These ships will be manned by civilian MSTS crews with a small Army detachment carried on board to service the vehicles.

FDL Concept *Department of Defense*

41 TANK LANDING SHIPS (LST)

Name	*No.*	*Name*	*No.*
LST 47	T-LST 47	**LST 537**	T-LST 587
LST 117	T-LST 117	**LST 590**	T-LST 590
LST 176	T-LST 176	**LST 607**	T-LST 607
LST 222	T-LST 222	**LST 613**	T-LST 613
LST 230	T-LST 230	**LST 623**	T-LST 623
LST 276	T-LST 276	**LST 626**	T-LST 626
LST 277	T-LST 277	**LST 629**	T-LST 629
LST 287	T-LST 287	**LST 630**	T-LST 630
LST 399	T-LST 399	**LST 643**	T-LST 643
LST 456	T-LST 456	**LST 649**	T-LST 649
LST 488	T-LST 488	**LST 664**	T-LST 664
LST 491	T-LST 491	**DAVIESS COUNTY**	T-LST 692
LST 530	T-LST 530	**DE KALB COUNTY**	T-LST 715
CHASE COUNTY	T-LST 532	**HARRIS COUNTY**	T-LST 822
LST 546	T-LST 546	**NEW LONDON COUNTY**	T-LST 1066
LST 550	T-LST 550	**NYE COUNTY**	T-LST 1067
CHESTERFIELD COUNTY	T-LST 551	**ORLEANS PARISH**	
LST 566	T-LST 566	(ex-MCS 6)	T-LST 1069
LST 572	T-LST 572	**LST 1072**	T-LST 1072
LST 579	T-LST 579	**PLUMAS COUNTY**	T-LST 1083
LST 581	T-LST 581	**PULASKI COUNTY**	T-LST 1088

Displacement, tons	LST 511-1152: 1 653 standard; 4 080 full load
	LST 1-510: 1 625 light; 4 050 full load
Dimensions, feet	328 oa × 50 × 14
Main engines	Diesels (General Motors); 1 700 shp; 2 shafts = 11·6 knots

Former Navy-manned tank landing ships now employed to carry cargo in the Western Pacific. T-LST 287, 532, 551, 590, 626, 643, 664, 692, 822, 1066, 1067, 1069, 1072, and 1088 (14 ships) are manned by South Korean personnel; all others by Japanese personnel. See Amphibious Warfare Ships for detailed data.

RECLASSIFICATION. The *Orleans Parish* was fitted to support minesweepers and reclassified a Mine Countermeasures Support Ship (MCS 6) on 19 Jan 1959; subsequently reclassified T-LST on 1 June 1966 and assigned to Military Sea Transportation Service.

DISPOSALS

LST **600** stricken on 1 June 1969.

EXPERIMENTAL, RESEARCH, AND SURVEYING SHIPS

TWO EXPERIMENTAL SURFACE EFFECT SHIPS

The Navy and the Maritime Administration announced the award of research and development contracts for two 100-ton experimental surface effect ships on 28 January 1969. The test craft will be built by the Aerojet-General Corp of El Monte, California, and the Bell Aerosystems Co., of Buffalo, New York.

The test craft are a major phase in the Navy-Maritime Administration long-range efforts to determine the feasibility of building and operating large, high-speed surface effect ships of 4,000 to 5,000 tons, and capable of 80-knot or high speeds.

The Bell craft will be propelled by supercavitating propellers driven by gas turbine engines; the Aero-General craft will use waterjet propulsion with gas turbine engines. The test craft will provide information on alternate design configurations, structural, lift, and flexible seal features as well as propulsion schemes. The craft will ride on a "cushion" or "bubble" of air as do the Navy's Patrol Air Cushion Vehicles (PACV) (see section on Patrol, Coastal and Riverine Craft).

A Joint Surface Effect Ships Programme Office (JSESPO) has been established to co-ordinate the Navy and Maritime Administration efforts in this area and to administer the contracts awarded to Aerojet-General and Bell.

1 CRUISER (AG): PROPOSED SONAR TEST SHIP

SPOKANE AG 191 (ex-CLAA 120)

Displacement, tons	6 000 standard; 8 200 full load
Dimensions, feet	530 wl; 541 oa × 53·2 × 25
Main engines	Geared turbines (Westinghouse); 75 000 shp; 2 shafts
Boilers	4 (Babcock & Wilcox)
Speed, knots	32

Formerly a light anti-aircraft cruiser of the "Juneau" class. Scheduled for conversion to a sonar test ship, but project deferred because of funding constraints; remains in reserve.
Built by Federal Shipbuilding, Kearny, New Jersey; laid down 15 Nov 1944, launched 22 Sep 1945, commissioned 17 May 1946. Placed in reserve shortly after completion.

ARMAMENT. Armament as CLAA consisted of 12 5 inch 38 cal DP guns in twin mounts and 28 40 mm AA guns in four quad and six twin mounts.

RECLASSIFICATIONS AND DISPOSALS

Acquisition of **AG 155** (C-4 cargo type) was cancelled; **Hunting** (AG 156, ex-EAG 398, ex-LSM 398) stricken in 1962; **King County** (AG 157, ex-LST 857) stricken with cancellation of Regulus II missile programme; AG **158** was to be research ship; **Oxford** (AG 159) reclassified AGTR 1; **AG 160-161** reclassifeid AGM 1-2; **Glover** (AG 163) reclassified AGDE 1; **AG 165-168** reclassified AGTR 2-5; **Lieutenant J. E. Robinson** (AG 170) reclassified T-AK 274; **T-AG 172-174** are in service as cargo ships; **AG 179-190** assigned to 12 "Victory" ships to have been used as floating depot ships; project cancelled. The **AG 335** is the former LSM 335, employed as a cargo ship and listed with Logistic Support Ships. **Peregrine** (AG 176, ex-MSF 373) stricken on 1 Feb 1969; **Shearwater** (T-AG-177) returned to US Army on 14 June 1967 (now used at Army Transportation Corps School in Virginia).

1 HYDROGRAPHIC RESEARCH SHIP (AG): "FLYER" TYPE

FLYER (ex-SS *American Flyer*, ex-SS *Water Witch*) T-AG 178

Displacement, tons	7 360 light; 11 000 full load
Dimensions, feet	459·2 oa × 63 × 28
Main engines	Turbines; 6 000 shp = 17 knots
Boilers	2
Complement	14 officers, 41 enlisted men

Acquired from Maritime Administration on 9 Feb 1965. CS-2-B1 type.
Operated by MSTS for Naval Electronic Systems Command; civilian manned.

FLYER (T-AG 178) *US Navy (MSTS)*

1 SURVEYING SHIP (AG): C1-M-AVI TYPE

SERGEANT CURTIS F. SHOUP T-AG 175

Displacement, tons	3 000 light; 7 410 full load
Dimensions, feet	339 × 50 × 21
Main engines	Diesel; 1 750 bhp = 11·5 knots
Complement	11 officers, 33 enlisted men, 42 technicians

CI-M-AVI Type. Fitted for gravity and magnetic survey. Fitted with helicopter platform forward.
Operated by MSTS for Naval Oceanographic Office; civilian manned.

SERGEANT CURTIS F. SHOUP (T-AG 175) *US Navy (MSTS)*

2 SPECIAL MISSION SHIPS (AG): C1-M-AVI TYPE

PRIVATE JOSE E. VALDEZ (ex-*Round Splice*, ex-*Joe J. Martinez*) T-AG 169 (ex-*T-APC* 119)

SERGEANT JOSEPH E. MULLER (ex-*Check Knot*) T-AG 171 (ex-*T-APC* 118)

Displacement, tons	2 460 light; 7 460 full load
Dimensions, feet	338·5 × 50 × 21
Main engines	Diesel; 1 750 bhp = 11·5 knots
Complement	15 officers, 148 enlisted men in *Valdez*; 16 officers, 153 enlisted men in *Mueller*

These are special mission ships which collect oceanographic, associated electro-magnetic radiation information, and meteorological observations in support of marine environmental programmes.
Operated by Military Sea Transportation Service for Naval Communications Command; civilian crews.
C1-M-AVI type.

SERGEANT JOSEPH E. MULLER (T-AG 171) *United States Air Force*

1 HYDROGRAPHIC RESEARCH SHIP (AG) "KINGSPORT" TYPE

KINGSPORT (ex-*Kingsport Victory*, T-239) T-AG 164

Displacement, tons	7 190 light; 10 680 full load
Dimensions, feet	455 oa × 62 × 24
Main engines	Geared turbines; 1 shaft; 8 500 shp = 17 knots
Boilers	2
Complement	14 officers, 61 enlisted men, 13 technicians

VC2-S-AP3. Built in 1944 by the California Shipbuilding Corp, Los Angeles. Former cargo ship in the MSTS fleet. Name shortened, ship reclassified, and converted in 1961-62 by Willamette Iron & Steel Co, Portland, Oregon, into the world's first satelite communications ship, for Project Advent, involving the promotion of a terminal to meet the required military capability for high capacity, world-wide radio communications, using high altitiude hovering satellites, and the installation of ship-to-shore communications, facilities, additional electric power generating equipment, a helicopter landing platform, aerological facilities, and a 30-ft parabolic communication antenna housed in a 53-ft diameter plastic radome abaft the superstructure. Painted white for operations in the tropics. Project Advent Syncom satellite relay operations were completed in 1966, and *Kingsport* was reassigned to hydrographic research. Antenna sphere now removed.
Operated by MSTS for Naval Electronic Systems Command; civilian manned.
Broadside view appears in 1968-1969 edition; note antenna mast on helicopter platform in photograph; exhaust ducts fitted to funnel.

KINGSPORT (T-AG 164) *United States Navy (MSTS)*

Experimental, Research & Surveying Ships—*continued*

1 SOUND TESTING SHIP (AG): CONVERTED OILER

MISSION CAPISTRANO (ex-*AO* 112) T-AG 162

Displacement, tons	17 000
Dimensions, feet	523·5 oa × 68 × 30·9
Main engines	Turbo-electric; 10 000 shp = 16 knots
Boilers	2
Complement	14 officers, 46 enlisted men, 25 technicians

Former oiler of T2-SE-A2 type converted by Todd Shipyards, New Orleans in connection, with operations of Texas Tower Argus Island off Bermuda. Fitted with a sound transducer assembly five stories high. Used to test the huge sonar transducer in sonar system for detecting submarines at long range. The transducer, aft of bridge, can be raised and lowered as desired. Project "Artemis". Built in 1944. Operated by MSTS for Office of Naval Research; civilian manned.

MISSION CAPISTRANO (T-AG 162) *United States Navy (MSTS)*

1 POLARIS-POSEIDON TEST SHIP (AG)

OBSERVATION ISLAND (ex-*YAG* 57, ex-SS *Empire State Mariner*) AG 154

Displacement, tons	17 600 full load
Measurement, tons	15 000
Dimensions, feet	529·5 wl; 563 oa × 76·2 × 29
Main engines	Geared turbines (General Electric); 1 shaft; 19 250 shp = 20 knots
Boilers	2
Complement	350

Built by New York Shipbuilding Corp, Camden, New Jersey. Converted by Norfolk Naval Shipyard, Portsmouth, Virginia. Commissioned on 5 Dec 1958. Experimental vessels for firing "Polaris" Fleet Ballistic Missile (FBM); subsequently fitted to fire the improved Poseidon FBM.

MISSILE TESTING. The ship is fitted for complete missile testing, servicing and firing system. She fired the first ship-launched Polaris missile, at sea on 27 Aug 1959. She was fitted with the second "Polaris" missile launching tube in Sep 1959 at Norfolk Naval Shipyard. Now fitted to fire Poseidon missile.

OBSERVATION ISLAND (AG 154) *United States Navy*

OBSERVATION ISLAND (AG 154) *United States Navy*

1 EXPERIMENTAL NAVIGATION SHIP (AG)

COMPASS ISLAND (ex-*YAG* 56, ex-SS *Garden Mariner*) AG 153

Displacement, tons	16 076 full load
Measurement, tons	17 600
Dimensions, feet	529·5 pp; 563 oa × 76·2 × 29
Main engines	Geared turbines (General Electric); 1 shaft; 19 250 shp = 20 knots
Boilers	2

Built by New York Shipbuilding Corp, Camden, New Jersey. Converted by New York Naval Shipyard, Brooklyn, and commissioned on 3 Dec 1956 for the development of the Fleet Ballistic Missile guidance and ship navigation systems. Her mission is to assist in the development and evaluation of a navigation system independent of shore-based aids. (See *Navigation* notes on SINS, Ship Inertial Navigational System, in the 1957-58 to 1963-64 editions). The ship was acquired by the Navy from the Maritime Administration. She was modernised to provide excellent living spaces for her crew and accommodation for a large number of scientists to work and live aboard. Navy manned.

STABILIZATION. One of the most comfortable riding ships in the Navy. She has the best automatic steering available, and has activated fins for roll stabilization. This system was developed by Sperry Gyroscope Co. When her sister ships roll 15 degrees, *Compass Island*, in the same seaway rolls about 1·5 degrees.

1 HYDROFOIL RESEARCH SHIP (AGEH)

PLAINVIEW AGEH 1

Displacement, tons	310 full load
Dimensions, feet	212 oa × 40·5 × 10 (foils extended), 26 (withdrawn)
ASW weapons	2 triple torpedo launchers (Mk 32)
Main engines	2 gas turbines (General Electric); 30 000 hp; 2 diesels; 1 200 hp
Complement	20 (6 officers, 14 men)

Aluminium hull experimental hydrofoil. Three retractable foils, 25 ft in height, each weighing 7 tons, fitted port and starboard and on stern, and used in waves up to 15 feet. Initial maximum speed of about 50 knots, with later modifications expected to raise the speed to 80 knots. Fitted with the largest titanium propellers made. The two 15 000 hp gas turbines are General Electric J-79 jet aircraft engines modified for marine use. Power plant and transmission designed to permit future investigation of various types of foils. Built by Lockheed Shipbuilding & Construction Co, Seattle, Washington. Laid down on 8 May 1964, launched on 28 June 1965, and completed in 1968. Delayed because of engineering difficulties. In service vice being in commission.

Two photographs of *Plainview* being fitted out appear in the 1968-1969 edition. The views below show her on builder trials in Puget Sound.

HYDROFOIL PROGRAMME. The US Navy has four ocean-going hydrofoils: the large experimental ship *Plainview*, the experimental *High Point* (PCH 1), and the hydrofoil gunboats *Flagstaff* (PGH 1) and *Tucumari* (PGH 2). The latter ships are listed in the section on Patrol Coastal and Riverine Craft.

PLAINVIEW (AGEH 1) *1968, Lockhead Shipbuilding*

PLAINVIEW (AGEH-1) *1968, Lockhead Shipbuilding*

Experimental, Research, and Surveying Ships—*continued*

2 ENVIRONMENTAL RESEARCH SHIPS (AGER)

BANNER (ex-AKL 25, ex-FS 345) AGER 1
PUEBLO (ex-AKL 44, ex-FS 344) AGER 2
PALM BEACH (ex-AKL 45, ex-FS 217) AGER 3

Displacement, tons	906 full load
Dimensions, feet	176·5 oa (*Banner* 180) × 32 × 10
Main engines	1 diesel; 1 000 shp; 1 shaft = 13 knots
Guns	*Pueblo:* 3—·50 cal MG; others rearmed with 20 mm guns
Complement	*Pueblo:* 6 officers, 75 enlisted men, 2 civilian hydrographers

These ships are former Army freight and supply ships, converted for passive intelligence operations. *Banner* acquired by the Navy in 1965; *Pueblo* and *Palm Beach* in 1966; all reclassified AGER on 1 June 1967. Fitted for electronic intelligence (ELINT) and sonar equipment for submarine noise signature identification and hydrographic work. Note differing configurations; *Pueblo* resembles *Banner* (photograph of *Pueblo* in 1968-1969 edition).

STATUS. The *Pueblo* was boarded and captured by North Korean forces in reportedly international waters off the port of Wonsan in January 1968. At this writing the ship was still interned by North Korea. At the time of capture her military complement included a 28-man intelligence group.

PALM BEACH (AGER 3) *1967, US Navy*

BANNER (AGER 1) *1968, US Navy*

1 RANGE INSTRUMENTATION SHIP (AGM): POSEIDON PROGRAMME

The Fiscal Year 1969 ship conversion programme provided $20 000 000 for the conversion of a ship to a Range Instrumentation Ship (RIS) to support development of the Poseidon Fleet Ballistic Missile (FBM). Further details were not available when this page closed; presumably the Poseidon RIS will be converted from a merchant ship hull currently in the Maritime Administration reserve fleet.

3 RANGE INSTRUMENTATION SHIPS (AGM): T2-SE-A2 TYPE

VANGUARD (ex-*Mussle Shoals*, ex-*Mission San Fernando*) T-AGM 19 (ex-T-AO 122)
REDSTONE (ex-*Johnstown*, ex-*Mission de Pala*) T-AGM 20 (ex-T-AO 114)
MERCURY (ex-*Flagstaff*, ex-*Mission San Juan*) T-AGM 21 (ex-T-AO 126)

Displacement, tons	21 626 full load
Dimensions, feet	595 oa × 75 × 25
Main engines	Turbine-electric; 1 shaft; 10 000 shp = 16 knots
Boilers	2 (Babcock & Wilcox)
Complement	*Vanguard* 19 officers, 71 enlisted men, 108 technical personnel; others 20 officers, 71 enlisted men, 120 technical personnel.

Former "Mission" class tankers converted in 1964-1966 to serve as mid-ocean communications and tracking ships in support of the Apollo manned lunar flights.
All built in 1944 by Marinship, Sausalito, California, as tankers. T2-SE-A2 type. Converted to Range Instrumentation Ships (RIS) by General Dynamics, Quincy Division, Massachusetts; each ship was cut in half and a 72-foot mid-section was inserted, increasing length, beam, and displacement; approximately 450 tons of electronic equipment installed for support of lunar flight operations, including communications and tracking systems; helicopter hangar and platform fitted aft. Cost for converting the three ships was $90 000 000. All operated by MSTS for Air Force Western Test Range in Pacific and NASA (normally to support Apollo lunar missions one ship is stationed in the Indian Ocean off the coast of Africa, one in the Pacific, and one in the Atlantic); civilian crews.

REDSTONE (T-AGM 20) *1966, General Dynamics*

VANGUARD (T-AGM 19) *1966, General Dynamics*

MERCURY (T-AGM 21) *1968, NASA*

2 RANGE INSTRUMENTATION SHIPS (AGM): C1-M-AV1 TYPE

SWORD KNOT T-AGM 13
COASTAL CRUSADER T-AGM 16

Dimensions, feet	338·8 oa × 50·3 × 12
Main engines	Diesel; 1 shaft = 10 knots
Complement	12 officers, 30 enlisted men, 28 technical personnel (27 technical personnel in *Coastal Crusader*)

Former merchant ships converted by Air Force to range instrumentation ships. *Sword Knot* built in 1945 by Consolidated Steel Corp, Wilmington, California; *Coastal Crusader* built in 1945 by Leatham D. Smith SB Co, Sturgeon Bay, Wisconsin. C1-M-AV1 type. Both assigned to MSTS on 1 July 1964; *Sword Knot* operated in support of Air Force Western Test Range in Pacific and *Coastal Crusader* in support of Air Force Eastern Test Range in Atlantic; civilian crews.

DISPOSALS
Four ships of this type have been stricken from the Navy List: **Rose Knot** (T-AGM 14) to Maritime Administration on 26 Mar 1968; *Coastal Sentry* (T-AGM 15, ex-AK 212) stricken on 11 July 1968 (scrapped); **Timber Hitch** (T-AGM 17) to Maritime Administration on 5 Feb 1968; **Sampan Hitch** (T-AGM 18) to Maritime Administration on 24 June 1968.
American Mariner (T-AGM 12), an EC2 "Liberty" ship, was expended as a target in Chesapeake Bay in Oct 1966.

COASTAL CRUSADER (T-AGM 16) *United States Navy (MSTS)*

2 RANGE INSTRUMENTATION SHIPS (AGM): C4-S-A1 TYPE

GENERAL H. H. ARNOLD (ex-USNS *General R. E. Collan*) T-AGM 9 (ex-T-AP 139)
GENERAL HOYT S. VANDENBERG (ex-USNS *General Harry Taylor*) T-AGM 10 (ex-T-AP 145)

Displacement, tons	16 600 full load
Dimensions, feet	552·9 oa × 71·5 × 26·3
Main engines	Geared turbines; 1 shaft; 9 000 shp = 15 knots
Complement	21 officers, 68 enlisted men, 89 technical personnel

Former transports converted in 1962-1963 for monitoring Air Force missile firings and satellite launches.
Both ships built in 1944 by Kaiser Co, Richmond, California, as large troop transports. C4-S-A1 type. Upon conversion to range instrumentation they were placed in service in 1963 as Air Force ships; however, assigned to MSTS for operation on 1 July 1964 (T-AGM 9) and 13 July 1964 (T-AGM 10). Both ships operate in support of the Air Force Eastern Test Range in the Atlantic; civilian crews.

GEN. NOYTS. VANDENBERG *US Navy (MSTS)*

1 RANGE INSTRUMENTATION SHIP (AGM): AKL TYPE

RANGE RECOVERER (ex-FS 278) T-AGM 2 (ex-T-AG 161)

Displacement, tons	550
Dimensions, feet	176·5 oa × 32 × 11·5
Main engines	Diesel; 1 shaft = 14 knots
Complement	8 officers, 14 enlisted men, 8 technical personnel

Former Army small cargo ship modified for telementry of rocket firings from Wallops Station in Chesapeake Bay.
Built in 1944 by Wheeler SB Corp, Whitesone, New York. Assigned to MSTS on 6 Apr 1960; operated in support of NASA; civilian crew.

RANGE RECOVERER (T-AG 161) *US Navy (MSTS)*

7 RANGE INSTRUMENTATION SHIPS (AGM): "VICTORY" TYPE

RANGE TRACKER (ex-SS *Skidmore Victory*)	T-AGM 1 (ex T-AG 160)
LONGVIEW (ex-*Haiti Victory*)	T-AGM 3 (ex-T-AK 238)
SUNNYVALE (ex-*Dalton Victory*)	T-AGM 5 (ex-T-AK 256)
WATERTOWN (ex-SS *Niantic Victory*)	T-AGM 6
HUNTSVILLE (ex-SS *Knox Victory*)	T-AGM 7
WHEELING (ex-*Seton Hall Victory*)	T-AGM 8
TWIN FALLS (ex-*Twin Falls Victory*)	T-AGM 11

Displacement, tons	7 190 Navy light; 10 680 full load
Dimensions, feet	T-AGM 1, 6, 7: 455·8 oa × 62 × 28·6;
	T-AGM 3, 5, 8, 11: 455·3 oa × 62·2 × 28 (draft varies)
Main engines	Geared turbines; 1 shaft; 8 500 shp
Speed, knots	T-AGM 1, 6, 7: 16·2; T-AGM 3, 5, 8: 17; T-AGM 11: 15·2

All VC2-S-AP3 type; details vary. All extensively modified to serve as Range Instrumentation Ships (RIS) in support of American military and National Aeronautics and Space Administration (NASA) missile and space programmes.
Range Tracker built in 1945 by Oregon SB Corp, Portland, Oregon. Assigned to MSTS on 1 May 1961; operated in support of Air Force Western Test Range in Pacific; civilian crew of 12 officers, 44 enlisted men, plus 42 technical personnel.
Longview built in 1944 by Permanente Metals Corp, Richmond, California. Assigned to MSTS on 1 Mar 1950 (as T-AK 238); operated in support of Air Force Western Test Range in Pacific; civilian crew of 18 officers, 61 enlisted men, plus 30 technical personnel. Fitted with helicopter hangar and platform aft.
Sunnyvale built in 1944 by California SB Corp, Los Angeles. Assigned to MSTS on 6 Aug 1950 (as T-AK 256); operated in support of Air Force Western Test Range in Pacific; civilian crew of 18 officers, 61 enlisted men, plus 60 technical personnel. Fitted with helicopter hangar and platform aft.
Watertown built in 1944 by Oregon SB Corp, Portland, Oregon. Assigned to MSTS on 11 Aug 1960; operated in support of Air Force Western Test Range in Pacific and NASA; civilian crew of 14 officers, 55 enlisted men, plus 72 technical personnel.
Huntsville built in 1945 by Oregon SB Corp, Portland, Oregon. Assigned to MSTS on 1 Mar 1960; operated in support of Air Force Western Test Range in Pacific and NASA; civilian crew of 14 officers, 55 enlisted men, plus 72 technical personnel.
Wheeling built in 1945 by Oregon SB Corp, Portland, Oregon. Assigned to MSTS on 28 May 1964; operated in support of Navy Pacific Missile Range; civilian crew of 13 officers, 46 enlisted men, plus 62 technical personnel. Fitted with helicopter hangar and platform aft.
Twin Falls built in 1945 by Oregon SB Corp, Portland, Oregon. Assigned to MSTS on 1 July 1964; operated in support of Air Force Eastern Test Range in Atlantic; civilian crew of 17 officers, 43 enlisted men, plus 57 technical personnel.

DISPOSALS
Richfield (T-AGM 4, ex-T-AK 253) of this type transferred to Maritime Administration on 21 Nov 1968.

RANGE TRACKER (T-AGM 1) *United States Navy*

LONGVIEW *United States Navy*

WATERTOWN (T-AGM 6) *United States Navy (MSTS)*

WHEELING (T-AGM 8) *United States Navy (MSTS)*

Experimental, Research & Surveying Ships—*continued*

1 OCEANOGRAPHIC RESEARCH SHIP (AGOR): CATAMARAN TYPE

T-AGOR 16

Displacement, tons	3 080 full load
Dimensions, feet	246·5 oa × 75 (see *Design* notes) × 18·8
Main engines	Geared diesels; 2 400 shp; 2 shafts = 15 knots
Complement	44 + 25 scientists

Authorised in Fiscal Year 1967 new construction programme. The T-AGOR 16 will be the second class of modern US naval ships to have a catamaran hull, the first being the ASR 21 class submarine rescue ships. Under construction at Todd Shipyards, Seattle, Washington; to be completed in 1971. Estimated cost is $15 900 000.
The ship will be operated by MSTS for the Office of Naval Research under the technical control of the Oceanographer of the Navy; civilian crew.

DESIGN. Catamaran hull design provides large deck working area, centre well for operating equipment at great depths, and removes laboratory areas from main propulsion machinery. Each hull is 246·5 feet long and 24 feet wide (maximum). There are three 36-inch diameter instrument wells in addition to the main center well.

In Oct 1965 the Chief of Naval Research had proposed that the minelayer *Terror* (MMF 5) be converted to an AGOR to provide a ship of this size; however, the plan was dropped because of excessive conversion costs and a new design was undertaken, resulting in the T-AGOR 16.
The T-AGOR 16 differs in appearance from the ASR 21 class ships by the oceanographic ship having a small deck working space aft of the bridge structure and the absence of stern helicopter platform of the rescue ships.

ENGINEERING. Fitted with controllable pitch propellers. An auxiliary 165-shp diesel is fitted in each hull to provide "creeping" speed of 2 to 4 knots.

T-AGOR 16 *Official Navy drawing*

2 OCEANOGRAPHIC RESEARCH SHIPS (AGOR): NEW CONSTRUCTION

Name	*No.*	*Laid down*	*Launched*	*Completed*
MELVILLE	AGOR 14	12 July 1967	10 July 1968	May 1969
KNORR	AGOR 15	9 Aug 1967	21 Aug 1968	June 1969

Displacement, tons	1 915 tons
Dimensions, feet	244 oa × 46 × 14·9
Main engines	Diesel; 2 500 shp; 2 cycloidal propellers = 12 knots
Complement	9 officers, 16 enlisted men, 25 scientists

Oceanographic research ships of an advanced design. AGOR 14 and AGOR 15 authorised in Fiscal Year 1966 new construction programme; AGOR 19 and AGOR 20 of this type in FY 1968 programme, but construction of the latter ships was cancelled. The *Melville* and *Knorr* built by Defoe Shipbuilding Co, Bay City, Michigan. *Melville* operated by Scripps Institution of Oceanography and *Knorr* by Woods Hole Oceanography Institution for the Office of Naval Research; under technical control of the Oceanographer of the Navy.

DESIGN. Fitted with internal wells for lower equipment; underwater lights and observation ports. Facilities for handling small research submersibles. Enlarged and improved version of earlier "Conrad" class.

ENGINEERING. First US Navy ocean-going ships with cycloidal propellers. One propeller is fitted at each end of the ship, providing movement in any direction and optimum station keeping without use of thrusters.

NOMENCLATURE. Oceanographic research ships and surveying ships generally are named for naval oceanographers, hydrographers, and explorers. (Converted ships generally retain original names).

JAMES M. GILLISS (T-AGOR 4) *United States Navy*

9 OCEANOGRAPHIC RESEARCH SHIPS (AGOR): "CONRAD" TYPE

Name	*No.*	*Laid down*	*Launched*	*Delivered*
ROBERT D. CONRAD	AGOR 3	19 Jan 1961	26 May 1962	29 Nov 1962
JAMES M. GILLISS	T-AGOR 4	31 May 1961	19 May 1962	5 Nov 1962
CHARLES H. DAVIS	T-AGOR 5	15 June 1961	30 June 1962	25 Jan 1963
SANDS	T-AGOR 6	23 Aug 1962	14 Sep 1963	8 Feb 1965
LYNCH	T-AGOR 7	7 Sep 1962	17 Mar 1964	22 Oct 1965
THOMAS G. THOMPSON	AGOR 9	12 Sep 1963	18 July 1964	1965
THOMAS WASHINGTON	AGOR 10	12 Sep 1963	1 Aug 1964	1965
DE STEIGUER	T-AGOR 12	12 Nov 1965	21 Mar 1966	28 Feb 1969
BARTLETT	T-AGOR 13	18 Nov 1965	24 May 1966	15 Apr 1969

Displacement, tons	1 200 standard; 1 380 full load
Dimensions, feet	191·5 wl; 208·9 oa × 37·4 × 15·3
Main engines	Diesel-electric; 1 shaft; 10 000 hp = 13·5
Complement	9 officers, 17 enlisted men, 15 scientists (except *De Steigeur* and *Bartlett*, 8 officers, 18 enlisted men)

This is the first class of ships designed and built by the US Navy for oceanographic research. Fitted with instrumentation and laboratories to measure the earth's gravity and magnetic fields, water temperature, sound transmission in water, and the geological profile of the ocean floor.
Special features include 10 ton capacity boom and winches for handling over-the-side equipment; bow thruster propulsion unit for precise manoeuvrability and station keeping; 620 hp gas turbine (housed in funnel structure) for providing "quiet" power when conducting operations in which use of main engines would generate too high a noise level (gas turbine also can drive the ship at 6·5 knots); endurance of 12 000 miles at 12 knots.
Robert D. Conrad built by Gibbs Corp, Jacksonville, Florida. Operated by Lamont Geological Observatory of Columbia University under technical control of the Oceanographer of the Navy; civilian crew.
James H. Gilliss and *Charles H. Davis* built by Christy Corp, Sturgeon Bay, Wisconsin. Operated by MSTS for Naval Oceanographic Office; civilian crew.
Sands and *Lynch* built by Marietta Manufacturing Co, Point Pleasant, West Virginia. Operated by MSTS for Naval Oceanographic Office; civilian crew.
Thomas G. Thompson built by Marinette Marine Corp, Marinette, Wisconsin. Operated by University of Washington (state) under technical control of the Oceanographer of the Navy; civilian crew.
Thomas Washington built by Marinette Marine Corp, Marinette, Wisconsin. Operated by Scripps Institution of Oceanography (University of California) under technical control of the Oceanographer of the Navy; civilian crew.
De Steiguer and *Bartlett* built by Northwest Marine Iron Works, Portland, Oregon. Operated by MSTS for Naval Oceanographic Office; civilian crew.

SANDS (T-AGOR 6) *United States Navy (MSTS)*

THOMAS WASHINGTON (AGOR 10) *United States Navy*

2 OCEANOGRAPHIC RESEARCH SHIPS (AGOR): Ex-SALVAGE SHIPS

Name	*No.*	*Launched*	*Commissioned*
CHAIN	AGOR 17 (ex-ARS 20)	3 June 1943	31 Mar 1944
ARGO (ex-*Snatch*)	AGOR 18 (ex-ARS 27)	8 Apr 1944	11 Dec 1944

Displacement, tons	*Chain:* 2 100 full load *Argo:* 2 079 full load
Dimensions, feet	207 wl; 213·5 oa × 39 × 15
Main engines	Diesel-electric (4 Cooper Bessemer diesels); approx 3 000 shp; 2 shafts = 14 knots
Complement	*Chain:* 29 + 26 scientists *Argo:* 40 + 28 scientists

Both ships converted from Navy salvage ships built by Basalt Rock Co, Napa, California. Commission dates as ARS. (See "Escape" class ARS). *Chain* converted to oceanographic research ship by Savannah Machine & Foundry in 1958; *Snatch* converted by Puget Sound Bridge and Drydock Co in 1959-1960. Both ships are versatile research craft fitted with laboratories and equipment for a variety of oceanographic tasks. The *Chain* is operated by the Woods Hole Oceanographic Institute for the Office of Naval Research and the *Argo* by the Scripps Institution of Oceanography for ONR; both under technical control of the Oceanographer of the Navy.

ENGINEERING. The *Chain* has an auxiliary 250 hp outboard propulsion unit for maneuvering at low speeds (up to 4·5 knots).

ELECTRONICS. Both ships equipped with extensive navigation, communication, and echo sounding equipment (last includes SQS-4 sonar in *Argo*).

NOMENCLATURE. *Argo* renamed upon conversion for mythological ship in which Jason sailed in search of the Golden Fleece; the *Chain* retains her Navy ARS name.

ARGO (AGOR 18) *United States Navy*

Experimental, Research, and Surveying Ships—*continued*

2 OCEANOGRAPHIC RESEARCH SHIPS (AGOR): Ex-CARGO SHIPS

Name	*No.*	*Launched*	*Delivered*
ELTANIN	T-AGOR 8 (ex-T-AK 270)	16 Jan 1957	2 Aug 1957
MIZAR	T-AGOR 11 (ex-T-AK 272)	7 Oct 1957	22 Nov 1957

Displacement, tons	2 036 light; 4 942 full load
Measurement, tons	2 486 gross; 1 300 deadweight
Dimensions, feet	256·8 wl; 262·2 oa × 51·5 × 18·7; (*Mizar* 22·8)
Main engines	Diesel-electric (ALCO diesels, Westinghouse electric motors); 2 shafts; 3 200 bhp = 12 knots
Complement	*Eltanin:* 12 officers, 36 enlisted men, 38 scientists *Mizar:* 11 officers, 30 enlisted men, up to 15 scientists

Built for MSTS by Avondale Marine Ways, New Orleans, La. Designed for Arctic operation with hull strengthened against ice. C1-ME2-13a type. Delivered as T-AK to MSTS.
As research ships the *Eltanin* is operated by MSTS for National Science Foundations, *Mizar* by MSTS for Naval Research Laboratory, latter ship under technical control of the Oceanographer of the Navy; civilian crews.

CONVERSION. *Eltanin* was converted in 1961 into a scientific laboratory for Antarctic research programme for the National Science Foundation. Equipped to study meteorology, the upper atmosphere, marine and terrestial biology, physical oceanography, submarine geology, and geomagnetic conditions. Reclassified from T-AK 270 to T-AGOR 8 on 15 Nov 1962.
Mizar converted in 1962 into deep sea research ship. Equipped with centre well for lowering oceanographic equipment including towed sensor platforms, fitted with laboratories and elaborate photographic facilities, hydrophone system and computer for seafloor navigation and tracking towed vehicles. The *Mizar* had key roles in the searches for the nuclear submarines *Thresher* and *Scorpion*, and recovery of the H-bomb lost off Palomares, Spain.
Other views of both ships are in 1968-1969 edition.

MIZAR (T-AGOR 11) *United States Navy (MSTS)*

ELTANIN (T-AGOR 8) *United States Navy (MSTS)*

1 OCEANOGRAPHIC RESEARCH SHIP (AGOR): Ex-SEAPLANE TENDER

JOSIAH WILLARD GIBBS (ex-*San Carlos*) T-AGOR 1 (ex-AVP 51)

Displacement, tons	1 750 standard; 2 800 full load
Dimensions, feet	300 wl; 310·8 oa × 41·2 × 13·5
Main engines	Diesels (Fairbanks-Morse); 2 shafts; 6 080 shp = knots
Complement	14 officers, 33 enlisted men, 24 scientists

Former seaplane tender converted for oceanographic research. Built by Lake Washington Shipyard, Houghton, Wash. Laid down on 7 Sep 1942, launched on 20 Dec 1942, and commissioned on 21 Mar 1944.

CONVERSION. Converted by Mobile Ship Repair Inc, Mobile, Alabama, in 1958. Fitted with special instrumentation winches, and laboratories for oceanographic research. Auxiliary propeller fitted for precise manoeuvring at speeds to four knots (subsequently removed).
Operated by MSTS for Naval Research Laboratory under technical control of the Oceanographer of the Navy; civilian manned.

TRANSFER. AGOR 2 was the *H. U. Sverdrup*, built in Norway with US funds.

JOSIAH WILLARD GIBBS (T AGOR 1) *United States Navy (MSTS)*

ADVANCED HYDROGRAPHIC SURVEYING SHIPS: PROPOSED

An advanced class of hydrographic surveying ships is planned which will be capable of surveying 1 000 square miles and produce finished charts within a five-day period. Ship construction tentatively is planned for Fiscal Year 1974-76 new construction programmes.

1 SURVEYING SHIP (AGS): Ex-SEAPLANE TENDER

REHOBOTH AGS 50 (ex-AVP 50)

Displacement, tons	1 766 standard; 2 800 full load
Dimensions, feet	300 wl; 310 oa × 41·2 × 13·5
Main engines	Diesels (Fairbanks-Morse); 2 shafts; 5 120 shp = 18 knots
Complement	169 (12 officers, 157 men)

Former seaplane tender. Reclassified as AGS and assigned to duties as deep-sea hydrographic-surveying ships under the technical control of the Oceanographer of the Navy. Built by Lake Washington Shipyard; laid down on 3 Aug 1942, launched on 8 Nov 1942, commissioned on 23 Feb 1944. Original armament of one 5 inch gun and eight 40 mm guns (2 twin, 1 quad) removed. Navy manned.

DISPOSAL
San Pablo (AGS 30, ex-AVP 30) decommissioned on 1 July 1969 and slated for disposal.

REHOBOTH (AGS 50) *United States Navy*

2 SURVEYING SHIPS (AGS): "KELLAR" TYPE

Name	*No.*	*Laid down*	*Launched*	*Delivered*
KELLAR	T-AGS 25	20 Nov 1962	30 July 1964	5 Feb 1969
S. P. LEE	T-AGS 31	27 June 1966	19 Oct 1967	13 Dec 1968

Displacement, tons	1 200 standard; 1 400 full load
Dimensions, feet	191·5 wl; 209 oa × 39 × 15
Main engines	Diesel-electric; 1 shaft; 1 200 hp = 15 knots
Complement	8 officers, 18 enlisted men, 15 scientists

This is the first class of ships designed and built for the US Navy for surveying operations. Same design as the "Conrad" class oceanographic research ships with different instrumentation and equipment. Special features include bow propulsion unit for precise manoeuvrability and station keeping; endurance of 12 000 miles at 12 knots.
Kellar built by Marietta Manufacturing Co, Point Pleasant, West Virginia, but completed by Boland Machine Manufacturing Co, New Orleans (Marietta contract terminated on 14 May 1965; Boland contract awarded 30 July 1966). She was sunk by a hurricane in Sept 1965, further delaying completion.
S. P. Lee built by Defoe SB Co, Bay City, Michigan. Authorised in Fiscal Year 1962 and 1965 shipbuilding programmes, respectively.
Both ships operated by MSTS for Naval Oceanographic Office; civilian crews.

Experimental, Research & Surveying Ships—*continued*

2 SURVEYING SHIPS (AGS): "CHAUVENET" TYPE

Name	*No.*	*Laid down*	*Launched*	*Delivered*
CHAUVENET	T-AGS 29	24 May 1967	13 May 1968	Oct 1969
HARKNESS	T-AGS 32	30 June 1967	12 June 1968	Dec 1969

Displacement, tons: 4 200 full load
Dimensions, feet: 393·2 oa × 54 × 16
Main engines: Diesel; 1 shaft; 3 600 hp = 15 knots
Complement: 19 officers, 245 enlisted men, 8 scientists

A new class of large ships designed to undertake extensive military hydrographic and oceanographic surveys, supporting coastal surveying craft, amphibious survey teams, and helicopters. Fitted with helicopter hangar and platform.
Chauvenet authorised in Fiscal Year 1965 new construction programme; *Harkness* in FY 1966 programme. Both ships built by Upper Clyde Shipbuilders, Govan Division, Glasgow, Scotland.
These ships will be operated by MSTS for the Naval Oceanographic Office with Navy detachments on board.

4 SURVEYING SHIPS (AGS): "BENT" CLASS

Name	*No.*	*Laid down*	*Launched*	*Delivered*
SILAS BENT	T-AGS 26	2 Mar 1964	16 May 1964	1965
KANE	T-AGS 27	19 Dec 1964	20 Nov 1965	1967
WILKES	T-AGS 33	18 July 1968	July 1969	1970
WYMAN	T-AGS 34	18 July 1968	Sep 1969	1970

Displacement, tons: 1 935 standard; *Silas Bent* and *Kane* 2 558 full load; *Wilkes* 2 540 full load; *Wyman* 2 420 full load
Dimensions, feet: 285·3 oa × 48 × 15·1
Main engines: Diesel-electric; 1 shaft; 3 600 hp = 14 knots
Complement: 12 or 13 Officers, 36 enlisted men, 30 scientists

Designed specifically for surveying operations. Special features include seafloor mapping equipment; bow propulsion unit for precise manoeuvrability and station keeping. All four ships operated by MSTS for Naval Oceanographic Office; civilian crews. *Silas Bent* built by American SB Co, Lorain, Ohio; *Kane* built by Christy Corp, Sturgeon Bay, Wisconsin; *Wilkes* and *Wyman* built by Defoe SB Co, Bay City, Michigan.

SILAS BENT (T-AGS 26) — *United States Navy (MSTS)*

1 SURVEYING SHIP (AGS): Ex-FLEET TUG

SERRANO AGS 24 (ex-ATF 112)

Displacement, tons: 1 240 standard; 1 640 full load
Dimensions, feet: 205 oa × 39 × 17
Main engines: Diesel-electric; 2 000 shp; 1 shaft

Former fleet ocean tug of the "Apache" class; built by United Engineering Co, Alameda, California; launched on 24 July 1943, commissioned on 22 Sep 1944, reclassified from ATF to AGS on 15 June 1960.

SERRANO (AGS 24) — *United States Navy*

1 SURVEYING SHIP (AGS): Ex-MINESWEEPER

SHELDRAKE AGS 19 (ex-AM 62)

Displacement, tons: 890 standard; 1 250 full load
Dimensions, feet: 215 wl; 221·2 oa × 32·2 × 10·8
Main engines: Diesel-electric; 2 shafts; 2 000-3 450 shp = 15 knots
Complement: 100

Former Fleet Minesweeper. Built by Gen Eng & DD Co, Alameda, California. Launched on 12 Feb 1942, commissioned on 14 Oct 1942; reclassified as surveying ship in 1952. Sister ship *Pursuit* AGS 17 (ex-AM 108) disposed of in 1960, *Prevail* AGS 20 (ex-AM 107) on 10 Jan 1964; *Requisite* AGS 18 (ex-AM 109) on 1 Apr 1964; *Towhee* AGS 28 (ex-AM 388) on 1 May 1969.

SHELDRAKE (AGS 19) — *1966 United States Navy*

3 SURVEYING SHIPS (AGS): "VICTORY" TYPE

BOWDITCH (ex-SS *South Bend Victory*) T-AGS 21
DUTTON (ex-SS *Tuskegee Victory*) T-AGS 22
MICHELSON (ex-SS *Joliet Victory*) T-AGS 23

Displacement, tons: 4 512 full load
Dimensions, feet: 455·2 oa × 62·2 × 25
Main engines: Turbine; 8 500 shp; 1 shaft = 15 knots
Boilers: 2

VC2-S-AP3 type built in 1945, *Bowditch* and *Michelson* by Oregon Shipbuilding Co; *Dutton* by South Coast Co, Newport Beach California. All converted to support the Fleet Ballistic Missile Programme, *Dutton* and *Michelson* at Philadelphia Naval Shipyard 8 Nov 1957 to 16 Nov 1958 and 1 Mar 1958 to 31 Dec 1958, respectively, and *Bowditch* at Charleston Naval Shipyard 10 Oct 1957 to 30 Sep 1958. Operated by MSTS for Naval Oceanographic Office; civilian crews. Designed to chart the ocean floor and to record magnetic fields and gravity to enable vessels to establish locations within a few yards of their actual positions.

MICHELSON (T-AGS 23) — *United States Navy (MSTS)*

2 SURVEYING SHIPS (AGS): Ex-ATTACK CARGO SHIPS

MAURY (ex-*Renate*) AGS 16 (ex-AKA 36)
TANNER (ex-*Pamina*) AGS 15 (ex-AKA 34)

Displacement, tons: 4 203 standard; 6 500 full load
Dimensions, feet: 400 wl; 426 oa × 58 × 17
Main engines: Turbo-electric (Westinghouse); 2 shafts; 6 000 bhp = 17 knots
Boilers: 2 (Wickes)
Complement: 701 (35 officers, 666 enlisted men)

Former Attack Cargo Ships. S4-SE2-B1 type. Both built by Walsh-Kaiser Co Inc, Providence, RI. *Maury* launched on 31 Jan 1945, commissioned on 28 Feb 1945; *Tanner* launched on 5 Jan 1945, commissioned on 10 Feb 1945; converted to surveying ships in 1946.

Helicopter flight deck on stern. Guns removed except for several machine guns. Navy manned.

DISPOSALS
The Navy's last coastal surveying ship, **Littlehales** (AGSC 15, ex-YF 854), was stricken in 1968 (sunk as target).

TANNER (AGS 15) — *1965, United States Navy*

Experimental, Research & Surveying Ships—*continued*

2 TECHNICAL RESEARCH SHIPS (AGTR): "VICTORY" TYPE

BELMONT (ex-*Iran Victory*) AGTR 4 (ex-AG 167)
LIBERTY (ex-*Simmons Victory*) AGTR 5 (ex-AG 168)

Displacement, tons	7 190 light; 10 680 full load
Dimensions, feet	455 oa × 62 × 24
Main engines	Turbine; 1 shaft; 8 500 shp = 18 knots
Complement	280
Guns	20 mm and ·50 calibre MG

Modified "Victory" ships. Conversion by Williamette Iron & Steel, Portland, Ore, commissioned 2 Nov and 30 Dec 1964, respectively. Mobile bases for research in communications and electromagnetic radiation. Considered Electronic Intelligence (ELINT) ships. *Liberty* severely damaged by Israeli air and torpedo boat attack in Eastern Mediterranean on 8 June 1967. She was decommissioned on 28 June 1968; in reserve. A photograph of the *Liberty* taken on 9 June 1967 appears in the 1968-1969 edition as does a view taken in 1964.

BELMONT (AGTR 4) *1966, US Navy*

3 TECHNICAL RESEARCH SHIPS (AGTR): "LIBERTY" TYPE

OXFORD (ex-*Samuel R. Aitken*, MCE 3127) AGTR 1 (ex-AG 159)
GEORGETOWN (ex-SS *Robert W. Hart*) AGTR 2 (ex-AG 165)
JAMESTOWN (ex-SS *J. Howland Gardner*) AGTR 3 (ex-AG 166)

Measurement, tons	7 330
Dimensions, feet	441·5 oa × 57 × 23
Main engines	Triple expansion; 1 shaft; 2 500 hp = 12·5 knots
Guns	20 mm and ·50 calibre MG
Complement	275 (18 officers, 257 men)

Modified "Liberty" ships. *Oxford* began conversion in Sep 1960 by New York Naval Shipyard and commissioned on 8 July 1961. For research and experiments in communications and electromagnetic radiations. *Georgetown* and *Jamestown*, built by New England Shipbuilding Corp in 1945, were converted by Newport News Shipbuilding & Dry Dock Co and commissioned on 9 Nov 1963 and 13 Dec 1963, respectively. All reclassified as AGTR on 1 Apr 1964.

OXFORD (AGTR 1) *1964, United States Navy*

GEORGETOWN (AGTR 2) *1964, United States Navy*

1 GUIDED MISSILE SHIP (AVM) CONVERTED SEAPLANE TENDER

NORTON SOUND AVM 1 (*ex*-AV 11)

Displacement, tons	9 106 standard; 15 170 full load
Length, feet (*metres*)	543·25 (*165·2*) oa
Beam, feet (*metres*)	71·6 (*21·5*)
Draft, feet (*metres*)	23·5 (*7·15*)
Guns	1—5 in (*127 mm*) 54 cal experimental (see *Gunnery* notes)
Missiles	1 twin launcher for standard testing 1 Basic Point Defence Missile System (BPDMS) launcher for Sea Sparrow missiles (see *Missile* notes)
Main engines	2 geared turbines (Allis-Chalmers) 12 000 shp; 2 shafts
Boilers	4 (Babcock & Wilcox)
Speed, knots	19·2
Complement	292 (22 officers, 270 enlisted men)

NORTON SOUND (AUMI) *US Navy*

The *Norton Sound* serves as a seagoing weapons laboratory and test centre under the operational control of Commander, Cruiser-Destroyer Force, Pacific Fleet. She was originally a seaplane tender (AV 11) of the "Currituck" class; fitted with helicopter platform forward and missile launching ramp aft during late 1940s and reclassified as Guided Missile Test Ship (AVM 1) on 8 Aug 1951. Subsequently served as test ship for several guided missile systems and, lately, for advanced gun systems. During August and September of 1958 the *Norton Sound* launched missiles which exploded three nuclear weapons at an altitude of about 300 miles to determine effects of nuclear explosions in space on missile defenses (Project ARGUS).
From 1963 until 1966 the *Norton Sound* served as test ship for the Typhon advanced fleet air defense system.

CONSTRUCTION. Built by Los Angeles Shipbuilding & Dry Dock Co, San Pedro, Calif. Laid down 7 Sep 1942; launched 28 Nov 1943; commissioned 8 Jan 1945. As built the *Norton Sound* had a 30-ton capacity boom atop her large, amidships aircraft hangar and a second 30-ton boom on her fantail; second boom removed when fitted with missile launching ramp. Original armament consisted of four 5 inch guns, two in single mounts forward and two in single mounts atop hangar, and 20 40 mm AA guns; forward 5 inch guns removed to make space for helicopter platform; all other armament removed prior to modification as Typhon test ship.

GUNNERY. Fitted in 1969 with light-weight 5 inch/54 cal gun and associated Mark 86 Gunfire Control System for operational test and evaluation. The light-weight Mark 45 gun is intended for new-construction ships. It has a rate of fire of 20 rounds per minute, weighs 50 000 pounds, and is operated by a five-man crew, none of whom are in the mount. The mount captain initially can fire 20 rounds in the gun's loader drum without the use of ammunition handlers. The gun offers a significant increase in reliability over previous guns of this calibre.

MISSILES. The *Norton Sound* has served as a test platform for several ship-launched rockets and missiles. Currently a twin surface-to-air missile launcher is installed aft for tests of the Standard missile as is a "pepper box" BPDMS launcher for the Sea Sparrow missile.

TYPHON. In 1963-64 the *Norton Sound* was converted to serve as test ship for the Typhon fleet air defense system. The conversion was undertaken at the Maryland Shipbuilding and Dry Dock Company, Baltimore, Maryland; recommissioned on 20 June 1964. A large, dome-shaped radar installation was erected atop the bridge structure (see photographs in 1968-1969 edition). Typhon system was designed to counter aircraft and guided missile threats of the 1970s. A single, high-powered radar was to automatically and simultaneously search, acquire target, track, and guide ship-launched

Experimental, Research & Surveying Ships—*continued*

missiles; system includes high-speed digital computers. However, Typhon was cancelled because of large size, high cost, and relative ineffectiveness. The radar equipment was evaluated in the *Norton Sound*; removed in July of 1966 at Long Beach Naval Shipyard (California). Complement while Typhon test ship was approx 450 officers and enlisted men.

PHOTOGRAPHS. Note single funnel, telementary antenna aft of funnel, signal yard atop bridge, Standard and Sea Sparrow missile launchers aft. The light-weight 5 inch gun was not installed when these photographs were taken. Compare with photograph of *Currituck* (AV 7) on earlier page.

1 ELECTRONICS TEST SHIP (AVT): Ex-AIRCRAFT CARRIER

BUNKER HILL AVT 9 (ex-CVS 17)

Displacement, tons	27 100 standard
Length, feet (*metres*)	888 (*270·7*) oa
Beam, feet (*metres*)	93 (*28·3*)
Draft, feet (*metres*)	31 (*9·4*)
Width, feet (*metres*)	147·5 (*44·9*) extreme
Complement	1 officer, 25 enlisted men, 36 scientists

The *Bunker Hill* is a former "Essex" class aircraft carrier employed as an electronics test platform for the Naval Electronics Laboratory Centre at San Diego, California. The inactivated ship is moored off the North Island Naval Air Station in San Diego Harbour.

She was completed as a fast carrier in 1943 and saw extensive action in World War II. She was severely damaged by a Japanese suicide plane attack in May 1945 and was not fully rejuvinated. After helping transport allied troops after the war, she was decommissioned on 9 Jan 1947 and placed in the reserve fleet at Bremerton, Washington.
In 1965 the *Bunker Hill* was towed from Bremerton to San Diego and moored off NAS North Island. She was officially stricken from the Navy List on 1 Nov 1966.

EXPERIMENTAL. Portions of the *Bunker Hill* have been converted into working areas for scientists and a number of electronic systems have been installed in the ship. Essentially, she is being used as a test and evaluation platform for the development of integrated electronic systems for naval vessels.
One of the more advanced systems being investigated in the *Bunker Hill* is a computer-controlled message handling and distribution system which receives, transmits, stores, and distributes information.

PHOTOGRAPH. The photograph of the *Bunker Hill* shows her being moved by tugs; a number of antennas subsequently have been installed on her island structure and flight deck. She is moored with non-metallic, dacron lines to alleviate the effect of metal anchor chains on the ship's electromagnetic characteristics. As she has been stricken from the Navy List, no flag is flown

BUNKER HILL (AVT9) AT NAS NORTH ISLAND *US Navy*

1 EXPERIMENTAL TARGET SHIP (IX): CONVERTED LIGHT CRUISER

ATLANTA IX 304 (ex-CL 104)

Converted from a "Cleveland" class light cruiser to target ship for studies of the effects of high-energy air explosions on naval ships (Operation SAILOR HAT conducted off Kahoolawe Island, Hawaii, in 1965). Converted at the San Francisco Naval Shipyard and fitted with representative deck houses, masts, antennas, fire control equipment, and weapon launchers of surface warships. Used as target ship in three explosions of TNT "stacks" during which she was manned by selected crewmen and scientific personnel. Complement as test ship was 169 Navy operating crew and 60 scientific personnel.
Built by New York Shipbuilding Corp, Camden, New Jersey, laid down on 25 Jan 1943, launched on 6 Feb 1944, and commissioned on 3 Dec 1944. Decommissioned on 1 July 1949 and placed in reserve at San Francisco.
Stricken from the Navy List on 1 Oct 1962 but reinstated as IX 304 on 15 May 1964. Now hulk.

PHOTOGRAPH. A photograph of the *Atlanta* as configured for the SAILOR HAT tests appears in the 1968-1969 edition.

1 TEST RANGE SUPPORT SHIP (IX): CONVERTED LANDING SHIP

Name	*No.*	*Builder*	*Commissioned*
ELK RIVER	IX 501 (ex-LSMR 501)	Brown SB Co (Houston, Texas)	27 May 1945

Displacement, tons	1 100 full load
Dimensions, feet	225 oa × 50 × 9·2
Main engines	Diesels; 1 400 shp; 2 shafts = 11 knots
Complement	25
Technical personnel	20

The *Elk River* is a former rocket landing ship specifically converted to support Navy deep submergence activities on the San Clemente Island Range off the coast of Southern California. The ship is capable of supporting the following activities: (1) deep diving for man-in-the-sea programmes (SEALAB), (2) deep diving for salvage programmes, (3) submersible test and evaluation, (4) underwater equipment testing, and (5) deep mooring operations.

CONVERSION. The *Elk River* was withdrawn from the Reserve Fleet and converted to a range support ship in 1967-1968 at Avondale Shipyards Inc. Westwego, Louisiana, and the San Francisco Bay Naval Shipyard.
The basic LSMR hull was lengthened and eight-foot sponsons were added to either side to increase deck working space and stability; superstructure added forward. An open centre well was provided to facilitate lowering and raising equipment; also fitted with 65-ton-capacity gantry crane (on tracks) to handle submersibles and active positioning mooring system to hold ship in precise location without elaborate mooring and permit shifting within the moor. Five anchors including stern anchor.

DIVING. Fitted with prototype Mk 2 Deep Diving System (see new-construction submarine rescue ships).

OPERATIONAL. As part of test programmes will carry special vans containing integrated medical and command facilities (for man-in-the-sea experiments), salvage operational control centre (for salvage work), and rescue control centre (for use with rescue submersibles). The photograph shows the *Elk River* with the command and medical vans developed to support Man-in-the-Sea experiments.

ELK RIVER (IX 501) *1968 US Navy*

2 RESEARCH SHIPS (YAG): Ex-MINESWEEPERS

GEORGE EASTMAN YAG 39
GRANVILLE S. HALL (ex-*Iro Nelson Morris*) YAG 40

Displacement, tons	6 000 light, 11 600 full load
Dimensions, feet	422·7 oa × 57 × 34·7 max
Main engines	Steam reciprocating; 1 shaft; 2 500 hp = 11 knots
Accommodation	19 officers, 150 men

Liberty ships of the EC-2-S-C1 type built in 1943-1944, acquired by the Navy in 1952-1953 as Experimental Minefield Sweepers. Several ships of this type have been used as guinea-pig ships in sweeping minefields. Remote engine room controls on bridge. Helicopter platform forward. Replaced in service in 1962. Assigned their former merchant ship names in 1963. Now used as special project and research ships.

NOMENCLATURE. Both ships officially were assigned their former merchant hull names in 1963.

DISPOSALS
The experimental minefield sweeper **YAG 37** (ex-*John L. Sullivan*) was scrapped in 1958, **YAG 36** (ex-*Floyd W. Spencer*) and **YAG 38** (ex-*Edward Kavanagh*) were stricken in 1960. The Fleet X-ray examination ship **Whidbey** AG 141, was stricken on 1 May 1959.

GEORGE EASTMAN (YAG39) *1966 US Navy*

Experimental, Research & Surveying Ships—*continued*

1 EXPERIMENTAL HYDROFOIL: "HIGH POINT" TYPE

HIGH POINT PCH 1

Displacement, tons	110
Dimensions, feet	115 oa × 31; draught 6 to 17
Guns	2—·50 cal MG (twin). See *Gunnery* notes
A/S weapons	4—21 in torpedo launchers (2 twin); DCT
Main engines	2 Bristol Siddeley Marine Proteus gas turbines; 2 shafts; 6 200 shp = 48 knots max Auxiliary diesel propulsion; 600 bhp = 12 knots cruising
Complement	13 (1 officer, 12 enlisted men)

Experimental hydrofoil submarine chaser. Aluminium hull. Four propellers, two pushing, two pulling, fitted on retractable hydrofoils. Forward foil single strut, after foil two struts. Struts extend over 14 ft below hull. With foils retracted draft is about 6 ft. Diesel with retractable propeller. Sonar equipment installed. Provided for under the Fiscal Year 1960 Programme. Cost $3 700 000. Named after High Point, North Carolina.

CONSTRUCTION. Designed by W. C. Nickum & Sons, Seattle, Wn. Built jointly by Boeing Aircraft Corpn, Seattle, Washington, and J. M. Martinac, Tacoma, Washington, at Martinac's Tacoma Yard. Laid down on 27 Feb 1961. Launched on 17 Aug 1962. Completed and placed in service on 3 Sep 1963.

GUNNERY. A single 40 mm gun was mounted forward in 1968; subsequently removed. Machine guns are not normally mounted.

HIGH POINT (PCH 1) *1968, The Boeing Co.*

HIGH POINT (PCH 1) *The Boeing Co.*

1 EXPERIMENTAL HYDROFOIL: "DENISON" TYPE

DENISON

Displacement, tons	90 max
Length, feet	104·5 (117 with tail foil down)
Beam, feet	23 (hull), 45 with foils down
Draft, feet	6·2 with foils up, 15·4 with foils down
Main engines	Gas turbines; 875 hp hull borne, 14 500 hp foil borne = 62 kts
Complement	8

Hydrofoil craft built as a test vehicle for $5 000 000 by Grumman Aircraft Engineering Corp, Bethpage, Long Island, NY, for Maritime Administration in 1962. Powered gas turbines by General Electric Corp. All aluminium hull, lightweight machinery. Transferred to the US Navy at Oyster Bay, Long Island, New York, on 27 Aug 1965 and assigned to Pacific Missile Range, Pt Mugu, Calif. Used to transport personnel and supplies to offshore islands and in the sea test range in area clearance and rescue work, until placed in reserve.

DENISON *United States Navy.*

DENISON *United States Maritime Administration*

7 TRAINING-EXPERIMENTAL CRAFT (PCE-PCER)

	PCE	*Launched*		PCER	*Launched*
AMHERST	853	18 Mar 1944	**REXBURG**	855	10 Apr 1944
WHITEHALL	856	21 Apr 1944	**MARYSVILLE**	857	4 May 1944
HAVRE	877	11 Aug 1943			
ELY	880	27 Oct 1943			
PORTAGE	902	28 Aug 1943			

Displacement, tons	640 standard; 903 full load
Dimensions, feet	180 wl; 184·5 oa × 33 × 9·5
Guns PCE	1—3 in dp; 6—40 mm AA; 4 DCT
PCER	Removed
Main engines	Diesel; 2 shafts; 1 800 to 2 400 bhp = 15 knots
Complement	60 (5 officers, 55 men)

Built by Pulman Standard Mfg Co, Albina Engine & Machinery Works and Willamette Iron and Steel Corpn. During the Second World War the "PCER" type carried hospital equipment and personnel, with accommodation for 57 patients were used to rescue survivors of convoy sinkings.
The surviving PCE and PCER were named on 15 Feb 1956. *Whitehall* is a former PCER. The remaining PCEs are training ships on the Great Lakes; the *Rexburg* and *Marysville* are experimental-hydrographic ships. A photograph of the *Fairview* (PCER 850) appears in the 1968-1969 edition.

TRANSFERS. *Eunice*, PCE 846, and *Pascagoula*, PCE 874, to Ecuador in 1960, several PCE to China, Cuba and Mexico, PCEC 873, PCEC 882, PCEC 896 and PCEC 898 to Korea, PCEC 873 and PCEC 898 to Korea in 1956 and PCEC 882 and PCEC 396 in Feb 1955, *Crestview* PCE 895 to Vietnam on 29 Nov 1961, *Batesburg* PCE 903, *Diana* PCE 870, *Marfa* PCE 842, and *Somerset* PCE 892, to Korea on 9 Dec 1961, *Lamar*, PCE 899 to the Coast Guard on 1 June 1964, *Worland* PCE 845 to the State of North Carolina on 6 June 1964, *Farmington* PCE 894 to Burma on 31 May 1965, *Battleboro* to Vietnam in 1966. *Rockville* PCER 851 stricken on 21 Dec 1968 and transferred to Columbia.

DISPOSALS
Skowhegan PCE 843, **Groton** PCE 900 and **Gettysburg** PCE 904, were stricken on 1 Feb 1960, **Banning** PCE 886 on 1 May 1961 (subsequently transferred to Hood River, Oregon, as a memorial), **Somersworth**, EPCER 849, on 1 Apr 1966. **Fairview** PCER 850 stricken on 1 May 1968 (target).

1 TRAINING CRAFT (PCS)

HOLLIDAYSBURG PCS 1385

Displacement, tons	251 standard; 338 full load
Dimensions, feet	136 × 24·5 × 8·5
Guns	1—3 in dp; 1—40 mm AA; 2—20 mm AA
A/S weapons	DCT
Main engines	2 GM diesels; 1 000 bhp = 14 knots
Complement	60

The survivor of a class of 52 units which were completed in 1944. All PCS were named on 15 Feb 1956. Several converted to mine sweepers and mine hunters. Employed as a Naval Reserve training ship.

TRANSFERS. PCS 1426 and PCS 1448 were loaned to Republic of Korea Navy on 9 June 1952 and PCS 1445 and PCS 1446 on 26 May 1952, but PCS 1426 was returned to the US Navy in Apr 1963 and stricken.

DISPOSALS
Attica, PCS 1383, and **Coquille**, PCS 1400, were scrapped in 1957. **Conneaute**, PCS 1444, **Deming**, PCS 1392, **Eufaula**, PCS 1384, **Provincetown**, PCS 1378, **Rushville**, PCS 1380, and **Winder**, PCS 1378, were stricken from the Navy List in 1957. **Hampton**, PCS 1386, was stricken on 1 July 1959. **Elsmere**, PCS 1413 was disposed of in 1961. **Prescott**, PCS 1423, was stricken on 1 Mar 1962, **McMinnville**, PCS 1401 in Aug 1962, **Grafton**, PCS 1431, on 1 June 1965, **Beaufort**, PCS 1387, on 18 July 1967.

HOLLIDAYSBURG (PCS 1385) *United States Navy*

SPECIALISED AUXILIARY SHIPS AND SERVICE CRAFT

1 NAVAL YACHT (AG)

SEQUOIA AG 23

Displacement, tons 110 light
Dimensions, feet 105 × 21 × 5
Main engines 1 diesel; 400 shp

Built in 1925 by J. H. Mathis Co. Assigned to the Secretary of the Navy. The Navy has several small sail training boats at the United States Naval Academy, Annapolis, Maryland. *Highland Light* (IX 48) stricken on 1 Apr 1965 and sold; *Royono* (IX 235) stricken on 1 July 1967 and sold; and *Freedom* (IX 43) stricken in 1968 *Saluda* (IX 87, ex-Odyssey) reclassified as YAG 87.

SEQUOIA (AG 23) *United States Navy*

36 Non-Self-Propelled Barracks Craft (APL)

APL 2	**APL 10**	**APL 20**	**APL 29**	**APL 42**	**APL 50**
APL 3	**APL 11**	**APL 21**	**APL 30**	**APL 43**	**APL 53**
APL 4	**APL 15**	**APL 23**	**APL 31**	**APL 44**	**APL 54**
APL 5	**APL 17**	**APL 25**	**APL 32**	**APL 45**	**APL 55**
APL 8	**APL 18**	**APL 26**	**APL 34**	**APL 46**	**APL 57**
APL 9	**APL 19**	**APL 27**	**APL 41**	**APL 47**	**APL 58**

Displacement, tons approx 2 660 full load
Dimensions, feet 261·2 oa × 49·2 × 8·5
Main engines 3 diesels (for ships service)
Complement 71 (5 officers, 66 enlisted men; designed)
Troops 600 to 800

All completed 1944-1945. Several are in service including the *APL 26* which is assigned to the Mobile Riverine Force (Task Force 117) in South Vietnam.

2 CABLE SHIPS (ARC): "AEOLUS" CLASS

AEOLUS (ex-*Turandot*) ARC 3 (ex-AKA 47)
THOR (ex-*Vanadis*) ARC 4 (ex-AKA 49)

Displacement, tons 7 040 full load
Dimensions, feet 400 wl; 438 oa × 64 × 16
Main engines Westinghouse turbo-electric; 6 000 shp = 16·9 knots

Aeolus (laid up in the Maritime Administration Reserve Fleet since June 1946) was reacquired by the Navy on 4 Nov 1954. Both converted to Cable Laying or Repair Ships by the Key Highway Plant of Bethlehem Steel, Baltimore, Maryland. *Aeolus* commissioned in May 1955. *Thor*, built by Walsh Kaiser Company, Providence, commissioned on 3 Jan 1956. Unarmed. Helicopter platform aft. Note that the *Aeolus* now has same pole and antenna masts aft as the *Thor*. Both ships are active.

THOR (ARC 4) *1964, United States Navy*

AEOLUS (ARC 3) *United States Navy*

2 CABLE SHIPS (ARC): "NEPTUNE" TYPE

NEPTUNE (ex-*William H. G. Bullard*) ARC 2
ALBERT J. MYER T-ARC 6

Displacement, tons 7 387 full load
Measurement, tons 3 929 gross; 4 860 deadweight
Dimensions, feet 322 wl; 370 oa (T-ARC 6 is 362 oa) × 47 × 18
Main engines Reciprocating Unaflow engines; 2 shafts; 4 800 hp = 14 knots
Complement T-ARC 6, 18 officers, 54 enlisted men, 19 scientists

Built by Pusey and Jones Corpn, Wilmington, Del. *Neptune* was launched in 1945 and completed in Feb 1946. Acquired from the Maritime Administration in 1953. Sister ship *Albert J. Myer*, US Army Cable Ship, on loan to the Military Sea Transportation Service, was acquired by the Navy in 1966 and designated T-ARC 6. Both of the S3-S2-BP1 type. Unarmed. Both ships are active. *Albert J. Myer* is used for hydrographic research, operated by MSTS for the Naval Electronic Systems Command; civilian manned.

TRANSFER. *Portunus* ARC 1 (ex-LSM 275) was transferred to Portugal on 1 May 1959.

DISPOSALS
The cable repair ship **Nashawena** YAG 35 (ex-AG 142) was stricken in 1960.
The cable repair ship **Yamacraw** ARC 5 (ex-USCG WARC 333, ex-ACM 9, ex-*Trapper*) originally an Army minelayer and subsequently a US Navy auxiliary minelayer, afterwards employed as a US Coast Geard cable layer, then a US Navy cable repair ship until 1959, was stricken on 1 July 1965 and transferred to the Maritime Administration.

NEPTUNE (ARC 2) *United States Navy*

ALBERT J. MYER (T-ARC 6) *US Navy (MSTS)*

1 SAIL FRIGATE (IX)

CONSTITUTION IX 21 launched 21 Oct 1797

Displacement, tons 2 200
Dimensions, feet 175 pp × 43·5
Guns 28—24 pounders; 10—12 pounders
Speed, knots 13 (under sail)

The oldest ship of the US Navy remaining on the Navy List. "In service" status as a relic at Boston. One of six sail frigates authorised by act of Congress approved on 27 Mar 1794. Completed in 1798 and saw action in Quasi-War with France, against Barbary pirates, and in War of 1812 with Britain. After 1812 success against HMS *Java* she was referred to as "Old Ironsides". Renamed *Old Constitution* from 1 Dec 1917 to 24 July 1925. Periodically she is taken out into Boston Harbour and "turned around".
The sail frigate *Constellation* which survives under private ownership at Baltimore, Maryland, was long thought to be the *Constitution's* sister ship launched in 1797. However, it now appears that the surviving *Constellation* was built at the Norfolk Navy Yard in 1853-1854 as the last sailing man-of-war for the US Navy. The previous *Constellation* was broken up at Norfolk in 1852.

CONSTITUTION (IX 21) *1963, United States Navy*

Special Auxiliary Ships and Service Craft—*continued*

1 TRAINING SHIP (IX): Ex-MINESWEEPER

PROWESS IX 305 (ex-MSF 280)

Employed as Naval Reserve training ship at Buffalo, New York.

DISPOSALS
Burleson (IX 67, ex-APA 67) stricken from the Navy List on 20 Nov 1968, transferred to Maritime Administration and scrapped; **Targeteer** (YV 3, ex-LSMR 508) decommissioned on 31 Dec 1968, stricken in 1969.

11 HARBOUR UTILITY CRAFT (YFU)

YFU 71 **YFU 72** **YFU 73** **YFU 74** **YFU 75** **YFU 76** **YFU 77** **YFU 78** **YFU 80** **YFU 81** **YFU 82**

Dimensions, feet	125 oa × 36 × 7·5
Main engines	diesels = 8 knots
Guns	2—·50 cal MG

Militarised versions of a commercial lighter design. Used for off-loading large ships in harbours and ferrying cargo from one coastal port to another. Built by Pacific Coast Engineering Co, Alameda, California; completed 1967-1968. Can carry more than 300 tons cargo; considerable cruising range. YFU 79 transferred to South Vietnam in Nov 1968.
YFU 83 under construction.

30 HARBOUR UTILITY CRAFT (YFU): FORMER LANDING CRAFT

YFU 4 (ex-LCU 562)
YFU 5 (ex-LCU 592)
YFU 7 (ex-LCU 629)
YFU 8 (ex-LCU 664)
YFU 18 (ex-LCU 869)
YFU 20 (ex-LCU 960)
YFU 24 (ex-LCU 980)
YFU 25 (ex-LCU 1056)
YFU 36 (ex-LCU 1250)
YFU 37 (ex-LCU 1283)
YFU 39 (ex-LCU 1363)
YFU 44 (ex-LCU 1398)
YFU 45 (ex-LCU 1411)
YFU 47 (ex-LCU 1330)
YFU 50 (ex-LCU 1486)
YFU 52 (ex-LCU 743)
YFU 53 (ex-LCU 1446)
YFU 54 (ex-LCU 509)
YFU 55 (ex-LCU 637)
YFU 56 (ex-LCU 646)
YFU 57 (ex-LCU 709)
YFU 58 (ex-LCU 716)
YFU 59 (ex-LCU 776)
YFU 60 (ex-LCU 851)
YFU 61 (ex-LCU 916)
YFU 62 (ex-LCU 973)
YFU 63 (ex-LCU 989)
YFU 84 (ex-LCU 649)
YFU 85 (ex-LCU 715)
YFU 86 (ex-LCU 1373)

Former utility landing craft employed primarily as harbour and coastal cargo craft (see section on Landing Craft for basic data). YFU 39 is assigned to Mine Force, Pacific Fleet, and is based at Long Beach, California, to support and sow practice mines for MSBs; YFU 44 is assigned to Naval Undersea Research and Development Centre at Long Beach and is fitted with an open centre well for lowering equipment; YFU 53 also is assigned to the Centre and has an open centre well for handling the CURV tethered torpedo recovery device.

CLASSIFICATIONS. YFU 1-70 and 84-86 all were former utility landing craft. Several reverted to LCU designations at various times and three were modified for salvage work: YFU 2, 16, and 33 to YLLC 5, 2, and 3, respectively.

DISPOSALS
Recent YFU/LCU disposals include **YFU 12** (ex-LCU 686) stricken in May 1968.

15 NAVIGATION TRAINING CRAFT (YP)

YP 654 **YP 655** **YP 656** **YP 659** **YP 658** **YP 657** **YP 660** **YP 661** **YP 662** **YP 663** **YP 664** **YP 665** **YP 666** **YP 667** **YP 668**

Displacement, tons	56 standard; 60 full load
Dimensions, feet	80 oa × 17·6 × 5
Main engines	Diesel; 2 shafts; 320 bhp

YP 654-663 were built by Stephen Bros Inc, Stockton, Calif; launched July 1957-Mar 1958 and completed Mar 1958-Nov 1958. YP 664 and 665 were built by Elizabeth City Shipbuilders, Inc, Elizabeth City, North Carolina. Floating classrooms for training midshipmen in seamanship and navigation at the United States Naval Academy Wooden hull construction with aluminium deck houses. Surface search radar, gyro and magnetic compass, navigational plotting equipment. Potential patrol craft for national emergency. YP 666 and 667 were built by Stephens Bros. Five other patrol vessels, YP 584, 585, 587, 588, 591, are also used for training at Annapolis. YP 647, 648, 649, 650 and 651 were stricken on 1 Mar 1960, and YP 586, 589 and 590 on 1 Aug 1964. YP 584 and 591 were reinstated in 1966. YP 668 built by Peterson Boatbuilding Co, Tacoma, launched on 24 Feb 1968. YP 654 fitted for oceanographic research and training.

2 HEAVY SALVAGE LIFT CRAFT (YHLC)

CRILLY YHLC 1
CRANDALL YHLC 2

Former German salvage lifting ships; non-self-propelled. Acquired for use in Southeast Asia. Named for Frank W. Crilly and Orson L. Crandall, US Navy divers who won the Medal of Honour, the nation's highest award.

PHOTOGRAPH. *Crandall* (left) and *Crilly* (right) are shown raising the hull of the French steamer *Paul Bert* from the My Tho harbour in South Vietnam. The steamer, sunk during World War II, was salvaged in 1966 to allow establishment of a US Navy patrol boat base.

CRANDALL (YHLC 2), CRILLY (YHLC 1) *1966, United States Navy*

2 MEDIUM SALVAGE LIFT CRAFT (YMLC): Ex-ARSD

SALVAGER YMLC 3 (ex-ARSD 3, ex-LSM 551)
WINDLASS YMLC 4 (ex-ARSD 4, ex-LSM 552)

Converted during World War II from medium landing ships to salvage craft; non-self-propelled. Reclassified from ARSD to YMLC on 1 Nov 1967. Now on loan to commercial operator. See AG 335 listing for details on original configuration (listed with Logistic Support Ships).

4 MEDIUM SALVAGE LIFT CRAFT (YMLC): Ex-ROYAL NAVY

YMLC 5 (ex-LC 23)
YMLC 6 (ex-LC 24)
YMLC 7 (ex-LC 26)
YMLC 8 (ex-LC 27)

Former British lift craft on loan to US Navy for use in Southeast Asia; non-self-propelled. The YHLC and YMLC are numbered in the same series; the YLLC (below) form another numerical series.

4 LIGHT SALVAGE LIFT CRAFT (YLLC): FORMER LANDING CRAFT

YLLC 1 (ex-LCU 1348)
YLLC 2 (ex-YFU 16, ex-LCU 788)
YLLC 3 (ex-YFU 33, ex-LCU 1195)
YLLC 5 (ex-YFU 2, ex-LCU 529)

Former utility landing craft now rigged for salvage lift and employed in Southeast Asia. These ships retain their propulsion machinery and are self-propelled (see listing on Landing Craft for specific data).
YLLC 4 (ex-LCU 1459) struck a mine and sunk in the Ham Luong River, South Vietnam, on 15 Nov 1968 and was stricken from the Navy List on 1 Jan 1969.

HAKE (AGSS 256) after being salvaged from 100 feet of water in Chesapeake Bay by personnel of Service Squadron Eight. The stricken submarine was scuttled on 5 May 1969 and subsequently used in submarine rescue and salvage exercises. In the US Navy's first submarine salvage operation since 1939 when the *Squalus* (SS 192) sank in 240 feet of water, the *Hake* was partially raised and then towed to shallow water where she again ground at a depth of 60 feet; subsequently she was raised to the surface (shown above) and towed to Norfolk for future use in salvage training. The round objects near the submarine are YSP wooden salvage pontoons; the craft in the background is the salvage craft tender YRST 2.

DEEP SUBMERGENCE VEHICLES

The US Navy acquired its first deep submergence vehicle with the purchase of the bathyscaph *Trieste* in 1958. The *Trieste* was designed and constructed by Professor Auguste Piccard, the noted Swiss physicist and aeronaut. The US Navy sponsored research dives in the Mediterranean Sea with the *Trieste* in 1957 after which the bathyscaph was purchased outright and brought to the United States.
The *Trieste* reached a record depth of 35 800 feet (*10 910 metres*) in the Challenger Deep off the Marianas on 23 Jan 1960, being piloted by Lieutenant Don Walsh, USN, and Jacques Piccard (son of Auguste). The *Trieste* subsequently was used in the search for wreckage of the nuclear-powered submarine *Thresher* (SSN 593) which was lost in 1963.

Late in 1963 the *Trieste* was rebuilt, the "new" craft being named *Trieste II*. She was employed in 1969 to examine the remains of the nuclear-powered submarine *Scorpion* (SSN 589).

During this period the US Navy sponsored development of the *Alvin*, a deep submergence research vehicle, which served as prototype for the later *Turtle* and *Sea Cliff* submersibles. The *Alvin* subsequently was accidentally lost at sea on 16 Oct 1968.

After the loss of the *Thresher* the US Navy initiated an extensive deep submergence programme which includes development of a series of Deep Submergence Rescue Vehicles (DSRV) and Deep Submergence Search Vehicles (DSSV).

Finally, in collaboration with the Atomic Energy Commission, the Navy developed the nuclear-powered ocean engineering and research vehicle NR-1.
The Navy has chartered several commercial deep submergence vehicles for research and evaluation, notably the General Dynamics-Electric Boat STAR III, Grumman-Piccard *Benjamin Franklin* (ex-PX-15), Lockheed *Deep Quest* Perry Cubmarine PC3B, Perry-Link *Deep Diver*, Reynolds *Aluminaut*, and Westinghouse *Deepstar 4000*. (The US Air Force operates the Perry Cubmarine PC3A in support of Pacific missile range activities). The following deep submergence vehicles are Navy-owned craft.

2 + 4 DEEP SUBMERGENCE RESCUE VEHICLES

No.	*Builder*	*Completion*
DSRV-1	Lockhead Missiles and Space Co.	Dec 1969
DSRV-2	(Sunnyvale, Caif)	Mar 1970

Weight in air, tons	35
Length, feet	49·2 oa
Diameter, feet	8
Propulsion	Electric motors, propeller mounted in control shroud and four ducted thrusters
Speed, knots	5 (maximum)
Endurance	12 hours at 3 knots
Operating depth, feet	5 000
Complement	3 (pilot, co-pilot, rescue sphere operator) +24 rescuees

The Deep Submergence Rescue Vehicle is intended to provide a quick-reaction, world-wide, all-weather capability for the rescue of survivors in a disabled submarine. The DSRV will be transportable by road, aircraft (in C-141 and C-5 jet cargo aircraft), surface ship (on ASR 21 class submarine rescue ships), and specially modified submarines (SSN type).
Upon notification that a submarine is disabled on the ocean floor the DSRV and its support equipment (all necessary check-out equipment and spare parts being housed in a mobile van) will be loaded in cargo aircraft and flown to a port near the disabled submarine. The DSRV and van will then be towed to a pier and loaded aboard a "mother" submarine, which had proceeded to the port upon notification that a submarine was disabled.
The mother submarine, with the DSRV attached to her main deck (aft of the sail structure), will then proceed to the disabled submarine and serve as an underwater base for the DSRV which will shuttle back and forth between the disabled submarine and the mother submarine. On each trip the DSRV will carry up to 24 survivors from the disabled submarine. The mother submarine will launch and recover the DSRV while submerged and, if necessary, while under ice. A total of six DSRVs are planned, to be based at three locations in the United States.

DESIGN. The DSRV outer hull is constructed of formed fibreglass. Within this outer hull are three interconnected spheres which form the main pressure capsule. Each sphere is 7·5 feet in diameter and is constructed of HY-140 steel. The forward sphere contains the vehicle's control equipment and is manned by the pilot and co-pilot; the centre and after spheres accommodate 24 passengers and a third crewman. Under the DSRVs centre sphere is a hemispherical protrusion or "skirt" which seals over the disabled submarine's hatch. During the mating operation the skirt is pumped dry to enable personnel to transfer between the DSRV and disabled or mother submarine.

ENGINEERING. Propulsion and control of the DSRV are achieved by a stern propeller in a movable control shroud and four ducted thrusters, two forward and two aft. These, plus a mercury trim system, permit the DSRV to maneuver and hover with great precision, and to mate with submarines lying at angles up to 45 degrees from the horizontal. An elaborate Integrated Control and Display (ICAD) system employs computers to present sensor data to the pilots and transmit their commands to the vehicle's control and propulsion system.

ELECTRONICS. Elaborate search and navigational sonar, and closed-circuit television (supplemented by optical devices) are installed in the DSRV to determine the exact location of a disabled submarine within a given area and for pinpointing the submarine's escape hatches. Side-looking sonar will be fitted for search missions.

OPERATIONAL. The completion dates above indicate when the DSRV-1 and DSRV-2 would be available for emergency submarine rescue. However, long-range, rapid-reaction rescue requires the use of shore facilities, support ships, aircraft, and other related equipment.
The first of 24 nuclear-powered submarines now scheduled to be fitted as "mother" submarines to carry and support a DSRV are the *Finback* (SSN 670) and *Hawkbill* (SSN 666), both of which will be completed early in 1970.
When a six-vehicle DSRV force is completed two vehicles will be based at each Rescue Unit Home Port (RUHP) in San Diego, California; Charleston, South Carolina; and New London, Connecticut.

DSRV "landing" on mother submarine *United States Navy*

1 DEEP SUBMERGENCE SEARCH VEHICLE

DSSV-1

Weight in air, tons	35
Length, feet	50 oa
Diameter, feet	11 (maximum)
Propulsion	Electric motors (powered by fuel cells)
Speed, knots	5 (maximum)
Endurance	30+ hours at 3 knots
Operating depth, feet	20 000
Complement	4 (2 operators, 2 relief operators)

The Deep Submergence Search Vehicle is intended to perform object location and small object recovery missions on the ocean floor to depths of 20 000 feet (an area which encompasses some 80 per cent of the ocean floor). The DSSV will be transportable by aircraft (in C-5 jet cargo aircraft), surface ships, and specially configured support submarines.
Two Search and Recovery Forces have been proposed, each to consist of two DSSVs, one set of Unmanned Instrument Platforms (UIP), a specially configured "mother" submarine, and a surface support ship.
A contract for final design and construction of the DSSV-1 was awarded to the Lockheed Missiles and Space Company, Sunnyvale, California. Estimated completion is Fiscal Year 1978 with a significant post-completion period planned for tests and evaluation.

ELECTRONICS. To be fitted with side-looking sonar and essentially the same electronics-control "package" as the DSRV rescue submersible.

DESIGN. The external hull of the DSSV will be fabricated of light-weight, corrosion-resistant materials; the internal pressure hull will house two operators, two relief crewmen, control equipment (similar to the ICAD of the DSRV), and the required life-support equipment. A manipulator will be fitted to perform light work, lift objects, and attach surface lift lines.

1 NUCLEAR POWERED OCEAN ENGINEERING AND RESEARCH VEHICLE (NR)

NR-1

Displacement, tons	400 submerged
Length, feet	140 oa
Diameter, feet	12 maximum
Machinery	Electric motors, 2 propellers; four ducted thrusters
Reactor	1 pressurised-water cooled
Complement	3 officers, 2 enlisted men, 2 scientists

The NR-1 was built primarily to serve as a test platform for a small nuclear propulsion plant; however, she additionally provides an advanced deep submergence ocean engineering and research capability. The NR-1 was built by the Electric Boat Division of General Dynamics Corp, Groton, Connecticut. Authorised in Fiscal Year 1965 shipbuilding programme; laid down on 10 June 1967; launched on 25 Jan 1969; scheduled for completion late in 1969. Commanded by an officer-in-charge vice commanding officer.
Vice Admiral Hyman Rickover, US Navy (Retired), Deputy Commander for Nuclear Propulsion, Naval Ship Systems Command, has stated: "The (NR-1) will be able to perform detailed studies and mapping of the ocean bottom, temperature, currents, and other oceanographic parametres for military, commercial, and scientific use. The development of a nuclear propulsion plant for an oceanographic research vehicle will result in greater independence from surface support ships and essentially unlimited endurance of propulsion and auxiliary power for detailed exploration of the ocean.
"The submarine (NR-1) will have viewing ports for visual observation of its surroundings and the ocean bottom. In addition, a remote grapple will be installed to permit collection of marine samples and other items. With its depth capability, the NR-1 is expected to be capable of exploring areas of the Continental Shelf, an area which appears to contain most accessible wealth in mineral and food resources in the seas. Such exploratory charting may also help the United States in establishing sovereignty over parts of the Continental Shelf".

DESIGN. The NR-1 is fitted with wheels beneath the hull to permit "bottom crawling". This will obviate the necessity of hovering while exploring the ocean floor. Submarine wheels, a concept proposed as early as the first decade of this century by submarine inventor Simon Lake, were tested in the small submarine *Mackerel* (SST 1).
The NR-1 is fitted with external lights, external television cameras, a remote-controlled manipulator, and various recovery devices. Credited with a 30-day endurance.

ENGINEERING. The NR-1 reactor plant was designed by the Atomic Energy Commission's Knolls Atomic Power Laboratory. She is propelled by two propellers driven by electric motors outside the pressure hull with power provided by a turbine generator within the pressure hull. Four ducted thrusters, two horizontal and two vertical, are provided for precise manouvering.

CONSTRUCTION. The Navy originally contemplated constructing the NR-1 using "state of the art" equipment, with the cost of such a vehicle estimated to be $30 000 000 in March 1965. During detailed design of the NR-1 the Navy determined that improved equipment had to be developed and a larger hull than originally planned would be required. Consequently, in July 1967 the Navy obtained Congressional approval to proceed with construction of the NR-1 at an estimated cost of $58 000 300. The final estimated ship construction cost at time of launching was $67 500 000 plus $19 900 000 for oceanographic equipment and sensors, and $11 800 000 for research and development (mainly related to the nuclear propulsion plant), for a total estimated cost of $99 200 000.

Deep Submergence Vehicles—*continued*

NR-1 *1969, General Dynamics Electric Boat*

2 DEEP SUBMERGENCE RESEARCH VEHICLES: "ALVIN" TYPE

SEACLIFF (ex-*Autec I*)
TURTLE (ex-*Autec II*)

Weight in air, tons	21
Length, feet	25 oa
Beam, feet	8
Propulsion	Electric motors, trainable stern propeller; 2 rotating propeller pods
Speed, knots	2·5
Endurance	8 hours at 2 knots
Operating depth, feet	6 500
Complement	2 (pilot, observer)

Both submersibles built by Electric Boat Division of General Dynamics Corp, Groton, Connecticut. Intended for deep submergence research and work tasks. Designated *Autec I* and *Autec II* during construction, but assigned above names in dual launching on 11 Dec 1968. Completed in 1969.
The *Sea Cliff* is operated by the Woods Hole Oceanographic Institution in support of the Office of Naval Research; the *Turtle* supports the Navy's Atlantic Undersea Test and Evaluation Centre (AUTEC) off Andros Island in the Tongue-of-the-Ocean.

CONSTRUCTION. Three pressure spheres were fabricated for the *Alvin* submersible programme, one for installation in the *Alvin*, a spare, and one for testing. The second and third spheres subsequently were allocated to new-construction submersibles.

DESIGN. Twin-arm manipulator fitted to each submersible.

LOSS. The smaller submersible *Alvin* of this design accidentally sank in 4 500 feet of water some 120 miles south of Cape Cod on 16 Oct 1968 when a cable broke on her catamaran support ship *Lulu*. Her access hatch was open and the submersible flooded; there were no casualties.

SEA CLIFFE *1968, General Dynamics, Electric Boat*

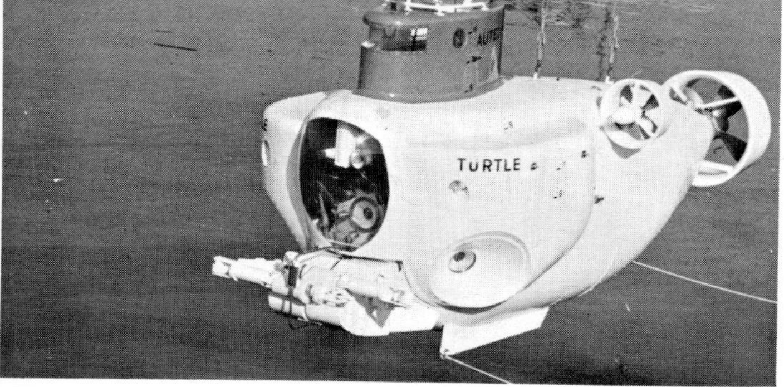

TURTLE *1968, General Dynamics, Electric Boat*

1 BATHYSCAPH RESEARCH VEHICLE

TRIESTE II

Weight in air, tons	50
Displacement, tons	303 submerged
Length, feet	78·6
Beam, feet	15·3
Propulsion	Electric motors, 2 propellers aft, ducted thruster forward
Speed, knots	2
Endurance	5 hours at 2 knots
Operating depth, feet	12 000 (see *Design* notes)
Complement	3 (2 operators, 1 observer)

The *Trieste II* is the extensively rebuilt *Trieste I* which the US Navy purchased in 1958 from Professor Auguste Piccard. The bathyscaph is essentially an underwater "elevator" with extremely limited horizontal maneuvrability. The bathyscaph is normally towed to the dive site with a towing speed of 7 knots.
The vehicle is operated by Submarine Development Group One at San Diego, California, and is used primarily as a test bed for underwater equipment and to train deep submergence vehicle operators (hydronauts).

DESIGN. The *Trieste II* is essentially a large float with a small pressure sphere attached to the underside. The float, which is filled with 66 000 gallons (US) of aviation petrol, provides buoyancy. The Terni sphere fitted to the *Trieste II* is 7 feet in diameter and constructed of Ni-Cr-Mo forged steel; designed operating depth is 20 000 feet but dives have been limited to approximately 12 000 feet. (The record-setting Challenger Deep dive was made with a Krupp sphere which has a virtually unlimited depth capability). Fitted with external television cameras and mechanical manipulator.

TRIESTE II *1965, United States Navy*

TRIESTE II *1964, United States Navy*

UNITED STATES COAST GUARD

Command

Commandant, United States Coast Guard: Admiral Willard J. Smith

Assistant Commandant: Vice Admiral Paul E. Trimble

Chief of Staff: Rear Admiral Thomas R. Sargent 3rd

Commander, Eastern Area: Rear Admiral Mark A. Whalen

Commander, Western Area: Rear Admiral Chester R. Bender

Establishment

The United States Coast Guard was established by an Act of Congress approved Jan 28, 1915, which consolidated the Revenue Cutter Service (founded in 1790) and the Life Saving Service (founded in 1878). The act of establishment stated the Coast Guard "shall be a military service and branch of the armed forces of the United States at all times. The Coast Guard shall be a service in the Treasury Department except when operating as a service in the Navy".

The Congress further legislated that in time of national emergency or when the President so directs, the Coast Guard operates as a part of the Navy. The Coast Guard did operate as a part of the Navy during the First and Second World Wars.

The Lighthouse Service (founded in 1789) was transferred to the Coast Guard on July 1, 1939.

The Coast Guard was transferred to the newly established Department of Transportation on March 1, 1967.

Missions

The current missions of the Coast Guard are to (1) enforce or assist in the enforcement of applicable Federal laws upon the high seas and waters subject to the jurisdiction of the United States; (2) administer all Federal laws regarding safety of life and property on the high seas and on waters subject to the jurisdiction of the United States, except those laws specifically entrusted to other Federal agencies; (3) develop, establish, maintain, operate, and conduct aids to maritime navigation, ocean stations, icebreaking activities, oceanographic research, and rescue facilities; and (4) maintain a state of readiness to function as a specialised service in the Navy when so directed by the President.

An analysis of current Coast Guard activity prepared in 1968 showed that 70 per cent of the service's funding is related to multi-purpose search, rescue, navigational, port security, and law enforcement activities; 13 per cent to oceanography, meteorology, icebreaking, and other marine sciences; 13 per cent to military activities; and 4 per cent to merchant marine inspection and safety.

The US Navy's five icebreakers (AGB) were transferred to the Coast Guard in 1965-1966 to consolidate this mission under a single service.

Cutters

All Coast Guard vessels are referred to as "cutters". Cutter names are preceded by USCG. Cutter serial numbers are prefixed with letter designations, the first letter being "W". The first two digits of serial numbers for cutters less than 100 feet in length indicate their approximate length over all.

Personnel

1966 Fiscal Year Strength: 32,519 officers and enlisted men
1967 Fiscal Year Strength: 34,546 officers and enlisted men
1968 Fiscal Year Strength: 36,563 officers and enlisted men
1969 Fiscal Year Strength: 37,565 officers and enlisted men
1970 Fiscal Year Strength: 4,277 officers, 1,250 warrant officers, 32,067 enlisted men (aggregate 37,594) plus 840 cadets at Coast Guard Academy

Aviation

The Coast Guard operates a small air arm to support Coast Guard operations. As of June 30, 1969, the Coast Guard operated 64 fixed-wing aircraft and 112 helicopters. Ninety-five of the helicopters were HH-52A; HH-3F helicopters are being procured to replace HU-16 Albatross amphibians.

There are 13 large and 13 small Coast Guard air stations located in the Continental United States; Barbers Point, Oahu, Hawaii; Kodiak and Annette, Alaska; Sangley Point, Philippines; San Juan, Puerto Rico; and Naples, Italy.

Vietnam Operations

A number of Coast Guard Cutters have been developed to Southeast Asia to supplement US Navy forces in the Vietnamese War. These vessels remain units of the US Coast Guard but are under the operational direction of the Commander US Naval Forces Vietnam. Five high endurance cutters form Coast Guard Squadron Three based in Subic Bay, Republic of the Philippines. Twenty-four 82-foot cutters form Coast Guard Squadron One based in South Vietnam. (These vessels are painted gray). All 29 cutters are assigned to Operation MARKET TIME which seeks to halt the Communist infiltration of men and arms into South Vietnam by sea.

Fiscal Year 1970 Programme

The Fiscal Year 1970 programme for the Coast Guard as presented by the Secretary of Transportation provided for one additional high endurance cutter of the "Hamilton" class. The Congress added two additional ships of this type to the programme for a total of three ships in FY 1970.

The large oceanographic research cutter (WHEO 701) previously approved for construction was cancelled in May of 1969.

HIGH ENDURANCE CUTTERS

11 + 3 HIGH ENDURANCE CUTTERS (WHEC): "HAMILTON" (378) CLASS

	No.	*Launched*	*Completed*
BOUTWELL	WHEC 719	17 June 1967	14 June 1968
CHASE	WHEC 718	20 May 1967	1 Mar 1968
DALLAS	WHEC 716	1 Oct 1966	1 Oct 1967
GALLATIN	WHEC 721	18 Nov 1967	20 Dec 1968
HAMILTON	WHEC 715	18 Dec 1965	20 Feb 1967
MELLON	WHEC 717	11 Feb 1967	22 Dec 1967
MORGANTHAU	WHEC 722	10 Feb 1968	14 Feb 1969
RUSH	WHEC 723	Nov 1968	3 July 1969
SHERMAN	WHEC 720	23 Sep 1967	23 Aug 1968
	WHEC 724		
	WHEC 725		

Displacement, tons	2 716 standard; 3 050 full load
Dimensions, feet	350 wl; 378 oa × 42 × 20
Guns	1—5 in, 38 cal; 2—81 mm mortars; 2—·50 cal MG
A/S weapons	2 Hedgehogs; 2 triple torpedo launchers (Mk 32)
Aircraft	One HH-52A helicopter
Main engines	2 Fairbanks Morse diesels, 2 Pratt & Whitney gas turbines; 2 shafts; 36 000 shp = 29 knots
Complement	15 officers, 185 enlisted men

Large, attractive multi-mission ships with good sea-keeping qualities.
All built by Avondale Shipyards Inc at a cost of $10 000 000 each for earlier ships. Aluminium superstructure.
Rescue equipment includes gas turbine powered motor lifeboats.
Three additional ships in Fiscal Year 1970 programme.

DESIGN. These ships have clipper bows, twin funnels enclosing helicopter hangar, helicopter platform aft. Fitted with oceanographic laboratories, elaborate communications capabilities, meteorological data gathering facilities.

MELLON (WHEC 717) *1968, United States Coast Guard*

High Endurance Cutters—*continued*

ENGINEERING. First large US government ships to be fitted with gas turbine engines. Engine and propeller pitch control consoles on navigation bridge and bridge wing stations as well as engine room control booth. Endurance on diesel propulsion plant is 11 500 miles at 20 knots; endurance on gas turbine plant is 3 000 miles at 25 knots.

CANCELLATION. The cancelled oceanographic cutter WHEO 701 was to have been similar in design and appearance.

NOMENCLATURE. The 378 and 327 classes of high endurance cutters honour former Secretaries of the Treasury.

BOUTWELL (WHEC 719) *1968, United States Coast Guard*

12 HIGH ENDURANCE CUTTERS (WHEC): "OWASCO" (255) CLASS

Name	*No.*	*Launched*	*Completed*
ANDROSCOGGIN	WHEC 68	16 Sep 1945	20 Sep 1946
CHAUTAUQUA	WHEC 41	14 May 1944	4 Aug 1945
ESCANABA (ex-*Otsego*)	WHEC 64	25 Mar 1945	20 Mar 1946
KLAMATH	WHEC 66	2 Sep 1945	5 Sep 1946
MENDOTA	WHEC 69	29 Feb 1944	2 June 1946
MINNETONKA (ex-*Sunapee*)	WHEC 67	21 Nov 1945	20 Sep 1946
OWASCO	WHEC 39	18 June 1944	18 May 1945
PONTCHARTRAIN (ex-*Okeechobee*)	WHEC 70	29 Apr 1944	28 July 1945
SEBAGO (ex-*Wachusett*)	WHEC 42	28 May 1944	20 Sep 1945
WACHUSETT (ex-*Huron*)	WHEC 44	5 Nov 1944	23 Mar 1946
WINNEBAGO	WHEC 40	2 July 1944	21 June 1945
WINONA	WHEC 65	22 Apr 1945	15 Aug 1946

Displacement, tons	1 563 standard; 1 913 full load
Dimensions, feet	254 oa × 43 × 17
Guns	1—5 in, 38 cal dual-purpose; 2—40 mm (twin) in some ships
A/S weapons	2 triple torpedo launchers (Mk 32) hedgehog
Main engines	Westinghouse geared turbines; electric drive; 1 shaft; 4 000 shp = 18·4 knots
Boilers	2
Oil fuel, tons	350
Complement	140

Rated as 255 ft Cutters. Employed as ocean station ships. All built by Western Pipe & Steel Co, except *Mendota* and *Pontchartrain*, by Coast Guard Shipyard. Named after Indian tribes. *Klamath, Wachusett* and *Winnebago* fitted with oceanographic research equipment.
Designation of high endurance cutters (through WHEC 719) changed from WPG to WHEC on 1 May 1966.

GUNNERY. As built these ships each mounted four 5-inch guns (twin), four 40 mm anti-aircraft guns (twin), and four 20 mm anti-aircraft guns; subsequently reduced. (Original depth charge racks also removed.)

WACHUSETT (WHEC 44) *United States Coast Guard*

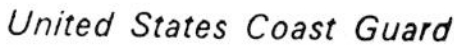

DISPOSAL
Iroquois WPG 43 was stricken in 1955.

6 HIGH ENDURANCE CUTTERS (WHEC): "CAMPBELL" (327) CLASS

Name	*No.*	*Launched*	*Completed*
BIBB (ex-*George M. Bibb*)	WHEC 31	14 Jan 1937	19 Mar 1937
CAMPBELL (ex-*George W. Campbell*)	WHEC 32	3 June 1936	22 Oct 1936
DUANE (ex-*William J. Duane*)	WHEC 33	3 June 1936	16 Oct 1936
INGHAM (ex-*Samuel D. Ingham*)	WHEC 35	3 June 1936	6 Nov 1936
SPENCER (ex-*John C. Spencer*)	WHEC 36	6 Jan 1936	13 May 1937
TANEY (ex-*Roger B. Taney*)	WHEC 37	3 June 1936	19 Dec 1936

Displacement, tons	2 216 standard; 2 414 full load
Dimensions, feet	308 wl; 327 oa × 41 × 15
Guns	1—5 in, 38 cal dual-purpose
A/S weapons	2 triple torpedo launchers (Mk 32) hedgehog
Main engines	Westinghouse geared turbines; 2 shafts; 6 200 shp = 19·8 knots
Boilers	2 (Babcock & Wilcox)
Oil fuel, tons	572
Complement	202

Rated as 327 ft Cutters. Employed as ocean station ships and deployed to Southeast Asia with Coast Guard Squadron 3. All built by Philadelphia Navy Yard except *Bibb* by Charleston Navy Yard and *Spencer* by New York Navy Yard.
The *Alexander Hamilton* (WPG 34) was lost during World War II.

GUNNERY. All originally mounted two 5-inch guns and several 40 mm and 20 mm anti-aircraft guns; only one 5 inch gun retained.

ENGINEERING. Endurance is 8 000 miles at 12·5 knots and 12 300 miles at 11 knots.

INGHAM (WHEC 35) *United States Coast Guard*

High Endurance Cutters — *continued*

DUANE (WHEC 33) *1967, United States Coast Guard*

12 HIGH ENDURANCE CUTTERS (WHEC)

1 OCEANOGRAPHIC CUTTER (WAGO): "CASCO" (311) CLASS

Name	*No.*	*Builder*	*Launched*	*Navy Comm.*
ABESECON (ex-*AVP* 23)	WHEC 374	Lake Washington Shipyard	8 Mar 1942	28 Jan 1943
BARATARIA (ex-*AVP* 33)	WHEC 381	Lake Washington Shipyard	2 Oct 1943	13 Aug 1944
BERING STRAIT (ex-*AVP* 34)	WHEC 382	Lake Washington Shipyard	15 Jan 1944	19 July 1944
CASTLE ROCK (ex-*AVP* 35)	WHEC 383	Lake Washington Shipyard	11 Mar 1944	8 Oct 1944
CHINCOTEAGUE (ex-*AVP* 24)	WHEC 375	Lake Washington Shipyard	15 Apr 1942	12 Apr 1943
COOK INLET (ex-*AVP* 36)	WHEC 384	Lake Washington Shipyard	13 May 1944	5 Nov 1944
GRESHAM (ex-*Willoughby*, ex-*AGP* 9, ex-*AVP* 57)	WHEC 387	Lake Washington Shipyard	21 Aug 1942	18 June 1944
HALF MOON (ex-*AVP* 26)	WHEC 378	Lake Washington Shipyard	12 July 1942	15 June 1943
HUMBOLDT (ex-*AVP* 21)	WHEC 372	Boston Naval Shipyard	17 Mar 1941	7 Oct 1941
McCULLOCH (ex-*Wachapreague*, ex-*AGP* 8, ex-*AVP* 56)	WHEC 386	Lake Washington Shipyard	10 July 1942	17 May 1944
ROCKAWAY (ex-*AVP* 29)	WAGO 377	Associated Shipbuilders	14 Feb 1942	6 Jan 1943
UNIMAK (ex-*AVP* 31)	WHEC 379	Associated Shipbuilders	27 May 1942	31 Dec 1943
YAKUTAT (ex-*AVP* 32)	WHEC 380	Associated Shipbuilders	2 July 1942	31 Mar 1944

Displacement, tons	1 766 standard; 2 800 full load
Dimensions, feet	311 oa × 41 × 14
Guns	1—5 in, 38 cal dual-purpose (removed from *Rockaway*)
A/S weapons	2 triple torpedo launchers (Mk 32) some ships also have hedgehog
Main engines	Diesel; 2 shafts; 6 080 bhp = 19 knots
Complement	215

These are the survivors of 18 former seaplane tenders transferred to the Coast Guard from the Navy.
Most employed as ocean station ships. *Dexter* was refitted with four new Fairbanks-Morse diesels in 1957 and was recommissioned in July 1958 for duty as West Coast Training Ship. *Unimak* is East Coast Training ship. *Rockaway* was adapted as oceanographic ship in 1966. *McCulloch* is in reserve.

GUNNERY. Original anti-aircraft armament of 40 mm and 20 mm guns removed; ASW weapons installed in Coast Guard service.

DESIGNATION. The designation of all these ships was changed from WAVP to WHEC on 1 May 1966.

ENGINEERING. Endurance is 22 000 miles at 11 knots; 8 000 miles at 19 knots.

PHOTOGRAPHS. Coast Guard orange identification slash and service name adopted in 1967. Patrol boats operating in Vietnam area are gray; larger cutters retain white, "peacetime" colour.

DISPOSALS
Coos Bay (WHEC 376, ex-AVP 36) returned to the Navy in *1967* and sunk as target ship; **Dexter** (WHEC 385, ex-AGC 18, ex-AVP 11), **Mackinac** (WHEC 371, ex-AVP 13), and **Matagorda** (WHEC 373, ex-AVP 22) all returned to the Navy in mid-1968 and expended as targets. **Casco** (WHEC 370, ex-AVP 12) returned to Navy in 1969 and expended as target.

ROCKAWAY (WAGO 377) *1967, United States Coast Guard*

GRESHAM (WHEC 387) *United States Coast Guard*

MEDIUM ENDURANCE CUTTERS

16 MEDIUM ENDURANCE CUTTERS (WMEC): "RELIANCE" (210) CLASS

Name	No.	Launched	Name	No.	Launched
ACTIVE	WMEC 618	31 July 1965	**DURABLE**	WMEC 628	29 Apr 1967
ALERT	WMEC 630	Oct 1968	**RELIANCE**	WMEC 615	25 May 1963
CONFIDENCE	WMEC 619	8 May 1965	**RESOLUTE**	WMEC 620	30 Apr 1966
COURAGEOUS	WMEC 622	18 Mar 1967	**STEADFAST**	WMEC 623	24 June 1967
DAUNTLESS	WMEC 624	21 Oct 1967	**VALIANT**	WMEC 621	14 Jan 1967
DECISIVE	WMEC 629	14 Dec 1967	**VENTUROUS**	WMEC 625	11 Nov 1967
DEPENDABLE	WMEC 626	16 Mar 1968	**VIGILANT**	WMEC 617	24 Dec 1963
DILIGENCE	WMEC 616	20 July 1963	**VIGOROUS**	WMEC 627	4 May 1968

Displacement, tons	950 standard, 1 000 full load
Dimensions, feet	210·5 oa × 34 × 10·5
Guns	1—3 in, 50 cal
Main engines	2 combination turbo-charged diesels (5 000 hp) and gas turbines (2 000 hp); 2 shafts; = 18 knots
Complement	64 (7 officers, 57 men)

A new class of cutters designed by the US Coast Guard. Primarily intended for search and rescue duties, the superstructure is arranged on three levels forward of midship, affording the wheelhouse 360 degree visibility. Another feature is a flight deck aft suitable for operating rescue helicopter (no hangar provided). Conspicuously missing is the conventional funnel, which is eliminated by the use of the exhaust vent in the stern. Equipped with facilities for ocean towing of vessels up to 10 000 tons gross. Air conditioned throughout except engine room; high degree of habitability.

Programmes:—1962 *Diligence, Reliance*; 1963 *Vigilant*; 1964; *Active, Confidence*; 1965 *Courageous, Dauntless, Resolute, Steadfast, Valiant, Venturous*; 1966 *Alert Decisive, Dependable, Durable, Vigorous.*

ENGINEERING. These ships cruise on diesel portion of propulsion plant; use gas turbines for maximum speed. Endurance is 5 000 miles at 15 knots. Engine room is unmanned during operation.

RECLASSIFICATION. Designation was changed from WPC (Patrol Craft) to WMEC on 1 May 1966.

BUILDERS. WMEC 615-617 built by Todd Shipyards; WMEC 618 built by Christy Corporations; WMEC 619, 625, 628 629 built by Coast Guard Yard (Curtis Bay, Baltimore, Maryland); WMEC 620-624, 626, 627, 630 by American Shipbuilding.

VIGILANT (WMEC 617) *United States Coast Guard*

DISPOSALS OF OTHER CLASSES
Of the "Argo" class, **Triton** (WMEC 116, ex-WPC 116) stricken in Jan 1967, **Aurora** (WMEC 103, ex-WPC 103) stricken in Jan 1968, **Ariadne** (WMEC 101, ex-WPC 101) stricken in Jan 1969.

1 MEDIUM ENDURANCE CUTTER (WMEC): "ALERT" (125) CLASS

MORRIS WMEC 147 (ex-WPC 147)

Displacement, tons	220 standard; 290 full load
Dimensions, feet	125 oa × 23·5 × 9
Guns	1—40 mm anti-aircraft
Main engines	Diesels; 2 shafts; 800 bhp = 13 knots

The lone survivor of a class of 27 steel patrol boats launched in 1926-1927. All were re-engined in 1939-1942.

Eight cutters disposed of prior to 1959; *Bonham* (WPC 129) was stricken in 1959, *Diligence* (WPC 135) in 1961, *Active* (WPC 125), *Marion* (WPC 145), *Travis* (WPC 153) in 1962, *Boutwell* (WPC 130) in 1963, *Cuyahoga* (WPC 157) in 1964, *Frederick Lee* (WPC 139) in 1965, *Ewing* (WMEC 137) in 1967, *Cahoone* (WMEC 131), *Cartigan* (WMEC 132), *General Greene* (WMEC 140), *Kimball* (WMEC 143), *Legare* (WMEC 144), *McLane* (WMEC 146) in 1968, *Alert* (WMEC 127), *Agassiz* (WMEC 126), *Yeaton* (WMEC 156) in 1969.

ICEBREAKERS

7 ICEBREAKERS (WAGB): "WIND" CLASS

Name		Launched
BURTON ISLAND	WAGB 283 (ex-AGB 1, ex-AG 88)	30 Apr 1946
EASTWIND	WAGB 279	6 Feb 1943
EDISTO	WAGB 284 (ex-AGB 2, ex-AG 89)	29 May 1946
NORTHWIND	WAGB 282	25 Feb 1945
SOUTHWIND (ex-*Atka*)	WAGB 280 (ex-AGB 3)	8 Mar 1943
STATEN ISLAND (ex-*Northwind*)	WAGB 278 (ex-AGB 5)	28 Dec 1942
WESTWIND	WAGB 281	31 Mar 1943

Displacement, tons	3 500 standard; 6,515 full load
Dimensions, feet	250 pp; 269 oa × 63·5 × 29
Aircraft	Two helicopters
Guns	*Eastwind*: 2—3 in, 50 cal (twin) *Northwind*: 2—5 in, 38 cal (twin) *Burton Island, Staten Island*: None Other three: 1—5 in, 38 cal
Main engines	6 diesel-electric; 2 shafts; 13 300 bhp = 16 knots
Endurance, miles	38 000 range at economical speed of 10·5 knots
Complement	21 officers, 195 men (*Burton Island* 15 and 196)

All built by the Western Pipe & Steel Co, San Pedro, California. Construction is entirely welded, with double hull and exceptionally heavy plating designed to crush ice 9 ft thick. Forward shafts were removed. All ships have helicopter flight deck and telescopic or rigid hangar aft. *Northwind* (first ship, ex-AGB 5), *Southwind* (*Severini Veter*) and *Westwind* (*Severini Polius*) were lent to the Soviet Navy in 1945, *Southwind* was returned in 1950, other two in Dec 1951. The four 40 mm guns in *Northwind* and *Westwind* and the four 20 mm guns in *Eastwind* were removed in 1962.

STATUS. The *Eastwind* is in reserve; all other Coast Guard icebreakers are operational.

TRANSFERS. It was officially announced in June 1965 that all five of the US Navy icebreakers would be transferred to the Coast Guard to consolidate a responsibility divided between the USN and USCG. *Edisto* was transferred on 20 Oct 1965, *Staten Island* on 1 Feb 1966, *Glacier* on 30 June 1966, *Akta* (again renamed *Southwind* in Jan 1967) on 20 Oct 1966 and *Burton Island* on 15 Dec 1966.

NORTHWIND (WAGB 282) *1968 U.S. Coast Guard*

BURTON ISLAND (WAGB 283) *As Navy AGBI* *1965 U.S. Navy*

Icebreakers—*continued*

NORTHWIND *1967*

1 ICEBREAKER (WAGB): "GLACIER" TYPE

GLACIER WAGB 4 (ex-AGB 4)

Displacement, tons	8 449 full load
Dimensions, feet	310 × 74 × 29
Aircraft	2 Helicopters
Guns	2—5 in, 38 cal (twin)
Main engines	10 Fairbanks-Morse diesels and 2 Westinghouse 10 500 hp electric motors; 2 shafts 21 000 shp = 18·3 knots
Endurance, miles	25 000 at cruising speed of 12 knots
Complement	15 officers, 226 enlisted men

Designed and built by Ingalls Shipbuilding Corporation, Pascagoula, Mississippi. Laid down on 3 Aug 1953, launched on 27 Aug 1954 and commissioned on 27 May 1955. Designed for breaking ice more than 20 feet thick. Her bow is heavily armoured for driving the ship on top of the ice field and crushing it by sheer weight. Helicopters are carried to spot the best course through the ice. Largest and highest powered American icebreaker yet built. Has largest capacity single-armature DC motors ever built and installed in a ship. Carries an LCVP in addition to five boats and rafts for entire ship's company. Thick double hull. Transferred from Navy (AGB 4) to Coast Guard on 30 June 1966.

GLACIER (WAGB 4) *1968 U.S Coast guard*

1 ICEBREAKER (WAGB): "MACKINAW" TYPE

MACKINAW (ex-*Manitowac*) WAGB 83

Displacement, tons	5 252
Dimensions, feet	290 oa × 74 × 19
Aircraft	1 helicopter
Main engines	Diesel; with electric drive; 3 shafts (1 forward, 2 aft); 10 000 bhp = 18·7 knots
Endurance, miles	60 000 range at economical speed of 9 knots

Built by Toledo Shipbuilding Co, Ohio. Laid down on 20 Mar 1943. Launched on 6 Mar 1944. Commissioned on 20 Dec 1944. Completed in Jan 1945. Specially designed and constructed with 1·6 in. plating for service as icebreaker on the Great Lakes. Equipped with two 12-ton cranes. Clear area for helicopter is provided on the quarter deck.

MACINAN (WAGB 83) *1966 U.S. Coast Guard*

1 ICEBREAKER (WAGB): "STORIS" TYPE

STORIS (ex-*Eskimo*) WAGB 38

Displacement, tons	1 715 standard; 1 925 full load
Dimensions, feer	230 oa × 43 × 15
Guns	1—3 in, 50 cal
Aircraft	1 helicopter
Main engines	Diesel-electric; 1 shaft; 1 800 bhp = 14 knots

Built by Toledo Shipbuilding Co, Ohio. Launched in 1942. Ice patrol tender. Helicopter platform aft. Strengthened for ice navigation. Employed on Alaskan service. Search, rescue and law enforcement are primary duties. Makes supply runs to isolated Coast Guard installations within her patrol area. Her designation was changed from WAG to WAGB on 1 May 1966.

PATROL BOATS

26 PATROL BOATS (WPB): 95 ft CLASS

CAPE CARTER	95309	**CAPE HORN**	95322
CAPE CORAL	95301	**CAPE JELLISON**	95317
CAPE CORWIN	95326	**CAPE KNOX**	95312
CAPE CROSS	95321	**CAPE MORGAN**	95313
CAPE CURRENT	95307	**CAPE NEWAGEN**	95318
CAPE FAIRWEATHER	95314	**CAPE ROMAIN**	95319
CAPE FOX	95316	**CAPE SHOALWATER**	95324
CAPE GEORGE	95306	**CAPE SMALL**	95300
CAPE GULL	95304	**CAPE STARR**	95320
CAPE HATTERAS	95305	**CAPE STRAIT**	95308
CAPE HEDGE	95311	**CAPE UPRIGHT**	95303
CAPE HENLOPEN	95328	**CAPE WASH**	95310
CAPE HIGGON	95302	**CAPE YORK**	95332

CG 95321—95335	**CG 95312—95314, 95316—95320**	**CG 95300—95311**
"C" Class (built 1958-59)	"B" Class (built 1955-56)	"A" Class (built 1953)

Displacement, tons	106 (B); 105 (A); 98 (C)
Dimensions, feet	95 oa × 19 × 6
Guns	1—20 mm or 1—40 mm
Main engines	4 diesels; 2 shafts (2 engines in tandem each shaft); 2 200 bhp = 21 knots max
Endurance miles	1 500 cruising range
Complement	14 (1 officer, 13 enlisted men)

Rated as 95 ft Cutters. Designed and built at Coast Guard Yard, Curtis Bay, Maryland for port security, search and rescue. Steel hulled, twin screws. "C" class boats, for search and rescue, have less armament, electronics and displacement.

TRANSFERS. Nine boats of this type were transferred to the South Korean Navy in 1968: *Cape Falcon* (95330), *Cape Providence* (95335), *Cape Rosier* (95333), *Cape Sable* (95334), *Cape Trinity* (95331), *Cape Darby* (95323), *Cape Florida* (95325), *Cape Kiwanda* (95329), and *Cape Porpoise* (95327).

CAPE CARTER (WPB 95309) *1968 U.S. Coast Guard*

POINT YOUNG (WP8 82303) *United States Coast Guard*

Patrol, Boats—*continued*

77 PATROL BOATS (WPB): 82ft CLASS

Name	No.	Name	No.
POINT ARDEN*	82309	POINT KNOLL	82367
POINT ARENA	82346	POINT LEDGE	82324
POINT BAKER	82342	POINT LOBOS	82366
POINT BANKS*	82327	POINT LOMAS*	82321
POINT BARROW	82348	POINT LOOKOUT	82341
POINT BATAN	82340	POINT MAST*	82316
POINT BENNETT	82351	POINT MONROE	82353
POINT BONITA	82347	POINT MORONE*	82331
OINT BRIDGE	82338	POINT NOWELL	82363
OINT BROWN	82362	POINT ORIENT*	82319
OINT CAUTION*	82301	POINT PARTRIDGE*	82305
OINT CHARLES	82361	POINT RICHMOND	82370
OINT CHICO	82339	POINT ROBERTS	82332
OINT CLEAR*	82315	POINT SAL	82352
OINT COMFORT*	82317	POINT SLOCUM*	82313
OINT COUNTESS	82335	POINT SPENCER	82349
OINT CYPRESS*	82326	POINT STEELE	82359
OINT DIVIDE	82337	POINT STUART	82358
OINT DUME*	82325	POINT SWIFT	82312
OINT ELLIS*	82330	POINT THATCHER	82314
OINT ESTERO	82344	POINT TURNER	82365
OINT EVANS	82354	POINT VERDE	82311
OINT FRANCIS	82356	POINT WARDE	82368
OINT FRANKLIN	82350	POINT WELCOME*	82329
OINT GAMMON*	82328	POINT WELLS	82343
OINT GLASS	82336	POINT WHITE*	82308
OINT GLOVER*	82307	POINT WHITEHORN	82364
OINT GRACE*	82323	POINT WINSLOW	82360
OINT GREY*	82324	POINT YOUNG*	82303
OINT HANNON	82355		
OINT HERRON	82318	POINT BARNES	82371
OINT HEYER	82369	POINT BROWER	82372
OINT HIGHLAND	82333	POINT CAMDEN	82373
OINT HOPE	82302	POINT CARREW	82374
OINT HUDSON*	82322	POINT DORAN	82375
OINT HURON	82357	POINT HARRIS	82376
OINT JEFFERSON*	82306	POINT HOBART	82377
OINT JUDITH	82345	POINT JACKSON	82378
OINT KENNEDY*	82320	POINT MARTIN	82379

CG 82332—82370 ;" class (built 1962-63 and 1965-67)

CG 82318—82331 "B" Class (built 1961)

CG 82301—82317 "A" Class (built 1960-61)

CG 82371—82379 " Class (built 1969-70)

Displacement, tons	64 standard; 67 full load
Dimensions, feet	78·1 wl; 83 oa × 17·2 × 5·8
Guns	1—81 mm/·50 cal MG and 2 to 4—·50 cal MG or 1—20 mm
Main engines	A/B classes: 2 diesels; 2 shafts; 1 200 bhp = 16·8 knots C/D classes: 2 diesels; 2 shafts; 1 600 bhp = 22·9 knots
Complement	8 to 10

ted as 82 ft Cutters. Designed and built at Coast Guard Yard, for law enforcement, rch and rescue. Steel hulls, unmanned engine room controlled from the bridge, wer steering and air conditioning. "C" class modifications (also 82318) include rease in bhp to 1 600 and speed to 22·9 knots. In 1965 26 of these craft were de-yed with the Navy and transferred to duty in Vietnam (they have a double action consisting of a ·50 cal machine gun mounted on top of an 81 mm mortar, re-cing the former 20 mm gun). As a result 17 replacement cutters were added to construction programme plus nine already planned. Of the latter, *Point Arena, nt Barrow, Point Bonita, Point Franklin, Point Judith* and *Point Spencer* were lt under the Fiscal Year 1965 Programme by Martinac SB, Tacoma, Wash, and 351 to 82370 in the 1966 programme. Nine "D" class cutters built by Coast Guard d with first, *Point Barnes*, completed on 19 Dec 1969.

tters assigned to Coast Guard Squadron One in Vietnam are indicated by asterisk r name. Two of the cutters in Vietnam, the *Point Garnet* (WPB 82310) and *Point gue* (WPB 82304) were transferred to the South Vietnamese Navy in May 1969.

MENCLATURE. CG 82301-82344 were assigned "Point" names in Jan 1964, d redesignated patrol craft instead of patrol boats.

TRAINING SHIPS

1 TRAINING SHIP (WTR): Ex-RADIO SHIP

URIER WTR 410 (ex-WAGR)
x-*Coastal Messenger*, ex-USS *Doddridge, AK* 176)

splacement, tons	5 800 standard; 7 500 full load
easurement, tons	5 926 deadweight
mensions, feet	338·5 × 50·3 × 21
ain engines	Diesel; direct drive; 1 700 bhp = 11 knots
adius, miles	Approximately 14 500

/I-AVI type, launched in 1945. Built as a naval cargo ship but not used by the Navy. uired by the US Coast Guard from the US Maritime Commission in 1951, fitted as an overseas radio relay base, manned by the Coast Guard and operated for the ed States Information Agency as a relay station for the "Voice of America" broad-s from 7 Sep 1952 until 17 May 1964. She was virtually a seagoing radio broad-ng station wirh transmitting equipment the most powerful of its kind ever installed ny vessel. She commissioned on 15 Feb 1952 and began broadcasts on 7 Sep 2, being stationed at Island of Rhodes, Greece. She returned to the USA in 1964 was decommissioned on 25 Aug 1964, but was converted and recommissioned July 1965 and employed as a training "cutter" for the reserve at Yorktown, Va. special communication equipment has been removed.

Training Ships—*continued*

COURIER (WTR 410) *1967, United States Coast Guard*

1 TRAINING SHIP (WTR): Ex-PATROL ESCORT

LAMAR (ex-USS PCE 899) WTR 899

Displacement, tons	640 standard; 903 full load
Dimensions, feet	180 wl; 184·5 oa × 33 × 9·5
Guns	1—3 in, 50 cal dp; 6—40 mm AA (3 twin). Original armament
Main engines	GM diesels; 2 shafts; 2 000 bhp = 15 knots
Complement	60 (5 officers, 55 men) Navy allowance. Accommodation for 9 officers, 90 men

Former escort, 180 ft steel type, acquired from the US Navy in 1965, converted for use as Coast Guard Reserve training ship and commissioned in 1965. Built by Willamette Iron & Steel Corp, Portland, Oregon. Laid down 11 Jan 1943. Launched on 11 Aug 1943. Completed (first commission) on 17 Mar 1945.

The yacht *Petrel* was sold in 1966.

LAMAR (WTR 899) *United States Coast Guard*

1 TRAINING SHIP (WTR): Ex-MINESWEEPER

TANAGER (ex-USS *MSF* 385) WTR 385

Displacement, tons	890 standard; 1 077 full load
Dimensions, feet	215 wl; 221 oa × 32·2 × 10·8
Main engines	Diesel-electric; 2 shafts; 3 474 bhp = 18 knots
Complement	5 officers, 34 men (80 reserve trainees)

Former fleet minesweeper, large steel-hulled type, acquired from the US Navy in 1964 as a Coast Guard Reserve training ship, at Yorktown, Va. Her minesweeping equipment was removed and a living compartment added. Built by American Ship-building Co, Lorain, Ohio. Laid down on 29 Mar 1944. Launched on 9 Dec 1944

TANAGER (WTR 385) *United States Coast Guard*

SEAGOING TENDERS

3 SEAGOING TENDERS (WLB): Ex-MINELAYERS

IVY (ex-*Barbican*)	WLB 329 (ex-ACM 5)
MAGNOLIA (ex-*Barricade*)	WLB 328 (ex-ACM 3)
WILLOW (ex-*Picket*)	WLB 332 (ex-ACM 8)

Displacement, tons	1 054 standard; 1 250 full load
Dimensions, feet	188·7 oa × 37 × 12
Main engines	Triple expansion; 2 shafts; 1 200 ihp = 12 knots

Ex-Army mineplanters, ex-US Navy ACM. Launched in 1942. Redesignated Seagoing Tenders, WLB instead of WAGL on 1 Jan 1965.
Heather (WLB 331, ex-ACM 7) stricken in 1967, *Jonquil* (WLB 330, ex-ACM 6) stricken in 1969.

HEATHER (WLB 331) — *1966, US Coast Guard*

38 SEAGOING TENDERS (WLB): "CACTUS" AND "IRIS" CLASSES

20 Marine Iron SB Co, Duluth

BASSWOOD	388	
BLACKHAW	390	18 June 1943
BLACKTHORN	391	20 July 1943
BUTTONWOOD	306	28 Nov 1942
CACTUS	270	25 Nov 1941
CITRUS	300	15 Aug 1942
CLOVER	292	1942
CONIFER	301	3 Oct 1942
COWSLIP	277	1942
EVERGREEN	295	
HORNBEAM	394	15 Aug 1943
MESQUITE	305	14 Nov 1942
PAPAW	308	
PLANETREE	307	
SASSAFRAS	401	1943
SEDGE	402	1943
SPAR	403	2 Nov 1943
SUNDEW	404	8 Feb 1944
SWEETBRIAR	405	30 Dec 1943
SWEETGUM	309	1943

17 Zenith Dredge Co, Duluth

ACACIA (ex-*Thistle*)	406	7 Apr 1944
BALSAM	62	1942
BITTERSWEET	389	1943
BRAMBLE	392	1943
FIREBUSH	393	1943
GENTIAN	290	1942
IRIS	395	10 Mar 1944
LAUREL	291	4 Aug 1942
MADRONA	302	11 Nov 1942
MALLOW	396	1943
MARIPOSA	397	7 Jan 1944
SAGEBRUSH	399	30 Sep 1943
SALVIA	400	15 Sep 1943
SORRELL	296	28 Sep 1942
TUPELO	303	28 Nov 1942
WOODBINE	289	
WOODBRUSH	407	1944

1 Coast Guard Shipyard, Curtis Bay

IRONWOOD	297	Mar 1943

Displacement, tons	935 standard; 1 025 full load
Dimensions, feet	180 oa × 37 × 14
Guns	1—3 in, 50 cal *
Main engines	Diesel electric; 1 200 bhp = 12 knots (*Citrus, Clover, Conifer, Cowslip, Evergreen, Tupelo, Woodbine*, 1 000 bhp = 11 knots) Some have Sundew diesels 1 800 bhp

Builders and launch dates above. *Cactus* and *Evergreen* are used as oceanographic cutters and designated WAGO; painted white.
The *Cowslip* was fitted with controllable pitch transverse bow propeller in 1961, *Bittersweet* with bow thruster propeller in 1966. All to be so fitted.
Photographs of *Cactus* (converted to WAGO in 1967) and *Firebush* appear in the 1959-60 to 1964-65 editions.
*3 inch gun being removed and ·50 cal MG installed, except in *Citrus, Cowslip, Evergreen, Sedge* and *Sorrel.*

EVERGREEN (WAGO 295) — *1966, US Coast Guard*

BITTERSWEET (WLB389) — *United States Coast Guard*

Seagoing Tenders —*continued*

SORREL (WLB296) — *1968, United States Coast Guard*

COASTAL TENDERS

3 COASTAL TENDERS (WLM): "HOLLYHOCK" CLASS

FIR WLM 212 — **HOLLYHOCK** WLM 220 — **WALNUT** WLM 252

Displacement, tons	989
Dimensions, feet	175 × 32 × 12
Main engines	Diesel reduction; 2 shafts; 1 350 bhp = 12 knots

Launched in 1937 (*Hollyhock*) and 1939 (*Fir* and *Walnut*). *Walnut* was re-engined by Willamette Iron & Steel Co, Portland, Oregon, in 1958. Redesignated Coastal Tenders, WLM, instead of Buoy Tenders, WAGL on 1 Jan 1965.

WALNUT — *1963, United States Coast Guard, Official*

1 COASTAL TENDER (WLM): "JUNIPER" TYPE

JUNIPER WLM 224

Displacement, tons	794
Dimensions, feet	177 × 23·7 × 9·2
Main engines	Diesel, with electric drive; 2 shafts; 900 bhp = 11 knots

Launched on 18 May 1940. Redesignated WLM vice WALG on 1 Jan 1965.

DISPOSALS
Several coastal tenders of various types have been stricken: **Hemlock** (WAGL 217) in 1958, **Violet** (WAGL 250) in 1962, **Arbutus** (WLM 203, ex-WAGL 203) in 1967, **Mistletoe** (WLM 237, ex-WAGL 237) in 1968.

JUNIPER (WLM 224) — *Added 1967, Official*

1 COASTAL TENDER (WLM): "LILAC" TYPE

LILAC 227

Displacement, tons	770
Dimensions, feet	172 × 32 × 8·5
Main engines	Reciptocaring; 2 shafts; 1 000 ihp = 11·5 knots

Launched in 1933. No. WLM (ex-WAGL) 227. Redesignated WLM on 1 Jan 1965. Scheduled for decommissioning in 1971.

3 COASTAL TENDERS (WLM): "RED" CLASS

RED BEECH WLM 686 — **RED BIRCH** WLM 687 — **RED WOOD** WLM 685

Displacement, tons	471 standard
Dimensions, feet	157 oa × 32 × 6
Main engines	2 diesels; 2 shafts; 1 800 bhp = 14 knots
Radius, miles	3 000 at 12 knots cruising range
Complement	32

Red Wood was laid down in 1963 and commissioned on 4 Aug 1964 at the Coast Guard Yard, Curtis Bay, Md, where *Red Beech* was commissioned on 20 Nov 1964 and *Red Birch* was commissioned on 7 June 1965. Controllable pitch propeller. Bow thruster unit to give high manoeuvrability. Hull reinforced for light icebreaking. Steering and engine control on bridge wings as well as in pilothouse.

Coastal Tenders—*continued*

RED WOOD (WLM 685) *1965, United States Coast Guard*

7 COASTAL TENDERS (WLM): "WHITE" CLASS

WHITE BUSH WLM 542
WHITE HEATH WLM 545
WHITE HOLLY WLM 543
WHITE LUPINE WLM 546
WHITE PINE WLM 547
WHITE SAGE WLM 544
WHITE SUMAV WLM 540

Displacement, tons	435
Dimensions, feet	133 *oa* × 30 × 10
Main engines	Diesel; 600 bhp = 10 knots

All launched in 1943. All eight ships are former US Navy YFs, adapted for the Coast Guard. The *White Alder* (WLM 541) was sunk in a collision on 7 Dec 1968.

DISPOSALS
Of the two "Hawthorne" class coastal tenders, **Hawthorne**, WLM 215 (ex-WAGL 215) was decommissioned on 24 July 1964, and **Oak** WLM 239 (ex-WAGL 239) on 1 Sep 1964. Both were officially deleted from the list in 1965. They were replaced by **Red Beech** and **Red Wood**, see above. The larger but older **Cedar** was sold in June 1955.

WHITE HOLLY (WLK 543) *1968, U.S. Coast Guard*

INLAND TENDERS

9 INLAND TENDERS (WLI): 100 ft CLASS

AZALEA (18 Feb 1948)
BARBERRY (14 Nov 1942)
BLUEBELL
BUCKTHORN
COSMOS (11 Nov 1942)
PRIMROSE
RAMBLER
SMILAX
VERBENA

Displacement, tons	178
Dimensions, feet	100 × 24 × 4·5
Main engines	Diesel; 2 shafts; 300 bhp = 8·5 knots
Complement	15 (1 officer, 14 enlisted men)

Launch dates above. Eight are of "A" Class. *Azalea* WLI 641, of "B" Class, laid down on 1 Oct 1957 and commissioned on 23 May 1958, was built at the Coast Guard Yard Curtis Bay, Maryland, to replace the old *Palmetto*. She is air-conditioned and has a pile driver in the bow. She cost $500 000. *Buckthorn* WLI 642, of "C" Class, built at a Coast Guard Yard, commissioned on 17 July 1964.

DISPOSALS
Brier of this class stricken.
Several inland tenders of various types stricken: **Hickory** in 1967, **Linden** in 1969, **Elm** in 1969, **Wistaria**, **Columbine.**

BUCKTHORN *1966, United States Coast Guard, Official*

Inland Tenders—*continued*

16 INLAND TENDERS (WLI)

TAMARACK

Displacement, tons	400
Dimensions, feet	124 × 29 × 7·5
Main engines	Diesel, with electric drive; 600 bhp = 10 knots

Launched in 1934. Redesignated Inland Tender, Large, WLI on 1 Jan 1965.

MAPLE **NARCISSUS** **ZINNIA**

Displacement, tons	342 (*Maple*, 350)
Dimensions, feet	122 × 27 × 6·5
Main engines	Diesel; 2 shafts; 400 bhp = 10 knots

All launched in 1939. Redesignated Inland Tenders, Large, WLI on 1 Jan 1965.

DISPOSALS
Of the two ships of the "Aster" class, **Thistle** decommissioned in 1957, and was sold in 1959 and **Aster** was decommissioned on 15 Aug 1962 to be sold.

CLEMATIS (1944)
SHADBUSH (1944) } 93 tons

Small buoy tenders. Redesignated Inland Tenders, Small, WLI on 1 Jan 1965.

DISPOSALS
Blackrock was sold to Haiti in Nov 1945. **Palmetto** was decommissioned in June 1958 and sold in 1958; she was replaced by **Azalea** (see "100-ft" class above) in 1958. **Rhododendron** was decommissioned for sale in 1958. **Poinciana** decommissioned on 17 Aug 1962. **Althea** on 10 Nov 1962, **Beech** on 23 Jan 1963, **Myrtle** on 8 Feb 1963, **Birch** on 24 Feb 1963, **Dahlia** on 9 Oct 1964, **Cherry** on 1 Dec 1964, **Bluebonnet** and **Jasmine** on 18 Jan 1965, **Elm** in 1969.

ANVIL (1962)
AXE (1966)
CLAMP (1964)
HAMMER (1962)
HATCHET (1966)
MALLET (1962)
SLEDGE (1962)
SPIKE (1966)
VISE (1962)
WEDGE (1964)

Rated as Construction Tenders, Inland, Small (WLIC). All 145 tons, 75 feet.

SLEDGE (WLIC 75303) PUSHING BARGE *U.S. Coast Guard*

RIVER TENDERS

28 RIVER TENDERS (WLR)

FOXGLOVE (1944)
SUMAC (1944)
FERN (6 Nov 1942) } 350 tons

DOGWOOD (1942)
FORSYTHIA (1940)
SYCAMORE (1940) } 230 tons
GOLDENROD (1938)
POPLAR (1939) } 193 tons

Rated as River Tenders, Large (WLR). *Goldenrod* was rebuilt and re-engined in 1960. *Foxglove* was refitted in 1961 with three 400 bhp diesels.

LANTANA (1943) 273 tons, 80 ft
OLEANDER (1940) 80 tons, 73 ft
GASCONADE (1964)
MUSKINGUM (1965)
WYACONDA (1965)
CHIPPEWA (1965)
CHEYENNE (1966)
KICKAPOO (1967) } 145 tons, 75 ft
OUACHITA (1960)
CIMARRON (1960) } 139 tons, 65 ft
OBION (1962)
SCIOTO (1962)
OSAGE (1962)
SANGAMON (1962) } 139 tons, 65 ft
BAYBERRY
BLACKBERRY
CHOKEBERRY
ELDERBERRY
HACKBERRY
LOGANBERRY } 65 ft

Rated as River Tenders, Small (WLR). "Berry" class are of recent construction.

BAYBERRY (WLR 65400) *U.S. Coast Guard*

SUPPLY SHIP

1 SUPPLY SHIP (WAK): CI-M-AVI TYPE

KUKUI (ex-USS *Colquitt*, AK 174) WAK 186

Displacement, tons	4 900 light; 7 450 full load
Measurement, tons	5 900 gross
Dimensions, feet	320 wl; 338·5 oa × 50 × 21
Main engines	Nordberg diesel; 1 750 bhp = 11·5 knots

Former naval cargo ship based at Honolulu to perform logistic services for US Coast Guard stations in the Pacific. Built in 1945 by Froemming Bros, Milwaukee, Wisc, Launched in 1944. Maritime Administration type CI-M-AVI.

TRANSFERS. The cable layer, *Yamacraw* WARC 333, was transferred to the US Navy on a loan basis in 1959, but was stricken from the Navy list on 1 July 1965 and transferred to the Maritime Administration Reserve Fleet; cargo ship *Nettle* WAK 169, ex-FS 396, transferred to Philippines in 1968.

KUKUI (WAK 186) *1965, United States Coast Guard*

1 TRAINING BARK (IX)

EAGLE (ex-*Horst Wessel*) WIX 327

Displacement, tons	1 634; 1 816 full load
Dimensions, feet	265·8 pp; 295·2 oa × 39·3 × 17
Sail area, sq ft	21 351
Height of masts, feet	150
Speed	As high as 18 knots under full sail alone
Main engines	Auxiliary diesel; 1 shaft; 740 bhp = 10 knots
Oil fuel, tons	48
Endurance, miles	3 500 at 10 knots with diesel
Complement	280

Former German training ship for 200 naval cadets. Built by Blohm & Voss, Hamburg. Launched on 13 June 1936. Taken by the United States as part of reparations after the Second World War for employment in US Coast Guard Practice Squadron. Taken over at Bremerhaven in Jan 1946. Arrived at home port, New London, Conn in July 1946. Has made several cruises to European waters to train Coast Guard cadets.

CLASS. Sister ship, *Albert Leo Schlageter*, was also taken by the USA in 1945 but was sold to Brazil in 1948 and re-sold to Portugal in 1962.

EAGLE (WIX 327) *United States Coast Guard*

OCEANGOING TUGS

2 OCEANGOING TUGS (WAT): ARS TYPE

ACUSHNET (ex-*Shackle*) WAT 167 **YOCONA** (ex-*Seize*) WAT 168

Displacement, tons	1 557 standard; 1 945 full load
Dimensions	207 wl; 213·5 oa × 39 × 15·5
Main engines	Diesel-electric; 2 shafts; 3 000 hp = 13 knots

Former US Navy ARS type. Launched on 1 Apr 1943 and 8 Apr 1944, respectively.

ACUSHNET *1965, United States Coast Guard, Official*

4 OCEANGOING TUGS (WAT): ATF TYPE

AVOYEL (9 Aug 1944) WAT 150 **CHILULA** (1 Dec 1944) WAT 153
CHEROKEE (10 Nov 1939) WAT 165 **TAMAROA** (13 July 1943) WAT 166

Displacement, tons	1 170
Dimensions, feet	195 wl; 205·2 oa × 38·5 × 16
Guns	1—3 in, 50 cal
Main engines	Diesel-electric; 3 000 hp = 16 knots

Avoyel and *Chilula* have been on loan from the United States Navy since 1956; transferred on 1 June 1969. All former ATF with same hull numbers. Launch dates given above.

AVOYEL (WAT 150) *1964, United States Coast Guard*

AUXILIARY OCEAN TUGS

2 AUXILIARY OCEAN TUGS (WATA)

COMANCHE (ex-*Wampanaog*) WATA 202 **MODOC** (ex-*Bagaduce*) WATA 194

Displacement, tons	534 standard; 860 full load
Dimensions, feet	134·5 wl; 143 oa × 34 × 12
Guns	1—20 mm
Main engines	Diesel-electric; 1 500 bhp = 13 knots
Complement	4 officers, 40 enlisted men

Equipped for search, rescue, firefighting and icebreaking. *Comanche* was on loan since 25 Feb 1959 from the US Navy: transferred on 1 June 1969. *Modoc* was transferred from the Maritime Administration to the Coast Guard on 15 Apr 1959, replacing *Bonham*.

MODOC (WATA 194) *1956, United States Coast Guard*

UNION OF SOVIET SOCIALIST REPUBLICS

Administration

Commander-in-Chief of the Navy and First Deputy Minister of Defence: Admiral of the Fleet of the Soviet Union Sergei Georgiyevich Gorshkov

First Deputy Commander-in-Chief of Navy: Admiral of the Fleet Vladimir Afanasevich Kasatonov

Strength of the Fleet

65 Nuclear Powered Submarines
320 Conventionally Powered Submarines
2 Cruiser Helicopter Ships
25 Cruisers, including missile ships
100 Destroyers, including missile ships
100 Escorts, small frigate type
275 Coastal Escorts, patrol vessels
350 Minesweepers
125 Missile Patrol Boats
350 Motor Torpedo Boats
230 Landing Craft excluding LCMs

Support ships, auxiliaries and service craft run into thousands.

Diplomatic Representation

Naval Attaché in London:
Rear-Admiral B. D. Yashin

Naval Attaché in Washington:
Captain Aleksandr Romanovich Astafiev

Nomenclature

Cruisers after statesmen, admirals or heroes
Destroyers after adjectives
Escorts after birds and winds
Minesweepers after weapons and equipment
Minelayers after rivers and lakes
Survey Ships after astronomical terms and explorers
Depot Ships after towns and rivers
Icebreakers after statesmen and Arctic explorers

The hull or side numerals of warships change periodically, although apparently the pennant numbers of auxiliaries may not change.

State

Most ships are of recent construction. Most modern ships not being refitted are fully manned and operational, but some of the older ships are in reserve. Cruisers, destroyers, submarines and many smaller craft are fitted for minelaying.

Appearance

Combatant Ships: Painted light grey all over
Auxiliaries: Painted somewhat darker grey
Surveying Ships: Black hulls with red waterlines, yellow funnels with black tops

Personnel

1969: 500,000 (50,000 officers and cadets, 450,000 ratings)

Mercantile Marine

Lloyd's Register of Shipping
4,206 vessels of 12,061,833 tons gross

Silhouettes

Scale 150 feet = 1 inch

Cruisers, Leaders

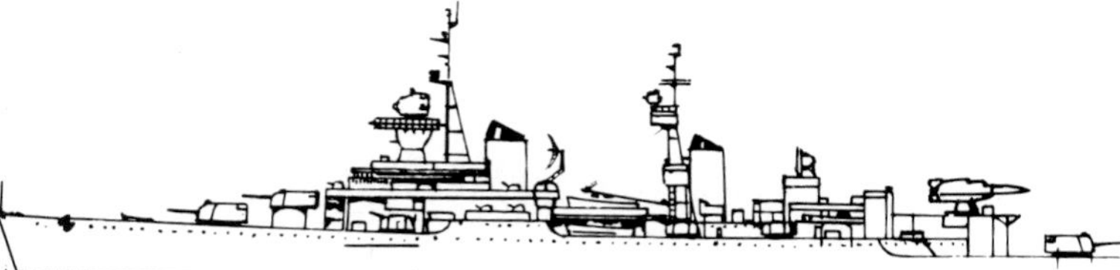
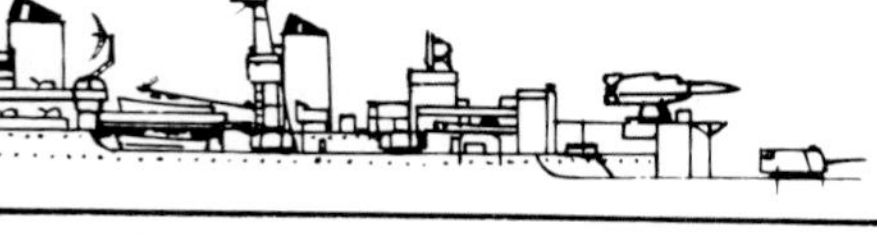

DZERZHINSKI

ZHELEZNYAKOV

KRESTA *Class*

KYNDA *Class*

KASHIN *Class*

KRUPNY *Class*

KILDIN *Class*

KOLA *Class*

Destroyers, Frigates

SAM KOTLIN *Class*

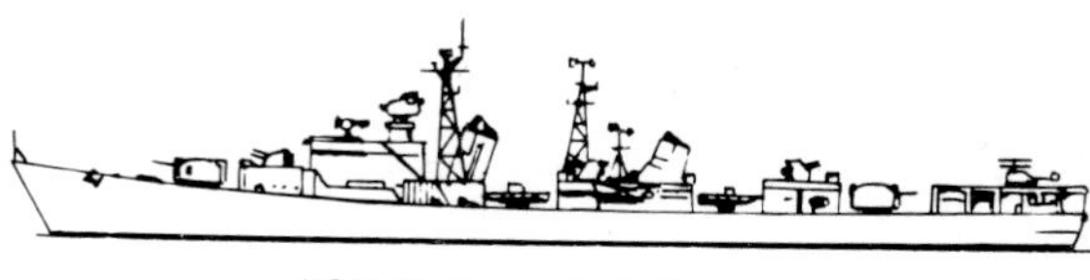

KOTLIN *Class* with helicopter deck

KOTLIN *Class*

TALLIN *Class*

Modified SKORY *Class*

SKORY *Class*

RIGA *Class*

SUBMARINES (*Podvodnye Lodki*)

Programme

There are about 375 effective submarines, of which half are medium range and the remainder large oceangoing types.
It is policy to maintain a four-theatre submarine fleet for operations in the Atlantic, Pacific, Baltic and Black Sea. Some submarines are armed with far-ranging surface rockets with nuclear and hydrogen warheads.

NEW CONSTRUCTION. About 30 submarines are being built in Soviet dockyards. These are reported to be of five different types including a nuclear powered class of over 300 feet started at the Gorky yard in 1967 and a new missile class with 16 launching tubes.

Nuclear Powered Submarines

CRUISE MISSILE TYPES

"C" CLASS

Described as a nuclear powered attack submarine with a large bulbous bow. May have a short range missile system of eight topside tubes, four to port and four starboard. (A new type of submarine officially announced in 1968 has prominent steel bulge around the conning tower).

25 "E II" CLASS

Displacement, tons	5 000 surface, 5 600 submerged
Dimensions, feet	393·7 × 33 × 27
Missiles	8 "Shaddock" launching tubes
Torpedo tubes	6—21 in (bow)
Main engines	Nuclear reactors, steam turbines
Speed, knots	22 max; 14 cruising
Complement	100

The "E II" sub-group design is a development of that of the "E I" sub-group lengthened to accommodate two more missile launchers.

5 "E I" CLASS

Displacement, tons	4 600 surface; 5 000 submerged
Dimensions, feet	385 × 33 × 27
Missiles	6 "Shaddock" launching tubes
Torpedo tubes	2—21 in (bow)
Main engines	Nuclear reactors, steam turbines; 20 knots max; 12 knots cruising
Complement	92 (12 officers, 80 men)

Long range submarines, with six cruise missiles in launching tubes elevated from the flush deck, with launchers two abreast. Cruise missiles have a range of 180 nautical miles. "E" class submarines in the Pacific were built at Komsomolsk.

BALLISTIC MISSILE TYPES

5 "H II" CLASS

Displacement, tons	3 700 surface; 4 100 submerged
Dimensions, feet	344 × 33 × 25
Missiles	5 launching tubes
Main engines	Nuclear reactors, steam turbines; 1 500 shp = 25 knots

A new class of ocean ranging streamlined submarines similar to the "H I" class but with missile equipment like that in the diesel powered "G" class submarines.

10 "H I" CLASS

Displacement, tons	3 500 surface; 4 000 submerged
Dimensions, feet	344 × 32·9 × 24·7
Missiles	3 launching tubes
Torpedo tubes	6—21 in (bow)
Main engines	Nuclear reactors, steam turbines; 15 000 shp = 25 knots
Complement	90

Fast long range submarines with three ballistic missile tubes in the large "sail", or conning tower. The earlier missiles had a range of 380 nautical miles, but later ballistic missiles have a range of 600 miles.

ANTI-SUBMARINE TYPE

15 "N" CLASS

Displacement, tons	3 500 surface; 4 000 submerged
Dimensions, feet	360 × 32 × 24
Torpedo tubes	6—21 in (bow)
Main engines	Nuclear reactors, steam turbines; 15 000 shp = 25 knots
Complement	88

Fast fleet submarines designed as submarine hunter-killers. The "N" class programme ended in 1965 after 15 units were built, including *Leninsky Komsomol*.

Missile submarine No. 788 — 1966

'N' Class — 1968, S. Breyer

LENINSKY KOMSOMOL, No. 270, "N" Class — 1967

"Z" Class — 1968

Submarines—*continued*

"N" Class Nuclear Powered Type *USSR*

"Z" Class *1969, MOD, RN, Official*

"Z V" Class Guided Missile Type *S. Breyer*

Missile submarine No. 780 (side opening hatches open) ***1966***

Submarines—*continued*

Missile Submarines

10 "J" CLASS

Displacement, tons	1 800 surface; 2 500 submerged
Dimensions, feet	328 × 27 × 20
Missiles	4 "Shaddock" launching tubes; 2 before and 2 abaft the low and extended sail or conning tower
Torpedo tubes	6—21 in (bow)
Main engines	Diesels = 19 knots surface; Electric motors = 15 knots submerged

Medium sized long range submarines with a long superstructure fin and high surface freeboard. The prototype, launched in 1962, is reported to have left the Baltic in 1963, and several completed since.

"J" Class *1969, S. Breyer*

25 "G" CLASS

BALLISTIC MISSILE TYPE

Displacement, tons	2 350 surface; 2 800 submerged
Dimensions, feet	320 × 28 × 22
Missiles	3 launching tubes
Torpedo tubes	6—21 in (bow)
Main engines	3 diesels; 3 shafts; Total 6 000 hp = 17·6 knots surface; Electric motors = 17 knots submerged
Radius, miles	22 700 surface cruising
Complement	86 (12 officers, 74 men)

This class has a very large conning tower fitted with three vertically mounted tubes and hatches for launching ballistic missiles. Built at Komsomolsk and Severodvinsk. Construction commenced in 1958.

"W" Class "Long Bin" Guided Missile Type *1968, S. Breyer*

6 "Z" CLASS

BALLISTIC MISSILE TYPE

Displacement, tons	2 100 surface; 2 600 submerged
Dimensions, feet	295·2 × 29 × 19
Missiles	2 launching tubes
Torpedo tubes	6—21 in
Main engines	Diesels; 2 shafts; 10 000 bhp = 22 knots surface; Electric motors 3 500 hp = 16 knots submerged
Complement	85

These are basically of "Z" class design but converted to ballistic missile submarines with larger conning towers and two vertical tubes for missile launching. Six boats were converted by 1961.

12 "W" CLASS

GUIDED MISSILE TYPE

Some of the "W" class are equipped with inclined missile launchers. Others were converted to "Shaddock" missile carrying submarines with twin cylinders on deck abaft the conning tower. See additional photograph of a "Long Bin" on following page.

"W" Class Twin Cylinder Guided Missile Type *1968, S. Breyer*

"G" Class missile submarine No. 783 *1966*

"Z" Class No. 515 *1966, col Borg*

Submarines—*continued*

Fleet Submarines

40 "F" CLASS.

LARGE ATTACK TYPE

Displacement, tons	2 000 surface; 2 300 submerged
Dimensions, feet	300 × 27 × 19
Tubes	8—21 in (20 torpedoes carried)
Main engines	Diesels; 3 shafts; 10 000 bhp = 20 knots surface; Electric motors; 4 000 hp = 15 knots submerged
Complement	70

Improved versions of the "Z" class. There is no longer currentness in listing numbers as the side numerals are so frequently changed or do not appear on the conning tower at all.

A starboard broadside surface view of an "F" class submarine appears in the 1963-64 to 1967-68 editions and a port bow surface view of No. 238 in the 1965-66 to 1967-68 editions.

20 "Z" CLASS.

LARGE OCEANGOING TYPE

Displacement, tons	1 900 surface; 2 200 submerged
Dimensions, feet	295 × 26 × 19
Tubes	8—21 in (6 bow, 2 stern). 24 torpedoes carried (or 40 mines)
Main engines	Diesel-electric; 2 shafts Diesels: 10 000 bhp = 20 knots surface; Electric Motors: 3 500 hp = 15 knots submerged
Radius, miles	20 000 to 26 000
Complement	70

Oceangoing type. Completed from 1954 to 1960. General appearance is streamlined with a complete row of rapid flooding holes along the casing. This class was stationed in the Baltic and Far East. The first of the class was laid down in 1951 and most were commissioned during 1954-60. Eighteen were built by Sudomekh Shipyard, Leningrad, in 1952-55 and others at Severodvinsk.

A large port quarter ablique aerial view of "Z" Class No. 958 and a port bow surface view appear in the 1960-61 to 1967-68 editions.

15 "R" CLASS

MEDIUM RANGE TYPE

Displacement, tons	1 100 surface; 1 600 submerged
Dimensions, feet	246 × 24 × 14.5
Tubes	6—21 in bow
Main engines	Diesels: 4 000 bhp = 18.5 knots surface Electric motors: 2 500 hp = 15 knots submerged
Complement	65

These are of an improved "W" type design with modernised superstructure, conning tower, and sonar installation. Reported to number 13 boats by the end of 1967

25 "Q" CLASS

SHORT RANGE TYPE

Displacement, tons	650 surface; 740 submerged
Dimensions, feet	185 × 18 × 13
Tubes	4—21 in
Main engines	Diesel: 1 shaft; 3 000 bhp = 18 knots surface Electric motors; 2 500 hp = 16 knots submerged
Oil fuel, tons	50
Radius, miles	7 000 cruising range
Complement	40

Short range, single screw submarines. Built from 1954 to 1960. Thirteen were constructed in 1955 by Sudomekh Shipyard, Leningrad.

"F" Class  1968

"R" Class 1968, Skyfotos

"Q" Class 1955, Col Breyer

"W" Class 1968

Submarines—*continued*

150 "W" CLASS. PATROL TYPE

Displacement, tons	1 030 surface; 1 180 submerged
Dimensions, feet	240 × 22 × 15
Tubes	6—21 in (4 bow, 2 stern); 18 torpedoes carried (or 40 mines)
Main engines	Diesel-electric; 2 shafts; Diesels: 4 000 bhp = 17 knots surface; Electric motors: 2 500 hp = 15 knots submerged
Radius, miles	13 000 to 16 500
Complement	60

Medium range submarines built from 1950 to 1957 in yards throughout the Soviet Union. Stationed in considerable numbers in the Baltic, the North, the Black Sea and the Far East. Equipped with snort. Fitted for minelaying.

PHOTOGRAPHS. Photographs of No. 12, No. 25, W III class, appear in the 1959-60 to 1966-67 editions.

"W" Class — *1968, Skyfotos*

"W" Class No. 372 — *1967, Skyfotos*

SEVERYANA   SLAVYANKA

Displacement, tons	1 000 surface; 1 100 submerged
Dimensions, feet	240 × 22 × 15
Main engines	Diesels: 4 000 bhp = 17 knots surface; Electric Motors: 2 500 hp = 15 knots submerged

Converted "W" class submarines specially fitted out for scientific research. *Severyanya* is attached to the Soviet Institute for Fisheries and Oceanographic Research. Torpedo compartment converted into a laboratory. Observation portholes, top and bottom echo sounders, sonar, long range searchlight, underwater television camera.

"K" CLASS

The few minelaying submarines of the "K" class which survived the Second World War were deleted from the list in 1963-64.

"MV" CLASS

28 boats of the "M V" class, M 205, 206, 209, 211, 212, 214, 215, 216, 219, 234, 235, and 237 to 253, were for disposal in 1962. M 200, 201, 202, 203, 254, 255, 256, 257 and 258 were deleted from the list in 1963, M 204 in 1964, M 259 to M 268 in 1966, and M 269, 270, 271, 272, 273, 274, 275, 276, 277, 278, 279, 280, 281, 282 and 283 in 1986. They are no longer operational A few may be used for static training but these boats are of no further fighting value.

"W" Class — *1966, Skyfotos*

"SHCH" CLASSES

The 19 submarines of the "Shch IV" class were deleted from the list in 1964. The 50 boats of the "Shch" class, including most of the "Sch" I, II and III classes, having become obsolete and worn out, were scrapped in 1960.

"W" Class — *1967, Skyfotos*

"S(C)" CLASS

The 30 old submarines of the "S(C)" class were discarded in 1963.

"M IV" CLASS

The 18 coastal submarines of the "M IV" class were discarded in 1963.

EX-GERMAN TYPES

The old ex-German submarines N 27 (ex-U 2529), N 28 (ex-U 3035), N 29 (ex-U 3041) and N 30 (ex-U 3515) of the "XXI" types; S 81 (ex-U 1057), S 82 (ex-U 1058), S 83 (ex-U 1064) and S 84 (ex-U 1305) of the VII type and N 31 (ex-U 2353) of the "XXIII" type all taken over by the Soviet Navy as war prizes. were in 1963 reported to have been scrapped.

OTHER CLASSES

For detailed list of disposals of older submarines discarded since the USSR has built so many submarines of her own designs in her own yards, see 1962-63 and earlier editions.

"W" Class "Long Bin" Guided Missile Type ("Kynda" class missiles cruiser in background) *1967*

CRUISER HELICOPTER SHIPS

2 "MOSCOW" CLASS

NEW CONSTRUCTION

LENINGRAD **MOSKVA**

Displacement, tons	15 000 standard ; 18 000 full load
Length, feet	600 wl ; 645 oa
Flight deck, feet	270 to 295 aft of superstructure
Aircraft	20 ASW helicopters ; 30 helicopters max capacity
Missiles	3 surface-to-air systems of twin launchers
Guns	4—57 mm (2 twin)
A/S weapons	2 mortars on forecastle
Torpedo tubes	5 trainable 21 inch
Main engines	Steam propulsion = 30 knots max

Both built at Nikolayev. The prototype *Moskva*, reported pennant number 851, ran her sea trials in July 1967. Would appear to be designed for anti-submarine warfare and support of land operations. Described as combination helicopter carriers and guided missile cruisers. The foremost dual arm launcher, for either surface or anti-submarine missiles are directed by sonar. The other two dual arm launchers are directed by the surface-to-air pedestals on the steps of the bridge superstructure. Ships are fitted with variable depth sonar.

MOSKVA *1969 MOD, RN, Official*

MOSKVA *1969, S. Breyer*

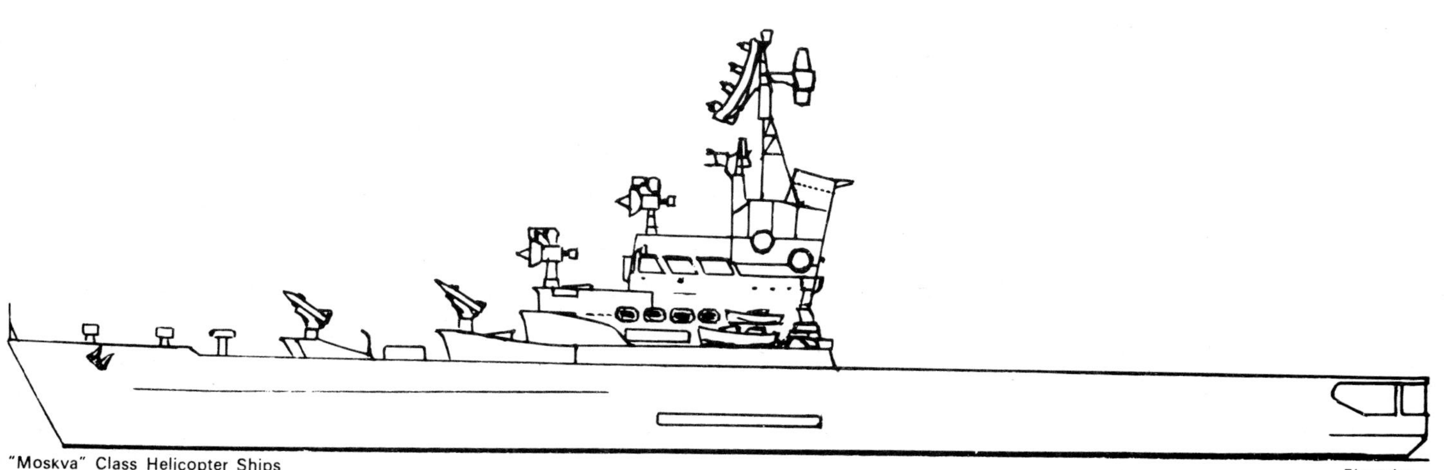

"Moskva" Class Helicopter Ships *Elevation*

Cruiser Helicopter Ships—*continued*

MOSKVA

1969, USN Official

SVERDLOV Class

1969, MOD, RN, Official

CRUISERS

12 "SVERDLOV" CLASS

ADMIRAL LAZAREV	MIKHAIL KUTUSOV
ADMIRAL SENJAVIN	MURMANSK
ADMIRAL USHAKOV	OKTYABRSKAYA REVOLUTSIYA
ALEXSANDR NEVSKII	SVERDLOV
ALEKSANDR SUVOROV	ZHDANOV
DMITRI POZHARSKIY	
DZERZHINSKI	

Displacement, tons	15 450 standard; 19 200 full load
Length, feet (*metres*)	656 (*200·0*) pp; 689 (*210·0*) oa
Beam, feet (*metres*)	70 (*21·3*)
Draught, feet (*metres*)	24·5 (*7·5*) max
Armour	Belts 3·9—4·9 in (*100—125 mm*); fwd and aft 1·6—2 in (*40—50 mm*); turrets 4·9 in (*125 mm*); C.T. 5·9 in (*150 mm*); decks 1—2 in (*25—50 mm*) and 2—3 in (*50—75 mm*)
Missiles, AA	Twin "Guideline" launcher aft in *Dzerzhinski* (see *Guided Missiles*)
Guns, surface	12—5·9 in (*150 mm*), 4 triple
Guns, dual purpose	12—3·9 in (*100 mm*), 6 twin
Guns, AA	32—37 mm ,16 twin mounts (see *Gunnery*)
Torpedo tubes	10—21 in (*533 mm*), 2 quintuple (see *Torpedoes*)
Mines	140 to 250 capacity
Boilers	4
Main engines	Geared turbines 130 000 shp; 2 shafts
Speed, knots	34
Radius, miles	5 000 at 20 knots
Oil fuel (tons)	4 000
Complement	1 050

Of the 24 ships of this class originally projected, 20 keels were laid and 17 hulls were launched from 1951 onwards, but only 14 ships were completed by Dec 1960. There were two slightly different types. *Sverdlov* and others had the 37 mm AA guns near the fore-funnel one deck higher than in later cruisers. Most ships were fitted for minelaying. Mine stowage was on the second deck. It is reported that the number of units in this class is being reduced by scrapping.

CONSTRUCTION. Originally designed for a displacement of 12,800 tons standard and 17 000 tons full load.

GUIDED MISSILES. In 1961-62 *Dzerzhinski* was fitted with a long range missile twin launcher aft in place of No. 3 or "X" turret.

GUNNERY. *Dzerzhinski* has only nine 6 inch guns in three triple turrets, "X" turret having been replaced by guided missile launcher.

TORPEDOES. *Oktyabrskaya Revolutsia* and *Murmansk* no longer have tubes

DRAWING. Port elevation and plan. Scale: 128 feet = 1 inch.

APPEARANCE. The first ships had their anti-aircraft bridge near the fore-funnel one deck higher than in later ships. *Oktyabrskaya Revolutsiya* no longer has torpedo tubes. *Murmansk* has low anti-aircraft bridge near the fore-funnel and no torpedo tubes.

PHOTOGRAPHS. Photographs of *Admiral Ushakov, Aleksandr Suvorov* and *Sverdlov* appear in the 1953-54 to 1957-58 editions, of *Oktyabrskaya Revolutsiya* (as *Molotovsk*) in the 1957-58 to 1959-60 editions (also large photograph showing midship details) and in the 1962-63 edition (port bow oblique view), of *Sverdlov* (counter view showing minelaying stern) in the 1961-62 and 1962-63 editions, of *Murmansk* (as *Zhdanov*) in the 1957-58 to 1964-65 editions. of *Dzerzhinski* in the 1965-66 and 1966-67 editions (port quarter view showing twin guided missile launcher), of *Oktyabrskaya Revolutsiya* in the 1961-62 to 1966-67 editions.

PROTECTION. Deep and thick side belts of armour from the fore turret to the after turret, tapering to the bow and the stern.

NOMENCLATURE. The ship first named *Molotovsk* was renamed *Oktyabrskaya Revolutsiya* in 1957. The ships to have been named *Dmitri Donskoi* and *Kosma Minin* apparently never materialised.

TRANSFER. *Ordzhonikidze* of this class was transferred to the Indonesian Navy in Oct 1962 and renamed *Irian*.

DISPOSALS

The uncompleted hulls of four "Sverdlov" class cruisers were reported to have been broken up at Leningrad. Several completed ships now surplus to naval requirements are scheduled to be discarded in the near future, and the number of cruisers of this class in commission will gradually be reduced and replaced on active service by the large guided missile armed destroyers or "rocket-cruisers" recently completed. *Admiral Nakhimov* was deleted from the list in 1969.

MURMANSK *1967*

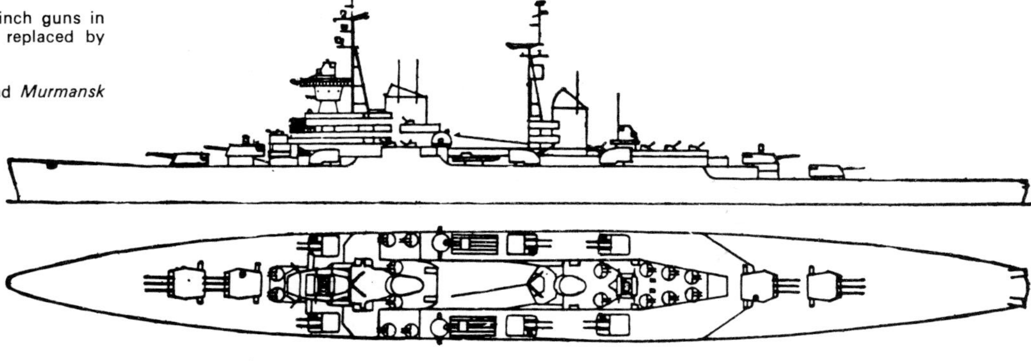

DZERZHINSKI *1967, col Breyer*

Cruisers—*continued*

SVERDLOV Class *1969*

DZERZHINSKI (see previous page) *1968*

DZERZHINSKI (showing midship arrays) ***1968, S. Breyer***

Cruisers—*continued*

2 "CHAPAEV" CLASS

KOMSOMOLETS (ex-*Chkalov*) **ZHELEZNYAKOV**

Displacement, tons	11 500 standard; 15 000 full load
Length, feet (*metres*)	656 (*200·0*)
Beam, feet (*metres*)	64·7 (*19·7*)
Draught, feet (*metres*)	21 (*6·4*)
Guns, surface	12—5·9 in (*150 mm*), 4 triple
Guns, dual purpose	8—3·9 in (*100 mm*), 4 twin
Guns, AA	28—37 mm, 14 twin
Mines	100 to 200 capacity
Boilers	6
Main engines	Geared turbines, with diesels for cruising speeds; 113 000 shp
Speed, knots	34
Radius, miles	4 500 at 20 knots
Oil fuel (tons)	3 500
Complement	834

Laid down in 1939-40. Launched during 1941-47. All work on these ships was stopped during the war, but was resumed in 1946-47. Completed in 1948-50. Catapults were removed from all ships of this type. *Zheleznyakov* serves as a training ship.

GUNNERY. Turret guns are in separate sleeves allowing independent elevation to at least 50 degrees.

APPEARANCE. Heavy director on control tower, pole foremast and tripod mainmast forward of after funnel. Vertical funnels. Higher freeboard and funnels than "Kirov" class. Resemble "Sverdlov" class but forecastle deck breaks abreast forefunnel instead of at quarter deck.

NOMENCLATURE. *Chkalov* was reported to have been renamed *Komsomolets* in 1961.

DRAWING. Port elevation and plan. Scale: 128 feet = 1 inch.

PHOTOGRAPHS. A port quarter view of *Zheleznyakov* appears in the 1952-53 to 1957-58 editions.

DISPOSALS

Chapaev, Frunse and *Kuibyshev* of this class were discarded.

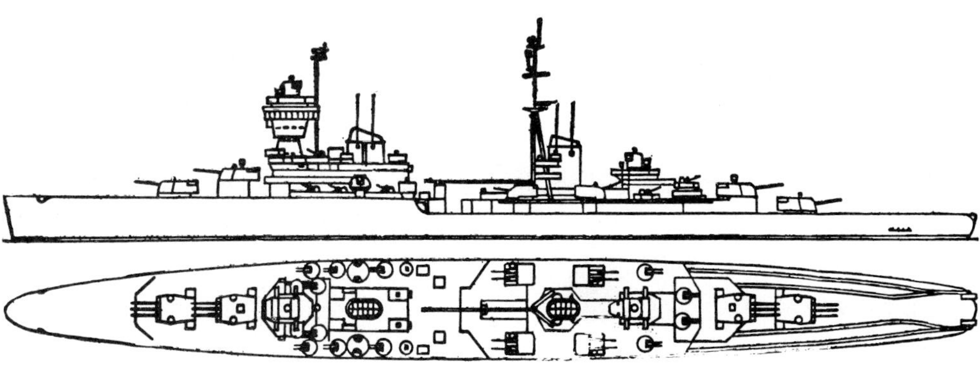

ZHELEZNYAKOV

Antonov Rogov

2 "KIROV" CLASS

Displacement, tons	8 800 standard; 11 500 full load
Length, feet (*metres*)	613·5 (*187·0*)pp; 626·7 (*191·0*) oa
Beam, feet (*metres*)	59 (*18·0*)
Draught, feet (*metres*)	20 (*6·1*) max
Armour	Side 3 in (*75 mm*); deck 2 in (*50 mm*); C.T. and gunhouses 3·9 in (*100 mm*)
Guns, surface	9—7·1 in (*180 mm*)
Guns, dual purpose	8—3·9 in (*100 mm*)
Guns, AA	16—37 mm; 6—13 mm
Torpedo tubes	6—21 in (*533 mm*)
Mines	60—90 capacity
Boilers	6 Yarrow or Normand
Main engines	Geared turbines, with diesels for cruising speeds; 110 000 shp
Speed, knots	34
Radius, miles	3 500 at 19 knots
Oil fuel (tons)	2 500
Complement	734

Design and technical direction of construction by Ansaldo. Of this class *Ordzhonikidze* under construction at Nikolayev, was wrecked by high explosives before the enemy occupied that port in Aug 1941.

APPEARANCE. *Kirov* has very long forecastle, heavy tripod mast stepped abaft forebridge, light tripod stepped abaft second funnel, very large funnels. Remaining vessels had high director tower on forebridge, light tripod foremast abaft bridge, heavy tripod mainmast stepped abaft second funnel, smaller funnels, and generally lighter appearance.

Name	*Builders*	*Laid down*	*Launched*	*Completed*
KIROV	Putilov DY	1934	1 Dec 1936	26 Sep 1938
SLAVA (ex-*Molotov*)	Marti Yard, Nikolaye	1935	23 Feb 1939	1944

PHOTOGRAPHS. Starboard bow and quarter views of *Kirov*, appear in the 1960-61 to 1962-63 editions, and a port oblique aerial view in the 1959-60 to 1967-68 editions.

GUNNERY. Triple guns are mounted in one sleeve and are incapable of individual elevation. Maximum elevation 40 degrees. For her role as a training ship *Kirov* has 9—7·1 inch, 6—3·9 inch, 8—37 mm and 2 older guns and no torpedo tubes.

NOMENCLATURE. *Molotov* was reported to have been renamed *Slava* in 1962.

DRAWING. Port elevation and plan of *Kirov*. Scale: 128 feet = 1 inch.

TRANSFER. *Kaganivotch* was reported to have been transferred to the Chinese Communist Navy.

DISPOSALS

Kalinin, Maksim Gorki and *Voroshilov* are reported to have been scrapped.

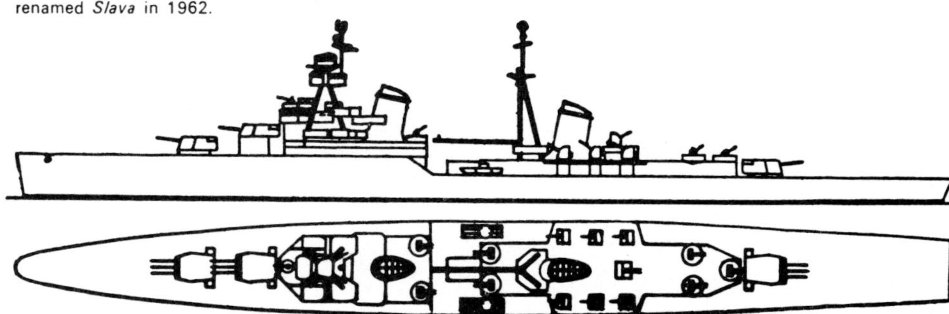

KIROV

1966

GUIDED MISSILE ARMED DESTROYER LEADERS (LIGHT CRUISERS)

2 "KRESTA" CLASS

Displacement, tons	6 000 estimated
Length, feet (*metres*)	508·5 (*155·0*)
Beam, feet (*metres*)	55·8 (*17·0*)
Draught, feet (*metres*)	20 (*6·1*)
Missiles, surface	2 twin "Shaddock" launchers
Missiles, AA	2 twin "Goa" launchers
A/S weapons	2 12-barrelled launchers; 2 6-barrelled launchers
Torpedo tubes	4 (two twin)
Aircraft	Helicopter
Guns	4—57 mm (2 twin)
Main engines	Gas turbines; 100 000 shp; diesels for cruising
Speed, knots	34
Complement	400

New construction dual purpose anti-submarine warfare and guided missile armed destroyer leaders or cruisers.

The design is a combination of that of the "Kashin" and "Kynda" classes and a logical follow-on to the "Kashin" class. Provided with a helicopter hangar and flight apron aft. Two ships of the class were reported building at the Zhdanov Shipyard, Leningrad. The prototype ship was laid down in Sep 1964, launched in 1965 and carried out sea trials in the Baltic in Feb 1967. The second ship was launched in 1966. "Kresta" is the NATO designation for the class.

KRESTA Class — *1969, MOD, RN, Official*

KRESTA Class — *1969, S. Breyer*

KRESTA Class Prototype

GUIDED MISSILE ARMED DESTROYER LEADERS (Light Cruisers) —*continued*

4 "KYNDA" CLASS

ADMIRAL GOLOVKO **GROZNY**
GROM **VARYAG**

Displacement, tons	4 800 standard; 6 000 full load
Length, feet (*metres*)	492 (*150·0*)
Beam, feet (*metres*)	51 (*15·5*)
Draught, feet (*metres*)	19 (*5·8*)
Aircraft	Apron for helicopter on stern
Missiles, surface	2 "Shaddock" quadruple mounts, 1 fwd, 1 aft
Missiles, AA	1 twin "Goa" launeher on forecastle
A/S	2—12 barrel rocket launchers on forecastle
Guns, AA	4—3 in (*76 mm*) 2 twin
Torpedo tubes	6—21 in (*533 mm*) 2 triple, amidships
Boilers	4 high pressure
Main engines	2 sets combined steam and gas turbines; 85 000 shp; 2 shafts
Speed, knots	35
Complement	390

The first vessel of the class was laid down in June 1960, launched in Apr 1961 at Zhdanov Shipyard, Leningrad, and completed in June 1962. The second ship was launched in Nov 1961 and fitted out in Aug 1962. Two enclosed towers, instead of masts, stepped forward of each raked funnel. Two screws and two rudders. Helicopter landing apron on the stern.

PHOTOGRAPHS. A starboard broadside aerial view of No. 898 appears in the 1963-64 and 1964-65 editions, and a port broadside surface view of No. 202 in the 1965-66 and 1966-67 editions.

KYNDA Class No. 810 *1969, USN Official*

KYNDA Class *1968*

KYNDA Class No. 299 *1967*

GUIDED MISSILE ARMED DESTROYERS

10 "KASHIN" CLASS

BOIKI
OBRAZTSOVYI
PROVEDYONNY
PROVORNYI
SLAVNY
SOOBRAZITELNYI
STEREGUSHCHYI

Displacement, tons	4,300 standard; 5 200 full load
Length, feet (*metres*)	475 (*144·8*)
Beam, feet (*metres*)	53 (*16·1*)
Draught, feet (*metres*)	19 (*5·8*)
Missiles, AA	Twin "Goa" launchers in "B" and "X" positions
Guns, AA	4—3 in (*76 mm*), 2 twin, "A" and "Y" positions
Torpedo tubes	5—21 in (*533 mm*) quintuple, amidships
Main engines	4 sets gas turbines; 100 000 shp
Speed, knots	35

A class of guided missile armed destroyers with anti-aircraft and anti-submarine propensities. Four separate towers carrying radar for missile guidance, anti-aircraft direction, search and gunnery direction.

PHOTOGRAPHS. **A starboard broadside view of No. 078 appears in the 1964-65 and 1965-66 editions.**

KASHIN Class No. 11 — *1966, col Breyer*

KASHIN Class No. 383 — *1968*

KASHIN Class — *1969, S. Breyer*

Guided Missile Armed Destroyers— *continued*

6 "KRUPNY" CLASS

GNEVNYI	**GREMYASHCHYI**
GORDYI	**PLAMYONNY**

Displacement, tons	3 650 standard; 4 650 full load
Length, feet (*metres*)	453 (*138·0*)
Beam, feet (*metres*)	44 (*13·4*)
Draught, feet (*metres*)	16·5 (*5·0*)
Missiles, surface	2 "Strela"; 1 forward, 1 aft
Guns, AA	16—57 mm, 4 quadruple; 2 amidships, 1 forward, 1 aft
Torpedo launchers	6 (2 triple) for A/S torpedoes
Boilers	4 high pressure water tube
Main engines	Geared steam turbines 80 000 shp; 2 shafts
Speed, knots	34
Complement	360

Flush-decked destroyers designed to carry guided missiles. Helicopter spot landing apron on the stern. Initial construction started in 1958 at Leningrad. Two were converted to surface-to-air missiles in 1967-68.

PHOTOGRAPHS. A port broadside aerial view of No. 526 appears in the 1961-62 to 1963-64 editions, a port broadside surface view of No. 700 in the 1962-63 and 1963-64 editions, a starboard bow surface view of No. 700 in the 1962-63 to 1964-65 editions, and a starboard broadside view in the 1963-64 to 1965-66 editions, and a starboard quarter surface view of No. 703 in the 1962-63 to 1966-67 editions.

2 "KANIN" CLASS

Displacement, tons	3 650 standard; 4 500 full load
Dimensions, feet	456 × 44 × 16
Missile launchers	1 forward, 1 aft for surface-to-air
Boilers	4 water tube
Main engines	Geared steam turbines; 80 000 shp; 2 shafts = 34 knots
Complement	350

Basically of the same design and construction as the "Krupnyi" class, but converted to launch surface-to-air missiles in 1967-68.

GNEVNYI *1969, MOD, RN, Official*

GNEVNYI *1969, MOD, RN, Official*

KRUPNY Class No. 700 *1966, col Borg*

Guided Missile Armed Destroyers—*continued*

KOTLIN SAM Class

1969, MOD, RN, Official

2 "KOTLIN" SAM CLASS

Displacement, tons	2 850 standard; 3 885 full load
Length, feet (*metres*)	425 (*129·5*) oa
Beam, feet (*metres*)	41·5 (*12·6*)
Draught, feet (*metres*)	16 (*4·9*) max
Missiles, AA	1 twin "Goa" launcher aft
Guns, dual purpose	2—3·9 in (*100 mm*), twin
Guns, AA	4—57 mm, quadruple
A/S	6 side thrown DC projectors
Boilers	4 high pressure
Main engines	Geared turbines 80 000 shp; 2 shafts
Speed, knots	36
Complement	285

"Kotlin" class modified with a surface-to-air missile launcher in place of the main twin turret aft and anti-aircraft guns reduced to one quadruple mounting. Two of the "Kotlin" class have been converted with surface-air-missiles, first in 1960, second in 1966.

PHOTOGRAPHS. A starboard bow view appears in the 1963-64 to 1965-66 editions.

KOTLIN SAM Class No. 165

KOTLIN SAM Class No. 935

1966, col Breyer

KOTLIN SAM Class

Guided Missile Armed Destroyers— *continued*

4 "KOTLIN" CLASS

Displacement, tons 3 000 standard; 4 000 full load
Length, feet (*metres*) 426·5 (*130·0*)
Beam, feet (*metres*) 42·7 (*13·0*)
Draught, feet (*metres*) 15·5 (*4·7*)

Missiles, surface 1 "Strela" launcher aft
A/S 2—16 barrel rocket launchers on forecastle
Guns, AA 16—45 mm, 4 quadruple
Boilers 4 high pressure
Main engines Geared turbines 80 000 shp; 2 shafts

Speed, knots 35 maximum designed continuous
Complement 300 officers and men (normal)

Large destroyers with the "Kotlin" type hull, but redesigned as guided missile armed destroyers with a launcher installed in place of the after gun mountings. Identified by NATO designation as the "Kildin" class.

KILDIN Class *1969, S. Breyer*

KILDIN Class ***1964***

KOTLIN Class No. 858 with helicopter aft (see next page) *S. Breyer*

KOTLIN Class (helicopter platform aft) *1969, MOD, RN, Official*

DESTROYERS

25 "KOTLIN" CLASS

BESSLEDNYI
BURLIVYI
NAPORISTYI
NASTOYCHIVYI
PLAMENNYI
SPRAVETLIVYI
SVETLIVYIARE
SVETLYI
VDOKHNOVENNYII
VOZMUSHCHENNY

Displacement, tons	2 850 standard; 3 885 full load
Length, feet (*metres*)	425 (*129·5*) oa
Beam, feet (*metres*)	41·5 (*12·6*)
Draught, feet (*metres*)	16 (*4·9*) max
Guns, dual purpose	4—5·1 in (*130 mm*) 2 twin
Guns, AA	16—45 mm, 4 quadruple
A/S	6 side thrown DC projectors
Torpedo tubes	10—21 in (*533 mm*)
Mines	80 capacity
Boilers	4 high pressure
Main engines	Geared turbines 80 000 sgp; 2 shafts
Speed, knots	36
Complement	285

Improved versions of the "Tallin" type with similar hulls but differing features. These fast anti-aircraft and anti-submarine destroyers, built in 1954-57, were designed for mass production. *Nastoychivyi* means Persistent.

MODERNISATION. Many of the "Kotlin" class have been modernised, with extensive modifications in anti-submarine and anti-aircraft armament. Several fitted with helicopter platform abaft the after mounting. Two fitted with surface-to-air twin missile launcher aft, installed atop a deckhouse in place of the after guns; with missile radar and tower fitted forward of the after funnel, see previous page.

SVETLYI, No. 168 with helicopter platform aft — *1968, col Borg*

KOTLIN Class — *1965, Skyfotos*

ANTI-SUBMARINE WARFARE. The six depth charge throwers in *Nastoychivyi* are welded to the deck, three on each beam at the stern, affording only transverse throw. They are apparently charged from deck magazines.

PHOTOGRAPHS. Another photograph of a "**Kotlin**", a port near broadside surface view at sea, appears in the 1957-58 to 1960-61 editions, and starboard broadside view of No. 82 in the 1958-59 to 1964-65 editions.

KOTLIN Class No. 774 — *1966, Skyfotos*

"TALLIN" CLASS

NEUSTRASHIMYI

Displacement, tons	3 200 standard; 4 300 full load
Length, feet (*metres*)	433 (*132·0*) oa
Beam, feet (*metres*)	44 (*13·4*)
Draught, feet (*metres*)	16 (*4·9*)
Guns, dual purpose	4—5·1 in (*130 mm*) semi-automatic
Guns, AA	16—45 mm, 4 quadruple
A/S	2 DC rocket launchers
Torpedo tubes	10—21 in (*533 mm*), 2 quintuple
Mines	70 to 90 according to size
Boilers	4 water tube
Main engines	Geared turbines 100 000 shp; 2 shafts
Speed, knots	38
Radius, miles	2 500 at 18 knots
Oil fuel (tons)	1 000
Complement	340

A multi-purpose anti-aircraft, anti-submarine and mine-laying flushdecked prototype destroyer for fleet escort and flotilla leader duties. *Neustrashimyi* means Unfearing.

GUNNERY. The 5·1 inch (*130 mm*) guns in two twin turrets, including firing directors, are fully stabilised. This was the first time such an armament had been contrived in a ship of destroyer size, an experiment in top weight.

CLASS. It is understood that there is only one destroyer of the "Tallin" class, a prototype for the "Kotlin" class, but several different pennent numbers have been observed, including No. 76, see photograph in the 1956-57 to 1960-61 editilons.

NEUSTRASHIMYI — *1961, Skyfotos*

Destroyers—*continued*

50 "SKORY" CLASS

BESSMENNYI **BEZUKORIZNENNYI**

Normally in the Black Sea

OTCHAYANNYI **OZHESTOCHENNYI**
OTVETSTVENNYI **OZHIVLENNYI**

Normally in the Arctic

SERIDTYI **SPOSOBNYI**
SERIOZNYI **STATNYI**
SMELYI **STEPENNYI**
SMOTRYASHCHYI **STOJKYI**
SOKRUSHITELNYI **STREMITELNYI**
SOLIDNYI **SUROVYI**
SOVERSHENNYI **SVOBODNYI**

Normally in the Baltic

VDUMCHIVYI **VRAZUMITELNYI**

Normally in the Far East

Displacement, tons	2 600 standard; 3 500 full load
Length, feet (*metres*)	393·7 (*120·0*) pp; 420 (*128·0*) oa
Beam, feet (*metres*)	41 (*12·5*)
Draught, feet (*metres*)	15 (*4·6*)
Guns, surface	4—5·1 in (*130 mm*), 2 twin
Guns, AA	2—3 in (*76 mm*); 7—37 mm (8—37 mm, twin mounts in some) see *Modernisation*
A/S	4 DCT
Torpdeo tubes	10—21 in (*533 mm*)
Mines	80 capacity
Boilers	4 high pressure
Main engines	Geared turbines 70 000 shp; 2 shafts
Speed, knots	36
Radius, miles	4 000 at 15 knots
Complement	260

There were to have been 85 destroyers of this class, but construction beyond 75 units was reported to have been discontinued in favour of later types of destroyers and the number has been further reduced to 50 by transfers to other countries, translations to other types, and disposals.

SVOBODNYI *1968*

MODERNISATION. Some ships of the "Skoryi" class have been modified under the fleet rehabilitation and modernisation programme, including extensive alterations to anti-aircraft armament, electronic equipment and anti-submarine weapons.

NOMENCLATURE. The names of "Skory" class destroyers are apparently based on their fleet assignment. Those in the Black Sea have names beginning with B, those in the Northern Fleet have names beginning with O, those in the Baltic have names beginning with S and those in the Pacific have names beginning with V.

APPEARANCE. There are three differing types in this class, the anti-aircraft guns varying with twin and single mountings; and two types of foremast, one vertical with all scanners on top and the other with one scanner on top and one on a platform half way.

GUNNERY. Equipped with modern target finding and gun sighting radar for the 5·1 inch guns.

PHOTOGRAPHS. Photographs of *Stepennyi, Sposobnyi* and *Surovyi* appear in the 1954-55 to 1957-58 editions, a large broadside view of *Smotryahchy* in the 1957-58 to 1959-60 editions, a starboard bow view of *Ozhestochennyi* in the 1957-58 to 1962-63 editions, a port broadside view of *Otchaiannyi* in the 1958-59 to 1962-63 editions, a port bow oblique aeriel view of *Svabodnyi* (No. 14) and a starboard broadside surface view of *Otretsvennyi* in the 1957-58 to 1966-67 editions.

TRANSFERS. Of this class *Skoryi* and *Smetlivyi* were transferred to the Polish Navy in 1957-58. Two were transferred to the Egyptian Navy in 1956. Four more units were transferred to the Indonesian Navy in 1959.

SVOBODNYI *1967*

OTCHAYANNYI *Added 1967*

ESCORTS

15 "MIRKA" CLASS

Displacement, tons	900 light (approx)
Length, feet (*metres*)	262 (*79·9*) oa
Beam, feet (*metres*)	29·5 (*9·0*)
Draught, feet (*metres*)	9·2 (*2·8*)
A/S	4—12 barrel rocket launchers
Guns, AA	4—3 in (*76 mm*) 2 twin
Torpedo tubes	5 anti-submarine (see notes)
Main engines	Gas turbines
Speed, knots	28
Complement	90

Successors and anti-submarine versions of the "Petya" class, of similar design, but with teething problems eradicated. Two built in the Baltic, three others built at Kalingrad in 1964. Two ships fitted with two quintuple 16 inch A/S torpedo tubes instead of rocket launchers aft, the forward rocket launchers being retained, have two 3 inch single guns and two 12-barrelled rocket launchers. Pennant numbers include 891.

"Mirka" Class No. 68 *1968*

35 "PETYA" CLASS

Displacement, tons	1 050 standard; 1 200 full load
Length, feet (*metres*)	250 (*76·2*) wl; 262·5 (*80·0*) oa
Beam, feet (*metres*)	32 (*9·8*)
Draught, feet (*metres*)	9·8 (*3·0*)
A/S weapons	4—16 barrell rocket launchers, see notes
Guns, dual purpose	4—3 in (*76 mm*) 2 twin
Torpedo tubes	5—21 in (*533 mm*) see notes
Main engines	2 diesels, total 4 000 hp 2 gas turbines, total 10 000 hp 2 shafts
Speed, knots	30
Complement	100

Escort patrol vessels with a low wide funnel. The first ship reported to have been completed in 1961. Built by Kaliningrad, Nikolaiev. Fitted with two mine rails. Later versions are fitted with two sets of torpedo tubes and two 12-barrelled rocket launchers. "Petya" class pennant numbers include 844, 846, 847, 849.

"Petya" Class *1969, Col Borg*

6 "KOLA" CLASS

Displacement, tons	1 500 standard; 2 000 full load
Length, feet (*metres*)	295 (*90·0*) pp; 305 (*93·0*) oa
Beam, feet (*metres*)	32·8 (*10·0*)
Draught, feet (*metres*)	11·5 (*3·5*)
Guns, dual purpose	4—3·9 (*100 mm*) single
Guns, AA	4—37 mm
A/S	DCT's and racks
Torpedo tubes	3—21 in (*533 mm*)
Boilers	2
Main engines	Geared turbines 30 000 shp; 2 shafts
Speed, knots	31
Complement	190

In design this class of flushdecked destroyer escort appears to be a combination of the former German "Elbing" type torpedo boat destroyers, with a similar hull form, and of the earlier Soviet "Birds" class frigates. The four 3·9 inch guns were mounted as in the "Gordyi" class destroyers.

"Kola" Class *1969, S. Breyer*

50 "RIGA" CLASS

Displacement, tons	1 200 standard; 1 600 full load
Length, feet (*metres*)	278·5 (*84·9*) pp; 295 (*90·0*) oa
Beam, feet (*metres*)	31·5 (*9·6*)
Draught, feet (*metres*)	11 (*3·4*)
Guns, dual purpose	3—3·9 in (*100 mm*) single
Guns, AA	3—37 mm
A/S weapons	2—16 barrelled rocket launchers; 4 DC projectors
Torpedo tubes	3—21 in (*533 mm*)
Boilers	2
Main engines	Geared turbines 25 000 shp; 2 shafts
Speed, knots	28
Complement	150

Successors to the "Kola" class escorts, of which they are lighter and less heavily armed but improved versions. Fitted with mine rails. The two 16-barrelled rocket launchers are mounted just before the bridge, abreast "B" gun. A photograph of No. 645 appears in the 1956-57 to 1962-63 editions, of No. 168 in the 1962-63 to 1965-66 editions.

"Riga" Class No. 375 *1966, col Breyer*

"BIRDS" CLASSES.
The three of the improved "Birds" class, *Albatros*, *Chaika* (Seagull), and *Krechet* (Buzzard); the seven of the "Birds" class, *Berkut* (Golden Eagle), *Grif* (Griffin), *Kondor*, *Korshun* (Kite), *Orel* (Eagle), *Voron* (Raven) and *Yastreb* (Hawk) were discarded.

ANSALDO TYPE. The two Ansaldo type vessels, *Dzerzhinski* (ex-PS 8) and *Kirov* (ex-PS 26), were deleted from the list on account of age obsolescence or being worn out.

"Riga" Class *1968*

SUPPORT SHIPS

NUCLEAR SUPPORT TYPE

3 "UGRA" CLASS

No. 82

Displacement, tons	6 000 light; 9 000 full load
Length, feet (*metres*)	370 (*112·8*) pp; 420 (*128·0*) oa
Beam, feet (*metres*)	65 (*19·8*)
Draught, feet (*metres*)	20 (*6·1*)
Aircraft	Provision for helicopter
Guns, dual purpose	8—2·3 in (*57 mm*), 4 twin mounts, 2 forward, 2 aft
Main engines	Diesels, 7 000 hp, 2 shafts
Speed, knots	17

Support and escort ships of the maintenance and repair, supply and depot type probably for servicing nuclear powered submarines. Built on warship lines. Equipped with workshops and staterooms. Provided with a helicopter platform. Fitted with comprehensive radar. Carries a large derrick to handle torpedoes and warheads. Has mooring points in hull about 100 feet apart, but has side doorways, possibly for coastal craft and submarines.

MISSILE SUPPLY TYPE

3 "LAMA" CLASS

No. 44

Displacement, tons	5 000 light; 7 000 full load
Length, feet (*metres*)	330 (*100·0*) pp; 370 (*112·8*) oa
Beam, feet (*metres*)	60 (*18·3*)
Draught, feet (*metres*)	19 (*5·8*)
Guns, dual purpose	8—57 mm, 2 quadruple, 1 forward, 1 aft
Main engines	Diesels, 5 000 hp, 2 shafts
Speed, knots	15

Support and escort ship of the depot and freighting type. Her features indicate a possible missile supply role. Engines sited aft to allow for a very large and high hangar or hold amidships for carrying missiles or weapon spares. The main erection is about 12 feet high above the main deck. There are doors at the forward end with rails leading in. This is surmounted by a turntable gantry or travelling cranes for transferring armaments to combatant ships.

PM 131

Displacement, tons	5 000 light; 7 000 full load
Length, feet (*metres*)	330 (*100·0*) pp; 370 (*112·8*) oa
Beam, feet (*metres*)	60 (*18·3*)
Draught, feet (*metres*)	19 (*5·8*)
Guns, AA	8—57 mm, 2 quadruple, 1 on the forecastle, 1 on the break of the quarter deck
Main engines	Diesels, 5 000 bhp 2 shafts
Speed, knots	15

Support and repair ship for missile armed surface ships. Can apparently be used for salvage and towing. Mooring points along the hull for low vessels such as submarines to come alongside. There appears to be a turntable on the deck, which is built up 2 feet above the main deck. The two cranes are in the stowed position and there appear to be pulleyed lifting arrangements, apparently intended to service the well deck and overside. The well deck is about 40 feet long, enough for a missile to fit horizontally before being lifted vertically for loading in submarines.

OCEANGOING SUBMARINE SUPPORT TYPE

6 "DON" CLASS

DMITRI GALKIN **MAGOMET GADZHIEV**
FEDOR VIDYAEV **VIKTOR KOTELNIKOV**

Displacement, tons	4 750 standard; 6 000 full load
Length, feet (*metres*)	426·5 (*130·0*)
Beam, feet (*metres*)	49 (*14·9*)
Draught, feet (*metres*)	17 (*5·2*)
Aircraft	Provision for helicopter in No. 701
Guns, dual purpose	4—3·9 (*100 mm*)
Guns, AA	8—45 mm
Mines	80 capacity
Main engines	Diesels
Speed, knots	20
Complement	300

Support ships, all named after officers lost in WW II. The design is interesting as a hybrid. It has been described as cruiser, frigate, minelayer, training ship, escort vessel, supply ship, and depot ship.

A photograph of *Viktor Kotelnikov*, No. 701, modified version with helicopter deck aft instead of guns, appears in the 1965-66 to 1967-68 editions.

OCEANGOING ICEBREAKER TYPE

1 "PURGA" CLASS

Displacement, tons	2 250 standard; 3 000 full load
Length, feet (*metres*)	325 (*99·0*)
Beam, feet (*metres*)	40 (*12·2*)
Draught, feet (*metres*)	17 (*5·2*)
Guns, dual purpose	4—3·9 in (*100 mm*) singles
Guns, AA	8—37 mm, twin; 4—25 mm, twin
Mines	50 capacity
Main engines	Diesel
Speed, knots	18
Complement	200

Sturdy oceangoing vessel of the frigate type equipped for minelaying and icebreaking. Fitted with directors similar to those in the "Riga" class frigates.

"Ugra" Class No. 82 — *1964, Skyfotos*

"Lama" Class No. 44 — *1964*

Later "Lama" Class No. PM-131 — *1964, Skyfotos*

MAGOMET GADZHIEV — *1968*

No. 551

FLEET MINESWEEPERS

30 "YURKA" CLASS

Displacement, tons	500 standard; 550 full load
Dimensions, feet	164 × 28 × 7
Guns	4—25 mm AA (2 twin)
Main engines	2 diesel; 4 000 bhp = 15 knots

A new class of medium minesweepers designed in 1964. Built of steel.

20 "T 58" CLASS

Displacement, tons	600 standard; 700 full load
Dimensions feet	220 × 29·5 × 9
Guns	4—57 mm AA
Main engines	Diesels; 2 shafts; speed = 18 knots

A class of fleet minesweepers built from 1959 onwards. Several of this class were converted to submarine rescue ships with armament and sweep gear removed.

T 58 Class No. 4 *1968*

120 "T 43" CLASS

Displacement, tons	500 standard; 600 full load
Dimensions, feet	200 × 27·5 × 9
Guns	4—37 mm AA; 8—13 mm AA MG
Main engines	Diesels; 2 shafts; speed = 17 knots

A handy type of moderately fast medium minesweepers built in 1948-57 in shipyards throughout the Soviet Union. Of the original 175 ships ten were transferred to Poland, eight to Albania, six to Egypt, four to Indonesia, three to Bulgaria, and two to Syria. Some of this class were converted into radar pickets (see photographs of No. 55 in the 1965-66 to 1967-68 editions).

"T 43" Class No. 8 *1968*

"T 43" Class *1969, MOD, RN, Official*

"T 43" Class No. 252 *1968*

MINELAYERS

1 + 1 NEW CONSTRUCTION. "ALESHA" CLASS

MMF 075

MMF 075 is the Soviet Navy's only modern fleet minelayer. Said to have been specifically designed and built as a minelayer from the keel up in 1967, but it seems very doubtful that she is intended primarily as a minelayer. She is in service and stationed in the Black Sea. Has capacity for 400 mines below decks, with four mine tracks to provide stern launchings. This prototype may be the first of several units of the same class which are eventually scheduled for construction.

The Soviet Navy is capable of a considerable mine-laying effort. In general, all ships and submarines other than surface ships fitted with missiles, can lay mines. Minelaying has always been a highly specialised branch of the Soviet Navy.

The old minelayers *Voroshilovsk*, *Elizabeta* (ex-*Marty*, ex-*Shtandart*), former Imperial Yacht, and the former Japanese *Kamishima* were deleted in 1963. *Ural* (ex-*Felix Dzerzhinski*) was reported to have returned to the Merchant Navy. The mining tenders *MU 41, 42, 43, 44, 45, 46, 48, 50, 51, 52, 53* and *54* were also deleted.

COASTAL ESCORTS

70 "POTI" CLASS

Displacement, tons	350 standard
Dimensions, feet	200 × 28 × 10
Guns	2—57 mm AA (1 twin mounting)
Tubes	4 anti-submarine
A/S weapons	2—12 barrelled rocket launchers
Main engines	Gas turbines; speed = 28 to 30 knots

This class of coastal escort vessels or patrol vessels of the submarine chaser type is reported to have been under construction since 1961.

"Poti" Class *1966, col Breyer*

100 "SOI" CLASS

Displacement, tons	215 light; 250 normal
Dimensions, feet	138 pp; 147 oa × 20 × 10 max
Guns	4—25 mm (2 twin mountings)
A/S weapons	4 five-barrelled ahead throwing rocket launchers
Main engines	3 diesels; 3 500 bhp = 28 knots
Complement	30

Built since 1957. Apparently the design is an enlarged version of the ex-US "110-foot" class of SCs built during the Second World War. Steel hulled.

"SO I" Class No. 58 *1968*

100 "KRONSTADT" CLASS

Displacement, tons	300 standard; 350 full load
Dimensions, feet	167·3 × 19·3 × 9
Guns	1—3·9 in; 2—37 mm AA; 3—20 mm AA
A/S weapons	Depth charge projectors
Main engines	Diesels; 2 shafts = 23 knots
Complement	40

Built in 1948-56. Flush-decked, large squat funnel, slightly raked, massive block bridge structure. Now gradually being taken out of service due to age.

"Kronstadt" Class No. 497

COASTAL MINESWEEPERS

40 "VANYA" CLASS

Displacement, tons	250 standard
Dimensions, feet	144·4 × 20 × 6·9
Guns	2—25 mm (1 twin) AA
Main engines	2 diesels; speed = 15 knots

A new class with wooden hulls of a type suitable for series production. Basically similar to NATO type coastal minesweepers.

"Vanya" Class *1968, S. Breyer*

35 "SASHA" CLASS

Displacement, tons	180 standard; 250 full load
Dimensions, feet	147 × 20 × 7.
Guns	1—57 mm dp; 4—25 mm AA (2 twin)
Main engines	Diesels; speed = 18 knots

Basically similar to NATO inshore minesweepers, but of steel construction. This series did not run into the number at first anticipated, construction having been discontinued in favour of later types.

"Sasha" Class No. 143 *1968, S. Breyer*

60 "T 301" CLASS

Displacement, tons	130 standard; 180 full load
Dimensions, feet	100 × 16 × 4·5
Guns	2—37 mm AA; 2—25 mm AA
Main engines	Diesel; 2 shafts; 480 bhp = 10 knots

Built from 1946 to 1956. Several were converted to survey craft, and many adapted for other purposes or used for port duty and auxiliary service. Now gradually being withdrawn from service due to age.

No. 223. *1962*

"P 8" Class *en flotille* (see next col) *1969, S. Breyer*

TORPEDO BOATS

20 "SHERSHEN" CLASS

Displacement, tons	150 normal
Dimensions, feet	132 × 32 × 6·5
Guns	4—25 mm AA (2 twin)
Tubes	4—21 in (single)
Main engines	Diesels; 7 500 bhp = 40 knots

These large torpedo boats have basically the same hull and layout as the "Osa" class missile boats, but with tubes on the launcher sites.

250 "P 6" "P 8" "P 10" CLASSES

Displacement, tons	66 standard
Dimensions, feet	85·3 × 20 × 6
Guns	4—25 mm AA
Tubes	2—21 in (or mines, or depth charges)
Main engines	Diesels; 5 000 bhp = 45 knots

The "P 6" class was of a standard medium type running into series production. Launched during 1951 to 1960. Known as "MO VI" class in the submarine chaser version. The later versions are known as the "P 8" and P" 10" classes. Some are powered with gas turbines.

25 "PCHELA" CLASS

Displacement, tons	80
Dimensions, feet	90 × 15
Guns	2—25 mm AA
Main engines	Diesels; 6 000 bhp = 50 knots

This class of hydrofoils, probably submarine chasers, are reported to have been built since 1964-65.

50 "P 4" CLASS

Displacement, tons	25
Dimensions, feet	82 × 16·8 × 5·6
Guns	2—25 mm AA
Main engines	Diesels; 2 000 bhp = 42 knots

A numerically large class of boats with aluminium alloy hulls. Launched in 1951-58.

"Shershen" Class *1966, col Breyer*

"P 8" Class No. 9 *1968, col Breyer*

"P 6" Class No. 312 *1966, col Borg*

"P 6" Class *1966, Col Breyer*

MISSILE BOATS "OSA" CLASS SERIES

"Osa" Class *1969, S Breyer*

"Osa" III Type (cylindrical missile launchers) *1969, S. Breyer*

"Osa" Class *1969, Col Borg*

"Osa" Class *1969*

"Osa" Class *1969*

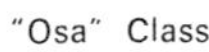

"Osa" Class *1969*

MISSILE BOATS

75 "OSA" CLASS

Displacement, tons	160 standard; 200 full load
Dimensions, feet	131·5 oa × 23 × 6·5
Missiles, surface	"Styx" launchers in two pairs abreast
Guns	4—25 mm; (2 twin, 1 forward, 1 aft)
Main engines	3 diesels; 4 800 bhp = 35 knots

These boats, built since 1959, have a larger hull and four large hood type launchers in two pairs as compared with one pair in the MTB conversions. They are reported to have a surface-to-surface missile range of about 15 to 18 miles.

"Osa" Class *1967, col Breyer*

50 "KOMAR" CLASS

Displacement, tons	75 standard; 100 full load
Dimensions, feet	82 oa × 20 × 6
Missiles, surface	2 "Styx" launchers with 15 miles range
Guns	2—25 mm AA (1 twin forward)
Main engines	3 diesels; 4 800 bhp = 40 knots

A smaller type of boats converted from "P 6" class motor torpedo boats. Fitted with two surface-to-surface launchers aft in a hooded casing approximately 45 degrees to the deck line. Built since 1960-61.

"Komar" Class *1968*

INTELLIGENCE TRAWLERS

ALIDADA	**BAROMETR**	**IZMIRITEL**	**REDUCTOR**
AMPERMETR	**DEFLEKTOR**	**KRENOMETR**	**PROTRACTOR**
AMTR	**EKHOLOT**	**LINZA**	**VAL**
BAROGRAPH	**GIDROFON**	**LOTLIN**	**VERTIKAL**
	GIROSKOP	**LOTZMAN**	**ZOND**

Measurement, tons	684 gross; 226 net; 502 gross; 197 net; 334 gross; 89 net; 293 gross; 88 net; and various other measurements
Dimensions, feet	Length 165 (ships vary)

Reported to be fitted with electronic interception equipment, with a layout designed for intelligence collection. A considerable number of observation trawlers, equipped with radio aerials and direction-finding apparatus have been sighted by British and American warships during international combined sea and air exercises. *Izmiritel* is of "Dnepr" class.

TYPICAL "LENTRA" CLASS TRAWLER *1968, Mr Michael D. J. Lennon*

LANDING SHIPS

20 "VYDRA" TYPE

These newest landing vessels are reported to be of the LSM type.

2 "ALLIGATOR" TYPE

Displacement, tons	4 000 standard
Dimensions, feet	328 × 50 × 14 max
Guns	2—57 mm AA
Main engines	Speed = 15 knots

Largest type of Soviet landing ship built in the USSR to date. LST type. First ship built in 1965-66 and commissioned in 1966. These ships have ramps on the bow *and* stern. Carrying capacity near 2 400 tons. "Alligator" is the NATO code name.

"Alligator" type *1967, col Breyer*

25 "POLNOCNY" TYPES

Displacement, tons	1 000
Dimensions, feet	246 × 39·3 × 9·8
Armament	Rocket projector (30 mm AA in "Polnochny II type)
Main engines	Diesels; 4 000 bhp = 15 knots

A new type of amphibious vessel basically similar to the US medium landing ship, rocket (LSMR) type. Can carry 8 to 10 tanks. "Polnocny II" type has a modified mast and 30 mm AA turret before the bridge.

"Polnocny II" Type *1969, S. Breyer*

20 "MP 8" TYPE

Displacement, tons	800
Dimensions, feet	236·2 × 36 × 13
Guns	4—57 mm (2 twin)
Main engines	Diesels; speed = 15 knots

Old type of landing ship with a short and low quarter deck abaft the after castle and a waist between the gun mounting before the bridge and the gun mounting on the high forecastle. Can carry 8 or more tanks.

10 "MP 6" TYPE

Displacement, tons	1 800
Dimensions, feet	246 × 40 × 10.5
Guns	4—47 mm (1 quadruple)
Main engines	Diesels; speed = 10 knots

Two masts, one stepped from the superstructure aft and one in the forecastle. King posts. Mounting in the bandstand on the forecastle has two pairs of barrels in the vertical plane. Can carry 8 to 10 tanks.

LANDING CRAFT

40 "MP 10" TYPE

Displacement, tons	200
Dimensions, feet	157·5 × 19·7 × 6·5
Main engines	Diesels; speed = 10 knots

A type of landing craft basically similar to the British LCT (4) type in silhouette and layout. Can carry 4 tanks.

30 "MP 4" TYPE

Displacement, tons	800
Dimensions, feet	180·5 × 23 × 9
Guns	4—25 mm (2 twin)

Of the small freighter type in appearance. Two masts, one abaft the bridge and one in the waist. Gun mountings on poop and forecastle. Can carry 6 to 8 tanks.

15 "MP 2" TYPE

Displacement, tons	600
Dimensions, feet	190 × 25 × 8·2
Guns	4—25 mm (2 twin)
Main engines	Diesels; 1 200 bhp = 16 knots

Basically similar to the British LCT (8) type. Gun mountings on after shelter deck abaft funnel and on forecastle. Can carry four tanks.

DEPOT SHIPS

6 "ATREK" CLASS

ATREK **AYAT** **BAKHMUT**

Displacement, tons	3 500 standard; 6 700 full load
Measurement, tons	3 258 gross
Dimensions, feet	336 × 49 × 20
Main engines	Expansion and exhaust turbines; 1 shaft; 2 450 hp = 13 knots
Boilers	2 water tube
Radius, miles	3 500 at 13 knots

Built in 1956-58, and converted to naval use from "Kolomna" class freighters. There are six of these vessels employed as submarine tenders and replenishment ships.

ATREK, V(B)-272 *1959, Sergei Romanov*

5 "DNIEPER" CLASS

PM 17

Displacement, tons	3 000 standard; 4 220 full load
Dimensions, feet	325 × 45 × 14
Main engines	Diesels; speed = 12 knots

Bow lift repair and depot ships for fleet support and maintenance. Built in 1957-66 as tenders and multi-purpose ships, equipped with workshops and servicing facilities.

PM 17 *1965*

PAYSHERD (ex-*Otto Wünche*)

Displacement, tons	4 730
Dimensions, feet	433 × 52·5 × 14·5
Guns	4—4·1 in; 2—37 mm; 12—20 mm
Main engines	4 MAN diesels; 2 shafts; 12 400 bhp = 20 knots

Ex-German. *Paysherd* was built by Howaldt, Kiel. Launched in 1941.

KUBAN (ex-*Waldemar Kophamel*)

Displacement, tons	4 726
Dimensions, feet	446 × 52·5 × 14·5
Guns	2—4·1 in; 2—37 mm AA
Main engines	4 MAN diesels; 2 shafts; 12 400 bhp = 20 knots

Ex-German. Launched in 1939. Submarine tender. Salvaged in 1950-51 after being sunk in shallow water by bombing in WW II. Repaired in 1951-1957.

Ex-**TEREK** (ex-*Elbe*)

Displacement, tons	820 standard; 1 600 full load
Dimensions, feet	157·5 × 28 × 11
Guns	1—3·5 in; 1—20 mm AA
Main engines	2 Linke-Hofmann-Busch diesels; 2 shafts; 1 600 bhp = 15 knots
Complement	48

Launched in 1931. Ex-German fishery protection vessel. Supply ship for "Z" class submarines. A photograph appears in the 1946-47 to 1963-64 editions.

The depot ships, ex-*Adolf Luderitz: Volga* (ex-*Juan Sebastian de Elcano*) and ex-*Donetz*, ex-*Weichsel*, ex-*Syra*, are reported probably scrapped.

3 "TOVDA" CLASS

INZA (ex-*Novoshaktinsk*) **TOVDA** **VYJEGRA**

Displacement, tons	3 000 standard; 4 000 full load
Dimensions, feet	282 × 39 × 16
Guns	6—45 mm AA (3 twin mountings)
Main engines	2 diesels; 7 000 bhp = 16 knots
Radius, miles	7 000 at 16 knots

Polish built ex-tankers converted in 1958 to 1960. Depot and repair ships. Also known as the "Soldek" class, but the NATO designation is "Tovda" class.

V(B) 415 *1959*

2 "DESNA" CLASS

CHAZHMA **CHUMIKAN**

Displacement, tons	5 300
Dimensions, feet	485·6 × 57 × 20·3
Aircraft	1 helicopter
Main engines	Triple expansion; 4 000 ihp = 18 knots

Soviet Missile Range Instrumentation Ships (SMRIS). The "Desna" class have a larger hull than the "Sibir" class and are better equipped. Active since 1963.

4 "SIBIR" CLASS

CHUKOTKA **SAKHALIN** **SIBIR** **SUCHAN**

Displacement, tons	4 000 standard; 5 000 full load
Measurement, tons	3 767 gross (*Chukotka* 3 800, *Suchan* 3 710)
Dimensions, feet	475·7 to 493·5 × 56·1 × 20 (ships vary)
Guns	6—45 mm AA; 2 MG
Main engines	Triple expansion; 2 shafts; 3 300 ihp = 15 knots
Radius, miles	3 300 miles at 12 knots

Converted bulk ore carriers employed as Missile Range Ships in the Pacific. *Sakhalin* and *Sibir* have three bubble-like domes forward and aft, and carry helicopters. *Suchan* is also equipped with a helicopter flight deck. Launched in 1957-59. All active since 1959.

IRTYSH (ex-*Kronstadt*)

Displacement, tons	5 880
Dimensions, feet	328 × 46 × 19·5
Guns	4—3 in; 3—45 mm AA; 2 MG
Main engines	Triple expansion; 1 shaft; 1 500 ihp = 12 knots
Coal, tons	430
Radius, miles	1 500 at 12 knots
Complement	240

Parent ship and general supply ship for submarines in the Baltic. Launched in 1931.

SARATOV
Submarine tender and depot ship of the "Anadyr" class

ANGARA (ex-*Hela*)

Displacement, tons	2 115 standard; 2 500 full load
Dimensions, feet	323 × 42·5 × 11
Guns	2—4·1 in; 1—37 mm AA; 2—20 mm AA
Main engines	4 MAN diesels; 2 shafts; 6 300 bhp = 18 knots
Radius, miles	2 000 at 15 knots

Former yacht built by Stülcken, Hamburg. Launched in 1939. In the Black Sea. A photograph of *Angara* appears in the 1947-48 to 1965-66 editions.

KOMMUNA (ex-*Volkhov*)

Displacement, tons	2 400
Main engines	Diesels; 2 shafts; speed = 8 knots

Former submarine salvage vessel. Launched in 1913. Repair ship. Double hull. Refitted and modernised at De Schelde Yard, Flushing, Netherlands during May 1950 to July 1951.

ELBRUS

Displacement, tons	2 600
Dimensions, feet	302 × 39 × 13·5
Guns	2—3 in; 1—45 mm AA
Main engines	Diesel-electric; 2 800 hp = 13 knots
Oil fuel, tons	180
Complement	150

Repair and depot ship. Latterly reported to be confined to harbour service.

SALVAGE VESSELS

"NEPA" CLASS

Displacement, tons	3 500
Dimensions, feet	Length: 426·5

New type of submarine rescue and salvage ship, similar to the "Prut" class but has a high stern which extends out over the water.

6 "PRUT" CLASS

MB 21 **MB 22** **MB 23**

Displacement, tons	2 000 standard; 3 500 full load
Dimensions, feet	344·5
Guns	4—57 mm (quadruple) forward
Main engines	Speed = 18 knots

Large rescue vessels with raked down flush deck and mainmast derrick. Built since 1960.

MB 23 *1965*

10 SUBMARINE RESCUE TYPE

GIDROLOG **VALDAY**

Ten "T 58" class fleet minesweeper hulls were completed as submarine rescue ships at Leningrad.

4 "PAMIR" CLASS

AGATAN **ALDAN** **ARBAN** **PAMIR**

Measurement, tons	1 443 to 2 032 gross
Dimensions, feet	256 oa × 42 × 13·5
Main engines	Two 10 cyl 4 str diesels; 2 shafts; 4 200 bhp = 17 knots

Salvage tugs built at AB Gävie, Varv, Sweden, in 1959-60. Equipped with strong derricks, powerful pumps, air compressors, diving gear, fire fighting apparatus and electric generators.

"OKHTENSKEY" CLASS TUGS

MB 24 **MB 25** **MB 26**

Displacement, tons	835
Dimensions, feet	134·5 wl; 143 oa × 34 × 15
Guns	1—3 in dp; 2—20 mm AA
Main engines	2 BM diesels; 2 electric motors. 2 shafts; 1 875 bhp = 14 knots
Oil fuel, tons	187
Complement	34

MB 24 *Photo A. Kull*

SIGNAL

Displacement, tons	680
Dimensions, feet	Speed = 14 knots

Launched in 1936. Fitted with powerful pump and other apparatus for salvage. In the Baltic. Other numbers reported are A 2, 480, 481, 490, 495, 515, 525, 580, 610, 612, 621 and 663. Salvage vessels are designated MSB.

TRANSPORTS

KAMCHATKA **MONGOL**

"Lake" class. Pennant numbers P-380 and P-242, respectively.

SHIM **OLGA** **USSURIJ** (ex-*Okhotsk*)
OB **SHILKA** **VISHERA**

Nos. P-247 (*Ob*), P 274 (*Shilka*), P-365 (*Ussurij*), P-379 (*Vishera*). *Olga* and *Ishim* are Coast Guard transports. *Ob* is 1 194-ton diesel electric Antarctic support ship.

The former Japanese cargo ships and military transports ex-*Hayasaki*, ex-*No. 13* and ex-*No. 137*, and the former Italian supply ship ex-*Montecucco*, ex KT 32, were deleted from the list in 1968, having been discarded on account of age or obsolescence.

MISSILE DETECTION SHIPS

KOSMONAUT VLADIMIR KOMAROV

Measurement, tons	8 000 approximately

Launched in 1966. Built at the Leningrad Shipyard. Designed for the Soviet Academy of Sciences as a research vessel to study higher layers of atmosphere in the tropical zone of the western part of the Atlantic Ocean. Prominent features of the ship are the unusual hull sponsons and the massive plastic spheres enclosing radar arrays. The ship is named in honour of the Soviet astronaut who died when his space craft crashed in 1967.

KOSMONAUT VLADIMIR KOMAROV *1969, Skyfotos*

KOSMONAUT VLADIMIR KOMAROV *1969, S. Breyer*

TRAINING SHIPS

2 "SEDOV" TYPE

KRUZENSTERN **SEDOV**

Barques. Built in 1921. Measurement: 3 064 tons gross. Employed as sail training ship for midshipmen, cadets and junior seamen. A photograph of *Sedov* appears in the 1968-69 edition.

TOVARISCH (ex-*Gorch Foch*)

Displacement, tons	1 350
Dimensions, feet	242·8 × 39·3 × 15
Guns,	2—20 mm AA
Main engines	MAN diesel; 1 shaft; 520 bhp = 8 knots
Oil fuel, tons	25
Radius, miles	3 500 at 8 knots
Complement	260

Barque. Ex-German training ship. Built by Blohm & Voss, Hamburg. Launched in 1933. Sail area: 2 150 sq yds. A photograph appears in the 1968-69 edition.

ENISEJ **PRAKTIKA** (ex-*Passat*) **TOBOL** **UCHEBA** (ex-*Mousson*).

Three masts. 300 tons displacement. In the Baltic. Sailing vessels for training cadets, boys and volunteers. There are about ten three-masted schooners of 300 tons with one square sail on the foremast of the same class as the *Pratika* and *Ucheba*, built in Finland. Th · are described as very nice little ships.

NYEMAN (ex-*Isar*, ex-*Puma*)

Displacement, tons	3 850
Dimensions, feet	319 × 45·5 × 13
Guns	4—37 mm
Main engines	Triple expansion; 2 shafts; 2 000 ihp = 12 knots

Built by Bremen-Vulcan. Launched in 1930. Converted merchant vessel. Former Submarine Depot Ship. Now a training ship in the Baltic. *Nyeman* is the name of a river in Western Russia.

Ex-**CRISTOFORO COLOMBO**, Ex-Z 18

Displacement, tons	2 787
Dimensions, feet	218 pp; 257 oa × 48·5 × 20·3
Sail area	18 700 sq ft
Main engines	2 Tosi diesels with electric drive to 2 Marelli motors. 2 shafts; 1 600 hp = 10 knots
Oil fuel, tons	103
Radius, miles	6 000 at 8 knots
Complement	280

Built at Castellammare. Launched on 4 Apr 1928. Assigned to the Soviet Navy by the Italian Peace Treaty. Delivered to the USSR in Feb 1949.

None of the above training ships are rated as naval ships.

The old training ship *Aurora* was deleted in 1963 as although she still exists as a prestige tourist relic (famous to the USSR as the cruiser from which the first round of the October Revolution was fired) she is no longer of military value.

SURVEY SHIPS

MICHAIL LOMONOSOV

Displacement, tons	5 960
Measurement, tons	3 897 gross; 1 195 net
Main engines	Speed = 13 knots

Built by Neptune, Rostock, in 1957. Operated not by the Navy but by the Academy of Science. Equipped with 16 laboratories. Carries a helicopter for survey.

MICHAIL LOMONOSOV *1968, Mr Michael D. J. Lennon*

VITYAZ

Displacement, tons	5 700
Main engines	Speed = 14·5 knots
Range, miles	18 400 at 14 knots
Complement	137 officers and men including 73 scientists

Oceanographic research ship. Equipped with 13 laboratories. Another non-nav oceanographic research ship, *Nereida*, was reported to be on operational servic in Apr 1965.

NEVELSKOYE

Displacement, tons	275 × 50 × 13

A naval hydrographic survey ship designed and built in the USSR

A2 and A

11 "NIKOLAI" ZUBOV CLASS

A. CHIRIKOV
A. VILKITSKIJ
BORIS DAVIDOV
F. BELLINSGAUSEN
F. LITKE
GAVRIL SARITSHEV
KHARITON LAPTEV
NIKOLAI ZUBOV
S. CHELYUSKIN
S. DEZHNEV
V. GOLOVNIN

Displacement, tons	2 674 standard; 3 021 full load
Dimensions, feet	295·2 × 42·7 × 15
Main engines	2 diesels; speed = 16·7 knots
Complement	108 to 120, including 70 scientists

"Nikolai Zubov" class, oceanographic research ships were built at Szczecin Shipyard, Poland in 1964. *Nikolai Zubov* visited London in 1965. Employed on survey in the Atlantic.

NIKOLAI ZUBOV

GAVRIL SARITSHEV *1966, courtesy Mr Michael D. J. Lennon*

AISBERG — OKEANOGRAF

Trawlers converted for surveying. Not in the Navy. Visited Glasgow in 1964.

"SAMARA" CLASS

AZIMUT
GIGROMETR
GLOBUS
GORIZONT
HIGROMETR
KOMPAS
P. MERKURYA
TROPIK
ZENIT

Measurement, tons	1 276 gross; 1 000 net

The sister ships of the "Samara" class have been built at Gdansk, Poland, since 1962 for hydrographic surveying and research.

HIGROMETR *1968, Mr Michael D. J. Lennon*

ZENIT *1968, Mr Michael D. J. Lennon*

3 "POLYUS" CLASS

BAIKAL — **BALKASH** — **POLYUS**

1 217 gross; 448 net

These ships of the "Polyus" class were built in East Germany in 1962-64.

AYTODOR

Measurement, tons

Built at Budapest. Naval survey supply (ex-merchant) ship of the "Keyla" class.

AYTODOR *1965, Mr Michael D. J. Lennon*

3 "MURMAN" CLASS

MURMAN — **OKEAN** — **OKHOTSK**

Displacement, tons	1 500 standard; 3 200 full load
Dimensions, feet	265·8 × 42·5 × 18·2
Guns	3—5·1 in; 2—3 in; 2 MG
Main engines	Triple expansion; 2 shafts; 2 400 ihp = 14 knots
Complement	160

Launched in 1937-38. In the Far East. Former minelayers converted into survey ships. A photograph of *Okhotsk* appears in the 1955-56 to 1965-66 editions.

"MOMA" CLASS

TAYMYR

Coastal survey ship reported to be in service in 1969.

BOOM DEFENCE VESSELS

18 "NEPTUN" TYPE

Displacement, tons	700
Dimensions, feet	170 × 36 × 12·5
Main engines	Oil fuel; speed = 12 knots

Boom defence vessels or netlayers built in 1957-60 by Neptun, Rostock.

"Neptun" Class No. 13

CABLE SHIPS

INGUL **JANA**

Displacement, tons	6 900
Measurement, tons	3 400 deadweight
Dimensions, feet	427·8 × 52·5 × 17
Main engines	Wärtsila Sulzer 6 MH 51 diesels; 4 300 shp = 14 knots
Complement	118

Built by Wärtsila, Helsingforsvarvet, Finland. Laid down on 10 Oct 1961 and 4 May 1962 and launched on 14 Apr 1962 and 1 Nov 1962 respectively.

JANA 1968

OILERS

4 "Uda" Type

DUNAY **TEREK** **SVIR**

Displacement, tons	circa 3 500
Dimensions, feet	344·5 × 47·2 × 13·1
Guns	6—25 mm AA (3 twin, 1 forward, 2 aft)
Main engines	Diesels; 2 shafts; speed = 13 knots

A new type of Soviet supply ships. Built in 1964-65. Ships vary.

"Uda" Type *1966, col Breyer*

"KONDA" CLASS

KONDA **ROSHOH**

V(B)-19

Oilers—*continued*

CRYPTON

Measurement, tons	1 769 gross; 559 full load

Naval fuel tanker. Built in 1965 when she went into Atlantic service.

CRYPTON *1965, Mr Michael D. J. Lennon*

"PEVEK" CLASS

OLEKMA **POLYARNIK** **ZOLOTOY ROG**

Length, feet:	400
Guns	8—45/57 mm (2 quadruple)

A type similar to the United States AOG gasolene carriers.

20 "Khobi" Class

KHOBI **SEYMA**

Of this class numerous units are reported to have been built from 1957 to 1959.

ALATYR **IRBIT** **JAHROMA** **KRASNOARMEETS** **KRASNOFLOTETS** **ROSSOSH**

Pennant Nos.: P-256 (*Irbit*), P-260 (*Polyarnik*), P-384 (*Rossash*) and P-335 (*Krasnoflotets*). The latter is a Coast Guard tanker.

"Kazbek" Class

VOLKHOV

Volkhov of "Leningrad" or "Kazbejk" class taken over by the Navy as an oiler. *Alatyr* has pennant number P 393.

NAVAL TANKER 1968

FLEET TUGS

KAPITAN V. FEDETOV

A large and powerful tug with a comprehensive array of radar and radio aerials.

There are numerous other tugs in the Fleet, see under Salvage Vessels on previous page, but numbers of tugs formerly listed have been deleted as they change or are suppressed from time to time according to geographical location or operational requirements.

KAPITAN V. FEDETOV 1963

OCEAN TUG 1968

ICEBREAKERS

2 PROJECTED. NUCLEAR POWERED

To be built from the same plans as *Lenin* but will have only two reactors, equal to 30 000 shp, and will be lighter by some 1 000 tons.

2 NEW CONSTRUCTION. NUCLEAR POWERED

ARKTIKA

Displacement, tons	25 000
Dimensions, feet	525 × 82 × 29
Aircraft	10 helicopters
Main engines	2 nuclear reactors; steam turbines; 30 000 shp = 25 knots

The largest icebreakers ever designed. Under construction. Equipped with hangar.

ARKTIKA (Sketch) *1967*

1 LARGE NUCLEAR POWERED TYPE

LENIN

Displacement, tons	16 000
Dimensions, feet	440 × 90·5 × 25
Aircraft	2 helicopters
Main engines	3 pressurised water-cooled nuclear reactors. 4 steam turbines; 3 shafts (no shaft in bow); 44 000 shp = 18 knots max

The world's first nuclear powered surface ship to put to sea. Built at the Kirov Elektrosia Works, Leningrad. Launched on 5 Dec 1957. Completed and commissioned on 15 Sep 1959. Reported to have accommodation for 1 000 personnel.
The nuclear reactors enable her to steam for 18 months without refuelling. Fuel consumption is reported to be only five ounces daily. The turbines were manufactured by the Kirov plant in Leningrad. Three propellers aft, but no forward screw.
With her reinforced prow she is able to force a 100 ft wide ice-free swathe and move continually through solid pack ice 8 feet thick at 3 to 4 knots.

LENIN *Added 1966*

VLADIVOSPOCK KIEV LENINGRAD MOSKVA MURMANSK

Displacement, tons	12 840 standard; 15 360 full load
Dimensions, feet	368·8 wl; 400·7 oa × 80·3 × 31 (normal); 34·5 max
Aircraft	2 helicopters
Main engines	8 Suplzer diesel-electric; 3 shafts; 22 000 shp = 18 knots
Oil fuel, tons	3 000
Radius, miles	20 000
Complement	145

Largest diesel-electric icebreakers in the world. Designed to stay at sea for a year without returning to base. Built by Wärtsilä-Koncernen A/B Sandvikens Skeppsdocka, Helsinki. The concave embrasure in the ship's stern is a housing for the bow of a following vessel when additional power is required. There is a landing deck for helicopters and hangar space for two machines. *Moskva* was launched on 10 Jan 1959 and completed in June 1960. *Leningrad* was laid down in Jan 1959. Launched on 24 Oct 1959, and completed in 1962. *Kiev* was completed in 1966. *Murmansk* was launched on 14 July 1967.
Eight generating units of 3 250 bhp each comprising eight main diesels of the Wärtsilä-Sulzer 9 MH 51 type which together have an output of 26 000 electric hp. Four separate machinery compartments. Two engine rooms, four propulsion units in each. Three propellers aft. No forward propeller. Centre propeller driven by electric motors of 11 000 hp and each of the side propellers by motors of 5 500 hp. Two Wärtsilä-Babcock & Wilcox boilers for heating and donkey work.
Moskva has four pumps which can move 480 metric tons of water from one side to the other in two minutes to rock the icebreaker and wrench her free of thick ice.

MOSKVA *1960, Wärtsilä-Koncernen A/B Sandvikens Skeppsdocka*

1 NEW CONSTRUCTION

It is reported that the Soviet Union is planning to order an icebreaker of 36 000 hp from the Wärtsila yard in Helsinki, Finland.

Name	Measurement	Launched	Completed
KAPITAN BELOUSOV	5 360 tons gross	1954	1955
KAPITAN MELECHOV	4 000 tons gross	19 Oct 1956	1957
KAPITAN VORONIN	3 416 tons gross	1955	1956

Displacement, tons	4 375 to 4 415 standard; 5 350 full load
Dimensions, feet	265 wl; 273 oa × 63·7 × 23
Main engines	Diesel-electric; 6 Polar 8 cyl; 10 500 bhp = 14·9 knots
Oil fuel, tons	740

Kapitan Belousov was laid down at the end of 1952 and completed in Sep 1954. All built by Wärtsilä-Koncernen A/B, Sandvikens Skeppsdocka, Helsinki. The ships have four screws, two forward under the forefoot and two aft.

KAPITAN BELOUSOV *1966*

POLLUKS (ex-*Pollux*)

Displacement, tons	4 500
Dimensions, feet	262·5 × 63 × 23
Main engines	Triple expansion; 6 000 ihp = 13 knots
Boilers	4

Built in the Netherlands by Smit, Rotterdam, in 1943. *Pollux* was German name.

ALIOSHA POPOVICH (ex-German *Eisvogel*)

Displacement, tons	2 090
Dimensions, feet	200 × 49·2 × 21·7
Main engines	2 Triple expansion; 3 200 ihp = 13·5 knots
Boilers	1

Former German icebreaker. Built by Aalborgs. Launched in 1941. In the White Sea.

ILIYA MUROMETS (ex-German *Eisbar*)

Displacement, tons	1 918
Dimensions, feet	180·5 × 49·5 × 21·7
Main engines	Triple expansion; 1 600 ihp = 15 knots
Boilers	1

Former German icebreaker. Built by Eriksberg, Gothenburg. Launched in 1941.

Name	Builders	Launched	Completed
ADMIRAL LAZAREV (ex-*Yosif Stalin*)	Baltic Works, Leningrad	14 Aug 1937	1939
LAZAR KAGANOVICH	Baltic Works, Leningrad	30 Apr 1937	1938
MIKOYAN (ex-*Otto Schmidt*)	Nikolayev	1938	1939

Displacement, tons	11 000
Measurement, tons	4 866 gross
Dimensions, feet	335·8 pp; 351 oa × 75·5 × 22
Aircraft	1 helicopter
Main engines	Triple expansion with diesel-electric propulsion for cruising; 3 shafts; 10 050 hp = 15·5 knots
Boilers	9
Fuel, tons	4 000 coal; and diesel oil
Complement	142

3 aircraft and 1 catapult were included in the design. All in the White Sea. *Admiral Makarov* (ex-*Vyacheslav Molotov*, was reported in 1967 being scrapped in Spain.

MIKOYAN after refit *1965, col Breyer*

Icebreakers—*continued*

PERESVET (ex-*Castor*)

Displacement, tons	5 150
Dimensions, feet	295·2 × 69 × 22
Main engines	Triple expansion; 3 shafts; 9 600 ihp = 15 knots
Boilers	4 Wagner

Former German icebreaker. Built by Schichau, Danzig. Launched in 1939. A photograph of *Peresvet* appears in the 1959-60 to 1966-67 editions.

SIBIRYAKOV (ex-*Jäakarhu*)

Displacement, tons	4 825
Dimensions, feet	246 × 63 × 21
Main engines	Triple expansion; 3 shafts; 9 200 ihp = 15 knots
Boilers	8; oil fuel

Launched by Smit, Rotterdam in 1926. Formerly Finnish. Appropriated by USSR.

SIBIRYAKOV *P. Bronsveld*

KRASSIN (ex-*Sviatogor*)

Displacement, tons	9 300
Measurement, tons	4 902 gross
Dimensions, feet	297 wl; 323·2 oa × 71 × 26
Main engines	3 sets triple expansion; 3 shafts; 10 000 ihp = 15 knots
Boilers	10 single-ended
Fuel, tons	3 200 coal
Complement	190

Built by Armstrong and launched in 1917. In the Baltic. Reported to have been converted into a floating museum at Archangel. Photograph in 1951-52 and earlier editions.

VLADIMIR ILYICH (ex-*Lenin*, ex-*Aleksandr Nevskii*)

Displacement, tons	6 260
Measurement, tons	3 828 gross
Dimensions, feet	273 wl; 281 oa × 64 × 19 (mean); 20·5 (max)
Main engines	3 sets triple expansion; 3 shafts; 8 000 ihp = 12 knots
Boilers	8
Fuel, tons	1 200 coal
Complement	122

Launched by Armstrong in 1917. Refitted on the Mersey in 1946-47. In the Baltic.

VLADIMIR ILYICH *Keith P. Lewis*

MALYGIN (ex-*Voima*)

Displacement, tons	2 070
Dimensions, feet	210·7 × 46·5 × 16·8
Main engines	Triple expansion; 1 shaft; 4 100 ihp = 13·5 knots

Former Finnish icebreaker. Built by Sandvikens and launched in 1917. In the Baltic. Photograph in the 1957-58 and earlier editions.

Most of the above icebreakers are immensely strong in framing and scantlings, with exceptionally thick plating, and decks strengthened for mounting guns in war.

Also reported are the icebreaker **PURGA** and the small icebreaker **VYUGA**.

LEDOKOL 1 **LEDOKOL 2** **LEDOKOL 3** **LEDOKOL 5** **LEDOKOL 6** **LEDOKOL 8**
VLADIMIR RUSANOV (ex-*Ledokol 7*) **VASILY POYARKOV** (ex-*Ledokol 4*)
YIRI LISYANSKY (ex-*Ledokol 8*)

Displacement, tons	2 500 standard
Measurement, tons	2 305 gross
Dimensions, feet	223 × 59 × 18
Main engines	3 shafts; speed = 13 knots

All built at Leningrad between 1961 and 1965. Divided between the Baltic, Black Sea and Far East. Name *V. Pronchischev* is also reported.

YIRI LISYANSKY *1968, Mr Michael D. L. Lennon*

VLADIMIR RUSANOV *Mr Michael D. J. Lennon*

DOBRINYA NIKITICH

Displacement, tons	2 460 standard
Measurement, tons	1 664 gross
Dimensions, feet	200 pp; 211 oa × 50·5 × 20
Main engines	Triple expansion; 2 shafts; 4 000 ihp = 14 knots
Boilers	6
Fuel, tons	370 coal

Built by Swan Hunter and Wigham Richardson, Ltd, Wallsend-on-Tyne, and launched in 1916. In the Black Sea. Photograph in the 1951-52 and earlier editions.

VOLYNETS (ex-*Suur Töll*, ex-*Vainamoinen*, ex-*Volynets*, ex-*Tsar Mikhail Fyodorovich*)

Displacement, tons	4 000
Dimensions feet	236·5 × 57 × 18·8
Main engines	3 sets triple expansion; 3 shafts; 5 800 ihp = 13·5 knots
Fuel, tons	800 coal

Former Estonian icebreaker. Launched in 1914. In the Baltic. Photograph in the 1957-58 and earlier editions.

SADKO (ex-*Lintrose*)

Displacement, tons	2 000
Measurement, tons	1 613 gross
Dimensions, feet	255 × 37·5 × 21
Main engines	Triple expansion; 3 500 ihp = 14 knots
Boilers	4

Built by Swan, Hunter and Wigham Richardson, Ltd, Wallsend-on-Tyne. Launched in 1913. Transferred from the Canadian Government in 1915. Sunk during the First World War off the Arctic coast of the USSR where she lay for many years until raised and refitted in the White Sea. Photograph in the 1957-58 and earlier editions.

GEORGII SEDOV (ex-*Beothic*)

Displacement, tons	3 217
Measurement, tons	1 383-1 588 gross
Dimensions, feet	240·5 × 36 × 16·5
Main engines	Triple expansion; 3 000 ihp = 13·5 knots
Fuel, tons	500 coal

Built in 1909 by D. & W. Henderson & Co. Purchased in 1915. In the White Sea. Sister ship *Vladimir Rusanov* (ex-*Bonaventure*) was scrapped.

Davidov (ex-*Krasnyi Oktyabr*, ex-*Nadyazhnyi*) was discarded in 1959 when *Fyodor Litke* (ex-*Kanada*, ex-*Earl Grey*) was also scrapped, *Vladimir Rusano* (ex *Bonaventure*) was scrapped about 1963, and *Yermak* in 1965. *Sevmorput*, *Stepan Makarov*, *Taimyr*, *Montcalm*, and ex-*Krisjans Valdemaras* were deleted from the list in 1969 as no longer operational or unfit for further service on account of age or obsolescence.

URUGUAY

Administration

Inspector General of the Navy:
Rear Admiral Pedro Torres Negreira

Diplomatic Representation

Naval Attaché in Washington:
Captain Eduardo A. Laffitte

Mercantile Marine

Lloyd's Register of Shipping
42 vessels of 131 123 tons gross

DESTROYER ESCORTS

Name	*No.*	*Builders*	*Launched*	*Completed*
ARTIGAS (ex-USS *Bronstein DE* 189)	DE 2	Federal SB & DD Co, Pt. Newark	14 Nov 1943	13 Dec 1943
URUGUAY (ex-USS *Baron, DE* 166)	DE 1	Federal SB & DD Co Pt. Newark	9 May 1943	5 July 1943

2 Ex-US DESTROYER ESCORT TYPE (ESCORT VESSELS, DE) "BOSTWICK CLASS

Displacement, tons	1 240 standard; 1 900 full load
Length, feet (*metres*)	306 (*93·3*) oa
Beam, feet (*metres*)	37 (*11·3*)
Draught, feet (*metres*)	17 (*5·2*)
Guns, dual purpose	3—3 in (*76 mm*)
Guns, AA	2—40 mm (see *Gunnery* notes)
A/S	Hedgehog; 8 DCT; 1 DCR (see *Torpedo Tubes* notes)
Main engines	Diesel-electric 6 000 bhp; 2 shafts
Speed, knots	19
Radius, miles	8 300 at 14 knots
Oil fuel (tons)	315 (*95* per cent)
Complement	159

ARTIGAS *Uruguayan Navy, Official*

Former United States destroyer escorts of the "Bostwick" class, transferred to Uruguay in 1951.

GUNNERY. Formerly also mounted ten 20 mm anti-aircraft guns, but these have been removed.

TORPEDO TUBES. The theee 21-inch torpedo tubes in a triple mounting, originally carried, were suppressed.

APPEARANCE. Practically identical, but *Uruguay* can be distinguished by the absence of a mainmast, whereas *Artigas* has a diminutive pole mast aft.

URUGUAY *Uruguayan Navy, Official*

FRIGATE

1 Ex-BRITISH CORVETTE TYPE TRAINING SHIP (*BUQUE ESCUELA*) **"CASTLE" CLASS**

MONTEVIDEO (ex-HMCS *Arnprior*, ex-HMS *Rising Castle*) PF 1

Displacement, tons	1 010 standard; 1 600 full load
Length, feet (*metres*)	251·8 (*76·7*)
Beam, feet (*metres*)	36·7 (*11·2*)
Draught, feet (*metres*)	17·5 (*5·3*) max
Guns, dual purpose	1—3 in (*76 mm*)
Guns, AA	2—40 mm; 4—20 mm
A/S	Hedgehog; 4 DCT; 1 DCR
Boilers	2 water tube
Main engines	Triple expansion, 190 rpm 2 750 ihp
Speed, knots	17
Radius, miles	5 400 at 9·5 knots
Oil fuel (tons)	480 max
Complement	90

Former successively British and Canadian "Castle" class corvette (frigate). Employed as a training ship.

MONTEVIDEO *Uruguayan Navy, Official*

ESCORT

COMMANDANTE PEDRO CAMPBELL, MSF 1 (ex-USS *Chickadee, MSF* 59)

Displacement, tons	890 standard; 1 250 full load
Dimensions, feet	215 wl; 221·2 oa × 32·2 × 10·8
Guns	1—3 in, 50 cal dp; 2—40 mm AA
Main engines	Diesel electric; 2 shafts; 3 118 bhp = 18 knots
Complement	105

Former United States fleet minesweeper of the "Auk" class. Built by Defoe B. & M. Works. Launched on 20 July 1942. Transferred on loan and commissioned at San Diego, Calif on 18 Aug 1966. Employed as PCE, escort patrol vessel, or corvette.

SURVEY SHIP

CAPITAN MIRANDA AGS 10

Displacement, tons	516 standard; 549 full load
Dimensions, feet	148 pp; 179 oa × 26 × 10·5
Main engines	1 MAN diesel; 500 bhp = 11 knots
Oil fuel, tons	37
Complement	52

Built by Sociedad Española de Construccion Naval, Matagorda, Cadiz. Launched in 1930. Used as general utility tender. A photograph appears in the 1932 to 1957-58 editions.

PATROL VESSELS

1 Ex-US PC TYPE

MALDONADO (ex-USS *PC* 1234) PC 1 (ex-B 1)

Displacement, tons	280 standard; 450 full load
Dimensions, feet	165 pp; 170 wl; 173·7 oa × 23 × 10·8
Guns	1—3 in dp; 1—40 mm; 3—20 mm
A/S weapons	1 MT; 4 DCT
Main engines	2 GM diesels; 2 shafts; 3 750 bhp = 19 knots
Complement	65

Former United States submarine chaser. Built in New York. Launched on 3 Apr 1943. Transferred from the US Navy in 1944.

MALDONADO *Uruguayan Navy, Official*

2 "PAYSANDU" CLASS

RIO NEGRO PR 3 **SALTO** PR 2

Displacement, tons	150 standard; 180 full load
Dimensions, feet	137 × 18 × 10
Guns	1—40 mm AA
Main engines	2 Germania diesels; 1 000 bhp = 17 knots
Oil fuel, tons	18
Radius, miles	4 800 at 10·7 knots
Complement	26

Training ships. Built by Cantieri Navali Riuniti, Ancona, Italy. Launched on 22 Aug 1935 and 11 Aug 1935, respectively. Sister ship *Paysandu* was stricken in 1963.

RIO NEGRO *courtesy Dr Giorgio Arra*

RESCUE LAUNCH
(*Lancha de Rescate*)

AR 1

Displacement, tons	25 standard
Dimensions, feet	63 × 15 × 3·8
Guns	4 MG
Main engines	2 sets Hall-Scott Defender engines 1 260 bhp = 33·5 knots
Radius, miles	600 at 15 knots
Complement	8

British type rescue motor launch. Launched on 4 July 1944. A photograph of AR 1 appears in the 1953-54 to 1957-58 editions.

OILER

PRESIDENTE ORIBE AO 9

Measurement, tons	17 920 gross; 28 267 deadweight
Dimensions, feet	587·2 pp; 620 oa × 84·3 × 33
Main engines	1 Ishikawajima turbine; 12 500 shp = 16·75 knots
Boilers	2 Ishikawajima-Harima Foster Wheeler type
Radius, miles	16 100 at 16 knots
Complement	76

Built by Ishikawajima-Harima Ltd, Japan. Delivered to the Uruguayan Navy on 22 Mar 1962.

PRESIDENTE ORIBE *Uruguayan Navy, Official*

TUG

YTL 589 (ex-US No.)

Transferred from the United States Navy in Sep 1965 under the Military Aid Programme

VIETNAM (NORTH)

Administration

Commander-in-Chief of the Navy: Rear Admiral Ta Xuan Thu

Strength of the Fleet

3 Patrol Vessels	4 Minesweeping Boats
15 Motor Torpedo Boats	30 Patrol Craft
28 Motor Gunboats	24 Landing Craft

Personnel

1969: 3 000 (270 officers and 2 730 men)

Mercantile Marine

Lloyd's Register of Shipping: 4 vessels of 2 255 tons gross

PATROL VESSELS

3 USSR "SOI" TYPE

Displacement, tons	215 light; 250 normal
Dimensions, feet	138 pp; 147 oa × 20 × 10 max
Guns	4—25 mm (2 twin mountings)
A/S weapons	4 ahead throwing rocket launchers; 2 DCT
Main engines	3 diesels; 3 500 bhp = 28 knots
Complement	30

Four submarine chasers of Soviet "SOI" type transferred to North Vietnam, two in 1960-61 and two in 1964-65, but one was sunk by US Navy aircraft 1 Feb 1966.

TORPEDO BOATS

3 USSR "P 6" TYPE

Displacement, tons	50 standard
Dimensions, feet	82 × 16·8 × 5·5
Guns	4—25 mm AA (2 twin)
Tubes	2—21 in (single)
Mines	4
Main engines	Speed = 40 knots

Wooden hulled MTBs of the "P 6" class built in China and transferred in 1957 and 1964.

12 USSR "P 4" TYPE

Displacement, tons	50 standard
Dimensions, feet	85·5 × 20 × 6
Guns	4—25 mm AA (2 twin)
Main engines	Diesels; 2 000 bhp = 42 knots

Aluminium hulled MTBs transferred from USSR in 1961 and 1964. A fast patrol boat, PTF 1, was also reported.

MOTOR GUNBOATS

4 Ex-CHINESE "SHANGHAI" TYPE

Displacement, tons	100 full load
Dimensions, feet	83·5 × 20 × 6
Guns	4—37 mm (2 twin); 2—12·7 mm
A/S weapons	8 depth charges
Main engines	4 diesels; 4 800 bhp = 40 knots
Complement	17

Received from the People's Republic of China (Communist) Navy in May 1966.

24 USSR "SWATOW" TYPE

Displacement, tons	67 full load
Dimensions, feet	83·5 × 20 × 6
Guns	2—37 mm; 2—20 mm
A/S weapons	8 depth charges
Main engines	4 diesels; 4 800 bhp = 40 knots
Complement	17

30 "Swatow" class motor gunboats built in China were transferred in 1958, and 20 in 1964 to replace those lost in action. Pennant numbers run in a 600 series.

MINESWEEPING BOATS

4 PATROL TYPE

Four vessels for sweeping, patrol and general purpose duties have been reported.

PATROL CRAFT

30 MOTOR LAUNCH TYPES

Reported to have been incorporated into the North Vietnam Navy before May 1966.

SERVICE TENDERS

10 GENERAL UTILITY TYPES

Tenders and launches commandeered to serve the fleet and naval establishments.

7 US LSM TYPE

Displacement, tons	743
Guns	2—40 mm AA (1 twin); 4—20 mm AA
Speed	12 knots

5 US LSSL TYPE

Displacement, tons	250
Guns	1—3 in; 4—40 mm AA; 4—20 mm AA
Speed	14 knots

There are also reported to be 5 of LCI/L31L, 1 of LCT(6) and 6 of LCT(7) types.

VENEZUELA

Administration

Commander General of the Navy:
(*Chief of Naval Operations*)
Rear-Admiral Jesus Carbonnell Izquierdo
Chief of Naval Staff:
Rear-Admiral Luis Ramirez Aranda

Personnel

1969: 3 500 naval officers and men

4 000 Marine Corps

Diplomatic Representation

Naval Attaché in London:
Captain Jaime Pirela Luengo

Naval Attaché in Washington:
Rear-Admiral Miguel Benatuil Guastini

Strength Of the Fleet

1 Submarine (Diesel Powered)
3 Destroyers
6 Fast Frigates (Light Destroyers)
10 Patrol Vessels (Submarine Chasers)
1 Large Landing Ship
4 Medium Landing Ships
23 Support Ships and Service Craft

Mercantile Marine

Lloyd's Register of Shipping:
89 vessels of 350,591 tons gross

SUBMARINES

1 Ex-US "BALAO" CLASS

CARITE S 11 (ex-USS *Tilefish*, SS 307)

Displacement, tons	1 526 standard; 1 816 surface; 2 425 submerged
Length, feet (*metres*)	312 (*91·8*) oa
Beam, feet (*metres*)	27 (*8·2*)
Draught, feet (*metres*)	17 (*5·2*)
Torpedo tubes	10—21 in (*533 mm*), 6 bow, 4 stern
Main engines	Diesels, 6 400 bhp, 2 shafts Electric motors, 4 600 hp
Speed, knots	20 on surface; 10 submerged
Radius, miles	12 000 at 10 knots
Oil fuel (tons)	300
Complement	80

Former United States submarine of the "Balao" class. Built by Mare Island Naval Shipyard, California. Launched on 25 Oct 1943. Commissioned on 28 Dec 1943. Purchased by Venezuela in 1960 after a three to four months overhaul in the United States. Transferred from the US Navy at San Francisco on 4 May 1960. Overhauled in San Francisco Navy Yard in 1962.

TRANSFER. The transfer of a second submarine by the USA to Venezuela was approved by the US House Armed Service Committee in Aug 1965. but has now been rescinded.

PHOTOGRAPHS. A starboard bow surface view of *Carite* appears in the 1962-63 to 1964-65 editions, and a port quarter oblique aerial view in the 1965-66 to 1968-69 editions.

CARITE *1969, Venezuelan Navy, Official*

DESTROYERS

3 "NUEVA ESPARTA" CLASS

Name	*No.*	*Builders*	*Laid down*	*Launched*	*Completed*
ARAGUA	D 31	Vickers Ltd, Barrow	29 June 1953	27 Jan 1955	14 Feb 1956
NUEVA ESPARTA	D 11	Vickers Ltd, Barrow	24 July 1951	19 Nov 1952	8 Dec 1953
ZULIA	D 21	Vickers Ltd, Barrow	24 July 1951	29 June 1953	15 Sep 1954

Displacement, tons	2 600 standard; 3 300 full load
Length, feet (*metres*)	384 (*117·0*) wl; 402 (*122·5*) oa
Beam, feet (*metres*)	43 (*13·1*)
Draught, feet (*metres*)	19 (*5·8*)
Guns, dual purpose	6—4·5 (*114 mm*), 3 twin
Guns, AA	16—40 mm, 8 twin
A/S	2 DCT; 2 DC racks (Squids in D 11 and D21)
Torpedo tubes	3—21 in (*533 mm*), triple
Boilers	2 Yarrow
Main engines	Parsons geared turbines 50 000 shp; 2 shafts
Speed, knots	34·5
Radius	5 000 miles at 11 knots
Complement	254 (18 officers, 236 men)

All built in Great Britain by Vickers, Barrow-in-Furness. *Nueva Esparta* and *Zulia* were ordered in 1950. Cost of these first two ships was £5 000 000. Air conditioned. Two engine rooms and two boiler rooms served by a single uptake. The 4·5 inch guns are fully automatic. *Nueva Esparta* and *Zulia* were refitted at the Palmers Hebburn Works of Vickers in May—Dec 1959, and modernised at New York Navy Yard in 1960 to improve anti-submarine and anti-aircraft capabilities. *Aragua* was refitted by Palmers Hebburn in 1964-65, *Nueva Esparta* was again refitted at Cammell Laird in 1968-69.

A photograph of *Nueva Esparta* appears in the 1962-63 to 1965-66 editions.

ARAGUA *1969, Venezuelan Navy, Official*

ZULIA ***1966, Venezuelan Navy, Official***

FAST FRIGATES

6 "ALMIRANTE CLEMENTE" CLASS

(Light Destroyer Type)

Name	No.	Laid down	Launched	Completed
ALMIRANTE CLEMENTE	D 12	5 May 1954	12 Dec 1954	1956
ALMIRANTE JOSÉ GARCIA	D 33	12 Dec 1954	12 Oct 1956	1957
ALMIRANTE BRION	D 23	12 Dec 1954	4 Sep 1955	1957
GENERAL JOSÉ DE AUSTRIA	D 32	12 Dec 1954	15 July 1956	1957
GENERAL JOSÉ TRINIDAD MORAN	D 22	5 May 1954	12 Dec 1954	1956
GENERAL JUAN JOSÉ FLORES	D 13	5 May 1954	7 Feb 1955	1956

Displacement, tons	1 300 standard; 1 500 full load
Length, feet (*metres*)	325·11 (*99·1*) oa
Beam, feet (*metres*)	35·5 (*10·8*)
Draught, feet (*metres*)	12 (*3·4*)
Guns, dual purpose	4—4 in (*102 mm*) 2 twin
Guns, AA	4—40 mm; 8—20 mm, modified group 40 mm only
A/S	2 Squid, 4DCT and 2 racks in original group; 1 Lanciabas, 4 DCT and 2 racks in modified group
Torpedo tubes	3—21 in (*533 mm*) triple original group only
Boilers	2 Foster Wheeler
Main engines	2 sets geared turbines 24 000 shp; 2 shafts
Speed, knots	34
Radius, miles	3 500 at 15 knots
Oil fuel (tons)	228
Complement	162 (12 officers, 150 men)

All built in Italy by Ansaldo, Leghorn. The first three were ordered in 1953. Three more were ordered in 1954. Aluminium alloys were widely employed in the building of all superstructure. All the ships are fitted with Denny-Brown fin stabilisers and air conditioned throughout the living and command spaces.

MODERNISATION. *Almirante José Garcia, Almirante Brion* and *General José de Austria* were refitted by Ansaldo, Leghorn, in 1962 to improve their anti-submarine and anti-aircraft capabilities, and this group are known as "Modified Almirante Clemente" type. *Almirante Clemente* and *General José Trinidad Moran* are being refitted by the Cammell Laird/Plessey group during 1969.

GUNNERY. The 4 inch anti-aircraft guns are fully automatic and radar controlled.

PHOTOGRAPHS. A photograph of *Almirante Clemente* appears in the 1957-58 edition, of *General Juan José Flores* in the 1957-58 to 1961-62 editions, of *General José de Austria* in the 1962-63 to 1964-65 editions, of *General José Trinidad Moran* in the 1962-63 to 1965-66 editions.

"FLOWER" CLASS

Of the former Canadian "Flower" type frigates *Carabobo* (ex-*Kamsack*) was lost on passage from Canada. *Libertad* (ex-*Battleford*) ran aground off western Venezuela on 12 Apr 1949 and was discarded, *Independencia* (ex-*Dunvegan*) was stricken from the Navy list in 1953, *Federacion* (ex-*Amherst*) was stricken in 1956, and *Constitucion* (ex-*Algoma*), *Patria* (ex-*Oakville*) and *Victoria* (ex-*Wetaskiwin*) were officially deleted from the Navy List in 1962.

GENERAL JUAN JOSÉ FLORES — *1966, Venezuelan Navy, Official*

ALMIRANTE JOSE GARCIA (modified group) — *1969, Venezuelan Navy, Official*

PATROL VESSELS

ALBATROS	(ex-USS PC 582) P-04	**GAVIOTA**	(ex-USS PC 619) P-10
ALCATRAZ	(ex-USS PC 565) P-03	**PETREL**	(ex-USS PC 1176) P-05
CALAMAR	(ex-USS PC 566) P-02	**PULPO**	(ex-USS PC 465) P-07
CAMARON	(ex-USS PC 483) P-08	**MEJILLON**	(ex-USS PC 487) P-01
CARACOL	(ex-USS PC 1170) P-06	**TOGOGO**	(ex-USS PC 484) P-09

Displacement, tons	280 standard; 430 full load
Dimensions, feet	170 wl; 173·7 oa × 23 × 10·8
Guns	1—3 in dp; 2—40 mm AA twin; 2—20 mm AA
A/S weapons	Provision for 4 DCT
Main engines	2 Fairbanks-Morse diesels; 2 shafts; 2 800 bhp = 20 knots
Complement	65

Mejillon was refitted and overhauled by Diques y Astilleros Nacionalis, Venezuela, prior to commissioning in the Venezuelan Navy, and from 1962 onwards more ships of this type underwent similar preparation to join the fleet. Altogether twelve of these former United States submarine chasers of the steel-hulled "173-ft" type were purchased from the USA in Oct 1960 for anti-smuggling patrols, namely:—*Cooperstown* PC 484, *Dalhart* PC 619, *Edenton* PC 1077, *Gilmer* PC 565, *Honesdale* PC 566, *Larchmont* PC 487, *Lenoir* PC 582, *Minden* PC 1176, *Paragould* PC 465, *Rolla* PC 483, *Tarrytown* PC 1252 and *Tooell* PC 572, and with these the Navy is assuming Coast Guard functions.

CALAMAR — *1969, Venezuelan Navy, Official*

MEDIUM LANDING SHIPS

LOS FRAILES T 15 (ex-USS *LSM* 544) **LOS ROQUES** T 14 (ex-USS *LSM* 543)
LOS MONJES T 13 (ex-USS *LSM* 548) **LOS TESTIGOS** T 16 (ex-USS *LSM* 545)

Displacement, tons	743 beaching; 1 095 full load
Dimensions, feet	196·5 wl; 203·5 oa × 34·5 × 8·3
Guns	1—40 mm AA; 4—20 mm AA
Main engines	Direct drive diesels; 2 shafts; 2 800 bhp = 12 knots
Radius	9 000 miles at 11 knots
Complement	59

All built by Brown Shipbuilding Co, Houston, Texas, in 1945. (The former United States medium landing ships LSM 370, LSM 542, LSM 543, LSM 544, LSM 545 and LSM 548 were sold to Venezuela under MAP in Aug 1958, but only the latter four have been commissioned in the Venezuelan Navy).

LOS TESTIGOS — *1962, Venezuelan Navy, Official*

COAST GUARD VESSELS

8 "RIO" CLASS

RIO APURE **RIO CABRIALES** **RIO GUARICO** **RIO NEVERI**
RIO ARAUCA **RIO CARONI** **RIO NEGRO** **RIO TUY**

Displacement, tons	38
Dimensions, feet	82 × 15 × 4
Main engines	2 Mercedes-Benz MB 820 Bb diesels; 1 400 rpm; 1 350 bhp = 27 knots; 24—25 knots cruising

All built by the Chantiers Navales de l'Estereles, Cannes, during 1954-56.

RIO CABRIALES *1956 Venezuelan Navy, Official*

RIO SANTO DOMINGO

Displacement, tons	40
Dimensions, feet	70 × 15 × 6
Main engines	2 GM diesels; 1 250 bhp = 24 knots

RIO TURBIO

Displacement, tons	40
Dimensions, feet	81·3 × 15 × 7·5
Main engines	4 GM diesels; 880 bhp = 20 knots

GOLFO DE CARIACO

Displacement, tons	37
Dimensions, feet	65 × 18 × 9
Main engines	Diesels; speed = 19 knots

TORBES (ex-*Felipe Santiago Esteves*, LC 12, ex-*Brion* CS 2) LA 12

Displacement, tons	47
Dimensions, feet	83 × 16 × 4
Guns	1—20 mm; 4 DCT
Main engines	2 petrol engines; 2 shafts; 1 200 bhp = 15 knots
Complement	10

Launched in 1937. Ex-US Coast Guard cutter 56196. Acquired in 1944. Of wooden construction. *Brion* was renamed *Felipe Santiago Esteves* in 1957 when LC pennant number was allocated and renamed *Torbes* No. LA 12, in 1962.

The survey launch *Torbes*, and the repair launch BT 1 were officially stricken from the list in 1962. *Caribe* was scrapped in 1956.

Antonio Diaz LC 11 (ex-CS 1, ex-56193), *Arismendi* LC 14 (ex-CS 4, ex-56194) and *Briceno Mendez* LC 13 (ex-CS 3, ex-56195) were stricken in 1960.

TRANSPORTS

PUNTA CABANA T 17 **T 19**

Three small troop carriers of about 3 000 tons with a speed of 17 knots are reported for the Army.

LAS AVES (ex-*Dos de Diciembre*) T 12

Guns	4—20 mm (2 twin)
Main engines	2 diesels; 2 shafts; 1 600 bhp = 15 knots
Radius, miles	2 600 at 11 knots

Launched by Chantiers Dubigeon, Nantes-Chantenay, France, in Sept. 1954 Light transport for naval personnel. Originally named *Dos de Diciembre*. Redesignated T 12 in 1958. Renamed *Las Aves* in 1961.

LAS AVES *Venezuelan Navy, Official*

SURVEY SHIPS

3 "PUERTO" CLASS

PUERTO DE NUTRIAS (ex-USS *Tunxis*, AN 90) H-01
PUERTO MIRANDA (ex-USS *Waxsaw*, AN 91) H 02
PUERTO SANTO (ex-USS *Marietta*, AN 82) H-03

Displacement, tons	650 standard; 785 full load
Dimensions, feet	146 wl; 168·5 oa × 33·9 × 10·2 max
Guns	1—20 mm AA
Main engines	Bush-Sulzer diesel-electric; 1 shaft; 1 500 bhp = 12 knots
Complement	46

Former US Navy netlayers of the "Cohoes" class. *Puerto Santo* was built by Commercial Iron Works, Portland, Oregon. Laid down on 17 Feb 1945 and launched on 27 Apr 1945. Transferred on loan from USA in Jan 1961 under MAP and converted into a hydrographic survey vessel and buoy tender by the United States Coast Guard Yard, Curtis Bay, Maryland, in Feb 1962. All ships originally carried one 3-inch 50 cal dual purpose gun. *Puerto du Nutrias* and *Puerto Miranda* were built by Zenith Bridge Co, Duluth, Minn, launched in 1944 and completed in 1945. They were leased-loaned to Venezuela in 1963 under the Military Aid Programme. A photograph of *Puerto Santo* appears in the 1966-67 and 1968-69 editions.

TRANSPORT LANDING SHIPS

Ex-ARL TYPE

GUAYANA T 18 (ex-USS *Quirinus*, ARL 39, ex-*LST* 1151)

Displacement, tons	1 625 light; 3 960 trials; 4 100 full load
Dimensions, feet	316 wl; 328 oa × 50 × 11·2 max
Guns	8—40 mm AA (two quadruple mountings)
Main engines	GM diesels; 2 shafts; 1 800 bhp = 11·6 knots
Complement	21 officers, 60 men

Former US Navy landing craft repair ship. Built by Chicago Bridge and Iron Co, Seneca, Illinois. Laid down on 3 Mar 1945. Loaned to Venezuela in June 1962 and now used as a transport in the Venezuelan Navy, it is officially stated.

GUAYANA *1969, Venezuelan Navy, Official*

TUGS

FELIPE LARRAZABAL R 11 (ex-USS *Tolowa*, ATF 116)

Displacement, tons	1 235 standard; 1 675 full load
Dimensions, feet	195 wl; 205 oa × 38·5 × 15·5 max
Guns	1—3 in; 4—40 mm AA; 2—20 mm AA
Main engines	4 diesels with electric drive; 3 300 bhp = 16·5 knots
Radius	11 500 miles at 12 knots
Complement	85

Former United States fleet ocean tug of the "Apache" class. Built by United Engineering Co, Alameda, California. Laid down on 28 July 1943, launched on 17 May 1944, and completed on 26 Dec 1944. Transferred on loan from the US Navy in Feb 1962. The former tug *Felipe Larrazabal* (ex-USS *Discoverer*, ex-USCG *Auk* AM 38) was stricken in 1962 and *Esteban Rojas*, *Dina* and *Caracas* in 1958.

FELIPE LARRAZABAL *1962, Venezuelan Navy, Official*

FERNANDO GOMEZ (ex-USS *Dadley*, YTM 744, ex-*Diana*, ex-US *Army* ST 873) **R 12**

Displacement, tons	161
Dimensions, feet	80 × 19 × 8
Main engines	Clark diesel, 6-cyl, 315 rpm; 380 bhp = 15 knots
Complement	10

A photograph of this tug appears in the 1952-53 to 1957-58 editions.

GENERAL JOSE FELIX RIBAS R 13 (ex-USS *Oswegatchie*, YTM 778, ex-YTB 515)

Large harbour tug. Transferred on 4 June 1965 at San Diego, Calif. There are also medium harbour tugs ex-USS *Sassacus* (YTM-193) and TYM 385 loaned by USA.

VIETNAM

Administration

Commander-in-Chief:
Rear Admiral Nguyen Nuc Van

Chief of Naval Operations:
Commodore Tran Van Chon

Strength of the Fleet

6	Escorts	10	Landing Ships
2	Patrol Vessels	21	Landing Craft
3	Minesweepers	12	Mine Launchers
20	Gunboats	20	Auxiliaries

Diplomatic Representation

Naval, Military and Air Attaché in Washington:
Colonel Nguyen Vinh Xuan

Personnel

1969: 16 000 officers and men

Mercantile Marine

Lloyd's Register of Shipping: 23 vessels of 15 526 tons gross

ESCORTS

DONG DA II (ex-USS *Crestview, PCE* 895) HQ 07
NGOC HOI (ex-USS *Brattleboro, EPCER* 852) HQ 12

Displacement, tons	640 standard; 903 full load
Dimensions, feet	180 wl; 184·5 oa × 33 × 9·5
Guns	1—3 in, 50 cal dp; 6—20 mm AA
Main engines	GM diesels; 2 shafts; 2 000 bhp = 15 knots
Complement	7 officers, 83 men

Dong Da II was built by the Willamette Iron and steel Corp, Portland, Oregon. Laid down on 2 Dec 1942, launched on 18 May 1943, completed on 30 Oct 1944. Served successively in the US Navy as escort vessel, submarine chaser, weather ship, reserve training ship and anti-submarine warfare evaluation ship. Transferred at Philadelphia Naval base on 29 Nov 1961 and renamed *Dong Da II*. *Ngoc Hoi* was built by Pullman Standard Car Mfg Co, Chicago, laid down on 28 Oct 1943, launched on 1 Mar 1944, completed on 26 May 1944. Formerly on experimental rescue, escort ship in the US Navy, she was transferred on 11 July 1966.

DONG DA II — *1963, Vietnamese Navy, Official*

CHI LANG II (ex-USS *Gayety, MSF* 239) HQ 08 19 Mar 1944
KU HOA (ex-USS *Sentry, MSF* 299) HQ 09 15 Aug 1943
NHUT TAO (ex-USS *Serene, MSF* 300) HQ 10 31 Oct 1943
CHI LINH (ex-USS *Shelter, MSF* 301) HQ 11 14 Nov 1943

Displacement, tons	650 standard; 945 full load
Dimensions, feet	180 wl; 184·5 oa × 33 × 9·8
Guns	1—3 in, 50 cal dp; 2—40 mm AA; 8—20 mm AA (4 twin)
A/S weapons	2 DCT
Main engines	Diesels; 2 shafts; 1 710 bhp = 14 knots
Complement	7 officers, 83 men

Built by Winslow Marine Railway and Shipbuilding Co, Winslow, Washington. Laid down on 14 Nov 1943, 16 May 1943, 8 Aug 1943 and 16 Aug 1943, and completed on 23 Sep 1944, 30 May 1944, 24 June 1944 and 9 July 1944 respectively. Launch dates above. *Gayety* was transferred in June 1962 and renamed *Chi Lang II*. *Sentry* was converted into a patrol vessel by the Sun Shipbuilding and Dry Dock Co, Chester, Pennsylvania, the minesweeping gear replaced by increased depth charge storage, and transferred at Philadelphia, Pa in Aug 1962. *Serene* and *Shelter* were transferred on 16 Jan 1964. Employed as escort patrol vessels, not as minesweepers.

KY HOA — *1963, Vietnamese Navy, Official*

PATROL VESSELS

TUY DONG (ex-*Trident*, ex-USS *PC* 1143) HQ 04 25 Sep 1943
VAN DON (ex-*Anacortes, PC* 1569) HQ 06 9 Dec 1944

Displacement, tons	280 standard; 380 normal; 450 full load
Dimensions, feet	170 wl; 173·7 oa × 23 × 10·8
Guns	1—3 in dp; 1—40 mm; 4—20 mm AA
A/S weapons	2 DC; 2 RL
Main engines	Diesel; 2 shafts; 2 800 bhp = 19 knots
Complement	6 officers, 54 men

Tuy Dong was built by Defoe SB Corp, Bay City, Mich, *Van Don* by Letham D. Smith SB Co. Launch dates above. Laid down on 17 Apr 1943 and 26 Sep 1944 respectively, and completed on 16 May 1944 and 14 Mar 1945. *Tuy Dong* is a former French *escorteur cotier* transferred in 1956. *Dan Don* was transferred at Seattle, Washington, on 23 Nov 1960. *Dong Da* (ex-French *Ardent*, ex-USS PC 1167) was stricken in 1961 and *Chi Lang* (ex-French *Mousquet* P633, ex-USS PC 1144) in 1961, their names allocated to larger vessels, *Tay Ket* HQ 05 (ex-French *Glaive*, ex-USS PC 1146) and *Van Kiep* HQ 02 (ex-French *Intrepide*, ex-USS PC 1130) on 10 July 1965 and 1 July 1965, respectively.

VAN DON — *1966, Vietnamese Navy, Official*

MOTOR GUNBOATS

20 Ex-US PGM TYPE

DINH HAI	HQ 610	**KIM QUI**	HQ 605	**THAI BINH**	HQ 612
HOA LU	HQ 608	**MAY RUT**	HQ 606	**THI TU**	HQ 613
KEO NGUA	HQ 604	**MINH HOA**	HQ 602	**TIEN MOI**	HQ 601
KIEN VANG	HQ 603	**NAM DU**	HQ 607	**TO YEN**	HQ 609
		PHU DU	HQ 600	**TRUONG SA**	HQ 611
					HQ 614

Displacement, tons	95 standard; 143 full load
Dimensions, feet	101 wl; 110 oa × 21 × 6
Guns	1—40 mm AA; 2—20 mm AA (1 twin); 2 MG
Main engines	Diesels, 2 shafts; 1 900 bhp = 16 knots

Built in the United States, the first ten, HQ 600-609, five by J. M. Martinac Shipbuilding Corp, Tacoma, Washington (the last of which, PGM 63 was delivered in 1963), and five by Marinette Marine Corp, Wisconsin. The US hull numbers of the above names were PGM 69, 62, 68, 67, 59, 60, 66, 61, 64, 72, 73, 65, 63, 70, respectively.

Thai Binh (ex-PGM 72), *Thi Tu* (ex-PGM 73) and HQ 614 (ex-PGM 74) were transferred on 10 Jan 1966. PGM 74, 80, 81, 82, 83, 91 are building in USA for transfer (names reported: *Lam Giang*, *Le Trong Dam*, *Nguyen Van Tru*).

PHU DU — *1963, Vietnamese Navy, Official*

COASTAL MINESWEEPERS

3 Ex-US MSC TYPE

CHU'O'NG-DU'O'NG II (ex-*MSC* 282)	HQ 115
BACH DANG II (ex-*MSC* 283)	HQ 116
HAM TU II (ex-*MSC* 281)	HQ 114

Displacement, tons	320 standard; 370 full load
Dimensions, feet	138 pp; 144 oa × 28 × 9
Guns	2—20 mm AA
Main engines	2 diesels; 2 shafts; 1 200 bhp = 13 knots
Complement	4 officers, 41 men

United States coastal motor minesweepers of the "Bluebird" class, non-magnetic type, of wooden construction, transferred under the Mutual Defence Assistance Programme in 1959 and 1960.

HAM TU II — *1960, Vietnamese Navy, Official*

CHU'O'NG-DU'O'NG II — *1964, Vietnamese Navy, Official*

DISPOSALS
Of the three coastal minesweepers of the ex-US YMS type transferred from the French Navy on 11 Feb 1954, **Ham Tu** HQ 111 (ex-*Aubepine*, ex-D 315, ex-YMS 28) was removed from the effective list in 1958. **Bach Bang** HQ 113, (ex-*Belledone*, ex-D 318, ex-YMS 78) in 1963, and *Chu'o'ng-Du'o'ng* HQ 112 (ex-*Digitale*, ex-D 326, ex-YMS 83) in 1964.

TRAINING SHIP

1 Ex-US FS TYPE

HOA GIANG (ex-*Dinr An*, ex-*Ingenieur en Chef Girod*, ex-*FS* 287, ex-*Governor Wright*) HQ 451

Displacement, tons	950
Dimensions, feet	176 × 32·3 × 10·2
Main engines	2 GM diesels; 1 shaft; 1 000 bhp = 10 knots
Complement	4 officers, 36 men

Former French survey vessel (ex-US Army freighter), sold to Vietnam in Dec 1955. Formerly rated as a light cargo ship (AKL), or supply vessel, but adapted and reclassified as a training ship in 1966.

HOA GIANG — *1963, Vietnamese Navy, Official*

LANDING SHIPS

CAM RANH (ex-USS *Marion County*, *LST* 975)	HQ 500
DA NANG (ex-USS *Maricopa County*, *LST* 938)	HQ 501
THI NAI (ex-USS *Cayugo County*, *LST* 529)	HQ 502

Displacement, tons	2 366 beaching; 4 080 full load
Dimensions, feet	316 wl; 328 oa × 50 × 14
Guns	8—40 mm AA
Main engines	GM diesels; 2 shafts; 1 700 bhp = 11 knots
Complement	7 officers, 103 men

Cam Ranh and *Da Nang* were built by Bethlehem Steel Co, Hingham, Mass. Laid down on 1 Dec 1944 and 14 July 1944, launched on 6 Jan 1945 and 15 Aug 1944, and completed on 3 Feb 1945 and 9 Sep 1944, respectively. Transferred in June 1962. *Thi Nai*, built by Jeffersonville B. & M. Co, Jefferson, Ind, laid down on 8 Nov 1943, launched on 17 Jan 1944 and comoleted on 29 Feb 1944 was transferred at Guam on 16 Dec 1963.

CAM RANH — *1963, Vietnamese Navy, Official*

HAU GIANG (ex-*LSM* 276)	HQ 406
HAN GIANG (ex-*LSM* 9012 ex-US *LSM* 110)	HQ 401
HAT GIANG (ex-*LSM* 9011, ex-US *LSM* 335)	HQ 400
LAM GIANG (ex-*LSM* 226)	HQ 402
HUONG GIANG (ex-USS *Oceanside*, *LSM* 175)	HQ 404
NINH GIANG (ex-*LSM* 85)	HQ 403
TIEN GIANG (ex-*LSM* 313)	HQ 405

Displacement, tons	743 beaching; 1 095 full load
Dimensions, feet	196·5 wl; 203·5 oa × 34·5 × 8·3
Guns	2—40 mm AA; 4—20 mm AA
Main engines	Diesel; 2 shafts; 2 800 bhp = 12 knots
Complement	5 officers, 70 men

Designed primarily to carry assault troops. First four were transferred to the French Navy for use in Indo-China, Jan 1954. *LSM* 9011, 9012 transferred to Vietnam Navy, Dec 1955. LMS 9014, 9017, 9018, returned to USA in 1955. *Oceanside* LSM 175, was transferred at Los Angeles, California, on 1 Aug 1961, and LSM 313 in 1962, *Hau Giang* (ex-LSM 276) on 10 June 1965. *Hat Giang* was converted into a hospital ship (LSMH) in 1966

HAN GIANG — *1965, Vietnamese Navy, Official*

DOAN NGOC TANG (ex-*LSSL* 9)	HQ 228	15 Sep 1965
LE VAN BINH (ex-*LSSL* 10)	HQ 227	15 Sep 1965
LINH KIEM (ex-*Arquebuse*, ex-*LSSL* 9022)	HQ 226	
LUU PHU THO (ex-*LSSL* 101)	HQ 229	2 Oct 1965
NO THAN (ex-*Framee*, ex-*LSSL* 105)	HQ 225	
NGUYEN DUC BONG (ex-*LSSL* 129)	HQ 231	19 Feb 1966
NGUYEN NGOC LONG (ex-*LSSL* 96)	HQ 230	8 Dec 1965

Displacement, tons	227 standard; 383 full load
Dimensions, feet	158 × 23·7 × 5·7
Guns	1—3 in; 4—40 mm; 4—20 mm; 4 MG
Main engines	Diesel; 2 shafts; 1 600 bhp = 14 knots
Complement	6 officers, 54 men

Of the LSSLs transferred from the USA in 1951 for service in Indo-China, *Arquebuse* was transferred by France to Vietnam in 1955 and *Frame* in 1957. The dates of other transfers of LSSLs from USA are shown after names above; these were formerly transferred to Japan by USA; they were renamed after Vietnamese officers who died for their country.

NO THAN — *1965 Vietnamese Navy, Official*

Landing Ships—*continued*

5 Ex-US LSIL TYPE

LOI CONG	(ex-*LSIL* 9034, ex-US 699)	HQ 330
LONG DAO	(ex-*LSIL* 9029, ex-US 698)	HQ 327
TAM SBT	(ex-*LSIL* 9033, ex-US 871)	HQ 331
THAN TIEN	(ex-*LSIL* 9035, ex-US 702)	HQ 328
THIEN KICH	(ex-*LSIL* 9038, ex-US 872)	HQ 329

Displacement, tons	227 standard; 383 full load
Dimensions, feet	158 × 22·7 × 5·3
Guns,	1—3 in; 1—40 mm; 2—20 mm; 4 MG; and 4 army mortars (2—3·1 in; 2—60 mm)
Main engines	Diesel; 2 shafts; 1 600 bhp = 14·4 knots
Complement	6 officers, 49 men

Former US ships. 9030-9033 were ceded to France at Bremerton, Washington, on 2 Mar 1951, and 9029 and 9034-39 in 1953 and stationed in Indo China. Similar to preceding class. LSIL 9030 (ex-715) was scrapped in 1955. The above vessels were transferred from France to Vietnam in 1956.

THIEN KICH *1962, Vietnamese Navy, Official*

UTILITY LANDING CRAFT

7 Ex-US LCU TYPE

HQ 533 (ex-*LCU* 9076) ex-US 1479
HQ 534 (ex-*LCU* 9089) ex-US 1480
HQ 535 (ex-*LCU* 9086) ex-US 1221
HQ 537 (ex-*LCU* 9887) ex-US 1501
HQ 538 (ex-*LCU*) ex-US 1594

Displacement, tons	180 light; 360 full load
Dimensions, feet	115 wl; 119 oa × 34 × 6
Guns	2—20 mm AA
Main engines	3 diesels; 3 shafts; 675 bhp = 10 knots

Built in the USA and transferred under MDAP. Acquired in 1954 from French reparations. All LCT (7) type except HQ 535 (LCT (6) type). The landing ships and landing craft from "naval attack divisions" (*Division navale d'assault*) most of which have one LSSL or LSIL as flagships.

DISPOSALS
One **LCU** (and one **LSSL**) are reported scrapped or lost, but the names/numbers are not specified.

HQ 536 *1962, Vietnamese Navy, Official*

HQ 536 (ex-*LCU* 9074, ex-US 1466)
HQ 539 (ex-*LCU*, ex-US 1502)

Displacement, tons	160 light; 320 full load
Dimensions, feet	119 oa × 33 × 5
Guns	2—20 mm AA
Main engines	3 diesels; 3 shafts; 675 bhp = 10 knots

Built under the offshore programme and transferred under the Military Aid Programme.

MINOR LANDING CRAFT

There were also 32 landing craft (*commandament*) of the LCM Type, 10 light monitors, 53 LCVP, and 46 FOM. A total of 150 boats of these types were assigned to the River Force in June 1965. These numbers have been much varied by transfers from the USN, as local conditions require.

MOTOR LAUNCH MINESWEEPERS

12 Ex-US MLMS TYPE

MLMS 150	**MLMS 153**	**MLMS 156**	**MLMS 159**
MLMS 151	**MLMS 154**	**MLMS 157**	**MLMS 160**
MLMS 152	**MLMS 155**	**MLMS 158**	**MLMS 161**

Converted 50 foot motor launches acquired from the United States in 1963.

SUPPORT SHIPS

18 AMPHIBIOUS LOGISTIC TYPES

Various landing ships, landing craft and auxiliaries adapted for fleet support.

RIVER ASSAULT CRAFT

200 ARMOURED TYPES

A mixed force of various small vessels, see under minor Landing Craft; also River Patrol Boats of the USN PBR Mk 1 and 3, and "Swift" type fast Patrol Craft. Numbers transferred vary as requirements dictate.

AUXILIARY GUNBOATS

500 JUNK TYPES

A Coastal Force of motorised junks was organised with United States assistance. This junk fleet was armed with ·50 and ·30 cal machine guns. The junk Force was established on 12 Apr 1960, with 100 junks, 28 groups of junks having been formed by June 1962. Mass production of improved design junks was undertaken to control infiltration of South Vietnam coastal waters by North Vietnamese forces. The latest junks were fitted with armour plate and fibre glass to protect the wooden hull against marine borers, and have diesels equal to speeds up to 15 knots. In June 1969 there were about 500 junks crewed by nearly 4 000 men. The sail junks were disposed of.
The Coastal Force (ex-Junk Force) became part of the Vietnamese Navy, and no longer a para-military organisation in July 1965.

OILERS

3 Ex-US YOG TYPE

HQ 470 (ex-*L'Aulne*, ex-US *YOG* 80)
HQ 471 (ex-*YOG* 33) (ex-US *YOG* 67)

Displacement, tons	450
Capacity, tons	700 deadweight

HQ 470 is a former US oiler ceded to France on 2 Mar 1950, and transferred from the French Navy to the Vietnamese Navy in 1956, and rated as a regional supply ship. HQ 471 was transferred from the USA to Vietnam in 1963. Ex-USS YOG 67, transferred under MAP March 1967.

SUPPLY VESSELS

2 TRAWLER TYPE

HA LONG HQ 452 **LONG HAI** HQ 453

Supply vessels of the trawler type taken into national service.

WATER CARRIER

1 Ex-US YW TYPE

YW 152

Former United States self-propelled water barge transferred under the Military Aid Programme.

TUGS

2 Ex-US YTM TYPE

YTM 193 (ex-USS *Sassacus*) **YTM 385** (ex-USS *Wannalancet*)

Medium harbour tugs transferred to Vietnam by the USA in Jan 1963. (The large harbour tug USS *Oswegatchie* YTB 515, was transferred to Venezuela and not to Vietnam as originally intended).

12 Ex-US YTL TYPE

HQ 9500 (ex-*YTL* 152)
HQ 9501 (ex-*YTL* 245)
HQ 9502 (TID type)
HQ 9503 (ex-*YTL* 200)
HQ 9504 (ex-*YTL* 206)

YTL 203 **YTL 423** **YTL 446** **YTL 451** **YTL 455** **YTL 587** **YTL 590**

Former United States small harbour tugs transferred from the US Navy under the MAP. Nos. 423, 446, 451, 455 and 590 were transferred in Jan 1963, and 587 leased and activated in 1968.

YUGOSLAVIA

Administration

Assistant Secretary of State for National Defence for the Navy:
Admiral Mate Jerkovic

Commander-in-Chief of the Fleet:
Vice-Admiral Ljubo Truta

Personnel

1969: 27 000 officers and ratings

Diplomatic Representation

Defence Attaché in London:
Colonel Svetozar Oro

Assistant Defence Attaché (Naval) in London:
Commander Zvonimir D. Kostic

Naval, Military and Air Attaché in Washington:
Colonel Milan Mavric

Strength of the Fleet

4 Submarines	20 Patrol Vessels
3 Destroyers	38 Minesweepers
2 Frigates	100 Torpedo Boats
1 Minelayer	26 Support Ships

Mercantile Marine

Lloyd's Register of Shipping:
337 vessels of 1,266,592 tons gross

SUBMARINES (*Podmornice*)

4 "SUTJESKA" CLASS

HEROJ **SUTJESKA**
NERETVA **ULJANIK**

Displacement, tons	550 standard; 700 surface 945 submerged
Length, feet (*metres*)	197 (*56·0*) pp
Beam, feet (*metres*)	21·3 (*6·5*)
Draught, feet (*metres*)	16 (*4·9*)
Torpedo tubes	6—21 in (*533 mm*)
Main engines	Diesels; electric motors 1 800 hp
Speed, knots	14 on surface; 9 submerged
Radius, miles	4 800 at 8 knots
Complement	38

Sutjeska was launched on 28 Sep 1958 at Uljanik Shipyard, Pula. The first submarine to be built in a Yugoslav yard. Commissioned on 16 Sep 1960.

PENNANT NUMBERS. Numbered in an "810" series, see 811 and 812 in photographs.

ULJANIK — *1969, Dr Giorgio Arra*

SUTJESKA — *1963, Yugoslavian Navy, Official*

"L" TYPE

The old modified "L" type submarine *Tara* (ex-*Nebojsa*) was scrapped in 1958.

SAVA (ex-*Nautilo*) Pennant No. 802

Displacement, tons	747 standard; 905 surface; 1 068 submerged
Length, feet (*metres*)	207·1 (*63·1*)
Beam, feet (*metres*)	22·8 (*6·9*)
Draught, feet (*metres*)	16 (*4·9*)
Torpedo tubes	6—21 in (*533 mm*)
Main engines	Diesels; electric motors 2 400 hp
Speed, knots	16 on surface; 8 submerged
Complement	55

Formerly Italian. Built by CRDA, Monfalcone. Laid down on 3 Jan 1942. Launched on 20 Mar 1943. Completed on 26 July 1943. Sunk on 9 Jan 1944. Salvaged. Reconstructed with new conning tower.

SAVA — *1966, Dr Giorgio Arra*

DESTROYERS (*Razarac*)

Name	*No.*	*Builders*	*Laid down*	*Launched*	*Completed*
KOTOR (ex-*Kempenfelt*, ex-*Valentine*: Leader)	R 21	John Brown & Co Ltd, Clydebank	24 June 1942	9 May 1943	25 Oct 1943
PULA (ex-*Wager*)	R 22	John Brown & Co Ltd, Clydebank	20 Nov 1942	1 Nov 1943	14 Apr 1944

2 Ex-BRITISH "W" CLASS

Displacement, tons	1 730 standard; 2 525 full load
Length, feet (*metres*)	339·5 (*103·5*) pp; 362·8 (*000·0*) oa
Beam, feet (*metres*)	35·7 (*10·9*)
Draught, feet (*metres*)	17 (*5·2*)
Guns, surface	4—4·7 in (*120 mm*)
Guns, AA	1—40 mm *Kotor*; 3—40 mm *Pula*
A/S	4 DCT
Torpedo tubes	8—21 in (*533 mm*)
Boilers	2 Admiralty 3-drum
Main engines	Parsons geared turbines 40 000 shp
Speed, knots	36·75 designed; 31·25 sea speed
Radius, miles	2 800 at 20 knots
Oil fuel (tons)	580
Complement	186

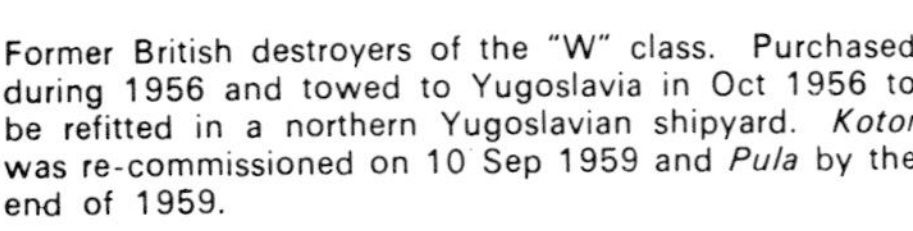
Former British destroyers of the "W" class. Purchased during 1956 and towed to Yugoslavia in Oct 1956 to be refitted in a northern Yugoslavian shipyard. *Kotor* was re-commissioned on 10 Sep 1959 and *Pula* by the end of 1959.

CLASS. Sister ships of *Wessex*, renamed *Jan van Riebeeck* and *Whelp*, renamed *Simon van der Stel*, in South African Navy, and original sister ships of *Wakeful*, *Whirlwind* and *Wizard* in the British Navy, and *Wrangler* in the South African Navy, converted to frigates, see earlier pages.

APPEARANCE. One director on bridge not so large as in later classes. Tall foremast in both. Single Bofors mounting high up abaft funnel in superfiring position.

PHOTOGRAPHS. A starboard view of *Pula* appears in the 1957-58 edition, and another photograpn of *Kotor* in the 1957-58 to 1961-62 editions.

PULA — *1962, Yugoslavian Navy, Official*

KOTOR — *1966, Yugoslavian Navy, Official*

Destroyers—*continued*

Name	No.	Builders	Laid down	Launched	Completed
SPLIT (ex-*Spalato*, ex-*Split*)	11	Brodogradiliste "3 Maj", Rijeka	July 1939	1940	4 July 1958

Displacement, tons	2 400 standard; 3 000 full load
Length, feet (*metres*)	376·3 (*114·7*)
Beam, feet (*metres*)	36·5 (*11·1*)
Draught, feet (*metres*)	12·3 (*3·8*)
Guns, surface	4—5 in (*127 mm*)
Guns, AA	12—40 mm
A/S	2 Squids, 6 DCT, 2 DCR
Torpedo tubes	5—21 in (*533 mm*)
Boilers	2
Main engines	Geared turbines 50 000 shp; 2 shafts
Speed, knots	31·5
Oil fuel (tons)	590

The original ship was laid down by Chantieres de Loire, Nantes, in 1939 at Split Shipyard. Launched in 1940. Carried out extensive trials in 1958. Ready for operational service in 1959. The original design provided for an armament of 5—5·5 inch guns, 10—40 mm AA guns and 6—21·7 inch torpedo tubes (tripled), but the plans were subsequently modified. Mine capacity: 40.

SPLIT *Official*

FAST FRIGATES (Light Destroyer Type)

Name	No.	Builders	Laid down	Launched	Completed
BIOKOVO (ex-*Aliseo*)	RE 52	Navalmeccanica, Castellammare	16 Sep 1941	20 Sep 1942	28 Feb 1943
TRIGLAV (ex-*Indomito*)	RE 51	Cantiere del Tirreno, Riva Trigoso	10 Jan 1942	6 July 1943	4 Aug 1941

2 "TRIGLAV" CLASS

Displacement, tons	1 204 standard; 1 709 full load
Length, feet (*metres*)	270·5 (*82·5*) pp; 293·0 (*89·3*) oa
Beam, feet (*metres*)	32·5 (*9·9*)
Draught, feet (*metres*)	9·5 (*2·9*)
Guns, dual purpose	3·9 in (*100 mm*) 47 cal. *Biokovo*: 2 *Triglav*: 3
Guns, AA	20 mm *Biokovo* 10 *Triglav*: 11
A/S	4 DCT
Torpedo tubes	4—17·7 in (*450 mm*) 2 twin
Boilers	2—3-drum type
Main engines	2 Tosi geared turbines 16 000 shp; 2 shafts
Speed, knots	26
Radius, miles	3 500 at 15 knots
Oil fuel (tons)	430
Complement	175

Ex-Italian large oceangoing torpedo boats or escort destroyers.

The former Italian large oceangoing torpedo boat or small destroyer *Ucka* (ex-*Balestra*) RE 54, latterly rated as a fast frigate, damaged by bombs on 25 Feb 1945, but completed by Yugoslavia in 1949, was officially removed from the active list in 1968.

The former Italian large oceangoing torpedo boat or small destroyer *Durmitor* (ex-*Ariete*), the only survivor of her class, afterwards reclassified as a fast frigate, was removed from the active list in 1963 and scrapped.

BIOKOVO *Yugoslavian Navy, Official*

TRIGLAV *Yugoslavian Navy, Official*

MINELAYER Training Ship (*Skolski Brodovi*)

GALEB (ex-*Kuchuck*, ex-*Ramb III*) M 11

Displacement, tons	5 182
Measurement, tons	3 667 gross
Length, feet (*metres*)	385 (*117·3*)
Beam feet (*metres*)	51 (*15·2*)
Draught, feet (*metres*)	18 (*5·5*)
Guns, AA	6—40 mm
Main engines	2 diesels; 2 shafts
Speed, knots	17

Ex-Italian. Launched in 1938. Refloated and completed in 1952. Now training ship. Also Presidential Yacht. Former armament was four 3·5 inch, four 40 mm and 24—20 mm (six quadruple) guns.

GALEB *1966, Yugoslavian Navy, Official*

PATROL VESSELS

MORNAR 551

Displacement, tons	330 standard; 400 full load
Dimensions, feet	170 × 23 × 6·5
Guns	2—3 in; 2—40 mm AA; 2—20 mm AA
A/S weapons	2 DCT; 2 DC racks
Main engines	4 diesels; 3 240 bhp = 24 knots max; 16 knots sea speed
Radius, miles	3 000 at 12 knots
Complement	60

Completed on 10 Sep 1959. Design is basically similar to that of PBR 581, see next page.

MORNAR *1968, Yugoslavian Navy, Official*

Patrol Vessels —*continued*

PBR 581 (ex-P6)

Displacement, tons	325 standard; 400 full load
Dimensions feet	170 pp × 23 × 6·5
Guns	2—40 mm AA; 2—20 mm AA
A/S weapons	1 Hedgehog; 4 DCT; 2 DC racks
Main engines	4 Pielstick SEMT diesels; 3 240 bhp = 18·7 knots
Radius, miles	3 000 at 12 knots; 2 000 at 15 knots
Complement	62

USA offshore procurement. Ordered in France. Built by F. C. Mediterranee (Graville). Launched on 1 June 1954. Transferred to Yugoslavia in 1956.

PBR 581 *Official*

PC 134

Displacement, tons	85 standard
Dimensions, feet	91·9 × 14·8 × 8·3
Guns	1—20 mm AA; 1—12·7 mm MG
Main engines	2 diesels; 900 bhp = 13 knots sea speed

Patrol boat (Patrolni camac) of new Type 134.

No. 134 *1968, Yugoslavian Navy, Official*

COASTAL MINESWEEPERS

HRABRI M 151 (ex-*D* 25) **SMELI** M 152 (ex-*D* 26)
SLOBODNI M 153 (ex-*D* 27) **SNAZNI** M 154

Displacement, tons	365 standard; 424 full load
Dimensions, feet	140 pp; 152 oa × 28 × 8·2
Guns	1—40 mm AA; 1—20 mm AA
Main engines	SIGMA free piston generators; 2 shafts. 2 000 bhp = 15 knots
Oil fuel, tons	48
Radius, miles	3 000 at 15 knots
Complement	40

First three were built in France by A Normand as United States "Off-shore" orders, launched on 27 Feb 1956, 26 May 1956 and 26 June 1956, respectively, and allocated to the Yugoslav Navy at Cherbourg in Sep 1957. *Snazni* was built in Yugoslavia in 1960.
A photograph of *Smeli* appears in the 1958:59 to 1965-66 editions.

SLOBODNI *1966, Yugoslavian Navy, Official*

TORPEDO BOATS (*Torpedni Camci*)

90 TYPE "108"

102, 103, 108, 115, 116, 119, 120, 122, 124, 125, 126, 127, 157, 159, 162, 164, 165, 167, 170, 174, 199, 201

Displacement, tons	55 standard; 60 full load
Dimensions, feet	69 pp; 78 oa × 21·3 × 7·8
Guns	1—40 mm AA; 4—12·7 mm MG
Tubes	2
Main engines	3 Packard motors; 3 shafts; 5 000 bhp = 36 knots
Complement	14

The total number of motor torpedo boats is reported to have reached 100. Under recent programmes if was planned to raise the total to 110. Several boats of the Soviet "Shersken", "Osa" and "Komar" classes have been observed but it has not been officially confirmed if these are outright acquisitions, lent, or merely on a mission from the USSR.

TRANSFERS. Two of the "108" class were transferred to Ethiopia in 1960 and renamed *Barracuda* P 22 and *Shark* P 21.

MTB 174 *Yugoslavian Navy, Official*

MTB 119 *Yugoslavian Navy, Official*

TRAINING SHIP

JADRAN

Displacement, tons	720
Dimensions, feet	190 × 29·2 × 13·8
Sail area, sq ft	8 600
Main engines	1 Linke-Hofman Diesel; 375 hp = 8 knots

Topsail schooner. Launched in 1932. Accommodation for 150 Cadets. Name means "Adriatic". While in Italian hands she was named *Marco Polo*.

JADRAN *1966, Yugoslavian Navy, Official*

MINING TENDERS
The three mining tenders of the Yarrow class, *M 31* (ex-*Meljine*), *M* 32, and *M 33* (ex-*Mljet*), were officially removed from the list in 1968.

RIVER PATROL VESSEL

KRAJINA (ex-*Dragor*)

Displacement, tons	250
Dimensions, feet	164 × 26·2 × 3·8
Main engines	480 hp = 10 knots

Launched in 1923. This vessel formerly served as the Royal Yacht on the Danube.

PATROL BOATS

"KRALJAVICA" CLASS SUBMARINE CHASERS

16 PBR 501-508 AND 509-516 TYPES

PBR 509
PBR 510
PBR 511
PBR 512
PBR 513
PBR 514
PBR 515
PBR 516

This second batch of submarine chasers launched in 1957-59 are an improvement on the PBR 501-508 series below, but of similar basic particulars.

PBR 512 — *Yugoslavian Navy, Official*

PBR 501
PBR 502
PBR 503
PBR 504
PBR 505
PBR 506
PBR 507
PBR 508

Displacement, tons	190 standard; 245 full load
Dimensions, feet	134·5 × 20·7 × 7
Guns	1—3 in; 1—40 mm AA; 4—20 mm AA
A/S weapons	DC
Main engines	Diesel; 2 shafts; 3 300 bhp = 20 knots
Oil fuel, tons	15
Radius, miles	1 500 at 12 knots
Complement	54

These submarine chasers of the "500" class were launched from 1953 to 1956.

PBR 508 — *1969, Dr Giorgio Arra*

SALVAGE VESSEL (*Brod za Spasavanje*)

PS II SPASILAC

Displacement, tons	740
Dimensions, feet	174 × 26·2 × 13
Main engines	Triple expansion; 2 000 hp = 15 knots

Built by Howaldt, Kiel. Launched in 1929. Name means "Salvador". While in Italian hands she was called *Intangible*.

SPASILAC — *1966, Yugoslavian Navy, Official*

YACHT (*Jahta*)

ISTRANKA (ex-*Vilax-Dalmata*)

Displacement, tons	230
Main engines	325 hp = 12 knots

Istranka means Nymph. Named *Fata* whilst in Italian hands during 1941-45.

WATER CARRIERS (*Vodonosci*)

PV 6 **PV 11** **PV 12**

There are 8 water carriers of various types. Also PT 12 and PO 54.

INSHORE MINESWEEPERS (*Minolovci*)

4 NEW CONSTRUCTION

ML 117 **ML 118** **ML 119** **ML 121**

Displacement, tons	120 standard; 131 full load
Dimensions, feet	98·4 × 18 × 4·9
Guns	1—40 mm AA; 2—12·7 mm MG
Main engines	2 GM diesels; 1 000 bhp = 12 knots

A new type of small minesweepers built in Yugoslav shipyards.

M 121 — *1968, Yugoslavian Navy, Official*

4 US MSI TYPE

M 141 **M 142** **M 143** **M 144**

Displacement, tons	123 standard; 164 full load
Dimensions, feet	100 × 21·8 × 5·5
Guns	1—40 mm AA or 1—20 mm AA
Main engines	2 Paxman diesels; 1 100 bhp = 13 knots
Complement	15

Built for transfer to Yugoslavia under the Military Aid Programme. The US Navy hull numbers were MSI 98, 99, 100 and 101.

M 142 — *1968, Yugoslavian Navy, Official*

12 TYPE 101

M 103
M 105
M 106
M 109
M 111
M 112
M 113
M 114
M 115
M 116
M 120
M 140

Displacement, tons	90 standard; 95 full load
Dimensions, feet	82 × 19·5 × 6·2
Guns	1—40 mm; 1—20 mm
Main engines	Diesel; 135-175 bhp = 12 knots

Built during 1950-56 in Yugoslav shipyards. Vary in detail. Some used for patrol. M 101, M 102, M 104, M 107, M 108 and M 110 were scrapped in 1966.

M 109 — *Yugoslavian Navy, Official*

ITALIAN TYPE. The six inshore minesweepers of the former Italian type 301, *ML 301* (ex-*RD* 6), *ML 302* (ex-*RD* 16), *ML 303* (ex-*RD* 21), *ML 304* (ex-*RD* 25), *ML 305* (ex-*RD 27*) and *ML 306* (ex-*RD* 28) were officially removed from the list in 1968. Sister ship *ML 307* (ex-*RD* 29) was scrapped in 1955.

RIVER MINESWEEPERS

14 RML 300 TYPE

M 301
M 302
M 303
M 304
M 305
M 306
M 307
M 308
M 309
M 310
M 311
M 312
M 313
M 314

Displacement, tons	38
Guns	1—20 mm
Main engines	Speed = 12 knots

All launched in 1951-53. A photograph of M 313 appears in the 1956-57 and 1957-58 editions.

DESPATCH VESSEL

JADRANKA (ex-*Bjeli Orao*)

Displacement, tons	567 standard; 660 full load
Dimensions, feet	197 pp; 213·2 oa × 26·5 × 9·3
Guns	2—40 mm AA; 2 MG
Main engines	2 Sulzer diesels; 1 900 bhp = 18 knots

Built by C. R. dell Adriatico, San Marco, Trieste; launched on 3 June 1939. Was used as Admiralty yacht and yacht of Marshall Tito. While in Italian hands was named *Alba* for some days only, then *Zagabria*.

JADRANKA *1966, Dr Giorgio Arra*

LANDING CRAFT

D 230

Displacement, tons *circa* 500

Capable of carrying at least two, possibly three of the heaviest tanks. Unlike other tank landing craft in that the lower part of the stern drops to form a ramp down which the tanks go ashore, underneath the prow, which is rigid.

D 230 *courtesy B. Hinchliffe, Esq*

Catamaran Type

Displacement, tons *circa* 50

A smaller craft consisting of two pontoons some feet apart, secured to each other by cross-girders on which stand the bridge and cabins, etc. This vessel appears to be capable of carrying one medium tank, to be put ashore by two bridge members which can be seen quite clearly, folded back on the deck.

Catamaran type *courtesy B. Hinchcliffe, Esq*

DTK 221

Displacement, tons	410
Dimensions, feet	144·3 × 19·7 × 7
Guns	1—20 mm AA; 2—12·7 mm
Main engines	Speed = 10 knots
Complement	15

D 221 *Yugoslavian Navy, Official*

D 206 (ex-*MZ* 713) **D 219** (ex-*MZ* 717)

Displacement, tons	225 and 239
Guns	1—20 mm AA; 2 MG AA
Main engines	Speed = 11 knots

Ex-Italian landing craft. Launched in 1942. Capable of carrying three tanks. A photograph of D 219 appears in the 1959-60 to 1965-66 editions.

D 203 **D 204**

Displacement, tons	220
Guns	1—3·4 in (88 mm); 2—20 mm AA
Main engines	Speed = 10 knots

Ex-German landing craft. Two landing craft were launched in 1956.

OILERS

PN 17

Displacement, tons	420 standard; 650 full load
Dimensions, feet	141·5 × 22·8 × 13·5
Main engines	300 bhp = 7 knots

There are also the small oilers *Kit* and *Uljesura*, displacement 250 tons.

PN 17 *1962, Yugoslavian Navy, Official*

4 PN 13 TYPE

PN 13 (ex-*Lovcen*)

Displacement, tons	560 and 695
Main engines	Speed = 8·5 knots

PN 13 (ex- *Lovcen*) was launched in 1932. For fleet servicing and freighting.

TRANSPORTS

2 PT 71 TYPE

PT 71 **PT 72**

Displacement, tons	310 standard; 428 full load
Dimensions, feet	141·5 × 22·2 × 16
Main engines	300 bhp = 7 knots

The transport *Tunj* PT 21 (ex-*Krk*, ex-*Kt.* 6) was removed from the list in 1963.

PT 71 *1966, Yugoslavian Navy, Official*

TUGS (*Remorkeri*)

PR 52 (ex-*San Remo*)

Displacement, tons	170
Main engines	350 hp = 9 knots

Former Italian tug and multi-purpose vessel. Launched in 1937.

PR 58 (ex-*Molara*)

Displacement, tons	118
Main engines	250 hp = 8 knots

Former Italian tug. Launched in 1937, now used as general transport and towing vessel.

PR 51 (ex-*Porto Conte*)

Displacement, tons 226

Former Italian tug. Launched in 1936. A photograph appears in the 1951-52 to 1957-58 editions.

PR 55 (ex-*Snazi*)

Displacement, tons	100
Main engines	300 hp = 10 knots

Launched in 1917. Name means "Strong". The Italian name was *Resistance*.

PR 54 (ex-*Ustrajni*)

Displacement, tons	160
Main engines	250 hp = 9 knots

Launched in 1917. Name means "Durable". The Italian name was *Duratero*.

LR 11 (ex-*Basiluzzo*)

Displacement, tons	108
Main engines	130 hp = 8 knots

Former Italian tug. Launched in 1915. There is also the very old tug PP 1.

ZAMBIA

The Tank Landing Craft of the LCT(8) type, ex-HMS *Bastion*, L 4040, purchased on 15 Sep, 1966 was put up for sale by public tender in 1969.

NAVAL STRENGTHS

ALL THE WORLD'S FIGHTING SHIPS

	Large Aircraft Carriers	Light Aircraft Carriers	Escort Carriers, Heli-copter Carriers, Com-mando Carriers	Command Ships, Commu-nications Ships, Amphib-ious Force Flag ships	Nuclear Powered Sub-marines	Conven-tionally Powered Sub-marines	Cruisers	Leaders, Large Destroy-ers, Frigates (DLG)	Destroy-ers	Destroy-er Escorts, Frigates, Escorts (and APD)	Corvettes (includ-ding PCE)	Patrol Vessels, Sub-marine Chasers (PC)	Missile Boats, Torpedo Boats, Motor Gun-boats, Fast Patrol Boats	Fleet Mine-layers, Fast Mine-layers, Mine Support Ships
ARGENTINA		2				2	3		9	2	2	9	2	
AUSTRALIA		1	1			4		3	5	9				
BELGIUM														
BRAZIL		1				2	2		11	5	10			
BULGARIA						2				2		8	8	
BURMA										1	2	5	5	
CANADA		1				4				22				
CEYLON										1				
CHILE						2	2		4	4	2	2	4	
CHINA						33			4	17		22	290	
COLOMBIA									3	3				
CUBA										4	2	14	42	
DENMARK						4				6	4		16	4
DOMINICAN R									1	3	3	7		
ECUADOR										3	2			
EGYPT						13			8	4	2	8	65	
FINLAND										3	2	4	15	
FRANCE		3	1			19	2	2	18	28		14		
GERMANY (E)										4		24	72	
GERMANY (W)						12			11	21	6		40	2
GREECE						2			8	4		7	8	
INDIA		1				4	2		3	16				
INDONESIA						12	1		7	11	1	12	64	
IRAN									1	5	5			
IRAQ												3	12	
ISRAEL						4			2			1	16	
ITALY						8	4	4	4	13	24	7	16	
JAPAN						9			23	16		20	10	
KOREA (N)						2						18	42	
KOREA (S)									3	13	11	6		
MALAYSIA										2			4	
MEXICO										8	21	1		
NETHERLANDS						6	2		12	6	9			
NEW ZEALAND											4			
NORWAY						15				5		2	47	
PAKISTAN						1	1		5	2				
PARAGUAY														
PERU						4	2		2	3	2			
PHILIPPINES										1	7	7		
POLAND						11			3			8	25	
PORTUGAL						4				12	1	13		
RUMANIA												3	13	
SOUTH AFRICA									2	6				
SPAIN			1			8	1		19	6	6	2	3	6
SWEDEN						24	1		8	7			42	1
TAIWAN									7	17	5	23	48	
THAILAND										5		14		
TURKEY						10			10		18	6	8	1
UNITED KINGDOM	2	2	2		8	33	3	8	11	68			4	1
URUGUAY										3		4		
USA	33	2	21	9	90	100	35	35	343	238	9	25	29	13
USSR			2		65	320	25		100	100		275	475	
VENEZUELA						1			3	6		12		
VIETNAM											6	2	14	
YUGOSLAVIA						4			3	2		2	100	1

Note—Figures include vessels in reserve, but not ships under construction

TABLE SHOWING THE NUMERICAL STRENGTH OF EACH COUNTRY

Ocean Mine-sweepers, Fleet Mine-sweepers	*Coastal Mine-sweepers, Mine Hunters*	*Inshore Mine-sweepers Mine-sweeping Boats*	*Motor Launches, Motor Patrol Craft, River Gun-boats*	*Landing Ships*	*Landing Craft*	*Boom Defence Vessels, Net-layers*	*Survey Ships*	*Depot Ships, Repair Ships Maintenance Ships*	*Trans-ports*	*Supply Ships*	*Oilers*	*Training Ships*	*Tugs*	*Miscella-neous*	
4	6		12	5	3		2		5		4	2	15	2	ARGENTINA
	6	3	20				5	1			1		3	10	AUSTRALIA
7	22	16	7					3					1	14	BELGIUM
	2		7				6	2	4		9	1	2	2	BRAZIL
2	4	22			10							1	1	22	BULGARIA
1			34		8				1					2	BURMA
	6		3			5	7	3		3	2		27	70	CANADA
			27										1	1	CEYLON
				3	3		1		2		1	1	11	3	CHILE
20	6		22	44	26	6	2	1		8	5		11	375	CHINA
			25				1		6		3		13	3	COLOMBIA
			27										1	6	CUBA
	8	4	13					3			2			7	DENMARK
			7	1	2						2		5	2	DOMINICAN R
			8	2									2	2	ECUADOR
6		2			24				1					14	EGYPT
		5	13						9				3	11	FINLAND
15	71	15	13	9	10	12	9	10	10	16	10	4	20	50	FRANCE
20		24	60		18		3				3	2	10	22	GERMANY (E)
	24	51	24		26		8	16		6	10	3	18	40	GERMANY (W)
5	14			14	8	1	2	2			7		14	10	GREECE
	4	2	5	1	1		4	1			3		1	10	INDIA
6	15		66	6	7		2	3	4		4	2	5	2	INDONESIA
	4	2	23		3			1			2		1	5	IRAN
			22										1	2	IRAQ
			4		6									2	ISRAEL
4	37	20		3	23	2	2	1	6		2	4	26	80	ITALY
	40	6	32	4	6			3			2	10	3	100	JAPAN
10		24	15											70	KOREA (N)
	11	1		20				1	1	6	4		2	6	KOREA (S)
	6	2	25				1							2	MALAYSIA
			8				1		1		2			1	MEXICO
	41	16	5		10	1	3	1		2	1	3	7	40	NETHERLANDS
2			12				1			1				2	NEW ZEALAND
	10						1	2				1		9	NORWAY
	8		6				1				2		4	3	PAKISTAN
			8											1	PARAGUAY
	2		17	4					3		4		2	3	PERU
	2		28	6			1	1	1		1		4	5	PHILIPPINES
21	4	27	36		22		1				3	2		9	POLAND
5	12		42		4		6	2			2	3		55	PORTUGAL
4		30										2		30	RUMANIA
1	0		6			1	1				1		1	2	SOUTH AFRICA
13	12		18	8		1	3		3		4	1	10	20	SPAIN
	18	17	31		23		12	2		1	3	2		19	SWEDEN
5	8		50	45	38		2	3	6		5		5	60	TAIWAN
1	4		8	5	8		1		1		4	1	5	3	THAILAND
	13	3	30			6		2			4	1	2	5	TURKEY
	66	22	4	2	26	20	13	8		11	38	4	70	185	UNITED KINGDOM
							1				1			2	URUGUAY
93	31	46	400	150	126	4	26	70	40	125	75	2	250	940*	*USA
70	135	45	120	100	130	18	55	50	25	20	50	20	40	900†	†USSR
			12	4			3	1	1				2	3	VENEZUELA
	3			10	23					1	2		14	10	VIETNAM
	4	34	18		7				2		6	1	8	20	YUGOSLAVIA

*Includes Coastguard

† Round figures are estimated

ADDENDA

New "KANIN" Class SAM Destroyer — *July 1969, S. Breyer*

U.S.S.R.

Submarines

Page 534

Ten nuclear powered submarines reported to have been completed during past year.

Guided Missile Destroyers

Page 547

KANIN Class SAM DDG (ex-KRUPNI Class)

Displacement, tons	3 600 standard; 4 600 full load
Length, feet (*metres*)	456·0 (*139·0*)
Beam, feet (*metres*)	48·9 (*14·9*)
Draught, feet (*metres*)	18·0 (*5·5*)
Missiles, AA	1 twin "SA-N-1" launcher aft
A/S weapons	3 12-barrelled rocket launchers
Guns	8—57 mm (2 quad uple forward)
Torpedo tubes	10—21 in (*533 mm*) A/S (2 quintuple)
Main engines	80 000 shp
Speed, knots	34

Conversion from 1967-68 onwards. The first two ships in service since 1969. Baltic Fleet. New armament. Larger helicopter platform. See photograph above.

Minelayer

Page 554

ALESHA Class

Displacement, tons	3 600 standard; 4 300 full load
Length, feet (*metres*)	321·5 (*98·0*)
Beam, feet (*metres*)	45·9 (*14·0*)
Draught, feet (*metres*)	14·8 (*4·5*)
Guns, AA	4—57 mm (1 quadruple forward)
Main engines	4 diesels; 8 000 bhp
Speed, knots	20
Complement	150 approx

In service since 1965. Probably carries exercise mines. Reported to be only one ship.

Coastal Escorts

Page 554

STENKA Class

Displacement, tons	170 standard; 210 full load
Length, feet (*metres*)	131·2 (*40·0*)
Beam, feet (*metres*)	23·0 (*7·0*)
Draught, feet (*metres*)	6·6 (*2·0*)
Guns, AA	4—30 mm (2 twin)
Torpedo tubes	4—16 in (406 mm) A/S
A/S weapons	2 DCT racks
Main engines	3 diesels; 10 000 bhp
Speed, knots	40
Complement	25

Submarine chasers of a new type. Built from 1967/68 onwards. Five units in service. See photograph below.

Landing Craft

Page 557

VYDRA Class

Displacement, tons	300 standard; 500 full load
Length, feet (*metres*)	164·0 (*50·0*)
Beam, feet (*metres*)	26·2 (*8·0*)
Draught, feet (*metres*)	7·2 (*2·2*)
Main engines	2 diesels

A new class of medium landing ships. Built from 1967 onwards. No armament.

VITTORIO VENETO as completed — *July 1969, Italian Navy*

ARTEMIZ (ex-HMS *Sluys*) — *July 1969, Vosper Thornycroft Group*

New STENKA Class — *July 1969, S. Breyer*

IRAN

Destroyers

Page 157

ARTEMIZ (ex-HMS *Sluys*)

Modernisation completed by Vosper Thornycroft Group, Portsmouth and Southampton. See Photograph above.

ITALY

Guided Missile Cruiser/Helicopter Carrier

Page 165

VITTORIO VENETO

Completed for operational service. See photograph above.

LATE ADDENDA

GREECE

Page 134

Submarines

Four submarines of 1 000 tons being built in West Germany.

Page 134

Fast Gunboats

Four fast gunboats of 220 tons and 40 knots ordered from Constructions Mécaniques de Normandie, Cherbourg. Similar to those already delivered to Israel.

INDONESIA

Page 151

Ships removed from the effective list:
Destroyers: *Siliwangi, Sanjaja, Singamangaradja, Gadjah Mada.*
Submarines: *Tjakra, Nanggala.*
Frigates: *Mongonsidi.*
Patrol Vessels: *Lapai, Madidihinang, Tjutjut, Momare, Lumba-Lumba, Tongkol, Bubara.*
Torpedo Boats: *Adjak, Singa, Angin Ribut, Angin Kumbang, Angin Passat.*
Coastal Minesweepers: *Palau Roma, Pulau Roti, Pulau Raas, Pulau Rempang, Pulau Enggano.*
Survey Ships: *Dewa Kembar.*
Landing Craft: *Teluk Wadjo, Teluk Weda.*
Auxiliary Patrol Craft: *Ampis, Merbabu*
Oilers: *Sambu, Bunju, Tjepu, Pladju.*
Salvage Vessels: *Triton.*

Ships scrapped:
Corvettes: *Banteng, Patiunus, Radjawali.*
Training Ships: *Nanusa.*

SINGAPORE

Page 263

Fast Patrol Craft

INDEPENDENCE

First of six Vosper Thornycroft type launched at Portsmouth, England, on 15 July 1969.

UNITED KINGDOM

Page 304

Flag Officers

Flag Officer, Medway, and Admiral Superintendent H.M. Dockyard, Chatham:
Rear Admiral Frederick Charles William Lawson, DSC & Bar, CEng, MIMechE (*August 1969*)

Senior Appointments

Director of Warship Design:
Mr Norman Hancock, CEng, MRINA, RCNC

U.S.A.

To page 382: Ship Listings
add to SSN Nuclear Powered Attack Submarines:
678 Archerfish
680 Redfish
add to SS Submarines:
341 Chivo
342 Chopper

To page 403: Aircraft Carriers, CVA, Hancock Class
Nineteen "Essex" class carriers remain on the Navy List: 4 attack carriers, 11 ASW carriers, 1 training carrier, and 3 amphibious assault ships. The *Ticonderoga* is scheduled to become a CVS in 1970 (for *Midway*), the *Hancock* in 1972 (for *Nimitz*), the *Bon Homme Richard* in 1974 (for CVAN 69), and the *Oriskany* in 1976 (for CVAN 70).

To page 415: "Mitscher" Class
Electronics: SQS-26 bow-mounted sonar installed in *Willis A. Lee* (DL 4) and *Wilkinson* (DL 5); SQS-23 sonar in *Mitscher* (DDG 35) and *John S. McCain* (DDG 36).

To page 417: Guided Missile Destroyers (DDG) "Charles F. Adams" Class
ELECTRONICS: SPS-39 radar to be replaced by SPS-52.

To page 425: Destroyers (DD) "Allen M. Sumner" Class
Maddox decommissioned in 1969.
Modernised "Fletcher" Class
Five ships were placed in reserve in 1969; *Cony*, DD 508, *Eaton* DD 510, stricken on 2 July 1969; *Taylor* DD 468, *Walker*, DD 517, stricken on 2 July 1969 and transferred to Italy; *Jenkins* DD 447 stricken in 1969.

To page 454: Amphibious Transport Submarine (LPSS) "Sealion" Type
Growler conversion to LPSS cancelled because of high cost.

To page 457

Pic of WHITE RIVER (LFR 536)

1969, US Navy by P. HAN Stephen L. Howk

To page 485: Fleet Minesweepers (MSF) "Auk" Class
Steady (MSF 118) to Taiwan China in 1968
Coastal Minesweepers (MSCO) "Albatross" Class
Seven of the class in reserve were stricken.

To page 488: Ammunition Ships (AE) "Lassen" Class
Shasta (AE 6) stricken in 1969.

To page 489: Store Ships (AF) C2-S-E1 Type *Hyades* in reserve.
Stores Issues Ships (AKS)
Altair (AKS 32) transferred to reserve.

To page 490: Oilers (AO) T3-S2-A1 Type
Cimarron (AO 22) was decommissioned in 1968 and scrapped.

To page 493: Netlaying Ships
Naubuc reacquired and redesignated YRST 4 on April 1 1968.

To page 491: Net Laying Ship
Butternut stricken 18 July 1969.

To page 503: Cargo Ships (AK)
The *Betelgeuse* (AK 260) is Navy manned, not HSTS.
Alcor (AK 259) fitted as FBM support ship, was stricken on 30 Dec 1968.
T-AK 282 being converted from *Marshfield Victory.*

To page 505: Light Cargo Ships (AKL/IX)
Add *New Bedford* IX 308 (ex-FS 289, ex-AKL-17).

HARRY E. HUBBARD DD 748 *1967, US Navy*

NAVAL AIRCRAFT

NAVAL AIRCRAFT

SHIP BORNE AIRCRAFT

Br 1050 ALIZE Breguet (France)

Carrier-borne 3-seat anti-submarine aircraft

Max speed at S/L	400 knots
Max Speed at 10 000 ft (*3 050 m*)	450 knots
Patrol speed	210-320 knots
Service ceiling	26 250 ft (*8 000 m*)
Normal range	1 350 n. miles
Normal endurance	5 hr 10 min
Max endurance	7 hr 40 min
Armament	Internal Bay: 3 × 353 lb depth charges or one torpedo Wing racks: 6 × 5-in rockets or 2 × AS12 ASM's
Max T-O weight	18 100 lb (*8 200 kg*)
Wing span	51 ft 2 in (*15·60 m*)
Width folded	23 ft 0 in (*7·00 m*)
Length	45 ft 6 in (*13·86 m*)
Height	16 ft 5 in (*5·00 m*)
Power plant	1 × 2 100 shp Dart R.Da 21 Turbo-prop.

75 were built for the French Navy to equip three squadrons; 12 were supplied to the Indian Navy for service aboard "Vikrant".

Alize of the French Navy with underwing rocket rails

Courtesy, J. Fricker

BUCCANEER S. Mk 2 Hawker Siddeley (UK)
Carrier-borne 2-seat all-weather strike aircraft

Max speed at S/L	Mach 0·92 approx.
Tactical radius	500 n. miles plus
Armament	Internal Bay: Nuclear or conventional weapons (4 × 1 000 lb bombs) or camera pack Wing mounts: 4 × Bullpup missiles or 4 × Martel missiles or 4 × 1 000 lb bombs or 4 × rocket packs or combinations of foregoing
Max T-O weight	62 000 lb approx
Wing span	42 ft 4 in (*12·90 m*)
Width folded	19 ft 11 in (*6·07 m*)
Length, overall	63 ft 5 in (*19·33 m*)
Length folded	51 ft 10 in (*15·79 m*)
Height overall	16 ft 6 in (*5·03 m*)
Height folded	16 ft 8 in (*5·08 m*)
Power plant	2 × 11 255 lb (*5 105 kg*) st RB.168 Spey Mk. 101 Turbojets

Equips four Squadrons of the Fleet Air Arm and is still in production now for the RAF to which the Fleet Air Arm aircraft will eventually go. A land-based version, designated S.50, was built for the South African Air Force to a total of sixteen. An earlier version, the S.1 powered by 2 × 7 100 lb (*3220 kg*) BS Gyron Junior turbojets remains in second-line service with the FAA.

Hawker Siddeley Buccaneer S.Mk.2—No. 809 Sqdn, Royal Navy *Courtesy, J. D. R. Rawlings*

A-7 CORSAIR II Ling-Temco-Vought (USA)

Carrier-borne single-seat attack aircraft

Max speed at S/L	502 knots
Max range (ferry)	3 560 n. miles
Radius of action	620 n. miles
Other performance details	Secret
Armament	Fuselage: 2 × 20 mm guns Wing mounts (6): 4 000 lb (*1 815 kg*) normal bomb load increasing to 15 000 lb (*6 800 kg*) on short missions.
Max T-O weight	32 500 lb (*14 750 kg*)
Wing span	38 ft 9 in (*11·80 m*)
Width folded	23 ft 9 in (*7·24 m*)
Length	46 ft 1·5 in (*14·06 m*)
Height	16 ft 2 in (*4·93 m*)
Power plant	A-7A 1 × P. & W. TF30-P-6 of 11 350 lb (5 150 kg) st A-7B 1 × P. & W. TF-30P-8 of 12 000 lb (*5 443 kg*) A-7D: 1 × Allison TF-41-A-1 of 14 250 lb (*6 465 kg*)

A-7A entered service with US Navy in November 1967, followed by A-7B. A-7E is a version of A-7B with integrated Light Avionics System (ILAAS), 151 A-7Es being ordered.

Bomb-laden A-7A Corsair II's of Sqdn. VA-97 of the US Navy

SHIP BORNE AIRCRAFT

F-8 CRUSADER

Ling-Temco-Vought (USA)

Carrier-borne single-seat fighter

Max speed	F-8A, B, C: 870 knots plus F-8D, E, H, J: Mach 1·7
Combat radius (F-8A)	521·05 n. miles (*965 km*)
Other performance details	Secret
Armament	Fuselage: 4 × 20 mm Colt cannon and 2 × Sidewinder missiles (4 on F-8D, E, H, J) Wing Mounts: (2) on F-8E, E (FN), H and J only): 2 × 2 000 lb bombs or Bullpup A or B ASM's or 24 Zuni rockets
Max weight (catapult-launch)	34 000 lb (*15 420 kg*)
Wing span	F-8A, B: 35 ft 8 in (*10·87 m*) F-8C, D, E, H, J: 35 ft 2 in (*10·72 m*)
Length	F-8A, B, C, D: 54 ft 3 in (*16·54m*) F-8E, H, J: 54 ft 6 in (*16·61 m*)
Width folded	22 ft 6 in (*6·86 m*)
Height	15 ft 9 in (*4·80 m*)
Power plant	F-8A, B: 1 × Pratt & Whitney J57-P-4A of 16 200 lb (*7 327 kg*) st turbojet F-8C: 1 × P. & W. J57-P-16 of 16 900 lb (*7 665 kg*) st F-8D, E, H, J: 1 × P. & W. J-57-P-20 of 18 000 lb (*8 165 kg*) st turbojet

Crusader F-8E (FN) of Fl. 14 of the French Navy *Courtesy, J. D. R. Rawlings*

In service with the US Navy since 1957. F-8H and J are reworked D's and E's. F-8E(FN) is version for French Navy. Reconnaissance versions are RF-8A & RF-8G

ETENDARD IV-M

Dassault (France)

Carrier-borne single-seat strike aircraft

Max speed at 36,000 ft (*11 000 m*)	Mach 1·02
Max cruising speed at 25,000 ft (*7 600 m*)	Mach 0·90
Service ceiling	49 200 ft (*15 000 m*)
Combat range low level	320 n. miles
Combat range med. level	870 n. miles
Armament	Fuselage: 2 × 30 mm Cannon Wing Mounts (4): Up to 3 000 lb (*1 060 kg*) of rockets, bombs, Sidewinder AAM's or AS.30 ASM's
Max T-O weight	22 650 lb (*10 275 kg*)
Wing span	31 ft 6 in (*9·60 m*)
Width folded	25 ft 7 in (*7·80 m*)
Length	47 ft 3 in (*14·40 m*)
Height	14 ft 1 in (*4·30 m*)
Power plant	1 × Atar 8 turbojet of 9 700 lb (*4 400 kg*) st

Etendard IVM of Fl. 11 of the French Navy *Courtesy, A. Van Haute*

Entered service with French Navy for "Clemenceau" & "Foch" carriers in 1962. 75 aircraft were built. 21 additional aircraft were built as IV-P's as dual-role tanker and reconnaissance aircraft with nose and ventral camera positions and flight refuelling equipment.

F-14

Grumman (USA)

Carrier-borne two-seat all-weather fighter

Max speed	Mach 2 plus
Gross weight	50 000 lb (approx)
Armament	1 nose-mounted M-61 six-barrelled cannon, Phoenix, Sidewinder and Sparrow missiles
Power plant	F-14A 2 × Pratt & Whitney TF30-P-12 of 20 000 lb (*7 067 kg*) st turbofans F-14B 2 × Pratt & Whitney TF30-P-401 turbofans. F-14C, 2 new engines yet to be developed

This aircraft is at present at the advanced development stage as a replacement for the Phantom II in the US Navy. A mock-up has been built.

Grumman F-14A—US Navy

SHIP BORNE AIRCRAFT

GANNET AEW Mk 3 — Westland (UK)

Carrier-borne three-seat early-warning aircraft

Max speed	220 knots approx
Endurance	5-6 hours at 120 knots
Equipment	Early-warning electronics for long-range ship and aircraft detection
Max loaded weight	22 000 lb (*10 000 kg*) approx
Wing span	54 ft 4 in (*16·56 m*)
Width folded	19 ft 11 in (*6·07 m*)
Length	44 ft 0 in (*13·41 m*)
Height	16 ft 10 in (*5·13 m*)
Power plant	1 × Roll-Royce Bristol Double Mamba 102 turboprop of 3 875 ehp

Entered service with the Fleet Air Arm in 1959, equips No. 849 Squadron which provides early-warning flights on each carrier.

Westland Gannet AEW Mk 3 of the Royal Navy's No. 849 Sqdn — *Courtesy, J. D. R. Rawlings*

GANNET AS.4

A small number of this variant remain in service with the FAA on COD duties and for training, together with the T.5 version.

C-2A GREYHOUND — Grumman (USA)

Carrier-borne COD (Carrier On-board Delivery) Transport Aircraft

Max speed at 11 000 ft (*3 450 m*)	286 knots
Cruising speed at 27 300 ft (*8 320 m*)	266 knots
Range at cruising speed and height	1 320 n. miles
Capacity	39 troops, 20 litters with 4 attendants or 15 000 lb (*6 818 kg*) of freight
Max T-O weight	54 830 lb (24 922 *kg*)
Wing span	80 ft 7 in (*24·56 m*)
Length	56 ft 6 in (*17·22 m*).
Width folded	29 ft 4 in (*8·94 m*)
Height	15 ft 11 in (*4·85 m*)
Power plant	2 × Allison T56-A-8 turboprops of 4 050 ehp

A small number (17) of these COD transports have been built, developed from the E-2A Hawkeye, for service aboard US Navy carriers.

Grumman C-2A Greyhound of US Navy's Sqdn VR-30 — *Courtesy, D. A. Kasulka*

E-2A HAWKEYE — Grumman (USA)

Carrier-borne five-seat early-warning aircraft

Max speed at S/L	258 knots
Max speed at optimum altitude	306 knots
Service ceiling	28 800 ft (*8 780 m*)
Combat range	1 428 n. miles
Endurance, max fuel	7 hours
Equipment	Early-warning and command electronics including Airborne Tactical Data System (ATDS)
Max T-O weight	49 638 lb (*22 564 kg*)
Wing span	80 ft 7 in (*24·56 m*)
Width folded	29 ft 4 in (*8·94 m*)
Length	56 ft 4 in (*16·9 m*)
Height	15 ft 11 in (*4·85 m*)
Power plant	2 × Allison T56-A-8 turboprops of 4 050 ehp

59 produced for service with Squadrons VAW-11 and VAW-12 of the US Navy in 1964. A development, designated the E-2B with more advanced avionics, first flew in February, 1969.

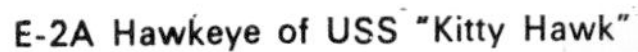

E-2A Hawkeye of USS "Kitty Hawk"

SHIP BORNE AIRCRAFT

A-6A INTRUDER Grumman (USA)

Carrier-borne two-seat strike and reconnaissance aircraft

Max speed at S/L	Mach 0·95
Service ceiling	41 660 ft (*12 700 m*)
Max range (ferry)	2 800 n. miles
Armament	Weapon mounts (5): Each mount is of 3 600 lb (*1 633 kg*) capacity to carry bombs or Bullpup missiles
Max T-O weight	60 626 lb (*27 500 kg*)
Wing span	53 ft 0 in (*16·15 m*)
Width folded	25 ft 2 in (*7·67 m*)
Length	54 ft 7 in (*16·64 m*)
Height overall	15 ft 7 in (*4·75 m*)
Height folded	15 ft 10 in (*4·82 m*)
Power plant	2 × P & W J52-P-8A turbojets of 9 300 lb (*4 218 kg*) each

This attack aircraft uses a digital integrated attack navigation system and serves with five US Navy and one Marine Corps squadrons. It has been developed into the EA-6A electronic countermeasures aircraft and further into the four-seat EA-6B for the same task.
Developments being produced are the A-6B, a special purpose missile carrier, the A-6C with TRIM electro-optical equipment, the KA-6D tanker version and the A-6E with Norden radar.

A-6A Intruder of Sqdn VA-165

F-4B PHANTOM II McDonnell (USA)

Carrier-borne two-seat all-weather fighter

Max speed	Mach 2·5
Combat ceiling	71 000 ft (*21 640 m*)
Combat radius	782 n. miles (*1 450 km*)
Ferry range	2 000 n. miles (*3700 km*)
Armament	Fuselage: 4 mountings for Sparrow III and/or Sidewinder AAM's Wings: 2 mountings for Sparrow III or Sidewinder AAM s Alternatively, 5 mounts for nuclear or conventional bombs and/or missiles up to 16 000 lb (*7 250 kg*)
Max T-O weight	54 600 lb (*24 765 kg*)
Wing span	38 ft 5 in (*11·70 m*)
Width folded	27 ft 6·5 in (*8·39 m*)
Length	58 ft 3 in (*17·76 m*)
Height	16 ft 3 in (*4·96 m*)
Power plant	F-4B, G: 2 × GE J79-GE-2A turbojets of 16 150 lb (*7 325 kg*) st each F-4J: 2 × GE J79-GE-10 turbojets of 16 500 lb (*7 485 kg*) st F-4K: 2 × RR Spey RB.168-25R turbofans of 12 500 lb (*5 670 kg*) st dry

Phantom FG.Mk.1 (F-4K) of Royal Navy

Courtesy, J. D. R. Rawlings

In service with the US Navy and Marines since 1962 in the F-4B form, together with the reconnaissance version, the RF-4B. The F-4G is a development of the F-4B with AN/ASW-21 data link communications equipment; the F-4J is a developed F-4B with more powerful engines, control improvements and advanced electronics; 24 of F-4K version, a developed F-4B, are in service as the Phantom FG 1 with the British Fleet Air Arm.

SEA HAWK Hawker Siddeley (UK)

Carrier-borne single-seat fighter

Max Speed at S/L	450 knots
Radius of action	250 n. miles
Armament	Fuselage: 4 × 20 mm cannon Wing mounts (4): 2 × 500 lb bombs and/or RP
Max gross weight	16 200 lb (*7 355 kg*)
Wing span	39 ft 0 in (*11·89 m*)
Width folded	13 ft 4 in (*4·04 m*)
Length	39 ft 8 in (*12·09 m*)
Height overall	8 ft 8 in (*2·64 m*)
Height folded	16 ft 10 in (*5·13 m*)
Power plant	1 × RR Nene 103 turbojet of 5 400 lb (*2 450 kg*) st

The type is operational with the Indian Navy for the carrier "Vikrant".

A Mk 50 Sea Hawk of the Indian Navy

SHIP BORNE AIRCRAFT

SEA VIXEN FAW Mk 2 — Hawker Siddeley (UK)

Carrier-borne two-seat all weather fighter

Max speed at 10 000 ft (*4 545 m*)	Mach 0·93
Service ceiling	Approx 48 000 ft (*14 630 m*)
Armament	Fuselage: 2 pods each containing 28 × 2 in rockets Wing mounts: (6) Combination of up to 4 Red Top or Bullpup AAM's, bombs, rocket pods or RP
Max Gross weight	36 000 lb (*16 300 kg*) approx
Wing span	50 ft 0 in (*15·24 m*)
Width folded	22 ft 3 in (*6·78 m*)
Length overall	55 ft 7 in (*16·68 m*)
Length folded	50 ft 2·5 in (*15·30 m*)
Height overall	11 ft 0 in (*3·35 m*)
Height folded	14 ft 11·[illegible] in (*4·55 m*)
Power plant	2 × RR Avon Ra.24 Mk 208 turbojets of 11 250 lb (*5,100 kg*) st

In service with the Fleet Air Arm since 1959, it equips three first-line squadrons.

Hawker Siddeley Sea Vixen FAW.Mk.2 of No. 892 Sqdn — *Courtesy, J. D. R. Rawlings*

SKYHAWK — McDonnell/Douglas (USA)

Carrier-borne single-seat attack bomber

Max speed at S/L	590 knots (A-4E version)
Max range	1 740 n. miles plus
Armament	Fixed: 2 × 20 mm cannon in wings. Fuselage and Wing Mounts (5): Up to 8 200 lb (*3 723 kg*) assorted bombs, rockets, Sidewinder AAM's Bullpup ASM's, Zuni or Mighty Mouse pods, gun pods, torpedoes or ECM equipment
Max T-O weight	24 500 lb (*11 113 kg*) (A-4E version
Wing span	27 ft 6 in (*8·38 m*)
Length	40 ft 3·5 in (*12·59 m*) (A-4E version)
Height	15 ft 0 in (*4·57 m*)
Power plant	A-4A: 1 × Wright J-65-W-4 turbojet of 7 200 lb (*3 493 kg*) st A-4B, C: 1 × Wright J65-W-16A of 7 700 lb (*3 493 kg*) st A-4E: 1 × P & W J52-P-6A of 8 500 lb (*3 855kg*) st A-4F, G: 1 × P & W J52-P-8A of 9 300 lb (*4 218 kg*) st

In service with the US Navy since 1956. A-4C and subsequent models have all-weather capability. A-4F improved controls. A-4G in service with the Royal Australian Navy since 1967 (8 aircraft). Also supplied to Argentina, Israel and R.N.Z.A.F. Re-ordered into production in 1969 for 50 A-4M's for the US Navy with a more powerful J52-P-400 engine.

A-4G Skyhawk—805 Sqdn, Royal Australian Navy

SHIP BORNE AIRCRAFT

A-3 B SKYWARRIOR McDonnell/Douglas (USA)

Carrier-borne 3-seat attack bomber

Max speed at 10 000 ft (*4 545 m*)	550 knots
Service ceiling	45 000 ft (*13 780 m*)
Range, Normal	2 500 n. miles
Armament	Fuselage: Weapons bay for bombs, torpedoes, etc. Tail-mounted barbette with 2 × 20 mm cannon
Gross weight	73 000 lb (*33 181 kg*)
Wing span	72 ft 5 in (*22·07 m*)
Length	76 ft 4 in (*21·46 m*)
Height	22 ft 8 in (*6·91 m*)
Power plant	A-3B: 2 × P & W J57-P-10 turbojets of 10 500 lb (*4 760 kg*) st

Entered service with the US Navy in 1957, the A-3B has provision for flight-refuelling. Electronic counter-measures version redesignated EA-3B and thirty RA-3B's entered service with cameras in the weapons bay.

McDonnell/Douglas Skywarrior—Sqdn VAH-13 of USS "Kitty Hawk"

Courtesy, G. S. Williams

E-1B TRACER Grumman (USA)

Carrier-borne four-seat early-warning aircraft

Max speed at S/L	230 knots
Endurance at 10 000 ft (*4 545 m*) and 156 knots	8 hr
Equipment	a 20 × 30 ft (*6·1 × 9·1 m*) radar antenna used in conjunction with the APS-82 early-warning system
Normal T-O weight	27 000 lb (*12 250 kg*)
Wing span	72 ft 7 in (*22·04 m*)
Length	45 ft 4 in (*13·82 m*)
Height	16 ft 10 in (*5·13 m*)
Power plant	2 × Wright R-1820-82 piston engines of 1 525 hp

Developed from the S-2 Tracker. 64 aircraft were built for the US Navy and entered service first in 1960.

Grumman E-1B Tracer

S-2 TRACKER Grumman (USA)

Max speed at S L	243 knots (S-2E)
Patrol speed at 1 500 ft (*450 m*)	130 knots
Service ceiling	21 000 ft (*6 400 m*)
Max range	1 172 n. miles
Max endurance	9 hrs
Armament (S-2D version)	Fuselage bomb bay: 2 × homing torpedoes or 4 × 385 lb depth charges or 1 × Mk 101 depth bomb Wing mounts (6): torpedoes or rockets or 250 lb bombs or sonobuoys
Max T-O weight	29 150 lb (*13 222 kg*)
Wing span	72 ft 7 in (*22·13 m*)
Width folded	27 ft 4 in (*8·33 m*)
Length	43 ft 6 in (*13·26 m*)
Height	16 ft 7 in (*5·06 m*)
Power plant	2 × Wright R-1820-82W piston engines of 1 525 hp each

The original variant, the S-2A, entered production in 1953 and was supplied to Japan (60), Italy (40), Brazil (12) and the Royal Netherlands Navy (26) in addition to the US Navy. The S-2C had enlarged weapons bays as did the S-2D which also had increased wingspan. The S-2E is an S-2D with improved ASW equipment, 14 of which are being supplied to the Royal Australian Navy. This aircraft was built under licence in Canada with the designations CS2F-1 (S-2A equivalent) and CS2F-2 and CS2F-3 which are developed versions. These are in service with the Royal Canadian Navy and the CS2F-1 with the Royal Netherlands Navy.

C-1A TRADER

Developed from the S-2 Tracker is the C-1A Trader which is used by the US Navy as a COD transport with accommodation for nine passengers or 3 500 lb (*1 590 kg*) of freight.

SHIP BORNE AIRCRAFT

Grumman S-2A Tracker—Royal Dutch Navy

Courtesy, J. D. R. Rawlings

A-5 VIGILANTE North American (USA)

Carrier-borne two-seat reconnaissance aircraft

Max speed at 40 000 ft	Mach 2·1
Service ceiling	64 000 ft (*19 500 m*)
Normal range	2 000 n. miles
Armament	Fuselage weapons bay: thermo-nuclear and conventional bombs Wing mountings: variety of weapons
Max T-O weight	approx 80 000 lb (*36 285 kg*)
Wing span	53 ft 0 in)*16·15 m*)
Width folded	42 ft 0 in (*12·80 m*)
Length, overall	75 ft 10 in (*23·11 m*)
Length folded	65 ft 4·8 in (*19·93 m*)
Height	19 ft 4·8 in (*5·91 m*)
Power plant	2 × GE J79-GE-8 turbojets of 10 900 lb (***4 944 kg***) st

In service as the A-5A with the US Navy from 1961. The A-5B was a long-range version with extra fuel in the enlarged fuselage. The RA-5C is a reconnaissance version of the A-5B, carrying cameras and side-looking radar in a ventral fairing. All A's and most B's have been converted to RA-5C standard.

RA-5C Vigilante

HELICOPTERS
Drone Helicopter

QH-50 Gyrodyne (USA)

Max speed	80 knots
Cruising speed	60 knots
Service ceiling	QH-50C: 16 500 ft (*5 030 m*) QH-50D: 25 000 ft (*7 620 m*)
Hovering ceiling	QH-50C: 11 300 ft (*3 445 m*) QH-50D: 16 000 ft (*4 875 m*)
Range	60 n. miles
Armament	2 × Mk 46 torpedoes or 1 torpedo and 1 sonobuoy
Max T-O weight	QH-50C: 2 300 lb (*1 043 kg*) QH-50D: 2 350 lb (*1 066 kg*)
Rotor Diameter	20 ft 0 in (*6·10 m*)
Power plant	QH-50C: 1 × Boeing T50-BO-8A of 300 shp QH-50D: 1 × Boeing T50-BO-10 of 300 shp) turbine engine

The DASH System (Drone Anti-Submarine Helicopter), of which the QH-50 is the mobile weapon-carrying unit, is carried aboard many US Navy vessels. The QH-50C went into se.vice in 1962 and the QH-50D in 1965. Take-off and landing are visually controlled by the Deck Control Officer who hands the helicopter over to the control information centre in the ship which flies the drone to the target, actuates the arming and weapon release switches and returns the drone to the ship. Sixteen are being supplied to the Japanese MSDF.

Helicopters

AGUSTA A.106 Agusta (Italy)

Ship-borne single-seat ASW light helicopter

Max speed	108 knots
Cruising speed	100 knots
Hovering ceiling	6 560 ft (*2 000 m*)
Max range	152 n. miles
Endurance	2 hrs
Armament	2 × Mk 44 torpedoes, or rockets or bombs
Max T-O weight	3 000 lb (*1 360 kg*)
Main rotor diameter	31 ft 2 in (*9·50 m*)
Length overall	36 ft 0 in (*10·97 m*)
Length folded	22 ft 8 in (*6·90 m*)
Power plant	1 × Turbomeca-Agusta TAA-230 shaft-turbine engine of 300 shp

Built as a private venture anti-submarine helicopter for operation from light naval vessels the prototype first flew in 1966. It is in production for and service with the Italian Navy.

Agust A.106 light helicopter—Italian Navy *Courtesy. M. Fricke*

HELICOPTERS

AGUSTA-BELL 204B

Agusta (Italy)

Ship-borne ASW helicopter

Max speed at S/L	120 knots
Cruising speed	104 knots
Hovering ceiling	4 400 ft (*1 340 m*)
Max range	327 n. miles
Equipment	Dipping Sonar
Armament	2 × Mk 44 torpedoes
Max T-O weight	9 500 lb (*4 310 kg*)
Main rotor diameter	48 ft 0 in (*14·63 m*)
Length overall	57 ft 0 in (*17·37 m*)
Power plant	1 × Lycoming T53-L-11A shaft-turbine engine of 1 100 shp; alternatively 1 × Rolls-Royce Bristol Gnome H.1200 of 1 200 shp

The Bell UH-1B built under licence in Italy, this aircraft is in service with the Dutch, Italian and Spanish navies.

Agusta-Bell 204B —Royal Dutch Navy *Courtesy, S. P. Peltz*

SE.3160 ALOUETTE III

Sud Aviation (France)

Carrier-borne seven-seat general-purpose helicopter

Max speed at S/L	114 knots
Cruising speed at S/L	102 knots
Service ceiling	13 950 ft (*4 250 m*)
Range with 1 400 lb (*635 kg*) payload	162 n. miles
Equipment	Sikorsky-Hamilton Standard auto-pilot with hover stabilisation, Doppler radar, quick-mooring harpoon
Max T-O weight (standard version)	4 630 lb (*2 100 kg*)
Main rotor diameter	36 ft 1 in (*11·0 m*)
Length overall	42 ft 0·8 in (*12·82 m*)
Length folded	33 ft 4·5 in (*10·17 m*)
Height	9 ft 9 in (*2·97 m*)
Power plant	1 × Turbomeca Artouste IIIB shaft-turbine engine of 870 shp derated to 550 shp

Developed from the standard Alouette III, this version is intended for "plane guard" duties aboard French Navy carriers. It first flew in 1964. It also serves with 29 air forces.

Alouette III of L'Aeronavale *Courtesy, Stephen P. Peltz*

HUEYCOBRA AH-1G

Bell (USA)

Two-seat close-support helicopter

Max speed (in dive)	199 knots
Cruising speed	150·9 knots
Service ceiling	20 000 ft (*6 096 m*)
Hovering ceiling	11 900 ft (*3 627 m*)
Range	386·36 n. miles
Gross weight	9 500 lb (*4 309 kg*)
Main rotor diameter	44 ft 0 in (*13·41 m*)
Length	53 ft 1·25 in (*16·18 m*)
Power plant	1 × Lycoming T53-L-5 of 960 shp

49 in service with the US Marine Corps. Over 800 on order for the US Army as the AH-1G.

Bell AH-IG Hueycobra—US Army

HELICOPTERS

BELL 47G Bell (USA)

Two-seat communications light helicopter

Max speed	95·45 knots
Cruising speed at 5 000 ft (*1 525 m*)	80 knots
Service ceiling	18 400 ft (*5 610 m*)
Hovering ceiling	12 300 ft (*3 758 m*)
Range	236·36 n. miles
Gross weight	1 848 lb (*838 kg*)
Main rotor diameter	37 ft 1·5 in (*11·32 m*)
Length	43 ft 7·5 in (*9·62 m*)
Height	9 ft 3·75 in (*2·83 m*)
Power plant	1 × Lycoming VO-540-BIB six-cylinder engine of 310 hp

In use with Chilean, Italian, Mexican, Peruvian and Uruguayan Navies.

Bell 47G *Courtesy, P. R. March*

Ka-15 (code-name "Hen") Kamov (USSR)

Ship-borne two-seat general-purpose light helicopter

Max speed	81 knots
Cruising speed	67·5 knots
Service ceiling	9 840 ft (*3 000 m*)
Hovering ceiling	2 230 ft (*680 m*)
Max range	252 n. miles
Max endurance	4 hrs
Gross weight	2 500 lb (*1 136 kg*)
Main rotor diameter	32 ft 9 in (*9·97 m*)
Length	19 ft 6 in (*6·0 m*)
Power plant	1 × Ivchenko AI-14V radial piston-engine of 255 hp

In service with the Soviet Naval Airfleet

Kamov Ka-15—Soviet Naval Airfleet

Ka-25 (code-name "Hormone") Kamov (USSR)

Ship-borne anti-submarine strike helicopter

Max speed	130 knots
Other performance details	secret
Equipment	Search radar under nose
T-O weight	11 500 lb (*5 000 kg*)
Main rotor diameter	51 ft 8 in (*15·5 m*)
Power plant	2 × 900 shp Glushenkov shaft-turbine-engines

In service with the Soviet Naval Airfleet

Kamov Ka-25 "Hormone" anti-submarine helicopter

S-55 Sikorsky (USA)

Carrier-borne and land-based general-purpose helicopter

Max speed at S/L	97 knots
Cruising speed	79 knots
Hovering ceiling	2 300 ft (*700 m*)
Range	315 n. miles
Gross weight	7 900 lb (*3 319.19 kg*)
Main rotor diameter	53 ft 0 in (*16·16 m*)
Length (fuselage)	42 ft 3 in (*12·88 m*)
Height	13 ft 4 in (*4·07 m*)
Power plant	1 × Wright R-1300-3 radial piston-engine of 800 hp

The S.55 is still in service with the US Navy as the UH-19F and the Marine Corps as the CH-19E and with Japanese and Netherlands Navies for plane guard, transport and search and rescue duties.

HELICOPTERS

Sikorsky S-55

Courtesy, M. Takeda

S-56 CH-37C

Sikorsky (USA)

Land-based two-crew assault transport helicopter

Max speed at S/L	112 knots
Cruising speed	100 knots
Hovering ceiling	1 100 ft (*335 m*)
Service ceiling	8 700 ft (*2 650 m*)
Range	130 n. miles
Capacity	20 passengers or 1 900 cu ft (*53·8 m³*) of cargo space
Main rotor diameter	72 ft 0 in (*21·95 m*)
Length, fuselage	64 ft 10 in (*19·76 m*)
Height	22 ft 0 in (*6·71 m*)
Normal T-O weight	31 000 lb (*14,100 kg*)
Power plant	2 × P & W R-2800-54 piston engines of 2 100 hp each

Approx 60 aircraft were built for the US Marines, commencing 1955, some remain in service.

A US Marines CH-37C

S-58 SEABAT

Sikorsky (USA)

Carrier-borne and land-based anti-submarine and general-purpose helicopter

Max speed at S/L	106 knots
Cruising speed	85 knots
Hovering ceiling	2 400 ft (*730 m*)
Service ceiling	9 500 ft (*2 900 m*)
Normal range	215 n. miles
Capacity	16-18 passengers
Max T-O weight	14 000 lb (*6 350 kg*)
Main rotor diameter	56 ft 0 in (*17·07 m*)
Length	56 ft 8 in (*17·27 m*)
Height	15 ft 11 in (*4·85 m*)
Power plant	1 × Wright R-1820-84 piston engine of 1 525 hp

In service with the US Navy as the SH-34G and SH-34J Seabat, the LH-34D for cold-weather operation, UH-34G and UH-34J utility aircraft. UH-34D is the US Marines version, also UH-34E amphibious version and VH-34D VIP transport. The S-58 is in service with other navies including the Argentine Navy, Belgian Navy (five, Sud-built), Indonesian Navy, Royal Netherlands Navy and the French Navy, the latter's aircraft being built in France by Sud-Aviation.

Sikorsky S-58—US Marine Corps

HELICOPTERS

SH-3 SEA KING

Sikorsky (USA)

Carrier-borne and land-based amphibious all-weather ASW and Transport helicopter

Max speed	135 knots
Cruising speed for max range	118 knots
Hovering ceiling	8 200 ft (*2 500 m*)
Service ceiling	14 700 ft (*4 480 m*)
Range with max fuel	550 n. miles
Equipment	Bendix AQS-13 sonar. Hamilton autostabilisation equipment with sonar coupler. Doppler radar
Armament	Up to 840 lb (*382 kg*) of weapons including homing torpedoes
Max T-O weight	20 500 lb (*9 300 kg*)
Main rotor diameter	62 ft 0 in (*18·90 m*)
Length overall	72 ft 8 in (*22·15 m*)
Width folded	16 ft 4 in (*4·98 m*)
Height	16 ft 10 in (*5·13 m*)
Power plant	2 × GE T58-GE-10 shaft turbines of 1 400 shp each

Two versions built by Sikorsky, the SH-3A, with GE T58-GE-8B engines which is also in service with the Japanese MSDF and, under the designation CHSS-2, with the Royal Canadian Navy; and the SH-3D, also in service with the Spanish and Italian Navies and, built under licence by Westland Aircraft, with the Fleet Air Arm, this latter using the RR Bristol Gnome 1400 engine.

SH-3D Sea King

Courtesy, J. D. R. Rawlings

SEA KNIGHT

Boeing-Vertol (USA)

Carrier-borne and land-based three-crew transport and utility helicopter

Max speed	146 knots
Cruising speed	144 knots
Hovering ceiling	5 600 ft (*1 707 m*)
Service ceiling	14 000 ft (*4 265 m*)
Range	200 n. miles
Capacity	25 troops or 15 stretchers plus 2 attendants
Max T-O weight	23 000 lb (*10 430 kg*)
Main rotor diameter	50 ft 0 in (*15·24 m*)
Length, fuselage	44 ft 10 in (*13·66 m*)
Height	16 ft 8·5 in (*5·09 m*)
Power plant	2 × GE T58-GE-10 shaft-turbine engines of 1 250 shp each

In service with the US Marine Corps since 1962 as the CH-46A and US Navy for shore to ship and ship to ship duties as the UH-46A, uprated in 1966 to CH-46D and UH-46D. Three in service with the Royal Swedish Navy as the HKP-4 using Bristol Siddeley Gnome H1200 and thirty-six for the Japanese MSDF.

Boeing-Vertol UH-46A Sea Knight of the US Navy

SEASPRITE

Kaman (USA)

Ship-borne two-crew all-weather rescue and general-purpose helicopter

Max speed at S/L	140 knots
Cruising speed	132 knots
Hovering ceiling	5 100 ft (*1 555 m*)
Service ceiling	17 400 ft (*5 300 m*)
Max range	580 n. miles
Capacity	11 passengers
Max T-O weight	10 200 lb (*4 625 m*)
Main rotor diameter	44 ft 0 in (*13·41 m*)
Length	52 ft 2 in (*15·90 m*)
Height	13 ft 6 in (*4·11 m*)
Power plant	1 × GE T58-GE-8B shaft turbine engine of 1 250 shp

Entered service with the US Navy in 1962 as the UH-2A, followed by the UH-2B "fair weather" version. A twin-engined version, the UH-2C with two T58 engines, is being introduced into service by retrospective modifications of UH-2A's and B's. Twelve UH-2C's redesignated HH-2C's, are being converted into gunships with a chin Minigun, 2 additional machine-guns and additional armour.

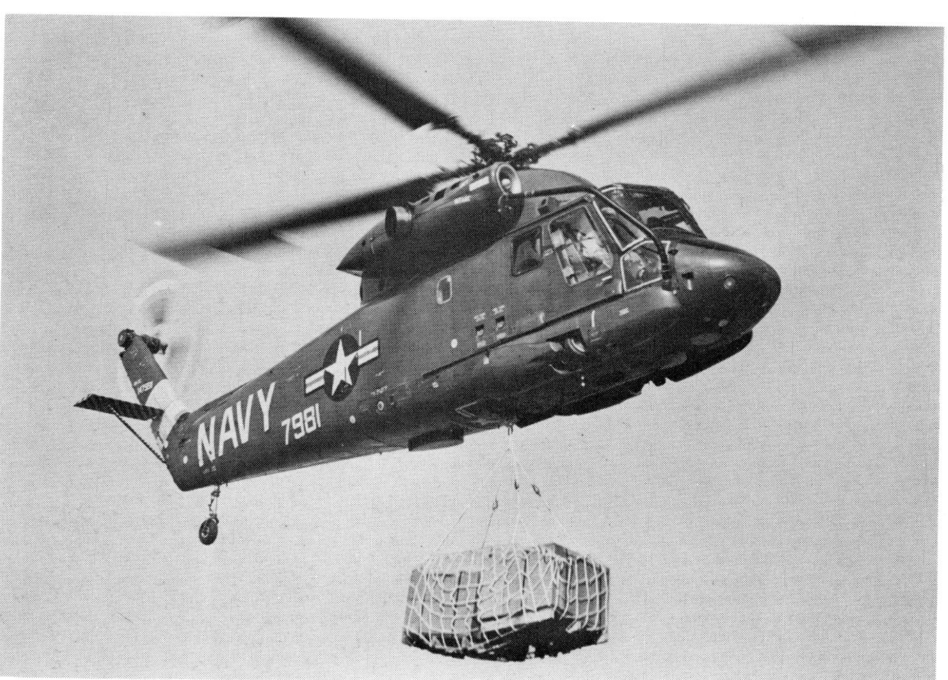

Kaman UH-2C, twin-engined Seasprite

HELICOPTERS

SEA STALLION

Sikorsky (USA)

Carrier-borne and land-based three-crew heavy assault and transport helicopter

Max speed	170 knots
Cruising speed	150 knots
Hovering ceiling	4 800 ft (*1 460 m*)
Service ceiling	18 550 ft (*5 655 m*)
Range, with 4 000 lb payload	222 n. miles
Capacity	38 passengers, 24 stretchers or 8 000 lb (*3 630 kg*) of internal or external cargo
Max T-O weight	42 000 lb (*19 050 kg*)
Main rotor diameter	72 ft 3 in (*22·02 m*)
Length	88 ft 3 in (*26·92 m*)
Width, folded	15 ft 6 in (*4·72 m*)
Height	24 ft 11 in (*7·60 m*)
Power plant	2 × GE T64-GE-6 shaft turbine engines of 2 850 shp each

Entered service with the US Marine Corps as the CH-53A in 1966, becoming operational in Vietnam in January 1967.

Sikorsky CH-53A of the US Marine Corps

Courtesy, B. M, Service

SA.321 SUPER FRELON

Sud-Aviation (France)

Land-based two - crew heavy assault and anti-submarine helicopter

Max speed at S/L	143 knots
Cruising speed	134 knots
Hovering ceiling	2 625 ft (*800 m*)
Service ceiling	14 100 ft (*4 300 m*)
Range with 3 000 kg payload	270 n. miles
Range, ferry	750 n. miles
Capacity	30 troops, 15 stretchers or 9 920 lb (*4 500 kg*) payload
Max T-O weight	26 450 lb (*12 000 kg*)
Main rotor diameter	62 ft 0 in (*18·90 m*)
Length	76 ft 7 in (*23·0 m*)
Width folded	17 ft 1 in (*5·20 m*)
Height	21 ft 11 in (*6·60 m*)
Power plant	3 × Turbomeca Turmo IIIC3 shaft-turbine engines of 1 500 shp each

In service with the French Navy as the SA-321D for ASW duties, the SA-321E for "Clemenceau" at the Pacific test centre, and the SA-321Ga and SA-321Gb, developments of the E and D respectively.

SA-321D Super Frelon—French Navy

Courtesy, B. M. Service

HELICOPTERS

UH-1E

Bell (USA)

Land-based single-crew assault support helicopter

Max speed	140 knots
Cruising speed	120 knots
Hovering ceiling	11 800 ft (*3 600 m*)
Service ceiling	21 000 ft (*6 400 m*)
Range, max fuel	250 n. miles
Capacity	12-14 passengers
Max T-O weight	9 500 lb (*4 300 kg*)
Main rotor diameter	44 ft 0 in (*13·41 m*)
Length	53 ft 0 in (*16·15 m*)
Height	12 ft 8·5 in (*3·87 m*)
Power plant	1 × Lycoming T53-L-13 shaft-turbine engine of 1 400 shp

Entered service with the US Marine Corps in 1964; the UH-1E is the Marine version of the Iroquois which is in widespread military service. Nine UH-1D's are in service with the Royal Australian Navy. Licence-built by Dornier, 27 UH-1D's will serve with the German Navy. The US Navy is to have 45 TH-IL trainers and 8 UH-1L.

One of the many US Marine Corps UH-1E's

WASP

Westland (UK)

Ship-borne two-crew anti-submarine helicopter

Max speed at S/L	105 knots
Cruising speed	96 knots
Hovering ceiling	8 900 ft (*2 715 m*)
Range	235 n. miles
Armament	2 × 44 Mk homing torpedoes
Max T-O weight	5 500 lb (*2 496 kg*)
Main rotor diameter	32 ft 3 in (*9·83 m*)
Length	40 ft 4 in (*12·29 m*)
Width folded	8 ft 8 in (*2·64 m*)
Height	11 ft 3 in (*3·43 m*)
Power plant	1 × RR Bristol Nimbus 103 shaft turbine engine of 710 shp

In service with the Fleet Air Arm since 1963 aboard anti-submarine frigates. Also with the navies of Australia, Brazil, Netherlands, New Zealand and South Africa.

Westland Wasp HAS 1

Courtesy, J. D. R. Rawlings

WESSEX

Westland (UK)

Ship and carrier-borne two-crew anti-submarine assault and general-purpose helicopter

Max speed at S/L	115 knots
Cruising speed	105 knots
Hovering ceiling	HAS.1: 3 600 ft (*1 100 m*) HU.5: 4,000 ft (*1 220 m*)
Service ceiling	HAS.1: 14 100 ft (*4 300 m*)
Normal range	HAS.1: 340 n. miles HU.5: 260 n. miles
Equipment	HAS.1: Doppler radar and dipping sonar HAS.3: as HAS.1 plus new search radar
Armament	HAS.1, 3: 1 or 2 homing torpedoes on fuselage side mounts, alternatively 4 × SS.11 ASM's HU.5: 4 × SS.11 ASM's alternatively various gun/rocket combinations
Capacity	HAS.1, 3: two additional A/S crew members HU.5: up to 13 troops
Max T-O weight	HAS.1: 12 600 lb (*5 715 kg*) HU.5: 13 500 lb (*6 120 kg*)
Main rotor diameter	56 ft 0 in (*17·07 m*)
Length	65 ft 9 in (*20·03 m*)
Length folded	38 ft 6 in (*11·73 m*)
Width, folded	13 ft 4 in (*4·06 m*)
Height	16 ft 2 in (*4·93 m*)
Power plant	HAS.1: 1 × Napier Gazelle NGa. 13 Mk 161 shaft turbine engine of 1 450 shp HAS.3: 1 × Napier Gazelle NGa. 13 Mk 165 shaft turbine engine of 1 600 shp HU.5: 2 × RR Bristol Gnome 112/113 shaft turbine engines of 775 shp each

In service with the Fleet Air Arm on anti-submarine duties since 1961 (HAS.1) and 1967 (HAS.3), also with Royal Australian Navy as HAS.31, identical to HAS.1 (27 aircraft, some modified to HAS-31B, with new search radar). The HU.5 version is a Marine Commando assault version, in service since 1964 with the Commando carriers.

HELICOPTERS

Westland Wessex HU Mk. 5—No. 845 Sqdn, Royal Navy *Courtesy, J. D. R. Rawlings*

WHIRLWIND Westland (UK)

Land-based and Carrier-borne two-crew rescue and general-purpose helicopter

Max speed at S/L	122 knots
Cruising speed	120 knots
Hovering ceiling	6 900 ft (*2 100 m*)
Service ceiling	16 600 ft (*5 060 m*)
Normal range	260 n. miles
Capacity	Up to 10 troops or 6 stretchers
Armament	4 × SS.11 ASM's
Max T-O weight	8 000 lb (*3 630 kg*)
Main rotor diameter	53 ft 0 in (*16·15 m*)
Length, fuselage	44 ft 2 in (*13·46 m*)
Height	13 ft 2·5 in (*4·03 m*)
Power plant	1 × RR Bristol Gnome H.1000 shaft turbine of 1 050 shp

This aircraft is in service with the Fleet Air Arm as the HAR.9 for plane guard and SAR duties and with RAF Coastal Command as the HAR.10 for SAR duties.

Westland Whirlwind HAR 9—Royal Navy

Courtesy, J. D. R. Rawlings

LAND-BASED AIRCRAFT

HU-16 ALBATROSS

Grumman (USA)

Land-based five-crew general purpose amphibian

Max speed at S/L	205 knots
Max cruising speed	195 knots
Service ceiling	21 500 ft (*6,550 m*)
Range	2 500 n. miles
Equipment (ASW version)	MAD gear, nose AS radome, ECM radome in wing
Armament (ASW version)	Torpedoes, depth charges or rockets
Max T-O weight	37 500 lb (*12 500 kg*)
Wing span	96 ft 8 in (*29·42 m*)
Length	62 ft 10 in (*19·12 m*)
Power plant	2 × Wright R-1820-76A radial piston engines of 1 425 hp each

In service with the US Navy as HU-16D and Coast Guard as HU-16E, developed from earlier HU-16C, many of which were converted. Supplied to a number of foreign countries and a special ASW version produced in 1961 and supplied to Norway and Spain. CSR-110 is a modified HU-16 with Wright R-1820-82 engines for SAR duties in Canada.

Grumman HU-16A Albatross—No. 333 Sqdn, Royal Norwegian Air Force *Courtesy, S. P. Peltz*

CP-107 ARGUS

Canadair (Canada)

Fifteen-crew long-range maritime reconnaissance aircraft

Max speed	250 knots
Cruising speed	150-175 knots
Service ceiling	20 000 ft (*6 100 m*) plus
Max range	5 037 n. miles at 194 knots
Armament	15 600 lb of weapons (bombs, torpedoes, missiles) stowed 8 000 lb internally and 3 800 lb under each wing
T-O weight	148 000 lb (*67 130 kg*)
Wing span	142 ft 3·5 in (*43·38 m*)
Length	128 ft 3 in (*39·09 m*)
Height	36 ft 8·5 in (*11·19 m*)
Power plant	4 × Wright R-3350-EA-1 turbo-compound radial piston engines of 3 700 hp each

In service with three squadrons (Nos. 404, 405, 415 Sqdns) of the Canadian Armed Forces in both Mk 1 and Mk 2 versions which differ in equipment.

Canadair Argus—No. 415 Sqdn. CAF

Br.1150 ATLANTIC

Breguet (France)

Twelve-crew long-range maritime reconnaissance aircraft

Max speed	330 knots
Max range	3 600 n. miles at 170 knots
Max endurance at 169 knots (patrol speed)	18 hours
Armament	Fuselage weapons bay: carries standard NATO bombs, 385 lb depth charges, homing torpedoes Wing mounts (4): HVAR rockets, or Martel ASM's
Max T-O weight	95 900 lb (*43 500 kg*)
Wing span	119 ft 1 in (*36·3 m*)
Length	104 ft 2 in (*31·75 m*)
Height	37 ft 1 in (*11·3 m*)
Power plant	2 × RR Tyne R.Ty.20 Mk 21 turboprop engines of 6 105 ehp each

In service since 1966 with French Navy (40 aircraft), German Navy (20 aircraft), Netherlands (9 aircraft), Italian (18 aircraft).

Breguet Atlantic—Fl. 22 French Navy

Courtesy, J. D. R. Rawlings

LAND-BASED AIRCRAFT

BERIEV M-12 (code-name "Mail") Beriev (USSR)

Maritime-reconnaissance amphibian

Max speed	304 knots
Max Altitude (record attempt)	39 977 ft (*12 185 m*)
Gross weight	65 000 lb (*20 545 kg*)
Equipment	Nose radome and MAD gear in tail
Span	108 ft 0 in (*32·8 m*)
Length	96 ft 0 in (*28·8 m*)
Power plant	2 × Ivchenko AI-20D turboprop engines of 4 015 shp each

In service with the Soviet Naval Airfleet

Beriev M-12 "Mail" of the Soviet Naval Airfleet

OV-10A BRONCO North American (USA)

Light armed-reconnaissance and forward air control aircraft

Max speed	255·45 knots
Combat radius	207·27 n. miles
Ferry range	1 298·3 n. miles
Max T-O weight	14 466 lb (*6 563 kg*)
Wing span	40 ft 0 in (*12·19 m*)
Length	41 ft 7 in (*12·67 m*)
Height	15 ft 2 in (*4·62 m*)

76 in service with the US Marine Corps.

Lockheed KC-130F—US Marines

C-130 HERCULES Lockheed (USA)

Medium-range transport and reconnaissance aircraft

Max level speed	318 knots
Max cruising speed	305 knots
Service ceiling	23 000 ft (*7 010 m*)
Range with max load	2 000 n. miles
Capacity	92 troops, 64 paratroops, or 74 stretchers
Max T-O weight	155 000 lb (*70 310 kg*)
Wing span	132 ft 7 in (*40·25 m*)
Length	97 ft 9 in (*29·78 m*)
Height	38 ft 3 in (*11·66 m*)
Power plant	4 × Allison T56-A-7A turboprop engines of 4 050 eshp each

This transport is in widespread service with eleven air forces and with the US Navy as C-130E, LC-130F (for ski operation), the Marine Corps as KC-130F (with flight refuelling equipment) and with the US Coast Guard as HC-130C for SAR duties.

A32 LANSEN SAAB (Sweden)

Two-seat all-weather and attack fighter and reconnaissance aircraft

Max speed at S/L	620 knots
Cruising speed at 36 000 ft (*11 000 m*)	470 knots
Service ceiling	52 500 ft (*16 000 m*)
Normal range	750 n. miles
Max range	1 737 n. miles
Armament	Fuselage: 2 × 20 mm cannon Wing mounts (2): 2 × Rb 04 ASM's or 2 200 lb of bombs or up to 24 rockets
T-O weight	29 750 lb (*13 500 kg*)
Wing span	42 ft 8 in (*13·00 m*)
Length	47 ft 7 in (*14·50 m*)
Height	15 ft 3 in (*4·65 m*)
Power plant	1 × Svenska Flygmotor R.M 5 (RR Avon) turbojet of 9 920 lb st

In service with the Swedish Air Force as the A32A attack fighter, J32B all-weather fighter and S32C photo-reconnaissance aircraft.

Saab A32A Lansen

LAND-BASED AIRCRAFT

MB 326K Aermacchi (Italy)

Two-seater Trainer-ground attack

Max speed	476·36 knots
Cruising speed	450 knots
Service ceiling	39 000 ft (*11 900 m*)
Radius of action (fully loaded)	68·2 n. miles
Gross weight	10 000 lb (*4 535 kg*)
Wing span	35 ft 7 in (*10·85 m*)
Length	34 ft 11·25 in (*10·65 m*)
Height	12 ft 2·5 in (*3·72 m*)
Power plant	1 × Rolls Royce Bristol Viper 20 of 3 410 lb (*1 547 kg*) st
Armament	Max of 3 075 lb (*1 395 kg*) underwing stores on six mounts

Six of this version built as light attack fighters for the Argentine Navy.

The Aermacchi MB 326G from which the MB 326K has been developed for the Argentine Navy

P-2 NEPTUNE Lockheed (USA)

Seven-seat long-range maritime-reconnaissance aircraft

Max speed	350 knots
Patrol speed at 1,000 ft (*305 m*)	150-180 knots
Service ceiling	22 000 ft (*6 700 m*)
Max range	3 200 n. miles
Armament	Fuselage Weapons Bay: Up to 8 000 lb (*5 000 kg*) of bombs, torpedoes, depth charges. Wing mounts (2): 16 × 0·5 in rockets. Optional dorsal turret with 2 × 0·5 guns
Max T-O weight	79 895 lb (*36 497·73 kg*)
Wing span (inc. tiptanks)	103 ft 10 in (*31·65 m*)
Length	91 ft 8 in (*27·94 m*)
Height	29 ft 4 in (*8·94 m*)
Power plant	2 × Wright R-3350-32W radial piston engines of 3 500 hp each PLUS 2 × Westinghouse J34 turbojet engines of 3 400 lb st each

This aircraft is in widespread service with the US Navy as the P-2H and with the French Navy, Royal Netherlands Navy, Royal Canadian Air Force, Royal Australian Air Force and with Argentine and Spain. With Brazil and Portugal it serves as the P-2E without the auxiliary turbojets.
A highly-modified version, the Kawasaki P-2J serves with the Japanese MSDF. It is powered by two 2 850 shp IHI/General Electric T64-GE-10 turboprops plus two 3 080 lb st IHI J3-IHI-7C auxiliary turbojets. It has an extended front fuselage and new sensor systems.

Lockheed Neptune—Royal Dutch Navy *Courtesy, J. D. R. Rawlings*

HS.801 NIMROD MR.1 Hawker Siddeley (UK)

Eleven-seat long-range maritime-reconnaissance aircraft

Performance details	Secret
Wing span	114 ft 10 in (*35·00 m*)
Length	126 ft 9 in (*38·025 m*)
Height	29 ft 8·5 in (*8·9 m*)
Power plant	4 × RR RB168 Spey Mk 250 turbofan engines of 11 500 lb st (*5 217 kg*) each
Equipment	Rear weapons bay for active and passive sonobuoys: forward bay for bombs, mines, depth charges and/or torpedoes. 2 wing mounts for Nord AS.12 or Martel ASM

38 aircraft are in production for service with RAF Strike Command.

Hawker Siddeley Nimrod MR.Mk.1
Courtesy, J. D. R. Rawlings

LAND-BASED AIRCRAFT

P-3 ORION Lockheed (USA)

Twelve-seat maritime-reconnaissance aircraft

Max speed at 15 000 ft (*4 570 m*)	413 knots
Patrol speed at 1 500 ft (*450 m*)	200 knots
Max range	4 993 n. miles
Max mission radius	2 200 n. miles
Max endurance, 2 engines at 1 500 ft	17·0 hrs
Equipment	Sonobuoys, MAD gear, ECM d/f, etc.
Armament	Fuselage weapons bay: accommodates mines, depth bombs, torpedoes Wing mounts (10): torpedoes, mines or rockets singly or in pods
Max T-O weight	127 200 lb (*57 697 kg*)
Wing span	99 ft 8 in (*30·37 m*)
Length	116 ft 10 in (*35·61 m*)
Height	33 ft 8·5 in (*10·29 m*)
Power plant	4 × Allison T56-A-14 turboprop engines of 4 910 eshp each (P-3B version)

Produced for US Navy as P-3A (Allison T56-A-10W engines) and P-3B and in current service. P-3B also serves with Royal Australian Air Force and Royal New Zealand Air Force. P-3C under development with A-NEW data processing systems, for introduction in 1969.

P-3C Orion—US Navy

SHACKLETON MR Mk 3 Hawker Siddeley/Avro (UK)

Ten-seat long range maritime-reconnaissance aircraft

Max speed at 12 000 ft (*3 660 m*)	260 knots
Service ceiling	19 200 ft (*5 850 m*)
Range at 150 knots at 1 500 ft (*450 m*)	3 200 n. miles
Max endurance	24 hrs
Armament	2 × 20 mm cannon in nose (optional) Weapons bay for bombs, mines, depth charge torpedoes, etc Wing mounts (8) for unguided rockets on SAAF aircraft only
Gross weight	100 000 lb (*45 360 kg*)
Wing span	119 ft 10 in (*36·52 m*)
Length	92 ft 6 in (*28·19 m*)
Height	23 ft 4 in (*7·11 m*)
Power plant	4 × RR Griffon 57A in-line piston engines of 2 455 hp each RAF Phase 3 versions have additionally 2 × RR Bristol Viper 203 turbojet engines of 2 500 lb st in outboard nacelles

In service with the South African Air Force in the MR Mk 3 version and the RAF in the MR Mk 3 Phase 3 version and MR Mk 2 which is an earlier tail-wheel version with less tankage.

Hawker Siddeley Shackleton MR 3 Phase 3—No. 42 Sqdn RAF

LAND-BASED AIRCRAFT

SHIN MEIWA PS-1 Shin Meiwa (Japan)
Anti-submarine flying-boat

Max speed at 5 000 ft (*1 500 m*)	309·1 knots
Cruising speed at 5 000 ft (*1 500 m*)	178·2 knots
Service ceiling	29 500 ft (*9 000 m*)
Normal range	1 224 n. miles
Gross weight	86 862 lb (*39 400 kg*)
Wing span	107 ft 7·5 in (*32·8 m*)
Length	109 ft 11 in (*33·5 m*)
Height	31 ft 10 in (*9·7 m*)
Equipment (Internal)	Dipping Sonar, AQA-3 Jezebel passive acoustic search equipment with 20 sonobuoys, Julie active acoustic echo ranging with 30 charges, four 330 lb (*150 kg*) anti-submarine bombs and smoke bombs
(External)	Two underwing pods each containing two homing torpedoes and two wingtip launchers for three 5 in (*12·7 m*) air-to-surface missiles

In production for the JMSDF.

C-121 CONSTELLATION Lockheed (USA)
Long-range transport and electronic reconnaissance aircraft

Max speed at 20 000 ft (*6 000 m*)	281 knots
Max range	4,000 n. miles
Capacity	72 troops in transport version 27 crew in electronic recce. version
Gross weight	143 600 lb
Wing span	126 ft 2 in (*42·03 m*)
Height	24 ft 9 in (*8·25 m*)
Length	116 ft 2 in (*38·69 m*)
Power plant	4 × Wright R-3350-91 radial piston engines of 3 250 hp each

In service with the US Navy as the C-121J transport, EC-121K, EC-121L, EC-121M for early-warning duties with dorsal and ventral radomes, and WC-121N for weather reconnaissance. The earlier version of the Constellation, the L749A, went into SAR service with the French SGAC, and the Indian Air Force is using one squadron of L1049's for maritime reconnaissance.

Lockheed Constellation—US Navy EC-121K

VIGGEN SAAB (Sweden)
Single-seat multi-mission combat aircraft

Max speed at 36 000 ft (*10 800 m*)	Mach 2 plus
Armament	External mounts (fuselage 3, wings 2): Carries Rb04 ASM, Rbo5A ASM, rockets, bombs, 30 mm gun packs or mines
Normal T-O weight	35 275 lb (*16 000 kg*) approx
Wing span	34 ft 9·2 in (*10·60 m*)
Length	53 ft 5·8 in (*16·30 m*)
Height overall	18 ft 4·5 in (*5·60 m*)
Height, fin folded	13 ft 1·5 in (*4·00 m*)
Power plant	1 × Svenska Flygmotor (P & W JT-8D) RM8 turbojet of 26 450 lb st with reheat

This important new aircraft forms the airborne component of System 37 to cover the attack, interceptor and reconnaissance needs of the Swedish Air Force. The prototypes are now flying and 175 aircraft are to be delivered between 1971-1974.

A development Viggen with Rb 04 ASM's

TU-16 (Code-name "Badger") Tupolev (USSR)
Long-range medium bomber/reconnaissance aircraft

Max speed at 35 000 ft (*10 700 m*)	510 knots
Cruising speed	430 knots
Service ceiling	42 650 ft (*13 000 m*)
Range, max bomb load	2,600 n. miles
Max range	3 450 n. miles
Armament	Fuselage: 19 800 lb (*9 000 kg*) bombs carried internally or "Kipper" stand-off bomb under fuselage. 2 × 23 mm cannon in forward dorsal, ventral and rear turrets and 1 × 23 mm cannon in starboard nose position Wing mounts (2): 2 × "Kennel" ASM's
Normal T-O weight	150 000 lb (*68 000 kg*) approx
Wing span	110 ft 0 in (*33·5 m*)
Length	120 ft 0 in (*36·5 m*)
Height	35 ft 6 in (*10·8 m*)
Power plant	2 × Mikulin AM-3M turbojet engines of 20 900 lb st each

In service with the Soviet Naval Airfleet since 1956 and the Indonesian Air Forces since 1961.

LAND-BASED AIRCRAFT

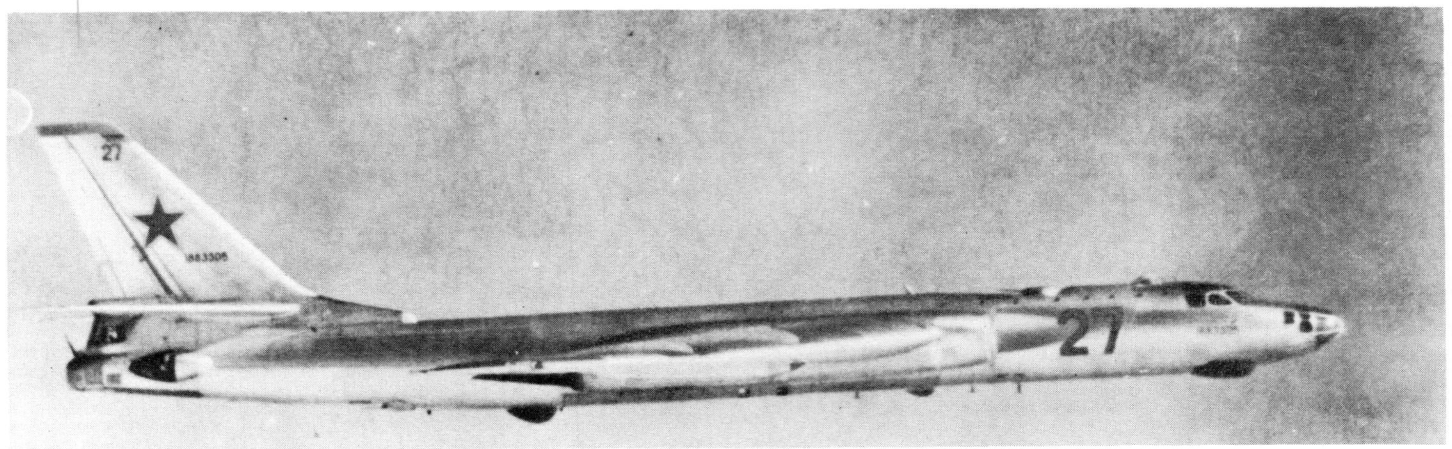

Tuplev Tu-16 "Badger" twin-jet bomber

TU-20 (code-name "Bear") Tupolev (USSR)

Long-range strategic bomber/reconnaissance aircraft

Max speed at 41 000 ft (*12 500 m*) 435 knots
Cruising speed at 32 000 ft (*10 000 m*) 410 knots
Range with max bomb load 6 800 n. miles
Armament Fuselage weapons bay: 25 000 lb (*11 300 kg*) of bombs
Fuselage external mounts: "Kangaroo" ASM. 2 × 23 mm cannon in dorsal, ventral and tail turrets
Loaded weight 340 000 lb (*154 220 kg*)
Wing span 164 ft (*50 m*)
Length 151 ft (*46 m*)
Power plant 4 × Kuznetsov NK-12M turboprop engines of 14 795 shp each

In service with the Soviet Naval Airfleet, largely for strategic reconnaissance and ECM roles.

Tupolev Tu-20 "Bear"

TU-22 (code-name "Blinder") Tupolev (USSR)

Medium-range supersonic strike and reconnaissance bomber

Max speed at 36,000 ft (*12 000 m*) Mach 1·5
Cruising speed 550 knots
Service ceiling 59 000 ft (*18 000 m*) plus
Range 1 250 n. miles
Armament Fuselage: "Kitchen" ASM part-recessed in bomb bay, alternatively internal bomb load
Loaded weight 180 000 lb (*82 000 kg*)
Wing span 80 ft 0 in (*24·4 m*)
Length 130 ft 0 in (*39·6 m*)
Power plant 2 × unspecified turbojet engines developing 19 200 lb st and 26 500 lb st with reheat

In service with the Soviet Naval Airfleet

Tupolev Tu-22 "Blinder"

NAVAL MISSILES

NAVAL MISSILES

Long-range Surface-to-Surface

MSBS Sereb (France)

Submarine-borne intermediate range ballistic missile (IRBM)

This two-stage solid propellent missile with 500-kiloton nuclear warhead is being prepared in France to equip the "Redoutable" class of nuclear-powered submarines from 1969 onwards, each of 4 submarines carrying 16 missiles becoming operational in 1970. The first stage has 10 tons of powder propellent in a Norma 904 rocket motor; the second stage is a Sud Aviation solid-propellent rocket of 8 820 lb (*4 000 kg*) weight. The MSBS has inertial guidance. It has the same body diameter as the M-112 (see below).

M-112 Sereb (France)

Test vehicle for MSBS

This test vehicle has been used particularly in developing methods of launching from submerged submarines, the M-112 being used from a submerged tube and from the test submarine "Gymnote" at the CERES firing range. It is a two-stage rocket with a solid-propellent first stage motor of 22 050 lb (*10 000 kg*) weight and an inert second-stage.

Length	33 ft 3·2 in (*10·14 m*)
Body diameter	4 ft 11 in (*1·50 m*)
Firing weight	39 725 lb (*18 005 kg*)

M-112, missile for France's submarine IRBM

POLARIS A2 and A3 UGM-27B and C Lockheed (USA)

Submarine-borne fleet ballistic missile

Both versions are in service as long-range two-stage solid propellent missiles with nuclear warhead. All 41 nuclear-powered submarines are operational, each with 16 Polaris missiles, 28 with A3 and 13 with A2. The submarine is positioned by a Ship Inertial Navigation System (SINS), thereafter the missile, after firing relies on its own inertial guidance system. The first stage ignites as the missile breaks surface, having been ejected by a gas/steam mixture produced by a small solid propellent rocket motor. The British Royal Navy is to deploy Polaris A3 on four submarines.

POSEIDON C3 ZUGM-73A Lockheed (USA)

Submarine-borne fleet ballistic missile

This is a larger and twice as powerful missile to replace Polaris with twice the payload and longer range. Operational target date is 1970/71 to equip 31 existing Polaris submarines with Poseidon. First test firing, at Cape Kennedy, was on 16th August, 1968 and first vessel to be equipped with Poseidon will be USS "James Madison" which will be operational in the early 1970s.

Length	34 ft 0 in (*10·36 m*)
Body diameter	6 ft 0 in (*1·83 m*)
Firing weight	60 000 lb (*27 200 kg*) approx
Range	2 726 n. miles

SURFACE-TO-SURFACE MISSILES

SAWFLY (NATO code-name) (USSR)

Appearing first in 1967 this missile would seem to be a research version of a second-generation IRBM with a range of approx 2 000 miles. It is thought to be a two-stage solid propellent rocket.

Length overall	42 ft 0 in (*12·8 m*) approx
Body diameter	5 ft 9 in (*1·75 m*) approx

Sawfly missile

Short-Range Surface-to-Surface

RB.08A SAAB (Sweden)

Surface-to-surface cruise missile

This missile is a modification of the French Nord CT.20 target drone for coastal defence duties. It is ramp-launched by two jettisonable rocket-boosters and thence propelled by a Turbomeca Marbore IID turbojet. The warhead is Swedish-designed, and it is both land-based and destroyer-based.

Length	18 ft 9 in (*5·71 m*)
Body diameter	2 ft 2 in (*0·66 m*)
Wing span	9 ft 10·5 in (*3·01 m*)
Launch weight	1 958 lb (*900 kg*)

Performance details are not publishable, however the following details on the almost identical CT20 are available:—

Speed at 32 800 ft (*10 000 m*)	500 knots
Endurance at 32 800 ft (*10 000 m*)	45 mins
Practical range	135 n. miles

SS-11 (B.1) Nord (France)

Close-range surface-to-surface wire-guided missile

Developed from the AS-11 (B.1) ASM this missile is in use by French Navy and Army and differs from the AS-11 in launching systems only. It is powered by a solid propellent rocket with cruciform swept wings on a cylindrical body and can be fitted with a range of warheads for anti-tank, perforating/Exploding or anti-personnel work. The guidance is visual/manual, with a gyrostabilised optical sighting system, through wires from the control. By July, 1967 over 120 000 SS-11 missiles had been ordered, with production at 1 200 per month and are used by 21 nations.

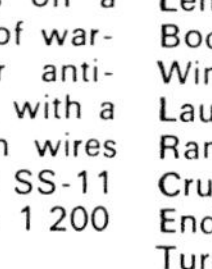

Length	3 ft 11 in (*1·200 m*)
Body diameter	6·4 in (*0·16 m*)
Wing span	1 ft 8 in (*0·500 m*)
Launch weight	66 lb (*30 kg*)
Range	9 840 ft (*3 000 m*)
Cruising speed	313 knots
Endurance	20 21 secs
Turning circle	3 300 ft (*1 000 m*)

SS-12M Nord (France)

Close-range surface-to-surface wire-guided missile

A larger and more powerful derivative of the SS-11, it is used from a twin shipboard launcher and is being developed to use the TCA automatic guidance system of the Harpon anti-tank missile. It is used aboard three Royal Libyan Navy patrol boats.

Length	6 ft 2 in (*1·875 m*)
Body diameter	7 in (*0·18 m*)
Wing span	2 ft 1·5 in (*0·65 m*)
Launch weight	167 lb (*75 kg*)
Range	19 650 ft (*6 000 m*)
Endurance	32 sec
Impact speed	182·36 knots

SS-11 and SS-12

GABRIEL (Israel)

Little is known of this weapon, reported to be a small short-range ship-borne surface-to-surface missile but it is reported that the Imperial Iranian is interested in acquiring this weapon system for its new patrol boats and frigates.

SEA KILLER MARK I Contraves Italiana (Italy)

Short-range surface-to-surface missile, ship-borne

This missile is installed in a five-round multiple launcher aboard the fast patrol boat "Sqetta" of the Italian Navy. Single-stage solid-propellent rocket of 4,400 lb (*2 000 kg*) thrust propels this missile with movable cruciform control surfaces and stabilising tailfins. Guidance is from beam rider/radio command/radar altimeter systems and the warhead is a high-explosive fragmentation type with proximity and/or contact fuses.

Length	12 ft 3 in (*3·73 m*)
Body diameter	7·87 in (*0·20 m*)
Wing span	2 ft 9·5 in (*0·85 m*)
Launch weight	370 lb (*168 kg*)
Speed at burn-out	Mach 1·9
Min/max range	1·6/5·4 n. miles (*3/10 km*)

SURFACE-TO-SURFACE MISSILES

Sea Killer Mk 1

SEA KILLER MARK 2 Contraves Italiana (Italy)

A two-stage version of the Mark I, to increase operational range. This missile was originally known as the Vulcan. The booster is also a solid propellent rocket which is separated from the rocket by an aerodynamic drag section. The missile has the same specification as the Mark 1 except for length increased to 14 ft 9 in (*4·50 m*), launching weight to 530 lb (*240 kg*), and max. effective range to over 11·5 miles (*18·5 km*).

TERNE Mk. 8 Kongsberg (Norway)

Short-range ship-borne surface-to-surface missile. Brought to production status by Kongsberg Vaapenfabrikk this anti-submarine missile was originated by the Norwegian Defence Research Establishment for the Royal Norwegian Navy, who now use it operationally. It is a rocket-propelled depth charge with a 110 lb (*50 kg*) warhead, having an ogival nose cone, and cruciform stabilising fins. Propulsion is by two concentric solid-propellent rocket motors and detonation of the warhead by an acoustic proximity and time fuse.
The system is so installed operationally that a full salvo of six missiles can be fired in 5 seconds.

Length	6 ft 4·75 in (*1·95 m*)
Body diameter	8·0 in (*20·3 cm*)
Launching weight	298 lb (*135·2 kg*)

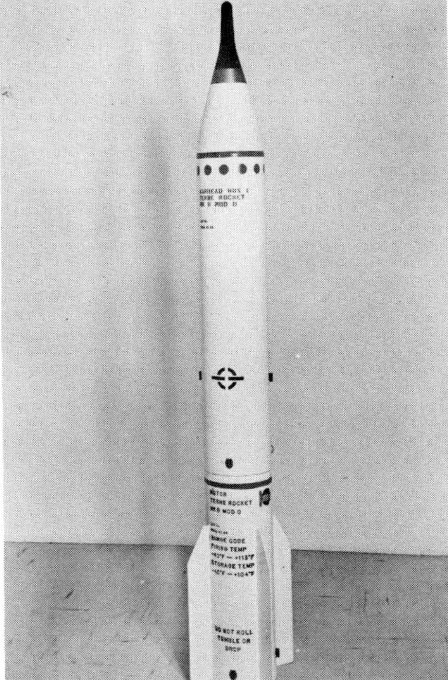

Terne Mk.8 surface-to-surface missile

SEA LANCE XMGM-52B LTV (USA)

Ship-borne surface-to-surface close-range missile

In 1961 development of the Sea Lance as a landing force support weapon for shore bombardment duty from US Navy ships began from the US Army Lance. It is designed to use the Mk 5 twin-launcher already installed on US Navy ships and is propelled by a Rocketdyne storable liquid-propellent engine. It can use interchangeable conventional and nuclear warheads.

Length	20 ft 0 in (*6·10 m*)
Body diameter	1 ft 10 in (*0·56 m*)
Launching weight	3 200 lb (*1 450 kg*)
Min/max range	2·6/26 n. miles

"STYX" (NATO code-name) (USSR)

Ship-borne surface-to-surface rocket missile

Used for ship-to-ship action this missile has stub wings and a tri-tail with control surfaces. Carried on a twin-rail launcher it is propelled by a solid-propellent rocket with a jettisonable booster. It is carried aboard the "Komar" and "Osa" class fast patrol boats of which more than 100 serve with the Soviet Navy and others with the Cuban, Indonesian, Polish and Egyptian Navies. Styx missiles from the latter were used to sink the Israeli destroyer "Eilat" on 21st October 1967.

Length	20 ft (*6·10 m*) approx
Wing span	8 ft 10 in (*2·70 m*) approx
Range	13 n. miles plus

"SHADDOCK" (NATO code-name) (USSR)

Medium-range surface-to-surface cruise missile

Designed in the same category as "Styx" but at least twice as large, little is known about this missile. It appears to have one main nozzle and two jettisonable booster rockets. The length of the missile is approximately 40 ft (*12·2 m*)

Air-to-Surface Missiles

AS-11 (B.1) Nord (France)

Airborne wire-guided missile

This is identical with the SS-11 (B.1) (which see) except that it is air-launched and this increases its range. It is carried by 14 different types of aircraft (fixed and rotary-wing) of 20 nations including all the ASW aircraft of the NATO countries.

AS-12 Nord (France)

Airborne wire-guided missile

This missile is a companion to the SS-12M (which see) and is already supplementing and replacing the AS-11 (B.1). It is being prepared for automatic guidance with the TCA system for the Harpon missile.

"Styx" surface-to-surface missile

AIR-TO-SURFACE MISSILES

AIRBORNE WIRE-GUIDED MISSILE

AS-30 Nord (France)

Tactical air-to-surface missile

This missile has a two-stage solid propellent rocket power plant and is directed by a pilot-operated radio-command guidance system whereby the pilot aims on his weapon sight and corrections are made by an infra-red tracker and axial gyroscope feeding into the radio-command system. It is in production for the French Air Force, the RAF, German, Swiss and South African air forces. It normally carries a 510 lb (*230 kg*) HE warhead.

Length	12 ft 9·5 in (*3·90 m*)
Body diameter	1 ft 1·5 in (*0·34 m*)
Wing span	3 ft 3·5 in (*1·00 m*)
Launch weight	1 146 lb (*520 kg*)
Speed at impact	1 475/1 640 ft/sec (*450/500 m/sec*)
Range	6·5 n. miles

Nord AS-30 (inboard) and AS-20 (outboard)

AS-30L Nord (France)

Tactical air-to-surface missile

A developed lighter version of the AS-30 for smaller, lighter aircraft. Warhead reduced to 253 lb (*115 kg*).

Length	11 ft 9·5 in (*3·60 m*)
Body diameter	1 ft 1·5 in (*0·34 m*)
Wing span	2 ft 11·5 in (*0·90 m*)
Launch weight	838 lb (*380 kg*)

AS-30 KORMORAN Nord/Bolkow (France/Germany)

A version of the AS-30 being developed against a German Navy requirement. It uses an inertial guidance system based on that of the AS-33.

AS-37/AJ.168 MARTEL Nord/HSD (France/UK)

Air-to-surface television-guided stand-off missile

Developed jointly by Matra and Hawker/Siddeley Dynamics the Martel is in two forms, an anti-radar, all-weather attack missile or a television-guided missile operated by a weapon operator aboard the parent aircraft. The anti-radar version can be launched in a variety of height and mission profiles. Immediately after launch the missile homes automatically on the target radar, the parent aircraft being independent. Its range of tens of miles gives it a stand-off capability. The TV version is guided in the final stages of its run by the weapon operator in the launch aircraft reading from a TV monitor in the aircraft displaying the missile's target field.

Martel is to be operational with the British Fleet Air Arm and RAF on Phantom, Buccaneer and Nimrod aircraft and the French services on Mirage III-E, Jaguar and Atlantic aircraft.

Length	12 ft (*3·6 m*) teleguidance 13 ft (*3·9 m*) anti-radar
Wing span	3 ft 8 in (*1·09 m*)
Body diameter	1 ft 3 in (*0·39 m*)

AIR-TO-SURFACE MISSILES

HELLCAT Short Bros & Harland (UK)

An air-to-surface version of the Seacat (which see), being developed for use by the Royal Navy's Wasp and Wessex helicopters. It is operated through a radio link from the left hand (co-pilot's) seat using a sighting head projecting through the cabin roof.

Martel being launched from the outboard wing pylon of a Royal Navy Sea Vixen FAW. Mk.2

Rb.04 Robotavdelningen (Sweden)

All-weather anti-shipping air-to-surface missile

This missile has been operational for nine years with the Swedish Air Force but has been under a continuous improvement programme to up-date it to modern needs. It equips the four attack wings flying A32A Lansens as the Rb.04D and will also be used with the Viggen in a later version, the Rb.04E. It is powered by a solid-propellent rocket motor giving it a subsonic performance carrying a 660 lb (*300 kg*) warhead.

Details apply to the Rb.04C

Length	14 ft 7 in (*4·45 m*)
Body diameter	1 ft 7·5 in (*0·50 m*)
Wing span	6 ft 8 in (*2·04 m*)
Launch weight	1 320 lb (*600 kg*)
Guidance	High-efficiency homing system

Rb.05A SAAB (Sweden)

Being developed for the Viggen and Sk.60, this missile is intended for the strike role but can also be used air-to-air. With long-chord cruciform wings and aft-mounted cruciform control surfaces it is powered by a pre-packed liquid propellent rocket motor built by Svenska Flygmotor. Guidance is by radio command signals from a pilot-operated micro-wave radio link, based on simultaneous observation of both target and missile by the pilot.

Length	11 ft 7 in (*3·52 m*)
Body diameter	1 ft 0 in (*0·30 m*)
Wing span	2 ft 8 in (*0·80 m*)
Launch weight	approx 660 lb (*300 kg*)

"KENNEL" (NATO code-name) (USSR)

Air-to-surface turbojet-powered missile

This anti-shipping missile, similar to the US Navy Regulus I, is operational on the Tu-16 "Badger" aircraft of the Soviet Naval Airfleet and the Indonesian Air Force. It is turbojet-powered and appears to use a radar homing device mounted above its air intake. It is also used as a surface-to-surface coastal defence missile by Poland Cuba and Egypt.

Length	28 ft 0 in (*8·5 m*)
Wing span	16 ft 0 in (*4·0 m*)

Two "Kennel" anti-ship missiles loaded beneath the wings of a Tu-16 bomber

AIR-TO-SURFACE MISSILES

"KIPPER" (NATO code-name) (USSR)

Air-to-surface anti-shipping missile with stand-off capability

Operational with the Tu.16 "Badger" since at least 1961 this missile has a swept-wing aircraft layout with an underslung power plant, presumably a turbojet. Nose radar implies a radar homing device.

Length	31 ft 0 in (*9·5 m*) approx

"KITCHEN" (NATO code-name) (USSR)

Little is known about this advanced missile, carried by the Tu-22 "Blinder". It appears to be a stand-off bomb with delta wings and cruciform tail and to be about 36 ft (*11 m*) long.

BULLPUP AGM-12B Maxson (USA)

Air-to-surface radio-guided missile

In production and service with the USAF and Navy, the Bullpup has cruciform wings at rear and nose-mounted control planes. Power plant is a Thiokol pre-packaged liquid-propellent motor of 12 000 lb (*5 440 kg*) st. It is radio-controlled by the pilot in flight with visual flares for guidance. Also with FAA for Buccaneer and Sea Vixen.

Length	10 ft 6 in (*3·20 m*)
Body diameter	1 ft 0 in (*0·30 m*)
Wing span	3 ft 1 in (*0·94 m*)
Launch weight	571 lb (*260 kg*)
Cruising speed	Mach 1·8
Range	6·7 n. miles

Bullpup about to be loaded under the wing of an A-4 Skyhawk

BULLPUP AGM-12C Maxson (USA)

Larger and more powerful version of AGM-12B above

Length	13 ft 7 in (*4·14 m*)
Body diameter	1 ft 6 in (*0·45 m*)
Wing span	4 ft 0 in (*1·22 m*)
Launch weight	1 785 lb (*810 kg*)
Range	8·7 n. miles

Bullpup B version with interchangeable nuclear and conventional warheads.

CONDOR AGM-53A North American (USA)

Air-to-surface TV-guided stand-off missile

This missile is under development as a future stand-off weapon for the US Navy for use on the A-6A Intruder and A-7 Corsair II. Its television-guidance system enables its parent aircraft to return to its carrier whilst controlling the missile. It is powered by a Thiokol rocket engine and carries a conventional high-explosive warhead. No dimensions or performance details are known other than a reported range of approx 35 n. miles.

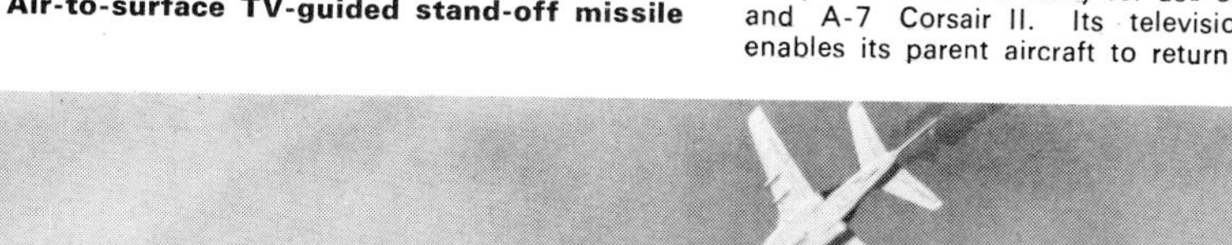

Artist's impression of the US Navy's Condor stand-off missile

AIR-TO-SURFACE MISSILES

SHRIKE AGM-45A

NOTS (USA)

Air-to-surface anti-radar missile

Built for carrier-based aircraft this anti-radar missile has Texas Instrument's guidance system and has been in service with the US Navy since 1964. Power is provided by a Rocketdyne Mk. 39 Mod 3 solid-propellent rocket motor and it carries a high-explosive warhead.

Length	10 ft 0 in (*3·05 m*)
Body diameter	8 in (*0·204 m*)
Launch weight	390 lb (*177 kg*)
Range	8·7 n. miles approx

Shrike anti-radar missile—US Navy

STANDARD ARM

NOTS (USA)

Advanced anti-radar missile

Developed from the Standard SAM rocket this missile is to replace Shrike in the anti-radar role. It will have a better homing head, longer range and more effective protection against ECM. See Standard under Surface-to-Air Missiles.

A Standard ARM fitted to the outboard pylon of a US Navy A-6 aircraft.

WALLEYE GW Mk 1 Mod-0

Martin (USA)

Television-guided glide-bomb missile

This is an unpowered 1 100 lb (*500 kg*) missile which is released from the parent aircraft and glides to its target with its homing system locked on by television. The guidance system is powered by electrical and hydraulic power from a ram-air turbine and a conventional high-explosive warhead is fitted.

Length	11 ft 3 in (*3·43 n.,*
Body diameter	1 ft 3 in (*0·38 m*)
Wing span	3 ft 9 in (*1·14 m*)

Walleye missile—US Navy

Surface-to-Air

The Goa missile which is used as a ship-borne SAM

Two Masurca missiles on the launcher of the French Navy's guided missile frigate "Suffren"

"GOA" (NATO code-name) (USSR)

Ship-borne anti-aircraft missile

This missile is standard anti-aircraft equipment aboard ships of the Soviet Navy, notably two destroyers of the "Kotlin" class, six of the "Kashin" class and five of the "Kresta" class. It is a two-stage solid-propellent missile with cruciform wings on both stages and movable control surfaces on the second stage.

Length	20 ft 0 in (*6·0 m*)
Body diameter (2nd stage)	1 ft 6 in (*0·45 m*)
Body diameter (1st stage)	2 ft 3 in (*0·7 m*)
Wing span	4 ft 0 in (*1·22 m*)

MASURCA Mk 2 Marine Francaise (France)

Developed to equip the guided missile frigates "Suffren" and "Duquesne" of the French Navy this missile is a two-stage solid-propellent missile, the first stage being jettisonable. The second stage has controllable tail surfaces in cruciform configuration, in line with the low-aspect ratio wings. A high-explosive warhead with a proximity fuse is fitted. The guidance system comprises CSF and CFTH tracking and semi-active homing radars.

Length	28 ft 2·5 in (*8 600 m*)
Body diameter	1 ft 4 in (*0·405 m*)
Booster fin Span	4 ft 11 in (*1·500 m*)
Launch weight	4 080 lb (*1 850 kg*)
Range	21·7 n. miles plus

SURFACE-TO-AIR MISSILES

SEA DART Hawker Siddeley (UK)

Medium-range ramjet powered surface-to-air missile

Under development for equipping the Royal Navy's Type 82 and Type 42 destroyers, this missile is a two-stage vehicle with an IMI solid-propellent first stage booster and a second stage comprising the warhead powered by a Rolls-Royce Bristol Odin ramjet. The air duct for this is in the nose with interferometer aerials for the guidance systems around it; it employs semi-active radar homing using the target illuminating radar Type 909.

Length	14 ft 3·5 in (*4·36 m*)
Body diameter	1 ft 4·5 in (*0·42 m*)
Wing span (max)	3 ft 0 in (*0·91 m*)
Range	20 n. miles

Hawker Siddeley Sea Dart

SEACAT Short Bros & Harland (UK)

Short-range anti-aircraft missile

Seacat is in widespread service and production. It is standard armament aboard the Royal Navy's "Daring", "Tribal", "County" and "Battle" classes and is also ordered for the Royal Australian Navy, Royal New Zealand Navy, Royal Netherlands Navy, Royal Swedish Navy (with whom it is designated Rb 07) Chilean, Brazilian, Federal German, Indian, Argentinian, Iranian and Royal Malaysian navies. It is also under development for use from fast patrol-boats and in a surface-to-surface anti-shipping role. It is propelled by a two-stage solid-propellent IMI rocket and has a high-explosive warhead with contact and proximity fuses. A number of different fire control systems are in use:— Mk 20 Visual (British, Australian and Brazilian navies), Mks 21 and 22 Radar Director (British and New Zealand Navies), M4/3 Radar director (Swedish and Chilean Navies). Normally mounted in a four-round launcher.

Length	4 ft 10·3 in (*1·48 m*)
Body diameter	7·5 in (*0·19 m*)
Wing span	2 ft 1·5 in (*0·64 m*)

Short Seacat Missile

SURFACE-TO-AIR MISSILES

SEASLUG Mk 1/Mk 2 Hawker Siddeley (UK)

Medium-range anti-aircraft missile

The Seaslug, in its Mk 1 and Mk 2 forms, equips the "County" class destroyers of the Royal Navy, initially the Mk 1 with the first four ships although they will be retrospectively fitted with Mk 2 as will be the later ships initially. During test firings a success rate of 90% has been achieved at heights up to 50 000 ft (*15 250 m*) plus. It has a solid-propellent sustainer rocket which is made by ICI, with four solid-propellent booster rockets around the rear body. Its guidance system is beam-riding in conjunction with Type 901 Radar. The Mk 2 is an improved weapon working on the Type 901M radar, has transistorized electronics, longer range, better low-level capability and an increase in length of 4 in.

Length (Mk 1)	19 ft 8 in (*5·995 m*)
Body diameter	1 ft 4 in (*0·41 m*)
Wing span	4 ft 8·5 in (*1·438 m*)
Tail span	5 ft 6·5 in (*1·69 m*)

A Seaslug being fired during trials

SEA WOLF BAC (UK)
Short-range anti-aircraft missile

Being developed by BAC and Marconi (for the guidance and control system) the Sea Wolf, originally designated PX 430, intended as the Royal Navy's Seacat replacement for the 1970's. No further details can be published.

SEA SPARROW Raytheon (USA)

Short-range supersonic anti-aircraft missile

A ship-launched version of the Sparrow III AAM, it is a possible addition to the US Navy's armoury. It is a single-stage rocket powered by a Raytheon Mk 38 Mod-2 solid-propellent motor and its guidance system is also Raytheon-built, a continuous-wave semi-active radar. It has a cylindrical body with pivoted cruciform wings and tailfins. Successful test firings have been made from USS "Enterprise".

Length	12 ft 0 in (*3·66 m*)
Body diameter	8 in (*0·20 m*)
Wing span	3 ft 4 in (*1·02 m*)
Launch weight	400 lb (*181 kg*)
Speed	Mach 2·5 approx
Range	6·9 n. miles plus

STANDARD RIM-66A/67A General Dynamics (USA)
Medium-long range supersonic ship-to air-missile

This missile is being developed in two versions, medium-range and extended-range, as a replacement for Tartar and Terrier; 50 destroyers, frigates and escort vessels of the US Navy are scheduled to receive it. Little modification is needed to fit it to the older launchers for the Tartar and Terrier. The MR version is a single-stage integral dual-thrust rocket whilst the ER version has a two-stage motor with jettisonable booster. Both versions have all-electric controls and solid-state electronics and an adaptive autopilot. Standard Missile has a semi-active homing system.

Length	ER: 26 ft (*8·0 m*) plus MR: 14 ft (*4·3 m*) plus
Launch weight	ER: 3 000 lb (*1 360 kg*) MR: 1 300 lb (*590 kg*)
Range	ER: 30·4 n. miles plus MR: 13 n. miles plus

Single-stage Standard missile

SURFACE-TO-AIR MISSILES

TALOS RIM-8G-AAW and RGM-8-H-ARM Bendix (USA)

Long-range Ramjet surface-to-air / surface-to-surface missile

Entered service on USS "Galveston" in 1959 and has since equipped six other cruisers including USS "Long Beach" for which General Electric has developed a special launching and handling system using a computer mechanism by means of which all operations from selecting the particular warhead below decks to the firing of the missile are done automatically. It is a two-stage vehicle with a 40 000 hp Bendix 28 inch (*710 mm*) ramjet sustainer and an Allegany Ballistics jettisonable solid-propellent booster. It is a beam-riding missile using a semi-active Sperry SPG-49 "lamp" radar and can carry either a nuclear or high-explosive warhead. It can also be used surface-to-surface.

Length	31 ft 3 in (*9·53 m*)
Body Diameter	2 ft 6 in (*0·76 m*)
Wing span	9 ft 6 in (*2·90 m*)
Launch weight	7 000 lb (*3 175 kg*)
Speed at burn-out	Mach 2·5
Slant Range	56·4 n. miles plus

TALOS

TARTAR on a twin-launcher

TARTAR RIM-24 General Dynamics (USA)

Supersonic surface-to-air missile

This weapon is in service with the US Navy, the aim being to equip 36 guided missile and several heavy cruisers. In addition it is aboard 4 French "Surcouf" destroyers, two Italian destroyers, three destroyers of the Royal Australian Navy and the Japanese destroyer "Amatsukaze". It is secondary armament on the larger ships and primary on the smaller ships and has a single-stage solid-propellent Aerojet motor with an initial high-thrust firing followed by a longer low-thrust period maintaining a supersonic speed to the target. It is effective at target heights from 1 000 to 40 000 ft (*305* to *12 200 m*). It employs a Raytheon guidance system of the homing type.

Length	15 ft 0 in (*4·57 m*)
Body diameter	13·4 in (*0·34 m*)
Launch weight	1 200 lb (*545 kg*) plus
Speed at burn-out	Mach 2·5 plus
Range	8·7 n. miles plus
Height effectiveness	1 000 to 40 000 ft (*305* to *12 200 m*)

ADVANCED TERRIER RIM-2 General Dynamics (USA)

Ship-borne Supersonic anti-aircraft missile

Developed from the Terrier the Advanced Terrier is in widespread service and production. As well as 39 ships of the US Navy, 3 cruisers of the Italian Navy and one of the Dutch Navy are equipped with this missile which is especially effective against low-flying aircraft. Allegany Ballistics supply both the solid-propellent sustainer and the dual boosters for this missile and it uses a homing guidance system in conjunction with SPS-48 search radar, the Mk 76 fire control system and the Naval Tactical Data System (NTDS).

Length	27 ft 0 in (*8·23 m*)
Body diameter, missile	1 ft (*0·305 m*)
Body diameter, boosters	1 ft 4 in (*0·406 m*)
Wing span	1 ft 8 in (*0·51 m*)
Launch weight	3 000 lb (*1 360 kg*)
Range	17·3 n. miles plus

AIR-TO-AIR MISSILES

MATRA R-530 — Matra (France)

Interceptor missile

In quantity production for the French Air Force and Navy, which latter uses it on its F-8E (FN) Crusaders; it is also supplied to Israel and the South African and Royal Australian Air Forces. It has a cylindrical body with cruciform delta wings, two with ailerons and cruciform tail controls and is powered by a two-stage Hotchkiss-Brandt solid-propellent motor of 18 740 lb (*8 500 kg*) static thrust.

It has interchangeable Hotchkiss-Brandt warheads with semi-active radar or infra-red homing, both containing high-explosive warhead of 60 lb (*27 kg*).

Length	10 ft 9·2 in (*3·28 m*)
Body diameter	10·2 in (*0·26 m*)
Wing span	3 ft 7·2 in (*1·10 m*)
Launch weight	430 lb (*195 kg*)
Max speed	Mach 2·7
Range	9·5 n. miles
Operational heights	0-69 000 ft (*21 000 m*)

FIRESTREAK — Hawker Siddeley Dynamics (UK)

Interceptor missile

The current standard British air-to-air weapon is used by the RAF on Lightnings and the Fleet Air Arm on Sea Vixens. It has a cylindrical metal body, cruciform wings and tail. It is propelled by a solid-propellent rocket and is homed by an infra-red guidance system and controlled by a proportional navigation system. The 50 lb (*22·7 kg*) warhead can be detonated at a pre-determined range.

Length	10 ft 5·5 in (*3·19 m*)
Body diameter	8·8 in (*0·225 m*)
Wing span	2 ft 5·5 in (*0·75 m*)
Launch weight	300 lb (*136 kg*)
Cruising speed	Mach 2 plus
Range	0·7/4·35 n. miles

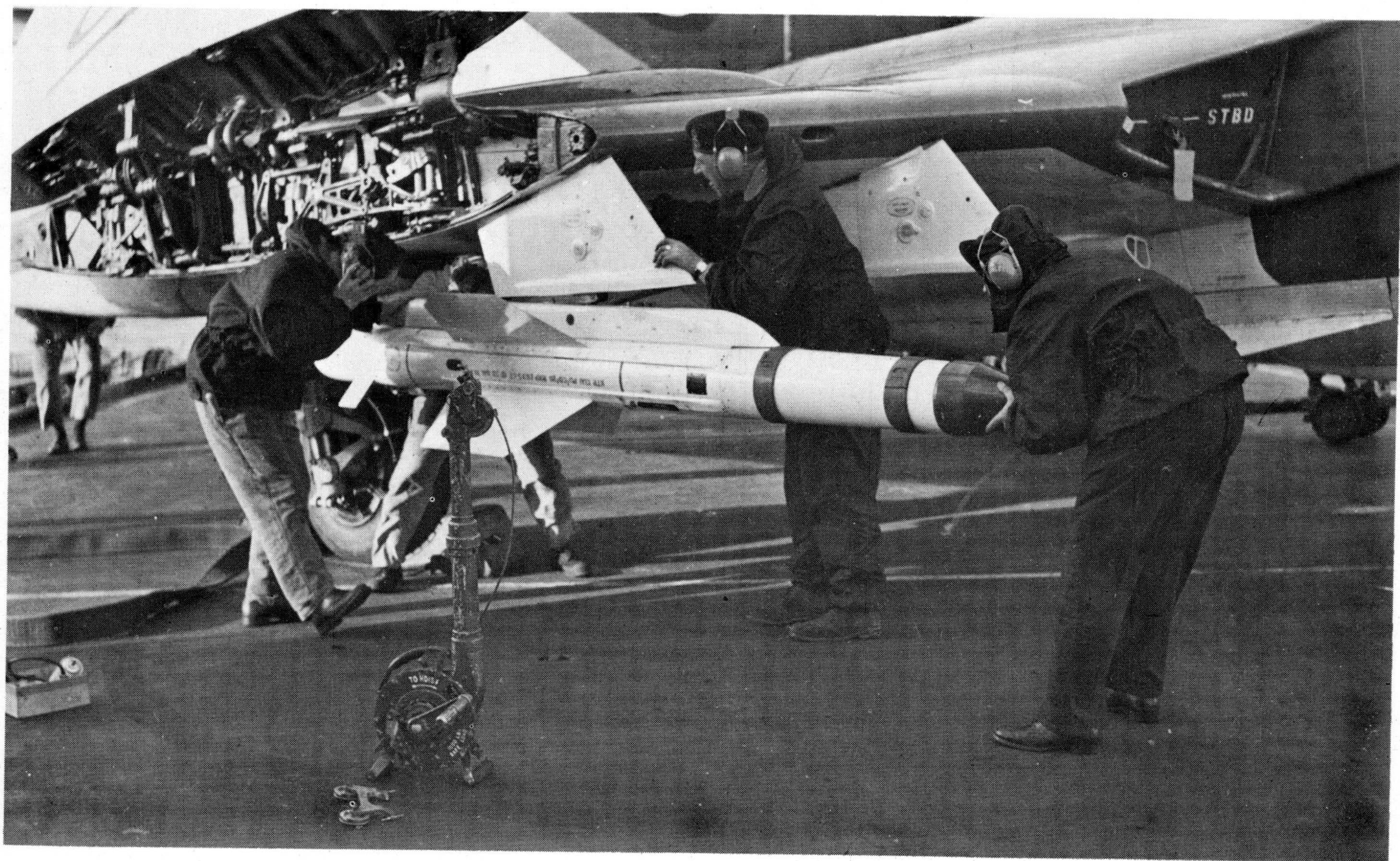

A Firestreak AAM being loaded on a Sea Vixen aboard HMS Victorious

RED TOP — Hawker Siddeley Dynamics (UK)

This is in effect a vastly-improved Firestreak with larger wings and control surfaces and a new infra-red guidance unit not limited to pursuit-course attack. Warhead is increased in weight to 68 lb (*31 kg*). The rocket motor is increased in power also. This missile is used by the RAF on Lightnings and the Fleet Air Arm on Sea Vixen FAW.2's.

Length	11 ft 5·7 in (*3·50 m*)
Body diameter	8·8 in (*0·225*) *m*
Wing span	2 ft 11·8 in (*0·91 m*)
Cruising speed	Mach 3
Range	6 n. miles

Red Top missiles

AIR-TO-AIR MISSILES

PHOENIX XAIM-54A Hughes (USA)

Long-range air-to-air missile

The F-111B aircraft was in mind when the Phoenix was being dèveloped and its future is now in question, although it is likely to be developed for the Grumman F-14. It has a cylindrical body with long-chord cruciform wings and tail controls. It is powered by a Rocketdyne solid-propellent motor. It is radar-guided (AN/AWG-9) and all-weather operation is envisaged with particular application to long-range targets.

Launch weights	1 000 lb (*455 kg*) approx
Range	35 n. miles plus

An experimental firing of the Phoenix missile

SIDEWINDER 1A AIM-9B and AIM-9E NOTS

Interceptor missile

Accent in the Sidewinder is on simplicity, with fewer than two dozen moving parts and unsophisticated radio equipment. It is powered by a Naval Propellent Plant solid-propellent rocket and has a 10 lb (*4·5 kg*) warhead. Control surfaces are at the nose in cruciform configuration, indexed by similar tailfins. It has had limited success in action. As well as being used by the USAF and US Navy it has been exported to Nationalist China, Australia, Japan, Philippines, Spain, Sweden and nine NATO countries and is under licence production in Germany

Length	9 ft 2 in (*2·79 m*)
Body diameter	5 in (*0·13 m*)
Fin Span	1 ft 9 in (*0·53 m*)
Launch weight	159 lb (*72 kg*)
Speed	Mach 2·5
Range	1·6 n. miles

Sidewinder missile mounted on an A-7A of Sqdn VA-97

SIDEWINDER 1C AIM-9C/D NOTS (USA)

Interceptor missile

A developed version of the 1A the 1C is in production for the US Navy and the UK. Power is from the Rocketdyne Mk 36 Mod-5 solid-propellent motor and the aerofoil surfaces have been revised. The AIM-9D version is equipped with infra-red homing guidance (the US Navy and UK version) and the -9C with semi-active radar guidance.

Length	9 ft 6·5 in (*2·91 m*)
Body diameter	5 in (*0·13 m*)
Fin span	2 ft 1 in (*0·64 m*)
Launch weight	185 lb (*84 kg*)
Range	1·6 n. miles plus

All figures relate to AIM-9D version.

AIR-TO-AIR MISSILES

SPARROW IIIB AIM-7E Raytheon (USA)

All-weather interceptor missile

The Sparrow IIIB is in service with 4-FB and F-4C aircraft with the US Navy and USAF respectively and will equip the F-4K (Fleet Air Arm) and F-4M (RAF) versions in the UK. It is also carried by the F-104S of the Italian Air Force. Powered by a Rocketdyne Mk 38 Mod-2 solid-propellent motor it is of standard cylindrical shape with cruciform wings and tail fins. Homing is by means of a Raytheon continuous-wave semi-active homing system and a 60 lb (*27 kg*) warhead is fitted.

Length	12 ft 0 in (*3·66 m*)
Body diameter	8 in (*0·20 m*)
Wing span	3 ft 4 in (*1·02 m*)
Launch weight	400 lb (*181 kg*)
Speed	Mach 2·5
Range	7 n. miles plus

An advanced version, designated AIM-7F, is being developed.

Anti-submarine systems

ASROC RUR-5A Honeywell (USA)

Surface ship-launched anti-submarine ballistic missile

The complete system comprises a Librascope precision fire control computer fed with data from a Sangamo Electric underwater sonar detector, the Asroc missile and an 8-missile launcher. The missile comprises a ballistic solid-propellent rocket with the weapon (torpedo or depth charge) affixed by a frame. Following a ballistic trajectory after firing, the rocket is jettisoned at a pre-determined point and the weapon continues to its target. If a torpedo a parachute opens to lower it into the target area and when submerged behaves as any other homing torpedo. If a depth charge it sinks to a pre-determined depth before detonating.

It is operational aboard cruisers, destroyers and escort vessels of the US Navy and the Japanese destroyer "Amatsukaze".

Length	15 ft 0 in (*4·57 m*)
Diameter	1 ft 0 in (*0·3 m*)
Fin Span	2 ft 6 in (*0·76 m*)
Launch weight	1 000 lb (*450 kg*)
Range	0·9/5·2 n. miles

Asroc anti-submarine missile

ANTI-SUBMARINE SYSTEMS

IKARA Dept of Supply (Australia)

Long-range anti-submarine weapon system

The actual weapon is a dual-thrust, solid-propellent rocket-propelled missile carrying an acoustic homing torpedo launched from a surface ship. Target information from a ship's Variable Depth Sonar or a helicopter's Dunking Sonar feeds into the Action Data Automation system which, with radar/radio tracking and guidance, ensures that the American Type 44 acoustic homing torpedo, separated from the missile and lowered by parachute, enters the sea in the immediate vicinity of the target. The torpedo has an active life of 20 mins for acoustic detection and homing. It is operational in the three "Charles F. Adams" destroyers and Type 12 frigates of the Royal Australian Navy and will be fitted to the Type 82 destroyers in the Royal Navy.

Length	11 ft 0 in (*3·35 m*)
Wing span	5 ft 0 in (*1·50 m*)
Range	7/1[illegible] n. miles

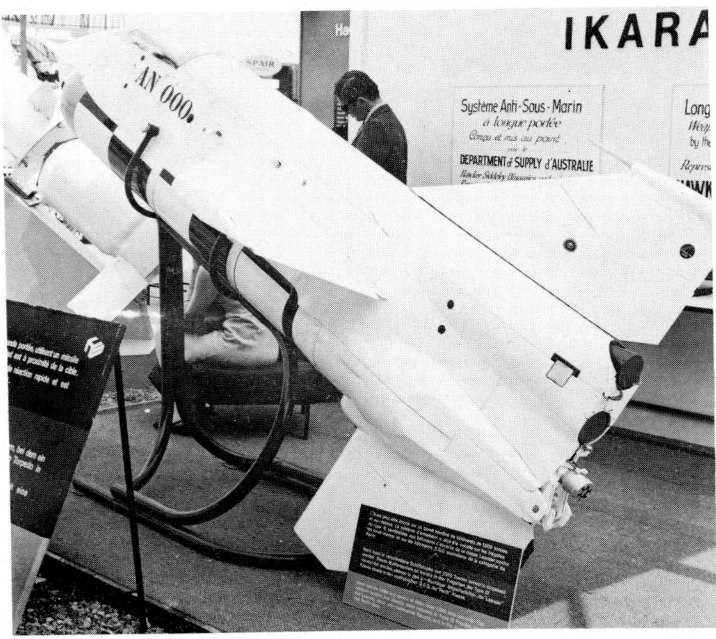

IKARA

MALAFON Mk.2 Latecoere (France)

Long-range anti-submarine weapon system

It comprises a cylindrical body containing a 21 inch (*0·533 m*) acoustic homing torpedo and with wings and tail, this weapon is ramp-launched by two solid-propellent rocket boosters which jettison after 3 sec. The weapon then glides at a height fixed by radio-altimeter. Sonar-detected data is fed into the device so that 875 yards short of its target the torpedo is jettisoned by parachute enters the water and homes on its target. It is in service with the French Navy installed in the anti-submarine vessel "La Galisonniere" and subsequently the frigates "Suffren" and "Duquesne", five T-47 class destroyers and five new corvettes.

Length	19 ft 8 in (*6·00 m*)
Body diameter	1 ft 9 in (*0·53 m*)
Wing span	9 ft 10 in (*3·0 m*)
Launch weight	2 865 lb (*1 300 kg*)
Speed	447·2 knots
Range	9·5 n. miles

Subroc anti-submarine missile.

SUBROC UUM-44A Goodyear (USA)

Submarine-launched long-range anti-submarine missile

Subroc is part of a complex weapons system including advanced long-range sonar and a specially designed fire control system for use aboard approx 25 US Navy hunter/killer submarines. It is fired conventionally from a submarine's torpedo tube, after which the solid-propellent rocket motor ignites under water at a safe distance from the submarine. Thrust-vectoring controls set the missile on its course, its angle of emergence from the water and control its stability in flight. At a pre-determined speed the rocket separates from the depth bomb which continues to its target supersonically, controlled by the inertial guidance system. Upon re-entering the water a shock-mitigating device cushions the impact, the bomb sinks and explodes.

Length	21 ft 0 in (*6·40 m*)
Max diameter	1 ft 9 in (*0·5333 m*)
Launching weight	4 000 lb (*1 815 kg*)
Max range	21·7/26 n. miles

NAVAL STAFFS

ARGENTINA

SHIPS
Commanding Officers

1ST. DIVISION DESTROYERS
Captain Enrique L. Carranza

2ND. DIVISION DESTROYERS
Captain V. H. Pereyra Murray

3RD. DIVISION DESTROYERS
Captain Eduardo P. Aratti

SUBMARINE DIVISION
Senior Lieutenant Dario José Goñi

SUPPORT DIVISION
Captain Luis Manrique

PATROL DIVISION
Senior Lieutenant Jorge I. Almiron

MINESWEEPER DIVISION
Commander Boris I. Marienhoff

ANTARCTIC NAVAL GROUP
Captain Gerardo F. Ojanguren

AIRCRAFT CARRIER A.R.A. "INDEPENDENCIA"
Captain Nelson A. Frigerio

AIRCRAFT CARRIER A.R.A. "25 DE MAYO"
Captain Tirso Brizuela

AIRCRAFT CARRIER A.R.A. "GENERAL BELGRANO"
Captain Gonzalo Bustamante

CRUISER A.R.A. "9 DE JULIO"
Captain Enrique G. Martinez

DESTROYER A.R.A. "ENTRE RIOS"
Commander Eduardo Sanguineti

DESTROYER A.R.A. "SAN JUAN"
Commander Norberto C. Bonesana

DESTROYER A.R.A. "SANTA CRUZ"
Commander Humberto J. Barbuzzi

DESTROYER A.R.A. "BROWN"
Commander Edgardo J. Segura

DESTROYER A.R.A. "ESPORA"
Commander Luis M. Casanova

DESTROYER A.R.A. "ROSALES"
Commander Isaac Jorge Anaya

DESTROYER A.R.A. "BUENOS AIRES"
Commander Hector A. Silva

DESTROYER A.R.A. "SAN LUIS"
Commander Jorge A. Gopcevich

DESTROYER A.R.A. "MISIONES"
Commander Pedro A. Santamaria

SUBMARINE A.R.A. "SANTA FE"
Commander José E. Cortines

SUBMARINE A.R.A. "SANTIAGO DEL ESTERO"
Commander Julio A. Torti

ICEBREAKER A.R.A. "GENERAL SAN MARTIN"
Commander A. Gonzalez Riesco

TRAINING SHIP FRIGATE A.R.A. "LIBERTAD"
Captain Fernando Vazquez Maiztegui

NAVAL ATTACHES

UNITED STATES OF AMERICA AND CANADA
Rear-Admiral Fernando Alberto Milia
1816 Corcoran Street, N.W.—Washington 9 D.C., U.S.A.

GREAT BRITAIN AND THE NETHERLANDS
Rear-Admiral Luis Maria Iriart
171 Victoria Street, London, S.W.1., England.

BRAZIL
Captain Ramón Jorge G. Poch
Rua Farani 29, Rio de Janeiro, Brasil.

CHILE
Captain Luis María Mendia
Ahumada 339—Piso 5° Santiago, Chile.

SPAIN
Captain Raymundo C. Suarez
Avda. La Castellana 63—3° piso, Madrid, Spain.

FRANCE AND WEST GERMANY
Captain Ricardo Guillermo Franke
6 Rue de Cimarosa, Paris 16 éme, France.

PERU
Captain Jorge Ernesto Chevalier
Av. Wilson 911—10° piso, Lima, Peru.

URUGUAY
Captain Alfredo E. Iglesias
Ramon Massini 3234, Montevideo, Uruguay.

ITALY
Captain Carlos Roberto Uhalde
Piazza del Esquilino 2, Rome, Italy.

BOLIVIA
Captain Juan Antonio Valente
Argentine Embassy, Azpiazu y Sanchez Lima, La Paz, Bolivia.

JAPAN
Captain Julio Alberto Aureggi
11-76 Chome Roppongi Minato-Ku, Tokyo, Japan.

PARAGUAY
Captain Gerardo Agustin Sylvester
Comando de la Armada, Hernandarias y Palma, Asunción, Paraguay.

SOUTH AFRICA
Captain Alfredo Galmarini
From January to June
Argentine Embassy, Colonial Mutual building, 97 St. George's St. 10th Floor, Cape Town, South Africa.
From July to December
1059 Church Street, East Pretoria, South Africa.

NAVAL BASE
Commanding Officers

NAVAL BASE—PUERTO BELGRANO
Rear-Admiral Leon M. Scasso

NAVAL BASE—MAR DEL PLATA
Captain Ricardo Alonso

NAVAL BASE—USHUAIA
Captain Justo Padilla

MARINE CORPS BASE—BATERIAS
Captain (IM) Aldo Bachmann

NAVAL AIR BASE—PUNTA INDIO
Commander Julio Garavaglia

NAVAL AIR BASE—COMMANDANTE TOMAS ESPORA
Commander Jorge M. Grau

NAVAL AIR BASE—TRELEW
Commander Carlos A. Suarez

NAVAL SCHOOLS

DIRECCION DE INSTRUCCION NAVAL (Director of Naval Instruction)—Rear-Admiral Eduardo Daviou
Comodoro Py y Corbeta Uruguay—Buenos Aires

ESCUELA DE GUERRA NAVAL (School of Naval Warfare)—Rear-Admiral Carlos Peralta
Libertador General San Martin 8071—Buenos Aires.
Telephone: 707474

ESCUELA NAVAL MILITAR (Naval and Military School)—Rear-Admiral Ruben Giavedoni
Rio Santiago—F.C.G. Roca—Pcia. de Buenos Aires
Telephone: Ensenada 780

ESCUELA POLITECNICA NAVAL (Naval Polytechnic)—Captain Adriano J. Roccatagliata
Rio Santiago—F.C.G. Roca—Pcia. de Buenos Aires

ESCUELA DE GUERRA DE INFANTERIA DE MARINA (School for Infantry and Marine Warfare)—Captain (IM) Pedro Calvo Paz
Avda. Antártida Argentina 1355—Buenos Aires
Telephone: 32-7985

ESCUELA DE SUBMARINOS (Submarine School)—Commander Luis F. Pita
Base Naval Mar del Plata—Pcia. de Buenos Aires
Telephone: 80062

ESCUELA DE AVIACION NAVAL (School of Naval Aviation)—Commander Raul Fitte
Base Aeronaval Punta Indio—Pcia. de Buenos Aires
Telephone: Magdalena 82

ESCUELA DE SUBOFICIALES DE AVIACION NAVAL (School of Naval Aviation NCOs)—Commander Sergio Trenchi
Base Aeronaval Punta Indio—Pcia. de Buenos Aires

ESCUELA BASICA DE INFANTERIA DE MARINA (School of Infantry and Marine Basic Training)—Commander (IM) Mario Robles
Base Naval Puerto Belgrano—Pcia. de Buenos Aires

ESCUELA DE SUBOFICIALES DE INFANTERIA DE MARINA (School for Infantry and Marine NCO's)—Commander (IM) Adolfo J. Roemhild
Base Naval Mar del Plata—Pcia. de Buenos Aires
Telephone: Punta Alta 168

ESCUELA DE MECANICA DE LA ARMADA (School of Naval Engineering)—Captain J. Gomez Davila
Avda. Libertador General San Martin—Buenos Aires
Telephone: 70-4143

LICEO NAVAL ALMIRANTE BROWN)Naval Lyceum-Admiral Brown)—Captain G. Carminatti
Rio Santiago—F.C.G. Roca—Pcia. de Buenos Aires

NAVAL AIR FORCES AND MARINE CORPS BRIGADE
Commanding Officers

NAVAL AIR FORCE No. 1
Captain José Luis Nicolini

NAVAL AIR FORCE No. 2
Captain R. A. Kolliker Frers

NAVAL AIR FORCE No. 3
Captain Ruben A. Iglesias

MARINE CORPS FORCE No. 1
Captain Abel Lizaso

MARINE CORPS BRIGADE No. 1
Captain José Cesar Scala

ARGENTINE NAVY

COMANDANTE OPERATIVO NAVAL (Naval Operative Commandant)—Vice-Admiral J. C. Gonzalez-llanos
Base Naval Puerto Belgrano, Pcia. de Buenos Aires

COMANDANTE NAVAL (Naval Commandant)—Rear-Admiral Carlos Coda
Base Naval Puerto Belgrano, Pcia. de Buenos Aires

COMANDANTE DE AVIACION NAVAL (Naval Aviation Commandant)—Captain Aldo Mariuzzo
Base Naval Puerto Belgrano, Pcia. de Buenos Aires

COMANDANTE DE INFANTERIA DE MARINA (Marine Corps Commandant)—Captain (IM) Eduardo Casado
Base de Infantería de Marina, Baterías, Pcia. de Buenos Aires

JEFE DEL SERVICIO DE HIDROGRAFIA NAVAL (Chief of Naval Hydrographic Service)—Captain José A. Ledesma
Avenida Montes de Oca 2120/24 Buenos Aires

JEFE DEL SERVICIO DE TRANSPORTES NAVALES (Chief of Naval Transport Service)—Captain Luis R. Segura
Bartolome Mitre 430 (6° piso), Buenos Aires

DIRECTOR GENERAL DE ADMINISTRACION NAVAL (Director General of Naval Administration)—Rear-Admiral Manuel Leone
Paseo Colon 1457, Buenos Aires

DIRECTOR GENERAL DEL PERSONAL NAVAL (Director General of Naval Personnel)—Rear-Admiral Raul Francos
Comodoro Py y Corbeta Uruguay, Buenos Aires

DIRECTOR GENERAL DEL MATERIAL NAVAL (Director General of Naval Material)—Vice-Admiral Jorge A. Desimoni
Comodoro Py y Corbeta Uruguay, Buenos Aires

JEFE DEL SERVICIO DE INTELIGENCIA NAVAL (Chief of Naval Intelligence Service)—Captain Jorge E. Zimmermann
Bartolome Mitre 1465, Buenos Aires

COMANDANTE EN JEFE DE LA ARMADA (Commander-in-Chief of the Navy)—Admiral Pedro A. Gnavi

JEFE DEL ESTADO MAYOR GENERAL NAVAL (Chief of Naval Stat)—Vice-Admiral C. G. Arguelles

JEFE DE POLITICA Y ESTRATEGIA (Chief of Policy and Strategy)—Rear-Admiral E. Fuenterosa

JEFE DE LOGISTICA (Chief Logistic Officer)—Vice-Admiral R. Sanchez-Sañudo

JEFE NAVAL (Naval Chief)—Rear-Admiral Horacio Barilari

JEFE DE AVIACION NAVAL (Chief of Naval Aviation)—Rear-Admiral Hermes Quijada

JEFE DE INFANTERIA DE MARINA (Chief of the Marine Corps)—Captain (IM) Pedro R. Irigoin

JEFE DE ORGANICA (Chief of the Organic Dept)—Rear-Admiral Julio Vazquez

SECRETARIO GENERAL NAVAL (Naval Secretariat General)—Rear-Admiral Alberto J. Oliver

JEFE DEL SERVICIO DE COMUNICACIONES NAVALES (Chief of Naval Communications Service)—Captain Leon Resio

JEFE DEL SERVICIO NAVAL DE INVESTIGACION Y DESARROLLO (Chief of Naval Investigation and Development)—Captain Victor Angel Poggi

All based at:—

Edificio del Comandante en Jefe de la Armada, Avenida Madero y Cangallo, Buenos Aires

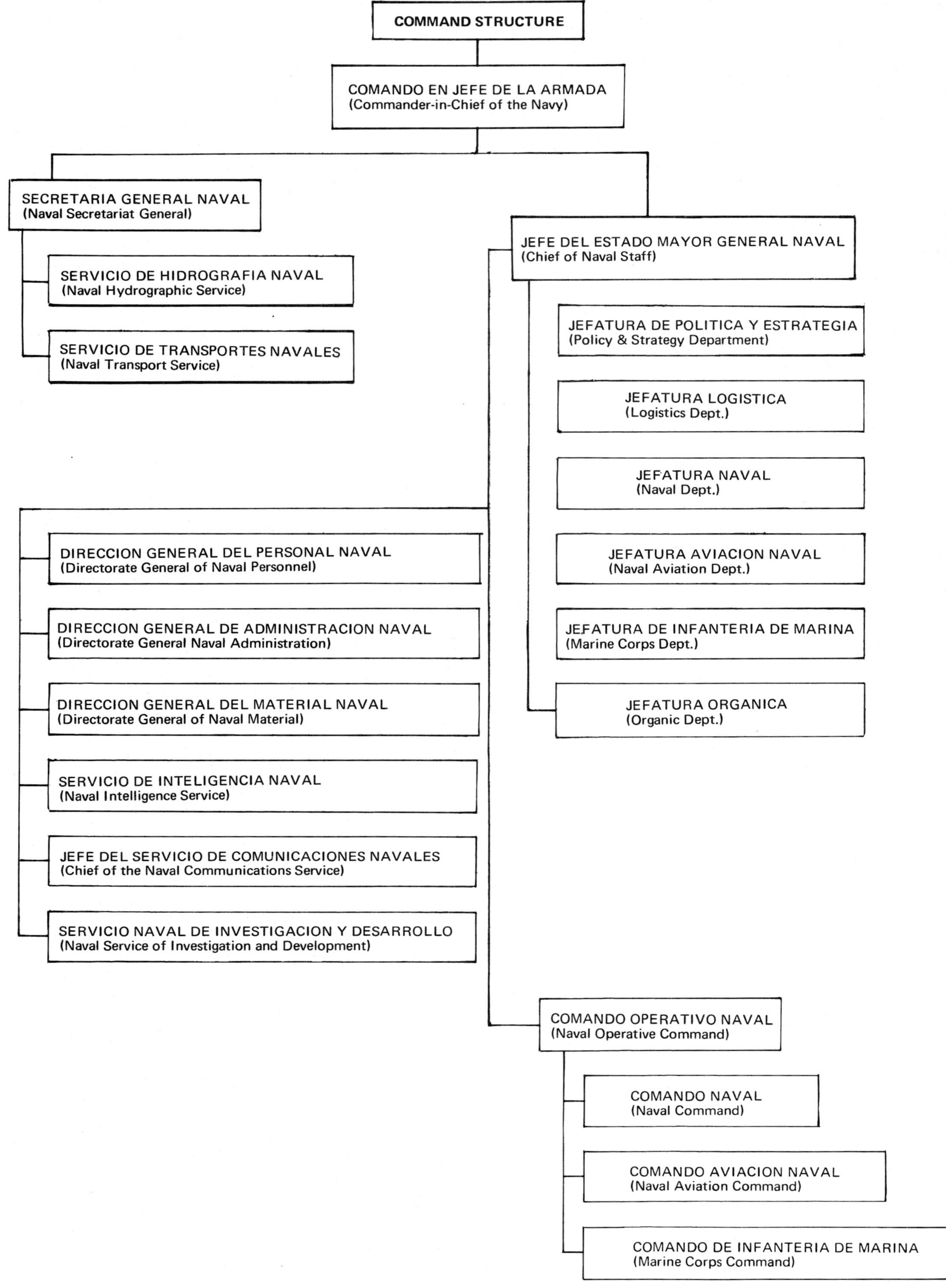
COMMAND STRUCTURE
COMANDO EN JEFE DE LA ARMADA
(Commander-in-Chief of the Navy)
SECRETARIA GENERAL NAVAL
(Naval Secretariat General)
SERVICIO DE HIDROGRAFIA NAVAL
(Naval Hydrographic Service)
SERVICIO DE TRANSPORTES NAVALES
(Naval Transport Service)
JEFE DEL ESTADO MAYOR GENERAL NAVAL
(Chief of Naval Staff)
JEFATURA DE POLITICA Y ESTRATEGIA
(Policy & Strategy Department)
JEFATURA LOGISTICA
(Logistics Dept.)
JEFATURA NAVAL
(Naval Dept.)
JEFATURA AVIACION NAVAL
(Naval Aviation Dept.)
JEFATURA DE INFANTERIA DE MARINA
(Marine Corps Dept.)
JEFATURA ORGANICA
(Organic Dept.)
DIRECCION GENERAL DEL PERSONAL NAVAL
(Directorate General of Naval Personnel)
DIRECCION GENERAL DE ADMINISTRACION NAVAL
(Directorate General Naval Administration)
DIRECCION GENERAL DEL MATERIAL NAVAL
(Directorate General of Naval Material)
SERVICIO DE INTELIGENCIA NAVAL
(Naval Intelligence Service)
JEFE DEL SERVICIO DE COMUNICACIONES NAVALES
(Chief of the Naval Communications Service)
SERVICIO NAVAL DE INVESTIGACION Y DESARROLLO
(Naval Service of Investigation and Development)
COMANDO OPERATIVO NAVAL
(Naval Operative Command)
COMANDO NAVAL
(Naval Command)
COMANDO AVIACION NAVAL
(Naval Aviation Command)
COMANDO DE INFANTERIA DE MARINA
(Marine Corps Command)

BELGIUM

CHEF DE L'ETAT-MAJOR DE LA FORCE NAVALE (Chief of Staff and Commander of Naval Force)—Commodore L.J.J. Lurquin

GROUPS

Le Groupement Opérationnel, Ostend
Le Groupement Instruction et Entraînement à Ste Croix (Bruges)
Le Groupement Logistique, Ostend.

NAVAL, MILITARY AND AIR ATTACHES

LONDON
Lt Colonel R. C. Close

PARIS
Col Ch. F. J. Laurent

LE HAGUE
Col Avi. J. A. J. Mathys

BONN
Col Avi. P. M. de Rijcker

WASHINGTON
Col Avi. F. B. F. van Rolleghem

CANADA

MARITIME COMMAND

In January 1966, headquarters of the integrated maritime command was established at Halifax with a Pacific sub-command at Esquimalt, B.C. Approximately two-thirds of the maritime force is on the east coast.

All seaborne and maritime air elements are under control of the maritine commander. The ASW air arm of maritime command includes five squadrons equipped with long-range Argus Aircraft which are land-based; one squadron of Tracker aircraft and one squadron of Sea King helicopters, all of which operate from carriers or ashore. Several squadrons of fixed and rotary wing aircraft operate in the support role.

HALIFAX BASED SHIPS
Special Duties

CVL 22 BONAVENTURE, (aircraft carrier)
Capt R. H. Falls (8 Apr 69 Capt. J. M. Cutts)

AOR 508 PROVIDER, (operational support ship)
Capt. W. J. Stewart

ARE 101 CAPE SCOTT, (repair ship)
Lt. Cdr. F. J. Copas

PCS 781 CORMORANT, (patrol craft)

DE 320 GRANBY, (diving tender)
Lt. Cdr. A. Sagan

FHE 400, (hydrofoil) Bras D'Or
Cdr. C. Cotaras

PROTECTEUR
Capt. P. R. Hinton

First Canadian Escort Squadron

DDH 206 SAGUENAY (helicopter-destroyer)
Cdr. R. O. Yanow

DDE 258 KOOTENAY (destroyer escort)
Cdr. G. C. McMorris (14 Apr 69 Cdr. NSTC Norton)

DDH 266 NIPIGON (helicopter-destroyer)
Cdr. R. C. Brown

Third Canadian Escort Squadron

DDH 207 SKEENA (helicopter-destroyer)
Cdr. W. G. Brown

DDE 259 TERRA NOVA (destroyer escort)
Cdr. J. M. Reid

DDH 265 ANNAPOLIS (helicopter-destroyer)
Cdr. D. Ross

DDE 257 RESTIGOUCHE (destroyer escort)
Cdr. P. L. McCulloch

Fifth Canadian Escort Squadron

DDH 205 ST. LAURENT (helicopter-destroyer)
Cdr. M. Barrow

DDE 236 GATINEAU (destroyer escort)
Cdr. W. A. Hughes

DDH 233 FRASER (helicopter-destroyer)
Cdr. F. W. Crickard

Seventh Canadian Escort Squadron

DDH 229 OTTAWA (helicopter-destroyer)
Cdr. P. E. Simard

DDH 234 ASSINIBOINE (helicopter-destroyer)
Cdr. G. L. Edwards

DDH 230 MARGAREE (helicopter-destroyer)
Cdr. R. I. Hitesman

First Canadian Minesweeping Squadron
(In reserve until April 1969, then activated for summer training)

MSC 164 CHALEUR (coastal minesweeper)

MSC 160 CHIGNECTO (coastal minesweeper)

MSC 159 FUNDAY (coastal minesweeper)
Lt. Cdr. R. G. Campbell

MSC 161 THUNDER (coastal minesweeper)

First Canadian Submarine Squadron

SS72 OJIBWA (Oberon class submarine)
Lt. Cdr. J. C. Wood

SS73 ONONDAGA (Oberon class submarine)
Lt. Cdr. L. G. Temple

SS74 OKANAGAN (Oberon class submarine)
Lt. Cdr. N. G. Frawley

In Reserve

LOON, MALLARD AND BLUE HERON (Patrol craft)

PORTE ST. JEAN AND PORTE ST. LOUIS (Gate vessels)

ESQUIMALT (B.C.) BASED SHIPS
Second Canadian Escort Squadron

DDE 261 MACKENZIE (destroyer escort)
Cdr. O. J. Cavenagh

DDE 262 SASKATCHEWAN (destroyer escort)
Cdr. H. Rusk

DDE 264 QU'APPELLE (destroyer escort)
Cdr. J. Allan

DDE 263 YUKON (destroyer escort)
Cdr. P. G. May

DDE 256 ST. CROIX (destroyer escort)
Cdr. J. M. Cumming

Fourth Canadian Escort Squadron

DDE 260 COLUMBIA (destroyer escort)
Cdr. T. C. Shuckburgh

DDE 235 CHAUDIERE (destroyer escort)
Lt. Cdr. P. G. Bissell

MSC 162 COWICHAN (coastal minesweeper)

MSC 163 MIRAMICHI (coastal minesweeper)

YMG 184 PORTE DE LA REINE (gate vessel)
Lt. Col. J. Hannam

YNG 185 PORTE QUEBEC (gate vessel)

QW 3 ORIOLE (sail training yacht)
Lt. Cdr. G. S. Hilliard

Special Duties

SS75 RAINBOW (EX–USS ARGONAUT) (submarine)
Lt. Cdr. C. E. Falstrem

In Reserve

ALGONQUIN AND CRESCENT (destroyers) CAPE BRETON (repair ship) and SS71 GRILSE (submarine) (pending return to USN)

NAVAL ATTACHES–OTTAWA

Captain H. E. Howard Naval Adviser
British High Commission, 80 Elgin Street, Ottawa 4, Ontario

Lieutenant Colonel P. R. Cazaillet
Air Naval and Military Attache
Embassy of France, 42 Sussex Drive, Ottawa 2, Ontario

Colonel E. G. Stamp
Air, Military and Naval Attache
Embassy of the Federal Republic of Germany, 1 Waverley Street, Ottawa 4, Ontario

Colonel V. Zamboni
Air, Military and Naval Attache
Embassy of Italy, 43 Blackburn Avenue, Ottawa 2, Ontario

Colonel D. van Dijk
Air, Military and Naval Attache
The Royal Netherlands Embassy, 12 Marlborough Avenue, Ottawa 2, Ontario

Colonel Z. Lisowski
Military, Naval and Air Attache
Embassy of Poland, 10 Range Road, Ottawa 2, Ontario

Brigadier I. S. Guilford
Military, Naval and Air Attache
Embassy of South Africa, 15 Sussex Drive, Ottawa 2, Ontario

Colonel J. Juega
Air, Naval and Military Attache
Embassy of Spain, The Rockliffe Arms, 124 Springfield Road, Apt 308, Ottawa 2, Ontario

Major O. Saka
Air, Naval and Military Attache
Embassy of Turkey, 197 Wurtemburg Street, Ottawa 2, Ontario

Colonel V. F. Groshev
Military, Naval and Air Attache
Embassy of the Union of Soviet Socialist Republics, 285 Charlotte Street, Ottawa 2, Ontario

Captain B. L. Garbow
Naval Attache & Naval Attache for Air
United States Embassy, P.O. Box 1514, Station 'B', Ottawa, Ontario

Colonel V. Maldonado
Military, Naval and Air Attache
Embassy of Venezuela, Victoria Building, Suite 708, 140 Wellington Street, Ottawa 4, Ontario

CHILE

PRINCIPAL NAVAL OFFICERS

COMMANDER-IN-CHIEF OF THE NAVY
Admiral Fernando Porta

DIRECTOR GENERAL COMPTROLLER
Vice-Admiral René Roman

DIRECTOR GENERAL BUREAU OF PERSONNEL
Rear-Admiral Francisco Suarez

COMMANDER-IN-CHIEF OF THE FLEET
Rear-Admiral Hugo Tirado

COMMANDER-IN-CHIEF 1ST. NAVAL DISTRICT
Rear-Admiral Quintilio Rivera

COMMANDER-IN-CHIEF 2ND. NAVAL DISTRICT
Rear-Admiral Enrique O'Reilly

COMMANDER-IN-CHIEF 3RD. NAVAL DISTRICT
Rear-Admiral Guillermo Barros

DIRECTOR OF COASTLINE AND MERCHANT NAVY
Rear-Admiral Augusto Geiger

DIRECTOR OF ARMAMENTS
Rear-Admiral José T. Merino

DIRECTOR OF SHIPYARDS
Rear-Admiral Ismael Huerta

COMMANDANT GENERAL OF MARINE CORPS
Rear-Admiral Luis Urzua

DIRECTOR OF SUPPLIES AND ACCOUNTANCY
Rear-Admiral Marcelo Malaree

GENERAL JUDGE ADVOCATE
Rear-Admiral Rodolfo Vio

DIRECTOR OF HEALTH
Rear-Admiral Miguel Versin

CHIEF OF THE GENERAL NAVAL STAFF
Rear-Admiral Patricio Carvajal

DIRECTOR OF ENGINEERING
Rear-Admiral Luis De La Maza

DIRECTOR OF NAVAL SCHOOL
Captain Hugo Cabezas

DIRECTOR OF NAVAL WAR COLLEGE
Captain Hugo Castro

DIRECTOR OF HYDROGRAPHIC INSTITUTE
Captain Raúl Herrera

COMMANDANT OF NAVAL AIR BRANCH
Captain Carlos Borrowman

COLOMBIA

NAVAL COMMAND STRUCTURE

COMANDANTE ARMADA NACIONAL (Commander of The Navy)
Contralmirante Jaime Parra Ramirez

JEFE DE OPERACIONES NAVALES (Chief of Naval Operations)
Contralmirante Eduardo Wills Olaya

JEFE ESTADO MAYOR NAVAL (Chief of Staff, Navy)
Contralmirante Jaime Barrera Larrarte

AGREGADO NAVAL EN LIMA (Naval Attaché–Lima)
Capitán de Navío Hernando Martinez Erazo

COMANDANTE FUERZA NAVAL DEL ATLANTICO (Commander–Atlantic Fleet)
Capitán de Navío Magin Ortiga Sanclemente

DIRECTOR ESCUELA NAVAL DE CADETES (Director of Naval School)
Capitán de Navío Eduardo Melendez Ramirez

OFFICER COMMANDING TUMACO
Capitán de Navío Manuel Torres Guzman

AGREGADO NAVAL EN WASHINGTON (Naval Attaché–Washington)
Capitán de Navío Ciro Fernandez Gutierrez

COMMANDER NAVAL BASE BARRANQUILLA
Capitán de Navío Luis Diaz Rodriguez

COMMANDER NAVAL BASE 1 CARTAGENA
Capitán de Navío Gilberto Barona Silva

OFFICER COMMANDING GLORIA
Capitán de Navío Benjamin Alzate Reyes

COMANDANTE INFANTERIA DE MARINA (Commander of Marine Corps)
Teniente Coronel IM Elias Niño Herrera

COMANDANTE FUERZA NAVAL DE SUR (Commander Southern Fleet)
Capitán de Fragata Jorge Vera Pineda

OFFICERS COMMADING

20 DE JULIO
Capitán de Fragata Alberto Ramirez Posse

BARRANCA
Capitán de Fragata Luis F. Mantilla Duarte

7 DE AGOSTO
Capitán de Fragata Luis H. Camacho Landinez

COVEÑAS
Capitán de Corbeta Luis A. Gomez Velasquez

ANTIOQUIA
Capitán de Corbeta Rafael E. Grau Araujo

PADILLA
Capitán de Corbeta Jaime Gaviria Becerra

MAMONAL
Capitán de Corbeta Campo E. Gonzalez Guevara

OFFICER COMMANDING BASE NAVAL NR. 2 BUENAVENTURA
Mayor de I.M. Arnold E. Arnedo Cardona

DENMARK

SENIOR NAVAL APPOINTMENTS

COMMANDER-IN-CHIEF ROYAL DANISH NAVY
Vice-Admiral S. S. Thostrup

CHIEF OF NAVAL STAFF
Rear-Admiral O. Brinck-Lund

CHIEF OF NAVAL OPERATIONAL FORCES
Rear-Admiral A. Helms

CHIEF OF NAVAL MATERIEL COMMAND
Rear-Admiral S. J. Valentiner

CHIEF OF NAVAL STATION COPENHAGEN
Rear-Admiral E. J. Saabye

CHIEF OF NAVAL STATION FREDERIKSHAVN
Captain P. Würtz

CHIEF OF NAVAL STATION KORSOR
Captain E. Wolfhagen

NAVAL ATTACHES

LONDON
Colonel H. R. H. Prince Georg of Denmark, CVO R.

WASHINGTON
Captain O. Felding

ECUADOR

ADMINISTRATION
MINISTRO DE DEFENSA NACIONAL (Minister of National Defence)
General (R) Rafael Andrade Ochoa

COMANDANTE GENERAL DE MARINA (Commandant General of The Navy)
CPNV EM Jorge Cruz Polanco

JEFE DE ESTADO MAYOR DE LA ARMADA (Chief of Naval Staff)
CPNV EM Reinaldo Vallejo Vivas

COMANDANTE DE LA I ZONA NAVAL (Commandant of No. 1 Zone)
CPNV EM Guillermo Jarrín Negrete

COMANDANTE EN JEFE DE LA ESCUADRA (Commandant in Chief of Squadrons)
CPNV EM Wilson Larrea Torres

DIRECTOR DE LA MARINA MERCANTE Y DEL LITORAL (Director of Merchant Marine and Stores)
CPNV EM Alfredo Poveda Burbano

DIRECTOR DEL MATERIAL (Director of Materials)
CPNV EM Wilson Arroyo Boada

NAVAL ATTACHES

WASHINGTON
CPNV EM Octavio Jarrín Salgado

PERU
CPNV EM Angel Benavídez Chávez

CHILE
CPNV EM Homero Muñoz Estrella

ESTABLISHMENTS

NAVAL WARFARE ACADEMY
Guayaquil

NAVAL AND MILITARY COLLEGE
Salinas

NAVAL BASES

Guayaquil, Galápagos, Salinas and San Lorenzo

EIRE

IRISH NAVAL SERVICE

COMMANDING OFFICER NAVAL SERVICE AND DIRECTOR NAVAL SERVICE
Captain T. McKenna

ASSISTANT DIRECTOR, NAVAL SERVICE
Comdr. P. O. Kavanagh

OFFICER COMMANDING NAVAL BASE
Comdr. C. J. Byrne

ENGINEER MANAGER, NAVAL DOCKYARD
Comdr. L. Ahern

OFFICER COMMANDING L. E. "Macha"
Lt. Cdr. Moloney

OFFICER COMMANDING L. E. "CLIONA"
Lt. Cdr. L. Brett

OFFICER COMMANDING L. E. "MAEV"
Lt. Cdr. J. Deasy

ADDRESSES
Naval Headquarters, Department of Defence Parkgate, Dublin

Naval Base, Haulbowline, Cobh, Co. Cork.

FINLAND

SENIOR OFFICERS FINNISH NAVY

COMMANDER-IN-CHIEF FINNISH NAVAL FORCES
Rear-Admiral J. K. Pirhonen

CHIEF OF NAVAL STAFF
Commodore O. Knaapi

COMMANDING OFFICER NAVAL SQUADRON
Commodore L. Pauhakari

MILITARY, NAVAL AND AIR ATTACHES

USA
Colonel M. Frick

U.K.
Captain F. N. K. Ruusuvuori

FRANCE
Colonel L. Boldt

U.S.S.R.
Colonel Y. Tehola

POLAND
Lt. Colonel A. Kantola

NORWAY
Lt. Colonel P. Laamanen

SWEDEN
Lt. Colonel B. Nordgren

FRANCE

COMMAND STRUCTURE

CHEF D'ETAT-MAJOR DE LA MARINE (Chief of the Naval Staff)
Admiral Andre Patou

SOUS-CHEF D'ETAT-MAJOR OPERATIONS (Deputy Chief of Staff Operations)
Rear-Admiral de Joybert

SOUS-CHEF D'ETAT-MAJOR MATERIEL (Deputy Chief of Staff Equipment)
Rear-Admiral Clotteau

SOUS-CHEF D'ETAT-MAJOR PLANS (Deputy Chief of Staff Plans)
Rear-Admiral Laure

PREFECT MARITIME PREMIERE REGION (Naval Superintendant First Region)
Vice-Admiral d'Escadre Rousselot

PREFECT MARITIME DEUXIEME REGION (Naval Superintendant Second Region)
Admiral La Haye

PREFECT MARITIME TROISIEME REGION (Naval Superintendant Third Region)
Vice-Admiral d'Escadre De Soitivaux de Greishe

GERMANY

FEDERAL GERMAN NAVY COMMAND STRUCTURE

CHIEF OF NAVAL STAFF FEDERAL GERMAN NAVY
Vice-Admiral Gert Jeschonnek

DEPUTY CHIEF OF NAVAL STAFF FEDERAL GERMAN NAVY
Rear-Admiral Erich Topp

COMMANDER IN CHIEF GERMAN NAVAL FORCES
Vice-Admiral Karl Hetz

COMMANDER GERMAN NAVAL FORCES NORTH SEA SUB-AREA
Rear-Admiral Armin Zimmermann

CHIEF OF GENERAL NAVAL OFFICE
Rear-Admiral Günter Kuhnke

NAVAL ATTACHE

LONDON
Capt. K. T. Raeder

WASHINGTON
Captain Paul Brasack

INDIA

NAMES OF ADMINISTRATIVE AUTHORITIES

FLAG OFFICER COMMANDING-IN-CHIEF WESTERN NAVAL COMMAND
Vice-Admiral S. M. Nanda

FLAG OFFICER COMMANDING-IN-CHIEF EASTERN NAVAL COMMAND
Rear-Admiral K. R. Nair

FLAG OFFICER COMMANDING WESTERN FLEET
Rear-Admiral V.A. Kamath

COMMODORE COMMANDING SOUTHERN NAVAL AREA
Commodore Inder Singh

NAVAL ADIVSERS

UNITED KINGDOM
Commodore K. K. Sanjana
Commander R. P. Bhalla (Deputy)

PAKISTAN
Captain L. Gomes I.N.

NAVAL ATTACHES

U.S.S.R.
Commodore S. Prakash

INDONESIA
Captain K. M. V. Nair, I.N.

WEST GERMANY
Commodore T. J. Kunnenkeri

ITALY

AMMIRAGLI DI SQUADRA (Squadron Commanders)

COMNAVSOUTH MALTA
Amm. Sq. Giuseppe Roselli Lorenzini

CAPO DI STATO MAGGIORE DELLA MARINA
Amm. Sq. Virgilio Spigal

PRESIDENTE SEZIONE MARINA DEL CONSIGLIO SUPERIORE DELLE FF. AA.
Amm. Sq. Raffaele Barbera

COMEDCENT NAPLES COM. TE IN CAPO DI MARIDIPART NAPLES
Amm. Sq. Giovanni Cantù

COM. TE IN CAPO DI MARIDIPART ANCONA
Amm. Sq. Luigi Longanesi Cattani

COM. TE IN CAPO DELLA SQUADRA NAVALE
Amm. Sq. Gino Birindelli

SOTTOCAPO DI STATO MAGGIORE DELLA MARINA
Amm. Sq. Francesco Brunetti

STAMADIFESA—PRESIDENTE CENTRO ALTI STUDI MILITARI
Amm. Sq. Vincenzo Vaccarisi

CAPO DEL SERVIZIO INFORMAZIONI DIFESA
Amm. Sq. Eugenio Henke

STATO MAGGIORE DIFESA-PRESIDENTE DEL CONSIGLIO TECNICO SCIENTIFICO
Amm. Sq. Enzo Zanni

SOTTOCAPO DI STATO MAGGIORE DIFESA
Amm. Sq. Giuseppe Pighini

COMANDANTI DI COMANDI NAVALI COMPLESSI (Commanders of Naval Divisions)

COM. TE LA 1ˆ DIVISIONE NAVALE
Amm. Div. Franco Micali Baratelli

COM. TE RAGGRUPP. SUBACQUEI ED INCURSORI "T. TESEI" LA SPEZIA
Amm. Div. Giovanni Giometti

COM. TE DEI DRAGAMINE
Amm. Div. Giovanni Peraldo Gianolino

COM. TE LA 3ˆ DIVISIONE NAVALE
Amm. Div. Ferdinando Valsecchi

COM. TE LA 2ˆ DIVISIONE NAVALE
Amm. Div. Gino De Giorgi

COM. TE LA 4ˆ DIVISIONE NAVALE
Contramm. Giovanni Fiorini

COM. TE DEI SOMMERGIBILI
Contramm. Antonio Mondaini

CAPI DI CORPO (Corp Captains)

CORPO DEL GENIO NAVALE
Gen. Isp. G. N. Giovanni Di Mento

CORPO DELLE ARMI NAVALI
Gen. Isp. A. N. Luciano Perona

CORPO SANITARIO MARITTIMO
Ten. Gen. Med Luigi Campanelli

CORPO DI COMMISSARIATO MILITARE MARITTIMO
Ten. Gen. Comm. Pietro Achilli

CORPO DELLE CAPITANERIE DI PORTO
Ten. Gen. Porto Mario Battaglieri

DIRETTORI GENERALI (Directorate General)

D.G. DI MARIPERS
Amm. Div. Ennio Ciuffo

D.G. DI NAVALCOSTARMI
Generale Ispettore G.N. Goivanni Di Mento

PRESIDENTI DEI COMITATI PROGETTI E STUDI (President of Progress and Study Committees)

PRES. MARICOMINAV
Ten. Gen. G.N. Antonio Siena

PRES. MARIOMITARMI
Gen. Isp. A.N. Ettore Santarcangelo

JAMAICA

OFFICER COMMANDING

Lieutenant Commander G. B. L. Copland
Jamaica Defence Force Coast Guard, Up Park Camp, Kingston, Jamaica

COMMANDING OFFICERS

HMJS DISCOVERY BAY
Lieutenant L. B. Scott

HMJS HOLLAND BAY
Lieutenant H. A. Robinson

HMJS MANATTEE BAY
Lieutenant A. I. Collins

The Coast Guard is expected to move to Port Royal, a new base, in the near future.

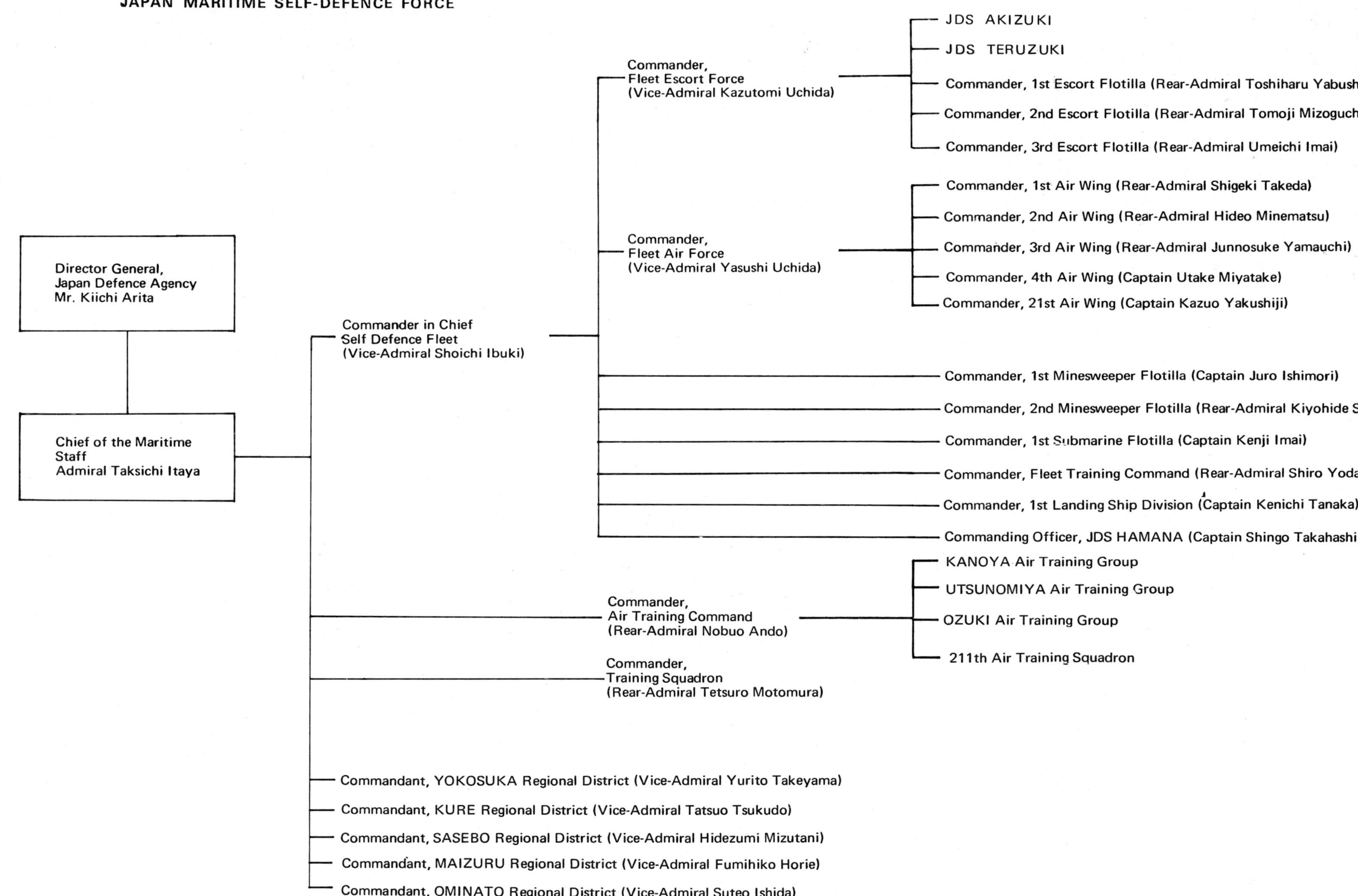

JAPAN MARITIME SELF-DEFENCE FORCE
Director General, Japan Defence Agency Mr. Kiichi Arita
Chief of the Maritime Staff Admiral Taksichi Itaya
Commander in Chief Self Defence Fleet (Vice-Admiral Shoichi Ibuki)
Commander, Fleet Escort Force (Vice-Admiral Kazutomi Uchida)
JDS AKIZUKI
JDS TERUZUKI
Commander, 1st Escort Flotilla (Rear-Admiral Toshiharu Yabushita)
Commander, 2nd Escort Flotilla (Rear-Admiral Tomoji Mizoguchi)
Commander, 3rd Escort Flotilla (Rear-Admiral Umeichi Imai)
Commander, Fleet Air Force (Vice-Admiral Yasushi Uchida)
Commander, 1st Air Wing (Rear-Admiral Shigeki Takeda)
Commander, 2nd Air Wing (Rear-Admiral Hideo Minematsu)
Commander, 3rd Air Wing (Rear-Admiral Junnosuke Yamauchi)
Commander, 4th Air Wing (Captain Utake Miyatake)
Commander, 21st Air Wing (Captain Kazuo Yakushiji)
Commander, 1st Minesweeper Flotilla (Captain Juro Ishimori)
Commander, 2nd Minesweeper Flotilla (Rear-Admiral Kiyohide Seki)
Commander, 1st Submarine Flotilla (Captain Kenji Imai)
Commander, Fleet Training Command (Rear-Admiral Shiro Yoda)
Commander, 1st Landing Ship Division (Captain Kenichi Tanaka)
Commanding Officer, JDS HAMANA (Captain Shingo Takahashi)
Commander, Air Training Command (Rear-Admiral Nobuo Ando)
KANOYA Air Training Group
UTSUNOMIYA Air Training Group
OZUKI Air Training Group
211th Air Training Squadron
Commander, Training Squadron (Rear-Admiral Tetsuro Motomura)
Commandant, YOKOSUKA Regional District (Vice-Admiral Yurito Takeyama)
Commandant, KURE Regional District (Vice-Admiral Tatsuo Tsukudo)
Commandant, SASEBO Regional District (Vice-Admiral Hidezumi Mizutani)
Commandant, MAIZURU Regional District (Vice-Admiral Fumihiko Horie)
Commandant, OMINATO Regional District (Vice-Admiral Suteo Ishida)

JAPAN

DIPLOMATIC RESPRESENTATION

DEFENCE ATTACHE IN LONDON
Captain Goro Yoshimura
Japanese Embassy 46, Grosvenor Street, London, W.1

DEFENCE (NAVAL) ATTACHE IN U.S.A.
Captain Fumiro Shimizu
Japanese Embassy 2520, Masachusetts Avenue, N. W., Washington D.C. 20008

DEFENCE ATTACHE IN TURKEY
Captain Hajime Ohori
Ambassade du Japon, Resit Galip Caddesi, No. 81 Gazi Osman Pasa, Mah., Ankara

MALAYSIA

ROYAL MALAYSIAN NAVY
Senior Naval Appointments

CHIEF OF THE NAVAL STAFF
Commodore K. Thanabalasingam, AMN, RMN

PRINCIPAL STAFF OFFICER
Captain M. A. Higgs, RN

STAFF OFFICER GRADE 1 PLANS, OPERATION AND WEAPONS POLICY
Commander J. I. Quinn, RNZN

STAFF OFFICER GRADE 1 TECHNICAL
Commander J. P. B. Drake, RN

STAFF OFFICER GRADE 1 LOGISTICS AND FINANCE
A/Commander Khoo Tee Ghuan, AMN, RMN

STAFF OFFICER GRADE 1 PERSONNEL AND TRAINING
Lieutenant Commander D. J. H. Robinson, RMN

STAFF OFFICER RESERVES
Lieutenant Commander Syed Halim bin Syed Abu Hassan, AMN, RMN (Retd.)

NAVAL OFFICER-IN-CHARGE, WEST MALAYSIA
Captain R. M. Burgoyne, RN

NAVAL OFFICER-IN-CHARGE, EAST MALAYSIA
A/Commander Ismail bin Hassan, AMN, RMN

COMMANDING OFFICER, KD HANG JEBAT
Commander Cheah Leong Voon, AMN, RMN

COMMANDING OFFICER KD HANG TUAH
A/Commander Charles Thong Yin Sin, AMN, RMN

COMMANDING OFFICER KD MALAYA
Commander B. E. I. Hyde-Smith, KMN, RMN

MEXICO

SECRETARY OF STATE FOR THE NAVY
Almirante C.G. Antonio Vazquez del Mercado

UNDER SECRETARY FOR THE NAVY
Almirante C.G. Antonio J. Aznar Zetina

PERMANENT UNDER SECRETARY
Licenciado Fernando Castro y Castro

COMMANDER IN CHIEF OF THE NAVY
Vicealmirante C.G. Gabriel Lagos Beltran

CHIEF OF THE NAVAL GENERAL STAFF
Vicealmirante C.G. Federico Romero Ceballos

DIRECTOR OF SERVICES
Contralmirante C.G. Angel Ramos Ramirez

COMMANDER OF THE FIRST NAVAL ZONE TAMPICO. TAMPS
Contralmirante C.G. Carlos Valenzuela Moncayo

COMMANDER OF THE SECOND NAVAL ZONE PUERTO CORTES, B.C.
Contralmirante C.G. Ignacio Saenz Gutierrez

COMMANDER OF THE THIRD NAVAL ZONE VERACRUZ, VERA
Vicealmirante C.G. Jose Abelardo Cerdan Muñoz

COMMANDER OF THE FOURTH NAVAL ZONE GUAYMAS, SON
Contralmirante C.G. Felix Morell Peyrefitte

COMMANDER OF THE FIFTH NAVAL ZONE CD. DEL CARMEN, CAMP
Contralmirante C.G. Alfredo Marquez Ricaño

COMMANDER OF THE SIXTH NAVAL ZONE, MANZANILLO, COL
Vicealmirante C.G. Pedro Calderon Lozano

COMMANDER OF THE SEVENTH NAVAL ZONE ISLA MUJERES, Q.ROO
Vicealmirante C.G. Ruben de Gante y Mendoza

COMMANDER OF THE EIGHTH NAVAL ZONE ICACOS, GRO
Almirante C.G. Rigoberto Otal Briseño

COMMANDER OF THE ENSENADA, B.C. NAVAL SECTOR
Capitan de Navío C.G. Raul Alcala Martinez

COMMANDER OF THE LA PAZ, B.C. NAVAL SECTOR
Capitán de Navío C.G. Pedro Toledo Astorga

COMMANDER OF THE MAZATLAN, SIN. NAVAL SECTOR
Contralmirante C.G. Lorenzo del Peon Alvarez

COMMANDER OF THE ISLA SOCORRO, COL. NAVAL SECTOR
Capitán de Navío C.G. Roberto Maupome Ruiz

COMMANDER OF THE SALINACRUZ, OAX. NAVAL SECTOR
Capitán de Navío C.G. Victor M. Chapa Zamudio

COMMANDER OF THE CHETUMAL Q.R. NAVAL SECTOR
Contralm P.A. Jose Blanco Peyrefitte

COMMANDER OF THE PROGRESCO, YUC. NAVAL SECTOR
Capitán de Navío C.G. Miguel Portela Cruz

COMMANDER OF THE COATZACOALCOS, VER. NAVAL SECTOR
Capitán de Fragata C.G. Alfonso Vaca Betancourt

COMMANDER OF THE TUXPAN, VER. NAVAL SECTOR
Capitán de Navío C.G. Jose Guardado Dominguez

COMMANDER OF THE MATAMOROS, TAMPS. NAVAL SECTOR
Capitán de Navío C.G. Fernando Magana Verdugo

DIRECTOR OF LA HEROICA NAVAL SCHOOL ANTON LIZARDO, VER
Contralmirante C.G. Fernando Piana Lara

DIRECTOR OF THE FLEET AIR ARM SCHOOL, LAS BAJADAS, VER
Capitán de Fragata P.A. Manuel Moreno Corzo

DIRECTOR OF THE TRAINING CENTRE VERACRUZ. VER
Contralmirante C.G. Fernando Gonzalez Ruiz

DIRECTOR OF THE SCHOOL FOR OFFICERS AND SEAMEN, ON BOARD THE TRANSPORT "DURANGO"
Capitán de Navío C.G. Mauricio Scheleske Sanchez

COMMANDER OF THE FIRST COMPANY SUBMARINE COMMAND—ICACOS, GRO
Capitán de Corbeta C.G. Luis Ordoñez Gonzalez

COMMANDER OF THE FIRST FLEET AIR ARM SQUADRON—LAS BAJADAS, VER
Capitán de Navío P.A. Estanislao Lopez Arreola

COMMANDER OF THE SECOND FLEET AIR ARM SQUADRON—MEXICO, D.F.
Capitán de Navío P.A. Fidencio Gonzalez Carrasco

COMMANDER OF THE THIRD FLEET AIR ARM SQUADRON—LAS BAJADAS, VER
Capitán de Fragata P.A. Vidal Preciado Ruiz

COMMANDER OF THE AIR SQUADRON OF BUSQUEDA Y SALVAMENTO—VERACRUZ, VER
Capitán de Fragata P.A. Federico Carballo Jimenez

NAVAL ATTACHES

U.S.A.
Vicealmirante C.G. Miguel Manzarraga Zamudio

ITALY
Vicealmirante P.A. Diego Mugica Naranjo

BRAZIL
Contralmirante C.G. Jose Maria Rivas Sanz

FRANCE
Contralmirante C.G. Ruben Montejo Sierra

COMMANDING OFFICERS

TEHUANTEPEC
Capitán de Fragata C.G. German Tejera Reyes

CALIFORNIA
Capitán de Fragata C.G. Mario Dominguez Genel

PAPALOAPAN
Capitán de Fragata C.G. Venancio Delgado Yepez

USUMACINTA
Capitán de Fragata C.G. Gildardo Alarcon Lopez

DURANGO
Capitán de Navío C.G. Mauricio Scheleske Sanchez

QUERETARO
Capitán de Fragata C.G. Rodrigo del Peon Alvarez

GUANAJUATO
Capitán de Fragata C.G. Mario Gonzalez Laine

POTOSI
Capitán de Fragata C.G. Marcial l'Eglise Muttio

MINESWEEPER 01
Capitán de Corbeta C.G. Luis Lopez Mancilla

MINESWEEPER 02
Capitán de Corbeta C.G. Manuel Monroy Gutierrez

MINESWEEPER 03
Teniente de Navío C.G. Alejandro Maldonado Mendoza

MINESWEEPER 04
Capitán de Corbetta C.G. Ambrosio Ariza Lopez

MINESWEEPER 05
Teniente de Navío C.G. Ruben Carrillo Pozo

MINESWEEPER 06
Capitán de Corbeta C.G. Guillermo Garcia Santillana

MINESWEEPER 07
Capitán de Corbeta C.G. Augusto Esparza Rodriguez

MINESWEEPER 08
Teniente de Navío C.G. Antonio Cordova Gomez

MINESWEEPER 09
Teniente de Navío C.G. Jose M. Gonzalez Sanchez

MINESWEEPER 10
Teniente de Navío C.G. Alvaro Perez Ortega

MINESWEEPER 11
Teniente de Navío C.G. Rodolfo Rodriguez Jurado

MINESWEEPER 12
Teniente de Navío C.G. Leopoldo Diaz Gonzalez Rcca

MINESWEEPER 13
Capitán de Corbeta C.G. Alvaro Sandoval Peralta

MINESWEEPER 14
Teniente de Navío C.G. Ildefonso Consejo Loperena

MINESWEEPER 15
Capitán de Corbeta C.G. Mario Rodriguez Esperon

MINESWEEPER 16
Capitán de Corbeta C.G. Felix J. Perez y Elias

MINESWEEPER 17
Capitán de Corbeta C.G. Miguel Viveros Parker

MINESWEEPER 18
Teniente de Navío C.G. Eugenio Magaña Gayou

MINESWEEPER 19
Capitán de Corbeta C.G. Fernando Magaña Gayou

MINESWEEPER 20
Teniente de Navío C.G. Jorge Lagos Kintzy

VIRGILIO URIBE
Capitán de Corbeta C.G. Gandhi Zilli Viveros

GC 38
Teniente de Navío C.G. Arturo Rosas Montero

ZACATECAS
Teniente de Navío C.G. Jose H. Orozco [illegible]lta

TLAXCALA
Teniente de Navío C.G. Jose Ramon Lorenzo Franco

AGUASCALIENTES
Capitán de Corbeta C.G. Alberto de la Cruz Ramos

AZUETA
Teniente de Fragata C.G. Agustin Flores Gonzalez

VILLALPANDO
Teniente de Navío C.G. Manuel Peyrot Gonzalez

POLIMAR UNO
Teniente de Navío C.G. Eduardo Luna Roma

POLIMAR DOS
Teniente de Navío C.G. Manuel Zermeño del Peon

POLIMAR TRES
Teniente de Navío C.G. Manuel Garcia Carmona

SOTAVENTO
Teniente de Navío C.G. Gabriel Serrano Franco

PROGRESO MARITIMO
Teniente de Fragata E.M. Rafael Gonzalez Gonzalez

NORWAY

COMMAND STRUCTURE

The Operational Command of all the Services is vested in the Chief of Defence. The Commander-in-Chief of the Navy is broadly responsible for all logistic services in the Navy (personnel, maintenance and finance) and for training. He is assisted by a deputy Commander-in-Chief who is also the operational naval commander in South Norway (Naval Commander South Norway—COMNAVSONOR) and as such, responsible to the Chief of Defence.

The Headquarters, Royal Norwegian Navy, has six divisions:
Plans, Policy and Operations,
Coast Artillery,
Personnel,
Logistics,
Finance and
Medical Services.

The country is divided into five Naval Commands—East, South, West, Tróndelag and North Norway. All Naval Commanders, except North Norway, is operationally responsible to COMNAVSONOR, otherwise to the Commander-in-Chief, Royal Norwegian Navy.

The Naval Commander, North Norway, is operationally responsible to the Force Commander, North Norway, who commands all the operational forces in the north.

The main base is Haakonsvern, near Bergen. Here is also found the Chief of Naval Logistics Services and the Naval Training Establishment.

The Naval Academy is in the neighbourhood of Bergen, while the Naval Staff College is in Oslo.

SENIOR OFFICERS

COMMANDER-IN-CHIEF ROYAL NORWEGIAN NAVY
Vice-Admiral M. Braadland
Sjøforsvarets Stab, H.Q. Royal Norwegian Navy

DEPUTY COMMANDER-IN-CHIEF, ROYAL NORWEGIAN NAVY
Rear-Admiral H. Skjong

CHIEF OF STAFF, PLANS, POLICY AND OPERATIONS
Captain O. B. Hatlem, (acting)

INSPECTOR GENERAL, COAST ARTILLERY
Commodore A. H. Furre

CHIEF OF STAFF, PERSONNEL
Commodore R. Thomesen

CHIEF OF STAFF, LOGISTICS
Commodore E. Bakke

CHIEF OF STAFF, FINANCE
Commodore A. E. Erichsen

MEDICAL DIRECTOR GENERAL
Commodore O.A. Mortensen

NAVAL COMMANDERS

EAST NORWAY
Rear-Admiral T. Holthe

SOUTH NORWAY
Commodore R. M. Sars

WEST NORWAY
Rear-Admiral H. Voltersvik

TRÖNDELAG
Commodore H. Sverdrup

NORTH NORWAY
Rear-Admiral R. A. Tamber

CHIEF OF NAVAL LOGISTICS SERVICES
Commodore Th. Pettersen

DIRECTOR OF NAVAL TRAINING ESTABLISHMENT
Commodore S. Ostervold

DIRECTOR OF NAVAL ACADEMY
Captain B. Helle (acting)

DIRECTOR OF NAVAL STAFF COLLEGE
Captain E. Zachariassen

NAVAL ATTACHES

U.S.A. AND CANADA
Captain Ch. O. Herlofsen
Royal Norwegian Embassy, 2720 34th Street, N.W., Washington D.C. 20008

GREAT BRITAIN AND EIRE
Captain O. Aslaksrud (Joint Naval, Army and Air Attaché)
Royal Norwegian Embassy, 25 Belgrave Square, London S.W.1.

FEDERAL REPUBLIC OF GERMANY AND SWITZERLAND
Lieutenant Colonel B. Muggerud (Joint Naval, Army and Air Attaché) domiciled in Bonn
Köiglich Norwegische Botschaft, Gotenstrasse 163, Bad Godesberg, Deutschland.

UNION OF SOVIET SOCIALIST REPUBLICS AND POLAND
Captain B. E. Ytterhorn (Joint Naval, Army and Air Attaché)
Kgl. Norsk Ambassade, Ulitsa Vorovskovo 7, Moscow

SWEDEN
Lieutenant Colonel : Folge (Joint Naval, Army and Air attaché)
Kgl. Norsk Ambassade, Strandvägen 113, Stockholm

FINLAND
Lieutenant Colonel E. Lund (Joint Naval, Army and Air Attaché)
Kgl. Norsk Ambassade, Rehbindervägen 17, Helsingfors

PERU

NAVAL AND MILITARY ATTACHES

ARGENTINE
Sr. Captain Dn. Javier Pinillos Cabada, (Naval Attaché)
Address: Av. del Libertador 4776-4° "A"
Telephone: 772-3102
Embassy: Libertador San Martín 1720—Buenos Aires
Telephone: 836-592

BRAZIL
Sr. Captain Dn. Jose Conterno Montani (Naval Attaché)
Address: Rua Paula Freitas 42-AP-101 Rio de Janeiro
Telephone: 364-358
Embassy: Av. Rui Barbosa 314—Rio de Janeiro
Telephone: 258-565

COLOMBIA
Sr.Captain Dn. Armando Figueroa Roggero (Naval and Military Attaché)
Address: Carrera 11A-93B-30—Bogota
Telephone: 36-2063
Embassy: Calle 67 No. 16-05 Bogota 2—Colombia
Telephone: 494-279

CHILE
Sr. Captain Dn. Jorge Mazure Gamboa (Naval Attaché)
Address: Av. Los Leones 605 Santiago
Telephone: 49-6009
Embassy: Huérfanos 1376-12° Piso (Edif. "El Solde Chile")
Telephone: 712-532

ECUADOR
Sr. Leiutenant Dn. Carlos Chipoco Vargas (Military Naval and Air Attaché)
Address: Av. Los Pinos 130—Quito 2
Telephone: 34-567
Embassy: Calle 9 de Octubre 151 Quito
Telephone: 32-246

U.S.A.
Sr. Rear-Admiral Dn. Fernando Elias Aparicio (Naval Attaché)
Address: 11114 Stephalle Lane-Lux-Manor Rookville M.D. 20852 U.S.A.
Telephone: 881-4418
Embassy: 1315-16 Th. Street N.W. Washington D.C. 20036 U.S.A.
Telephone: 234-3432 234-7043

SPAIN
Sr. Captain Dn. Jorge Parodi Galliani (Military, Naval and Air Attaché)
Embassy: Calle Gral. Mola 36 Madrid 1—España
Telephone: 275-9353

FRANCE
Sr. Rear-Admiral Dn. Guillermo de las Casas Frayssinet (Military and Naval Attaché)
Embassy: 50 Avenue Klevel—Paris XVI Poin Caro 3453
Telephone: 3453-3658

U.K. AND NETHERLANDS
Sr. Captain Dn. Ramon Arrospide Mejia (Naval Attaché)
Address: 89 Piccadilly, London S.W.1. England
Embassy: 52 Sloane Street London S.W.ı. (Peruvian Embassy)
Telephone: BEL-8340

COMMAND STRUCTURE

CMDTE. GRAL. DE LA ESCUADRA
C. Alm. Pedro Vargas Prada Zoller

CMDTE. FLOTILLA ANTISUBMARINA
C. de N. Guillermo Faura Gaig

CMDTE. FLOTILLA DESEMBARCO
C. de N. Ernesto Palacio Valdivieso

CMDTE. FLOTILLA AUZILIARES
Vacant

CMDTE. FLOTILLA SUBMARINOS
C. de N. Francisco Quiroz Tafur

CMDTE. FLOTILLA PATRULLERAS
C. de F. Juan Bergelund Remy

CMDTE. FLOT. CANONERAS—TORP
C. de F. Jorge Villalobos Urquiaga

COMMANDING OFFICERS

"ALMIRANTE GRAU"
C. de N. Jaime Vasques Bejares

"CORONEL BOLOGNES"
C. de N. Isaias Paredes Arana

"VILLAR"
C. de F. Ricardo Zevallos Newton

"GUISE"
C. de F. Geronimo Cafferata Marazi

"CASTILLA"
C. de F. Alfonso Castillo Jordan

"AGUIRRE"
C. de F. Guillermo Angulo Denegri

"RODRIGUEZ"
C. de F. Luis Murgia Benvenuto

"DIEZ CANSECO"
C. de C. Armando Pereira Rios

"GALVEZ"
C. de C. Jorge O'Hara Neyra

"DOS DE MAYO"
C. de F. Armando Vidal Martinez

"ABTAO"
C. de F. Willy Harm Esparza

"ANGAMOS"
C. de F. Romulo Aste Baptista

"IQUIQUE"
C. de F. Jorge Telaya Hidalgo

PHILIPPINES

CENTRAL NAVAL STAFF

CHIEF NAVAL STAFF AND CONCURRENT VICE CMDR.
Captain Hilario M. Ruiz

NAVAL COMPTROLLER
Captain Regalado Montecillo

PERSONNEL (N-1)
Lt. Cmdr. Rodolfo Punsalang

INTELLIGENCE (N-2)
Lt. Cmdr. Brillante Ochoco

OPERATIONS (N-3)
Cmdr. Pedro Velasco

LOGISTICS (N-4)
Lt. Cmdr. Loreño Aldea

PLANNING (N-5)
Cmdr. Socrates Viloria

SHIPS AND YARDS (N-6)
Lt. Cmdr. Gregorio Abad

COMMUNCIATIONS AND ELECTRONICS (N-7)
Lt. Artemic Tadiar

SECRETARY NAVAL STAFF
Cmdr. Ponciano Bautista

PORTUGAL

CHIEF NAVAL APPOINTMENTS

MINISTRO DA MARINHA
Contra-almirante Manuel Pereira Crespo

CHEFE DO ESTADO-MAIOR DA ARMADA (Chief of Naval Staff)
Vice-almirante Armando Júlio de Roboredo e Silva

VICE-CHEFE DO ESTADO-MAIOR DA ARMADA (Vice-Chief of Naval Staff)
Contra-almirante Laurindo Henriques dos Santos

SUBCHEFE DO ESTADO-MAIOR DA ARMADA (Assistant Chief of Naval Staff)
Comodoro Jaime Lopes

SUPERINTENDENTE DOS SERVICOS DO PESSOAL (Superintendant of Health Services)
Contra-almirante Fernando Eduardo Pinto de Ornelas e Vasconcelos

SUPERINTENDENTE DOS SERVICOS DO MATERIAL (Superintendant of Equipment Services)
Contra-almirante Luiz Bogarin Ribeiro Correia Guedes

DIRECTOR GERAL DA MARINHA
Contra-almirante António Morgado Belo

DIRECTOR DO INSTITUTO HIDROGRAFICO (Director of the Hydrographic Institute)
Contra-almirante Aníbal B. Almeida Graça

COMANDANTE NAVAL DO CONTINENTE (Naval Commandant for the Continent)
Contra-almirante Francisco Ferrer Caeiro

COMANDANTE NAVAL DOS ACORES (Naval Commandant for the Azores)
Comodoro António Garcia Braga

COMANDANTE NAVAL DE CABO VERDE (Naval Commandant-Cape Verde Islands)
Contra-almirante José Casimiro Alcobia Freitas Ribeiro

COMANDANTE NAVAL DE ANGOLA (Naval Commandant—Angola)
Contra-almirante Eugénio Ferreira de Almeida

COMANDANTE NAVAL DE MOCAMBIQUE (Naval Commandant—Mozambique)
Contra-almirante António Tierno Bagulho

COMANDANTE DA DEFESA MARITIMA DA GUINE (Commandant for Naval Defence in Guinea)
Comodoro Luciano Ferreira Bastos da Costa e Silva

INTENDENTE DOS SERVICOS DE ADMINISTRACAO FINANCEIRA DA MARINHA
Comodoro AN Ernesto Carneiro Allen Júnior

DIRECTOR DO INSTITUTO SUPERIOR NAVAL DE GUERRA (Director of Institute of Naval Warfare)
Contra-almirante Rogério de Castro e Silva

DIRECTOR E PRIMEIRO COMANDANTE DA ESCOLA NAVAL (Director and Chief Commandant of the Naval College)
Contra-almirante Lino Paulino Pereira

DIRECTOR DAS CONSTRUCOES NAVAIS (Director of Naval Construction)
Comodoro ECN Rogério Silva d'Oliveira

DIRECTOR DO SERVICO DO PESSOAL
Comodoro Fernando da Silva Soares Branco

DIRECTOR DO SERVICO DE SAUDE NAVAL (Director of Health Services)
Comodoro MN Rui Terenas Latino

DIRECTOR DO SERVICO DE MAQUINAS (Director of Engineering Services)
Comodoro EMQ Pedro Conceiçao Mouzinho

NAVAL ATTACHES

RIO DE JANEIRO
Lt.-Colonel (Air) António Celorico Borba de Silva.

MADRID
Captain José Augusto Barahona Fernandes

PARIS
Commander Mário Dias Martins

LONDON
Commander José Baptista Pinheiro Azevedo

WASHINGTON AND OTTAWA
Commander Vasco António Martins Rodrigues

BONN
Commander Manuel Eduardo Leal Vilarinho

SAN SALVADOR

NAVAL COMMANDERS

COMANDANTE DE LA MARINA NACIONAL
Lieut. Cnel Gonzalo Anselmo Argumedo
Avenida España 1009, San Salvador

COMANDANTE DE LAS UNIDADES NAVALES, LA UNION
Lieut. Cnel. Ernesto Cayetano Gallo

PORT CAPTAINS

La UNION
Lieut. Cnel. Mauricio Aquiles Funes

ACAJUTLA
Lieut. Cnel. Carlos Arturo Azucena

LA LIBERTAD
Lieut. Cnel. Juan Francisco Menéndez

EL TRIUNFO
Lieut. Mario Enrique Acevedo

SOUTH AFRICA

COMMAND STRUCTURE

Administration

MINISTER OF DEFENCE
The Honourable P. W. Botha M.P.

Command

COMMANDANT-GENERAL S. A. DEFENCE FORCE
General R. C. Hiemstra, SSA, SM

COMMANDER MARITIME DEFENCE AND CHIEF OF THE NAVY
Vice-Admiral H. H. Biermann, SSA, OBE

CHIEF OF NAVAL STAFF
Rear-Admiral M. R. Terry-Lloyd, SM

DIRECTOR OF PERSONNEL
Commodore S. C. Biermann, SM

DIRECTOR OF TECHNICAL SERVICES
Commodore J. R. Nortier, SM, MBE, AMI(SA) Mech E. C. Eng, AMI Prod. E.

DIRECTOR OF STORES
Commodore W. G. Crosby, SM

DIRECTOR OF ADMINISTRATION
Commodore J. C. Goosen,SM

SENIOR OFFICER AFLOAT
Commodore J. Johnson, SM, DSC

DIPLOMATIC REPRESENTATION (NAVAL)

ARMED FORCES ATTACHE IN BUENOS AIRES
Commodore B. V. Hegarty, DSC

NAVAL ATTACHE IN LONDON
Commander R. D. Kingon

NAVAL ATTACHE IN PARIS
Commander A. S. Davis

NAVAL ATTACHE IN BELGIUM
CHEF DE L'ETAT-MAJOR DE LA FORCE NAVALE (Commander-in-Chief, Naval Forces)
Commodore L. J. J. Lurquin

GROUPS

Le Groupement Opérationnel à Ostende

Le Groupement Instruction et Entraînement à Ste Croix (Bruges)

Le Groupement Logistique à Ostende

DIPLOMATIC REPRESENTATION
Military, Naval and Air Attaché

LONDON
Lt. Colonel R. C. Close

WASHINGTON
Lt. Général Avi. van Rolleghens

PARIS
Colonel Ch. F. J. Laurent

BONN
Col. Avi. P. M. de Rijcker

SPAIN

COMMANDING OFFICERS

CHIEF OF NAVAL STAFF
Admiral A. Baturone

2ND CHIEF OF NAVAL STAFF
Vice-Admiral I. Martel

GENERAL SECRETARY
Admiral E. Barbudo

CHIEF OF THE DEPARTMENT OF PERSONNEL
Vice-Admiral J. Pery

CHIEF OF LOGISTIC SUPPORT
Vice-Admiral G. Diaz

DIRECTOR OF NAVAL TRAINING
Rear-Admiral F. Nuñnez

CHIEF OF ESCORT COMMAND
Rear-Admiral E. Vázquez

CHIEF OF AMPHIBIOUS COMMAND
Rear-Admiral J. Moscoso

FLEET TRAINING COMMANDER
Rear-Admiral F. Pita da Veiga

COMMANDER OF MINESWEEPING GROUP
Captain J. L. Rodríguez

COMMANDER-IN-CHIEF, CADIZ NAVAL BASE
Admiral M. A. García Agulló

COMMANDER-IN-CHIEF, EL FERROL NAVAL BASE
Admiral A. Lostau

COMMANDER-IN-CHIEF, CARTAGENA NAVAL BASE
Admiral M. Gamboa

COMMANDER 11 DESTROYER SQUADRON
Captain G. Díaz del Río

COMMANDER 21 DESTROYER SQUADRON
Captain M. Pieltain

COMMANDER 31 DESTROYER SQUADRON
Captain J. A. Peral

COMMANDER 41 CORVETTE SQUADRON
Captain M. Durán

COMMANDER 51 FRIGATE SQUADRON
Captain V. Alberto

CAPTAIN OF CRUISER CANARIAS
Captain E. Arévalo

CAPTAIN OF T/A CASTILLA
Captain L. Leal

CAPTAIN OF T/A ARAGON
Captain P.C. Rey

CAPTAIN OF HELICOPTER CARRIER DEDALO
Captain J. Díaz

NAVAL ATTACHES

U.S.A.
Captain J. García-Parreño
1669 Columbia Road, N.W. 110-111, Washington, D.C. 20009

ARGENTINE CHILE AND URUGUAY
Captain M. Romero
Rodriguez Peña 2053, 6° A, Buenos Aires

BRAZIL
Captain G. Matéu
Rua Ministro Viveiros de Castro 62, Rio de Janeiro

FRANCE, BRUSSELS AND HOLLAND
Captain J. M. de la Guardia
11 Avenue Marceau, Paris, 8e

ITALY AND GREECE
Captain C. González-Aller
Lungotevere dei Mellini 7/5 Rome

PORTUGAL
Rua do Salitre 1, Lisbon

GREAT BRITAIN AND SWEDEN
Captain J. C. Muñoz-Delgado
3 Hans Crescent, London S.W.1.

SWEDEN

COMMAND STRUCTURE

COMMANDER-IN-CHIEF ROYAL SWEDISH NAVY
Vice Admiral Ü. F. Lindemalm

CHIEF OF NAVAL STAFF
Major General (CA) B. L. A. Westin

DIRECTOR NAVAL MATERIAL DEPARTMENT
Commodore (E) H.W. Hallberg

COMMANDER-IN-CHIEF ACTIVE FLEET
Rear Admiral D. Arvas

CHIEF OF STAFF ACTIVE FLEET
Commodore A. Berggren

1ST DESTROYER FLOTILLA
Commodore P. Y. Rudberg

1ST SUBMARINE FLOTILLA
Commodore S. R. V. Skedelius

NAVAL BASE COMMANDERS

EAST
Rear Admiral C. E. Blidberg

SOUTH
Commorodre E. H. R. Gottfridsson

WEST
Commodore N. G. Arnell

COAST ARTILLERY DEFENCE DISTRICT COMMANDERS

NORRLAND
Colonel (CA) P. J. O. Beckman

STOCKHOLM
Colonel (CA) K. L. Karlberg

GOTLAND
Colonel (CA) K. E. Lyth

BLEKINGE
Colonel (CA) B. Engwall

GOTEBORG
Colonel (CA) P. H. L. Carleson

(CA=Coastal Artillery)

NAVAL SCHOOLS

ROYAL NAVAL COLLEGE NÄSBY TÄBY
Commodore W. Edenberg

NAVAL TRAINING CENTRE, BERGA
Commodore T. L. Norinder

NAVAL TRAINING CENTRE, KARLSKRONA
Commodore H. G. Petrelius

COAST ARTILLEY SCHOOL SUNDBYBERG
Colonel (CA) K. E. F. Werner

NAVAL ATTACHES

WASHINGTON AND OTTAWA
Captain N. L. Lindgren

LONDON AND THE HAGUE
Captain S. L. Ahrén

COPENHAGEN AND BONN
Captain N. P. M. Flodérus

MOSCOW AND WARSAW
Commander E. O. Stenberg

THAILAND

NAVAL COMMAND STRUCTURE

DEPUTY COMMANDER-IN-CHIEF
Admiral Ananda Nateroj

ASSISTANT COMMANDER-IN-CHIEF
Admjral Siri Grachangnetara

CHIEF OF STAFF
Admiral Tavil Rayananon

COMMANDER-IN-CHIEF OF THE FLEET
Admiral Nai Nopakun

DEPUTY COMMANDER-IN-CHIEF OF THE FLEET
Vice-Admiral Cherdchai Thomya

CHIEF OF STAFF OF THE FLEET
Vice-Admiral Kawee Singha

COMMANDANT ROYAL THAI MARINE CORPS
Rear-Admiral Sophon Suyarnsettakorn

NAVAL ATTACHES

U.S.A.
Captain Tada Ditbanjong, RTN (Attaché)
Commander Pote Sattaboos RTN (Assistant)
Office of the Thai Naval Attache, 6820 Millwood Road Kenwood Park, Bethesda, Maryland 20034

UNITED KINGDOM
Captain Ampol Nabangchang RTN (Attaché)
Commander Prasarn Chuchinda RTN (Assistant)
Office of the Thai Naval Attache Royal Thai Embassy, 30 Queen's Gate, London S.W.7

FRANCE
Captain Vichit Vanavichai RTN (Attaché)
Ambassade de Royale de Thailande Bureau de IL'Attache Naval, 8 Rue Greuze, Paris XVIe

JAPAN
Captain Boonnuk Budhichun RTN
Office of the Naval Attache, No. 8-21, 2-Chome, Yoyogi Uehara-cho, Shiburya-ku, Tokyo

TAIWAN
Captain Kitti Nakages, RTN (Attache)
Office of the Naval Attache Royal Thai Embassy, 106 West Ningpo Street, Taipei

PHILIPPINES
Captain Prapat Krisanacharn RTN (Attache)
Office of the Naval Attache Royal Thai Embassy, 6th Floor, Oledan Building Ayala Avenue, Makati, Rizal

INDIA
Captain Talang Charntanaprayoon RTN (Attaché)
Office of the Naval Attaché Royal Thai Embassy Chanakyapuri

UNITED KINGDOM

ADMIRALS OF THE FLEET

H. R. H. THE DUKE OF WINDSOR

LORD TOVEY OF LANGTON MATRAVERS

LORD FRASER OF NORTH CAPE

SIR ALGERNON USBORNE WILLIS

H. R. H. PRINCE PHILIP, DUKE OF EDINBURGH

SIR GEORGE ELVERY CREASY

THE EARL MOUNTBATTEN OF BURMA, PERSONAL AIDE-DE-CAMP TO THE QUEEN AND COLONEL COMMANDANT, ROYAL MARINES

SIR CASPAR JOHN
Ministry of Defence Main Building, Whitehall London S.W.1.

SIR VARYL CARGILL BEGG
Ministry of Defence Main building, Whitehall, London S.W.1.

ADMIRALS

CHAIRMAN OF THE NORTH ATLANTIC MILITARY COMMITTEE (Oct. 68)
Sir Nigel Stuart Henderson
Ministry of Defence, Main Building, Whitehall, London S.W.1.

CHIEF OF NAVAL STAFF AND FIRST SEA LORD (Aug. 68)
Sir Michael Le Fanu
Ministry of Defence, Main Building, Whitehall, London S.W.1

COMMANDER IN CHIEF, NAVAL HOME COMMAND (July 69)
Sir John Byng Frewen
Admiralty House, H.M. Dockyard, Portsmouth

SECOND SEA LORD AND CHIEF OF NAVAL PERSONNEL (Aug. 67)
Sir Frank Roddam Twiss
Ministry of Defence, Main Building, Whitehall, London S.W.1.

COMMANDER IN CHIEF, WESTERN FLEET, ALLIED COMMANDER IN CHIEF, CHANNEL AND COMMANDER IN CHIEF, ALLIED FORCES, EASTERN ATLANTIC (Oct. 67)
Sir John Fitzroy Duyland Bush
Eastbury Park, Northwood, Middx.

CONTROLLER OF THE NAVY (July 65)
Sir Horace Rochfort Law
M.O.D. Whitehall

COMMANDER IN CHIEF, FAR EAST (Mar. 69)
Sir Peter Hill-Norton
R.N.H.Q. Singapore

VICE ADMIRALS

VICE CHIEF OF THE DEFENCE STAFF (Nov. 67)
Sir Ian Leslie Trower Hogg
M.O.D. London

CHIEF OF ALLIED STAFF, NAVAL HEADQUARTERS SOUTHERN EUROPE (Oct. 67)
Sir Patrick Uniacke Bayly
Headquarters, Allied Naval Forces, Southern Europe, Malta, G.C.

FLAG OFFICER MEDWAY AND ADMIRAL SUPERINTENDENT, HM DOCKYARD, CHATHAM (July 66)
Wilfred John Parker
H.M.S. Pembroke, Chatham

FLAG OFFICER, NAVAL AIR COMMAND (Oct. 68)
Hugh Richard Benest Janvrin
Wykeham Hall, Lee-on-Solent, Hants.

FLAG OFFICER, SCOTLAND AND NORTHERN IRELAND, COMMANDER NORTHERN SUB-AREA, EASTERN ATLANTIC AND COMMANDER, NORE SUB-AREA CHANNEL (June 68)
Sir Ian Lachlan Mackay McGeogh
Maritime Headquarters, Rosyth, Scotland

COMMANDER FAR EAST FLEET
Sir William Donough O'Brien (until Sept 1969) then Acting Vice-Admiral Leslie Dereck Empson
R.N. H.Q. Singapore

FLAG OFFICER SUBMARINES AND COMSUBEASTLANT (Dec. 67)
Sir Michael Patrick Pollock
Fort Blockhouse, Gosport, Hants.

CHIEF OF FLEET SUPPORT (May 68)
Arthur Francis Turner
M.O.D. London

VICE CHIEF OF NAVAL STAFF (Dec. 68)
Edward Beckwith Ashmore
M.O.D. London

DEPUTY SUPREME ALLIED COMMANDER, ATLANTIC (Aug. 68)
Peter Marwell Compston
M.O.D. Northwood, Middx.

FLAG OFFICER, FLOTILLAS, WESTERN FLEET
Andrew MacKenzie Lewis (until Nov 1969) then Rear Admiral John Ernle Pope
R.N.H.Q. Plymouth

COMMANDANT JOINT SERVICES STAFF COLLEGE (March 68)
Dennis Howard Mason
Latimer, Bucks.

FLAG OFFICER, PLYMOUTH (Sep. 69)
Anthony Templer Frederick Griffith Griffin
H.M.S. Drake, Devonport

CHIEF NAVAL ENGINEER OFFICER AND SENIOR NAVAL REPRESENTATIVE, BATH (Feb. 68) AND DIRECTOR GENERAL SHIPS (May 68)
Robert George Raper
R.N.H.Q. Bath, Somerset

MEDICAL DIRECTOR-GENERAL OF THE NAVY
Surgeon Vice Admiral Eric Blackburn Bradbury
M.O.D. London

REAR ADMIRALS

FLAG OFFICER ROYAL YACHTS (Mar. 65)
Patrick John Morgan
H.M.S. Britannia, Portsmouth

HYDROGRAPHER OF THE NAVY (Jan. 66)
George Stephen Ritchie
M.O.D. London

CHIEF OF STAFF TO THE COMMANDER-IN-CHIEF WESTERN FLEET AND CHIEF-OF-STAFF TO CINCEASTLANT (Dec. 67)
Peter William Beckwith Ashmore (until Dec. 1969) then Ian Wyndham Jamieson
Plymouth, Devon

NAVAL DEPUTY TO CINCAFNORTH (July 66)
George Hammond Evans
M.O.D. London

ADMIRAL SUPERINTENDENT HM DOCKYARD, ROSYTH (Sept. 66)
William Terence Colborne Ridley
Scotland

ADMIRAL SUPERINTENDENT, HM DOCKYARD, DEVONPORT (Oct 66)
Denis Bryan Harvey Wildish
Devon

DIRECTOR-GENERAL NAVAL PERSONAL SERVICES (Sept. 68)
John Edward Ludgate Martin
M.O.D. London

DIRECTOR-GENERAL DOCKYARDS AND MAINTENANCE (Aug. 67)
William Allen Haynes
M.O.D. London

HMS ST ANGELO, MALTA
Dudley Leslie Davenport (former Flag Officer, Malta)
M.O.D. London

ASSISTANT CHIEF OF NAVAL STAFF (OPERATIONS AND AIR)
Douglas Granger Parker (July 69)
M.O.D. London

DIRECTOR-GENERAL AIRCRAFT (NAVAL) (Jan. 67)
John Bayley Holt
Louis Edward Stewart Holland Le Bailly
M.O.D. London

FLAG OFFICER, AIRCRAFT CARRIERS AND AMPHIBIOUS SHIPS (Sept. 68) AND COMCARSTRIKGRUTWO (June 68)
Michael Frampton Fell
Fort Southwick, Fareham, Hants.

DIRECTOR, MANAGEMENT AND SUPPORT (INTELLIGENCE) (Feb. 69)
George Archer Henderson
M.O.D. London

DIRECTOR-GENERAL NAVAL MANPOWER (May 67)
Frank Douglas Holford
M.O.D. London

CHIEF OF STAFF TO COMMANDER-IN-CHIEF FAR EAST (June 67)
Michael Donald Kyrle-Pope
Headquarters, Far East Command, Phoenix Park, Singapore

NAVAL SECRETARY (Nov. 67)
David Arthur Dunbar-Nasmith
M.O.D. London

DEPUTY CONTROLLER OF AIRCRAFT (ROYAL NAVY) MINISTRY OF TECHNOLOGY (Feb. 69)
Philip Holden Crothers Illingworth
Millbank Tower, London S.W.1.

ASSISTANT CHIEF OF STAFF (LOGISTICS) ON STAFF OF SUPREME ALLIED COMMANDER EUROPE (July 1969)
Arthur Frederick Caswell
Northwood Middx.

CHIEF STAFF OFFICER (TECHNICAL) TO COMMANDER IN CHIEF WESTERN FLEET AND INSPECTOR GENERAL FLEET MAINTENANCE (Aug. 67)
Gambier John Byng Noel
R.N.H.Q. Portsmouth, Hants

REPRESENTATIVE IN EUROPE OF SUPREME ALLIED COMMANDER ALLIED FORCES, ATLANTIC (July 68)
George Cunningham Leslie
M.O.D. Northwood, Middx.

FLAG OFFICER, SECOND-IN-COMMAND, FAR EAST FLEET (Aug 69)
Terence Thornton Lewin
H.M.S. Terror, Singapore

FLAG OFFICER NAVAL FLYING TRAINING (Feb. 68)
Cedric Kenelm Roberts
H.M.S. Heron, Yeovilton, Somerset

SENIOR-NAVAL MEMBER AND VICE-PRESIDENT (NAVAL) OF THE ORDNANCE BOARD (Feb. 68)
Desmond Noble Callaghan
M.O.D. London

CHIEF OF STAFF TO COMMANDER, FAR EAST FLEET (Dec. 67)
Ian David McLaughlan
R.N.H.Q. Singapore

ADMIRAL COMMANDING RESERVES AND DIRECTOR-GENERAL NAVAL RECRUITING (Feb. 68)
Basil Charles Godfrey Place V.C., D.S.C.
M.O.D. London

DUTY WITH CHIEF OF NAVAL SUPPLIES AND TRANSPORT AND VICE-CONTROLLER (April 68)
John Douglas Trythall
M.O.D. London

FLAG OFFICER, GIBRALTAR ADMIRAL SUPERINTENDENT, HM DOCKYARD, GIBRALTAR (April 68)
Ian Wyndham Jamieson (until Oct. 1969) then Arthur Rodney Barry Sturdee

DIRECTOR-GENERAL WEAPONS (NAVAL) (May 68)
Ian Steward McIntosh
M.O.D. London

ADMIRAL SUPERINTENDENT, HM DOCKYARD, PORTSMOUTH (July 68)
Arthur MacKenzie Power
Hants

ASSISTANT CHIEF OF NAVAL STAFF (OPERATIONAL REQUIREMENTS) (May 68)
John Rae McKaig
M.O.D. London

ASSISTANT CONTROLLER (POLARIS) (Aug. 68)
George Francis Allan Trewby
HMS Neptune, Clyde, Scotland

ADMIRAL PRESIDENT, ROYAL NAVAL COLLEGE, GREENWICH (Sept. 68)
Edward Findlay Gueritz
Greenwich, London

REAR-ADMIRAL ENGINEERING ON STAFF OF FLAG OFFICER NAVAL AIR COMMAND (Jan. 69)
Richard Douglas Roberts
M.O.D. London

FLAG OFFICER, ADMIRALTY INTERVIEW BOARD (Jan. 69)
Charles Courtney Anderson
M.O.D. London

SENIOR, ROYAL NAVY MEMBER, IMPERIAL DEFENCE COLLEGE (Jan. 69)
Edward Gerard Napier Mansfield

FLAG OFFICER SEA TRAINING (May 69)
John Anthony Rose Troup
M.O.D. London

Frederick Charles William Lawson (former Admiral Superintendent, Dockyard, Singapore)
M.O.D. London

ASSISTANT CHIEF OF NAVAL STAFF (POLICY) (June 69)
Ian Easton
M.O.D. London

FLAG OFFICER, MALTA AND NATO COMMANDER SOUTH EASTERN AREA, MEDITERRANEAN (June 1969)
Rear-Admiral Derrick George Kent
H.M.S. St. Angelo, Malta, G.C.

COMMAND MEDICAL OFFICER AND MEDICAL OFFICER IN CHARGE, RN HOSPITAL, HASLAR (June 69)
Surgeon Rear-Admiral Nicol Sinclair Hepburn

COMMAND MEDICAL OFFICER AND MEDICAL OFFICER IN CHARGE, RN HOSPITAL, PLYMOUTH (Oct. 66)
Surgeon Rear-Admiral Stanley Miles

DIRECTOR OF NAVAL DENTAL SERVICES (Feb. 68)
Surgeon Rear-Admiral (D) William Ivan Forrest
RN Hospital, Haslar

DIRECTOR OF THE NAVAL EDUCATION SERVICE
Instructor Rear Admiral Albert John Bellamy
M.O.D. London

COMMANDANT-GENERAL, ROYAL MARINES
Lieutenant General Peter William Cradock Hellings
M.O.D. London

CHAPLAIN OF THE FLEET
The Venerable Archdeacon Ambrose Walter Marcus Weekes
M.O.D. London

COMMODORES

COMMODORE-IN-CHARGE AND QUEEN'S HARBOUR MASTER, HONG KONG
Phillip Roger Canning Higham

COMMANDER NAVAL FORCES, BAHREIN PERSIAN GULF
Kenneth Lee-White

COMMODORE SUPERINTENDENT, SINGAPORE
Michael Harold Griffin

COMMODORE-IN-CHARGE, CLYDE, SCOTLAND
Peter George La Nieve

COMMODORE AMPHIBIOUS WARFARE
Thomas Wathen Stocker

SENIOR BRITISH NAVAL OFFICER, RSA NAVY HQ, SIMONSTOWN SOUTH AFRICA
Thomas Evelyn Fanshawe

SENIOR NAVAL OFFICER IRELAND ISLAND, BERMUDA, WEST INDIES
Martin Noel Lucey

MAJOR SHIPS IN COMMISSION
Aircraft Carriers

EAGLE
Captain J. D. Treacher

HERMES
Captain P. M. Austin

Commando Ships

ALBION
Captain M. S. Ollivant

BULWARK
Captain J. A. Templeton-Cotill

Command Ships

BLAKE
Captain R. F. Plugge DSC

County Class

HAMPSHIRE
Captain R. P. Clayton

LONDON
Captain P. G. Loasby DSC

GLAMORGAN
Captain S. L. McArdle MVO, GM

FIFE
Captain W. D. S. Scott

NORFOLK
Captain B. H. G. M. Baynham

Assault Ships

FEARLESS
Captain J. R. S. Gerard-Pearce

INTREPID
Captain J. H. F. Eberle

Fleet Submarines

VALIANT
Commander G. R. King

WARSPITE
Commander J. B. Hervey

Polaris Armed Submarines

RESOLUTION
Commander R. H. Mann (Port Crew) and Cdr. G.A.S. Paul (Starboard Crew)

REPULSE
Commander J. R. Wadman (Port Crew) and Cdr. A. J. Whetstone (Starboard Crew)

c/o BFPO Ships London

U.S.A.

Names in parenthises indicate second or additional duty assignment; asterisks indicate naval aviators (Flag Officers only); # indicates Captains selected for promotion to Rear-Admiral.
Restricted line and staff corps designations:

AED	Aeronautical Engineering Duty
CEC	Civil Engineer Corps
DC	Dental Corps
ED	Engineering Duty
JAGC	Judge Advocate General's Corps
CHC	Chaplain Corps
MC	Medical Corps
SC	Supply Corps
SD	Special Duty
OED	Ordnance Engineering Duty

OFFICE OF THE SECRETARY OF THE NAVY
The Pentagon, Washington, DC 20350

SECRETARY OF THE NAVY
Hon. John H. Chafee

UNDER SECRETARY OF THE NAVY
Hon. John W. Warner

ASSISTANT SECRETARY OF THE NAVY (Manpower & Reserve Affairs)
Hon. J. D. Hittle

ASSISTANT SECRETARY OF THE NAVY (Installations & Logistics)
Hon. Frank Sanders

ASSISTANT SECRETARY OF THE NAVY (Financial Management); Comptroller
HON. Charles A. Bowsher

ASSISTANT SECRETARY OF THE NAVY (Research & Development)
Hon. Robert A. Frosch

DEPARTMENT OF THE NAVY STAFF OFFICES

ADMINISTRATIVE OFFICER
John H. Walter

DIRECTOR, CIVILIAN MANPOWER MANAGEMENT
Robert H. Willey

COMPTROLLER
Charles A. Bowsher

DEPUTY
Rear-Admiral Eli T. Reich (October 1967)

DIRECTOR OF BUDGETS & REPORTS
Rear-Admiral Walter D. Gaddis (July 1968)

DIRECTOR OF FINANCIAL MANAGEMENT
Rear-Admiral Kenneth E. Wheeler (July 1967)

AUDITOR GENERAL; DIRECTOR, NAVAL AUDIT SERVICE
Rear-Admiral Roland Rieve (SC) (June 1969)

JUDGE ADVOCATE GENERAL; DEPARTMENT OF DEFENSE REPRESENTATIVE IN LAW OF THE SEA MATTERS
Rear-Admiral Joseph B. McDevitt (JAGC) (April 1968)

DEPUTY
Rear-Admiral Donald D. Chapman (JAGC) (May 1968)

CHIEF OF LEGISLATIVE AFFAIRS
Rear-Admiral Means Johnston, Jr. (January 1969)

CHIEF OF NAVAL RESEARCH; ASSISTANT OCEANOGRAPHER FOR OCEAN SCIENCES
Rear-Admiral Thomas B. Owen (ED) (July 1967)

DIRECTOR, OFFICE OF PROGRAM APPRAISAL
Rear-Admiral Raymond E. Peet (June 1969)

OCEANOGRAPHER OF THE NAVY
Rear-Admiral Odale D. Waters, Jr. (September 1965)

ASSISTANT OCEANOGRAPHER FOR OCEAN SCIENCES
(Rear-Admiral Thomas B. Owen)

ASSISTANT OCEANOGRAPHER FOR OCEAN ENGINEERING & DEVELOPMENT
Rear-Admiral Thomas D. Davies

ASSISTANT OCEANOGRAPHER FOR OPERATIONS
Vacant

OFFICE OF THE CHIEF OF NAVAL OPERATIONS (OPNAV)
The Pentagon, Washington, D.C. 20350

CHIEF OF NAVAL OPERATIONS
Admiral Thomas H. Moorer* (August 1967)

VICE CHIEF OF NAVAL OPERATIONS
Admiral Bernard A. Clarey (January 1968)

ASSISTANT VICE CNO/DIRECTOR OF NAVAL ADMINISTRATION
Rear-Admiral Paul E. Hartmann* (May 1968)

DIRECTOR, NAVAL HISTORY DIVISION
Rear-Admiral Ernest M. Eller (Retired) (September 1956)

DIRECTOR, NAVY PROGRAM PLANNING
Vice-Admiral C. Edwin Bell

DIRECTOR GENERAL PLANNING & PROGRAMMING DIVISION

DIRECTOR INFORMATION SYSTEMS DIVISION
Rear-Admiral Roger W. Paine, Jr. (January 1968)

ASSISTANT CNO (INTELLIGENCE); COMMANDER NAVAL INTELLIGENCE COMMAND
Rear-Admiral Frederick J. Harlfinger II (August 1968)

DIRECTOR, LONG RANGE OBJECTIVES GROUP
Rear-Admiral Evan P. Aurand* (April 1967)

ASSISTANT CNO (COMMUNICATIONS & CRYPTOLOGY); COMMANDER NAVAL COMMUNICATIONS COMMAND
Rear-Admiral Francis J. Fritzpatrick (July 1968)

DIRECTOR ANIT-SUBMARINE WARFARE PROGRAMS
Vice-Admiral Turner F. Caldwell Jr,* (October 1967)

DIRECTOR SYSTEMS ANALYSIS DIVISION
Rear-Admiral John B. Davis, Jr. (August 1968)

DIRECTOR STRATEGIC OFFENSIVE AND DEFENSIVE SYSTEMS
Rear-Admiral Geroge H. Miller (February 1967)

ASSISTANT CNO (SAFETY)
Rear-Admiral Norvell G. Ward (October 1968)

CHIEF OF INFORMATION
Rear-Admiral Lawrence R. Geis* (September 1968)

NAVAL INSPECTOR GENERAL
Vice-Admiral Arthur R. Gralla (May 1969)

DEPUTY CNO (MANPOWER & NAVAL RESERVE)
Vice-Admiral Charles K. Duncan (April 1968)

ASSISTANT DEPUTY CNO (MANPOWER)
Rear-Admiral Burton H. Shupper (July 1968)

ASSISTANT DEPUTY CNO (RESERVE)
Rear-Admiral Julian T. Burke Jr. (January 1968)

DEPUTY CNO (FLEET OPERATIONS & READINESS)
Vice-Admiral Ralph W. Cousins* (July 1969)

ASSISTANT DEPUTY CNO (FLEET OPERATIONS & READINESS)
Rear-Admiral Robert E. Riera* (June 1968)

PROGRAM, CO-ORDINATOR DX/DXG PROGRAM
(Rear-Admiral Thomas R. Weschler) (March 1967)

ANTI-SHIP MISSILE DEFENSE CO-ORDINATOR
Rear-Admiral John E. Dacey (April 1968)

CVAN PROGRAM CO-ORDINATOR
(Rear-Admiral James L. Holloway) (February 1968)

DIRECTOR PLANS & PROGRAMS DIVISION
Captain J. T. Alexander

DIRECTOR SUBMARINE WARFARE DIVISION
Rear-Admiral Harold E. Shear (April 1969)

DIRECTOR ASW & OCEAN SURVEILLANCE DIVISION
Rear-Admiral Leslie J. O'Brien Jr. (June 1967)

DIRECTOR FLEET OPERATIONS DIVISION
Rear-Admiral Pierre N. Charbonnet Jr.* (September 1969)

DIRECTOR STRIKE WARFARE DIVISION
Rear-Admiral James L. Holloway III* (March 1969)

DIRECTOR ELECTRONIC WARFARE & TACTICAL COMMAND SYSTEMS DIVISION
Rear-Admiral George S. Morrison* (September 1969)

DIRECTOR SHIP CHARACTERISTICS DIVISION; CHAIRMAN, SHIP CHARACTERISTICS BOARD; PROGRAM CO-ORDINATOR, DX/DXG PROGRAM
Rear-Admiral Thomas R. Weschler (May 1968)

DIRECTOR FLEET READINESS & TRAINING DIVISION
Rear-Admiral Ben B. Pickett (July 1969)

DEPUTY CNO (LOGISTICS)
Vice-Admiral Earl R. Crawford (June 1969)

ASSISTANT DEPUTY CNO (LOGISTICS)

EXECUTIVE & PRESIDENT, NAVY BOARD OF INSPECTION & SURVEY
Rear-Admiral John D. Bulkeley (June 1967)

DIRECTOR LOGISTIC PLANS DIVISION
Rear-Admiral Fillmore B. Gilkeson* (July 1968)

DIRECTOR MATERIAL DIVISION
Captain J. B. Kaye

DIRECTOR INTERNATIONAL LOGISTICS DIVISION
Captain Strauss Leon

DIRECTOR SHIPS MATERIAL READINESS DIVISION
Rear-Admiral Emery A. Grantham (ED)

DIRECTOR SHORE INSTALLATIONS DIVISION
Rear-Admiral Lawrence G. Bernard (May 1969)

DEPUTY CNO (AIR)
Vice-Admiral Thomas F. Connolly* (November 1966)

ASSISTANT DEPUTY CNO (AIR)
Rear-Admiral Frederick H. Michaelis* (August 1968)

ASSISTANT DEPUTY CNO (MARINE AVIATION)
(Major General Keith B. McCutcheon)

DIRECTOR AVIATION PLANS & REQUIREMENTS DIVISION
Rear-Admiral William D. Houser* (November 1968)

DIRECTOR AVIATION PROGRAMS DIVISION
Rear-Admiral Robert B. Baldwin* (April 1969)

DEPUTY CHIEF OF STAFF (AIR) MARINE CORPS
Major-General Keith B. McCutcheon* (USMC)

ASSISTANT DEPUTY CHIEF OF STAFF (AIR) MARINE CORPS
Brigadier General William G. Johnson* (USMC)

DIRECTOR FLIGHT OPERATIONS DIVISION
Captain Glenn E. Lambert*

DIRECTOR AVIATION TRAINING DIVISION
Captain John M. Thomas*

DEPUTY CNO (PLANS & POLICY)
Vice-Admiral Francis J. Blouin (June 1968)

ASSISTANT DEPUTY CNO (PLANS & POLICY)
Rear-Admiral Frederick H. Schneider, Jr. (June 1969)

DIRECTOR STRATEGIC PLANS & POLICY DIVISION
Rear-Admiral John P. Weinel* (June 1969)

ASSISTANT DIRECTOR STRATEGIC PLANS & POLICY DIVISION
Rear-Admiral George C. Talley Jr.* (February 1968)

DIRECTOR POLITICO-MILITARY POLICY DIVISION
Rear-Admiral William W. Behrens Jr. (August 1968)

DIRECTOR PAN AMERICAN AFFAIRS & ADVISORY GROUPS DIVISION
Rear-Admiral Dean L. Axene (June 1969)

DIRECTOR FOREIGN MILITARY ASSISTANCE DIVISION
Captain George M. Hagerman

DEPUTY CNO (DEVELOPMENT)
Rear-Admiral Edward A. Ruckner (May 1967)

ASSISTANT DEPUTY CNO (DEVELOPMENT)
Rear-Admiral William N. Leonard* (February 1969)

DIRECTOR TECHNICAL ANALYSIS & ADVISORY GROUP
Dr. Robert O. Burns

DIRECTOR DEVELOPMENT PLANNING DIVISION
Captain Robert C. Gillette

DIRECTOR UNDERSEA AND STRATEGIC WARFARE DIVISION
Rear-Admiral Vincent P. Healey (April 1969)

DIRECTOR AIR SURFACE & ELECTRONIC WARFARE DIVISION
Rear-Admiral John K. Beling* (October 1967)

DIRECTOR ATOMIC ENERGY DIVISION
Captain J. G. Whiteaker

DIRECTOR NAVY SPACE PROGRAMS DIVISION
Rear-Admiral William J. Moran* (November 1968)

DEPARTMENT OF DEFENSE
Assignments held by Navy Flag officers

DIRECTOR WEAPONS SYSTEMS EVALUATION GROUP (WSEG)
Vice-Admiral Kleber S. Masterson (August 1966)

DEPUTY ASSISTANT SECRETARY OF DEFENSE (MANPOWER & RESERVE AFFAIRS)
Vice-Admiral William P. Mack (January 1969)

DEPUTY DIRECTOR (ADMINISTRATION EVALUATION & MANAGEMENT), OFFICE OF THE DIRECTOR DEFENSE RESEARCH & ENGINEERING (DDR&E)
Vice-Admiral Vincent P. de Poix* (February 1969)

DEPUTY DIRECTOR FOR INSPECTION SERVICES, OFFICE OF THE SECRETARY OF DEFENSE
Rear-Admiral Donald M. White* (July 1969)

SENIOR NAVAL MEMBER MILITARY STUDIES & LIAISON DIVISION, WSEG
Rear-Admiral Roy G. Anderson (March 1967)

DIRECTOR POLICY PLANNING STAFF, OFFICE OF THE SECRETARY OF DEFENSE (INTERNATIONAL SECURITY AFFAIRS) (ISA)
Rear-Admiral William E. Lemos* (March 1969)

DIRECTOR EAST ASIA & PACIFIC REGION, OFFICE OF THE SECRETARY OF DEFENSE (ISA)
Rear-Admiral Tazwell T. Shepard Jr.* (July 1968)

MILITARY ASSISTANT TO DEPUTY DIRECTOR (STRATEGIC & SPACE SYSTEMS) DDR&E
Rear-Admiral Kenneth C. Wallace (July 1968)

MILITARY ASSISTANT TO ASSISTANT SECRETARY OF DEFENSE (PUBLIC AFFAIRS) (PA)
Rear-Admiral Shannon D. Cramer Jr. (July 1968)

DEPUTY COMMANDER MILITARY TRAFFIC MANAGEMENT & TERMINAL SERVICES
Rear-Admiral Elliott Bloxom (SC) (July 1967)

DEPARTMENT OF DEFENSE REPRESENTATIVE IN LAW OF THE SEA MATTERS
(Rear-Admiral Joseph B. McDevitt)

NAVY DEPUTY TO THE DEPARTMENT OF DEFENSE MANAGER FOR MANNED SPACE FLIGHT SUPPORT OPERATIONS
Rear-Admiral Philip S. McManus (August 1968)

DEFENSE ATOMIC SUPPORT AGENCY (DASA)
T Building, Washington, D.C. 20350

DIRECTOR DEFENSE ATOMIC SUPPORT AGENCY
Vice-Admiral Lloyd M. Mustin (July 1968)

DEPUTY COMMANDER, FIELD COMMAND (WEAPONS & TRAINING)
Rear-Admiral William H. Livingston* (August 1969)

DEFENSE INTELLIGENCE AGENCY (DIA)
The Pentagon, Washington, D.C. 20350

DEPUTY DIRECTOR DEFENSE INTELLIGENCE AGENCY
Vice-Admiral Vernon L. Lowrance (November 1966)

ASSISTANT CHIEF OF STAFF FOR PLANS & PROGRAMS
Rear-Admiral Donald M. Showers (SD) (July 1966)

DEPUTY ASSISTANT DIRECTOR, INTELLIGENCE PRODUCTION
Rear-Admiral Daniel E. Bergin Jr. (July 1968)

DEFENSE COMMUNICATIONS AGENCY (DCA) 8th & South Courthouse Road, Arlington, Virginia 22204

VICE DIRECTOR DEFENSE COMMUNICATIONS AGENCY
Rear-Admiral Robert H. Weeks (April 1968)

DEPUTY DIRECTOR PLANS
#Captain Jon L. Boyes (July 1969)

DEFENSE SUPPLY AGENCY (DSA)
Alexandria, Virginia 22314

ASSISTANT DIRECTOR PLANS PROGRAMS & SYSTEMS
Rear-Admiral Ira F. Haddock (SC) (September 1967)

DEPUTY DIRECTOR FOR CONTRACT ADMINISTRATIVE SERVICES
Rear-Admiral Joseph L. Howard (SC) (July 1968)

EXECUTIVE DIRECTOR TECHNICAL & LOGISTIC SERVICES
Rear-Admiral John P. Sager (AED) (July 1969)

COMMANDER DEFENSE FUEL SUPPLY CENTER (ALEXANDRIA, VIRGINIA)
Rear-Admiral Fowler W. Martin (SC) (November 1966)

COMMANDER DEFENSE INDUSTRIAL SUPPLY CENTER (PHILADELPHIA, PENNSYLVANIA)
Rear-Admiral Grover C. Heffner (SC) (August 1967)

JOINT SERVICE STAFF AND COMMAND ACTIVITIES Assignments held by Navy Flag Officers

COMMANDER-IN-CHIEF ATLANTIC (CINCLANT); COMMANDER-IN-CHIEF US ATLANTIC FLEET (CINCLANT FLEET); SUPREME ALLIED COMMANDER ATLANTIC (SACLANT)
Admiral Ephraim P. Holmes (June 1967)

CHIEF OF STAFF, CINCLANT
(Vice-Admiral William I. Martin)

COMMANDER-IN-CHIEF PACIFIC (CINCPAC)
Admiral John S. McCain Jr. (July 1968)

DEPUTY CHIEF OF STAFF FOR MILITARY ASSISTANCE LOGISTICS & ADMINISTRATION
Rear-Admiral Frederick E. Janney (June 1969)

ASSISTANT CHIEF OF STAFF FOR PLANS
Rear-Admiral Walter L. Curtis Jr. (September 1967)

DEPUTY ASSISTANT CHIEF OF STAFF FOR INTELLIGENCE
Rear-Admiral Maurice H. Rindskopf (September 1967)

DIRECTOR JOINT STAFF JOINT CHIEFS OF STAFF (JCS)
Vice-Admiral Nels C. Johnson (July 1968)

DIRECTOR J-4 (LOGISTICS)
Vice-Admiral Lot Ensey (September 1967)

SPECIAL ASSISTANT FOR STRATEGIC MOBILITY
Rear-Admiral John H. Maurer (July 1968)

DEPUTY DIRECTOR J-5 (PLANS & POLICY)
Rear-Admiral Frank W. Vannoy (July 1968)

CHIEF FAR EAST DIVISION J-5 (PLANS & POLICY)
Rear-Admiral Horace H. Epes Jr.* (July 1968)

DIRECTOR J-1 (PERSONNEL)
Rear-Admiral Percival W. Jackson* (January 1968)

DEPUTY DIRECTOR NATIONAL MILITARY COMMAND CENTER, J-3
Rear-Admiral Oliver H. Penny Jr. (July 1969)

CHIEF JOINT COMMAND & CONTROL REQUIREMENTS GROUP
Rear-Admiral Leslie H. Sell (August 1968)

DEPUTY DIRECTOR NATIONAL MILITARY COMMAND CENTER, J-3
Rear-Admiral Ward S. Miller* (June 1969)

VICE DIRECTOR J-3 (OPERATIONS)
Rear-Admiral Frederic A. Bardshar* (June 1969)

CHIEF OF STAFF US EUROPEAN COMMAND (CINCEUR)
Vice-Admiral John A. Tyree Jr. (July 1968)

DIRECTOR COMMUNICATIONS-ELECTRONICS CINCEUR; CHIEF DEFENSE COMMUNICATIONS AGENCY EUROPE
Rear-Admiral William E. Kuntz (June 1968)

DEPUTY DIRECTOR INTELLIGENCE
Rear-Admiral James C. Longino Jr.* (July 1967)

DEPUTY DIRECTOR JOINT STRATEGIC TARGET PLANNING STAFF
Vice-Admiral Noel A. M. Gayler* (September 1967)

COMMANDER US TAIWAN DEFENSE COMMAND
Vice-Admiral John L. Chew (July 1967)

NAVAL MEMBER JOINT LOGISTIC REVIEW BOARD
Vice-Admiral Edwin B. Hooper (March 1969)

CHIEF JOINT US MILITARY GROUP-MILITARY ASSISTANCE ADVISORY GROUP SPAIN
Rear-Admiral James O. Cobb* (November 1968)

CHIEF OF STAFF COMMANDER-IN-CHIEF US STRIKE COMMAND
Rear-Admiral John J. Lynch* (December 1968)

DEPUTY COMMANDANT NATIONAL WAR COLLEGE
Rear-Admiral David B. Bell (July 1968)

COMMANDER ICELAND DEFENSE FORCE
Rear-Admiral Mayo A. Hadden Jr.* (January 1969)

DEFENSE SUPPLY AGENCY MEMBER JOINT LOGISTICS REVIEW BOARD
Rear-Admiral John W. Bottoms (SC) (May 1969)

CHAIRMAN'S STAFF GROUP OFFICE OF THE CHAIRMAN JCS
Captain Robinson C. Rembrandt (March 1969)

COMMANDER MIDDLE EAST FORCE
Rear-Admiral Ed R. King (June 1968)

COMMANDER SOUTH ATLANTIC FORCE
Rear-Admiral James A. Dare (July 1968)

NORTH ATLANTIC TREATY ORGANIZATION
Assignments held by Navy Flag Officers

SUPREME ALLIED COMMANDER ATLANTIC (SACLANT)
(Admiral Ephraim P. Holmes)

COMMANDER-IN-CHIEF ALLIED FORCES SOUTHERN EUROPE (CINCSOUTH)
Admiral Horacio Rivero Jr. (February 1968)

COMMANDER STRIKING FLEET ATLANTIC
(Vice-Admiral Benedict J. Semmes)

CHIEF OF STAFF SACLANT
Vice Admiral James W. O'Grady* (September 1968)

COMMANDER, IBERIAN ATLANTIC COMMAND; CHIEF MILITARY ASSISTANCE ADIVSORY GROUP PORTUGAL
Rear-Admiral Eugene B. Fluckey (July 1968)

COMMANDER MARITIME AIR MEDITERRANEAN
(Rear-Admiral Allan F. Fleming)

ASSISTANT CHIEF OF STAFF FOR LOGISTICS CINCSOUTH
Rear-Admiral Arthur G. Esch (July 1968)

DEPUTY COMMANDER NAVAL STRIKING & SUPPORT FORCES SOUTHERN EUROPE
Rear-Admiral George L. Cassell* (November 1968)

DEPUTY CHIEF OF STAFF & ASSISTANT CHIEF OF STAFF FOR PLANS POLICY & OPERATIONS SACLANT
Rear-Admiral Marmaduke G. Bayne (August 1968)

US ATLANTIC FLEET
Norfolk, Virginia 23511

COMMANDER-IN-CHIEF ATLANTIC FLEET
(Admiral Ephraim P. Holmes)

DEPUTY & CHIEF OF STAFF
Vice-Admiral William I. Martin* (August 1968)

COMMANDER AMPHIBIOUS FORCE
Vice-Admiral Luther C. Heinz (July 1968)

COMMANDER SUBMARINE FORCE
Vice-Admiral Arnold F. Schade (November 1966)

COMMANDER ASW FORCE
Vice-Admiral Paul Masterton* (October 1967)

COMMANDER, NAVAL AIR FORCE
Vice-Admiral Robert L. Townsend (March 1969)

COMMANDING GENERAL FLEET MARINE FORCE; COMMANDING GENERAL II MARINE EXPEDITIONARY FORCE
Lieutenant-General Richard G. Weede (USMC)

COMMANDER CRUISER-DESTROYER FORCE; COMMANDER NAVAL BASE NEWPORT RHODE ISLAND
Rear-Admiral John N. Shaffer (July 1969)

COMMANDER SERVICE FORCE
Rear-Admiral Richard E. Pratt (April 1969)

COMMANDER TRAINING COMMAND
Rear-Admiral John R. Wadleigh (June 1969)

COMMANDER AMPHIBIOUS TRAINING COMMAND
Captain Edwin K. Snyder (August 1969)

COMMANDER MINE FORCE
Rear-Admiral Douglas C. Plate (November 1968)

FLEET MAINTENANCE OFFICER & ASSISTANT CHIEF OF STAFF MAINTENANCE & LOGISTIC PLANS; MAINTENANCE OFFICER CINCLANT & CINC WESTERN ATLANTIC
Rear-Admiral John W. Dolan Jr. (ED) (October 1967)

FLEET SURGEON & ASSISTANT CHIEF OF STAFF MEDICINE
Rear-Admiral Walter Welham (MC) (October 1966)

FLEET SUPPLY OFFICER & ASSISTANT CHIEF OF STAFF SUPPLY
Rear-Admiral Stuart H. Smith (SC) (July 1967)

ASSISTANT CHIEF OF STAFF FOR FACILITIES ENGINEERING
(Rear-Admiral Paul E. Seufer)

FLEET DENTAL OFFICER & ASSISTANT CHIEF OF STAFF DENTISTRY; DIRECTOR DENTAL ACTIVITIES; 5th NAVAL DISTRICT; COMMANDING OFFICER DENTAL CLINIC NORFOLK; DENTAL OFFICER NAVAL BASE NORFOLK
Rear-Admiral Maurice E. Simpson (DC) (July 1967)

INSPECTOR GENERAL
Rear-Admiral Michael V. Moore (June 1969)

DEPUTY CHIEF OF STAFF & DEPUTY CHIEF OF STAFF FOR PLANS & OPERATIONS
Rear-Admiral Robert B. Erly (June 1969)

DEPUTY CHIEF OF STAFF FOR LOGISTICS & MANAGEMENT
Rear-Admiral Lucien B. McDonald (November 1968)

FLEET CHAPLAIN
Captain Francis L. Garrett (CHC) (July 1969)

COMMANDER SECOND FLEET; COMMANDER STRIKING FLEET ATLANTIC
Vice-Admiral Benedict J. Semmes Jr. (April 1968)

COMMANDER SIXTH FLEET
Vice-Admiral David C. Richardson* (August 1968)

COMMANDER ASW FORCE SIXTH FLEET
(Rear-Admiral Allan F. Fleming)

COMMANDER CRUISER-DESTROYER FLOTILLA

CRUDESFLOT 2
Rear-Admiral Ernest W. Dobie Jr. (October 1968)

CRUDESFLOT 4
Rear-Admiral John D. Chase (July 1969)

CRUDESFLOT 6
Rear-Admiral Lester E. Hubbell (April 1969)

CRUDESFLOT 8
Rear-Admiral Frank H. Price Jr. (September 1968)

CRUDESFLOT 10
Rear-Admiral Parker B. Armstrong (March 1969)

CRUDESFLOT 12
Rear-Admiral Isaac C. Kidd Jr. (August 1968)

COMMANDER SUBMARINE FLOTILLA

SUBFLOT 2
Rear-Admiral Eugene P. Wilkinson (June 1969)

SUBFLOT 6
Rear-Admiral James B. Osborn (January 1969)

SUBFLOT 8; CPMMANDER SUBMARINE MEDITERRANEAN
Rear-Admiral Oliver Hazard Perry Jr.

COMMANDER AMPHIBIOUS GROUP
PHIBGRU 2
Rear-Admiral William R. McKinney (August 1968)

PHILBGRU 4
Rear-Admiral Philip A. Beshany (May 1969)

COMMANDER CARRIER DIVISION
CARDIV 2
Rear-Admiral Jack M. James* (May 1969)

CARDIV 4
Rear-Admiral William H. House* (March 1969)

CARDIV 6
Rear-Admiral William M. Harnish* (August 1969)

CARDIV 14
Rear-Admiral Frank B. Stone* (February 1969)

CARDIV 16
Rear-Admiral James L. Abbot Jr.* (July 1969)

CARDIV 20
(Rear-Admiral Joseph B. Tibbets)

COMMANDER, INSHORE UNDERSEA WARFARE GROUP 2
Captain C. W. Ward

COMMANDER DESTROYER SQUADRON
DESRON 2
Captain F. C. Dunham Jr.

DESRON 4
Captain F. E. McKenzie

DESRON 6
Captain A. H. McCain

DESRON 8
Captain C. E. Landis

DESRON 10
Captain R. N. Moss

DESRON 12
Captain J. E. Murphy

DESRON 14
Captain S. L. Rusk

DESRON 16
Captain R. Dicori

DESRON 18
Captain J. F. Ackerman

DESRON 20
Captain R. W. Allen

DESRON 22
Captain W. B. Morrow

DESRON 24
Captain R. S. Lewellen

DESRON 26
Captain B. E. Gustafson

RESERVE DESRON 30
Captain W. J. Millar

DESRON 32
Captain J. H. Hooper

RESERVE DESRON 34
Captain C. F. Allen

DESRON 36
Captain P. L. Murphy

OMMANDER ESCORT SQUADRON
CORTON 6
Captain M. M. Zenni

CORTRON 8
Commander D. E. Pauly

CORTRON 10
Commander W. L. Read

OMMANDER DESTROYER DEVELOPMENT GROUP 2
aptain D. D. Ansel

OMMANDER AMPHIBIOUS SQUADRON
PHIBRON 2
Captain Robert F. Stanton

PHRIBRON 4
Captain J. F. Riley

PHIBRON 6
Captain Eugene M. Masica

PHIBRON 8
Captain John G. Now

PHIBRON 10
Captain J. P. Gutting

PHIBRON 12
Captain A. R. Trottier

COMMANDER SUBMARINE SQUADRON
SUBRON 2
Captain J. M. Snyder, Jr.

SUBRON 4
Captain H. R. Hanssen

SUBRON 6
Captain J. F. Heaid

SUBRON 8
Captain J. D. Eaton

SUBRON 10
Captain Frank T. Rawlings Jr.

SUBRON 12
Captain C. K. Schmidt

SUBRON 14
Captain B. F. Sherman Jr.

SUBRON 18
Captain W. M. Adams Jr.

COMMANDER SUBMARINE DEVELOPMENT GROUP 2
Captain C. E. Woods

COMMANDER SERVICE SQUADRON
SERVON 2
Captain K. C. Gummerson

SERVON 4
Captain E. S. Jackson

SERVON 6
Capt. H. W. Dawson

SERVON 8
Captain, Walter D. Chadwick

COMMANDER TACTICAL AIR CONTROL GROUP 2
Captain R. J. Dunn

COMMANDER BEACH GROUP 2
Captain V. J. Vaughan

COMMANDER SPECIAL WARFARE GROUP ATLANTIC
Captain F. M. Symons

US PACIFIC FLEET
Pearl Harbor, Hawaii
(Fleet Post Office, San Francisco, 96610)

COMMANDER-IN-CHIEF PACIFIC FLEET
Admiral John J. Hyland* (November 1967)

DEPUTY & CHIEF OF STAFF
Vice-Admiral Walter H. Baumberger (March 1967)

COMMANDER NAVAL AIR FORCE
Vice-Admiral Allen M. Shinn* (November 1966)

COMMANDER ASW FORCE
Vice-Admiral Harold G. Bowen Jr. (July 1967)

COMMANDER AMPHIBIOUS FORCE
Vice-Admiral John V. Smith (May 1968)

COMMANDER AMPHIBIOUS TRAINING COMMAND
Rear-Admiral David M. Robel (July 1969)

COMMANDER MINE FORCE; COMMANDER NAVAL BASE LOS ANGELES CALIFORNIA
Rear-Admiral Horace V. Bird (May 1967)

COMMANDER CRUISER-DESTROYER FROCE
Rear-Admiral Mason B. Freeman (March 1967)

COMMANDER TRAINING COMMAND
(Rear-Admiral Mason B. Freeman)

COMMANDER, SERVICE FORCE
Rear-Admiral Walter V. Combs Jr. (February 1968)

COMMANDER SUBMARINE FORCE
Rear-Admiral Walter L. Small Jr. (June 1968)

COMMANDING GENERAL FLEET MARINE FORCE
Lieutenant General Henry W. Buse Jr. (USMC)

DEPUTY CHIEF OF STAFF FOR PLANS & OPERATIONS
Rear-Admiral James D. Ramage* (October 1967)

FLEET SURGEON
Rear-Admiral Frank B. Voris* (MC) (July 1969)

FORCE SUPPLY OFFICER SERVICE FORCE PACIFIC; FLEET SUPPLY OFFICER
Rear-Admiral Elton W. Sutherling (SC) (June 1967)

FORCE CHAPLAIN SERVICE FORCE; FLEET CHAPLAIN
Rear-Admiral Henry J. Rotrige (CHC) (October 1968)

FLEET DENTAL OFFICER
Captain Victor J. Niiranen (DC)

INSPECTOR GENERAL
Rear-Admiral Joseph W. Williams Jr. (September 1967)

FLEET MAINTENANCE OFFICER; MAINTENANCE OFFICER SERVICE FORCE
Rear-Admiral David H. Jackson (ED) (July 1968)

COMMANDER FIRST FLEET
Vice-Admiral Bernard F. Roeder (July 1966)

COMMANDER SEVENTH FLEET
Vice-Admiral William F. Bringle* (November 1967)

COMMANDER ATTACK CARRIER STRIKING FORCE; COMMANDER CARRIER DIVISION 5
Vice-Admiral Maurice F. Weisner* (July 1969)

COMMANDER CRUISER-DESTROYER GROUP; COMMANDER CRUISER-DESTROYER FLOTILLA 3
Rear-Admiral Thomas J. Rudden Jr. (January 1968)

COMMANDER PATROL FORCE; COMMANDER FLEET AIR WING 1
Rear-Admiral William T. Rapp* (July 1968)

COMMANDER CRUISER-DESTROYER FLOTILLA
CRUDESFLOT 3
(Rear-Admiral Thomas J. Rudden Jr.)

CRUDESFLOT 7
Rear-Admiral Lloyd R. Vasey (October 1968)

CRUDESFLOT 9
Rear-Admiral Robert L. Baughan Jr. (August 1969)

CRUDESFLOT 11
Rear-Admiral Herbert H. Anderson (April 1969)

COMMANDER AMPHIBIOUS GROUP
PHIBGRU 1
Rear-Admiral Victor A. Dybdal (August 1969)

PHIBGRU 3
Rear-Admiral Edwin M. Rosenberg (December 1968)

COMMANDER ASW GROUP
ASW GROUP 1
Rear-Admiral Jerome H. King Jr. (July 1968)

ASW GROUP 3
Rear-Admiral Norman C. Gillette Jr.* (January 1969)

ASW GROUP 5
Rear-Admiral Herman J. Trum III* (June 1969)

COMMANDER CARRIER DIVISION
CARDIV 1
Rear-Admiral Malcolm W. Cagle* (June 1968)

CARDIV 3
Rear-Admiral Gerald E. Miller* (September 1968)

CARDIV 5
(Vice-Admiral Maurice F. Weisner)

CARDIV 7
Rear-Admiral Roy M. Isaman* (April 1969)

CARDIV 9
Rear-Admiral William R. McClendon* (August 1969)

COMMANDER DESTROYER FLOTILLA 5
Captain R. R. Law

COMMANDER COASTAL FLOTILLA 1
Captain R. F. Hoffman

COMMANDER LANDING SHIP FLOTILLA 1
Captain R. B. Perez

COMMANDER MINE FLOTILLA 1
Captain A. J. Kodiz

COMMANDER MINE FLOTILLA 3
Captain H. R. Moore

COMMANDER RIVER ASSAULT FLOTILLA 1; COMMANDER RIVER SUPPORT SQUADRON 7
Captain Carvel H. Blair

COMMANDER RIVER PATROL FLOTILLA 5
Captain Joseph R. Faulk

COMMANDER SUBMARINE FLOTILLA
SUBFLOT 1
Captain Roy H. Gallemore

SUBFLOT 5
Captain A. G. Newton

SUBFLOT 7
Captain L. G. Yeich

COMMANDER SUBMARINE GROUP SAN FRANCISCO BAY
Captain Clifford M. Esler

COMMANDER UNDERSEA WARFARE GROUP 1
Captain Robert Fitzgerald

COMMANDER SERVICE GROUP 1
Captain John S. Oller Jr.

COMMANDER SERVICE GROUP 3
Rear-Admiral Robert L. J. Long (Sept. 1968)

COMMANDER DESTROYER SQUADRON
DESRON 1
Captain A. T. Emerson Jr.

DESRON 3
Captain W. N. P. Homer

DESRON 5
Captain J. C. Berriman

DESRON 7
Captain R. H. Rossell

DESRON 9
Captain J. M. Mason

DESRON 11
Captain G. W. Fromknecht

DESRON 13
Captain B. D. Gaw

DESRON 15
Captain L. D. Cummins

DESRON 17
Captain C. P. Rozier

DESRON 19
Captain J. W. Smith

DESRON 21
Captain E. J. Cummings Jr.

DESRON 23
Captain J. J. Doak Jr.

DESRON 25
Captain A. G. Russillo

RESERVE DESRON 27
Captain J. J. Hoblitzell III

DESRON 29
Captain R. A. Rowe

DESRON 31
Captain R. Kirk

COMMANDER ESCORT SQUADRON
CORTRON 5
Commander W. W. Erikson

CORTRON 7
Commander J. F. Murphy

COMMANDER LANDING SHIP SQUADRON
LANSHIPRON 1
Commander S. J. Sowinski

LANSHIPRON 2
Commander C. H. Cross

LANSHIPRON 3
Commander Richard D. Gillham

LANSHIPRON 9
Captain Paul B. Perez

COMMANDER AMPHIBIOUS SQUADRON
PHIBRON 1
Captain James E. McCauley

PHIBRON 3
Captain John B. Randolph

PHIBRON 5
Captain George W. Stroud

PHIBRON 7
Captain B. R. Dodson

PHIBRON 9
Captain A. L. Battson

PHIBRON 11
Captain L. Savadkin

COMMANDER SUBMARINE SQUADRON
SUBRON 1
Captain R. B. Cowdrey

SUBRON 3
Capt. Lewis H. Neeb

SUBRON 5
Captain Fred T. Berry

SUBRON 7
Captain A. G. Newton

SUBRON 15
Captain Cleo N. Mitchell Jr.

COMMANDER SUBMARINE DEVELOPMENT GROUP 1
Captain R. H. Gautier

COMMANDER SERVICE SQUADRON
SERVRON 1
(Captain A. F. Betzel)

SERVRON 3
(Rear-Admiral R. L. J. Long)

SERVRON 5
Captain R. F. Reilly

SERVRON 7
(Captain J. S. Oller Jr.)

SERVRON 9
Captain Russell B. Dodge Jr.

FLEET AIR COMMANDS

COMMANDER FLEET AIR JACKSONVILLE (NAS JACKSONVILLE, FLORIDA)
Rear-Admiral Robert J. Stroth* (October 1967)

COMMANDER FLEEET AIR QUONSET (NAS QUONSET POINT, RHODE ISLAND)
Rear-Admiral Joseph B. Tibbets* (October 1969)

COMMANDER FLEET AIR ALAMEDA (NAS ALAMEDA, CALIFORNIA)
Rear-Admiral James Ferris* (June 1969)

COMMANDER FLEET AIR SAN DIEGO (NAS NORTH ISLAND, CALIFORNIA)

COMMANDER FLEET AIR WHIDBEY (NAS WHIDBEY ISLAND, OAK HARBOR, WASHINGTON)
Rear-Admiral

COMMANDER FLEET AIR ALASKA (NS KODIAK, ALASKA)
(Rear-Admiral Eugene G. Fairfax)

COMMANDER FLEER AIR ARGENTIA (NS ARGENTIA, NEWFOUNDLAND)
Captain G. L. Talveton

COMMANDER FLEET AIR AZORES (NAF LAJES, AZORES)
Captain Norman D. Hodson

COMMANDER FLEET AIR BERMUDA (NS BERMUDA)
Captain D. K. Peterson

COMMANDER FLEET AIR CARIBBEAN (NS ROOSEVELT ROADS, PUERTO RICO)
(Rear-Admiral Alfred R. Matter)

COMMANDER FLEET AIR HAWAII (NAS BARBERS POINTS, HAWAII)
(Rear-Admiral Donald C. Davis)

COMMANDER FLEET AIR KEFLAVIK (KEFLAVIK, ICELAND)
(Rear-Admiral Mayo A. Hadden Jr.)

COMMANDER FLEET AIR KEY WEST (NAS KEY WEST, FLORIDA)
(Rear-Admiral Frederick J. Brush)

COMMANDER FLEET AIR MEDITERRANEAN; COMMANDER ASW FORCE SIXTH FLEET; COMMANDER MARITIME AIR FORCE MEDITERRANEAN
Rear-Admiral Allan F. Fleming* (June 1969)

COMMANDER FLEET AIR MARAMAR (NAS MIRAMAR, CALIFORNIA)
Captain C. N. Conetser

COMMANDER FLEET AIR MOFFETT (NAS MOFFETT FIELD, CALIFORNIA)
Rear-Admiral Charles S. Minter Jr.* (August 1969)

COMMANDER FLEET AIR NORFOLK (NAS NORFOLK, VIRGINIA)
Captain J. R. Kincaid

COMMANDER FLEET AIR WINGS PACIFIC
Rear-Admiral Charles S. Minter Jr.* (July 1969)

COMMANDER FLEET AIR WINGS ATLANTIC; COMMANDER FLEET AIR WING 5
Rear-Admiral Ralph Weymouth* (July 1968)

COMMANDER FLEET AIR WESTERN PACIFIC
Rear-Admiral Harvey P. Lanham* (March 1968)

COMMANDER NAVAL AIR TEST CENTER; COMMANDER FLEET AIR PATUXENT RIVER (NAS PATUXENT RIVER, MARYLAND)
Rear-Admiral Henry L. Miller* (October 1968)

MILITARY SEA TRANSPORTATION SERVICE (MSTS)
Building T-8, Washington, D.C. 20390

COMMANDER MILITARY SEA TRANSPORTATION SERVICE
Vice-Admiral Lawson P. Ramage (March 1967)

DEPUTY COMMANDER & CHIEF OF STAFF
Rear-Admiral Thomas S. King (July 1969)

COMMANDER ATLANTIC AREA
Rear-Admiral Walter F. Schlech Jr. (July 1968)

COMMANDER PACIFIC AREA
Rear-Admiral Russell Kefauver (May 1967)

COMMANDER FAR EAST AREA
Rear-Admiral Sam H. Moore (October 1968)

COMMANDER EASTERN ATLANTIC & MEDITERRANEAN AREA
Captain D. G. Bryce

COMMANDER MEDITERRANEAN SUB-AREA
Captain Albert C. Ansorge Jr.

COMMANDER GULF SUB-AREA
Captain J. D. Miller

NAVAL FORCES

COMMANDER-IN-CHIEF US NAVAL FORCES EUROPE (LONDON)
Admiral Waldemar F. A. Wendt (July 1968)

DEPUTY CHIEF OF STAFF & AIDE
Rear-Admiral Leroy V. Swanson* (June 1969)

COMMANDER NAVAL FORCES SOUTHERN COMMAND; COMMANDANT 15th NAVAL DISTRICT
Rear-Admiral Charles D. Nace

COMMANDER NAVAL FORCES PHILIPPINES
Rear-Admiral Draper L. Kauffman (July 1968)

COMMANDER NAVAL FORCES MARIANAS
Rear-Admiral Philip P. Cole (August 1968)

COMMANDER NAVAL FORCES VIETNAM; CHIEF NAVAL ADVISORY GROUP MILITARY ASSISTANCE COMMAND VIETNAM
Rear-Admiral Elmo R. Zumwalt Jr. (September 1968)

DEPUTY
Rear-Admiral William R. Flanagan* (January 1969)

COMMANDER NAVAL FORCES KOREA; COMMANDER NAVAL COMPONENT UNITED NATIONS COMMAND KOREA; COMMANDER NAVAL COMPONENT US FORCES KOREA; CHIEF NAVAL ADIVISORY GROUP ROK NAVY; US NAVY ADVISOR TO ROK NAVY
Rear-Admiral George P. Steele II (July 1968)

COMMANDER NAVAL SUPPORT FORCE ANTARCTICA
Rear-Admiral David F. Welch (June 1969)

COMMANDER NAVAL FORCES JAPAN
Rear-Admiral Daniel P. Smith Jr.* (June 1968)

COMMANDER KEY WEST FORCE; COMMANDER NAVAL BASE KEY WEST; COMMANDER FLEET AIR KEY WEST
Rear-Admiral Frederick J. Brush* (April 1967)

COMMANDER OPERATIONAL TEST & EVALUATION FORCE
Rear-Admiral Alexander S. Goodfellow Jr. (June 1969)

COMMANDER NAVAL FORCES ICELAND
Captain R. W. Hart Jr.

COMMANDER NAVAL FORCES AZORES
Captain N. D. Hodson

SEA FRONTIERS

COMMANDER CARIBBEAN SEA FRONTIER
Rear-Admiral Alfred R. Matter* (June 1967)

COMMANDER WESTERN SEA FRONTIER
Rear-Admiral William H. Groverman Jr. (June 1967)

COMMANDER HAWAIIAN SEA FRONTIER; COMMANDANT 14th NAVAL DISTRICT COMMANDER FLEET AIR HAWAII
Rear-Admiral Donals C. Davis* (June 1969)

COMMANDER ALASKAN SEA FRONTIER; COMMANDANT 17th NAVAL DISTRICT; COMMANDER FLEET AIR ALASKA
Rear-Admiral Eugene G. Fairfax* (July 1969)

COMMANDER EASTERN SEA FRONTIER
(Vice-Admiral John M. Lee)

NAVAL DISTRICTS & BASES

COMMANDANT NAVAL DISTRICT WASHINGTON D.C.
Rear-Admiral George P. Koch* (June 1969)

COMMANDANT 11th NAVAL DISTRICT; COMMANDER NAVAL BASE SAN DIEGO CALIFORNIA
Rear-Admiral Marshall E. Dornin (September 1967)

COMMANDANT 13th NAVAL DISTRICT
Captain Patrick J. Hannifin (September 1969)

COMMANDANT 3rd NAVAL DISTRICT; COMMANDER NAVAL BASE NEW YORK
Rear-ADmiral Francis D. Foley* (September 1967)

COMMANDANT 9th NAVAL DISTRICT (GREAT LAKES III)
Rear-Admiral Henry A. Renkin (September 1967)

COMMANDANT 5th NAVAL DISTRICT; COMMANDER NAVAL BASE NORFOLK VA.
Rear-Admiral James C. Dempsey (May 1968)

COMMANDER NAVAL BASE KEY WEST FLA.
(Rear-Admiral Frederick J. Brush)

COMMANDANT 1st NAVAL DISTRICT; COMMANDER NAVAL BASE BOSTON MASS.
Rear-Admiral Joseph C. Wylie, Jr. (December 1968)

COMMANDANT 15th NAVAL DISTRICT
(Rear-Admiral Charles D. Nace)

COMMANDANT 6th NAVAL DISTRICT; COMMANDER NAVAL BASE CHARLESTON S.C,
Rear-Admiral Herman J. Kossler (August 1968)

COMMANDANT 4th NAVAL DISTRICT; COMMANDER NAVAL BASE PHILADELPHIA
Rear-Admiral Kenneth L. Veth (November 1968)

COMMANDANT, 8th NAVAL DISTRICT (NEW ORLEANS LA.)
Rear-Admiral Robert A. MacPherson* (September 1968)

COMMANDANT 14th NAVAL DISTRICT
(Rear-Admiral Donald C. Davis)

COMMANDER US NAVAL BASE SUBIC BAY PHILIPPINES
Rear-Admiral Valdemar G. Lambert* (June 1968)

COMMANDANT 12th NAVAL DISTRICT; COMMANDER NAVAL BASE SAN FRANCISCO CALIF.
Rear-Admiral Leo B. McCuddin* (January 1968)

COMMANDER NAVAL BASE GUANTANAMO BAY CUBA
Rear-Admiral James B. Hildreth (July 1968)

NAVAL SHIPYARDS

COMMANDER NAVAL SHIPYARD PEARL HARBOR
Captain R. E. Barnhart (ED)

COMMANDER NAVAL SHIPYARD PORTSMOUTH (N.H.)
Captain D. H. Kern (ED)

COMMANDER NAVAL SHIPYARD NORFOLK (Va.)
Rear-Admiral James A. Brown (ED) (June 1965)

COMMANDER NAVAL SHIPYARD BOSTON (MASS.)
Captain Robert C. Gooding (ED) (August 1968)

COMMANDER NAVAL SHIPYARD PHILADELPHIA (PA.)
Captain F. W. Gooch (ED)

COMMANDER NAVAL SHIPYARD CHARLESTON (S.C.)
Captain Charles N. Payne (ED)

COMMANDER NAVAL SHIPYARD SAN FRANCISCO BAY
Rear-Admiral Norbert Frankenberger (ED) (July 1968)

COMMANDER NAVAL SHIPYARD PUGET SOUND (SEATTLE WASH.)
Rear-Admiral William F. Petrovic (ED) (March 1967)

COMMANDER NAVAL SHIPYARD LONG BEACH (CALIF.)
Captain C. M. Hart (ED)

BUREAU OF NAVAL PERSONNEL (BUPERS)

CHIEF OF NAVAL PERSONNEL
(Vice-Admiral Charles K. Duncan)

DEPUTY CHIEF OF NAVAL PERSONNEL
Rear-Admiral Dick H. Guinn* (June 1969)

ASSISTANT CHIEF FOR PERSONNEL CONTROL
Rear-Admiral Damon W. Cooper* (August 1968)

ASSISTANT CHIEF FOR PLANS & PROGRAMS
Rear-ADmiral Robert R. Crutchfield (August 1967)

CHIEF OF CHAPLAINS
Rear-Admiral James W. Kelly (CHC) (July 1965)

ASSISTANT CHIEF FOR NAVAL RESERVE
Rear-Admiral Edelen A. Parker* (September 1966)

ASSISTANT CHIEF FOR EDUCATION & TRAINING
Rear-Admiral Sheldon H. Kinney (May 1969)

BUREAU OF MEDICINE & SURGERY NAVAL MEDICAL & DENTAL ACTIVITIES

CHIEF, BUREAU OF MEDICINE & SURGERY; SURGEON GENERAL OF THE NAVY
Vice-Admiral George M. Davies Jr. (MC) (February 1969)

ASSISTANT CHIEF FOR DENTISTRY; CHIEF DENTAL DIVISION
Rear-Admiral Edward C. Raffetto (DC) (July 1968)

DEPUTY CHIEF
Rear-Admiral John W. Albrittain (MC) (March 1969)

ASSISTANT CHIEF FOR PERSONNEL & PROFESSIONAL OPERATIONS
Rear-Admiral Frank T. Norris (MC) (June 1966)

ASSISTANT CHIEF FOR PLANS & LOGISTICS
Rear-Admiral Harry S. Etter (MC) (July 1967)

ASSISTANT CHIEF FOR RESEARCH & MILITARY MEDICAL SPECIALITIES
Rear-Admiral Ralph E. Faucett (July 1969)

INSPECTOR GENERAL MEDICAL
Rear-Admiral Felix P. Ballenger (MC) (September 1967)

INSPECTOR GENERAL DENTAL
Rear-Admiral Myron G. Turner (DC) (July 1968)

SPECIAL PROJECT
Vice-Admiral George G. Burkley (MC) (Retired) (January 1969)

COMMANDING OFFICER NAVAL AEROSPACE MEDICIAL CENTER PENSACOLA FLA; STAFF CHIEF NAVAL AIR RESERVE TRAINING
Rear-Admiral Edward P. Irons (MC) (June 1969)

COMMANDING OFFICER NAVAL HOSPITAL PORTSMOUTH VA.; DISTRICT MEDICAL OFFICER 5th NAVAL DISTRICT
Rear-Admiral Joseph L. Yon (MC) (November 1964)

COMMANDING OFFICER NATIONAL NAVAL MEDICAL CENTER
Rear-Admiral Robert O. Canada Jr. (MC) (March 1968)

COMMANDING OFFICER NAVAL HOSPITAL SAN DIEGO; COMMANDING OFFICER NAVAL HOSPITAL CORPS SCHOOL SAN DIEGO
Rear-Admiral Horace D. Warden (MC) (December 1964)

COMMANDING OFFICER NAVAL HOSPITAL OAKLAND CALIF.; DISTRICT MEDICAL OFFICER 12th NAVAL DISTRICT; DIRECTOR & ADVISOR ON MEDICAL MATTERS TO COMMANDER WESTERN SEA FRONTIER
Rear-Admiral Harry P. Machin (MC)

COMMANDING OFFICER NAVAL HOSPITAL GREAT LAKES Ill; DISTRICT MEDICAL OFFICER 9th NAVAL DISTRICT: COMMANDING OFFICER HOSPITAL CORPS SCHOOL GREAT LAKES
Rear-Admiral John H. Cheffey (MC) (February 1969)

COMMANDING OFFICER NAVAL HOSPITAL CAMP LE JEUNE NORTH CAROLINA
Captain Willard P. Arenpzen (MC)

COMMANDING OFFICER NAVAL HOSPITAL ST. ALBANS NEW YORK
Captain George H. Tarr Jr.

ATTENDING PHYSICIAN TO CONGRESS; STAFF NATIONAL NAVAL MEDICAL CENTER
Rear-Admiral Rufus J. Pearson Jr. (MC) (November 1966)

DIRECTOR DENTAL ACTIVITIES 11th NAVAL DISTRICT
Rear-Admiral Frank M. Kyes (DC) (July 1968)

COMMANDING OFFICER NAVAL HOSPITAL, PHILDELPHIA, PENNSYLVANIA
Captain Loy T. Brown (MC)

COMMANDING OFFICER NAVAL HOSPITAL, NATIONAL NAVAL MEDICAL CENTER, BETHESDA, MARYLAND
Captain David P. Osborne (MC)

COMMANDING OFFICER, NAVAL HOSPITAL, CAMP PENDLETON, CALIFORNIA
Captain Herbert G. Stoecklin (MC)

NAVAL MATERIAL COMMAND (NAVMAT)
Main Navy Building, Washington, D.C. 20360

CHIEF OF NAVAL MATERIAL
Admiral Ignatius J. Galantin (May 1966)

VICE CHIEF OF NAVAL MATERIAL
Vice-Admiral Jackson D. Arnold (AED) (August 1967)

DEPUTY CNM (PROGRAMMES & FINANCIAL MANAGEMENT)
Rear-Admiral Donald G. Baer (December 1967)

DEPUTY CNM (PROCUREMENT & PRODUCTION)
Captain R. G. Freeman III

DEPUTY CNM (DEVELOPMENT)
Rear-Admiral Thomas D. Davies* (May 1969)

DEPUTY CNM (LOGISTIC SUPPORT)
Rear-Admiral George E. Moore II (SC) (July 1969)

DEPUTY CNM (MANAGEMENT & ORGANIZATION)
Captain J. G. Smith

PROJECT MANAGER STRATEGIC SYSTEMS PROJECT (SSP)
Rear-Admiral Levering Smith (AED) (February 1965)

PROJECT MANAGER SURFACE MISSILES SYSTEMS PROJECT
Captain M. H. Sappington

COMMANDER ASW SYSTEMS PROJECT
Rear-Admiral William C. Abhau (May 1967)

PROJECT MANAGER ALL-WEATHER CARRIER LANDING SYSTEM (ACLS) PROJECT
Captain F. R. Fearnow

PROJECT MANAGER RECONNAISSANCE ELECTRONIC WARFARE SPECIAL OPERATIONS & NAVAL INTELLIGENCE PROCESSING (REWSON)
Rear-Admiral Albert H. Clancy Jr. (AED) (December 1968)

AIR TRAFFIC CONTROL RADAR BEACON SYSTEM; IFF; MILITARY SECURE SYSTEMS (AIMS) PROJECT
Captain J. S. Elmer

PROJECT MANAGER OMEGA (NAVIGATION SYSTEM)
Captain M. X. Polk

PROJECT MANAGER DEEP SUBMERGENCE SYSTEMS PROJECT (DSSP)
Captain William H. Nicholson (ED)

PROJECT MANAGER NAVAL INSHORE WARFARE SYSTEMS (NIWS) PROJECT
Captain W. P. Holden

DIRECTOR HIGH SPEED/LATER DESIGN SUBMARINE PROJECT
Rear-Admiral Paul L. Lacy, Jr. (January 1969)

PROGRAMME COORDINATOR DX/DXG PROGRAM
(Rear-Admiral Weschler)

PROGRAMME COORDINATOR CVAN PROGRAM
(Rear-Admiral Holloway)

COMMANDER NAVAL AIR SYSTEMS COMMAND (NAVAIR)
Rear-Admiral Thomas J. Walker* (February 1969)

VICE COMMANDER
Rear-Admiral Paul A. Holmberg (AED) (November 1968)

DEPUTY COMMANDER PLANS & PROGRAM COMPTROLLER
Rear-Admiral Thomas R. McClellan* (March 1969)

ASSISTANT COMMANDER FOR CONTRACTS
Captain J. E. Harvey Jr.

ASSISTANT COMMANDER FOR RESEARCH & TECHNOLOGY
Rear-Admiral Raymond J. Schneider (AED) (November 1968)

ASSISTANT COMMANDER FOR LOGISTIC/FLEET SUPPORT
Henry Suerstedt, Jr.* (July 1968)

ASSISTANT COMMANDER FOR MATERIAL ACQUISITION
Rear-Admiral Kenan C. Childers Jr. (AED) (May 1967)

INSPECTOR GENERAL & DIRECTOR OF ADMINISTRATION
Captain L. C. Powell

NAVAL AIR SYSTEMS COMMAND REPRESENTATIVE PACIFIC
Rear-Admiral James H. Smith, Jr. (AED) (August 1967)

NAVAL AIR SYSTEMS COMMAND REPRESENTATIVE ATLANTIC
Rear-Admiral Daniel K. Weitzenfeld (AED) (July 1967)

COMMANDER NAVAL ELECTRONIC SYSTEMS COMMAND (NAVELEX)
Rear-Admiral Joseph E. Rice (ED) (May 1966)

VICE COMMANDER
Rear-Admiral Burton H. Andrews (ED' ugust 1968)

DEPUTY COMMANDER PLANNING PROGRAMING & RESOURCES MANAGEMENT
Captain K. W. Cramp

DIRECTOR OF CONTRACTS
Captain C. A. Appleby

DIRECTOR OF RESEARCH & TECHNOLOGY
Comander N. D. Harding Jr.

DEPUTY COMMANDER ACQUISITION ENGINEERING
Captain F. H. Lamartin Jr.

DEPUTY COMMANDER LOGISTICS
Captain L. G. Cutchall

COMMANDER NAVAL FACILITIES ENGINEERING; COMMAND (NAVFAC); CHIEF OF CIVIL ENGINEERS
Rear-Admiral Walter M. Enger (CEC) September 1969)

DEPUTY COMMANDER FOR ACQUISITION
Captain H. L. Bowman (CEC)

DEPUTY COMMANDER FOR MANAGEMENT
Rear-Admiral Spencer R. Smith (CEC) (August 1968)

DIRECTOR OF PROGRAMS & COMPTROLLER
Captain C. F. Krickenberger Jr. (CEC)

ASSISTANT COMMANDER FOR CONTRACTS
(Captain H. L. Bowman)

ASSISTANT COMMANDER FOR RESEARCH & DEVELOPMENT
Captain E. M. Saunders (CEC)

ASSISTANT COMMANDER FOR ENGINEERING & DESIGN
Captain W. A. Walls (CEC)

ASSISTANT COMMANDER FOR CONSTRUCTION
Captain W. B. Jones (CEC)

ASSISTANT COMMANDER FOR MILITARY READINESS
Captain B. W. Van Leer (CEC)

ASSISTANT COMMANDER FOR REAL PROPERTY MANAGEMENT
Captain R. E. Dunnells (CEC)

ASSISTANT COMMANDER FOR FAMILY HOUSING
Captain G. A. Goetzke (CEC)

ASSISTANT COMMANDER FOR OPERATIONS & MAINTENANCE
Captain J. E. Powell (CEC)

ASSISTANT COMMANDER FOR FACILITIES PLANNING
Captain C. Bittenbring III (CEC)

COMMANDER PACIFIC DIVISION NAVFAC
Rear-Admiral William Heaman (CEC) (January 1966)

COMMANDER SOUTHWEST DIVISION NAVFAG; CIVIL ENGINEER 11th NAVAL DISTRICT
Rear-Admiral Robert R. Wooding (CEC) (January 1967)

COMMANDER ATLANTIC DIVISION NAVFAC; FLEET CIVIL ENGINEER ATLANTIC FLEET; ASSISTANT CHIEF OF STAFF FOR FACILITIES ENGINEERING ATLANTIC FLEET
Rear-Admiral Paul E. Seufer (CEC) (October 1968)

DEPUTY COMMANDER PACIFIC DIVISION NAVFAC SOUTHEAST ASIA; OFFICER-IN-CHARGE CONSTRUCTION VIETNAM
Rear-Admiral Henry J. Johnson (CEC) (July 1968)

COMMANDER NAVAL ORDANCE SYSTEMS COMMAND (NAVORD)
Rear-Admiral Mark W. Woods (June 1969)

DIRECTOR PERSONNEL & ADMINISTRATION
Commander G. W. Pace (acting)

DIRECTOR SYSTEMS ENGINEERING & QUALITY
Captain P. P. Vail Jr.

DEPUTY COMMANDER PLAN & RESOURCES
Rear-Admiral Thomas Christman (DED) (August 1968)

DIRECTOR OF CONTRACTS
Captain D. G. Aitken

ASSISTANT COMMANDER RESEARCH & TECHNOLOGY
Captain C. J. Flessner

ASSISTANT COMMANDER FLEET SUPPORT
Captain B. W. Frese

DEPUTY COMMANDER UNDERSEA WARFARE SYSTEMS
Captain T. C. Buell

DEPUTY COMMANDER ANTI-AIR WARFARE SYSTEMS
Captain M. H. Sappington

INSPECTOR GENERAL
Captain C. B. Cates Jr.

DEPUTY COMMANDER SURFACE WARFARE SYSTEMS
Captain R. L. Cochrane

COMMANDER NAVAL SHIP SYSTEMS COMMAND (NAVSHIPS)
Rear-Admiral Nathan Sonenshein (ED) (July 1969)

VICE COMMANDER
Rear-Admiral Frank C. Jones (ED) (January 1967)

DEPUTY COMMANDER PLANS PROGRAMS & FINANCIAL MANAGEMENT
Captain Van Dyke Johnson

DIRECTOR OF CONTRACTS
Captain R. H. Diggle

DEPUTY COMMANDER RESEARCH
Captain Frederick A. Hooper

DEPUTY COMMANDER FLEET MAINTENANCE & LOGISTIC SUPPORT
Rear-Admiral Robert E. Adamson Jr. (September 1967)

DEPUTY COMMANDER SHIP ACQUISITION
Rear-Admiral Jamie Adair (ED) (May 1966)

COMMANDER SHIP ENGINEERING CENTER
Rear-Admiral Harry C. Mason (ED) (August 1968)

DEPUTY COMMANDER SHIPYARD MANAGEMENT; PROGRAM DIRECTOR FOR SHIPYARD MODERNIZATION
Rear-Admiral James J. Stilwell (ED) (April 1967)

DEPUTY COMMANDER NUCLEAR PROPULSION
(Vice-Admiral Rickover)

INSPECTOR GENERAL
Rear-Admiral Edgar H. Batcheller (ED) (July 1968)

COMMANDER NAVAL SUPPLY SYSTEMS COMMAND (NAVSUP)
Rear-Admiral Bernhard H. Bieri, Jr. (SC) (August 1967)

VICE COMMANDER
Rear-Admiral Kenneth R. Wheeler (SC) (July 1969)

DEPUTY COMMANDER PROGRAMMING & FINANCIAL MANAGEMENT
Captain W. McHenry Jr. (SC)

DEPUTY COMMANDER PURCHASING
Captain G. S. Young (SC)

DEPUTY COMMANDER SUPPLY OPERATIONS
Rear-Admiral Paul F. Cosgrove, Jr. (SC) (August 1967)

DEPUTY COMMANDER TRANSPORTATION
Captain G. C. Nelson (SC)

DEPUTY COMMANDER PLANNING & POLICY
Rear-Admiral Roland Rieve (SC) (August 1967)

DEPUTY COMMANDE ADMINISTRATION & ORGANIZATION
Captain E. R. Joshua Jr. (SC)

DEPUTY COMMANDER FOR RESALE PROGRAMS
(Rear-Admiral Lyness)

DIRECTOR OF SUPPLY CORPS PERSONNEL
Captain John A. Scott (SC)

MAJOR NAVAL SUPPLY ACTIVITIES

COMMANDING OFFICER NAVAL SUPPLY CENTER LONG BEACH CALIF.
Rear-Admiral Howard F. Kuehl (SC) (June 1966)

COMMANDING OFFICER NAVAL SUPPLY CENTER NORFOLK VA.
Rear-Admiral Ira F. Haddock (SC) (May 1969)

COMMANDING OFFICER NAVAL SUPPLY CENTER SAN DIEGO CALIF.; DISTRICT SUPPLY OFFICER 11th NAVAL DISTRICT
Rear-Admiral Stephen Sherwood (SC) (June 1967)

COMMANDING OFFICER NAVAL AVIATION SUPPLY OFFICE PHILADELPHIA
Rear-Admiral Harry J. P. Foley, Jr. (SC) (July 1966)

COMMANDING OFFICER NAVAL SUPPLY CENTER OAKLAND CALIF
Rear-Admiral Jack J. Appleby (SC) (August 1968)

COMMANDING OFFICER SHIPS PARTS CONTROL CENTER MACHANICSBURG PA.
Rear-Admiral Frederick W. Corle (SC) (July 1966)

COMMANDING OFFICER NAVAL SHIPS STORE OFFICE BROOKLYN N.Y.; DISTRICT SUPPLY OFFICER 3rd NAVAL DISTRICT; DEPUTY COMMANDER FOR RESALE PROGRAMS NAVSUP
Rear-Admiral Douglas H. Lyness (SC) (September 1968)

COMMANDING OFFICER NAVAL SUPPLY CENTER CHARLESTON S.C.
Rear-Admiral Wallace R. Dowd Jr. (SC) (August 1968)

COMMANDING OFFICER NAVAL FLEET MATERIAL SUPPORT OFFICE MECHANICSBURG PENNSYLVANIA
Captain Vincent A. Lascara (SC)

MISCELLANEOUS NAVY FLAG OFFICER ASSIGNMENTS

VICE CHAIRMAN US DELEGATION UNITED NATIONS MILITARY STAFF COMMITTEE; COMMANDER EASTERN SEA FRONTIER
Vice-Admiral John M. Lee (March 1969)

CHIEF OF NAVAL AIR TRAINING
Vice-Admiral Bernard M. Strean* (July 1968)

PRESIDENT NAVAL WAR COLLEGE
Vice-Admiral Richard G. Colbert (August 1968)

CHIEF OF STAFF & AIDE NAVAL WAR COLLEGE
Vice-Admiral Fred G. Bennett (August 1969)

DIRECTOR DIVISION OF NAVAL REACTORS US ATOMIC ENERGY COMMISSION; DEPUTY COMMANDER FOR NUCLEAR PROPULSION NAVYSHIPS
Vice-Admiral Hyman G. Rickover (ED) (Retired) (February 1949)

US DEFENSE ATTACHE; US NAVAL ATTACHE & US NAVAL ATTACHE FOR AIR UNITED KINGDOM
Rear-Admiral Louis J. Kirn* (April 1967)

CHIEF OF NAVAL AIR TECHNICAL TRAINING
Rear-Admiral Ernest E. Christensen* (June 1967)

COMMANDER PACIFIC MISSILE RANGE
Rear-Admiral Howard S. Moore* (June 1969)

CHIEF OF NAVAL AIR RESERVE TRAINING
Rear-Admiral William S. Guest* (March 1967)

PRESIDENT NAVY BOARD OF INSPECTION & SURVEY
Rear-Admiral John D. Bulkeley (June 1967)

SUPERINTENDENT NAVAL POSTGRADUATE SCHOOL
Rear-Admiral Robert W. McNitt (October 1967)

CHIEF OF NAVAL AIR BASIC TRAINING
Rear-Admiral Herbert S. Matthews Jr.* (August 1969)

SUPERINTENDENT US NAVAL ACADEMY
Rear-Admiral James F. Calvert (July 1968)

COMMANDER NAVAL RESERVE TRAINING COMMAND
Rear-Admiral George R. Muse (October 1967)

DEPUTY
Rear-Admiral Edwin J. Zimmermann, Jr. (February 1968)

COMMANDER NAVAL SUPPORT ACTIVITY DANANG SOUTH VIETNAM
Rear-Admiral Emmett P. Bonner (December 1968)

MANAGER APOLLO PROGRAM KENNEDY SPACE CENTER NATIONAL AERONAUTICS & SPACE ADMINISTRATION (NASA)
Rear-Admiral Roderick O. Middleton (August 1967)

COMMANDER NAVAL TRAINING CENTER SAN DIEGO CALIF.
Rear-Admiral Allen A. Bergner (November 1967)

COMMANDER NAVAL SECURITY GROUP COMMAND; EXECUTIVE ASSISTANT FOR CRYPTOLOGY OPNAV
Rear-Admiral Ralph E. Cook (SD) (June 1967)

DIRECTOR INTERNATIONAL STAFF INTER-AMERICAN DEFENSE BOARD
Rear-Admiral John B. Johnson (June 1969)

GOVERNOR NAVAL HOME PHILADELPHIA PA.
Rear-Admiral Michael F. D. Flaherty (Retired) (October 1966)

CHIEF NAVAL SECURITY AGENCY PACIFIC
Rear-Admiral Lester R. Schulz (Retired) (June 1968)

COMMANDANT OF MIDSHIPMEN US NAVAL ACADEMY
Rear-Admiral Lawrence Heyworth Jr.* (August 1967)

CHIEF NAVY SECTION JOINT US MILITARY MISSION FOR AID TO TURKEY
Rear-Admiral John M. Barrett (August 1968)

CHIEF NAVY SECTION MILITARY GROUP BRAZIL
Rear-Admiral Clarence A. Hill Jr.* (March 1969)

CHIEF OF NAVAL AIR ADVANCED TRAINING
Rear-Admiral Frederick C. Turner* (October 1968)

COMMANDER 3rd NAVAL CONSTRUCTION BRIGADE
Rear-Admiral John G. Dillon (CEC) (March 1969)

DEPUTY CHIEF OF STAFF FOR RESOURCES MANAGEMENT NAVAL RESERVE TRAINING COMMAND
Rear-Admiral John B. Johnson (July 1967)

DIRECTOR INTER-AMERICAN DEFENSE COLLEGE
Rear-Admiral Gene R. La Rocque (August 1969)

HEADQUARTERS MARINE CORPS
Arlington Annex, Arlington, Virginia

COMMANDANT US MARINE CORPS
General Leonard F. Chapman Jr.

ASSISTANT COMMANDANT
General Lewis W. Walt

CHIEF OF STAFF
Lieutenant General William J. Van Ryzin

DEPUTY CHIEF OF STAFF (PLANS & PROGRAMS)
Lieutenant Frank G. Tharin

ASSISTANT DEPUTY CHIEF OF STAFF (PLANS)
Major General Frederick E. Leek

ASSISTANT DEPUTY CHIEF OF STAFF (PROGRAMS)
Major General John R. Chaisson

DEPUTY CHIEF OF STAFF (MANPOWER); DIRECTOR OF PERSONNEL
Lieutenant General Louis B. Robertshaw

DEPUTY CHIEF OF STAFF (RESEARCH DEVELOPMENT & SUPPORT)
Major General Louis Metzger

DEPUTY CHIEF OF STAFF (AIR)
Major General Keith B. McCutcheon*

ASSISTANT CHIEF OF STAFF G-1 (PERSONNEL)
Major General Jonas M. Platt

DEPUTY ASSISTANT CHIEF OF STAFF G-1 (PERSONNEL)
Brigadier General Kenneth J. Houghton

ASSISTANT CHIEF OF STAFF G-2 (INTELLIGENCE)
Colonel Stone W. Quillian

ASSISTANT CHIEF OF STAFF G-3 (OPERATIONS)
Brigadier General Webb D. Sawyer

DEPUTY ASSISTANT CHIEF OF STAFF G-3 (OPERATIONS)
Brigadier General Webb D. Sawyer

ASSISTANT CHIEF OF STAFF G-4 (LOGISTICS)
Brigadier General George C. Axtell

DEPUTY ASSISTANT CHIEF OF STAFF G-4 (LOGISTICS)
Brigadier General Herman H. Poggemeyer Jr.

INSPECTOR GENERAL
Brigadier General Lawrence F. Snoddy Jr.

DIRECTOR MARINE CORPS RESERVE
Brigadier General Charles F. Widdecke

DEPUTY DIRECTOR OF PERSONNEL
Major General Earl E. Anderson

FLEET MARINE FORCE ATLANTIC (FMFLANT)

COMMANDING GENERAL; COMMANDING GENERAL II MARINE EXPEDITIONARY FORCE
Lieutenant General Frederick E. Leek

DEPUTY COMMANDER
Major General Norman J. Anderson

COMMANDING GENERAL 2nd MARINE DIVISION
Major General Michael P. Ryan

COMMANDING GENERAL 2nd MARINE AIRCRAFT WING
Major General Marion E. Carl*

FLEET MARINE FORCE PACIFIC (FMFPAC)

COMMANDING GENERAL
Lieutenant General Henry W. Buse Jr.

DEPUTY COMMANDER FMFPAC; COMMANDING GENERAL V MARINE EXPEDITIONARY FORCE
Major General Paul J. Fontana

COMMANDING GENERAL III MARINE AMPHIBIOUS FORCE
Lieutenant Harman Nickerson Jr.

DEPUTY COMMANDER III MARINE AMPHIBIOUS FORCE
Major General Carl A. Youngdale

COMMANDING GENERAL 1st MARINE DIVISION
Major General Ormond R. Simpson

COMMANDING GENERAL 3rd MARINE DIVISION
Major General William K. Jones

COMMANDING GENERAL 5th MARINE DIVISION
Brigadier General Ross T. Dwyer Jr.

COMMANDING GENERAL 1st MARINE AIRCRAFT WING
Major General William G. Thrash*

COMMANDING GENERAL 3rd MARINE AIRCRAFT WING
Major General Robert G. Owens Jr.

COMMANDING GENERAL 9TH MARINE AMPHIBIOUS BRIGADE; COMMANDING GENERAL FMF 7TH FLEET
Brigadier General Robert B. Carney Jr.

HEADQUARTERS COAST GUARD
13th & Pennsylvania Avenue, N.W., Washington, D.C.

COMMANDANT US COAST GUARD
Admiral Williard J. Smith

ASSISTANT COMMANDANT
Vice-Admiral Paul E. Trimble

SCIENCE ADVISOR
Dr. Charles C. Bates

MEDICAL ADVISOR
Rear-Admiral Howard D. Fishburn (US Public Health Service)

CHIEF OF STAFF
Rear-Admiral Thomas R. Sargent III

CHIEF OFFICE OF PUBLIC & INTERNATIONAL AFFAIRS
Rear-Admiral Roderick Y. Edwards

CHIEF OFFICE OF BOATING SAFTEY
Rear-Admiral J. J. McClelland

COMPTROLLER
Captain Harold J. McCormack

CHIEF OFFICE OF ENGINEERING
Rear-Admiral D. B. Henderson

CHIEF OFFICE OF THE CHIEF COUNSEL
Rear-Admiral William L. Morrison

CHIEF OFFICE OF MERCHANT MARINE SAFETY
Rear-Admiral Charles P. Murphy

CHIEF OFFICE OF OPERATIONS
Rear-Admiral Robert W. Goehring

CHIEF OFFICE OF PERSONNEL
Rear-Admiral Joseph P. Scullion

CHIEF OFFICE OF RESEARCH & DEVELOPMENT
Rear-Admiral C. A. Richmond Jr.

CHIEF OFFICE OF RESERVE
Rear-Admiral John D. McCubbin

COAST GUARD DISTRICTS AND OPERATING FORCES

COMMANDER EASTERN AREA
Rear-Admiral Mark A. Whalen

COMMANDER WESTERN AREA
Rear-Admiral Chester R. Bender

COMMANDANT COAST GUARD DISTRICT

CGD 1
Rear-Admiral William B. Ellis

CGD 2
Rear-Admiral Russell A. Waesche Jr.

CGD 3
(Rear-Admiral Mark A. Whalen)

CGD 5
Rear-Admiral Edward C. Allen

CGD 7
Rear-Admiral Paul G. Prins

CGD 8
Rear-Admiral Ross P. Bullard

CGD 9
Rear-Admiral William F. Rea III

CGD 13
Rear-Admiral Frank V. Helmer

CGD 14
Rear-Admiral Benjamin F. Engel

CGD 17
Rear-Admiral R. E. Hammond

COMMANDER COAST GUARD ACTIVITIES VIETNAM
Captain Ralph W. Niesz

COMMANDER COAST GUARD SQUADRON 1
Lieutenant Commander Stanley J. Walden

COMMANDER COAST GUARD SQUADRON 3
Captain Daniel J. Scalabrini

STRATEGIC WARFARE SHIPS

GEORGE WASHINGTON SSBN 598
Blue Commander O. Smith
Gold Commander G. C. Merritt

PATRICK HENRY SSBN 599
Blue Commander R. Z. Test
Gold Commander G. A. Barunas Jr.

THEODORE ROOSEVELT SSBN 600
Blue Commander A. B. Crabtree
Gold Commander Francis L. Wadsworth

ROBERT E LEE SSBN 601
Blue Commander L. B. Hebbard Jr.
Gold Commander R. M. Hoover

ABRAHAM LINCOLN SSBN 602
Blue Commander S. M. Jenks
Gold Commander J. D. Leonard Jr.

ETHAN ALLEN SSBN 608
Blue Commander R. E. Chidley
Gold Commander R. L. Hart

SAM HOUSTON SSBN 609
Blue Commander H. A. Glovier Jr.
Gold Commander A. C. Bivens

THOMAS A. EDISON SSBN 610
Blue Commander W. A. Brooks
Gold Commander M. L. Philpot

JOHN MARSHALL SSBN 611
Blue Commander D. E. Kniss
Gold Commander M. C. Ritz

LAFAYETTE SSBN 616
Blue Commander C. D. Pollak
Gold Commander C. G. Foster Jr.

ALEXANDER HAMILTON SSBN 617
Blue Commander W. A. Miller
Gold Commander W. A. Williams III

THOMAS JEFFERSON SSBN 618
Blue Commander P. G. White Jr.
Gold Commander W. H. Purdum

ANDREW JACKSON SSBN 619
Blue Commander T. K. Demun
Gold Commander L. G. Valade

JOHM ADAMS SSBN 620
Blue Commander E. H. Mortimer
Gold

JAMES MONROE SSBN 622
Blue Commander R. T. Wright
Gold Commander J. C. Harris

NATHAN HALE SSBN 623
Blue Commander W. F. Sullivan
Gold Commander R. B. Hamilton

WOODROW WILSON SSBN 624
Blue Commander E. A. Tin
Gold Commander J. R. Ramzy

HENRY CLAY SSBN 625
Commander A. A. Young III

DANIEL WEBSTER SSBN 626
Commander W. E. Roberts

JAMES MADISON SSBN 627
Commander R. B. Miller Jr.

TECUMSEH SSBN 628
Blue Commander R. N. Williams
Gold

DANIEL BOONE SSBN 629
Blue Commander R. D. Rawlins
Gold

JOHN C. CALHOUN SSBN 630
Blue Commander T. A. Jewell
Gold

ULYSSES S. GRANT SSBN 631
Blue Commander T. U. Sisson Jr.
Gold Commander R. E. Engle

VON STEUBEN SSBN 632
Blue Commander G. R. Bryan Jr.
Gold Commander B. R. Clements

CASIMIR PULASKI SSBN 633
Blue Commander H. D. Hukill Jr.
Gold Commander J. P. Forsyth

STONEWALL JACKSON SSBN 634
Blue Commander J. P. Keone
Gold Commander E. L. McCutcheon

SAM RAYBURN SSBN 635
Blue Commander C. A. H. Trost
Gold Commander J. B. Orzalli

NATHANAEL GREENE SSBN 636
Blue Commander W. J. Coakley Jr.
Gold Commander L. E. Diley

BENJAMIN FRANKLIN SSBN 640
Blue Commander Robert M. Morrison
Gold Commander M. P. Alexich

SIMON BOLIVAR SSBN 641
Blue Commander J. T. Bush
Gold Commander J. J. Badgett

KAMEHAMEHA SSBN 642
Blue Commander F. W. Kelly
Gold Commander J. A. Sagerholm

GEORGE BANCROFT SSBN 643
Blue Commander S. N. Levey
Gold Commander J. W. McKinster

LEWIS AND CLARK SSBN 644
Blue Commander D. F. Limroth
Gold Commander K. A. Porter

JAMES K. POLK SSBN 645
Blue Commander P. Durbin
Gold Commander C. B. Shellman Jr.

GEORGE C. MARSHALL SSBN 654
Blue Commander J. C. Hay
Gold Commander C. L. Gooding Jr.

HENRY L. STIMSON SSBN 655
Blue Commander D. P. Hall
Gold Commander J. W. Ailes IV

GEORGE WASHINGTON CARVER SSBN 656
Blue Commander R. D. Tomb
Gold Commander D. R. Briggs

FRANCIS SCOTT KEY SSBN 657
Blue Commander L. D. Yarger
Gold Commander J. B. Logan

MARIANO G. VALLEJO SSBN 658
Blue Commander K. W. Curl
Gold Commander A. C. Johnson

WILL ROGERS SSBN 659
Blue Commander R. L. Kelsey
Gold Commander M. S. Greer

COMMAND & COMMUNICATION SHIPS

NORTHAMPTON CC1
Captain J. W. Short

WRIGHT CC2
Captain H. E. Thornhill

ANNAPOLIS AGMR 1
Captain K. C. Miller

ARLINGTON AGMR 2
Captain A. P. Carpenter

VALCOUR AGF 1
Commander S. M. Beck

AIRCRAFT CARRIERS

YORKTOWN CVS 10
Captain W. F. Chaires

INTREPID CVS 11
Captain H. N. Moore Jr.

HORNET CVS 12
Captain J. A. Stockton

TICONDEROGA CVA 14
Captain R. E. Fowler

LEXINGTON CVT 16
Captain W. E. Hammett

WASP CVS 18
Captain John F. Gillobly

HANCOCK CVA 19
Captain N. P. Foss

BENNINGTON CVS 20
Captain W. B. Barrow

BON HOMME RICHARD CVA 31
Captain D. W. Alderton

KEARSARGE CVS 33
Captain Leonard M. Nearman

ORISKANY CVA 34
Captain J. S. Kenyon

SHANGRI-LA CVS 38
Captain W. S. Nelson

MIDWAY CVA 41

FRANKLIN D. ROOSEVELT CVA 42
Captain J. O. Mayo

CORAL SEA CVA 43
Captain S. G. Gorsline

FORRESTAL CVA 59
Captain James W. Nance

SARATOGA CVA 60
Captain Warren H. O'Neil

RANGER CVA 61
Captain J. P. Moorer

INDEPENDENCE CVA 62
Captain B. B. Forbes Jr.

KITTY HAWK CVA 63
Captain J. F. Davis

CONSTELLATION CVA 64
Captain J. S. Christiansen

ENTERPRISE CVAN 65
Captain F. S. Petersen

AMERICA CVA 66
Captain R. E. Rumble

JOHN F. KENNEDY CVA 67
Captain J. S. Lake Jr.

FLEET ESCORT SHIPS

GALVESTON CLG 3
Captain R. B. Pettitt

LITTLE ROCK CLG 4
Captain W. F. V. Bennett

OKLAHOMA CITY CLG 5
Captain W. D. surface

PROVIDENCE CLG 6
Captain E. E. Hollyfield

SPRINGFIELD CLG 7
Captain L. W. Zech Jr.

LONG BEACH CGN 9
Captain W. A. Spencer

ALBANY CG 10
Captain A. P. Slaff

CHICAGO CG 11
Captain Joseph E. Feaster

COLUMBUS CG12
Captain D. J. J. Downey

FARRAGUT DLG 6
Commander W. A. Cockell

LUCE DLG 7
Commander J. D. Stevens

MACDONOUGH DLG 8
Commander Robert R. Clarke

COONTZ DLG 9
Commander D. P. Roane

KING DLG 10
Commander J. D. Scull

MAHAN DLG 11
Commander D. M. Altwegg

DAHLGTEN DLG 12
Commander Jack E. McQuestion

WILLIAM V. PRATT DLG 13
Commander F. J. Reeg

DEWEY DLG 14
Commander Virgil C. Snyder

PREBLE DLG 15

LEAHY DLG 16
Captain W. B. Murray

HARRY E. YARHELL DLG 17
Captain W. G. Lessmann

WORDEN DLG 18
Captain H. R. Youman Jr.

DALE DLG 19
Captain J. C. Linville

RICHMOND K. TURNER DLG 20
Captain C. R. Worley

GRIDLEY DLG 21

ENGLAND DLG 22
Captain G. A. Mitchell

HALSEY DLG 23
Captain W. E. Harper Jr.

REEVES DLG 24

BAINBRIDGE DLGN 25
Captain J. H. Doyle Jr.

BELKNAP DLG 26
Captain J. H. Aldrich

JOSEPHUS DANIELS DLG 27
Captain W. R. St. George

WAINWRIGHT DLG 28
Captain Pierre H. Vining

JOLETT DLG 29
Captain R. C. Barnhardt Jr.

HORNE DLG 30
Captain A. L. Lupia

STERETT DLG 31
Captain C. L. Tyler

WILLIAM H. STANDLEY DLG 32
Captain W. M. A. Greene

FOX DLG 33
Captain M. D. Ward

BIDDLE DLG 34
Captain A. R. Olsen Jr.

TRUXTUN DLGN 35
Captain D. D. Work

NORFOLK DL 1
Captain Charles D. Allen Jr.

WILLIS A. LEE DL 4
Commander W. J. Moredock

WILKINSON DL 5
Commander G. Van Hook

CHARLES F. ADAMS DDG 2
Commander J. L. Jones

JOHN KING DDG 3
Commander O. C. Chisum

LAWRENCE DDG 4
Commander D. J. Costello

CLAUDE V. RICKETTS DDG 5
Commander Jerome Rapkin

BARNEY DDG 6
Commander A. D. Branch

HENRY B. WILSON DDG 7
Commander H. C. Mustin

LYNDE McCORMICK DDG 8
Commander Gerald M. Carter Jr.

TOWERS DDG 9
Commander E. W. Carter III

SAMPSON DDG 10
Commander T. J. Bigley

SELLERS DDG 11
Commander R. D. Hoffman

ROBISON DDG 12
Commander P. K. Collins

HOEL DDG 13
Commander R. K. Fontaine

BUCHANAN DDG 14
Commander R. N. Congdon

BERKELEY DDG 15
Commander T. M. Ward Jr.

JOSEPH STRAUSS DDG 16
Commander L. Layman

CONYNGHAM DDG 17
Commander W. R. Shafer

SEMMES DDG 18
Commander Gerard F. Rogers

TATTNALL DDG 19
Commander R. A. Donnelly

GOLDSBOROUGH DDG 20
Commander P. A. Lautermilch

COCHRANE DDG 21
Commander J. F. Adams

BENJAMIN STODDERT DDG 22
Commander E. B. Talyor

RICHARD E. BYRD DDG 23
Commander C. S. Bird

WADDELL DDG 24
Commander L. O. Armel II

Decatur DDG 31
Commander J. B. Allen

JOHN PAUL JONES DDG 32
Commander L. R. Lester Jr.

PARSONS DDG 33
Commander R. E. Morris

SOMERS DDG 34
Commander H. L. Webster

MITSCHER DDG 35
Commander R. R. Robertson Jr.

JOHN S. McCAIN DDG 36
Commander David N. Denton

FLETCHER DD 445
Commander H. F. Boyle

RADFORD DD 446
Commander J. A. Maxwell

NICHOLAS DD 449
Commander John B. Hurd

O'BANNON DD 450
Commander

RENSHAW DD 449
Commander Samuel B. Wilson

CONWAY DD 507
Commander R. L. Logner

MULLANY DD 528
Commander D. O. Maxwell

TRATHEN DD 530

TWINING DD 540
Commander D. R. Brainard

BOYD DD 544
Commander Jack W. Davis

COWELL DD 547
Commander R. P. Good

PRICHETT DD 561
Commander J. E. Fernandes

STODDARD DD 566
Commander J. E. Lacy

SHIELDS DD 596
Commander R. J. Forsyth

BRAINE DD 630
Commander R. D. Van Antwerp

COWIE DD 632

COGSWELL DD 651
Commander F. W. Kraft

INGERSOLL DD 652
Commander J. M. Redfield

CHARLES J. BADGER DD 657

HICKOX DD 673

HOPEWELL DD 681
Commander R. F. Wilson

PORTERFIELD DD 682
Commander J. H. Bres

WEDDERBURN DD 684
Commander Dale W. Duncan

PICKING DD 685
Commander J. H. McLeavy

UHLMANN DD 687
Commander R. L. Adams

ALLEN M. SUMNER DD 692
Commander J. A. Meacham

MOALE DD 693
Commander J. Scoville

INGRAHAM DD 694
Commander R. M. Gowing

ENGLISH DD 696
Commander C. V. Lavin

CHARLES S. SPERRY DD 697
Commander R. W. Wright

AULT DD 698
Commander J. C. MacKinnon III

WALDRON DD 699
Commander L. Cywin

HAYNSWORTH DD 700
Commander J. C. Kittrell

JOHN W. WEEKS DD 701
Commander F. L. Etchison

HANK DD 702
Commander A. A. Strunk

WALLACE L. LIND DD 703
Commander J. S. Mitchell

BORIE DD 704
Commander J. R, Pouliot

COMPTON DD 705
Commander James M. Ford Jr.

GAINARD DD 706
Commander R. T. McDonald

SOLEY DD 707
Commander R. A. Baldwin

HARLAN R. DICKSON DD 708
Commander R. H. Loyd

HUGH PURVIS DD 709
Commander William K. Mallinson

GEARING DD 710
Commander A. F. Jefferis

EUGENE A. GREENE DD 711
Commander E. F. Wasniewski

GYATT DD 712
Commander A. J. Personette

KENNETH D. BAILEY DD 713
Commander Harold M. J. Lewis, Jr.

WILLIAM R. RUSH DD 714
Commander T. W. Lyons Jr.

WILLIAM M. WOOD DD 715
Commander C. L. R. Anderson

WILTSIE DD 716
Commander W. V. Powell

THEODORE E. CHANDLER DD 717
Commander T. L. Meeks

HAMNER DD 718
Commander J. M. Hoye

EPPERSON DD 719
Commander Leighton D. Smith

WALKE DD 723
Commander T. W. Watson

LAFFEY DD 724
Commander T. R. Cotten Jr.

O'BRIEN DD 725
Commander W. H. C. Self

DE HAVEN DD 727
Commander E. J. Casey Jr.

MANSFIELD DD 728
Commander P. L. Anderson

LYMAN K. SWENSON DD 729
Commander L. J. Brown

COLLETT DD 730
Commander W. R. Beck

HYMAN DD 732
Commander S. C. Gamache

PURDH DD 734

FRANK KNOX DD 742
Commander J. G. Baker

SOUTHERLAND DD 743
Commander W. E. Kennedy

BLUE DD 744
Commander H. W. Bademan

BRUSH DD 745
Commander C. R. Norton Jr.

TAUSSIG DD 746
Commander R. E. Adler

SAMUEL N. MOORE DD 747
Commander D. J. Mattson

HARRY E. HUBBARD DD 748
Commander R. E. McCoy

ALFRED A. CUNNINGHAM DD 752
Commander J. C. Uehlinger

JOHN R. PIERCE DD 753
Commander C. L. Meserve

JOHN A. BOLE DD 755
Commander F. C. Collins Jr.

BEATTY DD 756
Commander S. W. Jones

PUTNAM DD 757
Commander F. E. Beck Jr.

STRONG DD 758
Commander G. C. Lowry

LOFBERG DD 759
Commander J. E. White

JOHN W. THOMASON DD 760
Commander T. E. Vines

BUCK DD 761
Commander P. J. Mode

HENLEY DD 762
Commander W. C. Nation

WILLIAM C. LAWE DD 763
Commander J. H. Lytle

LLOYD THOMAS DD 764
Commander L. B. Wensman

KEPPLER DD 765
Commander R. P. Lensham

LOWRY DD 770
Commander R. L. Blanding

WILLARD KEITH DD 775
Commander H. G. Ehleringer

JAMES C. OWENS DD 776
Commander S. C. Montgomery

ZELLARS DD 777
Commander J. J. Zable

MASSEY DD 778
Commander W. V. Garcia

DOUGLAS H. FOX DD 779
Commander J. L. Wilson

STORMES DD 780
Commander W. C. Darwin

ROBERT K. HUNTINGTON DD 781
Commander L. J. Zvanovec

ROWAN DD 782
Commander F. R. Johns

GURKE DD 783
Commander E. B. Ackerman

McKEAN DD 784
Commander William D. Hart

HENDERSON DD 785
Commander P. V. Borlaug

RICHARD B. ANDERSON DD 786
Commander D. B. Robertson

JAMES E. KYES DD 787
Commander A. J. Tallet

HOLLISTER DD 788
Commander W. A. Knopp

EVERSOLE DD 789
Commander R. R. Pohli

SHELTON DD 790
Commander H. F. Nelson

PRESTON DD 795
Commander J. A. Coiner

CHEVALIER DD 805
Commander G. L. Palatini

HIGBEE DD 806
Commander J. D. Standard Jr.

BENNER DD 807

DENNIS J. BUCKLEY DD 808
Commander A. G. Luskin

CORRY DD 817
Commander C. S. Snodgrass

NEW DD 818
Commander H. C. Arnold

HOLDER DD 819
Commmander T. E. Wynkoop

RICH DD 820
Commmander E. C. Whelan Jr.

JOHNSTON DD 821
Commander D. F. Anglim Jr.

ROBERT H. McCARD DD 822
Commander G. W. M. Brown

SAMUEL B. ROBERTS DD 823
Commander S. O. Jones Jr.

BASILONE DD 824
Commander H. S. Keller Jr.

CARPENTER DD 825
Commander N. H. Kay

AGERHOLM DD 826
Commander R. T. Shultz

ROBERT A. OWENS DD 827
Commander R. F. Ackerman

MYLES C. FOX DD 829
Commander J. D, McLuckie

EVERETT F. LARSON DD 830
Commander A. W. Rilling

GOODRICH DD 831
Commander R. H. Baysinger Jr.

HANSON DD 832
Commander R, J. Raffaele

HERBERT J. THOMAS DD 833
Commander J. W. Bowen

TURNER DD 834
Commander A. Chertarian

CHARLES P. CECIL DD 835
Commander K. L. Meek

GEORGE K. MACKENZIE DD 836

SARSFIELD DD 837
Commander R. J. Reeder

ERNEST G. SMALL DD 838
Commander R. E. Mann

POWER DD 839
Commander D. C. Murphy

GLENNON DD 840
Commander G. M. Johnson

NOA DD 841
Commander H. D. Mann Jr.

FISKE DD 842
Commander J. S. Brunson

WARRINGTON DD 843
Commander E. J. Reiher

PERRY DD 844
Commander Curtis A. Sorenson

BAUSELL DD 845
Commander R. F. Stadler Jr.

OZBOURN DD 846
Commander R. L. Grove

ROBERT L. WILSON DD 847
Commander W. P. St. Lawrence Jr.

RICHARD E. KRAUS DD 849
Commander M. B. Humber

JOSEPH P. KENNEDY JR. DD 850
Commander Thomas A. Rodgers

RUPERTUS DD 851
Commander L. W. Freerman

LEONARD F. MASON DD 852
Commander Roger E. Ekman

CHARLES H. ROAN DD 853
Commander M. L. Slankard

BRISTOL DD 857
Commander Joseph E. Guion

FRED T. BERRY DD 858
Commander C. D. Armond

NORRIS DD 859
Commander W. J. Longhi

McCAFFERY DD 860
Commander A. F. Martin

HARWOOD DD 861
Commander C. D. Hopkins

VOLEGESANG DD 862
Commander R. A. Campbell

STEINAKER DD 863
Commander H. H. Sacks

HAROLD J. ELLISON DD 864
Commander I. K. Heyward IV

CHARLES R. WARE DD 865
Commander F. W. Cronin

CONE DD 866
Commander A. Codey

STRIBLING DD 867
Commander S. W. Coston Jr.

BROWNSON DD 868
Commander W. C. Glovanetti

ARNOLD J. ISBELL DD 869
Commander F. S. Adair

FECHTELER DD 870
Commander L. A. Dwyer

DAMATO DD 871
Commander L. T. Furey

FORREST ROYAL DD 872
Commander W. B. Latham

HAWKINS DD 873
Commander M. H. Lasell

DUNCAN DD 874
Commander C. R. Stephan

HENRY W. TUCKER DD 875
Commander S. D. Kully

ROGERS DD 876
Commander G. L. Hart

PERKINS DD 877
Commander L. H. Hamel

VESOLE DD 878
Commander P. H. Orvis

LEARY DD 879
Commander R. G. Clark

DYESS DD 880
Commander W. F. Sheeham Jr.

BORDELON DD 881
Commander T. D. Shearer

FURSE DD 882
Commander M. T. Greeley

NEWMAN K. PERRY DD 883
Commander C. W. Streightiff

FLOYD B. PARKS DD 884

JOH R. CRAIG DD 885
Commander C. L. Bekkedahl

ORLECK DD 886
Commander R. O. Gooden

BRINKLEY BASS DD 887

STICKELL DD 888
Commander Alvin J. Buchanan Jr.

O'HARE DD 889
Commander M. Gode

MEREDITH DD 890
Commander J. E. Withrow Jr.

FORREST SHERMAN DD 931
Commander R. E. Flynn

BARRY DD 933
Commander T. H. Sherman Jr.

DAVIS DD 937
Commander E. J. Mountford

JONAS INGRAM DD 938
Commander L. L. Hawkins

MANLEY DD 940
Commander W. R. Yetman

DU PONT DD 941
Commander R. H. Small

BIGELOW DD 942

BLANDY DD 943
Commander D. W. Simons

MULLINNIX DD 944
Commander D. W. Knutson

HULL DD 945
Commander F. N. Hannegan

EDSON DD 946
Commander J. S. Holmes

MORTON DD 948
Commander W. P. Hughes Jr.

RICHARD S. EDWARDS DD 950
Commander J. E. Murray Jr.

TURNER JOY DD 951
Commander R. M. Sudduth

ATTACK SUBMARINES

TANG SS 563
Lieutenant Commander E. R. Easton

TRIGGER SS 564
Lieutenant Commander C. H. Garrison

TROUT SS 566
Lieutenant Commander J. H. Slough

GUDGEON SS 567

HARDER SS 568
Lieutenant Commander W. A. Coll

SAILFISH SS 572
Commander J. P. Gleason

SALMON SS 573
Commander A. A. Hastoglis

DARTER SS 576
Commander D. E. Donovan

BARBEL SS 580
Lieutenant Commander J. W. Renard

BLUEBACK SS 581
Lieutenant Commander M. H. Munsey

BONEFISH SS 582
Lieutenant Commander J. W. Blanchard

NAUTILUS SSN 571
Commander N. E. Griggs

SEAWOLF SSN 575
Commander R. D. Griffiths

SKATE SSN 578

SWORDFISH SSN 579
Commander R. C. Bilyeu

SARGO SSN 583
Commander K. L. Highfill

SEADRAGON SSN 584
Commander A. S. Glazier

SKIPJACK SSN 585
Commander J. R. Devereaux Jr.

TRITON SSN 586

HALIBUT SSN 587
Commander C. E. Moore

SCAMP SSN 588
Lieutenant Commander D. M. Smith

SCULPIN SSN 590
Commander P. W. Lyon

SHARK SSN 591
Commander D. L. Self

SNOOK SSN 592

PERMIT SSN 594
Commander F. H. Kollmorgen

PLUNGER SSN 595

BARB SSN 596

TULLIBEE SSN 597

POLLACK SSN 603
Commander D. D. Boyle

HADDO SSN 604
Commander G. W. Muench

JACK SSN 605
Commander D. G. Smith

TINOSA SSN 606
Commander F. W. Victor

DACE SSN 607

GUARDFISH SSN 612
Commander H. A. Benton

FLASHER SSN 613
Commander J. C. Johnson

GREELING SSN 614
Commander A. B. Scott Jr.

GATO SSN 615
Commander L. Burkhardt III

HADDOCK SSN 621
Commander S. J. Anderson

STURGEON SSN 637

WHALE SSN 638
Commander W. M. Wolff Jr.

TAUTOG SSN 639
Commander B. G. Balderston

GRAYLING SSN 646
Commander C. R. Baron

POGY SSN 647

ASPRO SSN 648
Commander R. R. Wight

SUNFISH SSN 649
Commander R. L. Thompson

PARGO SSN 650

QUEENFISH SSN 651
Commander J. B. Richard

PUFFER SSN 652
Commander J. M. Will Jr.

RAY SSN 653
Commander J. S. Hurt

SAND LANCE SSN 650

LAPON SSN 661
Commander C. M. Mack

GURNARD SSN 662

HAMMERHEAD SSN 663
Commander E. F. Murphy Jr.

SEA DEVIL SSN 664
Commander R. A. Currier

GUITTARRO SSN 665

HAWKBILL SSN 666
Commander Christopher H. Brown

BERGALL SSN 667

SPADEFISH SSN 668

SEAHORSE SSN 669

FINBACK SSN 670

NARWHAL SSN 671

PINTADO SSN 672

FLYING FISH SSN 673

TREPANG SSN 674

BLUEFISH SSN 675

BILLFISH SSN 676

DRUM SSN 677

FIRE SUPPORT SHIPS

NEW JERSEY BB 62
Captain J. E. Snyder Jr.

BOSTON CA 69
Captain R. A. Komorowski

CANBERRA CA 70
Captain W. H. Bagley

ST. PAUL CA 73
Captain Hugh G. Nott

NEWPORT NEWS CA 148
Captain Joseph E. Bonds

COAST GUARD CUTTERS

BIBB WHEC 31
Commander Ralph R. Pruett

CAMPBELL WHEC 32
Commander Sydeny M. Shuman

DUANE WHEC 33
Commander Roger F. Erdmann

INGHAM WHEC 35
Captain N. D. Westfall

SPENCER WHEC 36
Captain Marc Welliver II

TANEY WHEC 37
Commander R. E. Ogin

OWASCO WHEC 39
Commander Charles F. Juechter

WINNEBAGO WHEC 40
Commander Daniel S. Bishop

CNAUTAUQUA WHEC 41
Commander Robert b. Grant

SEBAGO WHEC 42
Commander D. C. Goodwin Jr.

WACHUSETT WHEC 44
Commander Nathaniel C. Spadafora

ESCANABA WHEC 64
Commander P. C. Gaucher

WINONA WHEC 65
Commander Rrobert A. Moss

KLAMATH WHEC 66
Commander R. C. Donaldson

MINNETOKA WHEC 67
Commander David F. Lauth

ANDROSCOGGIN WHEC 68
Commander Milo A. Jordan

MENDOTA WHEC 69
Captain C. S. Marple

PONTCHARTRAIN WHEC 70
Commander C. Reinberg Jr.

CHINCOTEAGUE WHEC 375
Commander G. P. Sherburne

ABSECON WHEC 374
Commander P. W. Meyer

ROCKAWAY WAGO 377
Commander William T. Adams

YAKUTAT WHEC 380
Commander William c. Nolan

BARATARIA WHEC 381
Commander Joseph W. E. Ward

BERING STRAIT WHEC 382
Commander John P. Mihlbauerk

CASTLE ROCK WHEC 383
Commander Thomas F. McKenna Jr.

COOK INLET WHEC 384
Commander Richard K. Simonds

McCULLOCH WHEC 386
Commander K. D. Albritton

GRESHAM WHEC 387
Commander N. E. Fernald

UNIMAK WHEC 379
Commander Henry A. Cretella

HAMILTON WHEC 715
Captain James H. B. Morton

DALLAS WHEC 716
Captain Walter F. Guy

MELLON WHEC 717
Captain Ottis H. Abney

CHASE WHEC 718
Commander Wayne E. Caldwell

BOUTWELL WHEC 719
Captain Robert A. Schulz

SHERMAN WHEC 720
Captain Paul A. Lutz

GALLANTIN WHEC 721
Captain Kevin L. Mosher

MORGENTHAU WHEC 722
Captain James H. MacDonald

RUSH WHEC 723
Captain Randolph Ross Jr.

GLACIER WAGB 4
Captain E. E. McCroy

STORIS WAGB 38
Commander J. H. Byrd Jr.

MACKINAW WAGB 83
Captain D. F. Unsinn

STATEN ISLAND WAGB 278
Captain Eugene F. Walsh

SOUTHWIND WAGB 280
Commander Edward D. Cassidy

WESTWIND WAGB 281
Captain J. S. Thuma

NORTHWIND WAGB 282
Captain D. J. McCann
BURTON ISLAND WAGB 283
Captain F. J. Hancox

EDISTO WAGB 284
Captain Henry E. Steel

RELIANCE WMEC 615
Commander P. T. Anderson

DILIGENCE WMEC 616
Commander E. H. Daniels

VIGILANT WMEC 617
Lieutenant commander Ralph W. Eustis

ACTIVE WMEC 618
Commander William E. Smith

CONFIDENCE WMEC 619
Commander C. J. Blondin

RESOLUTE WMEC 620
Commander J. L. Smith
VALIANT WMEC 621
Commander K. R. Meade

COURAGEOUS WMEC 622
Commander J. C. Morrow

STEADFAST WMEC 623
Commander S. B. Vaughan

DAUNTLESS WMEC 624
Commander H. H. Istock

VENTUROUS WMEC 625
Commander J. L. Steinmetz Jr.

DEPENDABLE WMEC 626
Commander R. P. Cueroni

VIGOROUS WMEC 627
Commander George H. Wagner

DURABLE WMEC 628
Commander P. E. Schroeder

DECISIVE WMEC 629
Commander Eugene A. Delaney

ALERT WMEC 630
Commander Charles F. McFadden

VENEZUELA

NAVAL HIGH COMMAND

COMMANDER IN CHIEF OF THE NAVY
Rear-Admiral Jose Constantino Seijas Villalobos

CHIEF OF NAVAL STAFF
Rear-Admiral Alfredo Garcia Landaeta

FLEET COMMANDER
Rear-Admiral Miguel Benatuil Guastini

COMMANDER OF NAVAL BASE NO. 1
Rear Admiral Armando Perez Leffmans

U.S.A.

DILLON, REAR-ADMIRAL (SELECTEE) JOHN "G" (CIVIL ENGINEER CORPS)
CURRENT DUTY STATION: Commander, 3rd Naval Construction Brigade (March 1969)
DATE OF BIRTH: 1919
EDCUATION: 1960 Naval War College
FIRST COMMISSIONED: 16th June, 1942
PROMOTED TO: Rear Admiral, selected for promotion 6th June, 1968
COMMANDS: 1944 89th Naval Construction Battalion; 1966-1967 Southeast Division, Naval Facilities Engineering Command/District Civil Engineer and O-in-C of Construction, 6th Naval District
HOME ADDRESS: 3904 Terrace Drive, Annandale, Virginia 22003

ITALY

DI MENTO, GENERALE ISPETTORE GENIO NAVALE G. ITALIAN NAVY
DECORATIONS: Medaglia Mauriziana Grande Officiale; 1 Croce al merito di guerra Medaglia comm. guerra 1940-1943 (3 campagne); Medaglia comm. guerra liberazione 1943-1945 (2 campagne)
DATE OF BIRTH: 27 July, 1905
DATE OF PROMOTION: 22 September, 1965
OFFICIAL ADDRESS: Navalcostarmi, Rome

THAILAND

DITBANJONG, CAPTAIN T., ROYAL THAI NAVY
DECORATIONS: Knight Commander (Second Class) of The Most Noble Order of The Crown of Thai 1968; Commander (Third Class) of The Most Exalted Order of The White Elephant 1964; The Chakra Mala Medal 1959; The 25th Century of Buddhism Medal 1957; The Coronation Medal 1950
PRESENT APPOINTMENT: The Thai Naval Attache, Washington, D.C. 1 September, 1968
DATE OF BIRTH: 18 January 1926
EDUCATION: Royal Thai Naval Academy; U.S. Fleet Gunnery and Torpedo School (Anti-Aircraft Control Course); Royal Thai Naval Officer College (Staff Course) U.S. Naval War College (Naval Command Course); Royal Thai Armed Forces Staff College
DATE OF PROMOTION: 1 October, 1964
PRINCIPAL COMMANDS AT SEA: 1956-1957 Commanding Officer, HTMS Chumphone; 1958 Commanding Officer, HTMS Maeklong
OTHER PREVIOUS APPOINTMENTS OF NOTE: O/C, Operations Section, Fleet Headquarters 1961; O/C Training Section, Operations Department, RTN Headquarters 1964; Deputy Commander, Fleet Training Command 1966
OFFICIAL ADDRESS: Royal Thai Embassy. 2300 Kalorama Road, N.W. Washington, D.C. 20008 *Telephone:* 667-1446
PRIVATE ADDRESS: 6820 Millwood Road, Bethesda, Maryland, 20034

U.S.A.

DOBIE, REAR-ADMIRAL ERNEST WILLIAM, JR. US NAVY
CURRENT DUTY STATION: Commander, Cruiser-Destroyer Flotilla 2 (October 1968)
DATE OF BIRTH: 1916
EDUCATION: 1940 Naval Academy; 1946 Naval Academy, Naval Postgraduate School; 1960 Naval War College
FIRST COMMISSIONED: 6th June, 1940
PROMOTED TO; Rear Admiral 1st December, 1965
COMMANDS: 1952-1954 Lofberg DD 759; 1960-1961 Destroyer Division 112; 1961-1962 MT Baker AE 4; 1963-1964 Destroyer Squadron 2
HOME ADDRESS: 1632 Dempsey, McLean, Virginia 22101

U.S.A.

DOLAN, REAR-ADMIRAL JOHN WILLIAM, JNR., (ENGINEERING DUTY) US NAVY
CURRENT DUTY STATION: Commander-in-Chief, Atlantic Fleet (October 1967)
DATE OF BIRTH: 1915
EDUCATION: 1939 Naval Academy; 1944 Massachusetts Institute of Technology; 1957 Naval War College
FIRST COMMISSIONED: 1st June, 1939
PROMOTED TO: Rear Admiral 1st January, 1967
COMMANDS: 1963-1965 San Francisco Naval Shipyard; 1965-1967 Long Beach Naval Shipyard

U.S.A.

PORTUGAL

D'OLIVEIRA, COMMODORE R. S. Portuguese Navy
DECORATIONS: Military Merit 1st Class; Grand Officer of AVIS Order; Medal of V centenary of Infante D. Henrique
PRESENT APPOINTMENT: Director of Naval Construction
DATE OF BIRTH: 15 October, 1921
EDUCATION: Degree, Naval Academy; Degree in Naval Architecture, Royal Naval College, Greenwich; Degree in Civil Engineering, University of London Promotion Courses
DATES OF PROMOTION: Joined the Navy, Cadet 16 September, 1940; Ensign 16 September, 1943; Lieutenant Junior Grade 16 September, 1944; Lieutenant 30 August, 1952 Lieutenant Commander 30 August, 1956; Commander 20 October, 1957; Captain 6 September, 1964; Commodore 28 June, 1966
OTHER PREVIOUS APPOINTMENTS OF NOTE: Professor of the Naval Academy; Chief Inspector for the Construction of D.E'S.
OFFICIAL ADDRESS: Director of Naval Construction, Ministério da Marinha, Lisbon
PRIVATE ADDRESS: Av. Luís Bivar, 87-30, Lisbon 1

U.S.A.

DONALDSON, REAR-ADMIRAL JAMES CARMICHAEL, JR. (NAVAL AVIATOR) US NAVY
CURRENT DUTY STATION: Director of Fleet Operations Division, Office of the Chief of Naval Operations (December 1967)
DATE OF BIRTH: 1921
EDUCATION: 1942 Naval Academy; 1953 Naval War College; 1963 Industrial College of the Armed Forces
FIRST COMMISSIONED: 19th June, 1942
PROMOTED TO: Rear Admiral 1st August, 1968
COMMANDS: 1953-1956 Fighter Squadron 71; 1959-1960 Carrier Air Group 1; 1964-1965 Hermitage LSD 34; 1965-1966 Hancock CVA 19
HOME ADDRESS: 3406 Rose Lane, Falls Church, Virginia

U.S.A.

DORNIN, REAR-ADMIRAL MARSHALL EDGAR, US NAVY
CURRENT DUTY STATION: Commandant, 11th Naval District/additional duty; Commander, Naval Base, San Diego (September 1967)
DATE OF BIRTH: 1908
EDUCATION: 1930 Naval Academy; 1939 Naval Academy, Naval Postgraduate School; 1943 Fleet Sound School, Key West; 1951 Naval War College
FIRST COMMISSIONED: 5th June, 1930
PROMOTED TO: Rear Admiral 1st January, 1958
COMMANDS: 1943-1944 Abbot DD 629; 1949-1950 Destroyer Division 162; 1953-1954 Mellette APA 156; 1956-1957 Des Moines CA 134; 1959-1961 Destroyer Flotilla 3 and Destroyer Development Group, Pacific; 1961-1963 Superintendent, Naval Postgraduate School, Monterey; 1963-1965 Cruiser-Destroyer Force, Pacific Fleet; 1965-1967 Operational Test and Evaluation Force

PORTUGAL

DOS SANTOS, REAR-ADMIRAL L. H., PORTUGEUSE NAVY
DECORATIONS: MMo/sd c/p 1965; MMp/sd, 1955; MM/mm 1a cl. 1947; g. of. Aviz 1959; MMo/ce 1959; of. OLMA 1960; g. of. OMNB 1967; MMTB 1967; g. cr. OMNE d. br. 1966; com OLHF 1961; of. OCR 1937; MSNp/cah 1940; OCVA 1937; MCo/IDH 1960; MC/C-NA 1965
PRESENT APPOINTMENT: Vice-Chief of Naval Staff,Portugal (1965)
DATE OF BIRTH: 3 November, 1904
EDUCATION: Naval Academy; Gunnery Specialization; Elementary course on Naval Warfare; Senior course on Naval Warfare
DATES OF PROMOTION: 1923 Midhsipman; 1926 Ensign; 1928 Lieutenant Junior; 1936 Lieutenant; 1946 Lieutenant Commander; 1953 Commander; 1959 Captain; 1960 Commodore; 1963 Rear-Admiral
PRINCIPAL COMMANDS AT SEA: 1942-1943 Aux. ship Almirante Schultz; 1950-1953 D.E. Douro; 1959-1960 F.F. Afonso de Albuquerque; 1960 Escort's Flotilla; 1961 Flag Officer, Cabo Verde and Guiné Area; 1963-1965 Flag Officer, Angola Area
OTHER PREVIOUS APPOINTMENTS OF NOTE: Naval War Institute, teacher on Tactics 1943-1945; teacher on Strategy 1955-1957; Inspector of Gunnery, England 1932-1934 and 1938; Chief of Staff to Home Naval Force 1953-1954; Naval Attache in Washington and Ottawa 1957-1959; President of the Joint Portuguese Commission to the Peninsular Staffs 1965-1969
OFFICIAL ADDRESS: Estado-Maior da Armada—Lisbon 2 Portugal *Telephone:* 368961
PRIVATE ADDRESS: Rua Dom Joao V, 27 r. c. E.—Lisbon 2, Portugal *Telephone:* 682252

U.S.A.

DOWD, REAR-ADMIRAL (SELECTEE) WALLACE RUTHERFORD, JNR. (SUPPLY CORPS) US NAVY
CURRENT DUTY STATION: Commanding Officer, Naval Supply Center, Charleston, South Carolina
DATE OF BIRTH: 1921
EDUCATION: 1942 Naval Supply Corps School, Harvard University; 1949 Stanford University; 1955 Naval War College
FIRST COMMISSIONED: 11th July, 1942
PROMOTED TO: Rear Admiral, selected for promotion 6th June, 1

U.K.

DUFFAY, COMMANDER G. R. T., ROYAL NAVY
PRESENT APPOINTMENT: Office of Naval Secretary
DATE OF BIRTH: 28 January, 1927
EDUCATION: Monkton School
DATES OF PROMOTIONS: Commander 30 December, 1964
PRINCIPAL COMMANDS AT SEA: Urchin 1963-1964; Rhyl 1967-1969
OTHER PREVIOUS APPOINTMENTS OF NOTE: Training Commander, BRNC, Dartmouth 1964-1967

UNITED KINGDOM

DUNBAR-NASMITH, REAR-ADMIRAL D. A., ROYAL NAVY
DECORATIONS: D.S.C. November 1942
PRESENT APPOINTMENT: Naval Secretary 2 November, 1967
DATE OF BIRTH: 21 February, 1921
EDUCATION: Lockers Park; RNC Dartmouth
DATES OF PROMOTIONS: Lieutenant 16 April 1940; Lieutenant Commander 16 April 1948; Commander 30 June 1961; Captain 30 June 1958; Rear-Admiral 7 July, 1967
PRINCIPAL COMMANDS AT SEA: 1951-1952 HMS Enard Bay; 1954-1956 HMS Alert; 1961-1963 HMS Berwick
OTHER PREVIOUS APPOINTMENTS OF NOTE: Director of Defence Plans, Ministry of Defence 1963-1965; Commodore Amphibious Forces 1966-1967
OFFICIAL ADDRESS: Ministry of Defence, Main Building, Whitehall, London S.W.1.
PRIVATE ADDRESS: Glen Rothes, Rothes, Morayshire

U.S.A.
DUNCAN, VICE-ADMIRAL CHARLES KENNEY, US NAVY
CURRENT DUTY STATION: Chief of Naval Personnel/Deputy Chief of Naval Operations (April 1968)
DATE OF BIRTH: 1911
EDUCATION: 1933 Naval Academy; 1948 Armed Forces Staff College
FIRST COMMISSIONED: 1st June, 1933
PROMOTED TO: Rear Admiral 1st July, 1959; Vice Admiral 1st June, 1965
COMMANDS: 1943-1944 Wilson DD 408; 1951-1952 Destroyer Division 62; 1955-1956 Chilton APA 38, 1958-1959 Amphibious Group 1; 1959-1961 Amphibious Training Command, Pacific Fleet; 1961-1962 US Naval Base, Subic Bay, Philippines; 1964-1965 Cruiser Destroyer Force, Atlantic Fleet; 1965-1976 Amphibious Force, Atlantic Fleet; 1967-1968 2nd Fleet

U.K.
DUNN, COMMANDER A. J. ROYAL NAVY
PRESENT APPOINTMENT: Staff of R.N.T.S. 30 June, 1969
DATE OF BIRTH: 1 June, 1931
EDUCATION: RNC Dartmouth
DATES OF PROMOTIONS: Commander 30 June 1967
PRINCIPAL COMMANDS AT SEA: HMS Pellew 1967-1969
OTHER PREVIOUS APPOINTMENTS OF NOTE: 1st Lieutenant HMY Britannia 1963-1965
OFFICIAL ADDRESS: RNTS Woolwich SE18
PRIVATE ADDRESS: Burley, Harbour Way, Chidham, Chichester, Sussex

U.S.A.
DYBDAL, REAR-ADMIRAL VICTOR ASLE, US NAVY
CURRENT DUTY STATION:
Commander, Amphibious Group 1 (August 1969)
DATE OF BIRTH: 1914
EDUCATION: 1938 Naval Academy; 1949 Fleet Sonar School, San Diego; 1950 Armed Forces Staff College; 1954 Naval War College; 1958 National War College; 1964 George Washington University
FIRST COMMISSIONED: 2nd June, 1938
PROMOTED TO: Rear Admiral; 1st January, 1967
COMMANDS: 1944-1945 Drayton DD 366; 1946-1948 Fleet Gunnery and Torpedo School, San Diego; 1948-1949 Fleet Training Center, San Diego; 1950-1951 Damato DDE 871; 1955-1957 Escort Squadron 16; 1961-1962 Destroyer Squadron 7
OFFICIAL ADDRESS: FPO New York
HOME ADDRESS: 420 Underhill Place, Alexandria, Virginia 22305

UNITED KINGDOM
EASTON,.REAR-ADMIRAL, I., ROYAL NAVY
DECORATIONS: O.B.E. 1945; D.S.C. 1942; A.F.C. 1942
PRESENT APPOINTMENT: Assistant Chief of the Naval Staff (Policy) 12 June, 1969
DATE OF BIRTH: 27 November 1917
EDUCATION: RNC Dartmouth
DATES OF PROMOTIONS: Rear-Admiral 7 July, 1969
PRINCIPAL COMMANDS AT SEA: 1968-1969 HMS Triumph
OTHER PREVIOUS APPOINTMENTS OF NOTE: BJSM Weshington 1955-1957; Staff of Flag Officer Aircraft Carriers 1958-1960; Assistant Director of Tactical Weapons Policy 1960-1962; HMAS Watson 1962-1964; Templer Committee, Rationalisation of Air Power 1965; Director of Naval Tactical Weapons Policy 1966-1968
OFFICIAL ADDRESS: Ministry of Defence, Main Building, Whitehall, London SW1 *Telephone:* 01-930 7022 ext. 6070
PRIVATE ADDRESS: Causeway Cottage, Freshwater, Isle of Wight

U.S.A.
EDWARDS, REAR-ADMIRAL RODERICK YERKES, US NAVY
CURRENT DUTY STATION: Chief, Office of Public and International Affairs (June 1967)
DATE OF BIRTH: 1909
EDUCATION: 1941 New York Teachers College
FIRST COMMISSIONED: 5th December, 1933
PROMOTED TO: Rear Admiral 1st July, 1967
COMMANDS: 1943-1945 Merchant Marine Details; 1957 Marine Inspection Office, Philadelphia; 1963-1966 Marine Inspection, 12th Coast Guard District, San Francisco
HOME ADDRESS: 4501 Arlington Blvd., Arlington, Virginia

PERU
ELIAS, REAR ADMIRAL F. APARICIO, PERUVIAN NAVY
DECORATIONS: Caballero del Libertador; Venezuela, 1945; Commendador de la Orden Naval Almirante Padilla; Columbia 1960;Orden al Mérito Naval Segunda Clase, Venezuela 1962; Gran Oficial de la Orden Militar de Ayacucho, Peru 1967 Gran Oficial de la Cruz Peruana al Mérito Naval, 1967
PRESENT APPOINTMENT: Naval Attaché, Embassy of Peru, 1 November, 1968
DATE OF BIRTH: 12 April, 1914
EDUCATION: Peruvian Naval Academy; Submarine School in Perú; Student in the U.S.N., Hydrography Office in Suitland, Md.; USN Submarine School at New London, Conn.; PCO Submarine School; Student in the Peruvian Naval War College; Student in the Peruvian National War College (CAEM)
DATES OF PROMOTION: Midshipman March 25 1930; Ensign 30 December, 1936; Lieutenant Jg. 12 February, 1940; Senior Lieutenant 2 February 1942; Lieutenant Commander 1 February, 1946; Commander 1 February 1953; Captain 1 February 1959; Rear Admiral 1 January 1967
PRINCIPAL COMMANDS AT SEA: B.A.P. Tiburon; Commandidng Officer Cruiser B.A.P. Bolognesi
OTHER PREVIOUS APPOINTMENTS OF NOTE: General Secretary of the Ministry of Marine President of the Pedrmanent Court Martial of the Navy Staff of the Peruvian National War College (CAEM) Director of Hydrography; Chief of the Staff of the Peruvian Navy; General Inspector of the Peruvian Navy
OFFICIAL ADDRESS: 1315-16th St. N.W. Suite 105 234-3432
PRIVATE ADDRESS: 1114 Stephalee Lane, Luxmanor, Rockville, Md. 20852. *Telephone:* 881-4418

U.S.A.
ELLIS, VICE-ADMIRAL WILLIAM BROMFIELD, US NAVY
CURRNET DUTY STATION: Commander, 1st Coast Guard District, Boston (June 1968)
DATE OF BIRTH: 1914
EDUCATION: 1936 Coast Guard Academy
FIRST COMMISSIONED: 6th August, 1936
PROMOTED TO: Rear Admiral 1st July, 1966
COMMANDS: 1943-1945 Pettit; 1945 Escort Division 20; 1951-1952 Lowe; 1956-1958 Coos Bay

UNITED KINGDOM
EMPSON, REAR-ADMIRAL L. D., ROYAL NAVY
DECORATIONS: C.B. 1969
PRESENT APPOINTMENT: Assistant Chief of Naval Staff (Operations and Air) 1968-1969. Appointed Commander, Far East Fleet in acting rank of Vice Admiral to take effect in September 1969
DATE OF BIRTH: 29 October, 1918
EDUCATION: Eastbourne College and Clare College, Cambridge (B.A.)
DATES OF PROMOTIONS: 1952 Commander; 1957 Captain; 1967 Rear-Admiral
PRINCIPAL COMMANDS AT SEA: 1959-1960 HMS Apollo; 1963-1965 HMS Eagle
OTHER PREVIOUS APPOINTMENTS OF NOTE: Naval Assistant to First Sea Lord (Admiral Mountbatten) as Captain 1957-1959; Flag Officer Aircraft Carrier 1967-1968
OFFICIAL ADDRESS: M.O.D. Main Building, London S.W.1. *Telephone:* 01-930-7022 ext. 6657
PRIVATE ADDRESS:.Deep Field, West Street, Hambledon, Hants.

U.S.A.
ENGEL, REAR-ADMIRAL ARTHUR BRIGHT, US NAVY
CURRENT DUTY STATION: Superintendent, Coast Guard Academy (June 1967)
DATE OF BIRTH: 1914
EDUCATION: 1938 Coast Guard Academy; 1945 Massachusetts Institute of Technology
FIRST COMMISSIONED: 2nd June, 1938
PROMOTED TO: Rear Admiral 1st July, 1967
COMMANDS: 1959-1961 Klamath; 1965-1967 Coast Guard Yard, Curtis Bay

U.S.A.
ENGEL, REAR-ADMIRAL BENJAMIN FRANKLIN (NAVAL AVIATOR) US NAVY
CURRENT DUTY STATION: Commander, 14th Coast Guard District, Honolulu (April 1967)
DATE OF BIRTH: 1914
EDUCATION: 1938 Coast Guard Academy; 1957 Naval War College
FIRST COMMISSIONED: 2nd June, 1938
PROMOTED TO: Rear Admiral 1st May, 1967
COMMANDS: 1953-1955 Air Detachment, Kodiak; 1955-1957 Air Station, Traverse City; 1960-1963 Coast Guard Air Station, Brooklyn

U.S.A.
ENGEN, REAR-ADMIRAL (SELECTEE) DONALD DAVENPORT, US NAVY
CURRENT DUTY STATION: Head, Aviation Plans Branch, Office of the Deputy Chief of Naval Operations (September 1968)
DATE OF BIRTH: 1924
EDUCATION: 1948 University of California at Los Angeles; 1951 General Line School; 1966 Naval Justice School, Naval War College
FIRST COMMISSIONED: 9th June, 1943
PROMOTED TO: Rear Admiral, selected for promotion on 6th June, 1969
MAJOR AWARDS: Navy Cross
COMMANDS: 1960-1961 Fighter Squadron 21; 1962-1963 Carrier Air Group 11; 1964-1965 Kaimai AE 16; 1966-1967 America CVA 66
OFFICIAL ADDRESS: The Pentagon, Washington, DC 20350
HOME ADDRESS: 1740 Casa Grande, Pasadena, California

U.S.A.
ENGER, REAR-ADMIRAL WALTER MELVIN (CIVIL ENGINEER CORPS) US NAVY
CURRENT DUTY STATION: Commander, Naval Facilities Engineering Command & Chief of Civil Engineers of the Navy (September 1969)
DATE OF BIRTH: 1941
FIRST COMMISSIONED: 27th August, 1941
PROMOTED TO: Rear Admiral 10th August, 1965
HOME ADDRESS: 1200 N. Nash Street, Arlington, Virginia 22209

U.S.A.
ENSEY, VICE-ADMIRAL LOT, US NAVY
CURRENT DUTY STATION: Director, J-4 (Logistics), Joint Chiefs of Staff (September 1967)
DATE OF BIRTH: 1908
EDUCATION: 1930 Naval Academy; 1948 Armed Forces Staff College; 1952 Naval War College
FIRST COMMISSIONED: 5th June, 1930
PROMOTED TO: Rear Admiral 1st February, 1958; Vice Admiral 1st September, 1964
COMMANDS: 1942 Upshur DD 144; 1942-1943 Corry DD 817; 1944-1945 Blue DD 744; 1948-1949 Destroyer Division 172; 1949 Destroyer Division 112; 1954-1955 Achernar AKA 53; 1955-1956 Destroyer Squadron 2; 1963-1964 Cruiser-Destroyer Flotilla 9
OFFICIAL ADDRESS: The Pentagon, Washington, DC 20301
HOME ADDRESS: Quarters "A", Navy Yard, Washington, DC

U.S.A.
EPES, REAR-ADMIRAL HORACE HARDAWAY, JNR., (NAVAL AVIATOR) US NAVY
CURRENT DUTY STATION: Chief, Far East Division, J-5, Joint Chiefs of Staff
DATE OF BIRTH: 1917
EDUCATION: 1937 College of Engineering, New York University; 1948 General Line School; 1959 Naval War College
FIRST COMMISSIONED: 26th October, 1940
PROMOTED TO: Rear Admiral 1st October, 1966
COMMANDS: 1948-1951 Fighter Squadron 33; 1953-1954 Air Development Squadron 5; 1954 Carrier Air Group 15; 1961-1963 Thetis Bay LPH 6; 1963-1964 Kitty Hawk CVA 63; 1967-1968 Carrier Division 1
OFFICIAL ADDRESS: The Pentagon, Washington, DC 20301
HOME ADDRESS: 115 Loring Avenue, Pelham, New York

U.S.A.
ERLY, REAR-ADMIRAL ROBERT BROUSSARD, US NAVY
CURRENT DUTY STATION: Deputy Chief of Staff and Deputy Chief of Staff for Plans & Operations, Atlantic Fleet (June 1969)
DATE OF BIRTH: 1914
EDUCATION: 1937 Naval Academy; 1953 Armed Forces Staff College; 1963 National War College
FIRST COMMISSIONED: 3rd June, 1937
PROMOTED TO: Rear Admiral 1st July, 1965
COMMANDS: 1944-1945 Phelps DD 360; 1950-1952 James C. Owens DD 776; 1958-1959 Paul Revere APA 248; 1961-1962 Amphibious Squadron 5; 1965-1966 Amphibious Group 3
OFFICIAL ADDRESS: Norfolk, Virginia 23511
HOME ADDRESS 608 East Beach, Gulfport, Mississippi

U.S.A.
ESCH, REAR-ADMIRAL ARTHUR GERALD, US NAVY
CURRENT DUTY STATION: Assistant Chief of Staff for Logistics, Commander-in-Chief Allied Forces Southern Europe (July 1968)
DATE OF BIRTH: 1917
EDUCATION: 1940 Naval Academy; 1949 Naval Postgraduate School; 1964 National War College
FIRST COMMISSIONED: 6th June, 1940
PROMOTED TO: Rear Admiral 1st January, 1969
COMMANDS: 1951-1952 Power DD 839; 1959-1960 Destroyer Division 282; 1964-1965 Destroyer Squadron 2
OFFICIAL ADDRESS: (Naples, Italy) FPO New York 09524
HOME ADDRESS: 204 Catherine, Washington, Illinois

U.S.A.
ETTER, REAR-ADMIRAL HARRY STOUGH (MEDICAL CORPS) US NAVY
CURRENT DUTY STATION: Assistant Chief for Plans and Logistics, Bureau of Medicine and Surgery (July 1967)
DATE OF BIRTH: 1915
EDUCATION: 1940 Duke University; 1956 Naval War College
FIRST COMMISSIONED: 20th March, 1941
PROMOTED TO: Rear Admiral 1st January, 1967
OFFICIAL ADDRESS: Potomac Annex, Washington, DC 20390
HOME ADDRESS: 27 North Washington Street, Shippensburg, Pensylvania

UNITED KINGDOM
EVANS, REAR-ADMIRAL G. H., ROYAL NAVY
DECORATIONS: C.B. 1968
PRESENT APPOINTMENT: Naval Deputy, Allied Forces Northern Europe, 1966
DATE OF BIRTH: 15 January, 1917
DATES OF PROMOTIONS: 1951 Commander; 1957 Captain; 1966 Rear-Admiral
PRINCIPAL COMMANDS AT SEA: HMS Eggesford 1943-1945; HMS Nepal 1949-1950; HMS Modeste 1954-1955
OTHER PREVIOUS APPOINTMENTS OF NOTE: Director of Naval Recruiting, 1962-1964
OFFICIAL ADDRESS: Allied Forces Northern Europe, Köksas, Norway
Telephone: 55 66 90
PRIVATE ADDRESS: Vale Cottage, North Berwick, East Lothian

U.S.A.
FAHY, REAR-ADMIRAL EDWARD JOSEPH (ENGINEERING DUTY) US NAVY
CURRENT DUTY STATION: Commander, Naval Ship Systems Command (May 1966)
DATE OF BIRTH: 1910
EDUCATION: 1934 Naval Academy; 1943 Naval Postgraduate School
FIRST COMMISSIONED: 31st May, 1934
PROMOTED TO: Rear Admiral 1st April, 1962
COMMANDS: 1944 Plunger SS 179; 1953-1956 Naval Underwater Sound Laboratory New London, Connecticut; 1962-1965 Mare Island Naval Shipyard Vallejo, California; 1965-1966 San Francisco Bay Naval Shipyard
OFFICIAL ADDRESS: Main Navy Building, Washington, DC 20360
HOME ADDRESS: 1454 Shakespear Avenue, Bronx, new York

U.S.A.
FAIRFAX, REAR-ADMIRAL EUGENE GEORGE, (NAVAL AVIATOR) US NAVY
CURRENT DUTY STATION: Commander, Alaskan Sea Frontier: additional duty: Commandant, 17th Naval District; Commander, Fleet Air Alaska (July 1969)
DATE OF BIRTH: 1916
EDUCATION: 1939 Naval Academy; 1948 Naval War College
FIRST COMMISSIONED: 1st June, 1939
PROMOTED TO: Rear Admiral 1st August, 1966
COMMANDS: 1943-1945 Fighting Squadron 11; 1945-1946 Fighting Squadron 98; 1946 Fighting Squadron 11; 1960-1961 Passumpsic AO 107; 1961-1962 Ticonderoga CVA 14
OFFICIAL ADDRESS: FPO Seattle, Washington 98790
HOME ADDRESS 1701 East Blount Street, Pensacola, Florida

U.K.
FARQUHARSON-ROBERTS, S. M.,
DECORATIONS: OBE 1959
PRESENT APPOINTMENT: In command HMS Berry Head 13 January, 1969
DATE OF BIRTH: 3 June, 1922
EDUCATION: Brighton College Courses: Long TAS RNSC, JSSC, SOWC
DATES OF PROMOTIONS: Lieutenant Commander 31 March 1951; Commander 30 June, 1955; Captain 31 December, 1963
PRINCIPAL COMMANDS AT SEA: MTBs 1950-1951; Brocklesby 1952-1953; Berry Head 1969
PREVIOUS APPOINTMENTS: Joined first seagoing ship September 1940; mainly destroyers in Atlantic; TAS Sub specialisation; 1950-1951 Coastal Forces; 1954-1955 Senior Instructor JASS 1954-1955; Loan service Pakistan Navy 1956-1958; BNA, Cairo and Khartoum

U.S.A.
FAUCETT, REAR-ADMIRAL (SELECTEE) RALPH EUGENE (MEDICAL CORPS) US NAVY
CURRENT DUTY STATION: Assistant Chief for Research & Military Medical Specialities, Bureau of Medicine & Surgery (July 1969)
DATE OF BIRTH: 1916
EDUCATION: 1938 Indiana University; 1942 Earlham College, Indiana; 1948 Postgraduate
FIRST COMMISSIONED: 16th January, 1943
PROMOTED TO: Rear Admiral, selected for promotion on 19th June, 1968
OFFICIAL ADDRESS: Potomac Annex, 23rd & E Streets, NW Washington, DC
HOME ADDRESS: Box 41, Perrysville, Indiana

UNITED KINGDOM
FELL, REAR-ADMIRAL M. F., ROYAL NAVY
DECORATIONS: C.B. 1969; D.S.O. 1943; D.S.C. 1944; Bar 1952
PRESENT APPOINTMENT: Flag Officer Carriers and Amphibious Ships (NATO Title Commander Carrier Striking Group Two)
DATE OF BIRTH: 17 January 1918
EDUCATION: Harrow
DATES OF PROMOTIONS: 1952 Commander; 1958 Captain; 1967 Rear-Admiral
PRINCIPAL COMMANDS AT SEA: 1957-1958 HMS Puma; 1961-1963 HMS Loch Killisport; 1965-1966 HMS Ark Royal
OTHER PREVIOUS APPOINTMENTS OF NOTE: Wing Leader No. 7 Naval Fighter Wing 1943-1944; Air Group Commander No. 20 Carrier Air Group, Royal Australian Navy 1950-1952; Commanding Officer, Royal Naval Air Station Lossiemouth 1958-1961; Chief of Staff to the Commander-in-Chief Portsmouth 1963-1965; Flag Officer Gibraltar 1967-1968
OFFICIAL ADDRESS: Fort Southwick, Fareham, Hants.
PRIVATE ADDRESS: Jeremy's Stoughton, Chichester, Hants.

U.S.A.
FERRIS, REAR-ADMIRAL (SELECTEE) JAMES (NAVAL AVIATOR) US NAVY
CURRENT DUTY STATION: Commander, Fleet Air Alameda (June 1969)
DATE OF BIRTH: 1919
EDUCATION: 1955 General Line School; 1959 Industrial College of the Armed Forces
FIRST COMMISSIONED: 5th August, 1942
PROMOTED TO: Rear Admiral, selected for promotion on 6th June, 1969
COMMANDS: 1956-1958 Fighter Squadron 33; 1960-1961 Carrier Air Group 8; 1963-1965 Replacement Carrier Air Wing 4; Commander, Fleet Air Detachment Cecil Field, Florida; 1965-1966 Truckee AD 147; 1968-1969 Coral Sea CVA 43
OFFICIAL ADDRESS: Naval Air Station, Alameda, San Francisco, California 94501
HOME ADDRESS: 154 Columbia Avenue, Nutley, New Jersey

ITALY
FIORINI, CONTRE AMMIRAGLIO G.
DECORATIONS: Medaglio argento and Medaglio bronzo
DATE OF BIRTH: 13 October, 1912
DATE OF PROMOTION: Rear-Admiral 31 December, 1965
OFFICIAL ADDRESS: Comdinav Quattro, Nave Vesuvio, Marinopost, Rome

U.K.
FIRTH, CAPTAIN T. M. B. ROYAL NAVY
PRESENT APPOINTMENT: Senior Officer Reserve Ships (Portsmouth) and Commanding Officer HMS Bellerophon October 1966
DATE OF BIRTH: 25 February, 1923
EDUCATION: Wellington College, Berks
DATES OF PROMOTIONS: Commander 31 December, 1955; Act. Captain 3 October, 1966
PRINCIPAL COMMANDS AT SEA: HMS Hotham 1946; HMS Barrosa 1956-1957; HMS Dainty 1964
OTHER PREVIOUS APPOINTMENTS OF NOTE: HMS Anson 1942-1943; HMS Scourge 1944-1945; Long TAS course HMS Vernon 1947; 2nd & 5th Frigate Squadrons HMS Pelican 1949-1950; HMS Sea Eagle (Londonderry) 1951-1952; Executive Officer RNC Dartmouth 1958-1959; Admiralty 1960-1961; South Atlantic and South American Stn. 1962-1963; NATO C-in-C Channel Staff 1965-1966
OFFICIAL ADDRESS: HMS Bellerophon, Portsmouth. *Telephone:* 22351, ext. 23171 (7)
PRIVATE ADDRESS: Red Thorn, Shawford, Winchester

U.S.A.
FITZPATRICK, REAR-ADMIRAL FRANCIS JOHN, US NAVY
CURRENT DUTY STATION: Assistant Chief of Naval Operations (Communications and Cryptology) and Commander, Naval Communications Command (July 1968)
DATE OF BIRTH: 1916
EDUCATION: 1939 Naval Academy; 1944 Naval Postgraduate School; 1958 Industrial College of the Armed Forces
FIRST COMMISSIONED: 1st June, 1939
PROMOTED TO: Rear Admiral 1st June, 1967
COMMANDS: 1951-1953 Arnold J. Isbell DD 869; 1961-1962 Magoffin APA 199; 1964-1965 Wright CC2
OFFICIAL ADDRESS: The Pentagon, Washington, DC 20350
HOME ADDRESS: Kemmerer, Wyoming

U.S.A.
FLAHERTY, REAR-ADMIRAL (RETIRED) MICHAEL FRANCIS DONALD (NAVAL AVIATOR) US NAVY
CURRENT DUTY STATION: Governor, Naval Home, Philadelphia, Pennsylvania (October 1966)
DATE OF BIRTH: 1904
EDUCATION: 1928 Naval Academy; 1950 Naval War College
FIRST COMMISSIONED: 28th June, 1928
PROMOTED TO: Rear Admiral 1st August, 1956
COMMANDS: 1943 Airship Squadron 23; 1943-1944 Blimp Squadron 14; 1944-1945 Fleet Airship Wing 2; 1950-1951 Noble APA 218; 1953-1954 Wisconsin BB 64; 1957 Cruiser Division 6; 1957-1958 Cruiser Division 2; 1958-1959 Middle East Force; 1961-1962 Cruiser Force Atlantic Fleet, Cruiser Division 6; 1962-1963 Cruiser-Destroyer Flotilla 12; 1963-1966 Training Command, Atlantic Fleet; Commander, Fleet Training Group, Norfolk
OFFICIAL ADDRESS: 24th and Grays Ferry Avenue Philadelphia, Pennsylvania
HOME ADDRESS: 16 Hall Street, North Adams, Massachusetts

U.S.A.
FLANAGAN, REAR-ADMIRAL (SELECTEE) WILLIAM ROBERT (NAVAL AVIATOR) US NAVY
CURRENT DUTY STATION: Deputy Commander, Naval Forces, Vietnam (January 1969)
DATE OF BIRTH: 1921
EDUCATION: 1944 Naval Academy; 1961 Naval War College
FIRST COMMISSIONED: 9th June, 1943
PROMOTED TO: Rear Admiral, selected for promotion 6th June, 1968, authorized to assume title of Rear Admiral
COMMANDS: 1957-1958 Attack Squadron 192; 1964-1965 Montrose APA 212; 1967-1968 Constellation CVA 64
OFFICIAL ADDRESS: FPO San Francisco, California 96626
HOME ADDRESS: Athens, Georgia

U.S.A.
FLEMING, REAR-ADMIRAL ALLAN FOSTER (NAVAL AIVATOR) US NAVY
CURRENT DUTY STATION: Commander, Fleet Air Mediterranean; additional duty: Commander, ASW Force Sixth Fleet; Commander, Fleet Air Meditteranean (June 1969)
DATE OF BIRTH: 1912
EDUCATION: 1936 Naval Academy; 1954 Naval War College
FIRST COMMISSIONED: 4th June, 1936
PROMOTED TO: Rear Admiral 1st October, 1963
COMMANDS: 1944-1946 Naval Radar Training School, St. Simons Island, Georgia; 1950-1952 Air Development Squadron 4; 1958-1959 Pine Island AV12; 1959-1960 Saratoga CVA 60; 1964-1965 Carrier Division 4; Task Force 60
OFFICIAL ADDRESS: FPO New York 09524
HOME ADDRESS: Richland, Wisconsin

U.S.A.
FLUCKEY, REAR-ADMIRAL EUGENE BENNETT, US NAVY
CURRENT DUTY STATION: Commander, Iberian Atlantic Command and Chief, Military Assistance Advisory Group, Portugal (July 1968)
DATE OF BIRTH: 1913
EDUCATION: 1935 Naval Academy; 1943 Naval Postgraduate School; 1959 National War College
FIRST COMMISSIONED: 6th June, 1935
PROMOTED TO: Rear Admiral 1st July, 1961
MAJOR AWARDS: Medal of Honour, Navy Cross with 3 gold stars in lieu of subsequent awards
COMMANDS: 1944-1945 Barb SS 220; 1947-1948 Halfbeak SS 352; 1954-1955 Sperry AS 12; 1955 Submarine Squadron 5; 1955-1956 Submarine Group, Western Pacific; 1956 Submarine Squadron 5; 1960-1961 Amphibious Group 4; 1964-1966 Submarine Force, Pacific Fleet
OFFICIAL ADDRESS: (Lisbon, Portugal) APO New York 09678
HOME ADDRESS: 4306 Newport Avenue, San Diego, California

U.S.A.
FOLEY, REAR-ADMIRAL FRANCIS DRAKE (NAVAL AVIATOR) US NAVY
CURRENT DUTY STATION: Commandant, 3rd Naval District; Commander Naval Base New York (September 1967)
DATE OF BIRTH: 1910
EDUCATION: 1932 Naval Academy; 1953 Naval War College
FIRST COMMISSIONED: 2nd June, 1932
PROMOTED TO: Rear Admiral 24th July, 1958
COMMANDS: 1949-1950 Helicopter Squadron 2; 1955-1956 Salisbury Sound AV 13; 1956-1957 Shangri-La CVA 38; 1960-1961 Carrier Division 1
OFFICIAL ADDRESS: 90 Church Street, New York City 10007
HOME ADDRESS: Jacksonville, Florida

U.S.A.
FOLEY, REAR-ADMIRAL HARRY JOHN PATRICK (SUPPLY CORPS) US NAVY
CURRENT DUTY STATION: Commanding Officer, Naval Aviation Supply Office, Philadelphia, Pennsylvania (July 1966)
DATE OF BIRTH: 1916
EDUCATION: 1938 Naval Academy; 1947 Naval War College
FIRST COMMISSIONED: 2nd June, 1938
PROMOTED TO: Rear Admiral 1st June, 1965
COMMANDS: 1963-1964 Naval Supply Depot, Seattle, Washington
OFFICIAL ADDRESS: 700 Robbins Avenue, Philadelphia, Pennsylvania
HOME ADDRESS: 263 South Olden Avenue, Trenton, New Jersey

U.S.A.
UNITED KINGDOM
FORREST, SURGEON REAR-ADMIRAL W. I. N., ROYAL NAVY
DECORATIONS: Q.H.D.S. 1966
PRESENT APPOINTMENT: Director Naval Dental Services 1968
DATE OF BIRTH: 8 June, 1914
EDUCATION: Christ's Hospital; Guy's Hospital
DATES OF PROMOTIONS: Surgeon (D) 1937; 1960 Surgeon Captain (D); 1968 Surgeon Rear-Admiral (D)
PREVIOUS APPOINTMENT OF NOTE: HMS Birmingham 1937-1940; RN Hospital Bermuda 1947-1949; HMS Eagle 1952-1954; RN Hospital, Haslar 1955-1958; RN Hospital, Malta 1961-1963; Command Dental Surgeon, Portsmouth 1964-1968
OFFICIAL ADDRESS: M.O.D. Empress State Building, London S.W.6 *Telephone:* 385 1244 ext. 2079
PRIVATE ADDRESS: 8 Queen's Road, Waterlooville, Hants.

U.S.A.

FRANKENBERGER, REAR-ADMIRAL NORBERT (ENGINEERING DUTY) US NAVY
CURRENT DUTY STATION: Commander, San Francisco Bay Naval Shipyard (July 1968)
DATE OF BIRTH: 1918
EDUCATION: 1940 Naval Academy; 1945 Naval Postgraduate School; 1961 Naval War College
FIRST COMMISSIONED: 6th June, 1940
PROMOTED TO: Rear Admiral 1st October, 1967
OFFICIAL ADDRESS: Vallejo, California 94592
HOME ADDRESS: Washington, DC

U.S.A.

FREEMAN, REAR-ADMIRAL MASON BEHR, US NAVY
CURRENT DUTY STATION:
Commander, Cruiser-Destroyer Force, Pacific Fleet (March 1967); additional duty: Commander, Training Command, Pacific Fleet (June 1969)
DATE OF BIRTH: 1914
EDUCATION: 1935 Naval Academy; 1942 Naval Postgraduate School; 1950 Naval War College; 1957 National War College
FIRST COMMISSIONED: 6th June, 1935
PROMOTED TO: Rear Admiral 1st July, 1963
COMMANDS: 1948-1949 William R. Rush DD 714; 1952-1954 Conecuh AOR 110; 1959-1961 Destroyer Squadron 16; 1963-1964 Cruiser-Destroyer Flotilla 2
OFFICIAL ADDRESS: San Diego, California 92132
HOME ADDRESS: Oak Park, Illinois

PORTUGAL

FREITAS, REAR ADMIRAL J. C. RIBEIRO, PORTUGUESE NAVY
DECORATIONS: MMp/sd 1959; MM/mm la. Cl. 1968; 2MM/mm 2a. Cl. 1960-1962; MMo/ce 1963; MSNp/cah 1941; MC/I 1958; MCp/IDH 1960
PRESENT APPOINTMENT: Comandante Chefe das Forças Armadas de Cabo Verde 9 December, 1967; Comandante Naval de Cabo Verde 29 November 1967
DATE OF BIRTH: 8 October, 1908
EDUCATION: EN. Escola Naval 1927; Av. Especialização em Aviação 1935; CENG. Curso Elementar Naval de Guerra 1948; NCSO. Curson Controle Naval da Navegação 1956; ASAN. Curson Tactica Anti-Submarine Aeronaval 1956; CSNG. Curson Superior Naval de Guerra 1962
DATES OF PROMOTIONS: Aspirante Marinha 1927; Guarda Marinha 1930; 2o. Tenente 1932; lo. Tenente 1938; Capitão Tenente 1953; Capitã de Fragata 1956; Capitã de mar et Guerra 1960; Commodore 1965; Rear Admiral 1968
PRINCIPAL COMMANDS AT SEA: Comandante do Centro de Aviação Naval de Lisboa 1937; Comandante do NRP Macau 1939; Comandante de Centro de Aviação Naval de Macau 1941; Comandante do NRP. DAO 1956; Comandante de NRP. João de Lisboa 1957; Comandante da Defesa Maritima de Lisboa 1959; Comandante Naval dos Açores 1965; Comandante Chefe das Forças Armadas e Comandante Naval de Cabo Verde 1967
OTHER PREVIOUS APPOINTMENTS OF NOTE: Viajem Lisboa-Calshot-Lisboa num Hidro-aviäo Blackburn-Shark 1936; Chefe Brigada Aerea da Missào Hidrografica de Cabo Verde 1946; Chefe Brigada Aerea de Missão Geo-Hidrografica da Guiné Portuguesa 1948; Capitão do Porto de Macau 1950; Capitão do Porto de Lisboa 1963
OFFICIAL ADDRESS: Ministerio da Marinha. *Telephone:* 368961 Lisboa 2
PRIVATE ADDRESS: Rua Dom Constantino de Bragança 45 *Telephone:* 611714 Lisboa 3;

JAPAN

FUKUDA, REAR-ADMIRAL S.
DECORATIONS: Fifth Class Order of the Sacred Treasure; Sixth Class Order of the Rising Sun
PRESENT APPOINTMENT: Chief, Supply and Accounts Division, Maritime Staff Office 20 January, 1968
DATE OF BIRTH: 12 January, 1917
EDUCATION: Graduated from the Imperial Japanese Naval Academy, Supply and Accounts March 1937
DATES OF PROMOTIONS: Lieutenant Commander October 1953; Commander February 1955; Captain July 1962; Rear Admiral January 1967
PREVIOUS APPOINTMENTS OF NOTE: Staff Officer of Self Defence Fleet January 1955; Chief, Supply & Accounts Division, Yokosuka Regional District Headquarters August 1960; Chief, Account Section, Maritime Staff Office January 1964; Deputy Chief, Supply and Accounts Division, MSO January 1966
OFFICIAL ADDRESS: Maritime Staff Office, Japan Defence Agency, 9-7-45, Akasaka, Minato-Ku, Tokyo, Japan
PRIVATE ADDRESS: 1-28 Hanamidai, Hodogaya-Ku, Yokohama-Shi, Kanagawa-Ken, Japan

U.S.A.

GADDIS, REAR-ADMIRAL WALTER DONALD, US NAVY
CURRENT DUTY STATION: Director, Budget and Reports, Navy Comptroller (July 1968)
DATE OF BIRTH: 1917
EDUCATION: 1941 Naval Academy; 1946 Naval Postgraduate School and 1949; 1953 Armed Forces Staff College; 1959 Naval War College
FIRST COMMISSIONED: 7th February, 1941
PROMOTED TO: Rear Admiral 20th January, 1968
COMMANDS: 1953-1954 Kenneth D. Bailey DDR 713; 1959-1960 Destroyer Division 302; additional duty Destroyer Squadron 30; 1962-1963 Yosemite AD 19; 1965-1966 Destroyer Squadron 8
OFFICIAL ADDRESS: The Pentagon, Washington, DC 20350
HOME ADDRESS: 703 South 6th Street, Laramie, Wyoming

U.S.A.

GALANTIN, ADMIRAL IGNATIOUS JOSEPH, US NAVY
CURRENT DUTY STATION: Chief of Naval Material (May 1966)
DATE OF BIRTH: 1910
EDUCATION: 1933 Naval Academy; 1955 National War College
FIRST COMMISSIONED: 1st June, 1933
PROMOTED TO: Rear Admiral 1st August, 1958; Vice Admiral 1st March, 1965; Admiral 19th May, 1967
MAJOR AWARDS: Navy Cross
COMMANDS: 1942-1943 R-11 SS 88; 1943-1944 Halibut SS 232; 1949 Submarine Division 51; 1952-1953 Navasota AO 106; 1953-1954 Submarine Squadron 7; 1959-1960 Cruiser Division 2
OFFICIAL ADDRESS: Navy Department, Main Navy Building, Washington, DC 20360
HOME ADDRESS: Quarters "H", Washington Navy Yard, DC

SPAIN

GARCIA-PARREO, y KADEN
DECORATIONS: Campaign Medal 1936-1939; Military Medal, War Cross, Naval Cross of Merit, white badge, 2nd Class 1951 Cross of "san Hermenegildo" 1958; Plaque of "San Hermenegildo" 1968; Order of "Infante D. Henrique of Portugal" 1960
PRESENT APPOINTMENT: Naval Attache to the Embassy of Spain 6 September, 1968
DATE OF BIRTH: 20 January, 1916
EDUCATION: Colegio de Neustra señora del Pilar, Madrid Spain; Escuela Naval Militar, San Fernando, Cádiz, Spain
DATES OF PROMOTIONS: Lieutenant Junior Grade 11 November, 1939; Lieutenant 1 September, 1943; Lieutenant Commander 15 April, 1948; Commander 16 June, 1959; Captain 24 November, 1967
PRINCIPAL COMMANDS AT SEA: 1944-1945 "L.T.—22"; 1955-1956 "Meteoro"; 1960-1961 "Ulloa"; 1962-1963 "Legazpi"
OTHER PREVIOUS APPOINTMENTS OF NOTE: 1949-1951 Aide to the Minister of the Spanish Navy
OFFICIAL ADDRESS: 1669 Columbia Road, NW—111, Washington, DC 20009. *Telephone:* 387-7612
PRIVATE ADDRESS: 5916 Walhonding Road, N.W., Washington, DC 20016

U.S.A.

GARRETT, REAR-ADMIRAL (SELECTEE), FRANCIS LEONARD, (CHAPLAIN CORPS.) US NAVY
CURRENT DUTY STATION: Fleet Chaplain, Atlantic Fleet (July 1969)
DATE OF BIRTH: 1919
EDUCATION: Wofford College, Spartanburg, South Carolina 1940, Emory University, Georgia 1943; Wofford College 1967
DATE OF COMMISSION: 11th February 1944
PROMOTED TO: Rear Admiral selected for promotion in June 1969
OFFICIAL ADDRESS: Norfolk, Virginia 23511
COMMANDS: Force Chaplain, 3rd Marine Amphibious Force 1965-1966

U.S.A.

GAY, REAR-ADMIRAL DONALD, JNR. (NAVAL AVIATOR) US NAVY
CURRENT DUTY STATION: Commander, Fleet Air Wings, Pacific Fleet (November 1966)
DATE OF BIRTH: 1914
EDUCATION: 1937 Naval Academy; 1950 Armed Forces Staff College
FIRST COMMISSIONED: 3rd June, 1937
PROMOTED TO: Rear Admiral 1st July, 1964
COMMANDS: 1947-1948 Fighting Squadron 3B; 1948 Fighting Squadron 41; 1952-1953 Carrier Air Group 3; 1959-1960 Floyds Bay AVP 40; 1960-1961 Ranger CVA 61; 1963-1964 Carrier Division 18
OFFICIAL ADDRESS: Naval Air Station, Moffett Field, California 94035
HOME ADDRESS: BOX 501, Oak Harbor, Washington

U.S.A.

GAYLER, VICE-ADMIRAL NOEL ARTHUR, (NAVAL AVIATOR) US NAVY
CURRENT DUTY STATION: Director, National Security Agency (1969)
DATE OF BIRTH: 1914
EDUCATION: 1935 Naval Academy
FIRST COMMISSIONED: 6th June, 1935
PROMOTED TO: Rear Admiral 1st July, 1961; Vice Admiral 28th September, 1967
MAJOR AWARDS: Navy Cross with 2 gold stars in lieu of second and third Navy Crosses
COMMANDS: 1944-1945 Fighter Squadron 12; 1951-1954 Air Development Squadron 3; 1956-1957 Greenwich Bay AVP 41; 1959-1960 Ranger CVA 61; 1962-1963 Carrier Division 20
OFFICIAL ADDRESS: Fort Meade, Maryland
HOME ADDRESS Offutt Air Force Base, Nebraska 68113

U.S.A.

GEIS, REAR-ADMIRAL LAWRENCE RAYMOND (NAVAL AVIATOR) US NAVY
CURRENT DUTY STATION: Chief of Information (September 1968)
DATE OF BIRTH: 1916
EDUCATION: 1939 Naval Academy; 1959 National War College
FIRST COMMISSIONED: 1st June, 1939
PROMOTED TO: Rear Admiral 1st July, 1965
COMMANDS: 1947-1948 Fighting Squadron 3A; 1948-1949 Fighting Squadron 31; 1951-1952 Carrier Air Group 4; 1957-1958 Air Development Squadron 3; 1961-1962 Duxbury Bay AVP 38; 1962-1963 Forrestal CVA 59; 1967-1968 Carrier Division 4
OFFICIAL ADDRESS: The Pentagon, Washington, DC 20350
HOME ADDRESS: Arlington, Virginia

UNITED KINGDOM
GERARD-PEARSE, CAPTAIN J. R. S., ROYAL NAVY
PRESENT APPOINTMENT: Commanding Officer HMS Fearless, 1969
DATE OF BIRTH: 10 May, 1924
EDUCATION: Clifton College
DATES OF PROMOTIONS: 1960 Commander; 1966 Captain
PRINCIPAL COMMANDS AT SEA: 1957 HMS Tomutt; 1958-1959 HMS Grafton; 1964-1966 HMS Defender
OTHER PREVIOUS APPOINTMENTS OF NOTE: Captain Mine Countermeasures and Captain Fishery Protection 1966-1968
OFFICIAL ADDRESS: HMS Fearless, BFPO Ships, London
PRIVATE ADDRESS: Enbrook House, West Malling, Kent

ARGENTINA
GIAVEDONI, REAR ADMIRAL R. R. ARGENTINE NAVY
PRESENT APPOINTMENT: Director de la Escuela Naval Militar y Jefe de la Región Naval Rìo Santiago, 5 February, 1968
DATE OF BIRTH: 26 January, 1921
EDUCATION: Escuela Naval 1938-1942; Escuela de Aplicación para Oficiales 1948 Escuela de Guerra Naval 1954
DATES OF PROMOTIONS: Guardiamarina December, 1942; Teniente de Corbeta December, 1944; Teniente de Fragata December, 1946; Teniente de Navio December, 1948; Capitán de Corbeta December 1952; Capitán de Fragata December, 1956; Capitán Navio December 1962; Rear Admiral December, 1967
PRINCIPAL COMMANDS AT SEA: Capitán de Corbeta Buque Oceanográfico ARA Bahía Blanca 1956; Capitán de Fragata Buque Tanque ARA Punta Médanos 1960; Capitán de Fragata Destructor ARA Entre Rios 1961; Capitán de Navio Crucero ARA 9 July 1966
OTHER PREVIOUS APPOINTMENTS OF NOTE: Capitán de Fragata Jefe de Operaciones de la Flota de Mar 1962; Capitán de Navio Jefe del Estado Mayor de la Flota de Mar 1963; Capitán de Navio Agregado naval en Inglaterra y Holanda y Jefe de la Comisión Naval en Europa 1964-1965
OFFICIAL ADDRESS: Escuela Naval Militar Rio Santiago Provincia de Buenos Aires, República Argentina
PRIVATE ADDRESS: Calle Vicente López 1037, La Lucila, Provincia de Buenos Aires, República Argentina

U.S.A.
GILKESON, REAR-ADMIRAL FILLMORE BOLLING (NAVAL AVIATOR) US NAVY
CURRENT DUTY STATION: Director, Logistics Plans Division, Office of the Chief of Naval Operations (July 1968)
DATE OF BIRTH: 1915
EDUCATION: 1937 Naval Academy; 1949 Naval Postgraduate School
FIRST COMMISSIONED: 3rd June, 1937
PROMOTED TO: Rear Admiral 1st July, 1965
COMMANDS: 1942-1943 Air Anti-Submarine Squadron 2D-10; 1943-1944 Scout Observation Service Unit 2; 1944-1945 Torpedo Squadron 33; 1955-1957 Air Development Squadron 5; 1959-1960 Caloosahatchee AO 98; 1960-1961 Shangri-La CVA 38; 1965-1966 Anti-Submarine Warfare Group 3; 1966-1968 Naval Base, Subic Bay
OFFICIAL ADDRESS: The Pentagon, Washington, DC 20350
HOME ADDRESS: Red Acres, Orange, Virginia

U.S.A.
GILLETTE, REAR-ADMIRAL NORMAN CAMPBELL, JNR. (NAVAL AVIATOR) US NAVY
CURRENT DUTY STATION: Commander, Anti-Submarine Warfare Group 3 (January 1969)
DATE OF BIRTH: 1915
EDUCATION: 1936 Naval Academy; 1957 Naval War College
FIRST COMMISSIONED: 4th June, 1936
PROMOTED TO: Rear Admiral 1st June, 1964
COMMANDS: 1944-1945 Patrol Bombing Squadron 71; 1957 US Naval Activities Rota Spain and Commanding Officer Naval Air Station Rota; 1958-1959 Thetis Bay CVHA 1; 1960-1961 Fleet Air Wing 3; 1961-1963 Naval Air Station Norfolk, Virginia; 1963-1964 Fleet Air Wings, Atlantic Fleet; 1964-1966 Chief, Joint US Military Group/Military Assistance Advisory Group, Madrid, Spain
OFFICIAL ADDRESS: FPO San Francisco, California 96601
HOME ADDRESS: Chicago, Illinois

ITALY
GIOMETTI, REAR-ADMIRAL GIOVANNI
DECORATIONS: Ufficiale dell'Ordine al Merito della Repubblica Italiana; 3 Croci di Guerra al Valor Militare; 2 Croci al Merito di Guerra; Medaglia d'Oro per lunga navigazione
PRESENT APPOINTMENT: Comando Militare Marittimo in Sardegna
DATE OF BIRTH: 2 June, 1914
DATE OF LAST PROMOTION: 31 December, 1964
SERVICE ADDRESS: Marisardegna Cagliari

CANADA
GODBEHERE, CAPTAIN (SR) C. R., ROYAL CANADIAN NAVY
DECORATIONS: Canadian Volunteer Service Medal 1945; and Clasp Atlantic Star, 1945; 1939-1945 medal 1945; War Medal 1945; Canadian Forces Decoration 1958; Centennial Medal 1967
PRESENT APPOINTMENT: Commanding Officer, HMCS Chippawa 1966
DATE OF BIRTH: 28 May, 1922
EDUCATION: Sir George Williams University, Senior matriculation 1941; McGill University Extension 2 years management and administration (cert.); Queen's University, School of Business Executive summer school course (cert.)
DATES OF PROMOTIONS: Sub Lieutenant March 1943; Lieutenant March 1944; Lieutenant Commander December 1958; Commander January 1965; Captain September 1968
PRINCIPAL COMMANDS AT SEA: HMC Fairmile 115
OTHER PREVIOUS APPOINTMENTS OF NOTE: Training Officer, HMCS Donnacona 1951-1953; Training Officer, HMCS Nonsuch 1953-1957; Training Officer, HMCS Chippawa 1957-1966
OFFICIAL ADDRESS: HMCS Chippawa, 51 Smith Street, Winnipeg 1, Manitoba

U.S.A.
GOEHRING, REAR-ADMIRAL ROBERT WILLIAM, US NAVY
CURRENT DUTY STATION: Chief, Office of Operations, Coast Guard Headquarters
DATE OF BIRTH: 1917
EDUCATION: 1939 Coast Guard Academy; 1951 Harvard Graduate School of Business
FIRST COMMISSIONED: 29th May, 1939
PROMOTED TO: Rear Admiral, 1st July, 1967
COMMANDS: 1957-1958 Castle Rock; 1962-1965 Coast Guard Base, Boston

U.S.A.
GOODFELLOW, REAR-ADMIRAL ALEXANDER SCOTT, JNR. US NAVY
CURRENT DUTY STATION: Commander, Operational Test and Evaluation Force (June 1969)
DATE OF BIRTH: 1917
EDUCATION: 1940 Naval Academy; 1945 Naval Postgraduate School; 1957 National War College
FIRST COMMISSIONED: 6th June, 1940
PROMOTED TO: Rear Admiral 1st October, 1966
COMMANDS: 1953-1955 Frank Knox DDR 742; 1959-1960 Destroyer Division 112; 1961-1962 Paul Revere APA 248; 1965-1965 Galveston CLG 3; 1965-1966 Cruiser-Destroyer Flotilla 9; 1966-1967 Cruiser-Destroyer Flotilla 7
OFFICIAL ADDRESS: Naval Base, Norfolk, Virginia 23511
HOME ADDRESS: 300 6th Street, Coronado, California

U.S.A.
GOODING, REAR-ADMIRAL (SELECTEE) ROBERT CARPENTER (ENGINEERING DUTY) US NAVY
CURRENT DUTY STATION: Commander, Boston Naval Shipyard, Supervisor of Shipbuilding Conversion and Repair, 1st Naval District and Staff, Commandant, 1st Naval District (August 1968)
DATE OF BIRTH: 1918
EDUCATION: 1942 Naval Academy; 1946 Massachusetts Institute of Technology
FIRST COMMISSIONED: 19th December, 1941
PROMOTED TO: Rear Admiral, selected for promotion in 6th June, 1969
OFFICIAL ADDRESS: Boston, Naval Shipyard, Massachusetts
HOME ADDRESS: 204 West Alexandria Avenue, Alexandria, Virginia

SWEDEN
GOTTFRIDSSEN, COMMODORE H., ROYAL SWEDISH NAVY
DECORATIONS: Svàrdsorden with star 1967; Dannebrogen (Danish) 1945
PRESENT APPOINTMENT: Chief of Naval Base South 1966
DATE OF BIRTH: 14 April, 1914
EDUCATION: Royal Swedish Naval Academy, Submarine School; Royal National Defence College
DATES OF PROMOTIONS: Sub-lieutenant 1935; Captain 1957; Commodore 1960
PRINCIPAL COMMANDS AT SEA: Commanding Officer in several submarines 1943-1948
OTHER PREVIOUS APPOINTMENTS OF NOTE: Inspector of submarines 1960-1964
OFFICIAL ADDRESS: Chepu M Sydhustens orbrgsbas, 37100 Karslsbrona
PRIVATE ADDRESS: Landbrogatan 7, 37100 Karlsbrona

THAILAND
GRACHANGNETARA, ADMIRAL S., ROYAL THAI NAVY
DECORATIONS: Legion d'honeur Grand Officer 1957; Knight Grand Cross (First Class) of the Most Exalted Order of The White Elephant 1961; Knight Grand Cordon (Special Class) of the Most Noble Order of the Crown of Thailand 1965; Knight Grand Commander (Second Class, higher grade) of The Most Illustrious Order of Chula Chom Kloa 1966
PRESENT APPOINTMENT: Assistance C-in-C, RTN 14 June, 1966
DATE OF BIRTH: 17 February 1912
EDUCATION: 1932 Royal Thai Naval Accademy; 1949 H.M.S. Excellent Royal Navy; 1961 Naval War College DATES OF PROMOTIONS: 1935 Sub-Lieutenant; 1944 Lieutenant Commander; 1952 Captain; 1963 Admiral
PRINCIPAL COMMANDS AT SEA: 1946-1947 C.O.H.T.M.S. Sukothai; 1948-1949 C.O.H.T.M.S. Sri Ayudhya and Acting Chief of Staff, Gunboat Division
OTHER PREVIOUS APPOINTMENTS OF NOTE: Naval Attaché to Paris 1954-1957; C-in-C, Royal Thai Fleet 1962-1965
OFFICIAL ADDRESS: Royal Thai Navy Headquarters, Thon Buri *Telephone:* 61488
PRIVATE ADDRESS: 100 Soi Senanikom 1, Paholyothin Rd., Bangkok

AUSTRALIA
GRAHAM, RADM W. D. H., ROYAL AUSTRALIAN NAVY
DECORATIONS: C.B.E. June 1967
PRESENT APPOINTMENT: Fourth Naval Member of Naval Board January 1966
DATE OF BIRTH: 3 September, 1916
EDUCATION: Southport School, Queensland, 1930-1934
DATES OF PROMOTIONS: Commander (S) 31 December, 1951; Captain 31 December 1957; Rear-Admiral 7 January, 1967
PREVIOUS APPOINTMENTS OF NOTE: Captain of the Port, Sydney 1963-1965; Imperial Defence College 1962; Secretary to Chief of Naval Staff 1958-1961
OFFICIAL ADDRESS: Navy Office, Canberra, A.C.T. 2600 *Telephone:* 653401
PRIVATE ADDRESS: 4 Anstey Street, Pearce, A.C.T. 2607

U.S.A.
GRALLA, REAR-ADMIRAL ARTHUR ROBERT, US NAVY
CURRENT DUTY STATION: Naval Inspector General (May 1969)
DATE OF BIRTH: 1913
EDUCATION: 1934 Naval Academy; 1943 Naval Postgraduate School; 1950 Armed Forces Staff College; 1953 Naval War College
FIRST COMMISSIONED: 31st May, 1934
PROMOTED TO: Rear Admiral 1st July, 1960
COMMANDS: 1946-1947 Dennis J. Buckley DD 808; 1953-1954 Destroyer Division 202; 1956-1957 Naval Ordnance Test Unit Air Force Missile Test Center, Patrick AFB, Florida; 1957-1958 Norton Sound AVM 1; 1959-1961 Destroyer Flotilla 2; 1964-1966 South Atlantic Force; 1966-1969 Naval Ordnance Systems Command, Washington, DC
OFFICIAL ADDRESS: Arlington Annex, Washington, DC 20370
HOME ADDRESS: 606 Grove Street, Far Rockaway, Long Island, New York

ARGENTINA
GRAN, COMMANDER J. M. ARGENTINE NAVY
PRESENT APPOINTMENT: Commander, Cte. Espora Naval Air Station
DATE OF BIRTH: 22 December, 1924
EDUCATION: Graduate, Argentine Naval Academy
DATES OF PROMOTIONS: Guardiamaria 3 Děcember, 1947; Guardiamarina (Naval Aviator) 31 December, 1948; Teniente de Corbeta 31 December, 1949; Teniente de Fragata 31 December, 1951 Teniente de Navio 31 December, 1953; Capitan de Corbeta 31 December, 1958; Capitan de Fragata 31 December 1964;
PRINCIPAL COMMANDS AT SEA: Commander, Naval Air Antisubmarine Squadron 1962-1963; Commander, Naval Air Wing 4 1968
OTHER PREVIOUS APPOINTMENTS OF NOTE: Transition to S2 A/C, USA, RAG Squadron and A/S Faetupac Courses 1961-1962
OFFICIAL ADDRESS: Base Aeronaval Comandante Espora *Telephone:* 24305, Int. 412
PRIVATE ADDRESS: Cramer 2285, Buenos Aires, Argentine Republic

U.S.A.
GRANTHAM, REAR-ADMIRAL EMERY ARDEN (ENGINEERING DUTY) US NAVY
CURRENT DUTY STATION: Director, Ships Material Readiness Division, Office of the Chief of Naval Operations (October 1967)
DATE OF BIRTH: 1914
EDUCATION: 1937 Naval Academy; 1941 Naval Postgraduate School
FIRST COMMISSIONED: 3rd June, 1937
PROMOTED TO: Rear Admiral 1st October, 1964
OFFICIAL ADDRESS: The Pentagon, Washington, DC 20350
HOME ADDRESS: Albany, Texas

U.S.A.
GREER, REAR-ADMIRAL (SELECTEE) HOWARD EARL, US NAVY
CURRENT DUTY STATION: Chief of Staff and Aide, Commander, Naval Air Force Pacific (February 1969)
DATE OF BIRTH: 1921
EDUCATION: 1944 Naval Academy; 1961 Industrial College of the Armed Forces; 1965 Naval Postgraduate School
FIRST COMMISSIONED: 9th June, 1943
PROMOTED TO: Rear Admiral, selected for promotion on 6th June, 1969
COMMANDS: 1957-1958 Fighter Squadron 64; 1961-1962 Carrier Air Group 10; 1966-1967 Ponchatoula AO 148; 1967-1969 Hancock CVA 19
OFFICIAL ADDRESS: Naval Air Station North Island, San Diego
HOME ADDRESS: 807 Pinedale Place, Tyler, Texas

U.K.
GRIFFIN, VICE-ADMIRAL A. T. F. G., ROYAL NAVY
DECORATIONS: CB Military 1967
PRESENT APPOINTMENT: Flag Officer Second in Command Far East Fleet August 1968
DATE OF BIRTH: 24 November, 1920
EDUCATION: RNC Dartmouth 1934
DATES OF PROMOTIONS: Sub Lieutenant 1941; Lieutenant Commander 1949; Commander 31 December, 1951; Captain 31 December, 1956; Rear Admiral 7 January, 1966; Vice Admiral 13 November 1968
PRINCIPAL COMMANDS AT SEA: HMS Woodbridge Haven (Inshore Flotilla) 1959-1960; HMS Ark Royal 1964-1965
OTHER APPOINTMENTS OF NOTE: Executive Officer HMS Eagle 1955-1956; Deputy Director Plans 1960-1962; Imperial Defence College 1963; Naval Secretary 1966; Assistant Chief of Naval Staff (Warfare) 1966-1968; Flag Officer Plymouth 1969
OFFICIAL ADDRESS: Far East Fleet, BFPO 164
PRIVATE ADDRESS: Shedfield Cottage, Shedfield, Southampton Hants.

U.S.A.
GROVERMAN, REAR-ADMIRAL WILLIAM HEALD, JNR. US NAVY
CURRENT DUTY STATION: Commander, Western Sea Frontier (June, 1967)
DATE OF BIRTH: 1909
EDUCATION: 1932 Naval Academy; 1939 Naval Postgraduate School; 1951 Naval War College
FIRST COMMISSIONED: 2nd June, 1932
PROMOTED TO: Rear Admiral 1st February. 1961
COMMANDS: 1943-1944 Philip DD 498; 1945-1946 De Haven DD 727; 1951-1952 Destroyer Division 122 (Commander Task Group 95.21); 1956-1957 Mississinewa AO 144; 1957-1958 Des Moines CA 134; 1963-1965 Cruiser-Destroyer Flotilla 3
OFFICIAL ADDRESS: Naval Station, Treasure Island, San Francisco, California
HOME ADDRESS: 33A Newcomb Boulevard, New Orleans, Louisiana

U.S.A.
GUEST, REAR-ADMIRAL WILLIAM SELMAN (NAVAL AVIATOR) US NAVY
CURRENT DUTY STATION: Chief of Naval Air Reserve Training (March 1967); additional duty Commander Naval Air Reserve Forces (March 1969)
DATE OF BIRTH: 1913
EDUCATION: 1935 Naval Academy; 1955 Naval War College; 1950 Air War College
FIRST COMMISSIONED: 6th June, 1935
PROMOTED TO: Rear Admiral 1st August, 1963
MAJOR AWARD: Navy Cross
COMMANDS: 1948-1949 Patrol Squadron 48; 1957-1958 Salisbury Sound AV 13; 1960-1961 Oriskany CVA 34; 1962-1964 Fleet Air Whidbey; Naval Air Base, 13th Naval District; 1964-1965 Carrier Division 9
OFFICIAL ADDRESS: Box 1, Naval Air Station, Glenview, Illinois 60026
HOME ADDRESS: Colvin Road, Fort Worth, Texas

U.S.A.
GUINN, REAR-ADMIRAL DICK HENRY (NAVAL AVIATOR) US NAVY
CURRENT DUTY STATION: Deputy Chief of Naval Personnel (June 1969)
DATE OF BIRTH: 1918
EDUCATION: 1941 Naval Academy; 1960 National War College
FIRST COMMISSIONED: 7th February, 1941
PROMOTED TO: Rear Admiral 1st December, 1965
MAJOR AWARD: Navy Cross
COMMANDS: 1947-1948 Fighting Squadron 2A; 1952-1953 Composite Squadron 3; 1956-1957 Carrier Air Group 6; 1961-1963 Rigel AF 58; 1963-1964 Forrestal CVA 59; 1965-1967 Carrier Division 4; 1967-1969 Naval Air Basic Training
OFFICIAL ADDRESS: Arlington Annex, Washington, DC 20370
HOME ADDRESS: 1840 Grandview Avenue, El Paso, Texas

U.S.A.
HADDEN, REAR-ADMIRAL MAYO ADDISON, JNR. (NAVAL AVIATOR) US NAVY
CURRENT DUTY STATION: Commander, Iceland Defense Force (January 1969)
DATE OF BIRTH: 1916
EDUCATION: 1938 Hope College, Holland Michigan; 1947 General Line School; 1954 Naval War College; 1961 National War College
FIRST COMMISSIONED: 14th October, 1941
PROMOTED TO: Rear Admiral 1st April, 1969
COMMANDS: 1948-1949 Fighting Squadron 73; 1963-1964 Graffias AF 29; 1964-1965 Hornet CVS 12
OFFICIAL ADDRESS: Box 1, Fleet Post Office New York, 09571
HOME ADDRESS: 276 Pine Avenue, Holland, Michigan

U.S.A.
HADDOCK, REAR-ADMIRAL IRA FREDERICK (SUPPLY CORPS) US NAVY
CURRENT DUTY STATION: Commanding Officer, Naval Supply Center, Norfolk (May 1969)
DATE OF BIRTH: 1914
EDUCATION: 1938 Naval Academy; 1951 Naval Postgraduate School
FIRST COMMISSIONED: 2nd June, 1938
PROMOTED TO: Rear Admiral 1st July, 1964
COMMANDS: 1961-1964 Naval Ships Parts Control Center Mechanicsburg, Pennsylvania; 1966-1967 Defense Construction Supply Center Columbus, Ohio
OFFICIAL ADDRESS: Norfolk, Virginia 23512
HOME ADDRESS: Akron, Ohio

FINLAND
HAIKALA, COMMODORE O., FINNISH NAVY
DECORATIONS: VR 4; VR 3; VR 2
PRESENT APPOINTMENT: Commandant Naval Academy 6 January 1969
DATE OF BIRTH: 7 April, 1912
EDUCATION: Naval Academy 1930-1933; War College (Naval Section) 1947-1949
DATES OF PROMOTIONS: Sub-Lieutenant 1933; Lieutenant 1935; Lieutenant Commander 1940; Commander 1943; Captain 1954; Commodore 1964
PRINCIPAL COMMANDS AT SEA: Commanding Officer Naval Squadron 1966-1969
OFFICIAL ADDRESS: Naval Academy, Helsinki 19

SWEDEN
HALLBERG, COMMODORE (E) H. W., ROYAL SWEDISH NAVY
PRESENT APPOINTMENT; Chief of the Naval Material Department in the Material Administration of the Armed Forces, 1 October 1968
DATE OF BIRTH: 11 May, 1922
EDUCATION: Royal Institute of Technology 1947
DATES OF PROMOTIONS: Ensign (E) 1947; Commander (E) 1957; Commodore (E) 1966
OFFICIAL ADDRESS: Fŕsvarets Materielverk, Marinmaterielfŕvaltningen S-104 50, Stockholm 80, Sweden. *Telephone;* 08/679560
PRIVATE ADDRESS: Tjçdervçgen 8, S-181 40 Liding, Sweden

U.S.A.
HAMMOND, REAR-ADMIRAL ROBERT EARL (NAVAL AVIATOR) US NAVY
CURRENT DUTY STATION: Commander, 17th Coast Guard District, Juneau, Alaska (July 1968)
DATE OF BIRTH: 1918
EDUCATION: Coast Guard Academy 1940; 1943 Naval Air Station, Pensacola; 1948 Army Air Force Engineering School, Charmite Field
FIRST COMMISSIONED: 20th May, 1940
PROMOTED TO: Rear Admiral 1st April, 1968
COMMANDS: 1962-1964 Coast Guard Air Station, Kodiak; 1964-1966 Coast Guard

U.S.A.
HELMER, REAR-ADMIRAL FRANK V., US NAVY
CURRENT DUTY STATION: Commander, 13th Coast Guard, District Seattle (June 1967)
DATE OF BIRTH: 1913
EDUCATION: 1935 Coast Guard Academy
FIRST COMMISSIONED: 27th May, 1935
PROMOTED TO: Rear Admiral 1st July, 1965
COMMANDS: 1944-1945 Vance; 1945 Cambria; 1946 Escanaba; 1951-1952 Koiner; 1952-1956 Chief, Aids to Navigation Section, 13th Coast Guard District; 1959-1961 Taney; 1965-1966 Comptroller, Coast Guard Headquarters

U.S.A.
HANNIFIN, REAR-ADMIRAL (SELECTEE) PATRICK "J", US NAVY
CURRENT DUTY STATION: Commandant, 13th Naval District (1969)
DATE OF BIRTH: 1923
EDUCATION: 1945 Naval Academy; 1968 Industrial College of the Armed Forces
FIRST COMMISSIONED: 7th June, 1944
PROMOTED TO: Rear Admiral, selected for promotion on 6th June, 1969
COMMANDS: 1955-1957 Diodon SS 349; 1963-1965 Lafayette SSBN 616; 1968-1969 Submarine Squadron 15
OFFICIAL ADDRESS: Naval Air Station Sandy Point, Seattle, Washington
HOME ADDRESS: 700 South Lea Avenue, Roswell, New Mexico
PROMOTIONS: 1930 Cadet; 1937 Acting Paymaster Sub Lieutenant; 1938 Paymaster Lieutenant; 1941 Acting Paymaster Lieutenant Commander 1946 Lieutenant Commander (confirmed); 1951 Commander; 1961 Captain

UNITED KINGDOM
HARKNESS, COMMODORE J. P. K.
DECORATIONS: I.D.C; P.S.C.; S.O.W.C.; Mentioned in despatches for service in HMS Exeter in Java Sea 1942
PRESENT APPOINTMENT: Commodore Naval Drafting June 1966
DATE OF BIRTH: 28 November, 1916
EDUCATION: Stubbington House, RN College, Dartmouth
OTHER PREVIOUS APPOINTMENTS OF NOTE: Supply Officer, HMS Forth 1955; Staff of Flag Officer Air (Home) 1958; Supply Officer, HMS Ark Royal 1959; Assistant Director of Plans (Warfare), Admiralty 1962; HMS Centurion as Commodore Naval Drafting 1966
OFFICIAL ADDRESS: Commodore Naval Drafting, HMS Centurion, Lythe Hill House, Haslemere, Surrey *Telephone:* Haslemere 4022
PRIVATE ADDRESS: Alverstoke

U.S.A.
HARLFINGER, REAR-ADMIRAL FREDERICK JOSEPH, II, US NAVY
CURRENT DUTY STATION: Assistant Chief of Naval Operations (Intelligence) and Commander, Naval Intelligence Command (August 1968)
DATE OF BIRTH: 1913
EDUCATION: 1935 Naval Academy; 1952 Armed Forces Staff College; 1955 Armed Forces Industrial College
FIRST COMMISSIONED: 6th June, 1935
PROMOTED TO: Rear Admiral 1st April, 1964
MAJOR AWARD: Navy Cross
COMMANDS: 1943-1944 S-32 SS 137; 1944-1945 Trigger SS 237; 1945-1947 Sirago SS 485; 1950-1952 Submarine Division 43; 1955-1957 US Naval Attaché and Naval Attaché for Air, Bonn, Germany; 1957-1958 Mauna Loa AE; 1958-1959 Submarine Squadron 12; 1962-1964 Submarine Flotilla 1; 1967-1968 South Atlantic Force, US Atlantic Fleet
OFFICIAL ADDRESS: The Pentagon, Washington, DC 20350
HOME ADDRESS: Berbenfields, East Nassau, New York

U.S.A.
HARNISH, REAR-ADMIRAL WILLIAM MAX (NAVAL AVIATOR) US NAVY
CURRENT DUTY STATION: Director, Office of Program Appraisal, Navy Department (September 1967)
DATE OF BIRTH: 1919
EDUCATION: 1943 Naval Academy; 1951 Naval Postgraduate School; 1958 Naval War College
FIRST COMMISSIONED: 19th June, 1942
PROMOTED TO: Rear Admiral 1st August, 1968
COMMANDS: 1955-1957 Fighting Squadron 21; 1964-1965 Chipola AO 63; 1966 Ranger CVA 61
OFFICIAL ADDRESS: The Pentagon, Washington, DC 20350
HOME ADDRESS: 718 South Lynn Street, Champaign, Illinois

U.S.A.
HARTMANN, REAR-ADMIRAL PAUL ELLSWORTH (NAVAL AVIATOR) US NAVY
CURRENT DUTY STATION: Assistant Vice Chief of Naval Operations and Director of Naval Administration (May 1968)
DATE OF BIRTH: 1941
EDUCATION: 1937 Naval Academy; 1950 Naval War College
FIRST COMMISSIONED: 3rd June, 1937
PROMOTED TO: Rear Admiral 1st July, 1964
COMMANDS: 1947-1949 Medium Patrol Squadron 8; 1958-1959 Floyds Bay AVP 40; 1960-1961 Antietam CVS 36; 1963-1966 Fleet Air Western Pacific; additional duty Naval Air Bases Japan; 1966-1967 Carrier Division 20
OFFICIAL ADDRESS: The Pentagon, Washington, DC 20350
HOME ADDRESS: Boston, Massachusetts

U.S.A.
HARTY, REAR-ADMIRAL HARRY LAFAYETTE, JNR. (NAVAL AVIATOR) US NAVY
CURRENT DUTY STATION: Deputy Assistant Chief for Staff for Plans & Policy, Supreme Allied Commander Europe (September 1967)
DATE OF BIRTH: 1917
EDUCATION: 1939 naval Academy; 1958 Industrial College of the Armed Forces
FIRST COMMISSIONED: 1st June, 1939
PROMOTED TO: Rear Admiral 14th May, 1967
COMMANDS: 1944-1945 Patrol Squadron 210; 1961-1962 Greenwich Bay AVP 41; 1962-1963 Randolph CVS 15; 1966-1967 Anti-Submarine Warfare Group 3
OFFICIAL ADDRESS: (Paris) APO New York 09055
HOME ADDRESS: 616 Park Avenue, Sikeston, Missouri

PAKISTAN
HASAN REAR-ADMIRAL M.
DECORATION: S.K.
PRESENT APPOINTMENT: Chief of Staff 1969
DATE OF BIRTH: 1 February, 1921
DATE OF PROMOTIONS: 1964 Commodore; 1969 Rear Admiral
PRINCIPAL COMMANDS AT SEA: 1963 PNS Babur in Command; 1965 Commodore Commanding PNS Flotilla
OFFICIAL ADDRESS: Naval Headquarters, Napier Barracks, Karachi, (West Pakistan) 515413

PAKISTAN
HASAN, REAR-ADMIRAL M., PAKISTAN NAVY
DECORATIONS: S.K. 1965
PRESENT APPOINTMENT: Chief of Staff
DATE OF BIRTH: 1 February, 1921
EDUCATION 1941 B.Sc; 1948 Long 'C'; 1956 J.S.S.C.
DATES OF PROMOTIONS: 1944 Lieutenant; 1952 Lieutenant Commander; 1958 Commander; 1963 Captain; 1964 Commodore; 1969 Rear-Admiral
PRINCIPAL COMMANDS AT SEA: Destroyer Tughrill; Light Cruiser Babur; Commodore Commanding PN Flotilla
OTHER PREVIOUS APPOINTMENTS OF NOTE: Flag Lieutenant to C-in-C Pakistan Navy; Naval Adviser to Pakistan High Commissioner, London; Naval Officer-in-Charge, Chittagong; Principal Staff Officer to Naval H.Q.
OFFICIAL ADDRESS: Chief of Staff, Naval H.Q. Karachi

JAPAN
HASHIMOTO, VICE-ADMIRAL M.
PRESENT APPOINTMENT:Commandant, Ominato Regional District 1 July, 1969
DATE OF BIRTH: 24 November, 1914
EDUCATION: Graduated from Tokyo Mercantile Marine College May 1940
PRINCIPAL COMMANDS AT SEA: Commander Eighth Escort Division April 1961-March 1962; Commander Tenth Escort Division March 1962-December 1964; Commander First Minesweeper Squadron April 1966-July 1967
OTHER PREVIOUS APPOINTMENTS OF NOTE: Instructor Educational Affairs Division MSDF Staff College December 1957-April 1961; Staff National Defense College December 1964-April 1966
OFFICIAL ADDRESS: 7-45, 9-chome, Akasaka Minato-ku, Tokyo-to *Telephone:* Tokyo 408-5211 ext. 2840
PRIVATE ADDRESS: 11-13, 22-2 chome, Higashiyama Meguro-ku, Tokyo-to

U.K.
HASLAM, CAPTAIN D. W. ROYAL NAVY
DECORATION: O.B.E. June 1964
PRESENT APPOINTMENT: In Command H.M.S. Hecla 12 February, 1968
DATE OF BIRTH: 26 June, 1923
EDUCATION: Bromsgrove School 1937-1941
DATES OF PROMOTIONS: Commander December 1956; Captain December 1965
PRINCIPAL COMMANDS AT SEA: HMS Dalrymple; HMS Dampier; HMS Owen; HMS Hecla
OTHER PREVIOUS APPOINTMENTS OF NOTE: Hydrographer Royal Australian Navy 1966-1967; Commander RN Barracks Chatham
PRIVATE ADDRESS: 183 Duffield Road, Derby

U.S.A.
HEALEY, REAR-ADMIRAL, VINCENT PATRICK, US NAVY
CURRENT DUTY STATION: Director, Undersea & Strategic Warfare Development Division, Office of the Chief of Naval Operations (April 1969)
DATE OF BIRTH: 1918
EDUCATION: 1940 Naval Academy; 1949 Naval Postgraduate School; 1959 Industrial College of the Armed Forces
FIRST COMMISSIONED: 6th June, 1940
PROMOTED TO: Rear Admiral 1st November, 1967
COMMANDS: 1945-1946 Dyson DD 572; 1951-1952 Gyatt DD 712; 1962-1963 Pyro AE 24; 1963-1965 Destroyer Squadron 3; 1967-1969 Cruiser-Destroyer Flotilla 6
OFFICIAL ADDRESS: The Pentagon, Washington, DC 20350
HOME ADDRESS: 1032 Ogden Avenue, Bronx, New York

U.S.A.
HEAMAN, REAR-ADMIRAL WILLIAM McPHERSON (CIVIL ENGINEER CORPS) US NAVY
CURRENT DUTY STATION: Commander, Pacific Division, Naval Facilities Engineering Command (January 1966)
DATE OF BIRTH: 1910
EDUCATION: 1935 University of Washington; 1947 Armed Forces Staff College
FIRST COMMISSIONED: 10th September, 1941
PROMOTED TO: Rear Admiral 1st July, 1965
COMMANDS: 1962-1963 Construction Battalions, US Atlantic Fleet; 1963-1966 Director, Southeast Division, Bureau of Yards and Docks, Naval Base, Charleston, South Carolina
OFFICIAL ADDRESS: FPO San Francisco, California 96610
HOME ADDRESS: 6101 Crockett Street, Seattle, Washington

UNITED KINGDOM
HEATH, COMMANDER R. J. P., ROYAL NAVY
PRESENT APPOINTMENT: HMS Renown 1966; Port Crew 1968
DATE OF BIRTH: 17 March, 1929
EDUCATION: RNC Dartmouth
DATES OF PROMOTIONS: Lieutenant 1950; 1958 Lieutenant Commander; 1963 Commander
PRINCIPAL DOMMANDS AT SEA: 1957-1958 HMS Seascout; 1961 HMS Alcide; 1961-1962 Acheron; 1963-1964 Flotilla Tactical Officer—Staff of Flag Officer Submarines; 1964-1966 Staff Officer—Submarines on Staff of Commander British Navy Staff, Washington
OTHER PREVIOUS APPOINTMENTS OF NOTE: BRNC Dartmouth; Head of Seamanship Department and River Officer 1958-1960
OFFICIAL ADDRESS: HMS Renown, BFPO Ships

UNITED KINGDOM
HELLINGS, LIEUTENANT-GENERAL P. W. C., ROYAL NAVY
DECORATIONS: C.B. 1966; D.S.C. 1940; M.C. 1943
PRESENT APPOINTMENT: Commandant General Royal Marines (1968)
DATE OF BIRTH: 6 September, 1916
EDUCATION: Nautical College, Pangbourne
DATES OF PROMOTIONS: 1942 Captain; 1944 Acting Lieutenant Colonel; 1956 Lieutenant Colonel; 1963 Acting Brigadier; 1964 Major General; 1967 Lieutenant General
PREVIOUS APPOINTMENTS OF NOTE: Officer Commanding 41 and 42 Commandos 1945-1946; Served Italy, NW Europe, Far East during World War II; ADC to HM the Queen 1963; Chief of Staff to Commandant General Royal Marines 1968
OFFICIAL ADDRESS: Ministry of Defence, Main Building, Whitehall, London S.W.1. *Telephone:* 01-930-7022 ext. 7675
PRIVATE ADDRESS: The Leys, Milton Combe, Yelverton, Devon

U.S.A.
HENDERSON, REAR-ADMIRAL DOUGLAS BRUCE, US NAVY
CURRENT DUTY STATION: Chief, Office of Engineering (January 1968)
DATE OF BIRTH: 1910
EDUCATION: 1936 Coast Guard Academy; 1943 Massachusetts Institute of Technology
FIRST COMMISSIONED: 8th June, 1936
PROMOTED TO: Rear Admiral 1st July, 1966
COMMANDS: 1943-1946 Technical Division Office of Navy Supervisor of Shipbuilding, San Pedro; 1950-1951 Klamath; 1955-1959 Power Laboratory, Coast Guard Academy; 1959-1961 Ingham

UNITED KINGDOM
HENDERSON, ADMIRAL SIR N. S., ROYAL NAVY
DECORATIONS: G.B.E. 1968; K.C.B. 1962
PRESENT APPOINTMENT: Chairman NATO Military Committee 1968
DATE OF BIRTH: 1 August, 1909
EDUCATION: Cheltenham College
DATES OF PROMOTIONS: 1942 Commander; 1948 Captain; 1957 Rear-Admiral; 1960 Vice Admiral; 1963 Admiral
PRINCIPAL COMMANDS AT SEA: 1953-1954 HMS Protector; 1955-1957 HMS Kenya
OTHER PREVIOUS APPOINTMENTS OF NOTE: C-in-C Plymouth 1962-1965; Head British Defence Staff Washington and UK Rep. to NATO Standing Group and Military Committee
OFFICIAL ADDRESS: 56 Rue Jules Lejeune, Brussels 6 *Telephone:* 41-43-93
PRIVATE ADDRESS: Hensol, Castle Douglas, Scotland

U.S.A.
HEFFNER, REAR-ADMIRAL, GROVER CHESTER (SUPPLY CORPS) US NAVY
CURRENT DUTY STATION: Commander, Defense Industrial Supply Center, Philadelphia (August 1967)
DATE OF BIRTH: 1919
EDUCATION: 1940 University of Washington; 1950 Stanford University Graduate School of Business; 1964 National War College
FIRST COMMISSIONED: 25th May, 1940
PROMOTED TO: Rear Admiral 1st August, 1967
COMMANDS: 1964-1966 Naval Supply Center, Long Beach California
OFFICIAL ADDRESS: 700 Robbins Avenue, Philadelphia, Pennsylvania
HOME ADDRESS: 308 H. Street, Bremerton, Washington

U.S.A.
HEINZ, VICE-ADMIRAL LUTHER CARL, US NAVY
CURRENT DUTY STATION: Commander, Amphibious Force, Atlantic Fleet (July 1968)
DATE OF BIRTH: 1912
EDUCATION: 1933 Naval Academy; 1951 Naval War College
FIRST COMMISSIONED: 1st June, 1933
PROMOTED TO: Rear Admiral 1st July, 1961; Vice Admiral 1st September, 1965
COMMANDS: 1946-1947 Norris DD 859; 1951-1952 Destroyer Division 601; 1954-1955 Menifee APA 202; 1958-1959 Boston CAG 1; 1960-1963 Cruiser-Destroyer Flotilla 12
OFFICIAL ADDRESS: Naval Amphibious Base, Norfolk, Virginia 23520
HOME ADDRESS: 4405 Higbee Street, Philadelphia, Pennsylvania

ITALY
HENKE, AMMIRAGLIO DI SQUADRA EUGENIO, ITALIAN NAVY
DECORATIONS: 2 Medaglie d'argento al V.M.; 6 medaglie di bronzo al V.M.; 1 crose de guerra al V.M.; 1 avanzamento per merito di guerra; Grande Ufficiale Ordine Militare R.I.; Cavaliere di Gran Magistero del S.M.O.M.; Medaglia Mauriziana; Medaglia al merito di lunga navigazione M.M.
PRESENT APPOINTMENT: Capo del SID (Servizio Informazioni Difesa)
DATE OF BIRTH: 15 November 1909
DATE OF LAST PROMOTION: 1 January, 1968
OFFICIAL ADDRESS: Ministero della Difesa, Via XX settembre, Roma

CANADA
HENNESSY, VICE ADMIRAL R. L., CANADIAN ARMED FORCES
DECORATIONS: DSC 1942; CD 1948
PRESENT APPOINTMENT: Chief of Personnel, Canadian Forces Headquarters January 1969
DATE OF BIRTH: 5 September, 1918
EDUCATION: Cadet entry
PROMOTIONS: Cadet 28 August, 1936; Midshipman 1 May, 1937; A/Slt 1 May, 1939; Lieutenant 1 February, 1940; Assistant Lieutenant Commander 2 October, 1943; Lieutenant Commander 1 February, 1947 Commander 1 January, 1949; Captain 1 July, 1953; Commodore 30 June, 1960; Vice Admiral 16 July, 1966
PRINCIPAL COMMANDS AT SEA: HMCS Kings, HMCS Gatineau, HMCS Assiniboine February 1944-September 1945; HMCS Micmac September 1945-March 1947; HMCS Algonquin also Commander First Canadian Escort Squadron August 1954-June 1956
PREVIOUS APPOINTMENTS OF NOTE: HMCS Assiniboine as Executive Officer June 1941-October 1943; Royal Canadian Air Force Staff Course March 1947-September 1947; Naval Headquarters as Assistant Chief of Naval Personnel April 1948-June 1949; HMCS Quebec as Executive Officer January 1952-September 1953; National Defence College Course September, 1953-August 1954; HMCS Niobe in Command and Chief Staff Officer to Naval Member Canadian Joint Staff (London) and Alternate Naval Member to Military Agency for Standardization June 1966-September 1958; Commodore Personnel Atlantic Coast, Officer-in-Charge RCN Depot and on staff of the Flag Officer Atlantic Coast as Chief of Staff Personnel and Training Canadian Forces Headquarters as Comptroller General 1966-January 1969
OFFICIAL ADDRESS: Chief of Personnel, Canadian Forces Headquarters, Cartier Square, Ottawa 4, Ontario

UNITED KINGDOM
HEPBURN, SURGEON REAR-ADMIRAL N. S., ROYAL NAVY
DECORATIONS: C.B.E. 1968
PRESENT APPOINTMENT: MO i/c, RN Hospital, Haslar July 1969
DATE OF BIRTH: 2 February, 1913
EDUCATION: Broughton, Edinburgh, M.B. Cl. B. Ed. Univ. 1935; DPH (London) 1948; D.I.H. (London) 1952; Barrister-at-Law, Gray's Inn, 1956
DATES OF PROMOTIONS: 1941 Sgn. Lt. Cmdr; 1947 Surgn. Cmdr.; 1959 Surgn Captain; 1966 Sqn. Commodore; SRA 1969
OTHER PREVIOUS APPOINTMENTS OF NOTE: NMOH Ceylon 1948-1951; SMO HM Dluyd. Plymouth 1952-1955; SMO HMD Portsmouth 1955-1957; NMOH, Portsmouth 1959-1962; NAMOH, Malta 1962-1965; Deputy MDG 1966-1969
OFFICIAL ADDRESS: RN Hospital, Haslar, Gosport, PO12 2AA *Telephone:* Portsmouth 22351 ext. 91320
PRIVATE ADDRESS: Same as Official Address

U.K.
HEPWORTH CAPTAIN D., ROYAL NAVY
PRESENT APPOINTMENT: In Command HMS Ajax and Captain (D), Second Far East Destroyer Squadron
DATE OF BIRTH: 6 June, 1923
EDUCATION: Banbury Grammar School, Oxfordshire
DATES OF PROMOTIONS: Captain 31 December, 1964; Commander 31 December, 1958
PRINCIPAL COMMANDS AT SEA: HMS Ajax; HMS Ashanti; HMS Stalker and Senior Officer Submarines, Londerry; HM Submarine Truncheon; HM Submarine Thorough; HM Submarine Tudor
OTHER PREVIOUS APPOINTMENTS: Deputy Director Undersea Warfare, Naval Staff, Ministry of Defence (Navy)
OFFICIAL ADDRESS: HMS Ajax
PRIVATE ADDRESS: 73 Pine Hill, Epsom, Surrey *Telephone:* 21668

CHILE
HERRERA CAPTAIN R. A., CHILEAN NAVY
PRESENT APPOINTMENT: Director Instituto Hidrográfico de la Armada de Chile, 21 November, 1966
DATE OF BIRTH: 21 November, 1919
EDUCATION: Naval Academy of Chile (Naval Officer); Naval Polytechnical Academy of Chile (Navigator Specialist); USC and GS (Hydrographer)
DATES OF PROMOTIONS: Midshipman 1 January, 1940; Captain 30 April, 1966
PREVIOUS APPOINTMENTS OF NOTE: Member of Scientific Committee Oceanographic Research (SCOR); PIGH; Comisión Nacional de Geografia, Geodesía y Geogísica; Instituto Antárco Chileno; Instituto du Fomento Pesquero; Instituto de Recursas Naturales, Sociedad Clentífica
OFFICIAL ADDRESS: Casilla 324; Valparaiso, Chile. *Telephone:* 7531
PRIVATE ADDRESS: Los Plátanos 2636, Viña del Mar, Chile

UNITED KINGDOM
HERVEY, COMMANDER J. B., ROYAL NAVY
PRESENT APPOINTMENT: Commanding Officer, HMS Warspite 1968
DATE OF BIRTH: 14 May, 1928
EDUCATION: Marlborough College
DATES OF PROMOTIONS: 1964 Commander
PRINCIPAL COMMANDS AT SEA: 1956-1957 HMS Aeneas; 1959-1962 HMS Ambuse; 1962-1964 HMS Oracle; 1966-1967 HMS Cavalier
OTHER PREVIOUS APPOINTMENTS OF NOTE: Commanding Officer, 6th Submarine Division, Halifax, Nova Scotia 1964-1966
OFFICIAL ADDRESS: HMS Warspite, BFPO Ships, London
PRIVATE ADDRESS: c/o Westminster Bank, 26 Haymarket, London S.W.1.

GERMANY
HETZ, VICE ADMIRAL, KARL, GERMAN NAVY
DECORATIONS: Ehrenblattspange der Marine Deutsches Kreuz in Gold; Eisernes Kreuz 1 Klasse; Eisernes Kreuz 2 Klasse; Zerstörerkriegsabzeichen
PRESENT APPOINTMENT: Flag Officer Germany (NATO); C-in-C German Fleet (National) 1 January, 1966
DATE OF BIRTH: 11 May, 1920;
EDUCATION: Final High School Examination 1929;
PRINCIPAL COMMANDS: Flag-Lieutenant of the Fleet 1938-1939; Executive Officer Destroyer Jacobi 1939-1940; Destroyer Commands Staff Officer 1941-1943; Commanding Officer Z 34 North Norway and Baltic 1943-1945; After the war, military expert in English and American Services; Reactivated in Bundesmarine 1956; MOD-Section Bonn 1956-1960; Commander 3rd Destroyer Squadron 1960-1962; Deputy Chief of Naval Staff Germany 1963-1966; C-in-C German Fleet 1 October, 1966
DATES OF PROMOTIONS: Lieutenant October 1933; Lieutenant Commander April 1943; Commander January 1956; Captain January 1958; Rear Admiral i.G. January 1963; Rear Admiral 1964; Vice Admiral 1966
OFFICIAL ADDRESS: Flag Officer Germany, 2392 Glücksburg-Meierwik, Postfach 800
PRIVATE ADDRESS: Vice Admiral Karl Hetz, 239 Flensburg, Am Schützenhof 10

U.S.A.
HEYWORTH, REAR-ADMIRAL LAWRENCE, JNR. (NAVAL AVIATOR) US NAVY
CURRENT DUTY STATION: Commandant of Midshipmen, Naval Academy (August 1967)
DATE OF BIRTH: 1921
EDUCATION: 1930 Naval Academy; 1958 Naval War College
FIRST COMMISSIONED: 5th June, 1930
PROMOTED TO: Rear Admiral, selected for promotion on 6th June, 1968
COMMANDS: 1958-1958 Fighter Squadron 81; 1958-1959 Attack Squadron 81; 1959-1960 Carrier Air Group 8; 1963-1964 Pawcatuck AO 108; 1965-1966 America CVA 66
OFFICIAL ADDRESS: Naval Academy, Annapolis, Maryland 21402

UNITED KINGDOM
HIGHAM, COMMODORE P. R. C., ROYAL NAVY
PRESENT APPOINTMENT: Commodore-in-Charge, Hong Kong
DATE OF BIRTH: 9 June, 1920
EDUCATION: RN Dartmouth
DATES OF PROMOTIONS: Commander 1953; 1961 Captain; 1968 Commodore
PREVIOUS APPOINTMENTS OF NOTE: Experimental Commander HMS Excellent 1957-1959; Naval Attaché Middle East 1962-1964; Deputy Chief Polaris Executive 1965-1968; Imperial Defence College 1965
OFFICIAL ADDRESS: Office of the Commodore-in-Charge, Royal Navy, Hong Kong
PRIVATE ADDRESS: Holmwood House, Emsworth, Hampshire

U.S.A.
HILDRETH, REAR-ADMIRAL JAMES BERTRAM, US NAVY
CURRENT DUTY STATION: Commander, US Naval Base, Guantanamo Bay, Cuba (July 1968)
DATE OF BIRTH: 1920
EDUCATION: 1940 University of California (NROTC); 1947 General Line School; 1957 Armed Forces Staff College; 1961 Naval War College
FIRST COMMISSIONED: 25th May, 1940
PROMOTED TO: Rear Admiral 1st March, 1969
COMMANDS: 1947-1948 George DE 697; 1952-1954 Hopewell DD 681; 1961-1962 Destroyer Division 72; 1964-1965 Springfield CLG 7
OFFICIAL ADDRESS: Box 34, FPO New York 09593
HOME ADDRESS: 358 Jerome Avenue, Piedmont, California

U.S.A.
HILL, REAR-ADMIRAL (SELECTEE) CLARENCE ARTHUR, JNR. (NAVAL AVIATOR) US NAVY
CURRENT DUTY STATION: Chief, Navy Section, Military Group, Brazil (March 1969)
DATE OF BIRTH: 1920
EDUCATION: 1944 Naval Academy; 1957 Naval Postgraduate School; 1962 Naval War College
FIRST COMMISSIONED: 9th June, 1943
PROMOTED TO: Rear Admiral, selected for promotion on 6th June, 1968. Authrorzed to assume title of Rear Admiral
COMMANDS: 1960-1961 Attack Squadron 72; 1964-1965 Wrangell Ae 12; 1967-1969 Independence CVP 62
OFFICIAL ADDRESS: APO New York 09676

UNITED KINGDOM
HILL-NORTON, ADMIRAL SIR P., ROYAL NAVY
DECORATIONS: K.C.B. 1967
PRESENT APPOINTMENT: Commander-in-Chief, Far East 8 March, 1969
DATE OF BIRTH: 8 February, 1915
EDUCATION RNC Dartmouth; RNC Greenwich
DATES OF PROMOTIONS: 1948 Commander; 1953 Captain; 1962 Rear-Admiral; 1965 Vice Admiral; 1968 Admiral
PRINCIPAL COMMANDS AT SEA: 1955-1956 HMS Decoy; 1959-1961 HMS Ark Royal; 1964-1966 FO2 Far East Fleet
OTHER PREVIOUS APPOINTMENTS OF NOTE: ACNS 1962-1964; DCDS (P & L) 1966; Second Sea Lord 1967; VCNS 1967-1969
OFFICIAL ADDRESS: H.Q. Far East Command, Phoenix Park, c/o GPO Singapore
PRIVATE ADDRESS: King's Mill House, South Nutfield, Surrey

UNITED KINGDOM
HOGG, VICE-ADMIRAL SIR I., ROYAL NAVY
DECORATIONS: K.C.B. 1968; D.S.C. (Crete 1941 and Bar, Normandy) 1944
PRESENT APPOINTMENT: Vice Chief of Defence Staff November 1967
DATE OF BIRTH: 30 May, 1911
EDUCATION: Cheltenham 1925-1929; Special entry cadet
DATES OF PROMOTIONS: Captain December 1953; Rear-Admiral January 1963; Vice Admiral April 1966
PRINCIPAL COMMANDS AT SEA: HMS Sluys 1950-1952
OTHER PREVIOUS APPOINTMENTS OF NOTE: British Defence Staff, Washington 1955-1957; Flag Officer Medway and Admiral Superintendent, Chatham 1963-1966
OFFICIAL ADDRESS: Ministry of Defence, Main Building, Whitehall,

UNITED KINGDOM
HOLFORD, REAR-ADMIRAL F. D., ROYAL NAVY
DECORATIONS: D.S.C.
PRESENT APPOINTMENT: Director General Naval Manpower 1967
DATE OF BIRTH: 28 June, 1916
EDUCATION: RNC Dartmouth
DATES OF PROMOTIONS: 1951 Commander; 1957 Captain; 1967 Rear-Admiral
PREVIOUS APPOINTMENTS OF NOTE: Deputy Director Surface Weapons 1957-1960; Commander-in-Charge, Hong Kong (Guided Weapons) 1965-1967
OFFICIAL ADDRESS: M.O.D. (Navy) Old Admiralty Building Whitehall S.W.1. *Telephone:* 930-9000 1233
PRIVATE ADDRESS: Great Down Cottage, Soberton, Hants.

U.S.A.
HOLLOWAY, REAR-ADMIRAL JAMES LEMUEL, III (NAVAL AVIATOR) US NAVY
CURRENT DUTY STATION: Director, Strike Warfare Division, Office of the Chief of Naval Operations and CVAN Program co-Ordinator (March 1969; February 1968, respectively)
DATE OF BIRTH: 1922
EDUCATION: 1943 Naval Academy; 1962 National War College
FIRST COMMISSIONED: 19th June, 1942
PROMOTED TO: Rear Admiral 1st July, 1967
COMMANDS: 1956-1958 Attack Squadron 83; 1962-1963 Salisbury Sound AV 13; 1965-1967 Enterprise CVAN 65
OFFICIAL ADDRESS: The Pentagon, Washington, DC 20350
HOME ADDRESS: 924 South 26th Street, Arlington, Virginia

U.S.A.
HOLMBERG, REAR-ADMIRAL PAUL ALGODTE (AERONAUTICAL ENGINEERING DUTY) US NAVY
CURRENT DUTY STATION: Vice Commander, Naval Air Systems Command
DATE OF BIRTH: 1915
EDUCATION: 1939 Naval Academy; 1947 Naval Postgraduate School
FIRST COMMISSIONED: 1st June, 1939
PROMOTED TO: Rear Admiral 10th August, 1965
MAJOR AWARDS: Navy Cross with Gold Star in lieu of second award
COMMANDS: 1961-1963 Pacific Missile Range Facility Kwajalein
OFFICIAL ADDRESS: Main Navy Building, Washington, DC 20360
HOME ADDRESS: 3760 North Upland Street, Arlington, Virginia

U.S.A.
HOLMES, ADMIRAL EPHRAIM PAUL, US NAVY
CURRENT DUTY STATION: Commander in Chief, Atlantic; US Atlantic Fleet and Supreme Allied Commander, Atlantic (June 1967)
DATE OF BIRTH: 1908
EDUCATION: 1930 Naval Academy; 1938 Naval Postgraduate School; 1951 Naval War
FIRST COMMISSIONED: 5th June, 1930
PROMOTED TO: Rear Admiral 1st July, 1957; Vice Admiral 25th February, 1963; Admiral 17th June,1967
COMMANDS: 1943-1944 Stockham DD 683; 1952-1953 Sanborn APA 193; 1955-1956 Northampton CLC 1; 1959-1960 Cruiser Divison 4; 1963-1964 Amphibious Force, Pacific Fleet 1964 First Fleet
OFFICIAL ADDRESS: Norfolk, Virginia 23511
HOME ADDRESS: 101 Alma Street, Palo Alto, California

UNITED KINGDOM
HOLT, REAR-ADMIRAL J. B., ROYAL NAVY
DECORATIONS: C.B. 1969; B.Sc. Tech C.Eng FIEE
PRESENT APPOINTMENT: Director General Aircraft (Naval), Ministry of Defence, Navy Department January 1967
DATE OF BIRTH: 1 June, 1912
EDUCATION: William Hulme Grammer School, Manchester; Manchester University
DATES OF PROMOTIONS: 1948 Commander; 1958 Captain; 1967 Rear-Admiral;
PREVIOUS APPOINTMENTS OF NOTE: Command of the Air Electrical Establishment; 1961-1963 HMS Ariel; 1964-1966 Director of Officer Appointments (Engineers); 1965-1967 Naval A.D.C. to HM The Queen
OFFICIAL ADDRESS: Ministry of Defence (Navy Dept.), Old Admiralty Building, Whitehall, London S.W.1 *Telephone:* 01-930-9000 ext. 1415
PRIVATE ADDRESS: Rowley Cottage, Thursley, Near Godalming, Surrey

U.S.A.
HOOPER, VICE-ADMIRAL EDWIN BICKFORD, US NAVY
CURRENT DUTY STATION: Naval Mamber, Joint Logistics Review Board (March 1969)
DATE OF BIRTH: 1909
EDUCATION: 1931 Naval Academy; 1940 Naval Postgraduate School; 1953 National War College
FIRST COMMISSIONED: 4th June, 1931
PROMOTED TO: Rear Admiral 1st October, 1959; Vice Admiral 5th March, 1969
COMMANDS: 1945 Anti-Aircraft Training Center, Oahu Hawaii; 1949-1950 Waccamaw AO 109954-1955 Sierra AD 18; 1958-1959 Destroyer Squadron 26; 1961-1962 Amphibious Group 1; 1965-1968 Service Force, Pacific Fleet
OFFICIAL ADDRESS: Tempo A 2nd & T St., N.W. Washington, DC 20315
HOME ADDRESS: Chevy Chase, Maryland

JAPAN
HORIE, VICE-ADMIRAL F.
PRESENT APPOINTMENT: Commandant, Maizuru Regional District 1st April 1968, retired 1 July, 1969
DATE OF BIRTH: 20 February, 1912
EDUCATION: Graduated from the Imperial Japanese Naval Academy Engineering November 1933
DATE OF PROMOTIONS: Captain August 1955; Rear Admiral July 1963; Vice Admiral January 1967
PREVIOUS APPOINTMENTS: Deputy Chief, Supply and Accounts Division June 1962; Vice President, MASDF Staff College; Chief, J-4 Division. JSO March 1965; Superintendent, MSDF Officer Candidate School July 1966; Commandant, Maizuru Regional District April 1968
OFFICIAL ADDRESS: Maizuru Regional District, O-Banchi, Amarube, Maizuru-Shi, Japan. *Telephone:* Maizuru 2-2250
PRIVATE ADDRESS: MSDF Official House, 1 Amarube, Maizuru-Shi, Kyoto-Fu, Japan

U.S.A.
HOUSE, REAR-ADMIRAL WILLIAM HIRAM, US NAVY
CURRENT DUTY STATION: Commander, Carrier Division 4 (March 1969)
DATE OF BIRTH: 1916
EDUCATION: 1940 Naval Academy; 1953 Armed Forces Staff College; 1961 Naval War College
FIRST COMMISSIONED: 6th June, 1940
PROMOTED TO: Rear Admiral 1st October, 1967
MAJOR AWARD: Navy Cross
COMMANDS: 1948-1949 Attack Squadron 115; 1955-1957 Carrier Air Group 11; 1962-1963 Kennebec AO 36; 1963-1965 Oriskany CVA 34
OFFICIAL ADDRESS: FPO New York, New York 09501
HOME ADDRESS: 951 Cabrillo Avenue, Coronado, California

U.S.A.
HOUSER, REAR-ADMIRAL WILLIAM DOUGLAS, US NAVY
CURRENT DUTY STATION: Director, Aviation Plans and Requirements Division, Office of the Chief of Naval Operations (November 1968)
DATE OF BIRTH: 1921
EDUCATION: 1942 Naval Academy; 1959 Naval War College
FIRST COMMISSIONED: 19th December, 1941
PROMOTED TO: Rear Admiral 1st July, 1967
COMMANDS: 1959-1960 Fighter Squadron 124; 1963-1965 Mauna Loa AE 22; 1965-1966 Constellation CVA 64
OFFICIAL ADDRESS: The Pentagon, Washington, DC 20350
HOME ADDRESS: Miami, Florida

U.K.
HOWARD, CAPTAIN, H. E., ROYAL NAVY
DECORATIONS: DSC 1943
PRESENT APPOINTMENT: Naval Adviser to the British High Commissioner in Canada 1 September, 1968; The Royal Naval Liaison Officer, British Defence Liaison Staff Canada 1 September, 1968; Commanding Officer, HMS Howard 1 September, 1968
DATE OF BIRTH: 3 March, 1923
EDUCATION: Royal Naval College Dartmouth
DATES OF PROMOTIONS: Commander June, 1959; Captain December 1967
OTHER PREVIOUS APPOINTMENTS OF NOTE: ecutive Officer Hartland Point 1963; Executive Officer Ganges 1965; National Defence College Canada 1967
OFFICIAL ADDRESS: British High Commission Building, 80 Elgin Street, Ottawa 4, Canada. *Telephone:* 237-1530 ext. 412
PRIVATE ADDRESS: c/o Coutts and Co., 440 Strand, London, WC2

U.S.A.
HOWARD, REAR-ADMIRAL JOSEPH LEON (SUPPLY CORPS) US NAVY
CURRENT DUTY STATION: Deputy Director for Contract Administrative Services, Defense Supply Agency (July 1968)
DATE OF BIRTH: 1917
EDUCATION: 1949 University of California Berkeley Naval War College
FIRST COMMISSIONED: 23rd October, 1940 Naval Reserve; 20th April 1943 US Navy
PROMOTED TO: Rear Admiral 1st July, 1967
OFFICIAL ADDRESS: Cameron Station, Alexandria, Virginia 22314
HOME ADDRESS: 4005 Mill Creek Drive, Annandale, Virginia

U.S.A.
HUBBELL, REAR-ADMIRAL LESTER EARLE, US NAVY
CURRENT DUTY STATION: Commander, Cruiser-Destroyer Flotilla 6 (April 1969)
DATE OF BIRTH: 1916
EDUCATION: 1938 Georgia School of Technology (NROTC); 1951 Armed Forces Staff College; 1961 National War College
FIRST COMMISSIONED: 11th June, 1938
PROMOTED TO: Rear Admiral 1st July, 1966
COMMANDS: 1944-1945 Rolf DE 362; 1953-1955 Owen DD 536; 1956-1957 Destroyer Division 262; 1957-1958 Destroyer Squadron 26; 1958-1960 Fleet Air Defense Training Center Dam Neck, Virginia Beach, Virginia; 1961-1962 Yosemite AD 19; 1962-1963 Destroyer Squadron 15
OFFICIAL ADDRESS: FPO New York 09501
HOME ADDRESS: 500 Deal Lake Drive, Asbury Park, New Jersey

NEW ZEALAND
HUTCHINGS, W., ROYAL NEW ZEALAND NAVY
PRESENT APPOINTMENT: *Secretary of Defence (1 February, 1966)
DATE OF BIRTH: 7 December, 1911
EDUCATION: University Entrance
APPOINTMENTS OF NOTE: Assistant Navy Secretary 1951-1962; Navy Secretary 1964-1965
OFFICIAL ADDRESS: MOD GPO Box 295, Wellington NZ *Telephone:* 49-800
PRIVATE ADDRESS: 46 Penrose Street, Lower Hutt, NZ

U.S.A.

HYLAND, ADMIRAL JOHN JOSEPH (NAVAL AVIATOR) US NAVY
CURRENT DUTY STATION: Commander in Chief, US Pacific Fleet (November 1967)
DATE OF BIRTH: 1912
EDUCATION: 1934 Naval Academy; 1954 National War College
FIRST COMMISSIONED: 31st May, 1934
PROMOTED TO: Rear Admiral 1st July, 1960; Vice Admiral 1st December, 1965; Admiral 1st December, 1967
COMMANDS: 1944-1945 Carrier Air Group 10; 1956-1957 Onslow AVP 48; 1958-1959 Saratoga CVA 60; 1959-1960 Airborne Early Warning Wing, Atlantic/Commander, Fleet Air Argentina (Newfoundland); 1962-1963 Carrier Division 4; 1965-1967 Seventh Fleet
OFFICIAL ADDRESS: (Pearl Harbor) FPO San Francisco 96610
HOME ADDRESS: Union Street, Deep River, Connecticut

AUSTRALIA
HYLAND, MR. M. T., AUSTRALIAN NAVY
DECORATIONS: OBE 1969
PRESENT APPOINTMENT: First Assistant Secretary, Finance and Material (1964)
DATE OF BIRTH: 20 February, 1920
EDUCATION: A.A.S.A.; Imperial Defence College 1966
PREVIOUS APPOINTMENTS: Assistant Secretary 1960
OFFICIAL ADDRESS: Department of the Navy, Russell Offices, Canberra A.C.T. *Telephone:* 653204
PRIVATE ADDRESS: 83 Jacka Crescent, Campbell Canberra A.C.T.

JAPAN
IBUKI, VICE-ADMIRAL, JMSDF S.
DECORATIONS: The Fifth Class Order of Golden Kite Medal 29 April, 1940; The Sixth Class Order of the Rising Sun Medal 29 April, 1940; The Fifth Class Order of the Secret Treasure Medal 16 February, 1944
PRESENT APPOINTMENT: CINC Self Defence Fleet 1 January, 1969
EDUCATION Imperial Japanese Naval Academy 1934;
DATE OF BIRTH: 1 January, 1913
DATES OF PROMOTIONS: Captain 16 August, 1957; Rear Admiral 1 July, 1963; Vice Admiral 1 January, 1967
PRINCIPAL APPOINTMENTS OF NOTE: Commander Training Air Command 16 January, 1967; Commander Fleet Air Force 1 January, 1968; CINC Self Defence Fleet 1st January, 1969
OFFICIAL ADDRESS: CINC Self Defence Fleet, 7-73 Funakoshi-cho, Yokosuka-shi
PRIVATE ADDRESS: 196-386 Okazu-cho Yokohama-shi

ARGENTINA
IGLESIAS, CAPTAIN R. A., ARGENTINE NAVY
PRESENT APPOINTMENT: Commander Third Naval Aviation Force 14 February, 1969
DATE OF BIRTH: 1 April, 1925
EDUCATION: Escuela Anexa a la Universidad de la Plata 1932-1937; La Plata National College 1937-1941; Naval School, Rió Santiago 1942-1946; Naval Air School, Comandante Espara Air Naval Base; Naval War School 1958 and 1967
DATES OF PROMOTIONS: Ensign, December 1946; Lieutenant Junior grade December, 1948; Lieutenant Senior grade December 1953; Lieutenant Commander December 1960; Captain December 1966
PRINCIPAL COMMANDS: 2nd Attack Squadron, Punta Indio Air Naval Base 1957; 2nd Scout and A/S Squadron, Puerto Belgrano Naval Air Base 1959; 2nd Air Naval Wing of 2nd Naval Aviation Force, Comandante Espora Air Naval Base, 1963; Espora Naval Air Base 1964
OTHER PREVIOUS APPOINTMENTS OF NOTE: Operations Officer of ARA Independencia 1961; Overhaul and Repair Ships Director 1962; Chief of Operations Department 1965-1967; Chief of Staff, Naval Aviation Command 1967; Intelligence; Department Chief, Joint Armed Forces Staff, 1968
OFFICIAL ADDRESS: Fuerza Aeronaval No. 3, Base Aeronaval Ezeiza Provincia de Buenos Aires, Argentina
PRIVATE ADDRESS: Casa No. 3 La Valentina, Aerodromo Ezeiza, Provincia de Buenos Aires, Argentina

JAPAN
IMAI, CAPTAIN K.
DECORATIONS: 6th Class Order of the Sacred Treasure
PRESENT APPOINTMENT: Commander of Submarine Flotilla 1 16 December, 1968
DATE OF BIRTH: 17 December, 1918
EDUCATION: Naval Academy 1939; Naval Submarine School
DATE OF PROMOTIONS: Lieutenant November 1943; Commander August 1957; Captain July 1964
PRINCIPAL COMMANDS AT SEA: Commanding Officer SS "RO 68" March 1944; Commanding Officer SS "I 202" August 1944 Commanding Officer of LSSL "Ran" January 1953; Commanding Officer of DD "Asakaze" December 1961; Commander of Submarine Division 2 January, 1968
OTHER PREVIOUS APPOINTMENTS OF NOTE: C/S Escort Flotilla 2 December 1962; C/S Submarine Flotilla 1 February, 1963; AC/S for Operation, Self Defense Fleet December, 1965
OFFICIAL ADDRESS: Submarine Flotilla 1 c/o Kure Submarine Base, Showa-dori, Kure-Shi, Japan
PRIVATE ADDRESS: Official Residence No. 38, 13-Chome Miyahara-dori, Kure-Shi, Japan

U.S.A.
IRONS, REAR ADMIRAL, EDWARD PACE (MEDICAL CORPS) US NAVY
CURRENT DUTY STATION:
Commanding Officer, Naval Aerospace Medical Center; additional duty: Staff, Chief of Naval Air Training (June 1969)
DATE OF BIRTH: 1913
EDUCATION: 1939 University of Illinois College of Medicine
DATE OF COMMISSION: 14th August, 1939
PROMOTED TO: Rear Admiral 1st July, 1965
COMMANDS: 1964-1966 Naval Hospital, Yokosuka, Japan; additional duty; Staff, Medical Officer, US Naval Forces Japan; Staff Advisor to Commander, US Forces Japan
OFFICIAL ADDRESS: Pensacola, Florida 32512
HOME ADDRESS: 614 North 12th Street, Mt. Vernon, Illinois

U.S.A.

ISAMAN, REAR-ADMIRAL, ROY MAURICE (NAVAL AVIATOR) US NAVY
CURRENT DUTY STATION: Commander, Carrier Division 7 (April 1969)
DATE OF BIRTH: 1917
EDUCATION: 1947 University of Idaho, General Line School; 1959 Industrial College of the Armed Forces
DATE OF COMMISSION: 21st April, 1941
PROMOTED TO: Rear Admiral, 1st December, 1965
COMMANDS: 1951-9153 Attack Squadron 15; 1960-1962 Shasta AE 6; 1962-1963 Midway CVA 41; 1965-1967 PATROL Force 7th Fleet/US Taiwan Patrol Force/Fleet Air Wing 1
MAJOR AWARDS: Navy Cross
OFFICIAL ADDRESS: FPO San Francisco, California 96601
HOME ADDRESS: Jacksonville, Florida

JAPAN
ISHIDA, VICE-ADMIRAL S., JAPANESE MARITIME SELF DEFENCE FORCE
DECORATIONS: The Fifth Order of Sacred Treasure 1943; The Sixth of Rising Sun 1939 Legion of Merit Officer 1963;
PRESENT APPOINTMENT: Vice Chief of the Maritime Staff 1 July, 1969
DATE OF BIRTH: 22 April, 1916
EDUCATION: Naval Academy, Etajima
DATE OF PROMOTIONS: Lieutenant Commander 15 October, 1944; Lieutenant Commander JMSDF 1 May, 1952; Commander JMSDF 16 August, 1953; Captain JMSDF 16 February, 1958; Rear Admiral JMSDF 1 January, 1965; Vice Admiral JMSDF 1 July, 1968
PRINCIPAL COMMANDS AT SEA: Commanding Officer PF 297 Shii April 1954-September 1954; Commander Mine Sweeper Flotilla 1 (March 1965-April 1966);
OTHER PREVIOUS APPOINTMENTS OF NOTE: Yokosuka Regional Headquarters May 1952-August 1954; Headquarters Escort Flotilla 2 September 1954-March 1955 Student, Maritime Staff College March 1955-February 1956; Naval Attache Japanese Embassy USA February 1959-September 1962; Head Plans and Program Section, Maritime Office February 1963-March 1965; Chief Administrations Division, Maritime Staff Office May 1966-June 1968
OFFICIAL ADDRESS: 2-50 Ominato-machi, Mutsu-shi, Aomori-ken
PRIVATE ADDRESS: 19-23 Uda-machi, Mutsu-shi, Aomori-ken

JAPAN
ISHIKUMA, VICE-ADMIRAL T.
DECORATION: Fifth Class Order of the Sacred Treasure; Sixth Class Order of the Rising Sun
PRESENT APPOINTMENT: Chief Administration Division, Maritime Staff Office
DATE OF BIRTH: 22 February, 1916
EDUCATION: Graduated from the Imperial Japanese Naval Academy March 1938; Graduated from Senior Officer Course, MSDF Staff College January 1957
DATE OF PROMOTIONS: Lieutenant Commander May 1952; Commander February 1954; Captain February 1959; Rear Admiral Janaury 1966; Vice Admiral July 1969
PREVIOUS APPOINTMENTS OF NOTE: Commanding Officer, PF Maki January 1957; Commander, 4th Escort Division August 1961; Commander, 2nd Escort Flotilla July 1965; Chief of Staff, Self Defence Fleet July 1966; Chief Plans and Program Sub-Section, Maritime Staff Office January 1963; Chief, Personnel Section, MSO February 1964; Chief Administration Division, MSO July 1968
OFFICIAL ADDRESS Maritime Staff Office, Japan Defence Agency, 9-7-45, Akasaka, Minato-Ku, Tokyo, Japan. *Telephone:* 408-5211 ext. 2780
PRIVATE ADDRESS: 3-3-5, Wakabayashi, Setagaya-Ku, Tokyo, Japan *Telephone:* 422-4230

JAPAN
ISHIMORI, REAR-ADMIRAL J.
PRESENT APPOINTMENT: Commander Mine Flotilla 1 JMSDF
DATE OF BIRTH: 10 September, 1917
EDUCATION: Graduated Naval Academy in 1938; MSDF Staff College in 1957
DATES OF PROMOTIONS: Lieutenant Commander 15 July, 1952; Commander 16 February, 1955; Captain 1 January, 1961; Rear Admiral 1 July, 1969
PRINCIPAL COMMANDS AT SEA: Commanding Officer DD Teruzuki February 1960—January 1961; Chief of Staff, The Fleet Escort Force September 1965— December 1966; Commander Mine Flotilla 1 January 1969
OTHER PREVIOUS APPOINTMENTS OF NOTE: Chief of Staff Maizuru, Regional District Headquarter 1966-1968
OFFICIAL ADDRESS: c/o Headquarters, Kure Regional District, JMSDF 3-Chome Saiwai-cho Kure-shi, Hiroshima-ken, Japan. *Telephone:* Kure 22-5511
PRIVATE ADDRESS: 4-54 Taura-cho Yokosuka-shi, Kanagawa-ken, Japan

JAPAN
ITAYA, ADMIRAL JMSDF T.
DECORATIONS: The Fifth Order of the Golden Kite 1937; The Fourth Order of the Sacred Treasure May 1943); Gran Estrella al Merito Militar (Chile) November 1966; The Legion of Merit Degree of Commander (USA) February 1967; Cruz Peruana al Merito Naval Gran Oficial (Peru) June 1967
PRESENT APPOINTMENT: Chairman, Joint Staff Council 1 July, 1969
DATE OF BIRTH: 20 August, 1911
EDUCATION: Graduated from the Imperial Japanese Naval Academy November 1932; Student, US Naval War College August 1957—July 1958
DATES OF PROMOTIONS: Ensign, IJN March 1934; Lieutenant Junior Grade November 1935; Lieutenant June 1938; Lieutenant Commander November 1942; Commander September 1945; Commander, JMSDF May 1952; Captain August 1954; Rear Admiral July 1962; Vice Admiral July 1964
PREVIOUS APPOINTMENTS OF NOTE: Commander, 1st Escort Division April 1956; Commander, Fleet Escort Force July 1964; Chief, Personnel Section, Maritime Staff Office September, 1954; Chief, Education Division, MSDF Staff College December 1959; Deputy Chief, Operations Division MSO July 1961; Chief Administration Division MSO July 1962; Commandant, Yokosuka Regional District Headquarter July 1965; Chief of the Maritime Staff April 1966
OFFICIAL ADRESS: Maritime Staff Office, Japan Defence Agency, 9-7-45 Akasaka, Minato-ku, Tokyo, Japan. *Telephone:* 408-5211
PRIVATE ADRESS: 2-1-7 Yagumo, Meguro-ku, Tokyo, Japan

U.S.A.
JACKSON, REAR-ADMIRAL, DAVID HENRY (ENGINEERING DUTY) US NAVY
CURRENT DUTY STATION: Fleet Maintenance Officer, Pacific Fleet; additional duty: Maintenance Officer, Service Force Pacific (July 1968)
DATE OF BIRTH: 1917
EDUCATION: 1941 Naval Academy; 1944 Naval Postgraduate School; 1958 Naval War College
DATE OF COMMISSION: 7th February, 1941
PROMOTED TO: Rear Admiral 1st March, 1969
COMMANDS: 1966-1968 Naval Ship Repair Facility, Subic Bay, Philippines
OFFICIAL ADDRESS: (Pearl Harbor) FPO San Francisco, California 96610
HOME ADDRESS: 1123 Catalpa, El Dorado, Arkansas

U.S.A.
JACKSON, REAR-ADMIRAL PERCIVAL WILLIAM (NAVAL AVIATOR) US NAVY
CURRENT DUTY STATION: Director, J-1 (Personnel), Office of the Joint Chiefs of Staff (January 1968)
DATE OF BIRTH: 1914
EDUCATION: 1936 Syracuse University; 1947 General Line School; 1956 Naval War College; 1964 National War College
DATE OF COMMISSION: 1st December, 1937
PROMOTED TO: Rear Admiral 11th October, 1966
COMMANDS: 1942-1943 Scouting Squadron 31; 1943-1945 Composite Squadron 27; 1945-1946 Fighting Squadron 11; 1953 Naval Auxiliary Air Station, Chincoteague, Virginia; 1959-1960 Orca AVP 49; 1960-1961 Kearsarge CVS 33; 1966-1967 Carrier Division 14
MAJOR AWARDS: Navy Cross
OFFICIAL ADDRESS: The Pentagon, Washington, DC 20301
HOME ADDRESS: 59 Grand Avenuse, Poughkeepsie, New York

U.S.A.
JAMES, REAR-ADMIRAL JACK MILTON (NAVAL AVIATOR) US NAVY
CURRENT DUTY STATION: Commander, Carrier Division 2 (May 1969)
DATE OF BIRTH: 1920
EDUCATION: 1942 Naval Academy; 1960 Naval War College; 1963 Industrial College of the Armed Forces
DATE OF COMMISSION: 19th December, 1941
PROMOTED TO: Rear Admiral 1st August, 1968
COMMANDS: 1952-1953 Fighter Squadron 81; 1957-1959 Carrier Air Group 6; 1963-1964 Salamonie AO 26; 1964-1965 Saratoga CVA 60
OFFICIAL ADDRESS: FPO New York 09501
HOME ADDRESS: 132 East Andrew Avenue, Wildwood, New Jersey.

U.K.
JANION, Captain H. P., ROYAL NAVY
PRESENT APPOINTMENT: Commanding Officer, HMS Aurora 4 December, 1968
DATE OF BIRTH: 28 September, 1923
EDUCATIONS: Britannia Royal Naval College, Dartmouth 1937-1940
DATES OF PROMOTIONS: Lieutenant Commander 16 March 1952; Commander 31 December, 1958; Captain 30 June, 1966
PRINCIPAL COMMANDS AT SEA: HMS Jewel (and as Senior Officer, 2nd Division Dartmouth Training Squadron) 1960-1961
OTHER PREVIOUS APPOINTMENTS OF NOTE: Senior Direction Officer HMS Ark Royal 1956-1958; Commander, Exchange Service with USN 1958-1960; Training Commander HMS Raleigh 1962-1964; Executive Officer, HMS Ark Royal 1964-1966; Captain, MOD (Navy) 1966-1968
OFFICIAL ADDRESS: HMS Aurora, BFPO Ships
PRIVATE ADDRESS: Greystones, Bath Road, Bradford-on-Avon, Wilts.

U.S.A.
JANNEY, REAR ADMIRAL, FREDERICK EMERY, US NAVY
CURRENT DUTY STATION:
Deputy Chief of Staff for Military Assistance, Logistics & Administration, Commander-in-Chief Pacific (June 1969)
DATE OF BIRTH: 1914
EDUCATION: 1937 Naval Academy; 1956 National War College
DATE OF COMMISSION: 3rd June, 1937
PROMOTED TO: Rear Admiral 1st July, 1965
COMMANDS: 1944-1945 Hackleback SS 295; 1946-1948 Raton SS 270; 1952-1954 Submarine Division 32; 1958-1959 Fulton AS 11; 1960-1961 Topeka CLG 8; 1965-1967 Service Group 3
OFFICIAL ADDRESS: Camp Smith, Oahu, Hawaii, FPO San Francisco, California, 96610
HOME ADDRESS: Greenwich, Connecticut

UNITED KINGDOM
JANVRIN, VICE-ADMIRAL SIR H. R. B.
DECORATIONS: D.S.C. 1940; C.B. 1965; K.C.B. 1969
PRESENT APPOINTMENT: Flag Officer Naval Air Command 1968
DATE OF BIRTH: 9 May, 1915
EDUCATION: RNC Dartmouth
DATES OF PROMOTIONS: 1945 Lieutenant Commander; 1948 Commander; 1954 Captain 1964 Rear-Admiral; 1967 Vice Admiral
PRINCIPAL COMMANDS: 1951-1953 HMS Broadsword; 1957-1958 (Capt. D 2nd TS) HMS Grenville; 1958 RNAS Brandy; 1959-1960 HMS Victorious; 1964-1966 Flag Officer
OTHER PREVIOUS APPOINTMENTS OF NOTE: RN Staff College 1948; CSO to FOAC 1955; IDC 1961; Director of the Tactical and Weapon Policy Divison 1962; 1966 Deputy Chief of the Naval Staff 1966
OFFICIAL ADDRESS: Office of the Flag Officer, Naval Air Command, Wykeham Hall, Lee on Solent, Hants PO13 9NY
PRIVATE ADDRESS: Allen's Close, Chalford Hill, near Stroud, Glos.
London S.W.1. *Telephone:* 01 930 7022
PRIVATE ADDRESS: Widcombe Hill House, Bath, Somerset

GERMANY
JESCHONNEK, VICE ADMIRAL G., GERMAN NAVY
DECORATIONS: Iron Cross, 2nd & 1st Class; War Service Cross with Crossed Swords; Naval Car Badge Service Badge, 4th Class Legion of Merit; Degree of Commander
PRESENT APPOINTMENT: Chief of Staff 1 October, 1967
DATE OF BIRTH: 30 October, 1912
EDUCATION: Naval Staff College 1943-1944; US Naval War College Newport 1956-1957
DATES OF PROMOTIONS: Cadet April 1930; Ensign 1 October, 1934; Lieutenant 1 April 1939; Lieutenant Commander 1 April, 1943; Commander (recommissioned by Federal Armed Forces) 19 November, 1955; Captain (N) 28 May, 1958; Rear Admiral (Laver Hall) 7 August, 1963; Rear Admiral (Upper Half) 31 March 1965; Vice Admiral 8 June, 1966
PRINCIPAL COMMANDS AT SEA: Artillery Officer on Schleswig-Holstein 1943-1944; served on Nuruberg & Lutzav Minesweeping Service 1945-1947
OTHER PREVIOUS APPOINTMENTS OF NOTE: Staff Officer Operations Division Naval High Command 1944-1945; Directorate of Shipping Dept. of Inland Waterways 1947-1948; Deputy Chief of Staff Operations and Training NAVCENT 1960-1962; Chief of Staff Fleet Command, Ghicksburg 1962-1963; Head of Branch Navy Staff, Bonn April 1963-1965; Deputy Commander Allied Forces, Baltic Approaches, Kamp, Denmark June 1965-September 1967
OFFICIAL ADDRESS: German Navy Headquarters, 53 Bonn 1 *Telephone:* 2 0161

U.S.A.
JOHNSON, REAR-ADMIRAL FRANK LESHER, US NAVY
CURRENT DUTY STATION: Commandant, 13th Naval District (July 1968)
DATE OF BIRTH 1907
EDUCATION: 1930 Naval Academy; 1937 Naval Postgraduate School; 1951 Naval War College
DATE OF COMMISSION: 5th June, 1930
PROMOTED TO: Rear Admiral 1st January, 1958
COMMANDS: 1942-1943 Fletcher DD 445; 1944-1945 Purdy DD 734; 1949-1950 Destroyer Division 52; 1954-1956 Seminole AKA 104; 1956-1957 Destroyer Squadron 30; 1957-1959 Military Sea Transportation Service, Eastern Atlantic and Mediterranean Area; 1959-1960 Destroyer Flotilla 6; 1964-1965 Military Sea Transportation Service, Atlantic Area; 1965-1968 Naval Forces, Japan
OFFICIAL ADDRESS: Seattle, Washington 98115
HOME ADDRESS: 85 Dixon Street, Newport, Rhode Island

U.S.A.
JOHNSON, REAR-ADMIRAL (SELECTEE) HENRY JOSEPH (CIVIL ENGINEER CORPS) US NAVY
CURRENT DUTY STATION: Deputy Commander, Pacific Division, Naval Facilities Engineering Command, Southeast Asia (1968) Authorised to assume the title of Rear Admiral
DATE OF BIRTH: 1916
EDUCATION: 1960 Brooklyn Polytechnica Institute, Armed Forces Staff College
DATE OF COMMISSION: 16th January, 1940
PROMOTED TO: Rear Admiral, selected for promotion on 19th June, 1968
COMMANDS: 1945 Grainger AK 184; 1954-1955 Amphibious Construction Battalion 2
OFFICIAL ADDRESS: APO San Francisco 96243
HOME ADDRESS: Milford, Connecticut

U.S.A.
JOHNSON, VICE-ADMIRAL NELS CLARENCE, US NAVY
CURRENT DUTY STATION:
Director, International Staff, Inter-American Defense Board (June 1969)
DATE OF BIRTH: 1912
EDUCATION: 1934 Naval Academy; 1956 National War College
DATE OF COMMISSION: 31st May, 1934
PROMOTED TO: Rear Admiral 1st July, 1962; Vice Admiral 8th May, 1967
COMMANDS: 1943-1944 McLanahan DD 615; 1946-1947 Witek EDD 848; 1951-1953 Destroyer Division 262; 1956-1957 Arneb AKA 56; 1959-1960 Helena CA 75; 1961-1963 Amphibious Group 3
OFFICIAL ADDRESS: 2600 16th Street, NW Washington, DC 20441
HOME ADDRESS: Manchester, New Hampshire

U.S.A.
JOHNSTON, REAR-ADMIRAL MEANS, JNR., US NAVY
CURRENT DUTY STATION: Chief of Legislative Affairs (January 1969)
DATE OF BIRTH: 1916
EDUCATION: 1939 Naval Academy; 1951 Naval Postgraduate School; 1959 National War College
DATE OF COMMISSION: 1st June, 1939
PROMOTED TO: Rear Admiral 1st August, 1966
COMMANDS: 1945-1946 Hanna DE 449; 1946 Halford DD 480; 1946 Frank E. Evans DD 754; 1951-1952 Beatty DD 756; 1957-1958 Destroyer Division 222; 1961-1962 Capricornus AKA 57; 1962-1963 Destroyer Squadron 26; 1966-1968 Naval Base Newport, Rhode Island; 1968-1969 Cruiser-Destroyer Flotilla 10; additional duty: Commander, Naval Base Newport, Rhode Island
OFFICIAL ADDRESS: The Pentagon, Washington, DC 20350
HOME ADDRESS: Greenwood, Mississippi

U.S.A.
JONES, REAR-ADMIRAL FRANK COX (ENGINEERING DUTY) US NAVY
CURRENT DUTY STATION: Vice Commander, Naval Ship Systems Command (January 1967)
DATE OF BIRTH: 1917
EDUCATION: 1938 Naval Academy; 1956 Naval Postgraduate School
DATE OF COMMISSION: 2nd June, 1938
PROMOTED TO: Rear Admiral 1st July, 1965
COMMANDS: 1962-1966 Boston Naval Shipyard; additional duty: Industrial Manager, 1st Naval District
OFFICIAL ADDRESS: Main Navy Building, Washington, DC 20360
HOME ADDRESS: 640 Holley Road, Charleston, West Virginia

CEYLON
KADIRGAMAR, REAR-ADMIRAL R., CEYLON NAVY
DECORATIONS: MVO 1954
PRESENT APPOINTMENT: Captain of the Navy and CNS 16 November, 1960
DATE OF BIRTH: 9 June, 1922
EDUCATION: Royal College, Ceylon University; Royal Navy, RN Staff College
DATES OF PROMOTIONS: Commander 1 March 1955; Captain 1 July, 1959; Commodore 16 November, 1960; Rear-Admiral 1 October, 1967
PRINCIPAL COMMANDS AT SEA: Minesweepers all Classes
OTHER PREVIOUS APPOINTMENTS OF NOTE: ADC to Govenor General of Ceylon
OFFICIAL ADDRESS: Naval Headquarters, Colombo, Ceylon *Telephone:* 23278
PRIVATE ADDRESS: Klippenkerg House, Flag staff St. Colombo 1 Ceylon

INDIA
KAMATH, REAR ADMIRAL V. A., INDIAN NAVY
PRESENT APPOINTMENT: Flag Officer Commanding, Western Fleet 2 January, 1969
DATE OF BIRTH: 31 March 1921
EDUCATIONS: Indian Mercantile Marine Training Ship Dufferin 1936-1938; Defence Services Staff College, Wellington 1950-1951; Imperial Defence College, London 1967
DATES OF PROMOTIONS: Commander 31 December, 1953; Captain 30 June, 1960; Ag. Rear Admiral 15 January 1968
PRINCIPAL COMMANDS AT SEA: INS Tir (Training Ship of Midshipment) 1951-1952; INS Trishul and Captain "F" 15th Frigate Squadron 1960-1961; INS Vikrant 1964-1966
OTHER PREVIOUS APPOINTMENTS OF NOTE: Director of Naval Plans 1952-1954 & 1963-1964; Chief Instructor (Navy) Staff College 1957-1959; Director of Naval Armanent Inspection 1961-1963; Chief of Material 1968;
OFFICIAL ADDRESS Fleet Office, Naval Dockyard, Bombay-1 *Telephone:* 255653
PRIVATE ADDRESS: "Fleet House" 40 Heneker Drive, Colaba, Bombay 5

U.S.A.
KAUFFMAN, REAR-ADMIRAL DRAPER LAURENCE, US NAVY
CURRENT DUTY STATION: Commander, Naval Forces, Philippines (July 1968)
DATE OF BIRTH: 1911
EDUCATION: 1933 Naval Academy; 1951 Naval War College
DATE OF COMMISSION: 7th November, 1941
PROMOTED TO: Rear Admiral 1st July, 1961
COMMANDS: 1942-1943 Officer-in-Charge, Bomb Disposal School Washington, DC; 1943-1944 Naval Combat Demolotion Unit Project, Amphibious Training Base, Fort Pierce, Florida; 1944 Team 5, Combat Demolotion and Experimental Base; 1948-1950 Gearing DD 710; 1953-1954 Destroyer Division 121; 1957-1958 Bexar APA 237; 1960-1961 Helena CA 75; 1961 Destroyer Flotilla 3; 1961-1962 Cruiser-Destroyer Flotilla 3; 1963-1965 Director, Department of the Navy Program Appraisal Office; 1965-1968 Superintendent, Naval Academy
MAJOR AWARDS: Navy Cross With Gold Star in lieu of second award
OFFICIAL ADDRESS: Box 38, FPO San Francisco, California 96652
HOME ADDRESS: 5704 Rockmere Drive, Sumner, Maryland

U.S.A.
KEFAUVER, REAR-ADMIRAL RUSSELL, US NAVY
CURRENT DUTY STATION: Commander, Military Sea Transportation Service, Pacific (May 1967)
DATE OF BIRTH: 1911
EDUCATION: 1933 Navy Academy; 1955 Naval War College
DATE OF COMMISSION: 8th October, 1935
PROMOTED TO: Rear Admiral 1st September, 1963
COMMANDS: 1940-1944 Tambor SS 198; 1944-1945 Springer SS 414; 1951-1952 Submarine Division 61; 1955-1956 Orion AS 18; 1956-1957 Submarine Squadron 4; 1960-1961 Providence CLG 6; 1963-1964 Service Squadron 3
MAJOR AWARDS: Navy Cross with Gold Star in lieu of second award
OFFICIAL ADDRESS: Naval Supply Center, Oakland, California 94625
HOME ADDRESS: Alexandria, Virginia

AUSTRALIA
KELLY, HON. C. R., M.P.
PRESENT APPOINTMENT: Minister for the Navy (28 February, 1968), President of the Naval Board
DATE OF BIRTH: 22 June, 1912
EDUCATION: Prince Alfred College, Adelaide
OFFICIAL ADDRESS: Parliament House, Canberra, A.C.T. 2600 *Telephone:* 72710
PRIVATE ADDRESS: 6 View Street, Burnside, South Australia 5066

U.S.A.

KELLY, REAR-ADMIRAL, JAMES WOODROW (CHAPLAIN CORPS) US NAVY
CURRENT DUTY STATION: Chief of Chaplains, Bureau of Naval Personnel (July 1965)
DATE OF BIRTH: 1913
EDUCATION: 1933 Ouachita College, Arkadelphia, Arkansas; 1952 Southern Seminary, Louisville, Kentucky
DATE OF COMMISSION: 22nd March, 1942
PROMOTED TO: Rear Admiral 1st April, 1963
OFFICIAL ADDRESS: Arlington Annex, Washington, DC 20370
HOME ADDRESS: Lonoke, Arkansas

U.K.

KEMPSELL, LIEUTENANT K. D., ROYAL NAVY
PRESENT APPOINTMENT: Commanding Officer, HMS Nurton 9 January, 1969
DATE OF BIRTH: 6 January, 1931
EDUCATION: Spiers School, Beith
DATES OF PROMOTIONS: Commissioned 1 December, 1956; Lieutenant 1 October, 1962
PRINCIPAL COMMANDS AT SEA: 1st Command
OTHER PREVIOUS APPOINTMENT OF NOTE: Clyde Diving Officer; Scotland Command Bomb and Mine Disposal Staff Officer, Dartmouth; 1st Lieutenant HMS Kirluton
PRIVATE ADDRESS: 21 Muirwood Drive, Currie, Midlothian *Telephone:* 031 449 2640

U.S.A.

KIDD, REAR-ADMIRAL ISAAC CAMPBELL, JNR., US NAVY
CURRENT DUTY STATION: Commander, Cruiser-Destroyer Flotilla 12 (August 1968)
DATE OF BIRTH: 1919
EDUCATION: 1941 Naval Academy; 1961 National War College
DATE OF COMMISSION: 19th December, 1941
PROMOTED TO: Rear Admiral 1st December, 1965
COMMANDS: 1952-1953 Ellyson DMS 19; 1956-1958 Barry DD 933; 1961-1962 Destroyer Division 322; 1962 Destroyer Division 182
OFFICIAL ADDRESS: FPO New York 09501
HOME ADDRESS: Annapolis, Maryland

U.S.A.

KING, REAR-ADMIRAL ED REUBEN, US NAVY
CURRENT DUTY STATION: Commander, Middle East Force (June 1968)
DATE OF BIRTH: 1913
EDUCATION: 1936 Naval Academy; 1956 National War College; 1963 Naval Postgraduate School
DATE OF COMMISSION: 4th June, 1936
PROMOTED TO: Rear Admiral 1st September, 1964
COMMANDS: 1943-1945 Black DD 666; 1949-1951 Massey DD 778; 1953-1955 John S. McCain DL 3; 1958-1959 Tuckee AO 147; 1959-1960 Destroyer Squadron 22; 1964-1965 Cruiser-Destroyer Flotilla 8; 1965 Cruiser-Destroyer Flotilla 12
OFFICIAL ADDRESS: (Persian Gulf) FPO New York 09501
HOME ADDRESS: 1668 Peach Avenue, Memphis, Tennessee

U.S.A.

KING, REAR-ADMIRAL JEROME HENRY, JNR., US NAVY
CURRENT DUTY STATION: Commander, Anti-Submarine Warfare Group 1 (July 1968)
DATE OF BIRTH: 1919
EDUCATION: 1941 Yale University; 1949 and 1951 Naval Postgraduate School; 1958 Naval War College
DATE OF COMMISSION: 17th June, 1941
PROMOTED TO: Rear Admiral 8th April, 1968
COMMANDS: 1953-1955 Bache DDE 470; 1960-1961 Destroyer Division 601; 1961-1962 Nuclear Weapons Training Center, Atlantic, Norfolk, Virginia; 1962-1963 Yellowstone AD 27; 1965-1966 Destroyer Squadron 1
OFFICIAL ADDRESS: FPO San Francisco, California 96601

U.S.A.

KING, REAR-ADMIRAL THOMAS STARR, JNR., US NAVY
CURRENT DUTY STATION:
Deputy Commander, Military Sea Transportation Service (July 1969)
DATE OF BIRTH: 1914
EDUCATION: 1936 Naval Academy; 1945 Naval Postgraduate School; 1952 Naval War College
DATE OF COMMISSION: 4th June, 1936
PROMOTED TO: Rear Admiral 1st August, 1964
COMMANDS: 1948-1949 Winslow AG 127; 1954-1955 Destroyer Division 202; 1959-1961 Observation Island EAG 154; 1961-1962 Destroyer Squadron 5 and Destroyer Division 51; 1962-1963 Destroyer Flotilla 5; 1965-1966 Cruiser-Destroyer Flotilla 11
OFFICIAL ADDRESS: Navy Department, Washington, DC 20390
HOME ADDRESS: Guemes Island, Anacortes, Washington

U.S.A.

KINNEY, REAR-ADMIRAL SHELDON HOARD, US NAVY
CURRENT DUTY STATION:
Assistant Chief for Education & Training, Bureau of Naval Personnel (May 1969)
DATE OF BIRTH: 1918
EDUCATION: 1941 Naval Academy; 1948 Naval Postgraduate School; 1960 National War College
DATE OF COMMISSION: 7th February, 1941
PROMOTED TO: Rear Admiral 1st July, 1967
COMMANDS: 1943 Edsall DE 129; 1944 Bronstein DE 189; 1951-1952 Taylor DDE 468; 1956-1958 Mitscher DL 2; 1962-1963 Mississinewa AO 144; 1963 Amphibious Squadron 12; 1967-1969 Cruiser-Destroyer Flotilla 11
MAJOR AWARDS: Navy Cross
OFFICIAL ADDRESS: Arlington Annex, Washington, DC 20370
HOME ADDRESS: 661 South Los Robles Avenue, Pasadena, California

U.S.A.

KIRN, REAR-ADMIRAL LOUIS JOSEPH (NAVAL AVIATOR) US NAVY
CURRENT DUTY STATION: US Defence Attaché; US Naval Attaché and Naval Attaché for Air, United Kingdom (April 1967)
DATE OF BIRTH: 1908
EDUCATION: 1932 Naval Academy; 1939 Naval Postgraduate School; 1948 Armed Forces Staff College; 1952 Naval War College; 1956 Imperial Defense College, London
DATE OF COMMISSION: 2nd June, 1932
PROMOTED TO: Rear Admiral 1st May, 1959
COMMANDS: 1941-1942 Scouting Squadron 3; 1942-1943 Bombing Squadron 4; 1943 Bombing Squadron 99 1956-1957 Currituck 7; 1957-1958 Randolph CVA 15; 1959-1960 Carrier Division 19; 1962-1963 Carrier Division 5; 1963-1964 Key West Force
OFFICIAL ADDRESS: (London) Box 36, FPO New York 09510
HOME ADDRESS: Milwaukee, Wisconsin

U.S.A.

KOCH, REAR-ADMIRAL GEORGE PRICE (NAVAL AVIATOR) US NAVY
CURRENT DUTY STATION: Commandant, Naval District Washington, DC (June 1969)
DATE OF BIRTH: 1910
EDUCATION: 1933 Naval Academy; 1948 Naval War College
DATE OF COMMISSION: 29th May, 1934
PROMOTED TO: Rear Admiral 1st July, 1961
COMMANDS: 1942-1943 Headquarters Squadron Patrol Wing 5; 1944-1945 Humboldt AVP 21; 1955-1957 Naval Air Station Barbers Point Oahu, Hawaii; 1958-1959 Fleet Air Wing 3; Fleet Air Wing North Atlantic (NATO); 1959-1961 Naval Air Station Norfolk, Virginia; 1961-1962 Carrier Division 18; Anti-Submarine Carrier Group 3; 1962-1963 Fleet Air Wings, Atlantic Fleet; Fleet Air Wing 5; 1963-1965 Chief, Naval Air Reserve Training, Glenview, Illinois; 1965-1966 Carrier Division 6; 1966-1969 US Naval Forces, Southern Command and Commandant, 15th Naval District; additional duty: Commander, Panama Sector, Caribbean Sea Frontier & Commander, Panama Sector, Western Sea Frontier
OFFICIAL ADDRESS: Navy Yard Washington, DC
HOME ADDRESS: Ruxton, Maryland

ARGENTINA

KOLLIKER FRERS, CAPTAIN R., ARGENTINE NAVY
PRESENT APPOINTMENT: Commanding Officer Naval Air Force No. 2 1 January, 1969
DATE OF BIRTH: 25 June, 1923
EDUCATION: Matura, Switzerland; Argentine Naval Academy; Command and Staff College; Naval War College (Superior Course)
DATES OF PROMOTIONS: Captain 1 January, 1965
PRINCIPAL COMMANDS AT SEA: 1957 Commanding Officer Torpedo Boat Flotilla; 1965 Commanding Officer Destroyer
OTHER PREVIOUS APPOINTMENTS OF NOTE: Commanding Officer Naval Air Force 1 1967-1968
OFFICIAL ADDRESS: Base Aeronaval Cte. Espora (FCR) Argentine

U.S.A.

KOSSLER, REAR-ADMIRAL HERMAN JOSEPH, US NAVY
CURRENT DUTY STATION: Commandant, 6th Naval District; additional duty: Commander, Naval Base, Charleston, South Carolina (July 1968)
DATE OF BIRTH: 1911
EDUCATION: 1934 Naval Academy; 1955 National War College
DATE OF COMMISSION: 31st May, 1934
PROMOTED TO: Rear Admiral 1st July, 1961
COMMANDS: 1943-1946 Cavalia SS 244; 1950-1951 Submarine Division 52; 1955-1956 Sanborn APA 193; 1956-1957 Submarine Squadron 2; 1959-1961 Amphibious Squadron 10; 1964-1966 Mine F[illegible]e, Atlantic Fleet; 1966-1968 Naval Forces, Philippines; Command[illegible]n-Chief Pacific Representative, Philippines
MAJOR AWARD: Navy Cross
OFFICIAL ADDRESS: Naval Base, Charleston, SC 29408
HOME ADDRESS: 31 Afton Parkway, Portsmouth, Virginia

JAPAN

KUHARA, VICE-ADMIRAL JMSDF K.
DECORATIONS: The Fifth Order of the Rising Sun December 1941; The Fifth Order of the Sacred Treasure December 1941; The Fourth Order of the Sacred Treasure June 1943
PRESENT APPOINTMENT: Vice Chief of the Maritime Staff, Retired 1 July 1969
DATE OF BIRTH: 15 July, 1911
EDUCATION: Graduated from the Imperial Japanese Naval Academy November 1932; Student, National Defence Staff College September 1958—November 1959
DATE OF PROMOTIONS: Ensign, IJN March 1934; Lieutenant Junior Grade November 1935; Lieutenant June 1938; Lieutenant Commander November 1942; Commander September 1945; Commander, JMSDF July 1954; Captain August 1955; Rear Admiral January 1962; Vice Admiral July 1965;
PREVIOUS APPOINTMENTS OF NOTE: Commander, 2nd Training Division November 1959; Commander, Training Squadron December 1963; Commander, Fleet Escort Force July 1965 Instructor, MSDF Service School August 1954; Instructor, Defence Academy September 1955; Chief, 2nd Intelligence Section Maritime Staff Office January 1957; Chief, J-2, Joint Staff Office January 1962; Commander, Fleet Training Command December 1964; Vice Chief of the Maritime Staff January 1967
OFFICIAL ADDRESS: Maritime Staff Office, Japan Defence Agency, 9-7-45 Akasaka, Minato-ku, Tokyo, Japan. *Telephone:* 408-5211
PRIVATE ADDRESS: 3-5-12 Akazutsumi, Setagaya-ku, Tokyo Japan

U.S.A.

KUNTZ, REAR-ADMIRAL WILLIAM EDWARD, US NAVY
CURRENT DUTY STATION: Director, Communications-Electronics, CINCEUR and Chief, Defense Communications Agency, Europe (June 1968)
DATE OF BIRTH: 1917
EDUCATION: 1939 Naval Academy; 1945 Naval Postgraduate School
DATE OF COMMISSION: 1st June, 1939
PROMOTED TO: Rear Admiral 1st July, 1967
COMMANDS: 1947-1948 Marsh DE 699; 1951-1953 Lyman K. Swenson DD729; 1956-1958 Escort Squadron 14; 1961-1962 Altair AKS 32; 1964-1965 Northampton CC1
OFFICIAL ADDRESS: (Brussels) APO New York 09128
HOME ADDRESS: East Main Street, Leipsic, Ohio

U.S.A.

KYES, REAR-ADMIRAL FRANK MYERS (DENTAL CORPS) US NAVY
CURRENT DUTY STATION: Director, Dental Activities, 11th Naval District (July 1968)
DATE OF BIRTH: 1908
EDUCATION: 1930 University of Southern California
DATE OF COMMISSION: 13th April, 1936
PROMOTED TO: Rear Admiral 1st July, 1961
OFFICIAL ADDRESS: San Diego, California 92130
HOME ADDRESS: 3594 4th Street, San Diego, California

U.K.

KYRLE POPE, REAR ADMIRAL M. D., ROYAL NAVY
DECORATIONS: MBE 1946
PRESENT APPOINTMENT: Chief of Staff to the Commander in Chief Far East June 1967
DATE OF BIRTH: 1 October, 1916
EDUCATION: Wellington College, Berkshire
DATES OF PROMOTIONS: Commander 30 June, 1951; Captain 30 June, 1958; Rear Admiral 7 July, 1967; CSO (1) Germany 1955-1957; CSO (1) to C-in-C Far East 1958-1960; S.N.O. Persian Gulf 1962-1964; Dep Dir. Naval Int., MOD 1965; Commodore (Int.) MOD 1966
OFFICIAL ADDRESS: HQ Far East Command, Phoenix Park, c/o GPO Singapore
PRIVATE ADDRESS: Homme House, Much Marde, Herefordshire

U.S.A.

LACY, REAR-ADMIRAL PAUL LINDSAY, JNR., US NAVY
CURRENT DUTY STATION: Director, Later Design Submarine Project, Naval Material Command, Main Navy Building, Washington (January 1969)
DATE OF BIRTH: 1920
EDUCATION: 1942 Naval Academy; 1947 Naval Academy, Naval Postgraduate School; 1959 Naval War College; 1949 Awarded degree of M.Sc. in Ordnance Engineering; Weapons Systems, University of California
DATE OF COMMISSION: 19th June, 1942
PROMOTED TO REAR ADMIRAL 1st July 1967
COMMANDS: 1950-1952 Entemedor SS 340; 1954 Guitarro SS 363; 1954-1956 Pickerel SS 524; 1961-1964 Ethan Allen SSBN 603; 1967-1968 Naval Support Activity, Da Nang, Vietnam; 1968-1969 Amphibious Group 3
HOME ADDRESS: 7002 Tyndale Street, McLean, Virginia 22101

U.S.A.

LAMBERT, REAR-ADMIRAL VALDEMAR GREENE (NAVAL AVIATOR) US NAVY
CURRENT DUTY STATION: Commander, Naval Base Subic Bay, Philippines (June 1968)
DATE OF BIRTH: 1915
EDUCATION: 1947-1948 Naval School (General Line), Newport, R.I.; 1953-1954 Naval War College
DATE OF COMMISSION: 1st January, 1938
PROMOTED TO: Rear Admiral 1st July, 1965
COMMANDS: 1942 Scouting Squadron 1-D4; 1942-1943 Scouting Squadron 36; 1943 Composite Squadron 52; 1943-1945 Torpedo Squadron 15; 1948-1949 Air Group 15; 1960-1961 Ashtabula (AO 51);1961-1962 Saratoga (CVA 60); 1966-1968 Carrier Division 6
MAJOR AWARDS: Navy Cross
HOME ADDRESS: 212 Moale Avenue, Naval Station, Mayport, Florida 32228

AUSTRALIA

LANDAU, MR. S., AUSTRALIAN NAVY
DECORATIONS: CBE 1966
PRESENT APPOINTMENT: Secretary, Dapartment of the Navy, and Secretary, Naval Board (1963)
DATE OF BIRTH: 19 January, 1915
EDUCATION: Master of Arts, University of Melbourne; Imperial Defence College 1958
OTHER PREVIOUS APPOINTMENTS: First Assistant Secretary, Department of Defence 1957-1963
OFFICIAL ADDRESS Department of the Navy, Russell Offices, Canberra A.C.T. *Telephone:* 653201
PRIVATE ADDRESS: 100, Blamey Crescent, Campbell, Canberra, A.C.T. 2601

U.S.A.

LANHAM, REAR-ADMIRAL HARVEY PETER, (NAVAL AVIATOR) US NAVY
CURRENT DUTY STATION: Commander, Fleet Air, Western Pacific (March 1968)
DATE OF BIRTH: 1913
EDUCATION: 1937 Naval Academy; 1958 National War College
DATE OF COMMISSION: 3rd June, 1937
PROMOTED TO: Rear Admiral 1st February, 1966
COMMANDS: 1944-1945 Bombing Squadron 81; 1945-1946 Carrier Air Group 81; 1948-1949 Carrier Air Group 21; 1949-1950 Carrier Air Group 5; 1959-1960 Pine Island (AV 12); 1960-1961 Independence (CVA 62); 1966-1968 Carrier Division 2
HOME ADDRESS: 114 Breezy Point Drive, Naval Air Station, Norfolk, Virginia 23511

U.S.A.

LA ROCQUE,REAR-ADMIRAL GENE ROBERT, US NAVY
CURRENT DUTY STATION:
· Director, Inter-American Defense College (August 1969)
DATE OF BIRTH: 1918
EDUCATION: 1951 Naval War College, Newport; 1960 Industrial College of the Armed Forces
DATE OF COMMISSION: 14th March, 1941
PROMOTED TO: Rear Admiral 11th October, 1966
COMMANDS: 1945-1946 Solar (DE 221); 1947-1948 Major (DE 796); 1953-1955 Miller (DD 535); 1964-1965 Providence (CLG 6); 1965-1967 Cruiser-Destroyer Flotilla 12/Additional duty: Cruiser-Destroyer Flotilla 4
OFFICIAL ADDRESS: 4th & P Streets, SW Washington, DC 20305
HOME ADDRESS: 5015 Macomb Street, Washington, DC 20016

U.S.A.

LASCARA, REAR-ADMIRAL (SELECTEE), VINCENT ALFRED (SUPPLY CORPS.) US NAVY
CURRENT DUTY STATION: Commanding Officer, Navy Fleet Material Support Office, Mechanicsburg, Pennsylvania (September, 1968)
DATE OF BIRTH: 1919
EDUCATION: 1942 College of William and Mary; 1951 Stanford University; 1967 Naval War College
DATE OF COMMISSION: 2nd December, 1942
PROMOTED TO: Rear Admiral selected for promotion in June 1969
OFFICIAL ADDRESS: Mechanicsburg, Pennsylvania 17055

NAVAL STAFFS

The preceding naval staffs lists have been supplied by official sources the date to which they have been corrected necessarily varies from navy to navy, generally it may be taken that appointments have been updated to May/June 1969.

COMMAND STRUCTURE

United States Navy

These lists have been updated to 15th July 1969 it should be noted that some of the latest appointments are not reflected in the entries in the *Who's Who* section which is updated to 1st June 1969

WHO'S WHO

This first occasion of publishing in Jane's what it is hoped will become in future years a complete *Who's Who* of senior naval officers of all navies, necessarily requires some degree of apology for its initial incompleteness and unevenness. The time factor of reaching active service officers with invitations to provide these brief biographical details is longer than the publishers had anticipated. However this will be remedied in the next edition. Sincere apologies are offered to those officers whose entries did not arrive in time for inclusion. Meanwhile the publishers wish to express their appreciation of the co-operation which so many naval officers have given.

WHO'S WHO

U.S.A.

ABBOT, REAR-ADMIRAL JAMES LLOYD, JNR. (NAVAL AVIATOR) US NAVY
CURRENT DUTY STATION: Commander, Carrier Division 16 (July 1969)
DATE OF BIRTH: 1918
EDUCATION: 1939 Naval Academy; 1953 Armed Forces Staff College; 1964 National War College
FIRST COMMISSIONED: 1st June, 1939
PROMOTED TO: Rear-Admiral 30th May, 1967
COMMANDS: 1943-1944 Scouting Squadron 66; 1946-1948 Fighting Squadron 4-B; 1948 Fighting Squadron 42; 1951-1952 Utility Squadron 4; 1960-1961 Valcour AVP 55; 1961-1962 Intrepid CVA 11
OFFICIAL ADDRESS: FPO New York.
HOME ADDRESS: 910 Government Street, Mobile, Alabama.

U.S.A.

ABHAU, REAR-ADMIRAL WILLIAM CONRAD, US NAVY
CURRENT DUTY STATION: Antisubmarine Warfare Systems Project Office, Naval Material Command (May 1967)
DATE OF BIRTH: 1912
EDUCATION: 1935 Naval Academy; 1953 Naval Postgraduate School; 1957 Naval War College
FIRST COMMISSIONED: 6th June, 1935
PROMOTED TO: Rear Admiral 1st July, 1964
COMMANDS: 1947-1948 Eugene A. Greene DD 711; 1957-1958 Waccamaw AO 109; 1961-1962 Helena CA 75
OFFICIAL ADDRESS: Main Navy Building, Washington, DC 20360
HOME ADDRESS: Scott Circle, Annapolis, Maryland.

ITALY
ACHILLI, TENENTE, GENERALE COMMISSARIO P. ITALIAN NAVY
DECORATIONS: Croce di Guerra al V.M. 1942
PRESENT APPOINTMENT: Directore Generale di the Commissanato della Difesa January 1967
DATE OF BIRTH: 6 February, 1905
DATES OF PROMOTIONS: General Staff 1 January, 1960; Lieutenant General 14 April, 1964
OFFICIAL ADDRESS: Direzione General di Commissanato della Difesa, Palazzo Marina, Rome

U.S.A.

ADAIR, REAR-ADMIRAL JAMIE (ENGINEERING DUTY) US NAVY
CURRENT DUTY STATION: Deputy Commander for Ships Acquisition, Naval Ship Systems Command (May 1966)
DATE OF BIRTH: 1916
EDUCATION: 1938 Naval Academy; 1944 Naval Postgraduate School; 1956 Naval War College
FIRST COMMISSIONED: 2nd June, 1938
PROMOTED TO: Rear Admiral 1st July, 1966
COMMANDS: 1965-1966 Long Beach Naval Shipyard
OFFICIAL ADDRESS: Main Navy Building, Washington, DC 20360
HOME ADDRESS: 46 Park Drive, Williamsville, New York.

U.S.A.

ADAMSON, REAR-ADMIRAL ROBERT EDWARD, JNR., US NAVY
CURRENT DUTY STATION: Deputy Commander for Fleet Maintenance and Logistics Support, Naval Ship Systems Command (September 1967)
DATE OF BIRTH: 1920
EDUCATION: 1943 Naval Academy; 1950 Naval Postgraduate School; 1959 Army Command and General Staff College
FIRST COMMISSIONED: 9th June, 1943
PROMOTED TO: Rear Admiral 1st August, 1968
COMMANDS: 1956-1958 Naifeh DE 352; 1959-1961 Wiltsie DD 716; 1961-1963 Mullany DD 528; 1963-1964 Destroyer Division 152; 1965-1967 Galveston CLG3
OFFICIAL ADDRESS: Main Navy Building, Washington, DC 20360
HOME ADDRESS: Annandale, Virginia.

NIGERIA
ADELANWA, COMMANDER M. A., NIGERIAN NAVY
PRESENT APPOINTMENT: Staff Officer Operations 8 October, 1968
DATE OF BIRTH: 24 December, 1937
EDUCATION: WASC Grade II
DATES OF PROMOTIONS: A/Sub. Lieutenant 1 January, 1962; Sub Lieutenant 4 February, 1963; Lieutenant 26 August, 1963; Lieutenant Commander 26 August, 1966; Commander 1 April, 1968
PRINCIPAL COMMANDS AT SEA: NNS Challenger 18 January, 1965-7 November, 1965; HNS Ogaja 12 November, 1965-20 July, 1966; HNS Nigeria 27 October, 1967-7 October, 1968
OFFICIAL ADDRESS: Nigerian Navy, Harbour Road, Apapa *Telephone:* 46641
PRIVATE ADDRESS: 4 Yola Close, Apapa

PAKISTAN
AHSAN, VICE-ADMIRAL S. M., PAKISTAN NAVY
DECORATIONS: H.Q.A. 1968; S.PK. 1966; D.S.C. 1940
PRESENT APPOINTMENT: Chief of Naval Staff and Commander-in-Chief, Pakistan Navy 1966
DATE OF BIRTH: 21 November, 1920
EDUCATION: Joint Services Staff College, U.K.
DATES OF PROMOTIONS: Sub-Lieutenant 1940 (Royal Indian Navy), Officer Commanding Babur
OTHER PREVIOUS APPOINTMENTS OF NOTE: A.D.C. to Earl Mountbatten of Burma 1947; A.D.C. to Quaid-e-Azan Mohammed Ali Jinna, First Governor General, Pakistan; Naval Attaché in Pakistan Embassy, Washington 1955-1956; Chief Military Planning Officer, SEATO, Bangkok 1960-1964
OFFICIAL ADDRESS: Naval Staff Branch, Naval Headquarters, Karachi

U.S.A.

AINSWORTH, REAR-ADMIRAL (SELECTEE) HERBERT SYLVAN (NAVAL AVIATOR) US NAVY
CURRENT DUTY STATION: Assistant Director and Chief, Program Administration and Appraisal Division, Department of the Navy, Office of Program Appraisal (December 1967)
DATE OF BIRTH: 1920
EDUCATION: 1944 Naval Academy; 1951 and 1963 Naval Postgraduate School; 1963 Naval War College
FIRST COMMISSIONED: 9th June, 1943
PROMOTED TO: Rear Admiral, Selected for promotion on 6th June, 1969
COMMANDS: 1959-1960 Patrol Squadron 21; 1965-1966 Matthews AKA 96; 1966-1967 Fleet Air Wing 8; Task Group 72.3
OFFICIAL ADDRESS: The Pentagon, Washington, DC 20350
HOME ADDRESS: 800 Glorietta Boulevard, Coronada, California.

U.S.A.

ALBRITTAIN, REAR-ADMIRAL JOHN WARREN (MEDICAL CORPS) US NAVY
CURRENT DUTY STATION: Deputy Chief, Bureau of Medicine and Surgery (March 1969)
DATE OF BIRTH: 1911
EDUCATION: University of Maryland
FIRST COMMISSIONED: 15th June, 1939
PROMOTED TO: Rear Admiral 1st July, 1965
COMMANDS: 1964-1966 Naval Hospital, St. Albans, New York; 1966-1969 Naval Hospital, Great Lakes, Illinois
OFFICIAL ADDRESS: Potomac Annex, 23rd & E Streets, N. W., Washington, DC 20390
HOME ADDRESS: Chesapeake, Virginia

PORTUGAL
ALLEN, COMMODORE E. C., JNR., Portugese Navy
DECORATIONS: Military Merit of 1st Class Medal; Grand-Officer of the Military Order of Aviz; Silver and Gold Military Medals of exemplary conduct; Silver Medals for distinguished services; Infante D. Henrique V centenary Commemorative Silver Medal
PRESENT APPOINTMENT: I.S.A.F. Marinha 10 March, 1967
DATE OF BIRTH: 22 February, 1909
EDUCATION: Escola Naval; Curso Superior Naval de Guerre (I.N.G.) & ICEF de Lisboa
DATES OF PROMOTIONS: G. Marinha 1 March, 1932; 2nd Lieutenant 31 July, 1934; 1st Lieutenant 11 June 1948; Cap. Teniente 1 July, 1955; Cap. Frigate 15 January, 1960; Cap. Mar e Guerre 27 April 1964; Commodore 10 March 1967
PREVIOUS APPOINTMENTS OF NOTE: Instructor, Naval Academy 1939; Head of the Supply Department of the Maritime Command of Azores 1941-1946; Head of the Supply Department of the Captaincy of Ponta Delgada 1948; Training in Centre of S.O. of the American Navy 1956; Head of the Navy Finance Department 1958; Professor, Naval Academy 1964; Director, Navy Supply Department Superintendent, Navy Administration Finance Department 1969 Head of the Logistic section of Iberlant (NATO Exercises—fallex 60); Head of control department 1964
OFFICIAL ADDRESS: Ministerio Marinha, Lisbon *Telephone:* 368 737
PRIVATE ADDRESS: Praca Joao do Rio, 8-3° Esp., Lisbon

U.S.A.

ALLEN, REAR-ADMIRAL EDWARD CARLTON, JNR, US NAVY
CURRENT DUTY STATION: Commander, 5th Coast Guard District, Portsmouth, Va. (June 1967)
DATE OF BIRTH: 1916
EDUCATION: 1934 College of William and Mary; 1938 US Coast Guard Academy; 1951 George Washinton University Law School
FIRST COMMISSIONED: 2nd June, 1938
PROMOTED TO: Rear Admiral 1st July, 1967
COMMANDS: 1954-1955 Sebago; 1959-1960 Rockaway; 1960-1961 Spencer; 1961-1962 Mediterranean Section, Naples

ARGENTINA
ALONSO, CAPTAIN, R.F.B.
PRESENT APPOINTMENT: Chief of the Naval Region and Commander of the Naval Base Mar del Plata March 1968, Armada Argentina
DATE OF BIRTH: 22 March, 1923
EDUCATION: Naval Academy 1941-45 Polytechnic School—Armament 1950; Course A/S Warfare Control Officer (O.C.A.S.) 1951; General Course-Naval War College 1958; Senior Course-Naval War College 1966
DATES OF PROMOTION: Midshipman 1945; Sub Lieutenant 1948; Junior Lieutenant 1950; Senior Lieutenant 1952; Lieutenant Commander 1956; Commander 1961; Captain 1965
PRINCIPAL COMMANDS AT SEA: 1957 Commander of the Corvette REPUBLICA; 1965 Commander of the Frigate AZOPARDO
OTHER PREVIOUS APPOINTMENTS OF NOTE: 1956-1959 Naval General Staff; 1961-1962 Argentine Naval Commission in USA; 1963 Professor—Naval War College; 1966-1967 Chief of the Public Relations Service of the Command-in-Chief of the Navy
OFFICIAL ADDRESS: Base Naval Mar del Plata, Argentina
PRIVATE ADDRESS: Arenales 1074—Acasusso—Pcia de Buenos Aires, Argentina

UNITED KINGDOM
ANDERSON, REAR-ADMIRAL C. C., ROYAL NAVY
PRESENT APPOINTMENT: Flag Officer, Admiralty Interview Board 1969
DATE OF BIRTH: 8 November, 1916
EDUCATION: Royal Naval College, Dartmouth
DATES OF PROMOTIONS: 1952 Commander; 1959 Captain; 1969 Rear-Admiral
PRINCIPAL COMMANDS AT SEA: 1939-1942 MTB's; 1944-1946 HMS Wivern, Loch Killisport, Loch Achray; 1949-1951 HMS Contest
OTHER PREVIOUS APPOINTMENTS OF NOTE: Naval Attaché Bonn 1962-1965
OFFICIAL ADDRESS: HMS Sultan, Gosport Hants. *Telephone:* Gosport 80331
PRIVATE ADDRESS: HMS Sultan, Gosport, Hants.

U.S.A.
ANDERSON, REAR-ADMIRAL HERBERT HENRY, US NAVY
CURRENT DUTY STATION: Commander, Cruiser-Destroyer Flotilla 11 (April 1969)
DATE OF BIRTH: 1918
EDUCATION: 1941 Naval Academy; 1958 National War College
FIRST COMMISSIONED: 7th February, 1941
PROMOTED TO: Rear Admiral 1st July, 1967
COMMANDS: 1946 George E. Davis DE 357; 1946-1947 George DE 697; 1953-1955 Zellars DD 777; 1963-1964 Halsey DLG 23; 1964-1965 Destroyer Squadron 17
OFFICIAL ADDRESS: FPO San Francisco, California 96601
HOME ADDRESS: 212 McMaster Street, Bath, New York.

U.S.A.
ANDERSON, REAR-ADMIRAL ROY GENE, US NAVY
CURRENT DUTY STATION: Senior Naval Member, Military Studies & Liaison Division, Weapons Systems Evaluation Group (March 1967)
DATE OF BIRTH: 1915
EDUCATION: 1940 Naval Academy; 1946 Naval Postgraduate School; 1963 Industrial College of the Armed Forces
FIRST COMMISSIONED: 6th June, 1940
PROMOTED TO: Rear Admiral 1st December 1965
COMMANDS: 1949-1951 Carbonero SS 337; 1955 Submarine Division 51; 1964-1965 Taconic AGC 17; 1965-1967 Amphibious Group 4
OFFICIAL ADDRESS: 400 Army Navy Drive, Arlington, Virginia
HOME ADDRESS: 220 East Maple Street, Neosho, Missouri.

U.S.A.
ANDREWS, REAR-ADMIRAL (SELECTEE) BURTON HOWELL (ENGINEERING DUTY) US NAVY
CURRENT DUTY STATION: Vice Commander, Naval Electronic Systems Command, Naval Material Command (August 1968)
DATE OF BIRTH: 1916
EDUCATION: 1941 Naval Academy; 1949 Naval Postgraduate School
FIRST COMMISSIONED: 7th February, 1941
PROMOTED TO: Rear Admiral, selection approved 6th June, 1968
COMMANDS: 1960-1964 Navy Underwater Sound Laboratory New London, Connecticut
OFFICIAL ADDRESS: Main Navy Building, Washington, DC 20360
HOME ADDRESS: 700 Briggs Avenue, Pacific Grove, California.

JAPAN
ANDO, REAR-ADMIRAL N.
DECORATION: A, Order of Sacred 1942
PRESENT APPOINTMENT: Commander, Air Training Command 1968
DATE OF BIRTH: 3 June, 1916
EDUCATION: Graduated from the Imperial Japanese Naval Academy March 1938; Graduated from MSDF Staff College December 1958; Graduated from US Naval War College June 1960
DATES OF PROMOTIONS: Lieutenant Commander January 1953; Commander August 1954; Captain August 1959; Rear Admiral July 1966
PREVIOUS APPOINTMENTS OF NOTE: Commanding Officer, LSSL Sumire March 1953; Commanding officer, 5th Air Squadron July 1956; Commander, 1st Air Wing May 1966 Executive Officer, Kanoya Air Station August 1960; Executive Officer, Iwakuni Flight Centre July 1961; Chief of Staff, Air Training Command September 1961; Chief Aviation Education Section, MSO January 1964; Deputy Chief, Operations Division, MSO January 1968
OFFICIAL ADDRESS: NAS Utsunomiya, Utsunomiya-Shi, Tochigi-Ken, Japan
PRIVATE ADDRESS: 2797 Tomioka-cho, Kanazawa-Ku, Yokohama-Shi, Kanagawa-Ken, Japan

U.S.A.
APPLEBY, REAR-ADMIRAL JACK JESTINY (SUPPLY CORPS) US NAVY
CURRENT DUTY STATION: Commanding Officer, Naval Supply Center, Oakland, California (August 1968)
DATE OF BIRTH: 1915
EDUCATION: 1938 University of California (NROTC); 1956 Naval War College
FIRST COMMISSIONED: 21st May, 1938
PROMOTED TO: Rear-Admiral 1st July, 1965
COMMANDS: 1960-1965 Navy Ship's Store Office Brooklyn, New York
OFFICIAL ADDRESS: Oakland, California 94625
HOME ADDRESS: Blyth, California.

MEXICO
ARIZA, CAPTAIN A. LOPEZ, MEXICAN NAVY
PRESENT APPOINTMENT: Commander of the Mine Sweeper "04" December, 1967
DATE OF BIRTH: 7 December, 1933
EDUCATION: Grammar School, High School, Naval Academy
DATES OF PROMOTIONS: Guardiamarina 1 January, 1955; Teniente de Corbeta 7 May, 1957; Teniente de Fragata 20 November, 1962; Teniente de Navío 20 November 1964; Capitán de Corbeta 20 November, 1968
PRINCIPAL COMMANDS AT SEA: Coast Guard 1967-1968; Mine Sweepers 1968-1969
OTHER PREVIOUS APPOINTMENTS OF NOTE: Coast Guärds Executive Officer 1962-1963; Gun Ship Executive Officer 1964-1966
OFFICIAL ADDRESS: Primera Zona Naval Militar, Tampico, Tamps. *Telephone:* 2-32-41
PRIVATE ADDRESS: Antonio Matienzo 102A, Tampico, Tamps

U.S.A.
ARMSTRONG, REAR-ADMIRAL PARKER BROADHURST US NAVY
CURRENT DUTY STATION: Commander, Cruiser-Destroyer Flotilla 10 (March 1969)
DATE OF BIRTH: 1918
EDUCATION: 1941 Naval Academy; 1948 Postgraduate; 1959 Industrial College of the Armed Forces
FIRST COMMISSIONED: 19th December, 1941
PROMOTED TO: Rear Admiral 1st August 1968
COMMANDS: 1954-1956 Southerland DDR 743; 1959-1960 Escort Squadron 14; 1964-2965 Norfolk DL 1; 1965-1966 Destroyer Squadron 36; 1966 Match Maker II Squadron
OFFICIAL ADDRESS: FPO New York 09501
HOME ADDRESS: 2420 Lancaster Court, Falls Church, Virginia.

U.S.A.
ARNOLD, VICE-ADMIRAL JACKSON DOMINICK (AERONAUTICAL ENGINEERING DUTY) (NAVAL AVIATOR) US NAVY
CURRENT DUTY STATION: Vice Chief of Naval Material (August 1967)
DATE OF BIRTH: 1912
EDUCATION: 1934 Naval Academy; 1948 Naval Postgraduate School
FIRST COMMISSIONED: 30th May, 1934
PROMOTED TO: Rear Admiral 1st February, 1964; Vice Admiral 7th February, 1969
MAJOR AWARDS: Navy Cross
COMMANDS: 1943-1944 Torpedo Squadron 2; 1944 Carrier Air Group 2; 1958-1961 Naval Air Material Center, Philadelphia, Pennsylvania
OFFICIAL ADDRESS: Main Navy Building, Washington, DC 20360
HOME ADDRESS: 258 Natalen Street, San Antonio, Texas.

U.S.A.
ARTHUR REAR-ADMIRAL (SELECTEE) JOHN PAUL, (DENTAL CORPS.) US NAVY
CURRENT DUTY STATION: Assistant Chief of Dental Division, Bureau of Medicine and Surgery (May 1967)
DATE OF BIRTH: 1917
EDUCATION: North Pacific College of Dentistry 1940
DATE OF COMMISSION: 16th December, 1940
PROMOTED TO: Rear Admiral selected for promotion in June 1969
OFFICIAL ADDRESS: Potomac Annex, Washington, DC 20390

UNITED KINGDOM
ASHMORE, VICE-ADMIRAL E. B., ROYAL NAVY
DECORATIONS: C.B. 1966; D.S.C. 1942
PRESENT APPOINTMENT: Vice Chief of Naval Staff (1969)
DATE OF BIRTH: 11 December, 1919
EDUCATION; RN College, Dartmouth
DATES OF PROMOTIONS: 1950 Commander; 1955 Captain; 1965 Rear-Admiral; 1968 Vice Admiral
PRINCIPAL COMMANDS AT SEA: 1952-1953 HMS Alert; 1958-1960 HMS Blackpool and 6th Frigate Squadron; 1963-1964 Senior Naval Officer West Indies; 1967-1968 Flag Officer 2nd in Command, Far East Fleet
OTHER PREVIOUS APPOINTMENTS OF NOTE: Director of Plans 1960-1962; Assistant Chief of Defence Staff Signals
OFFICIAL ADDRESS: M.O.D. Whitehall, London S.W.1. *Telephone:* 930-7022 ext. 6617
PRIVATE ADDRESS: South Cottage, Headley Down, Hants.

UNITED KINGDOM
ASHMORE, REAR-ADMIRAL P. W. B., ROYAL NAVY
DECORATIONS: C. B. 1968; M.V.O. 1948; D.S.C. 1941
PRESENT APPOINTMENT: Chief of Staff to the Commander-in-Chief, Western Fleet and NATO Commander-in-Chief Eastern Atlantic December 1967
DATE OF BIRTH: 4 February, 1921
EDUCATION: RNC Dartmouth
DATES OF PROMOTIONS: 1951 Commander; 1956 Captain; 1966 Rear-Admiral
OTHER PREVIOUS APPOINTMENTS OF NOTE: Captain (D) Dartmouth Training Squadron 1960-1961; Deputy Director, RN Staff College Greenwich 1956-1959; Imperial Defence College 1962; Director of Naval Plans 1964-1966; Flag Officer Admiralty Interview Board 1966-1967
OFFICIAL ADDRESS: C-IN-C Western Fleet, Northwood, Middx. *Telephone:* 26161

U.S.A.
AURAND, REAR-ADMIRAL EVAN PETER (NAVAL AVIATOR) US NAVY
CURRENT DUTY STATION: Director, Long Range Objective Group, Office of Chief of Naval Operations (April 1967)
DATE OF BIRTH: 1917
EDUCATION: 1938 Naval Academy; 1953 Air War College
FIRST COMMISSIONED: 2nd June, 1938
PROMOTED TO: Rear Admiral 1st July, 1965
MAJOR AWARD: Navy Cross
COMMANDS: 1943-1944 Fighter Squadron 76; 1947 Fighting Squadron 1-A; 1947-1948 Fighting Squadron 5-A; 1948-1949 Fighting Squadron 51; 1961 Greenwich Bay AVP 41; 1961-1962 Independence CVA 61; 1962-1965 Anti-Submarine Warfare Group 1
OFFICIAL ADDRESS: The Pentagon, Washington, DC 20350
HOME ADDRESS: 219 Orchard Street, Fairfax, Virginia.

U.S.A.
AXENE, REAR-ADMIRAL (SELECTEE) DEAN LANE US NAVY
CURRENT DUTY STATION:
Director, Pan-American Affairs, Naval Missions & Advisory Group Division, Office of the Chief of Naval Operations (June 1969)
DATE OF BIRTH: 1923
EDUCATION: 1945 Naval Academy; 1948 Naval Postgraduate School
FIRST COMMISSIONED: 7th June, 1944
PROMOTED TO: Rear Admiral, selected for promotion on 6th June, 1969
COMMANDS: 1955-1957 Croaker SS 246; 1961-1963 Thresher SSN 593; 1964-1966 John C. Calhoun SSBN 630 (Blue Crew)
OFFICIAL ADDRESS: The Pentagon, Washington, DC 20350
HOME ADDRESS: 2257 Oxford Road, Columbus, Ohio.

U.S.A.
BAER, REAR-ADMIRAL DONALD "G" US NAVY
CURRENT DUTY STATION: Deputy Chief of Naval Material (Programs & Financial Management) (December 1967)
DATE OF BIRTH: 1915
EDUCATION: 1937 Naval Academy; 1957 Industrial College of the Armed Forces
FIRST COMMISSIONED: 3rd June, 1937
PROMOTED TO: Rear Admiral 1st January, 1965
MAJOR AWARD: Navy Cross
COMMANDS: 1944-1946 Lapon SS 260; 1946-1947 Remora SS 487; 1947 Sea Cat SS 399; 1952-1954 Submarine Division 63; 1957-1958 Fulton AS 11; 1960-1961 Submarine Squadron 1; 1964-1966 US Naval Base, Subic Bay; 1966-1967 Submarine Flotilla 6
OFFICIAL ADDRESS: Main Navy Building, Washington, DC 20360
HOME ADDRESS: 5944 Oakdale Road, McLean, Virginia.

U.S.A.
BAGLEY, REAR-ADMIRAL (SELECTEE) DAVID HARRINGTON, US NAVY
CURRENT DUTY STATION: Authorized to assume the title of Rear-Admiral Commander, Cruiser-Destroyer Flotilla 9 (July 1968)
DATE OF BIRTH: 1920
EDUCATION: 1944 Naval Academy; 1954 Naval War College
FIRST COMMISSIONED: 9th June, 1943
PROMOTED TO: Rear Admiral, selection approved 6th June, 1968
COMMANDS: 1958-1959; Henderson DD 785; 1961 Luce DLG 7; 1966-1968 Oklahoma City CLG 5
OFFICIAL ADDRESS: FPO San Francisco, California 96601
HOME ADDRESS: 2721 Glenwick Place, La Jolla, California.

U.S.A.
BAGLEY, REAR-ADMIRAL (SELECTEE) WORTH HARRINGTON, US NAVY
CURRENT DUTY STATION: Commanding Officer, USS Canberra CA 70 (November 1968)
DATE OF BIRTH: 1924
EDUCATION: 1947 Naval Academy; 1950 Command and General Staff College; 1961 Naval War College
FIRST COMMISSIONED: 5th June, 1946
PROMOTED TO: Rear Admiral, selected for promotion on 6th June, 1969
COMMANDS: 1958-1960 Bridget DE 1024; 1963-1965 Lawrence DDG 4
OFFICIAL ADDRESS: FPO San Francisco, California 96601
HOME ADDRESS: 8601 La Jolla Scenic Drive, La Jolla, California.

NORWAY
BAKKE, COMMODORE E.
PRESENT APPOINTMENT: Chief of Staff Logistics, Royal Norwegian Navy
DATE OF BIRTH: 19 April, 1916
DATES OF PROMOTIONS: 1955 Captain: 1962 Commodore
OFFICIAL ADDRESS: Sjøforsvartes Stab, Oslo Mil., Oslo.
PRIVATE ADDRESS: Jongstubben 23, Sandvika. *Telephone:* 33 30 70, Ext. 6409

U.S.A.
BALDWIN, REAR-ADMIRAL (SELECTEE) ROBERT BEMUS (NAVAL AVIATOR) US NAVY
CURRENT DUTY STATION: Director, Aviation Programs Division, Office of Chief of Naval Operations (April 1969)
DATE OF BIRTH: 1923
EDUCATION: 1944 Naval Academy
FIRST COMMISSIONED: 7th June, 1944
PROMOTED TO: Rear Admiral, selection approved 6th June, 1968
COMMANDS: 1956-1958 Fighter Squadron 154; 1961-1962 Fighter Squadron 51; 1963-1964 Air Group 16; 1966-1967 Chipola AO 63; 1967-1969 Forrestal CVA 59
OFFICIAL ADDRESS: The Pentagon, Washington, DC 20350
HOME ADDRESS: 1438 8th Street, Fargo, North Dakota.

U.S.A.
BALLENGER, REAR-ADMIRAL FELIX PETTEY (MEDICAL CORPS) US NAVY
CURRENT DUTY STATION: Inspector General, Medical, Bureau of Medicine & Surgery (September 1967)
Commanding Officer, National Naval Medical Center
DATE OF BIRTH: 1914
EDUCATION: 1934 Texas Technological College; 1938 University of Texas Medical School
FIRST COMMISSIONED: 8th May, 1942
PROMOTED TO: Rear Admiral 1st July, 1967
COMMANDS: US Naval Hospital, Yokosuka, Japan 1965-1967
OFFICIAL ADDRESS: Bethesda, Maryland
HOME ADDRESS: 1723 13th Street, Lubbock, Texas

ITALY
BARBERA, AMMIRAGLIO DI SQUADRA, IN S.P.E., R.
DECORATIONS: Medaglie di Bronzo al Valor Militare; Croci di Guerra al Valor Militare
PRESENT APPOINTMENT: Consiglio Superiore delle Forze Armate—Presidente della Sezione Marina
DATE OF BIRTH: 14 June, 1907
DATE OF PROMOTION: Ammiraglio di Squadra 1 January, 1965
OFFICIAL ADDRESS: Mariconsup, Rome

U.S.A.
BARDSHAR, REAR-ADMIRAL FREDERIC ABSHIRE (NAVAL AVIATOR) US NAVY
CURRENT DUTY STATION: Vice Director, J-3. Joint Chiefs of Staff (1969)
DATE OF BIRTH: 1915
EDUCATION: 1938 Naval Academy; 1948 Naval War College
FIRST COMMISSIONED: 2nd June, 1938
PROMOTED TO: Rear Admiral 1st July, 1965
COMMANDS: 1944-1945 Fighting Squadron 27 and Commander, Air Group 27; 1950-1951 Air Transport Squadron 32; 1961 Pawcatuck AC 108; 1967-1969 Carrier Division 7
OFFICIAL ADDRESS: The Pentagon, Washington, DC 20301
HOME ADDRESS: Seattle, Washington

U.S.A.

BARRETT, REAR-ADMIRAL (SELECTEE) JOHN MICHAEL, US NAVY
CURRENT DUTY STATION: Chief, Navy Section, Joint US Military Mission for Aid to Turkey (August 1968). Authorized to assume the title of Rear Admiral
DATE OF BIRTH: 1920
EDUCATION: 1943 Naval Academy; 1958 Naval War College
FIRST COMMISSIONED: 19th June, 1942
PROMOTED TO: Rear Admiral, selection approved 6th June, 1968
COMMANDS: 1953-1956 Tirante SS 420; 1960-1961 Submarine Division 73; 1965-1966 Canopus AS 34; 1966-1967 Submarine Squadron 16; 1967-1968 Submarine Flotilla 1
OFFICIAL ADDRESS: APO New York, New York 09254
HOME ADDRESS: 948 "G" Avenue, Coronado, California

U.S.A.

BARTLETT, REAR-ADMIRAL JAMES VINCENT (CIVIL ENGINEER CORPS) US NAVY
CURRENT DUTY STATION: Deputy Commander, Planning, Naval Facilities Engineering Command (April 1969)
DATE OF BIRTH: 1917
EDUCATION: 1941 Naval Academy; 1945 Naval Postgraduate School
FIRST COMMISSIONED: 30th June, 1942
PROMOTED TO: Rear Admiral 1st August 1968
COMMANDS: 1953-1955 Naval Mobile Construction Battalion 4; 1966-1967 Chesapeake Division, Naval Facilities Engineering Command Washington, DC; 1967-1969 3rd Naval Construction Brigade
OFFICIAL ADDRESS: Yards & Docks Annex, Washington, DC
HOME ADDRESS: 847 Chester Road, Charleston, West Virginia.

U.K.
BARTON, CAPTAIN S. F., FIMechE, MIMarE, MBIM
PRESENT APPOINTMENT: Captain, HMS Sultan, 22 October, 1968
DATE OF BIRTH: 19 January, 1922
EDUCATION: Muish's Grammar School, Taunton; HMS Caledonia; Royal Naval Engineering College
DATES OF PROMOTIONS: Commander June 1954; Captain June 1963
PREVIOUS APPOINTMENTS OF NOTE: Development Overseer Steam Catapult 1949-1951; Executive Officer, HMS Caledonia 1958-1960; Engineer Officer, HMS Centaur 1960-1963; Director of Fleet Work Study and Management Service 1963-1966; Chief Staff Officer (T) to Flag Officer Aircraft Carriers 1966-1968
OFFICIAL ADDRESS: HMS Sultan, Gosport, Hants, PO12 3BY **Telephone** Gosport 80331
PRIVATE ADDRESS: Sultan House, HMS Sultan, Gosport, Hants, PO12 3BY

Tele- phone: Gosport 80331

PORTUGAL
BASTOS, COMMODORE LUCIANO
DECORATIONS: Military Order of Aviz, Commander (1956); Distinguished Service Military Medal, Silver (1968); Expeditionary Military Forces, Angola (1961-1963); Military Merit Medal, 2nd Class (1967); Naval Medal, "Infante Dom Henrique" (1960); Naval Merit Order, 3rd Class, Spain (1967); Military Merit Order Cross, 1st Class, Spain (1940)
PRESENT APPOINTMENT: Naval Commander, Portuguese Guinea Naval Forces, 28 February, 1969
DATE OF BIRTH: 24 October, 1913
EDUCATION: Naval Officer Course (4 Years, College plus Naval School); Hydrographic Engineer (4 Years of College, Portugal and U.S.A.)
DATES OF PROMOTIONS: Midshipman 1 September, 1934; 2nd Lieutenant 1 March, 1936; 1st Lieutenant 1 March, 1941; Lieut. -Commander 31 March, 1953; Commander 27 September, 1958; Captain 10 June, 1963; Commodore 24 January, 1969
PRINCIPAL COMMANDS AT SEA: Patrol Ship "p5" (1944); Naval Hydrographic Ship "Carvalho Araujo" I (1953-1959); Naval Hydrographic Ship "Carvalho Araujo" II (1959-1963)
OTHER PREVIOUS APPOINTMENTS OF NOTE: Assistant Director of Hydrographic Institute (1963-1966); Commander of Group n.r. of Schools (Naval Fusiliers, Gunnery, Communications) (1966-1968)
OFFICIAL ADDRESS: Comando de Defesa Maritima da Guine, Bissau, Guinçe (Portuguese Guinea); *Telephone:* 2388
PRIVATE ADDRESS: Rua da Imprensa Nacional, 41/2E, Lisboa, Portugal

ITALY
BATTAGLIERI, TEN. GEN. DI PORTO M., ITALIAN NAVY
DECORATIONS: C.G.V.M., C.M.G., Gr.Uff.R.I.
PRESENT APPOINTMENT: Ispettore Capitanerie di Porto 1967
DATE OF BIRTH: 27 October, 1905
EDUCATION: Nautical Institute and Naval Academy
DATE OF LAST PROMOTION: 13 February, 1967
OFFICIAL ADDRESS: Ispettorato Capitanerie di Porto—Roma

U.S.A.

BAUGHAN, REAR-ADMIRAL ROBERT LOUIS, JNR., US NAVY
CURRENT DUTY STATION:
Commander, Cruiser-Destroyer Flotilla 9 (August 1969)
DATE OF BIRTH: 1919
EDUCATION: Naval Academy 1941; 1947 and 1949 Naval Postgraduate School; 1966 Industrial College of the Armed Forces
FIRST COMMISSIONED: 7th February, 1941
PROMOTED TO: 1st March, 1969
COMMANDS: 1951-1952 Porterfield DD 682; 1962-1964 Leahy DLG 16; 1964-1965 Destroyer Squadron 6
OFFICIAL ADDRESS: FPO San Francisco, California
HOME ADDRESS: 69 Oakwood Road, Huntington, West Virginia.

U.S.A.

BAUMBERGER, VICE-ADMIRAL WALTER HARLEN, US NAVY
CURRENT DUTY STATION: Deputy and Chief of Staff, Commander-in-Chief, Pacific Fleet (March 1967)
DATE OF BIRTH: 1912
EDUCATION: 1934 Naval Academy; 1955 Naval War College
FIRST COMMISSIONED: 31st May, 1934
PROMOTED TO: Rear Admiral 1st July, 1962; Vice Admiral 17th March, 1967
COMMANDS: 1945-1946 English DD 696; 1946 Gainard DD 706; 1953-1954 Destroyer Division 282; 1957-1958 Truckee AO 147; 1960 Canberra CAG 2; 1961-1963 Cruiser-Destroyer Flotilla 3; 1965-1967 Cruiser-Destroyer Force, Pacific Fleet
OFFICIAL ADDRESS: Pearl Harbor, FPO San Francisco, California 96610
HOME ADDRESS: 412 Monticello Avenue, Clarksburg, West Virginia.

U.S.A.
BAYNE, REAR-ADMIRAL (SELECTEE) MARMADUKE GRESHAM, US NAVY
CURRENT DUTY STATION: Deputy Chief of Staff and Assistant Chief of Staff for Plans, Policy and Operations, Supreme Allied Commander Atlantic (August 1968)
DATE OF BIRTH: 1920
EDUCATION: 1942 University of Tennessee; 1947 General Line School; 1957 Armed Forces Staff College
FIRST COMMISSIONED: 16th June, 1942
PROMOTED TO: Rear Admiral, authorized to assume the title of Rear Admiral, Selection approved 6th June, 1968
COMMANDS: 1954-1955 Piper SS 409; 1955-1957 Trigger SS 564; 1961-1962 Submarine Division 62; 1965-1967 Submarine Flotilla 8; Commander Task Forces 64, 69, 442
OFFICIAL ADDRESS: Norfolk, Virginia 23511
HOME ADDRESS: 5329 Powhatan Avenue, Norfolk, Virginia

UNITED KINGDOM
BAYLY, VICE-ADMIRAL SIR PATRICK, ROYAL NAVY
DECORATIONS: K.B.E. 1968; C.B. 1965; D.S.C. & 2 bars 1943, 1943, 1953; U.S. Legion of Merit 1952
PRESENT APPOINTMENT: Chief of Allied Staff to Comnavsouth, Malta 1967
DATE OF BIRTH: 4 August, 1914
EDUCATION: Royal Naval College Dartmouth 1928-1932
DATES OF PROMOTIONS: 1948 Commander; 1954 Captain; 1961 Commodore; 1963 Rear-Admiral; 1967 Vice Admiral
PRINCIPAL COMMANDS AT SEA: 1951 Alacrity; 1953 Constance; 1957 Captain D6 Cavendish
OTHER PREVIOUS APPOINTMENT OF NOTE: IDC 1957; Saclant Staff, 1959-1961; Flag Officer Sea Training 1963-1965; President RNC Greenwich 1965-1967
OFFICIAL ADDRESS: Headquarters, Allied Naval Forces Southern Europe, Malta G.C. *Telephone:* Naval 9608
PRIVATE ADDRESS: Villa Messina, Guardamangia, Malta G.C.

SWEDEN
BECKMAN, COLONEL P. J. O., ROYAL SWEDISH NAVY
DECORATIONS: Commodore of Royal Swedish Sværdsordern 1967
PRESENT APPOINTMENT: Commanding Officer, Coastal Artillery 1 October, 1966 Svärdsordern 1967
DATE OF BIRTH: 1 May, 1918
EDUCATION: Naval College; Armed Forces Staff College; Swedish Defence College; U.S. Marine Senior School
PREVIOUS APPOINTMENTS OF NOTE: Staff Officer Naval Headquarters; Chief Instructor CA Gunnery School; Instructor Naval College; Chief of Staff CA Regiment; Chief of Staff, Armed Forces, Staff College
OFFICIAL ADDRESS: Norlands Kustartilleriförsvar 87103 Härnösand 3 *Telephone:* 0611 10500
PRIVATE ADDRESS: Lindstedtsvägen 4, 87101 Härnösand 1. *Telephone:* 0611 i12072

UNITED KINGDOM
BEGG, ADMIRAL OF THE FLEET V. C., ROYAL NAVY
DECORATIONS: G.C.B. 1965; P.M.N. 1965; D.S.O. 1952; D.S.C. 1941
PRESENT APPOINTMENT: Governor and Commander-in-Chief, Gibralter 17 April, 1969
DATE OF BIRTH: 1 October, 1908
EDUCATION: Malvern College
DATES OF PROMOTIONS: 1947 Captain; 1957 Rear-Admiral; 1960 Vice Admiral; 1963 Admiral; 1968 Admiral of the Fleet
PRINCIPAL COMMANDS AT SEA: 1950-1952 HMS Cossack; 1955-1957 HMS Truimph; 1958-1960 Flag Officer, Second in Command Far East Fleet
OTHER PREVIOUS APPOINTMENTS OF NOTE: Vice Chief of Naval Staff 1960-1963; Commander-in-Chief Far East 1963-1965; Commander-in-Chief Portsmouth and Allied Commander-in-Chief Channel 1965-1966; Chief of Naval Staff and First Sea Lord 1966-1968
OFFICIAL ADDRESS: The Convent, Gibraltar,
PRIVATE ADDRESS: The Cottage, Harpsden, Henley-on-Thames, Oxon.
Telephone: Henley on Thames 3022

U.S.A.
BEHRENS, REAR-ADMIRAL WILLIAM WOHLSEN, JNR., US NAVY
CURRENT DUTY STATION: Director, Politico-Military Policy Division, Office of the Chief of Naval Operations (1969)
DATE OF BIRTH: 1922
EDUCATION: 1944 Naval Academy; 1964 National War College
FIRST COMMISSIONED: 9th June, 1943
PROMOTED TO: Rear Admiral 1st August, 1968
COMMANDS: 1953-1954 Balao SS 285; 1954-1955 Harder SS 568; 1958-1960 Skipjack SSN 585; 1961-1963 Ethan Allen SSBN 608; 1967-1969 Amphibious Group 1
OFFICIAL ADDRESS: The Pentagon, Washington, DC 20350
HOME ADDRESS: 25501 Devonshire Road, Harrisburg, Pennsylvania.

U.S.A.
BELING, REAR-ADMIRAL JOHN KINGSMAN (NAVAL AVIATOR) US NAVY
CURRENT DUTY STATION: Director, Air, Surface and Electronics Warfare Division, Office of the Chief of Naval Operations (October 1967)
DATE OF BIRTH: 1919
EDUCATION: 1941 Stevens Institute of Technology, Hoboken, New Jersy; 1947 Naval Postgraduate School; 1961 Naval War College
FIRST COMMISSIONED: 6th June, 1941
PROMOTED TO: Rear Admiral 1st August 1968
COMMANDS: 1959-1960 Attack Squadron 72; 1960 Attack Squadron 43; 1964-1965 Alstede AF 48; 1966-1967 Forrestal CVA 59
OFFICIAL ADDRESS: The Pentagon, Washington, DC 20350
HOME ADDRESS: 1710 Fifth Avenue, Zephyrhills, Florida.

U.S.A.
BELL, REAR-ADMIRAL CLARENCE EDWIN, JNR. US NAVY
CURRENT DUTY STATION: Director, General Planning and Programming Division, Office of the Chief of Naval Operations (February 1968)
DATE OF BIRTH: 1916
EDUCATION: 1939 Naval Academy; 1947 and 1950 Postgraduate; 1951 Armed Forces Staff College; 1960 National War College
FIRST COMMISSIONED: 1st June, 1939
PROMOTED TO: Rear Admiral 1st July, 1965
COMMANDS: 1948-1950 Diodon SS 349; 1955-1956 Submarine Division 61; 1960-1961 Cambria APA 36 1963-1964 Little Rock CLG 4; 1967-1968 Amphibious Group 4
OFFICIAL ADDRESS: The Pentagon, Washington, DC 20350
HOME ADDRESS: 5412 Studeley Avenue, Norfolk, Virginia

U.S.A.
BELL, REAR-ADMIRAL DAVID BONAR, US NAVY
CURRENT DUTY STATION: Deputy Commandant, National War College (July 1968)
DATE OF BIRTH: 1913
EDUCATION: Naval Academy 1937; 1949 Naval Postgraduate School; 1961 National War College
FIRST COMMISSIONED: 3rd June, 1937
PROMOTED TO: Rear Admiral 1st October, 1964
MAJOR AWARDS: Navy Cross with Gold Star in lieu of second award
COMMANDS: 1943-1946 Pargo SS 264; 1946 Trumpetfish SS 425; 1949-1950 Dogfish SS 350; 1954-1955 Submarine Division 62; 1957-1958 Submarine Squadron 6; 1961-1962 Waccamaw 109; 1962-1964 Submarine Squadron 14
OFFICIAL ADDRESS: Fort Lesley J. McNair, Washington, DC 20305
HOME ADDRESS: 55 Abney Circle, Charleston, West Virginia.

UNITED KINGDOM
BELLAMY, INST. REAR-ADMIRAL A. J., ROYAL NAVY
DECORATIONS: C.B. 1968; O.B.E. 1956
PRESENT APPOINTMENT: Director, Naval Education Service 1965
DATE OF BIRTH: 26 February, 1915
EDUCATION: Hanley Carble Grammer School; Downing College, Cambridge
DATES OF PROMOTIONS: 1950 Commander; 1958 Captain; 1965 Rear-Admiral
PREVIOUS APPOINTMENTS OF NOTE: Dean, Royal Naval Engineering College 1956-1960; Director of Studies, HMS Collingwood 1963-1965
OFFICIAL ADDRESS: Ministry of Defence, Old Admiralty Building, Whitehall, London S.W.1. *Telephone:* 930 9000 ext. 612
PRIVATE ADDRESS: Coombdale, Barns Green, Horsham, Sussex

U.S.A.
BENDER, REAR-ADMIRAL CHESTER R. (NAVAL AVIATOR) US NAVY
CURRENT DUTY STATION: Commander, Western Area and Commander, 12th Coast Guard District, San Francisco (June 1967)
DATE OF BIRTH: 1914
EDUCATION: 1936 Coast Guard Academy
FIRST COMMISSIONED: 8th June, 1936
PROMOTED TO: Rear Admiral 1st July, 1964
COMMANDS: 1943-1944 Air Sea Rescue Squadron, Coast Guard Air Station, San Diego; 1954-1955 Coast Guard Air Station, Traverse City; 1955-1958 Chief, War Plans Section, Coast Guard Headquarters; 1958-1959 Coast Guard Air Detachment, Barbers Point, Hawaii; 1959-1961 Bering Strait; 1964-1965 9th Coast Guard District, Cleveland

U.S.A.
BENNETT, VICE-ADMIRAL FRED GROCH
CURRENT DUTY STATION: Director, Navy Program Planning, Office of the Chief of Staff & Aide, Naval War College (August 1969)
DATE OF BIRTH: 1915
EDUCATION: 1936 Naval Academy; 1944 Naval Postgraduate School; 1955 Naval War College
FIRST COMMISSIONED: 4th June, 1936
PROMOTED TO: Rear Admiral 1st May, 1964; Vice Admiral 17th January, 1968
COMMANDS: 1951-1952 Harwood DDE 861; 1955-1956 Destroyer Division 82; 1959-1960 Grand Canyon AD 28; 1960-1961 Newport News CA 148; 1965-1966 Cruiser-Destroyer Flotilla 8
OFFICIAL ADDRESS: Naval War College, Newport, Rhode Island 02840
HOME ADDRESS: Yazoo City, Mississippi.

U.S.A.
UNITED KINGDOM
BENNETT, COMMANDER N. T., ROYAL NAVY
DECORATIONS: A.F.C. 1968
PRESENT APPOINTMENT: Commanding Officer Interservice Hovercraft Unit 1968
DATE OF BIRTH: 28 May, 1930
EDUCATION: Berkhamstead School
DATES OF PROMOTION: 1952 Lieutenant; 1960 Lieutenant Commander; 1965 Commander
OTHER PREVIOUS APPOINTMENTS OF NOTE: Lieutenant Commander (Flying) HMS Eagle; Senior Pilot RN Test Squadron
OFFICIAL ADDRESS: Interservice Hovercraft Unit, HMS Daedalus, Lee-on-Solent, Hants, PO13 9NY. *Telephone:* Lee-on-Solent 79143, Extension 258
PRIVATE ADDRESS: 12 Solent Way, Alverstoke, Gosport, Hants.

U.S.A.
BERGIN, REAR-ADMIRAL (SELECTEE) DANIEL EDWARD, US NAVY
CURRENT DUTY STATION: Deputy Assistant Director, Intelligence Production, Defense Intelligence Agency (July 1968)
DATE OF BIRTH: 1919
EDUCATION: 1942 Naval Academy; 1964 National War College; 1964 Naval Postgraduate School
FIRST COMMISSIONED: 19th December, 1941
PROMOTED TO: Rear Admiral, selection approved 6th June, 1968. Authorized to assume the title of Rear Admiral
COMMANDS: 1947 Spangeberg DE 223; 1955-1956 Kidd DD 661; 1960-1961 Landing Ship Squadron 7; 1965-1966 Destroyer Squadron 3
OFFICIAL ADDRESS: The Pentagon, Washington, DC 20301
HOME ADDRESS: 1065 Nelson Avenue, New York, New York

U.S.A.
BERGNER, REAR-ADMIRAL ALLEN ALFRED, US NAVY
CURRENT DUTY STATION: Commander, Naval Training Center, San Diego (November 1967)
DATE OF BIRTH: 1916
EDUCATION: 1940 Naval Academy; 1948 Naval Postgraduate School; 1959 Naval War College
FIRST COMMISSIONED: 6th June, 1940
PROMOTED TO: Rear Admiral 1st December, 1967
COMMANDS: 1944-1945 S-47 SS 158; 1945-1946 Saury SS 189; 1950-1952 Pomodon SS 486; 1955-1956 Submarine Squadron 62; 1961-1962 Orion AS 18; 1964-1965 Submarine Squadron 6
OFFICIAL ADDRESS: San Diego, California 92133
HOME ADDRESS: San Diego, California

U.S.A.
BERNARD, REAR-ADMIRAL LAWRENCE GEORGE
CURRENT DUTY STATION: Deputy Naval Inspector General (February 1969)
DATE OF BIRTH: 1914
EDUCATION: 1937 Naval ACADEMY: 1960 Air War College
FIRST COMMISSIONED: 3rd June, 1937
PROMOTED TO: Rear Admiral 1st February, 1966
COMMANDS: 1943 Puffer SS 268; 1944-1945 R-2 SS 79; 1945-1946 Stickleback SS 415; 1946-1948 Brill SS 330; 1953-1954 Submarine Division 22; 1957-1958 Howard S. Gilmore AS 16; 1961-1962 Submarine Squadron 7; 1963-1965 Submarine Flotilla 1; 1967-1969 Submarine Flotilla 6
OFFICIAL ADDRESS: Arlington Annex, Washington, DC 20370
HOME ADDRESS: 5 Charles Street, Deadwood, South Dakota

U.S.A.

BESHANY, REAR-ADMIRAL PHILIP ARTHUR, US NAVY
CURRENT DUTY STATION: Commander, Amphibious Group 4 (May 1969)
DATE OF BIRTH: 1914
EDUCATION: 1938 Naval Academy; 1949 Naval Postgraduate School; 1960 Industrial College of the Armed Forces 1960
FIRST COMMISSIONED: 2nd June, 1938
PROMOTED TO: Rear Admiral 1st May, 1965
COMMANDS: 1945-1946 Billfish SS 286; 1949 Burrfisk SSR 312; 1949-1951 Amberjack SS 522; 1954-1955 Submarine Division 101; 1960-1961 Salamonie AO 26; 1961-1962 Submarine Squadron 4: 1963-1964 Submarine Squadron 16
OFFICIAL ADDRESS: FPO New York 09501
HOME ADDRESS: Scranton, Pennsylvania.

U.S.A.

BIERI, REAR-ADMIRAL BERNHARD HENRY, JNR. (SUPPLY CORPS) US NAVY
CURRENT DUTY STATION: Commander, Naval Supply Systems Command (August 1967)
DATE OF BIRTH: 1915
EDUCATION: 1937 Naval Academy; 1953 Naval War College; 1960 National War College
FIRST COMMISSIONED: 3rd June, 1937
PROMOTED TO: Rear Admiral 1st January, 1964
COMMANDS: 1961-1962 Naval Supply Depot, Seattle, Washington; (Vice Chief of Naval Material 1962)
OFFICIAL ADDRESS: Main Navy Building, Washington, DC 20360
HOME ADDRESS: Arlington, Virginia

U.S.A.

BIRD, REAR-ADMIRAL HORACE VIRGIL
CURRENT DUTY STATION: Commander, Mine Force, Pacific Fleet (May 1967)
DATE OF BIRTH: 1912
EDUCATION: 1933 Naval Academy; 1939 Naval Postgraduate School; 1954 Naval War College
FIRST COMMISSIONED: 1st June, 1933
PROMOTED TO: Rear Admiral 1st May, 1963
COMMANDS: 1949-1951 Rogers DDR 876; 1955-1957 Destroyer Squadron 22; 1963-1964 Cruiser-Destoyer Flotilla 11; 1964-1967 Naval Forces Marianas
OFFICIAL ADDRESS: Naval Station, Long Beach, California 90801
HOME ADDRESS: Quarters "D" Naval Station, Long Beach, California.

ITALY

BIRIUDELLI, ADMIRAGLIO DI SQUADRA G,
DECORATIONS: 1940 Medaglia d'oro; 1941 Madeglia d'argento
PRESENT APPOINTSMENT: Commander in Chief Italian Fleet
DATE OF BIRTH: 19 January, 1911
DATE OF PROMOTION: 31 December, 1966
OFFICIAL ADDRESS: Comando in Capo Squadra Navale 74100 Taranto Italy

CANADA

BLANCHARD, LIEUTENANT-COMMANDER B. E.
DECORATIONS: CD 1964; Centennial Medal (Canada) 1967
PRESENT APPOINTMENT: Honorary Aide-de-Camp to the Governor-General of Canada, April 1967
DATE OF BIRTH: 7 August 1932
EDUCATION: Bachelor of Arts, University of Ottawa, 1953; Bachelor of Philisophy, University of Ottawa, 1953; Bachelor of Civil Law, McGill University, 1959
DATES OF PROMOTIONS: Sub-Lieutenant RCNR 1 September, 1952; Lieutenant 1 September, 1954; Lieutenant-Commander 1 September, 1962;
OTHER APPOINTMENTS: 1962-1964 Commanding Officer, University Naval Training Division HMCS Donnacona, Montreal, Quebec, Canada
OFFICIAL ADDRESS: Robitaille, Dansereau, Blanchard, Quesnel & Dubé, Barristers and Solicitors, 180 Dorchester Blvd. East, Montreal, Quebec, Canada
PRIVATE ADDRESS: 105, 3rd Avenue South, Roxboro, Quebec, Canada

U.S.A.

BLOUIN, VICE-ADMIRAL FRANCIS JOSEPH, US NAVY
CURRENT DUTY STATION: Deputy Chief of Naval Operations (Plans and Policy) (June 1968)
DATE OF BIRTH: 1910
EDUCATION: 1933 Naval Academy; 1948 Naval War College
FIRST COMMISSIONED: 1st June, 1933
PROMOTED TO: Rear Admiral 1st July, 1960; Vice Admiral 27th July, 1966
COMMANDS: 1943-1945 Sterett DD 407; 1945-1946 Ingersoll DD 652; 1950-1952 Escort Destroyer Division 12; 1957-1958 Mt. McKinley AGC 7; 1958-1960 Amphibious Squadron 4; 1962-1963 Amphibious Group 1; 1966-1968 Amphibious Force, Pacific Fleet
OFFICIAL ADDRESS: The Pentagon, Washington, DC 20350
HOME ADDRESS: Naval Observatory, Washington, DC

U.S.A.

BLOXOM, REAR-ADMIRAL ELLIOTT (SUPPLY CORPS) US NAVY
CURRENT DUTY STATION: Deputy Commander, Military Traffic Management & Terminal Services (July 1967)
DATE OF BIRTH: 1916
EDUCATION: 1937 College of William & Mary, Williamsburg, Virginia; 1961 Naval War College
FIRST COMMISSIONED: 12th June, 1940
PROMOTED TO: Rear Admiral 15th December, 1967
COMMANDS: 1944-1945 Pinon AN 66; 1965-1967 Naval Supply Center, Pearl Harbor
OFFICIAL ADDRESS: Nassif Building, Washington, DC 20315
HOME ADDRESS: 105 Ridge Lane, Chapel Hill, North Carolina

U.S.A.

BONNER, REAR-ADMIRAL EMMETT PEYTON, US NAVY
CURRENT DUTY STATION: Commander, Naval Support Activity, Danang, South Vietnam (December 1968)
DATE OF BIRTH: 1918
EDUCATION: 1939 Naval Academy; 1947 Naval War College
FIRST COMMISSIONED: 1st June, 1939
PROMOTED TO: Rear Admiral 1st July, 1967
COMMANDS: 1952-1954 Cogswell DD 651; 1957-1958 Escort Squadron 12; 1960-1961 Norton Sound AVM 1; 1963-1964 Oklahoma City CLG 5; 1966-1967 Cruiser-Destroyer Flotilla 6; 1967-1968 Mine Force, Atlantic Fleet
OFFICIAL ADDRESS: FPO San Francisco, California 06695
HOME ADDRESS: Macon, Georgia

U.S.A.

BOWEN, VICE-ADMIRAL HAROLD GARDINER, JNR., US NAVY
CURRENT DUTY STATION: Commander, Antisubmarine Warfare Force, Pacific Fleet (July 1967)
DATE OF BIRTH: 1912
EDUCATION: 1933 Naval Academy; 1936 Postgraduate; 1942 Postgraduate; 1950 Naval War College
FIRST COMMISSIONED: 1st June, 1933
PROMOTED TO: Rear Admiral 1st June, 1961; Vice Admiral 7th July, 1967
COMMANDS: 1943-1944 Conway DD 507; 1945-1946 Samuel N. Moore DD 747; 1952-1953 Destroyer Division 92; 1956-1958 Neosho AO 143; 1959-1960 Northampton CLC 1; 1962-1963 Cruiser-Destroyer Flotilla 4
OFFICIAL ADDRESS: Pearl Harbor, FPO San Francisco, California 96610
HOME ADDRESS: 65 Arlington Avenue, Providence, Rhode Island.

U.S.A.

BOYES, REAR-ADMIRAL (SELECTEE) JON LIPPITT, US NAVY
CURRENT DUTY STATION:
Deputy Director, Plans, Defense Communications Agency (July 1969)
DATE OF BIRTH: 1921
EDUCATION: 1944 Naval Academy; 1951 Naval Postgraduate School; 1960 Armed Forces Staff College; 1964 National War College
FIRST COMMISSIONED: 9th June, 1943
PROMOTED TO: Rear Admiral, selected for promotion on 6th June, 1969
COMMANDS: 1954-1955 Sarda SS 488; 1955-1957 Albacore AGSS 569; 1962-1963 Submarine Division 71; 1966-1967 Submarine Squadron 10
OFFICIAL ADDRESS: Building 12, 8th & South Courthouse Road, Arlington, Virginia 22204
HOME ADDRESS: 3806 North Wakefield, Arlington, Virginia

U.K.

BRIDLE, CAPTAIN G. W., MIEE, ACGI, ROYAL NAVY
DECORATIONS: MBE
PRESENT APPOINTMENT: Commanding Officer HMS Collingwood 24 June, 1969
DATE OF BIRTH: 1923
EDUCATION: King Edwards Grammar School, Birmingham; Northern Grammar School, Portsmouth; Electrical fitter apprentice, Royal Dockyard School, Portsmouth;
DATES OF PROMOTIONS: Imperial College of Science and Technology, London (Whitworth Scholar)
DATES OF PROMOTIONS: Lieutenant 1945; Lieutenant Commander 1953; Commander 1957; Captain 1965
OTHER PREVIOUS APPOINTMENTS OF NOTE: Sea Dart Project Manager, Ministry of Technology 1965-1969
OFFICIAL ADDRESS: HMS Collingwood, Fareham, Hants.

U.S.A.

BRINGLE, VICE-ADMIRAL WILLIAM FLOYD (NAVAL AVIATOR) US NAVY
CURRENT DUTY STATIONS: Commander, 7th Fleet (November 1967)
DATE OF BIRTH: 1913
EDUCATION: 1937 Naval Academy; 1953 Naval War College
FIRST COMMISSIONED: 3rd June, 1937
PROMOTED TO: Rear Admiral 1st January, 1964; Vice Admiral 6th November, 1967
COMMANDS: 1942-1943 Composite Scouting Squadron 2; 1943-1944 Observation Fighting Squadron 1; 1944-1945 Composite Spotting Squadron 1; 1945-1946 Carrier Air Group 17; 1946 Fighter Squadron 17; 1948-1950 Air Group 1; 1957-1958 Heavy Attack Wing 2; 1961-1962 Kitty Hawk CVA 63; 1964-1965 Carrier Division 7
OFFICIAL ADDRESS: FPO San Francisco, California 96601
HOME ADDRESS: 1639 Peabody Street, Memphis, Tennessee

U.K.
BRITTAN, COMMANDER D. M. G., FIL, AMBIM, ROYAL NAVY
PRESENT APPOINTMENT: Commander-in-Charge, Royal Naval School of Management and Work Study October 1968
DATE OF BIRTH: 19 July, 1929
EDUCATION: RNC Dartmouth 1943-1947
DATES OF PROMOTIONS: Lieutenant Commander 1959; Commander 1966
PRINCIPAL COMMANDS AT SEA: HMS Pelandok 1953-1954
OTHER PREVIOUS APPOINTMENTS OF NOTE: Malay Interpreters' Course 1954-1955; RN Staff Course 1963
OFFICIAL ADDRESS: Royal Naval School of Management and Work Study, Royal Naval Barracks, Portsmouth, Hants, PO1 3HH *Telephone:* 22351 ext. 72600
PRIVATE ADDRESS: 9 Hoylake Road, Portsmouth

UNITED KINGDOM
BROWN, CAPTAIN E. G., ROYAL NAVY
PRESENT APPOINTMENT:In Command HMS Osprey; Flag Captain to Fost
DATE OF BIRTH: 13 September, 1919
EDUCATION: Ardwyn School, Aberystwyth
DATES OR PROMOTIONS: 1943 Acting Lieutenant Commander; 1949 Lieutenant Commander; 1953 Commander; 1961 Captain
PRINCIPAL COMMANDS AT SEA: 1955-1956 HMS Tintagel Castle; 1956-1957 HMS Pellew; 1964-1966 HMS Nubian
OTHER PREVIOUS APPOINTMENTS OF NOTE: 1966-1968 Chief Staff Officer to Flag Officer Aircraft Carriers
OFFICIAL ADDRESS: HMS Osprey, Portland, Dorset. *Telephone* Weymouth 2781
PRIVATE ADDRESS: Portland Castel, Portland Dorset

UNITED KINGDOM
BROWN, CAPTAIN E. M., ROYAL NAVY
DECORATIONS O.B.E. 1945; D.S.C. 1942; A.F.C. 1942
PRESENT APPOINTMENT: CO. R.N. Air Station, Lossiemouth 13 September, 1967
DATE OF BIRTH: 21 January 1919
EDUCATION: Royal High School, Edinburgh; Edinburgh University M.A.
DATES OF PROMOTIONS: Commander 31 December, 1953; Captain 31 December, 1960
OTHER PREVIOUS APPOINTMENTS OF NOTE: Deputy director, Gunnery Division 1961; Deputy Director of Naval Air Warfare 1962-1964; Naval Attache, Bonn 1965-1967
OFFICIAL ADDRESS: RNAS, Lossiemouth, Morayshire, Scotland *Telephone:* 2121
PRIVATE ADDRESS: Captain's House, RNAS Lossiemouth, Morayshire, Scotland

U.S.A.
BROWN, REAR-ADMIRAL JAMES ANDREW (ENGINEERING DUTY) US NAVY
CURRENT DUTY STATION: Commander, Norfolk Naval Shipyard (June 1965)
DATE OF BIRTH: 1914
EDUCATION: 1936 Naval Academy; 1941 Naval Postgraduate School
FIRST COMMISSIONED: 4th June, 1936
PROMOTED TO: Rear Admiral 1st October, 1963
COMMANDS: 1954-1955 Naval Ship Repair Facility, Subic Bay, Philippines; 1961-1963 Supervisor of Shipbuilding, New York Shipbuilding Corp, Camden, New Jersey
OFFICIAL ADDRESS: Portsmouth, Virginia 23709
HOME ADDRESS: Nashville, Tennessee.

U.S.A.
BROWN, REAR-ADMIRAL SAMUEL ROBBINS, JNR. (NAVAL AVIATOR) US NAVY
CURRENT DUTY STATION: Commander, Fleet Air Alameda (July 1968)
DATE OF BIRTH: 1913
EDUCATION: 1934 Naval Academy; 1957 National War College
FIRST COMMISSIONED: 1st June, 1934
PROMOTED TO: Rear Admiral 1st. July, 1962
COMMANDS: 1944-1945 Bombing Squadron 82; 1945 Carrier Air Group; 1952-1954 Bombing Fighter Squadron 11; 1957-1958 Orca AVP 49; 1959-1960 Forrestal CVA 59; 1963-1964 Carrier Division 4
OFFICIAL ADDRESS: Naval Air Station, Alameda, California 94501
HOME ADDRESS: 1011 Olive Avenue, Coronado, California.

ITALY
BRUNETTI, AMMIRAGLIO DI SQUADRA IN S.P.E., F,
DECORATIONS: Medaglia d'Argento al V.M.; Madaglia d'Argento al Valor di Mavina; Medaglia di Bronzo al V.M.; Croce di guerra al V.M.
PRESENT APPOINTMENT: Stato Maggiore della Marina. Sottocapo di Stato Maggiore
DATE OF BIRTH: 20 November, 1909
DATE OF PROMOTION: Ammiraglio di Squadra 17 January, 1967
OFFICIAL ADDRESS: Maristat

U.S.A.
BRUSH, REAR-ADMIRAL FREDERICK JAMES (NAVAL AVIATOR) US NAVY
CURRENT DUTY STATION: Commander, Key West Force; additional duty Commander, Naval Base Key West; Commander Fleet Air Key West (April 1967)
DATE OF BIRTH: 1908
EDUCATION: 1931 Naval Academy; 1952 Naval War College
FIRST COMMISSIONED: 4th June, 1931
PROMOTED TO: Rear Admiral 1st February, 1960
COMMANDS: 1944 Carrier Air Group 81; 1954-1955 Point Cruz CVE 119; 1956-1957 Bon Homme Richard CVA 31; 1961-1962 Carrier Division 6; 1962-1964 Fleet Air Mediterranean/Commander Naval Activities Mediterranean
OFFICIAL ADDRESS: Naval Base, Key West, Florida 33040
HOME ADDRESS: Arlington, Virginia.

U.S.A.
BRYAN, REAR-ADMIRAL (SELECTEE) CLARENCE RUSSELL (ENGINEERING DUTY) US NAVY
CURRENT DUTY STATION: Ship Acquisition Project Manager/Submarines (PMS 381) and Head, Submarine Maintenance Branch, Naval Ship Systems Command (November 1968)
DATE OF BIRTH: 1923
EDUCATION: 1945 Naval Academy; 1952 Massachusetts Institute of Technology
FIRST COMMISSIONED: 9th June, 1944
PROMOTED TO: Rear Admiral, selected for promotion on 6th June, 1969
OFFICIAL ADDRESS: Main Navy Building, Washington, DC 20360
HOME ADDRESS: 610 Boundary Street, Red Oak, Iowa.

U.K.
BUCHANAN, CAPTAIN P. W., ROYAL NAVY
PRESENT APPOINTMENT: Endurance April 1968
DATE OF BIRTH: 14 May, 1925
EDUCATION: Malvern College
DATES OF PROMOTIONS: Commander 30 June, 1961; Captain 30 June, 1967
PRINCIPAL COMMANDS AT SEA: Scarborough 1961-1962
OTHER PREVIOUS APPOINTMENTS OF NOTE: Exec. Victorious 1965-1967
OFFICIAL ADDRESS: HMS Endurance, BFPO Ships
PRIVATE ADDRESS: Whitewalls, The Square, Titchfield, Hants

U.K.
BUCKLEY, COMMANDER R. N., ROYAL NAVY
PRESENT APPOINTMENT: Commanding Officer, HMS Churchill
DATE OF BIRTH: 16 June, 1931
EDUCATION: The Leas, Hoylake; R.N. College, Dartmouth
DATES OF PROMOTIONS: Lieut.-Commander 16 August, 1961; Commander 30 June, 1968
PRINCIPAL COMMANDS AT SEA: HMS Sturdy; HMS Sealion
OTHER PREVIOUS APPOINTMENTS OF NOTE: R.N. Staff Course; Commanding Officer Submarine Attack Teacher
OFFICIAL ADDRESS: HMS Churchill, BFPO Ships
PRIVATE ADDRESS: c/o Lloyds Bank Ltd., West Kirby, Wirral, Cheshire

U.S.A.
BULKELEY, REAR-ADMIRAL JOHN DUNCAN, US NAVY
CURRENT DUTY STATION: President, Navy Board of Inspection and Survey (June 1967)
DATE OF BIRTH: 1911
EDUCATION: 1933 Naval Academy; 1950 Armed Forces Staff College
FIRST COMMISSIONED: 12th June, 1933
PROMOTED TO: Rear Admiral 1st February, 1964
MAJOR AWARDS: Medal of Honor, Navy Cross
COMMANDS: 1941 Motor Boat Sub Chaser Division 2; 1941 Motor Boat Sub Chaser Squadron 1; 1941 Motor Torpedo Boat Division 1; 1941-1942 Motor Torpedo Boat Squadron 3; 1942-1943 Motor Torpedo Boat Squadron 7; 1944 Motor Torpedo Boat Squadron 2; 1944 PT Squadron 122; 1944-1945 Endicott DD 495; 1945 Endicott DMS 35; 1945-1946 Stribling DD 867; 1952-1954 Destroyer Division 132; 1958 Tolovana AO 64; 1959-1960 Destroyer Squadron 12; 1966-1967 Cruiser-Destroyer Flotilla 8; 1963-1966 Naval Base, Guantanamo Bay, Cuba
OFFICIAL ADDRESS: Arlington Annex, Washington, DC 20370
HOME ADDRESS: Haas Road, Millington, New Jersey

U.S.A.
BULLARD, REAR-ADMIRAL ROSS P., US NAVY
CURRENT DUTY STATION: Commander, 8th Coast Guard, District, New Orleans
DATE OF BIRTH: 1914
EDUCATION: 1939 Coast Guard Academy; 1953 Navy Post Graduate School of Communications, Monterey
FIRST COMMISSIONED: 29th May, 1939
PROMOTED TO: Rear Admiral 1st July, 1967
COMMANDS: 1950-1951 Balsam; 1951-1952 Klamath; 1958-1960 Casco; 1960-1962 International Ice Patrol

U.S.A.
BURKE, REAR-ADMIRAL JULIAN THOMPSON, US NAVY
CURRENT DUTY STATION: Assistant Deputy Chief of Naval Operations (Naval Reserve) (January 1968)
DATE OF BIRTH: 1918
EDUCATION: 1940 Naval Academy; 1958 Naval War College
FIRST COMMISSIONED: 6th June, 1940
PROMOTED TO: Rear Admiral 1st July, 1967
COMMANDS: 1945-1946 Guardfish SS 217; 1950-1952 Sablefish SS 303; 1952-1953 Williamsburg AGC 369; 1953-1955 Harold J. Ellison DD 864; 1958-1960 Submarine Division 63; 1963-1964 Fremont APA 44; 1964-1965 Amphibious Squadron 6; 1966-1967 Amphibious Group 3; 1967-1968 Amphibious Group 1
OFFICIAL ADDRESS: The Pentagon, Washington, DC 20350
HOME ADDRESS: Alexandria, Virginia.

U.S.A.
BURKLEY, VICE-ADMIRAL GEORGE GREGORY (MEDICAL CORPS) (RETIRED) US NAVY
CURRENT DUTY STATION: Special Project, Bureau of Medicine and Surgery (January 1969)
DATE OF BIRTH: 1902
EDUCATION: University of Pittsburgh
FIRST COMMISSIONED: 6th November, 1941
PROMOTED TO: Rear Admiral 10th August, 1962; Vice Admiral 11th March, 1965
COMMANDS: 1959-1961 Naval Dispensary/Medical Officer Naval Administrative Unit, Potomac River Naval Command; 1961-1963 Assistant Physician to the President of the United States; 1963-1969 Physician to the President of the United States
OFFICIAL ADDRESS: Potomac Annex, Washington, DC 20390
HOME ADDRESS: Chevy Chase, Maryland

U.K.
BURN, CAPTAIN W. G. M., ROYAL NAVY
PRESENT APPOINTMENT: In Command HMS Caledonia 26 February, 1969
DATE OF BIRTH: 22 October, 1922
EDUCATION: Glasgow Academy
DATES OF PROMOTIONS: Commander 31 December, 1956; Captain 31 December, 1965
OTHER PREVIOUS APPOINTMENTS OF NOTE: Principal Technical Officer 2nd Submarine Squadron 1 November, 1962- November 1965; British Naval Adviser, New Delhi, December 1965-November 1967
OFFICIAL ADDRESS: HMS Caledonia, Rosyth, Fife
PRIVATE ADDRESS: 14 Comely Park, Dunfermline

U.K.
BUSH, ADMIRAL SIR J., ROYAL NAVY
DECORATIONS: KCB 1965; DSC** August 1941; 1st Bar January 1942; 2nd Bar April 1944
PRESENT APPOINTMENT: Commander-in-Chief, Western Fleet, Allied Commander-in-Chief, Channel; Allied Commander-in-Chief, Eastern Atlantic Area 6 October, 1967
DATE OF BIRTH: 1 November, 1914
EDUCATION: Clifton College
DATES OF PROMOTIONS: Special Entry Cadet January 1933; Commander December 1946; Captain June 1952; Rear Admiral January 1961; Vice Admiral November 1963; Admiral August 1968
PRINCIPAL COMMANDS AT SEA: HMS Belvoir 1942-1944; HMS Zephyr 1944; HMS Chevron 1945-1946; HMS Cadiz 1950-1965; Captain (F) 6th Frigate Squadron in HMS Undine 1955-1956; Flag Officer Flotillas; Mediterranean 1961-1963
OTHER PREVIOUS APPOINTMENTS OF NOTE: Deputy Secretary to Chiefs of Staff Committee; MOD 1953; Commondore, Royal Naval Barracks, Chatham 1957; Director of Plans 1959-1960; Commander, British Navy Staff, Washington 1963-1965; Vice Chief of Naval Staff 1965-1967
OFFICIAL ADDRESS: Admiralty House, Eastbury Park, Northwood, Middlesex. *Telephone:* Northwood 26161, ext. 656 or 657
PRIVATE ADDRESS: Greenways, Titchfield Road, Fareham, Hampshire

U.K.
BUTT, CAPTAIN R. D., ROYAL NAVY
PRESENT APPOINTMENT: HMS Dryad September 1967
DATE OF BIRTH: 3 August, 1923
EDUCATION: Kings School, Canterbury; RNC Dartmouth
DATES OF PROMOTIONS: Commander 31 December, 1957; Captain 31 December, 1964
PRINCIPAL COMMANDS AT SEA: Chichester 1958-1959; Arethusa 1965-1967
OTHER PREVIOUS APPOINTMENTS OF NOTE: Fleet Navigating Officer, East Indies 1955-1956

U.S.A.
BUTTS, REAR-ADMIRAL (SELECTEE) JOHN "L" JNR. (NAVAL AVIATOR) US NAVY
CURRENT DUTY STATION: Executive Assistant and Senior Aide to the Commander-in-Chief Pacific (June 1968)
DATE OF BIRTH: 1920
EDUCATION: 1967 California Western University; 1952 General Line School
COMMANDS: 1950-1951 Fighter Squadron 112; 1954-1956 Fighter Squadron 51; 1956-1957 Fleet Air Gunnery Unit, Pacific; 1957-1958 Advanced Training Unit 206; 1962-1964 Platte AO 24; 1964-1965 Kitty Hawk CVA 63
OFFICIAL ADDRESS: (Pearl Harbor) FPO San Francisco 96601
HOME ADDRESS: Miami, Florida

CHILE
CABEZAS, CAPTAIN H. VIDELA, CHILEAN NAVY
DECORATIONS: Third Class Military Medal (Chile 1948; Staff Officer Medal (Chile) 1956; Second Class Military Medal (Chile) 1958; Naval Merit Medal (Peru) 1958; Distinguish Service Medal (Peru) 1963; Interamerican Defense Board Medal 1967; First Class Military Medal (Chile)
PRESENT APPOINTMENT: Director of Naval School 10 March, 1969
DATE OF BIRTH 2 May, 1918
EDUCATION: Naval School-Executive Branch Course; Torpedo and A/S Warfare Branch Course for Specialist Officers; Naval War Academy-Course for Navy Staff Officers
DATES OF PROMOTIONS: Midshipman 1940; Sublieutenant 1941; Second Lieutenant 1944; First Lieutenant 1948; Lieutenant Commander 1952; Commander 1956; Captain 1966
PRINCIPAL COMMANDS AT SEA: ATA Sobenes 1955; B.E. Esmeralda 1963; CL. O'higgins 1968
OTHER APPOINTMENTS OF NOTE: Chief of Naval School Instruction Dept 1958 Subdirector of Naval School Plans and Policy Dept. Navy Staff 1964-1965; Maritime Strategy Professor Army War Academy 1964-1965; Staff Member-Interamerican Defence Board 1966-1967
OFFICIAL ADDRESS: Director Escuela Naval, Correo Naval, Valparaíso, Chile. *Telephone:* Nr. 54540 Valpso, Chile
PRIVATE ADDRESS: Residencia Director Escuela Naval Subida Artillería s/n Valparaíso, Chile

PORTUGAL
CAEIRO, REAR-ADMIRAL F. FERRER, PORTUGUESE NAVY
DECORATIONS: Valor Militar de Prata Com Palma 1967; Serviços Distintos de Prata 1960; Mérito Militar de 1a Classe 1968; 2 Mérito Militar de 2a Classe 1954 and 1960; Grande Oficial da Ordem Militar de Aviz 1960; Comendador da Ordem do Infante Dom Henrique 1965; Croix d'Officer de L'Ordre de Leopold de Belgique 1959; Comendador do Ordem de Mérito Naval do Brasil 1968; Cruz del Mérito Aeronautico de 2a classe de España 1959; Gran Cruz del Mérito Naval de España 1967; Officer of The Legion of Merit, U.S.A. 1960
PRESENT APPOINTMENT: Naval Commander of Continental Portugal (22 July 1968)
DATE OF BIRTH: 22 October, 1910
EDUCATION: Naval Academy
DATES OF PROMOTIONS: Cadet 1 October, 1929; Midshipman 1 September, 1932; Second Lieutenant 1 March, 1934; First Lieutenant 1 March, 1940; Lieutenant Commander 1 January, 1953; Commander 1 January, 1955; Captain 20 February, 1958; Commodore 12 December, 1965; Rear-Admiral 11 June, 1968
PRINCIPAL COMMANDS AT SEA: 1947-1948 Sloop JOAO DE LISBOA; 1964 Frigate BARTOLOMEU DIAS
OTHER PREVIOUS APPOINTMENTS OF NOTE: Graduation from Naval Aviation School 1936; Air Survey Team for Mapping in Angola 1937-1939; Instructor at the Naval Aviation School 1939-1947; Second Commander of the Naval Aviation School 1948-1953; Second Commander of Montijo Air Base 1953-1958; First Commander of Montijo Air Base 1958-1961; Naval War College, Newport, R.I. 1962-1963; Naval Commander of Portuguese Guinea 1964-1967; Chief of Naval Operations Deputy 1968
OFFICIAL ADDRESS: Ministério de Marinha, Lisbon 2 Portugal *Telephone;* 368965
PRIVATE ADDRESS: R. Jorge Ferriera Vasconcelos, 11-R/C-E Lisbon, 5 Portugal *Telephone:* 775934

U.S.A.
CAGLE, REAR-ADMIRAL MALCOLM WINFIELD (NAVAL AVIATOR) US NAVY
CURRENT DUTY STATION: Commander, Carrier Division 1 (1968)
DATE OF BIRTH: 1918
EDUCATION: 1941 Naval Academy; 1958 National War College
FIRST COMMISSIONED: 7th February, 1941
PROMOTED TO: Rear Admiral 11th October, 1966
MAJOR AWARD: Navy Cross
COMMANDS: 1948-1950 Fighting Squadron 63; 1963-1964 Suribachi AE 21; 1964-1965 Franklin D. Roosevelt CVA 42
OFFICIAL ADDRESS: FPO San Francisco, California 96601
HOME ADDRESS: 408 Wolfe Street, Alexandria, Virginia.

UNITED KINGDOM
CALDWELL, SURGEON VICE-ADMIRAL SIR D., ROYAL NAVY
DECORATIONS: K.B.E. 1969; C.B.E. 1965; Q.H.P. 1963
PRESENT APPOINTMENT: Medical Director General (Navy) 1966
DATE OF BIRTH: 6 July, 1909
EDUCATION: Edinburgh Academy; Edinburgh University
MEDICAL DISTINCTIONS: 1950 M.D.; 1956 M.R.C.P.; F.R.C.P. (Edin.) 1962; FRCP (Lond.) 1968
DATES OF PROMOTIONS: 1934 Joined RN; 1945 Surgeon Commander; 1957 Surgeon Captain; 1963 S.R.A.; 1966 S.V.A.
PREVIOUS APPOINTMENTS OF NOTE: Med. Spec. Hong Kong 1947; Sen. Med. Spec. RNH Haslar 1956; Consultant in Medicine 1962
OFFICIAL ADDRESS: M.O.D. Empress State Building, London S.W.6. *Telephone:* 385-1244 ext. 2086
PRIVATE ADDRESS: 9a, Holland Park Road, Kensington W.14.

U.S.A.

CALDWELL, VICE-ADMIRAL TURNER FOSTER JNR. (NAVAL AVIATOR) US NAVY
CURRENT DUTY STATION: Director, Antisubmarine Warfare Programs, Office of the Chief of Naval Operations (November, 1967)
DATE OF BIRTH: 1913
EDUCATION: 1935 Naval Academy; 1956 National War College
FIRST COMMISSIONED: 6th June, 1935
PROMOTED TO: Rear Admiral 1st April, 1963; Vice Admiral 1st November, 1967
COMMANDS: 1944 Fighting Squadron 79; 1944-1945 Night Carrier Air Group 41; 1945 Night Air & Combat Training Unit, Pacific; 1947-1948 Battle Carrier Air Group 3; 1948-1949 Carrier Air Group 4; 1958-1959 Valcour AVP 55; 1959-1960 Ticonderoga CVA 14; 1963-1964 Anti-Submarine Warfare Group 5
OFFICIAL ADDRESS: The Pentagon, Washington, DC
HOME ADDRESS: 2300 E. Street, Washington, DC

UNITED KINGDOM

CALLAGHAN, REAR-ADMIRAL D. N., ROYAL NAVY
PRESENT APPOINTMENT: Senior Naval Member and Vice President (Naval) Ordnance Board
DATE OF BIRTH: 24 November, 1915
EDUCATION: St. Antony's, Eastbourne; RNC Dartmouth
DATES OF PROMOTIONS: 1950 Commander; 1959 Captain; 1968 Rear-Admiral
PRINCIPAL SERVICE AT SEA: 1941 HMS Hereward sunk off Crete; 1941-1945 POW Italy; 1945 HMS Argonaut; 1946 HMS Glory;
OTHER PREVIOUS APPOINTMENTS OF NOTE: Commanding Officer HMS Caledonia 1962; Director of Weapons Material (Naval) M.O.D. Bath 1965
PRIVATE ADDRESS: 28 Boyn Hill Road, Maidenhead, Berks.

U.S.A.

CALVERT, REAR-ADMIRAL JAMES FRANCIS, US NAVY
CURRENT DUTY STATION: Superintendent, Naval Academy (July 1968)
DATE OF BIRTH: 1920
EDUCATION: 1942 Naval Academy; 1962 National War College
FIRST COMMISSIONED: 19th June, 1942
PROMOTED TO: Rear Admiral 1st February, 1966
COMMANDS: 1953-1955 Trigger SS 564; 1957-1959 Skate SSN 588; 1959-1961 Submarine Division 102; 1965 Service Group 3; 1967-1968 Cruiser-Destroyer Flotilla 8
OFFICIAL ADDRESS: Annapolis, Maryland 21402
HOME ADDRESS: Chevy Chase, Maryland.

U.K.

CANNING, COMMANDER W. R.
PRESENT APPOINTMENT: J.S.S.C.Latimer (Student), 24 March, 1969
DATE OF BIRTH: 17 November, 1940
EDUCATION: Sedburgh School and R.N. College, Dartmouth
DATES OF PROMOTION: Lieutenant 1 September 1953; Lieut.-Commander 1 September 1961; Commander 30 June, 1966
PRINCIPAL COMMANDS AT SEA: HMS Striker January 1963-January 1964; HMS Cambrian August 1966-March 1969
PRIVATE ADDRESS: Deers Leap, Hollycombe Close, Liphook, Hants.

ITALY

CANTU, ADMIRAL G., ITALIAN NAVY
DECORATIONS: Two War Crosses for Military Valour; Two War Crosses for Merit; Grand Officer of the Order of Merit of the Italian Republic; Knight of the Order of Saints Mauritius and Lazarus; Officer of the Order of Crown of Italy; Gold Medal for Long Service at Sea; Mauritian Medal for Long Service 50 years
PRESENT APPOINTMENT: Commander, Central Mediterranean Area NATO and C-in-C, Naval District Lower Tyrrhenian Sea 9 June, 1969
DATE OF BIRTH: 26 June, 1907
EDUCATION: Naval Academy Courses
DATES OF PROMOTIONS: Vice Admiral 27 February, 1965; Admiral 9 June, 1969

CHILE

CARAVAJAL, REAR-ADMIRAL P., CHILEAN NAVY
DECORATIONS: Commander Victorian Order C.V.O. 1965
PRESENT APPOINTMENT: Chief of Staff, Chilean Navy, 17 January, 1969
DATE OF BIRTH: 13 September, 1916
EDUCATION: Colegio des Verbo Divino
DATES OF PROMOTIONS: 1936 Midshipman; 1969 Rear-Admiral
PRINCIPAL COMMANDS AT SEA: 1953 Captain of A.T.F. Lautaro; 1960 Captain of B.E. Esmeralda; 1961 Captain of P.F. Covadonga; 1967 Captain of C.L. Prat
OTHER PREVIOUS APPOINTMENTS OF NOTE: Naval Attaché London 1964-1966
OFFICIAL ADDRESS: Ministerio de Defensa, Correo 15, Santiago de Chile *Telephone:* 68101
PRIVATE ADDRESS: Santo Domingo 3998, Santiago de Chile

MEXICO

CARBALLO, JIMENEZ, CAPITAN DE FRAGATA P.A., F., MEXICAN NAVY
PRESENT APPOINTMENT: Commander of the Air Squadron of Busgueda y Salvamento 16 March, 1969
DATE OF BIRTH: 11 February, 1924
EDUCATION: Primaria, Pre-Vocacional; Escuela Naval Militar; Curso de Entrenamiento para pilotos navales en Pensacola, Fla., USA; Curso de Helicopterista en Palo Alto, Calif.
DATES OF PROMOTIONS: Guardiamarina 1 January 1948; Teniente de Corbeta 1 February, 1949; Teniente de Fragata 1 June, 1952; Teniente de Navío 1 March 1958; Capitan de Corbeta 20 November 1963; Capitán de Fragata 20 November, 1967
PREVIOUS APPOINTMENTS OF NOTE: Primer Comandante del Tercer Escuadrón Aeronaval 1967-1968; Subdirector, Escuela de Aviación Naval 1964-1967
OFFICIAL ADDRESS: Escuadron de Busqueda y Salvamento, Las Bajadas, Ver. *Telephone:* 2-36-37
PRIVATE ADDRESS: Av Jardín 336 Esquina Chalchilumecan, Fracc. Virginia, H. Veracruz, Ver.

NEW ZEALAND

CAREY, COMMODORE L. B., M.Sc; MIEE, ROYAL NEW ZEALAND NAVY
PRESENT APPOINTMENT: Third Naval Member (1 December, 1966)
DATE OF BIRTH: 29 September, 1915
EDUCATION: Wellington College; Victoria University
DATES OF PROMOTIONS: Commander 30 June, 1954; Captain 30 June, 1962; Commodore 18 May, 1967
OTHER PREVIOUS APPOINTMENTS OF NOTE: HMNZ Dockyard, Auckland 1948-1951; DCNTS Navy Office, Wellington 1957-1959; Captain Superintendent, HMNZ Dockyard, Auckland 1962-1966
OFFICIAL ADDRESS: Navy Office, Ministry of Defence, Wellington 49800
PRIVATE ADDRESS: Tyucha, 16 Barton Road, Heretaunga, Wellington

ARGENTINA

CARMINATTI, CAPITAN DE NAVIO G. H., ARGENTINE NAVY
PRESENT APPOINTMENT: Liceo Naval 'Almirante Brown'
DATE OF BIRTH: 18 June 1921
EDUCATION: Escuela Aplicación 1948; Escuela de Guerra Naval 1963; Escuela Naval Militar July 1944
PREVIOUS APPOINTMENTS OF NOTE: Jefe Div. Máquinas Flota de mar 1958; Jefe Dto. Ing. Crucero 'General Belgrano' 1959; Comisión Naval Europa 1960-1961; Jefe Arsenal Pto. Belgrano 1964-1966; Director Liceo Naval 1967-1969
OFFICIAL ADDRESS: Liceo Naval—Río Santiago—Rep. Argentina
PRIVATE ADDRESS: Calle 8 No. 491—City Bell FNGRoca *Telephone:* 80-165

U.S.A.

CARMODY, REAR-ADMIRAL MARTIN DOAN (NAVAL AVIATOR) US NAVY
CURRENT DUTY STATION: Director, Electronic Warfare and Tactical Command System Division, Office of the Chief of Naval Operations (September 1967)
DATE OF BIRTH: 1917
EDUCATION: San Jose State College, California 1949; General Line School
FIRST COMMISSIONED: 14th October, 1941
PROMOTED TO: Rear Admiral 1st June, 1968
COMMANDS: 1946 Bombing Squadron 98; 1946 Attack Squadron 21-A; 1952 Fighter Squadron 87; 1952-1953 Fighter Squadron 124; 1957-1958 Carrier Air Group 8; 1963-1965 Zelima AF 49; 1965-1966 Kitty Hawk CVA 63
OFFICIAL ADDRESS: The Pentagon, Washington, DC 20350
HOME ADDRESS: 18200 Elwood Road, San Jose, California

U.S.A.

CASSELL, REAR-ADMIRAL (SELECTEE) GEORGE LOUIS (NAVAL AVIATOR) US NAVY
CURRENT DUTY STATION: Deputy Commander, Naval Striking and Support Forces, Southern Europe (NATO) (November 1968). Authorized to assume the title of Rear Admiral
DATE OF BIRTH: 1918
EDUCATION: Texas A&M, Southern Methodist University, 1948 General Line School; 1956 Armed Forces Staff College
FIRST COMMISSIONED: 14th March, 1942
PROMOTED TO: Rear Admiral selected for promotion on 6th June, 1968
COMMANDS: 1956-1957 Attack Squadron 126; 1965 Nitro AE 23; 1966 Coral Sea CVA 43
OFFICIAL ADDRESS: (Naples, Italy) FPO New York 09524
HOME ADDRESS: 6338 Goliad Street, Dallas, Texas

U.K.
CATLOW, COMMODORE T. N., ROYAL NAVY
DECORATIONS: C.B.E. 1969
PRESENT APPOINTMENT: Commodore Superintendent of Contract Built Ships, 4 April, 1966
DATE OF BIRTH: 4 December, 1914
EDUCATION: R.N. College, Dartmouth 1928-1932; R.A.F. Staff College 1959; Senior Officers War Course 1961
DATES OF PROMOTION: Commander 30 June, 1949; Captain 31 December, 1956; Commodore 4 April, 1966
PRINCIPAL COMMANDS AT SEA: L.23 1941; Lochinsh 1959-1960
OTHER PREVIOUS APPOINTMENTS OF NOTE: Executive Officer HMS Ocean 1952-1954; Deputy Director Naval Equipment 1957-1959; Naval Attache Rome 1961-1963; Chief of Staff Scotland and Ireland 1964-1966
OFFICIAL ADDRESS: Navy Offices, 128 Grainger Street, Newcastle upon Tyne, NE1 5BR. *Telephone;* Newcastle 25171, Ext. 1
PRIVATE ADDRESS: Gabriel Cottage, Tunstall, Nr. Carnforth, Lancs.

THAILAND
CHANTANAPRAYURE, CAPTAIN, ROYAL THAI NAVY
PRESENT APPOINTMENT: Naval Attache, Royal Thai Embassy, New Delhi, 30 April, 1967
DATE OF BIRTH: 15 November, 1925
EDUCATION: Royal Thai Naval Academy; Royal Thai Naval Staff College
DATES OF PROMOTIONS: Sub-Lieutenant 1950; Lieutenant (JG) 1952; Lieutenant 1956; Lieutenant Commander 1959; Commander 1963; Captain 1967
PRINCIPAL COMMANDS AT SEA: Commanding Officer, HTMS Rawi; Executive Officer, HTMS Klongyai; Commanding Officer, HTMS Sichang; Chief AA Guns Groups HTMS Sukhothai Gunnery Officer, HTMS Bangpakong; Assistant Gunnery Officer, HTMS Tachin; Gunnery Officer, HRMS Tachin; Executive Officer HTMS Bangpakong
OTHER PREVIOUS APPOINTMENTS OF NOTE: Supreme Command Headquarters; Naval Headquarters
OFFICIAL ADDRESS: Office of Naval Attache, Royal Thai Embassy, Chanakyapuri, New Delhi India 175, Soi Santi Petchkhasem Road, Thonburi, Bangkok-6 Thailand

U.S.A.
CHAPMAN, REAR-ADMIRAL DONALD "D" (JUDGE ADVOCATE GENERAL CORPS) US NAVY
CURRENT DUTY STATION: Deputy Judge Advocate General of the Navy (May 1968)
DATE OF BIRTH: 1917
EDUCATION: 1939 Texas Technological College; 1942 University of Texas; 1959 Army Advocate General School
FIRST COMMISSIONED: 24th December, 1942
PROMOTED TO: Rear Admiral 1st May, 1968
COMMANDS 1945-1946 PC 792
OFFICIAL ADDRESS: Arlington Annex, Washington, DC 20370
HOME ADDRESS: Thalia, Texas

U.S.A.
CHARBONNET, REAR-ADMIRAL PIERRE NUMA (NAVAL AVIATOR) US NAVY
CURRENT DUTY STATION:
Director, Fleet Operations Division, Office of the Chief of Naval Operations (September 1969)
DATE OF BIRTH: 1919
EDUCATION: 1941 Naval Academy; 1960 National War College
FIRST COMMISSIONED: 7th February, 1941
PROMOTED TO: Rear Admiral 30th November, 1965
COMMANDS: 1944-1945 Fighting Squadron 24; 1946 Bombing-Fighting Squadron 82; 1946-1948 Fighting Squadron 18-A; 1955-1956 Carrier Air Group 8; 1962-1963 Marias AO 57; 1965 Coral Sea CVA 43
OFFICIAL ADDRESS: The Pentagon, Washington, DC 20350
HOME ADDRESS: Pensacola, Florida

CANADA
CHARLES, REAR ADMIRAL, J. A., Canadian Armed Forces
DECORATIONS: CD 1949;
PRESENT APPOINTMENT: Deputy Commander Maritime Command and Commander, Maritime Forces Pacific August 1966
DATE OF BIRTH: 27 March, 1918
EDUCATION: Cadet Entry
DATES OF PROMOTIONS: Cadet 20 August, 1937; Assistant Sub Lieutenant 1 May, 1940; Lieutenant 1 January, 1941; Assistant Lieutenant Commander 2 October, 1945; Lieutenant Commander 1 July, 1947; Commander 1st July, 1950; Assistant Captain 6 February, 1954; Captain 1 July, 1954; Commodore 23 August, 1961; Rear Admiral 1 August, 1966
PRINCIPAL COMMANDS AT SEA: HMCS Crescent January 1948-November 1948; HMCS Haida also commander Canadian Destroyer Squadron, Far East October 1953- September 1954; HMCS Assiniboine, also Commander Second Canadian Escort Squadron August 1960-August 1961
OTHER PREVIOUS APPOINTMENTS OF NOTE: On staff of the Naval Member, Canadian Staff Washington January 1947-January 1948; Royal Naval Staff Course April 1949-September 1949; Joint Service Staff College Course January 1950-August 1950; Naval Headquarters as Director of Naval Communications October 1951- October 1953; Commandant, Canadian Services College Royal Roads September 1954- September 1957; Naval Headquarters as Director of Naval Plans and Operations September 1957-August 1960 Commodore, RCN, Esquimalt, B.C. August 1961-August 1963; National Defense College Course September 1963-July 1964; Canadian Forces Headquarters as Director General Corces Development December 1964-July 1966;
OFFICIAL ADDRESS: Commander, Maritime Forces Pacific, FMO Victoria, British Columbia

U.S.A.
CHASE, REAR-ADMIRAL (SELECTEE) JOWN DAWSON, US NAVY
CURRENT DUTY STATION: Commander, Naval Weapons Laboratory, Dahlgren, Virginia (July 1968)
DATE OF BIRTH: 1919
EDUCATION: 1940 Naval Academy; 1948 Naval Postgraduate School; 1954 Armed Forves Staff College; 1960 Industrial College of the Armed Forces
FIRST COMMISSIONED: 6th June, 1940
PROMOTED TO: Rear Admiral, selected for promotion on 6th June, 1969
COMMANDS: 1954-1956 Frank E. Evans DD 754; 1960-1961 Destroyer Division 191; 1965-1966 Boston CAG 1
OFFICIAL ADDRESS: Dahlgren, Virginia
HOME ADDRESS: 243 Termino Avenue, Long Beach, California.

INDIA
CHATTERJI, ADMIRAL A. K., INDIAN NAVY
PRESENT APPOINTMENT: Chief of the Naval Staff (4 March, 1966)
DATE OF BIRTH: 22 November, 1914
DATES OF PROMOTIONS: Commander 15 August, 1947; Captain 30 June, 1961; Rear-Admiral 5 March, 1960; Vice-Admiral 22 November, 1966; Admiral 1 March, 1968
PRINCIPAL COMMANDS AT SEA: 1950 Delhi; 1953 Delhi; 1962 Flag Officer Commanding, Indian Fleet
OTHER PREVIOUS APPOINTMENTS OF NOTE: Naval Adviser, London 1950; Commodore-in-Charge Bombay 1954; Dy Chief of Naval Staff 1958; Commandant, National Defence College 1964
OFFICIAL ADDRESS: Naval Headquarters, New Delhi II *Telephone:* 371400

U.S.A.
CHEFFEY, REAR-ADMIRAL JOHN HOWARD (MEDICAL CORPS) US NAVY
CURRENT DUTY STATION: Commanding Officer, Naval Hospital, Great Lakes, Illinois; District Medical Officer, 9th Naval District; Commanding Officer, Naval Hospital Corps School Great Lakes (February 1969)
DATE OF BIRTH: 1916
EDUCATION: 1938 University of Pittsburgh; Jefferson Medical College
FIRST COMMISSIONED: 15th June, 1942
PROMOTED TO: Rear Admiral 1st August, 1968
COMMANDS: 1950-1951 Company E, 1st Medical Battalion, 1st Marine Division; 1967-1968 Naval Hospital, Newport, Rhode Island
OFFICIAL ADDRESS: Great Lakes, Illinois
HOME ADDRESS: Barnesville, Ohio

U.S.A.
CHEW, VICE-ADMIRAL JOHN LOUIS, US NAVY
CURRENT DUTY STATION: Commander, US Taiwan Defense Command (July 1967)
DATE OF BIRTH: 1909
EDUCATION: 1931 Naval Academy; 1939 General Line School
FIRST COMMISSIONED: 4th June, 1931
PROMOTED TO: Rear Admiral 1st April, 1959; Vice Admiral 25th November, 1965
COMMANDS: 1947-1948 Stickell DD 888; 1956 Pawcatuck AO 108; 1956-1958 Roanoke CL 145; 1966-1967 Anti-Submarine Warfare Force, Pacific Fleet
OFFICIAL ADDRESS: (Taiwan) APO San Francisco, California 96363
HOME ADDRESS: 15 Southgate Avenue, Annapolis, Maryland

U.S.A.
CHILDERS, REAR-ADMIRAL KENAN CLARK (AERONAUTICAL ENGINEERING DUTY) US NAVY
CURRENT DUTY STATION: Assistant Commander for Material Acquisition, Naval Air Systems Command (May 1967)
DATE OF BIRTH: 1917
EDUCATION: 1939 Naval Academy; 1945 Naval Postgraduate School; 1946 California Institute of Technology
FIRST COMMISSIONED: 1st June, 1939
PROMOTED TO: Rear Admiral 1st June, 1967
COMMANDS: 1961-1964 Naval Missile Center, Point Mugu, California
OFFICIAL ADDRESS: Main Navy Building, Washington, DC 20360
HOME ADDRESS: McLean, Virginia

U.S.A.
CHRISTENSEN, REAR-ADMIRAL ERNEST EDWARD (NAVAL AVIATOR) US NAVY
CURRENT DUTY STATION: Chief of Naval Air Technical Training (June 1967)
DATE OF BIRTH: 1913
EDUCATION: 1934 Naval Academy; 1941 Naval Postgraduate School; 1952 Naval War College
FIRST COMMISSIONED: 31st May, 1934
PROMOTED TO: Rear Admiral 1st July, 1962
COMMANDS: 1944-1945 Rehoboth AVP 50; 1945 Naval Air Station, Traverse City, Michigan; 1945-1946 Special Weapons Test and Tactical Evaluation Unit, Mojave, California; 1959-1960 Hornet CVS 12; 1962-1963 Carrier Division 18
OFFICIAL ADDRESS: Naval Air Station, Millington, Tennessee 38054
HOME ADDRESS: Memphis, Tennessee.

U.S.A.
CHRISTMAN, REAR-ADMIRAL (SELECTEE) THOMAS JACKSON (ORDNANCE ENGINEERING DUTY) US NAVY
CURRENT DUTY STATION: Deputy Commander for Plans & Research, Naval Ordnance Systems Command (August 1968)
DATE OF BIRTH: 1922
EDUCATION: 1944 Naval Academy; 1948 Naval Postgraduate School
FIRST COMMISSIONED: 9th June, 1943
PROMOTED TO: Rear Admiral, selected for promotion on 6th June, 1968
COMMANDS: 1967-1968 Naval Ammunition Depot, Crane, Indiana
OFFICIAL ADDRESS: Main Navy Building, Washington, DC 20360
HOME ADDRESS: 3206 Greens Avenue, Orlando, Florida

ITALY
CIUFFO, REAR-ADMIRAL (UPPER HALF) E., ITALIAN NAVY
DECORATIONS: (n. 3) War Crosses
PRESENT APPOINTMENT: Chief of Bureau of Military Personnel
DATE OF BIRTH: 12 May, 1910
DATE OF LAST PROMOTION: 1 January, 1966
OFFICIAL ADDRESS: Direttore Generale di Maripers, Ministero Difesa, Marina, Roma

U.S.A.
CLANCY, REAR-ADMIRAL ALBERT HARRISON (AERONAUTICAL ENGINEERING DUTY) US NAVY
CURRENT DUTY STATION: Project Manager, Reconnaissance, Electronic Warfare, Special Operations and Naval Intelligence Processing, Naval Material Command (December 1968)
DATE OF BIRTH: 1919
EDUCATION: 1940 Naval Academy; 1949 University of California at Los Angeles
FIRST COMMISSIONED: 6th June, 1940
PROMOTED TO: Rear Admiral 1st November, 1967
COMMANDS: 1965-1967 Naval Air Engineering Center, Philadelphia, Pennsylvania
OFFICIAL ADDRESS: Main Navy Building, Washington DC 20360
HOME ADDRESS: 1915 San Mateo, Albuqerque, New Mexico

U.S.A.
CLAREY, ADMIRAL BERNARD AMBROSE, US NAVY
CURRENT DUTY STATION: Vice Chief of Naval Operations (January 1968)
DATE OF BIRTH: 1912
EDUCATION: 1934 Naval Academy; 1956 National War College
FIRST COMMISSIONED: 31st May, 1934
PROMOTED TO: Rear Admiral 1st July, 1959; Vice Admiral 5th June, 1964; Admiral 17th January, 1968
COMMANDS: 1944-1945 Pintado SS 387; 1952-1953 Submarine Division 52; 1958 Hassayampa AO 145; 1962-1964 Submarine Force, Pacific Fleet; 1966-1967 Second Fleet
OFFICIAL ADDRESS: The Pentagon, Washington, DC 20350
HOME ADDRESS: Navy Yard, Washington, DC

UNITED KINGDOM
CLAYTON, CAPTAIN R. P., ROYAL NAVY
PRESENT APPOINTMENT: HMS Hampshire 16 January, 1969
DATE OF BIRTH: 9 July, 1925
EDUCATION: Horris Hill; Dartmouth (13 year entry)
DATES OF PROMOTIONS: Commander 30 June, 1958; Captain 30 June, 1964

PRINCIPAL COMMANDS AT SEA: 1958-1959 HMS Puma; 1968 HMS Kent
OTHER PREVIOUS APPOINTMENTS OF NOTE: Assistant Director of Naval Plans 1964-1966
OFFICIAL ADDRESS: HMS Hampshire, BFPO Ships, London
PRIVATE ADDRESS: Chateau de Roaix, 84 Roaix, France

U.S.A.
COBB, REAR-ADMIRAL JAMES OUTTERSON (NAVAL AVIATOR) US NAVY
CURRENT DUTY STATION: Chief, Joint US Military Group Military Assistance Advisory Group, Spain (November 1968)
DATE OF BIRTH: 1911
EDUCATION: 1933 Naval Academy; 1948 Naval War College
FIRST COMMISSIONED: 1st June, 1933
PROMOTED TO: Rear Admiral 1st July, 1961
COMMANDS: 1942-1943 Patrol Squadron 91; 1957-1958 Yorktown CVS 10; 1961-1962 Carrier Division 19; 1965-1966 Carrier Division 2
OFFICIAL ADDRESS: (Madrid) APO New York, 09285
HOME ADDRESS: 1037 Adella Avenue, Coronado, California

ARGENTINA
CODA, REAR ADMIRAL C. G. N. ARGENTINE NAVY
PRESENT APPOINTMENT: Comandante Naval 28 February, 1969
DATE OF BIRTH: 24 December, 1918
EDUCATION: Escuela de Aplicación de Oficiales 1945; Escuela de Guerra Naval 1951
DATES OF PROMOTIONS: Guardiamarina 9 November 1940; Teniente de Corbeta 31 December, 1942; Teniente de Fragate 31 December, 1944; Teniente de Navío 31 December, 1946; Capitán de Corbeta 31 December, 1950; Capitán de Fragata 31 December, 1954; Capitán de Navío 31 December, 1959; Rear Admiral 31 December, 1965
PRINCIPAL COMMANDS AT SEA: Buque Tanque Punta Loyola 1952; Destructores La Rioja & Mendoza 1957; Destructor San Juan 1958; Crucero 9 De Julio, Portaaviones Independencia 1963-1964
OTHER PREVIOUS APPOINTMENTS OF NOTE: Estado Mayor de la Junta Interamericana de Defensa 1959-1960; Jefe del Estado Mayor de la Flota de mar 1964; Director de la Escuela de Guerra Naval 1965; Jefe Del Estado Mayor de Coordinacion 1966; Secretario General del Comando de Operaciones Navales 1967; Comandante Naval 1969
OFFICIAL ADDRESS: Comando Naval Base Naval Puerto Belgrano *Telephone:* 1686 Republica Argentina
PRIVATE ADDRESS: Ayacucho 1743, Buenos Aires, Republica Argentina

U.S.A.
COLBERT, VICE-ADMIRAL RICHARD GARY, US NAVY
CURRENT DUTY STATION: President, Naval War College (August 1968)
DATE OF BIRTH: 1915
EDUCATION: 1937 Naval Academy; 1956 Naval War College
FIRST COMMISSIONED: 3rd June, 1937
PROMOTED TO: Rear Admiral 1st February, 1965; Vice Admiral 1st September, 1968
COMMANDS: 1939-1944 Barker DD 213; 1944-1945 Meade DD 602; 1960-1961 Altair AKS 32; 1961-1963 Boston CAG 1; 1965-1966 Cruiser-Destroyer Flotilla 6
OFFICIAL ADDRESS: Newport, Rhode Island 02840
HOME ADDRESS: Chevy Chase, Maryland

U.S.A.
COLE, REAR-ADMIRAL (SELECTEE) PHILIP PATTEN, US NAVY
CURRENT DUTY STATION: Commander, US Naval Forces, Marianas (August 1968)
DATE OF BIRTH: 1919
EDUCATION: 1942 Naval Academy; 1947 Naval Postgraduate School; 1964 Naval War College
FIRST COMMISSIONED: 19th December, 1941
PROMOTED TO: Rear Admiral, selection approved on 6th June, 1968, authorized to assume the title of Rear Admiral
COMMANDS: 1951-1953 Burrfish SSR 312; 1958-1959 Submarine Division 72; 1964-1965 Canisteo AO 99; 1965-1966 Submarine Squadron 6
OFFICIAL ADDRESS: (Guam, Marianan Islands) FPO San Francisco, California 96630
HOME ADDRESS: 6044 River Road, Norfolk, Virginia

U.S.A.
COLWELL, VICE-ADMIRAL JOHN BARR, US NAVY
DATE OF BIRTH 1909
EDUCATION: 1931 Naval Academy; 1939 Naval Postgraduate School
FIRST COMMISSIONED: 4th June, 1934
PROMOTED TO: Rear Admiral 1st August, 1958; Vice Admiral 18th January, 1964
COMMANDS: 1944 Converse DD 509; 1954-1955 Elokomin AO 55; 1958 Galveston CLG 3; 1961-1962 Amphibious Group; 1964-1965 Amphibious Force, Pacific Fleet
OFFICIAL ADDRESS: The Pentagon, Washington, DC 20350
HOME ADDRESS: Pawnee City, Nebraska

U.S.A.
COMBS, REAR-ADMIRAL WALTER VINCENT, JR. US NAVY
CURRENT DUTY STATION: Commander, Service Force, Pacific Fleet (February 1968)
DATE OF BIRTH: 1914
EDUCATION: 1936 Naval Academy; 1953 Naval War College; 1961 National War College
FIRST COMMISSIONED: 4th June, 1939;
PROMOTED TO: Rear Admiral 1st July, 1964
COMMANDS: 1944-1946 Harrison DD 573; 1949 Putnam DD 757; 1949-1950 Borie DD 704; 1953-1954 Escort Squadron 11; 1958-1959 Hamul AD 20; 1959-1960 Los Angeles CA 135; 1966-1968 Cruiser-Destroyer Flotilla 3
OFFICIAL ADDRESS: (Pearl Harbor) FPO San Francisco, California 96610
HOME ADDRESS: 1045 West 23rd Street, Upland, California

U.K.
COMPSTON, VICE ADMIRAL P. M., ROYAL NAVY
DECORATIONS: C.B. 1967
PRESENT APPOINTMENT: Deputy Squadron Allied Commander, Atlantic
DATE OF BIRTH: 12 September, 1915
EDUCATION: Epsom College
DATES OF PROMOTIONS: Commander 1956; Captain 1956; Rear Admiral 1965; Vice Admiral 1968
PRINCIPAL COMMANDS AT SEA: HMS Orwell in Command & Captain D. Plymouth 1957-1959; HMS Victorious 1962-1964; FOF Western Fleet 1967-1968
OTHER PREVIOUS APPOINTMENTS OF NOTE: Naval Attaché, Paris 1960-1962; Chief British Naval, Washington, DC 1965-1967
OFFICIAL ADDRESS: Saclant Headquarters, Norfolk, Va, USA
PRIVATE ADDRESS: Holmerwood Cottage, Strond, Nr. Petersfield, Hants. *Telephone:* Petersfield 3518

U.S.A.
CONNOLLY, VICE-ADMIRAL THOMAS FRANCIS (NAVAL AVIATOR) US NAVY
CURRENT DUTY STATION: Deputy Chief of Naval Operations (Air) (November 1966)
DATE OF BIRTH: 1909
EDUCATION: 1933 Naval Academy; 1942 Naval Postgraduate School
FIRST COMMISSIONED: 1st June, 1933
PROMOTED TO: Rear Admiral 1st April, 1960; Vice Admiral 1st November, 1965
COMMANDS: 1942-1944 Patrol Squadron 13; 1951-1952 Composite Squadron 6; 1956-1957 Corregidor T-CVU 58; 1957 Hornet CVA 12; 1961-1962 Carrier Division 7; 1965-1966 Naval Air Force, Pacific Fleet
OFFICIAL ADDRESS: The Pentagon, Washington, DC 20350
HOME ADDRESS: Navy Yard, Washington, DC

U.S.A.
COOK, REAR-ADMIRAL RALPH EDWARD (SPECIAL DUTY) US NAVY
CURRENT DUTY STATION: Commander, Naval Security Group Command and Executive Assistant for Cryptology, Office of the Chief of Naval Operations (June 1967)
DATE OF BIRTH: 1915
EDUCATION: 1938 Montana State College; 1952 Naval Justice School
FIRST COMMISSIONED: 21st January, 1941
PROMOTED TO: Rear Admiral 1st February, 1968
OFFICIAL ADDRESS: Naval Security Station, 3801 Nebraska Avenue NW., Washington, DC 20390
HOME ADDRESS: Chevy Chase, Maryland

U.S.A.
COOPER, REAR-ADMIRAL DAMON WARREN (NAVAL AVIATOR) US NAVY
CURRENT DUTY STATION: Assistant Chief of Personnel Control, Bureau of Naval Personnel (August 1968)
DATE OF BIRTH: 1919
EDUCATION: 1941 Naval Academy; 1958 Naval War College; 1961 Naval War College
FIRST COMMISSIONED: 7th February, 1941 PROMOTED TO: Rear Admiral 1st July, 1967
COMMANDS: 1944-1945 Torpedo Squadron 24; 1951-1953 Fighter Squadron 821; 1953 Fighter Squadron 143; 1955-1956 Air Task Group 3; 1959-1960 Attack Squadron 44; 1963-1964 Pine Island AV 12; 1964-1965 Ticonderoga CVA 14; 1966-1968 Patrol Force 7th Fleet; US Taiwan Patrol Force; Fleet Air Wing 1
OFFICIAL ADDRESS: Arlington Annex, Washington, DC 20370
HOME ADDRESS: Elizabethtown, Kentucky

U.S.A.
CORLE, REAR-ADMIRAL FREDERICK WILLIAM (SUPPLY CORPS) US NAVY
CURRENT DUTY STATION: Commanding Officer, Ships Parts Control Center, Mechanicsburg, Pennsylvania (July 1966)
DATE OF BIRTH: 1916
EDUCATION: 1939 Naval Academy; 1953 Harvard University; 1960 Naval War College
FIRST COMMISSIONED: 1st June, 1939
PROMOTED TO: Rear Admiral 30th May, 1967
COMMANDS: 1965-1966 Navy Electronics Supply Office, Great Lakes, Illinois
OFFICIAL ADDRESS: Mechanicsburg, Pennsylvania7055
HOME ADDRESS: 111 North Virginia Street, Reno, Nevade

U.S.A.
COSGROVE, REAR-ADMIRAL PAUL FRANCIS, JNR. (SUPPLY CORPS) US NAVY
CURRENT DUTY STATION: Deputy Commander for Supply Operations, Naval Supply Systems Command (August 1967)
DATE OF BIRTH: 1918
EDUCATION: 1939 Georgia Institute of Technology; 1955 Naval War College
FIRST COMMISSIONED: 18th January, 1940
PROMOTED TO: Rear Admiral 1st July, 1967
COMMANDS: 1965-1966 Navy Fleet Material Support Office, Mechanicsburg, Pennsylvania
OFFICIAL ADDRESS: Main Navy Building, Washington, DC 20360
HOME ADDRESS: 72 Belmont Drive, Atlanta, Georgia

U.S.A.
COUSINS, VICE-ADMIRAL RALPH WYNNE (NAVAL AVIATOR) US NAVY
CURRENT DUTY STATION:
Deputy Chief of Naval Operations (Fleet Operations & Readiness) (July 1969)
DATE OF BIRTH: 1915
EDUCATION: 1937 Naval Avademy; 1963 National War College
FIRST COMMISSIONED: 3rd June, 1937
PROMOTED TO: Rear Admiral 7th December, 1964; Vice Admiral 3rd July, 1968
MAJOR AWARD: Navy Cross
COMMANDS: 1959-1960 Nantahala AO 60; 1960-1961 Midway CVA 41; 1965-1966 Carrier Division 9; 1967-1969 Attack Carrier Striking Force, 7th Fleet; Carrier Division 5
OFFICIAL ADDRESS: The Pentagon, Washington, DC 20350
HOME ADDRESS: Washington, DC

U.S.A.
COWAN, REAR-ADMIRAL JOHN STEPHEN, (MEDICAL CORPS.) US NAVY
DATE OF BIRTH: 1913
EDUCATION: University of Pennsylvania
DATE OF COMMISSION: 1st October, 1940
PROMOTED TO: Rear Admiral 1st August, 1966
COMMANDS: 1944 6th Medical Battalion, 6th Marine Division; 1946-1950 Navy Medical Field Research Laboratory, Camp Lejeune, North Carolina; 1964-1966 Naval Hospital, Philadelphia, Pennsylvania; additional duty: Medical Officer, 4th Naval District

U.S.A.
COWAN, REAR-ADMIRAL JOSEPH STEPHEN (MEDICAL CORPS) US NAVY
DATE OF BIRTH: 1913
EDUCATION: 1937 University of Minnesota
FIRST COMMISSIONED: 1st October, 1940
PROMOTED TO: Rear Admiral 11th October, 1966
COMMANDS: 1944-1946 6th Medical Battalion, 6th Marine Division; 1964-1966 Naval Hospital, Philadelphia
HOME ADDRESS: Honolulu, Hawaii

U.S.A.
COX, REAR-ADMIRAL (SELECTEE) DONALD VANCE, US NAVY
CURRENT DUTY STATION: Chairman, Working Panel, Surface-to-Surface Missile Pilot Study and Deputy Program Co-ordinator for Anti-Ship Missile Defense, Office of the Chief of Naval Operations (April 1968)
DATE OF BIRTH: 1921
EDUCATION: 1944 Naval Academy; 1950 Naval Postgraduate School; 1961 Air War College
FIRST COMMISSIONED: 9th June, 1943
PROMOTED TO: Rear Admiral, selected for promotion on 6th June, 1969
COMMANDS: 1961-1963 Robinson DDG 12; 1966-1968 Chicago CG 11
OFFICIAL ADDRESS: The Pentagon, Washington, DC 20350
HOME ADDRESS: Farragut, Iowa

U.S.A.
CRAMER, REAR-ADMIRAL SHANNON DAVENPORT, JNR., US NAVY
CURRENT DUTY STATION: Military Assistant to the Assistant Secretary of Defense (Public Affairs) (July 1968)
DATE OF BIRTH: 1921
EDUCATION: 1943 Naval Academy
FIRST COMMISSIONED: 9th June, 1943
PROMOTED TO: Rear Admiral 1st August, 1968
COMMANDS: 1954-1956 Sirago SS 485; 1958-1960 Swordfish SSN 579; 1961-1963 Submarine Division 102; 1963-1964 Patrick Henry SSBN 599
OFFICIAL ADDRESS: The Pentagon, Washington, DC 20301
HOME ADDRESS: 1120 East Haines Street, Philadelphia, Pennsylvania

U.S.A.
CRAWFORD, REAR-ADMIRAL EARL RUSSELL, US NAVY
CURRENT DUTY STATION:
Assistant Deputy Chief of Naval Operations (Logistics) (June 1969)
DATE OF BIRTH: 1913
EDUCATION: 1936 Naval Academy; 1955 Naval War College
FIRST COMMISSIONED: 4th June, 1936
PROMOTED TO: Rear Admiral 1st July, 1964
COMMANDS: 1939-1943 S-46 SS 157; 1945-1946 Roncador SS 301; 1946-1948 Blueback SS 326; 1957-1958 Tulare AKA 112; 1962-1963 Amphibious Squadron 1; 1964-1965 Amphibious Training Command, Atlantic Fleet; 1965-1966 Amphibious Group 2; 1966-1968 Naval Base, Guantanamo Bay, Cuba
OFFICIAL ADDRESS: The Pentagon, Washington, DC 20350
HOME ADDRESS: 264 East 6th Street, Peru, Indiana

PORTUGAL
CRESPO, VICE ADMIRAL M. P., (PORTUGEUSE NAVY)
DECORATIONS: Two 'Medalhas Militares de prata de Serviços Distintos' 'Medalah de Mérito Militar de la. Classe' 'Comendador de Ordem Militar de Avis'; 'Medalha Militar de Ouro de Comportamento exemplar'; 'Oficial da Ordem da Legiao de Honora da França'; 'Cruz da Ordem de Mérito de Espanha de 3a. Classe, com distintivo branco'; 'Grande Oficial da Ordem de Mérito Naval do Brasil'.
PRESENT APPOINTMENT: Minister of Marine since, 19 August, 1969
DATE OF BIRTH: 30 July, 1911
EDUCATION: Specialisation in Radio-Telegraphy and Communications, Naval Academy, Curso Geral Naval de Guerra (Promotion Course, Junior Officer); Curso Superior Naval de Guer ra (Staff Course, Senior Officer).
DATES OF PROMOTIONS: Midshipman 1 October, 1930; Ensigne 1 September, 1933; Lieutenant Junior Grade 1 March, 1935; Lieutenant 28 March 1940; Lieutenant Commander 31 March 1953; Commander 9 July, 1968; Captain 31 July 1961; Rear Admiral 14 September 1966; Vice Admiral 24 January, 1969
PRINCIPAL COMMANDS AT SEA: Commander of the Survey Ship Mandovi 1947-1948-1951-1956, concurrent with Chief of the Geo-Hy drographic Mission Portuguese Guinea; Commander of Patrol Vessel Sal 1950-1951; Commander of the Survey Ship Pedro Nunes 1956-1957 Commander of Minesweepers Flotilla 1963-1964
OTHER PREVIOUS APPOINTMENTS OF NOTE: Chief of the 2nd Division of Naval Staff 1959-1963; Chief of the 1st Division of Naval Staff 1964-1966; Teacher at the Supreme Naval College 1967-1968 concurrent with Assistant to the Chief of Naval Staff
OFFICIAL ADDRESS: Ministério da Marinha-Praça do Comercio, Lisbon
PRIVATE ADDRESS: Rua Dionísio Santos Matias, 10-20°. Esq. Paço de Acros, Portugal

U.S.A.
CRUTCHFIELD, REAR-ADMIRAL ROBERT REYNOLD, US NAVY
CURRENT DUTY STATION: Assistant Chief for Plans & Programs, Bureau of Naval Personnel (August 1967)
DATE OF BIRTH: 1918
EDUCATION: 1939 Randolph-Macon College; 1951 Harvard University; 1958 Naval War College
FIRST COMMISSIONED: 14th November, 1940
PROMOTED TO: Rear Admiral 15th December, 1967
COMMANDS: 1945 Buckley DE 51; 1945-1946 Jack W. Wilke De 800; 1953-1955 New DDE 818; 1960-1961 Destroyer Division 282; 1963-1964 Dale DLG 19; 1965 Destroyer Squadron 26
OFFICIAL ADDRESS: Arlington Annex, Washington, DC 20370
HOME ADDRESS: Montross, Virginia

U.S.A.
CURTIS, REAR-ADMIRAL WALTER LOUIS, JNR. (NAVAL AVIATOR) US NAVY
CURRENT DUTY STATION: Assistant Chief of Staff for Plans, Commander-in-Chief Pacific Fleet (September 1967)
DATE OF BIRTH: 1915
EDUCATION: 1936 Wake Forest College; 1948 Naval Postgraduate School; 1958 Industrial College of the Armed Forces
FIRST COMMISSIONED: 1st October, 1937
PROMOTED TO: Rear Admiral 1st February, 1965
COMMANDS: 1950-1952 Air Anti-Submarine Squadron 31; 1961-1962 Thetis Bay LPH 6; 1962-1963 Kitty Hawk CVA 63; 1966-1967 Carrier Division 9
OFFICIAL ADDRESS: (Pearl Harbor) FPO San Francisco, California 96610
HOME ADDRESS: Ahoskie, North Carolina

U.S.A.
DACEY, REAR-ADMIRAL JOHN ELMER, US NAVY
CURRENT DUTY STATION: Office of CNO-special assistant for Tactical Surface Warfare (April 1968)
DATE OF BIRTH: 1916
EDUCATION: 1938 US Naval Academy; 1947 US Naval Academy Postgraduate School; 1949 Naval Training School, Massachusetts Institue of Technology; 1958 National War College
FIRST COMMISSIONED: 2nd June, 1938
PROMOTED TO: Rear Admiral 1st March, 1965
COMMANDS: 1952-1954 Dyess DDR 880; 1958-1959 Destroyer Division 212; 1962-1963 Destroyer Development Group 2; 1963-1965 Chicago CG 11; 1967-1968 Cruiser Destroyer Flotilla 12
HOME ADDRESS: 5300 Sanger Avenue, Alexandria, Virginia 22311

U.S.A.
DARE, REAR-ADMIRAL JAMES ASHTON, US NAVY
CURRENT DUTY STATION: Commander, South Atlantic Force, FPO New York 09501 (July 1968)
DATE OF BIRTH: 1915
EDUCATION: 1939 Naval Academy; 1946 Naval Academy Postgraduate School; 1947 Naval Training Schools, Massachusetts Institute of Technology; 1962 National War College
FIRST COMMISSIONED: 1st June, 1939
PROMOTED TO: Rear Admiral 1st May, 1967
COMMANDS 1951-1953 USS Douglas H. Fox DD 779; 1956-1958 USS Compass Island EAG 153; 1964-1965 Amphibious Squadron 10; 1965-1966 Naval Ordnance Laboratory, White Oak, Md.
HOME ADDRESS: 405 S. Pitt Street, Alexandria, Virginia 22314

U.K.
DAVENPORT, COMMANDER J. N. F., ROYAL NAVY
PRESENT APPOINTMENT: Commanding Officer, HMS Naiad 1 January, 1968
DATE OF BIRTH: 14 February, 1928
EDUCATION: Royal Nautical College, Dartmouth 1941-1945
DATES OF PROMOTIONS: Lieutenant Commander 1 June 1957; Commander 30 June, 1964
PRINCIPAL COMMANDS AT SEA: HMS/M Subtle 1957; HMS/M Alaric 1961; HMS/M Orphes 1962-1963
OTHER PREVIOUS APPOINTMENTS OF NOTE: ANA Moscow 1958-1959 CO S/M Commanding Officers Qualifying Course 1963-1965; DN Plans 1965-1967
OFFICIAL ADDRESS: HMS Naiad, BFPO Ships
PRIVATE ADDRESS c/o Barclays Bank, Halesworth, Suffolk

U.S.A.
DAVIES, REAR-ADMIRAL THOMAS DANIEL, US NAVY
CURRENT DUTY STATION: Deputy Chief of Naval Material for Development and Chief of Naval Development (May 1969)
DATE OF BIRTH: 1914
EDUCATION: 1937 Naval Academy; 1962 National War College
FIRST COMMISSIONED: 3rd June, 1937
PROMOTED TO: Rear Admiral 1st July, 1965
COMMANDS: 1949 Task Force 66, Wash., DC; 1956-1958 Naval Air Engineering Facility; 1960-1961 Caliente AO 53; 1962-1963 Fleet Air Wing 3; 1963-1964 NAS, Norfolk, Va.; 1967-1969 Carrier Division 20
HOME ADDRESS: 5800 Kennedy Drive, Chery Chase, Maryland 20015

U.S.A.
DAVIS, REAR-ADMIRAL GEORGE MONROE, JNR. (MEDICAL CORPS) US NAVY
CURRENT DUTY STATION: Deputy Chief, Bureau of Medicine and Surgery, Wash., DC (March 1968)
DATE OF BIRTH: 1916
EDUCATION: 1947 Northwestern School of Medicine, Chicago
FIRST COMMISSIONED: 15th August, 1939
PROMOTED TO: Rear Admiral 1st July, 1965
COMMANDS: 1964-1966 Naval Hospital, National Naval Medical Center, Bethesda, Md. 1966-1968 National Naval Medical Center, Bethesda, Md.
HOME ADDRESS: Quarters "B", National Naval Medical Center, Bethesda, Maryland 20014

U.S.A.
DAVIS, REAR-ADMIRAL JOHN BLOUNT, JNR, US NAVY
CURRENT DUTY STATION:
Commander, Hawaiian Sea Frontier and Commandant, 14th Naval District; additional duty: Commander, Fleet Air, Hawaii; Commander, Naval Base Pearl Harbor (June 1969)
DATE OF BIRTH: 1919
EDUCATION: 1941 Naval Academy; 1944 Naval Training Station, Norfolk, Va.; 1946 Naval Academy, Postgraduate School; 1948 Cornell University, Ithaca; 1953 Naval War College; 1964 National War College; 1965 Fleet Anti-Submarine Warfare School, San Diego
FIRST COMMISSIONED: 19th December, 1941
PROMOTED TO: Rear Admiral 1st August, 1968
COMMANDS: 1955-1957 Brinkley Bass DD 887; 1964-1965 Prairie Ad 15; 1965-1966 Destroyer Squadron 7; 1967-1968 Cruiser-Destroyer Flotilla 9
HOME ADDRESS: 860 Country Club Lane, Coronado, California 92118

EIRE
DEASY, LIEUTENANT COMMANDER J. A.
PRESENT APPOINTMENT: Commanding Officer L.E. Maev, 30 October, 1968
DATE OF BIRTH: 19 April, 1932
EDUCATION: Leaving Certificate (Ireland); Dartmouth (Benbow); HMS Devonshire, Subs Courses, Greenwich; Long T.A.S. Course HMS Vernon, etc.
DATES OF PROMOTIONS: Sub-Lieutenant 11 December, 1954; Lieutenant 30 November, 1959; Lieut.-Commander 30 November, 1968
OFFICIAL ADDRESS: L.E. Maev, Haulbowline, Cobh, Co. Cork
PRIVATE ADDRESS: Haulbowline, Cobh, Co. Cork

U.S.A.
DEMPSEY, REAR-ADMIRAL JAMES CHARLES, US NAVY
CURRENT DUTY STATION: Commandant, 5th Naval District additional duty: Commander, Naval Base Norfolk, Norfolk, Va. (May 1968)
DATE OF BIRTH: 1908
EDUCATION: 1931 Naval Academy; 1939 Naval Academy Naval Postgraduate School; 1951 Naval War College
FIRST COMMISSIONED: 4th June, 1931
PROMOTED TO: Rear Admiral 1st November, 1959
MAJOR AWARDS: Navy Cross with Gold Star in lieu of 2nd award
COMMANDS: 1941-1942 S 37; 1942-1943 Spearfish SS 190; 1943-1944 Cod SS 224; 1945 Submarine Division 102; 1945-1946 Submarine Division 71; 1946 Submarine Division 72; 1951-1952 Submarine Squadron 1; 1956-1957 Waccamaw AO 109; 1957-1958 Submarine Flotilla 1; 1959-1961 Military Sea Transportation Service, Atlantic Area; 1961-1962 Amphibious Group 2; 1962-1964 Amphibious Training Command, Atlantic Fleet; 1964-1966 Chief, Navy Section, Joint US Military Mission for Aid to Turkey, Ankara, Turkey

U.K.
LAUNDERS, Captain J. S., ROYAL NAVY
DECORATIONS: DSC 1942; DSC* 1943; DSO 1944; DSO* 1945
PRESENT APPOINTMENT: Captain (SM), 7th Submarine Division & HMS Forth in Command 18 November, 1968
DATE OF BIRTH: 18 August, 1919
EDUCATION: Skinners Company's School, Tunbridge Wells (Secondary School)
DATES OF PROMOTIONS: Commander 30 June, 1957; A/Captain 5 May, 1966; Captain 30 June, 1966
PRINCIPAL COMMANDS AT SEA: SM Venturer 1943-1945; SM Alcide 1952-1954; Ex-German U 1407 (HMS Meteorite) 1945-1948
OFFICIAL ADDRESS: HMS Forth, c/o BFPO Ships
PRIVATE ADDRESS: 315 Ratus Road, Singapore 27

UNITED KINGDOM
LAW, ADMIRAL SIR HORACE R., ROYAL NAVY
DECORATIONS: K.C.B. 1967; O.B.E. 1950; D.S.C. Crete 1942
PRESENT APPOINTMENT: Controller of the Navy 1965
DATE OF BIRTH: 23 June, 1911
EDUCATION: Sherborne School
DATES OF PROMOTIONS: 1929 Entered Royal Navy; 1946 Commander; 1961 Rear-Admiral
PRINCIPAL COMMANDS AT SEA: Served as a gunnery officer on HMS Cairo in Norwegian Campaign and served in HMS Coventry during Crete Campaign during World War II; 1946 HMS Modeste; 1952 HMS Triumph; 1953 HMS Duchess; 1958-1960 HMS Centaur
OTHER PREVIOUS APPOINTMENTS OF NOTE: Fleet Gunnery Officer, Far East Fleet 1949; Director, Royal Naval Tactical School Woolwich 1956; Flag Officer Submarines 1963-1965
OFFICIAL ADDRESS: Controller of the Navy, Room 7115, Ministry of Defence, Whitehall, London S.W.1. *Telephone:* 01-930-7022 ext. 2299
PRIVATE ADDRESS: Cell Cottage, Petersfield, Hants.

UNITED KINGDOM
LAWSON, REAR-ADMIRAL F. C. W., ROYAL NAVY
DECORATIONS: D.S.C. 1942; and bar 1945
PRESENT APPOINTMENT: Flag Officer Medway and Admiral Superintendent HM Dockyard, Chatham September 1969
DATE OF BIRTH: 20 April, 1917
EDUCATION: Eastbourne College and R.N. Engineering College, Keyham
DATES OF PROMOTIONS: 1949 Commander; 1960 Captain; 1969 Rear-Admiral
PREVIOUS APPOINTMENTS OF NOTE: Commodore Superintendent, Singapore 1965-1969; Assistant Director of Dockyards, Ministry of Defence 1964-1965; Chief Staff Officer Technical to C-in-C, Plymouth 1962-1964
PRIVATE ADDRESS: c/o Lloyds Bank, Tavistock Road, Devonport, Devon

U.K.
LEATHES, Captain R. E. de M., ROYAL NAVY
PRESENT APPOINTMENTS: Nutrian 26 June, 1968
EDUCATION: Rugby
DATES OF PROMOTIONS Commander 30 June, 1960; Captain 31 December, 1967
PRINCIPAL COMMANDS AT SEA: HMS Alert
OTHER PREVIOUS APPOINTMENTS OF NOTE: SOO to FOFH 1962-1964; N of Eagle 1958-1959; Occan 1957; Hart 1950-1951; SG & N to 6FS (Venus undine) 1953-1955; 5th FRS Coquette 1951-1953;

UNITED KINGDOM
LE BAILLY, REAR-ADMIRAL, L. E. S. H., ROYAL NAVY
DECORATIONS: O.B.E. 1952; C.B. 1969
PRESENT APPOINTMENT: Naval Attaché and Commander British Navy Staff, Washington
DATE OF BIRTH; 18th July, 1915
EDUCATION: RNC Dartmouth; RNEC Keyham; F.I.Mech. E., M.I. Mar E., M.Inst. Pet.
DATES OF PROMOTIONS: Captain 30 December, 1957; Rear-Admiral 9 January, 1967
PREVIOUS APPOINTMENTS OF NOTE: Assistant Engineer in Chief (Personnel) 1958-1961 Naval Assistant to Controller of Navy 1961-1963; I.D.C. 1963; Deputy Director of Marine Engineering 1964-1967
OFFICIAL ADDRESS: Commander British Navy Staff, HMS Saker, BFPO 2 *Telephone:* 202 ext. 1940
PRIVATE ADDRESS: c/o Martin's Bank, 31 Curzon Street, London W.1.

U.S.A.
LE BOURGEOIS, REAR-ADMIRAL (SELECTEE) JULIEN JOHNSON, US NAVY
CURRENT DUTY STATION: Executive Assistant & Senior Aide to the Chief of Naval Operations (April 1968)
DATE OF BIRTH: 1923
EDUCATION: 1944 Naval Academy; 1959 Armed Forces Staff College; 1962 Industrial College of the Armed Forces, Washington
DATE OF COMMISSION: 7th June, 1944
PROMOTED TO: Rear Admiral selected for promotion 6th June, 1968
COMMANDS: 1959-1961 Norris DDE 859; 1965-1967 Halsey DLG 23
HOME ADDRESS: 3210 Hampden Lane, Bethesda, Maryland 20014

U.K.
LEE, COMMANDER J. M., ROYAL NAVY
PRESENT APPOINTMENT: HMS Eskimo in command
DATE OF BIRTH: 18 January 1930
EDUCATION: Royal Naval College, Dartmouth, 1943-1947; Royal Naval Staff College, Greenwich 1963
DATES OF PROMOTIONS: Sub-Lieutenant 1949, Lieutenant 1951; Lieutenant-Commander November 1959; Commander December 1964
PRINCIPAL COMMANDS AT SEA: SDML 3514 (Hong Kong Flotilla) 1951-1953; HMS Chelsham (232nd MSS) 1956; HMS Upton (100th MSS) 1957; HMS Pellew (2nd F.S.) 1965-1965; HMS Eskimo (3rd Div.) 1969
OTHER PREVIOUS APPOINTMENTS OF NOTE: SOO to FO2FEF 1965-1966; Commanding Officer HMS St. George (SD Officer's School) 1967-1968
OFFICIAL ADDRESS: HMS Eskimo, BFPO Ships
PRIVATE ADDRESS: Cedar House, Bacon Lane, Hayling Island, Hants. **Telephone;** Hayling Island 4444

U.S.A.
LEE, REAR-ADMIRAL (SELECTEE) KENT LISTON, (NAVAL AVIATOR) US NAVY
CURRENT DUTY STATION: Commanding Officer, Enterprise CVAN 65 (August 1967)
DATE OF BIRTH: 1922
EDUCATION: 1949 Columbia University; 1950 Naval School (General Line) Newport; 1954 Naval Postgraduate School, Monterey
DATE OF COMMISSION: 1st August, 1943
PROMOTED TO: Rear Admiral selected for promotion 6th June, 1968
COMMANDS: 1958-1959 Attack Squadron 46; 1962-1963 Carrier Group 6; 1964-1965 Alamo LSD 33
HOME ADDRESS: 77 Sharon Avenue, Piedmont, California 94611

U.S.A.
LEE, VICE-ADMIRAL JOHN MARSHALL, US NAVY
CURRENT DUTY STATION: Vice-Chairman, US Delegation, United Nations Military Staff Committee; additional duty: Commander, Eastern Sea Frontier (March 1968)
DATE OF BIRTH: 1914
EDUCATION: 1935 Naval Academy; 1949 Amphibious Warfare School, Marine Corps. School; 1957 National War College
DATE OF COMMISSION: 6th June, 1935
PROMOTED TO: Rear Admiral 1 July, 1960; Vice Admiral 17th February, 1967
COMMANDS: 1944 Terry DD 513; 1951-1952 Benner DDR 807; 1957-1958 Chilton APA 38; 1958-1959 Northampton CLC 1; 1963-1965 Amphibious Group 1
MAJOR AWARDS: Navy Cross

UNITED KINGDOM
LE FANU, ADMIRAL SIR M., ROYAL NAVY
DECORATIONS:
G.C.B. January 1968; D.S.C. 1941
PRESENT APPOINTMENT: Chief of Naval Staff and First Sea Lord
DATE OF BIRTH: 2 August, 1913
EDUCATION: Bedford School; RNC Dartmouth
DATES OF PROMOTIONS: 1927 Cadet; 1934 Sub Lieutenant; 1935 Lieutenant; 1942 Lieutenant Commander; 1944 Commander; 1949 Captain; 1958 Rear-Admiral; 1961 Vice Admiral; 1965 Admiral
PRINCIPAL COMMANDS AT SEA: 1951-1958 HMS Eagle; 1960-1961 FO2FEF
OTHER PREVIOUS APPOINTMENTS OF NOTE: Commander-in-Chief Middle East 1965-1967; Controller of the Navy 1961-1965; DGW 1958-1960
OFFICIAL ADDRESS: M.O.D. Main Building, Whitehall, London, S.W.1. *Telephone:* 944/7022

U.S.A.
LEMOS, REAR-ADMIRAL WILLIAM EDWARD, (NAVAL AVIATOR) US NAVY
CURRENT DUTY STATION: Director, Policy Planning Staff, Officer of the Secretary of Defense (International Security Affairs)
DATE OF BIRTH: 1917
EDUCATION: 1941 Naval Academy; 1949 Massachusetts Institute of Technology; 1958 National War College
DATE OF COMMISSION: 7th February, 1941
PROMOTED TO: Rear Admiral 1st December, 1965
COMMANDS: 1954-1955 Composite Squadron 9; 1955-1956 Heavy Attack Squadron 9; 1962-1963 Okinawa LPH 3; 1963-1964 Ranger CVA 61
HOME ADDRESS: 6706 Hazel Lane, McLean, Virginia 22101

U.K.
LENNOX, COMMANDER I. B., ROYAL NAVY
PRESENT APPOINTMENT: Experimental Commander, HMS Excellent, December 1968
DATE OF BIRTH: 1 January 1931
EDUCATION: Wellingborough School
PRINCIPAL COMMANDS AT SEA: HMS Sallyport 1956; HMS Llandaff 1967-1968
OTHER PREVIOUS APPOINTMENTS OF NOTE: Staff of Flag Officer Sea Training 1965-1967;
OFFICIAL ADDRESS: HMS Excellent, Whale Island, Portsmouth. *Telephone;* Portsmouth 22351, Ext. 5685
PRIVATE ADDRESS: 13 Down End Road, Drayton, Portsmouth

U.S.A.
LEONARD, REAR-ADMIRAL WILLIAM NICHOLAS (NAVA AVIATOR) US NAVY
CURRENT DUTY STATION: Assistant Deputy Chief of Naval Operations (Logistics) (February 1969)
DATE OF BIRTH: 1916
EDUCATION: 1938 Naval Academy; 1959 National War College
DATE OF COMMISSION: 2nd June, 1938
PROMOTED TO: Rear Admiral 10th August, 1965
COMMANDS: 1948-1950 Fighter Squadron 171; 1950-1951 Carrier Air Group 17; 1954-1955 Air Development Squadron 5; 1959-1960 Salamonie (AO 26); 1961-1962 Ranger CVA 61; 1963-1965 Carrier Division 14
MAJOR AWARDS: Navy Cross with 1 Gold Star in lieu of 2nd award
HOME ADDRESS: 5121 North 33rd Street, Arlington, Virginia 22207

UNITED KINGDOM
LESLIE, REAR-ADMIRAL G. C., ROYAL NAVY
DECORATIONS: O.B.E. 1944
PRESENT APPOINTMENT: Saclant Repeur (Saclants Representative in Europe) 16 July, 1968
DATE OF BIRTH: 27 October, 1920
EDUCATION: Uppingham School
DATES OF PROMOTIONS: Commander 30 June, 1952; Captain 30 June, 1958; Rear-Admiral 7 January, 1968
PRINCIPAL COMMANDS AT SEA: 1950-1951 HMS Wrangler; 1951 HMS Wilton; 1954-1955 HMS Surprise; 1961-1962 HMS Duncan and as Captain Fishery Protection Squadron; 1965-1967 HMS Devonshire
OTHER PREVIOUS APPOINTMENTS OF NOTE: Commodore HMS Drake 1964-1965; Flag Officer Admiralty Interview Board 1968
OFFICIAL ADDRESS: NATO HQ BFPO 49, Brussels 41 00 40
PRIVATE ADDRESS: 28 Dereymaekenlaan Tewinen Brussels

UNITED KINGDOM
LEWIN, REAR-ADMIRAL T. T., ROYAL NAVY
DECORATIONS: M.V.O. 1958; D.S.C. 1942
PRESENT APPOINTMENT: Assistant Chief of the Naval Staff Policy January 1968; Appointed Flag Officer, Second-in-Command, Far East Fleet August 1969
DATE OF BIRTH: 19 November, 1920
EDUCATION: Judd School, Tonbridge
DATES OF PROMOTIONS: Commander 31 December, 1952; Captain 30 June, 1958; Rear-Admiral 7 January, 1968
PRINCIPAL COMMANDS AT SEA: 1955-1956 HMS Corunna; 1961-1963 Captain (F) Dartmouth Training Squadron and in Command HMS Urchin and HMS Tenby; 1966-1967 HMS Hermes
OTHER PREVIOUS APPOINTMENTS OF NOTE: Director, Naval Tactics and Weapons Policy Division in Ministry of Defence 1964-1965
OFFICIAL ADDRESS: Flag Officer Second-in-Command, Far East Fleet, BFPO 164
PRIVATE ADDRESS: Pitfields, Blackham, Tunbridge Wells, Kent.

UNITED KINGDOM
LEWIS, VICE-ADMIRAL A. M., ROYAL NAVY
DECORATIONS: C.B. 1967
PRESENT APPOINTMENT: Flag Officer Flotillas Western Fleet 1 July, 1968
DATE OF BIRTH: 24 January, 1918
EDUCATION: Haileybury
DATES OF PROMOTIONS: Rear-Admiral July 1965; Vice Admiral 20 July, 1968
PRINCIPAL COMMANDS AT SEA: HMS Girdlenen; 1964-1965 HMS Kent
OTHER PREVIOUS APPOINTMENTS OF NOTE: Director of Plans 1961-1963; Director General Weapons 1965-1968
OFFICIAL ADDRESS: Flag Officer Flotillas, Western Fleet, BFPO Ships, London
PRIVATE ADDRESS: Colemans Farm, Finchingfield, Essex.

U.S.A.
LIVINGSTON, REAR-ADMIRAL (SELCTEE) WILLIAM HAROLD (NAVAL AVIATOR) US NAVY
CURRENT DUTY STATION:
Deputy Commander (Weapons & Training) Field Command, Defense Atomic Support Agency (August 1969)
DATE OF BIRTH: 1922
EDUCATION: 1949 Naval Postgraduate School; 1958 Naval War College
DATE OF COMMISSION: 21st January, 1943
PROMOTED TO: Rear Admiral selected for promotion on 6th June, 1969
COMMANDS: 1955-1957 Fighter Sqadron 41; 1958-1960 Director, Naval Test Pilot School, Patuxent River, Maryland; 1960-1962 Air Development Squadron 4 and Fleet Air Detachment, Point Mugu, California; 1966-1967 Aucilla AO 56
OFFICIAL ADDRESS: FPO San Francisco, California 96601
HOME ADDRESS: Vero Beach, Florida

UNITED KINGDOM
LOASBY, CAPTAIN P. G., ROYAL NAVY
DECORATIONS: D.S.C. 1941
PRESENT APPOINTMENT: Commanding Officer HMS London June 1969
DATE OF BIRTH: 25 July, 1919
EDUCATION: RNC Dartmouth
DATES OF PROMOTIONS: Commander December 1953; Captain December 1961
PRINCIPAL COMMANDS AT SEA: 1940-1941 Senior Officer 2nd ML, and 12th MGB Flotillas; 1957-1958 Barfleur; 1963-1964 Cassandra; 1965 Falmouth and as Captain (D) 30th Escort Squadron
OTHER PREVIOUS APPOINTMENTS OF NOTE: IDC 1966; Director (Commandant) R.N. Staff College 1967-1969
OFFICIAL ADDRESS: HMS London, BFPO Ships
PRIVATE ADDRESS: Holly Lodge, Saxmundham, Suffolk

U.S.A.
LONG, REAR-ADMIRAL (SELECTEE) ROBERT LYMAN JOHN, US NAVY
CURRENT DUTY STATION: Commander, Service Group 3 (September, 1968)
DATE OF BIRTH: 29th May, 1920
EDUCATION: 1943 Naval Academy; 1954 Naval War College
DATE OF COMMISSION: 9th June, 1943
PROMOTED TO: Rear Admiral selected for promotion 6th June, 1968
COMMANDS: 1954-1956 Sea Leopard SS 483; Patrick Henry SSBN 599, Gold Crew 1960-1963; 1963-1965 Casimir Pulaski SSBN 633, Blue Crew

U.S.A.
LONGINO, REAR-ADMIRAL JAMES CHARLES, JNR., (NAVAL AVIATOR) US NAVY
CURRENT DUTY STATION: Director of Intelligence, Deputy Commander in Chief, US Forces, Europe (July 1967)
DATE OF BIRTH: 1918
EDUCATION: 1940 Naval Academy; 1956 Columbia University (Exec. Off./Postrgraduate Student, School of International Affairs); 1963 National War College
DATE OF COMMISSION: 6th June, 1940
PROMOTED TO: Rear Admiral 1st November, 1967
COMMANDS: Fighting Squadron 40 1944-1945; 1951-1953 Fighter Squadron 61; 1963-1964 Canisteo AO 99; 1964-1965 Lake Champlain CVS 39
HOME ADDRESS: 1813 24th Street, N.W. Washington, DC 20008

U.S.A.
LOWRANCE, VICE-ADMIRAL VERNON LONG, US NAVY
CURRENT DUTY STATION: Deputy Director, Defence Intelligence Agency (November 1966)
DATE OF BIRTH: 1909
EDUCATION: 1930 Naval Academy; 1938 Naval Academy, Naval Postgraduate School; 1954 National War College
DATE OF COMMISSION: 5th June, 1930
PROMOTED TO: Rear Admiral 1st August, 1957; Vice Admiral 31st August, 1964
COMMANDS: 1940-1942 R-16 SS 93; 1942-1943 Kingfish SS 234; 1943-1945 Seadog SS 401; 1945 Submarine Squadron 4; 1945 Submarine Division 121; 1945 Submarine Division 91; 1945-1946 Submarine Division 72; 1950-1951 Submarine Squadron 8; 1954-1955 Rockbridge APA 228; 1955-1956 Macon CA 132; 1958-1959 Cruiser Division 3; 1959-1960 Training Command, Pacific Fleet
MAJOR AWARDS: Navy Cross
HOME ADDRESS: Naval Security Station, 3701 Nebraska Avenue, NW, Washington, DC 20016

MEXICO
LOPEZ ARREOLA, CAPITAN de NAVIO P. A., MEXICAN NAVY
PRESENT APPOINTMENT: Commander of the 1st Fleet Air Navy Squadron, September 1968
DATE OF BIRTH: 7 May, 1923
EDUCATION: Primaria Elemental, Secundaria; Escuela Naval Militar del Pacifico, Escuela de Aviación Naval, Mexico; Entrenamiento para Aviador Naval Corpus Christy, EUA & Pensacola, Fla.; Curso de Helicopteristas, Escuela de Aviación Naval, Mexico
DATES OF PROMOTIONS: Guardiamarina 1 September, 1943; Teniente de Corbeta October, 1944; Teniente de Navío January 1948; Capitán de Corbeta November 1956; Capitan de Fragata November 1961; Capitan de Navío November 1967
PREVIOUS APPOINTMENTS OF NOTE: Comandante de Avión, Isla Marganta Comandante del Avión del C. Secretario de Marina Jefe, Sección del Estado Mayor Naval Comandante de diferentes Escuadrones de Helicópteros
OFFICIAL ADDRESS: Primer Escuadrón Seronaval, Las Bajadas, Ver., Mexico. *Telephone:* 2-42-20
PRIVATE ADDRESS: Casa Núm 11-C, Col de la Armada, H. Veracruz, Ver., Mexico

UNITED KINGDOM
LUCEY, COMMODORE M. N., ROYAL NAVY
DECORATIONS: D.S.C. 1944
PRESENT APPOINTMENT: Senior Naval Officer, West Indies November 1968
DATE OF BIRTH: 21 January, 1920
EDUCATION: Gresham's School
DATES OF PROMOTIONS: Commander 30 June, 1953; Captain 30 June, 1961
PRINCIPAL COMMANDS AT SEA: 1964-1966 HMS Puma
OTHER PREVIOUS APPOINTMENTS OF NOTE: Director, Naval Officer Appointments (Seamen), 1966-1968
OFFICIAL ADDRESS: S.N.O.W.I., BFPO Ships
PRIVATE ADDRESS: Saint Cross, Weydown Road, Haslemere, Surrey

U.S.A.
LYNCH, REAR-ADMIRAL JOHN JOSEPH (NAVAL AVIATOR) US NAVY
CURRENT DUTY STATION: Chief of Staff, US Strike Command (December 1968)
DATE OF BIRTH: 1911
EDUCATION: 1947 Naval School, General Line School, Newport; 1955 Naval War College
DATE OF COMMISSION: 1st September, 1936
PROMOTED TO: Rear Admiral 1st October, 1964
COMMANDS: 1942-1944 Composite Squadron 33; 1947-1948 Attack Carrier Air Group 13; 1955-1957 Naval Auxiliary Air Station, Whiting Field, Milton, Florida; 1958-1959 Manatee AO 58; 1960-1961 Coral Sea CVA 43; 1964-965 Carrier Division 18; 1965-1967 Naval Air Basic Training
MAJOR AWARDS: Navy Cross

U.S.A.
LYNESS, REAR-ADMIRAL (SELECTEE) DOUGLAS HENRY, (SUPPLY CORPS.) US NAVY
CURRENT DUTY STATION: Commanding Officer, Naval Ships Store Office, Brooklyn; additional duty: Supply Office, 3rd Naval District; Deputy Commander for Resale Programs, Naval Supply Systems Command (September, 1968)
DATE OF BIRTH: 6th July, 1919
EDUCATION: 1949 Stanford University; 1964 Industrial College of the Armed Forces
DATE OF COMMISSION: 26th May, 1941
PROMOTED TO: Rear Admiral selected for promotion 1st March, 1969
COMMANDS: Naval Supply Depot, Seattle, Wash., Supply Officer, 13th Naval District 1964-1967; Fleet Material Support Office, Mechanicsburg, Pennsylvania 1967-1968

SWEDEN
LYTH, COLONEL K. E., ROYAL SWEDISH NAVY
DECORATIONS: His Majesty King Gustaf VI Adolf Medal 1967; Knight Royal Swedish Order of Sword 1962; Knight Royal Swedish Order of Vasa 1967; Knight Royal Norwegian Order of Olof 1949; Knight Commander of Royal Thai Crown Order 1965; Knight Liberian Order of African Deliberation 1962;
PRESENT APPOINTMENT: Commander of Gotland Coast- Artillery Defence (Chef Gotlands kustartilleriförsvar)
DATE OF BIRTH: 21 December, 1920
EDUCATION: Royal Swedish Naval College 1941-1943; Royal Swedish Naval Academy 1949-1952; US Marine Corps. Schools; Royal Swedish War Academy 1964
DATES OF PROMOTION: Officer 1943; Captain 1952; Major 1961; Lieutenant Colonel 1963; Colonel 1966
PREVIOUS APPOINTMENT OF NOTE: Operational Section of Defence staff 1962-1966
OFFICIAL ADDRESS 620 35 Farösund. *Telephone:* 21400
PRIVATE ADDRESS: Klintv. 6, 620 35 Farösund. *Telephone:* 21522

U.S.A.
McDEVITT, REAR-ADMIRAL JOSEPH BRYAN (JUDGE ADVOCATE GENERAL'S CORPS.) US NAVY
CURRENT DUTY STATION: Judge Advocate General, Department of the Navy (April 1968)
DATE OF BIRTH: 1918
EDUCATION: 1959 Naval War College
DATE OF COMMISSION: 31st March 1943
PROMOTED TO: Rear Admiral 1st April 1968
HOME ADDRESS: 732 Lawton Street, McLean, Virginia 22101

U.S.A.
McDONALD, REAR-ADMIRAL LUCIEN BERRY
CURRENT DUTY STATION: Deputy Chief of Staff for Logistics and Management; Commander-in-Chief Atlantic Fleet (November 1968)
DATE OF BIRTH: 1916
EDUCATION: 1938 Naval Academy; George Washington University Post-graduate Comptrollership Program 1956; Industrial College of the Armed Forces 1960
DATE OF COMMISSION: 2 June 1938
PROMOTED TO: Rear Admiral 10th August, 1965
COMMANDS: 1945 Lamprey SS 372; 1945 Octavia AF 46; 1947-1949 Cochino SS 345; 1954-1955 Submarine Division 42; Noble APA 218 1960-1961; Submarine Squadron 1/ Submarine Flotilla 5 1961-1962; Submarine Flotilla 1 1965-1966; 1966-1968 Military Sea Transporation Service, Far East

UNITED KINGDOM
McGEOCH, VICE-ADMIRAL SIR I. L. M., ROYAL NAVY
DECORATIONS: K.C.B. 1969; C.B. 1965; D.S.O. 1943; D.S.C. 1943
PRESENT APPOINTMENT: Flag Officer, Scotland and Northern Ireland 1968
DATE OF BIRTH: 26 March, 1914
EDUCATION: Nautical College, Pangbourne
DATES OF PROMOTIONS: 1947 Commander; 1955 Captain; 1964 Rear-Admiral; 1967 Vice Admiral
PRINCIPAL COMMANDS AT SEA: 1941 Submarines H43 and H34; 1942-1943 Submarine HMS Splendid; 1946-1947 Hunt Clan destroyer, HMS Fernie; 1956-1957 HMS Adamant; 1962-1964 HMS Lion
OTHER PREVIOUS APPOINTMENTS OF NOTE: Officer Commanding 4th Submarine Squadron, Australia 1949-1951; Officer Commanding 3rd Submarine Squadron 1956-1957; Admiral President, RNC Greenwich 1964-1965
OFFICIAL ADDRESS: Office of Fosni, Rosyth, Dunfermlin, Fife *Telephone:* 23436 ext. 25

UNITED KINGDOM
McINTOSH, REAR-ADMIRAL I. S., ROYAL NAVY
DECORATIONS: D.S.O. 1944; M.B.E. 1941; D.S.C. 1942
PRESENT APPOINTMENT: Director General Weapons (Naval) 6 May, 1968
DATE OF BIRTH: 11 October, 1919
EDUCATION: Geelong Grammar School, Australia
DATES OF PROMOTIONS: 1952 Commander; 1959 Captain; 1968 Rear-Admiral
PRINCIPAL COMMANDS AT SEA: 1942 HMS H44; 1943-1944 HMS Sceptre; 1946-1948 HMS Alberney; 1951-1952; HMS Aeneas; 1966-1968 HMS Victorious
OTHER PREVIOUS APPOINTMENTS OF NOTE: 2nd S/M Squadron 1961-1963
OFFICIAL ADDRESS: Ministry of Defence (Naval) Bath *Telephone:* 6933 ext. 4507
PRIVATE ADDRESS: Rowley Cottage, Farleigh, Hungerford, Wiltshire

EIRE
McKENNA, CAPTAIN T., IRISH NAVY
DECORATIONS: Commander, Argentine Order of Naval Merit 1957; Commandatore, Italian Order of Merit 1959; Commander, Spanish Order of Naval Merit 1960; Commander, German Order of Merit 1965; Commandeur French Order Merité Maritime 1967
PRESENT APPOINTMENT: Commanding Officer and Director of Irish Naval Service 1 December, 1956
DATE OF BIRTH: 14 May, 1913
EDUCATION: Master Mariner (F.G.)
DATES OF PROMOTIONS: Commissioned Ensign 17 August, 1940; Sub Lieutenant 2 September 1941; Lieutenant 16 November, 1943; Lieutenant Commander 6 June, 1946; Commander 15 September, 1947; Captain 24 April, 1957
COMMANDS AT SEA: OC MTB; OC Training Ship (Sail)
PREVIOUS APPOINTMENTS OF NOTE: Commanding Officer Naval Base and Superintendent of Naval Dockyard
OFFICIAL ADDRESS: Naval Headquarters, Department of Defence, Parkgate, Dublin, 8 *Telephone:* 771881
PRIVATE ADDRESS: 'Cliff House', Howth, Co. Dublin.

U.S.A.
McKINNEY, REAR-ADMIRAL WILLIAM RUSSELL US NAVY
CURRENT DUTY STATION: Commander, Amphibious Group 2 (August 1968)
DATE OF BIRTH: 1919
EDUCATION: 1940 Naval Academy; 1948 Naval Academy, Naval Post-graduate School, and Cornell University; 1953
DATE OF COMMISSION: 6th June, 1940
PROMOTED TO: Rear Admiral 1st July, 1967
COMMANDS: 1948-1951 Underwater Demolition Team 3; Underwater Demolition Teams, Pacific Fleet; 1953-1955 Joseph P. Kennedy, Jnr., DD 850; 1960-1961 Montrose APA 212; 1964-1965 Naval Weapons Annex, Naval Ammunition Depot, Charleston, S.C.; 1965-1966 Amphibious Squadron 7
MAJOR AWARDS: Navy Cross

U.S.A.
McMANUS, REAR-ADMIRAL (SELECTEE) PHILIP STANLEY US NAVY
CURRENT DUTY STATION: Navy Deputy to the Department of Defense, Manager for Manned Space Flight Support Operations (August 1968)
DATE OF BIRTH: 1919
EDUCATION: 1942 Naval Academy; 1950 Naval Academy, Naval Post-graduate School; 1951 John Hopkins University, School of Engineering; Naval War College 1961
DATE OF COMMISSION: 19th June 1942
PROMOTED TO: Rear Admiral selected for promotion 6th June, 1968
COMMANDS: 1956-1957 William M. Wood DDR 715; 1965-1966 Landing Ship Flotilla 1; 1966-1968 Amphibious Squadron 5

U.S.A.
McMORRIES, REAR-ADMIRAL (SELECTEE) EDWIN ELIOT, (SUPPLY CORPS.) US NAVY
CURRENT DUTY STATION: Director of Procurement, Office of the Assistant Secretary of the Navy (Installations & Logistics); additional duty: Director of Procurement Programs, Office of the Deputy Chief of Naval Material (Procurement and Production) (June 1967)
DATE OF BIRTH: 1921
EDUCATION: 1943 Duke University; 1950 Stanford University; 1967 Naval War College
DATE OF COMMISSION: 31st March, 1942
PROMOTED TO: Rear Admiral selected for promotion in June 1969
OFFICIAL ADDRESS: Washington, DC

U.S.A.
McNITT, REAR-ADMIRAL ROBERT WARING, US NAVY
CURRENT DUTY STATION: Superintendent, Naval Postgraduate School, Monterey; additional duty: Director Naval Management Sustems Center, Naval Postgraduate School (October 1967)
DATE OF BIRTH: 1915
EDUCATION: 1938 Naval Academy; 1945 Naval Academy, Naval Postgraduate School; 1947 Naval Training School, Massachusetts Institute of Technology; 1958 Industrial College of the Armed Forces
DATE OF COMMISSION: 2nd June, 1938
PROMOTED TO: Rear Admiral 1st June, 1965
COMMANDS: 1952-1954 Taylor DDE 468; 1958-1959 Destroyer Division 322; 1959-1961 Atlantic Fleet ASW School, Norfolk, Virginia; 1961-1962 Destroyer Squadron 25; 1967 Cruiser-Destroyer Flotilla 4
HOME ADDRESS: Naval Postgraduate School, Monterey, California 93940

NEW ZEALAND
MACDONALD, SURGEON CAPTAIN J.,
DECORATIONS: Honorary Physician to the Queen (February 1963)
PRESENT APPOINTMENT: Director of Naval Medical Services (June 1963)
DATE OF BIRTH: 24 January, 1915
EDUCATION: Bayble Public School, Nicholson Institute; Aberdeen University
DATES OF PROMOTIONS: Surgeon Lieutenant 1st class 1 March, 1940; 1946 Lieutenant Commander; 1957 Commander; 1963 Captain
OTHER PREVIOUS APPOINTMENTS OF NOTE: Surgeon Lieutenant of HMS Ajax during period of Matapan, Greece 1940-1942; PMO Royalist HMNZS 1958-1960
OFFICIAL ADDRESS: RNZN Hospital Auckland 9 NZ
PRIVATE ADDRESS: Rangimsana Oban Road, Brawn's Bay, Auckland NZ

UNITED KINGDOM
MACDONALD, CAPTAIN R.D.
DECORATIONS: C.B.E. 1967
PRESENT APPOINTMENT: HMS Galatea 1968; Captain (D) 1st DS, September, 1969
DATE OF BIRTH: 25 February 1921
EDUCATION: Fettes College
DATES OF PROMOTIONS: 1957 Commander; 1965 Captain
PRINCIPAL COMMANDS AT SEA: 1954-1956 HMS Leeds Castle; 1958-1959 S. O. 104th Minesweeping Squadron; 1961-1964 HMS Falmouth; Captain (D) Londonderry Squadron 1968-1969
OTHER PREVIOUS APPOINTMENTS OF NOTE: Commander Naval Forces, Borneo 1965-1966
OFFICIAL ADDRESS: HMS Galatea, BFPO Ships
PRIVATE ADDRESS: Spinner Ash, Tilmore, Petersfield, Hants.

U.S.A.
MACK, VICE-ADMIRAL, WILLIAM PADEN, US NAVY
CURRENT DUTY STATION: Deputy Assistant Secretary of Defense (Manpower and Reserve Affairs) (1968)
DATE OF BIRTH: 1915
EDUCATION: 1937 Naval Academy; 1944 West Coast Sound School, San Diego; 1956 National War College; 1964 George Washington University
DATE OF COMMISSION: 3rd June, 1937
PROMOTED TO: Rear Admiral, 1st July, 1964; Vice Admiral 28th January, 1969
COMMANDS: Woodworth DD 460 1944-1946; 1949-1950 Richard B. Anderson DD 786; 1956-1957 Destroyer Division 22;1961-1962 Destroyer Squadron 28; Destroyer Division 281; 1963-1966 Chief of Information, Department of the Navy; 1966-1967 Amphibious Group 2; 1967-1968 Chief of Legislative Affairs, Department of the Navy
HOME ADDRESS: 1109 Gaillard Street, Alexandria, Virginia 22304

U.K.
MACKAY, CAPTAIN I. S. S., ROYAL NAVY
PRESENT APPOINTMENT: Captain (D) Dartmouth Training Squadron, HMS Eastbourne December 1967
DATE OF BIRTH: 11 September, 1924
EDUCATION: Nautical College, Pangbourne
DATES OF PROMOTIONS: Commander June 1959 Captain June 1965
PRINCIPAL COMMANDS AT SEA: Senior Officer, 108th Minesweeping Squadron 1959-1960
OTHER PREVIOUS APPOINTMENTS OF NOTE: Naval Staff 1960-1963; Executive Officer, HMS Ark Royal 1963-1965; Weapons Directorate (Radio) 1965-1967
OFFICIAL ADDRESS: Staff of Commander Far East Fleet, S'pene BFPO 164
PRIVATE ADDRESS: Crofters, Itchenor Gate, Chichester, Sussex

U.S.A.
MACPHERSON, REAR-ADMIRAL ROBERT ANTHONY (NAVAL AVIATOR) US NAVY
CURRENT DUTY STATION: Commandant, 8th Naval District (September, 1968)
DATE OF BIRTH: 1910
EDUCATION: 1933 Naval Academy; 1949 Armed Forces Staff College; 1953 Industrial College of the Armed Forces
DATE OF COMMISSION: 1st June, 1933
PROMOTED TO: Rear Admiral 1st July, 1961
COMMANDS: 1942-1943 Observation Squadron 4; 1956-1957 Cape Esperance T CVU 88; 1957-1959 Hancock CVA 19; 1962-1964 US Taiwan Patrol Force/Fleet Air Wing 1; 1964-1965 Anti-Submarine Warfare Group 5; 1965-1968 Chief of Naval Air Advanced Training, NAS, Corpus Christi, Texas; additional duty: Commandant 8th Naval District

U.S.A.
MAHIN, REAR-ADMIRAL (SELECTEE) HARRY PAUL, (MEDICAL COPRS.) US NAVY
CURRENT DUTY STATION: Commanding Officer, Naval Hospital, Oakland, California (1969)
DATE OF BIRTH: 1916
EDUCATION: 1938 University of Iowa; 1942 University of Louisville
DATE OF COMMISSION: 10th March, 1942
PROMOTED TO: Rear Admiral selected for promotion in June 1969
OFFICIAL ADDRESS: Naval Hospital, Oakland, California

U.S.A.
McCAIN, ADMIRAL JOHN SIDNEY, JNR., US NAVY
CURRENT DUTY STATION: Commander-in-Chief, Pacific (July 1968)
DATE OF BIRTH: 17th January, 1911
EDUCATION: 1931 Naval Academy
DATE OF COMMISSION: 4th June, 1931
PROMOTED TO: Rear Admiral 1st April, 1959; Vice Admiral 1st September, 1963; Admiral 1st May, 1967
COMMANDS: 1941-1942 O-8 SS 69; 1942-1943 Gunnel SS 253; 1943-1944 Dentuda SS 335; 1944 Gunnel SS 253; 1944-1945 Dentuda SS 335; Submarine Division 71 1949 1949-1950 Submarine Division 51; 1953-1954 Submarine Squadron 6; 1954-1955 Monrovia (APA 31); 1957-1958 Albany CA 123; 1960 Command Information Bureau, NATO, Supreme Allied Commander Atlantic; 1960-1961 Amphibious Group 2; 1961-1962 Amphibious Training Command Atlantic 1962-1963 Chief, Office of Information, Department of the Navy; 1963-1965 Amphibious Force Atlantic Fleet; 1965-1967 Vice Chairman, US Delegation, United Nations Military Staff Committee, New York/Commander, Eastern Sea Frontier/Commander, Atlantic Reserve Fleet; 1967-1968 Commander-in-Chief, US Naval Forces, Eurpoe

U.S.A.
McCLELLAN, REAR-ADMIRAL THOMAS RUFUS (NAVAL AVIATOR) US NAVY
CURRENT DUTY STATION: Deputy Commander, Plans and Programs, and Comptroller, Naval Air Systems Command (March 1969)
DATE OF BIRTH: 1922
EDUCATION: 1942 Naval Academy; 1946 Naval Academy, Naval Postgraduate School; 1947 California Institue of Technology
DATE OF COMMISSION: 19th June, 1942
PROMOTED TO: Rear Admiral 1st August, 1968
COMMANDS: 1959-1961 Patrol Squadron 49; 1961-1962 Patrol Squadron 30; 1964-1965 Rockbridge APA 228; 1965-1966 Fleet Air Wing 3; 1967-1969 Carrier Division 14
HOME ADDRESS: 1303 24th Street, South Arlington, Virginia 22202

U.S.A.
McCLELLAND, REAR-ADMIRAL JOSEPH JAMES, US NAVY
CURRENT DUTY STATION: Chief, Office of Boating Safety (March 1969)
DATE OF BIRTH: 1916
EDUCATION: 1935 University of Washington; 1940 Coast Guard Academy; 1950 Stanford University; 1964 National war College; 1965 George Washington University
FIRST COMMISSIONED: 20th May, 1940
PROMOTED TO: Rear Admiral 31st January, 1969
COMMANDS: 1945-1946 Vance; 1946 Potomac and Mistletoe; 1946-1947 Jackson; 1950-1951 Ivy; 1961-1963 Bibb; 1967-1968 Operations Division, 3rd Coast Guard District

U.S.A.
McCLENDON, REAR-ADMIRAL WILLIAM ROGER (NAVAL AVIATOR) US NAVY
CURRENT DUTY STATION:
Commander Carrier Division 9, (August 1969)
DATE OF BIRTH: 1920
EDUCATION: 1950 US Naval School, General Line School, Newport; 1959 Naval War College; 1963 Naval Postgraduate School, Monterey
DATE OF COMMISION: 17th March, 1942
PROMOTED TO: Rear Admiral 5th July 1967
COMMANDS: Fighter Squadron 173 1954-1955; 1963-1964 Firedrake AE 14; 1964-1965 Bon Homme Richard CVA 31; additional duty: Task Group 77.4
OFFICIAL ADDRESS: FPO San Francisco, California
HOME ADDRESS: 1101 Clover Drive, McLean, Virginia 22101

U.S.A.

McCUDDIN, REAR-ADMIRAL LEO BOB (NAVAL AVIATOR) US NAVY
CURRENT DUTY STATION: Commandant, 12th Naval District; additional duty: Commander Naval Base, San Francisco (January 1968)
DATE OF BIRTH: 1917
EDUCATION: 1948 Georgetown University Law School; 1951 Air University, Air Command & Staff School; 1958 Naval War College
DATE OF COMMISSION: 3rd April, 1942
PROMOTED TO: Rear Admiral 1st August, 1968
COMMANDS: 1954-1956 Fighter Squadron 13; 1958-1960 Carrier Air Group 3; 1963-1965 Mattaponi AO 41; 1965-1966 Ranger CVA 61
MAJOR AWARDS: Navy Cross
HOME ADDRESS: 9124 Glenbrook Road, Fairfax, Virginia 22030

U.S.A.

McCUBBIN, REAR-ADMIRAL JOHN DELMOND (NAVAL AVIATOR) US NAVY
CURRENT DUTY STATION: Chief, Office of Reserve, Coast Guard Headquarters (March 1968)
DATE OF BIRTH: 1914
EDUCATION: 1935 North Texas Agriculture College; 1939 Coast Guard Academy; 1942 Naval Air Station, Pensacola
FIRST COMMISSIONED: 29th May, 1939
PROMOTED TO: Rear Admiral 13th December, 1967
COMMANDS: 1951-1953 Coast Guard Air Detachment, Kodiak; 1960-1963 Coast Guard Air Detachment, Hawaii

UNITED KINGDOM
MALIM, REAR-ADMIRAL N. H., ROYAL NAVY
DECORATIONS: M.V.O. 1960
PRESENT APPOINTMENT: Captain, Royal Naval Engineering College, Manadon Plymouth March 1967 Chief Staff Officer (Technical) to the Commander-in-Chief, Western August 1969
DATE OF BIRTH: 5 April, 1919
EDUCATION: Weymouth College
DATES OF PROMOTIONS: Commander 31 December, 1957; Captain 30 June, 1960; Rear-Admiral 7 July, 1969
PREVIOUS APPOINTMENTS OF NOTE: Engineer Officer HM Yacht Britannia 1958-1960; Assistant and Deputy Director, Marine Engineering 1962-1965; Imperial Defence College 1966
OFFICIAL ADDRESS: RNEC Manadon, Plymouth *Telephone:* 53740 ext. Manadon 203
PRIVATE ADDRESS: 68 Firgrove Hill, Farnham, Surrey

U.K.
MANN, COMMANDER R. H., ROYAL NAVY
PRESENT APPOINTMENT: HMS Resolution (Port) in command 24 April, 1969
DATE OF BIRTH: 17 July, 1969
PRINCIPAL COMMANDS AT SEA: HMS Astute 1959; HMS Excalibur 1962; HMS Porpoise 1963-1964; HMS Odin 1964-1965
OFFICIAL ADDRESS: HMS Resolution, Clyde Submarine Base, Faslane, Helensburgh, Dumbartonshire. *Telephone;* Helensburgh 4321
PRIVATE ADDRESS: Woodland Cottage, Stubbington Lane, Stubbington, Hampshire

U.S.A.

MAROCCHI, REAR-ADMIRAL (SELECTEE) JOHN LOUIS (SPECIAL DUTY—INTELLIGENCE) US NAVY
CURRENT DUTY STATION: Intelligence Officer, Commander-in-Chief, Pacific Fleet (August 1968)
DATE OF BIRTH: 1920
EDUCATION: 1942 Naval Academy; 1946 Naval Intelligence School; 1958 Naval War College; 1957 Naval Postgraduate School
DATE OF COMMISSION: 19th December, 1941
PROMOTED TO: Rear Admiral selected for promotion on 6th June, 1969
OFFICIAL ADDRESS: FPO San Francisco, California 96601
HOME ADDRESS: Clarksville, Tennessee

U.S.A.
MARSCHALL, REAR-ADMIRAL (SELECTEE), ALBERT RHOADES, (CIVIL ENGINEERING CORPS.) US NAVY
CURRENT DUTY STATION: Commanding Officer, Southeast Division, Naval Facilities Engineering Command; District Civil Engineer and Officer-in-Charge of Construction 6th Naval District (September, 1967)
DATE OF BIRTH: 1921
EDUCATION: 1944 Naval Academy; 1948 Rensselaer Polytechnic Institute; Armed Forces Staff College
DATE OF COMMISSION: 7th June, 1944
PROMOTED TO: Rear Admiral selected for promotion in June 1969
COMMANDS: 1966-1967 13th Naval Construction Regiment and Deputy Commander, 3rd Naval Construction Brigade
OFFICIAL ADDRESS: Charleston, South Carolina 29408

U.S.A.
MARTIN, REAR-ADMIRAL FOWLER WARD (SUPPLY CORPS.) US NAVY
CURRENT DUTY STATION: Commander, Defense Fuel Supply Center, Alexandria, Virginia (November, 1966)
DATE OF BIRTH: 1916
EDUCATION: 1950 Stanford University, Graduate School of Business
DATE OF COMMISSION: 15th August, 1938
PROMOTED TO: Rear Admiral 1st April, 1967
COMMANDS: 1954 Naval Ordnance Supply Office, Mechanisburg, Pa: Acting CO 1954; 1961-1963 Yards and Docks Supply Office, Port Hueneme, California
HOME ADDRESS: 406 Skyhill Road, Alexandria, Virginia 22314

UNITED KINGDOM
MARTIN, REAR-ADMIRAL J. E., ROYAL NAVY
DECORATIONS: C.B. 1969; D.S.C. 1943
PRESENT APPOINTMENT: Director General, Personal Services and Training (Navy) 1969
DATE OF BIRTH: 10 May, 1918
EDUCATION: RNC Dartmouth
DATES OF PROMOTIONS: 1951 Commander; 1957 Captain; 1966 Rear-Admiral
PREVIOUS APPOINTMENTS OF NOTE: Deputy Director, Naval Manpower Planning and Complementing at the Admiralty 1958-1960; Senior Naval Officer, West Indies and Commander British Forces, Caribbean 1963-1966; Flag Officer, Middle East 1966-1968; Director General Navy Personal Services 1968-1969
OFFICIAL ADDRESS: Ministry of Defence (Navy), Old Admiralty Building, Whitehall, London S.W.1. *Telephone:* 01-930-9000 ext. 1643
PRIVATE ADDRESS: Carr House, Soberton, Southampton, Hants.

U.S.A.
MARTIN, VICE-ADMIRAL WILLIAM INMAN, (NAVAL AVIATOR) US NAVY
CURRENT DUTY STATION: Deputy and Chief of Staff, Commander-in-Chief Atlantic Fleet, and Chief of Staff, Commander-in-Chief Atlantic (1968)
DATE OF BIRTH: 1910
EDUCATION: 1934 Naval Academy; 1951 Naval War College
DATE OF COMMISSION: 31st May, 1934
PROMOTED TO: Rear Admiral 1st July, 1959; Vice Admiral 10th April, 1967
COMMANDS: 1943 Bombing Squadron 20; 1943-1944 Torpedo Squadron 10 (Enterprise CV 6 CV 6); 1944-1945 Night Carrier Air Group 90 (Enterprise CV 6); 1953-1955 Fleet All Weather Training Unit, Pacific; 1955-1956 Saipan CVLE 48; 1953-1955 Fleet All Weather Training Unit, Pacific; 1955-1956 Saipan CVL 48; 1958-1959 Airborne Early Warning Wing, Atlantic/Fleet Air, Argentia; Carrier Division 19 1959-1960; Chief of Naval Air Reserve Training 1961-1963; 1963-1964 Carrier Division 2; 1967-1968 6th Fleet, and Naval Striking and Support Forces, Southern Europe

UNITED KINGDOM
MASON, VICE-ADMIRAL D. H., ROYAL NAVY
DECORATIONS: C.B. 1 January, 1967; A.D.C. 1965
PRESENT APPOINTMENT: Commandant, Joint Services Staff College March 1968
DATE OF BIRTH: 7 February, 1916
EDUCATION: RNC, Dartmouth
DATES OF PROMOTIONS: Commander 1 January, 1951; Captain 30 June, 1956; Rear-Admiral 7 July, 1965; Vice Admiral 1 October, 1968
PRINCIPAL COMMANDS AT SEA: Coastal Forces. Frigates and Destroyers. Ending up in Command of HMS Oakley during the war; Commanded Woodbridge Haven, Mermaid, Urania, Undaunted, the last being as Leader during the time of resuscitation of the Londonderry Squadron.
OTHER PREVIOUS APPOINTMENTS OF NOTE: NATO Allied Commander in Chief Channel 1956-1958; IDC 1958; Senior Naval Officer Northern Ireland and Director of Joint A/S School, Londonderry 1961-1963; Director of RN Tactical School 1963-1965; Chief of Staff to Commander Far East Fleet 1965-1967; J.S.S.C. 1968
OFFICIAL ADDRESS: Commandant's House, J.S.S.C., Latimer, Chesham, Bucks. *Telephone:* Little Chalfont 2761

U.S.A.

MASON, REAR-ADMIRAL HARRY CHARLES, (ENGINEERING DUTY) US NAVY
CURRENT DUTY STATION: Deputy Commander, Engineering Division, Naval Ship Systems Command (August, 1968)
DATE OF BIRTH: 1916
EDUCATION: 1938 Naval Academy; 1949 Naval Academy, Naval Postgraduate School
DATE OF COMMISSION: 2nd June, 1938
PROMOTED TO: Rear Admiral 1st February, 1966
COMMANDS: 1945-1946 Wadsworth DD 516; 1946 Ingersoll DD 652; 1951-1953 Nicholas DDE 449; 1962-1965 Commanding Officer and Director, Navy Electronics Laboratory, San Diego
HOME ADDRESS: 6300 Anneliese Drive, Falls Church, Virginia 22044

U.S.A.

MASTERSON, VICE-ADMIRAL KLEBER SANDLIN, US NAVY
CURRENT DUTY STATION: Director, Weapons Systems Evaluation Group, Office of the Secretary of Defense (August 1966)
DATE OF BIRTH: 1908
EDUCATION: 1930 Naval Academy; 1939 Naval Academy, Postgraduate School; 1953 Naval War College
DATE OF COMMISSION: 5th June, 1930
PROMOTED TO: Rear Admiral 1st December, 1957; Vice Admiral 17th April, 1964
COMMANDS: 1947-1948 Destroyer Division 102; 1953-1954 Lenawee APA 195; 1956-1957 Boston CAG 1; 1960-1961 Cruiser Division 1; 1962-1964 Chief, Bureau of Naval Weapons; 1964-1966 2nd Fleet
HOME ADDRESS: Potomac Annex, 2300 "E" Street, NW, Washington, DC 20037

U.S.A.

MASTERTON, VICE-ADMIRAL PAUL (NAVAL AVIATOR) US NAVY
CURRENT DUTY STATION: Commander, ASW Force, Atlantic Fleet (October 1967)
DATE OF BIRTH: 1911
EDUCATION: 1933 Naval Academy; 1939 Naval Academy, Naval Postgraduate School; 1949 Naval War College
DATE OF COMMISSION: 1st June, 1933
PROMOTED TO: Rear Admiral 1st July, 1961; Vice Admiral 1st November, 1967
COMMANDS: 1943-1945 Bombing Squadron 151; 1946-1948 Air Transport Squadron 3; NAAS, Whiting Field, Milton, Florida 1953-1955; 1958 Airborne Early Warning Wing Atlantic/Fleet Air, Argentia; 1958-1959 Intrepid CVA 11; 1960-1962 Navy Administrative Unit, Joint Strategic Target Planning Staff, Offutt Airforce Base, Nebraske; 1962-1963 Carrier Division 1
HOME ADDRESS: 453 Dillingham Boulevard, Maryland House, Naval Station, Norfolk, Virginia

U.S.A.

MATTHEWS, REAR-ADMIRAL (SELECTEE) HERBERT SPENCER, JNR., (NAVAL AVIATOR) US NAVY
CURRENT DUTY STATION: Commanding Officer, USS Independence (CVA 62) (August 1968)
DATE OF BIRTH: 1921
EDUCATION: 1951 Tulane University; 1951 Naval Postgraduate School; 1958 Naval War College
DATE OF COMMISSION: 18th August, 1943
PROMOTED TO: Rear Admiral selected for promotion on 6th June, 1969
COMMANDS: 1958-1959 Attack Squadron 113; 1962-1963 Carrier Air Group 2; 1967-1968 Hermitage LSD 34
OFFICIAL ADDRESS: FPO New York
HOME ADDRESS: Coronado, California

U.S.A.

MATTER, REAR-ADMIRAL ALFRED RICHARD, (NAVAL AVIATOR) US NAVY
CURRENT DUTY STATION: Commander Caribbean Sea Frontier; additional duty: Commandant, 10th Naval District and Commander, Antilles Defense Command (May 1967)
DATE OF BIRTH: 1910
EDUCATION: 1932 Naval Academy; 1947 Naval War College
DATE OF COMMISSION: 2nd June, 1932
PROMOTED TO: Rear Admiral 1st April, 1960
COMMANDS: 1943-1944 Torpedo Squadron 50; 1953-1954 Composite Squadron 4; 1955-1956 Point Cruz CVE 119; 1957-1958 Saratoga CVA 60; 1959-1960 Carrier Division 20; 1964-1967 Fleet Air Wings, Atlantic Fleet; additional duty: Fleet Air Wing 5
HOME ADDRESS: San Geronimo Naval Station, San Juan, Puerto Rico

U.S.A.

MAURER, REAR-ADMIRAL JOHN HOWARD, US NAVY
CURRENT DUTY STATION: Special Assistant for Strategic Mobility, Office of the Joint Chiefs of Staff (July 1968)
DATE OF BIRTH: 1912
EDUCATION: 1935 Naval Academy; 1955 National War College
DATE OF COMMISSION: 6th June, 1935
PROMOTED TO: Rear Admiral 1st December, 1962
COMMANDS: 1944-1947 Atule SS 403; 1951-1952 Submarine Division II additional duty: Submarine Group, Western Pacific; 1955-1956 Submarine Squadron 7; additional duty: Submarine Group, Western Pacific; 1958-1959 Hassayampa AO 145; 1959-1960 Saint Paul CA 73; 1964-1966 Middle East Force; 1966-1968 Submarine Force, Pacific
MAJOR AWARDS: Navy Cross

CHILE

MAZA DE LA MAZA, CONTRAALMIRANTE INGENIERO L. A. DE LA, CHILEAN NAVY
DECORATIONS: Medalla de la I. Municipalidad de Tomé, after the earthquake of 1939; Estrella Militar, for 15 years service; Estrella Militar, for 20 years service Gran Estrella al Méritor Militar, for 30 years service; Condecoración Presidente de la República
DATE OF BIRTH: 27 January, 1914
EDUCATION: Escuela Naval Arturo Prat
DATES OF PROMOTIONS: Cadete Escuela Naval 28 March 1929; Guardiamrina de 2a Ingeniero 10 January, 1933; Guardimarina de 1ra Ingeniero 7 August, 1937; Teniente 20 Ingeniero 7 August, 1941; Capitán de Corbeta Ingeniero 14 December, 1946; Capitán de Fragata Ingeniero 10 April 1953; Capitán de Navío Ingeniero 25 August, 1960; Contraalmirante Ingeniero 17 February 1969
PRINCIPAL COMMANDS AT SEA: Oficial Ingeniero de dotación de los siguientes buques; Acorazado Almirante Latorre 1933 & 1940-19444; Blindado O'Higgins 1934; Blindado Capitán Prat 1935-1937; Crucero Blanco Encalada 1938-1939; Jefe del Depto. de Ingeniería de los siguientes buques: Fragata Covadonga 1946; Petrolero Maipo 1948; Destructor Videla 1949; AKA Presidente Errázuriz 1950-1951; cl. Prat 1955 Ingeniero de Escuadra 1955-1956
OTHER PREVIOUS APPOINTMENTS OF NOTE: Arsenal Naval de Valparaíso 1954; Depto. de Obras Militares de la Armada 1956; Misión Naval de Chile en Washington 1957-1958; Arsenal Naval de Talcahauano 1959; Jefe de Depto. de Planes de Produccion y Administrador de Astilleros y Maestranzas de la Armada 1960-1965; Sub-Director y Director de la Dirección de Ingeniería de la Armada 1966-1969
OFFICIAL ADDRESS: Prat 620-50 piso-Valparaiso-Chile. *Telephone:* 55649
PRIVATE ADDRESS: Riveros Cruz 1053-Vina del Mar-Chile Casilla 501-Vina Del Mar-Chile

U.S.A.

MEHLE, REAR-ADMIRAL ROGER WILLIAM, (NAVAL AVIATOR) US NAVY
CURRENT DUTY STATION: Commander, Naval Safety Center (July, 1968)
DATE OF BIRTH: 1915
EDUCATION: 1937 Naval Academy
DATE COMMISSIONED: 3rd June, 1937
PROMOTED TO: Rear Admiral 15th October, 1964
COMMANDS: 1944-1945 Fighting Squadron 28; Air Group 28; 1957-1959 Cape Esperance T CVU 88; 1960-1961 Saratoga CVA 60; 1967 Carrier Division 1; 1967 Carrier Division 5; 1967-1968 Fleet Air, Norfolk

ITALY

MICALI, BARATELLI, AMMIRAGLIO DI DIVISIONE F. ITALIAN NAVY
DECORATIONS: Two Silver, five Bronze and one War Cross for Military Valour 1940-1945; Grande Ufficiale dell' Ordine al Merito della Republica Italiana 1968
PRESENT APPOINTMENT: Comandante Prima Divisione Navale 21 September, 1968
DATE OF BIRTH: 18 July, 1913
EDUCATION: Degree in Political Sciences, University of Rome
DATES OF PROMOTIONS: Ammiraglio di Divisione 31 December, 1968; Rear Admiral 1 January, 1964
OFFICIAL ADDRESS: c/o Maristat, Ministero Difesa Marina, Roma, Italy

U.S.A.

MICHAELIS, REAR-ADMIRAL FREDERICK HAYES, (NAVAL AVIATOR) US NAVY
CURRENT DUTY STATION: Assistant Deputy Chief of Naval Operations (Air) (1968)
DATE OF BIRTH: 1917
EDUCATION: 1940 Naval Academy; 1948 Naval Academy, Naval Postgraduate School; 1949 Massachusetts Institute of Technology; 1959 Naval War College
DATE OF COMMISSION: 1940
PROMOTED TO: Rear Admiral 1st December, 1965
COMMANDS: 1944-1945 Fighter Squadron 12 Randolph CV 15; 1945-1946 Bomber Fighter Squadron 5; 1951-1952 Naval Air Detachment, Armed Forces Special Weapons Project, Sandia Base, Albuquerque; 1952-1954 Naval Air Special Weapons Facility, Kirkland Air Force Base, Albuquerque; 1954-1955 Carrier Air Group II; 1959 Tolovana AO 64; 1963-1965 Enterprise CVA N 65; 1967-1968 Carrier Division 9
MAJOR AWARDS: Navy Cross
HOME ADDRESS: 924 South 26th Street, Arlington, Virginia 22202

CANADA

MICHENER, THE RIGHT HON. ROLAND
DECORATIONS: CC; CD Chancellor and Principal Companion of the Order of Canada, 1 July, 1967. Prior for Canada and Knight of Justice of the Most Venerable Order of the Hospital of St. John of Jerusalem, (9 June 1967)
PRESENT APPOINTMENT: Governor General and Commander-in-Chief of Canada (April, 1967)
DATE OF BIRTH: 19 April, 1900
DATES OF PROMOTIONS: Served with R.A.F. 1918; Commissioned Lieutenant, R.C.A. (Res.) 1942
EDUCATION: University of Alberta, B.A., 1920; Rhodes Scholar for Alberta 1919; Oxford University, B.A. 1920; B.C.L. 1923; M.A. 1929; Hon. LL.D.; Ottawa 1948; Queen's 1958; Laval 1960; Univ. of Alberta 1967; St. Mary's University Halifax 1968; University of Toronto 1968; Hon. D.C.L. Bishop's University Lennoxville 1968; Honorary Fellow Hertford College, Oxford 1961; Royal College of Physicians and Surgeons of Canda 1968; Royal Architectural Institute of Canada 1968; Honorary Member the Canadian Medical Association 1968; Honorary Bencher The Law Society of Upper Canada 1968; Honorary Fellow Trinity College, Toronto 1968
CAREER STRUCTURE: Barrister, Middle Temple (England) 1923; Ontario 1924; K.C. 1943; Practising lawyer in Toronto from 1924-1957, with firm Lang, Michener and others. Member of the Ontario Legislature for St. David, Toronto 1945-1948 and Provincial Secretary and Registrar for Ontario 1946-1948; Elected to House of Commons 1953; Re-elected 1957-1958. Elected Speaker of the House of Commons 1957-1958. Sworn of the Privy Council 1962; Member of Council, Commonwealth Parliamentary Association 1959-1961; General Secretary for Canada for the Rhodes Scholarships 1936-1964; Chairman of Manitoba Royal Commission of Local Government and Finance 1962-1964; High Commissioner to India; 1964-1967
OFFICIAL ADDRESS: Government House, Ottawa, Canada

U.S.A.

MIDDLETON, REAR-ADMIRAL RODERICK OSGOOD, US NAVY
CURRENT DUTY STATION: Manager, Apollo Program, National Aeronautics and Space Administration (August 1967)
DATE OF BIRTH: 1919
EDUCATION: 1941 Naval Academy; 1945 Naval Academy, Naval Postgraduate School; 1946 Harvard University
DATE OF COMMISSION: 7th February, 1941
PROMOTED TO: Rear Admiral 1st July, 1967
COMMANDS: 1954-1956 Benham DD 796; 1961-1962 Destroyer Division 142; 1963-1964 Observation Island EAG 154; 1964-1965 Little Rock CLG 4

UNITED KINGDOM
MILES, SURGEON REAR-ADMIRAL S., ROYAL NAVY
DECORATIONS: C.B. 1968; Q.H.P. 1966
PRESENT APPOINTMENT: Medical Officer in Charge RN Hospital Plymouth 1966
DATE OF BIRTH: 1911
EDUCATION: King Edward VII School, Sheffield University M.D. 1955; M.Sc 1934; D.T.M & H. 1949
DATES OF PROMOTIONS: Surgeon Captain 1960; 1966 Surgeon Rear-Admiral
PREVIOUS APPOINTMENTS OF NOTE: Service in China on Yangtse River Gunboat 1936-1938; Atlantic and Pacific Fleets 1939-1945; Research work at Chemical Defence Establishment Porton 1953-1955; Director of Naval Medical Research and Consultant in Physiology 1959-1966
OFFICIAL ADDRESS: RN Hospital, Plymouth, Devon *Telephone:* 53740 ext. 315
PRIVATE ADDRESS: Seven Sevens, Hill Head, Fareham, Hants

ARGENTINA
MILIA, REAR ADMIRAL F. A., ARGENTINE NAVY
DECORATIONS: Naval Merit Spain 1948; Naval Merit Mexico 1957; Military Merit Mexico 1957
PRESENT APPOINTMENT: Argentine Naval Attaché in Washinton, DC since 25 January, 1969
DATE OF BIRTH: 10 December, 1920
EDUCATION: High School Graduate Santa Fé National College; Rio Santiago Naval Academy 1941; Naval Politechnical School 1946; Naval War College (Junior Course) 1952; Naval War College (Senior Course) 1960
DATES OF PROMOTIONS: Ensign December 1943; Lieutenant (J.G.) December, 1945; Lieutenant December 1947; Lieutenant Commander December, 1951; Commander December 1955; Captain December 1961; Rear Admiral December 1967
PRINCIPAL COMMANDS AT SEA: First Destroyer Squadron 1965; ARA La Argentina 1964; ARA Hercules 1959; ARA Bahia Blanca 1954; ARA Comechingones 1945
OTHER PREVIOUS APPOINTMENTS OF NOTE: Head, President's Military Household 1962-1963; President, Argentine Armed Forces' Institute for Scientific and Technological Research 1966-1968; Member, National Council for Space Research 1966-1967; Head, Naval General Staff's Weapons System Department 1961-1962; Chief Weapons Service ,Fleet Staff 1957-1958; Naval and Air Attaché in Mexico 1956-1957; Chief, Weapons Analysis Bureau 1953
PUBLICATIONS: Constitución y Empleo del Poder Militar EGN EMGN., Buenos Aires 1961 (co author); Estrategia y Poder Militar IPN, Buenos Aires 1965
OFFICIAL ADDRESS: 1816 Corcoran Street, NW, Washington, DC 20009
PRIVATE ADDRESS: Temporary; 5070 Macomb Street, NW, Washington DC 20016, USA Permanent: Florida 801, Buenos Aires, Argentina

U.S.A.
MILLER, REAR-ADMIRAL GEORGE HAROLD
CURRENT DUTY STATION: Director, Strategic Offensive and Defensive Systems, Office of the Chief of Naval Operations (February 1967)
DATE OF BIRTH: 1911
EDUCATION: 1933 Naval Academy; 1939 Naval Academy, Naval Postgraduate School; 1947 Naval War College
DATE OF COMMISSION: 1st June, 1933
PROMOTED TO: Rear Admiral 1st July, 1959
COMMANDS: 1943 Brennan DE 13; 1949-1950 Hollister DD 788; 1954-1955 Destroyer Division 322; 1957-1958 Elokomin AO 55; 1958-1959 Cruiser Division 5
MAJOR AWARDS: Navy Cross
HOME ADDRESS: 3326 Stoneybrae Drive, Falls Church, Virginia 22044

U.S.A.
MILLER, REAR-ADMIRAL EDWIN SWAIN, US NAVY
CURRENT DUTY STATION: Chief, Military Assistance Advisory Group, Portugal; additional duty: Commander, Iberian Atlantic Command (January 1966)
DATE OF BIRTH: 1910
EDUCATION: 1933 Naval Academy; 1948 Naval War College; 1966 Defense Language Institute, East Coast Branch
DATE OF COMMISSION: 1st June, 1933
PROMOTED TO: Rear Admiral 1st May, 1960
COMMANDS: 1944-1947 Lowry DD 770; 1951-1952 Williamsburg AGC 369; 1956-1957 Yellowstone AD 27; 1957-1958 Destroyer Squadron 28; 1963-1965 Cruiser-Destroyer Flotilla 7; Task Force 71 (2)
MAJOR AWARDS: Navy Cross
HOME ADDRESS: Av. D. Afonso Henriques, 47, Estoril, Portugal

U.S.A.
MILLER, REAR-ADMIRAL GERALD EDWARD (NAVAL AVIATOR) US NAVY
CURRENT DUTY STATION:
Deputy Director, National Military Command Center (June 1969)
DATE OF BIRTH: 1st July, 1919
EDUCATIONS: 1941 Naval Academy; 1950 Stanford University
DATE OF COMMISSION: 19th December, 1941
PROMOTED TO: Rear Admiral 1st December, 1965
COMMANDS: Fighter Squadron 831 1952; 1952-1953 Fighter Squadron 153; 1958-1959 Carrier Air Group 17; 1962-1963 Wrangell AE 12; 1963-1964 Franklin D. Roosevelt CVA 42
OFFICIAL ADDRESS: The Pentagon, Washington, DC 20301

MILLER, REAR-ADMIRAL, HENRY LOUIS, (NAVAL AVIATOR) US NAVY
CURRENT DUTY STATION: Commander Naval Air Test Center, Patuxent River, Maryland; Fleet Air Patuxent (October 1968)
DATE OF BIRTH: 1912
EDUCATION: 1934 Naval Academy; 1953 Industrial College of the Armed Forces
DATE OF COMMISSION: 31 st May,
PROMOTED TO: Rear Admiral 1st July, 1960
COMMANDS: 1942-1944 Fighter Squadron 23; 1944-1945 Carrier Air Group 6; 1955-1957 Naval Air Bases Philippines; Naval Air Station, Sangley Point, Philippines; Fleet Air Philippines; 1959-1960 Hancock CV 19; 1961-1962 Carrier Division 15; 1964-1966 Carrier Division 3

U.S.A.
MILLER, REAR-ADMIRAL (SELECTEE) WARD SCOTT, (NAVAL AVIATOR) US NAVY
CURRENT DUTY STATION: Head, Retention Plans and Programs Division, Bureau of Naval Personnel (November 1967)
DATE OF BIRTH: 1918
EDUCATION: 1942 Naval Academy; 1961 Naval War College; 1964 Armed Forces Staff College; Naval Justice School
DATE OF COMMISSION: 19th December, 1941
PROMOTED TO Rear Admiral selected for promotion on 6th June, 1969
COMMANDS: 1945 Officer-in-Charge Fighter Squadron 97B; 1951-1952 Fighter Squadron 63; 1958-1960 Fighter Squadron 174; 1964-1965 Hyades AF 28; 1966-1967 Ticonderoga CVA 14
OFFICIAL ADDRESS: Arlington Annex, Washington, DC 20370
HOME ADDRESS: 400 Spring Lake Terrace, Fairfax, Virginia

U.S.A.
MINTER, REAR-ADMIRAL CHARLES STAMPS (NAVAL AVIATOR) US NAVY
CURRENT DUTY STATION:
Commander, Fleet Air Wings Pacific; Commander Fleet Air Moffett (July 1969)
DATE OF BIRTH: 1915
EDUCATION: 1937 Naval Academy; 1956 National War College
DATE OF COMMISSION: 3rd June, 1937
PROMOTED TO: Rear Admiral 1st July, 1964
COMMANDS: 1943-1944 Headquaters Squadron 9-1, Fleet Air Wing 9; 1950-1952 Patrol Squadron 28; 1958-1959 Albemarle AV 5; 1960-1961 Intrepid CVS II; 1964-1965 Superintendent, Naval Academy; additional duty: Commandant, Severn River Naval Command
OFFICIAL ADDRESS: Naval Air Station, Moffett, California

JAPAN
MIYATAKE, REAR-ADMIRAL Y.
PRESENT APPOINTMENT: Commander, 2nd Air Wing
DATE OF BIRTH: 4 February, 1917
EDUCATION: Graduated from the Imperial Japanese Naval Academy
DATE OF PROMOTIONS: Lieutenant Commander January 1955; Commander August 1957; Captain July 1963; Rear Admiral July 1969
PREVIOUS APPOINTMENTS OF NOTE: Commander, Ozuki Air Training Group February 1965; Chief of Staff, Fleet Air Force November 1965; Commander, 4th Air Wing December 1967
OFFICIAL ADDRESS: 2nd Air Wing, Takadate, Hachinohe-Shi, Aomori-Ken, Japan. *Telephone:* 01782-8-3011
PRIVATE ADDRESS: 1111 Kanshiya, Hibakari, Hachinohe-Shi, Aomori-Ken, Japan

U.K.
MOLAND, COMMANDER R. W., ROYAL NAVY
PRESENT APPOINTMENT: HMS Dainty in command, 1 August, 1968
DATE OF BIRTH: 27 September, 1931
EDUCATION: Solihull School; Royal Naval College, Dartmouth
DATES OF PROMOTIONS: Commander 30 June, 1968
PRINCIPAL COMMANDS AT SEA: HMS Rapid
OFFICIAL ADDRESS: HMS Dainty. BFPO Ships
PRIVATE ADDRESS: Beehives, Stedham, Midhurst, Sussex

U.S.A.
MOORE, REAR-ADMIRAL GEORGE EVERETT, (SUPPLY CORPS.) US NAVY
CURRENT DUTY STATION:
Deputy Chief of Naval Material (Logistic Support) (July 1969)
DATE OF BIRTH: 1918
EDUCATION: 1939 Naval Academy; 1961 Naval War College
DATE OF COMMISSION: 1st June, 1939
PROMOTED TO: Rear Admiral 1st August, 1966
COMMANDS: 1963-1966 Navy Ships Parts Control Center, Mechanicsburg, Pennsylvania
OFFICIAL ADDRESS: Main Navy Building, Washington, DC 20390
HOME ADDRESS: 605 Timber Branch Parkway, Alexandria, Virginia 22302

U.S.A.

MOORE, REAR-ADMIRAL (SELECTEE) HOWARD SHACKLEFORD (NAVAL AVIATOR) US NAVY
CURRENT DUTY STATION: Deputy Director, National Military Command Center, J-3, Joint Chiefs of Staff (July 1968)
DATE OF BIRTH: 1920
EDUCATION: 1942 Naval Academy; 1953 Naval War College; 1968 University of Oklahoma
DATE OF COMMISSION: 19th June, 1942
PROMOTED TO: Rear Admiral selected for promotion 6th June, 1968
COMMANDS: 1959-1960 Heavy Attack Squadron 5; 1963-1965 Platte AO 24; 1965-1966 Forrestal CVA 59
HOME ADDRESS: 3657 North Military Road, Arlington, Virginia 22207

U.S.A.

MOORE, REAR-ADMIRAL, MICHAEL USIS, US NAVY
CURRENT DUTY STATION: Director, International Staff, Inter-American Defense Board (August 1967)
DATE OF BIRTH: 1921
EDUCATION: 1942 Naval Academy; 1947 Naval Academy, Naval Post-graduate School; 1949 Massachusetts Institute of Technology; 1960 Naval War College
DATE OF COMMISSION: 19th June, 1942
PROMOTED TO: Rear Admiral 1st August, 1968
COMMANDS: 1953-1955 K-2 SSK 2; 1961-1962 Submarine Division 71; 1964-1967 Submarine Development Group 2
HOME ADDRESS: 1110 Fidler Lane, Silver Spring, Maryland 20910

U.S.A.

MOORE, REAR-ADMIRAL SAM HOWARD, US NAVY
CURRENT DUTY STATION: Commander, Military Sea Transportation Service, Far East (October 1968)
DATE OF BIRTH: 1918
EDUCATION: 1950 Naval School, General Line School, Monterey; 1958 Marine Corps. Schools, Quantico, Va.; 1967 National War College
DATE OF COMMISSION: 5th May, 1942
PROMOTED TO: Rear Admiral 1st August, 1968
COMMANDS: YNS 415 1944-1945; 1945-1946 Mine Squadron 102; 1946 Destiny AM 218; 1946-1947 Scout AM 296; 1955-1957 Cushing DD 797; 1962-1963 Destroyer Division 102; 1965-1966 Chicago CG 11; 1967-1968 Destroyer Flotilla 7

U.S.A.

MOORER, ADMIRAL THOMAS HINMAN (NAVAL AVIATOR) US NAVY
CURRENT DUTY STATION: Chief of Naval Operations (August 1967)
DATE OF BIRTH: 1912
EDUCATIONS: 1933 Naval Academy; 1953 Naval War College
DATE OF COMMISSION: 1st June, 1933
PROMOTED TO: Rear Admiral 1st August, 1958; Vice Admiral 5th October, 1962; Admiral 26th June, 1964
COMMANDS: 1943-1944 Bombing Squadron 132; 1956-1957 Salisbury Sound AV 13; 1959-1960 Carrier Division 6; 1962-1964 7th Fleet; 1964-1965 Commander-in-Chief, US Pacific Fleet; 1965-1967 Commander-in-Chief, Atlantic and Atlantic Fleet, Supreme Allied Commander, Atlantic
HOME ADDRESS: Admiral's House, Naval Observatory, Washington, DC 20390

JAPAN
MOTOMURA, REAR-ADMIRAL T.
DECORATIONS: The Fifth Order of the Sacred Treasure
PRESENT APPOINTMENT: Commander Training Squadron 16 November, 1968
DATE OF BIRTH: 9 October, 1917
EDUCATION: Naval Academy
DATES OF PROMOTIONS: Lieutenant Commander 15 July, 1952; Commander 1 August, 1954; Captain 1 February 1959; Rear Admiral 1 January 1966
PRINCIPAL COMMANDS AT SEA: Commanding Officer, PF Nire; Commanding Officer, PF Kashi; Commander, 1st Training Division 1963; Commander 3rd Escort Flotilla 1965
OTHER PREVIOUS APPOINTMENTS OF NOTE: Staff, Operations Division, Maritime Staff Office 1957; Staff Research Division, Staff College 1959; Chief, Education Division, Officer Candidate School 1961; Chief, Administration Section, Maritime Staff Office 1963; Vice Commandant, Yokosuka Regional District Headquarters 1967
OFFICIAL ADDRESS: Commander Training Squadron, c/o Yokosuka Regional District Headquarters, Nishihemi-Cho, Yokosuka-Shi., Japan
PRIVATE ADDRESS: 439, Tsunashima-Cho, Kohoku-Ku, Yokohama-Shi, Japan

U.S.A.

MORAN, REAR-ADMIRAL WILLIAM JOSEPH (NAVAL AVIATOR) US NAVY
CURRENT DUTY STATION: Director, Navy Space Program Division, Office of the Chief of Naval Operations (November, 1968)
DATE OF BIRTH: 1919
EDUCATION: 1949 Naval School, General Line School, Monterey; 1955 Naval War College; 1965 National War College
DATE OF COMMISSION: 8th October, 1941
PROMOTED TO: Rear Admiral 1st August, 1968
COMMANDS: 1953-1954 Fighter Squadron 23; 1965-1966 Rainier AE 5; 1966-1967 Randolph CVS 15; 1967-1968 Anti-Submarine Warfare Group 3

MEXICO
MORENO CORZO, CAPITAN DE FRIGATA, M., MEXICAN NAVY
PRESENT APPOINTMENT: Director, Escuela de Aviación Naval, 1 September, 1967
DATE OF BIRTH: 8 May, 1922
EDUCATION: Primaria Elemental; Secundaria; H. Escuela Naval Militar; Escuela de Aviacin Naval y Escuela de Aviacin Naval, Pensacola Fla., USA
DATES OF PROMOTIONS: Guardiamarina 1 September, 1945; Teniente de Corbeta 20 November, 1946; Teniente de Fragata 20 November, 1949; Teniente de Navío 20 November, 1952; Capitán de Corbeta 20 November 1956; Capitán de Fragata 20 November, 1962
PREVIOUS APPOINTMENTS OF NOTE: Comandante de Avión J2F6 Grumman 1950-1952; Flight Instructor, Escuela de Aviación Naval; 20 Comandante del Primer Escuadrón Aeronaval 1953-1956; Subdirector, Escuela de Aviación Naval 1956; Comandante del Primer Escuadrón Aeronaval 1963
OFFICIAL ADDRESS: Escuela de Aviación Naval, Las Bajadas, Ver., Mexico. *Telephone;* 2-36-42
PRIVATE ADDRESS: Grijalva 97, Fracc. Reforma, H. Veracruz, Ver., Mexico. *Telephone;* 2-40-93

UNITED KINGDOM
MORGAN, REAR-ADMIRAL P. J., ROYAL NAVY
DECORATIONS: C.B. 1967; D.S.C. 1942
PRESENT APPOINTMENT: Flag Officer Royal Yachts 1965
DATE OF BIRTH: 26 January, 1917
EDUCATION: RNC, Dartmouth
DATES OF PROMOTIONS: 1949 Commander; 1956 Captain; 1965 Rear-Admiral
PRINCIPAL COMMANDS AT SEA: 1953-1954 HMS Constance; 1963-1965 HMS Bulwark
OTHER PREVIOUS APPOINTMENTS OF NOTE: Naval Attaché, Ankara and Teheran 1958-1960; Assistant Chief of Staff (Plans and Operations) to the Commander-in-Chief, Eastern Atlantic 1961-1963
OFFICIAL ADDRESS: HM Yacht Britannia c/o BFPO Ships
PRIVATE ADDRESS: Conway House, The Fairway, Worplesdon, Guildford, Surrey.

U.S.A.
MORRISON, REAR-ADMIRAL GEORGE STEPHEN, (NAVAL AVIATOR)
CURRENT DUTY STATION:
Director, Electronic Warfare & Tactical Command System Division, Office of the Chief of Naval Operations (September 1969)
DATE OF BIRTH: 1919
EDUCATION: 1941 Naval Academy
DATE OF COMMISSION: 7th February, 1941
PROMOTED TO: Rear Admiral 1st July, 1967
COMMANDS: 1954-1955 Fighter Squadron 112; 1962-1963 Guadalupe AO 32; 1963-1964 Bon Homme Richard CVA 31

OFFICIAL ADDRESS: The Pentagon, Washington, DC 20350

U.S.A.

MORRISON, REAR-ADMIRAL WILLIAM L., US NAVY
CURRENT DUTY STATION: Chief Counsel for the US Coast Guard (January 1969)
DATE OF BIRTH: 1914
EDUCATION: 1939 Coast Guard Academy; 1949 George Washington University Law School
FIRST COMMISSIONED: 29th May, 1939
PROMOTED TO: Rear Admiral 1st January, 1968
COMMANDS: 1943-1945 Sellstrom; 1950-1951 Mackinac; 1951-1952 Port Security Unit, Ellis Island; 1959-1960 Yocana; 1960-1961 Dexter
HOME ADDRESS: 500 McCauley St, Washington Grove, Md.

U.K.
MOTT, CAPTAIN J. W., ROYAL NAVY
DECORATIONS: MVO 1956
PRESENT APPOINTMENT: In Command HMS Condor, RN Air Station Arbroath
DATE OF BIRTH: 5th March, 1917
EDUCATION: Royal Naval College, Dartmouth; RM Engineering College, Keyham, Devonport
DATES OF PROMOTIONS: Commander 1949; Captain 1960
OTHER PREVIOUS APPOINTMENT OF NOTE: HM Yacht Britannia 1952-1956; Command Engineer Officer, Flag Officer Naval Air Command 1DC 1964; Naval & Air attaché, Belgarde 1964-1966;
OFFICIAL ADDRESS: HMS Condor, Royal Naval Air Station, Arbroath. *Telephone:* Arbroath 2201

U.K.
MUCHLOW, COMMANDER H., ROYAL NAVY
DECORATIONS: M in D 1965
PRESENT APPOINTMENT: Commanding Officer HMS St George
DATE OF BIRTH: 10 December, 1927
EDUCATION: Royal Hospital School
DATES OF PROMOTIONS: Commander 31 December, 1969; Lieutenant Commander 1 April, 1966; Lieutenant 1 April, 1958
PRINCIPAL COMMANDS AT SEA: HMS Chawson 1963-1965; HMS Whitby 1967-1968
OTHER PREVIOUS APPOINTMENT OF NOTE: RN Staff Course 1966
OFFICIAL ADDRESS: HMS St George, Eastney, Portsmouth P04 9LL *Telephone:* Portsmouth Dockyard, ext. 6411
PRIVATE ADDRESS: 9 Esplanade Gdn., Eastney

CANADA
MURDOCH, REAR ADMIRAL R. W.
DECORATIONS: CD 1948
PRESENT APPOINTMENT: Canadian Military Representative to the Military Committee in Permanent Session, North American Treaty Organization, Brussels, Belgium October 1967
DATE OF BIRTH: 21 February, 1918
EDUCATION: Cadet Entry
DATES OF PROMOTIONS: Cadet 28 August, 1936; Midshipman 1 May, 1937; Assistant Sub-Lieutenant 1 May, 1939; Sub-Lieutenant 3 November, 1939; Lieutenant 1 January, 1940; Assistant Lieutenant Commander 15 February, 1946; Lieutenant Commander 15 July, 1948; Commander 1 July, 1951; Captain 1 January, 1957; Commodore 26 November, 1963; Rear Admiral 20 October, 1966
PRINCIPAL COMMANDS AT SEA: HMCS Beacon Hill April 1950-October 1951; HMCS Sioux September 1955-April 1957; HMCS Crescent, also Commander Third Canadian Escort Squadron September 1959-June 1961
PREVIOUS APPOINTMENTS OF NOTE: Canadian Staff College Course June 1946-July 1947; Communications duties with the United States Navy July 1947- July 1948; Naval Headquarters for duty with the Director of Naval Communications August 1948-February 1950; Naval Headquarters as Director of Naval Communications October 1953-September 1955; Naval Headquarters as Deputy Assistant Chief of Naval Staff (Air and Warfare). September 1957-September 1958; National Defence College Course September 1958-September 1959; Naval Headquarters as Director of Naval Intelligence June 1961-November 1963; Canadian Forces Headquarters as Director General Plans December 1964-October 1966; Canadian Forces Headquarters as Deputy Chief Plans October 1966-October 1967
OFFICIAL ADDRESS: NATO, Brussels, Belgium

U.S.A.
MURPHY, REAR-ADMIRAL CHARLES PATRICK, US NAVY
CURRENT DUTY STATION: Chief, Office of Merchant Marine Safety (June 1964)
DATE OF BIRTH: 1914
EDUCATION: 1935 Webb Institute of Naval Archecture
PROMOTED TO: Rear Admiral 8th July, 1964
HOME ADDRESS: Valley Drive, Glen Hills, Rockville, Md.

U.S.A.
MUSE, REAR-ADMIRAL GEORGE READ, US NAVY
CURRENT DUTY STATION: Commander, Naval Reserve Training Command (October 1967)
DATE OF BIRTH: 1915
EDUCATION: 1938 Naval Academy; 1950 Armed Forces Staff College; 1958 Naval War College
DATE OF COMMISSION: 2nd June, 1938
PROMOTED TO: Rear Admiral 1st January, 1967
COMMANDS: 1944-1945 Stephen Potter DD 538; 1952-1954 McCaffery DDE 860; 1961-1962 Oklahoma City CLG 5 1966-1967 Cruiser-Destroyer Flotilla 11
HOME ADDRESS: 404 Park Avenue, New Castle, Pennsylvania 16101

U.S.A.
MUSTIN, VICE-ADMIRAL LLOYD MONTAGUE, US NAVY
CURRENT DUTY STATION: Director, Defense Atomic Support Agency (July 1968)
DATE OF BIRTH: 1911
EDUCATION: 1932 Naval Academy; 1940 Naval Academy, Naval Postgraduate School
DATE OF COMMISSION: 2nd June, 1932
PROMOTED TO: Rear Admiral 1st July, 1958; Vice Admiral 21st August, 1964
COMMANDS: 1948-1950 Keppler DD 765; 1954-1955 Piedmont AD 17; 1955-1957 Destroyer Squadron 13; 1958-1959 Destroyer Flotilla 2; 1959-1960 Naval Base, Key West, Florida; 1967-1968 AmphibiousForce, Atlantic Fleet
HOME ADDRESS: 500 W. Taylor Run Parkway, Alexandria, Virginia 22314

U.S.A.
NACE, REAR-ADMIRAL CHARLES DERICK, US NAVY
CURRENT DUTY STATION: Commander, US Naval Forces, Southern Command; Commandant, 15th Naval District (June 1969)
DATE OF BIRTH: 1917
EDUCATION: 1939 Naval Academy; 1953 Armed Forces Staff College; 1958 National War College; 1962 Harvard University
DATE OF COMMISSION: 1st June, 1939
PROMOTED TO: Rear Admiral 10th August, 1965
COMMANDS: 1945-1946 Rasher SS 269; 1948-1950 Ronquil SS 396; 1954-1955 Submarine Division 72; Pickaway APA 222 1960-1961; 1962-1964 Submarine Flotilla 7; 1967-1969 Submarine Flotilla 2
OFFICIAL ADDRESS: FPO New York 09580
HOME ADDRESS: 7005 Southridge Drive, McLean, Virginia 22101

UNITED KINGDOM
NAIR, REAR-ADMIRAL
DECORATIONS: K.R.; P.V.S.M. 1969
PRESENT APPOINTMENT: Flag Officer Commanding-in-Chief, Eastern Naval Command
DATE OF BIRTH: 15 July, 1915
EDUCATION: Master of Science DATES OF PROMOTIONS: Commander June 1951; Captain December 1955; Rear-Admiral 22 November 1966
PRINCIPAL COMMANDS AT SEA: 1951-1953 Ins Rana; 1958-1960 Captain (D) 22
OTHER PREVIOUS APPOINTMENTS OF NOTE: 1960-1963 & 1965-1967 Chief of Naval Personnel; 1963-1965 Chief of Staff Indian Fleet
OFFICIAL ADDRESS: Flag Officer Commanding-in-Chief, Eastern Naval Command, Naval Base, Vishakhapatnam-5. *Telephone:* 3021 Ext. 211
PRIVATE ADDRESS: "The Retreat", Waltair Uplands, Vishakhapatnam-3 *Telephone:* 3507 or 3021 ext. 208

U.S.A.
NANCE, REAR-ADMIRAL (SELECTEE) JAMES WILSON, (NAVAL AVIATOR) US NAVY
CURRENT DUTY STATION: Commanding Officer, USS Forrestal CVA 59 (December 1968)
DATE OF BIRTH: 1921
EDUCATION: 1945 Naval Academy; 1958 Naval War College; 1967 National War College
DATE OF COMMISSION: 7th June, 1944
PROMOTED TO: Rear Admiral selected for promotion on 6th June, 1969
COMMANDS: 1960-1962 Attack Squadron 83; 1963-1964 Carrier Air Wing 8; 1967-1968 Raleigh LPD 1
OFFICIAL ADDRESS: FPO New York
HOME ADDRESS: 408 East Houston Street, Monroe, North Carolina

THAILAND
NATEROJ, ADMIRAL A., ROYAL THAI NAVY
DECORATIONS: Knight Grand Cross (First Class) of the Most Exalted Order of the White Elephant 1963; Knight Grand Cordon (Special Class) of the Most Noble Order of the Crown of Thailand 1965; Knight Grand Commander (Second Class, higher grade) of the Most Illustrious Order of Chula Chom Klao 1966
PRESENT APPOINTMENT: Deputy Commander-in-Chief
DATE OF BIRTH: 16 July, 1911
EDUCATION: 1933 Royal Naval Academy, Graduated; 1944 Naval Staff College, Graduated; 1953 Further training in USA; 1963 National Defence College, Graduated
DATES OF PROMOTIONS: 1933 Acting Sub-Lieutenant; 1950 Captain; 1962 Admiral
PRINCIPAL COMMANDS: 1943 C.O. HTMS Chang; 1944 C.O. HTMS Patani; 1945 C.O. HTMS Surath; 1946 Deputy Commandant, Naval Rating School; 1951 Staff Officer, Royal Thai Fleet; 1955 C.O. Fleet Training Command; 1957 C.O. Sattahip Naval Station; 1962 C-in-C, Royal Fleet; 1963 Assistant C-in-C, Royal Thai Navy; 1966 Deputy C-in-C, Royal Thai Navy
OFFICIAL ADDRESS: Naval Headquarters, Thonburi, Thailand *Telephone:* 60093
PRIVATE ADDRESS: 28 Soi 27-29 Sukhumvit Road, Phrakhanong, Bangkok, Thailand.

U.S.A.
NEEDHAM, VICE-ADMIRAL RAY CANNON, (NAVAL AVIATOR) US NAVY
CURRENT DUTY STATION: Naval Inspector Gereral (September 1965)
DATE OF BIRTH: 1908
EDUCATION: 1931 Naval Academy; 1952 National War College
DATE OF COMMISSION: 4th June, 1931
PROMOTED TO: Rear Admiral 1st July, 1958; Vice Admiral 1st August, 1963
COMMANDS: 1948-1949 Tarawa CV 40; 1952-1953 Duxbury Bay AVP 38; 1954-1956 Naval Air Station, Quonset Point, Rhode Isalnd; 1956-1957 Wasp CVS 18; 1960-1961 Carrier Division 2
HOME ADDRESS: Quarters "D", Naval Observatory, Washington, DC 20390

SWEDEN
NORINDER, COMMODORE T. L., ROYAL SWEDISH NAVY
DECORATIONS: C.R.V.O. 1956; C.O.N.M. (French) 1966; C.O.S. (Swedish) 1968
PRESENT APPOINTMENT: Commanding Officer Naval Training Centre, Berga (1 April, 1968)
DATE OF BIRTH: 28 June, 1911
DATES OF PROMOTIONS: 1932 Sub-Lieutenant; 1951 Commander; 1955 Captain
PRINCIPAL COMMANDS AT SEA: 1945–1960 Ten different Swedish destroyers; 1960–1961 Commander of destroyer flotilla; 1946 Staff Officer to the Admiral, Commander-in-Chief, Swedish Home Fleet
OTHER PREVIOUS APPOINTMENTS OF NOTE: Chief of Organisation Section, Naval Staff 1956–1959; Chief of Naval Section, Military Academy 1961–1963; Naval and Air Attaché, Paris 1963–1968
OFFICIAL ADDRESS: Berga Flogsskolor, 130 61 Harsfjarden, Sweden *Telephone:* 0750/2010
PRIVATE ADDRESS: Villa vägen 41, 13700 Vcsterhaninge, Sweden *Telephone;* 0750/25810

U.S.A.

NORRIS, REAR-ADMIRAL FRANK TURNER, (MEDICAL CORPS.) US NAVY
CURRENT DUTY STATION: Assistant Chief for Personnel and Professional Operations, Bureau of Medicine and Surgery (June 1966)
DATE OF BIRTH: 1915
DATE OF COMMISSION: 15th August, 1939
PROMOTED TO: Rear Admiral 1st February, 1966
COMMANDS: 2nd Medical Battalion, 2nd Marine Division 1952-1953; 1962-1965 Naval Hospital, Camp Lejeune, North Carolina
HOME ADDRESS: 1311 Elsinore Avenue, McLean, Virginia 22101

UNITED KINGDOM

NOTLEY, CAPTAIN B. H., ROYAL NAVY
PRESENT APPOINTMENT: Commanding Officer RNAS Culdrose
DATE OF BIRTH: 6 March, 1919
EDUCATION: Magdalen College School, Oxford
DATES OF PROMOTIONS: Commander 31 December 1956; Captain 31 December, 1962
PRINCIPAL COMMANDS AT SEA: 1958-1960 HMS Malcom; 1965-1967 Captain of 2nd Frigate Squadron; HMS Aurora 1965-1967
OTHER PREVIOUS APPOINTMENTS OF NOTE: Directorate Naval Air Warfare 1956-1958; Standing Group N.A.T.O. 1960-1963; National Defence College, India 1964
OFFICIAL ADDRESS: Hawke House, RNAS Culdrose, Helston *Telephone* 2571 ext. 1
PRIVATE ADDRESS: Thurland Cottage, Chetnole, Dorset

CANADA

O'BRIEN, VICE ADMIRAL J. C. CANADIAN ARMED FORCES
DECORATIONS: CD 1949
PRESENT APPOINTMENT: Commander Maritime Command and Commander Canadian Atlantic Sub Area July 1966
DATE OF BIRTH: 16 December, 1918
EDUCATION: Two Years Military College
DATES OF PROMOTIONS: Cadet 20 August, 1937; Midshipman 1 September, 1938; Assistant Sub-Lieutenant 1 May, 1940; Lieutenant 1 March, 1941; Assistant Lieutenant Commander 1 June, 1945; Lieutenant Commander 1 September, 1948; Commander 1 July, 1951; Captain 1 July, 1955; Commodore 22 September, 1961; Rear Admiral 19 July, 1966; Vice Admiral 15 September, 1968
PRINCIPAL COMMANDS AT SEA: HMCS Crescent December, 1946-January 1948; HMCS Bonaventure September 1959-September 1961; Senior Canadian Officer Afloat Atlantic August 1964-July 1966
PREVIOUS APPOINTMENT OF NOTE: Officer-in-Charge Communications School, HMCS Stadacona January 1948-September 1951; Royal Naval Staff Course September 1951-April 1952; Executive Officer, HMCS Magnificent June 1954-July 1955; Naval Headquarters as Director of Naval Training July 1955-August 1957; Naval Member, Candian Joint Staff (Washington) and Canadian Naval Attaché (Washington) September 1961-August 1964
OFFICIAL ADDRESS: Commander Maritime Command, FMO Halifax, Nova Scotia

U.S.A.

O'BRIEN, REAR-ADMIRAL LESLIE JOHN, JNR., US NAVY
CURRENT DUTY STATION: Director Anti- Submarine Warfare and Ocean Surveillance Division, Office of the Chief of Naval Operations (June 1967)
DATE OF BIRTH: 1915
EDUCATION: 1938 Naval Academy; 1953 Armed Forces Staff College; 1957 Industrial College of the Armed Forces
DATE OF COMMISSION: 2nd June, 1938
PROMOTED TO: Rear Admiral 10th August, 1965
COMMANDS: 1945-1946 Haraden DD 585; 1951 Robert L. Wilson DDE 847; 1951-1953 Willard Keith DD 775; 1959-1960 Tulare AKA 112; 1960-1963 Key West and Evaluation Detachment, Key West, Florida; 1963-1964 Destroyer Squadron 14; 1965-1967 Cruiser-Destroyer Flotilla 10
HOME ADDRESS: 6311 Mori Street, McLean, Virginia 22101

UNITED KINGDOM

O'BRIEN, VICE-ADMIRAL SIR W. D., ROYAL NAVY
DECORATIONS: A.C.B. 1969; C.B. 1966; D.S.C. 1942
PRESENT APPOINTMENT: Commander, Far East Fleet 1967
DATE OF BIRTH: 13 November, 1916
EDUCATION: RNC Britannia
DATES OF PROMOTIONS: 1940 Lieutenant; 1946 Lieutenant Commander; 1949 Commander; 1955 Captain; 1964 Rear-Admiral; 1967 Vice Admiral
PRINCIPAL COMMANDS AT SEA: 1943-1944 HMS Cottesmore; 1946-1948 HMS Venus; 1958 8th Destroyer Squadron; 1961-1964 HMS Hermes
OTHER PREVIOUS APPOINTMENTS OF NOTE: Served on Russian Convoys in HMS Otta 1942; Chief Staff Officer, Flag Officer Flotillas, Med. 195
OFFICIAL ADDRESS: HM Naval Base, Singapore 27 (BFPO 164)
PRIVATE ADDRESS: Drew's Mill, Potterne Road, Devizes, Wiltshire

U.S.A.

O'GRADY, REAR-ADMIRAL JAMES WADSWORTH (NAVAL AVIATOR) US NAVY
CURRENT DUTY STATION: Chief of Staff, Supreme Allied Commander, Atlantic (September 1968)
DATE OF BIRTH: 1912
EDUCATION: 1936 Naval Academy; 1953 Naval War College
DATE OF COMMISSION: 4th June, 1936
PROMOTED TO: Rear Admiral 1st November, 1963
COMMANDS: 1948-1949 Carrier Air Group II; 1956-1957 Valcour (AVP 55); 1959-1960 Independence CVA 62; 1963-1964 Carrier Division 20

JAPAN

OGURA, REAR-ADMIRAL JMSDF T.
PRESENT APPOINTMENT: Chief, Technical Div. MSO
DATE OF BIRTH: 19 September, 1916
EDUCATION: Graduated from Kyushu Imperial University (Naval Architecture Division)
DATE OF PROMOTIONS: Lieutenant Commander July 1954; Commander August 1955; Captain August 1960; Rear Admiral July 1966
PREVIOUS APPOINTMENTS OF NOTE: Chief, Ships Section, Yokosika Regional District HDQ January 1956; Chief, Technical Division, Kure Regional District HDQ August 1960; Chief, Ships Section, Maritime Staff Office September 1963; Deputy Chief, Technical Division, MSO July 1967; Chief Technical Division, MSO January 1968
OFFICIAL ADDRESS: Maritime Staff Office, Japan Defence Agency, 9-7-45 Akasaka, Minato-Ku, Tokyo, Japan. *Telephone:* 408-5211 ext. 2870
PRIVATE ADDRESS 49 Kinuta-Cho, Setagaya-Ku, Tokyo, Japan *Telephone:* 416-5506

U.K.

OLAND, COMMODORE B. S. C., ROYAL NAVY
DECORATIONS: ED; CD
PRESENT APPOINTMENT: Senior Naval Reserve Adviser
DATE OF BIRTH: 31 March, 1918
EDUCATION: Kings College School, Windsor, Nova Scotia; Beaumont College, Old Windsor, Berks, England; United Brewers Academy USA
DATES OF PROMOTIONS: Lieutenant 12 April, 1951; Lieutenant Commander 12 April, 1959; Commander 1 January, 1962; Captain 1 January, 1966; Commodore 15 November, 1967
OTHER PREVIOUS APPOINTMENTS OF NOTE: Commanding Officer, Scotian, 18 August, 1963; Senior Naval Reserve Advisor to the Deputy Chief of Reserves, 15 November, 1967; ACD to His Excellency, the Governor General of Canada, 15 November, 1967
OFFICIAL ADDRESS: Keith Hall, Hollis Street, Halifax, Nova Scotia. *Telephone:* 422-7301
PRIVATE ADDRESS: 870 Young Avenue, Halifax, Nova Scotia

U.S.A.

OSBORNE, REAR-ADMIRAL (SELECTEE) DAVID PAUL, (MEDICAL CORPS.) US NAVY
CURRENT DUTY STATION: Commanding Officer, Naval Hospital National Naval Medical Center, and Deputy Commanding Officer, National Naval Medical Center, Bethesda, Maryland (June 1967)
DATE OF BIRTH: 1915
EDUCATION: Pennsylvania State College 1938; 1942 Temple University
DATE OF COMMISSION: 14th June, 1941
PROMOTED TO: Rear Admiral selected for Promotion in June 1969
OFFICIAL ADDRESS: Bethesda, Maryland 20014

U.S.A.

OSBORN, REAR-ADMIRAL JAMES BUTLER, US NAVY
CURRENT DUTY STATION: Commander, Submarine Flotilla 6 (January 1969)
DATE OF BIRTH: 1938
EDUCATION: 1941 Naval Academy; 1948 Naval Postgraduate School; 1958 Naval War College
DATE OF COMMISSION: 19th December, 1941
PROMOTED TO: Rear Admiral 1st August, 1968
COMMANDS: 1945-1946 Perch SS 313; 1953-1955 Tunny SSG 282; 1955-1957 Guided Missile Unit 50; 1957 Guided Missile Unit 90; 1959-1962 George Washington SSBN 598; 1964-1966 Simon Lake AS 33; 1968-1969 Naval Support Activity, DaNang, South Vietnam
OFFICIAL ADDRESS: FPO New York 09501
HOME ADDRESS: Stockton, Missouri

U.K.

OSBORN, CAPTAIN J. H. S.
PRESENT APPOINTMENT: In command HMS Hecate
DATE OF BIRTH: 8 October, 1921
EDUCATION: Geelong Grammar School
DATES OF PROMOTION: Lieutenant 1942; Lieutenant Commander 1950; Commander 1960; Captain 1967
PRINCIPAL COMMANDS AT SEA: HMAS Barcoo 1954-1956; HMAS Warrego 1958-1960; HMAS Moresby 1964-1966; HMS Hecate 1968
OFFICIAL ADDRESS: HMS Hecate, c/o BFPO Ships
PRIVATE ADDRESS: 19 Glenhurst Court, Farquhar Road, Dulwich, London, S.E.19

U.S.A.
OWEN, REAR-ADMIRAL THOMAS BARRON (ENGINEERING DUTY) US NAVY
CURRENT DUTY STATION: Chief of Naval Research; additional duty: Assistant Oceanographer of the Navy for Ocean Science (July 1967)
DATE OF BIRTH; 1920
EDUCATION: 1940 University of Washington; 1950 Naval Postgraduate School; 1962 Industrial College of the Armed Forces; 1950 Cornell University
DATE OF COMMISSION: 25th May, 1940
PROMOTED TO: Rear Admiral 1st July, 1967
COMMANDS: 1965-1967 Naval Research Laboratory, Washington, DC
OFFICIAL ADDRESS: Main Navy Building, Washington, DC 20360
HOME ADDRESS: 727 13th Avenue, Seattle, Washington

CANADA
PADDON, REAR ADMIRAL S. E., CANADIAN ARMED FORCES
DECORATIONS: CD 1952
PRESENT APPOINTMENT: Commander, Canadian Defence Liaison Staff, Washington, Canadian Forces Attaché and Senior Liaison Officer Navy, Washington September 1966
DATE OF BIRTH: 10 October, 1917
EDUCATION: Bachelor of Arts degree in Mathematics and Physics
DATES OF PROMOTIONS: RCNVR May 1940-October 1945 Sub-Lieutenant; Lieutenant; Assistant Lieutenant Commander; Lieutenant Commander discharged RCN Lieutenant 17 June, 1946; Assistant Lieutenant Commander 18 June, 1946; Lieutenant Commander 15 August, 1947; Commander 1 July, 1951; Assistant Captain 27 December, 1955; Captain 1 January, 1956; Commodore 21 December, 1961; Rear Admiral 29 August, 1966
PREVIOUS APPOINTMENT OF NOTE: Naval Headquarters as Assistant Director of Electrical Engineering June 1946-March 1948; Senior Staff Officer HMC Electrical School, Halifax, N.S. March 1948-June 1950; Naval Headquarters as Staff Officer Electrical Personnel June 1950-July 1952; HMCS Ontario as Electrical Officer July 1952-June 1954; Manager Electrical Engineering Pacific Coast and Manager Electrical Engineering, HMC Dockyard, Esquimalt, B.C. June 1954-December 1955; Deputy Superintendant, HMC Dockyard, Esquimalt December 1955-April 1957; Naval Headquarters as Deputy Electrical Engineer-in-Chief June, 1957-May 1969; National Defence College Course August 1962-July 1963; Canadian Forces Headquarters as Director General Postings and Careers December 1964-September 1966
OFFICIAL ADDRESS: Commander, Canadian Defence Liaison Staff Washington, 2450 Massachusetts Ave. North, Washington, DC 20008

U.S.A.
PAINE, REAR-ADMIRAL ROGER WARDE, JNR. US NAVY
CURRENT DUTY STATION: Director, Navy Information Systems Division, Office of the Chief of Naval Operations (January 1968)
DATE OF BIRTH: 1917
EDUCATION: 1939 Naval Academy; 1949 Naval Postgraduate School; 1957 Naval War College
DATE OF COMMISSION: 1st June, 1939
PROMOTED TO: Rear Admiral 1st April, 1967
COMMANDS: 1943-1944 S-34 SS 139; 1945-1946 Cubera SS 347; 1946 Whale SS 239; 1951-1953 Cowell DD 547; 1957-1958 Destroyer Division 202; 1961-1962 Topeka CLG 8; 1966-1968 Cruiser-Destroyer Flotilla 10
OFFICIAL ADDRESS: The Pentagon, Washington, DC 20350
HOME ADDRESS: 4900 East Valley Road, Fort Smith, Arkansas

U.S.A.
PARKER, REAR-ADMIRAL EDELEN ALPHONSUS (NAVAL RESERVE) (NAVAL AVIATOR)
CURRENT DUTY STATION: Assistant Chief of Naval Personnel for Naval Reserve (September 1966)
DATE OF BIRTH: 1915
EDUCATION: 1937 Catholic University of America
DATE OF COMMISSION: 1st January, 1939
PROMOTED TO: Rear Admiral 10th August, 1965
COMMANDS: 1944-1945 Composite Squadron 71; 1963-1965 Naval Air Reserve Training Unit, Andrews Air Force Base, Washington, DC
OFFICIAL ADDRESS: Arlington, Annex Washington, DC 20370
HOME ADDRESS: Clinton, Maryland

UNITED KINGDOM
PARKER, VICE-ADMIRAL SIR W. J., ROYAL NAVY
DECORATIONS: K.B.E. 1969; C.B. 1965; O.B.E. 1954; D.S.C. 1943
PRESENT APPOINTMENT: Flag Officer Medway and Admiral Superintendent of HM Dockyard, Chatham July 1966
DATE OF BIRTH: 12 October, 1915
EDUCATION: Royal Naval College, Dartmouth 1929-1933; Qualified as Communications Specialist 1941 (Signals and Radio); Graduate, Naval Staff College, Greenwich, 1946; Joint Services Staff College, 1947; Imperial Defence College 1957
DATES OF PROMOTIONS: 1964 Rear-Admiral; 1967 Vice Admiral
PRINCIPAL COMMANDS AT SEA: During the latter part of the Korean War commanded the Destroyer Comus, and for a short while was Chief Staff Officer to the Flag Officer, Second in Command, Far East Station 1952-1954 Senior Naval Officer, West Indies, as a Commodore 1958-1960
OTHER PREVIOUS APPOINTMENTS OF NOTE: Director of Officer Recruiting 1954-1956; Captain of Royal Naval College, Dartmouth 1961-1963; Assistant Chief Defence Staff (Operational Requirements) 1963-1966
OFFICIAL ADDRESS: Medway House, HM Dockyard, Chatham. *Telephone:* Medway 44422 ext. 2001
PRIVATE ADDRESS: Nyewood Oaks, Rogate, near Petersfield, Hants.

FINLAND
PAUHAKARI, COMMODORE L. V. FINNISH NAVY
DECORATIONS: VR 4; VR 3; SVR R1
PRESENT APPOINTMENTS: Commanding Officer Naval Squadron 6 January, 1969
DATE OF BIRTH: 10 November, 1917
EDUCATIONS Naval Academy 1937-1939; War College (Naval Section) 1951-1953
DATES OF PROMOTIONS: Sub-Lieutenant 1937; Lieutenant 1940; Lieutenant Commander 1943; Commander 1954; Captain 1961; Commodore 1969;
PREVIOUS APPOINTMENTS OF NOTE: Chief of Staff Naval Squadron 1966-1969
OFFICIAL ADDRESS: Naval Squadron, Turku 15

UNITED KINGDOM
PAUL, COMMANDER E. A. S., ROYAL NAVY
PRESENT APPOINTMENT: Commanding Officer, HMS Resolution
DATE OF BIRTH: 23 May, 1929
EDUCATION: Roundhay School, Leeds; Beckenham Grammer School
DATES OF PROMOTIONS: 1961 Lieutenant Commander; 1968 Commander
PRINCIPAL COMMANDS AT SEA: 1961 HMS Artful; 1962 HMS Alaric; 1966-1967 HMS Olympus
OTHER PREVIOUS APPOINTMENTS OF NOTE: Joined Submarines 1953
OFFICIAL ADDRESS: HMS Neptune, BFPO Ships, London
PRIVATE ADDRESS: 4 Beech Grove, Rhil, Dunbartonshire

U.S.A.
PAYNE, REAR-ADMIRAL (SELECTEE) CHARLES NORVILLE, JNR., (ENGINEERING DUTY)
CURRENT DUTY STATION: Commander, Charleston Naval Shipyard; Supervisor of Shipbuilding, Conversion and Repair, 6th Naval District; and Staff, Commandant 6th Naval District (June 1968)
DATE OF BIRTH: 1919
EDUCATION: 1942 Naval Academy; 1948 Massachusetts Institute of Technology 1948; 1963 Naval War College
DATE OF COMMISSION: 19th December, 1941
PROMOTED TO: Rear Admiral selected for promotion on 6th June, 1969
OFFICIAL ADDRESS: Naval Shipyard, South Carolina
HOME ADDRESS: Arcadia, Louisiana

U.S.A.
PEARSON, REAR-ADMIRAL HELMER SHEPPARD, US NAVY
CURRENT DUTY STATION: Deputy Chief, Office of Engineering, Coast Guard Headquarters (July 1968)
DATE OF BIRTH: 1916
EDUCATION: 1941 Coast Guard Academy; 1943 Massachusetts Institute of Technology; 1949 Massachusetts Institute of Technology
FIRST COMMISSIONED: 19th May, 1941
PROMOTED TO: Rear Admiral 31st January, 1969
COMMANDS: 1945-1946 Mobile Loran Detachments "H" and "G"; 1950-1953 Electronics Engineering Station, Wildwood; 1953-1955 Yamacraw; 1960-1963 Coast Guard Mediterranean Section Office, Naples; 1963-1965 Duane

U.S.A.
PEARSON, REAR-ADMIRAL RUGUS JUDSON, JNR., (MEDICAL CORPS.)
CURRENT DUTY STATION: Attending Physician to Congress (November 1966); additional duty: Staff National Naval Medical Center, Bethesda, Maryland (November 1968)
DATE OF BIRTH: 1915
EDUCATION: University of Florida, Emory University, Atlanta, Georgia,
DATE OF COMMISSION: 13th May, 1942
PROMOTED TO: Rear Admiral 20th March, 1967
OFFICIAL ADDRESS: The Capitol, Washington, DC 20515
HOME ADDRESS: Coral Gables, Florida

AUSTRALIA
PEEK, REAR-ADMIRAL R. I.
DECORATIONS: OBE 1944; DSC 1945; US Legion of Merit 1952
PRESENT APPOINTMENT: Second Naval Member A.C.N.B. April 1968
DATE OF BIRTH: 30 July 1914
EDUCATION: R.A.N.C.
DATES OF PROMOTIONS: 1954 Captain; 1964 Rear-Admiral
PRINCIPAL COMMANDS AT SEA: 1951 S.O. 1st Frigate Squadron; 1956-1958 Captain DIO in Tobruk; 1962 Sydney; 1962-1963 Melbourne
OTHER PREVIOUS APPOINTMENTS OF NOTE: 4th Naval Member 1964; D.C.N.S. 1965-1966; FOCAF 1967
OFFICIAL ADDRESS: Navy Office Canberra A.C.T. 653358
PRIVATE ADDRESS: 6 Penrhyn Street, Red Hill A.C.T.

U.S.A.
PEET, REAR-ADMIRAL RAYMOND EDWARD
CURRENT DUTY STATION: Director, Office of Program Appraisal, Navy Department (June 1969)
BORN: 1921
EDUCATION: 1942 Naval Academy; 1948 Naval Postgraduate School; 1965 National War College
DATE OF COMMISSION: 19th June 1942
PROMOTED TO: Rear Admiral 1st July 1967
COMMANDS: 1956-1957 Barton DD 722; 1963-1964 Bainbridge DLGN 25; 1967-1968 Amphibious Group 2
OFFICIAL ADDRESS: The Pentagon, Washington, DC 20350
HOME ADDRESS: 18 Ely Street, Binghamton, New York

ARGENTINE
PERALTA, REAR ADMIRAL C. F.,
DECORATIONS: Cruz al Mérito Naval (Armada Espanola) Medalla Naval Conmemorativa del 5 Centenario de la Muerte del Infante D. Enrique (Marina de Portugal)
PRESENT APPOINTMENT: Director, Escuela de Guerra Naval 1968
DATE OF BIRTH: 5 April 1920
EDUCATION: Colegio Nacional de Buenos Aires; Escuela Naval Militar; Escuela de Aplicación para Oficiales; Escuela de Guerra Naval
DATES OF PROMOTIONS: Guardiamarina 1942; Teniente de Corbeta 1944; Teniente de Fragata 1946; Teniente de Navío 1948; Capitán de Corbeta 1952; Capitán de Fragata 1956; Capitán de Navío 1962; Rear Admiral 31 December, 1967
PRINCIPAL COMMANDS AT SEA: Comandante de la Escuadrilla de Lanchas Torpederas 1956; Comandante Fragata ARA Azopardo 1961; Comandante del Destructor ARA Rosales 1961-1962
OTHER PREVIOUS APPOINTMENTS OF NOTE: Director of the School of Naval Mechanics 1963-1965; Chief of Staff to the Fleet 1967
OFFICIAL ADDRESS: Avenida del Libertador 8071, Buenos Aires Argentine
PRIVATE ADDRESS: Floreniro Sarchez 1921, Vincent Lopez, Provincia de Buenos Aires

ITALY
PERONA, GENERAL ISPETTORE L. ITALIAN NAVY
DECORATIONS: Grande Officiale; 1 Croce al merito di guerra Medaglia comm guerra 1940-1943; Medaglia comm. guerra liberazione 1943-1945 (2 Campagne); Croce d'oro anzianità di servicio (40 years)
PRESENT APPOINTMENT: Vice Direttore Generale Navalcostarmi
DATE OF BIRTH: 5 December, 1913
DATE OF PROMOTION: 31 December, 1966
OFFICIAL ADDRESS: Navalcostarini, Rome

U.S.A.
PERRY, REAR-ADMIRAL (SELECTEE) OLIVER HAZARD
CURRENT DUTY STATION:
Deputy Director, National Military Command Center (July 1969)
DATE OF BIRTH: 1921
EDUCATION: 1944 Naval Academy; 1957 Armed Forces Staff College
DATE OF COMMISSION: 9th June 1943
PROMOTED TO: Rear Admiral selected for promotion on 6th June 1969
COMMANDS: 1954-1956 Bream SSK-243; 1956-1957 Caiman SS-323; 1961-1963 Theodore Roosevelt SSBN-600; 1964-1965 Sam Rayburn SSBN 635
OFFICIAL ADDRESS: The Pentagon, Washington, DC 20301
HOME ADDRESS: 895 North Belvedere, Memphis, Tennessee

U.K.
PERTWEE, CAPTAIN J. W. M., ROYAL NAVY
PRESENT APPOINTMENT: In Command HMS Euryalus
DATE OF PROMOTION: Captain 31 December, 1964
PRINCIPAL COMMANDS AT SEA: HMS Jaguar; HMS Carysfort
OTHER PREVIOUS APPOINTMENTS OF NOTE: Naval Staff Course 1954; Joint Services Staff Course 1961; Commander of BRNE Dartmouth 1962-1964; Commander Naval Forces C/Borneo 1964-1965
OFFICIAL ADDRESS: HMS Eurylaus, BFPO Ships
PRIVATE ADDRESS: Hilston, Denmead, Nr. Portsmouth, Hampshire

U.S.A.
PETROVIC, REAR-ADMIRAL WILLIAM FRANCIS (ENGINEERING DUTY)
CURRENT DUTY STATION: Commander, Puget Sound Naval Shipyard (March 1967)
DATE OF BIRTH: 1913
EDUCATION: 1935 Naval Academy; 1941 Naval Postgraduate School
DATE OF COMMISSION: 5th June 1935
PROMOTED TO: Rear Admiral 1st August 1963
COMMANDS: 1960-1962 Naval Repair Facility, San Diego; 1966 New York Naval Shipyard
OFFICIAL ADDRESS: Naval Shipyard, Bremerton, Washington 98314
HOME ADDRESS: Cleveland, Ohio

NORWAY
PETTERSEN, COMMODORE T., ROYAL NORWEGIAN NAVY
DECORATIONS: St. Olavs Medal with oakleaves 1945; Member of the Order of the British Empire 1942; Knight Commander of the Victoria Order 1962; Various decorations from other Nations
PRESENT APPOINTMENT: Chief of Naval Logistics Services
EDUCATION: Naval College R. No. N; Long torpedo course H.M.S. Vernon; Various qualifying schools & courses
DATE OF PROMOTION: 1959 Commodore
PRINCIPAL COMMANDS AT SEA: 1951-1952 Fishery Protection Squadron; 1952-1953 Frigates
OTHER PREVIOUS APPOINTMENTS OF NOTE: Director of Plans and Policy Section Naval Headquarters 1954-1955; Staff Officer Shape 1954-1957; Director for Technical Section N.H.Q. 1957-1960; Chief of Staff Logistics N.H.Q. 1960-1962
OFFICIAL ADDRESS: Naval Logistics Services, Haakonsvern, 5070 Mathopen, Norway
PRIVATE ADDRESS: Same as Official Address

AUSTRALIA
PHILPOTT, MR. T. S., AUSTRALIAN NAVY
DECORATIONS: OBE 1965
PRESENT APPOINTMENT: First Assistant Secretary (Establishments and General) 1964
DATE OF BIRTH: 1 March, 1918
EDUCATION: B.A. (Hons) University of Melbourne; Imperial Defence College 1962
OTHER PREVIOUS APPOINTMENTS OF NOTE: Deputy Secretary 1959-1964
OFFICIAL ADDRESS: Department of the Navy, Russell Offices, Canberra A.C.T. *Telephone:* 653203
PRIVATE ADDRESS: Flat 7/1 Northbourne Flats, Canberra A.C.T.

U.S.A.
PICKETT, REAR-ADMIRAL, BEN BROWN
CURRENT DUTY STATION:
Director, Fleet Readiness & Training Division, Office of the Chief of Naval Operations (July 1969)
DATE OF BIRTH: 1915
EDUCATION: 1938 Naval Academy; 1945 Naval Postgraduate School; 1950 Armed Forces Staff College; 1957 National War College
DATE OF COMMISSION: 2nd June 1938
PROMOTED TO: Rear Admiral 19th August 1965
COMMANDS: 1946-1948 Winslow AG 127; 1953-1955 Gyatt DD 712; 1962-1964 Albany CG 10; 1964-1965 Naval Weapons Station, Yorktown, Virginia; 1965-1966 Cruiser-Destroyer Flotilla 4
OFFICIAL ADDRESS: The Pentagon, Washington, DC 20350
HOME ADDRESS: Pocahontas, Arkansas

ITALY
PIGHINI, ADMIRAL G., ITALIAN NAVY
DECORATIONS: Medaglie d'Argento al VM; 2 Medaglie di Bronzo al VM; 4 Croci di Guerra al VM; 4 Croci di Guerra al VM; Commendatore dell' Ordine al Merito della Repubblica Italiana Medaglia Manriziana al mento di 10 Instri di carriera Militare
PRESENT APPOINT: General Staff of Defence
DATE OF BIRTH: 1 April, 1911
DATE OF PROMOTION: Ammiraglio di Squadra 31 December, 1968
OFFICIAL ADDRESS: Stato Maggiole della Difesa, 11, Via XX Settembre, 00187, Rome

FINLAND
PIRHONEN, REAR ADMIRAL J. K. E., FINNISH NAVY
DECORATIONS: Mmr 2; SL KI; VR 4; VR 3 tlk; VR 2; SVR 1
PRESENT APPOINTMENT: Commander in Chief, Naval Forces 7 August, 1966
DATE OF BIRTH: 13 December, 1915
EDUCATION: Naval Academy 1935-1937; War College (Naval Section) 1948-1949
DATES OF PROMOTIONS: Sub Lieutenant 1935; Lieutenant 1939; Lieutenant Commander 1941; Commander 1944; Captain 1956; Commodore 1961; Rear Admiral 1966
PRINCIPAL COMMANDS AT SEA: Commanding Officer, Naval Squadron 1964-1966
OFFICIAL ADDRESS: Naval hg., Helsinki 16

UNITED KINGDOM
PLACE, REAR-ADMIRAL B. C. G., ROYAL NAVY
DECORATIONS: V.C. 1943; D.S.C. 1943; Polish Cross of Valour 1941
DATE OF BIRTH: 19 July, 1921
PRESENT APPOINTMENT: Admiral Commanding Reserves and Director General of Naval Recruiting February 1968
EDUCATION: RNC, Dartmouth
DATES OF PROMOTIONS: 1952 Commander, 1958 Captain; 1968 Rear-Admiral
PRINCIPAL COMMANDS AT SEA: 1942 HMS X4 and X7; 1955-1956 HMS Tumult; 1957-1958 HMS Corunna; 1962-1963 HMS Rothesay and 25th Destroyer Squadron; 1964-1967 HMS Albion
OTHER PREVIOUS APPOINTMENTS OF NOTE: CSO to FOAC 1958-1960; Captain HMS Ganges 1963-1965
OFFICIAL ADDRESS: Old Admiralty Building, Ministry of Defence, Whitehall S.W.1. *Telephone:* 930 9000 ext. 378
PRIVATE ADDRESS: The Old Bakery, Corton Denham, Sherborne, Dorset

PLATE, REAR-ADMIRAL DOUGLAS CAULFIELD
CURRENT DUTY STATION: Commander, Mine Force, Atlantic Fleet (November 1968)
DATE OF BIRTH: 1920
EDUCATION: 1941 Naval Academy; 1953 Naval War College; 1960 Industrial College of the Armed Forces
DATE OF COMMISSION: 19th December, 1941
PROMOTED TO: Rear Admiral 1st May, 1968
COMMANDS: 1955-1956 Everett F. Larson DDR 830; 1958-1959 Mitscher DL 2; 1964-1965 DLG 20;1965-1967 Naval Destroyer School, Newport; 1967-1968 Cruiser-Destroyer Flotilla 2
OFFICIAL ADDRESS: Charleston, South Carolina 29408
HOME ADDRESS: Gracemere, Tarrytown, New York

UNITED KINGDOM
PLUGGE, CAPTAIN R. F., ROYAL NAVY
DECORATIONS: D.S.C. 1944
PRESENT APPOINTMENT: Commanding Officer, HMS Blake 1968
EDUCATION: Britannia RNC Dartmouth
DATES OF PROMOTIONS: Commander 1953; Captain 1961
PRINCIPAL COMMANDS AT SEA: 1943-1946 Senior Officer MTB Flotillas; 1949-1951 Senior Officer MTB Flotillas; 1957-1959 HMS Barrosa; 1964-1965 HMS Galatea
OTHER PREVIOUS APPOINTMENTS OF NOTE: Captain (D) 29th Escort Squadron 1964-1965; Deputy Director of Operations 1961-1963; Commanding Officer, HMS Terror, Singapore 1966-1968
OFFICIAL ADDRESS: HMS Blake, BFPO Ships, London
PRIVATE ADDRESS: 5 The Parade, HM Dockyard, Portsmouth

U.S.A.
POIX, REAR-ADMIRAL VINCENT PAUL DE (NAVAL AVIATOR) US NAVY
CURRENT DUTY STATION: Deputy Director (Administration, Evaluation and Management), Office of the Director of Defense Research and Engineering (February 1969)
DATE OF BIRTH: 1916
EDUCATION: 1939 Naval Academy; 1945 Naval Academy, Naval Postgraduate School; 1946 Naval Training Schools, Massachusetts Institute of Technology; 1964 National War College
FIRST COMMISSIONED: 1st June, 1939
PROMOTED TO: Rear Admiral 1st July, 1965
COMMANDS: 1948 Fighting Squadron 18A; 1948-1950 Fighting Squadron 172; 1957-1959 Air Development Squadron 4; 1959 Albemarle AV 5; 1960-1961 Enterprise CVA (N) 65; 1961-1963 Enterprise CVA (N) 65; 1966-1967 Carrier Division 7
HOME ADDRESS: 2782 North Wakefield Street, Arlington, Virginia 22207

NEW ZEALAND
PORRITT, HIS EXCELLENCY SIR A., NEW ZEALAND
DECORATIONS: Bt.; GCMG; KCVO; CBE
PRESENT APPOINTMENT: Governor-General and Commander-in-Chief, New Zealand, December 1967
DATE OF BIRTH: 10 August, 1900
EDUCATION: Wanganui Collegiate School, NZ; Otago University NZ; Oxford University & St. Mary's Hospital London
OTHER PREVIOUS APPOINTMENTS OF NOTE: Surgeon, appointments included Surgeon to H.M. Household; Sergeant-Surgeon to The Queen
OFFICIAL ADDRESS: Government House, Wellington, New Zealand

CHILE
PORTA ANGULO, VICE ADMIRAL F., CHILEAN NAVY
DECORATIONS: Estrella Militar for 15 years service (Chile 1946; Medalla Conmemorativa del Primer Centenario de la Fundación de Punta Arenas, awarded by the 1. Municipalidad de Magallanes (Chile) 1950; Condecoracion de la Orden al Mérito Naval en el grado de Comendador (Argentine) 1952; Estrella al Mérito Militar, for 20 years service (Chile) 1953; HM Elizabeth II Coronation Medal (England) 1953; Gran Estrella al Mérito Militar, for 30 years service (Chile) 1960
PRESENT APPOINTMENT: Condecoración Presidente de la República (Chile) 1965
PRESENT APPOINTMENT: Commander in Chief of the Armada 17 December, 1968
DATE OF BIRTH: 30 June, 1913;
EDUCATION: Escuela Naval; Royal Naval College, Greenwich; Panamá; Academia de Guerra Naval; Academia de Defensa Nacional
DATES OF PROMOTIONS: Guardiamraina de 2a Clase 1 January, 1932; Guardiamarina de la Clase 27 December, 1933; Teniente 2° 10 July, 1936; Teniente 10-10 July, 1940. Capitán de Corbeta 5 July, 1944; Capitan de Fragata 1 February, 1951; Capitán de Navío 12 November, 1957; Rear Admiral 16 March, 1965; Vice Admiral 30 October, 1968
PRINCIPAL COMMANDS AT SEA: RAM Janegueo 1945; RAM Cabrales 1948; RAM Colo-Colo 1949; DD Orella 1956-1957; AO Montt 1961; CL O'Higgins 1962; Comandancia en Jefe Escuadra 1968
OFFICIAL ADDRESS: Comandancia en Jefe de la Armada, Minsterio de Defensa Nacional, Santiago, Chile. *Telephone:* 68101
PRIVATE ADDRESS: Mariano sànchez Fontecilla 1552, Santiago. *Telephone:* 484264

UNITED KINGDOM
POWER, REAR-ADMIRAL A. M., ROYAL NAVY
DECORATIONS: M.B.E. 1952
PRESENT APPOINTMENT: Flag Officer Spithead 1969 and Admiral Superintendent Portsmouth 1968
DATE OF BIRTH: 18 June, 1921
EDUCATION: Rugby School
DATES OF PROMOTIONS: 1952 Commander; 1959 Captain; 1968 Rear-Admiral
PRINCIPAL COMMANDS AT SEA: 1955-1957 HMS Ursa; 1964-1965 HMS Rhyl; 1967-1968 HMS Bulwark
OTHER PREVIOUS APPOINTMENTS OF NOTE: Officer Commanding HMS Excellent 1965-1967
OFFICIAL ADDRESS: HM Dockyard, Portsmouth, Hants
PRIVATE ADDRESS: Gunnsmead, South Road, Portsmouth, Hants.

U.S.A.
PRATT, REAR-ADMIRAL RICHARD ROCKWELL
CURRENT DUTY STATION: Commander, Service Force, Atlantic Fleet (April 1969)
DATE OF BIRTH: 1914
EDUCATION: 1936 Naval Academy; 1950 Naval War College; 1960 National War College
DATE OF COMMISSION: 4th June, 1936
PROMOTED TO: Rear Admiral 1st June, 1964
COMMANDS: 1943-1946 Hudson DD 475; 1948-1949 Hank DD 702; 1955-1956 Destroyer Division 222;1960-1961 Norfolk DL 1; 1964-1965 Amphibious Group 3
MAJOR AWARDS: Navy Cross with Gold Star in lieu of second award
OFFICIAL ADDRESS: Norfolk, Virginia 23511
HOME ADDRESS: Wonalancet, New Hampshire

PRICE, REAR-ADMIRAL FRANK HOBLITZELL, JNR.
CURRENT DUTY STATION: Commander, Cruiser-Destroyer Flotilla 8 (September 1968)
DATE OF BIRTH: 1919
EDUCATION: 1941 Naval Academy; 1946 Naval Postgraduate School; 1957 National War College
DATE OF COMMISSION: 7th February, 1941
PROMOTED TO: Rear Admiral 1st August 1968
COMMANDS: 1951-1953 Beale DDE 471; 1959-1960 Destroyer Division 362; 1963-1966 Long Beach CGN 9
OFFICIAL ADDRESS: FPO New York 09501
HOME ADDRESS: 5105 Danbury Road, Bethesda, Maryland

U.S.A.
PRINS, REAR-ADMIRAL PAUL GELEFF, US NAVY
CURRENT DUTY STATION: Commander, 7th Coast Guard District, Miami (April 1967)
DATE OF BIRTH: 1913
EDUCATION: 1937 Coast Guard Academy
FIRST COMMISSIONED: 20th September, 1937
COMMANDS: 1946 Merrill and Escort Division 45; 1954-1956 Mendota; 1960-1963 Courier

U.S.A.
PUGH, REAR-ADMIRAL (SELECTEE) PAUL EDWARD (NAVAL AVIATOR)
CURRENT DUTY STATION: Deputy for Current Operations; Operations Division, Staff, Commander-in-Chief Pacific (August 1967)
DATE OF BIRTH: 1918
EDUCATION: 1941 University of California; 1952 General Line School; 1955 Naval War College; 1963 Industrial College of the Armed Forces
DATE OF COMMISSION: 10th October, 1941
PROMOTED TO: Rear Admiral, selected for promotion on 6th June 1969
COMMANDS: 1955-1957 Fighter Squadron 211; 1957-1958 Carrier Air Group 21; 1965-1966 Eldorado AGC 11; 1966-1967 Kitty Hawk CVA 63 and Attack Carrier Striking Group 77.5
OFFICIAL ADDRESS: (Camp Smith, Oahu, Hawaii), FPO San Francisco, California 96610
HOME ADDRESS: 9207 Gunn Avenue, Whittier, California

U.S.A.
PUGH, REAR-ADMIRAL (SELECTEE) WILIIAM MARR, II
CURRENT DUTY STATION: Deputy Director, Antisubmarine Warfare Programs, Office of the Chief of Naval Operations (October 1968)
DATE OF BIRTH: 1920
EDUCATION: 1942 Naval Academy; 1958 Naval War College; 1949 and 1951 Naval Postgraduate School
DATE OF COMMISSION: 19th December, 1941
PROMOTED TO: Rear Admiral, selected for promotion on 6th June, 1969
COMMANDS: 1952-1954 Uedregal SS 480; 1959-1960 Submarine Division 81; 1964-1965 Holland AS 32; 1967-1968 Submarine Development Group 2
OFFICIAL ADDRESS: The Pentagon, Washington D.C. 20350
HOME ADDRESS: 505 W. 25th Street, Wilmington, Delaware

U.S.A.
RAFETTO, REAR-ADMIRAL EDWARD CHARLES (DENTAL CORPS.)
CURRENT DUTY STATION: Assistant Chief for Dentistry and Chief, Dental Division, Bureau of Medicine and Surgery (July 1968)
DATE OF BIRTH: 1912
EDUCATION: University of Pennsylvania 1935
DATE OF COMMISSION: 5th October, 1936
PROMOTED TO: Rear Admiral 1st August, 1963
OFFICIAL ADDRESS: Potomac Annex, Washington, D.C. 20390
HOME ADDRESS: 115 Main Street, Manasquan, New Jersey

U.K.
RAM, COMMANDER T. G. A., ROYAL NAVY
PRESENT APPOINTMENT: HMS Hermione in Command
DATE OF BIRTH: 19 June 1930
EDUCATION: Eton College, special entry in 1948
DATE OF PROMOTION: Commander 30 December, 1966
PREVIOUS APPOINTMENT OF NOTE: Sub specialised in Gunnery 1957; Gunnery Officer HMS Centaur 1962-1963; First Lieutenant HMS Rhyl 1965-1966
PRIVATE ADDRESS: Carpenters, Finchdean, Horndean, Hants.

U.S.A.

RAMAGE, REAR ADMIRAL, JAMES DAVID (NAVAL AVIATOR)
CURRENT DUTY STATION: Deputy Chief of Staff for Plans and Operations, Commander-in-Chief, Pacific Fleet (October 1967)
DATE OF BIRTH: 1916
EDUCATION: 1939 Naval Academy; 1958 National War College; 1963 Naval Postgraduate School
DATE OF COMMISSION: 1st June, 1939
PROMOTED TO: Rear Admiral 1st July, 1967
COMMANDS: 1943-1944 Bombing Squadron 10;1944-1946 Bombing Squadron 98; 1952-1954 Carrier Air Group 19; 1954-1955 Composite Squadron 3; Transitional Training Unit, Pacific Fleet; 1958-1960 Heavy Attack Wing 1; 1960-1961 Salisbury Sound AV 13; 1963-1964 Independence CVA 62; 1967 Fleet Air, Whidbey; Fleet Air Wing 4
OFFICIAL ADDRESS: (Pearl Harbor), FPO San Francisco, California 96610
HOME ADDRESS: Honolulu, Hawaii

U.S.A.

RAMAGE, VICE-ADMIRAL LAWSON PATERSON
CURRENT DUTY STATION: Commander, Military Sea Transportation Service (March 1967)
DATE OF BIRTH: 1909
EDUCATION: 1931 Naval Academy; 1939 Naval Postgraduate School; 1950 Armed Forces Staff College; 1955 Naval War College
DATE OF COMMISSION: 4th June 1931
PROMOTED TO: Rear Admiral 1st July 1956; Vice Admiral 15th July, 1963
COMMANDS: 1942-1943 Trout SS 202;1943-1944 Parche SS 384; 1946-1947 Submarine Division 52; 1951-1953 Submarine Squadron 6; 1953-1954 Rankin AKA 103; 1958-1959 Cruiser Division 2; 1964-1966 First Fleet
MAJOR AWARDS: Medal of Honor, Navy Cross with Gold Star in lieu of second award
OFFICIAL ADDRESS: Washington, D.C. 20390
HOME ADDRESS: New London, Connecticut

UNITED KINGDOM

RAPER, VICE-ADMIRAL R. G., ROYAL NAVY
DECORATIONS: C.B. 1968
PRESENT APPOINTMENT: Director General Ships 1 May 1968, Chief Naval Engineer Officer 21 February, 1968
DATE OF BIRTH: 27 August, 1915
EDUCATION: RNC Dartmouth, RNEC Keyham and RNC Greenwich
DATES OF PROMOTIONS: 1966 Rear-Admiral; 1968 Vice Admiral
PRINCIPAL APPOINTMENTS AT SEA: 1940 Senior Engineer, HMS Edinburgh until sunk in 1942; 1952-1954 Engineer Officer, HMS Birmingham (Korea)
OTHER PREVIOUS APPOINTMENTS OF NOTE: Appointments in Admiralty Design Dept. 1948-1951; 1955-1957; 1962-1964; IDC 1958; Command of HMS Caledonia Apprentice Training 1959-1960; Director of Marine Engineering 1966-1968
OFFICIAL ADDRESS: Block 'G', Ministry of Defence Offices, Foxhill, Bath
PRIVATE ADDRESS: Innocks Lodge, Hinton Charterhouse, near Bath

U.S.A.

RAPP, REAR-ADMIRAL (SELECTEE) WILLIAM THEODORE, (NAVAL AVIATOR)
CURRENT DUTY STATION: Commander, Patrol Force, 7th Fleet; Commander, US Taiwan Patrol Force; Commander, Fleet Air Wing 1 (July 1968) Authorized to assume title of Rear Admiral
DATE OF BIRTH: 1920
EDUCATION: 1943 Naval Academy; 1962 Naval War College; 1964 Naval Postgraduate School
DATE OF COMMISSION: 19th June 1942
PROMOTED TO: Rear Admiral, selection approved 6th June, 1968
COMMANDS: 1958-1960 Patrol Squadron 10; 1964-1965 Rankin AKA 103; 1966-1967 Fleet Air Wing 3
OFFICIAL ADDRESS: FPO Seattle, Washington 98770
HOME ADDRESS: 238 North Munn Avenue, East Orange, New Jersey

U.K.

RAWBONE, CAPTAIN A. R., ROYAL NAVY
DECORATIONS: AFC 1951
PRESENT APPOINTMENT: HMS Dido 1 June, 1968
DATE OF BIRTH: 19 April, 1923
EDUCATION: Saltley Grammar School, Birmingham
PRINCIPAL COMMANDS AT SEA: 897 Squadron 1953-1955; Loch Killisport 1959-1960; Dido 1968-1969
DATES OF PROMOTIONS: Commander 31 December, 1958; Captain 31 December, 1964
OTHER PREVIOUS APPOINTMENT OF NOTE: Commanding Officer, 736 Squadron 1953-1955; JSSC 1958-1959; Commander (Air), Lossiemouth 1961-1962; Commander (Air), Ark Royal 1962-1963; CSO (air) to Fonac 1965-1967
OFFICIAL ADDRESS: HMS Dido, BFPO, Ships
PRIVATE ADDRESS: 32 Monckton Road, Alverstoke, Gosport, Hants.

NIGERIA

RAWE, CAPTAIN, R. J., NIGERIAN NAVY:
DECORATIONS: M.B.E. 1963; O.B.E. 1966
PRESENT APPOINTMENT: Chief of Staff (N.H.Q.) January 1968
DATE OF BIRTH: 14 July, 1925
EDUCATION: St. Aloysius College; Chelsea College of Technology and Science
DATES OF PROMOTIONS: Commander 28 January, 1965; Ag. Captain 13 April, 1968
PRINCIPAL COMMANDS AT SEA: 1957-1959 Survey Ship Pathfinder; 1960 NNS Nigeria (Algerine)
OTHER PREVIOUS APPOINTMENTS OF NOTE: Command of Naval Base, Apapa 1964-1969
OFFICIAL ADDRESS: Naval Headquarters, Apapa *Telephone:* 45194
PRIVATE ADDRESS: Naval Headquarters, Apapa *Telephone:* 46641

U.S.A.

REA, REAR-ADMIRAL WILLIAM FREELAND, US NAVY
CURRENT DUTY STATION: Commander, 9th Coast Guard District, Cleveland (July 1968)
DATE OF BIRTH: 1918
EDUCATION: 1938 Mississippi State College, 1941 Coast Guard Academy
FIRST COMMISSIONED: 19th December, 1941
PROMOTED TO: Rear Admiral 1st July, 1968
COMMANDS: 1953-1954 Koiner, 1958-1960 Tamaroa; 1964-1967 Marine Inspection Office, New York

U.S.A.

REICH, REAR-ADMIRAL ELI THOMAS
CURRENT DUTY STATION: Deputy Comptroller of the Navy (October 1967)
DATE OF BIRTH: 1913
EDUCATION: 1935 Naval Academy; 1950 Armed Forces Staff College; 1956 Industrial College of the Armed Forces
DATE OF COMMISSION: 6th June 1935
PROMOTED TO: Rear Admiral 1st February 1963
COMMANDS: 1944 Sealion SS 315; 1945 Compton DD 705; 1948-1949 Officer-in-charge, Submarine Functional Training Unit, Naval Group, American Mission for Aid to Turkey; 1951-1952 Stoddard DD 566; 1956-1957 Submarine Squadron 8; 1957-1958 Aucilla AO 56; 1960-1961 Canberra CAG 2; 1965-1967 Anti-Submarine Warfare Group 5
MAJOR AWARDS: Navy Cross with two Gold Stars in lieu of subsequent awards
OFFICIAL ADDRESS: The Pentagon, Washington, D.C. 20350
HOME ADDRESS: 2810 36th Place N.W.3, Washington, D.C.

U.S.A.

RENKEN, REAR-ADMIRAL HENRY ALGERNON
CURRENT DUTY STATION: Commandant, 9th Naval District (September 1967)
DATE OF BIRTH: 1908
EDUCATION: Naval Academy 1931; 1939 General Line School; 1945 Naval War College
DATE OF COMMISSION: 4th June, 1931
PROMOTED TO: Rear Admiral 1st October, 1959
COMMANDS: 1942-1944 Hambleton DMS 20; 1949-1950 Destroyer Division 102; 1955-1956 Mt. McKinley AGC 7; 1956-1957 Northampton CLC 1; 1960-1962 Service Squadron 3; 1965-1967 Service Force, Atlantic Fleet
OFFICIAL ADDRESS: Great Lakes, Illinois 60088
HOME ADDRESS: 5924 Oak Place, Bethesda, Maryland

SWEDEN

RHEBORG, COMMODORE Rolf S:son, ROYAL SWEDISH NAVY
DECORATIONS: R.S.O.; LKrVA; LKÖS
PRESENT APPOINTMENT: C-in-C Royal Swedish Naval College 1969
EDUCATION: Staff course MHS
DATE OF PROMOTIONS: 1943 Sub-lieutenant; Lieutenant Commander 1952; Commander 1960; 1963 Captain; 1969 Commodore
PRINCIPAL COMMANDS AT SEA: 1950, 1952, 1953 Captain S/M; 1964-1965 Captain S/M Flotilla
OTHER PREVIOUS APPOINTMENTS OF NOTE: Teacher in Naval Tacties; Royal Sw Naval Academy; Head of Planning Division Naval Staff 1966-1969
OFFICIAL ADDRESS: Royal Swedish Naval College, 183 03 Täby, Sweden *Telephone:* 08/765 02 40
PRIVATE ADDRESS Öingvägen38, 181 33 Lidingö Sweden

U.S.A.

RICE, REAR-ADMIRAL JOSEPH ENOCH (ENGINEERING DUTY)
CURRENT DUTY STATION: Commander, Naval Electronic Systems Command (May 1966)
DATE OF BIRTH: 1914
EDUCATION: 1936 Naval Academy; 1944 Naval Postgraduate School
DATE OF COMMISSION: 4th June, 1936
PROMOTED TO: Rear Admiral 1st May, 1964
COMMANDS: Industrial Manager, 10th Naval District 1952-1954; 1961-1964 Philadelphia Naval Shipyard and Industrial Manager, 4th Naval District; 1964-1965 Industrial Manager, Potomac River Naval Command; 1965-1966 Industrial Manager/Commander, Naval Shore Electronics Engineering Center and Assistant Chief, Bureau of Ships for Shore Electronics, Naval District, Washington, D.C.
OFFICIAL ADDRESS: Main Navy Building, Washington, DC 20360
HOME ADDRESS: 908 West Whitner Street, Anderson, South Carolina

U.S.A.

RICHARDSON, VICE-ADMIRAL DAVID CHARLES (NAVY AVIATOR) US NAVY
CURRENT DUTY STATION: Commander, Sixth Fleet (August 1968)
DATE OF BIRTH: 1914
EDUCATION: 1936 Naval Academy; 1946 Royal Naval Staff College; 1947 Naval War College
DATE OF COMMISSION: 4th June, 1936
PROMOTED TO: Rear Admiral 1st June, 1964; Vice Admiral 14th August, 1968
COMMANDS: Fighting Squadron 1 1944-1945; 1948-1949 Carrier Air Group 13; 1959-1960 Cimarron AO 22; 1960-1961 Hornet CVS 12; 1964-1966 Fleet Air Norfolk; Naval Air Bases, 4th and 5th Naval Districts; 1966 Carrier Division 7; 1966-1967 Carrier Division 5
OFFICIAL ADDRESS: FPO New York 09501

U.S.A.

RICHMOND, REAR-ADMIRAL CHESTER ARTHUR, JNR. (NAVAL AVIATOR) US NAVY
CURRENT DUTY STATION: Chief, Office of Research and Development, Coast Guard Headquarters (March 1969)
DATE OF BIRTH: 1917
EDUCATION: 1941 Coast Guard Academy; 1943 Naval Air Section, Pensacola; 1953 Navy Test Pilot School
FIRST COMMISSIONED: 19th May, 1941
PROMOTED TO: Rear Admiral 1st August, 1969
COMMANDS: 1945-1947 Coast Guard Air Detachment, Honolulu; 1959-1962 Coast Guard Air Detachment, Kodiak; 1962-1965 Air Station, St. Petersburg
HOME ADDRESS: 3131 Valley Lane, Falls Church, Va.

U.S.A.

RICKOVER, VICE-ADMIRAL HYMAN GEORGE (RETIRED) (ENGINEERING DDUTY) US Navy
CURRENT DUTY STATION: Director, Division of Naval Reactors, US Atomic Energy Commission (February 1949); additional duty: Deputy Commander for Nuclear Propulsion, Naval Ships Systems Command (May 1966)
DATE OF BIRTH: 1900
EDUCATION: 1922 Naval Academy; 1929 Naval Postgraduate School
DATE OF COMMISSION: 2nd June, 1922
PROMOTED TO: Rear Admiral 1st July 1953; Vice Admiral 24th October, 1958
COMMANDS: 1937 Fincham 9; 1945 US Naval Repair Base, Okinawa; Industrial Manager, Naval Operating Base, Okinawa
OFFICIAL ADDRESS: Main Navy Building, Washington, DC 20360
HOME ADDRESS: 4801 Connecticut Avenue, Washington, DC

UNITED KINGDOM
RIDLEY, REAR-ADMIRAL W. T. C., ROYAL NAVY
DECORATIONS: C.B. 1968; O.B.E. 1954
PRESENT APPOINTMENT: Admiral Superintendent, Rosyth 1966
DATE OF BIRTH: 9 March, 1915
EDUCATION: RN College Dartmouth; RN Engineering College Keyham; RN College Greenwich
DATES OF PROMOTIONS: Commander 31 December, 1947; Captain 31 December, 1957; Rear-Admiral 7 July, 1966
PREVIOUS APPOINTMENTS OF NOTE: Seaslug Project Officer, RAE Farnborough 1950-1954; Deputy Technical Chief Executive Dreadnought Project 1958-1962; Commanding Officer RNEngineering College Mauadou 1962-1964
OFFICIAL ADDRESS: HM Dockyard, Rosyth, Fife
PRIVATE ADDRESS: Castlandhill House, Rosyth, Fife

U.S.A.

RIERA, REAR-ADMIRAL ROBERT EMMETT, (NAVAL AVIATORN) US NAVY
CURRENT DUTY STATION: Assistant Deputy Chief of Naval Operations (Fleet Operations and Readiness) (June 1968)
DATE OF BIRTH: 1912
EDUCATION: 1935 Naval Academy; 1942 Naval Postgraduate School; 1951 Naval War College
DATE OF COMMISSION: 6th June, 1935
PROMOTED TO: Rear Admiral 1st April, 1963
COMMANDS: 1942-1943 Bombing Squadron 23; 1944-1945 Carrier Air Group 11; 1947-1948 Battle Carrier Air Group 1; 1958-1960 Greenwich Bay AVP 41; 1960-1961 Forrestal CVA 59; 1963-1964 Carrier Division 14; 1964-1966 Alaskan Sea Frontier. Additional Duty: Fleet Air Alaska; Naval Air Bases, 17th Naval District; Commandant, 17th Naval District; 1966-1968 Fleet Air Mediterranean Naval Activities, Mediterranean
MAJOR AWARDS: Navy Cross
OFFICIAL ADDRESS: The Pentagon, Washington, DC 20350
HOME ADDRESS Winter Haven, Florida

U.S.A.
RIEVE, REAR-ADMIRAL ROLAND (SUPPLY CORPS.) US NAVY
CURRENT DUTY STATION:
Auditor General of the Navy; additional duty: Director, Naval Audit Service (June 1969)
DATE OF BIRTH: 1919
EDUCATION: 1941 Naval Academy; Naval Postgraduate School 1955; 1952 Armed Forces Staff College; 1962 Industrial College of the Armed Forces
DATE OF COMMISSION: 7th February 1941
PROMOTED TO: Rear Admiral 15th December, 1967
COMMANDS: 1966-1967 Naval Supply Depot, Subic Bay, Philippines
OFFICIAL ADDRESS: The Pentagon, Washington, DC 20350
HOME ADDRESS: 647 Wilkie Avenue, Dunedin, Florida

RINDSKOPF: REAR-ADMIRAL MAURICE HERBERT (US NAVY)
CURRENT DUTY STATION: Deputy Assistant Chief of Staff for Intelligence, Commander-in-Chief, Pacific Fleet (September 1967)
DATE OF BIRTH: 1917
EDUCATION: 1938 Naval Academy; 1957 Naval War College
DATE OF COMMISSION: 2nd June, 1938
PROMOTED TO: Rear Admiral 1st July, 1967
COMMANDS: 1944 Drum SS 228; 1947-1949 Sea Cat SS 399; 1953-1955 Higbee DDR 806; 1955-1956 Submarine Division 11; Officer-in-Charge, Submarine School, New London 1958-1960; 1960-1961 Fulton AS 11; 1963-1964 Submarine Flotilla 2; 1964-1965 Submarine Flotilla 8
MAJOR AWARDS: Navy Cross
OFFICIAL ADDRESS: (Pearl Harbor) FPO San Francisco 96610
HOME ADDRESS: Huntington, New York

UNITED KINGDOM
RITCHIE, REAR-ADMIRAL G. S., ROYAL NAVY
DECORATIONS: C.B. 1967; D.S.C. 1942
PRESENT APPOINTMENT: Hydrographer of the Navy January 1966
DATE OF BIRTH: 30 October, 1914
EDUCATION: RNC, Dartmouth
DATES OF PROMOTIONS: 1957 Captain; 1966 Rear-Admiral
PRINCIPAL COMMANDS AT SEA: 1951-1953 HM Surveying Ships Challenger; HMNZ Survey Ship Lachlan 1953-1957; 1959-1960 Dalrymple; 1964-1965 Vidal
OTHER PREVIOUS APPOINTMENTS OF NOTE: Assistant Hydrographer 1961-1963
OFFICIAL ADDRESS Hydrographic Dept. Ministry of Defence, Taunton
PRIVATE ADDRESS: Sharpe House, Wiveliscombe, Somerset

U.S.A.

RIVERO, ADMIRAL HORACIO, JNR., US NAVY
CURRENT DUTY STATION: Commander-in- Chief, Allied Forces, Southern Europe (February 1968)
DATE OF BIRTH: 1910
EDUCATION: 1931 Naval Academy; 1940 Naval Postgraduate School; 1953 National War College
DATE OF COMMISSION: 4th June, 1931; Rear Admiral 1st July, 1956; Vice Admiral 1st October, 1962; Admiral 31st July 1964
COMMANDS: 1948-1949 William C. Lawe DD 763; 1951-1952 Noble APA 218; 1957-1958 Destroyer Flotilla 1; 1962-1963 Amphibious Force, Atlantic Fleet
OFFICIAL ADDRESS: (Naples, Italy), FPO New York 09524

U.S.A.

ROBINSON, REAR-ADMIRAL (SELECTEE), REMBRANDT CECIL US NAVY
CURRENT DUTY STATION: Staff, Officer of the Joint Chiefs of Staff (January 1969)
DATE OF BIRTH: 1924
EDUCATION: 1944 Naval Reserve Midshipmen School; 1949 General Line School; 1957 Armed Forces Staff College
DATE OF COMMISSION: 26th October 1944
PROMOTED TO: Rear Admiral, selected for promotion on 6th June 1969
COMMANDS: 1959-1960 Charles Berry DE 1035; 1960-1962 Bradford DD 545; 1968-1969 Destroyer Squadron 31
OFFICIAL ADDRESS: The Pentagon, Washington, DC 20301
HOME ADDRESS: 830 Old Town Road, Clearfield, Pennsylvania

U.S.A.

ROEDER, VICE-ADMIRAL BERNARD FRANKLIN US NAVY
CURRENT DUTY STATION: Commander, First Fleet (July 1966)
DATE OF BIRTH: 1911
EDUCATION: 1931 Naval Academy; 1950 Naval War College
DATE OF COMMISSION: 4th June, 1931
PROMOTED TO: Rear Admiral 1st August, 1958; Vice Admiral 25th March, 1965
COMMANDS: 1947 Lowry DD 770; 1947 Collett DD 730; 1950-1951 Destroyer Division 112; 1954-1956 Pickaway APA 222; 1956 Transport Division 12; 1956-1957 Amphibious Squadron 1; 1960-1961 Amphibious Group 3; 1965-1966 Amphibious Force, Pacific Fleet
OFFICIAL ADDRESS: FPO San Francisco, California 96601
HOME ADDRESS: 3905 Ingomar Street, Washington, DC

U.K.
ROGERS, COMMANDER J. A., ROYAL NAVY
PRESENT APPOINTMENT: Senior Officer, 6th MCM Squadron 4 October, 1967, and Commanding Officer, HMS Maxton 6 May, 1969
DATE OF BIRTH: 24 September, 1926
DATE OF PROMOTION: Commander 31 December, 1967
PRINCIPAL COMMANDS AT SEA: HMS Caunton (CMS); HMS Murray (FF); HMS Houghton (CMS)
OFFICIAL ADDRESS: HMS Maxton, BFPO Ships

CHILE

ROMAN, VICE ADMIRAL R. CHILEAN NAVY
DECORATIONS: Medalla otorgada por la 1. Municipalided de Tome, for work performed after the earthquake of 1939; Estre la militar, for 15 years' service; Maltese Cross; Estrella al Mérito Militar, for 20 Years' service Gran Estrella al Mérito Militar, for 30 years' service Condecoración Presidente de la República; Cruz al Mérito Naval; Condecoración Cruz Peruana al Mérito Naval en el grado de Commendador Medalla Junta Interamericana de Defensa; Legión al Mérito en el grado de Oficial, awarded by the United States government of North America
PRESENT APPOINTMENT: Director General de los servicios de la Armada, 22 January, 1969
DATE OF BIRTH: 30 August, 1913
EDUCATION: Oficial de Estado Mayor
PRINCIPAL COMMANDS AT SEA: Comandante barcaza Goicolea 1948; Comandante RAM Huemil 1950; Comandante RAM Janequeo 1950; Crucero O'Higgins, Jefe Estado Mayor y Oficial de Operaciones de la Escuadra 1955; Comandante Fragata Bagnedano 1958; Crucero O'Higgins, Jefe Estado Mayor dela Escuadra 1959; Comandante del Petrolero Almirante Montt 1962
OTHER PREVIOUS APPOINTMENTS OF NOTE: Estado Mayor General de la Armada, Jefe depto. Misión Naval de Chile en Washington (EE UU de NA); Alumno Curso Comando Naval 1956; Misión Naval de Chile en Washington Alumno Curso Comando Naval, Estado Mayor de la Defensa Nacional, Jefe de Departamento 1957; Adicto Naval a las Embajadas de Chile en los EE UU y Canadá, Jefe de la misión Naval de Chile en Washington y Delegado de la Armada ante la Junta Interamericana de Defensa 1966; Jefe del Estado Mayor de la Armada 1968
OFFICIAL ADDRESS: Dirección gral, de los Servicios de la Armada, Prat 620-20 Piso. *Telephone:* 2441 Valparaiso
PRIVATE ADDRESS: Av. Jorge Montt 2730, Casa 7 (Las Salinas). *Telephone:* 81804 Vina del Mar

ITALY

ROSELLI LORENZINI, ADMIRAL G., ITALIAN NAVY
DECORATIONS: Knight of the Military Order of Italy; 2 silver medals awarded for valour; 5 bronze medals awarded for valour; 2 crosses for Distinguished Service in War; Grand Officer of the Order of Merit of the Italian Republic; Commendatore of the Order of the Italian Crown; Knight of the Colonial Order of the Italian Star; Gold medal fof long navigation in the Navy; Mauritius medal of merit for 50 years' military service; Gold cross for seniority in the service
PRESENT APPOINTMENT: Commander, Allied Naval Forces Southern Europe, Malta
DATE OF BIRTH: 17 March, 1910
DATES OF PROMOTIONS: Admiral (seniority) 20 January, 1965
OFFICIAL ADDRESS: Comnavsouth, Malta

U.S.A.

ROSENBERG, REAR ADMIRAL (SELECTEE) EDWIN MILLER
CURRENT DUTY STATION: Commander, Amphibious Group 3 (December 1968); Authorized to assume title of Rear Admiral
DATE OF BIRTH: 1919
EDUCATION: 1942 Naval Academy; 1961 Industrial College of the Armed Forces
DATE OF COMMISSION: 19th December, 1941
PROMOTED TO: Rear Admiral, selected for promotion 6th June 1968
COMMANDS: 1951-1953 J. Douglas Blackwood DE 219; 1954-1956 Burke DD 783; 1963-1964 Destroyer Division 232; 1966-1967 Canberra CAG 2
OFFICIAL ADDRESS: FPO San Francisco, California 96610
HOME ADDRESS: Sarpy County, Nebraska

U.S.A.

ROTRIGE, REAR-ADMIRAL HENRY JOHN (CHAPLAIN CORPS.) US NAVY
CURRENT DUTY STATION: Force Chaplain, Commander, Service Force Pacific; additional duty: Fleet Chaplain, Commander-in-Chief, Pacific Fleet (October 1968)
DATE OF BIRTH: 1912
EDUCATION: 1938 Kenrick Seminary, Webster Grove, Missouri
DATE OF COMMISSION: 9th March 1942
PROMOTED TO: Rear Admiral 1st July, 1964
OFFICIAL ADDRESS: (Pearl Harbor), FPO San Francisco, California 96610
HOME ADDRESS: St. Louis, Missouri

U.K.

ROXBURGH, REAR-ADMIRAL J. C. Y., ROYAL NAVY
DECORATIONS: C.B. 1969; C.B.E. 1967; D.S.O. 1943; D.S.C. 1942, Bar 1945
PRESENT APPOINTMENT: Flag Officer, Plymouth, Commander Eastern Atlantic Sub-Area, and Commander Plymouth Channel Sub-Area, 28 May, 1969
DATE OF BIRTH: 29 June, 1919
EDUCATION: Britannia RN College, Dartmouth
DATES OF PROMOTIONS: Cadet 1933; Midshipman 1937; Sub-Lieutenant 1939; Lieutenant 1941; Lieutenant-Commander 1949; Commander 1952; Captain 1958; Rear-Admiral 1967
PRINCIPAL COMMANDS AT SEA: HM S/M H.43 1942; HM S/M United 1943; HM S/M Tapir 1945; HM S/M Turpin 1950; HMS Contest 1957; HMS Adamant 1960 (Capt. S/M); HMS Eagle 1965
OTHER PREVIOUS APPOINTMENTS OF NOTE: Department of Naval Equipment, Bath, 1954; Executive Officer, HMS Triumph (Cadet Training Ship) 1955; Executive Officer, HMS Ark Royal 1956; British Joint Services Mission, Washington (S/M Staff Officer) 1958; Imperial Defence College 1962; Deputy Director Defence Plans (Navy) 1963; Flag Officer Sea Training 1967
OFFICIAL ADDRESS: Admiralty House, Mount Wise, Devonport

U.S.A.

RUBEL, REAR-ADMIRAL (SELECTEE) DAVID MICHAEL US NAVY
CURRENT DUTY STATION:
Commander, Amphibious Training Command, Pacific Fleet (July 1969)
DATE OF BIRTH: 1917
EDUCATION: Naval Academy 1941; 1966 National War College
DATE OF COMMISSION: 7th February, 1941
PROMOTED TO: Rear Admiral, selected for promotion on 6th June 1969
COMMANDS: 1945-1946 Laub DD 613; 1950-1952 George DE 697; 1952-1954 Theodore E. Chandler DD717; 1963-1964 Norfolk DL 1; 1964-1965 Destroyer Squadron 20
MAJOR AWARDS: Navy Cross
OFFICIAL ADDRESS: Naval Amphibious Base, Coronado, San Diego, California 92155
HOME ADDRESS: San Diego, California

U.S.A.

RUCKNER, REAR-ADMIRAL EDWARD ABERLE US NAVY
CURRENT DUTY STATION: Deputy Chief of Naval Operations (Development) (May 1967)
DATE OF BIRTH 1909
EDUCATION 1932 Naval Academy; 1941 Naval Postgraduate School; 1951 Naval War College
DATE OF COMMISSION: 2nd June, 1932
PROMOTED TO: Rear Admiral 1st October, 1960
COMMANDS: 1949-1950 Eugene A. Greene DD 711; 1955-1956 Mississippi EAG 128; 1956-1957 Destroyer Division 36; 1961-1962 Cruiser Divisiion I; 1962 Cruiser-Destroyer Flotilla II; 1965-1967 Cruiser-Destroyer Force, Atlanctic Fleet
OFFICIAL ADDRESS: The Pentagon, Washington, DC 20350
HOME ADDRESS: Westwood, New Jersey

U.S.A.

RUDDEN, REAR-ADMIRAL THOMAS JOSEPH, JNR., US NAVY
CURRENT DUTY STATION: Commander, Cruiser-Destroyer Flotilla 3 (January 1968)
DATE OF BIRTH: 1915
EDUCATION: 1939 Naval Academy; 1946 Naval Postgraduate School; 1955 Naval War College
DATE OF COMMISSION: 1st June 1939
PROMOTED TO: Rear Admiral 10th August 1965
COMMANDS: 1947-1948 McCook DMS 36; 1952-1954 Cassin Young DD 793; 1957-1959 Destroyer Division 252; 1963-1964 Galveston CLG 3
OFFICIAL ADDRESS FPO San Francisco, California 96601
HOME ADDRESS: 14 Marion Avenue, Newark, New Jersey

U.S.A.

SAGER, REAR-ADMIRAL JOHN PARKE (AERONAUTICAL ENGINEERING DUTY) US NAVY
CURRENT DUTY STATION:
Executive Director, Technical & Logistics Services, Defense Supply Agency (July 1969)
DATE OF BIRTH: 1912
EDUCATION: 1934 University of Michigan; 1935 Naval Postgraduate School
DATE OF COMMISSION: 1st December 1936
PROMOTED TO: Rear Admiral 1st October 1964
OFFICIAL ADDRESS: Alexandria, Virginia 22314
HOME ADDRESS: 105 Division Street, Petoskey, Michigan

U.S.A.

SALZER, REAR-ADMIRAL (SELECTEE) ROBERT SAMUEL US NAVY
CURRENT DUTY STATION: Project Officer of the Future Professional Manpower Requirements Study, Office of the Chief of Naval Operations (November 1968)
DATE OF BIRTH: 1919
EDUCATION: Yale University 1940; 1960 Industrial College of the Armed Forces; 1961 Naval Postgraduate School
DATE OF COMMISSION: 23rd December, 1940
PROMOTED TO: Rear Admiral, selected for promotion on 6th June 1969
COMMANDS: 1943 Officer-in-Charge Summit AMc 106; 1943-1944 YMS-347; 1944-1945 LST-624; 1961-1963 Bryce Canyon AD-36; 1963 Destroyer Division 232;1963-1964 Destroyer Division 192; 1966-1967 Amphibious Squadron 4; 1967-1968 River Assault Flotilla 1; River Support Squadron 7; Riverine Assault Force (CTF 117)
OFFICIAL ADDRESS: The Pentagon, Washington, DC
HOME ADDRESS: 1010 5th Avenue, New York, New York

U.K.

SANDS, COMMANDER M., ROYAL NAVY
PRESENT APPOINTMENT: HMS Zulu in command, 2 January, 1969
DATE OF BIRTH: 19 December, 1930
EDUCATION: R.N.C., Dartmouth
DATES OF PROMOTIONS: Lieutenant-Commander 1 July, 1960; Commander 31 June, 1965
PRINCIPAL COMMANDS AT SEA: HMS Carysfort 1965-1966
OFFICIAL ADDRESS: HMS Zulu, BFPO Ships
PRIVATE ADDRESS: c/o Lloyds Bank, 38 Blue Boar Row, Salisbury, Wilts

ITALY

SANTARCANGELO, GENERALE ISPETTORE ARMI NAVALI E.
DECORATIONS:Grande Ufficiale dell'Ordine al merito della Repubblica Italiana; Commendatore dell'Ordine della Corona d'Italia; Croce al merito de guerra; Medaglia commemorativa della guerra 1940-1943; Medaglia commemorativa della guerra de Liberazione 1943-1945; Croce d'oro con stelletta per anzianità di servizio (40 years)
PRESENT APPOINTMENT: Comitato per i Progetti delle Armi Navali—Presidente
DATE OF BIRTH: 6 March, 1906
DATE OF PROMOTION: 1 January, 1966
OFFICIAL ADDRESS: Ministero della Difesa Marina Lungotevere delle Navi. 00196, Rome. *Telephone;* 31.59.28

U.S.A.

SARGENT, REAR-ADMIRAL THOMAS R., US NAVY
CURRENT DUTY STATION: Chief of Staff, US Coast Guard Headquarters (June 1968)
DATE OF BIRTH: 1914
EDUCATION: 1938 Coast Guard Academy; 1952 Rensselaer Polytechnic Institute
FIRST COMMISSIONED: 2nd June, 1938
PROMOTED TO: Rear Admiral 1st July, 1967
COMMANDS: 1944-1945 Sandusky; 1954-1956 Winnebago; 1967-1969 11th Coast Guard District
HOME ADDRESS: 10810 Hords St., Wheaton, Maryland

THAILAND

SATTABOOS, COMMANDER P., ROYAL THAI NAVY
DECORATIONS: Commander (Third Class) of the Most Noble Order of The Crown of Thai 5 December, 1966
PRESENT APPOINTMENT: Assistant Naval Attache 30 September, 1966
DATE OF BIRTH: 11 June, 1929
EDUCATION: Graduated, Royal Thai Naval Academy May 1952; Naval Staff College September 1964
DATES OF PROMOTIONS: Lieutenant (Jg.) 1 October, 1955; Lieutenant 1 October, 1957; LCDR 1 October, 1961; Commander 1 October, 1965
PRINCIPAL COMMANDS AT SEA: 1954-1955 Gunnery Officer HTMS Bangkeo; 1957 Commanding Officer HTMS Kut; 1961-1962 Aide to Deputy C-in-C Royal Thai Fleet
OTHER PREVIOUS APPOINTMENTS OF NOTE: Acting Executive Officer, Naval Preparatory School 1955-1957; Attached Naval Officer School 1958-1960; Instructor, Naval Academy 1960-1961; Head of Fleet Maintenance Control Section 1964-1965
OFFICIAL ADDRESS: Office of Naval Attache, Embassy of Thailand, 2300 Kalorama Road, N.W. Washington, D.C. 20008 *Telephone:* (301) 657-4658
PRIVATE ADDRESS: 10145 Dallas Avenue, Silver Spring, Md. 20901, U.S.A.

U.S.A.

SCHADE, VICE-ADMIRAL ARNOLD FREDERIC, US NAVY
CURRENT DUTY STATION: Commander, Submarine Force, Atlantic Fleet (November 1966)
DATE OF BIRTH: 1912
EDUCATION: 1933 Naval Academy; 1950 Armed Forces Staff College; 1955 National War College
DATE OF COMMISSION: 1st June, 1933
PROMOTED TO: Rear Admiral 1st July, 1961; Vice-Admiral 19th November 1966
COMMANDS: 1944-1946 Bugura SS 331;1948-1949 Submarine Division 12; 1952-1954 Submarine Group 1, Mare Island Group, Pacific Reserve Fleet; 1955-1956 Seminole AKA 104;1958-1959 Submarine Squadron 6; 1963-1964 Middle East Force
MAJOR AWARD: Navy Cross
OFFICIAL ADDRESS: Norfolk, Virginia 23511
HOME ADDRESS: Calistoga, California

U.S.A.

SCHLECH, REAR-ADMIRAL WALTER FREDERICK, JNR., US NAVY
CURRENT DUTY STATION: Commander, Military Sea Transportation Service, Atlantic (July 1968)
DATE OF BIRTH: 1915
EDUCATION: 1936 Naval Academy; Naval War College 1955
DATE OF COMMISSION: 4th June 1936
PROMOTED TO: Rear Admiral 7th July, 1964
COMMANDS: 1945-1948 Tilefish SS 307; 1951-1952 Submarine Division 41; 1955-1957 Officer-in-charge, Submarine School, New London; 1957-1958 Submarine Squadron 12; 1958-1959 Great Sitkin AE 17; 1961-1963 Submarine Squadron 14; 1963-1964 Submarine Flotilla 6; 1966-1968 Chief, Navy Section, Joint US Military Mission for Aid to Turkey, Anakara, Turkey
OFFICIAL ADDRESS: 58th Street and 1st Avenue, Brooklyn, New York
HOME ADDRESS: 14 Stoneleight Park, Westfield, New Jersey

U.S.A.

SCHNEIDER, REAR-ADMIRAL FREDERICK HENRY, JNR., US NAVY
CURRENT DUTY STATION: Assistant Deputy Chief of Naval Operations (Plans and Policy) (June 1969)
DATE OF BIRTH: 1914
EDUCATION: Naval Academy 1937; 1957 National War College
DATE OF COMMISSION: 3rd June, 1937
PROMOTED TO: Rear Admiral 1st December, 1964
COMMANDS: 1944-1946 Thorn DD 647; 1954-1955 Willis A. Lee DL 4; 1955-1956 Destroyer Division 22; 1959-1960 Vermilion AKA 107; 1960-1961 Saint Paul CA 73; 1964-1965 Cruiser-Destroyer Flotilla 10
OFFICIAL ADDRESS: The Pentagon, Washington, DC 20350
HOME ADDRESS: 4653 38th Place, Arlington, Virginia

U.S.A.

SCHNEIDER, REAR ADMIRAL, RAYMOND JOHN (AERONAUTICAL ENGINEERING DUTY) US NAVY
CURRENT DUTY STATION: Assistant Commander for Research and Technology, Naval Air Systems Command (November 1968)
DATE OF BIRTH: 1917
EDUCATION: Naval Academy 1940; 1946 Naval Postgraduate School; 1960 Industrial College of the Armed Forces
DATE OF COMMISSION: 6th June, 1940
PROMOTED TO: Rear Admiral 1st August, 1968
OFFICIAL ADDRESS: Main Navy Building, Washington, DC 20360
HOME ADDRESS: 1226 Overlook Road, Lakewood, Ohio

U.S.A.

SCHULZ, REAR ADMIRAL, LESTER ROBERT (RETIRED) (SPECIAL DUTY—COMMUNICATIONS) US NAVY
CURRENT DUTY STATION: Chief, National Security Agency, Pacific (June 1968)
DATE OF BIRTH: 1913
EDUCATION: 1934 Naval Academy
DATE OF COMMISSION: 31st May, 1934
PROMOTED TO: Rear Admiral 1st July, 1963
COMMANDS: 1961-1962 Director, Naval Security Group, Washington; Deputy Director, Naval Security Group, Washington; additional duty: Assistant Director, Naval Communications for Naval Security Group
OFFICIAL ADDRESS: Box 210, FPO San Francisco, California 96610
HOME ADDRESS: 609 South Wenona Avenue, Bay City, Michigan

FRANCE

SCITIVAUX de GREISHCHE, VICE ADMIRAL D'ESCADRE C. P., FRENCH NAVY
PRESENT APPOINTMENT: Préfet Maritime de la 1110 Région 15 September 1967
DATE OF BIRTH: 8 August, 1911
EDUCATION: Collèges Privés; Lycée St Louis
DATES OF PROMOTIONS: CV 1 January. 1952; CA 1 December, 1960; VA 1 March 1966; VAE 1 August 1968
PRINCIPAL COMMANDS AT SEA: Aviso Lapterouse 1948-1949; Porte-avious Bois Belleau 1957-1958
OTHER PREVIOUS APPOINTMENTS OF NOTE: Cdt. 340 Squadron 1941-1942; Cdt. Ban Port Lyantey, Cdt. Aéro 111; Cdt. Forces Françaires Pacifique; President CPE
OFFICIAL ADDRESS: Prefecture Maritime, 83 Toulon, France. *Telephone:* 922905
PRIVATE ADDRESS: 117 Bd. Bineau, 92 Neuilly

U.S.A.

SCOTT, REAR-ADMIRAL (SELECTEE), JOHN ALEXANDER, SUPPLY CORPS. US NAVY
CURRENT DUTY STATION: Director of Supply Corps Personnel, Naval Supply Systems Command and Supply Corps Plans Assistant, Bureau of Naval Personnel (July 1966)
DATE OF BIRTH: 1920
EDUCATION: Whittier College 1942; 1952 Stanford University; 1964 Industrial College of the Armed Forces
DATE OF COMMISSION: 29th April 1942
PROMOTED TO: Rear Admiral selected for Promotion in June 1969
OFFICIAL ADDRESS: Arlington Annex, Washington, DC 20370

UNITED KINGDOM

SCOTT, CAPTAIN W. D. S., ROYAL NAVY
PRESENT APPOINTMENT: Commanding Officer HMS Fife
DATE OF BIRTH: 5 April 1921
EDUCATION: Tonbridge School; Special Entry Dartmouth
DATES OF PROMOTION: Sub Lieutenant April 1941; Lieutenant February 1942; Lieutenant Commander February 1950; Commander June 1956
COMMANDS AT SEA: HM Submarines P35; Satyr; Andrew; Thermopylae; HMS Surprise; HMS Adamant
OTHER PREVIOUS APPOINTMENTS OF NOTE: Commanding Officer HMS Gateshead and Senior Officer Midget Submarine Class; Training, Commander, BRNC Dartmouth Deputy Director Defence Plans 1965-1967; Chief of Staff to FOSM 1967-1969
OFFICIAL ADDRESS: HMS Fife, BFPO Ships, London

U.S.A.

SCULLION, REAR-ADMIRAL JOSEPH RIDDICK, US NAVY
CURRENT DUTY STATION: Chief, Office of Personnel, Coast Guard Headquarters (August 1968)
DATE OF BIRTH: 1912
EDUCATION: 1931 University of Virginia; 1935 Coast Guard Academy; 1949 Armed Forces Staff College
FIRST COMMISSIONED: 27th May, 1935
PROMOTED TO: Rear Admiral 8th July,1964
COMMANDS: 1945-1946 Separation Center No. 5, Portsmouth, Va.; 1952-1954 Iroquois; 1957-1960 Coast Guard Group, Norfolk; 1966-1968 17th Coast Guard District, Juneau
HOME ADDRESS: 6329 Mori St., McLean, Va.

SMEDER, REAR-ADMIRAL ORVAN RONALD (NAVAL AVIATOR) US NAVY
CURRENT DUTY STATION: Assistant Chief of Staff for Ocean Science (December 1968)
DATE OF BIRTH: 1915
EDUCATION: 1935 Ean Claire State Teacher's College; 1939 Coast Guard Academy; 1944 Naval Air Station, Pensacola
FIRST COMMISSIONED: 29th May, 1939
PROMOTED TO: Rear Admiral 1st July, 1967
COMMANDS: 1947-1948 Buttonwood; 1952-1954 Chantagna; 1958-1960 Androscoggin; 1965-1967 Coast Guard Reserve Training Center, Yorktown

JAPAN
SEKI, REAR- ADMIRAL K.
DECORATIONS: The Fifth Class of the Sacred Treasure 1942; Decoration of Red Cross 1962; Legion of Merit (Degree of Officer), USA, 1967
PRESENT APPOINTMENT: Commander, 2nd Minesweeper Flotilla 16 July, 1968
DATE OF BIRTH: 3 November, 1916
EDUCATION: The naval academy, graduated on March 1938; Staff College JMSDF, graduated in 1956
DATE OF PROMOTIONS: Commander, 1 August, 1954; Captain, 1 August, 1959; Rear Admiral 1 January, 1967
PRINCIPAL COMMANDS AT SEA: Commanding Officer, "Yukikaze (DD 102)" 1958; Commander 2nd Minesweeper Flotilla 1968
OTHER PREVIOUS APPOINTMENTS OF NOTE: Chief of staff, 1st Escort Flotilla 1959; Defence Attaché (for Navy) in USA 1962-1966; Chief of the First Division (Admin.) Joint Staff Council 1966-1968
OFFICIAL ADDRESS: HQ. 2nd Minesweeper Flottilla, c/o Yokosuka Regional District Headquarter, Nishihemi-cho Yokosuka-shi, Japan (238)
PRIVATE ADRESS: 17-5-7, Akasaka Minato-ku, Tokyo (107)

U.S.A.
SELL, REAR ADMIRAL, LESLIE HALE US NAVY
CURRENT DUTY STATION: Chief, Joint Command and Control Requirements Group, Joint Chiefs of Staff (October 1968)
DATE OF BIRTH: 1921
EDUCATION: 1942 Naval Academy; 1963 Industrial College of the Armed Forces; 1949 Naval Postgraduate School
DATE OF COMMISSION: 19th June, 1942
PROMOTED TO: Rear Admiral 1st August 1968
COMMANDS: 1956-1958 Moale DD 693; 1963-1964 Destroyer Division 322; additional duty: Destroyer Squadron 32; 1965-1966 England DLG 22
OFFICIAL ADDRESS: The Pentagon, Washington, DC 20301
HOME ADDRESS: 201 West Holston Avenue, Johnson City, Tennessee

U.S.A.
SEMMES, VICE ADMIRAL, BENEDICT JOSEPH, US NAVY
CURRENT DUTY STATION: Commander, Second Fleet; additional duty: Commander Strike Force Atlantic (April 1968)
DATE OF BIRTH: 1913
EDUCATION: 1934 Naval Academy; 1958 National War College
DATE OF COMMISSION: 31st May, 1934
PROMOTED TO: Rear Admiral 1st July 1959; Vice Admiral 1st April, 1964
COMMANDS: 1944-1945 Picking DD 685; 1948-1949 Ault DD 698; 1953-1954 Destroyer Division 302; 1958 Shenandoah AD 26; 1958-1959 Destroyer Flotilla 3; 1962-1963 Middle East Force; 1963-1964 Cruiser-Destroyer Force, Atlantic Fleet; 1964-1968 Chief of Naval Personnel/ Deputy Chief of Naval Operations (Manpower and Naval Reserve)
MAJOR AWARDS: Navy Cross
OFFICIAL ADDRESS: FPO New York 09501
HOME ADDRESS: 1916 47th, Washington, DC

U.S.A.
SEUFER, REAR ADMIRAL PAUL ERNEST, (CIVIL ENGINEER CORPS.) US NAVY
CURRENT DUTY STATION: Commander, Atlantic Division, Naval Facilities Engineering Command; additional duty: Fleet Civil Engineer, Atlantic Fleet; Assistant Chief of Staff for Facilities Engineering, Commander in Chief Atlantic Fleet (October 1968)
DATE OF BIRTH: 1913
EDUCATION: Rensselear Polytechnic Institue, Harvard University
DATE OF COMMISSION: 14th July, 1941
PROMOTED TO: Rear Admiral 1st April, 1967
COMMANDS: 1960-1963 Navy Public Works Center, Norfolk
OFFICIAL ADDRESS: Norfolk, Virginia 23511

U.K.
SEX, COMMANDER T. J. F., ROYAL NAVY
PRESENT APPOINTMENT: HMS Chichester in command 5 November, 1968
DATE OF BIRTH: 25 May, 1934
DATE OF PROMOTION: Commander 31 December, 1968
OFFICIAL ADDRESS: HMS Chichester

U.S.A.
SHAFFER, REAR ADMIRAL, JOHN NEVIN US NAVY
CURRENT DUTY STATION:
Commander, Cruiser-Destroyer Force, Atlantic Fleet (July 1969)
DATE OF BIRTH: 1912
EDUCATION: 1935 Naval Academy; 1943 Naval Postgraduate School; 1952 Armed Forces Staff College
DATE OF COMMISSION: 6th June, 1935
PROMOTED TO: Rear Admiral 1st Novemeber, 1962
COMMANDS: 1950-1952 Stormes DD 780; 1952-1954 Clarksville Base, Tenessee; additional duty: Naval Adminstrative Unit, Clarksville Base; 1954-1955 Destroyer Division 242; 1958-1959 Yosemite AD 19; 1959-1961 Director, Atomic Energy Division; additional duty: Commander, Task Group 7.3 Office of the Chief of Naval Operations; 1961 Destroyer Squadron 6; 1964-1966 Cruiser-Destroyer Flotilla 2; 1966-1967 Mine Force, Atlantic Fleet
OFFICIAL ADDRESS: Newport, Rhode Island 02840 .
HOME ADDRESS: 649 S. Juliana Street, Bedford, Pennsylvania

U.S.A.
SHEAR, REAR ADMIRAL, HAROLD EDSON, US NAVY
CURRENT DUTY STATION: Director, Submarine Warfare Division, Office of the Chief of Naval Operations (April 1969)
DATE OF BIRTH:1918
EDUCATION: 1955 Naval Academy, Armed Forces Staff College; 1965 National War College 1965
DATE OF COMMISSION: 19th December, 1941
PROMOTED TO: Rear Admiral 1st July, 1967
COMMANDS: 1952-1954 Becuna SS 319; 1960-1962 Patrick Henry SSBN 599; 1965-1966 Sacramento AOE 1; 1967-1969 Chief, Navy Section, US Military Group, Brazil
OFFICIAL ADDRESS: The Pentagon, Washington, DC 20350
HOME ADDRESS: Shelter Island, New York

U.S.A.
SHEPARD, REAR ADMIRAL TAZEWELL TAYLOR, JNR., (NAVAL AVIATOR) US NAVY
CURRENT DUTY STATION: Director, East Asia and Pacific Region, Office of the Secretary of Defense (International Security Affairs) (July 1968)
DATE OF BIRTH: 1921
EDUCATION: Naval Academy; 1952 Naval Postgraduate School; 1960 Naval War College
DATE OF COMMISSION: 19th June, 1942
PROMOTED TO: Rear Admiral 1st August 1968
COMMANDS: 1958-1959 Heavy Attack Squadron 15; 1964-1965 Aucilla AO-56; 1966-1967 Princeton LPH 5
MAJOR AWARDS: Navy Cross
OFFICIAL ADDRESS: The Pentagon, Washington, DC 20301
HOME ADDRESS: 1108 Government Street, Mobile, Alabama

U.S.A.
SHERWOOD, REAR ADMIRAL, STEPHEN, (SUPPLY CORPS.) US NAVY
CURRENT DUTY STATION: Commanding Officer, Naval Supply Center, San Diego (June 1967); additional duty: District Supply Officer, 11th Naval District (October 1967)
DATE OF BIRTH: 1911
EDUCATION: 1935 Naval Academy; 1938 Navy Finance and Supply School; 1950 Industrial College of the Armed Forces
DATE OF COMMISSION: 6th June, 1935
PROMOTED TO: Rear Admiral 1st April, 1963
COMMANDS: 1959-1961 Ships Parts Control Center, Mechanicsburg, Pennsylvania; 1964-1965 Navy Supply Center, Pearl Harbor, Hawaii; additional duty: Staff Supply Officer, 14th Naval District; 1967 Naval Supply Center, San Diego
OFFICIAL ADDRESS: 937 N. Harbor Drive, San Diego, California 92131
HOME ADDRESS: White Plains, New York

U.S.A.
SHIFLEY, VICE ADMIRAL RALPH LOUIS, (NAVAL AVIATOR) US NAVY
CURRENT DUTY STATION: Deputy Chief of Naval Operations (Logistics) (August 1967)
DATE OF BIRTH 1910
EDUCATION: 1933 Naval Academy; 1952 Naval War College
DATE OF COMMISSION: 1st June, 1933
PROMOTED TO: Rear Admiral 1st July, 1961; Vice Admiral 1st September 1967
COMMANDS: 1943-1944 Bombing Squadron 8; 1944 Carrier Air Group 8; 1956-1957 Badoeng Strait CVE 116; 1958-1959 Franklin D. Roosevelt CVA 42; 1962-1963 Carrier Division 7
MAJOR AWARD: Navy Cross
OFFICIAL ADDRESS: The Pentagon, Washington, DC 20350
HOME ADDRESS: Mounds, Illinois

U.S.A.
SHINN, VICE ADMIRAL ALLEN MAYHEW, (NAVAL AVIATOR) US NAVY
CURRENT DUTY STATION: Commander, Naval Air Force, Pacific Fleet (November 1966)
DATE OF BIRTH: 1908
EDUCATION: 1932 Naval Academy; 1953 National War College
DATE OF COMMISSION: 2nd June, 1932
PROMOTED TO: Rear Admiral 1st April, 1960; Vice Admiral 1st November, 1966
COMMANDS: 1946-1948 Fleet Airborne Electronics Training Unit Atlantic; 1948 Carrier Airborne Early Warning Squadron 2; 1948-1949 Composite Squadron 12; 1955-1956 Saipan CVL 48; 1958-1959 Forrestal CVA 59; 1959-1961 Carrier Division 14; 1963-1964 Carrier Division 6; 1964-1966 Bureau of Naval Weapons; Naval Weapons Support Activity, Washington; 1966 Naval Air Systems Command, Washington DC
OFFICIAL ADDRESS: Box 1210, Naval Air Station North Island, San Diego, California 92135
HOME ADDRESS: Niles, California

U.S.A.

SHOWERS, REAR ADMIRAL DONALD MAC (SPECIAL DUTY—INTELLIGENCE) US NAVY
CURRENT DUTY STATION: Assistant Chief of Staff for Plans and Programs, Defense Intelligence Agency (July 1966)
DATE OF BIRTH: 1919
EDUCATION: 1941 University of Iowa; 1961 Naval War College
DATE OF COMMISSION: 12th September, 1941
PROMOTED TO: Rear Admiral 1st December 1965
OFFICIAL ADDRESS: The Pentagon, Washington, DC 20301
HOME ADDRESS: Iowa City, Iowa

U.S.A.

SHUPPER, REAR ADMIRAL, BURTON HERBERT, US NAVY
CURRENT DUTY STATION: Assistant Deputy Chief of Naval Operations (Manpower) (July 1968)
DATE OF BIRTH: 1915
EDUCATION: 1937 Naval Academy; 1949 Naval War College; 1960 National War College
DATE OF COMMISSION: 3rd June 1937
PROMOTED TO: Rear Admiral 1st July, 1965
COMMANDS: 1944-1945 Macdonough DD 351; 1945-1946 Bell DD 587; 1955-1957 Destroyer Division 601; 1962-1963 Providence CLG 6; 1966-1968 Anti-Submarine Warfare Group 5
OFFICIAL ADDRESS: The Pentagon, Washington, DC 20350
HOME ADDRESS: Aurora Hills, Arlington, Virginia

ITALY

SIENA, TENENTE GENERALE DEL GENIO NAVALE ANTONIO, ITALIAN NAVY
DECORATIONS: Commendatore dell'ordine al merito della Repubblica Italiana; Cavaliere dell'ordine della Corona d'Italia; Medaglia di Bronzo al valor militare; Croce al merito di guerra; Medaglia commemorativa della guerra 1940-1943; Croce d'oro per anzianità di servizio, 40 anni
PRESENT APPOINTMENT: Presidente del Comitato per i Progetti delle Navi della Marina Militare
DATE OF BIRTH: 29 January, 1908
DATE OF PROMOTION: 18 November, 1963
OFFICIAL ADDRESS: Maricominav, Ministero della Difesa Marina, Piazale della Marina, Roma. *Telephone:* 312441

U.S.A.

SIMPSON, REAR ADMIRAL MAURICE EUGENE (DENTAL CORPS.) US NAVY
CURRENT DUTY STATION: Fleet Dental Officer and Assistant Chief of Staff for Dentistry, Commander-in-Chief, Atlantic Fleet; additional duty: Director, Dental Activities, 5th Naval District; Commanding Officer, Dental Clinic, Norfolk; Dental Reserve Programs Officer, 5th Naval District; Dental Officer, Naval Base Norfolk (July 1967)
DATE OF BIRTH: 1909
EDUCATION: 1936 University of Minnesota Dental College
DATE OF COMMISSION: 6th October, 1937
PROMOTED TO: Rear Admiral 1st July, 1964
OFFICIAL ADDRESS: Norfolk, Virginia 23511
HOME ADDRESS: 990 Arlington Avenue, Plainfield, New Jersey

U.S.A.

SMALL, REAR ADMIRAL WALTER LOWRY, JNR., US NAVY
CURRENT DUTY STATION: Commander, Submarine Force, Pacific Fleet (June 1968)
DATE OF BIRTH: 1916
EDUCATION: 1934 Naval Academy; 1953 Armed Forces Staff College; 1958 Naval War College
DATE OF COMMISSION: 2nd June, 1938
PROMOTED TO: Rear Admiral 10th August, 1965
COMMANDS 1945 Batfish SS 310;1948-1949 Clamagore SS 343; 1953-1954 Van Valkenburgh DD 656; 1954-1955 Submarine Division 61;1959-1960 Sperry AS 12; 1962-1964 Submarine Squadron 10; 1967-1968 Middle East Force
OFFICIAL ADDRESS: Pearl Harbor, FPO San Francisco, California 96601
HOME ADDRESS: 204 Colonial Avenue, Elizabeth City, North Carolina

U.S.A.

SMITH, REAR-ADMIRAL, DANIEL FLETCHER JNR., (NAVAL AVIATOR) US NAVY
CURRENT DUTY STATION: Commander, Naval Forces, Japan (June 1968)
DATE OF BIRTH: 1910
EDUCATION: 1932 Naval Academy; 1949 Air War College; 1953 National War College
DATE OF COMMISSION: 2nd June 1932
PROMOTED TO: Rear Admiral 1st April, 1960
MAJOR AWARD: Navy Cross
COMMANDS: 1942-1943 Fleet Air Wing 11; 1943 Carrier Aircraft Service Unit 21; 1943-1945 Carrier Air Group 20; 1956-1957 Randolph CVA 15; 1960-1962 Chief of Navy Information, Department of the Navy; 1962-1963 Carrier Division 3; 1963-1965 Chief of Naval Air Basic Training; 1965-1968 Naval Air Test Center, Patuxent River, Maryland; additional duty: Fleet Air Patuxent River
OFFICIAL ADDRESS: FPO Seattle, Washington 98762
HOME ADDRESS: Pittsburgh, Texas

U.S.A.

SNYDER, REAR-ADMIRAL (SELECTEE) EDWIN KNOWLSON, US NAVY
CURRENT DUTY STATION:
Commander, Amphibious Training Command, Atlantic Fleet (August 1969)
DATE OF BIRTH: 1922
EDUCATION: 1944 Naval Academy; 1963 Industrial College of the Armed Forces; 1957 Naval Postgraduate School
DATE OF COMMISSION: 9th June, 1943
PROMOTED TO: Rear Admiral, selected for promotion on 6th June 1969
COMMANDS: 1954-1956 Irex SS 339; 1961-1962 Submarine Division 81; 1965-1966 Allagash AO 97
OFFICIAL ADDRESS: Norfolk, Virginia
HOME ADDRESS 823 Colonial Court, Birmingham, Alabama

U.S.A.

SMITH, REAR ADMIRAL, JAMES HERBERT JNR., (AERONAUTICAL ENGINEERING DUTY) US NAVY
CURRENT DUTY STATION: Naval Air Systems Command Representative, Pacific (August 1967)
DATE OF BIRTH: 1915
EDUCATION: 1939 Naval Academy; 1946 Naval Postgraduate School
DATE OF COMMISSION: 1st June, 1939
PROMOTED TO: Rear Admiral 30th May, 1967
OFFICIAL ADDRESS: Naval Air Station, North Island, San Diego, California 92135
HOME ADDRESS: Charleston, West Virginia

U.S.A.

SMITH, VICE ADMIRAL, JOHN VICTOR, US NAVY
CURRENT DUTY STATION: Commander, Amphibious Force, Pacific Fleet (May 1968)
DATE OF BIRTH: 1912
EDUCATION: 1934, Naval Academy; 1942 Naval Postgraduate School; 1950 Armed Forces Staff College; 1954 National War College
DATE OF COMMISSION: 31st May, 1934
PROMOTED TO: Rear Admiral 1st July, 1962; Vice Admiral 7th June, 1968
COMMANDS: 1943-1944 Shubrick DD 639; 1945 Brush DD 745; 1952-1953 Destroyer Division 112; 1956-1957 Rockbridge APA 228; 1959-1960 Newport News CA 148; 1963-1964 Cruiser-Destroyer Flotilla 8; 1967-1968 Senior Member, United Nations Command, Armistice Commission, Korea
OFFICIAL ADDRESS: Naval Amphibious Base, San Diego, California 92155
HOME ADDRESS: 2336 South Nash, Arlington, Virginia

U.S.A.

SMITH, REAR ADMIRAL, LEVERING (ORDNANCE ENGINEERING DUTY) US NAVY
CURRENT DUTY STATION: Director, Strategic Systems Projects Office, Naval Material Command (February 1965)
DATE OF BIRTH: 1910
EDUCATION: Naval Academy 1932; 1940 Naval Postgraduate School
DATE OF COMMISSION: 2nd June, 1932
PROMOTED TO: Rear Admiral 1st April, 1963
COMMANDS: 1954-1956 Naval Ordnance Missile Test Facility, White Sands Proving Ground, New Mexico; Senior Officer Present Southern New Mexico Subarea; Deputy for Navy to Commanding General, White Sands Proving Ground
OFFICIAL ADDRESS: Main Navy Building, Washington DC 20360
HOME ADDRESS: 1462 Waggaman Circle, McLean, Virginia

U.S.A.

SMITH, REAR-ADMIRAL SPENCER RINGGOLD (CIVIL ENGINEER CORPS) US NAVY
CURRENT DUTY STATION: Deputy Commander for Management, Naval Facilities Engineering Command (August 1968)
DATE OF BIRTH 1915
EDUCATION: 1937 Yale University
FIRST COMMISSION: 8th April, 1941
PROMOTED TO: Rear Admiral 1st February, 1968
COMMANDS: 1958-1959 Naval Mobile Construction, Battalion 3; 1965-1966 Naval Construction Battalions, Atlantic Fleet
OFFICIAL ADDRESS: Yards and Docks Annex, Washington DC 20390
HOME ADDRESS: Haddonfield, New Jersey

U.S.A.

SMITH, REAR ADMIRAL STUART HENRY (SUPPLY CORPS.) US NAVY
CURRENT DUTY STATION: Fleet Supply Officer and Assistant Chief of Staff for Supply, Commander-in-Chief Atlantic Fleet (July 1967)
DATE OF BIRTH: 1920
EDUCATION: 1941 University of California; Naval Postgraduate School; 1963 Industrial College of the Armed Forces
PROMOTED TO REAR ADMIRAL 8th April, 1968
COMMANDS: 1966-1967 Navy Supply Corps. School, Athens, Georgia
OFFICIAL ADDRESS: Norfolk, Virginia 23511
HOME ADDRESS: 850 Webster Avenue, Palo Alto, California

AUSTRALIA

SMITH, VICE ADMIRAL, V. A. T., ROYAL AUSTRALIAN NAVY
DECORATIONS: CB 1968; CBE 1963; DSC 1941
PRESENT APPOINTMENT: Chief of Naval Staff and First Naval Member of the Australian Commonwealth Naval Board, 4 April, 1968
DATE OF BIRTH: 9 May, 1913
EDUCATION: Chatswood School, Royal Australian Naval College
DATES OF PROMOTIONS: Commander 31 December, 1947; Captain 31 December, 1953; Rear Admiral 9 January, 1963; Vice Admiral 4 April, 1968
PRINCIPAL COMMANDS AT SEA: Captain 1st Frigate Squadron 1955-1956; Captain HMAS Melbourne 1961-1962; Flag Officer Commanding HM Australian Fleet 1966-1967
OTHER PREVIOUS APPOINTMENTS OF NOTE: Second Naval Member and Chief of Personnel 1962-1964 Fourth Naval Member and Chief of Supply 1965-1966; Depty Chief of Naval Staff 1967-1968
OFFICIAL ADDRESS: Chief of Naval Staff, Department of Navy, Russell Offices, Canberra, ACT 2600. *Telephone:* 653251
PRIVATE ADDRESS: 15 Fishburn Street, Red Hill, ACT 2603

U.S.A.

SMITH, ADMIRAL WILLARD JOHN (NAVAL AVIATOR)
CURRENT DUTY STATION: Commandant, US Coast Guard (June 1966)
DATE OF BIRTH: 1910
EDUCATION: 1933 Coast Guard Academy; 1951 Armed Forces Staff College
FIRST COMMISSIONED: 15th May, 1933
PROMOTED TO: Rear Admiral 1st July, 1962; Admiral 1st June, 1966
COMMANDS: 1946-1948 Coast Guard Air Station, Traverse City, Michigan; 1951-1952 Coast Guard Depot, Cunan Island, and Western Pacific Section; 1952-1954 Mackinair; 1965-1966 9th Coast Guard District, Cleveland
HOME ADDRESS: 6601 Kennedy Dr., Bethesda, Md.

U.S.A.

SONENSHEIN, REAR ADMIRAL NATHAN, (ENGINEERING DUTY) US NAVY
CURRENT DUTY STATION:
Commander, Naval Ship Systems Command (July1969)
DATE OF BIRTH: 1915
EDUCATION: 1938 Naval Academy; 1944 and 1964 Naval Postgraduate School
DATE OF COMMISSION: 2nd June, 1938
PROMOTED TO: Rear Admiral 1st May 1965
OFFICIAL ADDRESS: Main Navy Building, Washington, DC 20360
HOME ADDRESS: Passaic, New Jersey

ITALY

SPIGAI, AMMIRAGLIO DI SQUADRA IN S.P.E., V.
DECORATIONS: Cavaliere dell Ordine Militare d'Italia; Tre Medaglie di Bionzo of V.M.; Due Croci al Merito di Guerra
PRESENT APPOINTMENT: Stato Maggiore della Marina; Capo di Stato Maggiore
DATE OF BIRTH: 24 September, 1907
DATE OF PROMOTION: Ammiraglio di Squadra 27 December, 1964
OFFICIAL ADDRESS: Maristat

U.S.A.

SPREEN, REAR-ADMIRAL (SELECTEE) ROGER ELMORE, US NAVY
CURRENT DUTY STATION: Chief of Staff, Commander Cruiser Destroyer Force, Pacific Fleet (July 1968)
DATE OF BIRTH: 1920
EDUCATION: 1943 Naval Academy; 1950 Naval Postgraduate School; 1956 Joint Service Staff College, Buckinghamshire, England; 1964 Industrial College of the Armed Forces
DATE OF COMMISSION 19th June, 1942
PROMOTED TO: Rear Admiral, selected for promotion on 6th June, 1969
COMMANDS: Foss DE 59; 1958-1960 Bigelow DD 942; 1960-1962 Farragut DLG 6; 1962-1963 Destroyer Division 262; 1967-1968 Destroyer Squadron 23
OFFICIAL ADDRESS: FPO San Francisco, California
HOME ADDRESS: 214 South Street, Sidney, Ohio

UNITED KINGDOM

STACEY CAPTAIN M. L., ROYAL NAVY
PRESENT APPOINTMENT: HMS Andromeda, 1968
DATE OF BIRTH: 6 July, 1924
EDUCATION: Epsom College
DATES OF PROMOTIONS: 1942 Cadet; 1943 Midshipman; 1945 Sub Lieutenant; 1946 Lieutenant; 1954 Lieutenant Commander; 1958 Commander; 1966 Captain
PRINCIPAL COMMANDS AT SEA: 1947-1949 In command MTB and 1st MTB Squadron HMS Hornet; 1960-1961 In Command HM Blackpool; 1968 In Command HMS Andromeda
OTHER APPOINTMENTS OF NOTE: RN Staff College, Greenwich 1954; Joint Services Staff College, Latimer 1962; Deputy Director, Joint Anti-Submarine School, Londonerry 1963-1964;Chief Staff Officer to Admiral Commanding Reserves 1966-1968
OFFICIAL ADDRES: C/O Ministry of Defence (Navy), London
PRIVATE ADDRESS: 'Little Hintock', 40 Lynch Road, Farnham, Surrey

U.S.A.

STEELE, REAR-ADMIRAL (SELECTEE) GEORGE PEABODY, II, US NAVY
CURRENT DUTY STATION: Commander, US Naval Forces, Korea; Commander, Naval Component Command, United Nations Command, Korea; and Commander, Naval Component Command, US Forces Korea; additional duty: Chief, US Navy Advisory Group, ROK Navy, US Navy Advisor to the ROK Navy (July 1968) authorized to assume title of Rear Admiral
DATE OF BIRTH: 1924
EDUCATION: 1944 Naval Academy
DATE OF COMMISSION: 7th June, 1944
PROMOTED TO: Rear Admiral, selected for promotion on 6th June, 1968
COMMANDS: 1954-1957 Hardhead SS 365; 1959-1961 Seadragon SSN 584; 1964-1966 Daniel Boone SSBN 629
OFFICIAL ADDRESS: APO San Francisco, California 96301
HOME ADDRESS: 6405 Kenhowe Drive, Bethesda, Maryland

U.K.

STEWART, COMMANDER W. H., ROYAL NAVY
PRESENT APPONTMENT: Commanding Officer, HMS Llandaff 21 October, 1968
DATE OF BIRTH: 20 December, 1928
DATE OF PROMOTION: Commander 30 June, 1968
PREVIOUS APPOINTMENT OF NOTE: Operations Officer HMS Eagle 1965-1967
OFFICIAL ADDRESS: HMS Llandaff, BFPO Ships
PRIVATE ADDRESS: 28 Woodcote Drive, Crofton Place, Orpington, Kent

U.S.A.

STILWELL, REAR ADMIRAL, JAMES JOSEPH (ENGINEERING DUTY) US NAVY
CURRENT DUTY STATION: Deputy Commander for Shipyard Management and Program Director for Shipyard Modernization, Naval Ship Systems Command (April 1967)
DATE OF BIRTH: 1916
EDUCATION: 1938 Naval Academy; 1943 Naval Postgraduate School; 1958 Naval War College
DATE OF COMMISSION: 2nd June, 1938
PROMOTED TO: Rear Admiral: 11th October, 1966
COMMANDS: 1964-1967 Philadelphia Naval Shipyard; additional duty: Industrial Manager, 4th Naval District
OFFICIAL ADDRESS: Main Navy Building, Washing, DC 20360
HOME ADDRESS: Cleveland, Ohio

UNITED KINGDOM

STOCKER, COMMODORE THOMAS W., ROYAL NAVY
PRESENT APPOINTMENT: Commodore Amphibious Forces 17 November, 1968
DATE OF BIRTH: 29 July, 1920
EDUCATION: RN College, Dartmouth; Staff Course & JSSC
DATES OF PROMOTIONS: Commander 31 December, 1955; Captain 31 December, 1961; Commodore 14 November, 1968
PRINCIPAL COMMANDS AT SEA: HMS Hesperus; HMNZS Kaniere & Hawea; HMS Jutland; HMS Dido & Captain D1
OTHER PREVIOUS APPOINTMENTS OF NOTE: Commander, RNC Dartmouth; Naval Adviser, Canberra; DNE
OFFICIAL ADDRESS: Commodore Amphibious Forces, BFPO 164
PRIVATE ADDRESS: Rodney House, Woodstick Drive, Singapore 10
PRIVATE ADDRESS IN UK: Holway Mill, Sandford Orcas, Sherborne, Dorset

U.S.A.

STOECKLEIN, REAR-ADMIRAL (SELECTEE) HERBERT GEORGE (MEDICAL CORPS) US NAVY
CURRENT DUTY STATION: Commanding Officer, Naval Hospital, Camp Pendleton, California (August 1967)
DATE OF BIRTH: 1916
EDUCATION: 1939 University of Pittsburgh; 1943 Hahnemann Medical College
DATE OF COMMISSION: 17th March, 1942
PROMOTED TO: Rear Admiral selected for promotion in June 1969
OFFICIAL ADDRESS: Camp Pendleton, California

U.S.A.

STONE, REAR-ADMIRAL, FRANK BRADFORD (NAVAL AVIATOR) US NAVY
CURRENT DUTY STATION: Commander, Carrier Division 14 (February 1969)
DATE OF BIRTH: 1915
EDUCATION: 1937 Ursinus College, Collegeville, Pennsylvania; 1951 Naval Postgraduate School; 1958 Naval War College
DATE OF COMMISSION: 14th February, 1941
PROMOTED TO: Rear Admiral 1st July, 1967
COMMANDS: 1948-1949 Attack Squadron 85; 1963-1964 Chemung AO 30; 1964-1965 Hancock CVA 19; 1967-1969 Iceland Defense Force
OFFICIAL ADDRESS: FPO New York 09501
HOME ADDRESS: 1321 Avondale Avenue, Jacksonville, Florida

U.S.A.

STREAN, VICE ADMIRAL, BERNARD MAX, (NAVAL AVIATOR) US NAVY
CURRENT DUTY STATION: Chief of Naval Air Training (July 1968)
DATE OF BIRTH: 1910
EDUCATION: 1933 Naval Academy; 1950 Armed Forces Staff College; 1958 National War College
DATE OF COMMISSION: 1st June, 1933
PROMOTED TO: Rear Admiral 1st May, 1960; Vice-Admiral 1st August 1968
MAJOR AWARD: Navy Cross
COMMANDS: 1943-1944 Fighter Squadron 1; 1944-1945 Air Group 98; 1945-1946 Carrier Air group 75; 1951-1954 Air Transport Squadron 8; 1954-1956 Naval School, Pre-Flight, NAS Pensacola, Florida; 1956-1957 Kenneth Whiting AV 14; 1958-1959 Randolph CVA 15; 1960-1961 Fleet Air Whidbey; 1961-1962 US Taiwan Patrol Force; 1964-1965 Carrier Division 2
OFFICIAL ADDRESS: Naval Air Station, Pensacola, Florida 32508
HOME ADDRESS: Covington, Indiana

U.S.A.

STROH, REAR-ADMIRAL, ROBERT JOSEPH (NAVAL AVIATOR) US NAVY
CURRENT DUTY STATION: Commander, Fleet Air, Jacksonville (October, 1967) To retire November 1969
DATE OF BIRTH: 1907
EDUCATION: Naval Academy 1930; 1954 National War College; 1949 Air War College
DATE OF COMMISSION: 5th June, 1930
PROMOTED TO: Rear Admiral 1st April 1958
COMMANDS: 1942 Photographic Interpretation School, Anacostia, DC; 1943-1944 Fleet Air Photographic Squadron 3; 1949-1950 Tactical Air Group 2; 1950-1951 Valcour AVP 55; 1956 Saratoga CVA 60; 1962-1963 Carrier Division 6
OFFICIAL ADDRESS: Box 24, Naval Air Station, Jacksonville, Florida
HOME ADDRESS: 8380 118th Street, Long Island, New York

U.S.A.

SUERSTEDT, REAR-ADMIRAL, HENRY, JNR., US NAVY
CURRENT DUTY STATION: Assistant Commander for Logistics and Fleet Support, Naval Air Systems Command (July 1968)
DATE OF BIRTH: 1920
EDUCATION 1955 San Francisco City College, Armed Forces Staff College 1955
DATE OF COMMISSION: 8th October, 1941
PROMOTED TO REAR ADMIRAL: 1st May, 1969
COMMANDS: 1948-1949 Attack Squadron 213; 1953-1954 Fighter Squadron 54; 1964-1965 Union AKA 106; Task Group 76.3; Task Group 76.7; 1966-1967 Tripoli LPH 10
OFFICIAL ADDRESS: Main Navy Building, Washington, DC 20360
HOME ADDRESS: 6215 Florio Street, Oakland, California

U.S.A.

SUTHERLING, REAR-ADMIRAL, ELTON WOODROW (SUPPLY CORPS.) US NAVY
CURRENT DUTY STATION: Force Supply Officer, Commander Service Force Pacific; additional duty: Fleet Supply Officer. Commander-in-Chief, Pacific Fleet (June 1967)
DATE OF BIRTH: 1914
EDUCATION: 1935 University of Washington; 1949 Armed Forces Staff College; 1953 Naval Postgraduate School
DATE OF COMMISSION: 23rd May 1936
PROMOTED TO: Rear Admiral 1st November, 1963
COMMANDS: 1953-1955 Naval Supply Depot, Guantanamo Bay, Cuba; 1960-1963 Naval Ordnance Supply Office Mechanicsburg, Pennsylvania; 1963-1965 Naval Supply Center, Bayonne, New Jersey
OFFICIAL ADDRESS: (Pearl Harbor) FPO San Francisco, California 96610

U.S.A.

SWANSON, REAR-ADMIRAL, LEROY VINCENT (NAVAL AVIATOR) US NAVY
CURRENT DUTY STATION:
Deputy & Chief of Staff, Commander-in-Chief, US Naval Forces Europe (1969)
DATE OF BIRTH: 1915
EDUCATION: General Line School 1948; 1962 National War College
DATE OF COMMISSION: 1st January, 1939
PROMOTED TO: Rear Admiral 10th August, 1965
COMMANDS: 1944 Torpedo Squadron 50; 1948-1950 Attack Squadron 45; 1952-1954 Carrier Air Group 17; 1957-1958 Naval CIC School, Naval Air Station, Glynco, Georgia; 1960-1961 Haleakala AE 25; 1962-1963 Independence CVA 62; 1968-1969 Carrier Division 2
OFFICIAL ADDRESS: (London) FPO New York 09510
HOME ADDRESS: Oneida, Illinois

JAPAN

TAKEYAMA, VICE-ADMIRAL JMSDF Y.
PRESENT APPOINTMENT: Commandant, Yokosuka Regional District 1 January, 1969
EDUCATION: Imperial Japanese Naval Academy 1933; National Defence College 1955
DATE OF BIRTH: 21 April, 1913
DATES OF PROMOTIONS: Captain 16 February, 1955; Rear Admiral 1 January, 1963; Vice Admiral 1 July, 1966
PRINCIPAL COMMANDS AT SEA: Commander, 1st Training Division 1 September, 1957; Commander, 2nd Minesweeper Flotilla 16 January, 1963;
DECORATIONS: The Fifth Class Order of the Rising Sun Medal; The Fourth Class Order of The Secret Treasure Medal
OFFICIAL ADDRESS: Yokosuka Regional Headquarters, Nishi Hemi-cho, Yokosuka-shi, Kanagawa-ken
PRIVATE ADDRESS: 58 Gakuto, Lomae-cho, Kitatama-gun, Tokyo-to

U.S.A.

TALLEY, REAR-ADMIRAL, GEORGE CLYDE, JNR., (NAVAL AVIATOR) US NAVY
CURRENT DUTY STATION: Assistant Director, Stratetic Plans Division, Office of the Chief of Naval Operations (February, 1968)
DATE OF BIRTH: 1922
EDUCATION: 1943 Naval Academy; 1954 Naval War College
DATE OF COMMISSION: 9th June, 1943
PROMOTED TO: Rear Admiral 1st August, 1968
COMMANDS: 1958-1960 Attack Squadron 34; 1961-1962 Carrier Air Group 1; 1965-1966 Chilton APA 38; 1966-1967 Franklin D. Roosevelt CVA 42
OFFICIAL ADDRESS: The Pentagon, Washington, DC 20350
HOME ADDRESS: 1611 Atlantic Boulevard, Jacksonville, Florida

NORWAY

TAMBER, REAR-ADMIRAL R. A., ROYAL NORWEGIAN NAVY
DECORATIONS: All Norwegian War decorations; 4 British and U.S. Legion of Merit
PRESENT APPOINTMENT: Commander, Allied Naval Forces, North Norway (April 1966)
DATE OF BIRTH: 10 April, 1913
EDUCATION: Royal Norwegian Naval Academy; Royal Naval Staff College, Greenwich; Norwegian Defence College
DATES OF PROMOTIONS: 1936 Sub-Lieutenant; 1939 Lieutenant; 1944 Lieutenant Commander; 1948 Commander; 1954 Captain; 1956 Acting Commodore; 1959 Commodore; 1959 Acting Rear-Admiral; 1966 Rear-Admiral
PRINCIPAL COMMANDS AT SEA: After graduation from the Naval Academy in 1959, Admiral Tamber was given command of the FPB Ravn, and in 1940 C O of FPB Laks and 5th FPB Div. After the surrender in Norway he escaped to UK where he served as C O FPB 5 based at Dover and later Flotilla Commander of the 4. M/L Flotilla from 1940 to 1941 based at Weymouth. During the rest of the war he was assigned to ships and services as follows:—
1942 First Lieutenant of KNM (FF) Sleipner; 1942-1944 Flotilla Commander 30 FPB flotilla based at Lerwick Shetland; 1944-1945 First Lieutenant KNM (DD) Stord; He took part in various raids, i.e. Spitsbergen, Lofoten II etc. 1945-1948 Staff Appointment to RNON Headquarter; 1948-1949 C O of KNM (DD)Stord; 1949-1952 RNON Headquarters; 1952-1955 Assistant Naval Attaché at the Norwegian Military Mission in Washington D.C. 1955 he attended the Norwegian Defence College and later the same year he took command of KNM (DD) Bergen; 1956-1959 Commander Coastal Fleet; 1959-1962 Deputy Commander of RNON; 1962 Head of the Norwegian Military Mission in Washington D. C. and Norwegian member of MCPS
OFFICIAL ADDRESS: SKN Box 359, 8001 Bodö. *Telephone:* 23040
PRIVATE ADDRESS: SKN, Box 359, 8001 Bodö

SOUTH AFRICA

TERRY-LLOYD REAR ADMIRAL M. R., SOUTH AFRICAN NAVY
DECORATIONS: SM 1960
PRESENT APPOINTMENT: Chief of Naval Staff 1 July, 1966
DATE OF BIRTH: 29 July, 1913
EDUCATION: Matriculation, AIBSA and sundry courses
DATES OF PROMOTIONS: Sub-Lieutenant RNVR (SA) July 1934; Lieutenant RNVR (SA) 1 July, 1938; Lieutenant-Commander SA Naval Forces 1 October, 1943; Lieutenant-Commander SA Navy 1 May, 1946; Commander 1 January, 1953; Captain 1 December, 1957; Commodore 1 April, 1963; Rear Admiral 1 July, 1966
PRINCIPAL COMMANDS AT SEA: Mooivlei 1940; Southern Isles 1942; Southern Sea 1943; Good Hope 1948; Natal 1948; Simon van der Stel 1954, and Senior Officer: 6th Escourt Group; Vrystaat 1956 and Senior Officer; 10th Frigate Squadron; President Kruger 1962; and Senior Officer: 10th Frigate Squadron
OTHER PREVIOUS APPOINTMENTS OF NOTE: Naval Liaison Officer, London 1946-1948; Staff Officer Plans 1950-1951; General Staff Officer, Naval Headquarters 1952-1953; Officer Commanding, South African Naval Base, Salisbury Island, Durban 1955-1956 (Acting Captain)
OFFICIAL ADDRESS: SA Naval Headquarters, Simonstown. *Telephone:* 869 ext. 600

NORWAY
THOMESEN, COMMODORE R., ROYAL NORWEGIAN NAVY
DECORATIONS: Norwegian and British War Medals
PRESENT APPOINTMENT: Chief of Staff Personnel (September 1968)
DATE OF BIRTH: 25 June, 1918
EDUCATION: Naval Staff College, Defence College
DATES OF PROMOTIONS: 1943 Sub-Lieutenant; 1945 Lieutenant; 1950 Lieutenant Commander; 1953 Commander; 1959 Captain; 1968 Commodore
PRINCIPAL COMMANDS AT SEA: 1954 Destroyer Escort; 1959 Training Ship
OTHER PREVIOUS APPOINTMENTS OF NOTE: Saclant 1956-1958
OFFICIAL ADDRESS: Royal Norwegian Naval Headquarters, Bankplassen 2, Oslo Mil, Oslo 1, Norway *Telephone:* 33 30 70 ext. 6780
PRIVATE ADDRESS: Nadderudveien 156, Oslo 7, Norway

U.S.A.
TIBBETS, REAR-ADMIRAL JOSEPH BONAFIELD (NAVAL AVIATOR) US NAVY
CURRENT DUTY STATION: Commander, Fleet Air Quonset; additional duty: Commander, Carrier Division 20 (June 1969)
DATE OF BIRTH 1911
EDUCATION: 1934 Naval Academy; 1952 Naval War College
DATE OF COMMISSION: 31st May, 1934
PROMOTED TO: Rear Admiral 1st July, 1962
COMMANDS: 1956-1957 Orca AVP 49; 1959-1960 Randolph CVS 15; 1962-1963 Carrier Division 15; 1963-1966 Chief, Military Assistance Advisory Group, Portugal
OFFICIAL ADDRESS: Naval Air Station, Quonset Point, Rhode Island
HOME ADDRESS: Winter Haven, Florida

U.S.A.
TIGHE, REAR-ADMIRAL CHARLES (NAVAL AVIATOR) US NAVY
CURRENT DUTY STATION: Commander, 11th Coast Guard District, Long Beach (July 1968)
DATE OF BIRTH: 1911
EDUCATION: 1935 Coast Guard Academy; 1939 Naval Air Station, Pensacola
FIRST COMMISSIONED: 27th May, 1935
PROMOTED TO: Rear Admiral 17th March, 1965
COMMANDS: 1943-1944 Training Squadron 8 Able and Senior Seaplane Commander; 1950-1951 Coast Guard Air Station, Port Angeles; 1952-1955 Coast Guard Air Station, Miami; 1955-1958 Coast Guard Air Detachment, Kodiak and Search and Rescue Sector 2, North Pacific; 1966-1968 9th Coast Guard District, Cleveland

CANADA
TILLEY, CAPTAIN H. R.
DECORATIONS: CD
PRESENT APPOINTMENT: Senior Liaison Officer (Navy), Canadian Defence Liaison Staff London 23 December 1967
DATE OF BIRTH: 17 December, 1923
EDUCATION: Lakefield College School, Lakefield, Ontario; Royal Naval College, Dartmouth
DATES OF PROMOTIONS: Commander 1 January, 1958; Captain 1 January, 1964
PRINCIPAL COMMANDS AT SEA: 1954-1956 HMCS Jonquiere; 1961-1963 HMCS Saguenay; 1965 Commander Seventh Canadian Escort Squadron
OTHER PREVIOUS APPOINTMENTS OF NOTE: Captain Sea Training 1964; Deputy COS (Combat Readiness) Maritime Command 1966; 1967 Imperial Defence College
OFFICIAL ADDRESS: Canadian Defence Liaison Staff London, 1 Grosvenor Square, London, W.1. *Telephone:* 01-629-9492 ext. 402
HOME ADDRESS: Woodcote, 24A, St. George's Road, Bickley, Bromley, Kent

CANADA
TIMBRELL, REAR ADMIRAL R. W.
DECORATIONS: DSC 1940; CD 1949
PRESENT APPOINTMENT: Deputy Chief Plans, Canadian Forces Headquarters September 1967
DATE OF BIRTH: 1 February, 1920
EDUCATION: Cadet Entry
PROMOTIONS: Cadet 20 August, 1937; Midshipman 1 September, 1938; Sub-Lieutenant 1 May, 1940; Lieutenant 15 August, 1941; Lieutenant-Commander 15 August, 1949; Commander 1 July, 1952; Captain 1 July, 1958; Commodore 1 July, 1965; Rear Admiral 1 September, 1967
PRINCIPAL COMMANDS AT SEA: HMCS Swansea April 1948-February 1949; HMCS St Laurent, May 1955-January 1957 also Commander Third Canadian Escort Squadron from September 1956; HMCS Bonaventure August 1963-April 1965
PREVIOUS APPOINTMENT OF NOTE: HMCS Stadacona as Officer-in-Charge, Anti-Submarine School and on staff of the Flag Officer Atlantic Coast as Staff Officer Anti-Submarine April 1946-March 1948; Naval Headquarters as a Torpedo Anti-Submarine Staff Officer August 1949-February 1951; Canadian Services College Royal Roads as Vice Commandant and Officer Commanding Cadet Wing March 1952-July 1954; Royal Naval Staff Course September, 1954-May 1955; HMCS Shearwater as Executive Officer February 1957-September 1958; Naval Headquarters as Director of Undersea Warfare September 1958-August 1960; On staff of the Supreme Allied Commander Atlantic as Assistant Director Plans Defensive Operations August 1960-August 1963; Training Command as Commander Naval Component and later as Comptroller August 1965-September 1967
PRESENT ADDRESS: Deputy Chief of Plans, Canadian Forces Headquarters, Cartier Square, Ottawa 4, Ontario

GERMANY
TOPP, REAR ADMIRAL (UPPER HALF) E., GERMAN NAVY
DECORATIONS: Dipl. Ing. (graduated engineer); Iron Cross II & I Class; Knight's Cross of Iron Cross; Oak Leaf Cluster to Knight's Cross; Oak Leaf Cluster with Crossed swords to Knights Cross; Submarine War Badge with Diamonds, War Service Cross, II & I class
PRESENT APPOINTMENT: Deputy Chief of Staff, Navy, and Chief, Navy Staff, Federal German Ministry of Defence 1 October, 1966
DATE OF BIRTH: 2 July, 1914
EDUCATION: Studied architecture 1946-1950; Graduate Assistant at Tech. University, Hannover 1950-1952
DATES OF PROMOTIONS: Entered Navy 1 April, 1934; Lieutenant (Junior Grade) 1 April 1937; Lieutenant 1 April, 1938; Lieutenant Commander 1 September, 1941; Commander 12 August, 1942; Commander (Senior Grade) 1 December, 1944; Captain (Navy) 28 November 1959; Rear Admiral (Lower Half) 8 November 1965; Rear Admiral (Upper Half) 21 December, 1966
PRINICPAL COMMANDS AT SEA: Commanding Officer U57 & U552 1940-1942; Chief, 7th Submarine Flotilla 1942-1944; Chief, Submarine Test Group 1944; Commanding Officer of a Type XXI Submarine 1945
OTHER PREVIOUS APPOINTMENTS OF NOTE: Head of Navy Section, Staff of German Permanenet Military Representative, MC/PS Washington, German Liaison Officer with Saclant 1958-1960; Chief of Staff, German Permanent Military Representative 1961; Commander, Amphibious Forces 1962-1963; Chief of Staff, Fleet Command 1963-1965; Assistant Chief of Staff, Operations, Navy, Federal German Ministry of Defence 1965-1966
OFFICIAL ADDRESS: Ministry of Defence, 53 Bonn,, Postfach 161
PRIVATE ADDRESS: 53 Bonn-Vennsberg, Garréstr 16

U.S.A.
TOWNSEND, VICE-ADMIRAL ROBERT LEE (NAVAL AVIATOR) US NAVY
CURRENT DUTY STATION: Commander, Naval Air Force, Atlantic Fleet (March 1969)
DATE OF BIRTH: 1911
EDUCATION: 1934 Naval Academy; 1956 National War College
DATE OF COMMISSION: 31st May, 1934
PROMOTED TO: Rear Admiral 1st July, 1961; Vice Admiral 1st March, 1969
COMMANDS: 1950-1951 Composite Squadron 6; 1959-1960 Kearsarge CVS 33; 1960-1961 Carrier Division 17; 1964-1965 Carrier Division 6; 1966-1969 Naval Air Systems Command, Washington, DC
OFFICIAL ADDRESS: Naval Air Station, Norfolk, Virginia 23511
HOME ADDRESS: 1100 North 7th Street, Harlingen, Texas

UNITED KINGDOM
TREACHER, CAPTAIN J. D., ROYAL NAVY
PRESENT APPOINTMENT: Commanding Officer HMS Eagle 25 November, 1968
DATE OF BIRTH: 23 September, 1924
EDUCATION: Colet Court and St. Pauls School, London
DATES OF PROMOTIONS: Commander 31 December, 1956; Captain 30 June, 1962
PRINCIPAL COMMANDS AT SEA: 1952-1953 849 Squadron; 1964-1966 HMS Lowestoft
OTHER PREVIOUS APPOINTMENTS OF NOTE: Commander (Air) HMS Victorious 1959-1961; Naval Assistant to Controller of the Navy 1962-1964
OFFICIAL ADDRESS: HMS Eagle, BFPO Ships, London

U.K.
TREWBY, REAR ADMIRAL G. F. A., ROYAL NAVY
DECORATIONS: FI Mech. E; MI Mar E; MRINA
PRESENT APPOINTMENT: Assistant Controller (Polaris) August 1968
DATE OF BIRTH July, 1917
EDUCATION: RNC Dartmouth 1931-1934; RNEC Keyham 1935-1939
DATES OF PROMOTIONS: Commander June 1950; Captain December 1959; Rear Admiral July 1968
PREVIOUS APPOINTMENTS OF NOTE: Commanding Officer HMS Sultan 1963-1964; IDC 1965; Captain of Base, Portland and CSO (T) to Fost 1966-1968

U.S.A.
TRIMBLE, VICE-ADMIRAL PAUL EDWIN, US NAVY
CURRENT DUTY STATION: Assistant Commandant, US Coast Guard (July 1966)
DATE OF BIRTH: 1913
EDUCATION: 1936 Coast Guard Academy; 1942 Harvard School of Business Administration
FIRST COMMISSIONED: 8th June, 1936
PROMOTED TO: Rear Admiral 1st July, 1964; Vice Admiral 27th July, 1966
COMMANDS: 1943-1944 Hoguiam; 1944-1945 Sansalito and Escort Division 27; 1951-1953 Storis; 1959-1961 Duane; 1961-1962 Coast Guard Base, Boston
HOME ADDRESS: 109 Lucas Lane, Bethesda, Md.

UNITED KINGDOM
TROUP, REAR-ADMIRAL J. A. R., ROYAL NAVY
DECORATIONS: D.S.C. 1943; and Bar 1945
PRESENT APPOINTMENT: Flag Officer Sea Training 13 May, 1969
DATE OF BIRTH: 18 July, 1921
EDUCATION: HMS Worcester; RNC, Dartmouth
DATES OF PROMOTIONS: Commander 31 December, 1953; Captain 31 December, 1959; Rear-Admiral 7 January, 1969
PRINCIPAL COMMANDS AT SEA: Submarines; Third Submarine Squadron; HMS Intrepid
OTHER PREVIOUS APPOINTMENTS OF NOTE: Staff of FOSM; Executive Officer HMS Victorious; Naval Assistant to First Sea Lord Director of Naval Equipment; Captain of the Fleet, Home Fleet
OFFICIAL ADDRESS: HM Naval Base, Portland *Telephone:* Weymouth 2781

U.S.A.
TRUM, REAR-ADMIRAL, HERMAN JOHN III, (NAVAL AVIATOR) US NAVY
CURRENT DUTY STATION:
Commander, Anti-Submarine Warfare Group 5 (June 1969)
DATE OF BIRTH: 1917
EDUCATION: 1940 Naval Academy; 1958 Naval War College
DATE OF COMMISSION: 6th June, 1940
PROMOTED TO: Rear Admiral 1st July, 1967
COMMANDS: 1946 Combat Aircraft Service Unit (F) 48; 1946-1947 Fleet Aircraft Service Squadron 119; 1950-1952 Fighter Squadron 53; 1961-1962 Manatee AO 58; 1963-1964 Oriskany CVA 34; 1967-1969 Fleet Air Whidbey; Commandant 13th Naval District
OFFICIAL ADDRESS: FPO San Francisco, California 96601
HOME ADDRESS: 7335 Mercier Street, Kansas City, Missouri

JAPAN
TSUKUDO, VICE-ADMIRAL T.
DECORATIONS: The Fifth Order of the Rising Sun 1938; The Fifth Order of the Sacred Treasure 1938
PRESENT APPOINTMENT: Commandant, Kure Regional District JMSDF
DTE OF BIRTH: 20 February, 1916
EDUCATION: Graduated Naval Academy 1936
DATE OF PROMOTIONS: Commander 16 August, 1953; Captain 1 August, 1958; Rear Admiral 1 July 1965 Vice Admiral 31 December, 1968
PRINCIPAL COMMANDS AT SEA: Commanding Officer, The 1st Submarine Flotilla 1965-1966
OTHER PREVIOUS APPOINTMENTS OF NOTE: Chief of Sections, Joint Staff Office, Defence Agency 1966-1967; Superintendent, Maritime Officers Candidate School 1968
OFFICIAL ADDRESS: Headquarters Kure Rigional District JMSDF, 3-Chome Saiwai-cho Kure-Si Hirosima-Ken Japan, *Telephone* Kure 22-5511
PRIVATE ADDRESS: 17-5 5-Chome Siroganedai Minato-Ku Tokyo-To Japan

UNITED KINGDOM
TURNER, VICE–ADMIRAL A. F., ROYAL NAVY
DECORATIONS: C.B. 1966; D.S.C. 1945
PRESENT APPOINTMENT: Chief of Fleet Support 1967
DATE OF BIRTH: 23 June, 1912
EDUCATION: Stonyhurst College; Royal Naval Engineering College.
DATES OF PROMOTIONS: 1931 Entered RN; 1947 Commander; 1956 Captain; 1964 Rear-Admiral; 1968 Vice Admiral.
PREVIOUS APPOINTMENTS OF NOTE: DAMR 1960-1962; CSO(T) Med 1962-1964; DGA (Naval) 1965-1967
OFFICIAL ADDRESS: Ministry of Defence, Main Building, London, S.W.1 *Telephone:* 01-930 7022 ext. 2163
PRIVATE ADDRESS: 15 West Way, Rickmansworth, Herts.

U.S.A.
TURNER, REAR-ADMIRAL (SELECTEE) FREDERICK CHARLES (NAVAL AVIATOR) US NAVY
CURRENT DUTY STATION: Chief of Naval Air Advanced Training (October 1968), Authorized to assume title of Rear Admiral
DATE OF BIRTH: 1923
EDUCATION: 1954 General Line School; 1961 University of Maryland, Industrial College of the Armed Forces
DATE OF COMMISSION: 1st December, 1943
PROMOTED TO: Rear Admiral, selected for promotion on 6 June 1968
COMMANDS: 1961-1962 Fighter Squadron 32; 1962-1963 Carrier Air Group 3; 1965-1967 Sandoval APA 194; 1967-1968 America CVA 66
OFFICIAL ADDRESS: Naval Air Station, Corpus Christi, Texas 78419
HOME ADDRESS: 9 Kennedy Road, Morris Plains, New Jersey

U.S.A.
TURNER, REAR-ADMIRAL MYRON GEORGE (DENTAL CORPS.) US NAVY
CURRENT DUTY STATION: Inspector General, Dental, Bureau of Medicine and Surgery (July 1968)
DATE OF BIRTH: 1913
EDUCATION: 1936 Ohio State University
DATE OF COMMISSION: 15th August, 1938
PROMOTED TO: Rear Admiral 1st July, 1965
OFFICIAL ADDRESS: Potomac Annex, Washington, DC 20390
HOME ADDRESS: 108 Sixteenth Avenue, Columbus, Ohio

UNITED KINGDOM
TWISS, ADMIRAL SIR F. R., ROYAL NAVY
DECORATIONS: K.C.B. 1965; C.B. 1962; D.S.C. 1945
PRESENT APPOINTMENT: Chief of Naval Personnel and Second Sea Lord August 1967
DATE OF BIRTH: 7 July, 1910
EDUCATION: Royal Naval College, Dartmouth; Qualified in Gunnery 1935; Naval Staff Co. 1939; Imperial Defence College 1955
DATES OF PROMOTIONS: 1945 Commander; 1950 Captain; 1960 Rear-Admiral; 1963 Vice Admiral; 1967 Admiral
PRINCIPAL COMMANDS AT SEA: 1946-1947 HMS Porlock Bay; 1953-1954 HMS Coquette; Captain Fishery Protection and 5th Minesweeping Squadron; HMS Ceylon 1957-1960; 1962-1964 Flag Officer Flotillas, Home Fleet
OTHER PREVIOUS APPOINTMENTS OF NOTE: Naval Secretary 1960-1962; Commander Far East Fleet 1965-1967
OFFICIAL ADDRESS: Chief of Naval Personnel and Second Sea Lord, Room 7373, Ministry of Defence (Main Building), Whitehall, London, S.W.1.

U.S.A.
TYREE, VICE-ADMIRAL JOHN AUGUSTINE, JNR., US NAVY
CURRENT DUTY STATION: Chief of Staff, US European Command (July 1968)
DATE OF BIRTH: 1911
EDUCATION: 1933 Naval Academy; 1954 National War College
DATE OF COMMISSION: 1st June, 1933
PROMOTED TO: Rear Admiral 1st July, 1959; Vice Admiral 26th July 1968
MAJOR AWARDS: Navy Cross with gold star in lieu of subsequent award
COMMANDS: 1941-1944 Finback SS 230; 1940-1950 Submarine Division 82; 1954-1955 Botetourt APA 136; 1955-1956 Submarine Squadron 6; 1958-1959 Service Squadron 3; 1959-1960 US Naval Forces, Korea; 1962-1964 South Atlantic Force
OFFICIAL ADDRESS: Brussels, APO New York 09128
HOME ADDRESS: 6909 Oakridge Avenue, Chevy Chase, Maryland

JAPAN
UCHIDA, ADMIRAL K.
DECORATIONS: The Order of the Golden Kite; 4th Order of the Sacred Treasure; 5th Order of the Risen Sun
PRESENT APPOINTMENT: Chief of the Maritime Staff 1 July, 1969
DATE OF BIRTH: 8 June, 1915
EDUCATION: Graduated from the Imperial Japanese Naval Academy
DATES OF PROMOTIONS: Lieutenant Commander June, 1952; Commander August 1953; Captain August 1957; Rear Admiral July 1964; Vice Admiral July 1967
PREVIOUS APPOINTMENTS OF NOTE: Commander, 3rd Escort Flotilla September 1963; Chief, Intelligence Division, Maritime Staff Office July 1964; Chief, Operations Division, Maritime Staff Office July 1966
OFFICIAL ADDRESS: Commander, Fleet Escort Force, c/o Ykosuka Regional District Headquarters, Nishihemi-Cho, Yokosuka-Shi *Telephone:* 0469-61-8281
PRIVATE ADDRESS: Nishi 1-9-14, Fukuoka-Cho, Iruma-Gun, Saitama-Ken. *Telephone:* 0492-62-0987

JAPAN
UCHIDA, VICE-ADMIRAL Y.
DECORATIONS: 5th Imperial Order of the Sacred Treasure 1944
PRESENT APPOINTMENT: Commander, Fleet Air Force January 1969
DATE OF BIRTH: 8 February, 1916
EDUCATION: Imperial Japan Naval Academy
DATE OF PROMOTIONS: Lieutenant Commander 1 June, 1954; Commander 16 February, 1955; Captain 1 August, 1959; Rear Admiral 1 July, 1965; Vice Admiral 1 January, 1969
OTHER PREVIOUS APPOINTMENTS OF NOTE: Commanding Officer, 4 Air Wing; Commanding Officer 2 Air Wing; Deputy Chief, Operations Division; Commander Air Training Command
OFFICIAL ADDRESS: Shonan-cho Higashikatsushika-Gun Chiba, JAPAN

JAPAN
UMEICHI, REAR-ADMIRAL I.,
DECORATIONS: 6th Order of Merit
PRESENT APPOINTMENT: Commander, 3rd Escort Flotilla, 16 July, 1968
DATE OF BIRTH: 8 December, 1918
EDUCATION: Naval Academy
DATE OF PROMOTION: 1 January, 1969
PRINCIPAL COMMANDS AT SEA: Commanding Officer of the DD Shikinami 1959; Commander, 32nd Escort Division 1965
OTHER PREVIOUS APPOINTMENTS OF NOTE: Chief Staffs, 2nd Escort Flotilla 1961; Chief, Sub-Section Plans, Operations Planning Section, Operations Planning Division, M.S.O. 1964; Chief of Educational Department, Officer Candidate School, 1966
OFFICIAL ADDRESS: Amarube, Maizuru-shi, Kyoto-fu Maizuru District Headquarters
PRIVATE ADDRESS: 2-13, Sasuke, Kamakura-shi

DENMARK
VALENTINER, REAR-ADMIRAL S. J., ROYAL DANISH NAVY
DECORATIONS: Commander of the Order of Dannebrog (Danish) 1964; Commander of the Order of The Sword (Swedish) 1954; Commander of the Order of St. Olav (Norweigian) 1965; Commander of the Order of Oranje-Nassau (Dutch) 1954; Officer of the Order of Legion of Merit (U.S.A.) 1967; Knigh of the Order of The Sword (Swedish) 1935; Good Conduct Medal (Danish) 1951
PRESENT APPOINTMENT: Commander Naval Material Command 1967
DATE OF BIRTH: 27 November, 1907
EDUCATION: Naval Academy 1925-1929; Swed. Naval Staff Coll. 1935-1937
DATES OF PROMOTIONS: 1929 Commissioned; 1938 Lieutenant Commander; 1945 Commander; 1958 Captain; 1964 Rear-Admiral (Act.); 1968 Rear-Admiral
PRINCIPAL COMMANDS AT SEA: 1947 Command of 2nd Minesweeper Flotilla; 1958-1963 Commanding Officer Naval Ordnance and Gunnery; 1953-1955 Naval Attaché Stockholm and Oslo; 1963-1966 Naval Attaché Washington Ottawa
OTHER PREVIOUS APPOINTMENTS OF NOTE: Danish Member of The NATO Military Committee in Permanent Session and Danish Liaison Officer to Saclant 1964-1966
OFFICIAL ADDRESS: Søvaernets Materielkommando, Holmen, Copenhagen, Denmark
PRIVATE ADDRESS: 'Søvaesthuset', Overgaden o.V.6o, Copenhagen, Denmark

ITALY
VALSECCHI, REAR ADMIRAL F., ITALIAN NAVY
DECORATIONS: 1 bronze medal, 3 crosses of merit of war
PRESENT APPOINTMENT: Flag Officer, 3rd Naval division
DATE OF BIRTH: 15 June, 912
DATE OF PROMOTION: Rear Admiral 31 December, 1964
OFFICIAL ADDRESS: Comando 3 Divisione Navale, Nave Etna, Marinapost, Roma

U.S.A.
VAN ARSDALL, REAR-ADMIRAL CLYDE JAMES, JNR., US NAVY
CURRENT DUTY STATION:
Deputy Chief of Staff, Commander-in-Chief Europe (1969)
DATE OF BIRTH: 1913
EDUCATION: Naval Academy 1930; 1955 Naval War College
DATE OF COMMISSION: 31st May, 1934
PROMOTED TO: Rear Admiral 1st July, 1962
MAJOR AWARDS: Navy Cross
COMMANDS: 1944-1945 Anthony DD 515; 1945-1947 Perry DD 844; 1951-1952 Escort Squadron 10 1957-1958 Tidewater AD 31; 1958-1959 Destroyer Squadron 37; 1961-1963 Destroyer Flotilla 1; 1966-1967 South Atlantic Force
OFFICIAL ADDRESS: Brussels
HOME ADDRESS: Indianola, Mississippi

U.S.A.
VANNOY, REAR-ADMIRAL FRANK WILSON US NAVY
CURRENT DUTY STATION: Deputy Director, J-5 (Plans and Policy) Joint Chiefs of Staff (July 1968)
DATE OF BIRTH: 1915
EDUCATION: 1939 Naval Academy; 1955 Naval War College
DATE OF COMMISSION: 1st June 1939
PROMOTED TO: Rear Admiral 10th August, 1965
COMMANDS: 1953-1954 Watts DD 567; 1957-1958 Mine Squadron 8; 1961-1963 Vermillion AKA 107; 1963-1964 Amphibious Squadron 10; 1965-1967 Amphibious Training Command, Atlantic Fleet; 1967 Amphibious Group 1; 1967-1968 Amphibious Group 3
OFFICIAL ADDRESS: The Pentagon, Washington, DC 20301
HOME ADDRESS: 1829 Rupert Street, McLean, Virginia

U.S.A.
VASEY, REAR-ADMIRAL LLOYD ROLAND US NAVY
CURRENT DUTY STATION: Commander, Cruiser-Destroyer Flotilla 7 (October 1968)
DATE OF BIRTH: 1917
EDUCATION: 1939 Naval Academy; 1951 Naval Postgraduate School; 1957 National War College
DATE OF COMMISSION: 1st June, 1939
PROMOTED TO: Rear Admiral 1st December, 1965
COMMANDS 1948-1950 Capitaine SS 336; 1955-1956 Submarine Division 102; 1961-1962 Kawishiwi AO 146; 1964-1965 St. Paul CA 73
OFFICIAL ADDRESS: FPO San Francisco, California 96601
HOME ADDRESS: North Hollywood, California

U.S.A.
VETH, REAR-ADMIRAL KENNETH LEROY US NAVY
CURRENT DUTY STATION: Commandant, Fourth Naval District; additional duty: Commander Naval Base, Philadelphia (November, 1968)
DATE OF BIRTH: 1911
EDUCATION: 1935 Naval Academy; 1953 Naval War College
DATE OF COMMISSION: 6th June, 1935
PROMOTED TO: Rear Admiral 1st July, 1961
COMMANDS: 1949-1950 Everett F. Larson DDR 830; 1953-1954 Mine Division 2; 1954-1955 Monongahela T-AO 42; 1959-1960 Providence CLG 6; 1960-1961 Destroyer Flotilla 7; 1961-1964 Mine Force, Pacific Fleet; 1964-1965 Anti-Submarine Warfare Group 3; 1965-1967 Chief of Legislative Affairs, Navy Department; 1967-1968 US Naval Forces, Vietnam; Chief, US Naval Advisory Group, US Military Assistance Command, Vietnam
OFFICIAL ADDRESS: Naval Base, Philadelphia, Pennsylvania 19112
HOME ADDRESS: Minot, North Dakota

U.K.
VILLAR, CAPTAIN G. R. ROYAL NAVY
DECORATIONS: DSC 1943
PRESENT APPOINTMENT: Captain HMS Excellent January 1969
DATE OF BIRTH: 14 May, 1922
EDUCATION: Dartmouth
DATES OF PROMOTIONS: Commander 1955; Captain 1964
PREVIOUS APPOINTMENTS OF NOTE:BJSM Washington 1958-1960; HMS Lochinvar 1961-1962; Naval Staff-Gunnery Division 1963-1964; Naval Attaché Athens & Tel Aviv 1965-1968
OFFICIAL ADDRESS: HMS Excellent, Portsmouth, Hants.

U.S.A.
VORIS, REAR-ADMIRAL, FRANK BURKHART, (MEDICAL CORPS.) US NAVY
CURRENT DUTY STATION:
Fleet Surgeon, Pacific Fleet (July 1969)
DATE OF BIRTH: 1909
EDUCATION: 1933 University of Illinois
DATE OF COMMISSION: 10th July, 1941
PROMOTED TO: Rear Admiral 11, October, 1966
OFFICIAL ADDRESS: Pearl Harbor, Hawaii
HOME ADDRESS: Miami Beach, Florida

U.S.A.
WADLEIGH, REAR-ADMIRAL, JOHN REMEY US NAVY
CURRENT DUTY STATION:
Commander, Training Command, Atlantic Fleet (June 1969);
DATE OF BIRTH: 1915
EDUCATION: 1937 Naval Academy; 1944 Naval Postgraduate School; 1948 Armed Forces Staff College
DATE OF COMMISSION: 3rd June, 1937
PROMOTED TO: Rear Admiral 1st July, 1965
COMMANDS: 1950-1951 John R. Pierce DD 753; 1954-1955 Escort Squadron 16; 1958-1959 Grand Canyon AD 28; 1962-1963 Springfield CLG 7
OFFICIAL ADDRESS: Norfolk, Virginia 23511
HOME ADDRESS: Jamestown, Rhode Island

U.S.A.
WAESCHE, REAR-ADMIRAL RUSSELL RANDOLPH, JNR., US NAVY
CURRENT DUTY STATION: Commander, 2nd Coast Guard District, St. Louis (March 1968)
DATE OF BIRTH: 1913
EDUCATION: 1930 Massanutten Military Academy; 1936 Coast Guard Academy
FIRST COMMISSIONED: 8th June, 1936
PROMOTED TO: Rear Admiral 1st July, 1966
COMMANDS: 1943-1944 Majave; 1944-1945 Camp; 1947-1948 Ivy; 1952-1954 Casco; 1960-1962 Northwind

U.S.A.
WALKER, REAR-ADMIRAL, THOMAS JACKSON III, (NAVAL AVIATOR) US NAVY
CURRENT DUTY STATION: Commander, Naval Air Systems Command (February 1969)
DATE OF BIRTH: 1916
EDUCATION: 1939 Naval Academy; 1944 Naval Postgraduate School; 1956 Industrial College of the Armed Forces
DATE OF COMMISSION: 1st June, 1939
PROMOTED TO: Rear Admiral 1st July, 1965
COMMANDS: 1946-1948 Fighter Squadron 5-B; 1951-1953 Air Development Squadron 5; 1957-1958 Fleet All-Weather Training Unit, Pacific; 1958 All-Weather Fighter Squadron 3; 1960 Nitro AE 23; 1961-1962 Constellation CVA 64; 1966-1967 Carrier Division 3
OFFICIAL ADDRESS: Main Navy Building, Washington, DC 20360
HOME ADDRESS: Daytona Beach, Florida

U.S.A.
WALLACE, REAR-ADMIRAL, KENNETH CARROLL, US NAVY
CURRENT DUTY STATION: Military Assistant to Deputy Director (Strategic and Space Systems), Office of the Director of Defense Research & Engineering (July, 1968)
DATE OF BIRTH: 1920
EDUCATION: 1942 Naval Academy; 1952 Naval Postgraduate School; 1958 Army Command and General Staff College
DATE OF COMMISSION: 19th June, 1942
PROMOTED TO: Rear Admiral 1st August, 1968
COMMANDS: 1953-1955 George DE 697; 1960-1961 Manley DD 940; 1964-1965 Observation Island EAG 154; 1966-1968 Long Beach CGN 9
OFFICIAL ADDRESS: The Pentagon, Washington, DC 20301
HOME ADDRESS: 1127 Flora Avenue, Coronado, California

U.S.A.

WARD, REAR-ADMIRAL NORVELL GARDINER, US NAVY
CURRENT DUTY STATION: Assistant Chief of Naval Operations (Safety) October 1968
DATE OF BIRTH: 1912
EDUCATION: Naval Academy 1935; 1952 Armed Forces Staff College; 1958 National War College
DATE OF COMMISSION: 6th June, 1935
PROMOTED TO: Rear Admiral 1st August, 1963
MAJOR AWARDS: Navy Cross
COMMANDS: 1943-1944 Guardfish SS 217; 1945-1946 Irex SS 482; 1951-1952 Yarnall DD 541; 1955-1956 Nantahala AO 60; 1956-1957 Submarine Squadron 5; 1958-1961 Submarine Squadron 14; 1965-1966 Chief, Naval Advisory Group, US Military Assistance Command Vietnam; 1966-1967 US Naval Forces, Vietnam; additional duty: Chief, Naval Advisory Group US Military Assistance Command, Vietnam; 1967-1968 Service Group 3
OFFICIAL ADDRESS: The Pentagon, Washington, DC 20350
HOME ADDRESS: Roanoke, Virginia

U.S.A.

WARDEN, REAR-ADMIRAL HORACE DREHER, (MEDICAL CORPS) US NAVY
CURRENT DUTY STATION: Commanding Officer, Naval Hospital, San Diego, and Commanding Officer, Naval Hospital Corps. School, San Diego (December 1964)
DATE OF BIRTH: 1911
EDUCATION: 1933 Montana State University; 1938 Rush Medical College of University of Chicago
DATE OF COMMISSION: 15th July, 1939
PROMOTED TO: Rear Admiral 11th September, 1964
COMMANDS: 1962-1964 Naval Hospital, Charleston, South Carolina
OFFICIAL ADDRESS: San Diego, California 92134
HOME ADDRESS: Roundup, Montana

U.S.A.

WATERS, REAR-ADMIRAL ODALE DABNEY JNR., US NAVY
CURRENT DUTY STATION: Oceanographer of the Navy (September 1965)
DATE OF BIRTH: 1910
EDUCATION: 1932 Naval Academy; 1940 Naval Postgraduate School; 1950 Armed Forces Staff College
DATE OF COMMISSION: 2nd June, 1932
PROMOTED TO: Rear Admiral 1st October, 1960
COMMANDS: 1945-1946 Laffey DD 724; 1952-1953 Glynn APA 239; 1956-1957 Destroyer Squadron 2; 1957-1958 Naval Mine Depot, Yorktown, Virginia; 1958-1960 Naval Weapons Station, Yorktown; 1960-1962 Destroyer Flotilla 1; 1964-1965 Mine Forces, Pacific Fleet, Naval Base, Los Angeles
OFFICIAL ADDRESS: Madison Building, 732 N. Washington Street, Alexandria, Virginia 22314
HOME ADDRESS: 4820 Ft. Sumner Drive, Sumner, Maryland

UNITED KINGDOM
WEEKES, VENERABLE ARCHDEACON A. W. M., ROYAL NAVY
DECORATIONS: Q.H.C. 1969; A. K.C.
PRESENT APPOINTMENT: Chaplain of the Fleet and Archdeacon, Royal Navy 1969
DATE OF BIRTH: 25 April, 1919
EDUCATION: Rochester Cathedral Choir School; King's College London; Lincoln Theological College
OFFICIAL ADDRESS: Ministry of Defence, Northumberland House, Northumberland Avenue, London W.C.2. *Telephone:* 01 930 9000, Ext. 1486
PRIVATE ADDRESS: Fig Tree House, Queenborough, Kent

U.S.A.

WEEKS, REAR-ADMIRAL, ROBERT HARPER, US NAVY
CURRENT DUTY STATION: Vice Director, Defense Communications Agency (April 1968)
DATE OF BIRTH: 1909
EDUCATION: Naval Academy 1932; 1955 Naval War College
DATE OF COMMISSION: 2nd June, 1932
PROMOTED TO: Rear Admiral 1st July 1961
COMMANDS: 1947-1948 James C. Owens DD 776; 1953-1954 Sabine AO 25; 1957-1958 Destroyer Squadron 10; 1962 Cruiser Division 4; 1962-1963 Cruiser-Destroyer Flotilla 10
OFFICIAL ADDRESS: Washington, DC 20305
HOME ADDRESS: 77 Coggeshall Avenue, Newport, Rhode Island

U.S.A.

WEINEL, REAR-ADMIRAL JOHN PHILLIP (NAVAL AVIATOR) US NAVY
CURRENT DUTY STATION:
Director, Strategic Plans & Policy Division, Office of the Chief of Naval Operations (June 1969)
DATE OF BIRTH: 1916
EDUCATION: 1939 Naval Academy; 1963 National War College
DATE OF COMMISSION: 1st June, 1939
PROMOTED TO : Rear Admiral 1st July, 1967
COMMANDS: 1943 Composite Squadron 33; 1945-1946 Fighting Squadron 14; 1946 Bomber Fighter Squadron 98; 1946-1947 Fighting Squadron 22-A; 1954-1956 Carrier Air Group 5; 1961-1962 Great Sitkin AE 17; 1963-1964 Ticoderoga CVA 14; 1967-1969 Carrier Division 3
OFFICIAL ADDRESS: The Pentagon, Washington, DC 20350

U.K.
WEIR, CAPTAIN J. F. R.
DECORATIONS: Mentioned in Despatches 1941
PRESENT APPOINTMENT: HMS Raleigh, 12 February, 1969
DATE OF BIRTH: 5 June, 1923
DATE OF PROMOTION: Captain, 30 June, 1964
PRINCIPAL COMMANDS AT SEA: HMS Laertes 1953-1954
OTHER PREVIOUS APPOINTMENTS OF NOTE: CO KD Malaya and Naval Officer-in-charge West Malaysia 1964-1966. ACOS C-in-C Western Fleet and Eastlant 1967-1969
OFFICIAL ADDRESS: HMS Raleigh, Torpoint, East Cornwall. *Telephone:* Plymouth 53740

U.S.A.

WEISNER, REAR-ADMIRAL, MAURICE FRANKLIN, (NAVAL AVIATOR) US NAVY
CURRENT DUTY STATION: Deputy Chief of Naval Personnel (July 1968)
DATE OF BIRTH: 1917
EDUCATION: Naval Academy 1941; 1959 National War College
DATE OF COMMISSION: 7th February, 1941
PROMOTED TO: Rear Admiral 1st December, 1965
COMMANDS: 1950-1951 Patrol Squadron 46; 1954-1955 Fighter Squadron 193; 1959-1960 Fighter Squadron 101; 1960-1961 Guadalupe AO 32; 1961-1962 Coral Sea CVA 43; 1965-1967 Carrier Division 1
OFFICIAL ADDRESS: Arlington Annex, Washington, D.C. 20370
HOME ADDRESS: 314 Burwell Avenue, Knoxville, Tennessee

U.S.A.

WEITZENFELD, REAR-ADMIRAL, DANIEL KEHR, (AERONAUTICAL ENGINEERING DUTY) US NAVY
CURRENT DUTY STATION: Naval Air Systems Command Representative, Atlantic (July, 1967)
DATE OF BIRTH: 1917
EDUCATION: 1939 Naval Academy; 1946 Naval Postgraduate School
DATE OF COMMISSION: 1st June, 1939
PROMOTED TO: Rear Admiral 1st July, 1967
OFFICIAL ADDRESS: Naval Air Station, Norfolk, Virginia 23511
HOME ADDRESS: 526 Fifth Street, St. Petersburg, Florida

U.S.A.

WELCH, REAR-ADMIRAL, DAVID FIFE, US NAVY
CURRENT DUTY STATION:
Commander, Naval Support Force, Antarctica (June 1969)
DATE OF BIRTH: 1918
EDUCATION: 1948 Franklin College of Inidana, General Line School; 1961 Naval Postgraduate School; 1963 NATO Defense College
DATE OF COMMISSION: 15th May, 1941
PROMOTED TO: Rear Admiral 1st February, 1968
COMMANDS 1941-1943 PC 473; 1945-1946 Ray K. Edwards APD 96; 1946 Frybarger DE 705; 1948-1951 Underwater Demolition Team 1; 1954-1956 Bausell DD 845; 1961-1962 Mine Squadron 8; 1966-1967 Destroyer Squadron 10; 1967-1968 Amphibious Training Command, Atlantic Fleet
OFFICIAL ADDRESS: Building 210, Washington Navy Yard, Washington, DC 20390
HOME ADDRESS: Tri-Lakes, Columbia City, Indiana

U.S.A.

WELHAM, REAR-ADMIRAL, WALTER, (MEDICAL CORPS.) US NAVY
CURRENT DUTY STATION: Fleet Surgeon and Assistant Chief of Staff, Medicine, Commander-in-Chief, Atlantic Fleet (October 1966)
DATE OF BIRTH: 1907
EDUCATION: 1935 University of Pennsylvania, Temple University Medical School; 1937 Naval Postgraduate School; 1939 Deep Sea Diving School
DATE OF COMMISSION: 25th July, 1936
PROMOTED TO: Rear Admiral 1st January, 1964
OFFICIAL ADDRESS: Norfolk, Virginia 23511
HOME ADDRESS: 1532 Snyder Avenue, Philadelphia, Pennsylvania

U.S.A.

WENDT, ADMIRAL, WALDEMAR FREDERICK AUGUST, US NAVY
CURRENT DUTY STATION: Commander-in-Chief, US Naval Forces, Europe (July, 1968)
DATE OF BIRTH: 1912
EDUCATION: 1933 Naval Academy; 1939 Naval Postgraduate School; 1950 Naval War College
DATE OF COMMISSION: 1st June, 1933
PROMOTED TO: Rear Admiral 1st April 1960; Vice Admiral 9th August, 1965; Admiral 12th July, 1968
COMMANDS: 1943-1944 Monaghan DD 354; 1953-1954 Escort Destroyer Division 22; 1956-1957 Rankin AKA 103; 1957-1958 Destroyer Squadron 36; Destroyer Division 361; 1959-1961 Naval Forces Marianas; Commander-in-Chief Pacific Representative, Marianas-Bonin Islands; 1961-1962 Destroyer Flotilla 7; 1962 Cruiser-Destroyer Flotilla 7
OFFICIAL ADDRESS: London, FPO New York 09510
HOME ADDRESS: Waterloo, Illinois

U.S.A.
WESCHLER, REAR-ADMIRAL THOMAS ROBERT, US NAVY
CURRENT DUTY STATION: Director, Ship Characteristics Division, Office of the Chief of Naval Operations and Chairman, Ship Characteristics Board (May 1968); additional duty: Program Coordinator, DX/DXG Program (March 1967)
DATE OF BIRTH: 1917
EDUCATION: 1939 Naval Academy; 1946 Naval Postgraduate School; 1951 Naval War College; 1963 National War College
DATE OF COMMISSION: 13th December, 1940
PROMOTED TO: Rear Admiral 11th October, 1966
COMMANDS: 1953-1955 Clarence K. Bronson DD 668; 1963-1964 Montrose APA 212; 1965-1966 Amphibious Squadron 3; 1966-1967 Naval Support Activity, Danang, South Vietnam
OFFICIAL ADDRESS: The Pentagon, Washington, DC 20350
HOME ADDRESS: 1305 Greenfield Drive, Erie, Pennsylvania

SWEDEN
WESTIN, MAJOR GENERAL B. L. A., SWEDEN
DECORATION: RS Order of the Sword Commodore 1st Class
PRESENT APPOINTMENT: Chief of Naval Staff November 1968
DATE OF BIRTH: 12 September, 1913
EDUCATION: Studentexamen, RS Naval Academy; RS Naval College; National War College
DATES OF PROMOTIONS: 1937, 2nd Lieutenant; 1961 Colonel; 1965 Brigadier; 1966 Major General
OTHER APPOINTMENTS OF NOTE: Assistant Military Attaché Washington D.C. 1951-1953; Chief Section 2 Defence Staff 1961-1966; Deputy Chief of The Defence Staff 1966-1968
OFFICIAL ADDRESS: Marinstaben, 104 50 Stockholm 80 *Telephone:* 67 95 60
PRIVATE ADDRESS: Stjärnvägen 21, Lidingö

U.K.
WEY, REAR ADMIRAL J. E. A., ROYAL NAVY
DECORATIONS: OFR 1 October, 1964
PRESENT APPOINTMENT: Chief of the Naval Staff 24 March, 1964
DATE OF BIRTH: 7 March, 1918
EDUCATION: Government Class IV, AMI, MARE, C.Eng
DATES OF PROMOTIONS: Commander 6 March, 1962. Captain 25 June, 1963; Commodore 24 March, 1964; Rear Admiral 25 July, 1967
PREVIOUS APPOINTMENT OF NOTE: Naval Officer-in-Charge, Lagos 10 January, 1963
OFFICIAL ADDRESS: Naval Headquarters, Lagos. *Telephone:* 25112
PRIVATE ADDRESS: 14 Queens Drive, Ikoyi, Lagos

U.S.A.
WEYMOUTH, REAR-ADMIRAL, RALPH (NAVAL AVIATOR) US NAVY
CURRENT DUTY STATION: Commander, Fleet Air Wings, US Atlantic Fleet; additional duty: Commander, Fleet Air Wing 5 (July 1968)
DATE OF BIRTH: 1917
EDUCATION: 1938 Naval Academy; 1949 Naval Postgraduate School; 1952 Armed Forces Staff College; 1962 National War College
DATE OF COMMISSION: 2nd June, 1938
PROMOTED TO: Rear Admiral 1st July, 1965
MAJOR AWARDS: Navy Cross
COMMANDS: 1950 Fighter Squadron 112; 1950-1951 Carrier Air Group 11; 1959-1960 Duxbury Bay AVP 38; 1960-1961 Lake Champlain CVS 39; 1965-1967 Iceland Defense Force; additional duty: Barrier Force, Atlantic; Fleet Air Keflavik; 1967-1968 Anti-Submarine Warfare Group 1
OFFICIAL ADDRESS: Naval Air Station, Norfolk, Virginia 23511
HOME ADDRESS: 624 White Street, Key West, Florida

U.S.A.
WHALEN, REAR-ADMIRAL MARK ALEXANDER, US NAVY
CURRENT DUTY STATION: Commander, Eastern Area and Commander, 3rd Coast Guard District (June 1968)
DATE OF BIRTH: 1913
EDUCATION: 1933 Georgetown University; 1937 Coast Guard Academy; 1959 Naval Warfare College
FIRST COMMISSIONED: 21st September, 1937
PROMOTED TO: Rear Admiral 1st July, 1966
COMMANDS: 1944-1945 Modoc; 1950-1952 Humboldt; 1956-1958 Androscoggin; 1963-1965 Coast Guard Reserve Training Center, Yorktown

U.S.A.
WHEELER, REAR-ADMIRAL KENNETH RAY, (SUPPLY CORPS) US NAVY
CURRENT DUTY STATION:
Vice Commander, Naval Supply Systems Command (July 1969)
DATE OF BIRTH: 1918
EDUCATION: 1939 University of California; 1957 Naval War College
DATE OF COMMISSION: 21st August 1939
PROMOTED TO: Rear Admiral 10th August, 1965
COMMANDS: 1963-1965 Naval Ordnance Supply Office, Mechanicsburg, Pennsylvania
OFFICIAL ADDRESS: Main Navy Building, Washington, DC 20390
HOME ADDRESS: Fullerton, California

UNITED KINGDOM
WHETSTONE, COMMANDER A. J., ROYAL NAVY
PRESENT APPOINTMENT: HMS Repulse (Star'd Crew) in Command 5 February, 1968
DATE OF BIRTH: 12 June, 1927
EDUCATION: King Henry VIII School Coventry
DATES OF PROMOTIONS: Commander 31 December, 1963
PRINCIPAL COMMANDS AT SEA: 1955-1956 HMS Sea Scout; 1959-1961 HMS Artful
OTHER PREVIOUS APPOINTMENTS OF NOTE: Operations Officer to Flag Officer Submarines 1963-1965
OFFICIAL ADDRESS: HMS Repulse *Telephone:* Helensburg 4321
PRIVATE ADDRESS: 17 Anglesey Road, Alverstoke, Gosport, Hants.

U.S.A.
WHITE, REAR-ADMIRAL DONALD MORISON, (NAVAL AVIATOR) US NAVY
CURRENT DUTY STATION:
Deputy Director for Inspection Services, Office of the Secretary of Defense (July1969)
Alaska (April 1966)
DATE OF BIRTH: 1915
EDUCATION 1937 Naval Academy; 1956 Naval War College
DATE OF COMMISSION: 3rd June, 1937
PROMOTED TO: Rear Admiral 1st October, 1964
MAJOR AWARDS: Navy Cross
COMMANDS: 1942-1944 Torpedo Squadron 9; 1949-1951 Carrier Air Group 2; 1958-1959 Shasta AE 6; 1961-1962 Forrestal CVA 59; 1964-1966 Carrier Division 20
OFFICIAL ADDRESS: The Pentagon, Washington, DC 20301
HOME ADDRESS: Ruxton, Maryland

U.K.
WILDISH, REAR ADMIRAL D. B. H., ROYAL NAVY
DECORATIONS: CB 1968
PRESENT APPOINTMENT: Admiral Superintendent, HM Dockyard, Devonport 26 October, 1966
DATE OF BIRTH: 24 December, 1914
EDUCATION: Royal Naval College, Dartmouth; Royal Naval Engineering College
DATES OF PROMOTIONS: Commander 30 June, 1948; Captain 31 December, 1957; Rear Admiral 7 July, 1966
OTHER PREVIOUS APPOINTMENT OF NOTE: Commodore Naval Drafting 1964-1966
OFFICIAL ADDRESS: Admiral Superintendent, HM Dockyard, Devonport. *Telephone:* 53740, ext: CB2
PRIVATE ADDRESS: Admiral Superintendent's Residence, 1 The Terrace Morice Yard, Devonport

U.S.A.
WILKINSON, REAR-ADMIRAL EUGENE PARKS, US NAVY
CURRENT DUTY STATION: Commander, Submarine Flotilla 2 (June, 1969)
DATE OF BIRTH: 1918
EDUCATION: 1938 San Diego State College; 1958 Naval War College; 1947 General Line School; 1953 Armed Forces Staff College
DATE OF COMMISSION: 12 December, 1940
PROMOTED TO: Rear Admiral 1st July, 1965
COMMANDS: 1950-1951 Volador SS 490; 1952-1953 Wahoo SS 565; 1954-1957 Nautilus SSN 571 1958-1959 Submarine Division 102; 1961-1963 Long Beach CGN 9
OFFICIAL ADDRESS: FPO New York 09501
HOME ADDRESS: California

U.S.A.
WILLIAMS, REAR-ADMIRAL JAMES WELDON (NAVAL AVIATOR) US NAVY
CURRENT DUTY STATION: Deputy Assistant Secretary of Transportation for Administration, Washington, DC (May 1967)
DATE OF BIRTH: 1914
EDUCATION: 1934 University of Texas; 1938 Coast Guard Academy; 1943 Naval Air Station, Pensacola; 1948 Aircraft Maintenance School for Officers, Rantoul; 1951 Air Force Base Institute of Technology, College of Industrial Administration
FIRST COMMISSIONED: 2nd June, 1938
PROMOTED TO: Rear Admiral 1st May, 1967
COMMANDS: 1958-1960 Coast Guard Air Station, Miami; 1960-1962 Coast Guard Air Station, San Francisco; 1962-1964 Elizabeth City Aircraft Repair and Supply Base; 1964-1966 Air Base Complex, Elizabeth City

U.S.A.
WILLIAMS, REAR-ADMIRAL JOSEPH WARFORD, JNR., US NAVY
CURRENT DUTY STATION: Inspector General, Pacific Fleet (September, 1967)
DATE OF BIRTH: 1911
EDUCATION: 1933 Naval Academy; 1955 Naval War College
DATE OF COMMISSION: 1st June, 1933
PROMOTED TO: Rear Admiral 1st July, 1961
MAJOR AWARDS: Navy Cross
COMMANDS: 1943 Runner SS 476; 1943-1944 Spearfish SS 190; 1944-1946 Bumper SS 333; 1949-1950 Submarine Division 21; 1952-1953 Sperry AS 12; 1953-1954 Submarine Squadron 5; 1959-1960 Toledo CA 133; 1960-1961 Submarine Flotilla 2; 1961-1962 Military Sea Transportation Service, Eastern Atlantic and Mediterranean Area; 1962-1964 Military Sea Transportation Service, Pacific Area; 1964 US Naval Forces Korea; 1964-1965 Service Group 3; Task Force 73; 1966-1967 Submarine Flotilla 2
OFFICIAL ADDRESS: FPO San Francisco, California 96610
HOME ADDRESS: Martinsville, Indiana

U.S./
WITTMANN, REAR-ADMIRAL (SELECTEE) NARVIN OTTO, (AERONAUTICAL ENGINEERING DUTY) US NAVY
CURRENT DUTY STATION: Assistant Executive Director for Systems/ Director, Aircraft Weapon Systems Division, Material Acquisition Group/ Assistant Deputy Commander for Plans and Programs, and Comptroller, Naval Air Systems Command (August, 1966)
DATE OF BIRTH: 1919
EDUCATION: 1945 Naval Postgraduate School; 1946 Massachusetts Institute of Technology; 1959 Industrial College of the Armed Forces
DATE OF COMMISSION: 6th June, 1941
PROMOTED TO: Rear Admiral selected for promotion on 6th June, 1969
COMMANDS: Naval Air Turbine Test Station, Trenton, New Jersey 1961-1963
OFFICIAL ADDRESS: Main Navy, Washington, DC 20360
HOME ADDRESS: Winslow, Nebraska

DENMARK
WOLFHAGEN, CAPTAIN E., ROYAL DANISH NAVY
PRESENT APPOINTMENT: Officer Commanding Naval Base Korsør and Naval District Great Belt 1965; President of the Danish Naval Officers Club 1962
DATE OF BIRTH: 25 May, 1916
EDUCATION: Danish Naval Academy 1939
DATES OF PROMOTIONS: 1939 Sub. Lieutenant; 1940 Lieutenant; 1945 Lieutenant Commander; 1950 Commander; 1955 Commander (Sen. Grade); Captain 1 June, 1962
PRINCIPAL COMMANDS AT SEA: 1951-1953 Officer Commanding Destroyers; 1958-1962 Captain Coastal Forces
OTHER PREVIOUS APPOINTMENTS OF NOTE: ADC HM The King 1953-1955; Head of Personnel Naval Staff 1962-1965
OFFICIAL ADDRESS: Naval Base, Korsør Denmark *Telephone:* (03) 571881
PRIVATE ADDRESS: Kjaersvej 25, Korsør Denmark *Telephone:* (03) 571602

U.S.A.
WOODING, REAR-ADMIRAL ROBERT REYNOLDS, (CIVIL ENGINEER CORPS.) US NAVY
CURRENT DUTY STATION: Commander, Southwest Division, Naval Facilities Engineering Command; additional duty: Civil Engineer, 11th Naval District (January 1967)
DATE OF BIRTH: 1916
EDUCATION: 1936 Naval Academy; 1944 Naval Postgraduate School
DATE OF COMMISSION: 6th June, 1940
PROMOTED TO: Rear Admiral 1st October, 1966
COMMANDS: 1961-1963 Naval Public Works Center, Newport, Rhode Island; 1963-1965 Naval Construction Battalions, Atlantic Fleet; 1965 Southeast Division, Bureau of Yards and Docks, Charleston, South Carolina; 1965-1966 Pacific Division, Bureau of Yards and Docks,Saigon, South Vietnam
OFFICIAL ADDRESS: San Diego, California 92132
HOME ADDRESS: 24 Mather Avenue, Broomall, Pennsylvania

U.S.A.
WOODS, REAR-ADMIRAL MARK WILLIAM, US NAVY
CURRENT DUTY STATION:
Commander, Naval Ordnance Systems Command (June 1969)
DATE OF BIRTH: 1918
EDUCATION: 1942 Naval Academy; 1949 Naval Postgraduate School; 1952 Naval War College
DATE OF COMMISSION: 19th December, 1941
PROMOTED TO: Rear Admiral 1st July, 1967
COMMANDS: 1954-1956 Gearing DD 710; 1964-1966 Canberra CAG 2; 1966-1967 Cruiser-Destroyer Flotilla 9
OFFICIAL ADDRESS: Main Navy Building, Washington, DC 20360
HOME ADDRESS: 2745 Eastgate, Lincoln, Nebraska

U.S.A.
WYLIE, REAR-ADMIRAL, JOSEPH CALDWELL, US NAVY
CURRENT DUTY STATION: Commandant, 1st Naval District; additional duty: Commander, Naval Base Boston (December, 1968)
DATE OF BIRTH: 1911
EDUCATION: Naval Academy 1932; 1949 Naval War College
DATE OF COMMISSION: 2nd June, 1932
PROMOTED TO: Rear Admiral 1st December, 1960
COMMANDS: 1943 Trever DMS 16; 1944-1945 Ault DD 698; 1953-1954 Arneb AKA 56; 1958-1959 Macon CA 132; 1960-1961 Cruiser Division 3; Cruiser-Destroyer Flotilla 9
OFFICIAL ADDRESS: 495 Summer Street, Boston, Massachusetts
HOME ADDRESS: Sea Girt, New Jersey

U.S.A.
YATES, REAR-ADMIRAL (SELECTEE), EARL PRESTON, (NAVAL AVIATOR) US NAVY
CURRENT DUTY STATION: Commanding Officer, USS John F. Kennedy (CVA 67) (September 1968)
DATE OF BIRTH: 1923
EDUCATION: 1944 Naval Academy; 1951 Naval Postgraduate School; 1961 Air War College;
DATE OF COMMISSION: 9th June, 1943
PROMOTED TO: Rear Admiral selected for promotion on 6th June, 1969
COMMANDS: 1959-1960 Heavy Attack Squadron 9; 1961-1962 Carrier Air Group 8; 1965-1966 Raleigh LPD 1
OFFICIAL ADDRESS: FPO New York
HOME ADDRESS: Ransom Road, Winston-Salem, North Carolina

U.S.A.
YON, REAR-ADMIRAL, JOSEPH LANGHAM, (MEDICAL CORPS.) US NAVY
CURRENT DUTY STATION: Commanding Officer, Naval Hospital, Portsmouth, Virginia; additional duty: District Medical Officer, 5th Naval District (November, 1964)
DATE OF BIRTH: 1912
EDUCATION: 1937 University of Virginia Medical School
DATE OF COMMISSION: 16th July, 1938
PROMOTED TO: Rear Admiral 1st July, 1964
COMMANDS: 1960-1962 Naval Hospital, Naval Base, Newport, Rhode Island; 1962-1964 Naval Hospital, St. Albans, Long Island, New York
OFFICIAL ADDRESS: Naval Hospital, Portsmouth, Virginia 23708
HOME ADDRESS: Charlottesville, Virginia

JAPAN
YOSHIMURA, CAPTAIN G.
DECORATIONS: The Sixth Order of the Sacred Treasure 1945
PRESENT APPOINTMENT: Defence attaché, Japanese Embassy, London, October 1965
DATE OF BIRTH: 19 November, 1917
EDUCATION: Naval Academy 1939 Grtd; National Defence College 1963
DATE OF PROMOTION: Captain January 1963
OTHER PREVIOUS APPOINTMENTS OF NOTE: Instructor, Naval War College 1963; Fleet Staff 1960; Naval Intelligence Staff 1966
OFFICIAL ADDRESS: Japanese Embassy, 46 Grosvenor Square, London W.1
PRIVATE ADDRESS: 20A Holland Park Road, London W.14

ITALY
ZANNI, ADMIRAL E., ITALIAN NAVY
DECORATIONS: 2 Medaglie d'argento al Valor Militare Croce di Guerra al Valor Militare
PRESENT APPOINTMENT: President of the Consiglio Tecnico Scientifico della Difesa
DATE OF BIRTH: 10 April, 1909
DATES OF PROMOTIONS: Contrammiraglio 1 January, 1961; Ammiraglio di Divisione 31 December, 1965; Ammiraglio di Squadra 31 December, 1968
PRINCIPAL COMMANDS AT SEA: Capitano di Corvetta 1941; Capitano di Fregata 1947; Capitano di Vascello 1954
OTHER PREVIOUS APPOINTMENT OF NOTE: Campagne di Guerra, 1940-1943
OFFICIAL ADDRESS: Consiglio Tecnico Scientifico Difesa, Rome

MEXICO
ZILLI VIVEROS, CAPITAN DE CORBETA C. G. G. MEXICAN NAVY
DECORATIONS: Perseverancia de 5/A Y 4/A Clase
PRESENT APPOINTMENT: Comandante dela corbeta Cadete Virgilio Uribe 1 February, 1968
DATE OF BIRTH: 30 December, 1931
EDUCATION: Graduated H. Escuela Naval, December 1953;
DATES OF PROMOTIONS: Guardiamarina C. G. 1 January, 1954; Teniente de Corbeta C. G. 20 November, 1956; Teniente de Fragata C.G. 20 November, 1959; Teniente de Navio C.G. 20 Novmeber 1963; Capitán de Corbeta C.G. 20 November, 1968
PRINCIPAL COMMANDS AT SEA: Comandante del Guardacostas 36 1958;
OTHER PREVIOUS APPOINTMENT OF NOTE: Ayudante Naval del Presidente de la Republica de Mexico 1959-1964
OFFICIAL ADDRESS: Corbeta Cadete Virgilio Uribe, Veracruz, Ver, Mexico
PRIVATE ADDRESS: Calle I. La Católica 19 Fracc, Reforma, Veracruz, Ver, Mexico

Jane's Fighting Ships

Bibliography of principal Naval books published in 1968-69

ARCHIBALD, Edward Hunter Holmes
The Wooden fighting ship in the Royal Navy, A.D. 897-1860
174p. illus. facsims, plans, Blandford Press 1968, London, 90s

BARNABY, Kenneth Clores
Some ship disasters and their causes
272p. illus. plates, Hutchinson, London 1968

BAYNHAM, Henry
From the lower deck: the old Navy, 1780-1840
200p. illus. plates, Hutchinson, London 1969, 50s

BENNETT, G. M.
Naval battles of the first world war
320p. illus. plates, maps, plans, ports, Batsford, London, 1968, 50s

BENNETT, G. M.
Charlie B: a biography of Admiral Lord Beresford of Metemmeh and Curraghmore, G.C.B., G.C.V.O., LL.D., D.C.L.
378p. illus. plates, facsims, map, plans, ports, Dawnay, London 1968, 60s

BERGAUST, E.
Aircraft carriers in action
Putnam, New York 1968, $3.29

BONNETT, Stanley Hubert
The Price of Admiralty: an indictment of the Royal Navy 1805-1966
272p. illus., plates, facsim, ports, Hale, London 1968 42s

BONWICK, George James
Seamanship handbook for basic studies, Edited by G. J. Bowman and F. S. Campbell
4th revised edition
311p. illus, plate, plans, Maritime Press 1968, 22s 6d

BOWERS, P. M. and SWANBOROUGH G.
United States Navy Aircraft since 1911
illus., Putnam, London 1968

BROWN, J. D.
Carrier operations in World War II, Vol. I, The Royal Navy
192p. illus., I. Allan Shepperton 1968, 37s 6d

BROWN, Malcolm and MEEHAN, Patricia
Scapa Flow: The reminiscences of men and women who served in Scapa Flow in the two world wars
264p. illus., plates, facsims, map, ports, A. Lane, London 1968

CALDWELL, John Bernard
The future of naval architecture: an inaugural lecture delivered before the University of Newcastle upon Tyne
20p. illus., Newcastle 1968, 5s

CARRISON, Daniel Jordan Capt., USN
The United States Navy
262p., illus, plates, maps, ports, Praeger Library of US Government Departments and Agencies, Washington 1968, 50s

CHAPELLE, Howard Irving
The search for speed under sail, 1700-1855
453p. illus. plates, plans, Allen & Unwin, London 1968, 90s
(Originally published in New York, 1967)

CHASE, Hubert Frank
The boatswain's manual
313p. illus., plates, plans, Brown, Son & Ferguson 1968, 36s

CHEVALLIER, J.
Le prototype à terre du réacteur nucléaire pour sous-marins
(Extract from *Revue de Defense Nationale*)
16p. Paris, 1968

COLLEDGE, James Joseph
Ships of the Royal Navy: a historical index
Vol 1 Major ships (excluding trawlers, drifters, tugs etc.)
642p., David & Charles, Newton Abbot 1968, £5 5s

COTTER, C. M.
A history of nautical astronomy
342p. illus. Hollis & Carter London, 1968

COX, John George
Cox and the JuJu Coast: a journal kept aboard HMS *Fly* 1868-1869
88p. illus. plates, maps, drags, Ellison, 1968

FOX, William Jack
Marine auxiliary machinery: contributors include H. Hillier etc., 4th revised edition
492p. illus. Newnes London 1968, 50s

FRACCAROLI, Aldo
Italian warships of World War II
204p. illus. I. Allan, Shepperton 1968, 30s

GARDINER, Leslie
The British Admiralty
418p. illus. plates, map, ports, Blackwood Edinburgh 1968, 50s

GARDNER, John
Warships of the Royal Navy. 1st Series: Sail
59p. illus., H. Evelyn London 1968, 84s

GINGALL, Basil
Warships (*Illustrated News* boxed books No. 2)
52 cards, illus., ports, Joseph London 1968, 30s

GRENFELL, Russell
Horatio Nelson: a short biography
247p. illus, plates, plans, port, Faber London, 1968 25s

GRETTON, Vice Admiral Sir Peter
Former naval person: Winston Churchill and the Royal Navy
338p. illus., plates, ports, Cassell London, 1968, 50s

HAIGH, K. R.
Cableships and Submarine Cables
256p. illus., Adlard Coles London, 1968, 84s

HAMPTON, Trevor Arthur
The Sailor's World, illustrations by John Horsley
128p. illus., plates. charts, David & Charles Newton Abbot, 25s

HANSEN, Hans Jürgen (Editor)
Art and the seafarer: a historical survey of the arts and crafts of sailors and shipwrights) (Translated by James and Inge Moore)
296p. illus., Faber London, 1968, £8 8s

HERRICK, Cdr R. W. USN
Soviet Naval Strategy, fifty years of theory and practice
XXXIV, 198p., Annapolis Maryland, 1968

HOUGH, Richard
Dreadnought: a history of the modern battleship (Introduction by C. S. Forester)
2nd edition
268p. illus. plates, plans, Allen & Unwin London 1968, 80s

HOUGHTON, Philip
Land from the Masthead
224p. illus., maps, Hodder & Stoughton London 1968, 30s

IRVING, D.
The Destruction of Convoy PQ17
337p. illus., plates, facsims, maps, ports, Cassell London 1968, 42s

JELLICOE, John (Earl)
The Jellicoe papers: Selections from private and official correspondence of Admiral of the Fleet Earl Jellicoe
Vol 2, 1916-1935
497p. plate, port, Navy Records Society London, 1968

JOHNS, W. E. and KELLY, R. A.
No surrender: The story of William E. Johns DSM, and how he survived the sinking of HMS *Exeter* in March 1942
illus, Harrap London, 1969

LAFFIN, John
Jack Tar, the story of the British sailor
212p. illus., plates, ports, Cassells London, 1969, 36s

LANGLEY H. D.
Social reform in the United States Navy, 1798-1962
309p., University of Illinois Press, 1967, $8.50 (64s)

LANGMAID, K. Captain
Beat to quarters! Ten outstanding Naval exploits
207p. illus.. plates, maps, Jarrolds 1968, 25s.

LE MASSON, Henri (Editor)
Flottes de Combat Editions Maritime D'outre-Mer
430p. illus., Paris 1968

LENTON, Henry Trevor
American battleships, carriers and cruisers
160p., illus., plans, Macdonald London, 1968, 15s

LENTON, Henry Trevor
Royal Netherlands Navy
160p. illus., plans Macdonald London, 1968, 15s

LLOYD, Christopher
The British seaman 1200-1860, a social survey
319p. illus., plates, facsims, Collins London, 1968, 45s

LORD, Walter
Incredible victory
331p. illus., plates, maps, ports, H. Hamilton London, 1968, 42s

LUBBOCK, Adelaide
Owen Stanley R.N., 1811-1850, Captain of the *Rattlesnake*
290p., Heinemann London, 1968

MAAS, P.
The Rescuer (Vice Admiral C. B. Momsem and the rescue of US Submarine *Squalus* in 1937)
256p. illus., London 1968

MACINTYRE, Captain D. G. F. W.
Trafalgar, Nelson's greatest victory
80p. maps, illus., London 1968

McLACHLAN, Donald
Room 39: Naval Intelligence in action 1939-1945
438p. illus., plates, ports, Werdenfeld & Nicolson London 1968, 50s

MAY, Cdr W. and KENNARD, A. N.
Naval swords and firearms
22p. illus., National Maritime Museum London, 1968

Bibliography of principal Naval books published in 1968-69—*continued*

MELLERSH, H. E. L.
Fitzroy of the Beagle
307p. illus., plates, chart, maps, ports, R. Hart-Davis London 1968, 63s

MELTON, Maurice
The Confederate Ironclads
319p. illus., plates, plans, ports, Yoseloff London 1968, 50s

MITCHELL, W. H. and SAWYER L. A.
British standard ships of World War I; drawings by John S. Lindsay
178p. illus., plans, Journal of Commerce and Shipping London, 1968

MORISON, E. E.
Admiral Sims and the modern American Navy
Russell & Russell, USA 1968, $17.50

MORISON, Samuel Eliot
"Old Bruin", Cmdr. Matthew C. Perry 1794-1858
482p. illus., charts, maps, ports, OUP London, 1968, 65s

MORRISON, John Sinclair and WILLIAMS R. J.
Greek oared ships, 900-322 BC
356p. plates, illus., maps, Cambridge University Press, 1968, £6 6s

NASATIR, Abraham Phineas
Spanish war vessels on the Mississippi 1792-1796
359 p. illus., plan, Yale University Press, 1968, 72s

NASH, H. P.
The forgotten wars
Yoseloff New York, 1968, 42s

O'BRIEN, Thomas Prudhoe
The design of marine screw propellers, 1st edition, 2nd impression
397p. illus., plates, Hutchinson, London, 1968

OPPENHEIM, Michael
The maritime history of Devon: introduction by W. E. Minchintor
175p. illus, plates, facsims, maps, ports, University of Exeter, 1968, 42s

PADFIELD, Peter
Broke and the Shannon
246p. illus., facsims, plans, ports, Hodder & Stoughton London 1968, 42s

PATER, A. F. (editor)
United States battleships
Monitor Book Co USA 1968, $19.95

PATTERSON, A. Temple
Jellicoe
277p. illus, plates, ports, Macmillan London, 1969, 55s

PAULLIN, C. O.
Diplomatic negotiations of American naval officers, 1778-1883
P. Smith USA, 1967 $5.50

PAULLIN, C. O.
Paullins history of naval administration 1775-1911
US Naval Institute Washington 1968, $8.50

PEILLARD, Leonce
Sink the Tirpitz! Translated by Oliver Coburn from the French
360p. illus, plates, facsims. maps, plans, ports, Cape London 1968, 35s

POCOCK, Tom
Nelson and his world
143p. illus., facsims, ports, Thames & Hudson London, 1968, 35s

POUNDER, Cuthbert Coulson
Marine diesels engine
4th edition, 772p. illus., Newnes London, 1968, 80s

PRATO, Vice Admiral V.
Rivista Marittima, Almanacco Navale, Rome 1968

ROHWER, J.
Die U-Boot-Erfolge der Achsenmächte 1993-1945
276p. J. F. Lehmans Verlag, Munich 1968

ROSKLL, Stephen
Naval policy between the wars
Vol 1. The period of Anglo-American antagonism 1919-1928
639p., 31 plates, illus., maps, ports, Collins London, 1968, 70s

RUSSELL, Jack
Nelson and the Hamiltons
371p. illus., plates, ports, Blond London, 1969

SCHOFIELD, Vice-Admiral B. B. and MARTYN, L. F.
The Rescue ships.
172p. illus., plates, facsim, ports, Blackwood Edinburgh, 1968, 30s

SHANKLAND, Peter
The Phantom Flotilla; the story of the Naval African Expedition 1915-1916
224p. illus, ports., Collins London 1968, 30s

SIGWART, Emil Edward
Royal Fleet Auxiliary: its ancestry and affiliations, 1600-1968
221p. illus, plate, Adlard Coles London 1969, 75s

SMITH, Peter C.
Destroyer leader: The story of HMS *Faulkner*
191p. illus., plates, maps, ports, Kimber London, 1968, 50s

SOUTHWORTH, J. V.
War at Sea I
Twayne, New York 1968, $7.50

STAFFORD, Edward Peary
The Far and the Deep
382p. illus., plates, ports, Barker London, 1968
(originally published by Putnam, New York, 1967)

STEINBERG, Jonathan
Tirpitz and the birth of the German battlefleet: yesterday's deterrent
240p. illus., plates, facsims, plans, ports, Macdonald, London 1968, 18s

STOKOE, Edward Alan
Reed's naval architecture for marine engineers
2nd edition, 390p. illus, T. Reed London 1968, 45s

STOKOE, Edward Alan
Reed's ship construction for marine engineers
2nd edition, 152p. illus., T. Reed London 1968, 37s 6d

STUMPF, Richard
The private war of Seaman Stumpf: the unique diaries of a young German in the Great War
422p. illus., plates, map, ports, Frewin London 1969

THOMAS, David A.
Battle of the Java Sea
260p. illus., plates, plans, port, Deutsch London 1968, 42s

TUCKER, Ernest Edward
The story of fighting ships: men of war in the days of oar and sail
192p. illus, Lutterworth Press London 1969, 28s

US NAVAL ACADEMY
Naval operations analysis
US Naval Institute 1968, $7.50

US NAVAL ACADEMY
Naval Science Dept., Ops., Committee: Naval Operations Analysis XIV
327p. Annapolis, Maryland, 1968

US DEPT. OF NAVY (HISTORY DIVISION)
Aviation in the US Navy
3rd edition, 32p. illus., Washington 1968

WALLIN, Vice Admiral H. N. USN (Retd)
Pearl Harbour: Why, How, Fleet Salvage and Final Appraisal
363p. illus., US Dept. of Navy (History Division) Washington 1968 $4

WARNER, Oliver
Great sea battles
304p. illus., facsims, maps, ports, Spring Books 1968, 55s

WARNER, Oliver
The life and letters of Vice Admiral Lord Collingwood
276p. illus., plates, maps, ports., OUP London, 1968, 42s

WATERS, John Mayo
Bloody Winter
279p. illus., plates, maps, ports, Van Nostrand London, 1968, 65s

WEYER'S WARSHIPS OF THE WORLD
Compiled by Alexander Bredt
US Naval Institute, Annapolis Maryland, $15
(Translation of German publication *Weyer's Flottentaschenbuch* edited by Gerhard Albrecht)

GENERAL INDEX

(Named Ships only)

LATE ADDENDA **UNITED KINGDOM**

SUBMARINE

Page 317: Name of sixth Nuclear powered submarine under construction changed from **Superb** to **Courageous** officially announced 15 August 1969.

GENERAL INDEX

(Named Ships only)

Abbreviations in ( ) following the name of the ship indicates the country

AbD Abu Dhabi
Al Albania
A Argentine
Alg Algeria
R.A.N. Australia
B Belgium
Br Brazil
Bru Brunei
Bul Bulgaria
Bur Burma
Ca Cambodia
Cam Cameroon
R.C.N. Canada
Chi Chile
C China
Cey Ceylon
Co Congo
Col Colombia
C.R. Costa Rica
Cu Cuba
D Denmark
Dom Dominican
EA East Africa
Ec Ecuador
Eg Egypt
Ei Eire
ES El Salvador
Et Ethiopia
F France
Fin Finland
G Gaboon
Ger West Germany
GE East Germany
Gh Ghana
Gr Greece
Gu Guatemala
Gui Guinea
H.K. Hong Kong
Hon Honduras
Hun Hungary
I.C. Ivory Coast
Ice Iceland
In India
Ind Indonesia
Ir Iran
Ira Iraq
Is Israel
I Italy
Jam Jamaica
J Japan
K.N. Korea North
Ke Kenya
Kor Korea
Ku Kuwait
L Laos
Le Lebanon
Li Liberia
Lib Libya
Ma Madagascar
M Malaya
Mal Mali
Mex Mexico
Mor Morocco
N Netherlands
R.N.Z. New Zealand
Nic Nicaragua
Nig Nigeria
Nor Norway
Pa Pakistan
Pan Panama
Par Paraguay
P Peru
Ph Philippines
Po Poland
Por Portugal
R. Rumania
S.A. South Africa
Sau Saudi Arabia
Sen Senegal
S.L. Sierra Leone
Som Somalia
Sp Spain
Sw Sweden
Su Sudan
Sy Syria
T.C. Taiwan China
Th Thailand
To Togo
Tu Tunisia
T Turkey
U.K. United Kingdom
U.S.A. United States of America
Rus U.S.S.R.
Ven Venezuela
V.M. Viet Minh
V Vietnam
Y Yugoslavia
Z Zanzibar

A. CHIRIKOV—ALMIRANTE FERRANDIZ

INDEX

INDEX

BAURÚ—CAPE JELLISON

INDEX

INDEX

COWSLIP—ERIDAN

INDEX

INDEX

INDEX

INDEX

KIRKLISTON—LORAIN COUNTRY

L

INDEX

INDEX

MORGANTHAU—OZHIVLENNYI

INDEX

P. MERKURYA—PROTEO

INDEX

PROTET—SAKARYA

INDEX

INDEX

SOMERSET—THOR

INDEX

THOR—VLADIMIR RUSANOV

INDEX

VNETA—ZWROTNY